S0-BJQ-384

THE

Jewish Encyclopedia

A DESCRIPTIVE RECORD OF

THE HISTORY, RELIGION, LITERATURE, AND CUSTOMS OF THE JEWISH PEOPLE FROM THE EARLIEST TIMES TO THE PRESENT DAY

Prepared by More than Four Hundred Scholars and Specialists

UNDER THE DIRECTION OF THE FOLLOWING EDITORIAL BOARD

CYRUS ADLER, PH.D. (*Departments of Post-Biblical Antiquities and the Jews of America*).

GOTTHARD DEUTSCH, PH.D. (*Department of History from 1492 to 1902*).

LOUIS GINZBERG, PH.D. (*Department of Rabbinical Literature*).

RICHARD GOTTHEIL, PH.D. (*Departments of History from Ezra to 1492 and History of Post-Talmudic Literature*).

JOSEPH JACOBS, B.A. (*Departments of the Jews of England and Anthropology; Revising Editor*).

MARCUS JASTROW, PH.D. (*Department of the Talmud*).

MORRIS JASTROW, JR., PH.D. (*Department of the Bible*).

KAUFMANN KOHLER, PH.D. (*Departments of Theology and Philosophy*).

FREDERICK DE SOLA MENDES, PH.D. (*Chief of the Bureau of Translation; Revising Editor*).

HERMAN ROSENTHAL (*Department of the Jews of Russia and Poland*).

ISIDORE SINGER, PH.D. (*Department of Modern Biography from 1750 to 1902*).

CRAWFORD H. TOY, D.D., LL.D. (*Departments of Hebrew Philology and Hellenistic Literature*).

ISAAC K. FUNK, D.D., LL.D.
Chairman of the Board

FRANK H. VIZETELLY
Secretary of the Board

ISIDORE SINGER, Ph.D.
Projector and Managing Editor

ASSISTED BY AMERICAN AND FOREIGN BOARDS OF CONSULTING EDITORS

COMPLETE IN TWELVE VOLUMES

EMBELLISHED WITH MORE THAN TWO THOUSAND ILLUSTRATIONS

FUNK AND WAGNALLS COMPANY
NEW YORK AND LONDON

בסימנא טבא

אודך

בישר לבב בלמדי משפטי

צדקך

ספר שלשה עשר והוא ספר משפטים

הלכות שכירות

הלכות שאלה ופקדון

הלכות מלוה ולוה

J. E. Vol. VIII. Copyright, 1904, by Funk & Wagnalls Company, New York and London.

ILLUMINATED PAGE FROM MAIMONIDES' "YAD"

(FROM A MANUSCRIPT IN THE BRITISH MUSEUM, DATED 1472)

THE

Jewish Encyclopedia

A DESCRIPTIVE RECORD OF

THE HISTORY, RELIGION, LITERATURE, AND CUSTOMS OF THE JEWISH PEOPLE FROM THE EARLIEST TIMES TO THE PRESENT DAY

Prepared by More than Four Hundred Scholars and Specialists

UNDER THE DIRECTION OF THE FOLLOWING EDITORIAL BOARD

CYRUS ADLER, PH.D. (*Departments of Post-Biblical Antiquities; the Jews of America*).

WILHELM BACHER, PH.D. (*Departments of the Talmud and Rabbinical Literature*).

GOTTHARD DEUTSCH, PH.D. (*Department of History from 1492 to 1904*).

RICHARD GOTTHEIL, PH.D. (*Departments of History from Ezra to 1492; History of Post-Talmudic Literature*).

EMIL G. HIRSCH, PH.D., LL.D. (*Department of the Bible*).

JOSEPH JACOBS, B.A. (*Departments of the Jews of England and Anthropology; Revising Editor*).

KAUFMANN KOHLER, PH.D. (*Departments of Theology and Philosophy*).

HERMAN ROSENTHAL (*Department of the Jews of Russia and Poland*).

ISIDORE SINGER, PH.D. (*Department of Modern Biography from 1750 to 1904*).

CRAWFORD H. TOY, D.D., LL.D. (*Departments of Hebrew Philology and Hellenistic Literature*).

ISAAC K. FUNK, D.D., LL.D.
Chairman of the Board

FRANK H. VIZETELLY, F.S.A.
Secretary of the Board

WILLIAM POPPER, M.A., PH.D.
Associate Revising Editor; Chief of the Bureau of Translation

ISIDORE SINGER, Ph.D.
Projector and Managing Editor

ASSISTED BY AMERICAN AND FOREIGN BOARDS OF CONSULTING EDITORS

VOLUME VIII

LEON—MORAVIA

FUNK AND WAGNALLS COMPANY
NEW YORK AND LONDON

COPYRIGHT, 1904, 1910, BY
FUNK & WAGNALLS COMPANY
All rights of translation reserved

Registered at Stationers' Hall, London, England
[*Printed in the United States of America*]

6.10

LITERARY DIRECTORATE

EDITORIAL BOARD

CYRUS ADLER, Ph.D.

(*Departments of Post-Biblical Antiquities and the Jews of America.*)

President of the American Jewish Historical Society; Librarian, Smithsonian Institution, Washington, D. C.

WILHELM BACHER, Ph.D.

(*Departments of the Talmud and Rabbinical Literature.*)

Professor in the Jewish Theological Seminary, Budapest, Hungary.

GOTTHARD DEUTSCH, Ph.D.

(*Department of History from 1492 to 1904.*)

Professor of Jewish History, Hebrew Union College, Cincinnati, Ohio; Editor of "Deborah."

RICHARD GOTTHEIL, Ph.D.

(*Departments of History from Ezra to 1492 and History of Post-Talmudic Literature.*)

Professor of Semitic Languages, Columbia University, New York; Chief of the Oriental Department, New York Public Library.

EMIL G. HIRSCH, Ph.D., LL.D.

(*Department of the Bible.*)

Rabbi of Chicago Sinai Congregation, Chicago, Ill.; Professor of Rabbinical Literature and Philosophy, University of Chicago; Editor of "The Reform Advocate."

JOSEPH JACOBS, B.A.

(*Departments of the Jews of England and Anthropology; Revising Editor.*)

Formerly President of the Jewish Historical Society of England; Author of "Jews of Angevin England," etc.

KAUFMANN KOHLER, Ph.D.

(*Departments of Theology and Philosophy.*)

President of Hebrew Union College, Cincinnati, Ohio; Rabbi Emeritus of Temple Beth-El, New York.

HERMAN ROSENTHAL.

(*Department of the Jews of Russia and Poland.*)

Chief of the Slavonic Department, New York Public Library.

ISIDORE SINGER, Ph.D.

MANAGING EDITOR.

(*Department of Modern Biography from 1750 to 1904.*)

CRAWFORD HOWELL TOY, D.D., LL.D.

(*Departments of Hebrew Philology and Hellenistic Literature.*)

Professor of Hebrew in Harvard University, Cambridge, Mass.; Author of "The Religion of Israel," etc.

I. K. FUNK, D.D., LL.D.

(*Chairman of the Board.*)

Editor-in-Chief of the STANDARD DICTIONARY OF THE ENGLISH LANGUAGE, etc.

FRANK H. VIZETELLY, F.S.A.

(*Secretary of the Board.*)

Associate Editor of the STANDARD DICTIONARY, "The Columbian Cyclopedia," etc.

WILLIAM POPPER, M.A., Ph.D.

(*Associate Revising Editor; Chief of the Bureau of Translation.*)

Gustav Gottheil Lecturer in Semitic Languages, Columbia University, New York (1903-5); Author of "The Censorship of Hebrew Books."

AMERICAN BOARD OF CONSULTING EDITORS

BERNARD DRACHMAN, Ph.D.,

Rabbi of the Congregation Zichron Ephraim; Instructor in the Bible and in Hebrew Grammar, Jewish Theological Seminary of America, New York.

B. FELSENTHAL, Ph.D.,

Rabbi Emeritus of Zion Congregation, Chicago, Ill.; Author of "A Practical Grammar of the Hebrew Language."

GUSTAV GOTTHEIL, Ph.D.

(DECEASED),

Late Rabbi Emeritus of Temple Emanu-El, New York.

HENRY HYVERNAT, D.D.,

Head of the Department of Semitic and Egyptian Literatures, Catholic University of America, Washington, D. C.

MARCUS JASTROW, Ph.D.

(DECEASED),

Late Rabbi Emeritus of the Congregation Rodef Shalom, Philadelphia, Pa.; Author of "Dictionary of the Talmud."

MORRIS JASTROW, Jr., Ph.D.,

Professor of Semitic Languages and Librarian in the University of Pennsylvania, Philadelphia, Pa.; Author of "Religion of the Babylonians and Assyrians," etc.

J. FREDERIC McCURDY, Ph.D., LL.D.,

Professor of Oriental Languages, University College, Toronto, Canada; Author of "History, Prophecy, and the Monuments."

H. PEREIRA MENDES, M.D.,

Rabbi of the Shearith Israel Congregation (Spanish and Portuguese), New York; President of the Board of Jewish Ministers, New York.

MOSES MIELZINER, Ph.D., D.D.

(DECEASED),

Late President of the Hebrew Union College, Cincinnati, Ohio; Author of "Introduction to the Talmud."

GEORGE F. MOORE, M.A., D.D.,
Professor of Biblical Literature and the History of Religions in Harvard University, Cambridge, Mass.; Author of "A Commentary on the Book of Judges," etc.

DAVID PHILIPSON, D.D.,
Rabbi of the Congregation B'ne Israel; Professor of Homiletics, Hebrew Union College, Cincinnati, Ohio; President of Hebrew Sabbath School Union of America.

IRA MAURICE PRICE, B.D., Ph.D.,
Professor of Semitic Languages and Literatures, University of Chicago, Ill.; Author of "The Monuments and the Old Testament," etc.

SOLOMON SCHECHTER, M.A., Litt.D.,
President of the Faculty of the Jewish Theological Seminary of America, New York; Author of "Studies in Judaism."

JOSEPH SILVERMAN, D.D.,
President of Central Conference of American Rabbis; Rabbi of Temple Emanu-El, New York.

JACOB VOORSANGER, D.D.,
Rabbi of the Congregation Emanu-El, San Francisco, Cal.; Professor of Semitic Languages and Literatures, University of California, Berkeley, Cal.

EDWARD J. WHEELER, M.A.,
Editor of "The Literary Digest," New York; Author of "Stories in Rhyme," etc.

FOREIGN BOARD OF CONSULTING EDITORS

ISRAEL ABRAHAMS, M.A.,
Coeditor of "The Jewish Quarterly Review"; Author of "Jewish Life in the Middle Ages," etc.; Reader in Talmudic, Cambridge University, England.

M. BRANN, Ph.D.,
Professor in the Jewish Theological Seminary, Breslau, Germany; Editor of "Monatsschrift für Geschichte und Wissenschaft des Judenthums."

H. BRODY, Ph.D.,
Rabbi, Nachod, Bohemia, Austria; Coeditor of "Zeitschrift für Hebräische Bibliographie."

ABRAHAM DANON,
Principal of the Jewish Theological Seminary, Constantinople, Turkey.

HARTWIG DERENBOURG, Ph.D.,
Professor of Literal Arabic at the Special School of Oriental Languages, Paris; Member of the Institut de France.

S. M. DUBNOW,
Author of "Istoriya Yevreyev," Wilna, Russia.

MICHAEL FRIEDLÄNDER, Ph.D.,
Principal of Jews' College, London, England; Author of "The Jewish Religion," etc.

IGNAZ GOLDZIHER, Ph.D.,
Professor of Semitic Philology, University of Budapest, Hungary.

M. GÜDEMANN, Ph.D.,
Chief Rabbi of Vienna, Austria.

BARON DAVID GÜNZBURG,
St. Petersburg, Russia.

A. DE HARKAVY, Ph.D.,
Chief of the Hebrew Department of the Imperial Public Library, St. Petersburg, Russia.

ZADOC KAHN,
Chief Rabbi of France; Honorary President of the Alliance Israélite Universelle; Officer of the Legion of Honor, Paris, France.

M. KAYSERLING, Ph.D.,
Rabbi, Budapest, Hungary; Corresponding Member of the Royal Academy of History, Madrid, Spain.

MORITZ LAZARUS, Ph.D.
(DECEASED),
Late Professor Emeritus of Psychology, University of Berlin; Meran, Austria.

ANATOLE LEROY-BEAULIEU,
Member of the French Institute; Professor at the Free School of Political Science, Paris, France; Author of "Israël chez les Nations."

ISRAEL LÉVI,
Professor in the Jewish Theological Seminary; Editor of "Revue des Etudes Juives," Paris, France.

EUDE LOLLI, D.D.,
Chief Rabbi of Padua; Professor of Hebrew at the University, Padua, Italy.

IMMANUEL LÖW, Ph.D.,
Chief Rabbi of Szegedin, Hungary; Author of "Die Aramäischen Pflanzennamen."

S. H. MARGULIES, Ph.D.,
Principal of the Jewish Theological Seminary; Chief Rabbi of Florence, Italy.

H. OORT, D.D.,
Professor of Hebrew Language and Archeology at the State University, Leyden, Holland.

ABBÉ PIETRO PERREAU,
Formerly Librarian of the Reale Biblioteca Palatina, Parma, Italy.

MARTIN PHILIPPSON, Ph.D.,
Formerly Professor of History at the Universities of Bonn and Brussels; President of the Deutsch-Israelitischer Gemeindebund, Berlin, Germany.

SAMUEL POZNANSKI, Ph.D.,
Rabbi in Warsaw, Russia.

E. SCHWARZFELD, LL.D.,
Secretary-General of the Jewish Colonization Association, Paris, France.

LUDWIG STEIN, Ph.D.,
Professor of Philosophy, University of Bern, Switzerland; Editor of "Archiv für Geschichte der Philosophie," etc.

HERMANN L. STRACK, Ph.D.,
Professor of Old Testament Exegesis and Semitic Languages, University of Berlin, Germany.

CHARLES TAYLOR, D.D., LL.D.,
Master of St. John's College, Cambridge, England; Editor of "Sayings of the Jewish Fathers," etc.

SYSTEMS OF TRANSLITERATION AND OF CITATION OF PROPER NAMES*

A.—Rules for the Transliteration of Hebrew and Aramaic.

1. All important names which occur in the Bible are cited as found in the authorized King James version; *e.g.*, *Moses*, not Mosheh; *Isaac*, not Yiẓḥaḳ; *Saul*, not Sha'ul or Shaül; *Solomon*, not Shelomoh, etc.

2. The spellings of names that have gained currency in English books on Jewish subjects, or that have become familiar to English readers, are generally retained; cross-references are given when topics are treated under forms transliterated according to the system tabulated below.

3. Hebrew subject-headings are transcribed according to the scheme of transliteration; cross-references are made as in the case of personal names.

4. The following system of transliteration has been used for Hebrew and Aramaic:

א *Not noted at the beginning or the end of a word; otherwise* ' *or by dieresis; e.g., pe'er or Meïr.*

ב *b*	ז *z*	ל *l*	פּ *(with dagesh)*, *p*	שׁ *sh*
ג *g*	ח *ḥ*	מ ם *m*	פ *(without dagesh)*, *f*	שׂ *s*
ד *d*	ט *ṭ*	נ ן *n*	צ *ẓ*	ת *t*
ה *h*	י *y*	ס *s*	ק *ḳ*	
ו *w*	כ ך *k*	ע ʿ	ר *r*	

Note: The presence of dagesh lene is not noted except in the case of פּ. Dagesh forte is indicated by doubling the letter.

5. The vowels have been transcribed as follows:

◌ָ (ḳameẓ) *a*	◌ֻ *u*	◌ַ *a*	◌ֱ *e*	וֹ *o*
◌ָ (ḳameẓ ḥatuf) *o*				
◌ֵ *e*	◌ֶ *e*	◌ֳ *o*	◌ִי *i*	
◌ִ *i*	◌ְ *e*	◌ֲ *a*	וּ *u*	

The so-called "Continental" pronunciation of the English vowels is implied.

6. The Hebrew article is transcribed as *ha*, followed by a hyphen, without doubling the following letter. [Not *hak-Kohen* or *hak-Cohen*, nor *Rosh ha-shshanah.*]

B.—Rules for the Transliteration of Arabic.

1. All Arabic names and words, except such as have become familiar to English readers in other forms, as *Mohammed*, *Koran*, *mosque*, are transliterated according to the following system:

أ *See* א *above*	خ *kh*	ش *sh*	غ *gh*	ن *n*
ب *b*	د *d*	ص *ṣ*	ف *f*	ه *h*
ت *t*	ذ *dh*	ض *ḍ*	ق *ḳ*	و *w*
ث *th*	ر *r*	ط *ṭ*	ك *k*	ي *y*
ج *j*	ز *z*	ظ *ẓ*	ل *l*	
ح *ḥ*	س *s*	ع ʿ	م *m*	

2. Only the three vowels—a, i, u—are represented:

◌َ *a* ◌ِ *i* ◌ُ *u*

No account has been taken of the *imalah; i* has not been written *e*, nor *u* written *o*.

---

* In all other matters of orthography the spelling preferred by the Standard Dictionary has usually been followed. Typographical exigencies have rendered occasional deviations from these systems necessary.

3. The Arabic article is invariably written *al*, no account being taken of the assimilation of the *l* to the following letter; *e.g.*, *Abu al-Salt*, not *Abu-l-Salt; Nafis al-Daulah*, not *Nafis ad-Daulah*. The article is joined by a hyphen to the following word.

4. At the end of words the feminine termination is written *ah*; but when followed by a genitive, *at*; *e.g.*, *Risalah dhat al-Kursiyy*, but *Hi'at al-Aflak*.

5. No account is taken of the overhanging vowels which distinguish the cases; *e.g.*, *'Amr*, not *'Amru* or *'Amrun; Ya'ḳub*, not *Ya'ḳubun;* or in a title, *Kitab al-Amanat wal-I'tiḳadat*.

C.—Rules for the Transliteration of Russian.

All Russian names and words, except such as have become familiar to English readers in other forms, as *Czar*, *Alexander*, *deciatine*, *Moscow*, are transliterated according to the following system:

А а	*a*	Н н	*n*	Щ щ	*shch*
Б б	*b*	О о	*o*	Ъ ъ	mute
В в	*v*	П п	*p*	Ы ы	*y*
Г г	*h, v,* or *g*	Р р	*r*	Ь ь	half mute
Д д	*d*	С с	*s*	Ѣ ѣ	*ye*
Е е	*e* and *ye* at the beginning.	Т т	*t*	Э э	*e*
Ж ж	*zh*	У у	*u*	Ю ю	*yu*
З з	*z*	Ф ф	*f*	Я я	*ya*
И и І і	*i*	Х х	*kh*	Ѳ ѳ	*F*
К к	*k*	Ц ц	*tz*	Ѵ ѵ	*œ*
Л л	*l*	Ч ч	*ch*	Й й	*i*
М м	*m*	Ш ш	*sh*		

Rules for the Citation of Proper Names, Personal and Otherwise.

1. Whenever possible, an author is cited under his most specific name; *e.g.*, Moses Nigrin under *Nigrin;* Moses Zacuto under *Zacuto;* Moses Rieti under *Rieti;* all the Ḳimḥis (or Ḳamḥis) under *Ḳimḥi;* Israel ben Joseph Drohobiczer under *Drohobiczer*. Cross-references are freely made from any other form to the most specific one; *e.g.*, to Moses *Vidal* from Moses *Narboni;* to Solomon Nathan *Vidal* from Menahem *Meïri;* to Samuel *Kansi* from Samuel Astruc *Dascola;* to Jedaiah *Penini* from both *Bedersi* and *En Bonet;* to *John* of Avignon from Moses de *Roquemaure*.

2. When a person is not referred to as above, he is cited under his own personal name followed by his official or other title; or, where he has borne no such title, by "of" followed by the place of his birth or residence; *e.g.*, *Johanan* ha-Sandlar; *Samuel* ha-Nagid; *Judah* he-Ḥasid; *Gershom* of Metz; *Isaac* of Corbeil.

3. Names containing the words *d', de, da, di, van, von, y, of, ben, ha-, ibn** are arranged under the letter of the name following this word; *e.g.*, de Pomis under *Pomis*, de Barrios under *Barrios*, Jacob d'Illescas under *Illescas*. The order of topics is illustrated by the following examples:

Abraham of Augsburg	Abraham de Balmes	Abraham ben Benjamin Aaron
Abraham of Avila	Abraham ben Baruch	Abraham ben Benjamin Zeeb
Abraham ben Azriel	Abraham of Beja	Abraham Benveniste

* When IBN has come to be a specific part of a name, as IBN EZRA, such name is treated in its alphabetical place under "I."

NOTE TO THE READER.

Subjects on which further information is afforded elsewhere in this work are indicated by the use of capitals and small capitals in the text; as, ABBA ARIKA; PUMBEDITA; VOCALIZATION.

LIST OF ABBREVIATIONS

[Self-evident abbreviations, particularly those used in the bibliographies, are not included here.]

Abbreviation	Meaning
Ab	Abot, Pirke
Ab. R. N	Abot de-Rabbi Natan
'Ab. Zarah	'Abodah Zarah
ad loc	at the place; to the passage cited
A.H	in the year of the Hegira
Allg. Zeit. des Jud.	Allgemeine Zeitung des Judenthums
Am. Jew. Hist. Soc.	American Jewish Historical Society
Am. Jour. Semit. Lang	American Journal of Semitic Languages
Anglo-Jew. Assoc.	Anglo-Jewish Association
Apoc	Apocalypse
Apocr	Apocrypha
Apost. Const	Apostolical Constitutions
'Ar	'Arakin (Talmud)
Arch. Isr	Archives Israélites
Aronius, Regesten	Aronius, Regesten zur Geschichte der Juden in Deutschland
A. T	Das Alte Testament
A. V	Authorized Version
b	ben *or* bar *or* born
Bacher, Ag. Bab. Amor	Bacher, Agada der Babylonischen Amoräer
Bacher, Ag. Pal. Amor	Bacher, Agada der Palästinensischen Amoräer
Bacher, Ag. Tan.	Bacher, Agada der Tannaiten
B. B	Baba Batra (Talmud)
B.C	before the Christian era
Bek	Bekorot (Talmud)
Benzinger, Arch.	Benzinger, Hebräische Archäologie
Ber	Berakot (Talmud)
Berliner Fest-schrift	Festschrift zum 70ten Geburtstag Berliners
Berliner's Magazin	Berliner's Magazin für die Wissenschaft des Judenthums
Bibl. Rab	Bibliotheca Rabbinica
Bik	Bikkurim (Talmud)
B. Ḳ	Baba Ḳamma (Talmud)
B. M	Baba Meẓi'a (Talmud)
Boletin Acad. Hist.	Boletin de la Real Academia de la Historia (Madrid)
Brit. Mus	British Museum
Brüll's Jahrb	Brüll's Jahrbücher für Jüdische Geschichte und Litteratur
Bulletin All. Isr.	Bulletin of the Alliance Israélite Universelle
c	about
Cant	Canticles (Song of Solomon)
Cat. Anglo-Jew. Hist. Exh	Catalogue of Anglo-Jewish Historical Exhibition
Cazès, Notes Bibliographiques	Cazès, Notes Bibliographiques sur la Littérature Juive-Tunisienne
C.E	common era
ch	chapter or chapters
Cheyne and Black, Encyc. Bibl.	Cheyne and Black, Encyclopædia Biblica
Chwolson Jubilee Volume	Recueil des Travaux Rédigés en Mémoire du Jubilé Scientifique de M. Daniel Chwolson, 1846-1896
C. I. A	Corpus Inscriptionum Atticarum
C. I. G	Corpus Inscriptionum Græcarum
C. I. H	Corpus Inscriptionum Hebraicarum
C. I. L	Corpus Inscriptionum Latinarum
C. I. P	Corpus Inscriptionum Peloponnesi
C. I. S	Corpus Inscriptionum Semiticarum
comp	compare
Curinier, Dict. Nat	E. E. Curinier, Dictionnaire National des Contemporains
d	died
D	Deuteronomist
De Gubernatis, Diz. Biog	De Gubernatis, Dizionario Biografico degli Scrittori Contemporanei
De Gubernatis, Ecrivains du Jour	De Gubernatis, Dictionnaire International des Ecrivains du Jour
De le Roi, Juden-Mission	De le Roi, Geschichte der Evangelischen Juden-Mission
Dem	Demai (Talmud)
Derenbourg, Hist.	Derenbourg, Essai sur l'Histoire et la Géographie de la Palestine, etc.
De Rossi, Dizionario	De Rossi, Dizionario Storico degli Autori Ebrei e delle Loro Opere
De Rossi-Hamberger, Hist. Wörterb	De Rossi-Hamberger, Historisches Wörterbuch der Jüdischen Schriftsteller und Ihrer Werke
Driver, Introduction	S. R. Driver, An Introduction to the Literature of the Old Testament
E	Elohist
Eccl	Ecclesiastes
Ecclus. (Sirach)	Ecclesiasticus
ed	edition
'Eduy	'Eduyot (Talmud)
Eisenberg, Biog. Lex	Ludwig Eisenberg's Grosses Biographisches Lexikon der Deutschen Bühne im XIX. Jahrhundert
Encyc. Brit	Encyclopædia Britannica
Eng	English
Epiphanius, Hæres.	Epiphanius, Adversus Hæreses
'Er	'Erubin (Talmud)
Ersch and Gruber, Encyc.	Ersch and Gruber, Allgemeine Encyklopädie der Wissenschaften und Künste
Esd	Esdras
et seq	and following
Eusebius, Hist. Eccl.	Eusebius, Historia Ecclesiastica
Ewald, Gesch	Ewald, Geschichte des Volkes Israel
Frankel, Mebo	Frankel, Mebo Yerushalmi
Fürst, Bibl. Jud.	Fürst, Bibliotheca Judaica
Fürst, Gesch. des Karäert	Fürst, Geschichte des Karäerthums
Gaster, Hist. of Bevis Marks	Gaster, Bevis Marks Memorial Volume
Geiger, Urschrift	Geiger, Urschrift und Uebersetzungen der Bibel in Ihrer Abhängigkeit von der Inneren Entwicklung des Judenthums
Geiger's Jüd. Zeit.	Geiger's Jüdische Zeitschrift für Wissenschaft und Leben
Geiger's Wiss. Zeit. Jüd. Theol.	Geiger's Wissenschaftliche Zeitschrift für Jüdische Theologie
Gesch	Geschichte
Gesenius, Gr	Gesenius, Grammar
Gesenius, Th	Gesenius, Thesaurus
Gibbon, Decline and Fall	Gibbon, History of the Decline and Fall of the Roman Empire
Ginsburg's Bible	Ginsburg's New Massoretico-Critical Text of the Hebrew Bible
Giṭ	Giṭṭin (Talmud)
Graetz, Hist	Graetz, History of the Jews
Grätz, Gesch	Grätz, Geschichte der Juden
Güdemann, Gesch	Güdemann, Geschichte des Erziehungswesens und der Cultur der Abendländischen Juden
Hag	Haggai
Ḥag	Ḥagigah (Talmud)
Ḥal	Ḥallah (Talmud)
Hamburger, R. B. T	Hamburger, Realencyclopädie für Bibel und Talmud
Hastings, Dict. Bible	Hastings, Dictionary of the Bible
Heb	Epistle to the Hebrews
Hebr	Masoretic Text
Herzog-Plitt or Herzog-Hauck, Real-Encyc.	Herzog-Plitt or Herzog-Hauck, Real-Encyklopädie für Protestantische Theologie und Kirche (2d and 3d editions respectively)
Hirsch, Biog. Lex.	Hirsch, Biographisches Lexikon der Hervorragenden Aerzte Aller Zeiten und Völker
Hor	Horayot (Talmud)
Ḥul	Ḥullin (Talmud)
ib	same place
idem	same author
Isr. Letterbode	Israelitische Letterbode
J	Jahvist
Jaarboeken	Jaarboeken voor de Israeliten in Nederland
Jacobs, Sources	Jacobs, Inquiry into the Sources of Spanish-Jewish History
Jacobs and Wolf, Bibl. Anglo-Jud.	Jacobs and Wolf, Bibliotheca Anglo-Judaica
Jahrb. Gesch. der Jud	Jahrbuch für die Geschichte der Juden und des Judenthums
Jastrow, Dict	Jastrow, Dictionary of the Targumim, Talmudim, and Midrashim
Jellinek, B. H	Jellinek, Bet ha-Midrash
Jew. Chron	Jewish Chronicle, London
Jew. Encyc	The Jewish Encyclopedia
Jew. Hist. Soc. Eng.	Jewish Historical Society of England
Jew. World	Jewish World, London
Josephus, Ant	Josephus, Antiquities of the Jews
Josephus, B. J	Josephus, De Bello Judaico
Josephus, Contra Ap.	Josephus, Contra Apionem
Josh	Joshua
Jost's Annalen	Jost's Israelitische Annalen
Jour. Bib. Lit	Journal of Biblical Literature
J. Q. R	Jewish Quarterly Review
J. R. A. S	Journal of the Royal Asiatic Society
Justin, Dial. cum Tryph	Justin, Dialogus cum Tryphone Judæo
Kaufmann Gedenkbuch	Gedenkbuch zur Erinnerung an David Kaufmann
Kautzsch, Apokryphen	Kautzsch, Die Apokryphen und Pseudepigraphen des Alten Testaments
Kayserling, Bibl. Esp.-Port.-Jud.	Kayserling, Biblioteca Española-Portugueza-Judaica
Kayserling, Die Jüdischen Frauen	Kayserling, Die Jüdischen Frauen in der Geschichte, Literatur und Kunst
Ker	Keritot (Talmud)
Ket	Ketubot (Talmud)
K. H. C	Kurzer Hand-Commentar zum Alten Testament, ed. Marti
Ḳid	Ḳiddushin (Talmud)
Kil	Kilayim (Talmud)
Ḳin	Ḳinnim (Talmud)

Kohut Memorial Volume........Semitic Studies in Memory of A. Kohut
Krauss, Lehnwörter........Krauss, Griechische und Lateinische Lehnwörter im Talmud, Midrasch, und Targum
Kuenen, Einleitung..........Kuenen, Historisch-Kritische Einleitung in die Bücher des Alten Testaments
Larousse, Dict....Larousse, Grand Dictionnaire Universel du XIXe Siècle
l.c................in the place cited
Levy, Chal. Wörterb........Levy, Chaldäisches Wörterbuch über die Targumim
Levy, Neuhebr. Wörterb........Levy, Neuhebräisches und Chaldäisches Wörterbuch über die Talmudim und Midraschim
Lewysohn, Z. T....Lewysohn, Zoologie des Talmuds
lit................literally
Löw, Lebensalter Löw, Die Lebensalter in der Jüdischen Literatur
LXX..............Septuagint
m..................married
Ma'as..............Ma'aserot (Talmud)
Ma'as. Sh..........Ma'aser Sheni (Talmud)
Macc...............Maccabees
Maimonides, Moreh.Maimonides, Moreh Nebukim
Maimonides, Yad ..Maimonides, Yad ha-Ḥazaḳah
Mak................Makkot (Talmud)
Maksh............Makshirin (Talmud)
Mas................Masorah
Massek............Masseket
McClintock and Strong, Cyc....McClintock and Strong, Cyclopædia of Biblical, Theological, and Ecclesiastical Literature
Meg................Megillah (Talmud)
Me'i................Me'ilah (Talmud)
Mek................Mekilta
Men................Menaḥot (Talmud)
Mid................Middot (Talmud)
Midr...............Midrash
Midr. Teh.........Midrash Tehillim (Psalms)
Miḳ................Miḳwa'ot (Talmud)
M. Ḳ..............Mo'ed Ḳaṭan (Talmud)
Monatsschrift.....Monatsschrift für die Geschichte und Wissenschaft des Judenthums
Mortara, Indice....Mortara, Indice Alfabetico
Müller, Frag.Hist. Græc..........Müller, Fragmenta Historicorum Græcorum
Munk, Mélanges . Munk, Mélanges de Philosophie Juive et Arabe
Murray's Eng. Dict.A. H. Murray, A New English Dictionary
Naz................Nazir (Talmud)
n.d................no date
Ned................Nedarim (Talmud)
Neg................Nega'im
Neubauer, Cat. Bodl.Hebr.MSS. Neubauer, Catalogue of the Hebrew MSS. in the Bodleian Library
Neubauer, G. T....Neubauer, Géographie du Talmud
Neubauer, M. J. C..Neubauer, Mediæval Jewish Chronicles
n.p................no place of publication stated
N. T...............New Testament
Oest.Wochenschrift.Oesterreichische Wochenschrift
Oh.................Ohalot (Talmud)
Onḳ................Onḳelos
Orient, Lit.........Literaturblatt des Orients
O. T...............Old Testament
P..................Priestly Code
Pagel, Biog. Lex. Pagel, Biographisches Lexikon Hervorragender Aerzte des Neunzehnten Jahrhunderts
Pal. Explor. Fund..Palestine Exploration Fund
Pallas Lex.........Pallas Nagy Lexicon
Pauly-Wissowa, Real-Encyc.....Pauly-Wissowa, Real-Encyclopädie der Classischen Altertumswissenschaft
Pes................Pesaḥim (Talmud)
Pesh...............Peshito, Peshiṭta
Pesiḳ..............Pesiḳta de-Rab Kahana
Pesiḳ. R...........Pesiḳta Rabbati
Pirḳe R. El........Pirḳe Rabbi Eli'ezer
Proc...............Proceedings
Publ...............Publications
R..................Rab *or* Rabbi *or* Rabbah
Rahmer's Jüd. Lit.-Blatt.......Rahmer's Jüdisches Litteratur-Blatt
Regesty............Regesty i Nadpisi
R. E. J............Revue des Etudes Juives
Rev. Bib...........Revue Biblique
Rev. Sém..........Revue Sémitique
R. H...............Rosh ha-Shanah (Talmud)
Rios, Estudios....Amador de los Rios, Estudios Históricos, Políticos y Literarios, etc.
Rios, Hist. ....Amador de los Rios, Historia . . . de los Judios de España y Portugal
Ritter, Erdkunde. Ritter, Die Erdkunde im Verhältnis zur Natur und zur Geschichte des Menschen
Robinson, Later Researches Robinson, Later Biblical Researches in Palestine and the Adjacent Regions . . . 1852
Robinson, Researches Robinson, Biblical Researches in Palestine, Mt. Sinai, and Arabia Petræa . . . 1838
Roest, Cat. Rosenthal. Bibl. Roest, Catalog der Hebraica und Judaica aus der L. Rosenthal'schen Bibliothek
R. V...............Revised Version
Salfeld, Martyrologium.........Salfeld, Das Martyrologium des Nürnberger Memorbuches
Sanh...............Sanhedrin (Talmud)
S. B. E............Sacred Books of the East
S. B. O. T........(Sacred Books of the Old Testament) Polychrome Bible, ed. Paul Haupt
Schaff-Herzog, Encyc.........Schaff-Herzog, A Religious Encyclopædia
Schrader, C. I. O. T.......Schrader, Cuneiform Inscriptions and the Old Testament, Eng. transl.
Schrader, K. A. T. Schrader, Keilinschriften und das Alte Testament
Schrader, K. B.....Schrader, Keilinschriftliche Bibliothek
Schrader, K. G. F. Schrader, Keilinschriften und Geschichtsforschung
Schürer, Gesch.....Schürer, Geschichte des Jüdischen Volkes
Sem................Semaḥot (Talmud)
Shab...............Shabbat (Talmud)
Sheb...............Shebi'it (Talmud)
Shebu..............Shebu'ot (Talmud)
Sheḳ...............Sheḳalim (Talmud)
Sibyllines.........Sibylline Books
Smith, Rel. of Sem..Smith, Lectures on Religion of the Semites
Soc. Bibl. Arch... Transactions of the Society of Biblical Archæology
Stade's Zeitschrift Stade's Zeitschrift für die Alttestamentliche Wissenschaft
Steinschneider, Cat. Bodl.......Steinschneider, Catalogue of the Hebrew Books in the Bodleian Library
Steinschneider, Cat. Leyden....Steinschneider, Catalogus Codicum Hebræorum Bibliothecæ Academiæ Lugduno-Batavæ
Steinschneider, Cat. Munich....Steinschneider, Die Hebräischen Handschriften der K. Hof- und Staats-Bibliothek in München
Steinschneider, Hebr. Bibl......Steinschneider, Hebräische Bibliographie
Steinschneider, Hebr. Uebers...Steinschneider, Hebräische Uebersetzungen
Strack, Das Blut.. Strack, Das Blut im Glauben und Aberglauben der Menschheit
Suk................Sukkah (Talmud)
s.v................under the word
Ta'an..............Ta'anit (Talmud)
Tan................Tanḥuma
Targ...............Targumim
Targ. Onḳ..........Targum Onḳelos
Targ. Yer..........Targum Yerushalmi *or* Targum Jonathan
Tem................Temurah (Talmud)
Ter................Terumot (Talmud)
Test. Patr.........Testaments of the Twelve Patriarchs
Toh................Ṭohorot
Tos................Tosafot
Tosef..............Tosefta
Tr.................Transactions
transl.............translation
Tristram, Nat. Hist.Tristram, Natural History of the Bible
T. Y...............Ṭebul Yom (Talmud)
'Uḳ................'Uḳzin (Talmud)
Univ. Isr..........Univers Israélite
Virchow's Archiv Virchow's Archiv für Pathologische Anatomie und Physiologie, und für Klinische Medizin
Vulg...............Vulgate
Weiss, Dor.........Weiss, Dor Dor we-Dorshaw
Wellhausen, I. J. G.........Wellhausen, Israelitische und Jüdische Geschichte
Winer, B. R........Winer, Biblisches Realwörterbuch
Wisdom.............Wisdom of Solomon
Wolf, Bibl. Hebr...Wolf, Bibliotheca Hebræa
W. Z. K. M.........Wiener Zeitschrift für die Kunde des Morgenlandes
Yad................Yadayim (Talmud)
"Yad"..............Yad ha-Ḥazaḳah
Yalḳ...............Yalḳuṭ
Yeb................Yebamot (Talmud)
Yer................Yerushalmi (Jerusalem Talmud)
YHWH...............Yahweh, Jehovah
Zab................Zabim (Talmud)
Z. D. M. G........Zeitschrift der Deutschen Morgenländischen Gesellschaft
Z. D. P. V.........Zeitschrift des Deutschen Palästina-Vereins
Zeb................Zebaḥim (Talmud)
Zedner, Cat. Hebr. Books Brit.Mus. Zedner, Catalogue of the Hebrew Books in the British Museum
Zeit. für Assyr....Zeitschrift für Assyriologie
Zeit. für Hebr. Bibl.Zeitschrift für Hebräische Bibliographie
Zeitlin, Bibl. Post-Mendels........Zeitlin, Bibliotheca Hebraica Post-Mendelssohniana
Zunz, G. S.........Zunz, Gesammelte Schriften
Zunz, G. V.........Zunz, Gottesdienstliche Vorträge
Zunz, Literaturgesch..........Zunz, Literaturgeschichte der Synagogalen Poesie
Zunz, Ritus......Zunz, Die Ritus des Synagogalen Gottesdienstes
Zunz, S. P.........Zunz, Synagogale Poesie des Mittelalters
Zunz, Z. G.........Zunz, Zur Geschichte und Literatur

CONTRIBUTORS TO VOLUME VIII

A.............**Cyrus Adler, Ph.D.,**
President of the American Jewish Historical Society; President of the Board of Directors of the Jewish Theological Seminary of America; Librarian of the Smithsonian Institution, Washington, D. C.

A. B.........**A. Biram, Ph.D.,**
Berlin, Germany.

A. Bü........**Alexander Büchler, Ph.D.,**
Rabbi, Keszthely, Hungary.

A. Ep........**Abraham Epstein,**
Author of "Eldad ha-Dani" and of other works on rabbinical subjects; contributor of the article "Gaon" in Volume V.; Vienna, Austria.

A. Fe........**Alfred Feilchenfeld, Ph.D.,**
Principal of the Realschule, Fürth, Bavaria, Germany.

A. G.........**Adolf Guttmacher, Ph.D.,**
Rabbi, Baltimore, Md.

A. Ga......**Abraham Galante,**
Editor of "La Buena Esperanza," Smyrna, Asia Minor.

A. H. R.....**A. H. Rosenberg,**
New York City.

A. H. S......**A. H. Sayce, D.D., LL.D.,**
Professor of Assyriology, Oxford University, Oxford, England.

A. Ke........**A. Kecskemeti,**
Rabbi, Makow, Hungary.

A. Ki........**Alexander Kisch, Ph.D.,**
Rabbi, Prague, Bohemia, Austria.

A. L..........**Alfred Lévy,**
Chief Rabbi, Lyons, France.

A. M. F.....**Albert M. Friedenberg, B.S., LL.B.,**
Counselor at Law; Correspondent of "The Jewish Comment," Baltimore, Md.; New York City.

A. M. H.....**A. M. Hyamson,**
London, England.

A. P..........**A. Porter,**
Formerly Associate Editor of "The Forum," New York; Revising Editor "Standard Cyclopedia," New York City.

A. Pe........**A. Peiginsky, Ph.D.,**
New York City.

A. Pl.........**A. Plaut,**
Rabbi, Detmold, Lippe, Germany.

A. S. I........**Abram S. Isaacs, Ph.D.,**
Professor of German Literature, University of the City of New York, New York City.

A. S. W......**A. S. Waldstein, B. A.,**
New York City.

A. S. W. R..**A. S. W. Rosenbach,**
Philadelphia, Pa.

A. U.........**A. Ury,**
Chief Rabbi, Strasburg, Alsace, Germany.

A. V. W. J..**A. V. W. Jackson, Ph.D., Litt.D.,**
Professor of Indo-Iranian Languages, Columbia University, New York City.

A. W.........**Albert Wolf,**
Dresden, Saxony, Germany.

B. Ei........**Benzion Eisenstadt,**
New York City.

B. Fr........**B. Friedberg,**
Frankfort-on-the-Main, Germany.

B. L. B......**B. L. Benas,**
Liverpool, England.

C. D. S......**C. D. Spivak, M.D.,**
Denver, Col.

C. I. de S....**Clarence I. de Sola,**
President of the Federation of Canadian Zionists, Montreal, Canada.

C. L..........**Caspar Levias, M.A.,**
Instructor in Exegesis and Talmudic Aramaic, Hebrew Union College, Cincinnati, Ohio.

C. L. S.......**Cyrus L. Sulzberger,**
President of the Jewish Agricultural and Industrial Aid Society, New York City.

C. T..........**Charles Taylor, D.D., LL.D.,**
Master, St. John's College, Cambridge, England.

D.............**Gotthard Deutsch, Ph.D.,**
Professor of Jewish History, Hebrew Union College, Cincinnati, Ohio.

D. Ba........**David Bachrach,**
Baltimore, Md.

D. I. F.......**D. I. Freedman, B.A.,**
Rabbi, Perth, Western Australia.

D. P..........**David Philipson, D.D.,**
Rabbi, B'ne Israel Congregation; Professor of Homiletics, Hebrew Union College, Cincinnati, Ohio.

E. C..........**Executive Committee of the Editorial Board.**

E. G. H......**Emil G. Hirsch, Ph.D., LL.D.,**
Rabbi, Sinai Congregation; Professor of Rabbinical Literature and Philosophy, University of Chicago; Chicago, Ill.

E. I. N.......**E. I. Nathans,**
Philadelphia, Pa.

E. J..........**Emil Jelinek,**
Vienna, Austria.

E. K..........**Eduard König, Ph.D., LL.D.,**
Professor of Old Testament Exegesis, University of Bonn, Germany.

E. L..........**Eude Lolli,**
Chief Rabbi; Professor of Hebrew, University of Padua; Padua, Italy.

E. Ms.......**Edgar Mels,**
New York City.

E. N..........**Eduard Neumann, Ph.D.,**
Chief Rabbi, Nagy-Kanisza, Hungary.

E. N. S......**Elvira N. Solis,**
New York City.

E. Schr.....**E. Schreiber, Ph.D.,**
Rabbi, Emanu-El Congregation, Chicago, Ill.

E. Sd........**E. Schwarzfeld, LL.D.,**
Secretary of the Jewish Colonization Association, Paris, France.

E. Sl.........**E. Slijper,**
Rabbi, Amsterdam, Holland.

F. C..........**Frank Cramer, B.Sc.,**
New York City.

F. H. V......**Frank H. Vizetelly, F.S.A.,**
Associate Editor of the STANDARD DICTIONARY, and of the "Columbian Cyclopedia"; New York City.

F. K. S......**Frank Knight Sanders, Ph.D., D.D.,**
Professor of Biblical History and Archeology; Dean of the Divinity School, Yale University, New Haven, Conn.

F. L. C.....**Francis L. Cohen,**
Principal Rabbi, Sydney, N. S. W., Australia.

F. N. L......**Florence N. Levy,**
New York City.

F. T. H......**Frederick T. Haneman, M.D.,**
Brooklyn, N. Y.

G............**Richard Gottheil, Ph.D.,**
Professor of Semitic Languages, Columbia University, New York; Chief of the Oriental Department, New York Public Library; New York City.

G. A. B......**George A. Barton, Ph.D.,**
Professor of Biblical Literature and Semitic Languages, Bryn Mawr College, Bryn Mawr, Pa.

G. A. K......**George Alexander Kohut,**
Formerly Rabbi in Dallas, Texas; Assistant Librarian of the Jewish Theological Seminary of America, New York City.

G. D. R......**George D. Rosenthal,**
Electrical Engineer, St. Louis, Mo.

G. L.........**Goodman Lipkind, B.A.,**
Rabbi, New York City.

G. M.........**G. Margoliouth,**
Assistant Custodian, Oriental Department, British Museum, London, England.

G. Mo.......**Godfrey Morse,**
Counselor at Law, Boston, Mass.

G. W........**Gabriel Weiss,**
New York City.

G. We.......**Gotthold Weil,**
Berlin, Germany.

H. B.........**H. Brody, Ph.D.,**
Rabbi; Coeditor of the "Zeitschrift für Hebräische Bibliographie"; Nachod, Bohemia, Austria.

H. E. C.....**Herbert E. Choate,**
Athens, Ga.

H. G.........**Hubert Grimme, Ph.D.,**
Professor of Semitic Languages and Literature, University of Freiburg, Switzerland.

H. Gut.......**H. Guttenstein,**
New York City.

H. Hir.......**Hartwig Hirschfeld, Ph.D.,**
Professor, Jews' College, London, England.

H. M.........**Henry Malter, Ph.D.,**
Assistant Professor, Hebrew Union College, Cincinnati, Ohio.

H. P. M.....**H. Pereira Mendes, M.D., D.D.,**
President of the Union of Orthodox Congregations of the United States and Canada; Rabbi of the Spanish and Portuguese Congregation, New York City.

H. R.........**Herman Rosenthal,**
Chief of the Slavonic Department of the New York Public Library, New York City.

H. V.........**Hermann Vogelstein, Ph.D.,**
Rabbi, Königsberg, East Prussia, Germany.

I. A..........**Israel Abrahams,**
Reader in Rabbinic, University of Cambridge; Coeditor of "The Jewish Quarterly Review"; Cambridge, England.

I. Be.........**Immanuel Benzinger, Ph.D.,**
Professor of Old Testament Exegesis, University of Berlin, Germany; Jerusalem, Palestine.

I. Bl.........**I. Blumenstein, Ph.D.** (deceased),
Late Chief Rabbi of Luxemburg, Luxemburg.

I. Br.........**Isaac Broydé** (*Office Editor*),
Doctor of the University of Paris, France; formerly Librarian of the Alliance Israélite Universelle, Paris, France; New York City.

I. Co.........**I. Cohen,**
London, England.

I. D..........**Israel Davidson, Ph.D.,**
New York City.

I. Da.........**Israel Davis,**
Barrister at Law, London, England.

I. E..........**Ismar Elbogen, Ph.D.,**
Instructor ât the Lehranstalt für die Wissenschaft des Judenthums, Berlin, Germany.

I. G. D.......**I. George Dobsevage,**
New York City.

I. H..........**Isidore Harris, A.M.,**
Rabbi, West London Synagogue, London, England.

I. Kra........**I. Kracauer, Ph.D.,**
Frankfort-on-the-Main, Germany.

I. L. B.......**I. L. Bril,**
New York City.

I. Lev........**Isaac Lévy,**
Chief Rabbi, Bordeaux, France.

I. Lö.........**Immanuel Löw, Ph.D.,**
Chief Rabbi, Szegedin, Hungary.

I. M. C......**I. M. Casanowicz, Ph.D.,**
United States National Museum, Washington, D. C.

I. M. P......**Ira Maurice Price, Ph.D., LL.D.,**
Professor of Semitic Languages and Literature, University of Chicago, Chicago, Ill.

I. S. B.......**Isidor S. Beaumache,**
New York City.

I. Sch........**Isaac Schwab, Ph.D.,**
Rabbi, St. Joseph, Mo.

I. War.......**Isidor Warsaw,**
Rabbi, Woodville, Miss.

I. Zi..........**Izrael Ziony,**
New York City.

J..............**Joseph Jacobs, B.A.,**
Formerly President of the Jewish Historical Society of England; Corresponding Member of the Royal Academy of History, Madrid; New York City.

J. D. E......**J. D. Eisenstein,**
New York City.

J. F. McC...**J. Frederic McCurdy, Ph.D., LL.D.,**
Professor of Oriental Languages, University College, Toronto, Canada.

J. F. McL...**J. F. McLaughlin, M.A., B. D.,**
Professor of Oriental Languages and Literature, Victoria College, Toronto, Canada.

J. F. S.......**J. F. Schamberg, M.D.,**
Philadelphia, Pa.

J. G. L......**J. G. Lipman, Ph.D.,**
Assistant Agriculturist, New Jersey State Experiment Station, New Brunswick, N. J.

J. H. G......**Julius H. Greenstone,**
Rabbi, Philadelphia, Pa.

J. H. Ho....**J. H. Hollander, Ph.D.,**
Assistant Professor of Political Economy, Johns Hopkins University, Baltimore, Md.

J. H. M......**Julius H. Meyer,**
Milwaukee, Wis.

J. Hy........**J. Hyams,**
Bombay, India.

J. Ka........**Jacques Kahn,**
Rabbi, Paris, France.

J. L. La.....**J. L. Lait,**
Journalist, Chicago, Ill.

J. S..........**Joseph Silverman, D.D.,**
Formerly president of Central Conference of American Rabbis; Rabbi of Emanu-El Congregation, New York City.

J. So.........**Joseph Sohn,**
Contributor to "The New International Encyclopedia"; formerly musical critic on the New York "American and Journal"; New York City.

J. Sp.........**Jacob Spiro,**
Rabbi, Mährisch-Ostrau, Moravia, Austria.

J. S. R.......**J. S. Raisin,**
Rabbi, Gemilut Chesed Congregation, Fort Gibson, Miss.

J. T..........**J. Theodor, Ph.D.,**
Rabbi, Bojanowo, Posen, Germany.

J. Wo.......**Josef Wohlstein, Ph.D.,**
Rabbi, Malmö, Sweden.

J. Z. L.......**J. Z. Lauterbach, Ph.D.** (*Office Editor*),
Rabbi, New York City.

K..............**Kaufmann Kohler, Ph.D.,**
Rabbi Emeritus of Temple Beth-El, New York; President of the Hebrew Union College, Cincinnati, Ohio.

L. B..........**Ludwig Blau, Ph.D.,**
Professor, Jewish Theological Seminary; Editor of "Magyar Zsidó-Szemle," Budapest, Hungary.

L. C. H.......**L. C. Harby,**
New York City.

L. Er..........**L. Errera, Ph. D.,**
Professor of Plant-Anatomy, Plant-Physiology, and Botany, University of Brussels, Belgium.

L. G..........**Louis Ginzberg, Ph.D.,**
Professor of Talmud, Jewish Theological Seminary of America, New York City.

L. H. G.......**Louis H. Gray, Ph.D.,**
Assistant Editor of the "Orientalische Bibliographie"; formerly on the editorial staff of "The New International Encyclopedia"; Newark, N. J.

L. Hü.......**L. Hühner, A.M., LL.B.,**
Counselor at Law, New York City.

L. L..........**L. Löwenstein, Ph.D.,**
Rabbi, Mosbach, Baden, Germany.

L. La.........**Laura Landau,**
New York City.

L. M. F......**Leo M. Franklin, B.L.,**
Rabbi of Temple Beth-El, Detroit, Mich.

L. Mu.........**L. Munk, Ph.D.,**
Rabbi, Marburg, Germany.

L. N. D......**Lewis N. Dembitz, D.H.L.,**
Counselor at Law, Louisville, Ky.

L. V..........**Ludwig Venetianer, Ph.D.,**
Rabbi, Ujpest, Hungary.

L. Wy.......**L. Wygodsky,**
St. Petersburg, Russia.

M. A. N. L..**M. A. N. Lindo,**
London, England.

M. Bu........**Moses Buttenwieser, Ph.D.,**
Assistant Professor of Exegesis, Hebrew Union College, Cincinnati, Ohio.

M. Co........**Max Cohen,**
Counselor at Law, New York City.

M. Fi..........**Maurice Fishberg, M.D.,**
Surgeon to the Beth Israel Hospital Dispensary; Medical Examiner to the United Hebrew Charities, New York City.

M. Fr.........**M. Franco,**
Principal, Alliance Israélite Universelle School, Demotica, Rumelia, Turkey.

M. Frie......**M. Friedländer, Ph.D.,**
Vienna, Austria.

M. Gr........**M. Grunwald, Ph.D.,**
Rabbi, Vienna, Austria.

M. H. H.....**M. H. Harris, Ph.D.,**
New York City.

M. K..........**Meyer Kayserling, Ph.D.,**
Rabbi, Budapest, Hungary.

M. Kn........**M. Knafo,**
Rabbi, Mogador, Morocco.

M. L. B......**Moses Löb Bamberger, Ph.D.,**
Rabbi; Lecturer in Rabbinic, Jewish Seminary, Würzburg, Bavaria, Germany.

M. N.........**Max Nordau, M.D.,**
Paris, France.

M. R.........**Max Rosenthal, M.D.,**
Visiting Physician, German Dispensary, New York City.

M. Sa.........**Max Samfield, Ph.D.,**
Memphis, Tenn.

M. Sc.........**Max Schloessinger, Ph.D.,**
Librarian; Lecturer on Biblical Exegesis, Hebrew Union College, Cincinnati, Ohio.

M. Sel.......**Max Seligsohn** (*Office Editor*),
Doctor of the University of Paris, France; New York City.

M. W. L.....**Martha Washington Levy, B.A.,**
Contributor to "The New International Encyclopedia," New York City.

M. W. M....**Mary W. Montgomery, Ph.D.,**
New York City.

M. Z..........**M. Zametkin,**
New York City.

N. D..........**Newell Dunbar,**
Newark, N. J.

N. R..........**N. Rashkovski,**
Odessa, Russia.

N. Sl..........**N. Slouschz,**
Doctor of the University of Paris; Lecturer on Neo-Hebraic Literature, University of Paris, France.

N. T. L......**N. T. London,**
New York City.

O. J. S.......**O. J. Simon,**
London, England.

P. B..........**Philipp Bloch, Ph.D.,**
Rabbi, Posen, Germany.

P. Wi.........**Peter Wiernik,**
Journalist, New York City.

S.............**Isidore Singer, Ph.D.,**
Managing Editor, New York City.

S. B..........**Samuel Baeck, Ph.D.,**
Rabbi, Lissa, Posen, Germany.

S. Be.........**Simon Bernfeld, Ph.D.,**
Formerly Chief Rabbi of Servia; Berlin, Germany.

S. G..........**S. Gundelfinger, Ph.D.,**
Darmstadt, Germany.

S. Ho.........**S. Horovitz, Ph.D.,**
Professor, Jewish Theological Seminary, Breslau, Germany.

S. J...........**S. Janovsky,**
Counselor at Law, St. Petersburg, Russia.

S. J. L.......**S. J. Levinsohn,**
Brooklyn, N. Y.

S. K..........**S. Kahn,**
Rabbi, Nîmes, France.

S. Kr........**Samuel Krauss, Ph.D.,**
Professor, Normal College, Budapest, Hungary.

S. Led.......**Sampson Lederhändler,**
New York City.

S. M.........**S. Mendelsohn, Ph.D.,**
Rabbi, Wilmington, N. C.

S. Man......**S. Mannheimer, B.L.,**
Instructor, Hebrew Union College, Cincinnati, Ohio.

S. M. G......**S. M. Goldstein,**
Assistant Professor, Archeological Institute, St. Petersburg, Russia.

S. Mü........**S. Mühsam, Ph.D.,**
Chief Rabbi, Gratz, Styria, Austria.

S. Mün......**Sigmund Münz, Ph.D.,**
Vienna, Austria.

S. N. D......**S. N. Deinard,**
Minneapolis, Minn.

S. S..........**Solomon Schechter, M.A., Litt.D.,**
President of the Faculty of the Jewish Theological Seminary of America, New York City.

S. Sa.........**Sigismund Salfeld, Ph.D.,**
Rabbi, Mayence, Hesse, Germany.

S. Wo........**Simon Wolf,**
Counselor at Law; President, Independent Order B'nai B'rith, Washington, D. C.

T............. **Crawford Howell Toy, D.D., LL.D.,**
Professor of Hebrew, Harvard University, Cambridge, Mass.

U. C.........**Umberto Cassuto,**
Editor of "La Rivista Israelitica," Florence, Italy.

V. C.........**Vittore Castiglione,**
Chief Rabbi, Rome, Italy.

V. E..........**Victor Rousseau Emanuel,**
Laurel, Md.

W. B.........**Wilhelm Bacher, Ph.D.,**
Professor, Jewish Theological Seminary, Budapest, Hungary.

W. H. C..... **W. H. Cobb,**
Boston, Mass.

W. M........**William Milwitzky,**
Cambridge, Mass.

W. M. M....**W. Max Müller, Ph.D.,**
Professor of Bible Exegesis, Reformed Episcopal Theological Seminary, Philadelphia, Pa.

W. N........ **Wilhelm Nowack, Ph.D.,**
Professor of Old Testament Exegesis, University of Strasburg, Germany.

W. P..........**William Popper, M.A., Ph.D.,**
Gustav Gottheil Lecturer in Semitic Languages, Columbia University, New York City.

W. Pe........**W. Perkowski,**
New York City.

W. R.........**William Rosenau, Ph.D.,**
Rabbi of Eutaw Place Temple, Baltimore, Md.

W. Wi.......**W. Willner,**
Rabbi, Meridian, Miss.

Z. K..........**Zadoc Kahn,**
Chief Rabbi of France; Honorary President of the Alliance Israélite Universelle; Officer of the Legion of Honor; Paris, France.

LIST OF ILLUSTRATIONS IN VOLUME VIII

N. B.—In the following list subjects likely to be sought for under various headings are repeated under each heading. Cross-references in this list are to other items in the list, not to articles in the Encyclopedia.

THE
JEWISH ENCYCLOPEDIA

LEON (LEÃO): Spanish-Portuguese family having branches in Italy, Holland, Germany, England, southern France, the Orient, the West Indies, especially Jamaica, and Surinam.

1. Abraham Judah Leon: Assistant rabbi of the Spanish-Portuguese congregation in London from 1685 until his death in 1707.

BIBLIOGRAPHY: Gaster, *Hist. of Bevis Marks*, p. 40.

2. David de Isaac de Leon: Lived in Amsterdam in the eighteenth century. He published "Sermão da Boa Fama" (Amsterdam, 1767), an address in Portuguese delivered June, 1767; also some Hebrew verses in honor of his father's "Avizos Espirituaés," printed with that book.

3. Elijah de Leon: Son of **Michael Judah de Leon** (d. March 3, 1658) and nephew of Jacob Judah Leon. He was ḥakam of the benevolent society Gemilut Ḥasadim in Amsterdam and corrector for the press 1656–66. The Hebrew Bible printed by Joseph Athias in 1661 was corrected and provided with a preface by Elijah de Leon and Samuel de Caceres. Some Hebrew verses of Elijah's are given in the Spanish translation of the Psalms by his uncle Jacob Judah Leon.

BIBLIOGRAPHY: Steinschneider, *Cat. Bodl.* p. 2879 and cxxx.; Roest, *Cat. Rosenthal. Bibl.* Supplement, No. 2366; Kayserling, *Bibl. Esp.-Port.-Jud.* p. 37.

4. Isaac de Leon: Son of Eliezer ben Solomon ibn Zur; born probably in Spain; lived in Ancona; died there most likely. He was the author of "Megillat Esther"—a commentary on Moses b. Maimon's "Sefer ha-Miẓwot," written in the latter's defense against the attacks of Moses ben Naḥman (Venice, 1592; Amsterdam, 1660). He wrote also a rabbinical decision in the dispute between Solomon de Lolli and Jacob Catalano (Rome, 1546).

BIBLIOGRAPHY: Azulai, *Shem ha-Gedolim*, i. 105; Nepi-Ghirondi, *Toledot Gedole Yisrael*, p. 134; Fürst, *Bibl. Jud.* ii. 231 (who wrongly ascribes the decision to another Isaac de Leon); Zedner, *Cat. Hebr. Books Brit. Mus.* p. 383.

5. Isaac de Leon: Talmudist, and director of a Talmud school in Salonica about 1630 (Conforte, "Ḳore ha-Dorot," p. 46a).

6. Isaac de Leon: In conjunction with Samuel Athar, he published a collection of stories from the Midrashim and Haggadot (Venice, n.d.).

BIBLIOGRAPHY: Fürst, *Bibl. Jud.* ii. 232.

7. Isaac de Leon: Grammarian and teacher in Amsterdam. Together with Jacob de Solomon Hezekiah Saruco, he wrote "Avizos Espirituaés e Instrucçoéns Sagradas, para Cultivar o Engenho da Juventude no Amor e Temor Divino" (Amsterdam, 1766), containing twenty-four dialogues on Biblical history, the articles of faith, the ritual, the feast- and fast-days, and the special Sabbaths.

BIBLIOGRAPHY: Kayserling, *Bibl. Esp.-Port.-Jud.* p. 57.

8. Isaac (de) Leon Templo: Son of Solomon Raphael Judah Leon Templo; printer and publisher in Amsterdam 1727–38. He edited his father's "Masseket Halakah le-Mosheh mi-Sinai" (Amsterdam, 1734). See No. 20.

BIBLIOGRAPHY: Ersch and Gruber, *Encyc.* section II., part 28, p. 73; Kayserling, *Bibl. Esp.-Port.-Jud.* p. 59.

9. Jacob de Leon, and **(9a) Jacob Rodriguez de Leon:** Both probably of Amsterdam; lived in Jamaica, W. I., in 1698.

BIBLIOGRAPHY: *Publications Am. Jew. Hist. Soc.* v. 88.

10. Jacob Judah Aryeh Leon Templo: Ḥakam, translator of the Psalms, and heraldic expert; of Marano descent; son of Abraham de Leon; born in 1603 at Hamburg, where he taught Talmud for several years; died after 1675. He became ḥakam in Middelburg and, after 1643, in Amsterdam, where he was engaged also as teacher in the Talmud Torah. He vocalized the entire Mishnah which was printed in 1646 at the establishment of Manasseh ben Israel.

Jacob Judah caused a great stir by a plan, drawn by him, of Solomon's Temple, which was exhibited before Charles II. of England and of which the author published a short, comprehensive description in Spanish entitled "Retrato del Templo de Selomoh" (Middelburg, 1642). This was translated into Dutch in the same year; into French in 1643; and by himself into Hebrew in 1650, with the title "Tabnit Hekal." Duke August of Brunswick, and more particularly his wife Elizabeth, wished a German translation of this description and entrusted the task to Prof. Johann Saubert of Helmstädt. Some one else published such a translation in 1665, and Saubert therefore wrote a Latin translation in that year. An English version appeared in 1778, done by M. P. Decastro, a relative of Templo's, and in whose possession the plan was then held.

In 1647 Jacob Judah wrote "Tratado de la Arca del Testamento" (Amsterdam, 1653). His treatise on the cherubim, their form and nature, written in Latin in 1647, appeared in Spanish under the title "Tratado de los Cherubim" (Amsterdam, 1654); and his description of Moses' tabernacle, written in 1647 in Dutch, was published under the title "Retrato del Tabernaculo de Moseh" (Amsterdam, 1654), and in English (1675). His last work was a Spanish paraphrase of the Psalms, which was printed with the text, under the title "Las Alabanças de Santitad" (Amsterdam, 1671), and, as is stated in the introduction, was written in seven months. The work was dedicated to Isaac Senior Teixéyra, financial agent, in Hamburg, of Queen Christina of Sweden, and was extolled by many ḥakamim, scholars, and poets in Hebrew, Latin, and Spanish verses.

Jacob Judah wrote also a dialogue ("Colloquium Middelburgense") between a rabbi and a Christian scholar on the value of the Christian dogmas; and he left in manuscript "Disputaciones con Diferentes Theologos de la Cristiandad." He was a skilful draftsman. The coat of arms of the English Grand Lodge of Masons with the motto קדש ליהוה, now "Holiness to the Lord," is the work of the "famous and learned Hebrewist, architect, and brother, Rabi Jacob Jehudah Leon." He drew also more than 200 figures and vignettes to illustrate Talmudical subjects, which his son **Solomon** gave to Surenhusius for his Latin translation of the Mishnah.

Jacob Judah Aryeh Leon Templo.

BIBLIOGRAPHY: De Rossi-Hamberger, *Hist. Wörterb.* pp. 176 *et seq.*; Koenen, *Geschiedenis der Joden in Nederland*, p. 337; Jost, *Gesch. des Judenthums und Seiner Sekten*, iii. 233; Grätz, *Gesch.* x. 24, 200 *et seq.*; *Transactions Jew. Hist. Soc. Eng.* ii. 156 *et seq.*; Fürst, *Bibl. Jud.* ii. 232 *et seq.*; Kayserling, *Bibl. Esp.-Port.-Jud.* pp. 58 *et seq.*

11. Joseph de Leon: Rabbi in Jerusalem about 1587.

12. Joseph de Leon: Rabbi in Venice in 1694.

BIBLIOGRAPHY: Frumkin, *Eben Shemuel*, p. 73; Nepi-Ghirondi, *l.c.* p. 170.

13. Judah de Leon: Rabbi; died about 1830. He went to Rome about 1792 as emissary from Hebron, and at the desire of the community remained as rabbi. In 1811 he was chief rabbi of the Jewish consistory in Rome. Judah's is the first signature to a document protesting against the charge that religious reforms had been introduced into Italy. This document appeared in the "Letters of the Chief Rabbis in Italy" (Leghorn; German transl., Altona and Hamburg, 1796).

BIBLIOGRAPHY: Nepi-Ghirondi, *l.c.* p. 166; Vogelstein and Rieger, *Gesch. der Juden in Rom*, ii. 400 *et seq.*; Zedner, *Cat. Hebr. Books Brit. Mus.* p. 394.

14. Judah Ḥayyim Leão (Leon): Ḥakam and leader in prayer in the synagogue of the Portuguese community in Hamburg. After forty years of active service he was pensioned in 1656, and his son-in-law, Isaac Namias, was appointed his successor.

BIBLIOGRAPHY: Grunwald, *Portugiesengräber auf Deutscher Erde*, p. 106.

15. M. (P.) de Leon: Lived in Surinam. In collaboration with others, he wrote in 1791 "Geschiedenis der Kolonie van Suriname" (Amsterdam, 1791; 2d ed. *ib.* 1802).

BIBLIOGRAPHY: *Publications Am. Jew. Hist. Soc.* iv. 6.

16. Manuel de Leon (Leão): Marano; writer of Spanish and Portuguese poems; born in Leiria; died in Amsterdam after 1712. His published works are: "Triumpho Lusitano Aplausos Festivos . . . Nos Augustos Desposorios do Inclyto D. Pedro Segundo com a Ser. Maria Sofia Isabel de Baviera, Monarcas de Portugal" (Brussels, 1688), a poem consisting of ninety-three verses, with a description of festivities held at Lisbon Oct. 11–25, 1687, and dedicated to D. Geronimo Nuñez da Costa, Portuguese agent in Amsterdam; "El Duelo de los Aplausos, y Triumpho de los Triumphos, Retrato de Guilielmo III., Monarcha Britanico" (The Hague, 1691); "Examen de Obrigaçoens. Testifica hum Filho, que os Pays Engendrão, Amão, Doutrinão os Filhos por Dependencia. Discursos Morales Deduzidos da Sagrada Escritura" (Amsterdam, 1712); "Gryfo Emblematico, Enigma Moral. Dedicado a Diego de Chaves" (*ib.* 1712). His "Certamen de las Musas en los Desposorios de Francisco Lopes Suasso, Barão de Auverne" is extant in manuscript in Amsterdam.

BIBLIOGRAPHY: Barbosa Machado, *Bibl. Lusit.* iii. 293; Kayserling, *Sephardim*, pp. 315 *et seq.*; idem, *Bibl. Esp.-Port.-Jud.* p. 57.

17. Meïr de Leon: Lived in Amsterdam; translated Verga's "Shebeṭ Yehudah" into Spanish under the title "La Vara de Juda" (Amsterdam, 1640; 2d ed. *ib.* 1744).

18. Samuel de Leon (Lião): Member of the college Keter Torah in Amsterdam. He was the author of the "Questoins [Questões] com Suas Repostas, que Propor na Academia de Queter Tora," Hamburg, 1679, and of a writing preserved in manuscript, under the title "Libro de Diversas Questoins e Suas Repostas, Comp. por my . y Respond. em Yesiba."

BIBLIOGRAPHY: Steinschneider, *Catalog der Hebräischen Handschriften in der Stadtbibliothek zu Hamburg*, p. 167; Kayserling, *Bibl. Esp.-Port.-Jud.* p. 59.

19. Samuel Judah Leon Templo: Brother of Solomon Raphael Judah (No. 20), mentioned by

Daniel Levi de Barrios. In 1682 he was teacher at the school, founded by Abraham da Fonseca, of the society Maskil el Dal in Amsterdam.

20. Solomon Raphael Judah Leon Templo: Ḥakam, preacher, and press-corrector in Amsterdam; died *c.* 1733. He was a son of Jacob Judah Leon (No. 10); and a pupil of Isaac Aboab da Fonseca. Together with David Nuñes Torres, he corrected the enlarged edition of Maimonides' "Yad ha-Ḥazaḳah" which appeared in Amsterdam in 1703. His published works include, besides several sermons in Portuguese: "Resit Hohmá, Principio da Sciencia, ou Grammatica Hebrayca por hum Methodo Breve, Facil e Distincto para Uzo das Escolas" (*ib.* 1703); "Orden de las Oraciones y Rogativas Compuestas para Pedir Piedades Sobre las Enfermedades. Traduzido por Selomoh R. J. Leon Templo" (*ib.* 1727).

After his death his son Isaac published a little book by him entitled "Masseket Halakah le-Mosheh mi-Sinai" (Amsterdam, 1734), on the hermeneutical rules of the Talmud, at the end of which the regulations for the Passover feast are given in rimes of four lines.

Bibliography: Kayserling, *Bibl. Esp.-Port.-Jud.* p. 58.

D. M. K.

LEON DE BAGNOLS. See Levi b. Gershon.

LEON, DAVID CAMDEN DE: American physician and surgeon; born in South Carolina in 1813; died at Sante Fé, N. M., Sept. 3, 1872; brother of Edwin de Leon. He was educated in South Carolina and at the University of Pennsylvania (M.D. 1836). Shortly after graduation he entered the United States army as assistant surgeon (1838) and served with distinction in the Seminole war. For several years afterward he was stationed on the Western frontier. He served throughout the Mexican war, and was present at most of the battles. At Chapultepec he earned the sobriquet of "the Fighting Doctor," and on two occasions led a charge of cavalry after the officer commanding had been killed or wounded. For his distinguished services and for his gallantry in action he twice received the thanks of Congress. He was then assigned to frontier duty, and in 1856 he became surgeon, with the rank of major.

De Leon was personally opposed to secession; but, like most Southern officers in the regular army, he resigned his commission at the outbreak of the Civil war and tendered his services to the Confederacy. De Leon organized the medical department for the Confederate government and was its first surgeon-general. At the close of the war he went to Mexico, but soon returned to New Mexico, where he had been stationed for several years, and where he owned property. He continued in practise there until his death. He was a man of considerable general culture and was esteemed as a writer.

Bibliography: *American Annual Encyc.* 1872, p. 627, New York, 1873; *Appleton's Cyclopedia of American Biog.* New York, 1894; Wolf, *The American Jew as Patriot, Soldier, and Citizen*, p. 114, New York, 1895; *idem*, in *Publ. Am. Jew. Hist. Soc.* p. 34; *American Biography*, iii., New York; Lamb, *Biog. Dict. of U. S.* edited by John H. Brown, ii. 416, Boston, 1900.

A. L. Hü.

LEON, EDWIN DE: American diplomat and journalist; born at Columbia, S. C., 1818; died in 1891; brother of David Camden de Leon. His father, a physician, removed to Columbia, S. C., and was mayor of that city for several years. De Leon graduated from South Carolina College and studied law, but soon turned to literature and politics. He became an active collaborator on the "Southern Review," the "Magnolia," the "Southern Literary Messenger," and other periodicals. Removing to Savannah, Ga., he took editorial charge of the "Savannah Republican" and made it a political factor in the state; his next charge was the Columbia (S. C.) "Telegraph," a daily.

At the invitation of a committee of Southern members of Congress, De Leon established, in Washington, D. C., "The Southern Press," which soon became the organ of the Southern people and secured a large circulation during the early fifties. For his services during the Pierce campaign, that president appointed him consul-general to Egypt, which position he filled for two terms with marked success. At the commencement of the Crimean war, an order was issued by the Porte expelling all Greeks from the Ottoman dominion. The Greeks in Egypt appealed to De Leon, who took them under the protection of the American flag, guaranteed their good behavior, and insisted that they should not be interfered with. The home government approved his course, and Congress paid him the compliment of ordering the printing of his despatches. The King of Greece tendered him the grand cross of the Order of San Sauveur, but Leon declined on the ground that it was antirepublican.

De Leon rendered conspicuous services in protecting American missionaries at Jaffa, and for this he received for the second time the thanks of the State Department. Through his influence American commerce with Egypt was largely extended and American machinery introduced into that country. It was during his incumbency of the consul-generalship that he heard of the secession of his native state from the Union. He at once forwarded his resignation. Returning home, he ran the blockade and made his way to New Orleans. Thence he proceeded to Richmond and reported to Jefferson Davis, volunteering for military duty. Davis sent him instead on a confidential mission to Europe to secure the recognition of the Southern Confederacy by foreign powers. De Leon refused any salary or remuneration for his services, but advanced from his own purse considerable sums for the use of the Confederacy. He again ran the blockade, reached Nassau, and arrived in England in July, 1862. As diplomatic agent he was received in the highest circles, both in England and in France, and personally pleaded the cause of the Confederacy with Lord Palmerston and the emperor Napoleon.

His despatches to the Southern government were intercepted, however, and were published by order of Lincoln's secretary of state, Seward.

Through his friend Thackeray, De Leon became a member of the Garrick Club and a contributor to the "Cornhill Magazine." After the Civil war De Leon returned to America and settled in New York. He frequently contributed to the leading magazines, chiefly on Eastern topics. Among his works are: "Thirty Years of My Life on Three Continents";

"The Khedive's Egypt"; "Under the Star and Under the Crescent"; "Askaros Kassis, the Copt," a novel, republished in England.

BIBLIOGRAPHY: *American Biography*, iii., New York; Oscar Fay Adams, *A Dictionary of American Authors*, p. 95, New York, 1901; Lamb, *Biog. Dict. of U. S.* edited by John H. Brown, ii. 416, Boston, 1900; Allibone, *Dict. of Authors*, suppl. vol., p. 473.

A. L. Hü.

LEON JOSEPH OF CARCASSONNE: Physician; lived toward the end of the fourteenth century and at the beginning of the fifteenth. He devoted himself to the translation from the Latin into Hebrew of medical works. Among his numerous translations three are still extant in manuscript: (1) a commentary on the ninth book (Pathology) of Razi by Gerard de Solo; (2) "Meyashsher ha-Mathilim," a manual of medicine by Gerard de Solo; (3) a chapter on the relation between astronomy and medicine, attributed to Hippocrates.

BIBLIOGRAPHY: Steinschneider, *Cat. Munich*, p. 209; idem, *Hebr. Uebers.* p. 794; idem, *Hebr. Bibl.* viii. 48; Renan-Neubauer, *Les Ecrivains Juifs Français*, pp. 424 *et seq.*; Gross, *Gallia Judaica*, p. 616.

G. I. Br.

LEON, LEONTIN. See Judah ben Meïr ha-Kohen.

LEON HA-LEVI: Provençal Jew who wrote a Purim parody under the pseudonym **Labi ha-Levi** because he feared that the Orthodox Jews would condemn his work. The treatise, called "Megillat Setarim," on "Midrash ha-Nabi ha-Labi ha-Lewi" (Venice, 1552), contains three sections, entitled respectively "Pereḳ Ḥabaḳbuḳ," "Hakkol Ḥayyabin," and "Mi-she-Niknas Adar," and is similar in plan to a Talmud treatise with so-called Rashi and Tosafot. It is full of humor. Another work of his, "Sefer Ḥabaḳbuḳ" (*ib.* 1552), is a parody of the Pentateuch and the prophetic style, representing a contest between "Karmi" (wine) and "Be'eri" (water). This work was likewise intended for Purim.

BIBLIOGRAPHY: Benjacob, *Oẓar ha-Sefarim*, p. 202; Fürst, *Bibl. Jud.* ii. 215; idem, *Die Purim-Literatur*, in *Orient, Lit.* 1849, p. 157; Sommerhausen, *Die Purimliteratur*, *ib.* 1850, p. 851; Steinschneider, *Cat. Bodl.* col. 580; idem, *Purim und Parodie*, in *Israelietische Letterbode*, vii. 7, No. 18.

G. M. L. B.

LÉON LÉVY BRUNSWICH (LHÉRIE). See Brunswich, Léon Lévy.

LEON, MESSER DAVID BEN MESSER (known also as **David ben Judah**): Italian rabbi; flourished in the fifteenth and sixteenth centuries. He studied at Naples in the school of his father, Messer Leon, author of "Libnat ha-Sappir," and received at the age of eighteen his rabbinical diploma from German and French Talmudic authorities. Soon afterward he went to Padua, where he studied under Judah Minz, who granted him a new rabbinical diploma. He then betook himself to Turkey, and while sojourning at Salonica, where he prepared for publication his "'En ha-Ḳore," he was called to the rabbinate of Avlona at a salary of 70 florins a year. The community possessed three congregations of various nationalities, and Leon officiated successively in the three synagogues on every third Saturday. In the very first year of his rabbinate dissensions on account of a ritual question arose which caused the separation of the Portuguese and Catalonian Jews from the Castilians. Toward the end of his second year in Avlona a quarrel broke out among the Sephardim and the Portuguese. Leon, who sided with the Portuguese, had for antagonists Abraham Ḥarbon and Abraham de Collier. Excommunications were launched by both parties even on the Day of Atonement.

Leon was a prolific writer, and produced works in many branches of secular science, as well as on distinctively Jewish subjects. With the exception of two, all remained unpublished. Most of them are no longer extant, and are known only from quotations. Leon preferred to clothe his philosophy in the garb of the Cabala, in which he was an adept; but he was too much of a philosopher to become involved in the abysses of mysticism. In his cabalistic work "Magen Dawid," still extant in manuscript, he freely quotes the Greek and the Arabic philosophers. For him Plato was the greatest cabalist. This philosopher, Leon claimed, lived at the time of the prophet Jeremiah, who was his teacher.

His Works.

Leon wrote also the following works: "Abir Ya'aḳob," on medicine and other sciences; "Sefer ha-Derashot," sermons arranged in the order of the sections of the Pentateuch (according to Neubauer, it is identical with the "Tif'eret Adam" quoted in Leon's commentary on Lamentations); "Menorat ha-Zahab," also extant in manuscript, probably a haggadic commentary on Lamentations; "'En ha-Ḳore," a commentary on the "Moreh Nebukim," criticizing the commentary of Isaac Abravanel; "Miktam le-Dawid," a cabalistic work mentioned in the "'En ha-Ḳore"; "Sod ha-Gemul," in which he shows that the Israelites, unlike other nations, are not under a special sign of the zodiac; refutations of Albo's criticisms of Aristotle; "Shebaḥ ha-Nashim," still extant in manuscript (according to Steinschneider, "Hebr. Bibl." xix. 83, identical with the commentary on Prov. xxxi.); "Tehillah le-Dawid" (published by the author's grandson Aaron le-Bet David, Constantinople, 1577), in three parts: (1) on the excellence of the Law; (2) on the elements of faith, which latter is superior to speculative reasoning; (3) on the principles of God, the divine attributes, providence, free will, etc.; a halakic decision on the ritual question which caused the division of the various congregations of Avlona, published by S. Bernfeld, under the title "Kebod Ḥakamim," Berlin, 1899 (Meḳiẓe Nirdamim).

Leon was considered as a high Talmudic authority, and was consulted on halakic questions. Two of his decisions have been preserved (Elijah Mizraḥi, Responsa, No. 47; Neubauer, "Cat. Bodl. Hebr. MSS." No. 834). In one of his works Leon mentions a commentary of his own on Moses of Coucy's "Sefer Miẓwot Gadol" ("Semag"). Parma MS. de Rossi No. 1395 ("Cat. Perreau," No. 19) contains a scientific treatise by Leon. In the introduction to this treatise Leon says that he wrote many poems in Hebrew and in the "Christian language," meaning thereby Latin or Italian. Shabbethai Bass, without indicating any source, gives, in his "Sifte Yeshenim," the following titles of works attributed to Leon: "Bet Dawid"; "Kisse Dawid"; "Nefesh Dawid"; "Ḳol Adonai ba-Koaḥ"; and "Naḥal 'Adanim."

BIBLIOGRAPHY: Rossi, *Dizionario*, s.v.; Nepi-Ghirondi, *Toledot Gedole Yisrael*, p. 78; Steinschneider, *Cat. Bodl.* col. 867; idem, *Hebr. Bibl.* viii. 64; *idem*, in *Letterbode*, xii. 57 *et seq.*; Neubauer, *ib.* x. 10b *et seq.*; Schechter, in *R. E. J.* xxiv. 118 *et seq.*; Michael, *Or ha-Ḥayyim*, No. 727; Carmoly, *Histoire des Médecins Juifs*, § ciii.; S. Bernfeld, introduction to *Kebod Ḥakamim*.

G. I. Br.

LEON (JUDAH ARYEH) OF MODENA: Italian scholar, rabbi, and poet; son of Isaac of Modena and Diana Rachel; born April 23, 1571, at Venice; died there March 24, 1648. He was a descendant of a prominent French family. His grandfather **Mordecai** became distinguished both as a physician and as a philanthropist, and was raised by Charles V. to the rank of Knight of the Order of the Golden Fleece. Leon was a precocious child. His father, who was then in good circumstances, gave him a complete education, not neglecting even such worldly accomplishments as singing and dancing. Leon's masters were successively Azriel Bassola, Hezekiah Galico, Hezekiah Finzi, and Samuel Archevolti. At the age of twelve Leon translated into Hebrew verse the first canto of Ariosto's "Orlando Furioso," and about a year and a half later he wrote his dialogue against gambling, which passed through ten editions and was translated into Latin, French, German, and Judæo-German. Even at this early age he was not only well versed in Hebrew and rabbinical literature, but was conversant with the classics and possessed a fair knowledge of mathematics, philosophy, and natural history.

There was, however, one thing that nature had denied to this highly gifted youth—a stable character. Like all poets, he lived upon his emotions. By the irony of fate, Leon, who had fulminated against gambling, developed a passion for all games of hazard, and, being too weak to overcome it, attributed the fault to the astral influences under which he had been born. This passion, which is probably accountable for his inconsistencies, had a large share in the misfortunes which filled his life. He had scarcely reached maturity when his father became impoverished, and Leon had to seek his own livelihood. In 1590 he married, and won a living by teaching. After the death of his father, in 1592, he settled at Venice, where he was appointed (1594) member of the rabbinate and preacher. In the latter capacity he was especially successful; his addresses in Italian attracted large audiences, including Christian priests and noblemen. Leon's successes as an orator and poet won for him the consideration of the Christian scholastic world, and admitted him to the highest Venetian circles. He had among his pupils Louis Eselin (a nobleman of the French court), the Archbishop of Lodève, John Plantanit, Jacob Gaffarelli, and Giulio Morosini.

Besides preaching and teaching, Leon exercised not less than twenty-six professions (press-corrector, notary, bookseller, etc.); but all his resources were swallowed up in gaming, and his material condition was rendered thereby a source of perpetual anxiety. To his monetary troubles was added a series of family disasters. Of his three sons, **Mordecai,** who was endowed with great ability, died at the age of twenty-six; **Zebulon** was killed in a brawl with his comrades; the third, **Isaac,** after having led a life of dissipation, emigrated to Brazil, and was never thereafter heard from. Of his two daughters, one died during his lifetime; the second lost her husband, and she and her family became thereby dependent upon Leon for support. In 1641 Leon's wife became insane, and remained in that state until her death. Amid all these trials Leon continued to study, write books, compose poems, relieve the distresses of others, so far as that was in his power, and—gamble. This last occupation involved him, in 1631, in a struggle with the leaders of the community, who launched an excommunication against any that should play cards, or take part in any other game of hazard, within the period of six years. On this occasion Leon wrote a brilliant dissertation, in which he demonstrated that the leaders had acted against the Law; the excommunication was accordingly revoked.

Family Misfortunes.

Leon of Modena.

The community of Venice in the seventeenth century must have been animated by a spirit of tolerance, for Leon continued to remain a member of the rabbinate until his death, although no doubt could be entertained as to his anti-Talmudic sympathies after the publication, in 1635, of his "Bet Yehudah" (known also under the title "Ha-Boneh"). This work contains all the haggadot omitted by the "'En Ya'aḳob"; in the accompanying commentary Leon points out the differences between the religious customs of the Jews of Palestine and of those living in other countries, showing thereby that the rabbis and scholars of any period have the right to modify Talmudic institutions (Shab. i.). He derides the haggadot, although he concedes that some of them contain salutary moral teachings. In the "Bet Yehudah," Leon went no further than to show his preference for religious reform; but he attacked traditional Judaism in a pseudonymous work entitled "Ḳol Sakal"; this work, either because in the meantime he had actually changed his views, or because he desired more thoroughly to conceal its authorship, he later endeavored to refute in another work entitled "Sha'agat Aryeh," which remained unfinished.

The "Ḳol Sakal" comprises three treatises, subdivided into chapters. In the first treatise the author deals with the existence of God, the Creation, the purpose of the world, reward and punishment, and the divine origin of the Law. In the second treatise he criticizes rabbinical interpretation of the Law. He contends that, like the Karaites, the Rabbis often followed the letter of the Law to the neglect of its spirit. He asserts that the use of phylacteries is not commanded by Biblical law; that the operation of circumcision is not performed in the manner pre-

Attacks Traditionalism.

scribed; and that rabbinical interpretation is often in direct opposition to the Law. That there was no traditional interpretation before Antigonus is seen from the existence of various sects during the time of the Second Temple. The third treatise enumerates the laws which must be reformed in order to bring the later Judaism into harmony with the Law, and render it spiritual and Biblical. The author proposes the simplification of the prayers and synagogal service, the abolition of many rites, the relaxation of Sabbath festivals, of Passover, and even of the ritual of the Day of Atonement. Fasting should not be carried beyond the ordinary physical and spiritual powers of the individual concerned. The dietary laws should be abrogated, or at least simplified; the prohibition against drinking wine with those of other creeds, obedience to which exposed Jews to derision, should be abolished.

The "Ḳol Sakal" and "Sha'agat Aryeh" were published by Isaac Reggio under the title "Beḥinat ha-Ḳabbalah" (Göritz, 1852). A discussion arose at the time of its appearance as to whether the "Ḳol Sakal" was written by Leon himself or whether, as is pretended in the "Sha'agat Aryeh," it proceeded from a certain Amittai ibn Raz of Alkala. It has even been suggested with some plausibility that both these works, instead of being written by Leon, were merely attributed to him by I. S. Reggio (see Deutsch, "Theory of Oral Tradition," p. 39; "Epochs of Jewish History," pp. 23 *et seq.*, New York, 1894). But a comparison between the ideas expressed by Leon in his "Bet Yehudah" and elsewhere and those expounded in the "Ḳol Sakal" leaves little doubt as to his authorship. Indeed, several of the criticisms, as, for instance, those concerning circumcision and the second day of festivals, are found expressed in the same terms in Leon's "Magen we-Ẓinnah" (published by A. Geiger, Breslau, 1856), which contains answers to eleven objections to the rabbinical interpretation of the Law brought, according to Leon, by a Marano of Hamburg.

Attacks Cabala.

Though brilliantly written, these works are of comparatively little value; neither criticisms nor refutations are profound enough to survive thorough investigation. Far superior is Leon's "Ari Nohem" (published by Fürst, Leipsic, 1840), which contains an attack upon the Cabala. It is divided into three parts, comprising altogether thirty-one chapters. Leon first demonstrates that Cabala can not be considered as a science, and then shows that the Zohar, on which it is based, is a modern composition. In addition to the works cited, Leon wrote:

Sur me-Ra'. A dialogue between Eldad and Medad on games of hazard. Venice, 1596; Prague, 1615; Leyden, 1656. Translated into Latin by Aug. Pfeifer (Wittenberg, 1665) and by Thomas Hyde (Oxford, 1698, 1702, 1767); into German, with the Hebrew title "Ẓaḥḳan Mellumad we-Mithareṭ," by Fr. Abb. Christiani (Leipsic, 1683; Frankfort-on-the-Main, 1713; Fürth, 1723); into Judæo-German, with the Hebrew title "Ẓaḥḳan Mussari," by Asher Anshel (Amsterdam, 1698); into French by Carmoly (Paris, 1841).

Sod Yesharim. One hundred enigmas and remedies. Venice, 1594; Verona, 1647; Amsterdam, 1649; Frankfort-on-the-Main, 1702. Another edition gives neither date nor place of publication.

Ẓemaḥ Ẓaddiḳ. An ethical work, translated from the Latin, with moral sayings taken from Bible and Talmud. Venice, 1600; Wilna, 1855; New York, 1899.

Midbar Yehudah. Twenty-one sermons. Venice, 1602.

Galut Yehudah. Explanations, in Italian, of all the difficult expressions found in the Bible, in the sayings of the Fathers, and in the Haggadah of Passover; preceded by a number of grammatical rules. Venice, 1612. Republished at Padua and Venice in 1640, with an Italian-Hebrew vocabulary entitled "Pi Aryeh."

Leb Aryeh. A method of mnemonics applicable in all sciences, with the 613 commandments according to Maimonides. Venice, 1612; Wilna, 1886.

Bet Leḥem Yehudah. An index of the sources of all the passages found in the "'En Ya'aḳob." Venice, 1625; Prague, 1705.

Ẓebi Esh. An abridgment of Isaac Abravanel's commentary on the Haggadah of Passover, with an Italian translation. Venice, 1629, 1664, 1695; Sulzbach, 1774, 1834; with a German translation, Fürth, 1804.

Tefillot Yesharim. Prayers and seliḥot for all occasions.

Ben Dawid. Controverting the doctrine of metempsychosis. Included by Eliezer Ashkenazi in the "Ṭa'am Zeḳenim." Frankfort-on-the-Main, 1855.

Magen wa-Ḥereb. Attacks upon Christian dogmas. Published in part, together with the "Magen we-Ẓinnah," by A. Geiger, Breslau, 1856.

Ha-Abot bi-Yehudah. Commentary on the Pirḳe Abot.

Commentaries on the Pentateuch, the Five Scrolls, the books of Samuel, Proverbs, and the Passover Haggadah.

Rashi's commentaries on Proverbs and the books of Job and Daniel. Included in the "Biblia Rabbinica."

Pitron ha-Millot. Explanations of the special terms used in logic and philosophy.

Ḥibbur. Models of Hebrew composition; a Hebrew translation of Ecclesiastes and the books of Maccabees, etc.

Derashot. Four hundred sermons.

Commentary on the Hafṭarot.

Mibḥar Yehudah. The nature of the work is unknown.

Pesaḳim. Halakic decisions on synagogal music. Venice, 1605; Vienna, 1861. Published as a supplement to "Ben Chananja," 1861, No. 27. On the excommunication launched by the leaders of the community of Venice against all games of hazard. Venice, 1631. Contained also in "Paḥad Yiẓḥaḳ," *s.v.* חרם. On the use of ordinary straps for phylacteries. Included in the responsa "Debar Shemuel," of Samuel Aboab, No. 19.

Leḳeṭ Yehudah. Collection of halakic consultations.

Shire Yehudah. Collection of Hebrew poems. Neubauer, "Cat. Bodl. Hebr. MSS." No. 2185.

Ḥayye Yehudah. Autobiography; published in part by Isaac Reggio, in the introduction to the "Beḥinat ha-Ḳabbalah," and in part by Geiger.

Historia dei Riti Ebraici, Vita e Osservanze degli Hebrei di Questi Tempi. Paris, 1637; Venice, 1638, 1673, 1678, 1687, 1715. Written, at the request of an English nobleman, for James I.; translated into English by Ed. Chilmead (London, 1650) and by S. Ockley (*ib.* 1707, 1753); into French by Recared Simon (Paris, 1671, 1681, 1710); into Dutch by Aug. Gedaret (Amsterdam, 1683); into Latin by J. Val. Grossgebauer (Frankfort-on-the-Main, 1693); into Hebrew, under the title "Shulḥan 'Aruk," by Solomon Rubin, with notes by A. Jellinek (Vienna, 1867).

Ziḳne Yehudah. Responsa, cited by Moses Ḥagiz in his "Leḳeṭ ha-Ḳemaḥ." It is, perhaps, identical with "Leḳeṭ Yehudah."

Oẓar ha-Ḥayyim. On the Cabala.

The following are of doubtful authorship: "Or Ṭob," explanations of difficult Hebrew words (Amsterdam, 1675 [Venice, 1681, under the title "Or Luz"; *ib.* 1701, under the title "Or Lusṭru"]), and "Parashot ha-Kesef," a commentary on four sections of the Pentateuch (Neubauer, "Cat. Bodl. Hebr. MSS." No. 2549). Steinschneider attributes also to Leon the work on chess entitled "Ma'adanne Melek." Leon edited a great number of works, which he provided with prefaces, poems, and approbations; and he assisted the musical composer Solomon de Rossi in the publication of his work on synagogal music.

BIBLIOGRAPHY: Azulai, *Shem ha-Gedolim*; De Rossi, *Dizionario*, p. 231; Geiger, *Leon de Modena*, Breslau, 1856; Luzzatto, *Iggarot*, i. 288-293; Joseph Almanzi, *Higgayon be-Kinor*, p. 70, Venice, 1839; Isaac Reggio, *Iggarot*, ii. 74 *et seq.*; idem, in *Kerem Ḥemed*, ii. 156-158; Jost's *Annalen*, 1841, p. 68; *Orient*, No. 5; Soave, in *Corriere Israelitico*, 1863-65; *idem*, in *Arch. Isr.* 1877, p. 73; Steinschneider, *Cat. Bodl.*

col. 1351; *idem*, in *Monatsschrift*, xliii. 311; Neubauer, in *Letterbode*, iii. 99–109; *idem*, in *R. E. J.* xxii. 84; Zunz, *Literaturgesch.* p. 427; Libowitz, *Rabbi Yehudah Aryeh Modena*, Vienna, 1896; 2d ed., New York, 1901; Simon Stern, *Der Kampf des Rabbiner's Gegen den Talmud*, Breslau, 1902; Michael, *Or ha-Ḥayyim*, pp. 439–444; Simonsen, in *Berliner's Festschrift*, pp. 337 *et seq.*; M. H. Friedländer, in *Oesterreichische Wochenschrift*, 1902, p. 87.

G. I. Br.

LEON, MOSES (BEN SHEM-ṬOB) DE: Cabalistic writer; author, or redactor, of the Zohar; born at Leon, Spain, about 1250; lived in Guadalajara, Valladolid, and Avila; died at Arevalo in 1305, while returning to his home. He was familiar with the philosophers of the Middle Ages and with the whole literature of mysticism, and knew and used the writings of Solomon ibn Gabirol, Judah ha-Levi, Maimonides, etc. He knew how to charm with brilliant and striking phrases without expressing any well-defined thought. He was a ready writer and wrote several mystical and cabalistic works in quick succession. In the comprehensive "Sefer ha-Rimmon," written in 1287 and still extant in manuscript, he treated from a mystical standpoint the objects and reasons for the ritual laws, dedicating the book to Levi ben Todros Abulafia. In 1290 he wrote "Ha-Nefesh ha-Ḥakamah," or "Ha-Mishḳal" (Basel, 1608, and frequently found in manuscript), which shows even greater cabalistic tendencies. In this work he attacks the philosophers of religion and deals with the human soul as "a likeness of its heavenly prototype," with its state after death, with its resurrection, and with the transmigration of souls. "Sheḳel ha-Ḳodesh" (written in 1292), another book of the same kind, is dedicated to Todros ha-Levi Abulafia. In the "Mishkan ha-'Edut," or "Sefer ha-Sodot," finished in 1293, he treats of heaven and hell, after the apocryphal Book of Enoch; also of atonement. He wrote as well a cabalistic explanation of the first chapter of Ezekiel.

Toward the end of the thirteenth century Moses de Leon wrote or compiled a cabalistic midrash to the Pentateuch full of strange mystic allegories, and ascribed it to Simeon ben Yoḥai, the great saint of the Tannaim. The work, written in peculiar Aramaic, is entitled "Midrash de R. Shimeon ben Yoḥai," better known as the Zohar. The book aroused due suspicion at the outset. The story runs that after the death of Moses de Leon a rich man from Avila offered the widow, who had been left without means, a large sum of money for the original from which her husband had made the copy, and that she then confessed that her husband himself was the author of the work. She had asked him several times, she said, why he had put his teachings into the mouth of another, but he had always answered that doctrines put into the mouth of the miracle-working Simeon ben Yoḥai would be a rich source of profit. Others believed that Moses de Leon wrote the book by the magic power of the Holy Name. At any rate the contents of the book have been accepted and approved by all cabalists, and can by no means be regarded as mere inventions and forgeries of Moses de Leon.

Bibliography: *Ahimaaz Chronicle*, ed. London, pp. 95 *et seq.*; Jellinek, *Moses b. Schem-Tob de Leon und Seine Verhältniss zum Sohar*, Leipsic, 1851; Grätz, *Gesch.* vii. 231 *et seq.*; Geiger, *Das Judenthum und Seine Geschichte*, iii. 75 *et seq.*, Breslau, 1871; De Rossi-Hamberger, *Hist. Wörterb.* p. 177; Steinschneider, *Cat. Bodl.* cols. 1852 *et seq.*; idem, *Hebr. Bibl.* x. 156 *et seq.*

K. M. K.

LEON, THOMAS COOPER DE: Lecturer, journalist, author, and playwright; brother of Edwin de Leon; born at Columbia, S. C., 1839. He served in the Confederate army from 1861 to 1865, and after the Civil war edited "The Mobile Register" (1877), and "The Gossip" and the "Gulf Citizen" (both Mobile papers; 1873–96). He is the author of a number of works, among them being "Creole and Puritan" (1889), "The Puritan's Daughter," and "Four Years in Rebel Capitals" (1893).

Bibliography: Lamb, *Biographical Dict. of the United States*, Boston, 1900; Allibone, *Dict. of Authors*, Supplement; *Who's Who in America*, 1903–5.

E. C. L. Hü.

LEON DI LEONE. See Judah Leon di Leone.

LEONE EBREO. See Judah Leone b. Isaac Sommo.

LEONTE (JUDAH) BEN MOSES: Roman rabbi; died in 1216. In the name of the community of Rome he sent a halakic decision to Judah ben Kalonymus of Speyer for approval ("Shibbole ha-Leḳeṭ," ii. 75; comp. Buber's introduction, note 87). The Roman manuscript Maḥzor contains eleven seliḥot which bear the signature of Leonte. One of these, beginning with אנהים במר אידתי, for the seventeenth day of Tammuz, is included in the Roman printed Maḥzor.

Bibliography: Azulai, *Shem ha-Gedolim*, p. 68; Zunz, *Literaturgesch.* p. 314; Vogelstein and Rieger, *Gesch. der Juden in Rom*, i. 372.

G. I. Br.

LEONTOPOLIS (Greek, Λεόντων πόλις = "lion city"): Place in the nome of Heliopolis, Egypt, situated 180 stadia from Memphis; famous as containing a Jewish sanctuary, the only one outside of Jerusalem where sacrifices were offered. Aside from a somewhat uncertain allusion of the Hellenist Artapanus (in Eusebius, "Præparatio Evangelica," ix. 23), only Josephus gives information of this temple (more explicitly in his "Antiquities" of the Jews than in his "Jewish War"). The Talmudic accounts are entirely confused. The establishment of a central sanctuary in Egypt was not due to the disorders that arose in Palestine under Antiochus IV., Epiphanes, to the desecration of the sanctuary at Jerusalem, to the supplanting of the legitimate family of priests by the installation of Alcimus, nor to the personal ambition of Onias IV., but to the vast extent of the Jewish diaspora in Egypt itself.

It would appear from the account of Josephus in the "Jewish War" (i. 1, § 1), and more especially from the fact that Onias is called in the same work (vii. 10, § 2) "the son of Simon," that the temple of Leontopolis was built by Onias III., who drove the sons of Tobias from Jerusalem, and who fled to Egypt, Syria's ancient rival, when Antiochus IV. attacked that city. But this account is contradicted by the story that Onias III. was murdered at Antioch in 171 B.C. (II Macc. iv. 33). Josephus' account in the "Antiquities" is therefore more probable, namely, that the builder of the temple was a son of the murdered Onias III., and that, a mere youth at the time of his father's death, he had fled to the court of Alexandria in consequence of the Syrian persecutions, perhaps because he thought that salvation would come to his people from Egypt ("Ant." xii. 5, § 1; *ib.* 9, § 7). Ptolemy VI. Philometor was King of Egypt at that time. He probably had not yet given up his claims to Cœle-Syria and Judea, and gladly gave refuge to such a prominent personage of the neighboring country. Onias now requested the king and his sister and wife, Cleopatra, to allow him to build a sanctuary in Egypt similar to the one at Jerusalem, where he would employ Levites and priests of his own race (*ib.* xiii. 3, § 1); and he referred to the prediction of the prophet Isaiah (Isa. xix. 19) that a Jewish temple would be erected in Egypt ("Ant." *l.c.*). Josephus then quotes two documents: Onias' letter to the royal couple, and the king's answer to Onias. Both of these, however, appear spurious, on the following grounds: Onias refers in his letter to his military exploits in Cœle-Syria and Phenicia, although it is not certain that the general Onias and the priest Onias are identical. His assertion that a central sanctuary is necessary because a multiplicity of temples causes dissension among the Jews evidences imperfect knowledge of the Jewish religious life; and, finally, his request for the ruined temple of the goddess Bubastis, because a sufficient supply of wood and sacrificial animals would be found there, seems unwise and improbable for a suppliant who must first obtain compliance with his principal request. It seems strange, furthermore, that in the second letter the pagan king points out to the Jewish priest that the proposed building of a temple is contrary to the law, and that he consents only in view of Isaiah's prophecy. Both letters were apparently written by a Hellenistic Jew. Only this can be stated as a fact, that the temple of Leontopolis was built on the site of a ruined temple of Bubastis, in imitation of the temple at Jerusalem, though smaller and less elaborate (*ib.* xiii. 3, § 3). The statement in "B. J." vii. 10, § 2 of Onias' argument that by the building of this temple the whole Jewish nation would be brought to turn from the Syrians to the Ptolemies seems very plausible, and may have given rise to the assertion made in the letters that there were dissensions among the Jews. The "fortress" (ὀχύρωμα) of the temple of Bubastis may be explained by the statement, which seems credible, that Onias built a fortress (φρούριον) around the temple in order to protect the surrounding territory, which now received the designation "Oneion" ("B. J." vii. 10, § 3).

Founded by Onias IV.

Spuriousness of the Onias Letters.

The Onias temple was not exactly similar to the Temple at Jerusalem, being more in the form of a high tower; and as regards the interior arrangement, it had not a candelabrum, but a hanging lamp. The building had a court (τέμενος) which was surrounded by a brick wall with stone gates. The king endowed the temple with large revenues (*ib.*)—a fact that may have suggested to the writer of the letters mentioned above the wealth of wood and sacrificial animals.

The reputation which the temple of Onias enjoyed is indicated by the fact that the Septuagint changes the phrase "city of destruction" (Isa. xix. 18) to "city of righteousness" (πόλις ἀσεδέκ). It may be taken for granted that the Egyptian Jews sacrificed frequently in the temple of Leontopolis, although at the same time they fulfilled their duty toward the Temple at Jerusalem, as Philo narrates that he himself did ("De Providentia," in Eusebius, *l.c.* viii. §§ 14, 64).

Sacrifices Made There.

In the Talmud the origin of the temple of Onias is narrated with legendary additions, there being two versions of the account (Men. 109b). It must be noted that here also Onias is mentioned as the son of Simon, and that Isaiah's prophecy is referred to. In regard to the Law the temple of Onias (בית חוניו, handed down in the name of Saadia Gaon as חוני״י) was looked upon as neither legitimate nor illegitimate, but as standing midway between the worship of YHWH and idolatry (Men. 109a; Tosef., Men. xiii. 12-14); the possibility of the priests of Onias being admitted to officiate at Jerusalem was explicitly stated, while one passage even expresses the view that sacrificial worship was permissible in the temple of Onias (Meg. 10a). The opinion was prevalent among the Rabbis that the temple of Onias was situated at Alexandria—an error that is repeated by all the chroniclers of the Middle Ages. This temple is also sometimes confounded with the Samaritan temple on Mount Gerizim ("Yuḥasin," ed. London, pp. 11b, 13b; Azariah dei Rossi, "Me'or 'Enayim," ed. Mantua, xxi. 89a; Gans, "Ẓemaḥ Dawid," ed. Offenbach, ii. 10; Heilprin, "Seder ha-Dorot," ed. Warsaw, 1891, i. 116).

According to Josephus, the temple of Leontopolis existed for 343 years, though the general opinion is that this number must be changed to 243. It was closed either by the governor of Egypt, Lupus, or by his successor, Paulinus, about three years after the destruction of the Temple at Jerusalem; and the sacrificial gifts, or rather the interior furnishings, were confiscated for the treasury of Vespasian ("B. J." vii. 10, § 4), the emperor fearing that through this temple Egypt might become a new center for Jewish rebellion. No ruins have so far been discovered of this temple, once so famous; perhaps the present Tell al-Yahudi marks its site (Ebers, "Durch Gosen zum Sinai," pp. 497 *et seq.*).

BIBLIOGRAPHY: Grätz, *Gesch.* 4th ed., iii. 27 *et seq.*; Weiss, *Dor*, i. 130; Willrich, *Juden und Griechen*, pp. 146-150; Schürer, *Gesch.* 3d ed., iii. 97; Büchler, *Tobiaden und Oniaden*, pp. 239-276, Vienna, 1899 (this author's opinion, that originally a Samaritan temple was referred to, is not tenable).

G. S. KR.

LEOPARD (Heb. "namer"): A ferocious carnivorous mammal. Several allusions are found in the Old Testament to this animal and its characteristics; *e.g.*, its fierceness, Isa. xi. 6; its agility and swiftness, Hab. i. 8; its cunning, Jer. v. 6 and Hos. xiii. 7; its unchangeable spots as a type of immutability, Jer. xiii. 23; as an emblem of one of the "great monarchies," Dan. vii. 6. The leopard (*Felis pardus*) is still met with in the forest of Gilead, round the Dead Sea, and in the mountains; the chetah (*Gueparda jubata*) is of less frequent occurrence in Palestine. The former frequency of the leopard there may perhaps be inferred from the place-names "Beth-nimrah" (Num. xxxii. 3, 36) and "Nimrim" (Jer. xlviii. 34), the latter perhaps identical with the modern Nimerah (comp. also the "mountains of leopards," Cant. iv. 8).

In the Talmud the namer is classed with the wolf, lion, etc., for dangerousness and ferocity (Sanh. 2a and parallels). Following the ancient conception of the leopard as a hybrid between a panther or pard and the lioness (hence the name "leo-pardus"), some of the rabbis believed it to be the issue of the boar and lioness (comp. Bartenora to the admonition of Ab. v. 5: "Be firm like a leopard to do the will of thy Father in heaven"). The namer is a type of immodesty (Ḳid. 70a). Its term of gestation is said to be three years (Bek. 8a).

Bibliography: Tristram, *Nat. Hist.* p. 111; Lewysohn, *Z. T.* p. 71; comp. also W. R. Smith, *Kinship and Marriage in Early Arabia*, p. 204.

E. G. H. I. M. C.

LEPROSY (צרעת): Chronic skin-disease characterized by ulcerous eruptions and successive desquamations of dead skin.—**Biblical Data**: According to the Levitical text, the characteristic features of leprosy were: (1) bright white spots or patches on the skin the hair on which also was white; (2) the depression of the patches below the level of the surrounding skin; (3) the existence of "quick raw flesh"; (4) the spreading of the scab or scall.

Comparison with Modern Leprosy.

There are two forms of modern leprosy—the tubercular, or nodular, and the anesthetic, or nervous; generally both forms are present. The nodular form begins, as a rule, as round or irregularly shaped spots, commonly of a mahogany or sepia color. These often disappear, and are followed by the appearance of nodules. In an advanced stage the face is covered with firm, livid, nodular elevations: the nose, lips, and ears are swollen beyond their natural size, the eyelashes and eyebrows are lost, and the eyes are staring; the whole producing a hideous disfigurement. As the disease progresses, insensibility of the skin and paralysis ensue, and the fingers and toes may rot away.

In the Biblical description, one is immediately impressed by the absence of all allusion to the hideous facial deformity, the loss of feeling, and the rotting of the members. If such conspicuous manifestations had existed they could not possibly have escaped observation. The Levitical code prescribed that the several examinations of the person suspected should be made at intervals of seven days, thus enabling the priest to note the progress of the disease. Leprosy is an exceedingly slow disease, particularly in the beginning, and a fortnight would show absolutely no change in the vast majority of cases. Moreover, the "lepra Hebræorum" was a curable disease. When the leper was cured the priest made an atonement before the Lord, and expiatory sacrifices in the form of a sin-offering and a trespass-offering were made also. Modern leprosy is, except in isolated instances, incurable.

Nature of "Ẓara'at."

The probabilities are that "ẓara'at" comprised a number of diseases of the skin, which, owing to the undeveloped state of medical science at that period, were not distinguished. The white spots, upon which so much diagnostic stress was laid, were in all likelihood those of vitiligo, a disease quite common in tropical countries, and characterized by bright white spots, the hairs on which also become white. Vitiligo begins as small patches, which slowly spread, often involving ultimately large areas of the body's surface. The disease is harmless, but most disfiguring in those of swarthy complexion.

In the Septuagint "ẓara'at" is translated by "lepra." It is reasonable to assume that the Hebrews attached the same meaning to "ẓara'at" that the Greeks did to "lepra," which is derived from "lepros" (= "rough" or "scaly"). According to the medical writings of Ægineta, Ætius, Actuarius, Oribasus, and others, lepra was uniformly regarded as a circular, superficial, scaly eruption of the skin; in other words, their lepra was the psoriasis of modern times. There is absolutely nothing in the Greek description of lepra that suggests even in a remote manner the modern leprosy. The Greeks, in speaking of true leprosy, did not use the term "lepra," but "elephantiasis." It is evident, therefore, that they meant by "lepra" an affection distinct and apart from the disease of leprosy as now known. The confusion and obscurity that have enveloped this subject for centuries have resulted from the use of different terms in successive ages to designate the same disease, and from the total change in the meaning and application of the word "lepra."

Segregation.

There is much reason to believe that the segregation of lepers was regarded, at any rate at certain periods, more in the light of a religious ceremonial than as a hygienic restriction. Ẓara'at was looked upon as a disease inflicted by God upon those who transgressed His laws, a divine visitation for evil thoughts and evil deeds. Every leper mentioned in the Old Testament was afflicted because of some transgression. "Miriam uttered disrespectful words against God's chosen servant Moses, and, therefore, was she smitten with leprosy. Joab, with his family and descendants, was cursed by David for having treacherously murdered his great rival Abner. Gehazi provoked the anger of Elisha by his mean covetousness, calculated to bring the name of Israel into disrepute among the heathen. King . . . Uzziah was smitten with incurable leprosy for his alleged usurpation of priestly privileges in burning incense on the golden altar of the Temple" (Kalisch). It would have been quite natural for the people by a posteriori reasoning to have regarded persons afflicted with ẓara'at as transgressors; they had violated the laws of God and their transgressions had been great, else they would not have been so afflicted.

Writers who hold the view that the exclusion of lepers had chiefly a religious significance conclude from these facts that lepers were obliged to remain outside the camp because they were regarded as likely to morally infect others. As long as the signs of the disease remained upon them they were obliged to live outside the camp. It is reasonable to believe that, although Biblical and modern leprosy are, in all probability, not the same disease, the present custom of segregating lepers had its origin and stimulus in the Biblical example of segregating those afflicted with ẓara'at. Had the Bible never been written it is probable that lepers would to-day be permitted to go in and out among their fellows unhindered, for leprosy is a much less actively communicable disease than several other well-known affections in the case of which segregation is not practicable.

The Biblical description of leprosy of garments and houses is strikingly analogous in its wording to that of leprosy of persons. The passages in Leviticus (xiii. 47-59) are at present inexplicable in the light of modern science. The probabilities are that the description refers to stains upon garments produced by pus and blood from boils and ulcers of various kinds. Thus alone could the greenish and reddish stains be accounted for. That the description in Lev. xiv. 33-48 could not have applied to a leprosy of walls of houses is beyond reasonable doubt: such conceptions may possibly be ascribed to Oriental fancy and love of metaphor. Chemical incrustations and mildew were doubtless in this manner endowed with the symptoms of a living and spreading disease.

E. G. H. J. F. S.

——**In the Talmud:** The subject of leprosy is treated chiefly in the treatise Nega'im. The Talmud maintains that Lev. xiii. 1 *et seq.* refers generally to any disease that produces sores and eruptions on the skin (Sifra 60a). The following epitomizes the Talmudic treatment of leprosy:

1. Leprosy was not considered contagious. While all peoples of antiquity, from earliest times up to some centuries after the Talmudic period, held (as at the present day; Katzenelenson, in "Ha-Yeḳeb," p. 75, St. Petersburg, 1894) that leprosy was contagious, the Talmudic writers treated it as not contagious. The following evidences this: (1) The Mishnah does not consider a leprous pagan or an unnaturalized proselyte ("ger toshab") ritually unclean (Neg. iii. 1, xi. 1). (2) If a bridegroom, on his wedding-day, observes symptoms of leprosy on his skin, he is not required to submit himself for examination at once, but he may postpone it until the seven days of his nuptials are over. Similarly, one who is affected with it during the holy days may postpone examination until they are over (Neg. iii. 2). Under other circumstances, one afflicted with leprosy is forbidden intercourse with his wife (Ḥul. 141a). (3) The Mishnah says that doubtful cases (with two exceptions) are not to be considered unclean (Ḥul. 9b *et seq.*). (4) The Bible commands that if the priest finds white hair on the parts affected he shall declare the subject unclean, for the white hair is a certain symptom of leprosy. But the Mishnah says that if the hair is plucked out before the examination takes place the person is clean (Neg. viii. 4). It was not, then, fear of contagion that led to regarding the leper as unclean.

Not Contagious.

2. Talmudic tradition, basing its definitions on the etymology of the Biblical terms used, knows of four different degrees of white in cases of leprosy, but not of "neteḳ" (Lev. xiii. 30). "Baheret" is of the whiteness of snow; the second degree recognized is of the whiteness of lime; "se'et" is of the color of the white of an egg; and the next degree of whiteness is that of white wool. The Mishnah adds, also, some intermediate shades; but it calls "bahaḳ" all those beyond the four shades in question (Neg. i. 1-3).

3. While the Bible divides the disease into "white leprosy" and "ulcerous leprosy" ("miḥyah"), the Mishnah divides it into "limited" ("ḳeṭannah") and "extended" ("gedolah") leprosy (Neg. viii. 9). Accordingly it expounds Lev. xiii. 9-11 as referring to "limited" leprosy, and Lev. xiii. 12 *et seq.* as applying to "limited" leprosy which has extended, and as such has become clean.

Limited Leprosy.

Leprosy if "extended" at the outset is to be treated as limited leprosy (Neg. viii. 7); extension does not render leprosy clean, unless following upon a disease which has shown sure symptoms of real leprosy (Neg. viii. 3). Leprosy should, moreover, be considered extended only when it invades the face (Neg. x. 9) and, if the individual is bald and beardless, the scalp and chin (Neg. vi. 8, viii. 5). If, after the scales of leprosy have spread over nearly the whole body, a bleeding and scaleless ulcer (miḥyah) is observed, the subject is unclean. Similarly, if the scales, having covered almost the whole body, fall off in one place and uncover an old bleeding ulcer, the subject is unclean (Neg. viii. 2).

The bleeding ulcer must be of the size of a lentil in order to render one unclean, in cases both of "limited" and of "extended" leprosy. In case the ulcer develops on the extremities of the body, as on the fingers or toes, or on the ears, nose, breast, etc., the person is not considered unclean (Neg. vi. 7). But if this ulcer had once been covered with scales and had then become open again, the person is unclean, unless the remaining scales are smaller than a "gruel" ("geris"; Neg. viii. 1). Finally, the miḥyah does not make a person unclean if it invades a place previously affected by a "sheḥin" or a burn, or if it develops on the hairy parts of the body, or in the recesses and cavities (Neg. vi. 8). When it settles on parts from which the hair has fallen out, or on parts previously affected by sheḥin or a burn, but which have become entirely healed before the appearance of the leprosy, two cases are to be distinguished, according as the miḥyah has previously been covered with scales or not; in the latter case it does not render the subject unclean.

4. In regard to leprosy consequent upon sheḥin or a burn (Lev. xiii. 18-28), the Mishnah maintains: (1) If the sheḥin or the burn has not been healed before the appearance of the scales of leprosy, the person is clean (Neg. ix. 2). (2) Where these affections have become completely healed before the appearance of leprosy, only that is to be considered as leprosy which invades parts of the body never before diseased (*ib.*). (3) Finally, leprosy consequent upon sheḥin or a burn is not rendered unclean by the development of a miḥyah, and one so affected can be isolated for seven days once only, not twice, as in the case of an ordinary leper (Neg. iii. 4).

Consequent on Burns.

5. In regard to leprosy on the scalp and chin (Lev. xiii. 29 *et seq.*), the Mishnah contains the following:

(1) The symptoms of leprosy here (*i.e.*, leprous scales) may present any color; but in any other part of the body only one or more of the four degrees of white can be presented (Sifra 60a). (2) As the Mishnah distinguishes a "limited" and an "extended" leprosy, so it distinguishes a "limited" and an "extended" neteḳ (Neg. x. 9). (3) The neteḳ does not become unclean in consequence of the presence of a miḥyah, but through the presence of fine white or yellow hair, and through the extension of the disease ("pisyon"; Neg. x. 1). (4) Finally, if the hair of the head or of the chin has fallen out, those parts are to be treated like other parts of the body (Neg. x. 10).

In the Talmud the classification or definition of leprosy and of its symptoms seems to be determined not by medical ideas, but by a literal and indiscriminating adherence to the letter of the Levitical law; Talmudic sages were satisfied merely with communicating the Biblical decisions. The Rabbis appear at times even to confuse true leprosy with eczema.

Bibliography: Rabbinowicz, *La Médecine du Thalmud*, pp. 107 *et seq.*, Paris, 1880.

J. A. S. W.

——**In Modern Times:** Leprosy among Jews is seldom mentioned in modern medical literature. Zombacco ("Bul. de la Société d'Anthropologie de Paris," Oct., 1891) states that the disease is very frequent among the Jews of Constantinople. Buschan, quoting this statement ("Globus," lxvii. 61), argues that the predisposition of the Jews to leprosy is a racial characteristic hereditarily transmitted from the ancient Hebrews to the modern Israelites. In support of this he mentions that the Karaites of Constantinople have not been observed by Zombacco, during his twenty years of medical practise among them, to suffer from leprosy. These Jews Buschan considers Jews only by religion, not by virtue of blood-relationship to the Semites. Ethnically he considers them as derived from the Chazars and other peoples of "Finnic" blood. On the other hand, the Rabbinic Jews of Constantinople, who are derived from "Syro-Arabic Semitic" race, have been often observed by Zombacco to suffer from the disease. He further states that the Mohammedans, Christians, Greeks, Armenians, and other non-Jews in Constantinople are free from it, notwithstanding the fact that they come in contact with the Jews. All this tends to show that the alleged predisposition of the Jews to leprosy is an ethnic trait.

This allegation, based as it is on very scanty evidence, is not confirmed by any other observer. In Russia, where in some provinces leprosy is endemic, the Jews are not observed to be frequently affected, while in some Oriental countries the evidence available tends to show that, on the contrary, the Jews are peculiarly free from leprosy. Thus, Nicholas Senn, speaking of leprosy in Jerusalem, says: "Most of the lepers are Arabs; and the Jews are singularly free from this disease. . . . Among the 47 inmates [of the Jesus Hilfe Hospital] there is only one Jew. Dr. Einsler, during his long and extensive practise in Jerusalem, has seen only five Jews affected with leprosy; and of these one came from Salonica and of the remainder two from Morocco. It seems that the Jerusalem Jews have in the course of time acquired an immunity from this disease, notwithstanding the increase of poverty and unsanitary surroundings" (N. Senn, "The Hospitals in Jerusalem," in "American Medicine," iv. 509-512).

J. M. Fi.

LERIDA (Catalan, **Leyda; Ilerda**): City in Catalonia, which as early as the fourteenth century had an important Jewish community possessed of several privileges. Thus, it was exempted from the general obligation to provide the royal court, during its presence in the city, with beds and the necessaries of life. Again, the Jews of Lerida, at the earnest request of the representatives of the congregation, were not compelled to attend the conversion sermons of Maestre Huesca and other Dominicans. In 1306 the congregation was granted permission by the king to receive into its membership ten Jewish families driven from France. The Shepherd persecutions brought great affliction to the community. Seventy Jews surrendered their possessions to the commander of the city, "so that he might bring them in safety to Aragon; but when they got outside the city he slew them with his sword." Eight years later the Jews had to defend themselves against attacks upon their lives. The hatred of the Christians was a constant source of menace to them. In 1325 the right to prepare Passover cakes was refused to them, so that they had to turn to the king for assistance.

The Jews of Lerida engaged in industry and carried on an extensive commerce; they had one large synagogue and several small ones. In 1269 "Nasi Azday" (Ḥasdai) was appointed as rabbi, whom in the following year the king presented with a building-plot. In 1275 the communal laws ("taḳḳanot") were sanctioned by the king. The ominous year 1391 was for the Jews of Lerida one of great calamity. The massacre occurred there Aug. 13; seventy-eight Jews being killed, while most of the survivors accepted baptism. The neophytes transformed the synagogue into a church under the name "S. Maria del Milagro"; in the fifteenth century it was still almost exclusively attended by neophytes. With 1391 the real "aljama" in Lerida ceased; Jews in scant numbers probably continued to live in the city, enjoying the old privileges, but they no longer constituted a congregation. The city soon felt the decline of the taxes formerly paid by the Jews. In 1410 the city council entered into negotiations with the Jews for the purpose of reimposing part of these taxes; but this led to no result.

The poet Joseph bar Sheshet ben Latimi (1308) and the physician Abraham, who, Sept. 12, 1468, performed an operation on King Juan of Aragon for cataract, lived in Lerida.

Bibliography: Joseph ha-Kohen, *'Emek ha-Baka*, pp. 60, 67; Rios, *Hist.* ii. 155, 158, 380, 402; iii. 83; José Pleyan de Porta, *Apuntos de Historia de Lerida*, Lerida, 1873; Jacobs, *Sources*, Nos. 756, 941, 1062.

G. M. K.

LERMA, JUDAH BEN SAMUEL: Spanish Talmudist; flourished in the middle of the sixteenth century. He was the author of "Leḥem Yehudah," a commentary on Pirḳe Abot, and of "Derush 'al ha-Neshamah," a treatise on the soul, published together under the former title (Sabbionetta, 1554)

In the preface Lerma laments the burning of the Talmud in Italy, which occurred in 1554, under Pope Julius III. According to Zedner ("Cat. Hebr. Books Brit. Mus." p. 551), the 1554 edition is the second; in that case either the whole preface or the part relating to the burning of the Talmud is an addition. Judah ben Samuel Lerma must not be confounded with Judah Lerma, rabbi of Belgrade (as seems to have been done by Steinschneider and other authorities), who was a pupil of Jehiel Bassani and belonged, therefore, to the seventeenth century. Lerma was the author of a large number of responsa, which, with the exception of thirty, were destroyed by fire; these thirty were rescued from the flames by Lerma's pupil, Simḥah b. Gershon ha-Kohen, who published them, adding a preface, under the title "Peleṭat Bet Yehudah" (Venice, 1647).

BIBLIOGRAPHY: Conforte, *Ḳore ha-Dorot*, pp. 40b, 51b; Fuenn, *Keneset Yisrael*, p. 408; Fürst, *Bibl. Jud.* ii. 233; Steinschneider, *Cat. Bodl.* col. 1337.

J. M. SEL.

LERNER, ḤAYYIM ẒEBI: Russian grammarian and teacher of Hebrew; born at Dubno 1815; died at Jitomir 1889. His early education in Bible and Talmud he received from his father. At the age of thirteen he was married. In 1833, when Wolf ADELSOHN went to Dubno and gathered around him a circle of Maskilim, to whom he taught Hebrew grammar and philosophy, Lerner became one of his disciples. He went to Odessa in 1835 and entered the model school of Bezaleel Stern, where Simḥah Pinsker was his teacher in Hebrew grammar. In the same school he also acquired a thorough knowledge of the Russian, German, French, and Italian languages. In 1838 Lerner returned to Dubno and became a teacher of Hebrew; from 1841 to 1849 he taught in Radzivilov; on Nov. 16 of the latter year he was appointed government teacher of the Jewish public school of Berdychev; and in 1851 he was appointed teacher of Hebrew at the rabbinical school of Jitomir, in which position he remained until the school was closed by the government (July 1, 1873).

Lerner's reputation among Hebrew grammarians was founded on his "Moreh ha-Lashon." It is written in a pure, popular Hebrew, and follows the system of grammar of European tongues, enabling the student to acquire the language more easily than did the works of his predecessors. The first edition appeared in 1859; six editions were issued during Lerner's lifetime; and many more have appeared since his death. Lerner was criticized for having adopted his methods from his teacher Pinsker; he himself acknowledged his indebtedness in the second edition of his work (p. 136, note).

Besides this grammar, Lerner wrote "Diḳduḳ Lashon Aramit" (Warsaw, 1875), an Aramaic grammar; "Ma'amar Toledot ha-Diḳduḳ" (Vienna, 1876); and a translation of S. D. Luzzatto's "Diḳduḳ Leshon Talmud Babli" (St. Petersburg, 1880). He left in manuscript: "Yalḳut," a collection of commentaries on the Bible and Rashi, together with critical and literary articles; "Arba' Middot," on the Baraita of the thirty-two Middot; and a Hebrew translation of Young's "Night Thoughts" and other poems.

BIBLIOGRAPHY: *Ha-Meliẓ*, 1889, Nos. 76-79; Sokolov, *Sefer ha-Shanah*, i. 62; idem, *Sefer Zikkaron*, p. 66.

H. R. M. R.

LERNER, JOSEPH JUDAH (OSSIP): Russian journalist; born Jan. 1, 1849, at Berdychev; educated at the gymnasium of Jitomir. In 1866 he went to Odessa, where he studied law for a year, and then entered upon a journalistic career. He served for ten years on the staff of the "Odeski Vyestnik," acting as war correspondent for that paper during the Russo-Turkish war of 1877-78. In Bucharest he published during the war a daily paper, "Zapiski Grazhdanina." In 1880 he founded at Odessa a Jewish theater, for which he wrote many plays in Judæo-German. The years 1883 and 1884 he spent in Germany and France as correspondent of the Moscow daily "Russkiya Vyedomosti," writing articles for other Russian papers also. In Hebrew Lerner published: a short sketch on the Chazars (Odessa, 1866); "Ma'amar Biḳḳoret" (*ib.* 1867), a criticism upon Gottlobers; "Yamim mi-Ḳedem" (*ib.* 1868), a tale of Jewish life in Russia; and articles on various topics of the time. Of his dramas in Judæo-German may be mentioned "Zhidovka," "Ḥanukkah," and "Der Fetter Moshe Mendelssohn" (Warsaw, 1889).

Lerner wrote many articles in Russian on the Jewish question, a list of which is to be found in "Sistematicheski Ukazatel," etc., St. Petersburg, 1893. In 1902 Lerner published "Yevrei Novorossiskavo Kraya," a historical sketch of the life of the Jews in South Russia, which, however, is rather a memoir than a history.

Lerner, who has recently become a convert to Christianity, is now (1904) residing in Odessa.

BIBLIOGRAPHY: Sokolov, *Sefer Zikkaron*, p. 66.

H. R. M. R.

LERNER, MAIER: German rabbi; born in Galicia 1857. He studied in Berlin under Hildesheimer, became rabbi at Winzenheim, Alsace (1884–1890), and preacher for the Federation of Synagogues in London (1890–94), and, since 1890, has been chief rabbi of Altona. He wrote "Anlage und Quellen des Bereschit Rabba" (Berlin, 1882) and has contributed to various periodicals ("Berliner's Magazin für die Wissenschaft des Judenthums," "Der Israelit," "Jüdische Presse," "Jewish World," etc.). His literary work is devoted almost exclusively to the defense of Orthodox Judaism. Lerner married a daughter of Hirsch Plato, a son of Samson R. Hirsch.

BIBLIOGRAPHY: Dukesz, *Iwoh Lemoschaw*, Cracow, 1903.

D.

LEROY-BEAULIEU, HENRI JEAN BAPTISTE ANATOLE: French Christian historian; born at Lisieux in 1842. His first work was entitled "Une Troupe de Comédiens" and was followed by "Essai sur la Restauration de nos Monuments Historiques Devant l'Art et Devant le Budget" (1866). In 1867 he went to Russia to study the political and economic organization of the Slavic peoples, the result of his studies being published under the title "L'Empire des Tsars et les Russes" (3 vols., Paris, 1882-89). In 1881 he was appointed professor of contemporaneous history and of Oriental affairs at L'Ecole Libre des Sciences Politiques, and in 1887 he became a member of the Académie des Sciences Morales et Politiques. From 1883 to 1891 he represented the canton of Auberive in the Conseil Général of the department of Haute-Marne.

In 1879 Leroy-Beaulieu published a critical analysis of the political situation under the Second Empire, entitled "Un Empereur, Un Roi, Un Pape, Une Restauration," and in 1884, under the title "Un Homme d'Etat Russe. Nicolas Milutine," a historical novel vividly depicting the great reformation due to the emancipation of the Russian serfs by Alexander II. Of his other political writings may be mentioned: "Les Catholiques Libéraux, l'Eglise et le Libéralisme de 1830 à Nos Jours" (Paris, 1885); "La France, la Russie et l'Europe" (*ib.* 1888); "La Révolution et le Libéralisme" (*ib.* 1890); "La Papauté, le Socialisme et la Démocratie" (*ib.* 1892); "L'Antisémitisme" (*ib.* 1897); "Les Doctrines de la Haine, l'Antisémitisme, l'Antiprotestantisme, l'Anticléricalisme" (*ib.* 1902). Of chief interest to the Jewish world, however, is his work "Israël chez les Nations" (1893). In this work the author embodies the result of a thorough study of the conditions governing the Russian Jews, and, while he is not lavish of his praise of the oppressed, he is emphatic in maintaining that nothing but emancipation can improve them mentally and morally. "All the virtues that the Jews possess are their own, while their vices are largely due to persecutions by Christian nations."

In the beginning of 1904 Leroy-Beaulieu went to the United States to deliver a series of lectures at some of the American universities (Harvard, Pennsylvania, etc.). The Jewish community of New York, during his sojourn in that city, tendered him a testimonial of appreciation of his vigorous war against anti-Semitism in France, and of his scholarly defense of Jewish character and traditions. Leroy-Beaulieu is a chevalier of the Legion of Honor.

BIBLIOGRAPHY: *La Grande Encyclopédie*; *Meyers Konversations-Lexikon*; *Nouveau Larousse Illustré*; Curinier, *Dict. Nat.*; *American Hebrew* (New York), May 6, 13, 20, 1904; *Jewish Comment* (Baltimore), April 29, 1904.

S. F. C.

LESSEE. See LANDLORD AND TENANT.

LESSER, ADOLF: German physician and writer on medical jurisprudence; born at Stargard, province of Pomerania, Prussia, May 22, 1851; graduated from Berlin University in 1875. From 1877 to 1884 he was assistant in the pharmacological institute of that university, and from 1879 to 1886 physician at Klinnsmann's lunatic asylum. In 1881 he became privat-docent in pharmacology at the university. In 1886 he was appointed physician-in-chief ("Stadtphysikus") to the board of health of Breslau, at the university of which city he was appointed assistant professor in 1887.

Of Lesser's numerous essays contributed to the medical journals may be mentioned: "Experimentelle Untersuchungen über den Einfluss Einiger Arsenverbindungen auf den Thierischen Organismus," in Virchow's "Archiv"; "Ueber die Localen Befunde beim Selbstmorde Durch Erhängen" and "Ueber die Wichtigsten Sectionsbefunde bei dem Tode Durch Ertrinken in Dünnflüssigen Medien," in the "Vierteljahresschrift für Gerichtliche Medizin."

Lesser is the author also of the well-known "Atlas der Gerichtlichen Medizin," 1884–92, and "Zur Lehre vom Abort," "Zur Lehre von den Kopfverletzungen Neugeborener," and "Erkrankungen Sowie Præ- und Postmortale Verletzungen des Halses," in Neisser's "Stereoskopischer Medizinischer Atlas."

BIBLIOGRAPHY: Pagel, *Biog. Lexikon*, s.v., Vienna, 1901.

S. F. T. H.

LESSER, ALEXANDER: Polish painter; born at Warsaw 1814; died there 1884. He was educated at the Warsaw lyceum and studied art at Warsaw University, at the Academy of Dresden (1833–35), and at Munich under Cornelius and Schnorr (1842). He devoted himself mainly to painting scenes from Polish history; and in search of historical material he made extensive tours through Germany, France, Belgium, and England. Among his historical paintings the best known are: "Wincent Kadlubek," "Skarbek Habdank," "The Young Boleslaw," "The Wry-Mouthed," and "Wanda and Jadwiga." For his "forty portraits of Polish kings" (reproductions published at Warsaw in 1860) he was elected a member of the Cracow Academy of Science.

Lesser was also active as an art critic and as a writer of historical sketches, contributing to the Polish periodicals "Klosy," "Tygodrik Illustrowany," and others.

BIBLIOGRAPHY: Orgelbrand, *Encyklopedja Powszchna*, ix.

H. R. G. D. R.

LESSER, EDMUND: German physician; born at Neisse May 12, 1852; educated at the universities of Berlin, Bonn, and Strasburg (M.D. 1876). He became assistant at the dermatological clinic at Breslau; in 1882 established himself as privat-docent at the University of Leipsic; was appointed assistant professor in the University of Bonn in 1892; in 1896 became chief physician of the syphilitic department at the Charité Hospital at Berlin; and in 1897 was appointed chief of the newly founded dermatological and syphilitic dispensary of the university in that city.

Of Lesser's works may be mentioned, besides his "Lehrbuch der Haut- und Geschlechtskrankheiten" (10th ed. 1890): "Ueber Syphilis Maligna"; "Beiträge zur Lehre vom Herpes Zoster"; "Ueber Nebenwirkungen bei Injectionen Unlöslicher Quecksilberverbindungen"; "Ueber Syphilis Insontium"; "Ueber Ischias Gonorrhoica"; "Die Aussatzhäuser des Mittelalters"; and "Zur Geschichte des Aussatzes."

BIBLIOGRAPHY: Pagel, *Biog. Lex.*

S. F. T. H.

LESSER, LOUIS: German soldier; born at Neustadt about 1850; served in the Second Brandenburg Dragoons in the Franco-Prussian war. On Nov. 18, 1870, while on patrol work between Sens and Villeneuve, his comrades being dispersed in various directions, he was surprised by six of the enemy. He stood his ground, and on the return of his comrades advanced and captured the captain of the francs-tireurs who had attacked him.

BIBLIOGRAPHY: *Deutsches Heldenbuch*, p. 304; *Juden als Soldaten*, p. 105.

S. J.

LESSER, LUDWIG: German poet, editor, and publicist; born at Rathenow, province of Brandenburg, Prussia, Dec. 7, 1802; died at Berlin Dec. 2, 1867. When very young he went to Berlin, and became a regular contributor to most of the literary periodicals of that city (often under the pseudonym "Ludwig Liber"). The humorist Saphir was attracted by Lesser's work and personality, and secured him for his literary staff. The two became very firm friends, and in 1827 they founded the Literarische Sonntags-Verein. Lesser wrote "Chronik der Gesellschaft der Freunde in Berlin zur Feier Ihres Fünfzigjährigen Jubiläums" (Berlin, 1842).

A selection of Lesser's poems was published under the title "Ausgewählte Dichtungen," Berlin, 1870; and the gold medal for art and science was conferred upon him by King Frederick William III. A characteristic epigram by him, of which the following is a free translation, gives some measure of his power:

One thing to Life you owe:
Struggle, or seek for rest.
If you're an anvil, bear the blow;
If a hammer, strike your best.

Lesser was devoted to the interests of the Jews: he was one of the founders of the Jüdischer Kulturverein, of a society for the aid of Jewish teachers, and of the Berlin Reform congregation.

Bibliography: R. Lesser, in preface to *Ausgewählte Dichtungen.*

s. M. Co.

LESSING, GOTTHOLD EPHRAIM: German poet and critic; born Jan. 22, 1729, at Kamenz, Upper Lusatia; died Feb. 15, 1781, at Brunswick.

Toleration and a striving after freedom of thought led him to condemn all positive religions in so far as they laid claim to absolute authority, and to recognize them merely as stages of historical development. A natural consequence of this principle was his sympathetic attitude toward the Jews; for he deemed it inconsistent with the dictates of religious liberty to exclude for religious reasons a whole race from the blessings of European culture.

In his comedy "Die Juden," one of his earliest dramatic works, he stigmatized the dislike of the Gentiles for the followers of the Jewish religion as a stupid prejudice. He went herein further than any other apostle of toleration before or after him. The full development and final expression of his views on this problem, however, are found in his drama and last masterpiece, "Nathan der Weise" (1779), Lessing thus beginning and ending his dramatic career as an advocate of the emancipation of the Jews.

The figure of *Nathan*, modeled in the main on that of his friend Moses Mendelssohn, was bound to convince the world that the tenets of toleration and humanity could be enunciated even by a representative of the race so bitterly hated by the world. The legend of the three rings, in which Christianity, Islam, and Judaism are allegorically represented as brothers, each deeming to possess the original magic ring, but all of them having, in reality, been cheated of it, clearly indicates that Lessing wished to represent the Jew as a man, and not Judaism as a dogmatic system. The prize of supremacy is not awarded to this or that confession, but to humanity and morality, which are not bound to any particular faith.

Lessing's "Nathan" had a liberating effect on the Jews in more ways than one. In the first place, the mere fact that he chose the Jew *Nathan* as his mouthpiece could not pass unnoticed, and was sure to act as a hindrance to persecution; and, secondly, he stimulated the ethical consciousness of the Jews themselves, who could not fall below the standard set up by a noble non-Jew.

While Lessing condemned the belief in positive revelation, he accepted its general concept, seeing in the dogmatic teachings of both the Old and New Testaments efficient educational instruments for the moral elevation of mankind.

In short, Lessing raised Judaism in the esteem of the European nations not only by showing its close connection with Christianity, but also by demonstrating the importance of Mosaism in the general religious evolution of humanity. It was really Lessing who opened the doors of the ghetto and gave the Jews access to European culture. In a certain sense he awakened Moses Mendelssohn to the consciousness of his mission; and through Mendelssohn Lessing liberated Judaism from the most heavy chains of its own forging.

As a Biblical critic Lessing is equaled by none of his contemporaries, and by very few of his predecessors.

s. M. Frie.

LESSMANN, DANIEL: German historian and poet; born at Soldin, Neumark, Jan. 18, 1784; committed suicide at a place between Kropstadt and Wittenberg Sept. 2, 1831. He attended the Joachimsthal'sche Gymnasium in Berlin, and had begun the study of medicine when the war of the allied powers against Napoleon broke out in 1813. He fought in the ranks, was wounded at the battle of Lützen (May 2, 1813), and on recovering remained in the field until the end of the war. When peace was restored he resumed his medical studies. He went as private teacher to Vienna, and removed later to Italy, remaining some time in Verona.

In 1824 he settled in Berlin and devoted himself to literary work, contributing to various periodicals sketches of life in southern countries, historical studies, short stories, and poems. A collection of his poems was published under the title "Amathusia," Berlin, 1824. In 1826 his "Zwölf Wanderlieder eines Schwermüthigen" appeared in Berlin, and four years later another volume was issued under the title "Gedichte," *ib.* 1830. In his poetry there is easily discernible the influence of Heine, with whom he was on friendly terms, and in whose letters to Moser there are frequent references to Lessmann.

Lessmann's contributions to imaginative prose literature include the novels "Louise von Halling," 2 vols., *ib.* 1827, which attracted the attention of Goethe, and "Die Heidemühle," published in two volumes seven years after his death. To Lessmann belongs much of the credit for the introduction of modern Italian literature into Germany through his translation of Manzoni's "I Promessi Sposi," and of "La Monaca di Monza," by Giovanni Rossini.

His important historical work was the "Mastino della Scala: Ein Beitrag zur Gesch. der Oberitalienischen Staaten im Mittelalter," *ib.* 1828. In 1829 and 1830 appeared successively the two volumes of "Biographische Gemälde," which included historical studies of Philip the Beautiful, Alfonso Albuquerque, Innocent III., and Prince Michael Glinski. Much of the "Nachlass," 2 vols., *ib.* 1837–38, is devoted to valuable historical work. Lessmann left in manuscript a voluminous "Weltgeschichte des Alterthums," which has never been published.

His seven years of literary activity were years of profound melancholy. Lessmann had high aspirations and great ambition. He dreamed of securing some position of eminence; and it appears, from the answer of Moser to one of Heine's letters, that in 1824 Lessmann adopted Christianity in order that he might realize his hopes. Nothing came of all his efforts in this direction; and he fell into a state of despondency, which is reflected in his poetry and in his "Wanderbuch eines Schwermüthigen," 2 vols., *ib.* 1831–32. One day Lessmann left Berlin on the pretext of taking a pedestrian tour to Leipsic and Dresden, and was found hanged by his own act.

Bibliography: Gödeke, *Grundr. der Deutschen Literatur*, iii. 730-732; Gubitz, *Errinnerungen*, iii. 1-7, Berlin, 1869; L. Geiger, *Daniel Lessmann*, in *Allg. Deutsche Biog.* xviii. 451-453; Strodtmann, *Heine*, i. 319; Brümmer, *Dichterlexikon*.

s. M. Co.

LETTER-CARRIERS, JEWISH: Jews carried letters to their coreligionists, apart from the regular post. In those business centers where a large Jewish population existed, such as Hamburg, Prague, Gross Glogau, Polish Lissa, Breslau, and Frankfort-on-the-Main, Jews, and at times even Jewesses, are found acting as letter-carriers under state control. It was necessary to employ them in the postal service, as it was almost impossible for Christian letter-carriers to deliver letters addressed in Hebrew. Another reason may have been the fact that the Jews, in their relations with the post, were subject to exceptional laws.

The only detailed notices of Jewish letter-carriers are furnished by the archives of Breslau and Frankfort; but the position of the letter-carriers in these places was no doubt typical of their status elsewhere. The Jewish letter-carrier, or "Post-Jude," in Breslau, is first mentioned in a document dated Dec. 13, 1722, which, however, allows the inference that the office had existed for many years before that date. It was maintained until the Silesian wars, after which time Breslau was no longer included in the imperial postal district of Habsburg.

The Jewish letter-carrier of Breslau, as he neither took any oath of office nor received any salary, was not really a government official. His whole income consisted merely of the postage paid by the recipients of the letters. As, however, there were no fixed postal rates, the amount received was so small that the letter-carrier had to pursue in addition some other occupation. That the postal authorities tolerated this state of affairs is shown by the fact that when the letter-carrier was absent on other business, his wife was allowed to take his place.

The first mention of a Jewish letter-carrier in Frankfort-on-the-Main occurs in a decree dating from the middle of the eighteenth century, and setting forth the regulations which the Jews must observe in their relations with the Thurn and Taxis post; but in Frankfort, too, the office had existed before that time. From 1748 until 1846 it was held by members of the same family, and it was abolished owing to altered conditions. The nephew and assistant of the Jews' letter-carrier who was then in office remained in the Thurn and Taxis service with the same rights and duties, and in 1867 was taken over into the Prussian service.

In Frankfort, as in Breslau, the Jewish letter-carrier received no pay, but two kreutzers were collected from the addressee for every ordinary letter, and six kreutzers for a registered letter. In proportion as international commerce developed and the Jewish interests therein increased, the income of the letter-carrier became correspondingly larger. The last incumbent of the office had a yearly income of 5,000 gulden, out of which, in very busy times, he had to pay his assistants 150 florins each. Besides, when other posts, such as that of Hesse-Cassel, became united to that of Thurn and Taxis, he was required to pay Count Thurn and Taxis 400 gulden yearly. He ultimately retired on a pension of 1,600 florins.

Bibliography: Kracauer, *Die Judenbriefträger in Frankfurt-a.-M.* in *Frankfurter Zeitung*, 1890, No. 109; Landsberger, *Juden im Dienste der Kaiserlichen Post zu Breslau, etc.* in Braun's *Volkskalender*, 1901, p. 43; Kaufmann, *Die Memoiren der Glückel von Hameln*, p. 109; Grunwald, *Portugiesengräber auf Deutscher Erde*, p. 98.

G. I. Kra.

LETTER-WRITING AND LETTER-WRITERS: The art of conveying information by letter ("miktab," "iggeret," "sefer") was unknown to the Hebrews in the first stages of their history. From the times of the Patriarchs to those of King Saul the Bible mentions only messengers who transmitted orally the communications entrusted to them (comp. Num. xxiv. 12; Judges xi. 13; I Sam. xi. 9). The first letter recorded is that written by David to Joab and sent by the hand of Uriah (II Sam. xi. 23, 25). David and his successors had special secretaries ("soferim") charged with the writing of letters and circulars; and these secretaries occupied an exalted position in the state. The Kenites living at Jabez were noted for their skill in writing (comp. I Chron. ii. 55). As among the Greeks and Romans, it seems to have been customary among the ancient Hebrews to seal a letter sent to a prominent person. To show his slight respect for the prophet's personality, Sanballat sends an open letter to Nehemiah (Neh. vi. 5).

In Talmudic Times.

With the expansion of commerce in Talmudic times the use of letters became a necessity, and nearly every town had its official letter-writer (לבלר = "libellarius"). The Rabbis forbade a scholar to reside in a city where there was no such functionary (Sanh. 17a). The Talmud has preserved the original text of two letters: one was addressed by the community of Jerusalem to that of Alexandria and refers to the sojourn of Judah ben Ṭabbai in the latter city; the other was sent by Gamaliel I. to the Jews of Upper and Lower Galilee and treated of the intercalation of an additional month in the year (Yer. Ḥag. ii.; Sanh. 11b). Besides letters of information or of friendship, there are traces in the Talmud of consultatory letters dealing with scientific subjects (comp. Ḥul. 95a). To this class belongs that important branch of rabbinical literature which is known by the name "She'elot u-Teshubot" (Responsa), and which developed after the geonic period (see Joel Müller, "Briefe und Responsen in der Vorgaonischen Jüdischen Litteratur," in "Jahresbericht der Lehranstalt für Jüdische Wissenschaft," Berlin, 1886).

Style and Composition.

The epistolary style varied according to the country. In the East it was modeled after that of the Arabs, who exercised care in the elaboration of their letters. The first, often the greater, part of the letter, usually written in rimed prose and adorned with Biblical quotations, formed a kind of introduction in which the writer attributed to his correspondent all the virtues conceivable to the imagination of an Oriental. In western countries expression was more moderate; the use of titles, however, was general, as it still is among the conservative Jews in Russia, Poland, and Galicia. The least important rabbi is addressed as the "Great Gaon," "Great Light," "Wonder of the Generation," "Pillar of Israel," or with similar extravagant epithets. Like the Arabs, the Jews in the Middle Ages neglected to place the date at the head of their letters; in modern times the custom was established of giving, after the formula ב"ה (="With the help of God"), with which the letter began, the day of the week, the Sabbatical section (sometimes also the day of the month), and the place. "Friday" was usually followed by the abbreviation עש"ק (="eve of the holy Sabbath"). The secrecy of letters was assured in the tenth century by R. Gershon (Me'or ha-Golah), who declared under the ban any one who should open without permission a letter not addressed to him.

Celebrated Collections.

The most famous letters in Jewish literature—because of both their contents and the prominence of their writers—are: that of Ḥasdai ibn Shaprut to the king of the Chazars; "Iggeret R. Sherira Gaon," on the sequence of tradition and the redaction of the Talmud; the various letters of Maimonides inserted in the "Pe'er ha-Dor"; the letters exchanged between the French rabbis and scholars and those of Spain on the study of philosophy ("Minḥat Ḳena'ot"); "Iggeret al-Tehi ka-Aboteka," addressed by Profiat Duran to En Bonet; the collection of letters on Shabbethai Ẓebi published by Ẓebi Ashkenazi (Ḥakam Ẓebi), Moses Ḥagiz, and Jacob Emden. As a curiosity, mention may be made of the letter addressed by the rabbis of Jerusalem to the alleged descendants of Moses ("Bene Mosheh," Amsterdam, 1731). The most noteworthy letters of modern times are: those of Moses Mendelssohn ("Iggerot RaMaD," Vienna, 1792); of Naphtali Herz Wessely included in the "Megalleh Ṭamirin" (*ib.* 1819); of J. Perl written in the style of "Epistolæ Obscurorum Virorum"; "Iggeret YaSHaR," by Isaac Samuel Reggio (*ib.* 1834); "Iggerot ShaDaL," by Luzzatto (Przemysl, 1883); and "Miktabe YaGeL," by Judah Löb Gordon (Warsaw, 1894).

Formularies for Letters.

From the sixteenth century Jewish literature was enriched with a number of formularies of Hebrew and Judæo-German letters. The first of this kind was the "Iggeret Shelomim," published at Augsburg in 1534 and republished with a Latin translation by Buxtorf the Younger at Basel in 1603. The characteristic features of this formulary, as of all the others published until 1820, were the stilted and bombastic style, the misuse of Biblical and Talmudical quotations, and the extravagance of the headings of the letters. In the "'Iṭṭur Soferim" (see the list below), for instance, there is such a heading; which, rendered into English, it reads thus: "His [the correspondent's] cheeks are as a bed of spices [Cant. v. 13], a ladder on which angels of God are ascending and descending [Gen. xxviii. 12]. He is of a reliable character; keeps secrets; shows power to Jew and Gentile; he is a righteous man upon whom the world is based." As a model of a business letter, in which the writer has to inform his correspondent that some salt which had been purchased is on the road, the "Ẓaḥut ha-Meliẓah" (see below) gives the following: "And he looked back from behind him and became a pillar of salt on the road," etc. (comp. Gen. xix. 26). A new era in letter-writing was inaugurated by Shalom ha-Kohen. In his formula "Ketab Yosher" (see below) he endeavored to do away with the obsolete forms and to cause the young, for whom his formulas are intended, to adopt a modern style of writing. He was followed in this endeavor by many writers of talent who produced formularies of real literary value. The following is a list of formularies published up to the last years of the nineteenth century:

אגרת שלומים, anonymous. Augsburg, 1534; Basel, 1603.

בריפשטעללער, in Judæo-German, by Judah Löb Liondor. Wilna, 1820, 1844, 1846.

בריף לעהרער, in Judæo-German, by Hirsch Liondor. Wilna, 1855.

דביר, by Mordecai Aaron Günzburg. Wilna, 1844; 2d ed., 1855.

דברני ספר, by Abraham Israel Kukelstein. Wilna, 1895.

חליפות אגרות, by H. Baueli. Wilna, 1866.

יד ועט, by Tobias Shapiro. Wilna, 1891.

כתב יושר, by Shalom ha-Kohen. Vienna, 1820; Wilna, 1858.

כתב יושר החדש, anonymous. Warsaw, 1869, 1871.

כתב ישראל, by Israel Segal. Sudilkov, 1796.

כתב נבחר, by Moses of Lemberg. Cracow, 1659; Prague, 1705.

לשון למודים, by Eliakim Mellamed. Amsterdam, 1686.

מגלת ספר, by Eliezer Beër Silbermann. Johannisberg, 1854.

מבטח עוז, in Hebrew and Judæo-German, by Azriel Selig Galin, Warsaw, 1889.

מכתב לבני הנעורים, by Baer Friedmann. Berdychev, 1890.

מכתב משלש, in Hebrew, Judæo-German, and Russian, by Feigensohn. Wilna, 1882.

מכתב משלש עם מרוץ אגרת החדש, by Abraham Jacob Paperna. Warsaw, 1884.

מכתבי בני קדם, by M. Letteris. Vienna, 1867.

מכתבי נעורים, by Israel Beer Riesberg. Warsaw, 1887.

מכתבי עברית, in Hebrew and Judæo-German, by S. Neumann. Vienna, 1815, 1834.

מכתבי עברית, in Hebrew and Judæo-German, anonymous. Lemberg, 1860.

מכתבי עברית, by Israel Busch. Vienna, 1847.

מכתבי עברית, by Israel Knöpflemacher. Vienna, 1855.

מכתבי שפת קודש, by Emanuel Bondi. Prague, 1857.

מכתבים בספר, by Lazar Isaac Shapiro. Warsaw, 1871.

מכתבים ללמד, by Naphtali Maskileison. Warsaw, 1876.

מכתבי השלם, by Abraham Markus Pjurko. Warsaw, 1872.

מערכת מכתבים, by Paradiesthal. Warsaw, 1853.

מפתח בית דוד, by David Zamosc. Breslau, 1823.

מריץ אגרות, in Hebrew and Russian, by A. J. Paperna. Warsaw, 1874, 1876.

עט סופר, by Moses Cohen. Fürth, 1691.

עט סופר, by Ẓemaḥ Landau. Wilna, 1830, 1833.

עט סופר החדש, by Ẓemaḥ Landau. Wilna, 1835, 1844, 1848.

עט עברי, by Tobias Shapiro. Warsaw, 1878.

עטור סופרים, by Moses Landsberg. Hamburg, 1721, and many other editions.

צחות המליצה, by Wolf Buchner. Prague, 1805.

קביצת מכתבים, by Ḥayyim Wittkind. Warsaw, 1873.

קסת הסופר, by Jacob Lapin. Berlin, 1857.

קרית סופר, by Mordecai Aaron Günzburg. Wilna, 1835, 1847, 1855; Warsaw, 1837, 1883.

שבט סופר, by Mendel Dolitzky. Vienna, 1883.

תולדות אדם, anonymous. Frankfort-on-the-Main, 1736.

G. I. Br.

LETTERIS, MEÏR HALEVI (MAX): Austrian scholar and poet; born Sept. 13, 1800, at Zolkiev; died at Vienna May 19, 1871. He was a member of a family of printers that originally came from Amsterdam. At the age of twelve he sent a Hebrew poem to Nachman Krochmal, who was then living at Zolkiev. Subsequently he made the acquaintance of Krochmal, who encouraged him in his study of German, French, and Latin literature. In 1826 he entered the University of Lemberg, where for four years he studied philosophy and Oriental languages. In 1831 he went to Berlin as Hebrew corrector in a printing establishment, and later in a similar capacity to Presburg, where he edited a large number of valuable manuscripts, and to Prague, where he received the degree of Ph.D. (1844). In 1848 he settled finally in Vienna.

Meïr Halevi Letteris.

Letteris' chief poetical work in German, "Sagen aus dem Orient" (Carlsruhe, 1847), consisting of poetic renderings of Talmudic and other legends, secured for him, though for a short time, the post of librarian in the Oriental department of the Vienna Imperial Library. His reputation as the foremost poet of the Galician school is based on his volume of poems "Tofes Kinnor we-'Ugab" (Vienna, 1860), and especially on his Hebrew version of "Faust," entitled "Ben Abuya" (*ib.* 1865). He has exerted a considerable influence on modern Hebrew poetry. One of his best poems is his Zionistic song "Yonah Ḥomiyyah," which has become very popular. His numerous translations are of incontestable value, but his original poems are as a rule too prolix. His Hebrew prose is correct, though heavy.

Besides the works already mentioned the following deserve special notice: "Dibre Shir" (Zolkiev, 1822) and "Ayyelet ha-Shaḥar" (*ib.* 1824), including translations from Schiller and Homer, and poems by Letteris' father; "Ha-Ẓefirah" (Zolkiev and Leipsic, 1823), a selection of poems and essays; "Palge Mayim" (Lemberg, 1827), poems; "Gedichte" (Vienna, 1829), German translations from the Hebrew; "Geza' Yishai" (Vienna, 1835), Hebrew translation of Racine's "Athalie"; "Shelom Ester" (Prague, 1843), Hebrew translation of Racine's "Esther"; "Spinoza's Lehre und Leben" (Vienna, 1847); "Neginot Yisrael," Hebrew rendering of Frankel's "Nach der Zerstreuung" (*ib.* 1856); and "Bilder aus dem Biblischen Morgenlande" (Leipsic, 1870).

He was the editor of "Wiener Vierteljahrsschrift," with a Hebrew supplement, "Abne Nezer" (*ib.* 1853), and of "Wiener Monatsblätter für Kunst und Litteratur" (*ib.* 1853).

Bibliography: Fürst, *Orient, Lit.* 1849, pp. 633 *et seq.*; idem, *Bibl. Jud.* ii. 234; *Zikkaron ha-Sefer*, Vienna, 1869 (autobiographical notes by Letteris); *Allg. Zeit. des Jud.* 1871, p. 692; G. Bader, in *Aḥiasaf*, 1903; N. Slouschz, *La Renaissance de la Littérature Hébraïque*, pp. 51-53, Paris, 1902.

s. N. Sl.

LETTERS IN EVIDENCE. See Evidence.

LEVANDA, LEV OSIPOVITCH: Russian author; born at Minsk 1835; died at St. Petersburg 1888. Levanda graduated from the rabbinical school in Wilna in 1854; was appointed instructor in the government school of his native town; and held the position of adviser on Jewish affairs ("learned Jew") to the governor-general of Wilna. He began his literary career early in life. In the fifties he was a contributor to the "Minskiya Gubernskiya Vyedomosti"; in 1860 he published in "Razsvyet," edited by Osip Rabinovitch, his "Depo Bakaleinyikh Tovarov"; in 1861 he began to publish in "Sion" his "Drug Bernar." He contributed to many periodicals, among them "Vilenskiya Gubernskiya Vyedomosti," of which he was the editor; "St. Peterburgskiya Vyedomosti"; and "Vilenski Vyestnik." In the last-named appeared his story "Samuel Gimpels." In 1876 he published a collection of sketches under the title "Ocherki Proshlavo," followed later by a number of stories, such as "Chetyre Guvernera," "Lyubitelski Spektakl," "Iz Dobravo Staravo Vryemeni," etc., in "Russki Yevrei," "Yevreiskoe Obozrenie," and "Voskhod." In 1876, also, he took active part in the publication of Landau's "Yevreiskaya Biblioteka." To this period belong his "Goryacheye Vryemya," "Gnyev i Milost Magnata," and "Avraam Yosefovich." In the eighties Levanda continued his literary activities with great zeal, publishing many letters and articles bearing on the Jewish question, besides two novels, "Ispovyed Dyeltza" and "Bolshoi Remiz," and other stories in "Nedyelya" and elsewhere.

Most of Levanda's writings deal with Jewish life and Jewish problems. He took a deep interest in everything that concerned his coreligionists, and rendered many a service to the Jews of Lithuania. He exposed (1863) the false witnesses in a trial of several Jews of the government of Kovno on the charge of ritual murder. He was at first a warm advocate of assimilation, and upbraided the Jews for their apathy and ignorance, stating his views in a series of novels and belletristic sketches. Later, his views underwent a change, and Levanda began to see that the salvation of the Russian Jew was not in assimilation. Levanda was a keen observer, a skilful but dry narrator, and possessed an intimate knowledge of Jewish life. His best novels are those which have no object, as "Ocherki Proshlavo" (1875), "Tipy i Siluety" ("Voskhod," 1881), "Avraam Yosefovich" ("Voskhod," 1885, 1887), etc. In his novel "Goryacheye Vryemya" (Yevreiskaya Biblioteka, 1871–73), which treats of the Polish insurrection, the author combats the idea of assimilation, which had for a while carried away the Jews of Poland. After the riots of 1881 Levanda became an advocate of the Palestinian movement. His works are enumerated in the "Sistematicheski Ukazatel," etc., St. Petersburg, 1892.

BIBLIOGRAPHY: *Entziklopedicheski Slovar*, xvii. 428; N. S. Rashkovski, *Sovremenniye Russko-Yevreiskiye Deyateli*, p. 46, Odessa, 1899.

H. R. J. G. L.

LEVEN, MANUEL: French physician; born in 1831. He studied in Paris at the Lycée Henri IV., and in 1851 entered the Institut Agronomique at Versailles. In the following year this institution was suppressed on suspicion of republicanism, and Leven, while lecturing on science at the Lycée Bonaparte, began his medical studies (M.D. 1860; his thesis, "Rapports de l'Idiotie et du Crétinisme," gained a gold medal from the Société Médicopsychologique of Paris). In 1863 he was appointed physician to the Compagnie du Chemin de Fer du Nord, and in 1870–71 was ambulance-surgeon of the ninth arrondissement of Paris and of the Bataillon du Chemin de Fer du Nord, receiving the military ribbon of the Legion of Honor in 1871. From 1871 to 1878 he was a member of the Board of Health of Paris, and from 1873 to 1889 head physician of the Hôpital Rothschild. Leven is especially noteworthy for his work in gastric pathology. He is the author of "Traité des Maladies de l'Estomac," 1879; "L'Hygiène des Israélites," 1883; "Estomac et Cerveau," 1884; "La Névrose," 1887; "Système Nerveux et Maladies," 1893; and "La Vie, l'Ame, et la Maladie," 1902.

Leven is known also as a philanthropist. Together with Eugène Manuel he founded, in 1848, the first night-school for Jewish apprentices, which developed into a manual-training school; and he has been the president of its administrative council since 1879. He is also one of the founders of the Alliance Israélite Universelle, vice-president of the Comité des Ecoles Israélites, member of the Comité de Refuge du Plessis-Piquet (an agricultural school), and chevalier of the Order of Isabella the Catholic.

S. J. KA.

LEVEN, NARCISSE: French lawyer and communal worker; born at Urdingen, on the Rhine, Oct. 15, 1833; educated at the Lycée Henri IV. and at the Faculty of Law in Paris. For five years he was the secretary of Adolphe Crémieux, and he was an active member of the group which opposed Napoleon III. and which included Jules Ferry, Spuller, and Hérold. During the Franco-German war he was general secretary of the Ministry of Justice, but he resigned on the retirement of its minister, Adolphe Crémieux, and has since refused all government positions. From 1880 to 1887 he was a member of the Municipal Council of Paris, of which he became vice-president.

Leven took an active part in the founding of the Alliance Israélite Universelle, becoming successively its secretary, vice-president (1883–98), and, after S. Goldschmidt's death, president. He is, in a certain sense, the historian of the Alliance, both through his clear and exhaustive reports and through the orations he has delivered at the funerals of his colleagues. For thirty-six years he has been a member of the Jewish Consistory of Paris, becoming its vice-president on the death of Michel Erlanger. He is a member also of the committees of the Rabbinical Seminary and the Ecole de Travail, and is president of the Jewish Colonization Association.

S. J. KA.

LEVENSON, PAVEL YAKOVLEVICH: Russian lawyer; born at Kamenetz, Podolia, 1837; died at St. Petersburg Jan. 16, 1894. In 1863 he went to St. Petersburg, where he devoted himself chiefly to law. In 1871 he graduated at the university there, and in 1877 became an advocate in the circuit court of justice.

Levenson contributed articles on Jewish subjects to the "Voskhod" and to other journals, was one of the editors of the "Suebny Vyestnik," and was editor of the department of criminology of the "Journal Grazhdanskavo i Ugolovnavo Prava." He was also the author of the biographies of Boccaria and Benthan in "Pavlenkovs Biografii Zamyechatelnykh Lyudei." His brother was **Osip Levenson,** advocate in the circuit court of Moscow (d. 1895). Osip was the musical critic of the Moscow daily "Russkiya Vyedomosti"; his articles were afterward published in Moscow under the titles "V Kontzert Zalye" (1880–81) and "Iz Oblasti Muzyki" (1885).

BIBLIOGRAPHY: Brockhaus and Efron, *Entziklopedicheski Slovar*, xviii. 433, St. Petersburg, 1895.

H. R. A. S. W.

LEVENTRITT, DAVID: American lawyer and judge; born at Winnsboro, South Carolina, Jan. 31, 1845; A.B. 1864, Free Academy (now College of the City of New York), and LL.B. 1871, University of the City of New York. He practised law in New York, acting as special counsel for the city in important condemnation proceedings; and since Jan. 1, 1899, he has been a justice of the Supreme Court of the state of New York.

Leventritt was for a number of years vice-president of the Aguilar Free Library, and is associated with many of the Jewish charitable institutions in New York city.

BIBLIOGRAPHY: *The Bench and Bar*; *Who's Who in America*, 1903–5.

A.

LEVERTIN, OSKAR IVAR: Swedish poet and critic; born at Gryt, East Gotland, July 17, 1862; educated at the University of Upsala (Ph.D. 1882), where, in 1889, he was appointed docent; four years later he became professor of literature at the University of Stockholm. His early work, "From the Riviera: Sketches from the Coast of the Mediterranean," and the collections of stories, "Småmynt" and "Konflikter, Nya Noveller" (1885), though realistic in tendency, are distinguished for exuberance of imagination. "Lifvets Fiender" (1891) marks a change in manner, and in "Legender och Visor," a volume of poems, he appears as a pronounced romanticist. These poems attracted much attention by their sentiment and finished form, and the succeeding volume, "Nya Dikter," placed Levertin in the front rank of Swedish romantic poets. His novel "Magistrarne Österås" appeared also in Germany. He was also a critic and essayist, his principal productions in this field being: "Teater och Drama Under Gustaf III."; "Gustaf III., som Dramatisk Författare"; "Johan Welander"; "Fran

Gustaf III. Dagar"; "Svenska Gestalter"; "Diktare och Drömmare"; etc. He died Sept. 22, 1906.

S. J. Wo.

LEVETUS, CELIA (CELIA MOSS): English writer; born at Portsea 1819; died at Birmingham 1873; daughter of Joseph and Amelia Moss of Portsea. At the age of eighteen Celia, in conjunction with her sister **Marion,** published a volume of poems bearing the title "Early Efforts. By the Misses Moss of the Hebrew Nation" (1838; 2d ed. 1839). The work was dedicated to Sir George Staunton. The next joint work in which the sisters engaged was the "Romance of Jewish History" (1840). This was published by subscription, among the subscribers being Sir Edward Bulwer Lytton, to whom the work was dedicated, and Lord Palmerston. The "Romance" was followed by "Tales of Jewish History" (1843).

The above-mentioned works were written in London, where the two sisters had settled in order to take up the profession of teaching. Besides publishing various poems and short stories, the two sisters founded "The Sabbath Journal" (1855), which, however, had only a brief existence. Subsequently Celia Moss married Lewis Levetus of Birmingham, to which city she removed, and for a time her literary efforts ceased. Her last work, "The King's Physician" (London, 1873), was written during the long and painful illness which ended in her death.

J. I. H.

LEVI (לוי).—**Biblical Data:** Third son of Jacob by Leah and one of the twelve Patriarchs of the tribes of Israel; born at Padan-aram (Gen. xxix. 34, xxxv. 23; I Chron. ii. 1). The name is derived from לוה (= "to be joined"; "Now this time will my husband be joined unto me," Gen. xxix. 34). Levi joined Simeon in the destruction of the Shechemites to avenge the honor of their sister Dinah, for which both were severely censured by their father (Gen. xxxiv. 25–30). When Jacob called his sons together to bless them, Levi and Simeon, notwithstanding their plea that they had acted in defense of their sister, were again condemned (Gen. xxxiv. 31, xlix. 5–7). Levi had one daughter, Jochebed, the mother of Moses, and three sons; he emigrated with them to Egypt with his father and brothers, and died there at the age of 137 years (Gen. xlvi. 8, 11 *et seq.*; Ex. i. 1–2; ii. 1; vi. 16, 20).

J. M. Sel.

——**In Apocryphal and Rabbinical Literature:** Levi, as ancestor of the priestly tribe chosen to guard the Sanctuary and the Law, appears prominently in both apocryphal and rabbinical literature. At variance with Gen. xxix. 34 and Num. xviii. 2, 4, the name "Levi" is interpreted as "the one who joins the sons to their Father in heaven" (Gen. R. lxxi. 5; see another interpretation in Ex. R. i. 4). He was "separated" by his father, Jacob, in accordance with the latter's vow (Gen. xxviii. 22), as the tenth son, either by counting from the youngest upward or by some more complicated process, and so consecrated to the priesthood (Book of Jubilees, xxii. 3–10; Targ. Yer. to Gen. xxxii. 25; Gen. R. lxx. 7; comp. Epstein, "Mi-Ḳadmoniyyot ha-Yehudim," p. 97; comp. Pirḳe R. El. xxxvii., according to which he was consecrated by the archangel Michael). In the Testaments of the Twelve Patriarchs (Levi, 1–9) are described two visions Levi had — before and after he had avenged the crimes perpetrated by Hamor, the son of Shechem. In the first vision he saw the seven heavens with all their mysterious contents, and after the secrets of the Messianic time and the Judgment Day had been disclosed to him he received a sword and a shield with which to make war against the Amorites. In the vision following the extermination of the Shechemites he beheld seven angels bringing him the seven insignia of the priesthood, of prophecy, and of the judgment, and after they had anointed him and initiated him into the priesthood they disclosed to him the threefold glory of his house: the prophecy of Moses, the faithful servant of the Lord; the priesthood of Aaron, the high priest, and his descendants; and the possession of the royal scepter and the priesthood together (in the Maccabean dynasty) after the pattern of Melchizedek: high priests, judges, and scribes. His grandfather Isaac instructed him in the law of God and in the statutes of priesthood. In Jubilees, xxxi. 12–17, also, Levi is told by Isaac, with reference to John Hyrcanus, of the future greatness and threefold glory of his house (see Charles, "Book of Jubilees," p. 187; comp. Targ. Yer. to Deut. xxxiii. 11).

Visions.

The twofold rôle in which Levi is represented in Deut. xxxiii. 8–11 (verse 11 originally followed verse 7, Judah's blessing) appealed with special force to the age of John Hyrcanus, who was both high priest and warrior-king, victorious over the Gentiles. Accordingly, in the war of the sons of Jacob against the Amorites, which forms a parallel to the war of the Maccabees against the surrounding tribes, Levi also took part (see Midr. Wayissa'u in Jellinek, "B. H." iii. 1–5; "Chronicles of Jerahmeel," p. 83, Gaster's transl. 1899; Jubilees, xxxiv. 1–9; Test. Patr., Judah, 3–5). In the Prayer of Asenath Levi is described as a prophet and saint who forecasts the future while reading the heavenly writings and who admonishes the people to be God-fearing and forgiving. He was entrusted with the secret writings of the ancients by his father, Jacob, in order to keep them in his family for all generations to come (Jubilees, xlv. 16).

The epithet "thy pious [A. V. "holy"] one" given to Levi, and the whole passage of Deut. xxxiii. 8–10, furnish the haggadic support for the characterization of Levi, as well as of the tribe of Levi, as superior to the rest in piety. Accordingly it is said (Sifre, Deut. 349–351; Sifre, Num. 67; Tan., Beha'aloteka, ed. Buber, p. 13; Midr. Teh. to Ps. i. 14; Ex. R. xv. 1; Num. R. iii., vii. 2, xv. 9) that in Egypt and in the wilderness the Levites observed the Abrahamitic rite and the whole Law; in the Holy Land they even abstained from work in order to devote themselves to contemplation (θεωρία) and to prayer (Tan., Wayera, ed. Buber, p. 4; Num. R. v. 1). In other words, they were the ancient Ḥasidim, the elect ones (Num. R. iii. 2, 4, 8, 11; xv. 9). Levi, the father of the tribe, accordingly displayed this

The Tribe.

spirit of piety in his own household; he married Milkah, of the daughters of Aram, of the (holy) seed of the Terahites (Jubilees, xxxiv. 20; Test. Patr., Levi, 11). The names he gave to his sons—Gershon, Kehat, and Merari—are interpreted in the sight of their future destiny (*ib.* Levi, 11; Num. R. iii. 12). When his daughter Jochebed ("God giveth glory") was born to him he was already "the glorified of God" among his brethren (Test. Patr., Levi, 11).

J. K.

LEVI (לוי), **TRIBE OF.—Biblical Data:** The tribe of Levi was descended from the patriarch Levi, the third son of Jacob and Leah (Gen. xxix. 34). Levi shared in Simeon's treachery toward the men of Shechem (Gen. xxxiv. 25–30), in consequence of which, it was thought, his descendants were scattered in Israel (Gen. xlix. 5–7). At the time of the descent into Egypt there were only three sons of Levi (Gen. xlvi. 11); these had become at the time of the Exodus a numerous tribe, which then was chosen for the priesthood and the service of the sanctuary (Ex. vi. 16 *et seq.*; Num. i. 49–54, iii. 6 *et seq.*). According to Leviticus and Numbers a wide distinction existed at this time between the house of Aaron, which constituted the priesthood, and the remainder of the Levites, to whom the more menial duties of the religious service were assigned (comp. Num. xvi. 8–11, and LEVITES).

In the blessing of Moses, Levi is mentioned only in connection with priestly functions (Deut. xxxiii. 8–11). At the settlement the Levites are said to have received no definite domain (Josh. xiii. 14), but scattered cities were assigned them in territory belonging to other tribes. From the portion of Simeon and Judah they received Hebron, Libnah, Jattir, Eshtemoa, Holon, Debir, Ain, Juttah, and Beth-shemesh; in the territory of Benjamin their cities were Gibeon, Geba, Anathoth, and Almon; from Ephraim they took Shechem, Gezer, Kibzaim, and Beth-horon; from Dan, Eltekeh, Gibbethon, Aijalon, and Gath-rimmon (comp. I Chron. vi. 69, where two of these cities are ascribed to Ephraim and two are not mentioned); from the tribe of Manasseh, Tanach, Gath-rimmon, Golan, and Beeshterah; from Issachar, Kishon, Dabareh, Jarmuth, and En-gannim; from Asher, Mishal, Abdon, Helkath, and Rehob; from Naphtali, Kedesh, Hammoth-dor, and Kartan; from Zebulun, Jokneam, Kartah, Dimnah, and Nahalal; from Reuben, Bezer, Jahazah, Kedemoth, and Mephaath; and from Gad, Ramoth in Gilead, Mahanaim, Heshbon, and Jazer (Josh. xxi. 11–39; comp. I Chron. vi. 55–81). When these cities are compared with those said to have been left to the other tribes, one is impressed with the fact that, if the Levites received all these, together with their suburbs, they must have had a better and more commanding inheritance than had any of their brethren.

Cities of Levites.

In striking contrast with this splendid inheritance attributed to the Levites by Joshua and the Chronicler is the non-appearance of the Levites in any important rôle during the period of the Judges. They are not mentioned in the Song of Deborah, nor do they appear elsewhere in Judges until the appendix, where two individual Levites are mentioned (comp. Judges xvii. 7, xviii. 30, and xix. 1). Under David and Solomon, according to the accounts in Samuel and Kings, the Levites exercised the priestly functions, though not to the exclusion of others from such functions. For example, Samuel, an Ephraimite (I Sam. ix. 13), and the sons of David (II Sam. viii. 18) offered sacrifices. From this time to the Exile the Levitical priests held much the same position as they held in the time of Solomon. They exercised their priestly functions, but were by no means, except in rare instances, the dominating influence. In the post-exilic period, as Chronicles, Ezra, and Nehemiah show, they became a dominant element in the Jewish community.

In Early Sources.

——**Critical View:** The problem presented by the Biblical data is this: What is the relation of the clan mentioned in such passages as Gen. xlix. 5–7 to the priests of a later time? In seeking a solution of this problem it should be noted that in J, the oldest source, the patriarch Levi merited his father's curse, in consequence of which the tribe was divided and scattered (comp. Gen. xxxiv. 30, 31). In narrating a crisis in the life of Moses the same writer mentions the "sons of Levi" (Ex. xxxii. 26–28), but in such a way that the phrase may refer either to the descendants of the patriarch or to men who possessed the qualities of a "levi." Later, a narrative that is ascribed to J by some critics (*e.g.*, Moore, in "S. B. O. T.") tells how a Levite of Beth-lehem-judah became a priest at the shrine at Dan (Judges xvii. 9, xviii. 30). This representation of J would seem to mean that misfortune overtook a clan known as that of Levi, that its members became scattered, and that they were held in such high esteem as priests that they gradually appropriated the priestly offices.

E has almost nothing to say of Levites. According to him, apparently, Moses and Aaron were of one of the tribes of Joseph, and he uses "Levite" to describe not the member of a clan, but a man especially eligible to the priesthood, distinctly stating that one such man belonged to the clan Judah (Judges xvii. 7; comp. "S. B. O. T."). If the patriarch Levi was mentioned in this source, the passage in question has not been transmitted. E, apparently, knew no such patriarch, and supposed that a priest might come from any tribe and that he received the designation "Levite" for other reasons than those of descent.

In the Source E.

P, the latest of the sources in the Pentateuch, distinctly connects the tribe of Levi with the priesthood, bridging all the gaps with extensive genealogies, dividing the various services of the sanctuary among the different descendants of the patriarch, and assigning to each class of descendants its respective cities in Canaan (Josh. xxi.). Of these three representations, P's can not be correct. The whole tenor of the history in Judges and Samuel contradicts P's assertion that the Levites received all these cities at the time of the conquest, as well as his view that the religious office was, in any exclusive sense, in the hands of the Levites. Gezer, for example, was not in Israel's possession until the time of Solomon (I Kings ix. 16). Recent exploration has shown it to have been the site of a great temple of Astarte ("Pal. Explor. Fund, Quarterly Statement," Jan., 1903, pp. 23 *et seq.*).

Not in Possession of Gezer.

This temple, too, was on the level of the pre-exilic Israelitish city, and may have been used by the Hebrews of the period. Other Levitical cities in the list, like Kadesh in Naphtali, Ashtaroth in Bashan, and Hebron, can be proved to have been old shrines which in the pre-exilic period were still in use. If the information contained in the sources known were more complete, it probably could be shown that P's whole system of Levitical cities is a post-exilic explanation of the fact that important sanctuaries had existed at these points in pre-exilic times, and that they had thus become the centers where Levites resided in large numbers.

P's whole conception is, therefore, untrustworthy. Recent critics are divided in opinion, some believing, with J, that there was actually a tribe of Levi, which became scattered and gradually absorbed the priestly office, others adopting the apparent view of E that "levi" was a general term for a priest, and then supposing that the existence of the clan Levi was assumed in order to explain the origin of the priestly class. Lagarde ("Orientalia," ii. 20; "Mittheilungen," i. 54), Baudissin ("Priesterthum," p. 72), and Budde ("Religion of Israel to the Exile," pp. 80 *et seq.*) may be cited as critics who have advocated this latter view. If Hommel and Sayce were consistent, they might be placed in the same class, for if the term came from contact with the Minæan Jethro, as they believe, it would not be found in Israel before the time of Moses. This inference, however, they do not draw. The former view (which has been called the view of J), that there was an actual tribe of Levi, has the support of Wellhausen ("History of Israel," pp. 141–147; "Prolegomena zur Gesch. Israels," 5th ed., pp. 137–145), Stade ("Gesch." i. 152–157), Dillmann ("Commentary on Genesis," ii. 458; "Alttestamentliche Theologie," pp. 128 *et seq.*), Nowack ("Lehrbuch der Hebräischen Archäologie," ii. 92 *et seq.*), Cornill ("Hist. of Israel," p. 46), Marti (in Kayser's "Alttestamentliche Theologie," 3d ed., pp. 72, 95 *et seq.*), Guthe ("Gesch. des Volkes Israel," pp. 21–47 *et seq.*), and Holzinger ("Genesis," in Marti's "K. H. C." p. 257).

It is probable that there was an old clan which was overtaken by misfortune and scattered. Sayce points out ("Patriarchal Palestine," p. 239) that the "Lui-el" of the list of Rameses III. is parallel to "Joseph-el" and "Jacob-el" of Thothmes III.'s list, and so may point to a habitat of the tribe of Levi. It is quite possible that the priestly order originated quite independently of this tribe, however, and afterward was erroneously identified with it. In the present state of knowledge it is impossible to tell whether the view of J or of E more nearly represents the truth.

The origin of the name "Levi" has been quite variously explained. (1) In Gen. xxix. 34, J regards it as from the stem לוה ("to join"), and explains it by Leah's hope that her husband would now be joined to her. (2) Lagarde (*l.c.*) derives it from the same stem, but explains it as referring to Egyptians who, like Moses, attached themselves to the Israelites when they left Egypt. (3) Baudissin (*l.c.*) derives it in the same way, but refers it to those who were attached to, or accompanied, the ark. (4) Budde (*l.c.*) gives it the same derivation, but applies it to those who attached themselves to Moses in some great religious crisis. (5) Hommel ("Aufsätze und Abhandlungen," i. 30; "Süd-Arabische Chrestomathie," p. 127; "Ancient Hebrew Tradition," pp. 278 *et seq.*) derives it from the Minæan "lawi'u" (= "priest");

Origin of Name.

with this Mordtmann ("Beiträge zur Minäischen Epigraphik," p. 43) and Sayce ("Early Hist. of the Hebrews," p. 80) agree. (6) Wellhausen ("Prolegomena," 5th ed., p. 141) suggests that it is a gentilic name formed from the name of Levi's mother, Leah; in this opinion Stade ("Gesch." i. 152), Gray ("Hebrew Proper Names," p. 96), Nöldeke (hesitatingly; in "Z. D. M. G." xl. 167), Gunkel ("Genesis," p. 301), and Luther (Stade's "Zeitschrift," xxi. 54) concur. (7) Jastrow ("Jour. Bib. Lit." xi. 120 *et seq.*) connects "Levi" with "Laba" of the El-Amarna tablets. "Laba" he connects with the word לביא ("lion"), thus making Levi the "lion" tribe. (8) Skipwith (in "J. Q. R." xi. 264) connects "Levi" with "leviathan," making it refer to the coils of the serpent. This variety of opinion illustrates and emphasizes the present uncertainty concerning the origin and existence of the tribe, which results from the scanty evidence.

Bibliography: In addition to the works already cited, see Graf, *Gesch. des Stammes Levi*, in Merx, *Archiv*, i. 68–106, 208–236; Hümmelauer, *Das Vormosaische Priesterthum in Israel*; Eduard Meyer, *Gesch. des Altertums*, i. 377 *et seq.*

E. G. H. G. A. B.

LEVI I. See Levi b. Sisi.

LEVI II.: Palestinian scholar of the third century (third amoraic generation); contemporary of Ze'era I. and Abba b. Kahana (Yer. Ma'as. iii. 51a). In a few instances he is quoted as Levi b. Laḥma (Ḥama; comp. Yer. R. H. iv. 59a with R. H. 29b; Yer. Ta'an. ii. 65a with Ta'an. 16a; see Rabbinovicz, "Diḳduḳe Soferim," to Ber. 5a, Ta'an. *l.c.*, Zeb. 53b). In later midrashim the title "Berabbi" is sometimes added to his name (Pesiḳ. R. xxxii. 147b; Num. R. xv. 10; Tan., Beha'aloteka, 6; comp. Pesiḳ. xviii. 135a; Tan., *l.c.* ed. Buber, p. 11; see Levi bar Sisi). He quotes halakic and homiletic utterances by many of his predecessors and contemporaries; but as he quotes most frequently those of Ḥama b. Ḥanina, it may be conjectured that he was the latter's pupil, though probably he received instruction at Johanan's academy also. In this academy he and Judah b. Naḥman were alternately engaged to keep the congregation together until Johanan's arrival, and each was paid for his services two "selas" a week. On one occasion Levi advanced the theory that the prophet Jonah was a descendant of the tribe of Zebulun, deducing proof from Scripture. Soon after Johanan lectured on the same subject, but argued that Jonah was of the tribe of Asher. The next week being Judah's turn to lecture, Levi took his place and reverted to the question of Jonah's descent, proving that both Johanan and himself were right: on his father's side Jonah was descended from Zebulun; on his mother's, from Asher. This skilful balancing of their opposing opinions so pleased Johanan that he declared Levi capable of filling an independent lectureship, and for twenty-two years thereafter Levi successfully filled such an office (Gen. R. xcviii. 11; Yer. Suk. v. 55a). This incident seems to indicate that Levi's earlier years were spent in poverty; later, however, he seems to have been better circumstanced, for he became involved in litigations about some houses and consulted Johanan on the case (Yer. Sanh. iii. 21d).

Views About Jonah.

Levi's name but rarely appears in halakic literature, and then mostly in connection with some Scriptural phrase supporting the dicta of others (see Yer. Ber. i. 2c, 3d *et seq.*; Yer. Ter. iv. 42d [where his patronymic is erroneously given as "Ḥina"]). In the Haggadah, on the contrary, he is one of the most frequently cited. In this province he became so famous that halakists like Ze'era I., who had no special admiration for the haggadist (Yer. Ma'as. iii. 51a), urged their disciples to frequent Levi's lectures and to listen to them attentively, for "it was impossible that he would ever close a lecture without saying something instructive" (Yer. R. H. iv. 59b; Yer. Sanh. ii. 20b). In these lectures he would frequently advance different interpretations of one and the same text, addressing one to scholars and the other to the masses (Gen. R. xliv. 4; Eccl. R. ii. 2). Sometimes he would discuss one subject for months in succession. It is reported that for six months he lectured on I Kings xxi. 25—"There was none like unto Ahab, which did sell himself to work wickedness in the sight of the Lord." Then he dreamed that Ahab appeared to him and remonstrated with him: "Wherein have I sinned against thee and how have I offended thee that thou shouldst continually dwell on that part of the verse which refers to my wickedness and disregard the last part, which sets forth the mitigating circumstance — 'whom Jezebel his wife stirred up'?" (הסתה = "instigated," "incited"). During the six months following, therefore, Levi spoke as Ahab's defender, lecturing from the same verse, but omitting the middle clause (Yer. Sanh. x. 28b).

Fame as Haggadist.

Levi divided all haggadists into two classes: those who can string pearls (*i.e.*, cite apposite texts) but can not perforate them (*i.e.*, penetrate the depths of Scripture), and those who can perforate but can not string them. Of himself, he said that he was skilled in both arts (Cant. R. i. 10). Once, however, he so provoked Abba b. Kahana by what was a palpable misinterpretation that the latter called him "liar" and "fabricator." But it is authoritatively added that this happened once only (Gen. R. xlvii. 9). He and Abba were lifelong friends, and the latter manifested his admiration for his colleague's exegesis by publicly kissing him (Yer. Hor. iii. 48c).

String of Pearls.

To render Scriptural terms more intelligible Levi frequently used parallels from cognate dialects, especially from Arabic (Gen. R. lxxxvii. 1; Ex. R. xlii. 4; Cant. R. iv. 1); and to elucidate his subject he would cite popular proverbs and compose fables and parables. Thus, commenting on Ps. vii. 15 (A. V. 14), "He . . . hath conceived mischief, and brought forth falsehood," he says: "The Holy One having ordered Noah to admit into the ark pairs of every species of living beings, Falsehood applied, but Noah refused to admit him unless he brought with him his mate. Falsehood then retired to search for a mate. Meeting Avarice, he inquired, 'Whence comest thou?' and on being told that he too had been refused admission into the ark because he had no mate, Falsehood proposed that they present themselves as mates. But Avarice would not agree to this without assurance of material gain; whereupon Falsehood promised him all his earnings, and Avarice repeated the condition agreed upon. After leaving the ark Avarice appropriated all of Falsehood's acquisitions, and when the latter demanded some share of his own, Avarice replied, 'Have we not agreed that all thy earnings shall be mine?' This is the lesson: Falsehood begets falsehood" (Midr. Teh. to Ps. vii. 15; Hamburger ["R. B. T." *s.v.* "Fabel"] erroneously ascribes this fable and several others to Levi bar Sisi). Levi became known among his contemporaries as מרא דשמעתא (= "master of traditional exegesis"; Gen. R. lxii. 5).

BIBLIOGRAPHY: Bacher, *Ag. Pal. Amor.* ii. 296-436; Frankel, *Mebo*, p. 111a; Heilprin, *Seder ha-Dorot*, ii., s.v. *Levi b. Sisi*, with whom he erroneously identifies Levi II.; Weiss, *Dor*, iii. 135.

S. S. S. M.

LEVI, AARON. See MONTEZINOS, ANTONIO.

LEVI, ABRAHAM: German traveler; born at Horn, in the principality of Lippe, in 1702; died at Amsterdam Feb. 1, 1785. At the age of five he was sent to Brog, near Lemgo, for the sake of his studies, and he stayed there till 1714, when he returned home. He then acquired a passion for traveling, and in 1719, when only seventeen years old, he definitely left the parental home in order to execute his plan.

Levi traveled through Germany, Bohemia, Moravia, Hungary, Austria, and the whole of Italy. Full of youthful ardor, he did not leave unnoticed the most trivial circumstance. He mentions among other things the synagogues of Frankfort, and the riches of his relative Samson Wertheimer of Vienna. He wrote an account of his travels in Judæo-German (published by Roest in "Isr. Letterbode"), adding a Hebrew poem describing ten of the most noteworthy events and giving an acrostic on his name. The poem is followed by explanatory notes, also in Hebrew. Levi's narrative is interesting in that it gives statistics and customs of the Jews in small localities not mentioned by other historians or travelers.

BIBLIOGRAPHY: Roest, in *Isr. Letterbode*, x. 148 *et seq.*

S. S. M. SEL.

LEVI BEN ABRAHAM BEN ḤAYYIM: French encyclopedist; champion of the liberal party in Provence in the struggle for the study of secular sciences; born at Villefranche-de-Confluent, Roussillon, between 1240 and 1250; died at or near Arles soon after 1315. He was descended from a scholarly family. His father, ABRAHAM BEN ḤAYYIM, was a synagogal poet, and rabbi in Narbonne, which place he left about 1240 to settle finally in Villefranche. Levi's uncle Reuben ben Ḥayyim, also, like his grandfather, was a scholar. A son of this Reuben ben Ḥayyim was, probably, Samuel ben Reuben of Beziers, who took Levi's part, although in vain, in his conflict with the orthodox party in Provence. Levi himself was the maternal grandfather of the philosopher Levi ben Gershon of Bagnols.

Life.

Levi ben Abraham was instructed in Bible and Talmud, and in secular sciences as well, and was soon drawn into the rationalistic current of the time. One of his teachers was a certain R. Jacob, whom he cites as his authority for an astronomical explanation, and who may have been Jacob ben Machir ibn Tibbon. It is probable, also, that Levi was instructed by his uncle Reuben ben Ḥayyim, from whom he quotes an explanation of Gen. i. 3 (Vatican MS. cxcii. 56b).

Levi left his native city (probably on account of poverty, which oppressed him almost throughout his life), remained for a short time in Perpignan, and then went to Montpellier, where, in 1276, he was engaged in literary pursuits, and earned a scanty living by teaching languages and lecturing. During the heat of the controversy over the study of secular sciences he was at Narbonne, in the house of the wealthy Samuel Sulami, who was prominent both as a poet and a scholar. Levi enjoyed his hospitality until, yielding to the pressure of the opposing party, represented especially by Solomon ben Adret, Samuel Sulami asked his guest to leave. The latter then sought shelter with his cousin Samuel ben Reuben in Beziers (see "Minḥat Ḳena'ot," No. 41), but was persecuted, apparently, even there. He was excommunicated by the orthodox party, yet, after the conflict was over, in 1315, he found rest and quiet at Arles, where he remained until his death. He has been identified by some with Levi of Perpignan, whom Judah Mosconi, in his supercommentary to Ibn Ezra, characterizes as one of the most prominent of scholars (see Berliner's "Magazin," iii. 148 [Hebr. part, p. 41]).

Works.

Steinschneider points out that a large portion of the scientific works written in Arabic were made accessible in Hebrew translations in the first half of the thirteenth century, and that the entire realm of knowledge began to be treated in encyclopedias in the second half of the same century. Levi ben Abraham wrote two such encyclopedic works, which show the range of knowledge of an educated rationalistic Provençal Jew of that period. The first of these is the "Batte ha-Nefesh weha-Leḥashim," the title of which is taken from Isa. iii. 20. It is a rimed compendium, didactic in tone, of the various sciences, in ten chapters and 1,846 lines, with a few explanatory notes and a preface, also in rimed prose. In the preface to this work, which is frequently found in manuscripts, Levi demonstrates the usefulness of his compendium by pointing out the difficulties which those who are not well acquainted with general literature must surmount in order to acquire a knowledge of the sciences, which are scattered through all sorts of books. He had long cherished the thought of compiling an encyclopedia, but had always been deterred by the fear that the task would prove beyond his power; at last, in 1276, strength was promised him in a vision, whereupon he began the work at Montpellier.

His Encyclopedia.

Levi was compelled, by the nature of the work, to limit himself to giving the conclusions of the chief authorities, particularly of Maimonides, whom he follows step by step. Ch. i. treats of ethics. In the paragraphs treating of the history of the diffusion of learning, the author expresses the view that the Greeks and Arabs derived almost their entire scientific culture from the ancient Hebrews, a theory which justified the reading of Greco-Arabic ideas into the Bible (Steinschneider). The following chapters treat of logic (ii.), the Creation (iii.), the soul (iv.), prophecy and the Messianic period (v.; the coming of the Messiah will occur in the year 1345), the mystic theme of the "Merkabah," the divine throne-chariot (vi.), numbers (vii.), astronomy and astrology (viii.), physics (ix.), and metaphysics (x.). After the author himself had found it necessary to provide the difficult verses with explanatory notes (which are not found in all the manuscripts), Solomon de Lunas, probably identical with Solomon ben Menahem Prat (or Porat), wrote, about 1400, a commentary to the "Batte ha-Nefesh weha-Leḥashim."

His "Liwyat Ḥen."

The second work of Levi was the "Liwyat Ḥen" or "Sefer ha-Kolel," a "comprehensive book" (encyclopedia). The dates of its beginning and completion are unknown, but it must have been written before the outbreak of the controversy mentioned above. It is divided into two "pillars," called "Jachin" and "Boaz" (after I Kings vii. 21), the first containing five treatises, and the second one. Since no complete manuscript of this work has yet been discovered, any analysis of its contents is naturally uncertain. According to Steinschneider, its six treatises are as follows: (1) logic or arithmetic (?); (2) geometry; (3) astronomy and astrology; (4) physics (?), psychology, and the "theory of intellect"; (5) metaphysics; (6) theology, prophecy, the mysteries of the Law, and belief and the Creation. In the third treatise, the most complete (Paris MS. No. 1047; Vatican MS. No. 383; Neubauer, "Cat. Bodl. Hebr. MSS." No. 2028, and additamenta), the astrological writings of Abraham ibn Ezra are slavishly followed, and the prediction is made that the Messiah will appear in the year 1345. The last, or theological, treatise, which is extant at Oxford (Neubauer, "Cat. Bodl. Hebr. MSS." Nos. 1285, 2023), Parma (MS. de Rossi No. 1346), and Rome (Vatican MS. No. 2893), naturally had a greater circulation, and, on account of the author's rationalistic interpretation of the Scriptures, aroused much more opposition than the other sections of the work, which aimed at nothing original and included only what could be found elsewhere.

The teachings which Levi ben Abraham promulgated, both by pen and by speech, although not original with him, naturally aroused the anger of the orthodox. In his hands Abraham and Sarah became symbols of "matter" and "intellect"; the four kings against whom Abraham went to war represented the four faculties of man; Joshua's miracles were symbolically interpreted: they were not actual occurrences; the possibility of a supernatural revelation was doubted; and there were other and similar doctrines that poisoned the naively credulous and religious mind.

Opposition to His Views.

Orthodox resentment was first shown at Narbonne, where Levi was residing in the house of Samuel Sulami. It mattered little that Levi "was in general very reserved and was communicative only to those who shared his views" ("Minḥat Ḳena'ot," No. 121), and that it was not known with certainty whether he was to be reckoned among the orthodox or among the heretics; nor yet that he always put off Don Vidal Crescas, who, although he opposed his teachings, was his personal friend, and had often, but vainly, asked him for his writings. Equally unavailing were his observance of the ceremonial law and his pretense that he occupied himself with philosophical questions only for the sake of being able to cope with heretics (*ib.* No. 14). Poverty compelled Levi, "who was born under an unlucky star," to teach at this dangerous and critical period and thereby spread his doctrines. Solomon ben Adret, therefore, then the champion of the orthodox party, felt constrained to attack this "arch-heretic, condemned by the voices of all." "A Mohammedan is dearer far to me than this man," he wrote (*ib.* No. 14; see J. Perles, "R. Salomo ben Abraham ben Adereth," p. 25), "who is not ashamed to say openly that Abraham and the other patriarchs have ceased to exist as real personages and that their places have been filled by philosophical concepts. . . . Levi and his adherents are enemies not only of Judaism, but of every positive religion." In his reply to Levi's letter, in which the latter endeavored to clear himself of the charges brought against him, Solomon ben Adret advised Levi in friendly terms to confine himself to Talmudic sciences; this Levi plainly did not wish to do, and thus he brought excommunication upon himself.

Levi expanded and revised his "Liwyat Ḥen" in Sept., 1315, at Arles, and the manuscript (Vatican MS. No. cxcii.) was discovered by Steinschneider ("Hebr. Bibl." 1869, p. 24).

In addition to these works Levi wrote three others —"Sodot ha-Torah," "Sefer ha-Tekunah," and an astrological treatise. The "Sodot ha-Torah" (Paris MS. No. 1066), which probably was an exposition of the mysteries contained in the Ten Commandments, and which was written before 1276, is said to be lost, but it was probably incorporated, in a revised form, in his "Liwyat Ḥen." The "Sefer ha-Tekunah," on astronomy and chronology, consisted of forty chapters and was written in 1276. The treatise on predictive astrology is entitled "Sha'ar ha-Arba'im be-Koḥot ha-Kokabim," "the fortieth chapter" of the preceding book, although it forms a separate work. They were edited at the same time. The great dependence on Abraham ibn Ezra's astrological opinions shown in this treatise would suggest that it may be the compendium which Levi is said to have made of Ibn Ezra's works. All these smaller treatises seem to have been merely preparatory to the "Liwyat Ḥen," in which they are used.

BIBLIOGRAPHY: Carmoly, *La France Israélite*, p. 46; A. Geiger, in *Oẓar Neḥmad*, ii. 94 *et seq.*; idem, in *He-Ḥaluẓ*, ii. 12 *et seq.*; Grätz, *Gesch.* vii. 219, 223; Gross, in *Monatsschrift*, 1879, p. 428; idem, *Gallia Judaica*, pp. 83, 199, 329, 465; Renan-Neubauer, *Les Rabbins Français*, pp. 628 *et seq.*, 658 *et seq.*; J. Perles, *R. Salomo ben Abraham ben Adereth*, pp. 13, 22 *et seq.*, 70; Steinschneider, in Ersch and Gruber, *Encyc.* section ii., part 43, pp. 294 *et seq.* (where all the previous literature on the subject is given).

J. M. Sc.

LEVI, BENEDIKT: German rabbi; born at Worms Oct. 14, 1806; died at Giessen April 4, 1899; son of Samuel Wolf Levi, a member of the Sanhedrin of Paris and rabbi of Mayence from 1807 until his death in 1813. Benedikt Levi, who was destined for a rabbinical career, received his early Talmudic education from Rabbis Gumpel Weismann, Ephraim Kastel, and Löb Ellinger. Having prepared himself under the tuition of Michael Creizenach, he entered the University of Würzburg (1824) and attended at the same time the lectures on Talmud of Abraham Bing, rabbi in that city. Three years later he entered the University of Giessen, where he took the degree of Ph.D. When A. A. Wolf was called from Giessen to Copenhagen, Levi was appointed (1829) his successor, remaining in that rabbinate for sixty-seven years.

Levi, who was an advocate of moderate Reform, published, in addition to various addresses and sermons, the essays "Beweis der Zulässigkeit des Deutschen Choralgesanges mit Orgelbegleitung beim Sabbathlichen Gottesdienste der Synagoge" (in Weiss's "Archiv für Kirchenrecht," 1833; republished separately, Offenbach, 1833) and "Das Programm der Radicalen Reformgemeinde Giessens Beleuchtet" (Giessen, 1848). Several minor treatises by him appeared in "Allg. Zeitung des Judenthums," "Der Volkslehrer," and other periodicals.

BIBLIOGRAPHY: Kayserling, *Bibliothek Jüd. Kanzelredner*, ii. 25–39; *Allg. Zeit. des Jud.* pp. 63, 172 *et seq.*

S. M. K.

LEVI, BORACH (Joseph Jean François Elie): Convert to Christianity; born at Hagenau in 1721; son of a Jewish commissary. He went to Paris in March, 1751, to follow up a lawsuit, and while there became a convert to Christianity, and was baptized Aug. 10, 1752. He attempted to win over his wife, whom he had left behind at Hagenau, but she refused, though she was forced by the law of the time to surrender her two daughters; they were baptized ten years afterward. He endeavored to gain permission to marry again, though he refused to give a Jewish bill of divorce to his wife. He obtained from the bishops of Verdun and Metz canonical opinions that a baptized Jew might marry a Christian if his wife refuses to be converted with him, and he attempted to get the curé of his town to cry the banns for his marriage with one Anne Thaevert. The curé refused, and a long series of lawsuits ensued. The whole question of the validity of a Jewish marriage was raised, and the technical difficulty which presented itself to the canonical lawyers was the possibility of Levi's wife becoming Christian after he had married a Christian woman. Parliament refused to give him relief (Jan. 2, 1758).

No more is known of him, though several legal memorials were written on the curious case.

BIBLIOGRAPHY: Isidore Loeb, in *Annuaire de la Société des Etudes Juives*, 1884, pp. 275–334.

J.

LEVI, CARLO: Italian physiologist; born at Genoa March 26, 1866; educated at the University of Modena (M.D. 1889). In 1888 he was appointed tutor, and later assistant professor, of experimental physiology at the University of Modena; in 1893 he assumed charge of the classes in special physiology, and in 1897 of the classes in histology, at the veterinary college connected with the same institution. In 1904 he was appointed editor of "L'Idea Sionista"; he is also vice-president of the Modena chapter of the Dante Alighieri Society. He has written papers on Jewish medical statistics, on physical culture, and on other scientific subjects for various periodicals, including the "Congresso Medico Internazionale di Roma" (1894) and the "Congresso Internazionale di Fisiologia a Torino" (1901), and has published lectures on experimental, technical, and veterinary physiology.

S. U. C.

LEVI, DAVID: Italian poet and patriot; born at Chieri 1816; died at Venice Oct. 18, 1898. Educated at the Jewish schools of his native town and Vercelli, he for a short time followed a mercantile career. In 1835 he went to the University of Parma, and later to that of Pisa, but he had to leave the latter on account of a duel in which he wounded a fellow student whom he had challenged for having made an insulting remark about the Jews. Having passed his examination as doctor of law, he went in 1839 to Paris. The university ideals of a united, free Italy had found a strong follower in Levi, who had become a member of the Irredentist society La Giovane Italia. In Paris he belonged to the circle of Italian patriots; and, on returning to Italy, he soon became one of the leaders in the political movement for the secession of northern Italy from Austria and for the union of all the Italian states.

David Levi.

Settling in Venice, Levi took part in the Lombardic rebellion against Austria of 1848–49. In 1850 he removed to Turin. After the Franco-Italian-Austrian war of 1859, when the Italian provinces of Austria were united with the Italian kingdom (1860), he was elected to the Italian assembly at Florence, where as a member of the Liberal party he championed the cause of equality of rights and religious freedom. He was a member of the National Assembly until 1879, when, being defeated, he retired from politics.

Levi wrote many poems, especially during his stay at Venice, and a large number of political and war songs, among these the well-known ode to Pope Pius IX., who in 1846, upon his election to the papal chair, was hailed as liberator, but who in 1849 changed his political views and became strongly reactionary. Through all Levi's works his great love for Italy and for Judaism is evident.

Levi was the author of: "Patria ed Affetti" (Venice, 1849), a collection of poems; "Gli Martiri del 1799" (Turin, 1850), a drama; "Martirio e Redenzione" (*ib.* 1859); "Del Navarra a Magenta" (*ib.* 1866; revised ed., 1884, with a fantastic allegorical dialogue as a second part); "Vita di Pensiero" (Milan, 1875); "Vita d'Azione" (Turin, 1882); "Il Semitismo" (*ib.* 1884); "La Mente di Michelangelo" (*ib.* 1890); "Giordano Bruno" (*ib.* 1894).

Levi's principal work, however, is the great drama "Il Profeta." Its theme Levi describes in his introduction as follows: "I intend to hold a mirror before my contemporaries, in which they may see their errors, faults, and mistakes, and thereby learn to despise them; at the same time placing before them a high ideal, which they should strive to live up to." To this end he selected the story of Jeremiah. The drama treats in five acts of the war between Zedekiah and Nebuchadnezzar. *Jeremiah* foresees the fall of Jerusalem, if the people do not give up their worship of Baal, repent of their sins, and return to the only true God. *Jeremiah* the prophet and *Ananias*, the priest of Baal, respectively exhort and try to persuade the king and the Jews to follow them. *Ananias* is successful; *Jeremiah* is thrown into prison; and Jerusalem falls when attacked by the invading army. The Temple is destroyed, and the Jews are led into captivity. *Jeremiah's* prophecy is fulfilled.

When *Jeremiah* is thrown into prison his daughter *Rachel* falls into the hands of *Ananias*, who tries to win her for himself. His suit proving unsuccessful, he orders her to be sacrificed to Moloch, when God intercedes. Lightning kills *Ananias*, and *Rachel* is liberated by her lover, *Emanuel*. The last words of *Ananias* are: "Uno Infinito hai vinto" (end of Act 3). *Emanuel* joins the ranks of the defender of Jerusalem, is mortally wounded, and dies in the arms of his beloved. Spiritually Jewdom has conquered over heathendom, and *Rachel* has returned pure to her lover; but physically Jewdom is defeated. *Rachel* loses her lover and must go into exile; this exile will, however, purify not the Jews alone, but through them the world, and will prepare man for a better future.

The dialogue which follows the drama in the 1884 edition has very little connection with it. It is sustained by *Emanuel*, the representative of prophetism, and by *Ahasuerus*, the representative of mankind, and treats mainly of Rome.

BIBLIOGRAPHY: S. H. Margulies, *Dichter und Patriot*, Berlin, 1896; Levi's own works, *Vita di Pensiero* and *Vita d'Azione*, as above.

S. F. T. H.

LEVI, DAVID: Hebraist and author; born in London 1742; died 1801. He was destined by his parents for the rabbinate; but the design was abandoned, and he was apprenticed to a shoemaker. Subsequently he set up in business for himself as a hatter; but, meeting with considerable losses, he abandoned this business and turned his attention to dressing the material for men's hats. Meantime he continued to pursue his studies in Hebrew, especially in the Prophets.

From 1783 to 1797 Levi was busily engaged in issuing a series of works (a list of which is given below) dealing with Jewish theology, grammar, and ritual. He rendered great services to the London Jews in translating their prayers into English and in vindicating their faith against the onslaughts of Dr. Priestley and Thomas Paine. His works present a remarkable instance of industry and perseverance under adverse conditions. During the latter part of his life he followed the business of a printer.

David Levi.

Among Levi's literary works were: "Rites and Ceremonies of the Jews" (London, 1783); "Lingua Sacra" (3 vols., 1785–87), a Hebrew dictionary and grammar; letters to Dr. Priestley (1787–89) in reply to the latter's "Letters to the Jews"; "The Pentateuch in Hebrew and English" (1789). He wrote also "Translations of the Hebrew Prayers and Services into English" (1789–93), which he undertook at the request of the representatives of the Portuguese Jews; "Dissertations on the Prophecies" (vol. i. 1793). In controversy with believers and unbelievers he wrote "Letters to Mr. Halhed on the Subject of the Prophecies of Brothers" (1795) and "Letters to Thomas Paine, in Answer to His 'Age of Reason'" (New York, 1797). Here he attempts to show that the divine mission of the Prophets is fully established by the present dispersion of the Jews. In 1794 he published a translation of the Seder service.

Levi was also poet in ordinary to the synagogue, and furnished odes when required on several public celebrations, as, for instance, on the king's escape from assassination in 1795.

Bibliography: *Jew. Chron.* Sept. 3, 10, 1896; Lysons, *Environs of London*, Supplement, pp. 430–431; *European Magazine*, May, 1799; *Memoirs of B. Goldsmid*; Picciotto, *Sketches of Anglo-Jewish History*, pp. 228, 229; *Dict. Nat. Biog.*

J. G. L.

LEVI, EUGENIA: Italian authoress; born Nov. 21, 1861, at Padua; educated in that city, and in Florence and Hanover. In 1885 she was appointed professor at the Royal High School for Young Ladies at Florence.

She has written many essays and studies for the Italian journals and has published the following works: "Ricorditi," anthology of Italian prosaists and poets from Dante Alighieri to Giosuè Carducci (Florence, 1888; 5th ed. 1899); "Dai Nostri Poeti Viventi" (Florence, 1891; 2d ed. 1896); "Dai Giornale di Lia" (Rome, 1892); "Rammentiamocci" (Florence, 1893); "Dante . . . di Giorno in Giorno" (*ib.* 1894; 3d ed. 1898), a collection of quotations from Dante; "Pensieri d'Amore" (*ib.* 1894; 3d ed. 1900); "Fiorita di Canti Tradizionali del Popolo Italiano" (*ib.* 1895); "Deutsch," a translation of standard German works (*ib.* 1899).

S. F. T. H.

LEVI BEN GERSHON (RaLBaG, commonly called **Gersonides;** known also as **Leon de Bagnols,** and in Latin as **Magister Leo Hebræus):** French philosopher, exegete, mathematician, and physician; born at Bagnols in 1288; died April 20, 1344. Abraham Zacuto ("Yuḥasin," ed. Filipowski, p. 224) states that Levi died at Perpignan in 1370; but the exact date of his death is given as above by Petrus of Alexandria, who translated in 1345 a note by Levi on the conjunction of Saturn with Jupiter (see Steinschneider in "Hebr. Bibl." vii. 83–84). "Gershuni," the Hebrew equivalent of "Gersonides," was first used to designate Levi b. Gershon by David Messer Leon (*c.* 1500). Levi was a descendant of a family of scholars. According to Zacuto (*l.c.*), his father was Gershon b. Solomon, the author of "Sha'ar ha-Shamayim" (but see Steinschneider, "Hebr. Uebers." p. 9, and Gross, "Gallia Judaica," p. 94); according to Zacuto (*l.c.*), Ibn Yaḥya ("Shalshelet ha-Ḳabbalah," p. 83, Warsaw, 1889), Conforte ("Ḳore ha-Dorot," p. 19a), and Azulai ("Shem ha-Gedolim," i.), Naḥmanides was Levi's maternal grandfather. As Levi himself, in his commentary on the Pentateuch (on Ex. xxxiv. 9), quotes Levi ha-Kohen as his grandfather, and as Levi b. Gershon is not known to have been a priest, this Levi ha-Kohen was apparently his mother's father. It was therefore suggested by Carmoly (Jost's "Annalen," i. 86) that Naḥmanides was the maternal grandfather of Levi's father. Levi was doubly related to Simon b. Ẓemaḥ Duran. Besides being a cousin of Judah Delesfils, Duran's grandfather, he married the latter's sister (Duran, "Tashbeẓ," i., No. 134; see Steinschneider, "Hebr. Bibl." *l.c.*).

Very little is known of Levi's life beyond the fact that he lived now in Orange, now in Avignon, now in a town called in Hebrew עיר האזוב = "the city of hyssop" (comp. Isidore Loeb in "R. E. J." i. 72 *et seq.*, who identifies the last-named town with Orange). In spite of Ben Adret's ban on those who taught philosophy to the young, Levi was early initiated into all its branches; and he was not thirty years old when he began to write the "Milḥamot Adonai," the philosophical work which brought him so much renown. Isaac de Lattes (Preface to "Sha'are Ẓiyyon") writes: "The great prince, our master Levi b. Gershon, was the author of many valuable works. He wrote a commentary on the Bible and the Talmud; and in all branches of science, especially in logic, physics, metaphysics, mathematics, and medicine, he has no equal on earth." Though a distinguished Talmudist, Levi never held a rabbinical office. He earned a livelihood most probably by the practise of medicine.

His Versatility.

In his commentary on the Bible, Levi makes frequent comparisons of Hebrew and Arabic words, while he speaks of Latin as the language of the Christians (commentary on I Sam. xvi. 6). Neubauer ("Les Ecrivains Juifs Français," p. 249)

מארץ מולדתו וילך לארץ
כנען והנה

התועלת

אלה תולדות

פרשת לך לך

ויאמר יי' אל אברם לך לך

וגו' עד ויהי רעב בארץ

ביאור המלות

PAGE FROM THE FIRST EDITION OF LEVI BEN GERSHON'S COMMENTARY TO THE PENTATEUCH, MANTUA, BEFORE 1480.

(From the Sulzberger collection in the Jewish Theological Seminary of America, New York.)

concludes, contrary to the assumption of Isidore Weil ("Philosophie Religieuse de Lévi-ben-Gerson," p. 15, Paris, 1868), that Levi knew Latin well, but not Arabic.

Although Levi lived in Provence, where, under the protection of the popes, the Jews suffered less than in other provinces of France, yet he sometimes laments over the sufferings of the Jews, which, he says, "are so intense that they render meditation impossible" (Preface to "Milḥamot"). In an epilogue to his commentary on Deuteronomy written in 1338 (Paris MS. No. 244) he says he was unable to revise his commentary on the Pentateuch at Avignon, as he could not obtain there a copy of the Talmud.

His Works.

Levi was the author of the following philosophical works: (1) "Milḥamot Adonai" (Riva di Trenta, 1560), mentioned above, begun in 1317 and finished in 1329 (see below). (2) Commentary on the Pentateuch (Mantua, 1476–80). (3) Commentary on the Earlier Prophets (Leiria, 1494). The philosophical essence of these two commentaries was published separately under the title "To'aliyyot" (Riva di Trenta, 1550 and 1564 respectively). Commentaries (4) on Job (Ferrara, 1477), (5) on Daniel (n.d.; n.p.), on Proverbs (Leiria, 1492), (6) on Canticles, Esther, Ecclesiastes, and Ruth (Riva di Trenta, 1560); (7) "Sefer ha-Heḳḳesh ha-Yashar," a treatise on syllogisms; (8) commentary on the Middle Commentaries and the résumés of Averroes, all of them finished about 1321 (the part of this commentary which refers to Porphyry's Isagoge to the categories, and to the treatise on interpretation, was translated into Latin by Jacob Mantino and published in the first volume of the works of Aristotle with the commentaries of Averroes); (9) "Sefer ha-Mispar," called also "Ma'aseh Ḥosheb," a treatise on algebra, which Levi finished in 1321, when, he says, he was thirty-three; (10) a treatise on astronomy, originally forming the first part of the fifth section of the "Milḥamot," but omitted by the editor, who considered it a separate work (see below); (11) commentary on the introduction to, and books i., iii.–v. of, Euclid, probably the work referred to by Joseph Solomon Delmedigo (see Geiger, "Melo Ḥofnayim," p. 12, Hebr.). (12) "Dillugim," astrological note on the seven constellations, in which Levi refers to his "Milḥamot"; (13) "Meshiḥah," on a remedy for the gout (Parma MS. De Rossi No. 1189; Neubauer, "Cat. Bodl. Hebr. MSS." No. 2142, 37). Levi wrote also the following rabbinical works: (14) "Sha'are Ẓedeḳ," commentary on the thirteen hermeneutic rules of Ishmael b. Elisha, printed in the "Berit Ya'aḳob" of Jacob b. Abraham Faitusi (Leghorn, 1800). (15) "Meḥoḳeḳ Safun," commentary on the haggadah in the fifth chapter of Baba Batra, mentioned by Solomon b. Simeon Duran ("Milḥemet Miẓwah," p. 23). Neubauer (*l.c.* p. 253) considers it doubtful whether the authorship of this work can be correctly ascribed to Levi. (16) Commentary on Berakot, mentioned by Levi in his commentary on Deuteronomy. (17–18) Two responsa signed by Levi b. Gershon, one concerning "Kol Nidre" and mentioned by Joseph Alashkar of Tlemçen, the other mentioned by Isaac de Lattes (Responsa, i. 88), and its authorship declared doubtful by Neubauer (*l.c.*). The Parma MS. No. 919 contains a liturgical confession beginning אלהי בשתי and attributed to Levi.

The following works are erroneously attributed to Levi b. Gershon: commentary on Averroes' "De Substantia Orbis," which seems to have been written by Moses of Narbonne; "Awwat Nefesh," a commentary on Ibn Ezra's commentary on the Pentateuch (comp. Benjacob, "Oẓar ha-Sefarim," p. 31); "Magen Yeshu'ot," a treatise on the Messiah; "Yesod ha-Mishnah" (Wolf, "Bibl. Hebr." iii. 650); ritual institutions ("taḳḳanot"; Parma MS. De Rossi No. 1094); commentary on Bedersi's "Beḥinat 'Olam."

His Astronomy.

Some description may be given here of Levi's astronomical treatise. It has been said that this was originally included in the "Milḥamot." It is probably the one referred to under the title "Ben Arba'im le-Binah" by Abraham Zacuto ("Tekunnat Zekut," ch. vi.), in allusion to Levi's being forty years old when he finished it. Steinschneider (in Ersch and Gruber, "Encyc." section ii., part 43, p. 298) calls it simply "Sefer Tekunah." It consists of 136 chapters. After some general remarks on the usefulness of astronomy and the difficulties attending its study, Levi gives a description of an instrument which he had invented for precise astronomical observations and which he calls "megalleh 'amuḳḳot." In the ninth chapter, after having devoted to this instrument two poems (published by Edelmann in "Dibre Ḥefeẓ," p. 7), he exposes the defects of the systems of Ptolemy and Al-Bitruji, and gives at length his own views on the universe, supporting them by observations made by him at different times. He finished this work Nov. 24, 1328, but revised it later, and completed it by adding the results of observations made up to 1340. The ninety-ninth chapter includes astronomical tables, which were commented on by Moses Botarel. This work was highly praised by Pico de Mirandola, who frequently quoted it in his "Disputationes in Astrologiam." Its importance is also apparent from the fact that the part treating of the instrument invented by Levi (ch. iv.–xi.) was translated into Latin by order of Pope Clement VI. (1342). Later the whole work was translated into Latin, and the beginning was published by Prince Boncompagni ("Atti dell' Academia dei Nuovi Lincei," 1863, pp. 741 *et seq.*).

BIBLIOGRAPHY: Grätz, *Gesch.* 3d ed., vii. 315–322; Gross, *Gallia Judaica*, pp. 94 *et seq.*; Munk, *Mélanges*, pp. 497–501; De Rossi, *Dizionario*, i. 126 *et seq.*; Renan-Neubauer, *Les Ecrivains Juifs Français*, pp. 240–298; Steinschneider, *Cat. Bodl.* cols. 1607–1615; *idem*, in Ersch and Gruber, *Encyc.* section ii., part 43, pp. 295–301; *idem*, in Berliner's *Magazin*, xvi. 137 *et seq.*; idem, in *Mi-Mizraḥ umi-Ma'arab*, iv. 40 *et seq.*; idem, *Hebr. Uebers.* p. 27 *et passim.*

M. SEL.

——**As Philosopher:** The position of Levi ben Gershon in Jewish philosophy is unique. Of all the Jewish Peripatetics he alone dared to vindicate the Aristotelian system in its integrity, regardless of the conflict existing between some of its doctrines and the principal dogmas of Judaism. Possessed of a highly developed critical sense, Levi sometimes disagrees with Aristotle and asserts his own views in opposition to those of his master, Averroes; but when, after having weighed the pros and cons of a doctrine, he believes it to be sound, he is not afraid to profess it, even when it is directly at variance with an accepted dogma of Jewish theology. "The Law," he says, "can not prevent us from considering to be true that which our reason urges us to believe" (Introduction to the "Milḥamot," p. 6).

His Unique Position.

Coming after Maimonides, Levi treated only of those philosophical questions which the author of the "Moreh Nebukim," because of his orthodoxy, either solved in direct opposition to Aristotelian principles, or explained by such vague statements that the student was left in the dark as to Maimonides' real opinion on the subject. These questions are: the immortality of the soul; prophecy; God's omniscience; divine providence; the nature of the celestial spheres; and the eternity of matter. To the solution of these six philosophical problems Levi devoted his "Milḥamot Adonai." The work comprises six main divisions, each subdivided into chapters. The method adopted by Levi is that of Aristotle: before giving his own solution of the question under discussion he presents a critical review of the opinions of his predecessors. The first main division opens with an exposition of the theories of Alexander of Aphrodisias, Themistius, Averroes, and of certain philosophers of his time, concerning Aristotle's doctrine of the soul. Aristotle's own treatment of this subject is, indeed, very obscure; for while asserting ("De Anima," ii. 1) that the soul is the first entelechy of the organic body, and consequently can not be separated from it any more than form can be separated from matter, he maintains (*ib.* iii. 5) that of the two elements of the soul, the passive intellect and the active intellect, the latter is immortal. To reconcile these two conflicting statements, Alexander of Aphrodisias, in his paraphrase of Aristotle's book on the soul, makes a distinction between the material intellect (νοῦς ὑλικός), which, like matter, has only a potential existence, and the acquired intellect (νοῦς ἐπικτητός), which latter is the material intellect when, by study and reflection, it has passed from potentiality into actuality, and has assumed an effective existence. The cause of this transition is the universal intellect, which is God Himself. But as the relation between God and the soul is only temporary, divine intervention ceases at death, and the acquired intellect lapses into nothingness. This psychological system, in which a mere physical faculty of a substance that has nothing spiritual in its essence may by a gradual development become something immaterial and permanent, is rejected by Themistius.

Views on the Soul.

For him the intellect is an inherent disposition which has for its substratum a substance differing entirely from that of the body. Averroes, in his treatise on the intellect, combines the two systems, and enunciates the opinion that the intellect is a mere potentiality so long as it is in the body, but that it becomes an actual substance as soon as it leaves the body. According to some contemporaries of Levi the intellect is a faculty which is self-existent.

After a thorough criticism of these various opinions, Levi gives his own view on the nature of the intellect. The intellect, he says, which is born with man, is but a mere faculty that has for a substratum the imaginative soul, this latter being allied to the animal soul. This faculty, when put in motion by the universal intellect, begins to have an effective existence by the acquired ideas and conceptions with which it identifies itself; for the act of thinking can not be separated from the object of the thought. This identification of the intellect with the intelligible constitutes the acquired intellect ("sekel ha-nikneh"), which is to the original faculty what form is to matter. But does the acquired intellect cease to exist with the death of the body? This question is closely connected with that of the nature of universals. If, as asserted by the realists, universals are real entities, the acquired intellect, which consists of conceived ideas that have a real existence, may survive the body; but if, as maintained by the nominalists, nothing exists but individuals, and universals are mere names, immortality is out of the question. In opposition to Maimonides ("Moreh," iii. 18) Levi defends the theory of the realists and maintains thereby the principle of immortality.

The second division of the "Milḥamot" is devoted to philosophy. It was intended to supplement and correct some statements made by Aristotle in his unfinished work "De Sensu et Sensibili," which contains two chapters on divination. While Maimonides (*l.c.* ii. 32–48) treated only of the psychological side of the problem, "What are the requisites of prophecy?"

On Prophecy.

Levi considered also the metaphysical phase, "Is prophecy possible?"; "Is the admissibility of prescience not absolutely incompatible with the belief in man's freedom of will?" To answer the first question there is, according to Levi, no need of speculative demonstrations. That there are men endowed with the faculty of foreseeing the future is, he considers, incontestable. This faculty is found not only in prophets, but also in soothsayers, visionaries, and astrologers. He cites the case of a sick man personally known to him, who, though without any medical knowledge, dreamed of the remedy which would cure him. Levi himself claimed to have received in dreams, on many occasions, solutions to puzzling metaphysical problems.

But prescience implies also predestination. This, however, seems to conflict with freedom of the will. To refute this objection, Levi endeavors to demonstrate that, though all sublunary events are determined by the celestial bodies, man may by his freedom of will and his intelligence annul such determinations. After having reconciled prediction with the principle of free will, he defines the nature of prescience and establishes a distinction between prophecy and other kinds of divination. In prophetic visions, he says, it is the rational faculty which is put into communication with the universal intellect, and therefore the predictions are always infallible; while in divination the receptive faculty is the imaginative power, and the predictions may be often chimerical. Thus, like Maimonides, Levi holds that the origin of prophetic perceptions is the same as that of ordinary science—the universal intellect. But, while the author of the "Moreh" counts among the requisites of prophecy a fertile imagination, Levi maintains that the greatness of the prophet consists precisely in his faculty of so checking the exercise of imagination that it may not disturb the dictates of reason. Another point of disagreement between Maimonides and Levi is the question whether intellectual and moral perfections are alone sufficient to insure to their possessor prophetic vision. For Maimonides the special will of God is the sine qua non for prophecy; for Levi moral and intellectual perfections are quite sufficient.

The most interesting part of the "Milḥamot" is the third main division, which treats of God's omniscience. As is known, Aristotle limited God's knowledge to universals, arguing that if He had knowledge of particulars, He would be subject to constant changes. Maimonides rejects this theory, and endeavors to show that belief in God's omniscience is not in opposition to belief in His unity and immutability. "God," he says, "perceives future events before they happen, and His perception never fails. Therefore no new ideas can present themselves to Him. He knows that such and such an individual will be born at such a time, will exist for such a period, and will then return into non-existence. The coming into existence of this individual is for God no new fact; nothing has happened that He was unaware of, for He knew this individual, such as he now is, before his birth" ("Moreh," i. 20).

God's Omniscience.

As to the objections made by the Peripatetics to the belief in God's omniscience; namely, how is it conceivable that God's essence should remain indivisible, notwithstanding the multiplicity of knowledge of which it is made up; that His intelligence should embrace the infinite; that events should maintain their character of contingency in spite of the fact that they are foreseen by the Supreme Being—these, according to Maimonides, are based on an error. Misled by the use of the term "knowledge," men believe that whatever is requisite for their knowledge is requisite for God's knowledge also. The fact is that there is no comparison whatever between man's knowledge and that of God, the latter being absolutely incomprehensible to human intelligence. This theory is severely criticized by Levi, who affirms that not reason but religion alone dictated it to Maimonides. Indeed, Levi argues there can be no doubt that between human knowledge and God's knowledge there is a wide difference in degree; but the assumption that there is not the slightest analogy between them is unwarranted. When the nature of God is characterized by means of positive determinations, the soul is taken as the basis of reasoning. Thus science is attributed to God, because man also possesses it to a certain extent. If, then, as Maimonides supposes, there is, except in name, no likeness between God's knowledge and man's knowledge, how can man reason from himself to God? Then, again, there are attributes which can be predicated of God, as, for instance, knowledge and life, which imply perfection, and others which must be denied to Him, as, for instance, corporeality and motion, because these imply imperfection. But, on the theory of Maimonides, there is no reason for the exclusion of any attribute, since, applied to God, all attributes necessarily lose their significance. Maimonides is indeed consistent, and excludes all positive attributes, admitting only negative ones; but the reasons given by him for their distinction are not satisfactory.

Having thus refuted Maimonides' theories both of God's omniscience and of the divine attributes, Levi gives his own views. The sublime thought of God, he says, embraces all the cosmic laws which regulate the evolutions of nature, the general influences exercised by the celestial bodies on the sublunary world, and the specific essences with which matter is invested; but sublunary events, the multifarious details of the phenomenal world, are hidden from His spirit. Not to know these details, however, is not imperfection, because in knowing the universal conditions of things, He knows that which is essential, and consequently good, in the individual.

In the fourth division Levi discusses the question of divine providence. Aristotle's theory that humanity only as a whole is guided and protected by a divine providence, admits the existence of neither prophecy nor divination. Nor can every individual be the object of the solicitude of a special providence; for this is (1) against reason, because, as has been demonstrated, the divine intelligence embraces only universals, and it is inadmissible that evil can proceed from God, the source of all good; (2) against experience, because one often sees the righteous borne down by miseries, while the wicked are triumphant; (3) against the sense of the Torah, which when warning men that their rebellions will be followed by disasters, because God will hide His face from them, implies that the calamities which will overtake them will come as the consequence of their having been left without protection from the vicissitudes of fate. Levi, therefore, arrives at the conclusion that some are under the protection and guidance of the general providence, and others under a special, individual providence. It is incontestable, he says, that a general, beneficent providence cares for all sublunary beings. Upon some it bestows certain bodily organs which enable them to provide themselves with the necessaries of life and to protect themselves from danger; to others it gives a nature which enables them to avoid that which would harm them. It is also demonstrated that the higher a being stands in the scale of creation the more organs it possesses for its preservation and defense; in other words, the greater is the solicitude and protection bestowed upon it by the Creator. Those species of animals which more nearly resemble man participate in the solicitude of providence to a greater extent than that part of animality which forms the connecting-link between the animal and vegetable kingdoms. If, then, the degree of participation by a being in the protection of the divine providence is proportioned to the degree of its development, it is obvious that the nearer one comes to the active intelligence, the more is he the object of the divine solicitude. Thus those who strive to develop the faculties of the soul enjoy the care of a special, individual providence, while those who grope in ignorance are guarded only by the general providence.

Divine Providence.

Relation to the Intellect.

There is, however, one great objection to this theory; namely, there can be no question of a special providence if God knows only generalities. To meet this antinomy Levi defines the nature of the special providence. All the events, he says, all the phenomena of this world, good as well as evil, are due to the influences of the celestial bodies. The various effusions of these bodies are regulated by eternal, immutable laws; so that the demiurgic principle, which knows these laws, has a perfect knowledge of all the phenomena which affect this world, of the good and evil which are in store for mankind. This subjection to ethereal substances, however, is not absolute; for man by his free will can, as stated above, annul their determinations. But in order to avert their mischievous emanations he must be warned of the danger. This warning is given by the divine providence to mankind at large; but as it is perceived only by those whose intellect is fully developed, the divine providence benefits individuals only.

The fifth division comprises three parts treating respectively of astronomy, physics, and metaphysics.

Astronomy, Physics, and Metaphysics.

The astronomical part, which forms of itself a considerable work of 136 chapters, was not included in the published edition of the "Milḥamot," and is still in manuscript. As has been said above, it was translated by order of Pope Clement VI. into Latin and enjoyed such a high reputation in the Christian scientific world that the astronomer Kepler gave himself much trouble to secure a copy of it.

The second part is devoted to the research of the final causes of all that exists in the heavens, and to the solution of astronomical problems, such as whether the stars exist for themselves, or whether they are only intended to exercise an influence upon this world; whether, as supposed by Ptolemy, there exists above the starred spheres a starless one which imparts the diurnal motion to the inferior heavens, or whether, as maintained by Averroes, there is none; whether the fixed stars are all situated in one and the same sphere, or whether the number of spheres corresponds to that of the stars; how the sun warms the air; why the moon borrows its light from the sun and is not luminous of itself.

In the third part Levi establishes the existence first of an active intellect, then of the planetary intelligences, and finally the existence of a primary cause, which is God. According to him, the best proof of the existence of an efficient and final cause is the phenomenon of procreation. Without the intervention of an efficient intelligence there is no possibility of explaining the generation and organization of animated beings.

But is there only one demiurgic intelligence, or are there many? After reviewing the various existing opinions on the subject, Levi concludes: (1) that

The Spheres.

the various movements of the heavenly bodies imply a hierarchy of motive principles; (2) that the number of these principles corresponds to that of the spheres; (3) that the spheres themselves are animated and intelligent beings, accomplishing their revolutions with perfect cognition of the cause thereof. In opposition to Maimonides, he maintains that the various intelligences did not emanate gradually from the first, but were all the direct effect of the primary cause. Can not this primary cause, however, be identified, as supposed by Averroes, with one of the intelligences, especially with that which bestows motion upon the most exalted of the spheres, that of the fixed stars? This, says Levi, is impossible, first because each of these intelligences perceives only a part of the universal order, since it is confined to a limited circle of influences; if God, then, were the mobile of any sphere there would be a close connection between Him and His creatures.

The last division deals with creation and with miracles. After having refuted the arguments advanced by Aristotle in favor of the eternity of the world, and having proved that neither time nor

Creation.

motion is infinite, Levi demonstrates: (1) that the world had a beginning; (2) that it has no end; and (3) that it did not proceed from another world. In the order of nature, he says, the whole earth was covered by water, which was enveloped by the concentric sphere of air, which, in turn, was encompassed by that of fire. Was it, he asks, as Aristotle supposes, the absorbent heat of the sun which caused the water to recede and the land to appear? In that case the southern hemisphere, where the heat is more intense, ought to present a similar phenomenon. It is, therefore, obvious that it was due to the action of a superior agent. From the fact that the world had a beginning one must not, however, infer that it will have also an end; on the contrary, it is imperishable like the heavenly bodies, which are its sources of life and motion, and of which the substances, being immaterial, are not subject to the natural laws of decay.

Having thus demonstrated that the world is not eternal "a parte ante" and is eternal "a parte post," Levi gives his own view of creation. He chooses a middle position between the theory of the existence of a primordial cosmic substance and that of a creation "ex nihilo," both of which he criticizes. According to him, there existed from eternity inert undetermined matter, devoid of form and attribute. At a given moment God bestowed upon this matter (which till then had only a potential existence) essence, form, motion, and life; and from it proceeded all sublunary beings and all heavenly substances, with the exception of the separated intelligences, which were direct emanations of the Divinity.

In the second part of the last division Levi endeavors to demonstrate that his theory of creation agrees

Miracles.

with the account of Genesis; and he devotes the last chapters of the "Milḥamot" to the discussion of miracles. After having defined from Biblical inferences their nature, he demonstrates that the actual performer of miracles is neither God nor prophet, but the active intellect. There are, he says, two kinds of natural laws: those which regulate the economy of the heavens and by which the ethereal substances produce the ordinary sublunary phenomena, and those which govern the special operations of the demiurgic principle and by which are produced the extraordinary phenomena known as miracles. Like freedom of the will in man, this faculty was given by God to the active intellect as a corrective of the influences of the celestial bodies, which are sometimes too harsh in their inflexibility. The supernatural as literally understood does not exist, since even a prodigy is a natural effect of a primordial law, though it is distinguished from other sublunary events by its origin and its extreme rarity. Thus a man of a highly developed intellect may foresee the accomplishment of a certain miracle which is only the result of a providential law conceived and executed by the active intellect. Miracles are subjected, according to Levi, to the following laws: (1) their effect can not remain permanently and thus supersede the law of nature; (2) no miracle can produce self-contradictory things, as, for instance, an object that shall be both totally black and totally white at the same time; (3) no miracle can take place in the celestial spheres. When Joshua said, "Sun, stand thou still upon Gibeon" (Josh. x. 12), he merely expressed the desire that the defeat of the enemy should be completed while the sun continued to shine on Gibeon. Thus the miracle consisted in the promptness of the victory. Nor is the going backward of the shadow on the dial of Ahaz (II Kings xx. 9; Isa. xxxviii. 8) to be understood in the sense of the sun's retrogression: it was the shadow which went backward, not the sun.

Philosophy in His Commentaries.

The conclusions arrived at in the "Milḥamot" were introduced by Levi in his Biblical commentaries, where he endeavored to reconcile them with the text of the Law. Guided by the principle laid down but not always followed by Maimonides, that a philosophical or a moral teaching underlies every Biblical narrative, Levi adopted the method of giving the literal meaning and then of summing up the philosophical ideas and moral maxims contained in each section. The books of Job, Canticles, and Ecclesiastes are mainly interpreted by him philosophically. Jerusalem, according to him, symbolizes man, who, like that city, was selected for the service of God; "the daughters of Jerusalem" symbolize the faculties of the soul; and Solomon represents the intellect which governs all. Ḳohelet (Ecclesiastes) presents an outline of the ethics both of Aristotle and of his opponents, because moral truth can not be apodictically demonstrated. In opposition to the philosophical exegetes of his time, Levi, however, did not allegorize the historical and legislative parts of the Bible; but he endeavored to give a natural explanation of the miracles.

Opposition.

Levi's philosophical theories, some of which influenced Spinoza (comp. "Theologico-Politicus," ch. ii., where Spinoza uses Levi's own terms in treating of miracles), met with great opposition among the Jews. While Ḥasdai Crescas criticized them on philosophical grounds, others attacked them merely because they were not in keeping with the ideas of orthodoxy. Isaac ben Sheshet (Responsa, No. 45), while expressing admiration for Levi's great Talmudical knowledge, censures his philosophical ideas, which he considers to be heresies the mere listening to which is sinful in the eyes of a pious Jew. Abravanel (commentary on Josh. x.) blames Levi in the harshest terms for having been so outspoken in his heretical ideas. Some zealous rabbis went so far as to forbid the study of Levi's Bible commentaries. Among these were Messer Leon Judah and Judah Muscato; the latter, applying to them Num. i. 49, says: "Only thou shalt not number the tribe of Levi, neither bring his Commentaries among the children of Israel" (Commentary on the "Cuzari," p. 4). Shem-Ṭob perverted the title "Milḥamot Adonai" (= "Wars of God") into "Milḥamot 'im Adonai" (= "Wars with God"); and by this corrupted title Levi's work is quoted by Isaac Arama and by Manasseh ben Israel, who attack it in most violent terms.

BIBLIOGRAPHY: Munk, *Mélanges*, p. 498; Baer, *Philosophie und Philosophische Schriftsteller der Juden*, p. 113; Joël, *Levi ben Gerson als Religionsphilosoph*, Breslau, 1862; Renan, *Averroes et Averroïsme*, p. 194; Weil, *Philosophie Religieuse de Levi ben Gerson*, Paris, 1868.

K. I. BR.

LEVI, HERMANN: Musical director; born at Giessen, Germany, Nov. 7, 1839; died at Munich May 13, 1900. His mother was a pianist of distinction. He studied under Vincenz Lachner at Mannheim (1852–1855), and at the Leipsic Conservatorium, principally under Hauptmann and Rietz (1855–58). In 1859 he became musical director at Saarbrücken, and in 1861 conductor of the German opera at Rotterdam, from which city he was summoned in 1864 to Carlsruhe, where in his capacity as court kapellmeister he aroused general attention by his masterly conducting of the "Meistersinger" (Feb., 1869).

In 1872 Levi received the appointment of court kapellmeister at Munich; and it was his thoroughly conscientious and excellent work here—notably his production of "Tristan and Isolde" in Nov., 1881—that induced Richard Wagner to select him as the conductor of "Parsifal" at the Bayreuth Music Festival of 1882. Appointed "General-Musikdirektor" at Munich in 1894, he resigned this position in 1896 owing to ill health, and was pensioned by the government.

As the foremost director of his time, Levi conducted the musical performances during the Bismarck-Feier and also on the occasion of the tricentenary celebration of the birth of Orlando di Lasso. He was the first to produce the trilogy "Der Ring der Nibelungen" after its performance at Bayreuth in 1876; and his masterly interpretation of the Wagnerian dramas contributed to make Munich for many years a permanent musical center for these works. Levi was a convert to Christianity.

BIBLIOGRAPHY: Heinrich Porges, in *Musikalisches Wochenblatt*, pp. 334–336, Leipsic, 1900.

S. J. So.

LEVI, ISAAC, YOM-ṬOB, and JACOB: Sons of Abigdor ha-Levi Laniatore of Padua; founded a Hebrew printing establishment at Rome in 1518, which received special privileges from the pope through the intercession of Cardinal Egidio di Viterbo. There Elijah Levita's ס׳ הרכבה was printed within eighteen days (with imperfect letter-press, owing to haste, as the colophon complains); this was followed by his tables of inflections, now lost, and by his "Baḥur." The press soon closed. In 1525 Jacob published at Trino in Piedmont a prayer-book according to the Italian ritual.

Bibliography: Steinschneider, *Cat. Bodl.* col. 2901; Vogelstein and Rieger, *Gesch. der Juden in Rom*, ii. 115.

J. I. E.

LEVI ISAAC BEN MEÏR: Russian rabbi of the first half of the nineteenth century. After having been rabbi at Selichow and Pinsk, Levi Isaac was called to the rabbinate of Berdychev, where he wrote "Ḳedushshat Lewi" (Berdychev, 1816), the first part of which contains a homiletic commentary on the Pentateuch, with collectanea, the second being miscellaneous in character. He wrote also a commentary on the "Sefer ha-Zekirut," a compilation by Raphael b. Zechariah Mendel of ethical writings, based on the Biblical passages beginning with "Zakor" (Wilna and Grodno, 1835).

Bibliography: Benjacob, *Oẓar ha-Sefarim*, pp. 156, 517; Fürst, *Bibl. Jud.* ii. 243.

K. M. Sel.

LÉVI, ISRAEL: French rabbi and scholar; born at Paris July 7, 1856. He was ordained as rabbi by the Rabbinical Seminary of Paris in 1879; appointed assistant rabbi to the chief rabbi of Paris in 1882; professor of Jewish history and literature at the Paris Seminary in 1892; lecturer on Talmudic and rabbinic literature at the Ecole Pratique des Hautes Etudes in 1896.

During 1894–95 Lévi was director of "Univers Israélite." He is one of the leading spirits of the Société des Etudes Juives. On its organization in 1880 he was elected secretary and general manager of the "Revue des Etudes Juives," and in 1892 took charge of its bibliographical section. He has contributed to this journal papers on the Haggadah, the Talmudic and midrashic legends, Jewish folk-lore, the religious controversies between Jews and Christians, as well as on the history of the Jews in France.

Lévi has published in addition the following works: "La Légende d'Alexandre dans le Talmud et le Midrasch" (1884); "Trois Contes Juifs" (1885); "Le Roman d'Alexandre" (Hebrew text, with introduction and notes, 1887); "Les Juifs et l'Inquisition dans la France Méridionale" (1891); "Textes Inédits sur la Légende d'Alexandre" (in the "Steinschneider Festschrift"); "Relations Historiques dans le Talmud sur Alexandre" (in the "Kaufmann Gedenkbuch"); "Les Dix-huit Bénédictions et les Psaumes de Salomon"; "L'Ecclésiastique ou la Sagesse de Jésus, Fils de Sira," original Hebrew text, with notes and translation (part i., ch. xxxix. 15–xlix. 11; 1898; part ii., ch. iii. 6–xvi. 26; parts of ch. xviii., xix., xxv., and xxvi.; xxxi. 11–xxxiii. 3, xxxv. 19–xxxviii. 27, xlix. 11 to the end; 1901; the Académie des Inscriptions et Belles Lettres, on June 6, 1902, awarded to this last-named work one-half of the "Prix Delalande"); "Ecclesiasticus," class-room edition, Hebrew text, with English notes and English-Hebrew vocabulary, in "Semitic Studies Series," ed. Gottheil and Jastrow, 1903.

Bibliography: Moïse Schwab, *Répertoire des Articles Relatifs à l'Histoire et à la Littérature Juives Parus dans les Periodiques de 1783 à 1898*, pp. 228-231, Paris, 1899 (Supplement, 1903).

S. J. Ka.

LEVI BEN JAPHETH (HA-LEVI) ABU SA'ID: Karaite scholar; flourished, probably at Jerusalem, in the first half of the eleventh century. Although, like his father, he was considered one of the greatest authorities among the Karaites, who called him "Al-Shaikh" (the master), no details of his life are to be found in the Karaite sources. There even exists confusion in regard to his identity; in some of the sources he is confounded with his brother, or his son Sa'id (comp. Pinsker, "Liḳḳuṭe Ḳadmoniyyot," p. 119), and also with a Mohammedan scholar named Abu Hashim (Aaron ben Joseph, "Mibḥar," Paris MS.). Levi wrote in Arabic a comprehensive work on the precepts, parts of a Hebrew translation ("Sefer ha-Miẓwot") of which are still extant in manuscript (Neubauer, "Cat. Bodl. Hebr. MSS." No. 857; Steinschneider, "Cat. Leyden," No. 22; St. Petersburg MSS., Firkovich collection, No. 613). This work, which was used by nearly all the later Karaite codifiers, contains valuable information concerning the differences between the Karaites and the Rabbinites (in whose literature the author was well versed), and the dissensions among the Karaites themselves. Thus in the section dealing with the calendar, in which the year 1007 is mentioned, Levi states that in Irak the Karaites in their determination of New-Year, resembled the Rabbinites in so far as, like them, they took for their basis the autumnal equinox, while in some places the Karaites adopted the Rabbinite calendar completely.

Levi distinguishes between the views, in regard to the calendar, of the earlier and the later Rabbinites, and counts Saadia, whom he frequently attacks with the utmost violence, among the latter. In the treatise on ẓiẓit Levi says that he drew his material from the works of his father and of his predecessors. He excuses the inadequacy of treatment marking some parts of the work on the ground of the lack of sources and of the various trials and sicknesses he had suffered during its composition.

Levi's "Muḳaddimah," an introduction to the pericopes of the Pentateuch, is no longer in existence. A fragment, on Deut. i., of the Hebrew translation of Moses ben Isaiah Firuz was in the Firkovich collection and was published by Pinsker, but was lost during the Crimean war. He wrote also a short commentary on the Earlier Prophets, a fragment of which, covering the first ten chapters of Joshua, still exists (Brit. Mus. Or. No. 308). Steinschneider believes it possible that Levi was also the author of the short commentary on Psalms found in the British Museum (No. 336). According to Ali ben Sulaiman, Levi made a compendium of the lexicon "Agron" of David ben Abraham; however, this is contested by Abu al-Faraj, who asserts that the compendium was prepared by David himself.

Bibliography: Pinsker, *Liḳḳuṭe Ḳadmoniyyot*, p. 64 and Index; Fürst, *Gesch. des Karäert.* ii. 143 *et seq.*; Steinschneider, *Polemische und Apologetische Literatur*, p. 336; idem, *Hebr. Uebers.* p. 945; idem, *Die Arabische Literatur der Juden*, § 46.

K. I. Br.

LEVI, JEDIDIAH B. RAPHAEL SOLOMON: Rabbi at Alessandria and Sienna; died 1790; author of hymns for the reconsecration of the synagogue at Sienna 1786; these hymns were printed in "Seder Zemirot we-Limmud," Leghorn, 1786.

BIBLIOGRAPHY: Steinschneider, *Cat. Bodl.* col. 1289; Mortara, *Indice*, p. 33.

D. I. E.

LEVI, JUDAH: Influential Jew at Estella, Navarre, from 1380 to 1391. In 1380 and the following years he was commissioned, with Samuel Amarillo, to collect the tax of five per cent on all real estate in the district of Estella which within the preceding fifty years had been sold or rented by Jews to Christians or Moors without the permission of the king. In 1391 he, with Yuze Orabuena and Nathan Gabay, occupied the position of farmer-general of taxes. He was engaged also in banking and exchange. He appeared frequently at court in connection with business of the king's, and always took the part of his coreligionists. He was utterly impoverished during the last years of his life, as may be seen from the letter of Benveniste ibn Labi (Vienna MSS. p. 205). The king, in view of Levi's needy condition and in recognition of his services, granted him a yearly pension of sixty florins from the state treasury. After his death, which occurred about 1392, he was unjustly stigmatized as a heretic.

BIBLIOGRAPHY: Jacobs, *Sources*, Nos. 1458, 1477, 1533, 1536; Kayserling, *Gesch. der Juden in Spanien*, i. 57, 89; Grätz, *Gesch.* viii. 413.

G. M. K.

LEVI BEN LAḤMA: Palestinian haggadist of the third century. He seems to have been a pupil of Simeon ben Laḳish, whose haggadot he transmitted (Ber. 5a); but he transmitted some haggadot of Ḥama b. Ḥanina also (R. H. 29b; Zeb. 53b). Ta'an. 16a records three haggadic controversies between Levi b. Ḥama and Ḥanina, the former being supposed by Heilprin ("Seder ha-Dorot," ii.) and Bacher ("Ag. Pal. Amor." i. 354, *passim*) to be identical with Levi b. Laḥma. One of Levi's own haggadot asserts that Job was a contemporary of Moses, inferring this from a comparison of Ex. xxxiii. 16 with Job xix. 23 (B. B. 15a).

S. S. M. SEL.

LEVI, LEO NAPOLEON: American lawyer and communal worker; born Sept. 15, 1856, at Victoria, Texas; died in New York Jan. 13, 1904. Destined for a commercial career, Levi was sent to New York to take a commercial course, but manifesting no interest in his father's business, he returned to Victoria in 1871, and in 1872 entered the University of Virginia at Charlottesville, Va., to study law. He won the debater's medal and the essayist's medal in one year. Levi returned, after having finished his studies, to Texas, but being only slightly over twenty years old, he had to resort to proceedings to remove his disabilities so that he could without delay be admitted to the bar. In 1878 Levi stumped the state of Texas on behalf of Gustav Sleicher, who was running for Congress and was elected, defeating Judge Ireland. Although he refused to hold a political office, Levi always took an active interest in public affairs both in Texas and in New York, to which latter state he removed in 1899, establishing a law-office in New York city.

Leo Napoleon Levi.

His main activity, however, was as a communal worker, especially in his connection with the B'NAI B'RITH, of which he became president in 1900. In 1887 Levi addressed an "open letter" to the American rabbinate, under the title "Tell Us: What Is Judaism?" The replies being unsatisfactory, he answered his own interrogation in the pamphlet "Judaism in America." His last public act was in connection with the petition to the Russian government drawn up in protest against the Kishinef massacre of April 19–20, 1903 (see "Report of the Executive Committee of the I. O. B. B. for 1902–3"; Isidor Singer, "Russia at the Bar of the American People," 1904, ch. iii.; Cyrus Adler, "The Voice of America on Kishineff," 1904).

A. S.

LEVI, LEONE: English political economist; born in Ancona, Italy, in 1821; died in London May 7, 1888. Levi went to England at an early age, was converted to Christianity, and became a member of the English bar (1859). He devoted much time and energy to the organizing of chambers of commerce. In 1850 he published his "Commercial Law of the World"; in 1852 he was appointed to the chair of commercial law in King's College, London. Levi was an active member of the council of the Royal Statistical Society, and contributed to its journal many papers bearing on the industrial occupations of the people. In 1887 he attended the congress of European statisticians at Rome. It was owing to Levi's suggestion of the benefits which would result from the possession of an international commercial code that the acts were passed (1858) whereby the mercantile laws of the United Kingdom were made uniform on many points.

Levi was the author of: "Taxation, How It Is Raised and How It Is Expended" (1860); "History of British Commerce and of the Economic Progress of the British Nation from 1863 to 1870" (2d ed. 1878); "Work and Pay"; "War and Its Consequences." He also delivered a number of public lectures and contributed many economic articles to journals and magazines. He was created doctor of political and economic science by the University of Tübingen in 1861, and was a fellow of the Society of Antiquaries and of the Royal Geographical Society; the King of Italy conferred upon him the rank of cavalier of St. Maurice and St. Lazarus and the Order of the Crown of Italy.

BIBLIOGRAPHY: *The Times* (London), May 9, 1888; Boase, *Modern English Biography*, s.v. *Law Journal*, 1888.

J. G. L.

LEVI, LEONE: Italian author and journalist; born at Nizza-Monferrato in 1823; died at Turin Nov. 8, 1876; educated at the Collegio Foà at Vercelli. Although a man of affairs and a lawyer, he still found time to devote himself to literature, his most important work being his "Lampi della Società Contemporanea," a faithful delineation of modern life. His "Massime a Casaccio," as well as his "Il Tempio di Torino" (his last work), was published in the "Corriere Israelitico" of Triest.

BIBLIOGRAPHY: *Corriere Israelitico*, 1876–77, p. 185; Mortara, *Indice*.

S. U. C.

LEVI, LIONELLO: Italian philologist; born at Triest June 22, 1869; educated at the gymnasium of Triest and the universities of Pisa, Rome (Ph.D. 1891), and Berlin. He has been teacher of literature, later of classical philology, at the gymnasia of Benevento (1891–93), of Rome (1893–95), of Modena (1896), and of Parma since 1896. In 1895 he became lecturer on Greek literature at the University of Rome, and in 1896 of Bologna.

Levi has contributed to several journals essays on Greek and Latin literature, and is the editor of Lucian's "Peregrinus" (Berlin, 1892) and of three of the recently discovered odes of Bacchylides (Parma, 1899).

BIBLIOGRAPHY: De Gubernatis, *Dizionario Biografico*.

S. F. T. H.

LEVI, MORITZ: American educator; born Nov. 23, 1857, at Sachsenhausen, Waldeck; educated at the University of Michigan (graduated 1887) and at the Sorbonne, Paris. He became junior professor of the Romance languages at the University of Michigan in 1902. He has edited "L'Avare" of Molière (1900) and "I Promessi Sposi" of Manzoni (1901), and has compiled (with V. E. François) a French reader (1896).

A.

LEVI, MOSE GIUSEPPE: Italian physician; born at Guastalla 1796; died at Venice Dec. 27, 1859. He graduated as doctor of medicine from the University of Padua in 1817 and settled in Venice, where he practised until his death.

Levi was the author of: "Saggio Teorico-Pratico Sugli Aneurismi Interni," Venice, 1822, which essay received the prize from the Royal Academy of Naples; "Dizionario Compendiato delle Scienze Mediche," *ib.* 1827–32; "Dizionario Classico di Medicina e Chirurgia," *ib.* 1832–40 (the two last-named being translations from the French); "Enciclopedia delle Scienze Mediche," *ib.* 1834–47; "Ricordi Interno agl' Incliti Medici"; "Chirurghi in Venezia Dopo il 1740," *ib.* 1840; "Encyclopedia Anatomica," *ib.* 1847; "Dizionario Economico della Scienze Mediche," *ib.* 1856 (incomplete). He translated also: Albert's "Hautkrankheiten," Venice, 1835; the works of Hippocrates, with Latin text, *ib.* 1838; and Burdach's "Physiologie," *ib.* 1845. He further wrote the following biographical works: "Aglietti," 1836; "A. S. Ruggieri," 1836; "G. Tommasivi," 1847; and "J. Penolazzi," 1856.

BIBLIOGRAPHY: Hirsch, *Biographisches Lexikon*.

S. F. T. H.

LEVI, MOSE RAFFAELE: Italian physician; born at Triest Aug. 9, 1840; died at Florence March 10, 1886. After graduating from the University of Padua (1862) he became assistant at the General Hospital in Venice. In 1868 he was one of the founders of the maritime hospital for scrofulous children at the Lido of Venice, at which institution he was physician-in-chief till 1873; he then removed to Padua, where he became privat-docent at the university and practised medicine, treating especially the diseases of children.

In 1878 he was appointed chief departmental physician at the General Hospital at Venice, lecturing there upon pediatrics. This position he resigned on account of illness in 1881, and then left Venice. In 1884 he was appointed professor of pediatrics at the University of Florence.

Levi from 1864 was collaborator and from 1873 to 1879 editor-in-chief of the "Giornale Veneto di Scienze Mediche." He wrote many essays in the medical journals of Italy. Among his works may be mentioned: "La Patologia Cellulare Considerata ne' Suoi Fondamenti e nelle Sue Applicazioni," Venice, 1863 (German transl., Brunswick, 1864); "Della Frequenza della Tenia per l'Uso Medico della Carne," etc., *ib.* 1865; "Due Case di Sifilide Cerebrali," *ib.* 1879; "Della Emiglobinuria ad Accessi Freddo," *ib.* 1881.

BIBLIOGRAPHY: Cantani, in Hirsch's *Biographisches Lexikon*.

S. F. T. H.

LEVI, NATHANIEL: Australian merchant and politician; born at Liverpool, England, Jan. 20, 1830. In 1853 he went to the gold-fields in Victoria; in 1858, having settled in Melbourne, he joined the firm of John Levi & Sons. In 1860 he was elected member of the Legislative Assembly for Maryborough, being the first Jew elected to Parliament in Victoria. While in the Legislative Assembly he took great interest in the abolition of the tea and sugar duties, in the taxation of uncultivated lands, and in the forming of labor loan-laws. In 1892 he was elected member of the Legislative Council. In 1885 he founded "The Melbourne Daily News." Levi was treasurer and president of the Melbourne Hebrew Congregation for many years, and was connected with all the chief Jewish communal institutions of the city. He died Sept. 11, 1908.

BIBLIOGRAPHY: *Jewish World*, June 7, 1901.

J.

LEVI, RAPHAEL: German mathematician; died May 17, 1779, in Hanover, whither his father, Jacob Joseph Levi, a poor pedler, had gone with him, then a boy of eight years, and had died a few days after their arrival. The orphan lad was provided for at the Israelitische Armenschule. At one time Leibnitz had occasion to hear some of his observations in respect to building materials, and was struck by the strong intellectual power which they manifested. He became very much interested in him, and himself instructed him in the higher mathematics. A portrait of Levi has been preserved in the Leibnitzhaus.

Of Levi's published works the following may be mentioned: "Zwei Logarithmische Tafeln," Hanover, 1747; "Vorbericht vom Gebrauche der Neuerfundenen Logarithmischen Wechseltabellen mit Fortsetzung," Leipsic, 1748; "Supplement zu dem Vorbericht," etc., Hanover, 1748; "Tekunat ha-Shomayim: Ueber Astronomie und Kalender-kunde, Namentlich Commentirung der Talmudischen und Rabbinischen Aussprüche Darüber, um Hilkot Kiddush ha-Hodesh Maimuni's zu Verstehen. Dazu Noten und Glossen von Mose ben Jekutiel," Amsterdam, 1756; and "Neue Compendiöse Allg. Cours- und Wechsel-Tafeln," etc. Several of his minor writings remained unpublished; but, from material contained in them, Simon Waltsch (Simeon ben Nathan Naṭa') issued a commentary on Maimonides' rules for the calendar, Berlin, 1786.

BIBLIOGRAPHY: Brüll, in *Allg. Deutsche Biographie*, xviii. 505; Blogg, *Sefer ha-Ḥayyim*, p. 313, Hanover, 1848; Fürst, *Bibl. Jud.* ii. 236.

S. M. Co.

LEVI BEN SHEM-ṬOB: Portuguese convert; lived at the end of the fifteenth century; notorious for his hostility to his former coreligionists. According to Abraham b. Solomon of Torrutiel (Neubauer, "M. J. C." i. 113-114), it was Levi b. Shem-Ṭob (Shem Ra') who advised King Emanuel of Portugal to close all the synagogues and forbid the Jews to attend prayers. This order not proving effective, King Emanuel, on the advice of Levi, issued another (April, 1497), ordering the baptism of all Jewish children (Zacuto, "Yuḥasin," p. 227, ed. Filipowski). Levi is identified by some scholars with a certain Antonio who was chief surgeon of King John II., and who wrote a pamphlet entitled "Ajudo da Fé Contra os Judeos" (Kayserling, Gesch. der Juden in Portugal," p. 86).

BIBLIOGRAPHY: Grätz, *Geschichte der Juden*, 3d ed., viii. 381.

G. M. SEL.

LEVI, SIMḤAH ARYEH BEN EPHRAIM FISCHEL: Russian Hebraist and author of the nineteenth century; born at Hrubieszow, government of Warsaw. He wrote a double commentary on Job, preceded by a preface and two poems (Lemberg, 1833); and "Dibre Purim" (Zolkiev, 1834), an epic poem, the central figures in which are Ahasuerus and Esther. He began the compilation, on original lines, of a Hebrew dictionary entitled "Memalle," of which only the letter א appeared (Warsaw, 1839). Benjacob criticized this work severely in "Pirḥe Ẓafon" (ii. 201-208, Wilna, 1844).

BIBLIOGRAPHY: Zeitlin, *Bibliotheca Hebraica Post-Mendelssohniana*, p. 201.

H. R. M. SEL.

LEVI B. SISI (SISYI; SUSYI): Palestinian scholar; disciple of the patriarch Judah I. and school associate of his son Simeon ('Ab. Zarah 19a); one of the semi-tannaim of the last decades of the second century and of the early decades of the third. He assisted Judah in the compilation of the Mishnah and contributed baraitot (Yoma 24a). Many of Levi's baraitot were eventually embodied in a compilation known as "Ḳiddushin de-Be Lewi" (Ḳid. 76b; B. B. 52b). In the Babylonian Gemara Levi is seldom quoted with his patronymic, and neither in that nor in the Jerusalem Gemara nor in the Midrashim is he quoted with the title of "Rabbi." Keeping this in mind, the student of rabbinics will easily determine whether passages written under the name "Levi" without a patronymic must be credited to Levi bar Sisi or to a younger namesake who is almost always cited as "R. Levi" (see LEVI II). But although Levi bar Sisi is not given the title "Rab," he was highly esteemed among the learned, and in many instances where an anonymous passage is introduced with the statement למדין לפני חכמים (= "it was argued before the sages") it is to be understood that the argument referred to was advanced by Levi before Judah I. (Sanh. 17b; comp. Men. 80b; Me'i. 9b; see Rashi and Tos. *ad loc.*).

Judah I. later spoke of Levi bar Sisi as of an equal. But the latter did not always succeed in impressing the public. At the request of a congregation at Simonias to send it a man who could act at once as lecturer, judge, superintendent of the synagogue, public scribe, and teacher, and attend to the general congregational affairs, Judah I. sent Levi. When, however, Levi entered on office he signally failed to satisfy the first requirement. Questions of law and of exegesis were addressed to him, and he left them unanswered. The Simonias congregation charged the patriarch with having sent it an unfit man, but the patriarch assured it that he had selected for it a man as able as himself. He summoned Levi and propounded to him the questions originally propounded by the congregation; Levi answered every one correctly. Judah thereupon inquired why he did not do so when the congregation submitted those questions; Levi answered that his courage had failed him (Yer. Yeb. xii. 13a; comp. Yeb. 105a; Gen. R. lxxxi. 2). A late midrash speaks of him as a Biblical scholar and good lecturer (Pesiḳ. xxv. 165b).

After Judah's death Levi retired with Ḥanina b. Ḥama from the academy, and when Ḥanina received his long-delayed promotion Levi removed to Babylonia, whither his fame had preceded him (Shab. 59b; see ḤANINA B. ḤAMA). He died in Babylonia, and was greatly mourned by scholars. In the course of a eulogy on him delivered by Abba bar Abba it was said that Levi alone was worth as much as the whole of humanity (Yer. Ber. ii. 5c).

BIBLIOGRAPHY: Bacher, *Ag. Tan.* ii. 536; Frankel, *Mebo*, p. 110b; Halevy, *Dorot ha-Rishonim*, ii. 60a; Heilprin, *Seder ha-Dorot*, ii.; Weiss, *Dor*, ii. 192.

S. S. S. M.

LEVI BEN SOLOMON: Galician Talmudist; lived at Brody in the first half of the eighteenth century. He was the author of "Bet Lewi," halakic novellæ and explanations of the difficult passages in Rashi and Tosafot (Zolkiev, 1732).

BIBLIOGRAPHY: Steinschneider, *Cat. Bodl.* col. 1616.

S. S. I. BR.

LEVI, SOLOMON B. ISAAC: Rabbi and scholar of the sixteenth century. He was born in Smyrna, became director of the academy 'Eẓ Ḥayyim at Salonica, and went subsequently to Venice. He was versed in philosophy, natural sciences, and mathematics as well as in the Talmud and the Halakah, and was eminent as a preacher. He wrote a large number of devotional and halakic works, including the following: "Leb Abot," commentary to Abot (Salonica, 1565 and 1571); "Dibre Shelomoh," five sermons for each of the weekly sections and feast-days (Venice, 1596); "Leḥem Shelomoh," commentary to the Talmud, the Midrash, and the Zohar (*ib.*

1597); responsa to the Ṭur and the Shulḥan 'Aruk (Salonica, 1652); "Leb Shelomoh," similar in contents to the preceding.

BIBLIOGRAPHY: Nepi-Ghirondi, *Toledot Gedole Yisrael*, p. 351; Benjacob, *Oẓar ha-Sefarim*, passim; Steinschneider, *Cat. Bodl.* col. 2363.

G. I. E.

LÉVI, SYLVAIN: French Orientalist; born at Paris March 28, 1863. He received his education at the Ecole des Hautes Etudes, where he became "agrégé ès lettres" in 1886. Here, too, three years later he was appointed "maître de conférences" in Sanskrit; and in the following year his duties were so extended as to include lecturing on the religions of India in the section for the science of religion. Of both these departments he is now (1904) the director. In 1889 Lévi was promoted to be "chargé de cours" in Sanskrit in the Faculty of Letters; and the next year he received the degree of "docteur ès lettres," presenting as his thesis "Quid de Græcis Veterum Indorum Monumenta Tradiderint." The same year saw the publication of his "Théâtre Indien," which is the standard work on its subject. In 1894 Lévi was appointed professor of Sanskrit in the Collège de France, a position which he still holds.

In addition to the two works already mentioned, Lévi has edited and translated the first eight chapters of Kshemendra's "Bṛhatkathamanjari" (Paris, 1886), and has published a treatise entitled "La Doctrine du Sacrifice dans les Brahmaṇas" (*ib.* 1898). He is also the author of numerous briefer studies, especially in the "Journal Asiatique," as well as of many reviews of Oriental books; and he is a collaborator on the "Revue Critique" and "La Grande Encyclopédie," to which he has contributed a large number of articles dealing with the literature and religion of India.

Lévi has been president of the Société de Linguistique de Paris and of the Société des Etudes Juives; he is also a member of the committee of the Alliance Israélite Universelle. In 1897 he was sent on a mission to India by the Ministry of Public Instruction.

BIBLIOGRAPHY: *La Grande Encyclopédie.*

S. L. H. G.

LEVI-CATELLANI, ENRICO: Italian lawyer; born at Padua June 12, 1856; educated at the university there. In 1885 he was appointed assistant professor, and in 1890 professor, of international law at the same university. Levi-Catellani is a corresponding member of the Padua Regia Accademia di Scienze, Lettere ed Arti and of the Regio Istituto Veneto di Scienze, Lettere ed Arti, and a member of the Association for the Reform and Codification of International Law, at London, and of the Institut de Droit International. He is the author of the following works: "Le Colonie e la Conferenza di Berlino" (Turin, 1885); "Storia del Diritto Internazionale Privato" (*ib.* 1895); "Della Riforma agl' Istituti della Cittadinanza e della Naturalizazione," a paper read at the fourth congress of Italian lawyers; "La Dottrina Platonica delle Idee e il Concetto di Società Internazionale," in the Fr. Schupfer Memorial Volume; "Realtà ed Utopie delle Pace" (Turin, 1899); and numerous articles in literary and scientific journals.

BIBLIOGRAPHY: *Annuario della R. Università di Padova*, 1885-86 *et seq.*

S. U. C.

LEVI-CIVITA, TULLIO: Italian physicist; born at Padua March 29, 1873; educated at the university there (Ph.D). He was successively appointed assistant professor (1898) and professor (1902) of applied mechanics, and professor of higher mechanics. He is also (1904) instructor in applied mechanics in the Regia Scuola di Applicazione per gl' Ingegneri connected with the university.

BIBLIOGRAPHY: *Annuario della R. Università di Padova*, 1898-99 *et seq.*

S. U. C.

LEVI-PEROTTI, GIUSTINA: A poetess, supposed to be of Sassoferrato, and assumed, until recently, to have addressed to Petrarch a sonnet beginning "Io Vorrei pur Drizzar Queste Mie Piume." This poem, to which Petrarch is said to have replied with his sonnet "La Gola, il Sonno, e l'Oziose Piume," was published for the first time in 1504 by G. A. Gilio, who, however, attributed it to Ortensia di Guglielmo of Fabriano. It was republished by Tommasini, who attributed it to Giustina ("Petrarca Redivivus," p. 111). Subsequently it was included in various collections of poetry, down to 1885. Although Crescimbeni, Tiraboschi, and Zeno doubted the authenticity of the sonnet, scholars like Quadrio and, with some hesitation, Foscolo accepted it. Morici concludes that the sonnet is the work of some cinquecentist, and that Giustina Levi-Perotti never existed.

BIBLIOGRAPHY: Borgognoni, *Le Rime di Francesco Petrarca*, pp. 22 *et seq.*, Modena, 1711; Carducci, *Rime di Francesco Petrarca*, pp. 3-4, Leghorn, 1876; Crescimbeni, *Dell' Istoria della Volgar Poesia*, iii. 164 *et seq.*, Venice, 1730; Foscolo, *Opere Edite e Inedite*, x. 409, Florence, 1859; Kayserling, *Die Jüdischen Frauen*; Morici, *Giustina Levi-Perotti e le Petrarchiste Marchigiane*, in *Rassegna Nazionale*, Aug., 1899; Pesaro, *Donne Celebri Israelite*, in *Il Vessillo Israelitico*, 1880, p. 376; Quadrio, *Della Storia e della Ragione d' Ogni Poesia*, i.-ii. 187-188, 194, 195, Milan; Tiraboschi, *Storia della Letteratura Italiana*, v. 581, Florence; Zeno, *Dissertazioni Vossiane*, i. 257b.

J. U. C.

LEVIAS, CASPAR: American Orientalist; born in Szagarren Feb. 13, 1860; received his elementary education in Russia and his collegiate training at Columbia College, New York (A.M.), and Johns Hopkins University, Baltimore; he was fellow in Oriental languages at the former (1893-94) and fellow in Semitic languages at the latter university (1894-95). Since 1895 Levias has been instructor at the Hebrew Union College, Cincinnati, Ohio. His published works are as follows: "A Grammar of the Aramaic Idiom Contained in the Babylonian Talmud," Cincinnati, 1900; "The Justification of Zionism," 1899. Besides these, Levias has published a large number of essays, chiefly on philological subjects, in "The American Journal of Semitic Languages" (in which his Talmudic grammar first appeared) and in the "Hebrew Union College Journal."

A.

LEVIATHAN AND BEHEMOTH: Names of gigantic beasts or monsters described in Job xl. The former is from a root denoting "coil," "twist"; the latter is the plural form of "behemah" =

"beast."—**Biblical Data:** Ever since Bochart ("Hierozoicon," iii. 705), "behemoth" has been taken to denote the hippopotamus; and Jablonski, to make it correspond exactly with that animal, compared an Egyptian form, "p-ehe-mu" (= "water-ox"), which, however, does not exist. The Biblical description contains mythical elements, and the conclusion is justified that these monsters were not real, though the hippopotamus may have furnished in the main the data for the description. Only of a unique being, and not of a common hippopotamus, could the words of Job xl. 19 have been used: "He is the first [A. V. "chief"] of the ways of God [comp. Prov. viii. 22]; he that made him maketh sport with him" (as the Septuagint reads, *πεποιημένον ἐγκαταπαίζεσθαι*; A. V. "He that made him can make his sword to approach unto him"; comp. Ps. civ. 26); or "The mountains bring him forth food; where all the beasts of the field do play" (Job xl. 20). Obviously behemoth is represented as the primeval beast, the king of all the animals of the dry land, while leviathan is the king of all those of the water, both alike unconquerable by man (*ib.* xl. 14, xli. 17–26). Gunkel ("Schöpfung und Chaos," p. 62) suggests that behemoth and leviathan were the two primeval monsters corresponding to Tiamat (= "the abyss"; comp. Hebr. "tehom") and Kingu (= Aramaic "'akna" = serpent") of Babylonian mythology. Some commentators find also in Isa. xxx. 6 ("bahamot negeb" = "beasts of the south") a reference to the hippopotamus; others again, in Ps. lxxiii. 22 ("I am as behemoth [= "beasts"; A. V. "a beast"] before thee"); but neither interpretation has a substantial foundation. It is likely that the leviathan and the behemoth were originally referred to in Hab. ii. 15: "the destruction of the behemoth [A. V. "beasts"] shall make them afraid" (comp. LXX., "thee" instead of "them").

E. G. H. K.

——**In Rabbinical Literature:** According to a midrash, the leviathan was created on the fifth day (Yalḳ., Gen. 12). Originally God produced a male and a female leviathan, but lest in multiplying the species should destroy the world, He slew the female, reserving her flesh for the banquet that will be given to the righteous on the advent of the Messiah (B. B. 74a). The enormous size of the leviathan is thus illustrated by R. Johanan, from whom proceeded nearly all the haggadot concerning this monster: "Once we went in a ship and saw a fish which put his head out of the water. He had horns upon which was written: 'I am one of the meanest creatures that inhabit the sea. I am three hundred miles in length, and enter this day into the jaws of the leviathan'" (B. B. *l.c.*). When the leviathan is hungry, reports R. Dimi in the name of R. Johanan, he sends forth from his mouth a heat so great as to make all the waters of the deep boil, and if he would put his head into paradise no living creature could endure the odor of him (*ib.*). His abode is the Mediterranean Sea; and the waters of the Jordan fall into his mouth (Bek. 55b; B. B. *l.c.*).

The body of the leviathan, especially his eyes, possesses great illuminating power. This was the opinion of R. Eliezer, who, in the course of a voyage in company with R. Joshua, explained to the latter, when frightened by the sudden appearance of a brilliant light, that it probably proceeded from the eyes of the leviathan. He referred his companion to the words of Job xli. 18: "By his neesings a light doth shine, and his eyes are like the eyelids of the morning" (B. B. *l.c.*). However, in spite of his supernatural strength, the leviathan is afraid of a small worm called "kilbit" (כלבית), which clings to the gills of large fishes and kills them (Shab. 77b).

The leviathan is prominent in the haggadic literature in connection with the advent of the Messiah.

In the Messianic Times.

Referring to Job xl. 30 (Hebr.), "and the pious ones [חברים] shall make a banquet of it," R. Johanan says that at the time of the resurrection a banquet will be given by God to the righteous, at which the flesh of the leviathan will be served (B. B. *l.c.*). Even the hunting of the leviathan will be a source of great enjoyment to the righteous. Those, says R. Judan bar Simon, who have not taken part in pagan sports will be allowed to participate in the hunting of the leviathan and of the behemoth (Lev. R. xiii. 3). Gabriel will be charged with the killing of the monster; but he will not be able to accomplish his task without the help of God, who will divide the monster with His sword. According to another haggadah, when Gabriel fails, God will order the leviathan to engage in a battle with the ox of the mountain ("shor habar"), which will result in death to both of them (B. B. 75a; Pesiḳ. p. 188b). Not only will the flesh of the leviathan furnish food for the table of the righteous, but there will be a great supply of it in the markets of Jerusalem (B. B. *l.c.*). From the hide of the leviathan God will make tents for the pious of the first rank, girdles for those of the second, chains for those of the third, and necklaces for those of the fourth. The remainder of the hide will be spread on the walls of Jerusalem; and the whole world will be illuminated by its brightness (*ib.*).

These haggadot concerning the leviathan are interpreted as allegories by all the commentators with the exception of some ultraconservatives like Baḥya ben Asher ("Shulḥan Arba'," ch. iv., p. 9, col. 3). According to Maimonides, the banquet is an allusion to the spiritual enjoyment of the intellect (commentary on Sanh. i.). The name, he says, is derived from לוה ("to join," "to unite"), and designates an imaginary monster in which are combined the most various animals ("Moreh," iii., ch. xxiii.).

Symbolical Interpretation.

In the cabalistic literature the "piercing leviathan" and the "crooked leviathan" (Isa. xxvii. 1), upon which the haggadah concerning the hunting of the animal is based, are interpreted as referring to Satan-Samael and his spouse Lilith ("'Emeḳ ha-Melek," p. 130a), while Ḳimḥi, Abravanel, and others consider the expressions to be allusions to the destruction of the powers which are hostile to the Jews (comp. Manasseh ben Israel, "Nishmat Ḥayyim," p. 48; see also Kohut, "Aruch Completum," *s.v.* "Leviathan," for other references, and his essay in "Z. D. M. G." vol. xxi., p. 590, for the parallels in Persian literature). The haggadic sayings obtained a hold on the imagination of the poets, who introduced allusions to the banquet of the leviathan into the liturgy.

S. S. I. Br.

——**In Apocryphal Literature:** Both leviathan and behemoth are prominent in Jewish eschatology. In the Book of Enoch (lx. 7–9), Enoch says:

"On that day [the day of judgment] two monsters will be produced: a female monster, named 'Leviathan,' to dwell in the depths of the ocean over the fountains of the waters; but the male is called 'Behemoth,' who occupies with his breast a waste wilderness named 'Dendain' [read "the land of Naid" after LXX., ἐν γῇ Ναίδ = בארץ נוד, Gen. iv. 16], on the east of the garden, where the elect and the righteous dwell. And I besought that other angel that he should show me the might of these monsters; how they were produced on one day, the one being placed in the depth of the sea and the other in the main land of the wilderness. And he spake to me: 'Thou son of man, dost seek here to know what is hidden?'" (Charles, "Book of Enoch," p. 155; comp. "the secret chambers of leviathan" which Elihu b. Berakel the Buzite will disclose, Cant. R. i. 4).

According to II Esdras vi. 49–53, God created on the fifth day the two great monsters, leviathan and behemoth, and He separated them because the seventh part of the world which was assigned to the water could not hold them together, and He gave to the behemoth that part which was dried up on the third day and had the thousand mountains which, according to Ps. l. 10, as understood by the haggadists ("the behemoth [A. V. "cattle"] upon a thousand hills"; comp. Lev. R. xxii.; Num. R. xxi.; and Job xl. 20), furnish behemoth with the necessary food. To the leviathan God gave the seventh part of the earth filled with water; and He reserved it for the future to reveal by whom and at what time the leviathan and the behemoth should be eaten.

In the Syriac Apocalypse of Baruch, xxix. 4, also, the time is predicted when the behemoth will come forth from his seclusion on land and the leviathan out of the sea, and the two gigantic monsters, created on the fifth day, will serve as food for the elect who will survive in the days of the Messiah.

Behemoth and leviathan form in the Gnostic system of the Ophites and others two of the seven circles or stations which the soul has to pass in order to be purged and to attain bliss (Hippolytus, "Adversus Omnes Hæreses," v. 21; Origen, "Contra Celsum," vi. 25). As if the meat of the "wild ox" behemoth and the fish leviathan were not deemed sufficient for the great banquet of the righteous in the future, a fowl was added, *i.e.*, the "ziz" (A. V. "the wild beasts" of the field), mentioned in Ps. l. 11 after the account of the behemoth in verse 10, and understood by the Rabbis to signify a gigantic bird (B. B. 73b). Thus the Apocalypse of Simeon b. Yoḥai (Jellinek, "B. H." iii. 76) has the three animals, the monster ox behemoth, the fish leviathan, and the gigantic bird ziz, prepared for the great banquet. This tradition, however, indicates Persian influence, for it is of the Parsee cosmology that the existence of such primeval representatives of the classes of animals is a part. There are four such species mentioned in "Bundahis," xviii.–xix.: (1) "the serpent-like Kar fish, the Arizh of the water, the greatest of the creatures of Ahuramazda," corresponding to the leviathan; (2) the three-legged ass Khara, standing in the midst of the ocean ("Yasna," xli. 28); it is mentioned in the Talmud as the "unicorn ḳeresh," "ṭigras" (*i.e.*, "thrigaṭ" = "three-legged"), the gazel of the heights (Ḥul. 59b), and forms, under the name "Ḥarish," in Mohammedan eschatology a substitute for behemoth and leviathan (see Wolff, "Muhammedanische Eschatologie," 1872, pp. 174, 181); (3) the ox Hadhayosh, from which the food of immortality is prepared, and which forms the parallel of behemoth; and (4) the bird Chamrosh, the chief of the birds, which lives on the summit of Mount Alburz (comp. "Bundahis," xix. 15); compare also Simurgh (Avesta "Saena Meregha," eagle-bird, griffin, Hebraized "Bar Yokneh"), the fabulous giant-bird, which the Rabbis identified with ziz (see Windischman, "Zoroastrische Studien," pp. 91–93; West, "Pahlavi Texts," in Max Müller, "S. B. E." v. 65–71).

Among the Gnostics.

Bibliography: The commentaries of Dillmann, Delitzsch, and others on Job; Gunkel, *Schöpfung und Chaos*, Göttingen, 1895; Eisenmenger, *Entdecktes Judenthum*, ii. 296 *et seq.*, 873 *et seq.*; Weber, *System der Altsynagogalen Theologie*, 1880, p. 195; Hastings, *Dict. Bible*; Cheyne and Black, *Encyc. Bibl.*

E. G. H. K.

LEVIN, EMANUEL BORISOVICH: Russian teacher and communal worker; born at Minsk Dec. 15, 1820; educated at the Molodechensk school for the nobility (1836–41). He taught in G. Klaczko's private school at Wilna from 1842 to 1844, and at the public schools of Minsk from 1846 to 1851. Having passed his examinations in 1848, he received an appointment in the Jewish government school at Proskurov, Podolia (1851–52), and subsequently in the rabbinical school at Jitomir (1853–57).

In 1859 Levin settled in St. Petersburg, where he became one of the first members of the Society for the Promotion of Culture Among the Jews of Russia, of which he acted as secretary until 1872, when he became an honorary member. Since 1895 Levin has been a member of the historical committee of the society and one of the collaborators of the "Regesty i Nadpisi." Levin was elected a member of the Imperial Russian Geographical Society in 1870; and he is also a member of the Society for the Promotion of Commerce and Industry. In 1895 Levin was made an honorary citizen by the Russian government for his "Code of Laws Concerning the Jews."

Levin's other works include: a Russian grammar in Hebrew, Wilna, 1846; "Moiseyevo Brachnoye Pravo," St. Petersburg, 1875, on the marriage laws according to the Talmud and the rabbinical literature, translated from Hebrew sources; "Svod Uzakoneni o Yevreyakh, *ib.* 1885; "Perechen Ogranichitelnykh Zakonov o Yevreyakh v Yevreyakh o Rossii" (*ib.* 1890), both on the disabilities of the Jews in Russia; "Sboraik Ogranichitelnikh Zakonov o Yevreyakh," *ib.* 1902, on the same subject. He published also the text of the Pirḳe Abot with Russian translation and notes, *ib.* 1868.

H. R. S. M. G.

LEVIN, HIRSCHEL BEN ARYEH LÖB (called also **Hirschel Löbel** and **Hart Lyon**): German rabbi; born at Rzeszow, Galicia, in 1721; died at Berlin Aug. 26, 1800. His father (known also as Saul Levin) was rabbi at Amsterdam; and on his mother's side Hirschel was a nephew of Jacob

Emden. Although he occupied himself also with secular sciences and philosophy, Levin paid special attention to Hebrew grammar and literature, and composed several Hebrew poems. Levin was a distinguished Talmudist, and in 1751, when he was only thirty years old, he threw himself into the struggle between Emden and Eybeschütz, naturally siding with the former. His epistles against Eybeschütz made such an impression that in 1756 he was elected chief rabbi of the London congregation of German and Polish Jews. In 1760 Jacob Ḳimḥi having published at Altona a responsum in which he charged the London butchers ("shoḥeṭim") with negligence in regard to their duties, Levin warmly defended them. The wardens of his synagogue, however, refused him permission to make a public reply to Ḳimḥi's charges; he therefore resigned in 1763, and accepted the rabbinate of Halberstadt. It would appear, from the letter in which the community of Halberstadt offered him the rabbinate, that Levin's resignation was occasioned by the neglect of Biblical and Talmudic studies by the Jews of London. He afterward became rabbi of Mannheim; and in 1772 he was appointed chief rabbi of Berlin. He was a great friend of Mendelssohn.

Hirschel Levin.

In 1778 Levin gave his approbation to Mendelssohn's German translation of the Pentateuch. In the preceding year the Prussian government had ordered Levin to make a résumé in German of the Jewish civil laws, such as those on inheritance, guardianship, and marriage, and to present it to the royal department of justice. Levin, not having a thorough knowledge of the German language, applied to Mendelssohn to do the work. Mendelssohn, accordingly, wrote his "Ritualgesetze der Juden," printed under Levin's superintendence, 1778.

Despite his toleration and enlightenment, Levin, instigated by the rabbis of Glogau and Lissa, began in 1782 to persecute Naphtali Herz Wessely for his "Dibre Shalom we-Emet" (Landshuth, "Toledot Anshe ha-Shem," p. 85; Kayserling, "Mendelssohn," p. 307). He prohibited the printing of that work, and insisted upon the expulsion of the author from Berlin. But Wessely's friends prevailed on Levin to desist from attacking Wessely, while Mendelssohn at the same time gave Levin to understand that the press in Germany was free to everybody.

Levin wrote: Epistles against Eybeschütz, printed by one of Emden's pupils, in the "Sefat Emet u-Leshon Zehorit," Altona, 1752; glosses on Pirḳe Abot, printed with Emden's commentary to Pirḳe Abot, Berlin, 1834; notes to the "Sefer Yuḥasin" and "Sefer ha-Ḥinnuk," some of which were published in Kobak's "Jeschurun." Some of his poetry was published in "Ha-Maggid" (xiv.) under the title "Naḥalat Ẓebi." Finally, three manuscript volumes of his responsa are to be found in the library of the London Bet ha-Midrash, bearing the numbers 24 to 26.

Bibliography: Grätz, *Gesch.* 2d ed., xi. 41, 89, 151; H. Adler, in *Publ. Anglo-Jew. Hist. Exhibition*, 1887, pp. 280 *et seq.*; Landshuth, *Toledot Anshe ha-Shem*, pp. 72-78; Kayserling, *Moses Mendelssohn*, pp. 282, 291, 311; Auerbach, *Gesch. der Israelitischen Gemeinde Halberstadt*, pp. 89 *et seq.*, Halberstadt, 1866; Fuenn, *Keneset Yisrael*, p. 284.

S. S. M. Sel.

LEVIN, ISRAEL SOLOMON: Danish grammarian and linguist; born in Randers 1810; died in Copenhagen 1883. He graduated from Randers high school, and afterward was employed as editor of a critical journal and as a translator of novels.

Levin was the author of several works on Danish grammar, notably "Dansk Lyd og Kjönslære" (1844), and of two novels, "Krigsfortællinger for Menigmand" and "Nogle Træk af Livet i Hamburg" (1848).

Bibliography: C. F. Bricka, *Dansk Biografisk Lexicon.*

S. F. C.

LEVIN, JACOB: Galician Hebraist; born at Brody in 1844. In 1865 he became coeditor with Werber on the Hebrew paper "'Ibri Anoki," in which he published a series of articles on the position of the Jews in Russia before Alexander II. In 1880 he produced a didactic poem entitled "Hitpatteḥut Tebel," on the evolution of religion and philosophy. Levin had previously translated into Hebrew Schiller's "Die Braut von Messina" under the title "Medanim Ben Aḥim" (Brody, 1868).

Bibliography: Sokolov, *Sefer ha-Zikkaron*, p. 63, Warsaw, 1889; Zeitlin, *Bibl. Post-Mendels.* p. 202.

S. M. Sel.

LEVIN, JOSHUA HÖSCHEL BEN ELIJAH ZEEB: Lithuanian Talmudist and author; born at Wilna July 22, 1818; died at Paris Nov. 15, 1883. After studying Talmud and rabbinics under Elijah Kalischer, Levin settled in Volozhin, where he lectured on Talmud and wrote several works. In 1871 he was called to the rabbinate of Praga, near Warsaw. Toward the end of his life Levin went to Paris with the intention of proceeding thence to the Holy Land; but at the request of Israel Salant he remained in the French capital and became preacher for the Russo-Polish community there.

Levin was the author of many works, of which the following have been published at Wilna: "Haggahot," notes on the Midrash Rabbah; "'Aliyyot Eliyahu" (1856), a biography of Elijah Wilna; "Ma'yene Yehoshua'," a commentary on Pirḳe Abot, printed in the "Ruaḥ Ḥayyim" of Ḥayyim Volozhin (1859); "Ẓiyyun Yehoshua'" (1859), a complete concordance to both Talmuds; "Tosefot Sheni le-Ẓiyyon," glosses to the Mishnah; "Peleṭat Soferim" (1863), novellæ and essays; "Dabar be-'Itto" (1878), discussions and explanations on halakic matters.

Bibliography: *Univ. Isr.* xxxix. 156; *Ha-Meliẓ*, 1883, col. 1423; *Ha-Asif*, i., section 1, p. 141.

S. S. M. Sel.

LEVIN, JUDAH LÖB (JEHALEL): Hebrew poet; born at Minsk, Russia, 1845. He studied Talmud under Rabbi Ḥayyim Selig and other prominent rabbis. At the age of sixteen he read through the entire Talmud. He was then married to the daughter of a Ḥasid; and under the influence of his new surroundings he began the study of the Zohar and other mystical literature. In 1868 he went to Kiev as teacher in the house of Lazar Brodski, where he studied German and Russian. He was also made treasurer of the Brodski flour-mills. In 1887 he was appointed treasurer of the Brodski sugar-refinery in Tomashpol, Podolia, where he is now (1904) residing.

Levin began to write Hebrew poetry at the age of ten; and he has contributed extensively during the last thirty years to the Hebrew periodicals "Ha-Meliẓ," "Ha-Ẓefirah," "Ha-Maggid," "Ha-Asif," and "Ha-Shaḥar." His first collection of verse, entitled "Sifte Renanim" (Jitomir, 1871), contains mostly occasional poems. In 1877 his "Kishron ha-Ma'aseh" appeared, first in "Ha-Shaḥar" (vols. vii., xviii.), and then in book form. It contains four large poems throwing light on the social condition of the Jews of Russia. They are socialistic in tendency. In another volume of "Ha-Shaḥar" (lxxx.) he published "Elḥanan," an epic poem in three parts, also concerning the social condition of the Russian Jews. Levin's style is affected and lacks brilliancy. In 1883 he translated Disraeli's "Tancred" into Hebrew under the title "Nes la-Goyim." The translation was much criticized by Frischman in "'Al ha-Nes," Warsaw, 1883.

BIBLIOGRAPHY: Zeitlin, *Bibl. Post-Mendels.*; Lippe, *Bibliographisches Lexicon*; Klausner, *Novo-Yevreiskaya Literatura*; Frischman, *Tohu wa-Bohu*, Warsaw, 1883.

H. R. J. G. L.

LEVIN, LEWIS CHARLES: American politician and writer; born at Charleston, S. C., Nov. 10, 1808; died in Philadelphia March 14, 1860. When still a youth he went to Woodville, Miss., where he became a school-teacher and studied law. After having been wounded in a duel he left that town and practised law successively in Maryland, Kentucky, Louisiana, and Pennsylvania. In 1838 he settled in Philadelphia and was there admitted to the bar. There he edited the "Temperance Advocate," and soon became known as a writer and speaker in the interest of the Temperance party. He was instrumental in the formation of the Native American party in 1843, and founded in its support in Philadelphia the "Sun," of which daily paper he became the editor. In 1845 he was elected to Congress, retaining his seat until 1851. He became a member of several committees and was chairman of the committee on naval affairs.

BIBLIOGRAPHY: C. Adler, in *American Jewish Year Book*, 5661 (1900-1).

A. F. T. H.

LEVIN, MENDEL (called also **Lefin** and **Satanower**): Polish scholar and author; born in Satanow, Podolia, about 1741; died in Mikolayev, in the same province, 1819. He was educated for a Talmudist, but became interested in secular studies after reading J. S. Delmedigo's "Elim," which opened for him the hitherto unknown world of science. He went to Berlin, and there, being attracted by the brilliant circle of Jewish scholars of which Moses Mendelssohn was the central figure, he remained for several years. From Berlin he went to Brody, where he exerted much influence over Perl, Krochmal, and other early representatives of the HASKALAH in Galicia. Later he lived in the palatial home of Joshua Zeitlin in Ustye, government of Moghilef, at the same time that BARUCH BEN JACOB resided there. He removed thence to Mikolayev, which belonged to the estate of Prince Adam Czartoryski, who engaged him as teacher for his children. M. Letteris saw an essay on Kant's philosophy written by Mendel in French for Czartoryski.

Levin's works are: "Moda' la-Binah," with an approbation by Mendelssohn (Berlin, 1789); "Refu'ot ha-'Am" (Zolkiev, 1794; 2d ed. Lemberg, 1851), popular medicine translated from the French by Tisot; "Ḥeshbon ha-Nefesh" (Lemberg, 1809; Wilna, 1844; Warsaw, 1852), practical ethics, after Franklin; "Masse'ot ha-Yam" (Zolkiev, 1818), travels on the sea, after Campe. His paraphrase of Tibbon's translation of the "Moreh Nebukim" in popular rabbinical Hebrew was published by M. Suchastover (Zolkiev, 1829), and his introduction to that work, entitled "Elon Moreh," by H. S. Slonimski (Odessa, 1867). Mendel was also the author of a Yiddish translation of Proverbs (Tarnopol, 1816), which innovation called forth a satirical work against him by Tobiah Feder ("Ḳol Meḥaẓeẓim," Berdychev, 1816). He translated also Ecclesiastes into the same dialect; but the work was not published till long after his death (Odessa, 1873).

BIBLIOGRAPHY: Fuenn, *Ḳiryah Ne'emanah*, pp. 277–278, Wilna, 1860; idem, *Safah le-Ne'emanim*, p. 140, Wilna, 1881; *Ha-Meassef* (Letteris ed., 1862), i. 96–97; Stanislavski, *Mendel Levin*, in *Voskhod*, 1881, No. 3, pp. 116–127; Zeitlin, *Bibl. Post-Mendels.* pp. 202–204.

H. R. P. Wi.

LEVIN, MORITZ: German rabbi; born 1843 at Wongrowitz, Posen. He studied at the University of Berlin, and was prepared for his rabbinical career by private teachers. After officiating as rabbi for a short time at Zurich, he went in 1872 in a similar capacity to Nuremberg. Since 1884 he has been preacher of the Reform congregation in Berlin.

Levin is the author of: "Gott und Seele nach Jüdischer Lehre," Zurich, 1871; "Der Gottesdienst des Herzens. Israelitisches Gebetbuch für Oeffentliche und Privatandacht," 2 vols., 1872; "Lehrbuch der Biblischen Geschichte und Literatur," 3d ed., 1897; "Iberia," Berlin, 1892; "Bar Kochba," 1892 (2d ed., 1904); "Lehrbuch der Jüdischen Geschichte und Literatur," 3d ed., 1900; "Die Israelitische Religionslehre, Systematisch Dargestellt," 1892 (2d ed., 1900); "Die Reform des Judentums. Festschrift zur Feier des 50-Jährigen Bestehens der Jüdischen Reformgemeinde in Berlin," 1895. S.

LEVIN, POUL THEODOR: Danish author; born in Copenhagen June 17, 1869; educated at the University of Copenhagen (Ph.D. 1898). Levin, who has become widely known as a literary critic, has written two dramatic works—"Antoinette" and "Sejr" (Copenhagen, 1895 and 1899). In 1894 he published "Dansk Litteraturhistorie i Omrids," a history of Danish literature, followed later by several general essays in the same field, among which are "Ovid's Ungdomsdigtning" (1897) and "Egne og Stæder" (1899).

BIBLIOGRAPHY: *Salmonsen's Store Illustrerede Konversations-Lexikon.*

S. F. C.

LEVIN (ROBERT), RAHEL ANTONIE FRIEDERIKE: German writer; born at Berlin June 19, 1771; died there March 7, 1833. Her home life was uncongenial, her father, a wealthy jeweler, being a strong-willed man and ruling his family despotically. She was very intimate with Dorothea and Henriette, daughters of Moses Mendelssohn. Together with them she knew Henriette Herz, with whom she later became most intimately associated, moving in the same intellectual sphere. Rahel's home became the meeting-place of men like Schlegel, Schelling, Steffens, Schack, Schleiermacher, Alexander and Wilhelm von Humboldt, Lamotte-Fouqué, Baron Brückmann, Ludwig Tieck, Jean Paul Richter, and F. von Gentz. During a visit to Carlsbad in 1795 she was introduced to Goethe, whom she again saw in 1815, at Frankfort-on-the-Main.

Rahel Levin.

After the death of her father in 1806 she lived successively in Paris, Frankfort-on-the-Main, Hamburg, Prague, and Dresden. This period was one of misfortune for Germany; Prussia was reduced to a small kingdom and her king was in exile. Secret societies were formed in every part of the country with the object of throwing off the tyranny of Napoleon; Rahel herself belonged to one of these societies. In 1814 she married, in Berlin, Karl August Varnhagen von Ense (b. Feb. 21, 1785, at Düsseldorf; d. at Berlin Oct. 10, 1858), after having been converted to Christianity. At the time of their marriage, Varnhagen, who had fought in the Austrian army against the French, belonged to the Prussian diplomatic corps, and their house at Vienna became the meeting-place of the Prussian delegates to the Vienna Congress. She accompanied her husband in 1815 to Vienna, and in 1816 to Carlsruhe, where he was Prussian representative. After 1819 she again lived in Berlin, where Varnhagen had taken up his residence after having been retired from his diplomatic position.

Though not a productive writer herself, Rahel was the center of a circle of eminent writers, scholars, and artists in the Prussian capital. A few of her essays appeared in print in "Das Morgenblatt," "Das Schweizerische Museum," and "Der Gesellschafter," and in 1830 her "Denkblätter einer Berlinerin" was published in Berlin. Her correspondence with David Veit and with Varnhagen von Ense was published in Leipsic, in 1861 and 1874–75 respectively.

Rahel always showed the greatest interest in her former coreligionists, endeavoring by word and deed to better their position, especially during the anti-Semitic outburst in Germany in 1819. On the day of her funeral Varnhagen sent a considerable sum of money to the Jewish poor of Berlin.

The poet **Ludwig Robert** was a brother of Rahel, and with him she corresponded extensively; her sister **Rosa** was married to Karl Asser.

BIBLIOGRAPHY: Schmidt-Weissenfels, *Rahel und Ihre Zeit*, Leipsic, 1857; Mrs. Vaughan Jennings, *Rahel, Her Life and Letters*, London, 1876; Assing, *Aus Rahels Herzensleben*, *ib.* 1877; Kayserling, *Die Jüdischen Frauen*, pp. 208 *et seq.*, Leipsic, 1879; Varnhagen, *Rahel, ein Buch des Andenkens für Ihre Freunde*, Berlin, 1833; idem, *Galerie von Bildnissen aus Rahel's Umgang und Briefwechsel*, Leipsic, 1836; Berdrow, *Rahel Varnhagen: Ein Lebens- und Zeitbild*, Stuttgart, 1900.

S. F. T. H.

LEVIN, ZEBI HIRSCH. See Levin, Hirschel ben Aryeh Löb.

LEVINSOHN, ANNA HENRIETTE: Danish operatic singer; born in Copenhagen Jan. 8, 1839; died there March 22, 1899. She made her début at the Kongelige Theater in Copenhagen on Dec. 20, 1860, when she, as *Nannette* in "Den Lille Rödhætte," completely won the hearts of her audience by her sympathetic impersonation of the guileless girl. She became "royal actress" in 1866, and was, on her retirement in 1879, appointed court singer ("Kongelig Kammersangerinde"). Her repertoire included: *Rosina* in "Barberen," *Susanna* in "Figaro's Bryllup," *Papagena* in "Trylleflöjten," *Anna* in "Jægerbruden," *Benjamin* in "Joseph og Hans Brödre," *Siebel* in "Faust," and *Venus* in "Tannhäuser."

BIBLIOGRAPHY: *Salmonsen's Store Illustrerede Konversations-Lexicon.*

S. F. C.

LEVINSOHN, ISAAC BAER: Russian-Hebrew scholar and writer; born at Kremenetz Oct. 13, 1788; died there Feb. 12, 1860. His father, Judah Levin, was a grandson of Jekuthiel Solomon, who settled in Kremenetz and acquired considerable wealth, and a son of Isaac, who had married the daughter of Zalman Cohen, famed for his wealth and scholarship. Levinsohn's father was a wealthy merchant and was popular among Jews and Gentiles alike. He was a master of Polish, wrote fluently in classical Hebrew (at that time a rare accomplishment), and was a thorough Talmudic scholar. At the age of three Levinsohn was sent to the ḥeder, where he soon manifested unusual aptitude for learning; and at nine he composed a cabalistic work that elicited the praise of scholars and rabbis ("Bet Yehudah," ii. 126, note 2). At ten he was versed in Talmudic lore, and knew the Old Testament by heart. He also studied and mastered the Russian language, an unusual achievement for a Russian Jew of that time. Thanks to his great mental power and industry, he rapidly familiarized himself with the rabbinical literature. At eighteen he married and settled in Radzivilov, supporting himself by teaching and translating; his married life, however, was unhappy, and he divorced his wife.

Some of Levinsohn's first literary efforts were in the domain of Hebrew poetry. Among others, he wrote a patriotic poem on the expulsion of the French from Russia, which was transmitted to the minister of the interior by General Giers, the commandant of the Radzivilov garrison. Levinsohn himself regarded his verses as mere literary exercises, did not attempt to print them, and the greater part of them were lost. Excessive study brought on nervous disorders, and Levinsohn journeyed to Brody, then the

His Verse.

center of the Jewish Haskalah, in order to consult the local physicians. There the future reformer of the Russian Jews found a congenial atmosphere in the circle of the Maskilim. He soon made the acquaintance of Dr. Isaac Erter, the Hebrew satirist, and later of Solomon Löb Rappoport. Though engaged as a bookkeeper in the local bank, he found time to continue his studies. Before long he passed the teacher's examinations and was appointed to teach Hebrew at the gymnasium of Tarnopol. There he soon became intimate with the scholar Joseph Perl, through whose influence he secured an instructorship at the Hebrew college of Brody.

Levinsohn's new position brought him into close relations with Nachman Krochmal of Zolkiev, an authority on all questions of rabbinical learning and Jewish custom. In 1817 he submitted to Krochmal his first critical studies, entitled "Ha-Mazkir," and Krochmal was so favorably impressed with the work that he offered to contribute toward the expense of publication. Unfortunately, it was never printed, and only a part of it was incorporated in "Te'uddah" and "Bet Yehudah." In 1820 Levinsohn prepared, for the benefit of the Russian youth, the first Hebrew grammar, entitled "Yesode Lashon Russiya." The necessary means being lacking, this was never published and the manuscript was lost.

His Writings.

About this time he wrote a satire on the Ḥasidim entitled "Dibre Ẓaddiḳim." Returning to Kremenetz in the same year, he began his "Te'uddah be-Yisrael," a work destined to leave an indelible impression on a whole generation of Russian Jews. It was finished in 1823, but was not published until 1828. The book attempted to solve many problems of contemporary Jewish life in Russia. It urged the study of the Scriptures before the Talmud, and the necessity of studying secular languages, particularly that of the Fatherland. It urged also the study of science and literature, and the great importance for the Jews of engaging in agricultural and industrial work. It strongly counseled the abandoning of petty trading and of other uncertain sources of livelihood.

Levinsohn's good advice, however, did not please the Ḥasidim, who opposed him in many ways and so embittered his existence that he was compelled to leave Kremenetz. Repairing to Berdychev, he became private tutor in the family of a wealthy Jew, and, gathering about him a circle of progressive friends, he organized a society for the promotion of culture. Regarding it as his special mission to carry enlightenment to the young generation, he resided successively in Ostrog, Nemirov, and Tulchin. On his way to the last-named place Levinsohn stopped at Kaminka, the estate of Prince Witgenstein, the Russian field-marshal. When the prince heard of Levinsohn's arrival he invited him to his house, assigned him a suite of rooms, and kept him there through the entire summer. The field-marshal liked to pass his evenings in conversation with the learned Jew, and often followed the latter's advice.

Isaac Baer Levinsohn.

In 1823 Levinsohn was compelled by failing health to return to Kremenetz. Soon after his arrival there he was confined to his bed by a sickness that kept him bedridden for twelve years. Notwithstanding this he never resigned himself to mental inactivity, and during these long years of suffering he made himself familiar with Arabic, Greek, and Syriac, and studied the classics, political economy, and philosophy.

In 1827, a year before the appearance of "Te'uddah," Levinsohn presented the manuscript, with an explanatory statement, to the Russian government, which accepted it with much favor, and awarded Levinsohn, on the representations of D. N. Bludov, a thousand rubles "for a work in Hebrew having for its object the moral education of the Jewish people." In the same year the minister of public instruction, Prince Lieven, submitted to Levinsohn thirty-four questions on Jewish religion and history, among them the following: "What is the Talmud?" "Who was the author of it?" "When, where, and in what language was it written?" "Have the Jews other books of such authority?" "Is there anything sensible in the Talmud? It is stated that it is full of improbable legends and fables." "How could the authors of the Talmud permit themselves to add to, or detract from, the commandments of the Torah, which forbids that?" "What is the object of the numerous rites that consume so much useful time?" "Is it true that the Jews are the descendants of those Pharisees whom the lawgiver of the Christians had accused of lying and superstition?" "Is it true that the Talmud forbids the Jews the study of foreign languages and science, as well as the pursuit of agricultural occupations?" "What is Ḥasidism, and who was its founder?" "In what towns mainly do the Ḥasidim reside?" "Do the Jews possess schools or learned books?" "How do the Jewish masses regard their schools?" "Can the condition of the Jews be improved? and, if so, by what means?" "What Messiah is it that the Jews are expecting?" "Is it true that the Jews expect to rule the entire world when the Messiah arrives, and that members of other religions will be excluded from participation in the after-life?" "How can a Jew be admitted into Christian society and be accorded full civic rights when he keeps himself aloof from the Christians and takes no interest in the welfare of the country where he resides?" Levinsohn referred the minister to his "Te'uddah" and to other works in various languages, transmitted to him concise answers to his questions, and promised to write a book in which these questions would be discussed in detail.

Questioned by Prince Lieven.

In 1828 "Te'uddah" saw the light. "It was not the yearning for fame," says Levinsohn in the preface, "that impelled me to write this book. . . . Friends seeking truth and light asked me to point out to them the true way of life; they wish to know what learning, aside from the Talmud and its commentaries, it is necessary for a Jew to acquire for the perfection and refinement of his nature as a man and a Jew."

Levinsohn now undertook his larger work, "Bet Yehudah," which was "to expose to Christian eyes the world of Jewish spiritual life founded on the principles of highest morality, a world then unknown to Russian Christians." He wished, also, to make his work of educational value to the Jewish people, so that uninstructed coreligionists would see Judaism in its true light. At the same time he found himself obliged to exercise great care in the treatment of the subject in order to avoid creating undue antagonism. Levinsohn presents in his "Bet Yehudah" a wonderfully clear and logical exposition of Jewish religious philosophy. According to him the Jewish religion may be summed up in two principles of belief: faith in one God, which involves the negation of idol-worship; and love of one's neighbor. He shows by numerous citations that the latter means the love not only of one Jew for another, but the love for any neighbor, irrespective of faith. He presents a history of the various Jewish sects, enumerates the contributions of the Jews to learning and civilization, and at the end suggests a plan for the reorganization of Jewish education in Russia. He urges the necessity of founding rabbinical seminaries fashioned after the German institutions, training the Jewish youth in religious and secular learning, opening elementary Jewish schools throughout the Pale, abolishing the institution of melammedim, and establishing agricultural and industrial schools.

Scope of His "Bet Yehudah."

"Bet Yehudah" exerted a powerful influence on the Jews of Russia and gave a plan of action to the progressive elements in the Russian Jewry. The book acquired renown outside of Russia also. It was translated into Polish, and the scholar Geiger read several chapters of it before an audience in the Breslau synagogue. But though "Bet Yehudah" was completed in 1829, it remained unpublished until 1838.

About this time the Jewish community of Zaslavl in Volhynia was accused of ritual murder; many families were imprisoned, and the entire community was in despair. Levinsohn's opponents then laid aside their enmity and turned to him as the only man capable of proving the falsity of the accusation. In spite of his sickness Levinsohn began his "Efes Dammim," in defense of the accused Jews. But the necessary means not being forthcoming, he was obliged to spend his own money in collecting material and information. "The purpose of my book," says Levinsohn, "is to acquit the Jews before the eyes of Christians, and to save them from the false accusation of using Christian blood." "Efes Dammim" is written in the form of a dialogue between a patriarch of the Greek Church in Jerusalem, Simias, and the chief rabbi in the Jewish synagogue there. The book shows the remarkable dialectic talent of the author. It was completed in 1834, published in 1837, republished three times, and was translated into English at the time of the "Damascus Affair" in 1840, at the instance of Sir Moses Montefiore and Crémieux. It was translated also into Russian (1883) and German (1884; another German edition appeared in 1892). In another polemical work, "Yemin Ẓidki," Levinsohn proves the absurdity of the accusations against Judaism and the Talmud. This work was left by him in manuscript.

Refutes Charges of Blood Accusation.

Other polemical works written by Levinsohn are "Aḥiyyah Shiloni ha-Ḥozeh" (Leipsic, 1841) and "Ta'ar ha-Sofer" (Odessa, 1863). "Aḥiyyah Shiloni ha-Ḥozeh" is directed against the work of the English missionary McCaul entitled "The Paths of the World" (London, 1839), and constitutes an introduction to Levinsohn's larger work "Zerubbabel," completed in 1853. This latter work was published, in part, by his nephew David Baer Nathansohn (Leipsic, 1863); the entire work was published later in Warsaw (1876). This work, which occupied twelve years, and was continued through sickness and suffering, was not only a defense of Judaism, but also an exposition of the value of traditional law in the Jewish religion, and of the great wisdom and moral force of its expounders and teachers. The "Ta'ar ha-Sofer" is directed against the Karaites.

In addition to these, Levinsohn wrote on Hebrew etymology and comparative philology. In this field he published "Bet ha-Oẓar," the first and second parts of which appeared in Wilna in 1841; the first part is entitled "Shorashe Lebanon," and includes studies of Hebrew roots; the second part comprises articles on various subjects, and "Abne Millu'im," a supplement to "Bet Yehudah." After Levinsohn's death Nathansohn published "Toledot Shem" (Warsaw, 1877) and "Ohole Shem" (Warsaw, 1893), both containing philological studies arranged in alphabetical order, and also corrections of Ben Zeb's "Oẓar ha-Shorashim," which was republished by Letteris. Levinsohn left a number of works in manuscript, including "Pittuḥe Ḥotam," on the period of the Canticles; "Yizre El," miscellaneous essays; "Be'er Yiẓḥaḳ," correspondence with contemporary scholars; "Eshkol ha-Sofer," letters, poetry, and humorous papers.

Levinsohn as a Philologist.

Levinsohn labored assiduously for the well-being of his coreligionists in Russia. He worked out and submitted to the government various projects for the amelioration of the condition of the Jews, such as the plan he submitted to the crown prince Konstantin in 1823, his memorandum to the minister of education in 1831, his project in regard to the censorship of Jewish books in 1833, and his plan for the establishment of Jewish colonies in 1837. Nicholas I. gave the last careful consideration. It is known, also, that the emperor wrote Levinsohn a personal letter in regard to this plan, but its contents are not known. The establishment of Jewish agricultural colonies in Bessarabia in 1838–39 and later and the organization of Jewish educational institutions undoubtedly owed much to Levinsohn's suggestions. The government appreciated his services, and, besides monetary rewards, offered him important positions, which he declined. The failure of his health compelled him to decline also appointment as member of the Jewish commission that sat in St. Petersburg in 1843, and in 1853 he again refused an appointment as member of the special commission on Jewish affairs. The following words were inscribed, at his own request, on his tombstone: "Out of nothing God called me to life. Alas, earthly life has passed, and I shall sleep again on the bosom of Mother Nature, as this stone testifies. I have fought the enemies of God not with the sharp sword, but with the Word. That I have fought for truth and justice before the Nations, 'Zerubbabel' and 'Efes Damim' bear witness." Levinsohn has been called "the Mendelssohn of Russia."

BIBLIOGRAPHY: Fuenn, *Keneset Yisrael*, p. 633, Warsaw, 1886; Zinberg, *Isaac Baer Levinsohn*, in *Galereya Yevreiskikh Dyeyatelei*, No. 3, St. Petersburg, 1900; Nathansohn, *Biographical Notes on Levinsohn*; Hausner, *I. B. Levinsohn*; Alabin, in *Russkaya Starina*, 1879, No. 5.

H. R.

LEVINSON-LESSING, FEODOR (FRANZ) YULYEVICH: Russian geologist; born 1861. He graduated from the physico-mathematical faculty of the University of St. Petersburg in 1883, was placed in charge of the geological collection in 1886, and was appointed privat-docent at St. Petersburg University in 1889. In 1892 he became professor, and the next year dean, of the physico-mathematical faculty of Yuryev University. Aside from his work on petrography he published also essays in other branches of geology, the result of scientific journeys throughout Russia. In various periodicals more than thirty papers have been published by him, the most important being the following: "Olonetzkaya Diabazovaya Formatziya" (in "Trudy St. Peterburgskavo Obschestva Yestestvovyedeniya," xix.); "O Fosforitnom Chernozyome" (in "Trudy Volnoekonomicheskavo Obschestva," 1890); "O Nyekotorykh Khimicheskikh Tipakh Izvyerzhonykh Porod" (in "Vyestnik Yestestvoznaniya," 1890); "Geologicheskiya Izslyedovaniya v Guberlinskhikh Gorakh" (in "Zapiski Mineralnavo Obschestva"); "Die Variolite von Yalguba" ("Tscherm. Mineral. Mitt." vi.); "Die Mikroskopische Beschaffenheit des Jordanalit" (*ib.* ix.); "Etudes sur le Porphirite de Deweboyu" (in "Bulletin de Société Belge de Géologie"); "1 et 2 Notes sur la Structure des Roches Eruptive" (*ib.*); "Note sur les Taxites et les Roches Elastiques Volcaniques" (*ib.*); "Les Ammonée de la Zone à Sporadoceras Munsteri" (*ib.*); "Petrographisches Lexicon" (2 parts, 1893–95); "Tablitzy dlya Mikroskopicheskikh Opredeleni Porodoobraznykh Mineralov." The last was published in English by Gregory.

BIBLIOGRAPHY: *Entziklopedicheski Slovar.*

H. R. J. G. L.

LEVINSTEIN, GUSTAV: German manufacturer and writer; born in Berlin May, 1842. After graduating from the Köllnisches Gymnasium in Berlin he went to England, where he and his brothers founded an anilin-dye factory at Manchester. Returning to Berlin, he entered the university and studied philosophy. He owns factories in southern France, though living in Berlin. He has at various times taken up his pen in behalf of Judaism and Jewish rights. Of his works the following may be mentioned: "Wissenschaftlicher Antisemitismus," directed against Paulsen (Berlin, 1896); "Der Glaube Israels" (*ib.* 1896); "Die Taufe" (*ib.* 1899); "Professor Paulsen und die Judenfrage" (*ib.* 1897); "Die Forderung des Sonntag-Gottesdienstes: Antwort auf das Gutachten des Rabbinats und den Beschluss der Repräsentanten-Versammlung," in support of supplementary Sunday services (*ib.* 1898); "Ueber die Erlösung des Judenthums," against Benediktus Levita (*ib.* 1900); "Professor Ladenburg und der Unsterblichkeitsgedanke im Judenthum" (*ib.* 1904).

S. M. K.

LEVINTHAL, BERNHARD LOUIS: Russian-American rabbi; born at Kovno, Russia, May 12, 1864. He was educated at the rabbinical schools of Kovno, Wilna, and Byelostok, and received rabbinical diplomas from Rabbi Isaac Elchanan Spector and Rabbi Samuel Mohilever in 1888. He emigrated to the United States in 1891, and shortly after his arrival there was appointed minister of six Russian congregations in Philadelphia. Levinthal helped to found various communal institutions in Philadelphia and is vice-president of the Union of Orthodox Rabbis of America, and honorary vice-president of the Federation of American Zionists.

BIBLIOGRAPHY: *American Jewish Year Book*, 1903-4, p. 74.

A. F. H. V.

LEVIRATE MARRIAGE (Hebr. "yibbum"): Marriage with a brother's widow. This custom is found among a large number of primitive peoples, a list of which is given by Westermarck ("History of Human Marriage," pp. 510–514). In some cases it is the duty of a man to marry his brother's widow even if she has had children by the deceased, but in most cases it occurs when there are no children, as among the Hindus ("Institutes of Manu," v. 59–63). Among the Hebrews marriage with a brother's widow was forbidden as a general rule (Lev. xviii. 16, xx. 21), but was regarded as obligatory (Deut. xxv. 56) when there was no male issue, and when the two brothers had been dwelling on the same family estate. The surviving brother could evade the obligation by the ceremony of ḤALIẒAH. The case of Ruth is not one of levirate marriage, being connected rather with the institution of the GO'EL; but the relations of Tamar with her successive husbands and with Judah are an instance (Gen. xxxviii.). If the levirate union resulted in male issue, the child would succeed to the estates of the deceased brother. It would appear that later the levirate marriage came to be regarded as obligatory only when the widow had no children of either sex. The Septuagint translates "ben" (son) in the passage of Deuteronomy by "child," and the Sadducees in the New Testament take it in this sense (Mark xii. 19; comp. Josephus, "Ant." iv. 8, § 23).

By Talmudic times the practise of levirate marriage was deemed objectionable (Bek. 13a), and was followed as a matter of duty only. To marry a brother's widow for her beauty was regarded by Abba Saul as equivalent to incest (Yeb. 39b). Bar Ḳappara recommends ḥaliẓah (Yeb. 109a). A difference of opinion appears among the later authorities, Alfasi, Maimonides, and the Spanish school generally upholding the custom, while R. Tam and the

Northern school prefer ḥaliẓah (Shulḥan 'Aruk, Eben ha-'Ezer, 165). The marriage was not necessary if the brother left a child by another marriage, even if such a child were on the point of death (*l.c.* 157). A change of religion on the part of the surviving brother does not affect the obligation of the levirate, or its alternative, the ḥaliẓah (Isaac b. Sheshet, Responsa, i. 2), yet the whole question has been profoundly affected by the change from polygamy to monogamy due to the taḳḳanah of Gershom ben Judah (see MARRIAGE).

The Samaritans followed a slightly different course, which may indicate an earlier custom among the Hebrews; the former practised the levirate only when the woman was betrothed and the marriage had not been consummated (Ḳid. 65b). The Karaites appear to have followed the same practise, and Benjamin Nahawendi, as well as Elijah Bashyaẓi, favored it ("Adderet Eliyahu, Nashim," p. 93a).

It has been suggested by Kalisch ("Leviticus," ii. 362–363) that the prohibition in Leviticus is of later date than the obligation under certain conditions in Deuteronomy, but it is equally possible that the Leviticus prohibition was a general one, and the permission in Deuteronomy only an exception when there was no male issue. J. F. Maclennan ("Studies in Ancient History," i. 109–114) suggested that the existence of levirate marriage was due to polyandry among the primitive Hebrews, and has been followed by Buhl ("Sociale Verhaltnisse," p. 34) and Barton ("Semitic Origins," pp. 66–67); but this is rather opposed to the Hebraic conditions, for it would be against the interests of the surviving brother to allow the estate to go out of his possession again. There is, besides, no evidence of polyandry among the Hebrews.

BIBLIOGRAPHY: Geiger, in *Jüdische Zeitschrift*, 1862, pp. 19–39.

S. S. J.

LEVISOHN, GEORGE (MORDECAI GUMPEL LEIVE): German surgeon; born in Berlin of a family known as "Schnaber"; died in Hamburg Feb. 10, 1797. He evinced an early aptitude for study, and attended the school of David Fränkel, chief rabbi of Berlin. Levisohn chose the medical profession, to which he devoted himself with enthusiasm. He left Germany for England, and, after studying under John Hunter, was appointed physician at the hospital of the Duke of Portland. Being called to Sweden by Gustavus III., he occupied for some time the position of professor at the University of Upsala. Gustavus thought highly of him, and he translated, at the king's command, from English into Swedish his medical and polemical works. Levisohn left the court in 1781 and returned to Germany, where he published German translations of most of his English medical works. Three years later (1784) he went to Hamburg, and, being well received, settled there and followed his profession with remarkable success.

The large number of his daily patients did not prevent him from prosecuting with zeal his medical, philosophical, and theological studies. In 1785–86 he published two medical journals, and during the following years labored at his great work on religious philosophy. He was then engaged for five years in physical researches. His works are: "Ma'amar ha-Torah we-Ḥokmah" (London, 1771), a philosophical treatise (this work caused its author to be regarded in the light of a dangerous innovator); "An Essay on the Blood" (*ib.* 1776); "Epidemical Sore Throat" (*ib.* 1778); "Beschreibung der Londonischen Medicinischen Praxis den Deutschen Aerzten Vorgelegt . . . mit einer Vorrede von T. C. A. Theden" (Berlin, 1782); "The Passions and Habits of Man, and Their Influence on Health" (Brunswick, 1797–1801); "Derek ha-Ḳodesh ha-Ḥadashah," a Hebrew grammar.

BIBLIOGRAPHY: Schröder, *Hamburgische Schriftsteller*; Carmoly, *Les Médecins Juifs*, pp. 217, 219; Picciotto, *Sketches of Anglo-Jewish History*, p. 147; *British Museum Catalogue*.

J. G. L.

LEVISOHN, MORDECAI GUMPEL. See LEVISOHN, GEORGE.

LEVISON, ESAIAS: Danish educationist and author; born in Copenhagen April 22, 1803; died there March 23, 1891; educated at the University of Copenhagen (B.A. 1823). In 1824 Levison was appointed tutor at the Jewish school in Copenhagen, in which position he remained till within two years of his death. He published several religious educational works, of which the following may be mentioned: "Kortfattet Forklaring over Lærebogen i Religionen for Ungdommen af den Mosaiske Troesbekjendelse" (Copenhagen, 1825); "Bibelske Fortællinger" (*ib.* 1827); a Jewish prayer-book, with Hebrew text and Danish translation (*ib.* 1833). Levison translated into Danish Bulwer Lytton's "Paul Clifford." For two years (1837–38) he acted as coeditor of "Borgervennen," a Danish political periodical, to which he contributed several articles. In 1837 the University of Kiel conferred upon him the honorary degree of Ph.D.

BIBLIOGRAPHY: *Erslew's Forfatter-Lexicon.*

S. F. C.

LEVISON, FERDINAND EMANUEL: Danish physician; born in Copenhagen Nov. 9, 1843; educated at the University of Copenhagen (M.D. 1868). He was successively assistant physician at Frederik's Hospital, the Lying-in Hospital, and the Almindeligt (Communal) Hospital in Copenhagen. In 1887 he was appointed guardian of the poor, which position he still (1904) occupies. Levison is an energetic advocate of cremation; the first Danish society for cremation was founded (1881) at his initiative, and he has ever since officiated as its president.

BIBLIOGRAPHY: C. F. Bricka, *Dansk Biografisk Lexicon.*

S. F. C.

LEVITA, ELIJAH (known also as **Elijah ben Asher ha-Levi Ashkenazi, Elijah Baḥur, Elijah Medaḳdeḳ,** and **Elijah Tishbi**): Grammarian, Masorite, and poet; born at Neustadt, near Nuremberg, in 1468; died at Venice Dec., 1549.

From his childhood Elijah showed a predilection for Biblical studies and Hebrew grammar. He settled early in Venice; but in 1504 he was at Padua, earning a livelihood by instructing Jewish children in Hebrew. At the request of his pupils he wrote a commentary to Moses Ḳimḥi's "Mahalak"; but a

ספר התשבי
לאליהו התשבי
שרשיו כמנין
תשבי

ורובם הם שרשים ׃ מלפנים אינם מפורשים ׃
ומורגלים בדברי רבותינו ׃ בתלמוד ומדרשים
בראשית רבא וילמדנו ׃ ולא יהיה שרש
בכל הספר ׃ שאינו דבר חדש מספר ׃
ועל זה פסוק אחד אשיר ׃ על
דרך מליצת השיר ׃ אין בית
אשר אין שם מת חדש
איזה דבר ׃ אשר
לא נשמע
כבר ׃

TITLE-PAGE FROM THE FIRST EDITION OF ELIJAH LEVITA'S "TISHBI," ISNY, 1541.

(From the Sulzberger collection in the Jewish Theological Seminary of America, New York.)

certain Benjamin Colbo, to whom Elijah had given the manuscript to transcribe, published the work at Pesaro under his own name. Colbo interspersed the annotations with excerpts from another work; and in this form Elijah's first production was most incorrectly printed. In spite of this, however, it became the favorite manual for students of the Hebrew language, both among Jews and Christians. It was soon reprinted several times at Pesaro, and made its way into Germany and France, where also it was reprinted; it was translated into Latin by Sebastian Münster (Basel, 1531, 1536). It was not until 1546 that Elijah, urged by his friends, claimed the authorship of the work and published a corrected edition of it at Venice. During his stay in Padua, Elijah published in German a version of the Baba Buch.

The relatively happy circumstances enjoyed by Elijah at Padua did not long continue. In 1509 the city was taken and sacked by the army of the League of Cambray, and Elijah, losing everything he possessed, had to leave the place. He betook himself to Rome, and having heard of the scholarly and liberal-minded Ægidius of Viterbo, general of the Augustine Order, who was studying Hebrew, he called upon him. This prelate, in exchange for Hebrew lessons from Elijah, offered to maintain him and his family. For thirteen years Elijah remained in the palace of the cardinal, writing works which spread his reputation, giving lessons in Hebrew, and, in turn, taking lessons in Greek from the cardinal. During this period Elijah produced the "Sefer ha-Baḥur," a grammatical treatise written at the request of the cardinal, to whom it was dedicated, and first published at Rome in 1518 (2d ed. Isny, 1542, and many subsequent reissues). As the author explains in his preface, he called the work "Baḥur" because that was his surname, and further because the word denoted both "youth" and "excellent." The treatise is divided into four parts, each of which is subdivided into thirteen sections, corresponding to the thirteen articles of the Jewish creed; while the total number of sections, fifty-two, represents the numerical value of "Elijah," his name. The first part discusses the nature of the Hebrew verbs; the second, the changes in the vowel-points of the different conjugations; the third, the regular nouns; and the fourth, the irregular ones.

Grammarian.

In the same year (1518) Elijah published tables of paradigms for beginners, entitled "Luaḥ be-Diḳduḳ ha-Po'alim weha-Binyanim"; and a work, on the irregular words in the Bible, entitled "Sefer ha-Harkabah." Desiring to explain every intricacy and anomaly in the Hebrew language, but fearing that too many digressions might prevent his grammar from becoming a popular manual, he in 1520 published dissertations on various grammatical subjects under the general title "Pirḳe Eliyahu." This he divided into four parts: the first, "Pereḳ Shirah," discussing in thirteen stanzas the laws of the letters, the vowel-points, and the accents; the second, "Pereḳ ha-Minim," written in prose, treating of the different parts of speech; the third, "Pereḳ ha-Middot," discussing the various parts of speech; and the fourth, "Pereḳ ha-Shimmushim," treating of the servile letters. Like his preceding works, it was translated into Latin and published by Sebastian Münster.

In 1527 misfortune again overtook Elijah; he was driven from his studies when the Imperialists sacked Rome, and lost all his property and the greater part of his manuscripts. He then returned to Venice, and was engaged by the printer Daniel Bomberg as corrector of his Hebrew press. To the income derived from this employment was added that earned by tuition. Among his pupils was the French ambassador George de Selve, afterward Bishop of Lavaur, who by generous pecuniary assistance placed Elijah in a position to complete his great Masoretic concordance "Sefer ha-Zikronot," on which he had labored for twenty years. This work, which De Selve, to whom it was dedicated, sent to Paris to be printed at his expense, has for some unknown reason never been published, and is still extant in manuscript in the Bibliothèque Nationale, Paris. An attempt to edit it was made by Goldberg in 1875, but he got no farther than אנמי. The introduction and the dedication to it were published by Frensdorf in Fraenkel's "Monatsschrift" (xii. 96–108). Still the "Sefer ha-Zikronot," to which Elijah often refers as his chef-d'œuvre, made a good impression in Paris, and Elijah was offered by Francis I. the position of professor of Hebrew at the university there, which he declined, being unwilling to settle in a city forbidden to his coreligionists. He declined also invitations from several cardinals, bishops, and princes to accept a Hebrew professorship in Christian colleges.

Proof-Reader and Tutor.

Two years after the completion of the "Sefer ha-Zikronot" Elijah published his Masoretic work "Massoret ha-Massoret" (Venice, 1538), divided into three parts, respectively denominated "First Tables," "Second Tables," and "Broken Tables," each with an introduction. The "First Tables" is divided into ten sections, or commandments ("'Aseret ha-Debarim"), dealing with the "full" and "defective" writing of syllables. The "Second Tables" treats of the "ḳere" and "ketib," "ḳameẓ" and "pataḥ," "dagesh," "mappiḳ," "rafe," etc. The "Broken Tables" discusses the abbreviations used by the Masorites. In the third introduction Elijah produces an array of most powerful arguments to prove that the vowel-points in the Hebrew Bibles were invented by the Masorites in the fifth century of the common era. This theory, although suggested by some Jewish scholars as early as the ninth century, provoked a great outcry among the Orthodox Jews, who ascribed to the vowel-points the greatest antiquity. They were already dissatisfied with Elijah for giving instruction in Hebrew to Christians, since the latter openly confessed that they studied the Hebrew language with the hope of finding in the Hebrew texts, especially in the Cabala, arguments against Judaism. To this Elijah replied in the first introduction to the "Massoret ha-Massoret" that he taught only the elements of the language and did not teach Cabala at all. Moreover, he pointed out that Christian Hebraists generally defended the Jews against the attacks of the fanatical clergy. Elijah's theory concerning the modernity

"Massoret."

of the vowel-points caused still greater excitement among Christians, and for three centuries it gave occasion for discussions among Catholic and Protestant scholars, such as Buxtorf, Walton, De Rossi, and others. The "Massoret ha-Massoret" was so favorably received that in less than twelve months after its appearance it was republished at Basel (1539). In this edition Sebastian Münster translated into Latin the three introductions, and gave a brief summary of the contents of the three parts. The third part, or the "Broken Tables," was republished separately at Venice in 1566, under the title "Perush ha-Massoret we-Ḳara Shemo Sha'are Shibre Luḥot." This part of the book was again republished, with additions, by Samuel ben Ḥayyim at Prague in 1610. The three introductions were also translated into Latin by Nagel (Altdorf, 1758–71). In 1772 the whole book was translated into German by Christian Gottlob Meyer, and in 1867 into English by Christian D. Ginsburg.

In 1538, also, Elijah published at Venice a treatise on the laws of the accents entitled "Sefer Ṭub Ṭa'am." Meanwhile David Bomberg's printing-office had ceased to exist, and Elijah, although at that time seventy years of age, left his wife and children and departed in 1540 for Isny, accepting the invitation of Paul Fagius to superintend his Hebrew printing-press there. During Elijah's stay with Fagius (until 1542 at Isny and from 1542 to 1544 at Constance) he published the following works: "Tishbi," a dictionary containing 712 words used in Talmud and Midrash, with explanations in German and a Latin translation by Fagius (Isny, 1541); "Sefer Meturgeman," explaining all the Aramaic words found in the Targum (*ib.*); "Shemot Debarim," an alphabetical list of the technical Hebrew words (Isny, 1542); a Judæo-German version of the Pentateuch, the Five Megillot, and Hafṭarot (Constance, 1544); and a new and revised edition of the "Baḥur." On returning to Venice, Elijah, in spite of his great age, still labored on the edition of several works, among which was David Ḳimḥi's "Miklol," to which he added notes of his own ("nimuḳim").

Lexicographer.

Bibliography: Wolf, *Bibl. Hebr.* iii. 97; Azulai, *Shem ha-Gedolim*, s.v.; G. B. de Rossi, *Dizionario*, s.v.; *Orient, Lit.* 1848, Nos. 4–6; Frensdorf, in *Monatsschrift*, xii. 96 *et seq.*; Gesenius, *Gesch. der Hebräischen Sprache*, Leipsic, 1815; Brüll's *Jahrb.* viii. 188; S. Buber, *Toledot Eliyahu*, 1856; Steinschneider, *Cat. Bodl.* col. 934; idem, *Bibliographisches Handbuch*, Nos. 1159–1167; Grätz, *Gesch.* viii. 199; Kahana, in *Ha-Shaḥar*, xii. 498 *et seq.*; C. D. Ginsburg, *The Masoreth ha-Masoreth of Elias Levita*, London, 1867; I. Davidson, in *Modia' la-Ḥadashim*, ii. 21 *et seq.*; J. Levi, *Elia Levita*, Breslau, 1888; Bacher, in Ersch and Gruber, *Encyc.* s.v. *Levita*; idem, *Elija Levita's Wissenschaftliche Leistungen*, in *Z. D. M. G.* xliii. 206–272; idem, *Zur Biographie Elija Levita's*, in *Monatsschrift*, xxxvii. 398 *et seq.*

J. I. Br.

LEVITAN, ISAAC (ISAAC ILYICH): Russian painter; born near Eidtkuhnen Aug. 18, 1860; died at Moscow July 22, 1900. His father, who earned a livelihood by giving private tuition, removed to Moscow when Levitan was still a boy and gave him a good home training. About 1875 Levitan entered the Moscow School of Art, where he finished the course. Living in great poverty, and at times in actual want, he still continued his work, and at the age of nineteen displayed considerable talent in his "An Autumn Day at Sokolniki." This picture was purchased by the well-known connoisseur Tretyakov. In 1880 Levitan exhibited "The Plowed Field," which attracted much favorable comment. As late as 1886, notwithstanding the reputation which he had acquired, he still continued to derive only a very small income from his profession.

The period 1887–97 was the most happy of Levitan's life, and to it belong his best works. He was a tireless worker and painted a very large number of pictures. Twenty-five of his paintings are to be seen in the Tretyakov gallery alone. He probably produced in all about 1,000 paintings and studies, most of them in the decade 1887–97. In 1892, when Levitan was already widely known and after the award to him of the first prize for his picture "Twilight" at the Art Lovers' Exhibition, the notorious May Laws were enforced in Moscow, and he was permitted to remain there only owing to the influence of powerful friends. His nearest relatives, however, were compelled to leave the city, their business was ruined, and Levitan had to render them material aid to the end of his life. In 1897 Levitan was elected an active member of the Munich society Secession, and the Academy of Art selected him an academician.

Levitan's paintings are marked by a thorough knowledge of Russian scenery and types. They possess a decided originality; at the same time they convey an expression of sadness. In his funeral oration Count A. E. Lvov said of Levitan: "He was an artist-poet. He not only painted pictures—in his paintings there was something besides; we not only saw his pictures, we also felt them. He knew how to interpret Nature and her mysteries as no other man." Even the "Novoye Vremya" (July 29, 1900), an organ decidedly anti-Semitic in its policy, admitted that "this full-blooded Jew knew, as no other man, how to make us realize and love our plain and homely country scenes."

Among the works of Levitan may be mentioned: "Over Eternal Rest"; "The Neglected Graveyard"; "A Tatar Graveyard"; "Relics of the Past—Twilight in Finland"; "The Golden Autumn"; "Vladimirka"; "March"; "After the Rain"; "Forest"; "Evening"; "The Peaceful Retreat"; "The Hay Harvest"; and two lake scenes. A picture by Levitan, entitled "A Convent on the Eve of a Holiday," was exhibited at the Columbian Exposition, Chicago, in 1893.

Bibliography: S. Vermel, *Voskhod*, xxii. 34.

H. R. J. G. L.

LEVITES (Temple Servants).—**Biblical Data:** Of the Levites, Aaron and his sons were chosen for the priestly office (Ex. xxviii. 1 *et seq.*); the menial services of the Tabernacle were assigned to the rest of the tribe (Num. i. 47 *et seq.*). The Kohathites were to bear the sacred furniture of the Tabernacle; the Gershonites, its curtains; and the Merarites, its boards, pins, and poles (Num. iv. 4–16, 22–28, 29–33). It is distinctly stated that the Levites shall not approach the most holy things (Num. iv. 19)—that is, they shall not act as priests, a function which the context reserves for Aaron and his sons.

In Deuteronomy the representation is quite different; "priests" and "Levites" are there synonymous terms, and the one is regularly placed in apposition with the other. In Deut. xviii. 1, apparently, every Levite is a potential priest. In Joshua, as in Numbers, the Levites consist of the clans of Kohath, Gershon, and Merari, and to each clan a large number of cities is assigned (comp. Josh. xxi.; see Levi, Tribe of). The Levites, as the servants of the Temple, appear next in I Chronicles, where David is represented as dividing them into "courses" to wait on the sons of Aaron by doing the menial work of the Temple because they were no longer needed to carry the Tabernacle (comp. I Chron. xxiii., especially 26–28). He also appointed some to be doorkeepers of the Temple, some to have charge of its treasure, and some to be singers (I Chron. xxv.–xxvi.).

Ezekiel, however, gives a somewhat different impression of the personnel of the Temple service in pre-exilic times. In ch. xliv. 9–13 he declares that in future no uncircumcised foreigner shall enter the Temple, and that the Levites who have served at idolatrous shrines shall be deposed from the priesthood and perform the menial services of the sanctuary, such as keeping the gates and slaying the offerings. This seems to imply that before the Exile this service had been performed not by Levites, but by foreigners (an impression which Josh. ix. 23 deepens), and that those who were accounted Levites in this subordinate sense had formerly exercised a priesthood, of which Ezekiel did not approve.

After the Exile the Temple organization, as reflected in the books of Ezra and Nehemiah, is the same as that portrayed in Chronicles. The plan of Ezekiel was not altogether carried out, for the Nethinim, who were descended from slaves whom David had given to the Temple (Ezra viii. 20), shared with the Levites the subordinate work of the sanctuary (Ezra vii. 24). In later times it would seem that the distinction between Levites and Nethinim gradually disappeared; present information on this point consists solely of the fact that the Nethinim were given genealogies along with the Levites (Ezra ii. 40 *et seq.*). At the beginning of the common era the Levites were an important class of religious officials (comp. Luke x. 32; John i. 19).

——**Critical View:** The Biblical data thus present two inconsistent views. According to Leviticus, Numbers, the greater part of Joshua, and Chronicles, the priesthood was confined to the house of Aaron from the first, and the Levites existed as a menial class for the performance of the subordinate work of the sanctuary from the time of Moses. The portions of Leviticus, Numbers, and Joshua which contain this point of view are all from the P stratum of the Hexateuch—a post-exilic document, as the Graf-Wellhausen school believes. Chronicles, too, is a work written some time after the Exile.

In the older books of Judges, Samuel, and Kings the priestly offices are represented as not exclusively performed by Levites, who, however, were from the first preferred for these services and gradually monopolized them (see Levi, Tribe of). These services were not confined to any one sanctuary, but were performed in temples all over the land (comp. Judges xviii. 30). This condition of affairs apparently continued until Josiah, in 621 B.C., instituted a reform on the basis of the Deuteronomic law (II Kings xxiii.), when all sanctuaries except that at Jerusalem were abolished. This left a large number of priests without a vocation, and they were consequently recommended to the charity of their brethren along with the widow, the fatherless, and the resident alien (Deut. xii. 18, 19; xiv. 27, 29; xvi. 11, 16). In this code every Levite is still regarded as a possible priest, however, and it is distinctly stipulated that if one of them goes to Jerusalem he shall have the same privileges in the exercise of the priestly office as are enjoyed by any other Levite (Deut. xviii. 6–7). But the influence of the Jerusalem priesthood seems to have been so great that even Josiah could not enforce this provision, and the provincial priests were never accorded in fact the privileges in the Temple on Zion which Deuteronomy had granted them (comp. II Kings xxiii. 9). Ezekiel's plan for the reorganization of the Temple services proposed to utilize these men for the menial work of the sanctuary; this proposal was actually embodied in the legislation of P and became a part of the post-exilic religious organization.

Earlier Accounts.

The view of the Graf-Wellhausen critical school is that last outlined—that the cleavage between priests and Levites was not begun until the time of Josiah, that it received a further impetus from Ezekiel, and that it became a real feature of the permanent religious organization after the return from Babylon. This view is strengthened by the fact that J in Josh. ix. 23 represents Joshua as presenting the foreign Gibeonites to the Temple as slaves, "hewers of wood and drawers of water," and that Ezekiel shows that foreigners continued to fill the menial offices down to the time of the Exile. Van Hoonacker ("Le Sacerdoce dans la Loi et dans l'Histoire des Hébreux," 1899) contends that Chronicles records pre-exilic conditions (comp. Baudissin in "Theologische Literaturzeitung," 1899, cols. 359–363). The picture of the Levites given in Leviticus, Numbers, the P portions of Joshua, and Chronicles is thought by others to be a projection by the writers of the institutions of their own times into the distant past.

After Josiah.

Bibliography: Wellhausen, *Prolegomena zur Gesch. Israels*, 5th ed., 1899, ch. iv.; Baudissin, *Die Gesch. des Alttestamentlichen Priestertumes*, 1889; H. Vogelstein, *Der Kampf Zwischen Priestern und Leviten seit den Tagen Ezechiels*, 1889; Nowack, *Hebräische Archäologie*, 1894; Benzinger, *Hebräische Archäologie*.

E. G. H. G. A. B.

LEVITICUS.—Biblical Data: The English name is derived from the Latin "Liber Leviticus," which is from the Greek (τὸ) Λευιτικόν (*i.e.*, βιβλίον). In Jewish writings it is customary to cite the book by its first word, "Wa-yiḳra." The book is composed of laws which treat of the functions of the priests, or the Levites in the larger sense. It is in reality a body of sacerdotal law. The various laws comprising this collection are represented as spoken by Yhwh to Moses between the first day of the first month of the second year after the Exodus and the first day of the second month of the same year (comp. Ex. xl. 17 and Num. i. 1). There is no note

Illuminated Page of Leviticus.

(From a manuscript formerly in the possession of the Duke of Sussex.)

of a definite time in Leviticus itself, but from the references cited it is clear that in the continuous narrative of the Pentateuch this is the chronological position of the book.

Ch. i.–vii.: A collection of laws relating to sacrifices. It falls into two portions: (1) ch. i.–vi. 7 (Hebr. i.–v.) and vii. 22–34 are laws addressed to the people; (2) ch. vi. 8–vii. 21 (Hebr. vi. 1–vii. 21) are addressed to the priests. Ch. i. contains laws for burnt offerings; ch. ii., for meal-offerings; ch. iii., peace-offerings; ch. iv., sin-offerings; ch. v. 1–vi. 7 (Hebr. ch. v.), trespass-offerings; ch. vi. 8–13 (Hebr. vi. 1–6) defines the duties of the priest with reference to the fire on the altar; ch. vi. 14–18 (Hebr. vi. 7–11), the meal-offering of the priests; ch. vi. 19–23 (Hebr. vi. 12–16), the priests oblation; ch. vi. 24–30 (Hebr. vi. 17–23), the trespass-offering; ch. vii. 1–7, trespass-offerings; ch. vii. 8–10, the portions of the sacrifices which go to the priests; ch. vii. 11–18, peace-offerings; ch. vii. 19–21, certain laws of uncleanness; ch. vii. 22–27 prohibits eating fat or blood; ch. vii. 28–34 defines the priests' share of the peace-offering. Ch. vii. 35–38 consists of a subscription to the preceding laws.

Contents.

Ch. viii.–ix.: The consecration of Aaron and his sons; though narrative in form, they contain the precedent to which subsequent ritual was expected to conform.

Ch. x. contains two narratives: one shows that it is unlawful to use strange fire at YHWH's altar; the other requires the priests to eat the sin-offering. Between these narratives two laws are inserted, one prohibiting intoxicating drink to the priests, the other giving sundry directions about offerings (8–15).

Ch. xi. contains laws in regard to clean and unclean animals, and separates those which may from those which may not be used for food.

Ch. xii. contains directions for the purification of women after childbirth. A distinction is made between male and female children, the latter entailing upon the mother a longer period of uncleanness.

Ch. xiii. and xiv. contain the laws of leprosy, giving the signs by which the priest may distinguish between clean and unclean eruptions.

Ch. xv. contains directions for the purifications necessary in connection with certain natural secretions of men (2–18) and women (19–30).

Ch. xvi. contains the law of the great Day of Atonement. The chief features of this ritual are the entrance of the high priest into the Holy of Holies and the sending of the goat into the wilderness (see AZAZEL).

Ch. xvii.–xxvi. contain laws which differ in many respects from the preceding and which have many features in common. They are less ritualistic than the laws of ch. i.–xvi. and lay greater stress on individual holiness; hence the name "Holiness Code," proposed by Klostermann in 1877 for these chapters, has been generally adopted. Ch. xvii. contains general regulations respecting sacrifice; ch. xviii. prohibits unlawful marriages and unchastity; ch. xix. defines the religious and moral duties of Israelites; ch. xx. imposes penalties for the violation of the provisions of ch. xviii. In ch. xxi. regulations concerning priests are found (these regulations touch the domestic life of the priest and require that he shall have no bodily defects); ch. xxii. gives regulations concerning sacrificial food and sacrificial animals; ch. xxiii. presents a calendar of feasts; ch. xxiv. contains various regulations concerning the lamps of the Tabernacle (1–4) and the showbread (5–9), and a law of blasphemy and of personal injury (10–23); ch. xxv. is made up of laws for the Sabbatical year and the year of jubilee (these laws provide periodical rests for the land and secure its ultimate reversion, in case it be estranged for debt, to its original owners); ch. xxvi. is a hortatory conclusion to the Holiness Code.

Holiness Code.

Ch. xxvii. consists of a collection of laws concerning the commutation of vows. These laws cover the following cases: where the vowed object is a person (1–8); an animal (9–15); a house (14–15); an inherited field (16–21); a purchased field (22–25); a firstling (26–27). Then follow additional laws concerning persons and things "devoted" (28–29) and concerning tithes (30–33). Verse 34 is the colophon to the Book of Leviticus, stating that these laws were given by YHWH as commands to Moses at Mount Sinai.

E. G. H. G. A. B.

——**Critical View:** In the critical analysis of the Pentateuch it is held that Leviticus belongs to the priestly stratum, designated by the symbol P. To this stratum the laws of Leviticus are attached by their nature and also by linguistic affinities (comp. PENTATEUCH, and J. Estlin Carpenter and G. Harford Battersby, "Hexateuch" [cited hereafter as "Hex."], i. 208–221). This priestly stratum was formerly regarded as the "Grundschrift," or oldest stratum of the Pentateuch, but by Graf and Wellhausen, whose views now receive the adherence of the great majority of scholars, it has been shown to be on the whole the latest. Leviticus as it stands is not, however, a consistent code of laws formulated at one time, but is the result of a considerable process of compilation. It has already been noted that chapters xvii. to xxvi. have a distinct character of their own and a distinct hortatory conclusion, which point to an independent codification of this group of laws. Within this same group many indications that it is a compilation from earlier priestly sources may also be found. Ch. xviii. 26, xix. 37, xxii. 31–33, xxiv. 22, xxv. 55, xxvi. 46, and xxvii. 34 are all passages which once stood at the end of independent laws or collections of laws. Similar titles and colophons, which are best explained as survivals from previous collections, are found also in other parts of the book, as in vi. 7 (A. V. 14); vii. 1, 2, 37, 38; xi. 46, 47; xiii. 59; xiv. 54, 55; xv. 32, 33. It is necessary, therefore, to analyze these laws more closely.

Latest Stratum of Pentateuch.

It will be convenient to begin this analysis with ch. viii.–x., which are, as previously noted, narratives rather than laws. Ch. viii. relates the consecration of Aaron and his sons to the priesthood. That consecration is commanded in Ex. xl. 12–15, just as the erection of the Tabernacle is commanded in Ex. xl. 1–11. As the erection of the Tabernacle is described in Ex. xl. 17–38, it is probable that Lev. viii., recounting the consecration of Aaron and his sons, immediately followed Ex. xl. Ch. i.–vii. have by editorial changes been made to separate this narrative from its context. Lev. viii. is based on Ex. xxix., relating its fulfilment, just as Ex. xxxv.–xl. is based on Ex. xxv.–xxviii. and xxx., xxxi. It has been shown (comp. Exodus, Book of, Critical View I.) that Ex. xxxv.–xl. is a later expansion of a briefer account of the fulfilment of the commands of xxv.–xxxi.; it follows accordingly that Lev. viii. probably belongs to a similar late expansion of a shorter account of the fulfilment of the commands of ch. xxix. Lev. viii. is not so late as Ex. xxxv.–xl., since it knows but one altar.

Chapters viii.-x.: Narratives.

Ch. ix. resumes the main thread of the original priestly law-book. It relates to the inaugural sacrifice of the Tabernacle—the real sequel to Ex. xxv.–xxix. Probably it was originally separated from those chapters by some brief account of the construction and erection of the sanctuary and the consecration of the priesthood. The editor's hand may be detected in verses 1 and 23.

Ch. x. 1–5 is the continuation of ch. ix. and is from the same source. The regulations in verses 6–20 are loosely thrown together, though verses 6, 12–15, and 16–20, are, as they stand, attached to the main incident in verses 1–5. Verses 10, 11 are allied to ch. xvii.–xxvi., the Holiness Code (comp. Driver in "S. B. O. T." *ad loc.*). Verses 16–20 are a late supplement, suggested by the conflict between the procedure of ix. 15 and the rule of vi. 24–30.

Ch. i.-vii.: Laws of Offerings.

Ch. i.–vii., as already noted, consist of two parts: i.–v. (A. V. vi. 7), addressed to the people, and vi.–vii. (A. V. vi. 8–vii. 36), addressed to the priests. It is not a unitary, harmonious code: the two parts have a different order, the peace-offering occurring in a different position in the two parts.

Ch. i.–iii. were compiled from at least two sources, and have been touched by different hands. Ch. iii. should follow immediately after ch. i.

Ch. iv., which graduates a scale of victims for the sin-offering according to the guilt of the sinner, is later than i.–iii. It is regarded by all critics as a late addition to the ritual. The altar of incense, v. 7, is unknown to the older ritual (comp. Ex. xxix. 10–14); and the ritual of the high priest's sin-offering is much more elaborate than in Ex. xxix. 10–14 or Lev. ix. 8–11. The sin-offering, which in other laws is a goat (Lev. ix. 15, xvi. 8, and Num. xv. 24), is here a bullock. The ritual is throughout heightened, perhaps beyond all actual practise.

Ch. v.–vi. 7 (A. V. v.) afford no indications of so late a date as ch. iv., although it is clearly a combination of laws from various sources (comp. verse 14 and v. 20 (A. V. vi. 1). The oldest nucleus seems to be v. 1–6, in which there are no ritual directions. Verses 7–10 and 11–13 are later and perhaps successive additions. Though united later, they are probably genuine laws.

The rules for the guidance of the priests (vi. [A. V. vi. 8–vii.]) are also compiled from previous collections, as is shown by the different headings (comp. vi. 1, 13, 18 [A. V. vi. 8, 19, 24]). They also are genuine laws from an older time.

Ch. xi.: Clean and Unclean Animals.

Ch. xi. defines the clean and unclean animals. Because several of these laws are similar to the Holiness legislation (comp. verses 2–8, 9–11, 20, 21, and 41, 42), it has been inferred by many critics that ch. xi. is a part of that legislation, that it is in reality the law which xx. 25 implies. Others, as Carpenter and Harford Battersby, regard it as an excerpt from a body of priestly teaching which once had an existence independent of the Holiness Code. The chapter is not a unit. Verses 24–31 seem to be an expansion of v. 8, while verses 32–38 appear to be a still more recent addition.

Ch. xii. contains directions for the purification of women after childbirth. In v. 2 reference is made to ch. xv. 19. As the rules in xii. are cast in the same general form as those of xv., the two chapters are of the same date. It is probable that xii. once followed xv. 30. Why it was removed to its present position can not now be ascertained. For date see below on ch. xv.

Ch. xiii. and xiv.: Laws of Leprosy.

The extreme elaboration of the rules for Leprosy has led some scholars to regard the compilation of ch. xiii. and xiv. as late, especially as it has been inferred from Deut. xxiv. 8 that when Deuteronomy was compiled the rules concerning leprosy were all still oral (comp. "Hex." ii. 158, note). Moore, on the other hand (in Cheyne and Black, "Encyc. Bibl."), points out that the ritual of xiv. 2–8 is very primitive (comp. Smith, "Rel. of Sem." pp. 422, 428 [note], 447), and that there is no reason to doubt the early formulation of such laws. These chapters are not, however, all of one date. The original draft of the law included only xiii. 2–46a, xiv. 2–8a, and the subscription in 57b; xiii. 47–59, which treats of leprosy in garments, was codified separately, for in verse 59 it has a colophon of its own. Ch. xiv. 10–20 is clearly a later substitute for 2–8a. Ch. xiv. 33–53, which treats of fungous growths on the walls of houses, is often classed with the rules for leprosy in garments; but since it has a new introductory formula (33) it is probably independent of that section. Since it adopts (49) the mode of cleansing of xiv. 2–8a, it is also independent of xiv. 9–32. As it makes mention of atonement while xiv. 2–8a does not, it is also later than that. Thus three hands at least worked on these chapters.

The rules for purification after the discharge of secretions of various kinds (ch. xv.) are often regarded as late. The language is tediously repetitious. The sacrificial ritual (verses 14, 29) is parallel to that of the sin-offering in ch. v. It is probable that a shorter earlier law on the subject has been expanded by a later hand; but it seems impossible now to separate the original from the later material.

Much discussion has been expended upon the account of the great Day of Atonement (ch. xvi.). Its opening words connect it with the incident of Nadab and Abihu (x. 1–5). These words are regarded as editorial by some, but the subsequent material, which denies the priests free approach to the sanctuary, makes such a connection fitting. Not all of the chapter, however, treats of this subject. With various prohibitions against entering the holy place, there is combined a curious ritual concerning the sending of a goat into the wilderness to AZAZEL. As this ritual is given before the directions for the observance of the day, Benzinger (in Stade's "Zeitschrift," ix. 65-89) has argued that in verses 4-28 two accounts have been combined, one of which dealt with entrance into the sanctuary, and the other with the Azazel ritual. The former of these consisted of verses 1-4, 6 (or 11), 12, 13, and 34b, which were perhaps followed by 29-34a. This original law prescribed a comparatively simple ritual for an annual day of atonement. With this verses 5, 7-10, 14-28 were afterward combined. This view has not escaped challenge (comp. "Hex." ii. 164, note); but on the whole it seems probable.

Ch. xvi.: The Day of Atonement.

The Day of Atonement appears, however, not to have been provided for by the priestly law-book in the time of Nehemiah; for, whereas the celebration of the Feast of Tabernacles, beginning with the fifteenth of the seventh month (Neh. viii. 14 *et seq.*), which was followed on the twenty-fourth by a confession of sin (*ib.* ix. 1 *et seq.*), is described, no mention is made of a day of atonement on the tenth. Probably, therefore, ch. xvi. and other passages dependent upon it (*e.g.*, Lev. xxiii. 26-32 and Ex. xxx. 1-10) are of later date (comp. "Hex." i. 156 *et seq.*). Even if this ritual be a late addition to the Book of Leviticus, however, there is good reason to believe that it represents a primitive rite (comp. Smith, "Rel. of Sem." 2d ed., pp. 411 *et seq.*, especially p. 414, and Barton, "Semitic Origins," pp. 114, 289).

Ch. xvii.-xxvi., as already pointed out, form a group of laws by themselves. Ch. xxvi. 3-45 contains an address of YHWH to the Israelites, setting forth the blessings which will follow if these laws are observed, and the disasters which will ensue if they are violated. The character of the discourse and its resemblance to Deut. xxviii. prove that Lev. xxvi. once formed the conclusion of a body of laws. The peculiar phraseology and point of view of this chapter recur a number of times in earlier chapters (comp. xviii. 1-5, 24-30; xix. 2, 36b, 37; xx. 7, 8, 22-26; xxii. 31-33). Ch. xviii.-xxvi. are therefore bound together as one code. Recent criticism regards ch. xvii. as originally a part of the same legislation. As the "Book of the Covenant," Ex. xx. 24-xxiii. 19, and the Deuteronomic Code, Deut. xx.-xxvi., each opened with a law regulating the altar ceremonies, it is probable that the Holiness Code (H) began in the same way, and that that beginning now underlies Lev. xvii. The regulations of this code sometimes resemble those of Deuteronomy, sometimes those of P; and as it traverses at times the legislation of both, there can be no doubt that it once formed a separate body of laws.

Ch. xvii.-xxvi.: The Holiness Code.

This code was compiled from various sources by a writer whose vocabulary possessed such striking characteristics that it can be easily traced. Some of his favorite phrases are, "I YHWH am holy"; "I am YHWH"; "my statutes and ordinances"; "who sanctifies you [them]"; "I will set my face against them"; etc. (comp. Driver, "Leviticus," in "S. B. O. T." p. 83, and "Hex." i. 220 *et seq.*). As the work now stands the laws have been somewhat interpolated by P; but these interpolations can for the most part be easily separated.

In ch. xvii. P has added verses 1, 2, 15, and 16, and all references to "the tent of meeting" and "the camp" in verses 3, 4, 5, and 6; probably, also, the last clause of verse 7. The original law required every one who slaughtered an animal to bring the blood to the sanctuary (comp. I Sam. xiv. 33-35), a thing perfectly possible before the Deuteronomic reform had banished all local sanctuaries. This law is, therefore, older than the centralization of the worship in 621 B.C. (comp. II Kings xxiii.). As P by his additions has left the law in Lev. xvii., it could have been observed by only a small community dwelling near Jerusalem.

Interpolations.

In ch. xviii. P has transmitted H's law of prohibited marriages and unchastity, prefixing only his own title.

Ch. xix. contains laws which are, broadly speaking, parallel to the Decalogue, though the latter portion, like the Decalogue of J in Ex. xxxiv., treats of various ritualistic matters. P's hand is seen here only in verses 1, 2a, 8b, 21, and 22.

Ch. xx. opens with a law against Moloch-worship. Verse 3 is contradictory to verse 2. Probably the latter is the old law and the former is from the pen of the compiler of H (comp. Baentsch in Nowack's "Hand-Kommentar," 1903). In verses 11-21 laws against incest, sodomy, approach to a menstruous woman, etc., are found. They are parallel to ch. xviii. and from a different source. H embodied both chapters in his work. P prefixed verse 1 to the chapter.

Ch. xxi. contains regulations for priests. Originally it referred to all priests; but P has interpolated it in verses 1, 10, 12b, 16a, 21, 22, and 24, so as to make it refer to Aaron and his sons.

The laws of sacrificial food and sacrificial animals have been modified by many glosses. Some of these are anterior to H. P has added the references to Aaron and his sons in verses 1, 2, 3, 4, and 18. In this chapter two originally independent calendars of feasts have been united. From P came verses 1-9, 21, 23-38, 39a, 39c, and 44; from H, verses 10-20, 39b, and 40-43. A later hand added verse 22, and perhaps other glosses (for details comp. "Hex." and Baentsch *ad loc.*).

Ch. xxiv. 1-9, which treats of the lamps and the showbread, belongs to the P stratum, but is out of place here. Verses 10-13, 23 deal with blasphemy. They are quite unrelated to verses 15-22 except as a partial doublet, and belong, perhaps, to a secondary stratum of P. Verses 15-22 are a part of the Holiness Code.

The law of the Sabbatical year and of jubilee in ch. xxv. is now composite. The earlier portion was a part of the Holiness Code. Driver sees this portion in verses 2b-9a, 10a, 13-15, 17-22, 24, 25, 35-39, 43,

47, 53, 55. P has added the portions which introduce a complicated reckoning, viz.: verses 1, 9b, 10b–12, 16, 23, 26–34, 40, 42, 44–46, 48–52, 54 (for other analyses comp. Baentsch and "Hex." *ad loc.*).

Ch. xxvi., as already noted, is the hortatory conclusion of the Holiness Code. It has escaped serious interpolation from later hands, except perhaps in verses 34 *et seq.*, where references to the Exile may have been inserted.

Leviticus now concludes with a chapter on vows, which belongs to a late stratum of P. It is later than the institution of the year of jubilee, and introduces a law, not mentioned elsewhere, concerning the tithe of cattle.

From what has been said concerning the absence of ch. xvi. from the Pentateuch of Nehemiah it is clear that some of the material of Leviticus was added to it later than Nehemiah's time. It is probable that P in its main features was in the hands of Ezra and Nehemiah. Leviticus is, however, not the work of the P who wrote the account of the sacred institutions, but of an editor who dislocated that work at many points, and who combined with it the Holiness Code and other elements.

Date and Place of Composition of P.

It is commonly supposed that the priestly laws were collected in Babylonia and were brought back to Palestine by Ezra. Haupt goes so far as to claim that the Levitical ritual is influenced by Babylonian institutions (comp. Haupt, "Babylonian Elements in the Levitical Ritual," in "Jour. Bib. Lit." xix. 55–81), and that a number of the words are Babylonian loan-words. Any deep Babylonian influence may well be doubted, however. It has been seen that the laws of Leviticus were collected little by little in small codes, and that they were united into their present form after the time of Nehemiah. If any of these collections were made during the Exile, it must have been the desire of the priests who collected them to preserve the sacred ritual of the Temple at Jerusalem. Like Ezekiel, they may have proposed reforms, but it is hardly likely that they would deliberately copy heathen practises. The Levitical terms which are identical with Babylonian no more prove borrowing from Babylonia than the similarities between the code of Hammurabi and the Hebrew codes prove a similar borrowing there. All that is proved in either case, when radical differences are given proper weight, is that in both countries the laws and the ritual were developed from a common basis of Semitic custom.

It is generally held that the Holiness Code is younger than Ezekiel, though this is opposed by Dillmann ("Exodus und Leviticus") and Moore (in "Encyc. Bibl." *s.v.*). That there are many resemblances between H and Ezekiel all agree. Ezekiel dwells again and again upon offenses which are prohibited in the code of H. Compare, *e.g.*, the laws of incest, adultery, and of commerce with a woman in her uncleanness (Lev. xviii. 8, xx. 10–17, and Ezek. xxii. 10, 11). A list of such parallels will be found in "Hex." i. 147 *et seq.* The same writers point out (*ib.* pp. 149 *et seq.*) that there is a similarity between Ezekiel and the hortatory portions of H so striking as to lead Colenso to regard the former as the author of those exhortations. Equally striking differences make Colenso's theory untenable; and it remains an open question whether Ezekiel influenced H, or H influenced Ezekiel. Those who regard H as the later (Wellhausen, Kuenen, Baentsch, and Addis) lay stress on the references to exile in xxvi. 34–44, while Dillmann and Moore regard such phenomena as the work of later hands. When one remembers how many hands have worked on Leviticus it must be admitted that the references to exile may well be additions; and if the antiquity of the law of the altar in ch. xvii. be recalled—a law which is clearly pre-Deuteronomic—the probability that H is really earlier than Ezekiel becomes great.

Date and Place of Composition of the Holiness Code.

Comparisons of the laws of H with those of Deuteronomy have often been instituted, but without definite results. Lev. xix. 35, 36 is, it may be urged, more developed than Deut. xxv. 13–15, since the measures and weights are more definitely specified; but the point is not of sufficient significance to be decisive. On the other hand, the implication of many sanctuaries in ch. xvii. points to H's priority to Deuteronomy. At any rate it seems probable that H and Deuteronomy were collected quite independently of each other. The hortatory form of each is similar. This, together with resemblances to the language and thought of Jeremiah, points to the same general period as the date of their composition. Whether H is not the older of the two must be left an open question, with a slight balance of argument in favor of its greater antiquity. This view makes it probable that the Holiness Code was compiled in Palestine.

BIBLIOGRAPHY: Dillmann, *Exodus und Leviticus*, 3d ed., 1897; Graf, *Die Geschichtlichen Bücher des Alten Testaments*, 1866; Nöldeke, *Untersuchungen zur Kritik des Alten Testaments*, 1869; Colenso, *The Pentateuch and the Book of Joshua*, 1872, vi.; Kuenen, *Hexateuch*, 1886; Wellhausen, *Die Composition des Hexateuchs*, 3d ed., 1899; Driver, *Introduction*, 6th ed., 1897; idem, *Leviticus*, in Haupt, *S. B. O. T.* 1898; Bacon, *Triple Tradition of the Exodus*, 1894; Addis, *Documents of the Hexateuch*, 1898; Carpenter and Harford Battersby, *Hexateuch*, 1900; Baentsch, *Exodus-Leviticus-Numeri*, in Nowack's *Hand-Kommentar*, 1903; Paton, *The Original Form of Lev. xvii.–xix.* in *Jour. Bib. Lit.* xvi. 31 *et seq.*; idem, *The Original Form of Lev. xxi.–xxii.* ib. xvii. 149 *et seq.*; Haupt, *Babylonian Elements in the Levitical Ritual*, ib. xix. 55 *et seq.*

E. G. H. G. A. B.

LEVY. See EXECUTION.

LEVY, AARON: Revolutionary patriot; founder of Aaronsburg, Pa.; born in Amsterdam in 1742; died in Philadelphia Feb. 23, 1815. He went to America at an early age and settled in Pennsylvania, his name appearing in the first tax-assessment lists of Northumberland county. He engaged in trade with the Indians and furnished supplies to the proprietary government, and, during the war of the Revolution, to the colonial army. In 1778 Levy signed a memorial of the inhabitants of Northumberland county asking help on account of the British and Indian ravages in the vicinity. In the same year he removed to Lancaster, engaging in business with Joseph Simon. He speculated in land in Pennsylvania, and soon became one of the largest landed proprietors, owning immense tracts in nearly every county in the state. During the war he released to the state twelve tracts in Luzerne county; later he petitioned the government requesting that they be either paid for or returned to him (see letter dated Aug. 26, 1801, in Pennsylvania State Archives, second series, xviii. 347, 442).

Robert Morris, the financier of the Revolution, was Levy's partner in many of these speculations, and borrowed considerable sums of money from him, acknowledgment of the indebtedness being made at the time of Morris' bankruptcy. Through the influence of Morris, Levy loaned a large amount of money to the Continental Congress for the purpose of carrying on the war. This money was never fully repaid (see letter in reference to these loans in the Journals of Congress, March 29, 1781). It was after the war that he engaged in his greatest speculation in land, with which his name will always be connected. In 1779 he bought a large tract of land in Center county, Pa., upon which he laid out the town of Aaronsburg, the earliest town in the county, the plan of which was recorded at Sunbury on Oct. 4, 1786; it is the first town in the United States that was planned by, and named after, a Jew. Aaron Levy was one of the original members of the Congregation Mickvé Israel, Philadelphia. He died without issue. See AARONSBURG.

BIBLIOGRAPHY: Isabella H. Rosenbach and Abraham S. Wolf Rosenbach, in *Publ. Am. Jew. Hist. Soc.* No. 2, 1894, pp. 157-163; *Pennsylvania Colonial Records*; *Pennsylvania Archives*; John Blair Linn, *History of Center County*.

A. A. S. W. R.

LEVY, ABRAHAM HIRTZEL: Alsatian martyr; born at Wittolsheim; executed at Colmar, Alsace, Dec. 31, 1754. He was accused with three other Jews of having stolen property amounting to three thousand livres from the house of a widow named Madeline Kafin. Notwithstanding that they all proved an alibi, he was condemned to "the ordinary and extraordinary question." He did not confess and was broken on the wheel the next day. The chief Jews of Alsace, convinced of his innocence, brought the case on appeal before the Privy Council of Paris, which reversed the verdict and proclaimed Levy innocent June 16, 1755. His remains were removed from the gallows, enveloped in a ṭallit, and buried in the Jewish cemetery of Jungholtz.

BIBLIOGRAPHY: I. Loeb, *Annuaire de la Société des Etudes Juives*, i. 123-161.

D. J.

LÉVY, ALBERT: French sculptor; born at Paris May 4, 1864. A pupil of Etienne Leroux, he exhibited for the first time in 1886, his work being a portrait medallion.

Lévy's sculptures include: "Rêverie," 1887; "La Prière" and "Fillette," 1888; "Etude d'Enfant," 1889; "Jeune Paysanne à la Source," 1891; "La Chanson," 1892; "Jeune Trouveur," 1893; "Portrait de Simon," 1894; "Eve," 1895; "Jean de Rotrou à Vingt Ans," 1896; "Sans Permis," 1898. He has executed also busts of several well-known persons.

BIBLIOGRAPHY: Curinier, *Dict. Nat.* ii. 126.

S. F. T. H.

LÉVY, ALFRED: French rabbi; born at Lunéville Dec. 14, 1840. He studied at the Collège de Lunéville and entered (1860) the Paris Rabbinical Seminary. On leaving it in 1866 he was appointed rabbi at Dijon, where he remained for two years. He then occupied for twelve years the rabbinate of his native town, and in 1880 became chief rabbi of the consistory of Lyons. He is a chevalier of the Legion of Honor.

Lévy has published the following writings: "Le Deuil et les Cérémonies Funèbres chez les Israélites," Paris, 1879; "Notice sur les Israélites du Duché de Lorraine," 1885; "Notice sur les Israélites de Lyon," 1894; "Les Doctrines d'Israel, Recueil de Sermons," Lyons, 1896. S.

LÉVY, ALPHONSE: French painter; born at Marmoutier, Alsace, in 1843; educated at the Strasburg lyceum. At the age of seventeen he went to Paris, where he studied under Gérôme. As an illustrator, Lévy has drawn for all the great Parisian journals, devoting himself almost exclusively to scenes of Jewish life. Among his illustrations the most important are those for the Jewish stories of Sacher Masoch, his "Jewish Life," and especially his latest collection of thirty drawings lithographed by himself. He is now (1904) engaged on a series of sketches of Jewish life in Algiers to parallel his drawings of the Ashkenazic Jews. In the Salon of the Société Nationale des Beaux-Arts and at the International Exposition of 1900 Lévy won prizes, and the committee, Gérôme, Dagnan, Bouveret, Henri Bouchot, and Gustave Geffroy, recommended him for the cross of the Legion of Honor. He has been made also an officer of the Academy.

S. J. KA.

LEVY, AMY: English novelist and poet; born Nov. 10, 1861, in London; died there Sept. 10, 1899. Verse written by her before she was eight years of age gave evidence of high literary talent. By the time she had entered her teens she had produced a considerable number of verses, essays, plays, and short stories characterized by a steady and rapid increase in significance and power; one of her poems written at the end of that period was published in the quarterly known as the "Pelican." In 1876 the family moved to Brighton, where she attended the high school. It was while at school that she wrote "Xantippe," a scathing defense in verse of Socrates' spouse from a modern standpoint—a remarkable achievement for a school-girl in her teens.

On leaving school Amy Levy spent two years at Girton College, Cambridge, working fitfully at the prescribed studies, but doing much reading and writing. During her first term there a story of hers came out in "Temple Bar," and a little later "Xantippe and Other Poems" was published in three volumes. Then came a winter in Dresden, and on her return to London she occupied herself with teaching and writing. "The Minor Poet," published in 1882, is tinged with sadness and with suggestions of autobiography. The third and last volume of her poems, "A London Plane Tree," appeared after her death. As pure literature all three volumes have a distinctive charm. Her first novel, the "Romance of a Shop," and a short story, "Miss Meredith," were published in 1886, after a winter spent in Florence; and in 1888 "Reuben Sachs" appeared. The last-named work presents some of the less pleasing aspects of the Jewish character, and the vivid writing of the exquisitely imagined story makes regret more keen that the author's outlook on her people was so limited.

BIBLIOGRAPHY: *Dictionary of National Biography.*

J.

LÉVY, ARMAND (ABRAHAM): French mathematician and mineralogist; born at Paris 1794; died there June 26, 1841. He was a graduate of the Ecole Normale, where he became teacher of mathematics (1814-15). He went to England, where he lived till 1828, and then to Belgium. Here he was lecturer at the University of Liége, and became a member of the Academy of Sciences at Brussels. Returning to France in 1830, he was appointed professor of mineralogy at the Collége Charlemagne.

Lévy published essays in the "Correspondance Mathématique" of Quételet (1828-30), in the "Annals of Philosophy," and in the "Philosophical Magazine," and was the author of: "De Différentes Propriétés des Surfaces de Second Ordre"; "Sur une Nouvelle Manière de Mesurer la Pesanteur Spécifique des Corps"; "Sur Quelques Propriétés des Systèmes de Forces."

BIBLIOGRAPHY: *La Grande Encyclopédie*; *Nouveau Larousse Illustré.*

S. F. T. H.

"Blessing of the New Moon."
(From a drawing by Alphonse Lévy.)

LEVY, ASSER (ASSER LEVY VAN SWELLEM): One of the first Jewish settlers of New Amsterdam, as New York city was known under the Dutch; probably born in Amsterdam; died in 1680. He is first mentioned as one of the Jews who went to New Netherlands in 1654, probably as refugees from Brazil. From the start Levy was one of the champions of his people, never permitting an injury, however slight, to pass without protest. In 1655 Peter Stuyvesant, the governor of the colony, was ordered to attack the Swedes on the Delaware, and accordingly issued orders for the enlistment of all adults. Several Jews, among whom was Asser Levy, appear to have been ready to serve; but the governor and council passed an ordinance "that Jews can not be permitted to serve as soldiers, but shall instead pay a monthly contribution for the exemption." Levy and his comrades at once refused to pay, and on Nov. 5, 1655, petitioned for leave to stand guard like other burghers or to be relieved from the tax. The petition was rejected with the comment that if the petitioners were not satisfied with the law they might go elsewhere. Levy successfully appealed to Holland, and was subsequently permitted to do guard duty like other citizens.

As Levy appears also as a prominent trader at Fort Orange (Albany), it is likely that he was responsible for the rebuke given to Stuyvesant by the directors in Holland during the same year because of his refusal to permit Jews to trade there. Levy was also one of the first licensed butchers in the colony. In 1657 the burgher right was made absolutely essential for certain trading privileges, and within two days of a notice to that effect Asser Levy appeared in court requesting to be admitted as a burgher. The officials expressed their surprise at such a request. The record reads: "The Jew claims that such ought not to be refused him as he keeps watch and ward like other burghers, showing a burgher's certificate from the city of Amsterdam that the Jew is a burgher there." The application was denied, but Levy at once brought the matter before Stuyvesant and the council, which, mindful of the previous experience, ordered that Jews should be admitted as burghers (April 21, 1657).

As early as 1661 Levy purchased real estate at Albany; he was also the earliest Jewish owner of real estate in New York city, his transactions there commencing in June, 1662, with the purchase of land on South William street. Within ten years of his arrival Levy had become a man of consequence, and when, in 1664, the wealthiest inhabitants were summoned to lend the city money for fortifications against the English, he was the only Jew among them: he lent the city 100 florins.

It is as a litigant, however, that Levy figures most prominently in the Dutch records, his name often appearing for days in succession. He invariably argued his own case and was almost invariably successful. Only on two or three occasions did he figure as defendant. No other Jew seems to have had so many dealings with Christians, or to have been on more intimate terms with them. As a litigant he is named also in the records of Gravesend in 1674. Levy's trading relations extended to New England, and he frequently appeared as attorney for merchants in Holland. In 1671 he lent the money for building the first Lutheran church in New York. About 1678 he built a slaughter-house in the east end of what is now known as Wall street, where he appears to have been the owner of a famous tavern.

Instead of being unpopular on account of his many lawsuits, the contrary seems to have been the case. The confidence reposed in his honesty by his Christian fellow citizens appears frequently from the court records. Property in litigation was put into his custody; he is named as executor in the wills of Christian merchants, and figures as both administrator and trustee in colonial records. His influence was not confined to New York; in the colonial records of Connecticut he appears as intervening to obtain the remission of a fine imposed upon a Jew there. The court remitted the fine with the comment that it did so "as a token of its respect to the said Mr. Asser Levy." He left a considerable estate, over which there was a long legal contest. A second **Asser Levy** appears in the Connecticut records as late as 1725, and a third, presumably a grandson, was an officer in a New Jersey regiment during the American Revolution.

BIBLIOGRAPHY: *The Records of New Amsterdam*, ed. B. Fernow, New York, 1897; Leon Hühner, *Asser Levy*, in *Publications Am. Jew. Hist. Soc.*; Thomas F. De Voe, *The Market Book*, i. 45, 46, 49, 54, 55; E. B. O'Callahan, *Hist. of New Netherlands*, ii. 286, New York, 1848; *Calendar of New York Historical Manuscripts (Dutch)*, *1630-1664*, pp. 151, 155, 184, 310; Simon W. Rosendale, *An Early Ownership of Real Estate*, in *Publications Am. Jew. Hist. Soc.*; *Valentine's Manual*, 1865, pp. 691, 701; *The Public Records of the Colony of Connecticut*, Hartford, 1872; *Documents Relating to Colonial History*, ed. Brodhead, xii. 96, xiv. 341, 351, Albany, 1877; J. Pearson, *Early Records of the City of Albany*, passim; Daly, *Settlement of the Jews in North America*, New York, 1893; F. B. Heitman, *Historical Register of Officers of the Continental Army*, p. 262.

A. L. Hü.

LÉVY, AUGUST MICHEL: French engineer, geologist, and mineralogist; born at Paris Aug. 17, 1844; son of Michel Lévy. In 1862 he entered the Ecole Polytechnique, and two years later the school of mines, becoming engineer in 1867, and engineer-in-chief in 1883. After 1876 he took an important part in the preparation of the detailed geological map of France published by the ministry of public works. In 1887 he became director of this important undertaking, and in the following year took charge also of the underground topographic survey. In addition to articles and notes scattered in various scientific periodicals, he wrote: "Mémoire sur les Divers Modes de Structure des Roches Eruptives Etudiées au Microscope," Paris, 1876; "Mémoire pour Servir à l'Explication de la Carte Géologique Détaillée de la France," *ib.* 1879; "Introduction à l'Etude des Roches Eruptives Françaises," *ib.* 1879; "Synthèse des Minéraux et des Roches," *ib.* 1882 (the three preceding in collaboration with Foqué); "Les Minéraux des Roches," *ib.* 1888; "Etude Géologique de Serrania de Ronda," *ib.* 1888 (with Bergeron); "Tableaux des Minéraux des Roches," *ib.* 1890 (with Lacroix); "Etude sur la Détermination des Feldspaths dans les Plaques Minces," *ib.* 1894; "Structure et Classification des Roches Eruptives," *ib.* 1899. He died Jan. 2, 1908.

S. J. Ka.

LEVY, BENJAMIN: Coloinal resident of Philadelphia. On Nov. 7, 1765, he signed, with other citizens of Philadelphia, the celebrated agreement not to import merchandise from England until the repeal of the Stamp Act. On Dec. 27, 1776, he was appointed, upon the recommendation of the treasurer of the United States, an authorized signer of the bills of credit (see "Journal of the Continental Congress").

BIBLIOGRAPHY: Rosenbach, *The Jews in Philadelphia Prior to 1800*, p. 13, Philadelphia, 1883; *Publications Am. Jew. Hist. Soc.* i. 60, 86.

A. A. S. W. R.

LÉVY, EDUARD CONSTANTIN: German musician; born March 3, 1796, at Sanct Avold, Lorraine; died June 3, 1846, at Vienna. He received his first lessons in music from his father, a musician to the Duke of Zweibrücken. As the protégé of a French officer he entered, at the age of fourteen, the Paris Conservatoire, where he became proficient in the bugle (which he chose as his favorite instrument), the cello, and the violin. He joined the French army in 1812, served with the Old Guard through the Waterloo campaign, and at the Restoration was appointed bandmaster and drum-major. After retiring from the service he went on concert tours through France and Switzerland, married at Basel, and in 1824 went to Vienna, where he became soloist in the K. K. Hof-Oper. In 1834 he was appointed professor at the Vienna Conservatorium, and in 1835 became a member of the Imperial Hofkapelle.

Levy's three children inherited his musical talent: **Karl** was a pianist, **Melanie** a harpist, and **Richard Eduard** a cornetist. In 1838 they accompanied their father on concert tours through Russia and Germany.

BIBLIOGRAPHY: Riemann, *Musikalisches Lexikon*.

S. E. J.

LEVY, ELEAZAR: Colonial resident of New York city prior to the Revolution. He fled from New York on account of the British occupation and took up his residence in Philadelphia, where he engaged in business. On Aug. 26, 1779, he presented a memorial to the Continental Congress, claiming that the United States had erected fortifications on lands at West Point on which he held a mortgage, and asking for compensation for his loss. On May 23, 1783, it is recorded that a congressional committee reported that in its opinion "it is not convenient to take any order therein." During the Revolutionary war Levy took the oath of allegiance to the state of Pennsylvania. In 1785 he acted as one of the administrators of the estate of Haym Solomon (see "Pennsylvania Journal," Jan. 15, 1785).

BIBLIOGRAPHY: Friedenwald, *Memorials Presented to the Continental Congress*, in *Publications Am. Jew. Hist. Soc.* ii. 123-126; Westcott, *Test Laws of Pennsylvania*, Philadelphia, 1885.

A. A. S. W. R.

LEVY, EMIL: German philologist; born at Hamburg Oct. 23, 1855; educated at the universities of Heidelberg and Berlin (Ph.D. 1880). The following two years he spent in Paris and Montpellier; he became privat-docent at the University of Freiburg-im-Breisgau in 1883, and was appointed assistant professor in 1887.

Levy is known principally as the author of the great dictionary, begun in 1894 and still (1904) unfinished, entitled "Provenzalisches Supplement-Wörterbuch. Berichtigungen und Ergänzungen zu Raynouards Lexique Roman" (vols. i.-iv. covering A to L). Among his other works are "Der Troubadour Bertolome Zorzi," Halle, 1883, and "Bemerkungen zum Engadinischen Hiob," Freiburg-im-Breisgau, 1895.

S. F. T. H.

LÉVY, ÉMILE: French rabbi; born at Marmoutier, Alsace, Jan. 28, 1848. Educated at the lyceum at Strasburg and the seminary at Paris, he became rabbi of Verdun in 1876, which position he held until 1892; in that year he became chief rabbi of Bayonne.

Lévy was a contributor to the "Revue des Etudes Juives" and is the author of "La Monarchie chez les Juifs en Palestine," Paris, 1885. In collaboration with M. Bloch he has written also "Histoire de la Littérature Juive Depuis l'Origine Jusqu'à Nos Jours." He died in December, 1907.

S. F. T. H.

LEVY, ERNST: German physician; born at Lauterburg, Alsace, March 5, 1864; educated at the universities of Strasburg, Heidelberg, and Paris (M.D. 1887). Settling in Strasburg, he became privat-docent in hygiene at the university there in 1891 and assistant professor in 1897.

Levy has written several monographs and essays in the German and French medical journals, and is the author also of the two following works: "Grundriss der Klinischen Bacteriologie," Berlin, 1894 (2d ed. 1898); "Bacteriologischer Leitfaden," Strasburg, 1897 (2d ed. 1901).

BIBLIOGRAPHY: Pagel, *Biog. Lex.*

S. F. T. H.

LEVY FAMILY (of America): The following is a genealogical tree of the family descended from Benjamin Levy of Philadelphia:

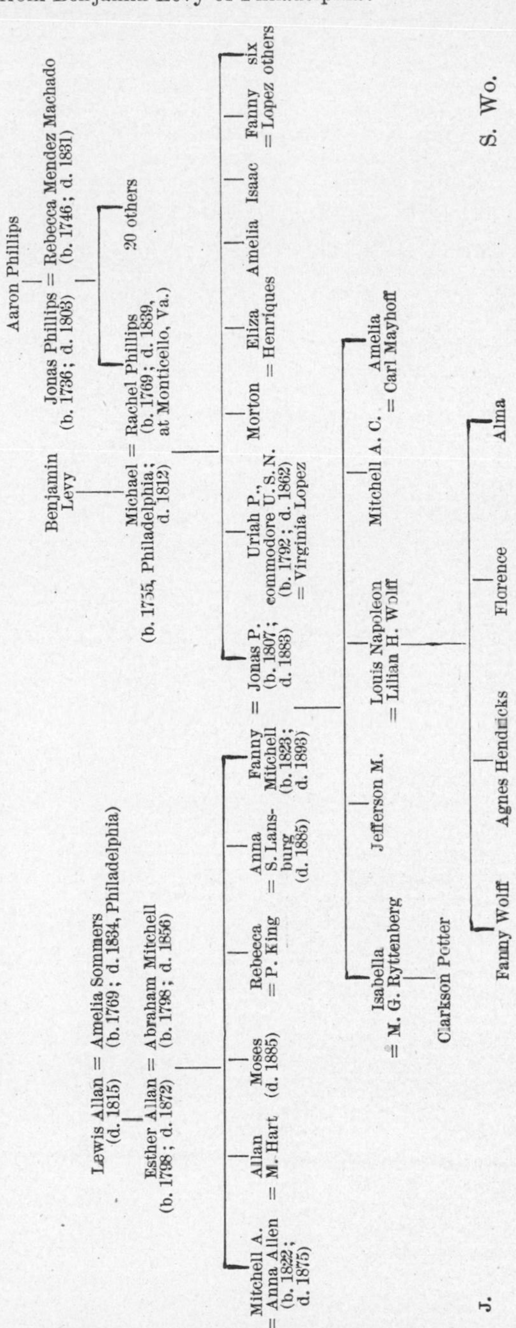

J. S. Wo.

LÉVY, GUSTAVE: French engraver; born at Toul June 21, 1819; died at Paris in 1894; a pupil of Geille. He exhibited first at the Salon of 1844, and engraved the portraits of Madrazzo, Rigaud, and a number of others. Special mention may be made of the following engravings by him: "The Family of Concina" (from the Veronese in the

Dresden gallery); Raphael's "Sistine Madonna" and "Diademed Virgin"; Caracci's "Madonna of Silence"; Couture's "Damocles"; and Rembrandt's "Good Shepherd." Still more popular are his engravings of the King of the Belgians (from Winterhalter's portrait), Béranger, the poet Ventura de la Vega, and the engraver Wille. The plate of Lévy's last engraving, "The Fair Gardener," was framed on his tombstone in the cemetery of Montmartre.

S. J. Ka.

LEVY, HAYMAN: Colonial merchant of New York; born in 1721; died in New York in 1789. He engaged in business at an early age, and is mentioned as the owner of a privateer and as engaged in the fur trade in 1760 (see "New York Mercury," Aug. 17, 1761). In 1765 the signature "Hayman Levy, Junior," was appended to the Non-Importation Resolutions drawn up by merchants in Philadelphia, but it can not be said with certainty that it was the signature of the Hayman Levy treated here. In 1770 Levy signed in New York resolutions of a similar but more stringent character. In 1768 he failed in business, but soon recovered his losses. The occupation of New York by the British caused him to remove to Philadelphia. On July 20, 1776, he is mentioned in the Journal of the Continental Congress. Hayman Levy was one of the founders of the Congregation Mickvé Israel, organized in 1782, and served on the first board of trustees. In 1784 he returned to New York and aided in the reestablishment of the congregation in that city. He was one of the most widely known merchants of New York, and was probably the first employer of John Jacob Astor. He had sixteen children, some of whom were prominent citizens of New York.

Bibliography: *Publications Am. Jew. Hist. Soc.* i. 14, 60, 88; iii. 81; iv. 89, 210; vi. 130, 135; ix. 88; x. 13, 62; Daly, *The Settlement of the Jews in North America*, pp. 52, 53.

A. A. S. W. R.

LÉVY, HENRI LÉOPOLD: French painter; born at Nancy Sept. 23, 1840; pupil of the Ecole des Beaux-Arts and of Picot, Cabanel, and Fromentin. His first exhibit was "Hecuba Finding the Body of Her Son Polydorus on the Shore," at the Salon of 1865; at the following Salons he exhibited "Joash Saved from the Massacre of the Grandsons of Athaliah" (1867); "Hebrew Captive Weeping over the Ruins of Jerusalem" (1869); "Herodias" (1872); "Sarpedon"; "The Sermon." For the Church of Saint Merri in Paris he painted mural pieces of scenes in the life of Saint Denis; these were exhibited at the Exposition of 1878. His "Coronation of Charlemagne" is a mural piece for the Panthéon at Paris. At the International Exposition in 1900 Lévy won a gold medal for his "Eve Plucking the Apple," "Deucalion and Pyrrha," and "Samson and Delilah." He died Jan. 2, 1905.

S. J. Ka.

LÉVY, ISAAC: French rabbi; born Jan. 20, 1835, at Marmoutier, in the old department of Bas-Rhin (Alsace). When sixteen years old he entered the rabbinic school of Metz, and was graduated thence at the age of twenty-three, receiving the diploma of a chief rabbi. In Feb., 1858, he was called as rabbi to Verdun (Meuse); in 1865 to Lunéville (Meurthe); and in 1869 to Colmar as chief rabbi of the district of Haut-Rhin.

When Alsace was annexed by Germany, Lévy decided to remain a Frenchman; and the French government created a new chief rabbinate for him at Vesoul (Haute-Saône). Here he officiated for fifteen years, and then (1887) went as chief rabbi to Bordeaux. Lévy is a chevalier of the Legion of Honor and an officer of public instruction. Besides a number of single sermons he has published the following: "Veillées du Vendredi" (2d ed., Paris, 1869); "Récits Bibliques" (2d ed., Paris, 1873); "Défense du Judaïsme" (*ib.* 1867); "Histoire Sainte" (*ib.* 1869 *et seq.*); "Alsatiana" (*ib.* 1873); "Nathan le Sage" (Vesoul, 1881); "Les Récréations Israélites" (2d ed., Paris, 1899); "Développement des 13 Articles de Foi" (*ib.* 1895); "Heures de Recueillement" (*ib.* 1898).

Lévy edited also a supplement, entitled "Le Foyer Israélite" (1862-65), to the periodical for the young, "La Vérité Israélite." S.

LEVY, JACOB: German rabbi and lexicographer; born May, 1819, at Dabrzyze, Posen; died at Breslau Feb. 27, 1892. Having received his Talmudic education from his father, Isaac Levy, who was district rabbi at Schildberg, and from Akiba Eger, he entered the Matthias Gymnasium at Breslau, after leaving which he studied philosophy and oriental languages at Breslau University, and received his doctor's degree from the University of Halle in 1845.

He accepted a call to Rosenberg, Upper Silesia, where he officiated as rabbi until 1850. Wishing to live in an intellectual center, he moved to Breslau without any prospect of employment. In 1857 he became associate rabbi of the Breslau community; in 1864 he was appointed admonitor to the local court, his duty being to admonish the Jews who had to take the oath "More Judaico"; and in 1878 he was appointed instructor at the Mora-Salomon Leipziger Stiftung, an office which he continued to hold till his death.

Levy published in 1867-68 at Leipsic his "Chaldäisches Wörterbuch über die Targumim" (3d ed., *ib.* 1881), with notes by Prof. H. Fleischer. In recognition of this work the Prussian ministry granted him in 1875 the title of "Königlicher Professor." His chief work, however, is his "Neuhebräisches und Chaldäisches Wörterbuch über die Talmudim und Midraschim" (with notes by Fleischer; 4 vols., *ib.* 1876-89).

Levy was the first to apply modern scientific methods to rabbinic lexicography; and he aided considerably toward rousing Christian scholars to an interest in rabbinical literature. All subsequent work in the field of Talmudic lexicography has been based on Levy's labors (comp. "Z. D. M. G." xlvii. 494 *et seq.*).

Bibliography: Schwab, *Répertoire*, s.v.; *Allg. Zeit. des Jud.* 1892, No. 11.

S. C. L.

LEVY, JONAS PHILLIPS: American merchant; son of Michael Levy and Rachel Phillips; born in Philadelphia 1807; died in New York 1883. He was granted the freedom of the country by the government of Peru for signal services rendered in the navy of that country. He commanded the U. S. S. "America" during the Mexican war, and was assigned to the transportation of troops to Vera Cruz, at the surrender of which port he was appointed its captain by Gen. Winfield Scott. He left three sons (**Jefferson M., Louis Napoleon,** and **Mitchell A. C.**) and two daughters.

A. S. Wo.

LEVY, JOSEPH HIAM: English economist; born 1838; educated at the City of London School and City of London College. He entered the British Civil Service, was assigned to the Board of Education in 1862, and rose to the position of examiner of school accounts. He was one of the most important members of the National Liberal Club; he founded its Economic Circle, became its chairman, and edited its "Transactions." Levy was lecturer and examiner in economics at the Birkbeck Institute and City of London College. He was editor of "The Individualist" and of "Personal Rights," the organ of the Personal Rights Association, and has written much on economic and social topics. He retired from the Board of Education in 1902.

Bibliography: *Jew. Chron.* Nov. 1, 1901; *American Jewish Year Book*, 1904.

J.

LEVY, JOSEPH LEONARD: American rabbi; born Nov. 24, 1865, in London; educated at Jews' College and University College (B.A.), London, at Bristol University, England, and at Western University of Pennsylvania (D.D.). Levy was rabbi of the Bristol Hebrew Congregation (1885–89) and of Bnai Israel Congregation, Sacramento, Cal. (1889–1893); associate rabbi of the Keneseth Israel Congregation, Philadelphia (1893–1901); and, since 1901, has been rabbi of the Rodeph Shalom congregation, Pittsburg. In 1898 he was elected chaplain of "Keegan's Brigade," with which he served through the Spanish-American war. Levy was the organizer of a number of charitable and religious societies among the Jews of Philadelphia. He is the author of a translation of the tractate Rosh ha-Shanah of the Babylonian Talmud (Philadelphia, 1895). He published also "The Greater Lights" (*ib.* 1895); "Home Service for the Passover" (*ib.* 1896); "The Nineteenth Century" (*ib.* 1901); "A Book of Prayer" (Pittsburg, 1902); "The Jew's Beliefs" (*ib.* 1903); "The Children's Service and Hymnal" (*ib.* 1903); "Text-Book of Religion and Ethics for Jewish Children" (*ib.* 1903); "Sabbath Readings" (*ib.* 1904); and eight volumes of Sunday lectures. Levy is the editor of the "Jewish Criterion," published at Pittsburg.

Bibliography: *American Jewish Year Book*, 1904.

A. I. G. D.

LEVY, JOSEPH MOSES: Founder and proprietor of the London "Daily Telegraph"; born Dec. 15, 1812; died at Ramsgate Oct. 12, 1888. He was educated in London and Germany. After spending the earlier part of his life in commercial pursuits he became the owner of a printing establishment near Fleet street. In this way he became connected with the "Sunday Times," of which he was chief proprietor in 1855. The "Daily Telegraph and Courier" was founded in June, 1855, and by September had come entirely under Levy's management, who reduced its price, making it the first London penny daily paper; and it was through his genius that it became a great power in journalism. When he assumed the proprietorship of the paper its fortunes were at so low an ebb that the purchase-money was only £1,000. Levy worked in the interests of the paper with unflagging zeal, many members of his family also becoming connected with it; and he collected round him a band of able writers, including Sir E. Arnold and G. A. Sala. In politics the paper was Liberal until 1886, when Liberal-Unionist principles were adopted.

Levy left several children. His eldest son, **Edward,** who assumed the name of "Lawson," became chief proprietor of the "Daily Telegraph," and was created a baronet in 1892, and a peer in 1902 with the title of Lord Burnham.

Bibliography: *Daily Telegraph*, Oct. 13, 1888; *Jew. Chron.* Oct. 19, 1888; *Times* (London), Oct. 13, 1888; *Dict. Nat. Biog.*

J. G. L.

LEVY, JUDAH: Tunisian rabbinical author; lived at Tunis and died there in the middle of the nineteenth century; son of Nathan Levy. He was originally from Gibraltar. He published under his own name only one Hebrew work, "Maḥane Lewiyyah." This work consists of four parts; namely: (1) a commentary on the treatise "Hilkot Semaḥot" of Meïr of Rothenburg; (2) a collection of rules on the duties of the "Nezirim"; (3) a treatise entitled "Ma'amar Nezirut Shimshon"; (4) a treatise on questions of Levitical impurities, "Hilkot Ṭum'ah." He published also, in collaboration with David Bonan, two works with the same title, "De Ḥesheb" (Leghorn, 1857), responsa and studies on the treatise Sanhedrin.

Bibliography: Cazès, *Notes Bibliographiques*, pp. 44–50, 237–239.

S. S. M. Fr.

LEVY, JUDITH: English philanthropist; born in London 1706; died there Jan. 20, 1803; a daughter of Moses Hart, founder of the Great Synagogue, London; married Elias Levy, a wealthy financier and government contractor. This lady, who lived to a great age, enjoyed after her husband's death an income of £6,000 a year, and dwelt in great splendor at a house formerly belonging to Heydigger, master of the revels to King George II. She frequented many of the nobility's social gatherings and played half-guinea quadrille with the Countess of Yarmouth, Lady Holdernesse, Lord Stormont, and other persons of rank.

Judith Levy was a generous benefactress to her coreligionists, and in 1790 contributed £4,000 toward the cost of rebuilding the Great Synagogue. The last years of her life were spent in seclusion, now at Bath, sometimes at Richmond, and occasionally in Albermarle street, where she died. She died intestate, leaving a sum of £125,000 at her bankers; and was buried on Jan. 21 in the Jewish cemetery at Mile End.

Bibliography: Lysons, *Environs of London*, Supplement, p. 68; *Cat. Anglo-Jew. Hist. Exh.* 1887; *Notes and Queries*, 2d series, xii.; Picciotto, *Sketches of Anglo-Jewish History*, p. 96.

J. G. L.

LEVY, LOUIS (ASHER BEN MOSES): Poet and cantor of the Berlin synagogue; died Jan. 25, 1853. He wrote "Teḳufat ha-Shanah" (Berlin, 1842), poems on the four seasons, in imitation of Thomson's "Seasons." The preface includes "Na-'al Yad," a translation of Schiller's "Handschuh." He wrote also some songs for festivals.

BIBLIOGRAPHY: Steinschneider, *Cat. Bodl.* col. 1619; Fürst, *Bibl. Jud.* ii. 242.

S. M. Sc.

LEVY, LOUIS EDWARD: American photochemist; born at Stenowitz, Bohemia, Oct. 12, 1846. He went to America in early life, and was educated at Detroit; he studied especially mathematics and astronomy at Michigan University in 1866, and optics at Detroit. He was connected with the meteorological observatory of the United States Lake Survey District in 1866, and engaged in researches in microscopic photography during 1869 and 1870. This led to his invention of a method of photochemical engraving, the "Levytype," which was patented in 1875. He established a company in Baltimore, but removed to Philadelphia in 1877, in which year he invented the "Levy line-screen," which was perfected by his brother Max. For this he received the John Scott Legacy medal at the Franklin Institute in 1897. He invented a new process of intaglio engraving, the "photo-mezzotint," in 1889. In 1896 he invented a new method of etching, the "Levy acid blast," for which he received the Elliott Cresson gold medal at the Franklin Institute in 1899. He was awarded a medal and diploma at the World's Columbian Exposition in 1893, and decorations and diplomas from the Imperial Photographic Society of Moscow and at the recent Paris Exposition.

From 1887 to 1890 Levy was publisher and editor of the Philadelphia "Evening Herald," and at the same time of the "Mercury," a Philadelphia Sunday paper. In 1896 he edited and published "Cuba and the Cubans." He is the author of "The Russian Jewish Refugees in America" (1895), an English version of Cabrera's "Cuba y sus Jueces," and "Business, Money, and Credit" (1896), a brochure on the relations of exchange to the medium of exchange. He has contributed to many technical journals, and represented the Franklin Institute at the Scientific Congress of the Paris Exposition. In Jewish matters he is associated with many communal organizations, and he was editor, author, and publisher of "The Jewish Year" (1895) and of other publications.

BIBLIOGRAPHY: *Who's Who in America.*

A.

LEVY, LUDWIG: German architect; born March 14, 1852, at Landau. After his return from Italy, where he completed his studies, he was entrusted with the building of the new synagogue in Kaiserslautern. He was the architect also of the church at Olsbrücke near Kaiserslautern, of the synagogues in St. Johann, Strasburg (Alsace), and Kleinwälde near Kaiserslautern.

Levy is at present (1904) professor in the Baugewerkschule at Carlsruhe. S.

LÉVY, MAURICE: French engineer and member of the Institut; born at Ribeauville, Alsace, Feb. 28, 1838. Educated at the Ecole Polytechnique and the Ecole des Ponts et Chaussées, he became an engineer in 1863. During the Franco-German war (1870–71) he was entrusted by the Government of National Defense with the control of a part of the artillery. During the next decade he held several educational positions, becoming professor at the Ecole Centrale in 1875, member of the commission of the geodetic survey of France in 1879, and professor at the Collège de France in 1885.

In 1888 Lévy inaugurated a system of boat-traction by means of overhead cables. A trial system was installed between Joinville-le-Pont and Saint-Maurice; it consisted of an endless cable which was kept in motion by powerful steam-engines and to which boats were attached and thus kept at a speed of four kilometers an hour. The system proved unsatisfactory, however.

Lévy is the author of several works, of which may be mentioned: "La Statistique Graphique et Ses Applications à l'Art des Constructions" (1874; 2d ed. 1887); "Sur le Principe d'Energie" (1888); "Etude des Moyens de Traction des Bateaux: Le Halage Funiculaire" (with M. G. Pavie, 1894). He has written also papers on kinematics, mechanics, physical mathematics, geometry, etc., in the "Comptes-Rendus de l'Académie des Sciences," the "Journal de l'Ecole Polytechnique," and the "Journal des Mathematiques Pures et Appliquées."

He is an officer of the Legion of Honor and of public instruction, and a member of the Academy of Sciences and of the Royal Academy of Sciences of Rome.

BIBLIOGRAPHY: Curinier, *Dict. Nat.*

S. V. E.

LEVY, MAX: American inventor; born at Detroit 1857. He invented the etched screen and the machinery for producing it now generally used in the half-tone process of photoengraving. After serving an apprenticeship of three years with an architect, he became chief draftsman in his brother's (Louis E. Levy's) photoengraving establishment at Baltimore during the early struggle to establish and perfect that branch of the graphic arts. He accompanied his brother to Philadelphia, and for a time was in charge of the entire business. After the introduction of the half-tone process he spent over two years of constant and close application devising and perfecting the mechanism of his new invention. Levy is also an inventor in other lines, and is a constant and indefatigable experimenter.

A. D. Ba.

LEVY, MEYER: German jurist; born in Wollstein, province of Posen, Jan. 17, 1833; died in Berlin Oct. 18, 1896. After practising as an assessor in Berlin, he received the appointment of "Rechts-Anwalt" in Fraustadt, where he at once began his literary activity, delivering lectures on legal subjects. Among his writings of this period are to be noted: "Der Staat und die Juden im Norddeutschen Bunde: Ein Mahnruf an das Norddeutsche Parlament," Lissa, 1867, and "Die Zweite Instanz in Bürgerlichen Rechtsstreitigkeiten," Berlin, 1871. In 1872 he returned to Berlin and engaged in practise there, first at the Stadtgericht, then at the Landgericht, finally gaining admission to the Kammergericht. He secured a very large and influential clientage. Levy was president of the Berlin Bar Association. He was killed by a robber.

Of Levy's works other than the above-mentioned may be cited the following: (with G. von Wilmowsky) "Civilprozessordnung und Gerichtsverfassungsgesetz für das Deutsche Reich," Berlin, 1877–1878 (2d ed. 1880; 6th ed. 1892); "Zur Practischen Anwendung der Deutschen Civilprozessordnung," *ib.* 1880; "Handausgabe der Civilprozessordnung," *ib.* 1884 (2d ed. 1889; 3d ed. 1894).

s. M. Co.

LÉVY, MICHEL: French publisher; born at Pfalzburg Dec. 20, 1821; died in Paris May 6, 1875. In 1836 he settled in the latter city, where, together with his brothers Calman and Nathan, he engaged in the publishing business. His firm soon became one of the most important publishing-houses in France and the center of modern belletristic literature. The most noteworthy of its publications are the works of the elder and the younger Dumas, George Sand, Balzac, Alfred de Vigny, Lamartine, and Victor Hugo, and the scientific writings of Guizot, Renan, and Michelet. Lévy published also the collections "La Bibliothèque Dramatique," "Le Théâtre Contemporain," "La Bibliothèque Contemporaine," and "La Collection Michel Lévy."

Of famous foreign authors whose works were published by the Lévy firm may be mentioned: Heine, Thackeray, and Macaulay. After Lévy's death the business was continued by his brother **Calman Lévy** (b. in Pfalzburg Oct. 19, 1819; d. at Paris June 18, 1891), and since the death of the latter it has been conducted by Calman's three sons, Paul, Georges, and Gaston.

Bibliography: *Nouveau Larousse Illustré*; *Meyers Konversations-Lexikon.*

s. F. C.

LÉVY, MICHEL: French physician; born at Strasburg Sept. 28, 1809; died at Paris March 13, 1872; educated at the University of Montpellier (M.D. 1834). In 1836 he became professor of hygiene at the Val-de-Grâce in Paris; in 1845 he was appointed professor of pathology at Metz; two years later he returned in this capacity to the Val-de-Grâce, of which medical school he became director in 1856. In the Crimean war he had for a few months charge of a hospital in Constantinople. He was the author of "Traité d'Hygiène Publique et Privée," Paris, 1843–45 (5th ed. 1869); "Sur la Rougeole des Adultes," *ib.* 1847; "Histoire de la Méningite Cérébro-Spinale Observée au Val-de-Grâce en 1848 et 1849," *ib.* 1850; "Sur l'Hygiène Militaire," *ib.* 1867; "Sur les Hôpitaux-Baraques," *ib.* 1871.

Bibliography: *La Grande Encyclopédie*; *Nouveau Larousse Illustré.*

s. F. T. H.

LEVY, MORITZ ABRAHAM: German Orientalist; born at Altona March 11, 1817; died at Breslau Feb. 22, 1872. Having received a rabbinical education, he became teacher in the Synagogen-Gemeinde of Breslau, where he was active for nearly thirty years. For his scientific labors he received from the King of Prussia, in 1865, the title of professor.

Levy was preeminent in the field of Semitic paleography. He was the first person after Gesenius to treat the subject in a comprehensive manner. In the deciphering and interpretation of Phenician, old Hebrew, Punic, Aramaic, Himyaritic, and later Hebrew coins, seals, gems, and monuments his peculiar intuition guided him more surely than mere philological knowledge did others; such, for example, was the case with his deduction from the inscriptions found on the Hauran that at the beginning of the Christian era an Arabic people lived there which used the Aramaic language and alphabet.

Levy's first published essay, in 1855, was on the inscriptions on certain Aramean bowls ("Z. D. M. G." ix. 465 *et seq.*). This was followed by the first and second parts of his "Phönizische Studien" (Breslau, 1856 and 1857); his decipherment of the Eshmunazar inscription won him immediate recognition. He next published a study in Jewish history, "Don Joseph Nasi, Herzog von Naxos, Seine Familie und Zwei Jüdische Diplomaten Seiner Zeit" (Breslau, 1859). In 1860 and 1861 other essays by him appeared ("Z. D. M. G." xiv. 365 *et seq.*, 594, 710 *et seq.*; xv. 615 *et seq.*, 623 *et seq.*; xvii. 75), dealing with Phenician numismatics. In 1862 was published "Die Gesch. der Jüdischen Münzen Gemeinfasslich Dargestellt" (Breslau). "Eine Lateinisch-Griechisch-Phönizische Inschrift aus Sardinien" appeared in "Z. D. M. G." (xviii. 53 *et seq.*). In 1863 he published the third part of his "Phönizische Studien," and in 1864 his "Phönizisches Wörterbuch" (Breslau). In 1865 Levy edited, at the request of the Deutsche Morgenländische Gesellschaft, the material which Osiander had left bearing on Himyaritic paleography and archeology ("Z. D. M. G." xix. 159 *et seq.*, xx. 205 *et seq.*; an essay on Jewish gravestones in Aden appears in xxi. 156 *et seq.*). His "Systematisch Geordnetes Spruchbuch als Leitfaden für den Jüdischen Religionsunterricht" was published in Breslau in 1867; "Siegel und Gemmen mit Aramäischen, Phönizischen, Althebräischen, Himyarischen, Nabathäischen und Altsyrischen Inschriften Erklärt" appeared in 1869. In 1870 he published the fourth part of his "Studien," and "Die Biblische Gesch. nach den Worten der Heiligen Schrift der Israelitischen Jugend Erzählt," both at Breslau. "Das Mesa Denkmal und Seine Schrift," and various essays in "Z. D. M. G." (xxv. 429 *et seq.*, xxvi. 417), appeared in the following year.

Bibliography: Siegfried, in *Allgemeine Deutsche Biographie.*

s. F. T. H.

LEVY, MORITZ MARCUS (CARL EDVARD MARIUS): Danish physician; born in Copenhagen Sept. 8, 1808; died there Dec. 30, 1865. He graduated as M.D. from the University of Copenhagen in 1833, having in 1830 won the university gold medal for a medical essay.

From 1833 till 1836 Levy traveled abroad, making a special study of obstetrics, and upon his return to Copenhagen he became resident physician of the Nursery Institute ("Plejestiftelsen").

In 1838 Levy accepted baptism and assumed the name "Carl Edvard Marius," thereby removing an obstacle in the way of his becoming a university professor. In 1840 he was appointed lector, in 1841 assistant professor, and in 1850 professor at Copenhagen University; and at the same time he became obstetrician to the city of Copenhagen.

Levy was a prolific scientific writer. Of his publications the following may be mentioned: "De Sympodia seu Monstrositate Sireniformi, cum Anatomica Ejusmodi Monstri Descriptione," Copenhagen, 1833; "Om Collisionen Imellem Perforation og Kaisersnit. Et Bidrag til Undersögelsen: De Jure Vitæ et Necis quod Competit Medico in Partu," *ib.* 1840; "Udtog af Födselsvidenskaben som Lærebog for Jordemödre," *ib.* 1843. Levy was coeditor of the "Journal for Medicin og Chirurgie," to which he contributed extensively. A number of essays and treatises from his pen have appeared also in the German and the English medical periodicals.

BIBLIOGRAPHY: C. F. Bricka, *Dansk Biografisk Lexicon*; *Erslew's Forfatter-Lexicon*.

S. F. C.

LEVY, NATHAN: Founder of the first Jewish cemetery in Philadelphia; born in Feb., 1704; died in Philadelphia Dec. 23, 1753. He probably went there from New York, for in 1730 a merchant of his name was a member of the Shearith Israel congregation of the latter city. Upon his arrival in Philadelphia he engaged in the general commission business with David Franks under the firm name of Levy & Franks, and continued in that business until his death. According to a letter of Richard Peters dated Sept. 20, 1738, there was laid out by Mr. Thomas Penn ("proprietary governor of Pennsylvania"), "for a burying-place for Mr. Nathan Levy and family," a plot of ground on Spruce street near Ninth street. Peters was evidently mistaken in the date, for it was on Sept. 25, 1740, that Nathan Levy obtained the first grant of thirty feet square; on June 27, 1752, he secured from the proprietary government the adjoining lot, thirty feet wide and sixty feet in depth. It was evidently the intention of Levy to permit the cemetery to be used by the Jews of his adopted city, and not to retain it for the use of his family alone. He had the ground boarded in. In 1751 he complained to the "Pennsylvania Gazette" that "unthinking persons had fired several shots against the Jews' burying-ground"; he had therefore enclosed it with a brick wall. At his death, two years later, his remains were interred in the cemetery he had founded. It is now the property of the Congregation Mickvé Israel (see PHILADELPHIA).

BIBLIOGRAPHY: Morais, in *Publications Am. Jew. Hist. Soc.* 1893, i. 20-21; Rosenbach, *The Jews of Philadelphia Prior to 1800*, pp. 8-9, Philadelphia, 1883.

A. A. S. W. R.

LEVY, SAMSON: Colonial merchant of Philadelphia. He was one of the originators, in 1748, of the City Dancing Assembly, a famous social organization of Philadelphia. In Nov., 1765, he signed, with other merchants of the city, including six Jews, the celebrated resolutions not to import goods from England until the Stamp Act had been repealed. He had two sons, **Moses** and **Samson.** Moses Levy (b. Philadelphia 1757; d. there May 9, 1826) was educated at the University of Pennsylvania, from which he graduated in 1776. On March 19, 1778, he was admitted to the bar; from 1802 to 1822 he was recorder of Philadelphia; from 1822 to 1825, presiding judge of the district court for the city and county of Philadelphia. At one time he was a member of the Pennsylvania legislature, and he was a trustee of the University of Pennsylvania for twenty-four years. Samson Levy (b. Philadelphia 1761; d. there Dec. 15, 1831) studied law with his brother Moses Levy, was admitted to the bar on June 9, 1787, and became one of the best-known lawyers of the city. He was one of the incorporators of the Pennsylvania Academy of the Fine Arts.

BIBLIOGRAPHY: Brown, *The Forum*; Martin, *The Bench and Bar of Philadelphia*; Morais, *The Jews of Philadelphia*; Rosenbach, *The Jews of Philadelphia Prior to 1800*; *Publications Am. Jew. Hist. Soc.* i. 60.

A. A. S. W. R.

LEVY, SARA: German philanthropist; born in Berlin June, 1761; died there March 11, 1854. She was a daughter of Daniel ITZIG, and was well educated according to the fashionable French standards of her time. Her husband was Samuel Levy, one of the first bankers of Berlin. During the time following the battle of Jena she was much sought after by Bignon, the French ambassador to Berlin, and the other French officials. She retained her Judaism, though most of her relatives deserted their faith; at her death she left thirty thousand thalers to the Jewish Orphan Asylum of Berlin, and bequeathed her house to King Frederick William IV.

BIBLIOGRAPHY: Kayserling, *Jüdische Frauen*, pp. 228 *et seq.*

S. J.

LÉVY, SIMON: French rabbi; born in 1829 at Lauterbourg, Alsace; died at Bordeaux Nov. 29, 1886. He studied first under Solomon ULMANN, and then at the Rabbinical School at Metz, which he left in 1853 to accept the rabbinate of Lunéville. In 1864 he was called as chief rabbi to Bordeaux, where he remained until his death. Besides a pamphlet, "Renan et la Synagogue," Lévy wrote "Moïse, Jésus, Mahomet," which work was published posthumously.

BIBLIOGRAPHY: *Archives Israélites*, Dec. 9, 1886.

S. I. LEV.

LEVY, URIAH PHILLIPS: American naval officer; born in Philadelphia April 22, 1792; died in New York March 22, 1862. Levy was a cabin-boy before the age of eleven; he was apprenticed as a sailor in 1806; in 1810 he became second mate of a brig, and later first mate of another. He purchased a one-third interest in the schooner "George Washington," of which he was master until 1812. On Oct. 23, 1812, he received a commission as sailing-master in the United States navy, serving on the ship "Alert," and later on the brig "Argus," bound for France. The "Argus" captured several prizes, and Levy was placed in command of one, but

Uriah Phillips Levy

the prize was recaptured by the English, and Levy and the crew were kept as prisoners in England for sixteen months. In 1816 he was assigned as sailing-master to the "Franklin," 74 guns, and in March, 1817, he was appointed lieutenant, his appointment being confirmed by the Senate.

Levy had many difficulties in the navy, possibly due to anti-Jewish prejudice. He fought a duel, killed his opponent, was court-martialed six times, and finally dropped from the list as captain, to which rank he had been promoted. He defended his conduct before a court of inquiry in 1855, was restored to the navy as captain, and subsequently rose to the rank of commodore.

Tombstone of Uriah Phillips Levy, Cypress Hills Cemetery, New York.
(From a photograph.)

Levy always acknowledged his Jewish allegiance. He was a great admirer of Thomas Jefferson; he purchased Monticello, the home of Jefferson (still owned by Levy's descendants), and presented to the United States government a statue of Jefferson, which is now in the Capitol at Washington. The freedom of the city of New York was voted to him by the common council on Feb. 6, 1834, as a testimonial to his character, patriotism, and public spirit. He is buried in that portion of Cypress Hills Cemetery in use by the Congregation Shearith Israel, and on his tombstone is recorded that "he was the father of the law for the abolition of the barbarous practise of corporal punishment in the United States navy."

BIBLIOGRAPHY: *American Jewish Year Book*, 1902-3, pp. 42-45.

A. S. Wo.

LÉVY-BACRAT, ABRAHAM: Rabbinical author of the beginning of the sixteenth century. Expelled from Spain in 1492, he settled at Tunis, where in 1507 he wrote "Sefer ha-Zikkaron," a supercommentary on Rashi. The manuscript remained unprinted till 1845, when it was discovered in a Jewish library in Tunis. The work has several prefaces, one of which, written by the author himself, recounts his sufferings at the time of the expulsion from Spain.

BIBLIOGRAPHY: Cazès, *Notes Bibliographiques*.

S. S. M. Fr.

LÉVY-BRUHL, LUCIEN: French philosopher; born at Paris April 10, 1857; educated at the Lycée Charlemagne and the Ecole Normale Supérieure. In 1879 he received the degree of "agrégé en philosophie," and was at once called to a professorship in philosophy at the Lycée of Poitiers, which he resigned two years later for a professorship at Amiens. In 1884 he received the degree of Ph.D., and the year following was appointed professor of philosophy at the Lycée Louis-le-Grand, succeeding Burdeau. For several years he held the same chair at the Séminaire Israélite de France, which he resigned in 1895 to become "maître de conférences" at the Ecole Normale Supérieure. In 1899 he was appointed to a similar position at the University of Paris, where, in 1902, he became "chargé de cours" of the history of modern philosophy. Since 1886 Lévy-Bruhl has lectured, at the Ecole Libre des Sciences Politiques, on the history of political movements and on the development of public spirit in Germany and England during the last two centuries.

Lévy-Bruhl has written: "L'Idée de Responsabilité" and "Quid de Deo Seneca Senserit" (Paris, 1884; his two graduating theses); "L'Allemagne Depuis Leibnitz" (*ib.* 1890); "Essai sur la Formation de la Conscience Nationale en Allemagne" (*ib.* 1890); "La Philosophie de Jacobi" (*ib.* 1894); "History of Modern Philosophy in France" (Chicago, 1899); "Lettres Inédites de John Stuart Mill à Auguste Comte" (Paris, 1899; containing the answers of Comte); "La Philosophie d'Auguste Comte" (*ib.* 1900); "La Morale et la Science des Mœurs" (*ib.* 1903). Lévy-Bruhl is a chevalier of the Legion of Honor.

S. J. Ka.

LEVYSOHN, SALOMON FREDERIK: Danish musician and critic; born in Copenhagen Oct. 14, 1858. He studied at the University of Copenhagen and at the Polytechniske Institut until 1878, when he decided to devote himself to the study of music. From 1884 to 1896 he was conductor of the Academical Song-Society (Studenter-Sangforeningen); in 1891 he was appointed keeper of the archives of music at the Kongelige Theater in Copenhagen.

Levysohn has translated into Danish the texts of several operas, including "Don Juan" and "Othello." He has written also a number of critical essays in "Morgenbladet" and in other Danish dailies.

BIBLIOGRAPHY: *Salmonsen's Store Illustrerede Konversations-Lexicon.*

S. F. C.

LEWALD, FANNY: German authoress; born May 24, 1811, in Königsberg, Prussia; died Aug. 5, 1889, in Dresden. In her seventeenth year she entered the Evangelical Church. In 1831, in company with her father, she made a tour through Germany and France, prolonging her stay in Breslau and Berlin. In 1834, to while away the hours of an invalid sister, she wrote a book of fairy-stories. It was not, however, until 1841 that she entered the literary arena with a novel entitled "Der Stellvertreter," published in serial form in the "Europa," a paper owned by a relative likewise named Lewald. Subsequently were published anonymously: "Klementine," 1842; "Jenny," 1843; "Eine Lebensfrage," 1845; "Das Arme Mädchen," 1845. In the spring of 1845 she made a tour of Italy, after which she settled in Berlin, where she married (1854) Adolph Stahr, the literary critic. In company with her husband she undertook a series of tours through Europe, her mind storing a wealth of impressions which were later to be called into requisition. Her literary productiveness during the years following upon this extended tour knew no bounds. One book followed another in quick succession, astonishing the reading public by their variety of subject and fertility of resource: "Italienisches Bilderbuch," 1847; "Diogena Roman von Iduna Gräfin H.-H.," giving a humorous portraiture of the Countess Hahn-Hahn; "Prinz Louis Ferdinand," 1849; "Erinnerungen aus dem Jahre 1848"; "Liebesbriefe," 1850, previously published 1845; "Dunen- und Berggeschichten," 1850; "Reisetagbuch Durch England und Schottland," 1852; "Das Mädchen von Hela," 1853; "Meine Lebensgeschichte," 1861; "Von Geschlecht zu Geschlecht," a novel in eight volumes, 1863–65; "Osterbriefe für die Frauen," 1863; "Erzählungen," in three volumes, 1866–68; "Villa Riunione," 1868; "Sommer und Winter am Genfer See," a diary, 1869; "Für und Wider die Frauen," letters, 1870; "Nella," Christmas story, 1870; "Die Erlöserin," a novel, 1873; "Benedikt," 1874; "Benvenuto," a novel from the world of art, 1875; "Reisebriefe aus Italien, Deutschland, und Frankreich," 1880; "Helmar," a novel, 1880; "Vater und Sohn," a novel, 1881; "Vom Sund zum Posilipp," letters of travel, 1883; "Stella," a novel, 1884; "Die Familie Darner," a novel, 1887; "Zwölf Bilder nach dem Leben," 1888; etc. These are only a few of the productions of this versatile writer. In all more than fifty volumes can be accredited to a pen never idle. Fanny Lewald is remarkable for her keen observation of men and manners, for the firmness with which her characters are outlined, for the grace and finish of her style; a harsh realism, however, pervades her works. This tendency to realism prompts her to seek an ideal in the dispassionate man of affairs, who according to her standpoint may be relied upon to solve the problem of human existence. As a rule, this view precludes the possibility of frequent excursions into the world of the imagination, and except in rare cases is apt to stamp the work of the writer as devoid of that poetic charm so essential to the highest literary achievement. Her activity was not confined to literature. She was one of Germany's foremost leaders in the movement for the emancipation and advancement of women, favoring the opening to them of new fields of employment. S.

LEWANDOWSKI, LOUIS: German composer of synagogal music; born at Wreschen, province of Posen, April 23, 1823; died Feb. 4, 1894, at Berlin. At the age of twelve he went to Berlin to study pianoforte and singing, and became solo soprano in the synagogue. He afterward studied for three years under A. B. Marx and also attended the school of composition of the Berlin Academy, where his teachers were Rungenhagen, Bach, and Grell. Graduated with high honors, he was appointed in 1840 choirmaster of the Berlin synagogue, in which capacity he rendered invaluable services in behalf of ritualistic music. His principal works are: "Ḳol Rinnah u-Tefillah," for chorus; "Todah u-Zimrah," for mixed chorus, solo, and organ; 40 psalms, for solo, chorus, and organ; symphonies, overtures, cantatas, and songs.

Louis Lewandowski.

In 1866 he received the title of "royal musical director," and shortly afterward was appointed choirmaster in the Neue Synagoge, Berlin, for which he composed the entire musical service. His arrangements of ancient Hebrew melodies for choir, cantor, and organ are considered masterly productions, and are characterized by great simplicity and a profound religious sentiment. Many of Lewandowski's pupils have become prominent cantors. Lewandowski was the principal founder of the Institute for Aged and Indigent Musicians, an institution which prospered under his management.

BIBLIOGRAPHY: Mendel, *Musikalisches Konversations-Lexikon*; Champlin, *Cyclopedia of Music and Musicians*; Riemann, *Musik-Lexikon.*

S. J. So.

LEWENTAL, FRANCIS DE SALES (SOLOMON): Polish publisher; born at Wloclawek, Russian Poland, 1839; died at Wiesbaden Sept. 24, 1902. In 1862 Lewental, the son of poor Jewish parents, bought with his accumulated savings the press of the Warsaw publisher John Glücksberg (d. 1859), and began his career with the "Kalendarz Ludowy," a popular almanac, which he continued until 1866. In 1865, in conjunction with others, he founded "Klosy," an illustrated weekly, which in the next year became his exclusive property. Under Lewental's management and under the editorship of Adam Plug "Klosy" became the most widely circulated illustrated weekly in Poland, and contributed in no small measure to the popularizing of Polish art and to the development of Polish wood-engraving. In 1871 Lewental bought the "Kolko Domowe," a home magazine, and transformed it into the popular "Tygodnik Romansow i Powiesci" (discontinued in 1900). Lewental was the proprietor also of the "Swit," edited for a few years by Mary Konopnicka. In 1871, also, he issued an edition of the works of Korzeniowski, which proved so popular that it led later to similar editions of the works of Kraszewski, Kremer, Rzewuski, Skarbek, Fredro, Syrokomla, Eliza Orzeszko, Kaczkowski, Balucki, etc.

In 1874 Lewental commenced the publication of the best productions of European literature under the title "Biblioteka Najcelniejszych Utworow Literatury Europejskiej." They were edited with the greatest care by Peter Chmielowski and, after him, by Stanislaus Krzeminski. The "John Matejko Album" and many other well-known works were issued from his press. In 1887 Lewental became one of the proprietors of the "Kuryer Warszawski." Though he avoided politics he did not succeed in escaping a conflict with the Russian government; he was arrested in 1900, was compelled to discontinue all his publications, and was sentenced to deportation for three years to Odessa. After a year there he obtained a passport for foreign travel. Lewental enjoyed the friendship of many literati, among them being J. I. Kraszewski, for whose release from imprisonment at Magdeburg he offered to furnish the bail required by the Prussian government.

H. R. W. Pe.

LEWI, JOSEPH: American physician; born at Radnitz, Bohemia, Aug. 17, 1820; died at Albany, N. Y., Dec. 19, 1897; educated at the universities of Prague and Vienna. After graduating from the latter university (M.D. 1846) he was appointed assistant at the Vienna Lying-in Hospital. In 1847 he began to practise in Radnitz, but in the following year, that of the Revolution, emigrated to America, settling in Albany in 1849. There he was appointed on the staff of the Albany hospital, and became a member and later president of the Albany County Medical Society, and senior censor of the State Medical Society. Lewi was one of the forty-two citizens of Albany who organized, in 1863, the Union League in that city.

Thirteen of Lewi's fourteen children survived him. The oldest son is the journalist **Isidor Lewi** (b. Albany May 9, 1850). He was educated at the Albany Academy, became connected with several newspapers, and is at present (1904) an editorial writer on the "New York Tribune" and publisher of the "New Era Illustrated Magazine." Another son, **Maurice J. Lewi** (b. Albany Dec. 1, 1857), is a physician in New York city. He graduated from the Albany Medical College in 1877. After a postgraduate course in Heidelberg and Vienna he began to practise in his native town (1880). He became lecturer at the Albany Medical College and professor of medical jurisprudence at the Albany Law School. In 1891 he was appointed secretary of the state board of medical examiners, which office he still (1904) occupies. In 1892 he removed to New York city.

A. F. T. H.

LEWIN, ADOLF: German rabbi and author; born at Pinne, Posen, Sept. 23, 1843. Lewin was educated at the Jewish Theological Seminary and at the University of Breslau. In 1872 he was appointed rabbi in Kozmin, later in Coblenz, and in 1886 was called to the rabbinate of Freiburg-im-Breisgau. He wrote: "Die Religionsdisputation R. Jehiels," a prize essay (Breslau, 1869); "Die Makkabäische Erhebung," a dissertation (*ib.* 1870); "Zur Judenfrage: Naturwissenschaft oder Judenhass" (*ib.* 1880); "Juden in Freiburg-im-Breisgau" (Treves, 1890); "Das Judenthum und die Nichtjuden" (*ib.* 1891); "Geschichte, Geographie, und Reiselitteratur der Juden" (in Winter and Wünsche, "Die Jüdische Litteratur," ii. 287–473).

S. M. K.

LEWIN, GEORG RICHARD: German dermatologist; born at Sondershausen April 25, 1820; died at Berlin Nov. 1, 1896. He was educated at the universities of Halle and Berlin, graduating as doctor of medicine in 1845. After a postgraduate course at the universities of Vienna, Würzburg, and Paris he settled in Berlin, where he practised as a specialist first in otology, and later in dermatology and syphilis. In 1862 Lewin was admitted to the medical faculty of his alma mater as privat-docent in otology. In 1865 he became chief physician in the department of dermatology and syphilis at the Charité Hospital, and in 1868 was appointed assistant professor.

In 1880 Lewin became a member of the imperial department of health, and in 1884 received the title of "Geheimer Medicinalrat." In the same year, through the influence of Bismarck, Lewin's clinic was divided into two departments, Lewin retaining the class in syphilis, while Schweninger, Bismarck's physician, was appointed chief physician for dermatology. This action of the government aroused much indignation in the medical faculties of most of the universities of Germany, and much public sympathy was expressed for Lewin.

Lewin was very successful in his profession. He introduced several new methods in the treatment of syphilis and in dermatology, among which may be mentioned the subcutaneous injection of mercuric chlorid and the spray application in diseases of the throat.

He was an industrious writer, and contributed many essays to the medical journals. He was also the author of the following works: "Klinik der Krankheiten des Kehlkopfes," 2d ed., Berlin, 1863; "Inhalationstherapie und Krankheiten der Respirationsorgane," 2d ed., *ib.* 1865; "Behandlung der Syphilis Durch Subcutane Sublimatinjectionen," *ib.* 1869.

Bibliography: Pagel, *Biog. Lex.*; *Meyers Konversations-Lexikon.*

S. F. T. H.

LEWIN, LOUIS: German pharmacologist and toxicologist; born at Tuchel, West Prussia, Nov. 9, 1850. He received his education at the gymnasium and the University of Berlin (M.D. 1876). The two years following his graduation he spent at Munich, in the laboratories of Voit and Pettenkofer. Returning to Berlin, he in 1878 became assistant at the pharmacological institute of the university, which position he resigned in 1881. In the same year he was admitted to the medical faculty at the university as privat-docent, and in 1897 he was appointed professor.

Lewin is a prolific writer. Among his many essays may be mentioned:

"Ueber Morphium-Intoxication," in "Deutsche Zeitschrift für Praktische Medizin," 1874, No. 26; "Experimentelle Untersuchungen über die Wirkungen des Aconitin auf das Herz," in "Centralblatt für die Medizinische Wissenschaft," 1875, No. 25; "Ueber die Verwerthung des Alkohols in Fieberhaften Krankheiten," in "Deutsches Archiv für Klinische Medizin," 1876; "Ueber Maximale Dosen der Arzneimittel," in "Transactions of the International Medical Congress," ninth session, Washington, 1887; "Ueber Allgemeine Hautvergiftung Durch Petroleum," in Virchow's "Archiv," cxii., 1888; "Ueber Anhalonium Lewinii und Andere Cacteen," in "Archiv für Experimentelle Pathologie und Pharmakologie," 1894; "Die Behandlung der Lepra," in "Deutsche Medizinische Wochenschrift," 1898; "Die Untersuchungen von Blutflecken," *ib.* 1899; "Die Vergiftungen in Betrieben," *ib.* 1890 (also translated by Pannier in "Bulletin Général de Thérapeutique," 1902); "Ueber die Behandlung der Lepra," *ib.* 1900.

Lewin is also the author of: "Die Nebenwirkungen der Arzneimittellehre," Berlin, 1881, 2d ed. 1893 (translated into Russian); "Lehrbuch der Toxicologie," Vienna, 1885, 2d ed. 1897 (translated into French by Pouchet, Paris, 1902); "Ueber Piper Methysticum (Kawa Kawa)," Berlin, 1886; "Ueber Areca Catechu, Chavica Detle, und das Betelkauen," Stuttgart, 1889.

s. F. T. H.

LEWINSKY, ABRAHAM: German rabbi; author; born March 1, 1866, at Loslau, Upper Silesia. He entered the University of Breslau in 1884 and from that time until 1887 he studied there, and was graduated (Ph.D.). At the same time he pursued his rabbinical studies at the Jewish Theological Seminary of that city. In 1890 he was called as district rabbi to Weilburg-on-the-Lahn; and two years later he took charge of the district rabbinate of Hildesheim, which position he still (1904) occupies.

Lewinsky has published: "Beiträge zur Kenntniss der Religionsphilosophischen Anschauungen des Flavius Josephus"; "Der Hildesheimer Rabbiner Samuel Hameln" (in "Kaufmann Gedenkbuch" and printed separately); and "Aus dem Hildesheimer Stadtarchive." S.

LEWINSOHN, JOSHUA: Russian teacher and writer; born 1833 at Vyeshiuti, government of Kovno. He received his Talmudical education at Zhagory, in the house of his uncle Simon Hurvitz, and graduated in 1865 from the gymnasium at Mitau, remaining there until 1874, when he was appointed inspector of the Jewish school at Tukum, Courland. His first articles in Hebrew appeared in "Ha-Maggid" in 1857; and since then he has contributed extensively to that paper and to "Ha-Meliẓ," "Ha-Shaḥar," and other Hebrew periodicals. He was also for many years a contributor to the German "Rigasche Zeitung."

Lewinsohn has published: "Ereẓ Russia u-Melo'ah" (Wilna, 1868), a geography and topography of Russia; "Toledot Anshe Shem be-Yisrael," biographies of about fifty Jewish authors; and "Toledot Seḥar ha-Yehudim" (in "Ha-Shaḥar"), a history of Jewish commerce. He has likewise written numerous articles on Jewish history which have appeared in various periodicals.

Bibliography: Sokolov, *Sefer Zikkaron*, p. 64.
H. R. J. G. L.

LEWINSTEIN, JOSEPH: Russian rabbi and author; born at Lublin, Russian Poland, 1840. He is a member of a family of rabbis and Talmudists which includes the author of the "Lebushim" and of "Pene Yehoshua'." At the age of twenty he became rabbi of Karol, in the government of Plotzk; in 1868, rabbi of Zaklikov, in the government of Lublin; since 1875 he has been rabbi of Serotzk, government of Lomza.

Lewinstein has written "Birkat Abraham," on Pesaḥim, Beẓah, and Ḥagigah; "Pene Abraham," commentary on Genesis; a commentary on the Haggadah of Passover; "Dor Dor we-Dorshaw," a collection of 6,600 names of the great of Israel of all generations, with the dates of their deaths. He has contributed biographical articles, which are of special genealogical value and which have won him recognition as an authority in this field, to "Ha-Goren" (ed. Horodetzky), to "Ha-Eshkol," and to other periodicals. He has written also appendixes to "'Ir Gibborim" and "'Ir Tehillah."

Bibliography: B. Z. Eisenstadt, *Dor Rabbanaw we-Soferaw*, i. 36, Warsaw, 1895.
H. R. A. S. W.

LEWIS, DAVID: English merchant and philanthropist; born in London 1823; died in Liverpool Dec. 4, 1885. Settling in Liverpool in 1840, he by 1856 had accumulated sufficient capital to commence business on his own account as a boys' clothier in Bold street. Subsequently he opened a second establishment; and thereafter he gradually developed one of the largest retail businesses of the kind in England, erecting an establishment of the "Universal Provider" or department store class. Similar ones were founded by him in Manchester, Sheffield, and Birmingham. No firm in the provinces did more than his to bring cheap and durable clothing within the reach of the masses.

Lewis' ample means were freely given in aid of charitable and philanthropic works. He headed the local subscription list for the persecuted Jews of Russia with a donation of £1,000 ($5,000), and gave large sums in support of the synagogue. For many years he held the position of warden and treasurer of the Old Hebrew Congregation, Liverpool. At his death he bequeathed very large sums (nearly a half-million sterling) for the erection of hospitals and other philanthropic institutions, which constitute some of the most important in Liverpool.

Bibliography: *Jew. Chron.* and *Jew. World*, Dec. 11, 1885; *Liverpool Leader*, Dec. 6, 1875.
J. G. L.

LEWIS, SIR GEORGE HENRY: English lawyer; born in London April 21, 1833; educated at University College, London. In 1850 he was articled to his father, **James Graham Lewis** (1804–1869), founder of Lewis & Lewis, one of the best-known firms of solicitors in the city of London. George was admitted in Hilary term in 1856, and was subsequently taken into partnership by his father and uncle. He first made his name in prosecuting the directors of the Overend and Gurney Bank, who had caused the disastrous panic of 1866, and for a time he devoted special attention to financial cases. In criminal cases he drew public attention to himself by his cross-examination in the Bravo case in 1875, and from that time onward was connected with most criminal "causes célèbres," being conspicuous in the prosecution of fraudulent persons like Madame Rachel and Slade the medium. Among other cases may be mentioned the Hatton Garden diamond robbery case; Belt versus Lawes; and the Baccarat case, in which the Prince of Wales's name was mentioned; and he was selected by the Parnell commission to conduct the case for Charles Stuart Parnell and the Irish party against the London "Times." Lewis has by far the largest practise in financial cases of any lawyer in London, and is especially expert in libel cases, being retained by some of the chief newspapers. He has shown himself especially skilful in exposing the practises of usurious money-lenders. Lewis was knighted in 1893, and raised to the rank of baronet in 1902.

Arms of Sir George Henry Lewis.

Bibliography: *Men and Women of the Times*; *Who's Who*; Burke's *Peerage, Baronetage, and Knighthood*, 1903.

J.

LEWIS, HARRY S.: English author and communal worker; born in London in 1861; educated at King's College School and St. John's College, Cambridge (B.A. 1884). At Cambridge he was one of the earliest to take honors in the Semitic languages tripos (1886) and was Hebrew scholar at his college. After leaving college he took residence at Toynbee Hall, Whitechapel, and devoted himself to social work among the Jews of the East End. In connection with this he published, with E. J. Russel, "The Jew in London" (London, 1900). He edited "The Targum on Isaiah i. 5, with Commentary" (*ib.* 1889).

Bibliography: *Jewish Year Book*, 5664 (1904).

J.

LEWIS, LEOPOLD DAVIS: English dramatist; born in London 1828; died there Feb. 23, 1890. Lewis was educated at the King's Collegiate School, London, and upon graduation became a solicitor, practising as such from 1850 to 1875. In 1871 he translated Erckmann-Chatrian's "Le Juif Polonais," giving it the name "The Bells," under which name it was produced by Henry Irving at the Lyceum Theatre, London, Nov. 25, 1871. Original plays from the pen of Lewis are: "The Wandering Jew" (Adelphi Theatre, April 14, 1873); "Give a Dog a Bad Name" (*ib.* Nov. 18, 1873); and "The Foundlings" (Sadler's Wells Theatre, Oct. 8, 1881). From February to December of 1868 he and Alfred Thompson conducted a monthly, "The Mask," which failed. In addition to the plays mentioned Lewis wrote a number of tales under the title "A Peal of Merry Bells" (1880).

Bibliography: *Dict. National Biog.* xxx. 191; *The Times* (London), Feb. 25, 1890; *The Era* and *St. Stephen's Review* (ib.), March 1, 1890.

J. E. Ms.

LEWIS, SAMUEL: English money-lender and philanthropist; born in Birmingham 1837; died in London Jan. 13, 1901. Lewis began work when thirteen years old. He became a salesman of steel pens, then opened a jeweler's shop, and finally entered the business with which his name was most identified, that of money-lending. He became the most fashionable money-lender of his day. Nearly every noble family in Great Britain is said to have been more or less in business connection with Lewis. He left nearly twenty million dollars, of which five millions are to go to charity on the death of his widow, Ada Davis Lewis, a sister of Hope Temple, the composer.

Bibliography: *Jew. Chron.* Jan. 18, 1901; *The Sketch* (London), Jan. 23, 1901.

J. E. Ms.

LEWIS, SAMUEL A.: American politician and philanthropist; born in New York city 1831. He early engaged in business, and was so successful that he retired with a competency in 1862. In 1868 he was elected a member of the board of education of the city of New York, serving as school commissioner and chairman of the financial committee. When in 1869 the legislature changed the board from elective to appointive, Lewis was confirmed in his office of school commissioner, and in 1870 was reappointed for a term of five years. In 1871, however, he was compelled to retire. One of his first acts as a school commissioner was to abolish corporal punishment. In 1874 Lewis was elected alderman at large, and later in the same year president of the aldermanic board, holding the presidency for two consecutive terms.

Lewis is one of the founders of the Mount Sinai Hospital, and has served, since its organization in 1852, on its board of management as secretary, director, and vice-president, resigning the last-named office in 1873. He founded (1872) the School-Teachers' Life Assurance Society, and was in 1874 chairman of the relief association for the Ninth Ward. In 1851 the Ladies' Benevolent Society presented him with a gold medal in acknowledgment of the valuable aid he had rendered that body. From 1868 to 1873 Lewis acted as a trustee of the College of the City of New York.

Bibliography: *New York Public School Journal*, Feb. 18, 1871, April 6, 1872; *New York Herald*, March 13, 1874; *Jewish Messenger*, April 17, 1874; *Daily Graphic*, Jan. 22, 1875.

A. F. C.

LEWISOHN, LEONARD: American merchant and philanthropist; born in Hamburg Oct. 10, 1847; died in London March 5, 1902. His father, **Samuel Lewisohn**, a prominent Hamburg merchant, sent him to the United States in 1863; about three years later he was joined by his younger brother, and they formed the firm of Lewisohn Brothers in Jan., 1866. As early as 1868 the firm turned its attention to the metal trade, becoming prominent dealers in lead during that year. Recognizing the commercial future of electricity and the need of copper for conducting-wires, Lewisohn specialized in that metal, and by 1879 was recognized as an important holder of "Lake Copper." Thenceforward his firm occupied a leading position in the copper markets of the world. He was also president of the United Metals Selling Company.

Lewisohn was equally prominent in the sphere of philanthropy. He contributed largely to the Alliance colony in New Jersey, founded in 1882, and to almost every philanthropic institution in New York, regardless of creed. He likewise acted as treasurer of the Hebrew Sheltering Guardian Society in New York, to which institution he gave his counsel and large sums of money. He was one of the largest contributors to the Jewish Theological Seminary of America and to the Montefiore Sanatorium for Consumptives.

A. J.

LEWITA, GUSTAW: Polish pianist; born at Plock, Poland, 1855; died at Paris Feb., 1889. After graduating from the Vienna Conservatorium with distinction, he went to Paris, where he became a member of the orchestra of the Pas de Loup concerts. In 1882 Lewita was called to a professorship in the Conservatorium at Warsaw, and in 1885 was invited to Vienna to give a concert at the court of the archduke Charles. He then went to America, where he gave concerts in the most important cities and before the Emperor of Brazil.

BIBLIOGRAPHY: *Ha-Asif*, 1893, p. 134; *Encyklopedja Powszechna*, ix. 281, Warsaw, 1901.

H. R. A. S. W.

LEWY, BERGNART (BERNHARD) CARL: Danish chemist; born in Copenhagen July 5, 1817; died there Jan. 1, 1863. He obtained the degree of graduate of pharmacy in 1835, and then studied chemistry for three years at the polytechnic school. In 1839 he studied in Berlin (Ph.D.), and spent the winter of 1839–40 in Rome. He then obtained a position as assistant in the private laboratory of J. B. Dumas in Paris.

Lewy soon proved himself to be the possessor of great experimental ability; so that the Académie des Sciences in 1841 entrusted him with the task of studying the atmospheric conditions around the North and Baltic seas, as well as in Copenhagen. Later he made a comparative test of the atmospheric conditions in Paris and in the surrounding country.

In 1847 Lewy was appointed professor of chemistry at Bogota, New Granada, where he enjoyed great popularity and filled many honorary offices. He was decorated by the King of Denmark, and in 1859 was awarded the gold medal of honor. His writings have appeared in "Annales de Chimie et de Physique," "Comptes Rendus" of the French Institute (Académie des Sciences), and in "Forhandlinger ved de Skandinaviske Naturforskeres 4, Möde" (1844).

BIBLIOGRAPHY: C. F. Bricka, *Dansk Biografisk Lexicon*.

S. F. C.

LEWY, ISRAEL: German scholar; born at Inowrazlaw in 1847; educated at the Jewish Theological Seminary and the University in Breslau. In 1874 he was appointed docent at the Lehranstalt für die Wissenschaft des Judenthums in Berlin, and in 1883, on the death of David Joël, he was called to the seminary at Breslau. Lewy's knowledge of Talmudic literature is unusually wide; he is endowed also with an exceptionally acute and dispassionate critical spirit and with a faculty for grasping the proper importance of details. His first publication was "Ueber Einige Fragmente aus der Mischna des Abba Saul" (Berlin, 1876), in which he showed that the Mishnah collections of the foremost teachers in the period before the final redaction of the Mishnah itself, including that of Abba Saul, agreed as regards all the essential points of the Halakah. "Ein Wort über die Mechilta des R. Simon" (Breslau, 1889) is likewise an authoritative work in the field of halakic exegesis. Lewy has published also "Interpretation des Ersten, Zweiten und Dritten Abschnitts des Palästinischen Talmud-Traktates Nesikin" (*ib.* 1895–1902), and "Ein Vortrag über das Ritual des Pesach-Abends" (*ib.* 1904).

S.

LEWYSOHN, ABRAHAM: Hebraist and rabbi of Peiskretscham, Upper Silesia; born Dec. 6, 1805; died Feb. 14, 1860. He left a large number of manuscripts—several hundred sermons in Hebrew and German, novellæ on the Talmud, verses, a German work on Hebrew grammar, and a work entitled "Ḳorot Tannaim wa-Amoraim," a history of the Tannaim and Amoraim, the introduction to which, entitled "Parnasat Ḥakme ha-Talmud," was published in Kobak's "Jeschurun" (i., part 3, p. 81). His published works are: "Meḳore Minhagim" (Berlin, 1846), a critical essay on religious customs according to the Talmud, Poseḳim, and Midrashim (this work was afterward plagiarized by Finkelstein, Vienna, 1851); "Shete Derashot" (Gleiwitz, 1856), sermons; "Toledot R. Yehoshua' ben Ḥananyah," biography of R. Joshua b. Hananiah (in Keller's "Bikkurim," 1865); "Toledot Rab," biography of Rab or Abba Arika (Kobak's "Jeschurun," vi. and vii.). Lewysohn was also a contributor to "Ha-Maggid" and to Klein's "Jahrbuch."

BIBLIOGRAPHY: Ludwig Lewysohn, in *Ha-Maggid*, vii. 364; Zeitlin, *Bibl. Post-Mendels.* pp. 208–209.

S. M. SEL.

LEWYSOHN, LUDWIG: German rabbi; born April 15, 1819, at Schwersenz, Posen; died at Stockholm May 26, 1901. Graduating from the Realgymnasium, Berlin, in 1843, he studied Orientalia in that city, and received his doctor's degree from the University of Halle in 1847, his dissertation being "De Sacrificiis Veteris Testamenti." In 1848 he became preacher at Frankfort-on-the-Oder. Three years later he was called as rabbi to Worms, where he officiated until 1858. He then accepted a call to Stockholm, where he labored from 1859 to 1893, in which year he resigned. Besides numerous contributions to Jewish periodicals (especially "Ha-Maggid"), he published "Nafshot Ẓaddiḳim" (Frankfort-on-the-Main, 1855), on the epitaphs at Worms, and "Zoologie des Talmuds" (*ib.* 1858).

BIBLIOGRAPHY: Reines, *Tableaux Historiques*, i. 123 *et seq.*; Zeitlin, *Ḳiryat Sefer*, i. 209.

S. M. L. B.

LEX TALIONIS. See RETALIATION.

LEXICOGRAPHY. See DICTIONARIES.

LEYDEN. See NETHERLANDS.

LHÉRIE. See BRUNSWICK, LÉON LÉVY.

LIADY, BÄR OF. See LADIER, DOB BÄR B. SHNEOR ZALMAN.

LIBATION. See SACRIFICE.

LIBAU: Russian city in the government of Courland. It has a population (1897) of 64,505, including 9,700 Jews. Among the latter are 3,225 artisans (1,309 being masters) and 117 day-laborers. Among its educational institutions are a government school for Jews (105 pupils), a Jewish general school for girls (90 pupils), and a Talmud Torah (108 pupils). The public schools have 333 Jewish children on their rolls. A Jewish loan and savings association was organized in 1901.

H. R. S. J.

LIBEL AND SLANDER. See SLANDER.

LIBERTINES. See SLAVES AND SLAVERY.

LIBIN, Z. See HUREWITZ, ISRAEL.

LIBOSCHÜTZ, JACOB: Russian physician; born in 1741; died at Wilna Feb. 10, 1827. After studying at the University of Halle he went to St. Petersburg. His religious belief, however, rendered it impossible for him to settle there, and he established himself at Wilna, where he became celebrated. When the famous physician Professor Frank was leaving Wilna and was asked in whose charge he had left the public health, he answered, "In the charge of God and the Jew" ("Deus et Judeus," meaning "God and Liboschütz"). Liboschütz was celebrated also as a diplomat and philanthropist (Fuenn, "Ḳiryah Ne'emanah," p. 260, Wilna, 1860).

H. R. A. S. W.

LIBOSCHÜTZ, OSIP YAKOVLEVICH: Russian physician; died at St. Petersburg in 1824; probably the son of Jacob LIBOSCHÜTZ. He studied medicine at Dorpat (M.D. 1806, his graduating thesis being "De Morbis Primi Paris Nervorum"). He then settled at St. Petersburg, where he became court physician, and founded a hospital for sick children. Liboschütz wrote: "Tableau Botanique des Genres de Plantes Observés en Russie" (Vienna, 1811); "Description de Mousses Qui Croissent aux Environs de St. Pétersbourg et de Moscou" (St. Petersburg, 1811; with Trinius); "Flore des Environs de St. Pétersbourg et de Moscou" (*ib.* 1811).

BIBLIOGRAPHY: *Entziklopedicheski Slovar*, xvii. 642, St. Petersburg, 1895.

H. R. A. S. W.

LIBOWITZ, NEHEMIAH SAMUEL: Russian Hebrew scholar and author; born Jan. 3, 1862, at Kolno, government of Lomza (Lomzha). He studied Talmud under R. Elijah Ḥasid and then under his own father, Isaac Libowitz; in addition he devoted himself to Hebrew literature, reading especially works on criticism. In 1881 he emigrated to the United States and settled in New York, where he still (1904) resides, devoting his time in part to business and in part to literature.

Libowitz is the author of: "Iggeret Biḳḳoret" (New York, 1895), against I. H. Weiss; "Rabbi Yehudah Aryeh Modena" (Vienna, 1896; 2d ed., New York, 1901), his most important work, a collection of materials for a biography of Leon of Modena; "Ephraim Deinard" (*ib.* 1901), a harsh criticism of Deinard; and several other pamphlets. Libowitz has also contributed to the Hebrew periodicals in the United States: "Ner Ma'arabi," "Ha-Modia' la-Ḥadashim," and "Yalḳuṭ Ma'arabi."

BIBLIOGRAPHY: Benzion Eisenstadt, *Ḥakme Yisrael be-Ameriḳa*, p. 62, New York, 1903.

H. R. A. S. W.

LIBRARIES: Very little is known concerning the methods employed by Jews in the collection and preservation of books. The Biblical writings are silent on this point. That there were royal archives in Jerusalem may be surmised with some show of reason, even though the terms "mazkir" (A. V. "recorder"; II Sam. viii. 16, xx. 24, and several other passages) and "sofer" (A. V. "scribe"; *ib.* viii. 17, and often elsewhere) do not necessarily point to the office of archivist. Nor does the place-name Kirjath-sepher (Josh. xv. 16; Judges i. 11-12), which the Septuagint translates Πόλις Γραμμάτων (Vulgate, "Civitas Litterarum" = "Book Town"), afford any further evidence; though Quatremère in 1842 deduced from it the existence of a library there, and Sayce in 1895 called it "the literary center of the Canaanites in the south of Palestine" ("Patriarchal Palestine," p. 220; "Higher Criticism and the Monuments," p. 54).

Nor is there any fuller information with regard to Talmudic times and the Middle Ages. The scrolls seem to have been kept in a cover or sheath of leather or of metal (תיק; θήκη; see passages in Krauss, "Lehnwörter," ii. 588), a custom which was observed in Eastern countries for many centuries.

Preservation of Books.

Sambari (*c.* 1672) speaks of the scroll in the synagogue of Al-Maḥallah in a metal תיק (Neubauer, "M. J. C." i. 119, 10), which still exists. The old and much-venerated Samaritan Pentateuch at Nablus is likewise in a metal cover. The scrolls were kept in a case (תיבה), of which there were three kinds, שידה, תיבה, and מגדל. In the catacombs of Rome there have been found representations of Jesus with a case of scrolls at his feet. The cases were usually made of wood, though sometimes of leather, glass, bone, or metal. It has been shown that such cases were the usual form of the Roman bookcase. That they were used by the Jews also is seen from the fact that the earliest representations of the Ark upon glass, dating from the third century, are in this form (see Blau, "Studien zum Althebräischen Buchwesen," pp. 176 *et seq.*; Jacobs, in "J. Q. R." xiv. 738). Sometimes the scrolls were placed in a sort of cupboard, which stood upon a pediment and had a cover. Openings were made at the top and at the side. See ARK OF THE LAW.

That catalogues of collections of Hebrew books were drawn up in early days is evidenced by the recent finds made chiefly in the Fostat Genizah. Such catalogues were sometimes sale-lists of book-traders—*e.g.*, the Adler manuscript in Arabic ("R. E. J." xxxix. 199); the Adler manuscript containing a sale-list of a certain 'Abd al-'Aziz of the thirteenth

Catalogues.

century (*ib.* xl. 56, 264); the list found on the back of the manuscript copy of Saadia's "Amanat" in Arabic (*ib.* xxxii. 126); the Adler manuscript of the twelfth century giving a list in Arabic of over 100 books ("J. Q. R." xiii. 52, 324; JEW. ENCYC. iii. 619a, *s.v.* CATALOGUES); and the Frankfort manuscript, also from the genizah ("J. Q. R." xv. 76; for other lists see "Zeit. für Hebr. Bibl." vii. 181)—and sometimes catalogues of real collectors, such as the genizah fragment containing a list of the books of Nathan b. Jeshuah (*ib.* vii. 184; "J. Q. R." xiv. 247) or the catalogue of the library of Leon Mosconi ("R. E. J." xxxix. 242, xl. 62; see also CATALOGUES).

That care was taken in the preservation of books is seen from the advice which is given by various writers. The author of the "Sefer Ḥasidim" (13th cent.) advises his readers to pay particular attention to the manner in which their books are kept. Especial weight is laid upon the duty of lending books to those whose means do not allow them to purchase them. Books were scarce in those days; the want of them is bewailed by such men as Isserlein and J. Kolon (Güdemann, "Gesch." ii. 191, iii. 65). Judah ibn Tibbon (12th cent.) gives much sage counsel to his son, to whom he left his collection of Arabic and Hebrew books. He bids him make his books his companions, and to take good care of his book-chests (ארגז) and bookcases (תיבה) and his garden.

"Take good care of thy books; cover thy shelves with a fine covering; guard them against damp and mice. Examine thy Hebrew books on the first of every month; thy Arabic ones once every two months; thy pamphlet-cases [כרכים קשוריכ] once every three months. Arrange them all in good order, so that thou weary not in looking for a book when thou needest it. . . . Write down the titles of the books in each row [בית] of the cases [ארגזים] in a separate fascicle [אגרת], and place each in its row, in order that thou mayest be able to see exactly in which row any particular book is without mixing up the others.

"Do the same with the cases. Take good care of the individual leaves [עלים] which are in the convolutes [כרכים] and fascicles; . . . look continually into the catalogue [מזכרת] in order to remember what books thou hast. . . . When thou lendest a book record its title before it leaves the house; and when it is brought back draw thy pen through the memorandum. Restore all loaned books on Pesaḥ and Sukkot" ("Ermahnungsschreiben des Jehudah ibn Tibbon," ed. Steinschneider, pp. 6, 12, Berlin, 1852; transl. in Güdemann, *l.c.* i. 28).

This care in the binding and handling of books is inculcated by Profiat Duran (of Catalonia, 14th cent.) also, as is seen in the preface to his "Ma'aseh Efod" (ed. Friedländer and Kohn, p. 19), and by Solomon Alami (1415): "Take good care of the writing and the arranging of thy books" ("Iggeret Musar," ed. 1854, p. 14).

Alcove in the Public Library, Parma, Italy.
(From a photograph.)

In earliest times the libraries were directly connected with the batte midrashot, each of such institutions having a collection of its own. This practise continued down through the Middle Ages. At times books of especial value were kept in the synagogue in a sort of cupboard, a custom which prevailed especially in Egypt. The contents of these school libraries must have varied in different countries. In the western French and German schools of the Middle Ages they probably contained little more than what was necessary for the almost exclusively Talmudic curriculum that was followed; but in Italy and Spain, where the curriculum embraced also philosophy, mathematics, and the natural sciences, the libraries must have been more varied and much larger.

The tradition thus begun has been kept up. Such libraries of distinctively Jewish books are now attached to seminaries and to theological schools and serve as Jewish university libraries. The chief collections may here be mentioned:

Austria: Library of the Israelitisch-Theologische Lehranstalt, Vienna; Hungary: library of the Landesrabbinerschule, Budapest (20,000 vols., of which 10,000 are Judaica; 41 incunabula; 50 MSS.).

England: Library of Jews' College (in all 25,000 vols., made up of the original Jews' College collection 4,000; the A. L. Green Library 7,000; the Montefiore Library 4,000; the A. Löwy Library 10,000; in addition 600 MSS., mainly from the Zunz and Halberstam collections), and that of the bet ha-midrash, London (the Herschel MSS.).

France: Library of the Séminaire Israélite, Paris.

Germany: Libraries of the Lehranstalt für die Wissenschaft des Judenthums and the Rabbinische Seminar in Berlin; of the Jüdisch-Theologische Seminar (about 23,000 printed vols.; 248 MSS.) in Breslau.

Holland: Libraries of the Portuguese Rabbinical Seminary; of the Bet ha-Midrash 'Ez Ḥayyim (20,000 vols.; 1,000 pamphlets; 300 portraits); of the Netherlands Israelitish Seminary.

Italy: Library of the Rabbinical Seminary, Florence.

United States: Library of the Hebrew Union College (about 15,000 vols.), Cincinnati, and that of the Jewish Theological Seminary of America, New York (14,500 vols.; 750 MSS.).

In the course of time these libraries have not proved sufficient. They served, in the main, theological purposes. An attempt at establishing a national Jewish library was made in the Abarbanel Library at Jerusalem, founded by Joseph Chazanowicz and now containing more than 20,000 vols. Next to this may be mentioned that of the Alliance Israélite Universelle in Paris, largely founded by Isidor Loeb and supported by donations and legacies from L. L. Rothschild (22,000 vols.; 200 MSS.; made up largely of the collections of Isidore Loeb and Bernard Lazare); the Bibliothek des Deutsch-Israelitischen Gemeindebundes (recently founded; 5,000 vols.) in Berlin; and the library of the B'nai B'rith in New York (Maimonides' Library; but this is not a solely Jewish collection).

The Italian Jewish communities seem to have been the first to establish libraries for their own use; *e.g.*, Mantua (in 1767, 4,500 vols.) and Pitiliono in Tuscany. In England the North London bet ha-midrash has its private collection; the Vienna community possesses a children's library; and Warsaw has its Synagogenbibliothek. Of late years the communal libraries have grown, especially in Germany. Breslau has its Bibliothek der Synagogengemeinde; Dettmold, its Lehrerbibliothek and Schülerbibliothek; Gleiwitz, its Jugendbibliothek; Homburg, its Israelitische Gemeindebibliothek Mendelssohn; Carlsruhe, its Jüdische Bibliothek der Israelitischen Genossenschaft; Kozmin, its Jüdische Gemeindebibliothek; Mayence, its Klingensteinische Bibliothek für Hessische Lehrer; Neckar-Bischofsheim, its Israelitische Gemeindebibliothek; Nuremberg, its Bibliothek und Leseverein; Ratibor, its Israelitische Bibliothek; Schwerin, its Gemeindebibliothek; Stettin, its Jüdische Bibliothek; Stuttgart, its Gemeindebibliothek; Parel, its Schul- und Gemeindebibliothek; and Wiesbaden, its Gemeindebibliothek.

Communal Libraries.

Few of the seminary libraries mentioned above can, however, rival the great collections gathered in the large national and public libraries. These antedate the seminary libraries; and, having been the first in the field, and commanding larger pecuniary resources, have been able to progress much further. The leading public collections are here cited. In many cases they are dealt with in separate articles in this encyclopedia or are referred to in the articles treating of the cities in which the collections are located.

Austria: Hofbibliothek, Vienna.

England: British Museum, London (15,000 vols.; 1,400 MSS.); Bodleian Library, Oxford (2,900 MSS.); Cambridge University Library.

France: Bibliothèque Nationale, Paris (1,390 MSS.).

Germany: Königliche Bibliothek, Berlin (5,000 vols.; 300 MSS.); Königliche Bibliothek, Munich (2,000 MSS.); Stadtbibliothek and Universitätsbibliothek, Leipsic; Stadtbibliothek, Frankfort-on-the-Main: Stadtbibliothek, Strasburg.

Holland: Academy of Sciences, Leyden (15,000 vols.); Bibliotheca Rosenthaliana in University Library, Amsterdam.

Italy: Vatican Library, Rome; Bibliotheca Casanatensis, Rome; Public Library, Parma; Bibliotheca Palatina and Bibliotheca Medicio-Laurentiana, Florence; Public Library, Turin; Bibliotheca Marciana, Venice; and Bibliotheca Ambrosiana, Milan. In addition there are smaller collections in the Biblioteca Vittorio Emanuele and the Biblioteca Angelica, Rome, and in the University Library, Bologna.

Russia: Friedland Library, in the Asiatic Museum of the Imperial Academy of Sciences, St. Petersburg (10,000 vols.; 300 MSS.); the University Library and the Synodal Library in the same city; the collection of Karaitica belonging to the Odessa Society for History and Antiquities.

United States: The Jewish collection in the New York Public Library (Schiff foundation; about 17,000 vols.), and that in the Library of Columbia University (gift of Temple Emanu-El; 5,000 vols.).

Most of the foregoing collections are based upon the private libraries of Jewish book-collectors, which have either been given to or bought for the institutions. Thus the British Museum in 1759 acquired by gift from Solomon da Costa a collection which had originally been gathered during the Commonwealth, had fallen to Charles II. at the Restoration, and had finally been purchased by the bookseller who sold it to Da Costa. The British Museum secured also (1848) the printed books in the library of H. I. Michael of Hamburg, which had consisted of 7,000 volumes, including manuscripts. The latter came into the possession of the Bodleian Library, which had previously (1829) been enriched through the purchase of the famous Oppenheimer collection. This consisted of 7,000 printed volumes and 1,000 manuscripts, nearly all Hebraica; it had been founded by the court Jew Samuel Oppenheimer of Vienna with the aid of his patron, Prince Eugene, and had passed into the possession of Samuel's son David, then into that of Hirschel Oppenheimer, and finally into that of Isaac Cohen of Hamburg. Similarly many other private collections have been acquired by various public libraries; *e.g.*, Michael Joseph's went (1849) to Jews' College, London, and Halberstam's to the Judith Montefiore College and later to Jews' College. The manuscripts of Joseph Almanzi went to the British Museum; his printed books, to Temple Emanu-El, New York, and finally to Columbia University in that city. Raphael Emanuel Mendola's books formed the basis of the Congregational Library at Mantua (1767); while the collection of L. Rosenthal of Hanover was presented by his son to Amsterdam University Library. A. Geiger's library enriched the Lehranstalt in Berlin, as did Saraval's and Beer's the sister institution in Breslau, and David Kaufmann's large collection, that in Budapest. The collection of A. Berliner, containing many liturgical works, is now the property of the Frankfort Stadtbibliothek. The library of David Montezinos in Amsterdam, especially rich in Judæo-Spanish productions and in incunabula, is in the Portuguese Seminary of that city, while the pride of Parma is the collection made by the Christian scholar G. B. de Rossi. Samuel Adler's library was given to the Hebrew Union College, Cincinnati, and the collection of M. Sulzberger, so rich in incunabula, to the Jewish Theological Seminary of America, where it has been added to the David Cassel and Halberstam libraries already in that institution. See BOOK-COLLECTORS.

Library Classification.

There is no information in regard to the classification of Hebrew books in olden times. In the above-mentioned genizah fragment of a catalogue, published in "J. Q. R." xiii. 52 *et seq.*, the books are classified as follows: Bible, Mishnah, Talmud, Theology, Halakah, and Liturgy. Some such general division as this must have sufficed. The first to attempt a classification upon a scientific basis was Shabbethai Bass (1641–1718) in the introduction to his "Sifte Yeshenim." Though this was undertaken for bibliographic rather than for library purposes, it deserves a place here. He divides Hebrew literature into two great categories, Biblical and Post-Biblical; and each of these into ten subdivisions as follows:

Biblical Literature: (1) The Bible.

(2) Works Explanatory of the Wording of Scripture:—Bible Lexicography; Dictionaries; Grammars; Explanations of the Text of the Targumim and of the Zohar; Commentaries on the whole Bible; Commentaries on portions of the Bible; Targumim; Cabalistic Commentaries on the Torah and on the Books of Ruth and Lamentations; Works on the Zohar; Lexicography of the Zohar, Recanati, and Baḥya; Philosophical Works Bearing on the Torah, the Megillot, Psalms, and Job; Grammar of the Torah; Supercommentaries on Ibn Ezra; Supercommentaries on Mizraḥi; Commentaries on Midrash Rabbot; Supercommentaries on Rashi to the Torah; Commentaries ("peshaṭ") and Homiletic Explanations ("derashot") arranged according to the sections of the Torah; Commentaries on the Megillot as a whole, and upon each Separate Scroll; Commentaries on the Hafṭarot; Commentaries and Homiletic Explanations on the Prophets and Hagiographa as a Whole and upon the Individual Books; Homilies.

(3) Books of Prayer and Song for the Synagogue Service (Liturgy); Other Poetry; Commentaries on the Liturgy; Commentaries on the Passover Haggadah; Books Dealing with the Writing of Pentateuchs and Mezuzot; of Legal Documents and Bills of Divorce.

(4) Letter-Writing and Rhetoric; Biography and History; Geography; Proverbs and Maxims.

(5) Kawwanot in Connection with the Liturgy and Religious Ordinances; Cabalistic Works Not Arranged According to the Sections of the Pentateuch.

(6) Grammatical Works Not Dealing Directly with the Torah; Masorah; Logic.

(7) Works on Salvation, Redemption, and the Resurrection; Books on the Future Life and the Soul.

(8) Works on Variant Readings, Corrections, and Mistakes in the Bible; Similar Works Dealing with Post-Biblical Literature.

(9) Ethics, Piety, and Religion.

(10) Introductions and Reference Works on the Bible.

Post-Biblical Literature:

(1) Mishnah.

(2) Commentaries on the Mishnah; Explanations and Novellæ to the Gemara, Rashi, and the Tosafot; Commentaries on "'En Ya'aḳob," Other Haggadot, and the Yerushalmi; Commentaries on Pirḳe Abot.

(3) Mathematics (Arithmetic, Algebra, Geometry, etc.); the Calendar; Astronomy and Astrology; Works on Philosophy, Not Arranged According to the Sections of the Pentateuch; Works on Chiromancy, etc. (שרטוטי היד והפרצוף); Works on Casting of Lots and Horoscopes; Works on Evil Spirits and Necromancy; Dreams and their Interpretation; Music; Works on the Other Sciences.

(4) Theology and the Thirteen Dogmas; Religious Discussions and Polemics.

(5) Minhagim (Rituals); Introductions and Works of Reference Regarding Minhagim and the Gemara.

(6) Responsa on Ritual Matters; Responsa on Philosophical Matters.

(7) Medicine (Human and Animal); Lapidaries (סגולות מאבנים טובים).

(8) Works on Initial Letters ("Rashe Tebot"), Gemaṭria, and Noṭariḳon.

(9) Commentaries and Novellæ According Either to the Arrangement of the Gemara or of Alfasi; Commentaries According to the Arrangement of the Arba' Ṭurim, Shulḥan 'Aruk, and "Lebushim"; Commentaries According to the Arrangement of the Mishneh Torah of Maimonides; Decisions and Explanations According to the (Sifre) Miẓwot; Decisions and Laws According to Various Arrangements; Decisions and Laws According to Various Halakot in the Different Portions of the Ṭurim.

(10) Talmudic Methodology; Works on the Building of the Tabernacle, on the Temple, and on its Vessels; Works Printed in the German Language (Judæo-German); Pedagogy.

In modern general libraries the books on Jewish subjects are not always shelved apart from the main collection, special sections for Jewish subjects being provided for merely in the various general sections. As a type of classification that adopted by the Bodleian Library may be cited.

BODLEIAN LIBRARY, OXFORD.

CLASSIFICATION OF BOOKS ON JEWISH SUBJECTS.

[The system of spelling in this list is that adopted by the library authorities.]

Shemitic Mythology and Folk-Tales.

Comparative Religion—Shemitic—General and Miscellaneous.

Judaism: Ancient History; Modern History; Ritual; Talmud; Liturgies and Prayers; Devotional Poems and Hymns; Sermons; General or Mixed Treatises; Encyclopædias; History, Biography, and Methodology of the Subject (Including Jewish Study of the Bible); Targums.

Missions to Jews.

Jewish Attacks on Christianity.

Christian Replies to Them.

Voyages and Travels: Syria and Palestine—Ancient and Mediæval—General and Miscellaneous; Jerusalem; Modern—General and Miscellaneous; Jerusalem.

Ethnography: "Anglo-Israel"; Shemitic.

Climatology and Topography of Health, Mortality, and Medicine: Syria and Palestine—Ancient and General; Mediæval and Modern; Modern Jewish.

General Descriptions and Statistics of Manners (Including General Antiquities) and Characteristics: Syria and Palestine—Ancient; Mediæval and Modern; Modern Jews Outside Palestine.

Chronology—the Hebrew Calendar.

History—General Mediæval; Crusades.

The Jews—In Palestine and General: History and Biography of the Study; General Materials; General Histories—Ancient Writers (Josephus, etc.); Modern Writers; to the Entry into Canaan; to the Secession of Israel; Kingdom of Judah and Judah ± Israel; Kingdom of Israel; Later Samaritan History; Captivity to the Rise of the Maccabees; Maccabees to A.D. 135; Since.

The Jews in Dispersion: History and Biography of the Study (General and Special); General Materials and Histories; Asia E. of the Indies; Asia W. of the Indies; Africa; Spain (and Spain ± Portugal); Portugal; Italy; France and Belgium; Switzerland; Austria-Hungary; Balkan Peninsula and Greece; Slavonic Countries; Scandinavian Countries; Germany; Holland; United Kingdom; America; Australasia; Works on Their Re-Migration to Palestine.

Writing and Illumination: Moabite; Old Israelite; Samaritan; Aramean and Palmyrene, etc., and Rabbinical Hebrew.

Bibliography: Bibliographies of Special Literatures (MSS. as well as printed books)—Hebrew; Bibliographies of Special Subjects—History—the Jews; Catalogues and Histories of Libraries in Syria and Palestine; Law, Jewish.

Miscellaneous Biography: Jews—Ancient; Mediæval and Modern (general and special).

Genealogy and Monuments: Ancient—Jewish.

History, Biography, and Description of General Education: Ancient Jewish; Modern Jewish (general).

Philosophy in General—History, Biography, and Criticism: Kabala.

Philosophy in General—Works: Kabalistic.

Proverbs: Shemitic.

The other great English library, that of the British Museum, has a special classification for its Jewish printed books, elaborated by Zedner; they are divided into fifteen regular sections, with three extra ones dealing with works not considered directly a part of Hebrew literature, as follows:

(1) Bibles; (2) Commentaries on Bible; (3) Talmud; (4) Commentaries on Talmud; (5) Codes of Law; (6) Decisions; (7) Midrash; (8) Cabala; (9) Sermons; (10) Liturgies; (11) Divine Philosophy; (12) Scientific Works; (13) Grammars; Dictionaries; (14) History; Geography; (15) Poetry; Criticism.

In addition: (1) Translations of Post-Biblical Hebrew Works; (2) Works in Arabic, Spanish, German, etc., in Hebrew Characters; (3) Bibliography.

The Vienna Kaiserliche Hofbibliothek has its manuscripts divided into the following categories:

(1) Bible Editions; (2) Masorah; (3) Targumim; (4) Bible Exegesis; (5) Midrash; (6) Talmud; (7) Decisions; (8) Legal Literature; (9) Responsa; (10) Liturgy; (11) Religious Philosophy; (12) Ethics; (13) Cabala; (14) Grammar; (15) Lexicography; (16) Rhetoric; (17) Aristotelian Philosophy; (18) Platonic Philosophy; (19) Ghazali's Philosophy; (20) History of Ḥai ibn Yuḳthan; (21) Medicine; (22) Astronomy; (23) Astrology.

Some of the public libraries have, however, a special division for Hebraica and Judaica. As specimens, the classifications used in the Frankfort Stadtbibliothek and in the Hebrew Union College at Cincinnati may be cited.

Frankfort Scheme.

In the following plan of the first-named library, where the rubrics are quite general, it will be seen that a special rubric is devoted to the history of the Jews of Frankfort.

(1) Hebrew and Jewish Journals; (2) Hebrew Philology (General Works; Lexica; Grammars); (3) Hebrew Bibliography and History of Literature; (4) Old Testament in Hebrew; (5) Anonymous Hebrew Works; (6) Hebrew Literature ("Auctores Hebraici Nominati"); (7) Judæo-German Literature; (8) Jewish Synagogal Music; (9) Secular Music of the Jews; (10) Jewish Literature and History in Other Languages than Hebrew; (11) Literature and History of the Frankfort Jews.

The scheme used by the Hebrew Union College contains a special rubric for manuscripts and rare editions (No. xxiv.), and makes provision also for a certain number of non-Jewish books which find their way by gift into the collection. The Roman numerals represent the alcoves into which the collection is divided.

Hebrew Union College.

I. Bibles in Various Languages; Koran; Zendavesta, etc.; II. Exegetics and Biblical History; III. Talmud; IV. Casuistics; V. Responses and Calendars; VI. Commentaries and Critical Works on the Talmud; VII. Religious History; Theology; Religious Philosophy; Ethics, etc.; VIII. Periodicals; IX. Philology; Literature; School-Books; X. Pre-Talmudic Literature; XI. Midrashim; Homiletics; Sermons; Zohar, etc.; XII. Special History; Philosophy of History; Biography; Travels; XIII. Universal, Oriental, Jewish, Grecian, Roman, and French History; XIV. Lexicography; XV. Philosophy; Logic; Political Economy; Education; XVI. Catalogues and Works on Biography; XVII. Law; XVIII. Mathematics; Natural Sciences; Music; XIX. Fiction; XX. Liturgy; Prayer-Books; XXI. Orientalia; XXII. Government and State Reports; XXIII. Reports of Colleges and Schools; Newspaper Almanacs; XXIV. Manuscripts and Rare Editions; XXV. Literature.

A peculiar system of designating the various classes of books is followed by the Landesrabbinerschule in Budapest. The signatures (A, B, Bi, etc.) are taken from the actual word designation of each class, as follows:

(1) A = Agada (or Haggadah); (2) B = Bible; (3) Bi = Bibliography; (4) C = Codices (*i.e.*, of the Talmudic Literature); (5) Chr = Christian Literature; (6) D = "Decisoren" (*i.e.*, Codes); (7) Di = "Diarien" (*i.e.*, Newspapers, Journals, and Collected Works in Non-Hebrew Tongues); (8) DI = "Diarien" (*i.e.*, Newspapers, Journals, and Collected Works in Hebrew); (9) E = Exegesis; (10) G = Grammar of Hebrew and Aramaic Languages; (11) H = Homiletical Literature in Hebrew; (12) HI = Historical Literature in Hebrew; (13) Hi = Historical Literature of the Jews, General and Special; Biographies in non-Hebrew Languages, Arranged According to Special Groups; (14) I = "Isagogik" (*i.e.*, Introductions); (15) L = Liturgy; (16) Lh = Hebrew, Aramaic, and Talmudic Lexicography; (17) Le = General Lexicography; (18) Nov = Talmudic Novellæ; (19) Nh = Neo-Hebraic Literature; (20) O = Orientalia; (21) P = Jewish Religious Philosophy; (22) Pr = "Predigt Literatur" (*i.e.*, Sermons); (23) R = Talmudic Responsa; (24) T = Talmud, Mishnah, and Introductions to the Same.

There is also a special signature, LG, for German and other literature, the books being arranged according to certain groups. Furthermore, the library of Samuel Löw Brill, presented to the seminary by the Jewish community of Pesth in 1897, is kept separate from the other books and is arranged according to the size of the books (duodecimo, quarto, octavo, etc.) and the alphabetical order of the authors' names. This system, which can be seen also in the catalogues of the Berlin Royal Library, is said to have peculiar advantages.

The most complete classification of works in a Jewish collection is, however, the following, made for the New York Public Library by A. S. Freidus, and reproduced by permission of the director, Dr. John S. Billings.

NEW YORK PUBLIC LIBRARY.

THE JEWISH COLLECTION—GENERAL DIVISIONS.

[The system of spelling in this list is that adopted by the library authorities.]

Manuscripts; Book Rarities; Works of Reference; Bibliography; Literary History; General Works; Hebrew Language and Aramaic; Hebrew Bible; Archæology; Pre-Talmudical Literature and Sects; Christianity; Talmudical Literature; Halacha; The Ritual; Homiletical Literature; Ethics; Doctrinal Theology; Post-Talmudical Schisms and Dissensions; Philosophy; Kabbala and Chasidism; Folk-Lore; Belles-Lettres; Dialects and Their Literatures, and Languages; Secular Sciences; Geography, General History, and Biography; Jewish History; The Jewish Race Ethnologically and Sociologically; Jews and Gentiles.

BIBLIOGRAPHY. LITERARY HISTORY.

Periodicals; Paleography (see also Regulations for Scribes); Catalogues of Manuscripts; History of Printing; Catalogues of Booksellers; Catalogues of Private Libraries; Public Libraries; Catalogues of Public Libraries; Bibliographies: Countries, Authors (see also Biography), Subjects; Literary History: Special Subjects, Modern, Judæo-German, Relation of Jewish Literature to Other Literatures.

GENERAL WORKS.

Periodicals in Hebrew; in Judæo-German (see also Judæo-German Literary Periodicals); in German; in English (American); in English (British); in French; in Other Languages; in Russian; Societies' Publications in Hebrew; Societies' Publications in Modern Languages; Collections (Polyglot); Collections in Hebrew (see also Literary Collections); Collected Works of Individual Authors in Hebrew (see also Collected Literary Works); Collections in Judæo-German (see also Judæo-German Literary Collections), Collections in Latin; Collections in German; Collections in English; Collections in Other Languages; Collections in Russian; Other General Works: Cyclopedias (see also Dictionaries of the Bible; Talmudical Works of Reference).

HEBREW LANGUAGE. ARAMAIC.

Biblical: General Works; Elementary Readers; Chrestomathies (see also Elementary O. T. Histories; Catechisms; Manuals of Judaism); Grammars (in Hebrew; see also Grammatical Notes on the Liturgies); Grammars (in Other Languages); Orthography (Including Alphabet, Vowel-Points, Accents) (see also Masora), Parts of Speech, Syntax, Rhetoric and Prosody (see also Poetry of the Hebrew Bible); Dictionaries (see also Concordances); Names; Synonyms; Miscellaneous. *Post-Biblical:* Chrestomathies; Grammar; Dictionaries; Foreign Terms (see also Dialects); Abbreviations. *Modern:* Letter-Writers (see also Legal Forms). *Aramaic* (see also Targums): Chrestomathies; Grammar.

HEBREW BIBLE.

General Works; Criticism; Introductions; Dictionaries; Helps; Poetry (see also Prosody); Prophecy; Whole Hebrew Bibles; Parts; Selections; Concordances; Masora (see also Grammar); Textual Criticism, Various Readings; Targums (see also Aramaic); Other Versions; Exegetics (see also General Works on Homiletics); Collected Commentaries; Rashi; Ibn Ezra; Other Hebrew Commentaries; Commentaries in Modern Languages; Collective Biography; Individual Biography; Old Testament History (only elementary works or such as have chiefly an exegetical interest go here; for works of historical interest see Pentateuchal Traditions; Entire O. T. Period; see also Fiction Relating to Biblical Times).

ARCHÆOLOGY.

(See also Calendar; Education; Geography [Biblical and Talmudical]; Medicine Among the Jews; Palestine; Ten Tribes; Woman.)

Periodicals, Societies, Collections; General Works; Inscriptions (see also Epitaphs); Numismatics; Metrology; Social and Economic Conditions; Slavery; Government (see also Jurisprudence); Sacred Antiquities (see also Ancient Judaism; Mythology; Idolatry of the Ancient Hebrews; Orach Chayim Laws; Prophecy; The Ritual): Festivals, Sacrifices, Priesthood, Temples; Art; Music; Costumes; Other Special Subjects.

PRE-TALMUDICAL LITERATURE AND SECTS.

(See also History—Return from Babylon to Completion of Talmud.)

General Works: Literature (see also Targums); Apocrypha: Ecclesiasticus, Other Books; Pseudepigrapha; Philo Judæus (see also Alexandrian School of Philosophy); Other Hellenistic Literature (see also Josephus). *Sects* (see also Post-Talmudical Schisms and Dissensions; Sabbathai Zebi; Chasidism); Samaritans (see also Samaritan Text of the Bible; Samaritan Targum); Sadducees, Pharisees, Essenes, Therapeutæ.

CHRISTIANITY.

General Works (see also The Messiah). *Historico-Literary Subjects:* Lives of Jesus (Jewish); Lives of Jesus (Christian) (for Jewish Contemporary History see Return from Babylon to the Close of the Talmud); New Testament; New Testament Parts; New Testament and Jewish Literature; The Fathers and Jewish Literature; Synagogue and Church. *Theologico-Controversial Subjects:* Missionary Periodicals; Missionary Societies; Christian Doctrine; Christian Liturgies; Jews in Christian Theology; Restoration of the Jews (see also Restoration of the Jews [in Jewish Theology]; Zionism); Conversion of the Jews; Conversion of the Jews, Works Against; Converted Jews (Missionaries); Converted Jews (Missionaries, Individual); Miscellaneous Missionary Writings; Evidences of Christianity; Christian Polemics (see also Unfavorable Criticism of the Oral Tradition); Jewish Apologetics and Polemics (see also Apologies of the Jews [against Anti-Semites]; Apologies of the Oral Tradition; The Messiah); Judaism and Christianity (see also Jews and Gentiles; Judaism and Other Religions).

TALMUDICAL LITERATURE.

The Oral Tradition: Unfavorable Criticism (see also Anti-Semitic Writings; Gentiles in Jewish Law and Literature; Christian Polemics), Apologies, Introductions, Essays, Methodology, Helps, Works of Reference (see also Dictionaries of Post-Biblical Hebrew; Indexes to the Agada), Collective Biography, Individual Biography, History (see also History; Return from Babylon to the Close of the Talmud); Mishna (see also Aboth); Commentaries; Literature of the Mishna Period; Jerusalem Talmud; Babylonian Talmud: Parts, Minor Treatises, Translations, Selections (see also Agada), Textual Criticism, Commentaries; Pilpul.

HALACHA.

General Works; The 613 Precepts; Codes of Law (to Maimonides); Maimonides; Jacob ben Asher (and other writers before Caro); Joseph Caro; Later Works; Codes of Special Laws: Orach Chayim Laws (see also The Ritual; Sacred Antiquities), Special Laws, Yoreh Deah Laws, Dietary Laws (for modern works see Dietary Laws, *s.v.* Jewish Race, Ethnologically and Sociologically), Purification (see also Codes in Judæo-German), Regulations for Scribes (see also Massecheth Soferim, under Minor Treatises of the Talmud; Paleography), Other Special Laws; Eben ha-Ezer Laws (for modern works see Special Laws): Divorce; Choshen ha-Mishpat Laws (see also Government of the Ancient Hebrews; Non-Jewish Law): Modern Works, Special Laws (see also Slavery), Legal Forms (see also Letter-Writers); Codes in Judæo-German and Judæo-Spanish; Decisions of Several Authors; Decisions of Individual Authors.

THE RITUAL.

(See also Orach Chayim Laws; Sacred Antiquities.)

General Works; Special Customs; Minhagim (see also Superstitions); Synagogue (see also Ecclesiastical Polity; Synagogue and Church); Reading of the Law. *Liturgies:* Works on the Liturgy; Collections of Liturgies; Daily Prayers (see also Christian Liturgies; Karaite Liturgies): Commentaries and Grammatical Notes, Rite of Reformed Jews; Saturday Prayers; Festival Prayers: Hagadah; Fastday Prayers: Lamentations; Benedictions; Occasional Prayers: Prayers for the Sick and the Dead (see also Folk-Medicine); Miscellaneous; Devotionals; Meditations; Private Hymnals; Readings; Synagogue Music.

HOMILETICAL LITERATURE.

(See also Agada.)

General Works (see also Exegetics). *Midrashim:* Collections of Midrashim; Midrash Raboth; Other Midrashim to Biblical Books; Other Midrashim (for Halachic Midrashim see Literature of the Mishna Period; for Kabbalistic Midrashim see Early Kabbalistic Literature); Yalkutim. *Sermons:* Sermons in Hebrew; Judæo-German; German; English; French; Italian; Other Languages; Slavic; Sabbath Sermons; Festival Sermons; Confirmation Sermons; Marriage Sermons; Funeral Sermons; Sermons on Other Occasions; Political and Patriotic.

ETHICS.

Works on Jewish Ethics; Aboth (see also Minor Treatises of the Talmud): Translations, Commentaries; Miscellaneous Writers; Judæo-German Writers; Judæo-Spanish Writers; Non-Jewish Writers; Special Subjects (see also Charity; Gentiles in Jewish Law); Etiquette (see also Massecheth Derech Erez [Minor Treatises of the Talmud]); Poetical Works; Maxims (see also Proverbs); Ethical Wills; Asceticism; Hortatory Theology.

DOCTRINAL THEOLOGY.

General Works; Ancient Judaism (see also Mythology; Idolatry [of the Ancient Hebrews]; Sacred Antiquities); Modern Judaism: Works in Modern Languages (see also Reformed Judaism); Manuals; Catechisms; Special Subjects: Eschatology (see also Sadducees; Pharisees), Restoration of the Jews (see also Palestine; Restoration of the Jews [in Christian Theology]; Zionism), The Messiah (see also Christianity); Judaism and Other Religions (see also Judaism and Christianity; Religions): Proselytism, Proselytes.

POST-TALMUDICAL SCHISMS AND DISSENSIONS.

General Works (see also Pre-Talmudical Sects); Works on the Karaites; Karaite Literature: Liturgies; Minor Sects; Reformed Judaism (see also Assimilation; Modern Jewish History): Works Against Reform, Works for Reform, Special Subjects (see also Rite of Reformed Jews); Dialogues, Irenics.

PHILOSOPHY.

(Works for and against the study of Philosophy go here.)

Terminology; Logic; General Works; Non-Jewish Philosophers; Alexandrian School (see also Philo Judæus); Saadiah; Gabirol; Judah ha-Levi; Maimonides; Other Philosophers; Spinoza; Modern Works; Psychology (for Modern Psychology see Psychology, *s.v.* Secular Sciences); Other Special Subjects.

KABBALA. CHASIDISM.

(Polemics against the Kabbala and works in its defense go here.)

General Works; Collections; Sefer Yezirah; Other Early Literature; Zohar; Later Literature; Miscellaneous (see also Transmigration); Sabbathai Zebi; Eybschuetz-Emden Controversy; Frank. *Chasidism:* Chasidaic Works; Chasidaic Legends.

FOLK-LORE.

General Works (see also Prophecy); Religions (except Judaism and Christianity) (see also Judaism and Other Religions); Mythology, Idolatry (of the Ancient Hebrews); Agada (see also Homiletical Literature): Indexes (see also Talmudical Works of Reference), Selections (see also Selections from the Talmud), Commentaries; Superstitions (see also Minhagim); Transmigration, Magic, Folk-Medicine (see also Prayers for the Sick), Other Special Subjects; Customs (see also Etiquette; Minhagim: Orach Chayim Laws; The Ritual); Games; Legends (see also The Blood Accusation; Chasadaic Legends): Wandering Jew; Tales (see also Fiction); Fables; Proverbs (see also Maxims); Riddles; Other Popular Literature.

BELLES-LETTRES.

(See also Dialects and Their Literatures.)

Hebrew: General works (see also History of Modern Literature); Collections; Selections (see also General Collections); Collected Works of Individual Authors (see also Collected Works of a General Character); Poetry (see also Ethical Poetry; Liturgies; Poetry of the Hebrew Bible; Prosody): Collections, Individual Mediæval Authors, Individual Modern Authors; Drama; Fiction; Humor and Satire; Parody; Miscellany. *Modern Languages:* General Works (see also Anti-Semitic Belles-Lettres; Delineation of the Jew in Literature); Poetry; Drama; Fiction Relating to Biblical Times; Fiction Relating to Modern Times; Humor and Satire; Miscellany.

DIALECTS AND THEIR LITERATURES. LANGUAGES.

(See also Aramaic; Foreign Terms Used in Post-Biblical Hebrew.)

Reserved for Dialects as yet Unrepresented in the Collection; Judæo-French; Judæo-Spanish (see also Codes in Judæo-Spanish); Judæo-German (for Bibliography see Bibliography, Subjects; for Literary History and Criticism see Bibliography and Literary History, Judæo-German): Dictionaries, Literary Periodicals (see also General Judæo-German Periodicals), Literary Collections (see also General Judæo-German Collections), Poetry (Collections), Poetry (Individual Authors), Fables, Drama, Stage, Fiction, Humor and Satire, Parodies, Miscellanies (see also Codes in Judæo-German; Devotionals for Women; Judæo-German Ethical Writers).

LANGUAGES.

Russian; English.

SECULAR SCIENCES.

(Works on the cultivation of the sciences among the Jews go here.)

General Works; Mathematics Among the Jews; Mathematical Works: Arithmetic; Other Mathematical Works; Astronomy (for Astrology see under Folk-Lore: Superstitions, Other Special Subjects); Works on the Calendar; Calendars; Natural Science; Natural History; Medicine Among the Jews; Physicians; Medical Works (see also Folk-Medicine); Hygiene; Psychology (for Metaphysical Psychology see Philosophy: Psychology); Music; Fine Arts; Useful Arts: Cookery, Book-Keeping, Commerce; Sociology and Economics; Socialism; Government; Law. (Other non-Jewish subjects are: Christianity; Games; Geography; History; Jewish Literature and Other Literatures; Judaism and Other Religions; Languages; Logic; Mythology; Philosophy; Religions; Travels; Wandering Jew.)

GEOGRAPHY. GENERAL HISTORY. BIOGRAPHY.

Geography: Biblical and Talmudical Geography; Palestine (see also Archæology; Jews in the Orient; Restoration of the Jews [in Christian Theology]; Restoration of the Jews [in Jewish Theology]; Zionism); Travels. *General History:* Special Countries; America; United States. *Non-Jewish Biography:* Non-Jewish Biography (Individual). *Jewish Biography:* Epitaphs (see also Inscriptions); Genealogy; Biographical Material (see also Bibliographies of Authors; Ethical Wills; Funeral Sermons; Legends; Legends of Chasidim; Names); Collective Biography (see also Converted Jews; O. T. Biography: Physicians; Talmudical Biography; Woman); Collections of Portraits; Individual Portraits; Individual Biography (see also Eybschuetz-Emden Controversy; Frank; Individual Converted Jews; Individual O. T. Biography; Individual Talmudists; Lives of Jesus; Proselytes; Sabbathai Zebi).

JEWISH HISTORY.

Periodicals; Societies; Collections; Historical Miscellanies (see also Archæology; Blood Accusation; Epitaphs; Karaism; Palestine; Travels); Josephus; Chronicles; General Jewish History.

DIVISION BY PERIODS.

Pentateuchal Traditions; Entire O. T. Period (for elementary works see Old Test. History, *s.v.* Hebrew Bible; see also Ancient Judaism; O. T. Biography; Prophecy: Ten Tribes); Return from Babylon to the Close of the Talmud (see also Pre-Talmudical Literature and Sects; Talmudical Biography and History); Middle Ages to the Latter Half of the 18th Century (see also Sabbathai Zebi; Eybschuetz-Emden Controversy); Modern (see also Chasidism; Emancipation; Reformed Judaism; Zionism).

DIVISION BY COUNTRIES.

(See also Bibliographies of Countries; Epitaphs.)

Orient (see also Palestine); Balkan Peninsula; Italy; Spain and Portugal (see also Judæo-Spanish); France (see also Judæo-French); Great Britain; Minor European Countries; Germany; Austria-Hungary; Poland; Russia; America; United States and Canada; Other Countries.

THE JEWISH RACE ETHNOLOGICALLY AND SOCIOLOGICALLY.

General Works; Anthropology; Ethnology (see also Assimilation); Ten Tribes (see also History of the O. T. Period); Circumcision (for the Halacha of this subject see Other Special Laws, *s.v.* Halacha, for the Liturgies see under Occasional Prayers); Dietary Laws (for the Halacha of this subject see under Halacha); Woman (see also Codes in Judæo-German; Devotionals for Women; Eben ha-Ezer Laws; Purification); Statistics; Occupations; Trades; Commerce; Agriculture (see also Social and Economic Conditions of the Ancient Hebrews); Trade Unions (see also Socialism); Mutual Aid Associations; Communal Organization (see also Synagogue); Charity; Crime; Education (see also Hebrew Readers; Letter-Writers; Post-Biblical Hebrew Readers; Elementary O. T. Histories; Elementary Works on Judaism): Educational Institutions (see also Libraries).

JEWS AND GENTILES.

(Works of this class relating to the Jews of a particular country go with the history of the Jews in that country, an exception being made in the 7th [Blood Accusation] and last two sections in this division, which take *all* works relating to those subjects.)

General Works; Delineation of the Jew in Literature and Art (see also Belles-Lettres; Jews in Christian Theology; Wandering Jew); Works on Anti-Semitism; Anti-Semitic Writings (see also Unfavorable Criticism of the Oral Tradition); Anti-Semitic Belles-Lettres; Gentiles in Jewish Law and Literature; The Blood Accusation; Apologetic Writings (see also Apologetics of Judaism Against Christianity; Apologies of the Oral Tradition); The Jewish Question: Various Solutions, Toleration, Emancipation (see also Modern Jewish History), Assimilation and Mixed Marriages (see also Ethnology; Reformed Judaism), Zionism (see also Jews in the Orient; Palestine; Restoration of the Jews [in Christian Theology]; Restoration of the Jews [in Jewish Theology]).

BIBLIOGRAPHY: Steinschneider, *Vorlesungen über die Kunde Hebräischer Handschriften*, in *Beihefte zum Centralblatt für Bibliothekswesen*, vii., Leipsic, 1897; Blau, *Studien zum Althebräischen Buchwesen*, Budapest, 1902; Schwab, *The Library of the Alliance Israélite Universelle*, in *Jewish Comment*, June, 1904.

G.

LIBYA: District in the north of Africa. The name "Libya" was often used by the ancients, sometimes to designate the whole of northern Africa (with the exception of Egypt), sometimes to denote a single province west of Egypt. According to Josephus ("Ant." i. 6, § 2), Libya was founded by Phut (comp. Gen. x. 6), and the eponymous hero Libys was a son of Mesraios, *i.e.*, of Egypt. Another old tradition says that Eofres (*i.e.*, Epher; Gen. xxv. 4) conquered Libya and that the land was called "Africa" after him (Josephus, *l.c.* i. 15; comp. Eusebius, "Præparatio Evangelica," ix. 20, § 2; "Chronicon Paschale," i. 66; Suidas, *s.v.* Ἄφροι; "Yuḥasin," ed. London, p. 233).

The Biblical data are more historical. Shishak (Shoshank), whose name is claimed to be Libyan, had Libyans in his army (A. V. "Lubims," II Chron. xii. 3); King Asa defeated a whole army of Cushites and Libyans (*ib.* xvi. 8; comp. xiv. 11); and the celebrated Egyptian Thebes also had Libyans in its pay (Nahum iii. 9). In all these passages the Septuagint has Λίβυες. In Dan. xi. 43, Egyptians, Libyans, and Cushites appear together.

In the Greco-Roman period Libya coincided approximately with Cyrene and the territory belonging to it. Jews lived there ("Ant." xvi. 6, § 1); and Augustus granted them certain privileges through Flavius, the governor of the province (*ib.* § 5). The Christian apostles also prepared themselves to extend their mission into Libya (Acts ii. 10). The great Jewish war of the year 70 had its aftermath in Libya; and the rebellious Jonathan was denounced to the governor of the Libyan Pentapolis (Josephus, "B. J." vii. 11, § 1). The Jews of Libya also took part in the rebellion under Trajan and Hadrian (see CYRENE).

Modern investigation is inclined to connect Lehabim (Gen. x. 13; I Chron. i. 11) with the Libyans, as did the Jerusalem Targum in rendering it by the Greek Λιβυκοί. Many proselytes came from Libya (Yer. Shab. 7b; Yer. Kil. 31c); hence Judaism must have carried on its propaganda there. The Rabbis mention beans (Löw, "Aramäische Pflanzennamen," p. 234) and asses from Libya (Bek. 5b; Shab. 51b).

The once flourishing province corresponds to the present Barka, which, under Islamic dominion, has become a desert.

BIBLIOGRAPHY: Knobel, *Die Völkertafel der Genesis*, pp. 282, 295-305, Giessen, 1850; Boettger, *Topographisch-Historisches Lexicon zu den Schriften des Flavius Josephus*, p. 163; Kohut, *Aruch Completum*, v. 5.

G. S. KR.

LICHTENBERG, CORNEL: Hungarian aurist; born in 1848 at Szegedin; studied at Budapest and Vienna (M.D. 1873). On receiving his degree he returned to Budapest, where he established himself at the university as docent in diseases of the ear (1883). The same year he was one of the founders of the polyclinic, of which institution he was appointed director in 1891. In recognition of his services he was decorated in 1895 with the "Ritter-Kreuz" of the Order of Francis Joseph.

Lichtenberg is the author of: "Az Ideges Süketség" (Budapest, 1879), on nervous deafness; "Ueber Subjective Gehörsempfindungen" (*ib.* 1882); and "Ein Fremdkörper im Ohre mit Cerebralen Erscheinungen" (*ib.* 1883).

BIBLIOGRAPHY: *Pallas Lex.*; Szinnyei, *Magyar Irók Elete.*

S. L. V.

LICHTENBERG, LEOPOLD: Violinist; born at San Francisco, Cal., Nov. 22, 1861. He studied under Beaujardin, and made his first appearance in concert when eight years of age. At twelve he became a pupil of Wieniawski, whom he accompanied on a tour through the United States. Some time afterward he spent six months in Paris under Lambert, and then rejoined Wieniawski at Brussels, where he studied unremittingly for three years. After winning the prize at the national "concours" held at Brussels, he made a successful tour through Holland. Upon his return to America he played with Theodor Thomas' orchestra in New York, and gave a number of recitals in other cities. After spending three years more in Europe Lichtenberg gave another series of concerts in America, after which he settled for some time in Boston, Mass., as a member of the Symphony Society. He next went to New York city to take charge of the department of violin at the National Conservatory. His fine technique and beautiful tone entitle him to high rank among violinists.

BIBLIOGRAPHY: Baker, *Biographical Dictionary of Musicians.*

A. J. So.

LICHTENFELD, GABRIEL JUDAH: Polish mathematician and author; born at Lublin 1811; died at Warsaw March 22, 1887. He was a descendant of Moses Isserles, and, true to the family tradition, showed early ability as a Talmudic scholar. He later became familiar with Latin, German, French, and Polish, and made a special study of philosophy and mathematics.

In the Hebrew periodical "Ha-Shaḥar," vol. iii. *et seq.*, there appeared a series of Hebrew articles by Lichtenfeld which attracted attention. His reputation was enhanced by his series of articles, in the Polish periodical "Izraelita," on Jewish mathematicians. Lichtenfeld is known also by his polemics with Slonimski on mathematical subjects.

Lichtenfeld was the author of: "Yedi'ot ha-Shi'urim" (Warsaw, 1865); "Ẓofnat Pa'neaḥ" (*ib.* 1874), a critical review of S. Slonimski's "Yesode Ḥokmat ha-Shi'ur"; "Tosefot" (*ib.* 1875), polemic against S. Slonimski; "Kohen Lelo Elohim" (*ib.* 1876), mathematical criticisms; "Sippurim be-Shir," etc. (*ib.* 1877), a collection of poems and rimed prose by himself and by his son-in-law Leon Peretz.

BIBLIOGRAPHY: Fuenn, *Keneset Yisrael*, ii. 356; Zeitlin, *Bibl. Post-Mendels.* p. 209.

H. R. J. G. L.

LICHTENSTADT, MOSES ABIGDOR: Polish Hebraist and Talmudist; born at Lublin, Russian Poland, July 15, 1787; died at Odessa Jan. 17, 1870. He was noted as well for his charities, especially in assisting poor students, as for his Biblical and Talmudic scholarship. He was one of the founders of the public school for Jewish children at Odessa. He contributed a number of articles on Biblical and Talmudic subjects to "Ha-Meliẓ," "Ha-Karmel," and "Ha-Maggid," and wrote "Mi-Moḥorat ha-Shabbat" (Vienna, 1860), on Pentecost, directed against the Karaites.

BIBLIOGRAPHY: *Ha-Meliẓ*, 1870, p. 19; Gottlober, in *Ha-Maggid*, 1864, p. 212; Zedner, *Cat. Hebr. Books Brit. Mus.* p. 436.

H. R. A. S. W.

LICHTENSTADT (LASH, from the Hebrew abbreviation ל״ש**), SIMEON BEN JUDAH:** Bohemian Talmudist; lived at Prague in the first half of the nineteenth century. He was the author of "Shesh ha-Ma'arakah," a commentary on the six Mishnaic orders, each order having a separate title as follows: (1) "Derek Emunah" (Presburg, 1840); (2) "Dabar be-'Itto" (*ib.* 1841); (3) "Ḥosen Rab" (*ib.* 1843), preceded by a sermon delivered at Prague on the first of the Penitential Days, 1836; (4) "Ma'yan ha-Yeshu'ah" (*ib.* 1846); (5) "Ḥokmat Adam" (Prague, 1852).

BIBLIOGRAPHY: Benjacob, *Oẓar ha-Sefarim*, p. 612, No. 1309; Fürst, *Bibl. Jud.* ii. 245, s.v. *Lichtenstadt.*

S. S. M. SEL.

LICHTENSTEIN, HILLEL: Hungarian rabbi; born at Vecs 1815; died at Kolomea, Galicia, May 18, 1891. After studying at the yeshibah of Moses Sofer he married, in 1837, the daughter of a well-to-do resident of Galantha, where he remained until 1850, when he was elected rabbi of Margarethen (Szent Margit). In 1854 he was elected rabbi of Klausenburg, but the opposition of the district rabbi, Abraham Friedmann, made it impossible for him to enter upon the duties of the office; finally he was expelled from Klausenburg by the authorities. Having lived for some time at Grosswardein, he was recalled to Margarethen, where he remained until about 1865, when he was called to Szikszo. Thence he went, in 1867, to Kolomea, where he remained until his death. Lichtenstein was the outspoken leader of the Orthodox extremists in Hungary: he not only resisted the slightest deviation from the traditional ritual, as the removal of the ALMEMAR from the center of the synagogue, but even vigorously denounced the adoption of modern social manners and the acquisition of secular education. He bitterly opposed the Hungarian Jewish congress of 1868–69 and the establishment of the rabbinical seminary in Budapest. In 1865 he called a rabbinical convention at Nagy-Mihaly, which protested against the founding of a seminary and sent a committee to the emperor to induce the government to prohibit its establishment. In his religious practise he surpassed the rigorism of the most Orthodox Hungarian rabbis, even going so far as to keep a she ass in order to be able to fulfil the law of the redemption of the first-born of the ass (see Ex. xiii. 13). He kept a sheep also in order to be able to give the first fleece to a kohen (Deut. xviii. 4), from whom subsequently he bought it back to make ẓiẓit from it. Lichtenstein was an ardent admirer of the Ḥasidim and made pilgrimages to the famous miracle-worker Ḥayyim Halberstam of Sandec. He offered his own intercession through prayer to people in distress, but declined any gifts.

Lichtenstein was a powerful preacher and a popular writer, and the resistance to modern tendencies among the Jews of northern Hungary is largely due to his influence. He inveighed against the use of other than traditional Jewish names; he denounced not only secular education, but even the playing of musical instruments and innocent social games, like chess and checkers; and he condemned those who relied on reason, for the ideal Jew should live up to the principle of Psalm lxxiii. 22, "I was as a beast before thee" ("'Et la-'Asot," p. 118a, Lemberg, 1881). He was a decided opponent also of all agitation for the political emancipation of the Jews, saying that it is the duty of the Jews to suffer the tribulations of the Exile until God finds them ripe for Messianic redemption.

Of the numerous works which Lichtenstein wrote, some of them being in Hebrew and others in Judæo-German, the most important are "Maskil el Dal" (Lemberg, 1867), "'Et la-'Asot" (*ib.* 1881), and "Abḳat Rokel" (*ib.* 1883), all of which have been repeatedly reedited. They are all devoted to the denunciation of liberal Judaism. In Hebrew Hillel signs his name ל״ש (Lash), which is an abbreviation for ליכטענשטיין (Lichtenstein).

BIBLIOGRAPHY: Hirsch Heller, *Bet Hillel*, Munkacs, 1893.

S. D.

LICHTHEIM, LUDWIG: German physician; born Dec. 7, 1845, at Breslau, where he was educated at the gymnasium. He then studied medicine at the universities of Berlin, Zurich, and Breslau, graduating in 1868. From 1869 to 1872 he was assistant in the medical hospital at Breslau; from 1872 to 1873 in the surgical hospital at Halle; and from 1873 to 1877 again at Breslau in the medical polyclinic. He became privat-docent at Breslau University in 1876; assistant professor at Jena in 1877; was called in 1878 to Bern University as professor of medicine and chief of the medical clinic; and has held a similar position since 1888 in the University of Königsberg.

Lichtheim has written many essays in the medical journals, among which may be mentioned: "Ueber Behandlung Pleuritischer Exsudate," in "Sammlung Klinischer Vorträge," 1872; (with Cohnheim) "Ueber Hydrämie und Hydrämisches Oedem," in Virchow's "Archiv," lxix.; "Ueber Periodische Haemoglobinurie," in "Sammlung Klinischer Vorträge," 1878; "Die Antipyretische Wirkung des Phenols," in "Breslauer Aerztliche Zeitschrift," 1881; "Ueber Tuberkulose," in "Rapport des Kongresses für Innere Medizin," 1883; "Die Chronischen Herzmuskelerkrankungen und Ihre Behandlung," *ib.* 1888; "Zur Diagnose der Meningitis," in "Berliner Klinische Wochenschrift," 1895. He is the author also of "Die Störungen des Lungenkreislaufs und Ihr Einfluss auf den Blutdruck" (Berlin, 1876).

BIBLIOGRAPHY: Pagel, *Biog. Lex.* Vienna, 1901.

S. F. T. H.

LICHTSCHEIN, LUDWIG: Hungarian rabbi; born in Komorn; died at Ofen in 1886. He studied at Papa, and was rabbinical assessor of Austerlitz, Gross Kanizsa, and Esztergom. From 1876 until his death he was rabbi at Somogy-Csurgó.

Lichtschein was the author of the following works: "A Zsidók Közép és Jelenkori Helyzetök" (Gross Kanizsa, 1866), on the condition of the Jews in medieval and modern times; "Die Dreizehn Glaubensartikel" (Brünn, 1870), a sermon; "Der Targum zu den Propheten" (in Stern's "Ha-Meḥaḳḳer," i.); "Der Talmud und der Socialismus" (*ib.* iii.); "Kossuth Lajos és a Sátoraljaúhelyi Rabbi" (in "Magyar Zsidó Szémle," 1885), on Kossuth and the rabbi of Sátoralja-Ujhely.

BIBLIOGRAPHY: Petrik, *Könyvészet*; Szinnyei, *Magyar Irók*; Lippe, *Biographisches Lexikon*, i. 288.

S. L. V.

LICHTSTEIN, ABRAHAM B. ELIEZER LIPMAN: Polish rabbi and author; lived at the end of the eighteenth and at the beginning of the nineteenth century; grandson of R. Kalman of Byelostok. He was rabbi and preacher at Prassnysz, in the government of Plotzk, Poland.

Lichtstein was the author of "Kanfe Nesharim," a commentary on the Pentateuch in several parts, each having a separate name, viz.: "Ḳiryat Sefer," an introduction to each book of the Pentateuch; "To-'aliyyot ha-Ralbag," treating of the doctrines deduced by Levi b. Gershon from passages of the Torah; "Abaḳ Soferim," miscellanea; "Maḥazeh Abraham," consisting of sermons on each section of the Torah; "Ner Miẓwah," treating of the number of the precepts according to Maimonides; "Shiyyure Miẓwah," treating of the additional precepts according to Naḥmanides, Moses b. Jacob of Coucy, and Isaac of Corbeil; "Milḥemet Miẓwah," on the disputes among various authorities concerning the numbering of the precepts by Maimonides; "Torat ha-Ḳorbanot," on the Levitical laws of offerings and on the order of the high priest's service in the sanctuary on the Day of Atonement; and "Sha'are Ẓiyyon," orations on theological subjects. The whole work was published together with the text of the Pentateuch, Josefow, 1829, and republished without the text, Wilna, 1894. Lichtstein was the author also of a commentary on the "Sefer ha-Tappuaḥ" which was published together with the text in the Grodno edition of 1799.

BIBLIOGRAPHY: *Kanfe Nesharim*, 2d edition; Benjacob, *Oẓar ha-Sefarim*, pp. 636, 660.

S. S. N. T. L.

LICHTSTEIN, ABRAHAM JEKUTHIEL SALMAN BEN MOSES JOSEPH: Rabbi of Plonsk, government of Warsaw, in the eighteenth century. He was the author of a work entitled "Zera' Abraham" (Dyhernfurth, 1811), a commentary on the Sifre, followed by Biblical and Talmudical indexes, and accompanied with the text. Lichtstein wrote also a preface and added a homily to his son's "Shoshannat 'Amaḳim."

BIBLIOGRAPHY: Walden, *Shem ha-Gedolim he-Ḥadash*, i. 15; Steinschneider, *Cat. Bodl.* col. 699; Zedner, *Cat. Hebr. Books Brit. Mus.* p. 437.

S. S. M. Sel.

LIEBEN, ADOLF: Austrian chemist; born at Vienna Dec. 3, 1836. He studied at the universities of Vienna, Heidelberg (Ph.D. 1856), and Paris, and subsequently held the positions of privat-docent at the University of Vienna (1861), and professor in the universities of Palermo (1863), Turin (1867), and Prague (1871). Since 1875 he has held the chair of general and pharmacological chemistry at the University of Vienna, and is a member of the Vienna Academy of Sciences.

Lieben has published many essays in "Liebig's Annalen der Chemie" ("Ueber die Einwirkung Schwacher Affinitäten auf Aldehyd," 1861; "Ueber das Iodbenzol," 1869; "Ueber Festes-Benzoylchlorid," 1875; etc.), "Sitzungsberichte den Kaiserlichen Akademie der Wissenschaften in Wien" ("Untersuchungen über Milchzucker," "Einwirkung von Cyangus auf Aldehyd," "Ueber den Formaldehyd und dessen Umwandlung in Methylalkohl," "Reduction des Exotonchlorals," etc.), "Monatshefte für Chemie," "Comptes-Rendus de l'Académie de Paris," "Berichte der Deutschen Chemischen Gesellschaft Berlin," "Gazzetta Chimica Italiana Palermo," etc.

S. F. T. H.

LIEBERMANN, AARON (ARTHUR FREEMAN): Russian writer; born at Wilna about 1840. Persecuted because of his participation in revolutionary movements, he fled to America, and died by his own hand at Syracuse, N. Y., Nov. 8, 1880. He was the editor of "Ha-Emet," a Hebrew monthly of communistic tendencies (Vienna, 1877), only the prospectus and two numbers of which appeared; and he was the first to organize socialist societies among the Jews in London.

Bibliography: Zeitlin, *Bibl. Post-Mendels.* p. 211.

D. S. Man.

LIEBERMANN, BENJAMIN: German manufacturer; born at Märkisch Friedland Feb. 4, 1812; died in Berlin Jan. 15, 1901. In 1825 his family moved to the latter city; and Liebermann, after completing a school course, entered the employ of a firm in London. Upon his return to Berlin he was taken into his father's business, which he soon developed into the largest calico-manufactory in Germany. That his ability was recognized is shown by the fact that he was elected to the presidency of the German merchants' association (Deutscher Handelstag). According to an anecdote he introduced himself to King Frederick William IV. as "the Liebermann who drove the Englishmen from the Continental calico market." For many years he held the office of president of the Gesellschaft der Freunde, and he was treasurer of the Lehranstalt für die Wissenschaft des Judenthums at the time of its foundation.

Bibliography: *Allg. Zeit. des Jud.* Jan. 25, 1901; *Mittheilungen aus dem Verein zur Bekämpfung des Antisemitismus*, 1901, p. 29.

S. D.

LIEBERMANN (LIBERMANN), ELIEZER: Talmudist of the first half of the nineteenth century. According to G. Wolf, in his biography of Isaac Noah Mannheimer (p. 10, Note), he was a native of Austria; Jost ("Culturgesch." iii. 24) says that he pretended to be a Hungarian rabbi; but in the preface to "Or Nogah," Liebermann signs himself "son of Zeeb Wolf, rabbi of Hennegau" (probably Hagenau, Alsace). He was the agent of the patrons of the Reform Temple at Hamburg, in defense of which he published "Nogah ha-Ẓedeḳ," a collection of the views of Shem-Ṭob Samun of Leghorn, R. Jacob Vita Ricanati of Pesaro, R. Moses Kunitz, or Kunitzer, of Budapest, and R. Aaron Chorin of Arad. The indorsement by the rabbinates of Leghorn and Jerusalem, which was added to that of Shem-Ṭob Samun, was afterward declared to be fictitious.

The "Nogah ha-Ẓedeḳ" was followed by "Or Nogah" (Dessau, 1818), in which Liebermann gives a lengthy and learned exposition of his own views in favor of Reform. It is prefaced by two eulogistic poems, one from Chorin and another signed "Ze'ebi." In refutation of this book the Hamburg rabbinate published "Eleh Dibre ha-Berit," a collection of the views of prominent Orthodox rabbis, and containing a declaration of Aaron Chorin revoking his former opinion (Altona, 1819). On the title-page of "Or Nogah" Liebermann claims the authorship of "'Ir Dammeseḳ," which work does not seem to have been printed.

In 1819 Liebermann traveled in Austria to propagate Reform ideas and, according to the statement of the chief of police Sedlnitzky, to found for that purpose a journal called "Syonia." Nothing else is known of Liebermann's life. According to Wolf and Graetz, Liebermann became a convert to Roman Catholicism; but there is nothing positive to corroborate this assertion.

Bibliography: Fürst, *Bibl. Jud.* ii. 248; Grätz, *Gesch.* xi. 420-424, Leipsic, 1870; Jost, *Culturgesch.* iii. 24-25, Berlin, 1847; Schreiber, *Reformed Judaism*, pp. 76-77, Spokane, 1892; Steinschneider, *Cat. Bodl.* col. 964; Moses Sofer, *Responsa*, vi. 91.

D. S. Man.

LIEBERMANN, ELIEZER DOB: Russian writer; born in Pilvischok, government of Suwalki, April 12, 1820; died in Byelostok April 15, 1895. His father was a shoḥeṭ and gave him the usual Jewish education. At the age of twelve he was sent to his uncle R. Elijah Schick ("Reb Elinke Lider"), then rabbi of Amstibove, who instructed him in Talmud and rabbinical literature. In 1838 he went to Wilna and joined the Maskilim; about 1844 he settled as a teacher in Byelostok; in 1867 he removed to Suwalki, remained there about twenty years, and then returned to Byelostok. Liebermann is the author of "Megillat Sefer," a collection of short stories, essays, fables, and letters (Johannisberg, 1854), and of "Ẓedeḳ u-Mishpaṭ," a Hebrew adaptation of S. D. Luzzatto's "Lezioni di Teologia Morale Israelitica" (Wilna, 1867). He wrote also "Ge Ḥizzayon" (Warsaw, 1889), several works still in manuscript, and a number of articles which he published in various Hebrew periodicals.

Bibliography: *Aḥiasaf*, vol. iii. (necrologies, in which he is erroneously called "Jacob"); Sokolov, *Sefer Zikkaron*, pp. 57-58, Warsaw, 1890; Zeitlin, *Bibl. Hebr. Post-Mendels.* p. 211.

H. R. P. Wi.

LIEBERMANN, FELIX: German historian; born July 20, 1851, in Berlin. Destined for a commercial career, he began business life in a Berlin bank in 1869. There he remained for some time, but ultimately went to England, going to Manchester in 1871. Not very long afterward he returned to Germany, where he devoted himself almost exclusively to the study of early English constitutional history under Waitz and Pauli, at Göttingen.

On this subject he has published several monographs, beginning with "Anglonormannische Geschichtsquellen" (Berlin, 1879) and culminating in his monumental edition of the "Gesetze der Angelsachsen" (Berlin, 1898–1903; published by the Savigny Fund). Many of the essays contained in this great work had been published previously by Liebermann, either separately (*e.g.*, "Quadripartitus," 1893; "Leges Edwardi," 1896; etc.) or in journals, as the "English Historical Review," "Transactions of the Royal Historical Society," etc. He contributes an annual review of the publications on English medieval history to the "Jahresbericht für Geschichtswissenschaft." In recognition of his contributions to English history the University of Cambridge conferred upon him the honorary degree of LL.D. (1899), and the Prussian government the title of professor.

BIBLIOGRAPHY: Kürschner, *Deutscher Literatur-Kalender*; C. Gross, *Sources of English History*, 1900, p. 589.

J.

LIEBERMANN, MATTATHIAS BEN ASHER LEMLE: Rabbi and preacher in Prague in the second half of the seventeenth century; died there 1709. He was the author of "Mattat Yah," a collection of sermons on the Pentateuch, reaching only to Numbers xxxiii. (Frankfort-on-the-Oder, 1696). Another collection of sermons by him, entitled "Peri Megadim," is preserved in manuscript.

BIBLIOGRAPHY: Azulai, *Shem ha-Gedolim*; Benjacob, *Ozar ha-Sefarim*, pp. 390, 495; Fürst, *Bibl. Jud.* ii. 248; Steinschneider, *Cat. Bodl.* col. 1682; Hock, *Die Familien Prags*, p. 397, Presburg, 1892.

D. S. MAN.

LIEBERMANN, MAX: German painter; born at Berlin July 29, 1849. After studying law at Berlin University for a year, he abandoned it and took up the study of painting at Weimar in 1869 under Thumann and Pawels. In 1872 he went to Paris, and during 1876–77 resided in Holland; after living for some time in Munich he finally returned to Berlin.

His paintings include: "Gänserupferinnen"; "Amsterdamer Waisenmädchen"; "Das Tischgebet"; "Strasse in Zandvoort"; "Kleinkinderschule in Amsterdam"; "Münchner Bierkonzert"; "Die Spinnerinnen"; "Die Konservenmacherinnen"; "Stille Arbeit"; "Die Schweinefamilie"; "Altmännerhaus in Amsterdam"; "Trauergottesdienst"; "Holländische Dorfstrasse"; "Der Weber"; "Netzeflickerinnen"; "Spitalgarten in Leiden"; "Biergarten in München"; "Flachsscheuer in Holland"; "Frau mit Ziegen"; "Bürgermeister Petersen"; "Viehmarkt in Haarlem." Some of these works are in private collections; others are in the Kunsthalle, Hamburg; the Nationalgallerie, Berlin; the Neue Pinakothek, Munich; the Strasburg Museum; the Leipsic Museum; and various other public galleries of Europe.

Max Liebermann.

Liebermann at first expressed the extreme tendencies of the modern realistic school, and illustrated the darker sides of life; his earlier works were exhibited in Paris in 1875, 1876, and 1877 ("Runkelrübenernte," "Arbeitssaal im Amsterdamer Waisenhaus," etc.), and at Munich in 1879 ("Jesus im Tempel"). In later years, however, he has turned toward the naturalistic school, producing a number of genre paintings and expositions of Dutch rural life. He has excelled also as an etcher. Liebermann won medals at the Berlin, Munich, and Paris (1889) expositions.

BIBLIOGRAPHY: Kämmerer, *Max Liebermann*, Leipsic, 1893; *Meyers Konversations-Lexikon*; *Allgemeines Künstler-Lexicon*, Frankfort-on-the-Main, 1898.

S. F. T. H.

LIEBERMANN'SCHE JAHRBUCH, DAS. See YEAR-BOOKS.

LIEBLING, EMIL: German pianist; born at Pless, Silesia, April 12, 1851. After a course in piano at the Neue Akademie der Tonkunst, Berlin, under Ehrlich and Kullak, he continued his studies with Dachs at Vienna and with Liszt at Weimar. In 1867 he went to America, where, until 1871, he taught music in a Kentucky seminary. In 1874 he revisited Europe and spent the summer at Weimar with Liszt. Upon his return to America he settled at Chicago, where he has since established a high reputation as pianist, teacher, and composer. Liebling has played in New York, Chicago, and other cities, and has made concert tours with Wilhelmj, Miss Cary, Miss Kellogg, and others.

The following are a few of Liebling's principal compositions: "Gavotte Moderne," Op. 11; "Florence Valse," Op. 12; "Albumblatt," Op. 18; two romances, Op. 20 and 21; "Cradle Song," Op. 23; "Canzonetta," Op. 26; "Mazurka de Concert," Op. 30; and several songs.

BIBLIOGRAPHY: Champlin, *Cyclopedia of Music and Musicians*, s.v.

A. J. So.

LIEBRECHT, FELIX: German folklorist; born at Namslau, Silesia, March 13, 1812; died at St. Hubert Aug. 3, 1890. He studied philology at the universities of Breslau, Munich, and Berlin, and in 1849 became professor of the German language at the Athénée Royal at Liége, Belgium. He resigned his chair and retired into private life in 1867. The following translations by him may be mentioned: Giambattista Basiles, "Pentamerone," with introduction by Jakob Grimm (Berlin, 1846); Johannes Damascenus, "Baarlam und Josaphat" (Münster, 1847); Dunlop, "Gesch. der Prosadichtung" (Berlin, 1851); an edition of Gervasius of Tilbury's "Otia Imperialia" (Hanover, 1856). A collection of original essays by him was published at Heilbronn in 1879, under the title "Zur Volkskunde."

BIBLIOGRAPHY: *Meyers Konversations-Lexikon.*

S. F. T. H.

LIEBREICH, OSKAR MATTHIAS EUGEN: German physician and pharmacologist; born at Königsberg, East Prussia, Feb. 14, 1839;

younger brother of Richard LIEBREICH. He studied first chemistry in Wiesbaden and Berlin and then, after nearly two years in Africa, medicine at the universities of Tübingen, Königsberg, and Berlin, graduating as doctor of medicine in 1865. In 1867 he became assistant at the pathological institute of Berlin University, and in 1868 joined the medical faculty of the same university as privat-docent in pharmacology. He was elected assistant professor in 1868 and appointed professor and chief of the pharmacological institute in 1872. In 1891 he received the title of "Geheime Medicinalrath."

Liebreich has added many new remedies to the pharmacopœia. In 1869 he discovered the narcotic effect of chloral hydrate; in 1873 he introduced platin-iridium cannulas for the hypodermic syringe; he showed the anesthetic effect of ethylene chlorid and butyl chlorid, the use of hydrargyrum formamidatum in the treatment of syphilis, the healing properties of lanolin (1885), of erythrophlein (1888), of cantharidin (1891), of creosol, tolipyrin, formalin, methylene blue, and many other drugs. He is a prolific writer, and has written many essays and monographs on his discoveries; especially noteworthy are those on: the presence of protogon in the brain as the chief chemical compound of phosphorus, the examination of lupus through phaneroscopic illumination, the use of strychnin as an antidote for chloral hydrate, the oxidation of neurin and the synthesis of oxyneurin (both discovered by him). His writings are very diverse; they deal not only with chemistry and pharmacology, but also with syphilology, dermatology, hygiene, and balneology. Since 1887 he has edited the "Therapeutische Monatshefte."

Liebreich is the author also of: "Das Chloralhydrat, ein Neues Hypnotikum," Berlin, 1869 (3d ed. 1871); "Encyclopädie der Therapie," *ib.* 1895; with Langgaard, "Kompendium der Arzneiverordnung," 5th ed. *ib.* 1900.

BIBLIOGRAPHY: Pagel, *Biog. Lex.*

S. F. T. H.

LIEBREICH, RICHARD: English ophthalmologist; born at Königsberg, East Prussia, June 30, 1830; brother of Oskar Liebreich. He received his education at the universities of Königsberg, Berlin, and Halle (M.D. 1853). After a postgraduate course at Utrecht under Donders, and at Berlin under Brücke, he became assistant in the ophthalmological institute of Berlin University from 1854 to 1862. In the latter year he established himself as an ophthalmologist in Paris, whence he removed to London in 1870. There he became lecturer and clinicist in ophthalmology at St. Thomas' Hospital.

Since about 1895 he has given up his hospital duties and reduced his private practise, spending most of his time in researches in art, especially the technique of the old masters.

Liebreich has constructed two ophthalmoscopes, which are universally used—a larger one, more elaborate and heavy, and a portable one. The latter especially supplied a long-felt want. Following Helmholtz's invention, Liebreich added two convex lenses to the small concave reflex mirror.

Of Liebreich's writings may be mentioned: "Atlas der Ophthalmoskopie," Berlin, 1863 (3d ed. 1885); "Ophthalmoskopische Notizen," in Albrecht von Graefe's "Archiv für Ophthalmologie," i., iv., v., vii.; "Ein Fall von Scheinbarer Myopie, Bedingt Durch Accommodationskrampf," *ib.* viii.; "Modification des Schieloperation," *ib.* xii.; (with Laqueur) "Recueil des Travaux de la Société Médicale Allemande de Paris," Paris, 1865; "Eine Neue Methode der Cataractextraction," Berlin, 1872; "On the Use and Abuse of Atropin," London, 1873; "Clinical Lecture on Convergent Squint," *ib.* 1874; "School Life in Its Influence on Sight and Figure," *ib.* 1877 (2d ed. 1878).

BIBLIOGRAPHY: Pagel, *Biog. Lex.*

J. F. T. H.

LIEGNITZ. See SILESIA.

LIEN. See MORTGAGE OR HYPOTHEC.

LIFE.—Biblical Data: The word "ḥayyim" (= "life") denotes first of all the animal existence which, according to Scripture, begins when "the breath [or spirit] of God" ("ruaḥ," "neshamah," or "nefesh") is first inhaled through the nostrils (Gen. i. 30, ii. 7, vii. 22; Job xxxiii. 4), and ceases when God withdraws His breath (Ps. civ. 29, cxlvi. 4; Job xxxiv. 14; Eccl. xii. 7). Life is the gracious gift of God (Job x. 12; Ps. xxx. 6 [A. V. 5]); with God is "the fountain of life" (Ps. xxxvi. 10 [A. V. 9]). Physical life is valued by the Hebrew as a precious good, given that he may "walk before God in the land [or "in the light"] of the living" (Ps. lvi. 14 [A. V. 13], cxvi. 9; comp. Isa. xxxviii. 11; Job xxxiii. 30). A long life, in ancient times, was regarded as the reward of virtue and piety (Ex. xx. 12; Deut. xxii. 7, xxxii. 47; Ps. xxxiv. 16; Prov. iii. 2, iv. 10, ix. 11, xii. 28, xxi. 21). The expressions "fountain of life" and "tree of life" (Prov. xi. 30, xiii. 12, xv. 4) point to the paradise legend (Gen. ii. 9–10) and possibly refer to a higher life. The brevity of life is a theme frequently dwelt upon by the poets (Ps. xxxix. 6 [A. V. 5], xc. 9–10, ciii. 15; Job ix. 5, xiv. 1 2).

But it is the ethical view of life which is chiefly characteristic of Judaism. Life is sacred, and it should accordingly be guarded and treated with due regard and tenderness in every being, man or beast (Gen. ix. 6; Lev. xix. 16; Deut. xxii. 7, xxv. 4; see CRUELTY). The "righteous man regardeth the life of his beast" (Prov. xii. 10). The whole Law is summed up in the words: "I have set before you life and death, blessing and cursing; therefore choose life" (Deut. xxx. 19); and the law of conduct toward others is stated in the words: "Let thy brother live with thee" (Lev. xxv. 35–36, Hebr.). The entire object of the Law is the preservation of life: "Ye shall keep my statutes and my ordinances, which if a man do he shall live by [A. V. "in"] them" (Lev. xviii. 4, Hebr.).

——**In Rabbinical Literature:** The same appreciative view of physical, or earthly, life prevails also among the Rabbis. A long life is regarded as Heaven's reward for certain virtues (Meg. 27b, 28a; Ber. 54b, 55a; Men. 44a; Yoma 87a). "He who performs only one meritorious act will have his life prolonged" (Ḳid. i. 10, 39b). "The object of the Law is the preservation of life, and not its destruction"; hence, ordinarily, one should rather transgress a commandment than incur death; only in regard to the three capital sins—idolatry, murder, and incest —should man give up his life rather than desecrate God's law (Sifra, Aḥare Mot, xiii.). "Better to extinguish the light on Sabbath than to extinguish life, which is God's light" (Shab. 30b).

"Ḥayye 'olam" (eternal life; Dan. xii. 2; Enoch, xxxvii. 4, xl. 9) occurs often in rabbinical terminology as "ḥayye 'olam ha-ba" (the life of the world to come; Tosef., Sanh. xiii. 3; Ber. 48b, 61b; M. Ḳ. 9a; Ket. 62a; Targ. I Sam. xxv. 29). At a later time, owing probably to the martyrdoms under Syrian and Roman persecution, earthly life was less esteemed (Wisdom iii. 17; iv. 7-8, 14; Philo, "De Abrahamo," § 46). Characteristic are these rabbinic sayings: "The pious live even in death; the wicked are dead even in life" (Ber. 18b). "Life" for "eternal life" (Psalms of Solomon, ix. 9, xiv. 6; II Macc. vii. 14; comp. vii. 9). "Ten are called living," that is, possess eternal life: (1) God (Jer. x. 10); (2) the Torah (Prov. iii. 18); (3) Israel (Deut. iv. 5); (4) the righteous (Prov. xi. 30); (5) paradise (Ps. cxvi. 9); (6) the tree of life (Gen. ii. 9); (7) the Holy Land (Ezek. xxvi. 20); (8) benevolent works (Ps. lxiii. 4 [A. V. 3]); (9) the wise (Prov. xiii. 15); (10) the fountain of waters in Jerusalem (Zech. xiv. 8; Ab. R. N. xxxiv. [ed. Schechter, p. 103]). "Dost thou wish life? Look to the fear of God, which increases the number of man's days; look for affliction; look to the study of the Torah and observe the commandments" (comp. Prov. iii. 18, iv. 4, vi. 23, x. 27). The Torah is called "medicine of life" (Sifre, Deut. 45; Yoma 72b; see also BOOK OF LIFE).

Life Eternal.

K.

LIGHT (Hebr. "or"): The primal element of Creation in all ancient cosmogonies; the first creation of God.—**Biblical Data:** "God said, Let there be light": and out of the primeval chaos there came forth "light" (Gen. i. 2-3). In the Creation psalm, God, before "stretching out the heavens like a curtain," "wraps Himself in light as in a mantle" (Ps. civ. 2, Hebr., whence "the Father of lights" of James i. 17). He is the Former of light and the Creator of darkness (Isa. xlv. 7). "No one knows the way to the light," which has its seat in heaven (Job xxxviii. 19, Hebr.); it emanates from the face of God (Ps. iv. 7 [A. V. 6], xliv. 4 [A. V. 3], lxxxix. 16 [A. V. 15]), whose whole being is luminous (Ex. xiii. 21, xxiv. 10; Ps. xxxvi. 10 [A. V. 9]; Job xxxvi. 30, xxxvii. 3). Gradually this light of God assumed a spiritual or symbolical meaning, in such passages as "God is light," to those who walk in darkness (Isa. ix. 2; x. 17; lx. 1-3, 19-20; Micah vii. 8; Ps. xxvii. 1, xxxvi. 10 [A. V. 9]).

The sun, moon, and stars, the luminaries placed in heaven to reflect their light upon the earth (Gen. i. 14-17), are supposed to have received, or to still receive, their light from the heavenly light created on the first day. Prophecy, therefore, speaks of the time when "the light of the moon will be like that of the sun, and that of the sun sevenfold like the light of the seven days of Creation" (Isa. xxx. 26, Hebr.; the commentators who failed to understand this meaning wished to eliminate from the text the words "ke-or shib'at ha-yamim"; but see Gen. R. iii. 6, xi. 2). Similarly, Isa. lx. 19-20: "Not sun nor moon, but the Lord, shall be for thy everlasting light" (Hebr.). The Avesta also speaks of the "endless lights" in heaven in which the good souls shall dwell ("Vendidad," ii. 131; "Yast," xx. 15; "Vistasp Yast," 61).

The Heavenly Light.

Light is often used as the symbol of life and joy (Job xviii. 5-6, xxxiii. 28; Ps. xlix. 20 [A. V. 19], xcvii. 11; Esth. viii. 16). It is likened to the word of instruction (Ps. cxix. 105; Prov. vi. 23).

K.

——**In Apocryphal and Rabbinical Literature:** Here also light takes a prominent position as a cosmic power. Wisdom is represented as the radiance of the everlasting light, the unspotted mirror of the power of God, more beautiful than the sun, and superior to the light which it resembles (Wisdom vii. 26, 29). God's majesty being surrounded with light to make Him invisible to all beings (Meg. 19b), the Rabbis speak of "the radiance of the Shekinah" ("ziw ha-Shekinah"; Ber 64b; Shab. 30a; B. B. 10a; comp. Ḥag. 14b and Heb. i. 3—"the brightness of his glory"). This was believed to be reflected in the new moon (Sanh. 42a, "Keillo mekabbel pene ha-Shekinah" = "he who sees the new moon is like one who greets the Divine Majesty"). The "radiance" ("ziw") of wisdom is reflected also in great men (Soṭah ix. 15). According to the cosmogony of Slavonian Enoch (xxv. 1-5) God made Adoel (Hadriel?), a fiery angel of great brightness, spring forth first as a visible being out of the invisible; and as Adoel burst asunder, there came forth a great light; and then God made a throne for Himself, and sat upon it, and placed the light above the throne to be the foundation of all things on high.

Similar is the "secret lore" of the Rabbis: The first act of Creation was when God robed Himself in light while the radiance of His glory ("ziw hadaro") illumined the world from one end to the other (Gen. R. iii.; Pirḳe R. El. iii.). "The light of the first day was such that by it the first man could see from one end of the world to the other; but, finding that wicked men would arise on earth, God removed this light to reserve it for the righteous in the world to come" (Ḥag. 12a; Gen. R. *l.c.*). The luminaries receive their light from the spark of that light of heaven, which is one hundred times as bright as the light visible on earth (Tan., Beha'aloteka, ed. Buber, p. 10). According to Targ. to Isa. xxx. 26 and Judges v. 31, the light of the future will be 343 ($7 \times 7 \times 7$) times as bright as the sun. The righteous alone desire it, not the wicked, who are as the bat in the fable, of whom the cock demands, "What is the light of day to thee, who preferrest the night?" (Sanh. 98b). Enoch (xlv. 4) speaks of "the eternal light" brought forth in the Messianic time: "The great light of heaven shone forth in splendor until Adam sinned; but on account of the Sabbath God would not withdraw the light before the day was over. Then when darkness set in Adam became afraid: 'Shall Satan henceforth overpower me?' Whereupon God set before him two bricks, from which Adam drew forth sparks of light by striking one against the other; and he blessed God for the

Primitive Light.

light which he thus obtained by his own hands" ('Ab Zarah 8c; Gen. R. xii.; Pesiḳ. R. xxiii.; comp. Pirḳe R. El., where the story is somewhat differently rendered; see HABDALAH).

God is in no need of light; the light kindled in the Sanctuary was to testify that the light of the Shekinah is in the midst of Israel (Men. 86b); therefore in the Temple of Solomon the windows were narrowed from without to indicate that the light streams forth from within (Tan., Teẓawweh, ed. Buber, p. 4). The light kindled before God was to be like the lantern carried by the blind for the one who sees; Israel is to aid in the spreading of the light of God on earth (Tan., Beha'aloteka, ed. Buber, p. 5; Ex. R. xxxvi.). When Moses was born the house was filled with light; hence it is said of him, as of the light of Creation, "he was 'good'" ("ṭob"; A. V. "goodly"; Ex. ii. 1; Soṭah 12a). In the ark Noah used a precious stone which illuminated all the surroundings (Gen. R. xxxi.; Sanh. 108b; comp. Meg. 12a).

The righteous in the world to come shall shine like the light of sun and stars, each in different luster (Sifre, Deut. 10, 47; Midr. Teh. to Ps. xi. 6; comp. I Cor. xv. 41). God had in view the righteous of the type of Abraham when He said "Let there be light" (comp. Ps. xcvii. 11; Ta'an. 15a; Tan., Teẓawweh, ed. Buber, p. 4); whereas the wicked of the type of Esau are sons of darkness (comp. Job xviii. 5; Gen. R. ii. 111). "The righteous who have loved God's name shall be clad in shining light" (Enoch, cviii. 12; comp. Dan. xii. 3 and Targ. to Judges v. 31: "they that love Him shall be as the sun"; Shab. 88b). Accordingly, the righteous are called "the generation of light," in contrast to the wicked, who are born (clothed?) in darkness (Enoch, cviii. 11); hence also the New Testament term, "sons of light" (Luke xvi. 8; John xii. 36; Ephes. v. 8; I Thess. v. 5; Col. i. 12).

Light is the symbol of the Torah (Meg. 16b, after Prov. vi. 23), of God (Tan., Teẓawweh, ed. Buber, p. 5, after Ps. xviii. 29), of the soul (*ib.* ed. Buber, p. 4, after Prov. xx. 27). "God says: 'If you conscientiously keep My light burning in your soul, I shall keep your light; if you kindle My lights in the Sanctuary, I shall kindle the great light for you in the future'" (*ib.* ed. Buber, pp. 2, 4–5; Ex. R. xxxvi.; Lev. R. xxxi.). In regard to Sabbath lights see LAMP, SABBATH. K.

LIGHT AND AIR. See NEIGHBORING LANDOWNERS.

LIGHT OF TRUTH. See PERIODICALS.

LIGHTFOOT, JOHN: English Christian divine and Talmudist; born at Stoke-upon-Trent 1602; died at Ely 1675. He passed through Christ's College, Cambridge, and later took orders, serving for the rest of his life as curate, rector, and canon. From 1650 till his death he was master of St. Catherine Hall (now College), Cambridge. He was parliamentarian, Presbyterian, and a leading member of the Westminster Assembly. It was through the influence of Sir Rowland Cotton (himself a Hebraist) that Lightfoot entered on the study of Hebrew, to which, including rabbinical Hebrew, he thenceforth devoted his leisure. His first publication was the tract "Ervbhin, or Miscellanies Christian and Judaicall, and Others, Penned for Recreation at Vacant Houres" (London, 1629). He is best known by his "Horæ Hebraicæ et Talmudicæ," composed in Latin, giving Talmudic parallels on the Gospels and I Corinthians, Acts, and some chapters of Romans, which appeared at intervals from 1658 to 1674, except the part on Acts and Romans, which was brought out later by Kidder, afterward Bishop of Bath and Wells (1691). The work was reproduced at Leipsic by Carpzov, the "Horæ" on the Gospels in 1675 (2d ed. 1684), and the rest in 1679; and at Oxford, in English, by Gandell in 1859. Lightfoot's collected works were first published in English (London, 1684), in two folio volumes, the one edited by George Bright, and the other by John Strype. Afterward they were published in Latin at Rotterdam (1686), and at Franeker (1699). The latest edition of his works is by J. R. Pitman (London, 1822–25).

By some critics, as Simon, Lightfoot's method in the "Horæ" was disparaged as "quelquefois trop rabbinique," but in general it found favor; and it was adopted by later writers, as Schöttgen, Meuschen, and Gill. He showed considerable acquaintance with Talmud and Midrash, greater perhaps than any non-Jew has shown before the present day. He corresponded with the younger Buxtorf, and helped Walton and others in their literary undertakings. He left his library to Harvard College, but nearly the whole collection was destroyed by fire in 1764.

BIBLIOGRAPHY: *Dict. Nat. Biog.*; Lightfoot's *Works*, ed. Pitman, as above.

T. C. T.

LIGHTNING, BENEDICTION ON: The Mishnah (Ber. ix. 2) prescribes, "At the sight of shooting stars or of lightning, and at hearing earthquakes, thunder, and storms, the benediction 'Blessed be He whose power and might fill the world' should be recited. At the sight of great mountains, seas, and deserts one recites the benediction 'Blessed be He who hath made the work of Creation.'" The suggestion was made at the Babylonian school that the latter benediction is in place also on the occasions previously mentioned; and this was accepted by both Abbaye and Raba, who declared that both benedictions should be recited (Ber. 59a). However, Isaac Alfasi and Maimonides ("Yad," Berakot, x. 14) understand the Talmudic passage to mean that either benediction may be recited on the occasion of lightning and the other phenomena mentioned.

This view is accepted also by Asheri and his son Jacob (Ṭur Oraḥ Ḥayyim, 227); and by Joseph Caro (Shulḥan 'Aruk, Oraḥ Ḥayyim, 227, 1). General custom, however, decided that while for thunder the former benediction, expressive of God's might, should be recited, the benediction for lightning should be, "Blessed be He who hath made the work of Creation" (see "Ṭure Zahab" and "Be'er Heṭeb" to Shulḥan 'Aruk, Oraḥ Ḥayyim, *l.c.*). Accordingly, the ordinary prayer-books have this arrangement as a fixed rule. K.

LILIEN, EPHRAIM MOSES: Austrian artist; born at Drohobicz, Galicia, in 1874. Lilien's artistic inclinations became evident early in life. He was apprenticed to a sign-maker, with whom he worked in return for meager board, and subsequently attended the academies of art in Cracow and Munich. He later removed to Berlin, where he is at present (1904) residing.

At first Lilien's work was deficient in individuality. Even "Der Zöllner von Klausen," one of the most admired of his earlier works, is vague, colorless, and feeble. Lilien began with the illustration of books and newspapers, but soon pushed himself to the front; a number of his earlier efforts appeared in the "Jugend" and in the "Vorwärts." His later productions, though not overladen with sentiment, are rich in pathetic touches. The best and most characteristic of his work is to be found in the book "Juda" (1900), which contains his "Jesaia," "Passach," and "Sodom's Ruinen." He illustrated also the "Lieder des Ghetto" of Morris Rosenfeld (1903). His "Gedenkblatt des Fünften Zionisten-Kongresses in Basel" has attracted wide attention. Other notable illustrations are: "Ex Libris E. M. Lilien," "Auf Zarten Saiten," "Der Jüdische Mai," "Ex Libris Ruben Brainin," "Ex Libris D. Simonson," "Ex Libris des Reichstagsabgeordneten R. Fischer," "Ein Salomonisches Urtheil," "In Rosenketten," "Heimatlos," "Chanukalichter," "Signet des Jüdischen Kunstverlages Phönix."

BIBLIOGRAPHY: *Ost und West*; *Jüdische Künstler*; *The Maccabæan*, March, 1904.

S. S. LED.

"ISAIAH."
(From the drawing by Ephraim Moses Lilien.)

LILIENBLUM, MOSES LÖB: Russian scholar and author; born at Keidany, government of Kovno, Oct. 22, 1843. From his father he learned the calculation of the course of the stars in their relation to the Hebrew calendar ("Ḥaṭṭot Ne'urim," i. 15). At the age of thirteen he organized a society of boys for the study of "'En Ya'aḳob" (*ib.* i. 14); and at the age of fifteen he married and settled at Wilkomir.

A change in the fortunes of his father-in-law throwing him upon his own resources, Lilienblum established a yeshibah in Wilna in 1865, and another in the year following (*ib.* i. 53-54). The advance of years, however, wrought a great change in the attitude of Lilienblum toward Judaism. He had read the writings of the Maskilim, particularly those of Mapu and M. A. Ginzburg, and these produced in him a feeling of dissatisfaction with Talmudic studies and of abhorrence for the ignorance and superstition surrounding him; he decided, therefore, to combat these faults. In an article entitled "Orḥot ha-Talmud," in "Ha-Meliẓ," 1868, he arraigned the superstitious beliefs and practises of his people, demanded the reform of Judaism, and insisted upon the necessity of establishing a "closer connection between religion and life."

Changed Views.

This article, followed by others of the same nature, stirred up the Jewish communities in Russia, and a storm of indignation against him arose among the ultra-Orthodox; he was denounced as a freethinker and continued residence in Wilkomir became impossible. He then went to Odessa (1869), where he intended to prepare himself for the university ("Ḥaṭṭot Ne'urim," ii. 3), but after a hard struggle he was compelled to give up that design.

The anti-Jewish riots of 1880 and 1881 aroused Lilienblum to a consciousness of the unsafe position of the Jews "in exile," and he gave utterance to his apprehensions in an article entitled "Obshcheyevreiski Vopros i Palestina" (in "Razsvyet," 1881, Nos. 41, 42), in which he points to the reestablishment of the Jews in Palestine as the only solution of the Jewish question. This article did not remain without results; the idea was hailed as practical, and many set themselves to realize it. In 1883 a committee was organized at Odessa for the colonization of Palestine, Lilienblum serving as secretary and Dr. L. Pinsker, author of "Autoemancipation," as president; at the famous conference at Kotowitz, where representatives of all European Jewries met and discussed plans of colonization in Palestine, the foundation was laid for the Zionist movement, in which Lilienblum, as secretary, has taken the most earnest and energetic part ("Derek la-'Abor Golim," p. 16).

Moses Löb Lilienblum.

Zionism.

Lilienblum's activity thus covers two distinct periods in the history of Russian Jewry. In the period of the Haskalah he followed the example of the Maskilim in demanding the reform of Judaism; but he differed from the Maskilim in that he was much less extravagant, his style being free from the flowery "meliẓah" used by them, and his ideas being marked by soberness and clearness. His "Orḥot ha-Talmud," mentioned above, and his "Ḥaṭṭot Ne'urim" (Vienna, 1876), a description of his material and spiritual struggles, both made a marked impression upon that period. His influence in the second period also, that of national reawakening, which he practically initiated, was due to his characteristic style. In his article on the Jewish question and Palestine, already mentioned, as well as in his "O Vozrozhdenii Yevreiskavo Naroda" (Odessa, 1883), the latter including the former and other essays of a similar character, he clearly and soberly presents the anomalous position held by Israel among the nations and logically demonstrates its hopelessness except through national independence.

Lilienblum wrote also: "Ḳehal Refa'im," a poem describing the different types of Russian Jewry of the time, as they appear in the nether world (Odessa, 1870); "'Olam ha-Tohu," on some phases of Hebrew literature (in "Ha-Shaḥar," 1873); "Biḳḳoret Kol Shire Gordon," on J. L. Gordon as a poet (in "Meliẓ Eḥad Mini Elef," St. Petersburg, 1884); "Zerubbabel," a historical drama in Yiddish (Odessa, 1888); "Derek la-'Abor Golim," a history of the Chovevei Zion movement up to the time of the ratification by the Russian government of the committee for the colonization of Palestine (Warsaw, 1899); "Derek Teshubah," an addition to "Ḥaṭṭot Ne'urim," describing the transition of the author from the negative period of the Haskalah to the positive period of national reawakening; "Pyat Momentov Zhizhni Moiseya" (in Russian; *ib.* 1901), a psychological analysis of some important moments in the life of Moses. Lilienblum also edited "Kawweret," a collection of articles in Hebrew (Odessa, 1890), and the "Luaḥ Aḥiasaf," 1901. He was the author of a number of other articles, of which the most important is "O Neobkhodimosti Reform v Yevreiskoi Religii" (in "Voskhod," 1882–83).

Works.

Bibliography: Lilienblum, *Haṭṭot Ne'urim*, Vienna, 1876; idem, *Derek Teshubah*, Warsaw, 1899; idem, *Derek la-'Abor Golim*, ib.; Mordecai b. Hillel ha-Kohen, in *Luaḥ Aḥiasaf*, ib. 1893; Berdychevsky, *Dor Dor*, ib. 1901; N. Slouschz, *Littérature Hébraïque*, pp. 166 *et seq.*, Paris, 1903; Wiener, *Yiddish Literature*, p. 238, New York, 1899.

H. R. A. S. W.

LILIENTHAL, MAX: Rabbi and educator; born at Munich Nov. 6, 1815; died at Cincinnati, Ohio, April 5, 1882; educated at the University of Munich (Ph.D. 1837). In 1839 he accepted the office of principal in the newly established Jewish school of Riga, where he was appointed preacher also. The school was opened Jan. 15, 1840. In recognition of the sentiments expressed in the sermon with which Lilienthal opened the school the emperor Nicholas presented him with a diamond ring. In Dec., 1841, at the instance of Uvarov, minister of public instruction, to whom he was recommended by Count Maltitz, the Russian ambassador to Holland, Lilienthal was sent from St. Petersburg on an official mission. It was the intention of the government to establish Jewish schools for secular and religious instruction, and the duty assigned to Lilienthal was to determine the attitude of the Jews in regard to them and to quiet their fears as to the intentions of the government; for the plans of the latter were regarded with suspicion among the Jewish masses, who believed that the real purpose of the proposed schools was to lead the Jews gradually to conversion to Christianity. Lilienthal repaired to Wilna, where the community, acting on his assurances, appropriated 5,000 rubles for school purposes, and promised Lilienthal that more money would be supplied when necessary. But notwithstanding Lilienthal's assurances, the mistrust toward him of the Jews in Lithuania increased. At Minsk, whither he had gone at the invitation of the local ḳahal, he was given to understand that the Jews of Lithuania had no confidence in him. His stay in Minsk was rendered unpleasant by the resentment of the Jewish masses, and he even had to invoke the protection of the police. On his return to Wilna, Lilienthal found distrust of him growing there; thereupon, discouraged, he returned to St. Petersburg.

After several months' arduous work in the offices of the Ministry of Education and with Count Uvarov, he returned to Wilna and prepared a circular letter to the Jews of Russia, published under the title "Maggid Yeshu'ah." When a council of rabbis and other prominent Jews was convoked at St. Petersburg, consisting of Rabbi Isaac ben Ḥayyim of

Volozhin, Rabbi Mendel Shneersohn of Lubavich, Bezaleel Stern of Odessa, and Israel Heilprin of Berdychev, Lilienthal was appointed secretary of a senatorial committee of fourteen. During the sessions Stern had many an encounter with Lilienthal and was even provoked to accuse him of ignorance of the Talmud. In the autumn of 1842 Lilienthal went to Odessa with letters of recommendation from Uvarov to Count M. S. Vorontzov. The Odessa community received him warmly, and appointed him their rabbi. Lilienthal was soon convinced, however, that his efforts in behalf of the Russian Jews would not yield the desired results; as a foreigner it was difficult for him to gain a true insight into their traditions, hopes, and aspirations. He did not understand them, nor they him; and he was placed in an awkward and delicate position by the distrust of the Jews on the one hand, and, on the other hand, by the efforts of the government to effect their assimilation without according them full rights of citizenship.

His "Maggid Yeshu'ah."

Lilienthal left Russia suddenly in 1844 and went to the United States. Settling in New York, he became rabbi of the Congregation Anshe Chesed, Norfolk street, and, later, rabbi of Shaar ha-Shomayim, Attorney street. His somewhat advanced views led to considerable friction. He resigned his position in 1850 and established an educational institute with which he attained considerable success. In 1854 he became correspondent of the "American Israelite," and in the following year removed to Cincinnati and became associate editor of that journal and rabbi of the Congregation Bene Israel. His activity in Cincinnati extended over a period of twenty-seven years. He organized the Rabbinical Literary Association, serving as its president, and was at first instructor and later professor of Jewish history and literature at Hebrew Union College. He was prominent, also, in the Jewish press as the founder and editor of the "Hebrew Review," a quarterly, and the "Sabbath-School Visitor," a weekly, and as a frequent contributor to the "Israelite," the "Occident," "Deborah" (founded by him), the "Asmonean," "Volksblatt," and "Volksfreund." He published a volume of poems entitled "Freiheit, Frühling und Liebe" (1857), several volumes of addresses and sermons, and left three dramas in manuscript—"Die Strelitzen Mutter," "Rudolf von Habsburg," and "Der Einwanderer."

Associate Editor of "American Israelite."

Lilienthal took an active interest in the affairs of the municipality. As member of the Cincinnati board of education, and as director of the Relief Union and of the university board, he contributed much to the welfare of his adopted city. He was a reformer by nature; he was instrumental in introducing reforms in his own congregation in Cincinnati, constantly preached tolerance, and urged a more liberal interpretation of Jewish law.

Bibliography: A. Ehrlich, *Entwickelungsgeschichte der Israelitischen Gemeindeschule zu Riga*, pp. 9-14; *Leket Amarim*, supplement to *Ha-Meliz*, 1888, pp. 86-89; Kayserling, *Gedenkblätter*, p. 50; *Ha-Pardes*, pp. 186, 198; *Jüdisches Volksblatt*, 1856, No. 36; Lilienthal, *My Travels in Russia*, in *American Israelite*, vols. i. and ii.; *Independent*, New York, xlviii. 343; Wunderbar, *Gesch. der Juden in Liv- und Kurland*, pp. 14-15, Mitau, 1853; Morgulis, in *Yevreiskaya Biblioteka*, i.; *Yevreiskiya Zapiski*, 1881, p. 9; *Vyestnik Russkikh Yevreyev*, 1871, No. 26.

H. R.

LILIENTHAL, OTTO: German mechanical engineer and experimenter in aerial navigation; born May 23, 1848, at Anklam; died Aug. 9, 1896, at Rhinow. Lilienthal's theory was that artificial flight must follow the principles of bird-flight. His experiments, which were made with the assistance of his brother **G. Lilienthal,** extended over a period of twenty-five years; in the summer of 1891 he made, with a pair of curved wings designed for soaring, the first practical demonstration of man's ability to fly. He made the flight successfully several times, but finally met death during an experiment at Rhinow.

Otto Lilienthal Experimenting with His Flying-Machine: Starting from a Platform.

(From a photograph.)

Lilienthal was a member of the German Society for the Advancement of Aerial Navigation. He was the author of "Der Vogelflug als Grundlage der Fliegekunst" (Berlin, 1889), in which he explained the theoretical reasons for the form of his aerial machine; and "Die Flugapparate."

Bibliography: Chanute, *Progress in Flying Machines*, pp. 202-211, New York, 1899; Kohut, *Berühmte Israelitische Männer und Frauen*, No. 15, pp. 246-247; Vallentine and Tomlinson, *Travels in Space*, pp. 252 *et seq.*, London, 1902; *Report of the Smithsonian Institution*, pp. 189-199, Washington, 1893.

S.

LILITH (לִילִית: LXX. Ὀνοκένταυροι; Symmachus, Λάμια; Vulg. "Lamia"): Female demon. Of the three Assyrian demons Lilu, Lilit, and Ardat Lilit, the second is referred to in Isa. xxxiv. 14. Schrader ("Jahrb. für Protestantische Theologie," i. 128) takes Lilith to be a goddess of the night; she is said to have been worshiped by the Jewish exiles in Babylon (Levy, in "Z. D. M. G." ix. 470, 484). Sayce ("Hibbert Lectures," pp. 145 *et seq.*), Fossey ("La Magie Assyrienne," pp. 37 *et seq.*), and others think that "Lilith" is not connected with the Hebrew "layil" (night), but that it is the name of a demon of the storm, and this view is supported by the cuneiform inscriptions quoted by them. It must, however, be assumed that the resemblance to the Semitic "layil" materially changed the conception of Lilith among the Semites, and especially among the Jews. No definite conclusions can be drawn from the passage in Isaiah, where it is said of the devastated palaces of Edom that wild animals shall dwell in them "and the satyr shall cry to his fellow; the screech-owl also shall rest there, and find for herself a place of rest" (Isa. xxxiv. 14; see Cheyne's note *ad loc.*). Baudissin connects Lilith with Zech. v. 9.

In Talmud and Midrash.

Lilith is more fully described in post-Biblical literature, where she appears as a demon of the night, as suggested by her Hebrew name. Three classes of demons are mentioned: spirits, devils, and "lilin" (Targ. Yer. to Deut. xxxii. 24; Targ. Sheni to Esth. i. 3; *passim*). The first have neither body nor form; the second appear in complete human shape; the third in human shape, but with wings (Rashi to Sanh. 109a). Adam procreated all the spirits while he was under a spell (Gen. R. xx. 11; 'Er. 18b). Similarly, Eve bore demons to male spirits for the space of 130 years. This corresponds to the view that the demons are half human (Ḥag. 16a). Hence an abortion which has the shape of Lilith may be a child, though it has wings (Nid. 24b). Lilith is a seductive woman with long hair ('Er. 100b); she is the Queen of Zemargad (Targ. Job i. 15; comp. Bacher and Kohut [see bibliography]); Ahriman is her son (B. B. 73a). She goes about at night, fastening herself upon any one sleeping alone in a room (Shab. 151b). "The Lord will protect thee" (Num. vi. 24) means, according to Targ. Yer., ". . . from lilin." The meteor-stone is her arrow and is a remedy against disease (Giṭ. 69b). Kohut's assumption that Agrat bat Maḥlat ("daughter of the dancer"), who roams at night with myriads of demons (Pes. 112b, bottom), is the queen of the lilin, is not verified. King Solomon, who commanded all spirits, had the lilin dance before him (Targ. Sheni Esth. i. 3).

Kohut identifies Lilith with the Parsee Bushyansta, and the Arabic translators render the word in Isa. xxxiv. 14 by "ghul," which is identical with the "lamia" of the Vulgate. In the Talmud, however, there is nothing to indicate that Lilith is a vampire. The Arabians, on the contrary, are said to regard Lilith, under the form of Lalla, as a "holy dame" (Schwab, "Les Coupes Magiques et l'Hydromancie dans l'Antiquité Orientale," p. 11). The name "Lilith" is found also on amulets with terra-cotta figures (*idem*, "Coupes à Inscriptions Magiques," p. 62). In the later Middle Ages the mystics systematically amplified demonology on the basis of the traditions and the current European superstitions, and they

Middle Ages and Modern Times.

also assigned a more definite form to Lilith (see the quotations in Eisenmenger, "Entdecktes Judenthum," ii. 417 *et seq.*). The superstitions regarding her and her nefarious doings were, with other superstitions, disseminated more and more among the mass of the Jewish people. She becomes a nocturnal demon, flying about in the form of a night-owl and stealing children. She is permitted to kill all children which have been sinfully begotten, even from a lawful wife. If a child smiles during the night of the Sabbath or the New Moon, it is a sign that Lilith is playing with it. One should then strike the nose of the child three times and drive Lilith away by the prescribed rough words (Joseph Cohen, "'Emeḳ ha-Melek," p. 84b; comp. Grunwald, "Mitteilungen der Gesellschaft für Jüdische Volkskunde," v. 62). Lilith likewise appears to men in their dreams; she is the bride of Samael (Schwab, "Angélologie"; comp. Zohar ii. 267b). It is said in a Judæo-German book ("Hanhagat ha-Ḥasidim") printed at Frankfort-on-the-Main in the beginning of the eighteenth century that Lilith deceives men and has children by them; infant mortality is regarded as a consequence of this miscegenation (comp. Grunwald, *l.c.* v. 10, 62). In a certain legend she appears as the Queen of Sheba, who in the guise of a beautiful woman seduced a poor Jew of Worms (Grunwald, *l.c.* ii. 30 *et seq.*). As she was eager to seize new-born infants, mother and child were provided with amulets, which since early times were regarded as an efficient protection against magic and demons; Lilith is the chief figure on the "childbirth tablets" still hung on the walls of the lying-in room in the East and in eastern Europe (see AMULETS). The name "Lilith" occurs also in non-Jewish superstitions (Lammert, "Volksmedicin," p. 170; Grunwald, *l.c.* vii., col. 2, n. 4). The conception that she was Adam's first wife (comp. Gen. R. xxiv.; Yer. 'Er. 18b) appears to have been spread through Buxtorf's "Lexicon Talmudicum," *s.v.* Lilith is a clear instance of the persistence of popular superstitious beliefs.

BIBLIOGRAPHY: W. M. Menzies Alexander, *Demoniac Possession in the N. T.* pp. 15-16, 26, 44, 55, Edinburgh, 1902; Bacher, *Lilith, Königin von Smargad*, in *Monatsschrift*, 1870, xix. 187-189; W. W. Baudissin, *Studien zur Semitischen Religionsgesch.* i. 128, Leipsic, 1876; *Bar Bahlul's Syrisches Wörterb.*; G. Brecher, *Das Transcendentale*, etc., pp. 47, 50, 54, Vienna, 1850; Eisenmenger, *Entdecktes Judenthum*, ii. 413 *et seq.*; C. Fossey, *La Magie Assyrienne*, pp. 26, 37 *et seq.*, Paris, 1902; M. Grunwald, *Mitteilungen der Gesellschaft für Jüdische Volkskunde*, ii. 68, 74; v. 10, 62; vii. 104; F. Hommel, *Vorsemitische Kultur*, p. 367; idem, *Die Semiten*, etc., p. 368, Leipsic, 1881; A. Kohut, *Ueber die Jüdische Angelologie und Dämonologie*, pp. 86-89, *ib.* 1866; M. Schwab, *Vocabulaire de l'Angélologie*, p. 162, Paris, 1897; idem, *Les Coupes Magiques et l'Hydromancie dans l'Antiquité Orientale*, in *Tr. Soc. Bibl. Arch.* April, 1890; idem, *Coupes d Inscriptions Magiques*, ib. June, 1891.

E. G. H.—S. S. L. B.

LILY: Rendering in the Bible of the Hebrew word שׁוֹשַׁן (I Kings vii. 19) or שׁוֹשַׁנָּה (II Chron. iv. 5; Cant. ii. 1; Hosea xiv. 5), which is probably a loanword from the Egyptian "s-sh-sh-sh-n" = "lotus"; the white lily, *Lilium candidum* Linn., growing wild in the Lebanon and other regions of northern Palestine. In a figurative sense the word "shoshan" is used of the capitals of the pillars and of the molten sea in the Temple (I Kings vii. 19, 26), and in the Mishnah of a nail-head and the knob on the ETROG; in the Targum it connotes "flower" in general.

Sometimes, however, Targumic diction, followed by the Zohar, gives "shoshan" the meaning of "rose."

The first account of the lily is given by Ibn Ezra in his commentary on the Song of Solomon (comp. Salfeld, "Das Hohelied Salomo's bei den Jüdischen Erklärern des Mittelalters," 1879, p. 68), and is one of the few descriptions of plants in Jewish literature. It runs thus: "It is a white flower of sweet but narcotic perfume, and it receives its name because the flower has, in every case, six [שש] petals, within which are six long filaments." The Midrash alludes once to the abundance of its sap, and David Ḳimḥi says that it has no roots. Abravanel says that dew makes the lily bloom, but rain destroys it. The heart of this flower is directed upward, even though it be among thorns, thus symbolizing the trust in God which should be felt by Israel amid all afflictions (Lev. R. xxiii. 1; Cant. R. ii. 2). The Zohar speaks of the thirteen leaves of the lily which surround the flower as the thirteen attributes of God which encompass Israel. This number is evidently derived from the description of Ibn Ezra with its six petals, six stamens, and one pistil. In the "Tiḳḳunim" (xxv., end; xxvi., beginning) the theme is varied, the "shoshannah" being taken as denoting both the lily and the rose. The lilies among which the beloved feeds (Cant. ii. 16) are the morning and evening Shema'; the five leaves of the rose are the first five words of the Shema'; and the thirteen leaves of the lily the numerical equivalent of "eḥad," the last word.

Described by Ibn Ezra.

The identifications of the "lily-of-the-valleys" (*ib.* ii. 1) and the "royal lily" of the Syriac translation of Ecclus. (Sirach) xxxix. 14 and the Mishnah (Kil. v. 8; "Tiḳḳunim," iii. 78, l. 2) are uncertain, although the latter has been regarded plausibly as a species of *Fritillaria.*

The lily as the chief of flowers seems to have been represented on the shekels and half-shekels ascribed to Simon the Hasmonean; and was common on coats of arms in medieval Spain and in modern times.

About this flower a rich and abundant symbolism has gathered. The faces of the righteous are as the lily, and exist only for redemption as the lily for perfume; so that the later cabalists employ the flower as a symbol of the resurrection (Gamaliel di Monselice on Pirḳe Shirah, ed. Mantua, p. 96a). Yet most of all the lily typifies Israel. As it withers in the sunlight, but blooms beneath the dew, so Israel withers away except God becomes as dew for her (Hos. xiv. 5), and she is renowned among the nations as the lily among the flowers. The lily among thorns is likened to Rebekah, who remained pure amid evil surroundings (Bacher, "Ag. Pal. Amor." ii. 243), and to the sons of Korah (Ps. xlv. 1 [A. V., heading]). While it was as difficult to save the Israelites from the Egyptians as a lily from the thorns (Bacher, *l.c.* ii. 76), yet they remained faithful among those that worshiped strange gods, as the lilies keep their beauty despite gashes and wounds (Targ., Cant. ii. 1). The title of Ps. lxxx. is supposed by Aḥa of Lydda to refer to the lily; and the passage in Ps. cxxx. 1, "Out of the depths," is explained by him as an allusion to the lily-of-the-valley. The phrase "set about with lilies" (Cant. vii. 2) is applied by the Haggadah to the words of the Law; but it is more usually regarded as alluding to the seventy elders of the Sanhedrin. In a funeral oration R. Simeon b. Laḳish (Bacher, *l.c.* i. 401) interprets Cant. vi. 2 thus: "My beloved" is God, who has descended into "his garden," the world, to the "beds of spices," Israel, to feed in "the gardens," the nations of the world, and to gather the "lilies," the righteous whom he removes by death from the midst of them. Similar allegorical interpretations are common, even as late as Enoch Zundel Luria in the middle of the nineteenth century. The symbolism of the lily has passed from the Jews to the Christians, so that the angel of the Annunciation is conventionally represented as bearing lilies without filaments.

Typical Application.

Bibliography: Fonck, *Streifzüge Durch die Biblische Flora,* pp. 53 *et seq.*, Freiburg-im-Breisgau, 1900.

E. G. H. I. Lö.

LIMA, MOSES B. ISAAC JUDAH: Lithuanian rabbinical scholar, one of the so-called Aharonim; born in the second decade of the seventeenth century; died about 1670. When a comparatively young man he successively occupied the rabbinates of Brest-Litovsk and Slonim. His fame as a scholar soon reached Wilna, whither he was called, in 1650, to fill the office of chief rabbi. Lima was of a retiring and diffident disposition, which probably accounts for the paucity of his writings. He left a manuscript commentary on Shulḥan 'Aruk, Eben ha-'Ezer, which his son Raphael published (1670) under the title of "Ḥelḳat Meḥoḳeḳ," and which, while betraying profound erudition, was so condensed that the editor deemed it necessary to provide it with explanatory notes. Lima did not carry even this work to completion; it covers only the first 126 chapters of the Eben ha-'Ezer.

Bibliography: Azulai, *Shem ha-Gedolim*, i. and ii., s.v. *Ḥelḳat Meḥoḳeḳ*; S. Bäck, in Winter and Wünsche, *Die Jüdische Litteratur,* ii. 519; Gans, *Ẓemaḥ Dawid*, p. 596; Grätz, *Gesch.* x. 61 *et seq.*; Jost, *Gesch. des Judenthums und Seiner Sekten*, iii. 244.

H. R. S. M.

LIMERICK: Seaport town in Ireland, in which Jews began to settle about 1881, after the Russian exodus. A synagogue was founded in 1889 in Colooney street, and in the same year a biḳḳur ḥolim. In 1901 it was found necessary to establish a Jewish board of guardians. On Jan. 11, 1904, Father Creagh, of the Redemptorist Order, delivered a violent sermon against the Jews, accusing them of ritual murder, of blaspheming Jesus, and of robbing the people of Limerick. On the following day there was a riot in which the Jews were attacked by mobs, and this was followed by a general boycott by the local Roman Catholic confraternity, numbering about 6,000 members. The chief ground for complaint against the Jews was the "weekly-instalment plan" by which they sold their goods. The outburst against the Jews drew forth many protests from Protestant and Roman Catholic clergy and laymen. The Jews of the locality suffered much from the boycott. Limerick has a population of 45,806, of which about 300 are Jews.

Bibliography: *Jewish Year Book*, 1904; *Jew. Chron.* 1904, Jan. 22 and succeeding numbers.

J.

LIMOGES. See FRANCE.

LINCOLN: County town of Lincolnshire, England; formerly the second town of importance in the country, and on that account largely populated by Jews in the preexpulsion period. They appear to have settled on the Steep Hill, between the old Roman colony and the new castle and cathedral. The earliest mention of them occurs in 1159, when the sheriff of Lincolnshire renders count of £40 for the Jews of Lincoln in the pipe-roll of that year.

Aaron of Lincoln conducted his extensive operations from this town as a center; and his house, though considerably "restored," still remains as one of its earliest antiquities (see AARON OF LINCOLN). He took in pledge the plate of Lincoln Minster (Giraldus Cambrensis, "Opera," ed. Dymock, vii. 36). During the outbreaks against the Jews at the beginning of the reign of Richard I. the Lincoln Jews saved themselves by seeking refuge in the castle. The influence of St. Hugh, Bishop of Lincoln, may have had some effect in restraining the mob. At any rate, Jews mourned his death sincerely in 1200 (Jacobs, "Jews of Angevin England," p. 207). It would appear that Moses b. Isaac, author of the "Sefer ha-Shoham," was the son of a Lincoln Jew, his mother being Contessa of Cambridge. Much business was done not only by Aaron of Lincoln, but also by Benedict fil Isaac, as well as by Aaron's brothers Senior and Benedict, and his sons Elias, Abraham, and Vives. In the Nottingham "donum" of 1194 Lincoln comes second in point of tribute—£287 4s. 11d., as against £486 9s. 7d. for London—but the number of Jewish names mentioned in Lincoln is the largest. Aaron and his family possessed a considerable number of houses in the precincts of the Bail. Those belonging to Aaron himself escheated to the crown on his death, and were declared to be above 60s. in value. The houses of his brother Senior also became the property of the crown; but their value was only 10s.

About 1220 a raid seems to have been made upon the Jews' houses in Lincoln, Mosse de Ballio, as well as Sara, the wife of Deulacresse, having been murdered in that year. In the middle of the thirteenth century the most important Lincoln Jew was Benedict fil Mosse, who is undoubtedly to be identified with BERECHIAH DE NICOLE mentioned among the Tosafists. There is also a Joce de Nicole mentioned; and in the celebrated case of Hugh of Lincoln reference is made to the school of Peitevin, from which it seems probable that there was a bet ha-midrash at Lincoln. Several Hebrew "sheṭarot" exist dealing with the transactions of the Jews of Lincoln, mainly with the Abbey of Neusome. When Henry III. tailaged the Jews of Lincoln, several men were made responsible for the tallage, among them Leo of Lincoln, said to be, at the time, one of the six richest Jews in England. He was also concerned with the debts of the Abbey of Neusome. Leo was condemned for some crime; and his house in the parish of St. Martin's escheated to the crown in 1275. In 1255 occurred the case of HUGH OF LINCOLN, which resulted in considerable loss of life to the Jewish community. Many of these victims are referred to in later deeds with the title "ha-ḳadosh" or "martyr."

Thirteenth Century.

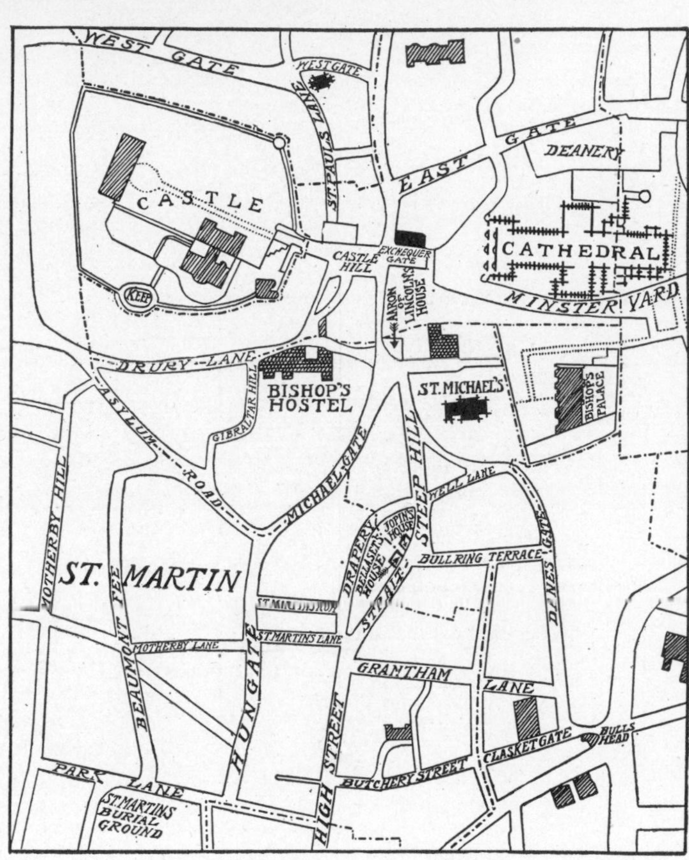

The Jewish Quarter, Lincoln, Circa 1290.
(From Jacobs' "Jewish Ideals.")

During the uprising of the barons in 1266 the "disinherited" attacked the Jewry of Lincoln, mainly for the purpose of destroying the deeds of indebtedness which tended to put the baronage in the king's power. It is probable that the chest of the chirographers of Lincoln was burned at this time ("Select Pleas," ed. Rigg, p. 41). Berechiah de Nicole had a son, Ḥayyim or Vives, and a daughter, Belaset, probably identified with the Belaset of Wallingford whose house is the better known of the two Jews' houses at Lincoln. She was executed in 1287 for clipping coin. The betrothal deed of her daughter still exists, in which an elaborate written copy of the Hebrew Scriptures is one of the most important items of the dowry.

At the expulsion in 1290 no less than sixty-six householders of Lincoln left deeds, bonds for money, corn, or wool, aggregating in money £423 15s.; in corn £601 9s. 4d.; and in wool £1,595 6s. All of these fell into the hands of the king, besides thirty houses the exact value of which can not be ascertained. Most of the houses were in the Brauncegate or in St. Martin's parish, where indeed the ghetto seems to have been. No Jewish community has been formed in Lincoln since 1290.

BIBLIOGRAPHY: Jacobs, *Jews of Angevin England*, passim; M. D. Davis, in *Archæological Journal*, xxxviii. 178 *et seq.*; Freeman, *English Towns*, p. 216; *Trans. Jew. Hist. Soc. England*, ii.

J.

LINDAU, BARUCH BEN JUDAH LÖB: German mathematician; born at Hanover in 1759; died at Berlin Dec. 5, 1849. He wrote: "Reshit Limmudim," a text-book of natural science (part i., physics and geography, Berlin, 1789; Brünn, 1796; Cracow, 1820; part ii., natural philosophy, with additions by Wolf ben Joseph [Joseph Wolf of Dessau], Dessau, 1810; complete ed. Lemberg, 1869); "Shir Ha-tunnah," epithalamium in honor of Judah ben Solomon of Hanover (n.d., n.p.).

BIBLIOGRAPHY: Fürst, *Bibl. Jud.* ii. 250; Steinschneider, *Cat. Bodl.* col. 1624; Zeitlin, *Bibl. Post-Mendels.* p. 212.

D. S. MAN.

Jew's House, Steep Hill, Lincoln.
(From a drawing of the eighteenth century, in the British Museum.)

LINDO: One of the oldest and most esteemed of London Sephardic families; it traces its descent back to Isaac Lindo, who died in 1712. For eight successive generations a member of the family has been a sworn broker of the city of London. See family chart on following page.

LINDO, ALEXANDER: English merchant; died in London in 1818. He was connected with the West India trade, and in this connection entered into relations with Napoleon after the Treaty of Amiens, arranging for the shipment of goods to the value of £260,000 to the French West Indies for the use of the troops commanded by General Leclerc. The latter drew a draft on Paris for the amount, but this was dishonored on a frivolous pretext, and Lindo does not appear to have ever obtained his money. He died in financial difficulties; his bequest to the Bevis Marks Synagogue was never paid. His son **Abraham Alexander Lindo** wrote a pamphlet entitled "A Word in Season" (London, 1839), but he was prohibited by the Mahamad from publishing anything more.

BIBLIOGRAPHY: Picciotto, *Sketches of Anglo-Jewish History*, pp. 273-328, London, 1875.

J.

LINDO, DAVID ABARBANEL: English communal worker; born in London Aug. 14, 1772; died there Feb. 26, 1852. He was an uncle of Lord Beaconsfield, whom he initiated into the covenant of Abraham, and was intimately connected with the Bevis Marks Congregation, representing the rigidly legal standpoint against the struggle for Reform. At its beginning in 1838 he helped to found and became chairman of a society called "Shomere Mishmeret Akodesh," formed to resist all innovations and oppose Reform tendencies; but the Yehidim ordered the dissolution of the society as likely to lead to disunion. Lindo had no less than eighteen children, eight of whom married into well-known Sephardic families.

BIBLIOGRAPHY: *Catalogue of the Anglo-Jewish Historical Exhibition*, pp. 56, 70; Gaster, *Hist. of Bevis Marks*, pp. 171-175, London, 1902.

J.

LINDO, ELIAS HAYYIM: English author and historian; born in 1783; died in London June 11, 1865. He spent the first half of his life in the island of St. Thomas, where he married and became one of the leading merchants. He was president of the Hebrew congregation and acted also in the honorary capacity of mohel for many years.

Lindo settled in England about 1832 and began a series of literary labors. He translated the "Conciliador" of Manasseh ben Israel (London, 1842). In 1832 he published his "Calendar," a reissue of which appeared in 1860. The tables are preceded by an essay on the structure of the Jewish calendar; and appended is a collection of general information. His last published work was the "History of the Jews of Spain and Portugal" (*ib.* 1849), for which he visited the Iberian Peninsula and obtained

Isaac, m. Leah Lindo
(d. 1712) (d. 1713)

* Elias, m. (1708) Rachel Lopes Fereira
(d. 1728) (d. 1755)

* Isaac, m. (1729) Bath-sheba de Ephraim Abarbanel
(d. 1767) (d. 1772)

* Elias, m. (1757) Grace Lumbroso de Mattos
(d. 1785) (d. 1788)

- David Abarbanel, m. (1794) Sarah de Abraham Mocatta
  (b. 1772; d. 1852) (b. 1777; d. 1852)
  - Elias (b. 1796), m. Susan Lyon
  - Grace (b. 1799), m. Judah Aloof
  - Jacob (b. 1804), m. Esther Levy, St. Thomas, W. I.
  - Nethaneel (b. 1810; d. 1889), m. Sarah da Costa Lindo
  - Zechariah (b. 1813), m. Isabel Levy
  - Sarah (b. 1814), m. Edward Henry
    - Bilhah (b. 1836), m. Benjamin Lindo
    - Esther, m. Isaac A. Joseph
    - Jemima, m. (1) Samuel de Sola (2) Lawrence Jacob
    - David (b. 1851), m. Re Henry
    - Abraham (b. 1859), m. Mabel Halford
  - Daniel (b. 1816), m. Hannah Garcia
  - Jemima (b. 1819), m. Joshua Alexander
  - and ten others
- * Moses de Eliahu, m. (1783) Sarah de Moses da Costa
  (d. 1837) (d. 1835)
  - * Moses da Costa, m. (1813) Leah Norsa (b. 1792;
    (b. 1784; d. 1866) d. 1847)
    - †Nethaneel, m. (1835) Sarah da Costa Lindo
      (b. 1810; d. 1889) (b. 1814; d. 1900)
      - * Joseph Norsa (b. 1837), m. (1861) Esther Benoliel (b. 1841; d. 1885)
        - Moses Albert Norsa (b. April 27, 1862), m. (1892) Constance Mary Elkin (b. 1865)
          - 2 children
      - Gabriel (b. 1838; d. 1908) m. (1861) Miriam Mendes da Costa (d. 1875)
      - Arthur (b. 1839), m. (1864) Selina Spyer

* Sworn brokers of the city of London.

† Identical with Nethaneel, son of David Abarbanel.

J.

M. A. N. L.

PEDIGREE OF THE LINDO FAMILY.

much of his information from original sources; it still retains some value. He furthermore made manuscript translations into English of some of the masterpieces of Hebrew literature, including Baḥya's "Ḥobot ha-Lebabot"; Judah ha-Levi's "Cuzari"; Isaac Aboab's "Menorat ha-Ma'or." The manuscripts are now in the possession of Jews' College, London.

Lindo was several times warden of the Portuguese congregation of London, and compiled a complete catalogue of all the works in its library, with biographical memoranda of their authors.

BIBLIOGRAPHY: *Jew. Chron.* June 23, 1865.

J. G. L.

LINDO, MARK PRAGER: Dutch writer; born in London Sept. 18, 1819; died at The Hague March 9, 1879. He went to Holland in 1838 as teacher of English, first at Arnhem, and then at the Military Academy at Breda; and he studied Dutch literature at Utrecht University (D.Litt. 1854). He was inspector of schools in South Holland from 1865 until his death. Lindo took a somewhat important position in Dutch literature as a mediator between Holland and England. He translated Dickens, Thackeray, Fielding, Sterne, and Scott in versions which were more distinguished for vigor than accuracy. He wrote a number of novels under the pseudonym "De Oude Heer Smits," among them being "Afdrukken van Indrukken" (1854; his most popular work; written in conjunction with Lodewyk Mulder); "Brieven en Ontoezemingen" and "Familie van Ons" (1855); "Typen" (1871). With Lodewyk Mulder also he published the weekly "Nederlandsche Spectator." Lindo wrote a history of England in Dutch (2 vols., 1868–74). His collected works, edited by Mulder, appeared in five volumes (Amsterdam, 1879).

BIBLIOGRAPHY: *Encyc. Brit.* 10th ed., Supplement.

S. J.

LINDO, MOSES: Planter and merchant in South Carolina; born probably in England; died at Charleston, S. C., April 26, 1774. He seems to have been considered one of the foremost experts in the cochineal and indigo trade in London. Becoming interested in the prospects of the indigo industry of South Carolina, he removed to Charleston in Nov., 1756, and at once announced his intention of purchasing indigo for the foreign market. His advertisements appear repeatedly in the "South Carolina Gazette" for 1756. He soon became a wealthy planter and slave-owner and ranked among the prominent merchants of Charleston. He did more than any other individual to encourage and advance the indigo industry of the colony, among the most important industries in South Carolina in prerevolutionary times. His transactions were enormous, and in 1762 he was appointed "Surveyor and Inspector-General of Indigo, Drugs, and Dyes," an office he resigned in 1772.

Lindo seems to have been a man of scientific attainments, and his experiments with American dyes commenced as early as 1757. He maintained a correspondence with Emanuel Mendez da Costa, librarian of the Royal Society and one of the foremost naturalists of his day. The "Philosophical Transactions of the Royal Society" (liii. 238, paper 37) contains "An account of a New Die from the Berries of a Weed in South Carolina: in a letter from Mr. Moses Lindo dated at Charlestown, September 2, 1763, to Mr. Emanuel Mendez da Costa, Librarian of the Royal Society."

An item in the "South Carolina Gazette" (March 15, 1773) states that Lindo purchased a stone which he believed to be a topaz of immense size, and that he sent it to London by the Right Hon. Lord Charles Greville Montague to be presented to the Queen of England. A number of Lindo's advertisements and of items concerning him in the "South Carolina Gazette" have recently been collected by Rev. B. A. Elzas, and reprinted in the "Charleston News and Courier," Jan. 18, 1903.

BIBLIOGRAPHY: Kayserling, *Zur Gesch. der Jüdischen Aerzte*, in *Monatsschrift*, vii. 165; Hühner, *The Jews of South Carolina Prior to 1800*; N. Taylor Phillips, *Publications Am. Jew. Hist. Soc.* ii. 51–52.

A. L. Hü.

LINEN: Cloth made of flax. The Biblical terms are "bad" (LXX. λίνεος; A. V. "linen"), "shesh," and "buẓ" (LXX. βύσσος or βύσσινος; A. V. "fine linen"). In the construction of the Tabernacle linen was used for the inner cover (Ex. xxvi. 1); the hanging or screen closing the entrance to the Tabernacle (Ex. xxvi. 36); the veil which divided the "Holy" from the "Holy of Holies" (Ex. xxvi. 31); and the hangings of the court together with the curtain for the entrance to it (Ex. xxvii. 9, 16, and parallels). It was used also in the priests' vestments (Ex. xxviii. 42, xxxix. 27–29; Lev. xvi. 4). According to II Chron. iii. 14 (comp. ii. 14), a curtain of buẓ also divided the Holy of Holies ("debir") from the Holy in the Temple of Solomon; and from I Macc. (i. 22, iv. 51) and Josephus ("B. J." v. 5, §§ 4 *et seq.*) it can be seen that in the two succeeding Temples both the Holy and Holy of Holies were divided by curtains of byssus.

From Ex. xxxix. 27–29, compared with Ex. xxviii. 42 and Lev. xvi. 4, it would appear that "bad" and "shesh," the latter being identified with Coptic "shens" and first mentioned in connection with Egypt (Gen. xli. 42), are, if not identical, manufactural varieties of the same substance. "Buẓ," again, which occurs only in later books, is assumed to be a later equivalent of "shesh" (comp. II Chron. ii. 14, iii. 14, v. 12 with Ex. xxv. 4, xxvi. 31, xxviii. 42, etc.); in I Chron. xv. 27 it corresponds to "bad" in II Sam. vi. 14. It may also be a different local name for the same fabric (comp. Ezek. xxvii. 7 and 16).

The view of many modern exegetes that the Hebrew terms denote "linen" is supported not only by the Septuagint renderings of λίνεος and βύσσος, which latter generally means "linen" (comp., for instance, Herodotus, ii. 86; Thomson, "Mummy Cloths of Egypt," in "London and Edinburgh Philosophical Magazine," 3d series, vol. v., p. 355; Budge, "The Mummy," p. 190, Cambridge, 1893), but also by the facts that in the Temple of Ezekiel the priests, while ministering, wore linen garments (Ezek. xliv. 17), and that cotton is mentioned in the Old Testament under the name of "karpas" (Esth. i. 6). Still, as the ancients did not always sharply distinguish between linen and cotton, it is possible that both were used in the Sanctuary and that the terms designate in general "white stuff."

It was enacted that garments should be made of only one kind of stuff (Lev. xix. 19), and later tradition (Josephus, "Ant." iii. 6, §§ 1 *et seq.*; 7, §§ 1 *et seq.*; *idem*, "B. J." v. 5, § 7; Philo, "De Vita Moysis," ii. 151; *idem*, "Duo de Monarchia," ii. 225 [ed. Mangey]) and the Talmud have it that only wool (for the variegated ornaments) and linen entered into the textiles used in the Tabernacle and Temple (comp. Yoma 34b; Kil. ix. 1; comp. also Ibn Ezra on Ex. xxv. 4). According to Josephus ("Ant." xx. 9, § 6), Agrippa II. permitted the Levites also to wear linen garments (comp. II Chron. v. 12; see Sha'atnez).

Bibliography: John Braun, *De Vestitu Sacerd. Hebr.* i., ch. vi., Amsterdam, 1680; J. R. Forster, *De Bysso Antiquorum*, London, 1776; Haneberg, *Die Religiösen Alterthümer der Bibel*, p. 536, Munich, 1869; Tristram, *Nat. Hist.* pp. 440, 465, London, 1867; Yates, *Textrinum Antiquorum*, London, 1843.

E. G. H. I. M. C.

LINETZKI, ISAAC JOEL: Russo-Yiddish humorist; born at Vinnitza Sept. 8, 1839, in which town his father, Joseph Linetzki, was a Ḥasidic rabbi. At the age of eighteen Isaac ran away from home and went to Odessa. Thence he intended to go to Breslau to study at the rabbinical seminary, but was intercepted at the frontier by his father's fanatical friends, who forced him to return home. Linetzki then attended the rabbinical school at Jitomir (1862–63); and while there he wrote his first poems, which were published in his "Beizer Marshelik" (Odessa, 1868). Zweifel and Slonimsky took a great interest in Linetzki, who on the latter's recommendation obtained a position in the office of M. Weinstin at Kiev.

In 1866 Linetzki became a contributor to "Ḳol Mebasser," a Yiddish weekly published in Odessa, and in 1868 he began the publication of his famous novel "Das Polische Jüngel." The success of this work was unprecedented in Yiddish literature. Being a true account of the life of a Ḥasidic youth and entirely based upon actual experience, "Das Polische Jüngel" is, in the opinion of the most eminent critics, one of the best humoristic works in Yiddish (L. Wiener, "Hist. of Yiddish Literature," p. 165).

In 1875 Linetzki published at Lemberg conjointly with Goldfaden a Judæo-German weekly, "Yisrolik." In 1876–77 he published his "Pritshepe" and "Statek," and the first number of his calendar, which he continued to issue for a number of years. In the period between 1882 and 1888 he published several works, including "Amerika zi Erez Isroel"; a geography of Palestine; and translations of Lessing's "Nathan der Weise" and Grätz's "Gesch. der Juden." His "Worem Chrein," a sequel to "Das Polische Jüngel," was published as a serial in the "Jüdische Volksbibliotek" (1888, vol. i.). Shorter sketches from his pen have appeared in the "Familienfreund," in the "Hausfreund," and in the "Volksfreund."

Bibliography: *Linetzki Yubileum*, Odessa, 1891; Wiener, *Hist. of Yiddish Literature*, New York, 1899; *Voskhod*, 1884, No. 2.

H. R. M. Z.

LION.—Biblical Data: There are several names for the lion in the Old Testament (comp. Job iv. 10 *et seq.*): "aryeh," or "ari," which is the most general name; "labi'" and "lebiyah," for the old lion and lioness; "kefir" and "gur," for the young, strong lion and whelp respectively; while "layish" and "shaḥal" occur in more poetic diction.

The lion is one of the most frequently mentioned animals in the Bible, which would indicate its former abundance in Palestine. Its favorite haunts were the bushy environments of the Jordan (Jer. xlix. 19, l. 44; Zech. xi. 3), caves and thickets (Jer. iv. 7, xxv. 38; Ps. x. 9, xvii. 12), in general the woods (Jer. xii. 8; Amos iii. 8) and the desert (Isa. xxx. 6). Place-names which may be connected with the lion are: Arieh (II Kings xv. 25), Lebaoth and Beth-lebaoth (Josh. xv. 32, xix. 6), Chephirah (Josh. ix. 17, xviii. 28; Ezra ii. 25; Neh. vii. 29), and Laish, the original name of northern Dan (Judges xviii. 29).

Many habits of the lion are incidentally mentioned in the Old Testament. The male assists in the rearing and training of the young (Ezek. xix. 2; Nah. ii. 13); it lies in wait in secret places (Deut. xxxiii. 22; Lam. iii. 10); growls over its prey (Isa. xxxi. 4); breaks the bones of its victims (Isa. xxxviii. 13), and carries them to its lair (Gen. xlix. 9). It not only was the terror of flocks (Mic. v. 8), but also attacked men (I Kings xiii. 24, xx. 36; II Kings xvii. 25). It was, however, fought by shepherds with sling and staff (I Sam. xvii. 34; Amos iii. 12), and was sometimes killed by daring men (Judges xiv. 5; II Sam. xxiii. 20). From Ezek. xix. 4, 8 it may be inferred that the usual manner of catching the animal alive was by pit and net. The custom of Oriental kings of throwing those fallen into disgrace to lions which were kept in dens, is illustrated in Dan. vi. 8 *et seq.*

The lion is the emblem of strength, courage, and majesty (Prov. xxii. 13, xxvi. 13, xxx. 30). Judah is compared to a lion (Gen. xlix. 9); so also are Gad and Dan (Deut. xxxiii. 20, 23), Saul and Jonathan (II Sam. i. 23), Israel (Num. xxiii. 24, xxiv. 9), and even God Himself (Isa. xxxi. 4; Hos. v. 14, xi. 10). Similes are derived from its terrific visage (I Chron. xii. 9), and especially from its terror-inspiring roar. The latter is ascribed to enemies (Isa. v. 29; Zeph. iii. 3; Ps. xxii. 13; Prov. xxviii. 15); to false prophets (Ezek. xxii. 25); to the wrath of a king (Prov. xix. 12, xx. 2); to God (Jer. xxv. 30; Joel iv. 16; Amos i. 2, iii. 8). In the Psalter the lion is often the symbol of the cruel and oppressive, the mighty and rich (*e.g.*, Ps. x. 9, xxxiv. 11, xxxv. 17).

As an element of decorative art the figure of the lion entered into the design of the brazen Laver in the Temple of Solomon and of Solomon's throne (I Kings vii. 29, x. 20, and parallels).

E. G. H. I. M. C.

——**In Rabbinical Literature:** The Talmud states six names of the lion, namely: "aryeh," "kefir," "labi'," "layish," "shaḥal," and "shaḥaf" (Sanh. 95a; Ab. R. N. xxxix., end). The most general terms, however, are "are," "arya'" (B. Ḳ. 4a), and "aryeh"; for the lioness, "lebiyah" (B. Ḳ. 16b), "guryata" (Shab. 67a), and "kalba" (Yalḳ. ii. 721); and for the young lion, "gurya"

(Sanh. 64a). In Ḥul. 59b an animal called "ṭigris" is defined as "the lion of Be-'Ilai" (א׳ דבי עילאי). By "Be-'Ilai" is probably meant a mountain height or mountain forest, perhaps specially the Lebanon (comp. "bala," *ib.* 80a, and see GOAT); and if by "ṭigris" the tiger is meant, it would appear that the Talmudical writers did not know this animal from personal observation, and it was therefore endowed by them with fabulous proportions and qualities. Thus it is said in the same passages that the distance between the lobes of its lungs was nine cubits, and that its roar at a distance of 400 parasangs brought down the walls of Rome. Kohut ("Ueber die Jüdische Angelologie und Dämonologie," etc., p. 103; comp. also *idem*, "Aruch Completum," iv. 15) surmises that "ṭigris" is the Persian "thrigaṭ," *i.e.*, the mythical three-legged animal (comp. also Schorr in "He-Ḥaluẓ," vii. 32).

The lion is often enumerated among the dangerous animals (B. Ḳ. 15b and parallels). It is especially dangerous in rutting-time (Sanh. 106a). It begins to devour its prey alive (Pes. 49b), carrying part of it to the lair for the lioness and the whelps (B. Ḳ. 16b; Sanh. 90b). Sometimes, however, the lion will stay among flocks without injuring them (Ḥul. 53a); it attacks man only when driven by hunger (Yeb. 121b), and never two men when they are together (Shab. 151b). Though the lion can be tamed (Sanh. 15b; comp. the expression "ari tarbut," B. Ḳ. 16b), it is, on account of its dangerousness, kept in a cage (Shab. 106b), and when so confined is fed with the flesh of wild asses (Men. 103b). It is forbidden to sell lions to the pagans because the latter use them in their circuses ('Ab. Zarah 16a). In passing a lion's den ("gob") one should recite a benediction of thanksgiving in memory of the miracle which happened to Daniel when he was thrown into such a den (Ber. 57b). The term of gestation of the lion is three years (Bek. 8a). Its tormentor is the "mafgia'," or little Ethiopian gnat (Shab. 77b). For the medicinal use of the milk of the lioness see Yalḳ. 721.

The Talmud makes about the same figurative use of the lion as does the Old Testament. The lion is the king of animals (Ḥag. 13b) and the symbol of true mental greatness; and in this regard it is contrasted with the fox (Shab. 111b; Ab. iv. 15; Giṭ. 83b); it is the type of strength and awe (Pes. 112a; Shebu. 22b; B. Ḳ. 85a). The sound of God's voice is likened to the roaring of the lion (Ber. 3a, b). The name of the lion is applied to God, Israel, and the Temple (comp. Isa. xxix. 1: "ariel"; Pesiḳ. R. 28 [ed. Friedmann, p. 133] and parallels). The lion also symbolizes the mighty spirit of temptation and seduction to idolatry (Sanh. 64a; comp. I Peter v. 8). The Temple of Ezekiel is compared to the lion in its structure, both being broad in front and narrow behind (Mid. iv. 7). The lion is also the fifth sign ("Leo") of the zodiac, corresponding to the fifth month, Ab (Pesiḳ. R. *l.c.*; Yalḳ., Ex. 418).

BIBLIOGRAPHY: Tristram, *Nat. Hist.* p. 115; Lewysohn, *Z. T.* pp. 68 and 70.

S. S. I. M. C.

LION, HENRI JULIUS: Dutch journalist; born March 23, 1806, at Elberfeld; died Oct. 19, 1869. In 1824 he entered the Prussian army, and in 1830 that of Holland. In 1834 he went to India, and was honorably discharged as an officer at his own request in 1841. After this he devoted himself to industrial enterprises, having acquired a great practical knowledge of Indian affairs. He was the Nestor of Indian journalism, being the founder of the "Bataviaasch Handelsblad." To his great perseverance must be ascribed the appointment of a committee to consider the establishment of a railway in Java.

BIBLIOGRAPHY: Van der Aa, *Biographisch Woordenboek*, xxi.

S. E. SL.

LION, ISAAC JACOB: Dutch journalist; born at Amersfort Dec. 17, 1821; died at The Hague Aug. 27, 1873. Settling in Amsterdam, he occupied himself with literary work, and became in 1840 editor of the "Handelsblad." In 1849 he applied himself to stenography, and in the following year was appointed shorthand writer to the Second Chamber (Tweede Kamer der Staten Generaal). Jointly with the lawyer D. Leon he established in 1850 the weekly "De Gemeente Stem." He was also correspondent for several weeklies and dailies. In 1856 he became editor of the "Indier," and in 1860 proprietor of the "'sGravenhaagsche Nieuwsbode," which paper he combined with the "Indier" and published as the "Dagblad van 'sGravenhage en Zuid-Holland." This paper is still (1904) in existence.

BIBLIOGRAPHY: Van der Aa, *Biographisch Woordenboek*, xxi. (gives list of works covering 3 pages); *Dagblad van 'sGravenhage*, Aug. 28, 1873.

S. E. SL.

LIPINER, SIEGFRIED: Austrian poet; born at Yaroslav, Galicia, Oct. 24, 1856; educated at the gymnasia in Tarnow and Vienna and at the universities of Leipsic and Strasburg. In 1881 he was appointed librarian to the Austrian Reichsrath, which post he still occupies (1904). In 1894 the title of "Regierungsrath" was conferred upon him. Lipiner has written: "Der Entfesselte Prometheus" (1876); "Renatus" (1878); "Das Buch der Freude" (1880); "Totenfeier" (1887), all published at Leipsic. In 1883 he translated the "Pan Thaddeus" of Mickiewitz, and in 1886 wrote the libretto for Goldmark's "Merlin."

BIBLIOGRAPHY: *Meyers Konversations-Lexikon*.

S. F. T. H.

LIPKIN: Russo-Jewish family which derives its origin from Dob Bär Lipkin, rabbi of Plungian in the first half of the eighteenth century (see Ezekiel Katzenellenbogen, "Keneset Ezekiel," No. 7). The pedigree of the most important members of the family will be found on the following page.

Israel Lipkin (known as **Rabbi Israel Salanter,** after his place of residence, Salaty): Russian rabbi; born at Zhagory at the beginning of the nineteenth century; died at Königsberg, Prussia, Feb. 2, 1883. He received his first training from his father, Zeeb Wolf, who was rabbi at Zhagory. After his marriage Lipkin settled at Salaty, where he continued his studies under Rabbi Hirsch Broda and Rabbi Joseph Zundel (died in Jerusalem 1866). Zundel exerted a deep influence on the development of Lipkin's character; and the latter showed his appreciation of his teacher by referring to him in the preface to his periodical "Tebunah" as the light which he followed all his days.

In 1842 Lipkin was called to Wilna as head of the yeshibah Tomeke Torah. During his incumbency he established a new yeshibah at Zarechye, a suburb of Wilna, where he lectured for about three years.

Lipkin's great service lay in his insistence on the practical application of the moral teachings of Judaism and in his emphasis of the necessity of manual labor on the part of the Jews. He established societies for the study of religious ethics, with but little regard for worldly affairs; and at his suggestion the works on religious ethics of Moses Ḥayyim Luzzatto, Mendel Lefin, and Solomon ibn Gabirol were reprinted at Wilna.

When, in 1848, the Russian government established the rabbinical school at Wilna, Lipkin declined an invitation to become instructor in Talmud and rabbinical law. He settled in Kovno and established a yeshibah, connected with the bet ha-midrash of Hirsch Naviazsky, of which he retained charge until 1857, when failing health compelled him to remove to Germany for medical treatment. He remained in the house of the philanthropists, the Hirsch brothers of Halberstadt, until his health improved, and then (in 1861) began the publication of the Hebrew monthly "Tebunah," devoted to rabbinical law and religious ethics. On account of his failing health this periodical was discontinued at the end of a year, and Lipkin again lived for a time the life of a wanderer, visiting yeshibot and offering advice to teachers and students wherever his assistance was sought. Toward the end of his life Lipkin was called to Paris to organize a community among the Russian immigrants, and he remained there for two years.

Lipkin was a singular combination of the ultra-Orthodox Jew and the man of the world, particularly in regard to the duties of citizenship. He preached love for the fatherland and respect for the laws of the country. When the ukase making military service universally obligatory appeared, Lipkin wrote an appeal to the rabbis and community leaders urging them to keep lists of recruits so as to leave no pretext for the contention that the Jews shirked such service. He was considered one of the most eminent Orthodox rabbis of the nineteenth century because of his broad Talmudic scholarship, his deep piety, and his personal influence for good; and he was probably the only rabbi of his time that exerted a wide influence on his fellow rabbis and on the Jewish communities of Russia. His disciples collected and published some of his sayings, commentaries, and sermons in "Eben Yisrael" (Warsaw, 1853) and in "'Eẓ Peri" (Wilna, 1880).

BIBLIOGRAPHY: Fuenn, *Keneset Yisrael*, p. 697, Warsaw, 1886; H. M. Steinschneider, *'Ir Wilna*, p. 128; Feldberg, in *Ḳedosh Yisrael*, Wilna, 1884.

H. R. J. G. L.

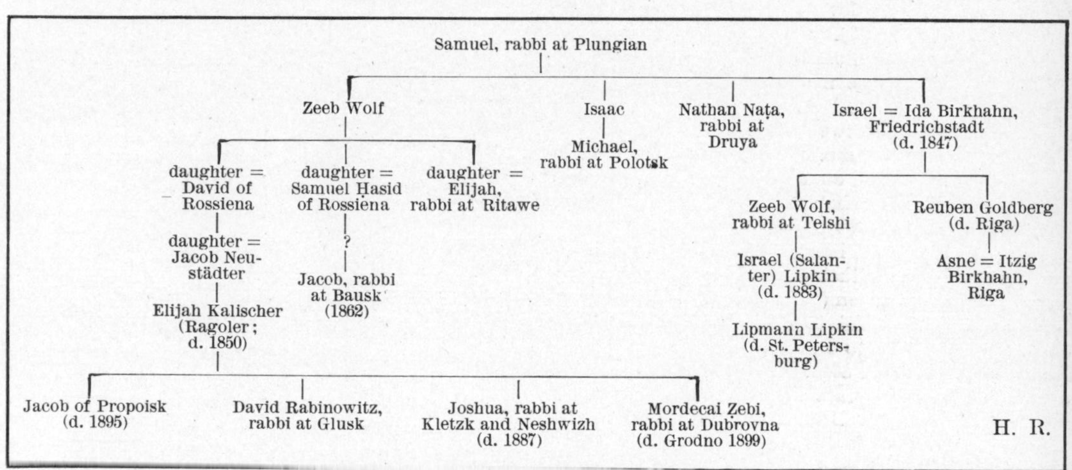

PEDIGREE OF THE LIPKIN FAMILY.

Lipmann Lipkin: Russian mathematician; born at Salaty, government of Kovno, 1846; died at St. Petersburg Feb. 9 (21), 1876; son of Israel Salanter. Lipkin's early training consisted in the study of the Bible, the Talmud, and other religious books. At an early age he began to show a decided inclination for scientific subjects, particularly mathematics. Not knowing any European language, he had to derive his information from Hebrew books alone. Notwithstanding the incomplete nature of such sources, and without other aid, Lipkin not only succeeded in mastering the elementary sciences, but also acquired a knowledge of the higher mathematics. He also began the study of modern languages, especially German and French. Subsequently he went to Königsberg, where through the influence of Professor Rischelo he was admitted to the lectures. Somewhat later Lipkin entered the Berlin Gewerbe-Academie, and then Jena University, where he received the degree of Ph.D., his dissertation being "Ueber die Räumlichen Strophoiden." From Jena Lipkin went to St. Petersburg, and because of his great ability was permitted to take the examination for master of mathematics in spite of the fact that he possessed only the degree of "candidate," had not studied in any Russian school, and was not even thoroughly conversant with the Russian language. In 1873 he passed his examination brilliantly. His dissertation was almost completed when he was attacked by smallpox, of which he died.

Lipkin's name first became known in the mathematical world through his mechanical device for the change of linear into circular motion, this mechanism having been invented by him while he was still a pupil at the technical high school. He described his invention in the journal of the Russian Academy ("Mélanges Mathématiques de l'Académie Impériale à St. Petersbourg," 1870), under the title "Ueber eine Gelenkgeradeführung von L. Lipkin." The Russian mathematician Chebyshev had tried to show that an exact solution was impossible; and his views were accepted until Lipkin's discovery proved the contrary. This invention has been described in numerous text-books, such as Collignon's "Traité de Mécanique, Cinématique" (Paris, 1873), where it is called "Lipkin's Parallelogram."

A model of Lipkin's invention was exhibited at the exposition at Vienna in 1873, and was later secured from the inventor by the Museum of the Institute of Engineers of Ways of Communication, St. Petersburg.

Lipkin never lost his deep interest in purely Jewish affairs, as is shown by his contributions to "Ha-Ẓefirah."

Bibliography: *Yevreiskaya Biblioteka*, v. 191 (translated into German in *Allg. Zeit. des Jud.* 1876, p. 13); *Ha-Ẓefirah*, 1876.

H. R. J. G. L.

LIPMAN, CLARA: American actress; born in Chicago. She made her début as an ingénue with Modjeska in 1888, and subsequently played similar parts in A. M. Palmer's company. She created the principal rôle in "Incog" (1891), but before this had interpreted leading parts in classic drama in various English and German companies. In 1898 she created the part of *Julie Bon Bon* in "The Girl from Paris." With her husband, Louis Mann, she starred for five years, appearing in "All on Account of Eliza," "The Red Kloof," "The Telephone Girl," "The Girl in the Barracks," "Master and Pupil," etc. During the season of 1902-3 she withdrew from the stage on account of an accident to one of her arms. Clara Lipman is the author of a play entitled "Pepi" (1898).

A. F. H. V.

LIPMAN, SAMUEL PHILIPPUS: Dutch jurist; born in London April 27, 1802; died at Hilversum July 7, 1871. He was educated at Glueckstadt, Hamburg, and Amsterdam; studied law at Leyden (1819–22), and in 1823 established himself as a lawyer at Amsterdam, where he soon became famous as a pleader. In May, 1852, he was converted to Roman Catholicism. He then removed to The Hague, and devoted himself after 1862 entirely to religious study.

Lipman published, besides many pamphlets (a complete list of which is given in "Levensberichten"): "Geschiedenis van de Staatkunde der Voornaamste Mogendheden van Europa Sedert den Val van Napoleon," 2 vols., Zutphen, 1834; "Het Nieuwe Testament Vertaald," 's Hertogenbosch, 1859; "Constitutioneel Archief van Alle Koninklijke Aanspraken en Parlementaire Adressen," 4 vols., 1847–63 (2d ed., The Hague, 1864).

Bibliography: *De Tijd*, July 18, 1871; *De Wachter*, Aug. 1, 1871; *Levensberichten van de Maatschappij soor Letterkunde*, 1872; Van der Aa, *Biographisch Woordenboek*, xxi.

S. E. Sl.

LIPMANN-MÜLHAUSEN, YOM-ṬOB BEN SOLOMON: Austrian controversialist, Talmudist, and cabalist of the fourteenth and fifteenth centuries. According to Bishop Bodecker of Brandenburg, who wrote a refutation of Lipmann's "Niẓẓaḥon," Lipmann lived at Cracow. But Naphtali Hirsch Treves, in the introduction to his "Siddur," calls him Lipmann-Mülhausen of Prague, adding that he lived in the part of the town called "Wyschigrod." Manuscript No. 223 in the Halberstam collection contains a document issued at Prague in 1413 and signed by Lipmann-Mülhausen, as dayyan.

His Attainments. It is seen from his "Niẓẓaḥon" that, besides his rabbinical studies, Lipmann occupied himself with the study of the Bible, that he was acquainted with Karaite literature, that he read the New Testament, and that he knew Latin. His authority in rabbinical matters is shown by his circular to the rabbis warning them against the use of any shofar not made of a ram's horn (comp. Luzzatto in "Kerem Ḥemed," vii. 56). There are also responsa addressed to him by Jacob b. Moses Mölln (Neubauer, "Cat. Bodl. Hebr. MSS." No. 907, 5), and Israel Isserlein mentions him ("Terumat ha-Deshen," No. 24) as one of five scholars who met at Erfurt. In 1399 (Aug. 16) Lipmann and many other Jews were thrown into prison at the instigation of a converted Jew named Peter, who accused them of insulting Christianity in their works. Lipmann was ordered to justify himself, but while he brilliantly refuted Peter's accusations, as a result of the charges seventy-seven Jews were martyred on Aug. 22, 1400, and three more, by fire, on Sept. 11 in the same year. Of the accused Lipmann alone escaped death.

His Works. Lipmann was the author of: "Sefer ha-Niẓẓaḥon," a refutation of Christianity and Karaism and a demonstration of the superiority of rabbinical Judaism; "Zikron Sefer ha-Niẓẓahon," a refutation of Christianity, an abstract in verse of the preceding work (pp. 107–117 in the "Tela Ignea Satanæ" of Wagenseil, who supplied a Latin translation and added a long refutation, Freiburg, 1681; Geiger, in Bresslauer's "Deutscher Volkskalender," iii. 48, declares Lipmann's authorship of this poem doubtful); a commentary to the "Shir ha-Yiḥud" (Freiburg, 1560). In Samson b. Eleazar's "Baruk she-Amar" (Shklov, 1804) there is a cabalistic treatise on the Hebrew alphabet, entitled "Sefer Alfa Beta," the author of which is given as מהר"ל שלי"ו. Sachs and Steinschneider concluded that the author was Lipmann-Mülhausen. This work discusses: (1) the form of the letters, (2) the reason for their form, (3) the mystery of their composition, order, and numerical value, and (4) the cabalistic explanation of their form. In this work the author frequently mentions a cabalistic work entitled "Sefer ha-Eshkol" and a commentary to the "Sefer Yeẓirah." Menahem Ẓiyyoni's "Ẓefune Ẓiyyoni" is ascribed, in a pamphlet quoted by Reuben Hoshke (Yalḳ., Reubeni, section "Naso"), to a certain R. Ṭabyomi, whom Steinschneider ("Cat. Bodl." col. 1411) identifies with Lipmann-Mülhausen. Lipmann promises, in his "Niẓẓaḥon" (§ 197), a commentary to Pirḳe Abot, but such a work is not extant. Finally, it may be added that Manuscript 820 in Oppenheimer's collection was supposed to be a Biblical commentary by the author of the "Sefer ha-Niẓẓaḥon," but Dukes ("Orient, Lit." xi. 299) declares that it is nothing else than the "Niẓẓaḥon" itself.

Lipmann's reputation is dependent, mainly, upon his "Niẓẓaḥon." That a rabbi in the fifteenth century should occupy himself with Latin and the New Testament was certainly a rare thing. Lipmann was compelled to justify himself (§ 3) by referring to the saying of R. Eliezer, "Know what thou shalt answer to the heretic" (Abot ii. 14). The whole work consists of 354 paragraphs, the number of days in the lunar year, each paragraph, with the exception of the last eight, beginning with a passage of the Bible, upon which the author founds his argument. Thus his arguments rest upon 346 passages taken from all the books of the Old Testament. The last eight paragraphs contain his dispute with the convert Peter. In the introduction Lipmann says that he divided the work into seven parts to represent the seven days of the week. The part for the first day contains the arguments against Christians; that for the second day those against the Karaite interpretation of the Bible; those for the remaining five days contain severally interpretations of obscure Biblical passages that are likely to mislead students; the reasons for the commandments; arguments against atheists; arguments against the Karaites and their rejection of the Talmud; and an account of the sixteen things which comprehend the whole of Judaism and which, after being indicated in the Pentateuch, are repeated in the Prophets and Hagiographa.

Contents of the "Niẓẓaḥon."

Very characteristic is Lipmann's refutation of the assumed miraculous birth of Jesus, as well as his demonstration of the falsity of the conclusions of the Christians who claim that the birth of Jesus was foretold by the Prophets. He constantly quotes Maimonides, Ibn Ezra, Naḥmanides, Saadia, Rashi, Shemariah of Negropont, and other ancient scholars. Lipmann must have written his "Sefer ha-Niẓẓaḥon" before 1410, for he expressed a hope that the Messiah would arrive in that year (§ 335). It was first published by Hackspan (Altdorf, 1644), who with great difficulty obtained the manuscript from the rabbi of Schneittach. Wagenseil published, at the end of his "Sota" (Altdorf-Nuremberg, 1674), corrections of Hackspan's edition under the title of "Correctiones Lipmannianæ." Later, the "Niẓẓaḥon" was reprinted, with the addition of Ḳimḥi's "Wikkuaḥ," in Amsterdam (1709 and 1711) and Königsberg (1847). Sebald Snelle published the Hebrew text with a Latin translation and refutation of the paragraph (§ 8) denying the miraculous birth of Jesus (Altdorf, 1643); and at various dates he published Latin translations of the paragraphs directed against Christianity. A Latin translation of the whole work, with the exception of the passages taken from the Pentateuch, was made by John Heinrich Blendinger (Altdorf, 1645). As will be readily understood, the work gave rise to many polemics and called forth replies from Christians. The first was Stephen Bodecker, Bishop of Brandenburg, a younger contemporary of Lipmann, who wrote a refutation of the "Niẓẓaḥon" (comp. Wolf, "Bibl. Hebr." i. 736). The following other refutations are published: Wilhelm Schickard, "Triumphator Vapulans sive Refutatio," etc. (Tübingen, 1629); Stephen Gerlow, "Disputatio Contra Lipmanni Nizzachon" (Königsberg, 1647); Christian Schotan, "Anti-Lipmanniana" (Franeker, 1659), giving also the Hebrew text of the "Niẓẓaḥon."

Translations and Refutations.

Bibliography: Fuenn, *Keneset Yisrael*, p. 443; Fürst, *Bibl. Jud.* ii. 403; Grätz, *Gesch.* 3d ed., viii. 71–72; Sachs, in *Kerem Ḥemed*, viii. 206 *et seq.*; Steinschneider, *Cat. Bodl.* cols. 1410–1414; idem, *Jewish Literature*, pp. 113, 129, 145; Wolf, *Bibl. Hebr.* i., iii., No. 1364; Zunz, *Z. G.* pp. 124, 129, 194, 380.

D. M. Sel.

LIPOVETZ: Town in the government of Kiev, Russia. In 1897 it had a total population of 6,068, of which 4,500 were Jews. There were 670 Jewish artisans and 71 Jewish day-laborers; of the latter 25 engaged in field-work during the harvest season. The economic condition of the Jews there has been unfavorably affected by the abolition of annual and weekly fairs, and in 1900 the poverty of the population became so great that a mob of several hundred collected at the house of the local police official and demanded bread and the reestablishment of the fairs. The Jewish artisans are engaged extensively in the manufacture of a new kind of footwear, one variety of which, worn by the peasantry, is known as "postaly," and another, worn by the more prosperous, as "skorokhody." The 25 ḥadarim afforded instruction to 475 children, and 59 Jewish pupils attended the city school. The Talmud Torah, founded in 1898, had 97 pupils. In 1768 Lipovetz suffered with other Ukrainean towns from the attacks of the Haidamacks.

Bibliography: *Voskhod* (monthly), 1890, ii. 94; *Voskhod* (weekly), 1900, Nos. 12, 17.

H. R. S. J.

LIPPE (Lippe-Detmold): Small sovereign principality in northwest Germany, with a Jewish population of 750; total population (1895) 123,515. The earliest traces of Jewish settlement in Lippe date back to the beginning of the fourteenth century. The Jews in the principality of Lippe seem to have enjoyed more privileges and greater security than in other German states. Thus the town council of Lemgo in a document dated 1419 refers to a Jew named Moses as "our fellow citizen." The contribution of the Jewry to the city treasury amounted in 1507 to one hundred florins ($40), a considerable sum in those days. Besides, it had to pay a Jew-tax, which in 1511 was fixed at eighteen gulden. In the year 1500 the "Edelherrn" Bernhard VII. and Simon V. (father and son) permitted Antzell the Jew, with his wife and servants, to reside in Detmold.

A Jewish community was not formed in Detmold until the second half of the seventeenth century. Religious differences seem to have led to a split in the community, for in 1723 the Jews of Detmold asked permission to build a second synagogue. These synagogues, however, were merely rented rooms. In 1742 the community evidently reunited, for it acquired a house and a barn, and constructed out of the latter a synagogue, which is still in use. In 1810, during the regency of the princess Pauline, the Jews in Lippe received family names and were regularly registered. At this time there were 175 Jewish families in Lippe; twenty-seven of these families were resident in Detmold, under Rabbi Abraham Löb Färnbach, succeeded by his son Dr. Enoch Färnbach (Fahrenbach), who officiated until his death (Oct. 5, 1872). The civic rights of the Jews, as well as their systems of school and synagogue, were regulated afresh by the laws of 1858 and 1879. From 1872 (Oct.) to 1879 (March) the rabbinate was provisionally filled by the teacher Leseritz of Detmold and, afterward, by Rabbi Klein of Lemgo.

After this period, consequent upon the steady decrease in the size of the community, the rabbinical position was left vacant. The supervision of religious instruction in the twelve congregations of the principality, comprising about 900 members, some 250 of whom belonged to Detmold, was entrusted to the teacher and preacher Abraham Plaut of Detmold. Detmold is the birthplace of Leopold Zunz and of Dr. Abraham Treuenfels, while Dr. Hermann Vogelstein, at present (1904) rabbi in Stettin, is a native of Lage in the principality of Lippe.

As a benefactor to the Jews in Lippe, and, particularly, of the Detmold community, may be mentioned the court commissioner Solomon Joel Herford (d. Sept. 21, 1816). He was the founder of the Joel Herfordsche Schule, the Joel Herfordsche Milden Stiftungen, and the Jüdische Militär-Unterstützungskasse.

D. A. Pl.

LIPPE, CHAIM DAVID: Austrian publisher and bibliographer; born Dec. 22, 1823, at Stanislawow, Galicia; died Aug. 26, 1900, at Vienna. For some time he was cantor and instructor in religion at Eperies, Hungary, but he left that town for Vienna, where he conducted a Jewish publishing-house, which issued several popular works. He himself edited a bibliographical lexicon of modern Jewish literature ("Ch. D. Lippe's Bibliographisches Lexicon der Gesammten Jüdischen Literatur der Gegenwart und Adress-Anzeiger," Vienna, 1881; 2d ed. 1900).

S. E. J.

LIPPMANN, EDOUARD: French engineer; born at Verdun Feb. 22, 1833. Educated at his native town, the lycée at Metz, and the Ecole Centrale des Arts et Manufactures at Paris, he graduated as engineer in 1856. Joining the firm of Degousé & Laurent, architects, he resided in the French capital and took an active part in the defense of Paris as captain of the volunteer engineer corps during the Franco-Pussian war. In 1878 he established himself in Paris, founding the house of Edouard Lippmann & Company. He became especially interested in the boring of deep wells (one bored by his firm at the Place Herbert at Paris was 718 meters deep), especially petroleum-wells, and in the building of bridges, canals, and roads in various parts of the world.

Lippmann has published several essays in the professional papers, especially in the "Genie Civil," and is the author of "Petit Traité de Sondage." He has received several honorable mentions at the international expositions; *e.g.*, at Amsterdam in 1883, and at Paris in 1867, 1878, 1889, and 1900.

Lippmann is an officer of the Legion of Honor.

Bibliography: Curinier, *Dict. Nat.* ii. 127.

S. F. T. H.

LIPPMANN, EDUARD: Austrian chemist; born at Prague Sept. 23, 1842; educated at the gymnasium of Vienna and the universities of Leipsic and Heidelberg (Ph.D. 1864). He took a postgraduate course at Paris, and in 1868 became privatdocent at the University of Vienna. During 1872 he took charge of the classes of Professor Linnemann at the technical high school at Brünn; in 1875 he was appointed assistant professor of chemistry at Vienna University and chief of the third chemical institute; and in 1877 he was appointed professor of analytical chemistry at the Vienna Handelsakademie, which position he resigned in 1881. He is at present (1904) lecturer of chemistry at the Vienna technical high school.

Lippmann has contributed many essays to the reports of the Vienna Imperial Academy of Sciences and to the professional journals of Europe.

Bibliography: Eisenberg, *Das Geistige Wien*, ii., Vienna, 1895.

S. F. T. H.

LIPPMANN, GABRIEL: French physicist; born at Hollerich, Luxemburg, in 1845. After being educated at the Ecole Normale and in Germany, he went to Paris, taking the degree of D.Sc. in 1875. During his stay in Germany he had given special attention to electricity, and subsequently invented the capillary electrometer, an electrocapillary motor, etc. In 1891 he discovered the process of color-photography, which discovery he amplified in 1892. He prepared glass slides, which were covered with a very finely granulated bromid-of-silver solution, and which, when dried, were placed in a concave frame filled with quicksilver, giving a mirror-like surface to the solution. When the photograph is taken the light-rays form a wave of light in the solution in conjunction with the rays from the quicksilver-mirror, giving light "maxima" and dark "minima." These when reproduced give, by reflected light, a true picture in the original colors. However, the very long exposure necessary (about ten minutes) makes the process unsatisfactory. This discovery won him recognition. In 1883 he succeeded Briot as professor of physical mathematics at the Sorbonne, and in 1885 he became professor of experimental physics at the same institution. In 1886 he was elected member of the Académie des Sciences, succeeding Dessain. Lippmann has contributed many essays to the professional journals, and is the author of "Cours de Thermodynamique," Paris, 1886, and "Cours d'Acoustique et d'Optique," *ib.* 1888.

Bibliography: *Nouveau Larousse Illustré.*

S. F. T. H.

LIPPMANN, GABRIEL HIRSCH: German rabbi; born at Memmelsdorf, Bavaria; died at Kissingen May 26, 1864. He went in his early youth to Burgpreppach, where he studied the Talmud under Rabbi Abraham Moses Mayländer. He continued his studies at the yeshibah at Fürth and, under the guidance of Chief Rabbi Hillel Sondheimer, at Aschaffenburg; he received his Ph.D. degree from the University of Würzburg. He then accepted a call as preacher to Aurich, and later became district rabbi in Kissingen.

Lippmann was the editor of: "Sefer Ẓaḥot. Ueber die Feinheiten der Hebräischen Sprache. Grammatische Forschungen von Abraham ibn Esra. Neue Ausgabe mit Hebräischem Commentar," Fürth, 1827; "Sefer ha-Shem. Ueber das Tetragrammaton," *ib.* 1834; "Safah Berurah. Ueber Hebr. Grammatik . . . Abr. ibn Esra, mit Hebr. Commentar," *ib.* 1839; "Sefat Yeter. Beleuchtung Dunkler Bibelstellen . . . von Abraham ibn Esra, mit Hebr. Commentar und Vorwort von I. M. Jost," Frankfort-on-the-Main, 1843.

BIBLIOGRAPHY: Bamberger, *Gesch. der Juden in Aschaffenburg*, p. 78; *Ben Chananja*, 1864, No. 22.

S. M. L. B.

LIPPMANN, MAURICE: French engineer; born at Ville d'Avray (Seine-et-Oise) Sept. 27, 1847. He received his diploma as bachelor of law in 1869. During the siege of Paris in 1870 he served in the artillery. In 1874 Lippmann was appointed director of the state manufactory of weapons ("manufacture nationale d'armes") at St. Etienne, which position he held for ten years. Resigning in 1884, he retired to private life, living at Bracquemont, near Dieppe. In 1889 he was appointed a member of the commission of military art for the French Exposition of 1890.

Lippmann has published: "L'Art dans l'Armure et dans les Armes." He is an officer of the Legion of Honor.

BIBLIOGRAPHY: Curinier, *Dict. Nat.* ii. 144.

S. F. T. H.

LIPPOLD: German physician and financier; born at Prague; lived at Berlin in the sixteenth century. He was in great favor with the elector Joachim II., acting as his financial adviser and as administrator of Jewish affairs. After the sudden death of Joachim (1571), his son and successor, Johann Georg, accused Lippold of having poisoned the elector. Being put to the torture of the rack, he confessed this crime; and, although he afterward retracted, he was executed Jan. 28, 1573, the Jews of Berlin and of the province of Brandenburg being expelled from the country in the same year.

BIBLIOGRAPHY: Ludwig Geiger, *Gesch. der Juden in Berlin*, p. vi., Berlin, 1871; Grätz, *Gesch.* 2d ed., ix. 474.

D. S. MAN.

LIPSCHITZ, RUDOLF: German mathematician; born May 14, 1832, at Königsberg, East Prussia; died at Bonn Oct. 8, 1903. Educated at his native town (Ph.D. 1853), he established himself in 1857 as privat-docent in the University of Bonn, becoming professor of mathematics in the University of Breslau in 1862, and in that of Bonn in 1864.

Lipschitz was the author of: "Wissenschaft und Staat," Bonn, 1874; "Die Bedeutung der Theoretischen Mechanik," Berlin, 1876; "Lehrbuch der Analysis," Bonn, 1877–80; "Untersuchungen über die Summen von Quadraten," *ib.* 1886.

BIBLIOGRAPHY: *Brockhaus Konversations-Lexikon.*

S. F. T. H.

LIPSCHÜTZ (LÜPSCHÜTZ, LIPSCHITZ, LIBSCHITZ): Name of a family of Polish and German rabbis; derived from "Liebeschitz," name of a town in Bohemia.

Aryeh Löb Lipschütz: Austrian rabbi and author; lived in the second half of the eighteenth and in the first half of the nineteenth century; died in Brigul, Galicia, before 1849. He was the pupil of Aryeh Löb (author of "Ḳeẓot ha-Ḥoshen") and son-in-law of Moses Teitelbaum, rabbi at Ujhely. He held the office of rabbi in several cities in Galicia, and at last went to Brigul, where he remained till his death. He was the author of "Ari She-be-Ḥaburah" and "Geburot Ari," novellæ on Ketubot, mentioned in "'Emeḳ Berakah," by Joseph Saul Nathanson. Besides these works he wrote "Aryeh debe-'Ilai," containing novellæ on Ḳiddushin, Yoma, Menaḥot, Ḳinnim, and Niddah, as well as responsa on the four parts of the Shulḥan 'Aruk. This work was published in Lemberg.

BIBLIOGRAPHY: Walden, *Shem ha-Gedolim he-Ḥadash*, i. 82, ii. 16; Eliezer Cohen, *Ḳin'at Soferim*, p. 104b (note 1733), and p. 110a.

S. S. N. T. L.

Baruch Isaac Lipschütz: Son of Israel Lipschütz; born in Dessau; died in Berlin Dec. 18, 1877. He was at first rabbi at Landsberg, and then district rabbi in Mecklenburg-Schwerin, but was obliged to resign both positions in consequence of disagreements with his congregations. Thereafter he lived in private at Hamburg. He wrote "Torath Sch'muel, ein Erbauungsbuch für Israeliten" (Hamburg, 1867).

S. M. K.

Baruch Mordecai b. Jacob Lipschitz (Libschitz): Russian rabbi and author; born about 1810, died at Siedlce, Poland, March 30, 1885. At an early age he became known for his wide Talmudical learning; and later he ranked with the leading rabbinical authorities of his time. Rabbis from all parts applied to him for decisions in regard to difficult questions, and his responsa were characterized by clearness and sound sense. He officiated as rabbi for forty-three years in various cities, including Semiatitz, Wolkowisk, Novogrudek, and finally Siedlce, where he remained till his death.

Lipschitz was the author of: "Berit Ya'aḳob" (Warsaw, 1876–77), responsa on the four parts of the Shulḥan 'Aruk; "Bet Mordekai," sermons; "Minḥat Bikkurim," novellæ on the Shulḥan 'Aruk; and novellæ on the Jerusalem Talmud. The last three works remain in manuscript.

BIBLIOGRAPHY: *Ha-Ẓefirah*, 1885, No. 14; *Ha-Asif*, 1885, p. 758; H. N. Steinschneider, *'Ir Wilna*, p. 164.

S. S. N. T. L.

Eliezer ben Solomon Lipschütz: German rabbi; died at Neuwied about 1748. At the age of thirty he became rabbi at Ostrow, where he gathered many pupils about him. Several years later he accepted a rabbinate elsewhere, but differences with

Warhafftige Abconterfeyung oder gestalt/des angesichts Leupolt Jüden/
sampt fürbildung der Execution/welche an jhme/seiner woluerdienten grausamen vnd vnmenschlichen thaten halben (so er an dem vnschüldigen Christlichen Blut begangen) den 28. Jenners/1573. zu Berlyn/nach innhalt Göttliches vnd Kayserliches Rechten/vollnzogen worden ist.

Darneben kürtzlich seine vnd anderer Jüden tirannen/so etwan von jhnen wider alle menschliche Affecten/vnd mitleiden
gegen den Christen menschen geübt/aus glaubwirdigen Historien/allen frommen Christen zu gut vnd warnung (Auff das sie sich für solchen blut-Eglen desto fürderlicher wissen zuhüten) in Reimen gestelt/vnd an tag geben.
L. T. Z. T.

EXECUTION OF LIPPOLD, 1573.
(From a contemporary copperplate.)

his congregation soon compelled him to resign. He wandered about until finally he went to Cracow, where he obtained a rabbinate through the influence of his wife's uncle, Simon Jolles. There, too, he had many enemies, and on the death of Jolles he was obliged to leave Cracow. After some time he became rabbi at Neuwied, where he remained until his death. He wrote "Heshib R. Eli'ezer we-Siaḥ ha-Sadeh," responsa, published together with a number of responsa by his son Israel Lipschütz (Neuwied, 1749), and "Dammeseḳ Eli'ezer," novellæ (to Shulḥan 'Aruk, Yoreh De'ah and Ḥoshen Mishpaṭ) and responsa, among the latter being some written by his brother Ephraim Lipschütz (*ib.* 1749).

BIBLIOGRAPHY: Preface to *Heshib R. Eli'ezer we-Siaḥ ha-Sadeh*; Dembitzer, *Kelilat Yofi*, ii. 133, Cracow, 1893.

S. M. K.

Gedaliah ben Israel Lipschütz: Rabbi at Obrzizk, near Posen; flourished in the eighteenth and nineteenth centuries (d. 1826). He was the author of the following works: "Regel Yesharah" (Dyhernfurth, 1776), explanations of Rashi and tosafot to the section Neziḳin, notes on Abot de-Rabbi Natan and on the small tractates of the Talmud, with two supplements treating of weights, measures, and geometry in the Talmud, and explaining the calculations found in Kilayim iii., v.; "Ḥumre Matnita" (Berlin, 1784), divided into six parts ("ḳinnim"), containing a commentary on the Talmud, explanations of all the foreign words found in the Talmud, a commentary on Asheri (Rosh), notes on Alfasi, a commentary on Targum Onḳelos, and explanation of the difficult mishnayot; "Keneset Yisrael" (Breslau, 1818), notes on the Mishnah and on various Talmudical subjects, extracted from several works left by Gedaliah in manuscript, and published by his son Israel Lipschütz.

BIBLIOGRAPHY: Steinschneider, *Cat. Bodl.* col. 1003; Fürst, *Bibl. Jud.* ii. 275; Fuenn, *Keneset Yisrael*, s.v.

S. S. I. BR.

Gedaliah ben Solomon Lipschütz: Polish scholar; lived at Lublin in the sixteenth and seventeenth centuries. He was a relative and also a pupil of Meïr of Lublin, whose responsa he edited, adding to them an index (Venice, 1618). He wrote a commentary to Albo's "'Iḳḳarim," entitled "'Eẓ Shatul" (*ib.* 1618). This commentary may be considered a double one; in "Shorashim" the commentator explains the text of Albo, while in the part called "'Anafim" he gives an exposition of Albo's views, comparing them with the views of other philosophers. In the preface, Lipschütz says that he composed the commentary in his twenty-sixth year, but that for various reasons he could not publish it. Later, at the request of friends, he revised his work, which revision he completed at Lublin, Feb. 12, 1617. He compiled an index to the Biblical and Midrashic passages in Albo's text.

BIBLIOGRAPHY: Fuenn, *Keneset Yisrael*, p. 213; Fürst, *Bibl. Jud.* ii. 230; Nissenbaum, *Le-Ḳorot ha-Yehudim be-Lublin*, p. 46.

S. S. M. SEL.

Ḥayyim ben Moses Lipschütz: Polish rabbi of the seventeenth century; born at Ostrog about 1620. He wrote "Derek Ḥayyim" (Sulzbach, 1702), a book containing prayers and ritual laws for persons who are traveling, published by some of his pupils. Although the book contains prayers which show that the author was a follower of Shabbethai Ẓebi, it is interesting to know that it had the approbation of eight of the most renowned rabbis of the time.

BIBLIOGRAPHY: Wiener, *Ḳehillat Mosheh*, p. 297; Emden, *Torat ha-Ḳena'ot*, p. 144, Lemberg, 1870; Steinschneider, *Cat. Bodl.* col. 830.

D. B. FR.

Israel Lipschütz: Son of Eliezer Lipschütz; rabbi at Cleve. There he became notorious in connection with a "geṭ" controversy which attracted the attention of a large number of contemporary Jewish scholars. The dispute arose over a divorce granted by him in August, 1766, which was declared invalid and which the rabbinate of Frankfort-on-the-Main opposed with such persistence and vehemence that it became a "cause célèbre." Israel Lipschütz was severely criticized and stoutly defended. Toward his own defense he published (Cleve, 1770) seventy-three similar decisions, under the title "Or Yisrael," to counterbalance the "Or ha-Yashar" published by Simon Kopenhagen in the previous year at Amsterdam.

BIBLIOGRAPHY: M. Horovitz, *Frankfurter Rabbiner*, iii. 67 *et seq.*, Frankfort-on-the-Main, 1884.

Israel Lipschütz: Son of Gedaliah Lipschütz; born 1782; died Sept. 19, 1860. He was rabbi first at Dessau and then at Danzig. He led the life of an ascetic, frequently fasted three days in succession, and studied incessantly. He wrote "Tif'eret Yisrael," a commentary on the Mishnah, in which he applied to the orders a nomenclature of his own: Zera'im he called "Zera' Emunah"; Ṭohorot, "Ṭa'am wa-Da'at" (Hanover, 1830); Neziḳin, "Kos Yeshu'ot" (Danzig, 1845). His ethical will ("Ẓawwa'ah"; 1861) contains twenty-eight paragraphs, consisting chiefly of moral and ascetic precepts. He left in manuscript many notes ("derashot") to Caro's Shulḥan 'Aruk and to Maimonides' Yad ha-Ḥazaḳah, a comprehensive treatise on the order Ṭohorot, and many responsa.

BIBLIOGRAPHY: Walden, *Shem ha-Gedolim he-Ḥadash*, i. 406, Warsaw, 1864; Steinschneider, *Hebr. Bibl.* iv. 27.

Joshua Aaron Lipschütz: Rabbi at Bützow, Mecklenburg-Schwerin; born in Poland in 1768. He was a correspondent of Jacob Emden ("She'elat Ya'abeẓ," pp. 50 *et seq.*).

S. M. K.

Judah Löb b. Isaac Lipschütz: Austrian rabbi and author of the seventeenth century; rabbi at Eidlitz, Bohemia. He wrote: "Hanhagot Adam," a collection of rules from other works, on daily religious practises (Fürth, 1691; Amsterdam, 1717; Zolkiev, 1770); "Ẓaddiḳ Tamim," a redaction of the former work with many additions (Fürth, 1699; an abridgment of the book was seen in manuscript by Nepi, in Padua); "We-Zot li-Yehudah," explanations added to Jacob Weil's "Sheḥiṭot u-Bediḳot," on the rules of slaughtering cattle (Fürth, 1699; Frankfort-on-the-Main, 1820).

BIBLIOGRAPHY: Fürst, *Bibl. Jud.* i. 225, 226; Zedner, *Cat. Hebr. Books Brit. Mus.* p. 439; Benjacob, *Oẓar ha-Sefarim*, pp. 141, 506, 571.

L. G. N. T. L.

Moses ben Noah Isaac Lipschütz: Polish rabbi, and the author of the commentary "Leḥem Mishneh," on the orders Zera'im, Mo'ed, and Ḳodashim (published, according to Azulai, in 1596). He wrote a commentary also to the treatise Abot (Lublin, 1612; reprinted at Cracow in 1637 and included in the edition of the Mishnah published at Amsterdam in 1726).

BIBLIOGRAPHY: Azulai, *Shem ha-Gedolim*, ii. 71.

S. M. K.

Noah b. Abraham Lipschütz (called **Noah Mindes**): Polish rabbinical scholar; died in Wilna Dec. 22, 1797. He was a prominent member of the Jewish community of Wilna, and married a daughter of Elijah Pesseles. Lipschütz's daughter married Abraham, son of Elijah, gaon of Wilna. Lipschütz was the author of two cabalistic works, "Parpera'ot le-Ḥokmah" (Shklov, 1785), on the Pentateuch, and "Nifla'ot Ḥadashot" (Grodno, 1797), which latter includes cabalistic explanations by R. Samson Ostropoler. Both works were published anonymously. Noah died about three months after Elijah Gaon and was buried near him.

BIBLIOGRAPHY: Fuenn, *Ḳiryah Ne'emanah*, pp. 170-171, Wilna, 1860.

H. R. P. Wi.

Solomon ben Moses Lipschütz: German cantor; born at Fürth about 1675; died at Metz after 1708. He studied at Nikolsburg in the yeshibah of David Oppenheim, and for some time acted as cantor, shoḥeṭ, and teacher at Wallerstein. He then went to Pfersee, and thence to Prague, where he became chief cantor in the Phinehas and Zigeuner synagogues. In 1706 he retired to Frankfort-on-the-Main, but in the following year accepted the position of cantor at Metz, where he died. Lipschütz was the author of "Te'udat Shelomoh" (Offenbach, 1708), a book of morals and laws for cantors, published with the approbation of the rabbi and parnas of Metz.

D. B. Fr.

LIPSCHUTZ, SOLOMON: American chess-player; born at Ungvar, Hungary, July 4, 1863. At the age of seventeen he emigrated to New York, where he soon became known in chess circles. In 1883 he was chosen as one of a team to represent New York in a match with the Philadelphia Chess Club, and won both of his games. In 1885 he won the championship of the New York Chess Club, and in the following year took part in the international tournament held in London, where he succeeded in defeating Zukertorf and Mackenzie, among others. At the Masters' Tournament at New York in 1889 Lipschutz gained the sixth place, he being the only American player to secure a prize. In 1890 he won the championship of the United States, and repeated his success in 1892. He secured for the Manhattan Chess Club the absolute possession of the "Staats-Zeitung" challenge cup by winning it three times in succession (one tie against Steinitz). Twice pitted against Lasker, he has drawn his games on each occasion. Several of the games played by Lipschutz have been published in "Examples of Chess Master-Play" (New Barnet, 1893). Lipschutz revised "The Chess-Player's Manual," and he edited "The Rice Gambit," New York, 1901.

BIBLIOGRAPHY: *Chess Monthly*, Dec., 1890.

A. A. P.

LISBON: Capital of Portugal. It had the largest Jewish community in the country and was the residence of the chief rabbi ("arraby mor"). It had several "Judarias" or Jewish streets, one of them in the part of the city called "de Pedreira," between the cloisters do Carmo and da Trinidade; another, laid out later, was in the quarter da Conceiçaõ. In 1457 a third Judaria was created, the de Alfama, near the Pedro gate. In the Rua Nova, passing through the most beautiful and the liveliest part of the city, resided the rich and prominent Jews, the large synagogue being in the same thoroughfare. A small synagogue was erected by Joseph ibn Yaḥya about 1260, at his own expense.

For a long period the Jews of Lisbon were left undisturbed. The first storm broke upon them during the war between Dom Ferdinand of Portugal and Henry II. of Castile. The Castilian army forced its way into Lisbon; several Jews were killed, and the Rua Nova was plundered and destroyed by the rapacious soldiery (1373). The grand master of the Knights of St. Bennett of Aviz, later King John I., successor of Dom Ferdinand, protected the Jews in the capital against pillage. As a sign of their gratitude, the Jews, in addition to their contribution to the gift of 10,000 livres made to the king by the city, presented to him 70 marks and made him a loan of 1,000 reis.

The Jews of Lisbon, who in 1462 paid for "serviço real" alone 50,000 reis (about 3,500 francs), were engaged in various mercantile pursuits and trades. When Dom Duarte imposed restrictions upon free intercourse between Jews and Christians, representatives of the Jewish community at Lisbon applied to the king for the removal of the restrictions, and the king granted the request in a letter to the community dated Dec. 5, 1436. The prosperity and consequent luxury of the Jews aroused the envy and hatred of the Christians, even to the point of violence. Toward the end of the year 1449 some young men maltreated several Jews at the fish-market, and the royal corregidor had them publicly whipped. This aroused the anger of the people against the Jews, who were attacked, and a number of whom were killed, despite their brave resistance. Probably the fight would have ended in a terrible massacre but for the armed intervention of the Count de Monsanto. The attack was renewed, and the king was compelled to adopt severe measures against persons convicted of aggressions against the Jews. The profound hatred against the latter was increased by the arrival of immigrants from Castile, who sought shelter at Lisbon.

Outbreaks Against Lisbon Jews.

In 1482 the populace again assailed the Jews, plundered their stores, and destroyed their dwellings; it was at this time that Isaac Abravanel lost his entire possessions, including his valuable library. To increase their troubles, the pestilence broke out simultaneously with the immigration of their coreligionists from Spain. By order of the city council the refugees from Spain were required to leave the city at once; though, through the intervention of the king, John II., the city council was compelled to grant to Samuel Nayas, procurator of the Castilian Jews, the right to stay there, and to the Castilian physician Samuel Judah the right to practise medicine (Rios, "Hist." iii. 338-349). In 1497, by order of King Emanuel, the Jews were driven out of Portugal; the Lisbon community ceased to exist, and the large synagogue was transformed into a church.

Lisbon Scholars.

The number of Jewish scholars of Lisbon is not especially large. Besides the members of the old families Ibn Yaḥya and Negro, who were born in the Portuguese capital and lived and studied there, there were the chief rabbis Judah and Moses Navarro, Judah Cohen, and others, as well as the rabbis Joseph and Moses Ḥayun and a certain Don Abraham, who was a physician and, in 1484, became also rabbi at Lisbon. Lisbon is the birthplace of Isaac Abravanel and his sons, and of Jacob ibn Ḥabib, and at Lisbon lived Joseph Vecinho (physician to King John II.), Abraham Zacuto, and Abraham Ẓarẓar. The learned Eliezer Toledano in 1485 established in this city a Hebrew printing-press, of which several books were the product. Among these was the Pentateuch with the commentary of Moses ben Naḥman (1489). In Lisbon Samuel ben Yom-Ṭob wrote (1410) a Torah roll now preserved in Bern; Samuel de Medina, in 1469, a Pentateuch; and Eliezer, son of Moses Gagos, in 1484, a ritual work for Isaac, son of Isaiah Cohen.

After their expulsion from Lisbon no Jews resided there openly, but there was a large number of "secret Jews," or "Christaõs Novos" (New Christians), who were compelled to attend the Church ceremonies, but in secret lived in accordance with Jewish precepts. The Portuguese people hated these New Christians, or MARANOS, far more than the confessed Jews, though King Emanuel favored them in order to win them by kindness to the Christian faith. But the king was powerless to protect them in face of the incendiary speeches of fanatical priests.

New Christians at Lisbon.

On May 25, 1504, Whitsunday, a number of New Christians happened to meet in the Rua Nova, and were chatting together, when suddenly they were surrounded by a crowd of turbulent youths who insulted and reviled them. One of the New Christians finally drew his sword and injured some of the tormentors. A tumult ensued, which soon was checked by the appearance of the governor of the city with an armed guard. Forty of the rioters were arrested and condemned to be whipped and to be exiled for life to the island of St. Thomas, but through the intervention of the queen they were pardoned.

This uprising was the forerunner of the terrible massacre of the secret Jews in Lisbon which occurred in April, 1506. During the celebration of the Jewish Passover on the night of April 17 in that year, a party of New Christians was suddenly attacked and seventeen of them were arrested, but were set at liberty after two days. The people, enraged at this act, talked of bribery, and were ready to burn all New Christians at the stake. Two days later, on April 19, a number of Christians and New Christians attended a service in the Church of the Dominicans, in order that they might beseech God to stop the terrible, devastating pestilence. Suddenly, in a side chapel called the "Jesus Chapel," a crucifix radiating an extraordinary brightness attracted the attention of the Christians, who saw therein a miracle. One of the secret Jews was incautious enough to express his lack of faith in the wonder. This was the spark that caused the conflagration. The people were excited to the highest pitch and committed most fearful deeds of violence. The unbelieving New Christian was seized by the hair, dragged out of the church, and killed forthwith by the infuriated women, and his body was burned on a hastily erected pile on the Rocio Praça. Two Dominican monks, Joaõ Mocho, from Evora, and Bernaldo, an Aragonese, marched through the streets carrying the crucifix, calling aloud "Heresiã! Heresia!" and exhorting the people to extirpate all heretics. The mob was soon joined by German, Dutch, and French sailors, and a terrible massacre began. On the first day, over five hundred New Christians were killed and burned; next day the brutalities were renewed in even worse form. Babies in the cradle were not spared; women seeking shelter in the church were dragged from the altar, outraged, and flung into the flames. The day's work ended with the murder of the tax-farmer Joaõ Rodriguez Mascarenhas, the richest and most hated New Christian; he was dragged to the Rua Nova, killed by the populace, and burned amid great rejoicing. Over two thousand (according to other authorities, four thousand) secret Jews were killed during the course of forty-eight hours.

The king, who was far from the capital at the time, was deeply incensed, and proceeded with severity against the criminals. The ringleaders were hanged, and many others were quartered or decapitated. The two Dominican monks who stirred up the people were expelled from their order and garroted, and their bodies were burned. Every resident of the city of Lisbon (which thereafter was no longer allowed to call itself "the most faithful") who was found guilty of either robbery or murder was punished corporally and subjected to loss of property (Damião de Goes, "Cron. de D. Manoel," pp. 141 *et seq.*; Garcia de Resende, "Miscellanea," xi. 6; Pina, "Chron. de D. Affonso," v. 130; "Shebeṭ Yehudah," p. 93; Usque, "Consolaçam," p. 200; hence the statement in "'Emeḳ ha-Bakah," p. 90; Herculano, "Inquisicaõ em Portugal," i. 142 *et seq.*; De Mendoça, "Historia de Portugal," vi. 955; Rios, "Hist." iii. 363 *et seq.*; Kayserling, "Gesch. der Juden in Portugal," pp. 145 *et seq.*; Grätz, "Gesch." ix.).

After the catastrophe a number of secret Jews left the country; the greater part of these fugitives returned to Lisbon, however, and for a time they were protected by the king, but were always hated by the people. The arrival of David Reubeni at the capital of Portugal produced a feverish excitement among the secret Jews. They believed him to be their savior and honored him as the expected Messiah. A New

לוח לדעת סימני השנים מתחלת
מחזור רסט עד סוף מחזור רפג

PAGE FROM THE "ABUDARHAM," LISBON, 1489.

(From the Sulzberger collection in the Jewish Theological Seminary of America, New York.)

Christian of Lisbon, a young man of twenty-four, Diogo Pires, who held a government position, openly confessed the Jewish faith and, calling himself "Solomon Molko," became an adherent of Reubeni. By means of large money payments, the rich New Christians in Lisbon were able to postpone, but not prevent, the introduction of the Inquisition.

Visit of Reubeni.

Lisbon was the seat of a congregation called "The Brotherhood of San Antonio," which existed among the secret Jews; it met in the Rūa de Moneda, in a house which contained a secret synagogue, where Diaconus Antonio Homem conducted the service. He suffered for his attachment to Judaism by death at the stake on May 5, 1624. Not a few of the secret Jews who were distinguished as poets, physicians, and scholars, and who in Italy and Holland openly avowed themselves to be Jews, called Lisbon their birthplace, or resided there at some time. In this city Duarte Pinhel, or Abraham Usque, wrote his Latin grammar (1543), and Amatus Lusitanus and Abraham Farrar practised medicine. Moses Gideon Abudiente, Manuel de Pina, and others were born at Lisbon (see AUTO DA FÉ; INQUISITION; PORTUGAL).

BIBLIOGRAPHY: Kayserling, *Gesch. der Juden in Portugal*, Leipsic, 1867; J. Mendes dos Remedios, *Os Judeos em Portugal*, i., Coimbra, 1895; Rios, *Hist.* ii. 274, 281; iii. 179, 337.
G. M. K.

——**Modern:** Besides the Maranos who continued to reside in Lisbon after the expulsion, the city has at all times contained a certain number of avowed Jews also, mainly from neighboring Africa. This is evidenced by the edict issued Feb. 7, 1537, by John III., in which the Jews were ordered to wear badges so that they might be distinguished from Christians. A greater spirit of tolerance toward the Jews began to prevail in government circles with the accession of the Braganza dynasty (1640), which had been considerably assisted by Jewish financiers in its struggles against Philip IV. of Spain. But, owing to the fear of the Inquisition, which continued to persecute the Neo-Christians or Maranos, and to the fanaticism of the populace, only a few Jews ventured to settle in Lisbon. It was only toward the middle of the eighteenth century that a Jewish community began to be formed by the inflow of Jews from Gibraltar, who, as British subjects, could practise their religion freely, though privately. The decrees of 1773 and 1774, which were issued by King Joseph under the influence of his minister, the Marquis de Pombal, and which deprived the Inquisition of all tyrannical and arbitrary powers, gave a new impulse to the settlement of Jews at Lisbon, and toward the close of the eighteenth century there were a considerable number of them in the Portuguese capital, and the need of a near-by burial-place began to be keenly felt. For this purpose a small piece of ground was leased, in 1801, in the English cemetery situated in the Rua da Estrella, and the first to be buried there was a certain Jose Amzalaga (d. Feb. 26, 1804). The lease, which had been made privately without special legal sanction, was renewed, in 1833, at an annual rental of 1,000 reis.

Eighteenth Century.

At the beginning of the nineteenth century there were in Lisbon several widely known Jewish firms, which rendered great services to Portugal by supplying grain during a famine that occurred about 1810. In recognition of these services the government agreed to permit the foundation of a synagogue, although hitherto the laws of the country had not permitted the practise of any form of religion other than the Roman Catholic. The synagogue, under the name "Sha'ar ha-Shamayim," was founded in 1813 by R. Abraham Dabella; the Jews, however, had no legal status; they were only tolerated. According to the information given in 1825 by the prelate Joaquim José Feireira Gardo to the French historian Capefigue, there were in Lisbon at that time about 500 Jews, the majority of whom were engaged in brokerage and in foreign trade, and they owned three private synagogues.

Synagogue Founded 1813.

Although by the law the Jews were considered as foreigners, some of them took part in the political movements of the country. Levy Bensabath and his son Marcos Bensabath distinguished themselves by their struggles against the absolute government of Dom Miguel I. (1828–1834). Later Marcos Bensabath became an officer in a regiment of light infantry. In 1853 R. Abraham Dabella died, and his synagogue was managed by a committee composed of Leão Amzalak, Levy Bensabath, Abraham Cohen, Fortunato Naure, and Mair and Moisés Buzaglo. Several years later occurred the death of Salamão Mor José, and the two congregations then existing were united (about 1855). The union was of short duration, and a new synagogue was erected in 1860 in the Alley dos Apostolos; it is still the principal prayer-house in Lisbon. About that time Jacob Toledano of Tangiers was called to the rabbinate of Lisbon and officiated there until 1899. An important event for the Jews of Lisbon was the recognition of their religion by the government Oct. 30, 1868, when the community was authorized to use as a burial-place a plot of ground it had acquired for the purpose in 1865. On June 30, 1892, the government sanctioned the constitution of the charitable society Gemilut Ḥasadim.

Distinguished Jews of Lisbon.

In 1890 a plan for the complete organization of the community of Lisbon was adopted, according to which all the Orthodox Jews, both Sephardim and Ashkenazim, were to form one congregation. An interesting article (No. 31) of their constitution runs as follows: "Should the Portuguese Jews disappear from this town and from the kingdom, the German Jews here at that time may take under their care and for their own use the synagogues, estates, portable objects, and other things of value then in the possession of the Portuguese Jews or accruing to them later; but the German Jews shall restore the whole to the Portuguese congregation should it be reestablished." Besides the Gemilut Ḥasadim Society, there exists at Lisbon a useful benevolent association known as the Somej Nophlim, founded in 1865; this institution, in 1900, established a kasher restaurant for the poor, and is now (1904) contemplating the establishment of an asylum for Jewish travelers. On May 25, 1902, was laid the corner-stone of the new Sha'are Tiḳwah synagogue, which has replaced the various synagogues formerly in use. In accordance with the law, the new building is situated in an enclosure and bears no outward sign of being a place of worship.

The community of Lisbon now numbers about 400 persons in a total population of 357,000; they are mostly natives of Gibraltar, Morocco, or the Azores, and the majority of them are ship-owners and merchants. Among those Jews who have become widely known in connection with science, letters, or the arts are the following: Alfred Benarus, professor of fine arts; Bensaude, professor at the Industrial Institute; Joseph Benoliel, professor at the Marques de Pombal Industrial School; Jacob Bensaude, professor of English at the Collège du Porto; Salancão Saragga, a distinguished Hebraist; Dr. Raul Bensaude, consulting physician to the King of Portugal, and officiating rabbi since the death of Jacob Toledano in 1899. The ḥazzan of the community is Levy ben Simon of Jaffa.

Bibliography: Kayserling, *Gesch. der Juden in Portugal*, pp. 338 *et seq.*; Lindo, *History of the Jews in Spain and Portugal*, pp. 374 *et seq.*; Bail, *Les Juifs au Dix-Neuvième Siècle*, p. 126, Paris, 1816; *Revue Orientale*, i. 274; *Allg. Zeit. des Jud.* 1841, p. 681; Cardozo de Bethencourt, in *J. Q. R.* xv. 251 *et seq.*

D. I. Br.

——**Typography:** Hebrew printing flourished in Lisbon for the three years from 1489 to 1492, the first work, the commentary of Naḥmanides on the Pentateuch, being produced by Eliezer Toledano in July, 1489. The next year he produced a "Ṭur Oraḥ Ḥayyim" and two sections of the Bible. Eliezer Alantansi, who had a printing-press also at Ixar, printed the "Abudarham" at Lisbon, and two other works were produced here—Joshua Levi's "Halikot 'Olam" and an edition of the Proverbs; the printer of the last-named is not known. Toledano was one of the earliest to use borders. It has been suggested that the printer Ibn Yaḥya carried the Lisbon types to Constantinople and either printed from them there or used them as models for new types. J.

LISBONNE, EUGENE: Lawyer, and a member of the French Senate; born at Nyons, near Avignon, Aug. 2, 1818; died at Montpellier Feb. 6, 1891. He was a lawyer at Montpellier under the government of July, 1830, and became attorney of the republic at Béziers. On Dec. 10, 1848, he was dismissed, and at the coup d'état (Dec. 2, 1851) was deported. After the accession of Napoleon III. he returned to Montpellier and took an active part in the struggles of the republican party against the empire. From the revolution of Sept. 4 to April 23, 1871, he was prefect of the department of Hérault, where he energetically opposed the "Government of Moral Order." On Feb. 20, 1876, he was elected to represent the second district of Montpellier in the Chamber of Deputies, where he was one of the leaders of the Republican Union. After the crisis of May 16, 1877, he was reelected (Oct. 14). In 1887 he introduced the measures which established almost complete freedom of the press in France. The elections of Aug. 21, 1887, compelled Lisbonne to retire from public life; he soon reentered it, however (Jan. 5, 1888), and as senator from Hérault introduced a measure in restriction of those of 1887. This was carried by the Senate, but was defeated in the Chamber of Deputies.

Bibliography: *La Grande Encyclopédie*,

s. J. Ka.

LISKER, ABRAHAM BEN ḤAYYIM: Russian rabbi of the seventeenth century; native of Brest-Litovsk. After studying in the yeshibot of Lublin and Cracow, Lisker was called to the rabbinate of Rossiena, in the government of Kovno. He was the author of "Be'er Abraham," a commentary on the six orders of the Mishnah and based upon preceding commentaries, to which he added his own novellæ under the title "Me Be'er." Only that part of his commentary that deals with the first three orders has been published: Zera'im (Frankfort-on-the-Oder, 1665) and Mo'ed and Nashim (*ib.* 1683).

Bibliography: Benjacob, *Oẓar ha-Sefarim*, p. 381; Michael, *Or ha-Ḥayyim*, No. 95.

s. s. M. Sel.

LISSA (called formerly **Polnisch Lissa**): Town of Prussia. Originally a village, it was incorporated in 1534; and soon afterward the first Jews settled there, with the authorization of Count Andreas Lescynski (1580–1606). Many of these Jewish settlers were probably of German origin, as the names "Auerbach" and "Oldenburg" frequently occur. The first privilege granted to them is dated March 10, 1626. In that year there already existed a synagogue at Lissa, also a cemetery, the plot for which had been presented by Count Lescynski. The earliest extant tombstone is dated 1662. At that date the community was fully organized and the schedule of taxation determined. Communal expenses were defrayed by taxes on slaughtering, dowries, the sale of houses, the ritual bath, and legacies. The Jews of Lissa not only engaged in commerce, but also followed trades: there were tailors, furriers, shoemakers, goldsmiths, lacemakers, locksmiths, tanners, barbers, embroiderers in gold, jewelers, buttonmakers, dyers, and turners. Most of these trades were organized into gilds, each of which generally had its own rabbi. The strong competition between the Jewish artisans and merchants and the Christians often led to sanguinary conflicts.

The Jews of Lissa suffered much during the wars in which Poland engaged, and more especially from the Cossack persecutions under Bogdan Chmielnicki. On the partition of Poland Lissa was annexed to Prussia.

In its most prosperous days Lissa contained between 4,000 and 5,000 Jews. It became the seat of a famous yeshibah which attracted students even from distant parts of Germany ("Memoiren der Glückel von Hameln," ed. Kaufmann, pp. 231–234). The first rabbi of Lissa was Isaac Eilenburg (1648), whose successors were: Jacob Isaac ben Shalom (d. 1675); Isaac ben Moses Gershon (d. 1695); Ephraim Kalisch; Mordecai ben Ẓebi Hirsch (d. 1753); Hirsch's brother, Abraham b. Ẓebi Hirsch (died as rabbi of Frankfort-on-the-Main, 1768); Phoebus Heilman (rabbi of Bonn; died at Metz); Aryeh ben Samuel; Tebele Horachow (d. 1792); and Jacob

Lissa (died at Stry in 1832). After Jacob Lissa's death the rabbinate remained vacant until 1864, when the present incumbent, Dr. S. Bäck, was elected. Among the many Talmudic scholars of Lissa was Akiba Eger, the younger (subsequently rabbi at Posen), who lived there from 1770 to 1791. The present (1904) population of Lissa is about 14,000, including about 1,200 Jews.

D. S. B.

LISSACK, MORRIS: English author and communal worker; born at Schwerin-on-the-Wartha, grand duchy of Posen, in 1814; died in London Jan. 13, 1895. He emigrated to England in 1835, and in 1839 settled as a "teacher of languages and dealer in jewelry" at Bedford, where he lived for nearly a half-century. In 1851 he published a book entitled "Jewish Perseverance, or The Jew at Home and Abroad," an autobiography with pious meditations and moral reflections. Lissack became a trustee of the Harpur Charity, Bedford, and took advantage of his position to secure concessions in favor of Jewish pupils. He was also an active worker in the cause of Jewish emancipation.

BIBLIOGRAPHY: *Jew. Chron.* and *Jew. World*, Jan. 18, 1895.

J. G. L.

LISSAUER, ABRAHAM: German physician and anthropologist; born at Berent, West Prussia, Aug. 29, 1832; educated at the gymnasium of his native town and at the universities of Vienna and Berlin (M.D. 1856). He practised in Neidenburg till 1863, when he removed to Danzig; but gave up his practise in 1892 upon his appointment as custos and librarian of the Anthropological Society of Berlin.

Lissauer has written several essays on medical and anthropological subjects, among which may be mentioned: "Zur Antipyretischen Behandlung des Typhus Abdominalis," in Virchow's "Archiv," liii.; "Ueber den Alkoholgehalt des Bieres," in "Berliner Klinische Wochenschrift," 1865; "Ueber das Eindringen von Canalgasen in die Wohnräume," in "Deutsche Vierteljahresschrift für Oeffentliche Gesundheitspflege," 1881; "Untersuchungen über die Sagittale Krümmung des Schädels," in "Archiv für Anthropologie," 1885, xv.; "Die Prähistorischen Denkmäler der Provinz West-Preussen," 1887; "Altertümer der Bronzezeit in der Provinz West-Preussen."

BIBLIOGRAPHY: Pagel, *Biog. Lex.* Vienna, 1901.

S. F. T. H.

LISSAUER, HEINRICH: German physician; born at Neidenburg Sept. 12, 1861; died at Hallstadt, Upper Austria, Sept. 21, 1891; son of Abraham Lissauer. He studied medicine at the universities of Heidelberg, Berlin, and Leipsic, receiving his diploma in 1886. Settling as a physician in Breslau, he became assistant at the psychiatric hospital and clinic of the university, which position he continued to hold until his death.

He wrote several essays in the medical journals, especially on pharmacology and on the anatomy and pathology of the nerves. Among these may be mentioned: "Beitrag zum Faserverlauf im Hinterhorn des Menschlichen Rückenmarks und zum Verhalten Desselben bei Tabes Dorsalis," in "Archiv für Psychiatrie," xvii.; "Ein Fall von Seelenblindheit Nebst einem Beitrag zur Theorie Derselben," *ib.* xxi.; "Sehhügelveränderungen bei Progressiver Paralyse," in "Deutsche Medizinische Wochenschrift," 1890.

BIBLIOGRAPHY: Pagel, *Biog. Lex.* Vienna, 1901.

S. F. T. H.

LISSER, ELEAZAR BEN SOLOMON (ZALMAN): Polish scholar; lived at Kleczewo in the eighteenth and nineteenth centuries. He was the author of a twofold commentary on Jedaiah Bedersi's "Beḥinat 'Olam," published with the text at Frankfort-on-the-Oder (1792). The first part, entitled "Migdenot Eleazar," deals with the interpretation of the text; the second, entitled "Ha-Mazkir," contains the vocabulary. Eleazar wrote twofold commentaries also, under similar titles, on Benjamin Musafia's "Zeker Rab" and on Abraham ibn Ezra's "Ḥidah," which he published with the text, the former at Altona (1807), and the latter, under the general title "Ḥomat Esh," at Breslau (1799), with an appendix containing literary essays by Eleazar and also enigmas.

BIBLIOGRAPHY: Steinschneider, *Cat. Bodl.* col. 914; Zedner, *Cat. Hebr. Books Brit. Mus.* p. 439; Fuenn, *Keneset Yisrael*, p. 142.

H. R. I. Br.

LISSER, JOSHUA FALK: Prominent rabbi and Talmudist of the second half of the eighteenth century; a descendant of Joshua Falk Kohen of Lemberg and of R. Liwa (MaHRaL) of Prague, and a pupil of R. Moses Zarah Eidlitz of Prague, author of "Or la-Yesharim." He was dayyan or judge at Lissa while R. David Tebele was chief rabbi there, and was, therefore, a member of the council which in 1782, under the presidency of David Tebele, condemned and burned Naphtali Herz Wessely's letter entitled "Dibre Shalom we-Emet." Lisser wrote commentaries on the minor tractates Abot de-Rabbi Natan, Semaḥot, and Derek Ereẓ Rabbah we-Zuṭa, with textual emendations ("Binyan Yehoshua'," Dyhernfurth, 1788); the commentary on the Abot de-Rabbi Natan was reprinted in the Wilna (1897) edition of the Talmud. In the preface he apologizes for his textual emendations by referring to Solomon Luria and Samuel Edels, who had likewise suggested variants in their commentaries.

S. S. J. Z. L.

LITERATURBLATT DES ORIENTS. See Orient, Der.

LITERATURE, HEBREW: Under this designation may be comprised all the works written by Jews in the Hebrew and the Aramaic tongue. Works written in Hebrew by non-Jews are too few to require consideration here. The term "Jewish literature" should be used in a broader sense, as including works written by Jews upon Jewish subjects, irrespective of the language in which they may be expressed, while the term "Judaica" should be applied to works written by Jews or non-Jews upon Jewish subjects, but in languages other than Hebrew. An exception is made in the case of Aramaic, not only because of its intimate philological connection with Hebrew, but also because at an early date it became practically a second mother tongue for the Jews, and was used in the Bible, in many of the Talmudic discussions, in the prayer-book, and in the

Cabala. Works written by Jews but not upon Jewish subjects and not in Hebrew are treated under the names of their respective authors. See also JUDÆO-GERMAN; JUDÆO-GREEK; JUDÆO-SPANISH.

The most significant characteristic of Hebrew literature is that the greater part of it is directly or indirectly the outgrowth of the Bible. There is a marked continuity in the development of the later from the earlier literary forms, all of them going back to the first source—the Bible. In other words, Hebrew literature is chiefly a religious literature, secular writings, produced mostly under the influence of foreign literatures, forming but a minor part of it. It seems, therefore, that, aside from dividing Hebrew literature into periods, as is usually done in histories, it will be best to give a sketch here under the categories into which the Bible itself may be divided, showing what part of the literature may be traced back to the Bible and what must be traced to foreign influence. These categories are "Law," "Prophecy and Wisdom Literature," "History," and "Psalmody." For more detailed information see subjects referred to throughout this article.

The Law.

The Law as a literature has continued its development from the earliest times down to the present day, and has been of greater influence upon the life of the Jews than any other branch of literature. It owes its growth chiefly to the doctrine, long inculcated in the Jewish mind, that along with the written law Moses received also an oral law, which was faithfully handed down by an unbroken chain of teachers and leaders to the men of the Great Synod and by them to succeeding generations. This gave rise to the Talmudic law, or HALAKAH, which deals, like the Biblical law, not only with man's civil and public life, but also with his private habits and thoughts, his conscience, and his morality. Traces of the Halakah are discoverable even in the Later Prophets, but its period of full development lies between 300 B.C. and 450 C.E. (see MISHNAH; TALMUD). In the latter half of the fifth century the Babylonian schools declined and the teachers of the Law no longer assumed authority. They confined their teachings to the comparison and explanation of the laws that came down to them from previous generations, allowing themselves to introduce only methodological and mnemonic signs into the Talmud. This sums up literary activity in the line of the Law during the period following the close of the Talmud. See SABORAIM.

The development of the Halakah in the subsequent period received impetus from the fact that the Babylonian schools once more raised themselves to an important position, owing, perhaps, to Arabic dominion in that country. The Geonim, as the teachers of this period are called, did not produce independent halakah, but continued to promote the study of the Talmud. What the Bible was to the Tannaim and Amoraim that the Talmud became, in its turn, to the Geonim and later teachers. It lay before them as an object of exposition, investigation, and discussion. The succeeding period was one of systematization, condensation, and elucidation; introductions, commentaries, compendiums, and dictionaries were the outcome of the study of the Talmud in those days. A new epoch commenced with the activity of Maimonides. His "Mishneh Torah" embraces the whole field of Halakah, and became an object of much discussion and explanation. In the fourteenth century the halakic literature began to deteriorate, and instead of being the guide of conduct it became a mere play of the intellect. In the sixteenth century, however, it again received a fresh impetus through the Shulḥan 'Aruk of Joseph Caro, which is still the standard work of traditional Judaism. Works on the Halakah are to be found in various forms, viz., in the form of commentaries **(Perushim; Ḳunṭresim)**, glosses **(Nimuḳim)**, additions (TOSEFOT), novellæ (ḤIDDUSHIM), collections **(Liḳḳuṭim)**, compilations **(Ḳobeẓim)**, compendiums **(Ḳiẓẓurim)**, decisions **(Pesaḳim)**, and judgments **(Dinim)**, as well as in independent codes and responsa.

Prophecy and Wisdom Literature.

From the prophetic utterances to the preachings and homilies of later days was but a short step, and accordingly public preaching for general instruction and moral edification was instituted among the Jews in very early times. This gave rise to the Haggadah, which did for the spirit what the Halakah did for the practise of Judaism. Just as the Halakah embraces various kinds of law, so does the Haggadah embrace different forms of thought. In a restricted sense, however, the Haggadah may be said to deal with ethics and metaphysics, and it is in this sense that it may be regarded as the natural issue of the earlier prophecies. In its ethical characteristics the Haggadah was greatly influenced by the Wisdom literature of the Bible, but in its metaphysical tendencies it shows the influence of Hellenistic philosophy. To the ethical Haggadah belong a few apocryphal books, such as BEN SIRA, the Apocalypse of Zerubbabel, and the Wisdom of Solomon, and the still more important works Pirḳe ABOT, Abot de-Rabbi Natan, and Masseket Derek Ereẓ. The metaphysical Haggadah did not develop into a separate literature until a much later date. See MIDRASH; TARGUM.

About the middle of the eighth century Arabic philosophy began to exercise a strong influence over the Jewish mind, and owing to the rationalistic character of that philosophy the Midrash ceased to grow, and its place was taken by theological and philosophical works of a systematic nature. The prophetic spirit is no longer so clearly discernible as before, owing to the large intermixture of foreign thought, but, on the other hand, the prodigious development of Hebrew literature in the Middle Ages must be ascribed to this foreign influence, for its presence is felt in almost every branch of thought cultivated in those days. It is seen in the rise of Karaism, in the development of philology and exegesis, as well as in the cultivation of general sciences among the Jews. Later, again, when Jewish thought came in touch with Christian mysticism, the developed Cabala sprang into existence in place of the metaphysical Haggadah (see CABALA). Finally, a great part of the large controversial literature owes its existence to the conflict between Judaism and Mohammedanism.

The theological literature previous to the twelfth

century is very fragmentary, and consists mostly of partial translations from the Arabic. Though the beginning of this literature dates from the days of Saadia Gaon, there is no independent work of the kind in Hebrew until a much later date, and even the earliest among the prominent men in this field, IBN GABIROL (11th cent.), JUDAH HA-LEVI and MAIMONIDES (12th cent.), wrote in Arabic, as had Saadia. The first important theological writers in Hebrew were LEVI BEN GERSHON (14th cent.), Joseph ALBO (15th cent.), and Elijah DELMEDIGO (15th cent.).

Philosophic Haggadah.

The ethical literature was continued in the works of Gabirol and BAḤYA BEN JOSEPH (11th cent.), Halevi (12th cent.), Isaac Aboab and ELEAZAR BEN JUDAH (13th cent.), Jedaiah BEDERSI (14th cent.), Leon of Modena (16th cent.), and Moses Ḥayyim LUZZATTO (18th cent.), as well as in the large literature of ethical WILLS and correspondence current throughout the Middle Ages.

The metaphysical Haggadah assumed under the influence of Arabic philosophy the aspect of a systematic philosophy, and through the influence of Christian mysticism it became a sort of theosophy which looked for the hidden and disregarded the evident meaning of the Law, and which, under the name of Cabala, began to develop an extensive literature, first in Italy and in Provence, and later in the East. The founder of the Cabala was R. ISAAC THE BLIND (12th cent.), who was followed, in the thirteenth century, by a host of eminent scholars. To the same century undoubtedly belongs the most famous cabalistic work, the Zohar, which is ascribed by all critics to Moses de Leon. The cabalistic literature of the fourteenth and fifteenth centuries is mostly anonymous and not original. But a new epoch opens with the teachings of R. Isaac Luria in the sixteenth century. He inaugurated the "practical" Cabala. No longer content to be restricted to the world of thought, this Cabala assumed to interfere in the world of action and to direct man's conduct in life. Luria's chief disciple was Ḥayyim VITAL, who committed the teachings of his master to writing. In the latter part of the seventeenth century this "practical" Cabala was at the root of the Shabbethaian movement, and in the eighteenth century it was the cause of the extravagances of the Ḥasidim, the chief of whom were Israel Ba'al Shem, Bär of Meseritz, and Salman of Liadi.

With the rise of systematic theology there came into existence an extensive literature of controversy. For although traces of this literature may be found in the Talmud, it was not until Judaism came into conflict with its two sister religions and with Karaism that religious controversy became a significant part of Hebrew literature. The first great work of this kind is the "Cuzari" of Judah ha-Levi, which is directed mainly against Mohammedanism and Karaism. But the most fruitful period for religious controversy was the fourteenth and fifteenth centuries, and the leading authors of that period were Profiat DURAN, Joseph ALBO, Isaac ABRAVANEL, and Yom-Ṭob Lipmann HELLER. In the sixteenth century two strong polemics were written against Christianity: the "Hoda'at Ba'al Din" of Joseph NASI and the "Ḥizzuḳ Emunah" of Isaac ben Abraham TROKI. In modern times Isaac Baer Levinsohn wrote many controversial works.

Polemical Literature.

Another product of the influence which Arabic philosophy exerted over Judaism is Karaism. It took its origin in the latter part of the eighth century and came early under the influence of Mohammedan dogmatism. Its literature dates from the same period, and consists mainly of dogmatics, exegesis, and grammatical works; its most prominent authors are: Judah HADASSI (12th cent.); Aaron the Elder (13th cent.); AARON BEN ELIJAH, author of "'Eẓ ha-Ḥayyim" and "Gan 'Eden" (14th cent.); Elijah BASHYAẒI (15th cent.); and Zerah TROKI (17th cent.). In the nineteenth century the most prominent Karaite scholar was Abraham ben Samuel FIRKOVICH. To the influence of Arabic literature must be ascribed also the scientific development of Hebrew grammar, which in turn greatly affected Biblical exegesis; both form important branches of Hebrew literature, but they can not be discussed here.

"The meager achievements of the Jews in the province of history do not justify the conclusion that they are wanting in historic perception. The lack of Jewish writings on these subjects is traceable to the sufferings and persecutions that have marked their path. Before the chronicler had had time to record past afflictions, new sorrows and troubles broke upon them" (G. Karpeles, "Jewish Literature, and Other Essays," p. 23). Though real historical works, in the modern sense of the term, are a very late product in Hebrew literature, the elements of history were never absent therefrom. The traditional nature of the Halakah created a demand for chronology and genealogy, while the Haggadah often enlarged upon the historic material of the Bible for purposes of its own. The most important historic documents of the Talmudic period are the Seder 'Olam Rabbah (1st cent.) and the Megillat Ta'anit (2d cent.; though in its present state, however, perhaps the product of the eighth century). From the geonic period there are a number of historic documents, *e.g.*, Seder 'Olam Zuṭa, Seder Tannaim we-Amoraim, and the Letter of Sherira Gaon. From the tenth century there is the "Yosippon," and from the eleventh the "Sefer ha-Ḳabbalah" of ABRAHAM IBN DAUD. Besides these there are some notable books of travel to be mentioned, as the "Sefer Eldad ha-Dani" (11th cent.), the "Sibbub Rab Petaḥyah" (12th cent.), and the "Massa'ot" of Benjamin of Tudela (12th cent.). The fifteenth, sixteenth, and seventeenth centuries produced notable chroniclers like Solomon IBN VERGA (15th cent.), Abraham ZACUTO (16th cent.), JOSEPH HA-KOHEN (16th cent.), David GANS (16th cent.), David CONFORTE (17th cent.), and Jehiel HEILPRIN (17th cent.). Azariah dei ROSSI (16th cent.) may be regarded as the first critical literary historian, and his work is authoritative even to-day. In the eighteenth century Ḥayyim Joseph David Azulai is the most prominent literary historian, while in the nineteenth century the chief works on history and the history of literature are those of Rapoport, Schorr, I. H. Weiss, Frankel, and Isaac Halévy. See HISTORIOGRAPHY.

History.

The literature devoted to the liturgy of the Synagogue extends over a long period. Although in the Bible there is no mention made of any composition specially written for the purpose of prayer, it is not unlikely that many Psalms were recited in the Temple service and then adopted as prayers. And inasmuch as the oldest prayers are largely mosaics, made up of quotations from the Scriptures, the liturgy may justly be regarded as a development of the Psalm literature. It was due to this Biblical origin also that the language of the old prayers was in most cases Hebrew and the style fluent and forcible. The later development of the liturgy, however, was closely connected with the development of the Midrash. This is evident from the fact that the additions which grew up around the old nucleus of the prayer were in the spirit of the Midrash, until finally the Midrash itself entered into the liturgy. Under the influence of the new forms of poetry in the Arabic period the daily prayers, and still more those of the festivals, assumed various forms. Liturgical poems adapted for special occasions were produced and new technical names invented. By degrees even dogmatic theology and halakah were versified and introduced into the liturgy. The important occasions of life—birth, marriage, and death—were made the subject of synagogal poetry. The literature of the liturgy is so large that no attempt is made to record names. It will be sufficient to state that although a skeleton of much of the ritual was already fixed in Talmudic times additions to it were made as late as the sixteenth century. See LITURGY; PIYYUṬ.

Psalmody.

From religious to secular poetry is but a step, yet it was only in the middle of the tenth century that secular poetry began to flourish. In this as in other branches of literature, Arabic influence was strongly felt from the days of Ḥasdai (10th cent.) down to those of Immanuel of Rome (14th cent.). From the fifteenth to the seventeenth century inclusive, Hebrew poetry declined, and was not revivified until the beginning of the eighteenth century, when it came under the influence of modern literatures. The period from Moses Ḥayyim Luzzatto to that of Naphtali Wessely may be called the Italian period, and that from Wessely to Abraham Bär Lebensohn, the German period. Judah Löb Gordon, though he came under the influence of foreign literatures, made the foreign taste subservient to the Jewish spirit. He is also the first poet to deal with real life, while the recent school of poets, under the influence of the national movement, shows a tendency to return to romanticism. Owing also to the influence of modern literatures, Hebrew has developed a literature of fiction and essays which deserves general recognition.

Secular Poetry.

Finally, a word must be said of the works written in Hebrew that deal with the arts and sciences. Originally, the sciences developed among the Jews as a branch of Halakah, receiving recognition only by virtue of some religious function which they were made to serve, as, for example, astronomy in connection with the fixing of the calendar, upon which depended the observance of the festivals. Later, however, when the Jews came in contact with Arabic civilization, the sciences came to be cultivated for their own sake, and since the middle of the tenth century many books have been written on the various arts and sciences, irrespective of their religious bearing. See also DICTIONARIES; DRAMA; FABLES; FOLK-SONGS; FOLK-TALES; GRAMMAR, HEBREW; HEBREW LANGUAGE; POETRY, DIDACTIC; SEMITIC LANGUAGES; TRANSLATIONS.

BIBLIOGRAPHY: Abrahams, *Chapters on Jewish Literature*, Philadelphia, 1899; D. Cassel, *Lehrbuch der Jüdischen Gesch. und Literatur*, Leipsic, 1879 (2d ed., Frankfort-on-the-Main, 1896); idem, *Manual of Jewish History and Literature*, London, 1883; J. W. Etheridge, *Jerusalem and Tiberias: Sora and Cordova*, an introduction to the study of Hebrew literature, London, 1856; A. S. Freidus, *A Scheme of Classification for Jewish Literature in the New York Public Library*, New York, 1901; Grätz, *Gesch.* passim; G. Karpeles, *Gesch. der Jüdischen Literatur*, Berlin, 1886; idem, *Ein Blick in die Jüdische Literatur*, Prague, 1895; idem, *Jewish Literature, and Other Essays*, Philadelphia, 1895; S. Levy, *Is There a Jewish Literature?* in *J. Q. R.* xv. 583-603; M. Steinschneider, *Jüdische Literatur*, in Ersch and Gruber, *Encyc.* section ii., part 27; idem, *Jewish Literature*, London, 1857; H. L. Strack, *Bibliographischer Abriss der Neuhebräischen Literatur* (C. Siegfried and H. L. Strack, *Lehrbuch des Neuhebräischen Sprache*, pp. 93-132, New York, 1884); Weiss, *Dor*; Winter and Wünsche, *Die Jüdische Litteratur*; Zunz, *G. S.*; *What Is Jewish Literature?* by W. Bacher, A. Wolf, and S. Levy, in *J. Q. R.* xvi. 300-329; *Hebrew Literature, Translations from the Talmud, Midrash, and Kabbala*, with introduction by M. H. Harris, in *Universal Classic Library*, Washington and London, 1901; *Hebrew Literature, Comprising Talmudic Treatises, Hebrew Melodies, and the Kabbalah Unveiled*, with introduction by E. Wilson, in *The World's Great Classics*, New York and London, 1901. See also JEW. ENCYC. iii. 199, *s.v.* BIBLIOGRAPHY.

J. I. D.

LITERATURE, MODERN HEBREW: Modern Hebrew literature (1743–1904), in distinction to that form of Neo-Hebraic literature known as rabbinical literature (see LITERATURE, HEBREW), which is distinctly religious in character, presents itself under a twofold aspect: (1) humanistic, relating to the emancipation of the language by a return to the classical models of the Bible, leading to the subsequent development of modern Hebrew; (2) humanitarian, dealing with the secularization of the language with a view to the religious and social emancipation of the Jews of the ghetto. These two tendencies are expressed by the word HASKALAH, a term denoting the movement which predominated in Hebrew literature from the second half of the eighteenth century down to the death of Smolenskin in 1885.

Beginning with the seventeenth century, many attempts were made to emancipate Hebrew from the forms and ideas of the Middle Ages. Italy, with critics and poets like Azariah dei Rossi, Leon of Modena, Francis, etc., who were inspired by the Italian Renaissance, led in this period of transition in Hebrew literature. But it was not until the appearance of Moses Ḥayyim Luzzatto that Hebrew poetry shook off the medieval fetters which hindered its free development. His allegorical drama "La-Yesharim Tehillah" (1743), which may be regarded as the first product of modern Hebrew literature, is a poem that in its classic perfection of style is second only to the Bible. In the less advanced countries especially it has contributed to the regeneration of Hebrew and has stimulated a host of imitators among writers removed from modern literary centers.

Period of Transition in Italy.

At Amsterdam, Luzzatto's pupil, David Franco Mendes (1713–92), in his imitations of Racine ("Gemul 'Atalyah") and of Metastasio ("Yehudit"), continued his master's work, without, however, equaling Luzzatto's poetic inspiration and originality. In Germany, where, in consequence of the ideas promulgated by the encyclopedists, the Jews developed more normally, and where, moreover, in the middle of the eighteenth century, Hebrew was still almost the only literary language accessible to the masses, another successor of Luzzatto, Naphtali Hartwig Wessely (1725–1805), inaugurated the haskalah movement. His "Shire Tif'eret," or "Mosiade," which, though falling short of poetic inspiration, is written in a pure, oratorical style and is marked by a lofty, moral tone, made him, so to speak, poet laureate of the period.

Under the stimulus of Mendelssohn, literary societies were formed by the Maskilim in the large communities, which undertook to propagate modern ideas among the Jews and to familiarize them with modern secular life. Two schools or parties, which were more or less distinct, undertook this work: (1) the BIURISTS, a group of commentators and translators of the Bible who, under the leadership of Mendelssohn, desired to replace the Judæo-German dialect with pure German and to provide a more rational interpretation of the sacred text; (2) the Me'assefim, scholars connected with the first literary collection in Hebrew, "Ha-Me'assef," which was established in 1785 at Breslau by Isaac Eichel and B. Lindau, and which became the organ of the haskalah and a bond of union among the Hebraists.

First German Maskilim.

Wessely may be regarded as the spiritual leader of the Me'assefim. Although a devout believer himself, he did not hesitate to meet the objections which the Orthodox rabbis of Austria and Germany opposed to all educational and civic reforms advocated by the government of Joseph II. In his eight messages (1784), "Dibre Shalom we-Emet," he emphasized the necessity, even from the standpoint of the Talmud, of these reforms as well as of secular studies, especially the study of modern languages and classical Hebrew and of manual training. Despite the opposition of the Orthodox rabbis of Germany and Austria, the aid of the liberal Italian rabbis enabled him to arouse public opinion in favor of the haskalah, and thus to prepare the way for the Me'assefim. "Ha-Me'assef" was discontinued after an existence of seven years, the French Revolution and the downfall of the old order of things destroying the interest in the Hebrew language, which was the only relic left to the emancipated Maskilim. The literary and scientific value of "Ha-Me'assef" is very doubtful. In their instinctive aversion to everything medieval and rabbinic, the Me'assefim went to the other extreme and adopted the affected style of the "meliẓah," which was cultivated by their successors, and which often ended in mere artificial juggling with words. As regards their content most of the pieces in the collection have only a slight interest, being merely puerile imitations of German pseudo-romanticism. Having broken with the Messianic ideal of traditional Judaism, and being unable to replace it with another ideal more in conformity with modern ideas, the Me'assefim ended in advocating assimilation with the surrounding people. But the importance of this first secular periodical in Hebrew was such that it imposed its name upon the entire literary movement of the second half of the eighteenth century, which is called "the period of the Me'assefim."

Among the Me'assefim, I. Eichel is noteworthy for his uncompromising attitude, unusual at that time, toward rabbinism, and Baruch Lindau is known for his works on the subject of natural science and written in Hebrew. The most influential, however, was the rabbi Solomon Pappenheim (1776–1814), an eminent philologist, whose sentimental elegy, "Arba' Kosot," was the book of the day and contributed much to the dissemination of the meliẓah. The most valuable contributors to "Ha-Me'assef" were, perhaps, the Me'assefim of Polish origin, especially the grammarian and stylist S. Dubno; S. Maimon, the commentator of Maimonides; the eccentric but gifted Isaac Satanow, author of the maxims "Mishle Asaf"; and the grammarian Judah Ben-Zeeb (Bensew) of Cracow.

In short, although the Me'assefim lacked originality, they accomplished the double task which they had set themselves. Hebrew, which had been almost entirely neglected in the Slavic countries, was again studied, giving rise to a literature more or less worthy the name and producing the Maskilim, a class of secular scholars who were active during the following century in awakening the masses from their medieval slumbers and in disputing, in the name of science and modern life, the authority of the Rabbis over the people (see HASKALAH).

Influence of the Me'assefim.

The nineteenth century did not open auspiciously for Hebrew literature, especially in western Europe. Hebrew disappeared more and more as a living language among the emancipated Jews, who had broken with their national ideals and were ambitious of assimilating themselves entirely with their neighbors. It is true that the Napoleonic wars gave birth to a whole literature of odes and hymns, many of which were sung in the synagogue, the most poetical and characteristic being Elie Ḥalfan Halévy's "Ha-Shalom" (Paris, 1804); but the few rabbis who continued to use Hebrew did not influence the masses. In Italy, however, there was still an ardent band of Hebrew scholars, among them the poet E. Luzzatto. About this time the center of literary activity was definitively transferred to the Slavic countries, where was witnessed a remarkable revival of Hebrew letters. The lead which Austria, followed by Italy, took in the movement at the beginning of the nineteenth century was later yielded to Russia; and that country has maintained its leadership down to the present time.

At the close of the eighteenth century Polish Judaism, which for a long time had been politically isolated and had devoted itself entirely to pious observance and to the study of the Talmudic law, came in contact with modern ideas, and awakened from its centuries of slumber. Galicia became a center for the haskalah. The "Me'assef,"

Poland and Austria.

which had been edited in a new series in Germany by Solomon ha-Kohen (Dessau, 1809–11), but without much success, was revived at Vienna and later in Galicia, and succeeded, first under the title of "Bikkure ha-'Ittim" (1820–31), and then under that of "Kerem Ḥemed" (1833–42), in gathering together many writers, the larger proportion of whom were Polish. In Poland, however, where the Jewish population lived apart, and could not even aspire to the dreams of equality and liberty of the German writers, the Maskilim were confronted with very complicated problems. On the one hand, political upheavals, modern instruction, and military service had paved the way for the mysticism of the Ḥasidim, which seized the masses despite the efforts of the liberal rabbis aided by writers like D. Samoscz and Tobias Feder.

On the other hand, light literature and romantic imitations could not satisfy scholars saturated with Talmudic study. In order to meet these needs Hebrew literature descended from its heights to devote its attention to the necessities of daily life. Joseph Perl, a Mæcenas and himself a scholar, encouraged this movement, and published the parody "Megalleh Ṭemirin," directed against the superstitions and the cult of the Ḥasidic ẓaddiḳim. Solomon Judah Rapoport (1790–1867), who began by translating Racine and Schiller, now turned to the critical study of the past. By his able reconstruction of the lives and the scientific work of the masters of the Middle Ages, by his careful critical method, and by his devotion to the Law and the Jewish spirit, Rapoport created the SCIENCE OF JUDAISM.

But this science, which was warmly received especially by the cultivated minds of western Europe, could not satisfy the poor Polish scholars, living in entirely Jewish surroundings, and, no longer contented with the reasons advanced by the medieval masters, anxiously questioning the wherefore of the present and future existence of Israel. Then a master mind arose, to give an answer at once ingenious and adapted to the time. Nachman Krochmal, teaching gratuitously in his obscure corner of Poland, succeeded in uniting the propositions of modern critics with the principles of Judaism by the bond of nationalism, as it were, thus creating a Jewish philosophy in conformity with modern thought. Starting with Hegel's axiom of real and of absolute reason, Krochmal sets forth in his essays and in his ingenious Biblical and philosophic studies that the Jewish people is a concrete national organism, a separate unity, whose existence is justified, as the existence of all other nationalities is justified. But, at the same time, as the people of the Prophets, it has in addition a spiritual reason for its existence, which transcends national boundaries, and will join the entire human race in one bond.

Nachman Krochmal (1785-1840).

Many poets, scholars, and popular writers besides Rapoport and Krochmal contributed to the dissemination of Hebrew and to the emancipation of the Jews of Galicia. The satirical poet Isaac Erter (1792–1841), whose collection of essays, "Ha-Ẓofeh le-Bet Yisrael," is one of the purest works of modern Hebrew literature, attacked Ḥasidic superstitions and prejudices in a vigorous and classical style, marked by bright fancy and a cutting sarcasm which heaped ridicule upon the rabbi and satire upon the ẓaddiḳ.

Meïr Halevy Letteris acquired merited renown and was for a long time considered poet laureate of the period by reason of his numerous translations, both in prose and in poetry, including "Faust" and works by Racine and Byron, and also on account of original lyric poetry, his song "Yonah Homiyyah" being a masterpiece. The popularizer of Galician history and geography, Samson Bloch, also won a reputation, although his insipid and prolix style does not warrant the success achieved by his works. The Galician scholar Judah Mises is noted especially for his violent attacks on rabbinical tradition and for his extreme radicalism, his work being continued by I. A. Schorr, the daring editor of "He-Ḥaluẓ."

The Galician School.

Outside of Galicia, where the scholars issued their works, and where periodicals multiplied, some of which were published at Vienna, as "Kokebe Yiẓḥaḳ" (ed. Stern), "Oẓar Neḥmad" (ed. Blumenfeld), Kerem Ḥemed, etc., groups of Maskilim or individual scholars were to be found toward the middle of the century in all the countries of Europe. In Germany the campaign for and against religious reform gave opportunity to certain scholars and rabbis to conduct their polemics in Hebrew. Zunz, Geiger, Z. Frankel, Jellinek, Carmoly, Fürst, J. Schwarz, and others, also published part of their works in Hebrew. Moses Mendelssohn of Hamburg, a pupil of Wessely and author of the maḳamat "Pene Tebel" (Amsterdam, 1872), may be considered as the epigone of the Me'assefim. In the Netherlands, especially at Amsterdam, there was also a circle of epigones, including the poet Samuel Molder (1789–1862). In Austria, Vienna was the depot for publishing Hebrew books and periodicals, and Prague became an active center for the haskalah. The best known among the Maskilim here is J. L. Jeiteles (1773–1838), author of witty epigrams ("Bene ha-Ne'urim") and of works directed against the Ḥasidim and against superstition, and director of the "Bikkure ha-'Ittim." There were scholars in Hungary also, the most gifted among them being Solomon Lewison of Moor (1789–1822), a remarkable stylist, whose classical "Meliẓat Yeshurun" places him above all the poets of the period. Gabriel Südfeld, father of Max Nordau, and Simon BACHER, may also be mentioned. The reflex of this movement was felt even in Rumania (J. Barasch, etc.). Galicia, however, the center of the haskalah, finally succumbed to Ḥasidism, while the moderns gave up Hebrew, and ended by more or less openly advocating assimilation. A few circles of Maskilim barely succeeded in perpetuating the Hebrew tradition, but had no influence on the masses.

Decadence of the School.

The Italian school exercised a more pronounced influence. I. S. Reggio (1784–1854) endeavored in his "Ha-Torah weha-Filosofiah" to reconcile modern thought with the Jewish law, while in his numerous writings and publications he openly sided with the German religious reformers. Joseph Almanzi, Ḥayyim Salomon, S. Lolli, and others wrote poems on the grandeur of the Law and the glory of Israel; these contained, however, not a spark of originality. More interesting perhaps is the only poetess of the period, Rachel Morpurgo (1790–1860), whose poems evince religious piety and a mystic faith in Israel's future. The most original and gifted Italian writer of the period is Samuel David Luzzatto (SHeDaL, 1800–65), whose influence reached beyond Italy and beyond his time. Gifted with an encyclopedic mind, Luzzatto did good work alike in poetry ("Kinnor Na'im"), in philology ("Bet ha-Oẓar" and "Betulat Bat Yehudah"), in philosophy, and in general literature. At the same time Luzzatto was the first modern writer to introduce religious romanticism into Hebrew and to attack northern rationalism in the name of religious and national feeling.

Italy: Luzzatto.

"True Jewish science is founded on faith. . . . Faith is the only arbiter of supreme morality which gives us true happiness. The happiness of the Jewish people, the people of morality, does not depend on its political emancipation, but on faith and on morality. . . ." These ideas led Luzzatto into polemics with his northern friends, but they also helped to familiarize the believers in Russia with modern literature. Luzzatto thus found the key to the heart of the masses; and it was due to him that the work of the Maskilim, which had failed of permanent results in the West, in the East led to the development of a national literature. But in Italy also Hebrew declined more and more, even among scholars; and by the second half of the century it was almost entirely forgotten in the civilized countries of Europe.

The large bodies of Jews in the Polish districts annexed to Russia were entirely removed from all political and social life, and vegetated in a kind of profound resignation or in mystical piety. At the Europeanized city of Odessa, however, Galician Jews formed a circle of Maskilim, which, though active, was restricted in its influence. Here in the middle of the century were the scholars S. Pinsker and S. Stern, who were soon joined by the Karaite Firkovich and by the poet Jacob Eichenbaum. The acknowledged leader of these Maskilim of southern Russia was Isaac Bär Levinsohn, the apostle of humanism in Russia, whose influence penetrated even into government circles, but whose literary work has been overestimated. His personal endeavors, as well as his books ("Te'udah be-Yisrael" and "Bet Yehudah"), in which he recommends to the Orthodox the study of the sciences and the pursuit of manual employments, contributed to general emancipation rather than to that of Hebrew literature in particular.

Russia.

Lithuania, an eminently Jewish country, was more favored by circumstances; and here the haskalah was destined to lead to the unfolding of a literature. At Shklov, the first city to come in contact with the outside world, a group of humanists arose as early as the beginning of the century. But it was at Wilna, the capital of the country, abandoned by its native population and entirely removed from outside influence, that the Hebrew language flourished to an extraordinary degree. It was due to the enlightened tolerance of the gaon Elijah Wilna and the zeal of his pupils that Wilna became, toward the end of the eighteenth century, the home of excellent grammarians and stylists. About 1820 or 1830 a circle of Maskilim, called "Berliner," and evidently inspired by the writers of Germany, was formed, which assiduously cultivated modern Hebrew literature. Two eminent scholars lent special luster to this new literary movement. M. A. GÜNZBURG well deserves his title "the father of prose," which he won for himself through his numerous translations, histories, and scientific compilations, his picturesque narration of the ritual murder at Damascus, his realistic autobiography "Abi'ezer" (a glowing criticism of customs of the past), and especially through his style, which is at once temperate, realistic, and modern. At the same time Abraham Bär LEBENSOHN, called "the father of poetry," lent new radiance and vigor to Hebrew verse.

A. Bär Lebensohn.

The touching lyric quality of some of his poems, the profound pessimism, the plaint over life, and the fear of death, which betray the feelings of the Jew tried by the ordeal of ghetto life, all stamp him as the veritable poet of the ghetto. The simplicity of his ideas, his rabbinical dialectic and even his frequent prolixity only added to his popularity. His poems "Shire Sefat Ḳodesh" were extraordinarily successful; and his elegant, limpid, and often energetic style is still justly admired.

It was due to these two masters that modern Hebrew literature was widely disseminated throughout Lithuania, circles devoted to the haskalah being formed nearly everywhere. Hebrew became the language of daily life, the literary language, and, what is still more characteristic, the language of folk-lore. In fact, the list of popular Hebrew poems by known or unknown authors is too long to be noted here. The unhappy political situation of the Russian Jews under Nicholas I.—a period of persecutions of all kinds and of terror—had particularly contributed to produce this state of mind in the harassed people; and while Ḥasidism completed its work of producing intellectual obscurantism and hopeless resignation in the province of Poland and in southern Russia, mysticism found in Lithuania a redoubtable enemy in the sentimentality of the unfolding Hebrew literature.

The diffusion of the affected style of the meliẓah and the return to the language of the past awakened among this unhappy people a regret for the glorious Biblical times and a romanticism that was to bear rich fruit. Popular Hebrew poetry had become fundamentally Zionistic, as is evident from the anonymous poems then written ("Shoshannah," "Ẓiyyon, Ẓiyyon," etc.). Literary romanticism soon followed upon this romantic tendency.

Popular and Literary Romanticism.

The Lithuanian writers, sharing the life and patriotic thoughts of the people, and encouraged by the example of S. D. Luzzatto, who united modern culture with ardent patriotism, turned to romanticism. The prolific popularizer Kalman Schulman (1826–1900) inaugurated romantic fiction and introduced the romantic form into Hebrew through his Hebrew version of "Les Mys tères de Paris" ("Mistere Paris"); and he became one of the civilizers of the ghetto through his numerous popular scientific works and especially through his studies of the Jewish past. His pure, flowing, meliẓah style, his extreme sentimentalism as well as his naive romanticism in all matters touching Judaism, won for him great influence. For fully half a century he, in spite of his lack of originality, ranked as a master. The young and gifted writer Micah Joseph LEBENSOHN (1828–52), the first true artist and romantic poet in Hebrew, has left poems that are perfect in style, including an admirable translation of the "Æneid," lyrics of love, of nature, and of sorrow. But his masterpieces are romantic poems ("Moses," "Judah ha-Levi") dealing with Israel's glorious past.

The creator of the Hebrew novel was Abraham Mapu (1808-67), whose historical romance "Ahabat Ẓiyyon" exercised an important influence on the development of Hebrew. This novel, which deals with the golden age of Judah, that of Isaiah, and is couched in the very language of that prophet, is rather a succession of poetic pictures reconstructing the civilization of ancient Judea than a connected story. Simple and primitive in his thoughts, Mapu was so imbued with the spirit of the Bible that, although unconsciously, he was translated to ancient times, and, guided by a marvelous intuition, he succeeded in reconstructing the free, agricultural life of ancient Judah, in the land of the prophets, of justice, and of truth, the land of love and of the joy of life. This past, to renew which was the ambition of scholars and people, superimposed itself upon the present, and it was due to Mapu's novel that an entire people came forth from its long lethargy, to be reborn. Another novel ("Ashmat Shomeron") by Mapu served to increase his popularity.

Many imitators of these leaders of Hebrew romanticism appeared, and at a time when the political outlook checked all hopes of a better life: the Maskilim demanded, in the name of the prophetic past, the rights of civilization and progress. Many persons, also, were won over to the reading of secular literature. When in 1856 Silbermann founded at Lyck the first political journal in Hebrew, "Ha-Maggid," he met with unexpected success and had many imitators. In Austria, Russia, and even in Palestine, periodicals, more or less successful, appeared, furthering the cause both of Hebrew and of emancipation. Among these journals were "Ha-Karmel," founded by the scholar Samuel Joseph Fuenn; "Ha-Ẓefirah," founded by the popularizer of science C. Z. Slonimsky; and "Ha-Meliẓ," founded by A. Zederbaum.

Official Liberalism and Radicalism.

The accession of Alexander II. radically changed the condition of the Russian Jews. A wave of liberty and radicalism swept through the empire, and for the first time the Russian Jews could hope for a lot similar to that of their western coreligionists. Awakened from their century-long sleep, the backward people of the ghetto began to shake off religious and other fetters, becoming imbued with modern ideas and adopting modern modes of life. In the large centers there was no serious opposition to emancipation, and the Jews flocked in masses to the schools and sought secular employments. The scholars themselves, encouraged by the government and by the notables of the great cities, decided to attack all the "domains of darkness" of the past, and to occupy themselves with the affairs of the day; and when the small provinces, less disturbed by the economic and moral upheavals, bitterly opposed this social emancipation—which led to forgetfulness of the Law and endangered the faith—the Maskilim knew no limits to their fury against the fanatics of the ghetto. Hebrew literature, at first realistic, attacking customs and superstitions in the name of utility and the reality of things, became more and more antirabbinical as it opposed religious tradition. Mapu led the way in his novel "'Ayiṭ Ẓabua'," which, though a failure from a literary point of view, depicts the backward types of the ghetto, the Tartuffes, and the enemies to progress, with a realism intentionally exaggerated. ABRAMOWITSCH, then a young man, described in his novel "Ha-Abot we-ha-Banim" the customs of the Ḥasidim and the struggles of their progressive sons. The aged poet Abraham Bär Lebensohn published his drama, "Emet we-Emunah" (written twenty-five years previously), in which he satirized cabalistic hypocrisy and mysticism. The number of popularizers of science, critics of belated customs, and belittlers of the religious past became legion.

Leon Gordon (1830-92).

The most distinguished among these writers was the poet Leon GORDON, an implacable enemy of the Rabbis, who personified in himself this realistic epoch. He began by writing romantic poems in imitation of the two Lebensohns. But when the horizon widened for the Russian Jews, he was filled with pity for the deplorable state of the Orthodox masses, to whom he addressed his "Hakiẓah 'Ammi"—"Awake, my people, to a better life," *i.e.*, "to the life of those about you." Of a mettlesome spirit, he unmercifully attacked the rabbinical law, the dead letter, the religious yoke weighing upon the masses. He regarded rabbinism as the greatest misfortune of the Jewish people, which killed the nation by delivering it up to the more secular Romans, and which hindered its participation in the realities of modern life. Gordon's activity covered all branches of literature. He ranks foremost in Hebrew literature as a satirical poet and critic of manners; and as a writer of fables he has no equal. But in spite of his apparent severity and his extreme skepticism, he remained at heart a patriot; and when he criticizes he does so in order to elevate the social life of the Jews, while grieving for the misery of the Messianic nation. Even in his historical poems, "Ẓidḳiyahu be-Bet ha-Peḳudot" and "Bi-Meẓulot Yam," he displays all his love for his people, which became more pronounced during the years of persecution and misery in Russia. But even then he believed that rabbinism was the enemy which prevented a national renascence. Gordon was among the first successfully to introduce Talmudisms into poetry.

The hopes of the Maskilim were not realized: Russia did not continue its radical reforms; and a reaction began between 1865 and 1870. Disappointed in their dreams of equality, writers now bent all their energies to the work of the emancipation of individuals from among the masses, by disseminating instruction and by advocating the pursuit of trades as being necessary to fit the Jews to deal with the exigencies of life and to take part in the battle for subsistence incident to the economic changes of the time.

In Galicia a circle of scholars, under the leadership of Schorr, director of "He-Ḥaluẓ," and A. Krochmal, advocated religious reforms, boldly attacking tradition and even the law of Moses. But in Russia, especially in Lithuania, the scholars did not go so far. The ideology of the Maskilim was not accepted by the scholars who came in closer contact with the masses; and instead of attacking principles, they advocated practical reforms and changes in conformity with the needs of daily life. Utilitarianism succeeded to the ideology of the earlier scholars. Abraham Kowner in his pamphlet "Ḥeḳer Dabar," etc. (1867) attacked the masters of Hebrew for being idealists, and the press because it ministered neither to the strict necessities of daily life nor to the material well-being of the masses. Paperna and others were also pronounced realists. Moses Lilienblum inaugurated a campaign in favor of the union of life and faith—an endeavor perilous to its author and his emulators, but noteworthy as being the last attempt of rabbinic Judaism to adapt itself to the needs of modern life without giving up its minute observances. In his instructive volume "Ḥaṭṭot Ne'urim," Lilienblum has left a curious document describing the inner conflicts of a young Talmudist of the ghetto who has passed through all the stages between the simple life of an Orthodox believer and that of a skeptical freethinker. Viewing the life of the modern Jew, emancipated and indifferent to all that is Jewish, he is shaken in his highest convictions and cries out, "The Law will never go hand in hand with life." Lilienblum himself at last became a utilitarian, seeking in Jewish life nothing but individual material well-being, and testifying regretfully to the downfall of the haskalah by reason of an excess of ideology. "Young men must think and work for their own lives only." This became the watchword of the last Maskilim toward 1870.

Utilitarianism.

The ghetto, however, had not yet spoken its final word. Within the confines of traditional Judaism itself the modernization of Hebrew and of the religious spirit was accentuated, leading to a compromise between faith and life. Orthodox journals were beginning to be the mouthpieces of a conservative party more in touch with modern ideas. Side by side with the realistic press—"Ha-Meliẓ," the organ of the realists; "Ha-Ẓefirah," a popular scientific journal; "He-Ḥaluẓ," an antireligious paper; and others—there were "Ha-Maggid" and "Ha-Lebanon," in which Orthodox rabbis enthusiastically advocated the cultivation of Hebrew and boldly offered plans for its rejuvenation as well as for the colonization of Palestine. Michel Pines, the antagonist of Lilienblum, published in 1872 his "Yalde Ruḥi," a treatise displaying deep faith, and in which he bravely defends traditional Judaism, insisting that ritual and religious observances are necessary to a maintenance of the harmony of faith, which influences the mind as well as the morals. Reforms are unnecessary, because believers do not feel the need of them, and freethinkers no longer cherish any beliefs. Like the mass of believers, Pines does not share the pessimism of the realists, but he firmly believes in the national renascence of Judaism. Any understanding between the two parties seemed impossible, the realists no longer believing in the future of Judaism, and the conservatives refusing all attempts at religious reform. Even skeptics like Gordon were alarmed to see "the young people leave without returning." Then, once again, a man arose to undertake the work of mingling the humanistic and the romantic currents and of leading the haskalah back to the living sources of national Judaism. This was Perez Smolenskin, the initiator of the progressive national movement. He, also, began his career, in 1867, with a critical article of pronounced realism, "Biḳḳoret Teḥiyyah." But, disheartened by the fanaticism of the ancients and by the indifference and narrowness of the moderns, he left Russia and traveled first through Austria and later through the other western countries, sorrowfully noting the decadence of Judaism and of his patriotic ideal. At Vienna he issued in 1868 "Ha-Shaḥar," whose object it was to attack medieval obscurantism and modern indifference. For eighteen years Smolenskin continued this laborious campaign. In his "'Am 'Olam" (1872) he appears as the champion of the national preservation of Israel and of the realization of the rabbinical ideal freed from all mysticism. This secularization of an ideal which had constituted Israel's power of resistance had important results. In the first place it restored to Judaism and to Hebrew the best among the young men, who, while still profoundly attached to Judaism and to the life of the masses, had no longer any faith. This prepared the way for Zionism. But this was not all. Smolenskin recognized that one of the chief factors in the process of assimilation was the idea set forth by Mendelssohn and especially by his disciples (Geiger and others) that Judaism does not constitute a nation but a religious confession, an idea which would naturally induce the assimilation of the freethinkers. Smolenskin attacked this idea in a series of articles, which, though violent and often unjust, were yet needed to point out the priority of the national factor over the religious factor in the conservation of Judaism.

M. Pines.

P. Smolenskin (1842-85).

For eighteen years "Ha-Shaḥar" was the rallying-point for daring ideas and campaigns against the obscurantists and the moderns. It was especially noted for the realistic novels of Smolenskin, which, despite their technical shortcomings, take a high place in Hebrew literature. Side by side with character sketches of the ghetto and violent attacks on obscurantism appear a profound love for the masses and an ardent faith in Israel's future and in the apotheosis of young scholars endowed with the soul of prophecy, veritable dreamers of the

"Ha-Shaḥar."

ghetto. For the first time the Hebrew language, as modernized by Smolenskin, took immense strides. "Ha-Shaḥar" published only original work; and through the support and influence of its editor there arose a whole school of realists who wrote in Hebrew. In addition to Gordon and Lilienblum, there were Brandstädter (the clever creator of the short story in Hebrew), S. Mandelkern, J. L. Levin, Ben Ẓebi, M. Cohn, Silberbusch, Mandelstam, and others. Science was represented by S. Rubin, D. Kohan, Heller, D. Müller, etc.

The influence of "Ha-Shaḥar" was felt throughout Hebrew literature. The popular poet and scholar of the south, A. B. Gottlober, founded his review "Ha-Boḳer Or" (1876) for the purpose of defending Mendelssohn and the haskalah. Gottlober himself contributed character sketches of the Ḥasidim, while the gifted writer R. A. Braudes began in its pages his novel "Ha-Dat weha-Ḥayyim," in which he depicts with masterly hand the struggle for the union of life and faith. Even America boasted a Hebrew journal, "Ha-Ẓofeh be-Ereẓ Nod," published by Sobel. A converted Jew, Salkinson, produced an admirable Hebrew translation of Shakespeare and of Milton, and the socialist Freiman published a review in Hebrew entitled "Ha-Emet" (1878). More important, however, was the great work by I. H. Weiss, "Dor Dor we-Dorshaw," dealing with the evolution of religious tradition. The sciences were taken up by H. Rabbinowitz, Pories, S. Sachs, Reifman, Harkavy, Gurland, J. Halevy, A. Epstein, Zweifel, Popirna, Buber, etc. Even the style was modernized, although the meliẓah did not disappear, as is seen by the writings of Schulman, Friedberg, and others.

Smolenskin's ideas bore fruit. With the return of the national ideal, Hebrew as the national language was again revived. Leon Gordon's literary jubilee was enthusiastically celebrated in St. Petersburg, and after his return from a journey through Russia in 1880, he was everywhere received as the national author, even by the students of the capitals. The appearance of anti-Semitism, the renewed persecutions, and the terrible years 1881 and 1882 finally destroyed the ideals of the haskalah, whose last Hebrew followers were forced to admit that Smolenskin was right.

When the first colonies in Palestine had been founded, and there existed no longer a belief in the possibility of religious reform without an upheaval of Judaism as a whole, it was commonly admitted that the work of Israel's national rebirth should be encouraged. The Hebrew press undertook especially to support the "Ḥobebe Ẓiyyon" (Chovevei Zion), as the Zionists were then called. Hebrew modern literature, which for a century had been progressive and secularizing, now became the instrument of patriotic propaganda. Often those who had formerly advocated reforms now urged the abandonment of modern ideas in order to conciliate the masses. Smolenskin alone did not abandon his civilizing mission, and remained a progressive realist. He finally succumbed to overwork and died in 1885. On his death "Ha-Shaḥar" ceased publication, just one century after the appearance of "Ha-Me'assef" (1785). This was the end of the haskalah. It now gave place to Zionism, which was at first hesitating, but gradually arose to the realization and assertion of its full strength.

Contemporary Literature (1885-1904).

The changing attitude in the profession of faith among Hebrew scholars and the young men who had returned to the national ideal and to the prophetic dreams was of advantage to Hebrew, which now came to be considered as the national language of the Jewish people and the tie uniting the Jews of all countries. While E. Ben-Judah at Jerusalem, through personal example and through propaganda in his journal "Ha-Ẓebi," restored Hebrew as a living language in Palestine, there was an increasing demand for Hebrew books in Russia, and the modernized Jews became ambitious to cultivate the national language. The success of the great literary collection "Ha-Asif" (edited by the writer N. Sokolow), which succeeded "Ha-Shaḥar," soon called forth other publications, noteworthy among which was the Zionistic work "Keneset Yisrael" by the historian S. P. Rabbinowitz, and the more scientific "Oẓar ha-Sifrut."

Daily Press.

In 1886 L. Kantor began the publication of "Ha-Yom," the first Hebrew daily paper; and soon after "Ha-Meliẓ" and "Ha-Ẓefirah" were changed into dailies. A political press, also, was established, and contributed largely to the propagation of Zionism and to the modernization of Hebrew style. The founding of two large publishing-houses (the "Aḥiasaf" and "Tushiyyah"), through the efforts of Ben-Avigdor, finally regulated the conditions for the progress of Hebrew, and created a class of paid writers. Journals, more than other forms of literature, are multiplying, and there are a number even in America.

Literary activity was resumed after a short interval, now on an entirely national basis and in agreement with the many needs of a nationalist group. All the branches of letters, science, and art were assiduously cultivated, without neglecting the renascence of the Jewish people in the land of their fathers. In the field of poetry, besides Mandelkern and Gottlober, both converted to Zionism, are to be found Dolitzky, author of Zionistic songs describing the miseries of the Russian Jews; the two Zionist poets Isaac Rabinowitz and Sarah Shapira, and the gifted lyric poet M. H. Mané, who died at an early age. Perhaps the most noteworthy was C. A. Shapira, an eminent lyric poet, who, embittered by indignation, introduced a new note into Hebrew poetry—hatred of persecution. There is, finally, N. H. Imber, the poet of renascent Palestine and the author of popular songs. Bialik is a lyric poet of much vigor, an incomparable stylist, and a romanticist of note, while his younger contemporary Saul Tschernichowsky is proceeding along new lines, introducing pure estheticism, the cult of beauty and of love, in the language of the Prophets. The most gifted among the younger poets are S. L. Gordon, N. Pinés, A. Lubochitzky, Kaplan, Lipschütz, and A. Cohan.

In the field of belles-lettres Ben-Avigdor is the creator of the new realistic movement; this he expounds in his psychologic stories and especially in his "Menaḥem ha-Sofer," in which he attacks, in the name of modern life, national chauvinism. Braudes became prominent as a romanticist. The aged A. J. Abramowitsch, who has returned to Hebrew, delights his readers by his artistic satires. I. L. Perez has in his songs, as in his poetry, a tendency toward symbolism. M. J. Berdyczewski attempts to introduce Nietzschian individualism into his stories and articles. Feierberg expresses the sufferings of a young scholar seeking truth. Goldin is a pleasing but sentimental writer of stories. Bershadsky is an outspoken realist and close observer. Others deserving mention are: J. Rabinovitz; Turov; A. S. Rabinovitz; Epstein; Asch; J. Steinberg; Goldberg; Brener; the Galicians Silberbusch and Samueli; the poet and prose-writer David Frischman, the translator of "Cain"; J. Ch. Tawjew, who is a distinguished feuilletonist and writer on pedagogics; A. L. Levinsky, the story-teller, author of a Zionist Utopia ("Travels in Palestine in 5800"); and J. L. Landau, the only dramatic poet. As Landau is a poet rather than a psychologist, his "Herod" and other plays are not intended for the theater. The Orientalist Joseph Halévy has published a volume of patriotic poems.

The reaction of 1890 in the work of colonizing Palestine and the evident necessity of taking some steps to meet such a reaction produced the work of "Aḥad ha-'Am" (Asher Ginzberg). He is notably a critic of manners; and in the name of pure ideology he attacked first actual colonization and then political Zionism. Judaism before everything, and not the Jews; a moral and spiritual, not an economic and a political center; a national ideal taking the place of faith—such, in the rough, is the idea of this acute and paradoxical publicist. A number of young men, influenced by his collection "Ha-Pardes" and the review "Ha-Shiloaḥ," founded by him and continued by Klausner, have followed in his lead. Quite opposite in tendencies is Zeeb Ya'beẓ, the editor of "Ha-Mizraḥ," a remarkable stylist and religious romanticist. L. Rabinovitz, the director of "Ha-Meliẓ," in his articles "Ha-Yerushshah weha-Ḥinnuk" also shows himself to be a defender of Jewish tradition, while Ben-Judah, the author of "Hashḳafah" (Jerusalem), constantly opposes obscurantism. N. Sokolow, by the power of his genius, forces Hebrew and modern ideas even upon the Ḥasidim. The critic Reuben Brainin is a close observer, an admirable stylist, and a charming story-teller. The historian S. Bernfeld is a scholarly popularizer of Jewish science.

Pedagogics and juvenile literature also have their periodicals and worthy representatives. Among these are: Lerner, S. L. Gordon, Madame Ben-Judah, Yellin, Grosovsky, and Berman. Many scholars have devoted themselves to science, as the late philosopher F. Misés; the grammarian J. Steinberg, who is an admirable writer; the anatomist, archeologist, and author of popular stories Katzenelenson; Neimark; and Hurvitz. There are, in addition, many translators and compilers who have rendered into Hebrew Longfellow, Mark Twain, Zola, and even De Maupassant; and this work is being actively carried forward. There is a steady increase in the number of daily and weekly journals, all of which, though Zionistic, are none the less progressive. With the emigration of the Russian Jews to foreign countries, Hebrew is finding new centers. In 1904 a course in modern Hebrew literature was instituted at the Sorbonne. Palestine is in a fair way to become the home of Hebrew as a living language, and in America and in England there are numerous publications in Hebrew. Even in the Far East, Hebrew books and periodicals are to be found in increasing numbers, stimulating national and social regeneration. But it must be remembered that the future of Hebrew is intimately connected with Zionism, which is accepted by the masses only by reason of the ideal of national renascence. Faithful to its Biblical mission, the Hebrew language alone is able to revive moral vigor and prophetic idealism, which have never failed where the sacred language has been preserved.

Bibliography: N. Schlousz, *La Renaissance de la Littérature Hébraïque, 1743–1885*, Paris, 1903; R. Brainin, *Mapu, Smolensky* (in Hebrew), Warsaw; S. Bernfeld, *Dor Ḥakam*, Warsaw, 1896; idem, *Da'at Elohim*, *ib.* 1897–98; J. Klausner, *Hebrew Literature in the Nineteenth Century* (in Russian); M. Mendelssohn, *Pene Tebel*, Amsterdam, 1872.

G. N. Sl.

LITHUANIA (Russian or Polish, **Litwa**; in Jewish writings ליטא): Formerly a grand duchy, politically connected more or less intimately with Poland, and with the latter annexed to Russia.

Lithuania originally embraced only the waywodeships of Wilna and Troki; but in the thirteenth century it augmented its territory at the expense of the neighboring principalities and included the duchy of Samogitia (Zhmud; זמיט).

In the first half of the fourteenth century, when Russia was already under the Tatar yoke, the Lithuanian grand duke Gedimin (1316–41) still further increased his possessions by family alliances and by conquest until they came to embrace the territories of Vitebsk, Kiev (1321), Minsk, etc. Under Olgerd and Keistat, sons of Gedimin, the Russian principalities of Chernigov-Syeversk, Podolia (1362), and Volhynia (1377) were also added to Lithuania; and the territory thus extended from the Baltic to the Black Sea.

As early as the eighth century Jews lived in parts of the Lithuanian territory. Beginning with that period they conducted the trade between South Russia, *i.e.*, Lithuania, and the Baltic, especially with Danzig, Julin (Vineta or Wollin, in Pomerania), and other cities on the Vistula, Oder, and Elbe (see Georg Jacob, "Welche Handelsartikel Bezogen die Araber des Mittelalters aus Baltischen Ländern?" p. 1).

When Duke Boleslaw I. of Poland sent Bishop Adalbert of Prague in 997 to preach the Gospel to the heathen Prussians (Lithuanians), the bishop complained that Christian prisoners of war were sold for base money to Jews, and that he was not able to redeem them. Records, of that time, of Jewish residents in Kiev are still extant. About the middle of the twelfth century Rabbi Eliezer of Mayence referred to some ritual customs of the Russian, *i.e.*, Lithuanian, Jews ("Eben ha-'Ezer," p. 74a, Prague, 1710), and in the same century mention was made also of Moses of Kiev. In the thirteenth century Jews lived in Chernigov, Volhynia, and Smolensk.

Among them there were men of learning, as is evidenced by a manuscript in the Vatican Library (Codex 300) dated 1094, and consisting of a commentary on the Bible written in "Russia." Another commentary, dated 1124, also written in Russia, is preserved in Codex Oppenheim Additamenta, Quar. No. 13, at present in the Bodleian Library, Oxford. About the same time there lived in Chernigov ITZE (Isaac), who is probably identical with Isaac of Russia. In the first half of the fourteenth century there lived in Toledo, Spain, a Talmudic scholar, Asher ben Sinai, who came from Russia (Asheri, Responsa, part 51, No. 2; Zunz, "'Ir ha-Ẓedeḳ," p. 45). These isolated cases do not prove, however, that Talmudic learning had, at the period in question, become widely diffused in the Lithuanian-Russian territory. As Harkavy has pointed out, the individual efforts of the Russian Talmudists to spread Jewish knowledge did not meet with success until the sixteenth century. In a letter written by Eliezer of Bohemia (1190) to Judah Ḥasid it is stated that in most places in Poland, Russia, and Hungary there were no Talmudic scholars, chiefly because of the poverty of the Jews there, which compelled the communities to secure the services of men able to discharge the three functions of cantor, rabbi, and teacher ("Or Zarua'," p. 40, § 113, Jitomir, 1862). These references to Russia do not necessarily always apply to Lithuania, since Galicia also was designated by that name in Hebrew writings of the Middle Ages, while the Muscovite territory of that time was referred to as "Moskwa." The mention of the name "Lita" first occurs in a responsum of the fifteenth century by Israel Isserlein. He refers to a certain Tobiah who had returned from Gordita (Grodno ?) in Lithuania, and states that "it is rare for our people from Germany to go to Lithuania" (Israel Bruna, Responsa, §§ 25, 73).

Origin of Lithuanian Jews.

The origin of the Lithuanian Jews has been the subject of much speculation. It is now almost certain that they were made up of two distinct streams of Jewish immigration. The older of the two entered Lithuania by way of South Russia, where Jews had lived in considerable numbers since the beginning of the common era (see ARMENIA; BOSPORUS; CRIMEA; KERTCH). The fact that these had adopted the Russian language (the official language of the Lithuanians) and the customs, occupations, and even the names of the native population, serves to prove that they came from the East rather than from western Europe. The later stream of immigration originated in the twelfth century and received an impetus from the persecution of the German Jews by the Crusaders. The blending of these two elements was not complete even in the eighteenth century, differences appearing at that time in proper names, in the pronunciation of the Judæo-German dialect, and even in physiognomy.

The peculiar conditions that prevailed in Lithuania compelled the first Jewish settlers to adopt a different mode of life from that followed by their western coreligionists. In the Lithuania of that day there were no cities in the western sense of the word, no Magdeburg Rights or close gilds.

Some of the cities which later became the important centers of Jewish life in Lithuania were at first mere villages. Grodno, one of the oldest, was founded by a Russian prince, and is first mentioned in the chronicles of 1128. Novogrudok was founded somewhat later by Yaroslav; Kerlov in 1250; Voruta and Twiremet in 1252; Eiragola in 1262; Golschany and Kovno in 1280; Telshi, Wilna, Lida, and Troki in 1320.

With the campaign of Gedimin and his subjection of Kiev and Volhynia (1320-21) the Jewish inhabitants of these territories were induced to spread throughout the northern provinces of the grand duchy. The probable importance of the southern Jews in the development of Lithuania is indicated by their numerical prominence in Volhynia in the thirteenth century. According to an annalist who describes the funeral of the grand duke Vladimir Vasilkovich in the city of Vladimir (Volhynia), "the Jews wept at his funeral as at the fall of Jerusalem, or when being led into the Babylonian captivity." This sympathy and the record thereof would seem to indicate that long before the event in question the Jews had enjoyed considerable prosperity and influence, and this gave them a certain standing under the new régime. They took an active part in the development of the new cities under the tolerant rule of Gedimin.

The Charter of 1388.

Little is known of the fortunes of the Lithuanian Jews during the troublous times that followed the death of Gedimin and the accession of his grandson Witold (1341). To the latter the Jews owed a charter of privileges which was momentous in the subsequent history of the Jews of Lithuania. The documents granting privileges first to the Jews of Brest (July 1, 1388) and later to those of Troki, Grodno (1389), Lutsk, Vladimir, and other large towns are the earliest documents to recognize the Lithuanian Jews as possessing a distinct organization. The gathering together of the scattered Jewish settlers in sufficient numbers and with enough power to form such an organization and to obtain privileges from their Lithuanian rulers implies the lapse of considerable time. The Jews who dwelt in smaller towns and villages were not in need of such privileges at this time, as Harkavy suggests, and the mode of life, the comparative poverty, and the ignorance of Jewish learning among the Lithuanian Jews retarded their intercommunal organization. But powerful forces hastened this organization toward the close of the fourteenth century. The chief of these was probably the cooperation of the Jews of Poland with their Lithuanian brethren. After the death of Casimir the Great (1370), the condition of the Polish Jews changed for the worse. The influence of the Catholic clergy at the Polish court grew; Louis of Anjou was indifferent to the welfare of his subjects, and his eagerness to convert the Jews to Christianity, together with the increased Jewish immigration from Germany, caused the Polish Jews to become apprehensive for their future. On this account it seems more than likely that influential Polish Jews cooperated with the leading Lithuanian communities in securing a special charter from Witold.

The preamble of the charter reads as follows:

"In the name of God, Amen. All deeds of men, when they are not made known by the testimony of witnesses or in writing, pass away and vanish and are forgotten. Therefore, we, Alexander, also called Witold, by the grace of God Grand Duke of Lithuania and ruler of Brest, Dorogicz, Lutsk, Vladimir, and other places, make known by this charter to the present and future generations, or to whomever it may concern to know or hear of it, that, after due deliberation with our nobles we have decided to grant to all the Jews living in our domains the rights and liberties mentioned in the following charter."

has loaned money to a Christian, but has no witnesses to prove it, the latter may clear himself by taking an oath. (5) Jews may make loans on any personal property except blood-stained articles or articles employed in religious service. (6) Where a Christian asserts that an article pawned to a Jew has been stolen from a Christian, the Jew, after swearing that he was ignorant of the robbery, is relieved of responsibility to the owner of the article, and need not return it until the sum advanced by him, with the interest, has been repaid. (7) Where a Jew loses pawned property by fire or robbery he is relieved from responsibility for articles so lost if he takes an oath that such articles were lost together with his own. (8) A suit be-

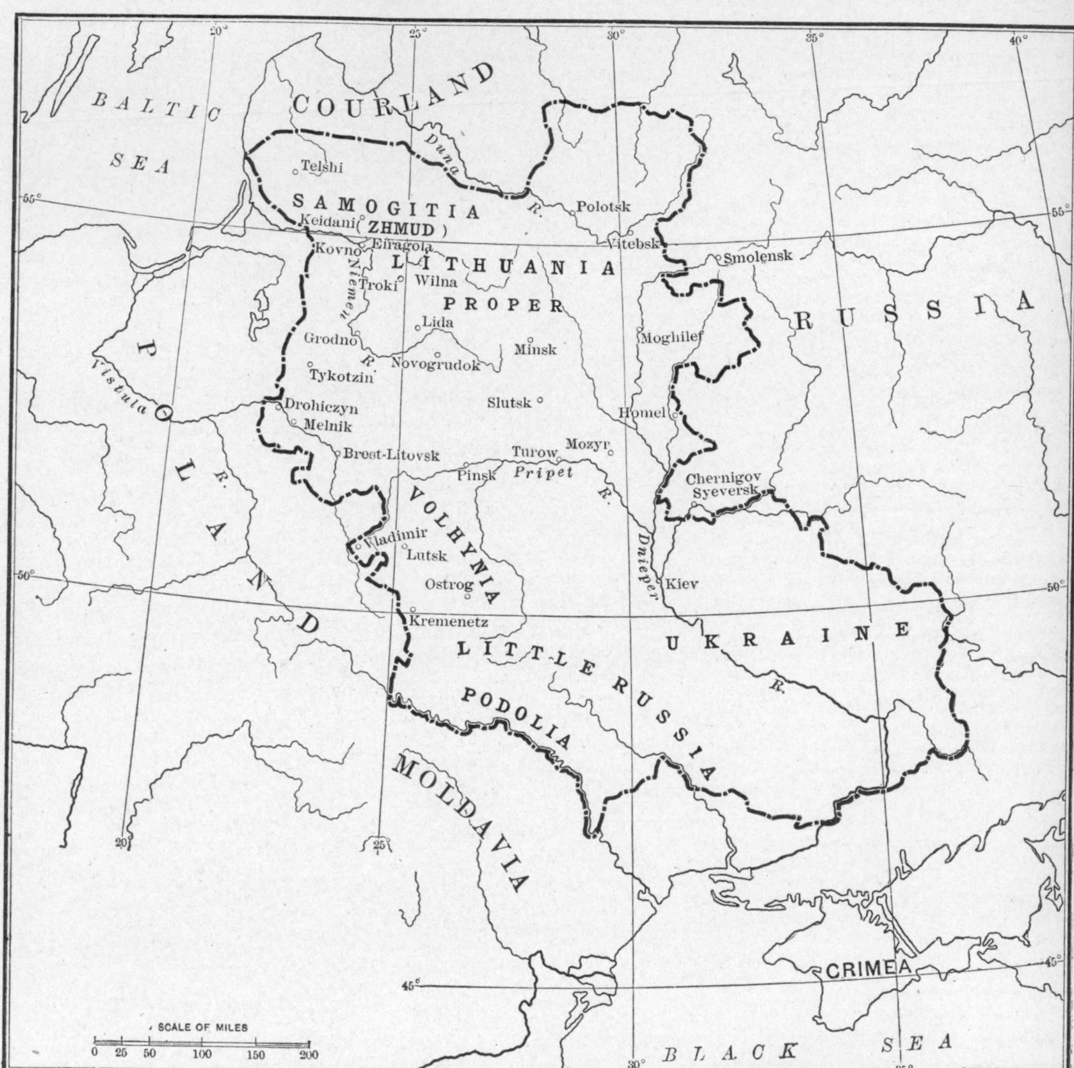

GRAND DUCHY OF LITHUANIA AT ITS GREATEST EXTENT, SHOWING CITIES WHERE JEWS LIVED.

The charter contains thirty-seven sections, which may be summarized as follows:

(1) In criminal or other cases involving the person or property of a Jew, the latter can not be convicted on the testimony of one Christian witness; there must be two witnesses—a Christian and a Jew. (2) Where a Christian asserts that he has placed an article in pawn with a Jew, and the Jew denies it, the latter may clear himself by taking the prescribed oath. (3) Where a Christian claims that he has pawned an article with a Jew for a sum less than that claimed by the latter, the Jew's claim shall be allowed if he take the usual oath. (4) Where a Jew claims he

tween Jews may not be decided by a city judge, but must be submitted in the first instance to the jurisdiction of the subwaywode, in the second instance to the waywode, and finally to the king. Important criminal cases are subject to the jurisdiction of the king alone. (9) A Christian found guilty of inflicting wounds upon a Jewess must pay a fine to the king and damages and expenses to the victim, in accordance with the local regulations. (10) A Christian murdering a Jew shall be punished by the proper court and his possessions confiscated to the king. (11) A Christian inflicting injuries upon a Jew, but without shedding blood, shall be punished in accordance with local law. (12) A Jew may travel without hindrance within the limits of the country, and when he carries merchandise he shall pay the same duties as the local burghers. (13) Jews may transport the bodies of their dead free of taxation. (14) A Christian injuring a Jewish cemetery shall be punished in accordance with the local law and his property confiscated. (15) Any person throwing stones into the synagogue shall pay to the waywode a fine of two pounds. (16) A Jew failing to pay to the judge the fine called "wandil" shall pay the anciently established fine. (17) Any Jew not appearing in court after being twice summoned shall pay the customary fine. (18) A Jew inflicting wounds on another Jew shall be fined in accordance with local custom. (19) A Jew may take an oath on the Old Testament in important cases only, as where the claim exceeds in value fifty "griven" of pure silver, or where the case is brought before the king. (20) Where a Christian is suspected of killing a Jew, though there were no witnesses, and the relatives of the victim declare their suspicion, the king is to give the Jews an executioner for the accused. (21) Where a Christian assaults a Jewess he shall be punished according to local usage. (22) A subwaywode may not summon Jews to his court except on a regular complaint. (23) In cases concerning Jews the court is to sit either in the synagogue or in a place selected by the Jews. (24) Where a Christian pays the sum advanced to him on any article when due, but omits to pay the interest, he shall be given a written extension of time, after which the sum unpaid shall be subject to interest until paid. (25) The houses of Jews are free from military quartering. (26) When a Jew advances to a noble a sum of money on an estate, the Jew is entitled, if the loan be not repaid on maturity, to the possession of the property, and shall be protected in its possession. (27) A person guilty of stealing a Jewish child shall be punished as a thief. (28) If the value of an article pawned with a Jew by a Christian for a period less than a year does not exceed the amount advanced upon it, the pawnbroker, after taking the article to his waywode, may sell it; but if the article is of greater value than the sum advanced the Jew shall be obliged to keep it for a further period of one year and one day, at the expiration of which time he shall become its possessor. (29) No person may demand the return of pawned property on Jewish holy days. (30) Any Christian forcibly taking an article pawned with a Jew, or entering a Jewish house against the wish of its owner, shall be subject to the same punishment as a person stealing from the common treasury. (31) To summon a Jew to appear in court is allowed only to the king or the waywode. (32) Since the papal bulls show that Jews are forbidden by their own law to use human blood, or any blood whatever, it is forbidden to accuse Jews of using human blood. But in the case of a Jew accused of the murder of a Christian child, such accusation must be proved by three Christians and three Jews. If the Christian accuser is unable to prove his accusation he shall be subjected to the same punishment that would have been inflicted on the accused had his guilt been proved. (33) Loans made by Jews to Christians must be repaid with interest. (34) The pledging of horses as security on loans made by Jews must be done in the daytime; in case a Christian should recognize a horse stolen from him among horses pawned with a Jew, the latter must take an oath that the horse was received by him in the daytime. (35) Mint directors are forbidden to arrest Jews, when the latter are found with counterfeit coin, without the knowledge of the king's waywode, or in the absence of prominent citizens. (36) A Christian neighbor who shall fail to respond at night when a Jew calls for help shall pay a fine of thirty "zloty." (37) Jews are permitted to buy and sell on the same footing as Christians, and any one interfering with them shall be fined by the waywode.

The charter itself was modeled upon similar documents granted by Casimir the Great, earlier by Boleslaw of Kalisz, to the Jews of Poland. These in their turn were based on the charters of Henry of Glogau (1251), King Ottokar of Bohemia (1254–67), and Frederick II. (1244), and the last-mentioned upon the charter of the Bishop of Speyer (1084). The successive remodelings of the different documents were made necessary by the characteristic customs and conditions of the various countries; and for this reason the charter granted by Witold to the Jews of Brest and Troki is distinguished from its Polish and German models by certain peculiarities. The chief digressions are in §§ 8, 21, 28, 33, and 35. The distinctive features were made more manifest in the later issues of these privileges by the attempt to conform them to the needs of Lithuanian-Russian life. While the earlier charters of Brest and Troki were evidently framed upon western models for a class of Jews largely engaged in money-lending, the charters of Grodno (June 18, 1389 and 1408) show the members of that community engaged in various occupations, including agriculture. The charter of 1389 indicates that the Jews of Grodno, the residence of Witold, had lived there for many years, owning land and possessing a synagogue and cemetery near the Jewish quarter. They also followed handicrafts and engaged in commerce on equal terms with the Christians.

As the Jews of Germany were servants of the rulers ("Kammerknechte"), so the Lithuanian Jews formed a class of freemen subject in all criminal cases directly to the jurisdiction of the grand duke and his official representatives, and in petty suits to the jurisdiction of local officials on an equal footing with the lesser nobles ("Shlyakhta"), boyars, and other free citizens. The official representatives of the grand duke were the elder ("starosta"), known as the "Jewish judge" ("judex Judæorum"), and his deputy. The Jewish judge decided all cases between Christians and Jews and all criminal suits in which Jews were concerned; in civil suits, however, he acted only on the application of the interested parties. Either party who failed to obey the judge's summons had to pay him a fine. To him also belonged all fines collected from Jews for minor offenses. His duties included the guardianship of the persons, property, and freedom of worship of the Jews. He had no right to summon any one to his court except upon the complaint of an interested party. In matters of religion the Jews were given extensive autonomy.

The "Starosta."

Under these equitable laws the Jews of Lithuania reached a degree of prosperity unknown to their Polish and German coreligionists at that time. The communities of Brest, Grodno, Troki, Lutsk, and Minsk rapidly grew in wealth and influence. Every community had at its head a Jewish elder. These elders represented the communities in all external relations, in securing new privileges, and in the regulation of taxes. Such officials are not, however, referred to by the title "elder" before the end of the sixteenth century. Up to that time the documents merely state, for instance, that the "Jews of Brest humbly apply," etc. On assuming office the elders declared under oath that they would discharge the duties of the position faithfully, and would relinquish the office at the expiration of the appointed term. The elder acted in conjunction with the rabbi, whose jurisdiction included all Jewish affairs with the exception of judicial cases assigned to the court of the deputy, and by the latter to the king. In religious affairs, however, an appeal from the decision of the rabbi and the elder was permitted only to a council consisting of the chief rabbis of the king's cities. The cantor, sexton, and shoḥeṭ were subject to the orders of the rabbi and elder.

The favorable position of the Jews in Lithuania during the reign of Witold brought to the front a number of the wealthier Jews, who, besides engaging in commerce, also leased certain sources of the ducal revenues or became owners of estates. The first known Jewish farmer of customs duties in Lithuania was "Shanya" (probably Shakna), who was presented by Witold with the villages Vinnike and Kalusov in the district of Vladimir. The good-will and tolerance of Witold endeared him to his Jewish subjects, and for a long time traditions concerning his generosity and nobility of character were current among them. He ruled Lithuania independently even when that country and Poland were united for a time in 1413. His cousin, the Polish king Ladislaus II., Jagellon, did not interfere with his administration during Witold's lifetime.

Under the Jagellons.

After Witold's death Ladislaus assumed active sovereignty over a part of Lithuania. He granted (1432) the Magdeburg Rights to the Poles, Germans, and Russians of the city of Lutsk, while in the case of the Jews and Armenians the Polish laws were made effective (see POLAND). This policy toward his Jewish subjects in Poland was influenced by the clerical party, and he attempted to curtail the privileges granted to them by his predecessors. However, his rule in Lithuania was too short to have a lasting effect on the life of the Lithuanian Jews.

Swidrigailo, who became Grand Duke of Lithuania at the death of Witold (1430), strove to prevent the annexation of Volhynia and Podolia to the Polish crown. He availed himself of the service of Jewish tax-farmers, leasing the customs duties of Vladimir to the Jew Shanya and those of Busk to the Jew Yatzka. There is, however, reason for the belief that he was not always friendly toward the Jews, as is shown by his grant of the Magdeburg Rights to the city of Kremenetz and the placing of all the inhabitants, including the Jews, under the jurisdiction of the German waywode Yurka (May 9, 1438). The latter act may have been prompted by his desire to retain the allegiance of the German inhabitants of Volhynia. Swidrigailo was assassinated in the year 1440, and was succeeded by Casimir Jagellon.

As Grand Duke of Lithuania (1440–92) Casimir Jagellon pursued toward his Jewish subjects the liberal policy of Witold. In 1441 he granted the Magdeburg Rights to the Karaite Jews of Troki on conditions similar to those under which they were granted to the Christians of Troki, Wilna, and Kovno; giving the Troki Karaites, however, a wider autonomy in judicial matters and in communal affairs, allowing them one-half of the city revenues, and presenting them with a parcel of land. The Troki and Lutsk Karaites were descendants of 380 families brought, according to tradition, by Witold from the Crimea at the end of the fourteenth century, when Rabbinite Jews were already established in Troki (see Graetz, "History," Heb. transl. by Rabinowitz, vi. 225). Settling originally in New Troki, the Karaites subsequently spread to other Lithuanian and Galician towns. The poorer among them were, like most of the Rabbinite Jews, engaged in agriculture and handicrafts, while the richer members were, like the wealthier Rabbinites, leaseholders and tax-farmers. The Lithuanian rulers of that time did not make any distinction between Rabbinites and Karaites, designating both in their decrees merely as "Jews" ("Zidy"). See KARAITES.

Jews as Tax-Farmers.

In 1453, for services rendered to him, Casimir granted to the Jew Michael of Hrubieszów, his wife, and their son Judah, exemption from all taxes and customs duties throughout the country. Between 1463 and 1478 he presented to Levin Schalomich certain lands in the waywodeship of Brest, together with the peasants living on them. In 1484 he awarded the lease of the customs duties of Novgorod for three years to the Troki Jews Ilia Moiseyevich, Ruwen Sakovich, Avraam Danilovich, and Jeska Schelemovich. In 1485 he ordered the waywode of Troki to see that the Jewish part of the town paid its taxes separately, this arrangement being made in response to a petition from the Jews themselves. In 1486 he leased the customs of Kiev, Wischegorod, and Jitomir for a term of three years to Simha Karvchik, Sadke and Samak Danilovich, Samaditza, and Ryzhka, who were Jews of Kiev and Troki. In the same year the customs duties of Bryansk were leased to Mordecai Gadajewich and Perka Judinovich of Kiev; certain taxes of Grodno and Meretz to Enka Jatzkovich and his sons of Grodno; and the customs duties of Putivl to Jews of Kiev and Troki. In 1487 the customs duties of Brest, Drohycin, Byelsk, and Grodno were leased to Astaschka Ilyich, Onatani Ilyich, and Olkan, Jews of Lutsk, and the customs duties of Lutsk to Shachna Peisachovich and Senka Mamotlivy. In 1488 certain taxes of Grodno and Meretz were again leased to Jatzkovich and his sons, and the customs duties of Zvyagol to the Lutsk Jews Israel, Yeska, and Judah. In the following year the customs duties of Minsk were leased to the Jew of Troki, Michael Danilovich; the customs duties of Vladimir, Peremyshl, and Litovishk to the Jews of Brest and Hrubieszów; and the customs duties of Kiev and Putivl to Rabei and other Jews of Kiev. In 1490 certain revenues of Putivl were leased to Merovach and Israel of Kiev and Abraham of Plotzk. These leases prove that throughout Casimir's reign the important commercial and financial affairs of the grand duchy were largely managed by Jewish leaseholders, to whom he was heavily indebted. At times his treasury was depleted to such an extent as to compel him to pawn the queen's robes and his silverware, but the Jews came to his aid in time of need.

Commercial Relations.

According to the Polish historian Jaroszewicz in his "Obraz Litwy," the Jews of Lithuania after the reign of Casimir Jagellon were intimately connected with the development of the country's commerce. Their business ventures reached far beyond Lithuania, most of the export trade to Prussia and the Baltic Sea being in their hands.

Historians are agreed that Casimir was not a strong and just ruler. He did not scruple to give contradictory promises to Poland and Lithuania, and his frequent favors to the Jews do not necessarily show that he was their friend. At most he considered them as useful agents in his financial undertakings.

The influential Jewish tax-farmers often encountered difficulties with foreign merchants. The Russian Grand Duke Ivan Vassilivich III. repeatedly made representations to Casimir in regard to the high-handed treatment of Muscovite merchants and ambassadors by the tax-collectors Shan (the son-in-law of Agron), Simha, Ryabchik, and others. The king upheld his Jewish tax-farmers on the ground that the Russian merchants attempted to evade payment of customs duties by choosing rarely traveled roads. From these documents it is also clear that the Jewish customs officials had under them armed men to arrest violators of the regulations. At Casimir's death (1492) many of his Jewish creditors were left unpaid.

Casimir was succeeded as king of Poland by his son John Albert, and on the Lithuanian throne by his younger son, Alexander Jagellon. The latter confirmed the charter of privileges granted to the Jews by his predecessors, and even gave them additional rights. His father's Jewish creditors received part of the sums due to them, the rest being withheld under various pretexts. Jewish tax-farmers continued to lease the customs duties in the important cities, as is exemplified by a lease of those of Brest, Drohoczyn, Grodno, and Byelsk (Oct. 14, 1494) to four Jews of Brest. The favorable attitude toward the Jews which had characterized the Lithuanian rulers for generations was unexpectedly and radically changed by a decree promulgated by Alexander in April, 1495. By this decree all Jews living in Lithuania proper and the adjacent territories were summarily ordered to leave the country.

Expelled by Alexander.

The expulsion was evidently not accompanied by the usual cruelties; for there was no popular animosity toward the Lithuanian Jews, and the decree was regarded as an act of mere wilfulness on the part of an absolute ruler. Some of the nobility, however, approved Alexander's decree, expecting to profit by the departure of their Jewish creditors, as is indicated by numerous lawsuits on the return of the exiles to Lithuania in 1503. It is known from the Hebrew sources that some of the exiles migrated to the Crimea, and that by far the greater number settled in Poland, where, by permission of King John Albert, they established themselves in the towns situated near the Lithuanian boundary. This permission, given at first for a period of two years, was extended "because of the extreme poverty of the Jews on account of the great losses sustained by them." The extension, which applied to all the towns of the kingdom, accorded the enjoyment of all the liberties that had been granted to their Polish brethren (Cracow, June 29, 1498). The expelled Karaites settled in the Polish town of Ratno.

The causes of the unexpected expulsion have been widely discussed. It has been suggested by Narbut and other Lithuanian historians that the decree was the outcome of Alexander's personal animosity toward the Jews, he having been educated by the Polish historian Dlugosc (Longinus), an avowed enemy of the Jews. Others have held that it was instigated by the grand duchess Helena, daughter of Ivan III. of Russia. Legend has it that she was at first very friendly toward the Jews, but having been rendered barren by a Jewish midwife through the aid of witchcraft, her father demanded the punishment of the witches, and the decree of expulsion followed. The improbability of this story has been demonstrated by Bershadski ("Litovskie Yevrei," p. 251), who shows that the marriage took place in Feb., 1495, and that the expulsion occurred in April of the same year. Bershadski and Harkavy suggest as a probable motive the pressure put upon Alexander by the Catholic clergy. He may have been influenced by the expulsion of the Jews from Spain (1492). This view is strengthened by his continued favors to the baptized Jews, as exemplified by his lease to Simsha of Troki (who had adopted the Christian faith); of the customs at Putivl in the same year to Feodor, "the newly baptized," and his son-in-law Peter; and the grant to the former tax-farmer of Putivl, "the newly baptized" Ivan, of one-third of the income from these customs duties; and above all by the very marked favors shown by him to Abraham Jesofovich after his baptism, Alexander going so far as to create him a member of the hereditary nobility. These favors indicate that if the expulsion was due to animosity on Alexander's part, such animosity was a religious rather than a racial one. Another motive suggested by Bershadski was the financial embarrassment of the grand duke, then heavily indebted to the wealthy Jewish tax farmers and leaseholders. During the settlement with his Jewish creditors (Dec., 1494), *i.e.*, four months before the expulsion, it was noticed that Alexander was much troubled over the condition of his finances, as was evidenced by his repudiation for one reason or another of a part of his debts ("Russko-Yevreiski Arkhiv," i., No. 26). Alexander's extravagance was commonly known; and it was said of him that "he pawned everything that he did not give away." The depleted condition of his treasury may have driven him to adopt drastic measures. By confiscating the estates of the Jews the grand duke became the owner of their property. He presented a part of these estates to monasteries, charitable institutions, and baptized Jews "for certain considerations," and turned the proceeds into the grand-ducal treasury. A third motive assumed by Bershadski was the desire to replace the Jews by German settlers. As to the second and third of these possible motives, documents show that, while they may have helped Alexander to reach his decision, yet there was a certain foundation for the popular tradition concerning the influence of Grand Duchess Helena in the matter. As the daughter of Ivan III. she must have been aware of the grave apprehensions created in Moscow by the successful propaganda of the Judaizing sect, and the probable fear of the Lithuanian clergy that the Judaizing Heresy would spread to Lithuania. The success of the new teaching was impressed upon it by the conversion of Helena's sister-in-law the Princess Helena of Moscow (daughter-in-law of Ivan III.), the Russian secretary of state Kuritzyn, and the Metropolitan of Moscow Zosima. The clergy, alarmed at the success of the new heresy, probably convinced Alexander that its encouragement by Ivan III. and his court would create a grave political danger for Lithuania.

Soon after the promulgation of the decree the Jewish tax-farmers hastened to adjust their affairs and to render their accounts to Alexander, but evidently they could collect only a small portion of the sums due to them. The more valuable of the real property left by them was soon disposed of by the grand duke. In June, 1495, he presented his furrier Sova with an estate near Troki, together with the cattle, grain, and all else pertaining to it, which had belonged to the Jew Shlioma. On June 26 of the same year he presented the nobleman Soroka and his brother with estates belonging to the Jews Enko Momotlivy and Itzchak Levanovich and situated in the district of Lutsk. On July 15 the Bishop of Wilna was granted the houses and estates of the Jews Bogdan Chatzkovich and Ilia Kunchich, while the city of Wilna received as a gift the house formerly belonging to the Jew Janushovski. On Aug. 10 the farm of the Konyukovich brothers in the district of Grodno was given by Alexander to his secretary Lyzovy, and on Aug. 30 he presented a house in Lutsk, once the property of the Jew Enka, to his stableman Martin Chrebtovich. On March 12, 1496, the nobleman Semashkowich received the farm in Volhynia belonging to the Jews Nikon and Shlioma Simshich, and on March 21 all the properties left vacant by the Jews in Grodno. On Oct. 4 the estates of the brothers Enkovich of Brest were presented to Alexander's secretary Fedka Janushkovich; on Jan. 27, 1497, the estate of Kornitza, formerly belonging to the Jew Levon Shalomich, was given to Pavel, magistrate of Brest-Litovsk. In July of the same year all the unoccupied properties left by the Jews of Lutsk were presented to the elders of the city, in order to encourage new settlers. This distribution of Jewish property by Alexander was continued until the middle of 1501.

Escheat of Jewish Property.

Soon after Alexander's accession to the throne of Poland he permitted the Jewish exiles to return to Lithuania. Beginning March, 1503, as is shown by documents still extant, their houses, lands, synagogues, and cemeteries were returned to them, and permission was granted them to collect their old debts. The new charter of privileges permitted them to live throughout Lithuania as heretofore. It also directed the vice-regent of Wilna and Grodno, Prince Alexander Juryevich, to see that the Jews were restored to the enjoyment of their former property and assisted in the collection of debts due to them. The privilege was accorded them of repurchasing also the property originally owned by them at the price paid by their successors to the grand duke. They were likewise to pay all expenses for improvements and for the erection of new buildings, and were obliged to pay all mortgages. Moreover, they were required to equip annually a cavalry detachment of 1,000 horsemen besides paying large annual sums to the local authorities.

Return to Lithuania.

The return of the Jews and their attempt to regain their old possessions led to many difficulties and lawsuits. Alexander found it necessary to issue an additional decree (April, 1503), directing his vice-regent to enforce the law. In spite of this some of the property was not recovered by the Jews for years.

The tax-farmers returned to their old occupations, and were shown many marks of favor by Alexander. He could not, however, obliterate the remembrance that he had robbed the Jews. The permission given the exiles to return is ascribed to the depleted condition of his treasury and to the impending war with Russia, combined with the efforts of the influential Jews of Poland and the baptized Jews of Lithuania to secure their return.

The improvement in the condition of the Jews was especially marked in the reign of Alexander's youngest brother, Sigismund I. (1506–48). Among his first decrees was one (Dec. 22, 1506) which relieved the two synagogues of Lutsk—the Rabbinite and the Karaite—from the annual tax of 12 kop groschen imposed upon them by the city authorities. In January of the following year he confirmed, at the request of the Lithuanian Jews, the grant of privileges made by Witold in 1388. This was modeled after the original charter of Brest and was included in the first Lithuanian statute of 1529. Numerous other examples of his good-will toward the Jews show that while being a good Catholic he was free from fanaticism and religious intolerance. He looked upon his Jewish subjects as a class of men contributing by their usefulness to the welfare of the country, and as being entitled to the protection of equitable laws.

Sigismund I.

Like his predecessors, Sigismund availed himself extensively of the services of the wealthy tax-farmers. He borrowed large sums from them and in return accorded them special privileges. The most influential among the tax-farmers at his court, at the beginning of his reign, was Michael Jesofovich. When, in 1508, Prince Glinski rebelled against Sigismund, and by an agreement with the rulers of Moscow attempted to effect the annexation of portions of Poland and Lithuania to the Muscovite empire, two Jews of Brest, Itzko and Berek, aided the prince in his undertaking, and furnished him with secret information. Michael Jesofovich excommunicated them with the blowing of the shofar and with great public solemnity. In recognition of Michael's services, and prompted also by the desire to establish a more perfect system of tax-collection, Sigismund appointed him prefect over all the Lithuanian Jews (1514). This was a similar appointment to that of Abraham of Bohemia as prefect of the Polish Jews (1512). Like Abraham, Michael was invested with wide powers. He had the right to communicate directly with the king on important Jewish matters, and with the aid of a learned rabbi to administer justice among his coreligionists in accordance with their special laws. Michael's actual authority concerned the collection of taxes rather than the internal communal administration; and whatever his religious powers may have been, he certainly was not chief rabbi of the Lithuanian Jews, as some Jewish historians have stated.

This and similar acts, accompanied by the strengthening of the communal organizations, added to the prosperity of the Lithuanian communities. The most flourishing among them at the time were those of Brest, Grodno, Troki, Pinsk, Ostrog, Lutsk, and Tykotzin. The members of the communities found themselves in a better position legally than the burghers, although in practise the Jews were often deprived of the full enjoyment of their rights. According to the Lithuanian statutes of 1529 the murder of a Jew, a nobleman, or a burgher was punishable by death, and compensation was to be paid by the family of the murderer to that of the victim. But while the life of a Jew or a nobleman was valued at 100 kop groschen, that of a burgher was valued at only 12 kop groschen. Proportionate compensation was provided for personal injuries. The prominent Jewish tax-farmers frequently exceeded their legal powers, as is shown by complaints to the authorities. Thus in 1538 Goshko Kozhchich, a Jew of Brest, was fined 20 kop groschen for the illegal imprisonment of the nobleman Lyshinski. Similarly in 1542 the Jew Zachariah Markovich was ordered to pay 12 kop groschen as compensation for assaulting the king's boyar Grishka Kochevich. On the other hand, numerous instances are recorded of the friendly intercourse between Jews and Christians. They drank and ate in common, and the Jews took part in the Christian festivals and even vied with their Christian neighbors in athletic feats. But with the exception of a few wealthy Jewish tax-collectors, the Jews of Lithuania were not a great economic or political force. In their mode of life they were not markedly different from the rest of the population, and the names of the Jewish middle class are rarely met with in official documents. The rich Jews, however, are frequently mentioned in connection with their official business.

Prosperity of the Congregations.

About 1539, rumors were spread by a baptized Jew that many Christians had adopted the Mosaic faith and had found refuge and protection among the Jews of Lithuania. An investigation was ordered by Sigismund, but it failed to disclose anything incriminating the Jews. None the less, in the course of the inquiry the king's nobles subjected the Jews to great annoyance. They unjustly arrested them on the highways, broke into their houses, and otherwise maltreated them. Before the conclusion of the investigation another rumor was spread ascribing to the Lithuanian Jews the intention to emigrate to Turkey and to take the new converts with them. New inquiries accompanied by similar excesses and abuses were made. The Jews sent numerous deputations to the king, protesting their innocence. Their assertions were substantiated by the findings of a special commission; and Sigismund hastened to declare the Jews free from any suspicion (1540).

Rumors of Converts to Judaism.

In the last years of Sigismund's reign, and even during part of that of Sigismund August, Bona Sforza shared in their government, sometimes assuming absolute authority. The energetic queen was herself eager to make and to save money. Among the many decrees issued by her in her own name are two of special interest, as evidencing the occurrence of internal conflicts in Jewish communities. These deal with the quarrel in the community of Grodno between the powerful Judah family (Yudichi) and the rest of the community, due to the appointment of a rabbi in opposition to the wishes of a majority of the congregation. This rabbi was Mordecai, son-in-law of Judah Bogdanovich, and he is probably identical with Mordecai ben Moses Jaffe, rabbi of Cracow, who died about 1568. He should not be confounded with Mordecai ben Abraham Jaffe, author of "Lebushim" (1530–1612), who also was rabbi of Grodno (1572). Queen Bona decreed that the opposing faction be permitted to appoint a rabbi of its own, who was not to be related to the Judah family, and that the members of the latter should not call themselves "elders" of the Jews, a title that should be assumed only with the consent of the entire community. Accordingly, Moses ben Aaron was elected rabbi by opponents of the Judah family. This case tends to show that Mordecai Jaffe represented the Bohemian party, and Moses ben Aaron the Lithuanian-Polish faction.

Sigismund II., August, only son of Sigismund I., succeeded as Grand Duke of Lithuania (1544) before the death of his father. He succeeded to the Polish throne in 1548. Liberal in his rule and in his treatment of his Jewish subjects, he accorded them the same tolerance as he did the Lutherans and Calvinists, who were then beginning to grow in numbers both in Poland and in Lithuania. Like all the Jagellons, he was a great spendthrift and of loose morals, but was none the less mindful of the welfare of his people. At the beginning of his reign the power of the lesser nobles ("Shlyakhta") was still limited. They did not participate in the legislative, judicial, or administrative affairs of Lithuania. Until then the rights of the nobility, and of the Jews had differed but slightly. Thus the rabbi of Brest, Mendel Frank, was styled "the king's officer," and the Jew Shmoilo Israilevich was appointed deputy to the governor of Wilna. The more prominent Jews were always called in official documents "Pany" ("Sirs"). Like the nobility, the Jews carried swords, and were ready to fight whenever the occasion warranted. They wore also golden chains, and rings on which were engraved coats of arms. Until the union of Lublin (1569) the Jews of Lithuania, with few exceptions, lived on grand-ducal lands, and as subjects of the king enjoyed his protection. Thus the king ordered the reigning prince, Juri Semionovich of Slutsk, to pay damages for illegal acts against certain Jews, instructing the local authorities in case of opposition on the part of the prince to place the Jews in possession of his estates. The Jews could also collect debts not only from the Lithuanian lords, but even from such prominent persons as the Grand Duke of Ryazan. King Sigismund even entered into a diplomatic correspondence with the Grand Duke of Moscow urging the restoration of merchandise confiscated in Russia from Lithuanian Jewish merchants. The relations between the Jews and the local authorities were governed partly by their charters of privileges and partly by custom. The Jews, for instance, made presents to the magistrate or elder, but were quite independent in their dealings with them. The local officials were answerable to the king for illegal acts.

Under Sigismund II.

The middle of the sixteenth century witnessed a

growing antagonism between the lesser nobility and the Jews. Their relations became strained, and the enmity of the Christians began to disturb the life of the Lithuanian Israelites. The anti-Jewish feeling, due at first to economic causes engendered by competition, was fostered by the clergy, who were then engaged in a crusade against heretics, notably the Lutherans, Calvinists, and Jews. The Reformation, which had spread from Germany, tended to weaken the allegiance to the Catholic Church. Frequent instances occurred of the marriage of Catholic women to Jews, Turks, or Tatars. The Bishop of Wilna complained to Sigismund August (Dec., 1548) of the frequency of such mixed marriages and of the education of the offspring in their fathers' faiths. The Shlyakhta also saw in the Jews dangerous competitors in commercial and financial undertakings. In their dealings with the agricultural classes the lords preferred the Jews as middlemen, thus creating a feeling of injury on the part of the Shlyakhta. The exemption of the Jews from military service and the power and wealth of the Jewish tax-farmers intensified the resentment of the Shlyakhta. Members of the nobility, like Borzobogaty, Zagorovski, and others, attempted to compete with the Jews as leaseholders of customs revenues, but were never successful. Since the Jews lived in the towns and on the lands of the king, the nobility could not wield any authority over them nor derive profit from them. They had not even the right to settle Jews on their estates without the permission of the king; but, on the other hand, they were often annoyed by the erection on their estates of the tollhouses of the Jewish tax-collectors.

Rise of Opposition.

Hence when the favorable moment arrived the Lithuanian nobility endeavored to secure greater power over the Jews. At the Diet of Wilna in 1551 the nobility urged the imposition of a special poll-tax of one ducat per head, and the Volhynian nobles demanded that the Jewish tax-collectors be forbidden to erect tollhouses or place guards at the taverns on their estates. In 1555 the illegal treatment of the Jews by Zhoslenski, the magistrate of Wilna, led Sigismund August to announce that a fine of 300 kop groschen would follow any repetition of such an excess of power. In 1559 the nobility of Samogitia complained of abuses by Jewish tax-collectors and demanded that the collection of customs duties be entrusted to them on the same terms as to the Jews. In 1560 the king found it necessary to prohibit the magistrates of Volhynia from assuming jurisdiction over the clerks of the tax-collector Mendel Isakovich. In 1563 the Lithuanian nobility demanded that the Jews furnish 2,000 foot-soldiers and an even greater number of sharpshooters. In 1564 Bernat Abramovich, clerk of the prominent tax-collector Isaac Borodavka, was arrested and tried on the accusation of having murdered a Christian child. The royal chamberlain testified that he had heard the confession of Bernat shortly before his execution, and that he had solemnly declared his innocence. Investigation proved the falseness of the charge, which had been prompted by enmity toward Borodavka.

Action of the Nobles.

A similar unfounded accusation of two other servants of Borodavka in 1566 led Sigismund August to declare the innocence of the accused, and to reaffirm the decree of Aug. 9, 1564, by which all Jews accused of the murder of Christian children or of desecrating the host were to be tried by the king himself before the assembled Diet. Until the time of trial the accused were to be surrendered for safe-keeping to two of their coreligionists. The guilt of the accused could be declared only on the testimony of four Christian and three Jewish witnesses. The failure to prove the accusation rendered the accuser liable to loss of life and property. In this decree the king also reminded the Christians of the grand duchy that previous charters and papal bulls had amply proved that Jews were not in need of Christian blood for the purposes of their ritual.

The opposition to the Jews was finally crystallized and found definite expression in the repressive Lithuanian statute of 1566, when the Lithuanian nobles were first allowed to take part in the national legislation. Paragraph 12 of this statute contains the following articles: "The Jews shall not wear costly clothing, nor gold chains, nor shall their wives wear gold or silver ornaments. The Jews shall not have silver mountings on their sabers and daggers; they shall be distinguished by characteristic clothes; they shall wear yellow caps, and their wives kerchiefs of yellow linen, in order that all may be enabled to distinguish Jews from Christians." Other restrictions of a similar nature are contained in the same paragraph. However, the king checked the desire of the nobility to modify essentially the old charters of the Jews.

The Act of 1566.

Twenty years later the royal veto was ineffective against the increasing power of the nobility; but by that time the attitude of the latter toward the Jews had undergone such a complete change that instead of adding new restrictions the nobility abolished most of the regulations which had been so objectionable.

Through the union with Lithuania, Poland gained in power and exerted a greater influence on the former country. The introduction of the reformed faith (the teachings of Calvin) met with ready acceptance by the nobility and middle classes. The new religious ideas brought in their wake a taste for science and literature, and Jewish and Christian children sought learning in the same schools. A number of young men went to Germany and Italy for the study of medicine and astronomy. The inmates of the yeshibot (of Lithuania especially) were acquainted with the writings of Aristotle, as is evidenced by the complaint of Solomon Luria that Rabbi Moses Isserles was responsible for much free thought. He had noticed in the prayer-books of the scholars (baḥurim) the prayer of Aristotle. Cardinal Commendoni testifies that many Russian and Lithuanian Jews had distinguished themselves in medicine and astronomy. The Jews of Lithuania were, like their Catholic neighbors, affected by the broader spiritual atmosphere of the day. The Polish Calvinists, among them Prince Radziwil, enjoyed extensive influence at court, and Radziwil was almost

After the Union of Lublin.

successful in causing Sigismund August to renounce allegiance to the papal authority. The extreme Calvinists, like the Socinians and the followers of Simon Budny, attacked the doctrine of the Trinity as a form of polytheism. Therefore they were styled Unitarians or anti-Trinitarians, and were frequently referred to by their opponents as "half-Jews." The influence of the religious unrest of the times on Jewish thought is evidenced by the discussions which took place between the Jews and the dissenters (see Czechowic). The learned Karaite Isaac ben Abraham of Troki took a prominent part in such discussions. His polemical experience is described in his work "Ḥizzuḳ Emunah" (translated into Latin by Wagenseil and published with the Hebrew text in 1681, and later translated into Spanish, German, and French). This work is frequently cited by the French encyclopedists in their attacks on Catholicism. The French Duke Henry of Anjou, one of the leaders in the massacre of St. Bartholomew, was elected to succeed Sigismund August on the thrones of Poland and Lithuania. He was an enemy of the Jews notwithstanding the fact that he largely owed his election to the efforts of Solomon Ashkenazi. He planned strict measures against his Jewish subjects, and blood accusations occurred during his short reign. Fortunately he escaped to France in 1574 to assume the crown left vacant by the death of his brother. After the short interregnum which followed, the Polish people elected the Transylvanian Duke Stephen Bathori. During the latter's equitable rule of eleven years the condition of the Polish and Lithuanian Jews was greatly improved. In July, 1576, he ordered by decree that all persons making false blood accusations or baseless charges of desecration of the host, then being spread in Lithuania, should be severely punished, his own investigations having convinced him that such accusations were instigated merely to incite riots. He found not only that the Jews were innocent and beyond suspicion, but also that the Shlyakhta who had made the accusations had themselves been misled by fanatical agitators. He declared that "whosoever shall disobey this decree shall be severely punished irrespective of his position in society; and whoever shall spread such rumors shall be considered a calumniator; and he who shall make such false charges before the authorities shall be punished by death." In the same month he confirmed by decree all of the ancient privileges of the Lithuanian Jews. At the beginning of his reign Mordecai Jaffe (author of the "Lebushim") went to Lithuania. He at first officiated in Grodno, and built the large synagogue which is still standing there and which has on its ark an inscription showing that the building was completed in 1578. Mordecai Jaffe by his great rabbinical erudition and secular knowledge played an important rôle in the Council of Four Lands and in the development of the methodical study of rabbinical literature in Lithuania and Poland. See also Bathori, Stephen.

Under Stephen Bathori.

The long reign of Sigismund III. (1587–1632) witnessed gradual but decisive changes in the relations of the Lithuanian Jews to the rest of the population. Born in the Protestant family of the Vasas, Sigismund was educated by his father, John III., in the Catholic faith with a view to his future occupation of the Polish throne. The Jesuit training of Sigismund was reflected in his attitude toward his non-Catholic subjects. The severe measures which he took against the dissenters affected the Jews also. In the attack of the Jesuits on Protestants and Greek Catholics the Jesuits caused the promulgation of numerous decrees restricting the ancient privileges of the Lithuanian Jews. They secured complete control of the education of the Polish-Lithuanian youth and instilled into the future citizens a religious intolerance hitherto unknown in Lithuania and which later made the existence of the Jewish subjects almost unbearable. A return to medieval methods was prevented only by the unsettled political and social condition of the country and the independence of the Shlyakhta. This independence, however, gradually vanished, and in the political degeneration which followed, the lesser nobility became a tool in the hands of a few reactionary leaders.

Sigismund III. and Ladislaus IV.

The king himself, following in the footsteps of his predecessors, attempted to pose as the protector of the Jews. He confirmed their charters of privileges (1588), and frequently took their part in their struggle with the Christian merchant gilds; but more often he sacrificed them to the self-assumed power of the city magistrates. The commercial rivalry between the Jews and the burghers, and the disregard by the latter of the ancient rights of the Jews, led Sigismund to issue several special decrees declaring the inviolability of Jewish autonomy in religious and judicial matters. The first of these decrees was due to the efforts of Saul Judich, representing the Jews of Brest (1593), and was called forth by the illegal assumption of authority over the Jews by the magistrates of Brest in matters reserved to the jurisdiction of the ḳahals or the king. The object of the magistrates was the collection of excessive fees and other extortions. This Saul Judich was one of the most prominent farmers of taxes and customs duties in Lithuania, and as "servant of the king" was in a position to render important services to his coreligionists. He is first mentioned in a decree of 1580 as having, in company with other communal leaders, strongly defended the rights of the Jews of Brest against the Christian merchants. As Bershadski shows, he is the Saul Wahl, the favorite of Prince Radziwil, who, according to legend, was made King of Poland for one night.

In the same year (1580) Sigismund granted the Jews of Wilna, as a protection against the oppressive measures of the city magistrates, a charter permitting them to purchase real estate, to engage in trade on the same footing as the Christian merchants, to occupy houses belonging to the nobles, and to build synagogues. As tenants of the nobility they were to be exempt from city taxes, and in their lawsuits with Christians they were to be subject to the jurisdiction of the king's waywodes only. A few days later the king accorded them the additional right to establish in the lower portion of the city a syna gogue, cemetery, and bath-house, as well as stores for the sale of kasher meat. The burghers naturally resented the grant of these privileges and used every effort to secure their curtailment. Their endeavors evidently met with success, for in 1606 the Jews of Wilna found it necessary to petition the king for protection.

Later decrees of Sigismund show that ultimately anti-Jewish influences prevailed at his court. In 1597 he granted the Magdeburg Rights to the city of Vitebsk, but denied by a legal technicality the right of the Jews to reside permanently in the city. Another decree provided that no synagogue should be built without the king's permission. In the carrying out of this enactment the Jews were practically compelled to secure the permission of the Catholic clergy also whenever they desired to build a synagogue. Still another decree, which was later incorporated into the statutes, provided for the elevation to nobility of Jewish converts to Christianity. The rapidly growing number of the so-called "Jerusalem nobles" later caused alarm among the Polish nobility, and in 1768 the law was repealed.

With the permanent establishment of the Jesuits in Poland and in Lithuania, the ramification of their intrigues and their active participation in politics and in legislation gave them a predominating influence in the affairs of the country. Having come to Lithuania in the reign of Sigismund II., August, the Jesuits at first kept free from politics, and occupied themselves with educational work, science, and literature. Stephen Bathori had no fear of their intrigues, and even entrusted them with the management of the newly established academy in Wilna. However, aided by the demoralized condition of the country, they soon succeeded in arraying the religious factions against one another. Bribery was rampant at the court and among the city officials. The masses were unruly and licentious, the Shlyakhta wilful, the clergy fanatical, and the magistrates lawless. The Jews were frequently made to suffer in these factional struggles. The restrictions put upon them grew constantly; they were forbidden to engage in retail trade, handicrafts, and other remunerative callings, and they were practically outlawed. The only occupation in which they were to any extent safe from the rapacity of city officials was the keeping of taverns in the townlets and villages. There, their only masters were the nobles, whom it was easier to please than the numerous functionaries and Shlyakhta. Thus the Jews unfortunately became in some parts of Lithuania useful tools in the hands of the nobility for the exploitation of the peasantry. The lords then found it expedient to take the Jews under their protection. Prominent among them were the Radziwils in Lithuania, and the Wishnevetzkis in the Ukraine.

Influence of Jesuits.

Ladislaus IV. (1632-48) was not a zealous Catholic, and he had no love for the Jesuits. He attempted to make peace between the warring religious factions, and sought to revive the ancient rights of the Jews. On March 11 and 16, 1633, he confirmed the charters of privileges of the Jews of Lithuania, and decreed that all suits between Jews and Christians should be tried by the waywodes and elders and not by the city magistrates, who were the avowed enemies of the Jews, and often discriminated against them. He also checked the anti-Jewish student demonstrations, instigated by Jesuit teachers. All appeals in suits between Jews were to be brought before the king or his vice-regent.

Notwithstanding his religious tolerance, however, Ladislaus lacked the energy to resist the power of the clergy and the merchants, and was vacillating in his policy. At times he supported the Jews; at other times he yielded to the influence of their opponents. In 1633 and again in 1646 he confirmed the decree of his father (July, 1626) expelling Jews from the central portion of Moghilef and assigning them new quarters in the lower portion of the city. At the instigation of the Christian merchants of Wilna he also limited the rights of the Jews of that city. Aided by the propaganda of the clergy, the burghers caused new acts to be introduced, known as "De Judæis." It was decreed, for instance, that Jews should not appear on the main streets or in the marketplaces on Christian holidays; that Jewish physicians should not attend Christian patients; and that Jewish barbers should neither shave nor cup Christians. Fortunately for the Jews, on account of the powerful protection of the nobility, enactments could not always be carried out. Moreover these decrees, advocated by the lesser clergy and the Jesuits, were opposed by other powerful Church magnates, the bishops and the archbishops, who, as landed proprietors, availed themselves of the services of the Jews. Thus in the Catholic Church itself there were two parties, one favorable and the other antagonistic to the Jews; and it is often found that the archbishops and bishops were in opposition to the Church councils.

On the whole, the animosity toward the Jews produced by various economic evils had taken such deep root that Ladislaus, well-meaning as he was, found himself unable to stem the tide of class dissensions. The Jews themselves felt grateful for whatever efforts he made in their behalf, as was thus voiced by one of the leading rabbis of his time, Shabbethai ben Meïr ha-Kohen of Wilna (SHaḲ): "He was a righteous king, worthy to be counted among the just; for he always showed favor to the Jews, and was true to his promise." The Jewish masses, who had found safety on the estates of the landed nobility, ultimately became scapegoats in the bitter struggle of the Greek Catholic peasantry with the Polish nobles and Roman Catholic clergy, a struggle which culminated in the Cossacks' Uprising.

The fury of this uprising destroyed the organization of the Lithuanian Jewish communities. The survivors who returned to their old homes in the latter half of the seventeenth century were practically destitute. The wars which raged constantly in the Lithuanian territory brought ruin to the entire country and deprived the Jews of the opportunity to earn more than a bare livelihood. The intensity of their struggle for existence left them no time to reestablish the conditions which had existed up to 1648. John Casimir (1648-68) sought to ameliorate their condition by granting various concessions to the Jewish communities of Lithuania.

Effect of Cossacks' Uprising.

attempts to return to the old order in the communal organization were not wanting, as is evident from contemporary documents. Thus in 1672 Jewish elders from various towns and villages in the grand duchy of Lithuania secured a charter from King Michael Wishnevetzki (1669–73), decreeing "that on account of the increasing number of Jews guilty of offenses against the Shlyakhta and other Christians, which result in the enmity of the Christians toward the Jews, and because of the inability of the Jewish elders to punish such offenders, who are protected by the lords, the king permits the kahals to summon the criminals before the Jewish courts for punishment and exclusion from the community when necessary." The efforts to resurrect the old power of the ḳahals were not successful. The impoverished Jewish merchants, having no capital of their own, were compelled to borrow money from the nobility, from churches, congregations, monasteries, and various religious orders. Loans from the latter were usually for an unlimited period and were secured by mortgages on the real estate of the ḳahal. The ḳahals thus became hopelessly indebted to the clergy and the nobility.

Numerous complaints to King John Sobieski (1674–96) by the Jews of Brest against their communal leaders, led him (May, 1676) to grant the rabbi of Brest, Mark Benjaschewitsch, jurisdiction in criminal cases over the Jews of his community, and to invest him with the power to impose corporal punishment and even the sentence of death. Under this ruler the Lithuanian communities saw a partial restoration of their old prosperity, and the authority of the Lithuanian Council served to bring some order out of the chaotic condition of the Lithuanian Jewry. Still the real stability of the old communities was destroyed, and frequent conflicts arose in regard to the territorial limits of the jurisdiction of the ḳahals. In the middle of the eighteenth century all the Lithuanian ḳahals were insolvent (see Jew. Encyc. vii. 410b, *s.v.* Ḳahal).

In 1792 the Jewish population of Lithuania was estimated at 250,000 (as compared with 120,000 in 1569). The whole of the commerce and industries of Lithuania, now rapidly declining, was in the hands of the Jews. The nobility lived for the most part on their estates and farms, some of which were managed by Jewish leaseholders. The city properties were concentrated in the possession of monasteries, churches, and the lesser nobility. The Christian merchants were poor. Such was the condition of affairs in Lithuania at the time of the second partition of Poland (1793), when the Jews became subjects of Russia.

The founding of the yeshibot in Lithuania was due to the Lithuanian-Polish Jews who studied in the west, and to the German Jews who migrated about that time to Lithuania and Poland. Very little is known of these early yeshibot. No mention is made of them or of prominent Lithuanian rabbis in Jewish writings until the sixteenth century. The first known rabbinical authority and head of a yeshibah was Isaac Bezaleel of Vladimir, Volhynia, who was already an old man when Luria went to Ostrog in the fourth decade of the sixteenth century. Another rabbinical authority, Kalman Haberkaster, rabbi of Ostrog and predecessor of Solomon Luria, died in 1559. Occasional references to the yeshibah of Brest are found in the writings of the contemporary rabbis Solomon Luria (d. 1585), Moses Isserles (d. 1572), and David Gans (d. 1589), who speak of its activity. Of the yeshibot of Ostrog and Vladimir in Volhynia it is known that they were in a flourishing condition at the middle of the sixteenth century, and that their heads vied with one another in Talmudic scholarship. Mention is also made by Gans of the head of the Kremenetz yeshibah, Isaac Cohen (d. 1573), of whom but little is known otherwise. For other prominent scholars in Lithuania at that time see Brest-Litovsk; Grodno; Kremenetz; Ostrog; Wilna.

Judicial Function of the Rabbis.

At the time of the Lublin Union, Solomon Luria was rabbi of Ostrog, and was regarded as one of the greatest Talmudic authorities in Poland and Lithuania. In 1568 King Sigismund ordered that the suits between Isaac Borodavka and Mendel Isakovich, who were partners in the farming of certain customs taxes in Lithuania, be carried for decision to Rabbi Solomon Luria and two auxiliary rabbis from Pinsk and Tykotzin.

The far-reaching authority of the leading rabbis of Poland and Lithuania, and their wide knowledge of practical life, are apparent from numerous decisions cited in the responsa. They were always the champions of justice and morality. In the "Etan ha-Ezraḥi" (Ostrog, 1796) of Abraham Rapoport (known also as Abraham Schrenzel; d. 1650), Rabbi Meïr Sack is cited as follows: "I emphatically protest against the custom of our communal leaders of purchasing the freedom of Jewish criminals. Such a policy encourages crime among our people. I am especially troubled by the fact that, thanks to the clergy, such criminals may escape punishment by adopting Christianity. Mistaken piety impels our leaders to bribe the officials, in order to prevent such conversions. We should endeavor to deprive criminals of opportunities to escape justice." The same sentiment was expressed in the sixteenth century by R. Meïr Lublin (Responsa, § 138). Another instance, cited by Katz from the same responsa, likewise shows that Jewish criminals invoked the aid of priests against the authority of Jewish courts by promising to become converts to Christianity.

The decisions of the Polish-Lithuanian rabbis are frequently marked by breadth of view also, as is instanced by a decision of Joel Sirkes ("Bet Hadash," § 127) to the effect that Jews may employ in their religious services the melodies used in Christian churches, "since music is neither Jewish nor Christian, and is governed by universal laws."

Decisions by Solomon Luria, Meïr Katz, and Mordecai Jaffe show that the rabbis were acquainted with the Russian language and its philology. Jaffe, for instance, in a divorce case where the spelling of the woman's name as "Lupka" or "Lubka" was in question, decided that the word is correctly spelled with a "b," and not with a "p," since the origin of the name was the Russian verb "lubit" = "to love," and not "lupit" = "to beat" ("Lebush ha-Buz we-Argaman," § 129). Meïr Katz ("Geburat Anashim," § 1) explains that the name of Brest-

Litovsk is written in divorce cases "Brest" and not "Brisk," "because the majority of the Lithuanian Jews use the Russian language." It is not so with Brisk, in the district of Kujawa, the name of that town being always spelled "Brisk." Katz (a German) at the conclusion of his responsum expresses the hope that when Lithuania shall have become more enlightened, the people will speak one language only—German—and that also Brest-Litovsk will be written "Brisk."

The responsa throw an interesting light also on the life of the Lithuanian Jews and on their relations to their Christian neighbors. Benjamin Aaron Solnik states in his "Mas'at Binyamin" (end of sixteenth and beginning of seventeenth century) that "the Christians borrow clothes and jewelry from the Jews when they go to church."

Items from the Responsa.

Joel Sirkes (*l.c.* § 79) relates that a Christian woman came to the rabbi and expressed her regret at having been unable to save the Jew Shlioma from drowning. A number of Christians had looked on indifferently while the drowning Jew was struggling in the water. They were upbraided and beaten severely by the priest, who appeared a few minutes later, for having failed to rescue the Jew.

Rabbi Solomon Luria gives an account (Responsa, § 20) of a quarrel that occurred in a Lithuanian community concerning a cantor whom some of the members wished to dismiss. The synagogue was closed in order to prevent him from exercising his functions, and religious services were thus discontinued for several days. The matter was thereupon carried to the local lord, who ordered the reopening of the building, saying that the house of God might not be closed, and that the cantor's claims should be decided by the learned rabbis of Lithuania. Joseph Katz mentions ("She'erit Yosef," § 70) a Jewish community which was forbidden by the local authorities to kill cattle and to sell meat—an occupation which provided a livelihood for a large portion of the Lithuanian Jews. For the period of a year following this prohibition the Jewish community was on several occasions assessed at the rate of three gulden per head of cattle in order to furnish funds wherewith to induce the officials to grant a hearing of the case. The Jews finally reached an agreement with the town magistrates under which they were to pay 40 gulden annually for the right to slaughter cattle. According to Hillel ben Herz ("Bet Hillel," Yoreh De'ah, § 157), Naphtali says the Jews of Wilna had been compelled to uncover when taking an oath in court, but later purchased from the tribunal the privilege to swear with covered head, a practise subsequently made unnecessary by a decision of one of their rabbis to the effect that an oath might be taken with uncovered head.

The responsa of Meïr Lublin show (§ 40) that the Lithuanian communities frequently aided the German and the Austrian Jews. On the expulsion of the Jews from Silesia, when the Jewish inhabitants of Silz had the privilege of remaining on condition that they would pay the sum of 2,000 gulden, the Lithuanian communities contributed one-fifth of the amount.

The influence in communal life of prominent rabbinical scholars, such as Mordecai Jaffe, Moses Isserles, Solomon Luria, and Meïr Lublin, proved but a slight check to the growing misrule of the ḳahals. The individuality of the Lithuanian Jew was lost in the ḳahal, whose advantages were thus largely counterbalanced by the suppression of personal liberty. The tyranny of the ḳahal administration and the external oppression drove the great mass of the Lithuanian Jewry to seek consolation in the dry formalism of Talmudic precepts. The Talmud and its endless commentaries became the sole source of information and instruction. Every Jew was compelled by the communal elders to train his children in Talmudic lore. The Halakah offered a solution for every question in Jewish life, while the poetry of the Haggadah supplied alleviation for sorrow and hope for the future. Reformers arising among the Lithuanian Jews were forced by the ḳahal elders either to leave the community or to bend to the will of the administration. All was sacrificed to the inviolability of customs sanctioned by tradition or by the letter of the Law. The ties of friendship and family relationship were subordinated to the interests of the community. Hence it is little to be wondered at that the Cabala found fertile soil in Lithuania. The marked indications of approaching political anarchy were the chief causes of the organization of the LITHUANIAN COUNCIL.

BIBLIOGRAPHY: Antonovich, *Monografii po Istorii Zapadnoi i Yugo-Zapadnoi Rossii*, vol. i., Kiev, 1885; Bershadski, *Litovskie Yevrei*, St. Petersburg, 1883; idem, *Russko-Yevreiski Arkiv*, 2 vols., *ib.* 1882; Czacki, *Rozprava o Zydach i Karaitach*, Wilna, 1807; idem, *O Litewskich i Polskich Prawach*, Warsaw, 1800; Dubnov, *Yevreiskaya Istoriya*, vol. ii., *s.v.*, Odessa, 1897; Graetz, *History of the Jews*, Hebrew ed., vols. vii. and viii., *s.v.*; Harkavy, in *Russische Revue*, vols. xxii., xxiii., St. Petersburg, 1883–84; Jaroszewicz, *Obraz Litwy . . . od Czasow Najdawniejszych do Konca Wieku*, xviii., Wilna, 1844; Kraushaar, *Historya Zydów w Polsce*, 2 vols., Warsaw, 1865–66; Leontovich, *Istoricheskoe Izslyedovanie o Pravakh Litovsko-Russkikh Yevreyev*, Kiev, 1864; Maciejowski, *Zydzi w Polsce na Rusi i Litwie*, Warsaw, 1878; Narbutt, *Dzieje Narodu Litewskiego*, part viii., p. 490; Neubauer, *Aus der Petersburger Bibliothek*, Leipsic, 1866; *Regesty i Nadpisi*, vol. i., St. Petersburg, 1899; Sternberg, *Geschichte der Juden in Polen*, Leipsic, 1878; *Sistematicheski Ukazatel*, s.v., St. Petersburg, 1893; *Sbornik Budushchnosti*, i. 244.

H. R.

LITHUANIAN COUNCIL (Hebr. **Wa'ad Medinot Lita,** or **Wa'ad ha-Medinot ha-Rashiyyot de-Lita**): Long before the Union of Lublin, probably with the beginning of the sixteenth century, the Jews of Poland and Lithuania were taxed as a single body, the pro rata assessment being made by the Jews themselves. In 1613 Sigismund III. decreed separate assessments for the Jews of Lithuania and Poland. The former were obliged to pay 9,000 gulden and the latter 7,000 gulden, the per capita payment being the same in each case. In order to assure an equitable distribution of the taxes among the several communities, and because of the desire to secure uniform legislation in religious matters and to protect their communal interests, the Jews of Lithuania organized, in 1623, a separate council of their own, this council being known as the "Wa'ad ha-Medinot ha-Rashiyyot de-Lita." Previously, from the Union of Lublin in 1569 until 1623, the Jews of Lithuania, not being, perhaps, in urgent need of a council of their own, had their representatives in the Council of Three Countries (Poland,

Russia, Lithuania), or in the Council of Five Lands (see Council of Four Lands).

It was customary for the Lithuanian delegates to hold preliminary meetings at Brest-Litovsk before taking part in the deliberation of the general councils. It has not yet been determined, however, to what extent the Lithuanian Jews were governed by the decisions of these councils; only this much is certain, that while they were well represented at the councils' sessions they occasionally refused to obey their rulings. The Lithuanian councils were originally composed of delegates from the three most important communities—Pinsk, Brest, and Grodno. Wilna was added in 1652, and Slutsk in 1691. The councils were designated in accordance with the number of communities represented, as "Wa'ad Shalosh [Arba', or Ḥamesh] Medinot Rashiyyot de-Lita" (= "Council of Three [Four, or Five] Main Districts of Lithuania"). The Lithuanian Council in time became an authoritative body in all local Jewish affairs; but, while practically an independent body, it assumed a subordinate position to the Council of Four Lands. At times the two councils worked in unison in matters of common interest during the sessions of the Council of Four Lands, but where differences occurred, the authority of the latter prevailed. Thus, in the dispute in regard to Tykotzin, in the government of Lomza, a boundary town between Poland and Lithuania, it was decided to place the town under the jurisdiction of the Council of Four Lands, although formerly it had been regarded as Lithuanian territory. Similarly, in the dispute between Tykotzin and Grodno concerning the less important neighboring communities of Zabludov, Horodok, and Khvoroshcha, the latter were assigned by the Council of Four Lands to Tykotzin. In this case, however, the decision was not accepted as final ("Sefer ha-Yobel," pp. 257–259).

Relation to Council of Four Lands.

The Lithuanian Council, like that of the Four Lands, had no fixed meeting-place; it assembled biennially or triennially at Zabludov, Seltzy, or elsewhere. Like that of the Four Lands, also, it served to cement the interests of the Lithuanian and other Russo-Polish Jews at a time when dissolution and demoralization reigned in the Polish kingdom, and it acted as a bulwark against the rancor of the Christian clergy, especially the Jesuits, who made continuous attacks on the Jews. The records of the Lithuanian Council are better preserved than those of the Council of Four Lands. There is extant a complete list of the meetings held by the Lithuanian Council from 1623 to 1762, when it was abolished, after over 1,000 regulations ("taḳḳanot") had been adopted. These taḳḳanot were made with the following ends in view:

(1) To encourage and endear to the people the study of the Talmud by establishing yeshibot, and to supervise the conduct of students. (2) To protect the interests of the Jewish people as a whole and as individuals against the malice of non-Jews, by pleading the cause of the Jews in the Polish Diets. (3) To supervise the conduct of the communities as well as of individuals, in order to prevent them from rousing the antagonism of their neighbors by indulging in improper and illegal trades. (4) To determine and properly distribute the government taxes imposed upon Jews. (5) To determine the boundaries of each ḳahal district. (6) To determine the duties of each community and its share in the common efforts and expenditures in cases where blood accusations were to be contested. (7) To determine the right of membership to be granted to new settlers in the communities ("ḥeskat yishshub"): as each Jewish community stood responsible for the conduct of its individuals, restrictions were necessary to regulate the granting of membership to newcomers. (8) To aid poverty-stricken communities and individuals. (9) To maintain and aid poor settlers in Palestine.

Of the regulations enacted at the meetings of the Lithuanian Council the following deserve mention, since they afford an insight into the state of culture of the Lithuanian Jews and into the character of the council itself: "Every community shall carefully guard against card- and dice-playing, and offenders shall be fined and subjected to corporal punishment" (1623; No. 51). "Beggars invading Lithuania and Russia [meaning White Russia], especially those who disguise themselves as scholars and pious persons while committing secretly various wicked acts, shall not be allowed to remain in any one community more than twenty-four hours" (1623; No. 87). "It shall be the duty of the communal leaders to expose any attempts at fraud which may be discovered on the part of Jews borrowing money or goods from a 'shlakhtitz' [peasant], or leasing from lords estates, taxes, and other sources of revenue. On the refusal of the parties likely to be defrauded to heed the warning of the communal leaders, the latter shall declare the transaction void, using force if necessary, in order that the Christians concerned may not suffer loss" (No. 26). "It is incumbent upon the three chief communities of Lithuania to arrange annually for the marriage of thirty poor girls, giving each a dowry of thirty gulden."

Among the taḳḳanot there are also regulations regarding competition in business, against luxury, and against expensive and gaudy dresses.

In 1654–56, when the Russians invaded Lithuania, the activities of the Lithuanian Council relaxed. It convened less frequently, and the regulations adopted between 1656 and 1670 deal in the main with financial accounts. After 1670, however, it resumed its former energy.

The Lithuanian Council was abolished about 1762, at the same time and for the same reason as the Council of Four Lands. Thenceforward taxes were no longer imposed on Lithuania as a whole, but on each community separately, the prime motive for the union of the communities being thus abolished.

H. R.

LITTAUER, LUCIUS NATHAN: American congressman and manufacturer; born in Gloversville, N. Y., Jan. 20, 1859. He graduated from Harvard University in 1878, after which he engaged in the glove-manufacturing business with his father, whom he succeeded in 1882. He was elected in 1896 to the 55th Congress as Republican representative of the 25th District of New York and has been reelected to each succeeding Congress. He has served as a member of the Committee on Appropriations.

Bibliography: *The Congressional Directory of the 58th Congress*; *American Jewish Year Book*, 1902–3.

A.

LITTE OF REGENSBURG. See Judæo-German Literature.

LITTHAUER, ISSACHAR BÄR: Polish-German Talmudist; flourished at the beginning of the nineteenth century. He wrote: "Iggeret Yissakar," on morality and religion, in the form of a letter to his son (Budapest and Lemberg, 1826); "Da'at Yissakar," commentary on Rashi to the Pentateuch and the Five Megillot (Budapest, 1827).

BIBLIOGRAPHY: Fuenn, *Keneset Yisrael*, p. 184, Warsaw, 1886; Fürst, *Bibl. Jud.* ii. 253; Steinschneider, *Cat. Bodl.* No. 5281.

H. R. A. S. W.

LITTLE RUSSIA. See RUSSIA.

LITURGISCHE ZEITSCHRIFT. See PERIODICALS.

LITURGY: The Jewish religious service falls, generally, into two main divisions—instruction and prayer. This division of the service has existed since the earliest times. In the time of Isaiah the people gathered in the courts of the Temple to receive instruction from the Prophets and to pray (Isa. i. 12–15), while on the day of the New Moon and on the Sabbath women also visited them (II Kings iv. 23). At the Feast of Tabernacles in the Sabbatical year the Law was read to the assembled people (Deut. xxxi. 10–13), and Ezra recited passages from the Pentateuch to the community (Neh. viii. 5–8). In the course of time this led to the custom of reading certain portions of the Scripture, especially of the Pentateuch, to the people on the Sabbath, on feast-days, and even on Mondays and Thursdays, as well as on New Moon and fast-days, and by the first century of the common era this was regarded as an ancient usage (Josephus, "Contra Ap." ii. 17, end; Acts xv. 21; B. Ḳ. 82a *et passim*; comp. Philo, ed. Mangey, ii. 568, 630; Winer, "B. R." ii. 549; Zunz, "G. V." pp. 1–7). This part of the worship is described under HAFTARAH; MEGILLOT; LAW, READING FROM THE. The second division, that of prayer, is still more ancient, and is frequently mentioned in the Bible (I Sam. i. 10; I Kings viii. 12 *et seq.*; II Kings xx. 2 *et passim*), while Deutero-Isaiah speaks of the house of God as a "house of prayer for all people" (Isa. lvi. 7; on the form of prayer and posture see Guthe, "Kurzes Bibelwörterbuch," pp. 82 *et seq.*, and other dictionaries; also ADORATION, FORMS OF). In general, it may be said that in the earliest times the prayers were short, and were used only occasionally in private devotion, and that no ritual was developed in the pre-exilic period. Formal prayers are found only in Deut. xxvi. 5–13 and Lev. xvi. 21.

Divisions of Divine Service.

In view of the position which the Temple occupied, it may be assumed that after the exile the public worship there influenced the liturgy, and in great part even created it; the prayers just mentioned were part of the Temple worship. The Levites recited prayers of thanksgiving and praise during the morning and evening sacrifices (I Chron. xxiii. 30), and Neh. xi. 17 indicates that this was an established ceremony. The threefold repetition of the daily prayer (Dan. vi. 11; Ps. lv. 18 [A. V. 17]) is likewise connected with the Temple service, the second prayer corresponding perhaps with the sacrifices which were offered by individuals between the official morning and evening sacrifices. The Talmud says, with correct historical insight, that the prayers were instituted to correspond with the sacrifices (Ber. 24b, *passim*). The fact that in prayer the face was turned toward the Temple (Dan. vi. 10; II Chron. vi. 34; Ber. 4b–5a, *passim*), as well as the contents of the prayer, together with various other indications, clearly shows that the synagogal liturgy was derived primarily from the Temple worship.

Influence of the Temple on the Liturgy.

In the Temple itself, side by side with the sacrificial cult, there existed a liturgy whose most splendid remnants are the Psalms, which constituted the hymnal of the Second Temple and now occupy an "important position in the synagogal liturgy. Those Psalms which are cast in the form of prayers and hymns soon took their place as hymns in the service of the sanctuary, even though they were not originally composed for this purpose, and they were sung, especially on feast-days, in the synagogue and in private gatherings. In its descriptions of Temple festivities the Book of Chronicles alludes to them, especially to the eighteen 'Hallelujah,' 'Hallel,' and 'Hodu' Psalms (Ps. cv.–cvii., cxi.–cxviii., cxxxv., cxxxvi., cxlvi.–cl.). . . . Prophecy and psalmody were gradually typified in two persons, Moses and David. . . . Even after the destruction of the Temple these united elements left their impress upon the Synagogue: the readings were devoted to the Law and the discourses to the Prophets, while entire psalms, or verses from them, were used as prayers" (Zunz, "S. P." pp. 4 *et seq.*). The place which many Psalms occupied in the worship may still be recognized from their form (final verses, notes on the mode of recitation, etc.) or from their contents (see the commentaries to the Psalms by Olshausen, Hupfeld, and others, and especially by Graetz). The authors of the superscriptions and concluding words of the Psalms recognize the collection as liturgical (Ps. lxxii., end: "The prayers of David . . . are ended"), and tradition frequently alludes to this fact (*e.g.*, Tamid, end). In the ritual of the Synagogue the Psalms retain their ancient position, at least as regards the text of the prayers. "In the Sabbath and festival discourses the wise man becomes the prophet, and the leader in prayer the psalmist" (Zunz, *l.c.*).

In addition to the sacrifice, which was in the care of the priests, and the singing of the Psalms, which was performed by the Levites, the Temple had its special liturgy for the third class of the people, the Israelites. The entire nation had been divided into twenty-four sections, so that to each division of priests there corresponded one of Levites and one of Israelites. Each section served for a week in the Temple, and this period was a time of fasting, for the Israelites assigned to the section doing service, both those who were in Jerusalem and those who had remained in their country homes. Every day they read a prescribed portion of the first chapter of Genesis. These details are recorded in Ta'an. iv. 1, in both Talmuds *ad loc.*, and in Tosef., Ta'an., iv., which seem to assign the beginnings of synagogal worship to the Temple; that there was some foundation for their account is shown by the fact that Joshua b. Hananiah, a teacher living in the time of the Temple, is mentioned. It is possible, however, that the reading of the Torah was taken over into the Temple ritual from an already existing synagogal ritual.

Fast-Day Services.

The services in periods of drought constitute an independent source for the liturgy of the Synagogue. The frequent scarcity of rain greatly distressed the people, for it meant famine and death to man and beast. At such times public assemblies for fasting and prayer were held as early as the time of the Prophets, in which old and young, the bride and the groom, took part (Joel i.; ii. 16–17; Jer. viii., especially verse 11). An entire treatise of the Mishnah (Ta'anit) is devoted to the regulations in regard to fasting, and its second chapter discusses the liturgy in detail. The prayer consisted of twenty-four benedictions, of which eighteen were those of the daily prayer and six were additional (see Schürer, "Gesch." 3d ed., ii. 490; Israel Lévi, in "R. E. J." xlvii., where the sources and bibliography are given). The final evening prayer, "Ne'ilah," recited on this occasion, has been preserved only in the service for the Day of Atonement. The liturgy for the fast was developed long before the common era, and it is highly probable not only that it was evolved independently of the Temple, but that it influenced the beginnings of the daily form of worship.

It is certain, however, that the institution of the reading of the "Shema'" (Deut. vi. 4–9) originated entirely in the Temple service. At the morning sacrifice the priests read the Ten Commandments and the "Shema'" and recited several benedictions (Tamid v.). Contrary to the custom in all other ceremonies, the day for the Temple service began with sunrise, and not with evening or with the appearance of the moon, and since the first rays of the sun were awaited before beginning the morning sacrifice there was some danger lest it might be held that the sun-god was being worshiped. Hence the congregation was addressed as follows: "Hear, O Israel, the Eternal is our God; the Eternal is One." It may have

The Reading of the "Shema'."

become customary, therefore, as early as the Persian period to recite the first sentence of the "Shema'" in the Temple before beginning the sacrifice, the other verses, including Deut. xi. 13–21, being added in the course of time. The requirement that it should be recited outside the Temple and before sunrise (Ber. v. 1 *et passim*) points to the origin of this usage. Its antiquity may be inferred from the fact that Josephus ("Ant." iv. 8, § 13) seems to ascribe it to Moses and that in traditional literature it is explained as a Biblical custom. At that time it must have been in existence for some centuries, for its genesis had been forgotten. The reading of the "Shema'" in the evening must have been introduced somewhat later, since it was not recited in the Temple, and the rules governing it were less rigorously defined. The reading of the Decalogue probably became customary in the Greek period in order to guard, by the solemn utterance of the first two commandments, against the imminent danger from Hellenistic polytheism (see Blau in "R. E. J." xxxi. 179–201, where the history of the benedictions in the "Shema'" is discussed). In ancient times the "Shema'" was not recited in the manner now customary in the synagogue, but either with the leader, verse by verse alternately, or in some other way. As it was Israel's solemn confession of faith, each one knew it by heart (Ta'an. 26a), and it was recited in the synagogue "with one mouth, one voice, one song" (Cant. R. viii. 14). It might be read in any language (Soṭah vii. 1 and parallels), and a scribe once heard it in Greek (Yer. Soṭah 21b, below). It was sometimes read backward (Ber. ii. 4 and parallels), a custom which is reminiscent of magic practises (see SHEMA').

"Shemoneh 'Esreh."

The second and doubtless later division of the daily liturgy is the prayer consisting of eighteen benedictions, named the "Tefillah" κατ᾽ ἐξοχήν in the sources. This petition, which is still included in every Jewish prayer-book, is called SHEMONEH 'ESREH (eighteen prayers) even in the earliest sources (Ber. vi. 3; Ta'an. ii. 2). Rabbi Johanan (d. 279), the famous director of the school of Tiberias, who was distinguished also for his knowledge of the historical traditions, ascribes the introduction of these benedictions, the emphasizing of the sanctity of the Sabbath, the feast-days, and the benedictions at their close, to the Great Synagogue (Ber. 33a). Four kinds of liturgy, in the widest sense of the word, are here mentioned: "berakot," "tefillot," "ḥiddushot," "habdalot." In the benedictions are included, *e.g.*, the sentences of thanksgiving recited after meals, which are probably very ancient (see Maimonides, "Yad," Tefillah), and which are explained as Biblical, as well as all blessings spoken on partaking of fruit, executing commands, and the like. The beginnings of these prayers, perhaps, date back to the Persian period, their brevity and pure, simple Hebrew favoring this view. Their development, doubtless, was gradual and occupied several centuries. This may be assumed even in the case of the "Shemoneh 'Esreh," of which the first and last three benedictions constitute the foundation and hence are the oldest portion; and they are mentioned in the Mishnah with special names designating the several sentences (R. H. iv.; Tamid v. 1; R. H. 32a). "The ancient regulation which designates that portion for all the days of the year, while the other passages of the 'Tefillah' are excluded on the Sabbath and on festivals, is almost certainly a proof of greater age" (Zunz, "G. V." 2d ed., p. 380). The intermediate twelve sentences are of later date, and Zunz ascribes them to various periods. Different versions of one and the same prayer were apparently differentiated and included as independent benedictions. These, however, never received a stereotyped form for general use, and each has its own history (Elbogen, in "Monatsschrift," 1902). Even before the destruction of the Temple the twelfth benediction was added expressly against apostates and traitors ("birkat ha-minim"), and later was the cause of various changes in the "Shemoneh 'Esreh" (Zunz, *l.c.* p. 382; Elbogen, *l.c.*). This prayer can not have been directed exclusively against Judæo-Christians, for at the time of its composition they can have been neither powerful nor antinomian in Palestine (see MINIM.)

On account of its age the "Shema'" was much more widely known than the "Tefillah" which has just been outlined. This is clear from the fact that the "Tefillah" is regarded as a rabbinical, while the "Shema'" is regarded as a Biblical, prayer. As late as 100 C.E. a prominent scribe asserted that the entire "Tefillah" was unnecessary and that the evening "Tefillah" was not binding, in consequence of which view he became involved in a controversy with the patriarch Gamaliel II. (Ber. 28a, *passim*; Elbogen, *l.c.*). On account of its length it was not suitable for the mass of the people. As a matter of fact, only seven, nine, or ten benedictions are included in the "Tefillah" for the feast-days, although they are of earlier date and of greater importance, in view of the occasion. On these days, also, the daily benediction was very short, consisting probably only of a few words, perhaps as follows: "Cleanse our hearts that we may serve Thee faithfully" (Frisch, in "Magyar-Zsidó Szemle," 1892, pp. 264 *et seq.*, where the importance of a short prayer is shown; comp. *ib.* pp. 313 *et seq.*, where the same author attempts to sketch the historical development of the "Tefillah"). Probably both because it was the custom of the Temple and because they were ignorant of the "Tefillah," the people themselves did not pray, but listened to the ḥazzan, the "delegate of the community," and punctuated his sentences with "Amen" (R. H. 32a; Elbogen, *l.c.*).

"Shema'" and "Tefillah."

In the sanctuary the people later responded with another formula, mentioned below. They were educated for prayer only by centuries of practise, and the original formulas, consisting of one or two words, remained as distinctive signs in the amplified invocations. The "Hallel" and "Hodu" formulas, which are in fact found only in passages from the Psalms included in the synagogal ritual, are characteristic of the oral worship of the sanctuary. The "Hosanna" is likewise derived from the Temple, and the "Baruk" formula is probably taken from the same source, although the latter soon became predominant and was repeated frequently both in public and in private worship. Prayers for week-days, Sabbaths, and fast-days, the liturgy for fast-days, and grace before and after meals, as well as all kinds of benedictions and prayers of thanksgiving, have retained the same fixed form to the present day, and may, therefore, be discussed in some detail here, together with their historical development. As regards their external form, all the prayers designated by the Talmud, in the passage cited above (Ber. 33a), as "benedictions, prayers, sanctifications and habdalahs," are merely berakot.

In the earliest times the people prayed only occasionally, and the benedictions likewise were merely incidental utterances of thanks for mercies vouchsafed, as for rescue from danger, etc. The different forms of the root "barak" occur frequently in the Bible, even in the oldest portions. The word meant originally "to bend the knee" (comp. "berek" = "knee" in Ps. xcv. 6), and hence in general "to praise," "to pray," because the ancients commonly knelt on such occasions. In this sense the participle ("baruk") is used in the "ḳal," and all the other forms ("berek," "meborak," etc.) in the "pi'el" and "pu'al."

The adjuration "Praise God!" was probably addressed to the people of earlier times only in the flush of victory after deliverance from the dangers of war (Judges v. 2, 9), but later, when a regular Temple cult had been instituted, it may have been uttered daily, so that it became a liturgical formula with which divine worship was generally concluded (Ps. lxviii. 27 [A. V. 26], c. 4, *passim*). In Ps. cxxxv. (comp. also cxviii. 2–4) Israelites, priests, Levites, and the pious are summoned by groups to "bless the Lord!" and it is noteworthy that this invitation is placed at the conclusion of the Psalm. The final verse, "Blessed be the Lord out of Zion, which dwelleth at Jerusalem. Praise ye the Lord," constituted the benediction spoken by those who had been summoned. The benedictions that conclude the closing chapters of the five books of Psalms (xli., lxxii., lxxxix., cvi., cl.), all being in substance one and the same eulogy, may represent synagogal formulas from the time of the Temple which the people intoned after completing the singing of the several books. Occasionally, however, the people concluded with a simple "Amen" (comp. the Psalms quoted and I Chron. xvi. 36). It may also be assumed that such benedictions were not reserved for public worship exclusively, but were also pronounced in private: "I will bless the Lord at all times: his praise shall continually be in my mouth" (Ps. xxxiv. 2; comp. cxv. 18, cxlv. 2). Mention is made of supplications at "evening and morning, and at noon" (Ps. lv. 18 [A. V. 17]), and of praise offered seven times a day (Ps. cxix. 164), while in another passage only praise rendered in the morning is mentioned (Ps. lix. 17).

Doxologies During Public Worship.

The origin of this liturgical usage was the custom, on joyful occasions, of praising God for His goodness. A few examples may be given here in their Biblical order. Thus Noah says, "Blessed be the Lord God of Shem" (Gen. ix. 26); Eliezer prays, "Blessed be the Lord God of my master Abraham, who hath not left destitute my master of his mercy and his truth" (Gen. xxiv. 27); and Jethro exclaims, "Blessed be the Lord, who hath delivered you out of the hand of the Egyptians, and out of the hand of Pharaoh" (Ex. xviii. 10). Similar utterances are found in I Sam. xxv. 32 (David to Abigail) and xxv. 39 (where David says of Nabal's death, "Blessed be the Lord, that hath pleaded the cause of my reproach") and II Sam. xviii. 28 (Ahimaaz). Solomon thanks God in similar phraseology for having placed him on the throne of his father (I Kings i. 48, viii. 15; comp. viii. 56), and Hiram, King of Tyre, uses the same formula in rejoicing that God had given David such a wise son over this great people (*ib.* v. 7). The Queen of Sheba says to Solomon, "Blessed be the Lord thy God, which delighted in thee, to set thee on the throne of Israel" (*ib.* x. 9). This formula is used also in Zech. xi. 5; II Sam. xxii. 47 (Ps. xviii. 47 [A. V. 46]); Ps. xxviii. 6, cxliv. 1; Ezra vii. 27; II Chron. ix. 8. It is interesting to note that in Ruth iv. 14 the women address Naomi with the same formula, which shows that

Private Benedictions the Model.

it was transferred to the liturgy from popular speech.

The doxology in all these passages is really a prayer of gratitude to God for blessings bestowed, either on the speaker or on another.

Form.

The occasion of the thanksgiving is stated at the end and is generally introduced by the relative pronoun "asher" (also by "ki," Ps. xxviii. 6), or by a participle preceded by an article (comp., however, Zech. xi. 5). The same order occurs also in the benedictions prescribed by the Talmud. The benediction proper is expressed in most cases by "baruk," which generally constitutes the first word. An exception is found in I Kings x. 9 (II Chron. ix. 8), which has "Yehi Adonai Eloheka baruk," imitating the phraseology of "Yehi Shem Adonai meborak" (Job i. 21; Ps. cxiii. 2). Neither of these formulas is found elsewhere in the Bible. The Tetragrammaton alone designates the name of God in Ex. xviii. 10; Ruth iv. 14; I Sam. xxv. 39; I Kings viii. 56; Zech. xi. 5; Ps. xxviii. 6, lxxxix. 53, cxxiv. 6, cxxxv. 21 (once "Adonai," Ps. lxviii. 20 [A. V. 19], and twice "Elohim," Ps. lxvi. 20, lxviii. 36 [A. V. 35]). Usually "Elohim," "Elohe Yisrael," or some similar expression is added to the Tetragrammaton, so that God is generally named in the third person. The phrase "Baruk Attah Adonai, lammedeni ḥuḳḳeka" (Ps. cxix. 12) is an exception, and the benedictions in the Talmud have, curiously enough, this form also, although only as regards the use of the second person, since "Elohenu Melek ha-'Olam" is normally added to the Tetragrammaton. This use of the second person indicates a later origin, like "Elohe Abotenu" (Ezra vii. 27; comp. "Abinu," I Chron. xxix. 10), which occurs also in the first benediction of the "Shemoneh 'Esreh." The earliest form of the Torah benediction is found in Ps. cxix. 12, which is also the only one that is a prayer and not an expression of gratitude. The benediction "U-baruk Shem Kebodo le-'olam" (Ps. lxxii. 19) is identical with the preceding "Baruk Adonai," for "Shem Kebodo" indicates the Tetragrammaton (comp. Deut. xxviii. 58, "ha-Shem ha-Nekbad"; Neh. ix. 5, "Shem Kebodeka"; and Ps. xxiv. 7–10, "Melek ha-Kabod"). This gave rise to the later formula "Baruk Shem Kebod Malkuto le-'olam wa-'ed" (which was, however, used in the Temple), in which "Adonai Elohim" is paraphrased by three words in order that the people should not pronounce the real names of God. The benediction is once called "berakah" in the Bible—"And blessed be thy glorious name, which is exalted above all blessing and praise" (Neh. ix. 5). The words "'olam" and "'olam wa-'ed," which with variations are added to the benedictions, are of later origin and belong to the liturgical formula. They occur only in the Psalms and in Chronicles (Ps. xli. 14 [A. V. 13], lxxii. 19, lxxxix. 53 [A. V. 52], cvi. 48, cxiii. 9, cxv. 18, cxlv. 1; I Chron. xvi. 36, xxix. 10). This formula seems to have been used only when the congregation was assembled as a whole.

The significance of the benediction steadily increased in the course of centuries until it finally was used on the occasion of every manifestation of nature and of human life. While it appears in the Bible only in connection with public worship and on a few special occasions, in the traditional literature it accompanies all the expressions of individual life, and sanctifies all functions of the body and the soul.

Difference Between Bible and Talmud.

The pious Jew, on going to sleep and on awakening, and on all intervening occasions, uttered, and still utters, words of praise to God. God is praised for His mercy on occasions of joy or sorrow, on satisfying the needs or desires of the body, on studying the Law, or on fulfilling the ordinances of religion. The benediction, like the entire religion, is individualized and specialized. It continually reminds the Jew of God, and only when unclean, before he has bathed or purified himself in some other way, is he forbidden to utter it. The fact that the treatise Berakot, devoted to it, precedes all the other treatises, indicates its extent and importance, and its popularity is shown by the minute questions referring to it, which were discussed even by the earliest scribes. "The benedictions of a man indicate whether he is a scholar" (Ber. 50a; comp. Ta'an. 16a). Some examples are selected here from the mass of material, which may show the variety of these utterances and their nature.

There were persons who were very exact in regard to the benedictions and watched their neighbors closely (*ib.* נקדנין).

General Doxology.

If any one made a mistake in the form in use during worship, the entire congregation corrected him (*ib.* 51a). He who deviated from the form laid down by scholars was remiss in his duty, although in a certain case the short sentence of a shepherd—who was the prototype of ignorance among the Talmudists—was approved (*ib.* 40b). Prayers and doxologies might be recited in any language (Soṭah 32a *et passim*). Weekdays and feast-days, as well as all kinds of food, had their special benedictions (Ber. 40a, below). A blessing might not be pronounced over anything that had been "accursed" ("min ḳelalah," unsound fruit, etc.; *ib.* 40b), nor in case of nocturnal pollution, nor unnecessarily (*ib.* 20b, 33a). The doxology is pronounced before fulfilling any of the commandments (Pes. 7b; comp. Tosef., Ber. vii. 1).

One hundred benedictions a day shall be pronounced by every one (Men. 43b, below), but whoever writes them down sins as grievously as if he had burned the Torah (Shab. 115b). The Tetragrammaton and a reference to God as the King of the World are essential to every benediction (Ber. 12a, 40b, 49a). While Johanan b. Zakkai still used the Biblical form and in a doxology referred to God in the third person (Ḥag. 14b, "Baruk Adonai Elohe Yisrael she-natan," etc.), only the second person is used in the later doxologies ("Baruk Attah Adonai Elohenu Melek ha-'Olam"). The last three words are omitted in certain cases (Ber. 46a, below). The knee shall be bent on uttering "baruk" (*ib.* 12b), although this rule refers only to prayer and not to other benedictions (comp. also *ib.* 34b, relating to the king and high priest). One person may pronounce the benediction for all the other persons assembled (*ib.* 53a). The principal person at table is entitled to say grace (*ib.* 47a, 45b), to which the others respond with "Amen," which is regarded as more important than the pronouncing of the berakah itself (*ib.* 53b), and it is even praiseworthy to say "Amen" after one's own eulogy. One should not pronounce a "rapid, chopped, or orphaned 'Amen,' nor speak the benediction too quickly," nor lift the voice at the "Amen" above the voice of the speaker (*ib.* 45a, b, 47a). The form of some benedictions depends on the number of those present (*ib.* 49b). "Thou shalt praise God for evil fortune as well as for good" (*ib.* ix. 1). One should say, even in the house of mourning, "Blessed be the Merciful One who granteth good things" ("Baruk ha-Ṭob weha-Meṭib"). Akiba, however, says, "Blessed be the Just Judge" ("Baruk Dayyan Emet," *ib.* 46b, 54b, 60b). After a successful journey by sea or desert, after recovery from illness, or after release from prison, one should say, "Blessed be He who granteth favors" ("Baruk gomel ḥasadim," *ib.* 54b). There was also a special blessing for a person who had been bled (*ib.* 60a). See BENEDICTION.

God was praised at the crowing of the cock for having given it understanding to distinguish between day and night, and there were special benedictions for every act of dressing, which are now collected at the beginning of the book of daily prayer (Ber. 60b). "Whoso profits aught from this world without reciting a benediction defrauds it" (*ib.* 35a). Everything that may be enjoyed (fruits of the earth, etc.) has a corresponding benediction; only the words "everything came into being at His word" may be applied to them all (*ib.* 40a). There is even a berakah for perfume (*ib.* 43b, where individual rules are given for other things). Bread and wine, being the most important articles of food, have special benedictions (*ib.* vi. 1). The seven kinds of fruit of the Holy Land enjoy certain prerogatives, and the oil of the patriarch and of the emperor is especially honored (*ib.* 40b, 43a, 44a). Most of the regulations refer to the prayer after meals, which is often called "the three benedictions." It had to be spoken and might not be recited mentally (*ib.* 15a, b). It was obligatory also upon women, slaves, and children, who might pronounce it in place of the head of the family, and did so if he was unacquainted with Hebrew (*ib.* 20b). This and the Torah benediction alone were regarded as Biblical, while the introduction of the others was ascribed to the Great Synagogue (*ib.* 33a, 48b; Meg. 17a). The first benediction of the prayer at meals, it is said, was composed by Moses, the second by Joshua, and the third by David and Solomon (Ber. 48b); Moses was the first one who could praise God for the food offered (the manna), Joshua the first who could praise him for the Holy Land, and David and Solomon the first who could praise him for Jerusalem, which was delivered into their hands. The fourth benediction ("Ha-Ṭob weha-Meṭib"), it was said, was introduced at Jabneh in thanksgiving for the burial of those who had been killed in the great war with Rome (70 C.E.). These four benedictions, according to a "heavenly voice" (see BAT ḲOL), are worth forty denarii (Ḥul. 87b). The blessing at meals had to be pronounced while sitting (Ber. 51b), and there are ten regulations regarding the wine used in connection with it (*ib.* 51a). It is dangerous, on account of the demons, to drink two cups of wine, or any even number (*ib.* 51b). The benediction pronounced over bread is also mentioned in the New Testament (Matt. xv. 36; John vi. 11; Acts xxvii. 35) and by Philo (ed. Mangey, ii. 481).

Daily Benedictions.

The Torah benediction and the reading of the "Shema'" (Deut. vi. 4–8) are likewise explained as being Biblical, while the "Shemoneh 'Esreh" is regarded as a rabbinical institution (Ber. 21a). As the doxologies preceding the "Shema'" are really Torah benedictions, they also are declared to be Biblical (comp. *ib.* 11b, 48b, and the interesting passage, Shab. 88a, referring to the "threefold" Torah). The following is considered the best berakah: "Blessed be the Lord who hath given the doctrine" (*ib.* 11b). The division of the benedictions into Biblical and rabbinical is important for the matter of chronology, the first group being earlier in origin. The most important doxologies of the prayer are "Yehi Shemo ha-gadol meborak" (*ib.* 21a = Job i. 21 and Ps. cxiii. 2; Aramaic, "Yehe Shemeh rabba meborak," Ber. 57a; Shab. 119b; Suk. 38b, 39a; Targ. Yer. to Gen. xlix. 2; Deut. vi. 4) and the "Baruk Shem kebod malkuto le-'olam wa-'ed" already mentioned (Pes. 56a; Deut. R. ii. 31, 36). In the sanctuary the people pronounced this blessing, but no "Amen" (Ta'an. 16; Ber. 54a).

The following rules and customs deserve special notice from a historical and religious point of view:

Benedictions of Historical Interest.

A special berakah was pronounced at the circumcision of a proselyte (Shab. 137b, "le-mul et ha-gerim"). "Amen" may be said after the benediction of a Samaritan only if one has heard the whole of it (Ber. viii. 1); the blessing for light may not be recited for the light beheld at the end of the Sabbath in a city inhabited mostly by Samaritans (*ib.* 53a). At Jabneh a special berakah against Judæo-Christians (Minim) was composed after the destruction of the Temple (*ib.* 28b). If the ḥazzan commits an error in reciting this passage he is removed (*ib.* 29a). "Any one who says, 'The pious praise Thee,' is guilty of heresy" (Meg. iv. 9), while, according to R. Judah, any one uttering a benediction on seeing the sun is also guilty of heresy (Tosef., Ber. vii. 6). This mishnaic teacher ordains that one should praise God every day "that Thou hast not created me a heathen or a woman or a slave" (Men. 43b, below; comp. Gal. iii. 28; Diogenes Laertius, i. 1, § 7; James Darmesteter, "Une Prière Judéo-Persane," p. 9, Paris, 1891; "Monatsschrift," xxxvii. 14; "Magyar Zsidó Szemle," x. 100). On seeing a Hermes one should say, "Blessed be He who is lenient toward them that break His law," and on beholding a place where an idol has been destroyed, "Blessed be He who destroyeth idols in our land; as He hath destroyed it in this place, so may He destroy all in the land of Israel, and lead the hearts of their worshipers back unto His service." In a foreign country, however, one should say nothing, for the majority of the inhabitants there are heathen (Ber. 57b; comp. x. 1). "Any one beholding a place where miracles have been vouchsafed to Israel should say, 'Blessed be He who hath shown marvelous things unto our fathers on this spot'" (*ib.*), together with benedictions applying to manifestations of natural phenomena. One who sees Jewish sages should say, "Blessed be He who hath granted of His wisdom to His followers"; and whoever sees pagan sages should say, "Blessed be He who hath granted of His wisdom to His creatures."

At the sight of Jewish or pagan kings praise was rendered to God, who granted of His dignity to His followers or to His creatures (*ib.* 58a). On beholding graves of Jews one should praise God, who created them and who will finally raise them up again (*ib.* 58b). He who sees the Euphrates from the bridge of Babylon or the Tigris from the bridge of Shebistena should praise the Creator (*ib.* 59b), for it was believed that these streams had arisen at these places and were therefore still in their original state, although a Babylonian amora of the early part of the fourth century indicates another place as the source of the Euphrates, the Persians having diverted it from its channel. God should receive praise and thanksgiving from any one beholding a ford of the sea, of the Jordan, or of the River Arnon (where Israel beheld marvels); beholding hailstones (Ex. ix. 33), the cliff of Beth-horon (Josh. x. 11), the stone which Og, King of Bashan, wished to hurl upon Israel, the rock on which Moses sat when Joshua fought with Amalek (Ex. xvii. 12), the wife of Lot, or the fallen walls of Jericho (Ber. 54a). All these objects were still to be seen at the time of the composition of this baraita, about the second century.

Difference Between Christian and Jewish Benedictions.

Although the benedictions of the priests, and the benedictions pronounced in the house of mourning, and at betrothals, weddings, etc., are mentioned, there are no indications that they were regarded as exercising any material influence on persons or things, *i.e.*, that they were sacramental as the Christian Church has taught and still teaches (Herzog-Hauck, "Real-Encyc." ii. 588). They are merely utterances of praise and thanksgiving, and it can no longer be determined whether originally they had the force which the Church ascribes to them. It is certain, however, that the idea of sacramentalism was foreign to Judaism. Several passages in the New Testament in praise of God are called "doxologies" (*e.g.*, Rom. xvi. 27; see Hastings, "Dict. Bible," i. 620).

The principal component parts of public worship are the "Shema'" and the "Tefillah," the preceding recitation from the Psalms, etc., having only the force of custom. As late as the time of Maimonides morning prayer began with "Ḳaddish" before "Bareku" and ended with it ("Yad," Tefillah, ix.), and this practise still obtains in the Sephardic ritual.

Origin and Development.

In the course of time additions to the liturgy were multiplied. The ritual, even in its simpler portions, took definite form only by degrees. The earliest elements of synagogal worship were developed from the Temple service and the custom of sacrificial watches ("Ma'amad"), as well as from private and public worship—from psalms and prayers which were composed at different times for special occasions. The benedictions at the beginning of the "Ma'amad" and the prayers at the end became respectively the "Shema'" and the "Tefillah" (Rapoport, "Kalir"; Zunz, "G. V." pp. 367 *et seq.*). The latter, which about 100 C.E. had neither definite redaction nor general binding force, probably consisted at first of only six numbers for week-days and seven for Sabbath and feast-days; in the remaining numbers either a Ḥasidic or a political origin may be traced. Even in the second century the final benedictions for public fast-days still varied (Ta'an. 17a); in the third the whole assembly was not yet accustomed to go to the synagogue at "Musaf" (Yer. R. H. iv. 8; Rapoport, "'Erek Millin," p. 164), and the attendance was generally small (Zunz, "G. V." p. 339). It took centuries before the order of prayer as found in the Babylonian Talmud became established: it was neither desired nor was it possible to give it a fixed and definite form (Zunz, "Ritus," pp. 1 *et seq.*).

Private Prayer.

Private prayer existed side by side with the official liturgy. A large number of prayers composed by scribes and recited on special occasions are mentioned in traditional literature, and prayers by laymen are also quoted. In general, an important place was assigned to prayer, although its thoughtless drawling was condemned. Thus, it is said, "Prayer is more pleasing to God than good works and sacrifice" (Ber. 32b and parallels); while Johanan felt, "Would that prayer lasted the entire day." Worship was held to be equivalent to prayer, and indeed the ritual was actually modeled upon the sacrificial cult (Sifre, Deut. xi. 14; Ta'an. 2a; Ber. 28b). There were many rules regarding prayer (*ib.* 28, 31; Sanh. 22; Ab. ii. 18, etc.). He who prays should drop his eyes, but lift up his heart (Yeb. 105b), although he should not raise his voice (Ber. 24, 31). The saying "God wisheth the heart" (Sanh. 106b) has become a proverb. The suppliant knelt, or fell on his face, stretching out his hands and his feet (prostration; Ber. 34b *et passim*), although this is now done only on the Day of Atonement at the "'Abodah" (see ADORATION). The pious made themselves ready an hour before prayer, and stood still for an hour after it (Ber. 31b). A drunken man was not allowed to pray ('Er. 64; see the eight prescriptions which, according to "Yad," Tefillah, v. 1, must be observed). All faces were turned toward the sanctuary (Ber. 30a), and Maimonides ordained (*l.c.* v. 6, following Ber. 31) that the windows should be opened during prayer. The hands were washed before praying (Ber. 16, 26; Shab. 10), a custom with which the construction of synagogues on the banks of rivers is connected. Ten adults were required to be present at worship (Meg. 34a), a custom which still obtains. On the other hand, the entire congregation did not pray, as it does to-day; but the leader in prayer, the "messenger of the congregation," the most learned among them (Ta'an. 17b), standing in a depression, prayed for all (Ps. cxxx. 1; Ber. 10b): "to step down before the Tabernacle" is equivalent to "leading in prayer" (R. H., end).

Among the people various superstitions arose in connection with the recitation of prayers. The reader of the "Shema'" must not blink his eyes, nor compress his lips, nor point with his fingers (Yoma 19). It is forbidden to pray with phylacteries in the hand or with a Torah roll on the arm (Ber. 23b). He who is unwilling to lead the prayers in a colored garment may not lead when dressed in white, and he who will not lead in sandals may not lead barefoot (Meg. 24b; for other examples see Blau, "Altjüdisches Zauberwesen," pp. 146 *et seq.*).

The Jewish liturgy at first completely dominated the Christian. The three benedictions—still placed at the head of the morning prayer—in which the Jews praise God that he has not created them heathen, or slaves, or women (Men. 43b), express, as their brevity indicates, ancient Jewish views; and therefore they are not to be regarded as imitations of similar Greek formulas (Diogenes Laertius, i. 1, § 7). A striking allusion to this prayer is found in Paul's Epistle to the Galatians, iii. 28: "There is neither Jew nor Greek, there is neither bond nor free, there is neither male nor female: for ye are all one in Christ Jesus." A similar view is expressed in a Parsi prayer ("Monatsschrift," xxxvii. 14 *et seq.*; "Magyar Zsidó Szemle," x. 113 *et seq.*). For early forms of liturgy see "J. Q. R." x. 654 *et seq.*

Influence on Early Christian Liturgy.

The early Christian liturgy, in the reading of the Scriptures, in prayer, and in the singing of the Psalms, was modeled on synagogal practises. The fact that no complete Christian liturgical specimens of the first three centuries are extant indicates that the liturgy in use during that period may have been borrowed from that current in the synagogue. The earliest extant Christian prayers, the pseudo-Cyprianic (text in Michel, "Gebet und Bild in Frühchristlicher Zeit," pp. 3 *et seq.*, Leipsic, 1902), written after 300, are still Jewish in form and content. One of them begins with the "Ḳedushshah" and continues with the introductory formula of the "Shemoneh 'Esreh," and mentions also "purity of heart," which was and is still the main point in the seventh or middle benediction for the Sabbath and feast-days. After the "Shema'" the Jewish ritual placed the "salvation benediction" ("ge'ullah"); and Christian circles, in harmony with folk-beliefs, derived from this benediction various prayers for deliverance from the persecutions of the devil. Satan is mentioned in Jewish prayers also (*e.g.*, morning prayer), although not in the official liturgy nor in the obligatory prayers.

Jewish Prayers and Early Christian Art.

The liturgy of the fasts, which is the oldest, assumed definite form long before the common era (I. Lévi, in "R. E. J." xlvii. 161-171; Michel, *l.c.* pp. 44 *et seq.*). Its formulas took the deepest hold upon the people on account of its antiquity and its peculiar solemnity. This explains why the views of the early Christian Church show the dominant influence of this liturgy and why its prayers contain for the most part not New Testament but Old Testament phraseology. The liturgy naturally dominated early Christian art as well. The subjects for the figures in the catacombs, on stained glass, etc., were borrowed as a rule from those Biblical stories which were found also in the Jewish festival literature; as, for example, the sacrifice of Isaac, Daniel in the lion's den, the three Hebrews in the fiery furnace, and scenes from the story of Jonah (comp. Kaufmann in "R. E. J." xiv. 33-48, 217-253). The prayers do not always observe the chronological order of events; in one prayer the name of Job follows immediately upon that of Abraham, the author evidently sharing the Jewish view that Job was the contemporary of Abraham (see Michel, *l.c.*, where extensive bibliography is given).

History of the Ritual.

The history of the ritual is eventful and varied. At first there were no written prayers; a scribe of the end of the first century says, "The writers of benedictions are as those that burn the Torah." A man who was caught copying some at Sidon threw a bundle of his copies into a washtub (Shab. 115b and parallels; comp. Blau, "Altjüdisches Zauberwesen," p. 93). In no case was written matter used during public worship. Prayer-books appear about the seventh century. "The prayer-books are doubtless older than the prayer 'orders,' which date from the eighth century. However, the first book of this kind of which definite mention is made was composed by Gaon Kohen Ẓedeḳ (843); a generation later appeared the Siddur of Amram Gaon, which was much used after the eleventh century and formed the foundation for benedictions and Siddur collections" (Zunz, "Ritus," p. 18). Prayer-books ("siddur") were composed also by Saadia, Hai, Nissim, and Rashi (extant in MSS.; Buber, in "Ha-Ẓefirah," 1904, No. 8), by Rashi's pupil Simḥah ("Maḥzor Vitry," ed. Hurwitz, Berlin, 1892), and by others (Zunz, "Ritus," pp. 19, 25). The most important work of the twelfth century in this direction, and one highly extolled in later times, was

Siddur and Maḥzor.

"the Yad ha-Ḥazaḳah of Maimonides, in which, for the first time, the texts of prayers and the ritual were arranged in masterly order by a scholar" (Zunz, *l.c.* pp. 26 *et seq.*).

Between 1180 and 1320 an immense amount of work was done in Europe in systematizing the worship, the prayer-books of this period forming the foundation for the ritual of the succeeding centuries. There were, also, Arabic forms of siddurim. Until 1300 the Halakah and the Haggadah, current practises, poetry, mysticism, and philosophy, all contributed toward the shaping of the ritual, the poetic material not being increased to any extent after this period (Zunz, *l.c.* pp. 27-30). The word "maḥzor" (shortened from "maḥzor tefillim"), denoting "prayer-book," means literally astronomical or yearly cycle. The Syrians use the term "maḥzor" to denote the breviary. While the Sephardim apply it to those collections which contain all the prayers for the year, the Ashkenazim apply it to the prayer-books containing the festival ritual only. Spanish, Italian, and French maḥzorim were issued sometimes in octavo and smaller sizes, and were often written in small script and handsomely bound. In Germany the various collections were seldom issued in quarto, but generally in folio, with the exception of the Siddur proper, which was issued in smaller size. In contrast to these heavy and expensive volumes for public worship, the 12mo or 16mo Siddur was used for private devotions after the thirteenth century. The latter often contained much superstitious matter, part of which, in the course of time, found its way into the regular prayer-books and was then accepted as part of the ritual service (*ib.* p. 84).

The Cabala, which had taken deep root by 1500, effected material changes in the Siddur. "In the beginning of the seventeenth century Isaiah Horowitz and others, with their following of the school of Luria, began to introduce new prayers, strange words, and unintelligible meditations ["kawwanot"], with which they deluged public and private worship. All the siddurim and maḥzorim from Tlemçen to Kaffa are filled with mystic alterations and additions; even amulet-formulas were included and thus introduced among the people. This cabalistic-ascetic movement progressed from Palestine to Italy and Poland, from Poland to Germany and Holland, and from Jerusalem and Leghorn to Barbary. Based on ancient customs, it introduced fasting on the 'Small Day of Atonement' and on the eve of New-Moon, early-morning devotions, regular societies which held meetings for prayer and fasting on Mondays and Thursdays, and others which assembled nightly to lament over the Exile, and the like. . . . Through the dissemination of the printed Siddur, of formulas for grace at meals, and of 'tikkun' of all kinds, prayers, either old and obsolescent or new, found their way from foreign rituals and from the works of the cabalists into the ritual of the communities, and there they were retained, modifying to a considerable degree public worship" (*ib.* pp. 149 *et seq.*). On commentaries to the prayers, and on ritual books, etc., see Zunz, *l.c.* pp. 21 *et seq.*, 153 *et seq.*; Abudarham, p. 30; for the varieties of prayer-books used after 1180 see Zunz, "Ritus," p. 33; for mystic vigil order, etc., after 1580, evening assembly at the Feast of Weeks and the "HOSHA'NA RABBAH," etc., see *ib.* pp. 151 *et seq.*

Influence of Cabala.

On the whole, the original prayers, as handed down by the Talmud and the Geonim, agree in all the rituals with Amram's Siddur, although this, as regards the position of the Psalms and of the "Baruk she-Amar," or the wording of individual phrases and clauses, coincides sometimes with the Roman and sometimes with the German or the Spanish Maḥzor. The various rituals are divided into two chief groups, the Arabian-Spanish and the German-Roman. In the former group, the Spanish, or, more correctly, the Castilian, ritual has been preserved in the purest form. This group includes the rituals of Aragon, Catalonia, Avignon, Algeria, Tunis, Tlemçen, Majorca (Catalonio-African), Provence, Carpentras, Sicily (various rituals), and Tripoli (for further details see *ib.* pp. 38 *et seq.*). "Saadia's Siddur apparently contained the substance of the old prayer-order of Egypt, his version of the 'Tefillah' in particular being the one used in that country. . . . After 1200, however, the use of Maimonides' prayer-order became prevalent in Egypt, Palestine, Maghreb, and among the Mozarabic communities generally, the members of which were subsequently called 'Moriscos'" (*ib.* p. 55). At Saragossa and Traga the "Musaf Tefillah" on New-Year's Day was not recited by the congregation alone before its recitation by the ḥazzan, but together with the latter, the ignorance of the majority of the congregation being assigned as the reason for this practise (*ib.* p. 41). As Spain was a center for the first group of rituals, so was Germany for the second. The several rituals may vary in details, but they agree in essentials. The Jews of Germany, Bohemia, Moravia, Silesia, Poland, Prussia, and Hungary have one and the same order of prayer (*ib.* p. 75). The French ritual is really that of Burgundy, and the English communities had probably the same or a similar one (*ib.* pp. 63 *et seq.*). The Roman ritual was widely disseminated, and the "Romanian" or Greek ritual exists in the Romanian Maḥzor, which dates from some period after 1520 (*ib.* pp. 76–79). The Romanian group includes also the rituals of Corfu and Kaffa, while the Palestinian ritual, which varied to some extent in the earlier period, lost its independence in the twelfth century (*ib.* pp. 82–84). The interrelation of the various rituals appears in individual portions of the service, chiefly in those which were not based on ancient usage, such as the dirges ("ḳinot") for the Ninth of Ab and the "Hosha'not."

Two Main Groups of Rituals.

"The Day of Atonement did not always have the somber coloring given it in the Middle Ages. Even in the time of the Soferim the people danced in the vineyards on that day, and as late as the beginning of the fourth century it does not seem to have been customary in Palestine for every one to spend the whole day in the synagogue (Ḥul. 101b). The form of the 'TEFILLAH' had not been definitely fixed by the third century; it occasionally ended with 'NE'ILAH,' omitting the evening prayer . . . ''Abodah' and 'Seliḥah' were considered as the most important divisions, even though the form of the latter was by no means invariable." Amram's Siddur does not refer to the "Kol Nidre," which is designated in the later redaction as of Spanish origin, and was recited only by the ḥazzan (Zunz, "Ritus," pp. 95 *et seq.*; on 'ABODAH and ABINU MALKENU in antiquity see *ib.* pp. 101, 118). The second and the fifth day of the week (comp. Luke xviii. 12) were set apart even in antiquity as lesson-days, on which the people went to the synagogue. In the early Middle Ages the pious began to consider these as penitential days. Penitence consisted in prayer and fasting, there being no fast-day without a prayer of atonement ("SELIḤAH"), while to utter this without fasting was considered unseemly. The ten days of penance between New-Year and the Day of Atonement were observed, however, in antiquity, which, as stated above, possessed a definitely fixed fast-day liturgy (Zunz, "Ritus," pp. 120–130; *idem*, "S. P." p. 83).

Day of Atonement.

Toward the end of the Middle Ages there were many changes in the form of worship, for reasons both internal and external. "Gutenberg and Luther no less than the Cabala and the Inquisition influenced the ritual of the Synagogue. After the first decades of the fifteenth century the minute regulations of the ritual manuals allowed scarcely any initiative to the ḥazzan, who had, moreover, lost his former high position, being now neither a poet nor a teacher of the

Changes in the Prayer-Books.

Law, nor was he either of these at any time in Germany or Poland. When the art of printing made manuals and prayer-books accessible to all, the editor took the place of the ḥazzan. Printing imposed restrictions. . . . The similarity of the copies in the hands of the people produced uniformity; the 'Minhag' conformed to the printed editions. Within forty or fifty years printed Hebrew prayer-books were current in the countries in which there were Jews and printing-presses. The German ritual was the first one printed (grace at meals, 1480; 'Seliḥah,' n.d. and 1496; prayer-book, 1508; Maḥzor, *c.* 1521); then followed the Roman ritual (prayer-book and Maḥzor, 1486; 'Seliḥah,' 1487; 'Hosha'na,' 1503), the Polish (prayer-book, 1512; Maḥzor, 1522; 'Yoẓerot,' 1526; 'Seliḥah,' 1529; all printed at Prague), and those of Spain (n.d. and 1519), Greece (1520), Catalonia (1527), Aragon (n.d.), and the Karaites (1528)" (Zunz, "Ritus," p. 145; for further details on commentaries, translations, editions of prayer-books, and the ritual of the Karaites, *ib.* pp. 153–162; on the last-named see also Zunz, "G. V." pp. 439 *et seq.*; and comp. Lady McDougall, "Hymns of Jewish Origin," in "Songs of the Church," London, 1903).

After the expulsion of the Jews from Spain in 1492 the Spanish ritual was more widely introduced and became an important factor. The "informers" caused material changes in the Maḥzor. Even in the Middle Ages they brought charges against the prayer-books as well as the Talmud, and consequently their owners in alarm erased passages, cut out entire leaves, and changed single words here and there. The Kol Nidre and the 'Alenu were special objects of attack as early as the fourteenth century; in the second half of the following century the persecutions steadily increased, especially on the part of the preaching friars, and soon the Inquisition began to act in the same direction. "When printing and a knowledge of the language facilitated examination of the liturgical prayers, the Roman Church being at the same time endangered by the Reformation, the books were watched more carefully, and a censorship which constantly increased in severity fettered the prayer-books also. Certain expressions were no longer allowed in the editions. . . . Since that time some prayers have disappeared entirely and others have been mutilated. . . . The Herdenheim edition of the 'Seliḥah' (1546) removed 'all offensive and dangerous matter.' Thenceforth not only the Siddur and Maḥzor, but all Jewish printed books, were subject to constant attack from the Dominicans, who employed converted Jews. . . . In the year 1559 the prayer-books of the community of Prague were taken to Vienna to be examined." These mutilations increased in the course of time (Zunz, "Ritus," pp. 145 *et seq.*, and appendix vi.; comp. also *idem*, "G. S." iii. 239; Berliner, "Einfluss des Ersten Hebräischen Buchdrucks auf den Cultus und die Cultur der Juden," Frankfort-on-the-Main, 1896; Popper, "The Censorship of Hebrew Books," New York, 1899).

The reform of worship began with Moses Mendelssohn as a result of the general readjustment in Jewish life and learning. Wolf Heidenheim especially rendered enduring services to this reform by the correctness of his editions, his excellent notes, and the translations adapted to his time. The editions of the Siddur by Landshuth (Königsberg, 1845) and Baer (Rödelheim, 1868) are also valuable. Liturgy was and is still the field on which the different parties within Judaism—Orthodox, Progressive, and Reform—fight their battles with more or less bitterness. Among these conflicts the Hamburg Temple controversy, in 1819, and the Reform prayer-book controversy of the Berlin community are especially noteworthy. Reform is still progressing in this department and is not likely to reach a conclusion in the near future.

Reforms in the Nineteenth Century.

Leopold Zunz (1794–1886) investigated all branches of the liturgy with astonishing assiduity. In his first great work, "Gottesdienstliche Vorträge" (Berlin, 1832), which is the earliest product of modern Jewish science and which contains a complete history of the liturgy, he advocates the abolition of many old prayers and the introduction of appropriate new ones (pp. 494 *et seq.*). Reform, however, was not content with removing external abuses; it investigated the earliest prayers of the liturgy, the recitation of which had been declared to be obligatory as early as the time of the Talmud. It considered the views which gave rise to these prayers in connection with modern ideas and has abandoned the prayers, either partly or entirely. See Benedictions; Grace at Meals; Habdalah; Habinenu; Ḥad Gadya; Hafṭarah; Haggadah (Shel Pesaḥ); Haḳḳafot; Hallel; Halleluiah; Happiness; Ḥazzan; Heidenheim, Wolf; Holiness; Maḥzor; Megillot, The Five; Music, Synagogal; Prayer-Books; Reform; etc.

Bibliography: L. Zunz, *G. V.*; idem, *Ritus*; idem, *S. P.*: idem, *Literaturgesch.* (with Supplement, 1867); Steinschneider, *Jüdische Litteratur*, in Ersch and Gruber, *Encyc.* section ii., part 28 (English ed., *Jewish Literature*, London, 1857; Hebrew ed., *Sifrut Yisrael*, Warsaw, 1897); Schürer, *Gesch.* 3d ed., Leipsic, 1901–2 (see Index, s.v. *Gebet*); Benjacob, *Oẓar ha-Sefarim*, iii. 660, 722-885 (editions of the prayer-books). Some of the many other works on liturgical literature are quoted in the body of the article.

A. L. B.

LITWACK or LITTWACK, JUDA: Dutch mathematician; born in Poland about 1760; died Jan. 15, 1836; buried at Ouerveen. A disciple of Moses Mendelssohn, he removed to Amsterdam, where he became one of the most important members of the 'Adat Yeshurun congregation. With C. Asser and Lemon he was appointed a deputation to the Sanhedrin at Paris, where he delivered a discourse in the German language (Feb. 12, 1807).

Litwack was a member of the Mathesis Artium Genetrix society. He wrote "Verhandeling Over de Proefgetallen Gen. 11," Amsterdam, 1817 (2d ed., 1821).

Bibliography: Bierens de Haan, *Bibliographie Neerlandaise*; *Collection des Procès Verbaux*, ii.; Grätz, *Gesch.* xi. 298; *Jaarboeken*, 1836, p. 86; *Vaderlandsche Letteroefeningen*, 1817, p. 482.

s. E. Sl.

LIVER (כבד): A glandular organ situated, in man, to the right beneath the diaphragm and above the stomach. In six passages of the Bible in which the liver is mentioned the expression יותרת הכבד is met with in reference to the part of the organ which had to be sacrificed as a fatty piece (Ex.

xxix. 13, 22, *et passim*). The meaning of this expression has not been successfully established. Both Onkelos and pseudo-Jonathan translate it חצרא דכבדא, or in the Hebrew form חצר הכבד, which is met with in the Talmud. The Authorized Version, following Jerome, renders it "the caul above the liver"; and it seems that Rashi gave the same interpretation. But the Septuagint renders it by "the lobe of the liver," which shows that the piece sacrificed was a part of the liver itself. The interpretation "caul" or "flap around the liver" seems to be based on the Aramaic חצר, taken in the sense of "surrounding." But Bochart ("Hierozoicon," i. 562, Leipsic, 1793–96) has proved the error of such an interpretation, referring to Saadia's Arabic rendering "za'idah" (= "excrescent"). Kohut ("Aruch Completum," *s.v.* אצבע and חצר הכבד) draws attention to a passage in Tamid (31a) in which "the finger of the liver" is spoken of (see Rashi *ad loc.*). Kohut therefore supposes that the Aramaic חצרא is the equivalent of the Arabic "khanṣar" = "little finger." His supposition is confirmed by Isaac ibn Ghayyat, who quotes Hai Gaon (Dukes, in "Orient, Lit." ix. 537) to the effect that the expression חצר הכבד comes from the Arabic and that the liver is composed of pieces similar to fingers. According to Naḥmanides (Responsa, No. 162), if this part of the liver is perforated, the flesh of the animal may be eaten (see also Dillmann on Lev. iii. 4; Driver and White, "Leviticus," p. 65; Nowack, "Archäologie," i. 228; comp. Caul; Fat).

Neither man nor beast can live without a liver ('Ar. 20a). If the liver is missing from an animal, its flesh may not be eaten (Ḥul. 42a). Therefore if any one dedicates to the sanctuary the value of his head or of his liver, he must pay the value of his entire person ('Ar. 20a; B. M. 114a). On liver complaints see Maimonides, "Yad," Shehiṭah, vi. 1, 8, 9; vii. 4, 19, 21; viii. 16.

The liver is the seat of life. The archers pierced the liver with their arrows (Prov. vii. 23), thereby quickly causing death. Johanan (d. 279) says: "He smote him under the fifth rib" (II Sam. ii. 23), *i.e.*, in the fifth partition, where liver and gall are connected (Sanh. 49, above). Johanan does not mean to imply that liver and gall are in the chest, as Ebstein infers ("Medicin des N. T. und des Talmuds," ii. 129), but merely that liver and gall were wounded. The tradition (I Kings xxii. 34; II Chron. xviii. 33) that the arrow struck the king between the ribs ("debaḳim") likewise refers to the fifth partition (see also Sanh. 63b; Kohut, "Aruch Completum," iv. 182b). A tannaite living at Rome about 150 recommends the membrane of the liver of a mad dog as a remedy against hydrophobia, and Galen also approves of this remedy; but the Palestinian teachers forbade it because its efficacy had not been proved (Yoma viii. 5; 84a, b; see Blau, "Altjüdische Zauberwesen," pp. 80 *et seq.*). Tobit vi. 8, viii. 2, however, shows that fumigating with fish-livers was considered a means of exorcising evil spirits in Palestine.

On the functions of the liver there is only a single passage in the Bible, namely, Lam. ii. 11: "Mine eyes do fail with tears, my bowels are troubled, my liver is poured upon the earth, for the destruction of the daughters of my people." On the functions of the several organs of the human body this observation is found in the Talmud: "The liver causes anger; the gall throws a drop into it and quiets it" (Ber. 61, above).

The augural significance of the liver, hepatoscopy, is mentioned only once in the Bible, and then as a foreign custom. Ezekiel (xxi. 21) says of Nebuchadnezzar: "For the king of Babylon stood at the parting of the way, at the head of the two ways, to use divination: he made his arrows bright, he consulted with images, he looked into the liver" (see Jew. Encyc. iv. 624a, *s.v.* Divination). Levi (3d cent.) remarks on this passage: "as the Arabian, who slaughters a sheep and inspects the liver" (Eccl. R. xii. 7).

S. S. L. B.—M. Sel.

LIVERPOOL: Chief seaport in the northwest of England, situated on the Mersey, and in the county of Lancashire. There was a primitive settlement of Jews in the town about 1750, but this later became extinct. Tombstones with Hebrew inscriptions were discovered beneath some structures between Derby street and Cumberland street, an old portion of the city. The synagogue with cemetery attached is marked in a map of Liverpool for 1796; but at the time of Harwood's large survey in 1803 it had disappeared. It became a Sandemanian chapel (W. Robinson, "History of Liverpool," 1810, p. 388).

Early Settlements.

It seems that the first Jewish settlers were mainly recruited from the Portuguese Jews of Bevis Marks, London, and were of those who were about to proceed to Ireland, Dublin being then an established Jewish center.

About 1780 the Jews again assembled for worship in Turton Court, on the site of the present custom-house. From their names, as given in a Liverpool directory of 1790, they appear to have been a medley of Germans, Poles, and Londoners, mostly itinerant dealers and venders of old clothes. Here and there a Sephardi is recorded as a merchant; but the Polish element must have predominated, as the early minute-books of the community are written in Judæo-German with square, not cursive, characters.

The next removal, in Dec., 1789, was to Frederick street, the Liverpool corporation assigning to the Jews for religious purposes a building with a garden in the rear for a cemetery. At the extreme end of this synagogue, which could hold sixty or seventy worshipers, was a glass roof evidently intended for a sukkah or tabernacle. In the basement was a "miḳweh," or ritual bath. In 1806 the corporation presented the Jews with another site in Seel street, where the Old Hebrew Congregation met from 1807 until 1874, when it removed to the present handsome building on Prince's Boulevard. In 1835 the town had encroached on the cemetery in Oakes street, and a burial-ground was purchased in Fairfield (Deane road), then quite rural; this in turn became inadequate, and a new one in Broad Green was opened in June, 1904.

The Seel street synagogue was the first in the United Kingdom in which sermons were delivered in English; this happened in 1806, the preacher being Tobias Goodman. D. W. Marks acted as secretary and preacher to the congregation in 1833. He subsequently became chief minister of the Berkeley Street (London) Congregation of British Jews. There were probably 250 Jewish families in Liverpool in 1838, when a secession took place in the community. At first the seceders held divine service in a small building in Hardman street, now used as a temperance hall. In 1857 they erected a handsome building in Hope place. They also purchased a cemetery in Green lane, Tuebrook, which is still (1904) in use.

New Congregation.

In 1846 a few numbers of a monthly Jewish magazine entitled "Kos Yeshu'ot" appeared in Liverpool.

The first organization in Great Britain in connection with the Alliance Israélite Universelle was founded in Liverpool in 1868, three years before the Anglo-Jewish Association was established in London, with which, however, it later amalgamated. In 1882 the extensive emigration to America was organized and directed from Liverpool; and during the year of the Russo-Jewish persecutions 6,274 persons were sent, at a cost which amounted to over £30,000 ($150,000), to the United States and Canada in thirty-one steamships.

It is computed that there are at present about 1,500 Jewish families in Liverpool in a total population of about 685,000. Owing to the great influx of Russian and Polish Jews, a number of ḥebras have sprung into existence, as well as two considerable congregations: (1) Bet ha-Midrash, situated in Crown street; (2) the Fountains Road Congregation, situated in the suburb of Kirkdale.

A Hebrew school was founded in 1842, commencing with ten pupils. Subsequently a building was erected in Hope place to accommodate eighty pupils; it has since been enlarged so as to provide room for more than 700 children.

Among the many Jewish organizations may be mentioned: the Philanthropic Society, Provident Society, Tontine Benefit Society, Board of Guardians, Jewish Shelter, Ladies' Benevolent Charity, Branch of the Anglo-Jewish Association.

BIBLIOGRAPHY: B. L. Benas, in *Proceedings of the Historic Society of Lancashire and Cheshire* (1900), vol. xv.

J. B. L. B.

LIVONIA. See RIGA.

LIVORNO. See LEGHORN.

LIWA BEN BEZALEEL. See JUDAH LÖW BEN BEZALEEL.

LIZARD: A saurian or lacertilian reptile. About forty species and twenty-eight genera of lizards found in Palestine have been enumerated, the most common of which are the green lizard (*Lacerta viridis*) and its varieties, and the wall-lizard belonging to the genus *Zootoca*. It is therefore generally agreed that besides "leṭa'ah," traditionally rendered by "lizard," the following terms, enumerated among the "creeping things that creep upon the earth" (Lev. xi. 29 *et seq.*), also denote some kinds of lizard: "zab" (Arabic, "ḍabb"), identified with the *Uromastix spinipes* (A. V. "tortoise"; R. V. "great lizard"); "anaḳah" with the gecko, of which six species are found in Palestine (A. V. "ferret"; R. V. "gecko"; see FERRET); "koaḥ" (Vulgate and Ḳimḥi, "stellio") with the monitor (A. V. "chameleon"; R. V. "land-crocodile; see CHAMELEON); "ḥomeṭ" with the sand-lizard (A. V. "snail"; R. V. "sand-lizard"); "tinshemet," by reason of the etymology of the name (= "breathing," "blowing"), with the chameleon (A. V. "mole"; R. V. "chameleon"; see CHAMELEON); "semamit" (Prov. xxx. 28), the same word which the Targum Yerushalmi uses for "leṭa'ah," and the Samaritan version for "anaḳah," the meaning of the passage being that the lizard may be held in the hand with impunity (A. V. "spider"; R. V. "lizard").

In the Talmud "leṭa'ah" is the general term for the *Lacertilia*. It is described as having a thick but soft and separable skin (Shab. 107a, b; Ḥul. 122a), and its eggs have the white and yolk unseparated ('Ab. Zarah 40a [Rashi]). A case of resuscitation of an apparently dead lizard by pouring cold water on it is related in Pes. 88b. In Shab. 77b the semamit is mentioned as inspiring terror in the scorpion and also as serving as a cure for its bite, with which may be compared Pliny, "Historia Naturalis," xxix. 4, 29. In Sanh. 103b it is related that King Amon, after abolishing the Temple service, placed a semamit upon the altar. The chameleon is considered to be intended by "zeḳita" in Shab. 108b. This may be connected with "ziḳa" (= "wind"), meaning properly "the windy," the ancients believing the chameleon to live on air (comp. Pliny, *l.c.* viii. 33, 35).

BIBLIOGRAPHY: Tristram, *Nat. Hist.* pp. 266 *et seq.*; L. Lewysohn, *Z. T.* pp. 221 *et seq.*

E. G. H. I. M. C.

LOANS: In the commonwealth of Israel, as among other nations of antiquity, loans of money, or of corn or like commodities, were made as a matter of favor by the wealthy to those standing in need, and but seldom, if ever, in the way of furnishing capital necessary for enterprises in trade or agriculture. At least in all passages of Scripture lender and borrower stand, at the time of the loan, in the attitude of benefactor and dependent (Ps. cxii. 5); after the loan, in that of master and servant (Prov. xxii. 7); and, when the lender enforces his demand, in that of tyrant and sufferer (II Kings iv. 1). It is made the duty of the well-to-do Israelite to lend of his affluence to his poor brother (*i.e.*, fellow Israelite) according to the borrower's wants, at least when a pledge is offered (Ex. xxii. 25; Deut. xv. 8), and that without claiming interest (see USURY); and he should not refuse even when the approach of the year of release endangers the recovery of the loan (Deut. xv. 9), and though the security of the pledge is much weakened by the lender's duty of returning it when the debtor needs it (see PLEDGE). In truth, to lend is regarded in Scripture (*ib.* 1–11) as an act of benevolence the reward for which must be expected only from God.

In the Bible.

R. Ishmael, of the time of Hadrian (see Mek., Ex. xxii. 25), reckons the command to lend to the poor as one of the affirmative precepts; and the Talmud (B. M. 71a) derives from Ex. xxii. 25 the rule that between the Gentile who offers interest and the Israelite from whom it is not allowed to be accepted, the latter should have the preference; between the rich and the poor, one should lend to the poor; between kinsmen and townsmen, lend to kinsmen first, but give the preference to townsmen over those from a distance. To lend is deemed more meritorious than to give (Maimonides, "Yad," Malveh, i. 1); for by a timely loan the receiver may be saved from beggary.

In the Talmud.

The lender or creditor is bidden also, on inferential Scriptural grounds (*ib.*; Deut. xv. 2–3), not to press the borrower or debtor when he knows that the latter can not pay; which admonition was so extended by the Rabbis that they forbade the creditor to show himself to the unfortunate debtor, in order that he might not put the latter to shame ("Yad," *l.c.* xiii. 3).

On the other hand, it is a most sacred duty of the borrower to pay if he can. To withhold payment is wickedness (Ps. xxxvii. 21), and, according to the Rabbis, the debtor, when able to pay, must not even put the creditor off, telling him to come again; nor must he waste the borrowed money or lose it recklessly, so that he can not repay it.

Under the written law (Deut. xv.) all debts arising from a loan are canceled by the passage of the year of release over them, on the last day (last of Elul) of that year. The text (*ib.* verse 9) warns earnestly against the baseness of not lending to the poor from fear of such release; yet in the days of King Herod this kind of baseness prevailed among the well-to-do Jews to such an extent that Hillel the Elder, who according to rabbinical tradition was at that time president of the Sanhedrin, in order "that the door might not be shut in the face of borrowers" thought it best to contrive a fiction whereby to nullify the Scriptural law (see Sheb. viii. 2–3; Sifre, *ad loc.*). He authorized the creditor to execute a deed, known as the "prosbul," in some such words as these: "I, A. B., hereby deliver to you [giving the names], judges of the court at [naming the place] all the claims which I own, so that I may collect them at any time I may choose"; which instrument was signed by the judges and by two witnesses, and the bonds were then handed over to the court. The act of Hillel was justified on the ground that the year of release being indissolubly connected with the year of jubilee and the restoration of lands to their former owners, and the latter being in the second commonwealth no longer feasible, the release of debts ceased to be a Scriptural and became only a rabbinical law, and for good cause might therefore be modified, or even abrogated, by the Great Sanhedrin (see Talmud Yerushalmi on above mishnah). The Sabbatical year, as far as it affected seed-time and harvest, was meant only for the Holy Land; neither did it ever work the release of debts beyond the boundaries of that country. Joseph Caro says, in his code, that as a rabbinical institution the law of the year of release operates in all times and places; but the gloss of Moses Isserles declares that in "these countries," meaning northern Europe, it had fallen entirely into desuetude.

Cancelation of Loans.

A debt arising from the sale of goods or of land or from liability for wrongs done, the wages of labor, or the hire of lands or of animals, whether liquidated by the written law or unliquidated, was not affected by the year of release; but if the parties agreed upon the amount due or that should be paid, and upon the length of time of forbearance, such debt or liability became a loan in the eyes of the law, and was then regarded as a subject of release, unless kept alive by the prosbul (Sheb. viii. 2; Sifre, Deut. 15).

The fear that a literal enforcement of the Scriptural law against lenders would "shut the door in the face of borrowers" led to its relaxation in other respects also. Thus, strictly speaking, creditors should have the debtors' worst lands ("zibburit") allotted to them in satisfaction; but as such a rule would discourage loans, it was modified so as to allot middle-grade lands for their satisfaction (Giṭ. 49b; see Appraisement).

S. L. N. D.

LOANS or LOANZ (לואנץ), ELIJAH BEN MOSES ASHKENAZI: German rabbi and cabalist; born at Frankfort-on-the-Main 1555; died at Worms July, 1636. He belonged to the Rashi family, and on his mother's side was the grandson of Johanan Luria, and on his father's of Joselmann of Rosheim. After having studied in his native city under the direction of Jacob Ginzburg and Akiba Frankfort, Loans went to Cracow, where he attended the lectures of Menahem Mendel. While there he prepared for publication the "Darke Mosheh" of Moses Isserles. At the beginning of the seventeenth century Loans was called to the rabbinate of Fulda, which he left in 1612, occupying sucessively the rabbinates of Hanau, Friedberg (1620), and Worms (1630), in which last named city he remained until his death.

Loans was a diligent student of cabala, and for this reason was surnamed "Ba'al Shem." Besides his great learning he possessed many accomplishments, such as music and calligraphy; and all kinds of legends circulated regarding his personality. He was the author of the following works: "Rinnat Dodim" (Basel, 1600), a commentary on Canticles; "Miklol Yofi" (Amsterdam, 1695), a commentary on Ecclesiastes; "Wikkuaḥ Yayin 'im ha-Mayim" (*ib.* 1757), a poem with a commentary; "Ma'agle Ẓedeḳ" (Neubauer, "Cat. Bodl. Hebr. MSS." No. 1832), a commentary on Baḥya's "Ḥobot ha-Lebabot"; "Ẓofnat Pa'aneah" (*ib.* No. 1830), a commentary on the "Tiḳḳune Zohar"; a commentary on Genesis Rabbah (*ib.* No. 149); "Adderet Eliyahu" (*ib.* 1829), a commentary on the Zohar.

Loans also edited the "'Ammude Shelomoh" of Solomon Luria on the "Semag" (Basel, 1599), and the "Sha'are Dura" of Isaac ben Meïr of Dueren, to which he wrote a preface (*ib.* 1600).

Bibliography: Moses Mannheimer, *Die Juden in Worms*, p. 61, Frankfort-on-the-Main, 1842; L. Lewysohn, *Nafshot Ẓaddiḳim*, p. 59, *ib.* 1855; Carmoly, in Jost's *Annalen*, i. 94; Steinschneider, *Cat. Bodl.* col. 942; Zunz, *Z. G.* p. 402; Michael, *Or ha-Ḥayyim*, No. 401.

K. I. Br.

LOANS, JACOB BEN JEHIEL: Physician in ordinary to the German emperor Frederick III. (1440–93), and Hebrew teacher of Johann Reuchlin; died at Linz about 1506. Loans rendered lifelong faithful service to the emperor, by whom he was knighted. At Linz in 1492 Reuchlin, who had been sent to the emperor's court by his protector Eberhard of Württemberg, met Loans; and the latter became his first teacher in Hebrew grammar. Reuchlin always held him in grateful remembrance; he cites him as "præceptor meus, mea sententia valde doctus homo Jacobus Jehiel Loans Hebræus" ("Rudimenta Hebraica," p. 249) or "humanissimus præceptor meus homo excellens" (*ib.* p. 619). Geiger supposes that Reuchlin took Loans as a model for the Jewish scholar *Simon*, one of the three disputants in Reuchlin's "De Verbo Mirifico."

BIBLIOGRAPHY: Ludwig Geiger, *Johann Reuchlin*, pp. 105 *et seq.*; Grätz, *Gesch.* ix. 47, 83, 147; Gross, *Gallia Judaica*, p. 273; Steinschneider, *Jewish Literature*, p. 208; Winter and Wünsche, *Die Jüdische Litteratur*, ii. 225.

G. M. Sc.

LOANZ, JOSEPH. See JOSEL (JOSELMANN, JOSELIN) OF ROSHEIM.

LÖB ARYEH BEN ELIAH OF BOLOCHOW: Russian rabbi; born at Satanov, government of Podolia, 1801; died at Zaslavl, government of Volhynia, Sept. 2, 1881; a descendant of Rabbi Joshua Höschel of Cracow (1654-64), author of "Sefer Toledot Aharon." Löb Aryeh, in addition to his studies in rabbinic literature, had a thorough knowledge of the Bible and of Hebrew grammar, and he became a fluent writer in Hebrew. He had a fair knowledge of mathematics also. He was rabbi of Zaslavl for about twenty years, and published "'Arugat ha-Bosem," commentaries to the Yoreh De'ah, Wilna, 1870, and "Shem Aryeh," commentaries to other parts of the Shulḥan 'Aruk, Wilna, 1873.

BIBLIOGRAPHY: Preface to *Shem Aryeh*; Walden, *Shem ha-Gedolim he-Ḥadash*, pp. 66, 72; *Ha-Ẓefirah*, 1881, No. 36.

L. G. H. R.

LÖB ARYEH HA-KOHEN OF STYRIA: Rabbi at Rozniatow and afterward at Styria; died in 1813. He was the author of the following works: "Ḳeẓot ha-Ḥoshen," a casuistic commentary in two volumes on the Ḥoshen Mishpaṭ of Joseph Caro's Shulḥan 'Aruk, published in 1788 and later; "Abne Millu'im," a similar commentary in two volumes on the Eben ha-'Ezer of the same work (Lemberg, 1815, and Zolkiev, 1825); and "Sheb Shema'tata," novellæ on the Talmud (Lemberg, 1804). The first volume of the "Abne Millu'im" contains an appendix, entitled "Meshobeb Netibot," in which the author defends his first works against the attacks of Jacob of Lissa.

BIBLIOGRAPHY: Walden, *Shem ha-Gedolim he-Ḥadash*, p. 79; Zedner, *Cat. Hebr. Books Brit. Mus.* p. 54.

S. S. I. BR.

LÖB ARYEH BEN MEÏR: Lithuanian rabbi; lived in the seventeenth and eighteenth centuries. His notes on Rashi and on Elijah Mizraḥi's commentaries on the Pentateuch were published, under the title "Ḥiddushe Maharsha" (Hanover, 1716), with Samuel Edel's novellæ on the Pentateuch, by his brother **Ẓebi Hirsch b. Meïr.**

BIBLIOGRAPHY: Wolf, *Bibl. Hebr.* iii., No. 353d; Steinschneider, *Cat. Bodl.* col. 745.

S. S. M. SEL.

LÖB ARYEH BEN TOBIAH: Lithuanian Talmudic scholar and printer; died at Wilna Oct. 24, 1812. He enjoyed great consideration in Wilna on account of his learning and of the assistance rendered by him to Talmudic students. He was the first (in partnership with Tobiah b. Abraham Abele) to establish a Hebrew printing-house at Wilna (1799). The first work printed there was Saadia's "Ma'amar ha-Teḥiyyah weha-Pedut." Owing to competition the establishment existed a short time only.

BIBLIOGRAPHY: Fuenn, *Ḳiryah Ne'emanah*, pp. 199, 225.

J. M. SEL.

LÖB BEN BARUCH BENDET: Rabbi of Byelostok, Russia, in the eighteenth and nineteenth centuries; author of "Sha'agat Aryeh" (Byelostok, 1805), novellæ on the treatise Makkot. The author quotes frequently his father's "Ner Tamid" (Grodno, 1789); and in the preface he states that he has written novellæ on the whole Talmud.

BIBLIOGRAPHY: Benjacob, *Oẓar ha-Sefarim*, p. 553; Walden, *Shem ha-Gedolim he-Ḥadash*, p. 79.

H. R. M. SEL.

LÖB, ELIEZER: German rabbi; born at Pfungstadt, grand duchy of Hesse, 1837; died at Altona Jan. 23, 1892. He was educated at the gymnasium of Darmstadt and at the University of Giessen, and received his rabbinical instruction chiefly under Benjamin H. AUERBACH, rabbi of Darmstadt, whose daughter he married. At first he was principal of the Jüdische Realschule in his native city, founded by him (1857-61). Subsequently he was called to the rabbinate of Ichenhausen, Bavaria, where he remained until 1873, when he was called to succeed Jacob Ettlinger as chief rabbi of Altona. He contributed to the "Jüdische Presse," and prepared for publication H. J. Michael's bibliographical work "Or ha-Ḥayyim," but ill health prevented him from completing his labor, which was finished by A. Berliner. A rabbinical work by him, "Dammeseḳ Eli'ezer," remained in manuscript. He was a devoted worker for Orthodox communal affairs and was for years a trustee of the Hildesheimer Seminary at Berlin.

BIBLIOGRAPHY: Dukesz, *Iwoh, Iwoh le-Moshab*, pp. 133-136, Cracow, 1903.

S. D.

LÖB B. JOSEPH (REB LÖB SARAH'S): Early Ḥasidic rabbi; died in Yaltushkov, Podolia, about 1797. His was the strangest and most mysterious character of the many miracle-working rabbis of the Ḥasidim of the latter part of the eighteenth century. He continually traveled from one Polish city to another, spending money lavishly, but never accepting anything from his adherents. Most of the wonderful stories which are still told about him connect him with kings and princes and with successful efforts to influence the authorities in behalf of Jews. This caused Gottlober to suspect that he was in the secret service of the Polish or the Austrian government, a view seemingly absurd, although a letter by R. Bär of Meseritz, stating that "R. Löb Sarah's of Rovno is to be assisted and implicitly believed, for he is rendering important services to Jews, and will himself orally explain things which can not be put down in writing" (Primishlauer's "Darke Yesharim," Jitomir, 1805), lends some slight support to the supposition. The story of an eye-witness that R. Löb Sarah's passed the guards unnoticed and entered the royal palace of Warsaw on the day of the coronation of Stanislaus Poniatowski (1764), and the account of his seven years' struggle with Emperor Joseph II., on whom he inflicted terrible sufferings, are characteristic examples of the miracles ascribed to him by the superstitious people. R. Azriel of Kozin (near Kremenetz), his pupil (according to Gottlober, his driver), was considered as his successor.

Bibliography: Eleazar ha-Kohen, *Kin'at Soferim*, p. 75a, Lemberg, 1892; Gottlober, in *Ha-Boker Or*, v. 386-388, vi. 1-2; *Seder ha-Dorot he-Hadash*, pp. 43-49; Walden, *Shem ha-Gedolim he-Hadash*, p. 81, Warsaw, 1882.

H. R. P. Wi.

LÖB JUDAH B. EPHRAIM: Rabbi of the second half of the seventeenth century; probably born in Wilna, from which city his father, Ephraim b. Jacob ha-Kohen, fled to Buda (Ofen, incorporated into the present Budapest) during the Cossack uprising of 1655; died in Palestine after 1686. Löb remained in Buda until 1684, when he went to Jerusalem, and there, with the assistance of Moses Galanti the younger, began to prepare for publication his father's work "Sha'ar Efrayim." When Charles of Lorraine wrested Buda from the Turks in 1686, the members of Löb's family lost all their possessions and removed to Prague. Löb returned from Palestine to that city; and wealthy people there assisted him to publish the "Sha'ar Efrayim," with his own notes and an appendix (Sulzbach, 1686). He went again to the Holy Land, and died in Safed (according to others, in Jerusalem).

Bibliography: Azulai, *Shem ha-Gedolim*, s.v. *Ephraim of Wilna*; Fuenn, *Kiryah Ne'emanah*, pp. 84-85, Wilna, 1860; idem, *Keneset Yisrael*, p. 399, Warsaw, 1886; Eleazar ha-Kohen, *Kin'at Soferim*, p. 55a, Lemberg, 1892.

S. S. P. Wi.

LÖB JUDAH B. ISAAC: Polish rabbi; died in Cracow about 1730; grandson of R. Joshua, author of "Maginne Shelomoh." He officiated as rabbi at Shidlow, Poland, being at the same time a representative of Cracow in the Council of Four Lands. After 1715 he became rabbi and president of the yeshibah at Cracow, where he remained till his death.

Löb Judah is known by his approbations to many books, among which may be mentioned "Panim Me'irot," by Meïr Eisenstadt (Amsterdam, 1714), and "Berit Shalom," by Phinehas b. Pelta (Frankfort-on-the-Main, 1718).

Of his family are known only two sons: **David Samuel,** who succeeded his father, first in Shidlow and afterward in Cracow, and **Isaac,** rabbi of Tarnow, Galicia.

Bibliography: Zunz, *'Ir ha-Zedek*, pp. 159-160; Friedberg, *Luhot Zikkaron*, pp. 25, 26.

H. R. N. T. L.

LÖB JUDAH BEN JOSHUA: Bohemian scholar; lived at Prague in the middle of the seventeenth century. He filled the office of secretary to Simon Spira, chief rabbi of Prague, and he published, under the title "Milhamah be-Shalom," an account of the siege of Prague by the Swedes in 1648 and of the suffering of the Jews on that occasion. Printed first at Prague, it was reproduced later, with a Latin translation by Wagenseil, in "Exercitatio Tertia," and republished in the "Bikkure ha-'Ittim," iv. 103 *et seq.*

Bibliography: Zunz's notes to Asher's edition of *Benjamin of Tudela*, p. 284; idem, *Z. G.* p. 300, No. 242; Steinschneider, *Cat. Bodl.* col. 1324; Zedner, *Auswahl Historischer Stücke*, p. 138, Berlin, 1840.

D. I. Br.

LÖB HA-LEVI OF BRODY: Galician rabbi of the beginning of the nineteenth century; held office first at Podhajce, then at Brody. Among his contemporaries was Ephraim Zalman Margaliot, chief rabbi of Brody, in whose "Bet Efrayim" occurs a responsum of Löb's. He was the author of "Leb Aryeh" (Lemberg, 1820), a commentary on Hullin.

Bibliography: Benjacob, *Ozar ha-Sefarim*, p. 253; Walden, *Shem ha-Gedolim he-Hadash*, p. 82.

D. M. Sel.

LÖB BEN MEÏR. See Judah ben Meïr.

LÖB MOKIAH OF POLONNOYE: Polish preacher and leader of the Hasidic party in the second half of the eighteenth century. Löb was a pupil of Israel Ba'al Shem-Tob and of Bär of Meseritz, and contributed much to the former's thaumaturgy. Several wonderful things are narrated about him in the "Shibhe Ba'al Shem-Tob." Löb was the author of a work entitled "Kol Aryeh" (Korzec, 1802), homiletic annotations on the Pentateuch.

Bibliography: Rodkinson, *Toledot Ba'ale Shem-Tob*, p. 38, Königsberg, 1876; Walden, *Shem ha-Gedolim he-Hadash*, p. 79.

H. R. M. Sel.

LÖB BEN MOSES HA-KOHEN: Polish rabbi of the eighteenth century; author of "Pene Aryeh" (Novidvor, 1787), novellæ on the Talmud, to which is added a pamphlet entitled "Kontres Mille de-Abot," novellæ by Löb's father and father-in-law.

Bibliography: Benjacob, *Ozar ha-Sefarim*, p. 486; Fürst, *Bibl. Jud.* ii. 265.

H. R. M. Sel.

LÖB OF POLONNOYE. See Löb Mokiah.

LÖB BEN SAMUEL ZEBI HIRSCH: Russian rabbi; born probably at Pinczow, government of Kielce, Poland, about 1630; died at Brest-Litovsk 1714. Löb was on his father's side the grandson of Joel Sirkes and stepson of David ben Samuel ha-Levi, of whom he was also the pupil. He studied besides under Joshua Höschel, author of "Maginne Shelomoh," and under Yom-Tob Lipmann Heller. He was rabbi successively of Swirz, Galicia (before 1663), Kamorna, Stobnitz, Zamosc (1679–89), Tiktin, Cracow, and finally Brest-Litovsk (1701–14). He was considered by his contemporaries so great a Talmudic authority that in 1669 he was sent with his stepbrother Isaiah ha-Levi to Constantinople to investigate the claims of Shabbethai Zebi. His responsa were published later, under the title "Sha'agat Aryeh" (Neuwied, 1736), by his grandson Abraham Nathan Meisels, who added some of his own under the title "Kol Shahal." Other responsa of Löb's are to be found in the "Shebut Ya'akob," No. 107 edited by his grandson, and in "Teshubot Geonim Batra'e," published first in Turkey by the author of "Ma'ane Elihu," and afterward in Prague (1816).

Bibliography: Friedberg, *Luhot Zikkaron*, pp. 24, 25; Azulai, *Shem ha-Gedolim*, ii. 138; Michael, *Or ha-Hayyim*, No. 527; M. Zunz, *'Ir ha-Zedek*, pp. 150 *et seq.* and note 64.

H. R. M. Sel.

LÖB OF SHPOLA: Early Ḥasidic rabbi; died at an advanced age Oct. 4, 1810. It is said that he was a poor "melammed" or teacher in his younger days, and that he did not assume the title of rabbi because, unlike other "ẓaddiḳim" of that period, he was not the pupil or disciple of a great ẓaddiḳ. Although his only claim to prominence in the Ḥasidic world was a visit which he paid once to R. Israel Ba'al Shem-Ṭob, the nominal founder of Ḥasidism, both R. Baruch of Medzhibozh and R. Naḥman of Bratzlave (the first a grandson and the second a great-grandson of the Ba'al Shem) developed a fierce antagonism to him. He was popularly known as "the Shpoler Zeide" (grandfather of Shpola), and was revered for his great piety. He led a very simple, almost ascetic, life, and distributed in charity most of the money given him by his numerous adherents. He left no writings, and if his detractors are to be believed, he did not possess the knowledge and intelligence to produce anything of value; but he so impressed his contemporaries that his name is still preserved among the Ḥasidim, especially those of southern Russia, as that of one of the saintly, miracle-working rabbis of the first period of Ḥasidism.

Bibliography: Gottlober, in *Ha-Boḳer Or*, v. 384-388; Rodkinson, *Toledot Ba'ale Shem-Ṭob*, pp. 39-40, Königsberg, 1876.

H. R. P. Wi.

LÖB (ARYEH) BEN ZACHARIAH (called also **Hocher R. Löb**): Polish rabbi; born at Cracow about 1620; died there 1671. When a young man he was called as rabbi to Vienna, where he officiated for a fèw years. Thence he went to Przemysl, Galicia, and in 1665 he became rabbi at his native place, where he remained until his death. He was the author of "Tiḳḳune Teshubah," an ethical work in Judæo-German, Cracow, 1666.

Bibliography: Zunz, *'Ir ha-Ẓedeḳ*, p. 115, Lemberg, 1874; H. N. Dembitzer, *Kelilat Yofi*, i. 78b; Joel Dembitzer, *Mappelet 'Ir ha-Ẓedeḳ*, p. 25.

H. R. B. Fr.

LOBATO: Marano family, several of whose members lived at Amsterdam. The best-known members of the family are:

Diego Gomez Lobato (called also **Abraham Cohen Lobato**): Portuguese Marano; born at Lisbon, where he was living in 1599; cousin and countryman of the poet Paul de Pina (Rehuel Jeshurun). When the latter was going to Rome, intending to enter a monastery there, Lobato gave him a letter, dated April 3, 1599, addressed to Elijah Montalto (subsequently physician to Maria de Medici), who was then living at Leghorn, asking Elijah to dissuade Paul from his purpose. Paul de Pina was in fact induced by Montalto to desist from carrying out his intention. He became an enthusiastic follower of Judaism, and lived, like Diego Gomez Lobato, at Amsterdam.

Isaac Cohen Lobato: Portuguese Marano; born at Lisbon; died at an advanced age in Amsterdam; a relation of Diego Gomez Lobato. At the performance in the first synagogue of Amsterdam of Rehuel Jeashurun's antiphonal poem "Dialogo delos Siete Montes" (composed in 1624), in which the mountains of the Holy Land are introduced as speakers, Lobato took the leading part of *Mt. Zion.* In 1678 he, together with David Mendes Coutinho, founded the philanthropic society Sha'are Ẓedeḳ at Amsterdam.

Rehuel Cohen Lobato: Sephardic author; lived at Amsterdam; father of Isaac Cohen Lobato. Together with Moses Belmonte he issued a new Spanish translation of the Pirḳe Abot, entitled "Perakym" (Amsterdam, 1644).

Bibliography: Grätz, *Gesch.* ix. 520, x. 4; Kayserling, *Sephardim*, p. 176; idem, *Bibl. Esp.-Port.-Jud.* pp. 27, 64, 89.

G. M. K.

LOBATTO, REHUEL: Dutch mathematician; born at Amsterdam June 6, 1797; died at Delft Feb. 9, 1866. He sprang from a Portuguese Marano family which had gone to Holland in 1604. From his mother, a Da Costa, he acquired a complete knowledge of the south-European languages; and while yet a schoolboy he displayed remarkable talent for mathematics. Littwack and Van Swindern were his teachers, and at Brussels Quetelet, with whom he edited the "Correspondance Mathématique et Physique." In 1823 he published "Wiskundige Mengelingen." In 1828 he was appointed gager at Delft; afterward he became inspector-general of the gaging-office there; and in 1842 he was appointed teacher of higher mathematics in the same city.

Lobatto was the author of a great number of articles in scientific periodicals and of various schoolbooks. From 1828 till 1849 he was editor of the official annual of statistics. In 1841 he was appointed by Minister Rochussen member of a commission for the conversion of the public debt. The Order of the Netherlands Lion was conferred upon him; he received the degree of doctor "honoris causa" from Groningen University, and was a member of the Royal Academy of Sciences.

Bibliography: Matthes, in *Jaarboek Köninklijke Akademie voor Wetenschappen*, Amsterdam, 1866 (gives complete lists of Lobatto's works); *Spectator* (The Hague), 1866; Bierens de Haan, *Bibliographie V. d. Aa Woordenboek*, xxi.

D. E. Sl.

LÖBEL, ARTHUR: Austrian physician; born at Roman, Rumania, May 15, 1857; educated at the gymnasium of Czernowitz and the universities of Vienna and Paris (M.D., Vienna, 1883). During the year 1884 he served as assistant at the General Hospital, Vienna, and in 1885 settled as a physician at the watering-place of Dorna, where he practises during the summer months, spending the winters in Vienna. In 1898 he received the title of "Kaiserlicher Rath."

Löbel is the author of: "Das Balneotherapeutische Verfahren Während der Menstruation," Berlin, 1880; "Der Curgebrauch mit Mineralwässern Während der Gravidität," *ib.* 1888; "Das Bukowinaer Stahlbad Dorna," Vienna, 1889; "Die Curdiätetik im Eisenbade," Vienna and Leipsic, 1890; "Die Moorbäder und Deren Surrogate," Vienna, 1890; "Zur Thermalbehandlung der Endometritis," Leipsic, 1891; "Die Neueren Behandlungsmethoden der Metritis Chronica," *ib.* 1892; "Kosmetische Winke," Leipsic and Vienna, 1894; "Zur Behandlung der Oophoritis Chronica," Berlin, 1895; "Geschichtliche Entwicklung des Eisenbades Dorna," Vienna, 1896; "Das Diätetische Verhalten Während der Menstruation," Kreuznach, 1897; "Die Balneologischen Curmethoden bei Behandlung der Chronischen Para- und Perimetritis," Halle, 1898; "Die Balneo- und Diätotherapie der Arterioklerose," Vienna, 1899; "Zur Puerperalbehandlung mit Trink- und Badekuren," Berlin, 1900; "Die Leistungen der Physikalischen Herzheilmethoden," Vienna, 1902; "Studien über die Physiologische Wirkungen der Moorbäder," *ib.* 1904.

S. F. T. H.

LÖBEL, HIRSCHEL. See LEVIN, HIRSCHEL.

LÖBELE OF PROSSNITZ. See PROSSNITZ, LÖBELE.

LOBO, MOSES JESHURUN: Spanish poet; lived at Amsterdam in the seventeenth century. He was one of the poets who celebrated the martyrdom of Abraham Nuñez Bernal in 1655; and his elegies form a part of the "Elogios" (Amsterdam, 1655). Daniel de Barrios ("Relacion de los Poetos," p. 56 = "R. E. J." xviii. 285) speaks of "an excellent Spanish poet, Custodio Lobo, otherwise called Moses Jeshurun Ribero" (died at Leghorn), some anti-Christian verses by whom he quotes. The similarity of their names induced Wolf ("Bibl. Hebr." iii., No. 1579d) to suppose the two poets to be identical.

BIBLIOGRAPHY: Fürst, *Bibl. Jud.* ii. 254; Kayserling, *Sephardim*, p. 262; idem, *Bibl. Esp.-Port.-Jud.* p. 64.

G. M. SEL.

LOCK. See KEY.

LOCUST: Of all the insects the locust is most frequently mentioned in the Old Testament. It occurs under the following nine names, which probably denote different species; but there is no certain clue by which the exact species intended by each name can be identified: (1) "arbeh" (A. V. sometimes "grasshopper"), the most common term, comprising the whole genus; (2) "sol'am," derived by Ibn Ezra from "sela'" = "rock" (rock-locust; A. V. "bald locust"); (3) "ḥargol" (A. V. "beetle"; R. V. "cricket"; Jewish exegetes, "grasshopper"; comp. Arabic "ḥarjal" = "a troop of horses," or "locust," from "ḥarjala" = "to hop," "to jump"); (4) "hagab" (A. V. usually "grasshopper"; seems likewise to be used in a general sense in Num. xiii. 33; Isa. xl. 22); (5) "ḥasil" (I Kings viii. 37; Ps. lxxviii. 46); (6) "gazam" (Joel i. 4; Amos iv. 9), usually rendered "palmer-worm"; (7) "yeleḳ" (Jer. li. 27; Nahum iii. 15; LXX. and Vulgate, "bronchos"; R. V. "canker-worm"); (8) "ẓelaẓal" (Deut. xxviii. 42) may be an onomatopœic designation of locusts in general; (9) "gebim" and "gobai" (Nahum iii. 17; Amos vii. 1; A. V. "grasshopper"; R. V. margin to the latter passage, "green worms") are probably also general terms. The first four species are enumerated among the "winged creeping things" which are allowed to be eaten, and are described as having "legs above their feet to leap withal upon the earth" (Lev. xi. 21 *et seq.*).

Upward of forty orthopterous insects have been discovered in Palestine. The *Acrydium lineola*, *A. peregrinum*, and the *Œdipoda migratoria* are counted among the most destructive, and are therefore the most dreaded.

The term "locusts" is sometimes used figuratively; *e.g.*, for swarming hordes and mighty hosts (Judges vi. 5, vii. 12; Jer. xlvi. 23; Prov. xxx. 28); for prancing horses (Joel ii. 4; Job xxxix. 20); as an emblem of voracious greed (Isa. xxxiii. 4; Amos vii. 1); of feebleness, insignificance, and perishableness (Num. xiii. 33; Isa. xl. 22; Ps. cix. 23; Nahum iii. 17).

The Talmud points out as the marks of the clean locust: four feet, two hopping legs, and four wings which are large enough to cover the body (Ḥul. 59a). Besides the species mentioned in the Old Testament the Talmud refers to many others (comp. Ḥul. 65). Public prayers were instituted against the plague of locusts (Ta'an. 14a, 19a). Some locusts, probably variegated, were the playthings of children (Shab. 90b). The egg of the ḥargol carried in the ear relieves earache (*ib.* 65a); while the left part of the "ẓipporat keramim" worn on the left side of the body preserves one's knowledge (*ib.* 90b; Tristram, "Nat. Hist." p. 306; Lewysohn, "Z. T." p. 285; Burckhardt, "Notes on the Bedouins," p. 269).

E. G. H. I. M. C.

LODÈVE: Small town in the department of Hérault, France. A Jewish community was founded here as early as the fifth century. It was under the jurisdiction of the bishop, to whom it paid an annual tax. In 1095 Bishop Bernard, in conformity with an old decision of the councils, forbade marriages between Jews and Christians, on pain of excommunication for the latter. In 1188 King Philip Augustus of France confirmed the bishop's rights and privileges relating to the Jews. Several Lodève Jews were living at Montpellier in 1293 and 1294, and at Perpignan in 1413 and 1414. A Paris manuscript (Bibliothèque Nationale, No. 242), containing Levi b. Gershon of Bagnol's commentary on Genesis and Exodus, refers to two rabbis of Lodève (לוטבה), Eleazar and Isaac קיטון or ביטון (= "Botin," according to Carmoly), or Isaac del Portal or de la Porte (מן השער). This name is probably derived from "Portale" (Latin, "Portalis"), in the department of Vaucluse. It may, however, be derived from "Portes," a village in the department of the Gard. A Jew named Isaac de Portes lived at Nîmes in 1306.

Rabbi Solomon Ezobi of Carpentras corresponded with the Bishop of Lodève, Jean Plantavit de la Pause, author of the work entitled "Planta Vitis seu Thesaurus Synonymicus Hebræo-Chaldæo-Rabbinicus"; about 1629 he addressed three Hebrew poems to the bishop.

BIBLIOGRAPHY: Carmoly, *Revue Orientale*, iii. 340; Dom Vaissète, *Histoire Générale de Languedoc*, vol. i., book xv.; vol. iii., book lxx.; Gross, *Gallia Judaica*, pp. 158, 274, 611; *R. E. J.* xiv. 66, 73, 75; xxii. 265; Saige, *Les Juifs du Languedoc*, vii. 3, 12, 14.

G. S. K.

LODZ (LODZI): City in the government of Piotrkow, Russian Poland, about 90 miles west of Warsaw. As late as 1821 it was only a village of 800 inhabitants, when the manufacture of woolens was first introduced there by Germans. Later, cotton-mills were added. The population of Lodz gradually increased until in 1872 it amounted to 50,500; and in 1876 it reached a total of nearly 80,000, including about 15,000 Jews.

Lodz is now considered the second city of Poland, both in population and in the importance of its cotton-mills; indeed, it is styled "the Manchester of Poland." The rapid growth of the city is due no more to the Germans than to the Jews, who introduced numerous spindles and hand-looms in almost every household, and, being satisfied with small profits, were able to compete with the largest manufacturers both in Moscow and in other cities of Russia. The expulsion of the Jews from Moscow in 1891 helped to increase the volume of business in Lodz. In 1898 the keen competition abroad compelled the Jewish merchants of Lodz to adopt desperate measures to retain business by making also a cheap grade of goods to imitate woolens. This new stuff was called "shoddy," being a mixture of waste from cotton and woolen stuffs which was formerly discarded as of no value. The Polish newspaper "Rozowj" lamented this new attempt of the Jews to "spoil the market."

Introduction of Shoddy.

The question of employing Jewish operatives was a very difficult one. In the first place, they could not subsist on the small wages paid to the mill-hands. Secondly, when the factories were built and machinery was introduced the Jews could not work together with non-Jewish operatives on Saturday, and the establishments were closed on Sunday. Israel Posnanski, the richest manufacturer of Lodz, in order to utilize Jewish labor, solved the problem by setting aside a factory for Jewish employees. Later, Rabbis Meisels and Jelski prevailed upon other Jewish manufacturers to open similar factories.

The Jewish community of Lodz was organized before Lodz was recognized as a town. Hillel, the first rabbi, died in 1823; his successor, Ezekiel, died in 1851; and the present (1904) rabbi, Elijah Ḥayyim Meisels, was elected in 1873.

There is in Russia no Reform congregation; but it has what is known as "German" congregations. These are attended by the rich members of the community; strict decorum is observed; a cantor with trained choir conducts the service; and an academical rabbi delivers his sermons in pure German or Russian. Lodz has such a congregation. Adolph M. Radin, now in New York, was elected its rabbi in 1884, and was succeeded by the present rabbi, Israel Jelski. The congregation completed its new temple in 1888 at a cost of 500,000 rubles.

Congregations and Synagogues.

There are two synagogues, one on the Old Bazaar and one in Wulke, the Jewish quarter. The leaders of the community are Michael Adolph Cohen, attorney at law; Herzberg; Pinkus; and Wachs.

The Hebrew Free School (Talmud Torah) has been under the management of Herman Konstadt since 1877. The Jewish hospital was founded by Israel Posnanski, who donated 40,000 rubles for it in 1879. The building was finished in 1883.

The Free Loan Society (Gemilut Ḥasadim) was organized in 1883 by J. S. Goldman and Isaac Mondiecki. In the same year Isaiah Rosenblatt established the Free Lodging Society (Haknasat Oreḥim). There are also a home for the aged (Bet Maḥseh li-Zeḳenim), and an asylum for poor girls. Marcus Silberstein is the founder of the Orphan Asylum, opened in 1895 with 64 children. The report of 1897 shows an average expenditure of 14,960 rubles per annum. A Hebrew technical school, organized by J. K. Posnanski, Bernhard Dobronicki, and S. Jarazinski, has an attendance of 300 pupils. The Jewish clerks employed in the factories formed a mutual aid society in 1896. Isidor Kempinski shortly before his death (1900) founded a secular school for Jewish children.

Institutions.

The Jews of Lodz have contributed liberally to charitable institutions abroad. For example, they gave 10,000 rubles to Rabbi Hildesheimer toward a Hebrew school for Russian Jewish immigrants in Berlin in 1883; and it is estimated that in the same year they expended in charity more than 1,000,000 rubles. They contributed also a large sum to help their Christian neighbors build a Russian church in Lodz.

Among the Jewish celebrities who are natives of Lodz is David Janowski, the champion chess-player of France. On his visit to his native city in 1900 the authorities recognized his successes by presenting him with a gold medal. The artists Herschenberg, Glitzenstein, and Pilichowski also were born in Lodz. The last-named received a gold medal at the Paris Exposition of 1900 for his painting "The Wandering Jew." Another gold medal was awarded to Emanuel Sadokierski of Lodz for excellency in bookbinding and for articles made of papier-mâché ("Currier Warszawski," 1900, No. 239). The Jews of Lodz, however, refused to send a manufacturing exhibit to the Paris Exposition, thereby marking their indignation at the proceedings in the Dreyfus affair. Among Jewish writers of Lodz are David Fischman, the Hebrew novelist, and Sarah Feige Foner, author of the Hebrew novels "Beged Bogedim" and "Ahabat Yesharim." She organized in Lodz the Bat Ẓiyyon Society for teaching girls the Hebrew language and Jewish history and literature.

Distinguished Natives.

The present (1904) population is about 300,000, including 75,000 Jews. The statistics of 1896 give 1,827 births, 1,856 deaths, and 564 marriages among the Jews of Lodz in that year.

H. R. J. D. E.

LOEB, ISIDORE: French scholar; born at Sulzmatt (Soultzmatt), Upper Alsace, Nov. 1, 1839; died at Paris, June 3, 1892. The son of Rabbi Seligmann Loeb of Sulzmatt, he was educated in Bible and Talmud by his father. After having followed the usual course in the public school of his native town, Loeb studied at the college of Rufach and at the lycée of Colmar, in which city he at the same time attended classes in Hebrew and Talmud at the preparatory rabbinical school founded by Chief Rabbi Solomon Klein. In 1856 he entered the Central Rabbinical School (Ecole Centrale Rabbinique) at Metz, where he soon ranked high through his knowledge of Hebrew, his literary ability, and his proficiency in mathematics. In 1862 he was graduated, and received his rabbinical diploma from the Séminaire Israélite de France at Paris, which had replaced (1859) the Metz Ecole Centrale Rabbinique.

Loeb did not immediately enter upon a rabbinical career, but tutored for some years, first at Bayonne and then at Paris. In 1865 he was called to the rabbinate of St. Etienne (Loire). His installation sermon, on the duties of the smaller congregations ("Les Devoirs des Petites Communautés"), is one of the best examples of French pulpit rhetoric.

Soon, however, he felt a desire to extend the field of his activity. He went to Paris, where he was appointed (June 1, 1869) secretary of the Alliance Israélite Universelle, which position he held until his death. It was largely due to Loeb's labors that this association became an important factor in the progress of Oriental Judaism; and he created the library of the Alliance, which is one of the most valuable Jewish libraries in existence. Meanwhile he continued his historical and philological researches, and developed an extensive literary activity. The chair of Jewish history in the Rabbinical Seminary of Paris having become vacant through the resignation of Albert Cohn (1878), Loeb was appointed his successor. He held this position for twelve years. His main activity, however, was devoted to the Société des Etudes Juives, which was organized in Paris in 1880. Beginning with the first number, he successfully edited the "Revue des Etudes Juives," the organ of that society, and was, moreover, a voluminous and brilliant contributor thereto.

Isidore Loeb.

The following works published by Loeb deserve especial notice: "La Situation des Israélites en Turquie, en Serbie, et en Roumanie" (1869); "Biographie d'Albert Cohn" (1878); "Tables du Calendrier Juif Depuis l'Ere Chrétienne Jusqu'au XXXe Siècle"; "Les Juifs de Russie" (1891); "La Littérature des Pauvres dans la Bible"; and "Réflexions sur les Juifs." The two last-named works have been published by the Société des Etudes Juives.

BIBLIOGRAPHY: I. Lévi, list of Loeb's works, in *R. E. J.* vol. xxiv.; Z. Kahn, biographical sketch, *ib.*

S. Z. K.

LOEB, JACQUES: American biologist; born in Germany April 7, 1859; educated at the universities of Berlin, Munich, and Strasburg (M.D. 1884). He took a postgraduate course at the universities of Strasburg and Berlin, and in 1886 became assistant at the physiological institute of the University of Würzburg, remaining there till 1888, when he went in a similar capacity to Strasburg. During his vacations he pursued biological researches, at Kiel in 1888, and at Naples in 1889 and 1890. In 1892 he was called to the University of Chicago as assistant professor of physiology and experimental biology, becoming associate professor in 1895, and professor of physiology in 1899. In 1902 he was called to fill a similar chair at the University of California.

The main subjects of his works are: animal tropisms and their relation to the instincts of animals; heteromorphosis, *i.e.*, substitution at will of one organ of an animal for another; toxic and antitoxic effects of ions; artificial parthenogenesis; and hybridization of the eggs of sea-urchins by the sperm of starfish.

Among Loeb's works may be mentioned: "Heliotropismus der Thiere und Seine Identität mit dem Heliotropismus der Pflanzen," Würzburg, 1889; "Physiologische Morphologie," part i., *ib.* 1890; part ii., *ib.* 1891; "Vergleichende Physiologie des Gehirns und Vergleichende Psychologie," Leipsic, 1899; edition in English, New York, 1900.

A. F. T. H.

LOEB, LOUIS: American artist; born at Cleveland, Ohio, Nov. 7, 1866. At the age of thirteen he was apprenticed to a lithographer in his native city, and in 1885 went to New York, where he studied in the night-schools of the Art Students' League, of which he became vice-president in 1889. Loeb went to Paris in 1890, and studied under Gérôme, obtaining honorable mention at the Paris Salon in 1895, and third medal in 1897.

From 1893 Loeb contributed to the chief magazines of the United States some of their most important illustrations. He is a member of the Society of American Artists and associate of the National Academy of Design, and has contributed many noteworthy paintings to their exhibitions. Among the most important are the portraits of I. Zangwill (1898), J. H. Schiff (1904), Eleanor Robson (1904); and the following pictures: "Temple of the Winds," 1896 (silver medal, Pan-American Exposition, Buffalo, 1903); "The Breeze" (1900); "The Joyous Life" (1903); and "The Dawn," 1903 (Webb prize).

BIBLIOGRAPHY: *Who's Who in America*; *The Bookman*, Feb., 1900.

A.

LOEB, MORRIS: American chemist; born at Cincinnati, Ohio, May 23, 1863; son of Solomon Loeb; educated at the New York College of Pharmacy and at the universities of Harvard, Berlin, Heidelberg, and Leipsic. In 1888 he became private assistant to Professor Gibbs of Newport, R. I., and a year later docent at Clark University, Worcester, Mass. He has been professor of chemistry at New York University since 1891, and director of the chemical laboratory there since 1894.

Loeb has largely occupied himself with matters of Jewish interest and holds offices in many charitable associations and other communal organizations. He is president of the Hebrew Technical Institute, president of the (N. Y.) Hebrew Charities Building Fund, director of the Jewish Theological Seminary of America and of the Educational Alliance (1892–97). He is the author of various scientific articles, chiefly on physical and inorganic chemistry.

A.

LOEWE, LOUIS: English Orientalist and theologian; born at Zülz, Prussian Silesia, 1809; died in London 1888. He was educated at the yeshibot of Lissa, Nikolsburg, Presburg, and at the University of Berlin. Stopping at Hamburg on his way to London, he was entrusted with the classification of the Oriental coins in the Sprewitz cabinet. Soon after his arrival in London he was introduced to the Duke of Sussex, who in 1839 appointed him his "Orientalist." He then traveled in the East, where he studied Arabic, Persian, Coptic, Nubian, Turkish, and Circassian. In Cairo he was presented to the khedive, Mohammed Ali Pasha, for whom he translated some hieroglyphic inscriptions. While in Palestine he was attacked by Bedouins, who took everything he had with him, including his collections and note-books. On his return he met at Rome Sir Moses and Lady Montefiore, who invited him to travel with them to the Holy Land. When in 1840 Sir Moses went on his Damascus expedition, Loewe accompanied him as his interpreter. In the firman granted for the relief of the accused, Loewe discovered that the word "pardon" ("'afw") was used instead of "acquittal," and it was due to Sir Moses' exertions that the change to "acquittal" was made.

Altogether, Loewe accompanied Sir Moses Montefiore on nine different philanthropic missions. When Jews' College was opened in 1856, he was nominated principal; and when Sir Moses Montefiore opened a theological college at Ramsgate in 1869, he made his friend principal of that institution, which position Loewe retained until three years after the death of his patron.

Loewe wrote: "The Origin of the Egyptian Language," London, 1837; a translation of J. B. Levinsohn's "Efes Dammim," *ib.* 1841; a translation of David Nieto's "Maṭṭeh Dan," *ib.* 1842 (awarded the York Medal); "Observations on a Unique Coptic Gold Coin," 1849; a dictionary of the Circassian language, 1854; as well as several sermons and a Nubian grammar (the latter still in manuscript).

Bibliography: *Celebrities of the Day*, April, 1881; J. H. Loewe, *A Catalogue of the Library of the Late Dr. L. Loewe*, 1890.

J. H. Hir.

LOEWE, LUDWIG: German manufacturer, philanthropist, and member of the Reichstag; born at Heiligenstadt Nov. 27, 1837; died at Berlin Sept. 11, 1886. The son of a poor teacher, he attended the gymnasium in his native city, and then went to Berlin. While still a young man he accidentally made the acquaintance of Ferdinand Lassalle before the period of the latter's socialistic agitation, and was admitted to his brilliant social circle.

Loewe first entered upon a mercantile career as a dealer in woolens, then became a machinist, and in 1864 established a manufactory of sewing-machines in Berlin. In 1870 he visited the United States to study the construction of machinery, and on his return to Germany founded a factory for the production of tool-machinery in accordance with American methods, utilizing American machinery that had never before been introduced into Germany. He brought the manufacture to such a pitch of perfection that the Prussian War Department arranged with him for the establishment of a factory for the production of weapons. Under a guaranty from the government, Loewe established a remarkable plant to supply not only weapons for the army, but also machinery for expositions.

From 1864 until his death Loewe was a member of the Berlin Municipal Council, and was particularly influential in developing the school system. He was elected a member of the Prussian Abgeordnetenhaus in 1876, and two years later a member of the Reichstag; here he identified himself at first with the "Fortschrittspartei," being a devoted follower of Johann Jacoby, and afterward with the progressive party ("Deutsch-Freisinnige"). Subsequently his contracts with the government in connection with the furnishing of small arms were the subject of calumnious animadversions by the anti-Semite Hermann Ahlwardt. Loewe having died, his brother Isidor, then at the head of the firm, insisted upon a complete investigation, which resulted in the demonstration of the utter baselessness of the charges made by the anti-Semitic leader. These charges were nothing less than that the Loewes were members of an international Jewish conspiracy to secure control of the entire world; that the greatest obstacle to gratifying this ambition being the obstinacy of the Germans, the surest means of breaking that obstinacy was by the defeat of the Germans in war; that this could be most effectually secured by arming the German soldiers with defective weapons; and that to this end the Loewes had, by fraud and bribery, foisted upon the German military authorities nearly half a million guns that would explode in battle, maiming and disabling those who carried them and frightening their comrades, thus causing stampedes and routs.

Loewe was for some time president of the Jewish congregation in Berlin.

Bibliography: *Allg. Zeit. des Jud.* 1886, pp. 614-615, 632-638; Ahlwardt, *Neue Enthüllungen: Judenflinten*, Dresden, 1892; *Judenflinten*, part ii., *ib.* 1892.

S. M. Co.

LOEWENTHAL, EDUARD: German writer and editor; born March 12, 1836, at Ernsbach, Württemberg; educated at the high school at Stuttgart and at the University of Tübingen, where he studied jurisprudence and philosophy (Ph.D. 1859). He founded at Frankfort-on-the-Main the "Allgemeine Deutsche Universitätszeitung" and became assistant editor on Max Wirth's "Der Arbeitgeber." Soon afterward he became editor of Payne's "Die Glocke" at Leipsic, and established there the "Zeitgeist." In 1873 he became editor-in-chief of the "Neue Freie Zeitung," and in the following year founded the Deutscher Verein für Internationale Friedenspropaganda.

After having served two terms in prison as the result of press lawsuits, Loewenthal went to Brussels, London (where he remained for a year), and Paris. In the last-named city he founded the "Weltbühne, Deutsche Pariser Zeitung," and a French monthly, "Le Monde de l'Esprit." In 1888 he returned to Berlin, Emperor Frederick III. having proclaimed an amnesty for political offenders.

Among Loewenthal's works may be mentioned: "System und Gesch. des Naturalismus" (6th ed. 1868; Engl. transl. 1897); "Gesetz der Sphärischen Molekularbewegung" (also an English edition); "Napoleon III. and the Commune of Paris" (drama); "Eine Religion ohne Bekenntniss" (1865); "Der Militarismus als Ursache der Massenverarmung" (1868; translated into French, at the expense of the Société des Amis de la Paix, 1869); "Grundzüge zur Reform und Kodification des Völkerrechts" (1872; translated into English and French); "Le Cogitantisme ou la Religion Scientifique" (1886); "Der Staat Bellamy's und Seine Nachfolger" (1892); "Grundriss der Gesch. der Philosophie" (1896); "Die Religiöse Bewegung im 19. Jahrhundert" (1900); "Die Fulguro-Genesis im Gegensatz zur Evolutionstheorie" (1902); "Gesch. der Friedensbewegung" (1903).

s. L. La.

LOEWY, EMANUEL: Austrian archeologist; born at Vienna Sept. 1, 1857; educated at the gymnasium and university of his native city (Ph.D. 1882). He is now (1904) professor of archeology at the University of Rome.

Loewy is the author of: "Untersuchungen zur Griechischen Künstlergeschichte" (1883); "Inschriften Griechischer Bildhauer" (1885); "Lysipp und Seine Stellung in der Griechischen Plastik" (1891); "Die Naturwiedergabe in der Aeltesten Griechischen Kunst" (1900).

s. F. T. H.

LOEWY, MAURICE: Astronomer; born at Vienna, Austria, April 15, 1833. A descendant of a Hungarian family, he received his education at his native city, where he was employed at the observatory. In 1860 he was called to the Paris Observatory as assistant astronomer, being appointed astronomer in 1864. In 1865 he became a French citizen. In 1872 he was appointed a member of the Bureau des Longitudes; in 1873 he was elected to the French Institute (Académie des Sciences); in the same year he became assistant director and in 1896 director of the Paris Observatory.

Maurice Loewy.

Loewy since 1878 has been editor of "Ephémérides des Etoiles de Culmination Lunaire," and since 1896 of the "Rapport Annuel sur l'Etat de l'Observatoire de Paris." He invented several important astronomical instruments, among which is especially well known his "equatorial coudé" or elbow-telescope, with which he secured the best photographs of the moon. He published with Puiseux since 1896 the "Atlas Photographique de la Lune."

Among Loewy's numerous essays and works may be mentioned: "Nouvelles Méthodes pour la Détermination des Orbites des Comètes," 1879; "Des Eléments Fondamentaux de l'Astronomie," 1886; "De la Constance de l'Aberration et de la Réfraction," 1890; "Du Coefficient de l'Elasticité," 1892 (with Tresca); "De la Latitude et des Positions Absolues des Etoiles Fondamentales," 1895. Loewy's "Memoires" have been published in the "Comptes Rendus de l'Académie des Sciences" and in the "Annales de l'Observatoire." He died Oct. 15, 1907.

Bibliography: Curinier, *Dict. Nat.* iii. 12; *La Grande Encyclopédie*, xxii. 415; *Nouveau Larousse Illustré*, v. 730; *Meyers Konversations-Lexikon*.

s. F. T. H.

LOGIC: The science of correct thinking; the science of the principles governing the comparative and constructive faculties in the pursuit and use of truth. Although, judging from the principles that were propounded by the Tannaim for the deduction of halakot from the Biblical text, it can be surmised that the Rabbis were acquainted with the laws of syllogisms, analogies, etc., no mention of logical science is made in Jewish literature prior to the Judæo-Arabic period (see Talmud). It was only with the transplantation of the Arabo-Greek philosophy to Jewish soil that the Aristotelian "Organon," as propounded by the Arabs, became the vade-mecum of every Jewish student, and was regarded as indispensable to the acquisition of metaphysical and psychological knowledge. The Hebrew terms adopted for "logic" were חכמת הדבר, which is the literal translation of the Arabic "'ilm al-kalam," and חכמת ההגיון, corresponding to the Arabic "'ilm al-manṭiḳ," each signifying both "the science of speech" and "the science of thinking." The term "hokmat higgayon" was, according to Shem-Ṭob ("Sefer ha-Emunot," p. 45), first so employed by the Tibbonides. It is found also in the Talmud, but in the sense of "recitation." Eliezer said to his pupils, "Restrain your children from הגיון" (Ber. 28b), intending thereby to warn them against parading a superficial knowledge of the Bible gained by verbal memorization. The anti-Maimonists, however, interpreted the word "higgayon" in the sense of "logic," and saw in Eliezer's saying a warning against the study of that science.

First Jewish Work on Logic.

The first work on logic written by a Jew was the "Maḳalah fi Ṣana'at al-Manṭiḳ" of Maimonides (12th cent.), translated into Hebrew by Moses ibn Tibbon under the title "Millot ha-Higgayon." It is divided into fourteen chapters containing explanations of 175 logical terms. The Hebrew terminology used by the translator has been adopted by all subsequent writers on Hebrew philosophical literature. The eight books of the "Organon," without counting Porphyry's introduction, are enumerated. The "Millot ha-Higgayon" was first published with two anonymous commentaries at Venice in 1552, and has since passed through fourteen editions. Commentaries upon it were written by Mordecai Comtino (15th cent.) and by Moses Mendelssohn. A Latin translation was published by Sebastian Münster (Basel, 1527); and German ones were made by M. S. Neumann (Venice, 1822) and Heilberg (Breslau, 1828).

During the thirteenth and fourteenth centuries Jewish literature was enriched with several writings on logic. The works of Al-Farabi and of Averroes were translated and commented upon; and the translations have survived the originals. Of Al-Farabi's essays on logic the following are still extant in Hebrew manuscripts in various European libraries: the introduction (Arabic, "Tauṭiyah"; Hebr. הצעה), in three versions; the "Isagoge of Porphyry"; "Hermeneutics"; "Posterior Analytics," the translation of which is attributed to Moses ibn Tibbon; "Topics," in two versions; and "Syllogisms," an abridgment of which was made by Jacob ben Abba Mari Anatoli under the title "Sefer Heḳesh Ḳaẓer." A commentary on Al-Farabi's five chapters on logic was written in the fifteenth century by the Karaite Abraham Bali. Of Averroes' Short Commentary there are two Hebrew versions: one made by Jacob ben Machir of Montpellier in 1189 and published under the title "Kol Meleket Higgayon" at Riva di Trenta in 1559, and the other made by Samuel Marsili ben Judah of Tarascon in 1329. A Latin translation of Jacob ben Machir's version was made by Abraham de Balmes. A commentary on the Short Commentary was written by Moses Narboni (1340–55). Of Averroes' Middle Commentaries those on Porphyry's introduction, "Categories," "Interpretation," "Syllogisms," and "Demonstration" were translated by Jacob ben Abba Mari Anatoli; on "Topics" and "Sophistical Refutations," by Kalonymus ben Kalonymus of Arles in 1313; on "Rhetoric" and "Poetics" by Todros Todrosi of Trinquetaille in 1337. Anatoli's translation of the first five books was used by Joseph Caspi, who wrote an abridgment of the books on logic under the title "Ẓeror ha-Kesef." A translation from the Greek of Aristotle's logic was made in the fourteenth century by Shemariah ben Elijah Ikriti of Negropont. At the end of the same century Joseph ben Moses Kilti treated, in his work "Minḥat Yehudah," of Aristotle's logic in the fashion of the aphorisms of Hippocrates. Shortly after appeared a work on Aristotle's logic written by Elijah ben Eliezer of Candia. Another original work of the same period was the "Kelale Higgayon" of David ibn Bilia.

Translations of Al-Farabi.

Averroes' Middle Commentaries were much commented upon during the fourteenth and fifteenth centuries. The oldest supercommentary known is that found in the Vatican Library (MS. No. 337). It dates from 1316 and deals with Porphyry's "Isagoge," "Categories," and "Hermeneutics." The other known supercommentaries of the fourteenth century are those of: Jedaiah Bedersi, mentioned by Moses Ḥabib; Levi ben Gershon, a Latin translation of which is still extant in manuscript in the Vatican Library (see "Atti dell' Academia dei Nuovi Lincei," Rome, 1863); Judah ben Samuel Abbas; and Abraham Abigdor ben Meshullam (Bonet). A rimed résumé of Porphyry's introduction and the "Categories" was given by Moses Rieti in his "Miḳdash Me'aṭ."

To the writings on logic of the fifteenth century belong: the supercommentary on Averroes' Middle Commentaries, and the abridgment of Logic, entitled "Miklol Yofi," by Messer Leon (Judah ben Jehiel); the abridgment of the "Categories," "Syllogisms," and "Demonstration" by Abraham Farissol; the commentary on the "Isagoge" by Joseph ben Shem-Ṭob; the commentaries on the "Isagoge," "Categories," and "Interpretation" by Elijah Habillo; the annotations on Averroes' Middle Commentary on the "Categories" and "Interpretation" by Manoah Sho'ali; and several anonymous commentaries on various books on logic. A supercommentary on the "Posterior Analytics" was written by Abraham Bibago. Of Averroes' questions on the "Organon," contained in the "Masa'il fi al-Ḥikmah," one portion was translated by Kalonymus ben Kalonymus, and the whole by Samuel ben Meshullam in 1320 under the title "Ha-She'elot ha-Dibriyyot weha-Derushim Asher le-Pilusufim." A commentary on two portions was written by Levi ben Gershon. From Samuel's translation proceeded the Latin version made by Abraham de Balmes, which was first published in 1550. Another Latin translation of six portions was made by Elijah Delmedigo. Samuel ben Judah translated into Hebrew other questions on logic proceeding from the Arabic writers Abu al-Ḳasim ben Idris, Abu al-Ḥajjaj ibn Ṭalmus, Abu al-'Abbas Aḥmad ben Ḳasim, and 'Abd al-Raḥman ben Ṭahir. These questions also were rendered into Latin by Abraham de Balmes. An original writer on logic of the fifteenth century was Mordecai Comtino.

Commentaries on Logic.

Like the other branches of philosophy, the study of logic has since the sixteenth century been neglected by the Jews, and no important work on this science has been published in Hebrew. Among the Jewish logicians of modern times the most notable was Solomon Maimon, who wrote "Versuch Einer Neuen Logik" (Berlin, 1794), in which he attempted to expound an algebraic or symbolic system of logic.

BIBLIOGRAPHY: Munk, *Mélanges*, p. 108 *et passim*; Renan, *Averroès et l'Averroïsme*, pp. 184 *et seq.*; Steinschneider, *Hebr. Uebers.* pp. 43 *et seq.*; idem, *Al-Farabi*, Index.

J. I. Br.

LOGOS, THE. See MEMRA; PHILO; WISDOM.

LOLLI, DAVID: Italian physician; born at Göritz 1825; died at Triest 1884; son of Samuel Vita Lolli; studied medicine at Padua and Vienna. On the outbreak of the Italian war for liberation he abandoned his studies, hastened to Padua to join the volunteers, took part in the unsuccessful attempt to hold Vicenza, and then joined the garrison guarding Venice. When the cholera broke out in the besieged city, Lolli also was stricken. On his recovery he returned to his native city, but subsequently established himself as a physician at Triest. He continued to agitate for the independence of Italy (in which he included Göritz and Triest), and often incurred great danger in consequence.

Lolli wrote much, especially on psychology and magnetism. Most of his works remained in manuscripts; but the following were published: "Sul Magnetismo Animale, Pubblicato Nell' Occasione di Conseguire la Laurea," Padua, 1850; "Sulla Migliare, Due Parole di Occasione," Triest, 1857; "Sii Forte e Sarai Libero (Seneca): Sii Libero e Sarai Forte," Milan, 1860, published anonymously for political reasons; "I Numi," Milan, 1866, a symbolical story, published under the pseudonym "Aldo Apocalissio"; "Sul Cholera," Triest, 1866; and "L'Amore dal Lato Fisiologico, Filosofico, e Sociale," Milan, 1883.

S. E. L.

LOLLI, EUDE: Italian rabbi; born at Göritz Aug. 23, 1826; died at Padua, Dec. 15, 1904; educated in his native town and at the rabbinical college of Padua, graduating thence in 1854. In 1865 he was appointed professor of the college, a position he held until the institution was definitely closed in 1871. In 1869 he was elected chief rabbi of Padua, and in 1877 he became lecturer in, and in 1886 professor of, Hebrew and Chaldaic at the University of Padua.

Lolli was the author of: "Dizionario del Linguaggio Ebraico-Rabbinico," Padua, 1869; "Prelezione ad un Corso di Lingua Ebraica e Caldaica," 1877; "Corso di Grammatica della Lingua Ebraica," *ib.* 1878. He also contributed a large portion to S. D. Luzzatto's "La Sacra Bibbia Volgarizzata," Rovigo, 1872. He died Dec. 15, 1904.

BIBLIOGRAPHY: De Gubernatis, *Diz. Biog.*
S. F. T. H.

LOM (LOM-PALANK): Town in Bulgaria, situated at the mouth of the River Lom. It has a population of about 8,000, of which approximately 700 are Jews, chiefly artisans and traders in grain. On March 20, 1904, a riot broke out against the Jews in connection with the disappearance of a young Bulgarian, whom the Jews were accused of murdering for ritual purposes. Through the timely measures taken by the government, a massacre was averted, and the riot subsided after a number of stores and dwelling-houses and the synagogue had been sacked. The young Bulgarian was afterward found drowned.

BIBLIOGRAPHY: *Entziklopedicheski Slovar*, xvii. 945, St. Petersburg, 1895; *Budushchnost*, 1904, Nos. 13–14.
D. A. S. W.

LOMAZY: Town in the district of Bialy, near Brest-Litovsk, Russia. Though in 1566 there was no Jew among its 400 house-owners, its customs revenues were farmed out to Jews. In 1589 the customs and mills were leased to the Jews Leibka, Wolfovich, and Itzka. According to Samuel ben Phoebus ("Ṭiṭ ha-Yawen") 200 Jews were killed in Lomazy during the Cossack uprising (1648–49). In 1897 the Jews of Lomazy numbered 1,100 in a total population of 3,200.

BIBLIOGRAPHY: *Russko-Yevreiski Arkhiv*, ii., No. 232; *Regesty*, i., Nos. 669, 671; Samuel ben Phoebus, *Ṭiṭ ha-Yawen*.
H. R. G. D. R.

LOMBROSO (LUMBROSO): Sephardic family, members of which lived in Tunis, Marseilles, and Italy. The two forms of the family name are doubtless due to different readings of the Hebrew לומברוזו.

Abram Lumbroso, Baron: Tunisian physician and scientist; born in Tunis 1813; died in Florence 1887. After completing his classical studies in Florence and receiving his M.D. degree at Pisa, he became physician-in-chief to the Bey of Tunis and afterward director of the state sanitary service. In 1846 he accompanied the bey to Paris, receiving from King Louis Philippe the Order of the Legion of Honor.

In Tunis Lumbroso founded a scientific society, of which he was president; and he was one of the most ardent assistants of the bey, who was interested in the promotion of culture. Lumbroso distinguished himself not only by his skill as a physician, but also by his philanthropic acts. As a reward for his valuable services during the cholera epidemic, rendered to foreigners and to natives without regard to sect or creed, King Victor Emanuel II. of Italy bestowed upon him the title of baron, with remainder to his eldest son. He was decorated also by the Sultan of Turkey with the Order of the Medjidie.

Of Lumbroso's published works may be cited: "Schizzo Storico Scientifico sul Colera Asiatico che Invase la Reggenza di Tunisi nel 1849 e 1850," Marseilles, 1850; "Lettere Medico-Statistiche sulla Reggenza di Tunisi," *ib.* 1850.

BIBLIOGRAPHY: De Gubernatis, *Piccolo Dizionario dei Contemporanei*, Rome, 1895; *Resoconto sulle Opere del Barone Dr. Abram Lumbroso Letta all' Accademia Reale di Medicina di Torino nel Anno 1866.*

David Lumbroso: Tunisian political agent; born in Tunis 1817; died in Leghorn 1880. He was a highly respected merchant in the Italian colony of the former city, and was much trusted by the Tunisian government, to which he was of service on many critical occasions.

Giacomo Lumbroso: Brother of Abram Lumbroso; head of a prominent business house at Marseilles, where he was consul for Tunis till the latter came under the protectorate of France.

Giacomo Lumbroso, Baron: Son of Abram Lumbroso. He studied law in Tunis, graduating with honors, but devoted himself principally to historical and archeologic researches, upon which he has written many important works. He was professor of ancient history, first in the University of Pisa and afterward in that of Rome. He resigned the latter position and retired to private life. Baron Giacomo is a member of the Accademia dei Lincei.

BIBLIOGRAPHY: De Gubernatis, *Piccolo Dizionario dei Contemporanei*, Rome, 1895.

Giacomo Lumbroso: Italian physician; born in Leghorn 1859. He was privat-docent in neuropathology and electrotherapeutics at the Institute of Florence, and physician-in-chief at the united royal hospitals of Leghorn.

BIBLIOGRAPHY: De Gubernatis, *Piccolo Dizionario dei Contemporanei*, Rome, 1895.
S. E. L.

Isaac Lumbroso: Chief rabbi of Tunis and rabbinical author; died in 1752. He was prominent in the Tunisian Jewry, being judge of the community about 1710—an epoch coinciding with the schism which divided the Jews of the city into two camps, native Tunisians and Gournis or Italians. Lumbroso was appointed rabbinical judge of the latter; and, being a man of means, he filled at the same time the position of receiver of taxes to the bey as well as that of caid, being the representative official of his community.

From a literary point of view, Lumbroso, who was one of the most brilliant pupils of Rabbi Ẓemaḥ Ẓarfati, was the most important among the Tunisian rabbis of the eighteenth century. He encouraged and generously assisted his fellow rabbis; and his reputation as a Talmudist and cabalist has survived to the present day.

Lumbroso was the author of "Zera' Yiẓḥaḳ," published posthumously at Tunis in 1768. This work, the only one which has as yet been printed in that city, is a commentary on the different sections of the Talmud. Several funeral orations, pronounced by Lumbroso on divers occasions, are appended thereto.

BIBLIOGRAPHY: Cazès, *Notes Bibliographiques*, pp. 240-246.

S. S. M. Fr.

Isaac Vita Lumbroso: Father of Abram Lumbroso; born in Tunis 1793; died in Leghorn 1871. He was well known because of his philanthropy. For thirty years he was president of the Portuguese consistory in Tunis, and for four years judge of the Court of Appeals.

S. E. L.

Jacob Lombroso: Italian rabbi and physician, of Spanish origin; lived at the beginning of the seventeenth century in Venice, where he published a notable Bible having an exhaustive introduction and explanations together with Spanish translations of the more difficult passages. By some he is considered to be the author of the "Propugnaculum Judaismi," written in defense of Judaism against the attacks in the fifth book of Grotius' "De Veritate Religionis Christianæ." Mortara, however ("Indice," p. 35), observes that Lombroso himself ascribes this work to Isaac Orobio.

BIBLIOGRAPHY: De Rossi, *Dizionario*.

D. E. L.

LOMBROSO, CESARE: Italian alienist and criminologist; born Nov. 18, 1835, at Verona. Both his paternal and his maternal ancestors belonged to the tribe of Levi. On his father's side he was descended from a family which for many generations had been rich in rabbis and Hebraists. His maternal ancestors were chiefly manufacturers and bankers who had long been established at Chieri, Piedmont. But in this branch of his family, also, there were many men of great talent, among others the poet David Levi, who took an important part in the Italian struggle for liberty, first as a Carbonaro, and afterward as a deputy.

Cesare Lombroso.

Under Professor Marzolo, Lombroso studied Hebrew, Aramaic, Arabic, and Chinese, intending to devote himself wholly to philology. He afterward studied medicine at Padua, Paris, and Vienna, and from the very beginning showed an especial preference for the study of insanity. While still a student he wrote two essays—one on insanity in antiquity, and one on the insanity of Cardan—in which, for the first time, was pointed out the connection between madness and genius.

Lombroso served as physician in the Austro-Italian war (1859). The scientific results of his military service were two papers on amputation (which were awarded the Riberi prize, the only official academic reward he has ever received), and a work on Calabrian folk-lore, which subject he had an opportunity of studying after the conclusion of peace, when he and his regiment were transferred to Calabria. As this regiment was composed of soldiers from all parts of Italy, Lombroso took advantage of the opportunity thus afforded him to study the ethnical types of the Italian people, and to lay the foundation for an ethnographical-anthropological chart of Italy. Some time later he was sent from Calabria to Pavia, where he asked permission to visit the insane asylum regularly, in order to acquire greater knowledge in his specialty. This permission being refused, he abandoned the military career.

Studies in Ethnology.

His experience during the following year was a very trying one. He taught at the University of Pavia, and served as a physician in the insane asylum; but in both cases he gave his services gratuitously; and at night, in order to earn a bare subsistence, he had to make translations from the German. It was under such circumstances that he produced, among other works, his Italian edition of Moleschott's well-known work, "Kreislauf des Lebens," under the title "Il Circuito della Materia." At length, after a year of extreme want, he was made professor of psychiatry at Pavia, with a yearly salary of 2,000 francs ($400), at that time a very considerable sum to him. His first two pamphlets, which he wrote during two sleepless nights, deal with genius and madness, and contain in embryo all the ideas afterward developed in his great work "L'Uomo di Genio" (see below). During the first year of his professorship he wrote "L'Uomo Bianco e l'Uomo di Colore," a work treating of the development of the human race, which development is conceived entirely from the point of view of the theory of evolution, and is filled with Darwinian ideas, although at that time Lombroso knew neither Darwin nor Herbert Spencer.

In Pavia, also, Lombroso began his studies of pellagra, a peculiar skin-disease prevalent in northern Italy and the origin of which was totally unknown. He showed conclusively that it was due to a poison developed in old, moldy corn, the only food of the poor agricultural laborers of the country. On account of his discovery of the real cause of this malady he was denounced by the landed proprietary to the government as a madman; and it was demanded that he should be deprived of his professorship. Years later, however, his theory of pellagra was accepted by the whole profession. On the skull of a criminal executed at Pavia, he noticed the fossa occipitalis media, an atavic feature which he was the first to observe.

Lombroso was transferred from Pavia University to that of Turin, where he is now (1904) professor of psychiatry and medical jurisprudence. He made a collection of criminals' skulls and photographs, of writings and works of art by lunatics and condemned criminals, as well as of prison appliances, which is one of the most extensive and instructive of its kind. He has many disciples, who are called collectively in Italy "La Scuola Lombrosiana." Many of these (*e.g.*, Enrico Ferri, Baron Garofalo Roncoroni, Patrizi, Ferrero, Zerboglio, and Carrara) have as a result of their investigations attained to national and even world-wide renown.

Lombroso's name is chiefly connected with two theories: (1) that genius is a peculiar, psychical form of larvate epilepsy; (2) that there is a degenerate class of human beings, distinguished by anatomical and psychical characteristics, who are born with criminal instincts and who represent a reversion to a very primitive form of humanity. He made a rich collection of materials for the investigation of his theory that genius is a form of epilepsy. Both he and his pupils carefully studied the best-known geniuses of all nations, ages, and spheres of activity; they brought together everything pertaining to their lives, works, appearance, hereditary characteristics, illnesses, idiosyncrasies, habits, etc., and noted all traits that could make it seem probable that the subjects had suffered from epileptic disturbances.

Theories of Genius and Crime.

In his theory of the born criminal, Lombroso recognized crime as a phenomenon of degeneration, and placed the criminal among those abnormal types of the human species which, according as their development is either defective or excessive, present examples of atavism or of evolution—*i.e.*, become on the one hand idiots or criminals; on the other, saints, martyrs, altruists, revolutionists, artists, or poets. The effect of this theory was felt chiefly in the field of criminal jurisdiction. It gave rise to a distinct science—criminal anthropology; and it effected a revolution in the mode of viewing both the criminal and the crime which has found expression in the newer penal codes.

Of Lombroso's works may be mentioned: "L'Uomo Delinquente in Rapporto alla Antropologia, alla Giurisprudenza ed alle Discipline Carcerarie" (3 vols., 4th ed. Turin, 1889; German transl. by Fränkel, "Der Verbrecher in Anthropologischer, Aerztlicher und Juristischer Beziehung," 2 vols., Hamburg, 1887–90; Atlas, 1895); "L'Uomo di Genio" (*ib.* 1889; 6th ed. 1894; German transl. by Fränkel, "Der Geniale Mensch," Hamburg, 1890; translated into French, Spanish, Portuguese, Russian, etc.); (with Guglielmo Ferrero, afterward Lombroso's son-in-law) "La Donna Delinquente" (*ib.* 1893; German transl. "Das Weib als Verbrecherin und Prostituirte," Hamburg, 1894); (with Laschi) "Il Delitto Politico" (2 vols., *ib.* 1890); "Le Crime, Causes et Remèdes"; "L'Antisemitismo e le Scienze Moderne" (*ib.* 1894; German ed., Leipsic, 1894); "Grafologia" (Milan, 1894); "Gli Anarchisti" (*ib.* 1894; German transl., Hamburg, 1895).

Lombroso was associate editor of the "Archivio di Psichiatria, Antropologia Criminale e Scienze Penali." He died Oct. 19, 1909.

Bibliography: Gubernatis, *Ecrivains du Jour*; *La Grande Encyclopédie*; *Meyers Konversations-Lexikon*; Kurella, *Cesare Lombroso und die Naturgeschichte des Verbrechens*, Hamburg, 1892.

S. M. N.

LOMZA (LOMZHA): Capital of the government of Lomza, Russian Poland; situated on the left bank of the River Narev. In 1897 it had a total population of 26,075, including 9,822 Jews. The earliest known references to an organized Jewish community in Lomza date from the beginning of the nineteenth century. The first rabbi recorded is Solomon Zalman Ḥasid, a cabalist, who corresponded with Akiba Eger. He was rabbi of the Lomza community for thirty years, and died there about 1840. He was succeeded by R. Benjamin Diskin (who officiated until 1848) and the latter, by his son Joshua Löb Diskin (b. Grodno 1818; d. Jerusalem 1898). Abraham Samuel Diskin, another son of Benjamin Diskin, was born at Lomza in 1827, and became rabbi of Volkovisk (government of Grodno), where he died in 1887. He was the author of "Leb Binyamin." Joshua Löb Diskin was succeeded by R. Elijah Ḥayyim Meisels, now (1904) rabbi at Lodz. The fifth rabbi was Eliezer Simḥah Rabinowitz (1879), now at Kalvariya. The present rabbi is Malchiel Ẓebi Tennenbaum, author of "Dibre Malkiel."

In 1884 a destructive fire rendered eighty families homeless. In 1885 a yeshibah was established in Lomza by R. Eliezer Shulawitz, the pupil of R. Israel Salanter. The institution is attended by hundreds of boys, who are provided there with food and clothing. Among the prominent members of the Lomza community may be mentioned Dr. Ephraim Edelstein, son-in-law of Lazar Rosenthal of Yasenovka.

Besides the general schools, Lomza has special Jewish schools, including 20 ḥadarim (430 pupils), and 1 Talmud Torah (180 pupils). The yeshibah has about 250 students. The charitable institutions include a hospital, a poor-house, a free-loan association, and a society for aiding the poor. Manufacturing and trading have been but little developed in Lomza. In 1897 there were 1,327 Jewish artisans there.

Bibliography: *Ha-Asif*, i., iv. 5; *Ha-Ẓefirah*, 1877, No. 11; 1879, No. 26; 1883, No. 31; 1884, p. 266; 1887, p. 10; 1889, p. 1133.

H. R. J. G. L.—S. J.

LONDON: Capital city of England. According to William of Malmesbury, William the Conqueror brought certain Jews from Rouen to London about 1070; and there is no evidence of their earlier existence in England. Besides these settlers from Rouen, London was visited by Jews from the Rhine valley, one of whom, from Mayence, had a friendly dispute, about 1107, with Gilbert Crispin, Abbot of Westminster. Another Jew was even converted to Christianity by Anselm ("Opera," III., epist. cxvii.). The earliest reference to a collective Jewish settlement is in the "Terrier of St. Paul's," of about 1115, where mention is made of some land in the "Jew street," which from its description corresponds to a part of Old Jewry. In 1130 the Jews of London incurred a fine of £2,000—an enormous sum in those days—"for the sick man whom they killed"; possibly some charge of magic was involved. Among the persons paying this fine was "Rubi Gotsce" (Rabbi Josce or Joseph), whose sons Isaac and Abraham were the chief members of the London community toward the end of the century, and whose house in Rouen was in possession of the family as late as 1203 ("Rot. Cart." 105b). In 1158 Abraham ibn Ezra visited London and wrote there his letter on the Sabbath and his "Yesod Mora." Up to 1177 London was so far the principal seat of Jews in England that Jews dying in any part of the country had to be buried in the capital, probably in the cemetery known afterward as "Jewin Garden," and now as "Jewin street." The expulsion of the Jews from the Isle of France in 1182 brought about a large acquisition to the London community, which was probably then visited by Judah Sir Leon, whose name occurs as "Leo le Blund" in a list of London Jews who contributed to the Saladin tithe Dec., 1185. This list includes Jews from Paris, Joigny, Pontoise, Estampes, Spain, and Morocco.

Massacre of 1189.

The massacre of the Jews at the coronation of Richard I. Sept. 3, 1189 (see England), was the first proof that the Jews of England had of any popular ill-will against them. Richard did practically nothing to punish the rioters, though he granted a special form of charter to Isaac fil Joce, the chief London Jew of the time, "and his men," which is the earliest extant charter of English Jews. In 1194 the Jews of London contributed £486 9s. 7d. out of £1,803 7s. 7d. toward the ransom of the king: in the list of contributors three Jewish "bishops" are mentioned—Deulesalt, Vives, and Abraham. In the same year was passed the "Ordinance of the Jewry," which in a measure made London the center of the English Jewry for treasury purposes, Westminster becoming the seat of the Exchequer of the Jews, which was fully organized by the beginning of the thirteenth century. Meanwhile anti-Jewish feeling in London had spread to such an extent that King John found it necessary in 1204 to rebuke the mayor for its existence. After the massacre of 1189, it would appear, the Jews began to desert Old Jewry, and to spread westward into the streets surrounding the Cheape, or market-place, almost immediately in front of the Guildhall. To a certain extent the Jews were crowded out from Old Jewry by the Church, which during the twelfth century established there the monastery of St. Thomas of Acon, St. Mary Colechurch, and at the back St. Martin Pomary, looking upon Ironmonger lane, where, it would seem, the Jews' College, or high school of all the English Jews, was located.

Old Jewry.

Escheats and purchases tended also to drive the Jews away from this quarter, the corner houses of Ironmonger lane being taken from Jews by the Earl of Lancaster and the Earl of Essex respectively. The Jewish dwellings spread along Gresham street, Milk street, and Wood street. The fact that the chief noblemen of the time were anxious to obtain them shows these houses to have been strongly built, as was indeed the complaint at the time of the riots.

Besides their predominant position, due to the existence of the Exchequer of the Jews, and which brought to London all the Jewish business of the country, the Jews of the capital had also spiritual domination, inasmuch as their presbyter or chief rabbi held a position analogous to that of the archbishop (see Presbyter).

The chief synagogue of the London Jewry at this date appears to have been on the site of Bakewell Hall. It probably continued to be used down to the Expulsion, though for certain reasons it was in private hands from 1283 to 1290. Another synagogue, in the northeast corner of Old Jewry, was handed over to the Fratres de Sacca, while still another was given to St. Anthony's Hospital, on the site of which is now the City Bank. Reference to more than one synagogue among the Jews of London is distinctly seen in the proclamations which were ordered to be made in the "synagogues" to determine whether or not a person was in debt to the Jews (see "Select Pleas of the Jewish Exchequer," ed. Rigg, p. 9).

The Jews of London suffered from their position as buffer between the king and the barons. In 1215 the barons opposing John sacked the Jewish quarter and used the tombstones of the Jewish cemetery to repair Ludgate (Stow, "Survey of London," ed. Thoms, p. 15). Similarly, in the trouble with Simon de Montfort, in 1263, the barons looted the London Jewry in pursuance of their opposition to the oppression of the king, into whose hands fell the debts of the Jews in London and elsewhere. This outburst had been preceded in 1262 by a popular riot against the Jews in which no less than 700 had been killed. A curious suit which followed the death of a Jew on this occasion is given in "Select Pleas," pp. 73–76, from which it appears that some of the Jews of that time took refuge in the Tower of London. It is a mistake, however, to suppose that there was a separate Jewry in that neighborhood. Most of the trials that took place with regard to ritual or other accusations were held in the Tower (see Norwich). Nevertheless the Tower continued to be the main protection of the Jews against the violence of the mob; and they are reported to have been among its chief defenders in 1269 against the Earl of Gloucester and the disinherited.

In the Barons' War.

In 1244 London witnessed an accusation of ritual murder, a dead child having being found with gashes upon it which a baptized Jew declared to be in the shape of Hebrew letters. The body was buried with much pomp in St. Paul's Cathedral, and the Jews were fined the enormous sum of 60,000 marks (about £40,000). Later on, in 1279, certain Jews of Northampton, on the accusation of having murdered a boy in that city, were brought to London, dragged at horses' tails, and hanged.

Toward the later part of their stay in London the Jews became more and more oppressed and degraded, and many of them, to avoid starvation, resorted to doubtful expedients, such as clipping. This led at times to false accusations; and on one occasion a Jew named Manser fil Aaron sued for an inquiry concerning some tools for clipping which had been found on the roof of his house near the synagogue (1277). In the following year no fewer than 680 Jews were imprisoned in the Tower, of whom 267 were hanged for clipping the coinage. On another occasion the lord mayor gave orders that no meat declared unfit by the Jewish butchers should be exposed for sale to Christians (Riley, "Chron." p. 177).

Disputes as to jurisdiction over the Jews often occurred between the Jewish Exchequer and the lord mayor. Thus in the year 1250 pleas of disseizin of tenements of the city of London were withdrawn from the cognizance of the justice of the

Jews and assigned for trial in the mayor's court, though they were reassigned to the Exchequer in 1271. In that year Jews were prevented from acquiring any more property in London, on the ground that this might diminish the Church tithes ("De Antiquis Legibus Liber," pp. 234 *et seq.*). The Church was very careful to prevent any encroachment on its rights; and it endeavored to curtail those of the Synagogue as much as possible. In 1283 Bishop Peckham caused all synagogues in the diocese of London to be closed; and it is for this reason that there exists no record of any synagogue falling into the hands of the king at the Expulsion (1290), though it is probable that the house held by Antera, widow of Vives fil Mosse of Ironmonger lane, was identical with the synagogue and was used for that purpose.

Synagogues Closed.

At the Expulsion the houses held by the Jews fell into the hands of the king, and were with few exceptions transferred to some of his favorites. In all, the position of about twenty-five houses can still be traced (see accompanying map), though it is doubtful whether the 2,000 Jews of London could have been accommodated in that small number of dwellings. As will be seen, the houses were clustered around the Cheape or market. Many of their owners were members of the Hagin family, from which it has been conjectured Huggin lane received its name (but see HAGIN DEULACRES). Traces of the presence of Jews are found also in surrounding manors which now form part of London, as West Ham, Southwark, etc.

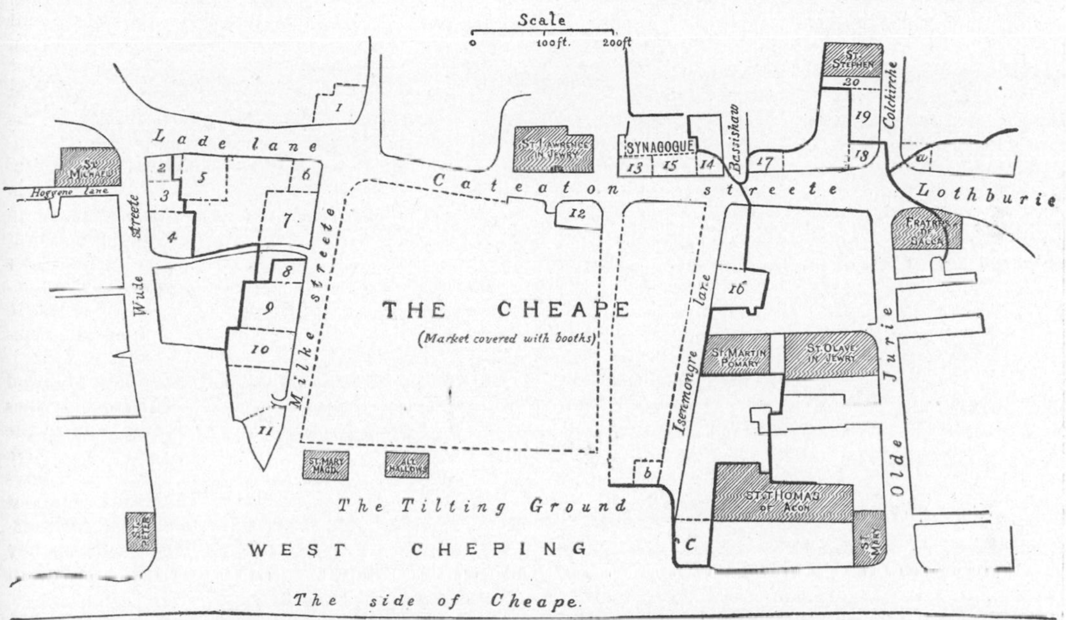

THE LONDON JEWRY, 1290. NUMBERED PLOTS BELONGED TO JEWS.
(From Jacobs' "Jewish Ideals.")

From the Expulsion to the seventeenth century London was only occasionally visited by Jews, mainly from Spain. In 1542 a certain number of persons were arrested on the suspicion of being Jews. Indeed, their presence appears to have become so common that in an old play ("Every Woman in Her Humour," 1609) a citizen's wife thus advises any one desirous of going to court: "You may hire a good suit at a Jew's." From this it would appear that Jewish traffic in old clothes had already begun.

The Return.

Toward the middle of the reign of Charles I. a number of Spanish Jews, headed by Antonio Fernandez CARVAJAL, settled in London in order to share in the benefits of the trade between Holland and the Spanish colonies. They passed as Spaniards, and attended mass at the chapel of the Spanish embassy; but when the Independents, with Cromwell at their head, became predominant in English affairs, several of these Jews assisted him in obtaining information about Spanish designs (see INTELLIGENCERS). Meanwhile MANASSEH BEN ISRAEL attempted to secure formal permission for the return of the Jews to England. At the conference at Whitehall on Dec. 18, 1655, the matter was left undecided; but it was put to a practical test in the following year by the ROBLES case, as a result of which Cromwell granted the lease of a burial-ground at Mile End for 999 years ("Jew. Chron." Nov. 26, 1880). Even previous to this the Jews had met for worship in a private house fitted up as a synagogue in Creechurch lane, Leadenhall street; and it is possible to assume the existence of a second meeting-place at St. Helens in the same neighborhood by 1662. These places of worship were fairly well known to the general public, though they were protected by treble doors and other means of concealment. Thomas Greenhalgh visited the one in Creechurch lane in 1664; and from the number of births in that year it would appear that about 280 Jewish souls resided in London at the beginning of the reign of Charles II. These must have increased considerably by 1677, when more than fifty Jewish names occur in the first London directory (Jacobs and Wolf, "Bibl. Anglo-Jud." pp. 59-61), implying a population of at least 500 Jewish souls. There is evidence of a number of aliens pretending to be Jews in that very year (L. Wolf, in "Jew. Chron." Sept. 28, 1894, p. 10).

Much opposition was directed against the Jews by the citizens of London, who regarded them as formidable rivals in foreign trade. Besides a petition of Thomas Violett against them in 1660, attempts were made in 1664, 1673, and 1685 to put a stop to their activity and even to their stay in England. On the last occasion the ingenious point was made that the grants of denization given to the London Jews by Charles II. had expired with his death, and that their goods were, therefore, liable to alien duty (Tovey, "Anglo-Judaica," pp. 287-295); and this contention was ultimately sustained. The more important merchants of London, however, recognized the advantages to be derived from the large Jewish trade with the Spanish and Portuguese colonies and with the Levant, to which, indeed, England was largely indebted for its imports of bullion. Rodriques Marques at the time of his death (1668) had no less than 1,000,000 milreis consigned to London from Portugal. Accordingly individual Jews were admitted as brokers on the Royal Exchange, though in reality not eligible by law. Solomon Dormido, Manasseh ben Israel's nephew, was thus admitted as early as 1657, and others followed, till the south-eastern corner of the Exchange was definitely set aside for the Jewish brokers. In 1697 a new set of regulations was passed by a committee of the Exchange appointed by the aldermen, which limited the number of English brokers to 100, of alien brokers to 12, and of Jewish brokers to 12. Of the 12 Jews admitted all appear to have been Sephardim except Benjamin Levy, who was probably an Ashkenazi. A petition in 1715 against the admission of Jews to the Exchange was refused by the board of aldermen.

Spanish and Portuguese Cemetery, Mile End Road, London.
(From a photograph.)

Organization.

The Sephardim soon established communal institutions, following, it may be conjectured, the example of Amsterdam, from which city most of them had emigrated. The Gates of Hope School was founded as early as 1664; and this was followed by the Villa Real Schools in 1730. The Sephardic Orphan Asylum had been established as early as 1703, and a composite society, whose title commenced with "Honen Dalim," was founded in 1704 to aid lying-in women, support the poor, and to give marriage portions to fatherless girls. In 1736 a Marriage Portion Society was founded, and eleven years later the Beth Holim, or hospital, came into existence, this in turn being followed in 1749 by the institution known as "Mahesim Tobim." Thanks to these and other minor institutions, the life of a Sephardic Jew in London was assisted at every stage from birth, through circumcision, to marriage, and onward to death, while even the girls of the community were assisted with dowries. This unfortunately had a pauperizing effect, which came to be felt toward the beginning of the nineteenth

INTERIOR OF THE NEW SYNAGOGUE, GREAT ST. HELEN'S, LONDON.

(From an old engraving.)

century. All these institutions centered round the great Sephardic synagogue built in Bevis Marks Sept., 1701 (see BEVIS MARKS SYNAGOGUE). This was a center of light and learning, having the society Etz Haim (founded as early as 1664) for the study of the Law. Later this was merged with the yeshibah into one institution called the "Medrash," which is still in existence. In the early days of the community almost all the names of importance were connected with Bevis Marks, *e.g.*, the Cortissos, Lagunas, Mendes, Pimentels, Samudas, Salvadors, Sarmentos, Suassos, and Villa Reals; the Nietos and the Azevedos likewise represented a high state of culture and Hebrew learning. By the middle of the eighteenth century these and other families, such as the Franks, Treves, Seixas, Nunes, Lamegos, Salomons, Pereiras, and Francos, had accumulated considerable wealth, mainly in foreign commerce; and in a pamphlet of the time it was reckoned that there were 100 families with an income ranging between £1,000 and £2,000, while the average expenditure of the 1,000 families raised above pauperism was estimated at £300 per annum. The whole community was reckoned to be worth £5,000,000 ("Further Considerations of the Act," pp. 34–35, London, 1753). The Jews were mainly concerned in the East-Indian and West-Indian trades and in the importa-

EXTERIOR OF THE GREAT SYNAGOGUE, DUKE'S PLACE, LONDON.
(From a photograph.)

tion of bullion. The Jamaica trade was almos monopolized by them (*ib.* pp. 44–49). The mos important member of the community was Samso GIDEON, who by his coolness during the crisis of tl South Sea Bubble and the rising of 1745 rendere great service to the government and acquired larg means for himself. The riots that followed the pa sage of the bill of 1753 for the naturalization of Jew had in many ways a disastrous effe upon the Sephardic section of tl community. Despairing of emancip tion, a large number of the wealthie and most cultured either were ba tized themselves or had their children baptize Gideon leading the way in the latter expedien

Social Condition in 1750.

His son became Lord Eardley in the Irish peerag One consequence of the rejection of the naturaliz tion bill of 1753 was the formation of the Board Deputies, then known as the "Deputados of t Portuguese Nation," really an extension of t Committee of Diligence formed to watch the pa sage of the naturalization bill through the Irish Pa liament in 1745. The Board of Deputies came in existence as a sort of representative body whose fi business was to congratulate George III. on l accession. As indicated by its earlier name, i membership was confined to Sephardim, though l rrangement representatives of the "Dutch Jews" were allowed to join in their deliberations (see LONDON BOARD OF DEPUTIES).

Meanwhile the "Dutch Jews" or Ashkenazim had rom the beginning of the century been slowly inreasing in numbers and importance. They had established a synagogue as early as 1692 in Broad treet, Mitre square; and thirty years later the congregation was enabled by the generosity of Moses Iart (Moses of Breslau) to remove to a much more pacious building in Duke's place, Aldgate, still known as the "Great Shool." His brother, Aaron Iart, was established as the chief rabbi; and his daughter, Mrs. Judith Levy, contributed liberally o the synagogue's maintenance. Three years later a schism occurred, and the HAMBRO' SYNAGOGUE was founded. It was not till 1745 that the Jews of he German ritual found it necessary to establish any charity. The Hakenosath Berith was then organized, to be followed as late as 1780 by the Meshivath Nephesh. Rigid separation existed between he two sections of the community. Even in death hey were divided: the Ashkenazic cemetery was at Alderney road, Mile End.

The social condition of the Ashkenazim toward he end of the eighteenth century was by no means atisfactory. Apart from a very few distinguished merchants like Abraham and Benjamin Goldsmid, Levy Barent Cohen, and Levy Salomons, the bulk of the Ashkenazic community consisted of petty traders and hawkers, not to speak of the followers of more disreputable occupations. P. Colquhoun, in his "Treatise on the Police of the Metropolis" (London, 1800), attributes a good deal of crime and vice to their influence; and his account is confirmed by less formal sketches in books like P. Egan's "Life in London" and by the caricatures of Rowlandson and his school. The lower orders of the Sephardic section also were suffering somewhat from demoralization. Prize-fighters like Aby Belasco, Samuel Elias, and Daniel Mendoza, though they contributed to remove some of the prejudice of the lower orders, did not help to raise the general tone.

JEWS' HOSPITAL AND ORPHAN ASYLUM, WEST NORWOOD, LONDON.
(From a photograph.)

Ashkenazic Institutions.

The revelations of Colquhoun led earnest spirits within the community to seek for remedies; and Joshua van Oven with Colquhoun's assistance drafted a plan for assisting the Jewish poor which was destined to bear fruit fifty years later in the Board of Guardians. Attention was directed to the education of the poor in 1811, when the Westminster Jews' Free School was established; and six years later the Jews' Free School was founded in Ebenezer square, and replaced a Talmud Torah founded in 1770. The first head master was H. N. Solomon, who afterward founded a private school at Edmonton which, together with that of L. Neumegen at Highgate, afterward at Kew, educated most of the leaders of the Ashkenazim during the first two-thirds of the nineteenth century. Even earlier, care had been taken of orphans. By the exertions of Abraham and Benjamin Goldsmid the sum of £20,000 was collected between 1795 and 1797, with which in 1806 the Jews' hospital, called "Neveh Zedek," was opened June 28, 1807, at Mile End for the support of the aged poor and for the education of orphan children. This was removed to Norwood in 1863 to a building erected on ground presented by Barnett Meyers. A similar institution, the Jews' Orphan Asylum, founded in 1831, was amalgamated with the Neveh Zedek in 1876; and these were supplemented by the National and Infant schools founded in 1836, and by the Jews' Infant School founded in 1841 by Walter Josephs. Provision for the aged poor was made by the Aged Needy Society, founded in 1829, and by the almshouse established by Abraham Moses and Henry Salomon nine years later. The blind were cared for from 1819 onward by the Institution for the Relief of the Indigent Blind. The poor were cared for by a committee of the three London synagogues—the Great, the Hambro', and the New.

Jews' College, Queen's Square, London.
(From a photograph.)

Meanwhile echoes of the Mendelssohnian movement had reached London, besides which the general wealth of the Sephardic community had brought its members in contact with the main currents of culture. One of the Sephardim, Emanuel Mendes da Costa, had been secretary of the Royal Society; and his brother Solomon had presented to the newly founded British Museum 200 Hebrew books, which formed the nucleus of the magnificent Hebrew collection of that library. Moses Mendez had proved himself a poetaster of some ability; and Oliver Goldsmith in his "Haunch of Venison" depicted a Jewish journalist of his time as a characteristic figure. But the "mahamad" of Bevis Marks went on in its old way without regard to any changes, spiritual or otherwise, in the community which it ruled; inflicting fines, and repelling many of the most promising members who were getting in touch with more refined methods of worship. Many of them ceased their connection with the Synagogue, either formally by becoming baptized or by resigning and allowing their children to be brought up in the dominant faith. Among the families thus deserting the Synagogue at the beginning of the nineteenth century may be enumerated the Basevis, D'Israelis, Ricardos, Samudas, Uzziellis, Lopezes, and Ximines. Not that the Sephardim were left without some important figures: Hananel de Castro, David Abravanel Lindo, Jacob and Moses Mocatta, not to mention Sir Moses Montefiore, were still left to uphold the more rigid traditions of Bevis Marks (Gaster, "Hist. of Bevis Marks," p. 172, London, 1901).

Second Sephardic Defection.

The hegemony in the community was thus transferred to the Ashkenazic section, which had been reenforced by the powerful personality of Nathan Meyer Rothschild, who had removed from Manchester to London in 1805 and who thenceforth became the central figure of the community. By his side stood the venerable figure of the "Rav," Solomon Herschel. Even in the literary sphere the Ashkenazim began to show ability. Whereas David Levi had been almost their sole representative at the end of the eighteenth century, in the first third of the nineteenth Michael Josephs, Moses Samuels, and Hyman Hurwitz treated the various branches of Hebrew learning; and the arts were represented by John Braham in secular, and by the two Aschers in sacred, music. Against these names the Sephardim could only show those of Elias Hyam Lindo and race Aguilar in letters and that of Carlo Delpini a drama.

Though the parliamentary struggle for emancipaon was intended for the benefit of all British Jews, ıd has, therefore, been described in some detail under ENGLAND, it centered mainly around London. The influence of the Jews in the city had increased. David Salomons was one of the founders of the London and Westminster Bank; e London Docks began their great career through e influence of the Goldsmids; the Alliance Insurıce Company was in large measure the creation of r Moses Montefiore and his brother-in-law, Nathan othschild. These and similar institutions brought wish merchants into ever-widening relations with en of influence in the city. Their bid for justice as widely supported by the citizens of London. hus, at the first attempt to pass the "Jew Bill" in 30 the second reading was supported by a petition no fewer than 14,000 citizens of London; and this as supplemented at the second attempt in 1833 by petition of 1,000 influential names from Westminer. Again, the Sheriffs' Declaration Bill of 1835 as in reality concerned with the shrievalty of Lonon, for which the popular David Salomons was aking a gallant fight; in this he succeeded that ar, to be followed two years later by Moses Monfiore, who was soon afterward knighted by Queen ictoria. In the same year (1835) Salomons was ected alderman, but was unable to occupy that fice owing to his religion. For ten years he urged e right of his coreligionists to such a position, l at last he succeeded in getting a bill passed alwing Jews to become aldermen in the city of Lonon and, thereby, eligible as lord mayor. Saloons was the first Jewish sheriff (1835), the first wish alderman (1847), and the first Jewish lord ayor (1855) of London. He was clearly destined be the first Jew elected member of Parliament, ough, appropriately enough, it was Baron Lionel othschild who first actually took his seat as mem-r for the city of London, which had shown so much mpathy for Jewish emancipation (see ENGLAND).

Struggle or Emancipation.

The sympathy thus attracted to Jews in the city as prominently shown during the DAMASCUS AFAIR, when a Mansion House meeting was held uly 3, 1840) to protest against the threatened dister. Incidentally, the struggle for Reform aided opening out new careers for the disfranchised ws of London. Francis Goldsmid, one of the ost strenuous fighters for the cause, was admitted the bar in 1833, though there were doubts as to s eligibility. He was followed in 1842 by John fterward Sir John) Simon, who was ultimately one the last sergeants-at-law.

Reform Movement.

Meanwhile the community in both its sections was nt by a schism which left traces almost to the end of the century. Alike among the Ashkenazim and the Sephardim the more cultured members had been increasingly offended by the want of decorum own both at Bevis Marks and the "Great Shool." otests were made in 1812 and 1828 in the former nagogue, and in 1821 and 1824 in the latter; but Dec. 4, 1836, matters were brought to a crisis by a definite proposal for Reform presented to the mahamad by a number of the "Yehidim." The petition was rejected as were similar ones in 1839 and in 1840, so that in 1840 twenty-four gentlemen, eighteen of the Sephardic and six of the Ashkenazic section of the community, determined to organize a congregation in which their ideas as to decorum in the service should be carried out. The new congregation dedicated its synagogue in Burton street Jan. 27, 1842, notwithstanding a "caution" which had been issued Oct. 24, 1841, against the prayer-book to be used by it, and a "ḥerem" issued five days before the inauguration of the synagogue against all holding communion with its members. This ban was not removed till March 9, 1849. For the further history of the movement see REFORM JUDAISM. The schism produced disastrous effects upon the harmony of the community. The older congregations would not even allow deceased members of the new one to be buried in their graveyard; and it was necessary to establish a new cemetery at Ball's Pond (1843). The Board of Deputies, under the influence of Sir Moses Montefiore, refused to recognize the new congregation as one qualified to solemnize valid Jewish marriages; and a special clause of the Act of 1856 had to be passed to enable the West London Synagogue of British Jews to perform such marriages.

The Jewish Press.

It is not without significance that the beginnings of the Jewish press in London coincided in point of time with the stress of the Reform controversy. Both "The Voice of Jacob," edited by Jacob Franklin, and "The Jewish Chronicle," edited by D. Meldola and Moses Angel—the latter of whom had in the preceding year become head master of the Jews' Free School, over which he was to preside for nearly half a century—came into existence in 1841. About the same time a band of German Jewish scholars established themselves in England and helped to arouse a greater interest in Jewish literature on scientific principles than had been hitherto displayed. Among these should be especially mentioned Joseph Zedner, keeper of the Hebrew books in the British Museum; the eccentric but versatile Leopold Dukes; H. Filipowski; L. Loewe; B. H. Ascher; T. Theodores; Albert Löwy; and Abraham Benisch, who was to guide the fortunes of "The Jewish Chronicle" during the most critical years of its career. The treasures of Oxford were about this time visited by the great masters Zunz and Steinschneider. They found few in England capable of appreciating their knowledge and methods, Abraham de Sola, David Meldola, and Morris Raphall being almost the only English Jews with even a tincture of rabbinic learning. On the other hand, the native intellect was branching out in other directions. Showing distinction in the law were James Graham Lewis, Francis Goldsmid, and John Simon; in dramatic management, Benjamin Lumley; in song, Mombach in the synagogue, and Henry Russell outside it; in music, Charles Sloman, Charles K. Salaman, and Sir Julius Benedict; in painting, Solomon Alexander Hart, the first Jewish R.A., and Abraham Solomon; in commerce, besides the Rothschilds and Goldsmids, the Wormses, Sassoons, Sterns, and

Sir Benjamin Phillips were rising names distinguished both within and without the community. J. M. Levy and Lionel Lawson were securing a large circulation for the first penny London newspaper, the "Daily Telegraph." Confining their activities within the community were men like Barnet Abrahams, dayyan of the Sephardim; Sampson Samuel; H. N. Solomon; N. I. Valentine; the Beddingtons; Louis Merton; and Sampson Lucas. All these may be said to have flourished in the middle of the century, toward the end of the struggle for complete independence.

JEWISH BOARD OF GUARDIANS BUILDING, LONDON.
(From a photograph.)

With them, but of a later generation, were growing up men who were destined between 1850 and 1880 further to consolidate the London community, now firmly established in the respect and confidence of the other citizens.

Further Consolidation (1856-1871).

The chief rabbi, N. M. Adler, began the process by establishing Jews' College for the training of Jewish ministers, in 1860 following it up, in cooperation with Dayyan Barnet Abrahams, with the establishment of the Jewish Association for the Diffusion of Religious Knowledge. Ephraim Alex with the aid of the energetic Lionel L. Cohen founded in 1859 the Board of Guardians for the Relief of the Jewish Poor to revise the system of charity conducted joint by the three synagogues according to the treat of 1805. This body soon developed loan, industria apprenticeship, visitation, and immigration con mittees, and for eighteen years (1862–79) too medical care of the Jewish poor, mainly under tl supervision of Dr. A. Asher. Lionel Cohen, togeth with the last-mentioned, then devoted his attentio to the solution of the financial and other problen brought about by the western extension of the Lo don ghetto up to the middle of the century. Tl Jews of London had remained concentered in tl Whitechapel district with the classic "Petticoa lane" as a nucleus; but as wealth increased amon the Ashkenazic Jews a steady western exodus too place, so that it was necessary as early as 1855 to es tablish, under the ministry of the Rev. A. L. Greer in Great Portland street, a branch synagogue c the "Great Shool." Synagogues at Bayswater (1863 in the Borough (1867), and at North London (186 were further evidences of the dispersion tendency and it became necessary to secure harmony in divir service and consolidation in financial responsibility b bringing these synagogues under one management

At the suggestion of Chief Rabbi N. M. Adle the three city synagogues—the Great, the Hambro

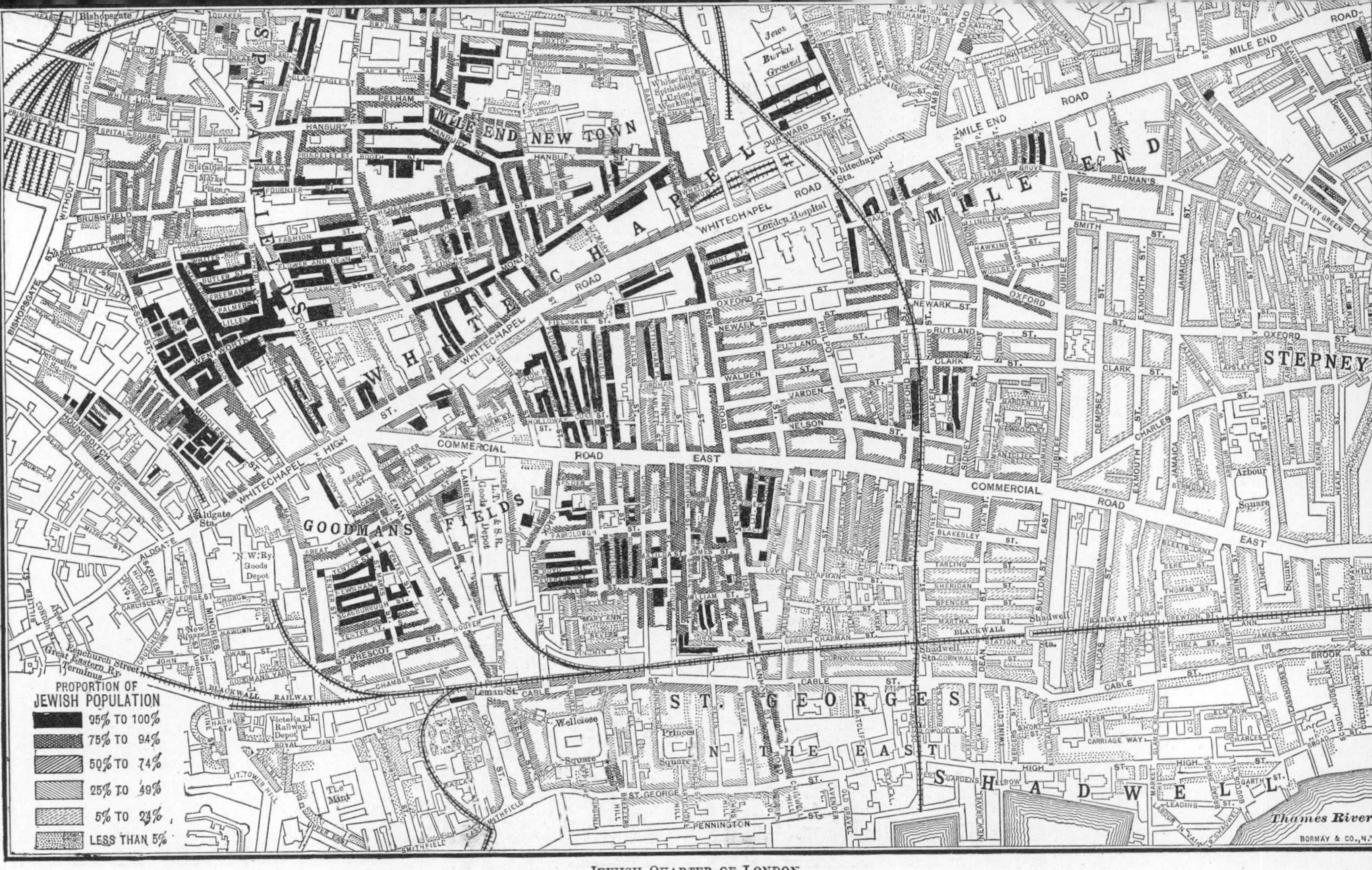

JEWISH QUARTER OF LONDON.
(After Russel and Lewis, "The Jew in London.")

and the New—with their western branches at Portland street and Bayswater agreed to a scheme (April 19, 1868), which was submitted to the Charity Commissioners of England and embodied by them in an Act of Parliament. This was passed July 14, 1870, although the legislature hesitated to establish the Synagogue just at the time when it was disestablishing the Irish Church. The original five synagogues have since been joined by ten others (see UNITED SYNAGOGUE). One of the consequences of this arrangement, which upon the face of it appears to be merely financial, was to give a certain pontifical importance to the chief rabbi, without whose consent, according to a special declaration attached to but not forming part of the Act of Parliament, no changes in ritual could be undertaken by any constituent synagogue.

WENTWORTH STREET, FORMERLY "PETTICOAT LANE," LONDON.
(From a photograph.)

Indeed, one of the characteristic features of the London community has always been the importance of the chief rabbi (called among the Sephardim "haham") of the prominent congregation, around whom as a sort of center of crystallization the community has rallied. At first the Sephardim held this position, which had been secured by the important work of David Nieto, who became chief of the Sephardim in 1702 and was one of the most distinguished Jews of his time, being equally noted as philosopher, physician, mathematician, and astronomer. His predecessors, Jacob Sasportas (1656–66) and Solomon Ayllon (1689–1701), were not suited either by character or by attainments to acquire great influence. David Nieto was succeeded by his son Isaac, who in turn was followed by Moses Gomez de Mesquita (d. 1751). Moses Cohen d'Azevedo again raised the position of haham to some consequence during his rule (1765–84). Of his successors, Raphael Meldola (1805–28), Benjamin Artom (1866–1879), and Moses Gaster, the present incumbent (elected in 1887), have been the most distinguished.

The Rabbinate.

But by the end of the eighteenth century the "Ravs" or chief rabbis of the Ashkenazim had begun to vie in importance with the hahamim of the Sephardim. The first of these was Aaron Hart (Uri Phoebus), brother of Moses Hart, founder of the Great Synagogue. He was succeeded by Hirschel Levin (sometimes called "Hirschel Löbel" and "Hart Lyon") who held office only seven years (1756–63), and then returned to the Continent. He was succeeded by David Tebele Schiff, who was chief rabbi from 1765 to 1792, and who founded a hereditary rabbinate for the next century, though his successor, Solomon Herschell (1802–42), was related to Schiff's predecessor, Hirschel Levin. Chief Rabbi N. M. Adler, who followed Herschell, was a relative of Schiff, and did much for the harmonizing of the London community; Jews' College, the United Synagogue, and, to a certain extent, the Board of Guardians owe their existence to his initiative. He was succeeded by his son, Herman Adler, the present (1904) incumbent of the post.

Besides Jews' College, the Board of Guardians, and the United Synagogue, the same generation arranged for a more efficient performance of its duties toward Jews oppressed in other lands. This function would naturally have fallen to the Board of Deputies; but, owing to its action with regard to the Reform Synagogue, certain members of this latter, especially Sir Francis Goldsmid and Jacob Waley, determined to form an independent institution to act for the British dominions in the same way that the Alliance Israélite Universelle had acted for the Continent. Owing to the Franco-Prussian war the Alliance had lost all support in Germany, and increased support from England had become necessary; this was afforded by the ANGLO-JEWISH ASSOCIATION, founded in 1871 with Albert Löwy as its secretary, who was instrumental also in founding the Society of Hebrew Literature in 1873.

By the beginning of the last quarter of the nineteenth century the London Jewish community had fully overcome the difficulties which had beset it at the beginning of the century; and it now organized all branches of its activity in a systematic and adequate manner. A series of remarkably able public servants—Asher Asher at the United Synagogue, A. Benisch at the "Jewish Chronicle," Moses Angel at the Jews' Free School, A. Löwy at the Anglo-Jewish Association, S. Landeshut at the Board of Guardians, and S. Almosnino, secretary of the Bevis Marks Synagogue and of almost all the Sephardic institutions—gave a tone of dignity as well as of efficiency to communal affairs. They were supported by leaders, some of whom, as Sir Julian Goldsmid and Baron Henry de Worms (afterward Lord Pirbright), had shown their capacity in national affairs, while others, like Lionel L. Cohen and his brother Alfred, Barrow Emanuel, David Benjamin, and Charles Samuel (to mention only those who are dead), had devoted their great abilities and administrative capacity to the internal needs of the community. Other members of the community were attaining distinction in the various branches of professional life. Sir George Jessel was the most distinguished judge, Judah P. Benjamin the most renowned barrister, and George Lewis the most noted solicitor practising English law. In medicine Ernest Hart, Henry Behrend, and R. Liebreich were noted; and in chemistry Ludwig Mond had become distinguished. Taste and capacity for literature were being shown by Sydney M. Samuel and Amy Levy; Frederic H. Cowen and in a less degree Edward Solomon were gaining distinction in music; and David James was famous in acting.

Social Condition About 1880.

It was estimated about the year 1883 that the total Jewish population of London then numbered 47,000 persons. Of these, 3,500 were Sephardim (including 500 "Reformers"); 15,000 could trace their descent from the Ashkenazim of the eighteenth century; 7,500 from Jews who had settled in England in the early part of the century; 8,000 were of German or Dutch origin; and the remaining 13,000 were Russian and Polish. What might be called the native element thus outnumbered the foreign contingent by 26,000 to 21,000 (Jacobs, "Jewish Statistics," iii.). The various social classes into which they were divided were summarized by the same observer as follows, the numbers of the first four classes being determined from estimates of Jewish names in the "London Directory," of the last three from the actual statistics of Jewish charitable institutions; the number of shopkeepers and petty traders also were based on the last-mentioned source (*ib.* ii.):

Position.	Individuals.	Family Income.
Professional and retired living W.	1,200	100 at £10,000
Rich merchants living W	5,400	1,400 " 1,000
Merchants with private houses living N., S., and E.	3,600	800 " 500
Professional and retired living N., S., and E.	800	200 " 250
Shopkeepers	12,500	3,000 " 200
Petty traders	11,000	2,000 " 100
Servants, etc.	500	 30
Board of Guardians, casuals and chronic	7,911	1,000 " 50 1,884 " 10
Other paupers and afflicted	2,242	
Russian refugees	1,947	 10

The total income was about £3,900,000, or an average per head of £82.

As regards their occupations, an examination of the London directory for those merchants sufficiently important to appear in its pages resulted in the following classification (*ib.* v.):

Class.	No. of Trades or Professions.	Individuals.	Class.	No. of Trades or Professions.	Individuals.
Merchants and factors	84	689	Leather	17	81
Clothing	68	799	Iron	13	70
Furniture	49	640	Instruments	11	33
Food	33	348	Tobacco	9	104
Stationery	19	111	Money-dealers	5	33
Jewelry	17	245	Toys	4	51
			Professions	15	154

There were but three occupations having over one hundred names: Stock Exchange brokers, 138; general merchants, 131; and tailors, 123. Then came clothiers, 89; bootmakers, 80; city of London brokers, 78; diamond-cutters, 78; furniture-brokers, 60; watchmakers, 57. The trades in which Jewish merchants had the largest representation were those in coconuts, oranges, canes and umbrellas, meerschaum pipes, and valentines.

Unfortunately this prosperous condition of the community was rudely disturbed by the Russian persecutions of 1881; these mark an epoch in Anglo-Saxon Jewry, upon whose members has fallen the greatest burden resulting from them. On Jan. 11 and 13, 1882, appeared in "The Times" of London an account of the persecution of the Jews in Russia, written by Joseph Jacobs, which drew the attention of the whole world to the subject and led to a Mansion House meeting (Feb. 1) and to the formation of a fund which ultimately amounted to more than £108,000 for the relief of Russo-Jewish refugees. This was supplemented by a further sum of £100,000 in 1890, when a similar indignation meeting was held at the Guildhall to protest against the May Laws (see MANSION HOUSE AND GUILDHALL MEETINGS).

The Russian Exodus.

The circumstances of the case, however, prevented the Russo-Jewish Committee, even under the able chairmanship of Sir Julian Goldsmid, from doing much more than supplement the work of the Board of Guardians, upon which fell the chief burden of the Russian exodus into England. But the publicity of the protest made on these occasions, and the large sums collected, naturally made the London community the head of all concerted attempts to stem the rising tide of Russian oppression, and gave London for a time the leading position among the Jewish communities of the world. As passing events which helped to confirm the consciousness of this proud position may be mentioned the centenary in 1885 of Sir Moses Montefiore's birth, celebrated throughout the world, and the Anglo-Jewish Historical Exhibition (suggested and carried out by Isidore Spielmann) at the Albert Hall, London, in 1887. This exhibition led, six years later, to the foundation of the Jewish Historical Society of England.

The number of refugees permanently added to the London Jewish community—most of them merely passing through on their way to America—was not of very large proportions; but an average of about 2,500 in a condition of practical destitution annually added to a community of less than 50,000 souls naturally taxed the communal resources to the utmost. To prevent evils likely to result from the landing of refugees unacquainted with the English language and customs, the Poor Jews' Temporary Shelter and the Jewish Association for the Protection of Girls and Women were founded in 1885.

Exterior of the New West End Synagogue, London.
(From a photograph.)

The newcomers generally showed a tendency to reject or neglect the religious supremacy of the English chief rabbi; and to check this and to serve other purposes a Federation of East End Synagogues was effected in 1887 under the auspices of Samuel (afterward Sir Samuel) Montagu. The want of capacity and technical skill among the newcomers, or "greeners," caused them to fall into the hands of hard taskmasters, and resulted in their becoming victims of the "sweating system," which formed the subject of a parliamentary inquiry (1888–90), due to the not overfriendly efforts of Arnold White. The poverty resulting from this system led to serious evils in the way of overcrowding with resulting immorality. Several remedial institutions were founded to obviate these evil results in the case of boys, the most prominent of which were the Jewish Lads' Brigade (1885) and the Brady Street Club for Working Boys. It was nevertheless found necessary in 1901 to establish an industrial school for Jewish boys who had shown criminal tendencies.

The increased tide of alien immigration became especially noticeable as it was mainly directed into one administrative district of East London, that of Stepney. The overcrowding which already existed in this district was accentuated; and a certain amount of displacement of the native inhabitants took place owing to the excessive rise in rents, producing a system of "key money," by which a bonus was paid by the incoming tenant for the privilege of paying rent. Certain branches of the tailoring, shoemaking, and carpentering trades tended to become monopolized by the Russo-Polish Jews settled in Stepney. Toward the end of the nineteenth century a certain amount of objection began to be raised to this and other tendencies of the immigrants. A special organization known as "The British Brothers' League," headed by Major Evans Gordon, raised an agitation against any further immigration of the kind; and owing in large measure to its clamor, a royal commission was appointed to examine into the alleged effects of unrestricted immigration. Though nominally directed against all aliens, it was almost without disguise applied chiefly to aliens of the Jewish faith. A previous commission, appointed to consider the same subject in 1889, had decided that the evils, if any, were so insignificant that they did not require any special legislation.

INTERIOR OF THE NEW WEST END SYNAGOGUE, LONDON.
(From a photograph.)

The commission, on which Lord Rothschild sat as member, devoted a considerable amount of attention to the subject, holding forty-nine public meetings mostly with regard to the London Jews of the East End. On the whole, it gave a fairly favorable account of the alien immigrant. He was acknowledged to be fairly healthy and reasonably clean on arrival, thrifty and industrious, and law-abiding. His children were especially bright and assimilative of English ways. It was not proved to the satisfaction of the commission that any severe displacement of labor had been caused by the "greener," who on his part tended to introduce new though less highly efficient methods of production in the clothing and furniture industries. The one true indictment found against the immigrant was that of overcrowding; and the recommendations of the commission were chiefly directed against this. It suggested that any district in which aliens congregated should be declared a prohibited area, and no alien should be admitted thereto for a period of two years after his arrival; and that to insure this all immigrants should be registered. Legislation intended to carry this out was introduced into Parliament in 1904, but withdrawn. An unfortunate admission of Leonard L. Cohen, president of the Board of Guardians, that his institution found it necessary to send back a certain number of "undesirables," weakened the possible resistance of the London community to the proposal that the repatriation of such undesirables should be undertaken by the government.

Commission on Alien Immigration.

During the last quarter of the nineteenth century a certain revival of interest in Jewish literature and history occurred among native London Jews. A small study circle associated with the Rev. A. L. Green in the early part of the seventh decade, and a series of public lectures in connection with Jews' College, gave opportunities for young men of promise to display their ability. These efforts have been more recently seconded by those of Jewish literary societies spread throughout London, and of a Jewish Study Society founded in 1900, mainly in imitation of the American Council of Jewish Women. "The Jewish Quarterly Review," founded by C. G. Montefiore and edited by him and by Israel Abrahams, has gradually become one of the most important scientific journals connected with Jewish science. Both of these gentlemen have been connected from time to time with movements intended to render religious worship more free from traditional trammels. The latest of these movements was that of the Jewish Religious Union in the year 1902, which was eminently a year of unions, as it saw also the formation of the Jewish Literary Societies Union, the Union of Jewish Women, and the Jewish Congregational Union.

Intellectual Progress.

One more movement may be referred to as characteristic of the London Jewry. About 1885 a number of the younger intellectual workers in the community were collected around Asher I. Myers, editor of "The Jewish Chronicle," in an informal body; they called themselves "The Wandering Jews," and included S. Schechter, I. Zangwill, Israel Abrahams, Joseph Jacobs, Lucien Wolf, and others. These met for several years in one another's houses for the informal discussion of Jewish topics, and this ultimately led to the foundation of the Maccabæans, an institution intended to keep professional Jews in touch with their coreligionists. This mixing with the outer world while still retaining fellowship with Israel is most characteristic of London, as indeed of the whole of English, Jewry.

Recent immigration has tended to divide London Jewry into two diverse and to a certain extent antagonistic elements; but the experiences and the administrative policy of the past decade have tended to bridge over the gap and reunite the two classes in communal organization. The beginning of the twentieth century finds difficulties similar to those found at the beginning of the nineteenth. Former experience shows that it is within the power of the community to remedy its own shortcomings.

This sketch of the history of the institutions and the prominent men that have made up the London community may be concluded with a list of the latter, from 1700 onward, including many who could not otherwise be specifically referred to. Persons whose date of birth alone is given are still living.

Name.	Date.	Description.
Abraham, Abraham......	d. 1863....	Author and communal worker.
Abrahams, Abraham.....	1801-80....	Hebrew writer on sheḥiṭah.
Abrahams, Barnett.......	1831-63....	Dayyan.
Abrahams, Barnett Lionel	b. Dec. 9, 1869.	Communal worker.
Abrahams, Israel.........	b. 1858....	Author and communal worker.
Abrahams, Louis Barnett.	b. 1842....	Head Master, Jews' Free School.
Adler, Elkan Nathan.....	b. 1861....	Communal worker; bibliophile.
Adler, Very Rev. Hermann.	b. May, 1839.	Chief rabbi of the United Hebrew Congregations of the British Empire.
Adler, Rev. Michael......	b. July 27, 1868.	Minister of Central Synagogue.
Adler, Nathan Marcus....	1803-90....	Chief rabbi of England.
Aguilar, Ephraim Lopez Pereira, Baron d'.	1739-1802..	Eccentric and miser.
Aguilar, Grace...........	1816-47....	Novelist.
Alex, Ephraim...........	1800-82....	Founder Jewish Board of Guardians.
Alexander, Abraham.....	1718-86....	Author and printer.
Alexander, David L......	b. 1842....	President, Board of Deputies.
Alexander, Levy..........	1754-1853?	Author and printer.
Alexander, Lionel L.....	1852-1901..	Honorary Secretary, Board of Guardians.
Almeida, Joseph d'.......	1716-88....	Stockbroker.
Almeida, Manuela Nuñez d'.	fl. c. 1720..	Poetess.
Almosnino, Ḥasdai.......	d. 1802....	Dayyan.
Almosnino, Isaac.........	d. 1843....	Ḥazzan.
Almosnino, Solomon......	1792-1878..	Secretary, Bevis Marks Synagogue.
Angel, Moses............	1819-98....	Educationist.
Ansell, Moses...........	d. 1841....	Secretary, Great Synagogue.
Ansell, Zalman...........	fl. 1790....	Dayyan.
Aria, Mrs. David B.......	b. Aug. 11, 1866.	Journalist.
Artom, Benjamin........	1835-79....	Haham.
Ascher, B. H.............	1812-93....	Rabbi and author.
Ascher, Joseph...........	1829-69....	Musical composer.
Ascher, Simon...........	1789-1872..	Ḥazzan.
Asher, Asher............	1837-89....	First Secretary, United Synagogue.
Avigdor, Elim d'.........	d. 1895....	Communal worker.
Avigdor, Countess Rachel d'.	1816-96....	Communal worker.
Avigdor - Goldsmid, Osmond Elim d'.	....	Communal worker.
Azevedo, Moses Cohen d'.	d. 1784....	Haham.

Name.	Date.	Description.
Ballin, Mrs. Ada Sara		Journalist.
Barnato, B. I	1852–97	Financier.
Barnett, A. L	1797–1878	Dayyan.
Barnett, Morris	1800–56	Dramatist and actor.
Baruh, Raphael	d. 1800	Author.
Beddington, Alfred H	1835–1900	Communal worker.
Beddington, Ed. Henry	1819–72	Communal worker.
Beer, Mrs. Rachel		Journalist.
Behrend, Henry	1828–93	Physician, author, and communal worker.
Belais, Abraham	1773–1853	Hebrew author.
Belasco, Aby	b. 1797	Pugilist.
Belasco, David (David James).	1839–93	Actor.
Belisario, Isaac Mendes	d. 1791	Preacher.
Belisario, Miriam Mendes.	d. 1885	Authoress.
Belmonte, Bienvenida Cohen.	fl. c. 1720	Poetess.
Benedict, Sir Julius	1804–85	Composer and musician.
Benham, Arthur	1875–95	Dramatist.
Benisch, Abraham	1811–78	Hebraist and journalist.
Benjamin, David	1815–93	Communal worker.
Benjamin, Judah Philip	1811–84	American statesman and English barrister.
Bensusan, Samuel Levy	b. Sept. 29, 1872.	Journalist.
Bentwich, Herbert	b. May 11, 1856.	Communal worker.
Bernal, Ralph	d. 1854	Politician and art-collector.
Bischoffsheim, Mrs. H. L.		Communal worker.
Blank, Joseph E	b. 1866	Communal secretary.
Bolaffey, Hananiah	b. 1779	Hebraist and author.
Braham, John	1774–1856	Composer and singer.
Buzaglo, Abraham	d. 1788	Inventor and author.
Carvajal, Antonio Fernandez de.	d. 1659	Founder of London Jewish community.
Castello, Daniel	1831–83	Communal worker.
Castello, Manuel	b. Mar. 21, 1827	Communal worker.
Castro, Hananel de	1794–1849	Communal worker (Sephardic).
Castro, Jacob de	b. 1758	Comedian.
Castro, Jacob de	1704–89	Physician and surgeon.
Chapman, Rev. John	b. 1845	Communal worker and educationist.
Cohen, Alfred L	1836–1903	Communal worker.
Cohen, Arthur	b. 1830	Communal worker and King's counsel.
Cohen, Benjamin Louis	b. 1844	Member of Parliament.
Cohen, Rev. Francis L	b. Nov. 14, 1862.	Minister, Borough New Synagogue.
Cohen, Leonard L	b. April 17, 1858.	President, Board of Guardians.
Cohen, Levy Barent	1740–1808	Communal worker.
Cohen, Lionel Louis	1832–87	Communal worker, financier, and politician.
Cohen, Louis Louis	1799–1882	Financier.
Cohen, Nathaniel Louis	b. 1847	Communal worker.
Cohen, Samuel Isaac	b. Jan. 1, 1861.	Communal secretary.
Cortissos, Don José	1656–1742	Army contractor.
Costa, Benjamin Mendez da.	1704–64	Philanthropist.
Costa, Emanuel Mendez da.	1717–91	Librarian to the Royal Society and scientific writer.
Costa, Solomon da	fl. c. 1760	Donor of Hebrew library to British Museum.
Cowan, Phineas	1832–99	Public worker.
Cowen, Frederic H	b. Jan. 29, 1852.	Composer and conductor.
Dainow, Hirsch	1832–77	Maggid.
Davids, Arthur Lumley	1811–32	Orientalist.
Davidson, Ellis Abraham.	1828–78	Technologist.
Davis, David Montague		Composer.
Davis, Felix Arthur	b. Aug. 14, 1863.	Communal worker.
Davis, Frederick	1843–1900	Antiquary.
Davis, Israel	b. 1847	Proprietor "Jewish Chronicle."
Davis, James		Playwright and journalist.
Davis, Maurice	1821–98	Physician and communal worker.
Davis, Myer David	b. 1830	Anglo-Jewish historian.
Delpini, Carlo Anton	d. 1828	Clown and theatrical manager.
Deutsch, Emanuel Oscar	1831–73	Orientalist.
Disraeli, Benjamin, Earl of Beaconsfield.	1804–81	Statesman.
D'Israeli, Isaac	1766–1848	Author.
Dolaro, Selina	1852–89	Actress.
Duparc, M	b. 1852	Secretary, Anglo-Jewish Association.
Dyte, D. M	fl. c. 1800	Saved life of George III.
Eichholz, Alfred	b. Nov. 26, 1869.	Educationist.
Eisenstadt, Jacob	fl. c. 1770	Author of "Toledot Ya'akob."
Eliakim b. Abraham	fl. c. 1794	Hebrew author.
Elias, Samuel ("Dutch Sam").	1775–1816	Pugilist.
Ellis, Sir Barrow Helbert.	1823–87	Indian statesman.
Emanuel, Barrow	1842–1904	Communal worker.
Emanuel, Charles Herbert Lewis.	b. Jan. 10, 1868.	Secretary, Board of Deputies.
Emanuel, Frank L	b. 1866	Artist.
Emanuel, Joel	d. 1842	Philanthropist.
Emanuel, Lewis	1832–98	Secretary, Board of Deputies.
Emanuel, Walter L	b. 1869	Litterateur.
Evans, Samuel ("Young Dutch Sam").	1801–43	Pugilist.
Falk, Ḥayyim Samuel Jacob ("Ba'al Shem").	1708–82	Cabalist.
Farjeon, B. L	1833–1903	Novelist.
Faudel, Henry	d. 1863	Worker for emancipation.
Faudel-Phillips, Sir George, Bart.	b. 1840	Communal worker.
Fay, Rev. David	b. April, 1854.	Minister, Central Synagogue.
Fernandez, Benjamin Dias.	c. 1720	Author.
Franklin, Ellis A	b. Oct., 1822	Communal worker.
Franklin, Ernest Louis	b. Aug. 16, 1859.	Communal worker.
Franklin, Jacob Abraham	1809–77	Journalist and philanthropist.
Freund, Jonas	d. 1880	Physician and founder of the German Hospital.
Friedländer, Michael	b. April 29, 1833.	Principal, Jews' College.
Gaster, Anghel	b. 1863	Physician.
Gaster, Very Rev. Moses	b. 1856	Haham of the Spanish and Portuguese Congregation.
Gideon, Samson	1699–1762	Financier.
Goldsmid, Abraham	1756–1810	Financier and philanthropist.
Goldsmid, Albert Edward W.	1846–1904	Colonel; communal worker and Zionist.
Goldsmid, Anna Maria	1805–89	Authoress and communal worker.
Goldsmid, Benjamin	1755–1808	Financier and philanthropist.
Goldsmid, Sir Francis, Bart.	1808–78	Philanthropist and politician.
Goldsmid, Sir Isaac Lyon, Bart.	1778–1859	Financier and philanthropist.
Goldsmid, Sir Julian	1838–96	Communal leader.
Goldstücker, Theodor	1821–72	Professor of Sanskrit, King's College.
Gollancz, Rev. Hermann.	b. Nov. 30, 1852.	Professor of Hebrew, University College.
Gollancz, Israel	b. 1864	Secretary, British Academy.
Gollancz, S. M	1822–1900	Ḥazzan.
Gompertz, Benjamin	1779–1865	Actuary and mathematician.
Gompertz, Ephraim	fl. 1860	Economist and mathematician.
Gompertz, Isaac	1774–1856	Poet.
Gompertz, Lewis	d. 1861	Founder of "Animals' Friend."
Goodman, Edward John	b. Dec. 19, 1836.	Journalist.
Goodman, Tobias	fl. 1834	Preacher and author.
Gordon, Lord George	1751–93	Convert to Judaism.
Gordon, Samuel	b. September, 1871.	Novelist.
Green, Rev. A. A	b. 1860	Minister, Hampstead Synagogue.
Green, Rev. Aaron Levy	1821–83	Minister and preacher.
Greenberg, L. J		Communal worker and Zionist.
Guedalla, Henry	b. c. 1820	Communal worker.
Guedalla, Judah	1760–1858	Moroccan merchant and philanthropist.
Harris, Henry	1819–99	Communal worker.
Harris, Rev. Isidore	b. June 6, 1853.	Minister, West London Synagogue of British Jews.
Hart, Aaron	1670–1756	Chief rabbi.
Hart, Ernest	1836–98	Physician.
Hart, Moses	d. 1756	Founder of Duke's Place Synagogue.
Hart, Solomon Alexander.	1806–81	Artist.
Hartog, Cécile Sarah		Musician.

Name.	Date.	Description.
Hartog, Numa Edward	1846–71	Senior wrangler.
Henriques, David Quixano	1804–70	Prominent reformer.
Henry, Emma	1788–1870	Poetess.
Henry, Michael	1830–75	Journalist and mechanician.
Herschell, Solomon	1762–1842	Chief rabbi.
Hirsch, S. A.		Hebraist and journalist.
Hirschfeld, Hartwig		Arabist.
Hurwitz, Hyman	1770–1844	Professor of Hebrew and author.
Hyams, Henry H.	b. 1852	Communal secretary.
Isaac, Benjamin	d. 1750	Founder of Hambro' Synagogue.
Isaac, Samuel	1812–86	Promoter of the Mersey tunnel.
Isaacs, Sir Henry Aaron	b. Aug. 15, 1830.	Municipal worker; lord mayor.
Isaacs, Rufus D.		King's counsel.
Jackson, Harry	1836–85	Actor.
Jacobs, Joseph	1813–70	Wizard and prestidigitator.
Jessel, Albert Henry	b. Oct. 31, 1864.	Communal worker.
Jessel, Sir Charles James, Bart.	b. May 11, 1860.	Director of public companies.
Jessel, Right Hon. Sir George.	1824–83	Master of the rolls.
Joseph, Delissa	b. 1859	Communal worker; architect.
Joseph, Rev. Morris	b. 1848	Senior delegate minister, West London Synagogue.
Joseph, N. S.	b. 1834	Communal worker; architect.
Josephs, Michael	1763–1849	Hebraist.
Kalisch, Marcus M.	1828–85	Hebraist and Bible commentator.
Keeling, Henry L.	1805–80	Philanthropist.
Keizer, Moses	1831–93	Ḥazzan.
Ḳimḥi, Jacob	1720–1800	Hebraist and pedler.
King, John	d. 1824	Author.
Kohn-Zedek, Joseph	1827–1904	Hebraist.
Laguna, Daniel Israel	1660–1720	Hebraist and poet.
Lamego, Moses	fl. 1737	Philanthropist.
Landau, Hermann	b. 1844	Communal worker.
Landeshut, Samuel	1825–77	Secretary, Board of Guardians.
Lara, Isidore de	b. Aug. 9, 1858.	Musician.
Lasker, Emanuel	b. Dec. 24, 1868.	Chess champion of the world.
Laurence, John Zechariah	1828–70	Ophthalmic surgeon and author.
Lawson, Lionel	1823–79	Newspaper proprietor.
Lee, Sidney	b. Dec. 5, 1859.	Author and Shakespearean scholar.
Leon, Hananel de	fl. c. 1821	Physician.
Levetus, Celia	d. 1873	Authoress.
Levi, David	1742–1801	Hebraist and author.
Levisohn, George (Gompertz).	d. 1797	Surgeon and author.
Levy, Abraham	b. Sept. 7, 1848.	Educationist and communal worker.
Levy, Amy	1862–89	Poetess and novelist.
Levy, Benjamin	fl. 1750	Financier.
Levy, Jonas	d. 1894	Vice-chairman, London and Brighton Railway.
Levy, Joseph Hiam	b. July 17, 1838.	Political economist.
Levy, Joseph Moses	1812–88	Proprietor of "Daily Telegraph."
Levy, Rev. Solomon	b. 1872	Minister, New Synagogue.
Lewis, Sir George Henry	b. April 21, 1833.	Solicitor.
Lewis, Harry S.	b. 1861	Communal worker.
Lewis, James Graham	d. 1873	Solicitor.
Liebreich, Richard	b. June 30, 1830.	Surgeon and ophthalmologist.
Lindo, Abigail	1803–48	Hebrew lexicographer.
Lindo, Algernon	b. 1863	Musician.
Lindo, David Abarbanel	1765–1851	Communal worker.
Lindo, Elias Haim	1783–1865	Jewish historian.
Lindo, Frank	b. Oct. 30, 1865.	Actor.
Lindo, Gabriel	b. July, 1839.	Communal worker.
Lindo, Moses Albert Norsa	b. April 27, 1862.	Communal worker.
Loewe, James H.	b. 1852	Communal worker.
Loewe, Louis	1809–88	Orientalist; first principal Judith Montefiore College.
Lopez, Sir Manasseh, Bart.	d. 1831	Politician.
Löwenthal, J. J.	1810–76	Chess-player.
Löwy, Rev. Albert	b. December, 1816.	Communal worker.
Lucas, Alice (Mrs. Henry Lucas).		Authoress and communal worker.
Lucas, Sampson	1821–79	Communal worker.
Lumley, Benjamin	1811–75	Theatrical director.
Lyon, George Lewis	1828–1903	Journalist and communal worker; editor, "Jewish World."
Lyon, Hart	1721–1800	Chief rabbi.
Maas, Joseph	1847–86	Musician and singer.
Magnus, Lady	b. 1844	Authoress and communal worker.
Magnus, Laurie	b. Aug. 5, 1872.	Author and journalist.
Magnus, Sir Philip	b. Oct. 7, 1842.	Educationist and communal worker.
Marks, B. S.		Artist and communal worker.
Marks, David Woolf	b. Nov. 22, 1811.	Chief minister, West London Synagogue.
Marks, Harry Hananel	b. 1855	Member of Parliament; journalist; "Financial Times."
Medina, Sir Solomon de	fl. 1711	Army contractor.
Meldola, David	1797–1853	Dayyan.
Meldola, Raphael	1754–1828	Haham.
Meldola, Raphael	b. July 19, 1849.	Chemist.
Mendes, Abraham	fl. 1718	Thieftaker.
Mendez, Moses	d. 1758	Banker and poet.
Mendoza, Daniel	1763–1836	Champion pugilist.
Merton, Louis	1840–74	Financier.
Meyers, Barnett	1814–89	Communal worker.
Middleman, Judah	fl. 1847	Hebrew author.
Mocato, Moses	fl. 1677	Merchant and author.
Mocatta, Abraham	1797–1880	Communal worker.
Mocatta, Abraham Lumbrozo de Mattos	1730–1800	Merchant and communal worker.
Mocatta, A. de Mattos	1853–91	Communal worker.
Mocatta, Frederick David	b. Jan. 15, 1828.	Philanthropist.
Mocatta, Jacob	1770–1825	Communal worker.
Mocatta, Moses	1768–1857	Author.
Mombach, Julius (Israel) Lazarus.	1813–80	Musician and composer.
Mond, Ludwig	b. March 7, 1839.	Chemist.
Montagu, Hyman	1845–95	Numismatist.
Montagu, Sir Samuel, Bart.	b. 1832	Communal worker.
Montefiore, Claude G.	b. 1858	Author and communal worker.
Montefiore, Sir Francis Abraham, Bart.	b. Oct. 10, 1860.	Communal worker and Zionist.
Montefiore, Horatio	1798–1867	Communal worker.
Montefiore, Joseph Barrow.	1803–93	Communal worker.
Montefiore, Joseph Mayer	1816–80	Communal worker.
Montefiore, Sir Joseph Sebag.	1822–1901	Communal worker.
Montefiore, Judith, Lady	1784–1862	Philanthropist.
Montefiore, Leonard	1853–79	Author.
Montefiore, Sir Moses, Bart.	1784–1885	Philanthropist.
Mosely, Alfred	b. 1855	South-African pioneer.
Moses, Joseph Henry	1805–75	Philanthropist.
Myers, Asher I.	1848–1902	Journalist and communal worker.
Neumegen, Leopold	1787–1875	Schoolmaster.
Newman, Alf. Alvarez	1851–87	Metal-worker and art-collector.
Newman, Selig	1788–1871	Hebraist and teacher.
Nieto, David	1654–1728	Haham.
Nieto, Isaac	d. 1755	Haham.
Nonski, Abraham	fl. 1785	Hebrew writer on vaccination.
Oppenheim, Morris Simeon.	d. 1882	Barrister.
Pacifico, Emanuel		Founder of almshouses.
Palgrave, Sir Francis Cohen.	1788–1861	Historian.
Pereira, Jonathan	1804–53	Physician.
Phillips, Sir Benjamin	1811–89	Lord mayor of London.
Picciotto, James	1830–97	Anglo-Jewish historian.
Picciotto, Moses Haim	1806–79	Communal worker.
Pimentel, Abraham Jacob Henriques.	fl. 1720	Author.
Pimentel, Sara de Fonseca y.	fl. 1720	Poetess.
Pinto, Thomas	d. 1773	Violinist.
Pirbright, Baron	1840–1902	Member of Parliament.
Price, Julius Mendes		Artist; journalist; traveler.
Pyke, Joseph	1824–1902	Communal worker.

Name.	Date.	Description.
Pyke, Lionel E.	1855–99.	Queen's counsel.
Raphall, Morris Jacob	1798–1868.	Preacher and author.
Rausuk, Samson	1793–1877.	Hebrew poet.
Rebello, David Alves	d. 1796.	Merchant and numismatist.
Ricardo, David	1772–1823.	Economist and politician.
Rintel, Meïr	fl. 1817.	Hebrew author.
Rosebery, Lady	1851–90.	Political and social leader.
Rothschild, Sir Anthony de, Bart.	1810–76.	Financier and communal worker.
Rothschild, Baroness Charlotte de.	1836–84.	Philanthropist.
Rothschild, Baron Ferdinand de.	1839–98.	Philanthropist; member of Parliament.
Rothschild, Lord	b. Nov. 8, 1810.	Communal worker.
Rothschild, Baroness Hannah de.	1782–1850.	Communal worker
Rothschild, Baroness Juliana de.	d. 1877.	Philanthropist.
Rothschild, Lady	....	Communal worker.
Rothschild, Leopold de	b. 1845.	Communal worker.
Rothschild, Baron Lionel de.	1808–79.	Financier and politician.
Rothschild, Hon. Lionel Walter.	b. Feb. 8, 1868.	Communal worker; Member of Parliament.
Rothschild, Baron Mayer de.	1818–74.	Financier and sportsman.
Rothschild, Baron Nathan Mayer.	1777–1836.	Financier.
Russell, Henry	1813–1900.	Composer and singer.
Salaman, Chas. Kensington.	1814–1901.	Musician.
Salaman, Malcolm Charles	b. Sept. 6, 1855.	Author and journalist.
Salomons, Annette A.	d. 1879.	Authoress.
Salomons, Sir David, Bart.	1797–1873.	Lord mayor and politician.
Salomons, Sir David Lionel, Bart.	b. June 28, 1851.	Engineer.
Salomons, Levi	1774–1843.	Financier.
Salvador, Joseph	fl. 1753.	Philanthropist.
Samuda, Isaac de Sequera.	fl. 1721.	Physician.
Samuda, Jacob	1811–74.	Civil engineer.
Samuda, Joseph d'Aguilar	1813–84.	Politician and shipbuilder.
Samuel, Baron Denis Moses de.	1782–1860.	Financier.
Samuel, Charles	1821–1903.	Communal worker.
Samuel, Sir Harry S	b. 1853.	Member of Parliament; communal worker.
Samuel, Herbert	b. 1870.	Member of Parliament.
Samuel, Sir Marcus, Bart.	b. 1853.	Lord mayor of London.
Samuel, Moses	1795–1860.	Author.
Samuel, Sampson	1804–68.	Secretary to the Board of Deputies.
Samuel, Stuart M	b. 1856.	Member of Parliament; communal worker.
Samuel, Sydney M.	1848–84.	Author.
Samuels, Moses	fl. 1830.	Biographer of Mendelssohn.
Sarmento, Jacob de Castro.	1692–1762.	Physician.
Sassoon, Sir Albert	1818–97.	Anglo-Indian merchant and philanthropist.
Schiff, David Tebele	d. 1792.	Chief rabbi.
Schloss, David Frederick.	b. 1850.	Communal worker.
Schloss, Leopold	b. Nov. 5, 1824.	Communal worker.
Sebag, Solomon	1828–92.	Hebrew teacher.
Seligman, Isaac	b. Dec. 2, 1834.	Communal worker.
Semon, Sir Felix	b. Dec. 8, 1849.	Laryngoscopist.
Sequera, Isaac Henriques.	1738–1816.	Physician.
Serra, Isaac Gomes	d. 1818.	Philanthropist.
Simon, Sergeant Sir John.	1818–97.	Communal worker, lawyer, and politician.
Simon, Oswald John	b. Sept. 3, 1855.	Communal worker.
Singer, Rev. Simeon	b. 1848.	Minister, New West End Synagogue.
Sloman, Charles	1808–70.	Musical composer and improvisator.
Sloman, Henry	1793–1873.	Actor.
Snowman, Isaac	b. 1874.	Artist.
Sola, Abraham de	1825–52.	Preacher; professor of Hebrew.
Sola, Samuel de	1839–66.	Ḥazzan.
Solomon, Abraham	1824–62.	Artist.
Solomon, Henry Naphtali	1796–1881.	Educationist and Hebraist.
Solomon, Selim	b. April 28, 1843.	Secretary, West London Synagogue of British Jews; communal worker.
Solomon, Solomon Joseph	b. Sept. 16, 1860.	Artist.
Spielmann, Isidore	b. July 21, 1854.	Communal worker.
Spielmann, Marion H.	b. May 22, 1858.	Author and publicist.
Stern, David, Viscount de	d. 1877.	Financier.
Stern, Sir Edward David	b. c. 1860.	Communal worker.
Stern, Baron Hermann de	1815–87.	Financier.
Stern, Rev. J. F.	b. Jan. 2, 1865.	Minister, East London Synagogue.
Strauss, Gustave Lewis Maurice.	1807–87.	Author.
Suasso, Isaac (Antonio) Lopez, Baron Avernes de Gras.	1693–1775.	Financier.
Sydney, Algernon Edward	b. Jan. 8, 1834.	Solicitor and communal worker.
Sylvester, J. J.	1814–97.	Mathematician; professor.
Symons, Baron Lyon de	fl. 1800.	Communal worker.
Tuck, Adolf	....	Communal worker.
Valentine, Nathan Isaac	fl. 1806.	Hebrew author.
Van Oven, Barnard	1797–1860.	Physician.
Van Oven, Joshua	1766–1838.	Surgeon.
Van Strahlen, Samuel	b. 1845.	Hebrew librarian, British Museum.
Villa Real, Isaac da Costa	d. 1730.	Founder of Villa Real School.
Villiers, John Abraham Jacob de.	b. 1863.	Writer and communal worker.
Waley, Jacob	1819–73.	Conveyancer; professor of political economy.
Wandsworth, Baron	b. 1845.	Politician.
Wasserzug, H.	d. 1882.	Ḥazzan and composer.
Wolf, Lucien	b. Jan. 20, 1857.	Journalist and Anglo-Jewish historian.
Wolff, Joseph	1795–1862.	Traveler and Christian missionary.
Worms, Baron de	b. Feb. 16, 1829.	Politician.
Worms, Maurice Benedict de.	1805–67.	Financier.
Worms, Baron Solomon de	1801–82.	Financier.
Ximenes, Sir Morris	b. 1762.	Financier.
Zangwill, Israel	b. 1864.	Man of letters.
Zangwill, Louis	b. 1869.	Novelist.
Zedner, Joseph	1801–71.	Hebraist.
Zimmer, N. L. D.	1831–95.	Hebraist and cabalist.
Zukertort, J. H.	1842–88.	Chess-player.

——**Present Conditions (Statistics):** It is possible to ascertain with some accuracy the Jewish population of London owing to the fact that statistics of Jewish deaths and marriages have been recorded with some completeness by the United Synagogue and the Board of Deputies for the last thirty years. To the information from these sources may be added the reports of the number of Jewish children attending the Jewish schools, given by Jacobs and Harris in successive issues of the "Jewish Year Book" with ever-increasing fulness. The following table gives these data at intervals of five years for the last thirty years:

Population.

Year.	Deaths.	Marriages.	School-Children.
1873	847	331	....
1878	985	377	....
1883	959	381	7,383
1888	1,129	589	....
1893	1,792	788	15,964
1898	1,765	1,096	19,442
1902	2,233	1,478	31,515

From the last-given data the number of Jews in London in the middle of 1902 can be ascertained with some degree of probability. The general death-rate of London for the year 1902 was 17.6 per thousand, but since the Jewish population is composed so largely (three-quarters as against one-half in the general London population) of young men and women of the most viable ages, 15-60, it is unlikely that the death-rate was higher than 15 per thousand (the same as that in the Jewish quarter of the borough of Stepney in 1901). This would give a Jewish population in London of 148,866 in 1902, an estimate which is confirmed by the number of marriages, 1,478, which, at 10 per thousand—a very high rate indeed—would give 147,800. The number of school-children, however, would point to an even higher total. Of these, 31,515, out of a total of 761,729, were in board and voluntary schools. If the proportion of school-children to population held with regard to the Jewish children as to the total population (4,536,541) within the school board area, this would imply a Jewish population of about 187,427. But these statistics are for a year later than that of the death-rate figures quoted above, and besides it is probable that more Jewish children are entered on the school-books, and more of those entered attend, than with the general population, so that the figures are somewhat misleading. Altogether it is likely that the Jewish population of London in the middle of 1902 was about 150,000, of whom at least 100,000 were in the East End of London, half of these being in the borough of Stepney ("Alien Immigration Commission," iii. 90). Of the remainder the majority are well-to-do residents in the Maida Vale, Bayswater, and Hammersmith districts, though subordinate ghettos have been created in Soho and Southwark. From the above-cited figures it would seem probable that the London Jewish population trebled during the years between 1883 and 1902. Part of this increase is doubtless due to the excess of births over deaths and to migration from the provinces, but at least 50,000 have been added by foreign immigration during that period, an average of 2,500 per annum.

Synagogues.

This increase has been met by a corresponding increase in the number of seat-holders in the London synagogues—2,289 in 1873; 3,397 in 1883; 5,594 in 1893; and 9,556 in 1902. Altogether there are 65 synagogues to meet the religious needs of the Jews of London; of these 15 belong to the **United Synagogue.** They are as follows, with the number of their seat-holders and their income for 1902, and are arranged in the order of their reception within the ranks of the United Synagogue:

Synagogue.	Total Income.	Seats Let.	Synagogue.	Total Income.	Seats Let.
Great	£2,923	437	New West End.	£4,613	320
Hambro'	489	200	Dalston	2,186	361
New	1,458	302	Hammersmith..	934	211
Bayswater	4,259	363	Hampstead	4,896	464
Central	3,710	350	South Hackney.	1,190	354
Borough	794	178	Stoke Newington	800	....
St. John's Wood	3,020	378			
East London	1,202	353			
North London..	1,318	187	Total	£33,792	4,458

Besides these there are 38 minor synagogues combined in the **Federation of Synagogues,** of which the chief are Cannon St. Road, London Chevra Torah, Sandy's Row, and West End Talmud Torah. Outside these two great associations stand the Spanish and Portuguese Congregation with its center at Bevis Marks, and the West London Synagogue of British Jews at Berkeley street (see Reform Judaism). Of the remaining 10 synagogues the most interesting is the Western, in St. Alban's place; it was founded in 1797 and was for a long time the only synagogue outside the "city." Altogether the expenditure of these 65 synagogues may be reckoned at something like £50,000 per annum, while besides these there is a very large number of "ḥebrot" scattered throughout the Jewish quarter. Many London Jews, however, still remain unattached to any prominent synagogal organization, and for the chief holidays of the New-Year, in the autumn, a large hall in the East End is hired, where the services are attended by no less than 5,000 persons. A large proportion of the Jewish inhabitants of London makes use of one or other of the numerous charitable institutions. In 1883 the proportion was one-fourth (Jacobs, "Jewish Statistics," p. 14), though it is probably not so high at present. From 1895 to 1901 an annual average of 851 cases of foreigners arriving during the year applied to the Board of Guardians, or Russo-Jewish Committee ("Alien Immigration Commission," iii. 93). As a case includes on an average 3 persons, this would imply that nearly the whole of the 2,500 persons arriving during the year have reason to apply, for one cause or another, to the Board of Guardians. On the other hand, the assistance needed and given is often very slight, and the proportion of those who remain chronically connected with the charitable institutions is fairly small, probably not more than 5 per cent of the whole Jewish population.

Charity.

Almost every need of a Jewish person from birth to burial is provided for by one or other of the metropolitan Jewish charities, of which the following is a classified list, with the amounts expended during the year 1902; in most cases dates of foundation are given in parentheses:

	£	s.	d.
Orphans.			
Jews' Hospital and Orphan Asylum, West Norwood (1795)	10,506	10	10
Spanish and Portuguese Orphan Society (for children of Sephardim only; 1703)	625	0	0
Hayes Industrial School (exclusive of grants earned)	600	0	0
Girls.			
Domestic Training Home (1894)	1,161	2	1
Deaf and Dumb and Blind.			
Deaf and Dumb Home (1863)	2,145	8	3
Institution for the Indigent Blind (1819)	1,913	0	0
Apprenticeship.			
Mahasim Tobim (for Sephardim only; 1749)	138	0	0
Labor Registry.			
Location and Information Bureau (1892)	1,023	4	10
Emigration.			
Emigration Society (1852)	668	14	9

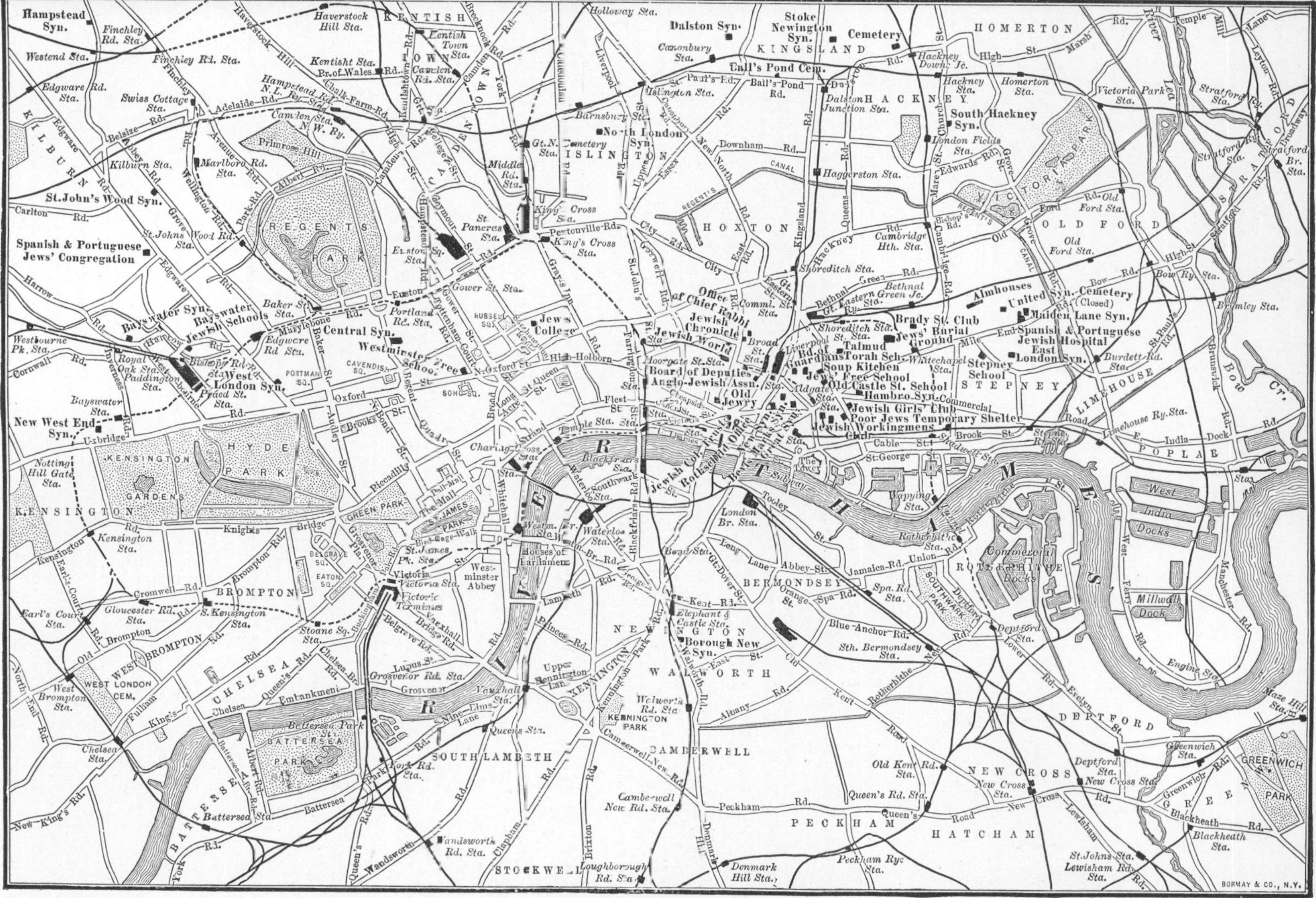

MAP OF LONDON SHOWING LOCALITIES OF JEWISH INTEREST.

LOANS.

	£	s.	d.
Ladies' Benevolent Loan Society (1844)	2,476	0	0
Western Jewish Philanthropic Society (1827)	247	3	6
Excelsior Fund (1862)	150	0	0

RELIEF IN KIND.

(a) *Meals.*

	£	s.	d.
Soup-Kitchen for the Jewish Poor (1854)	2,099	6	6
Society for Providing Penny Dinners (at Board and Jewish Schools; 1883)	406	5	2
Society for Providing Sabbath Meals (1869)	269	6	10

(b) *Clothing.*

	£	s.	d.
Jewish Ladies' Clothing Association (upon Investigation by Visiting Committee; 1892)			
Jewish Schools' Boot Fund (1889)	359	4	4

(c) *Bread, Meat, Coal, and Groceries.*

	£	s.	d.
East End Bread, Meat, and Coal Charity (1896)	331	13	5
Metropolitan Promoters of Charity (1860)	474	16	0
Meshivath Nephesh (1780)	2,455	0	0
North London Grocery Fund (1890)	579	4	7

NURSING FOR INVALIDS.

	£	s.	d.
Sick-Room Helps Association	1,136	19	3
Ladies' Society for Helping the Poor and Sick	30	0	0

LYING-IN INSTITUTIONS.

	£	s.	d.
Ladies' Benevolent Institution	2,500	0	0
Honen Dalim, Menahem Abelim, Hebrat Yetomot, and Hebrat Moalim (for Sephardim only; 1724)	245	0	0
Lying-in Charity	163	0	0

CONVALESCENT HOMES.

	£	s.	d.
Baroness de Hirsch Convalescent Home (1898)	2,000	9	5
Jewish Convalescent Home (1862)	1,208	2	3

INCURABLES.

	£	s.	d.
Home and Hospital for Jewish Incurables (1889)	3,171	8	1

THE AGED.

(a) *Homes.*

	£	s.	d.
Home for Aged Jews (1894)	2,773	6	8
Beth Holim Hospital (in connection with the Spanish and Portuguese Congregation; 1747)	1,190	0	0
Salomons' Almshouses (in connection with the United Synagogue; 1862).			
J. H. Moses' Almshouses (Jewish Board of Guardians; 1862).			
Abraham Lyon Moses' and Henry Solomon's Almshouses, Devonshire street, Mile End, E. (1838).			
Joel Emanuel's Almshouses, Wellclose square.			

(b) *Pensions.*

	£	s.	d.
Society for Relieving the Aged Needy (1829)	1,474	15	0
Jews' Hospital and Orphan Asylum, West Norwood (1795)	374	0	10

WIDOWS.

	£	s.	d.
City of London Benevolent Society for Assisting Widows of the Jewish Faith (1867)	329	4	8
Israelite Marriage Portion and Widows' Pension Society	150	0	0

MARRIAGE PORTIONS.

	£	s.	d.
Marriage Portion Society (1850)	61	19	4
Society for Granting Marriage Portions to Orphans (for Sephardim only).			

CHILDREN.

	£	s.	d.
Jewish Branch of Children's Country Holiday Fund (1889)	464	0	4
Initiation Society (1745)	514	14	4
Jewish Crêche (1897)	483	14	5

PREVENTIVE AND RESCUE WORK.

	£	s.	d.
Jewish Association for the Protection of Girls and Women (1885)	942	4	0

GENERAL.

	£	s.	d.
Hebrew Society for Brotherly Help (1896)	260	0	0
Poor Jews' Temporary Shelter (1885)	3,690	7	2
Spanish and Portuguese Jews' Board of Guardians (1837)	1,637	10	1
Jewish Ladies' West End Charity (1842)	970	8	9
South London (1902)	69	16	6
Tradesmen's Benevolent Society (1858)	522	0	0

Board of Guardians for the Relief of the Jewish Poor (1859):

	£	s.	d.
Relief	£20,301	11	9
Sanitary Department	216	3	0
Loans	19,465	11	11
Workrooms	112	15	0
Industrial	2,887	18	5
Russo-Jewish Committee	2,214	3	6
Administration	3,104	11	9
Almshouses	44	2	6
	48,346	17	10

United Synagogue Charities (exclusive of contribution to Board of Guardians; 1870):

	£	s.	d.
Pensions	£885	17	2
Grants	340	0	0
Relief in Kind	719	13	3
Marriage Portions	104	0	0
Ministers' Augmentation	200	0	0
Special Bequests	146	15	4
Festival Distributions	472	13	0
Mazzot	582	0	7
Visitation Committee	600	0	0
Talmud Torah	29	2	8
Mikwah and Poor of Holy Land	40	0	0
Charity Funerals	1,027	15	1
Free Religious Services	473	12	11
Educational Institutions	996	3	4
	6,617	13	4

	£	s.	d.
Jewish contribution to Hospital Sunday Fund, 1903.	1,679	10	1
Total	£111,639	3	5

From this total should be deducted the figures of the loan department of the Board of Guardians and of the other loan societies, amounting to £22,338 15s. 5d., leaving a total expenditure of £89,300 8s. 0d. for the charity budget of the London Jewry in 1902, apart from private donations. Among such a large body of persons it is natural that a certain proportion of them should fall by the way, either from weakness or wickedness. Comparatively speaking, these are few in number. Only 1,909 found it necessary to apply for Poor Law relief throughout London in 1901, at least four-fifths of these being merely applicants for medicine. Records have been kept of the number of Jewish inmates of public institutions in and around London for the last thirty years, from which may be compiled the following table showing the number received annually:

Defectives and Delinquents.

Year.	Asylums.	Hospitals.	Workhouses.	Prisons.	Reformatories.	District Schools.
1873	88	66	4	81	2	..
1878	46	383	12	186	3	2
1883	20	506	23	227	3	4
1888	48	776	78	247	4	1
1893	51	1,190	299	388	13	..
1898	106	1,609	351	514	20	2
1902	129	2,391	458	796	9	37

The prisoners were held mostly for minor offenses. Thus in 1902, while 796 were received, the maximum number of inmates at any one time was 233, showing that, in the majority of instances, they served very short sentences. As regards other undesirable qualities the Alien Immigration Commission recorded only 93 bankruptcies among alien Jews in the London district during the three years ending March 31, 1903 ("Report," i. 835).

Education. Nine-tenths of all the Jews who reside in London send their children to the ordinary public schools, one-third of these going to the voluntary and the remainder to the Board schools. The chief Jewish voluntary schools are given in the following list, with the number attending them in 1903:

School.	Boys.	Girls.	Infants.	Total.
Jews' Free School...	2,289	1,310	.....	3,599
Infant schools.......	.....	.....	1,727	1,727
Stepney Jewish......	406	271	182	859
Bayswater Jewish...	135	95	81	311
Westminster Jewish.	315	322	.....	637
Norwood Asylum....	150	132	30	312
Deaf and Dumb.....	25	16	.....	41
South London.......	109	72	53	234
Thrawl Street........	.....	153	170	323
Hayes Industrial....	57	.....	.....	57
Total............	3,486	2,371	2,243	8,100

Of the children attending the Jewish voluntary schools about one-fifth were born abroad, one-eighth in England of native parents, and the rest were born in England of foreign parents. The greatest of Jewish schools is the Jews' Free School, Bell lane, one of the largest institutions of its kind in the world. The total expenditure of these schools is about £52,000 per annum. Quite a large majority of Jewish children in London go to other than purely Jewish schools, the proportion being shown by the following table:

School.	Boys.	Girls.	Infants.	Total.
Board schools.......	6,189	6,416	8,741	21,346
Voluntary schools (Jewish)...........	3,486	2,371	2,243	8,100
Voluntary schools (non-Jewish)......	.....	.....	.....	2,069
Total............				31,515

In addition English instruction for adult Russian refugees is provided by the English evening classes in connection with the Russo-Jewish Committee.

Social Institutions. A somewhat higher grade of educational effort is indicated by the many social clubs and institutions intended to link together Jewish lads and young men. The central body of this kind is the Jewish Workingmen's Club, Great Alie street, Aldgate, founded in 1872. As a preparation for this there are a certain number of clubs for Jewish working boys, the chief of which is the Brady Street Club, founded in 1896. There are similar clubs for girls—the Jewish Girls' Club, founded in 1886, and the West Central Jewish Girls' Club, founded in 1887.

For specifically Jewish instruction the provision in London is somewhat small. Each division of the community has a bet ha-midrash, the Sephardic institution of that name being instituted as far back as 1664. The Ashkenazic institution is under the auspices of the United Synagogue, and the present building was opened in 1876. Local institutions

of a similar character exist in North and Northeast London. The Jews' College still remains the center of Jewish learning in London, though large provision is now made for more popular lectures and instruction by the Jewish Study Society and its various offshoots, which are combined in the Union of Jewish Literary Societies, founded in 1902.

Occupations. It is impossible to give any full account of the occupations of London Jews, but in the census of 1901 there is a list of occupations of Russians and Poles in London, which at any rate enables the statistician to determine the most popular occupations among the least-favored individuals of the London Jewry. It is as follows:

			MALES.	FEMALES.
Total..			28,574	24,863
Under ten years............	1,927	1,959		
Over " "	26,647	22,904		
Of whom earn their living..	24,164	5,358		
Clothing trades..................................			14,666	3,698
Tailors......................	10,070	2,603		
Women's tailors............	36	454		
Capmakers..................	707	214		
Furriers.....................	319	167		
Shoemakers.................	2,890	120		
Slipper-makers.............	150	6		
Miscellaneous..............	494	134		
Furniture trades................................			2,550	12
Cabinet-makers..............	1,894	4		
Polishers....................	55	1		
Carpet-makers..............	135	..		
Turners......................	220	2		
Miscellaneous..............	246	5		
Painters..			226	1
Carpenters..			210	..
Watchmakers.....................................			158	1
Goldsmiths..			143	..
Tobacco-workers.................................			342	331
Tobacco-dealers..................................			150	12
Workers and dealers in food produce...........			1,399	177
Pedlers..			464	69
Tradespeople......................................			609	44
Travelers..................	313	16		
Agents.....................	163	25		
Others.....................	133	3		
Teachers..			219	36
Servants..			16	551
Barbers (probably not Jewish)..................			519	14
Others...			2,570	1,729

With regard to the classes which have been longest settled in the country, the proportions, though probably not the numbers, of those employed in the various occupations are not likely to be much different from the estimate made in 1883 and given above.

Friendly and Benefit Societies. A large number of societies for mutual assistance exist in the London Jewry, no less than 140 being recorded in the last issue of the "Jewish Year Book," besides many separate branches of the larger orders, like the Grand Order of Israel, the Ancient Order of Mount Sinai, the Hebrew Order of Druids, the orders Achei Ameth and Achei Berith, and the Order of Ancient Maccabæans. In addition, most of the ḥebrot are also benefit societies, and there have existed altogether about 39 Jewish trade-unions in London (see Halpern, "Die Jüdischen Arbeiter in London," pp. 66–68). Many of these latter, however, exist only for a short time, and occasionally are created simply for the purposes of a strike. The most prominent of them appear to be the United Ladies' Tailoresses, founded in 1891, and the Independent Cabinet Makers' Association, founded in 1895. The aim of Jewish workmen to become masters on their own account seems to stand in the way of their becoming trade-unionists.

Zionism.

London is one of the chief centers of Zionism, which was taken up with great enthusiasm. It is the seat of THE JEWISH COLONIAL TRUST, and the Fifth Zionist Congress was held there. Of Zionist societies, 23 exist there, besides the English Zionist Federation, of which Sir Francis Montefiore is the president. No less than 51 Zionists' share clubs exist in London to enable Zionists of small means to become shareholders in the Jewish Colonial Trust.

BIBLIOGRAPHY: Jacobs, *Jews of Angevin England*, 1894; Margoliouth, *History of the Jews in Great Britain*, vol. iii., London, 1851; Halpern, *Die Jüdischen Arbeiter in London*, 1902; C. Russel and H. S. Lewis, *The Jew in London*, 1900; Jacobs and Harris, *Jewish Year Book*, various years; *Transactions Jew. Hist. Soc. Eng.*; Jacobs, *Studies in Jewish Statistics*, London, 1891; *Report of the Alien Immigration Commission*, 1903; *Report from the Committee of the House of Lords on the Sweating System*, London, 1889; *Report from the Select Committee on Immigration and Emigration (Foreigners)*, London, 1889; Evans Gordon, *The Alien Immigrant*, London, 1904; Picciotto, *Sketches of Anglo-Jewish History*, 1902; Jacobs and Wolf, *Bibl. Anglo-Jud.*

——**Typography:** The earliest Hebrew printing in the city of London was done by Christian printers, the first book being an edition of the Psalms in four languages which appeared in London in 1643. Steinschneider suggests that the Hebrew was printed from incised wooden blocks. The printer's name was Thomas Harper. An edition of Abot with punctuated text was published at London in 1651, the printing being done by Thomas Roycroft, who appears also to have printed the Walton polyglot of 1653–57. The first book printed for and by a Jew in London appears to have been the "Urim we-Tummim" by Uri Phoebus (1707). It is doubtful whether Johanan ben Isaac's attack upon this work was printed in London; the continuation was certainly done in Amsterdam. The Christian printer Thomas Ilive printed a few Hebrew works, among others the "Maṭṭeh Dan," 1715, of David Nieto. Similarly, about 1770, three Jews, Isaac ben Jedidiah, Moses ben Gershon, and Jacob Cohen, published a certain number of works printed by William Tooke. The first regular printer and publisher may be regarded as David ben Mordecai Levi (1794–99), though previous to this the ALEXANDERS had begun their series of prayer-books (from 1770 onward), to be succeeded by the Valentines, who have published most of the rituals of the London community. For a long period the firm of Wertheimer, Lea & Company published most books in London requiring Hebrew type, apart from the Bible and the books of the conversionist societies. Filipowski may be here mentioned as having had printed the various works he edited in new and very clear though small type, in the middle of the nineteenth century.

BIBLIOGRAPHY: Steinschneider, in Ersch and Gruber, *Encyc.* section ii., part 28, p. 91; *Cat. of the Anglo-Jewish Historical Exhibition*, p. 43.

J.

LONDON COMMITTEE OF DEPUTIES OF BRITISH JEWS (more commonly **London Board of Deputies**): A body formed to safeguard the interests of British Jews as a religious community. It can be traced to a committee called "The Committee of Diligence," which committee was formed to watch the progress through the Irish Parliament, in 1745, of the bill for Jewish naturalization. After the rejection of the Naturalization Bill of 1753, and on the accession of George III. in 1760, "deputados of the Portuguese nation" were appointed to attend court and express the loyalty of the British Jews, which they did on Nov. 19, 1760. The German, or "Dutch," Jews were not formally represented on the committee, but arrangements were made by which they should cooperate in important cases. The board was established to protect the interests of British Jews not only in the British Isles, but in the colonies. It was appealed to from Jamaica in 1761 and from the Balearic Isles in 1766. Meetings were held sporadically in 1778 and 1789. In the latter year Moses I. Levi was elected as president, and in 1812 the German members of the board became regularly connected with it. The deputies watched over all the legislation relating to marriages, labor laws, and other matters which might affect Jews prejudicially, and aided considerably in the struggle for Jewish emancipation. In 1835 Sir Moses Montefiore was elected president, and he remained in that office until his death, being supported by Sampson Samuel as secretary (appointed 1838), and later by Lewis Emanuel (d. 1898), who was succeeded by his son Charles, the present (1904) secretary. The committee took an active part in the Damascus Affair as well as in the early struggle for Reform; as president, Sir Moses, throughout his incumbency of the office, vetoed every attempt at opposition on the part of the representatives from the West London Synagogue.

Beginning in 1838, attempts were made to get the provincial congregations to appoint representatives on the board, with varying but on the whole increasing success, the arrangement generally being for the provincial congregation to select as its representative a London resident — if possible, one of the congregation who had settled in London. The board had much to do with the foundation of the Morocco Fund as well as of the Rumanian Committee, but since the formation of the Anglo-Jewish Association in 1871 it has worked conjointly with that body wherever any communication with the Foreign Office or with a foreign government is concerned. It helped also to found the Russo-Jewish Committee in 1882. The elections are held triennially, the latest occurring in May, 1904, when sixty-five deputies were selected, thirty-one from eighteen metropolitan synagogues, thirty-two from provincial synagogues, and two from colonial congregations. The expenses are borne pro rata by the various synagogues and congregations.

BIBLIOGRAPHY: Picciotto, *Sketches of Anglo-Jewish History*, ch. xiii., xiv.; *Jewish Year Book*, 5664, pp. 58–60.

J.

LONDON, JACOB BEN JUDAH ḤAZZAN: English scholar; born in London at the beginning of the eighteenth century. When quite young he went to Amsterdam, where he lived for a long time. Later he traveled through Italy, and in the course of his journey had the misfortune to be taken for a spy, on account of the numerous papers—the con tents of which were unintelligible to the police—he had with him.

London was the author of an ethical work entitled "Hista'arut Melek ha-Negeb 'im Melek ha-Ẓafon" (Amsterdam, 1737); the work is explained by two accompanying commentaries, "Sinai" and "Boẓeẓ," the former being a general interpretation of the text, the latter containing definitions of the difficult words. London was also the editor of the "Shib'ah 'Enayim" (Leghorn, 1745), containing editions of various works by Naḥmanides, Aboab Isaac de Leon, and Abraham Bolat.

Bibliography: *Revue Orientale*, ii. 334; Steinschneider, *Cat. Bodl.* col. 1230; Zedner, *Cat. Hebr. Books Brit. Mus.* p. 302.

J. I. Br.

LONDON, SOLOMON B. MOSES RAPHAEL: Russian author and publisher; lived at Novogrudok, Lithuania, in the first half of the eighteenth century. He was the pupil of Samuel Schotten, rabbi at Frankfort-on-the-Main. He edited the following works: "Zoker ha-Berit," on the rite of circumcision (Amsterdam, 1710?); the "Ẓeri ha-Yagon" of Shem-Ṭob ibn Falaquera (Hanau, 1716); "Maṭṭeh Mosheh," by Moses b. Abraham Mat, rabbi of Przemysl (Frankfort-on-the-Main, 1720); "Minḥah Ḥadashah," on the Pirḳe Abot, containing extracts from Rashi, Maimonides, and the "Pirḳe Mosheh" and "Leb Abot" of Michael Moraftschek (*ib.* 1722); "Tiḳḳun Shelomoh," the order of Sabbath prayers according to Isaac Luria (Venice, 1733; Amsterdam, 1775; Dyhernfurth, 1806); "Orḥot Ẓadiḳim," with a Judæo-German translation (Amsterdam, 1735); the "Agur" of Jacob Landau (Offenbach, 1738); "Ḳehillat Shelomoh," a collection of rites, prayers, and "dinim," with a small Hebrew and Judæo-German vocabulary under the title "Ḥinnuk Ḳaṭan" (Amsterdam, 1744; Frankfort-on-the-Oder, 1799; Hanover, 1830); the "Sefer ha-Gan," moral exhortations of Judah Ḥasid, and the "Hadrakah" of Johanan Luria (Fürth, 1747).

Bibliography: Preface (by London) to *Maṭṭeh Mosheh*, Frankfort-on-the-Main, 1720; Approbation, *ib.* by Samuel Schotten; Fürst, *Bibl. Jud.* ii. 255; Zedner, *Cat. Hebr. Books Brit. Mus.* pp. 364, 498, 566, 698.

H. R. N. T. L.

LONG BRANCH. See New Jersey.

LONGO, SAADIA BEN ABRAHAM: Turkish Hebrew poet; lived at Constantinople about the middle of the sixteenth century. A manuscript in the Bodleian Library (Neubauer, "Cat. Bodl. Hebr. MSS." No. 1986) contains a collection of Longo's poems on various subjects; letters written by him to contemporary scholars and by them to him; a poetical correspondence between Longo and David Onkeneira; and a paper entitled "Naḥal Ḳedumim," in prose interspersed with verse in which occur 1,000 words beginning with א, an arrangement similar to that which was followed in the "Elef Alfin" of Ibn Laṭimi.

Some of Longo's dirges were published under the title "Shibre Luḥot" (Salonica, 1594). To them is prefixed a chronicle of Jewish writers and their works, entitled "Seder Zemannim." Longo wrote, besides, poems on many works of his contemporaries; these poems are printed at the beginning of the works to which they refer.

Bibliography: Fürst, *Bibl. Jud.* ii. 255; Steinschneider, *Cat. Bodl.* col. 2227.

G. M. Sel.

LONZANO, ABRAHAM BEN RAPHAEL DE: Austrian grammarian; lived at the beginning of the eighteenth century. He was baptized at Idstein and took the name of **Wilhelm Heinrich Neumann.** His Hebrew grammar, "Ḳinyan Abraham," was published in Zolkiev in 1723 (De le Roi, "Die Evangelische Christenheit und die Juden," i. 93; Steinschneider, "Cat. Bodl." col. 699).

T. M. Sc.

LONZANO, MENAHEM BEN JUDAH BEN MENAHEM DE: Palestinian Masoretic and midrashic scholar, lexicographer, and poet; died after 1608 in Jerusalem. His nativity is unknown, but it has been supposed that he was born in Italy. According to Jellinek, who identified Lonzano (לונזאנו or לונצאנו) with Longano, a seaport of Messenia, his home was Greece; it may, however, have been Longono, a port of Tuscany near Leghorn. In early childhood Lonzano lost both father and mother, and throughout his entire life he was haunted by poverty, care, and sickness ("Shete Yadot," p. 81a).

Poverty and Travels.

In his youth he went to Jerusalem and married there, but in consequence of the treachery of one of his friends, Gedaliah Cordovero, he was compelled to leave the city; he went to Constantinople, where he enjoyed the hospitality of a certain Solomon ("Ṭobah Tokaḥat," pp. 140, 148).

There also he met Samuel di Modena, whom he calls "teacher," and under whom he studied for some time (Conforte, "Ḳore ha-Dorot," p. 44a). From Constantinople he returned to Jerusalem: he was compelled to travel continually to earn his bread. In old age, again driven by poverty, he returned to Italy, having spent altogether about forty years of his life in Jerusalem. Though paralyzed in both feet and with the sight of one eye entirely lost, he preached twice in an Italian synagogue and gave the community cause to marvel at his unusual knowledge of midrashic literature. A fund was raised by the congregation to support him and to enable him to return to Jerusalem, and a petition was sent to a wealthy man asking him for a generous contribution. This letter (Mortara, No. 12) has been published by David Kaufmann ("J. Q. R." viii. 525 *et seq.*). Lonzano died in the outskirts of Jerusalem and was buried there (comp. "Shibḥe Yerushalayim," p. 3a; "Ḥibbat Yerushalayim," p. 42b; Luncz, "Jerusalem," i. 115).

Lonzano had three children; a son, Adonikam, died at an early age. He was the father-in-law of the historian David Conforte ("Ḳore ha-Dorot," *l.c.*); Lonzano of Florence (1716), author of a responsum mentioned in "Shemesh Ẓedaḳah" (i., No. 15, p. 27a), may be one of his descendants (Landshuth, "'Ammude ha-'Abodah," p. 184).

Lonzano's first work, composed and printed in his youth, probably in Constantinople about 1572, contains "Derek Ḥayyim," a moral poem of

315 verses; "Pizmonim u-Baḳḳashot," hymns and prayers; and "'Abodat Miḳdash," a poetical description of the daily sacrifice in the Temple (comp. Steinschneider, "Cat. Bodl." col. 1728).

He wrote commentaries to most of his poems; this was, indeed, often necessary on account of the obscurity of his verses, especially where they are cabalistic in content and employ the cabalistic terminology. He generally indicates the meters of the piyyuṭim, many of which were set to Arabic melodies because these, the author thought, were better adapted, on account of their melancholy, to arouse feelings of devotion and humility ("Shete Yadot," p. 65b); or, as he says farther on in the same work (p. 142a), because they sound more solemn than any others. He is well aware of the fact that high authorities objected to the use of foreign melodies for religious hymns, but he does not share their view, although he objects most strongly to the practise of imitating the sound of foreign words by means of Hebrew assonants. He condemns, for instance, "Shem Nora," imitating the title of the Italian song "Seniora"; and he felt compelled to declare solemnly before God and Israel that he used foreign terms only to praise the Lord and not for profane or frivolous purposes (*ib.* p. 122a).

From the point of view of literary history the passage in "Shete Yadot" (p. 137b) in which he names those payyeṭanim he preferred is valuable. He considers a good religious poem one that would cheer and gladden him while it would also make him weep; that would break the haughtiness of his heart and inspire him with love for God (comp. Sachs, "Die Religiöse Poesie der Juden in Spanien," p. 257). Although his own poems display little taste or beauty, the cabalists were fond of quoting them, and some of his piyyuṭim became part of the Sephardic Maḥzor (comp. Maḥzor Sefarad for "Shalosh Regalim," ed. Vienna, 1836, pp. 21–22; Reubens, "Catalogue Ḥesheḳ Shelomoh," p. 83, No. 573, Amsterdam, 1857; Landshuth, "'Ammude ha-'Abodah," p. 181).

Lonzano called his chief work "Shete Yadot" (= "Two Hands"; Venice, 1618), taking the title from Ex. xxvi. 17; and, keeping to the same figure, he divided these two "hands" into five "fingers" ("eẓba'ot") each. The five fingers of the first part, called "Yad 'Ani" ("Hand of the Poor"; comp. Ezek. xvi. 49), are severally entitled "Or Torah," "Ma'arik," "'Abodat Miḳdash," "Derek Ḥayyim," and "Ṭobah Tokaḥat."

Masorah.

(1) "Or Torah," Masoretic studies, and emendations of the Masoretic text of the Pentateuch. For this he used old Pentateuchal manuscripts, from which he took much valuable material not found in other sources. He possessed some very valuable unprinted midrashim, among them some which even the author of the 'Aruk and of the Yalḳuṭ had never seen. To aid him in collecting his splendid library his friends wrote to the communities of Jerusalem, Aleppo, and Damascus, and he obtained books from those cities. An illustration of Lonzano's scientific spirit is found in the passage in which he says: "I have made this correction on the strength of ten or more manuscripts, not one of which could be copied [now] for 100 ducats, and some of which are more than five or six hundred years old, namely: the 'Massoret Seyag la-Torah' of Meïr ben Todros ha-Levi Abulafia (a manuscript of the Masorah), the 'Ḳiryat Sefer' of Meïri, the ''Eṭ Sofer' of David Ḳimḥi, the 'Shemen Sason,' and various others. Accordingly, if any one is in doubt as to the reading of any passage in the Bible, with God's help I will resolve his perplexity, especially if I am at home." Lonzano could not endure the thought that this scientific material was lying idle or that it might perish with him. He therefore determined to publish the book, even at an expense of a hundred ducats for printing, although he was well aware that he was acting cruelly toward his needy family in Jerusalem, to which he could send no money. The "Or Torah" was afterward published separately (Amsterdam, 1659; Hamburg, 1738; Berlin, 1745; Zolkiev, 1747; see Benjacob, "Oẓar ha-Sefarim," p. 28).

Lexicography.

(2) "Ma'arik," explanations in alphabetical order of foreign words in the Talmuds, the Midrashim, and the Zohar. His knowledge of Arabic and Greek, gained during his toilsome journeys, proved of great service in his philosophical investigations. In the introduction to this part he speaks, not without humor, of his new method of treating these loan-words and of the way he came to adopt it. Thus Lonzano actually reintroduced into lexicography the rational, scientific spirit of the old, classic Hebræo-Arabic philologists, despite the opposition of his contemporaries and against the authority of old, recognized teachers, including even the author of the 'Aruk. The summary of the "Ma'arik" by Philippe d'Aquin, the author of the lexicon "Ma'arik ha-Ma'areket" (Paris, 1629), like the whole of the work "Shete Yadot," is as valuable as it is rare. It has been published in modern times by A. Jellinek (Leipsic, 1853), and is printed in the Lemberg edition of the 'Aruk of Nathan ben Jehiel of Rome under the title "Arba'ah Sefarim Niftaḥim" (1857).

(3) The "'Abodat Miḳdash" and (4) "Derek Ḥayyim" are reprints, with additions, from his first work, mentioned above; the "'Abodat Miḳdash" was published also by Judah Perez in his collection "Sha'are Raḥamim" (Venice, 1710), by Jacob Emden (Leghorn, 1767), by Azriel of Wilna (Fürth, 1726), and at Venice at the end of the sixteenth century (see Fürst, "Bibl. Jud." ii. 256; Zedner, "Cat. Hebr. Books Brit. Mus." p. 528).

(5) "Ṭobah Tokaḥat," didactic poems, written at the house of Solomon, his patron in Constantinople. These are largely borrowed from a collection of short moral proverbs, entitled "Sefer Toẓe'ot Ḥayyim," by a certain Moses ben Nathanael ibn Solomon.

The second part of the "Shete Yadot," called "Yad ha-Melek," and also divided into five "fingers," is a collection of old midrashic works, some of which appeared here for the first time; others afforded more complete and correct texts than any previously known. Lonzano himself, on account of lack of money, could print only: (1) "Haggadat Bereshit"; of the remaining four "fingers" of the "Yad ha-Melek," (2) "Midrash Agur" was published, according to Benjacob ("Oẓar ha-Sefarim,"

p. 299), in 1626, at Safed or Kefar 'Ain Zeitun; but Steinschneider ("Cat. Bodl." col. 1778) denies that it ever appeared in print. The other three "fingers" exist only in manuscript: (3) "Tanna debe Eliyahu"; (4) "Abot de-Rabbi Natan," "Masseket Derek Ereẓ," "Otiyyot de R. Akiba"; (5) "Sefer ha-Tashlumin," containing the remaining portions of Genesis Rabbah, and supplements to Midrash Yelammedenu, Sifra, Sifre, and Tanḥuma.

Lonzano wrote also: "'Adi Zahab," glosses to the "Lebush" of Mordecai Jaffe (see Azulai, "Shem ha-Gedolim," ii. 106); "Imre Emet," notes on Ḥayyim Vidal's Cabala; "'Omer Man," commentary on Idra Zuṭa, a part of the Zohar, published with a refutation by Naphtali ben David (Amsterdam, 1729); and lexicographical observations on the Yerushalmi (published by S. Buber in "Ha-Asif," ii. 320 *et seq.*).

Characterization.

In spite of physical infirmities, Lonzano was an eager combatant, and not only defended his own conclusions with energy, but also aggressively attacked both his predecessors and his contemporaries. At the same time he always felt conscious that their worth was as far above his as the "heaven is above the earth" ("Shete Yadot," p. 83). He assails the author of the midrashic commentary "Mattenat Kehunnah," attacks Israel ben Moses Najjara on account of blasphemous illustrations and expressions in his "'Olat Ḥodesh," disputes with Abraham Monson concerning Vidal's Cabala, with Solomon Norzi concerning the Masorah, and with others. It can easily be understood that in his single-minded devotion to the truth, "to which all owe the highest regard" ("Shete Yadot," p. 81b), Lonzano made many personal enemies. In only one respect does he seem to have been in harmony with the spirit of the time, and that was in his love for the Cabala and his hostility toward philosophy.

Bibliography: A. L. Frumkin, *Toledot Ḥakme Yerushalayim*, pp. 103 *et seq.*; D. Kaufmann, *Notes on the Life of Menahem di Lonsano*, in *J. Q. R.* viii. 525; Landshuth, *'Ammude ha-'Abodah*, i. 178 *et seq.*; Jellinek, *Ma'arik*, Preface; Delitzsch, *Zur Gesch. der Jüdischen Poesie*, p. 56; Zunz, *S. P.* p. 357.

S. S. M. Sc.

LOOKING-GLASS. See Mirror.

LOPEZ: A family of Sephardic Jews several of whom were distinguished for scholarly attainments.

Eliahu Lopez: Dutch ḥakam of the seventeenth century. He received his rabbinical education, together with Isaac Nieto and others, in the Yeshiba de los Pintos at Rotterdam, and then at Amsterdam, in which city he was for some years ḥakam. At the dedication of the large synagogue he delivered an oration, which was printed together with the other orations delivered on that occasion. While still a young man Lopez went as ḥakam to Barbados.

Bibliography: Kayserling, *Bibl. Esp.-Port.-Jud.* p. 64; *idem*, in *Publ. Am. Jew. Hist. Soc.* iii. 19.

Isaac Lopez: Ḥakam at Amsterdam. He issued a new and revised edition of Aboab's "Nomologia" (Amsterdam, 1727).

Isaac Henriquez Lopez: Haham in London at the beginning of the eighteenth century. At the inauguration of the society known as "Sahare Ora Vaawi Yethomim" he delivered a discourse which was printed under the title "Oracion . . . Que se Hizieron en la Celebridad de la Fundacion de la Santa y Pia Hermandad de Sahare Ora Vaawi Yethomim" (London, 1703).

G. M. K.

LOPEZ, SIR MANASSEH MASSEH: English politician; born in Jamaica Jan. 22, 1755; died at Maristow House, Devonshire, 1831; descended from ancient Sephardic stock. Both he and his father, Mordecai Rodriguez Lopez, became converts to Christianity in 1802. In the same year Manasseh Lopez was returned to Parliament as member for New Romney, and was created a baronet Oct. 5, 1805, with remainder to his nephew Ralph Franco. At the next election Lopez secured a seat for Barnstaple, for which borough he was again returned in 1818. On March 18, 1819, he was found guilty of having bribed the electors of the borough of Grampound to secure his election, and on conviction was sentenced to two years' imprisonment with a fine of £1,000 ($5,000). On Nov. 13 he was again prosecuted for a similar offense, and on conviction was sentenced to another fine and term of imprisonment. Notwithstanding this, Lopez was once more returned to Parliament, in 1823, as member for the borough of Westbury. He was reelected in 1826, but resigned to make room for Sir Robert Peel, who had been rejected at Oxford University.

Subsequently Lopez filled the office of recorder of Westbury, in addition to being a magistrate for two counties.

Bibliography: Picciotto, *Sketches of Anglo-Jewish History*, pp. 304, 305; *Dict. Nat. Biog.*; *Gentleman's Magazine*, 1831.

J. G. L.

LOPEZ, RODRIGO: Court physician to Queen Elizabeth; born in Portugal about 1525; executed June 7, 1594, for having attempted to poison the queen. He settled in London in 1559, and in 1571 was residing in the parish of St. Peter le Poer. Previous to this he had become a member of the College of Physicians, and was selected in the last-mentioned year to read the anatomy lecture at the college—an honor which he declined. Before 1584 he had become body-physician to the Earl of Leicester; and he was accused of assisting that nobleman in removing some of his enemies by poison. Two years later he became chief physician to Queen Elizabeth, who in 1589 granted him the monopoly of importing aniseed and sumac into England.

Relations with Don Antonio.

At court Lopez became acquainted with the Earl of Essex, and was thus brought into relations with Don Antonio, the pretender to the crown of Portugal, and with Antonio Perez, the discharged secretary of Philip II. He assisted them in inducing the queen to permit the attempted invasion of Portugal in 1589, and suffered some loss of influence through its failure. An indiscreet revelation of some of Essex's ailments set that nobleman against him; and about 1590 Lopez began intriguing against Antonio with the court of Spain, at first with the connivance of Walsingham, who hoped through Manuel de Andrada, one of Lopez's adherents, to obtain useful information of Spanish projects. Andrada brought back a diamond and ruby ring worth £100 as an earnest of the reward Lopez would get if he removed Don Antonio. Lopez offered the ring to the queen, who refused it, presumptive evidence, according to Major Hume, that she knew it came from Philip II. Later on, the ring was used as evidence of Lopez's designs against the queen.

In Oct., 1593, one Esteban de Gama was seized in Lopez's house on a charge of conspiring against Don Antonio; and shortly afterward a person named Gomez d'Avila was likewise seized on landing at Dover. He proved to have mysterious correspondence relating to "the price of pearls" and to musk and amber, and to be in some relation with Lopez. A third conspirator, Ticino, was induced to come over from Brussels with an invalid safe-conduct. By confronting the prisoners some evidence was elicited leading to the conclusion that the "price of pearls" referred to a plot against the queen, in which Lopez was implicated. He was seized and examined by the Earl of Essex, who failed, however, to find any definite cause for suspicion. Later, confessions of the minor conspirators led to Lopez being put on the rack, where he confessed to having entertained suggestions as to poisoning the queen for the sum of 50,000 ducats, but, as he alleged, merely with the design of cozening the King of Spain and of getting as much money out of him as possible. This excuse was not accepted; and, after lingering some time in the Tower, he, with D'Avila and Ticino, was hanged, drawn, and quartered as a traitor, declaring with his last breath amid the derision of the spectators that he loved the queen as well as he loved Jesus Christ.

His Execution.

Lopez Conspiring to Poison Queen Elizabeth.
(From Carleton's "Thankful Remembrances," 1624.)

His trial created a great sensation at the time. References are made to it in Marlowe's "Faustus," Dekker's "Whore of Babylon," and Middleton's "Game at Chess"; while it has been suggested by Sidney Lee that he was the original *Shylock* in "The Merchant of Venice," a version of which appears to have been put on the stage about two months after Lopez's execution. The fact that Shakespeare was on the side of the Earl of Essex, and that *Antonio* is adopted as the name of the hero, lends some plausibility to this suggestion. See SHYLOCK.

Historians are divided as to the exact amount of criminality involved in Lopez's connection with Spanish plots. Dimock ("English Historical Review," 1894, pp. 440–472) denies his innocence on the ground that he kept the negotiations secret. Major Hume ("Treason and Plot," pp. 115–152, New York, 1901) considers his guilt unproved, as he had been permitted to make similar false suggestions with the connivance of Walsingham in 1590.

BIBLIOGRAPHY: S. Lee, in *Gentleman's Magazine*, Feb., 1880; *idem*, in *Tr. New Shakespeare Society*, 1887–92, pt. ii., pp. 158–162; *idem*, in *Dict. Nat. Biog.* s.v.; H. Graetz, *Shylock in der Sage, im Drama, und in der Gesch.* Krotoschin, 1880; Forneron, *Philippe II.* vol. ii., Paris, 1890; Hume, *Treason and Plot*, p. 116, note.

J.

LOPEZ-LAGUNA. See LAGUNA.

LOPEZ ROSA: Portuguese Marano family of Lisbon, which owned a printing establishment there in 1647.

Duarte Lopez Rosa: Physician; born at Beja. Duarte was condemned by the Inquisition at Lisbon (Oct. 10, 1723) as an adherent of Judaism.

Moses Duarte Lopez Rosa: Physician and poet of the seventeenth century; born at Beja, stayed for a time at Rome, and then settled in Amsterdam, where in 1680 he openly professed Judaism, taking the name of Moses. He was a member of the Akademia de los Floridos at Amsterdam. Especially attached to the Portuguese royal couple, he addressed sonnets and a longer poem to the royal bride elect, a princess of Neuburg, and to the bridesman, D. Manuel Telles da Silva; and some years later he wrote a pæan on the birth of an infante.

The published works of Lopez Rosa include: "Alientos de la Verdad en los Clarines de la Fama," etc., Amsterdam, 1688; "Soneto Dedicado a la . . . Princeza de Neuburgo D. Maria Sofia, Agora Rainha de Portugal, em Sua Felice União com el Rey D. Pedro II." n.d., n.p.; "Soneto ao exc. Senhor Principe Senescal de Ligue," n.d., n.p.; "Panegyrico Sobre la Restauracion de Inglaterra en la Coronacion de las Magestades de Guillelmo III. y Ser[a] Maria por Reyes de la Gran Bretaña," *ib.* 1690; "Elogios ao Felice Nacimiento do Infante de Portugal, Filho de D. Pedro II. e de D. Maria Sofia," *ib.* 1691. The following remained unprinted: "Luzes de la Idea y Academicos Discursos Que Se Proposieron en la Ilustre Academia de Amsterdam en el Año de 1683, Intit. Los Floridos de la Almendra, con Otros Flores del Ingenio"; and "Novellas Espanholes."

BIBLIOGRAPHY: Barbosa Machado, *Bibliotheca Lusitana*, i. 733; Kayserling, *Bibl. Esp.-Port.-Jud.* p. 95; idem, *Gesch. der Juden in Portugal*, p. 319.

Ruy (Ezekiel) Lopez Rosa: Astrologer; born in Portugal; lived at Amsterdam in the seventeenth century. He gave an exposition of the "seven weeks" of Daniel ix. 25.

Bibliography: Barrios, *Relacion de los Poetas*, p. 54; Kayserling, *Bibl. Esp.-Port.-Jud.* p. 95; Steinschneider, *Cat. Bodl.* col. 3044.

Simon Lopez Rosa (called also **Abraham Farrar**): Physician, and director of the oldest Spanish-Portuguese congregation (Bet Ya'aḳob) in Amsterdam; died Dec. 14, 1618 (his wife died nine days later). He was not an orthodox Jew. He spoke slightingly of the Haggadah and the Cabala, and converted many members of the community to his liberal views. A precursor of Uriel Acosta, Lopez Rosa opposed the rulings of the Rabbis, thus occasioning a quarrel in the congregation, which led to the founding in 1618 of a new congregation (Bet Yisrael). R. Joel Sirkes of Brest-Litovsk, to whom the rabbis of Amsterdam carried the case, advised them to excommunicate Lopez Rosa.

Bibliography: Kayserling, *Bibl. Esp.-Port.-Jud.* p. 44; *idem*, in *R. E. J.* xliii. 275 *et seq.*

G. M. K.

LORD'S PRAYER, THE: Name given by the Christian world to the prayer which Jesus taught his disciples (Matt. vi. 9-13; Luke xi. 1-4). According to Luke the teaching of the prayer was suggested by one of Jesus' disciples who, on seeing him holding communion with God in prayer, asked him to teach them also to pray, as John the Baptist had similarly taught his disciples a certain form of prayer. Obviously, then, the latter was of a similar character. From the Talmudic parallels (Tosef., Ber. iii. 7; Ber. 16b-17a, 29b; Yer. Ber. iv. 7d) it may be learned that it was customary for prominent masters to recite brief prayers of their own in addition to the regular prayers; and there is indeed a certain similarity noticeable between these prayers and that of Jesus.

As the following extracts from the Revised Version show, the prayer in Luke is much shorter than that in Matthew, from which it differs, too, in expression. Possibly both were in circulation among the early Christians; the one in Matthew, however, is of a later origin, as is shown below:

Matthew.	Luke.
Our Father which art in heaven, Hallowed be thy name.	Father, Hallowed be thy name.
Thy Kingdom come. Thy will be done, as in heaven so on earth.	Thy Kingdom come.
Give us this day our daily [Greek: apportioned or needful] bread.	Give us day by day our daily [apportioned] bread.
And forgive us our debts, as we also have forgiven our debtors.	And forgive us our sins; for we ourselves also forgive every one that is indebted to us.
And bring us not into temptation, but deliver us from the evil one. [Addition in many manuscripts: For thine is the kingdom, and the power, and the glory, for ever. Amen.]	And bring us not into temptation.

The prayer is a beautiful combination or selection of formulas of prayer in circulation among the Hasidæan circles; and there is nothing in it expressive of the Christian belief that the Messiah had arrived in the person of Jesus. On the contrary, the first and principal part is a prayer for the coming of the kingdom of God, exactly as is the Ḳaddish, with which it must be compared in order to be thoroughly understood.

Original Form and Meaning.

The invocation "Our Father" = "Abinu" or Abba (hence in Luke simply "Father") is one common in the Jewish liturgy (see Shemoneh 'Esreh, the fourth, fifth, and sixth benedictions, and comp. especially in the New-Year's ritual the prayer "Our Father, our King! Disclose the glory of Thy Kingdom unto us speedily"). More frequent in Hasidæan circles was the invocation "Our Father who art in heaven" (Ber. v. 1; Yoma viii. 9; Soṭah ix. 15; Abot v. 20; Tosef., Demai, ii. 9; and elsewhere: "Yehi raẓon mi-lifne abinu she-ba-shamayim," and often in the liturgy). A comparison with the Ḳaddish ("May His great name be hallowed in the world which He created, according to His will, and may He establish His Kingdom . . . speedily and at a near time"; see Baer, "'Abodat Yisrael," p. 129, note), with the Sabbath "Ḳedushshah" ("Mayest Thou be magnified and hallowed in the midst of Jerusalem . . . so that our eyes may behold Thy Kingdom"), and with the "'Al ha-Kol" (Massek. Soferim xiv. 12, and prayer-book: "Magnified and hallowed . . . be the name of the supreme King of Kings in the worlds which He created, this world and the world to come, in accordance with His will . . . and may we see Him eye to eye when He returneth to His habitation") shows that the three sentences, "Hallowed be Thy name," "Thy Kingdom come," and "Thy will be done on earth as in heaven," originally expressed one idea only—the petition that the Messianic kingdom might appear speedily, yet always subject to God's will. The hallowing of God's name in the world forms part of the ushering in of His kingdom (Ezek. xxxviii. 23), while the words "Thy will be done" refer to the time of the coming, signifying that none but God Himself knows the time of His "divine pleasure" ("raẓon"; Isa. lxi. 2; Ps. lxix. 14; Luke ii. 14).

The problem for the followers of Jesus was to find an adequate form for this very petition, since they could not, like the disciples of John and the rest of the Essenes, pray "May Thy Kingdom come speedily" in view of the fact that for them the Messiah had appeared in the person of Jesus. The form reported to have been recommended by Jesus is rather vague and indefinite: "Thy Kingdom come"; and the New Testament exegetes explain it as referring to the second coming of the Messiah, the time of the perfection of the kingdom of God (comp. Luke xxii. 18). In the course of time the interpretation of the sentence "Thy will be done" was broadened in the sense of the submitting of everything to God's will, in the manner of the prayer of R. Eliezer (1st cent.): "Do Thy will in heaven above and give rest of spirit to those that fear Thee on earth, and do what is good in Thine eyes. Blessed be Thou who hearest prayer!" (Tosef., Ber. iii. 7).

The rest of the prayer, also, stands in close relation to the Messianic expectation. Exactly as R. Eliezer (Mek.: "Eleazar of Modin") said: "He who created the day created also its provision; wherefore he who, while having sufficient food for the day, says: 'What shall I eat to-morrow?' belongs to the men of little faith such as were the Israelites at the giving of the manna" (Mek., Beshallaḥ, Wayassa', ii.; Soṭah 48b), so Jesus said: "Take no thought for your life, what ye shall eat or . . . drink. . . . . O ye of little faith. . . . Seek ye first the Kingdom of God, . . . and all these things shall be added to you" (Matt. vi. 25–34; Luke xii. 22–31; comp. also Simeon b. Yoḥai, Mek. *l.c.*; Ber. 35b; Ḳid. iv. 14). Faith being thus the prerequisite of those that wait for the Messianic time, it behooves them to pray, in the words of Solomon (Prov. xxx. 8, Hebr.; comp. Beẓah 16a), "Give us our apportioned bread" ("leḥem ḥuḳḳi"), that is, the bread we need daily.

Relation to Messianic Expectation.

Repentance being another prerequisite of redemption (Pirḳe R. El. xliii.; Targ. Yer. and Midr. Leḳah Ṭob to Deut. xxx. 2; Philo, "De Execrationibus," §§ 8–9), a prayer for forgiveness of sin is also required in this connection. But on this point special stress was laid by the Jewish sages of old. "Forgive thy neighbor the hurt that he hath done unto thee, so shall thy sins also be forgiven when thou prayest," says Ben Sira (Ecclus. [Sirach] xxviii. 2). "To whom is sin pardoned? To him who forgiveth injury" (Derek Ereẓ Zuṭa viii. 3; R. H. 17a; see also Jew. Encyc. iv. 590, *s.v.* Didascalia). Accordingly Jesus said: "Whensoever ye stand praying, forgive, if ye have aught against any one; that your Father also which is in heaven may forgive you your trespasses" (Mark xi. 25, R. V.). It was this precept which prompted the formula "And forgive us our sins ["ḥobot" = "debts"; the equivalent of "'awonot" = "sins"] as we also forgive those that have sinned ["ḥayyabim" = "those that are indebted"] against us."

Directly connected with this is the prayer "And lead us not into temptation." This also is found in the Jewish morning prayer (Ber. 60b; comp. Rab: "Never should a man bring himself into temptation as David did, saying, 'Examine me, O Lord, and prove me' [Ps. xxvi. 2], and stumbled" [Sanh. 107a]). And as sin is the work of Satan (James i. 15), there comes the final prayer, "But deliver us from the evil one [Satan]." This, with variations, is the theme of many Hasidæan prayers (Ber. 10b–17a, 60b), "the evil one" being softened into "yeẓer ha-ra'" = "evil desire," and "evil companionship" or "evil accident"; so likewise "the evil one" in the Lord's Prayer was later on referred to things evil (see commentaries on the passage).

The doxology added in Matthew, following a number of manuscripts, is a portion of I Chron. xxix. 11, and was the liturgical chant with which the Lord's Prayer was concluded in the Church; it occurs in the Jewish ritual also, the whole verse being chanted at the opening of the Ark of the Law.

On closer analysis it becomes apparent that the closing verses, Matt. vi. 14–15, refer solely to the prayer for forgiveness. Consequently the original passage was identical with Mark xi. 25; and the Lord's Prayer in its entirety is a later insertion in Matthew. Possibly the whole was taken over from the "Didache" (viii. 2), which in its original Jewish form may have contained the prayer exactly as "the disciples of John" were wont to recite it.

Bibliography: F. H. Chase, *The Lord's Prayer in the Early Church*, in *Texts and Studies*, 3d ed., Cambridge, 1891; Charles Taylor, *Sayings of the Jewish Fathers*, 1897, pp. 124–130; A. Harnack, *Die Ursprüngliche Gestalt des Vaterunser*, in *Sitzungsberichte der Königlichen Academie der Wissenschaften*, Berlin, 1904.

K.

LORD'S SUPPER (called also **The Last Supper**): Name taken from I Cor. xi. 20, and given by the Christian world to the rite known as the eucharist, the partaking of the cup of wine and the bread offered in memory of Jesus' death and brought into connection with the story of his last meal, which he is said to have taken with his disciples on the eve of his crucifixion. According to the synoptic Gospels (Matt. xxvi. 26–29; Mark xiv. 23–25; Luke xxii. 15–18, 19), Jesus was partaking of the Passover meal with his disciples on the fourteenth of Nisan, before his capture by the officers of the high priest. The Gospel of John, however, knows nothing of the institution and assigns the crucifixion to the fourteenth day of Nisan, the day when the Passover lamb is sacrificed. This discrepancy shows that the identification of the "crucified Christ" with the "lamb of God which taketh away the sin of the world" (John i. 29 [adapted from Isa. liii. 7]; I Peter i. 19; Acts viii. 32; Rev. v. 6; and elsewhere) gradually led to an identification of Jesus with the Passover lamb also (see I Cor. v. 7).

Subsequently the mystic love-meals of the Mithra-worshipers, who also broke bread and drank the soma-wine in memory of Mithra's last supper (see T. Cumont, "Die Mysterien des Mithra," pp. 99–101, 118–119, Leipsic, 1903), caused the love-feasts of the early Christians to be celebrated as actual remembrances of the last supper eaten by Jesus; and so a special passage was inserted (I Cor. xi. 23–28, interrupting the context, and contradictory to *ib.* x. 4) in which the apostle rather oddly declares that he had received from Jesus by inspiration the statement that he had instituted the eucharist on the night of his betrayal, giving the formulas for the bread and the cup which, with some variations, appears in each of the three synoptic Gospels. Incompatible with the whole story, however, is the fact that the Christian Didache (ix. 1–4; comp. Jew. Encyc. iv. 587) gives the eucharist formulas for the cup and the wine used in Christian circles without any reference to the crucifixion or to the last supper. This makes it probable that the institution had developed out of the Essene communion-meals and was only at a later time referred to Jesus.

The original idea of the Essene communion-feasts, borrowed from Parseeism, remained attached to it: the hope for the banquets (of leviathan) in paradise; wherefore Jesus is reported as having especially referred to wine in the Kingdom of God (Matt. xxvi. 29; Mark xiv. 25; Luke xxii. 18, 30).

The whole story of the Passover celebration by Jesus on the eve of his crucifixion thus arose in circles where real familiarity with Jewish law and life no longer existed. It has, however, been argued that the ritual of the mass or communion service is derived from that of the Passover eve service (see Bickell, "Messe und Pascha"). K.

LORIA. See Luria.

LORIA, ACHILLE: Italian political economist; born at Mantua March 2, 1857; educated at the lyceum of his native city and the universities of Bologna, Pavia, Rome, Berlin, and London. He became professor of political economy in the University of Sienna in 1881; and he has held a similar appointment in the University of Padua since 1891.

Loria is the author of: "La Rendita Fondiaria e le Sue Elisione Naturale," Milan, 1880; "Le Basi Economiche della Costituzione Sociale," Turin, 1886 (translated into French 1893, German 1895, and English 1899); "Analisi della Proprietâ Capitalista," 2 vols., *ib.* 1889 (received the royal prize); "L'Opera Postuma di Carlo Marx," Rome, 1895; "Problemi Sociali Contemporanei," Milan, 1896 (translated into French 1897); "La Costituzione Economica Odierna," Turin, 1899.

Bibliography: Conrad, *Handwörterb. der Staatswissenschaften.*

s. F. T. H.

LORIA, GINO: Italian mathematician; born at Mantua May 19, 1862; educated at the Mantua lyceum and at the University of Turin, becoming doctor of mathematics in 1884. The same year he was appointed demonstrator in mathematics in the University of Turin; in 1886, teacher at the military academy, Turin; and in 1887, assistant professor in the University of Genoa, where since 1891 he has held the chair of descriptive geometry.

Loria's publications treat of pure mathematics and its history, and have appeared in Italian and foreign magazines. He is also the author of "Il Passato ed il Presente delle Principali Teorie Geometriche," 2d ed. 1896 (translated into German, Polish, and English).

s. F. T. H.

LORKI, IBN VIVES. See Ibn Vives al-Lorqui.

LORM, HIERONYMUS. See Landesmann, Heinrich.

LORRAINE. See Metz.

LOS ANGELES: Commercial and manufacturing city in the state of California; situated on the left bank of the river of the same name, and about 14 miles from the Pacific Ocean. Jews first settled in Los Angeles in 1849; and they increased in number so rapidly that within a few years they organized a congregation and erected a house of worship. They also obtained from the city the grant of a tract of land for a cemetery, and established a charitable organization to afford decent burial for the poor.

At present (1904) the Jews number about 3,000 in a total population of about 120,000. There are a number of Jewish educational and charitable institutions, of which may be mentioned: Ladies' Hebrew Benevolent Society, Los Angeles Lodge I. O. B. B. and two other B'nai B'rith lodges, Kaspare Cohn Hospital Association, and Ladies' Aid Society. The congregation has had five rabbis: A. W. Edelman, E. Schreiber, A. Blum, M. G. Solomon, and S. Hecht, the present incumbent.

The Jewish contingent of the population has taken an active part in promoting the business interests of the city, and a number of Jews are prominent as bankers, manufacturers, real-estate dealers, wholesale-grocery merchants, etc. There are also several Jewish physicians, lawyers, architects, and mechanics. See Jew. Encyc. iii. 511, *s.v.* California.

A.

LOST PROPERTY. See Finder of Property.

LOT (לוט).—**Biblical Data:** Son of Haran, Abraham's brother, and, consequently, nephew of Abraham; emigrated with his grandfather, Terah, from Ur of the Chaldees to Haran (Gen. xi. 31). Lot joined Abraham in the land of Canaan, and in the time of famine went with him to Egypt (*ib.* xii. 4, xiii. 1). Owing to Lot's riches in flocks and tents a quarrel arose between his herdsmen and those of Abraham, the result of which was the separation of uncle and nephew. Lot chose the fertile plain of the Jordan, and extended his tents to Sodom (*ib.* xiii. 5–12). After the defeat of the King of Sodom and his allies in the valley of Siddim, Lot, who had been dwelling among them, was taken prisoner, with all his family and property, by Chedorlaomer; but he was rescued by Abraham (*ib.* xiv. 12–16).

In Gen. xix. Lot is represented as the counterpart of Abraham in regard to hospitality: like Abraham, he rose to meet the angels, whom he took for men, bowing to them; and, like Abraham, too, he "pressed" them to enter his house and "made them a feast" (*ib.* xix. 1–3). When his dwelling was surrounded by the profligate people of Sodom, Lot placed his duty as a host above that as a father and offered them his two unmarried daughters. The angels then announced to him that their mission was to destroy the guilty cities, and urged him to leave the place. Lot tried, but unsuccessfully, to persuade his sons-in-law to leave also. He himself hesitated to flee, and the angels took him, his wife, and his two daughters by the hand, "the Lord being merciful unto him," and led him out of the city. They then enjoined him to flee to the mountain without looking behind him; but the mountain being so far off Lot requested them to spare the small city of Zoar in order that he might find refuge there; and his request was granted. During the flight to Zoar, Lot's wife, who looked behind her, was turned into a pillar of salt (*ib.* xix. 4–22, 26).

Lot, fearing that Zoar, also, might be destroyed eventually, went up to the mountain and dwelt in a cave, where, by an incestuous intercourse with his two daughters, he became the ancestor of the two nations Moab and Ammon (*ib.* xix. 30–38). Lot is twice mentioned in the expression "children of Lot," applied to Ammon and Moab (Deut. ii. 19; Ps. lxxxiii. 8).

E. G. H. M. Sel.

——**In Rabbinical Literature:** Lot is generally represented by the Rabbis in an unfavorable light. When the quarrel arose between his shepherds and those of Abraham (Gen. xiii. 7), there was a quarrel between Abraham and Lot also. The latter sent his flocks to graze in fields that did not belong to him; and when Abraham, induced by the complaints of the wronged owners, remonstrated,

Lot showed himself rebellious (Targ. of pseudo-Jonathan and Yer. to Gen. xiii. 7; Pesiḳ. R. 3 [ed. Friedmann, pp. 9b–10a]; Gen. R. xli. 6–7). Lot, while separating himself from Abraham, separated himself from God also, saying, "I have no desire either in Abraham or in his God" (Gen. R. xli. 9–10). It was only after the wicked ("rasha'") Lot had left Abraham that God spoke again to the latter (Pesiḳ. R. *l.c.*; comp. Gen. xiii. 14). Lot was given over to lust; therefore he chose Sodom as his residence (Pesiḳ. R. *l.c.*; Gen. R. xli. 9), and his daughters' act of incest was due to his neglect. The account of it was therefore read every Saturday in the synagogues as a warning to the public (Nazir 23b; Gen. R. li. 12).

The above-mentioned incident of the flocks shows that Lot was not too conscientious; he was besides very greedy of wealth; and at Sodom he practised usury (Gen. R. li. 8). His hesitation to leave the city (comp. Gen. xix. 16) was due to his regret for his great wealth which he was obliged to abandon (Gen. R. l. 17). The Rabbis cited the drunkenness of Lot as an example of the degree of intoxication which renders a man irresponsible ('Er. 65a). All the special favors which Lot received from God were granted through the merit of Abraham; otherwise he would have perished with the people of Sodom (Gen. R. xli. 4; Midr. ha-Gadol to Gen. xiii. 11). His being spared at the time of the destruction of Sodom is recorded also as a reward for not having betrayed Abraham when the latter told Pharaoh that Sarah was his sister (*ib.* li. 8).

Lot's Wife Turned into a Pillar of Salt.
(From the Sarajevo Haggadah of the fourteenth century.)

The Pirḳe Rabbi Eli'ezer, however, shows a much milder attitude toward Lot, interpreting the word "ẓaddiḳ" of Gen. xviii. 23 as referring to him (Pirḳe R. El. xxv.). Besides passing over in silence Lot's shameful deeds, it records the hospitality which, in imitation of Abraham, he practised at Sodom: even after the people of Sodom had proclaimed that any hospitable person would be burned, he continued to practise it under cover of night. This trait is mentioned also in Gen. R. (l. 8); but it is there narrated in a manner which renders Lot's merits insignificant. It is further said (*ib.* l. 9; Lev. R. xxiii.) that Lot pleaded the whole night in favor of the people of Sodom. The Alphabet of Ben Sira (ed. Bagdad, pp. 2b, 17b, 19b), apparently borrowing from the Koran (suras vii. 78–82, xxii. 43), calls Lot "a perfectly righteou man" ("ẓaddiḳ gamur") and prophet (comp. I Peter ii. 7, 8; Epstein, "Mi-Ḳadmoniyyot ha-Yehu dim," 121).

Genesis Rabbah (l. 14) concludes that Lot had a the time of the destruction of Sodom four daugh ters, two married and two betrothed, and that th latter escaped with their father. But he had previ ously had a daughter named Peloṭet, who was mar ried to one of the inhabitants of Sodom. Sh secretly practised hospitality, but being one day discovered by the people of Sodom, was sentence to be burned (Pirḳe R. El. *l.c.*; "Sefer ha-Yashar," "Lek Leka," ed. Leghorn, p. 23a). Lot's wife called "'Irit" or "'Idit," desirous to see whether he other two daughters followed her, looked behin her; but she then saw the back of the Shekinal and was accordingly punished for her imprudenc (Pirḳe R. El. *l.c.*). She was turned into a pillar o salt because sh had previously sinned by no giving salt t strangers (Targ pseudo-Jona than and Yer. t Gen. xix. 26 comp. Gen. R li. 7). Accordin to a legend, oxen used to consum every day th pillar of salt by licking it dow to the toes, bu it was restore by the mornin (Pirḳe R. El *l.c.*; Sefer ha Yashar, "Wa yera," p. 28a, b) Lot's wife, be ing turned int a pillar of salt was not con sidered as a dead body, contact with which ren dered one unclean (Niddah 70b). The transfor mation was one of those miraculous occurrence at sight of which one must recite a benedictio (Ber. 54a).

S. S. M. Sel.

——**Critical View:** Lot is regarded by the critics a an eponym representing the supposed common an cestor of the two tribes or nations of Moab and Am mon. His relation to Abraham is in this view intended to mark the ethnographic connection o these two tribes with the Israelites; and his choic of an eastern location may be taken as indicating a voluntary relinquishment of all claims of the Moab ites and Ammonites to Canaan. His relations wit his daughters probably represent some rough pleas antry common among the Israelitish folk and indica ting their scorn for their nearest neighbors. Fenton however ("Early Hebrew Life"), suggests that in a matriarchal state such unions would not be indeco rous, since in social stages where descent was trace only through the mother the father would be no relation to the children.

The story about Lot's wife, also, bears marks of popular origin, and is regarded by critics and travelers as a folk-legend intended to explain some pillar of crystallized rock-salt resembling the female human form. Owing to its composition, such a pillar would soon dissolve. One in the neighborhood of the Dead Sea was identified by Josephus ("Ant." i. 11, § 4) as that of Lot's wife; and another (or the same) had that name at the time of Clement of Rome (I Cor. xi. 2).

As Lot is declared to have dwelt in a cave (Gen. xix. 30), Ewald ("History of Israel," i. 313) and Dillmann (*ad loc.*) identify him with Lotan, the leader of one of the tribes of Horites or cave-dwellers (Gen. xxxvi. 22, 29). The Dead Sea is still called "Baḥr Luṭ."

E. G. H. J.

LOTS: Means of determining chances. Primitive peoples, and occasionally those on a higher plane of culture, resort to lots for the purposes of augury. They spin a coconut or entangle strips of leather in order to obtain an omen. Thieves especially are detected by the casting of lots, etc. (Tylor, "Primitive Culture," German ed., i. 78–82). The pagans on a ship with Jonah under stress of a storm cast lots in order to find out who among them had incurred the Divine anger (Jonah i. 7). Haman resorted to the lot when he intended to destroy the Jews (Esth. iii. 7). The Greek heroes cast their lots into Agamemnon's helmet in order to ascertain who should fight with Hector ("Iliad," vii. 171). In ancient Italy oracles with carved lots were used.

In Ancient Israel.

The ancient Israelites likewise resorted to the lot for the most varied purposes. Rhabdomancy was known as late as Hosea (Hos. iv. 12); and Ezekiel (Ezek. xxi. 26 *et seq.*) mentions the arrow-oracle of the King of Babylon, which was still used a thousand years later among the pagan Arabians (Wellhausen, "Reste Arabischen Heidenthums," 2d ed., pp. 126 *et seq.*, comp. Sprenger, "Leben und Lehre des Mohammed," i. 259 *et seq.*; Huber, "Ueber das Meiser-Spiel der Heidnischen Araber," Leipsic, 1883). As the priestly lot-oracles are discussed under EPHOD, URIM AND THUMMIM, and TERAPHIM, the present article deals merely with the lot in secular life. Joshua discovers the thief, and Saul the guilty one, by means of the lot (Josh. vii. 16 *et seq.*; I Sam. xiv. 42; comp. I Sam. x. 20 *et seq.*). Primitive peoples divide land and other common property by means of the lot. In Hebrew the word for "lot" ("goral") has retained the meaning of "share"; it has also acquired the more general meaning of "fate" (Isa. xvii. 14, lvii. 6; Jer. xiii. 25; Ps. xvi. 5; Dan. xii.). The land west of the Jordan is divided among the several tribes by lot (Num. xxvi. 55 *et seq.*, xxxiii. 54, xxxiv. 13, xxxvi. 2; Josh. xiii. 6, xiv. 2, xv. 1, xvii. 1, xviii. 6–10, xix. 51, xxiii. 4; Ps. lxxviii. 55, cv. 11; comp. Ezek. xlv. 1, xlvii. 22). Jewish tradition, finding offense in this kind of allotment, declared that the land was really divided under the inspiration of the Holy Spirit, the lot being merely the visible means of confirming the division for the people (Sifre, Num. 132; B. B. 122a). Prov. xvi. 33 and xviii. 18 indicate that lots were cast in legal controversies. The wicked "part my garments among them, and cast lots upon my vesture" (Ps. xxii. 19; comp. Matt. xxvii. 35; John xxix. 24). Booty of war is divided by lot (Joel iv. 3; Nahum iii. 10; Ob. 11; see also Judges xx. 9; Neh. x. 35, xi. 1; I Chron. xxiv. 5, xxv. 8, xxvi. 13 (see Herzog-Hauck, "Real-Encyc." 3d ed., xi. 643 *et seq.*).

According to the etymology of the word "goral," the lots were probably small stones, or sticks, as Hos. iv. 12 indicates. They were thrown, or possibly shaken (Prov. xvi. 33, "into the lap"), so that one fell out, whereby the case in question was decided. It can not be ascertained whether a tablet with writing on it is meant in Lev. xvi. 8, as the Mishnah assumes (Yoma iii. 9, iv. 1). At the time of the Second Temple the lot was prominent in the Temple cult, and customs were developed, after Biblical example, whereby the several offices were apportioned by lot.

In Talmud and Midrash.

The priests drew lots in all cases where differences might arise (Yoma 37a, 39a–41a, 62a–63b, 65b; Zeb. 113b; Men. 59b; Ker. 28a). In Tamid i. 2 the overseer of the Temple calls for the lot; and Yoma 24b records a discussion whether the priests shall draw lots in holy or in secular garments. Lots were cast four times in succession (Yoma iv. 1). The Prophets increased the four classes of priests that returned from the Diaspora to twenty-four; they mixed up the names of the additional ones and placed them in an urn (κάλπη) and then let each of the four original classes of priests draw five names (Tosef., Ta'an. ii. 1, and parallel passages). The urn was originally made of cypress-wood; but the high priest Ben Gamala had one which was made of gold (Yoma iii. 9); hence drawing lots from it created a sensation (Yer. Yoma 41b, below). In the sanctuary the lots were taken out by hand (Yoma 39b, 40a). The lot was either a black or a white pebble (Yer. Yoma iv., beginning), or was made of olive-, nut-, or cypress-wood (Yoma 37a). A third kind, consisting of pieces of paper with writing on them (πιττάκιον), is frequently mentioned.

Many facts seem to indicate that choosing by lot was common in post-Biblical times. Moses chose the seventy elders (Num. xi. 26) by selecting six men from each of the twelve tribes, and then placing seventy-two pieces of paper (πιττάκιον), of which two were blank, into an urn, one being drawn by each man. He proceeded similarly in determining the 273 first-born who were to pay each five shekels ransom, 22,273 tickets in all being drawn (Yer. Sanh. 19c, below, and parallel passages). Eldad and Medad were, according to Targ. Yer. to Num. xi. 26, among the elders who drew lots. Jacob's sons also drew lots to decide who should take Joseph's coat to their father (Gen. R. lxxxiv.). Achan attempted to bring the casting of lots into discredit when he said to Joshua: "If I order you and the high priest Eleazar to draw lots, one of you will certainly be pronounced guilty" (Sanh. 43b). Nebuchadnezzar's casting of lots (Ezek. xxi. 25 *et seq.*) is mentioned; but, according to the vernacular of the time, the Greek word κλῆρος is used, which occurs also in

Acts i. 26 (Lam. R., Preface, No. 5; Midr. Teh. x. 6; comp. *ib.* x. 5 on casting of lots among the Romans, and Krauss, "Lehnwörter," ii. 545b).

In Palestine brothers divided their patrimony by lot as late as, and probably much later than, the second century (B. B. 106b). Apparently the lot was also occasionally used in ordaining teachers (Yer. Bik. 65d, l. 24). Under Grecian influence the drawing of lots degenerated into dice-playing. "No one is accepted as witness who plays with little stones [ψῆφος]," *i.e.*, gambles professionally (Yer. Sanh. iii. 6 and parallel passages). The same regulation applies to the dice-player (κυβευτής and κυβεία), who is frequently referred to (see passages in Krauss, *l.c.* ii. 501).

In the Middle Ages and in Folk-Lore.

The drawing of lots and its companion practise, the throwing of dice, were common in the Middle Ages; and they are even in vogue at the present time. Moses of Coucy (*c.* 1250) mentions xylomancy. Splinters of wood the rind of which had been removed on one side, were tossed up, and according as they fell on the peeled or the unpeeled side, augured favorably or unfavorably (Güdemann, "Gesch." i. 82). An Italian teacher denounced the casting of lots (*ib.* ii. 221). Dice-playing was especially in vogue among the Italian Jews of the Middle Ages, and was, as well as other games of hazard, frequently forbidden (*ib.* ii. 210). In Germany there was a game of chance, called "Rück oder Schneid," in which a knife was used (Berliner, p. 22). Many books on games of chance originated in the later Middle Ages (see bibliography below). The present writer has in his possession a Bokhara manuscript containing a "Lot-Book of Daniel." It mentions also means ("segullot") for detecting a thief. The Jews of the present day, likewise, are not unacquainted with the various modes of casting lots found among all peoples and used for various and generally harmless purposes; but among these remnants of ancient superstition customs that are Jewish in origin are probably to be found only in Ḥasidic circles and in the East.

Bibliography: T. W. Davies, *Magic, Divination, and Demonology*, pp. 74 *et seq.*, London and Leipsic, 1898; Hastings, *Dict. Bible*, iii. 152 *et seq.*; Thomas Gataker, *Von der Natur und dem Gebrauche der Loose*, 1619; H. Guthe, *Kurzes Bibelwörterb.* p. 397, Tübingen and Leipsic, 1903; Hamburger, *R. B. T.* i. 723; A. Lehmann, *Aberglaube und Zauberei*, p. 40, Stuttgart, 1898; Lenormant, *Magie und Wahrsagekunst*, etc., Jena, 1878; Herzog-Hauck, *Real-Encyc.* 3 ed., xi. 643 *et seq.*; B. Stade, *Gesch. Israels*, i. 471 *et seq.*; E. B. Tylor, *Primitive Culture*, Index; Germ. ed., i. 78 *et seq.*, Leipsic, 1873; I. Wellhausen, *Reste Arabischen Heidenthums* 2d ed., pp. 132 *et seq.*; Winer, *B. R.* ii. 31. On medieval and modern lot-books: Benjacob, *Oẓar ha-Sefarim*, pp. 90 *et seq.* A. Berliner, *Aus dem Leben der Deutschen Juden im Mittelalter*, Berlin, 1900; M. Grunwald, *Mittheilungen der Gesellschaft für Jüdische Volkskunde*, v. 12; M. Güdemann *Gesch.* i., ii.; Steinschneider, *Loosbücher*, in *Hebr. Bibl.* v. 120; idem, *Jüdische Literatur*, ch. xxii., end.

A. L. B.

LOTTERIES. See Gambling.

LOUISVILLE. See Kentucky.

LOUSADA (OF PEAK HOUSE): Name of a family that has held for many generations large possessions in Jamaica. A member of the family was created Duke de Lousada and Marquis di San Miniato. It is the only Jewish family that has held so exalted a title. Its members claim to be descendants of the original Spanish grandees of that name. Isaac de Lousada was confirmed, in 1848, in the titles that had been borne by his "ancestor" the Duke de Lousada, grand chamberlain to Charles III., King of the Two Sicilies. This monarch, when crowned King of Spain, created the duke a grandee of the first class. Isaac de Lousada died in 1857, and was succeeded by his eldest son, Emanuel, second duke (b. 1809; d. 1884). Emanuel was succeeded by his nephew, Horace Francis, the third and present (1904) duke, son of Count Francis (d. 1870), the second son of the first duke. Count Francis married Marianne, daughter of Sir Charles Wolsely; he was created Marquis di San Miniato by the Grand Duke of Tuscany in 1846. Following is a pedigree of the family:

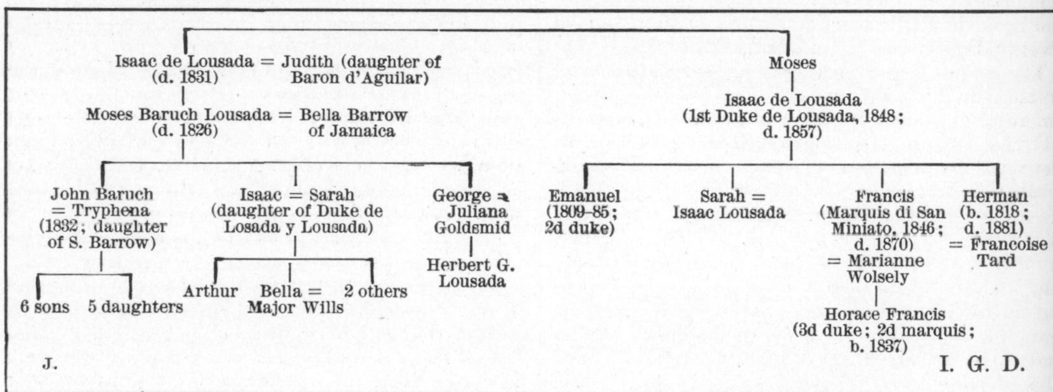

Bibliography: Debrett, *Peerage*, 1901, p. 928; Isaac da Costa *Israel en de Volken*, p. 465, Utrecht, 1876; Burke, *Landed Gentry*, 1868, i. 900; Rietstap, *Armorial General*, i. 10 Gouda, 1884.

J. H. Gut.

LOVE (אהבה): The deep affection by which one person feels closely drawn to another and impelled to give up much, or do much, for him without regard of self.—**Biblical Data:** While the word אהבה, like the Greek ἀγάπη, denotes also sensual love (Hos. ii. 7, 9, 12; Ezek. xxiii. 5, 9; Judges xvi. 4; II Sam. xiii. 15), it becomes, owing to the higher ethical spirit pervading Judaism, more and more expressive of the purer sentiment so exquisitely characterized in Cant. viii. 6-7: "Love is strong as death. . . . Many waters can not quench love either can the floods drown it: if a man would give ll the substance of his house for love, it would ut- erly be contemned." Besides love of man for wom- n, "ahabah" denotes parental love (Gen. xxv. 28, xxvii. 3), and it is transferred to that love of man or man which is better termed friendship, and which exemplified in the love of David and Jonathan nd characterized by the former in the words, "My rother Jonathan, very dear [A. V. "pleasant"] ast thou been unto me; thy love to me was won- erful, passing the love of women" (II Sam. i. 26, Iebr.). Hence "lover" becomes identical with friend" (Prov. xviii. 24; Ps. xxxviii. 12 [A. V. 1], lxxxviii. 19 [A. V. 18]). Gradually the entire ystem of life is permeated by the principle of love, nd the relation between God and man as well as etween man and man is based upon it.

It is the prophet Hosea who, chastened by his ex- erience in his own life, gives to love a deeper and urer meaning, while finding that God loves Israel otwithstanding its backslidings (Hos. xi. 1). It is love of free will (*ib.* xiv. 5 [A.V. 4]). Upon love euteronomy builds its entire system. God loved ne fathers (Deut. x. 15), and because He transferred nis love to their descendants, the entire people of srael, He chose them, though not on account of neir own merit, to be His own peculiar (missionary) ation and shielded them against their foes (*ib.* vii. 8, xxiii. 6). He therefore demands their love in eturn (*ib.* vi. 5; x. 12; xi. 1, 13, 22; xiii. 4; xix. 9; xx. 6, 16, 20). He loves also the stranger, and emands love for the stranger in return (*ib.* x. 18– 9). The love of God for Israel is declared by eremiah to be "an everlasting love" (Jer. xxxi. 3), nd both the exilic seer and the last of the prophets ccentuate this love of God (Isa. lxiii. 9; Mal. i. 2).

The love of God for mankind in general is not ex- ressed in Scripture by the term "love," but by mercy" (Ps. cxlv. 9); it is, however, extended to ll who observe His commandments (Ex. xx. 6; eut. vii. 9), who follow righteousness and speak right" (Prov. xv. 9, xvi. 13; Ps. cxlvi. 8), because Ie loves righteousness and justice (Isa. lxi. 8; Ps. l. 7, xcix. 4). Nor is the love of God for Israel avoritism. "Whom the Lord loveth He chasten- th" (A. V. "correcteth"; Prov. iii. 12). Love be- ng the essence of God's holy nature, the law of hu- nan life culminates in the commandment "Thou halt love thy neighbor as thyself" (Lev. xix. 18). This love includes the enemy (Ex. xxiii. 4–5). The ords "Thou shalt not hate thy brother in thy eart: thou shalt not bear sin against [A. V. "suffer in upon him"] him . . . nor bear any grudge gainst the children of thy people" (Hebr.) show n what manner the enemy can be loved—one must emove the cause of hatred in order to be able to ove his neighbor (Lev. xix. 17). This includes the tranger (Lev. xix. 34); the criminal also is called thy brother" (Deut. xxv. 3; see BROTHERLY LOVE).

—**In Apocryphal and Rabbinical Litera- ure:** Love as a divine principle was especially eveloped among the Ḥasidim, who made love of God and love of man the guiding principles of their ives (Philo, "Quod Omnis Probus Liber," § 12; see ESSENES). To them God appeared as "the spirit of love for all men" (Wisdom i. 6). "Thou lovest all things that are. . . . Never wouldst Thou have made anything if Thou hadst hated it. . . . Thou sparest all, for they are Thine, O Lord, Thou Lover of souls" (*ib.* xi. 24–26). Philo also ("De Opificiis Mundi," i. 4; comp. Müller, "Buch von der Welt- schöpfung," 1841, p. 150) finds love, or goodness, to be the principle and motive power of the divine creation. So God says to Ezra, as he complains about the ills of the world, "Thou canst not love My creation more than I do" (IV Esdras viii. 45). Love for God and man is accordingly declared to be the principle of conduct in the DIDACHE and in the Testaments of the Twelve Patriarchs (Simeon, 3, 4; Issachar, 5; Zebulun, 8; Dan, 5; Gad, 7; Benjamin, 8). Love of all creatures is taught by Hillel (Abot i. 12; Wisdom xii. 19; Philo, "De Humanitate," §§ 12– 14; comp. BROTHERLY LOVE and GOLDEN RULE).

Justice the Fundamental Principle.

The Rabbis also declare that the world was cre- ated by the divine principle of love (Gen. R. xii. 15) and that the human world is founded on mercy (Ab. R. N. iv.). "Beloved is man by God, in whose likeness he is made; es- pecial love was shown him in being made aware of this godlikeness of his" (Ab. iii. 14). Still, a deeper con- ception of the Rabbis made justice the fundamental principle of life, and not mere love. "When God saw that the world could not stand on rigid justice, then only He tempered it with love" (Gen. R. *l.c.*). Love pardons but fails to eradicate sin in individuals or society at large. Upon justice, truth, and peace the world is founded (Ab. i. 15; Deut. R. v. 1). Love is not strong and firm enough to form the foundation of life, whether in individ- uals, who must strive for character, or in society at large, which can not afford to tolerate wrong-doing (see HOLINESS; JUDGMENT, DIVINE). Love pre- vails only where God is recognized as Father, and this tender relation works for pity and forgiveness (Ber. 7a). All depends then upon whether that state has been attained in which the will of God is done from mere love.

The Broader Hellenistic View.

Whether the heathen as well as Jews may attain this state of true God-childship is a question at is- sue between the Hellenistic and a few of the more liberal Palestinian rabbis on the one hand and the greater majority of the rabbis on the other. The former insist that Job and Enoch attained this state as well as Abraham; the latter deny it, asserting that fear and not love of God was the motive power of the ancient heathen (comp. Testament of Job, i. 24 [in Kohut Memorial Volume, p. 171], Enoch, lxxi. 14, and Slavonic Enoch, lxiv. 5, with Soṭah v. 5 and Gen. R. xxv.). Christianity was partly influenced by the broader Hellenistic views in stating that "God is love" and that all men are children of God (I John iii. 1; iv. 7–8, 11–20; v. 3). Still, the prevailing view in the New Testament is that of Paul, according to whom it is the Holy Spirit which, through baptism, works love and renders the believers "sons of God," for whom there would otherwise be only salvation by right- eousness (Rom. viii. 14–31; comp. i. 17). In other words, only through belief in the especial God-son-ship of the crucified Christ does the Christian obtain the title of God's son and the right to claim His fatherly love. This view is maintained also in John v. 20–24, x. 17, xv. 9, xvii. 26.

This conception of a divine love bought by sacrificial blood was combatted by the rabbis; R. Akiba, for instance, declares: "Beloved are the Israelites inasmuch as they are called children of God"; especially did that love manifest itself in making known to them that they are children of God (Abot iii. 15, with reference to Deut. xiv. 1). The entire relation between Israel and God is found by R. Akiba to be typified in the Song of Songs, which to him is "the holiest of all books," because it allegorizes the divine love (Yad. iii. 5; Cant. R., Introduction). Whether Israel may claim God's love as His children when disregarding His commandments is a matter of dispute between R. Meïr (who affirms) and R. Judah (who denies; Sifre, Deut. 96).

God's Love for Israel.

The love of God means the surrounding of life with His commandments (Men. 43b) and is conditioned by the love of the Torah (R. H. 4a); God loves Israel in a higher degree than He does the Gentiles (Sifre, Deut. 144; Yoma 54a) because through the Torah they stand closer to Him (Pesiḳ. ii. 16–17); they love Him, giving their very lives for the observance of His commandments (Mek., Yitro, 6, to Ex. xx. 6). Indeed, love of God is voluntary surrender of life and all one has for God's honor (Sifre, Deut. 32; Ber. 54a). It is unselfish service of God (Abot i. 3; 'Ab Zarah 19a). There are chastisements of love for the righteous to test their piety (Ber. 5a; comp. Rom. v. 3). It is this unequaled love, braving suffering and martyrdom, which established the unique relation between God and Israel, so that "none of the nations can quench this love" (Cant. R. viii. 7). This unique love is echoed also in the liturgy (see Ahabah Rabbah). To be a true "lover of God," however, means "to receive offense, and resent not; to hear words of contumely, and answer not; to act merely from love, and rejoice even in trials as tests of pure love" (Shab. 88b; Soṭah 31a; comp. Rom. viii. 28).

The Highest Aim of Life.

Love as the highest aim of life is especially emphasized in Tanna debe Eliyahu R. xxvi.: "Love should be perfectly unselfish, and regulate the conduct of man toward man." In the same sense it is accentuated as the highest incentive of action by Baḥya ibn Paḳuda, in "Ḥobot ha-Lebabot" (see Jew. Encyc. ii. 454). Maimonides, in his Yad ha-Ḥazaḳah, devotes the whole tenth chapter of Hilkot Teshubah, with reference to Abot i. 3, to love as the motive which gives all human action its true ethical and religious value. Similarly, Naḥmanides in his commentary to Deut. vi. 4, with reference to Sifre, *l.c.*, declares that love of God involves the study and observance of the Law without regard to gain or expectation of reward; so also Baḥya ben Asher, in his "Kad ha-Ḳemah," under "Ahabah."

R. Eleazar of Worms, in his ethical work "Rokeaḥ," begins with the chapter on love, referring to Sifre, Deut. 32, 41, 48; Ber. 54a; Yoma 86a; Ned. 62a; Soṭah 31a; Tanna debe Eliyahu xxvi.; Midr. Teh. to Ps. xiii. 2 ("I love Thee; that is, 'I lov Thy creatures'"); and Midr. Tadshe xii., and statin that he who truly loves God subordinates all othe desires and cares to the one great object of life—th fulfilment of God's will in joy. Still more exten sively does Elijah de Vidas, in his ethical wor "Reshit Ḥokmah" (part 2), dwell on love as th highest aim and motive of life. He also quotes th Zohar (i. 11b; ii. 114, 116a; iii. 68a, 264b, 267a; an other passages), where it is frequently stated tha pure love is suppression of all care for self, an through such love true union of the soul with Go is effected. This union is said by the cabalists t take place in the celestial "palace of love" (Zoha i. 44b, ii. 97a).

As Cosmic Principle.

Still greater importance was attached to lov when it was rendered a cosmic principle in the philo sophical systems of Ḥasdai Crescas and, through him of Spinoza. Instead of rendering th creative intellect the essence of th Deity, as did Maimonides and all th Aristotelians, Crescas, like Philo o old, makes love the essential quality of God. Lov is divine bliss, and hence love of God is the sourc of eternal bliss for mortal man ("Or Adonai," i. 3 5; comp. Spinoza's "Amor Intellectualis," v. 32–36 see Joël, "Don Chasdai Creskas' Religionsphiloso phische Lehren," 1866, p. 37; *idem*, "Spinoza's The ologisch-Politischer Tractat," 1870, pp. ix.–xi.).

But, more than Crescas, it was probably Do Judah Isaac Abravanel, known as Leo Hebræus from whom Spinoza borrowed the idea of "intellec tual love" as a cosmic principle, and who, followin the Platonic and pantheistic tendency of the perio of the Italian Renaissance, made (in his "Dialogh di Amore") the "amore intellectivo" and "amor mentale" or "rationale" the essence of God and th central force and end of the world. "Love links a things together in the cosmos, but while love in th natural world is sensual and selfish, divine love i unselfish and uplifting. God's love created th world and brings about the perfection of all things especially of man, who, when good, is God-lovin as well as God-beloved, and whose love of God lead him to eternal bliss, which is identical with divin love." This intellectual love is identical with th Biblical "to him [God] shalt thou cleave" (Deut. x 20, xi. 22, xiii. 5; Sifre, Deut. 49; Soṭah 14a) an gives rise to the "imitatio Dei." It is highest per fection and supreme joy (B. Zimmels, "Leo He bræus," 1886, especially pp. 51, 67, 74–79, 89 100). Leo Hebræus' view of love as the princip of the world appears to have exerted some influenc also upon Schiller in his "Philosophische Briefe (1838, x. 289; Zimmels, *l.c.* pp. 8–11).

Bibliography: Grünbaum, *Der Grundzug und Dessen Ent wicklung der Liebe im Judenthume*, in Geiger's *Wis Zeit. Jüd. Theol.* ii. 285, iii. 59, 180; Schenkel's *Bibellexicon*

K.

LOVE-FEAST. See Agape.

LOVEMAN, ROBERT: American poet; bor at Cleveland, Ohio, April 11, 1864; educated and no (1904) residing at Dalton, Ga.; M.A., University o Alabama. He has published the following volume of verse, which have won for him recognition fro contemporary critics: "Poems," Tuscaloosa, Ala

889; "Poems," *ib.* 1893; "Poems," Philadelphia, a., 1897; "A Book of Verses," *ib.* 1900; "The ates of Silence," New York, 1903.

BLIOGRAPHY: *Who's Who in America*, 1903–5; Stedman, *An American Anthology*, New York, 1900; Adams, *Dict. of Authors*.

A.

LÖVINSON, ERMANNO (formerly **Her-ann**): German historian; born in Berlin June 3, 863; educated at Berlin University (Ph.D. 1888). nce 1889 he has lived in Italy, and since 1895 has een assistant archivist of the royal state archives at ome.

Lövinson's published works in German include: Beiträge zur Verfassungsgeschichte der Westfälihen Reichsstiftsstädte," Paderborn, 1889; "Die indensche Chronik des Busso Watensted, eine Fälhung Paullinis," *ib.* 1890; and "Ist die Gesch. ne Wissenschaft?" Berlin, 1892 (translated from e Italian of P. Villari); in Italian: "Cristoforo olombo Nella Letteratura Tedesca," Rome, 1893; Giuseppe Garibaldi e la Sua Legione Nello Stato omano 1848–49," *ib.* 1902. S.

LOVY, ISRAEL: French cantor and synaogal composer; born near Danzig Sept., 1773; died Paris Jan. 7, 1832. He received a Talmudic and cular education at Glogau, where his father was azzan. Lovy traveled extensively, visiting the reatest cantors of the time, and studying the works the greatest masters, especially those of Haydn d Mozart. In 1799 he settled at Fürth, where became accomplished in violin, violoncello, and iano, and proficient in French and Italian. After aving served for short terms congregations in ayence, Strasburg, and London, he was called in 818 to Paris, where he officiated as cantor until his eath. Lovy was gifted with a voice of unusual rength, compass, and sweetness, and the greatest asters of vocal music at Paris attended the Jewish rvices to hear him sing. He received attractive fers from the stage, but the Jewish Consistory of aris elected him for life and thus induced him to main as cantor. In March, 1822, his congregation edicated a new temple and introduced an organ and oys' chorus. Lovy wrote all the music for the gan and the new choir, and it was mainly the eauty of his compositions that silenced the opposion of the Orthodox element of the community, hich at first protested against the innovation.

BLIOGRAPHY: Mendel and Reismann, *Musikalisches Conversations-Lexikon*, Berlin, 1878; *Arch. Isr.* 1850 (biography by his grandson Eugène Manuel).

S. I. War.

LOW, A. MAURICE: Anglo-American wrir; born in London July 14, 1860. Educated at ing's College School in that city, and afterward Austria, he devoted himself to journalism. Since 888 he has been correspondent at Washington, . C., for the "Boston Globe," and since 1896 for e London "Daily Chronicle," being the first Washgton correspondent to be appointed by an English aper.

Low's journalistic positions have been many. nce 1896 he has edited the American department the London "National Review"; he wrote "The nited States and Its Dependencies" for the "Anal Register" (London, 1901); and is a contributor to the majority of the more influential magazines in England and America, including "Collier's Weekly," "Harper's Weekly," "The Forum," "North American Review," "Scribner's," "McClure's," and "The Fortnightly Review." He is the author of "The Supreme Surrender," a novel (New York, 1901).

A.

LÖW, ASHER BEN ARYEH LÖB: Chief rabbi of Carlsruhe; born at Minsk in 1754; died at Carlsruhe July 23, 1837. He studied under his father, Aryeh Löb, rabbi of Metz; and when the latter had become blind he assisted him in conducting his yeshibah or rabbinical college. In 1783 Asher was elected rabbi of Niederwerrn, and in 1785 rabbi of Wallerstein. When in 1809 the Grand Duke of Baden organized the Jewish congregations of his country upon the Napoleonic model, Asher was elected member of the consistory and chief rabbi ("Oberrath" and "Landrabbiner") of the grand duchy. He accepted these positions in 1810, and occupied them until his death, declining a call to Paris and, later, one to Metz. Asher was a strict Talmudist of the old school, and very orthodox in his views, though at the same time tolerant of those of others.

In his last years his health was very precarious, and the work of the rabbinate was done by his assistant, Elias Willstätter. Shortly before his death he sent various manuscripts dealing with rabbinical subjects to Wilna; but only some responsa were published—in a work of his father, "She'elot u-Teshubot Sha'agat Aryeh ha-Ḥadashot," Wilna, 1873. One of his sons, who adopted the family name "Ascher," was rabbi of Bühl, and died there Feb. 20, 1838.

BIBLIOGRAPHY: *Allg. Zeit. des Jud.* 1837, pp. 252, 260.

J. S. Man.

LÖW, BENJAMIN WOLF: Polish-Hungarian rabbi; born in Wodzislaw, government of Kielce, Poland, 1775; died at Verbo, Hungary, March 6, 1851. His father, Eleazar Löw, instructed him in Talmudic literature, and at an early age he became rabbi of a Polish congregation. In 1812, following his father to Austria, he became rabbi of Kolin, Bohemia. In 1826 he was called as rabbi to Gross-Tapolcsany, Hungary, and in 1836 to Verbo, where he spent the remainder of his life. His only work is "Sha'are Torah," a treatise on the principles of Talmudic law which shows the author's methodical mind and vast knowledge of Talmudic literature. Three parts of the work appeared in print (Vienna, 1821 and 1850; Satoralja-Ujhely, 1872), while the fourth part is still in manuscript. Wolf Löw was twice married; his first wife, from whom he obtained a divorce, was the daughter of Ephraim Zalman Margolioth of Brody; the second was the daughter of Isaac Landau, rabbi of Auschwitz. Löw's son **Jeremiah,** rabbi in Satoralja-Ujhely, was the recognized leader of the Orthodox party in Hungary and its spokesman in an audience which its deputation obtained with the emperor in order to protest against the establishment of a rabbinical seminary ("Allg. Zeit. des Jud." 1864, p. 292). He was nevertheless opposed to the secession of the Orthodox from the whole body of Judaism and therefore refused to take part in a congress planned by the Orthodox (*ib.* 1870, p. 786). Upon his death in 1872 he was succeeded by his son Eleazar, who was later called to the rabbinate of Unghvar, of which he is still (1904) the incumbent. Other grandsons of Wolf Löw are **Abraham** and **Benjamin Singer,** joint authors of "Ha-Madrik," a pedagogic anthology of the Talmud. Moses Löb Bloch was Wolf Löw's nephew and pupil.

Bibliography: Münz, *Rabbi Eleasar, Genannt Schemen Rokeach*, pp. 90-100, Treves, 1895.

D.

LÖW, LEOPOLD: Hungarian rabbi; born at Czernahora, Moravia, May 22, 1811; died at Szegedin Oct. 13, 1875. He received his preliminary education at the yeshibot of Trebitsch, Kolin, Leipnik, and Eisenstadt (1824–35), and then studied philology, pedagogics, and Christian theology at the Lyceum of Presburg and at the universities of Pesth and Vienna (1835–41). After having been a teacher at Prossnitz, he succeeded to the rabbinate of Gross-Kanizsa (Sept. 10, 1841).

Löw early in his career acquired a knowledge of Hungarian, and was the first to introduce it into the synagogue service, his first sermon in that language being printed in 1845. In 1844 he began his literary activity in behalf of the emancipation of the Hungarian Jews, taking the lead in that struggle until its object was attained (1867). The periodical "Ben Chananja," edited by him from 1858 to 1867, was an especially influential factor in this movement.

Leopold Löw.

In 1846 Löw had been called to Papa, where he encountered many difficulties. After the revolution he was denounced by his enemies, and was arrested, but was pardoned by General Haynau (Dec. 14, 1849) and liberated after two months' imprisonment. In consequence of this persecution he accepted a call to Szegedin, where he was installed Dec. 10, 1850. He refused subsequent calls to Lemberg, Brünn, and Bucharest, as well as to the Hochschule für die Wissenschaft des Judenthums at Berlin.

Löw brought his thorough knowledge of history, theology, and esthetics to bear upon the reform of the ritual in agreement with modern views. He was the foremost preacher of Hungary, especially in the vernacular, and was invited to participate in nearly all the patriotic celebrations and synagogal dedications. His Hungarian sermons (1870) formed the first Jewish collection of the kind issued in that language. Löw combined the careful, logical arrangement of the Christian sermon with a clever analysis of complicated haggadic sentences. His studies, beginning with the history of the Halakah, subsequently included the entire Jewish archeology of post-Talmudic time. He endeavored to determine the development of Jewish life and law as it appears in the halakic literature, and to disprove, in the interest of Judaism, the view that Judais remained stationary in its manners and custor down to the beginning of the Reformation in Ge many. His most important archeological studies ar responsa were written for the purpose of proving t development of various institutions and of showir the influence, in many cases, of foreign customs.

Influence on Hungarian Reform.

Löw was a leading authority both from a scie tific point of view and in questions of practical th ology. The absolute (1850–66) as well as the cons tutional government (1867) of Austria and especial that of Hungary were guided by the replies I gave to their questions in matters referring to t organization of the Jewish ritual and schools. Je ish education throughout Hungary owes much him. Down to his death he was the leader of t progressive Hungarian Jews, especially after t general congress—which was convened against h advice and in which he did not take part—had r sulted in a schism among the Jews of Hungary inste of the union that had been anticipated.

Aside from his works on the Halakah, Löw le only one other larger work, "Ha-Mafteaḥ" (185 a history (in German) of exegesis among the Jew this is still authoritative. After t emancipation, when he gave up t editorship of "Ben Chananja," he d voted himself to larger archeological monographs, which the following were published: "Die Grapl schen Requisiten" (1870–71) and "Die Lebensalt in der Jüdischen Literatur" (1875). Fragmen of a third volume, "Der Synagogale Ritus," we published posthumously (1884). His smaller wor have appeared in five volumes (Szegedin, 1889–190 the last of which contains a complete bibliograpl of his works.

His Works.

Bibliography: Löw and Kulinyi, *A Szegedi Zsidók*, 1888, 172-251.

S.

Of Löw's sons, **Immanuel Löw,** a rabbi a Orientalist (born at Szegedin, Hungary, Jan. 2 1854), was educated at his native town and at Berli where he studied at the Lehranstalt für die Wisse schaft des Judenthums and at the university, grad ating as rabbi and as Ph.D. in 1878. The same ye he became rabbi in Szegedin, where he is still (190 officiating.

Among his books may be mentioned: "A mäische Pflanzennamen," Vienna, 1881; "A Szeg di Zsidók," Szegedin, 1885; "A Szegedi Chevra," 1887; "Alkalmi Beszédek," *ib.* 1891; "Az Ezred Nyolc Beszéd," *ib.* 1896; "Löw Immánuel Besz dei," *ib.* 1900; "Imádságok," 3d ed. *ib.* 1903; "V rösmarty Mihály," *ib.* 1900; "Szilágyi Dezsö," 1901; "Tisza Kálmán," *ib.* 1902; "Kossuth Lajos *ib.* 1902; "Templomszentelö," *ib.* 1903; "Deák F renc," *ib.* 1903. He has furthermore contribut articles on Syriac lexicography to various volum of the "Z. D. M. G.," and has edited the followi works: "Schwab Löw, Emlékeztetés a Vallásb Nyert Oktatásra," 5th ed. Szegedin, 1887; "Lö Lipót, Bibliai Történet," 10th ed. Budapest, 190 "Leopold Löw: Gesammelte Schriften," i.–v., Sze edin, 1889–1900.

s. F. T. H.

Another son, **Samuel Löw** (born Sept. 11, 1846, Papa; studied at Szegedin and Vienna [M.D. 1871 is a physician. In 1873 he went to Budapest, where three years later he founded the "Pester Medizinisch-Chirurgische Presse." In this periodical, of which he is (1904) the editor-in-chief, most of his scientific articles have appeared.

A third son, **Theodor Löw** (born Nov. 14, 1848, at Papa), is a lawyer in Budapest. The following are his chief works: "Iromány Példák az uj Magyar Csödeljáráshoz" (Budapest, 1882), on the new Hungarian bankruptcy proceedings, and "A Magyar Büntetö Törvénykönyv a Büntettekröl és Vétségekröl" (*ib.* 1884), on the Hungarian criminal and civil codes.

BIBLIOGRAPHY: Szinnyei, *Magyar Irók Elete*; Löw and Kulinyi, *A Szegedi Zsidók*, p. 218.

S. L. V.

A fourth son, **Tobias Löw**, was born June 5, 1844, at Gross-Kanizsa, Hungary, and died June 7, 1880, at Budapest, where he had been acting attorney-general. In 1874 he founded the "Magyar Igazságügy," a legal periodical in the interests of Hungarian jurisprudence and legislation. Löw took an active part in the preparation of the Hungarian penal code, for which he edited the material (1880).

A fifth son, **William Löw**, is a lawyer and editor in New York city.

BIBLIOGRAPHY: Szinnyei, *Magyar Irók Elete.*

S.

LÖW, MORITZ: Astronomer; born at Mako, Hungary, in 1841; died in Steglitz, Berlin, May 25, 1900; studied at the universities of Leipsic and Vienna, and received his Ph.D. degree from the University of Budapest (1867). After graduating he became an assistant at the Leipsic observatory, and in 1883 was appointed section chief in the Prussian geodetic institute at Berlin, with the title of professor.

Löw's principal works are: "Elemente der Planeten"; "Einfluss der Verbesserten Sternörter auf die Polhöhen der Gradmessung in Ostpreussen"; "Polhöhe von Helgoland"; "Zur Theorie der Passage-Instrumente im Ersten Vertikal"; "Astronomisch-Geodätische Ortsbestimmungen im Harz"; "Polhöhebestimmungen im Harzgebirge Ausgeführt 1887–91."

BIBLIOGRAPHY: *Allg. Zeit. des Jud.* June 8, 1900 (*Gemeindebote*, p. 2); *Univ. Isr.* June 15, 1900, p. 408.

S. N. D.

LÖW, SAMUEL (called also **Samuel Kollin, or Kelin**): Talmudist; son of Naṭe (נטע = Nathan) ha-Levi; born at Kolin, Bohemia, about 1720; died May 20, 1806, at Boskowitz, Moravia, where for nearly sixty years he had presided over a yeshibah. He wrote: "Maḥaẓit ha-Sheḳel," an extensive subcommentary on Abraham Abele Gombiner's "Magen Abraham" on Shulḥan 'Aruk, Oraḥ Ḥayyim (Vienna, 1807–8; 2d ed. 1817; several times reprinted); "Hilkot Niddah" (Lemberg, 1858); and "Hilkot Meliḥah" (*ib.* 1860). His son Wolf BOSKOWITZ delivered the sermon at his funeral ("Ma'amar Esther," Ofen, 1837). His descendant in the fifth generation, Dr. **Max Anton Löw**, a convert to Roman Catholicism, was the attorney of the anti-Semite DECKERT ("Mittheilungen der Gesell. zur Abwehr des Antisemitismus," 1896, pp. 45, 48; 1897, pp. 190, 246; "Oest. Wochenschrift," 1896, p. 65).

BIBLIOGRAPHY: Walden, *Shem ha-Gedolim he-Ḥadash*, ii. 44, Warsaw, 1880; Benjacob, *Oẓar ha-Sefarim*, p. 321; Fürst, *Bibl. Jud.* s.v. *Kollin, Samuel*; Zedner, *Cat. Hebr. Books Brit. Mus.* p. 417.

D. S. MAN.

LÖWE, AUGUST: Russian mathematician and author of mathematical works. Of his books the best known are: "Obscheponyatnaya Teoriya Perspectivy," 1858; "Obscheponyatnaya Prakticheskaya Geometriya," 2d ed. 1860; "Nizshaya Geodesiya," 2d ed. 1861; "Prakticheskaya-Arifmetika Dlya Dyevitz," 1862; "Kurs Arifmetiki i Sobraniye Arifmeticheskikh Zadach," 2d ed. 1871; "Nachalnyya Osnovaniya Geometrii," 2d ed. 1871; and "Arifmetika Dlya Nachalnykh Narodnykh Uchilishch," 1872.

BIBLIOGRAPHY: *Entziklopedicheski Slovar*, xvii. 430.

H. R. J. G. L.

LÖWE BEN BEZALEEL. See JUDAH LÖW BEN BEZALEEL.

LÖWE, JOEL: German commentator; born in 1760; died in Breslau Feb. 11, 1802. He signed his name in Hebrew writings as Joel בריל"ל (= "son of R. Judah Löb"). At the age of twenty he went to Berlin, where he received instruction from Isaac Satanow, who was a follower of Moses Mendelssohn. In Berlin Löwe met Mendelssohn, his acquaintance with whom soon ripened into friendship. Mendelssohn's influence was doubtless instrumental in securing for Löwe the position of tutor in the house of the influential David Friedländer. Löwe became a most intimate friend of another prominent Mendelssohnian, Isaac Abraham Euchel, whose first work, a Hebrew biography of Mendelssohn, contains a dedicatory letter addressed to Löwe. At the close of his life Löwe was principal of the Wilhelms-Schule in Breslau.

Löwe was an excellent Hebraist, grammarian, and exegete, and, like most Mendelssohnians, was also a "Schöngeist." Conjointly with Aaron Wolfsohn he edited "Ha-Meassef," in which periodical he published a large number of poems and essays. He belonged to the bi'urists who assisted Mendelssohn in his commentaries on the Bible. His own main work was a critical Hebrew commentary and an excellent introduction to the Psalms (1788), which latter forms a history of Biblical poetry; and he published, also, Mendelssohn's German translation of the Psalms in Hebrew letters. In company with Aaron Wolfsohn, Löwe published Mendelssohn's German translation of the Song of Solomon with a Hebrew commentary. He was the first to translate the "Haggadah shel Pesaḥ" into German (1785). Of his "'Ammude ha-Lashon," on the elements of the Hebrew language, only the first part was published (1794). He wrote also on chronology, and was a contributor to Eichhorn's "Allgemeine Bibliothek der Biblischen Literatur." His plan to publish a Hebrew grammar on a large scale did not materialize.

S. E. SCHR.

LÖWE, KONRAD: Austrian actor; born at Prossnitz, Moravia, Feb. 6, 1856. He took a law course at the University of Vienna, and then went on the stage (1878). After filling engagements in various Austrian and German cities he was called in

1895 to the Hofburgtheater, Vienna, of which company he has since been a member. He plays heroic parts.

Löwe has also been active as a writer and dramatist. He has published a volume of poetry entitled "Leben und Lieben" (Leipsic, 1890), and has adapted Grabbe's "Herzog Theodor von Gothland" (Vienna, 1892). S.

LÖWE, LUDWIG: German physician; born at Berlin March 11, 1844. After graduating from the gymnasium, he attended the universities of Jena, Würzburg, Strasburg, and Breslau, leaving the last institution with the degree of doctor of medicine in 1872. In the following year he became an assistant at the anatomical institute of the University of Strasburg, which position he held till 1875, when he became an assistant at the dermatological hospital and dispensary of the Charité at Berlin, resigning this position in 1876. In 1878 he was admitted to the medical faculty of the University of Bern as lecturer on anatomy. He finally returned to Berlin and established himself as a specialist in diseases of the ear, nose, and throat.

Löwe has contributed several essays to medical journals, and is the author of: "Beiträge zur Anatomie der Nase" (Berlin, 1878, 2d ed. 1883); "Beiträge zur Entwicklungsgeschichte des Nervensystems" (vol. i., Berlin, 1880 ; vol. ii., Leipsic, 1883); "Lehrbuch der Ohrenheilkunde," 1884.

BIBLIOGRAPHY: Pagel, *Biog. Lex.* 1901.

S. F. T. H.

LÖWE, MOSES SAMUEL (Johann Michael Siegfried Löwe): German painter and engraver; born at Königsberg, Prussia, June 24, 1756; died there May 10, 1831. Aided by the friendship and influence of the Friedländer family, he had achieved such a reputation by 1780 that the empress Catherine II. of Russia commissioned him to paint her portrait. His pictures were among the most popular in the German exhibitions, and he was one of the foremost miniaturists and pastel-painters of his time. He was also a master of the game of chess. His "Bildnisse Jetzt Lebender Berliner Gelehrten mit Selbstbiographien" (Berlin, 1806–7) was praised by Goethe ("Werke," xxviii. 60 *et seq.*).

BIBLIOGRAPHY: Aug. Hagen, *Neue Preussische Provinzialblätter*, iii. 317 *et seq.*; Jolowicz, *Gesch. der Juden in Königsberg*, p. 102.

D. M. K.

LÖWENBERG, JULIUS: German geographer; born at Strzelno, Prussia, 1800; died at Berlin Dec. 12, 1893. He was educated in Berlin, where he became acquainted with Alexander von Humboldt, who assisted him in various ways. He wrote: "Afrika" (1835); "Historisch-Geographischer Atlas" (1836–40); "Gesch. der Geographie" (1840); "Alexander von Humboldt" (1842); "Humboldt's Reisen in Amerika und Asien" (1844); "Gesch. der Geographischen Entdeckungen" (1882); "Die Entdeckungs- und Forschungsreisen in den Beiden Polarzonen" (1886). His last years he spent in the Jewish home for aged people in Berlin.

BIBLIOGRAPHY: *Allg. Zeit. des Jud.* Dec. 21, 1893; Kürschner, *Literatur-Kalender*, 1893.

J. D.

LÖWENFELD, LEOPOLD: German physician; born in Munich Jan. 23, 1847; educated at the gymnasium and university in his native city (M.D. 1870). During the Franco-Prussian war he was assistant physician in a Bavarian field-hospital. After several years of practise in the United States, he settled permanently in his native city (1875).

Löwenfeld has published: "Studien über Aetiologie und Pathogenese der Spontanen Hirnblutungen," 1886; "Sexualleben und Nervenleiden," 1891; "Pathologie und Therapie der Neurasthenie und Hysterie," 1893; "Lehrbuch der Gesammten Psychotherapie," 1897; "Der Hypnotismus: Handbuch der Lehre von der Hypnose und der Suggestion," 1901; "Die Psychischen Zwangserscheinungen, auf Klinischer Grundlage Dargestellt," 1904; "Die Moderne Behandlung der Nervenschwäche," 4th ed. 1904. S.

LÖWENGARD, MAX: German rabbi; born in Württemberg; died at Basel May 25, 1876. He was a friend of Berthold Auerbach and a diligent student of Schelling's philosophy. Though a fervent advocate of Reform in his youth, he became a zealous supporter of Orthodoxy in the latter part of his life, after having occupied rabbinates in Gebenhausen and other communities of Württemberg. He was the author of "Beiträge zur Kritik der Reformbestrebungen in der Synagoge" (Stuttgart, 1841); "Auch Einige Worte Ueber das Neue Gebetbuch im Hamburger Tempel" (Tübingen, 1842); and "Jehova, Nicht Moloch, War der Gott der Hebräer," a refutation of Ghillany's "Die Menschenopfer der Alten Hebräer" (Berlin, 1843). The first work appeared under the pseudonym "Juda Leon."

BIBLIOGRAPHY: Fürst, *Bibl. Jud.* ii. 269; Steinschneider, *Cat. Bodl.* col. 1629; Kayserling, *Sterbetage*, p. 22, Prague, 1891.

S. I. Br.

LÖWENSTAMM, LEVI SAUL. See Aryeh Loeb ben Saul.

LÖWENSTAMM, SAUL: Rabbi and Talmudist; born at Rzeszow 1717; died at Amsterdam June 19, 1790. He is known as the author of "Binyan Ariel" (Amsterdam, 1778), which title he chose as a pun on "Ben Aryeh." As he tells in the preface, he was appointed rabbi at לאקטש (Lakacz, Hungary?), and afterward at Dubno in succession to his father-in-law, Abraham Kahana (d. 1749); and in 1755 at Amsterdam, on the death of his father, Levi Saul Löwenstamm.

Besides "Binyan Ariel," Saul Löwenstamm wrote annotations on Niddah (Amsterdam, 1765), on the Shulḥan 'Aruk (*ib.* 1765), on the Pentateuch (*ib.* 1768–1777), on the Mishnah (*ib.* 1775), and many approbations and poems (1766–78). His "Binyan Ariel" is divided into three parts: (1) annotations on the Pentateuch; (2) on the Five Rolls; and (3) on some passages from the Talmud.

Löwenstamm devoted much attention to the bet ha-midrash founded by his father. The generosity of the members of the community enabled him to build a new home, which he occupied June 22, 1778.

Some of the memorial addresses delivered on his death have been published. He was succeeded by his son **Jacob Moses Löwenstamm.**

Bibliography: Landshuth, *Toledot Anshe Shem*, pp. 70, 118, Berlin, 1884; Buber, *Anshe Shem*, p. 39, Cracow, 1895; *She-'erit Yisrael* (transl. Polak), p. 617; Wagenaar, *Een Oud Gebouw*, Amsterdam, 1881; Koenen, *Geschiedenis der Yoden in Nederland*, p. 369.

D. E. Sl.

LÖWENSTEIN, BARUCH SOLOMON: Russian mathematician; born at Wolodarka, Russia, in the second quarter of the nineteenth century. He wrote: "Bikkure ha-Limmudiyyot," explanations of mathematical passages in the works of Abraham ibn Ezra, Moses Maimonides, and Joseph Delmedigo. He also annotated and published a second edition of "Shebile di-Reḳia'," by Elias ben Ḥayyim Kohen Höchheimer, on the rules of the calendar, with the elements of geometry, trigonometry, and astronomy (Warsaw, 1863).

Bibliography: Zeitlin, *Bibl. Post-Mendels.* p. 217.

D. S. Man.

LÖWENSTEIN, BERNHARD: Austrian rabbi; born at Meseritz, province of Posen, Feb. 1, 1821; died at Lemberg March 15, 1889. Upon the recommendation of Ludwig Philippson he was elected preacher in Szent Miklos, Liptau, Hungary (1845), where he became known as the pioneer of the modern synagogue service in Hungary. In 1857 he left Szent Miklos for the rabbinate of Butschowitz, Moravia, whence, shortly afterward, he was called as rabbi to Lemberg. Löwenstein was an impressive preacher and an indefatigable communal worker. He was twice decorated by the Emperor of Austria. In addition to some sermons, he published a volume of poems under the title "Jüdische Klänge" (Brünn, 1862).

Bibliography: Teller, *Shem 'Olam*, Cracow, 1889; Buber, *Anshe Shem*, p. 126, Cracow, 1895.

D.

LÖWENSTEIN, L. H.: Hebrew scholar; died at Frankfort-on-the-Main about 1850. He was reviser in the publishing-house of Isaac Lehrberger at Rödelheim, which office was afterward held by Seligman Baer. He published: The Book of Proverbs, edited from manuscripts, with a Hebrew commentary and a German metrical translation (Frankfort-on-the-Main, 1838); "Ḳol Bokim," the Book of Lamentations, with a Hebrew commentary and a German metrical translation, to which he added various dirges introduced into the liturgy of the Synagogue (*ib.* 1838); "Damascia: die Judenverfolgung zu Damascus und Ihre Wirkung auf die Oeffentliche Meinung, Nebst Nachweisungen über den Ursprung der Gegen die Juden Wiederholten Beschuldigung des Ritualmords" (Rödelheim, 1840; 2d ed. 1841); "Mizmor le-Todah," an ode addressed to Moses Montefiore on his return from the Orient (*ib.* 1841); "Stimmen Berühmter Christen über den Damascener Blutprozess" (*ib.* 1842). He also edited the Pentateuch with Targum Onḳelos, Rashi's commentary, and an explanation of the French words occurring in the last-named (2 vols., *ib.* 1848).

Bibliography: Fürst, *Bibl. Jud.* ii. 270; Steinschneider, *Cat. Bodl.* cols. 154, 1630.

D. S. Man.

LÖWENSTEIN, LEOPOLD: German rabbi; born in Gailingen, Baden, Dec. 1, 1843. He attended the gymnasium at Bischofsheim-on-the-Tauber, receiving at the same time instruction in the Talmud from his father, who was district rabbi there. He subsequently entered the University of Würzburg (1862), attending concurrently the Talmudic lectures of Rabbi Seligmann Bär Bamberger, and then went to the yeshibah of Rabbi Israel Hildesheimer at Eisenstadt, Hungary. In 1872 he became district rabbi in his native place, and exchanged that position in 1887 for his present one in Mosbach, Baden, where he officiates as rabbi for the three districts of Mosbach, Merchingen, and Wertheim. In 1891 he was decorated with the Zähringer Löwenorden.

Löwenstein published: "Gesch. der Juden am Bodensee" (1879), and "Beiträge zur Gesch. der Juden in Deutschland," i. 1895, ii. 1898; since 1900 he has edited the "Blätter für Jüdische Gesch. und Literatur," which appears as a supplement to "Der Israelit" of Mayence. S.

LÖWENSTEIN, RUDOLF: German author; born at Breslau Feb. 20, 1819; died at Berlin Jan. 6, 1891. When only nine years of age he was baptized. Educated at the gymnasium at Glogau and the universities of Breslau and Berlin, he received the degree of Ph.D. in 1843.

As early as 1836 some of Löwenstein's poems had been printed in the journals of Silesia; and his reputation was established by the appearance in 1840 of his "Der Kindergarten," a collection of songs for children. In 1848 he with David Kalisch and Ernest Dohm founded the well-known "Kladderadatsch," of which he became one of the chief editors.

The revolution of 1848 found Löwenstein on the liberal side, and he was expelled from Prussia in 1849 for his political activity. Returning to Berlin in 1850, he resumed the editorship of "Kladderadatsch" and continued in this capacity for thirty-seven years. In 1863 he became editor also of the political part of the "Gerichtszeitung." In 1887 he retired from public life.

Besides his "Der Kindergarten," he wrote "Ehret die Frauen," Berlin, 1874, and many songs, most of which were set to music.

His political poems in the "Kladderadatsch" gained him a wide reputation, especially those written during the eventful period 1860–80.

Bibliography: *Jew. Chron.* Jan. 9, 1891, p. 7; De le Roi, *Juden-Mission*, i. 354; Brümmer, *Deutsches Dichter-Lexikon*, Eichstädt and Stuttgart, 1876.

S. F. T. H.

LÖWENTHAL, JOHANN JACOB: Hungarian chess-master; born July, 1810, in Budapest; died at St. Leonard's-on-Sea, England, July 20, 1876. He was educated at the gymnasium of his native city, and received a civil appointment under the administration of Louis Kossuth. On the downfall of the latter, Löwenthal was expelled from Austria-Hungary, and he emigrated to America (1849). In 1851 he went to London, and thenceforward resided permanently in England. At the Manchester tourney of 1857 Löwenthal defeated Anderssen for first place; in 1858 he lost a match with Morphy; and in the same year he gained first prize at Birmingham.

Löwenthal was for some time chess editor of "The Illustrated News of the World" and of "The Era." He was editor also of "The Chess Players'

Magazine" (1863–67). In 1860 he published "Morphy's Games of Chess, with Analytical and Critical Notes." Under the influence of W. G. Ward, with whom he played chess, Löwenthal became a Roman Catholic.

Bibliography: *Dict. Nat. Biog.*

J. A. P.

LÖWENTHAL, NATHAN: Russian histologist; born in 1856; educated at the Academy for Physicians and Surgeons at St. Petersburg and at the universities of Kiev and Geneva. From 1881 to 1884 he was assistant to Schiff at Geneva, but he went to Lausanne in the latter year as assistant professor of histology, becoming professor in 1890.

Löwenthal is the author of the following monographs: "Ueber den Unterschied der Secundären Degeneration des Seitenstranges nach Hirn- und Rückenmarksverletzungen," in Pflüger's "Archiv für Physiologie," 1883; "Contribution Expérimentale à l'Etude des Atrophies Secondaires du Cordon Postérieur et de la Colonne de Clarke," in "Recueil Zoologique Suisse," 1885–86; (in collaboration with Herzen) "Trois Cas de Lésion Médullaire," etc., in "Archives de Physiologie Normale et Pathologique," 1886; "Experimentalisch-Anatomischer Beitrag zur Kenntniss der Bahnen im Rückenmark und Gehirn"; "Notiz über die Protoplasmastructur der Kornzellen des Eierstockes," and "Zur Kenntniss des Keimfleckes im Ureie Einiger Säuger," in "Anatomischer Anzeiger," 1887–95; "Die Spermatogenese bei Oxyuris Ambigua," "Die Befruchtung, Reifung, und Teilung des Eies von Oxyuris Ambigua," and "Die Harder'sche Drüse," all in "Internationale Monatsschrift für Anatomie," 1889–96; "Zur Frage über die Anwendung von Terpentinöl in der Histologischen Technik," in "Centralblatt für Physiologie," 1889; "Technisch-Histologische Notiz" and "Ueber eine Neue Alkoholische Carminlösung," in "Zeitschrift für Wissenschaftliche Mikroskopie," 1893–1902; "Contribution à l'Etude du Lobe Olfactif des Reptiles," in "Journal de l'Anatomie et de la Physiologie," 1894; "Drüsenstudien" and "Beitrag zur Kenntniss der Struktur und der Teilung von Bindegewebszellen," in "Archiv für Mikroskopische Anatomie," 1900–3; "Beitrag zur Kenntniss der Beziehungen der Taenia Semicircularis," in "Morphologisches Jahrbuch," 1902. He has written also two books: "Questions d'Histologie: La Cellule et les Tissus," Paris, 1901; and "Atlas zur Vergleicheden Histologie der Wirbeltiere," Berlin, 1904. S.

LÖWENTHAL, NAUMANN: German teacher and writer; born Feb. 25, 1819, at Schmiegel; died at Posen Feb. 28, 1855. He attended the gymnasium in Lissa and the universities of Berlin and Breslau, where he devoted himself principally to the study of philosophy, mathematics, and the natural sciences. He took his degree at Halle in 1841, and in 1844 passed the examination "pro facultate docendi" at Berlin. Löwenthal was the first Jew in Prussia to be appointed a head teacher, and that at a municipal technical school ("Realschule") in Posen. Besides many treatises in technical periodicals, he published "Die Physiologie des Freien Willens," Leipsic, 1843.

Bibliography: *Allg. Zeit. des Jud.* xix. 203.

S. M. K.

LÖWI, ISAAC: German rabbi; born at Adelsdorf, near Erlangen, Bavaria, Jan. 31, 1803; died at Fürth Dec. 26, 1873. He received his Talmudical training at the yeshibah of Wolf Hamburger at Fürth, and studied philosophy and philology at the University of Munich. He was rabbi of Uhlfeld from 1827 to 1830, when he was elected district rabbi of Fürth. Though his election was duly confirmed by the government (Dec. 1) the opposition of the Orthodox party rendered necessary a decree of installation by King Ludwig I. (March 10, 1831). As early as Dec. 30, 1831, and Feb. 29, 1832, his adversaries, among whom was his former teacher, Wolf Hamburger, petitioned the government to depose Löwi for teaching irreligious doctrines in his sermons and in the school and for introducing reforms into the divine services without regard to ancient customs and religious laws. For nearly eight years this suit was pending, until the government, by an order of Oct. 23, 1838 (renewed April 13, 1839), enjoined upon Löwi "to be more careful in his words and actions and to have more regard for those who conform to the true Mosaic ceremonials and who do not adhere to 'pernicious neology.'" Löwi was also sentenced to pay one-third of the costs of the suit; in the following year he was enjoined from performing the rite of confirmation. When the Orthodox party renewed its attacks, the government (1842) ordered a new election, which resulted in a strong majority for Löwi, after which he was allowed to perform the ceremony of confirmation.

Löwi's opponents nevertheless continued their complaints and insisted upon his dismissal; the government again decided in his favor, but allowed the dissatisfied members to elect for themselves an Orthodox rabbi who might officiate at weddings and decide religious questions. The agitation against Löwi gradually ceased. He stood in high esteem with King Ludwig II., who knighted him in 1869. In Löwi's last years Emil Neubürger became his assistant, succeeding him upon his death. From 1857 to 1872 the young congregation of Nuremberg was included in his rabbinical district. When, on Dec. 23, 1856, by order of the district government, the magistrate of Fürth requested him to serve as the spiritual guide of the Nuremberg Jews, Löwi declined, giving as his reason their religious indifference. But when the government insisted and a committee of the Jews of Nuremberg expressed regret for their former conduct, he accepted the added responsibility (Feb. 1, 1857). Löwi lent efficient aid in establishing the Nuremberg congregation and in regulating its religious affairs.

Bibliography: *Allg. Zeit. des Jud.* 1839, pp. 244 *et seq.*; 1841, p. 610; 1843, p. 48; 1844, p. 259; 1847, p. 598; 1869, p. 745; 1874, pp. 24, 44; *Orient*, 1844, pp. 141, 164; Barbeck, *Gesch. der Juden in Nürnberg und Fürth*, pp. 90, 98, Nuremberg, 1878; Jost, *Neuere Gesch.* i. 145; Ziemlich, *Die Israelitische Kultusgemeinde Nürnberg*, passim, Nuremberg, 1900.

D. S. Man.

LÖWINSOHN, JACOB MORDECAI BEN JUDAH LÖB: Russo-Polish scholar and journalist; born in Grodno 1832; died in Warsaw Feb. 13, 1878. A son of the rabbi of Grodno, he was trained in Talmud, and then studied Russian, German, Polish, and French, which he mastered in a very short time. Thus equipped he entered upon a journalistic career. He published numerous articles in Russian papers, and when, in 1862, Daniel Neufeldt founded the JUTRZENKA, Löwinsohn became an active collaborator on it, always defending the interests of his coreligionists. He was a great controversialist, and had heated discussions with R. Hirsch Kalischer in "Ha-Maggid," and with L. J. Shapiro in the "Jutrzenka."

He settled in Serhei, government of Suwalki, where he made the acquaintance of David Gordon, editor of "Ha-Maggid," and Rabbi Ḥayyim Fillippower. About 1868 he passed his examination at the Rabbinical Seminary of Wilna, where he was ordained rabbi; but he never accepted a rabbinate.

Of his first work, "Ha-Adam be-Ẓelem Elohim" (Königsberg, 1855), only a limited number of copies were printed, which he distributed among his friends. His numerous articles and essays on Jewish literature and science he published under the nom de plume ל.מ.י.

BIBLIOGRAPHY: L. J. Shapiro, in *Gan Peraḥim*, pp. 63-65, Warsaw, 1890; Shapiro and Gordon, in *Ha-Maggid*, 1878, No. 10, p. 80.

H. R. I. S. B.

LÖWISOHN, SOLOMON: Historian and poet; born in Mor, district of Stuhlweissenburg, Hungary, in 1788; died there April 27, 1821. He studied at the yeshibah of Prague, among his fellow students being his relative Moses Saphir, the humorist. He subsequently became a corrector in the printing establishment of Anton Edler von Schmid in Vienna.

Löwisohn's works include: "Siḥah be-'Olam ha-Neshamot" (Prague, 1811); "Meliẓat Yeshurun" (Vienna, 1816), poems; "Meḥḳere Ereẓ," treating of the topography of the Bible. He wrote also for the Mishnah edition published in 1815 an essay on the language of the Mishnah. Further, he translated and annotated the festival prayers, and part of the ritual for the 9th of Ab (Vienna, 1819). His most important work is "Vorlesungen über die Neuere Gesch. der Juden" (*ib.* 1820), of which the first volume only was published.

BIBLIOGRAPHY: Ignatz Reich, *Beth-El*, i. 72-77; A. Büchler, *A Moóri Chevra-Kadisa Története*, Budapest, 1891; A. Büchler, *Egy Magyar Zsido Költő*, in *Izraelita Magyar Evkönyve*, i. 387-403; *Pallas Lex.* xi.

S. A. Bü.

LÖWY, ADOLF: German physiologist; born in Berlin June 29, 1862; educated at the gymnasium and university of his native city (M.D. 1885), where he became privat-docent in physiology at the latter in 1895, and assistant professor in 1900. For his monograph "Untersuchungen über die Respiration und Circulation bei Aenderung des Druckes und des Sauerstoffgehaltes der Luft," Löwy received a prize from the Smithsonian Institution, Washington, in 1895. Numerous other publications of his have appeared in Pflüger's "Archiv für die Gesammte Physiologie," in the "Archiv für Anatomie und Physiologie," and in "Virchow's Archiv." S.

LÖWY, ALBERT: English rabbi and communal worker; born at Aussee, Moravia, Dec., 1816. He studied first at Olmütz, and then moved to Vienna, where under Professor Steinschneider he began a systematic study of Hebrew and Arabic. A few years after the formation of the Reform Synagogue in London, Löwy was appointed minister in association with the Rev. Professor Marks, whom he assisted in compiling the prayer-book of the congregation. He served for fifty years, retiring in 1892. From 1871 to 1889 he acted as secretary of the Anglo-Jewish Association, which, with Dr. Benisch, he had helped to found.

Löwy's knowledge of Samaritan literature enabled him to collect and catalogue the Samaritan manuscripts belonging to the Earl of Crawford and Balcarres. He printed in the "Trans. Soc. Bibl. Arch.," 1875, the first specimen of a dialect of Aramaic current among the Jews of Urmia; and his contribution gave rise to the subsequent literature on the subject. In 1891 he printed a "Catalogue of Hebraica and Judaica in the Library of the Corporation of the City of London," with a copious subject-index. In recognition of his researches, the University of St. Andrews conferred upon him in 1893 the honorary degree of LL.D.

Löwy helped to found the Society of Hebrew Literature; and was a frequent lecturer before the Society of Biblical Archeology and other learned associations. He died May 21, 1908.

BIBLIOGRAPHY: *Jew. Chron.* Dec. 4, 1876; *Jew. World*, Dec. 22, 1899; *Young Israel*, 1897.

J. G. L.

LÖWY, JACOB EZEKIEL: German rabbi and author; born at Hotzenplotz, Austrian Silesia, Aug. 24, 1814; died at Beuthen Nov. 20, 1864. After attending various yeshibot in his native country, he became a pupil of Wolf Löw in Nagy Tapolcsany, and then, inclining to Ḥasidism, he went successively to Lemberg and Brody in order to continue his rabbinical education. Finally he went to Berlin, where he acquired some secular learning. Having obtained after great difficulties a license to marry, he settled as a business man in Bielitz, and in 1846 was appointed district rabbi of Wadowice, with a seat at Oswiecin (Auschwitz). In 1854 he was elected rabbi of Beuthen, which position he continued to hold until his death.

Löwy was the author of "Biḳḳoret ha-Talmud: Kritisch-Talmudisches Lexikon" (vol. i., Vienna, 1863), containing 150 articles for a proposed Talmudic encyclopedia.

BIBLIOGRAPHY: *Die Neuzeit*, No. 1, Vienna, 1865.

S. D.

LUAḤ. See ALMANAC; CALENDAR.

LUBARSKY, HESCHEL ABRAMOVICH: Russian writer; born at Balta Sept., 1878. He was educated in a family of Ḥasidim, in the Odessa Commercial School, and in the Riga Polytechnical Institute. In 1897, while a student in the latter institute, he joined the Zionist movement. Shortly after he went to Palestine, where he visited the Jewish agricultural colonies, which he described in a series of articles under the title "V Stranye Predkov." Returning to Odessa in 1898, he wrote "Palestina," descriptive of the Holy Land and of the condition of the Jews there (Warsaw, 1900). In 1900 Lubarsky graduated from the Riga Polytechnical Institute (as engineer), and is now (1904) pursuing his studies in Berlin. He has contributed numerous articles to the Russo-Jewish periodicals, and, in 1903, published a pamphlet, "Shestoi Kongress Sionistov," on the subject of the Sixth Zionist Congress. His father, Abraham Elijah, is a well-known Zionist.

H. R. J. L. La.

LÜBECK: Free city of Germany; situated on the River Trave, not far from the Baltic Sea; it forms, with the surrounding territory, a free state. In 1900 it had a population of 82,813, including 663 Jews. Like most of the free cities of Germany, Lübeck did not tolerate the Jews. In 1350 the city council wrote to Duke Otto of Brunswick-Lüneburg requesting him to exterminate the Jews living in his territory, as they were responsible for the plague, which would not cease until all Jews had been killed. As the council does not mention any order to this effect in the city, it is clear that Jews could not have lived there before then. In 1499 the local chronographer, Reimer Kock, states expressly that "there are no Jews in Lübeck, as they are not needed here." The Thirty Years' war and, perhaps, the Chmielnicki persecutions in Poland seem to have caused a number of Jews to go to Lübeck. The gild of the goldsmiths complained in 1658 that "many Jews and other suspicious characters sneak daily into the city to deal in precious metals"; and the council decreed, April 15, 1677, that no Jew should be permitted to stay in the city overnight without the express permission of the senate, which was rarely given. In 1680 two "Schutzjuden" of the senate, Samuel Frank and Nathan Siemssens, are mentioned. But when the senate accepted Siemssen's son-in-law, Nathan Goldschmidt, as "Schutzjude," the citizens objected, and wherever he rented a house the neighbors protested to the senate. It was, perhaps, due to an intrigue that Goldschmidt was accused of having received stolen goods (Feb. 15, 1694); the trial dragged on for at least five years, and its result is not known. The gilds continued to demand of the council the expulsion of all Jews, and finally saw their wishes fulfilled (March 4, 1699). In spite of that victory of the gilds, Jews not only made brief visits to the city, but the council permitted, as early as 1701, one Jew to remain as "Schutzjude" in consideration of an annual payment of 300 marks courant ($84).

New Synagogue at Lübeck.
(From a photograph.)

Settlement in Neighborhood.

The great difficulties which stood in the way of prospective Jewish settlers in Lübeck suggested the evasion of the prohibition by a settlement in the neighboring territory of Denmark. A number of Jews, mostly Polish fugitives, settled in the village of Moisling as early as 1700, and, in spite of constant protests by the gilds, the council had to grant them, as Danish subjects, the right to enter the city, although under great restrictions. Desiring to obtain jurisdiction over the Jews in Moisling, the city of Lübeck acquired, in 1765, the estate whose owner had feudal rights over the inhabitants of that village; when, in 1806, the King of Denmark ceded the district that included Moisling, to Lübeck the Jews there became subjects of the latter city. But when Lübeck was annexed to France (Jan. 1, 1811) all discriminations ceased; the special taxes of the "Schutzjuden" were abolished, and many Jews of Moisling, as well as of other places, moved to Lübeck, where they at once purchased a lot for a synagogue. In the following years their numbers were rapidly augmented, especially in consequence of the expulsions during the siege of Hamburg. As soon, however, as the French domination had ceased, the senate began to debate the restriction of the Jews, to whom it proposed giving "an appropriate new constitution" (1815), while the gilds peremptorily demanded their expulsion. The Jews protested against this violation of their rights, and, together with the Jewish citizens of other free cities, appealed to the Congress of Vienna, engaging Carl August Buchholz as their advocate. But the city would not yield, in spite of the intercession of the Prussian chancellor Prince Hardenberg and of the Austrian chancellor Prince Metternich. The Congress of Vienna finally adopted Article 16 of the "Bundesakte," which guaranteed to the Jews in all German states the rights which they had obtained "from" the various states, instead of "in" the various states, as the original text read (June 8, 1815).

Expelled After Congress of Vienna.

Having thus obtained a free hand, the senate of Lübeck decreed (March 6, 1816) that all Jews should leave the city within four weeks. The Jews again protested, but finally were compelled to accept the proposition of the senate, which guaranteed to all Jews who would settle in Moisling the rights of Lübeck citizens, subject to certain limitations (Sept., 1821); in 1824 all Jews, with the exception of a few "Schutzjuden," had left the city. The senate now showed a certain amount of good-will toward its Jewish subjects by giving them a house in Moisling for their rabbi, and by building a new synagogue, for which the congregation was required to pay only a moderate annual rent.

Since 1831 the Jews have had to serve in the militia; in 1837 a parochial school, subsidized by the city, was opened; and in 1839 the senate issued an order which compelled the gilds to register Jewish apprentices. A commission appointed in 1842 reported that the condition of the Jews should be improved by an extension of their rights, but their emancipation did not become perfect until the law of Oct. 9, 1848, abolished all their disabilities. In 1850 a new synagogue was acquired. This brought to the young congregation considerable annoyance; the ill-disposed neighbors, who claimed that the ritual bath connected with it spread an unbearable smell of garlic, endeavored to obtain an injunction against it (this building gave way to a new synagogue in 1880). In 1859 the rabbi moved from Moisling to Lübeck, and in the same year a parochial school was opened in the city. In 1869 the school in Moisling was closed, and in 1872 the Moisling synagogue, which had not been used for some time, was demolished. A law of Aug. 12, 1862, modified the form of oath ("More Judaico") which Jews until that time had been compelled to use, and introduced a new form, which remained in force until the German law of 1879, regulating civil procedure, abolished it.

The Lübeck congregation has a parochial school of three grades, and religious instruction for Jewish children attending public schools has been made compulsory by the law of Oct. 17, 1885. The city pays to the congregation an annual subsidy. The rabbis of the congregation have been: Akiba Wertheimer (called also Akiba Victor; up to 1816; d. 1835, as rabbi of Altona); Ephraim Joël, an uncle of Manuel and David Joël (1825–51); Süssmann Adler (teacher and preacher, 1849–51; rabbi, 1851–1869); S. Carlebach, the present (1904) incumbent (since 1869). The congregation has a number of educational, devotional, and social organizations.

Bibliography: Jost, *Neuere Gesch. der Israeliten*, i. 32 *et seq.*; Grätz, *Gesch.* xi. 324 *et seq.*; Carlebach, *Gesch. der Juden in Lübeck und Moisling*, Lübeck, 1898; *Statistisches Jahrbuch*, 1903.

D.

LUBELSKI, PHILIPP: Polish physician; born at Zamosc 1788; died at Warsaw Feb. 3, 1879. He began his career as an army surgeon under Napoleon I., who created him an officer of the Legion of Honor. After the close of the Franco-Russian war Lubelski was appointed chief physician of the military hospital at Zamosc. From 1826 he resided permanently in Warsaw, where he engaged in private practise.

His son, **Wilhelm Lubelski** (born at Warsaw 1832; died there 1890), was likewise a physician. He studied medicine at Dorpat, Vienna, and Paris, and held the position of physician in ordinary at the hospital of the Orphan Asylum of Jesus at Warsaw. He published four medical works (1861–69).

Bibliography: *Encyklopedja Powszechna*, ix., Warsaw, 1901; Gurland, *Yevreiski Kalendar*, p. 117, St. Petersburg, 1880.

H. R. M. R.

LUBLIN: City of Russian Poland, in the government of the same name; situated 60 miles southeast of Warsaw; in importance the third city of Poland. Numbers of Jews were living in Lublin in the fourteenth century. They were not allowed to dwell in the city proper, but were restricted to the suburb of Kazimierz on the Bystrzyc, a tributary of the Wierprz. This suburb was named after Casimir III., by whose order it was assigned to the Jews in 1396. Later it became known as the "Piaski Zydowskie" (Jewish Strand). The Jews were allowed gradually to occupy a district within the city until the accession to the Polish throne of Sigismund II. (1518), who confined the settlement of the Jews to their original quarter. In the following year the king imposed upon them a special tax called "Striegeld," and, to please their competitors, the Christian merchants, restrained their commercial enterprises. The manufacture of beer, which was at that time exclusively in the hands of the Jews, was now restricted by the king to those who had acquired real property in the city. In 1552 he prohibited the Jews from dealing in food.

From the middle of the sixteenth to the middle of the eighteenth century Lublin was a great center of Jewish activity and the principal place of meeting of the Council of Four Lands.

Special Taxes and Restrictions.

At the end of the sixteenth century the Jews, in consideration of the payment of special taxes, were permitted to reside in the Podzance quarter of Lublin. The government record of licenses (part xxxvi., No. 14) of the year 1596 shows that there were then 100 Jewish houses in Podzance, and that the annual tax was fixed at 80 florins and 27 grivins. Sigismund August increased the tax on houses to 250 fl. Besides taxing the tenants of the houses 70 fl., he imposed the following additional taxes: for 16 butcher-shops, 53 fl. 6 gr.; for 20 hot-bath tubs, 80 fl.; for a bath-house and a liquor-shop at Podzance, 200 fl. The number of Jews in the city at that time may therefore be estimated at about 2,000. Their numbers steadily increased, and in 1630 the annual tax paid by them amounted to 300 Polish guilders. Ladislaus IV. confirmed (March 21, 1633) the privileges granted to the Jews by former kings of Poland.

Immediately prior to the COSSACKS' UPRISING in 1648 the Jesuits instigated a riot and attacked the Jewish quarter. Twenty houses were ransacked, eight Jews being killed and twenty wounded. The Jesuits were prosecuted before Ladislaus IV. and were severely punished. Later (1650) the Jesuits established in Lublin a printing-press which existed till 1670. They published many works hostile to the Jews, thus creating enmity between the latter and the Christian inhabitants. To the influence of the Jesuits is attributed also the decree of 1650, forbidding Jewish apothecaries to prepare medicine, and that of 1654, prohibiting performances by Jewish musicians not having a special permit from the government.

Persecutions and Massacres.

The Jewish population of Lublin in 1656 was about 2,000 families, and, including those who for safety fled from the neighboring villages, there must have been in the city at least 10,000 Jews, most of whom were massacred by the Cossacks. Among the martyrs were many prominent rabbis and scholars. Some entered the cemetery and, after engraving their names upon the wall, arranged to be buried alive rather than fall into the hands of the mob and be tortured. Rabbi Samuel b. David, in his "Ḥesed Shemuel" (ed. Amsterdam, 1699, pp. 2b, 43b), assigns the occurrence to the day preceding the Sukkot festival of 5417 (= Oct. 15, 1656), and describes his own miraculous escape (see COSSACKS' UPRISING).

Privileges for Jews.

Under the city magistrate Jan Carl Danielowicz the Jews of Lublin fared better than they had done at any previous time. In his charter of Nov. 21, 1675, concerning the rights of the Jews, Danielowicz reviews the privileges granted by the former Polish kings, which he declares to be a safeguard to Jewish life and property. He enumerates the following provisions: (1) The Jews of Lublin to contribute no more than the customary real-estate tax of 700 Polish guilders (this tax covered the dwellings, synagogues, charitable institutions, cemetery, shops, wax-factories, and bath-houses). (2) All contracts made between Christians and Jews residing in Podzance, regarding the purchase and sale of mead, beer, brandy, etc., to be valid. (3) The commercial tax on Jews to be no higher than the same tax on Christian citizens in proportion to their respective numbers. (4) Jews to be exempt from having soldiers quartered among them either permanently or temporarily. (5) Jews to be exempt from furnishing food and clothing supplies to the guard of the city hall. (6) No encroachment to be made on the Jewish cemetery. (7) In legal suits concerning chattels appeals to be made to the city magistrate; in other cases, to the Supreme Court. "I make," he says, "these provisions voluntarily, and promise to fulfil them for the benefit of the Jews who have petitioned me, and for the benefit of their descendants, so long as I live; and I pray that my successors shall follow my example."

King JOHN SOBIESKI in 1679 prohibited trading between Jews and Christians during Christian holidays, and ordered the confiscation of any goods sold on those days. King Augustus II. in 1720 further restricted Jewish commerce, and annulled the leases of shops to Jews in the Christian quarters of the town on the ground that the Jews were keen competitors of the Christian merchants. Augustus III. forbade (1736) Jews to act as agents of Christians. It is claimed that this restriction was formulated at the solicitation of the Jewish congregation against certain of its members, who, in order to shirk the communal tax, and also to avoid the special government tax, severed their connection with the synagogue and transacted business as the nominal agents of Christians, and shared the profits with them. Stanislaus Augustus Poniatowski, the last King of Poland, on his coronation in 1764, ordered the expulsion of Jews from Lublin and its suburbs. Later they were permitted to return subject to curtailed privileges and heavy taxes. The Russian army captured Lublin in 1831.

Communal Work.

Jewish communal life in Lublin began with the above-mentioned settlement of Jews in the suburb of Piaski, where they were permitted to form a congregation under a charter and with a seal bearing the emblem of a hornless deer. Not only were they allowed to have their own civil laws, but they were even appointed attorneys and judges in the general courts. Indeed, to such an extent was this the case that the waywodes of Warsaw specially assembled in 1540 to prohibit such appointments.

The Jewish cemetery, situated on the Gradzisk hill, was granted to the Jews by Tenczinski in 1555; but it had already been utilized as a Jewish burial-ground, as is evidenced by the record of a tombstone dated 1541.

The congregational minute-books, which had been placed in the government archives, were destroyed by fire in 1829. They contained valuable data for the history of the Lublin Jews and of the Council of Four Lands. There is left but one pinḳes of the ḥebra ḳaddisha beginning with 1685, interesting extracts from which are published in Nissenbaum, "Le-Ḳorot ha-Yehudim be-Lublin," p. 14. The record includes a proclamation of 1694 by the officers of the burial society excommunicating evil-minded persons who had denounced their Jewish neighbors for selfish purposes before Christian priests and noblemen. These persons were blacklisted by the members of the society, who pledged themselves not to give them a decent funeral nor to bury them within the Jewish cemetery. The offenders were, however, afforded the opportunity to retract their denunciations and to give a solemn promise never to repeat the offense (*ib.* p. 142).

Synagogues and Charitable Institutions.

Lublin possesses five synagogues: (1) The Meharshal Synagogue, the oldest in the town, formerly attended by Solomon LURIA. It has seats for about 3,000. (2) The Synagogue of Ẓebi b. Moses Doctor ("Doctor" meaning "Rabbi"; otherwise known as Jeleno [Hirsch] Doctorowicz), founded by Ẓebi in 1669 by permission of King Ladislaus IV. It appears that this synagogue was also rebuilt by Ẓebi to commemorate the victories of King John Sobieski in 1683. (3) The Synagogue of Saul Wahl (d. 1617). This synagogue is known also as the "Läufer [" runıers"] Synagogue," because it was formerly used by 'isitors and strangers. (4) The Kahal Synagogue, ›ften visited by Samuel EDELS (d. 1631). (5) The ?arnes Synagogue, founded by Abraham Parnes (d. .763). There are also a "Tailors' Synagogue" and everal others of recent date.

Among the charitable and educational institutions .re: the Jewish hospital, housed in a modern build-ıng, with 56 beds; an asylum for the aged, for vidows, and for orphans; a Hebrew free school Talmud Torah); and a Jewish school, in which the eaching of Hebrew and of secular knowledge is ombined under Jewish and non-Jewish masters.)n the yeshibot founded by various rabbis see Jacob ?OLLAK; Shalom SHACHNA; Solomon LURIA; Meïr ›en Gedaliah LUBLIN.

The government census of 1896 gave the total ›opulation as 48,758, of whom 23,788 were Jews. n 1899 the total Jewish population of the govern-ıent of Lublin was 186,787. Lublin is an industrial nd manufacturing town, containing 3 distilleries, 3 ›reweries, 4 tanneries, 6 brick-factories, 4 soap-and-andle factories, 3 tobacco-factories, 2 implement-actories, and 1 flour-mill; also factories of yarn and f linen and hemp goods. The Jews control most f these, and nearly all the mercantile and banking usiness.

IBLIOGRAPHY: Sierpinski, *Historyczny Obraz Miasta Lublina*, Lublin, 1849; Ziellinski, *Mono. Lublina*, ib. 1877; Dembitzer, *Miklele Bikkoret*, Letter ב Cracow, 1892; Friedberg, *Le-Toledot ha-Defus ha-'Ibri be-Lublin*, ib. 1901; Nissenbaum, *Le-Korot ha-Yehudim be-Lublin*, Lublin, 1900; *Jüdische Statistik*, Berlin, 1903; *Ha-Maggid*, 1852, No. 16; *Ha-Asif*, 1886, p. 393; Bershadski, in *Voskhod*, Oct., 1895.

H. R. J. D. E.

—**Typography:** The first Hebrew printing-ouse at Lublin was founded in 1547 by Joseph f Lublin, who printed the "Ketab Hitnazzelut le)arshanim" of David ha-Darshan (1548), and some ther books. In 1550 he obtained from Sigismund .ugust the monopoly of printing Hebrew books.

In 1558 a new printing-house was founded by acob b. Moses, Meshullam b. Solomon, Eliezer b. saac of Prague, Kalonymus b. Mordecai Jafe, and acob b. David Gutrat. The first work printed by ıem was the Pentateuch (1558); in the following ear they issued the Talmud treatises Shebu'ot and 'esaḥim, which were followed by many other books efore 1579. In that year printing was suspended ll 1590, when it was resumed and carried on till 1603.)uring that time the house printed Mordecai Jafe's Lebush" (1590), Jacob ben Asher's "Ṭur Oraḥ Iayyim" (1599), etc.

In 1606 Ẓebi Hirsch b. Kalonymus Jafe opened printing-house, where he printed the "Minḥat 'ehudah" of Judah Löb b. Obadiah Eulenburg 1609), and the "Tebu'ot Shor" of Ephraim Zalman hor (1615). In 1618 he began the printing of the 'almud, which was completed in 1628. In 1642 Kalonymus b. Ẓebi Jafe opened another printing-ouse, from which were issued, among other books, ıe "Yalkuṭ Shim'oni" (1643) and "Dammesek Eli'ezer" (1646). The wars which broke out in 'oland caused a suspension of the work.

Fourteen years later a new printing-house was ›unded by Jacob b. Abraham Jafe. He printed ıe "'Ammudeha Shib'ah" of Bezaleel of Slutsk 1662), and the "Ketonet Passim," on the Pesaḥ Haggadah, by Joseph b. Moses of Przemysl (1685), besides a great many pamphlets.

For nearly two hundred years the printing of Hebrew books at Lublin was suspended. In 1870 Hirschenhorn and Schneidemesser opened a new printing-house, and issued the collection of responsa known as "Noda' bi-Yehudah" and other books. In 1901 they printed a beautiful edition of the Bible with various commentaries.

BIBLIOGRAPHY: Wolf, *Bibl. Hebr.* ii.; Zunz, *Ozar ha-Sifrut*, p. 1; B. Friedberg, *Zur Gesch. der Hebr. Typographie in Lublin*, 1900; Ersch and Gruber, *Encyc.* section ii., part 28, p. 56; Steinschneider, *Cat. Bodl.* cols. 319, 1216, 1220, 1705, 2918, s. v. *Jafe*.

J. B. FR.

LUBLIN, MEÏR BEN GEDALIAH (MaHaRaM): Polish rabbi; born at Lublin (?) 1558; died there May 3, 1616. He was descended from a family of rabbis, and he speaks of his father as being an eminent Talmudist (Maharam, Responsa, No. 1). His principal teacher was his father-in-law, Isaac ha-Kohen Shapiro, rabbi of Cracow (*ib.* No. 105), and he distinguished himself so highly in the knowledge of the Talmud and Posekim that in 1587, when he was not yet thirty years old, he was invited to the rabbinate of Cracow. Up to that time he seems to have lived in Lublin; for in one of his responsa (No. 138), which bears neither date nor place, he writes, "all my tools [*i.e.*, books] are still at Lublin." According to Lewinstein ("Ha-Goren," i. 41–43), Lublin was from 1582 onward chief rabbi of Lublin, at the same time that Simon Wolf Auerbach was head of the yeshibah there (but see AUERBACH, SIMON [ZE'EB] WOLF). Owing to continual quarrels between the pupils of these two Talmudists, Lublin was ordered to leave the town.

It can not be said with certainty how long he remained at Cracow, as there is only one (undated) responsum (No. 50) which he wrote while holding that rabbinate. It seems certain, however, that he left Cracow after 1591 in order to become rabbi at Lemberg, a position which he held till 1613. In Lemberg he was engaged in continual controversies with Joshua Falk, author of "Me'irat 'Enayim"; particularly a bill of divorce issued by the latter at Vienna occasioned lengthy discussions between them (Maharam, Responsa, Nos. 123 *et seq.*; see also FALK, JOSHUA BEN ALEXANDER HA-KOHEN). Lublin speaks in his responsa (Nos. 68, 102–103) of a fire (referring to the fire of Lemberg) in which his work "Seder Gittin" was burned.

According to a tradition, Lublin was forced by the authorities of Lemberg, at the instigation of Abraham Schrenzel, to leave the town. The latter thus avenged his teacher, Joshua Falk, who had been insulted by Lublin.

Leaves Lemberg.

At this time (1613) the community of Lublin being in want of a rabbi, Meïr accepted the rabbinate, and he continued to hold it till his death. Wherever he settled Lublin organized a yeshibah, of which he was the head; and owing to his renown as a Talmudic scholar and casuist, the number of his pupils was considerable. Among them were Joshua Höschel of Cracow, author of "Maginne Shelomoh," and Isaiah Horowitz, author of "Shene Luḥot ha-Berit," besides many others who became prominent rabbis or heads of yeshibot. He took special interest in his yeshibah, and often he signed his responsa "the one who is much occupied with his pupils" (Responsa, Nos. 80, 81, *et passim*). He was consulted by rabbis even from Italy and Turkey (*ib.* Nos. 12, 13, 21, 89).

His printed works are: (1) "Meïr 'Ene Ḥakamim" (Venice, 1619), novellæ forming a casuistic commentary on the Talmud, Rashi, and Tosafot; published by his son Gedaliah. It has since been republished several times, and is now printed in all the principal editions of the Talmud under the heading "Maharam." (2) "Manhir 'Ene Ḥakamim" (*ib.* 1619), a collection of 140 responsa, published by his son Gedaliah, who in collaboration with his brother Isaac added a preface. His unpublished works include: "Ma'or ha-Gadol," a commentary on the four Ṭurim; "Ma'or ha-Ḳaṭon," a commentary on the "Sha'are Dura"; "Ner Miẓwah," a commentary on the "Sefer Miẓwot Gadol"; "Torah Or," a homiletic commentary on the Pentateuch; "Or Shib'at ha-Yamim," a collection, apparently unfinished, of orally transmitted laws.

Works.

The method employed by Lublin in his commentary on the Talmud was the opposite of that adopted by him when lecturing to his pupils in the yeshibah. In the latter case, as is usual with great casuists, he explained the passages of the Talmud, of Rashi, or of the Tosafot at great length, or, as he expressed himself, "by profound pilpul" (Maharam on 'Ab. Zarah 22a; Ḥul. 2b; Niddah 2b). But in his commentary or novellæ he for the most part adopted a short and simple explanation, giving as his reason for not expounding a passage at greater length that he did not wish to dwell on it too long (Ḥul. 9b, 81b). In certain cases where he employed pilpul, he justified himself by saying that he was obliged to do so as the students might otherwise interpret the passage wrongly (Shab. 48a), or because he wished to sharpen their minds (*ib.* 20a). He showed a great tendency to correct the text of the Talmud (comp. Maharam on Giṭ. 5, 6; Yeb. 59 *et passim*).

Being a fearless critic, Lublin did not spare even the Tosafists when their expressions seemed to him obscure (Maharam on Suk. 10; Beẓah 7). He was generally dogmatic both in his novellæ and in his responsa; he declared on several occasions that his interpretation was the right one and that the passage could not be rendered otherwise (Maharam on Shab. 67 *et passim*). He often attacked Solomon Luria and Samuel Edels, saying that their interpretations were erroneous and might mislead students (Shab. 58b; Ḥul. 28a *et passim*). In his responsa he took for his basis the Aḥaronim, whom he declared to be of greater authority than the Tosafists, Maimonides, or Mordecai b. Hillel (Responsa, Nos. 114, 133, 137). He violently attacked Joseph Caro's Shulḥan 'Aruk, declaring that it was a mixture of laws from different authorities and having no connection with one another (*ib.* No. 11; Isserles, Responsa, No. 135). Lublin paid little heed to the Cabala, though it is evident from his responsum No. 34 that he believed in the sacredness of the Zohar.

Method of Interpretation.

Bibliography: Buber, *Anshe Shem*, pp. 132-133; Grät *Gesch.* 3d ed., x. 53-54; Horodetzki, in *Ha-Goren*, i. 55-61 Lewinstein, *ib.* pp. 39-54; Nissenbaum, *Le-Ḳorot ha-Yehu dim be-Lublin*, pp. 31-34, Lublin, 1899; Steinschneide *Cat. Bodl.* col. 1705; J. M. Zunz, *'Ir ha-Ẓedeḳ*, pp. 28-42.
S. S. M. Sel.

LUBLINER, HUGO (pseudonym, **Hugo Bürger**): German dramatist; born at Breslau April 2 1846. He studied at the industrial school in Berlin and became manager of a cotton and woolen mil Inclination led him to dramatic composition. A first he wrote occasionally only, but with such suc cess that he at length gave up business and devote himself wholly to the production of plays.

Among the best-known of Lubliner's works are "Nur Nicht Romantisch" (1865), one-act comedy the only one of his earlier efforts that still holds th stage; "Der Frauenadvokat" (1873), three-act com edy, which has been performed at all the principa German theaters; "Die Modelle des Sheridan (1875), four-act comedy; "Die Florentiner" (1876 tragedy; "Die Adoptierten" (1877), drama; "Ga briele" (1878), drama; "Die Frau Ohne Geist (1879), comedy; "Auf der Brautfahrt" (1880), com edy; "Gold und Eisen" (1881); "Der Jour Fix (1882), comedy; "Aus der Grossstadt" (1883); "Di Mitbürger" (1884), comedy; (with G. von Mose "Glück bei Frauen"; (with Paul Lindau) "Fra Susanne"; "Gräfin Lambach" (1886); "Die Gläu biger des Glückes" (6th ed., Breslau, 1886); "Di Frau von Neunzehn Jahren" (*ib.* 1887), the last tw as parts of the romance-cycle "Berlin im Kaiser reich"; "Die Armen Reichen" (1886), comedy; "De Name" (1888), drama; "Im Spiegel" (1890), com edy; "Der Kommende Tag" (1891), drama; an the following comedies: "Das Neue Stück" (1894) "Aus der Menschlichen Komödie" (1895); "An de Riviera" (1895); "Die Junge Frau Arneck" (1895) "Roman eines Anständigen Mädchens" (1896) "Andere Luft" (1897); "Das Fünfte Rad" (1898); an "Splitter und Balken" (1899). Some of the forego ing pieces were collected in "Dramatische Werke (4 vols., Berlin, 1881-82).

Bibliography: *Brockhaus Konversations-Lexikon*; *Mey ers Konversations-Lexikon*.
S. N. D.

LUBLINER, OZIASZ LOUIS (LUDWIK) Polish writer; born 1809; died at Warsaw 1868. Afte the Polish revolution of 1831 he settled in Brussel where he published "Des Juifs en Pologne," an ex amination of the condition of the Jews in Russi from the historical, legislative, and political point of view. He wrote also, in Polish, "Obrona Zydow (Warsaw, 1858), a defense of the Jews living in Po lish territory; and a number of articles in Polis periodicals on the Jewish question. In 1861 he pub lished in Brussels a work entitled "Les Confiscation des Biens des Polonais," in which he reviewed th various ukases of Emperor Nicholas I. concernin Poland, and criticized the cruel treatment of th Polish Jews. In 1862 Lubliner was appointed libra rian at the University of Warsaw.

Bibliography: Orgelbrand, *Encyklopedja Powszechna*, vo ix.; *American Israelite*, ix. 102.
H. R. J. G. L.

LUBLINSKY, SOLOMON: German journalis and writer; born at Johannisberg, Prussia, Feb. 1

1868. He was occupied for a time as a clerk in a second-hand bookstore at Venice, after which he engaged in journalism at Berlin. He is now (1904) among the foremost Jewish writers. In addition to his journalistic work Lublinsky has written the following works, all published in Berlin: "Jüdische Charactere bei Grillparzer, Hebbel, und O. Ludwig" and "Literatur und Gesellschaft im 19ten Jahrhundert" (1899); "Multatuli" and "Der Imperator," dramas (1901); "Gescheitert," a novel (1901); "Hannibal," a drama (1902).

Bibliography: Kürschner, *Deutscher Literatur-Kalender*, p. 811; *Aḥiasaf*, 1898-99, p. 117.
H. R. A. S. W.

LUBOML: Town in the government of Volhynia, Russia. Jews lived there as early as the sixteenth century, though the attitude of the Christian inhabitants toward them was distinctly hostile. In 1557 the Jewish community resolved that none of its members should buy property within the city, for there was danger of its being attacked or set on fire by the Christian inhabitants. In 1576 this decision was reaffirmed by the leaders of the community with the indorsement of R. Abraham Polyak. Those who had violated this rule were warned to sell their property to Christians, under penalty of a fine or of some other punishment. Outside the town the Jews owned eight parcels of land; some of them leased grist mills, and others leased three lakes, paying for their leases in money, pepper, saffron, and salt fish to the total value of about 400 gold ducats. The population of Luboml in 1897 was 4,600, of whom 3,300 were Jews. It has 349 Jewish artisans and 52 Jewish day-laborers. The seventeen ḥadarim give instruction to 370 pupils, and 60 are instructed in the Talmud Torah (1898).

Bibliography: Katz, *Le-Ḳorot ha-Yehudim*, p. 7, Berlin, 1899; *Regesty i Nadpisi*, i. 241, St. Petersburg, 1899.
H. R. S. J.

LUCAS, LOUIS ARTHUR: African explorer; born in London Sept. 22, 1851; died at sea Nov. 20, 1876. After traveling in the United States (1872) and Egypt (1873), he organized an expedition to explore the Kongo. He left London Sept. 2, 1875, and arrived at Khartum in Jan., 1876, leaving that place in the following April. He next went with Colonel Gordon to the Albert Nyanza, and navigated the northern part of the lake in the first steamboat ever launched on it. He returned to Khartum in Aug., 1876, and reached Suakim on Nov. 18 of that year. In connection with this journey, Lucas compiled a vocabulary of Bisharin words, which was published in the "Journal of the Anthropological Institute."

In the same year (1876), against the advice of General Gordon and his staff, Lucas attempted to cross Africa, but, becoming sick and paralyzed, he soon had to return to Khartum. After lying ill for three months, he died on a steamboat between Suakim and Suez, and was buried at Jiddah.

Bibliography: *Times* (London), Dec. 26, 1876; *Jew. Chron.* Dec. 29, 1876; *Athenæum*, Dec., 1876; *Proceedings of the Royal Geographical Society*, 1876; *Dict. Nat. Biog.*
J. G. L.

LUCCA (Hebr. לוקא): City of Tuscany, Italy. Its Jewish community is known in literature especially through the Kalonymus family of Lucca, whose ancestor saved the life of the German emperor Otto II. after the battle of Cotrone in Calabria (982), and seems thereupon to have settled at Mayence, where the family had extensive privileges. In the twelfth century the community again appears in literature in the person of Abraham ibn Ezra, who lived at Lucca for a time while writing his grammatical works "Yesod" and "Sefat Yeter," as well as his commentary on the Pentateuch and Isaiah. He seems to have given instruction here in Hebrew grammar and Biblical science; one of his pupils, Ḥayyim, he mentions by name. The community was not a large one at that time; for Benjamin of Tudela, who visited it in 1165, found only forty Jews, under the leadership of R. David Samuel and R. Jacob.

In 1431 permission was granted to Angelo di Gaio, a Jew from Forli, to settle in Lucca and to open a bank for loans. A dispute arose, however, when King Sigismund, as he passed through Lucca, forcibly imposed a tax of 1,500 gold florins on the Jew, and Di Gaio left the city, while his son Gaietro opened a bank elsewhere. Later a similar permission was granted in Lucca to Isaac Manuelli & Co., who with others had settled in the city, and had a synagogue in a private house, besides a cemetery. Certain enemies of the Jews lodged a complaint against them with Pope Nicholas V.; but he, annulling the constitutions of Clement V. and a decree of the Bishop of Lucca, declared himself in favor of the Jews and confirmed their privileges. Other Jews who had banks in Lucca were David Dattali or da Tivoli and Vitale Isaac. In 1489, however, as a result of the anti-Jewish preaching of Bernardino da Feltre (in whose way many difficulties were placed at first in order to protect the Jews), the community decided to open a mont-de-pietà, and the Jews, who had objected to its establishment, were obliged to pay a fine of 1,300 florins.

Since their residence in Lucca was neither profitable nor secure, the Jews abandoned the city; according to some sources they were driven from it. After 1500 they returned, but they were in general not permitted to stay more than fifteen days consecutively. There are records, dated as late as May, 1728, of the names of Jews who had permission to make an extended residence in the city. After the French Revolution the Bacciochi family desired in vain to attract to the principality Jews who would buy property from the state.

Lucca has never had a Jewish community of any importance, and at present (1904) only about thirty Jews live there.

Bibliography: Aronius, *Regesten*, Nos. 70, 136; Rosin, *Die Religionsphilosophie des Abraham ibn Esra*, in *Monatsschrift*, xlii. 21; Benjamin of Tudela, *Itinerary*, ed. Asher, i. 37, ii. 16; Depping, *Die Juden im Mittelalter*, pp. 368 *et seq.*; *Regio Archivio di Stato di Lucca*, i. 208, 210-211, 362; iii. 387-388, s.v. *Ebrei*.
G. I. E.—V. C.

LUCENA (אליסאנה, אליסנה): City near Cordova, Spain, magnificently situated, and surrounded by strong walls and wide moats. In early times it was inhabited almost exclusively by Jews who had arrived together with its founders; hence it was called "Jews' City," an epithet applied also to

Granada and Tarragona. The Jews of Lucena, who carried on extensive trade and industries, were, according to an Arabic writer, richer than those of any other city. They enjoyed the same freedom as their coreligionists in the large Mohammedan cities. Their rabbi, who was elected by the entire community, was granted special privileges, and acted as judge in the civil and criminal cases arising in the community.

The Jews lived peaceably until the Almoravides came into power. A certain faḳih of Cordova pretended to have discovered a tradition according to which the Jews had entered into an agreement with Mohammed that they would embrace Islam at the end of the fifth century after the Hegira. Yusuf ibn Teshufin thereupon went to Lucena (1107) to induce the Jews of that city to fulfil the promises made by their ancestors. As the Jews suspected Yusuf of caring for their money rather than for their faith, they applied to Ibn Ḥamdin, the cadi of Cordova, or, according to Condé, to the vizier Abdallah ibn 'Ali, who induced the king to compromise the matter by accepting a very large sum of money. The Jews were glad to escape so easily. A worse fate befell them thirty-nine years later under the rule of the Almohades, whose leader, 'Abd al-Mu'min, persecuted and robbed them and forced them to accept Islam; and the flourishing and wealthy city, the seat of Jewish science, was destroyed (1146). At the beginning of the eleventh century several important scholars lived in Lucena, as also their most brilliant pupil, Abu al-Walid ibn Janaḥ. When Ferdinand III. of Castile conquered Andalusia he presented Lucena to the first bishop of Cordova, Don Lope, his former teacher. Isaac Alfasi founded a large Talmudic academy in Lucena, and here also Isaac ibn Ghayyat, Isaac ibn Albalia, and Joseph ibn Migash were prominent.

BIBLIOGRAPHY: Idrisi, *Geografia*, p. 265, Leyden, 1866; Condé, *Historia de la Dominacion de los Arabes en España*, ii., ch. xxiii.; Rios, *Hist.* i. 287 *et seq.*, 300, 365; Dozy, *Gesch. der Mauren in Spanien*, ii. 388; Grätz, *Gesch.* v. 116 *et seq.*, 187.

G. M. K.

LUCERNE: City of Switzerland, in the canton of the same name. Jews were living there as early as the middle of the thirteenth century. The earliest records of the town contain regulations for the sale of the flesh of animals slaughtered according to ritual: "When a Jew slaughters an animal, the meat shall be sold 'hinten an in der Schall,' and it shall also be stated that it belongs to the Jew." The regulations further say that the Jews who have obtained rights of sojourn or citizenship "shall offend no one, either by words or by deeds, either in the city or without it. And no one shall offend or injure the Jews 'von deheines Kindes wegen on des Rates wissende,' on pain of paying a fine of five pounds, without remission; and if the offender be so poor that he can not pay this fine, he shall nevermore set foot in the city." As elsewhere in Switzerland, the Jews in Lucerne were engaged in money-lending, they alone being privileged to charge interest on loans. In 1401 they were expelled from the city.

It was not until about 1864 that a Jew (from Endingen) again settled in Lucerne. The city has now (1904) a Jewish community numbering forty-two members. In 1900 there were 336 Jews in the entire canton.

BIBLIOGRAPHY: Ulrich, *Jüdische Geschichten in der Schweiz*, pp. 175 *et seq.*; Pfyffer, *Gesch. der Stadt und des Kantons Luzern*, p. 151; Kopp, *Geschichtsbilder der Schweiz*, i. 347 *et seq.*

G. M. K.

LUCIFER (Φωσφόρος): Septuagint translation of "Helel [read "Helal"] ben Shaḥar" (= "the brilliant one," "son of the morning"), name of the day, or morning, star, to whose mythical fate that of the King of Babylon is compared in the prophetic vision (Isa. xiv. 12–14). It is obvious that the prophet in attributing to the Babylonian king boastful pride, followed by a fall, borrowed the idea from a popular legend connected with the morning star; and Gunkel ("Schöpfung und Chaos," pp. 132–134) is undoubtedly correct when he holds that it represents a Babylonian or Hebrew star-myth similar to the Greek legend of Phaethọn. The brilliancy of the morning star, which eclipses all other stars, but is not seen during the night, may easily have given rise to a myth such as was told of Ethana and Zu: he was led by his pride to strive for the highest seat among the star-gods on the northern mountain of the gods (comp. Ezek. xxviii. 14; Ps. xlviii. 3 [A.V. 2]), but was hurled down by the supreme ruler of the Babylonian Olympus. Stars were regarded throughout antiquity as living celestial beings (Job xxxviii. 7).

The familiarity of the people of Palestine with such a myth is shown by the legend, localized on Mount Hermon, the northern mountain of Palestine and possibly the original mountain of the gods in that country, of the fall of the angels under the leadership of Samḥazai (the heaven-seizer) and Azael (Enoch, vi. 6 *et seq.*; see FALL OF ANGELS). Another legend represents Samḥazai, because he repented of his sin, as being suspended between heaven and earth (like a star) instead of being hurled down to Sheol (see Midr. Abḳir in Yalḳ. i. 44; Raymund Martin, "Pugio Fidei," p. 564). The Lucifer myth was transferred to Satan in the pre-Christian century, as may be learned from Vita Adæ et Evæ (12) and Slavonic Enoch (xxix. 4, xxxi. 4), where Satan Sataniel (Samael?) is described as having been one of the archangels. Because he contrived "to make his throne higher than the clouds over the earth and resemble 'My power' on high," Satan-Sataniel was hurled down, with his hosts of angels, and since then he has been flying in the air continually above the abyss (comp. Test. Patr., Benjamin, 3; Ephes ii. 2, vi. 12). Accordingly Tertullian ("Contra Marcionem," v. 11, 17), Origen ("Ezekiel Opera," iii 356), and others, identify Lucifer with Satan, who also is represented as being "cast down from heaven" (Rev. xii. 7, 10; comp. Luke x. 18).

BIBLIOGRAPHY: Cheyne, *Encyc. Bibl.*; Duhm, *Das Buch Jesaiah*, 1892, p. 96.

K.

LUCUAS: Toward the end of the reign of the emperor Trajan, in 116, the Jews of CYRENE rebelled, their leader being Lucuas according to Eusebius ("Hist. Eccl." iv. 2), Andreias according to Dio Cassius (lxviii. 32). These two statements can not be harmonized, as some historians have attempted to do by supposing that either of the two names was a symbolic one (Lucuas = "the bright or shining one,

Andreias = "the brave"); for the authors would not have passed over such an explanation in silence. Moreover, Eusebius and Dio Cassius refer to different phases of the rebellion. According to a later source, Abu al-Faraj, Lucuas sought refuge in Palestine, where he was defeated by Marcius Turbo. According to Eusebius he was proclaimed king; and the Papyrus Parisiensis No. 68 (published by Wilcken in "Hermes," xxvii. 464 *et seq.*) refers perhaps to him.

BIBLIOGRAPHY: Münter, *Der Jüdische Krieg*, p. 18; Krauss, in *R. E. J.* xxx. 206; Grätz, *Gesch.* 3d ed., iv. 115; Schürer, *Gesch.* 3d ed., i. 665.
G. S. Kr.

LUDASSY (GANS), MORIZ: Hungarian journalist; born at Komorn in 1825; died at Reichenau Aug. 29, 1885. As early as 1848 he was editor of the "Esti Lapok" in Budapest and of the "Magyar Világ," advocating in both periodicals the cause of the Conservatives. About fifteen years later he went to Vienna, where, with Georg Apponyi and Paul Sennyei, he founded the "Debatte," which advocated the establishment of a dual government in Austro-Hungary and the political equality of the two countries. When Count Julius Andrássy was premier, Ludassy was chief of the Hungarian press bureau and was at the same time ministerial councilor in the department of the interior. He returned to Vienna, however, where he was commissioned by Minister Beust to edit the "Tagespresse," the organ of the imperial court party during the war of 1870–71. In recognition of his services he was created a Hungarian noble.

One of his sons, **Julius Ludassy,** whose pen-name is "Julius Goose," is one of the editors of the "Fremdenblatt" in Vienna. He has written several comedies, among them "Maximen," "Spleen," and "Garrick."

BIBLIOGRAPHY: *Pallas Lex.* xi.; Agai, *Por és Hamu*, p. 320.
S. L. V.

LUKE. See New Testament.

LULAB: Name given to the festive palm-branch which with the Etrog is carried and waved on the Feast of Tabernacles (Sukkot). The three constituents of the lulab are: (1) a shoot of the palm-tree in its folded state before the leaves are spread out; this must be at least three handbreadths long, so that it may be waved, and must be bound round with a twig or tendril of its own kind; (2) three twigs of myrtle of the species which has its leaves in whorls of three; and (3) two willow-branches of the kind of which the wood is reddish and the leaves are long and entire (Suk. 29b, 32b, 34a). The myrtle-twigs and willow-branches are tied to the lower end of the palm-branch—the former on the right, and the latter on the left—by means of three rings of palm-strips. These branches constitute with the etrog the "four species" ("arba'at ha-minim").

Coin of Bar Kokba Bearing a Lulab.
(After Madden.)

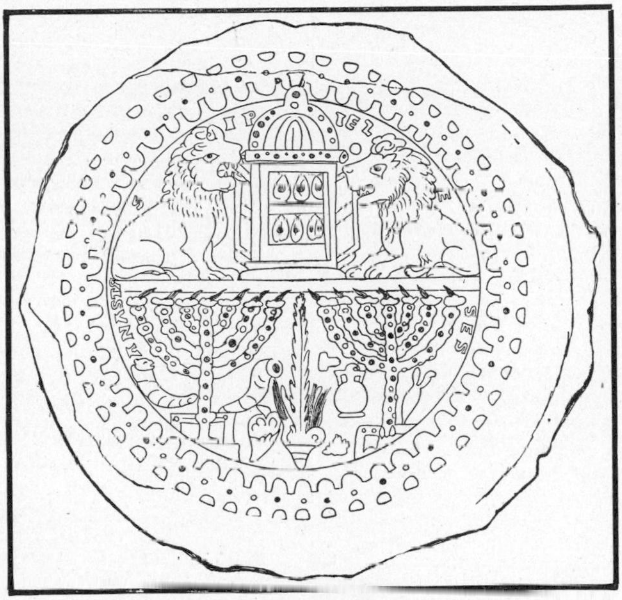

Representation of a Lulab on a Glass Dish Found in the Jewish Catacombs at Rome.
(In the Museo Borgeano at Rome.)

The use of the lulab is closely connected with the reciting of the Hallel (Ps. cxiii.–cxviii.). In the Second Temple it was waved during the recitation of the passages expressive of thanksgiving or prayer, viz., Ps. cxviii. 1–4, 25 (Suk. 37b). The manner of waving was as follows: Facing east and holding the lulab in the right hand and the etrog in the left, the worshiper shook the former in the directions east, south, west, and north, upward and downward, forward and backward; this was in acknowledgment of God's sovereignty over nature (*ib.*). After the additional sacrifices of the day had been offered the lulab and etrog were carried in procession around the altar in the court while Ps. cxviii. 25, or the refrain אני והו הושיעהנא, was chanted.

In the Temple.

On each of the first six days one such processional circuit ("haḳḳafah") was made; on the seventh day seven circuits took place, and at the end the etrogs were eaten by the children (Suk. 45a; see also Hosha'na Rabbah). According to tradition, the carrying of the lulab was observed in the Temple throughout the seven days of the feast, but outside of it on one day only. After the destruction of the Temple, R. Johanan ben Zakkai ordained that the practise should be observed everywhere during seven days, "in remembrance of the Temple" (Suk. 41a, 43b).

This ordinance is observed in the synagogue (except on Sabbath). The mode of carrying and waving the lulab and etrog is the same as it was in the Temple, but the first waving takes place before the commencement of Hallel, while the usual formula of benediction is recited: "Blessed art thou . . . concerning the holding of the lulab." After the Musaf service (which takes the place of the additional sacrifices in the Temple) the processional circuits, the precentor or ḥazzan leading, are made around the reading-desk, or bemah, on which the Torah-scroll is held in an upright position, while the hosannas (hymns beginning and closing with the words הושע נא) are chanted, in the same manner as in the Temple.

In the Synagogue.

The ordinance is binding on every observant Jew. One should not break fast before carrying it out. In countries where, owing to the cost, not every household can afford a lulab and an etrog, the poor are allowed the use of those belonging to their wealthy brethren. Usually the congregation owns a lulab and an etrog which are carried from house to house, so that children and feeble persons who can not come to the synagogue may observe the commandment and be allowed to break their fast in due time.

Lulab.
(After Picart.)

The ordinance of the lulab is derived from Lev. xxiii. 40: "And ye shall take you on the first day the fruit of goodly trees, branches of palm-trees, and the boughs of thick trees, and willows of the brook: and ye shall rejoice before the Lord your God seven days." Aside from the palm-branch and the willows the passage does not specify what shall be used; and the interpretation of the "fruit of goodly trees" and the "boughs of thick trees" to mean the etrog and myrtle respectively, as also the precise manner of using the four species, rests on tradition. A question as to the correctness of the accepted interpretation of the passage is raised in Lev. R. xxx. 15 (comp. also Tan., Emor, 20); and the answer is, quoting Prov. xxx. 24, "There be four things which are little upon the earth, but they are exceeding wise," that the "wise" explained the four species to mean etrog, lulab, myrtle, and willow-branches. A justification is attempted in Suk. 32b on the ground that "boughs of thick trees" implies a tree whose leaves cover the branches, and that this is characteristic of the myrtle, or a tree whose fruit and wood taste alike (have the same aroma), which again is a peculiarity of the myrtle. The presence of the latter characteristic is given as justification for the choice of the etrog also (*ib.* 37a). In Ta'an. 2b the four species are put in close relation with the prayers for the annual rainfall (comp. also Lev. R. xxx. 13), which was believed to be determined upon on the Feast of Tabernacles (R. H. 16a; comp. Suk. 37b); and it is added that the choice of them is suitable, for as "they can not exist without water, so also the world can not exist without water."

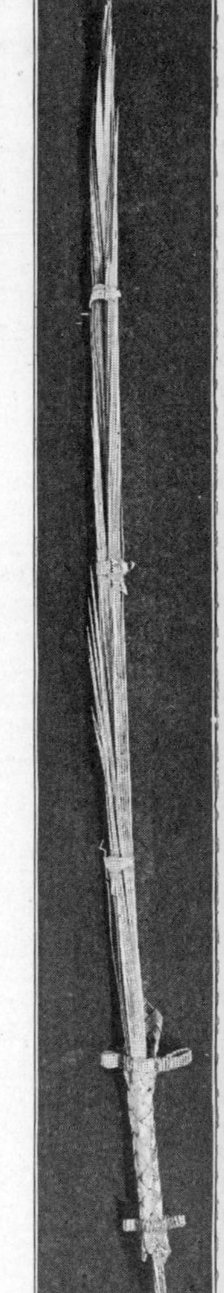

Lulab.
(From a photograph.)

In addition to these explanations, the Midrash (*ib.* 9–14; comp. Tan., Emor, 17) indulges in many symbolical explanations of the four species, *e.g.*, they refer to God Himself in His various attributes and activities; they remind one of the three patriarchs and Joseph, or of the four mothers of Israel; they represent the great Sanhedrin with the scholars and their disciples and scribes attached to it; or the whole people of Israel in its four divisions of (1) pious and learned, (2) learned but not pious, (3) pious but not learned, and (4) those who are neither; and lastly they symbolize the four chief constituents of the human body—the spinal column, the heart, the eye, and the mouth. The Samaritans and Karaites refer the passage in Leviticus to the parts constituting the booth ("sukkah"), pointing to Neh. viii. 15, where, however, some different species ("olive-branches" and "branches of wild olive") are enumerated.

The assumption—drawn from the fact that Plutarch ("Symp." iv. 6, 2) and Josephus ("Ant." xiii. 13, § 5: "for it is the custom among the Jews for each to have on the Feast of Booths a thyrsus of palms and citrons"; comp. also II Macc. x. 7) refer to the lulab as "thyrse" (θύρσος), and the latter, in "Ant." iii. 10, § 4 ("carrying in their hands a bunch of myrtle, willow-branches, palms, and citrons"), as εἰρεσιώνη—that the carrying of the lulab was connected with the Bacchic celebrations, or with the Pyanepsia and Thargelia, ignores the spirit and tendency of the Judaism of the Maccabean period. It s repudiated, in his manner, even by Tacitus "Hist." v. 5).

BIBLIOGRAPHY: Haremberg, in *Biblioth. Lubec.* iii. 434; A. Büchler, in *R. E. J.* xxxvii. 181-202 (on the passages in Plutarch, Josephus, and Tacitus).

A. I. M. C.

LULIANI BEN ṬABRIN: Palestinian scholar of the beginning of the fourth century. The name, which is the equivalent of "Julianus ben Tiberianus," has been corrupted into יולימנא בן עבדי in Pesiḳ. R. 7 (ed. Friedmann, p. 26a). His father's name, the usual form of which is טברין, is written also טבריינאי (Ex. R. xliv.) and טורין (Gen. R. xcviii. 4). Luliani is particularly known as the transmitter of haggadot of his teacher, Isaac Nappaḥa. He is frequently mentioned in pre-Talmudic literature and in the Midrash. There is, however, one haggadah ascribed to Luliani himself: "When the lesser people listen to the great and yet the latter do not alleviate the burden of the former, they shall account for it to God" (Ruth R., Introduction, 6); but a similar sentence is ascribed to R. Isaac in Deut. R. i. 8. The statement of Midrash Tehillim (to Ps. viii. 29) that Luliani transmitted a haggadah of R. Ishmael is apparently a mistake due to the abbreviation ר"י. Luliani is mentioned also as having asked his teacher Isaac a halakic question (Yer. Meg. 75c). Luliani was the father of the Ḥiyya b. Luliani who is frequently mentioned in the Jerusalem Talmud and who is stated to have caused rain to fall in time of drought (Ta'an. 25a).

BIBLIOGRAPHY: Bacher, *Ag. Pal. Amor.* ii. 210 *et passim*; Heilprin, *Seder ha-Dorot*, ii.

S. S. M. SEL.

LUMBROSO. See LOMBROSO.

LUMBROZO, JACOB or **JOHN**: Physician, planter, and trader resident in the palatinate of Maryland, America, in the middle of the seventeenth century; born at Lisbon; died between Sept. 24, 1665, and May 31, 1666. From Portugal he removed to Holland, and ultimately established himself in Maryland Jan. 24, 1656. His arrival formed, directly or indirectly, an important event in the life of the province. He early exercised his profession, and apparently enjoyed a lucrative practise. On Sept. 10, 1663, letters of denization were issued to him, together with certain privileges, enabling him to take up land under the liberal terms established by the proprietary—a privilege of which he promptly availed himself. A "Mistress Lumbrozo" was living in Sept., 1663, having arrived in Maryland in the preceding year. She was probably not of Jewish descent. Lumbrozo appeared as a witness in a lawsuit in 1657, and served as a juror in 1663. In 1665 he was granted a commission to trade with the Indians. He seems to have been in active intercourse with London merchants and to have corresponded with a sister in Holland. He amassed considerable wealth both in real and in personal property.

Although Jews were resident in Maryland probably from its settlement, Lumbrozo is the first Israelite—indeed the only one of that time—of whose faith there is documentary evidence. He was one of the earliest medical practitioners in the palatinate, and for nearly a decade continued to be an important figure in its economic activity. His career is of widest interest in its relation to the history and nature of religious toleration in Maryland. After living for at least two years in undisturbed quiet as a recognized Jew, and probably as a professed one, he was in 1658, through the activity of zealots and in consequence of his own indiscretion, arrested, under the provisions of the so-called Toleration Act of 1649, for "blasphemy," that is, for denial of the doctrine of the Trinity, thus becoming liable to punishment by death and forfeiture of lands and goods. The general amnesty proclaimed in the province ten days later, upon the accession of Richard Cromwell to the English protectorate, gave him freedom. Whether in consequence of his high economic importance or because of the milder interpretation put upon the statute in the case of discreet unbelievers, no further attempt was made to vindicate the letter of the law; and thereafter Lumbrozo gradually succeeded in exercising most of the rights of a fully naturalized citizen.

Record exists of a **John Lumbrozo**, born in June, 1666, who apparently was a posthumous child of Jacob's. But the widow married very soon after his birth; and the name "Lumbrozo" figures no more in Maryland colonial records.

BIBLIOGRAPHY: Hollander, *Some Unpublished Material Relating to Dr. Jacob Lumbrozo of Maryland*, in *Publ. Am. Jew. Hist. Soc.* No. 1 (1893), pp. 25-39; idem, *Civil Status of the Jews in Maryland, 1634-1776*, ib. No. 2 (1894), pp. 33-44, and references therein cited.

A. J. H. HO.

LUMLEY, BENJAMIN: Director of Her Majesty's Theatre, Drury Lane, London; born in Canada 1811; died in London March 17, 1875. He was the son of Louis Levy, a Canadian merchant who died in London about 1831. Benjamin was educated at King Edward's School, Birmingham, and early in life assumed the name "Lumley." In 1832 he became a solicitor in London, and from 1837 to 1842 was a parliamentary agent, publishing in 1838 a standard book on "Parliamentary Practise on Passing Private Bills." From 1836 to 1841 he superintended the finances of Her Majesty's Theatre for Laporte, and on Sept. 25, 1841, succeeded him in the management. He transformed the whole system of opera, and employed artists like Grisi, Persiani, Mario, Tamburini, and Lablache in grand opera, and Taglioni, Cerito, and Elssler in the ballets. These latter he made much more elaborate, introducing the famous "pas-de-quatre" in 1845. In 1847, however, as the result of many quarrels with his "stars," a rival opera-house was opened in Covent Garden, and Lumley was saved from ruin only by securing the services of Jenny Lind. On her retirement from the stage in 1849, Lumley's fortunes became embarrassed; and his attempt at controlling the Paris Opera House in 1850-51 led to further pecuniary difficulties. After the burning of Covent Garden Theatre in 1856 Lumley resumed the management of the Drury Lane house; but he failed to make it pay, and finally became reduced to such circumstances that he accepted the results of two benefit performances (1863). He introduced into England over thirty Italian operas, including Donizetti's "La Favorita," Verdi's "Ernani" and "La Traviata," and Auber's "Masaniello."

Lumley wrote two fantastic works of fiction: "Sirenia," 1862; and "Another World," 1873; the latter, describing a utopia in the planet Mars, had some success, and ran through three editions. He published also his "Reminiscences," 1864.

BIBLIOGRAPHY: *Times* (London), March 19, 1875; *Illustrated Sporting and Dramatic News*, March 21, 1875; Boase, *Modern English Biog.*; *Dict. Nat. Biog.*

G. L.—J.

LUNCZ, ABRAHAM MOSES: Russian scholar and editor; born Dec. 9, 1854, at Kovno, Russia; went when very young to Jerusalem, where he still (1904) lives. Luncz, who has been blind for many years, has founded, in conjunction with Dr. Koisewski, an institution for the blind at Jerusalem.

In the exploration of the Holy Land, Luncz has rendered great services from the historical, geographical, and physical standpoints, through his guide-books for Palestine, his Palestine annuals, and his Jerusalem almanac: (1) "Netibot Ẓiyyon we-Yerushalayim: Topography of Jerusalem and Its Surroundings" (vol. i., 1876); (2) "Jerusalem, Jahrbuch zur Beförderung einer Wissenschaftlich Genauen Kenntnis des Jetzigen und des Alten Palästina" (Hebrew and German, 6 vols., 1881–1903); (3) "Literarischer Palästina-Almanach" (Hebrew; since 1894). He owns a Hebrew printing-press, from which he has begun the issue of a Palestinian library, Estori Farḥi's "Kaftor wa-Feraḥ" and Schwarz's "Tebu'ot ha-Areẓ" being the first works published. He has now (1904) in the press a new edition of the Jerusalem Talmud with commentary and introduction.

BIBLIOGRAPHY: *Sokolow Sefer Zikkaron*, p. 184.

S. M. L. B.

LUNEL (Hebr. לוניל): Chief town of the department of Hérault, France; at times it is called מגדל ירחו and בקעת יריחו (see Zerahiah Gerundi, preface to "Ma'or," and I. de Lattes, "Sha'are Ẓiyyon," p. 75). The Jewish community here is an ancient one; important in the eleventh century, it became still more prominent in the twelfth. Benjamin of Tudela, who visited it in 1166, says ("Itinerary," i. 3) that it consisted of 300 members, some of whom were very learned and wealthy and took pleasure in offering hospitality to poor students eager to attend its famous academy. This institution had become so important in the twelfth century that it was at times called the "dwelling-place of the Torah" ("Ma'or" to Pes. vii.), and the "vestibule of the Temple" ("Temim De'im," No. 7).

The lords of Lunel were in general very well disposed toward the Jews. In 1252 one of them, Gaucelin, employed two Jews of his dominion as intermediaries to consult the Spanish Jewish doctor Ibrahim in behalf of Alphonse of Poitiers, whose eyesight had become seriously affected. In 1295 Rosselin of Lunel, in spite of the interdictions of the Church councils, pawned the revenues of his barony to a Jew named Thauros. In 1319 the Jews of Lunel were arrested, and the property was seized of those among them who were charged with having, during the preceding Holy Week, "in outrageous mockery" carried a crucifix through the streets of Lunel and trailed it in the dust (MS. Aubais, in the Nîmes Library, fol. 60).

At present there is not a single Jewish famil in Lunel, and only a few vestiges of the synagogu remain in the former Hôtel de Bernis (now belong ing to A. Ménard) in the Rue Alphonse Ménarc According to a document in the municipal archive (case 5, book i., No. 2319) the cemetery was situ ated on the Mas Desports road.

The following scholars, or "sages of Lunel," ar mentioned in the twelfth and thirteenth centuries Meshullam b. Jacob, a very learned man; Judah l Saul ibn Tibbon, physician and translator; Samu ibn Tibbon, translator of Maimonides' "Moreh N bukim"; the Talmudists Zerahiah b. Isaac ha-Le (Gerundi), Jonathan b. David ha-Kohen, and Man ah; Abba Mari b. Moses b. Joseph (Don Astruc c Lunel), author of the "Minḥat Ḳena'ot," a colle tion in which he preserved the letters exchange from 1303 to 1306 between the champions of orth doxy and the advocates of science and philosoph (among the former were the Lunel rabbis Isaac l Abigdor Simeon b. Joseph, called "En Duran of Lu nel," and Meïr b. Isaiah; among the latter, Solomo b. Isaac, called the "prince," who was commissione in 1286, together with several other Jews, to colle the taxes imposed by King Philip the Fair upon th Jews in the jurisdiction of the seneschal of Carca sonne); the physician Solomon, who is probabl identical with Maestro Solomon Davin, author of work on fever; Sen Samuel, commentator of th "Moreh Nebukim"; and the astronomer Salmor and in the fourteenth century, the philosoph Asher b. Abraham Cohen.

Several scholars from Lunel bore the surnam "Yarḥi" (= "of Lunel"), among them: Abraha b. Nathan ha-Yarḥi, David ha-Yarḥi, Aryeh Ju dah ha-Yarḥi b. Levi (Zunz, "Literaturgesch." p 495; *idem*, "Z. G." p. 469), and Solomon b. Abb Mari ha-Yarḥi, who lived in the second half of th fourteenth century and wrote a Hebrew gramma entitled "Leshon Limmudim." The name "Lunel is still a very common one among the Jews c southern France.

BIBLIOGRAPHY: Saige, *Les Juifs du Languedoc*, passim; R nan-Neubauer, *Les Rabbins Français*, pp. 512 *et seq.*; idem *Les Ecrivains Juifs*, pp. 401, 404 *et seq.*; Bédarrides, *L Juifs en France*, pp. 100, 143, 144; Abbé A. Rouet, *Noti sur la Ville de Lunel au Moyen Age*, pp. 13–77; Thom Millerot, *Histoire de la Ville de Lunel*, pp. 27, 40 *et se* Dom Vaissète, *Histoire Générale du Languedoc*, iv. 16 Grätz, *Gesch.* vii. 28 *et seq.*; S. Kahn, *Les Ecoles Juives et l Faculté de Médecine de Montpellier*, pp. 7, 11; Gross, *Gall Judaica*, pp. 277 *et seq.*

G. S. K.

LUNTSCHITZ, SOLOMON EPHRAIM See EPHRAIM, SOLOMON BEN AARON.

LUNTZ: Name of a family descended from th Loans, or Loanz, family of Worms. According t a family tradition, Elijah, the sixth in line of direc descent from Moses, son of Joselman Loans, em grated from Worms and settled in the little town c Kelm (Chelm; now in the government of Kovnc about the year 1700, and became its rabbi. He le a son, Meïr (b. 1709), whose first son, Elijah c Krozhe (Krozher; 1723?–1814), was a wealthy an pious Talmudist, and whose descendants adopted th name of Rabinowitz. His second son, Ezekiel, b came rabbi of Shavli about 1749, and continued i that position until his death in 1808. One of Ez kiel's sons, Moses, enjoyed the rare distinction c eing magistrate of Shavli. Another son, Getzel, vas the great-grandfather of Wolf Luntz of Riga, well-known communal worker and one of the ounders of the Zionist movement in Russia. Abraam Moses Luncz of Jerusalem does not belong to his family, whose pedigree follows:

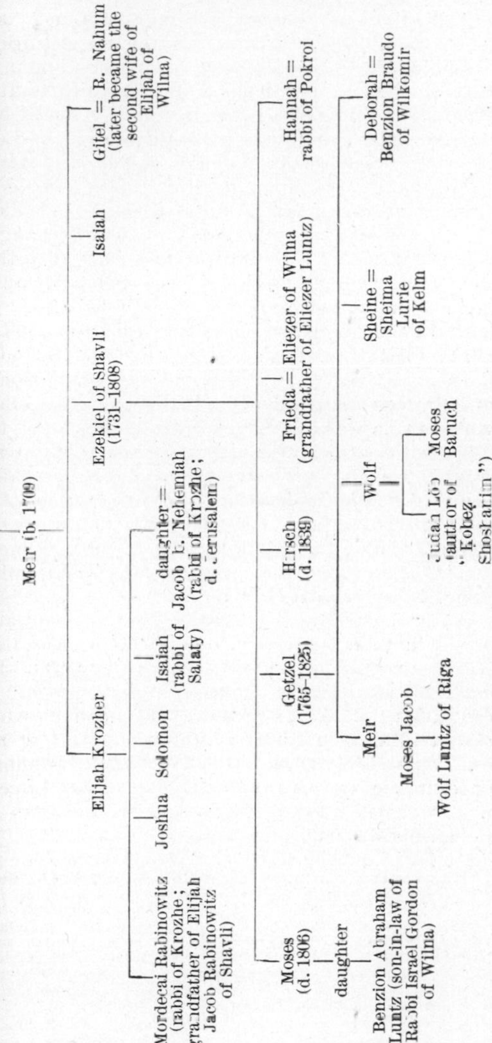

BIBLIOGRAPHY: Judah Löb Luntz, *Ḳobeẓ Shoshanim*, pp. 58–64, Warsaw, 1891.

H. R. P. Wi.

LUPERIO (LUPERCIO), ISAAC: A Jew, perhaps a Marano, of Spanish descent; lived at Smyrna. His apology, written in Spanish and directed against a monk at Seville, and an interpretation by him of Daniel's "seventy weeks," entitled "Apoloxia Repuesta y Declaracion de las Setenta Semanas de Daniel, Contra lo Que Escrivio una Persona Residente en Ruan," appeared in a Latin translation at Basel, 1658.

BIBLIOGRAPHY: Kayserling, *Bibl. Esp.-Port.-Jud.* p. 64; De Rossi, *Bibliotheca Judaica Antichristiana*, p. 58; De Rossi-Hamberger, *Hist. Wörterb.* p. 186.

G. M. K.

LÜPSCHÜTZ. See LIPSCHITZ; LIPSCHÜTZ.

LURIA: A family with wide ramifications and several of whose members were distinguished for mystical tendencies and rabbinical knowledge.

Abraham b. Nissan Luria: Russian rabbi and grammarian of the first half of the nineteenth century. He was rabbi of Skod (Shad ?) in Lithuania, and is known chiefly through his grammatical work "Nisyonot Abraham" (Wilna, 1821). It consists of two parts, of which the first is on the grammatical passages in Rashi's commentary on the Bible, and the second on similar passages occurring in the older commentaries on the Mishnah and Talmud.

BIBLIOGRAPHY: Fürst, *Bibl. Jud.* ii. 257; Fuenn, *Safah le-Ne'emanim*, p. 149, Wilna, 1881.

David b. Aaron Luria: Russian educator; born in Minsk about 1800; died in Königsberg, Prussia, July, 1873. The son of wealthy parents, he was given a liberal Jewish education, which he later supplemented by the acquisition of a knowledge of the secular sciences. After Lilienthal's failure (1842) to induce the Jews of Minsk to establish a school for Jewish children, Luria took up the work and succeeded beyond all expectations. At first opposed by the Orthodox, he soon overcame all opposition, and in 1843 gained control of the Talmud Torah of Minsk. As its superintendent, he transformed it into a modern institution; and his admirable management won the recognition not only of the local authorities, but even of the central government (see "Journal of the Ministry of Public Education," vol. 53, i. 40).

Luria's success not only turned his former antagonists into warm supporters, but induced the well-to-do Jewish merchants to open a school for their children so that they might be enabled to receive as good an education as was given to the orphans in the Talmud Torah. Thus a merchants' school was founded, also under Luria's management; but it failed on account of circumstances over which he had no control. The support it had received, however, encouraged him to establish the Midrash Ezraḥim or citizens' school, for children of the middle class, which proved a great success, although its fees were more than double those of the local gymnasium. But all his hopes were destroyed when his classes in the Talmud Torah and his Midrash Ezraḥim were closed by order of the government, to make room for the government schools which were then being established in Jewish communities. Greatly disappointed, "his only rewards being a gold medal from the czar and a short poem by Gottlober" ("Ha-Niẓẓanim," p. 214, Wilna, 1850), he retired to his books and his studies, and for the rest of his life took but little interest in public affairs.

Luria was the author of "'Omer ba-Sadeh" (Wilna, 1853), a book for the young, in which Biblical passages are explained in a moral and patriotic sense.

BIBLIOGRAPHY: *Yevreiskaya Biblioteka*, iii. 360 *et seq.*; *Ha-Shaḥar*, iv. 569; Zeitlin, *Bibl. Post-Mendels.* pp. 220–221.

Enoch Zundel b. Isaiah Luria: Russian preacher and author; died in Brest-Litovsk Feb. 13, 1847. He lived for several years in Wilna, and later became successively preacher in New Zhagory and Novogrudok, both in the government of

Kovno. He wrote "Kenaf Renanim" on "Perek Shirah" (Krotoschin, 1842; Presburg, 1859; Warsaw, 1888). He wrote also "Moṭot Kenafayim," sermons and addenda to his former work, but it remained in manuscript. A review of the "Kenaf Renanim" is given in "Orient, Lit." 1842, No. 26.

BIBLIOGRAPHY: Fuenn, *Keneset Yisrael*, p. 312; Feinberg, *'Ir Tehillah*, p. 228, Warsaw, 1886.

H. R. P. Wi.

Isaac ben Solomon Ashkenazi Luria (ARI): Founder of the modern Cabala; born of German parents at Jerusalem in 1534; died at Safed Aug. 5, 1572. While still a child he lost his father, and was brought up by his rich uncle Mordecai Francis, tax-farmer at Cairo, who placed him under the best Jewish teachers. Luria showed himself a diligent student of rabbinical literature; and, under the guidance of Bezaleel Ashkenazi, he, while quite young, became proficient in that branch of Jewish learning. At the age of fifteen he married his cousin, and, being amply provided for, was enabled to continue his studies undisturbed. When about twenty-two years old, becoming engrossed with the study of the Zohar, which had recently been printed for the first time, he adopted the life of a hermit. He removed to the banks of the Nile, and for seven years secluded himself in an isolated cottage, giving himself up entirely to meditation. He visited his family only on the Sabbath, speaking very seldom, and always in Hebrew. Such a mode of life could not fail to produce its effect on a man endowed by nature with a lively imagination. Luria became a visionary. He believed he had frequent interviews with the prophet Elijah, by whom he was initiated into sublime doctrines. He asserted that while asleep his soul ascended to heaven and conversed with the great teachers of the past.

Lives as Hermit.

In 1569 Luria removed to Palestine; and after a short sojourn at Jerusalem, where his new cabalistic system seems to have met with but little success, he settled at Safed. There he formed a circle of cabalists to whom he imparted the doctrines by means of which he hoped to establish on a new basis the moral system of the world. To this circle belonged Moses Cordovero, Solomon Alḳabiẓ, Joseph Caro, Moses Alshech, Elijah de Vidas, Joseph Ḥagiz, Elisha Galadoa, and Moses Bassola. They met every Friday, and each confessed to another his sins. Soon Luria had two classes of disciples: (1) novices, to whom he expounded the elementary Cabala, and (2) initiates, who became the depositaries of his secret teachings and his formulas of invocation and conjuration. The most renowned of the initiates was Ḥayyim Vital of Calabria, who, according to his master, possessed a soul which had not been soiled by Adam's sin. In his company Luria visited the sepulchers of Simeon ben Yoḥai and of other eminent teachers, the situation of which had been revealed to him by his constant mentor, the prophet Elijah. Luria's cabalistic circle gradually widened and became a separate congregation, in which his mystic doctrines were supreme, influencing all the religious ceremonies. On Sabbath Luria dressed himself in white and wore a fourfold garment to signify the four letters of the Ineffable Name. His follower looked upon him as a saint who had the power t perform all kinds of miracles, while he himself pre tended to be Messiah ben Joseph, the forerunner o Messiah ben David.

Disciples.

Luria used to deliver his lectures extempore and with the exception of some cabalistic poems in Ara maic for the Sabbath service, did not write anything The real exponent of his cabalistic sys tem was Ḥayyim Vital. He collecte all the notes of the lectures whic Luria's disciples had made; and fron these notes were produced numerous works, th most important of which was the "'Eẓ Ḥayyim," i six volumes (see below). At first this circulated i manuscript copies; and each of Luria's disciple had to pledge himself, under pain of excommunica tion, not to allow a copy to be made for a foreig country; so that for a time all the manuscripts re mained in Palestine. At last, however, one wa brought to Europe and was published at Zolkiev i 1772 by Satanow. In this work are expounded bot the speculative Cabala, based on the Zohar, and th practical or miraculous Cabala (קבלה מעשית), o which Luria was the originator.

His Utterances.

The characteristic feature of Luria's system in th speculative Cabala is his definition of the Sefirot an his theory of the intermediary agents, which h calls "parẓufim" (from πρόσωπον = "face"). Befor the creation of the world, he says, the En Sof fille the infinite space. When the Creation was decide upon, in order that His attributes, which belon to other beings as well, should manifest them selves in their perfection, the En Sof retired int His own nature, or, to use the cabalistic term, con centrated Himself (צמצם את עצמו). From this con centration proceeded the infinite light. When in it turn the light concentrated, there appeared in th center an empty space encompassed by ten circle or dynamic vessels ("kelim") called "Sefirot," b means of which the infinite realities, though form ing an absolute unity, may appear in their diver sity; for the finite has no real existence of itsel However, the infinite light did not wholly desert th center; a thin conduit (צינור) of light traversed th circles and penetrated into the center. But whil the three outermost circles, being of a purer sul stance because of their nearness to the En Sof, we able to bear the light, the inner six were unable t do so, and burst. It was, therefore, necessary to re move them from the focus of the light. For th purpose the Sefirot were transformed into "figures ("parẓufim"). The first Sefirah, Kete was transformed into the potentiall existing three heads of the Macr prosopon ("Erek Anfin"); the secon Sefirah, Ḥokmah, into the active masculine princip called "Father" ("Abba"); the third Sefirah, Bina into the passive, feminine principle called "Mother ("Imma"); the six broken Sefirot, into the male chil ("Ze'er"), which is the product of the masculi active and the feminine passive principles; the tent Sefirah, Malkut, into the female child ("Bat"). Th proceeding was absolutely necessary. Had G in the beginning created these figures instead the Sefirot, there would have been no evil in t

The Sefirot.

orld, and consequently no reward and punish- ent; for the source of evil is in the broken Sefirot ' vessels, while the light of the En Sof produces ıly that which is good. These five figures are und in each of the four worlds; namely, in the orld of emanation (עולם האצילות); in that of crea- on (עולם הבריאה); in that of formation (עולם היציר); and in that of action (עולם העשיה), which presents the material world.

Luria's psychological system, upon which is based s practical Cabala, is closely connected with his etaphysical doctrines. From the five figures, he ys, emanated five souls, Neshamah, Ruaḥ, Ne- sh, Ḥayyah, and Yeḥidah; the first of these being e highest, and the last the lowest. Man's soul is e connecting-link between the infinite and the ite, and as such is of a manifold character. All e souls destined for the human race were created gether with the various organs of Adam. As there e superior and inferior organs, so there are superior d inferior souls, according to the organs with hich they are respectively coupled. Thus there e souls of the brain, souls of the eye, souls of the nd, etc. Each human soul is a spark ("niẓoẓ") from dam. The first sin of the first man caused confu- on among the various classes of souls: the superior termingled with the inferior, good with evil; so at even the purest soul received an admixture of il, or, as Luria calls it, of the element of the shells" ("ḳelipot"). From the lowest classes of uls proceeded the pagan world, while from the gher emanated the Israelitish world. But, in con- quence of the confusion, the former are not wholly prived of the original good, and the latter are not together free from sin. This state of confusion, hich gives a continual impulse toward evil, will ase with the arrival of the Messiah, who will estab- sh the moral system of the world upon a new basis. ntil that time man's soul, because of its deficien- es, can not return to its source, and has to wander ot only through the bodies of men and of animals, it even through inanimate things such as wood, vers, and stones.

To this doctrine of metempsychosis Luria added the eory of the impregnation ("'ibbur") of souls; that to say, if a purified soul has neglected some relig- us duties on earth, it must return to the earthly fe, and, attaching itself to the soul of a living man, unite with it in order to make good such neglect.

Return of the Soul.

Further, the departed soul of a man freed from sin appears again on earth to support a weak soul hich feels unequal to its task. However, this nion, which may extend to three souls at one time, n only take place between souls of homogeneous aracter; that is, between those which are sparks of e same Adamite organ. The dispersion of Israel ıs for its purpose the salvation of men's souls; and e purified souls of Israelites unite with the souls of en of other races in order to free them from demo- acal influences. According to Luria, man bears on s forehead a mark by which one may learn the na- re of his soul: to which degree and class it belongs; e relation existing between it and the superior orld; the wanderings it has already accomplished; e means by which it can contribute to the estab- lishment of the new moral system of the world; how it can be freed from demoniacal influences; and to which soul it should be united in order to become purified. This union can be effected by formulas of conjuration.

Luria introduced his mystic system into religious observances. Every commandment had for him a mystic meaning.

Influence on Ritual.

The Sabbath with all its ceremonies was looked upon as the embodiment of the Divinity in temporal life; and every ceremony performed on that day was considered to have an influence upon the superior world. Every word, every syllable, of the prescribed prayers contain hidden names of God upon which one should meditate devoutly while reciting. New mystic ceremonies were ordained and codified under the name of "Shulḥan 'Aruk shel Ari." This tendency to substitute a mystic Judaism for the rabbinical Judaism, against which Luria was warned by his teacher of Cabala, David ibn Abi Zimra, became still stronger after Luria's death. His disciples, who applied to him the epithets "Holy" and "Divine," sank further in mysticism and paved the way for the pseudo-Messiah Shabbethai Ẓebi.

The following are the works attributed to Luria by his disciples, given in the order of their publication:

1595. Marpe Nefesh, on the purification of the soul. Venice.
1600. Tiḳḳune ha-Teshubah, on penitence. Published by Elijah Moses de Vidas. Venice.
1615. Seder we-Tiḳḳun Ḳeri'at Shema', mystic explanations of the Shema'. Prague.
1620. Sefer ha-Kawwanot, mystic explanations of the prayers. Venice. (With corrections by Pethahiah ben Joseph, Hanau, 1624; Amsterdam, 1710; Jessnitz, 1723; abridged, under the title "Zot Ḥuḳḳat ha-Torah," by Abraham Ḥazzeḳuni, Venice, 1659.)
1624. Tiḳḳune Shabbat, mystic poems for Sabbath, and explanations of the Sabbath ceremonies. Venice.
1652. Sefer Ma'yan ha-Ḥokmah, on Creation and on the union between the higher and lower spheres, first published by Abraham Ḳalmanḳes. Amsterdam.
1663. Derek Emet, annotations on the Zohar and the "Sefer ha-Tikkunim." In three parts, Venice, 1663.
1663. Notes on the "Zohar he-Ḥadash," with text. Venice.
1680. Shulḥan 'Aruk, mystic explanations of many religious ceremonies.

Mubḥar she be-Abot, cabalistic commentary on Pirḳe Abot.

1710. Re'amim u-Re'ashim, prognostications. Constantinople.
1715. Notes on the Zohar, with text. Amsterdam.
1719. Perush Sefer Yeẓirah, commentary on the "Sefer Yeẓirah." Amsterdam.
1728. Tiḳḳun Ashmurot, midnight prayers termed "ḥaẓot." Amsterdam.
1737. Golel Or, on metempsychosis. Published by Meïr ben Ḥalifah Bikayim. Smyrna.
1766. Ḥadrat Melek, commentary on the Zohar. Published by Shalom ben Moses Buzaglio. Amsterdam.
1781. Seder ha-Tefillah, a book of prayer. Published by Aryeh ben Abraham. Zolkiev.
1785. Liḳḳuṭe Shas, cabalistic dissertations on several Talmudic treatises. Korzec.
1785. Zohar ha-Raḳia', commentaries on the Zohar, with the text. Korzec.
1785. Ḳol be-Ramah, on the Idra Rabba, with additions by Jacob ben Ḥayyim Ẓemaḥ. Korzec.
1788. Kelalot Tiḳḳunim we-'Aliyyot ha-'Olamot, on the ascension of the soul. Lemberg.
1839. Ma'or we-Shemesh, cabalistic collectanea. Published by Judah ben Abraham Raphael Koriat. Leghorn.

Ḥayyim Vital, as stated above, produced from the notes of Luria's lectures a work entitled "'Eẓ Ḥayyim" (Korzec, 1784), in six volumes: (1) "Oẓerot Ḥayyim," containing twenty-one cabalistic essays; (2) "Sefer Derushim," cabalistic explanations of the Bible; (3) "Sefer Kawwanot," mystic explanations of the prayers; (4) "Ṭa'ame ha-Miẓwot," on the precepts; (5) "Sefer ha-Gilgulim," on metempsychosis; (6) "Sefer Liḳḳuṭim," miscellanea. According to Azulai, Luria wrote in the earlier part of his life novellæ on Zebaḥim and Beẓah. A halakic consultation addressed by Luria to Joseph Caro is inserted in "Abḳat Rokel" (§ 136).

Bibliography: Solomon Shelemiel ben Ḥayyim, *Shibḥe ha-Ari*, Korzec, 1785; *Orḥot Ẓaddiḳim*, Leghorn, 1785; Naphtali Herz ben Jacob Elhanan, *Toledot ha-Ari*, published with the *'Emeḳ ha-Melek*, Amsterdam, 1648; Ḥayyim Cohen, *Ma'aseh ha-Ari*, in the introduction to his *Meḳor Ḥayyim*, ib. 1655; *Sefer Sedah ha-Ari*, ib. 1720; *Ma'aseh Nissim shel ha-Ari*, ib. 1720; Azulai, *Shem ha-Gedolim*, i. 104; Conforte, *Ḳore ha-Dorot*, p. 40b; Rossi, *Dizionario*, p. 186; Steinschneider, *Cat. Bodl.* col. 1133; idem, *Jewish Literature*, p. 456; D. Ch. Ginsburg, *The Kabbalah*, p. 134, London, 1865; Grätz, *Gesch.* ix. 436 *et seq.*; Fuenn, *Keneset Yisrael*, p. 630.

K. I. Br.

Johanan ben Aaron ben Nathanael Luria: Alsatian Talmudist; lived successively at Niedernheim and Strasburg at the end of the fifteenth century and in the beginning of the sixteenth. After having studied for many years in German yeshibot, he returned to Alsace and settled in Strasburg, where he founded a yeshibah by permission of the government. Luria was the author of an ethical work entitled "Hadrakah" (Cracow, *c.* 1579) and of "Meshibat Nefesh" (Neubauer, "Cat. Bodl. Hebr. MSS." No. 257), a haggadic and mystical commentary on the Pentateuch, founded on Rashi. To this commentary was appended a dissertation in which Luria refuted the arguments advanced by Christians against Judaism.

Bibliography: Carmoly, *Itinéraires de la Terre Sainte*, p. 345; Zunz, *Z. G.* pp. 106-130; *Orient, Lit.* xi. 546; Steinschneider, *Cat. Bodl.* col. 1398.

K. I. Br.

Solomon b. Jehiel Luria: Rabbi and author; born in Brest-Litovsk, Lithuania, 1510; died at Lublin Nov. 7, 1573. When still a youth his parents sent him to Posen, where he studied under the guidance of his grandfather Rabbi Isaac Klauberia. He left Posen in 1535, owing to an extensive fire which destroyed his grandfather's property. On his return to his native place he assiduously continued his studies. Here he married Lipka, daughter of Rabbi Kalonymus. After some time he was elected rabbi of Brest, and established a yeshibah there. About 1550 he received the appointment of rabbi and head of the yeshibah at Ostrog, and in 1555 he moved to Lublin, where he became head of the famous yeshibah.

Concerning his method of study and teaching he says: "I was painstaking always to trace the last source of the Halakah, which I used to discuss with my friends and pupils, spending sometimes a week in research and close reasoning till I came upon the root of the matter; then I used to put it down in my book. And it was always my habit to quote all the opinions of my predecessors, according to their rank of authority, also the decisions and rulings of those who compiled the responsa, in order to avoid the suspicion of plagiarism or the reproach that I had overlooked the opinion of some great authority.

His Method of Study.

In two years I did not reach in my studies further than half of the tractate Yebamot. I spent a whole year on two chapters of the tractate Ketubot; and the chapter 'Miẓwat Ḥaliẓah' [Yebamot] took me half a year." It is therefore not surprising that Luria was very independent, and was not afraid to say in public: "Do not take an notice of what people have been accustomed t now to consider as permitted; for most of the used to read only the 'Ṭur Oraḥ Ḥayyim' by Rab Jacob ben Asher. He gave permission in the name his father, Rabbi Asher; and in his introduction l even asserts that whenever he quotes the ruling his father, it should be considered as decisive f practise. And, indeed, many people took it f granted that it is to be looked upon as the last ar absolute decision, as though it were handed dow to us as a tradition of Moses from Mount Sinai. Tl fact that he agrees with his father does not pled us to agree with him; indeed, so it is in many ritu matters that the general usage is against him." N does he spare even Joseph Caro, whom he accus of having occasionally expressed merely superfici views in his effort to harmonize conflicting laws, well as of having sometimes based his decisions the reading of corrupt texts.

With even more asperity he speaks of Benjam Zeeb and his responsa, "Binyamin Ze'eb," whi he warns the public are worthless and full of pl giarisms. Of some of the rabbis of his time l says as follows: "The ordained are many; b those who know something are few. The numb of overbearing ones is steadily increasing, none whom knows his place. As soon as they are c dained they begin to domineer and, by means their wealth, to gather about themselves disciple just as lords hire slaves to run before them. Th rule over the scholars and the congregation. Th excommunicate and anathematize, and they orda pupils who did not study under them, and recei therefor money and reward. They are always see ing their own interests."

Though Luria was not on very good terms wi most of his contemporaries, yet he formed an in

Friendship with Isserles.

mate friendship with Rabbi Mos Isserles of Cracow, as may be se from their correspondence. But tl friendship did not prevent Luria fro remonstrating with Isserles when learned that the latter was devoted to the study philosophy, for he exhorted him with the word "Thou art turning to the wisdom of the uncircu cised Aristotle. Wo unto my eyes that they ha seen such a thing! This is a sin for such a prince Israel." The adherents of the Cabala he censur severely, saying: "These modern ones pretend belong to the sect of the cabalists. . . . They c not see in the light of the Zohar, which they do n understand. . . . Therefore, do not go in th ways. Have nothing to do with things secret."

Luria's works include: (1) "Ḥokmat Shelomo (Cracow, 1582), critical notes on the Talmud and earlier commentaries; it has been appended to t later editions of the Talmud; (2) Responsa (Lu lin, 1574); (3) "Yam shel Shelomoh" (Prague, 161 and later), novellæ on different treatises of the T mud: on Baba Ḳamma; on Ḥullin (Cracow, 164 on Yebamot (Altona, 1740); on Beẓah (Lubl 1636); on Ḳiddushin (Berlin, 1766); and on Giṭ (*ib.* 1766); (4) "Yeri'ot Shelomoh," supercommenta on the commentary of Elijah Mizraḥi on Ras prepared for print by his pupil Jehiel ben Mesh m; (5) "'Ammude Shelomoh" (Basel, 1600), commentary on the book of precepts by Rabbi Moses Coucy; (6) "'Aṭeret Shelomoh"; (7) "Zemirot" enice, 1602), commentary on the "Sha'are Dura" Isaac of Düren (Lublin, 1598), liturgical songs; d others. Many of Luria's works are still extant manuscript.

BLIOGRAPHY: *Pascheles Israelitischer Volkskalender*, x. 49; *Der Orient*, ix. 568; *Ha-Maggid*, p. 27, Lyck, 1858; Horodezky, in *Ha-Goren*, i. 95; idem, *Kerem Shelomoh* (1896); Rabbinowicz, *Ma'amar*, p. 56, Munich, 1877; Steinschneider, *Cat. Bodl.* cols. 23–65; Nissenbaum, *Le-Ḳorot ha-Yehudim be-Lublin*, p. 20, Lublin, 1899; Epstein, *Die Familie Lurie*, p. 14, Vienna, 1901; Feinstein, *'Ir Tehillah*, p. 198, Warsaw, 1886; Kohn-Zedeḳ, *Shem u-She'erit*, p. 21, Cracow, 1895; Güdemann, *Quellenschriften zur Gesch. des Unterrichts*, p. 59, Berlin, 1891; Grätz, *Gesch.* ix. 436; *Ha-Asif* (Warsaw), v. 127; *Isr. Letterbode*, xi. 165.

S. S. B. Fr.

LUSITANUS, AMATUS. See Juan Rodrigo e Castel-Branco.

LUST. See Yeẓer ha-Ra'.

LUSTRATION. See Ablution.

LUTHER, MARTIN*: German church reormer; born at Eisleben Nov. 10, 1483; died there eb. 18, 1546. The Reformation originated in the enaissance, being due partly to the general critical camination of traditional doctrines, and partly to e study of ancient languages, particularly of Greek d Hebrew, a study which was advocated and stered by the Humanists, and the necessity of hich was implied in the fundamental principle Luther that Scripture alone is the infallible uide in religious belief. Luther attempted from e start to win over Reuchlin, the author of the rst Hebrew grammar written by a Christian and e defender of rabbinical literature against the tacks of the apostate Pfefferkorn and against the ominicans who supported him; but while Menchthon, Reuchlin's nephew, was Luther's truest iend, and while he did not succeed in winning euchlin over to his cause, he incurred the enmity f Reuchlin's foes, one of them being the Dominin friar, Hoogstraten.

Scant Knowledge of Hebrew.

While Luther always upheld the Bible as the asis of belief, and while he speaks very highly of ebrew, which he calls the best, the richest, and at the same time the plainest language, he himself did not go back to the original text; indeed, he admits that he was not a Hebrew scholar, and especially that he knew nothing of Herew grammar (*ib.* lxii. 313). A Hebrew book he had ceived, he gave to a friend, saying, "Excedit im vires meas" ("Luther's Sämmtliche Werke," . 612, "Briefe"). His exegetical principle is one hich reveals the context by inspiration rather than y grammatical exposition, and while he speaks ery highly of Moses and David Ḳimḥi, whose orks he knew through Nicholas de Lyra and aulus of Burgos, he often inveighs, in his characristically coarse manner, against what he calls the erversions of the rabbinical exegetes who "versuhen, drehen, deuten, martern fast alle Wort" *b.* xxxii. 174 ["Von den Juden und Ihren Lügen"] nd lxii. 311–317; see Geiger, "Das Studium der Hebr. Sprache in Deutschland," pp. 5–7, 132, Breslau, 1870). He speaks highly of the Jews as having been chosen by God as the instruments for the promulgation of His message to the world. "The Jews," he says, "are of the best blood on earth" (Luther, *l.c.* xxv. 409); "through them alone the Holy Ghost wished to give all books of Holy Scripture to the world; they are the children and we are the guests and the strangers; indeed, like the Canaanitish woman, we should be satisfied to be the dogs that eat the crums which fall from their master's table" (xxv. 260).

In Luther's attitude toward the Jews two periods have to be distinguished. During the earlier, which lasted until 1537 or shortly before, he is full of compassion for their misery and enthusiastic for their conversion to Christianity; in the later, toward the end of his life, he denounces them in unmeasured terms, saying that it is useless to convert any Jew, and accusing them of a relentless hatred of Christianity and of all the crimes which their enemies ever charged them with—well-poisoning, ritual murder, cowardly assassinations of their patients, etc. He wishes the princes to persecute them mercilessly and the preachers to set the mob against them. What caused this change of attitude is not exactly known. Luther himself speaks of polemical works written by Jews in which they blasphemed Jesus and Mary, of the propaganda which they made among Christians and which caused quite a number of Christians in Moravia to embrace Judaism, and of three Jews who had come to him to convert him.

"Dass Jesus ein Geborner Jude Sei."

The first of Luther's works dealing with the Jews is a pamphlet entitled "Dass Jesus ein Geborner Jude Sei," which appeared in 1543 and was republished seven times in the same year (*ib.* xxix. 45–74). The occasion for publishing the pamphlet was the accusation hurled against Luther, evidently by his Catholic opponents, that he had denied the supernatural birth of Jesus. After defending himself against the charge of being a Jew at heart, he speaks of the Jews and of the way to convert them to Christianity. "Our fools, the popes, bishops, sophists, and monks, these coarse blockheads ["die groben Eselsköpfe"], dealt with the Jews in such a manner that any Christian would have preferred to be a Jew. Indeed, had I been a Jew and had I seen such idiots and dunderheads [Tölpel und Knebel] expound Christianity, I should rather have become a hog than a Christian" (*ib.* xxix. 46–47). The accusation that Roman Catholicism presented Christianity in such a repulsive form that Jews could not be won over by it occurs repeatedly in his works. "If I were a good Jew, the pope could never persuade me to accept his idolatry. I would rather ten times be racked and flayed" ("ehe wollte ich mich zehen Mal lassen raedern und aedern"; *ib.* lxii. 355). In another passage he tells the anecdote, derived from Boccaccio, of a Jew who desired to embrace Christianity but wished first to see the pope. When the Jew returned from Rome he asked a priest to baptize him, "for the God of the Christians must indeed be a God who forgives all iniquity if he suffers all the rogueries of Rome"

*This article is limited to the presentation of Luther's reation to Jews and Judaism.

(*ib.* lxii. 377). "If the Apostles had dealt with the heathen as the Christians deal with the Jews, none ever would have been converted to Christianity" (*ib.* xxix. 47).

Luther closes this remarkable pamphlet with the following appeal: "I would advise and beg everybody to deal kindly with the Jews and to instruct them in the Scripture; in such a case we could expect them to come over to us. If, however, we use brute force and slander them ["gehen mit Luegentheiding umb"], saying that they need the blood of Christians to get rid of their stench, and other nonsense of that kind, and treat them like dogs, what good can we expect of them? Finally, how can we expect them to improve if we prohibit them to work among us and to have social intercourse with us, and so force them into usury? If we wish to make them better we must deal with them not according to the law of the pope, but according to the law of Christian charity. We must receive them kindly and allow them to compete with us in earning a livelihood, so that they may have an opportunity to witness Christian life and doctrine; and if some remain obstinate, what of it? Not every one of us is a good Christian" (*ib.* xxix. 74).

Hope of Conversion of Jews.

This book was undoubtedly written with the purpose of winning the Jews over to Christianity, as may be inferred from the fact that he sent it in the year of publication to a converted Jew named Bernhard (Geiger, "Jüd. Zeit." vii. 24 *et seq.*). Luther was an enthusiastic believer in the Christianity of the apostle Paul, and therefore expected from the Reformed Church the fulfilment of Paul's prophecy that all Israel shall be saved (Rom. xi. 26). "If this prophecy has not been fulfilled yet, it is because papacy has presented such a perverted Christianity that the Jews have been repulsed by it." It is very probable that Luther expected the attestation of the truth of Christianity by a general conversion of the Jews, and, being disappointed, changed his attitude toward them. In one of his letters he speaks of a Polish Jew who had been hired to assassinate him, but this was most likely merely a vague rumor in which he did not himself believe (Geiger, "Jüd. Zeit." vii. 26). In 1537, when Duke John Frederick of Saxony, who was a strong supporter of the Reformation, ordered the expulsion of the Jews from his country, Josel Rosheim, the advocate of the Alsatian Jews, armed with a letter of introduction from Luther's friend Capito, asked Luther to intercede with the duke in behalf of his coreligionists. Luther, however, refused to act, saying that the Jews had not appreciated the kindness he had shown them in his book and that they were "doing things which are unbearable to Christians." The somewhat obscure allusions of this letter seem to indicate that he was incensed at the Jews for their refusal to become Christians (*ib.* v. 78-80; Geiger, "Jüd. Zeit." v. 28; "R. E. J." xiii. 112).

Two books published by Luther in 1544 are especially marked by bitterness—"Von den Juden und Ihren Luegen" and "Vom Schem Hamphoras und vom Geschlecht Christi," both printed in Wittenberg (*ib.* xxxii. 99-358). The occasion for writing the first book was, as he states, the audacity with which the Jews attacked the Christian dogmas and espe cially the Christological exposition of the Ol Testament. The bitterness noticeable in the wri

"Von den Juden und Ihren Luegen."

tings of his last years and which wa due to disappointment at the slov progress of his work, to the dissen sions among his followers, and, no the least, to his physical ailments, i evident to a degree which is grievou to his most ardent admirers. He must have bee influenced by some converts from Judaism, such a Antonius Margaritha and Bernhard Ziegler (*il* xxxii. 357), probably the Bernhard referred t above, for he attacks the views expressed in th prayer-book as blasphemous, and repeats the ol accusations that the Jew does not consider th "goyim" as human beings, that he prays for thei misfortune (*ib.* xxxii. 193), and that when a Chris tian comes to his house he says to him "Sche willkomm," which the Christian understands as welcome, though in reality the Jew is calling him "devil" (*ib.* xxxii. 222). Luther praises the "dea Emperor Charles" for having expelled the Jews fro Spain (*ib.* xxxii. 231, evidently meaning Ferdinand Charles V.'s grandfather), and expresses great satis faction at a recent edict of expulsion from Bohemia He repeatedly urges that their synagogues be burned and is sorry that he can not destroy them with hel fire. He further advises that their houses be tor down, their books taken from them, their rabbi prohibited from teaching; that no safe-conduct b granted them; that their usury be prohibited; tha their public worship be interdicted; that they b forced to do the hardest labor; and he admonishe everybody to deal with them in a merciless manne "even as Moses did, who slew three thousand o them in the wilderness." The invectives which h uses against them are vile even for sixteenth-cen tury standards. After admonishing his readers no to have the slightest intercourse with the Jews, h says: "If that which you already suffer from th Jew is not sufficient strike him in the jaw." The mos fanatic statement is the following: "If I had powe over them I would assemble their most prominen men and demand that they prove that we Christian do not worship the one God, under the penalty o having their tongues torn out through the backs o their necks" (*ib.* xxxii. 257).

"Shem Hamphoras."

His "Shem Hamphoras" was written to refute statement made by some Jews that Jesus performe his miracles with the aid of magic art He attacks cabalistic and rabbinica literature, saying that if Jews posses the knowledge of magic art they mus have had it from Judas Iscariot (*il* xxxii. 342 *et seq.*). In both works he repeatedly de clares it useless to attempt the conversion of an Jew, for a Jewish heart is so "stocksteineisenteufel hart" that it can never be changed (*ib.* xxxii. 276) He also quotes, in his "Table-Talks," a report tha in a church of Cologne is the statue of a dean wh was a convert from Judaism and who had ordere the statue to be made with a cat in one hand and mouse in the other, because just as mouse and ca will never live in harmony, neither will Jew an Christian (*ib.* lxii. 371).

These books aroused grave fears among the Jews, and Josel Rosheim asked the city council of Strasburg to allow him to publish a book in refutation of Luther's pamphlets (July 11, 1543); but this the council considered unnecessary. Josel complains that although he made seven attempts to see Luther he was never admitted, and in his memoirs, written in the year following Luther's death, he speaks with bitterness of the great reformer's attitude toward the Jews, expressing the hope that he was in hell, both body and soul ("R. E. J." xvi. 92; see also, on Josel's relations with Luther, Feilchenfeld, "Rabbi Josel von Rosheim," p. 121, Strasburg, 1898). Luther often referred to the Jews in his commentaries on the Bible, as in his exposition of the 109th Psalm, in which he explains the reference to the lot of the wicked to be a prophecy of Israel's misery. The argument that the sufferings of the Jews are the just punishment for their rejection of Jesus is as common with him as with all medieval theologians. The totally different attitudes which he took at different times with regard to the Jews made him, during the anti-Semitic controversies of the end of the nineteenth century, an authority quoted alike by friends and enemies of the Jews.

Bibliography: *Luther's Sämmtliche Werke*, 67 vols., Erlangen and Frankfort-on-the-Main, 1826–57 (the edition used for the references given in the text); Herzog-Hauck, *Real-Encyc.* s.v. *Bibelübersetzungen Deutsche* and *Luther*; Grätz, *Gesch.* 3d ed., ix. 196, 304 et seq., 311 et seq.; Geiger, *Jüd. Zeit.* v. 23–29.
D.

LUTSK (LUTZK): District city in the government of Volhynia, Russia, situated on the right bank of the Styr at its junction with the Gizhtza. Between the years 1224 and 1227 about 300 Karaite families removed from Wilna to Volhynia, and some of them settled in Lutsk. About the same time a number of Rabbinite Jews also came to Volhynia. Lutsk Jews are mentioned in Witold's charter of privileges granted to the Jews of Lithuania July 1, 1388. Reference is made to them also in the grant of the Magdeburg Rights to the burghers of Lutsk by Ladislaus Jagellon Oct. 31, 1432, whereby the Jews and Armenians of that city are accorded the same rights as those of Cracow and Lemberg, except as regards the collection of customs duties, which the king reserves for himself. Toward the end of the fifteenth century the Jewish community of Lutsk had acquired considerable wealth and influence, and some of its members figured prominently as tax-farmers.

In the Fourteenth and Fifteenth Centuries.

The records of that time mention the names of the brothers Ostashka and Jonathan Ilyich, Shakna Novakhovich, Israel, Esko, Judah, Enka Momotlivy, and Olkon. The last-named is probably the Alkan Danilevich to whom King Casimir Jagellon at the time of his death owed 415 kop groschen, a debt partly repudiated by his heir, Alexander Jagellon.

On the expulsion of the Jews from Lithuania in 1495 the extensive estates owned by the wealthy Jews of Lutsk were distributed among Alexander's favorites. Thus on June 26, 1495, he presented to the Polish nobles Soroka and his brother two estates in the district of Lutsk belonging to the Jews Enka Momotlivy and Itzkhak Levanovich; on March 12, 1496, he gave the estate of Topoli, formerly the property of the Jew Simchich, to the alderman of Lutsk; on June 5, 1496, he presented another Jewish estate to Prince Ostrozhski; and on July 31, 1497, for the encouragement of Christian settlers, he made to the Christian inhabitants of Lutsk a general grant of the vacant lands and houses belonging to the exiled Jews. On the return of the Jews to the city in 1503 they organized two separate communities, one Rabbinite and the other Karaite, having their respective synagogues, as appears from a decree issued by King Sigismund Dec. 22, 1506, by which he grants the petition of the Jews of Lutsk for the removal of the burdensome tax of 12 kop groschen on each of the two synagogues.

Jewish Tax-Collectors.

To some extent at least the Jews regained their former wealth and influence, becoming prominent as before in the farming of the taxes and as leaseholders, and engaging in important commercial undertakings. The more important of them were Shamakh Danilevich and Missan Kozka (1507); Mishko Polchekovich, Abraham Shakhnovich, Mordas Chagadayevich, Frush, Nissan Shimchich, and Rebinko Leveyevich (1509). In 1509 the collection of taxes in Lutsk and in other towns was awarded to the Jew Michael Jesofovich, who again farmed the taxes on salt and wax in Lutsk from 1520 to 1526.

During the first half of the sixteenth century the Jews of Lutsk continued to share in the prosperous condition of their coreligionists throughout Poland and Lithuania. They were often granted special privileges and exemptions, as is evidenced by a number of contemporary documents. By a royal decree dated July 18, 1528, the Jews equally with the burghers were freed from the payment of taxes to the crown for a period of ten years, and of municipal taxes for five years. This decree was issued in response to a petition for such exemption on account of a destructive fire which had devastated the city. Similarly in 1551 the Jews of Lutsk, in common with those of other towns, were exempted from the payment of the special tax called "SchErebschisna"; and on July 30, 1556, King Sigismund August exempted them from the payment of customs duties on all commodities except wax and salt, on the same conditions as the Christian inhabitants.

Documents of the middle of the sixteenth century bear witness to the growing friction between the Jewish community of Lutsk and the local authorities.

In the Sixteenth Century.

In 1545 both the Rabbinite and the Karaite community made complaint that Prince Matvei Chetvertinski, ignoring the privileges granted to the Jews of Lutsk by the king, had blocked the road to their cemetery and cut off access to a certain pond. An inspector sent to investigate the case reported thereon to King Sigismund August, who ordered the prince to reopen the road and to abstain from further obstructing it. As time went on the friction increased, due largely to the great power of the Jewish leaseholders and tax-farmers, who were under the immediate jurisdiction of the king, and who naturally refused to acknowledge the authority of the local officials. For instance, in 1560 Mendel Isakovich, a Lutsk Jew, complained to the king that the authorities of Volhynia had placed under their jurisdiction his (Mendel's) secretaries and other employees engaged in the collection of the taxes. The king ordered that henceforth these officials should not be interfered with. Again, in 1561, the burgomaster and alderman of Lutsk complained in the name of the burghers that the agents of the Jewish leaseholder Yeska Shlomich had caused them great damage by collecting during the fair of St. Simon large sums for the privilege of selling spirituous liquors, in consequence of which the visitors had departed and the burghers "were obliged to wander in the villages like Gipsies." Moreover, the same agents had prohibited the burghers from leaving the town with spirituous liquors in their possession, thereby causing them pecuniary loss. In 1566 the burghers of Lutsk descended on the royal estate of Guidovskoye and seized the Jew Shmoila Gooshich, whom they put to death notwithstanding the protest of the other employees on the estate. In 1569 the alderman of Lutsk, Prince Koritzki, imprisoned the Jews of the city on account of the non-payment of their share of the tax levied on the Jews of Lithuania. King Sigismund August, however, ordered their release, since they had already paid the poll-tax of 15 groschen determined upon by the Diet of Grodno. The king ordered also the removal of the seals which had been placed on the synagogue and other property of the Jews. In the same year the whole of Volhynia was added to Poland, and the members of both of the Jewish communities of Lutsk took the oath of allegiance (June 23, 1569).

A considerable number of legal documents dating from the latter half of the sixteenth century make mention of the Jews of Lutsk and of their relations to their neighbors. In 1571 John Stefanovich, the superior of the monastery of Derwansk, stated in his will that he had paid in behalf of the town secretary of Lutsk the sum of 2½ groschen to the Jews Izel and Yesko for the building of a cellar. In the list of property left by Andrei Rusin, Bishop of Pinsk and Turov, reference is made to certain documents belonging to a Jew and relating to three properties "at the end of the crooked bridge of Lutsk"; also to ten documents written in Hebrew. Among the servants of the bishop are enumerated several bought from this Jew. In 1583 Batko (Simeon) Misanovich, who had recently been baptized, requested the alderman of Lutsk to enter in the city records his bequest to his son Moshka of certain moneys due to him (Simeon).

A number of documents preserved in the central archives of Kiev, and dated 1563, afford interesting information concerning the life of the Jews of Lutsk at this time. Among these is the complaint of the Jew Yakhna Leveyevich, a soldier in the service of Prince Constantin Ostrozhski, against his father-in-law, Nissan Rabiyevich of Klevan, who in Yakhna's absence had visited his house, taken away his wife and his goods, and had then disappeared. The enumeration of the articles abstracted includes Turkish knives, a Hungarian sword with silver mountings, a silver dagger, saddles, and gold ornaments, besides household utensils.

In the Seventeenth Century.

In 1601 Prince Grigori Sangushko Koshirski presented for entry in the city records of Lutsk a copy of the lease to the Jews Abraham Shmoilovich of Turisk, Getz Pertsovich of Torchinsk, and their heirs, of his estates in the town of Gorokhov, the estate and village of old Gorokhov, and a number of other estates and villages. The lease was for a period of three years, and the lessees were permitted among other things to exercise complete jurisdiction over the peasants, even to the extent of inflicting the death penalty if necessary.

On March 6, 1625, Leib Israilevich and Ilia Abramovich, Jewish scholars of Lutsk, reported for entry in the city records an attack made upon them by the nobles Lesetzki and their followers while the complainants were accompanying to the cemetery the body of Leib Isakovich. The Lesetzkis had filled in the freshly dug grave, had destroyed the bridge leading to the cemetery, had nailed fast the cemetery gates, and had refused to allow the burial to take place until a debt due to one of them should have been paid. The priest, appealed to by the Jews, ordered the Lesetzkis not to molest the Jews; but the nobles collected an armed mob, drove off the Jews, many of whom were wounded, and threw the body of Isakovich into the ditch.

In Oct., 1637, the burghers of Lutsk lodged a complaint against all the Jews to the effect that they paid nothing into the city treasury, that they had freed many houses from local jurisdiction, that they had built many others on land belonging to the burghers, and had established on the city walls breweries and distilleries, thus diminishing the city's power of defense; further, that they had refused to perform military and guard duty, and that they had purchased liquor from the merchants of places outside of the city limits, reselling it within the city. Complaint of excessive taxation was also made by Jewish leaseholders and their representatives.

In 1647 one of the priests of Lutsk forbade the communicants of his church to buy meat from Jewish butchers. The matter was carried to the courts, and the priest was ordered to pay damages.

During the Cossack uprising under Chmielnicki (1648–49) the Jewish community suffered severely, and a number of Jews were killed. In 1662 the Diet of Volhynia exempted the Jews of Lutsk and other Volhynian towns from the payment of all taxes except that on braid.

In 1637 Lutsk possessed a yeshibah which was destroyed probably by the Cossacks in 1648. In the "Sefer Zikkaron" of the Karaites (Neubauer, "Ginze Petersburg," p. 130) is a statement concerning the Karaites of Lutsk and commencing as follows: "These are the names of the members of our community who were killed by the Cossacks." During the same uprising the prayer-houses were destroyed and all the books burned (Graetz, "Hist." Hebrew ed., vol. vii.). In 1699, at the request of Charles XII. of Sweden, Mordecai ben Nissan, sexton of a Karaite synagogue, went to Lutsk and wrote an account of his observations in "Lebush Malkut," in which he denounces the Rabbinite Jews.

Among the tombstones in the Jewish cemetery are those of: Hannah Ginzburg, died in 1317 (?); a woman who died in 1595; Rabbi Eliakim Getzel, died in 1715; Rabbi Mordeccai ben Shalom, died in 1723; Judah Zeeb ben Tobias, martyred in 1764; and the maggid of Lutsk, Meïr ben Ḥayyim, died in 1819 ("Ha-Meliẓ," 1860, No. 19).

In 1791, the year of its annexation to Russia, Lutsk contained only fifty houses owned by the burghers; the rest belonged to the Rabbinite Jews and the Karaites. In 1864 there were 3,423 Rabbinite Jews and 221 Karaites in a total population of 4,973; in 1895 the numbers were 12,007 and 72 respectively in a total population of 15,125. In the last-cited year the community possessed eighteen synagogues and prayer-houses besides a Karaite prayer-house, one Jewish hospital, and one Jewish dispensary. At the same date there were in the district of Lutsk, exclusive of the city, 42 Karaites and 18,775 other Jews in a total population of 188,636.

BIBLIOGRAPHY: *Regesty*, i., *passim*; *Russko-Yevreiski Arkhiv*, i., *passim*.

H. R.

LUTZYN: Russian town in the government of Vitebsk; it is situated near a chain of mountains and surrounded by lakes and streams. Lutzyn is an ancient city, and was fortified by the Livonian Order in the twelfth century. According to tradition and local inscriptions, Jews began to settle at Lutzyn in the fifteenth century; but when Ivan the Terrible conquered Polotsk, Lebezh, and Lutzyn, those of the Jews in the neighborhood who did not flee were exterminated. The Jews of Polotsk and Lebezh were drowned by the order of Ivan, but the Jews of Lutzyn, according to tradition, escaped, together with a number of the Poles and Catholic clergy. At the end of the sixteenth century, after the Russians had been driven out, Jews again commenced to settle in and around Lutzyn, but their number remained small until the second half of the eighteenth century. After the first partition of Poland (1772) the Jews of Lutzyn became the subjects of Russia, but they remained an unorganized community, without rabbi, charitable institution, or cemetery, until 1783. At this time a great misfortune befell them. Some Catholic priests and Jesuits attempted to convert the Jewish tailor Moses, and when the latter, during a dispute, answered in a way that was unpleasant to his opponents and reflected upon the Christian religion, he was burned alive. On the day after this crime was committed, the Jews collected the ashes of their martyr, buried them with impressive ceremonies on the spot where he had been burned, and decided to organize themselves; they finally succeeded in bringing to justice the murderers of their "ḳadosh" (martyr).

In 1795 David Ziony was appointed rabbi of Lutzyn; he held the rabbinate for two years, and died at the age of thirty-eight. His eldest son, Naphtali, succeeded him when not quite twenty years of age, and served his community more than fifty years. He established several charitable institutions, and, when he died in 1848, was succeeded by his eldest son, Aaron Selig. R. Aaron Selig died in 1875, after occupying the rabbinate for twenty-seven years. He was the author of "Sefer Ẓiyyoni" (Wilna, 1872), on various religious and theological subjects.

Aaron Selig was succeeded by Eleazar Don-Echi, a nephew, and his oldest son-in-law. The latter is the author of "Eben Shetiyah," and is the present (1904) rabbi of Lutzyn.

Blood Accusation. In the early spring of 1883 a Christian girl, who had been for several months a servant in the household of the Jew Zimel Lotzov, disappeared, and was afterward found drowned near the town. The procurator of the government, influenced by the clergy, made out a case against the Lotzov family and the whole community. Prince Urusoff, the Russian jurist and philanthropist, left St. Petersburg to defend the Jews, the result being that the jury declared them innocent of any connection with the drowning of the girl. But the procurator was not satisfied with this verdict and transferred the case to the courts of Vitebsk, where Lotzov and his wife were sentenced to Siberia—Lotzov to penal servitude for life in the government mines, his wife to imprisonment for six years. Prince Urusoff again defended them, but his eloquence, as well as the testimony of physicians and other witnesses, failed to save them, because the representatives of the government used every possible means, lawful and unlawful, to influence the minds of the Vitebsk judges. The Lotzovs were declared guilty, not as murderers themselves, but as the shelterers of murderers who had killed a Christian girl for some unknown reason.

The Jews of Lutzyn contributed materially to the establishment of Jewish agricultural colonies in Kherson, Yekaterinoslav, and northwestern Russia. In 1835 many Jews of Lutzyn sold their property for small sums and went to South Russia, where the government gave them farming land. A few decades after the migration to the Kherson and Yekaterinoslav colonies, two Jewish agricultural colonies were founded by the government near Lutzyn.

Lutzyn has a population of 6,000, half of which are Jews. Of these 310 are artisans and 65 day-laborers. The educational institutions consist of: a Jewish one-class school with 30 pupils, 20 ḥadarim with 150, and a Talmud Torah with 42; there are also 49 Jewish pupils attending the district and common schools.

BIBLIOGRAPHY: *Lyutzinskoye Dyelo Po Obvineniyu Lotzovykh, Gurevicha i Maukh v Ubistvye Marii Drich i Stenograficheski Otchet*, St. Petersburg, 1885.

H. R. I. Zi.

LUXEMBURG: Grand duchy of central Europe, its capital bearing the same name. The sources do not definitely indicate when Jews first settled in Luxemburg. The first record of a Jew residing there occurs in a document of the year 1276. At this time the Jewish population of the duchy seems to have been small and in indigent circumstances; for the impoverished nobility of Luxemburg transacted their money affairs with the Jews of Treves, Coblenz, Saarburg, and Wittlich.

Early History. During the entire Middle Ages the Jews lived in a ghetto, where there were a Jews' gate, a cemetery, and a synagogue. It appears that subsequently the cemetery ceased to exist; for down to the beginning of the nineteenth century the Jews buried their dead at Freudenburg, in the district of Saarburg, province of the Rhine. As elsewhere in the German empire, the Jews of Luxemburg were the "servi cameræ" of the German emperors, and as a source of income to the imperial exchequer they were placed by the emperors under the protection of the local princes. Thus, on May 7, 1350, at the time of the Black Death, Charles IV. ordered the governor and the provost of Luxemburg to look to the safety of the Jews living there. In 1370, when the Jews of Brussels were accused of having desecrated a holy wafer, Wenzel, Duke of Brabant and Luxemburg, expelled all the Jews from Brabant; and none are met with in the country during the next fifty or sixty years.

With the beginning of the Burgundian rule (1441) Jews are again found at Luxemburg; each of them had to pay two gulden for a protection that was merely nominal. In March, 1470, notwithstanding the presence of the governor and the militia, the townspeople attacked the Jews, plundered and demolished their houses, and maltreated them, so that they were barely able to flee to the castle on the Bockfelsen (Clausener Berg), to which they were admitted by the governor and whence they subsequently reached places of safety.

In the beginning of the sixteenth century there were Jews at Echternach, Luxemburg, Arlon, and Igel. But no Jews are mentioned after 1527, and probably none were living at Luxemburg from the time of the Spanish rule, 1555, to the end of the eighteenth century, although Maranos seem to have lived there in the seventeenth century.

In the Sixteenth Century.

All the more worthy of note is it that, as is shown by a tablet in the wall of the present fortress of the city, the famous citadel of Luxemburg was built by a Jewish engineer, Isaac de Traybac, in 1644. Little is known of the Maranos' occupations. They were probably engaged in retail business; for by a decree of the provincial council, dated April 15, 1513, they were forbidden to sell cloth otherwise than by the piece. They were never required to wear the so-called Jews' hat or yellow badge; and although they were compelled to take an oath "more Judaico" they were not required to submit to the humiliating ceremonies that usually accompanied it. A decree of Philip V., issued Sept. 6, 1703, determined the poll-tax that traveling Jews had to pay at the bridges of various cities, this decree being confirmed Sept. 20, 1720. These conditions seem to have obtained during the entire eighteenth century down to the beginning of the French Revolution; for as late as 1787 a Jew complained of this unjust tax, without receiving satisfaction.

By the laws of Jan. 28 and July 20, 1790, and Sept. 27 and Nov. 13, 1791, the Jews were granted equal civic rights with the other citizens. The community, numbering seventy-five persons, was organized by a law of March 17, 1808, and was placed under the jurisdiction of the consistory of Treves. When, on the termination of the French rule, Luxemburg was incorporated with the Netherlands (1815), the community was joined to the synagogue of Maestricht; and when Holland was separated from Belgium by the Belgian revolution of 1830 the grand duchy of Luxemburg became autonomous, and the Jewish community independent. A rabbinate, subventioned by the state, was organized,

In the Eighteenth and Nineteenth Centuries.

the first incumbent being Dr. Samuel Hirsch (1843-66), former rabbi of Dessau. As an advocate of religious reform he had to contend with many difficulties. He was succeeded by the French rabbi Sopher, of Dijon (1866-1870). In 1871 Dr. Isaac Blumenstein was elected rabbi, and upon his death (Aug. 3, 1903) Dr. Samuel Fuchs was called to the rabbinate. A new cemetery was laid out in 1884, and a handsome new synagogue was built in 1894. On Jan. 12, 1899, the supreme court declared the community, as represented by its president, to possess the rights of a corporation. There are also Jewish communities at Ettelbrück, Grevenmacher, Esch, and Medernach; and Jews are living in about twenty other smaller localities. The communities of Ettelbrück and Grevenmacher have each their own cemetery; at Esek a new synagogue was built in 1899.

The grand duchy has about 1,200 Jews in a total population of 236,543, and the capital 407, in 20,938. Only the community in the city of Luxemburg is officially recognized. It is under city and state supervision, and enjoys all the privileges accorded other ecclesiastical bodies. The affairs of the community are directed by a board of seven members, whose election is subject to confirmation by the government. Although legally the Jews of Luxemburg have full civic rights, they hold no government offices and are not represented in municipal councils. One exception, however, is to be recorded, due principally to local circumstances. In Hamm, near Luxemburg, the office of mayor is held by a Jew, Jules Godchaux, his predecessors having been his father, Samson, and the latter's cousin, Paul Godchaux. The Luxemburg Jews are engaged in industry, commerce, and agriculture. In their cloth-, glove-, and furniture-factories, they employ hundreds of working men, thus contributing materially to the national wealth. Socially, the Jews are on the same footing as the other citizens; and anti-Semitism has made no progress there, although clericalism in its organ "Luxemburger Wort" has occasionally started an anti-Jewish agitation. In one case the editor was fined 500 francs for libeling Jews and Judaism (April 2, 1889).

D. I. Bl.

LUZ: **1.** Older name of the city of Beth-el (Gen. xxviii. 19, xxxv. 6, xlviii. 3; Josh. xvi. 2, xviii. 13; Judges i. 23).

2. Name of a city in the land of the Hittites, built by an emigrant from Beth-el, who was spared and sent abroad by the Israelitish invaders because he showed them the entrance to the city (Judges i. 26). "Luz" being the Hebrew word for an almond-tree, it has been suggested that the city derived its name from such a tree or grove of trees. Winckler compares the Arabic "laudh" ("asylum"). Robinson ("Researches," iii. 389) identifies the city either with Luwaizah, near the city of Dan, or (*ib.* iii. 425) with Kamid al-Lauz, north of Heshbon (now Ḥasbiyyah); Talmudic references seem to point to its location as somewhere near the Phenician coast (Soṭah

46b; Sanh. 12a; Gen. R. lxix. 7). Legend invested the place with miraculous qualities. "Luz, the city known for its blue dye, is the city which Sennacherib entered but could not harm; Nebuchadnezzar, but could not destroy; the city over which the angel of death has no power; outside the walls of which the aged who are tired of life are placed, where they meet death" (Soṭah 46b); wherefore it is said of Luz, "the name thereof is unto this day" (Judges i. 26, Hebr.). It is furthermore stated that an almond-tree with a hole in it stood before the entrance to a cave that was near Luz; through that hole persons entered the cave and found the way to the city, which was altogether hidden (Gen. R. *l.c.*).

3. Aramaic name for the os coccyx, the "nut" of the spinal column. The belief was that, being indestructible, it will form the nucleus for the resurrection of the body. The Talmud narrates that the emperor Hadrian, when told by R. Joshua that the revival of the body at the resurrection will take its start with the "almond," or the "nut," of the spinal column, had investigations made and found that water could not soften, nor fire burn, nor the pestle and mortar crush it (Lev. R. xviii.; Eccl. R. xii.). The legend of the "resurrection bone," connected with Ps. xxxiv. 21 (A. V. 20: "unum ex illis [ossibus] non confringetur") and identified with the cauda equina (see Eisenmenger, "Entdecktes Judenthum," ii. 931–933), was accepted as an axiomatic truth by the Christian and Mohammedan theologians and anatomists, and in the Middle Ages the bone received the name "Juden Knöchlein" (Jew-bone; see Hyrtl, "Das Arabische und Hebräische in der Anatomie," 1879, pp. 165–168; comp. p. 24). Averroes accepted the legend as true (see his "Religion und Philosophie," transl. by Müller, 1875, p. 117; see also Steinschneider, "Polemische Literatur," 1877, pp. 315, 491; *idem*, "Hebr. Bibl." xxi. 98; *idem*, "Hebr. Uebers." p. 319; Löw, "Aramäische Pflanzennamen," 1881, p. 320). Possibly the legend owes its origin to the Egyptian rite of burying "the spinal column of Osiris" in the holy city of Busiris, at the close of the days of mourning for Osiris, after which his resurrection was celebrated (Brugsch, "Religion und Mythologie," 1888, pp. 618, 634).

BIBLIOGRAPHY: Jastrow, *Dict.*; Levy, *Neuhebr. Wörterb.*

K.

LUZKI, SIMḤAH ISAAC BEN MOSES: Karaite writer and bibliographer; born at Lutsk at the end of the seventeenth century; died, according to Firkovich, at Chufut-Kale, Crimea, or, according to another source, at Lutsk, March, 1766. He was well versed in rabbinical literature and was also a diligent student of Cabala. An indefatigable and able copyist, he went in 1751 to Chufut-Kale, where there was a flourishing Karaite community which possessed a rich library of Karaite manuscripts. He was received into the house of the Karaite writer Mordecai ben Berakah Yerushalmi, and succeeded Samuel Ḳala'i as teacher of the bet ha-midrash at Chufut-Kale. Luzki rendered great services to Karaite literature both as copyist and as writer. To his labors are due the preservation of many valuable works; and his book on bibliography (see below), although sometimes lacking critical sense, became an indispensable guide to the student of ancient Karaite literature.

Works. The following are Luzki's works in the chronological order of their composition, as given by himself in his "Oraḥ Ẓaddiḳim": "Be'er Yiẓḥaḳ," commentary on Judah Gibbor's "Minḥat Yehudah" on the Pentateuch; "Siaḥ Yiẓḥaḳ," commentary on the prayer אדני שפתי תפתח for the Day of Atonement; "Reshit Ḥokmah," commentary in three volumes on the daily prayers; "Me'irat 'Enayim," code in two volumes, of which the first, entitled "Ner Miẓwah," comprises the Commandments and their explanations, and the second, entitled "Ner Ẓaddiḳim," enumerates the differences between the Rabbinites and the Karaites and gives a genealogy of the Karaite scholars and a list of their works; "Sha'are Ẓedeḳ," on the calendar; "'Aḳedat Yiẓḥaḳ," on the laws concerning the slaughtering of animals, and on the ten Karaite articles of belief; "Kebod Elohim," commentary on Joseph ben Mordecai Troki's mystic prayer "Ha-Elef Leka"; "Arba' Yesodot," on the four dogmatic principles, namely, the creation of the world, the existence of an invisible God, His holiness and spirituality, and His unity; "Tefillah le-Mosheh," questions and answers exchanged between God and Moses; "Halikot 'Olam," description of the creation of the world and of the nature of all things according to their quantitative and qualitative attributes; "'Ene Yiẓḥaḳ," commentary on Elijah Bashyaẓi's calendric tables; "Toledot Yiẓḥaḳ," religious poems, enigmas, letters, etc., in two volumes; "Ṭure Zahab u-Neḳuddot ha-Kesef," on the precepts, in two volumes, of which the first, "Ṭure Zahab," enumerates in verse all the precepts, arranged in the order of the 620 letters of the Decalogue; the second, "Neḳuddot Kesef," being a commentary thereon; "Sefer Bereshit," a mystic explanation of the Creation; "Rekeb Elohim," on the mysteries of the Divine Chariot; "Kebod Melakim," a mystic explanation of the letters of the Hebrew alphabet; "Sefer ha-Tappuaḥ," on the Creation and on the Divine Chariot, according to the modern Cabala; "Libnat ha-Sappir," on the ten Sefirot.

The only two writings of Luzki's which have been printed are: (1) "Or ha-Ḥayyim" (Koslov, 1835), commentary on Aaron ben Elijah's philosophical work "'Eẓ Ḥayyim," and (2) "Oraḥ Ẓaddiḳim" (Vienna, 1837), which is an abridgment of the "Ner Ẓaddiḳim." Another redaction of the last-named work, prepared by Luzki in 1756 at the request of Mordecai ben Berakah Yerushalmi, and entitled "Iggeret Miḳra'e Ḳodesh," gives a fuller description of the works enumerated in the "Oraḥ Ẓaddiḳim."

Luzki was a strong believer in Cabala, which he defends in his "Or ha-Ḥayyim," "Libnat ha-Sappir," and "Sefer ha-Tappuaḥ." He asserts that the Zohar was composed before the Mishnah, although it became known only at the time of Joseph Gikatilla. Had Maimonides, he says, known this divine book he would not have spent his time on the futilities of philosophy; and when Luzki criticizes the Cabala it is only the practical and not the speculative Cabala. Luzki cites the great rabbinical authorities who believed in the authenticity of the Zohar, from Abravanel down to Joseph Delmedigo. According to him there were cabalists even among the Karaites. Luzki was the author also of many religious poems, five of which have been incorporated into the Karaite ritual (part iii., beginning).

BIBLIOGRAPHY: Firkovich, *Abne Zikkaron*, No. 451; Jost, *Gesch. des Judenthums und Seiner Sekten*, ii. 370; Fürst, *Gesch. des Karäert*. iii. 107 *et seq.*; Neubauer, *Aus der Petersburger Bibliothek*, pp. 82 *et seq.*; Gottlober, *Biḳḳoret le-Toledot ha-Ḳara'im*, p. 203.

K. I. Br.

LUZZATTI, LUIGI: Italian statesman and political economist; born at Venice March 11, 1841; studied at the University of Padua (Doctor of Law 1863) and in Venice. While in the latter city he was strongly influenced by Politeo, professor of philosophy, and by Zanella, the lyric poet and teacher of literature from Vicenza. At the age of twenty Luzzatti had already given lectures on economics in Venice. He was an enthusiastic supporter of the doctrine of free trade. At twenty-two he became a teacher at the Istituto Tecnico in Milan; in 1867, professor of economics in the University of Padua; and in the same year the government appointed him commissioner for the Paris Exposition.

Luigi Luzzatti.

In 1869 he became general secretary under Minghetti in the agricultural department of the ministry. Shortly afterward he entered Parliament as deputy from Oderzo, and later was chosen as the representative of Padua.

Luzzatti has held his seat in Parliament uninterruptedly for more than thirty years. He is one of the leaders of the Right, and has repeatedly been president of the budget committee. In matters relating to economic development he has rendered his country incalculable service. He introduced the ideas of Schultze-Delitzsch into Italy, and made them national. He also labored in behalf of coöperative associations and for the establishment of postal and school savings-banks. He is an authority on all questions connected with the tariff, and has a firm grasp of the subject of commercial treaties.

Luzzatti is a tireless worker, speaker, and writer. At all times he upholds Italy's friendship with France. He has frequently been entrusted by successive Italian governments with delicate international negotiations. As one of the delegates who arranged (1902) the commercial treaty with France, he received the grand cross of the Legion of Honor. When in 1901 King Victor Emmanuel III. established the Order of Labor, Luzzatti, in recognition of his labors in behalf of the working classes, was the first to receive the new decoration. He fights against the Agrarians, who have now become so powerful in Germany; and he endeavors to make propaganda in favor of commercial treaties to prevent "Middle-Age economics" from invading Europe.

From Feb., 1891, to May, 1892, and from July, 1896, to June, 1898, Luzzatti was minister of the treasury in Rudini's cabinet. He then returned to his chair of economics at the University of Rome. At present (1904) he is minister of the treasury in the cabinet of Giolitti.

His works include the following: "Il Socialismo e le Questioni Sociali Innanzi ai Parlamenti d'Europa," 1883; "Schultze-Delitzsch," 1883; "Emulazione e Progressi delle Banche d'Emissione in Italia," 1886; "L'Abuso del Credito e la Finanza Italiana," 1889; "La Pace Sociale all' Esposizione di Parigi," 1890.

BIBLIOGRAPHY: Telesforo Sarti, *Il Parlamento Subalpino e Nazionale*, Terni, 1890; De Gubernatis, *Diz. Biog.*; Leone Carpi, *Il Risorgimento Italiano, Biografie Storico-Politiche*, vol. i., Milan, 1888; Luigi Branzi, *I Moribondi di Montecitorio*, Turin, 1889; *Nuova Enciclopedia Italiana*, 1895, Supplement, iv. 201; *Jew. Chron.* Nov. 6, 1903.

S. S. Mun.

LUZZATTO (LUZZATTI): Name of a family of Italian scholars whose genealogy can be traced back to the first half of the sixteenth century. According to a tradition communicated by S. D. Luzzatto the family descends from a German who immigrated into Italy from the province of Lausitz, and who was named after his native place ("Lausatia," "Lausiatus" = "Luzzatto"). The name "Luzzatti," which one branch of this family bears, can similarly be traced back to the plural form "Lausiati." The German rite is credibly reported to have been observed in the family synagogue (Scuola Luzzatto) in Venice.

The earliest member of the family of whom there is record is one Abraham Luzzatto, who lived at Safed at the beginning of the sixteenth century. His descendants may be grouped with some degree of probability in the following pedigree:

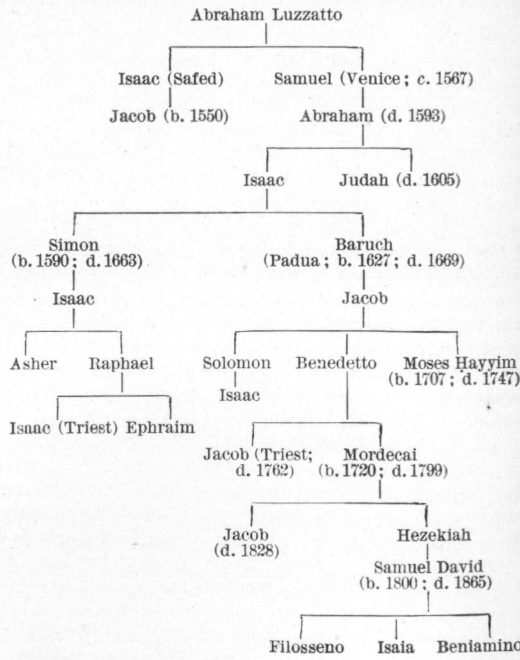

BIBLIOGRAPHY: *Autobiografia di S. D. Luzzatto Preceduta di Alcune Notizie Storico-Letterarie sulla Famiglia Luz-*

zatto a Datare del Secolo Decime Sesto, Padua, 1878-82; Brann, *Die Familie Luzzatto*, in *Samuel David Luzzatto: Ein Gedenkbuch zum Hundertsten Geburtstag*, Berlin, 1900; Mortara, *Indice*.
S. Be.—J.

Benedetto (Baruch) Luzzatto: Italian preacher and poet; flourished in the seventeenth century at Padua, where he was chief rabbi toward the close of his life. He united Talmudic learning with profound classical scholarship, and was especially well versed in history and philosophy. In 1636 he wrote a finished Italian sonnet for his friend Immanuel Porto Rapa's mathematical treatise "Porto Astronomico."

Luzzatto was highly esteemed by contemporary scholars. The anatomist and botanist Giovanni Weslingio was his intimate friend, and Leon of Modena in a list of his pupils praises his halakic learning. None of his works has been published.

Bibliography: S. D. Luzzatto, *Autobiografia*, p. 12; Brann, in *Samuel David Luzzatto, ein Gedenkbuch*, p. 36.
D. I. E.

Beniamino Luzzatto: Italian physician; born at Padua Dec. 3, 1850; died there June 22, 1893; son of Samuel David Luzzatto. Educated at the university of his native town (M.D. 1872), he became physician at the general hospital. In 1876 he was appointed lecturer on pathology, and in 1882 assistant professor and chief of the propædeutic clinic of Padua University.

Luzzatto wrote essays on the systolic murmur of the apex of the heart (Padua, 1875); on chronic broncho-pneumonia and tuberculosis (Milan, 1876); on tetanus traumaticus in pregnancy (Padua, 1876); and he was also the author of: "Embolia dell' Arteria Pulmonale," Milan, 1880; "Vade Mecum di Percussione," Padua, 1882; "Lezioni di Propedeutica Clinica," *ib.* 1883.

Bibliography: Pagel, *Biog. Lex.*
S. F. T. H.

Ephraim Luzzatto: Italian physician and poet; born at San Daniele, Friuli, in 1729; died at Lausanne, Switzerland, in 1792; studied medicine at the University of Padua, graduating in 1751. After practising in Italy for some years, he settled, in 1763, in London, where he was appointed physician in the hospital of the Portuguese congregation. In 1792 he left London, and was on his way to Italy when he died. Luzzatto was a highly gifted Hebrew poet, and he exercised his talent with equal success in national, mythological, moral, and sometimes amorous themes; the beauty of his style and the richness and delicacy of his vocabulary place his productions far above the average. He seems, however, to have lacked conviction and to have wavered sometimes between the extremes of religion and atheism, between Judaism and paganism.

Luzzatto wrote "Eleh Bene ha-Ne'urim," poems on various subjects (London, 1766), and "Ḳol Shaḥal" (Berlin, 1796). A second edition of the former work was published by Meïr Letteris (Vienna, 1839).

Bibliography: Carmoly, in *Revue Orientale*, i. 459; S. D. Luzzatto, in Busch's *Kalender*, p. 152; D. A. de Sola, in *Orient, Lit.* i. 7; Delitzsch, *Zur Gesch. der Jüdischen Poesie*, p. 92; *Kokebe Yiẓḥaḳ*, xxii. 20; Mortara, *Indice*, p. 36.
S. I. Br.

Filosseno (Philoxene) Luzzatto: Italian scholar; son of Samuel David Luzzatto; born at Triest July 10, 1829; died at Padua Jan. 25, 1854. Luzzatto (whose surname is the Italian equivalent of the title of one of his father's principal works, "Oheb Ger," which was written at the time of Filosseno's birth) showed from childhood remarkable linguistic aptitude, and having mastered several European languages, he devoted himself to the study of Semitic languages and Sanskrit. When a boy of thirteen he deciphered some old inscriptions on the tombstones of Padua which had puzzled older scholars. Two years later, happening to read D'Abbadie's narrative of his travels in Abyssinia, he resolved to write a history of the Falashas. In spite of his premature death, he wrote several important works: "L'Asia Antica, Occidentale e Media" (Milan, 1847); "Mémoire sur l'Inscription Cunéïforme Persane de Behistan," in "Journal de l'Institut Lombard" (*ib.* 1848); "Le Sanscritisme de la Langue Assyrienne" (Padua, 1849); "Etudes sur les Inscriptions Assyriennes de Persépolis, Hamadan, Van, et Khorsabad" (*ib.* 1850); "Notice sur Abou Jousouf Hasdai ibn Shaprout" (*ib.* 1852); "Mémoire sur les Juifs d'Abyssinie ou Falashas" (printed posthumously in "Arch. Isr." xii.-xv.). He also translated into Italian eighteen chapters of Ezekiel, adding to the same a Hebrew commentary. Luzzatto contributed to many periodicals, mostly on philological or exegetical subjects. Of special interest are his observations on the inscriptions in the ruins of the ancient Jewish cemetery in Paris ("Mémoires des Antiquités de France," xxii. 60).

Bibliography: S. Cahen, in *Arch. Isr.* xv. 270 *et seq.*; Fürst, *Bibl. Jud.* ii. 281; H. S. Morais, *Eminent Israelites*, pp. 218 *et seq.*, Philadelphia, 1880.
S. M. Sel.

Isaia Luzzatto: Italian notary; born at Padua Sept. 27, 1836; died there Nov. 7, 1898; son of S. D. Luzzatto; graduated in law at the university of his native city. He was for some time attorney for one of the principal Jewish families of the community. His life was saddened by illness and other troubles. Besides a small work, written in his youth, on the battle of Legnano, he wrote various books to serve as a guide for the publication of his father's writings: "Materiale per la Vita di S. D. Luzzatto" (extract from the "Corriere Israelitico"), Triest, 1877; "Index Raisonné des Livres de Correspondance de Feu S. D. Luzzatto de Trieste, Précédé d'un Avant-Propos et Suivi d'un Essai de Pensées et Jugements Tirés de Ses Lettres Inédites," Padua, 1878; "Materiale per la Illustrazione degli Scritti Editi e Inediti di S. D. Luzzatto," *ib.* 1878; "Catalogo Ragionato degli Scritti Sparsi di S. D. Luzzatto, con Riferimento Agli Altri Suoi Scritti, Editi e Inediti," *ib.* 1881.

Bibliography: *Vessillo Israelitico*, 1898, p. 380.
S. U. C.

Jacob ben Isaac Luzzatto: Oriental rabbi and preacher; flourished at Safed in the second half of the sixteenth century. In the pinḳes of Venice it is stated that a Jacob Luzzatto died in that city April 13, 1587, at the age of about sixty; he may well have been the subject of this article, though there is nothing to sustain the identification.

Luzzatto was the author of "Kaftor wa-Feraḥ" or "Yashresh Ya'aḳob" (Basel, 1580), containing besides some stories from the "Sefer Ḥasidim," 165 haggadot explained according to Rashi, the Tosafot, Solomon b. Adret, and R. Nissim; parallel passages being cited from the Yerushalmi, Midrashim, and cabalistic works. The particular object of this work was to defend the Haggadah against the attacks of ecclesiastical censors. As at the end of the book Luzzatto calls himself "corrector," S. D. Luzzatto concluded that it was Jacob Luzzatto who wrote the "Haggahot," or explanatory notes to the Talmud, printed at Basel, 1578–80, under the censorship of Marco Marino. The object of those notes was to show that the haggadot which seem to be directed against Christianity have really an allegorical meaning. Luzzatto wrote also "Ḳehillat Ya'aḳob" (Salonica, 1584), novellæ on the Talmud, and edited and supplied a preface and index to Solomon Molko's "Sefer ha-Mefo'ar" (Cracow, 1570) and to Menahem Recanati's "Ṭa'ame ha-Miẓwot" (Basel, 1581). From his preface (rimed) to the latter work, it is seen that though born at Safed, his Hebrew pronunciation was that of the German Jews, indicating his German origin.

Bibliography: Fuenn, *Keneset Yisrael*, p. 554; Fürst, *Bibl. Jud.* ii. 277; Jellinek, in *Orient, Lit.* vii. 221; S. D. Luzzatto, *Autobiografia*, in *Mosè*, i. 83–86; Steinschneider, *Cat. Bodl.* col. 1230.

S. M. Sel.

Moses Ḥayyim Luzzatto: Italian cabalist and poet; born at Padua 1707; died at Acre May 6, 1747. His father was the wealthy merchant Jacob Luzzatto, and his mother also was a descendant of the Luzzatto family. He was carefully educated by his father in Latin and in other languages. At the age of thirteen he entered the Talmud Torah of his native city, which was then widely known through the teachings of Judah Minz, and which numbered among its instructors Isaiah Bassani and Isaac Ḥayyim Cohen de Cantarini, with the former of whom Luzzatto was especially intimate. He read omnivorously in the library of the Talmud Torah, being attracted particularly by the cabalistic works he found there.

Benjamin ha-Kohen Vital of Reggio (comp. Kaufmann in "Monatsschrift," xli. 700 *et seq.*), a pupil of Moses Zacuto and father-in-law of Bassani, seems to have exerted a great influence on Luzzatto's development as poet and cabalist. Luzzatto soon took up Isaac Luria's works, endeavoring to master the practical Cabala by their aid; and he instructed his former teachers in its mysteries in a school which he opened in his own house after Bassani had moved to Reggio.

The Talmud and mysticism, however, did not satisfy Luzzatto's versatile mind; and at an early age he began a thorough study of the Hebrew language and of poetic composition. He wrote epithalamia and elegies, a noteworthy example of the latter being the dirge on the death of his teacher Cantarini, a lofty poem of twenty-four verses written in classical Hebrew. Before completing his twentieth year Luzzatto had begun his composition of one hundred and fifty hymns modeled on the Biblical Psalter. In these psalms, composed in conformity with the laws of parallelism, he freed himself from all foreign influences, imitating the style of the Bible so faithfully that his poems seem entirely a renaissance of Biblical words and thoughts. They provoked the criticism of the Rabbis, however, and were one of the causes of the persecutions to which Luzzatto was later subjected. R. Jacob Poppers of Frankfort-on-the-Main thought it unpardonable presumption to attempt to equal the "anointed of the God of Jacob." Only two psalms are known of which it can with certainty be said that they belonged to Luzzatto's psalter ("Bikkure ha-'Ittim," 1825, p. 56; 1826, p. 99); in addition seven hymns by him which were sung at the inauguration of the enlarged Spanish synagogue at Padua appeared in the work "Ḥanukkat ha-Maron" (Venice, 1729); but it is not certain whether they were taken from the psalter.

His Psalter.

As a youth Luzzatto essayed also dramatic poetry, writing at the age of seventeen his first Biblical drama, "Shimshon u-Felistim," of which only fragments have been preserved, in another work of his. This youthful production foreshadows the coming master; it is perfect in versification, simple in language, original and thoughtful in substance. This first large work was followed by the "Leshon Limmudim," a discussion of Hebrew style with a new theory of Hebrew versification, in which the author showed his thorough knowledge of classical rhetoric. It is in a certain sense a scientific demonstration of the neoclassic Italian style, in contrast with the medieval. There is a vast difference between Luzzatto's style, which recalls the simplicity, smoothness, and vigor of the Bible, and the insipid, exaggerated, and affected work of his contemporaries. The book, dedicated to his teacher Bassani, was printed at Mantua 1727, with a text which deviates from the manuscript formerly in the possession of M. S. Ghirondi.

In the same year or somewhat later, Luzzatto wrote his allegorical festival drama "Migdal 'Oz" (or "Tummat Yesharim"), on the occasion of the marriage of his friend Israel Benjamin Bassani. This four-act play, which shows Latin and Italian as well as Biblical influence, illustrates the victory of justice over iniquity. It is masterly in versification and melodious in language, the lyrical passages being especially lofty; and it has a wealth of pleasing imagery reminiscent of Guarini's "Pastor Fido." The drama was edited by M. Letteris, and published with notes by S. D. Luzzatto and prolegomena by Franz Delitzsch, Leipsic, 1837.

The Cabala, however, attracted Luzzatto more than did science or poetry; and he was seized with the illusion that he enjoyed the special favor of a heavenly genius ("maggid") which vouchsafed divine revelations to him as it had done to his cabalistic predecessors. He imagined that he beheld heavenly visions and that he conversed with the prophet Elijah, Adam, the Patriarchs, and others; and he finally became convinced that he was the Messiah, called to redeem humanity and more especially Israel. Many cabalistic works, including "Shib'im Tiḳḳunim," "Kelale Ḥokmat ha-Emet," "קל״ח Pitḥe Ḥokmah," "Ma'amar ha-Ge'ullah," "Liḳḳuṭe Kawwanot," "Ḥibbur 'al Ḳohelet," "Ma'amar ha-Wikkuaḥ," "Perush 'al 'Aseret ha-Dibrot," "Ma'amar 'al ha-'Iḳḳudim Asher be-Sefer ha-

Cabalistic Productions.

Zohar," "Perush la-Tiḳḳunim ha-Meyuḥasim le-RaSHBI," were the fruit of these aberrations of a great mind. He explained his teachings in pure, simple Hebrew reminiscent of the language of the Mishnah. In his cabalistic commentary on the Pentateuch, on the other hand, which he entitled "Zohar Tinyana," he imitated the language of the Zohar, thinking that this "second Zohar" would in time take the place of the first.

None of these works, however, was published; and only two sympathetic disciples, Isaac Marini and Israel Treves, were initiated by Luzzatto into his esoteric doctrine and were deemed worthy to meet him for daily cabalistic discussion. Chance revealed their secret. While Luzzatto was visiting his teacher Bassani at Reggio, a scholar by the name of (Raphael) Israel Ḳimḥi (author of the "'Abodat Yisrael") came to Padua for a few days, and Luzzatto's disciples showed him their master's writings. Ḳimḥi guarded his discovery while in Padua; but at Venice he told of it. Luzzatto's reputation as a cabalist soon spread far and wide, attracting many pupils, while his native city also began to awaken to his greatness and to honor him in various ways.

Among Luzzatto's pupils was a Pole, Jekuthiel b. Löb Gordon of Wilna, who had come to the university in 1729 to study medicine. At home he had given much time to the Talmud and to other Jewish literature; and now, putting his other studies aside, he took up the Cabala under Luzzatto. Fascinated by his teacher, he described his impressions, together with Luzzatto's visions, in a letter to Meïr H. Bösing, which, by a trick of fate, fell into the hands of the court agent Mordecai Jaffe of Vienna. Jekuthiel then wrote a letter to R. Joshua Höschel of Wilna, in which he enclosed a leaf from the "Zohar Tinyana." Luzzatto's reputation thus spread beyond Italy; and while the followers of the Cabala rejoiced in its new disciple, its opponents, who had not forgotten the troubles caused by Shabbethai Ẓebi, looked with apprehension upon Luzzatto's work. Chief among these was Moses Ḥagiz of Altona. The Venetian rabbis had still another cause for complaint against Luzzatto, for when Leon of Modena's anticabalistic work "Ari Noham" (or "Sha'agat Aryeh") fell into his hands he wrote the pointed reply "Ḥoḳer u-Meḳubbal" (or "Ma'amar ha-Wikkuaḥ"), in which he unsparingly attacked the famous Venetian rabbi. The other rabbis thereupon indignantly opposed Luzzatto, who now found himself unwillingly the center of public discussion. Every effort was made to condemn him; and letters and responsa multiplied in Padua, Venice, Leghorn, and Altona. No decisive steps were taken at the time in Italy itself; but the German rabbis, yielding to Luzzatto's enemies who were headed by Moses Ḥagiz, pronounced the ban upon any who should write in the language of the Zohar, in the name of the "faithful shepherd," or of other saints.

Opposition and Polemics.

The Venetian rabbis thereupon requested Bassani at Reggio to explain to Luzzatto the consequences of his actions, and to take an active part in the controversy generally. Bassani then went to Padua and induced Luzzatto to declare in writing before the delegates of the Venetian rabbinate that he would renounce the teachings of the Cabala, would not show his works to any one, and would publish nothing in future without the approval of his teacher Bassani and other reliable men. Luzzatto's works were locked up in a casket, one key of which was given to Bassani and another to the representatives of the Venetian rabbinate. Luzzatto himself received the title of rabbi.

He now seemed definitely to have renounced his connection with the Cabala, and he turned again to literature, producing his finest poems. He traveled, cultivated his friends, married the daughter of R. David at Mantua, and took part also in the business affairs of his relatives. Despite all this, he could not permanently resist the attractions of the Cabala. It seems that decreasing prosperity once more led him to mysticism; for, notwithstanding his promises, he composed the cabalistic works "Kelalim Rishonim le-Ḥokmat ha-Emet," "Tefillah we-Shir 'al Ge'ullat Miẓrayim," "Tefillah we-Shir 'al Mattan Torah," and "Wikkuaḥ ben ha-Sekel weha-Neshamah," and Bassani was weak enough to slur his duty and to refrain from opposition to this activity. The news reached the Venetian rabbis, who had been informed that Luzzatto intended also to publish his polemic against Leon of Modena. They lent a credulous ear to those who had been set to watch Luzzatto; and when he refused to take an oath that he would publish no more works without submitting them to the censorship of the Venetian rabbinate, the six rabbis of Venice pronounced (Dec., 1734) a ban upon him and his works, and made it incumbent upon every one who possessed any copies of his writings to deliver them to the rabbinate. News of the ban was sent to all the communities of Germany; and Ḥagiz was informed of the victory he had gained.

Renewed Cabalistic Activity.

It was now impossible for Luzzatto to remain in Italy; for he was abandoned by all except Bassani and a few faithful friends. He therefore decided to emigrate to Amsterdam. On the journey he did not neglect to exhort his pupils to endurance and harmony. In Frankfort-on-the-Main a deep humiliation awaited him: he had to promise under oath to give up his mystic studies and not to print or even write a sentence cabalistic in content. Not until his fortieth year would he be permitted to study the mysteries of the Cabala, and then only in the Holy Land in company with worthy men. This declaration was communicated to many rabbis in different countries; and Luzzatto's works were taken away from him.

Luzzatto was welcomed at Amsterdam with great honor. He was received into the house of the prominent Moses de Chaves, whose son he taught, and the Sephardic community offered him a salary; but, preferring his personal independence, he supported himself by grinding optical lenses. He devoted his spare time to study and teaching, and was soon able to send for his wife, son, and parents, who likewise were cordially received. Luzzatto now resumed his correspondence with Bassani and his pupils; he commended the latter to his teacher

At Amsterdam.

and exhorted them to remain faithful to the study of the Cabala. This correspondence became known to the Venetian rabbis, and as they could do nothing further to Luzzatto, they attacked Bassani, who was suspected of having opened the casket which contained Luzzatto's works (though perhaps the psalms were not included [Kahana, "Luzzatto," p. 10, note 2]) and of having restored them to him. This casket, which was supposed to be guarded by a cherub (Zunz, "Die Monatstage des Kalenderjahrs," p. 26), is said to have found its way to Prague after many vicissitudes (comp. Kaufmann, "Contributions à la Biographie de Mosé Hayyim Luzzatto, Yekutiel Gordon et Mosé Hages.—La Caisse des Manuscrits de Luzzatto et Jacob Cohen Popers," in "R. E. J." xxiii. 256-261). The ban was then renewed against those having forbidden works by Luzzatto in their possession and failing to deliver the same to the rabbinate of Venice.

Meanwhile Luzzatto's reputation was increasing at Amsterdam. He won the friendship of the foremost men there and displayed great activity as a teacher, still continuing his cabalistic studies. In that city he published the following works: "Mesillat Yesharim" (1740), a popular survey of religious ethics, which was widely read; the Talmudic and methodologic treatise "Derek Tebunot" (1743); the smaller works, dealing with various subjects, "Ma'amar ha-'Iḳḳarim," "Ma'amar 'al ha-Aggadot," "Derek Ḥokmah," "Ma'amar ha-Ḥokmah" (1743); and the allegorical drama "La-Yesharim Tehillah," written on the marriage of his pupil Jacob de Chaves—"a work of art unique in Neo-Hebraic literature, masterly in form, language, and thought, a monument to his great gifts, fitted to immortalize him and the tongue in which he composed it." This drama, which in its simple plot bears much resemblance to that of the "Migdal 'Oz," is closely connected in sentiment with the ethical works written by Luzzatto at Amsterdam and is filled with lofty thought. It was imitated by many on account of its style, which is modeled, though with great freedom, on that of the Bible. Luzzatto had only fifty copies printed, which he distributed among the prominent members of the Sephardic community of the city.

At Amsterdam Luzzatto lived quietly and comfortably for ten years, making one short visit to London. When his period of renunciation of the Cabala drew to a close he was filled with a longing for the Holy Land, and after many hardships he arrived with his wife and son at Safed. He exchanged some letters with his disciples at Padua, in which he spoke of his aims and hopes; but in the midst of his plans for the future he, together with his wife and son, died of the Plague in his fortieth year, and was buried at Tiberias beside R. Akiba.

BIBLIOGRAPHY: Jacob Emden, *Torat ha-Ḳena'ot*; M. S. Ghirondi, in *Kerem Ḥemed*, ii. 54 *et seq.*; J. Almanzi, *ib.* iii. 113 *et seq.*; Franz Delitzsch, *Zur Gesch. der Jüdischen Poesie*, pp. 89 *et seq.*; Jost, *Gesch. des Judenthums und Seiner Sekten*, iii. 179 *et seq.*; Grätz, *Gesch.* x. 369 *et seq.*; Zunz, *Literaturgesch.* p. 449; *Autobiografia di S. D. Luzzatto Preceduta di Alcune Notizie Storico-Letterarie sulla Famiglia Luzzatto*, Padua, 1882; Abraham Kahan, *Rabbi Ḥayyim Luzzatto*, Warsaw, 1899; Kaufmann, *Poésies de Moïse Hayyim Luzzatto*, etc., in *R. E. J.* xxxix. 133 *et seq.*; Halberstam, *ib.* 317 *et seq.*

S. E. N.

Samuel David (ShaDaL) Luzzatto: Italian philologist, poet, and Biblical exegete; born at Triest Aug. 22, 1800; died at Padua Sept. 30, 1865. While still a boy he entered the Talmud Torah of his native city, where besides Talmud, in which he was taught by Abraham Eliezer ha-Levi, chief rabbi of Triest and a distinguished pilpulist, he studied ancient and modern languages and profane science under Mordecai de Cologna, Leon Vita Saraval, and Raphael Baruch Segré, whose son-in-law he later became. He studied Hebrew also at home, with his father, who, though a turner by trade, was an eminent Talmudist.

Samuel David Luzzatto.

Luzzatto manifested extraordinary ability from his very childhood, so that while reading the Book of Job at school he formed the intention to write a commentary thereon, considering the existing commentaries to be deficient. In 1811 he received as a prize Montesquieu's "Considérations sur les Causes de la Grandeur des Romains," etc., which contributed much to the development of his critical faculties. Indeed, his literary activity began in that very year, for it was then that he undertook to write a Hebrew grammar in Italian, translated into Hebrew the life of Æsop, and wrote exegetical notes on the Pentateuch (comp. "Il Vessillo Israelitico," xxv. 374, xxvi. 16). The discovery of an unpublished commentary on the Targum of Onḳelos induced him to study Aramaic (preface to his "Oheb Ger").

Early Ability.

At the age of thirteen Luzzatto was withdrawn from school, attending only the lectures in Talmud of Abraham Eliezer ha-Levi. While he was reading the "'En Ya'aḳob" by Jacob ibn Ḥabib, he came to the conclusion that the vowels and accents did not xist in the time of the Talmudists, and that the ohar, speaking as it does of vowels and accents, ust necessarily be of later composition. He pro- ounded this theory in a pamphlet which was the rigin of his later work "Wikkuaḥ 'al ha-Ḳab- alah."

In 1814 there began a most trying time for Luz- atto. His mother dying in that year, he had to do e housework, including cooking, and to help his ther in his work as a turner. Nevertheless, by e end of 1815 he had composed thirty-seven poems, hich form a part of his "Kinnor Na'im," and in 817 had finished his "Ma'amar ha-Niḳḳud," a trea- se on the vowels. In 1818 he began to write his Torah Nidreshet," a philosophico-theological work f which he composed only twenty-four chapters, e first twelve being published in the "Kokebe 'iẓḥaḳ," vols. xvi.-xvii., xxi.-xxiv., xxvi., and e remainder translated into Italian by M. Coen- orto and published in "Mosé," i.-ii. In 1879 Coen- orto published a translation of the whole work in ook form. In spite of his father's desire that he hould learn a trade, Luzzatto had no inclination for ne, and in order to earn his livelihood he was bliged to give private lessons, finding pupils with reat difficulty on account of his timidity. From 824, in which year his father died, he had to de- end entirely upon himself. Until 1829 he earned livelihood by giving lessons and by writing for the Bikkure ha-'Ittim"; in that year he was appointed rofessor at the rabbinical college of Padua.

At Padua Luzzatto had a much larger scope for is literary activity, as he was able to devote all his ime to literary work. Besides, while explaining ertain parts of the Bible to his pupils he wrote own all his observations. Luzzatto was the first ewish scholar to turn his attention to Syriac, con- idering a knowledge of this language necessary for he understanding of the Targum. His letter pub- ished in Kirchheim's "Karme Shomeron" shows his horough acquaintance with Samaritan. He was also he first Jew who permitted himself to amend the text of the Old Testament; and his emendations have met with the ap- proval of Christian scholars. Through a careful examination of the Book of Ecclesiastes, Luzzatto came to the onclusion that its author was not Solomon, but ome one who lived several centuries later and whose ame was Ḳohelet. The author, Luzzatto thinks, scribed his work to Solomon, but his contempora- ies, having discovered the forgery, substituted the orrect name "Ḳohelet" for "Solomon" wherever he latter occurred in the book. As to the Book of saiah, in spite of the prevalent opinion that chapters l.-lxvi. were written after the Captivity, Luzzatto naintained that the whole book was written by saiah. Difference of opinion on this point was one f the causes why Luzzatto, after having main- ained a friendly correspondence with Rapoport, urned against the latter. Another reason for the nterruption of his relations with the chief rabbi of Prague was that Luzzatto, though otherwise on ood terms with Jost, could not endure the latter's ationalism. He consequently requested Rapoport o cease his relations with Jost; but Rapoport, not

Critical Treatment of Bible.

knowing Luzzatto personally, ascribed the request to arrogance.

Luzzatto was a warm defender of Biblical and Talmudical Judaism; and his opposition to philo- sophical Judaism brought him many opponents among his contemporaries. But his opposition to philosophy was not the result of fanaticism nor of lack of un- derstanding. He claimed to have read during twenty-four years all the an- cient philosophers, and that the more he read them the more he found them deviating from the truth. What one approves the other disproves; and so the philosophers themselves go astray and mislead stu- dents. It is for this reason that while praising Maimonides as the author of the "Yad," Luzzatto blames him severely for being a follower of the Aristotelian philosophy, which, he says, brought no good to himself while causing much evil to other Jews ("Penine Shadal," p. 417). Luzzatto attacked Abraham ibn Ezra also, declaring that the latter's works were not the products of a scientific mind, and that as it was necessary for him in order to secure a livelihood to write a book in every town in which he sojourned, the number of his books cor- responded with the number of towns he visited. Ibn Ezra's material, he declared, was always the same, the form being changed sometimes slightly, and at other times entirely ("Kerem Ḥemed," iv. 131 *et seq.*). Luzzatto's pessimistic opinion of philosophy made him naturally the adversary of Spinoza, whom he attacked on more than one occasion.

Views on Philosophy.

During his literary career of more than fifty years, Luzzatto wrote a great number of works, both in Hebrew and in Italian. Besides he contributed to most of the Hebrew and Jewish periodicals of his time. His correspondence with his contemporaries is both voluminous and instructive; there being hardly any subject in connection with Judaism on which he did not write. The following is a list of Luzzatto's works:

In Hebrew.

Kinnor Na'im, collection of poems. Vol. i., Vienna, 1825; vol. ii., Padua, 1879.

Ḳinah, elegy on the death of Abraham Eliezer ha-Levi. Triest, 1826.

Oheb Ger, guide to the understanding of the Targum of Onḳelos, with notes and variants; accompanied by a short Syriac grammar and notes on and variants in the Targum of Psalms. Vienna, 1830.

Hafla'ah sheba-'Arakin of Isaiah Berlin, edited by Luzzatto, with notes of his own. Part i., Breslau, 1830; part ii., Vienna, 1859.

Seder Tannaïm wa-Amoraïm, revised and edited with variants. Prague, 1839.

Betulat Bat Yehudah, extracts from the diwan of Judah ha-Levi, edited with notes and an introduction. Prague, 1840.

Abne Zikkaron, seventy-six epitaphs from the cemetery of Toledo, followed by a commentary on Micah by Jacob Pardo, edited with notes. Prague, 1841.

Bet ha-Oẓar, collection of essays on the Hebrew language, exegetical and archeological notes, collectanea, and ancient poetry. Vol. i., Lemberg, 1847; vol. ii., Przemysl, 1888; vol. iii., Cracow, 1889.

Ha-Mishtaddel, scholia to the Pentateuch. Vienna, 1849.

Wikkuaḥ 'al ha-Ḳabbalah, dialogues on Cabala and on the antiquity of punctuation. Göritz, 1852.

Sefer Yesha'yah, the Book of Isaiah edited with an Italian translation and a Hebrew commentary. Padua, 1855-67.

Mebo, a historical and critical introduction to the Maḥzor. Leghorn, 1856.

Diwan, eighty-six religious poems of Judah ha-Levi corrected, vocalized, and edited, with a commentary and introduction. Lyck, 1864.

Yad Yosef, a catalogue of the Library of Joseph Almanzi. Padua, 1864.

Ma'amar bi-Yesode ha-Diḳduḳ, a treatise on Hebrew grammar. Vienna, 1865.

Ḥereb ha-Mithappeket, a poem of Abraham Bedersi, published for the first time with a preface and a commentary at the beginning of Bedersi's "Ḥotam Toknit." Amsterdam, 1865.

Commentary on the Pentateuch. Padua, 1871.

Perushe Shedal, commentary on Jeremiah, Ezekiel, Proverbs, and Job. Lemberg, 1876.

Naḥalat Shedal, in two parts; the first containing a list of the Geonim and Rabbis, and the second one of the payyeṭanim and their piyyuṭim. Berlin, 1878–79.

Yesode ha-Torah, a treatise on Jewish dogma. Przemysl, 1880.

Ṭal Orot, a collection of eighty-one unpublished piyyuṭim, amended. Przemysl, 1881.

Iggerot Shedal, 301 letters, published by Isaiah Luzzatto and prefaced by David Kaufmann. Przemysl, 1882.

Penine Shedal (see below). Przemysl, 1883.

In Italian.

Prolegomeni ad una Grammatica Ragionata della Lingua Ebraica. Padua, 1836.

Il Giudaismo Illustrato. Padua, 1848.

Calendario Ebraico. Padua, 1849.

Lezioni di Storia Giudaica. Padua, 1852.

Grammatica della Lingua Ebraica. Padua, 1853.

Italian translation of Job. Padua, 1853.

Discorsi Morali agli Studenti Israeliti. Padua, 1857.

Opere del De Rossi. Milan, 1857.

Italian translation of the Pentateuch and Hafṭarot. Triest, 1858–60.

Lezioni di Teologia Morale Israelitica. Padua, 1862.

Lezioni di Teologia Dogmatica Israelitica. Triest, 1864.

Elementi Grammaticali del Caldeo Biblico e del Dialetto Talmudico. Padua, 1865. Translated into German by Krüger, Breslau, 1873; into English by Goldammer, New York, 1876; and the part on the Talmudic dialect, into Hebrew by Ḥayyim Ẓebi Lerner, St. Petersburg, 1880.

Discorsi Storico-Religiosi agli Studenti Israeliti. Padua, 1870.

Introduzione Critica ed Ermenutica al Pentateuco. Padua, 1870.

Autobiografia (first published by Luzzatto himself in "Mosé," i.–vi.). Padua, 1882.

Isaiah Luzzatto published (Padua, 1881), under the respective Hebrew and Italian titles "Reshimat Ma'amare SHeDaL" and "Catalogo Ragionato degli Scritti Sparsi di S. D. Luzzatto," an index of all the articles which Luzzatto had written in various periodicals.

The "Penine Shedal" (= "The Pearls of Samuel David Luzzatto"), published by Luzzatto's sons, is a collection of eighty-nine of the more interesting of Luzzatto's letters. These letters are really scientific treatises, which are divided in this book into different categories as follows: bibliographical (Nos. i.–xxii.), containing letters on Ibn Ezra's "Yesod Mora" and "Yesod Mispar"; liturgical-bibliographical and various other subjects (Nos. xxiii.–xxxi.); Biblical-exegetical (Nos. xxxii.–lii.), containing among others a commentary on Ecclesiastes and a letter on Samaritan writing; other exegetical letters (Nos. liii.–lxii.); grammatical (Nos. lxiii.–lxx.); historical (Nos. lxxi.–lxxvii.), in which the antiquity of the Book of Job is discussed; philosophical (Nos. lxxviii.–lxxxii.), including letters on dreams and on the Aristotelian philosophy; theological (Nos. lxxxiii.–lxxxix.), in the last letter of which Luzzatto proves that Ibn Gabirol's ideas were very different from those of Spinoza, and declares that every honest man should rise against the Spinozists.

Bibliography: Bernfeld, in *Sefer ha-Shanah*, ii. 278 *et seq.*; idem, in *Gedenkbuch zum Hundertsten Geburtstag Luzzattos*, Berlin, 1900; *Educatore Israelita*, xiii. 313, 357, 368; xiv. 19; Geiger, in *Jüd. Zeit.* iv. 1–22; A. Kahana, in *Ha-Shiloaḥ*, iii. 58, 337; iv. 58, 153; J. Klausner, *ib.* vi. 117–126, 213–228, 299–305; S. D. Luzzatto, *Autobiografia*, Padua, 1882; *idem*, in *Ha-Maggid*, ii., Nos. 17–19, 22, 23, 30–33; iii., Nos. 1, 13, 14, 21, 22, 31–33; vi., Nos. 12, 15, 16, 21–23; H. S. Morais, *Eminent Israelites of the Nineteenth Century*, pp. 211–217, Philadelphia, 1880; Senior Sachs, in *Ha-Lebanon*, ii. 305, 327, 344.

S.

M. Sel.

Simeon (Simḥah) ben Isaac Luzzatto: Italian rabbi and apologist; born about 1580; died Jan. 6, 1663, at Venice, where he was rabbi. Luzzatto was one of the most prominent demagogues of his time, and when still a young man he had already acquired renown as a rabbi and scholar. He is styled "rabbi" at the head of a long responsum entitled "Mish'an Mayim," which he wrote in 1606 in regard to the "miḳweh" of Rovigo ("Mashbir Milḥamot," pp. 38b–56b). He shared the rabbinate of Venice with Leon of Modena, who held him in great esteem; according to Wolf ("Bibl. Hebr." iii. 1150), they wrote together a work on the Karaites. The above-mentioned responsum shows him to have been an authority in rabbinics; and he is quoted by Isaac Lampronti ("Paḥad Yiẓḥaḳ," i., *s.v.* אשה אינה מתקדשת), Raphael Meldola ("Mayim Rabbim," No. 11), Mordecai Jaffe ("Lebush," end of "Eben ha-'Ezer"), and other rabbinical authorities.

As may be seen from his Italian writings, Luzzatto was well acquainted with ancient literature and philosophy as well as with the literature of his time, while he is praised by Joseph Delmedigo as a distinguished mathematician (comp. Conforte, "Ḳore ha-Dorot," p. 50a).

His "Discorso."

Luzzatto wrote two important works in Italian—"Discorso Circa il Stato degli Hebrei" (Venice, 1638) and "Socrate" (*ib.* 1651). The former is a treatise on the position of the Jews, particularly of those that lived in Venice. It is an apology for the Jews in eighteen arguments, each of which forms a chapter. For instance, one chapter defends them on the ground of their usefulness in commerce; another explains the causes of decreases in certain revenues of a state and shows that encouragement of the activities of the Jews would tend to increase those revenues. He points out that the Jews are especially fitted for commerce; that they loyally observe the laws of the state; that the Venetian republic reaped great advantages from their relations with them. The chief merit of this book is its impartiality, for while Luzzatto depicts the better characteristics of the Jews he does not ignore their faults. He shows remarkable knowledge of the commerce of his time and of the political influences that affected it. According to him, the common people felt little antipathy toward the Jews, upon whom, to some extent, they depended for their living. It was among the patricians that the fanatical religious zealots were found who, out of envy, advocated restrictions and even banishment. Wolf translated the last three chapters into Latin; they comprise (1) an examination of Hebrew literature and of the various classes of Jewish scholars; (2) an account of the directions in which the Jews were permitted freedom, and of their sufferings; and (3) a survey of the Jews in non-Italian countries ("Bibl. Hebr." iv. 1115–1135). The thir enth chapter was translated into Hebrew by Regio in his "Iggeret Yashar" (i. 65–70).

In the second work, "Socrate," written in his outh, Luzzatto endeavors to prove the impotence f human reason when unaided by divine revelation. t is in the form of a parable, in which he puts his thoughts into the mouth of Socrates. Reason, being imprisoned by Orthodox Authority, appealed for liberation to the Academy of Delphi, which had een founded to rectify the errors of the human ntellect. The academy granted her petition notwithstanding the remonstrance of Pythagoras and ristotle, who argued that Reason, when free, would pread abroad most frightful errors. Liberated Reaon caused great mischief, and the academicians did ot know what to do, when Socrates advised ombining Reason with Revelation. It is apparent hat Luzzatto was a thinker and a believer as well; e did not share Manasseh b. Israel's dream that he ten tribes still exist together in some part of he world. He maintained that Daniel's revelation efers not to a future Messiah, but to past historical vents. This utterance of Luzzatto was either misnderstood or deliberately perverted by the convert amuel Nahmias (Giulio Morosini), who, in his "Via ella Fide," makes Luzzatto say that Daniel's reveation may perhaps point to Jesus as the Messiah comp. Wolf, *l.c.* iv. 1128).

His "Socrate."

Luzzatto, who dedicated this book to the doge nd Senate of Venice, stated that his ancestors had ettled in Venice two centuries previously. In the rst book (pp. 5a, 99a), Luzzatto quotes a work of is own entitled "Trattato dell' Opinioni e Dogmi egl' Hebrei e dei Riti Loro Piu Principali." Jacob boab asserts that he saw in Venice a collection of uzzatto's speeches and responsa, which included decision in regard to the use of a gondola on the abbath.

BIBLIOGRAPHY: Fürst, *Bibl. Jud.* ii. 283; Grätz, *Gesch.* 3d ed., x. 147 *et seq.*; S. D. Luzzatto, *Autobiografia* (in *Mosé*, i. 300 *et seq.*); Nepi-Ghirondi, *Toledot Gedole Yisrael*, pp. 316–317; Steinschneider, *Cat. Bodl.* col. 2597.

S. M. SEL.

LWOW, AARON MOSES BEN ẒEBI HIRSCH: Grammarian, scribe, and dayyan of emberg in the eighteenth century. He wrote: Shirah Ḥadashah" (Zolkiev, 1764), a Hebrew grammar in verse, divided into six poems with explanaions in prose, composed after the model of Elijah evita's "Pereḳ Shirah"; "Ohel Mosheh" (*ib.* 1765), complete Hebrew grammar in four parts, following Ḳimḥi's "Sefer ha-Zikkaron" and criticizing almana Hanau (RaZaH); also "Halakah le-Mosheh," ovellæ on the Talmud and decisions; and "Ohel Io'ed," a treatise on the Hebrew language, both of which works are still unpublished.

BIBLIOGRAPHY: Fürst, *Bibl. Jud.* ii. 284; Buber, *Anshe Shem*, p. 26.

H. R. M. SEL.

LYDDA or **LOD** (לוד): City in Palestine, later amed **Diospolis**; situated one hour northeast of Ramleh, about three hours southeast of Jaffa, and, ccording to the Talmud (Ma'as. Sh. v. 2; Beẓah a), a day's journey west of Jerusalem. It seems to ave been built originally by a descendant of Benjamin (I Chron. viii. 12), and to have been occupied again by Benjamites after the Exile (Ezra ii. 33; Neh. xi. 35). According to the Talmud (Yer. Meg. i. 1) it was a fortified city as early as the days of Joshua. At the time of the Syrian domination the city and district belonged to Samaria, and Demetrius II. (Nicator) apportioned it to Judea (I Macc. xi. 34; Josephus, "Ant." xiii. 4, § 9). Cestius Gallus, Roman proconsul under Nero, burned Lydda when he advanced upon Jerusalem from Cæsarea (Josephus, "B. J." ii. 19, § 1), but soon afterward it is named as the capital of one of the toparchies into which Judea was later divided, surrendering as such to Vespasian (*ib.* iii. 3, § 5; iv. 8, § 1). Josephus describes it as a "village" equal in size to a "city" ("Ant." xx. 6, § 2).

At a time which can not definitely be fixed, but which was during the Roman period, the name of the place was changed to Diospolis, which name is found on coins struck under Septimius Severus and Caracalla. The city is frequently mentioned by Eusebius and Jerome. It became a bishopric at an early date, its bishops signing at the various councils either as bishops of Lydda or as bishops of Diospolis (comp. Reland, "Palestina ex Monumentis Veteribus Illustrata," p. 877; Robinson, "Palästina," iii. 263 *et seq.*). At an early date Lydda was a center of the veneration of St. George, for both Antoninus Martyr (*c.* 600) and Benjamin of Tudela refer to it as the burial-place of the saint (comp. Reland, *l.c.*). On the varying fortunes of the city see Robinson, "Palästina" (*l.c.*). The present village of Lidd still preserves traces of the historical Lydda, which is described in tradition as second only to Jerusalem (comp. Van de Velde, "Reise Durch Syrien und Palästina," i. 332; Munk-Levy, "Palästina," pp. 148 *et seq.*; Schwarz, "Das Heilige Land," p. 104; Neubauer, "G. T." pp. 76 *et seq.*; Socin, "Palästina und Syrien," 2d ed., pp. 11 *et seq.*).

After the destruction of Jerusalem, Lydda was famous as a seat of Jewish scholarship, and the academy which flourished there is frequently mentioned in the Talmud and other works of traditional literature. The term "scholars of the South" ("ziḳne Darom," Ḥul. 132b; Zeb. 23a; "rabbanan di-Daroma," Lev. R. 20, 163b; "rabbanan mi-Daroma," Yer. M. Ḳ. iii. 82; and simply "Deromayya," Yer. Pes. v. 32) doubtless refers to the Lydda teachers of the Law, whose wisdom is recognized also in the sentence "Ha-roẓeh she-yaḥkim yadrim" = "Let him who wishes to attain to wisdom go to the South" (B. B. 25b; comp. also Schürer, "Gesch." ii. 302).

After the Fall of Jerusalem.

Rabbi Eliezer lived at Lydda (Yad. iv. 3; Sanh. 32b); R. Ṭarfon taught there (B. M. 49b); and it was also the scene of R. Akiba's activity (R. H. i. 6). Responsa from Lydda are often mentioned (Tosef., Miḳ. vii. [viii.], end); but despite the reputation which the teachers at the academy enjoyed, there seems to have been a certain feeling of animosity against them in consequence of their arrogance, and it was therefore denied that they possessed any deep knowledge of the Law (comp. Pes. 62b; Yer. Pes. 32a; Yer. Sanh. 18c, d; Bacher, "Ag. Pal. Amor." i. 60, iii. 16).

At Lydda, in the garret of one Nitsa, during the Hadrianic persecutions, was adopted the historical resolution that where martyrdom was the only alternative, all the religious laws, excepting three, might be transgressed, the three exceptions being the laws concerning idolatry, incest, and murder (Yer. Sheb. iv. 35; Sanh. 74a; Yer. Sanh. iii. 21; comp. Pesiḳ. xiii.). At another meeting held in Nitsa's garret the question whether the study of the Law is more important than the practise of the Law was unanimously decided in the affirmative (Ḳid. 40b; comp. Sifre to Deut. xi. 13 [ed. Friedmann, p. 79b] and parallels).

BIBLIOGRAPHY: Grätz, *Gesch.* 2d. ed., iv. 170, especially note 17; Jost, *Gesch. des Judenthums und Seiner Sekten*, ii. 80, 107.

J. E. N.

LYING (Hebr. "shaḳar," "kazab," "kaḥash," and "shaw"): Telling a falsehood with the intent of deceiving.—**Biblical Data:** Lying is most vigorously condemned in the Law: "Keep thee far from a false matter" (Ex. xxiii. 7); "Neither deal falsely, neither lie one to another" (Lev. xix. 11). Regarding the false oath see PERJURY. Lying on the witness-stand to harm another is a crime specially mentioned in the Decalogue (Ex. xx. 16), and the punishment is that the false witness be dealt with as the one witnessed against would have been dealt with if guilty (Deut. xix. 15-21). Regarding lying in fraudulent dealing see FRAUD AND MISTAKE.

Lying is abhorred throughout Scripture as an offense against the holy God who "lieth not" (I Sam. xv. 29; Ps. lxxxix. 34-35); it is "an abomination of the Lord" (Prov. xii. 29). "He that telleth lies shall not tarry in my sight" (Ps. ci. 7; comp. xxiv. 4 and xv. 2). "They speak falsely every one with his neighbor; with flattering lips and with a double heart. . . . The Lord shall cut off all flattering lips" (Ps. xii. 3-4, Hebr. [A. V. 2-3]). "Speak ye every one the truth to his neighbor . . . love no false oath: for all these are things that I hate, saith the Lord" (Zech. viii. 16-17). "The remnant of Israel shall not do iniquity, nor speak lies; neither shall a deceitful tongue be found in their mouth" (Zeph. iii. 13). With the Psalmist, one should "hate every false way" and "abhor lying" (Ps. cxix. 104, 128, 163).

——**In Apocryphal and Rabbinical Literature:** Ben Sira warns against the habit of lying as even worse than theft, because it brings ruin and disgrace (Ecclus. xx. 24-26; comp. vii. 12-14); he warns also against duplicity of tongue (*ib.* v. 9, 14; xxviii. 13), which "is a snare of death" ("Didache," i. 4). The spirit of lying is one of the seven evil spirits in man (Test. Twelve Patr., Reuben, 3). "Hate lying in order that the Lord may live among you and Belial flee from you," warns Dan (*ib.* Dan, 1-6). Especially emphatic are the Rabbis in condemning lying. "God's seal is truth" (Shab. 55a; Gen. R. lxxxi.). "He who changes his word acts as if he were worshiping other gods" (Sanh. 92a). Among the "three God hateth is he who speaks the thing he means not," "with duplicity of tongue" (Pes. 113b). "Liars can not behold the majesty of God" (Soṭah 42a). "To conceal the truth, or to deceive others by creating a false impression, even for a good purpose, is a transgression of the command, 'Thou shalt keep thee far from a false matter'" (Shebu. 31a). To pretend an affectionate feeling in order to win the good opinion of another is sinning against truth (Tos. to B. Ḳ. vii. 8). The Shammaites declared it sinful even to lavish, at the wedding-feast, laudations on a bride which are not in harmony with the truth, as, for instance, to call her beautiful when she is ugly (Ket. 17a). "In case of doubt, train thy tongue always to say 'I do not know,' lest thou be caught in an untruth" (Ber. 4a). "Never tell a child 'I shall give you so-and-so' unless you actually will give it to him; else the child will learn to utter untruths himself" (Suk. 46b). "Canaan, in his last will, told his children not to speak the truth" (Pes. 113b). "Let thy 'yea' be 'yea' and thy 'nay' 'nay'" (B. M. 49a). "Truth will abide; falsehood will not abide" (Shab. 104a). In case a life depends upon your telling a falsehood, as, for instance, when a robber or murderer inquires after one he pursues, the law permits lying (Ned. ii. 4; Shulḥan 'Aruk, Yoreh De'ah, 232, 14; see also under HYPOCRISY). In the Daily Prayers the silent prayer begins with the words, "My God, keep my tongue from evil and my lips from speaking falsehood!" (Ber. 17a); and at the beginning of the Morning Prayer are recited these words, taken from Tanna debe Eliyahu Rabbah 21: "At all times man should be God-fearing in secret also, and ever confess the truth and speak the truth in his heart."

BIBLIOGRAPHY: Hamburger, *R. B. T.* s.v. *Wahrhaftigkeit*; F. Perles, *Bousset's Religion des Judenthums*, pp. 71-74, Berlin, 1903.

K.

LYON, ABRAHAM DE: One of the first Jewish settlers in Georgia, U. S. A.; ancestor of the well-known family of that name which has figured prominently in the annals of that state. According to a family tradition he was born in Spain. The early records, however, invariably describe him as "a vineron from Portugal" and as having been for years prior to his emigration "a vineron in Portugal." He went to America in the same year that the colony of Georgia was founded by Oglethorpe and settled in 1733 in Savannah, where he soon became a freeholder.

The trustees of the colony were especially desirous of making Georgia a wine-producing country and De Lyon soon attracted the attention of their agents by his ability as a horticulturist and vine grower. He introduced viticulture and cultivated several kinds of grapes, among them the Porto and Malaga, to great perfection. He proposed to the trustees that if they would lend him £200 sterling he would employ that sum, with a further sum of his own, in importing from Portugal "vines and vinerons." His proposition was accepted, and the money was sent to Oglethorpe, who, however, gave only a part of it to De Lyon, claiming that "he had other uses for the money."

In his journal, under date of Dec., 1737, Col. William Stephens, the agent of the trustees, gives an elaborate description of De Lyon's vineyard.

De Lyon probably removed from Georgia about 1740, when the illiberal policy of the trustees caused both Jewish and Christian settlers to leave; and there is a definite record of Mrs. De Lyon's depar ure in that year in the trustees' journal. In all likelihood, however, De Lyon soon returned to Savannah and died there.

Bibliography: Charles C. Jones, *History of Georgia*, i. 378; *idem*, in *Publ. Am. Jew. Hist. Soc.* i. 10; Leon Hühner, *The Jews of Georgia in Colonial Times*, ib. x. 65–95, and authorities there cited.

A. L. Hü.

LYON, GEORGE LEWIS: English journalist and communal worker; born at Portsea, England, Dec. 11, 1828; died in London Feb. 14, 1904. After acting for a time as secretary of the Portsmouth Hebrew Benevolent Institution, Lyon went to London in the early fifties and became secretary of the Jews' and General Literary and Scientific Institution. On resigning this position he devoted himself to financial journalism, and became city correspondent of many London and provincial newspapers. In Feb., 1873, he founded and edited the "Jewish World," which journal, however, passed into other hands some years before his death.

Lyon was secretary of the Jews' Infant School and subsequently of the Jews' Emigration Society.

Bibliography: *Jewish Year Book*, London, 1903; *Jew. Chron.* Feb. 19, 1904.

J. G. L.

LYON, HART. See Hirsch, Levin Joseph.

LYON (LEONI), MYER: Operatic singer and hazzan; died at Kingston, Jamaica, about 1800; uncle of John Braham; both he and his nephew were choristers at the same time at the Great Synagogue, London. Lyon was also a public singer; and his voice was said to have surpassed that of his nephew in sweetness and melody. His first appearance was at Covent Garden (1775) in "Artaxerxes." He subsequently joined Giordani in the management of an English opera-house in Dublin, and was also engaged by Palmer for the Royalty Theatre. He finally became ḥazzan in the English and German Synagogue, Kingston, Jamaica, being the first qualified ḥazzan in the English colonies.

Lyon composed many morceaux for both theater and synagogue, particularly for the "Musaf" of Rosh ha-Shanah and Yom Kippur.

Bibliography: *Jew. Chron.* Dec. 26, 1873; Humphreys, *Memoirs of De Castro*, London, 1824; Picciotto, *Sketches of Anglo-Jewish History*; *Thespian Dict.*

J. G. L.

The name "Leoni" is given to the melody associated in English hymnals with the verses commencing "The God of Abraham praise." These were composed by Thomas Olivers, a Wesleyan minister London, on a Friday evening in 1770, and was deeply (1725–99). He had attended the Great Synagogue, moved by the service, carrying away a keen impression of the singing of Myer Lyon (Leoni) in the closing hymn Yigdal. Lyon afterward gave him the melody, and Olivers called it by his name. The hymn was an immediate success. Eight editions were called for in two years, and the thirtieth edition was reached in 1779.

The melody thus furnished was the tune then (and still) used by the English Jews for the concluding hymn in the Sabbath eve service. The characteristic and effective tune, of no great age, is also utilized among Continental Jews on the festivals. A tune by the late Sir John Stainer is now more often sung with Olivers' verses in the Church of England service.

Bibliography: A. Bär, *Ba'al Tefillah*, No. 760, Göteborg, 1877, and Frankfort, 1883; Cohen and Davis, *Voice of Prayer and Praise*, No. 28, London, 1899; *Hymns, Ancient and Modern*, No. 601, 1st tune, *ib.* 1875; *Jew. Chron.* Dec. 26, 1873; J. Julian, *Dictionary of Hymnology*, p. 1150, *ib.* 1892; Montgomery, *Christian Psalmody*, p. 28, *ib.* 1828.

J. F. L. C.

LYON, ROBERT: American journalist, born in London, England, Jan. 15, 1810; died in New York city March 10, 1858. After a brief business career in London, he emigrated to the United States (1844), and, meeting no success in a manufacturing enterprise, began to publish (Oct. 26, 1849) "The Asmonean," the first American Jewish weekly of its kind, which he conducted until his death. He edited at the same time the New York "Mercantile Journal," an organ devoted to trade. For a time Isaac M. Wise and other Jewish writers of the day were regular contributors to "The Asmonean," which, however, failed to win more than local fame.

Bibliography: Morais, *Eminent Israelites of the Nineteenth Century*, pp. 221–223.

A. A. S. I.

LYONS: City on the Rhône, France. Jews seem to have been established in the surrounding region at an early date. The fact that Pope Victor in the fifth century prohibited the Archbishop of Vienne (France) from celebrating Easter with the Jews shows not only that there were Jews in the towns surrounding Lyons, but also that the Christians were on terms of comparative intimacy with them.

It is chiefly in the ninth century that the presence of Jews in Lyons is incontestably demonstrated.

First Mention.

They then formed a prosperous community and lived in a special quarter situated at the foot of the Fourvière hill, of which one street is still called "Rue Juiverie." Protected by the King of France, Louis le Debonnaire, and by Judith, his wife, they were special objects of aversion to the bishop Agobard, who, however, succeeded only in alienating himself from his sovereign, and failed utterly in his struggle against them.

The Jews continued to live in Lyons until the middle of the thirteenth century. The arrival of Pope Innocent IV., who took refuge in the domain of the archbishop, seems to have been fatal to them. The council held at Lyons in 1245 under the presidency of the pope expressed indignation at the relations existing between Jews and Christians and tried to repress the former. Not only were they precluded from holding any office; they were also obliged to wear on their dress a piece of cloth of a special color and circular in form. About the same time Archbishop Philip of Savoy, setting an example which was to be imitated three years later by Jean, Bishop of Vienne, expelled them from Lyons.

For nearly a century there were no Jews, except temporary residents, in the whole district. A manuscript copy of a tariff of taxes paid to the archbishop or metropolitan chapter for merchandise in 1340 shows that every Jew who passed through Lyons was obliged to pay 12 deniers on entering the city or else to receive a blow ("Archives du Rhône," an inedited manuscript).

Beginning with the fourteenth century, official records show that Jews had returned to Lyons and were living there. The ordinance of Charles V., dated Sept. 27, 1364, decreeing that the Jews of Lyons should contribute to the common charges, clearly proves their presence in the city. At that time they lived in the same quarter, St. Georges, which their predecessors had occupied two centuries earlier. In 1379 Jean de Tabaru drove them out of the Rue Dorée, adjacent to the Rue Juiverie, and bade them settle in another quarter, situated on the right bank of the Rhône. Their number increased daily, as is seen from a document of the time in which the city complains of the benefits derived by the clergy from the Jews ("Archives du Rhône," carton CC, 290). In 1386 Charles VI. by letters patent renewed the ordinance of his father ordering the Jews to contribute to the expenses of the city ("Archives de la Ville de Lyon," CC, 290). They had then, as under Louis II., a conservator of their rights, the "magister Judæorum." In 1393 the archbishop claimed jurisdiction over the Jews, who protested, declaring themselves subject to the king. They lost their case, however, as is shown by a document of the fourteenth century in which are found the names of certain Jews of Lyons: Josson of Montmelian, Josson of Vermenton, Dalmon Moyses, Saussin, and Abraham Noblet ("Archives du Rhône," ch. metrop., fols. 116-119).

In the Fourteenth Century.

The edict of Sept. 17, 1394, by which Charles VI. expelled all Jews from France, did not immediately affect those at Lyons. Several historians give 1420 as the date of their definite departure from the city and of their arrival at Trevoux, whither they transferred the gold- and silver-thread industry. The names "Trefousse," "Dreyfus," etc., are probably Alsatian corruptions of "Trevoux," as certain malcontents among these Lyonnaise Jews were driven out later from Trevoux and took refuge in Alsace.

Expulsion.

From this time until the middle of the eighteenth century Jews were not allowed to live in Lyons. Two documents, dated respectively 1548 and 1571, show that their presence was at these dates considered a scandal to the city and the Christian religion.

Toward the end of the reign of Louis XV. several Jewish families again settled at Lyons. Some of them came from the cities of the south—Avignon, Carpentras, and Cavaillon; others, from Bordeaux or Alsace. At the very beginning of this reign the community numbered about fifteen families. A special vault was assigned to them for burial in the ground adjoining the hospital; and the mortuary records, still extant in the archives of the city, show that between the years 1767 and 1787 thirty-two bodies were interred there. The syndic of the new community was Elijah Rouget of Avignon. In a letter dated 1781 the lieutenant-general of the police of Lyons confers this dignity upon him and indicates to him the formalities to be observed before the magistrates by those Jews who live in the city and by those who are merely passing through Lyons. The successor of Elijah Rouget in the syndicate was Benjamin Naquet, who held the office for twenty years.

Syndic of the Community.

During the Revolution little attention was paid to the Jews of Lyons, since there was only a small number of them in the city, and they passed unnoticed. One of them, however, figures among the victims executed by the revolutionary tribunal which was instituted under the Reign of Terror: this was Azariah Vidal, executed in 1793.

After becoming French citizens by the decree of the convention of Sept. 27, 1791, the members of the Lyonnaise community in 1795 acquired for a cemetery, at a cost of 12,000 francs, a piece of land located at the Guillotière.

The history of the community during the first half of the nineteenth century includes nothing of particular interest. Numbering only 200 souls under the empire and 500 under the Restoration and the constitutional monarchy, it was controlled after 1808 by the consistory of Marseilles, its affairs being regulated by a board of administration. Of the numerous administrators may be mentioned Isaac Helf (1808–18), Isaac Cerf of Ricqlès (1828–38), and Nordheim (1838–51). Religious services were held in a modest prayer-house, first in the Rue Bellecordière, on the second floor of a house occupied by numerous tenants, then on the ground floor of one in the Rue du Peyrat. Until 1850 the service was performed by an officiating minister. In that year a decree of the president of the republic instituted a rabbinate at Lyons, which included in its jurisdiction the department of the Rhône, of the Isère, and of the Loire. On Dec. 26, 1850, Jacques Weinberg, rabbi at Ribeauville, was called to fill the post.

The Rabbinate.

In 1854 the suggestion was made to create a new consistory with Lyons as its center. This was effected Aug. 24, 1857: it comprises the departments of the Loire, the Ain, the Isère, the Jura, the Saône and Loire, and the Doubs. The consistory of Lyons has been represented at the central consistory by the Orientalist Salomon Munk (1858–67); by Michel Alcan, professor in the Conservatoire des Arts et Métiers (1867–77); by the poet Eugène Manuel (1877-1900); and by M. Camille Lyon, departmental chief in the council of state (the present representative). In the ten years succeeding its foundation the Israelitish population had become doubled. The consistory obtained from the municipal council of Lyons for the site of a synagogue a parcel of land situated in one of the most beautiful quarters, on the Quai Tilsitt, facing the hill of the Fourvière. On June 23, 1864, the new synagogue, built according to the plans of Abraham Hirsch, was inaugurated. It is considered to be one of the most beautiful in France. In 1864 a home for the aged was built. In 1870 a new cemetery, adjacent to the old one, was purchased. The various presidents of the consistory have been: J. Kuppenheim, Abraham Hirsch, Leon Kahn, and Henri Gaisman. M. Weinberg, who was the first to occupy the post of grand rabbi after the creation of the consistory, and who died in 1879, was succeeded by the present (1904) incumbent, Alfred Lévy, who was installed a

The Synagogue.

Lyons July 1, 1880, having previously been rabbi at Dijon (1867–69) and at Lunéville (1869–80).

Present Condition. The Jews of Lyons at present (1904) number about 1,500 in a total population of 466,767. The annual communal budget includes 40,000 francs for religious purposes and 25,000 francs for charities. Besides the home for the aged mentioned above, there are: a board of charities, destined especially to help poor travelers, of whom there are always a great number at Lyons; two women's charitable societies; a young women's society for the protection of poor girls; a young people's society for educating poor boys; and two mutual aid societies.

Among those members who hold honorable offices and render distinguished services to the state may be mentioned: Edouard Millaud, senator; Abraham Hirsch, honorary chief architect of the city of Lyons; Aron, councilor of the Court of Appeal; Aron, chief engineer of the Paris-Lyon-Mediterranean Railway Company; Brahm, solicitor of the Court of Appeal; Edmond Weil, professor in the faculty of medicine; Emmanuel Lévy, lecturer in the faculty of law; Lang, director of the Ecole la Martinière; Lévy Léon and Weil, professors at the Lycée; Seyewetz, subdirector of the school of chemistry; Marc Lévy, professor at the school of commerce; Isidore, commandant of artillery and subdirector of the arsenal.

BIBLIOGRAPHY: Menestrier, *Histoire Consulaire de Lyon*; Prudhomme, *Les Juifs en Dauphiné*, Grenoble, 1883; *Archives du Rhône*, carton CC; ib., *Actes Capitulaires*, E 1; *Archives de la Ville de Lyon*, carton BB; *Archives de Villefranche*, carton AA; A. Lévy, *Notice sur les Israélites de Lyon*, 1894; Baluze, *Opera Agobardi*, Paris, 1866; *Inauguration du Temple Israélite de Lyon*, Lyons, 1864; *MS. Lyons*, No. 1464.

G. A. L.

LYONS, ISRAEL: Hebrew teacher and author; born in Poland; died 1770. He emigrated to England and settled in Cambridge. Here he practised the craft of silversmith and acquired a reputation as a Hebrew scholar. This led to his appointment as "teacher of the Hebrew tongue" in the University of Cambridge. He wrote "The Scholar's Instructor, or Hebrew Grammar, with Many Additions and Emendations Which the Author Has Found Necessary in His Long Course of Teaching Hebrew," a second edition of which appeared in 1757 and a fourth in 1823, while his treatise "Observations and Enquiries Relating to Various Parts of Scripture History" was printed by the Cambridge Press in 1768 and published by subscription.

BIBLIOGRAPHY: Nichols, *Literary Anecdotes*, ii. 327, 419, London, 1812.

J. I. Co.

LYONS, ISRAEL: English astronomer, botanist, and mathematician; born at Cambridge 1739; died in London 1775; son of Israel Lyons. In his earliest youth he showed a remarkable aptitude for study, especially for mathematics. He began in 1755 the study of botany, which he continued till his death. In 1758 he published a "Treatise on Fluxions," dedicated to his patron, Dr. Smith, master of Trinity College; and in 1763 "Fasciculus Plantarum Circa Cantabrigiam Nascentium, Quæ post Raium Observatæ Fuere." Lyons was invited by Sir Joseph Banks, president of the Royal Society, who had received his earliest lessons in science from him, to lecture at Oxford in 1762, but he soon returned to Cambridge. He was appointed by the board to accompany Captain Phipps (afterward Lord Mulgrave) on a voyage to the north pole in 1773. On his return he married and settled in London, where he died in about a year. At the time of his death he was engaged in publishing some papers of Edmund Halley, secretary of the Royal Society.

BIBLIOGRAPHY: Nichols, *Literary Anecdotes*, ii. 327–328 and iii. 660, London, 1812; Maunders, *Treasury of Biography*; Carmoly, *Médecins Juifs*, Brussels, 1844; *Jew. Chron.* Nov. 27, 1863.

J. I. Co.

LYONS, JACQUES JUDAH: American minister; son of Judah and Mary Lyons; born in Surinam, Dutch Guiana, Aug. 25, 1814; died in New York Aug. 12, 1877. He was educated in Surinam, and was minister of the Spanish and Portuguese congregation there, Neweh Shalom, for five years. He left Surinam in 1837 and went to Richmond, Va., where for two years he was minister of the Congregation Beth Schalom. In 1839 he was elected minister of the Spanish and Portuguese congregation Shearith Israel, New York city, in succession to Isaac Seixas, and served the congregation thirty-eight years, successfully combating every movement to change the form of worship in his congregation.

Lyons was among those who founded The Jews' (now Mount Sinai) Hospital; he was actively concerned in founding the Jewish Board of Delegates and Hebrew Free Schools and was superintendent of the Polonies Talmud Torah School, in connection with his own congregation. For many years he was president of the Hebra Hased ve-Emet and of the Sampson-Simpson Theological Fund. Lyons was an ardent student and collected a library that is now in possession of the Jewish Theological Seminary of America. In 1857, in connection with the Rev. Dr. Abraham De Sola of Montreal, he prepared and published a Hebrew calendar covering fifty years, together with an essay on the Jewish calendar system.

A. F. H. V.

LYRA, NICOLAS DE: French exegete; born at Lyre, near Evreux, Normandy, about 1270; died at Paris Oct. 23, 1340. The only certain dates in connection with his life are furnished by his epitaph in the monastery of the Minorites at Paris, which has been edited by Wadding. He entered the Franciscan order at Verneuil in 1291 and studied later at Paris, where he became doctor of theology and taught at the Sorbonne until 1325, when he was appointed provincial of his order for Burgundy.

Lyra, who was later declared to be of Jewish descent, wrote an anti-Jewish work entitled "De Messia Ejusque Adventu Præterito." His most important activities, however, were exegetical. Of the four methods of interpretation indicated in the mnemonic verse

"Littera gesta docet, quid credas allegoria,
Moralis quid agas, quo tendas anagogia,"

he was the first to emphasize as the most important that dependent upon the literal sense ("sensus litteralis"), and he endeavored to apply this system of Biblical exegesis to the exclusion of all others. His chief work, to which he devoted himself from 1322 to 1330, is his "Postillæ Perpetuæ, sive Brevia Commentaria in Universa Biblia" (first printed at Rome 1471-72, Cologne 1478, Venice 1482, and often since, either in whole or in part). After his death his book was supplemented by such additions as the general introduction, "De Libris Canonicis et Non Canonicis," and by numerous prefaces. The "Postillæ" includes fifty books of commentary on the entire Old and New Testaments and the Apocrypha, which latter is regarded as less binding in character. There are also thirty-five books of "Moralities" ("Moralia"). The author presents his point of view in the three prologues to his work, especially in the second—"De Intentione Autoris et Modo Procedendi." Even in cases which tradition has interpreted mystically he still considers the literal meaning as the decisive one; he offers esoteric explanations but seldom, and then almost always with a Christological tendency, for he seeks to find the deeds of the New Testament the fulfilment of the words of the Old.

Lyra used the original texts of the Old and New Testaments rather than the corrupt Latin translations. His knowledge of Jewish tradition was drawn from Rashi, whom he transcribes almost word for word, and who also was an advocate of literal exegesis ("peshaṭ"). Raymond Martin was his authority for Aramaic and Arabic, and he was frequently indebted to many others, particularly to Thomas Aquinas on the Book of Job. During the Middle Ages, Lyra was highly esteemed and widely read on account of his sound scholarship, judicious interpretation, and freedom from dogmatic prejudice. Luther frequently used Lyra's works; to them he owed his rabbinical knowledge, especially his acquaintance with Rashi, and it is to this influence that the well-known verse alludes—"Si Lyra non lyrasset, Lutherus non saltasset."

Bibliography: Wadding, *Annales Minorum*, v. 264 *et seq.*, vii. 237 *et seq.*; Fabricius, *Bibliotheca Latina*, xiii. 350 *et seq.*, Hamburg, 1736; Herzog-Hauck, *Real-Encyc.* xii. 28 *et seq.*; *Nicolas von Lyra und Seine Stellung in der Gesch. der Mittelalterlichen Schrifterklärung*, in *Katholik*, ii. 940 *et seq.* (1859); Fischer, *Des Nicolas von Lyra Postillæ Perpetuæ*, in *Jahrbuch für Protestantische Theologie*, 1889; Siegfried, *Raschis Einfluss auf Nicolas von Lyra und Luther*, in *Archiv für Erforschung des Alten Testaments*, i. 428, ii. 36; Maschkowski, *Raschis Einfluss auf Nicolas von Lyra in der Auslegung des Exodus*, in Stade's *Zeitschrift*, 1891. See also the works of Richard Simon, Diestel, and Reuss.

T. G. We.

LYRE. See Harp and Lyre.

LYSIAS: Syrian statesman of royal descent; died 162 B.C. (I Macc. iii. 32; Josephus, "Ant." xii. 7, § 2). When Antiochus Epiphanes undertook a campaign against the Parthians in 166-165, he appointed Lysias regent and guardian of his heir, Antiochus V. (Eupator), who called Lysias brother (II Macc. xi. 22). The new viceroy was charged with the suppression of the Jewish revolt, and on the defeat of his generals he himself led a strong army against the rebels (165). He seems to have marched along the Palestinian coast to southern Judea, but he was defeated at Beth-Zur, south of Jerusalem, and was obliged to retreat to Antioch (I Macc. iii. 34-36, iv. 26-35; "Ant." xii. 7, § 5).

According to II Maccabees, which Niese regards as the best authority on the subject, this campaign took place after the consecration of the Temple by Judas Maccabeus. The same source states also that Lysias made peace with Judas and quotes the letter in which the former is supposed to have granted the demands of the Jews (II Macc. xi. 1-21).

According to I Maccabees, however, this peace was not concluded until a later date. After the death of Antiochus Epiphanes, Lysias went to Judea (163) with the young king Antiochus V. He again attacked from the south, besieged Beth-Zur, and thus compelled Judas to raise the siege of Acre and give battle. The Jewish army was defeated near Beth-Zechariah, and Beth-Zur fell into the hands of the victors. The Syrians had already laid siege to Jerusalem, then held by the Jews, who would, in all probability, have been utterly defeated had not Lysias been compelled to make war upon his rival Philip, who had been appointed guardian of Antiochus V. (I Macc. vi. 28-48; II Macc. xiii. 1-17; "Ant." xii. 9, §§ 3-5; *idem*, "B. J." i. 1, § 5). The regent found it advisable, therefore, to make peace with the Jews, whom he allowed to resume their former prerogatives (I Macc. vi. 55-62; II Macc. xiii. 23-26; "Ant." xii. 9, §§ 6-7).

Realizing that it was impossible to deprive the Jews of their religious freedom, Lysias proved himself a better politician than his king, Antiochus Epiphanes. He would have conquered Philip had not his own soldiers betrayed him and his ward, Antiochus V., to the pretender Demetrius I. (Soter), who put them both to death (162; I Macc. vii. 1-4; II Macc. xiv. 2; Appian, "Syrian War," § 47; "Ant." xii. 10, § 1).

Bibliography: Niese, in *Hermes*, xxxv. 468-476; Schürer, *Gesch.* i. 205, 213-216.

J. S. Kr.

LYSIMACHUS: Anti-Jewish Alexandrian writer; lived before Apion. Like the Stoic Chæremon, he went beyond even Manetho in his inimical account of the exodus of the Jews from Egypt. According to Lysimachus, the Jews, numbering 110,000, left Egypt in the reign of King Bokchoris, journeyed through the desert on the advice of a certain Moyses, and after many hardships finally arrived at Judea, where they founded the city of Hierosyla (= "Temple robbery"), which they subsequently called "Hierosolyma."

The fragments of Lysimachus found in Josephus ("Contra Ap." i. 34 *et seq.*), as well as in the works Θηβαϊκὰ Παράδοξα and Νόστοι, which are often quoted in ancient literature, have been collected by C. Müller in "Fragmenta Historicorum Græcorum," iii. 334-342 (see, also, Reinach, "Textes d'Auteurs Grecs," pp. 117 *et seq.*).

Bibliography: Josephus, *Contra Ap.* i. 34 *et seq.*; ii. 2, 14; Schürer, *Gesch.* iii. 403 *et seq.*; Westermann, in Pauly-Wissowa, *Real-Encyc.* iv. 1311.

G. M. K.

M

MAACAH: **1.** Small Aramean kingdom east of the Sea of Galilee (I Chron. xix. 6). Its territory was in the region assigned to the half-tribe of Manasseh east of the Jordan. Maacah, its king, became a mercenary of the Ammonites in their war against David (II Sam. x. 6). It is probable that the city Abel of Beth-maachah in Naphtali (*ib.* xx. 15) derived its name from its relation to this kingdom and people.

2. A wife of David, and daughter of Talmai, King of Geshur (*ib.* iii. 3), a near neighbor of the Maachathites.

3. King of Gath, to whose son, Achish, Shimei's servants fled early in Solomon's reign (I Kings ii. 39). About a half-century earlier than this event, David with 600 men had fled to Achish, son of Maoch, King of Gath (I Sam. xxvii. 2); but the identification of Maoch is doubtful, though kinship is exceedingly probable.

4. Wife of Rehoboam, King of Judah, and mother of Abijah; in I Kings xv. 2 she is called the daughter of "Abishalom," but of "Absalom" in II Chron. xi. 20, 21. She was removed from her position as queen mother by her grandson Asa (*ib.* xv. 16).

Other persons of this name are mentioned in Gen. xxii. 24; I Chron. ii. 48, vii. 15, viii. 29, xi. 43, xxvii. 16.

E. G. H. I. M. P.

MA'ALI IBN HIBAT ALLAH, ABU AL-: Egyptian physician; lived at Fusṭaṭ (Cairo) at the end of the twelfth century. He was the physician of Salaḥ al-Din (Saladin) and, after the death of the latter, of his brother Al-Malik al-'Adil. Ibn Abi Uṣaibi'ah, in his biographies of the Arabic physicians, speaks highly of Abu al-Ma'ali's learning, generosity, and great influence at court. He relates further that almost all his children embraced Islam. Al-Ma'ali wrote many works and essays on medicine, which are no longer in existence. Steinschneider is inclined to identify Ma'ali with the brother-in law of Maimonides and the secretary of the mother of the vizier Al-Faḍal. Ma'ali wrote a work on medicine entitled "Ta'aliḳ wa-Maghrabat."

Bibliography: Steinschneider, *Die Arabische Literatur der Juden*, § 155.

G. I. Br.

MA'AMAD. See Mahamad.

MA'ARABI (AL-MAGHREBI), ISRAEL BEN SAMUEL HA-DAYYAN: Karaite scholar; lived at Cairo in the thirteenth and fourteenth centuries; teacher of the Karaite physician and writer Japhet ibn Ẓaghir of Cairo. Ma'arabi wrote, in Arabic, a work on the precepts (probably "Kitab al-Fara'iḍ"), of which only the part dealing with the laws concerning the slaughtering of animals and the part treating upon the calendar (but in a Hebrew translation) are extant in manuscript, the former in London (Brit. Mus., Or. No. 2528), St. Petersburg (Firkovich collection, No. 640), and Strasburg (No. 50), the latter in Leyden (Nos. 25 and 60) and St. Petersburg (No. 716, where the name of the author is erroneously given as "Elijah ha-Dayyan"). A Hebrew translation of the part on the laws of slaughtering was published under the title "Hilkot 'Inyan Sheḥiṭah" at Vienna (1830); a Hebrew translation of the part treating upon the calendar was incorporated in the "Tiḳḳun ha-Ḳara'im," reproduced by Wolf in his "Bibliotheca Hebræa" (iv. 1077 *et seq.*). In addition to the work on the precepts, Ma'arabi wrote: "Tartib al-'Aḳa'id al-Sittah," on the six articles of belief (the belief in God, in His messenger [Moses], in the Prophets, in the Torah, in Jerusalem, in the Last Judgment); "Sharḥ 'Aseret ha-Debarim," a commentary on the Decalogue (St. Petersburg, Firkovich collection, No. 638); "Iggeret," a decision in a contested case of marriage (Fischl MSS., No. 59 E.); "Muḳaddimah," a commentary on Prov. iii. 13, or, according to Neubauer, a prayer for the dead ("ẓidduḳ ha-din").

Ma'arabi attacked, in his work on the precepts, the theories of the "Ba'ale ha-Rikkub" with regard to the laws of incest, and advocated the reform that had been preconized by Joseph ha-Ro'eh.

Bibliography: Munk, in Jost's *Annalen*, iii. 93; idem, *Notice sur Abulwalid Merwan ibn Djanah*, p. 8; Pinsker, *Liḳḳuṭe Ḳadmoniyyot*, pp. 148, 176, 233; Steinschneider, *Cat. Bodl.* col. 1168; idem, *Hebr. Bibl.* v. 51, xx. 91; idem, *Die Arabische Literatur der Juden*, § 184; Fürst, *Gesch. des Karäert.* ii. 252; Grätz, *Gesch.* vii. 322; Gottlober, *Biḳḳoret le-Toledot ha-Ḳara'im*, p. 186; Neubauer, *Aus der Petersburger Bibliothek*, pp. 25, 27.

J. I. Br.

MA'ARABI, NAHUM: Moroccan Hebrew poet and translator of the thirteenth century ("Ma'arabi," "Maghrabi" = "the western" or "the Moroccan"). His poems are found only in Moroccan collections. Two of them, of a liturgic character, were published by L. Dukes in "Zur Kenntniss der Hebräischen Poesie" (pp. 162–163), and they were translated into German by M. Sachs in "Die Religiöse Poesie" (p. 131). Ma'arabi translated from Arabic into Hebrew: (1) Maimonides' "Iggeret Teman," under the title "Petaḥ Tiḳwah," to which he added a preface in verse (Basel, 1631); (2) the commentary to the "Sefer Yeẓirah" by Isaac Israeli or Jacob b. Nissim, prefacing it with a poem (a fragment of it was published by L. Dukes in "Ḳontres ha-Massoret," pp. 5–10); (3) Joseph ibn Ẓaddiḳ's "Microcosmos," under the title "Ha-'Olam ha-Ḳaṭon" (the translation is anonymous, but see Steinschneider ["Hebr. Uebers." pp. 408–409]); (4) Saadia's commentary on the thirteen hermeneutic rules ("Shelosh 'Esreh Middot") of R. Ishmael.

Bibliography: Steinschneider, *Hebr. Uebers.* pp. 395, 409, 930, 935; idem, *Cat. Bodl.* col. 2021; idem, *Hebr. Bibl.* xv. 13; L. Dukes, *Ḳontres ha-Massoret*, pp. 5–10; idem, *Zur Kentniss*, pp. 162 *et seq.*; *Oẓar Ṭob*, 1885, p. 11.

G. M. Sel.

MA'ARIB: The evening prayer, from the first benediction in which the name is taken, the Talmudic term being "Tefillat 'Arbit"; one of the three daily prayers instituted in conformity with the practise of David ("Evening, and morning, and at noon, will I pray," Ps. lv. 18 [A. V. 17]) and Daniel (Dan. vi. 10). The Talmud ascribes to the Patriarchs the origin of the prayers, and credits Jacob with the "Ma'arib," because it is said: "And he lighted ["wa-yifga'"] upon a certain place . . . because the sun was set" (Gen. xxviii. 11), interpreting "wa-yifga'" as "and he prayed" (comp. "tifga'" = "make intercession," Jer. vii. 16).

In Biblical times prayers were devotional in character and were considered as voluntary offerings. But after the destruction of the Temple, prayers became obligatory as substitutes for the sacrifices: "So will we render as bullocks the offering of our lips" (Hos. xiv. 2, R. V.). But inasmuch as the offering of sacrifices in the Temple occurred only twice a day, morning and afternoon, only the corresponding two prayers became an obligation, while the "Ma'arib" still remained a voluntary prayer, according to the best authority (Ber. 27b). This of course refers to the standing-prayer, "Shemoneh 'Esreh," and not to the "Shema'," which it is obligatory to read morning and evening. Consequently in Talmudic times and in a greater part of the geonic period, as the "Seder R. Amram Gaon" clearly shows, the standing-prayer was omitted from the "Ma'arib" service. To replace the Eighteen Benedictions, eighteen scattered Biblical verses, each mentioning the name of God, were introduced at the end of the "Ma'arib" service. This composition, beginning with "Baruk Adonai le-'olam," was arranged by the rabbis of Babylonia and accepted by the rabbis of Palestine. Maimonides admits that the "Ma'arib" is only voluntary, but he claims that since the Jews everywhere, by common custom, consented to say the prayer regularly, it is equivalent to an obligation ("Yad," Tefillah, i. 6).

"Ma'arib" usually follows the "Minḥah" prayer at the synagogue, to avoid the trouble of a second gathering of the congregation. The time for the "Ma'arib" service begins when three stars are visible in the heavens. The time may be extended to midnight, and in case of an emergency to the rising of the morning star (Ber. i. 1). The service begins with "Wehu Raḥum" and "Baraku," and continues with the first benediction, "Asher bi-Debaro," the second benediction, "Ahabat 'Olam," "Shema'" (Deut. vi. 4–10, xi. 13–22; Num. xv. 37–41), the third benediction, "Emet we-Emunah," the fourth benediction, "Hashkibenu" (Ber. 4b), the eighteen verses mentioned above, "Yire'u 'Enenu," the standing-prayer, and the "'Alenu." If the "Ma'arib" service is conducted by a quorum of ten, the leader does not repeat the standing-prayer.

Order of Prayer.

On Friday evening the "Ma'arib" service commences somewhat earlier, preceded by "Leku Nerannanah." The Sephardim begin with "Wehu Raḥum," as usual, but the Ashkenazim omit this, as the Sabbath is a day of joy not to be disturbed with any supplication or devotional prayer of the character of "Wehu Raḥum." The Zohar gives another reason for the omission—that on Sabbath "the Higher Judgment must not be revoked" (Zohar, Terumah, p. 130a, ed. Wilna, 1882). The leader of the congregation repeats a part of the standing-prayer for Sabbath, "Magen Abot," "Bame Madliḳin" (the second chapter of Shabbat, relating to the lighting of Sabbath lights), the "Alenu," and "Yigdal." See Devotional Literature; Prayer.

Bibliography: *Shulḥan 'Aruk, Oraḥ Ḥayyim*, §§ 235-237; Yarḥi, *Minhagim*, pp. 22b *et seq.*, ed. Goldberg, Berlin, 1855; *Shibale ha-Leḳet*, §§ 43-48, ed. Buber; Dembitz, *Services in Synagogue and Home*, p. 80. For the text and English translation see Singer, *Authorized Daily Prayer-Book*, London.

J. J. D. E.

MAARSSEN, JOSEPH BEN JACOB: Dutch scholar and publisher; member of a family of printers; lived at Amsterdam in the seventeenth and eighteenth centuries. Maarssen published the following works: (1) A Judæo-German translation, by himself, from the Dutch of an account of the uprising that occurred at Amsterdam in 1696. It was edited (Amsterdam, 1707), under the title "Eine Beschreibung von die Rebelerei zu Amsterdam," by the translator's father, who had witnessed the events. (2) "Ḥanok la-Na'ar," models of Judæo-German letters, with a glossary containing more than one hundred Latin, French, and German words, compiled by him in collaboration with Moses Bendin (Amsterdam, 1714–15). (3) "Leshon Zahab," or "Miktam le-Dawid," by David Maarssen, models of Hebrew letters, published as a supplement to the preceding work (*ib.* 1714). (4) "Yehoshua' ben Sirak," the wisdom of Ben Sirah, translated by Maarssen into Judæo-German from the Dutch (*ib.* 1712). (5) "Schöne Artliche Geschichten," seven stories of Boccaccio's, translated, also by Maarssen, from the Dutch (*ib.* 1710). (6) "Tiḳḳun Soḥarim we-Tiḳḳun Ḥillufim," specimens of commercial notes and of the laws concerning commercial bills, compiled by him in collaboration with Ẓebi Hirsch ben Gershon Szczebrszeszyn and Moses Bendin (*ib.* 1714).

Bibliography: Steinschneider, in *Serapeum*, ix. 335, 345; x. 10; idem, *Cat. Bodl.* col. 1505; *idem*, in Ersch and Gruber, *Encyc.* section ii., part 28, p. 70.

D. I. Br.

MAAS, JOSEPH: English musician and singer; born at Dartford, Kent, Jan. 30, 1847; died at London Jan. 16, 1886. Maas acted as chorister for five years at Rochester Cathedral (from 1856) and studied under J. C. Hopkins and Madame Bodda-Pyne. When his voice broke he became a clerk in the dockyards at Chatham. In 1869 he went to Milan, returning to England in 1871, when he appeared at one of the Henry Leslie Choir Concerts at St. James's Hall; he sang in "Babil and Bijou" at Covent Garden in Sept., 1872. He made his reputation as an operatic singer in America, where he remained for a number of years, chiefly as first tenor in various English opera companies. On his return to England he was engaged by Carl Rosa, and appeared in "The Golden Cross" at the Adelphi Theatre in 1878. In 1879 he appeared at Her Majesty's Theatre as *Rienzi* in Wagner's opera of that name. In the ballad operas of Balfe and Wallace his popularity was unequaled; one of his best and most successful parts was that of the hero in Massanet's "Manon" at Drury Lane Theatre. Maas sang for a short time in Italian opera at Her Majesty's and Covent Garden theaters. On the concert platform he had few rivals in English ballads and as a soloist in Handel's oratorios.

Bibliography: *The Times* (London), Jan. 18 and 23, 1886.

J. G. L.

MAAS, MYRTIL: French mathematician; born in France in 1792; died in Paris Feb. 27, 1865. He early showed an aptitude for mathematics, and in 1813 entered the Ecole Normale at Paris, where he studied until the political upheaval of 1815 caused the suspension of the school. In that year, when walking with some of his schoolfellows in the Champ de Mars, where the troops were drilling, he was accidentally shot in the leg, and the wound never perfectly healed. Being a Jew, he was unable to obtain a chair in mathematics; but he found employment first in a porcelain factory and then as a private tutor. In 1818 he was employed as actuary by the Compagnie d'Assurances Générales of Paris. He then studied in London, returned to Paris, was chosen by the company from among three distinguished mathematicians, and soon became its vice-president. In 1828 he became president of a new life- and fire-insurance company, founded by the Foulds. Maas labored actively in the interests of the Jews; in 1830 he became a member of the Central Consistory, and thirteen years later its vice-president. His death was caused by a malady that developed from his wound. A eulogy upon him was read in the directors' room of the company, and his old schoolfellows had a medal engraved in his honor; this was delivered to his son, who assumed the position and responsibilities of his father.

Bibliography: Servi, *Israeliti d'Europa*, pp. 195, 196; *Archives Israélites*, March 15, 1865; *Univers Israélite*, April 8, 1865.

s. N. D.

MA'ASEH BERESHIT; MA'ASEH MERKABAH (literally, "work of Creation" and "work of the Chariot"): Talmudic terms for the esoteric doctrine of the universe, or for parts of it (comp. Cabala). Ma'aseh Bereshit, following Gen. i., comprises the cosmogony of the Talmudic times; Ma'aseh Merkabah, based on the description of the Divine Chariot in Ezek. i., and on other prophetic descriptions of divine manifestations, such as that in Isa. vi., is concerned with the theosophic views of those times. The secret doctrine might not be discussed in public. Ecclesiasticus (iii. 21-22) inveighs against its study: "Seek not out the things that are too hard for thee, neither search the things that are above thy strength. But what is commanded thee, think thereupon with reverence; for it is not needful for thee to see with thine eyes the things that are in secret." Ḥag. ii. 1 says: "Ma'aseh Bereshit must not be explained before two, nor Ma'aseh Merkabah before one, unless he be wise and understands it by himself"; Ḥag. 13a then goes on to explain that the chapter-headings of Ma'aseh Merkabah may be taught, as was done by R. Ḥiyya. According to Yer. Ḥag. ii. 1, the teacher read the headings of the chapters, after which, subject to the approval of the teacher, the pupil read to the end of the chapter. R. Zera said that even the chapter-headings might be communicated only to a person who was head of a school and was cautious in temperament. According to R. Ammi, the secret doctrine might be entrusted only to one who possessed the five qualities enumerated in Isa. iii. 3. A certain age is, of course, necessary. When R. Johanan wished to initiate R. Eliezer in the Ma'aseh Merkabah, the latter answered, "I am not yet old enough." A boy who recognized the meaning of חשמל (Ezek. i. 4) was consumed by fire (Ḥag. 13b), and the perils connected with the unauthorized discussion of these subjects are often described (Ḥag. ii. 1; Shab. 80b).

Creation Mystery.

Ḥag. 11b states that it is permissible to inquire concerning the events of the six days of Creation, but not regarding what happened before the Creation. In no case, then, is the entire cosmogony included in the term "Ma'aseh Bereshit," but only its more mystic aspects, nor can all the passages of the Talmud and the Midrash dealing with these problems be considered as parts of the doctrine. Thus, ideas like those regarding the ten agencies by means of which God created the world, or questions as to whether heaven or earth was first created, or concerning the foundations of the world, or as to whether there are two heavens or seven (all these problems being mentioned in connection with the interdiction against teaching the Ma'aseh Bereshit to more than one person), do not belong to the doctrine itself, for such arguments are forbidden by the dictum, "Thou mayest speak of the seven heavens, but of the things thereafter thou mayest not speak." The views which are found scattered throughout the Talmud, and especially in Gen. R. i.-xii., are generally haggadic in character; indeed the question arises whether anything more than mere allusions may be expected therein regarding the Ma'aseh Bereshit in so far as it is esoteric in content. Some information seems to be given, though only by intimation, in the well-known story in Ḥag. 14b-15b of the four scholars that entered paradise (that is, penetrated the mysteries of the secret doctrine), of whom only R. Akiba remained uninjured. R. Akiba's words at the beginning of the story (14b), "When ye reach the shining marble stone do not cry out 'Water, water,'" seem to point to those theories of Creation which assume water to be the original element.

Ben Yoma is represented as interested in the determination of the space between the upper and lower waters. Ḥag. ii. 1 also indicates this in the story of R. Judah b. Pazzi, who opened his discourse on Ma'aseh Bereshit with the words, "In the beginning the world was water in water." Thus the question of the primal elements undoubtedly belongs to this field. Here again one must distinguish haggadic and devotional from mystic and philosophical thought, and must not teach views such as that the world was created out of "tohu" and "bohu" and "ḥoshek," or that air, wind, and storm were the primal elements, as component parts of the doctrine of Creation. In like manner the cosmogonic conceptions of the Apocrypha and of geonic mysticism must not be considered as indications of the secret teachings of the Ma'aseh Bereshit.

Chariot of Fire.

Somewhat simpler is the question regarding the nature of the Ma'aseh Merkabah, which is designated as "an important matter" in the Talmud (Suk. 28a) and which, perhaps, occupies on the whole a more prominent position than the Ma'aseh Bereshit. Just as in the case of the latter, the purely haggadic explanations of Ezek. i., as found, for instance, in Ḥag. 13b, must not be taken into consideration. This chapter of Ezekiel, it is declared, may be studied even by young pupils, because a boy can seldom recognize the doctrines implied therein. The object, therefore, was to find special secrets in these verses. R. Akiba is said (Ḥag. 15b–16a) to have gathered his mystic deductions from Deut. xxxiii. 2 ("and he came with ten thousands of saints"), Cant. v. 10 ("the chiefest among ten thousand"), Isa. xlviii. 2 ("The Lord of hosts is his name"), and I Kings xix. 11, 12 (Elijah's great theophany). The Ma'aseh Merkabah, therefore, dealt with esoteric teachings concerning the visible manifestations of God, and hence with angelology and demonology, though not to the same degree as in Talmudic literature. As the story of R. Akiba indicates, the other theophanies mentioned in the Bible were used in the Ma'aseh Merkabah; Ḥag. 13b shows, *e.g.*, that this was the case with Isa. vi.

Practical Applications.

The Ma'aseh Merkabah seems to have had practical applications. The belief was apparently current that certain mystic expositions of the Ezekiel chapter, or the discussion of objects connected with it, would cause God to appear. When R. Eleazar b. 'Arak was discoursing upon the Ma'aseh Merkabah to R. Johanan b. Zakkai, the latter dismounted from his ass, saying, "It is not seemly that I sit on the ass while you are discoursing on the heavenly doctrine, and while the Divinity is among us and ministering angels accompany us." Then a fire came down from heaven and surrounded all the trees of the field, whereupon all of them together began to recite the hymn of praise. R. Jose ha-Kohen and R. Joshua (according to Yer. Ḥag. ii. 1, R. Simon b. Nathanael) had similar experiences. The belief in the appearance of God is indicated also in the popular idea that all who inquire into the mysteries of the Ma'aseh Merkabah without being duly authorized will die a sudden death. Such a divine interposition is expressly mentioned in connection with the "story of the Creation" in Sanh. 95b. Rab Hananiah and Rab Hoshaiah studied the "Sefer Yeẓirah" and the "Hilkot Yeẓirah" respectively every Sabbath evening and succeeded in creating a calf as large as a three-year-old ox.

This esoteric tendency, originating in pagan conceptions in connection with certain Bible stories, must have led often to pessimistic and nihilistic views, as is shown by the accounts of Aḥer or Elisha b. Abuyah (Ḥag. 15a, b), and the Mishnaic passage, "He who speaks of the things which are before, behind, above, and below, it were better he had never been born."

According to a tradition handed down by Jose b. Judah, a tanna of the second half of the second century (Tosef., Ḥag. ii. 2; Ḥag. 14b; Yer. Ḥag. ii. 1), Johanan b. Zakkai was the founder of the secret doctrine. In the same passage, in both Talmuds, it is said, however, that he refused to discuss it, even in the presence of a single person, although, as already stated, R. Eleazar b. 'Arak discoursed on it with him and was extravagantly praised by him; two other pupils of his, R. Joshua and R. Jose ha-Kohen, also discussed it with him. According to tradition, the second one to give instruction in these matters was R. Joshua, vice-president of the Sanhedrin under R. Gamaliel. He was succeeded by R. Akiba, and the last to teach them was R. Neḥunya b. ha-Ḳanah. R. Jose the Galilean and Pappus discussed the subject with R. Akiba (Ḥag. 14a; Gen. R. xxi.). The tradition, quoted above, of the four who studied the secret doctrine mentions, besides Akiba, Simeon b. 'Azzai, Simeon b. Zoma, and Elisha b. Abuyah. The fate of the last-named, who was driven from Judaism by his experience, is said to have given rise to restrictive measures. The study of profane books was forbidden (Sanh. 100), and an interdiction of the public discussion of these subjects was issued, only R. Ishmael objecting. In the time of R. Judah, R. Judah b. Pazzi and Bar Ḳappara delivered public discourses on these mysteries (Yer. Ḥag. ii. 1; Gen. R. i.). R. Levi regarding this as inadmissible, R. Ḥiyya declared that the chapter-headings might be taught. R. Judah ha-Nasi was at this time the authority to whom, as formerly to R. Johanan, such matters were referred. In later times the interdiction against public discussions of the story of the Creation was accepted without protest, but by way of warning this saying (Ḥag. 16a) of Resh Laḳish was added: "His eyes shall be dull who looketh on three things—the rainbow [because it resembles Ezekiel's vision], the king [because he resembles God in majesty], and the priest [because he utters the name of God]."

Source of Doctrines.

This Talmudic doctrine may well be connected with the old Jewish esoteric teachings of the time of the Second Temple, as partly preserved in the Apocrypha and the pseudepigrapha; but the theosophic and cosmogonic portions of this literature can not with certainty be regarded as the source of the Talmudic doctrine, nor can the literature of the so-called geonic mysticism, crystallized in the Ma'aseh Bereshit and the Ma'aseh Merkabah and designated in its literary form by these names, be regarded as the immediate continuation of Talmudic mysticism. Although much of the material found in the former may belong to the Talmud, yet the entire doctrine of the heavenly halls, angelology, and the doctrine of the Creation as it is found, for instance, in the "Sefer Yeẓirah," must not be regarded as Talmudic in origin. The very fact that there are so many Talmudic and midrashic parallels to the conceptions of the geonic period leads to the conclusion that they contain only a limited amount of original material from the ancient esoteric teachings. It may be mentioned, finally, that Maimonides interprets Ma'aseh Bereshit as referring to physics and Ma'aseh Merkabah as referring to metaphysics. See also Merkabah.

Bibliography: Hamburger, *R. B. T.* ii., s.v. *Geheimlehre*; Zunz, *G. V.* 2d ed., v. 171–173.
J. A. B.

MA'ASEH BOOKS: Books written in Judæo-German in Hebrew script, and containing stories, legends, and tales ("ma'asim") on various subjects, most of them relating to Jews and Judaism. They originated about the beginning of the fifteenth century, when Jews were living in the Rhenish provinces, and were further developed during the migrations to Russia and Poland. Like the name "ma'aseh buch" itself, this entire literature is a mixture of Jewish and German, both in language and in sub stance. The first products of Judæo-German literature, which is very voluminous, were principally translations of the prayer-books and the Bible, and devotional books. The ma'aseh books constitute a group by themselves; their object was to furnish entertainment and instruction for women and girls, who, unlike the men, were not in duty bound to learn Hebrew. Where the subject is a non-Jewish one, Hebrew words may be altogether lacking in the story, except the invariable formula at the end of the book—סליק and אכי"ר (אם כן יהי רצון), or a note in Hebrew regarding the author, and a Hebrew verse on the title-page. At first the writers generally chose non-Jewish stories, but as the literature developed, Jewish subjects were given the preference. It is to be noted, furthermore, that in the earlier period consecutive stories of considerable length were employed, while later the ma'aseh collections took the form of readers and anthologies containing short stories ending with a moral; for this reason fables also are included.

The non-Jewish subjects at first selected were various in nature. Indeed the Jews were led to make these collections by their acquaintance with the stories from the cycles of King Arthur, Dietrich of Bern, and the "Nibelungenlied," all of which were well known in the region of the Rhine. Thus a Judæo-German version was made of the poem "Ritter aus Provincienland, Sigmund Is Sein Name Genannt, und Magdalena, Tochter des Königs von England." In 1501 Elijah Levita composed at Venice the well-known BABA BUCH or "Bovo-Ma'aseh," a Judæo-German rimed version of the English romance of Bevis of Hampton, following Italian versions in which the hero is called "Bovo d'Antonia," the form of the name which gave Levita's rendering its title. Sources apparently the most remote were drawn upon for material, such as the facetiæ of Till Eulenspiegel, and even Boccaccio's frivolous tales, which found their way into Judæo-German from Dutch versions.

Subjects.

Side by side with this foreign material Jewish tales were developed and remodeled. The Bible, especially the stories of Joseph, David, and Samuel (the "Schmuel-Buch," Basel, 1612), offered rich material, while Jewish history and literature furnished an abundance of subjects. There are also Judæo-German historical works, such as the "Yosippon," "Shebeṭ Yehudah," and "She'erit Yisrael" (Grünbaum, "Jüdisch-Deutsche Chrestomathie," pp. 345, 357, 361). The stories of Judith and Esther, of the heroic wars of the Maccabees and the destruction of the Temple, were retold, mingled with many legends; and later works, such as the "Ben ha-Melek weha-Nazir" (Prince and Dervish), were also translated.

Modifications Introduced.

Jewish readers, curiously enough, preferred the books dealing with non-Jewish subjects (comp. Cornelius Adelkind's introduction to Levita's translation of the Psalms and the introduction to the ma'aseh book of 1602). Although Perles has shown ("Monatsschrift," 1876, pp. 351 *et seq.*) that in the stories belonging to the Dietrich cycle the passages with a Christian coloring were replaced by others, a change which was probably made also in other non-Jewish stories, yet such alterations did not suffice for the real purpose of the ma'aseh books, which was to furnish instruction in Jewish history and literature for those who were ignorant of Hebrew. To remedy this defect a pious Jew issued in 1602 a work known simply as "Ma'aseh-buch," purporting to be a collection of Jewish legends and historical tales and without any admixture whatever of foreign elements. The collector indicates his purpose in the preface as follows: "Here cometh a beautiful Ma'aseh Book, ye dear sirs and dames; now look upon the beautiful Ma'aseh Book, which has never before been published in the world, and contains some three hundred ma'asim, all made from the Gemara and also from the רבתא and Beḥai; and also from R. Judah Ḥasid's ma'asim ye will miss none; and also from the Sefer Ḥasidim, and the Sefer Musar, and the Yalḳuṭ, as ye may see below in my 'simanim.' Therefore, ye dear dames, ye now have the German books all before you, and ye have likewise the German Gemara, even as ye have 'kol hattoro kullo gor.'" Then in Hebrew: "By order of Jacob b. Abraham of blessed memory, of Meseritsch in Lithuania. Here at Basel the great [city], 362 [*i.e.*, 1602], by Herr Conrad Waldkirch."

Despite the author's intention, some non-Jewish stories found their way into this book. Steinschneider assumes that its compiler lived in western Germany in the last third of the sixteenth century. A German translation of it was published by Christoph Hellwig (Helvicus), together with notes that are anti-Jewish in tone (Giessen, 1612). The "Ma'aseh Adonai" and the "Ma'asehbuch" (Wilmersdorf and Rödelheim, 1752) from which Grünbaum published extracts ("Chrestomathie," pp. 385 *et seq.*), may also be noted here. All the works belonging to this class of literature are very similar in content, being compilations of an undigested series of anecdotes from various Jewish books, especially from the Babylonian Talmud, the Midrash, Yalḳuṭ, the Zohar, and such historical books as the "Yuḥasin," "Shalshelet ha-Kabbalah," and "Shebeṭ Yehudah." Each story begins with the words "Ma'aseh es geschach" or "Ma'aseh es wor einmal" ("a 'ma'aseh' happened," or "there was a 'ma'aseh' once upon a time"). The authors prefer to narrate instructive stories or miracles of anonymous ḥasidim, and they frequently tell tales of famous Jewish rabbis like Maimonides and Luria, or of earlier ones like Joshua ha-Levi and Akiba. Often the stories are noble and lofty and sincere in their religious feeling, and are told in simple, straightforward language. The ma'aseh books contain highly valuable material for the knowledge of the life and thought of the Jews of the Middle Ages, but as yet they have scarcely been studied from this point of view. A detailed bibliographical list of this literature is given by Steinschneider in his Bodleian catalogue.

BIBLIOGRAPHY: Steinschneider, *Cat. Bodl.* cols. 613-619; Grünbaum, *Jüdisch-Deutsche Chrestomathie*, pp. 385 *et seq.*, Leipsic, 1882; Steinschneider, *Hebr. Bibl.* vi. 22, vii. 42 *et seq.*, viii. 13-17, ix. 58; *idem*, in *Serapeum*, xxvii. 1-12; *idem*, in Gosche's *Archiv für Litteraturgesch.* ii. 1-21; Wiener, *History of Yiddish Literature in the Nineteenth Century*, pp. 2 *et seq.*, 42, New York and London, 1899.

A. G. WE.

MA'ASER. See TITHE.

MA'ASEROT (מעשרות = "tithes"): Seventh masseket of the Mishnah, Tosefta, and Palestinian Gemara, in the Talmudic order of Zera'im. It deals with the tithes of agricultural produce due to the Levites (Num. xviii. 21). In contradistinction to the tithe called "ma'aser sheni," which the owner must consume at Jerusalem (Deut. xiv. 22 *et seq.*), and to the triennial poor man's tithe (Deut. xiv. 28 *et seq.*, xxvi. 12 *et seq.*), called "ma'aser 'ani," the tithe treated in this masseket is denominated "ma'aser Lewi" (the Levite's tithe) or "ma'aser rishon" (first tithe; see Ma'as. Sh. v. 6, 10). The latter name was formerly applied to this treatise (see Joshua ha-Levi, "Halikot 'Olam," i. 1; Frankel, "Darke ha-Mishnah," p. 257), which is so styled in the Erfurt manuscript of Tosefta (ed. Zuckermandel). The treatise is divided into five chapters (three in the Tosefta), and its contents, briefly stated, are as follows:

Ch. i.: Whatever is edible, and is private property, and grows in the ground is subject to tithe. Plants that are edible while young as well as when full grown are subject to tithe before maturity (if any part of the crop is taken before maturity); but of plants that are not properly eatable before they reach a certain stage of ripeness one may eat, without separating the tithes, until they develop. The Mishnah then proceeds to designate the respective stages at which plants come under the general head of edibles and are consequently subject to tithe. As between picking for marketing and for domestic consumption a distinction is made: in the latter case one may use small quantities before bringing the mass under shelter (comp. iii. 5).

Ch. ii.-iv.: Under what circumstances a Ḥaber may eat of the produce of an 'Am ha-Areẓ without first separating the ma'aser. If a laborer, hired to assist in gathering figs, stipulates with his employer that he be allowed to eat of the fruit, he may eat without regard to tithing; but if his stipulation includes one of his dependents, or if he sends one of his dependents instead, the latter will not be privileged to partake of the fruit before the tithe is properly set aside. [The laborer is by law entitled to eat of the produce he handles (see B. M. vii. 2 *et seq.*), as a kind of charity; comp. B. M. 92a *et seq.*] After the crop reaches the employer's enclosed premises the laborer may eat thereof only if his employer has not promised to board him.

Ch. v.: Laws regarding cases in which one is required to pay tithes when he transplants vegetables; laws regarding the sale of crops to one who is suspected of non-observance; law regarding the paying of tithes in the case of vegetable fields purchased in Syria.

S. S. S. M.

MA'ASIYYOT. See Anecdotes.

MACCABÆAN, THE: Monthly magazine of Jewish life and literature published in New York; established Oct., 1901, as the outcome of a resolution unanimously passed at a convention of the societies affiliated with the Federation of American Zionists, held at Philadelphia in the June preceding.

Until June, 1902, "The Maccabæan" was issued partly in English and partly in Yiddish under the editorship of Louis Lipsky. By a resolution of the convention held in Boston in June, 1902, the Yiddish department was dropped, and the editorial chair has since been occupied by J. de Haas. In 1903 (Jan.) the publication was incorporated as a stock-company, the Federation holding the majority of the stock, and Prof. Richard Gottheil being appointed president of the company. The present (1904) president is G. H. Mayer; M. B. Laude, William Morris, and J. H. Lieberman are respectively vice-president, treasurer, and secretary.

G. S.

MACCABÆANS, THE: Association of English Jewish professional men and others; founded in 1892; its aim is social intercourse and cooperation among its members with a view to the promotion of the higher interests of the Jewish race. At first membership was not limited to any one class in the community, but shortly after the establishment of the club admission was restricted to Jewish professional men. The term "professional men" was, however, very widely interpreted, and subsequent legislation has empowered the committee to elect in any year ten Jews who have become prominent by reason of their public services or their connection with literature, science, or art. These specially elected members must not number more than one in four of the ordinary membership.

The establishment of the Maccabæans was primarily due to Herman Cohen, with whom the idea originated, and whose efforts were well supported by several professional friends, including Solomon J. Solomon, A.R.A. (first president); and Asher I. Myers (treasurer). Herman Cohen himself became first honorary secretary. The Maccabæans hold frequent meetings for the reading and discussion of papers of Jewish interest. Not only do these meetings offer a free platform on which all parties in the community meet and discuss controversial topics of general interest, but as a result of papers read before the Maccabæans the Jewish Lads' Brigade, the Jewish Athletic Association, and the Education Aid Society, among other movements, have been started.

J. A. M. H.

MACCABEES, THE (Greek, Οἱ Μακκαβαῖοι): Name given to the Hasmonean family. Originally the designation "Maccabeus" (Jerome, "Machabæus") was applied solely to Judas, the third son of Mattathias the Hasmonean (I Macc. ii. 4, iii. 1, *et passim*), Mattathias' other sons having different surnames; but as Judas became the leader of the party after his father's death, and as he was also the most heroic warrior, his surname was applied not only to all the descendants of Mattathias, but even to others who took part in the revolutionary movement under the leadership of the Hasmoneans. Hence the title "Books of the Maccabees."

The etymology of the name, in spite of the efforts of the scholars, who have advanced various theories on the subject, remains undetermined. According to Jerome ("Prologus Galeatus"), the First Book of the Maccabees was originally written in Hebrew. Origen (in Eusebius, "Hist. Eccl." book vi., last chapter) even gives the Hebrew title, שרבט שר בני אל; thus the Greek and Latin forms of the name must have been transliterations from the Hebrew.

But the original Hebrew text is lost; and there is

no mention of the name either in the Talmud or in the Midrash, where the family is always referred to as "the Hasmoneans." In later Hebrew writings the name occurs in two forms, מכבי, transliterated from the Latin, and מקבי, according to the Greek spelling. The latter form is generally explained as meaning "the hammer," a surname given to Judas on account of his heroism. Iken ("Symbolæ Litterariæ," i. 184, Bremen, 1744) derives it from the Arabic "manḳab" (= "general"), while, according to others, the name originated in the fact that Modin, where Mattathias dwelt, was in the territory of Gad (Reland, "Palästina," p. 901), the banner of which tribe bore the inscription מקב, the final letters of the names Abraham, Isaac, and Jacob.

מכבי is, however, the preferred form; it occurs in "Yosippon" (ch. xx.), and is explained by Gorionides as meaning "the hero," though it is not known in what way. Others explain it as composed of the initials of מי כמוך באלים יהוה (Ex. xv. 11), written on the banner of the Hasmoneans, or as the initials of מתתיהו כהן בן יוחנן. But the statement that it was the surname of Judas only is against these interpretations. Curtiss ("The Name Machabee," Leipsic, 1876) derives it from כבה = "to extinguish"; thus מכבי would mean "the extinguisher," which agrees with the interpretation of Gorionides. Finally, the following two opinions may be added: (1) that the Hebrew read מחבאי = "he who hides himself," referring to the fact that the Hasmoneans hid themselves in the mountains (I Macc. ii. 28); (2) that of Filosseno Luzzatto that it is a Greek word, an anagram of Βιαιομάχος = "violent warrior." For the history of the Maccabees see HASMONEANS; JUDAS MACCABEUS; MATTATHIAS MACCABEUS.

BIBLIOGRAPHY: A. Levi, in *Mossé*, ii. 6; E. Levi, in *Univers Israélite*, xlvi. 330; D. Oppenheim, in *Ha-Maggid*, xvii., Nos. 5, 6; P. Perreau, in *Vessillo Israelitico*, xxviii. 76, 113; Wetstein, in *Ha-Maggid*, xxiii., No. 19; Zipser, in *Ben Chanania*, iii. 497 *et seq.*; Winer, *B. R.* i. 631, s.v. *Judas*.

J. M. SEL.

MACCABEES, BOOKS OF: I. There are four books which pass under this name—I, II, III, and IV Maccabees. The first of these is the only one of the four which can be regarded as a reliable historical source.

I Maccabees: The First Book of the Maccabees covers the period of forty years from the accession of Antiochus (175 B.C.) to the death of Simon the Maccabee (135 B.C.). Its contents are as follows: Ch. i. 1–9 is a brief historical introduction; i. 10–ii. 70 treats of the rise of the Maccabean revolt; iii. 1–ix. 22 is devoted to the Maccabean struggle under Judas; ix. 23–xii. 53, to the fortunes of Israel under Jonathan; xiii. 1–xvi. 24, to the administration of Simon. The events are followed with intense interest and sympathy. At times the enthusiasm of the writer rises to a high pitch and breaks out into poetry of a genuine Semitic character (comp. iii. 3–9). The style is simple, terse, restrained, and objective, modeled throughout on that of the historical books of the Old Testament. The fact that just proportions are observed in treating the different parts of the narrative proves the author to have been a writer of considerable skill. He dates all events in terms of the Seleucid era.

It is clear from the Semitic idioms which occur throughout the work that it was composed in a Semitic language (see, for example, ii. 40, iv. 2), and certain passages indicate with great clearness that the original language was Hebrew (see ii. 39, iii. 19). To this fact Origen and Jerome also bear testimony, though it is possible that the version or paraphrase known to them was Aramaic.

Original Language.

The Hebrew original seems not to have borne the name "Maccabees," though it is not known what was its real designation. Eusebius ("Hist. Eccl." vi. 25) quotes Origen as authority for the name Σαρβὴθ Σαβαναι Ἐλ, a name which has been explained in many different ways. For some of these see Grimm ("Das Erste Buch der Makkabäer," p. xvii.). Dalman ("Grammar," p. 6), whom Torrey (Cheyne and Black, "Encyc. Bibl.") follows, takes the name as a corruption of ספר בית חשמנאי (= "Book of the Hasmoneans"). If this be the correct interpretation, an Aramaic translation of the book must have been made at an early time, and it was this translation which was known to Origen and Jerome—a view which does not seem improbable. Be this as it may, the Hebrew was translated very early into Greek, and the Greek only has survived. The Greek version seems to be a literal one, often preserving the Semitic, and sometimes even the Hebrew, idiom; but it is clear, and probably it is, on the whole, a satisfactory translation. It is transmitted in three uncial manuscripts of the Septuagint—the Codex Sinaiticus, the Codex Alexandrinus, and the Codex Venetus—as well as in several cursives.

Concerning the author no information is obtainable beyond that which may be inferred from the book itself. He was a devout and patriotic Jew who lived and wrote in Palestine. This latter fact is proved by his intimate and exact geographical knowledge of the Holy Land (comp. iii. 24; vii. 19; ix. 2–4, 33, 34, 43; xii. 36–40; xiii. 22, 23; xvi. 5, 6) and by his lack of accurate knowledge of any of the foreign countries which he mentions. The author was also a loyal admirer of the Hasmonean family; he believed that to it Israel owed her deliverance and existence. He admired not only the military deeds of Judas (comp. v. 63), but also those of Jonathan (comp. x. 15–21) and Simon (comp. xiv. 4–15). The narrative is told not as though deliverance came by miracle, but as though it was due to the military genius of these men, exercised under the favoring guidance of God (i. 64, iii. 8). Curiously enough the word "God" does not appear in the work, nor does the word "Lord." The idea is not lacking, however, as in the Book of Esther, but is represented by "Heaven," or by the pronoun "He." The author was a deeply religious man in spite of this mannerism. He was very zealous for the Law and for the national religious institutions (see i. 11, 15, 43; ii. 20–22; iii. 21), for the Scriptures (i. 56, iii. 48), and for the Temple (i. 21, 39; iii. 43).

Author.

It should be noted, also, that throughout the work the priesthood is represented in a favorable light. The renegade priests Jason and Menelaus are not mentioned—a fact in striking contrast with the treatment which the Second Book of the Maccabees accords them. From these facts Geiger conjectured that the author was a Sadducee, and most recent writers follow him in this opinion, although they consider him wrong in calling the First Book of the Maccabees a partizan document; its temperate and just tone certainly redeems it from such a stricture. The *terminus a quo* of the work is found in the fact that John Hyrcanus I., who began to reign in 135 B.C., is mentioned at the close of the book (xvi. 21–24).

Date.

As the Romans are throughout spoken of in terms of respect and friendliness, it is clear that the *terminus ad quem* must be sought at some time before the conquest of Jerusalem by Pompey in 63 B.C. As to whether the date can be more nearly determined scholars are not agreed. The determining fact is held by most to be the statement in xvi. 23, 24, that the "rest of the acts of John . . . are written in the chronicles of his high-priesthood." It is thought by many that this implies that John had died and that a sufficient time had elapsed since his death to permit the circulation of the chronicles. Bissell (Lange's "Commentary," p. 479) thinks that not more than a score or two of years had passed, while Schürer ("Hist. of the Jewish People," div. ii., vol. iii., p. 8) and Fairweather (in "Cambridge Bible" and Hastings, "Dict. Bible") think that not more than a decade or two had elapsed, and date the work in the first or second decade of the first century B.C. Torrey, on the other hand, thinks ("Encyc. Bibl.") that this reference to the chronicle of the priesthood is an imitation of well-known passages in the Books of Kings, that it was intended solely as a compliment to John, and that the work was composed early in his reign (*i.e.*, soon after 135 B.C.) by one who had been an interested spectator of the whole Maccabean movement. The vivid character of the narrative and the fact that it closes so abruptly after the death of Simon make this a very plausible view.

Those who maintain the later date of the work are obliged to account for the vivid details which it contains by supposing that the writer employed older sources, such as letters and memoranda. In Torrey's view no such sources are needed, as the author, where he did not have personal knowledge, could have talked with participants or eye-witnesses of the events. In either case the First Book of the Maccabees is one of the best sources known for the history of the Jews.

Sources and Integrity.

J. D. Michaelis held that Josephus used the Hebrew original of the book, which differed in some important particulars from the present text. Destinon ("Die Quellen des Josephus," 1882) revived this theory and endeavored to prove (pp. 80 *et seq.*) that ch. xiv.–xvi. were not contained in the edition used by Josephus. Destinon bases his argument on the fact that Josephus treats this portion very scantily in comparison with his treatment of the other material of the book, although these chapters contain quite as much and as interesting material. He has been followed by Wellhausen ("I. J. G." pp. 222 *et seq.*). But Torrey (in "Encyc. Bibl."), by utilizing the investigations of Mommsen, has shown that Josephus actually knew some of this material and introduced it at a later point in his work ("Ant." xiv. 8, § 5), in describing the history of Hyrcanus II. In all probability, therefore, the First Book of the Maccabees has retained its original form.

BIBLIOGRAPHY: Grimm, *Das Erste Buch der Makkabäer*, in *Kurzgefasstes Exegetisches Handbuch zu den Apokryphen*, 1853; Wace, *Apocrypha*; Bissell, *Apocrypha*, in Lange's *Commentary*; Fairweather and Black, *First Book of Maccabees*, in *Cambridge Bible for Schools and Colleges*; Kautzsch, *Apokryphen*; Torrey, *Schweizer's Hebrew Text of I Maccabees*, in *Jour. Bib. Lit.* xxii. 51-59.

II Maccabees: The Second Book of the Maccabees opens with two letters written by Jews resident in Palestine to brethren dwelling in Egypt. The first letter occupies ch. i. 1–10a; the second, ch. i. 10b–ii. 18. These letters, it is thought by some, formed no part of the original work. The preface is found in ch. ii. 19–32, and states that Jason of Cyrene had composed five books on the Maccabean revolt, which the writer undertakes to epitomize for his readers. Ch. iii. relates how the attempt of Heliodorus to plunder the Temple was miraculously thwarted; ch. iv. narrates the wickedness of the high priests Jason and Menelaus, and of Simon, the Temple overseer; ch. v., how Antiochus began the persecution of the Jews; ch. vi. and vii., the story of the martyrdom of Eleazar and the seven young men and their mother; while ch. viii.–xv. are occupied with the history of the wars of Judas Maccabeus.

The time covered by this material is barely fifteen years, from the very end of the reign of Seleucus IV., whose servant was Heliodorus, to the victory of Judas over Nicanor (175–160 B.C.). The reason why the book terminates here is to be found in its aim, which was to set before the Jews of the Diaspora the importance of observing the two Maccabean feasts—the Feast of the Dedication and the Feast of Nicanor. In no other way, the writer believed, could they share in the glory and the fruits of the great struggle for liberty. The author is so intent on this that though he has lauded Judas as a splendid example of religious patriotism he passes in silence over his death. The writer further takes occasion often to impress upon his readers the sacred character of the Temple at Jerusalem, which the Diaspora might easily undervalue. In contrast with I Maccabees, the language of II Maccabees is highly religious. God appears as the great "Sovereign" who miraculously delivers His people (see iii. 24 and, perhaps, ii. 21). The author is a religious teacher (see iii. 1 *et seq.*, iv. 15–17, v. 17–20, *et al.*); he did not write for the sake of the history as such. This places his work in a very different class from that of I Maccabees. In the earlier part he supplies some welcome information not contained in I Maccabees, and in nearly every chapter are interesting facts—some of them confirmed by Josephus—which may, with caution, be used. But his purpose, style, and temperament are such that, since the time of Ewald, it has been recognized that the work is not a sober and restrained history like I Maccabees, but is rhetorical and bombastic.

Historical and Religious Character.

One important fact to be noted is the writer's belief in the bodily resurrection of the dead (see vii. 9, 11, 14, 36; xiv. 16; and especially xii. 43–45). This, together with his attitude toward the priesthood as shown in his lifting the veil which I Maccabees had drawn over Jason and Menelaus, led Bertholdt and Geiger to regard the author as a Pharisee and the work as a Pharisaic party document. This much, at least, is true—the writer's sympathies were with the Pharisees. The author claims that he epitomized the work of Jason of Cyrene (ii. 23), which seems to have been his only source, unless he himself prefixed the two letters to his work. Jason is thought by Schürer (*l.c.* p. 212) to have compiled his work from hearsay shortly after 160 B.C. at Cyrene. If this is true, the work of Jason, like II Maccabees, concluded with the victory over Nicanor. There can be no doubt that both the work of Jason and that of his epitomizer (*i.e.*, the author of II Maccabees) were written in Greek, and that the latter was a Hellenistic Jew.

Sources.

There is a reference in ch. xv. 37 to the Book of Esther, which would preclude any earlier date of authorship than about 130 B.C. (see Cornill, "Einleitung," p. 252). On the other hand, II Maccabees was known to the author of the Epistle to the Hebrews (see Peak, in "The Century Bible," p. 223) and to Philo (see Schürer, *l.c.* p. 214). The work, therefore, must have been composed about the beginning of the common era.

The two letters prefixed to II Maccabees have excited much discussion. Some scholars regard them as the basis of the author's work, which he himself prefixed to it because they treat of the topics of which he wished to speak—the Temple at Jerusalem and the importance of observing its feasts. Others hold that the letters were placed in their present position by a later hand, while some believe them to be fabricated. There is in the letters nothing which is inconsistent with their belonging to the time from which they profess to come and there seems to be no good reason for doubting that it was the epitomist himself who prefixed them to the book. For details see the works mentioned below.

The Letters.

BIBLIOGRAPHY: Grimm, *Zweites, Drittes, und Viertes Bücher der Makkabäer*, in *Kurzgefasstes Exegetisches Handbuch zu den Apokryphen*; Wace, *Apocrypha*; Kautzsch, *Apokryphen*; Bruston, *Trois Lettres des Juifs de Palestine*, in Stade's *Zeitschrift*, 1890, x. 110 *et seq.*; Torrey, *Die Briefe 2 Makkabäer, i. 1–ii. 18*, ib. 1900, xx. 225 *et seq.*; Herkenne, *Die Briefe zu Beginn des Zweiten Makkabäerbuches*, 1904.

III Maccabees: The Third Book of the Maccabees has in reality nothing to do either with the Maccabees or with their times. It received its name probably because it is a fiction concerning the persecution of the Jews by a foreign king; that king was Ptolemy Philopator (222–205 B.C.). The story runs as follows: After Ptolemy's defeat of Antiochus III. in 217 B.C., at the battle of Raphia, the former visited Jerusalem and tried to enter the Temple, but was miraculously prevented (i. 1–ii. 24). Returning to Alexandria, he assembled the Jews in the hippodrome to be massacred, but the necessity of writing down their names exhausted the paper in Egypt, so that they escaped (ii. 25–iv. 21). Next the king devised a plan for having the Jews trampled to death by elephants; this also was frustrated in various improbable ways (v. 1–vi. 21). The king then underwent a change of heart and bestowed great favor on the Jews, and the day on which this occurred was ever after celebrated as a festival in memory of the deliverance (vi. 22–vii. 23).

The author of this fiction was certainly an Alexandrian Jew who wrote in Greek, for its style is even more rhetorical and bombastic than that of II Maccabees. The work begins abruptly and is thought to be but a fragment of a once larger whole. Whether there is any foundation for the story concerning Philopator with which the writer begins there is no means of knowing. If true, it is one of a very few grains of fact in the whole account. Josephus ("Contra Ap." ii. 5) tells how Ptolemy Physco (146–117 B.C.) cast the Jews of Alexandria, who, as adherents of Cleopatra, were his political opponents, to intoxicated elephants. When the elephants turned on his own people the king saw a sudden apparition and gave up his purpose. The Jews, it is added, celebrate the day of their deliverance. It would seem that the author of III Maccabees, anxious to connect this celebration with Jerusalem, has transferred it to an earlier Ptolemy and given it an entirely unhistorical setting. His narrative can not be regarded as a successful fiction, as it abounds in psychological as well as historical improbabilities.

Authorship and Character.

This work was written later than II Maccabees, for its author made use of that book (see ii. 9; comp. II Macc. vi. 18 *et seq.* and xiv. 35 with III Macc. iii. 25–33; see also Grimm, *l.c.* p. 220). He can not have written earlier, therefore, than the end of the first century B.C. On the other hand, he can not have written later than the first century C.E. or his work would not have been used by Christians. Ewald regarded this work as a polemic against Caligula and dated it accordingly about 40 C.E.; this view has been abandoned by more recent writers, since Philopator is not represented as claiming divine honors.

BIBLIOGRAPHY: In addition to the works cited in the bibliography to the second part of this article: Deissmann, *Bible Studies*, 1901, pp. 341-345; I. Abrahams, in *J. Q. R.* 1896-97, ix. 39 *et seq.*; Ewald, *Gesch. des Volkes Israel*, iv. 611-614.

IV Maccabees: The Fourth Book of the Maccabees, so called, is a semiphilosophic discourse, or sermon, on the "supremacy of the pious reason" (ch. i. 1). It consists of a prologue (i. 1–12) and of two principal parts. The first of these (i. 13–iii. 18) is devoted to the elucidation of the author's philosophical thesis, and the second (iii. 19–xviii. 24) to the illustration of the thesis by examples drawn from II Maccabees. In the latter portion of the work there is, first (iii. 19–iv. 26), a brief review of the sufferings of the Jews under Seleucus and his son (?) Antiochus Epiphanes; the conquering power of reason is illustrated (v. 1–vii. 23) by the example of Eleazar, drawn from II Macc. v. 18–31; by that of the seven brethren (vii. 24–xiv. 10), drawn from II Macc. vii. 1–23; and by that of their mother (xiv. 11–xvi. 25), taken from II Macc. vii. 25 *et seq.* In ch. xvii. and xviii. the author expresses his impressions with reference to these martyrdoms.

It appears, therefore, that the only connection this work has with the Maccabees is in the fact that the author's illustrations are drawn from the Second Book of the Maccabees.

Ch. xviii. 3–24 has been thought by several scholars to be the work of a later hand, but the opinion does not appear to be well founded.

Integrity and Character.

Ch. xvii. 2 would form a weak ending to the book, while xviii. 20–24 suits well the style of the author of the earlier parts, and the apparent incongruity of xviii. 6–19 would seem to be designed in this hortatory composition to make a strong impression on its hearers. This latter view is strengthened if it be remembered that the work is throughout a discourse addressed directly to listeners (comp. i. 1, 7; ii. 13; xiii. 19; xviii. 1). Ewald and Freudenthal called it a sermon and held that it is an example of Alexandrian synagogue preaching, but this view is now abandoned, for even in the Diaspora the sermon of the synagogue was usually founded on a passage from the Bible. This discourse, also, is too abstruse for an ordinary congregation; it is an address to a more select circle.

Its style is oratorical and ornate, though not so extravagant as that of III Maccabees. It contains a large philosophic element of the Stoic type, though its author possessed a taste for philosophy rather than real philosophical insight. It contains also a core of Judaism. The writer was a Jew who could clothe his religion in a philosophic garb in accordance with the tendency of the times. The Hellenic and the Jewish elements in his work both appear at their best and in a combination almost without a parallel; the nearest example is the New Testament Epistle to the Hebrews.

It is probable, therefore, that the author of IV Maccabees was an Alexandrian Jew. Eusebius ("Hist. Eccl." iii. 10) and Jerome ("De Viris Illustribus," xiii.) ascribe the work to Josephus—an opinion which was for a long time followed, and which has caused the text of IV Maccabees to be included in many editions of the works of Josephus.

Author and Date.

But the language and style of the work differ so radically from those of the writings of Josephus that it is clear that this is a mistaken opinion. Of some of its historical combinations, as in iv. 5 and v. 1, Josephus could hardly have been guilty. The writer of IV Maccabees had certainly come under the influence of the culture of Alexandria, even if he lived and wrote in some other city. As to the time when the book was written, the data for an opinion are the same as in the case of III Maccabees: it was written probably at the close of the last century B.C. or during the first century C.E., and before the time of Caligula, for the Jews seem to have been at peace at the time.

The writer is a strong believer in immortality, but he has abandoned the Pharisaic standpoint of II Maccabees, which recognizes a bodily resurrection, and holds to the view that all souls exist forever, the good being together in a state of happiness (xvii. 18), with the Patriarchs (v. 37) and with God (ix. 8 and xvii. 18).

Eschatology.

These views are the more striking as they are entwined with the same narratives which in II Maccabees express the more materialistic view. The writer holds, also, that the suffering of the martyrs was vicarious; by it they wrought deliverance for their nation (comp. i. 11, xvii. 19–23, xviii. 24).

BIBLIOGRAPHY: For the Greek text of *IV Maccabees*, as well as of the other books, see Swete, *The Old Testament in Greek*, vol. iii., 1894; for the translation, see Kautzsch, *Apokryphen*, ii. 152 *et seq.*; for introductions, see Bissell in Lange's *Commentary*, and Schürer, *History of the Jewish People*; see also Bensly, *The Fourth Book of Maccabees in Syriac*, 1895.

T. G. A. B.

II.* I Maccabees, now extant only in Greek, was originally composed in Hebrew or Aramaic, most probably the former; but the original can not have been long in circulation. The fragment of a Hebrew text of I Maccabees published by Chwolson (1896) and again by Schweizer (1901) is not part of the original; and it may well be that even

I Maccabees.

Origen knew only an Aramaic translation and not the original. He calls (Eusebius, "Hist. Eccl." vi. 25) I Maccabees *Σαρβηθ Σα(ρ)βαναιελ*, a title which has given rise to much conjecture. Only two suggestions need be named: Derenbourg's ספר בית שר בני אל ("Book of the Family of the Chief of the People of God"), given in his "Essai sur l'Histoire et la Géographie de la Palestine" (p. 450, Paris, 1867), and Dalman's ספר בית חשמנאי, in his "Grammatik des Jüdisch-Palästinischen Aramäisch" (p. 6, Leipsic, 1894). Of the name "Maccabees" it may be mentioned that in a text of the Megillat Anteyukas ("J. Q. R." xi. 291 *et seq.*) the reading is מקנאי (="the zealot"), which would be very acceptable were it better attested.

As to the date of the book, much turns on the meaning of the last two verses. Some critics, indeed, doubt the authenticity of the whole of the last section (xiv. 16–xvi. 24), but the trend of opinion is in favor of the integrity of the book. Schürer and Niese (in "Kritik der Beiden Makkabäerbücher," Berlin, 1900) maintain that the last verses imply that I Maccabees was written after the death of John Hyrcanus (105 B.C.), but there is good reason for holding that the reference is to the beginning (135 B.C.) and not to the end of Hyrcanus' reign (see "J. Q. R." xiii. 512 *et seq.*).

Critics are practically unanimous in attaching great value to I Maccabees as a historical record. "On the whole, the book must be pronounced a work of the highest value, comparing favorably, in point of trustworthiness, with the best Greek and Roman histories" (Torrey). This is high praise but it is fully deserved (comp. Schürer, "Gesch." iii. 141). Niese (*l.c.*) has done good service in vindicating the authenticity of Judas' embassy to Rome; and it is no peculiar demerit in I Maccabees that in the reports of the numbers engaged in battle, of speeches, and even of documents, its account is inexact and sometimes quite incredible. Such defects are shared by Thucydides and Livy. The substance, not the exact form, of documents was given by ancient historians. On the other hand, it differs somewhat from the Biblical histories in its standpoint. The divine element is not wanting, and success is ultimately traced (as in Mattathias' deathbed utterances) to God. Judas invariably sings psalms of thanksgiving for victory, and the key-note of the revolt is "Not unto us, O Lord, not unto us

*A second article on the Book of Maccabees is inserted as treating the subject from a Jewish standpoint.—J.

but unto thy name give glory" (Ps. cxv. 1). The period also, as many hold, gave rise to numerous new psalms. But in I Maccabees, nevertheless, history is written from the human standpoint. Victory is earned by endeavor as well as bestowed by grace. Partly because of this phenomenon, it was urged by Geiger ("Urschrift," 1857, pp. 200-230) that one may detect a dynastic purpose in the book and that its author was a Sadducean apologist for the Hasmoneans.

It is certainly true that the author is silent concerning the worst excesses of the (Sadducean) high priests, and attaches primary importance to the founder of the dynasty, Mattathias. Mattathias is unknown to II Maccabees, though the latter is supposed by Geiger to be a Pharisaic counterblast to the Sadducean I Maccabees. Yet, strangely enough, in the Pharisaic tradition of the Talmud and Synagogue Mattathias plays a large part, so large that Judas is thrown into the background.

On one important point some modern writers are unfair to the book. God is not "named" in it; the term "heaven" replaces the divine name. From this the inference has been drawn that "God was absolutely conceived as reigning in the remote heaven, and no longer as dwelling among the people by the Shekinah" (Fairweather and Black, "I Maccabees," Introduction, p. 47). This is as false an inference as would be a similar conclusion from the opening words of the Lord's Prayer, "Our Father who art in Heaven." God is not "named" throughout the Lord's Prayer. In I Maccabees the personal pronoun is most significantly used (iii. 22, 51; iv. 10, 55) with relation to the term "heaven"; and, more remarkable still, the pronoun is sometimes used (ii. 61) without any noun at all: "And thus consider ye from generation to generation, that none that put their trust in him shall want for strength." That there grew up a disinclination to "name" God is undoubted; but whatever the origin of this scrupulosity, it was not any sense of the remoteness of God (see discussion by Benjacob, "Im Namen Gottes," p. 164, Berlin, 1903). From the Maccabean period onward God becomes ever nearer to Israel. If there was a fault at all, it was not that God became too transcendent; the tendency was rather in the direction of overfamiliarity than of undue aloofness.

Unlike I Maccabees, the book known as II Maccabees was written in Greek. For the history of the war it is of less value than I Maccabees, though some recent writers (in particular Niese) have maintained the opposite opinion. It adds, however, important particulars regarding the events that led up to the Maccabean revolt. Besides this, II Maccabees, written quite independently of I Maccabees, is a strong support of the general truth of the familiar story of the revolt, though II Maccabees is embellished with angelical and miraculous ornament foreign to the first book. Its style is rhetorical, its purpose didactic. It emanated from Alexandria and was addressed to the Greek-speaking Jews of the Diaspora. It was designed to impress on them the unity of Judaism, the importance of Jerusalem as the center of religious life, and the duty of observing the two feasts of Ḥanukkah and Nicanor's Day (see Nicanor). That the book has a Pharisaic color is undoubted, but not in the sense of being a partizan pamphlet in reply to I Maccabees, which, indeed, the author of II Maccabees most probably did not know. Moreover, II Maccabees takes no account of Mattathias, nor, indeed, of any of the band of heroes except Judas; and this is not easily forced into evidence of Pharisaic partizanship. On the other hand, in II Macc. xiv. 6 Judas is represented as the leader of the Hasidæans, who have many points in common with the Pharisees, and from whom the Hasmoneans were soon alienated.

II Maccabees.

Of specifically non-Sadducean doctrines, II Maccabees has a very clear expression of belief in the resurrection. Death is a "short pain that bringeth everlasting life" (II Macc. vii. 36; comp. other passages in the same chapter and xiv. 46). Judas is represented (II Macc. xii. 43 *et seq.*) as making offerings for the dead because "he took thought of the resurrection." The reference to such offerings is, however, without parallel in Jewish literature, and nothing is otherwise known of such offerings being made at the Temple in Jerusalem (see Israel Lévi, "La Commemoration des Ames dans le Judaïsme," in "R. E. J." xxix. 48).

The book is usually held to belong to the latter part of the first century B.C.; Jason (of whose work it purports to be an epitome) wrote at least a century earlier. Niese places II Maccabees at the date 125-124 B.C., thus regarding it as older than, as well as superior to, I Maccabees. In this preference of the second to the first book, Niese stands practically alone, but he has done great service in vindicating the importance and value of the former (comp. also Sluys, "De Maccabæorum Libris I et II Quæstiones," Amsterdam, 1904). It remains to add that the authenticity of the letters prefixed to II Maccabees has been fiercely assailed. Yet it is coming to be recognized that the letters have a clear bearing on the design of the book, as explained above, and it is quite conceivable, though very improbable, that they were part of the original work of Jason. On these letters see, besides earlier literature, Herkenne, "Die Briefe zu Beginn des Zweiten Makkabäerbuchs," Freiburg, 1904.

One point remains. The martyrdoms described in II Maccabees, especially of the mother and her seven sons, have given the book undying value as an inspiration and encouragement to the faithful of all ages and creeds. As will be seen below (in connection with IV Maccabees), this feature of the Maccabean heroism made a special appeal to the Christianity of the first four centuries. "The figure of the martyr, as the Church knows it, dates from the persecution of Antiochus; all subsequent martyrologies derive from the Jewish books which recorded the sufferings of those who in that day were strong and did exploits" (E. Bevan, "House of Seleucus," 1902, ii. 175).

III Maccabees purports to record a persecution of the Jews in Alexandria during the reign of Ptolemy (IV.) Philopator (222-204 B.C.). The Jews are assembled in the hippodrome, and 500 infuriated elephants are to be let loose upon them. In the event the elephants turned against the persecutors, and the Jews not only escaped, but were treated with much honor by the king. That there is much of the fabulous in this story is obvious, and it may well be that the similar story told in Josephus ("Contra Ap." ii. 5) concerning Ptolemy (VII.) Physcon is, as most assume, the original of III Maccabees. The book would thus belong at the latest to the first century C.E.; at the earliest to the last century B.C. Recently important new light has been thrown on the book by the discovery of early Jewish settlements in the Fayum. On independent gounds, the present writer ("J. Q. R." ix. 39) and Prof. A. Büchler ("Tobiaden und Oniaden," pp. 172 *et seq.*, Vienna, 1899) have put forward the theory that the book refers to a persecution in the Fayum. Certainly, the rapid transference of Jewish allegiance from Egyptian to Syrian hegemony about 200 B.C. finds its explanation if the Jews of Egypt were then undergoing persecution. That the author was an Alexandrian is unquestionable. On the other hand, Willrich ("Hermes," 1904, xxxix. 244) disputes the Fayum theory and supports the view that the book is best explained as referring to Caligula.

III Maccabees.

The beautiful work known as IV Maccabees is a homily, not a history. As Freudenthal was the first to show, it is a sermon addressed to a Greek-speaking audience, and delivered probably on Ḥanukkah ("Die Flavius Josephus Beigelegte Schrift über die Herrschaft der Vernunft [IV Makkabäerbuch]," Breslau, 1869), the thesis being that, reason (religion) can control the passions; the author illustrates this from many examples, especially from the story of the Maccabean martyrdoms as related in II Macc. vi., vii. A very noble level of eloquence is reached by the writer, and the book is in many ways one of the best products of the syncretism of Hebraic and Greek thought.

IV Maccabees.

The authorship of IV Maccabees was at one time ascribed (as by Eusebius, Jerome, and other authorities) to Josephus, but this is clearly wrong. Nothing can with definiteness be asserted as to the date of the book; it belongs probably to the period shortly before the fall of Jerusalem. In its present form it contains possibly some Christian interpolations (*e.g.*, vii. 19, xiii. 17, xvi. 25), but they are certainly very few and insignificant. Later on, Christian homilists used the same topic, the martyrdoms, as the theme for sermons; the Church maintained a Maccabean feast (though not on the same date as the Jews) for at least four centuries. Homilies by Gregory Nazienzen and Chrysostom for the festival of Aug. 1 (the "Birthday of the Maccabees") are extant on this subject. On the "Maccabees as Christian Saints" see Maas in "Monatsschrift," xliv. 145 *et seq.*

V Maccabees, so called by Cotton ("Five Books of Maccabees," 1832), is known also as the Arabic II Maccabees. It is included in the Paris and London Polyglots. It has clear relations to II Maccabees, the Arabic "Yosippus," and the Hebrew "Yosippon." Late in origin and without historical value, the book is, however, of considerable importance from other points of view.

V Maccabees.

J. I. A.

MACEDONIA: Country of southeastern Europe; now a part of the Turkish empire. It is the native country of Alexander the Great, who is, therefore, called "Alexander the Macedonian" in rabbinical writings. In Dan. xi. 30 the Macedonians are mentioned under the name "Kittim" (R. V.), and Eusebius and the Hebrew Josephus or Gorionides (Knobel, "Völkertafel," p. 103) use the same designation.

In the apocalyptic literature this kingdom is known as the "fourth beast" (Dan. vii. 7). The First Book of the Maccabees, which originally was written in Hebrew, also uses the word "Kittim" for Macedonians, and mentions Philip and Alexander (i. 1), as well as Philip III. and his illegitimate son Perseus (viii. 5), as kings of the Macedonians. Since the Greek Syrians style themselves "successors of Alexander," these Syrians also are called "Macedonians" (II Macc. viii. 20).

The Rabbis, whose acquaintance with Greek life was one acquired during the Macedonian era, identified the Hebrew "Yawan" (Javan) with Macedonia (Targ. Yer. to Gen. x. 2; Targ. of I Chron. i. 5; Yoma 10a; Gen. R. xxxvii. 1), and to them, as to Daniel, Macedonia represented the eschatological kingdom (Mek. to Ex. xx. 18; Targ. of I Sam. ii. 4); with them the expression "Javan" is interchangeable with "Macedonia." They mention, probably in a figurative sense, the "jaundice" of Macedonia (Targ. Yer. to Deut. xxviii. 22); also the gold from the same country (Targ. to Esth. viii. 15; 2d Targ. to Esth. vi. 10).

Many Macedonian idioms, it is claimed, are found in the Jewish-Hellenistic language, especially as it appears in the Septuagint (Swete, "Introduction to the O. T. in Greek," p. 291, Cambridge, 1900). Cities having Macedonian names were founded on Palestinian soil, such as Berœa, Dion, Pella. Certain weapons of the Macedonians are referred to by Josephus ("B. J." v. 11, § 3).

Many Jews must have lived in Macedonia, since Christian doctrines found a ready and early acceptance there. Paul visited the Macedonian regions on his second missionary journey (Acts xvi. 9; comp. I Cor. xvi. 5); his fellow workers Silas and Timothy labored there (Acts xvii. 14, xviii. 5). Paul visited it again on his third journey (Acts xx. 1; II Cor. i. 16, ii. 13, vii. 5), stopping in the cities Philippi, Thessalonica, and Berœa. Jewish inscriptions have been found in Thessalonica ("R. E. J." x. 78), and the presence of Jews in Macedonia is proved also by Agrippa's letter to Caligula (Philo, "Legatio ad Caium," § 36 [ed. Mangey, ii. 587]).

For an account of the Jews in Macedonia in modern times see TURKEY.

BIBLIOGRAPHY: Schürer, *Gesch.* iii. 27; Krauss, *Lehnwörter*, ii. 349.

G. S. KR.

MACHADO: Name of a family of Maranos which appears to have emigrated to America from Lisbon. The name is met with in Mexico and the West Indies at a very early date. As early as 1600 during the course of the trial of Jorge de Almeida by the Inquisition in Mexico, **Isabel Machado** and her father, **Antonio Machado,** were charged with being Jews. **Abraham de Macado** is mentioned as a resident of Martinique in 1680, and **M. Machado** is known to have been a planter in Surinam, about 1690.

The most important family bearing the name in America is the one in New York. It is descended from **David Mendez Machado,** who went from Lisbon, as a refugee from the Inquisition, to England, where he joined the emigrants going to Georgia, arriving at Savannah in 1733. David Mendez Machado married Zipporah, daughter of Dr. Samuel Nuñez, one of the early settlers of Georgia, and shortly afterward left Savannah for New York; there, in 1734, he became ḥazzan of the Spanish and Portuguese congregation Shearith Israel, with which he remained until his death in 1753. **Aaron Machado,** presumably a brother, became a freeman in New York in 1739. David Mendez Machado had two children: **Rebecca,** born in New York, 1746, married at Philadelphia, in 1762, Jonas Phillips (see PHILLIPS); and **Sarah,** married Mr. Moses of Charleston, S. C. Among the distinguished descendants of David Mendez Machado may be mentioned Commodore Uriah P. Levy, Henry M. Phillips, Jonas B. Phillips, Mordecai M. Noah, and N. Taylor Phillips.

Following is a family tree of the Machado family of New York :

David Mendez Machado = Zipporah Nuñez
(d. 1753) (d. 1799)

Sarah = Mr. Moses
Israel Moses
Raphael Moses
Raphael Moses, Jr.

Rebecca = (1762) Jonas Phillips
(1746–1831) (1736–1803)
21 children

BIBLIOGRAPHY: N. Taylor Phillips, *Family History of the Rev. David Mendez Machado*; *Publications Am. Jew. Hist. Soc.* ii. 45 *et seq.*; iv. 3; vi. 47, 128.

A. L. Hü.

MACHÆRUS: Mountain fortress in Peræa, on the boundary between Palestine and Arabia. Alexander Jannæus first built a fortification there (Josephus, "B. J." vii. 6, § 2). His wife Salome Alexandra turned over to the Sadducean party all the citadels with the exception of Hyrcania, Alexandrium, and Machærus (Josephus, "Ant." xiii. 16, § 3), where the Hasmoneans had their treasures. Gabinius advanced upon Machærus; Alexander surrendered, and the fortification was razed to the ground by the former ("Ant." xiv. 5, §§ 2, 4). Shortly afterward Aristobulus fortified himself there, and Gabinius captured the position again after a siege of two days ("B. J." i. 8, § 6). Herod restored it as a frontier fort against the Arabs, founded a walled city there, and built towers, turning the whole mountain-top into a fortification. In the middle of the fortified space he built a splendid palace ("B. J." vii. 6, § 2). According to Pliny ("Historia Naturalis," v. 16, § 72), it was, next to Jerusalem, the strongest fortress in Palestine. In the war against the Romans it was occupied by Jews after the Roman garrison had retired from it ("B. J." *l.c.*).

Not till two years after the fall of Jerusalem did Lucilius Bassus advance upon Machærus with a Roman army. The fort was defended by a heroic youth called Eleazar; he fell into the hands of the Romans and was to have been crucified; but the Jews, to save him, surrendered the city on condition that they be allowed a safe retreat. The Romans, however, broke their word; about 1,700 men were killed, and the women and children were sold as slaves; 3,000 Zealots who had joined the fugitives from Machærus were killed in a bloody battle near the Jordan (*ib.* vii. 6, §§ 1–6).

Several wonderful features of Josephus' narrative can be explained through Talmudic accounts. According to Josephus, in the Herodian palace was a rue which grew as high as a fig-tree ("B. J." vii. 6, § 2); with this statement should be compared Yer. Peah vii. 4 and Ket. 111b (see Winer, "B. R." *s.v.* "Senf"). Josephus says that from two hills in the vicinity flowed two springs, one warm and the other cold, and that together they afforded an agreeable and healthful bath; allusion is made to these hills in the Talmud also when it declares that the goats in the mountains of Machærus grew fat upon the odors from the Temple (Tamid 30; Yoma 39b), meaning probably odors from the mountain of Machærus itself, which was used as a signal-fire station for the announcement of New Moon (R. H. 23b; Tosef., R. H. ii. 2).

The spelling of the name Machærus varies in the rabbinical writings between מכוור and מכבר, also מכאוור; it was pronounced "Mekhawar" (comp. *Μαχαβέρως*, "Machaveros" in writings of the Middle Ages). Accordingly, *Μαχαιροῦς* in Josephus is probably only a Greek form of the Semitic name, and is not connected with *μαχαίρα* (= "knife"). Strabo (xvi. 2, § 40) and Stephen of Byzantium also mention the place. John the Baptist is said to have been killed at Machærus ("Ant." xviii. 5, § 2). It is identified with the present Mukaur, east of the Dead Sea (Raumer, "Palästina," p. 264; Brann, in "Monatsschrift," 1873, p. 345).

BIBLIOGRAPHY: Böttger, *Lexicon zu Fl. Josephus*, p. 165; Grätz, *Gesch.* 4th ed., iii. 548; Neubauer, *G. T.* pp. 40, 42; Schürer, *Gesch.* 3d ed., i. 638; *Ha-Lebanon*, v. 359.

G. S. Kr.

MACHIM, MASAHOD COHEN: Moorish envoy to England, in 1813, from Mulai Sulaiman, Emperor of Morocco (1794–1822), in whose reign Christian slavery was abolished in Morocco. His son **Meïr Cohen Machim** visited England in the same capacity in 1827.

BIBLIOGRAPHY: Picciotto, *Sketches of Anglo-Jewish History*, p. 174; M. Margoliouth, *History of the Jews in Great Britain*, ii. 197.

J. I. Co.

MACHIR: 1. The first-born son of Manasseh (Josh. xvii. 1; I Chron. vii. 14); founder of the most important or dominant branch of the tribe of Manasseh. His importance is shown by the collocation of Ephraim and Machir (instead of Manasseh) in Deborah's Song (Judges v. 14), which seems to imply that the whole tribe was once known by his name. This is confirmed by the statement that Machir was the only son of Manasseh (Num. xxvi. 29). In Gen. l. 23 the children of Machir are said to have been "born upon Joseph's knees" (R. V.), that is, they were adopted by Joseph (Gunkel, "Genesis," p. 442; Stade's "Zeitschrift," 1886, pp. 145 *et seq.*).

Machir removed to the east of the Jordan, conquered Gilead (Num. xxxii. 39, 40; Deut. iii. 15), and added Bashan to his territory. Hence Machir is spoken of as the father of Gilead (I Chron. ii. 21, 23; vii. 14; Num. xxvi. 29), and Gilead is called the son of Machir (Num. xxvii. 36; Josh. xvii. 3; I Chron. vii. 17). The conquest of Gilead is generally regarded as made not during the first invasion of the lands east of the Jordan, but subsequently by a reflex movement from western Palestine.

The Midrash (Num. R. xiv. 19) mentions three sons of Machir, for whom the three whole offerings referred to in Num. vii. 57 were brought by the chief of the tribe of Manasseh. These sons inherited the possessions of their brother Jair, who died childless.

2. Son of Ammiel, who had an estate at Lo-debar, east of the Jordan, not far from Mahanaim (II Sam. ix. 4 *et seq.*, xvii. 27). He remained faithful to the house of Saul, giving refuge to the son of Jonathan, Merib-baal, or Mephibosheth. Later, however, he showed his loyalty to David by supplying his army at Mahanaim during the rebellion of Absalom (Smith, "Samuel," pp. 310, 356, New York, 1900).

J. E. I. N.

MACHIR: A Babylonian scholar who settled in Narbonne, France, at the end of the eighth century and whose descendants were for many generations the leaders of that important community. According to a tradition preserved by Abraham ibn Daud in his "Sefer ha-Ḳabbalah," Machir was a descendant of the house of David. He was sent to Narbonne by the calif Harun al-Rashid at the request of Charlemagne, who, it is said, received the Babylonian scholar with great honor, conferred upon him and his descendants the title of "king of the Jews," and gave him a section of the city of Narbonne. Although this relation between Machir and Charlemagne is probably legendary, it is a fact that the Machir family enjoyed for centuries many privileges and that its members bore the title of "nasi" (prince). Benjamin of Tudela, who visited Narbonne in 1165, speaks of the exalted position occupied by the descendants of Machir, and the "Royal Letters" of 1364 (Doat Collection, pp. 53 *et seq.*, 339–353) also record the existence of a Jewish "king" at Narbonne. The place of residence of the Machir family at Narbonne was designated in official documents as "Cortada Regis Judæorum" (Saige, "Hist. des Juifs du Languedoc," p. 44). Machir is said to have founded a Talmudical school there which vied in greatness with those of Babylonia and which attracted pupils from many distant points.

Bibliography: Zacuto, *Yuḥasin*, ed. London, p. 84; Gross, in *Monatsschrift*, 1878, p. 250; 1881, p. 451; idem, *Gallia Judaica*, p. 404; Neubauer, in *R. E. J.* x. 100–103; Renan-Neubauer, *Les Rabbins Français*, pp. 561, 743.

E. C. I. Br.

MACHIR BEN ABBA MARI: Author of a work entitled "Yalḳuṭ ha-Makiri," but about whom not even the country or the period in which he lived is known. Steinschneider ("Jewish Literature," p. 143) supposes that Machir lived in Provence; but the question of his date remains a subject of discussion among modern scholars. The work itself is similar in its contents to the "Yalḳuṭ Shim'oni," with the difference that while the latter covers the whole Bible, Machir extended his compilation of Talmudic and midrashic sentences only to the books of Isaiah, Jeremiah, Ezekiel, the twelve Minor Prophets, Psalms, Proverbs, and Job. In the introductions, apparently very similar, to these books, Machir gives the reason which induced him to undertake such a work: he desired to gather the scattered haggadic sentences into one group. He seems to have thought it unnecessary to do the same thing for the Pentateuch and the Five Scrolls, as it had been done already, to a certain extent, in the Midrash Rabbah; but it may be concluded that Machir intended to make such a compilation on the earlier prophetical books also. From his introduction to the part on Isaiah it would seem that he began with Psalms and finished with Isaiah, though in his introduction to the part on the Psalms he mentions the other parts.

Machir used the following sources in his compilation: the two Talmuds, the Tosefta, the minor treatises, the Sifra, the Sifre, the Pesiḳta, Midrash Rabbah on the Pentateuch, Midrash Ḳohelet, Midrash Tehillim, Midrash Mishle, Midrash Iyyob, Midrash Tanḥuma, a Midrash quoted as ע״דשחנו, Pirḳe Rabbi Eli'ezer, Seder 'Olam, and Haggadat Shir ha-Shirim, frequently quoting the last-named Midrash in the part on Isaiah. Machir had another version of Deuteronomy Rabbah, of which only the part on the section "Debarim" exists now (comp. S. Buber, "Liḳḳuṭim mi-Midrash Eleh ha-Debarim Zuṭa," Introduction). It is difficult to ascertain whether Machir knew of the Midrash Yelammedenu; he quotes only Midrash Tanḥuma, but the passages which he cites are not found in the present text of that work, so that it is possible that he took these passages from the Yelammedenu.

Only the following parts of the "Yalḳuṭ ha-Makiri" are extant: Isaiah, published by I. Spira (Berlin, 1894; comp. Israel Lévi in "R. E. J." xxviii. 300) from a Leyden manuscript; Psalms, published by S. Buber (Berdychev, 1899) from two manuscripts (one, previously in the possession of Joseph b. Solomon of Vyazhin, was used by David Luria, and its introduction was published by M. Straschun in Fuenn's "Ḳiryah Ne'emanah," p. 304; the other is MS. No. 167 in the Bodleian Library); the twelve Minor Prophets (Brit. Mus., Harleian MSS., No. 5704); Proverbs, extant in a MS. which is in the possession of Grünhut ("Zeit. für Hebr. Bibl." 1900, p. 41), and which was seen by Azulai ("Shem ha-Gedolim," ii., *s.v.* "Yalḳuṭ ha-Makiri").

Gaster ("R. E. J." xxv. 43 *et seq.*) attached great importance to Machir's work, thinking that it was older than the "Yalḳuṭ Shim'oni," the second part of which at least Gaster concluded was a bad adaptation from the "Yalḳuṭ ha-Makiri." Gaster's conclusions, however, were contested by A. Epstein ("R. E. J." xxvi. 75 *et seq.*), who declares that Machir's "Yalḳuṭ" is both inferior and later than the "Yalḳuṭ Shim'oni." Buber conclusively proved, in the introduction to his edition of the "Yalḳuṭ ha-Makiri," that the two works are independent of each other, that Machir lived later than the author of the "Yalḳuṭ Shim'oni," and that he had not seen the latter work. Poznanski thinks that Machir lived in the fourteenth century.

BIBLIOGRAPHY: Poznanski, in *R. E. J.* xl. 282 *et seq.*, and the sources mentioned above.

E. C. M. SEL.

MACHIR BEN JUDAH: French scholar of the tenth and eleventh centuries; born at Metz; brother of Gershom Me'or ha-Golah. He is known by his dictionary entitled "Alfa Beta de-R. Makir," not extant, but quoted often by Rashi, RaSHBaM, Eliezer b. Nathan, Jacob Tam, and other tosafists. As the title indicates, the dictionary was arranged in alphabetical order, and from the many quotations by Rashi in his commentary on the Talmud (Ḥul. 20b; Pes. 50a *et passim*) it seems that it dealt chiefly with the difficult words and passages of the Talmud; but (by Rashi) he is quoted also for the interpretation of the word "botnim," in Gen. xliii. 11. Machir adopted for the most part the interpretations of his brother, who was Nathan ben Jehiel's teacher. Still he sometimes differed from his brother in the interpretation of words, and in such cases Nathan often adopted the opinion of Machir (comp. Jacob Tam, "Sefer ha-Yashar," p. 58b), though he never quotes him in his "'Aruk." The quotations from Machir by Rashi and the other rabbis mentioned above were collected by Solomon L. Rapoport in his biography of Nathan b. Jehiel ("Bikkure ha-'Ittim," x. 8, xi. 82).

BIBLIOGRAPHY: Fürst, *Bibl. Jud.* ii. 285; Michael, *Or ha-Ḥayyim*, No. 1104.

T. M. SEL.

MACHLUP, ADOLF: Hungarian merchant and philanthropist; born at Eisenstadt in 1833; died at Budapest Jan. 1, 1895. He studied at Budapest, and at the Polytechnic School in Vienna, and took part in the revolutionary movement of 1848. In 1867 he and his brother Eduard built at Budapest the first leather-factory in Hungary, and in 1868 the first factory for stearin candles and soap. Both these enterprises did much to advance Hungarian industry and trade. Machlup left large sums to many Jewish as well as non-Jewish societies, including a bequest of 200,000 gulden to found a nonsectarian Home for Convalescents in the city of Budapest.

BIBLIOGRAPHY: *Pallas Nagy Lexicon*.

S. L. V.

MACHORRO (מאגורו; spelled also **Machorre, Maczoro, Magoro**): Name of a family of Sephardim that flourished in Brazil, Germany, Holland, Hungary, and Italy. Thirteen persons bearing the name are buried in Altona, the earliest epitaph being dated 1620 and the latest 1782. A Jac[ob] de Dan[iel] Machorre was one of the contributors to an album which contained the autographs and verses of thousands of persons who had inspected Prof. D. Mill's model of the Temple of Solomon at Utrecht (*c.* 1748–57). Mention is made of a Maczoro, in Temesvar, Hungary, in 1772 **Abraham, Moses,** and **Solomon Machorro** flourished at Amsterdam about the middle of the seventeenth century. The first two were members of the society Temime Derek. Abraham is highly praised by De Barrios as one skilled equally in the use of the flute and of the pen. **Elijah Machorro,** a kinsman of Abraham Machorro, lived in Brazil about the same time. **Moses ben Daniel Machorro** was rabbi in Venice about 1693. One of his decisions with reference to the cutting of the hair on the "middle days" of the festivals ("ḥol ha-mo'ed") is published in Moses Ḥagiz' "Leḳeṭ ha-Ḳemaḥ," on Yoreh De'ah (pp. 31–32, Amsterdam, 1706; see BEARD). A Portuguese version of this responsum, not known to bibliographers, seems to have been circulated in Amsterdam about 1704 (comp. "Catalogue Cardozo," p. 75, Amsterdam, 1870). It is well worth mention that one of the numerous Maranos figuring in the trial of Gabriel de Granada in Mexico (1642–45) was named Juan Pacheco de Leon, alias Solomon Machorro ("Publications Am. Jew. Hist. Soc." No. 7, p. 3).

BIBLIOGRAPHY: De Barrios, *Relacion de los Poetas y Escritores Españoles*, p. 58; Wolf, *Bibl. Hebr.* iii. 103; Rios, *Estudios*, p. 568; Nepi-Ghirondi, *Toledot Gedole Yisrael*, p. 251, Triest, 1853; Kayserling, *Sephardim*, pp. 296, 360, 361; *idem*, in *R. E. J.* xviii. 287 (1889); *idem*, in *Bibl. Esp.-Port.-Jud.* pp. 23, 65, Strasburg, 1890; Mortara, *Indice*, p. 36, Padua, 1886; M. Grunwald, *Portugiesengräber auf Deutscher Erde*, p. 115, Hamburg, 1902; the sources cited by G. A. Kohut in *Publications Am. Jew. Hist. Soc.* No. 3, pp. 108–109.

A. G. A. K.

MACHPELAH.—Biblical and Post-Biblical Data: Name of a field and cave bought by Abraham as a burying-place. The meaning of the name, which always occurs with the definite article, is not clear; according to the Targumim and the Septuagint it means "the double," while Gesenius ("Th."), with more reason, connects it with the Ethiopic for "the portion." It appears to have been situated near Mamre, or Hebron, and to have belonged to Ephron the Hittite. Abraham needed a burying-place for Sarah, and bought the field of the Machpelah, at the end of which was a cave, paying four hundred silver shekels. The cave became the family burying-place, Sarah being the first to be buried there; later, Abraham, Isaac, Rebekah, Leah, and Jacob were placed there (Gen. xxiii. 9, 16–20; xxv. 9; xlix. 30–31; l. 13). It is designated twice only as the "cave" of the Machpelah (Gen. xxiii. 9, xxv. 9); in the other instances it is called "the cave of the field of the Machpelah" or "the cave in the field of the Machpelah." No further reference is made to it or to the burying-place of the Patriarchs, though some scholars find an allusion to it in II Sam. xv. 7, 8.

Josephus speaks of the purchase of Ephron's field at Hebron by Abraham as a place of burial and of the tombs (Μνημεῖα) built there by Abraham and his descendants, without, however, mentioning the name "Machpelah" ("Ant." i. 14, 22). In the twelfth century the cave of the Machpelah began to attract visitors and pilgrims, and this aroused the curiosity and wonder of the natives. Benjamin of Tudela relates: "At Hebron there is a large place of worship called 'St. Abraham,' which was previously a Jewish synagogue. The natives erected there six sepulchers, which they tell foreigners are those of the Patriarchs and their wives, demanding money as a condition of seeing them. If a Jew gives an additional fee to the keeper of the cave, an iron door which dates from the time of our forefathers opens, and the visitor descends with a lighted candle. He crosses two empty caves, and in the third sees six tombs, on which the names of the three Patriarchs and their wives are inscribed in

Hebrew characters. The cave is filled with barrels containing bones of people, which are taken there as to a sacred place. At the end of the field of the Machpelah stands Abraham's house with a spring in front of it" ("Itinerary," ed. Asher, pp. 40–42, Hebr.). Samuel b. Samson visited the cave in 1210; he says that the visitor must descend by twenty-four steps in a passageway so narrow that the rock touches him on either hand ("Pal. Explor. Fund," Quarterly Statement, 1882, p. 212). Now the cave is concealed by a mosque; this was formerly a church, built by the Crusaders between 1167 and 1187 and restored by the Arabs (comp. Stanley, "Sinai and Palestine," p. 149). See Hebron.

E. G. H. M. Sel.

——**In Rabbinical Literature:** The name of "Machpelah" (= "the doubled one") belongs, according to the Rabbis, to the cave alone, their reasons for the name being various: it was a double cave, with two stories (Rab); it contained pairs of tombs (Samuel); it had a double value in the eyes of people who saw it; any one buried there could expect a double reward in the future world; when God buried Adam there He had to fold him together (Abahu; 'Er. 53a; Gen. R. lviii. 10). Adam and Eve were the first pair buried there, and therefore Hebron, where the cave was situated, bore the additional name of "Kirjath-arba" (= "the city of four"; *i.e.*, of the tombs of Adam and Eve, Abraham and Sarah, Isaac and Rebekah, Jacob and Leah ('Er. 53a; Soṭah 13a; comp. Gen. R. lviii. 4).

Tomb of Adam and Eve.

According to Pirḳe R. El. xxxvi., the cave of Machpelah was at Jebus, and the reason that induced Abraham to buy it was the following: When Abraham went to fetch the calf for his guests (comp. Gen. xviii. 7) it escaped to the cave of Machpelah. Abraham ran after it, and when he entered the cave he saw Adam and Eve lying in their beds as though they were sleeping, while lighted candles were around them, exhaling a fragrant odor. Abraham, filled with a desire to possess the cave, determined to buy it at any price. The Jebusites, however, refused to sell it to him until he had sworn that when his descendants conquered the land of Canaan they would spare the city of Jebus (Jerusalem). Abraham accordingly took the oath, and the Jebusites inscribed it on brazen idols which they placed in the markets of the city. This was the reason why the children of Benjamin did not drive out the inhabitants of Jebus (Judges i. 21). Abraham secured his purchase of the cave of Machpelah by a formal deed signed by four witnesses: Amigal, son of Abishua the Hittite; Elihoreph, son of Ashunah the Hivite; 'Iddon, son of Ahira the Gardite; Aḳdul, son of 'Abudish the Zidonite ("Sefer ha-Yashar," section "Ḥayye Sarah," p. 37a, Leghorn, 1870).

After Isaac's death, Jacob, desirous of becoming sole owner of the cave of Machpelah, acquired Esau's part of it in exchange for all the riches left him by his father. This sale was also ratified by a document, which Jacob put in an earthen vessel to preserve it from decay (*ib.* section "Wayesheb," p. 77b). Nevertheless, at the burial of Jacob the cave was the subject of a violent dispute between Jacob's children and Esau. The latter opposed the burial of Jacob in the cave on the ground that there was room only for four pairs, and that Jacob, by burying Leah, had filled up his part. Naphtali returned to Egypt for the title-deed, but meanwhile Hushim, the son of Dan, struck Esau on the head with a stick so that the latter's eyes fell on Jacob's knees (Soṭah *l.c.*; comp. "Sefer ha-Yashar," *l.c.* pp. 97a–98a, where it is said that Hushim cut off Esau's head, which was buried on the spot). There is another tradition, to the effect that Esau was slain by Judah in the cave of Machpelah at Isaac's burial (Midr. Teh. xviii.; Yalḳ., Gen. 162).

Title-Deeds.

S. S. M. Sel.

MACROCOSM. See Microcosm and Macrocosm.

MADAI. See Media.

MADRID: Capital of Spain. Jews lived there as early as the twelfth century. By the old municipal law ("Fuero de Madrid") they were given the same privileges as the other inhabitants, with the one exception that Christian butchers were forbidden to sell "carne trefa" (meat which the ritual laws forbid Jews to eat), or any other flesh of animals slaughtered by Jews, under penalty of a fine of 10 maravedis or of imprisonment. A certain Yuçaf de Don Salomon Aben Çahal (Sahal) in Madrid, in the year 1336, sold a vineyard belonging to him situated in Ensiniella, near Madrid, to Garcia de Canillas; the deed, bearing the date of March 21, 1336, signed by Leon Çag (Isaac) Çaragoçi as witness, is printed in the "Boletin de la Real Academia de la Historia" (x. 160). In the years 1343 and 1369 Jews were living in villages in the neighborhood of Madrid—Parla, Torrejon de Vedasco, Polvoranca, Alcavendas, Barajas, and Coveña. Undoubtedly they were numerically insignificant, for in the year 1474 the taxes of the Jews in Madrid, Ciempozuelos, Pinto, Barajas, and Torrejon de Vedasco amounted to only 1,200 maravedis. In the year 1384 the monastery of S. Domingo in Madrid received from King John I. an annuity of 3,000 maravedis, payable from the taxes of the Jews.

As was the case with the Jews in the remainder of Castile in 1391, of those in Madrid some were plundered and murdered and others were forcibly baptized. The city council, as in Valencia, demanded the punishment of the rioters and their leaders; some were captured, and others, among them Ruy Sanchez de Urosco, Lope Fernandez and Diego de Vargas, and Ruy Garcia de la Torre, took to flight; the government empowered the council to confiscate the property of those found guilty. The destruction of the Jewry in Madrid inflicted great loss upon the monastery of S. Domingo. The Jewry was situated in the Calle de la Fé, in the immediate vicinity of Las Damas street and next to the S. Laurencia Church; this street contained the synagogue, and until 1492 was known as "Synagogue street." After 1391 the Jewry was rebuilt. By an order of Ferdinand and Isabella of May 28, 1480, it was surrounded by a wall, the gates of which were locked at dusk.

Several Jewish physicians lived in Madrid. One of them, Rabbi Jacob, was privileged (Nov. 9, 1481) to live outside the Jewry, so that he might visit his patients at night unhindered. As physicians or surgeons there were appointed by the council, in 1481 and 1489, Don Juda and his son Maestre Zulema (Salomon) and Rabbi Jacob (probably the one already mentioned) and his son Rabbi Joseph. The Jews were compelled to take part in the public church festivals. At one of these festivals, held on June 22, 1480, both the Jews and the Moors in Madrid were compelled to give an exhibition of the dancing peculiar to their respective races.

Since 1869 Jews have again begun to live in Madrid, going there from Tunis, Mogador, Lisbon, Alexandria, and from various cities in France and elsewhere—about twenty families in all. They have not formed a congregation nor consecrated a cemetery; but they hold services on New-Year and on the Day of Atonement in a private house.

BIBLIOGRAPHY: Rios, *Hist.* i. 195, iii. 568, 591; Fidel Fida, *Estudios Historicos*, v. 77 *et seq.*; *R. E. J.* xiii. 245 *et seq.*

G. M. K.

MAFṬIR: 1. The reader of the concluding portion of the Pentateuchal section on Sabbaths and holy days in the synagogue. On regular Sabbaths that portion forms a part of the section read by the seventh reader, and is repeated by the one appointed to read the Hafṭarah. For special Sabbaths and holy days the maftir reads a separate Pentateuchal portion bearing on the occasion. Such was the custom established by Rashi and his teachers. But the general custom of the congregations in France was that the maftir on such occasions recited the last portion of the regular lesson besides reading the special one (Meg. 23a). All congregations have since accepted the decision of Rashi. The mafṭir is not counted in the quorum of readers, which must not be less than seven on Sabbaths or than five on holy days. Since the mafṭir repeats but a few sentences and is not counted in the necessary quorum, it was held that he received somewhat less honor than the other readers, and therefore he was compensated in Talmudic times by being granted the privilege of reading the "Shema'" and the "'Amidah" on the same day (Meg. iv. 6, 24a).

2. The reader of the Hafṭarah. He should not begin to read the Hafṭarah unless he has previously read a portion of the Torah (Meg. 23a); nor should he read the Hafṭarah until the scroll is rolled up (Soṭah 39b). The text of the Hafṭarah must not be less than twenty-one verses in the books of the Prophets, three verses being thus allowed for each of the seven readers of the Torah (Meg. 23a). The benedictions recited by the mafṭir (other than the two for the reading of the Pentateuchal portion) are five—one before and four after the Hafṭarah; they are mentioned in Soferim xiii. 9. The first benediction begins with "Praised be the Lord, . . . who chose goodly prophets and approved their words spoken in truth"; the end of the second benediction reads, "who is faithful in all His words"; the third ends with "who is building Jerusalem"; the fourth with "the shield of David"; the fifth with "who sanctified the Sabbath" (or "the holy days"). Maimonides copied the older version reading "building Jerusalem"; but R. Abraham ben David amends this to "who maketh Zion joyful through her children," which version has since been retained.

The reading of the Hafṭarah is generally reserved for a bar miẓwah, or for a bridegroom on the Sabbath before his marriage. On Shebu'ot, after the first benediction and before the Hafṭarah, the mafṭir recites a poem beginning "Yeẓib pitgam."

3. Sometimes, the usher or sexton whose duty it was to watch at the conclusion of the prayer-service at the synagogue and to gather and usher in the students in the bet ha-midrash. 'Awira Shammai was a mafṭir for the yeshibah of the "great teacher" (perhaps Judah ha-Nasi I.; Ḥul. 51a). See BAR MIẒWAH; HAFṬARAH; LAW, READING FROM THE.

BIBLIOGRAPHY: Dembitz, *Jewish Services in Synagogue and Home*, pp. 264, 276.

A. J. D. E.

MAGAZIN FÜR DIE WISSENSCHAFT DES JUDENTHUMS: Journal founded by Dr. Abraham Berliner Jan. 1, 1874. It appeared first as a bimonthly, in quarto form, under the title "Magazin für Jüdische Geschichte und Literatur," and contained a series of articles by Berliner on Hebrew manuscripts in the Italian libraries, besides studies in the history of Jewish culture, criticisms of new publications, extracts from midrashim, etc. Many of the most prominent Jewish scholars were contributors, and the success of the magazine justified Berliner in enlarging its scope. With its third volume (1876) it was changed to an octavo quarterly in order that lengthier and more strictly scientific articles (exegetical, philological, historical) might be admitted, its title became "Magazin für die Wissenschaft des Judenthums," a special Hebrew supplement ("'Oẓar Ṭob") was added to contain principally material from unpublished Hebrew manuscripts, and Dr. David Hoffmann became associated in the editorship. The excellence of the contributions, including many by the editors and by such scholars as Steinschneider, D. Kaufmann, D. Oppenheim, M. Wolff, Harkavy, A. Epstein, and Bacher, was maintained for twenty years, when pressure of other duties compelled the editors to suspend publication (1893).

J. W. P.

MAGDALA: Town in Palestine in the province of Galilee; probably the birthplace of Mary Magdalene. There is a Talmudic sentence which declares that Magdala was destroyed (by the Romans) on account of its immorality (Lam. R. ii. 2). Jesus once went to Magdala by ship on the Sea of Gennesaret (Matt. xv. 39; even if the reading Μαγαδάν [= Μαγαδάλ] be accepted in place of Μαγδαλά, it must be inferred that Magdala is meant). Because he made the journey by boat some have held that the town was on the eastern shore of the sea; such a conclusion is not necessary, however, and Magdala was more probably on the western shore, perhaps the present Al-majdal, a small village an hour and a quarter north of Tiberias.

Rabbinical accounts are clear only in indicating Magdala as situated near Tiberias. In Tosef., 'Er. vi. 13 (ed. Zuckermandel, p. 145; comp. Yer. 'Er. v. 22d, where the description is more detailed and accurate), it is true, Tiberias is placed near Gadara also, which latter place is known to have been situated east of the Jordan. But the proximity to Tiberias is noted also in Yer. Ma'as iii. 50c; and

Simeon ben Laḳish, who had a quarrel with the patriarch, fled to Magdala from the neighboring Tiberias (Yer. Sanh. ii. 19d; Hor. iii. 47a). There were in Magdala a seminary or a synagogue, and a school for children (Eccl. R. x. 8). In several passages in the Talmud and Midrash "Magdala" occurs as a variant of "Migdal Ẓabba'aya" (tower of the dyers). Neubauer is consequently of the opinion that the latter as well as other names compounded with "Migdal" refers to a quarter in the town of Magdala; but this is not the case. Only so much is certain, that a few teachers of the Law were born in Magdala—*e.g.*, R. Isaac (B. M. 25a) and Yudan (Yer. Ber. ix. 14a; Ta'an. i. 64b). In the Talmud besides the usual Aramaic name "Magdala" the Hebrew form "Migdol" occasionally occurs (*e.g.*, Tosef. 'Er. vi. 13). This is without significance, however, as is shown by the fact that the Biblical "Migdol" is regularly rendered by the Septuagint as Μάγδωλος (*e.g.*, in Num. xxxiii. 7).

Bibliography: Winer, *B. R.*; Neubauer, *G. T.* p. 217; Lightfoot, *Horæ Hebraicæ*, p. 136.

G. S. Kr.

MAGDEBURG: Capital of the Prussian province of Saxony; situated on the Elbe. It has a population of 229,633, of whom about 2,000 are Jews. There were Jews at Magdeburg as early as the tenth century. The district occupied by them lay without the city and was called "Judendorf zu Magdeburg" (Hagedorn, in "Geschichtsblätter für Stadt und Land Magdeburg," xx. 93). Politically as well as geographically they belonged to the archbishopric of Magdeburg rather than to the town; probably they never lived within the city itself. The first inflow of Jews to Magdeburg is supposed to have been from the Rhine district, but the date when this took place is unknown. The earliest mention of them there occurs in a document of Otto the Great, dated July 9, 965, in which the "Jews and other traders" living in the city are placed under the exclusive control and jurisdiction of the Archbishop of Magdeburg (Aronius, "Regesten zur Gesch. der Juden in Deutschland," p. 55). The way in which Jews are described in this and in a similar document of Otto II. dated June 4, 973 (Aronius, *l.c.* p. 56), justifies the inference that even at that period they formed a community of fair size and were of such importance commercially that they contributed materially to the prosperity of Magdeburg. If Westberg's view is correct that the word "Maznbrgh," found in an Arabic source, is a corruption of "Magdeburg," it was there that the Judæo-Arabic traveler Ibrahim ibn Ya'ḳub "the Israelite" appeared in 965 at the court of Otto the Great, perhaps as a member of an embassy from Cordova, and obtained from the emperor valuable information concerning the Slavs, which he used in the account of his travels, written in Arabic.

Under the Archbishop.

The history of the Jews in Magdeburg in the succeeding centuries resembles in all respects the record of other Jewish communities in Germany during the Middle Ages. It may be inferred that they were prosperous from the fact that many Jews of Magdeburg accompanied the funeral procession of Archbishop Walthard in 1012 and manifested their grief in lamentations (see Aronius, *l.c.* p. 61). On the other hand, the First Crusade (1096) is said to have caused the expulsion of the Jews from the Judendorf (Aronius, *l.c.* p. 93; comp. p. 111). In a communication from Pope Innocent III. to the clergy of the archbishopric of Magdeburg, dated Dec. 31, 1199, in which they are urged to come to the assistance of the Christians in the Orient, there is the provision that the secular arm shall compel the Jews to release their Christian debtors from paying interest and that, until they shall have done so, they shall not be permitted to have any intercourse with Christians (Aronius, *l.c.* p. 155). How far this regulation was observed is unknown. Archbishop Albrecht of Magdeburg, although friendly to the Jews, could not prevent the destruction of the Judendorf in 1213 by the troops of Otto IV. (A. Levy, "Gesch. der Juden in Sachsen," p. 8, Berlin, 1900). In 1261, on the Feast of Tabernacles of that year, when Jews from other cities were in the Judendorf, Archbishop Robert, finding it necessary to refill his empty coffers, seized their money and valuables, and held the richest of them for high ransoms. He seems to have done the same at Halle; no less than 100,000 silver marks are said to have been extorted from the Jews of the two cities (Aronius, *l.c.* p. 281; M. Spanier, "Zur Gesch. der Juden in Magdeburg," in "Zeitschrift für die Gesch. der Juden in Deutschland," v. 273). His successor as archbishop, Conrad of Sternberg, was unfriendly to the Jews on religious grounds.

Early Middle Ages.

Judendorf Destroyed 1213.

The religious fanaticism awakened by the Crusades and the desire of the cities for independence found vent at this time in wholesale persecutions of the Jews. When in 1301 a Christian girl from the Judendorf circulated the rumor that the Jews had nailed an image of Jesus to a cross, recrucifying him in effigy, the citizens fell upon the ghetto, plundered it, and killed some Jews and drove others away. A document of 1312 has been preserved, according to which the Jews bought four fields for the extension of their cemetery. At the time of the Black Death (1348) the citizens and peasants of the vicinity again fell upon the Judendorf, pillaged it, and burned many Jews in their houses. This time, however, Archbishop Otto and the magistrate Von Vorn took the Jews under their protection, so that the uprising gained little headway, although during it the rabbi of the community, Rabbi Shalom, died the death of a martyr (see Salfeld, "Martyrologium," p. 247; comp. p. 284). A tombstone in the old Jewish cemetery also names a martyr, Samuel, of the year 1356. Between 136[illegible] and 1367 Archbishop Dietrich employed a Jewish court banker, Schmoll or Shemuel. In 1385, according to a document, the cemetery was again enlarged. This fact, together with the names mentioned in this record, justifies the conclusion that the community was growing considerably at that time through additions from other cities.

Persecutions, 1301 and 1348.

In 1410 Archbishop Günther issued a patent to the Jews of Magdeburg, assuring them of his protection for six years, in return for which they were to pa[y] tax of 40 silver marks in half-yearly payments. 'his patent, however, which contains benevolent rovisions regarding the legal status of the Jewish ommunity, was not meant seriously, for in the fol-owing year Günther would have extorted money 'om the Judendorf had not the citizens of Magde-urg frustrated his design lest they should lose the ecurities they had deposited with the Jews. When rnst von Sachsen entered the city as archbishop in ie year 1476, the Jews also did homage to him; ut in 1492 the archbishop, yielding to the inflamed assions of the citizens and the clergy, decreed the banishment of the Jews from Magdeburg on account of an unimportant altercation between two Jews and two monks. The edict was enforced nine ionths later after the council of Sudenburg had aid the Jews the equivalent of their houses and oods. More than 1,400 emigrated. The syna-ogue of the Judendorf was turned into a chapel in onor of the Virgin Mary and named "Marienka-elle," and the name "Judendorf" was changed to Mariendorf" (see H. A. Erhard, "Das Judendorf ei Magdeburg und der Erzbischof Ernst zu Magde-urg, Judenverfolgung im Jahre 1493," in Lede-ur's "Archiv für die Geschichtskunde des Preussi-hen Staates," 1830, i. 318).

Banished 1492.

Of the internal life of the community up to the me of its banishment very little is known. It ibmitted religious questions to Meïr Rothenburg l. 1293; Responsa, No. 32, ed. Cremona, 1557) and various French scholars. At the time of Isaac en Moses of Vienna (1200-70) there lived in Mag-eburg a Rabbi Hezekiah ben Jacob, with whom ie former was in correspondence (Steinschneider, Hebr. Bibl." viii. 2). In the fifteenth century Ja-ob Mölln mentions a scholar, Rabbi Isaac, of Magde-urg ("Minhagim," Hilkot Ḥanukkah). At that me the community seems to have been active and ourishing and to have had a yeshibah which was ttended also by students from other places, who ere assured of safe-conduct by a patent of protec-on issued in 1410.

After the banishment (1493) no Jew was allowed ie right to settle in Magdeburg, whose magistrate, in a letter to the king dated Sept. 14, 1711, speaks of that right as "a high royal favor." It was not until 1720 that a Jew, Gumpert by name, ob-ained permission to reside in the Altstadt of Magde-urg, and up to 1806 only one protected Jew at a me enjoyed this privilege. If Jews attempted to emain in the Neustadt, the council of the city was oon forced to expel them, as is seen from the case f Lewin Bauer (see M. Spanier, *l.c.* pp. 392 *et seq.*).

Permission to Return.

The present community did not come into exist-nce until the third decade of the nineteenth century. s first preacher, who was also the principal of the ewly founded religious school of the community he first of its kind in North Germany), was udwig Philippson, who was rabbi from 1833 1862 (Kayserling, "Ludwig Philippson," pp. 47 *seq.*, Leipsic, 1898). Philippson, in his reminis-ences, speaks of an old rabbi named Salme, to whom e was for a time assistant. Philippson was suc-eeded as rabbi by M. Güdemann (1862-66) and M. Rahmer (1869-1904). A new synagogue was built in the city of Magdeburg in the years 1850-51. The community has a burial association, institutions for the support of invalids, widows, and orphans, various other benevolent foundations, a Jewish women's society, and a society for Jewish history and literature.

Bibliography: Güdemann, *Zur Gesch. der Juden in Magdeburg*, Breslau, 1866 (= *Monatsschrift*, xiv. 241 *et seq.*); *Statistisches Jahrbuch des Deutsch-Israelitischen Gemeindebundes*, 1903, p. 46.

D. M. Sc.

MAGDEBURG LAW (MAGDEBURG RIGHTS): General name for a system of privileges "securing the administrative independence of municipalities," which was adopted in many parts of Germany, Poland, and Bohemia ("Encyc. Brit."). Usually it was introduced into the Slavic countries at the instance and for the benefit of the German merchants and artisans, who formed the most important part of the population of many cities. Jews and Germans were always competitors in those cities, and as the Jews lived under special privileges and were not considered a part of the native population, not only were they excluded from participating in the benefits of the Magdeburg law, but their condition usually was rendered worse wherever it was introduced. In Wilna, where the Magdeburg law was granted to the municipality as early as the fourteenth century, the Jews were expressly excluded from its benefits, but in the near-by city of Troki the Jewish community secured from Grand Duke Casimir Jagellon the Magdeburg rights for itself, and independently of the Christian community, which had received the same rights earlier. This grant, dated March 27, 1444, gave the Jews of Troki equal rights with their Christian neighbors (see Lithuania).

One of the most interesting provisions of the Magdeburg law relating to Jews was that a Jew could not be made "Gewaersmann," that is, he could not be compelled to tell from whom he acquired any object which had been sold or pledged to him and which was found in his possession. This actually amounted to permission to buy stolen property.

Bibliography: Bershadski, *Litovskie Yevrei*, pp. 221, 234, 241 *et seq.*; Fuenn, *Ḳiryah Ne'emanah*, p. 6, Wilna, 1860.

H. R. P. Wi.

MAGEN DAWID ("David's shield"): The hexagram formed by the combination of two equilateral triangles; used as the symbol of Judaism. It is placed upon synagogues, sacred vessels, and the like, and was adopted as a device by the American Jewish Publication Society in 1873 (see illustration, Jew. Encyc. i. 520), the Zionist Congress of Basel (*ib.* ii. 570)—hence by "Die Welt" (Vienna), the official organ of Zionism—and by other bodies. The ḥebra ḳaddisha of the Jewish community of Johannesburg, South Africa, calls itself "Ḥebra Ḳaddisha zum Rothen Magen David," following the designation of the "red cross" societies.

The Jewish view of God, which permitted no images of Him, was and still is opposed to the acceptance of any symbols, and neither the Bible nor the Talmud recognizes their existence. It is noteworthy, moreover, that the shield of David is not mentioned in rabbinical literature. The "Magen Dawid," therefore, probably did not originate within

Rabbinism, the official and dominant Judaism for more than 2,000 years. Nevertheless, a David's shield has recently been noted on a Jewish tombstone at Tarentum, in southern Italy, which may date as early as the third century of the common

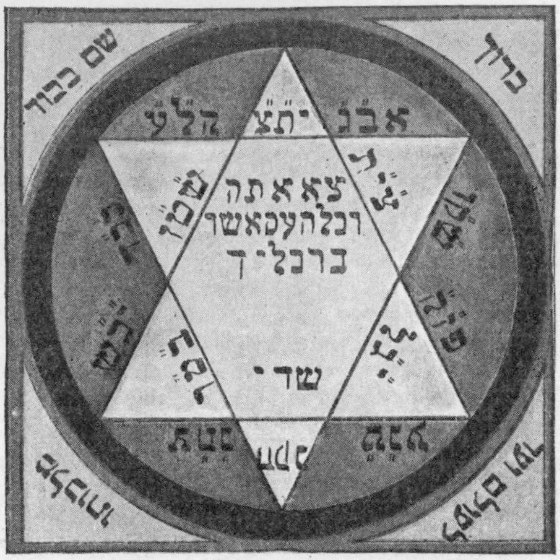

A "Magen Dawid" from a "Mizraḥ."

era (see Herbert M. Adler in "J. Q. R." xiv. 111). The earliest Jewish literary source which mentions it, the "Eshkol ha-Kofer" of the Karaite Judah Hadassi (middle of the 12th cent.), says, in ch. 242: "Seven names of angels precede the mezuzah: Michael, Gabriel, etc. . . . Tetragrammaton protect thee! And likewise the sign called 'David's shield' is placed beside the name of each angel." It was, therefore, at this time a sign on amulets.

Magic Papyri.

In the magic papyri of antiquity, pentagrams, together with stars and other signs, are frequently found on amulets bearing the Jewish names of God—"Sabaoth," "Adonai," "Eloai"—and used to guard against fever and other diseases (Wessely, "Neue Zauberpapyri," pp. 68, 70, and note). Curiously enough, only the pentacle appears, not the hexagram. In the great magic papyrus at Paris and London there are twenty-two signs side by side, and a circle with twelve signs, but neither a pentacle nor a hexagram (Wessely, *l.c.* pp. 31, 112), although there is a triangle, perhaps in place of the latter. In the many illustrations of amulets given by Budge in his "Egyptian Magic" (London, 1899) not a single pentacle or hexagram appears. The syncretism of Hellenistic, Jewish, and Coptic influences did not, therefore, originate the symbol. It is probable that it was the Cabala that derived the symbol from the Templars (see Vajda in "Magyar Zsidó Szemle," xvii. 314 *et seq.*; German reprint in Grunwald's "Mitteilungen der Gesellschaft für Jüdische Volkskunde," x. 138 *et seq.*). The Cabala, in fact, makes use of this sign, arranging the Ten Sefirot, or spheres, in it, and placing it on amulets (see illustrations, Jew. Encyc. i. 181, 550; iii. 475).

The pentagram, called **Solomon's seal,** is also used as a talisman, and Henry thinks that the Hindus derived it from the Semites ("Magie dans l'Ind Antique," p. 93, Paris, 1904), although the name b

Solomon's Seal.

no means proves the Jewish or Semiti origin of the sign. The Hindus lik wise employed the hexagram as means of protection, and as such i is mentioned in the earliest source, quoted abov In the synagogues, perhaps, it took the place of th mezuzah, and the name "shield of David" ma have been given it in virtue of its protective pow ers. The hexagram may have been employed orig nally also as an architectural ornament on syn agogues, as it is, for example, on the cathedrals o Brandenburg and Stendal, and on the Marktkirche a Hanover. A pentacle in this form, ✡, is found on th ancient synagogue at Tell Hum. Charles IV. pr scribed for the Jews of Prague, in 1354, a red fla with both David's shield and Solomon's sea while the red flag with which the Jews met Kin Matthias of Hungary in the fifteenth century showe two pentacles with two golden stars (Schwandtne "Scriptores Rerum Hungaricarum," ii. 148). Th pentacle, therefore, may also have been used amon the Jews. It occurs in a manuscript as early as th year 1073 (facsimile in M. Friedmann, "Seder Eliyah Rabbah we-Seder Eliyahu Zuṭa," Vienna, 1901).

Bibliography: M. Grunwald, *Jahrb. für Jüdische Gesc und Literatur*, vol. iv., Berlin, 1901; *Mitteilungen de Gesellschaft für Jüdische Volkskunde*, x. 137–140, Hambur 1902; B. Vajda, *Zur Gesch. des Davidsschildes*, in *Magyo Zsidó Szemle*, 1900, xvii. 310–322; Zunz, *Ritus*, p. 149 (th 67th Psalm on David's shield in the form of the menorah); Mayer, *Der Aberglaube des Mittelalters*, p. 257, Basel, 188

J. L. B.

MAGGID. See Cabala.

MAGGID: Itinerant preacher, skilled as a na rator of stories. A preacher of the more scholar sort was called "darshan" and usually occupied th official position of rabbi. The title of "maggi mesharim" (= "a preacher of uprightness"; a breviated מ"מ) probably dates from the sixteent century. There always have been two distin classes of leaders in Israel—the scholar and rabb and the preacher or maggid. That the popul prophet was sometimes called "maggid" is mai tained by those who translate "maggid mishne Zech. ix. 12, by "the maggid repeats" (Löw "Beḳoret ha-Talmud," p. 50). Like the Greek sop ists, the early maggidim based their preaching o questions addressed to them by the multitude. Th the Pesiḳta, the first collection of set speeches, usual begins with "yelammedenu rabbenu" (= "let o master teach us"). An excellent example is th Passover Haggadah, which is introduced by fo questions; the reciter of the answer is call "maggid." When there were no questions the ma gid chose a Biblical text, which was called th "petiḥah" (opening).

The greater popularity of the maggid as compar with the darshan is instanced by the fact that th

Popularity of the Maggid.

people left the lecture-room of R. Ḥiyya, the darshan, and flocked hear R. Abbahu, the maggid. To ap pease the sensitive Ḥiyya, Abbah modestly declared, "We are like tw merchants, one selling diamonds and the other sellin trinkets, which are more in demand" (Soṭah 40a 'almudists like R. Meïr combined the functions of darshan and a maggid (Sanh. 38b). When R. saac Nappaḥa was requested by one in his audience) preach a popular haggadah, and by another a alakic discourse, he answered, "I am like the man 'ho had two wives, one young and one old, and ich wishing her husband to resemble her in apearance; the younger pulled out his gray hair 'hile the older pulled out his black hair, with the esult that he became entirely bald." R. Isaac iereupon delivered a lecture that embraced both alakah and haggadah (B. Ḳ. 60b).

Levi ben Sisi, his son Joshua, and others were at ie head of a regular school of rabbinical maggidim. . Ze'era was opposed to their methods of twisting ud distorting the Biblical verses to suit their moientary fancy. In Ze'era's estimation their works 'ere of no more value than books on magic (Yer. Ia'as. iii. 9). In the geonic period and in the Midle Ages the principal of the yeshibah, or the rabbi, elivered a lecture before each festival, giving instructions in the laws governing the days of the festival. The maggid's function was to preach to the common people in the vernacular whenever ccasion required, usually on Sabbath afternoon, asing his sermon on the sidra of the week. The 'andering, or traveling, maggid then began to apear, and subsequently became a power in Jewry. lis mission was to preach morality, to awaken the ormant spirit of Judaism, and to keep alive the Mesanic hope in the hearts of the people. The maggidim's deliverances were generally lacking in literry merit, and were composed largely of current hrases, old quotations, and Biblical interpretations 'hich were designed merely for temporary effect; herefore none of the sermons which were delivered y them have been preserved.

In Geonic Times.

Maggidism reached a period of high literary activ:y in the sixteenth century. The expulsion of the ews from Spain in 1492 revealed a master magid in Isaac ABRAVANEL. His homiletic commenary on the Bible became an inexhaustible source of uggestion for future maggidim. In his method of xplaining every chapter, preceded by a number of uestions, he followed the early maggidim and ophists. His long argumentations in an easy and 'uent style were admirably suited to the purposes of maggid. Moses ALSHECH, a maggid in Safed, 'alestine, preached every Sabbath before large audinces. In his commentaries he followed closely the iethod of Abravanel. Alshech also became an auhority for the maggidim, who quoted him freuently.

The persecutions of the Jews brought forth a umber of maggidim who endeavored to excite the Messianic hope as a balm to the troubled and oppressed Jewry. Asher LEMMLEIN preached in Germany and Austria, announcing the coming of the Messiah in 1502, and found credence verywhere. Solomon MOLKO preached, without delaring the date of the advent, in both Italy and Tur:ey, and as a result was burned at the stake in Mantua n 1533. R. Höschel of Cracow (d. 1663) delighted n the elucidation of difficult passages in the midrash known as the "Midrash Peli'ah" (= "wonderful" or "obscure" midrash). H. Ersohn's biography of Höschel, in his "Ḥanukkat ha-Torah" (Pietrkov, 1900), gives a collection of 227 "sayings" gathered from 227 books by various writers, mostly Höschel's pupils. These sayings became current among the maggidim, who repeated them on every occasion. Some maggidim copied his methods and even created a pseudo-Midrash Peli'ah for the purpose of explaining the original ingeniously in the manner initiated by R. Höschel.

Relation to Messianism.

Elijah b. Solomon Abraham of Smyrna, in the beginning of the eighteenth century, published his "Shebeṭ Musar," which he divided into fifty-two chapters, one for each week. This book caused him to be known as the "Terror Maggid"; he preached moral and religious conduct as a safeguard against the terrible punishments of the day of judgment. Dante could not picture the horrors of hell and the punishments awaiting the wicked more minutely than did the author of the "Shebeṭ Musar." It established a new "fire and brimstone" school of maggidim. Judah Rosanes of Constantinople (d. 1727), in his "Parashat Derakim," combined the darshan with the maggid. He adopted a new method of harmonizing the acts of Biblical personages with the legal views of Talmudic scholars. For instance, Pharaoh, in refusing to release Israel from bondage, acted according to the contention of Abaye, while Moses insisted on Israel's release in accordance with the decision of Rabba. This far-fetched pilpulism had many followers, some of whom asserted that Ahasuerus concurred in the decision of Maimonides, and that Vashti coincided with the opinion of RaBaD.

The "Shebeṭ Musar."

Jacob Kranz of Dubno, the "Dubner Maggid" (d. 1804), author of "Ohel Ya'aḳob," adopted the Midrash's method of explaining by parables and the incidents of daily life, such as the relations between the man of the city and the "yeshubnik" (village man), between the bride, the bridegroom, and the "meḥuttanim" (contracting parents), and compared their relations to those between Israel and YHWH or between the Gentiles and the Jews. He drew also moral lessons from the "Arabian Nights" and from other secular stories in illustrating explanations of a midrash or a Biblical text. Moses Mendelssohn named Kranz the "Jewish Æsop." Kranz's pupil Abraham Bär Plahm and a host of other maggidim adopted this method. In the same period there were Jacob Israel of Kremnitz, author of "Shebeṭ mi-Yisrael," a commentary on the Psalms (Zolkiev, 1772); Judah Löw Edel of Slonim, author of "Afiḳe Yehudah," sermons (Lemberg, 1802); Ḥayyim Abraham Katz of Moghilef, author of "Milḥamak be-Shalom" (Shklov, 1797); Ezekiel Feiwel of Deretschin, author of "Toledot Adam" (Dyhernfurth, 1809) and maggid in Wilna (Levinsohn, "Bet Yehudah," ii. 149).

The "Dubner Maggid."

The most celebrated maggid during the nineteenth century was Moses Isaac ben Noah Darshan, the "Kelmer Maggid" (b. 1828; d. 1900, in Lida). He was among the "terror" maggidim of the "Shebeṭ Musar" school and preached to crowded synagogues for over fifty years in almost every city of Russian Poland. Another prominent maggid was Ḥayyim Ẓedeḳ, known as the "Rumsheshker" (Gersoni, "Sketches of Jewish Life and History," pp. 62–74, New York, 1873). The "philosophical" maggid is one who preaches from Arama's "Aḳedat" and Baḥya's "Ḥobot ha-Lebabot." Enoch Sundl Luria, the author of "Kenaf Renanim," on "Pirḳe Shirah" (Krotoschin, 1842), was a noted philosophical maggid.

Philosophical Maggidim.

Meïr Leibush Malbim (d. 1880), in his voluminous commentaries on the Bible, followed to some extent Abravanel and Alshech, and his conclusions are pointed and logical. Malbim's commentaries are considered to offer the best material for the use of maggidim.

From the "terror," or "Musar," maggid developed the "penitential" maggid, who, especially during the month of Elul and the ten days of penitence between New-Year's Day and Yom Kippur, urged the wicked to repent of their sins and seek God's forgiveness. Jacob Joseph, chief rabbi of the Russian Jews in New York (d. 1902), formerly maggid of Wilna, was one of these. In the middle of his preaching he would pause to recite with the people the "Shema'," the "Ḳolenu," and the "Ashamnu," raising the audience to a high pitch of religious emotion. The maggid usually ends his preaching with the words, "u-ba le-Ẓiyyon goel," etc. (a redeemer shall come to Zion speedily in our days; let us say "Amen"). Some of the wandering maggidim act also as meshullaḥim. The yeshibot in Russia and the charitable institutions of Jerusalem, especially the Wa'ad ha-Kelali, send abroad meshullaḥ-maggidim. The resident maggid who preaches at different synagogues in one city is called the "Stadt Maggid," as in Wilna and other large cities in Russia. The modern, or "maskil," maggid is called "Volksredner" (people's orator), and closely follows the German "Prediger" in his method of preaching. Ẓebi Hirsch Dainow (d. 1877) was the first of the modern type of maggid, which soon developed into that of the "national," or "Zionistic," maggid. Hirsch Masliansky and Joseph Zeff, both of New York, are representatives of the latter class. See HOMILETICS.

BIBLIOGRAPHY: G. Deutsch, *The Decline of the Pulpit*, in *American Hebrew*, 1899, No. 17; *Dor Dor u-Darshanim*, in *Ha-Yom*, 1887, No. 213.

J. J. D. E.

MAGGID (STEINSCHNEIDER), HILLEL NOAH: Russian genealogist and historian; a descendant of the family of Saul Wahl; born at Wilna 1829; died there Oct. 29, 1903. His father was a bibliographer, and his grandfather Phinehas was rabbi at Polotsk and Wilna, the emissary of Elijah of Wilna in his struggle with the Ḥasidim, and the author of nine exegetical works. Having lost his father at the age of eighteen, Maggid learned the calling of a lapidary, but not content with cutting epitaphs on tombstones and monuments, he occasionally composed inscriptions. He early joined the Progressionists of Wilna, among whom were Fuenn, Lebensohn, and M. A. Günzburg. He indulged his taste for general literature and published various articles and bibliographical papers in the current Hebrew periodicals. Among these may be noted his biography of David Oppenheim, rabbi of Prague (in "Gan Peraḥim," 1882), and his notes on the history of the Jewish community of Lemberg (in "Anshe Shem," 1895). Maggid also collaborated with Fuenn in the latter's history of the Jewish community of Wilna ("Ḳiryah Ne'emanah"). Maggid's most important work was "Ir Wilna," the first volume of which appeared in Wilna in 1900; it contains the biographies of more than three hundred prominent rabbis, preachers, and communal workers. The notes alone, referring to genealogical literature, show that the author was familiar with responsa literature as well as with general rabbinical and historical works in Hebrew literature. Maggid left in manuscript two other volumes, containing biographies of the important scholars and communal workers of Wilna in more recent times. The third volume contains also new material for the history of the Jews in Wilna and Lithuania, and includes numerous documents hitherto unpublished. A sketch of his life was written by Ben 'Ammi in his "Ocherki Litvye" (in "Voskhod"). Maggid's son is **David Maggid** of St. Petersburg, author of "Toledot Mishpaṭ," Günzburg.

BIBLIOGRAPHY: Halpern, in *Sbornik Budushchnost*, iv. 249, St. Petersburg, 1904; *Voskhod*, Nov., 1903.

H. R. J. G. L.

MAGGID MISHNEH. See PERIODICALS.

MAGHARIYYAH, AL-: Arabic name of a Jewish sect, meaning "Men of the Caves." According to the account given by Joseph al-Ḳirḳisani this sect was founded in the first century before the common era and derived its designation from the fact that it kept its books in caves. Except the writings of one named "the Alexandrinian," and a later work entitled "Sefer Yadua'," these books, he says, were of little value. The sect reckoned the months from the appearance of the new moon and prohibited games of every kind. It possessed strange commentaries on the Bible, and, contrary to the Sadducees, it was opposed to all anthropomorphisms. Believing God to be too sublime to mingle with matter, the sect rejected the idea that the world was created directly by Him, and invented an intermediary power. This power was an angel who produced the world, in which he is God's representative. The Law and all communications to prophets proceeded from this angel, to whom are referable all the anthropomorphic expressions concerning God found in the Bible.

This account of the tenets of the Maghariyyah agrees with that of the Jewish sect erroneously called by Shahrastani "Al-Muḳaribah," and coupled by him with that of the Yudghanites founded in the eighth century ("Kitab al-Milal wal-Nuḥal," ed. Cureton, p. 168). This confusion of names and dates led to the erroneous ascription of its foundation to Benjamin ben Moses al-Nahawendi, who was influenced by the writings of the Maghariyyah (some of them were still extant at the time of David ben Merwan al-Muḳammaẓ), as, according to Ḳirḳisani was also Arius, the founder of the Christian sect of the Arians.

Harkavy identifies the Maghariyyah with the Essenes. The reasons given by him for this identification are: (1) the name of the sect, which, according to him, does not refer to its books, but to its followers, who lived in caves or in the desert, this being known to have been the Essene mode of life; (2) the coincidence in the date of its foundation with that of the Essenes; (3) the theory of the angel, which is in keeping with the tenets of the Essenes; (4) Ḳirḳisani's omission of the Essenes from his list of the Jewish sects, which omission would be unaccountable had he not considered the Maghariyyah to be identical with the Essenes. Harkavy goes still further and identifies the "Alexandrinian" author with Philo, whose sympathies with the Essenes are well known, and sees in the theory of the angel a perfect analogy to Philo's "Logos."

BIBLIOGRAPHY: Jellinek, in *Orient, Lit.* xii. 410; Grätz, *Gesch.* vi. 192; Gottlober, *Biḳḳoret le-Toledot ha-Ḳera'im*, p. 100; Harkavy, *Le-Ḳorot ha-Kittot be-Yisrael*, in the Hebrew transl. of Grätz's *Gesch.* (iii. 496).

S. I. BR.

MAGI. See BABYLONIA.

MAGIC (כשפים): The pretended art of producing preternatural effects; one of the two principal divisions of occultism, the other being DIVINATION. The effects produced may be either physical (as a storm or death under conditions insufficient to explain its occurrence, or any phenomenon impossible in the ordinary course of nature) or mental, and the latter either intellectual (as preternatural insight or knowledge) or emotional (as love or hate arising or disappearing in obedience to the arbitrary will of the magician). The methods of producing these effects include on the one hand actions of various sorts, and on the other incantations, invocations, and the recitation of formulas. Even in the Talmud the act and the results produced by it are regarded as the criteria of magic, and these two factors appear in all forms of witchcraft as essential characteristics. Closely connected with magic are SUPERSTITION and DEMONOLOGY. In so far as gods are invoked (demons frequently being degraded gods), magic is akin to idolatry, and, in a certain sense, to ASTROLOGY.

In the Bible.

Jewish magic is mentioned as early as Deut. xviii. 10–11, where various classes of diviners, astrologers, and exorcists are named, their ceremonies being forbidden as idolatrous (comp. II Kings xxi. 6; II Chron. xxxiii. 6). Nor is there any doubt expressed as to the actual potency of magic, and the magician, who may misuse it, is accordingly feared and abhorred (Micah v. 11 [A. V. 12]; Jer. xxvii. 9; Ex. xxii. 17-23; *et al.*). The commonest form of magic was the love-charm, especially the love-charm required for an illicit amour. Such magic was practised especially by women, so that magic and adultery frequently are mentioned together (II Kings ix. 22; Nah. iii. 4; Mal. iii. 5). The law (Ex. xxii. 17 [A. V. 18]) which punishes sorcery with death speaks of the witch and not of the wizard. This was correctly interpreted by the Talmud (Sanh. 67a) as implying that magic was practised chiefly by women, and the context of the passages in Exodus which mention sorcery clearly shows that it was associated with sexual license and unnatural vices (Blau, "Das Altjüdische Zauberwesen," pp. 17-18, Strasburg, 1898; see WITCHCRAFT). The frequency of allusions to it in the Bible indicates that the practise of magic was common throughout ancient Israel.

In Talmudic Literature.

More abundant information is found in post-Biblical literature, especially in the Babylonian Talmud, where the great number of the passages alluding to magic furnishes incontrovertible evidence of its wide diffusion. It was, however, only the practise of witchcraft which was prohibited, for a knowledge of magic was indispensable to a member of the chief council or of the judiciary, and might be acquired even from the heathen. The most profound scholars were adepts in the black art, and the Law did not deny its power. The people, who cared little for the views of the learned, were devoted to witchcraft, though not so much as the Babylonians, Egyptians, Greeks, and Romans (Blau, *l.c.* pp. 17 *et seq.*). "Adultery and sorcery have destroyed everything" (Soṭah ix. 13); the majesty of God departed from Israel and His wrath came upon the world when the "wizards" became too numerous (Tosef., Soṭah, xiv. 3); Simon b. Sheṭah hanged eighty witches in a single day (Sanh. 45b); Ecclesiasticus (Sirach) xlii. 9–10 is quoted in Sanh. 100b with the addition of the words "When the daughter grows old she will probably deal in magic" (see further examples in Blau, *l.c.* pp. 23–26).

This ingrained belief in magic infected even the scholars; for although they did not practise witchcraft for gain or for unlawful ends, they occasionally counteracted black magic by white. They were even able to create a calf when they needed food (*ib.* pp. 26 *et seq.*). Healing by means of white magic is not condemned except when the means employed are pagan or idolatrous. Many scholars consumed men with a glance, or reduced them to a heap of bones, but since this magic was regarded as a punishment for sins which had been committed, the passages of the Talmud which mention it take no exception to it (Blau, *l.c.* pp. 49–61). EXORCISM also flourished, although not as widely as in Judæo-Christian circles (Acts viii. 9, xiii. 6–9). Jesus was regarded in the Talmud and by the ancient world generally as a magician (Sanh. 100b, Soṭah 17b; see JESUS IN JEWISH LEGEND). The Greco-Roman world regarded the Jews as a race of magicians (Juvenal, vi. 542–547; Suidas, *s.v.* Ἐζεκίας, *et passim*).

Magic Agencies.

The means adopted in witchcraft were manifold. The most potent was human speech, to which all peoples attribute invincible power. "Open not thy mouth for evil" (Ber. 19a and parallels). Those words of the magician are all-powerful which he utters at the right time and place and under proper conditions (Blau, *l.c.* pp. 68–82). Since official Judaism bitterly opposed black magic, there was a constant stream of prohibitions against it, and from these the existence of various forms of witchcraft can be inferred. The secret Jewish name of God was a powerful factor in incantation, as is shown by the Egyptian magic papyri written in Greek, in which heathen and Jewish names of the Deity are frequently found in juxtaposition or combination, termed משתף (= "union") by the Talmud (*ib.* pp. 117–146).

In addition to the magic word and the magic formula there were various magic objects (*ib.* pp. 156–165) which were used to avert the Evil Eye. Women and children, and even animals, as being weaker and less capable of resistance, were protected by Amulets and Talismans. These charms consisted either of natural objects or of papers with writing on them. Copies of the Bible had protective power and were carried especially on journeys, while the tefillin, as their Greek name, Phylacteries, implies, were also regarded as preservative, at least in Hellenistic circles, as were the slips of paper ("mezuzot") attached to the door-posts. Blau (*ib.* pp. 96–117) has edited, translated, and explained two Hellenistic exorcismal formulas, one of which was found in a grave in Hadrumetum (in the ancient Byzacium), in the Roman province of Africa.

Apocrypha.

In addition to the official sources from which the data given above are derived, the Apocrypha, in view of its antiquity, deserves attention in connection with the subject of magic. The general picture which it presents is the same as that given by the Bible and the Talmud. According to the Book of Enoch (ix. 7), the angels taught the daughters of men "incantations, exorcisms, and the cutting of roots, and revealed to them healing plants" (comp. viii. 1 *et seq.* with vii. 6, ix. 8; x. 7–8 with xiii. 2, xvi. 3, and lxix. 12 *et seq.*). The heart, liver, and gall are magic agencies, and the blind Tobit recovers his sight when his eyes are anointed with the gall of a fish (vi. 4 *et seq.*, viii. 2, xi. 10; see Sibyllines, iii. 220 *et seq.*, discussed in "Alter Orient," iii. 41; Ascensio Isaiæ, ii. 5; Syriac Apoc. Baruch, lx. 1, where the muttering of the incantations of the Ammonites is mentioned; see Kautzsch, "Apokryphen," ii. 435, note). Noah's book of healing (Jubilees, x.) was magical in character, as were the writings of Solomon and Moses, mentioned elsewhere.

Medieval Jewish Magicians.

In the Middle Ages, as in antiquity, the Jews were regarded as magicians, and many of them doubtless profited by the general delusion. In the ninth century a Jewish magician named Zambrio is found in Italy (Güdemann, "Gesch." ii. 40; comp. p. 255), and Sicilian sorcerers flourished even a century earlier (Zunz, "Z. G." p. 486; "Magyar Zsidó Szemle," xv. 47). The Arabic author Mas'udi speaks of a Jewish magician (Budge, "Egyptian Magic," p. 23). The Jews were considered sorcerers in Germany also (Güdemann, *l.c.* iii. 233; comp. "Israelitische Monatsschrift," 1899, No. 7; "Hebräische Bibliographie," 1903, No. 24; Micelle, p. 30, "Judæi . . . pessimi magici"; "Jüdische Wahrsager," in Van Vloten, "Recherches sur la Domination Arabe," pp. 55 *et seq.*, Amsterdam, 1894). In times of drought, during the Middle Ages, the people turned to the Jews, who were supposed to be able to cause rain, and they are still regarded by some peoples as magicians.

Sources of Jewish Magic.

The diversity existing within ancient Jewish magic and the essential contradiction between witchcraft and monotheism are in themselves evidences of foreign influence on the system. The scholars of the first centuries of the present era refer frequently and unanimously to Egypt as the original home of magic arts (Blau, *l.c.* pp. 37–49). In the Bible the real homes of all varieties of witchcraft are given as Egypt (Ex. vii. *et passim*) and Babylon (Isa. xlvii. 9–15). It is very probable that in this respect both countries influenced Israel; and their political power and high civilization made it inevitable that that influence should be deep, although the lack of historical data renders it impossible to determine its extent or trace its course. The influence of Egypt admits of no doubt as regards post-Biblical Judaism, which was for a long period under the control of the Ptolemies both in its civilization and its government. The Egypto-Hellenistic syncretism influenced first the Hellenistic Jews, especially those of Alexandria, and through them the Jews of Palestine. The Jewish and Judæo-Christian view as to the source of Hebrew magic is confirmed by the Books of Hermes and by the recently discovered Greek and Coptic magic papyri, in which the Jewish element is no small factor; and Jacob ("Im Namen Gottes") has recently proved that the belief in the almighty power of the name of God is Egyptian in origin. Although Assyro-Babylonian and other elements are not lacking, they are for the most part astrological and divinatory in character. Egypt, therefore, gave ancient Judaism its magic, and Babylonia gave it its divination, while Hellenism served as the connecting-link.

In view of the authority which the Talmud possessed for posterity the magic in it could not but influence later generations. There is no doubt that the majority of the theurgic and magic elements in the post-Talmudic literature which Jellinek collected in his "Bet ha-Midrash," date from Talmudic, and in part even from pre-Talmudic, times (see Gnosticism). This may be assumed also for the magical portions of the geonic literature in general, especially as the Geonim lived and worked in Babylonia. This ancient magic, blended with Hellenistic and medieval European elements, was incorporated in the "practical Cabala." At the close of the Middle Ages the Cabala influenced the Jewish and the Christian world alike. The "Nishmat Ḥayyim" of Manasseh ben Israel, chief rabbi in Amsterdam in the seventeenth century, is filled with superstition and magic, and many Christian scholars were deluded. The evil deeply and widely infected the people, and is still active, especially among the Ḥasidim. See Abracadabra; Abraxas; Asmodeus; Astrology; Asusa; Augury; Balaam; Bibliomancy; Blessing and Cursing; Cursing Death; Folk-Medicine; Hermes, Books of; Liver; Necromancy; etc.

Bibliography: Zimmern, *Beiträge zur Kenntnis der Babylonischen Religion*, Leipsic, 1896; Blau, *Das Altjüdische Zauberwesen*, Strasburg, 1898; Brecher, *Das Transcendentale, Magie, und Magische Heilarten im Talmud*, Vienna, 1850; Davies, *Magic, Divination, and Demonology Among the Hebrews and Their Neighbours*, London, 1898 (with extensive bibliography); Gaster, *The Sword of Moses*, ib. 1896; Güdemann, *Gesch.*; Jacob, *Im Namen Gottes*, Berlin, 1903; Reitzenstein-Poimandres, *Studien zur Griechisch-Aegyptischen und Frühchristlichen Literatur*, Leipsic, 1904; Schürer, *Gesch.* iii. 297–304 (extensive bibliography); Scholz, *Götzendienst und Zauberwesen bei den Alten Hebräern und den Benachbarten Völkern*, Ratisbon, 1877; Moïse Schwab, *Un Vase Judéo-Chaldéen*, in *R. E. J.* iv. 165; Smith, *Witchcraft and the Old Testament*, in *Bibliotheca Sacra*, 1902, pp. 26-35; *Zauberei*, in Winer, *B. R.*; *Magier*, *Magie* in Herzog-Hauck, *Real-Encyc.* xii. 55–70; Hastings, *Dict. Bible*; *Jüdische Magie*, in *Beilage zur Münchener Allgemeinen Zeitung*, 1898, No. 38.

J. L. B.

MAGINO, MEÏR DI GABRIELE: French silk-manufacturer; lived at Venice. In 1587 he went to Rome to promote the manufacture of silk, which had been begun in that city; and on June 4 of the same year the monopoly of silk-manufacture by his improved process was secured to him for sixty years, only the sister of the pope taking a share of the profits. He was also permitted to live outside the ghetto for fifteen years. In 1588 Magino printed his Italian lectures on the uses of silk and on its manufacture, dedicating the book to Pope Sixtus V. In the same year he received a privilege and patent for polishing mirrors and cut glass with a vegetable oil which he had discovered.

BIBLIOGRAPHY: Ranke, *Römische Päpste*, i. 455; Natale Ettore, *Il Ghetto di Roma*, p. 218; Vogelstein and Rieger, *Gesch. der Juden in Rom*, ii. 180 *et seq.*; Berliner, *Gesch. der Juden in Rom*, ii. 23.

D. I. E.

MAGISTER JUDÆORUM. See BISHOP OF THE JEWS; HOCHMEISTER.

MAGISTRATE. See JUDGE.

MAGISTRATUS, ELIJAH. See ELIJAH BEN SAMUEL BEN PARNES OF STEPHANOW; GENAZZANO, ELIJAH ḤAYYIM BEN BENJAMIN OF.

MAGNESIA. See MANISSA.

MAGNET. See PERIODICALS.

MAGNUS, EDUARD: German painter; born at Berlin Jan. 7, 1799; died there Aug. 8, 1872. After studying successively medicine, architecture, and philosophy, he finally adopted the profession of painting, attending the Berlin Academy of Fine Arts. From 1826 to 1829 he traveled in France and Italy, revisiting the latter country in 1831. In 1850–53 he again toured through France and also visited Spain. In 1837 he became a member of the Berlin Academy, and in 1841 received the title of professor. His general culture secured for him considerable influence in artistic circles. He is best known by his portraits, of which "Thorwaldsen," "Prince Radziwill as a Child," "Count Wrangel," "Mendelssohn-Bartholdy," "Gustav Magnus," "Countess Arnim," "Madame Egells," "Henrietta Sontag," "Jenny Lind" (National Gallery, Berlin), and "E. Mandel" are the most important. His genre pictures include: "The Fisher Boy of Nice," "The Returning Greek," "Italian Women," "Children Playing with Flowers," and "Italian Landscape" (a very poetic production). In recognition of his ability he was decorated with the ribbon of the Order of Michael, the Order of the Red Eagle of the fourth class, and several gold medals.

BIBLIOGRAPHY: Seybert, *Künstler-Lexikon*; *Meyers Konversations-Lexikon*.

S. J. So.

MAGNUS, HEINRICH GUSTAV: German chemist and physicist; born in Berlin May 2, 1802; died there April 4, 1870. He was graduated from the University of Berlin in 1827, afterward studying a year at Stockholm under Berzelius, and later spending some time in Paris under Gay-Lussac and Thénard. In 1831 Magnus began teaching as privat-docent in Berlin; in 1834 he became assistant professor of physics and technology in the university there, and in 1845 was appointed professor. The physical cabinet of the university was formed by him. He ceased teaching in Feb., 1869.

The first work published by Magnus was "Ueber die Selbstentzündlichkeit des Feinzerteilten Eisens" (1825). While at Stockholm in 1828 he discovered the compound known as "the green salt of Magnus." He discovered also sulfovinic, ethionic, and isethionic acids, and (with Ammermüller) periodic acid; investigated the diminution in density produced in garnet and vesuvianite by melting; and studied the property inherent in the blood of absorbing carbonic acid and oxygen (founding thereon the theory of the absorption of the blood). On Dec. 13, 1841, he published the results of his experiments upon the coefficient of the dilatation of gases (Regnault having published his results in the same field on Nov. 25 of the same year); in 1860 and 1861 he announced the results of his experiments on the transmission of heat through gases by conductibility and radiation, which led to a long controversy with Tyndall.

He made researches also in magnetic and in thermal electricity, hydraulics, the deflection of projectiles from firearms, the diathermal power of gases, the polarization of radiant heat, etc. The results of his experiments and researches may be found in Poggendorff's "Annalen" or in the publications of the Berlin Academy of Sciences.

BIBLIOGRAPHY: Helmholtz, *Rede zum Gedächtnis an G. Magnus*, Berlin, 1871; Hofmann, *Zur Erinnerung an G. Magnus*, ib. 1871; *Aus Jac. Berzelius' und G. Magnus' Briefwechsel*; *Allg. Deutsche Biographie*; Poggendorff, *Biographisch Literarisches Handwörterb.*; *Brockhaus Konversations-Lexikon*; *Meyers Konversations-Lexikon*; Larousse, *Dict.*; *La Grande Encyclopédie*; *Encyc. Brit.*; *Appleton's Cyclo. of Am. Biog.*; Johnson's *Encyc.*

S. N. D.

MAGNUS, LADY KATIE: English authoress and communal worker; born at Portsmouth May 2, 1844; daughter of E. Emanuel; wife of Sir Philip Magnus. She has been connected with various committees of the Berkeley Street Synagogue, has taken a great interest in the Jews' Deaf and Dumb Home, and is treasurer of the Jewish Girls' Club. Lady Magnus has written much on Jewish topics, beginning with "Little Miriam's Bible Stories" and "Holiday Stories," as well as two sketches of Jewish history—"About the Jews Since Bible Times" (London, 1881) and "Outlines of Jewish History"; the latter has run into three editions, and has been republished (with additional chapters on America) by the Jewish Publication Society of America (Philadelphia, 1900). She has contributed much to the periodicals, and a collection of her various papers was published under the title "Salvage" (1899). Those relating to Jewish topics are included in her "Jewish Portraits," which has run into a second edition (London, 1901). She is also the author of "First Makers of England," London, 1901.

BIBLIOGRAPHY: *Jewish Year Book*, 5664 (1903–4).

J.

MAGNUS, LAURIE: English author and publisher; son of Sir Philip Magnus; born in London in 1872; educated at Magdalen College, Oxford. He was the Berlin correspondent of the London "Morning Post" (1897–98) and leader-writer for the same paper. He is now (1904) joint managing director of George Routledge & Sons, Ltd. Magnus has edited a series of "Secondary Education Text-Books" for the publishing-house of John Murray, has published "A Primer of Wordsworth," translated the first volume of "Greek Thinkers" (from the German of Prof. T. Gomperz), and has edited "Prayers from the Poets" and "Flowers of the Cave" (in conjunction with Cecil Headlam). He has written "Aspects of the Jewish Question" (1902), reprinted and enlarged from the London "Quarterly Review."

BIBLIOGRAPHY: *Jewish Year Book*, 1901-2.

J. M. W. L.

MAGNUS, LUDWIG IMMANUEL: German mathematician; born in Berlin March 15, 1790; died there Sept. 25, 1861; cousin of Heinrich Gustav Magnus. His father died when he was young; and his mother induced him to enter his uncle's bank; after business hours he studied Euclid. In the Napoleonic wars he was a volunteer in the artillery, being soon promoted to the rank of gunner and serving from 1813 to 1815. On the conclusion of peace he again took up the business of banking in Berlin; in his leisure hours studying higher mathematics, and teaching that subject in the academy founded in 1816 by a brother of the sculptor Cauer. On the removal of the academy to Charlottenburg (1826) Magnus continued to be one of its regular staff of teachers; and he held that position until 1834, when Cauer died. Magnus then abandoned teaching, and spent the next nine years as head revenue officer in the recently founded Berliner Kassenverein, retiring in 1843 on a competency. Hard work had, however, broken his health, and he did nothing more for mathematics. During the latter part of his life he was an invalid, suffering from a disease of the eyes.

By 1834 Magnus' reputation as a mathematician had become established, and the University of Bonn conferred upon him the honorary degree of doctor. Magnus' mathematical writings appeared in Gergonne's "Annales des Mathématiques," vols. xi. and xvi. (1820-25); in Crelle's "Journal," vols. v., vii., viii., and ix. (1830-32); in the third part (1833) of Meier Hirsch's "Sammlung Geometrischer Aufgaben"; and in "Sammlung von Aufgaben und Lehrsätzen aus der Analytischen Geometrie des Raumes" (published in 1837, but written long before).

BIBLIOGRAPHY: *Allg. Deutsche Biographie*, xx. 91-92, Leipsic, 1884; Poggendorff, *Biog.-Literarisch Handwörterb.* Leipsic, 1863, *s.v.*

S. N. D.

MAGNUS, MARKUS: Elder of the Jewish congregation of Berlin in the first quarter of the eighteenth century; court Jew to the crown prince, afterward King Frederick William I. The Jewish community of Berlin was divided into two hostile camps by Magnus' quarrels with his rival, Jost Liebmann. Frederick I. favored the latter, while the crown prince supported Magnus. After the death of Liebmann his widow and sons continued these quarrels, which ended in the victory of Magnus. He induced the members of the congregation to substitute a public synagogue for the two private synagogues hitherto maintained by Liebmann, Veit, and Riess (see JEW. ENCYC. iii. 70-71, iv. 317). When the government (March 16, 1722) issued new regulation for the administration of the Berl Jewish congregation, Magnus and Moses Levi Gur pertz were appointed permanent chief elders with salary of 300 thalers each.

BIBLIOGRAPHY: Geiger, *Gesch. der Juden in Berlin*, i. 19-38, Berlin, 1871; Grätz, *Gesch.* x. 309-310, 350, Leipsic, 1868

D. S. MAN.

MAGNUS, PAUL WILHELM: German bo anist; born at Berlin Feb. 29, 1844; educated at th Werdergymnasium and the university of his nati city and at the University of Freiburg-im-Breisga (Ph.D. Berlin, 1870). He became in 1875 priva docent at his alma mater, where since 1880 he ha occupied the position of assistant professor of bo any. He was a member for botany of the Prussia commission for the exploration of the seas, and a such took part in the expeditions of 1871 in th Baltic Sea, of 1872 in the North Sea, and of 1874 o The Sley. He made reports of these expedition which were published by the government. Magnu contributed articles on botany to various scientif journals, and is the author of: "Beiträge zur Kenn niss der Gattung Najas," 1870; "Morphologie d Sphacelaricen," 1873; "Pilze des Kantons Gra bündten," 1890.

S. F. T. H.

MAGNUS, SIR PHILIP: English educatio ist; born in London Oct. 7, 1842; educated at Un versity College in that city, and at the University o London (B.A. 1863; B.Sc. 1864). Destined for th Jewish ministry, he pursued his studies in Berl (1865-66). On his return to England he became or of the ministers of the Berkeley Street Synagogu London. At the same time he did much priva teaching, and was professor of mechanics at th Catholic University. His "Lessons in Elementar Mechanics" (London, 1874) was for a long time th standard text-book on the subject. In 1880 he wa appointed secretary of the City and Guilds of Lo don Institute for the Advancement of Technica Education, and in that capacity became the leadin authority on technical education in the United King dom. He was a member of a royal commission fo this subject (1881-84), visiting in connection there with the chief educational centers of western Eu rope. In 1886 he was knighted in recognition o his services to education. In 1888 he published work on "Industrial Education," as one of a serie of text-books on education edited by him. He wa principal of the Finsbury Technical College fro 1883 to 1885, and a member of the London Schoo Board in 1890 and 1891. In 1900 he became fello of the senate of London University, and at the pre ent time (1904) is connected in an honorary capacit with many important educational institutions.

Magnus' work at the Guilds Institute cause him to resign his position in the Jewish ministry but he has retained his interest in many communa institutions, being vice-president of the Anglo-Jew ish Association, president of the Deaf and Dum Home, and a representative on the board of deputie of the Berkeley Street Synagogue, of which he ha been also a warden.

BIBLIOGRAPHY: *Men and Women of the Time*, 1894; *Who Who*, 1904.

J.

MAGOG. See Gog and Magog.

MAGREPHAH. See Music.

MAGYAR IZRAELITA. See Periodicals.

MAGYAR ZSIDÓ SZEMLE: Hungarian wish monthly review; established in 1884 by Josef non, secretary of the Jewish chancery, Wilhelm cher, and Josef Bánóczi, the two latter being prossors in the "Landesrabbinerschule" of Budapest. purpose is to promote the scientific knowledge Judaism, and at the same time to disseminate inmation concerning the social and legal conditions the Jews. The editorship was assumed by Báczi and Bacher, who retired in 1890 in favor of Blau and F. Mezey. The latter resigned at the d of 1895 after the Ungarisch-Israelitischer Litteraverein had been founded through the efforts of e "Magyar Zsidó Szemle," which thereafter beme a quarterly under the sole editorship of Blau. list of contributors includes Americans as well Europeans. It is the first and at present (1904) e only Jewish scientific periodical published in ıngarian, and has attracted a large number of conbutors from among the younger generation.

H. R. L. B.

MAGYAR ZSINAGOGA. See Periodicals.

MAH NISHTANNAH (lit. "wherein is disguished"): The opening words of the child's estions to the father in the Passover Haggadah; e whole of the domestic service of the Passover is metimes, familiarly, so named. The questions are ten chanted in the students' cantillation of the lmudical schools; the text thus intoned may be und in Jew. Encyc. iii. 550.

A. F. L. C.

MAHAMAD (more correctly **MA'AMAD** מעמד): The board of directors of a Spanish-Porguese congregation. The word is of Neo-Hebrew igin, and in the Talmud is applied to the repreentatives of the people present at the Temple rvice (Ta'an. 15b). The board consisted of four ardens and a treasurer, and its members were ected, or, more exactly, cooptated, from the "yedim"—those who had full rights of membership the synagogue. Whenever a vacancy occurred tween elections, which happened chiefly through ath, the remaining members, with eight ex-members, formed an electoral committee, and conferred on one of their number, by lot, the right to nomate a new colleague from the congregation. If the sembly approved of the choice, it held good. This system naturally resulted in a monopoly of the administration of the congregation by a limited number of families. That this oligarchic circle might t become too narrow, it was decided that no one uld be a member of the mahamad at the same time his son, grandson, son-in-law, stepson, brother, other-in-law, nephew, or cousin; and, furtherore, in order to insure just decisions, no one under venty-five could be elected treasurer of the mamad, and no one under forty could be warden, less he had already served as treasurer. This was e rule in the Bevis Marks Synagogue of London, and the regulations were practically the same in the other Portuguese communities.

Rules of Election.

The laws of the mahamad, according to which the affairs of the synagogue were administered, were called Ascamot. Basing its authority on them, the mahamad exercised over the members of the congregation a despotic control which degenerated into a sort of police supervision. No member could marry or be divorced without the consent of this board, nor could one bring a lawsuit against a fellow member without first consulting the mahamad on the subject, except in cases where such a delay in bringing complaint would cause him injury. No book, and no treatise of a religious or political nature, in any language whatsoever, could be printed without the permission of the mahamad. Thus Haham David Nieto published his "Maṭṭeh Dan" "con licencia de los Señores del Mahamad" (London, 1714), and Isaac Nieto dedicates his sermon on Yom Kippur "a los muy Ilustres SSrs. del Mahamad, y por su Orden Impresso" (*ib.* 1756). In London, for the greater political security of the congregation, every one was forbidden by the mahamad to join parties "which any of the people may form against the government, the ministry, or the judicial administration of the kingdom."

Despotic Rule.

In the synagogue, or in the law-court of the mahamad, no one might oppose an order of the mahamad or of the presiding officer who represented it, or criticize such an order, or write or circulate writings containing adverse criticisms of actions taken by it. The haham of the congregation enjoyed the same protection. No non-Portuguese Jew might pray in the Portuguese synagogue without the permission of the mahamad, nor might any one refuse an office or function in the services, or in the administration of synagogal affairs, which the mahamad or its president might assign him. According to the ascamot of the Bevis Marks Synagogue of London, any one who did not accept election as a member of the mahamad, or who had not shown his willingness to accept it before the expiration of eight days, was fined £40; if he had been elected treasurer, he was fined £30. The strict application of this rule, in 1813, led Isaac D'Israeli to sever his connection with the Bevis Marks Synagogue, since he would neither accept the office of warden nor pay the fine of £40. The board was especially strict in the observance of the first ascama, that no one might hold services outside the synagogue, except in a house of mourning during the first seven days thereof.

The mahamad was very prompt in imposing penalties where its regulations were ignored or violated, though excommunication, exclusion from the synagogue for a certain length of time, fines for the benefit of the poor-fund, withdrawal of all "miẓwot," forfeiture of the right to vote, and similar disciplinary measures began naturally in the course of time to lose their desired effect. Occasionally, moreover, the mahamad appealed to the secular authorities to execute its decrees, as in London in 1783, when it desired to remove those who, during the service on Purim, according to ancient

Disciplinary Measures.

custom, beat on the synagogue kettle-drums whenever the name of Haman was read from the Megillah. At Amsterdam, in the year 1670, the mahamad applied to the magistracy for confirmation and support in the execution of its decree that no one might sever his connection with the congregation even when under the strictest excommunication. A confession of repentance made by the delinquent before God and the congregation was sufficient to bring about a mitigation of the punishment or to secure a total revocation of the decree of excommunication.

The members of the mahamad were at the same time members of the tax-commission, and in this capacity were comprised among the "fintadores" (see JEW. ENCYC. v. 388b, *s.v.* FINTA).

In the Portuguese communities the affairs of the congregation and of the synagogue are still administered by a mahamad, although the disciplinary powers granted by the old ascamot have been very materially curtailed. The régime of the old mahamad of London is humorously described by Israel Zangwill in "The King of Schnorrers" (pp. 105 *et seq.*).

BIBLIOGRAPHY: *Jew. Chron.* June 11, 1897, p. 11; M. Gaster, *History of the Ancient Synagogue*, passim, London, 1901; J. Picciotto, *Sketches of Anglo-Jewish History*, Index, *ib.* 1875.

D. M. SC.

MAHANAIM: City on the east of the Jordan, near the River Jabbok; first mentioned as the place where Jacob, returning from Aram to southern Canaan, had a vision of angels (Gen. xxxii. 1–2). This implies that Mahanaim was a sanctuary at a very early period. In the records in the Book of Joshua of the allotments to the tribes Mahanaim is accounted a part of the inheritance of the tribe of Gad (xxi. 38). Apparently it was on the border between Gad and Manasseh, and it was assigned as a Levitical city (Josh. xiii. 26, 30; xxi. 38; comp. I Chron. vi. 80).

Mahanaim gained a temporary prominence in the days of the beginnings of the kingdom. It was then a stronghold, adapted to serve as a refuge for fugitives of importance (II Sam. xviii. 24). To it Abner, Saul's general, brought Ish-bosheth, Saul's son and successor (II Sam. ii. 8); during his brief and ill-starred reign Mahanaim was his capital. To Mahanaim David fled at the time of Absalom's rebellion (II Sam. xvii. 24, 27; I Kings ii. 8), and made it his residence until his recall to Jerusalem. Later on it was the headquarters of one of Solomon's commissary officers (I Kings iv. 14). According to Maspero ("The Struggle of the Nations," p. 773), Mahanaim was among the cities plundered by Shishak during his invasion (I Kings xiv. 25) of Israelitish territory. There is no subsequent reference to the city in the annals. It is not improbable that a vigorous resistance to Shishak or to some other invader brought about its utter demolition. The form of the name appears to be dual, hence the common rendering "two companies" or "camps." The narrator of Jacob's plan (Gen. xxxii. 7) for avoiding the loss of all his property so understood the name. Many scholars at the present day prefer to regard the termination in this case as the expansion of a shorter ending rather than as a sign of the dual.

The exact location of Mahanaim is very uncertain, the Biblical data being inconclusive. The city was certainly in northern Gilead and in a situation wh commanded an extensive view (II Sam. xviii. 2 it was approached from the south by way of Jordan valley and probably through a wadi t debouched into it (II Sam. ii. 29). Most explor agree in placing it at or near the wadi 'Ajlun.

BIBLIOGRAPHY: Conder, *Heth and Moab*; Merrill, *East of Jordan*; Van Kasteren, in *Z. D. P. V.* xiii. 205 *et seq.*; Bu *Geographie des Alten Palästina*, p. 257; G. A. Smith, *H Geog.* pp. 586–588.

S. F. K. S

MAHER-SHALAL-HASH-BAZ (ר שלל חש בז = "speeding for booty," "hastening to spoil"): Symbolic name of the son of Isaiah indi ting the sudden attack on Damascus and Syria the King of Assyria (Isa. viii. 3–4). Isaiah had fi been commanded by God to write it on a large (*ib.* viii. 1).

E. G. H. M. SEL.

MAHLER, ARTHUR: Austrian archeologi born in Prague Aug. 1, 1871. After completi his studies at the gymnasium in Prague, he stud the history of art and archeology at the universit of Prague and Vienna (Ph.D.), and in 1902 beca privat-docent in archeology at the German univers at Prague. He has contributed a number of articles the "Jahreshefte des Oesterreichischen Archäolo schen Institutes" (of which institute he is a cor sponding member), the "Revue Archéologique," a the "Journal d'Archéologie Numismatique." is the author of "Polyklet und Seine Schule: Beitrag zur Gesch. der Griechischen Plastik" (Le sic, 1902). He also delivered a series of lectures the American School for Archeology at Rome.

S.

MAHLER, EDUARD: Austrian astronom born in Cziffer, Hungary, 1857. He was graduat from the Vienna public school in 1876, and th studied mathematics and physics at the univers in that city, taking his degree in 1880. From N 1, 1882, till the death of T. Oppolzer (Dec., 18 Mahler shared in the latter's scientific labors. June 1, 1885, he was appointed assistant in the ro Austrian commission on measurement of degrees.

Mahler has devoted himself chiefly to chronolog In early life he paid considerable attention to cient Oriental history, Assyriology, and Egy ology, in which subjects he is at present priv docent at the University of Budapest. On Sept. 1889, he received the royal gold medal "litteris artibus" of Sweden and Norway; and since 1 he has been an official of the Hungarian Natio Museum.

Mahler has published: "Fundamentalsätze Allgemeinen Flächentheorie," Vienna, 1881; " tronomische Untersuchung über die in der Bi Erwähnte Aegyptische Finsterniss," *ib.* 1885; "I Centralen Sonnenfinsternisse," *ib.* 1885; "Untersu ung einer im Buche Nahum auf den Unterga Ninive's Bezogenen Finsterniss," *ib.* 1886; "Bibliso Chronologie und Zeitrechnung der Hebräer," 1887; "Fortsetzung der Wüstenfeld'schen V gleichungs-Tabellen der Mohammedanischen u Christlichen Zeitrechnung," Leipsic, 1887; "Ch nologische Vergleichungs-Tabellen," Vienna, 18 "Maimonides' Kiddusch-Hachodesch," *ib.* 1

anslated and explained); besides many papers Hungarian as well as contributions to various rman scientific journals, as "Zeitschrift der Deutnen Morgenländischen Gesellschaft," "Sitzungsrichte der Kaiserlichen Akademie der Wissennaften," "Journal Asiatique," "Zeitschrift für ssyriologie," "Zeitschrift für Mathematik und ysik," and "Zeitschrift für Aegyptische Sprache."

BLIOGRAPHY: Eisenberg, *Das Geistige Wien*, ii. 321-322.

s. N. D.

MAHLER, GUSTAV: Austrian composer; rn at Kalischt, Bohemia, July 7, 1860; studied at e gymnasiums at Iglau and Prague, and entered e University of Vienna in 1877. He attended also e conservatorium in that city, studying pianoforte th Epstein, and composition and counterpoint th Bruckner. After conducting theater orchestras Hall (Upper Austria), Laibach, and Cassel (where directed the grand musical festival as a leaveking), he was in 1885 appointed the successor of nton Seidl at Prague, where, among other works, conducted Wagner's "Ring der Nibelungen," Meistersinger," and "Tristan und Isolde," the symony of Bruckner, and the Ninth Symphony of eethoven. From 1886 to 1888 he was kapelleister at the Stadttheater in Leipsic, where, in e absence of Nikisch, he conducted the opera for x months. During the following years he contribed, by his splendid ability and skilful management, bring about a thorough reorganization of the yal Opera at Budapest, to which place he had en called in 1888. In 1891 he was appointed conctor at the Stadttheater in Hamburg, and held is position until 1897, when he accepted the posin of kapellmeister of the Royal Opera, Vienna, cceeding Wilhelm Jahn as director in October of e same year. Soon thereafter he was converted to nristianity.

While generally recognized as one of the greatest usical leaders of the day, Mahler has, within the st few years, aroused considerable interest also by s compositions, among which the following are the ost noteworthy: "Die Drei Pintos," an opera eipsic, 1888); symphony in D major (performed Budapest in 1891, and also at the Weimar Music estival); two symphonies, C minor (1895) and F ajor (1896); "Humoreske," for orchestra; "Das lagende Lied," for soli, choir, and orchestra; three oks of songs.

BLIOGRAPHY: Riemann, *Musik-Lexikon*; Baker, *Biographical Dictionary of Musicians*.

s. J. So.

MAHOMET. See Mohammed.

MAḤOZA (מחוזא, *i.e.*, "The City"): Babylonian ty on the Tigris, three parasangs south of Ctesiphon. ear it was the citadel of Koke (אקרא דכובי, Χώχη), hich was regarded as a part of Maḥoza. Owing its proximity to the royal canal, Nehar Malka, it as called also "Maḥoza Malka" (Maoga-Malcha). ahoza existed in the third century (see below) and ems to have been inhabited solely by Jews, for ne of the amoraim expressed his astonishment at ot seeing a "mezuzah" on the gates of Maḥoza Yoma 11a). Most of the Jews there were descendants of proselytes (Ḳid. 73a, b) and they are represented as given over to luxury, on account of which they were denounced as "children of Hell" (בני גיהנם; R. H. 17a), as "effeminate" (Shab. 109a), and as "drunkards" (Ta'an. 26a). The women of Maḥoza had a passion for jewelry, and when Levi b. Sisi promulgated a halakah permitting women to wear their jeweled head-dress on Sabbath, eighteen women of one street alone took advantage of that decision, while only twenty-four women in the whole city of Nehardea followed their example (Shab. 33a). On the other hand, the people of Maḥoza were intelligent (owing to their drinking the water of the Tigris; Ber. 59b) and charitable (B. Ḳ. 119a).

Maḥoza had an academy, seemingly founded about the middle of the third century by Joseph b. Ḥama, Raba's father, who was succeeded by Rabbah (Sherira, in Neubauer, "M. J. C." i. 29). The academy was most prosperous under Raba, who attracted thither many students and thereby caused the decline of Abaye's academy at Pumbedita. Thus Maḥoza, after Pumbedita, may with justice be called the home of the Talmud; but after Raba's death, owing to the lack of able successors, the academy of Maḥoza gave way to that of Pumbedita. Maḥoza was destroyed in 363 by the Romans under Julian the Apostate, during the war against the Persians. It was rebuilt, however, and became later the capital of a small Jewish state governed by the Prince of the Captivity (the "Rosh Galuta"). This Jewish independence did not last long, for the Jewish army, under Mar Zuṭra, the exilarch, was defeated by Kobad, King of Persia, and Mar Zuṭra, with his grandfather Mar Ḥanina, was executed on the bridge of Maḥoza (*c.* 520); the Jews there were taken captive by Kobad, and the family of the exilarch escaped to Judea.

About the middle of the sixth century Chosroes Nushirvan built in the vicinity of Maḥoza a town on the plan of Antioch; he called it "Antiocheia-Rumia," but the Arabs called it "Al-Maḥoza" (Gregory Bar Hebræus, "Ta'rikh al-Duwal," ed. Pokocke, Arabic text, p. 150). This town also had a large Jewish population, the greater part of which was put to death by the Persian general Mebodes when he captured the town in the beginning of the seventh century.

Bibliography: Fürst, *Kultur- und Litteraturgesch. der Juden in Asien*, p. 107, Leipsic, 1849; Grätz, *Gesch.* 2d ed., iv. 274-275, 351, 375; Neubauer, *G. T.* pp. 356-357.

E. C. M. Sel.

MÄHRISH-OSTRAU: Town in Moravia, Austria. The congregation of Mährish-Ostrau is one of the youngest in Moravia, for Jews were not allowed to settle there until 1792, and it was not until 1848, when general freedom of residence was granted, that the congregation began to grow rapidly. It is now the second largest Jewish congregation in Moravia, and embraces a number of smaller neighboring communities, including Oderberg; it numbers 6,500 souls. It became a chartered congregation in 1875 and dedicated its synagogue in 1879 (on which occasion Chief Rabbi Jellinek officiated). The first rabbi of the congregation was Dr. B. Zimmels, who died in 1893. He was followed, in 1894, by the present (1904) incumbent, Dr. Jacob Spira. The community, since 1871, has supported a parochial school, which has now 200 pupils.

Among its institutions are the Jewish Women's Society, the Bikkur Holim (with a membership of 220), and a bet ha-midrash. The community supports also a number of poor students.

D. J. Sp.

MAHZOR (plural, **Mahzorim**): Term applied to the compilation of prayers and piyyutim; originally it designated the astronomical or yearly cycle. By the Sephardim it was used for a collection which contains the prayers for the whole year, while the Ashkenazim employed it exclusively for the prayer-book containing the festival ritual. The Mahzor varies with the custom (מנהג) of the countries or cities in which it is used. Among the different European Mahzorim the oldest is the "Mahzor Romaniya," known also as "Hazzaniyya shel Romaniya," or "Grigos." It originated in the Byzantine empire (whence the name "Romaniya"), and differs from the Ashkenazic in that it contains fewer poetical compositions of Kalir. It was edited by Elijah ben Benjamin ha-Levi (who enriched it with poetical compositions of his own), and according to Zedner was published first at Venice, in the printing-office of Daniel Bomberg, and then at Constantinople (1573–1576). It is divided into two large volumes and contains, besides the prayers for the year and the piyyutim, the Five Scrolls, the Book of Job, the Haggadah of Passover, the beginnings and endings of the Sabbatical sections of the Pentateuch, and calendric rules.

From the Byzantine empire the use of piyyutim was introduced into southern Italy, and thence into Rome. The Romans adopted some parts of the Mahzor Romaniya, discarded others, and added much that was new, thus forming a new rite known by the name "Minhag Bene Roma," or "Minhag Lo'azim," or "Minhag Italyani." The Roman ritual was widely disseminated from Rome, and after 1520 the Greek ritual was based upon the Roman Mahzor, which served also as a basis for the rituals of Corfu and Kaffa. The Roman Mahzor was published first at Soncino in 1485. Johanan Treves wrote a commentary on it under the title "Kimha de-Abishona," which was published, together with the text, at Bologna in 1540. An Italian translation of the Mahzor was published at Bologna in 1538, at Vienna in 1823, and at Leghorn in 1837.

Roman Rite.

The use of piyyutim was introduced into northern Europe probably from Italy. There, again, the Mahzor underwent many changes, and a German ("Ashkenazi") ritual was established which is contained in the "Mahzor Ashkenaz," the "Mahzor Pehm [Bohemia] we-Polin [Poland]," and the "Minhag Zarfat" (= "French ritual"). Of these the first two only are now in use. The French ritual was never published; it is extant partly in manuscript and partly in the ritual of the three Italian communities of Asti, Fassano, and Moncalvo, where many French Jews settled after their expulsion from France in 1306 and 1394. The several Mahzorim included in the Ashkenazic ritual vary in some details, but agree in essentials. They are distinguished from those of other rituals in containing numerous piyyutim based upon the Halakah and Haggadah. The German ritual is used by the Jews in Germany, Bohemia, Morav or Silesia, Prussian Poland, Russia, Austria, Hungar France, and England. The Ashk nazic Mahzor was first published abo 1521, the Polish in 1522. Among t commentaries on the German and P lish Mahzor, which have often been published gether with the text, are those of: Benjamin b Meïr ha-Levi of Nuremberg (Tanhausen, 1540), Isa ben Jacob Jozebel (entitled "Hadrat Kodesh," Ve ice, 1554), an anonymous writer (entitled "Ma'a Zedek," Venice, 1568), Zebi Hirsch Zundels (Lubl 1579), Nathan Shapira (Cracow, 1604), Joseph Be leel Kaz Mehokek (Prague, 1616), a second anon mous writer (with additions entitled "Sefer ha-M bir," by Joseph עששא, and with glosses and no entitled "Masbir he-Hadash," by Moses Kosmar Amsterdam, 1667), Hirz Shatz (Wilhelmsdorf, 167 Benjamin Wolf Heidenheim (Rödelheim, 180 Uri Feibus ben Aryeh Löb (entitled "Keri'e Mo'e Breslau, 1805), Moses Israel Büdinger (Metz, 181 and Jehiel Michael ha-Levi (entitled "Matteh Lew Slobuta, 1827).

Ashkenazic Rite.

Translations of parts of the German Mahzor i the vernacular of the countries in which they w used began to be made as early as the fourteen century. In 1571 Abigdor ben Moses publishe Judæo-German translation of the Mahzor for Ne Year and the Day of Atonement. 1600 the Judæo-German translation the whole Mahzor was published Meïr Anshel ben Joseph Mordecai Posen. A German translation of t whole Mahzor was first published by Benjan Wolf Heidenheim, 1800. He was followed by Prosp of Alsace (Metz, 1817), Moses ben Israel Land (Prague, 1834), Moritz Frenkel (Berlin, 1838–4 I. N. Mannheimer (Vienna, 1840), Moses Pappe heimer and Jeremiah Heinemann (Berlin, 1840–4 Raphael Jacob Fürstenthal (Krotoschin, 1845), M ha-Levi Letteris (Prague, 1845), and Michael Sac (Berlin, 1855). A French translation of the wh Mahzor was published by Elhanan Durlacher (Par 1852).

Translations into German.

The first attempt to render the Mahzor into En lish was made by A. Alexander, who in 1787 pu lished the piyyutim for the eve of the Day of Ato ment, and in 1789 the whole service for New-Yea In 1794 David Levi published an English versi of the services for New-Year, the Day of Atonemen and the feasts of Tabernacles and Pentecost, and th teen years later gave a new version of the wh Mahzor. In 1860 a new English version was pu lished by David Aaron de Sola. A Dutch transl tion of the entire Mahzor was published by Gabr Isaac Pollack in 1841. The services for New-Ye and the Day of Atonement were rendered into Ru sian by Rabbi Hurwitz after 1880.

Spain, in the Middle Ages the home of Jewi poetry, could hardly be satisfied with the piyyut of Kalir, which had been introduc either from Babylonia with the "Si dur" of R. Amram Gaon, or fro Italy. These, therefore, were replaced by new pi yutim composed by Spanish poets, as Joseph b Abitur, Solomon Gabirol, Isaac Ghayyat, Judah b

In Spain.

Page from a Folio Manuscript Maḥzor of the Fourteenth Century.

(From the Sulzberger collection in the Jewish Theological Seminary of America, New York.)

Levi, and Abraham and Moses ibn Ezra. Indeed, the number of piyyuṭim composed by Spanish poets was so great that almost every Spanish city had its own ritual. After the Spanish exile the same ritual was adopted by all the Sephardim with the exception of the Catalonian and Aragonian congregations of Salonica, which still use their old Maḥzor for New-Year and the Day of Atonement.

The Maḥzor of the Sephardic ritual was first published at Venice in 1614. As representing distinct branches of the Sephardic ritual may be regarded: the Tripoli Maḥzor for New-Year and the Day of Atonement (published first at Venice in 1648, under the title "Sifte Renanot"); the Maḥzor of Tunis (published at Pisa); the Maḥzor of Algiers ("Minhag Algaza'ir," published first at Amsterdam in 1685); and the maḥzorim of Provence and Languedoc, four of which are still extant—those of Avignon, Carpentras, Cavaillon, and Montpellier. Many piyyuṭim of the Sephardim were incorporated into the Maḥzor of northern France, and some of them entered the German Maḥzor. Parts of the Spanish Maḥzor, like the "'Abodah" of Joseph ben Abitur, the "Azharot" of Solomon ibn Gabirol, and various poems by Isaac ibn Ghayyat, were annotated by Jacob Anatoli, Moses ibn Tibbon, Isaac ben Todros, Simon Duran, and by others. Jacob Tam compiled a maḥzor modeled upon the Spanish Maḥzor, and many liturgical poems of Spain are found in the Maḥzor Vitry, compiled by Simḥah ben Samuel of Vitry, pupil of Rashi.

The Spanish Maḥzor exerted an influence upon the Karaite ritual. Several rabbinical poems of Spanish origin were introduced into the Karaite service before it was arranged by Aaron ben Joseph. See LITURGY; POETRY; PRAYER-BOOKS.

BIBLIOGRAPHY: Luzzatto, *Mebo*; idem, in *Kerem Ḥemed*, iv. 23a; Zunz, *Ritus*, Berlin, 1859; *idem*, in *Allg. Zeit. des Jud.* 1838, pp. 580 *et seq.*; Steinschneider, *Jewish Literature*, pp. 164 *et seq.*; Benjacob, *Oẓar ha-Sefarim*, s.v. מחזור.

J. I. BR.

MAI, JOHANN HEINRICH (the elder): German Protestant theologian; born in Pforzheim Feb., 1653; died in Giessen Sept., 1719. In 1689 he became professor in the University of Giessen. Besides various Biblical exegetical works he wrote: "Synopsis Theologiæ Judaicæ" (Giessen, 1698); "Exercitatio . . . de Jure Anni Septimi" (ed. by his son, *ib.* 1707, and later printed along with Maimonides' tract on the subject); "Grammatica Rabbinica" (*ib.* 1710). His son **J. H. Mai** (the younger; b. March, 1688; d. June, 1732) was made professor of Greek and Oriental languages in the University of Giessen in 1709; he published, among other things: "Dissertatio . . . de Origine, Vita Atque Scriptis D. Isaac Abarbanielis" (Altdorf, 1708); "D. Isaaci Abarbanielis Preco Salutis in Ling. Latin. Translatus" (Frankfort-on-the-Main, 1712).

BIBLIOGRAPHY: *Universal-Lexicon*, Halle and Leipsic, 1739; Jöcher's *Gelehrten-Lexicon*.

T.

MAI, JOSEPH BEN MICHAEL: German printer; born at Dyhernfurth Dec. 29, 1764; died at Breslau Dec. 1, 1810. His father had a printing establishment at Dyhernfurth, to which Joseph and his brother succeeded. Mai was a Talmudic scholar and wrote prefaces to the works of his father-in-law, Isaiah Berlin, rabbi of Breslau. He wrote also in collaboration with his brother, notes to the four Ṭurim (Dyhernfurth, 1790).

BIBLIOGRAPHY: Berliner, *Rabbi Jesaja Berlin*, p. 13; Fuenn, *Keneset Yisrael*, p. 482; Löwenstamm, *Mispad Mar*, Breslau, 1833.

J. B. FR.

MAIER, JOSEPH VON: German rabbi; born Apr. 24, 1799; died at Stuttgart Aug. 19, 1873; rabbi at Stuttgart, 1833–73; president of the first rabbinical conference held at Brunswick in 1844; and he was also a member of the Jewish Consistory of Württemberg. In recognition of his action for reform in Jewish prayer and for organizing the Jewish communities he was ennobled by the King of Württemberg. This gave him the distinction of being the first German rabbi belonging to the nobility ("Allg. Zeit. des Jud." 1873, p. 585).

S. I. WAR.

MAIMING. See MAYHEM.

MAIMON (MAIMUN) BEN JOSEPH: Spanish exegete and moralist; born about 1110; father of Moses Maimonides. He studied under Joseph ibn Migash at Lucena, and became a dayyan. He was the author of a commentary, in Arabic, on the Pentateuch, fragments of which are quoted by his grandson Abraham. Maimon wrote in Arabic also on the "dinim" concerning the ritual and the festivals. It is, possibly, from this source that Maimonides quotes in his commentary on the Mishnah (Bek. viii. 7; 'Eduy. i. 3, iv. 7; and Sheb. vi. 7) and in his "Yad" (Sheḥiṭah, xi. 10). His only extant work, however, is a letter of consolation which has been identified with the "Iggeret ha-Shemad" attributed to his son; the Arabic text was edited and translated by L. M. Simmons ("J. Q. R." ii. 66–101). It was written in the year 1160, while Maimon and his son Moses were at Fez. They left Fez in 1165 and arrived at Jerusalem on Oct. 12 in that year (see MOSES BEN MAIMON).

BIBLIOGRAPHY: L. M. Simmons, in *J. Q. R.* ii. 62–64; Steinschneider, *Hebr. Bibl.* viii. 114; idem, *Die Arabische Literatur der Juden*.

J.

MAIMON, MOISEI LEIBOVICH: Russian painter; born at Wilkowiszk, government of Suwalki, Russian Poland, Feb. 4, 1860. After attending the schools of painting in Warsaw and Wilna he entered, in 1880, the Academy of Fine Arts at St. Petersburg; in 1881 he was awarded a silver medal for a painting from life, and in 1883 was graduated. At the exhibitions of the academy in 1884 and 1885 he was again awarded silver medals. In 1885 and 1886 Maimon executed portraits of the daughter of General Minkevitz and of the son of Baron Ungern von Sternberg. In October of the latter year he was awarded a gold medal by the academy for his "St. Irene Cures St. Sebastian," and for his "Ivan the Terrible Taking Orders Before His Death from the Metropolitan" the title of "Artist of the First Degree" was conferred upon him. He painted many portraits, among them those of the czar, czarina, the three princes, and Prof. Daniel Chwolson (1900; St. Petersburg Artists' Exhibition). His paintings include: "The House-Cleaner," "The Wagons at the Market-Place," "An Applicant," and "The Poli-

יהא אדם ירא שמים בסתר ומודה על האמת ודובר אמת בלבבו וישכים ויאמר: רבון כל
העולמים לא על צדקותינו אנחנו מפילים תחנונינו לפניך כי על רחמיך הרבים. מה אנו מה
חיינו מה חסדנו מה כחינו מה גבורתינו מה נאמר לפניך ייׄ אלדינו ואלדי אבותינו הלא כל
הגבורים כאין נגדך ואנשי השם כלא היו וחכמי כבלי מדע ונבוני כבלי השכל הלא כל מעשינו
תהו ובהו וימי חיינו הבל לפניך שכן כתוב בדברי קדשך ומותר האדם מן הבהמה אין כי ה
הכל הבל: אבל אנחנו עמך בני בריתך בני אברהם אוהבך שנשבעת לו בהר המוריה
זרע יצחק יחידך שנעקד על גבי מזבחך עדת יעקב בנך בכורך שמאהבתך שאהבת אותו ו
ומשמחתך ששמחת בו קראת אותו ישראל וישורון: לפיכך אנו חייבים להודות לך ול
ולשבחך ולפארך וליתן שבח והודאה לשמך וחייבים אנו לומר לפניך תמיד שמע בכל
יום אשרינו מה טוב חלקנו מה נעים גורלינו מה יפה מאד ירושתינו אשרנו שאנו משכימים
ומעריבים ערב ובקר תמיד בכל יום ומיחדים את שמך פעמים באהבה ואומרים שמע יש
ישראל ייׄ אלדינו ייׄ אחד: אתה הוא עד שלא נברא העולם ואתה הוא משנברא העולם
אתה הוא בעולם הזה ואתה הוא לעולם הבא קדש את שמך על מקדישי שמך קדש את שמ
שמך בעולמך ובישועתך תרים ותגביה קרננו ברוך מקדש שמו ברבים: אתה הוא
ייׄ אלדינו בשמים ממעל ושמי השמים העליונים אתה הוא ראשון ואתה הוא אחרון ומבלע
ומבלעדיך אין אלדים קבץ קויך מארבע כנפות הארץ יכירו וידעו כל באי העולם כי אתה
הוא האלדים לבדיך לכל ממלכות הארץ אתה עשית את השמים ואת הארץ ומי בכל מעשה
ידיך בעליונים או בתחתונים שיאמר לך מה תעשה אבינו שבשמים עשה עמנו בעבור כבוד
שמך האל הגדול הגבור והנורא וקיים עלינו מהרה מה שאמרת על ידי צפניה נביאך בעת
ההיא אביא אתכם ובעת קבצי אתכם כי אתן אתכם לשם ולתהלה לכל עמי הארץ בשובי
את שבותכם לעיניכם אמר ייׄ

ה

PAGE FROM THE FIRST EDITION OF THE MAHZOR, SONCINO, 1485.
(From the Sulzberger collection in the Jewish Theological Seminary of America, New York.)

ticians" (exhibited 1889 and 1891; these represent chiefly peasant types); "He Lost His Way," "An Old Man," "A Girl's Head," and "The Fishers" ("Blanc et Noir" exhibition of 1891); "A Corner in the Theater," "In the Kitchen," "Buying Groceries," and "Repairing His Property" (academy exhibition of 1892); "A Cheap Restaurant" (St. Petersburg Art Exhibition of 1892); "The Maranos" (1893; Academy of Fine Arts); "The Mushroom-Seller," "A Girl Student," and "The Peasant Elder" (St. Petersburg Artists' Exhibition of 1894); "The Invitation," "The Broken Heart" (1895); "A Prayer in the Woods," "The Bouquet Fading Away," "The Southern Girl," "The Servant-Girl," "An Old Man" (1896); "A Woman's Head" (St. Petersburg Exhibition, 1899, held in the palace of Baron Shtiglitz).

Maimon attained also considerable success in caricature. In 1900 he published two albums, one containing ten portraits of women, and the other ten portraits of men, all of persons mentioned in the Bible; some of these were copies from works of the great masters.

"The Maranos" represents a Passover night in a rich Marano home. The family is seated at the table, at the head of which an old man, clothed in white, is reading from the Haggadah. The door opens suddenly and a masked and armed force of the Inquisition enters. The family is horror-stricken, with the exception of the old man, who continues to read quietly, with his hand on the arm of the chair, and by his attitude seeming to say: "I will finish my reading and then I shall be ready." For this painting he was made "Academician and Titular-Rath."

Maimon contributed several articles to the weekly edition of the "Voskhod," and an article of his in Hebrew was presented, in the form of a pamphlet, by "Ha-Meliẓ" to its readers.

BIBLIOGRAPHY: *Sefer ha-Shanah*, 1901, pp. 72-81.

H. R. J. G. L.

MAIMON, SOLOMON BEN JOSHUA: Philosophical writer; born at Nieszwicz, Lithuania, in 1754; died at Niedersiegersdorf, Silesia, Nov. 22, 1800. Endowed with greaty ability, he became versed in rabbinical literature while still a child. He was married at the age of twelve, by his father, to the daughter of a widow of his native town; at the age of fourteen Maimon was a father. Pressed by his mother-in-law, with whom he was perpetually quarreling, to earn a livelihood, he became tutor to the family of an innkeeper in a neighboring village. His days were spent in expounding the Pentateuch to his unpromising pupils, and the greater part of his nights in studying Jewish philosophical literature. He derived special pleasure from speculative science. Maimonides' "Moreh Nebukim" became his guiding star, and it was in token of reverence for that great master that he assumed the name of "Maimon." He soon plunged into cabalistic mysticism, which he endeavored to place upon a philosophical basis, being convinced that the Cabala was an attempt, veiled in allegory and fable, at a scientific explanation of existence. This endeavor of Maimon's irritated the Ḥasidim with whom he associated, and he received rebukes instead of the expected compliments. Disillusioned, he turned to secular studies. Maimon began to study physics, especially optics, from old German books, which he procured at considerable pains. The further he advanced in the study the stronger grew his innate thirst for knowledge, and, being harassed both by his implacable mother-in-law and by his coreligionists, who began to regard him as a heretic, he decided to go to Germany and there study medicine. A pious merchant accorded him passage to Königsberg, and, after many struggles, at the age of twenty-five he reached Berlin.

Solomon Maimon.

Early Studies.

But a rude reception awaited the future philosopher, whose words Goethe was to treat with respect, and to whom Schiller and Kerner were to pay tributes of praise; he was refused admission as a vagabond by the Jewish gatekeeper. In his despair Maimon appealed to a rabbi he had met, showing him the manuscript of his commentary on the "Moreh." Unfortunately, the rabbi belonged to those for whom Maimonides' philosophical work is the symbol of heresy. For six months Maimon wandered about the country, in company with a professional beggar, until he reached Posen. There he was befriended by the pious rabbi Hirsch Janow, who, conceiving a high opinion of Maimon's rabbinical learning, furnished him with means of subsistence. After two years of comfortable life Maimon grew weary of his superstitious surroundings, and recklessly wounded the religious feelings of his Orthodox protectors. Again he went to Berlin; this time, owing to the protection of a countryman of his settled there, he was admitted. Soon a happy accident brought him into contact with Moses Mendelssohn. In reading Wolff's "Metaphysics" Maimon was quick to detect the deficiencies in his proofs of the existence of God; Maimon wrote a criticism of them and sent it to Mendelssohn, who, recognizing in him a profound thinker, took him under his protection.

Received in Berlin.

Maimon had now an excellent opportunity to begin an honorable career; but his mind, fed on metaphysical problems, had become inadaptable to any regular occupation. He abandoned his project of studying medicine and took up pharmacy; but after three years of study he was not in a position to exercise it professionally. He frequented bad society, acquired habits of intemperance, and made a profession of cynicism which scandalized his protectors. Finally he was abandoned by Mendelssohn and had to leave Berlin. Mendelssohn, however, gave him letters of recommendation which secured him a good reception in the leading Jewish circles of Holland, whither he went after a short stay in Hamburg. In Holland, again, his uncouth manners and unman-

PAGE FROM A MAḤZOR PRINTED AT PRAGUE, 1525.
(From the Sulzberger collection in the Jewish Theological Seminary of America, New York.)

ageable temper alienated his friends. In desperation he returned to Hamburg and, in order to improve his position, decided to embrace Christianity. Addressing a letter to a Lutheran clergyman, he expressed his readiness to abandon Judaism. Maimon, however, had a natural aversion to hypocrisy, and naively confessed that it was not religious conviction that made him prefer Christianity, for, he says, Judaism is more in keeping with reason than is Christianity. The honest clergyman naturally refused to baptize him, but procured him the means of entering the gymnasium of Altona in order that he might improve his knowledge of languages.

Resorts to Conversionists.

After two years Maimon left the gymnasium and returned to Berlin. His former friends, especially Mendelssohn, befriended him again, and sent him to Dessau, where he was to translate into Hebrew German scientific works intended for circulation among the Russian and Polish Jews. Their publication, however, was abandoned, and Maimon, dissatisfied with his friends, went to Breslau, where, through the assistance of Ephraim Kuh and Professor Grave, he found pupils. While there Maimon received a visit from his son, then twenty years of age, who demanded, in the name of his mother, that Maimon should return to his family or give her a letter of divorce. Maimon had refused a similar demand, made through a messenger, while he was still in Hamburg, because he hoped to be able in the near future to support his family in his native country; now that he could no longer entertain such a hope he endeavored to persuade his wife and son to join him in Germany. They refused, however, and Maimon finally gave the desired divorce.

In 1786 Maimon once more returned to Berlin, and, protected by Ben David, Asher, and Marcus Herz, devoted himself to literary-philosophic activities. In 1790 Count Kalkreuth gave him an asylum on his estate at Niedersiegersdorf. Until that year Maimon had published only philosophical articles. In 1788 he became acquainted with Kant's philosophy, and under its influence wrote "Versuch über die Transcendentale Philosophie" (Berlin, 1790), in reference to which Kant declared, in a letter to Marcus Herz, that of all his critics and opponents Maimon was the most acute. In 1791 Maimon published a philosophical lexicon, in which he had collected a series of dissertations on the principal points of philosophy. This work gave rise to a violent controversy between him and Reinhold; Maimon defended his views in "Streifereien im Gebiete der Philosophie" (*ib.* 1793).

Philosophic Essays.

After having published three historical and critical works on philosophy—"Ueber die Progresse der Philosophie" (*ib.* 1793); "Versuch einer Neuen Logik" (*ib.* 1794), in which he attempted to expound an algebraic or symbolic system of logic; and "Die Kategorien des Aristoteles" (*ib.* 1794), with explanatory notes—propædeutic to his theory of logic—Maimon produced his most important work, "Kritische Untersuchungen über den Menschlichen Geist" (*ib.* 1797), which secured him a prominent place among the historians of philosophy. Therein he originated that speculative monistic idealism which, during the first half of the nineteenth century, pervaded not only philosophy, but all sciences, and by which Fichte, Schelling, and Hegel were influenced. The great question at issue in Kant's analysis of the mind was, "Has man any ideas which are absolutely and objectively true?" the answer to which depends on another question, "Has man any ideas independent of experience?" for if all ideas depend on experience, there can be no question of objective ideas, experience being essentially subjective.

His "Kritische Untersuchungen."

Kant answered the second question in the affirmative, and the first in the negative. He showed that in consciousness certain elements are given which are not derived from experience, but which are necessarily true. However, these given elements or "things in themselves" man knows only as they appear to him, but not as they are "per se." This concept of "things in themselves" is rejected by Maimon, who holds that the matter of exterior objects which produce impression on man's sensibility is absolutely intelligible. He also contested the Kantian distinction between sensibility and understanding as well as the subjectivity of the intuitions of time and space. For him, sense is imperfect understanding, and time and space are sensuous impressions of diversity, or diversity presented as externality. In practical philosophy he criticized Kant for having substituted an unpractical principle for the only motive for action—pleasure. The highest pleasure is in knowing, not in physical sensation, and because it recognizes this fact the "Ethics" of Aristotle is much more useful than the Kantian.

Maimon's autobiography was published by K. Ph. Moritz (Berlin, 1793). In this work he gives a résumé of his views on the Cabala, which he had expounded in a work written while he was still in Lithuania. According to him the Cabala is practically a modified Spinozism, in which not only is the world in general explained as having proceeded from the concentration of the divine essence, but every species of being is derived from a special divine attribute. God, being the ultimate substance and the ultimate cause, is called "En Sof," because He can not be predicated by Himself. However, in relation to the infinite beings, positive attributes were applied to Him, and these attributes were reduced by the cabalists to ten—the ten sefirot. The ten "circles" correspond to the ten Aristotelian categories, without which nothing can be conceived. In the same work Maimon expresses his views on Judaism. He divides Jewish history into five main periods: (1) the period of natural religion, extending from the Patriarchs to Moses; (2) that of revealed or positive religion, from Moses to the Great Sanhedrin; (3) the mishnaic period; (4) the Talmudic period; (5) the post-Talmudic period. Maimon censures the Rabbis for having burdened the people with minute prescriptions and ceremonies, but praises their high moral standard. Only those, he says, who have not penetrated into the real spirit of the Talmud and who are not familiar with the custom of the ancients, especially of Orientals, of veiling their theological,

Autobiography.

ethical, and philosophical teachings in fable and allegory, can find in the old rabbinical writings matter for derision.

Maimon was the author of the following Hebrew works, of which only the first has been published: "Gib'at ha-Moreh," a commentary on the first part of Maimonides' "Moreh Nebukim," preceded by a sketch of the history of philosophy (Berlin, 1791); "Ta'alumot Ḥokmah," on mathematical physics; and "Ḥeshek Shelomoh." The last work is in four parts: (1) "Ma'aseh Nissim," on the twelve sermons of R. Nissim; (2) "'Ebed Abraham," on Ibn Ezra's commentary on the Pentateuch and Psalms; (3) "Ma'aseh Libnat ha-Sappir," reflections; (4) "Ma'aseh Ḥosheb," on algebra.

Bibliography: S. J. Wolff, *Maimoniana*, Berlin, 1813; J. H. Witte, *Solomon Maimon*, Berlin, 1876; Ed. Erdmann, *Gesch. der Neuern Philosophie*, iii., part 1, p. 510, Leipsic, 1853; Geiger's *Jüd. Zeit.* iv. 189; S. Bernfeld, in *Ha-Shiloaḥ*, 1901, p. 226; S. Hodgson, *Philosophy of Experience*, Preface; Venn, *Symbolic Logic*, Preface; Watson, *Salomon Maimon*, Toronto, 1890; Zangwill, *Dreamers of the Ghetto*.

K. I. Br.

MAIMONIDES, MAIMUNI. See Moses ben Maimon.

MAIMONISTS. See France; Moses ben Maimon.

MAINTENANCE. See Husband and Wife.

MAINZ. See Mayence.

MAISON, KARL: Bavarian merchant, manufacturer and deputy; born in Oberdorf, Württemberg, Sept. 18, 1840; died in Munich Sept. 29, 1896. He was educated at the primary and Latin schools at Oberdorf, and received a business training at Offenbach-on-the-Main. When Maison attained his twenty-fourth year he became a partner in the firm of A. Maison, established in Munich. In 1871 Maison was appointed a "Commerzienrat" and became a member of the Upper Bavarian Chamber of Commerce and Manufacture in 1875. Subsequently he was elected a director of that body and chosen Danish and Swedish-Norwegian consul. Maison represented Munich in the Chamber of Deputies from 1887 to 1896.

Bibliography: Bettelheim, *Biog. Jahrbuch*, 1900, pp. 40*, 41*.

S. N. D.

MAJOR, JULIUS: Hungarian composer of music; born Dec. 13, 1859, at Kaschau on the Hernad, chief town of Aber Uj Var district, Hungary. He commenced his studies at the Realschule in Pesth, intending to become an engineer, but left that institution and entered the Landesmusikakademie, where he was a pupil of Volkmann and Erkel. Subsequently he was appointed music-teacher in various institutions, and at the present time (1904) he holds the office of instructor in music at the Jewish teachers' seminary at Budapest. At the Pesth gymnasium he organized a pupils' orchestra; in 1894 he founded the Hungarian Women's Chorus; and in 1896 he established a school of music which enjoyed considerable popularity.

Major is an excellent pianist and has become known through his composition of chamber-music. His works include: two trios; several violin sonatas; a piano concerto; a serenade for stringed orchestra; a "Hungarian Sonata"; several songs; and choruses for female voices.

Bibliography: Riemann, *Musik-Lexikon*.

S. L. V.

MAJOR, SOLOMON IBN: Turkish rabbi; flourished toward the end of the sixteenth century at Salonica, where he was head of the yeshibah. Many distinguished rabbis were Major's pupils, among them being Joseph Florentin, Abraham Falcon, and his own son Moses ibn Major. He was the author of a number of responsa, some of which are printed in the "Teshubot" of Ḥayyim Shabbethai (Salonica, 1651), some in the latter's "Torat Ḥayyim" (*ib.* 1713), and some in Judah Lerma's "Peleṭat Bet Yehudah" (Venice, 1647).

Bibliography: Conforte, *Ḳore ha-Dorot*, pp. 44b, 46a; Fürst, *Bibl. Jud.* ii. 316.

D. M. Sel.

MAJORCA. See Balearic Islands.

MAJORITY (רוב): 1. More than half of a given number or group; the greater part: applied to opinions. In their endeavor to find a Biblical basis for every principle of law the Rabbis interpreted Ex. xxiii. 2 so as to derive the majority principle from it (Sanh. 3b). But since this passage stands in connection with laws regulating the administration of justice, the principle was applied only where a definite number (רובא דאיתא קמן) was concerned, as when a difference of opinion arose among the judges constituting a court of justice (see Acquittal); or as in the case, frequently quoted in the Talmud, where a piece of meat was found in a street that contained nine shops for kasher meat and one for ṭerefah, in which case it was held that the meat came from one of the kasher shops, since they were in the majority. Other Biblical passages and laws had to be employed in order to find a Mosaic basis for the majority principle where the numbers were not definite (רובא דליתיה קמן; Ḥul. 11a, b). The principle was followed in all legal and ritual enactments and gave rise to a number of maxims, by which the Rabbis were guided in the decision of various cases. For instance, the majority of women marry when they are virgins (Ket. 16a); most children are born after nine months of pregnancy (Yeb. 37a); most women give birth to healthy children (Yeb. 36a); the majority of idolaters are loose in their moral conduct (Ket. 13b); most of those engaged in the ritual slaughtering of animals are expert (Ḥul. 3b); most of the actions of minors are of no value (Ḥul. 86a); the majority of animals yield milk only after they have borne young (Bek. 20b); most sick people recover, while most of those who are dangerously sick ("goses") do not recover (Giṭ. 28a).

These and many similar maxims scattered throughout the Talmud were valuable not only in the decision of a doubtful case (see Ḥazaḳah), but also in determining the state of an object. There were, however, some rabbis who would not be guided entirely by the majority principle, holding that the case under consideration might belong to the exceptional minority (חייש למיעוטא). R. Meïr (Yeb. 61b) forbade a minor from performing the levirate rite or the ḥaliẓah, declaring that he might later be found to be impotent, although the majority of persons are not impotent. R. Jose (Yeb. 67a, b), R. Akiba (Bek. 20b), R. Ṭarfon (Mak. 7b; comp. Ḥul. 11b; Tos. Ḥul. 11b, *s.v.* "Laḥosh"), and many other tannaim and amoraim also, were careful to provide for the minority. But the consensus of opinion among the Rabbis was to follow the majority in all cases, even where capital punishment was involved (Sanh. 69a).

The performance of the greater part of an act was sometimes counted, on the majority principle, as equivalent to the performance of the whole act. If, in slaughtering an animal, one cuts through the greater part only of the esophagus and the windpipe, although the Law requires that both these be severed, the animal is ritually fit for food (Ḥul. 27a; see SHEḤIṬAH). Similarly, after the greater part of a child's body protrudes from the womb, the child is considered as born (Nid. 29a).

"Majority" of an Act.

When the principle of majority conflicted with the principle of ḥazaḳah the former took precedence (Ḳid. 80a). The same is the case when it conflicts with the principle of proximity ("ḳarob"; B. B. 23b). The principle of majority does not apply to monetary cases (B. B. 92b; B. Ḳ. 27b; Tos. B. Ḳ. 27b *s.v.* "Ko."). While in the case of a disagreement among the judges the opinion of the majority is followed (see ACQUITTAL), in the case of disagreeing witnesses majority is entirely disregarded. If a hundred witnesses testified to a certain fact and two witnesses refuted their testimony the testimony of none was believed (Mak. 5b; Maimonides, "Yad," 'Edut, xviii. 3; see EVIDENCE).

BIBLIOGRAPHY: Goitein, *Kesef Nibḥar*, s.v. רוב, Lemberg, 1895; Hamburger, *R. B. T.* s.v. *Mehrheit*; *Yad Malaki*, ii. 157, Berlin, 1857; Jalish, *Melo ha-Ro'im*, s.v. רוב, Halberstadt, 1859.

2. The age at which the law permits one to manage his own affairs; full age; maturity. No definite age of maturity is given in the Bible. To the army, only those above twenty years of age were admitted (Num. i. 3). This was also the age-limit for those who had to pay the half-shekel when the people were counted (Ex. xxx. 14). The Levites were admitted to service at the age of thirty (Num. iv. 23; comp. viii. 24, where twenty-five is given as the age-limit; in I Chron. xxiii. 27 and in Ezra iii. 8 the age-limit is put at twenty; comp. Ḥul. 24a), and were dismissed from service at the age of fifty (comp. *ib.*). In the case of vows to the sanctuary ("'arakin"), mention is made of various ages with regard to determining the assessment value of the individual (Lev. xxvii. 1-8; see ESTIMATE; VOW).

The Rabbis, however, reckoned the age of maturity from the time when the first signs of puberty appear (Nid. 52a), and estimated that these signs come, with women, about the beginning of the thirteenth year, and about the beginning of the fourteenth year with men. From this period one was regarded as an adult and as responsible for one's actions to the laws of the community. In the case of females, the rabbinic law recognized several distinct stages: those of the "ḳeṭannah," from the age of three to the age of twelve and one day; the "na'arah," the six months following that period; and the "bogeret," from the expiration of these six months. In the case of males, distinction was made in general only between the period preceding the age of thirteen and one day and that following it, although, as will be seen below, other stages were occasionally recognized.

The Age of Maturity.

The attainment of the age of majority, however, did not of itself render one an adult; the prescribed age and the symptoms of puberty together were necessary to establish the majority of a person. If there were no signs of puberty at the age of majority (*i.e.*, at the beginning of the thirteenth year in a female and at the beginning of the fourteenth in a male) the person retained the status of a minor until the age of twenty. If after that period signs of impotence developed, thus explaining the absence of the signs of puberty, the person was admitted to the status of an adult; if such signs did not develop, the person remained in the status of a minor until the age of thirty-five years and one day—the greater part of the time allotted to man on earth (comp. Ps. xc. 10). In the case of a woman, the bearing of children was regarded as sufficient to establish her majority (Yeb. 12b; Maimonides, "Yad," Ishut, ii. 9; comp. "Maggid Mishneh" and "Leḥem Mishneh" *ad loc.*; for the whole subject see Nid. v. 3-8; vi. 1, 11-12; "Yad," *l.c.* ch. ii.).

The ḳeṭannah might be given in marriage by her father, and the marriage was valid, necessitating a formal divorce if separation was desired. Her earnings and her findings, also, belonged to her father, and he could annul her vows and accept a divorce for her (Nid. 47a; Ket. 46b). In the absence of her father, her mother or her brothers might contract a marriage for her, but such a marriage might be annulled by her without any formality before she reached the age of maturity (see MI'UN). Illegitimate intercourse with her carried with it the regular punishment for the transgressor, although she could not be punished (Nid. 44b). The na'arah, however, although still under the control of her father (Ḳid. 41a), was considered a responsible person; her vows were valid (Nid. 45b). The bogeret was regarded as entirely independent of her father's will and was looked upon as an adult in all respects (Nid. 47a).

Marriage of Minors.

The Rabbis recognized in males a stage similar to that of the ḳeṭannah. A boy nine years of age was regarded as being of a nubile age, so that if he had illegitimate intercourse with a woman forbidden to him she would be liable to punishment, although he could not be punished until he reached the age of maturity—thirteen years and one day (Nid. 44a). His marriage, however, was not valid (Ḳid. 50b; "Yad," *l.c.* iv. 7), although he could acquire a "yebamah" through intercourse (Nid. 45a; B. B. 156b). A stage similar to that of the na'arah was recognized by the Rabbis in the case of the rebellious son (Deut. xxi. 18-21). The period during which one might become liable to the punishment inflicted upon the rebellious son was extended to include the three months (six months in Yer. Sanh. viii. 1) immediately succeeding the age of maturity (Sanh. 69a). After a boy had reached the age of maturity he was regarded a responsible person in all ritual and criminal matters, and the court inflicted punishment upon him for any transgressions. The Rabbis entertained the belief that heavenly punishment was not visited for sins committed before the age of twenty (Shab. 89b; comp. B. B. 121b; Maḥzor Vitry, ed. Hurwitz, p. 550; Ḥakam Ẓebi, Responsa, § 49; but comp. "Sefer Ḥasidim," ed. Wistinetski, § 16, where the opinion is expressed that the heavenly punishment does not depend on age but on the intelligence of the transgressor; see also Asher ben Jehiel, Responsa, xvi. 1).

Business Transactions of Minors.

According to the Mosaic law minors are unable to enter upon any business transaction. The Rabbis, however, provided that those who are above the age of six and manifest an appreciation of business dealings should be able to dispose of movable property (Giṭ. 59a, 65a). After they had reached the age of maturity they might dispose even of real property that came into their possession through gift or purchase, but they could not dispose of inherited immovable property until they reached the age of twenty (B. B. 155a, 156a; see CONSENT; GIFTS; INFANCY). The same principle was followed with regard to their testimony. After the age of thirteen and one day their testimony was admitted, though in general only when the disposition of movable property was involved. If, however, they showed signs of intelligence and of an appreciation of the value of their testimony, they might testify also in cases involving immovable property (B. B. 155b; "Yad," 'Edut, ix. 8). Minors were disqualified from testifying in any case, although the testimony of an adult with regard to incidents that he had witnessed in his minority was in some cases admitted into evidence (Ket. 28a; B. Ḳ. 88a; see EVIDENCE). For the age at which one might become a judge see JUDGE IN RABBINICAL LITERATURE.

Although the minor was considered not responsible for any act of his and could not be summoned to court for any injury caused to another by him or by his property, still when one of his animals showed signs of viciousness (see GORING OX) the court was obliged to appoint some one to take charge of the animal. There is a difference of opinion among the Rabbis as to what should be done if it caused damage after that, some thinking that the damage should be collected from the minor's property, and others that the trustee should pay the damages (B. Ḳ. 39a).

Religious Majority.

On arriving at the age of maturity the boy is obliged to observe all the commandments of Judaism (Ab. v. 21; comp. Maḥzor Vitry, *l.c.*; see BAR MIẒWAH). From that time on he may be counted as one of the ten needed for public worship (Shulḥan 'Aruk, Oraḥ Ḥayyim, 55, 9), and he may even act as ḥazzan in case of emergency, although, as a rule, the ḥazzan is required to have a full beard (Ḥul. 24b; Shulḥan 'Aruk, *l.c.* 53, 6–8). While the minor is regarded in many respects as incapable of performing religious observances (Kil. xvii. 15; Ṭoh. iii. 6; Maksh. vi. 1) and is placed in the same category as the deaf-mute and the idiot (see DEAF AND DUMB; INSANITY) still parents are enjoined to train their children in the observance of religious duties and customs even before they reach the age of maturity. On the Day of Atonement children of nine years of age should be made to fast part of the day, and those who have reached the age of eleven and are healthy should fast the whole day (Yoma 78b, 82a). In all other religious observances, as in making the pilgrimage to Jerusalem on every festival (Ḥag. 2a, 6a), in attending the general assembly on Sukkot following the Sabbatical year (Ḥag. 3a; see Deut. xxxi. 12), and in wearing ẓiẓit or tefillin ('Ar. 2b), the father is expected to train his child during various stages of its minority.

BIBLIOGRAPHY: Löw, *Die Lebensalter in der Jüdischen Literatur*, Szegedin, 1875; Mayer, *Die Rechte der Israeliten, Athener und Römer*, ii. 126, Leipsic, 1866; Mendelssohn, *Ritualgesetze der Juden*, pp. 83–85, Berlin, 1793; Mielziner, *Jewish Law of Marriage and Divorce*, pp. 71–74, Cincinnati, 1884.

S. J. H. G.

MAKAI, EMIL: Hungarian poet; born at Mako Nov. 17, 1871; died at Budapest Aug. 6, 1901; son of Rabbi A. E. Fischer. He was educated at the Rabbinical Seminary in Budapest and distinguished himself as a student by his poetical talent. Some of the medieval Hebrew poets, like Gabirol, Ha-Levi, Moses ibn Ezra, Al-Ḥarizi, and Immanuel of Rome, he made known by his happy renderings of their productions. He wrote also "Absalom," a Biblical drama; "Zsidó Költökböl" (1891), a collection from the Hebrew poets; and "Enekek Eneke" (1892); and he published a few volumes of lyric poetry.

S. A. KE.

MAKKEDAH: City situated, according to the Priestly description of tribal boundaries and groups of cities contained in the Book of Joshua (xv. 41), among the foot-hills bordering upon Judah and extending westward to the maritime plain. It is mentioned also several times in the narrative (Josh. x.) of the pursuit of the routed forces of the allied southern kings by the Israelites under Joshua, and once (xii. 16) in the list of the princes conquered during the southern campaign. Apparently Makkedah was a stronghold of some importance, being deemed worthy of especial mention side by side with Libnah, Lachish, and Hebron (x. 28–37). Near the city was a large cave in which the five allies sought refuge. When this was reported to Joshua he ordered the exit of the cave to be blocked by boulders and guarded. The army then followed the fleeing enemy and accomplished its utter defeat. On its return to Makkedah the five kings were led out and executed.

The site of Makkedah is much in doubt. Warren was the first to identify it with the modern Al-Mughar ("the cave"), several miles southwest from Ekron, and about eight miles from the sea and twenty-five miles from Gibeon. The determining reason for this identification is the presence of caves at Al-Mughar. According to Major Conder it is the only site in the Shefelah where caves are to be found. Eusebius declared that Makkedah was eight miles east of Eleutheropolis, but this seems incredible.

S. F. K. S.

MAKKOT (מכות = "blows," "punishments"): Treatise of the Mishnah, Tosefta, and Gemara (Palestinian and Babylonian). It is fifth in the order of Neziḳin ("Damages"), following Sanhedrin, to which in contents it is closely related and with which it was formerly united (see Maimonides, "Haḳdamah"). It is divided into three chapters (containing respectively 10, 8, and 16 mishnayot), and treats of the conditions under which false witnesses are pronounced guilty of, and punished for, conspiracy (Deut. xix. 16 *et seq.*); of the conditions under which the homicide is interned in a city of refuge (Ex. xxi. 13; Deut. xix. 4–5); of the penalty of flagellation (Deut. xxv. 1 *et seq.*), when incurred and how administered. Following is an epitome of its contents:

Contents of First Section.

I. According to the Pentateuchal law, the false witness suffers the penalty which he intended should fall on his guiltless brother (Deut. xix. 19). However, there are cases where the same penalty can not be inflicted, as where conspirators would degrade a priest by falsely declaring him to be the offspring of a union between a priest and a divorcée, a union that would debar him from participating in priestly functions (Lev. xxi. 13–14); or where they would bring about an innocent man's banishment to a city of refuge by falsely charging him with manslaughter. In either case the same penalty can not be imposed: in the first instance, because the witnesses' children, who are entirely innocent, would be tainted; in the second, because the cities of refuge are for the protection of the involuntary homicide only (see Homicide). Therefore the penalty is commuted from degradation or internment to flagellation. But in general the same penalty is meted out to false witnesses. Thus, where they conspire to have one adjudged indebted to another in a certain sum of money, and it is legally proved that their testimony is fabricated, they are jointly condemned to pay the accused a like sum. Or, where they testify that A had borrowed from B a certain sum to be repaid at the end of a month, and it is proved that the loan was made for ten years, they are jointly fined to the amount that would be given for the use of the sum in question for the period of ten years less the one month.

Where the penalty involved is capital or corporal punishment, each of the confuted witnesses is subjected to the full penalty. Thus, if they aver that a certain man had been sentenced to receive thirty-nine lashes, but had escaped before the execution of the sentence, and it is legally proved that their testimony is false, each of them will receive thirty-nine lashes. However, to subject the confuted witnesses to the penalty attached to the crime charged by them it must be legally demonstrated that they themselves could not possibly have witnessed the crime or the transaction concerning which they have testified, supposing it to have been committed, and it is necessary that the court should have pronounced their intended victim guilty, but should not have executed the sentence before the confutation. Nor can the false witnesses be found guilty of plotting and be subjected to the penalty involved by their accusation unless they constitute a legal number and a legal "set," and unless the whole set is confuted. (See Alibi.)

If among a large number of witnesses one is discovered to be debarred from testifying in the case before the court, or to be disqualified from bearing witness anywhere, the whole number is disqualified. An escaped convict, being recaptured and brought before the tribunal that had originally convicted him, can have no new trial, but is dealt with according to the sentence passed. If such a one is brought before another tribunal and a legal number of witnesses testify that in their presence a certain court had found him guilty of a certain crime, and that he had escaped before suffering the penalty, the latter court is bound to have the convict duly punished. The chapter concludes with sentiments opposed to capital punishment. A sanhedrin that averages one sentence of death in every seven years is a murderous tribunal; Eleazar b. Azariah is of opinion that it is such if it average one sentence of death in seventy years; and Ṭarfon and Akiba declare that they would never have permitted the execution of a human being. Simon b. Gamaliel, however, believes that removing the fear of punishment would contribute toward an increase in bloodshed.

Accusation of Accidental Homicide.

II. Accidental homicide subjects its author to exile in one of the cities assigned as cities of refuge. Every Israelite is subject to this law, no exception being made on account of descent or station or relationship. A parent accidentally killing a child, or vice versa, is subject to exile; and so is the high priest. The only exception allowed is in favor of the sightless. But as "accidents" admit of gradation, not all accidental homicides are subject to the penalty of exile (see Homicide). The number of the cities of refuge is six—three in Canaan and three beyond the Jordan (Num. xxxv. 13–14), and careful provision is made for their easy reach. On his way to the city the exile is accompanied by scholars whose duty it is to defend him against the avenger of blood. Once interned in one of the cities he remains there for life, or until the death of the high priest during whose term the accident occurred (Num. xxxv. 25 *et seq.*). If the high priest himself is the exile, the death of his successor does not release him; neither does the death of a high priest free an exile who has slain a high priest. If the exile goes beyond the bounds of the city, the avenger of blood may kill him with impunity (see Avenger). In case the exile again becomes subject to exile, he is transferred from the district in which he had resided to another, but he must not leave the city. If honors are offered the exile in his asylum, he must not accept them without first acquainting the people with the reason for his presence there; if then the people think him worthy he may accept. When, on the death of a high priest, he returns to his original home, all the property he had left there is restored to him; but he can not resume an office which he held at the time of his banishment.

III. The third chapter enumerates fifty-nine offenses, each entailing flagellation. Of these, three are marital sins of priests; four, prohibited intermarriages; seven, sexual relations of an incestuous nature; eight, violations of dietary laws; twelve, various violations of the negative precepts; twenty-five, abuses of Levitical laws and vows. When the offense has been persisted in, the punishment depends on the number of forewarnings (see HATRA'AH). The Mishnah gives thirty-nine as the maximum number of stripes the court may impose for any one misdemeanor; but the convict must be examined as to his physical ability to endure the full count without endangering his life. The convict is bound in bent position to a post, and the public executioner administers the punishment with a leather strap while one of the judges recites appropriate Scriptural verses (Deut. xxviii. 15, 29; xxix. 8; Ps. lxxviii. 38). Any one guilty of a sin which is punished by excision may be cleared by flagellation. The author of this midrash, Ḥanina b. Gamaliel, adds, "If by the commission of a sin one forfeits his soul before God, so much the more reason is there for the belief that, by a meritorious deed, such as voluntary submission to punishment, his soul is saved."

Penalty of Flagellation.

The tractate concludes with a few haggadic passages bearing upon the punishment awaiting the sinner and the reward reserved for the righteous. The Gemara, Jerusalem as well as Babylonian, elaborates the concise rules embodied in the Mishnah, citing opinions and counter-opinions, Scriptural texts to prove one or the other, and precedents. Haggadot also abound there, but chiefly in the Babylonian. The following is quoted from the Yerushalmi: Referring to the provision that the roads leading to the several cities of refuge must be kept in good order (ii. 5 [ed. Krotoschin, p. 8]), Eleazar b. Jacob asserts that there were signs bearing the direction "miḳlaṭ" (= "refuge," "asylum"), and Abun states more exactly that the roads were provided with sign-posts attached to which were index-hands inscribed with the word "miḳlaṭ." Thereupon Phinehas remarks, "From the consideration of such merciful provisions one can learn the meaning of the saying of the Psalmist, 'Good and upright is the Lord, therefore will He point sinners the way [to the city of refuge]'" (Ps. xxv. 8, Hebr.).

Gemarot.

S. S. S. M.

MAKO: Town in Hungary, in the county of Csanad. It has a total population of 33,722, of which 1,642 are Jews (1900). Jews began to settle there about the middle of the eighteenth century, under the protection of Stanislavich, the Bishop of Csanad, who, in 1740, assigned a special quarter to them. They soon formed a community, and by 1747 had established a ḥebra ḳaddisha. The first rabbi of Mako was Judah b. Abraham ha-Levi, who occupied the rabbinate from 1778 to 1824. He was succeeded by Salomon Ullman (1826–63). Ullman wrote a commentary on certain sections of Yoreh De'ah, under the title "Yeri'ot Shelomoh" (Vienna, 1854). He was followed by Anton Enoch Fischer (1864-96), former rabbi of Duna-Földvar. Fischer introduced German and (later) Hungarian in his sermons. Mako has a Jewish school (of which Marcus Steinhardt has been one of the teachers for forty years), established in 1851, a Jewish women's association, a Jewish students' aid society, and a Jewish women's lying-in hospital. The present (1904) incumbent is Dr. A. Kecskemeti.

D. A. KE.

MAKOWER, HERMANN: German jurist; born at Santomischel, Posen, March 8, 1830; died at Berlin April 1, 1898. His father, recognizing the inadequate educational facilities of the town, sent him, alone and almost penniless, at the age of nine, to win a living and an education in Berlin. There he attended the Französische Gymnasium, secured a position as chorister in a synagogue, and met Siegmund Meyer, a boy of the same age, with whom he formed a friendship that lasted throughout his life. Makower gave private lessons, and after graduation served as "Referendarius" and assessor, and ultimately became "Grundbuchrichter" at the Berlin city court, a position never before held by one of his coreligionists. In 1857 he published his first contribution to legal literature, "Die Stellung der Vertheidigung im Preussischen Strafverfahren" (Berlin, 1857). He gave up his prospects for judicial advancement for the more substantial rewards of a career as legal practitioner.

Makower's activities in the sphere of commercial law were inaugurated by his "Studien zur Konkursordnung vom 8. Mai 1855" (Berlin, 1861). In the following year appeared his great work, in the preparation of which his friend Siegmund Meyer cooperated with him—"Das Allgemeine Deutsche Handelsgesetzbuch, Nebst dem Preussischen Einführungsgesetze vom 24. Juni 1861, und der Instruktion vom 12. Dezbr. 1861, für den Praktischen Gebrauch aus den Quellen Erläutert" (Berlin, 1862; 11th ed., 1893); this was followed by "Zur Revision der Deutschen Konkursordnung" (*ib.* 1894), and by a number of minor writings on insurance companies and the protesting of bills and notes, and by discussions of various points in commercial law.

He enjoyed a very large and lucrative practise, and won for himself a clientele among the greatest men of his time. One of the celebrated causes with which he was identified was that of the historian Theodor Mommsen, charged with slandering Prince Bismarck. He opened his argument at one of the several trials of this case with these words: "Two princes represent antithetical views; one, a prince of diplomacy, the other, a prince of learning; one, a man who makes history, the other, a man who writes history"; after appealing to the highest courts of the empire Mommsen was finally acquitted (1883).

Makower was zealously interested in the communal and congregational life of the Jews in Berlin, and earnestly supported the efforts to sustain the Lehranstalt für die Wissenschaft des Judenthums. For its benefit he delivered a lecture, Jan. 10, 1881, entitled "Unsere Gemeinde" (Posen, 1881). Another contribution to the literature of Jewish communal affairs was his treatise on "Die Gemeinde-Verhältnisse der Juden in Preussen" (Berlin, 1873). He was instrumental in the publication of the "Regesten zur Geschichte der Juden im Deutschen Reich," and was one of the most active in collaboration on the "Grundsätze der Jüdischen Sittenlehre." From 1866 to 1892 he was a member of the board of the Jewish community of Berlin; from 1870 to 1892 he was its president.

BIBLIOGRAPHY: Bernhard Breslauer, *Hermann Makower*, in *Allg. Zeit. des Jud.* 1898, pp. 162–163, 173–175, 185–188, 200–202; Justizrath Meyer, *Justizrath Hermann Makower*, in *Deutsche Juristen Zeitung*, ii. 162–165.

S. M. Co.

MAḲRE DARDEḲE: Name given in the Middle Ages to Hebrew glossaries primarily intended for the use of students of the Bible; its literal meaning is "teacher of children." The first and most noteworthy work of this kind is the one published at Naples in 1488, the author of which is Perez Trévôt. The work gives every Hebrew vocable, accompanied by a translation into Italian and Arabic and a short explanation in Hebrew, at times quoting the French glosses occurring in the Bible commentary of Rashi and in the works of R. David Ḳimḥi. The work was composed in 1395, in southern Italy, with the purpose of promoting a better understanding of the Scriptures among the Italian Jews (who had neglected Biblical for Talmudic studies), in order to enable them to answer successfully Christian and Moslem attacks on Judaism. This work is of importance for the fourteenth-century Italian it contains. Similar works, based on this, were afterward produced in other countries, French, German, or Spanish being substituted for the original Italian and Arabic. The Italian glosses of the "Maḳre Dardeḳe" were published separately by M. Schwab in "R. E. J." (xvi. 253 *et seq.*).

BIBLIOGRAPHY: Bodek, in *Orient*, viii. 612–618; Grünbaum, *Jüdisch-Deutsche Chrestomathie*, pp. 521 *et seq.*; Güdemann, *Gesch.* ii. 206; Perles, *Beiträge zur Gesch. der Hebr. und Aram. Studien*, pp. 113–130.

G. C. L.

MAKSHAN, SAMUEL BEN PHINEHAS HA-KOHEN: Bohemian Talmudist of the sixteenth century; born in Prague. He wrote: "Tehillat Dibre Shemuel," commentary on the Targum of Esther (Prague, 1594 [according to Zunz, "Z. G." p. 278; 1601 according to other bibliographers]); "Bet Din shel Shemuel," commentary on Rashi to Esther and Ruth and on the Targum of the latter (Lublin, 1606); "Yegon Leb," commentary on Lamentations (Cracow, n.d.).

BIBLIOGRAPHY: Fürst, *Bibl. Jud.* ii. 318; Steinschneider, *Cat. Bodl.* col. 2435.

D. M. Sel.

MAKSHIRIN ("Predisposings"): Name of the eighth tractate, in the Mishnah and Tosefta, of the sixth Talmudic order Ṭohorot ("Purifications"). This tractate contains six chapters, divided respectively into 6, 11, 8, 10, 11, and 8 sections, while the Tosefta has only three chapters and 31 sections. It treats of the effects of liquids in rendering foods with which they may come into contact susceptible, under certain conditions, of Levitical uncleanness. It is based on the Scriptural provision, "If any water be put upon the seed, and any part of their carcass fall thereon, it shall be unclean" (Lev. xi. 38; see 34 *et seq.*). From this the Rabbis deduce (1) that foods are not susceptible of uncleanness by contact with the carcass of a reptile unless the foods have first been moistened (see Ḥul. 36a); and (2) that as Scripture, in the passage just cited, uses the expression כי יתן, which, when vowelless, may be read either "ki yuttan" (= "if it be put") or "ki yitten" (= "if one will put"), and as "putting" is necessarily the result of intention, "being put" also must be accompanied by intention (see B. M. 22b). Where this condition is absent the contact of liquid with foods will have no effect. Hence the general rule elaborated in the first chapter following.

Ch. i.: All liquids ("mashḳin"; see vi. 4 *et seq.*) when originally desired (expected to be beneficial) though ultimately unwelcome, or when the reverse is the case (not desired originally, but ultimately acceptable), predispose loose fruit moistened by them to Levitical uncleanness. Thus if one shakes a tree to bring down some fruit or a dead reptile, and at the same time some drops of water fall from the tree on fruit lying near by, the water does not come under the law of ki yuttan, or the fruit under liability to uncleanness by contact with a defiling object; but when one's intention is to shake off the rain-water or the dewdrops, the loose fruit moistened thereby becomes susceptible to uncleanness. Where water is used for other than its ordinary purposes, as where one submerges fruit or vegetables to secrete them from thieves, the effect is not to render the fruit liable to defilement. A precedent under this rule is cited from the history of the last days of Judea's struggle against the Romans, when some citizens of Jerusalem secured their fig-cakes from the sicarii by hiding them under water, the Rabbis deciding that under the circumstances, the submersion did not predispose the food to uncleanness. Similarly, fruit that is floated down a river is not subject to the rule of ki yuttan.

General Principle.

Ch. ii.: In doubtful cases, objects and conditions are classified by a majority rule. For example, the defiling effects of receptacles of waste water used in common by Jews and Gentiles will depend on the majority using them; if the majority are non-Jews the water will be considered Levitically unclean, but where the majority are Jews the water will be considered Levitically clean. Where these are equally divided the presumption of uncleanness will prevail. The majority rule is not limited to questions of clean and unclean; it serves as a criterion in other matters, ritual and even civil.

Doubtful Cases.

Ch. iii.–vi. 3 continue the discussion of the main subject in connection with the Scriptural expression "ki yuttan." Ch. vi. 4–8 enumerates the mashḳin which render loose fruit liable to Levitical uncleanness through contact with defiling objects. According to the Rabbis, the term "mashḳin" covers seven kinds of liquid: dew, water, wine, oil, blood, milk, and honey (see Tosef., Shab. viii. [ix.] 24–28, where Scriptural phraseology is adduced to prove the connotation of "mashḳeh"). "Water" includes discharges of the eye, ear, and other organs. There is no Gemara, Yerushalmi or Babli, to this treatise.

S. S. S. M.

MALABAR. See Cochin.

MALACH, ḤAYYIM. See Ḥayyim Mal'ak

MALACHI, BOOK OF.—Biblical Data: The ook of Malachi is the last in the canon of the Old 'estament Prophets. It has three chapters in the Iasoretic text, while in the Septuagint, the Vulate, and the Peshiṭta it has four. The King James 'ersion also, following the latter versions, has four hapters. As in the books of Isaiah, Lamentations, nd Ecclesiastes, the last verse in the Masoretic text a repetition of the last verse but one. The style f the book is more prosaic than that of any of the ther prophetical books; the parallelism met with in ie others is here less pronounced, and the imagery ften lacks force and beauty. The method of treatient is rather novel; it approaches the teaching iethod of the schools; Cornill speaks of it as "casutic-dialectic." Thus the prophet first states his roposition; then he follows with remonstrances iat might be raised by those he addresses; finally e reasserts his original thesis (comp. i. 2 *et seq.*, 6 *et q.*; ii. 13 *et seq.*, 17; iii. 8, 13 *et seq.*). This form dds vividness to the argument. The book may be ivided into three sections—(1) i. 1–ii. 9; (2) ii. 10–7; (3) iii. (A. V. iii. and iv.), the divisions given eing those of the Masoretic text.

Contents.

Ch. i. 2–ii. 9 represent Yhwh as Ruler and loving 'ather. It opens with a tender allusion to the love hown by Yhwh to Judah in the past; yet Judah cted faithlessly, deserting its benefactor. Malachi then addresses himself to the priests, those who are to lead the people in the way of Yhwh. He castigates them or being derelict in their duty by offering on 'hwh's altars polluted bread and animals that have lemishes. By doing so they show that they depise Yhwh (i. 6–10). But Yhwh can do without ieir worship, for the time will come when the 'hole heathen world will worship Him (i. 11–14). f the priests will not heed the admonition, dire unishment will be visited upon them (ii. 1–8).

Ch. ii. 10–17 speaks of Yhwh as the supreme God nd Father of all, and inveighs against those who ad left their Jewish wives and married heathen 'omen.

Ch. iii. (A. V. iii. and iv.) speaks of Yhwh as the ighteous and final Judge. It begins with the anouncement that the messenger of Yhwh will come prepare the way for Him by purifying the social nd religious life (1–4). Yhwh will call to judgient all those who have transgressed the moral law nd have been lax in the observance of the ritual; Ie invites all who have gone astray to return to Iim and receive His blessings (5–15). The faithful 'ill be blessed, while those who persist in disobeyig the law of God will be punished (16–21). The ook closes with a final exhortation to the godly.

Prophetic Tone.

Malachi, as opposed to the other prophetical ooks, lays much stress upon ceremonial observance . 6 *et seq.*, 13 *et seq.*; iii. 7 *et seq.*, 22): the priest is 'hwh's messenger (ii. 7, iii. 3 *et seq.*), and the law f Moses, with its statutes and observances, must be strictly observed (iii. 22). Yet he is not a formalist; the book breathes the genuine prophetic spirit. Thus, from the idea of the brotherhood of all sraelites he deduces the social duties which they we to one another (ii. 10). Ceremonial observance is of value in his eyes only so long as it leads to spiritual service. In scathing language he lays bare the moral degeneracy of his time, a time given over to adultery, false swearing, oppression of the hireling and the widow and the fatherless (iii. 5 *et seq.*). Especially severe is he toward those who had entered into wedlock with heathen women (ii. 11–16).

The conditions that existed under his predecessors Haggai and Zechariah seem to have existed at the time of Malachi. The Exile is a matter of the past; the Temple is built, and sacrifices are being offered (i. 10, iii. 1–10). Malachi describes most faithfully the temper of his generation. The people had strayed away from Yhwh, and sought, by an assumption of indifference and by mockery, to hide their restlessness. The exiles had been disillusioned when they found the land of their fathers a wilderness. Drought, locusts, failure of harvests (iii. 10 *et seq.*) had deepened their discontent. Yhwh's sanctuary had been rebuilt, but still their condition did not improve; they were growing impatient and were asking for proofs of Yhwh's love (iii. 13 *et seq.*). Under the pressure of these unfavorable circumstances, priests and people neglected to show Yhwh the honor due to Him (i. 2 *et seq.*). Malachi lays stress upon the inevitableness of the Day of Judgment, the coming of which would prove to the skeptical that devotion and fear of God are not in vain, but will be rewarded. The messenger of Yhwh and the Last Judgment form the closing theme of Malachi's prophecy. The messenger will come in the person of Elijah, who will regenerate the people and restore them to union with Yhwh.

——**In Rabbinical Literature:** Malachi is identified with Mordecai by R. Naḥman and with Ezra by Joshua b. Ḳarḥa (Meg. 15a). Jerome, in his preface to the commentary on Malachi, mentions that in his day the belief was current that Malachi was identical with Ezra ("Malachi Hebræi Esdram Existimant"). The Targum of Jonathan ben Uzziel to the words "By the hand of Malachi" (i. 1) gives the gloss "Whose name is called Ezra the scribe." According to Soṭah 48b, when Malachi died the Holy Spirit departed from Israel. According to R. H. 19b, he was one of the three prophets concerning whom there are certain traditions with regard to the fixing of the Jewish almanac. A tradition preserved in pseudo-Epiphanius ("De Vitis Proph.") relates that Malachi was of the tribe of Zebulun, and was born after the Captivity. According to the same apocryphal story he died young, and was buried in his own country with his fathers.

——**Critical View:** The name מלאכי is not a "nomen proprium"; it is generally assumed to be an abbreviation of מלאכיה (= "messenger of Yhwh"), which conforms to the Μαλαχίας of the Septuagint and the "Malachias" of the Vulgate. The Septuagint superscription is ἐν χειρὶ ἀγγέλου αὐτοῦ, for ביד מלאכי. Wellhausen, Kuenen, and Nowack consider ch. i. 1 a late addition, pointing to Zech. ix. 1, xii. 1. Cornill states that Zech. ix.–xiv. and Malachi are anonymous, and were, therefore, placed at the end of the prophetical books. Mal. iii. 1 shows almost conclusively that the term מלאכי was misunderstood, and that the proper name originated in a misconception of the word. The consensus of opinion seems to point to 432–424 B.C. as the time of the composition of the book. This was the time between the first and second visits of Nehemiah to Jerusalem. Some assert that the book was written before 458 B.C., that is, before the arrival of Ezra in Jerusalem.

BIBLIOGRAPHY: Boehme, in Stade's *Zeitschrift*, vii. 210 *et seq.*; Driver, *Introduction*; D. Knobel, *Prophetismus der Hebräer*, i. 386, Breslau, 1837; Bleek, *Introduction to the Old Testament*, 2d ed., i. 357; Cornill, *Einleitung in das Alte Testament*, pp. 205 *et seq.*, Freiburg, 1896; Cornill, *The Prophets of Israel*, p. 158, Chicago, 1895.

S. A. G.

MALACHI, ABRAHAM. See ABRAHAM MALAKI.

MALACHI B. JACOB HA-KOHEN: Prominent Talmudist and methodologist of the eighteenth century; the last of the great rabbinical authorities of Italy; died before 1790. He was dayyan at Leghorn, and apparently lived to an old age. A decision by him, dated Nisan, 1732, and referring to a civil case at Rome, is included in the responsa of Rabbi Isaiah Bassani of Reggio ("Todat Shelamim," No. 11, Venice, 1741). In the controversy between Eybeschütz and Emden he sided with the former (letter of the rabbinate of Leghorn in "Luḥot 'Edut," p. 22). He is especially famous for his "Yad Mal'aki" (Leghorn, 1767; Berlin, 1856; Przemysl, 1877), a methodological work in three parts: part one contains an alphabetical list of all the rules and technical terms found in the Talmud, with explanations; part two deals with rules regarding the codifiers; part three treats of the rules relating to legal decisions, explaining certain general principles of legal responsa. Malachi wrote also a liturgical work, "Shibḥe Todah" (Leghorn, 1744), containing prayers for the 22d of Shebaṭ, a fast-day instituted by the community of Leghorn.

BIBLIOGRAPHY: Azulai, *Shem ha-Gedolim*, i. 63; Steinschneider, *Cat. Bodl.* col. 1644.

S. S. J. Z. L.

MALAGA (מלקה, מאלקה, מאלאקה): Spanish Mediterranean seaport; capital of the province of Malaga; said to have been founded by the Phenicians. Malaga was an important place of commerce in the time of the Romans and had Jewish inhabitants at a very early date. During the Moorish supremacy the Jews there enjoyed complete equality and, especially in the time of Samuel ibn Nagdelah, were even held in high esteem, although under the Almohades they shared the sufferings of their brethren in the rest of Spain. The sources of information are very scanty concerning the Jewish community of Malaga, which, although not so large as those of Seville, Cordova, and Granada, was still of some importance. When the city was taken by the Spanish, Aug. 18, 1487, the Jews from Seville and Cordova, who had been baptized by force and had sought protection in Malaga from the persecutions of the Inquisition, were cruelly tortured and killed. All the Malaga Jews, 400 to 450 in number, mostly women who spoke Arabic and dressed like Moorish women, were taken captive and condemned to slavery with the remainder of the inhabitants. The young Solomon ibn Verga was sent to the Spanish communities to collect money for their ransom, and succeeded in raising 20,000 gold doubloons. Wi this sum, added to the money and jewels the ca tives themselves possessed, they were redeemed an sent to Africa in two sailing vessels by the chi tax-collector Don Abraham Senior, who had b come a Christian and who, probably because of h change of faith, is not mentioned by the contemp rary Jewish chroniclers. After the year 1492 Jew were no longer allowed to live in Malaga, thoug Maranos were still found there in the eighteent century. Malaga is the birthplace of Solomon ib Gabirol, and there lived Isaac ha-Levi ibn Ḥaka ha-Sofer (a contemporary of Isaac b. Sheshet Judah and Moses Alashkar, and others.

BIBLIOGRAPHY: Bernaldez, *Cronica de los Reyes Catolic* ch. lxxxvi. *et seq.*; Grätz, *Gesch.* viii. 348; Zacuto, *Sefer Y ḥasin*, p. 227a; Rios, *Hist.* iii. 299; *Shebeṭ Yehudah*, p. 1

G. M. K.

MALBIM, MEÏR LÖB BEN JEHIE MICHAEL: Russian rabbi, preacher, and Hebr ist; born at Volochisk, Volhynia, in 1809; died Kiev Sept. 18, 1879. The name "Malbim" is d rived from the initials of his name (מלבים), and b came his family name by frequent usage. Malbi was educated in Hebrew and Talmud by his fath and by his stepfather (R. Löb of Volochisk). H showed unusual talent from his early childhood, an his works indicate that he had a considerable knowledge of secular sciences. From 1838 to 1845 he was rabbi of Wreschen, district of Posen, and in the latter year was called to the rabbinate of Kempen, where he remained until 1860; he was thereafter known as "der Kempener." In 1860 Malbim became chief rabbi of Bucharest, Rumania. But he could not agree with the rich German Jews there; they wished to introduce the Reformed rite, and did not shrink even from violence in the pursuit of the aims. By intrigues they succeeded in throwing hi into prison, and though he was liberated throug the intervention of Sir Moses Montefiore, it w upon the condition that he leave Rumania.

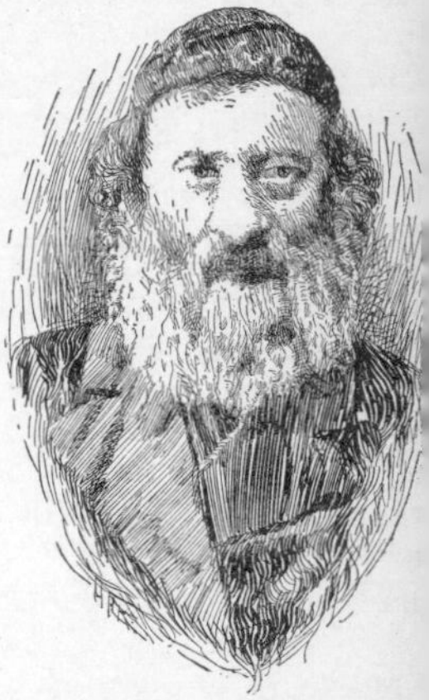

Meïr Löb Malbim.

Malbim went to Constantinople and complain to the Turkish government, but obtained no sati faction. After staying six months in Paris, he we to Lenczİza, government of Kalisz, Russian Polan as successor to his deceased father-in-law, Ḥayyi Auerbach (1866). Shortly after he was rabbi Kherson, and thence was called to the rabbina of Moghilef, on the Dnieper (1870). There, too, h lack of subservience provoked the resentment of t richer Jews; these denounced him as a political crim nal, and the governor of Moghilef ordered him leave the town. Malbim then went to Königsberg chief rabbi of the Polish community, but there h ared no better than in Bucharest and Moghilef; e was continually harassed by the German Jews. When Malbim passed through Wilna in 1879 the community there would have appointed him rabbi in place of Isaac Elijah Landau, but the governor of Wilna opposed the election on the ground that he could not sanction the appointment of a rabbi who had been expelled from Moghilef as a political criminal. In September of the same year Malbim was on his way to Krementchug, to the rabbinate of which town he had been appointed, when he fell sick and died at Kiev.

Malbim was the author of: "Arẓot ha-Ḥayyim," commentary and novellæ on the Shulḥan 'Aruk, Oraḥ Ḥayyim (Breslau, 1837); "Arẓot ha-Shalom," collection of sermons (Krotoschin, 1839); "Ha-Torah weha-Miẓwah," commentary on the Pentateuch and Sifra (Warsaw, 1874–80); "Miḳra'e Ḳodesh," commentary on the Prophets and Hagiographa ib. 1874; this commentary is double—on the words and on the sense; Malbim always endeavored to explain the different meanings of synonyms); "Mashal u-Meliẓah," dramatic philippic, in verse, against hypocrisy (Paris, 1867).

Bibliography: *Der Israelit*, 1879, p. 1079; S. Sachs, in *Ha-Lebanon*, ii. 92 *et seq.*, 106 *et seq.*

H. R. M. Sel.

MALCHA: Russian town, in the government of Grodno. A Jewish community existed in Malcha in 1685, when, in consequence of rumors current as to the killing of a Christian laborer by the Jews, the kahal of Malcha invited the constable of the district of Brest, Alexander Shavlovski, to visit Malcha and investigate the matter. No evidence being found to justify the rumor, the Jews made a formal protest against the spreading of the accusation. It has a total population (1903) of about 3,000, half of whom are Jews. Of the latter, 291 are artisans. In the ḥadarim 90 Jewish children are instructed, and in the two Talmud Torahs, 40. The charitable organizations consist of a biḳḳur ḥolim, a gemilut ḥasadim, etc.

Bibliography: *Regesty i Nadpisi*, p. 383, St. Petersburg, 1899.

H. R. S. J.

MALCHIN. See Mecklenburg.

MALCHUS (CLEODEMUS THE PROPHET): Hellenistic writer of the second century B.C. His Semitic name, "Malchus," a very common one in Phenicia and Syria but not met with among the Jews, combined with the pagan traditions abounding in his work, has given rise to discussions concerning his origin. Ewald supposes him to have been a Phenician; Herzfeld, a Syrian; Freudenthal endeavors to prove that he was a Samaritan; and Schürer holds that he must have been either a Jew or a Samaritan.

Cleodemus was the author of a history of the Jews in Greek, in which Jewish traditions are blended with Greek mythology. A short notice of his history, which is no longer in existence, is quoted by Josephus ("Ant." i. 15) from Alexander Polyhistor. Cleodemus relates that among the sons of Abraham and Keturah were three, Apher, Surim, and Japhran ('Αφέραν, 'Ασουρείμ, 'Ιάφραν), from whom the town of Aphra, the land of Assyria, and Africa derived their names. He relates further that these three sons helped Hercules in his fight against Libya and Antæus, and that Hercules married the daughter of Aphra, by whom he had a son, Didorus, from whose son Sophon the Sophacians derived their name.

Bibliography: Ewald, *Gesch.* vii. 91; Herzfeld, *Gesch. des Volkes Israel*, iii. 498, 575; Freudenthal, *Alexander Polyhistor*, p. 130 *et passim*; Schürer, *Gesch.* iii. 357 (Eng. transl. ii. iii. 209).

T. I. Br.

MALEA (MALEHA; MELEA), MEÏR DE: "Almoxarif mayor"; chief farmer of taxes of King Ferdinand III. (the Holy) of Castile, whose favor he gained through his honesty and zeal in the interest of the state. Don Meïr, who was versed in the Talmud and was held in high esteem by his coreligionists, is called by Moses ben Naḥman "the great prince, the learned Don Meïr Almoxarif." Ferdinand's son and successor, Alfonso X. (the Wise), whose finances, in consequence of the troubled condition of the state, were in great confusion, employed, after the death of Don Meïr, his sons Don Zag (Isaac) and Don Juzef, who inherited the influence and position of their father, to remove the financial difficulties. When Alfonso desired to subdue his vassal Aben Nathfot de Niebla, Don Zag undertook the provisioning and administration of the entire army, being given as security the lease of all the customs duties and taxes.

Don Zag remained the only lessee of taxes until 1276, when he met competitors in the persons of his brother-in-law Don Abraham ibn Xuxen (Shushan) and one Roy Fernandez of Sahagum, and was compelled to enter into partnership with them. For two years these three paid the king an annual rent of 80,000 gold maravedis. Don Zag, who possessed the complete confidence of the king, took, with his brother Don Juzef, in addition to the lease of the taxes, that of the fines, most of which were concerned with commerce and customs, and the officials of the king were placed at their disposal to recover such fines. They certainly rendered in this capacity great services to the state, but they nevertheless incurred in no small measure the anger of the population.

Don Zag, who was exceedingly wealthy, fell suddenly, through the following incident, from the height upon which he stood: When King Alfonso undertook the siege of the city of Algeziras, he ordered the almoxarif to employ in victualing the army the large sum which he had collected as tax-lessee. Just then Don Zag was accidentally met by the infante, Don Sancho, who was in conflict with his royal father, and the infante succeeded in taking the money from Don Zag under the pretext that he wished to send it to his mother, Donna Violante, living in separation from the king. The king, exceedingly enraged, ordered Don Zag and the other Jewish tax-lessees to be thrown into dark dungeons. When the infante returned to Seville from his victorious campaign against the Moors, in the autumn of 1280, the king had the unfortunate Don Zag dragged through the city and executed in the presence of the infante. The infante had endeavored to relieve the almoxarif, who was suffering on his account and who had rendered such valuable services to the state, but all his endeavors proved futile. One Sabbath shortly after, when all the Jews of Castile and Leon were in their synagogues, they were seized by order of Alfonso, who demanded 12,000 gold maravedis, and imposed a fine of another 12,000 for every day of delay. The deposition of Alfonso, which took place several years later, stands in no relation to the execution of Don Zag.

BIBLIOGRAPHY: Zuñiga, *Anales de Sevilla*, i. 297, 318; Marques de Mondejar, *Memorias Historicas del Rey Sabio*, pp. 297, 367; Moses b. Naḥman, *Responsa*, Nos. 284, 322; Rios, *Hist.* i. 488 *et seq.*; Grätz, *Gesch.* vi. 165; Kayserling, *Gesch. der Juden in Spanien*, i. 118, 218.

G. M. K.

MALEKAR, MOSES BAPUJEE: Beni-Israel soldier; born at Bombay about 1830. He enlisted in the 12th Regiment Native Infantry April 12, 1851; was made subahdar Jan. 1, 1865; subahdar-major Feb. 15, 1878. He received the second class Order of British India in 1879, and later that of the first class, with the title of "Sirdar Bahadur." He was present at the siege and capture of Kotah and at the action of Bunnas (awarded medal and clasp). On his retirement he was made justice of the peace.

J. J. HY.

MALICE. See INTENTION.

MALINOVSKI, JOSEPH. See TROKI, JOSEPH B. MORDECAI.

MALKA BEN AHA: Gaon of Pumbedita from 771 to 773. The only fact known concerning him is that, with ḤANINAI KAHANA BEN HUNA (765–775), he opposed Naṭronai ben Ḥabibai, who, for unknown reasons, endeavored to supplant the exilarch Zakkai ben Ahunai; the two geonim succeeded in compelling Naṭronai to leave Babylonia. Naṭronai probably settled in Kairwan.

BIBLIOGRAPHY: *Letter of Sherira Gaon*, in *M. J. C.* i. 36, 188; Halevy, *Dorot ha-Rishonim*, iii. 115a *et seq.*; Grätz, *Gesch.* v. 174, 2d ed., v. 420; Weiss, *Dor*, iv. 27, 29.

S. S. M. SC.

MALKI, EZRA BEN RAPHAEL: Rabbi of Rhodes in the seventeenth century; brother-in-law of Hezekiah de Silva, the author of "Peri Ḥadash." Malki was the author of "Malki ba-Ḳodesh" (Salonica, 1749). This work contains novellæ on the laws of Passover given in the Shulḥan 'Aruk (Oraḥ Ḥayyim) and in the "Bet Yosef"; commentaries on the Pesaḥ Haggadah and on the parts of the Yad ha-Ḥazaḳah which contain the laws concerning the Passover lamb, Rosh ha-Shanah, Yom Kippur, and lulab; novellæ on the "Sefer Miẓwot ha-Gadol"; and collectanea. He wrote also: "Shemen la-Ma'or" (Constantinople, 1760), novellæ on the first chapter of Baba Meẓi'a, in which he defends Zerahiah ha-Levi against the attacks of Naḥmanides; "'En Mishpaṭ" (*ib.* 1770), responsa; "'Enot Mayim" (Salonica, 1811), sermons.

BIBLIOGRAPHY: Azulai, *Shem ha-Gedolim*, ii., s.v. מלכי בקדש; Fürst, *Bibl. Jud.* ii. 320; Zedner, *Cat. Hebr. Books Brit. Mus.* p. 508.

S. M. SEL.

MALKI, RAPHAEL MORDECAI: Rabbinical scholar and physician of Palestine; lived at Safed about 1627. He was versed in astronomy and philosophy, and was the author of a commentary on the Pentateuch entitled "Perush 'al ha-Torah."

BIBLIOGRAPHY: Hazan, *Ha-Ma'alot li-Shelomoh*, p. 89.

S. M. FR.

MALKUT SCHLAGEN. See STRIPES.

MALTER, HENRY: American rabbi an scholar; born at Zabno, Galicia, March 23, 1867 educated at the Zabno elementary school, and a the universities of Berlin (1889–93) and Heidelber (Ph.D. 1894). He pursued his Jewish studies at th Veitel Heine-Ephraimsche Lehranstalt, Berlin (ur der Steinschneider) from 1890 to 1898, and at th Berlin Hochschule from 1894 to 1898, receiving hi rabbinical diploma from the latter institution. H acted as librarian of the scientific library of th Jewish community at Berlin in 1899, and in 190 was appointed professor of medieval philosophy an Arabic at the Hebrew Union College, Cincinnati since 1902 he has also filled the office of rabbi of th Sheerith Israel Congregation of Cincinnati. Hi publications include: "Sifrut Yisrael," a Hebrev edition of Steinschneider's "Jewish Literature, with additional bibliographical notes; "Die Be schneidung in der Neueren Zeit" (in Glasberg' "Die Beschneidung," Berlin, 1896); "Die Abhand lung des Abu Hamid al-Gazzali" (Frankfort-on-the Main, 1896); "Katalog der von Fischel Hirsc Nachgelassenen Bücher" (Berlin, 1899). He has als contributed to "Ha-Maggid," "Ha-Shiloaḥ," "Mi Mizraḥ umi-Ma'arab," "Jüdischer Volkskalender, "Deborah," "American Journal of Semitic Lan guages," and the "Hebrew Union College Journal and "Annual."

A.

MALVANO, GIACOMO: Italian diplomat born at Turin Dec. 14, 1841. In 1862 he entered th diplomatic service, and by 1887 had become envo extraordinary and minister plenipotentiary; tw years later he was appointed councilor of state, an shortly afterward became general secretary in th ministry of foreign affairs. In 1875–76 he forme one of a committee appointed to draft certain com mercial treaties; in 1879 he attended the monetar conference held at Paris, as the delegate of the Ital ian government. In 1891–92 he arranged a numbe of commercial treaties with Austro-Hungary, Ger many, and Switzerland. He was repeatedly nomi nated vice-president and member of council of th Italian Geographical Society; he still (1904) occu pies the latter position.

BIBLIOGRAPHY: De Gubernatis, *Diz. Biog.*

S. V. C.

MAMON (MAMMON): Mishnaic Hebrev and Aramaic for "riches." The word itself is give in the Sermon on the Mount: "Ye can not serv God and mammon" (Matt. vi. 24). There is no evi dence that there was a Syriac god of this name, th modern idea that such a god existed being derive from Milton's personification of the name—"Mam mon, the least erected spirit that fell from heaven ("Paradise Lost," i. 679). The word occurs i Abot ii. 12, where almsgiving is called "the salt o Mammon or riches." Gesenius suggests that the wor was derived from "maṭmon" ("treasure"), with as similation of the "ṭet." The spelling with three "m's, however, is apparently not justified; the Greek forr with two is held by most scholars to be correct.

J.

MAMRAN: A check; an expression used b Polish Jews from the end of the sixteenth to the be ginning of the nineteenth century. The word is derived from "membrana," Low Latin equivalent for "promissory note." It was first used by Mordecai Jafeh in "'Ir Shoshan" (ch. 48), and was recognized by the law of East Prussia of 1801. Later laws, declaring that in legal documents only the language of the country may be used, threw the term into disuse. There are various forms of the word—"mamre," "mamram," "mamrama," "mamrame," etc., and a number of false etymological derivations (*e.g.*, from המיר = "to exchange"; or from "Maharam" [Meïr] Lublin, supposed to have introduced it).

Bibliography: Bloch, *Der Mamran* (ממרן), *der Jüdisch-Polnische Wechselbrief*, in *Berliner Festschrift*, Berlin, 1903.

A. D.

MAMZER. See Bastard.

MAN, SON OF (Hebrew, "ben adam" or "ben enosh"; plural, "bene adam"; Aramaic, "bar enash," "bar nasha," or "bar nash"): Individual of the species man; synonym of "man." While "ben enosh" occurs only in Ps. cxliv. 3, the term "ben adam" is found exclusively in poetic (Num. xxiii. 19; Ps. viii. 5 [A. V. 4]) and prophetic passages (Isa. li. 12; Jer. xlix. 18). The expression is used with particular force about ninety times in Ezekiel, from ch. ii. 1 on, as the title by which the prophet is addressed by Yhwh, obviously to accentuate the great distance between him, the earth-born mortal, and the sublime God who speaks to him. Most of the Jewish commentators, whom modern exegetes follow, take the title in that sense. "God addressed him thus in order to make him feel that, though God speaks to him, he is still a frail human being" (comp. "bene adam" with "bene ish" [the former denoting the humbler, and the latter the higher, classes of men] in Ps. xlix. 3 [A. V. 2]).

In Daniel.

The expression "son of man" ("bar enash") has a peculiar use in Dan. vii. 13. Daniel in a vision sees "one like the son of man coming on [A. V. "with"] the clouds of heaven and appearing before the Ancient of Days," to receive from Him "the dominion, the glory, and the kingdom for all time" (Hebr.). There is no dispute among commentators that Israel is thereby meant; but they differ as to the question whether the "son of man" depicted is merely a personification of the people, or whether the writer had in mind a concrete personality representing Israel, such as the Messiah or Israel's guardian angel, the archangel Michael. The latter interpretation, proposed by Cheyne and adopted by others, has little in its favor compared with the older opinion that the person of the Messiah is alluded to—a view shared by the Rabbis (Sanh. 98a; Midr. Teh. to Ps. ii.; comp. the name "'Anani" in Targ. to I Chron. iii., and "bar nefele" [= "son of the clouds"] in Sanh. 96b) and the Apocalyptic as well as Christian writers (Enoch xxxvii.-lxxi.; IV Esdras xiii. 3; Justin Martyr, "Dialogus cum Tryphone," p. 31, and Ephraem Syrus in his commentary to Daniel, *l.c.*; see also the commentaries of Nowack and others to the passage).

It is this double use of the term "son of man" in the New Testament time and in New Testament documents which has caused great confusion to the recorders and translators as well as to the exegetes of the New Testament. As is seen in Enoch and IV Esdras (*l.c.*), "son of man" was among the Apocalyptic writers a favorite term for the Messiah, and accordingly it occurs frequently in Messianic apocalypses embodied in the New Testament (Matt. xxiv.-xxv.; Mark xiii. 26; Luke xxi. 27, 36) and in Messianic prophecies which are ascribed to Jesus regarded, in accordance with this conception, as the "son of man" in the clouds (of glory) (Matt. xii. 40; xiii. 27, 41; xvi. 27; xix. 28; xxvi. 64; Mark viii. 38, xiv. 62; Luke xii. 40; xvii. 22-30; xviii. 8, 31; xxii. 69; John i. 51, iii. 13, v. 27, vi. 62).

The term "son of man" has a quite different meaning in such sayings as "the son of man is lord even of the Sabbath day" (Matt. xii. 8 and parallels). It denotes simply man as master over the Sabbath in the same sense given it in the saying of the Rabbis, "The Sabbath is given over unto you, but not you unto the Sabbath" (Mek., Ki Tissa, 1).

Generalized Use of Term.

In many passages the expression "son of man" is used in the sense of "that person," or "myself," a use of it known to have been common in Talmudic times. Thus when Jesus says "the son of man hath not where to lay his head" (Matt. viii. 20), he means simply "myself"; and likewise when he speaks of his future suffering and betrayal, the term "son of man" has nothing to do with the Messianic title (Matt. xvii. 22 and parallels). Afterward the records confounded the two usages, and consequently Matthew uses the term promiscuously in a manner which has to this day puzzled most of the commentators (see Wellhausen, "Des Menschen Sohn," in "Skizzen und Vorarbeiten," 1899, pp. 187-215; and comp. Dalman, "Die Worte Jesu," 1898, pp. 191-218).

The following passage in Yer. Ta'an. ii. 65b is remarkable. Commenting on Num. xxiii. 19 ("God is not a man that he should lie, neither the son of man that he should repent"), R. Abbahu, who had frequent disputations with Christians in Cæsarea and was therefore acquainted with their terminology, said: "If a man says, 'I am God,' he lies; if he says, 'I am the son of man,' he will repent; if he says, 'I will ascend to heaven,' he will not succeed."

Bibliography: Cheyne, *Encyc. Bibl.*; Wellhausen, *Skizzen und Vorarbeiten*, 1899, pp. 187-215.

K.

MANASSEH: 1. The elder of two sons born before the famine to Joseph and Osnath, daughter of the priest of Heliopolis (Gen. xli. 50-51, xlvi. 20). Biblical etymology, deriving his name from נשה (= "to forget"), makes it signify "He who causes one to forget," and explains it in the passage "God . . . hath made me forget all my toil" (*ib.* xli. 51). According to Gen. xlviii. 5, Manasseh and Ephraim were put by the patriarch Jacob on an equality with Reuben and Simeon as progenitors of separate tribes. In the blessings invoked by Jacob on the heads of Manasseh and Ephraim, Manasseh, although the elder, was made subordinate to Ephraim (*ib.* xlviii. 14). Tradition does not tell what caused Jacob's preference for Ephraim (see Ephraim and Junior Right). Notwithstanding his subordination, Manasseh's blessing was not to be despised. Manasseh, like Ephraim, was to be protected by "the Angel which redeemed" Jacob "from all evil," and was to grow into a great people (*ib.* xlviii. 16, 19). Because Gen. xlviii. 20 reads, "in thee shall Israel bless, saying, God make thee as Ephraim and as Manasseh," the phrase "God make thee as Ephraim and as Manasseh" has been given a place in the benediction Jewish parents pronounce over their sons on the eves of Sabbaths and holy days. I Chron. vii. 14 reports that Manasseh was married to a Syrian concubine. Targums Jerushalmi and pseudo-Jonathan to Gen. xlii. 23 make the statement that Manasseh was steward in Joseph's house, acted as interpreter for Joseph when the latter talked to his brothers, and possessed extraordinary physical strength, which he displayed at the imprisonment of Simeon.

J. W. R.

2. One of the twelve tribes of Israel which received a portion in the land of Canaan; its eponym was a son of Joseph. While at the time of the Exodus Manasseh numbered 32,200 (Num. i. 35, ii. 21) against Ephraim's 40,500 (Num. i. 32-33, ii. 19), before Israel's entrance into Canaan forty years later Manasseh had increased to 52,700 (Num. xxvi. 34), and Ephraim had fallen to 32,500 (Num. xxvi. 37). This made Manasseh rank sixth in numerical importance, the tribes more numerous being Judah, Issachar, Zebulun, Dan, and Asher.

During the march through the Sinaitic desert Manasseh's position was, with Ephraim and Benjamin, on the western side of the Tabernacle (Num. ii. 18-24); the chief of the tribe was Gamaliel, son of Pedahzur (Num. i. 10, ii. 20, vii. 54).

The Targums of Jerusalem and pseudo-Jonathan to Num. ii. 18 report that the standard of the three Rachel tribes revealed the figure of a boy, with the inscription: "The cloud of the Lord rested on them until they went forth out of the camp"; and the Talmud mentions that Manasseh's tribal banner, during the journey to the Promised Land, consisted of a black flag with the embroidered figure of a unicorn. Among the twelve spies sent by Moses to report on Canaan, Manasseh was represented by Gaddi, son of Susi (Num. xiii. 11). Manasseh is recorded as prompting the enactment of laws regulating the possession of property in Canaan by daughters where the father had died without a son; the particular case in question was that of the daughters of Zelophehad (Num. xxvii. 1-8).

Manasseh was valorous. It took a prominent part in the defeat of the natives encountered on both sides of the Jordan. Reference is made to its prowess in Num. xxxii. 39; Deut. iii. 14; Josh. xvii. 1; and particularly in I Chron. v. 18-22. Its warriors Machir, Jair, and Nobah conquered the most difficult districts, Argob and the hills of Gilead. The fearless chieftains Gideon, who with a small army defeated the Midianites (Judges vi. 15), and Jephthah, who vanquished the Ammonites (Judges xi.), belonged to Manasseh.

The territory inhabited by Manasseh lay on both sides of the Jordan. The part east of the Jordan was acquired after the conquest of Gilead (Num. xxxii.), and was requested on the ground of being specially adapted for the grazing of cattle—the same argument as that urged by Reuben and Gad for preferring that section of Canaan. The boundaries of Eastern and Western Manasseh can not be given with exactness. Eastern Manasseh probably extended from the Jabbok to Mount Hermon (its northern portion consisting of Argob and Bashan), while Western Manasseh extended from Ephraim, lying directly south, to the slopes of Mount Carmel (comp. Josh. xvii. 15: "Get thee up to the wood country").

Territory of Manasseh.

Although more numerous than Ephraim shortly before the conquest of Canaan, Manasseh did not compare with Ephraim in wealth, power, and population in later times; Western Manasseh never completely expelled the natives (Josh. xvii. 12; Judges i. 27).

At the time of David's accession to the throne, Western Manasseh sent to Hebron 18,000, and Eastern Manasseh 120,000—Reubenites and Gadites included. After this event Eastern Manasseh gradually disappears and Western Manasseh lacks prominence, although both sections had separate rulers; Joel, son of Pedaiah, governed the latter, and Iddo, son of Zechariah, governed the former (I Chron. xxvii. 20-21).

Manasseh is heard of in the revival under Asa; in the Passover celebration in the days of Hezekiah; in the subsequent attack on idolatry; in the reform instituted by Josiah; and in the restoration of the Temple (II Chron. xv. 9; xxx. 1, 10-11, 18; xxxi. 1; xxxiv. 6, 9).

Like Reuben and Gad, Manasseh ultimately lost its identity; it became assimilated with the inhabitants of the country, whose idolatries it practised. The children of Manasseh "transgressed against the God of their fathers, and went a-whoring after the gods of the people of the land, whom God destroyed before them" (I Chron. v. 25). In Ps. lx. 9 (A. V. 7) and cviii. 8 Manasseh is called a most precious possession.

J. W. R.

3. According to II Kings xxi. 1, Manasseh, the successor of Hezekiah upon the throne of Judah, was but a boy of twelve at his father's death. His reign of fifty-three years is the longest recorded in the annals of Judah. There can be no doubt that Sennacherib, the King of Assyria, departed to his capital in the days of Hezekiah (II Kings xix. 36), regarding Judah as a conquered and tribute-paying province; and so it remained during the reigns of Esarhaddon and Assurbanipal, his successors upon the throne of Assyria. In their published inscriptions Manasseh of Judah is distinctly mentioned as a vassal king (Schrader, "K. B." ii. 148, 238). That these sovereigns cherished a real interest in their western domain is shown by their settlement of colonists in Samaria (Ezra iv. 2, 9-10). Each of them invaded and plundered Egypt and maintained protracted sieges of the strong cities of Phenicia.

In II Kings, written within a century or so of Manasseh's death, there is no hint of revolt. The Chronicler, however, declares (II Chron. xxxiii. 11) that in consequence of the deliberate unfaithfulness of Judah God brought upon the nation "the captains of the host of the King of Assyria," who took Manasseh in chains to Babylon. Thence, having truly repented, he was restored to his throne, where he demonstrated the genuineness of his change of heart by giving himself to measures of defense, administration, and religious reform. To harmonize the Chronicler's testimony with that of the Hebrew contemporary writings is even more difficult. The crying need in the days of Josiah, Manasseh's immediate successor, was religious reform; Jeremiah declared (xv. 4; comp. II Kings xxiii. 26) that Manasseh's sins had yet to be expiated.

Relations with Assyria.

The writer in Kings emphasizes three deplorable details of the reign of Manasseh: the religious reaction which followed hard upon his accession; its extension by the free adoption of foreign cults; and the bitter persecution of the prophetic party. During Manasseh's half-century the popular worship was a medley of native and foreign cults, the influence of which was slow to disappear (Ezek. viii.).

Such a reaction involved the persecution of those who had bitterly condemned the popular syncretism. The prophets were put to the sword (Jer. ii. 30). "Innocent blood" reddened the streets of Jerusalem (II Kings xxiv. 4). For many decades those who sympathized with prophetic ideas were in constant peril.

J. F. K. S.

4. Son of Johanan the high priest and brother of Jaddua; married Nicaso, daughter of Sanballat (Josephus, "Ant." xi. 7, § 2). In Neh. xiii. 28 he is referred to as "one of the sons of Joiada, the son of Eliashib the high priest," but is not mentioned by name. It is further said (*ib.*) that, owing to his being Sanballat's son-in-law, Nehemiah had deposed him from the priesthood.

Josephus describes this fact at greater length. He says that the high priest Jaddua, Manasseh's brother, was himself indignant at Manasseh on account of his marriage with a foreign woman, and, joining the people of Jerusalem, he gave Manasseh the alternative of divorcing his wife or of leaving the priesthood. Manasseh went to Sanballat, and declared to him that in spite of his love for his wife he gave the preference to the priesthood. Whereupon Sanballat promised him that if he would retain his wife he would obtain for him from the king the dignity of a high priest. He further promised that he would build with the king's approval a temple upon Mount Gerizim, where Manasseh should officiate as high priest. Manasseh, accordingly, remained with his father-in-law and became high priest in the Samaritan temple on Mount Gerizim ("Ant." xi. 8, § 2-4). Still, Josephus says (*ib.* xii. 4, § 1) that Manasseh officiated as high priest at Jerusalem between the priesthood of his nephew Eleazar and that of Onias II. (see SANBALLAT).

BIBLIOGRAPHY: Grätz, *Gesch.* ii. 161, 167, 242; Schürer, *Gesch.* 3d ed., i. 182.

G. M. SEL.

MANASSEH, PRAYER OF: Greek poetic composition attributed to Manasseh, son of Hezekiah, King of Judah, "when he was holden captive in Babylon" (II Chron. xxxiii. 11-13, 18-19). It is found among the Canticles which, in some of the Septuagint manuscripts, are appended to the Book of Psalms, and is placed at the end of II Chronicles in some Latin manuscripts (see Swete, "The Old Testament in Greek," ii., pp. viii. and xi., and iii., pp. vi. and 802-804; Sabatier, "Bibl. Lat." iii. 1038). It is found also in the "Apostolic Constitutions" (ii. 22) and in the "Didascalia" (where it follows a reference to II Chron. xxxiii.). The Latin translation found in some Vulgate manuscripts is not by Jerome, but is, according to Fritzsche, "certainly of more recent origin." The Prayer of Manasseh was never distinctly recognized as canonical by the Church; but it has been deservedly retained by Luther, and is included in the authorized English version, among the Apocrypha.

The Story.

In the "Apostolic Constitutions" (ii. 22) the whole story of Manasseh is given as an instructive lesson to bishops in their dealings with the erring and in the administration of justice. The story is based upon II Kings xxi. and II Chron. xxxiii. After recounting the sins of Manasseh it relates that he was taken captive to Babylon, bound in shackles of iron, and cast into prison. Bread made of bran and water mixed with vinegar was given him in small quantities, only so much as would keep him alive. In his great affliction he repented of his sins, humbled himself, and sought YHWH's forgiveness. Then follows the prayer, after which YHWH had compassion upon him. A flame of fire appeared about him, his chains and shackles melted, and he was restored to Jerusalem and to his kingdom. Thereafter he worshiped YHWH only and sought to undo the evil he had done in the earlier part of his reign. Julius Africanus (*c.* 221 C.E.), apparently, had read the story in this form, for he says that "while Manasseh was reciting a hymn his bonds burst asunder, iron though they were, and he escaped" (see Hastings, "Dict. Bible").

The Prayer.

The prayer opens with an invocation addressed to the "Lord, Almighty, God of our fathers, Abraham, Isaac, and Jacob, and of their righteous seed." His power, glory, and majesty are described, and His compassion, long-suffering, and grace to the repentant sinner. The passage following (not found in the Greek MSS. of the LXX.) declares that God has promised forgiveness to the transgressor and has "appointed repentance unto sinners, that they may be saved." He has not appointed repentance only to persons such as the Patriarchs, who have not sinned, but "unto me that am a sinner." There follows a confession of sin, couched for the most part in general terms. The only approach to specific statement is in the words, "I did not Thy will, neither kept I Thy commandments" (omitted by Codex A, "Apostolic Constitutions," and by Latin MSS.); "I have set up abominations and multiplied offenses." This, of course, may be understood as referring to his idolatrous practises. Next he pleads for forgiveness, and concludes with a confident expectation that God will save him and with an outburst of praise for His mercy.

Ewald and, more recently, Budde (Stade's "Zeitschrift," 1892, pp. 39 *et seq.*) have maintained the view that the Greek version of the prayer is a translation from a Hebrew original. This is not impossible, but it is not supported by sufficient evidence.

Authorship. The author was evidently a Jew, but the place and date of composition can not be definitely ascertained. The story in II Chronicles assumes the existence of a Prayer of Manasseh and of various details of his life in the "history of Hozai" (R. V.) or "of the seers" (LXX., ἐπὶ τῶν λόγων τῶν ὁρώντων). This history must have been lost, and the Greek prayer is, most probably, the attempt of some pious Jew of later times to reproduce it. Schürer ("Hist. of the Jewish People," division ii., vol. iii., p. 188) compares the interpolation of the prayers of Mordecai and Esther as supplements to the Book of Esther, and the Prayer of Azariah and the Song of the Three Holy Children as supplements to the Book of Daniel. There is, indeed, nothing in the conception of God's forgiving grace to the repentant sinner which is not implied in the story in Chronicles as well as in other still earlier Old Testament passages, as Ex. xxxiv. 6–7, and Ps. xxxiv. 18, li. 17. The emphasis, however, upon the fact that God is God of the penitent as well as of the righteous, and the conception of the Patriarchs as conspicuous examples of the latter, point to the later Judaism. F. C. Porter (Hastings, "Dict. Bible") thinks it is a Hellenistic composition. So does Swete ("Introduction to the O. T. in Greek," p. 253). Nestle ("Septuagintastudien," 1899, iii.) maintains that the text of the prayer in the Greek manuscripts of the Septuagint comes from the "Apostolic Constitutions," or from the "Didascalia," and that it is not, as has been commonly supposed, drawn by the latter from the Septuagint.

There appears to be no trace of the Prayer of Manasseh in Jewish tradition. The Jerusalem Talmud (Sanh. x. 2) relates that Manasseh was put into an iron mule, beneath which a fire was kindled. In his torture he prayed in vain to the idols he had formerly worshiped. At last he besought the God of his fathers, and was delivered (comp. Apoc. Baruch, vi. 4).

BIBLIOGRAPHY: Text: Fritzsche, *Vet. Test. Græc. Libri Apocryphi*, pp. xiv., 92; Swete, *Old Testament in Greek*, iii. 802–804; Nestle, *Septuagintastudien*, 1899, iii. Commentaries: Fritzsche, *Exegetisches Handbuch*, 1851; Ball, in *Speaker's Commentary* (*Apocrypha*, ii. 362 *et seq.*); Ryssel, in Kautzsch, *Apokryphen und Pseudepigraphen*, 1899 (transl. and notes).

T. J. F. McL.

MANASSEH BEN ISRAEL: Dutch polyhistor; born at La Rochelle about 1604 (see Bethencourt in "Jew. Chron." May 20, 1904); died at Middleburg, Netherlands, Nov. 26, 1657. After the auto da fé of Aug. 3, 1603, his parents had thought it prudent to leave Lisbon. They soon passed on from La Rochelle to Amsterdam, where Manasseh was brought up under Isaac Uzziel of Fez, the rabbi of the new congregation Neveh Shalom; the latter died in 1620 and was succeeded by Manasseh. Two years later Manasseh married Rachel Soeiro. He soon became distinguished as one of the best orators of the Amsterdam pulpit, rivaling even Isaac Aboab. The contrast between their preaching was acutely indicated by a Spanish priest of the time, Fra Antonio Vieyra, who reported, after hearing both, that "Manasseh said what he knew and Aboab knew what he said." Neither preaching nor private tuition being sufficient to provide him with a suitable livelihood, Manasseh started the first Hebrew press in Amsterdam (indeed, in all Holland), in which he produced a Hebrew prayer-book (Jan. 12, 1627) set up from entirely new type, an index to the Midrash Rabbah (1628), a Hebrew grammar of his teacher's, Isaac Uzziel (1628), and an elegant and handy edition of the Mishnah.

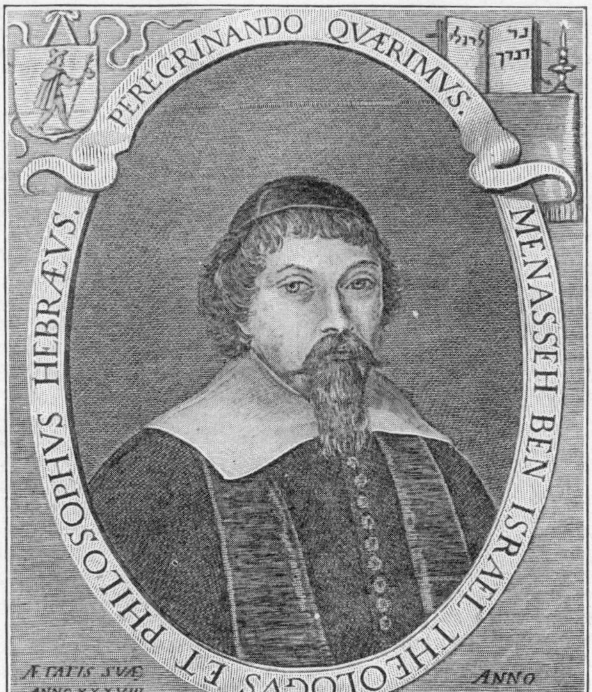

Manasseh ben Israel.
(From the engraving by Salom Italia.)

Meanwhile Manasseh ben Israel was occupied with the compilation of his chief work, "El Conciliador," a laborious enumeration and discussion of all the passages contained in the Old Testament which seem to conflict with one another. Manasseh brought his very extensive rabbinical knowledge to bear upon each of these, and wrote, in fluent Spanish, an exposition of the recognized Jewish method of reconciling the seeming inconsistencies. The book was almost the first written in a modern language by a Jew which had an independent interest for Christian readers, and it accordingly gave Manasseh a wide-spread reputation in the learned world. Some of the best scholars of his time had correspondence with him—

Isaac and Dionysius Vossius, Hugo Grotius, Caspar Barlæus, Cunæus Bochart, Huet, and Blondel; Anna Marie de Schurman consulted him. His Jewish acquaintance was even more numerous, and included Emanuel Frances, and the Buenos, Abravanels (relatives of his wife), Pintos, Abudientes, and Henriques. He corresponded also with Zacuto Lusitano, Daniel Caceres, and Diego Barrassa (to whom he dedicated one of his works), and assisted Joseph Delmedigo to publish a selection of his works at Amsterdam.

His Friendships.

Notwithstanding this wide fame, Manasseh ben Israel still found it difficult to obtain a living for himself, wife, and three children; he determined, therefore, on settling in Brazil, whither, in 1638, he had sent his brother-in-law, Ephraim Soeiro, on a joint venture. At this time the three synagogues of Amsterdam were reorganized, and, as seems probable, Manasseh ben Israel lost his position as rabbi of the Neveh Shalom. In preparation for his departure he dedicated the second part of the "Conciliador," which appeared about that time, to members of the Jewish community of Pernambuco. At this moment the brothers Pereira came to his aid and established a yeshibah, placing him at the head (1640). Manasseh was thus enabled to devote himself entirely to authorship and to his ever-widening correspondence with Jewish and Christian literati.

Menasseh ben Israel

(After the mezzotint by Rembrandt.)

Manasseh was most profoundly interested in Messianic problems, being convinced, for example, of the Davidic origin of the Abravanel family, from which his own wife was descended. He was full of cabalistic opinions, though he was careful not to expound them in those of his works that were written in modern languages and intended to be read by Gentiles. In particular, he was convinced that the restoration to the Holy Land could not take place until the Jews had spread into and inhabited every part of the world. In 1644 he came in contact with Antonio de Montesinos (Aaron Levi), who convinced him that the North-American Indians were the Lost Ten Tribes. He appears to have directed his attention to the countries in Europe where Jews were not permitted to live, trusting that by obtaining their admission the coming of the Messiah would be accelerated. He entered into correspondence with Christina, Queen of Sweden, ostensibly regarding matters of Hebrew learning, but probably with the design of getting her help in obtaining for the Jews admission into Sweden. But his chief attention was directed to securing the readmission of Jews into England, with many leading theologians of which country he was in active correspondence on this point.

Manasseh attracted the notice of many Protestant theologians who likewise were convinced of the speedy coming of the Messiah and who naturally desired to know the views of Jewish theologians on a topic so specifically Jewish. Among these Christian theologians were Abraham von Frankenberg, the Silesian mystic, and Johannes Mochinger. But it was especially several of the more mystical minded of the Puritans in England who had become interested in the question, and Manasseh entered into correspondence with several of them, including John Dury, Thomas Thorowgood, and Nathaniel Holmes. The first-named had written to Manasseh on the subject of the Israelitish descent of the American Indians, thereby redirecting his attention to Antonio de Montesinos' views. Manasseh determined, therefore, to write a treatise on the Lost Ten Tribes, and in support of the readmission of the Jews into England published his "Esperança de Israel" (Hope of Israel; 1650). This work appeared first in Spanish, then in a Latin translation; to the latter he wrote a prefatory epistle addressed to the Parliament or Supreme Court of England in order to gain its favor and goodwill for the Jews. The pamphlet aroused much interest in England, several replies being written, especially with regard to the identity of the North-American Indians with the Lost Ten Tribes. One of the replies, "An Epistle to the Learned Manasseh ben Israel" (London, 1650), was

Advocates Readmission of Jews into England.

written by Sir Edward Spencer, member of Parliament for Middlesex; another appeared anonymously under the title "The Great Deliverance of the Whole House of Israel" (*ib.* 1652). Both these replies insisted upon the need of conversion to Christianity before the Messianic prophecies about Israel could be fulfilled, and it was, perhaps, for this reason that the matter was dropped for a time.

Meanwhile Cromwell's attention had been drawn to the subject, and before the negotiations with Holland were broken off by the Navigation Act of 1652 Cromwell's representative at Amsterdam was put into communication with Manasseh; the latter addressed the English council of state on the subject of the readmission, and a pass was issued to enable him to go to England. After the cessation of the war between Holland and England, Manasseh sent his son Samuel and his nephew David Dormido to consult with Cromwell. They being unsuccessful, Samuel returned to Amsterdam in 1655 to persuade his father to attempt the task himself.

Manasseh arrived in London in October of that year, and immediately printed his "Humble Addresses to the Lord Protector," the result being a national conference held at Whitehall in December, 1655. It does not appear that Manasseh spoke at this conference, though his pamphlet was submitted to it. A formal declaration was made by the lawyers present at the conference that there was nothing in English law to prevent the settlement of Jews in England, though the question of its desirability was ingeniously evaded by Cromwell (see CROMWELL). Prynne wrote his "Short Demurrer" against the proposal, and this was answered by Manasseh ben Israel in his "Vindiciæ Judæorum" (London, 1656). Meanwhile the opening of the Robles case had brought the question to a practical issue, though not in the sense Manasseh was striving for. He appears to have quarreled with the London Jews, and had to go for help to Cromwell, who, at the end of 1656, made him a grant of £25, and in the following year gave him a pension of £100 a year. In September, 1657, his son Samuel died; with the aid of a grant from Cromwell, Manasseh took the body to Holland to be buried at Middleburg, where he himself died two months later. Though he had not succeeded in obtaining formal permission for the resettlement of the Jews in England, he had by the publicity of his appeal brought the subject prominently before the ruling minds of England, and thus indirectly led to the recognition of the fact that there was nothing in English law against the readmission.

The pamphlets connected with the return of the Jews to England have been republished, with an introduction, by Lucien Wolf through the Jewish Historical Society of England (London, 1901); the first part of the "Conciliador" appeared at Frankfort-on-the-Main in 1632; the remaining three parts at Amsterdam in 1641, 1650, and 1651. Manasseh wrote also: a series of works in Latin on various theological problems, giving the usual rabbinic solutions, all printed at Amsterdam —"De Creatione" (1635), "De Resurrectione Mortuorum" (1635), "De Termino Vitæ" (1639); an essay in Spanish, "De la Fragilidad Humana" (1642); and a list of the 613 commandments in Portuguese, entitled "Thesoro dos Dinim" (1645). Several of his works have been translated: "Conciliador" into Latin by Vossius (Amsterdam, 1632), and into English by E. H. Lindo (London, 1642; reprinted, Edinburgh, 1904). His "Esperança de Israel" was translated into English by M. Wall, and had three editions between 1650 and 1652; into German by M. Drucker (1651); into Hebrew by Eliakim ben Jacob (1697). His "Vindiciæ Judæorum" was translated into German, with a preface by Moses Mendelssohn (reprinted 1782). Manasseh contemplated writing a large number of other works "on the influence of tradition," "on the divine origin of the Mosaic law," "a summary of Jewish theology," a "bibliotheca rabbinica," and a "Hebrew-Arabic lexicon"; none of these works saw the light, nor did the "Historia Heroyca," which he intended as a sequel to Josephus. Of special interest is his book on the statue of Nebuchadnezzar—"Estatua de Nebuchanassar" (Amsterdam, 1657 ?). This was illustrated by four plates by Rembrandt, explained by Manasseh in his prefatory remarks. Rembrandt etched a portrait of Manasseh, and another engraving of him was executed by Salom Italia in 1642. There is a portrait by Rembrandt at St. Petersburg alleged to be of Manasseh, but its dissimilarity to the authorized portrait renders it impossible that the two can be of the same person.

His Works.

Manasseh claimed to read and understand ten languages, and printed works in five—Hebrew, Latin, Portuguese, English, and Spanish. His erudition was wide, but he had no claims to accuracy or thoroughness, and he is now chiefly remembered for his untiring labors toward the readmission of the Jews into England.

BIBLIOGRAPHY: M. Kayserling, in *Jahrb. für die Gesch. der Juden*, pp. 85–188 (transl. by F. de Sola Mendes, in *Miscellany of the Society of Hebrew Literature*, second series, pp. 96 *et seq.*, London, 1877; also separately); Lucien Wolf, Introduction to *Manasseh ben Israel's Mission to Oliver Cromwell*; Steinschneider, *Cat. Bodl.* Nos. 6205, 8703; D. P. Huet, *Huetiana*, pp. 225–227, Paris, 1722; Lady Magnus, *Jewish Portraits*, pp. 68–89; M. Weiskopf, in *Arch. Isr.* 1902, pp. 53–54, 61–62, 77–78; E. N. Adler, in *J. Q. R.* April, 1904.

J.

MANASSEH, JACOB: Turkish rabbinical writer and chief rabbi of Salonica, where he died in 1832. Among his works may be mentioned: "Ohel Ya'aḳob," an alphabetical collection of the laws of religion (Salonica, 1832); "Be'er ha-Mayim," responsa (*ib.* 1836); "'En ha-Mayim," commentary on Shulḥan 'Aruk, Yoreh De'ah (printed in Turkey in 5618 = 1858).

BIBLIOGRAPHY: Hazan, *Ha-Ma'alot li-Shelomoh*, pp. 6, 13, 44; Franco, *Histoire des Israélites de l'Empire Ottoman.*

S. M. FR.

MANASSEH BEN JOSEPH OF ILYE (known also as **Ben Porat**): Russian rabbinical writer and philosopher; born at Smorgony, government of Wilna, 1767; died at Ilye, in the same government, 1831. At seven years of age he was acquainted with some original sources in rabbinical literature, but his father would not permit him to study Hebrew grammar and the Bible lest these might interfere with his Talmudic studies. According to the custom of that time Manasseh was married early; at the age of thirteen he became the husband of the daughter of a wealthy citizen of

Smorgony; but he soon divorced her and married the daughter of a merchant in the village of Ilye, where he spent most of his life. His erudition early drew a circle of friends and disciples around him, and in discussing with them the rabbinical laws and regulations he did not hesitate to criticize such authorities as the Shulḥan 'Aruk and Rashi. He even dared to interpret some parts of the Mishnah in contradiction to the explanation given by the Gemara; for such daring he probably would have been put under the ban had not an influential rabbi, Joseph Mazel of Wyazyn, come to his rescue. The latter took great interest in Manasseh and threw open to him his extensive and valuable library of rabbinical and philosophical literature.

Relation to Elijah of Wilna.

Manasseh became acquainted also with Elijah Gaon of Wilna, whom he visited once a year; but when Elijah discovered that Manasseh visited Zalman of Liozna, the leader of the northern Ḥasidim, he credited those of his disciples who asserted that Manasseh showed Ḥasidic leanings, and held aloof from him, though Manasseh explained to the gaon that only a love of knowledge induced him to visit Zalman, and that his views differed widely from those of the Ḥasidim. Manasseh really sympathized somewhat with the latter, expecting that their movement might develop into something better than the existing rabbinical orthodoxy. In his writings Manasseh holds Elijah of Wilna in high esteem, declaring in "Binat Miḳra" (Grodno, 1818) that from him he had learned to interpret the Talmud by the simple philological method of the "peshaṭ," while the majority of Talmudic teachers used the less scientific methods of the "derash." He even says that but for Elijah of Wilna the Torah would have been forgotten in Israel ("Alfe Menashsheh," § 102; comp. § 177).

The suspicions of the Orthodox members of Manasseh's community increased when he began to study philosophy, mathematics, and astronomy. He had formed the resolution to go to Berlin for the purpose of becoming acquainted with the circle of Moses Mendelssohn; but at Königsberg he was stopped by some of his Orthodox coreligionists, who induced the Prussian authorities to refuse him a passport. Thus he was forced to return home, where, with the sole aid of some old manuals, he studied German, Polish, natural philosophy, and mechanics.

Shows Advanced Tendencies.

Manasseh had large ideas of educating the Russo-Jewish youth, but the rabbis of his time were not prepared to accept them. In his "Pesher Dabar" (Wilna, 1807) he complains "that the Jews are divorced from real life and its practical needs and demands; that the leaders of the Jews are short-sighted men who, instead of enlightening their followers, darken their intellect with casuistic restrictions, in which each rabbi endeavors to outdo his predecessors and contemporaries. The wealthy class thinks only of its profits, and is not scrupulous with regard to the means of getting money. Even those who are honest and endeavor to help their poorer brethren do it in such an unintelligent way that they do harm rather than good. Instead of educating the children of the poor to become artisans, they add to the number of idlers, and are thus responsible for the dangerous consequences of such an education." Plungiansky (see bibliography) is of the opinion that these words were directed against Elijah; and from the preface to "Pesher Dabar" it is evident that Manasseh desired to make peace between the leader of the Ḥasidim and the gaon. The consequences to the author of this daring appeal to the rabbis were serious: many rabbis destroyed his book, and some of his disciples and nearest friends left him.

Manasseh's father-in-law having lost his fortune, Manasseh left his native town and went to Brody, where he made the acquaintance of R. Jacob Landau, who expressed his disapproval of Manasseh's radical criticism of Rashi. He went next to Brest-Litovsk, where R. Aryeh Löb Katzenellenbogen engaged him as teacher to his sons, on the express condition that he adopt the interpretation of Rashi. Manasseh, however, could not abandon his critical methods, and, being dismissed, returned to Ilye. During his stay in Volhynia, on his way to Brody, Manasseh had begun to print his "Alfe Menashsheh," but when the printer became acquainted with the radical spirit of the work he threw both proofs and manuscript into the fire. Manasseh at once proceeded to rewrite his book, and owing to his remarkable memory was able to complete it; he published it in Wilna in 1827 (republished in Warsaw in 1860). In this work Manasseh demonstrates that in accordance with the rabbinical teachings the Rabbis have the power to amend certain Jewish legal decisions when there is a necessity for it. Manasseh was compelled to suppress the paragraph containing this (§ 20) because Samuel Katzenellenbogen threatened that if it were not withdrawn he would order the work publicly burned in the synagogue-yard.

When the Russian government ordered the establishment of rabbinical schools, Manasseh wrote a work on higher mathematics, mechanics, and strategics and asked his friends to induce some scholar to translate this work into Russian in order to show the government what a Jew could produce on those lines. His friend Joseph of Wyazyn feared, however, the unfavorable comment of the officials, who might say that the Jews, instead of working on farms, were preparing war plans. It was resolved therefore to burn the manuscript. Judah Löb of Kovno, Samuel Eliasberg, and Wolf Adelsohn may be mentioned among Manasseh's friends.

Manasseh was undoubtedly a great scholar, and his mind was remarkable for subtlety and power of analysis; he was also a friend of the people, and translated his "Samma-de-Ḥayye" into Judæo-German for the purpose of reaching them. In another work, "Sheḳel ha-Ḳodesh" (Shklov, 1823), he defends himself against the accusation of being an ambitious innovator. He says that his opponents can not even understand that one can risk his peace by antagonizing influential rabbis out of mere love for one's people. He asserts that he never sought wealth, fame, or pleasure, and that he lived on bread and water; but that the thirst for self-perfection would not allow him to rest until he had fulfilled his mission. In the same book he shows that it is erroneous to suppose that the earthly life is only a vale of tears and misery and the antechamber to a future life.

Manasseh was one of the first victims of the cholera epidemic of 1831. He did not live to realize any of his aspirations, but he prepared the ground for the Maskilim, who disseminated his ideas. Besides the above-named works Manasseh left one on mathematics and some other writings in manuscript.

BIBLIOGRAPHY: M. Plungiansky, *Sefer ben Porat*, Wilna, 1858; Golubov, *R. Manasseh ben Porat*, in *Voskhod*, 1900, xi. 77.
S. S. H. R.

MANCHESTER: City in Lancashire, England, and one of the chief British manufacturing centers. It has a population of 543,969, of whom about 25,000 are Jews (the second largest Jewish community in the British empire). The history of the Manchester Jewish community dates from about 1780, when Jews commenced to settle near Shudehill and Long Millgate. The first synagogue was founded by two brothers, Lemon and Jacob Nathan, from Liverpool, where a congregation had recently been organized. The upper part of a house in Long Millgate served as the first place of worship of the new community. Lemon Nathan became its first president and Rabbi Ahron (Aaron Jacobs) its first minister. A son of Rabbi Ahron, Alexander Jacobs, became an early president of the Manchester Jews, and in 1804 established their first local charity. It was known as the Manchester Jewish Philanthropic Society, and its object was to grant relief during the winter months to poor resident Jews. The original cemetery was opened in 1794, in the neighborhood of St. Thomas' Church, Pendleton. The congregation next worshiped in Ainsworth Court, Long Millgate, removing, in 1824, to Halliwell street, where it erected a synagogue for itself. Sixteen years later a schism occurred, in consequence of which a separate congregation was formed which worshiped in Miller's lane, acquiring a cemetery of its own at Miles Platting; after a time, however, the two congregations were reunited. A third cemetery was acquired at Prestwich, in 1843.

The appointment of Dr. Schiller-Szinessy as rabbi of the Halliwell Street Synagogue was productive of another schism, which led to the establishment, in 1856, of a Reform synagogue, under the auspices of Professor Theodores, Horatio Micholls, Dr. Hesse, Sigismund Schloss, and others. On the retirement of Dr. Schiller-Szinessy, in 1861, he was succeeded by Dr. Gustav Gottheil, who ministered at Manchester for thirteen years, until called to America to fill the pulpit of Temple Emanu-El, New York. Dr. Gottheil's most prominent successor at Manchester was the Rev. L. M. Simmons (d. 1900).

The Halliwell Street Congregation continued to grow, and in 1858 it removed to Cheetham Hill, where a magnificent place of worship was built, which became known as the "Great Synagogue" and is now the principal synagogue in Manchester. Prof. S. M. Isaacs of Liverpool—the first regular English preacher in Great Britain—became preacher of the Great Synagogue in that year, dividing his ministrations between the two cities. In 1863 he left Liverpool and thenceforth devoted himself entirely to the Manchester synagogue; he died in 1878, and was succeeded by the Rev. Dr. B. Salomon. In 1871 two new synagogues were established, one in Oxford road, for the Jews living in South Manchester, and another in York street, for the Spanish and Portuguese Jews. The rapid growth of the community since 1890 has necessitated the foundation of several new congregations, and there are now nearly thirty synagogues.

In 1838 the Manchester Hebrew Association had founded religious classes, and in 1842, as an outcome of these classes, a Jewish school was established through the instrumentality of Abraham Franklin and his brother Jacob Franklin (subsequently editor of the "Voice of Jacob"), Philip Lucas (who became the first president), and Eleazar Moses. A couple of rooms were engaged, in the first instance, at the Salford Lyceum Institution, and an enlarged building in York street was acquired in 1851. In 1869 the present structure in Derby street was erected. The school now (1904) has 2,300 scholars (800 in the boys' and girls' classes respectively, and 700 infants). The head master, Ephraim Harris, M.A., has occupied that position since 1869. The Jewish Board of Guardians was founded in 1867.

Other important Jewish institutions in Manchester are: the Hebrew Philanthropic and Loan Society (established 1861); the Sustentation Fund (connected with the Manchester Congregation of British Jews); the Visiting Committee (founded in 1885, in conjunction with Liverpool, for hospital and prison visitation); the United Sisters' Maternity Society; the Jewish Ladies' Visiting Association; the Children's Holiday Home; the Jewish Home for Aged and Needy Jews; the Hebrew Bread, Meat, and Coal Society; the Soup Kitchen for the Jewish Poor; the Talmud Torah School; the Jewish Working Men's Club (founded 1887); the Manchester Board of Shechita; the Manchester Naturalisation Society; the Manchester branch of the Jewish Lads' Brigade; and the Manchester Jewish Hospital. Zionism is also strongly represented in Manchester.

BIBLIOGRAPHY: *Jewish World*, Sept.-Nov., 1877; *Jew. Chron.* Aug.-Oct., 1903; *Jewish Year Book*, 1904.
J. I. H.

MANDÆANS: Eastern religious sect that professes and practises an admixture of Christian, Jewish, and heathen doctrines and customs. The members of the sect live in Lower Babylonia, in the territory of Wasiṭ and Bassora, near Khuzistan, and speak the languages of the localities in which they are settled (Arabic and Persian). Their sacred books are in an Aramaic dialect which has close affinities with that of the Talmud of Babylon, and they are written in peculiar characters resembling Old Palmyrenian script. Besides the name "Mandæans," derived from מנדא דחיא (= "word of life"), the most important figure in the Mandæan religious system, they take, in their dealings with other communions, the name of "Sabians," and call the wise and learned among them "Nasoræans" (נצוריא). To European scholars of the seventeenth century, who first heard of their existence through Christian missionaries, they were known under the erroneous appellation of "Christians of St. John" (the Baptist), on account

Language.

of the reverence in which St. John is held among the members of the sect and because of their frequent baptisms. The sacred books of the Mandæans consist of fragments, of various antiquity, derived from an older literature. Of these the most important is the גנזא (= "treasure") or סדרא רבא (= "the great book"), which dates from somewhere between 650 and 900 C.E. It is divided into two unequal parts: the larger, intended for the living, is termed ימינא (= "to the right hand"); the smaller, containing prayers to be read on the burial of priests, is called סמאלא (= "to the left hand"). In this book, and in some other works of lesser importance, is expounded the Mandæan religious system, in which Jewish influence is distinctly visible. It is essentially of the type of ancient Gnosticism, traces of which are found in the Talmud, the Midrash, and in a modified form in the later Cabala.

The גנזא gives three conflicting accounts of the Creation, the least complicated of which may be summarized as follows: A triad of divinities existed at the beginning of all things—Pira Rabba (= "the great fruit"), Ayar Ziwa Rabba (= "the ether of great brilliancy"), and Mana Rabba. (According to Joseph Halévy, Mana is the Biblical מן, which the Talmud and Midrash regarded as a celestial food.

Gnostic Elements.

The connection between Pira and Mana is easily explained by the Gnostic idea which compares the divine essence to the grain of a fig.) The last-named, the most prominent of the three, is the King of Light, from whom all things proceeded. From him emanated the Great Jordan, which permeates the whole ether, the domain of Ayar. (The idea that water, air [ether], and fire existed before the creation of the world is found in a Palestinian midrash of the fourth century; see Epstein, in "R. E. J." xxix. 77.) Then Mana called into existence Hayye Kadmaye ("primal life"), and, when the act was accomplished, withdrew into strictest privacy, being visible only to the souls of pious Mandæans.

As the revealed and governing deity, Ḥayye Ḳadmaye is entitled to the chief worship and adoration. Ḥayye Ḳadmaye produced, besides the numerous angels (עותריא) that arose from the further development and combination of these primary manifestations, Ḥayye Tinyane ("secondary life"), or Yushamin (= יה שמיא, the Jehovah of the Hebrews being considered by the Gnostics as a divinity of second rank). The next emanation after Yushamin was Manda de-Ḥayye (מנדא דחיא), the Primal Man (גברא קדמיא; in the Cabala, אדם קדמין). Then a revolution occurred in heaven. Yushamin attempted to seize the government, but failed, and was punished by ejection from the pure ethereal world into that of inferior light. (A similar story of the revolt of Satan and of his banishment to the subterranean regions is found in the haggadic literature; see Gen. R. iv.) Manda de-Ḥayye revealed himself to humanity in a series of incarnations,

Series of Revelations.

first taking the forms of the three brothers Hibil, Shitiel, and Anosh (the Biblical Abel, Seth, and Enoch). The most prominent of these is Hibil, who possesses the same attributes as Manda de-Ḥayye, with whom he is often confounded.

Among the "'utre" (angels) who emanated from Ḥayye Tinyane the most prominent is Ḥayye Tlitaye ("third life"), often called Abatur ("father of the 'utre"). He sits on the verge of the world of light that lies toward the lower regions, and weighs in his balance the deeds of the spirits ascending to him from the earthly life. Beneath him originally was an immense void, with troubled black water at the bottom in which his image was reflected, the reflection ultimately becoming solidified into Petaḥiel, called also Gabriel, who partakes of the nature of matter. Petaḥiel received the mission to build the earth and to people it. Accordingly he made Adam and Eve, but was unable to make them stand upright; whereupon Hibil, Shitiel, and Anosh were sent by Ḥayye Ḳadmaye to infuse into their forms spirit from Mana Rabba himself. Hibil then instructed man in the true religion, and apprised him that his Creator was not Petaḥiel, but the Supreme God who is far above him. Petaḥiel was then exiled to the under world, made up of four vestibules and three hells. Each of these vestibules has two rulers—Zartay and Zartanay, Hag and Mag (see Gog and Magog), Gaf and Gafan, Antan and Kin. In the highest hell rules the grisly king Shedum (in Haggadic literature, Ashmedai; see Asmodeus).

Invested with the power of Mana Rabba, Hibil descended into these lower regions and brought forth Ruḥa, the mother of falsehood and lies, the queen of darkness, and prevented her return to the nether world (see Lilith). She then bore the devil Ur; he in his pride sought to storm the world of light, but was overpowered by Hibil, who cast him into the black waters and imprisoned him within seven iron and seven golden walls. By Ur, Ruḥa bore three sets of sons, seven, twelve, and five respectively. They all were translated by Petaḥiel to the heavenly firmament, the seven forming the seven planets and the twelve the signs of the zodiac, while the fate of the remaining five is unknown.

According to the Mandæan belief the appointed duration of the world is four hundred and eighty thousand years, divided into seven epochs, in each of which one of the planets rules. The whole human race, with the exception of one

True and False Prophets.

single pair, has been destroyed three times. The Mandæans consider the Biblical saints as false prophets. Such were Abraham (who lived, according to their computation, 6,000 years after Noah, during the reign of the sun), Misha (Moses, in whose time the true religion was professed by the Egyptians, from whom the Mandæans claim to descend), and Shlimon (Solomon, son of David, to whom the devils yielded obedience; comp. Giṭ. 57a). A true prophet was Yaḥya (John), son of Zechariah, who was an incarnation of Hibil.

During forty years Yaḥya baptized myriads of men in the Jordan. By a mistake he baptized the false prophet Yishu Meshiḥa (Jesus), son of the devil Ruḥa Ḳadishta. Thereupon Hibil's younger brother Anosh descended from heaven, caused himself to be baptized, performed miracles, and brought about the crucifixion of the false Messiah. Then he preached the true religion, destroyed the city of Jerusalem ("Ur-Shalom" = "the devil finished it"), which had been built by Adonai, and dispersed over the world the Jews, who had put Yaḥya to death. It is interesting to note that the Mandæans accuse the Christians of using the blood of Jewish children in the preparation of hosts.

BIBLIOGRAPHY: Chwolson, *Die Ssebier und der Ssabismus*, i. 100, St. Petersburg, 1856; Nöldeke, *Mandäische Grammatik*, Introduction, Halle, 1875; A. J. H. Wilhelm Brandt, *Die Mandäische Religion*, Leipsic, 1889; Joseph Halévy, in *R. E. J.* xxii. 139 *et seq.*; K. Kessler, in Herzog-Hauck, *Real-Encyc.*

J. I. BR.

MANDEL, PAUL: Hungarian jurist and deputy; born at Nyirbator Jan. 6, 1839. He studied law in Budapest and Vienna, and in 1875 was elected to the Hungarian Parliament as representative of his native city. He has retained his seat from that time up to the present (1904); he became a member of the law committee in 1881, and has taken a prominent part in framing the laws concerning guardianship, copyright, and the office of royal notary public. His parliamentary speeches in 1878 against capital punishment aroused much attention, as did those in 1884 in the cause of religious freedom, and in 1885 against the anti-Semites.

BIBLIOGRAPHY: Sturm, *Orsvággyülési Almanach*, 1897; Szinnyei, *Magyar Irók*.

S. L. V.

MANDELKERN, SOLOMON B. SIMḤAH DOB: Russian poet and author; born in Mlynov, Volhynia, 1846; died in Vienna March 24, 1902. He was educated as a Talmudist. After his father's death he went to Dubno (he was then fourteen), where he continued his Talmudical studies. He became associated with the Ḥasidim in that community and with their "rabbi," Mendel of Kotzk, with whose son David he spent some time studying Jewish philosophy and Cabala. Later he became identified with the Haskalah movement. After his marriage he went to Wilna, entered its rabbinical school, and graduated as a rabbi. Mandelkern subsequently studied Oriental languages at St. Petersburg University, where he was awarded a gold medal for an essay on the parallel passages of the Bible. In 1873 he became assistant rabbi at Odessa, where he was the first to deliver sermons in Russian, and where he studied law at the university. The degree of Ph.D. was conferred upon him by the University of Jena. About 1880 he settled in Leipsic and occupied himself with literary work and with teaching. In 1900 he visited the United States; he returned to Leipsic in 1901, and was visiting Vienna when he suddenly became ill and died in the Jewish hospital of that city.

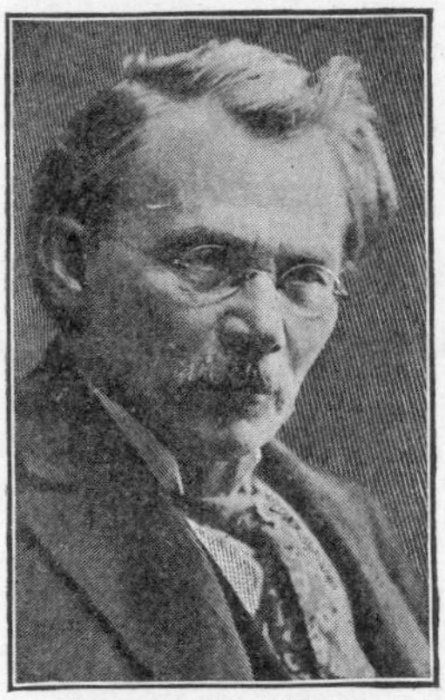

Solomon Mandelkern.

Mandelkern was a prolific writer in several languages, especially in Hebrew, in which he produced poetical works of considerable merit. His literary career began in 1886 with "Teru'at Melek Rab," ar ode to Alexander II., followed by "Bat Sheba'," ar epic poem, "Ezra ha-Sofer," a novel (transl. from the German by L. Philippson), and a satirical work en titled "Ḥizzim Shenunim" (all published in Wilna). Other works of his are: "Dibre Yeme Russiya," a history of Russia (Warsaw, 1875; written for the Society for the Promotion of Culture Among Russian Jews; for this work he was presented by the czar with a ring set with brilliants); "Shire Sefat 'Eber," Hebrew poems (2 vols., Leipsic, 1882 and 1889); and "Shire Yeshurun," a translation of Byron's "Hebrew Melodies" (*ib.* 1890). He published also: "Bogdan Chmelnitzki," in Russian, a translation of Hanover's "Yewen Meẓulah" (St. Petersburg, 1878; Leipsic, 1883); a Russian edition of Lessing's fables (*ib.* 1885); and "Tamar," a novel in German (*ib.* 1885; really a translation of Mapu's "Ahabat Ẓiyyon," without any mention of Mapu as the author). Sermons by him in Russian, and Russian and German translations of his Hebrew songs and articles, have appeared in various periodicals, and most Hebrew journals and year-books published within the last thirty years (especially "Ha-Shaḥar," "Ha-Asif") contain articles, poems, and epigrams by him.

Mandelkern's greatest work is the "Hekal ha-Ḳodesh," or "Veteris Testamenti Concordantiæ," a Hebrew-Latin concordance of the Hebrew and Chaldaic words found in the Bible (Leipsic, 1896), which has almost superseded all similar works of that nature. An abridged edition of this monumental work appeared under the title "Tabnit Hekal" (*ib.* 1897; for the various criticisms which were made of Mandelkern in connection with the two editions of the concordance, and for lists of errata, see Stade's "Zeitschrift," xviii. 165, 348; xix. 187–191, 350; xxi. 320; xxiii. 94, 352; xxiv. 146; etc.).

In his last years Mandelkern was engaged in the composition of a Talmudic and Midrashic concordance, part of which, probably, is among the many complete and incomplete works which he left in manuscript.

BIBLIOGRAPHY: Sokolow, *Sefer Zikkaron*, p. 67, Warsaw, 1890; Zeitlin, *Bibl. Post-Mendels.*; Lippe, *Bibliographisches Lexicon*; *Sistematicheski Ukazatel* (an index to Russian literature upon the Jews); Wiernik, in *Jewish Comment* Jan. 19, 1900; *Illustrirte Zeitung*, Feb. 15, 1896; April 1902; *Allg. Zeit. des Jud.* (May 16, 1902); *Jewish Exponent*, April 11, 1902.

H. R. P. WI.

MANDELLI, DAVID: Hungarian linguist; born about 1780 at Presburg; died at Paris Dec. 2?, 1836. He was one of the greatest linguists of his time, and is said to have excelled in his knowledge of foreign languages even the celebrated Cardinal Giuseppe Mezzofanti. The favorite studies of Mandelli were Hebrew, Arabic, Persian, Chinese, Greek, and Latin, from a combination of which he formed a language of his own (Oettinger, "Moniteur des Dates").

S. I. WAR.

MANDELSTAMM, BENJAMIN B. JOSEPH: Russian Hebraist and author; born in Zhagory about the end of the eighteenth century; died in Simferopol May 8, 1886. He was the eldest of several sons and received a liberal education.

the first part of his "Ḥazon la-Mo'ed" (Vienna, 1877) Benjamin describes a journey which he made from Zhagory to Moscow about 1835. The second part of the work consists of letters which he wrote from Wilna in 1841–43 in regard to LILIENTHAL's mission to Russia. Like most of the leading Maskilim of the time, Mandelstamm was at first very enthusiastic about the movement; but he was much disappointed at the results and expressed strong disapproval of Lilienthal's methods. The third part contains a description of the Crimea with plans for bettering the condition of the Russian Jews.

Mandelstamm was employed by the Günzburgs, with some intervals, for more than forty years, and from 1864 until the time of his death he was their representative in Simferopol. He visited Paris in 1875 and gave a graphic description, in Hebrew, of the French capital in his "Paris" (Warsaw, 1878). He furthermore wrote "Mishle Binyamin," which appeared in the first two volumes of "Ha-Asif" (published also separately), and contributed to "Ha-Meliẓ" (1892, Nos. 267–271) a very interesting description of the younger days of his brother Leon and to "Ha-Ẓefirah" (xv., Nos. 12 *et seq.*) an article on the anti-Jewish riots of 1881–82. He is considered one of the best of Hebrew prose-writers, although his too florid style and his continual deviations from the subject can hardly please a modern reader.

BIBLIOGRAPHY: *Ha-Asif*, iii. 117; *Ha-Shaḥar*, viii. 384; *Ha-Ẓefirah*, xiii., No. 26; *Keneset ha-Gedolah*, iv., part 2, pp. 30 *et seq.*; Zeitlin, *Bibl. Post-Mendels.* p. 227.

H. R. P. WI.

MANDELSTAMM, LEON (ARYEH LÖB) B. JOSEPH: Russian Hebraist, poet, and educator; born in Zhagory, government of Kovno, in 1809; died in St. Petersburg Sept. 12, 1889. He was the fourth son of Joseph Mandelstamm, a man of liberal and progressive views who had imbibed German ideas and collected German books during his business travels in Germany. Under the guidance of his father and older brothers Leon acquired a large amount of rabbinical and secular knowledge before he was fifteen years of age. He married while very young, and settled with his wife's parents in Keidany, government of Wilna; but his progressive thoughts and habits were considered heretical there, and he was compelled to divorce his wife after about six months of married life.

Mandelstamm then resumed his studies with renewed vigor, and about 1832 went to Wilna with the intention of entering its university; but that institution being about to be transferred to Kiev, he entered the University of Moscow instead. He graduated as a "candidate" (bachelor) in philology from the University of St. Petersburg in 1844, being the first Jew in Russia to attain that honor.

Mandelstamm acted as secretary to the rabbinical commission called at St. Petersburg in the summer of 1843 to draw up a system of education for the Jews of Russia. When LILIENTHAL, who had been selected to carry out the plans of the commission, or rather the plans of Uvarov, the Russian minister of public instruction, suddenly left Russia in 1845, Mandelstamm was appointed in his place and served under Uvarov and his successors until he retired in 1857. In these twelve years he wrote, edited, and published various books for use in Jewish schools, superintended the establishment of schools in various localities, including the rabbinical schools of Wilna and Jitomir, and appointed teachers for them (see Gottlober in "Ha-Maggid," xvii. 392). He had charge also of the disbursement of the candle-tax funds, which were for the purpose of supporting those schools; the conservative masses, hating both the tax and the purpose for which it was levied, saw in him the embodiment of all the evil of the new movement. The ill-feeling against him disappeared in later years (see Gurland in "Ha-Shaḥar," iv. 112).

After his retirement from the service of the government he engaged in various financial enterprises, but few of which were successful. He spent much time in Germany, especially in Berlin, where most of his works were published. His Russian translation of the Bible was at first prohibited in Russia, and was permitted later only on condition that it would not be sold without the Hebrew text ("Allg. Zeit. des Jud." 1870, pp. 438–439; *ib.* 1871, p. 340). His last years were spent in poverty and neglect. Having died suddenly on a ferry-boat, he was buried in a pauper's grave; several days afterward, however, he was disinterred and buried with proper honors in the Jewish cemetery of St. Petersburg. His library was taken to the United States by A. M. Bank and was sold to the New York Public Library, where it formed the nucleus of the Jewish department of that institution.

Mandelstamm was the author of: "Stikhotvoreniya," poems (Moscow, 1840); "Ḥinnuk Ne'arim," Hebrew and German text-book for schools, in two parts (Wilna, 1849–50); notes to the Bible, in the edition (24 vols.), with the German translation, printed (under his supervision) by the Russian government (St. Petersburg, 1852) and known as the "Mandelstamm edition" of the Bible; "Shene Peraḳim," better known as "Kebod Melek," in Hebrew and German (*ib.* 1852); "V Zashchitu Yevreyev" (*ib.* 1858); "Sefer Millim," Russian-Hebrew and Hebrew-Russian dictionary (*ib.* 1859); "Horæ Thalmudicæ," in German (Berlin, 1860); Russian translation of the Pentateuch (*ib.* 1862; 2d ed. 1871); "Die Bibel, Neu Uebersetzt und Erklärt" (the Book of Genesis and a dramatization of Canticles, both annotated; *ib.* 1862); "Biblische Studien," in two parts (*ib.* 1862); "Saratovskie Mucheniki," an account of a ritual-murder trial of 1857 (Berlin, 1863); "Einleitung in den Pentateuch" (*ib.* 1864); "Yevreiskaya Semyya," a drama (*ib.* 1864; 3d ed., St Petersburg, 1872); "O Zheleznikh Dorogakh," on Russian railroads (St. Petersburg, 1865–67); "Bibleiskoe Gosudarstvo," in "Yevreiskaya Biblioteka," for 1871; "Stimmen in der Wüste," German songs (London, 1880). He also contributed numerous articles to periodicals in various languages. A part of his "Horæ Thalmudicæ," under the title "Rabbi Joshua ben Hanania," appeared in an English translation (Berlin, n.d.). The four volumes of extracts from Maimonides' Yad ha-Ḥazaḳah, with German translation, published by the Russian government (St. Petersburg, 1851), were prepared, under Mandelstamm's supervision, by his townsman Ḥayyim Sack.

Mandelstamm had a son, **Joseph**, a physician, who

died long before him. A daughter, by a second marriage, is the wife of Dr. M. L. Zimmerman of Philadelphia.

Bibliography: Bloch's *Wochenschrift*, 1889, No. 46; Brockhaus-Efron, *Russian Encyclopedia*; *Jüdische Presse*, xx., No. 39; B. Mandelstamm, *Alumme Aryeh Mandelstamm*, in *Ha-Meliz*, 1892, Nos. 267–271; *Ha-Meliz*, 1889; *Moskovskiya Vyedomosti*, 1889, No. 276; *Voskhod* (weekly ed.), 1889, No. 36; *Ha-Meliz*, 1889, Nos. 198, 199, 201, 232.
H. R. P. Wi.

MANDELSTAMM, MAX (EMANUEL): Russian physician and Zionist; born in Zhagory, government of Kovno, in 1838. His father, Ezekiel Mandelstamm, younger brother of Benjamin and Leon Mandelstamm, taught him French and German, in addition to the usual studies of the "ḥeder." Later Max attended a school in Mitau for about a year, and the gymnasium at Wilna from 1850 to 1854. At the age of sixteen he entered the University of Dorpat as a medical student, and later studied at Kharkof, where he graduated in 1860. After practising medicine in Chernigov for about four years he went to Berlin (1864) and entered the university, where he studied ophthalmology under Graefe and pathology under Virchow. Later he studied for some time in Heidelberg under Helmholtz, and in 1866 he became assistant physician in Pagenstecher's hospital for eye-diseases in Wiesbaden. Two years later he settled in Kiev, where he still (1904) resides. He is considered one of the leading oculists in Russia. He was privat-docent at the University of Kiev for twelve years, and was thrice chosen professor; but the election was each time declared void on account of his being a Jew. He was for four years the head of the clinic for eye-diseases at the university, and is now the head of a private ophthalmic hospital which he established in 1880.

Max Mandelstamm.

Mandelstamm takes a prominent part in Jewish affairs both in Kiev and in Russia generally. He was president of a committee to assist emigration in 1881 and 1882, and was one of the two Jewish representatives who were permitted to plead the cause of the Jews before the commission which investigated Jewish affairs after the riots of 1881. He has taken a leading part also in Zionism since the inception of the movement, and has been a conspicuous figure at all the Zionist congresses held during recent years. Most of Mandelstamm's writings are on subjects relating to his scientific specialty, and have appeared in Graefe's "Archiv" (vols. xi., xiii., xix.) and "Centralblatt für Praktische Augenheilkunde"; only one essay has been translated into English, under the title "How Jews Live," London, 1900. His articles on Zionism appeared in "Welt" and "Ost u[nd] West."

Bibliography: Brainin, in *Aḥiasaf*, 1900, pp. 336–349.
H. R. P. Wi.

MANDL, CHRISTOF: Hungarian autho[r]; converted to Christianity in 1534. His godfath[er] was George, Margrave of Brandenburg, to who[m] Mandl dedicated his "Dass Jesus Christus Sey d[as] Ewig Wort" (1536), in which Jesus is represent[ed] as the Redeemer. His other works are "Rechnu[ng] der 70 Wochen Danielis" (1552) and another, pu[b]lished in 1557, in which Jesus is described as t[he] Messiah (Büchler, "A Zsidók Története Budapesten," Budapest, 1901).
D. A. Bü.

MANDL, LUDWIG LAZAR: Hungaria[n] anatomist and pathologist; born at Budapest Dec. 1812; died in Paris July 5, 1881; educated at V[i]enna and Budapest (M.D. 1836). He then settled [in] Paris to study microscopy. His researches in t[he] embryology of the higher mammalia attracted the a[t]tention of the Parisian Society of Physicians, whic[h] in 1845, requested him to prepare anatomical spec[i]mens. In 1846 he began to lecture on microscop[ic] anatomy at the Collège de France. In the sa[me] year he was made a knight of the Legion of Hono[r]. After 1862 he lectured before the Medical Clinic [of] Paris on diseases of the vocal organs.

Mandl was a prolific writer; the following a[re] among his principal works: "Sanguis Respect[u] Physiologico" (Budapest, 1836); "Anatomie Micr[o]scopique" (Paris, 1838–58); "Traité Pratique d[u] Microscope" (*ib.* 1839); "Mémoires d'Anatom[ie] Pathologique" (*ib.* 1840); "Manuel d'Anatomie G[é]nérale" (*ib.* 1843; awarded a prize by the Frenc[h] Academy in 1858); "Traité d'Anatomie Microsc[o]pique" (*ib.* 1847; awarded a prize by the Frenc[h] Institute in 1850); "Mémoires Concernant la Path[o]logie et la Thérapeutique des Organes de la Respir[a]tion" (*ib.* 1855); "Traité Pratique de Maladies [du] Larynx et de Pharynx" (*ib.* 1872).

Bibliography: *Jüdisches Athenäum*, p. 129 (inaccurate); *Allg. Deutsche Biog.* xx. 178; Reich, *Beth-El*, iv. 31; Szinyei, *Magyar Irók.*
S. L. V.

MANDL, MORITZ: Austrian dramatist an[d] journalist; born in Presburg May 13, 1840. H[e] went to Vienna and there joined the editorial sta[ff] of the "Wanderer" (1862) and later that of t[he] "Neue Freie Presse." Since 1877 he has been a[s]sistant editor of the "Fremdenblatt."

Mandl has written: "Deutschland und der Auge[n]blick" (Leipsic, 1861), a pamphlet that won so[me] attention; "Käthchen von Heilbronn" (Vienn[a], 1873), a German epic; a dramatic prologue to t[he] Vienna "Kleist-Feier" of 1876; and several plays.

Bibliography: Eisenberg, *Das Geistige Wien*, i. 336–337.
S. N. D.

MANE. See Weights and Measures.

MANESSIER DE VESOUL: French com[]munal leader; originally from Vesoul and probabl[y] of the family of Héliot of Vesoul, whose ledger ha[s] been published by Isidore Loeb (in "R. E. J." viii., ix.). He is chiefly known in connection with t[he] Paris community. It was he who negotiated f[or] the return of the Jews to France about the year 1358. He was appointed by the king "procureur général" of the Jews, with the function of granting or withholding the right of entrance into France to every individual Jew, being in turn responsible for their contributions to the treasury. He held this position as late as 1376. Associated with him about 1370 was one Jacob de Pont St. Maxence. After a time these two quarreled, and Jacob accused Manessier and Vivant (Manessier's brother) of certain malversations in his office, of having established a synagogue without the king's permission, and of having pronounced an edict of excommunication contrary to the provisions of the act of Parliament of Feb. 3, 1374. Manessier was imprisoned in the Châtelet, Paris. The king's proctor demanded a fine, with imprisonment until the fine had been paid. It is, however, probable that this was remitted, as Manessier afterward recovered his credit with the court, after having made peace with Jacob.

Bibliography: Isidore Loeb, in *Grätz Jubelschrift*, pp. 54-56.

G. J.

MANETHO (Greek, Μανεθώς or Μανεθών): Greco-Egyptian writer whose history of Egypt, forming a source of Josephus, especially in his book "Contra Apionem" (i. 14 *et seq.*; ed. Niese, §§ 73-105; 228-251), possesses special interest for the history of Israel.

Manetho was high priest of Sebennytus in the Delta (according to some, erroneously, of Heliopolis), and lived under the first two Ptolemies. His history was written after 271 B.C.; its importance rests on Manetho's ability to use hieroglyphic sources directly. Though he seems to have enjoyed considerable reputation among the contemporary Greeks, it does not appear that his history was much read in the first century of the common era. Josephus is the only writer who furnishes coherent extracts. After him, Julius Africanus (221) and Eusebius (326) extracted chronological tables of Egyptian dynasties and kings for their Biblical chronographies. Both extracts were preserved by Georgius Syncellus (*c.* 792). The confusion of facts and names in Josephus' extracts (especially on the Exodus, "Contra Ap." i. 26; ed. Niese, §§ 228 *et seq.*) is almost incredible. Some of the errors may be attributed to Josephus himself. What Josephus reports about the Hyksos (or Hykussos) dynasty contains valuable information; but the connection of those kings and the Israelites is an untenable theory. What remains of the Manethonian Exodus account after the correction of the most manifest blunders seems, however, to show that the writer used the Biblical narrative and tried to combine it with some popular Egyptian tales.

Bibliography: The extant fragments of Manetho have often been collected (by Rosellini, Bunsen, and others). They are most conveniently accessible in C. Müller, *Historici Græci Minores*, ii. 511; and the most valuable treatise on them is Unger, *Die Chronologie des Manetho*, 1867. For scattered literature see Wiedemann, *Gesch. Aegyptens*, p. 121.

T. W. M. M.

MANETTI, GIANNOZZO: Italian statesman and Christian Hebraist; born in Florence 1396; died at Naples Oct. 26, 1459. At the suggestion of Pope Nicholas V., who had made him one of his secretaries, Manetti learned Hebrew from a Jew named Manuel. He is said to have had a Jewish servant with whom he spoke Hebrew; and his son Agnolo from an early age was taught Hebrew besides Latin and Greek.

Manetti translated the Psalms at Nicholas' request, but had to defend the principles of his translation in a special treatise. In the hope of gaining the 5,000 ducats promised by the pope for the discovery of the original Hebrew of the Gospel of Matthew, Manetti collected many Hebrew manuscripts which are now in the Vatican. He also began a large apologetic work against the Jews.

Bibliography: Burckhart, *Renaissance in Italy*, i. 270; Steinschneider, in *Zeit. für Hebr. Bibl.* i. 87; Michaud, in *Biographie Universelle*; *Nuova Enciclopedia Italiana*.

T. J.

MANI, ELIJAH: Turkish rabbi; died in Hebron, Palestine, in the summer of 1899. He was a native of Bagdad, where he was held in great esteem for his piety and his knowledge of the Cabala. About 1856 he went to Jerusalem, and two years later settled in Hebron. When R. Moses Pereire of that city died, Mani succeeded him as rabbi of the Sephardim. For fourteen years he accepted no remuneration, but later was forced by poverty to overcome his scruples. He was very active in charitable and communal affairs, and his simple and noble life won for him the respect and admiration of all the inhabitants of that ancient city; Mohammedans as well as Jews thronged to his funeral. He is said to have written eleven works, which he refused to publish.

Bibliography: *Aḥiasaf*, 5661 (1900-1), pp. 385-386.

S. S. P. Wi.

MANISSA (the ancient **Magnesia ad Sipylum**): Town in the Turkish vilayet of Aidin, twenty-eight miles northeast of Smyrna. It has a population of 40,000, of whom 1,800 are Jews (against 1,200 in 1898). The community there is said to be older than that of Smyrna. Richard Pococke, who visited the city about 1733-34, says ("Description of the East," ii. 56): "Several Jews [of Manissa] exported goods to Smyrna and Europe. They also manufactured calicoes, and usually were rich. To-day they are the commercial leaders. As artisans, they are chiefly shoemakers, tinsmiths, etc. The young women have recently begun to learn the manufacture of Turkish rugs, and this industry is in quite a flourishing condition." When Tournefort visited the district in 1702 ("Voyage au Levant," ii. 490) he found three synagogues there; now there are five—named Shalom, Mayorca, Toledo, 'Ez Ḥayyim, and Talmud Torah. The oldest of these, Shalom, was destroyed by fire, but has been rebuilt.

Among its benevolent societies are the ḥebra ḳaddisha; the Hospital Society; the Mohar u-Mattan, which assists and dowers girls who wish to marry; the Ḥesed shel Emet, which provides for poor families in time of mourning; the Shilluḥim, to assist strangers and the poor to emigrate; and the 'Ozer Dallim, which provides the poor with shoes. The different societies have their own revenues.

There are two cemeteries, one old and the other

dating back about a century. In the former, tombstones dated 5406 (= 1646) have been found. A portion of the old cemetery was occupied for some years by Mohammedan refugees, who mistook it for vacant ground, and built houses there. To save the new cemetery from a similar fate, it was enclosed with walls in 1900 by the ḥebra ḳaddisha, which spent for this purpose 400 Turkish livres. The community has a small but well-organized hospital, which was founded in 1869 on the initiative of Rabbi Ḥayyim Maẓliaḥ and Rabeno Algranati. Before the establishment of schools by the Alliance Israélite Universelle (one for boys in 1892 and another for girls in 1896) the Talmud Torah was the only educational center. The school buildings stand on a fine estate belonging to the community. After the foundation of these schools the Talmud Torah ceased to exist, and modern ideas of progress have been adopted. Hebrew, French, and Turkish are taught in the schools, and a reading-room was established in 1895. Greek, Turkish, and Judæo-Spanish are the vernaculars. The community is governed by a chief rabbi, who is also the government representative. Since the abolition of the communal tax called "'arikah," the tax upon salt has met the communal needs and the salaries of the rabbis and shoḥeṭim.

The oldest of the chief rabbis of whom any mention is made was Aaron Lapapa, the author of the "Bene Aharon" (Smyrna, 1674), who was succeeded by Benjamin Melammed. After Melammed, the next rabbis known were Zerahiah Azulai, author of "Sukkat Dawid"; Raphael Abraham Maẓliaḥ, author of "Ma'amar ha-Melek" (Salonica, 1806); Joseph Maẓliaḥ, Abraham Maẓliaḥ, Joseph Ḥakim, Moses Maẓliaḥ, and David Gomel, the present (1904) rabbi. Two blood accusations have been brought against the Jews of Manissa, one in 1883 and the other in 1893. In 1837 two hundred Jews died of the Plague.

In a chest in the synagogue Shalom is preserved a parchment manuscript of eight books of the Bible, in three volumes. The first volume contains the books of Genesis and Exodus; the second those of Leviticus, Numbers, and Deuteronomy; and the third Joshua, Judges, and Isaiah. At the end of the last volume is the name of the copyist, Reuben bar Todros, and the date of the book, 5049 (1289). These books are greatly venerated. Some years ago the second volume was sent to Paris to be sold in order to obtain money for the needs of the community. As soon as the book had left Manissa there occurred a succession of sudden and premature deaths. Attributing these misfortunes to the removal of the volume, the community telegraphed for its immediate return.

Among the famous Jews born in Manissa was Samtob (Shem-Ṭob) Shikar, a composer of Oriental music.

About eighty years ago, in the time of Kara Oglu Osman, Chelebi Aaron Franco was the government treasurer; on the downfall of the former, Franco shared his disgrace; Franco's enemies went so far as to pass sentence of death on him, but he was saved through the efforts of Ḥayyim Palaggi, chief rabbi of Smyrna. One of the contemporaries of Franco was a certain Chelebi Abrahamaji Mayo, proprietor of a large estate. Samtob (Shem-Ṭob) Joseph is at present the veterinary surgeon of Manissa and its dependencies; several Jews are members of local tribunals, and David Franco is the present dragoman of the Italian vice-consulate.

D. A. Ga.

MANN, LOUIS: American actor; born in New York city 1865; son of Daniel and Caroline Mann. He began his career as an actor when but six years of age. In 1880 Mann went on tour with a small company, and subsequently was engaged by the elder Salvini (1881), by Lewis Morrison (1882), and by J. K. Emmett (1888). At the conclusion of these engagements Mann set out as a "barnstormer" in classical drama. Among the parts he has created may be mentioned that of *Utterson* the lawyer, in Robert Louis Stevenson's "Dr. Jekyll and Mr. Hyde," as presented by Daniel Bandmann (1887). Mann next appeared in "Incog," in which he took one of the leading parts (1891). His next conspicuous success was in 1896, in a burlesque of the character of *Svengali* in "The Merry World." Later he turned his attention to German comedy parts and originated those in "The Strange Adventures of Miss Brown" (1896), "The Girl from Paris" (1897), "The Telephone Girl" (1898), "All on Account of Eliza" (1901), and "Master and Pupil." Since then Mann has devoted himself especially to these and character parts. In 1902 he took the leading rôle in "The Red Kloof," and later joined Weber and Fields of New York, being associated with them in their productions until the dissolution of their partnership in 1904.

A. F. H. V.

MANNA (מן).—**Biblical Data**: The miraculously supplied food on which the Israelites subsisted in the wilderness. Its name is said to have originated in the question מן הוא ("What is it?" Ex. xvi. 15, R. V.; comp. Rashi *ad loc.*), asked by the Israelites when they first saw it. According to George Ebers ("Durch Gosen zum Sinai," p. 236), the name comes from the Egyptian "mennu" (= "food"). The manna is also designated "bread" (Ex. xvi. 4); it is called "the corn of heaven" and "the bread of the mighty" in Ps. lxxviii. 24–25, R. V., and, in a depreciative sense, "the light bread" in Num. xxi. 5. The manna descended in the night in the form of coriander-seed of the color of bdellium (Num. xi. 7), so that in the morning the ground looked as if it were covered with hoar frost. The grains were ground or pounded into flour, and then the flour was prepared and baked in the form of cakes, the taste of which was like that of "wafers made with honey" or "as the taste of fresh oil" (Ex. xvi. 31; Num. xi. 8).

The gathering of the manna was connected with several miracles: it was collected before sunrise, for, in spite of its hard substance, it melted in the sun. The quantity collected made exactly one omer for every person, whether one collected much or little. On Friday morning the portions were double, for the manna could not be found on Sabbath. The manna was eaten the day it was gathered; if it were left until the following morning it corrupted and bred worms, though the manna gathered on Friday and kept for the Sabbath remained fresh. It continued to descend during the forty years the Israelites were in the wilderness, but when they arrived at Gilgal, on the 14th of Nisan, and began to eat the grain grown there, the manna ceased to fall. In order to perpetuate the memory of this providence, Aaron was told to put an omer of manna in a vessel and lay it "before the testimony" (Ex. xvi. 17-35; Josh. v. 10-12). Num. xxi. 5 makes it appear that manna was the only food of the Israelites while they were in the wilderness, although references to provisions of fine flour, oil, and meat are met with elsewhere. It may be either that the manna constituted their main but not only food-supply during the whole forty years, or that it became their exclusive food after the provisions they took with them from Egypt were exhausted.

Israelites Gathering Manna in the Desert.
(From the Sarajevo Haggadah of the fourteenth century.)

Certain modern scholars attempt to identify the manna of Exodus with the exudation of the tamarisk-trees (named by Ehrenberg the "Tammarix mannifera") of the Sinaitic peninsula. The Arabs call it "mann al-sama" (= "heavenly manna"), and collect it and sell it to pilgrims. It has been identified also with the exudations of other trees found in those regions. A more recent view identifies the Biblical manna with lichen and allied species of plants found in Arabia and other parts of western Asia. The reports of modern travelers, however, are contradictory in regard to "manna."

E. C. M. Sel.

——**In Rabbinical Literature:** Manna was one of the ten things created on the first Friday of Creation, in the twilight (Abot v. 9; comp. Targ. pseudo-Jonathan to Ex. xvi. 4, 15). According to Zabdi b. Levi, the manna which fell near the camp of the Israelites in the wilderness covered an area two thousand cubits square; it remained on the ground until four hours after sunrise, when it melted. It fell to a depth of sixty cubits, or, according to Isi b. Akiba (Midr. Teh. to Ps. xxiii.), of fifty cubits, and the quantity which fell every day would have sufficed to nourish the people for two thousand years. The question why was it necessary that the manna should fall every day is answered by the Rabbis in different ways: the Israelites could not be encumbered with its burden; they needed warm food every day, and the manna was warm when it fell; they needed that their hearts should be turned to God for their daily bread. It was so conspicuous that all the kings of the East and West could see it from their palaces (Yoma 76a; Tan., Beshallaḥ, 21).

In order that the manna might remain clean, a north wind first swept the ground, and then rains washed it. Then, after the ground had been covered with a layer of dew, the manna fell upon it, and was itself then covered with dew (Mek., Beshallaḥ, Wayassa', 3; comp. Sifre, Num. 89). It so fell that the righteous had no trouble in gathering it, finding it at the doors of their tents; those of less firm belief had to go farther for it; the wicked had to go far from the camp to gather it (Yoma 75a). A very different statement, but of the same nature, is given in Tan., Beshallaḥ, 22: The diligent went out into the field to gather the manna; the less diligent went just outside their tents; but the indolent lay in their sleeping-places while the manna fell into their outstretched hands. Created only for the children of Israel, the heathen could not secure the smallest quantity of it, for when one stretched out his hand to pick it up, it slipped from his grasp (Sifre, Deut. 313; Midr. Abkir, in Yalḳ., Ex. 258); according to another opinion, it tasted bitter to the heathen (Tan., *l.c.*).

The melting of the manna formed streams which furnished drink to many deer and other animals, and when those animals were afterward killed by heathen, the latter recognized in the meat the taste of the manna (Tan., *l.c.*; comp. Targ. pseudo-Jonathan to Ex. xvi. 21). It was only in this way that the heathen could know the true taste of the manna, for the water itself was bitter to them (Tan., *l.c.*). With the manna precious stones fell every morning (Yoma *l.c.*). The manna was adapted to the taste of each individual; to the adult it tasted like the food of the adult, while to the sucking child it tasted like the milk of its mother's breasts. By wishing, one could taste in the manna anything desired, whether fowl or fruit; thus the statement that the people ground it, or pounded it, and then baked it (Num. xi. 8), is only figurative, for if one so wished it tasted like food made of flour ground or pounded, baked or cooked. According to a different interpretation, the wicked were compelled to grind it and prepare it until it was fit for food, while for the righteous it was ground by angels before it fell from heaven.

The manna exhaled a fragrant odor, and during the forty years the Israelites wandered in the wilderness it served the women as perfume. Being a heavenly food, the manna contained nutritious matter only, without any waste products, so that during the whole time the Israelites lived upon it the grossest office of the body remained unexercised. The Israelites, nevertheless, complained of it (comp. Num. xi. 6): "Shall a human being not discharge of what he eats? our bowels will surely be swollen" (Yoma *l.c.*; Sifre, Num. 87–89; Tan., *l.c.*).

Characteristics.

A miracle attended the collecting of the manna, in that the number of omers gathered by each family was found to correspond to the number of its members. This rendered the manna useful in solving most difficult problems. For instance, when two people came before Moses, one accusing the other of having stolen his slave and the other claiming to have bought the slave, Moses deferred his decision to the following morning, when the number of omers of manna in their respective houses showed to whom the slave belonged. In this way many otherwise inextricable complications could be unraveled (Yoma 75a).

The Rabbis disagreed as to the period of time for which the pot of manna was placed by Aaron "before the testimony." It was placed there only for the following generation; it was placed there for all future generations; it was to be kept there until the coming of the Messiah. It is one of the three things which will be restored by Elijah. Jeremiah, when remonstrating with the children of Israel for their neglect of the Torah, showed them the pot of manna: "See how God nourishes those that occupy themselves with the study of the Law." There is also a disagreement between the Rabbis with regard to the length of time after Moses' death in which the Israelites ate the manna—whether for forty days, seventy days, or for the fourteen years during which the land of Canaan was conquered and divided among the tribes. According to R. Joshua, the manna ceased to descend immediately after Moses' death, and the Israelites were compelled to eat what they had gathered previously (Mek., *l.c.*). The manna is reserved as the future food of the righteous, for which purpose it is ground in a mill situated in Sheḥaḳim, the third heaven (Ḥag. 12b; Tan., *l.c.*).

E. C. M. Sel.

MANNE, MORDECAI ẒEBI: Russian Hebrew poet and painter; born at Rodzkowitz, government of Wilna, 1859; died there in 1886. He received the Talmudic training usual in Poland, and was taught Hebrew grammar by his father. At thirteen he entered the yeshibah at Minsk, and he remained there until 1876, when he removed to Wilna, studied at the yeshibah there, and, on the advice of Joshua Höschel Levin, entered the school of painting and design. His first poetical writings also belong to that time. In 1880 he went to St. Petersburg and enrolled as a student at the Imperial Academy of Fine Arts, receiving, in 1882, a silver medal from the grand duke Vladimir for extraordinary progress.

Manne's poems, "Mebasser ha-Abib," "Ha-Abib," "Ha-Shoshannah," and "Mas'at Nafshi" (which has been set to music and is sung often in Zionist gatherings), place him among the foremost Hebrew poets. His best poems are somewhat didactic in character, as "Tiḳwah la-'Obed," a fragmentary work, depicting the contrast between hope and despair. Another fragmentary poem, "We-Zaraḥ ha-Shemesh u-Ba ha-Shemesh," is an elegy on the death of Emperor Alexander II. His first prose article, on the art of painting, especially among the Jews, appeared in "Ha-Ẓefirah" in 1882. This was followed by a whole series of papers on art, artists, and esthetics, including one on the art of poetry and a paper on the Jewish painter Oppenheim. His writings have been published in two volumes, under the title "Kol Kitbe Mordekai Ẓebi Manne" (Warsaw).

Bibliography: *Ost und West*, 1902, p. 195; *Kol Kitbe*, Warsaw, 1896.

H. R. J. G. L.

MANNHEIM: Town in the grand duchy of Baden, Germany. It has a population of 141,131, including 5,478 Jews (1900). Jews are not known to have lived in Mannheim before the middle of the seventeenth century. On Sept. 1, 1660, thirteen families, eleven of German and two of Portuguese origin, obtained permission from the elector Karl Ludwig to reside there. A deed dated 1656 mentions the first burial-ground, which in 1661 was exchanged for another; the latter was used until 1839. The first rabbi was Naphtali Herz (1657–71). His successor was Isaac Brilin (1671–78), who was appointed rabbi at Mannheim after the expulsion of the Jews from Hammelburg. Upon his death his son-in-law, Eliezer b. Jekuthiel, became rabbi; but, like his successor, Moses Grotwohl (1679), he held the office only a short time. Even at that early date there were 78 Jews in Mannheim, a fact which induced the municipal administration to submit a request to the government of the Palatinate not to grant any more permits to Jews. Isaac Aaron Worms of Metz was rabbi from 1685 to 1693. The devastation of the Palatinate by the French compelled the Jews of Mannheim, who had assisted in the defense of the city, to go elsewhere; nearly 70 families lost their homes by fire. Heidelberg received 26 families until their houses at Mannheim were rebuilt (1691). Among the new houses was the large quadrangular building erected by the court factor Emanuel Oppenheimer of Vienna, son of the famous Samuel Oppenheimer, and which, until 1729, was the temporary residence of the elector Karl Philipp. A concession granted in 1698, whose object was to bring about the reconstruction of the city as soon as possible, increased the number of Jewish inhabitants to 150 families. In 1701 the Jews obtained permission to extend their burial-place and to build a synagogue.

The first rabbi after the reconstruction of the city was Joseph David Ulf (1706–29). It was at this period that a Klaus was founded at Mannheim through the generosity of Lemle Moses Reinganum, with a capital of 100,000 gulden. The building, including a synagogue and bet ha-midrash, was dedicated in 1708, and, with some alterations, exists to-day. Similar institutions, but smaller, were established by

Michael May and Elias Haium. The rabbi at that time was Samuel Helmann (1726–51), an opponent of Jonathan Eybeschütz. On Helmann's appointment as rabbi at Metz, David (Tebele) Hess was elected chief rabbi in Mannheim. During his tenure of office occurred the notorious divorce dispute of Cleve, which involved a member of the Mannheim congregation and aroused a bitter controversy among the rabbis of Germany (1766; see "Or Yisrael," Cleve, 1770; Horovitz, "Frankfurter Rabbinen," iv. 27–31, Frankfort-on-the-Main, 1885; Lubetzki, "Bidḳe Battim," p. 44b, Paris, 1896). The elector Karl Theodor granted more Jews the right to live in Mannheim (1744), at the same time, however, ordering them to settle in the side streets, as they should not be allowed to own a house in the main street. For thirty-two years the chief rabbi at the klaus was Naphtali Hirsch Katzenellenbogen. The "Stadtrabbiner" was Hirschel Levin (1770–73), who left Mannheim for Berlin. In 1784 Michel Scheuer, from Mayence, was appointed "Stadtrabbiner"; he held the office for twenty-five years and died in 1809. His successors were: Gottschalk Abraham, who had been klaus rabbi and "Oberland" rabbi (d. 1824); Hirsch Traub (d. 1849); Moses Praeger (d. 1861), who introduced a Reform service (1856); B. Friedman (1863–79); and the present (1904) rabbi, M. Steckelmacher (since 1880). Mannheim contains many Jewish philanthropic institutions.

Bibliography: Löwenstein, *Gesch. der Juden in der Kurpfalz*, Frankfort-on-the-Main, 1895.

D. L. L.

MANNHEIMER (MAGYAR), GUSTAV: Hungarian painter; born at Budapest Feb. 27, 1854. He studied at the schools of drawing in Budapest, Munich, Vienna, and Rome. The best known of his paintings are: "On Flowery Mead," "Procession at Anacapri," "Young Tramps," and "Italian Evening Landscape."

Bibliography: Singer, *Allg. Künstler-Lexikon*, vol. iii.

S. N. D.

MANNHEIMER, ISAAC NOAH: Jewish preacher; born at Copenhagen Oct. 17, 1793; died at Vienna March 17, 1865. The son of a ḥazzan, he began the study of the Talmud at an early age, though not to the neglect of secular studies. On completing the course of the cathedral school at Copenhagen, he took up philosophy, Oriental languages, and theology at the university there, at the same time continuing his studies in Talmud and Jewish science. When the Jews of Denmark were emancipated in 1814 confirmation was made obligatory, and the office of catechist was instituted by the state, Mannheimer being the first incumbent (1816). The first confirmation took place May, 1817. In 1821 Mannheimer went to Vienna, where there was then no congregation, the community being divided into two opposing parties. Mannheimer, who was welcomed by both factions, soon succeeded in organizing a congregation, drafting a program and ritual on the traditional basis and harmonizing the views of the two parties. He returned to Copenhagen in December of the same year. Failing in his attempt to secure a new synagogue for Reform services, he accepted a call to the pulpit left vacant by Zunz in Berlin. German services, however, were interdicted in that city; the temple formerly under the ministry of B. Beer was closed, and the royal cabinet order of Dec. 26, 1823, obtained by the Orthodox party, frustrated the attempt to adapt the old ritual to new forms by delivering German sermons in the chief synagogue. Mannheimer therefore left Berlin and took temporary charge of the pulpit of Hamburg, preaching also at Leipsic during the fairs. In 1824 he married Liseke Damier, and in November of the same year he was called to the new synagogue of Vienna. As he could not receive the title of preacher or rabbi, he was inducted, in June, 1825, as "Direktor der Wiener K. K. Genehmigten Oeffentlichen Israelitischen Religionsschule"; he dedicated the new temple in April, 1826, and officiated there until 1829.

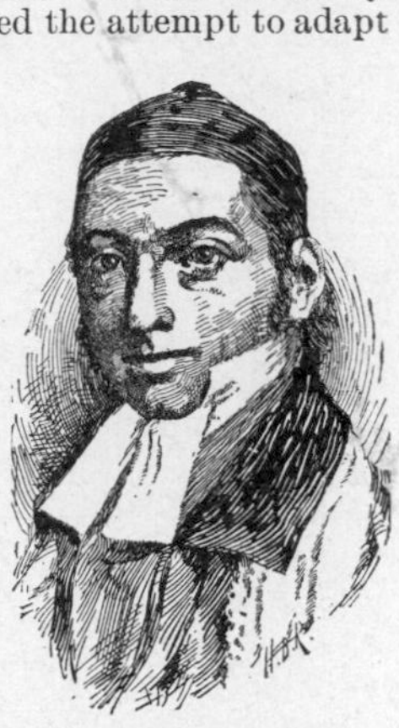

Isaac Noah Mannheimer.

Mannheimer's success was due in great measure to his oratorical gifts. His sermons were, for their time, models (Geiger, "Einleitung in das Studium der Jüdischen Theologie," in "Nachgelassene Schriften," ii. 31). His German translation of the prayer-book and of the fast-day prayers, and his arrangement of the fast-day liturgy, are of permanent importance for the ritual, the conservative spirit in which this work was undertaken leading to its adoption by many communities.

In 1848 Mannheimer was returned by Brody to the Austrian Reichstag, where he delivered two memorable speeches, one on the Jew-tax (Oct. 5, 1848) and the other on the abolition of capital punishment (Jan. 29, 1849). On his seventieth birthday the city of Vienna conferred honorary citizenship upon him. He devoted the gifts bestowed by the community upon him on that occasion to a foundation for the aid of rabbis, preachers, and teachers, which still bears his name.

Mannheimer published the following works: "Prædikener Holdte ved det Mosaiske Troes-Samfund's Andagts-Övelser i Modersmaalet i Sommerhalvaaret 1819" (Copenhagen, 1819); "Gottesdienstliche Vorträge Gehalten im Israelitischen Bethause zu Wien im Monate Tischri 5594" (Vienna, 1834); "Gottesdienstliche Vorträge für die Wochenabschnitte des Jahres," vol. i., Genesis and Exodus (*ib.* 1835; partly translated into Hebrew by E Kuttner, under the title מי נח, *ib.* 1865); a translation of the prayer-book and of the fast-day prayers according to the ritual of the Vienna Temple (1840; frequently reprinted). His polemics and responsa include: "Gutachten für das Gebetbuch des Hamburger Tempels" (1841); "Gutachten Gegen die Reformpartei in Frankfurt-am-Main in Angelegenheit der Beschneidungsfrage" (1843); "Einige Worte über Juden und Judenthum" (supplement to the "Oesterreichische Medicinische Wochenschrift," 1842, No. 34), directed against Professor Rosa's statements in reference to the Jewish question (1848). Two numbers of his "Gottesdienstliche Vorträge" appeared posthumously, edited by S. Hammerschlag (Vienna, 1876).

BIBLIOGRAPHY: G. Wolf, *Isak Noa Mannheimer, Prediger: Eine Biographische Skizze*, Vienna, 1863 (Italian transl. by Lelio della Torre, Triest, 1863); Kayserling, *Bibliothek Jüdischer Kanzelredner*, i. 285, and the bibliography there given.

J. E. N.

MANNHEIMER (HERSCHMAN), LOUISE: Writer and poetess; born at Prague Sept. 3, 1845. In 1866 she went with her parents to New York, where she became the wife of Prof. Sigmund Mannheimer. She wrote German and English poems, and articles and reviews for German and English periodicals. Zimmermann's "Deutsch in Amerika" (Chicago, 1894) contains some of her poems and a short biographical notice. Among her productions in English are "The Storm," a translation of one of Judah ha-Levi's poems, and "The Harvest," a prize poem (printed in "The American Jews' Annual," Cincinnati, 1897). In 1895 she published under the title of "The Jewish Woman" a translation of Nahida Remy's "Das Jüdische Weib" (2d ed. 1897). She is the author of "The Maiden's Song," and is the founder of the Cincinnati Jewish Industrial School for Boys and the inventor of the Pureairin Patent Ventilator.

A. S. MAN.

MANNHEIMER, SIGMUND: American educator; born at Kemel, Hesse-Nassau, May 16, 1835. Educated at the teachers' seminary at Ems, Nassau, he became teacher in the Jewish schools of Schierstein (1853) and Hegenheim (1858). In 1861 he entered the University of Paris (Bachelier ès Lettres, 1863), becoming professor of German in 1864. In 1865 he went to America and lived successively in Baltimore (to 1867), New York (to 1873), St. Louis (to 1876), and Rochester, N. Y. (where he became teacher at the Jewish school). In 1884 he was appointed professor of exegesis and Aramaic, and librarian, at Hebrew Union College, Cincinnati, Ohio.

Mannheimer has published: "Die Wahrheit über den Talmud" (Basel, 1858; translated from the French of T. Klein); "Hebrew Reader and Grammar" (New York, 1873; 4th ed., Cincinnati, 1903); "Anti-Semitism" (Cincinnati, 1897; translated from the French of Leroy-Beaulieu); "Iggeret Musar," an English translation of Solomon Alami's "Iggeret Musar" (*ib.* 1898).

A. F. T. H.

MANOAH B. JACOB: French Talmudist; lived at Lunel in the second half of the thirteenth century. He is sometimes quoted under the abbreviation ר"ם (= "R. Manoah"; Halberstam MSS., No. 345). Manoah often cites decisions in the name of his father. After a brief residence at Narbonne, where he studied with Meïr b. Simon and Reuben b. Ḥayyim, Manoah returned to Lunel. Like several of his contemporaries, he was a student of the works of Maimonides, and wrote a commentary on the latter's Yad ha-Ḥazaḳah, which is quoted in "Sha'are Ẓiyyon" under the title "Sefer ha-Manoaḥ," and in "Ḳore ha-Dorot," under the title "Sefer ha-Menuḥah." It was printed at Constantinople in 1518.

BIBLIOGRAPHY: Azulai, *Shem ha-Gedolim*, p. 60a; Conforte, *Ḳore ha-Dorot*, p. 17a; Isaac de Lattes, *Sha'are Ẓiyyon*, p. 75; Renan-Neubauer, *Les Rabbins Français*, p. 512; Fürst, *Bibl. Jud.*; Gross, *Gallia Judaica*, p. 285.

S. S. K.

MANOAH OF LUNEL. See MANOAH B. JACOB.

MANOAH B. SHEMARIAH HANDEL: Polish author; born at Brzeszticzka (ברעסטיצקא), Volhynia; died in 1612. He was the author of the following works: "Ḥokmat Manoaḥ," glosses to the Talmud (printed in the Cracow 1602–5 edition of the Talmud, and separately at Prague, in 1602, by his son); "Menoaḥ ha-Lebabot," commentary to Baḥya ben Joseph's "Al-Hidayah ila Fara'iḍ al-Ḳulub" (Lublin, 1596; frequently reprinted); "Manoaḥ Maẓa Ḥen," on the title-page of which the emperor Rudolph and King Matthias are mentioned. Manoah must have composed a number of other works, for his son, who preserved those already noted, speaks of his intention to publish "all" his father's works on the Talmud, the Cabala, and astronomy.

BIBLIOGRAPHY: Sternberg, *Gesch. der Juden in Polen*, p. 184, Leipsic, 1878; Steinschneider, *Cat. Bodl.* col. 1652, No. 6209.

S. S. G. WE.

MANRESA: Town in Spain, in the province of Barcelona. In the twelfth century it is said to have contained 500 Jewish families, most of which lived in a narrow lane named "Grau dels Jueus," near the town hall; their cemetery, still called "Fossana dels Jueus," was outside the city. In the thirteenth and fourteenth centuries the Jews there were engaged in manufacturing, in trading (including that in slaves), in money-lending (at the rate of 20 per cent, the usual interest at that time), and in the cultivation of their vineyards and estates. The hostility of the Christians toward the Jews which prevailed throughout Catalonia was manifested in Manresa also. In 1325 the Christian inhabitants of the town endeavored to prevent the Jews from baking their Passover bread, so that the latter were obliged to appeal to the king for protection. The Jews in Manresa did not escape the general persecution of 1391, and many of them professed to accept Christianity. After 1414 comparatively few Jews remained in the town, and in 1492 they sold their property for whatever they could get for it and left the country. At the beginning of the fifteenth century Manresa had 30,000 inhabitants; three centuries later it contained barely one-fifth of that number. Several members of the Zabarra (Sabara) family lived in Manresa. The town is not mentioned in the "Shebeṭ Yehudah."

BIBLIOGRAPHY: J. M. de Mas y Casas, *Memoria Historica de los Hebreos y de los Arabes en Manresa*, Manresa, 1837 (2d ed. 1882); Ed. Tamaro, *Los Judios de Manresa*, in Jacobs, *Sources*, pp. 154 *et seq.*; *R. E. J.* v. 286 *et seq.*, vi. 297; Rios, *Hist.* ii. 155, 402; iii. 310.

G. M. K.

MANSION HOUSE AND GUILDHALL MEETINGS: Meetings held at the summons of the lord mayor of London by citizens of the English metropolis to protest against the persecution of the Jews. The first of these was held on July 3, 1840, to protest against the blood accusation brought against the Jews of Damascus. A demand for this meeting was made by 210 important residents of the city. Speeches were delivered by Daniel O'Connell, Alderman Thompson, Dr. Bowring, and others, expressing their disbelief in the accusation and demanding the release of the accused. The resolutions of the meeting were sent by the lord mayor to the chief ambassadors of foreign powers residing in England, and an especially favorable reply was received from the Emperor of Russia. Over forty years later meetings were convened by the lord mayor of London to protest against the persecutions of the Jews in Russia. Attention had been called to these by articles in the London "Times" of Jan. 9 and 11, 1882, written by Joseph Jacobs, and a requisition was made for a Mansion House Meeting in consequence. The requisition was signed by thirty-eight persons, including the Archbishop of Canterbury, Cardinal Manning, Charles Darwin, John Tyndall, and eighteen members of Parliament. This meeting was followed by numerous others throughout the United Kingdom, including one at the University of Oxford.

The requisition for the Guildhall Meeting of Dec. 10, 1890, was signed by eighty-three persons, again headed by the Archbishop of Canterbury and Cardinal Manning, and including nineteen peers, twenty-seven members of Parliament, and the foremost representatives of nearly every learned profession. The following resolution, proposed by the Duke of Westminster and seconded by the Bishop of Ripon, was adopted: "That in the opinion of this meeting the renewed sufferings of the Jews in Russia from the operation of severe and exceptional edicts and disabilities are deeply to be deplored, and that in this last decade of the nineteenth century religious liberty is a principle which should be recognized by every Christian community as among the natural human rights." In the name of the citizens of London a memorandum was addressed to the czar to this effect, praying that the Jews of Russia should be granted political and social equality with the rest of his subjects. The czar refusing officially to receive the communication, it was returned through the foreign office.

As a consequence of the first of the two last-mentioned meetings, a Mansion House Fund was raised of £108,000 and was administered by a **Mansion House Committee**; this later took over the £100,000 collected after the Guildhall Meeting, when it became known henceforth as the **Russo-Jewish Committee.** In the early stages of its work the Mansion House Committee supervised the transportation of large numbers of Russo-Jewish refugees from Brody to America, having a branch committee at Liverpool presided over by B. L. Benas. The chairman of both committees was Sir Julian Goldsmith, and the honorary secretary was N. S. Joseph. The committee took part also in all the conferences held to consider the position of the Russian Jews and helped to found agricultural colonies at Moosomin, Canada; Painted Woods, N. Dak.; Vineland, N. J.; and elsewhere. None of these colonies, however, had a very long life. The Russo-Jewish Committee, besides assisting the Jewish Board of Guardians by arranging for the immigration, repatriation, and settlement of refugees, founded also in London a Location and Information Bureau as a labor registry, and evening classes in English for the refugees, so as to enable them to earn their living outside the congested districts.

BIBLIOGRAPHY: *The Times* (London), Feb. 2, 1882, and Dec. 11, 1890; *Publications of the Russo-Jewish Committee.*

O. J. S.—J.

MANṢUR MARZUḲ: Egyptian rabbi and author; settled at Salonica toward the close of the eighteenth century. He was the author of several works: "Ẓur Todah" (Salonica, 1783), a commentary on the Yad ha-Ḥazaḳah; "Ben Pedahẓur" (*ib.* 1786), sermons; "Ḳorban Eliẓur," a Talmudic commentary.

BIBLIOGRAPHY: Azulai, *Shem ha-Gedolim*; Franco, *Histoire des Israëlites de l'Empire Ottoman*, p. 127.

S. M. Fr.

MANTINO, JACOB BEN SAMUEL: Italian physician; died at Damascus in 1549. His parents—and perhaps Mantino himself—were natives of Tortosa, Spain, which place they left at the time of the banishment of the Jews from Spain (1492). Mantino studied medicine and philosophy at the universities of Padua and Bologna. Having graduated, he established himself at the latter place, and devoted his hours of leisure to the translation of scientific works from Hebrew into Latin. By these translations he soon acquired a high reputation, and he was befriended by the highest dignitaries of the court of Pope Clement VII.

The war of 1527 compelled Mantino to leave the Pontifical States. He settled at Verona, where the new bishop, Giberti, protected him. In 1528, when Giberti left Verona for Rome, Mantino decided to settle at Venice, where the Council of Ten exempted him from wearing the Jews' hat. This privilege was granted him, at first for a term of several months, upon the recommendation of the French and English ambassadors, the papal legate, and other dignitaries whom he numbered among his patients. At the expiration of the prescribed term Mantino found an influential protector in another of his patients, Théodore Trivulce, marshal of France and governor of Genoa; the latter, urging his own services to the Venetian Republic, insisted that the council should make the exemption perpetual.

The efforts of the English king Henry VIII. to get rid of his wife Catherine on the pretext that their marriage was contrary to the Biblical law, and that the dispensation obtained from Pope Julius II. was invalid, involved Mantino in difficulties. Henry sent Richard Croke to Italy in order to obtain opinions favorable to his case, and the latter addressed himself to Jewish as well as to Christian scholars. Pope Clement VII., in his turn, consulted Mantino, who decided against Henry. This decision created for Mantino many enemies in Venice, where Croke had won a favorable opinion from the famous physician and scholar Elijah Menahem Ḥalfon, among others. Meanwhile the Messianic dreamer Solomon Molko, whom Mantino had energetically opposed while he was in Venice, went to Rome, followed by Mantino. Having many friends and protectors at the court of Clement VII., Mantino soon acquired great influence in Rome, which he employed in crushing Molko. Mantino attained the zenith of his influence at the accession to the papal throne of Paul III. (1534), who appointed him his physician. This high position did not prevent Mantino from concerning himself with the affairs of the Jewish community of Rome, in whose records he appears as a member of the rabbinate, with the title "gaon." In 1544, for some unknown reason, Mantino returned to Venice, where again he was exempted from wearing the Jews' hat. Five years later he accompanied, as physician, the Venetian ambassador to Damascus, where he died soon after his arrival.

Mantino translated the following commentaries of Averroes: "Paraphrasis Averrois de Partibus et Generatione Animalium," with the commentary of Levi ben Gershon (dedicated to Pope Leo X.; Rome, 1521); commentary (the compendium) on Aristotle's "Metaphysics"; the "middle commentaries" on Aristotle's "Isagoge"—books i.–iv. of "Topics" and "Poetics" (Venice, 1550); commentary on Plato's "Republic" (dedicated to Pope Paul III.); proem to the large commentary on Aristotle's "Physics"; the large commentary on the third book of Aristotle on the soul; proem to book xii. of Aristotle's "Metaphysics"; the "middle commentary" on Aristotle's "Physics." He translated also Averroes' medical work "Colliget" ("Kullayot"), the first book of Avicenna's "Canon," and Maimonides' "Shemonah Peraḳim."

BIBLIOGRAPHY: Wolf, *Bibl. Hebr.* i. 606; Wüstenfeld, *Die Uebersetzungen Arabischer Werke in das Lateinische seit dem XI. Jahrhundert*, pp. 123 *et seq.*; Steinschneider, in *Zunz Jubelschrift*, pp. 13, 20; idem, *Cat. Bodl.* col. 1235; idem, *Hebr. Uebers.* pp. 145, 438, 673, 685, 976; Kaufmann, in *R. E. J.* xxvii. 30 *et seq.*; *Il Vessillo Israelitico*, 1885, p. 317; Renazzi, *Storia dell' Universita degli Studi di Roma*, ii. 110; Vogelstein and Rieger, *Gesch. der Juden in Rom*, ii. 94 *et seq.*

D. I. Br.

MANTLE OF THE LAW (מפה): The cover of the scroll of the Pentateuch. The Hebrew name "mappah" is derived from the Greek μάππα. Originally, a wrapping of fine silk was spread along the full length of the parchment, to protect the writing from dust and injury when the scroll was rolled up. The mantle is mentioned in Soferim iii. 16. "A scroll that has no mantle shall be turned face down, so as not to expose the writing" (Yer. Meg. i. 9). The custom of completely covering the writing with silk, when the mantle is not in use, is still practised by the Sephardim in the Orient. The color chosen is usually green. Probably, in earlier times the less expensive method was adopted of using a narrow strip of silk to cover the writing at the opening of the scroll, which would account for the word μάππα = "kerchief" or "napkin." Another kind of covering was called "miṭpaḥat," and was used to wrap the scroll after it had been rolled up. It appears from the Mishnah that all books or scrolls were provided with coverings (Kelim xxiv. 14). When Levi b. Samuel and Huna b. Ḥiyya were preparing coverings for the books of R. Judah, they thought the scroll of Esther did not require a miṭpaḥat, for which opinion they were rebuked by R. Judah (Sanh. 100a). In the Orient, mantles are often not used, carved wooden boxes being substituted for them.

Mantle of the Law, Velvet, Seventeenth Century.
(In the Victoria and Albert Museum, London.)

The "mantle of the Law," as it is popularly called, is made in the form of a bag, to fit the scroll after it is rolled up. It is open at the bottom and closed at the top except for two openings to allow the scroll-handles ("'eẓ ḥayyim") to pass through. The mantle is made of expensive material, which must not have been used for any other purpose. Old, worn-out mantles should not be thrown away, but should be stored in the genizah or sewed into a shroud for a corpse to be buried in (Shulḥan 'Aruk, Oraḥ Ḥayyim, 154, 4). Between the sectional readings of the Pentateuch at the synagogue the scroll is closed and covered with the mantle. On special occasions, when two scrolls are read from, e one first used must be rolled up and covered be-re the mantle is removed from the second scroll (*ib.* 7). The mantle of the Law is usually decorated embroidered with the CROWN OF THE LAW, the

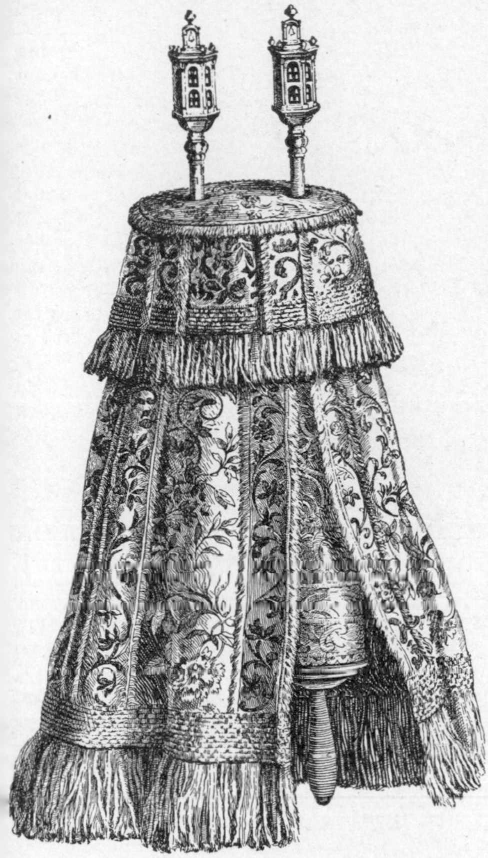

Mantle of the Law, Holland, Early Eighteenth Century. (From Picart.)

ion of Judah, and with tassels and ornaments. The antle is often made and presented to the syna-gogue by women, and sometimes bears the name of e donor or donors.

J. J. D. E.

MANTUA: Fortified Italian city, on the Mincio; apital of the duchy of Mantua. It has a popula-on of 29,160, including 1,100 Jews (1901). In 1858 had 2,523 Jews—the greatest number in its his-ry. The first mention of Jews in Mantua dates om the twelfth century, when Abraham ibn Ezra nished (1145) there his grammatical work "Ẓaḥot." pparently he was in that city again in 1153. There e no further references to Jews in connection with antua until they are mentioned in the new statutes f the city at the end of the fourteenth century, hen a large number seem to have lived there. In 459 a special tax of 2,000 ducats was imposed on e community, though by vigorous protest they acceeded in having it reduced to 600 ducats. The nportance of the community about that time is evi-ent from the fact that two famous rabbis, Joseph COLON and Judah da Napoli (Messer Leon), officiated in Mantua, although, on account of their inability to agree, both were expelled from the city in 1475. In the following year, with the consent of the pope, the Jews were permitted to lend money at interest, and eight years later Bernardino da Feltre founded a "monte di pietà" there, the granting of its charter being one of the first acts of the government of the new prince, Francesco Gonzaga (1466–1519), who was generally ill-disposed toward the Jews. In 1485 he ordered all of them, with their wives, to attend Bernardino's anti-Jewish sermons. In 1496, when the preachers again demanded that restrictions be placed on courtezans and Jews, the wife of the prince, during his absence, ordered the wearing of the Jewish badge.

Under the Gonzagas.

From this time the treatment of the Jews varied, and intermittently they were favored by the princes. Although Frederick Gonzaga, the first Duke of Mantua, had a Jewish physician, Abraham Portaleone, he forbade the Jews to keep Christian servants, an exception being made in regard to necessary services performed on the Sabbath. In 1531 the Marano Solomon Molko was burned publicly at the stake during the visit of Emperor Charles V. Although the congregation had received permission from Pope Clement VII. in 1530 to build an Ashkenazic synagogue, the duke did not confirm it until 1540, at the earnest solicitation of Isaac Porto; the last-named was called to the rabbinate of Mantua in 1550, as the first of an uninterrupted succession of rabbis whose names are preserved in the communal archives.

The condition of the Jews improved under Duke Frederick's successors. A decree of 1545 says: "We desire that the Jews shall be as free and secure in pursuing their business and professions in our city and in our duchy as the Christians." These were the best days of the community, the numbers of which probably were augmented by Portuguese immigrants. The Jewish merchants of Mantua carried on extensive business with foreign countries. Jews were often welcomed at court, and after 1542 the duke had Jewish musicians and Jewish actors. Nevertheless, oppressive measures were enacted against them; their cemetery was taken from them in

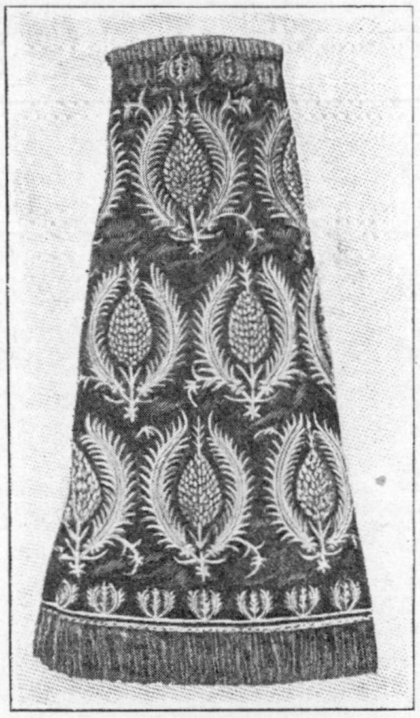

Mantle of the Law, Padua, Eighteenth Century. (From Frauberger.)

1549 that an extension to a monastery might be built in its place. Guglielmo Gonzaga, who was also the first Duke of Monferrato, confirmed their old privileges and suppressed a riot which threatened them in 1562. The security which the community enjoyed enabled it to interest itself in Jewish affairs at large, and it was instrumental in securing the reception of a delegation from the Jewish communities, in 1563, by the Council of Trent, which delegation obtained permission to print Hebrew books.

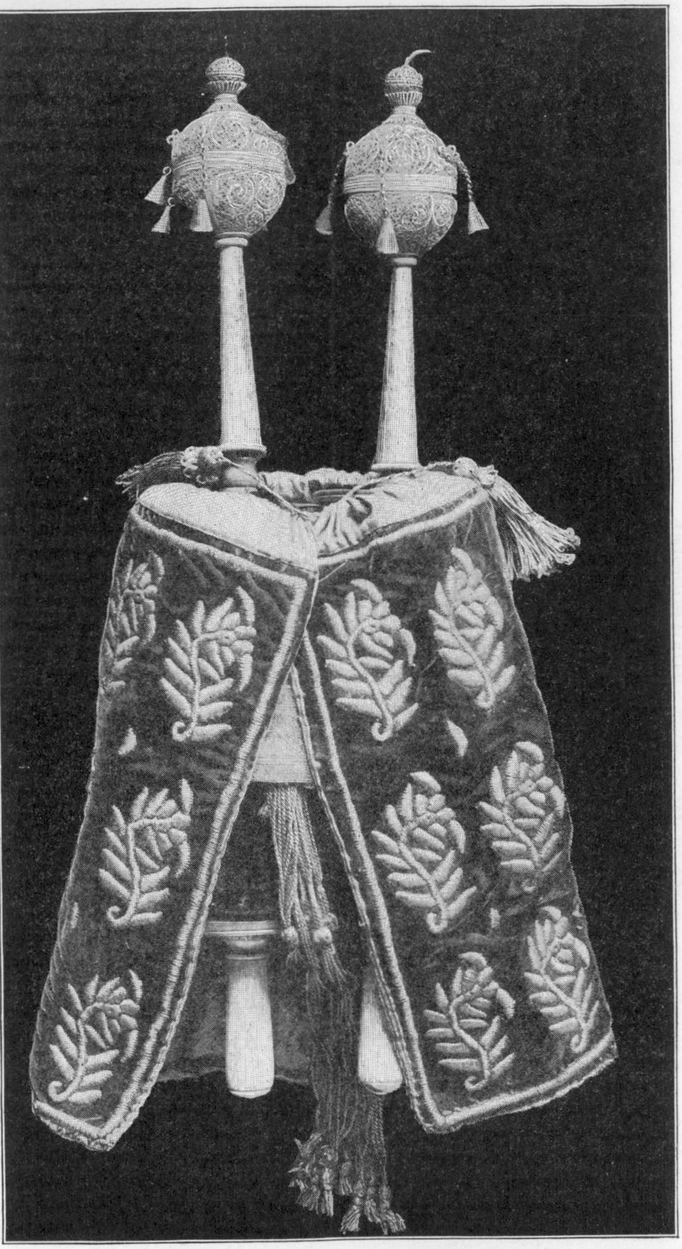

Mantle of the Law, Oriental.
(In the United States National Museum, Washington, D. C.)

In 1577 new edicts were issued regarding the wearing of the badge. Evil times came with Vincenzo Gonzaga (1587–1612), who, in 1590, expelled all foreign Jews from the city to prevent the increase of the Jewish population. In the following year this decree was reinforced by menaces against the entire community. On April 22, 1600, Giuditta Franchetti, eighty years of age, was publicly burned on a charge of witchcraft, and other members of the community were sentenced to heavy punishments. In 1602, however, in spite of these rigorous proceedings, the Franciscan monk Bartolomeo da Salutivo publicly accused the prince of leniency toward the Jews. As the populace was threatening them, Vincenzo was obliged to interfere sternly in their behalf (Aug. 14), although at the beginning of the year he had issued orders for the complete separation of Jews and Christians. He next forbade Jewish ph[y]sicians to treat Christians without special permissio[n] and, at the instance of Pope Clement VIII., decre[ed] (Nov. 7) that the Jews should sell all their real esta[te] within a year; he placed all their civic and comme[r]cial affairs und[er] the jurisdicti[on] of a special of[fi]cial terme[d] "commissar[io] degli Ebrei" and in certa[in] other relatio[ns] they were su[b]jected to eccl[e]siastical contr[ol]. This office [of] Jewish comm[is]sioner exist[ed] until 1765. [In] 1610 the esta[b]lishment of [a] ghetto was d[e]creed, and [in] Feb., 1612, t[he] Jews were co[m]pelled to mo[ve] into it. The ne[w] edict called t[he] "Tolleran[za] Generale" su[b]jected them [to] still more rig[or]ous treatmen[t]; it was renew[ed] every eig[ht] years, on pa[y]ment of a lar[ge] sum, and r[e]mained in fo[rce] until 1791.

Charles [of] Rethel, who su[c]ceeded to t[he] dukedom on t[he] extinction of t[he] house of Go[n]zaga in 1628, a[s]sured the Je[ws] of his favo[r]. During the sie[ge] of Mantua [by] Emperor Fer[di]nand II., in t[he] same year, th[ey] helped to fort[ify] and defend t[he] city, even brea[k]ing the Sabbat[h]; and when t[he] city was betrayed (1630) to the enemy 1,800 Je[ws] were expelled and their property confiscated; n[or] could they return until after many bitter experienc[es], as Abraham Masserani has recounted in his "Ha-G[a]lut weha-Pedut" (Venice, 1634). In 1699 the co[m]munity was released from the obligation of attendi[ng] 'hristian sermons, and about 1700 various Jews re-eived extensive industrial privileges, and were even ntiusted with the management of state domains.

When Mantua came into the possession of the Iapsburgs, after the war of the Spanish succession, he Austrian governors tried to protect the Jews rom the many petty annoyances which the latter ad to suffer through clerical intrigues; for the de-ree issued in 1740 by the grand inquisitor of the Roman Curia marked the culmination of the perse-ution and humiliation of the Jews by Rome. In Mantua they were permitted to institute a suit for compensation for annoyance on the street on the testimony of a single witness. To avoid being insulted by the students of the gymna-ium—it had become customary for the students to nsult Jews whenever they met them—the Jews nade a yearly payment in kind o the principal. On special occa-ions, as during ieges, large as-essments were evied upon the ommunity, which was espe-ially taxed dur-ng the reign of Maria Theresa, hough under er the civic tatus of the Jews began to mprove. In 752 the sani-ary laws were leclared to be qually binding upon Jews and Christians, and he restriction egarding Jew-sh physicians vas abrogated.

Under the Hapsburgs.

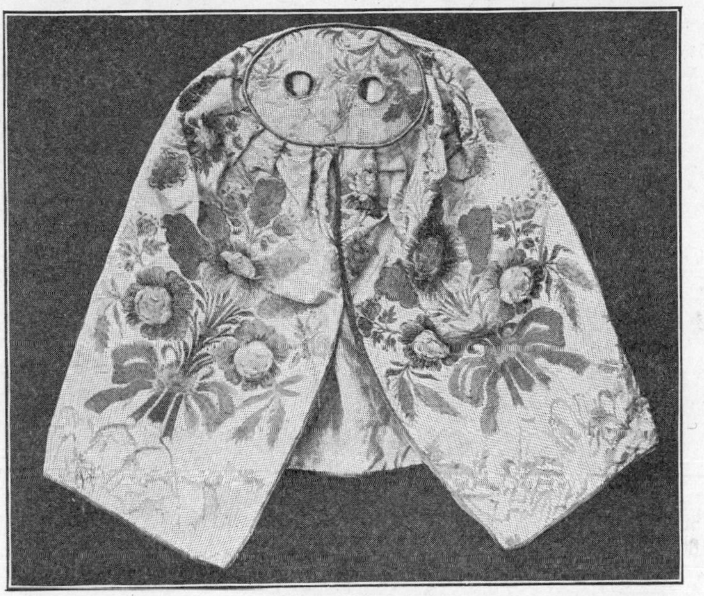

Mantle of the Law.
(In the British Museum.)

The condition of the Jews improved still further when Joseph II. was made coregent. In 1772 they vere allowed to loan money at the "monte-di-pietà," while in 1779 many of the ancient restrictions were repealed, the badge was abolished, Jews were ad-nitted to the public schools and were allowed to acquire real estate, and the tribunal of the Inquisi-ion was suppressed. Under Leopold II. (1790–92) a deputation sent to Vienna succeeded in having the "Tolleranza Generale" made permanent and in se-uring the repeal of all special taxes on the commu-nity, while the emperor declared that he would put the Jews on an equality with all other citizens in all points compatible with the general welfare. But under Francis I. (1792–1835) the Jews had more troub-ed times and were again heavily taxed.

The community of Mantua, like all other Italian communities, had a period of freedom in 1797, dur-ng the French invasion of Italy. Two Jews, David Pavia and Felice Coen, were made members of the municipal council, and the latter became also a member of the central administration of the district of the Mincio, while Rabbi Abraham de Cologna was a member of the cabinet of the Cisalpine Republic. The gates of the ghetto were torn down by the people in 1798, but in the following year the city was retaken by the Austrians, and the political suspects, including some Jews, were imprisoned. Zechariah Carpi has given an account of his sufferings in his "Toledot Yiẓḥaḳ" (Cracow, 1892). The French, however, soon retook the city, and Napoleon's pro-Jewish legislation went into force. Abraham de Cologna represented Mantua at the Congress of Lyons in 1801, and he took part also in the Convention of Notables at Paris, being made vice-president of the Sanhedrin (1806–7) and subsequently president of the consistory.

In 1814 Mantua again came under Austrian rule. The Jews retained their rights, but were not permitted to hold public offices, with the exception of those connected with the possession of real estate, and even this exception was declared to be revocable. The number of Jewish families was to be limited, special permission being necessary for immigration and for marriage. Francis I., however, declared that he would endeavor to place the Jews upon an equality with the other citizens, his desire being to see that all shared alike in the welfare of the state. He ordered that the rabbis of the community should give proof of sufficient secular and religious education. In 1821 Mantua proposed to the communities of Lombardy and Venice that a rabbinical seminary should be founded, and as a result the institute at Padua was opened in 1829. The community continued to suffer from its insecure legal status and from the enmity of the populace, and was imperiled by the riots of 1824 and 1842. The Jews did not obtain full civic liberty until Mantua was incorporated in the kingdom of Italy by the peace of 1866. One of the heroes of the Italian struggle for unity, Giuseppe Finzi, was a Mantuan Jew.

The community of Mantua repeatedly held an important position in Judaism. At the time of the Renaissance it was distinguished for the number of its scholars and liberal thinkers; it was the birthplace of Azariah dei Rossi. For a long time the community was obliged to furnish to the dukes of Gonzaga a company of actors who from 1525 to 1597 gave dramatic representations, which form an important chapter in the early history of the Italian stage. The dramaturge of the company, Leone Sommo, produced in his "Dialoghi sull' Arte Rappresentativa" the first work of its kind; in recognition of his merits as a poet he was made a knight, and a member of the Academy of Padua.

Scholars and Rabbis.

Among the Jewish musicians at the court of Mantua were the harpists Abraham dell' Aspra and his grandson; Isacchino Massarano was distinguished as a lutist, a singer, and a dancing-master; Solomon Rossi was known as a composer of religious and secular songs, while his sister Europa was a singer, and her son Anselmo and Davide Civitâ were esteemed as composers. Mordecai Finzi was a mathematician and Abraham Colorni an engineer. Mantua was foremost, also, in the sixteenth century in the field of Jewish science. As a century previously Joseph Colon had taught there, so now the brothers Moses and David Provençal were famous as Talmudists, founding the rabbinical academy which flourished down to modern times; while a third brother, Judah Moscato, was famous as a preacher and philosopher. The brothers Provençal were so enthusiastic in the cause of science that David and his son Abraham determined to establish a university in their house (1564), and issued a detailed prospectus inviting students ("Ha-Lebanon," v. 418 *et seq.*; "Berliner Festschrift," pp. 164 *et seq.*). Subsequently Mantua became the chief seat of the cabalists.

The community of Mantua has had many famous rabbis, and a number of rabbinical families whose members succeeded one another in office. The most noteworthy names are: Basilea, Brieli, Cases, Cologna, Fano, Jarè, Modena, Mortara, Moscato, Portaleone, Provençal, Dei Rossi, Romanelli, Saraval, Viterbi, and Zacuto. Marco Mortara officiated from 1842 until 1894, and was succeeded by Isaiah Levi.

Synagogues.

Since the sixteenth century the community has had six places of worship: Scuola Grande (built 1537), transferred a century later to its present site); Scuola Norsa Torazzo (founded 1513); Scuola Cases (founded 1590); Scuola Beccaria (founded in 1595 over a slaughter-house and named after it); Scuola Porto (founded 1540); and Scuola Ostiglia (founded 1558). In the first three the Italian ritual is followed, in the last three the German. Their foundations have recently been in part united. The community owns a large library containing numerous manuscripts and important archives, from which Stern has published a number of documents. Among Mantua's philanthropic institutions is the Casa di Ricovero, an asylum for the aged founded in 1825 and connected with a foundation for the promotion of trade and industry among the Jews and a home for apprentices. In 1834 Samuele Trabotti devoted his entire fortune to a fund for dowering Jewish brides, educating Jewish youths in the arts and sciences, establishing prizes for artisans, and relieving the sick and the poor. This richly endowed foundation absorbed the existing institutions of similar character.

BIBLIOGRAPHY: M. Gioia, *Statistica del Dipartimento del Mincio*, Milan, 1838; C. Diarco, *Studi Intorno al Municipio di Mantova*, Mantua, 1873; R. Rocco, in *Annali di Statistica*, 1884; L. Carnevali, *Gli Israeliti di Mantova*, Mantua, 1878; idem, *Il Ghetto di Mantova*, ib. 1884; Al. d'Ancona, *Origini del Teatro Italiano*, Turin, 1891; Ed. Birnbaum, *Jüdische Musiker am Hofe zu Mantua*, Vienna, 1893; M. Stern, *Urkundliche Beiträge über die Stellung der Päpste zu den Juden*, vol. i., Kiel, 1893; Mortara, *Indice*; Zunz, *Z. G.* pp. 249 *et seq.*

D. I. E.

——**Typography**: Mantua was among the earliest places at which Hebrew works were printed. The physician Abraham Conat started printing there as early as 1476, when he produced the Ṭur Oraḥ Ḥayyim; some of his productions may have been begun even in the preceding year. He had the merit of producing the only Hebrew incunabulum published during its author's lifetime—"Nofet Ẓufim." His wife, Estellina Conat, made herself responsible for the "Beḥinat 'Olam," issued from his press after his death. In the printing of Levi ben Gershon's Pentateuch, Conat was associated with Abraham of Cologne, possibly identical with the Abraham de Tintori who afterward emigrated to Bologna. Hebrew printing was resumed at Mantua in 1513 by Samuel Laṭif, who appears to have been forced from business a year later by the competition of the Soncinos. The next printers of Hebrew books were Christians—the Rufinellis and Philipponis (1561–97); their printer's sign was a peacock. A large number of Jewish workmen, including Meïr Sofer, his son, and his son-in-law, were employed by them. In the seventeenth century Eliezer de Italia started a Hebrew printing-press (1612), being followed by Judah di Perugia in 1622. In the eighteenth century Isaac Jarè and Raphael Ḥayyim di Italia printed at Mantua. For reproductions from books printed at Mantua see JEWISH ENCYCLOPEDIA, iv. 172, 173, 205; vii. 261.

BIBLIOGRAPHY: Steinschneider, in Ersch and Gruber, *Encyc.* section ii., part 28, pp. 34, 43–46; *Cat. Bodl.* col. 310.

J.

MANUEL, EUGÈNE: French educator and poet; born at Paris July 13, 1823; died there June 1, 1901. A grandson on his mother's side of the famous Paris ḥazzan Lovy, he remained throughout his brilliant career intimately attached to the faith of his ancestors. After having finished his studies at the Collège Charlemagne he entered the École Normale (1843-46), where he had as comrades Emile Burnouf, Paul Janet, Gaston Boissier, Caro, Alfred Mézières, and Pasteur, all of whom have become renowned in the world of letters and science. Manuel became professor of rhetoric successively at the colleges of Dijon, Grenoble, Tours, and in the lyceums Charlemagne (1849) and Saint-Louis and the Collège Rollin in Paris. After the Franco-Prussian war Jules Simon, having become minister of public instruction, appointed Manuel his "chef du cabinet" and in 1872 "directeur du secrétariat."

Soon after, Manuel became inspector-general of secondary public instruction (1876). He now began to devote much of his energy and time to literature. In 1852 he had already published an edition of the "Morceaux Choisis des . . . Œuvres Lyiques" of Rousseau. His second work, written in collaboration with his brother-in-law Lévi-Alvarès (1854–58), was in four volumes, and was entitled "La France sous l'Aspect Géographique, Historique et Administratif." His earliest poems, "Pages Intimes," date from the year 1866, and it was they which laid the foundation for his literary fame. The ring of patriotism in his "Poèmes Populaires," which appeared in 1871, rendered them very popular. "Henri Regnault," "Les Pigeons de la République," "En Voyage," and "Pendant la Guerre" have placed Manuel in the rank of the foremost poets of his time. This last dramatic poem and "Les Ouvriers" were played at the Théâtre Français with Coquelin and Sarah Bernhardt in the leading rôles (Jan. 17, 1870). About this time "L'Absent" and "Pour les Blessés" were represented at the Théâtre Français. Manuel made several unsuccessful attempts to gain admission to the Académie Française.

Those of Manuel's poems which bear a special relation to Judaism are: "La Place du Pauvre," dedicated to his friend Isidore Cahen, the director of the "Archives Israélites"; "Le Verset"; "La Prière"; "Caïn et Abel"; and "Les Trois Peuples" (Jerusalem, Athens, Rome). His biography of his grandfather Israel Lovy, in the "Archives Israélites" (1850), deserves special mention. For twenty years Manuel was professor of Greek and Latin literature at the Jewish Theological Seminary at Paris, and he was one of the six founders of the Alliance Israélite Universelle, remaining a member of that institution until his death. After the death of Michel Alcan, Manuel was elected to represent the Jews of Lyons in the Central Consistory of the Jews of France (1877). He was a commander of the Legion of Honor. On Oct. 27, 1901, the Société Historique d'Auteuil et de Passy, of which he was one of the founders, placed a memorial tablet on the house in which the poet died.

BIBLIOGRAPHY: *Archives Israélites*, June, 1901; *Univers Israélite*, June, 1901; *A la Mémoire de Eugène Manuel*, 1901; *A la Mémoire de Eugène Manuel*, 1902; M. Bloch, in *R. E. J.* xlvi.

S.

MANUSCRIPTS: The first materials used for writing were such substances as stone, wood, and metal, upon which the characters were engraved with a stylus. At a very early time, however, animal substances were employed, and letters were written upon them with various liquid preparations. The usual word for a written document, "sefer," which occurs 182 times in different forms in the Bible, and is to be supplied in many places, as, for instance, with "Torah," designates the skin of an animal, the writing material anciently employed by the Orientals, and not papyrus. The usual word for writing, "katab," the fundamental meaning of which is "to place signs in succession," is found in the Bible 220 times (Blau, "Studien zum Althebräischen Buchwesen," pp. 9 *et seq.*). For private writing in the first centuries of the common era various materials were used, including clay tablets for bills. Books might be written only on skins of animals, of which three kinds were prepared—"gewil," "ḳelaf," and "doksosṭos." Gewil is the plain hide with the hair scraped off (*i.e.*, leather); ḳelaf is parchment, made by paring away the skin, and which received the writing upon the flesh side (*i.e.*, a membrane); doksosṭos is another form of parchment (*ib.* pp. 22 *et seq.*).

Writing Material.

Parchment.

Copies of the Bible were, as a rule, made from whole skins, as at the present day, which were prepared from clean animals. To this the copyist ("sofer") himself generally attended. A gaon says, "We have never seen a Torah scroll which was written on parchment." There is a possibility, however, that in ancient times there were Biblical books written on papyrus; in regard to non-Biblical writings this supposition is even probable. The skin used for writing was ruled, and there were special regulations for margins and for the number of lines. Only black, effaceable ink, which was renewed when necessary, might be used for Biblical works. Metallic ink was known, but was forbidden. The Letter of Aristeas (§§ 176–179), however, relates that the copy of the Bible sent by the high priest to the Egyptian king Ptolemy was written in gold, and the Talmud also speaks of gold-writing, which may have been a Jewish invention (Blau, *l.c.* pp. 13, 150 *et seq.*; see Index).

Scroll and Codex.

Both the Jewish and the non-Jewish world in antiquity had books in the form of scrolls (Isa. xxxiv. 4; Job xxxi. 35–36; Jer. xxxvi.; Ezek. ii. 8–9; Ps. xl. 8; Zech. v. 1). In post-Biblical times the employment of such scrolls may be traced for a thousand years, and in copies of the Pentateuch for the synagogue this usage has survived until the present time. Both the Letter of Aristeas (*l.c.*) and I Macc. iii. 48 speak of scrolls. On the arch of Titus a man is depicted carrying on his back a long roll, undoubtedly a representation of the Torah scroll of the Temple of Jerusalem, which was taken to Rome (see Josephus, "B. J." vii. 5, § 5). The Talmud and Midrash know books only in this form (Blau, *l.c.* pp. 40–43), and the Christian documents of the first three centuries testify also to the use of rolls (Schulze, in "Greifswalder Studien Hermann Cremer Dargebracht," pp. 148-158). When and where the codex form first appeared among the Jews is as yet unknown. It is not impossible that the word "diftera," in Soferim iii. 6, designates a codex. The oldest complete and dated manuscript of the Bible, the codex of the Prophets at St. Petersburg, was written in 916. In ancient times school children had tablets for their first lessons in reading and writing, while wax tablets (πίναξ) were in general use among citizens, so that the prototype of the book was familiar from a very early period. There is, therefore, no need to assume foreign influence, whether Greco-Roman or Oriental and Christian, to explain the development of the scroll into the codex. The transition probably began in the seventh century and proceeded gradually, since no distinct mention of a codex has yet been discovered in the Talmud and Midrash.

The books of antiquity were always of small size (II Kings xxii. 8–10; II Chron. xxxiv. 15 *et seq.*; Neh. viii. 1 *et seq.*; see references from the Talmud, Midrash, and classic literature in Blau, *l.c.* pp. 72 *et seq.*), and people sat cross-legged when reading them.

The largest scroll, the official copy of the Torah, which was used in the Second Temple had at most a height of six and a diameter of two handbreadths (*ib.* pp. 76 *et seq.*). The smallness of the books was compensated by the minuteness of the characters (*ib.* p. 79 *et seq.*). The contents of a manuscript might be very small, as, for example, one of the Book of Obadiah, or the original roll of fasts (*c.* 100 C.E.), while the normal size probably never exceeded that of the collection of the Twelve Prophets. At the time of the first selection of the canon (*c.* 4th cent. B.C.) large scrolls could not have been popular, as is shown by the division of the Torah into five parts, by the division of the Book of the History of the Kings into the books of Samuel and Kings, by the separation of the books of Ezra and Nehemiah from the Chronicles, and by other instances. About the year 100 C.E., however, there were certainly collective scrolls which contained the three sections of the Bible in one roll each, while there were even some which included all the books of the Scriptures in one large roll. Such a one, probably, was the Hexapla of Origen. There was, moreover, no lack of copies of single portions, which contained a section of a book, such as the Roll of Jealousy (= Num. v. 11-23, etc.; Blau, *l.c.* pp. 46-70).

Size, Compass, and Distribution.

The preparation of books has had an eventful history. At the time of the chroniclers (*c.* 3d cent. B.C.) Bible copies were rare; they had been almost entirely destroyed by the Syrians before the Maccabean revolt. Afterward, however, their number increased steadily, since it was made incumbent on every one to write a copy of the Torah for himself, and each congregation owned at least one. In the Talmudic period there was an enormous number of copies, especially as it was customary to wear portions of the Bible (chiefly Torah rolls) around the arm as amulets. Manuscripts of the Bible were found also in heathen families, and pagans even liked to trade in these books, which they were able to write themselves. Christians converted from Judaism or paganism owned many Hebrew writings (*ib.* pp. 84-97). In consequence of the ever-increasing demand a kind of book-trade developed as early as the first century. In general, however, people ordered their manuscripts direct from the copyist, according to ancient custom. The Apocrypha, the original of which has been lost, and other non-Biblical Hebrew books, were not in special demand and did not circulate in large numbers.

Book-Trade.

The high value placed upon the Scriptures is evidenced by the great care taken for their preservation. The scrolls were wound on a stick, the Torah on two sticks. Coverings of various kinds served to protect them, and cases of various forms were used for keeping them. The rolls were firmly tied with a cord, and sometimes they were sealed to prevent any one from reading them without permission (*ib.* pp. 173-188 *et seq.*). When worn out the manuscripts of the Bible were protected against profanation by being placed in the coffins of dead scribes. In consequence of this custom not a single Biblical manuscript has been preserved from ancient times, nor is there any hope that one will ever come to light. Nevertheless, a few archetypes which existed in antiquity are mentioned. In the first rank among these stands the copy of the Torah of the Second Temple, already noted (I Macc., Introduction; II Macc. ii. 14; Josephus, "Ant." v. 1, § 17; Blau, *l.c.* pp. 99 *et seq.*). "The Book of the Court" (M. Ḳ. iii. 4a *et al.*) was the copy from which the high priest read on the Day of Atonement and which served as a model (Blau, *l.c.* p. 107).

Oldest Codices.

Three other codices from the Temple court are mentioned: "Sefer Me'on," "Sefer Za'aṭuṭe," and "Sefer Hi," and they still served as models at the beginning of the fourth century (*ib.* p. 104). After the destruction of the Temple the Torah of the celebrated copyist R. Meïr, the codex of Emperor Severus, and others (*ib.* p. 111) are mentioned, while from post-Talmudic times date the codices of Hillel, Sanbuki, and others. The most celebrated was the codex of Ben Asher, used by Maimonides (H. L. Strack, "Prolegomena Critica in Vetus Testamentum Hebraicum"). See BIBLE MANUSCRIPTS.

BIBLIOGRAPHY: L. Löw, *Graphische Requisiten bei den Juden*, Leipsic, 1870-71; L. Blau, *Studien zum Althebräischen Buchwesen und zur Biblischen Litteratur- und Textgeschichte*, Budapest and Strasburg, 1902 (where a full bibliography is given); idem, *Ueber den Einfluss des Althebräischen Buchwesens*, in *Berliner Festschrift*, Frankfort-on-the-Main, 1903 (also printed separately).

J. L. B.

It is now necessary to inquire how the Hebrew manuscripts collected in various public and private libraries were written, and in what form the material of which they consist was presented. The time over which the inquiry extends ranges, roughly speaking, from about the year 900 of the common era down to the present day, though in some instances, notably in the case of papyri, an earlier period is referred to. For inscriptions on stone, metal, and other hard substances see PALEOGRAPHY.

I. Materials Used to Receive Writing.—Papyrus (Greek, πάπυρος, from the ancient Egyptian word "p-apa"; but in Herodotus always βύβλος, no doubt also from an Egyptian term; Hebrew, "neyar," apparently representing the Arabic "naur"): The number of Hebrew papyri hitherto discovered is quite insignificant as compared with the numerous classical papyri recently brought into Europe from Egypt. There is the small number of Egyptian-Aramaic papyri belonging to the late Ptolemaic or early Roman period, of which the British Museum papyrus No. cvi.* is a good representative specimen (see the first specimen of writing on Plate I.; also "Proc. Soc. Bibl. Arch." xxv., parts 4 and 5). Some pieces dating from the sixth to the ninth century have been described by Steinschneider, Chwolson, and others (for references see bibliography below). The Cambridge University Library possesses a mutilated liturgical codex assigned to the ninth century. The papyrus of the Decalogue in the same library, first described by S. A. Cook ("Proc. Soc. Bibl. Arch." xxv., part i.; see JEW. ENCYC. iv. 493, *s.v.* DECALOGUE), may be assigned to the sixth or seventh century (see Pl. III., No. 59). A few Oxford fragments, probably of the sixth century, have been

Earliest Papyri.

described by A. Cowley in "J. Q. R." Oct., 1903 (see Pl. I., No. 2).

Skins (Hebrew, "'or," known also as "gewil"; Greek, *διφθέρα*, a term which in early times was transferred to papyrus, and was later on applied to vellum also): None of the skin was peeled off, but the hair was carefully rubbed away; for it was the hair side that was used for writing upon. The ancient rule of using only skins for Torah rolls has not, however, been universally followed in the period under consideration. The Yemenite rolls (Pentateuch, Esther, and קצת חנה) are indeed all of red skin; and the Pentateuch rolls written in the eighteenth century for the Jews of K'ai-Fung-Foo, China (*e.g.*, Brit. Mus. MS. Add. 19,250), are of white leather. The oldest Pentateuch roll (14th cent., Spanish origin) in the British Museum is also of leather; but there are many specimens on vellum belonging to the sixteenth century and onward. Of the forty-seven Karaite Pentateuch rolls in the Imperial Library, St. Petersburg, only five are of leather, the remaining forty-two being of vellum. This proportion no doubt represents the greater deviation among the Karaites from the old synagogue rolls. For the Book of Esther vellum appears to have been more largely used than for the Torah. A roll of the Hafṭarot on leather, written in Corfu in 1560, found its way into Europe a few years ago. For manuscripts in book form skins would in early times have been naturally superseded by parchment or vellum as material fitted for receiving writing on both sides.

Parchment and Vellum (Hebrew, "ḳelaf" and "doksosṭos," for the exact meaning of which see above): For practical purposes, that is to say, so far as the manuscripts now under consideration are concerned, it is enough to remark that "ḳelaf," not unlike the term "parchment" in its more restricted sense, signifies the rougher article, while by "doksosṭos," as by the term "vellum" the finer variety is meant. The Jews were no doubt at all times adepts in the art of producing parchment and vellum, as they had so much need of the materials, and as a religious intention during the manufacture was considered important; but their art would naturally be conditioned, to a large extent at any rate, by the degree of perfection attained in it in the countries where they were domiciled. The finest kinds of vellum used for Hebrew manuscripts were of Spanish and Italian origin. As examples of the former may be mentioned Brit. Mus. MS. Or. 5866 (liturgy, middle of 15th cent.: thin vellum, delicately worked, smooth surface), and Brit. Mus. MSS. Or. 2626-2628 (Bible, 1482-1483: stout, crisp, and pretty smooth). A fine specimen of Italian vellum of about the middle of the same century is furnished by Brit. Mus. MSS. Add. 19,444-19,445 (Florentine liturgy: material very carefully prepared and slightly tinted). Rougher sorts of material were to be found by the side of the finer kind in both countries.

Among representative codices of earlier times, the British Museum Pentateuch dating from the ninth century (MS. Or. 4445, apparently of Babylonian origin) consists of strong, crisp, and very smooth vellum. Brit. Mus. MS. Harley 5720 (probably of early part of 12th cent.; also of Eastern origin) is hard and strong, with surface not very smooth.

Examples of Old Vellum.

The British Museum copy of the Maḥzor Vitry (MSS. Add. 27,200-27,201: 12th cent.; French origin) is written on a very inferior sort of material. French as well as German vellum employed for Hebrew in the Middle Ages is, in fact, as a rule coarse as compared with the Spanish and Italian kinds; but Brit. Mus. MS. Add. 11,639 (collection of works, 12th cent.), from the south of France, is an example of exceedingly fine, smooth vellum. The vellum used for Hebrew charters in England in the twelfth and thirteenth centuries (note especially the large collection belonging to Westminster Abbey) is fairly good, though fineness of manufacture can not be expected in material used for this particular purpose. Some of the early examples of vellum (11th and 12th cent.) found in the Cairo Genizah are stout and smooth; other specimens are of a rougher manufacture. No example of purple-stained vellum, of which there are fair numbers among Greek and Latin manuscripts, has so far come to light among Hebrew ones. On the comparative use of vellum and paper see below.

Paper (Greek, *πάπυρος*, name taken over from "papyrus"; called also "charta bombycina," "charta Damascena," etc.; Hebrew, נייר, also taken over from the Hebrew name for papyrus): This material was known to the Chinese at a very early period; and the Arabs are said to have first learned its use at Samarcand about the middle of the eighth century (for an account of recent researches on this matter see "J. R. A. S." Oct., 1903, first article, where further references will be found). A Judæo-Persian document lately brought from Khotan, written (in Persian in Hebrew characters) on paper, appears to belong to the eighth century (see "J. R. A. S." Oct., 1903, fifth article). Another extant example of a Judæo-Persian document is dated 1020 ("J. Q. R." 1899, pp. 671 *et seq.*).

The Karaites, standing as they did in very close connection with the Arab world, and being also less tied by this kind of conservatism, appear to have used no other material than paper for their manuscripts in book form. Karaite collections of manuscripts are, therefore, an excellent means of studying the kinds of paper made in Palestine, Egypt, and Turkey during a practically uninterrupted period from the tenth century onward. Thus Brit. Mus. MS. Or. 2540 (Exodus: Hebrew text in Arabic characters; see the first two specimens on Pl. IV., col. 2) belongs to the tenth century. Among the dated Karaite manuscripts are found specimens belonging to 1004, 1024, 1027, 1211, 1331, 1564, 1614, 1700, 1744, and 1869.

Karaite Manuscripts.

Like early Oriental paper generally, the older kind of Karaite paper (apparently made for the most part of fine linen rag) is stout, of a yellowish tint, and with a glossy surface. In later times the yellowish tint gradually disappears, the texture becomes rougher, and the surface less smooth. The early specimens of paper used by the Karaites are, moreover, much finer than the Khotan Hebræo-Persian document (probably Chinese paper) already referred to. An early dated example of a Rabbinite manuscript on paper is Brit. Mus. MS. Or. 73 (1192; Rashi's commentary on Baba Meẓi'a, written in the East). A British Museum copy of the "Taḥkemoni" (MS. Add. 27,113; Spanish Oriental writing) is dated 1282. The last-named two manuscripts show the same kind of slight yellowish tint; but the paper of the second is thicker than that of the first. A specimen of Italian paper of 1363–64 is furnished by Cambridge University Library MSS. Dd. 11, 12; and Brit. Mus. MS. Add. 27,293 (also of about the middle of the 14th cent.) is a specimen of fairly early Spanish paper.

The European Jews were slow in allowing paper to displace vellum; for though several paper-factories are known to have existed in the thirteenth and fourteenth centuries (indeed, the earliest known mention of paper made in Europe occurs in the tract of Peter, Abbot of Cluny, 1122–50), there are comparatively few Hebrew paper manuscripts of the fourteenth century. There is a fair number of the following century; and the proportion kept on growing until the use of paper became quite common among the Jews from the seventeenth century onward.

Paper in Egypt.

Egypt as a center of Arab life would naturally abound in paper manuscripts fairly early; and the contents of the Cairo Genizah accordingly include specimens dated 832 (in the possession of E. N. Adler), 977, 1005, etc. (at the British Museum and elsewhere). In Yemen paper was used by the Jews pretty freely side by side with vellum from the fifteenth century and probably earlier. The older specimens of Yemenite paper often show an exaggerated kind of yellow tint. For the rest, the Jews of the different countries would naturally depend on the paper manufactured there; and the information contained, *e.g.*, in Sir E. M. Thompson's "Greek and Latin Palæography," will, therefore, be found to apply to Hebrew manuscripts also in so far as vellum can be shown to have in some degree given place to paper.

II. Writing-Fluids, etc.: The ink (Hebrew, "deyo"; Arabian variety, "ḥibr") used by the Jews during the period here considered would naturally be much the same as that used by their Gentile neighbors in different countries. On the manufacture of ink generally see Thompson, *l.c.* pp. 50, 51. The ink sanctioned by Maimonides, and no doubt used by him for writing his own scroll of the Law, was, according to a responsum discovered a few years ago, made of oil, pitch, resin, gum arabic, etc. By burning these substances a soot was formed which was mixed with gum and honey, and the thin slices formed of it were finally dissolved in an infusion of galls (see "J. Q. R." July and Oct., 1899). Vitriol (קלקנתום; *χάλκανθος*) is expressly excluded by Maimonides, though he does not absolutely forbid it. His point is that the ink should cleave firmly to the vellum, but that, at the same time, one should be able to erase it (on this point, as on the preparation of ink generally, see Löw, "Graphische Requisiten und Erzeugnisse bei den Juden," p. 145; and Ink).

Kinds of Ink.

With regard to the appearance of the ink actually used in the manuscripts now under observation, it should be noted that Torah rolls are all written with black ink (though early Samaritan scrolls are written with ink of a reddish hue). Brit. Mus. MS. Or. 4445 (9th cent.) and in fact many of the early manuscripts written in the East are in black or bluish black. Several of the finest Spanish codices show a yellow tint, while the finer sort of Italian manuscripts present a more or less violet one. German ink is generally black, though not very pronouncedly so. Early Cairo Genizah fragments often show a yellow tint; but Yemenite ink is usually black.

Red ink is sometimes, though but rarely, used alternately with the usual writing-fluid. Pigments of different kinds, though generally red, are sometimes used for initial words, etc. On the use of gold as a writing-fluid see p. 313 under "Illuminations."

With regard to writing-instruments, only the reed ("ḳulmos"; *κάλαμος*) and the quill pen need be considered here. It is difficult to say when the quill came into use, and for how long the reed was used alongside of it. Syrian scribes are known to have used the quill as far back as 509 (Wright, "Cat. Syriac MSS. in Brit. Mus." p. xxvii.); and the Ostrogoth Theodoric (*c.* 454–526) is reported to have used a quill for writing his name. The reed, on the other hand, continued in use to some extent through the Middle Ages, and appears to have survived in Italy into the fifteenth century (Thompson, *l.c.* p. 49). Several early Hebrew codices of Eastern origin appear to have been written with a reed; but the greater suitability of the more flexible quill pen could not have been overlooked by Jewish scribes even in comparatively early times.

Kinds of Pens.

III. Forms of Books: Apart from contracts of small size ("geṭ," "sheṭar ḥaliẓah," etc.), which would naturally be preserved flat, there call for consideration (1) the roll and (2) manuscripts in book form.

The Roll (Hebrew, "megillah"; Latin, "volumen"; used only for the five scrolls, the Torah roll itself being always called "Sefer Torah"): This consists of a number of strips of leather or vellum sewed together to form a continuous whole. It is, at one end, fixed to a stick round which it is rolled; and it is usually provided with a flat, round border-piece at top and bottom to keep the roll even. The number of columns to a strip varies considerably; and there is also great diversity in the height of rolls. Brit. Mus. MS. Harley 7619, which is about 26¾ ins. high, is probably one of the largest extant. Esther rolls are sometimes of very diminutive dimensions. A very remarkable and perhaps unique specimen of a roll is Brit. Mus. MS. Add. 26,883 (containing cabalistic prayers written in Italy in the 15th cent.), which, though measuring about 125 ins. from end to end (the height being about 4½ ins.), is all of one piece instead of consisting of strips sewed together. The vellum of this roll is very fine; and the workmanship in straightening out so long a piece must have been exceedingly elaborate. Rolls of Ruth, Lamentations, the Song of Solomon, and Ecclesiastes are far less frequent than those of Esther. The Yemenite rolls of the קצת חנה (to which the hafṭarah for the Ninth of Ab is found attached), as also a leather

Size of Rolls.

roll of 1560 containing the hafṭarot, have already been mentioned. For Karaite Torah rolls consult Harkavy and Strack, "Catalog der Hebräischen Bibelhandschriften zu St. Petersburg," Nos. 1-47. For Samaritan rolls see Harkavy, "Catalog der Hebräischen und Samaritanischen Handschriften der Kaiserlichen Oeffentlichen Bibliothek" (in Russian), St. Petersburg, 1875.

Manuscripts in Book Form: Manuscripts in book form date from the whole period under consideration, and were doubtless in use for a number of centuries before. Most of the early codices that have been preserved are very large. Thus Brit. Mus. MS. Or. 4445 measures about $16\frac{1}{2}$ ins. by 13 ins.; the St. Petersburg codex of 916, about $14\frac{3}{4}$ ins. by $12\frac{1}{6}$ ins.; the Vatican codex of the Sifra, dating from 1073, about $12\frac{3}{4}$ ins. by 10 ins.; the British Museum copy of the Maḥzor Vitry, about $15\frac{1}{2}$ ins. by 12 ins. Small sizes are, however, not wanting. German codices of the Bible and liturgy written in the thirteenth and fourteenth centuries are generally very large. Among manuscripts written in Italy the quarto and octavo sizes are much more common than in Germany. Spanish Bible codices of the thirteenth to the fifteenth century are as a rule handsome quartos; but the comparatively few Spanish service-books extant are usually very small, probably on account of the proscription under which Jewish worship lay in Spain, and owing to the fact that small volumes could be more easily hidden away. North-African manuscripts of the fourteenth and fifteenth centuries are more often octavos than quartos. Yemenite Bible codices are generally folios, and liturgies either folios or quartos. The Karaites had a great predilection for the octavo size.

Size of Books.

In the arrangement of quires (generally 8 or 10 leaves to a gathering), etc., Hebrew manuscripts do not differ from contemporary Latin and Greek ones; and the student may, therefore, be referred to general works on paleography. When a Hebrew vellum manuscript is opened, "the two pages before the reader have the same appearance, either the yellow tinge of the hair side or the whiter surface of the flesh side" (Thompson, *l.c.* pp. 62-63). There is usually at the end of each quire a catchword indicating the first word of the next quire. Signatures in Hebrew letters—in the case of Hebrew-Arabic works, sometimes in either Arabic letters or numerals—were generally placed in the left-hand lower corner on the last page of a quire, but occasionally in the right-hand upper corner of the first page. In some cases both methods were adopted. In Karaite manuscripts the signatures are often in the left-hand upper corner of the first page.

The ruling of Hebrew manuscripts is not different from that observable in contemporary classical ones. There are usually perpendicular lines to mark off the columns, besides the horizontal ruling. The prickings in the margin made to mark the distances between the horizontal lines have in many cases been cut away in the process of binding. The writing sometimes depends from the ruled line instead of standing on it; so, *e.g.*, Brit. Mus. MS. Or. 4445 (9th cent.; comp. Blau, "Studien zum Althebräischen Buchwesen," p. 147).

Ruling of Manuscripts.

The earlier codices of large size have usually either two (*e.g.*, St. Petersburg codex of the year 916) or three columns (*e.g.*, Brit. Mus. MS. Or. 4445) (see Blau, *l.c.* pp. 138-139). Manuscripts of small size generally exhibit but one column to a page. In later times the single column became much more frequent even in manuscripts of larger size.

IV. Styles of Writing: The style of writing Hebrew has in each country been influenced more or less by causes similar to those which produced what may fairly be called national differences in calligraphy generally. So far as Europe is concerned, Hebrew penmanship most probably was brought first to the countries of the southern coast, more especially to Spain and Italy; and spread thence into France, Germany, and divers other countries, assuming various modifications in its course. The locality in which a manuscript was written is, however, not always a safe guide to the kind of calligraphy used, as it sometimes happened that a scribe belonging to one part of the world prosecuted his profession for a longer or shorter time in a different country. It should also be remarked that after the introduction of printing there arose a tendency to copy from printed forms; so that, in Europe at any rate, the square character has for several centuries past been almost everywhere conforming to one particular form of calligraphy. The earlier printed books were, it is true, set up in types that were cut differently in different countries (compare especially the early Spanish with the early Italian printed books); but the Spanish forms soon superseded all the others, and they have on account of their greater regularity ever since maintained their ground both in printing and in writing.

Copying from Printed Forms.

In the following observations the specimens of writing given in the accompanying four plates are referred to their sources and localities, and attention is occasionally directed to some peculiarities of penmanship. As a rule, however, the specimens are left to speak for themselves.

A. Square Writing: This series is, for the sake of completeness, preceded by two lines taken from the above-mentioned British Museum papyrus No. cvi.* (belonging to the late Ptolemaic or early Roman period), as the Hebrew-Aramaic writing then used exhibits a close affinity with the Palmyrene character, and thus forms an important link in the transition to the square character. Then follow specimens of:

Early Oriental (Nos. 2-8): No. 2 is taken from an Oxford papyrus belonging to the sixth or seventh century ("J. Q. R." xvi., No. 61); No. 3, from the Hebræo-Persian document (apparently of the 8th cent.) lately brought from Khotan in central Asia and already referred to; No. 4, from Brit. Mus. MS. Or. 4445 (9th cent.); No. 5, from the St. Petersburg codex of the Later Prophets (dated 916); No. 6, from Codex Gaster No. 150 (belonging to about the same period); No. 7, from a contract (dated 980) on vellum, brought to the British Museum from the Cairo Genizah; No. 8, from Brit. Mus. MS. Or. 1467 (Per-

1 ומ שנת כומ שנה
יוחנן שמואל רטל

2 כוללון שלם נס
יקרלון די אמר

3 ייר כורת איאר באשר
וביסת נמח ביש קר

4 הערה וממפרסי
הפרסה את הגמל

5 נמוג פלשת כלך כי מצפון
עשן בא ואין בודד

6 נסעו איש למשפחתיו
על בית אבתיו

7 היו עלי עדים וקני מהני מעבשיו
למבורך בר קיאם להיות בידון

8 אלה מסעי בני ישראל אשר
מצרים לצבאתם ביד משה

9 צמאני אשאהו ברבהו אדיני
לבקר ולדרוש ולבלות מה פקיד

10 וגם על היין אל תתגבר
כור בוחן מעשה לטש

11 יהיב לך ית ארעא טבתא הדא
ארי עם קשי קדל את זכר

12 חזח ולא ראו ולא
הלכו בתורתו ובחקתיו

13 וימאסו בארץ חמדה לא האמינו לדברו
וירגנו באהליהם לא שמעו בקול יהוה

14 על המזבח בכפרך עליו
ומשחת אתו לקדשו

15 מקרב המחנה עד תמם ויהי
כאשר תמו כל אנשי המלחמה

16 איזן יהיה בית עדר א
ארום חביתי שלשה

17 דבקה לעפר נפשי חייני כדברך דרכי ספרתי
ותענני למדני חקיך דרך פקודיך הבינני

18 אתה בחרתנו מכל העמים אהבת אותנו
ורצית בנו ורוממתנו מכל הלשונות

19 וזרק משה ית דמא
על מדבחא סחור סחור

20 האלהים ויביאם ארץ
שנער בית אלהיו
ואת הכלים הביא בית

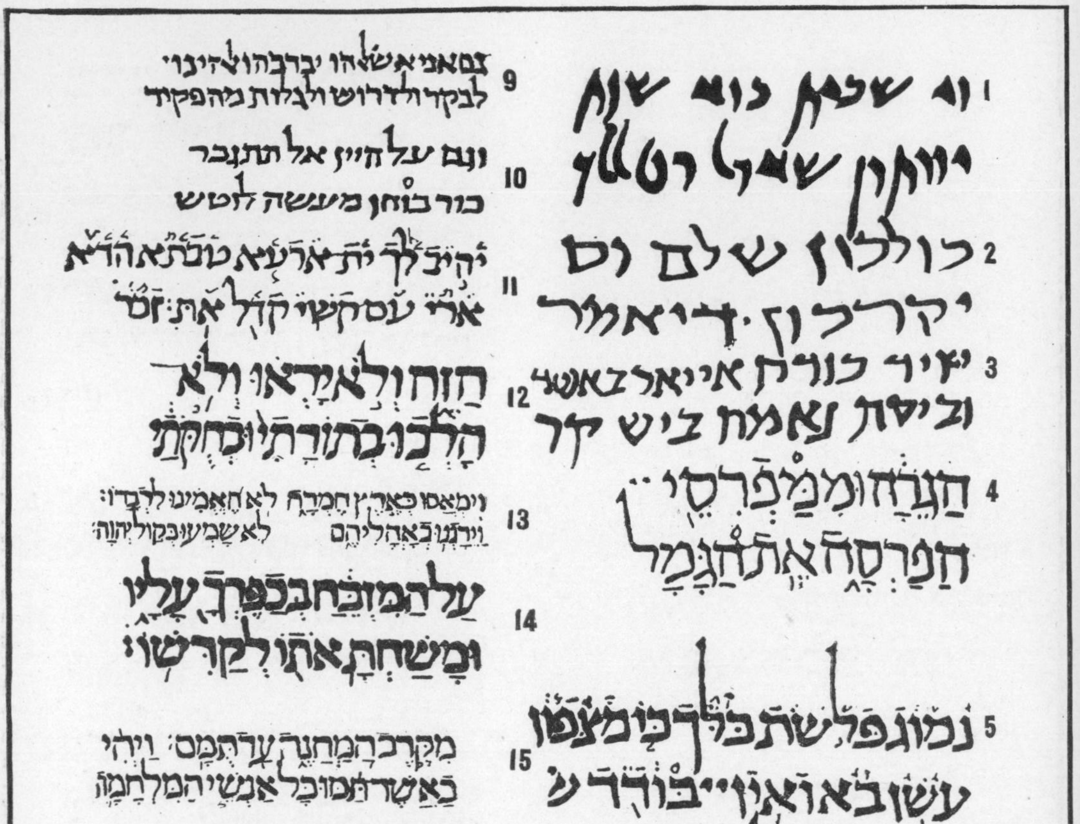

21 פקיד שר וכל שופט
יצאו ירד הוב ישפט

22 נשתלם זה ספר נביאים תרגומא
על ידי זרח בר יהודה ווטר

23 תשרי [illegible] ובשבת שלפניו
עם וילך משה צום גדליה

24 ויהי דבר יי אל יונה בן אמתי
לאמר קום לך אל נינוה

25 אך בחלקות תשית למו
איך היו לשמה כרגע

26 יהוה אשר עשו אבותינו לא
הוא ביניכו וביניכם חלילה לנו

27 עלי לארכביזם הזה ארימר ירדתן
עלי ולית דמחוי לי כד גזר בריעם

28 אשר לו נשאו כל איש מר נפש
עמו כארבע מאות איש וילך

29 כל בכור זכר לבני ישראל
ומעלה ושא את מספר

30 חרבי ותאחז במשפט
לצרי ולמשנאי אשלם

31 [illegible]

32 ריב שלום ממרומים קרונח
ממרום וברכות עד בלי די

33 שנאה לארון ואנשים גאוה ומשנאהם מעל יושבן
מלכות מגני לנוי תסוב בגלל חמס גאוה: מה יגאה

34 ידעים ולמלאת חכינו
פני בת יבלם ומשאותיכם

35 במותב תלתה הוינא בתלתה בשבא
שבט שנת אלפא ותלת מאה ועשרין

36 [illegible] נחדא ואולכה
שלמדנו ודבנו אדם נך [illegible]

37 נתן הכהן בר [illegible] הכה
במותב תלתא כחדא הוינא כד אתו

38 הוגה מספרי אני
משה ברבי מימון

39 [illegible]

40 [illegible]

41 [illegible]

42 נבחר [illegible] שבח לעולם
[illegible]

43 השביע עליו חמשה פעמים בין כפי
ואחת אמר ר׳ שמעון מה הטעם מפני
חמשה [illegible] אותו ואמרו לו הן לא

44 מפני חטאינו גלינו מארצנו זר׳
ונתרחקנו מעל אדמתינו
ואין אנו יכולין לעלות ולראות בבית

45 הוא היה אומ׳ אל תהי בז לכל אדם ואל תהי
מפליג לכל דבר שאין לך אדם שאין לו
שעה ואין לך דבר שאין לו מקום ׳

46 ומנין שמט חיה ועוף במקום אחד כיסוי אחד לכולן ״
חיות כיסוי אחד לכולן וחי״ב לברך על כסוי הדם ·
מזומן · כמ׳ סדורים בתורת כהנים ובתלמוד שלנו ·

47 כי הבאו יבול משבאו לעבר הירדן
אל הארץ אל הארץ המיוחדת יבול
מואב ועמון אשר אני נותן לכם

48 הר׳ לשם שבו׳
לתך שעודיה׳ ממיני מירות הוא׳
לאשר על המלוחה · כלי בגדים הנחבשים ·

49 ״נב׳ ויהפכו נערי דוד׳ ותחפר והלך
יסז מרכבותיה להלך׳ הר״ץ׳ דב׳ אל
כעש׳ חר״ס׳ בעברתו׳ חרוס שניכו

50 אז הקדם על ההרם נשבה
קם לך מנורה כשחל נבקעה

51 מס כיסודם נבנה ארמון
היתה עיר על לב איש תו

52 לתאניה ותאניה מן כתאבלתעשיר
עלום עצימה ותגג נסימה ובראהין

53 ותחת בעץ לתעהב למנקלה מן כור
לכלם פי פרשה דאת תהיה בעדרת
שרי בה׳ כתהיל בפרשת אחרי מורת

54 פה׳ עלי ערבין אחדהם פי רום
ארא כאן אולא כלמה אהחע

55 אני טוביה הסופר הצבל מאבי׳ל יניין
אויר המחמד ׳ וחוע סדר טהכים ׳ ובו
ימהללני זל׳ ותוספתי מליחם מה

56 [illegible]
[illegible]
[illegible]

57 כיאדראן וכדהיד אזמר אחסנתא אוי
ואגר עסת בראודראן נפיר אוי וכדהיד
בקראבת אוו און נזדיך תר באוי אז אוה

58 ואסף איש טהור את אפר הפרה והניח מחוץ למחנה
במקום טהור והיתה לעדת בני ישראל למשמרת למי
נדה חטאת הוא׃ וכבס האסף את אפר הפרה את

59 אשר טשחים תפלו אשר כאוץ
ופתחת לאיזלואת שתחיות לאת
סגר והיות אלאיך אלקנוא נה

60 פרק אשית׳ו נפלה החומה׃ אגדרא
אם בהרת קדמת לשער לבן טמא׳ ושער
לטומאה כדמתו והנה נהפך שער לבן

61 יקום אחד [illegible] וחצלה
יורא אדונא [illegible]
והו ישרח להם [illegible] ערבי

62 כל זית שיש לו שם בשדה כגון זית הנטופה
בשמו ובמעשיו ובמקומו בשמו שקיבה
במקומו שבוא עומד בכתל בגפו או בכתל

63 [illegible]
[illegible]
[illegible]
[illegible]

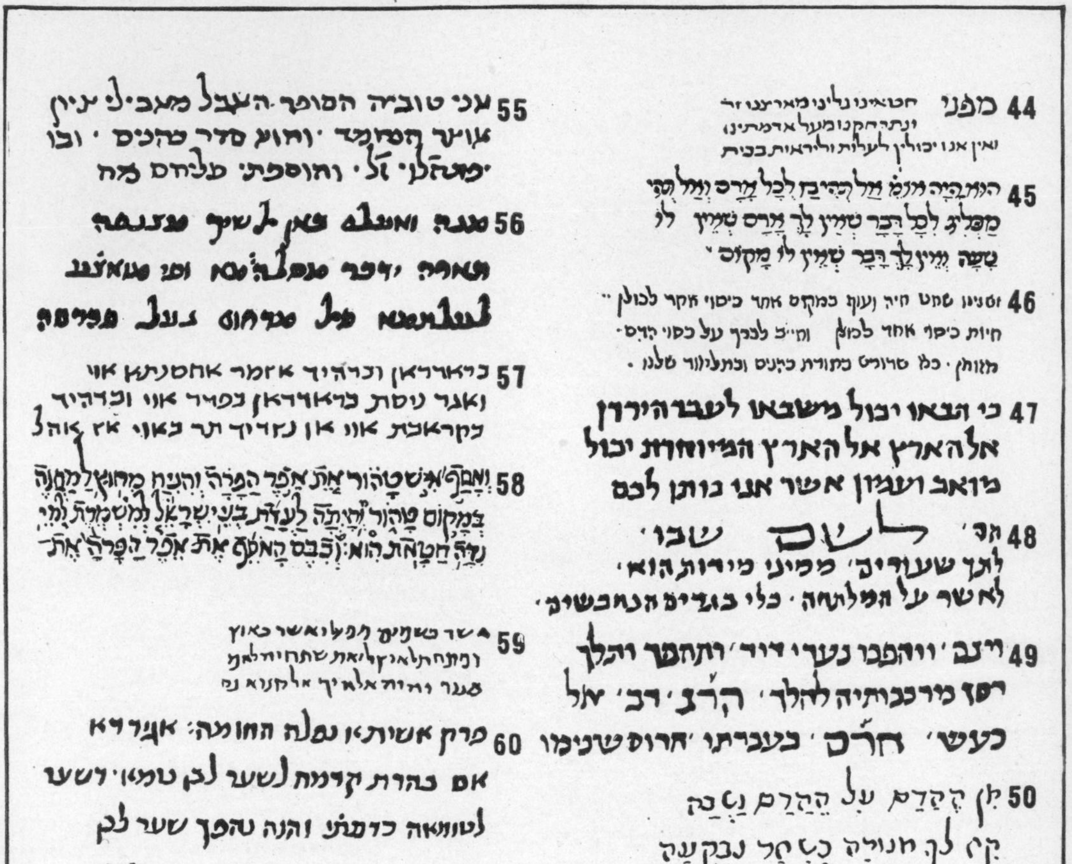

PLATE IV.

64

65

66

67

68

69 לאשתו דין ודברים אין לי בנכסיך
שהם נכסי המלוג הרי זה אוכל
פירות נכסיה בחייה ואם מתה

70

71

72 כי מובטח אני שאין אומות העולם
נאם הסופר אליהו בר אשר הלוי
המדקדק

73

74

75

76

77

78

79

80

81

82

83

84

85

86

sian origin, probably 11th cent.). With regard to No. 3 it should be noted that though the final "nun" (of which, however, no instance appears in the specimen) is long in the document, this is no mark of later date; for the long form of the letter appears in early papyri (as in specimen No. 2). In Nos. 4–6 the final "nun" is uniformly short. No. 8 shows the superlinear punctuation combined with the ordinary mode of accentuation.

Syro-Egyptian (Nos. 9–11): No. 9 is taken from a Hebrew letter, dated 1055, brought to the British Museum from the Cairo Genizah; No. 10, from the text of the Hebrew Ecclesiasticus (Sirach), also from the Cairo Genizah (11th–12th cent.); No. 11, from Pl. I. of Neubauer's portfolio of facsimiles (referred to hereafter as "Neubauer") printed to illustrate his catalogue of Oxford manuscripts (12th–13th cent.). In No. 9 note the peculiar combined form of אל (which is really Rabbinic). The mark over the second word of line 2 in No. 10 refers to a marginal note in the original. In No. 11 both the punctuation and the accentuation are superlinear.

Spanish (Nos. 12–15): No. 12 is taken from the Brit. Mus. MS. Harley 5720 (11th cent.); No. 13, from Brit. Mus. MS. Or. 2201 (dated 1246); No. 14, from a Bible codex belonging to the Earl of Leicester (13th cent.; see C. D. Ginsburg, "Facsimiles," London, 1898); No. 15, from Brit. Mus. MS. Or. 2626 (dated 1483). No. 12 may fairly be described as representing a transition stage from the early Oriental square writing to the Spanish.

Italian (Nos. 16–18): No. 16 is taken from Brit. Mus. MS. Arundel Or. 2 (dated 1216); No. 17, from Brit. Mus. MS. Or. 2736 (dated 1390); No. 18, from Brit. Mus. MS. Add. 18,692 (handwriting of Abraham Farissol, dated 1478). It should here be remarked that instead of the square writing in the proper sense of the word, Italian scribes often employ for Bible codices the semi-Rabbinic character exemplified in No. 45 (see below).

Franco-German (Nos. 19–21): No. 19 is taken from Brit. Mus. MS. Add. 10,455 (dated 1310); No. 20, from Cambridge University Library MSS. Ee, 8, 9 (dated 1347; see the "Oriental Series of the Palæographical Society" [hereafter referred to as "O. S."], Pl. XLI.); No. 21, from Neubauer, Pl. XI. (written before 1471). Note especially the sloping character of No. 20, a peculiar mark of German writing.

Greek (Nos. 22–24): No. 22 is taken from the Carlsruhe codex of the Prophets (dated 1105–6; "O. S." Pl. LXXVII.); No. 23, from Brit. Mus. MS. Add. 27,205 (dated 1179); No. 24, from Neubauer, Pl. XXI. (written before 1263).

Yemenite (Nos. 25–28): No. 25 is taken from Brit. Mus. MS. Or. 2373 (13th–14th cent.); No. 26, from Brit. Mus. MS. Or. 2370 (dated 1460–61); No. 27, from Brit. Mus. MS. Or. 2210 (dated 1468); No. 28, from Neubauer, Pl. XXXI. (dated 1561).

Varia (Nos. 29–31): No. 29 is taken from Brit. Mus. MS. Or. 2496, showing Karaite square writing of apparently the thirteenth century; No. 30, from a Pentateuch roll written for the Jews of K'ai-Fung-Foo, China (18th cent.; Brit. Mus. MS. Add. 19,250; showing the dependence of Chinese on Persian writing); No. 31, from Neubauer, Pl. XXXIX. (see Harkavy, "Neuaufgefundene Bibelhandschriften," Table II.—perhaps a forgery).

B. Square Rabbinic or Semi-Rabbinic Writing: This series shows an approximation in greater or less degree to the freer Rabbinic style of writing.

Syro-Egyptian (Nos. 32–38): No. 32 is taken from an Oxford papyrus of the sixth or seventh century (see "J. Q. R." xvi., No. 61); No. 33, from a manuscript of the above-mentioned Hebrew Ecclesiasticus (perhaps 9th cent.) belonging to E. N. Adler; No. 34, from the Genizah document Brit. Mus. MS. Or. 5538 (dated 1003); No. 35, from the Genizah document Brit. Mus. MS. Or. 5536 (dated 1015); No. 36, from the Genizah document Brit. Mus. MS. Or. 5545 (dated 1089); No. 37, from the Genizah document Brit. Mus. MS. Or. 5551 (dated 1151); No. 38, from Neubauer, Pl. IV. (signature of Maimonides). The Rabbinic tendency in No. 35 is only slight; but the ת is written freely, and the general appearance of the specimen shows affinity with semi-Rabbinic. It is necessary to note the slighter approximation of the square to the freer Rabbinic forms.

Spanish and North-African (Nos. 39–42): No. 39 is taken from Brit. Mus. MS. Harley 5530 (13th cent.); No. 40, from Brit. Mus. MS. Or. 5866 (middle of 15th cent.); No. 41, from Brit. Mus. MS. Or. 5600 (15th cent.); No. 42, from Brit. Mus. MS. Add. 19,780 (17th cent.). No. 40 appears to be of decidedly Spanish origin, the remaining three numbers being North-African (No. 42 can be definitely located as Algerian).

Italian (Nos. 43–46): No. 43 is taken from the Leyden copy of the Talmud Yerushalmi (dated 1281; see "O. S." Pl. LVI.); No. 44, from Brit. Mus. MS. Add. 18,690 (written between 1332 and 1350); No. 45, from Brit. Mus. MS. Add. 19,944 (dated 1441); No. 46, from Brit. Mus. MS. Or. 1081 (dated 1390). No. 46 appears to show French characteristics combined with Italian ones.

Franco-German (Nos. 47–50): No. 47 is taken from the Vatican copy of the Sifra (dated 1073; see "O. S." Pl. XC.); No. 48, from Brit. Mus. MS. Add. 27,214 (dated 1091); No. 49, from Brit. Mus. MS. Arundel Or. 51 (dated 1189); No. 50, from Brit. Mus. MS. Or. 5466 (dated 1690). In Nos. 47–49 the tendency to semi-Rabbinic is but slight.

Greek (No. 51): This specimen is taken from Brit. Mus. MS. Harley 5583 (15th–16th cent.).

Yemenite (Nos. 52–53): No. 52 is taken from Brit. Mus. MS. Or. 4837 (a fine copy of Ibn Janaḥ's "Kitab al-Uṣul," 14th cent.); No. 53, from Neubauer, Pl. XXXII. (dated 1491).

Karaite (Nos. 54–56): No. 54 is taken from Neubauer, Pl. XXXIV. (13th–14th cent.); No. 55, *ib.* Pl. XXXV. (written before 1353); No. 56, *ib.* Pl. XXXVI. (dated 1747).

Persian (Nos. 57–58): No. 57 is taken from Brit. Mus. MS. Or. 5446 (Pentateuch in Persian; dated 1319); No. 58, from Brit. Mus. MS. Or. 2451 (dated 1483).

C. Rabbinic Writing: This series exhibits various styles of writing of a decided Rabbinic character.

Early Oriental (Nos. 59–60): No. 59 is taken from the Decalogue papyrus referred to above (probably 6th or 7th cent.); No. 60, from Brit. Mus. MS. Or. 73 (perhaps written at Mosul; dated 1190).

Syro-Egyptian (Nos. 61–63): No. 61 is taken from

Brit. Mus. MS. Or. 5519 (12th cent.); No. 62, from Neubauer, Pl. III. (13th-14th cent.); No. 63, *ib.* Pl. VI. (14th cent.?).

Spanish (Nos. 64–65): No. 64 is taken from Brit. Mus. MS. Add. 14,763 (dated 1273); No. 65, from Brit. Mus. MS. Or. 5866 (middle of 15th cent.; for semi-Rabbinic forms from the same manuscripts see No. 40).

North-African, etc. (Nos. 66–68): No. 66 is taken from Brit. Mus. MS. Add. 27,113 (dated 1282); No. 67, from Neubauer, Pl. VII. (dated 1480; described as Syrian Rabbinic Maghrebi character); No. 68, *ib.* Pl. XIII. (15th cent.; described as Oriental Provençal).

Italian (No. 69): Specimen taken from Brit. Mus. MS. Or. 5024 (dated 1374).

Franco-German (Nos. 70–72): No. 70 is taken from Brit. Mus. MS. Add. 17,049 (dated 1394); No. 71, from Cambridge University Library MS. Add. 560 (dated 1401; see "O. S." Pl. LXVIII.); No. 72, from Brit. Mus. MS. Add. 27,199 (Elijah Levita's autograph; dated 1515).

Greek (Nos. 73–74): No. 73 is taken from Neubauer, Pl. XXIII. (written before 1184); No. 74, *ib.* Pl. XXV. (dated 1375).

D. Cursive Writing: This series is preceded by two specimens (Karaite) of writing in which the Hebrew text is written in the Arabic character and provided with Hebrew punctuation. No. 75 is taken from Brit. Mus. MS. Or. 2540 (10th cent.), and No. 76 from Brit. Mus. MS. Or. 2549 (11th cent.). No. 77 (Neubauer, Pl. XIX.; dated 1506) is Oriental. No. 78 (*ib.* Pl. X.; handwriting of Jacob b. Ḥayyim, early 16th cent.) is a specimen of Spanish cursive. Nos. 79–83 are Italian. No. 79, from Neubauer, Pl. XXIX., is old Italian; No. 80, from Brit. Mus. MS. Add. 27,096, is Mordecai Dato's writing (16th cent.). No. 81, from Brit. Mus. MS. Add. 27,148, is Judah Modena's autograph (1648); No. 82, from Brit. Mus. MS. Add. 26,991, is Solomon Portaleone's autograph (17th cent.); and No. 83, from Brit. Mus. MS. Add. 27,103, is Joseph Almanzi's autograph. Nos. 84 and 85 are German, the former being taken from Brit. Mus. MS. Add. 18,695 (a Maḥzor in a Judæo-German translation, dated 1504), and the latter from Neubauer, Pl. XVII. (Heidenheim's autograph). No. 86 is Karaite German cursive writing, dated 1826 (Neubauer, Pl. XXXVII.).

Specimens of Cursive.

Here may fitly be added a specimen of writing from

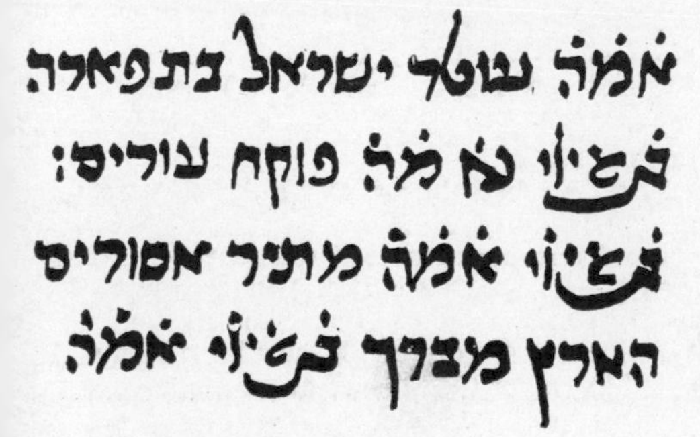
אמה שוטר ישראל בתפארה
מה פוקח עורים:
אמה מתיר אסורים

Codex Gaster 80, fol. 23b, which contains forms rarely found elsewhere. Remarkable is the abbreviation of אלהינו in line 2. The manuscript contains Maimonides' "Sefer ha-Madda'," and may belong to the fourteenth or to the thirteenth century. The writing appears to combine Yemenite with Persian characteristics (perhaps displaying the former more than the latter).

V. Illuminations: Illuminations in Hebrew manuscripts are far from being rare. Roughly speaking, the proportion of illuminated codices in a large and representative collection of Hebrew manuscripts would probably be found to be about seven or eight, if not more, in every hundred. On some early Eastern illuminations of Biblical codices (mostly in gold) see M. Gaster, "Hebrew Illuminated Bibles of the IXth and Xth Centuries (Codices Gaster 150, 151)." A fair specimen of early Persian chain-like ornamentation can be seen in "O. S." Pl. LIV. (Brit. Mus. MS. Or. 1467). Fine specimens of arabesque border illumination are found, *e.g.*, in Brit. Mus. MSS. Or. 2626–2628 of the year 1483–84, and in Brit. Mus. MSS. Harley 5698 and 5699, a page of which has been reproduced in colors for the present article (see frontispiece). In this instance, however, the arabesque form has been much modified. On Haggadah illuminations see HAGGADAH.

Comparative Frequency of Illuminations.

Spain and Provence seem to have been foremost in the last-named branch of illustration. Fine German illuminations are comparatively rare. The ornamentations, or what were meant for such, found in German copies of the Bible, etc., are as a rule grotesque rather than appropriate. Very interesting specimens of French illuminations, however, are found in Brit. Mus. MS. Add. 11,639 (12th and 13th cent.), containing a collection of Biblical, liturgical, and other texts. A finely ornamented page of an early Karaite Biblical text (10th cent.) has been reproduced in colors in G. Margoliouth, "Catalogue of the Hebrew and Samaritan MSS. in the British Museum," vol. i., Pl. V. (Brit. Mus. MS. Or. 2540).

VI. Palimpsests: Hebrew palimpsests, *i.e.*, manuscripts showing Hebrew written over erased or partly erased earlier writing, are rare. The Jews, as was only natural, did not, as a rule, like to utilize for sacred purposes material that had been used for other objects. Some notable examples of Hebrew palimpsests have, however, been found in the Cairo Genizah. From this source come the Oxford fragments containing Hebrew writing of apparently the twelfth century over Palestinian Syriac of the sixth and seventh, and eighth and ninth centuries (see Gwilliam and others in "Anecdota Oxoniensia," Semitic Series, 1893-96). More interesting still are the Cambridge palimpsests which contain Hebrew of the eleventh and twelfth centuries written over portions of Aquila's Greek version of the Old Testament and Origen's Hexapla (see F. C. Burkitt, "Fragments of the Books of Kings According to the Translation of Aquila," 1897; and C. Taylor, "Hebrew-Greek Cairo-Genizah Palimpsests," 1900). A page of palimpsest in which a Hebrew liturgical text of 1179 was written over Latin writing of the tenth century can be seen

Palimpsests and Colophons.

in "O. S." Pl. LXXVIII. (Brit. Mus. MS. Add. 27,205); see also Jew. Encyc. *s.v.* Aquila.

VII. Colophons: At the end of a manuscript, and sometimes also at the conclusion of parts of the same, a colophon (Greek, *κολοφών*) or "finishing stroke" is often found. In its fullest form the colophon contains (1) the title of the work, (2) the name of the scribe, (3) the name of the person for whom the manuscript was written, (4) the place of writing, (5) the date, and (6) precative and benedictive sentences, usually taken from the Bible (see Colophon).

The mention of the title in a colophon is, in the case of unknown or little-known works, helpful for identification, if, as not infrequently happens, the beginning of the manuscripts has been lost. The entries of scribes' names at times reveal long genealogies of families among which the profession of copying had descended from father to son for a number of generations. Scribes sometimes mark off their names also in the initial letters of one or more pages of the manuscripts. The complimentary epithets lavished by the scribe on his rich, or comparatively rich, employer are often conspicuous enough; but the more important references to descent and position are not wanting. There are also cases in which the scribe writes his manuscript for himself or for one or other of his children. The mention of the place of writing is, of course, useful for localizing the different styles of writing, though, as has already been mentioned, caution has to be exercised in this respect.

The manner of dating a manuscript demands special notice. For some points connected with the subject see Chronology and Era. Mention should be made first of the two specifically Jewish modes of dating, and then of eras borrowed from other nations.

Methods of Dating Manuscripts.

(1) The era of the Creation is in common use in manuscripts written in most parts of Europe; and as it appears to have been generally adopted about the middle of the tenth century of the common era, it was used in the entire period here dealt with. If the full number of years from the Creation is given, the reckoning is styled "peraṭ gadol" (abbreviated פ"ג); and the year of the common era is obtained by subtracting the number 3760 (or 3761, if the manuscript was written, or rather finished, in the first three months of the Jewish year). But the thousands are often omitted; and the reckoning is then called "peraṭ ḳaṭon" (abbreviated פ"ק). In such cases the number 1240 (or 1241) has to be added in order to obtain the date of the common era.

(2) Dating from the destruction of the Second Temple (*i.e.*, from the year 68) is comparatively rare in manuscripts, but it is not, as has been thought, strictly confined to Greece; for this mode of dating is found not only in the Carlsruhe copy of the Prophets, which was written in a Greek Ashkenazic hand in 1105–6 (דא תתסו ליצירה ובתתרלח לחרבן בית הבחירה = 4866 of the Creation or 1038 from the destruction of the Temple), but also in the Vatican copy of the Sifra written in a French hand in 1073, and (see below) in a manuscript from Yemen.

"Minyan Sheṭarot."

A very common mode of dating manuscripts written in the East is (3) by the Seleucidan or Greek era ("le-ḥeshbon ha-Yewanim," "le-minyan sheṭarot," or simply "li-sheṭarot"; sometimes considered to synchronize with the cessation of prophecy). In order to obtain the corresponding C.E. date, 311 (or 312 if the manuscript is dated within the first three months of the Jewish year) has to be subtracted. This era is by far the most common in Hebrew manuscripts written in Yemen, though the era of the Creation as well as the Mohammedan era is also occasionally met with, one era being sometimes followed by another. The Karaites use also the Greek era; but the reckoning from the Creation is more common in their colophons. The Karaites add the Mohammedan era more frequently than do the Jews of Yemen.

(4) The Mohammedan era just referred to is generally introduced under the designation "ḥeshbon ha-Yishme'elim"; but the expression "le-ḳeren ze'era" (in allusion to Dan. vii. 8) is also found.

(5) The common era is of very rare occurrence in Hebrew colophons; and it then only follows the year of the Creation previously given. Thus Brit. Mus. MS. Harley 5704 (containing a unique copy of the Yalḳuṭ Makiri on the Minor Prophets, written for Cardinal Ægidius) is dated "Tuesday, the 16th day of Ab, in the year 274 of the 'small reckoning' [ורחמך לפ"ק: this being at the same time an example of utilizing the numerical value of a Scriptural phrase for dating], and according to their reckoning 1514" (the term "li-yeẓirah" being then added by mistake). There are some instances where the Christian month is given side by side with the year of the Creation.

Multiple Dating.

A remarkable instance of multiple dating (though given at the beginning of the manuscript, and, therefore, not in the form of a colophon) is found in Brit. Mus. MS. Add. 27,294 (containing an Arabic commentary in Hebrew characters on Maimonides' Mishneh Torah, ch. i.–iv.; see "J. Q. R." xiii. 488) which was written by the scholarly Yemenite compiler Sa'id ibn Daud. It contains the following datings: (1) לחרבן ראשון אתתפט (1889 years since the destruction of the First Temple); (2) לחרבן שני אשצח (1398 since the destruction of the Second Temple); (3) ליציאת מצרים . . . (date of Exodus no longer legible); (4) לשטרות אתשעח (1778, according to the era of contracts); (5) ליצירה . . . (date of the Creation no longer legible); (6) לסלוק הנבואה אתשעח (1778 since the cessation of prophecy; the same as No. 4).

It should here be remarked that the date of a manuscript may, in the absence of a colophon, be computed from the table of calendar cycles of nineteen years that is sometimes (more especially in liturgical manuscripts) added to the text. Thus Brit. Mus. MS. Add. 27,205 must have been written about 1180; for the table of cycles commences with רסא, the two hundred and sixty cycles past yielding $260 \times 19 = 4940$ A.M. = 1180 C.E. In manuscripts containing digests of Talmudical law, the date may etimes be gathered from the year given in the ı of the letter of divorcement ("geṭ"), etc. curious addition, sometimes attached to colons (in certain cases standing by itself), is the ative phrase that the scribe should suffer no in- (לא יזק) "until an ass should mount on the lad- dreamed of by Jacob]" (עד שיעלה חמור בסולם אשר יעקב אבינו [; see "O. S." description of Pl. VIII).

III. Owners, etc.: A large number of manuots contain the names of those who at one time nother owned them. These are generally found ly-leaves at the beginning or at the end, but etimes also in the margin of inner leaves. Ocnally owners record the births of their children the fly-leaves, more rarely deaths and other ts. In a number of instances manuscripts are ked as having been obtained by an owner at the sion of his late father's or another testator's prop-. Contracts of transfer of manuscripts by sale also often found; and occasionally the pawning manuscript is recorded on one of its fly-leaves. money value that was at the time attached to manuscript is sometimes stated in the notices of

K. Censors: On this subject see CENSORSHIP HEBREW BOOKS. The following few remarks , however, be added to what is said in that arti- An instance of self-imposed censorship in nce, about 1291, is found in a Hebrew manuot at the British Museum (Add. 19,664). Brit. . MS. Add. 17,050 contains (in the form of a eaf) a document, dated Lugo, Feb. 16, 1610, by ch permission was given to carry the codex to ena. Brit. Mus. MS. Or. 74 contains an entry e for the censor by his notary. Very often the ies of several censors are found on the same page, manuscript having been from time to time subed to fresh examinations.

IOGRAPHY: In addition to the sources given in the article following may be cited: On papyri: Steinschneider, in *itschrift für Aegyptische Sprache*, xvii. 93; Chwolson, *I. H.* cols. 120-125; Erman and Krebs, *Aus den Papyri Königlichen Museums*, p. 290; *Mittheilungen aus der mmlung des Erzherzog Rainer*, i. 38-44. Catalogues: list in JEW. ENCYC. iii. 618 *et seq.* Facsimiles: Neuıer, *Facsimiles of Hebrew MSS. in the Bodleian Liıry*, Preface, 1886 (which has been largely drawn upon in accompanying plates); C. D. Ginsburg, *Series of XVIII. csimiles of MSS. of the Hebrew Bible*, London, 1898; *e Haggadah of Sarajevo*, Vienna, 1898; and *The Fragnts Hitherto Recovered of the Hebrew Text of Ecclesticus*, Oxford and Cambridge, 1901.

G. M.

he following list gives the number of known rew manuscripts in existence with the names of aries or private owners possessing them. The s in parentheses are those of the printed catanes of the collections.

ENGLAND.	
eian, Oxford (1886).	2,541
Adler	1,476
sh Museum (1893).	1,196
bridge University	762
' College (1903)	580
-Hamedrash (1884).	147
Ginsburg	80
ity College, Cambdge	29
st Church, Oxford	13

FRANCE AND SWITZERLAND.	
Paris, Bibliothèque Nationale (1866)	1,313
Baron Günzburg	900
Basel	20
Bern	20
Nîmes	15
Lyons	12
Elsewhere	9

RUSSIA.	
St. Petersburg	880
Friedlandiana	300

GERMANY AND AUSTRIA-HUNGARY.	
Munich (1897)	408
Hamburg (1878)	355
Berlin (1897)	259
Vienna (1847)	257
Breslau Seminary	190
Strasburg (1881)	51
Leipsic, Ratsbibliothek (1838)	43
Erfurt (1863)	17
Budapest Seminary	12
Geiger (Hochschule), Berlin	12

ITALY.	
Parma (1803, 1880)	1,634
Vatican, Rome (1756)	580
Turin (1874)	294
Mantua (1878)	178
Florence	130
Angelica, Rome (1878)	54
Bologna (1887)	28
Vittorio Emanuele, Rome (1878)	28
Modena	27
Venice (1886)	19

SPAIN AND PORTUGAL.	
Escurial	75
Toledo	42
Elsewhere	27

UNITED STATES.	
Jewish Theological Seminary, New York.	750
Columbia University	100
Sutro, San Francisco	135

HOLLAND AND SCANDINAVIA.	
Leyden (1858)	116
Upsala (1893)	38
Rosenthal	32
Copenhagen (1846)	16
Lund (1850)	6

Besides these there are other collections not yet catalogued; some in private hands, *e.g.*, those of Dr. M. Gaster of London, and of the late D. Kaufmann at Budapest, others in public libraries, as, for example, the Alliance Israélite Library. The fragments of the Cairo Genizah, numbering many thousands, and scattered in Cambridge, Oxford, London, and Paris, are not included. Many libraries, as the Bodleian and Bibliothèque Nationale, have received notable accessions since their catalogues were printed.

BIBLIOGRAPHY: Steinschneider, *Vorlesungen über die Kunde Hebräischer Handschriften*, pp. 68-90.

J.

MA'OZ ẒUR (מעוז צור): Commencement of the hymn originally sung only in the domestic circle, but now used also in the synagogue, after the kindling of the lights on the Feast of Dedication (ḤANUKKAH). The acrostic signature is that of Mordecai. Zunz ("Literaturgesch." p. 580) is inclined to place the author of this hymn in the middle of the thirteenth century. He may have been the Mordecai ben Isaac ha-Levi who wrote the Sabbath table-hymn "Mah Yafit" (Majufes), or even the scholar referred to in Tos. to Niddah 36a. Or, to judge from the appeal in the closing verse, now generally suppressed, he may have been the Mordecai whose father-in-law was martyred at Mayence in 1096.

The Traditional Tune.

The bright and stirring tune now so generally associated with "Ma'oz Ẓur" serves as the "representative theme" in musical references to the feast (comp. ADDIR HU; AḲDAMUT; HALLEL). Indeed, it has come to be regarded as the only Ḥanukkah melody, four other Hebrew hymns for the occasion being also sung to it (comp. Zunz, *l.c.* pp. 422, 429; D. Kaufmann, in "Ha-Asif," ii. 298), as well as G. Gottheil's paraphrase, "Rock of Ages," in the "Union Hymnal" (No. 107). It was originally sung for "Shene Zetim" ("Olives Twain"), the "Me'orah," or piyyuṭ, next preceding the SHEMA' in the Morning Service of the (first) Sabbath in the eight days of the Feast of Dedication. Curiously enough, "Shene Zetim" alone is now sometimes sung to a melody which two centuries ago was associated rather with "Ma'oz Ẓur." The latter is a Jewish-sounding air in the minor mode, and is found in Benedetto

Marcello's "Estro Poetico Armonico," or "Parafrasi Sopra li Salmi" (Venice, 1724), quoted as a melody of the German Jews, and utilized by Marcello as the theme for his "Psaim XV." This air has been transcribed by Cantor Birnbaum of Königsberg in the "Israelitische Wochenschrift" (1878, No. 51).

The present melody for the Ḥanukkah hymn has been identified by Birnbaum as an adaptation from the old German folk-song "So weiss ich eins, dass mich erfreut, das pluemlein auff preiter heyde," given in Böhme's "Altdeutsches Liederbuch" (No. 635); it was widely spread among German Jews as early as 1450. By an interesting coincidence, this folk-melody was also the first utilized by Luther for his German chorals. He set it to his "Nun freut euch lieben Christen gmein" (comp. Julian, "Dictionary of Hymnology," *s.v.* "Sing praise to God who reigns above"). It is familiar among English-speaking people as the tune for a translation by F. E. Cox of the hymn "Sei lob und ehr dem höchsten gut," by J. J. Schütz (1640-1730). As such it is called "Erk" (after the German hymnologist), and, with harmonies by Bach, appears as No. 283 of "Hymns, Ancient and Modern" (London, 1875). The earliest transcription of the Jewish form of the tune is due to Isaac Nathan, who set it, very clumsily indeed, to the poem "On Jordan's Banks" in Byron's "Hebrew Melodies" (London, 1815). Later transcriptions have been numerous, and the air finds a place in every collection of Jewish melodies. It was modified to the form now favored by English Jews by the delicate liturgical taste of Mombach, to whom is due the modulation to the dominant in the repetition of the first strain, shown in the transcription above.

MA'OZ ẒUR

BIBLIOGRAPHY: Ed. Birnbaum, *Chanuca-Melodie für Pianoforte, mit Vorbemerkung*, Königsberg, 1890; E. Breslaur, *Sind Originale Melodien bei den Juden Geschichtlich Nachweisbar?* p. 70, Leipsic, 1898; Cohen and Davis, *Voice of Prayer and Praise*, No. 294 (and especially Mombach, in Nos. 64 and 66), London, 1899; *Journal of the Folk-Song Society*, i. 36, London, 1900; *Jewish Chronicle* (London), No 1888; Dec. 20, 1889; Dec. 5, 1890; Dec. 25, 1891; L. Lewanski, *Chanukka-Hymne* (two voices and piano), Berlin; J senfeld, *Chanukka Hymne für Kinderstimmen*, Be D. Rubin, *Maoz Tsur für Chor und Orgel*; A. Schoen *Nationalgesang zur Erinnerung an die Siege der Ma bär*, Posen.

A. F. L. C

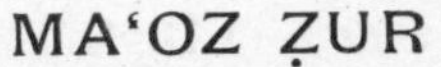

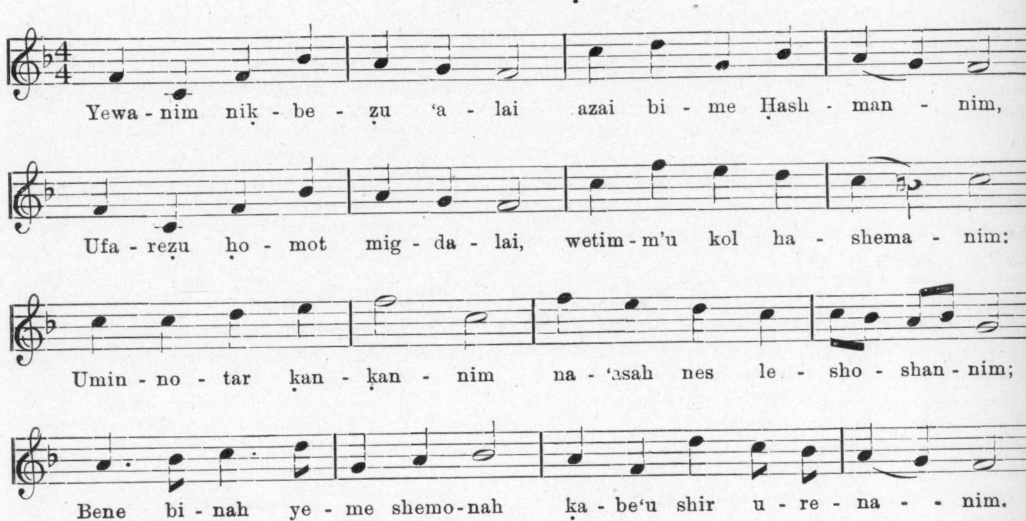

MAPU, ABRAHAM: Russian Hebrew no ist; born near Kovno Jan. 10, 1808; died at Kön berg Oct. 9, 1867. Mapu introduced the novel Hebrew literature. His early education in B and Talmud was received at the ḥeder, on leav which, at the age of twelve, he continued the stud the Talmud in private, and was so successful tha soon acquired the name of "'Illui" (Friedberg, " ronot," in "Hausfreund," i. 22). Moved thereto his own poetical and impulsive disposition and fluenced by his father, Jekuthiel, himself a my and cabalist, Mapu took up, at the age of fift the study of Cabala. According to an anecdote lated of him, he attempted to give his studies pra cal effect by endeavoring to render himself invisi Though he carefully followed cabalistic prescript he was cruelly disillusioned by being addressed a friend at the very moment when he thought l self secure from mortal observation (*ib.*). Mapu l studied Talmud and Cabala with Elijah Kali (Ragoler), rabbi at Slobodka (Mapu's birthpla In Kalisher's house he found a copy of the Psa with a Latin translation, and this awakened wi him a desire to study Latin, which he did from translation. A better opportunity to study L presented itself when he formed the acquaintanc a Catholic priest while teaching in a country sch and he made such good progress in the langu that he wrote a book in Latin (*ib.* i. 24).

From this time dates Mapu's devotion to sec studies, particularly to languages and literatu which he pursued henceforth assiduously. In forties he removed with his family to Rossieny, g ernment of Kovno; there he became acquainted w

scholar Senior Sachs, who greatly heightened his
e for ancient Hebrew history and literature and the beauties of Biblical diction, of which Mapu le later such good use in his romances (Brainin, "Abraham Mapu," p. 36). A few years later he became teacher in the house of Apatov Parnes at Wilna, and then was appointed teacher of Jewish religion and German at the gymnasium of Kovno. In 1860 his health began to fail; he suffered especially from palsy in his right hand, which made writing difficult for him; in 1867 he went for medical treatment to Königsberg, where he died (*ib.* i. 67).

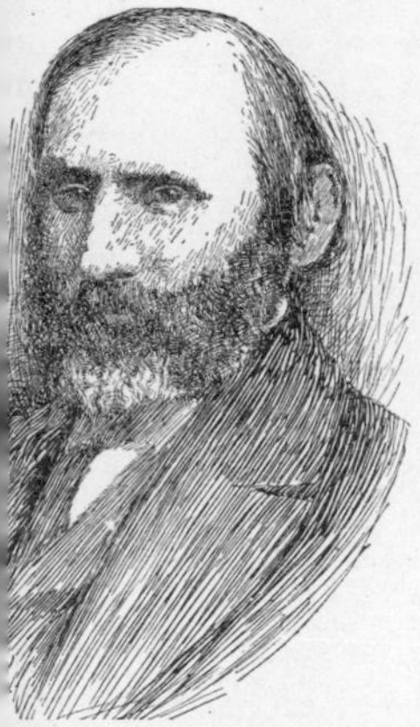

Abraham Mapu.

he literary activity of Mapu fell in a period of enness for Hebrew literature, as far as fiction concerned. Here and there a poem of moderate ıe, or a translation of a French romance, had apred, but there was not one original novel. His first book, "Ahabat Ẓiyyon," begun in 1831 and published at Wilna in 1853, is a romance of the time of King Hezekiah and Isaiah. In this as well as in his other works, one recognizes unmistakable influence of the French Romantic ol—of Victor Hugo, Dumas (père), and Eugène , particularly of the last-named, whom Mapu als admired (*ib.* i. 49). Perhaps through their influe Mapu succeeded in giving to his characters gene naïveté and naturalness, which combined with ghly successful use of Biblical diction to make work classic. "Ahabat Ẓiyyon" was translated German as "Tamar" by S. Mandelkern (2d Leipsic, 1897), without mention of Mapu's ıorship; into English, under the title "Amnon, ıce and Peasant," by Frank Jaffe (London, 1887), by Schapiro, under the title "In the Days of Isa" (New York, 1903); into Yiddish, in Warsaw '4). His second work, "Ashmat Shomeron" (Wil1865), is likewise a work of powerful imagina. It is a romance of the days of Ahaz, King of ah, and of Pekah b. Remaliah and Hosea b. Elah, gs of Israel, depicting the wild, orgiastic character amaritan society and setting against it the purity simplicity of Judean society. "'Ayiṭ Ẓabua'" lna, 1857–61) is a novel, in five parts, of modern picturing the struggle of the Maskilim against "painted vulture," or hypocrite—a standing epi; at that time for the ultra-Orthodox.

His Ahabat yyon."

lapu wrote also "Ḥozeh Ḥezyonot," a romance, en parts, of the times of Shabbethai Ẓebi; but ng to the intervention of the "hypocrites" of his n the manuscript was destroyed while on its to the minister of public instruction for apval, only a fragment being preserved. His other ·ks are "Ḥanok la-Na'ar" and "Amon Padagug," Hebrew text-books (Wilna, 1859, and Königsberg, 1868), and "Hausfranzose" (Wilna, 1861).

BIBLIOGRAPHY: A. Kaplan, *Ḥayye Mapu*, Vienna, 1870; Brainin, *Abraham Mapu*, Piotrokow, 1900; Friedberg, *Zikronot*, in *Hausfreund*, i. 21 *et seq.*; S. Sachs, *Le-Toledot Abraham Mapu*, in *Ha-Meassef*, pp. 13 *et seq.* (supplement to *Ha-Ẓefirah*, Warsaw, 1903); N. Slouschz, *Littérature Hebraïque*, pp. 104 *et seq.*, Paris, 1903.

H. R. A. S. W.

MAR (מר): Aramaic noun meaning "lord." Daniel addresses the king as "Mari" (= "my lord"; Dan. iv. 16 [A. V. 19]; comp. Hebr. "Adoni," used in speaking to the king). In the Palestinian schools "Mari" and "Rabbi" were customarily employed in addressing the sages. It is said of King Jehoshaphat that on seeing a scholar he rose from his throne, and saluted him with the words, "Abi, abi; rabbi, rabbi; mari, mari" (Ket. 103b; Mak. 24a). Jesus was addressed by his disciples both as "Mari" and as "Rabbi" (comp. Dalman, "Die Worte Jesu," i. 269 *et seq.*). In conversation, "Mari" was used as a respectful form of address in Palestine (comp. Yer. Pes. 21b, lines 48–49: איקריה דמרי, לא יבעום מרי); "Mar," in Babylonia (comp. Yoma 20b: לימא מר). In the latter country "Mar" became also a title preceding the name, and it was sometimes customary to call scholars "Mar" and not "Rab," particularly in the case of the two great contemporaries of Rab (Abba Arika)—Mar Samuel and Mar 'Ukba. When Abaye was speaking of his uncle and teacher Rabbah bar Naḥmani, he merely said "Mar," without adding any name (Pes. 101a). When Tabyomi, R. Ashi's son, cited in a lecture sentences by his father, he did not refer to him by name, but said "Abba Mari" (= "my father, my lord").

Tabyomi's contemporaries never referred to him by name, but called him "Mar"; in the Talmud he is, therefore, designated only as "Mar bar Rab Ashi." "Mar" and "Rab" (= "lord" and "master") together became a customary title of the Babylonian scholar in the geonic period. Sherira Gaon is the first one to use this combination, in the letter in which he refers to the first geonim—Mar Rab Hanan at Pumbedita and Mar Rab Mar at Sura (where "Mar" is already a proper name; see JEW. ENCYC. v. 568, *s.v.* GAON)—and he always prefixes the double title "Mar Rab" to their names (*ib.* v. 571). In the prayer "Yeḳum Purḳan," dating from the time of the Geonim, the scholars are designated as "Maranan we-Rabbanan" (= "our lords and masters"). The title "Mar Rab," also, was combined with the personal suffix of the first person plural, so that the Geonim were called "Marana Rabbana" (= "our lord, our master"). This seems to have been the official title in the headings of the questions addressed to the Geonim (comp. Harkavy, "Responsen der Gaonen," p. 149; Neubauer, "M. J. C." i. 41, etc.), and it is the exact ramaic counterpart of the Hebrew "Adonenu we-Rabbenu," by which, according to the tannaitic Halakah, the king was to be addressed (Tosef., Sanh. iv. 3). The gaon was called also simply "Marana" (Harkavy, *l.c.* pp. 83, 107, 140, 143), or the Hebrew "Adonenu" was used instead (*ib.* pp. 88, 187, 278, 314), which was rendered in Arabic by "Sayyiduna." "Mar Rab" was applied

Title and Name.

also to scholars who were not geonim (Harkavy, *l.c.* pp. 24, 172).

The title "Mar" was not customary in the West, so that Abraham ibn Daud, in his "Sefer ha-Ḳabbalah," refers to the Geonim merely as "Rab." Menahem Meïri distinguishes only the scholarly and noble Todros and his son Levi of Narbonne by the title "Marana we-Rabbana" (Neubauer, *l.c.* ii. 229). Isaac Lattes (*ib.* ii. 238) likewise designates certain scholars of Narbonne by the title "Maran" (מרן = מרנא), which also means "our lord." This is the title subsequently applied as a mark of respect to Joseph Caro, the author of the Shulḥan 'Aruk (comp. Azulai, "Shem ha-Gedolim," i. 82). One of Lattes' manuscripts has "Morenu" (מורנו) instead of "Maran." The title "Morenu," which originated in the fourteenth century, is developed from the older form "Marana" (Güdemann, "Gesch." iii. 31). The Hebrew form "Morenu" instead of "Marana" occurs sporadically even in the geonic period (comp. Harkavy, *l.c.* pp. 275 and 276, where the gaon Saadia is entitled "Morenu we-Rabbenu"). There are other indications, also, which show that the two words were regarded as synonymous (comp. Targ. to Prov. v. 13, where מורי is translated by מרוותי = "my lords, my masters"; Sanh. 98, where רבי ומרי is to be read instead of ר' ומורי; and Dalman, *l.c.* p. 268). Thus the old Hebrew title "Marana" was changed to "Morenu," with the meaning "doctor noster," perhaps under the influence of the custom which had become prevalent among Christian scholars of addressing one another with the title "doctor." As shown in the examples given above, מר itself designated the teacher and sage.

S. S. W. B.

MARAH (lit. "bitter"): The name of a station or halting-place of the Israelites in the wilderness (Ex. xv. 23; Num. xxxiii. 8), so called in reference to the water of the well found there. It was reached by the Israelites three days after crossing the Red Sea and after they had passed the valley of Shur and the wilderness of Athan. The well is variously identified with 'Ayun Musa, 'Ain Naba, or Al-Gharḳadah (comp. Holzinger, "Exodus," p. 55; Dillman, "Exodus," p. 177). The Talmud says that at Marah three laws were added to the seven commands already given to Noah—those regarding the institution of tribunals, Sabbath observance, and obedience to parents (Suk. 56b; Levy, "Neuhebr. Wörterb." iii. 244b).

J. E. I. N.

MARANO (plural, **Maranos,** generally written **Marranos**): Crypto-Jews of the Iberian Peninsula. The term, which is frequently derived from the New Testament phrase "maran atha" ("our Lord hath come"), denotes in Spanish "damned," "accursed," "banned"; also "hog," and in Portuguese it is used as an opprobrious epithet of the Jews because they do not eat pork. The name was applied to the Spanish Jews who, through compulsion or for form's sake, became converted to Christianity in consequence of the cruel persecutions of 1391 and of Vicente Ferrer's missionary sermons. These "conversos" (converts), as they were called in Spain, or "Christãos Novos" (Neo-Christians) in Portugal, or "Chuetas" in the Balearic Isles, or "Anusi (constrained) in Hebrew, numbered more t 100,000. With them the history of the Pyren Peninsula, and indirectly that of the Jews also, ters upon a new phase; for they were the im diate cause both of the introduction of the Inqu tion into Spain and of the expulsion of the J from that country. The wealthy Maranos, who gaged extensively in commerce, industries, agriculture, intermarried with families of the nobility; impoverished counts and marquises hesitatingly wedded wealthy Jewesses; and it happened that counts or nobles of the blood r became infatuated with handsome Jewish gi Beginning with the second generation, the N Christians usually intermarried with women of t own sect. They became very influential thro their wealth and intelligence, and were called to portant positions at the palace, in government cles, and in the Cortes; they practised medicine law and taught at the universities; while their c dren frequently achieved high ecclesiastical hon

Classes of Maranos.

The Maranos and their descendants may be divi into three categories. The first of these is compo of those who, devoid of any real affection for Ju ism, and indifferent to every form religion, gladly embraced the op tunity of exchanging their oppres condition as Jews for the brilli careers opened to them by the acceptance of Ch tianity. They simulated the Christian faith w it was to their advantage, and mocked at Jews Judaism. A number of Spanish poets belong this category, such as Pero Ferrus, Juan de Va dolid, Rodrigo Cota, and Juan de España of Tol called also "El Viejo" (the old one), who was c sidered a sound Talmudist, and who, like the m Diego de Valencia, himself a baptized Jew, in duced in his pasquinades Hebrew and Talmu words to mock the Jews. There were also m who, for the sake of displaying their new zeal, secuted their former coreligionists, writing bo against them, and denouncing to the authori those who wished to return to the faith of t fathers, as happened frequently at Valencia, Ba lona, and many other cities (Isaac b. Sheshet, sponsa, No. 11).

The second category consists of those who c ished their love for the Jewish faith in which t had been reared. They preserved the tradition their fathers; and, in spite of the high positi which they held, they secretly attended synagog and fought and suffered for their paternal relig Many of the wealthiest Maranos of Aragon belon to this category, including the Zaportas of Mon who were related by marriage to the royal hous Aragon; the Sanchezes; the sons of Alazar Y of Saragossa, who intermarried with the Cavalle and the Santangels; the very wealthy Espes; Paternoys, who came from the vicinity of Ver to settle in Aragon; the Clementes; the sons Moses Chamoro; the Villanovas of Calatayud; Coscons; and others.

The third category, which includes by far largest number of Maranos, comprises those yielded through stress of circumstances, but in t ome life remained Jews and seized the first opportu- ity of openly avowing their faith. They did not voluntarily take their children to the baptismal font; and if obliged to do so, they on reaching home washed the place which had been sprinkled. They e no pork, celebrated the Passover, and gave oil to e synagogue. "In the city of Seville an inquisi- r said to the regent: 'My lord, if you wish to know w the Maranos keep the Sabbath, let us ascend e tower.' When they had reached the top, the rmer said to the latter: 'Lift up your eyes and ok. That house is the home of a Marano; there is e which belongs to another; and there are many ore. You will not see smoke rising from any of em, in spite of the severe cold; for they have no e because it is the Sabbath.' Pretending that avened bread did not agree with him, one Marano e unleavened bread throughout the year, in order at he might be able to partake of it at Passover ithout being suspected. At the festival on which e Jews blew the shofar, the Maranos went into e country and remained in the mountains and in e valleys, so that the sound might not reach the ty. They employed a man specially to slaughter imals, drain away the blood, and deliver the meat their homes, and another to circumcise secretly" Shebeṭ Yehudah," pp. 96 *et seq.*). The Jews of at time judged the Maranos gently and indul- ntly; in Italy a special prayer was offered for them ery Sabbath, asking that "God might lead them om oppression to liberty, from darkness to the ght of religion" (אחיכו אנוסי ישראל הנתונים בצרה ובשביה המקום ירחמם ויחון אותם בעבור שמו הגד ויושיעם ויושיענו ויוציאם ויוציאנו מצרה לרוחה ומאפי א לאורה ונאמר; MS. Roman Maḥzor of the year 41). To the Maranos who lived in secret conform- y with the Jewish law, the Rabbis applied the lmudic passage: "Although he has sinned, he ust still be considered a Jew"; and Anusim, who ok the first opportunity of going to a foreign untry and openly professing Judaism, might act witnesses in religious matters according to rab- nic law. A distinction was frequently made be- een Spanish and Portuguese Maranos in regard to arriage and divorce (Isaac b. Sheshet, *l.c.* Nos. 4, ; Saadia ibn Danan, in Edelmann, "Ḥemdah enuzah," pp. 14 *et seq.*; Joseph b. Leb, Responsa, 15; the responsa of Moses ben Ḥabib, Samuel de edina, and many others).

'emporary Maranos.

The large numbers of the Maranos, as well as their ealth and influence, aroused the envy and hatred the populace, whom the clergy incited against em as unbelieving Christians and hypocrites. he Neo-Christians were hated much more than the ws, and were persecuted as bitterly as their former religionists had been. The first riot against them oke out at Toledo in 1449, and was accompanied ith murder and pillage. Instigated by two canons, an Alfonso and Pedro Lopez Galvez, the mob plundered and burned the houses of Alonso Cota, a wealthy Marano and tax-farmer, and under the leadership a workman they likewise attacked the resi- nces of the wealthy Neo-Christians in the quarter De la Magdelena. The Maranos, under Juan de la Cibdad, opposed the mob, but were repulsed and, with their leader, were hanged by the feet. As an immediate consequence of this riot, the Maranos Lope and Juan Fernandez Cota, the brothers Juan, Pedro, and Diego Nuñez, Juan Lopez de Arroyo, Diego and Pedro Gonzalez, Juan Gonzalez de Illescas, and many others were deposed from office, in obedience to a new statute. Another attack was made upon the Neo-Christians of Toledo in July, 1467. The chief magistrate ("alcalde mayor") of the city was Alvar Gomez de Cibdad Real, who had been private secretary to King Henry IV., and who, if not himself a "converso," as is probable, was at least the protector of the Neo-Christians. He, together with the prominent Maranos Fernando and Alvaro de la Torre, wished to take revenge for an insult inflicted by the counts de Fuensalida, the leaders of the Christians, and to gain control of the city. A fierce conflict was the result. The houses of the Neo-Christians near the cathedral were fired by their opponents, and the conflagration spread so rapidly that 1,600 houses were consumed, including the beautiful palace of Diego Gomez. Many Christians and still more Maranos perished in the flames or were slain; and the brothers De la Torre were captured and hanged.

n Spain.

The example set by Toledo was imitated six years later by Cordova, in which city the Christians and the Maranos formed two hostile parties. On March 14, 1473, during a procession in honor of the dedication of a society which had been formed under the auspices of the fanatical Bishop D. Pedro, and from which all "conversos" were excluded, a little girl seems to have accidentally thrown some dirty water from the window of the house of one of the wealthiest Maranos, so that it splashed over an image of the Virgin. Thousands immediately joined in the fierce shout for revenge which was raised by a smith named Alonso Rodriguez; and the rapacious mob straightway fell upon the Maranos, denouncing them as heretics, killing them, and plundering and burning their houses. To stop the excesses, the highly respected D. Alonso Fernandez de Aguilar, whose wife was a member of the widely ramified Marano family of Pacheco, together with his brother D. Gonzalo Fernandez de Cordova ("el gran Capitan"), the glory of the Spanish army, and a troop of soldiers, hastened to protect the Neo-Christians. D. Alonso called upon the mob to retire, but instead of obeying, the smith insulted the count, who immediately felled him with his lance. The people, blinded by fanaticism, regarded their slain leader as a martyr. Incited by Alonso de Aguilar's enemy, the knight Diego de Aguayo, they seized weapons and again attacked the Maranos. Girls were outraged; and men, women, and children were pitilessly slain. The massacre and pillage lasted three days; those who escaped seeking refuge in the castle, whither their protectors also had to retire. It was then decreed that, in order to prevent the repetition of such excesses, no Marano should thenceforth live in Cordova or its vicinity, nor should one ever again hold public office.

Riots at Cordova.

Like the persecution of the Jews in 1391, the attack on the Maranos in 1473 spread to other cities. At Montoro, Bujalance, Adamur, La Rambla, Santaella, and elsewhere, they were killed, and their houses were plundered. At Jaen the populace was so bitter against them that the constable Miguel Lucas de Iranzo, who undertook to protect them, was himself killed in church by the ringleaders (March 21, 22). The Maranos were fiercely attacked by the populace in Andujar, Ubeda, Baeza, and Almodovar del Campo also. In Valladolid the populace was content with plundering the Neo-Christians, but the massacre was very fierce at Segovia (May 16, 1474). Here the attack, instigated by D. Juan Pacheco, himself a member of a Marano family, was terrible; corpses lay in heaps in all the streets and squares, and not a Neo-Christian would have escaped alive had not the alcalde Andreas de Cabrera interfered. At Carmona every Marano was killed.

Introduction of Inquisition.

The introduction of the Inquisition was bitterly opposed by the Maranos of Seville and other cities of Castile, and especially of Aragon, where they rendered considerable service to the king, and held high legal, financial, and military positions. As D. Miguel Lucas de Iranzo, constable of Castile, had been slain in the cathedral of Jaen, so the inquisitor Pedro Arbues was assassinated twelve years later in the cathedral of Saragossa, the former by Christians, the latter by Maranos. The murderers of De Iranzo went scot-free, while those of the inquisitor were punished most cruelly. Together with the introduction of the Inquisition an edict was issued that henceforth the Jews must live within their ghetto and be separated from the Maranos. Despite the law, however, the Jews remained in communication with their Neo-Christian brethren. "They sought ways and means to win them from Catholicism and bring them back to Judaism. They instructed the Maranos in the tenets and ceremonies of the Jewish religion; held meetings in which they taught them what they must believe and observe according to the Mosaic law; and enabled them to circumcise themselves and their children. They furnished them with prayer-books; explained the fast-days; read with them the history of their people and their Law; announced to them the coming of the Passover; procured unleavened bread for them for that festival, as well as kasher meat throughout the year; encouraged them to live in conformity with the law of Moses, and persuaded them that there was no law and no truth except the Jewish religion." All these charges were brought against the Jews in the edict issued by Ferdinand and Isabella, and formed the grounds for their banishment from the country. The decree of expulsion materially increased the number, already large, of those who purchased a further sojourn in their beloved home by accepting baptism.

In Portugal.

The Portuguese Maranos or Christãos Novos clung much more faithfully and steadfastly than their Spanish brethren to the religion of their fathers, bearing the most terrible tortures for the sake of their faith. The scholar Simon Mimi of Lisbon, who would not renounce Judaism even in prison, his wife, his sons-in-law, and other Maranos were enclosed in a wall built up to their necks, t prisoners being left for three days in this agonizin situation. As they would not yield the walls we torn down, after six of the victims had died, ar Mimi was dragged through the city and slain. Tw Maranos who served as wardens in the pris buried the body of the martyr in the Jewish cem tery at the risk of their lives (Abraham Saba "Ẓeror ha-Mor," p. 105b; Grätz, "Gesch." viii. 398

The Portuguese, being even more fanatical th the Spaniards, hated the Maranos much more th the Jews, considering them neither Christians n Jews, but atheists and heretics. Many a Portugue preferred death to being treated by a Marano ph sician. The hatred which was felt for the Marano and which had long smoldered, broke out at Lisbo On April 17, 1506, several Maranos were discover who had in their possession "some lambs and pou try prepared according to Jewish custom; also u leavened bread and bitter herbs according to t regulations for the Passover, which festival th celebrated far into the night." Several of them we seized, but were released after a few days. T populace, which had expected to see them punishe swore vengeance. On the same day on which t Maranos were liberated, the Dominicans display in a side-chapel of their church, where several Ne Christians were present, a crucifix and a reliqua in glass from which a peculiar light issued. A Ne Christian, who was so incautious as to explain t ostensible miracle as being due to natural causes, w dragged from the church and was killed by an infu ated woman. A Dominican roused the popula still more; and two others, crucifix in hand, we through the streets of the city, crying "Heresy and calling upon the people to destr the Maranos.

Massacre at Lisbon.

All Neo-Christia found in the streets were killed; a a terrible massacre ensued. More th 500 Maranos were slain and burned on the first da and the scenes of murder were even more atrocio on the day following. The innocent victims popular fury, young and old, living and dead, we dragged from their houses and thrown upon t pyre. Even Christians who in any way resembl Maranos were killed. Among the last victims, a the most hated of all, was the tax-farmer Jo Rodrigo Mascarenhas, one of the wealthiest a most distinguished Maranos of Lisbon; his house w entirely demolished. In this manner at least 2,0 Maranos perished within forty-eight hours. Ki Manuel severely punished the inhabitants of t city. The ringleaders were either hanged or qu tered, and the Dominicans who had occasioned t riot were garroted and burned. All persons co victed of murder or pillage suffered corporal pu ishment, and their property was confiscated, wh religious freedom was granted to all Maranos twenty years.

The Neo-Christians of Portugal, who were d tinguished for their knowledge, their commerce, a their banking enterprises, but were bitterly hat despised, and reviled by the Christians, were led entertain better hopes for the future by the appe ance of a foreign Jew, David Re'ubeni. Not o was this Jew invited by King John to visit Por gal; but, as appears from a letter (Oct. 10, 1528) of D. Martin de Salinas to the infante D. Fernando, brother of the emperor Charles, he also received permission "to preach the law of Moses" ("Boletin Acad. Hist." xlix. 204). The Maranos regarded Re'ubeni as their savior and Messiah. The Neo-Christians of Spain also heard the glad news; and some of them left home to seek him. The rejoicing lasted for some time; the emperor Charles even addressed several letters on the matter to his royal brother-in-law. In 1528, while Re'ubeni was still in Portugal, some Spanish Maranos fled to Campo Mayor and forcibly freed from the Inquisition a woman imprisoned at Badajoz. The rumor spread at once that the Maranos of the entire kingdom had united to make common cause. This increased the hatred of the populace, and the Neo-Christians were attacked in Gouvea, Alemtejo, Olivença, Santarem, and other places, while in the Azores and the island of Madeira they were even massacred. These excesses led the king to believe that the Inquisition might be the most effective means of allaying the popular fury.

The Portuguese Maranos waged a long and bitter war against the introduction of the tribunal, and spent with some satisfactory results immense sums to win over to their cause the Curia and the most influential cardinals. The sacrifices made by both the Spanish and the Portuguese Neo-Christians were indeed astonishing. The same Maranos who from Toledo had instigated the riot of the communes in 1515, Alfonso Gutierrez, Garcia Alvarez "el Rico" (the wealthy), and the Zapatas, offered through their representative 80,000 gold crowns to Emperor Charles V. if he would mitigate the harshness of the Inquisition ("R. E. J." xxxvii. 270 *et seq.*). All these sacrifices, however, especially those made by the Mendes of Lisbon and Flanders, were powerless to prevent or retard the introduction of the Holy Office into Portugal. The Maranos were delivered over to the popular fury and to the heartless servants of the Inquisition. They suffered unspeakably. At Trancoso and Lamego, where many wealthy Maranos were living, at Miranda, Viseu, Guarda, Braga, and elsewhere they were robbed and killed. At Covilhão the people planned to massacre all the Neo-Christians on one day; and to achieve this the more easily, the prelates petitioned the Cortes in 1562 that the Maranos be required to wear special badges, and that the Jews in the cities and villages be ordered to live in ghettos as before.

Dispersion.

The Maranos, who were constantly threatened and persecuted by the Inquisition, tried in every way to leave the country, either in bands or as individual refugees. Many of them escaped to Italy, attracted thither by the climate, which resembled that of the Iberian Peninsula, and by its kindred language. They settled at Ferrara, and Duke Ercole I. d'Este granted them privileges, which were confirmed by his son, Alfonso I., to twenty-one Spanish Maranos, physicians, merchants, and others (*ib.* xv. 113 *et seq.*).

Spanish and Portuguese Maranos settled also at Florence; and Neo-Christians contributed to make Leghorn a leading seaport. They received privileges at Venice, where they were protected from the persecutions of the Inquisition. At Milan they materially advanced the interests of the city by their industry and commerce, although João de la Foya captured and robbed large numbers of them in that region. At Bologna, Pisa, Naples, Reggio, and many other Italian cities they freely exercised their religion, and were soon so numerous that Fernando de Goes Loureiro, an abbot from Oporto, filled an entire book with the names of the Maranos who had drawn large sums from Portugal and had openly avowed Judaism in Italy. In Piedmont Duke Emanuel Philibert of Savoy welcomed the Maranos from Coimbra, Pablo Hernando, Ruy Lopez, and Rodriguez, together with their families, and granted them commercial and industrial privileges, as well as the free exercise of their religion. Rome was full of Maranos. Pope Paul III. received them at Ancona for commercial reasons, and granted complete liberty "to all persons from Portugal and Algarve, even if belonging to the class of Neo-Christians." Three thousand Portuguese Jews and Maranos were living at Ancona in 1553. Two years later the fanatical Pope Paul IV. issued orders to have all the Maranos thrown into the prisons of the Inquisition which he had instituted. Sixty of them, who acknowledged the Catholic faith as penitents, were transported to the island of Malta; twenty-four, who adhered to Judaism, were publicly burned (May, 1556); and those who escaped from the Inquisition were received at Pesaro by Duke Guido Ubaldo of Urbino. As Guido was disappointed, however, in his hope of seeing all the Jews and Maranos of Turkey select Pesaro as a commercial center, he expelled (July 9, 1558) the Neo-Christians from Pesaro and other districts (*ib.* xvi. 61 *et seq.*). Many Maranos were attracted to Ragusa, formerly a considerable seaport. In May, 1544, a ship landed there filled exclusively with Portuguese refugees, as Balthasar de Faria reported to King John.

In France.

At this same period the Maranos were seeking refuge beyond the Pyrenees, settling at St. Jean de Luz, Tarbes, Bayonne, Bordeaux, Marseilles, and Montpellier. They lived apparently as Christians; were married by Catholic priests; had their children baptized, and publicly pretended to be Catholics. In secret, however, they circumcised their children, kept the Sabbath and feast-days as far as they could, and prayed together. King Henry III. confirmed the privileges granted them by Henry II., and protected them against such slanders and accusations as those which a certain Ponteil brought against them. Spanish and Portuguese Maranos petitioned Henry IV. to permit them to emigrate to France, saying that should he do so, a large number of their fellow sufferers, "good men all of them," would choose France as their home; but many Neo-Christians who entered French territory were obliged to leave within a short time. Under Louis XIII. the Maranos of Bayonne were assigned to the suburb of St. Esprit. At St. Esprit, as well as at Peyrehorade, Bidache, Orthez, Biarritz, and St. Jean de Luz, they gradually avowed Judaism openly. In 1640 several hundred Maranos, considered to be Jews, were living at St. Jean de Luz; and at St. Esprit there was a synagogue as early as 1660.

Next to Turkey the Maranos turned chiefly to Flanders, attracted by its flourishing cities, such as Antwerp, where they settled at an early date, and Brussels. Before the end of the sixteenth century Portuguese Maranos, under the leadership of Jacob Tirado, arrived at Amsterdam. So many others followed these that the city was called a new Jerusalem, while hundreds of Neo-Christian families settled at Rotterdam also. Maranos from Flanders, and others direct from the Pyrenean Peninsula, went under the guise of Catholics to Hamburg and Altona about 1580, where they established commercial relations with their former homes. Christian IV. of Denmark invited some Neo-Christian families to settle at Glückstadt about 1626, granting certain privileges to them and also to the Maranos who came to Emden about 1649.

In Flanders.

Large numbers of Maranos, however, remained in Spain and Portugal, despite the extensive emigration and the fate of countless victims of the Inquisition. The Neo-Christians of Portugal breathed more freely when Philip III. came to the throne and by the law of April 4, 1601, granted them the privilege of unrestricted sale of their real estate as well as free departure from the country for themselves, their families, and their property. Many, availing themselves of this permission, followed their coreligionists to Africa and Turkey. After a few years, however, the privilege was revoked, and the Inquisition resumed its activity. But the Portuguese who were not blinded by fanaticism perceived that no forcible measures could induce the Maranos to give up the religion of their fathers.

Individual Neo-Christians, as Antonio Fernandez Carvajal and several from Spain, Hamburg, and Amsterdam, went to London, whence their families spread to Brazil, where Maranos had settled at an early date, and to other countries of America. The migrations to Constantinople and Salonica, where refugees had settled after the expulsion from Spain, as well as to Servia, to Rumania and Bulgaria, and even to Vienna and Temesvar, continued down to the middle of the eighteenth century.

Whether there are still Maranos in Spain or not, this much is certain, that there are many persons in Barcelona, Saragossa, Madrid, Cordova, Toledo, and Burgos who, conscious of their Jewish descent, are well disposed toward the Jews. In Portugal there is a community of Maranos at Covilhã. See Inquisition.

Bibliography: Rios, *Hist.* iii. 147 *et seq.*; Isaac da Costa, *Israel und die Völker*, German transl. by Mann, p. 274; Kayserling, *Gesch. der Juden in Portugal*, pp. 262 *et seq.*, and bibliography given there; *R. E. J.* xi. 148, xv. 118, xvi. 61 *et seq.*, xliii. 259; *Allg. Zeit. des Jud.* liii. 402; Grunwald, *Portugiesengräber*, pp. 6 *et seq.*, 128 *et seq.*

J. M. K.

MARBE HASKALAH. See Society for the Promotion of Culture Among the Jews of Russia.

MARBLE (שיש): A stone composed mainly of calcium carbonate or of calcium and magnesium carbonates. It is mentioned in the Old Testament in three very late passages only. According to I Chron. xxix. 2, David prepared, among other materials, white "marble stones" for the building of the Temple. The account of the building in the Book of Kings does not mention the use of marble. In the Song of Solomon (v. 15) the author compares the legs of the bridegroom to marble pillars in golden sockets. Finally, Esther i. 6 speaks of marble columns and of a pavement of white and colored marble in the palace of the Persian king. In the last-cited passage it is not wholly certain if the text is intact in the versions; consequently there is doubt whether marble is really meant. In the other two passages also the correctness of the text has been doubted (see "Encyc. Bibl." *s.v.* "Marble").

Moreover, the fact that all the old authorities, especially the accounts of the building of the Temple, preserve complete silence on the subject shows that the Hebrews in olden times were not acquainted with the use of marble as a building-stone. Its employment for building purposes seems to have been very limited even among the Assyrians.

E. G. H. I. Be.

MARBURG: 1. Town in the Prussian province of Hesse-Nassau. Jews are first mentioned as living in Marburg in a document dated May 13, 1317, which indicates that they were then organized as a community and possessed a synagogue; also that they dwelt in a special quarter of the town. From a document of 1452 it appears that the synagogue was demolished in that year, and that the Jewish cemetery passed into Christian hands; hence the Jews must have been expelled from Marburg about that time. They gradually returned to the city; and in 1532 Landgrave Philipp revoked the decree of expulsion issued by him in 1524, and permitted the Jews provisionally to remain in his territory for a period of six years. Two Jews, named respectively Liebmann and Gottschalk, availed themselves of this permission in 1536.

As the Hessian cities repeatedly petitioned against the admission of Jews, the number of the latter remained very small: in 1744 there were only six Jewish families at Marburg; in 1776, eight. No one was permitted to harbor foreign Jews, except at the times of the fairs, on pain of being fined and of losing the privilege of protection. The Marburg community increased somewhat with the granting of freedom of residence; but even as late as 1902 it numbered only about 300 members in a total population of 16,668. It possesses a handsome synagogue (built in 1897), a parochial and a religious school, and a home for pupils and apprentices (opened in 1901) with seventy inmates.

Since 1823 Marburg has been the seat of the board of management of the union including the Jewish communities in the districts of Marburg, Kirchhayn, Frankenberg, and Ziegenhain. Marburg is the seat also of a district rabbinate, which includes not only the former districts, but also those of Biedenkopf and Wetzlar. The district rabbis have been: Moses Solomon Gosen, 1824–62; Liebmann Gersfeld, 1862–76; and Dr. Leo Munk, the present (1904) incumbent, appointed in 1876. There are a number of educational and philanthropic societies. Hermann Cohen has been for a number of years professor of philosophy at the University of Marburg.

D. L. Mu.

2. Austrian town, the second in the duchy of Styria. It has a population of 24,501, including about 100 Jews. Jews first settled at Marburg toward the end of the thirteenth century; gravestones of that period are still found there. According to the records they had a synagogue in their ghetto in 1277, as well as a school and a bath-house. The Jews of Marburg were respected merchants; they owned houses, fields, mills, and vineyards, and lived peaceably with their neighbors. They were not affected by the great persecutions of 1336 and 1338, and many Jews persecuted elsewhere found refuge at Marburg on payment of an annual tax of 40 gulden. In the old tax-records of Marburg the Jews are described as quiet and wealthy merchants who paid their taxes promptly. The Jews who were expelled from the territory of the neighboring city of Cilli in 1404 were received at Marburg, to the benefit of its commerce and industry. The decree of Frederick III. (1410–1493) relating to the importation of Hungarian wines was especially favorable to the Jewish wine-merchants. About this time R. Israel Isserlein, one of the foremost rabbis of the fifteenth century, and a native of Marburg, officiated there. Up to the middle of the fifteenth century the Jews of Marburg were generally respected; the Jew Elijah was one of its most prominent citizens, and Gerl, Jacob, and Aram Rorer were in the employ of noblemen as their treasurers. Mention is made also of the Jews Cham, who owned six, and Maul, who owned three, houses in Marburg. The wealthy money-lender Abraham b. Isaac advanced the money for part of the expenses of the Diet and contributed large sums for the equipment of the army. The Jews Hirsel, Süsskind, and Aaron b. Söldmann are mentioned among those who gave money to the Christian Church.

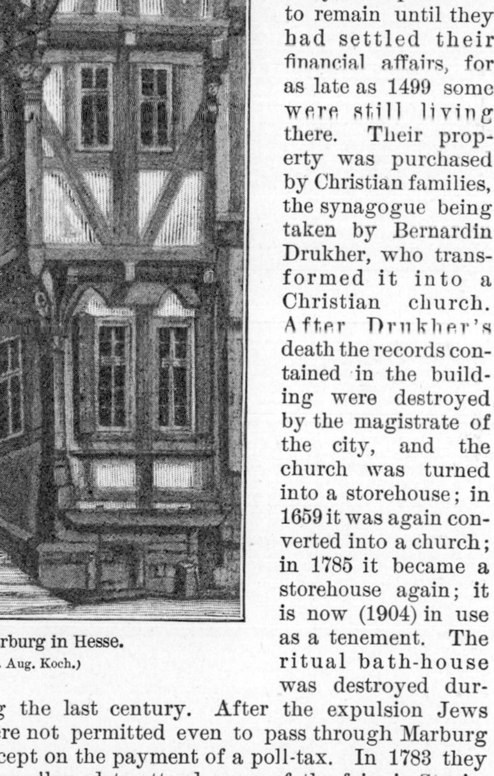

The "Judengasse" of Marburg in Hesse.
(From an old print by Joh. Aug. Koch.)

Marburg is one of the four cities of Styria the Jews of which had a special judge ("Judenrichter"), whose position was regarded as "very lucrative"; about 1440 it was held by the governor Sigmund von Rogendorf himself. There were special "Judenmeister" for internal Jewish affairs. Notes of debts held by Jews against Christians had to be indorsed by the city judge. In 1477, when the Jews of Marburg were building a new synagogue, David b. Aram, who had removed a short time before to Radkersburg, refused to pay the contribution of twelve gulden which the community levied upon him. The result was a tedious lawsuit, which Frederick III. finally settled by deciding that the defendant's assessment should be remitted, and that he should be neither excommunicated nor subjected to coercion of any other kind. The Jews of the city continued to enjoy the protection of the authorities and the good-will of their Christian fellow citizens until 1496, when the emperor Maximilian decreed the expulsion of all Jews from Styria. Those in Marburg, apparently, were permitted to remain until they had settled their financial affairs, for as late as 1499 some were still living there. Their property was purchased by Christian families, the synagogue being taken by Bernardin Drukher, who transformed it into a Christian church. After Drukher's death the records contained in the building were destroyed by the magistrate of the city, and the church was turned into a storehouse; in 1659 it was again converted into a church; in 1785 it became a storehouse again; it is now (1904) in use as a tenement. The ritual bath-house was destroyed during the last century. After the expulsion Jews were not permitted even to pass through Marburg except on the payment of a poll-tax. In 1783 they were allowed to attend some of the fairs in Styria, but not at Marburg. In 1811 three Jews were baptized in that city, but none settled there again until 1867, when the merchant Jacob Schlesinger was admitted. Some of the Jews now resident there are government and district officials.

Bibliography: Puff, *Marburg in Steiermark*, Graz, 1847; Muchar, *Gesch. des Herzogthums Steiermark*, 9 vols., *ib.* 1844–77.

D. S. Mu.

MARC, CHARLES CHRÉTIEN HENRI: French physician; born in Amsterdam Nov. 4, 1771; died in Paris Jan. 12, 1841. He took the degree of M.D. at Erlangen in 1792, and practised at Vienna, Bamberg, and in Bohemia. In 1795 he went to Paris, where with Fourcroy, Cabanis, Desgenelles, and others, he founded the Société Médicale d'Emulation. For several years he had a hard struggle, but by 1811 his position had become secure; his books won him fame, and he became a member of the Board of Health (1816) and of the Academy of Medicine (soon after its foundation, in 1820). In 1829, with Esquirol, Parent-Duchâtelet, Orfila, and others, he founded the "Annales d'Hygiène Publique et de Médecine Légale," to which he wrote the introduction. After the Revolution of July, 1830, he became first physician to Louis Philippe. He embraced Christianity.

Marc published: "Observations Générales sur les Poisons" (1795, translated into several languages); "Sur les Hémorrhoïdes Fermées" (Paris, 1804, translated from the German of Hildenbrand); "Manuel d'Autopsie Cadavérique Médico-Légale" (1808, translated from Roze); "Recherches sur l'Emploi du Sulfate de Fer dans le Traitement des Fièvres Intermittentes" (*ib.* 1810); "La Vaccine Soumise aux Simples Lumières de la Raison" (*ib.* 1810 and 1836); "De la Folie Considérée dans Ses Rapports avec les Questions Médico-Judiciaires" (2 vols., *ib.* 1840; one of the first works to show the connection between crime and insanity); etc. He contributed many articles to the "Bibliothèque Médicale," the "Dictionnaire de Médecine," the "Dictionnaire des Sciences Médicales," and to other journals.

BIBLIOGRAPHY: *La Grande Encyclopédie*; Larousse, *Dict.*

S. N. D.

MARC-MOSSÉ, JOSEPH: French poet and author; born in Carpentras about 1780; died in Paris Feb. 21, 1825. His name appears to have been originally "Moses"; he was known also under the pseudonyms "L'Ami" and "Lejoyeux de Saint Acre." At the age of six Joseph wrote verses, and at seven knew by heart the finer scenes of Racine's "Athalie," and had versified passages from Fénelon's "Télémaque." In 1787 he was kidnaped by the Catholic clergy, baptized, and shut up in a monastery, whence for five years his friends, notwithstanding great efforts, found it impossible to extricate him. In 1792, however, after the outbreak of the Revolution, he was restored to his family, transformed into a little "abbé galant"—diseased in body, depraved in taste, corrupt in morals, and given over to laziness and sensuality. He presently went to Paris, where he showed himself a born courtier and frequenter of the society of the great, and where he was much sought after and admired. The irregularities of his life gradually brought on consumption, and, rather than endure the trials that lay before him, he committed suicide, in company with his English wife.

Marc-Mossé wrote: "Chronique de Paris" (1819); "Archives des Lettres, des Sciences et des Arts" (1820–21); "Eucharis, ou les Sensations de l'Amour" (1824); "La Caninéide" (epic-satiric poem); "Le Printemps" (idyl read by the author at the Paris Athénée in 1810); "Odes" (to the refugees from Spain, to war, to Napoleon's marriage); "La France Consolée," etc.; a critical examination of Lamennais' "Essai sur l'Indifférence en Matière de Religion" (in defense of the Israelites). He wrote also many amatory poems, studies, and treatises upon the art of pleasing, the art of preserving and increasing beauty, the art of making oneself loved by women, etc. (1808–11), and he left a large number of works in manuscript.

BIBLIOGRAPHY: *La Grande Encyclopédie*; Servi, *Israelit d'Europa*, pp. 197–199.

S. N. D.

MARCELLO, BENEDETTO: Italian musician; born at Venice 1686; died there 1739. He is particularly celebrated for his settings to the Psalms, fifty of which, under the title of "Estro Poetico-Armonico, Parafrasi Sopra li Salmi," were published at Venice between 1724 and 1727, in eight volumes. These compositions, in the cantata form for from one to four voices, with accompaniments for organ, violoncello, two violas, or other obligato strings, are noble and dignified; and their grandeur and beauty have earned them republication in numerous editions. Important for the study of Hebrew melody is the circumstance that for the themes of eleven of the earlier Psalms, Marcello utilized Jewish airs, taking six from the German and five from the Spanish tradition. Some historians of music, led by Forkel, have fallen into the error of assuming that Marcello's selected melodies reproduce the ancient Temple intonations for the Psalms. The list of Hebrew originals, given by Marcello himself, should, however, have guarded against this. The themes utilized by Marcello are: (1) to Ps. ix., a chant of the Spanish Jews for Ps. clxiv.; (2) to Ps. xii., a German chant for Ps. cxiv.; (3) to Ps. xiv., a "Hallel" air used in the Spanish ritual; (4) to Ps. xvi., a German melody for "Ma'oz Ẓur"; (5) to Ps. xvii., a Spanish chant for Ps. xcvi. and xcvii. (comp. De Sola and Aguilar, "Ancient Melodies," No. 13; Cohen and Davis, "Voice of Prayer and Praise," No. 16); (6) to Ps. xviii., a Spanish hymn by Solomon ben Mazzal Ṭob, No. 233 in Soncino's collection (Constantinople, 1545), for the Sabbath when a bridegroom attends the synagogue; (7) to Ps. xviii., a German melody for the hymn "Ha-Mabdil"; (8) to Ps. xix., a Spanish melody to Ibn Gabirol's hymn "Sha'ar Asher Nisgar" (Dukes, Ehrensäulen," p. 76; F. H. Cowen has employed the same melody for the "Dance of the Reapers" in his oratorio "Ruth," composed for the Worcester Musical Festival of 1887); (9) to Ps. xx., a German melody for the Sabbath evening hymn "Lekah Dodi"; (10) to Ps. xxi., a German melody for Ibn Gabirol's hymn "Shofet Kol ha-Areẓ" (comp. Baer, "Ba'al Tefillah," Frankfort-on-the-Main, No. 1426); (11) to Ps. xxiii., a German air, in folk-song style, for the "Ḳaddish" at the conclusion of the service on the eve of the New Year.

BIBLIOGRAPHY: Ed. Birnbaum, in *Der Jüdische Kantor*, 348, Bromberg, 1883; J. Singer, *Marcello Benedetto, ein Christlicher Psalmen-Componist des 17. Jahrhunderts*, Vienna, 1885.

D. F. L. C.

MARCUS AURELIUS ANTONINUS. See ANTONINUS.

MARCUS, BRENTGEN: First Jewish court singer in Germany; flourished toward the end of the seventeenth century. She lived with her father, Isaac Marcus, in the town of Wesel in Brandenburg, where, in 1690, Frederick of Brandenburg, afterward King Frederick I. of Prussia, heard her sing. Admiring her voice, and desiring to secure for her a musical education, he sent her and her father to Berlin. On July 16 of that year he wrote to the Prince of Anhalt and the council notifying them of his discovery and his wishes concerning Brentgen, and commended her to the attention of his wife, the princess Sophie Charlotte, who, however, was not at Berlin when the singer arrived. On July 25 the Prince of Anhalt wrote to the crown prince that he and others had heard and admired her unusually fine voice, and that provision would be made for her in accordance with his wishes.

BIBLIOGRAPHY: Isaak Münz, *Eine Jüdische Hofsängerin vor 200 Jahren*, in *Der Israelit*, xxv., No. 54, Supplement.

S. M. Co.

MARCUS, LEWI (LEWIN): German lawyer; born Oct. 15, 1809, at Rhena, Mecklenburg; died Oct. 7, 1881, at Manchester, England. On account of his indefatigable exertions in behalf of his coreligionists he became known as the "Gabriel Riesser of Mecklenburg." He was the first Jewish deputy of the Mecklenburg Diet, of which he became vice-president. He was made honorary citizen of the city of Schwerin, and for seventeen years was acting president of its municipal council (Kayserling, "Gedenkblätter," Leipsic, 1892), and president of the Jewish community of Schwerin.

S. I. War.

MARCUS, LOUIS. See Markus, Ludwig.

MARCUSE, ADOLF: German astronomer; born Nov. 17, 1860, in Magdeburg; educated at the universities of Strasburg and Berlin (Ph.D. 1884). Before his graduation he took part, as assistant, in the German expedition (1882) to South Carolina to observe the transit of Venus. In 1885 he studied at the Russian observatory at Pulkova, near St. Petersburg; in 1886 he went to Santiago, Chile, as astronomer-in-chief to the national observatory, remaining there for two years; while in South America he visited the Argentine Republic, Brazil, and Peru. On his return to Germany he received an appointment at the royal observatory in Berlin, where in behalf of the Centralbureau der International Erdmessung he was engaged, until 1891, in making continuous observations of the periodical changes of latitude. In April, 1891, he was commissioned by the same society to conduct the astronomical-geodetic expedition to the Hawaiian Islands; as a result of his observations the investigation of the changes of geographical latitude was considerably advanced.

After his return from the South Sea Islands and from a journey to Samoa, Australia, and Ceylon, he constructed a large photographic zenith-telescope in Berlin for the purpose of improving the photographic method of determining the altitude of the pole, and of rendering it available for scientific purposes. His lectures at the Royal University of Berlin are chiefly on the determination of geographical and nautical locations by means of astronomy, with practical demonstrations at the observatory. He improved also the photographic method of determining locality by constructing a photographic instrument for purposes of travel. Since 1903 he has been one of the editors of the "Geographisches Jahrbuch" (Gotha).

Marcuse is a member of the international astronomical and of the geographical societies of Berlin, of the Free Photographic Association, and of the German society for the study of aerial navigation. Of his writings the following may be mentioned: "Die Physische Beschaffenheit der Cometen" (Berlin, 1884); "Beobachtungsergebnisse der Königlichen Sternwarte" (part 4, *ib.* 1888); "Die Hawaiischen Inseln" (*ib.* 1894); "Die Atmosphärische Luft" (*ib.* 1896); "Die Photographische Bestimmungsweise der Polhöhe" (*ib.* 1897); "Die Fehler der Sinneswahrnehmungen bei Präcisionsmessungen" (*ib.* 1897); "Beiträge zur Nautischen Astronomie" (*ib.* 1899); "Anwendung Photographischer Methoden zur Geographischen Ortsbestimmung" (*ib.* 1899); "Die Neuere Entwickelung der Geographischen Ortsbestimmung" (*ib.* 1901); "Physik der Erde" (*ib.* 1902); "Bearbeitung der Berliner Polhöhen 1889–1890 im Auftrage des Centralvereins der Internationalen Erdmessung" (*ib.* 1902); "Handbuch der Geographischen Ortsbestimmung" (Brunswick, 1904).

S.

MARCZALI, HEINRICH: Hungarian historian; born at Marczali April 3, 1856; educated at Raab, Papa, Budapest, Berlin, and Paris. In 1878 he became professor at the gymnasium of his native town. He became a member of the Hungarian Academy in 1893, and two years later he was appointed professor of Hungarian history at the University of Budapest. In addition to numerous contributions to specialist journals, he has written the following books: "A Földrajzi Viszonyok Befolyása Magyarország Történetére" (Budapest, 1874); "A Magyar Történet Kútfői" (*ib.* 1880; German transl. "Quellen der Ungarischen Gesch." Berlin, 1882); "Regesták a Külföldi Levéltarakból" (Budapest, 1882); "Ujkor Története" (*ib.* 1883-86); "Magyarorszóg Története II. Jozsef Korában" (*ib.* 1882-88); "Maria Theresia" (*ib.* 1891); "A Legujabb Kor Története" (*ib.* 1892); "Az Arpádok és Dalmáczia" (French transl. under the title "Les Relations de la Dalmatie du XI. au XIII. Siècle," Paris, 1898); the first, second, and eighth volumes of the great history of Hungary published by Szilágyi.

BIBLIOGRAPHY: *Pallas Lex.*

S. L. V.

MARETZEK, MAX: Austrian impresario; born at Brünn, Moravia, June 28, 1821; died at Pleasant Plains, New York, May 14, 1897. He was a pupil of Seyfried in Vienna, and also attended the university in that city. Several years later he became connected with Italian opera in London. In 1848 he went to New York, where he began his career as leader of the orchestra at the Italian opera. From 1849 to 1878 he was organizer and manager of grand opera at the Astor Place Opera House, the Academy of Music, and Pike's Opera House (now the Grand Opera House). He occasionally made professional tours to other cities of the United

States, and to Mexico and Cuba. In 1849 he brought to America the celebrated singer Mlle. Bertucca, who afterward became his wife.

In Oct., 1854, Maretzek leased the Academy of Music, and in the following year had a brilliant season, his company including La Grange, Brignoli, Vestvali, and Badiali. "Semiramide" and "Il Trovatore" were produced for the first time in America during that season. "Rigoletto" was brought out in 1855, and "Traviata" and "William Tell" in 1856. In 1858 Maretzek engaged Piccolomini, and on Nov. 24 of that year he introduced Adelina Patti. He controlled the Academy from 1864 until it burned down in 1866. Among his singers of that period were Gazzaniga, Clara Louise Kellogg, Ronconi, Adelaide Phillips, Mazzolini, and Succi. On Nov. 25, 1863, he conducted the first performance of "Faust" in America, the cast including Kellogg, Sulzer, Mazzolini, and Biacchi.

Upon the restoration of the Academy of Music in 1867, opera was given there under his direction, with Kellogg, Mazzolini, Ronconi, Minnie Hauck, and Antonicci in the cast. In the following year he leased Pike's Opera House, but returned to the Academy in 1869, where he brought out the French tenor Lefranc. It was here also that Lucca made her first appearance under Maretzek's management in 1872.

The list of operas introduced by Maretzek to the New York public, in addition to those already mentioned, includes the following: "Forza del Destino"; "Ione"; "Carneval de Venice"; "Don Sebastiano"; "Saffo"; Peri's "Judith"; "Fra Diavolo"; "Le Prophète"; "L'Africaine"; "Aroldo"; "I Masnadier"; "Medea"; "Crispino e la Comare"; "Romeo et Juliette"; "L'Etoile du Nord"; "Luise Müller"; "I Due Foscari"; "Attila"; "Roberto"; "Anna Bolena"; "Policlito"; "Maria di Rohan"; "Linda di Chamounix"; "La Favorita"; "Don Pasquale"; "Macbeth"; "Marino Faliero"; "Belisario"; "Betty"; "I Lombardi." During the latter part of his life Maretzek enjoyed great popularity as a teacher of singing in New York. On Oct. 12, 1889, his golden jubilee was celebrated, Mme. Lehmann, Herr Kalisch, Signor Perotti, Mme. Fursch-Madi, Miss Anna Juch, Herr Alvary, Herr Fischer, the Daly and Palmer companies, as well as several other artists, participating. Maretzek composed the operas "Hamlet" (Brünn, 1843) and "Sleepy Hollow" (Academy of Music, New York, 1879). He composed also orchestral and chamber music, pianoforte pieces, songs, etc., and wrote "Crotchets and Quavers," New York, 1857.

BIBLIOGRAPHY: *The Herald*, New York, May 15, 1897; Baker, *Biographical Dictionary of Musicians*.

S. J. So.

MARGALIOT, MARGALIOTH. See MARGOLIOTH.

MARGALITA, AARON: Polish convert to Christianity; born 1663 at Zolkiev. He was a learned rabbi, and traveled as a maggid in Poland and Germany, preaching in the synagogues. In Holland he remained for seven years teaching rabbinics at Leyden. He thus became intimate with Trigland, through whose influence he was converted to the Reformed Church, as Margalita himself relates in his work "Oblatio Aaronis seu Tractatus de Passionibus Christi," Frankfort-on-the-Oder, 1706.

Disappointed in his hope of receiving support which would enable him to study for an academic career, he left Holland and went to Berlin. Here he denounced the Talmudic Haggadah as containing blasphemies against the Christian religion, whereupon King Frederick I. of Prussia ordered that the copies of a new edition of the Midrash Rabbah, which had been published at Frankfort-on-the-Oder in 1705, should be placed under seal until the Christian theological faculty of that city should render an opinion upon the work. This opinion being favorable, the order of suspension was revoked and the sale of the book was permitted.

Through the protection of King Frederick, Margalita was appointed professor of rabbinic Hebrew at the University of Frankfort-on-the-Oder. Here he remained but a short time, and it is said that in 1712 he became a convert to the Lutheran Church at Hamburg. Jöcher says in his lexicon that for having expressed a desire to return to Judaism, Margalita was imprisoned at Copenhagen, where he died a few years later.

BIBLIOGRAPHY: Bischoff, *Thalmud-Uebersetzungen*, p. 171, note 11, Frankfort-on-the-Main, 1899; A. Fürst, *Christen und Juden*, pp. 192-193, Strasburg, 1892; Grätz, *Gesch.* x. 313-314; Jost, *Gesch. des Judenthums und Seiner Sekten*, viii. 298.

D. S. MAN.

MARGARITA, ANTONIUS: Convert to Christianity in the first half of the sixteenth century; born about 1500 at Ratisbon (Regensburg), where his father, Jacob Margolioth, was rabbi; died at Vienna; baptized in 1522 at Wasserburg, Bavaria. He was teacher of Hebrew successively at Augsburg, Meissen, Zell, Leipsic, and (from 1537 till his death) at the University of Vienna.

He wrote "Der Gantz Jüdisch Glaub mit Sampt ainer Gründlichen und Wahrhafften Anzaygunge, Aller Satzungen, Ceremonien, Gebetten, Haymliche und Offentliche Gebreuch, Deren sich dye Juden Halten, Durch das Gantz Jar, Mit Schönen und Gegründten Argumenten Wyder Jren Glauben," Augsburg, 1530; Frankfort-on-the-Main, 1544, 1561, 1689; Leipsic, 1705, 1713. The author ridicules Jewish ceremonies, accuses the Jews of usury and of sentiments hostile to Christians and Christianity, and argues against their Messianic hopes. He denounces the 'ALENU prayer as anti-Christian in tendency. Declaiming against the usury and idleness of the Jews, he appeals to the magistrates to remedy the evil and to force the Jews to perform manual labor. He charges the Jewish physicians with ignorance and greediness, and asserts that, despite their minuteness in ritual, the Jews are neither pious nor charitable, and that, notwithstanding their apparent aversion to proselytism, they are eager to gain adherents to their faith.

This libelous book had a great influence upon Luther, who made use of it in writing his "Von den Juden und Ihren Lügen." It was praised by Hoornbeck, B. Lutberus, and Joseph Müller; but Wagenseil speaks of it less favorably. When it appeared, JOSEL OF ROSHEIM, being at that time at Augsburg, made complaint to Emperor Charles V., who appointed a committee to examine the denunciations contained in the book. The author was imprisoned and later expelled from Augsburg.

BIBLIOGRAPHY: De le Roi, *Die Evangelische Christenheit und die Juden*, i. 221, Leipsic, 1884; A. Fürst, *Christen und Juden*, p. 191, Strasburg, 1892; Fürst, *Bibl. Jud.* ii. 330; Geiger, *Gesch. der Juden in Deutschland*, ii. 324–325, v. 310–312; Grätz, *Gesch.* ix. 190–191, 303–304, 314, note; Steinschneider, *Cat. Bodl.* No. 6263; Wolf, *Bibl. Hebr.* i., No. 335; G. Wolf, *Studien zur Jubelfeier der Wiener Universität*, pp. 28–29, Vienna, 1865.

D. S. MAN.

controversies with the author of "Noda' bi-Yehudah," among others. The most renowned of this branch of the Margolioth family was **Ephraim Solomon** of Brody (d. there Aug. 5, 1828). Ephraim Solomon was not a rabbi, but his numerous works were accepted in the rabbinical world as authoritative. There are numerous scholars bearing the name of Margolioth whose relationship to the family, though probable, can not be determined.

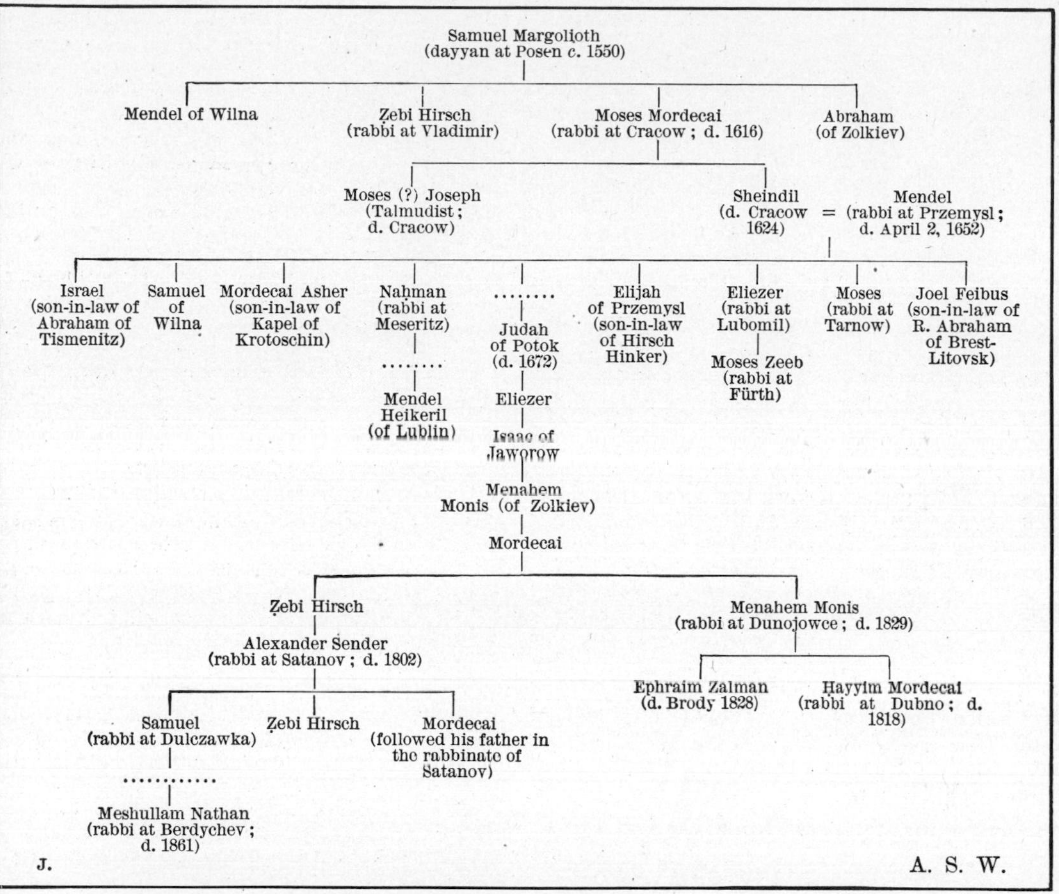

MARGOLIOTH PEDIGREE.

MARGOLIOTH; (מרגליות; the name occurs also as **Margaliot, Margolis, Margulies, Margolouth,** and in various other forms): Polish family of Talmudic scholars that traces its descent from Rashi, on the one side, and from the families of Shor and Samuel Edels on the other. The first Margolioth known was **Samuel,** dayyan at Posen about 1550; one of his sons, **Moses Mordecai,** was rabbi at Cracow. The daughter of R. Moses Mordecai married a relative, **Mendel Margolioth,** rabbi at Przemysl (d. April 2, 1652), and bore him eight sons, all of whom were distinguished Talmudists. It is not certain from which one of Mendel Margolioth's sons **Judah of Potok** (d. 1672) was descended. From **Mordecai b. Menahem Monis,** the great-great-grandson of Judah of Potok, descended a line of scholars. Mordecai himself was a cabalist and had Talmudic

BIBLIOGRAPHY: Walden, *Shem ha-Gedolim he-Ḥadash*, pp. 24–25, 53, 94–97, 111, Warsaw, 1888; *'Ir ha-Ẓedeḳ*, p. 42; Fuenn, *Keneset Yisrael*, p. 327; Buber, *Ḳiryah Nisgabah*, p. 8, Cracow, 1903.

J. A. S. W.

Abi Ezra Selig Margolioth: German Talmudist; flourished in the first half of the eighteenth century; born at Kalisch, where he was subsequently preacher. He preached also at Prague for a short time. He then went to HALBERSTADT, where he was prebendary of the "Klaus" founded by Berent Lehmann in 1703. According to Steinschneider, he then went with his wife to Palestine, Lehmann furnishing him with the necessary funds. Margolioth was the author of: "Kesef Nibḥar," commentary on the Pentateuch (Amsterdam, 1712); "Ḥibbure Liḳḳuṭim," novellæ and responsa (Venice, 1715).

Bibliography: Azulai, *Shem ha-Gedolim*, ii. 68; Steinschneider, *Cat. Bodl.* No. 2584; Auerbach, *Gesch. der Gemeinde Halberstadt*, p. 62.

D. A. Pe.

Abraham Elijah b. Nathan Margolioth: Rabbi of Nachod, Bohemia, where he was a "moreh ẓedeḳ" (acting rabbi) at the beginning of the eighteenth century. With Eliezer b. Pethahiah, ḥazzan of Worms, he wrote "Tefillah le-Kibbuẓ Galyotenu," published at Amsterdam in 1705 (Benjacob, "Oẓar ha-Sefarim," p. 661; Steinschneider, "Cat. Bodl." No. 3347; Wolf, "Bibl. Hebr." iii. 21).

D. P. Wi.

Alexander Margolioth: Polish rabbi; died in Satanov, Podolia, Jan. 3, 1802. He succeeded his father, Ẓebi Hirsch, as rabbi of Zbaraz, Galicia, and was there in 1774. Later he became rabbi of Satanov, where he remained until his death. He is spoken of very highly by contemporary rabbis like R. Ezekiel Landau and R. Aryeh Löb of Stry (author of "Keẓot ha-Ḥoshen"). A collection of his responsa from 1776 to 1791 was published more than half a century after his death, under the title "Teshubot ha-RAM." (Warsaw, 1859). He was the teacher of his nephew Ephraim Solomon Margolioth of Brody.

Bibliography: Eisenstadt-Wiener, *Da'at Ḳedoshim*, p. 73; Fuenn, *Keneset Yisrael*, p. 138.

H. R. P. Wi.

Asher Solomon Margolioth. See Judah Löb ben Asher Margolioth.

Ephraim Zalman Margolioth: Galician rabbi; born in Brody Dec. 19, 1762; died Aug. 24, 1828. He received his Talmudic education at different yeshibot, in which he distinguished himself for the acuteness of his intellect and for his astonishing memory. His correspondence with Ezekiel Landau and other leading Talmudists soon gained for him a high reputation. He established a banking-house which proved so successful that within a short time he became quite wealthy. In 1785 he published his responsa entitled "Bet Ḥadash ha-Ḥadashot"; and in the following year the rabbis of Brody elected him one of their number. Being of independent means, he opened in his house a yeshibah of which he was the head; and several of his pupils became eminent rabbis.

Margolioth was considered a high rabbinical authority. He published the following works: "Bet Efrayim" (2 vols., Lemberg, 1809–10), commentary on parts of the Yoreh De'ah; oration at the funeral of R. Meïr Kristianopoler (*ib.* 1815); "Bet Efrayim" (4 parts, *ib.* 1818), responsa on the four parts of the Shulḥan 'Aruk; "Yad Efrayim" (Dubno, 1820), commentaries on Shulḥan 'Aruk, Oraḥ Ḥayyim; "Sha'are Efrayim" (*ib.* 1820), on the rules pertaining to the reading of the Law; "Yad Efrayim" (Zolkiev, 1823), extensive commentaries on the names of men and of women to be employed in letters of divorce; "Shem Efrayim" (Berdychev, 1826), commentary on the Pentateuch; "Maṭṭeh Efrayim" (Zolkiev, 1834), on the ritual laws to be observed from the beginning of the month of Elul until after the Feast of Tabernacles, as well as on the regulations regarding the Ḳaddish of orphans; "Zera' Efrayim" (Lemberg, 1853), commentary on the Pesiḳta Rabbati. Many other works by him are still in manuscript.

Bibliography: Walden, *Shem ha-Gedolim he-Ḥadash*, p. 21, Warsaw, 1864; Kluger, *Toledot Shelomoh*, p. 33, Lemberg, 1888; S. J. Fuenn, *Keneset Yisrael*, p. 327, Warsaw, 1886; Zedner, *Cat. Hebr. Books Brit. Mus.* p. 511; *En Dinah* (oration delivered at Margolioth's funeral), Zolkiev, 1834.

S. S. B. Fr.

Ḥayyim Mordecai Margolioth: Polish rabbi; died at Dunajowce 1818; brother of Ephraim Solomon Margolioth. Ḥayyim Mordecai was at first rabbi at Brestitzki, and later became rabbi in Great Dubno, where he established a printing-office. He was among those who elected the three deputies sent to St. Petersburg to confer with the government upon Jewish affairs, and was the author of "Sha'are Teshubah," commentary to Shulḥan 'Aruk, Oraḥ Ḥayyim (Dubno, 1820); it contains extracts from other works and appears in most editions of the Shulḥan 'Aruk.

Bibliography: *'Ir Dubno we-Rabbaneha*, p. 26, Cracow, 1902; Steinschneider, *Cat. Bodl.* No. 4698; Fürst, *Bibl. Jud.* ii. 327.

Isaac ben Jacob Margolioth: Rabbi of Prague, where he died April 17, 1525; son of Jacob Margolioth, rabbi of Nuremberg. He is mentioned in connection with the Mintz-Margolioth affair, in which he sided with his father. He wrote the preface to his father's "Seder Giṭṭin wa-Ḥaliẓah."

Bibliography: Eisenstadt-Wiener, *Da'at Ḳedoshim*, pp. 17, 68, St. Petersburg, 1897–98; S. Rapoport, *Gal 'Ed*, p. 30, Prague, 1856.

E. C. A. S. W.

Jacob Margolioth of Nuremberg: German rabbi of the fifteenth century; died at an advanced age about 1492. His contemporaries Joseph Colon (Responsa, No. 26) and Judah Minz (Responsa, No. 13) speak of him as one of the greatest rabbis of his time, which caused Grätz ("Gesch." viii. 268) to hold that in all probability he presided over the meeting of German rabbis held in Nuremberg in 1474. Emperor Frederick III. ordered, in 1487, the two brothers Abraham and Solomon of Ulm to submit their disputes to Jacob Margolioth, "Hochmeister" of Nuremberg (see Wiener, "Regesten zur Gesch. der Juden in Deutschland," No. 126). In the quarrel between Moses Capsali and Joseph Colon, Margolioth sided with the former. Later, according to Grätz ("Gesch." viii. 58), he opposed Jacob Pollack, who is said to have been his pupil; but the above-quoted responsum of Judah Minz proves this to be only a surmise.

Zunz ("Z. G." p. 106), and after him Grätz and Fuenn, confounded this Jacob Margolioth with a younger contemporary at Ratisbon, of the same name, who corresponded with Reuchlin. It is probable that Jacob Margolioth "of Nuremberg" is identical with R. Jacob Margolioth "of Worms," and perhaps with R. Jacob Margolioth "of Lucca" (?) and Jacob Marmonda Margolioth (Moses Minz, Responsa, Nos. 73, 114). He is commonly accepted as the author of "Seder Giṭṭin wa-Ḥaliẓah," and, consequently, as the father of Isaac b. Jacob Margolioth of Prague (d. 1525), the editor of that work, which appeared together with the "Ṭib Giṭṭin" of Ephraim Zalman Margolioth (Zolkiev, 1823).

Bibliography: Eisenstadt-Wiener, *Da'at Ḳedoshim*, Appendix, pp. 67–68, 74, St. Petersburg, 1897–98; Fuenn, *Keneset Yisrael*, pp. 555–556, Warsaw, 1886; idem, *Ḳiryah Ne'emanah*, p. 328, Wilna, 1860; Wiener, in *Monatsschrift*, 1868, xvii. 345 *et seq.*

Jacob Margolioth of Ratisbon: German rabbi and Hebraist; flourished about 1500. He is known chiefly by a Hebrew letter addressed to Reuchlin, which is preserved in "Epistolæ Clarorum Virorum ad Reuchlinum" (see text in Fuenn, "Keneset Yisrael," pp. 555–556, where he is confounded with Jacob Margolioth, rabbi of Nuremberg). His son, the apostate Antonius MARGARITA, relates the great services which Jacob rendered his townsmen by interceding in their behalf with Siegmund von Rohrbach, who was imperial governor at Ratisbon from 1499 to 1512 (quoted by Wiener from Margarita's "Der Gantz Jüdisch Glaub," p. 138, Leipsic (1705). According to the same authority this Jacob Margolioth had another son, who was a musician in Prague; this led Wiener to believe that this musician may be identical with R. Isaac b. Jacob Margolioth of Prague (d. 1525), who edited his father's "Seder Giṭṭin wa-Ḥaliẓah" (see MARGOLIOTH, JACOB, OF NUREMBERG); but the supposition seems improbable.

BIBLIOGRAPHY: Wiener, in *Monatsschrift*, 1868, xvii. 345 *et seq.* (where all other sources are quoted and discussed).

D. P. WI.

Jacob Koppel b. Ẓebi Margolioth: Polish preacher and moralist of the seventeenth century; died 1673 (?). He came from Vladimir, Volhynia, where he was an eye-witness of the massacres of 1648–49, from which he escaped to Germany. He was the author of "Mar'ot Ya'aḳob," tables of ethical rules (Venice, 1662); "Mizbaḥ Ya'aḳob," a sermon on penitence and some haggadic novellæ (*ib.* 1662); and "Ḳol Ya'aḳob," on the Pentateuch and the Talmud, to which is appended an elegy on the victims of the above-mentioned massacres (Amsterdam, 1708).

BIBLIOGRAPHY: Fuenn, *Keneset Yisrael*, p. 556; Fürst, *Bibl. Jud.* ii. 328; Lewinstein, in *Dor Dor we-Dorshaw*, p. 109, Warsaw, 1899.

H. R. P. WI.

Judah Löb ben Asher Margolioth: Grandson of R. Mordecai Jaffe; died at Frankfort-on-the-Oder June 14, 1811. He was successively rabbi at Busnow, Szebrszyn, Polotsk, Lesla, and Frankfort-on-the-Oder, and wrote the following works: "Ḳorban Reshit," responsa and discussions on Rosh ha-Shanah (Frankfort-on-the-Oder, 1778); "Peri Tebu'ah," responsa (parts i. and ii., Novidvor, 1796; parts iii. and iv. are still in manuscript); "Tal Orot," treatises on the essence of the soul, on immortality, etc. (Frankfort-on-the-Oder, 1751); "Or 'Olam," treatises on natural philosophy, to which is appended Saadia Gaon's commentary on Canticles (*ib.* 1777); "Bet Middot," on ethics, in prose and verse (Dyhernfurth, 1778); "'Aẓe 'Eden," homilies on belief, philosophy, pride, and humility, with a criticism of Mendelssohn's "Jerusalem" (*ib.* 1802); "Amirah Ne'imah," on the Haggadah and the Pentateuch (in manuscript); "Iggeret ha-Meliẓah," on style (Novidvor, 1794); "Sefer Ṭob we-Yafeh," collection of poems on dogmatic, grammatical, and liturgical subjects (Frankfort-on-the-Oder, 1770). He was probably the first Judæo-Polish author to write on natural philosophy.

BIBLIOGRAPHY: *Ha-Zeman*, i. 97; Fuenn, *Keneset Yisrael*, p. 413, Warsaw, 1886; Steinschneider, *Cat. Bodl.* No. 5740; Fürst, *Bibl. Jud.* ii. 328; Zeitlin, *Bibl. Hebr.* p. 229.

E. C. A. S. W.

Meïr b. Ẓebi Hirsch Margolioth: Polish rabbi and author; born probably at Horodenka, Galicia; died at an advanced age at Ostrog, Volhynia, April 24, 1790. He was rabbi of the district of Lemberg for more than forty years (*c.* 1742–82), at the time when Lemberg had two rabbis, one for the city proper and one for the surrounding district. In 1782 he seems to have gone to Ostrog, where he remained until his death. Margolioth was a pupil of R. Israel Ba'al Shem Ṭob (BEShT), the reputed founder of Ḥasidism, and was probably the greatest Talmudical authority of the time to confess to such discipleship. He was the author of "Meïr Netibim," responsa and novellæ (Polnoi, 1791), "Sod Yakin u-Bo'az," on the Cabala (*ib.*), and "Derek ha-Ṭob weha-Yashar," on the Shulḥan 'Aruk (Polnoi and Shklov, 1799).

Margolioth left four sons: **Joseph Naḥman,** rabbi of Polnoi and father of R. Ḥayyim of Ostrog; **Bezaleel,** rabbi of Zwahil and successor to his father as rabbi of Ostrog; Saul, rabbi successively of Komorn, Zbaraz, and Lublin; and **Naphtali Mordecai.** Margolioth's daughter married Naphtali Herz ha-Kohen, rabbi of Scharigrod. Margolioth had also an older brother, **Isaac Dob Bär** (rabbi of Jazlowicz and the district of Podolia; author of "Be'er Yiẓḥaḳ"), who is mentioned in his works. Isaac Dob Bär was one of the three rabbis (the other two being R. Israel Ba'al Shem and R. Ḥayyim Cohen Rapoport of Lemberg) who represented the Talmudist position in the discussion with the Frankists under the auspices of Bishop Mikulski in 1759. Margolioth's mother was a sister of R. Aryeh Lebush b. Mordecai Auerbach of Stanislau (d. 1772).

BIBLIOGRAPHY: Buber, *Anshe Shem*, pp. 137–140, 202, Cracow, 1895; Lazar ha-Kohen, *Ḳin'at Soferim*, pp. 162–163, Lemberg, 1892; Walden, *Shem ha-Gedolim he-Ḥadash*, p. 87.

D. P. WI.

Moses b. Judah Löb Margolioth: Rabbi at Semnitz, Hungary, in the nineteenth century; son of Judah Löb Margolioth. He was the author of "Ḥaḳirat ha-Gemul," treatises on retribution and punishment, with an appendix under the title "Keter Malkut," a poem by W. Buchner (Budapest, 1829; Steinschneider, "Cat. Bodl." No. 6518).

Moses Mordecai ben Samuel Margolioth: Talmudist and cabalist; born probably at Posen, where his father was rabbi, about 1540; died at Cracow Nov. 21, 1616. On the death of Joseph Katz (1591) Moses Mordecai Margolioth became head of the yeshibah at Cracow, which office he retained over twenty years. He wrote: "Ḥasde Adonai," on the thirteen attributes of God (Cracow, 1589); "Seliḥah 'al ha-Ḳedoshim," prayer for the martyrs of 1596, published in an edition of seliḥot (Dyhernfurth, 1702); "Zohar Ḥadash 'im Midrash ha-Ne'lam" (Cracow, 1603).

BIBLIOGRAPHY: Zunz, *'Ir ha-Ẓedeḳ*, p. 42, Lemberg, 1874; Steinschneider, *Cat. Bodl.* No. 6517; Fürst, *Bibl. Jud.* ii. 330.

Naphtali Margolioth (Margaritha): Scholar and author; born at Vienna 1562. He embraced Christianity in 1603, taking the name of **Julius Conrad Otto,** and later became professor of Hebrew at Altorf. Subsequently he returned to Judaism. He wrote: "Usus Ebreæ Linguæ" (Nuremberg, 1604); "Grammatica Hebræa" (*ib.* 1605);

"Lexicon Radicale," a dictionary of rabbinical and Talmudic words (*ib.* 1607); "Gale Razaya," a work full of false Talmudic citations and of misinterpretations of Talmudic sayings regarding the Messianic idea and the doctrine of the Trinity (*ib.* 1605).

BIBLIOGRAPHY: Wolf, *Bibl. Hebr.* i. 480, iii. 365, iv. 845; De le Roi, *Evangelische Christenheit*, i. 133; Steinschneider, *Cat. Bodl.* No. 6702; Fürst, *Bibl. Jud.* ii. 330.
E. C. A. S. W.

Saul b. Meïr Margolioth: Polish rabbi; died in Lublin Dec. 13, 1800 (?); son of R. Meïr of Ostrog and Lemberg (author of "Meïr Netibim") and pupil of R. Israel Ba'al Shem-Ṭob. He was rabbi successively of Zbaraz, Galicia, and of Komorn, before he went to Lublin, where he remained until his death.

Saul is often mentioned in the records of the community of Lublin as the author of useful communal measures. He left no works, but is mentioned in the above-cited work of his father's. His son **Ẓebi Hirsch,** who married a daughter of R. Löb of Amsterdam, succeeded Saul b. Meïr as rabbi in the city of Lublin.

BIBLIOGRAPHY: Buber, *Anshe Shem*, p. 202, Cracow, 1895; Nissenbaum, *Le-Ḳorot ha-Yehudim be-Lublin*, pp. 91-94, Lublin, 1899; Lewinstein, in *Dor Dor we-Dorshaw*, p. 124, Warsaw, 1899.
H. R. P. Wi.

MARGOLIS, ISAAC BEN ELIAH: Russo-Polish rabbi and author; born in Kalvariya, government of Suwalki, Russian Poland, 1842; died in New York Aug. 1, 1887; son of the rabbi of Wizhajny, and a descendant of Yom-Ṭob Lipmann Heller of Prague.

His youth was devoted to the study of the Talmud; and in 1862 he settled in Meretz, government of Wilna, where later on he embarked in business. The zealots of that city and business reverses rendered his life there unpleasant; and in consequence he removed to Kovno, where he soon found employment as tutor in the house of Ezekiel Jaffe. Later he became rabbi of Druskeniki, government of Grodno. In 1884 he emigrated to the United States and became rabbi of the Congregation Anshe-Kalvariya, New York.

Margolis was the author of "Ma'oz ha-Talmud" (Warsaw, 1868), an apologetic work in defense of the Talmud and the Shulḥan 'Aruk against certain critics; "Ma'oz ha-Yam" (Wilna, 1870), a reply to the attacks of M. L. Lilienblum in "Megillah 'Afah"; and "Sippure Yeshurun" (Berlin, 1876), a collection of Talmudic and Midrashic legends, anecdotes, etc., written in an elegant Hebrew style. He also contributed largely to the Hebrew periodicals "Ha-Maggid," "Ha-Ẓefirah," and "Ha-Meliẓ."

BIBLIOGRAPHY: H. Herzmann, in *Ha-Asif*, iv.; M. Caplan, in *Ha-Ẓefirah*, No. 168; *American Hebrew*, Aug. 22, 1887, p. 8.
H. R. I. S. B.

MARGOLIS, MAX LEOPOLD: American philologist; born at Meretz, government of Wilna, Russia, Oct. 15, 1866; son of Isaac Margolis; educated at the elementary school of his native town, the Leibnitz gymnasium, Berlin, and Columbia University, New York city (Ph.D. 1891). In 1891 he was appointed to a fellowship in Semitic languages at Columbia University, and from 1892 to 1897 he was instructor, and later assistant professor, of Hebrew and Biblical exegesis at the Hebrew Union Colle[ge] of Cincinnati. In 1897 he became assistant profess[or] of Semitic languages in the University of Californi[a]; in 1898, associate professor; and since 1902 he h[as] been acting head of the Semitic department.

Of Margolis' works may be mentioned: "T[he] Columbia College MS. of Megillah," New Yor[k], 1892; "Notes on Semitic Grammar," parts i.-iii., [in] "Hebraica" ("American Journal of Semitic La[n]guages and Literatures"), 1894, 1896, 1902; "T[he] Theology of the Old Prayer-Book," in "Year Book [of] the Central Conference of American Rabbis," 189[.]; "The Theological Aspect of Reformed Judaism," Baltimore, 1904.

BIBLIOGRAPHY: *The American Israelite*, 1902.
A. F. T. H.

MARGOLIUT, MARGULIES, MARGU[-]LIOTH. See MARGOLIOTH.

MARGOLIUTH, MOSES: Convert to Chri[s]tianity; born in Suwalki, Poland, Dec. 3, 1820; di[ed] in London Feb. 25, 1881. He went to Liverpo[ol], England, in 1837, where he met a convert nam[ed] Lazarus, and the Rev. H. S. Joseph; the latter ba[p]tized Margoliuth in April, 1838. He entered Tri[n]ity College, Dublin, Jan., 1840; became curate of S[t.] Augustine, Liverpool, June 30, 1844; and had ma[ny] ecclesiastical appointments, ultimately becomi[ng] vicar of Little Linford, Buckinghamshire (1877-8[1]). He took the degree of Ph.D. at Erlangen in 18[5?]. In 1847 he started a Hebrew-Christian month[ly] magazine entitled "The Star of Jacob."

Margoliuth wrote the following works, all pu[b]lished in London: "Modern Judaism" (1843); "T[he] History of the Jews of Great Britain" (1857; a wo[rk] of some merit in the last two volumes); "A Pilgri[m]age to the Land of My Fathers" (1858); "The C[u]rates of Riverdale" (1860); "The Spirit of Prophec[y]" (1864); "The Poetry of the Hebrew Pentateuc[h]" (1871). Margoliuth was one of the revisers of t[he] English version of the Old Testament. He wr[ote] also a considerable number of minor works.

BIBLIOGRAPHY: *Jewish World*, London, March 4, 1881; *Jo[ur]nal of British Archæological Association*, 1881; M. Mar[go]liuth, *Some Triumphs and Trophies of the World* (18[8?]); *Autobiography* prefixed to *Modern Judaism*.
J. G. L.

MARGULIES, SAMUEL HIRSCH: Rab[bi]; born at Brzezan, Galicia, Oct. 9, 1858; a descenda[nt] of Rabbi Ephraim Zalman Margolioth; educated [at] the theological seminary at Breslau. He was fr[om] 1885 to 1887 rabbi of the Congregation Newe Sh[a]lom in Hamburg; till 1890, of the congregation [of] Weilburg, Hesse-Nassau; and since 1890 he has be[en] chief rabbi of Florence. In 1899 he was appoint[ed] principal of the Collegio Rabbinico Italiano, whi[ch] was later transferred from Rome to Florence.

Margulies has published several essays in B[er]liner's "Magazin" and in the "Monatsschrift," a[nd] is the author of: "Saadja Alfajûmi's Arabisc[he] Psalmen-Uebersetzung," Breslau, 1884; "Zw[ei] Pesach-Predigten," Frankfort-on-the-Main, 18[.]; "Dichter und Patriot," Treves, 1896. He is a[lso] (1904) editor of the "Rivista Israelitica."
S. F. T. H

MARḤAB IBN AL-ḤARITH: Jew[ish] Arabian warrior and poet; killed during Moha[mmed's] med's invasion of Khaibar about 628. Marḥab, who was of Himyarite descent, distinguished himself by his bravery in defending one of the forts of Khaibar. He is represented in the "Ta'rikh al-Hamis" (quoted by Caussin de Perceval) as a man of uncommon strength and audacity, wearing two cuirasses, a double turban and a helmet, and a sword at each side, and brandishing a three-pointed lance. According to the custom of Arab warriors, Marḥab sent a poem challenging any of Mohammed's heroes to single combat. Ali, Mohammed's cousin and third successor, answered the challenge, and Marḥab was killed. According to Ibn Hisham, Mohammed's biographer, it was Mohammed ibn Maslamah, who, wishing to avenge his brother, killed on the previous day, offered to fight Marḥab. Ibn Hisham further says that the two combatants kept a tree between them as a defense, and that the branches of the tree immediately over their heads were soon cut away. Marḥab accidentally dropping his sword, Mohammed seized the opportunity to deal him a fatal blow.

Bibliography: Caussin de Perceval, *Essai sur l'Histoire des Arabes*, iii. 195 *et seq.*; Grätz, *Gesch.* 3d ed., v. 105-106; Ibn Hisham, *Kitab Sirat Rasul Allah*, pp. 760-761, ed. Wüstenfeld, Göttingen, 1858.

J. M. Sel.

MARḤESHWAN. See Ḥeshwan.

MARI BEN DIMI: Second gaon of Pumbedita. When the Jewish scholars were compelled to leave the Babylonian academies, Mari, with others, went to Firuz-Shabur and there established a new academy which became associated with his name. After the death of the gaon Ḥanan of Isḳiya, in 609, he was elected successor in the gaonate. Two halakic decisions of his have been preserved—one, quoted by Judah Gaon, concerning two unknown plants mentioned in the Talmud (Chaim M. Horowitz, "Halachische Schriften der Geonim," ii. 56, Frankfort-on-the-Main, 1851; "Teshubot ha-Geonim," p. 45, ed. Lyck, 1864), and the other concerning the marriage of a "mamzer" ("Halakot Gedolot," ed. Vienna, p. 22a).

Bibliography: Grätz, *Gesch.* v. 12-13; Müller, *Einleitung in die Responsen der Babylonischen Geonen*, p. 62; Weiss, *Dor*, iv. 6; *Letter of Sherira Gaon*, in Neubauer, *M. J. C.* i. 35, ii. 187.

E. C. M. Sc.

MARIA THERESA. See Austria.

MARIAMNE: **1.** Wife of Herod the Great; the first of this name. She was the daughter of the Hasmonean Alexander, a son of Aristobulus II., who was conquered and put to flight by Herod's father, Antipater. Her mother was Alexandra, daughter of the reigning prince Hyrcanus II. When Herod, at that time tetrarch, entered Jerusalem in triumph in 42 B.C., Alexandra sought to bring about the marriage of her daughter to him, hoping thus to avoid the ruin of her house (Josephus, "Ant." xiv. 12, § 1; *idem*, "B. J." i. 12, § 3). The war, however, left Herod no leisure; and not until five years after his betrothal to Mariamne, and three years after he had become nominal king of Judea, did he leave the siege of Jerusalem, in 37 B.C., and celebrate his marriage in Samaria ("Ant." xiv. 15, § 14; "B. J." i. 17, § 8). Mariamne bore him three sons, Alexander, Aristobulus, and one who died young, and two daughters, Salampsio and Cypros.

The marriage proved an unhappy one. The king, indeed, loved the beautiful woman passionately; but the queen could not forget that Herod had been the murderer of all her family and that he had succeeded to the throne really at the cost of her paternal house. She displayed a natural pride toward this parvenu which was especially felt by Herod's mother and by his sister Salome, who wrought so much evil in the course of her life.

The queen ruled the king completely. This was made manifest when Alexandra insisted that her son, Mariamne's brother, should be made high priest. On the advice of Dellius, the friend of Antony—who wished to give the latter's passion another direction—she sent pictures of her two beautiful children to the Egyptian queen, Cleopatra. Antony had, in fact, designs on the youthful Aristobulus; and since Mariamne also asked the favor of the king, he found himself obliged to make the youth high priest (35 B.C.; "Ant." xv. 2, § 6; "B. J." i. 22, § 3), although, in reality, only to kill him on a suitable occasion. When, later, Herod was obliged to justify before Antony at Laodicea the killing of Aristobulus, he placed Mariamne under the protection of Joseph, his brother-in-law, commanding him to kill her in case he (Herod) should not return alive. As Joseph had occasion to associate a good deal with Mariamne in connection with governmental affairs, he good-naturedly told her of the boundless love the king felt for her and of the secret instructions which Herod had given him. A false report of Herod's death being circulated, Mariamne sought refuge with the Roman legions. Herod, however, was dismissed with the favor of Antony. On his return Salome accused Mariamne of adultery with Joseph. Herod at first would not believe the charge; but it chanced that the queen reproached him for the secret commission he had entrusted to Joseph, and this convinced Herod of the criminality of Joseph and Mariamne. In his anger he caused Joseph to be put to death immediately, and he would have similarly disposed of Mariamne had not his love for her been greater than his anger. He, however, threw Alexandra into prison (34 B.C.) as the instigator of the scandal ("Ant." xv. 3, §§ 5-9; "B. J." i. 22, §§ 4-5).

Left in Charge of Joseph.

In the spring of the year 30, Herod visited Augustus in Rhodes. He left Mariamne and her mother under the protection of a certain Joseph and of the Iturean Sohemus. Again he commanded that his wife should be killed in the event of his death. The king had hoped to find love on his return; instead he found himself hated and avoided. The king's mother and sister found him ready to listen to their slanders. Salome told him that Mariamne sought to poison him. Thereupon the king questioned Mariamne's favorite eunuch, who said he knew nothing of the poison, but that the queen was offended because of what Sohemus had told her in regard to his secret instructions. Sohemus met the same fate as had Herod's brother-

Falsely Accused by Salome.

in-law, and Herod caused Mariamne to be accused before a tribunal composed of his friends, which pronounced sentence of death. The king and some of the judges did not wish to hasten the execution, desiring merely to put Mariamne in prison; but Salome represented that the people might raise a disturbance and seek to release Mariamne, and the latter was consequently led to death. During the entire route to the place of execution her own mother, Alexandra, desiring to rehabilitate herself in Herod's eyes, reviled her, accusing her of adultery and of ingratitude toward Herod. Mariamne answered not a word, and died calm and composed ("Ant." xv. 6, § 5; 7, § 6), being about twenty-eight years of age (29 B.C.).

The fact that Mariamne was twice accused under similar circumstances of adultery with the regent, makes it probable that Josephus' account contains some inaccuracies, the more so as the second account is wholly lacking in "B. J." (Destinon, "Di Quellen des Josephus," p. 113). The second account, however, can not be a simple repetition on the part of Josephus of the first, since Josephus himself, in relating the second incident, refers to the first ("Ant." xv. 7, § 1). It is remarkable that Josephus mentions Joseph the second time without any further particulars (*ib.* 6, § 5), which looks, it is true, as though he had before him two parallel accounts which he tried to combine in this way. According to "B. J.," Mariamne was put to death in the first case—that is, in the year 34. But this is impossible, since she could not have borne five children between the years 37 and 34. Indeed on closer scrutiny the two incidents do not appear at all identical, since in the second case it is not the regent Phreroras with whom Mariamne is associated, but Sohemus, who was of comparatively low rank. Hence the two incidents are probably historical, and the omission of the second account in "B. J." is due to the fact that Josephus, as usual, has condensed his narration in that work. The historian Nicholas of Damascus believed in Mariamne's guilt ("Ant." xvi. 7, § 1).

Discrepancy in the Sources.

There is a Talmudic legend concerning the marriage and death of Mariamne, although her name is not mentioned. It is to the effect that when the whole house of the Hasmoneans had been rooted out, she threw herself from the roof and was killed (B. B. 3b). Out of love for her, Herod is said to have kept her body preserved in honey for seven years (*ib.*; S. Geiger, in "Oẓar Neḥmad," iii. 1). In the Talmud this sort of mental derangement is called a "deed of Herod" (Sanh. 66b). Josephus relates also that after her death Herod tried in hunting and banqueting to forget his loss, but that even his strong nature succumbed and he fell ill in Samaria, where he had made Mariamne his wife ("Ant." xv. 7, § 7). The Mariamne tower in Jerusalem, built by Herod, was without doubt named after her; it was called also "Queen" (Βασιλίς; "B. J." ii. 17, § 8; v. 4, § 3).

Talmudic Legends.

Josephus writes the name Μαριάμη, adding the inflectional ending to Μαριάμ (= מרים), the Septuagint form of the name. In some editions of Josephus Μαριάμμη stood with double "μ"; this was dissimilated to "mn" in the Middle Ages, and the name has so remained (S. Pape-Benseler, "Wörterbuch der Griechischen Eigennamen," 3d ed. 1870, *s.v.*).

BIBLIOGRAPHY: Grätz, *Gesch.* 4th ed., iii. 187, 200, 216; Derenbourg, *Hist.* p. 151; Schürer, *Gesch.* 3d ed., i. 358-386; Wellhausen, *I. J. G.* 4th ed., pp. 325, 328.

2. Wife of Herod the Great; the second of this name. She was held to be very beautiful; and Herod, on first seeing her, was seized with an ardent passion for her. Since he did not wish to obtain possession of her by force, he thought it best to marry her. He advanced her father, Simon the son of Boethus (a man of humble birth, originally from Alexandria, but at that time living in Jerusalem), to the position of high priest (25 B.C.) a few years after the execution of the first Mariamne (Josephus, "Ant." xviii. 5, § 4; comp. *ib.* xvii. 1, § 2; *idem*, "B. J." i. 28, § 4).

Mariamne bore Herod one son, also called Herod ("Ant." xvii. 1, § 2), who married Herodias (*ib.* xviii. 5, § 4), and who was in fact the destined heir to the throne ("B. J." i. 29, § 2; comp. *ib.* 30, § 3). Mariamne knew of Herod's intention in regard to her son (*ib.* 30, § 7). Josephus always writes Μαριάμη or Μαριάμμη, as he does also in the case of other persons of the same name.

BIBLIOGRAPHY: Grätz, *Gesch.* 4th ed., iii. 223; Schürer, *Gesch.* 3d ed., i. 407.

G. S. KR.

MARIAMPOL (Polish, **Marjampol**; called formerly **Staripole**): Town situated in the government of Suwalki, Russian Poland. The Jewish community there, like the town itself, is of comparatively recent date. At first the community was dependent, in communal affairs, upon the neighboring town of Kalvariya. Its first rabbi, Ḥayyim Shershaver, was elected in 1780, though the community was too poor to build a synagogue; and the rabbi then visited a number of towns in order to collect money for that purpose. In the Polish revolution of 1831 a Polish regiment passed through Mariampol and carried away four of the Jewish elders who were faithful to the Russians, and left them, bound in the forest. In the same year, on the occasion of an encounter between the Russians and the Poles at Mariampol, the latter locked all the Jews in the synagogue, with the result that only one Jew was killed. Mariampol has (1897) a total population of 6,298, of which over two thousand are Jews.

BIBLIOGRAPHY: *Yalḳuṭ Ma'arabi*, i. 116.

H. R. A. S. W.

MARIK, SOLOMON: Spanish surgeon, of whose life no details are known. He wrote in Spanish in Hebrew script a work entitled "Libro de la Cirogia," of which a fragment exists in a volume of miscellanea in the royal library at Munich.

David Marich or **Marik,** a physician and merchant, and **Abraham Marich,** both Spanish exiles, together with nineteen others, received permission from Duke Alfonso of Este on Feb. 1, 1493, to settle with their families at Ferrara ("R. E. J." xv. 120).

BIBLIOGRAPHY: Steinschneider, *Cat. Munich*, codex 291, 3; Kayserling, *Bibl. Esp.-Port.-Jud.* p. 65.

G. M. K.

MARINI, SOLOMON B. ISAAC: Italian rabbi of the seventeenth century; died in 1670. He was the only rabbi at Padua who survived the plague of 1631, which decimated the community. His wisdom and his eloquence contributed much to the restoration of order. He wrote a commentary to Isaiah entitled "Tiḳḳun 'Olam" (Verona, 1652). He was renowned as a scholar, teacher, and pastor, and among his pupils was the physician and rabbi Isaac Ḥayyim Cantarini. His brother, **Shabbethai b. Isaac Marini** (d. 1685), was a physician.

BIBLIOGRAPHY: Nepi-Ghirondi, *Toledot Gedole Yisrael*, pp. 336, 338 *et seq.*

D. I. E.

MARIX, ADOLPH: American naval commander; born Apr. 24, 1848, in Saxony. He went to America while still a boy, and in 1864 entered the United States Naval Academy at Annapolis, Md., graduating in 1868. In 1869 he was promoted to the rank of ensign, and in the following year was assigned to special duty on the U. S. S. "Congress." He was promoted master in 1870, served on the "Canandaigua" with the North Atlantic squadron during 1871–72, was commissioned lieutenant in 1872, and served thereafter on various ships in the North Atlantic and Asiatic stations until 1879, when he was assigned to service in the Hydrographic Office. In 1880 he was ordered to the training-ship "Minnesota," from which, in 1882, he was transferred to the battle-ship "Brooklyn," then with the South Atlantic squadron. From 1883 to 1886 he served again on the Asiatic station, after which he was assigned to special service in the judge-advocate-general's office. In connection with his duties in this department he was sent to Australia (1888), and on his return (1889) was ordered to the training-ship "Jamestown," from which he (1892) was transferred to the Hydrographic Office in New York. In 1893 he was promoted lieutenant-commander and assigned to the receiving-ship "Minnesota," until in 1895 he was transferred to the ill-fated battle-ship "Maine," on which he served until January, 1898, when he took command of the U. S. S. "Scorpion." He served as recorder of the Maine court of inquiry. In March, 1899, he was promoted to the rank of commander.

Commander Marix was by act of Congress advanced two numbers for "eminent and conspicuous conduct in battle in two engagements at Manzanillo July 1 and July 18, 1898," during the Spanish-American war.

BIBLIOGRAPHY: Hamersly, *Records of Living Officers of the U. S. Navy*, New York, 1898; *List of Officers of the U. S. Navy and of the Marine Corps 1775–1900*, pp. 351, 718.

E. C. F. C.

MARK. See SEAL; SIGNATURE.

MARK. See NEW TESTAMENT.

MARKENS, ISAAC: American writer; born in New York city Oct. 9, 1846; son of Elias Markens, a linguist and Orientalist. Isaac Markens was educated in the public schools of his native city. He became a merchant, and afterward private secretary to Railway Commissioner Albert Fink. Subsequently he entered the journalistic field, and wrote for the New York "Commercial Advertiser" and the "Mail and Express." In 1888 he published "The Hebrews in America," a series of historical and biographical sketches of value as being the first of their kind on American Jewish history.

Markens was for several years secretary to the board of arbitration of the Joint Executive Committee of Eastern and Western Railways.

A.

MARKS, B. S.: English artist; born in 1827 at Cardiff, where he received his art education and followed the profession of portrait-painter until his removal to London in 1867. As a native of Wales he became Royal Cambrian Academician. During the more than thirty years of his professional career in London he has executed commissions for many distinguished sitters, including the Prince of Wales, Lord Rothschild, Chief Rabbi N. M. Adler, the late Lord Shaftesbury, Lord Aberdare, and Field-Marshal Sir John Burgoyne. Marks is an active communal worker in connection with Jewish schools and institutions. He was a member of the committees of the Jews' Free School and of the Westminster and the Bayswater schools, and for a long period acted as honorary art teacher to the pupils and teaching staffs.

In the general community Marks has been active in the free-library and art-school movements, and contributed to the establishment of the Cardiff and Ealing libraries. His son, **Percy L. Marks,** is an architect, and has published "Principles of Planning" (London, 1901). His daughter, **Constance Isabella,** has shown considerable mathematical talent, having become editor of the mathematical department of the "Educational Times." Two other daughters, **Anne** and **Gertrude,** follow their father's profession, while another, **Helena,** has published several songs.

BIBLIOGRAPHY: *Young Israel*, Aug., 1898; *Jewish Year Book*, 1900–1 and 1903–4.

J. G. L.

MARKS, DAVID WOOLF: The "father" of Anglo-Jewish Reform; born in London Nov. 22, 1811; educated at the Jews' Free School, London. He acted as pupil-teacher at Solomon's boarding-school at Hammersmith for five years, and then became assistant reader at St. Alban's Synagogue, but resigned the latter position to go to Liverpool as assistant reader and secretary. At Liverpool his desire for Reform found expression in his refusal to read the Law on the second days of festivals. Meanwhile Marks devoted himself to general literature, and ultimately secured the appointment of professor of belles-lettres at Wigan College, Liverpool. About 1840 a movement was in progress in London for establishing a Reform synagogue, and the sympathy with Reform of which Marks had given evidence brought him under the notice of the founders of that movement; he was accordingly elected, at the age of twenty-nine, minister of the West London Synagogue of British Jews.

During his sixty years' ministration to that congregation Marks has effected important changes in the community. He was active in furthering educational projects, in instituting regular pulpit instruction, and in improving decorum in Jewish public worship. In 1848 he was appointed to the chair of Hebrew at University College, London, which he filled until 1898. He died May 3, 1909.

Marks published three volumes of sermons, and a pamphlet entitled "The Law is Light"; he was one of the editors of Smith's "Dictionary of the Bible," and he compiled and published the order of service used in the Reform synagogues.

BIBLIOGRAPHY: *Jew. Chron.* Nov. 22, 1895; *Young Israel*, Jan., 1898; Morais, *Eminent Israelites of the Nineteenth Century*; *Jewish Year Book*, 1903-4.

J. G. L.

MARKS, HENRY HANANEL: English journalist and politician; born April 5, 1855, in London; fifth son of the Rev. Prof. D. W. Marks; educated at University College, London, and at the Athenée Royale, Brussels. At the age of sixteen he went to the United States, where he entered the journalistic field, meeting with varying success. Finally, when his resources were at their lowest ebb, he returned to London (1883), and soon after established the "Financial News." Beginning in a very small way, he made the paper a power in the financial world. In 1889 Marks was elected member for Marylebone of the London County Council; three years later at the parliamentary election he contested the Northeast Bethnal Green division; and in 1895 he was elected member of Parliament for St. George's Tower Hamlets. He retained his seat until 1900.

BIBLIOGRAPHY: *Who's Who*, 1904; *The Jewish Year Book*, 1904.

J. E. Ms.

MARKS, MARCUS M.: American merchant; born at Schenectady, N. Y., March 18, 1858. In 1877 he started a business at Passaic, N. J., and later entered the wholesale clothing firm of his father, David Marks & Sons. He has held many prominent positions in connection with the clothing trade, being president of the Clothiers' Association of New York, president of the National Association of Clothiers, president of the Clothing Trade Association of New York, and chairman of the Hospital Saturday and Sunday Association Trade Auxiliary. He has served also as trustee of the Hospital Saturday and Sunday Association, director of the Educational Alliance, member of the Conciliation Committee of the National Civic Federation, director of the National Butchers' and Drovers' Bank, and is now (1904) organizing credit cooperation in several trades, with the view of establishing a central clearing-house for direct trade information. Marks has been a contributor to labor and trade journals on subjects of labor and conciliation and on credit cooperation.

A. F. H. V.

MARKS, SAMUEL: South-African pioneer; born in Germany about 1850. He went to Cape Colony about 1868 and commenced trading in the country. He entered the diamond trade, and, gaining the confidence of the diggers, bought claims and worked them. He was joined subsequently by his brothers; working harmoniously together, they amassed an enormous fortune. In 1884 Marks left the diamond-fields for the Transvaal, where he became acquainted with President Kruger, advanced the government considerable sums of money, and acquired numerous farms in the Transvaal. These farms turned out to be extensive and valuable coal-mines, and the Cape government contracted with the firm of Lewis & Marks for the supply of coal for its railway. The interests of the firm in South Africa at the end of the century were almost colossal. It gave great impetus to the trade of the country by its opening up of coal- and silver-mines and by its establishment of glass, jam, and other factories. It furthermore held the monopoly of the manufacture of spirits and possessed a distillery near Pretoria.

BIBLIOGRAPHY: *Jewish Chronicle*, June 28, 1895; March 17, 1899.

J. G. L.

MARKUS, LUDWIG: German Orientalist; born in Dessau Oct. 31, 1798; died in Paris July 15, 1843. He attended the Franzschule and the ducal gymnasium in Dessau; he was sent to the latter by the hereditary Prince of Anhalt-Dessau, his father having lost his means. He then studied medicine at Berlin University (1818–21), but when in the last year of his course he abandoned medicine for philosophy, and studied astronomy under Encke at the Berlin Observatory so ardently that his mind was for a time affected. When scarcely recovered he became a member of the Society for Jewish Culture and Science in Berlin. In its "Zeitschrift für die Wissenschaft des Judenthums" for 1822 (pp. 401–418) appeared his first publication, the beginning of a work on the natural history of Palestine, which was still unfinished when the periodical discontinued publication. He then began his life labor—a work on the foreign colonies in Abyssinia and Senaar from the seventh century B.C. to the fourth century C.E. In 1825 Markus went to Paris, where Cuvier appreciated his attainments; through Cuvier's influence Markus was engaged to edit part of the notes to Panckoucke's Latin-French edition of Pliny (1829). He steadily proceeded with his work on Abyssinia, though he was without means to publish it; but two extracts from it appeared in the "Journal Asiatique" for 1829. In 1830 Cuvier secured for him an appointment as teacher of German in the royal college at Dijon, where he wrote the elementary works needed by the pupils.

The loss of his devoted mother in 1835 having left Markus almost alone in the world (he already had lost nearly all his brothers and sisters), he fell into a state of melancholy which made teaching in Dijon distasteful to him. His work on the Vandals having been very well received, he resigned his position in Dijon and (1838) returned to Paris. It was one day about this time that Markus met Heine and a companion walking on the boulevard. Heine's companion, struck by Markus' somewhat ludicrous appearance, inquired, "Who is that man?" Heine, who had known the Orientalist at the university, replied, "That is the King of Abyssinia." This title, so thoughtlessly conferred, thereafter clung to him. Markus died in Dr. Pinel's asylum for the insane. Baroness de Rothschild bore the funeral expenses, and Heine wrote an obituary. Markus had a remarkable memory and was called the "walking library." He was very modest, and, in spite of his poverty, charitable to the extent of his means.

He wrote: "Storia dei Vandali" (1836); "Géographie Ancienne des Etats Barbaresques" (1842; translation of a part of K. Mannert's "Geographie er Griechen und Römer," with extensive notes and lditions); a comparative chronology of the princi-l nations of antiquity; and a prosody of the Greek d Latin languages.

BLIOGRAPHY: *Arch. Isr.* 1843, pp. 541-549 (obituary by S. Munk; translated into German by S. Heilberg, Breslau, 1847); Servi, *Israeliti d'Europa*, pp. 197-199; Heine, *Gesammelte Werke*, xiv. 179-202, Hamburg, 1876; *Allg. Zeit. des Jud.* 1843, Nos. 18 and 34.

S. N. D.

MARLI (מארלי), SAMUEL RAPHAEL EN MAZLIAH: Italian Talmudist and litur-st of the sixteenth and seventeenth centuries. ccording to S. D. Luzzatto, the name "Marli" eans "of Arles" (Steinschneider, "Hebr. Bibl." . 97, v. 46). Marli was the head of the yeshibah Mantua (Abraham Portaleone, "Shilṭe ha-Gib-rim," p. 20a), and was one of the rabbis that rticipated in the heated controversy over the Miḳwah" of Rovigo (Moses Porto, "Palge Mayim," 55).

BLIOGRAPHY: Nepi-Ghirondi, *Toledot Gedole Yisrael*, p. 337; Steinschneider, *Cat. Bodl.* col. 2435; Zunz, *Literatur-gesch.* p. 421.

D. M. SEL.

MARMOREK, ALEXANDER: Austrian ysician; born at Mielnica, Galicia, Feb. 19, 1865; ucated at a gymnasium and at the University of ienna (M.D. 1887). He removed to Paris, where became a pupil, later an assistant, at the Pas-ur Institute. He is the author of "Versuch einer heorie der Septischen Krankheiten," Vienna, 1894. In 1900 Marmorek claimed to have discovered an tidote (antistreptococcus serum) against puerperal ver; but his remedy did not prove efficacious. is still, however, used at the Pasteur Institute. gain, in 1903 he appeared before the French Acad-ny of Medicine in Paris, claiming to have found antidote for tuberculosis. He stated that the tu-rculin discovered by Koch was not the toxin (or ison) of the tubercle-bacillus, but a product which ly stimulates the cells to produce the toxin; that e real toxin had been found by him (Marmorek), d that he had discovered also the antituberculosis ccine. He claimed good results for his remedy, hich he had sent to Duyen of Paris and Von Mi-licz of Breslau. The first-named expressed him-lf in favor of Marmorek's antidote; the other con-mned it.

Marmorek is known also as an ardent Zionist. As student he had been a member of the Ḳadimah, e first students' Zionist society of Vienna; he is erefore one of the earliest of the modern Zionists. e was made an officer of the first Zionist Congress, d has held office in each succeeding one. He is at e head of the French Zionist Federation and is the under of the Jewish Popular University in Paris. e has taken an active part also in communal work Paris, and was one of the founders of the "Echo oniste," the Zionist monthly published in Paris. armorek has been decorated with the Legion Honneur

BLIOGRAPHY: The medical journals for Nov. and Dec., 1903; *Le Petit Journal* (Paris), Dec. 2, 1903.

S. F. T. H.

MARMOREK, OSKAR: Austrian architect; other of Alexander Marmorek; born at Skirta, Ga-ia, April 9, 1863. He studied at the polytechnic high school at Vienna and took a postgraduate course at Paris. Returning to Vienna in 1889, he settled there as an architect. Several important works have been undertaken by him, including the illuminated fountain at the Forestry Exposition of 1890 at Vienna, the music-hall at the Vienna Musical Exposition of 1892, and the plan of the villa district of Assee.

Marmorek, like his brother Alexander, is an enthusiastic Zionist, having been a member of the Vienna Ḳadimah. At the first Zionistic Congress he was appointed member of the Actions Committee, which office he has since held. In 1902 he was a member of the 'Arish Expedition.

At the Congress of Basel in 1901 Marmorek proposed to recognize the hospitality of Basel by erecting a Zionist Congress Home, and exhibited plans therefor which he had prepared.

BIBLIOGRAPHY: Eisenberg, *Das Geistige Wien*, Vienna, 1893.

S. F. T. H.

MARRIAGE.—Biblical Data: The earliest Hebrew literature represents a comparatively high development of social and domestic life. Of primitive conditions of polyandry, such as existed among the early Arabs, there is no certain evidence in the Old Testament. Even of the matriarchate, or reckoning of kinship through the mother, which W. Robertson Smith holds to have been originally the universal rule of Arabia ("Kinship and Marriage," 2d ed., pp. 145-190), there is no clear indication. Traces thereof have been supposed to remain in certain family connections, such as those of Milcah and Sarah, or in tribal groups, such as the sons of Leah and of Rachel, and also in the evidently closer and more intimate relationship between children of the same mother or with relatives on the maternal side. There is, however, probably nothing more in these than such distinctions as would necessarily arise in polygamous families and in the natural intimacy between full brothers and sisters. Polygamy, or, more correctly, polygyny, was the prevalent form of the marriage relation in Old Testament times. There seems to have been no limit to the number of wives or concubines a man might have, except his ability to maintain them and their children. As a matter of fact, however, only men of wealth, chiefs, or kings had many wives; the historian draws special attention to the large households of Gideon, David, and Solomon (Judges viii. 30; II Sam. v. 13; I Kings xi. 1 *et seq.*). The Patriarchs had not many wives; Isaac appears to have been content with one. Cases such as those of Elkanah (I Sam. i. 1-2) and Jehoiada (II Chron. xxiv. 3), each of whom had two wives, may have been common (comp. Deut. xxi. 15).

Forms of the Marriage Relation.

Not infrequently the Hebrew slave-girl became the wife or the concubine of her master. Instances are given of the wife voluntarily giving her maid to be wife to her husband (Gen. xvi. 3; xxx. 3, 9). The lot of the childless wife in such a home was evidently an unhappy one. The law of later times was designed to limit the practise and to correct the abuses of polygamy. The king is enjoined not to multiply wives, "that his heart turn not away"

(Deut. xvii. 17). A man may not "take a woman to her sister to be a rival to her" (Lev. xviii. 18, R. V.). The interests of the less loved, or the hated, wife and her children are guarded (Deut. xxi. 15–17). Even in the earliest legislation the slave-girl who is espoused by her master and the slave's wife are protected in their rights (Ex. xxi. 2–11; comp. Deut. xxi. 10 *et seq.*).

By the Prophets polygamy was discouraged. In the prophetic history monogamy is presented as the ideal original state (Gen. ii. 18 *et seq.*). Plurality of wives first occurs among the degenerate Cainites (Gen. iv. 23); but Noah is the husband of one wife, and so, apparently, is the patriarch Job. The idyllic pictures of II Kings iv., Ps. cxxviii., Prov. xxxi. 10 *et seq.*, are of monogamous homes. Hosea and Isaiah were monogamists. When the Prophets represent Jehovah's relation to Israel by the figure of marriage, it is as a jealous husband choosing and betrothing to himself one beloved wife (Hos. ii.; Isa. l. 1, liv. 5). The books of Proverbs and Ecclesiasticus exalt the place and character of the wife in the undivided home (Prov. xii. 4, xviii. 22, xix. 14, xxxi. 10 *et seq.*; Ecclus. [Sirach] xxv. 1, 8; xxvi. 1 *et seq.*, 13 *et seq.*; comp. Eccl. ix. 9). Monogamy was the rule among the Jews in Roman times, but there were notable exceptions. While the New Testament does not expressly prohibit, it discredits and discourages, polygamy (*e.g.*, Matt. xix. 4–5; I Tim. iii. 2, 12).

Kinship and Marriage.

In the earliest Hebrew history endogamy prevails; particular care is taken that Isaac and Jacob shall contract marriage only with their own kin. The Canaanite wives of Esau were "a grief of mind unto Isaac and to Rebekah" (Gen. xxvi. 34–35; comp. xxvii. 46). Some of the sons of Jacob also departed from this custom (Gen. xxxviii. 1–2, xli. 45). Moses married outside his own people, but he was a fugitive, and became an adopted member of his wife's tribe (Ex. ii. 21; comp. iv. 18). It was, nevertheless, looked upon as right and fitting that marriage should take place within the circle of one's own kindred (Gen. xxiv. 2–4, xxix. 19; comp. Judges xiv. 3).

However, the changed conditions subsequent to settlement in Canaan made an intermingling of races inevitable (see Judges iii. 6; Ruth i. 4; II Sam. xi. 3; I Kings vii. 14; I Chron. ii. 17; II Chron. xxiv. 26), and the custom of the kings in making foreign alliances by marriage favored this (II Sam. iii. 3; I Kings iii. 1, xi. 1, xvi. 31). The Deuteronomic law forbids marriage with the Canaanites, but, apparently, makes an exception to the endogamous rule in favor of the Edomites and Egyptians (Deut. vii. 3, xxiii. 7; comp. Ex. xxxiv. 16). The period of the Exile and the century following was also a period of laxity, but strict laws prohibiting marriage with the foreigner were enforced in the time of Ezra and Nehemiah (Ezra ix. 10; Neh. xiii. 23–30).

The older custom of intermarriage within the circle of kinship was governed by no strict rules. Of course marriage with a daughter or uterine sister was not tolerated, but there was no bar to union with close relatives on the father's side, and even down to the Babylonian exile such unions appear have been common (Gen. xx. 12; Ex. vi. 20; Nu xxvi. 59; II Sam. xiii. 13; Ezek. xxii. 10–1 Deuteronomy prohibits certain marriages with ne relatives (xxii. 30; xxvii. 20, 22–23), but the m elaborate legislation in this direction is found Leviticus (xviii. 7–17, xx. 11–21). According this law a man may not marry his mother, ste mother, mother-in-law, father's sister, mothe sister, paternal uncle's wife, half-sister, stepsis (daughter of stepmother and her former husban sister-in-law (brother's wife), living wife's sist daughter-in-law, stepdaughter, granddaughter, daughter of stepson or stepdaughter. It is cl that marriage with a deceased wife's sister is n forbidden, but it has been argued that the near re tives of the wife equally with those of the husba are within the forbidden degree to him and that, the wife's mother and daughter are barred, so al by analogy, is the wife's sister. Whatever anomalies or defects, there is no doubt that by t law a high ideal of domestic and social purity w maintained. The pre-Islamic Arabic custom, a thorized by Mohammed, was closely similar. S INCEST.

The ancient custom of levirate marriage requi to be considered here. According to the story Gen. xxxviii., it was an obligation resting upon man to take in marriage the childless widow o deceased brother and "to raise up seed to brother." The Deuteronomic law provides th where brothers live together, if one die without so the widow shall not marry a stranger, but that husband's brother shall take her, and that the fi born son shall be reckoned the son of the de brother and shall succeed to his inheritance. App ently there is a twofold purpose here—to perpetu the husband's name and to prevent the alienation the property. The widow is permitted to insult p licly an unwilling brother-in-law by loosing his sh and spitting in his face (see ḤALIẒAH). Thencefo his name is to be called in Israel "the house of h that hath his shoe loosed" (Deut. xxv. 5–10; com Matt. xxii. 24–25; Mark xii. 19; Luke xx. 28). slightly different example of the same custom presented in the Book of Ruth. Indeed, the cust has been shown to have been widely prevalent o side of Israel (Westermarck, "History of Hun Marriage," pp. 510–514). It is difficult to determ whether or not the law in Lev. xviii. 16 and xx. is intended as an abrogation of the old levirate la More probably Leviticus states the general rule which the levirate is a particular exception (Nowack, "Lehrbuch der Hebräischen Archäologi i. 346; Driver, "Deuteronomy," *ad loc.*). LEVIRATE MARRIAGE.

Duties of Husband and Wife.

The wife was regarded as property (see Ex. 17; comp. the Hebrew terms "ba'al" = "husbar and "be'ulah" = "wife"; literally, the "owner" "master" and the "owned"). S was, however, valuable property a was, as a rule, well cared for. S was not isolated as among the Moha medans, but had considerable freed and influence. In the wealthier homes she m often have had a large measure of independen and in the royal household she sometimes became an important power in the state. It will be sufficient to recall the stories of Sarah and Rebekah; of Deborah, a prophetess, the wife of Lappidoth, who judged Israel; of Jael, the wife of Heber the Kenite; of Abigail (Nabal's wife) and the Shunammite woman; of Jezebel and Athaliah. In the prophetic account of the Creation (Gen. ii., iii.) she is made a helpmeet for her husband, bone of his bone and flesh of his flesh. In the home the innermost apartment was hers, or, in some instances, a separate house (Judges xv. 1, xvi. 9; I Kings vii. 8). She performs the ordinary household duties or manages the affairs of her household and directs her servants (I Sam. ii. 19; Prov. xxxi. 10 *et seq.*). She must be chaste and obedient, and infidelity on her part is looked upon as a gross sin (Gen. iii. 16; Deut. xxii. 20 *et seq.*; Ezek. xvi.; John viii. 5–7). A false accusation against her is severely punished (Deut. xxii. 13 *et seq.*); a curious ordeal is prescribed in Num. v. 11–31 for testing the truth or falsity of a charge of infidelity. Adultery is strictly forbidden in the moral code and is denounced by the Prophets as a crime comparable to stealing, murder, false swearing, and idolatry (Ex. xx. 14; Jer. vii. 9, xxiii. 10; Hos. iv. 2; Mal. iii. 5). The husband must provide his wife with food and raiment. While greater laxity was evidently permitted to him than to the wife, yet conjugal fidelity was highly esteemed and sexual license regarded as foolish and even fatal (Judges xix.–xx.; II Sam. xi.–xii.; Prov. ii., v., vi., vii.). In the New Testament love and fidelity on the part of the husband, and obedience on the part of the wife, are inculcated (Acts xv. 29; Ephes. v. 22–33; Coloss. iii. 18–19; I Thes. iv. 3–6).

Betrothal and Nuptial Rites.

The first step toward marriage was betrothal, involving the consent of the parent or guardian of the girl and the payment of a price. The act of betrothal is expressed by the Hebrew word "aras"; the price paid, by "mohar" (see Gen. xxxiv. 12; Ex. xxii. 16–17; Deut. xx. 7, xxii. 29; Hos. ii. 19–20). The mohar may be in the form of service in the field or in war (Gen. xxix.; I Sam. xviii. 25). Probably it was customary, even in early times, to give the bride some portion of the mohar, or at least to give her presents (Gen. xxiv. 53, xxxi. 15, xxxiv. 12). After betrothal the bride might be taken to her husband's house and the nuptials celebrated either immediately or later (Gen. xxiv. 49–67; Judges xiv. 5 *et seq.*). The initial steps, it appears, were customarily taken by the parents of the suitor, who formally made the proposal (Gen. xxiv., xxxiv. 4–6; Judges xiv. 2, 10). Not infrequently, however, in the comparatively free social intercourse of those days, the young man and woman had met and formed a mutual attachment resulting in a love-match (Gen. xxix. 9–12, 18; I Sam. xviii. 20, 28).

The bride did not always go to her husband empty-handed. Sometimes she received gifts from her father, and a king's parting gift to his daughter was in one case a conquered city (Josh. xv. 16 *et seq.*; Judges i. 12 *et seq.*; I Kings ix. 16). In post-exilic times mention is made of a wife's dowry and of a woman being able, by her own wealth, to support her husband (Tobit viii. 21; Ecclus [Sirach] xxv. 22). Mention is made also of a written marriage-contract (Tobit vii. 14).

After betrothal the bride was subject to the same restrictions as a wife (Deut. xxii. 23–24). Of the marriage ceremonial little is known; it is not mentioned at all in the story of Isaac, while in that of Jacob (Gen. xxix.) a marriage-feast and a nuptial week are spoken of. The central features in later times were the wedding-procession and the wedding-feast. The bridegroom in festive attire and accompanied by his friends went to the home of the bride, whence she, likewise in bridal garments, veiled, and accompanied by her companions, was led to the house of his parents (Isa. lxi. 10; Judges xiv. 10–11; Jer. ii. 32; Isa. xlix. 18; Ps. xlv. 8–15). The procession was enlivened with songs by, or in praise of, the bride and bridegroom, and was lighted, if in the evening, by torches or lamps (Jer. vii. 34, xvi. 9, xxv. 10; I Macc. ix. 37–39; Matt. xxv. 1–12; comp. Ps. xlv. and the Canticles, possibly representing such wedding-songs). There followed the nuptial feast in the house of the bridegroom, and the subsequent festivities sometimes continued for several days (Matt. ix. 15, xxii. 1–14; John ii. 1).

Divorce.

The husband has the right to divorce his wife, but he was required by the Deuteronomic law to give her a writing of divorce (Deut. xxiv. 1). She may remarry, but if she is again divorced or is left a widow her former husband may not receive her again (Deut. xxiv. 2–4). Older practises are probably represented in Hos. ii. and II Sam. iii. 14. In two cases the right to divorce was withdrawn (Deut. xxii. 19, 29). The prophet Malachi protested most strongly against the practise (Mal. ii. 10–16). In the teaching of Jesus it is expressly condemned except on the ground of adultery (Matt. v. 31–32; Mark x. 2–12; Luke xvi. 18; comp. I Cor. vii. 11–13). See DIVORCE and GET.

BIBLIOGRAPHY: Benzinger, *Arch.* Freiburg, 1894; Nowack, *Lehrbuch der Hebr. Arch.* vol. i. *ib.* 1894; Keil, *Biblical Archæology*, vol. ii.; Stade, *Gesch. des Volkes Israel*, i. 371–395, Berlin, 1887; McLennan, *Primitive Marriage* (reprinted in *Studies in Ancient History*, London, 1876); W. Robertson Smith, *Kinship and Marriage in Early Arabia*, Cambridge, 1895 (new ed., London, 1903); Starcke, *The Primitive Family*, London, 1889; Westermarck, *History of Human Marriage*, London, 1891 (new ed., 1903); Cheyne and Black, *Encyc. Bibl.*; Hastings, *Dict. Bible.*

S. J. F. McL.

——**In Rabbinical Literature:** Wedded life was regarded by the Rabbis as the most natural and the most exalted state. The unmarried man lives without joy, without blessing, and without good; also, according to others, without the Torah, without a wall (protection), and without peace (Yeb. 62b; Gen. R. xvii. 2). R. Ḥisda, in interpreting the expression "in want of all things" as used in Deut. xxviii. 48, said that it meant "without a wife" (Ned. 41a). Another amora, R. Eleazar, referring to Gen. v. 2, wished to deprive the unmarried man of his manhood (Yeb. 63a). It is therefore permitted for one to sell a scroll of the Law if the money is needed for the purpose of getting married (Meg. 27a; Yer. Bik. iii. 6; comp. DESECRATION). At marriage all sins are forgiven (Yeb. 63a; Yer. Bik. iii. 3).

One should be careful in selecting a wife. A saying current among the Rabbis was, "Hasten to buy land; deliberate before taking a wife; descend one step in choosing a wife; ascend one step in choosing the best man" ("shushbin"; Yeb. 63a). One should first establish a home and plant a vineyard, and then marry (Soṭah 44a). The pursuit of the study of the Law, however, should be postponed until after marriage, when a man is settled in mind and can devote himself entirely to that vocation (Yoma 72b; Men. 110a; comp. Ḳid. 29b).

Choice of Wife.

To marry a woman for her wealth was deprecated by the Rabbis (Ḳid. 70a; "Seder Eliyahu Zuṭa," ch. iii., ed. Friedmann, Vienna, 1902; Shulḥan 'Aruk, Eben ha-'Ezer, 3, 1, Isserles' gloss; "Sefer Ḥasidim," §§ 1094, 1096, ed. Wistinetzki, Berlin, 1891; see Dowry). The daughter of a respectable family is most to be desired (B. B. 109b); especially should the brothers of the bride be good and respectable men, for the character of the children is like that of the brothers of the mother (B. B. 110a; "Sefer Ḥasidim," §§ 1092, 1099, 1100). One should sell all he possesses in order to marry the daughter of a learned man (Pes. 49a, b; Ket. 111b; Yalḳ., Ex. 269; comp. Yoma 71a). A marriage between the daughter of a priest or of a learned man and an ignoramus ("'am ha-areẓ") will not be a successful one (Pes. 49a). All the promises of the Prophets will be fulfilled upon him who gives his daughter in marriage to a learned man (Ber. 34b); it is as if he united himself with the divine presence itself ("Shekinah"; Ket. 111b). It is deemed advisable that the wife should not be of a higher rank than the husband, in accordance with the homely saying, "A shoe that is larger than my foot I do not desire" (Ḳid. 49a). The Rabbis were very much opposed to marriage between an old man and a young woman, or vice versa (Yeb. 44a; Sanh. 76a, b); they also advised against marrying a divorced woman or a widow (Pes. 112a). Marriage should be contracted with no other intention than that of doing the will of God (Soṭah 12a; "Seder Eliyahu Zuṭa," ch. iii.).

The acquisition of a good and virtuous wife was regarded by the Rabbis as one of the greatest blessings. The praise given to the virtuous woman in Prov. xxxi. is elaborated in Ecclesiasticus (Sirach), from which the Rabbis frequently quote the sentence: "Blessed is the man that hath a virtuous wife, for the number of his days shall be doubled" (xxvi. 1, Hebr.; comp. Yeb. 63b). He is rich who has a wife whose deeds are noble (Shab. 25b), for the wife can influence her husband more than he can influence her (see Gen. R. xvii. 1). In Palestine the custom was to address a man who had just been married with the question, "Maẓa o Moẓe?" referring to the initial words of two passages, Prov. xviii. 22 ("Whoso findeth a wife findeth a good thing") and Eccl. vii. 26 ("And I find more bitter than death the woman. . . ." (Ber. 8a; Yeb. 63b). The quarrelsome woman was abhorred by the Rabbis of the Talmud, so that one would rather have all the evils combined than a bad wife (Shab. 11b). Some of the prominent Rabbis are recorded as having suffered much from the spitefulness of their wives (Yeb. 63a; comp. B. B. 145b).

Influence of Wife.

Physical beauty in woman was highly appreciate by the Rabbis; a beautiful wife is one of the thing that contributes to man's happiness (Ber. 57b; com Yoma 74b). A woman that has beautiful eyes need no further recommendation (Ta'an. 24a). "Th highest attribute of a woman is her beauty" wa the song of the maidens of Jerusalem at their gath erings on the Fifteenth of Ab and the Day of Aton ment when wishing to attract the attention of th assembled youths (Ta'an. 31a). While it is com mendable to marry soon after betrothal (Mid Shemuel xvii. 4 and note, ed. Buber, Cracow, 1893 no one should marry a woman unless he has see her beforehand (Ḳid. 41a; "Sefer Ḥasidim," § 1143 Similarity in stature or in complexion between th man and the woman was regarded with disfavo A tall man should not marry a tall woman, nor short man a short woman; a dark man should n marry a dark woman, nor a fair-complexioned ma a fair-complexioned woman (Bek. 45b).

The proverb that "marriages are made in heaven is illustrated by a story in the Midrash. A Roma matron, on being told by R. Jose ben Ḥalafta th God arranges all marriages, said that this was a easy matter, and boasted that she cou do as much herself. Thereupon sh assembled her male and female slav and paired them off in couples; but o the morrow they all went to her wi complaints. Then she admitted that divine inte vention is necessary to suitable marriages (Gen. R lxviii. 3-4). Even God Himself finds it as difficu an undertaking as the dividing of the Red Se Forty days before a child is born its mate is dete mined upon (Gen. R. lxviii. 3-4; Soṭah 2a; San 22a; comp. M. Ḳ. 18b; "Sefer Hasidim," § 1128).

Marriages Made in Heaven.

R. Jose asked of Elijah, "The Bible calls the wi a helpmeet; in what manner does she assist h husband?" To this Elijah replied, "A man brin wheat to his house, but he would have to chew th grains of wheat; he brings flax to his house, but h would have to clothe himself in flax—were it not f the wife, who [in preparing these materials] enligh ens his eyes and helps him onto his feet" (Yeb. 63 Leḳaḥ Ṭob to Gen. ii. 18; comp. "Seder Eliyah Rabba," x. [ix.], where the story is given at great length). To the worthy man the wife is a helpmee to the unworthy man the wife is a hindrance (Ye 63a).

The term "ḳiddushin" (sanctification), by whi the act of marriage is designated in rabbinical wr tings, points to the reverence in which this cer mony was held. "He thus prohibits her to th whole world as a sacred object" is the explanati given to that term (Ḳid. 2b). Marriage was th symbol frequently employed by the Prophets designate the relation between God and Israel (Ho ii. 2-22; Isa. lxii. 4-5, liv. 6; Jer. iii. 1, 20; Eze xvi.; *et al.*). The love-songs of Canticles we taken by the Rabbis to refer to the love of God f Israel (see "Aggadat Shir ha-Shirim" to Cant. viii. "Seder Eliyahu Rabba," ch. vii. [vi.] and x. [ix. *et al.*); God betrothed Israel with few gifts in th world, but the marriage which will take place in th Messianic time will be attended with many gif (Ex. R. xvi. 30). The relation of Israel to the Tor s also symbolized as that of man to wife. The 'orah is betrothed to Israel and therefore forbidden o every other nation (Ex. R. xxxiii. 8; Sanh. 59a; 'es. 49b).

IBLIOGRAPHY: Buchholz, *Die Familie*, Breslau, 1867; Suwalski, *Ḥayye ha-Yehudi*, ch. liii., Warsaw, 1893.

S. S. J. H. G.

—**Statistics:** The number of marriages and the onditions under which they are contracted differ n the Jewish from those of the surrounding population. A smaller proportion marry, though these, or the most part, marry earlier than their neighbors. However, the changed social conditions in Germany in recent years are tending to modify the proportions. The number of Jews marrying to every thousand of the Jewish population (including children) s almost invariably less than among the general opulation, as may be seen from the following able:

Frequency.

Place.	Epoch.	Jews.	Christians.	Authority.
lgiers......	1878	105	75	"Annuaire Statistique de la France," 1881, p. 580.
ustria......	1864	46	83	Jeiteles, "Cultusgemeinde Wien," p. 50.
"	1870	53	98	Bergmann, "Beiträge," p. 69.
aden	1857–63	58	74	*Ib.*
avaria.......	1835–68	61	75	*Ib.*
ucharest....	1878	127	65	"Orasului Bucaresci," 1878.
'rance.......	1855–59	62	82	Legoyt, "Immunities," p. 68.
lungary.....	1864–73	64	105	Schwicker, "Ungarn," p. 99.
'russia.......	1822–40	72	89	Hoffmann, in "Jour. Stat. Soc." 1846, p. 78.
"	1820–76	75	88	Fircks, "Zeit. Preuss. Stat." 1884, p. 148.
"	1878-82	65	78	Ruppin, in "Jahrbücher für Nationalökonomie," 1902, p. 384.
"	1888-92	66	80	*Ib.*
"	1893-97	66	81	*Ib.*
ussia........	1852–59	82	95	Legoyt, *l.c.* p. 52.
"	1867	87	100	"Le Mouvement de la Russie en 1867," p. 19.
'uscany	1861	70	97	Legoyt, *l.c.* p. 60.
'ictoria (Australia).	1871–80	53	63	"Victorian Year-Book," 1881, p. 177.

Jews live generally in towns, and fewer town-wellers marry than country people. There is a arger preponderance of Jewesses over Jews in most f the countries of western Europe, where emigration emoves the young men, and this slightly reduces the ate of marriage. In fact, the rate is probably illuory because reckoned on the whole of the populaion, including children. The larger the number of narriages the larger the number of children, and, herefore, the larger the population. Thus because he number of marriages among Jews is really reater, it has the appearance of being smaller.

The age at which marriage is contracted affects nore than any other circumstance the physical, nental, and social characteristics of the offspring, letermining the average duration of a generation, the fertility of marriage, and the physical and mental health of children, and, it has been conjectured, the proortion of sex to sex in the offspring. The most nportant ages are those below 20 and those between 0 and 30, the latter being the normal and more desirable period for marriage. The following details are known with regard to Jewish marriages at these ages. The figures in parentheses refer to females.

Age.

Place.	Epoch.	Under 20.		20 to 30.	
		Jews.	Christians.	Jews.	Christians.
Austria	1861–70	(23.5)	(15.1)	68.6 (58.7)	58.6 (57.6)
Moscow.....	1868–72	6.2 (49.3)	4.0 (29.9)	76.6 (48.5)	55.9 (55.6)
Budapest ...	1858–70	(38.4)	(20.5)	67.6 (48.5)	51.0 (53.1)
Posen.......	1867–73	0.7 (17.8)	1.7 (17.1)	65.7 (69.1)	69.4 (63.2)
Russia......	1867	47.6 (63.2)	36.9 (56.7)	37.9 (29.4)	42.9 (33.7)
"	1897	5.9 (27.7)	31.2 (55.0)	77.7 (63.9)	54.5 (38.5)
St. Petersburg	1866–72	9.5 (56.9)	3.7 (27.3)	52.4 (30.6)	48.1 (51.4)

The relatively early marriage of Jews was noticed in 1841 by Hoffmann, who mentions that 78.6 per cent of Jewish marriages in Prussia between 1822 and 1840 occurred under the age of 40 as against 74.6 of the general population ("Jour. Stat. Soc." ix. 80). Körösi attempts to prove that Jews have the fewest abnormal marriages (that is, where the bride is under 18, or over 40, and the bridegroom over 40)—12 per cent as against 35 per cent among Catholics, and 33 per cent among Protestants ("Statistisches Jahrbuch," 1873, p. 37). In Russia, however, the general population appears to marry earlier than the Jewish. The proportion of protogamous marriages, or first marriages, is larger among Jews than among Gentiles, as may be seen from the following table giving the percentage of such marriages:

Place.	Epoch.	Jews.	Christians.	Authority.
Austria	1861–70	87 (93)	82 (89)	Schimmer, "Stat. der Jud." 1873, p. 6.
Budapest....	1858–75	88 (94)	86 (89)	Körösi, "Grandes Villes," p. 4.
Moscow	1868–72	88 (88)	83 (85)	*Ib.* p. 178.
Prague	1879–80	86 (96)	82 (92)	"Statist. Handbuch," 1881, p. 24.
Prussia (Eastern).	1867–73	91 (97)	83 (89)	Bergmann, *l.c.* p. 96.
Russia......	1870	74 (80)	82 (87)	"Jour. Stat. Soc." 1880, p. 363.
St. Petersburg.	1866–72	83 (78)	85 (87)	Körösi, *l.c.* p. 172.

This is probably due to the greater viability of Jews, since the longer husband and wife live the less likely either is to contract a second marriage. Thus among Jews in Budapest in 1870 no less than 66 per cent of those over 50 had husband, or wife, living, as against 51 per cent among Catholics and 53 per cent among Protestants ("Statist. Jahrb." 1873, p. 38). It is probable that Jews more frequently than others marry their cousins. Jacobs has shown this for England, where marriage of cousins occurs to the extent of 7.5 per cent of all marriages as against 2 per cent in the general population ("Studies in Jewish Statistics," ch. i.); Stieda has shown the same for Lorraine, where such marriages occur in the proportion of 23.02 per 1,000 among Jews as against 1.86 among Protestants, and 9.97 among Catholics.

Consanguineous Marriages.

The following table gives the proportion of intermarriages between Jews and Christians, and between Christians and Jewesses, at the times and places mentioned:

Place.	Epoch.	Jews–Christians.	Christians–Jewesses.	Authority.
Algeria....	1878	0.94	0.94	"Ann. Stat. France," 1881, p. 581.
Bavaria....	1876–80	1.57	2.19	"Zeit. Bay. Stat." 1881, p. 213.
Berlin.....	1881	7.95	4.91	"Statist. Jahrb." ix. 8.
"	1895–99	10.53	6.53	Ruppin, *l.c.* p. 761.
Budapest..	1881	0.96	0.10	"Pest in 1880," p. 12.
Prague.....	1878–80	1.14	0.20	"Statist. Handbuch," 1881, p. 24.
Prussia.....	1875–79	4.46	5.36	Fircks, "Zeit. Preus. Stat." 1880, p. 16.
Vienna....	1865–74	2.60	3.06	Körösi, *l.c.* p. 18.

Relatively speaking, mixed marriages are not very numerous (see INTERMARRIAGE).

The creeds professed by divorced persons are rarely given, so that it is difficult to ascertain whether Jews are divorced more frequently than others. In Bavaria, between 1862 and 1865, divorces were 5.1 per cent in Jewish marriages as against 6.1 per cent in Protestant and 5.7 per cent in Catholic marriages ("Annales de Demographie," 1882, p. 290). In Berlin, 1885–86, Jewish divorces were 2.7 as against 3.6 for Protestants and 2.7 for Catholics; ten years later the figures were—Jews, 3.3; Protestants, 4.7; Catholics, 3.3 (Ruppin, *l.c.* 1902, p. 385).

Divorces.

BIBLIOGRAPHY: Jacobs, *Studies in Jewish Statistics*, pp. 49–54.

J.

MARRIAGE-BROKER. See SHADKAN.

MARRIAGE CEREMONIES: Association of the sexes was much restricted among the Jews, and the BETROTHAL was generally brought about by a third person, often a professional match-maker ("shadkan"). The latter received a brokerage-fee fixed by law, as a rule a small percentage of the dowry, the sum being doubled when the contracting parties came from a distance. It was paid by either of the parties, or each paid one-half, at the betrothal or after the wedding. The rabbi, as a person enjoying special confidence, was also often employed as intermediary; it is well known that Jacob Levi of Mayence lived upon fees thus derived, while he devoted his income as rabbi to assisting his pupils. Although the marriage preliminaries were exclusively the concern of the parents and their agents, yet the young people were in nowise forced into the contract.

Early marriages were frequent; apart from moral considerations, they were often due to political conditions; in Russia, for example, the Jews were subject to conscription, but those who were married men were excused from military service. Social conditions also had some influence: a father, possessing the dowry for his child, urged the marriage so as to secure the dowry to her before one of the numberless persecutions robbed him of it. The betrothal was concluded, conditionally or definitely, as soon as the amount of the "ḳenas" (the penalty for breaking the contract) was fixed; however, it had, generally, no religious or legal significance, since the Talmudic custom of immediately connecting the betrothal ("ḳiddushin") and the nuptial ceremony ("erusin"), and of having the marriage proper follow later ("nissu'in"), fell more and more into disuse in the Middle Ages. At the betrothal the stipulations made by each party were fixed ("tena'im rishonim"), and a glass was thrown upon the floor, the broken pieces of which were saved to be laid upon the eyes of the espoused pair after death.

In Poland, even to-day, the bridegroom receives pastry ("chosenbrod") when he visits his betrothed.

Preliminaries.

During the week before the wedding-day the betrothed pair was allowed to leave the house only when accompanied. On Friday evening, or sometimes two Sabbaths, before the wedding, a feast was given in honor of the parents; this feast was commonly called "spinnholz" ("sponsalia" or "spindel"), or, in Poland, "vorspiel." On the day before the wedding the most prominent members of the community carried the presents of the groom to the bride with special ceremonies; as was customary also in non-Jewish circles, the presents consisted generally of a girdle, veil ("covering" before the ceremony still obtains, in conformity with Rebekah's example), mantle ("kursen"), and wreath, subsequently also of a "siflones tefillah," a prayer-book with the inscription אהבה ואחוה שלום ורעות ("Love, fraternity, peace, and good-fellowship"). Among the Greco-Turkish Jews a ring was included, called "nissu'in"; among the Greeks and Romans it was called "symbolum" (hence the Jewish "siflones"). The groom received a ring and shoes, later a ṭallit and a shroud. The rings were handed down in the family; the rings were formerly often of fine workmanship, having the miniature model of a synagogue carved on them and the inscription בטב גרא, later מזל טוב (= "good luck").

Two weddings on one day, especially of brothers or sisters, were avoided, and it was considered unlucky if the father-in-law and the son-in-law had the same name. In Talmudic times virgins were married preferably on Wednesday, and widows on Thursday (later, on Friday afternoon), a custom that still obtains in the East. A wedding in Mayence at the end of the fourteenth century took the following course: Early in the morning the "schulklopfer" invited the whole community to the ceremony. The leaders took the bridegroom, with music and candles, to the court of the synagogue; then the musicians and candle-bearers brought the bride with her friends and an escort of women. At the door of the synagogue the groom took the bride's hand, while the two were showered with wheat and coins (given afterward to the poor), and Ps. cxlvii. 14, and later Gen. i. 28 ("Be fruitful, and multiply"), were recited as a greeting; after this they sat for a short time, hand in hand, on the bench in front of the synagogue. Then the bride was escorted home, where she put on the festive robe of the married, and under it the shroud ("sargenes"). The groom also modified his festive appearance by drawing the hood ("gugel") over his head, which he strewed with ashes; even to-day the groom in

Day of Wedding.

eastern Europe wears the sargenes. With this sign of mourning for Zion even at the height of human felicity, belonged in Talmudic times another—the breaking of a glass, the pieces of which were gathered up by girls "for luck," while the "shammash" cried out "Zeh ha-ot" (="This is the sign"), and all present responded "Mazzal ṭob." The grief at Zion's loss appeared likewise in the mournful strains of the wedding-songs in the Talmud, as also in the poems of Judah ha-Levi, who first composed individual "carmina" on the model of Ps. xlv. and the "kallah" songs down to the eighteenth century.

As soon as the groom had sat down beside the Ark of the Law, the morning prayer began, after which the bride was led with music to the door of the synagogue; thence she was escorted by the rabbi and the elders of the community to the bemah (see ALMEMAR), taking her place at the right of the groom (comp. Ps. xlv. 10 [A. V. 9], in which

Marriage Ceremony.
(From a Passover Haggadah, Amsterdam, 1695.)

the last letters of the words נצבה שגל לימינך ["upon thy right hand did stand the queen"], taken in reverse order, spell כלה ["bride"]), where the mothers of the young couple stood. Bride and groom were covered with the ṭallit, or with the long end of the groom's gugel, and wedded. Later the wedding-tent ("ḥuppah") came into use; this was a reminiscence of the litter in which the bride was formerly carried or of the room in which the couple were left alone for a time. Then the groom was escorted home, and after him the bride, whom he met at the door and as she entered he placed her hand on the upper post, thus making her the mistress of the house. The wedding-festival proper, in the bride's house, did not begin until the evening; it lasted until Sunday morning, but was interrupted by the Sabbath morning service. At this, as at every service, the groom was the center of interest; in his honor songs were rendered that grew more numerous as marriages became less frequent, and more solemn as the social and political condition of the Jews was rendered more unfortunate. On returning home the groom handed to his young wife his mantle, girdle, and hat to signify that she shared his property.

The Ḥuppah.

The bridal procession (mentioned in Biblical writings) was headed, among the Spanish Jews, by mimes, fiddlers, and armed riders. In Egypt the bride was decked with helmet and sword, while the groom and his escort wore feminine garments and colored their finger-nails with henna, as women did. The women played the cymbals and danced. Even the most dignified scholars, also, danced in Talmudic times. Later, music was regarded as an essential part of the wedding, non-Jews being engaged to play on the Sabbath, while on the other hand Jewish musicians played at the festivities of Christians. The garlanding of the bridal pair, a custom of Biblical origin that was carried to an extreme of extravagance, ceased with the destruction of the Temple; yet the myrtle-wreath of the bride has been retained. Even in New Testament times young girls with torches escorted the pair (Matt. xxv.); in Arabia a pole to the top of which a light has been fastened is carried at the head of the procession. In Bagdad the groom is accompanied to the house of the bride by poor people carrying lamps, and he distributes for this service coins among them. On the way the poor thrust live sheep in front of him, and whenever he steps on the head of one he gives a certain amount to its owner. The bride is usually led seven times (or at least once) around the groom; or both sit while the people, old and young, dance around them. According to an ancient Persian custom in Talmudic times, nuts and flowers were strewn in the path of the pair, and they were showered with barley which had been planted in a pot shortly before the wedding (on the use of hops in this connection see Hehn, "Kulturpflanzen," p. 488; and on the use of rice among the Indians, whose wedding-customs are very similar to those of the Jews, see Dorville, "Gesch. der Verschiedenen Völker des Erdbodens"). On the birth of a boy a cedar was planted; on that of a girl, an acacia; and when the girl became a bride her litter was made from the branches of that acacia. In Germany the young couple's first meal consisted of milk and honey, and salt was sprinkled in the house (comp. Num. xviii. 19). In Ṭur Malka two hens are carried before the couple, and after the wedding chicken is placed before them ("chosenhühndel"). In the East they jump over a vessel containing a fish, and in Germany fish was formerly eaten on the second day of the wedding-week; all these customs are symbols of fertility.

Wedding-Feast.

The fasting of the bridal pair dates back to the Talmud; it is either due to the fact that their sins are forgiven or is intended to remind them of the duty of temperance. The wedding-songs were often in the form of riddles, following Biblical precedent (Samson's wedding), and were improvised especially by the jester ("marschalik"), who, however, at times moved his hearers to tears by serious speech, as he still does in eastern Europe. Plays also were given, a practise which prevailed otherwise only at Purim.

Before the fourteenth century the presence of the rabbi was not required; nor did he speak at the ceremony, though he did at the feast, when the groom likewise delivered a "derashah" (Talmudic discourse; hence the use of the word "derashah" for wedding-gifts). Weddings were occasionally celebrated in the open air in the Middle Ages, although the Talmud protested against the custom; it was done probably because of the limited space in the synagogue or in the bride's house; later the custom was interpreted symbolically (comp. Gen. xv. 5). At the synagogue service on the Sabbath after the wedding the congregation read to the groom the chapter on Isaac's marriage, a custom that ceased in Europe with the seventeenth century. In the East the Arabic translation is read in addition to the Hebrew.

During the seven blessings at the ceremony the bride and the groom, in accordance with a wide-spread superstition, each tried to secure the mastery in the household by putting one of the feet on the foot of the other. At the time of the Geonim (as occasionally to-day in the East) these seven blessings were uttered twice—once in the house of a relative of the bride, whither the latter had been taken from her father's house on the evening before the day of the wedding, and once in the house of the groom.

The ring, without stone or inscription, is put on the first finger of the bride's right hand. The marriage certificate, the wording of which varies according to time and place (Chorny, "Sefer ha-Massa'ot," p. 242; Rinman, "Mas'ot Shelomoh," pp. 156, 159; Kaufmann, in "Monatsschrift," 1897; S. Krauss, in "Zeit. für Hebr. Bibl." 1901; A. Berliner, in "Meḳiẓe Nirdamim," ix.), dates from the Hellenistic period; among the Sephardim, especially the Italian Sephardim, and in Cochin, it was artistically ornamented. In early times it often bore the portraits of the bridal pair. Among the Jews of the Caucasus it is sometimes put in the grave (Chorny, *l.c.* p. 26).

The "Ketubah."

The reports of travelers concerning the marriage ceremonies among the Oriental Jews are interesting. Thus Rinman tells of the White Jews at Cochin: If the contracting parties have come to an understanding, the couple are taken before the elders of the community, the eldest of whom asks the groom whether he consents to the union; if he has parents, he answers, "The will of my parents is my will"; if not, "I desire her." Then the bride is questioned, and if she also consents, the elder takes a cup of wine and drinks to the health of the pair, the others present doing likewise; then they partake of coffee and confectionery and leave. On the day of the wedding the groom wears a white turban and the bride a fine cap; after the ceremony both clothe themselves in red silk, and on the seventh day in green silk or in silk of some other color.

The costs of the feast are borne by the father of the bride, the father of the groom furnishing only wine and meat (often forty beeves during the fifteen days of the feast, although beef is given only to the servants, the guests being fed with fowl). The owner of the largest house in the community surrenders his apartments for the wedding festivities. On the Sabbath the groom spreads a feast for his friends; then the whole community goes to the house of the bride to escort her to the house of one of her relatives who serves coffee to them. At the end of the Sabbath the bride is led to the house in which the ceremony is to take place, and there the people eat and drink until after midnight. On the following evening the bride is led to the miḳweh, or ritual bath. On Tuesday morning the goldsmith comes to make the ring for the bride, which she wears until her death. While she puts the ring on, the women sing Malabarian songs. In the evening the groom is led with music to the synagogue, where he stands on the steps before the Ark of the Law and recites the evening prayer with the congregation. Then the whole community, with the sound of trumpets and drums, calls for the bride, who walks under a kind of sun-umbrella carried by her father, in accordance with a Talmudic law. She sits down with her bridesmaids to the right of the Ark; before her stands a silver inkstand, to be used by the signatories to the ketubah.

Customs of Cochin.

The groom, in the ṭallit, sits down opposite her with his two best men; the ḥazzan thereupon fills a golden cup with wine and gives it to the groom, receiving in return 7½ francs; and the groom, reciting the first blessing, drinks part of the wine and gives some to the bride. Then he hands her the ring, with the words: "Thou,——, daughter of——, art betrothed unto me, ——, son of ——, according to the law of Moses and Israel." Thereupon the ketubah is read to a certain melody, and the groom gives it to the bride, after having thrice repeated, "Here is thy ketubah." The ḥazzan then causes the groom to take hold of his ṭallit, and to promise that he "will fulfil his duties as husband." After the ḥazzan has pronounced the seven blessings, the bride is unveiled, to the song "Yafah kalebanah," based on Cant. vi. 10. Hand in hand, the young couple now proceed, with music and torch-bearers, and followed by the people, to the house in which the festivities are to be held. There the groom dances with his friends and the bride with hers, and all partake of refreshments. At 10 o'clock they sit down to the feast, the bridal couple at the head of the table, and next to them the leaders of the community, men on the one side and women on the other. The old people call out "Yeḥi he-ḥatan weha-kallah!" (Long live groom and bride!), and the young people answer, "Hep! Hep!" (This custom is derived from the Portuguese.) The ḥazzan then sings, the community responding, after which the elders sing, and the ḥazzan pronounces grace and intones Ps. cxi., "Eshet Ḥayil," and finally the seven blessings (a different elder of the community blesses the bride and groom on each of the seven wedding-days). Then the young people dance with the groom, clap their hands, and again sing Ps. cxi.

On Wednesday evening the groom goes to the bride, who has assumed a white gown, which the women take away as soon as the groom is gone. The next day the elder women, after a meal, gather to pass judgment on the virtue of the young wife. On the following Sabbath there is another feast. In the synagogue is read from a printed copy of the Torah the section, "And Abraham had reached the days," with the Aramaic translation. After the service

MARRIAGE CEREMONY AMONG NUREMBERG JEWS, EARLY EIGHTEENTH CENTURY.
(From Kirchner, "Jüdisches Ceremoniel," 1726.)

every one gathers in the house of festivity; the bride, in gorgeous garments, with a wreath of pearls on her head, stands in front of her throne, the women sing before her, the men eat, drink, and dance, and then all sit down to dinner. Smaller feasts are held daily until the following Wednesday. On Tuesday evening there is a greater feast, when the guests present their gifts. There is no difference between the weddings of the rich and the poor, since the rich give to the poor everything that is required for the occasion.

In Cochin and among the Cingalese the following order is observed: The bride counts seven days from the day on which the groom declares his intention of marrying her.

In Ceylon.

On the night before the eighth day she takes a bath, the women assisting her, and singing. The next night, called "kofa," she is led with music to the women's ritual bath, after which the rabbi sings a song beginning "Yafah kalebanah Torah" (an acrostic containing "Yiẓḥaḳ"); a Torah-roll, opened at the Decalogue, is placed before the bride, who kisses it while putting her hand to her eyes. Then the rabbi blesses her, placing his hand on her head. The people eat, and sing acrostics with the names "Abraham" and "Solomon"; after washing their hands they say grace and go home. On the following day they gather again in the wedding-house; the bride places the presents of the groom in a vessel, and the goldsmith examines the gold and silver to see that they are not below the minimum value of one "peruṭa" or mite each. Here, also, the women sing. At a second gathering on the same day the groom appears with his hair cut, having bathed and donned new garments, including a new turban; as soon as he comes to the table the guests sing Ps. cxxii., the groom is placed among them, and they recite Esth. viii. 15 *et seq.*; he is then blessed and sits down at table. This meal is called "ajni." After dinner the rabbi sings "Kalil ḥatan li-beraḳah," and the several blessings of grace are recited in turn by various guests. The next evening the people proceed with music and songs to the synagogue, where the groom and his best men ("shushbinim") light four wax candles; then the procession marches to the wedding-house, where the bride is waiting. She is placed on a chair, wrapped in a large cloth, and the groom stands in front of her and quotes again from the Book of Esther (viii. 15 *et seq.*). Then the groom himself, as is customary in Yemen, pronounces, according to the version of Maimonides, the first blessing over a cup of wine, to which a silver ring is attached by a white thread. He tastes the wine, takes off the ring, and gives the cup to the bride with the words "Ba ḳiddushiki." After drinking she gives the cup to some one in the circle. The groom next places the ring on the little finger of her right hand, using the same words as before, and the rabbi reads the marriage certificate, after having obligated the groom (by taking hold of his mantle—"meḳabbel ḳinyan"—three times) to fulfil the chief duties of the husband as stated in the certificate. The certificate is signed by the groom and two witnesses, and then given to the bride. Songs follow, the bride is unveiled and placed in a litter, and cups of wine are given to the groom and the rabbi, who pronounces the seven blessings. The ceremony ends with a song.

On the Sabbath morning the groom goes with his relatives to the synagogue, where he is received by the rabbi with the words of Ps. cxxii. He is called up as the eighth to read the Torah, while the leader in prayer recites a piyyuṭ—"'Arba'ah Kelilin." Before the second blessing the groom recites by heart from Gen. xxiv. After the Hafṭarah the words of Isa. lxi. 10 are pronounced before the blessings. When the groom leaves the synagogue the rabbi repeats Ps. cxix., etc. Arrived at home, the bride and groom are blessed by the rabbi, and the people eat and sing. On the eve of the seventh day of the wedding-week the bride and groom are led with music to the synagogue, the rabbi reads Ps. xliv., and the groom recites the evening prayer; then they go to the wedding-house, where the rabbi repeats "Yafah kalebanah," and the people feast and sing "Yismaḥ ḥatan ba-kallah."

In the town of Tilla on the Sabbath the passage Gen. xxiv. is read to the groom from a second Torah-roll, and the janitor of the synagogue renders the song "Mi Kamoka," by Judah ha-Levi (in the Sephardic maḥzor for Purim). On the morning of the third day the friends of the groom color his hands and feet red (the people go barefoot in Tilla); in the evening there is a great feast, after which they shave the groom's head and put on the turban the bride has given him, he, on his part, having presented his friends and the brothers of the bride with turbans; all then proceed, with dancing and singing and with torches, to the house of the bride. There the groom pronounces one blessing over a cup of wine and the others over a second cup; he takes a ring and coins of gold, copper, and (chiefly) silver, and says to the bride, in Aramaic: "Be hallowed and be betrothed unto me, ——, the bridegroom, thou, bride and virgin [divorcée or widow], by this cup of wine and by this coin; on account of them thou shalt pass into my possession, according to the law of Moses and of Israel." After having given her wine, he offers her the money and the ring, before witnesses, and translates from the Arabic the marriage certificate, which he also gives her. The congregation sings the seven blessings together with songs in honor of the couple, and the choir-leader recites Ps. iii., the people responding "Hallelujah." Then the groom says, "You have blessed me, may God bless you; you have made me glad, may God make you glad," and drinks the wine. On Friday evening there is a feast in the house of the bride, at which the groom gives her the wedding-gift. On the Sabbath she is taken to the house of the groom, where the festivities last for seven days, on each of which the seven blessings are recited. During this time the groom sits daily for one hour under the ḥuppah.

In Bagdad the palms and the soles of the bride and her friends are colored with henna the night before the wedding. The people make merry first in the house of the bride, then in that of the groom. The next day, about five hours before sunset, the "ḥakamim" accompany the groom and his relatives to the house of the bride. The ḥakam lifts the bride's veil in order to show her to the groom, but lets it fall

MARRIAGE PROCESSIONS AMONG GERMAN JEWS, EIGHTEENTH CENTURY.
(From Bodenschatz, "Kirchliche Verfassung," 1748.)

again immediately. In Bagdad also the celebration lasts seven days.

Chorny (*l.c.* p. 298) says that in the Caucasus the ceremony is always performed on Wednesday. On the preceding Thursday three or four girls, relatives of the bride, put on her clothes and invite other girls to sleep in a special room with her. Toward evening the groom sends meat and rice-flour to the bride and her friends. The latter go out to sprinkle the flour on the young people, who dance while the boys and girls clap their hands. On this evening also the groom spreads a feast for his friends. On Sabbath morning the friends of the bride, among whom there must be at least five grown persons, clad in the bride's garments, go from house to house leaving invitations to the feast and receiving wherever they may stop sugar, coffee, apples, or eggs.

In the Caucasus.

After the service, at which the groom is not called up for the Torah, which is read only after the ceremony, the guests accompany the pair to the house of the groom for a feast, and then to the house of the bride, where the men eat first and the women afterward, the girls furnishing music with harmonicas, trumpets, etc. On the Sabbath, as well as on the following day, the bride spreads a table for her friends; on Sunday the groom for his friends. On Monday and Tuesday the bride visits the friends of her household with her girl companions, who sing a Tatar song. She is clad in mourning to indicate her sorrow at leaving her parents' house. The visitors everywhere receive presents and refreshments. As they approach the house of the groom, his companions appear and pelt the procession with sand and small stones. The groom is similarly led about among his friends. If he is rich he is even obliged to have silk wedding-garments made for the members of his household.

On Tuesday evening the father of the groom spreads a feast for the whole community. On Wednesday the bride and groom fast. About noon the rabbi, with a male relative of the groom and some women, goes to the house of the bride in order to inspect the clothing which she has had made with the money of the groom. Quarrels often arise on this occasion. If the father is wealthy he adds a sum of money to that which has been provided by the groom.

MARRIAGE SCENE AT CRACOW.
(From "Oesterreichisch-Ungarische Monarchie in Wort und Bild.")

Then the groom and bride are taken to the sea for the bath, after which they put on the wedding-garments. The groom is preceded by young men, and the bride by girls, with drums and with hand-clapping and Tatar songs. While the hair of the weeping bride is being combed, the girls light the lamps; then the bride, kneeling, receives her mother's blessing. The brothers of the bride, if she has any, otherwise an uncle, lead her to the ceremony in the court of the synagogue, the girls following with lights, generally white candles ornamented with blossoms.

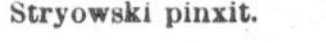

Stryowski pinxit.

MARRIAGE SCENE IN GALICIA.

The groom also is brought with songs from the sea; girls go to meet him in festive train, with dishes of confectionery, and with a branch hung with silken kerchiefs and coins. Arrived at home, he is kissed on the forehead by all the women; then, after having been blessed by his relatives, he is led with music to the court of the synagogue, where, under the ḥuppah, the rabbi with two pupils awaits the pair. The music ceasing, the groom goes under the ḥuppah, while the bride's parents are mourning at home for their child and those of the groom are preparing for the ceremony. The bride is led a few times around the groom, the bridesmaids and the others carrying lights. The ritual is that of the Sephardim; the rabbi sits during the ceremony, and both he and the groom hold a glass of wine during the blessings, drinking after each of them.

After the ceremony, guns and rockets are discharged; the bride, closely veiled by her attendants, is put on a horse, which a relative of the groom leads while another holds a mirror before her face; and with shouting and music the couple are led home, showered on the way with rice. Arrived at the house of the bride, the girls dance, and as soon as she crosses the sill the door-posts are smeared with honey, while a light burns over the door; at the same time the young men again discharge pistols. The musicians are then paid, and the wedding procession is ended.

Afterward the groom goes walking with his friends until the evening, when the men and the women eat in separate rooms without music. After the meal is finished the gifts, of gold only, are presented, the rabbi blessing each giver. The bride keeps with her in the room of the women only a sister and an aunt, if she has any, and a few friends. Late in the evening, after the guests have departed, the groom is led to the bride. After a time the young men call him out, discharging guns. The bride's mother must prepare for them a cock and a hen, or all her chickens will be stolen and killed. The bride and groom receive also money and fruit, the latter being eaten in the bride's room. The bride herself remains for twelve days behind a curtain, guarded by girls who demand pay from the groom.

In Grusia.

In Grusia (Georgia; Chorny, *l.c.* p. 129) the groom and bride are led in festive train from their homes to the synagogue, where they take their places beside the bemah. The ḥakam recites some piyyuṭim, translating them into Grusian, the ketubah also being written in Hebrew and Grusian. After a blessing upon the czar the groom covers himself and the bride with a ṭallit. While the ḥakam pronounces the first blessings the groom holds a ring and an earthen vessel containing wine. Then handing the ring to the bride, he breaks the vessel; covered by a cloth, the ends of which both hold, the bride and groom circle around the bemah, kiss the curtain of the Ark of the Law, and leave the synagogue.

A. M. Gr.

MARRIAGE LAWS: The first positive commandment of the Bible, according to rabbinic interpretation (Maimonides, "Minyan ha-Miẓwot," 212), is that concerning the propagation of the human species (Gen. i. 28). It is thus considered the duty of every Israelite to marry as early in life as possible. Eighteen years is the age set by the Rabbis (Ab. v. 24); and any one remaining unmarried after his twentieth year is said to be cursed by God Himself (Ḳid. 29b). Some urge that children should marry as soon as they reach the age of puberty, *i.e.*, the fourteenth year (Sanh. 76b); and R. Ḥisda attributed his mental superiority to the fact that he was married when he was but sixteen years old (Ḳid. *l.c.*). It was, however, strictly forbidden for parents to give their children in marriage before they had reached the age of puberty (Sanh. 76b). A man who, without any reason, refused to marry after he had passed his twentieth year was frequently compelled to do so by the court. To be occupied with the study of the Torah was regarded as a plausible reason for delaying marriage; but only in very rare instances was a man permitted to remain in celibacy all his life (Yeb. 63b; Maimonides, "Yad," Ishut, xv. 2, 3; Shulḥan 'Aruk, Eben ha-'Ezer, 1, 1–4; see Celibacy).

Age for Marriage.

The duty of marriage is discharged after the birth of a son and a daughter (Yeb. 61a). Still no man may live without a wife even after he has many children (*ib.*). Women are exempted from the duty of marriage, although, to avoid suspicion, they are advised not to remain single (*ib.* 65b; "Yad," *l.c.* 2, 16; *ib.* Issure Biah, xxi. 26; Eben ha-'Ezer, 1, 13; see Woman).

The consent of parents is not essential to the validity of a marriage (Shulḥan 'Aruk, Yoreh De'ah, 240, 25, Isserles' gloss). The Rabbis, however, urge great care in the choice of a wife. He who marries a woman unworthy of him is bound by Elijah and chastised by God; and concerning him Elijah writes, over the signature of God, "Wo unto him who profanes his children and degrades his family" (Ḳid. 70a; Derek Ereẓ R. i.). According to R. Akiba, he who marries a wife that is unworthy of him transgresses five Biblical commandments (Ab. R. N. xxvi. 4). While all families are presumptively pure and respectable, those that are at constant warfare with one another, or whose members are accustomed to call one another shameful names, or are known for their acts of cruelty and uncharitableness, are under suspicion of being of impure descent (Ḳid. 71b, 76b). The families most desirable for matrimonial alliances, according to the Rabbis, were classified in the following order: those of the scholar; the most prominent man of the community; the head of the congregation; the collector for charity; and the teacher of children. The family of the ignoramus ("'am ha-areẓ") is to be avoided, and one should not give his daughter in marriage to such a person (Pes. 49b; "Yad," Issure Biah, xxi. 32; Eben ha-'Ezer, 2; see 'Am ha-Areẓ).

To the degrees of prohibited marriages enumerated in the Bible (Lev. xviii. 6–18, xx. 11–21), the Rabbis added some new degrees, besides extending those mentioned in the ascending and the descending line. These additions are known in the Talmud by the name of "sheniyyot," *i.e.*, secondary, such as are given on the authority of the Soferim ("Scribes"). See Ḥaliẓah; Incest; Levirate Marriage.

Prohibitions of Marriage.

Prohibitions of marriage on grounds other than those of consanguinity refer to the following: (1) Mamzers, persons born of incest or of adultery; they are not permitted to marry Israelites (see Bastard; Foundling; Illegitimacy; Incest). (2) Ammonites or Moabites; they may not marry Israelitish women. (3) Egyptians or Idumeans to the third generation. (4) Nethinim or Gibeonites. The Rabbis declare: "Now all proselytes are permitted to marry Israelites; and we do not suspect that they are descendants of any of the nations forbidden in the Bible" ("Yad," Issure Biah, xii. 25; Tosef., Ḳid. v. 6; Yad. iv. 4; Ber. 28a; see Intermarriage; Proselytes). (5) Slaves. (6) Spadones, *i.e.*, persons forcibly emasculated, but not those that are born so. When the defect is the result of a disease, there is a difference of opinion among the authorities (Eben ha-'Ezer, 5).

Prohibited Degrees.

One who is suspected of having committed adultery with another man's wife is not permitted to marry her after she has been divorced or after she has become a widow (Soṭah 25a; Yeb. 24b; see Adultery). The Biblical prohibition forbidding one to remarry his divorced wife after she has been married to another (Deut. xxiv. 4) is extended by the Rabbis to the following cases: No one may remarry his divorced wife if he divorced her on suspicion of adultery, or because she had subjected herself to certain vows, or on account of her barrenness (see Divorce). Those who assist at a divorce proceeding, or the witnesses who testify to the death of an absent husband, may not marry the woman thus released (Yeb. 25a; Giṭ. 45a; "Yad," Gerushin, x. 13; Eben ha-'Ezer, 10, 3; 12, 1–2).

Besides the proselyte and the profane (Ḥalalah) or the divorced woman (Lev. xxi. 17 [A. V. 14]), the descendants of Aaron were forbidden to marry also the "ḥaluẓah," the woman who performed the ceremony of Ḥaliẓah ("loosening the shoe") upon her deceased husband's brother (Yeb. 24a). A priest's wife who had been criminally assaulted had to be divorced by her husband (*ib.* 56b). A woman captured by an enemy in time of war was under suspicion of having been assaulted by her captors, and hence priests were forbidden to marry her, unless witnesses who were with her during the whole time of her captivity testified that she had not been assaulted (Ket. 22a, 27a). The Rabbis insisted on the fulfilment of these laws even after the Temple had been destroyed and the priestly office abolished; and they compelled an Aaronite, under penalty of excommunication or other means, to divorce the woman that he had married contrary to the Law ("Yad," Issure Biah, xvii.–xx.; Eben ha-'Ezer, 6, 7; see Priestly Code).

There are some prohibitions which relate specifically to the woman's remarriage. A woman who was twice widowed, if both husbands died natural deaths, might not marry again (Yeb. 64b; "Yad," *l.c.* xxi. 31; Eben ha-'Ezer, 9). A widow or a divorced woman might not remarry before the expiration of ninety days from her husband's death or from the time when the bill of divorce was handed to her.

Remarriage.

This provision was made in order to ascertain whether she was pregnant, and that in the event of her being so the paternity of her child might be established. For the sake of uniformity the Rabbis required the woman to wait that length of time even when there could be no suspicion of pregnancy. If she was visibly pregnant, she might not remarry until after her delivery, and even then, if the child lived, she was required to wait until it was twenty-four months old. A woman who had an unweaned child was required to wait the same period. If the child died during the interval, she might remarry immediately (Yeb. 41a, 42a; "Yad," Gerushin, xi. 18–28; Eben ha-'Ezer, 13; see Divorce; Widow).

There are certain times during which marriage is forbidden. During the first thirty days of mourning after the death of a near relative no marriage may be entered upon. A widower may not remarry until three festivals have passed after the death of his wife. If, however, she left him with little children needing the care of a mother, or if he had not yet discharged his duty of propagating the species, *i.e.*, if he had no children (see above), he might remarry after a lapse of seven days (M. Ḳ. 23a; "Yad," Ebel, vi. 5; Yoreh De'ah, 392). No marriage might be entered upon on Sabbaths, holy days, or the week-days of the holy days, except in very urgent cases (Beẓah 36b; "Yad," Shabbat, xxiii. 14; *ib.* Ishut, x. 14; Eben ha-'Ezer, 64, 5; Oraḥ Ḥayyim, 339, 4, 524, 1, Isserles' gloss). The first nine days of the month of Ab were regarded as days of mourning and no marriage might then be performed. Some extended this prohibition to the three weeks intervening between the fast of the Seventeenth of Tammuz and that of the Ninth of Ab (Oraḥ Ḥayyim, 551, 2, 10, Isserles' gloss, and commentaries). The period between Passover and Shabu'ot ("Sefirat ha-'Omer") was also regarded as one of mourning; and no marriage might be performed during this time, except on a few specified days. In some places it was customary to refrain from marriage only until the thirty-third day of the Omer (*ib.* 493, 1, Isserles' gloss; see Mourning; Omer).

Conditions.

Marriage, being regarded also as a civil transaction, required the consent of the contracting parties in order to make it valid (see Consent). Hence idiots or imbeciles were considered incapable of contracting a legal marriage (see Insanity). The deaf-mute was also debarred from entering a legal marriage for the same reason, but the Rabbis sanctioned the marriage of a deaf-mute if contracted by means of signs (see Deaf and Dumb in Jewish Law). Minors (*i.e.*, such as have not reached the age of puberty which was held to begin at thirteen years in males and twelve in females), are also precluded from contracting marriages (see Majority). A daughter who was a minor could be given in marriage by her father; and such a marriage was valid. In the case of her father's death, her mother or her brother could give her in marriage, subject to her confirmation or annulment on her reaching the age of puberty (see MI'UN). A marriage contracted under certain conditions was valid when the conditions were fulfilled. The conditions had to be formulated in accordance with the general laws governing conditions (see CONDITIONS).

In rabbinic times there were two distinct stages in the marriage ceremony: (1) its initiation or the BETROTHAL ("erusin"), and (2) its completion or the marriage proper ("nissu'in"). These might or might not have been preceded by an engagement ("shiddukin"), although the prevailing custom was to have a formal engagement before marriage, when a contract ("tena'im") was drawn up in which the parties promised, under the penalty of a fine ("ḳenas"), to be married at an appointed time (see BREACH OF PROMISE OF MARRIAGE). The Rabbis regarded it as improper to marry without a previous engagement, and would punish one who did so, although the act itself was considered valid (Ḳid. 12b; "Yad," Ishut, ii. 22; Eben ha-'Ezer, 26, 4).

The betrothal was effected in any of the three following ways: (1) by the man handing a coin (a peruṭah, the smallest Palestinian coin, was sufficient for the purpose) or its equivalent to the woman in the presence of two competent witnesses, and pronouncing the words "Be thou consecrated to me," or any other phrase conveying the same idea; (2) by the man handing a contract ("sheṭar") to the woman containing the same formula; (3) by actual cohabitation between groom and bride. This last form of betrothal was discouraged by the Rabbis; and sometimes such a procedure met with severe punishment at the hands of the authorities. The manner of betrothal first mentioned seems to have been the most common, but later this was modified, so that instead of money the man gave his bride a ring, plain, and made of gold, the value of which was constant and well known (Tos., Ḳid. 9a, *s.v.* "Wehilketa"; Eben ha-'Ezer, 27, 1; 31, 2, Isserles' gloss; see BETROTHAL). The act of betrothal might be performed also by proxies appointed either by the bride or by the groom or by both; but it was recommended that the contracting parties be present at the ceremony ("Yad," Ishut, iii. 19; Eben ha-'Ezer, 35, 36). After betrothal the parties were regarded as man and wife; and the act could be dissolved only by death or by a formal bill of divorce. If the woman proved unfaithful during the period of betrothal she was treated as an adulteress, and her punishment (that of stoning; Deut. xxii. 23, 24; Sanh. 66b) was considered to be much more severe than that (strangulation) inflicted upon the unfaithful married woman (Deut. xxii. 22; Sanh. 52b). The parties were not, however, entitled to conjugal rights, nor were they bound by the obligations of married life (see HUSBAND AND WIFE).

After the lapse of a certain period from the time of betrothal (twelve months if the bride was a virgin and a minor, and thirty days if she was an adult or a widow; Ket. 57b), during which the bride could prepare her trousseau, the marriage proper was celebrated. This was attended with the ceremony of home-taking ("liḳḳuḥin" or "nissu'in") and isolation of the bridal pair in the bridal chamber ("ḥuppah"). From that time they became husband and wife, even if there was no cohabitation. Various ceremonies attended the act of marriage (see MARRIAGE CEREMONY). An important feature was the handing over of the marriage contract ("ketubah") to the bride. In later times the two stages of marriage were combined, a custom universally followed at the present time.

Besides the cross-references cited above see CONFERENCES; DOWRY; KETUBAH; PILEGESH; POLYGAMY.

BIBLIOGRAPHY: Hamburger, *R. B. T.* i., s.v. *Ehe*; ii., s.v. *Trauung*; Mayer, *Rechte der Israeliten, Athener, und Römer*, ii., sections 207–231, Leipsic, 1866; Saalschütz, *Das Mosaische Recht*, ch. cii.–cv., Berlin, 1853; Weill, *La Femme Juive*, Paris, 1874; Buchholz, *Die Familie*, Breslau, 1867; Duschak, *Das Mosaisch-Talmudische Eherecht*, Vienna, 1864; Fränkel, *Das Jüdische Eherecht*, Munich, 1891; Bergel, *Die Eheverhältnisse der Alten Juden*, Leipsic, 1881; Mielziner, *The Jewish Law of Marriage and Divorce*, Cincinnati, 1884; Bloch, *Der Vertrag*, sections 96–102, Budapest, 1893; Amram, *The Jewish Law of Divorce*, Philadelphia, 1896; Graszl, *Eherecht der Juden in Oesterreich*, Vienna, 1849; Fassel, *Das Mosaisch-Talmudische Civilrecht*, i., §§ 44–121, Vienna, 1852; Lichtenstein, *Die Ehe nach Mosaisch-Talmudischer Auffassung*, Leipsic, 1879; Fränkel, *Grundlinien des Mosaisch-Talmudischen Eherechts*, Breslau, 1860.

S. S. J. H. G.

MARRIAGE SETTLEMENT. See KETUBAH.

MARRIED WOMAN. See MARRIAGE; WOMAN.

MARSEILLES (מרשילייה or מרסיליא): Seaport of southern France with about 5,000 Jews in a population (1896) of 420,300. It had a Jewish colony as early as the fifth century, and in 567 a number of exiles from Clermont, Auvergne, sought refuge there from the intolerance of Bishop Avitus. Pope Gregory intervened in their behalf in 591, reproaching Theodore, Bishop of Marseilles, for having attempted to convert them by force and not by suasion. Benjamin of Tudela says ("Itinerary," i. 6) that when he passed through the city, about 1165, the Jewish community numbered 300 members, who worshiped in two synagogues. In the thirteenth century the Jews carried on an extensive commerce and had considerable relations with the East. While they are called "citizens of Marseilles" ("cives Massiliæ"), as appears from the compact made in 1219 between the city and the bishop in regard to the municipal franchises, and from the agreement between the inhabitants of Marseilles and the Duke of Avignon in 1257, this does not seem to denote that they had equal rights with their Christian fellow citizens. Their condition, which seems to have been favorable during the earlier parts of the Middle Ages, underwent a change in 1262, when the city was obliged to capitulate in consequence of an insurrection against the Duke of Anjou, Count of Provence, to whom the Jews were surrendered as property which he might tax at pleasure. The count, on the other hand, was well disposed toward the Jews, and in March, 1276, issued a severe edict against the inquisitors who had compelled them to wear a badge of greater size than the one worn by them since the Lateran Council of 1215, and extorted large sums from them under the pretext of fines.

Still, although theoretically the Jews were citizens, certain passages of the laws make it clear that they were not treated as such. After the age of seven they were obliged to have on their breasts a disk of some colored material, as large as the hand, while married Jewesses were required to wear special veils, "orales," under penalty of a fine of five

Disabilities.

sous. As in other cities of Provence, the Jews of Marseilles were forbidden to testify against Christians if their testimony was challenged, or to work on Sundays and Christian holy days. They were likewise prohibited from going to the baths more than once a week, from journeying to Alexandria, or from embarking in groups of more than four on the same ship. Jewish passengers on a vessel, moreover, were forced to refrain from meat on days when the Christian passengers abstained.

Toward the end of the thirteenth century a Jew living near the episcopal palace arranged some Purim games which the Christians regarded as a mockery of their religion, and the bishop, making the whole community responsible, imposed a heavy fine upon it (Ibn Adret, Responsa, iii. 389).

Fourteenth Century.

The fourteenth century was a golden age for the Jews, for they were placed under the absolute protection of the municipality. The municipal council did not permit the statutes to be construed in any way to their disadvantage, nor did it hesitate to oppose the guardian of the Jews appointed by the Count of Provence, or the most hostile of the clergy, to secure for the Jews the security promised them by the laws of the city. They were permitted to engage in the same trades as the Christians; most them were brokers, wine-, or cloth-merchants, or tailors. There was also one "magister lapidis" or stone-cutter. Another Jew, Crescas Davin, called Sabonerius, is said to have introduced the soap industry in 1371, and he was succeeded by his son Solomon Davin.

Although the majority of the Jews were engaged in commerce, there were also a number of physicians (Barthélemy, "Les Médecins à Marseille Avant et Pendant le Moyen Age," Marseilles, 1883; reprinted nearly entire in "R. E. J." vii. 293, 294).

The counts of Provence intervened in behalf of the Jews whenever occasion demanded. Thus, in 1320 King Robert enjoined his royal officers to afford special protection to the Jews, to assist them under all circumstances, and to receive them at need either in his castles and fortresses or in theirs; and in 1331 and 1332 Philippe de Sanguinet, seneschal of Provence, decreed that the Jewish communities in general and all Jews in particular should be protected against every vexation and that their property should be guarded by royal officers.

No complaint seems ever to have been brought against the community as a whole. In 1357 it helped to defend the city, threatened by a siege; in 1385 it contributed fifty florins to a loan which the citizens of Marseilles found themselves obliged to contract. In return, Queen Marie, in 1387, and her son Louis II. in 1389, confirmed the liberties, privileges, and immunities of the Jews.

Under Provençal Rule.

As long as Provence was independent the counts refused to listen to the exaggerated complaints against the Jews, who continued to live under benevolent municipal statutes and franchises. In 1422 Queen Yolande of Naples, Countess of Provence, forbade her royal officers to accept certain personal property from the Jews, under penalty of forfeiture of office and of payment of 100 marks fine silver. In 1463 King René, who ten years previously had entertained certain charges which had been brought against the Jews without investigating them, declared that they had a right to his special protection, since they could count on it alone, not being able to rely on that of the Church. In 1481, on the complaint of two Jewish deputies, Solomon Botarelli and Baron de Castres, René closed the baptistery of Saint-Martin, where a Christian woman had forcibly baptized a young Jewish girl, and he obliged the parishioners to have their children baptized in the Church of St. Jacques de la Corrigerie.

Projects of Expulsion.

In 1484 the lawless bands which overran the cities of Provence, attacking and pillaging the Jews, assailed the community of Marseilles, and in the following year the inhabitants of the city, accusing the Jews of usury and of various imaginary crimes, fell upon them and massacred a large number, demanding that King Charles VIII. immediately expel the remainder from Provence. The king, not daring to comply at once with a demand so contrary to the tolerance hitherto characterizing the rule of the counts of Provence, decreed that all Jews desiring to depart should be permitted to leave the city unmolested, provided they had fulfilled all their engagements with the Christians. The municipal council, ignoring this royal command, forbade any Jew or Jewess to leave with property. The Jews protested vigorously to the provost and the municipal council against this unjustifiable action, and demanded the protection of the magistrates. These protests must have been in so far effective as to secure them a respite, for in 1492 the community was still numerous enough to ransom 118 Aragonian Jews captured by the pirate Bartholemei Janfredi, paying the sum of 1,500 écus, which it borrowed from a Christian. Eight years later a royal decree of banishment from Marseilles was issued against the Jews, though it was not carried out completely until about 1501.

In the seventeenth and eighteenth centuries some Jews had again settled at Marseilles. Among them were Villaréal, who was expelled in 1682 for having induced some Jewish families to come to the city and having opened a synagogue in his house; Lopez, originally from Bordeaux, who was driven out in 1711; and Rouget, who, in virtue of a residence of fifteen years at Marseilles, claimed in 1771 the right of engaging in marine commerce.

Since 1808 Marseilles has been the seat of a consistory, whose administrative authority extends over all the Jewish communities of southern France.

Ghetto.

The Jewish quarter, with its principal street, which was called "Carreria Jusatarie" or "Carreria Judæorum," and its lanes and byways, formed a kind of island designated "Insula Juzatarie," and occupied a considerable area. In 1350 the Jews planned to leave their ghetto, but the inquisitor objected and obliged them to remain. When the city was taken by King Alphonso V. of Aragon, in 1423, the Jews suffered especially, and most of them fled from Marseilles, seeking refuge in various places of Provence. Some returned within a short time, under the protection of a safe-conduct, while the remainder were enjoined to return within fifteen days, under penalty of furnishing their coreligionists with a sufficient security to guarantee the payment of the communal debt incurred before the disasters of 1423.

Synagogues and Cemeteries.

The Jews had two synagogues in the Middle Ages, one "Scola Major," and the other "Scola Minor." A Latin document mentions a third synagogue in an entirely different quarter. The present temple was built in 1865. In medieval times the Jewish cemetery was situated on the Mont-Juif or Montjusieu, but after the expulsion of the Jews King Charles VIII. presented the site to a citizen of Marseilles. In 1783 Solomon de Silva and Mordecai Ḥay Darmon bought a plot in the Quartier du Rouet. This served as a cemetery for the Jews until 1804, when it no longer sufficed; and a larger piece of land was bought in the vicinity ("R. E. J." xiv. 302). At present (1904) the community of Marseilles owns two cemeteries, one, now closed, near the Place Castellane, and the other in the Quartier de St. Pierre.

The hospital was situated in the vicinity of the large synagogue, and the two almshouses were under the supervision of rectors. One of them was called "Saraca." The Jew Bonias Salemas left it in 1426 a bequest of four measures of pure wine annually as a perpetuity; to the other one he bequeathed, in a similar manner, a measure of oil to be delivered every year on the eve of the fast of Kippur. The women's bath, called "Lo Banhador de las Fennas," was also situated in the ghetto. The Jews had their own slaughter-house, called "Lo Masel de los Jusieus."

In the second half of the twelfth century Marseilles was an important center for Jewish studies.

Scholars.

Benjamin of Tudela styles it "the city of geonim and sages." In 1194 it was to these "scholars and learned men" that Maimonides addressed his letter on astrology (comp. Maimonides, "Iggerot," ed. Amsterdam, p. 6). The following are some of the scholars of Marseilles: twelfth century: Simeon b. Antoli or Anatole and his brother Jacob, Isaac b. Abba Mari, Moses b. Samuel ibn Tibbon; thirteenth century: Jacob b. Machir (called also Profatius Judæus), Shem-Ṭob b. Isaac, Joseph of Marseilles, Solomon Nasi b. Isaac Cayl, Jonathan, Isaac of Marseilles, Samuel b. Judah or Meles Bonjudas; fourteenth century: Solomon b. Joseph, Nissim b. Moses, Shem-Ṭob Falcon, and Joseph b. Johanan; fifteenth century: Judah b. David (called also Maestre Bonjudas Bondavi), and Jacob b. David Provençal. Of the modern rabbis may be noted Jonas Weyl (d. 1903) and his successor, the present (1904) incumbent, Honel Meiss.

BIBLIOGRAPHY: Aug. Fabre, *Hist. de Marseille*, i. 481–491; idem, *Anciennes Rues de Marseille*, pp. 99–109; Bédarride, *Les Juifs en France*, p. 228; Barthélemy, *Les Médecins à Marseille Avant et Pendant le Moyen Age*, pp. 13–29; idem, *La Savonnerie Marseillaise*, p. 8; Blancard, *Documents Inédits sur le Commerce de Marseille au Moyen Age*, i., 2d part, No. 55, p. 79, No. 314, p. 392; ii., No. 518, p. 76, No. 716, p. 161, Nos. 963, 964, p. 274; ii., 3d part, No. 23, p. 423; Beugnot, *Les Juifs d'Occident*, i. 135; C. Arnaud, *Essai sur la Condition des Juifs en Provence*, pp. 14, 15, 28 *et seq.*; Depping, *Les Juifs dans le Moyen Age*, pp. 198–200; Gregory of Tours, *Historia Francorum*, v. 11, vi. 17; Gross, in *Monatsschrift*, 1878, p. 155; idem, *Gallia Judaica*, pp. 366–384; Octave Teissier, *Marseille au Moyen Age*, pp. 43–155; Papon, *Histoire Générale de la Provence*, iii., 61, documents, xv.; Portal, *Un Procès en Responsabilité Médicale*, p. 5, Marseilles 1902; *R. E. J.* vii. 293; ix. 66; xii. 267; xiv. 310; xvi. 73; xvii. 96; xlvi. 1, 246; xlvii. 62; xlix. 301; Ruffi, *Hist. de Marseille*, xiii. 26, pp. 305-309; *Shebeṭ Yehudah*, ed. Hanover, p. 114.

D. S. K.

MARSHALL, LOUIS: American lawyer and communal worker; born at Syracuse, N. Y., Dec. 14, 1856; educated at the Syracuse high school and at the Columbia College Law School. He entered upon the practise of his profession in Syracuse in 1878, removing to New York city in 1894. As a member of the bar Marshall has attained a distinguished position. He was appointed by Governor Hill, in 1890, a member of the commission to revise the judiciary article of the constitution of New York, and was elected to the New York Constitutional Convention of 1894, serving as vice-chairman of the judiciary committee and chairman of the committee on "future amendments." He has served also as vice-president of the New York State Bar Association and has written numerous articles and essays on professional subjects.

Marshall is active also as a Jewish communal leader. He is a director and chairman of the executive committee of the Jewish Theological Seminary of America, and is a director of the Congregation Emanu-El, the Educational Alliance, and the Jewish Protection and Aid Society (all of New York), and of the New York branch of the Alliance Israélite Universelle. Marshall has taken especial interest in the establishment of a Jewish "protectory" for delinquent Jewish children, and has occasionally delivered addresses and lectures on Jewish subjects.

BIBLIOGRAPHY: Markens, *The Hebrews in America*, p. 229; *History of the Bench and Bar of New York*; Leslie, *History of New York*.

A.

MARTIN, RAYMUND: Spanish Christian theologian; born in the first half of the thirteenth century at Subirats in Catalonia; died after 1284. In 1250 he was selected by the provincial chapter, sitting in Toledo, to study Oriental languages at a Dominican school which had been founded for the express purpose of preparing its pupils to engage in polemics against Jews and Moors. Subsequently he lived for a long time in a monastery at Barcelona. In March, 1264, he was commissioned, with the Bishop of Barcelona, Raymund de Peñaforte, and two other Dominicans, Arnoldus de Sagarra and Petrus Janua, to examine the Hebrew manuscripts and books which the Jews, by order of the king, were to submit to them, and to cancel passages deemed offensive to the Christian religion. This is the first instance of Dominican censorship of the Talmud in Spain. Their report was not at all severe, however, since Raymund Martin declared that many passages were confirmatory of the truth of Christianity, and that the Talmud should not be burned entirely ("Pugio Fidei," ii. 14, § 8).

Martin was the author of two anti-Jewish books, one of which, the "Capistrum Judæorum," has never been printed. His chief work, the "Pugio Fidei," mentioned by Victor Salbaticis in 1520, was lost for a long time, but was finally brought to light by Justus Scaliger, and edited by Joseph de Voisin, with many notes, under the title "Pugio Fidei

Raymundi Martini Ordinis Prædicatorum Adversus Mauros et Judæos" (Paris, 1651). Better known than this edition is its reprint by J. B. Carpzov (Leipsic, 1667), with the anti-Jewish preface "Introductio in Theologiam Judaicam." The work treats of God's omniscience, the Creation, immortality, and the resurrection of the dead, and attempts to show the falsity of the Jewish religion; the latter part of the work is valuable on account of its extracts from the Talmud, the Midrash, and from other sources. Martin has been accused of forgery because of his quotations from Genesis Rabbah, which was not otherwise known; but Zunz defends him against this charge ("G. V." p. 300).

Martin was widely read in Hebrew literature, quoting not only from Talmudic and Midrashic works, but from Rashi, Ibn Ezra, Maimonides, and Ḳimḥi. His fundamental views, which he attempts to substantiate by his citations, are that Jesus is announced in rabbinical literature as the Messiah and son of God; that the Jewish laws, although revealed by God, are abrogated by the advent of the Messiah; that the Talmudists corrupted the text of the Bible, as is indicated by the "tiḳḳun soferim." Martin's work was for a long time the chief source for Dominican polemics.

Bibliography: Antoine Touron, *Histoire des Hommes Illustres de l'Ordre de St. Dominique*, i. 489-504, Paris, 1743; Jacob Quétif, *Scriptores Ordinis Prædicatorum*, i. 396-398, *ib.* 1719; Wolf, *Bibl. Hebr.* i. 1016-1018, iii. 989-991; Herzog-Plitt, *Real-Encyc.*; Grätz, *Gesch.* vii. 124, 150.

s. G. We.

MARTINET, ADAM: German Catholic Orientalist; born in Höchstädt, near Bamberg, in Jan., 1800; date of death uncertain. Martinet, who was a professor in the lyceum of Bamberg, was the author of "Tif'eret Yisrael," or "Hebräische Chrestomathie der Biblischen und Neueren Literatur, mit Anmerkungen und Glossar" (Bamberg, 1837), in which are given selections from the writings of Rapoport, Wessely, Friedländer, and other modern Hebrew authors.

Bibliography: Oettinger, *Moniteur des Dates*; *Allgemeine Deutsche Biographie.*

T.

MARTINEZ, FERRAND: Archdeacon of Ecija in the fourteenth century, and one of the most inveterate enemies of the Jewish people; lived at Seville, where among Christians he was highly respected for his piety and philanthropy. In his sermons and public discourses he continually fanned the hatred of the Christian population against the Jews, to whom he ascribed all sorts of vices. As vicar-general of Archbishop Barroso of Seville he arrogated to himself the right of jurisdiction over the Jews in his diocese, injuring them wherever he could, and demanding that the magistrates of Alcalá de Guadeyra, Ecija, and other places no longer suffer the Jews among them. The Jewish community of Seville, at that time the richest and most important community of the country, was forced to appeal to King Henry II., who commanded the archdeacon, in a letter dated Aug. 25, 1378, not to meddle in future with the affairs of his subjects the Jews; not to incite the people against them; and to abstain from deciding their lawsuits. The Jews were empowered to withdraw from the archdeacon's jurisdiction, and the royal officials of Seville and other cities were summoned to protect the Jews in their rights. But this made no impression on Ferrand Martinez; and the Jews were obliged, four years later, to complain to King John I. John severely reproved him (March 3, 1382), but to no effect. The king issued a new edict (Aug. 25, 1383) in which he commanded the archdeacon to desist, on pain of heavy punishment. Nothing, however, could keep Ferrand Martinez from pursuing his purpose of exterminating the Jews.

The community of Seville finally decided to summon the archdeacon before the highest tribunal. On Feb. 11, 1388, Ferrand Martinez, and the clothier Judah Aben Abraham, the representative of the community of Seville, together with their witnesses appeared before the "alcaldes mayores" Ferrand Gonzalez and Ruy Perez. Judah, referring to the two royal edicts, demanded in the name of the community that the archdeacon should desist once for all from any arbitrary and unlawful acts against the community; otherwise the community would immediately bring a complaint before the king.

Public Trial.

Ferrand Martinez declared in his written answer, read eight days later before the tribunal, that he would continue to preach and act as heretofore; that all he had done so far had been done on the advice of the archbishop and for the benefit of the Church and the welfare of the king. He asserted also that the Jews had offered him 10,000 doubloons for deciding an important case in their favor. The archiepiscopal chapter now interfered, sending two of its members to the king to say that the archdeacon was setting aside even the authority of the pope, and that the safety of the Jews was imperiled. The king, who was entirely ruled by his wife, Leonora, Ferrand Martinez's penitent, replied that matters should not be precipitated, and that the archdeacon's zeal was worthy of all praise; at the same time he declared that the Jews under his protection must not be maltreated.

Archbishop Barroso proceeded more energetically. Summoning a body of theologians and experts in canonical law, he called upon Martinez to recant. As Martinez refused to do so, he was forbidden to perform thenceforth any ecclesiastical function whatsoever, or to decide any case, on pain of excommunication. When Ferrand Martinez was deposed from office the Jews of Seville felt relieved, but their relief was of short duration. The archbishop Barroso and King John died within three months. The king was succeeded by Henry III., a child of eleven years, under the tutelage of his bigoted mother. The archiepiscopal chapter chose the excommunicated archdeacon for vicar-general. Ferrand Martinez immediately (Dec. 8, 139[illegible]) called upon the clergy of his diocese to demolish all synagogues in their parishes, and send to him without delay all lamps, Hebrew books, and scrolls of the Law found therein, on pain of excommunication.

Appointed Vicar-General.

The clergy of Ecija and Alcalá de Guadeyra obeyed at once; and the synagogues of Sor[illegible] and Santillana also came near being torn down.

The Jewish community of Seville turned in its consternation to the king (about Dec. 15, 1390), wh[illegible] seven days later sent a letter to the archiepiscopal chapter, holding it responsible for all damages done to the Jews, and commanding it to rebuild or to repair at its own expense all synagogues that had been torn down or damaged. He gave strict orders that the archdeacon should be at once deposed from office and placed where he could do no further harm. The chapter proceeded to obey the king's command; but Martinez declared that an ecclesiastic was subject to the Church and not to the king, and that the chapter had no right to depose him from office, or to demand that he rebuild the demolished synagogues.

Under Leonora's regency Martinez could defy even the king, receiving effective support from the people he had aroused. The first riots broke out in March, 1391, during which several Jews were killed. The great massacre occurred at Seville June 6, 1391, when several thousand Jews were killed and many forced to accept baptism. The people rose against the Jews throughout Castile, Aragon, and Majorca, many thousands being slain or forced into the Church. Ferrand Martinez was imprisoned at Seville in 1395 by command of Henry III., but was soon released. The people worshiped him as a saint. Before his death he presented his whole fortune to the hospital of San Maria at Seville, which he had founded.

BIBLIOGRAPHY: Zuniga, *Anales de Sevilla*, ii. 29 *et seq.*; Rios, *Hist.* ii. 338, 579 *et seq.*, Henry Ch. Lea, *Acta Capitular del Cabildo de Sevilla*, in *American Historical Review*, i. 220 *et seq.*; *R. E. J.* xxxviii. 260 *et seq.*

G. M. K.

MARTINI GEESE. See BARNACLE-GOOSE.

MARTINIQUE: Island in the West Indies, now constituting a French colony. In the beginning of the seventeenth century a number of Dutch Jews settled at Martinique and in the neighboring islands, and were in very prosperous circumstances when France took possession of the island in 1635. But in 1658 the Jesuits, jealous of the commercial supremacy of the Jews, induced the sovereign council of Martinique to issue an edict forbidding Jewish commerce in the islands. At the instance, however, of the home authorities the council revoked this decision, which menaced the interests of the colony, and consented to restore the Jews to their commercial rights.

This freedom was of short duration. In 1664 Governor-General Tracy was induced by the Jesuits to issue a decree forbidding "persons of the Jewish nation to buy or sell on the Sabbath-day [Sunday] . . . on pain of a fine of 300 pounds of petun, of which one-third shall go to the church, one-third to the poor, and one-third to the informer." The Jews thereupon appealed to the new governor, Baas, who restored to them the free exercise of trade and commerce. Their enemies then approached the governor, who, yielding to their importunities, forbade (1669) Jews "to perform on Saturday any ceremonies relating to their faith, . . . to work on Sunday, or to appear in public from Maundy Thursday to Easter Sunday." But, like his predecessor, Baas soon perceived the importance of Jewish commerce and industry and sent Colbert a report favorable to the Jews, requesting certain privileges for them, especially that of the free exercise of their religion. Colbert pleaded the cause of the Jews so well before the king that on May 23, 1671, Louis XIV. decreed that the Jews of Martinique should thenceforth enjoy not only religious liberty but also the same privileges as the other inhabitants. During the life of Colbert all hostile schemes against the Jews failed, despite the powerful support which their enemies found in Count de Blénac, who had succeeded Baas as governor. But with Colbert's death they lost their protector, and the governor, yielding to the Jesuits, on Sept. 24, 1683, during a visit to France, obtained from Louis XIV. an edict banishing the Jews from Martinique. This order, evidently, was not put into execution at once, since two years later a new decree was issued, known as the "Code Noir," which obliged the Jews to leave the island within three months. No exceptions were to be made, not even in favor of Benjamin d'Acosta, who had introduced the cultivation of the sugarcane in the island. In 1694 six Jewish families went to Martinique, but were at once expelled.

In the first half of the eighteenth century some Jews obtained permission to live in the colony. Laws were passed granting them a degree of legal existence, and the "Code Noir" was declared to apply only to foreign Jews. In 1722 David GRADIS of Bordeaux established an office at St. Pierre. In 1764 Count d'Estaing imposed a tax upon the Jews, who were then numerous in Martinique, some residing there under the protection of "naturalization papers" and others being merely tolerated. Wishing to have their position clearly defined, they appealed to their coreligionists of Bordeaux, with whom they were in family and business relations, to request Louis XVI. to extend to colonial Jews the privileges enjoyed by the Jews of Bordeaux. Jacob Rodrigues Pereire of Bordeaux took up the cause of the Jews of Martinique, and addressed an eloquent memorial to Minister Tartine, who, after investigating the matter for some months, declared against any change (1776). All subsequent attempts made to improve their condition were equally unsuccessful, and they continued to live under a régime of bare toleration down to 1789, when the French Revolution removed their disabilities.

BIBLIOGRAPHY: Abbé Grégoire, *Histoire des Sectes Religieuses*, vol. iii., book xi.; Moreau de Saint-Méry, *Lois et Constitutions des Colonies Françaises d'Amérique sous le Vent*, vols. i. and ii., *passim*, Paris, 1787; *R. E. J.* ii. 93, iv. 133, v. 80; Théophile Malvezin, *Histoire des Juifs à Bordeaux*, pp. 241-243.

D. S. K.

MARTYRDOM, RESTRICTION OF: True to the principle current in rabbinical literature—"live through them [the laws], but do not die through them" (Yoma 85b, based on Lev. xviii. 5)—the Rabbis endeavored to restrain the desire for martyrdom on the part of the zealous. During the period of the Hadrianic persecutions such a restraint was obviously necessary. Akiba is related to have courted martyrdom rather than give up the teaching of the Law, in spite of the warning given to him by Papus (Ber. 61b); as did also Hananiah b. Teradion, in spite of the counsel of Jose ben Ḳisma ('Ab. Zarah 18a). R. Ishmael, on the other hand, was of the opinion that one may even worship idols in order to save one's life, although he admits that martyrdom should be preferred to a public profession of idolatry (Sanh. 74a; 'Ab. Zarah 24b). Probably it was during this period that the following principle was adopted, at a sitting of rabbis in the house of a certain Nitzah in Lydia: "All negative commandments of the Bible, except those with regard to idolatry, adultery, and murder, may be transgressed if there is danger of life" (Sanh. 74a; Yer. Sanh. iii. 6; Yer. Sheb. iv. 1; comp. Pesiḳ. R., ed. Friedmann, p. 55a). At the same meeting the question whether the study of the Law is more important than the practise of the Law was decided in the affirmative, for the reason that study leads to practise (Ḳid. 40b; Cant. R. ii. 31; Sifre, Deut. 41). This question was of practical importance to the rabbis of that time, and the decision meant that one must submit to martyrdom rather than forsake the study and the teaching of the Law (see B. Ḳ. 17a). The later rabbis, while disregarding this last decision, adopted and developed to meet various cases the general principle governing submission to martyrdom for the practise of the Law (comp. Grätz, "Gesch." 3d ed., iv., note 17, ii.; Weiss, "Dor," ii. 131).

Conditions of Martyrdom.

If the intention of the persecutor is not so much to benefit himself as to compel the Jew to transgress the laws of Judaism in public (פרהסיא = παῤῥησία, explained to mean "in the presence of ten Israelites"), the Jew should rather submit to martyrdom than commit even the smallest transgression. In a time of general persecution of Jews one should prefer martyrdom when required to transgress a law even in private (Sanh. 74a, b; Maimonides, "Yad," Yesode ha-Torah, v. 1-3; Shulḥan 'Aruk, Yoreh De'ah, 157, 1). In a case in which a Jew is permitted to transgress a law when the alternative is death, he may submit to martyrdom, if he prefer martyrdom to the transgression; some authorities, however, forbid this, regarding it as a forfeiting of life to no avail ("Yad," Yesode ha-Torah, v. 4; comp. Mishneh le-Melek *ad loc.*; Yer. Sheb. iv. 2; 'Ab. Zarah 27b; Tos. *ib.* s.v. "Yakol"; Yoreh De'ah, *l.c.*). If he can redeem himself by giving up all his possessions he should part with all he has rather than transgress a negative law of the Bible (R. Nissim on Alfasi to Suk. iii. 2, *s.v.* "Dabar"; Isserles to Yoreh De'ah, *l.c.*; "Pitḥe Teshubah," *ad loc.*; comp. "Sefer Ḥasidim," ed. Wistinetzki, § 1365). One who transgresses the Law instead of submitting to martyrdom where martyrdom is enjoined, can not be punished in the courts, since the transgression is committed under duress, but he must be regarded as a defiler of God's name; and if he persists in living in the same place and in continuing the transgression when he can escape, he forfeits his portion in the future world and will be assigned to the lowest chambers of Gehenna ("Yad," *l.c.*). At no time is it permitted to a Jew to commit suicide or to kill his children in anticipation of religious persecution; he must wait until the persecutor comes and submit to the death inflicted upon him ("Be'er ha-Golah" to Yoreh De'ah, 157, 1, end, quoting the "Bedeḳ ha-Bayit").

Other Cases.

The same laws that apply to cases of religious persecution apply also to other cases which involve danger to life. At the order of a physician a sick man is permitted to break all the laws of the Bible except the three mentioned above—idolatry, adultery, and murder—if his life depends on the breaking of these laws (Pes. 25a; "Yad," *l.c.* v. 6-8). But, anxious for the chastity of Jewish women, the rabbis decided that even when adultery is not involved, as when the woman is unmarried, one should be left to die from the intensity of his passion rather than that the purity of a Jewish woman should be defiled. In an instance related in the Talmud conversation between the sick man and the object of his desire was forbidden (Sanh. 75b; "Yad," *l.c.* v. 9). Martyrdom is enjoined only when the transgression of the Law would involve a deliberate act. Thus, a woman is not obliged to undergo martyrdom if attacked with an immoral intent (comp. Sanh. 74b; Tos. *ib.* s.v. "Weha"; R. Nissim on Alfasi to Pes. ii. 1, *s.v.* "Ḥuẓ"; Isserles to Yoreh De'ah, *l.c.*).

If a number of Jews are threatened with death if they do not deliver one among them to be slain, they all should submit to the alternative of martyrdom. There is a difference of opinion, however, in a case where the one demanded is indicated by name. Some authorities hold the view that in such a case they may surrender the one thus specified in order to save themselves from death; while others are of the opinion that they may surrender him only when he is guilty of some act that involves the death-penalty. The same is true if one among a number of women is demanded for immoral purposes (Ter. viii. 12; Yer. Ter. viii. 4, end; Tosef. *ib.* vii. 23; comp. Rashi to Sanh. 72b, *s.v.* "Yaẓa"; "Yad," *l.c.* v. 5; and "Kesef Mishneh," *ad loc.*; Yoreh De'ah, *l.c.*; "Sefer Ḥasidim," §§ 253, 254).

In times of persecution a Jew may not say that he is a Gentile in order to save himself from death, although he may mislead his persecutors into an understanding that he is not a Jew (ROSh to 'Ab. Zarah ii. 4; Yoreh De'ah, 157, 2). In such a case it is permitted to the Jew to put on garments with "sha'atnez" (wool and flax) in them, or to shave his beard, and for a woman to attire herself in male garments, or in those worn by nuns, in order to deceive the persecutors ("Ḥatam Sofer" to Shulḥan 'Aruk, Oraḥ Ḥayyim, 159; "Sefer Ḥasidim," §§ 202–207, 259–262). Although it is forbidden to a Jew to be alone with a non-Jew ('Ab. Zarah 22a), in case of persecution a Jew may seek protection at the house of a non-Jew (ROSh, Responsa, xix. 17; Yoreh De'ah, *l.c.* 3; comp. "Sefer Ḥasidim," § 251).

BIBLIOGRAPHY: Hamburger, *R. B. T.* ii., s.v. *Rabbinismus*; Supplement, i., s.v. *Märtyrer*.

S. S. J. H. G.

MARTYROLOGY: Biography of martyrs. Early in its existence the Christian Church began to register the judicial proceedings against its martyrs and saints. These records, called "Acta Sanctorum," took the form of calendars, menologies, "menæa," or "legenda passionalia." Since the anniversaries of the deaths of the saints were celebrated by the sacrifice of the mass, the calendars were merely lists arranged according to the secular year and intended only for the use of individual churches. The martyrologies, which were introduced in the seventh century, were an amplification of the calendars, and contained short biographies, and lists of the festivals of other churches. The arrangement of these books clearly appears in the present official "Martyrologium Romanum." The third class of stories, the "Vitæ Sanctorum," had the alternative name of "legends," as being intended both for private and for public reading.

Jewish "Saints" or Martyrs.

Israel likewise has its "saints," though the word is used in an entirely different sense from that employed by the Christian Church. Only a brief portion of the liturgy is set aside for commemorating the martyrs of Israel, and the literature on the Jewish heroes of the faith is comparatively small. The "ḳedoshim," the saints of Israel, had merely fulfilled their religious duty when they steadfastly endured torture and death. Their widows did not marry again, since their murdered husbands still lived in liturgical poems, simple notices, or formal narratives, and in single lists; in Germany these lists were read at the HAZKARAT NESHAMOT to the community, which, on the Sabbaths before Pentecost and before the anniversary of the destruction of Jerusalem, as well as on the 9th of Ab, commended the souls of the martyrs to the mercy of God. The lists of the places of martyrdom and of the martyrs contained in the MEMOR-BOOKS may in a certain sense be called "martyrologies," although there were also independent works bearing this name. Schudt ("Jüdische Merkwürdigkeiten," iv. 1) has the following passage referring to the descendants of the martyrs persecuted by the Inquisition: "The 'Neuester Staat des Königreichs Portugall,' by an anonymous author, also shows that the Jews have special martyrologies and records of coreligionists whom they honor as martyrs since because of their religion they were executed by the Inquisition in Spain and Portugal. . . . It is also noteworthy that the Jews of Amsterdam have their own books of martyrs, in which they enter the names of those who were burned for the sake of their faith, and many Jews are marvelously steadfast when they face the Inquisition" (comp. also "Unschuldige Nachrichten auf das Jahr 1740," p. 10; Delitzsch, "Zur Gesch. der Jüdischen Poesie," p. 122).

Among the lists of martyrs made in Germany, the home of persecutions, are those of Worms of 1096 and 1349, preserved in several places; the Nuremberg list of 1349; and the lists in the memor-books of Sontheim, Heilbronn, Krautheim, Neustadt-on-the-Aisch, Sindringen, and Widdern (1298), dating from the time of the persecutions instigated in Franconia by the nobleman Rindfleisch. A detailed martyrology, however, is found in the memor-book of the famous old community of Nuremberg, which was composed in 1296 by Isaac b. Samuel of Meiningen; by request of the HISTORISCHE COMMISSION it was edited by Salfeld, under the title "Das Martyrologium des Nürnberger Memorbuches," and published in 1898 as the third volume of the "Quellen zur Gesch. der Juden in Deutschland." The compiler drew his material not only from ancient accounts of the persecutions, but also, in all probability, from lists which were kept in the Jewish communal archives of Nuremberg. In lapidary style he gives an eloquent account of the victims slain in Germany during the Crusades; during the persecution caused by a false accusation of profanating a host in Franconia; in 1298, during various local massacres; and at the time of the burning of the Jews in 1349. The account referring to this incident mentions only the victims at Nuremberg, while references to former persecutions are apparently complete. For the years 1298, 1338–39 (see ARMLEDER PERSECUTIONS), and 1349, also, the manuscript contains lists of those who died as martyrs for their faith. In addition to the accounts of the persecutions in Germany, there are lists of those at Blois (1171) and Troyes (1288), while the persecutions in England and in France are merely mentioned, with the exception of that at Corbeil, which is especially emphasized. The manuscript contains also notes on the sufferings and martyrdoms of converts to Judaism (Salfeld, "Martyrologium," p. 149) in the midst of the other martyrs; and these are followed by a list of places where martyrdoms occurred during the persecutions under Rindfleisch in 1298. The statements in the lists of martyrs are supported by contemporary accounts, especially by the historical elegies, of which eleven, taken from manuscripts and old editions, have been added to the work.

The Nuremberg Martyrology.

BIBLIOGRAPHY: Wetzer and Welte, *Kirchenlexicon*, i. 173 *et seq.*, s.v. *Acta Sanctorum*; Krauss, *Real-Encyclopädie der Christlichen Altertümer*, ii. 380, Freiburg-im-Breisgau, 1882; Salfeld, *Martyrologium*, pp. xviii., note 1, and xx., note 1; Neubauer, *Le Memorbuch de Mayence*, in *R. E. J.* iv. 1 *et seq.*; idem, *Isr. Letterbode*, viii. 89 *et seq.*; Jellinek, *Worms und Wien*, pp. 3 *et seq.* (comp. Neubauer in *Isr. Letterbode*, vi. 677, viii. 891); Jellinek, *Märtyrer- und Memorbuch*; Jaraczewsky, *Gesch. der Juden in Erfurt*; Kroner, *Festschrift zur Einweihung der Neuen Synagoge in Erfurt*, p. 16; Berliner, in *Ḳobeẓ al-Yad*, 1887, ii. 27 (containing the list of martyrs at Erfurt in 1221); Stern, in *Zeitschr. für die Gesch. der Juden in Deutschland*, ii. 195; Grotefend, *Die Frankfurter Judenschlacht von 1241*, in *Mittheilungen des Vereins für Gesch. und Altertumskunde in Frankfurt-am-Main*, vi. 63; Horovitz, *Frankfurter Rabbinen*; Carmoly, *Annuaire Israélite*, 1855–56, p. 100; Darmesteter, *Deux Elégies du Vatican*, in *Romania*, 1874, pp. 443–486; *L'Autodafé de Troyes*, in *R. E. J.* ii. 199 *et seq.*; Stern and Salfeld, *Nürnberg im Mittelalter*, pp. 172 *et seq.*; Lowe, *The Memorbook of Nürnberg* (German transl. by Rahmer), in *Litteraturblatt*, vol. x., Nos. 31-32.

J. S. SA.

MARTYRS, THE TEN: Among the numerous victims of the persecutions of Hadrian, tradition names ten great teachers who suffered martyrdom for having, in defiance of an edict of the Roman emperor, instructed their pupils in the Law. They are referred to in haggadic literature as the **'Asarah Haruge Malkut.** Popular imagination seized upon this episode in Jewish history and embellished it with various legends relating the virtues of the martyrs and the fortitude shown by them during their execution. These legends became in the geonic period the subject of a special midrash—the Midrash 'Asarah Haruge Malkut, or Midrash Eleh Ezkerah, of which there exist four versions, each differing from the others in various points of detail (see Jellinek, "B. H." i. 64, vi. 19). Contrary to the accounts given in the Talmud and in Midrash Rabbah ('Ab. Zarah 17b, 18a; Ber. 61b; Sanh. 14a; Lam. R. ii. 2; Prov. R. i. 13), which clearly state that there were intervals between the executions of the ten teachers, the Midrash 'Asarah Haruge Malkut, probably in order to produce a greater effect upon the mind of the reader, describes their martyrdom as occurring on the same day.

This midrash differs from the older sources in regard also to the accusation upon which they were condemned. It says that when a certain Roman emperor who had been instructed in the Law came to the Biblical passage, "And he that stealeth a man, and selleth him, or if he be found in his hand, he shall surely be put to death" (Ex. xxi. 16), he conceived the following mischievous device: He summoned Ishmael ben Elisha (perhaps the propounder of the "Thirteen Rules"; see Ab. R. N., ed. Schechter, p. 54b; comp. Ned. ix. 10), Simeon (certainly not Simeon ben Gamaliel II; see Ta'an. 29b), Ishmael, Akiba ben Joseph, Hananiah ben Teradion, Ḥuẓpit (the interpreter ["meturgeman"] of the Sanhedrin of Jamnia), Yeshebab (the secretary of the Sanhedrin), Eliezer ben Shammua' (in Midr. R. *l.c.* "R. Eliezer Ḥersanah," or "R. Tryphon"), Hananiah ben Ḥakinai (in Midr. R. *l.c.* "Judah ha-Neḥetam"), and Judah ben Baba, and demanded of them what was the punishment prescribed by the Law for stealing a man. They answered, "Death"; whereupon the emperor said, "Then prepare to die, for your ancestors [alluding to the history of Joseph and his brethren] committed such a crime, and you, as the representatives of the Jewish nation, must answer for it." The rabbis asked for a delay of three days that they might ascertain, by invoking the Ineffable Name, whether the punishment pronounced against them was ordained by Heaven. Ishmael ben Elisha, in his capacity as high priest, or as the son of a high priest, was chosen to make the inquiry, and after having ascertained that it was decreed by Heaven, the rabbis submitted to their fate.

Their Names.

Ishmael and Simeon were the first to be taken to the place of execution, where a dispute arose between them as to which should be executed first, each desiring to precede the other in order that he should be spared the sight of the martyrdom of his colleague. Thereupon the emperor ordered lots to be cast, and the lot fell on Simeon, whose head was stricken from his body with a sword. Ishmael was flayed; he suffered with great fortitude, and began to weep only when his executioners reached the place of the phylacteries. The third victim was Akiba, whose flesh was torn off with a carding-implement. While undergoing the torture he recited the Shema' with a peaceful smile on his face. Astonished at his extraordinary courage, his executioner asked him if he was a sorcerer that he could so easily overcome the pain he was suffering, to which Akiba replied, "I am no sorcerer, but I rejoice that I am permitted to love God with my life." He died at the last words of the Shema'—"God is One." The fourth martyr was Hananiah ben Teradion, who was wrapped in a scroll of the Law and placed on a pyre of green brushwood; to prolong his agony wet wool was placed on his chest. "Wo is me," cried his daughter, "that I should see thee under such terrible circumstances!" "I should indeed despair," replied the martyr, "were I alone burned; but since the scroll of the Torah is burning with me the Power that will avenge the offens against the Law will avenge me also." His disci ples then asked: "Master, what seest thou?" H answered: "I see the parchment burning while th letters of the Law soar upward." His disciples the advised him to open his mouth that the fire migh enter and the sooner put an end to his sufferings but he refused to do so, saying, "It is best that H who hath given the soul should also take it away no man may hasten his death." Thereupon th executioner removed the wool, fanned the flame thus accelerating the end, and then himself plunge into the fire.

The martyrdom of the remaining rabbis is note without details, with the exception of Judah be Baba, who is said to have been pierced by lance He was the last of the martyrs; according to th Talmud (Sanh. 14a), he was surprised by the Roman in the valley between Usha and Shefar'am, where h was secretly investing the seven remaining pupils c Akiba with the authority to continue the teachin of the Law. The martyrdom of the "Ten Teach ers" is commemorated in a seliḥah recited in th Musaf service of the Day of Atonement. It i entitled "Eleh Ezkerah," and is based upon the ac count given in the Midrash 'Asarah Haruge Malku With some difference in names it is treated also i the dirge for the Ninth of Ab entitled "Arze ha Lebanon."

Bibliography: Grätz, *Gesch.* iv. 161 *et seq.*; J. Derenbour, *Essai sur l'Histoire et la Géographie de la Palestine*, p 427 (note), 430 (note), 436, Paris, 1867.

s. I. Br.

MARX, ADOLF BERNHARD: Germa musical writer; born at Halle May 15, 1799; died a Berlin May 17, 1866. He had studied music fo some time with D. S. Türk when his father, wh had destined him for the law, sent him to the Un versity of Halle, where he matriculated. Shortl afterward, however, he rejected the offer of a leg appointment at Naumburg in order to devote him self entirely to music, and proceeded to Berlin, whe he became a pupil of Zelter, while gaining a livel hood by teaching. In conjunction with the wel known publisher Schlesinger, he founded (1824) tl "Berliner Allgemeine Musikalische Zeitung," whic he conducted until 1830. In 1827 the University o Marburg conferred on him the title of doctor o philosophy; and in this capacity he lectured on tl pedagogics of music at the University of Berli which institution in 1830 appointed him music director of its student choir.

With Kullak and Stern, Marx founded in 1850 tl Berliner Musikschule, now the Stern Musik Co servatorium, one of the most prominent music institutes of Berlin. Here he taught until 185 when he resigned in order to devote himself entire to literary and university work and to the teachi of composition. His long and intimate friendsh with Mendelssohn was ultimately severed becau of the latter's strictures upon Marx's composition which, indeed, have not withstood the test of tim His musical writings, however, are far more val able, and include: "Ueber Malerei in der Tonkuns" (1828); "Die Lehre von der Musikalischen Kompo tion" (Berlin, 1837-1847, 4 vols.; several times r printed); "Allgemeine Musiklehre" (1839; 9th ed., 1875; translated into English); "Die Musik des 19ten Jahrhunderts und Ihre Pflege" (1855); "Ludwig van Beethoven's Leben und Schaffen" (1858; 3d ed., 1875); "Gluck und die Oper" (1863, 2 vols.); "Erinnerungen aus Meinem Leben" (1865, 2 vols.); and several other writings of an analytical nature.

BIBLIOGRAPHY: Mendel, *Musikalisches Konversations-Lexikon*; Riemann, *Musik-Lexikon*.

S. J. So.

MARX, BERTHE: French pianist; born at Paris July 28, 1859. She began to study the pianoforte at the age of four, receiving her first instruction from her father, who for forty years was a violoncello-player in the Conservatoire and Grand Opera orchestras. In 1868 she entered the Conservatoire, where she became a pupil of Henri Herz, in whose class at the age of fifteen she gained the first prize. Upon completing her studies she undertook a series of concert tours through France and Belgium, everywhere meeting with a cordial reception. At Brussels she met Sarasate, who, recognizing her great talent, engaged her as soloist and accompanist, in which capacities she accompanied him on his tours through Europe and America, extending even to Mexico and California; she played in all in about 600 concerts. She has composed several "Rhapsodies Espagnoles," and has arranged Sarasate's Spanish dances for the piano.

BIBLIOGRAPHY: A. Ehrlich, *Celebrated Pianists of the Past and Present Time*.

S. J. So.

MARX, DAVID: Chief rabbi of Bordeaux, France; born at Landau, Bavaria, in 1807; died Feb., 1864. On his graduation from the Ecole Centrale Rabbinique at Metz he assumed charge of the Ecole Religieuse Israélite at Nancy; and in June, 1837, before he had attained the age required for the office, he was elected by the consistory of Bordeaux to succeed Chief Rabbi Abraham Andrade. In 1841 he proposed the introduction of confirmation at Bordeaux, a rite then regarded as a dangerous innovation. Marx organized numerous institutions in the community of Bordeaux, including a "salle d'asile" and an infirmary; and under his guidance the children of the community founded the Société de la Jeunesse Israélite de Bordeaux, for the relief of less fortunate children. At various times during his term of office he interfered in behalf of minors who had been kidnaped from their parents by Catholic proselytizers. In 1852 he was decorated by Napoleon III., then prince-president, with the cross of the Legion of Honor. On the day of his funeral Dounet, Cardinal Archbishop of Bordeaux, ordered the bells of all the churches in the city to be tolled. Marx, who was a remarkable preacher, published the following sermons: "Sermon sur le Culte Public" (Bordeaux, 1853); "Discours lors de l'Inauguration de la Synagogue de Clermont-Ferrand" (1862); "Sermon sur le Dogme et la Morale" (*ib.* 1863).

BIBLIOGRAPHY: Aristide Astruc, *Oraison Funèbre de D. Marx*, Paris, 1864.

S. J. Ka.

MARX, JACOB: German physician; born in Bonn 1743; died in Hanover Jan. 24, 1789; studied medicine in Halle (M.D. 1765). He traveled for scientific purposes in Holland and England, in the latter country making the acquaintance of Dr. John Fothergill. He finally settled in Hanover, where he made himself greatly beloved. He has been reproached with inability to free himself from the prejudices of his time when he opposed Herz for attacking the Jewish burial customs of the period. Marx wrote: "Dissertatio de Spasmis et Motibus Convulsivis Optimaque Iisdem Medendi Ratione" (Halle, 1765); "Observata Quædam Medica" (Berlin, 1772); "Observationes Medicæ" (Hanover, 1774–87), in three parts: part one was translated into German by Böhm (Berlin and Hanover, 1786), parts two and three by Marx himself (Hanover, 1787); "Abhandlung über die Lungenschwindsucht" (Hanover, 1784); "Gesch. der Eicheln und Erfahrungen über die Diät und Medizinischen Gebrauch Derselben" (1784); "Bestätigte Kräfte der Eicheln" (1787); "Ueber die Beerdigung der Toten" (Hanover, 1787); etc.

BIBLIOGRAPHY: *Allg. Deutsche Biog.*; *Allg. Zeitschrift des Judenthums*, 1840, p. 711.

S. N. D.

MARX, KARL: German socialistic leader and political economist; born at Treves May 5, 1818; died in London March 14, 1883. His father, a practising attorney at the Landgericht, adopted Christianity in 1824. Marx attended the gymnasium at Treves and the universities of Bonn and Berlin, graduated as doctor of philosophy, and then turned to journalism, becoming in 1842 editor of the "Rheinische Zeitung für Politik, Handel und Gewerbe," which was founded by the Liberal party at Cologne. It was the most radical journal of the time in Germany. Marx became involved in a number of controversies, particularly with the "Oberpräsident" of the Rhine province, concerning the condition of the peasantry of the Moselle district; and in 1843 he resigned his editorial position to study political economy. In that year also he married Jenny, daughter of Baron von Westphal.

Shortly after the marriage Marx, on the invitation of Arnold Ruge, went to Paris to aid in the publication of the "Deutsch-Französische Jahrbücher," of which, however, only one (double) number was issued (1844). It contained, besides other matter, the celebrated "Lobgesänge auf den König von Bayern," by Heine, and two articles by Marx himself, "Zur Kritik der Hegel'schen Rechtsphilosophie" and "Zur Judenfrage."

After the publication of the "Jahrbücher," Marx became associated with the "Vorwärts," also published in Paris. The Prussian government intimated to that of France its displeasure at certain utterances of the "Vorwärts"; and Guizot ordered those of its editors who were not French citizens to leave the country. An interpellation in the French Chamber led to a revocation of the order; but Marx decided to leave Paris, and in 1845 he went to Brussels.

In Paris Marx had become intimately connected with the Bund der Gerechten, which had been founded in Paris in 1836, and which afterward became the Kommunistenbund. Its leaders in London corresponded with him; and they formed a branch in Brussels from which to send representatives to the congress to be held in London in the summer and fall of 1847. Marx attended in November, and after expounding his ideas in a number of addresses, the "Kommunistische Manifest," prepared by himself and Engels, was finally adopted, its concluding words, "Proletarier aller Länder, vereiniget Euch!" becoming the battle-cry of the laboring classes throughout the world. Upon the outbreak of the Paris revolution, in Feb., 1848, Marx prepared to go to the scene of conflict, but was arrested and forced to return to Germany. From June 1, 1848, he edited the "Neue Rheinische Zeitung." As leader of the left wing of the democratic movement of the Rhine province he was an important factor in the revolution. He was a member of the Rheinische Kreisausschuss der Demokraten, and with Schaffer and Schneider, as a committee of the organization, signed a proclamation (Nov., 1848) in which the members of the Democratic Association were advised to resist the collection of all taxes and to organize a military force. Marx and his associates were arrested and placed on trial for incitement to rebellion; but a jury acquitted them. In 1849 the government felt itself strong enough to order his banishment (May 16); and he went once more to France.

Karl Marx.

When Marx arrived in Paris a number of petty revolutions were ripe, in which he undoubtedly took part, although his share in them does not seem clear. When the demonstration of June 13 came to an end he was directed to leave France; and he then sought refuge in England.

Freed from agitation and revolution, Marx had now about fourteen years of peaceful literary activity. He frequently contributed to the Anglo-American press. On Sept. 24, 1864, a great meeting was held in London, at which Professor Beesly, the positivist, presided, and it was finally determined to establish a permanent organization of the working people of the civilized world. The International Working Men's Association was thus founded. Mazzini and Marx were entrusted with the task of preparing the address and the constitution; and at the congress held in Geneva in 1866 the report of Marx was adopted. Until 1872 Marx dominated the organization at the congresses and in the executive committee. His purpose was that of propaganda alone; but the mistake of the leaders was that the influence of the association was not exerted to hinder the Paris Commune in 1871. Marx himself was guilty of an even worse mistake: he actually approved the Commune's operations, in his pamphlet "Der Bürgerkrieg in Frankreich," published in 1871 and reissued in 1876. In order to dissolve the Internationale without giving his opponents a chance to reorganize it, he in 1872 transferred the seat of the general council to New York, in care of his faithful follower F. A. Sorge; and so the association came to an end.

The great work of Marx's life, and that with which his fame is most enduringly identified, is "Das Kapital," of which the first volume was published in 1873; the second, edited by Engels, in 1885; and the third, in 1894. Of the first (4th ed., 1892) an English translation by Moore and Aveling was issued in London in 1886.

BIBLIOGRAPHY: Gustav Gross, *Karl Marx*, Leipsic, 1885; Eugen von Böhm-Bawerk, *Karl Marx*, transl. by Alice M. MacDonald, London, 1892; Georg Adler, *Die Grundlagen der Karl Marx'schen Kritik der Bestehenden Volkswirthschaft*, Tübingen, 1887 (contains a bibliography of Marx's writings); E. Aveling, *The Student's Marx*, London, 1892; Slonimski, *Karl Marx' Nationalökonomische Irrlehren*, transl. from the Russian, Berlin, 1897.

S. M. Co.

MARX, ROGER: French art critic; born in Nancy Aug 28, 1859. In 1878 he went to Paris, where he wrote for various theater and art journals. In 1883 he became art, and afterward literary, critic of the "Voltaire." He was later appointed secretary of the Academy of Fine Arts, which position he resigned on the death of the director, M. Castagnary, though he continued to act as inspector of the Academy. In 1886 the government sent him on a mission to Spain to study the methods of instruction followed in the schools of industrial art and of design. In 1889 he was appointed assistant inspector-general of museums and organized the centennial section of French art at the Exposition Universelle in 1900, when, on the occasion of the opening of the fine arts exhibits, he was made an officer of the Legion of Honor. As a writer he is an individualist.

Marx has published: "Les Jouets" and "Les Dimanches de Paris," two works of fiction; "Etude d'Art Lorrain" (1882); "L'Art à Nancy en 1882" (Nancy, 1883); "Henri Regnault" (1886); "La Décoration et l'Art Industriel à l'Exposition Universelle de 1889" (Paris, 1890); "Histoire de la Médaille Française Depuis Cent Ans" (1890); "The Painter Albert Besnard" (*ib.* 1893); "J. K. Huysmans" (*ib.* 1894); "La Collection des Goncourt" (1897); "Die Französischen Medailleure Unserer Zeit," a collection of 442 medals and plaquettes (Stuttgart, 1898); "Les Médailleurs Français de 1789" (Paris, 1898); "La Décoration et les Industries d'Art" (*ib.* 1901); "Les Médailleurs Modernes en France et à l'Etranger" (*ib.* 1901); "Handbuch für Leihbibliotheken."

BIBLIOGRAPHY: Larousse, *Dict.* 2d Supplement; *Arch. Isr.* July 4, 1889; *Univ. Isr.* May 4, 1900.

S. N. D.

MARX, SAMUEL: Chief rabbi of Bayonne, France; born in 1817 at Dürkheim, Bavaria; died in 1887; cousin of David Marx. On completing his studies at the Ecole Centrale Rabbinique at Metz, he became director of the Ecole Religieuse Israélite at Nancy and assistant to the chief rabbi of that city. In 1843 he was appointed rabbi of Saint-Esprit and Bayonne, becoming chief rabbi three years later. Marx published the following sermons: "Sermon Prononcé à la Synagogue de Nancy, le 16 Avril, 1842"; "Discours de l'Installation, 18 Décembre, 1846" (Bayonne); "Sermon sur la Mesousa" (*ib.* 1866); "Le Centenaire de Sir Moses Montefiore" (*ib.* 1884).

BIBLIOGRAPHY: Henry Léon, *Histoire des Juifs de Bayonne*, Paris, 1893.

S. J. Ka.

MARYLAND: One of the thirteen original States of the American Union. The history of the Jews in Maryland may be divided into three periods: the first extends from shortly after the establishment of the provincial government at St. Mary's, in 1634, to the expansion of trade and commerce in the middle of the eighteenth century; the second begins a decade before the Revolution and ends with the practical removal of political disabilities in 1826; the third covers the following seventy years of German immigration, congregational development, and communal growth.

The characteristic of the first, or provincial, period is the apparent absence of any single influx of Jews corresponding to those which occurred in New York, Newport, Savannah, and Charleston. Record is found of one Mathias de Sousa as early as 1639, fifteen years before the arrival of "David Israel and the other Jews" at New Amsterdam. If, indeed, credence is to be given to the distinctiveness of such names as Matthias de Costa, Isaac de Barrette, Hester Cordea, David Fereira, and Jacob Leah, it seems probable that Jews were resident in Maryland in appreciable numbers from the earliest days of the palatinate. Yet percolation rather than influx, and quiet exercise rather than open profession of faith, seem to distinguish the period.

From among the hazy forms which thus constitute the history of the Jews in provincial Maryland the figure of Jacob or John Lumbrozo stands forth in bold prominence. He is the first, indeed the only, Jew of whose faith there is documentary evidence. Subsequent data gather about him as a nucleus, and it is largely in his experience that the difficulties of the period must be solved. He is one of the earliest medical practitioners in Maryland; his arrival forms a distinct event in the life of the province, and for nearly a decade he continues an important figure in its economic activity. Names of a distinctively Jewish character appear at intervals in the accessible records from 1660 to the overthrow of the proprietary government in 1692, always without mention of any communal organization, without even a bare indication of the bearers' faith. Among these are the names of David Fereira, Francis Hyems, Abraham Hart, Daniel Mathena, Jacob Leah, Solimon Barbarah, Sarah Hayes, Philip Salomon, Joseph Lazear, Matthias de Costa, Isaac de Barrette, Hester Cordea, and Isaack Bedlo. Whatever such evidence may suggest, the positive conclusion to which it leads is that while the Jew in proprietary Maryland was, de jure, without civil rights, was denied freedom of residence, and was liable to punishment by death for the bare profession of his faith, he was, de facto, permitted undisturbed domicil and was gradually allowed the exercise of certain undefined rights.

Jacob Lumbrozo.

The reduction of the palatinate to a crown colony in 1692 led naturally to a Protestant church establishment, and ecclesiastical organization, it seems, tended to identify citizenship with church membership and to disfranchise the professed Jew in the province at large. The broader organization of the cities, whither the Jew would naturally gravitate, permitted some political recognition. Thus the charter of Annapolis, granted in 1708, conferred the suffrage upon any person possessing a freehold or a visible estate of twenty pounds sterling, and those of other cities and towns gradually followed with similar privileges. But even there the Jew could hold no office. The act of 1715 reorganizing the Protestant Church establishment provided that the oath of abjuration, terminating with the words, "upon the true faith of a Christian," should be administered to "all persons that already have, or shall hereafter be admitted to have or enjoy, any office or place of trust within this province." The exclusion was perfected in the following year by the addition of the oaths of allegiance and abhorrency, and the test; to the last two no conscientious Jew could subscribe. No essential modification was made in this requirement until sixty years later, when it was embodied in the fundamental law of the state.

Excluded from Office.

Whatever recognition the Jew could obtain, it is necessary to remember, was accorded entirely upon sufferance. Legally, profession of Judaism still remained punishable by death. In 1723 the spirit of the Toleration Act of 1649 was revived by an act (repealing an apparently similar measure of 1715) "to punish blasphemers, swearers, drunkards." It did much more than this, however, in the opening enactment, which declared that "if any person shall hereafter within this province . . . deny our Savior Jesus Christ to be the Son of God, or shall deny the Holy Trinity" he shall, for the first offense, be fined and have his tongue bored; for the second, fined and have his head burned; for the third, put to death.

This act also remained unrepealed until after the adoption of the state constitution.

From the restoration of the "lord proprietor" in 1715 until the outbreak of the Revolution, Jewish names are rarely mentioned. The Jewish settlements at Schaefersville and Lancaster seem to have contributed little to the stream of German immigration which flowed steadily from southeastern Pennsylvania into Frederick county, Md. Similarly, the Jewish communities of Philadelphia and New York do not appear to have yielded to the commercial inducements offered by the more southerly colony. The absence of such contact suggests either a deliberate avoidance of the province or the absence of public avowal of Jewish faith during residence therein. Church establishment terminated with the fall of proprietary rule and with the emergence of Maryland into statehood. With it fell, too, the force of the legislation which for a century and a half had declared profession of the Jewish faith a capital offense. The practical identification in men's minds of citizenship and church membership and the subscription to doctrinal oaths as a necessary preliminary to political office could not, however, be swept away so easily.

The Constitution of 1776.

In Sept., 1776, a declaration of rights and a formal constitution were submitted to the Provisional Convention by a committee of five members appointed a month before. As adopted, the thirty-fifth article of the declaration of rights provided: "That no other test or qualification ought to be required on admission to any office of trust or profit than such oath of support and fidelity to this state, and such oath of office, as shall be directed by this convention or the legislature of this state, and a declaration of belief in the Christian religion." The text of the oath of fidelity was given in the fifty-fifth article of the constitution, and the requirement that the person so appointed "shall also subscribe a declaration of his belief in the Christian religion" was repeated. Henceforth the Jew in Maryland was secure in his religious profession and vested with certain political privileges. But the largest civic recognition was still withheld, and not until half a century later, after a persistent struggle extending over more than half this interval, was the fullest equality in the eye of the law accorded him.

The gradual influx of Jews into Maryland during and immediately after the Revolutionary war must undoubtedly be attributed to the commercial and industrial advantages of Baltimore. There is hardly any detailed information concerning the number, time of arrival, or personal history of these early settlers; a considerable part of them seems to have come from Philadelphia, and almost all appear to have been persons in moderate circumstances.

The first formal legislative effort to effect the removal of the existing disability was made in 1797. On Dec. 13 in that year a petition signed by Solomon Etting, Bernard Gratz, and others was presented to the General Assembly at Annapolis; the petitioners averred "that they are a sect of people called Jews, and thereby deprived of many of the valuable rights of citizenship, and pray to be placed upon the same footing with other good citizens." The petition was read and referred to a committee of three persons, who upon the same day reported that they "have taken the same into consideration and conceive the prayer of the petition is reasonable, but as it involves a constitutional question of considerable importance they submit to the House the propriety of taking the same into consideration at this advanced stage of the session." This summary disposition of the petition put a quietus upon further agitation for the next five years. On Nov. 26, 1802, a petition "from the sect of people called Jews" specifically stating their grievance, namely, "that they are deprived of holding any office of profit and trust under the constitution and laws of this state," was referred to the General Assembly, which read it and referred it to a special committee of five delegates, including the two Baltimore representatives, with instructions to consider and report upon the prayer of the petitioners for relief. A month later the petition was refused by a vote of thirty-eight to seventeen. The attempt to secure the desired relief was repeated at the legislative session of 1803; again proving unsuccessful, it was renewed in the following year.

Beginnings of Civic Emancipation.

There is much similarity in these successive attempts as disclosed in the bare outline of formal records. In 1803 and in 1804, as in 1802, petitions for legislative relief were presented to the House of Delegates, read, and referred to special committees. As in 1802, bills to the desired effect were reported back from these committees and shelved at the second reading; in 1803 the further consideration of the bill at this stage was postponed till the following session of the assembly; in 1804 the bill was defeated by a decisive vote of thirty-nine to twenty-four. Four successive attempts had now been made to secure full civic recognition, and four successive defeats had been suffered. Some favorable advance in public sentiment becomes evident upon a comparison of the votes of 1804 and 1802, but general opinion still continued so pronouncedly hostile to the grant of relief that to the few determined spirits upon whom the brunt of the struggle had thus far fallen any further agitation seemed absolutely hopeless if not actually unwise. Accordingly with the legislative defeat of 1804 further formal agitation ceased until fourteen years later.

Within this period (1804–18) occurred three circumstances of prime importance with respect to further efforts to secure legislative relief: (1) the rise in material importance and communal influence of the Jews of Baltimore; (2) the actual hardship, as distinct from merely possible inconvenience, suffered from the operation of civil disabilities; (3) the enlistment of the keen sympathy and persistent efforts of certain distinguished men active in public affairs in Maryland in behalf of the struggle for the removal of civil disabilities of the Jews.

The first circumstance is largely connected with the arrival in Baltimore from Richmond, Va., in the year 1803, of the Cohen family, consisting of the widow and six sons of Israel J. Cohen. The eldest son, Jacob I. Cohen, Jr., became at an early age a successful business man, and the founder of the banking-house of Jacob I. Cohen, Jr., & Brothers, videly and honorably known in commercial circles. With Solomon Etting he was early recognized as a

The Cohen Family.

leader and representative figure in the local Jewish community. His interest in public affairs was keen and sustained, his intercourse and friendship with ersons engaged in public life large and intimate, nd his concern for the full emancipation of Jews n Maryland intense. He was the author of the suc-essive petitions for relief and the proposed consti-utional amendments that besieged every session of he General Assembly from 1816 to 1826. He was he moving spirit of the sharp legislative struggle hat followed each effort, and it was his personal riends, largely out of regard for him, who led in he successive contests.

The second circumstance, the actual as distinct rom the possible inconvenience entailed by civil isabilities, is closely associated with the rise in naterial importance of members of the Jewish com-nunity. The elder Cohen had in Richmond been conspicuous in all municipal movements, being hosen a magistrate and a member of the city coun-il"; his sons found that so humble an office as that f wood-corder in Baltimore required a preliminary eclaration of belief in the Christian religion. Reu-en Etting was deemed by Thomas Jefferson worthy f appointment as United States marshal for Mary-and, but for the office of constable or justice of the eace his religious persuasion was an absolute dis-ualification. Others who had served with distinc-ion in the defense of Baltimore in 1812 and in sub-equent military engagements were disqualified rom rising from the ranks, and while personal ravery and the esteem and admiration of associates aused the letter of the law to be ignored, the offi-er's commission was held nevertheless by tacit onsent and upon bare sufferance. These two onditions, the larger influence and wider intercourse f leading Jewish families of Baltimore and the ctual hardship suffered by the operation of civil isabilities, combined to enlist the sympathy and id of a group of men active in public life in Mary-nd, and these conducted the legislative struggle

Struggle in Legis-lature.

for full emancipation in the General Assembly in the years from 1816 to 1826. The most prominent figure in this group, which included Thomas Brackenridge, E. S. Thomas, General Vinder, Col. W. G. D. Worthington, and John V. . MacMahon, was Thomas Kennedy of Washing-on county.

The history of the legislative struggle for the re-oval of the obnoxious restriction can be indicated ere only in the barest outline. Beginning with the gislative session of 1818, and continuing until the esired end was attained in 1826, a deliberate and istained attempt was made at each successive ses-on of the General Assembly to secure legislation lieving the Jewish appointee to political or civil fice in Maryland of the necessity of subscribing to declaration of belief in the Christian religion. The gislative struggle attracted wide-spread attention roughout the United States. The important news-apers of the country characterized the test as a dis-raceful survival of religious intolerance and urged its prompt repeal. The Jew Bill became a clearly defined issue in Maryland politics. In the debate in the legislative session of 1819–20, a detailed account of which has been preserved in notes taken by Thomas Kennedy and communicated to Jacob I. Cohen, it was openly charged that certain members had failed of reelection because they had voted for the repeal of Jewish disabilities. On the other hand, a disposition favorable to Jewish emancipation be-came at an early date a sine qua non of election from Baltimore. In 1822 a bill to the desired effect passed both houses of the General Assembly; but the constitution of Maryland required that any act amendatory thereto must be passed at one session of the General Assembly and published and confirmed at the succeeding session of the legislature. Ac-cordingly recourse was necessary to the legislative session of 1823–24, in which a confirmatory bill was introduced, accompanied by a petition, marked by singular loftiness of sentiment and dignity of tone, from the Jews in Maryland. The bill was con-firmed by the Senate, but in the House of Delegates, after a stirring debate, the important speeches in which have been preserved, it was defeated, and all formal legislation hitherto enacted was rendered nugatory.

But the end was nearer, perhaps, than even the friends of emancipation dared hope. On the very last day of the following session of the legislature (Feb. 26, 1825) an act "for the relief of the Jews in Maryland," which had already received the sanction of the Senate, was passed by the House of Delegates by a vote of twenty-six to twenty-five, only fifty-one out of eighty members being present. The bill provided that "every citizen of this state professing

Act of 1825.

the Jewish religion" who shall be ap-pointed to any office of profit or trust shall, in addition to the required oaths, make and subscribe a declaration of his belief in a future state of rewards and punish-ments instead of the declaration now required by the government of the state. A year later the brief but effective statute was enacted "that an act passed at December session, 1824, entitled an 'act for the relief of the Jews in Maryland,' shall be, and the same is hereby, confirmed."

An epilogue to the history of the struggle thus sketched were the repeal in 1847, at the instance of Dr. Joshua I. Cohen and through the efforts of John P. Kennedy, of a curious surviving discrimination against the Jews in the existing laws of evidence, and the efforts made, also at the instance of Dr. Joshua I. Cohen, in the constitutional conventions of 1850 and 1867 to eliminate entirely the religious test. The removal of the civil disabilities of the Jews in Maryland was gracefully signalized by the prompt election in Baltimore (Oct., 1826), as mem-bers of the city council, of Solomon Etting and Jacob I. Cohen, both of whom had been throughout the moving spirits of the legislative struggle. Cohen was made president of the "First Branch," and subsequently was elected for a long series of years as a municipal representative of his ward.

Since 1825 the Jew in Maryland has suffered no formal disability with respect to political office, and he has been frequently appointed to positions of trust and influence. The later history of the Jews in Maryland has been in the main the history of the Jewish community of BALTIMORE. Small bodies of Jews are to be found in Cumberland (165 in 1901), Hagerstown (209 in 1902), and in many localities throughout the state. The Jewish population of Baltimore in 1902 was estimated at 25,000, and that of the twenty-three counties (including towns) outside of Baltimore, at 1,500, making the total Jewish population of the state 26,500.

BIBLIOGRAPHY: Hollander, *Some Unpublished Material Relating to Dr. Jacob Lumbrozo of Maryland*, in *Publications Am. Jew. Hist. Soc.* 1893, No. 1, pp. 25-39; idem, *Civil Status of the Jews in Maryland, 1634-1776*, ib. 1894, No. 2, pp. 33-44 (see also references therein cited); *Sketch of Proceedings in the Legislature of Maryland, December Session, 1818, on What Is Commonly Called the Jew Bill*, Baltimore, 1819; *Address to the Children of Israel in Maryland*, ib. 1820; *Speech of Thomas Kennedy, Esq., in the Legislature of Maryland on the Bill Respecting Civil Rights and Religious Privileges*, Annapolis, 1823; *Memorial of Jewish Inhabitants of Maryland to the General Assembly*, 1824 (n.p.); *Governor Worthington's Speech on the Maryland Test Act, 1824*, Baltimore, 1824; *Speeches on the Jew Bill in the House of Delegates in Maryland, by H. M. Brackenridge, Col. W. G. D. Worthington, and John S. Tyson, Esquire*, Philadelphia, 1829; *Winning the Battle; or One Girl in Ten Thousand*, ib. 1882; G. E. Barnett, in *American Jewish Year Book*, 1902-3, pp. 46-62; correspondence and records in the possession of Mr. Mendes Cohen, Baltimore, Md.

A. J. H. Ho.

MÄRZROTH (pseudonym of **Moritz Barach**): Austrian author; born in Vienna March 21, 1818; died at Salzburg in 1888. After leaving the University of Vienna in 1844 he entered the field of journalism, in which his influence helped to establish a more liberal régime. He founded several journals, including "Das Wiener Feuilleton" (1853; belles-lettres), "Der Komet" (Vienna, 1853; humor), and "Die Komische Welt," edited the comic album "Brausepulver" (Vienna and Leipsic, 1847 and 1848), and wrote for "Fliegende Blätter," "Ueber Land und Meer" ("Wiener Croquis," a humorous chronicle of Vienna life), "Bauerle's Theaterzeitung" (letters of travel from 1855), and other publications. Most of his poems are in dialect, of which he was a master, and many of his songs have been set to music. Toward the end of his life he left Baden bei Wien, where he had long lived, and settled at Salzburg.

The following works of Barach may be mentioned: "Bilder, Lieder, und Geschichten," in dialect (Berlin, 1854); "Liederbuch ohne Goldschnitt" (Dresden, 1856); "Satans Leier" (Prague, 1860); "Spottvögel (*ib.* 1864); "Geistergestalten aus dem Alten Wien" (Vienna, 1868); "Schattenspiele aus dem Alten und Neuen Wien" and "Bitt' Gar Schön, Singa Lass'n!" poems in the Salzburg dialect (1878); "Lachende Geschichten" (4 vols., 1880-81); "Weltlust: Historietten, Schwänke und Lieder eines Heitern Vagranten" (Leipsic, 1883); "Alt-Wien: Bilder und Geschichten" (*ib.* 1885); "Ein Neuer Decamerone" (*ib.* 1887); and the following comedies: "Fritz Nürnberger," "Die Frau Professorin," "Zur Statistik der Frauen" (*ib.* 1869, in one act), "Lucretia Borgia" (with Otto Prechtler), "Der Biberhof," "Eine Million für einen Erben" (with L. Feldmann).

BIBLIOGRAPHY: Wurzbach, *Biograph. Lex.*; Brümmer, *Dichter-Lex.*; Bornmüller, *Biograph. Schriftsteller-Lex.*

S. N. D.

MASADA: Strong mountain fortress in Palestine, not far west of the Dead Sea. The fortress was built by the high priest Jonathan (a statement which Schürer upon insufficient grounds holds to be false), who also gave it its name (Josephus, "B. J." vii. 8, § 3). The name is certainly Hebrew: "Meẓadah" = "mountain fortress." Josephus writes *Μασάδα* and *Μασαδά* (variant, *Μεσάδα*); Strabo (xvi. 2, § 44) corrupts it to *Μοασάδα*; while Pliny ("Historia Naturalis," v. 17, § 73) writes correctly "Masada" (comp. "Die Epitome des Solinus," ed. Mommsen, § 35). Helix, second in command under Cassius, took the fortress from the Herodians in 42 B.C. (Josephus, "Ant." xiv. 11, § 7; "B. J." i. 12, § 1). Later Herod took refuge here ("Ant." xiv. 13, § 8; "B. J." i. 13, § 7); Antigonus, who besieged the fortress, could not take it, in spite of the fact that the defenders suffered from a scarcity of water ("Ant." xiv. 14, § 6; 15, §§ 1-4; "B. J." i. 15, §§ 3-4). When Herod became king he repaired the fortress, building a wall with thirty-seven high turrets around the summit of the mountain, which was flat. Within the wall were dwelling-houses and a splendid palace for Herod, who wished the fortress to be a place of refuge from every danger. Grain, which was stored there, on account of the purity of the air did not spoil easily ("B. J." vii. 8, § 3).

Masada attained great importance in the war with the Romans. The Sicarii captured it and killed the Roman garrison ("B. J." ii. 17, § 2); Menahem took possession of the arms stored there by Herod (*ib.* § 8); Menahem's relative Eleazar b. Jair governed the fortress for about six years (*ib.* § 9); and Bar Giora also took refuge there for some time (*ib.* 22, § 2). From here the Sicarii harassed and plundered the whole vicinity, especially Engedi (*ib.* iv. 7, § 2). Not until three years after the fall of Jerusalem did a Roman army, under Silva, advance upon Masada. Josephus in this connection gives a detailed account of the situation of the fortress, which was almost inaccessible and inexpugnable (*ib.* vii. 8, § 3); there was only one spot upon which the Romans could place a battering-ram, and even there only with great difficulty. When, finally, a breach was made in the wall, the invaders were confronted by a newly erected bulwark, which, however, they succeeded in destroying by fire. Eleazar b. Jair persuaded the besieged to kill themselves, and when the Romans entered they found alive only two women (*ib.* 8, §§ 1-7; 9, § 2).

With the fall of Masada the war came to an end (on the 15th of Nisan, 73; 72 according to Niese in "Hermes," xxviii. 211).

Smith and Robinson ("Palästina," ii. 477) discovered Masada in the cliffs of Al-Sabbah. The account of Josephus has been completely confirmed by them and by Ritter ("Erdkunde," xv. 655); and the traces of the Roman camp may still be seen.

BIBLIOGRAPHY: Tuch, *Masada*, Leipsic, 1863; Boettger, *Topographisch-Historisches Lexicon zu den Schriften des Flavius Josephus*, p. 175; Conder and Kitchener, *The Survey of Western Palestine*, iii. 418-421; Schürer, *Gesch.* 3d ed., i. 391 note 68; 638, note 137.

G. S. KR.

MASARJAWAIH or **MASARJOYAH** or **MASARJIS**: One of the oldest Arabic Jewish physicians, and the oldest translator from the Syriac lived in Bassora about 883. His name, mutilated in every possible way, has been transmitted in European sources; nor has it yet been satisfactorily explained. Neuda (in "Orient, Lit." vi. 132) compares he name "Masarjawaih" with the Hebrew proper name "Mesharsheya"; but the ending "-waih" points to a Persian origin. The form "Masarjis" has been compared with the Christian proper name "Mar Serjis"; but it is not known that Masarjis embraced either Christianity or Islam.

Masarjawaih's son, who also was a translator, and was the author of two treatises (on colors and on foods), was called "'Isa," that is, "Jesus"; which name, of course, points to the fact that this son had been converted to Christianity.

Masarjawaih translated the pandects of the archdeacon or presbyter Aaron from the Syriac into

Mount Masada in Judea.
(From a photograph by Bonfils.)

rabic and added to the thirty chapters of this anslation two of his own. He also wrote in Arabic vo treatises, "The Virtues of Foods, Their Advantage and Their Disadvantage," and "The Virtues of the Medicinal Plants, Their Advantage and heir Disadvantage." None of these three writings as been preserved. Their contents, however, are nown to a certain extent by quotations. How uch Masarjawaih added to the translation of aron's pandects can hardly be decided, as the orks themselves are preserved in fragments only.

BLIOGRAPHY: Steinschneider, in *Z. D. M. G.* liii. 428 *et seq.*; dem, *Die Arabische Literatur*, § 16, pp. 13 *et seq.*

G. M. Sc.

MASHAL. See Parable.

MASHIAḤ, ḤASUN BEN: Karaite scholar; flourished in Egypt (or Babylonia) in the first half of the tenth century. According to Steinschneider, "Ḥasun" is a corrupted form of the Arabic name "Ḥusain," the ו being easily confounded in manuscript with the י. Ḥasun, or, as he is generally quoted by the Karaite authorities, Ben Mashiaḥ, was a younger contemporary of Saadia Gaon, whom, according to Sahl ben Maẓliaḥ in his "Tokaḥat Megullah," he once challenged to a religious controversy. Ḥasun was the author of a polemical work, written probably in Arabic, in which he refuted one of Saadia's unpublished anti-Karaite writings, which came into his possession after the death of the author. Owing to a misunderstanding of a passage (§ 258) in the "Eshkol ha-Kofer" of Hadassi, Ḥasun was erroneously credited with the authorship of the anonymous chapter, on the theodicy, entitled "Sha'ar Ẓedeḳ" (St. Petersburg, Firkovich MSS. Nos. 683, 685), in the religio-philosophical work "Zikron ha-Datot," and of "Ḳuppat ha-Rokelim." Simḥah Isaac Luzki attributes to Ḥasun also a work on the precepts ("Sefer ha-Miẓwot"). Abraham ibn Ezra, in his introduction to the commentary on the Pentateuch, quotes a Karaite scholar named Ben Mashiaḥ, who is probably identical with Ḥasun.

Bibliography: Pinsker, *Liḳḳuṭe Ḳadmoniyyot*, p. 114; Fürst, *Gesch. des Karäert.* ii. 46; Gottlober, *Biḳḳoret le-Toledot ha-Ḳera'im*, p. 168; Steinschneider, *Hebr. Bibl.* iv. 48; idem, *Cat. Bodl.* p. 2169; idem, *Cat. Leyden*, p. 390; idem, *Hebr. Uebers.* p. 460; idem, *Die Arabische Literatur der Juden*, § 41.

s. I. Br.

MASKIL (plural, **Maskilim**): **1.** A title of honor used principally in Italy. The word "maskil," with the meaning of "scholar" or "enlightened man," was used by Isaac Israeli, who died in 1326 ("my colleagues, the maskilim"; "Yesod 'Olam," ii. 11, Berlin, 1846). But in some places "maskil" meant one who held a secondary rabbinical position corresponding to that of dayyan, and Jehiel Heilprin ("'Erke ha-Kinnuyim," p. 45b, Dyhernfurth, 1806) so defines it. In the Orient the overseers of the poor, or "gabbai ẓedaḳot," are called "maskilim" (Hazan, "Kerub Mimshaḥ," p. 26b, Alexandria, 1895). In Italy, and especially in Tuscany, the title "maschil" is conferred on rabbinical students (see Panzieri in "Jewish Comment," vol. xiv., No. 18; "Il Corriere Israelitico," 1889, pp. 166–167), though in some parts of Italy the title given in such cases is "ḥaber." It may be said to correspond to the title "Morenu" among the German Jews; it is considered inferior to the rabbinical title "ḥakam" ("Il Vessillo Israelitico," 1900, p. 244). Azulai reports in his diary that in 1776 he experienced considerable difficulty in adjusting a trouble which had arisen in Ancona over the fact that the title "maskil" had been bestowed on the local ḥazzan ("Ma'agal Ṭob," p. 6b, Leghorn, 1879).

2. Among the Jews of the Slavonic countries "maskil" usually denotes a self-taught Hebrew scholar with an imperfect knowledge of a living language (usually German), who represents the love of learning and the striving for culture awakened by Mendelssohn and his disciples; *i.e.*, an adherent or follower of the Haskalah movement. He is "by force of circumstances detained on the path over which the Jews of western Europe swiftly passed from rabbinical lore to European culture" and to emancipation, and "his strivings and shortcomings exemplify the unfulfilled hopes and the disappointments of Russian civilization."

The Maskilim are mostly teachers and writers; they taught a part of the young generation of Russian Jewry to read Hebrew and have created the great Neo-Hebrew literature which is the monument of Haskalah. Although Haskalah has now been flourishing in Russia for three generations, the class of Maskilim does not reproduce itself. The Maskilim of each generation are recruited from the ranks of the Orthodox Talmudists, while the children of Maskilim very seldom follow in the footsteps of their fathers. This is probably due to the fact that the Maskil who breaks away from strictly conservative Judaism in Russia, but does not succeed in becoming thoroughly assimilated, finds that his material conditions have not been improved by the change, and, while continuing to cleave to Haskalah for its own sake, he does not permit his children to share his fate.

The quarrels between the Maskilim and the Orthodox, especially in the smaller communities, are becoming less frequent. In the last few years the Zionist movement has contributed to bring the Maskilim, who joined it almost to a man, nearer to the other classes of Jews who became interested in that movement.

The numerous Maskilim who emigrated to the United States, especially after the great influx of Russian immigrants, generally continued to follow their old vocation of teaching and writing Hebrew, while some contributed to the Yiddish periodicals. Many of those who went thither in their youth entered the learned professions. See Literature, Modern Hebrew.

Bibliography: Atlas, *Mah le-Fanim u-Mah le-Ahor*, pp. 56 *et seq.*, Warsaw, 1898; Brainin, in *Ha-Shiloaḥ*. vii. 43; Friedberg, *Zikronot*, ii. 27 *et seq.*, Warsaw, 1899; Gersoni, in *Independent*, New York, Jan. 12, 1893; Taviov, in *Ha-Meliẓ*, xxix., No. 77; Wiernik, in *New Era Illustrated Magazine*, Feb., 1904, pp. 34–43.

J. P. Wi.—D.

MASKILEISON, ABRAHAM B. JUDAH LÖB: Russian rabbi and author; born 1788; died at Minsk 1848. He was a descendant of R. Israel Jaffe of Shklov, author of "Or Yisrael." Maskileison officiated as rabbi in many cities, and in his late years went to Minsk, where he remained till his death. Having no desire to use his cabalistic knowledge for gain, as was done by the miracle-working rabbis, he devoted his whole life to study. He lived in comparative poverty, being satisfied with a small income. He wrote the following works: "Maskil le-Etan" (Shklov, 1818), novellæ on parts of Mo'ed and Ḳodashim, printed with the approbations of Saul Katzenellenbogen of Wilna and Manasseh Iliyer; "Be'er Abraham" (Wilna, 1848), novellæ on the remaining parts of the Talmud. After his death were published: "Naḥal Etan" (*ib.* 1859), novellæ on the first two parts of Maimonides' Yad ha-Ḥazaḳah; "Miẓpeh Etan" (Jitomir, 1858–64; Wilna, 1880–86), notes on the Talmud; "Yad Abraham" (Wilna, 1888), novellæ on Yoreh De'ah; notes on Sifre, some of which are published at the end of the Wilna edition (1865).

Bibliography: Fuenn, *Keneset Yisrael*, p. 41; Eisenstadt-Ben Zion, *Rabbane Minsk*, pp. 27–43; Benjacob, *Oẓar ha-Sefarim*, pp. 132, 133, 376, 395; preface (by Maskileison's son) to *Naḥal Etan*.

H. R. N. T. L.

MASKILEISON, NAPHTALI: Russian Hebrew author and book-dealer; born at Radashkovichi, near Minsk, Feb. 20, 1829; died at Minsk Nov. 19, 1897. His father, R. Abraham Maskileison, a Hebrew scholar of note and the author of "Maskil le-Etan," instructed him in Talmud. Study of the poetical works of Moses Luzzatto and N. Wessely awakened Maskileison's interest in Neo-Hebrew literature, then regarded with disfavor by the Orthodox circles in which he grew up. His first poetical production was the drama "Esther," which was praised by the poet A. B. Lebensohn. Later he published, in various Hebrew periodicals, some poems which are marked by beauty of form and depth of thought. His many prose articles, published in the Hebrew periodicals during a period of forty years, are likewise distinguished for their excellence, as is his "Miktabim le-Lammed," a collection of eighty-eight letters of varied content (Wilna 1870). One of Maskileison's most valuable undertakings was his revised edition of Jehiel Heilprin's "Seder ha-Dorot" (Warsaw, 1878–82). He system atized the work and corrected the errors and omissions that had rendered the chronology almost useless, and appended a biography of Heilprin. He left many works in manuscript. Maskileison represents the best type of the Maskilim.

BIBLIOGRAPHY: *Voskhod*, 1897, No. 49, p. 1367; *Aḥiasaf*, 1898, p. 345; Sokolow, *Sefer Zikkaron*, pp. 153 *et seq.*

H. R. J. G. L.

MASLIANSKY, ẒEBI HIRSCH B. ḤAYYIM: Russian preacher; born in Slutsk, government of Minsk, June 6, 1856. He received a thorough rabbinical education, spending two years in the yeshibah of Mir. Later he settled as a teacher in Pinsk, where he remained about fourteen years, occasionally preaching. In 1887 he went to Yekaterinoslaf, where also he taught and preached. In 1891 he went to Odessa, where his oratorical talent attracted the attention of the Zionist leader M. L. Lilienblum and others, who advised him to devote himself entirely to preaching. For the following three years he traveled through many parts of Russia, his Zionist speeches arousing much enthusiasm. In 1894 he went to England, and in 1895 to the United States, where he is recognized as a foremost Yiddish and Hebrew orator. Since 1898 he has lectured every Friday evening in the auditorium of the Educational Alliance, New York city. The "Yiddishe Welt," a daily Yiddish newspaper, was founded by him in 1902 in New York. He contributed also to the Hebrew periodicals "Ha-'Ibri" and "Ha-Pisgah," in which he described his Russian travels.

BIBLIOGRAPHY: Eisenstadt, *Dor Rabbanaw we-Soferaw*, ii. 30, Wilna, 1900; idem, *Ḥakme Yisrael be-Amerika*, pp. 70-71, New York, 1903; M. Zablotski and J. Massel, in *Ha-Yiẓhari*, Manchester, 1895.

H. R. P. Wi.

MASORAH: The system of critical notes on the external form of the Biblical text. This system of notes represents the literary labors of innumerable scholars, of which the beginning falls probably in pre-Maccabean times and the end reaches to the year 1425.

Etymology of the Name.

The name "Masorah" occurs in many forms, the etymology, pronunciation, and genetic connection of which are much-mooted points. The term is taken from Ezek. xx. 37 and means originally "fetter." The fixation of the text was correctly considered to be in the nature of a fetter upon its exposition. When, in course of time, the Masorah had become a traditional discipline, the term became connected with the verb מסר (= "to hand down"), and was given the meaning of "tradition." For a full discussion of the meaning and history of the word see Bacher in "J. Q. R.," iii. 785, and C. Levias in the "Hebrew Union College Annual" for 1904.

The entire body of the Masorah goes back to the Palestinian schools; but recently Dr. P. Kahle discovered a fragment of the Babylonian Masorah which differs considerably from the received text in its terminology (comp. Paul Kahle, "Der Masoretische Text des Alten Testaments nach der Ueberlieferung der Babylonischen Juden," Leipsic, 1902).

Language and Form.

The language of the Masoretic notes is partly Hebrew and partly Palestinian Aramaic. Chronologically speaking, the Aramaic is placed between two periods of the Hebrew; the latter appearing in the oldest, the pre-amoraic period, and in the latest, the Arabic period (which begins here about 800). To the oldest period belong terms like אות = "letter"; פרשה, "section"; פסוק, "verse"; טעם, "sense-clause"; מלא, "plene"; חסר, "defective"; מקרא, "Bible"; also מקרא סופרים, עטור סופרים, הכרע; the verb נקד = "to punctuate," and certain derivatives; not all of these terms, however, happen to occur in the remnants of tannaitic literature which have been preserved. The Aramaic elements may thus be dated roughly from 200 to 800.

The Masoretic annotations are found in various forms: (*a*) in separate works, *e.g.*, the "Oklah we-Oklah"; (*b*) in the form of notes written in the margins and at the end of codices. In rare cases the notes are written between the lines. The first word of each Biblical book is also as a rule surrounded by notes. The latter are called the **Initial Masorah;** the notes on the side margins or between the columns are called the **Small** or **Inner Masorah;** and those on the lower and upper margins, the **Large** or **Outer Masorah.** The name "Large Masorah" is applied sometimes to the lexically arranged notes at the end of the printed Bible, usually called the **Final Masorah,** in Hebrew literature **Masoretic Concordance** (מערכת המסורה, or מסורה מערכית).

The Small Masorah consists of brief notes with reference to marginal readings, to statistics showing the number of times a particular form is found in Scripture, to full and defective spelling, and to abnormally written letters. The Large Masorah is more copious in its notes. The Final Masorah comprises all the longer rubrics for which space could not be found in the margin of the text, and is arranged alphabetically in the form of a concordance. The quantity of notes the marginal Masorah contains is conditioned by the amount of vacant space on each page. In the manuscripts it varies also with the rate at which the copyist was paid and the fanciful shape he gave to his gloss.

The question as to which of the above forms is the oldest can not be decided from the data now accessible. On the one hand, it is known that marginal notes were used in the beginning of the second century of the common era; on the other, there is every reason to assume the existence of Masoretic baraitas which could not have been much later. The Small Masorah is in any case not an abbreviation of the Large Masorah. Like the latter, it occurs also arranged in alphabetical order.

Origin.

From the statements in Talmudic literature to the effect that there was deposited in the court of the Temple a standard copy of the Bible for the benefit of copyists, and that there were paid correctors of Biblical books among the officers of the Temple (Ket. 106a); from the fact that such a copy is mentioned in the Aristeas Letter (§ 30; comp. Blau, "Studien zum Althebr. Buchwesen," p. 100); from the statements of Philo (preamble to his "Analysis of the Political Constitution of the Jews") and of Josephus ("Contra Ap." i. 8) that the text of Scripture had never been altered; finally, from the fact that there seem to have been no differences of readings between Pharisees and Sadducees, it may be concluded that the Scriptural text, at least as much as then belonged to the canon, was already fixed, at the latest, about 200 B.C. and perhaps a century earlier.

While the text was thus early fixed, it took centuries to produce a tolerable uniformity among all the circulating copies. This is by no means astonishing when one considers that the standard copy deposited at the Temple could be of benefit only to those who were sufficiently near Jerusalem to make use of it. This was not the case with those living in the Diaspora. When to this is added the carelessness of some copyists, it will not seem strange that as late as the second century of the common era scholars found it necessary to warn against incorrect copies; and the conclusions usually drawn from differences in the late books between the Hebrew text and the Greek version lose much of their force.

In classical antiquity copyists were paid for their work according to the number of stichs. As the prose books of the Bible were hardly ever written in stichs, the copyists, in order to estimate the amount of work, had to count the letters. Hence developed in the course of time the **Numerical Masorah,** which counts and groups together the various elements and phenomena of the text. Thus וישחט (Lev. viii. 23) forms the half of the number of verses in the Pentateuch; all the names of Divinity mentioned in connection with Abraham are holy except אדני (Gen. xviii. 3); ten passages in the Pentateuch are dotted; three times the Pentateuch has the spelling לא where the reading is לו. The collation of manuscripts and the noting of their differences furnished material for the **Text-Critical Masorah.** The close relation which existed in earlier times (from the Soferim to the Amoraim inclusive) between the teacher of tradition and the Masorite, both frequently being united in one person, accounts for the **Exegetical Masorah.** Finally, the invention and introduction of a graphic system of vocalization and accentuation gave rise to the **Grammatical Masorah.**

Fixation of the Text.

The old Hebrew text was, in all probability, written in continuous script, without any breaks. The division into words, books, sections, paragraphs, verses, and clauses (probably in the chronological order here enumerated); the fixing of the orthography, pronunciation, and cantillation; the introduction or final adoption of the square characters with the five final letters (comp. NUMBERS AND NUMERALS); some textual changes to guard against blasphemy and the like; the enumeration of letters, words, verses, etc., and the substitution of some words for others in public reading, belong to the earliest labors of the Masorites. Since no additions were allowed to be made to the official text of the Bible, the early Masorites adopted other expedients: *e.g.*, they marked the various divisions by spacing, and gave indications of halakic and haggadic teachings by full or defective spelling, abnormal forms of letters, dots, and other signs. Marginal notes were permitted only in private copies, and the first mention of such notes is found in the case of R. Meïr (*c.* 100-150). The traditionally fixed text, especially with a view to its orthography, was called מסורת; the traditional pronunciation, מקרא; the division into sense-clauses, which underlies the proper recitation or cantillation, פיסוק טעמים or הכרע.

Tikkune Soferim.

Tannaitic sources mention several passages of Scripture in which the conclusion is inevitable that the ancient reading must have differed from that of the present text. The explanation of this phenomenon is given in the expression כנה הכתוב ("Scripture has used euphemistic language," *i.e.*, to avoid anthropomorphism and anthropopathism). R. Simon b. Pazzi, an amora of the third century, calls these readings "emendations of the Scribes" ("tikkune Soferim"; Gen. R. xlix. 7), assuming that the Scribes actually made the changes. This view was adopted by the later Midrash and by the majority of Masorites. In Masoretic works these changes are ascribed to Ezra; to Ezra and Nehemiah; to Ezra and the Soferim; or to Ezra, Nehemiah, Zechariah, Haggai, and Baruch. All these ascriptions mean one and the same thing: that the changes were made by the Men of the Great Synagogue (comp. Tan., Beshallah, on xv. 7). Ben Asher remarks that the proper expression would have been כנוי סופרים ("Dikduke ha-Te'amim," § 57), but, in the sense of the oldest sources, the only proper expression would have been כנוי הכתובים, a term which in an old variant has really been preserved (comp. Blau, "Masoretische Untersuchungen," p. 50).

The term "tikkun Soferim" has been understood by different scholars in various ways. Some regard it as a viva voce correction or modification of Biblical language authorized by the Soferim for homiletical purposes; *i.e.*, the Scribes interpret a supposed euphemism, and their interpretation is called "tikkun Soferim." Others take it to mean a mental change made by the original writers or redactors of Scripture; *i.e.*, the latter shrank from putting in writing a thought which some of the readers might expect them to express. Considering the various interpretations and the fact that neither the number nor the identity of the passages in question is definite (Mekilta counts 11, Sifre 7, Tanhuma 13, Masorah 15 or 18), S. Sachs (in "Kerem Hemed," ix. 57, note) and, without mentioning him, Barnes ("Journal of Theological Studies," i. 387-414) come to the conclusion that the tikkun tradition belongs rather to the Midrash than to the Masorah; *i.e.*, its true bearing is on exegesis, not on textual criticism. The tikkune Soferim are interpretations, not readings. The tikkun tradition is probably connected with the tradition which ascribes the redaction of several books of Scripture to the Great Synagogue.

There are, however, phenomena in the Biblical text which force one to assume that at some time textual corrections had been made. These corrections may be classified under the following heads:

(1) Removal of unseemly expressions used in reference to God; *e.g.*, the substitution of ברך ("to bless") for קלל ("to curse") in certain passages.

(2) Safeguarding of the Tetragrammaton; *e.g.*, substitution of "Elohim" for "YHWH" in some passages. Under this head some have counted such phenomena as the variants of the divine names in theophorous proper names; *e.g.*, "Joahaz" for "Je-

PAGE FROM A THIRTEENTH-CENTURY (?) MANUSCRIPT BIBLE BEARING MASORETIC NOTES WRITTEN TO FORM ORNAMENTAL DECORATIONS.

(In the British Museum.)

hoahaz," "Elijah" for "Eliyahu," etc., but compare on this point J. H. Levy in "J. Q. R." xv. 97 *et seq.*

(3) Removal of application of the names of false gods to Yhwh; *e.g.*, the change of the name "Ishbaal" to "Ishbosheth."

(4) Safeguarding the unity of divine worship at Jerusalem. Here belongs the change (Isa. xix. 18) עיר ההרם for עיר הצדק or עיר ההדם.

"Mikra" and "'Ittur."

Among the earliest technical terms used in connection with activities of the Scribes are (Ned. 37b) the "miḳra Soferim" and "'iṭṭur Soferim." In the geonic schools the first term was taken to signify certain vowel-changes which were made in words in pause or after the article; *e.g.*, אֶרֶץ, הָאָרֶץ; the second, the cancelation in a few passages of the "waw" conjunctive, where it had by some been wrongly read. The objection to such an explanation is that the first changes would fall under the general head of fixation of pronunciation, and the second under the head of "ḳere" and "ketib." Various explanations have, therefore, been offered by ancient as well as modern scholars without, however, succeeding in furnishing a satisfactory solution.

Undecided Constructions.

A number of words is mentioned—by the Talmud 5; by later authorities 8—which negatively expressed have no הכרע, but positively expressed have a השאה. According to Yer. 'Ab. Zarah ii. 8 (41c), this Masoretic note should be understood to mean that the Scribes had left undecided the question whether the affected words belonged to the preceding or to the following clause. But such an interpretation may be objected to for two reasons. First, the accentuation fixes the construction of those words in a very definite way. Even if one assumes that the accentuators had acted high-handedly and had disregarded tradition, which is not probable, it is impossible to conceive how in public worship the words were recited to indicate such doubtful construction. The reader must have connected them either with the first or with the second clause. Secondly, a still graver objection is that some of those words make sense in only one clause, the one in which the accentuators have put them. It must, therefore, be assumed that the tradition refers here to exegesis, not to textual criticism. It must refer to what is termed by later scholars עולה ויורד, a kind of construction *ἀπὸ κοινοῦ*, wherein the word is understood to follow itself immediately. Tradition was undecided whether these words were to be read merely as they stood, or understood also with the following word.

Suspended Letters and Dotted Words.

There are four words having one of their letters suspended above the line. One of them, מ̇נשה (Judges xviii. 30), is due to a correction of the original משה out of reverence for Moses. The origin of the other three (Ps. lxxx. 14; Job xxxviii. 13, 15) is doubtful. According to some, they are due to mistaken majuscular letters; according to others, they are later insertions of originally omitted weak consonants.

In fifteen passages in the Bible some words are stigmatized. The significance of the dots is disputed. Some hold them to be marks of erasur others believe them to indicate that in some collate manuscripts the stigmatized words were missin hence that the reading is doubtful; still others co tend that they are merely a mnemonic device to i dicate homiletical explanations which the ancient had connected with those words; finally, some mai tain the dots were designed to guard against th omission by copyists of text-elements which, at firs glance or after comparison with parallel passage seemed to be superfluous. Instead of dots som manuscripts exhibit strokes, vertical or else horizo tal. The first two explanations are unacceptabl for the reason that such faulty readings would b long to ḳere and ketib, which, in case of doubt, th majority of manuscripts would decide. The las two theories have equal probability.

Inverted Letters.

In nine passages of the Bible are found signs usu ally called "inverted nuns," because resembling th letter נ. Others find a resemblance in these sign to the letter ר or כ. S. Krauss (in Stade's "Zei schrift," xxii. 57) holds that the sign were originally obeli, and have tex critical value. He assumes that th correct reading in Massek. Soferim v 1, 2 is שיפור; but the original reading seems to b שילפר, a word of unknown etymology. If the wor stands for *ששפר it would be a synonym of ציון an mean simply "sign." But the reading שיפור ("ram's horn") yields a very good sense. It is th Greek *παράγραφος*, which had exactly such a sig and served the same purpose (comp. Perles, "Ety mologische Studien," p. 41, note 1; p. xiv., col. 3).

Marginal Readings.

Even in antiquity substitutions were made—a first only orally in public worship; later also in th form of marginal notes in private copies—of reading other than those found in the text. As Frankel ha shown ("Vorstudien," pp. 220 *et seq.*), even th Septuagint knew those readings an frequently adopted them. These var ants have various origins. Some o them represent variants in ancien manuscripts and have, therefore, a text-critica value (comp. Ḳimḥi, Introduction to Commentar on Joshua; Eichhorn, "Einleitung," § 148; also Jo seph ibn Waḳar, in Steinschneider, "Jewish Liter ature," p. 270, note 15). Others arose from the ne cessity of replacing erroneous, difficult, irregula provincial, archaic, unseemly, or cacophonous ex pressions by correct, simpler, current, appropriat or euphonious readings (comp. Abravanel, Introduc tion to Commentary on Jeremiah). A third clas may have been designed to call attention to som mystic meaning or homiletical lesson supposed to b embodied in the text (comp. Krochmal, "More Nebuke ha-Zeman," ch. xiii.; S. Bamberger, "Ein leitung zu Tobiah b. Eliezer's Leḳaḥ Ṭob zu Ruth, p. 39, note 1). A fourth class, finally, and this ver late, is due to variants found in Talmudic literatu (comp. "Minḥat Shai" on Isa. xxxvi. 12, Ps. xli 13, Eccl. viii. 10; Luzzatto, in "Ḳerem Ḥemed," i 9 on II Sam. xxii. 8). These variants are of a thre fold character: (1) words to be read ("ḳere") fo those written in the text ("ketib"); (2) words to b read for those not written in the text; (3) word written, but not to be read.

PAGE FROM A MANUSCRIPT BIBLE OF THE FOURTEENTH CENTURY CONTAINING MASORETIC NOTES.

(From the Sulzberger collection in the Jewish Theological Seminary of America, New York.)

A certain school of Masorites used for the term "ḳere" the synonymous term "sebirin." The readings of that school are usually registered by the Masorah disapprovingly with the addition "u-maṭ'in" = "and they are misleading."

To the Masorites belongs also the credit of inventing and elaborating graphic signs to indicate the traditional pronunciation, syntactical construction, and cantillation of the Biblical text.

History of Development.

The history of the Masorah may be divided into three periods: (1) creative period, from its beginning to the introduction of vowel-signs; (2) reproductive period, from the introduction of vowel-signs to the printing of the Masorah (1425); (3) critical period, from 1425 to the present time.

The materials for the history of the first period are scattered remarks in Talmudic and Midrashic literature, in the post-Talmudical treatises Masseket Sefer Torah and Masseket Soferim, and in a Masoretic chain of tradition found in Ben Asher's "Diḳduḳe ha-Ṭe'amim," § 69 and elsewhere. Masseket Soferim is a work of unknown date by a Palestinian author. The first five chapters are a slightly amplified reproduction of the earlier Masseket Sefer Torah, a compendium of rules to be observed by scribes in the preparation and writing of Scriptural rolls. Ch. vi. to ix. are purely Masoretic; the third part, commencing at ch. x., treats of ritualistic matter. While the work as a whole is perhaps not earlier than the beginning of the ninth century, its Masoretic portions probably go back to the sixth or seventh century. A comparison of this work with the Masoretic material found in Talmudic literature shows that the lists of marginal readings have been systematically enlarged. A critical comparison has been instituted between parallel passages in Scripture. Rules are now given, for the first time, as to the unusual form in which certain letters and words, of which the Talmud had taken special note, are to be written. The stichometrical form in which the Scriptural songs are to be arranged is described in fuller detail than it had been in the Talmud. It is also stated that in private copies the beginnings of verses used to be marked. Some readings in ch. xiii. 1 mention also accents; but these readings are doubtful (comp. Vocalization). In the chain of tradition quoted in Ben Asher the earliest name is a certain Naḳḳai, who is said to have emigrated under the persecutions of T. Annius Rufus from Palestine to Babylonia and spread Masoretic knowledge in the city of Nehardea. This would be about 140 of the common era, and the tradition, containing eight names, would date about 340.

Differences Between Babylonia and Palestine.

In the course of time differences in spelling and pronunciation had developed not only between the schools of Palestine and of Babylonia—differences already noted in the third century (comp. Ginsburg, "Introduction," p. 197)—but in the various seats of learning in each country. In Babylonia the school of Sura differed from that of Nehardea; similar differences existed in the schools of Palestine, where the chief seat of learning in later times was the city of Tiberias. These differences must have become accentuated with the introduction of graphic signs for pr nunciation and cantillation; and every localit following the tradition of its school, had a standa codex embodying its readings.

In this period living tradition ceased, and t Masorites in preparing their codices usually fo lowed the one school or the other, examining, how ever, standard codices of other schools and notir their differences. In the first half of the tenth ce tury Aaron b. Moses ben Asher of Tiberias an Ben Naphtali, heads of two rival Masoretic schools, each wrote a standard codex of the Bib embodying the traditions of their respective school Ben Asher was the last of a distinguished family Masorites extending back to the latter half of t eighth century. In spite of the rivalry of Ben Nap tali and the opposition of Saadia Gaon, the mo eminent representative of the Babylonian scho of criticism, Ben Asher's codex became recognize as the standard text of the Bible. Notwithstandin all this, for reasons unknown neither the printe text nor any manuscript which has been preserve is based entirely on Ben Asher: they are all eclecti Aside from Ben Asher and Ben Naphtali, the name of several other Masorites have come down; bu perhaps with the exception of one—Phinehas, t head of the academy, who is supposed by mo ern scholars to have lived about 750—neither the time, their place, nor their connection with the va rious schools is known.

Ben Asher and Ben Naphtali.

The two rival authorities, Ben Asher and Be Naphtali, practically brought the Masorah to a clos Very few additions were made by the later Maso rites, styled in the thirteenth and fou teenth centuries Naḳdanim, who re vised the works of the copyists, adde the vowels and accents (generally i fainter ink and with a finer pen) an frequently the Masorah. Considerable influence o the development and spread of Masoretic literatu was exercised during the eleventh, twelfth, an thirteenth centuries by the Franco-German scho of Tosafists. R. Gershom, his brother Machi Joseph b. Samuel Bonfils (Tob 'Elem) of Limoge R. Tam (Jacob b. Meïr), Menahem b. Perez Joigny, Perez b. Elijah of Corbeil, Judah of Pari Meïr Spira, and R. Meïr of Rothenburg made Ma oretic compilations, or additions to the subjec which are all more or less frequently referred to i the marginal glosses of Biblical codices and in th works of Hebrew grammarians.

Critical Study.

Jacob b. Ḥayyim ibn Adonijah, having collated vast number of manuscripts, systematized his mat rial and arranged the Masorah in the second Bom berg edition of the Bible (Venice, 1524-25). Beside introducing the Masorah into the margin, he com piled at the close of his Bible a concordance of th Masoretic glosses for which he could not find roo in a marginal form, and added an elaborate intr duction—the first treatise on the Masorah ever pr duced. In spite of its numerous e rors, this excellent work has generall been acknowledged as the "textus re ceptus" of the Masorah. Next to Ib Adonijah the critical study of the Masorah has bee most advanced by Elijah Levita, who publish h famous "Massoret ha-Massoret" in 1538. The 'Tiberias" of the elder Buxtorf (1620) made Levita's researches accessible to Christian students. Walton's eighth prolegomenon is largely a réchauffé of the "Tiberias." Levita compiled likewise a vast Masoretic concordance, "Sefer ha-Zikronot," which still lies in the National Library at Paris unpublished. The study is indebted also to R. Meïr b. Todros ha-Levi (RaMaH), who, as early as the thirteenth century, wrote his "Sefer Massoret Seyag la-Torah" (correct ed. Florence, 1750); to Menahem di Lonzano, who composed a treatise on the Masorah of the Pentateuch entitled "Or Torah"; and in particular to Jedidiah Solomon of Norzi, whose "Minḥat Shai" contains valuable Masoretic notes based on a careful study of manuscripts. Mention must also be made of J. C. Wolf, whose "Bibliotheca Hebræa" contains a treatise on the Masorah and a list of Masoretic authorities (part ii., book iii.). For less-known names consult the bibliography below.

In modern times knowledge of the Masorah has been advanced by the following scholars: W. Heidenheim, A. Geiger, S. D. Luzzatto, S. Pinsker, S. Frensdorff, H. Graetz, J. Derenbourg, D. Oppenheim, S. Baer, L. Blau, B. Königsberger, A. Büchler, J. Bachrach, I. H. Weiss, S. Rosenfeld, M. Lambert, J. Reach, A. Ackermann, L. Bardowicz, and W. Bacher. Among Christian scholars are to be mentioned: H. Hupfeld, Franz Delitzsch, L. H. Strack, C. D. Ginsburg (a Jew by birth), W. Wickes, Ad. Merx, F. Praetorius, and P. Kahle.

Masorah to Targum Onḳelos.

In imitation of the Masorah to the Hebrew text, a similar work exists to the text of Targum Onḳelos, first edited by A. Berliner (Leipsic, 1877), then by S. Landauer (Amsterdam, 1896). According to Berliner's opinion, it must have been compiled about the end of the ninth or the beginning of the tenth century.

BIBLIOGRAPHY: On the name: Paul de Lagarde, *Mittheilungen*, i. 1884; P. Haupt, *Proc. Am. Oriental Soc.* xvi., p. cvi.; S. D. Luzzatto, additamenta to הפלאה שבערמן, ii. 119b; Ed. König, *Lehrgebäude*, ii. 358, 491; idem, *Introduction*, p. 38; Ginsburg, *Masoretico-Critical Introduction*, p. 421, note 1; Blau, in *Zeit. für Hebr. Bibl.* iv. 62; especially Bacher, in *J. Q. R.* iii. 785; idem, *Aelteste Terminologie*, s. v.; comp. J. Bachrach, *Ishtaddelut 'im Shedal*, i. 20, notes 4, 34, 181.

Editions: In *Rabbinic Bible*, Venice, 1524-25, by Ibn Adonijah; in Basel edition by Buxtorf, 1618-19 (in some respects an improvement on its predecessor, although it exhibits many unwarrantable alterations); Frensdorff, *Ochlah we-Ochlah*, Hanover, 1864; idem, *Die Massora Magna*, i., *ib.* 1876; C. D. Ginsburg, *The Massorah*, London, 1880-85. S. Baer's *Masorah* is still unpublished.

Masoretico-grammatical works: Ben Asher, *Diḳduḳe ha-Te'amim*, ed. Baer and Strack, Leipsic, 1879; anonymous, *Horayot ha-Ḳore*, inedited; Joseph of Constantinople, *'Adat Dibburim*, inedited; Samson Punctator, *Ḥibbur ha-Ḳonim*, inedited; Moses Punctator, *Darke ha-Niḳḳud weha-Neginot*, ed. Frensdorff, Hanover, 1847; Jekuthiel Punctator, *'En ha-Ḳore*, ed. Heidenheim (in his Pentateuch *Me'or 'Enayim*, Rödelheim, 1818-21, and in his *Seder Yeme ha-Purim*, ib. 1826); anonymous, *Manuel du Lecteur*, ed. Derenbourg, Paris, 1870 (reprint from *Journal Asiatique*); anonymous, *Petite Grammaire Hébraïque*, ed. Neubauer, Leipsic, 1891.

Commentaries: M. A. Angel, *Masoret ha-Berit*, Cracow, 1629; Abraham b. Reuben of Ochrida, *Sefer Bet Abraham*, Constantinople, 1742; David Viterbi, *Sefer Em la-Masoret*, Mantua, 1748; Abraham b. Jeremiah of Calvary, *Sefer Seder Abraham*, Frankfort-on-the-Main, 1752; Asher Amshel of Worms, *Seyag la-Torah*, ib. 1766; Joseph b. David Heilbron of Eschweg, *Sefer Mebin Ḥidot*, Amsterdam, 1765 (a plagiarism from the preceding work); Solomon Dubno, *Tiḳḳun Soferim*, in Mendelssohn's Pentateuch *Netibot ha-Shalom*, Berlin, 1783; Phoebus b. Solomon, *Menorat Shelomoh*, and *Minḥat Kalil*, in Pentateuch edited in Dobrowno, 1804; Joseph b. Mordecai, *Masorah Berurah*, Berdychev (1820?); Joseph Ḳalman b. Solomon, *Sha'ar ha-Masorah*, Wilna, 1870.

Historico-critical works on the Masorah: Jacob b. Ḥayyim, *Introduction*, ed. Ginsburg, London, 1865; E. Levita, *Massoret ha-Massoret*, ed. Ginsburg, *ib.* 1867; H. L. Strack, *Prolegomena Critica*, Leipsic, 1873; Joseph Ḳalman b. Solomon, *Mebo ha-Massorah*, Warsaw, 1862 (2d ed., *ib.* 1890?); Geiger, *Jüd. Zeit.* iii. 78-119; J. H. Weiss, in *Gesch. der Jüdischen Tradition*, iv. and Index; S. Rosenfeld, introduction to his *Mishpaḥat Soferim*, Wilna, 1883; Ad. Merx, *Die Tschufutkaléschen Fragmente*, in *Verhandlungen des Fünften Internationalen Orientalischen Congresses*, part ii., section 1, pp. 188-225, Berlin, 1882; Isidore Harris, *The Rise and Development of the Massorah*, in *J. Q. R.* i. 128-142, 223-257; C. D. Ginsburg, *Introduction to the . . . Hebrew Bible*, London, 1897; W. Bacher, *Die Masorah*, in Winter and Wünsche, *Jüdische Literatur*, ii. 121-132; Hamburger, *Massora*, in his *R. B. T.* Supplement, iv. 52-68.

On special points: *Sefer Tagin*, ed. J. Bargès, Paris, 1866; *Midrash Ḥaserot wi-Yeterot*, ed. Berliner, in his *Peleṭat Soferim*, Breslau, 1872 (reedited in a more complete form by S. Wertheimer, Jerusalem, 1899); S. Rosenfeld, *Ma'amar bi-Ḳere u-Ketib*, Wilna, 1866; M. Lambert, *Une Serie de Qere-Ketib*, Paris, 1891; J. Reach, *Die Sebirin der Massoreten von Tiberias*, Breslau, 1895; L. Blau, *Masoretische Untersuchungen*, Strasburg, 1891; idem, *Zur Einleitung in die Heilige Schrift*, Budapest, 1894; B. Königsberger, *Aus Masorah und Talmudkritik*, i., Berlin, 1892; A. S. Weissmann, *Ḳedushshat ha-TNK*, Vienna, 1887; S. R. Edelmann, *Ha-Mesillot*, Wilna, 1875; L. Bardowicz, *Studien zur Geschichte der Orthographie des Althebräischen*, Frankfort-on-the-Main, 1894; A. Wedell, *De Emendationibus a Sopherim in Libris Sacris Veteris Testamenti Propositis*, Breslau, 1869.

For articles in periodical literature compare M. Schwab, *Répertoire*, s.v. *Accents*, *Division de la Bible*, *Massora*, *Massorètes*, *Sections de la Bible*, *Sedarim*, *Versets de la Bible*, *Tikkun Sofrim*, and פסקא. For older Christian literature compare the references in Strack's *Prolegomena*. For special points compare the literature under the various terms in C. Levias, *Dictionary of Philological Terminology*; also the bibliographies to ACCENTS IN HEBREW; BIBLE MANUSCRIPTS; NAḲDANIM; OKLAH WE-OKLAH; and VOCALIZATION.

T. C. L.

MASSACHUSETTS: A northeastern state in the American Union. The earliest record of a Jew in Massachusetts bears the date of May 3, 1649, and refers to a certain Solomon Franco, for whom an allowance was made pending his return to Holland; and recorded among the inhabitants of Boston, in 1695, there are "Samuell, the Jew," and "Raphaell Abandana" ("Publications Am. Jew. Hist. Soc." No. 11, pp. 78-80). On Sept. 13, 1702, Simon the Jew was baptized at Charlestown, taking the name of "Barns," and about the same time a certain Joseph Frazon or Frazier lived in Boston. An attempt to convert him was unsuccessful, and it is recorded that he died Feb. 4, 1704, and that his body was sent to Newport, R. I., for burial. In 1722 Judah MONIS was baptized; he was an instructor in Hebrew at Harvard College from 1723 to 1760.

The first considerable colony in Massachusetts resulted directly from the Revolutionary war. In 1777 Aaron Lopez and Jacob Rivera, with fifty-nine other Jews, left Newport to find a refuge from its invasion by the British troops, and established themselves at Leicester, Mass. Lopez was a man of great wealth and, according to Ezra Stiles, in the extent of his commercial dealings was probably surpassed by no merchant in America (*ib.* No. 10, p. 15). He purchased an estate at Leicester and erected upon it a substantial house, which since has become the home of the Leicester Academy. The colonists rigidly observed the customs of their faith. In spite of the high opinion in which Lopez was held, it appears that in 1762 the supreme court of Massachusetts refused to grant the application of himself and Isaac Lezur for naturalization (*ib.* No. 6, p. 71).

It is known that other Jews went to Boston during the seventeenth century, but owing to the intolerance of the Puritans, they either removed or embraced Christianity. This accounts for the numerous families of distinctively Jewish name found in many of the Massachusetts towns. Just prior to the War of the Revolution Moses Michael Hays went to Boston from Newport, taking with him his own family and his two nephews, Abraham and Judah Touro. Hays was a successful insurance underwriter, and for four years (1788 to 1792) was grand master of the Grand Lodge of Masons of Massachusetts; he died in 1805. It is not known that any of his descendants live there. Abraham Touro became a very wealthy merchant, and when he died in 1822 he bequeathed $10,000 to the Massachusetts General Hospital, and $5,000 each to the Asylum for Indigent Boys, the Massachusetts Humane Society, and the Boston Female Society. His brother Judah Touro went to New Orleans. Judah Hays, Isaac Solomon, and Abraham Solis were residents of Boston between 1780 and 1798.

In 1830 a number of Algerian Jews settled in Boston and occupied themselves in trading; some of them went to Newport to live; the others disappeared, and no trace of them is left. In 1840 a number of German and Polish Jews settled in Boston, and their descendants still live there (for the history of Boston Jews see BOSTON). After 1880, Russian and Rumanian Jews began to settle in the towns outside of Boston, and now there are estimated to be about thirty thousand Jews in various parts of the state, exclusive of those in the capital. The newcomers have become Americanized and take an interest in public affairs; many work in factories and mills; it is estimated that 30 per cent of them are successfully established in various branches of business; a few still follow the old custom of peddling. In Boston there are 40,000 Jews, 21 synagogues, 64 lodges, many charitable societies, and a large number of social and literary clubs.

STATISTICS.

The following statistics of Massachusetts cities and towns (exclusive of Boston) were obtained through inquiry of town officials or are based upon the "American Jewish Year Book" for 5661, and upon manuscript additions thereto in possession of the Jewish Publication Society of America:

Name of City or Town.	Number of Jewish Inhabitants.	Congregations.	Synagogues.	Lodges.	Other Institutions.
Attleboro	30	..	....	..	..
Brockton	300	1	1	2	1
Cambridge	....	1	....	..	2
Chelsea	2,000	4	2	4	1
Chicopee	50	..	....	..	..
Danvers	24	..	....	..	..
Fall River	5,000	3	3	8	3
Faulkner	....	1	....	..	..
Fitchburg	200	1	building	..	..
Gloucester	200	1	1	..	1
Haverhill	300	2	1	2	1
Holyoke	200	2	....	2	..
Lawrence	600	2	2	2	..
Lowell	750	2	2	1	..
Lynn	....	2	....	..	2
Malden	600	1	1	1	1
Marlboro	24	..	....	..	..
Medford	....	..	....	..	1
Millis	....	1	....	..	..
New Bedford	1,000	4	2	1	2
Newton	32	..	....	..	..
North Adams	80	2	1	1	1
Northampton	120	2	....	1	..
Pittsfield	350	2	2	1	..
Quincy	26	1	....	..	2
Revere	300	..	....	..	..
Salem	300	2	....	..	..
Springfield	300	4	....	..	6
Taunton	80	..	....	..	..
Watertown	25	..	....	..	..
Worcester	1,000	4	....	1	7

BIBLIOGRAPHY: Hühner, *The Jews of New England*, in *Publications Am. Jew. Hist. Soc.* No. 11, pp. 75 *et seq.*; Cyrus Adler, *The Menorah*, 1888, v. 256-260.
A. G. Mo.

MASSARANI (MASSARAN): Name of an Italian family which has been known since the latter part of the fifteenth century. Originally the name of the family was ממאסראן, from Massarano, a small town near Novara in Piedmont. Subsequently various members lived at Mantua, and still later at Milan. The earliest known bearer of the name was **Isaac Massaran,** who copied, in 1255, No. 23 of the Codex De Rossi; it is not certain, however, whether he belonged to this family or whether he was a native of Mazarron, in Spain. Two centuries later the copyist **Isaiah b. Jacob b. Isaiah Massaran** lived at Mantua and wrote Nos. 6 and 620 of the Codex De Rossi, No. 127 of the Codex Turin, and No. 4[illegible] of the Codex Montefiore. Azariah dei Rossi's scholarly brother-in-law, **Ḥayyim Massaran,** who owned a number of rare Talmudical works, lived at Mantua about 1560. At the same time **Bezaleel b. Samson, Levi b. Jacob, Samson b. Jehiel,** and **Samson b. Isaiah,** all belonging to the Massarani family, were living in this community. Among these Bezaleel b. Samson Massarani is especially noteworthy for his energetic efforts to save Hebrew books from the destruction with which the Inquisition threatened them. He was the chairman of the deputation of communal directors and rabbis that decided at Padua upon an anticipatory censorship in order to secure permission to reprint the Talmud. As the leader of this deputation Bezaleel went to Rome, to Pope Sixtus V., and obtained permission to print and own the Talmud after it had been censored and expurgated and the title changed. **Samson Massarani** was one of the deputies cited by the cardinals in 1590 before the Congregation of the Index Expurgatorius. Another **Samson,** a son of Bezaleel, was a pupil of R. Moses Provençal, with whom he corresponded on Talmudic subjects. In 1592 **Simon Massarani** published at Mantua Al-Ḥarizi's "Mishle Hakamim," with a rimed Italian translation, under the title "Motti di Diversi Saggi Tradotti di Lingua Hebræa in Volgare." Abraham b. Isaac Alluf described, in 1630, the expulsion of the Jews from Mantua. **Ephraim Massarani** was rabbi at Cento in 1676, and in correspondence with Isaac Lampronti. About the same time **Isaac Massarani** was rabbi at Salonica. Among the more recent members of this family may be mentioned **Giacobbe Massarani,** lawyer at Milan about 1850, whose son **Tullo,** one of the foremost writers of Italy, was formerly vice-president of the Italian chamber, and has been a member of the Senate since 1879.

BIBLIOGRAPHY: Zunz, in *Kerem Ḥemed*, v. 134; Mortara, *Indice*, p. 37; Stern, *Urkundliche Beiträge*, i., Nos. 131 *et seq.*
G. I. E.

MASSARANI, TULLO: Italian senator, author, painter; born at Mantua in 1826; died Aug. 4, 1905. He studied law at Pavia and took an active part in the Italian revolution of 1848, after the failure of which he fled to Frankfort-on-the-Main. From Paris he went to Switzerland, thence to Milan, where he became a member of Parliament (1860–67), and was afterward very efficient as a member of the municipal council. He is well known in Italy as a painter, his best-known painting being "The Warm Baths of Alexandria." His essay on Heine in "Crepuscolo" (1857) and his translation of the latter's works have made Heine very popular in Italy. Massarani was president of the international jury of art at the Paris Exposition of 1878. He is a member of the Lombard Institute for Arts and Sciences, of the Academy of Fine Arts, and honorary member of the Academy of San Luca. He is the author of the following works: "Quelques Mots sur la Défense de Venise" (Paris, 1849); "L'Idea Italiana Attraverso i Tempi" (*ib.* 1850); "Deutschland und die Italienische Frage" (Breslau, 1859); "L'Arte a Monaco e a Norimberga" (Florence, 1870); "Studii di Letteratura e di Arte" (*ib.* 1873); "Studii di Politica e di Storia" (*ib.* 1875); "Domeniche di Agosto" (*ib.* 1876); "Legnano, Grandi e Piccole Storie" (1876); "Eugenio Camerini e i Suoi Tempi" (*ib.* 1877); "L'Arte a Parigi" (Rome, 1879); "Sermoni" (Florence, 1880; 2d ed. 1884); "Il Libro di Giuda" (*ib.* 1882); "Saggi Critici" (2d ed. 1883); "Carlo Tenca e il Pensiero Civile del Suo Tempo" (*ib.* 1886); "Cesare Correnti Nella Vita e Nelle Opere" (*ib.* 1892); "L'Odissea della Donna," prose and verse (Rome, 1893); "Come la Pensava il Dottore Lorrenzi" (1894). He has collected and published the scattered writings of Cesare Correnti.

BIBLIOGRAPHY: *Nuova Enciclop. Italiana*, 4th Supplement; *Brockhaus Konversations-Lexikon*, xi. and Supplement; *Meyers Konversations-Lexikon*.
S. N. D.

MASSEKET or **MASSEKTA** (plural, **Massektot, Massektiyyot**; Num. R. xviii. 21; Midr. Teh. civ. 25): Any collection of rabbinic texts affecting any more or less complex subject. Literally the term means "a web" (from נסך = "to weave"; comp. Latin "textus"). It is applied indifferently to a treatise of the Mishnah (Shab. 3b; B. Ḳ. 102a), to a compilation of baraitot (Shab. 114a), or to a treatise of the Mishnah with Gemara (Hor. 10b). The whole of the Mishnah as now known comprises sixty-three massektot, though ancient authorities speak of sixty only, reckoning the three Babot (Baba Ḳamma, Baba Meẓi'a, and Baba Batra) as one and Sanhedrin and Makkot as one (Num. R. xviii. 21; see Straschun *ad loc.*, note 23; Cant. R. vi. 9; see Luria *ad loc.*). The Babylonian Gemara embraces thirty-seven massektot, and the Palestinian thirty-nine. Besides these there are appended to editions of the Babylonian Talmud many "minor massektot" ("massektot ḳeṭannot"), seven of which Raphael Kirchheim edited (Frankfort-on-the-Main, 1851); these seven are chiefly of a halakic nature. Latterly the term "masseket" was applied to any treatise, even if of comparatively small compass and of cabalistic type. See TALMUD.

BIBLIOGRAPHY: Kohut, *Aruch Completum*; Levy, *Chal. Wörterb.*; idem, *Neuhebr. Wörterb.*; Jastrow, *Dictionary*.
S. S. S. M.

MASSEL, JOSEPH: Russian Jewish Hebraist; born at Ujasin, government of Wilna, 1850. He emigrated to England in the nineties and settled at Manchester, where he opened a printing and publishing office. Massel has translated and published the following works: "Ha-Rokel," a novel, translated from the German (Warsaw, 1886); "Shimshon ha-Gibbor," a translation of Milton's "Samson Agonistes" (Manchester, 1895); "Mi-Kenaf ha-'Areẓ," original poems, and translations from the English (*ib.* 1898); "Dibre Aḥiḳar," translation of "Ahikar the Wise" (*ib.* 1898); "Yehudah ha-Makkabi," a translation of Longfellow's "Judas Maccabeus" (*ib.* 1900). He has published also "Ha-Maḳhelah," a collection of Hebrew poets from 1725 to 1903 (London, 1903).

BIBLIOGRAPHY: Zeitlin, *Bibl. Post-Mendels.* p. 232; Lippe, *Osaf ha-Mazkir he-Ḥadash*, p. 260, Vienna, 1899; *Jewish Year-Book*, 1904.
J. A. S. W.

MASTER AND SERVANT: The Pentateuch lays down the rule, in favor of the workman, that "the wages of him that is hired shall not abide with thee all night until the morning" (Lev. xix. 13); the preceding words of the same verse, "thou shalt not oppress thy neighbor" (R. V.), are also construed as forbidding the withholding of the workman's hire (B. M. 110). Even more strongly is this idea expressed in Deut. xxiv. 15: "In his day thou shalt give him his hire; neither shall the sun go down upon it" (R. V.).

Deut. xxiii. 25, which permits one who goes into the vineyard or the cornfield of his neighbor to pluck and eat grapes or ears of corn, though he may not use a vessel for the former nor a sickle for the latter, is by tradition (B. M. vii. 2–8) interpreted as applying only to the workmen who enter into the vineyard or field in the employment of the owner.

(1) What the Mishnah says about the rights and duties of workmen ("po'alim") applies mainly to those employed in husbandry; mechanics and carriers are specially treated as such. As in the law of rural leases (see LANDLORD AND TENANT), local custom was the principal standard in dealings with those hired for husbandry. The Mishnah (B. M. vii. 1) says, "He who hires workmen and asks them to work in early morning or in late evening at a place where early morning or late evening work is not customary can not compel them [to do so]. Where the custom is to feed, he must feed; to provide sweets, he must provide [them]—all according to the custom of the province." This applies also to the quality of the board, as R. Simeon ben Gamaliel points out in answer to the saying of R. Johanan ben Mattai, of whom the following is reported: He sent his son to hire laborers, and the son agreed to board them. When he returned to his father, the latter said: "My son, even if you provide for them a meal equal to the best of Solo-

Board as Wages.

mon's, you have not discharged your obligation to them, for they are the children of Abraham, Isaac, and Jacob. Before they begin to work, say to them: 'I shall give you bread and beans.'" Though R. Johanan's view is not correct, it shows the high regard in which even the lowly Israelite, depending on hired labor for his daily bread, was held by the sages (B. M. 83–87).

(2) The passages in Leviticus and Deuteronomy on the payment of hired laborers, one giving the entire day and the other the entire night in which to pay, are thus harmonized in the Mishnah (B. M. ix. 11): "He that is hired by the day receives [his wages] at any time in the [following] night; one hired by the night, at any time in the [following] day; one hired by the hour, at any time during the night and day following; one hired by the week, month, year, or week of years, if the time ends in the day, during the remainder of the day; if during the night, he receives it during that night or on the following day." The duty of the hirer to pay promptly is not confined to wages, but extends to payment for the use of cattle or implements (B. M. ix. 12), probably because these were often furnished by the workman, as is the case to-day with the teamster, who sets a price per day for himself and his team.

(3) In regard to the right to eat grapes or ears of corn in the master's field, the Mishnah (B. M. vii. 2–8) says: "The following eat according to Scripture: He that works on what is affixed to the ground eats at the time of finishing the work; he that works on what is separated from the ground eats before the work is complete [for after that it is subject to tithe] of those things which grow from the earth [which excludes esculent roots]." But those engaged in milking or cheese-making, for instance, do not eat of the produce they are handling. "He whose work is among figs has no right to eat from the grapes, or vice versa; but the man may restrain his appetite until he comes to the finest fruit." All this applies to men at ordinary work; but when the workmen are engaged in bringing back some of the master's lost property, they may eat while going from furrow to furrow, or while returning from the wine- or oil-press, or from what is on a beast of burden which they are unloading. The workman may eat cucumbers, or dates, or the like, irrespective of their market value; but he should be taught not to act greedily and thereby "close the door upon himself." The workman may, for a sum of money, surrender his right to eat, either on his own behalf, or on behalf of his wife, or of his grown children or slaves, but not on behalf of his infant children or infant slaves, or of his beasts.

User of Crop.

Those that watch the crops are according to Scripture not permitted to eat, but by custom are, nevertheless, allowed to do so. When one man watches the fields of several owners he may satisfy his hunger from the field of one alone (B. M. 87–93).

(4) Elsewhere (B. M. vi. 1–2) the Mishnah speaks of mechanics ("umanin"), ass-drivers, and teamsters, the hirer being not a master mechanic or master carrier, but a householder ("ba'al ha-bayit") who employs them in his own affairs. If, in the case of the hirer and the mechanic, one has led the other into error, the latter has no remedy beyond a "rebuke" ("tar'umet"). In the Gemara two possible cases of this sort are mentioned. In one the householder sends one workman to employ others, and the workman so sent engages them either at higher wages than authorized (which, of course, does not bind the employer), or at lower wages, which, to their loss, they accept. In the other, after work is begun, the master (or the workmen) refuses to continue. But where an ass-driver or teamster is hired under pressing circumstances, as for a wedding or a funeral, or where workmen are hired to bring in flax from the tanks, or to do similar tasks involving perishable matter, and they refuse to continue (after beginning the work), the hirer may employ others at the cost of the workmen so refusing, to the extent of the whole wage or any part thereof.

Mechanics.

When the mechanics who have been employed refuse to continue with the work (after doing part) they are at a disadvantage; the hirer may take out of their wages all the cost of employing others, even though the rate of wages has risen; but if the householder refuses to continue he is at a disadvantage; that is, he must pay them for what they have done plus the whole contract-price for the future work, less what it would cost to hire others, even though the rate of wages has fallen in the interval. In general, whoever recedes from a contract is at a disadvantage (lit. "his hand is the lower"). These rules naturally would apply to husbandry also (B. M. 75a; B. B. 153a).

(5) Whenever a workman in plying his trade has in his charge any chattel or animal of his employer, his liability for loss or damage is measured by that of a "keeper for hire" (B. M. vi. 6). See BAILMENTS.

BIBLIOGRAPHY: Maimonides, *Yad*, *Sekirut*, ix.; Caro, *Shulḥan 'Aruk*, *Ḥoshen Mishpaṭ*, 311–319.

S. L. N. D.

MAT, MOSES BEN ABRAHAM: Galician rabbi; born at Przemysl about 1550; died at Opatow 1606. After having studied Talmud and rabbinics under his uncle R. Ẓebi and Solomon Luria, he became rabbi of Beldza, where he had a large number of pupils. He retired from this rabbinate and lived privately for a time at Vladimir. He was then called to the rabbinate of Przemysl, and, in 1597, to that of Luboml. Toward the end of his life Mat became the chief of the community of Opatow and district rabbi of Cracow.

Mat was the author of the following works: "Taryag Miẓwot" (Cracow, 1581), a versification of the 613 commandments; "Maṭṭeh Mosheh" (*ib.* 1590–91), a treatise on the practical ritual laws; "Ho'il Mosheh" (Prague, 1611), a simple and homiletic commentary on the Pentateuch, in which he occasionally explains the commentary of Rashi. Some responsa of his are to be found in the responsa collections of his rabbinical contemporaries.

BIBLIOGRAPHY: Kohen Ẓedek, *Shem u-She'erit*, p. 40, Cracow, 1895; Steinschneider, *Cat. Bodl.* col. 1762; Fürst, *Bibl. Jud.* ii. 334.

S. S. B. FR.

MATAH MEḤASYA (MAḤSEYA): Town in southern Babylonia, near Sura (see Schechter,

"Saadyana," p. 63, note 1). Sherira Gaon regarded the two places as identical, for in his accounts of the geonim of Sura he uses the names of both Matah Meḥasya (or Meḥasya) and Sura to indicate the seat of the academy, the former name even being the more frequent of the two. In the passage where he describes the founding of the Academy of Sura by Rab he says expressly that Rab had come to "Sura, which is Matah Meḥasya" (ed. Neubauer, i. 29; variant, "Sura, called 'Matah Meḥasya'"). There is no doubt, however, that these names belonged to two distinct towns, which came to be regarded as one when the seat of the academy was mentioned. They are named together in Ber. 29a, where the different modes of speech of the peoples of the two places are noted. Other Talmudic passages clearly indicate that these were two different towns (B. M. 67b; Yoma 86a). Sherira Gaon himself says (i. 30) that in the second half of the third century Ḥuna's school (by implication the academy founded by Rab) was in the vicinity of Matah Meḥasya; Rab's colleague Ḥisda lived at Sura. It seems likely, therefore, that the school was situated between the two places.

When the academy entered upon a new period of prosperity, under Ashi, in the second half of the fourth century, its seat was at Matah Meḥasya, where Ashi lived, and most of the Talmudic references to this place, which, Ashi says (Ket. 4a), may not be called either a city or a borough, date from his time. He refers to its synagogue, which strangers visited on his account (Meg. 26a), and he claims to have saved the town from destruction by prohibiting the construction of houses higher than the synagogue (Shab. 11a). Ashi was wont to say that the non-Jewish inhabitants of Matah Meḥasya were hard-hearted, since they beheld the splendor of the Torah twice a year at the great Kallah assemblies, and yet not one of them was converted to Judaism (Ber. 27b).

Halevy assumes that Sura again became the seat of the academy after Ashi's death ("Dorot ha-Rishonim," ii. 599), and that Mar b. Ashi restored Matah Meḥasya to the position to which Ashi had raised it. From his time probably dates the maxim which the martyr Mashershaya gave his sons, contrasting the outward poverty of Matah Meḥasya with the splendor of Pumbedita: "Live on the dung-heaps of Matah Meḥasya and not in the palaces of Pumbedita!" (Ker. 6a; Hor. 12a). There were various differences of opinion between the scholars of Pumbedita and Matah Meḥasya regarding questions of civil law, the opinions being collected in Ket. 55a. Rabina, the last amora of the Academy of Sura, lived at Matah Meḥasya (see Yoma 86a; Ḳid. 33a; B. Ḳ., end). The Talmud refers to the destruction of Matah Meḥasya (Shab. 11a), but in post-Talmudic times the town lent its name to the Academy of Sura, as stated above.

Bibliography: A. Berliner, *Beiträge zur Geographie und Ethnographie Babyloniens*, p. 45, Berlin, 1883; I. H. Hirschensohn, *Sheba' Ḥokmot*, pp. 162 *et seq.*, 177, Lemberg, 1883; I. Halevy, *Dorot ha-Rishonim*, ii. 543 *et seq.*

S. S. W. B.

MATALON, JACOB BEN SOLOMON: Turkish rabbinical scholar; lived at Salonica in the sixteenth century. According to De Rossi ("Dizionario," i. 135) the name "Matalon" is the Hebrew equivalent of "one of Toulon," but Zunz (see Steinschneider, "Cat. Bodl." col. 1241) derives it from "Mataloni," the name of an Italian town. In spite of his premature death Matalon wrote several works, two of which were published (Salonica, 1597): "She'erit Ya'aḳob," sermons, and "Toledot Ya'aḳob," commentary on various haggadot in the Talmud and Midrashim.

Bibliography: Conforte, *Ḳore ha-Dorot*, p. 38a; Fürst, *Bibl. Jud.* ii. 334.

E. C. M. Sel.

MATALON, MORDECAI: Rabbi of Salonica in the sixteenth century; uncle of Jacob b. Solomon Matalon. Besides being a prominent Talmudist, Matalon was, according to his companion Samuel di Modena, who quotes him frequently in his responsa, well versed in secular sciences (Responsa on Ḥoshen Mishpaṭ, No. 40). He is quoted also by Isaac Adarbi in his "Dibre Ribot" (Nos. 217, 326). Matalon was the author of responsa inserted in the "Mishpeṭe Shemuel" of Samuel Ḳala'i (Venice, 1599).

Bibliography: Conforte, *Ḳore ha-Dorot*, pp. 38a, 40a, b; Fürst, *Bibl. Jud.* ii. 334.

S. M. Sel.

MAṬAṬRON. See Meṭaṭron.

MATER SYNAGOGUE. See Pater Synagogue.

MATHEMATICS: The science that treats of the measurement of quantities and the ascertainment of their properties and relations. The necessity of studying astronomy for calendric purposes caused the ancient Hebrews to cultivate various branches of mathematics, especially arithmetic and geometry, applications of which are frequent in the Mishnah and Talmud. With regard to arithmetic there occur the four rules, in both whole numbers and fractions; even the decimal system is alluded to by Rabba, who says that the Persians called the number 10 "one" (Ber. 60a). As to geometry, the treatises 'Erubin, Kelim, Ohalot, etc., contain many applications of planometry and stereometry. The terms "bigon," "trigon," "tetragon," and "pentagon" are found several times in the Talmud, both in their geometrical sense, signifying a figure of two, three, four, or five angles, and in their arithmetical sense, expressing the numbers 2, 3, 4, and 5. As early as the forty-ninth "middot" of R. Nathan $3\frac{1}{7}$ to 1 is given as the relation between the circumference and the diameter of a circle. The names which occur often in the Talmud in connection with mathematical propositions are Gamaliel, Joshua, Judah, and Samuel.

"Mishnat Middot."

Still, however rapid may have been the spread of mathematical knowledge among the Jews in the Talmudic times, no work on that science is known to have existed in Jewish literature prior to the Judæo-Arabic period, to which belongs probably the "Mishnat Middot," the oldest mathematical work in Hebrew known. According to Steinschneider, who first published it (Berlin, 1864), it is an imperfect endeavor to propound the elements of geometry.

With the expansion of the Greco-Arabic philosophy the Jews began to take part in the development of mathematics, which was regarded as a science introductory to philosophy. It was divided by the Arabian school into seven "disciplinæ"; namely, arithmetic (ח' החשבון), algebra (ח' התשבורת), geometry (ח' הנדסה or ח' המדידה), astronomy (ח' התכונה), astrology (ח' הנסיון), optics (ח' הראות), and music (זמרה). Of these only algebra and geometry are treated at length in this article, the others being dealt with under their respective names.

With the exception of the above-mentioned "Mishnat Middot," no work on algebra or geometry is known to have been written in Hebrew before the twelfth century; the few writings composed by Jews in these branches of mathematics, which in the Middle Ages were neglected in favor of astronomy and astrology, were in Arabic. The oldest Jewish writer on mathematics in its strict sense was the renowned astrologer Mashallah (more correctly Ma Sha Allah), who flourished at the end of the eighth century and at the beginning of the ninth.

Arabic Jewish Mathematicians.

A contemporary of his, Abu Othman Sahl ibn Bishr ibn Ḥabib ibn Ḥani, was the author of a work on algebra entitled "Al-Jabar wal-Muḳabalah." Another work on algebra, bearing the same title, and a commentary on the "Elements" of Euclid, were written about the same time by a Jewish convert to Islam, Sind ben 'Ali. To the same period belongs Sahl Rabban al-Ṭabari, who was considered one of the greatest geometers of his time. Among the writers of the tenth and eleventh centuries mention should be made of Bishr ben Phinehas ben Shu'aib and Jacob ben Nissim of Kairwan, the latter of whom wrote, under the title "Ḥisab al-Ghubar" (Hebr. חשבון האבק), a work on Indian mathematics. In the twelfth century works on algebra and geometry began to appear in Hebrew, mainly as translations from the Arabic.

The first known Hebrew writer on geometry was Abraham bar Ḥiyya ha-Nasi, who expounded its elements in a work entitled "Ḥibbur ha-Meshiḥah weha-Tishboret." This work, which probably formed a part of his encyclopedia "Yesode ha-Tebunah we-Migdal ha-Emunah," was edited by Steinschneider in the publications of the Meḳiẓe Nirdamim Society (1895, vol. xi.). A Latin translation of Abraham bar Ḥiyya's work was made about 1136 by Plato of Tivoli. Another prominent writer on geometry in that century was Samuel ibn 'Abbas, who, at the request of Sultan Abu al-Fatḥ Shah Ghazzi, composed in Arabic a work on the difficulties encountered by the geometer. As a translator of astronomical and mathematical works from the Arabic into Latin, in the same century, the Jewish convert known by the name of Johannes Hispalensis was distinguished. An English Jew is said to have written in Latin, in 1190, a work on mathematics under the title "Mathematica Rudimenta Quædam."

The thirteenth century was especially rich in mathematical productions. The writings of the Greek and Arabian mathematicians were translated into Hebrew and commented upon. Judah ben Samuel Cohen of Toledo (1238), in his encyclopedia—written originally in Arabic and translated by himself into Hebrew under the title "Midrash ha-Ḥokmah"—gives extracts from the "Elements"

In the Thirteenth Century.

of Euclid. In 1278 Euclid's entire work was translated from the Arabic probably by Moses ibn Tibbon. Another translation, entitled "Yesodot," or "Shorashim," and including Hypsicle's books, is supposed to have been made by Jacob ben Machir. Commentaries upon it by Arabian mathematicians, such as Al-Farabi and Ibn Haitham, were also rendered into Hebrew, probably by Kalonymus ben Kolonymus, who, according to the commentary of Simplicius, had translated Book xiv. and Ibn Haitham's commentary on the introduction to Book x. Among the other commentaries on the "Elements" still extant in manuscript in various European libraries are those by a pupil of Jacob ben Machir; by Abba Mari on the introduction to Book i.; by Levi ben Gershon on the propositions of Books i., iii., iv., and v.; by Abraham ben Solomon Yarḥi; and, according to Joseph Delmedigo, by Elijah Mizraḥi. Euclid's "Data" was rendered into Hebrew, from the Arabic version of Ḥunain ibn Isḥaḳ, by Jacob ben Machir, under the title "Sefer ha-Mattanah." Three new translations were made between 1775 and 1875. Euclid's works were published first by Abraham ben Joseph Minz, with annotations by Meïr of Fürth, under the title "Reshit Limmudim hu Sefer Iḳlides" (Berlin, 1795). Five years later a new translation of the first six books of the "Elements" was published by Baruch Schick (The Hague, 1780). In 1875 a new translation of Books xi. and xii. was published at Jitomir.

Jacob ben Machir, in the thirteenth century, translated from the Arabic the work on spherical

Translations from the Arabic.

figures of the Alexandrian mathematician Menelaus. Kalonymus ben Kalonymus twice translated the works of Archimedes on conoids and spheroids and on the measure of the circle under the titles "Be-Kaddur ube-Iẓṭawwonot" and "Sefer Arkimedes be-Meshiḥat ha-'Iggulah." He made the following translations also: "Sefer Meshalim be-Tishboret," on algebraic propositions; "Sefer ha-Temunah ha-Ḥittukit"; a work on geometry by Thabit ibn Ḳurra entitled "Al-Shakl al-Ḳaṭṭa'"; "Ma'amar be-Iẓṭawwonot webe-Ḥiddudim," a treatise on cylinders and cones by Abu al-Ḳasim Aṣbagh or Asba' ben Mohammed. In the fifteenth century Jewish literature was enriched with several important works on algebra and geometry. Mordecai Comtino, teacher of the rabbi and mathematician Elijah Mizraḥi, wrote a treatise, in two parts, on arithmetic and algebra, in which he followed partly the Greek and Latin authors, partly the Mohammedan; he also annotated the "Elements." Elijah Mizraḥi wrote on arithmetic, algebra, and geometry under the title "Meleket ha-Mispar." Mordecai ben Abraham Finzi translated from the Latin, under the title "Taḥbulat ha-Mispar," a work on algebra by Abu Kamil Shuja', and a work on geometry under the title "Ḥokmat ha-Medidah."

The most prominent representative of mathematical knowledge among the Jews in the sixteenth century was the historian David Gans, who wrote three works on mathematics—"Ma'or ha-Ḳaṭan," "Migdal

Dawid," and "Prozdor." Among the mathematicians of the seventeenth century the most renowned was Joseph Delmedigo, who in his "Bosmat Bat Shelomoh" gives a survey of geometry and devotes several chapters of his "Ma'yan Gannim" to trigonometry and algebra. In the eighteenth century the most noted mathematician among the Jews was Elijah Wilna, who wrote a work containing treatises on trigonometry, geometry, and some principles of astronomy and algebra. The following is a list of all the Hebrew works on algebra, geometry, and arithmetic published up to the last years of the nineteenth century:

Elijah Wilna.

אוקלידס, a new translation of Euclid, by Baruch Schick. The Hague, 1780.

אוקלידס, on Books xi. and xii. of the "Elements," by David Friesenhausen. Jitomir, 1875.

אילם, containing, among other scientific dissertations, treatises on arithmetic, algebra, geometry, and trigonometry, by Joseph Delmedigo. Amsterdam, 1629.

אנפאנגסגרינדע, arithmetic, in Judæo-German, by Faibus Hurwitz. Amsterdam, 1791.

ברורי המדות, on the geometrical propositions found in the Talmud, by Tobias Hurwitz. Prague, 1807.

ברית אברהם, arithmetic, according to Elijah Mizraḥi and non-Jewish sources, by Abraham Niederländer. Prague (1609?).

דרכי החשבון, arithmetic, by Jehiel Michael Epstein. Wilna, 1836.

חכמת המספר, arithmetic, by Moses Ḥayyim Eisenstadt. Dyhernfurth, 1712.

חכמת המספר, arithmetic and algebra, by Naḥman Hirsch Linder of Dubno. Warsaw, 1855.

חכמת השעורים, arithmetic, translated from the French by Jacob Eichenbaum. Warsaw, 1857.

ידיעת החשבון, arithmetic, in Judæo-German, by Aryeh Löb Shames. Amsterdam, 1690.

ידיעות השעורים, geometry, by Gabriel Judah Lichtenfeld. Warsaw, 1865.

יסוד עולם, containing, among other things, geometrical propositions, by Baruch Schick. Berlin, 1777.

יסודי ח' השעור, on the various branches of mathematics, by Ḥayyim Zelig Slonimski. Jitomir, 1865.

כליל החשבון, algebra, by David Friesenhausen. Berlin, 1797 (Zolkiev, 1835).

לוחות חמגבילים, logarithms, by David Friesenhausen. Königsberg, 1854.

מבחר החשבון, arithmetic, by Letableau. Warsaw, 1866 (*ib.* 1875).

מוסדות תבל, proofs on the eleventh proposition of Euclid, by David Friesenhausen. Vienna, 1820.

מלאכת החשבון, arithmetic, by Moses Samuel Neumann. Vienna, 1831.

מלאכת מחשבת, arithmetic and algebra, by Elijah ben Gershon of Pintschow, Zolkiev, 1740.

מלאכת מחשבת, in two volumes: the first, entitled עיר חשבון, deals with arithmetic and the elements of algebra; the second, בירורי מדור, treats of geometry, by Gershon Elias. Berlin, 1765 (Frankfort-on-the-Oder, 1766; Ostrog, 1806).

מלאכת מחשבת, arithmetic, in Judæo-German, by Goldenberg. Berdychev, 1823 (Sdilkov, 1834).

מלאכת מחשבת, arithmetic and algebra, in Hebrew and Judæo-German, by Moses Zerah Eidlitz. Prague, 1775. (In Hebrew only, Zolkiev, 1837, 1845.)

מלאכת מחשבת החדש, on all branches of mathematics, in three volumes, by Shalom Blenker. Berdychev, 1834.

מלאכת חמספר, arithmetic, algebra, and geometry, by Elijah Mizraḥi. Constantinople, 1534.

מפתח אלגיברא החדשה, algebra, by Asher Anshel Worms. Offenbach, 1722.

משנת המדות, on geometry, edited by Steinschneider. Berlin, 1864. (With a German translation and notes by Hermann Schapira, Leipsic, 1880.)

נאוה קודש, geometry and trigonometry, by Simeon Waltsch. Berlin, 1786.

עובר לסוחר, arithmetic, by Menahem Zion Porto. Venice, 1627.

עומק הלכה, on the mathematical propositions found in the Talmud, by Jacob Kopel. Cracow, 1598 (Amsterdam, 1710).

פרפראות לחכמה, dissertations on geometry, by Kopel Shacherles. Vienna, 1814.

צפנת פענח, criticisms on the mathematical works of Ḥayyim Zelig Slonimski, by Gabriel Judah Lichtenfeld. Warsaw, 1874.

צפנת פענח, arithmetic and algebra, by Joseph Schliffers. Wilna-Grodno, 1827.

קנה המדה, trigonometry, by Baruch Schick. Prague, 1784.

קצור מלאכת מחשבת, arithmetic. Wilna, 1830.

ראשית למודים, a commentary on the "Elements," by Abraham Joseph Minz. Berlin, 1775.

שבילי דרקיע, on the calendar, and on arithmetic and geometry, by Elijah Hechim. Warsaw, 1863.

שני ספרים בכרך אחד, logarithms, by Rabinowitsch. St. Petersburg, 1872.

BIBLIOGRAPHY: Poggendorff, *Handwörterb.* i. 458; Zuckermann, *Das Mathematische im Talmud*, in *Jahresbericht der Frankelschen Stiftung*, 1878; Eduard Mahler, *Die Irrationalitäten der Rabbinen*, in *Zeitschrift für Mathematik*, 1884; idem, *Zur Talmudischen Mathematik*, ib. 1886; Gurland, *Calendar*, vi. 112–118; Steinschneider, *Jewish Literature*, passim; *idem*, in *Bibliotheca Mathematica*, 1890; idem, *Hebr. Uebers.*; idem, *Die Arabische Literatur der Juden.*

J. I. Br.

——**Modern:** The number of mathematicians of Jewish origin in the nineteenth century is so great that a detailed list of all could hardly be given here. As there are, moreover, no data regarding the lives of the French, English, and Russian mathematicians the biographer frequently would be obliged to resort to conjecture. For example, it is believed that Lobatschewski, one of the discoverers of absolute geometry (pangeometry), was the son of Jewish parents, since his father, a native of Poland, is known to have been converted to the Orthodox Greek Church, and conversion from Catholicism is not likely. Similarly, the ancestry of the great astronomer Friedrich Bessel calls for investigation.

The following German mathematicians may be mentioned: M. Abraham (mathematical theory of electricity); Aronhold; Borchardt (algebra; editor of Crelles' "Journal für die Reine und Angewandte Mathematik"); Georg Cantor (author of the theory of transfinite numbers); Moritz Cantor (history of mathematics); Eisenstein; Fuchs; Gordan (basal principles of the theory of invariants); Hensel (continued Kronecker's investigations); Hurwitz (author of prominent works in various branches of mathematics); Hamburger (differential equations); Hirsch Meyer (source for all modern collections of elementary examples; properties of symmetrical functions); Jacobi; Jolles (geometry); König (algebra); Königsberger (transformation of hyperelliptical functions; biography of Helmholtz); Kronecker; Landau (theory of numbers); Landsberg (algebraic [Abel's] functions); Lipschitz (prominent in all departments of pure and applied mathematics); London (geometry); Minkowski (foremost living [1904] authority on the theory of numbers); Noether (algebra and Abel's functions); Pasch (critique of the principles of mathematics; important geometrical investigations on complexes); Pringsheim (modern theory of functions); Rosanes (geometrical transformation and apolarity); Rosenhain; Saalschütz (convergence; applied mathematics); Schlesinger (comprehensive text-book, and original investigations on differential equations); Schönflies (geometry); Schwarzschild (director of the observatory at Göttingen; mathematical astronomy); Wälsch (theory of invariants); Weingarten (foremost living authority on the theory of surfaces); Wolfskehl (theory of numbers).

Of Italian mathematicians the following are the most important, their chief distinction being won in analytic and synthetic geometry: Castelnuovo, Enriquez, Fano, Jung, Beppo Levi, Levi-Cività, Loria, Segre, Volterra (mathematical physics).

The most prominent Russian mathematicians are Schapiro (cofunctions; algebraic integration) and Slonimski (inventor of a well-known counting-machine and editor of Jewish calendars).

Of the Jewish mathematicians of France those who have gained especial prominence are: Hadamard (Hadamard's theorem); Halphen (reduction of linear equations to integrable form [obtained a prize from the French Academy]; spatial curves [obtained a prize from the Berlin Academy]; compare Stieltjes' biography of him in Halphen's "Traité des Fonctions Elliptiques," vol. iii.); Maurice Lévi (mathematical physics; president of the Institute).

The most noteworthy English mathematician is James Joseph SYLVESTER.

J. S. G.

MATHIAS OF CRACOW. See CALAHORA.

MATRIARCHY: A system of society in which descent and property are traced solely through females. It has been suggested that the prominence given to the mothers of kings in the Books of Kings and to the wives of the Patriarchs are survivals of this system. The fact that the tribes can be divided into tribes descended from Rachel and tribes descended from Leah has also been urged in favor of this view, especially as the name "Rachel" means "ewe," and the name "Leah" has been traced by Robertson Smith to a Semitic root meaning "antelope." The view is thus dependent upon the theory that the early Israelites had a totemistic tribal system (see TOTEMISM).

BIBLIOGRAPHY: W. Robertson Smith, *Kinship and Marriage in Early Arabia*, especially p. 219, Cambridge, 1885; Jacobs, *Studies in Biblical Archæology*, London, 1891.

A. J.

MATTANIAH. See ZEDEKIAH.

MATTATHIAS MACCABEUS: The originator of the Maccabean rebellion. His genealogy is given as follows in the First Book of Maccabees, the most authentic source: "Mattathias, the son of John, the son of Simeon, a priest of the sons of Joiarib, from Jerusalem; and he dwelt at Modin" (I Macc. ii. 1). Josephus ("Ant." xii. 6, § 1) traces the genealogy back for one generation further, mentioning Asamoneus (= Hasmonæus) after Simon. But this Hasmonæus should not be considered as Mattathias' great-grandfather, but merely as a distant ancestor of the whole house, since only so is it comprehensible why both Greek and rabbinical sources of the following period call the whole house that of the Hasmoneans. The fact, moreover, that the names John and Simeon recur in the family in the very next generation after Mattathias, while the name "Hasmonæus" is not found in historic times, is a proof that the first bearer of this name belongs to antiquity.

The rabbinical sources have a different account. In the Seder 'Olam Zuṭa, which, it is true, is not very reliable, Mattathias is given as the direct son of Hasmonai; and elsewhere also Hasmonai appears as a historic person who is very much in evidence. Thus, in Soferim xx. 8 occurs the reading: "Mattithiah, son of Johanan the high priest, and Hasmonai and his sons." The conjunction "and" must originally have stood also in the liturgical formula fixed for the Ḥanukkah feast, so that Mattathias and Hasmonai are to be regarded as two independent heroes who lived in the same period and who were probably relatives. In the Talmud, Hasmonai is even mentioned before Mattathias (Meg. 11a). A midrash to Deut. xxxiii. 11, quoted by Rashi, mentions the children of Hasmonai, among them Eleazar; as does also Jellinek "B. H." vi. 2. Hasmonai thus appears in these passages in the place of Mattathias.

Distinguished from Hasmonai.

The rabbinical sources never mention all of Mattathias' sons together, but only one at a time, sometimes Eleazar (who, according to most of the authentic sources, took only a subordinate part), sometimes John (who also is unimportant in the books of the Maccabees and in Josephus), and sometimes Judas. The First Book of Maccabees and Josephus enumerate the sons of Mattathias as follows: John Gaddis or Caddis (Johanan Gadi), Simon Thassi, Judas Maccabeus, Eleazar Avaran, and Jonathan Apphus. The Aramaic-sounding cognomens, which have not been fully explained, were probably given them by their father, with reference to contemporary events or to the respective characters of the sons themselves. The Second Book of Maccabees mentions still another brother, between Simon and Jonathan, called Joseph; but that is probably only a corrupt reading for "Johanan."

Mattathias belonged to the priestly tribe of Joiarib (comp. I Chron. xxiv. 7); the name is badly preserved in Josephus. From the statement that he was from Jerusalem, but resided in Modin, it is certain that he actually officiated in Jerusalem. The rabbinical sources which make him high priest are mistaken. Mattathias was already old when the religious persecution under Antiochus Epiphanes broke out. The king's soldiers under Apelles, who is mentioned by Josephus but not in the Book of Maccabees, came to Modin, a small city in Judea. They set up an altar to the heathen god, and ordered Mattathias, as the most influential citizen, whose example would be followed, to sacrifice in accordance with the king's command. But Mattathias said: "Though all the nations that are under the king's dominion obey him, . . . yet will I, and my sons, and my brethren, walk in the covenant of our fathers" (I Macc. ii. 19–20). And when a certain Jew was about to obey the command, Mattathias, who was filled with holy wrath, killed the offender and destroyed the altar, while his sons cut down the king's officer. Thereupon Mattathias called out: "Whoever is zealous for the Law, and maintaineth the covenant, let him follow me." His countrymen, abandoning all their possessions, followed him and hid in the mountains and desert places. Others, who had hidden themselves before, joined them. When Mattathias learned that the pious ones

Refuses to Sacrifice to Idols.

would rather be cut down by the king's soldiers than defend themselves on the Sabbath he commanded them to fight, when necessary, on that day. This practise, says Josephus, was continued in later days. It is evident from this that Mattathias had authority in religious matters also.

From his hiding-place he scoured the neighboring districts of Judea, drove out small bands of the king's troops, punished the renegade Jews, destroyed the heathen temples and altars, and brought children, who through fear had not been circumcised, into the covenant of Abraham. Josephus, whose account otherwise agrees with that of I Maccabees, differs from it in stating that Mattathias reigned one year and then became ill. Also in "B. J." (i. 1, § 3) Josephus speaks of Mattathias as a prince chosen by the people. According to both authorities, Mattathias before his death urged his sons and the people to continue steadfast in the defense of their ancestral religion. Of his sons he designated Simon as counselor and Judah as general. He died in 146 of the Seleucid era (166 B.C.), and was buried in Modin, amid the lamentations of all Israel. Niese has tried to prove from the fact that Mattathias does not appear in the Second Book of Maccabees that he never existed. This has been refuted by Schürer and Wellhausen. The importance of Mattathias is attested by the fact that rabbinical tradition mentions his name and even puts it in the Hanukkah prayer. The name Mattathias recurs in the person of his grandson, a son of Simon (I Macc. xvi. 14).

BIBLIOGRAPHY: Grätz, *Gesch.* ii.[2] 322-325; Niese, *Kritik der Beiden Makkabäerbücher*, pp. 44-47 (reprint from *Hermes*, 1900, vol. xxxv.); Schürer, *Gesch.* 3d ed., i. 202; Wellhausen, *I. J. G.* 4th ed., p. 257, note 1, Berlin, 1901; Krauss, in *R. E. J.* xxx. 215. For the sources of Josephus see Büchler, *ib.* xxxiv. 69-76.

G. S. Kr.

MATTATHIAS B. SIMON: Son of the Hasmonean prince Simon, whom he accompanied on his last journey, together with his brother Judah and his mother. Simon, with his sons, was invited by his son-in-law Ptolemy to a banquet in the fortress of Docus, near Jericho, where he was murdered, his sons being first put in fetters and then killed. The accounts in I Maccabees and in Josephus do not agree as to whether Mattathias was slain at the same time as his father, or later; Josephus, however, probably reports the affair more correctly, as he refers also to other sources.

BIBLIOGRAPHY: *I Macc.* xvi. 16; Josephus, *Ant.* xiii. 8, § 1; idem, *B. J.* i. 2, § 3; C. Werner, *Johann Hyrkan*, p. 10, note 22, Wernigerode, 1877; Grätz, *Gesch.* iii. 67 *et seq.*

G. M. K.

MATTERSDORF, JOAB BEN JEREMIAH: Hungarian rabbi; died about 1807. Through the influence of Aaron Chorin, a disciple of his father, he became rabbi of Deutschkreuz, near Mattersdorf, Hungary. He wrote "Ḥen Ṭob" (Zolkiev, 1806), commentary on a part of the code Eben ha-'Ezer, to which is added "Zebed Ṭob," on the same code, by his son-in-law Isaac (Eisik) ben Lippmann Fränkel. Joab wrote also: "Sha'are Binah," novellæ to Isaac ben Reuben Alfasi's "Sha'are Shebu'ot," Vienna, 1792. Like Joseph Caro, Marcus Benedict, and others, Mattersdorf mistook this Isaac ben Reuben for a grandson of Isaac Alfasi (see JEW. ENCYC. i. 377, *s.v.* ALFASI, ISAAC BEN REUBEN).

BIBLIOGRAPHY: Benjacob, *Oẓar ha-Sefarim*, p. 194; Fürst *Bibl. Jud.* ii. 334; Löw, *Gesammelte Schriften*, ii. 257 Steinschneider, *Cat. Bodl.* No. 5824; Zunz, in Geiger's *Wiss Zeit. Jüd. Theol.* iii. 57.

D. S. MAN.

MATTHÄI (SIMEON), ADAM RUDOLF GEORG: German convert to Christianity; born at Fürth 1715; died at Nuremberg 1779. After having studied Talmud at Prague under his father, Jaidel, who was lecturer on Talmud in the bet ha-midrash, Matthäi, whose name was then Simeon, returned to his native town. There he was appointed teacher in the Jewish high school and afterward lecturer in the bet ha-midrash. In April, 1748, Matthäi announced to the clergy of Fürth his intention of embracing Christianity, and on their advice he went to Nuremberg, where he was baptized on Sept. 20 of the same year, and where he was afterward appointed sacristan of the Dominican Church.

Matthäi wrote several works in German which, according to his admirers, were a defense of Christianity against the attacks of the Jews, but in reality were attacks on Judaism. It must be admitted, however, that he displayed in his writings a wide knowledge of rabbinical literature.

The following is a list of his works in their chronological order; with one exception they were published at Nuremberg:

Beschreibung des Jüdischen Sabbats. 1750.
Die Verderbniss des Heutigen Judenthums. 1752.
Beschreibung des Jüdischen Neujahrsfestes. 1755.
Beschreibung des Jüdischen Purimfestes. 1758.
Beschreibung des Jüdischen Jom Kippur. 1760.
Sammlung Talmudischer Lehrsätze. Schwabach, 1763.
Abhandlung von der Verleumdung. 17[illegible].
Sendschreiben an Rabbi Peloni aus der Stadt Lo-Theda. 1766.
Erneuerung des Taufbundes. 1768.
Kurzgefasste Talmudische Lehrsätze von der Nothwendigkeit Sich in den Ebestand zu Begeben. N.d.
Beweis von der Uebereinstimmung der Alten Israelitischen Kabbala mit der Lehre des Apostels Paulus. N.d.
Beweisgründe von der Uebereinstimmung der Altjüdischen Lehre mit der Lehre der Christen. 1770.
Christlich Gesinnte Erklärung der Kabbalisten Ueber das Hohelied. 1776.

BIBLIOGRAPHY: De le Roi, *Juden-Mission*, i. 398; Fürst, *Bibl. Jud.* ii. 335.

G. M. SEL.

MATTHEW. See NEW TESTAMENT.

MATTHIAS BEN MARGALOT: Associated with Judah ben Zippori in the instigation of an uprising against Herod the Great (Josephus, "Ant." xvii. 6, § 2; *idem*, "B. J." i. 33, § 2). See JUDAH BEN ZIPPORI.

S. S. KR.

MATTHIAS BEN THEOPHILUS: Name of two high priests. **1.** The successor of Simon ben Boethus, and, unlike the other high priests appointed by Herod, who were foreigners, a native of Jerusalem (Josephus, "Ant." xvii. 4, § 2). On the eve of a Day of Atonement—for the priest the most important time in the year—he had become ritually unclean, and consequently was unable to perform the duties of his office, which were discharged instead by his kinsman Joseph ben Ellem ("Ant." xvii. 6, § 4). This occurrence is mentioned in the Talmud (Tosef., Yoma, i. 4; Yoma 12b; Yer. Yoma 38d), although the name of Matthias ben Theophilus is omitted. His deposition, however, was not due to this cause, but to the fact that he was supposed to have been implicated in the insurrection when the golden eagle was pulled down from the gate of the Temple (see JUDAH BEN ZIPPORI). His tenure of office lasted only one or two years (5–4 B.C.).

2. A descendant, apparently, of the preceding, and the last high priest but one. He was in office in 65 C.E., when the war against the Romans broke out (Josephus, "Ant." xx. 9, § 7). During the troubles in Jerusalem which preceded the siege by Titus ("B. J." iv. 3, § 7) he was deposed, since he, like the other aristocrats, belonged to the peace party, one of his sons having even sought refuge with the Romans. Matthias was put to death as a dangerous character by the very Simon ben Gioras whom he had invited to Jerusalem to subdue the revolutionists ("B. J." vi. 2, § 2). According to Grätz, it is he who is referred to in a Talmudic story which relates that once, on a Day of Atonement, a high priest remained in the Holy of Holies a longer time than usual praying for the Sanctuary, which was in danger of destruction by the Zealots (Tosef., Yoma, ii. 5; Yoma 53b; Yer. Yoma 42c).

BIBLIOGRAPHY: Derenbourg, *Histoire de la Palestine*, p. 160; Grätz, in *Monatsschrift*, 1881, pp. 51 *et seq.*; Grätz, *Gesch.* 4th ed., iii. 737, 750; Schürer, *Gesch.* ii. 217–220.

S. S. KR.

MATTITHIAH B. HERESH: Roman tanna of the second century; born in Judea; probably a pupil of R. Ishmael, and certainly a contemporary and friend of his pupils R. Josiah and R. Jonathan. After his ordination Mattithiah went to Rome, apparently on account of the persecution by Hadrian; there he founded a school and a Jewish court which soon became prominent. Halakic sentences by him have been preserved which show his desire to make the Sabbath laws less rigorous in so far as their fulfilment by the sick was concerned. He seems, however, to have devoted himself chiefly to the Haggadah; a number of his homiletic sentences, especially to Exodus, are extant. He has a maxim in the Pirke Abot: "Meet each man with friendly greeting; be the tail among lions rather than the head among foxes" (iv. 15). He associated with the Palestinian scholars who visited Rome and sought instruction from them—from R. Simeon b. Yoḥai and R. Eleazar b. Jose, for instance. A later legend in the Midrash Abkir represents him as victoriously resisting a temptation placed in his path by Satan.

BIBLIOGRAPHY: Frankel, *Darke ha-Mishnah*, pp. 130 *et seq.*; Grätz, *Gesch.* 3d ed., iv. 285; Bacher, *Ag. Tan.* i. 385 *et seq.*; Vogelstein and Rieger, *Gesch. der Juden in Rom*, i. 110 *et seq.*

E. C. I. E.

MATTITHIAH B. ISAAC OF CHINON (קינו): French scholar of the end of the thirteenth century. He was a pupil of R. Perez of Corbeil and a contemporary of Mordecai b. Hillel, martyred at Nuremberg in 1298. He is sometimes wrongly identified with Mattithiah, the teacher of Eliezer b. Joel ha-Levi, author of the ritual work "Abi Asaf," who lived at the beginning of the thirteenth century.

BIBLIOGRAPHY: Mordecai, *Mo'ed Katan*, No. 936; idem, *Ketubot*, v., Nos. 184, 290; Gross, *Gallia Judaica*, p. 581.

E. C. S. K.

MATTITHIAH B. JOSEPH THE PRO-VENÇAL (פרובינ״ש): Chief rabbi of Paris and o France from 1360 to 1385; son of Joseph b. Johanar of Treves, rabbi of Marseilles; pupil of Perez b Isaac ha-Kohen and of Nissim b. Reuben of Gerona In 1360 King Charles V. appointed him chief rabbi o the community of Paris and of all the newly organ ized communities of France, exempting him an Manecier of Vesoul from wearing the Jewish badge Mattithiah founded a rabbinical school at Pari which soon attracted many pupils, eight of whon were called to various communities. He is proba bly identical with Mattithiah Treves (טרייבוש, th author of MS. No. 676, folio 147, containing a re sponsum, in the Paris Bibliothèque Nationale) an with Mattithiah "the Frank" (הצרפתי; author of a methodological treatise on the Talmud). Isaac be Sheshet (Responsa, No. 271) applies to him the titl of "Eben Boḥan" ("touchstone"), a term which ha been held to imply that he composed a work beari this name (Shabbethai Bass, "Sifte Yeshenim," x. No. 9). Zunz ("Literaturgesch.") mentions a liturgical poet by the name of Mattithiah b. Joseph "th administrator" ("ha-parnes"), but this latter epithe can apply neither to Mattithiah b. Joseph nor t his father.

BIBLIOGRAPHY: Brüll, *Jahrbücher*, i. 93; Carmoly, in *Arch Isr.* 1856, p. 261; Gross, *Gallia Judaica*, pp. 532–533; Léo Kahn, *Les Juifs à Paris*, p. 26; Grätz, *Gesch.* viii. 9; *Ordon nances des Roys de France*, v. 498; Zunz, *Z. G.* pp. 190, 19

S. S. K.

MATTITHIAH KARṬIN (known also a **Ibn Ḥarṭon**): Scholar of the fourteenth century He translated into Hebrew verse the "Moreh Nebu kim" of Maimonides in 1363 (comp. Wolf, "Bib Hebr." i., No. 1682). His work seems to have bee lost, unless this Mattithiah is identical with Matti thiah b. Shabbethai of Monte Politiano, a work o whose, in verse, is found in the library of the Vati can (No. 258). Steinschneider, after having declare ("Cat. Bodl." col. 1897) that Mattithiah versified th "Moreh Nebukim," says, in his "Jewish Literature (p. 147), that his work is a commentary, in Hebre verse, on the "Moreh." In the Vatican Library (MS No. 298) there is a poem of Mattithiah's, entitled "M bine 'Am," which is an acrostic containing his name Steinschneider thinks that this Mattithiah may b identified with the Italian liturgist called Mattithiah whose three dirges are found in the library of Pa ma (MS. De Rossi No. 1205). Zunz ("Literatu gesch." p. 579) supposes that the latter was a po of the sixteenth century.

BIBLIOGRAPHY: Steinschneider, *Hebr. Uebers.* p. 428.

J. M. SEL.

MATTITHIAH BEN MOSES BEN MAT TITHIAH: Spanish Talmudist; lived toward th end of the fourteenth century and at the beginnin of the fifteenth. He was a member of the Yizha family of Narbonne. As he himself relates, his a cestors on being banished from France (1306) settle together with other scholars in Catalonia and Ar gon. According to Neubauer, Mattithiah is ide tical with the rabbi of this name cited as one those who took part in the disputation at Tortos in 1413.

Mattithiah was the author of the followi

works: (1) "Derashot," homilies on the Pentateuch, no longer extant; (2) a commentary on Ps. cxix. (Venice, 1546; partly translated into Latin by Philippe d'Aquin, Paris, 1629); (3) a commentary on Pirke Abot, still extant in manuscript; (4) notes on Abraham ibn Ezra's commentary on the Pentateuch (Neubauer, "Cat. Bodl. Hebr. MSS." No. 236); (5) a philosophical commentary on the Pentateuch, still extant in manuscript; (6) "Parashiyyot," homilies; (7) "Derashot," no longer extant.

Bibliography: Loeb, in *R. E. J.* vii. 155, ix. 119; Neubauer, *ib.* vii. 154; Steinschneider, *ib.* ix. 118; Renan-Neubauer, *Les Ecrivains Juifs Français*, p. 432.
G. I. Br.

MATTITHIAH OF PARIS: Head of the Talmudic school of Paris in the eleventh century and doubtless identical with Mattithiah b. Moses, one of Rashi's pupils. He is occasionally called **Mattithiah the Great.** He corresponded with Samuel b. Meïr (RaSHBaM), who names him among the "ancients" of Paris.

Bibliography: Gross, *Gallia Judaica*, pp. 226, 508; *Maḥzor Vitry*, No. 280; *Or Zarua'*, i. 138b; *Shibbole ha-Leḳeṭ*, ii., Nos. 18, 136.
E. C. S. K.

MATURITY. See Majority.

MATZEL, ASCHER: Hungarian soldier and philanthropist; born 1763 at Stampfen, Hungary; died Nov. 22, 1842. At the age of seventeen he entered the service of the Jewish hospital in Vienna, of which he became the superintendent in 1799. Emperor Joseph II. appointed him during the war with the Turks superintendent of the hospital in the fortress of Leopoldstadt, which position he later exchanged for that of director of the hospital of Semlin. The emperor bestowed on him many tokens of his appreciation, among others a diamond ring with the emperor's initials.

After the close of the war Matzel returned to Vienna to resume charge of the Jewish hospital. In 1818 he received from Emperor Francis the gold medal of honor and from the Emperor of Russia the Order of Merit. In 1814 Matzel became manager of the military magazine of munitions, and in 1830, during the cholera epidemic, he became chief of the board of health of the Rossau, a suburb of Vienna.

Bibliography: *Jüdischer Plutarch*, ii. 194-196.
S.

MAURICE, CHARLES: Theatrical director; born at Agen, France, May 29, 1805; died in Hamburg Jan. 27, 1896. Maurice, who was of French descent, was educated in his native city, and until his twenty-second year, when he accompanied his father to Hamburg, was totally ignorant of the German language. Although unfamiliar with theatrical matters, Maurice assumed charge of a minor playhouse in Hamburg in 1831 and proved so successful that, when the great fire of 1842 destroyed the structure, aid came to him from all quarters, and he was enabled to replace it with the present Thaliatheater. In 1847 he assumed the management of the Stadttheater also, relinquishing it, however, in 1854. From that time on Maurice's energies were devoted to the Thaliatheater, which obtained world-wide fame under his direction. In 1885 he retired from active participation in its affairs, but in 1893 he was forced, by the death of his son and successor Gustav, to resume the management. Maurice celebrated in 1881 the fiftieth anniversary of his entry upon the theatrical field, and was the recipient of a series of remarkable felicitations.

Maurice was not merely a clever manager from the commercial point of view, but also a student of human nature remarkable for his discernment of histrionic talent. It was Maurice who developed the immature talent of Bogumil Dawison and of Friederike Gossman, and encouraged Emil Thomas, Marie Barkany, Franz Wallner, and others, when their fame was still embryonic.

Bibliography: Kohut, *Berühmte Israelitische Männer und Frauen*, pp. 245-249.
S. E. Ms.

MAUROGONATO, ISACCO PESARO: Italian legislator; born in Venice Nov. 26, 1817; died in Rome April 5, 1892. He was a member of a prominent family of Ferrara. His father, Israel Pesaro, removed to Venice on his marriage, and the son took the name of Maurogonato in addition to the family name in consequence of an inheritance left him by one of his mother's relatives. He studied law, and afterward finance and political economy. Maurogonato took an active part in the organization of the Venetian revolution of 1848-49; on its outbreak he was elected to the assembly, and was later made minister of finance. He succeeded in supplying an empty treasury with funds for carrying on the war, and was Manin's and Tommaseo's right hand. When the Austrians examined the municipal accounts after regaining possession of the city they found them absolutely correct. General Gorskowski exclaimed in surprise, "I never could have believed the rascally Republicans were so honest!" On the collapse of the revolution Maurogonato was one of the forty excepted from the amnesty; with Manin and Tommaseo he was compelled to leave the country. He went to the Ionian Islands, but in a few years was allowed to return to Italy and engage in business at Vicenza.

In 1866 Maurogonato again entered public life as a member of the chamber. When in 1884 the recognition of the loans made to the Venetian revolutionary government of 1848-49 was proposed in Parliament, Maurogonato—who thought the proposition a just one, but did not feel that he could conscientiously advocate it to his own gain—turned over his claims, before the discussion began, to the municipality of Venice. They brought about 16,000 francs, and that sum became the foundation of a fund for furnishing annual subsidies to the veterans of the revolution. He became vice-president of the chamber and was for a number of years a member of the general budget commission. The portfolio of finance was several times offered to him, Victor Emanuel even personally urging him to accept, but he steadily refused. On Oct. 27, 1890, King Humbert made him a senator. Both houses of Parliament, the government, and the municipal councils of Venice and of Rome took official notice of his death, and King Humbert sent his condolences to his family. Imposing public funeral services were held at Rome and at Venice, in which latter city he was buried. Throughout his life Maurogonato was devoted to the interests of his coreligionists.

Bibliography: *Arch. Isr.* 1892, pp. 156–157; *Il Vessillo Israelitico*, 1892, pp. 123–124.

s. N. D.

MAUSCHBERGER, LEOPOLD: Biblical scholar of the eighteenth century. He was the author of commentaries on the Pentateuch and the Earlier Prophets (Olmütz, 1757), and on the books of Chronicles, Ezra, Tobit, Judith, etc. (*ib.* 1758; Fürst, "Bibl. Jud."). T.

MAUTHNER, FRITZ: Austrian poet, novelist, and satirist; born in Horitz, Bohemia, Nov. 22, 1849. He attended the Piarist gymnasium in Prague and then ostensibly studied law at the university, though in reality he busied himself almost exclusively with philosophy and the history of art. He passed only the first state examination in jurisprudence, after which he was occupied for a short time in a lawyer's office in Prague. While there he published a collection of sonnets, under the title "Die Grosse Revolution" (1871), which almost brought upon him an indictment for treason. This was followed by "Anna" and several minor comedies, which were successfully produced. He then devoted himself exclusively to literature. After writing for a time for Prague publications, he removed, in 1876, to Berlin, where he wrote critical articles for various journals. Since 1895 he has written the dramatic articles for the "Berliner Tageblatt." Mauthner's works include: "Aus dem Märchenbuch der Wahrheit," satirical prose poems; "Nach Berühmten Mustern," parodies (Stuttgart, 1879); "Der Neue Ahasver," romance (Bern, 1881); "Dilettanten Spiegel, Travestie nach Horaz's Ars Poetica" (*ib.* 1883); "Credo" (Berlin, 1886); "Der Letzte Deutsche von Blatna" (*ib.* 1886); "Von Keller zu Zola" (*ib.* 1887); "Schmock, oder die Literarische Karrière der Gegenwart," a satire (*ib.* 1888); "Quartett Fanfare" (1888); "Xantippe" (Dresden, 1889); "Der Pegasus, eine Trago-Komische Geschichte" (Dresden, 1889); "Der Villenhof"; three romances published collectively under the title of "Berlin W" (1890); "Bekentnisse einer Spiritistin: Hildegard Nilson" (Berlin, 1891); "Hypatia," romance (Stuttgart, 1892); "Der Geisterseher," humorous romance (Berlin, 1894); "Kraft," "Die Bunte Reihe," and "Der Steinerne Riese," romances (1896); "Die Böhmische Handschrift" (1897); "Beiträge zu einer Kritik der Sprache: Sprache und Psychologie" (Stuttgart, 1901).

Bibliography: Eisenberg, *Das Geistige Berlin*; *Nord und Süd*, May, 1904.

s. N. D.

MAUTHNER, JULIUS: Austrian chemist; born in Vienna Sept. 26, 1852; educated at Vienna University (M.D. 1879), where he became privat-docent in experimental medical chemistry (1881) and assistant professor (June 3, 1885). He is a member of the Leopold and Caroline Academy of Naturalists and Chemists. He has published a number of scientific papers in the "Sitzungsberichte der Kaiserlichen Akademie der Wissenschaften," Liebig's "Annalen der Chemie," "Berichte der Deutschen Chemischen Gesellschaft," "Zeitschrift für Biologie," "Wiener Medicinische Blätter," and elsewhere.

Bibliography: Eisenberg, *Das Geistige Wien*, ii. 328–329; Schmidt, *Jahrb. der Gesammten Medicin.*

s. N. D.

MAUTHNER, LUDWIG: Austrian ophthalmologist; born in Prague April 13, 1840; died in Vienna Oct. 20, 1894; educated at the University of Vienna (M.D. 1861). He was admitted to the medical faculty of his alma mater as privat-docent in ophthalmology in 1864, and became professor in the University of Innsbruck in 1869. This position he resigned in 1877, returning with the title of professor to Vienna, where he again became privat-docent. In 1890 he was appointed assistant-chief physician in the eye dispensary; and four years later he was appointed professor. In 1899 a monument was erected in his honor in the "Arcaden" of Vienna University.

Mauthner wrote many essays upon neuropathy and ophthalmology for the medical journals. Among his works may be mentioned: "Die Bestimmung der Refractionsanomalien mit Hilfe des Augenspiegels," Vienna, 1867; "Lehrbuch der Ophthalmoskopie," *ib.* 1868; "Recherches sur la Structure du Système Nerveux," Paris, 1868; "Die Optischen Fehler des Auges," Vienna, 1872 (2d ed. 1876); "Die Syphilitischen Erkrankungen des Auges," in Zeissl's "Lehrbuch der Augenheilkunde," 1873; "Die Sympathischen Augenleiden," Wiesbaden, 1879; "Die Funktionsprüfung des Auges," *ib.* 1880; "Gehirn und Auge," *ib.* 1881; "Die Lehre vom Glaukom," *ib.* 1882; "Die Lehre von den Augenmuskeln," *ib.* 1883 (2d ed. 1889); "Die Nicht Nuclearen Augenmuskellähmungen," *ib.* 1886; "Diagnostik und Therapie der Augenmuskellähmungen," *ib.* 1889.

Bibliography: Pagel, *Biog. Lex.*

s. F. T. H.

MAUTNER, EDUARD: German author and journalist; born at Budapest Nov. 13, 1824; died in Baden, near Vienna, July 2, 1889. His father, who was a merchant in Budapest, died when Eduard was seven years old, whereupon his mother, with her children, of whom Eduard was the oldest, removed to Vienna. There he attended the elementary school and the gymnasium. After attending lectures on philosophy at the University of Prague (1843), where he published several poems and a tale in Glaser's "Ost und West," he returned to Vienna, began the study of medicine, exchanged it for that of law, and then dropped law for literature. In 1844 he removed to Leipsic, studied philosophy and ethics, and renewed friendships begun at Prague with Moritz Hartmann, Uffo Horn, and Alfred Meissner. To Lewald's "Europa," Herlosssohn's "Komet," Kuranda's "Grenzboten," and Oettinger's "Charivari" Mautner contributed poems, tales, and critical and literary articles, all of which were well received by the critics. He returned to Vienna in the autumn of 1847.

While visiting his mother in Triest, the revolutionary movement of 1848 began. Mautner hastened to Vienna, and during the revolution was active as a journalist, writing especially for Frankl's "Sonntagsblatt." He next acted as feuilletonist and dramatic critic for the "Ostdeutsche Post," the "Presse," and the "Wanderer." In 1851 his comedy, "Das Preislustspiel," took the second prize at the Hofburg Theater competition. In 1853 he traveled in Germany, Belgium, France, and England, returning to Vienna in 1854, to publish a series of sketches in the "Ostdeutsche Post" and in the "Familienbuch des Oesterreichischen Lloyd." From 1855 to 1864 he was officially connected with the Staatsbahngesellschaft; during that period he published several poetical works, and some minor comedies that were produced in Vienna. Early in 1865 he became assistant in the Imperial Court Library at Vienna, and afterward was engaged in the literary bureau of the Ministry of Foreign Affairs. He wrote: "Gräfin Aurora" (Vienna, 1852); "Kleine Erzählungen" (*ib.* 1858); "In Catilinam, ein Kranz Geharnischter Sonette," against Napoleon (*ib.* 1859); "Während der Börse" (Berlin, 1863; played at the court theater); "Eine Frau, die an der Börse Spielt" (produced at the Vienna Carltheater); "Eglantine," drama (Vienna, 1863); "Die Sanduhr" (Berlin, 1871); "Eine Kriegslist," comedy (1878); "Von der Aar zur Donau," festival play (1881); "Ausgewählte Gedichte" (Vienna, 1889).

BIBLIOGRAPHY: Wurzbach, *Biog. Lex.*; *Meyers Konversations-Lexikon*; *Jüdisches Athenäum.*

S. N. D.

MAXIMS (Legal): Short sayings in which principles of law of wide application are laid down. They are known to all systems of jurisprudence: thus, "Casus nocet domino" and "Ignorantia juris nocet" are maxims of Roman law; "Nobody can plead his own wrong" and "You can not come into a court of equity but with clean hands" are maxims of English law. Of the maxims which are current in the Talmud many belong to substantive law, others to the law of evidence and procedure. The following may be cited as examples:

כל שחבתי בשמירתו הכשרתי את נזקו ("I am bound to make good any damage caused by whatever I am bound to guard" [B. Ḳ. i. 2]). This applies to domestic animals, to a pit or any similar source of danger, and to fire. See ACCIDENT.

אדם מועד לעולם ("A man is always forewarned" [B. Ḳ. ii. 6]); that is, a man is, like the owner of a "forewarned ox," always liable for the whole damage arising directly from his acts.

חרש שוטה וקטן פגיעתן רעה ("A deaf man, a fool, and a child are bad to meet" [B. Ḳ. 87a]) because whoever harms them is liable for the damage done, while no compensation is recoverable from them for any damage done by them.

שלוחו של אדם כמותו ("A man's agent is, in effect, the man himself"). This is similar to the Roman principle "Qui facit per alium facit per se."

כל המשלם אינו לוקה ("Who pays is not flogged" [Mak. i. 2]); that is, wherever the law orders compensation paid for an unlawful act, and the payment is made, punishment by stripes can not be inflicted.

כל התדיר מחברו קודם לחברו ("Whenever one thing is more nearly permanent than another it has the preference" [Hor. iii. 6]) appears in the Gemara simply as תדיר קדים ("The permanent ranks first"), a rule derived from the often reiterated insistence of the Torah on the celebration of the daily sacrifice on festive days, when other sacrifices also are prescribed

אין מרחמים בדין ("They have no mercy in judgment" [Ket. ix. 2-3]) means that the courts do not act on the principle of modern equity known as "marshaling the assets," the principle of giving to the creditor having the weakest hold on other funds (הכושל) a stronger hold on the fund under dispute; every creditor must take his chance, according to the opinion of R. Akiba, which prevails over that of R. Ṭarfon.

חיזק ראייה שמיה היזק ("Damage by seeing is called damage" [Gemara; B. B. 2b]) expresses the right of a householder to privacy; that is, to be screened while in his house or courtyard from the view of his neighbors is a legal right.

אין בית דין אחד סותר דברי ב"ד חברו עד שגדול ממנו בחכמה ובמנין ("One court does not overrule the decision of another court unless it is greater in wisdom and numbers" ['Eduy. i. 5]) is a principle that, supplemented by the high regard in which the Tannaim (ending with R. Judah about 220) were held by succeeding generations, has done much to keep Jewish laws and customs in their old, sometimes obsolete, forms. See AḤARONIM.

יקוב הדין את ההר ("Let the judgment pierce the mountain" [Sanh. 6a, b]), corresponding to the Latin "Fiat justitia, ruat cœlum" (Let justice be done though the heavens fall), expresses a principle not much followed in practise, as the sages always desired a compromise between the litigants more than strict enforcement of the law.

Law of Evidence and Procedure.

אין אדם משים עצמו רשע ("No man can make himself out wicked" [Sanh. 25a]) means that no penalty, such as death, exile, or stripes, nor more than full restitution, nor even a fixed sum as damages to an injured party, can be awarded upon the admission or confession of the accused (see ACCUSATORY AND INQUISITORIAL PROCEDURE; see Ket. iii. 9). Two competent witnesses are indispensable.

לא ראינו אינו ראיה ("'We have not seen' is no proof" ['Eduy. ii. 2]). This principle was carried further in the Talmudic than it is in modern law, as the former was averse to the establishment of any fact by indirect evidence.

נכסים בחזקתן ("Property [abides] in its status" [B. B. ix. 8-9; see BURDEN OF PROOF]). In the absence of evidence either way, property remains with the owner in possession, and his heirs.

המוציא מחברו עליו הראיה ("He who desires to take anything from his companion must furnish the proof" [B Ḳ. iii. 11; see BURDEN OF PROOF]); that is, the party seeking recovery of money or property must prove his case. The English rule is that the burden of proof rests upon the party having the affirmative in any issue; the Talmudic rule will often prove at variance with this practice.

מודה במקצת חייב בשבועה ("He who admits a part is bound to make oath" [Shebu. vi. 1-3]). One that is sued for a given sum or thing of value, and admits that he owes a smaller sum, or thing, than that claimed, or admits facts tending to such a conclusion, can not by his mere denial in regard to the balance put his adversary to proof; but he must, if the latter calls for it, confirm his denial by an oath.

הפה שאסר הוא הפה שהתיר ("The mouth which bound [forbade] is the mouth that also loosened" ["permitted"; 'Eduy. iii. 6]). This maxim is given with this illustration:

Where it is known of a woman only by her own account that she has been a captive, and she says she was not defiled, her statement is taken, and she may marry into the priesthood; but if the proof of her captivity rests upon witnesses, and she claims that she was not defiled, the court would say לא על פיה אנו חיים ("We do not live on what she says"; see also, for the rule, Ket. ii. 5, and, for its counterpart, Ket. i. 6-9).

The general principle known as כלל, with which the discussion of a branch of law in its details sometimes ends, is to be distinguished from the ordinary legal maxim. An example is found at the end of the treatise Shebu'ot, the last chapter of which states all the cases in which a depositary, by swearing to an untrue statement of fact, incurs guilt, and concludes with: "This is the general principle: 'Whoever swears in order to make it easier for himself, is guilty; to make it harder for himself, is not guilty.'" Legal maxims are to be distinguished from such sayings of worldly wisdom as: "He who has read the letter, let him carry out its purpose."

S. L. N. D.

MAY, ISAAC: Rabbi of Lublin, Poland, in the latter half of the sixteenth century. Gaining the favor of Count Jenchinsky, the starost of Lublin, he secured in 1556 a very considerable parcel of land which adjoined his house, and which had formerly been covered by a mill-pond. Having filled in this uneven area, May made it available for the growth of the overcrowded Jewish quarter of Lublin. In time most of the land became covered with Jewish houses; but May reserved a portion of it, which he presented to the community for the establishment of a yeshibah. In this way he was largely instrumental in founding the first high-grade rabbinical school in Poland. The royal decree, secured Aug. 23, 1567, by Isaac May and other representatives of the community, contains a passage which, freely translated, reads as follows: "In compliance with the representations of some of his advisers and the humble petition of the Jews of Lublin, King Sigismund August permits the Jews to build at their own general expense ["sumpto communi Judæis"] a gymnasium for the instruction of persons in the Jewish religion, and near the gymnasium a synagogue, on the land of Isaac May, rabbi of Lublin, situated between the Jewish houses, near Lublin Castle, in the Jewish quarter . . ."

BIBLIOGRAPHY: Bershadski, in *Voskhod*, Dec., 1896, p. 13.

H. R. J. G. L.

MAY, LEWIS: American merchant and banker; born in Worms Sept. 23, 1823; died at Dobbs Ferry, N. Y., July 22, 1897. He went to the United States in 1840, and in 1845 established an independent business in Shreveport, La. In 1850 he effected an important copartnership for the purpose of carrying on trade in San Francisco, Cal., Portland, Ore., and, later, in New York. He took up his residence in the last-named city in 1856. In 1869 he retired from mercantile life and established the banking firm of May & King. He turned his business talents toward other enterprises also, serving for many years as trustee, treasurer, or director of various New York corporations.

May was treasurer and director of Mt. Sinai Hospital for nineteen years, was one of the organizers and the first president of the Young Men's Hebrew Association, and was trustee and president of Temple Emanu-El for thirty-three years. In recognition of his services the congregation of Temple Emanu-El, in 1888, presented him with a valuable testimonial, and after his death dedicated a memorial window in the Temple to him.

BIBLIOGRAPHY: *National Cyclopædia of American Biog.*; *The Metropolis*, part i.; *The American Hebrew*, July and Nov., 1897; Myer Stern, *The History of Temple Emanu-El*.

A. J. S.

MAY, MITCHELL: Member of the American House of Representatives; born in Brooklyn, N. Y., July 10, 1871; educated at the Brooklyn Polytechnic Institute and Columbia Law School. He was a member of the 56th Congress (1899 to 1901) and has held several positions in Jewish communal organizations.

A.

MAY LAWS: Temporary regulations concerning the Jews of Russia, proposed by Count Ignatiev, and sanctioned by the czar May 3 (15), 1882. They read as follows:

"(1) As a temporary measure, and until a general revision is made of their legal status, it is decreed that the Jews be forbidden to settle anew outside of towns and boroughs, exceptions being admitted only in the case of existing Jewish agricultural colonies.

"(2) Temporarily forbidden are the issuing of mortgages and other deeds to Jews, as well as the registration of Jews as lessees of real property situated outside of towns and boroughs; and also the issuing to Jews of powers of attorney to manage and dispose of such real property.

"(3) Jews are forbidden to transact business on Sundays and on the principal Christian holy days; the existing regulations concerning the closing of places of business belonging to Christians on such days to apply to Jews also.

"(4) The measures laid down in paragraphs 1, 2, and 3 shall apply only to the governments within the Pale of Jewish Settlement [that is, they shall not apply to the ten governments of Poland]."

These regulations, as is apparent from their phraseology, were intended only as temporary measures; and the government itself when it issued them was aware of the fact that such legislation would not suffice for the permanent adjustment of the legal status of the Russian Jews. But public excitement due to the riots in South Russia ran high; there was no time to weigh the practical consequences of the new regulations either to the Jews themselves or to their non-Jewish neighbors. The regulations were to remain in force until the final revision of the laws concerning the Jews. This revision was assigned to a special commission, under the chairmanship of Count Pahlen, which soon afterward completed its task; but no further action has been taken in the matter, and the "temporary regulations are still in force with no immediate prospect of their repeal.

The official motives for the enactments were stated

follows: "These laws are called into being by the ort of the government to improve the relations tween the Jews and the native population in the Pale of Settlement, and to protect the former from the hostility of the latter, which has manifested itself in outbursts against the person and property of the Jews; also to lessen the eco-mic dependence of the native population upon the ws." In a resolution of the Senate (Nov. 28, 1888) e government admitted that "the existing relations tween the Jews of the Pale and the native Rus-ns can not be considered normal, and the deter-ination of the legal status of the Jews in our untry urgently calls for a decisive and early set-ment, which, owing to its extent and complexity, d because of the importance of the interests in-lved, can be made only by a thorough revision of e entire existing legislation concerning the Jews." ie enactments, while not changing essentially and rmanently the existing laws concerning the Jews, ere intended to remove the main motives for a nflict between the Jews and the native popula-n ("Ryesheniya Obsch. Sobran. Senata," 1888, o. 25).

stensible nd Real Motives.

Such were ostensibly the reasons which led the vernment to pass the temporary regulations. As matter of fact they were merely the outcome of e Panslavist policy for the repression of the Jews. he views of the Ultra-Conservatives have not been alized; nevertheless it is certain that the May Laws ve resulted in great injury to the economic and litical life of Russia.

The temporary regulations have from the begin-ng given rise to different interpretations and end-ss misunderstandings and complaints. For in-ance, the phrase "to settle anew outside of towns d boroughs" has been a prolific source of official abuse. Some governments informed their officials that by this phrase must be understood not only change of residence by a Jew from one settlement to other, but also from one house to another in the me settlement. The Senate decided against this terpretation; but in the meantime it had become a urce of much annoyance to the Jews. As to the moval from one settlement to another, it appears at every Jew became interned in the village in hich he happened to be living at the time of the actment. Thus, while he was still accorded the ght to remove from village to city within the Pale, e lost the right to remove from village to village. this wise petty officials acquired the power to noy the Jews and to resort to extortion. Appeals the Senate have usually resulted in decisions vorable to the Jews; but the expenditure of time d money involved in them detract considerably om their effectiveness.

Applica-tions.

A few examples will suffice to show to what ngths local officials have gone in the interpreta-on of the May Laws. If one who had the right to side in a village left it temporarily, he encountered ouble on returning (see the decision of the Senate the case of Engelmann, May 12, 1895, No. 5120). ews who had served in the army encountered diffi-ulties, at the expiration of their terms of service, in resettling in the villages in which they had dwelt (*idem*, May 23, 1884; case of Reznikov, Jan. 13, 1885). Similar difficulties were experienced by Jews living in villages and employed in cities, whither they went daily, sometimes remaining there for a few days (*idem*, case of Feigin, Jan. 30, 1895, No. 1253), and by Jews privileged to live anywhere in the empire (*idem*, case of Elkin, Oct. 2, 1885). Misunderstandings occurred in the case of Jews living in the suburbs of cities also (*idem*, 1888, No. 18). Difficulties arose through conflicting decisions of the Senate as to what constituted a townlet (*idem*, July 27, 1887, No. 8849). A frequent source of annoyance was the illegal change by local administrations, without the permission of the minister of the interior, of townlets to villages (*idem*, March 22, 1894; Feb. 13, 1896, No. 1591; July 3, 1896, No. 6557; and many others). There are also numerous cases on record where local officials refused permission to Jews to visit villages temporarily for business purposes, although the law expressly states that Jews are only forbidden to "settle anew" (*idem*, 1895, No. 4025). A further limitation created by the May Laws is that Jews possessing the right of residence in villages have not the right to execute leases or contracts to purchase, the absurd condition being thus created of compelling the Jews to live under the open sky. This absurdity was finally removed by the Senate, which decided that Jews having such right of residence might rent rooms or might build houses of their own on land leased for the purpose (*idem*, Sept. 28, 1892, No. 11702). The Senate likewise decreed that Jews might rent for grazing purposes lands belonging to cities and located within the city limits (*idem*, Oct. 10, 1890). On the other hand, it has been decreed by the Senate department of appeals that even Jews who are privileged to reside anywhere in the empire have not the right to lease lands situated outside of cities and townlets (*idem*, 1889, No. 24).

The May Laws also limit the rights of Jews to become shareholders in stock companies, or directors, managers, or superintendents of real property belonging to corporations and situated outside of towns or townlets in the Pale. Jews may be admitted as members by a majority vote of the stockholders, but they may not hold appointments as officers of such companies. Only a certain proportion of Jews, moreover, may be admitted, the number being limited to one-tenth of the total number of shareholders (Collection of Laws, May 20, 1897, No. 51, p. 674).

Relation to Stock Companies.

The administration of the May Laws by petty officials who were very often ignorant of their meaning intensified abuses. The Senate had to instruct the officials in the most simple principles of law; for instance, that a law is in force only from the day of its publication. The attempts to define the phrase "new settlement" led to the taking of censuses of the Jewish residents, sometimes by semi-illiterate police officials; and grievous blunders resulted. Jews were registered as living in a certain village when they really lived in another, while the names of actual residents were omitted altogether. For instance, because he was not included in the registry list, Gdaliya Zeigermacher was expelled from the village of Puzheikovo, although it was proved that he had lived there for sixteen years. One Bondarchick was improperly registered as residing in the village of Baksha, and was therefore expelled from the village of Kapustyanka, where he had lived for twenty years. The misspelling of names, a very frequent occurrence, led to annoyance and expulsion; *e.g.*, "Gruzman" was entered as "Ruzman"; "Garvich" as "Gurovich"; and "Shmerka Dorfman" as "Shlyoma." A slight error made by a petty official, not to speak of various evil motives, sufficed to bring about the expulsion of the unfortunate Jew from his home and to bring terror and despair upon him.

ANCIENT REMAINS OF THE JEWISH CEMETERY AT MAYENCE.
(From a photograph.)

BIBLIOGRAPHY: Gessen, in *Yevreiskaya Biblioteka*, 1903, x. 318; Sbornik, *Budushchnosti*, i. 76; *Voskhod*, Jan.-Feb., 1883, p. 57; 1901, No. 78, Mysh, *Rukovodstvo k Russkim Zakonam o Yevreyakh*, St. Petersburg, 1898; *The Persecutions of the Jews in Russia*, issued by the Russo-Jewish Committee, London, 1890, contains a summary of the special and restrictive laws.

H. R.

MAY MARRIAGE. See OMER.

MAYBAUM, SIEGMUND: Rabbi in Berlin; born at Miskolcz, Hungary, April 29, 1844. He received his education at the yeshibot of Eisenstadt and Presburg, at the lyceum in the latter city, and at the university and the theological seminary of Breslau (Ph.D., Halle, 1869). From 1870 to 1873 he was rabbi at Alsó-Kubin, Hungary; from 1873 to 1881, at Saaz, Bohemia; and since 1881 he has held a sin ilar position in Berlin, where he is also docent at th Lehranstalt für die Wissenschaft des Judentums. A founder of the rabbinical society of Germany, whos president he at present (1904) is, he convened the firs congress of German rabbis at Berlin in 1884. He one of the most eloquent rabbis of Germany. In 190 he received the title of professor.

Maybaum is the author of the following works "Die Anthropomorphismen und Anthropopathiee bei Onkelos und den Späteren Targumim," Breslau 1870; "Die Entwickelung des Altisraelitische Priestertums," *ib.* 1880; "Die Entwickelung de Israelitischen Prophetentums," Berlin, 1883; "Pr digten," *ib.* 1892–94; "Jüdische Homiletik," *ib.* 1894 "Methodik des Jüd. Religionsunterrichtes," Breslau 1895; "Die Anfänge der Jüd. Predigt," Berlin, 1901

S. F. T. H.

MAYENCE: German city in the grand duch of Hesse-Darmstadt; on the left bank of the Rhine the seat of an archbishop, who was formerly one o the prince-electors of the Holy Roman Empire. I has a population of 84,251, of whom 3,200 are Jews Although there are no historical documents relatin to Jewish settlements while Mayence was unde Roman rule, it may be assumed that Jews followe the Roman legions to the Rhine in the first centurie of the common era. Legend reports that Charle magne called Kalonymus of Lucca as rabbi to th congregation of Mayence, but documentary evidence of the existence of Jews in Mayence does not antedate the first half of the tenth century, when Archbishop Frederick (937–954) made an unsuccessful attempt to restrict Jewish commercial activity. In 1012 the peace of the Jews of Mayence was disturbed by a religious persecution instigated by Henry II., and which led to apostasy or banishment. After a few months, however, the exiles returned to the city, and most of the converts to Judaism. In the following period of peace the intellectual life of the Jews of Mayence flourished as never before, under various members of the KALONYMUS family and under other Talmudic authorities, including in particular GERSHOM BEN JUDAH.

THE CEMETERY OF THE JEWISH COMMUNITY OF MAYENCE.
(From a photograph.)

In 1084 the Jews were accused of having caused conflagration which destroyed a large part of the ity, and many emigrated in consequence. These efugees were received by Bishop Rüdiger Huozıan of Speyer, who desired to build up his city. The charter dated 1090 and supposed to have been ssued by this bishop is a forgery of later times, ased on a document of Henry IV.) Under the eadership of Emicho of Leinigen the Crusaders atacked the Jews of Mayence May 27, 1096, massacring more than eleven hundred in the city and fifty-three who had fled to the neighboring Rüdesheim, in spite of their brave resistance and of the protection of Archbishop Ruthard. ncluded by Henry IV. in the "king's peace" of 103, the community slowly recovered, until in 1147 the Second Crusade claimed more victims, in consequence of the agitations of the monk Radulph. Persecutions which threatened the Jews in 1187 and 1188 were averted by the bishop and the emperor Frederick Barbarossa. Toward the end of the thirteenth century the accusation of ritual murder was raised at Mayence. In June, 1281, R. Meïr b. Abraham ha-Kohen was slain and the synagogue desecrated and burned; on April 19, 1283, ten Jews were slain by the populace. The persecutions spread throughout the vicinity, and in 1285 the Jews of Mayence, Worms, Speyer, Frankfort-on-the-Main, and the Wetterau decided to abandon their property and to emigrate to Palestine under the leadership of R. MEÏR OF ROTHENBURG. The real estate left at Mayence—in the most beautiful part of the city, the so-called "Judenerben"—was seized by the city in 1286, but was confiscated to the state by Archbishop Adolf II. in 1462. The Jews of Mayence escaped the massacres of 1298 under RINDFLEISCH and 1338–39 under ARMLEDER. In August, 1349, at the time of the Black Death, nearly the whole community perished, and the ghetto was set on fire. The community gradually revived, however, and lived in peace for nearly ninety years, until the Jews were expelled from the city July 25, 1438, in consequence of municipal quarrels; their cemetery and synagogue were confiscated, and the tombstones were used for building purposes. When the old city government was overthrown in 1414 the Jews were permitted to return by Archbishop Diether, who claimed them as his property. Ex-

Massacres During Crusades.

pelled again in 1462 by Archbishop Adolf, though soon readmitted, they were obliged to leave the city definitely in 1473, their synagogue being transformed into a chapel. On March 6, 1492, a Jew named Isaac was permitted to occupy and manage the "miḳweh" (ritual bath), which had been owned by the state for twenty years, and to bury in the "Judensand," mentioned as a cemetery as early as 1286, the Jewish dead brought into the city.

The sufferings of the Jews of the metropolis were shared by those in various localities in the archbishopric, where Jews had settled since the Carlovingian time. This is clear from the following partial summary of places which suffered: Aschaffenburg, persecutions in 1147, 1337, 1349; Amorbach, 1349; Bensheim, 1349; Bingen (mentioned in 1160–73), 1349; Dieburg, 1349; Eltville, 1349; Erfurt, 1221, 1266, 1349; Fritzlar, 1349; Heppenheim, 1349; Heiligenstadt-im-Eichsfeld, 1349; Klingenburg, 1298; Königheim, 1298; Königshofen, 1298, 1349; Krautheim, 1298; Külsheim, 1337; Lahnstein, 1287, 1349; Lorch, 1276, 1337; Miltenberg, 1349; Neudenau, 1298; Ostheim, 1298; Seligenstadt, 1349; Tauberbishofsheim, 1235, 1298, 1337, 1349.

In the Archbishopric.

In the beginning of the sixteenth century only one Jewish family was living at Mayence. In the diocese of Mayence, outside the city, Jews were living under the protection of Archbishop Uriel of Gemmingen, who, on June 2, 1513, appointed the "Jews' doctor" Beyfus to the position of "rabbi, 'Hochmeister,' corrector, and chief judge" of all the Jews in the diocese, assigning him the village of Weisenau near Mayence as his residence. A movement inaugurated by Archbishop Albrecht of Brandenburg in 1516 to expel all Jews from western Germany failed through the intervention of the emperor Maximilian. The few who found a domicil at Mayence in the sixteenth century were obliged to leave in 1579, together with those of the district of the Rhine. A new community was founded in 1583, which received accessions from Frankfort-on-the-Main in 1614, after the Fettmilch insurrection in that city, and from Worms in 1615, on the expulsion of the Jews there. Elijah Loans, who brought with him refugees from Hanau, reorganized the community of Mayence. A rabbi was officially appointed in 1630, and a new synagogue was built nine years later. While the French held Mayence (1644–48) the community was subjected to heavy burdens, and scarcely were these trials passed when the elector Johann Philipp decreed, Dec. 8, 1662, that only twenty Jews should be protected and be permitted in the city, this number being reduced to ten in 1671. These were compelled to move into a

Community Reorganized.

Interior of the Synagogue of the Israelitischen Religionsgesellschaft, Mayence.
(From a photograph.)

new Jews' street and to submit to the most humiliating restrictions, while the Jews who were permitted to settle in neighboring localities were equally hampered. Although subsequent electors permitted Jews to go to Mayence, only 101 "protected" Jews were allowed there during the electorate.

The government, inspired by the tolerant legislation of Joseph II. of Austria, endeavored, even before the outbreak of the French Revolution, to ameliorate the condition of the Jews in the archbishopric. The first steps taken were the inquiry of 1782 and the rescript of July 29, 1783, while the general rescript of Feb. 9, 1784, was intended to bring about a complete change. After determining the salary of the rabbi and of the Jewish provincial board at Aschaffenburg, declaring the German language to be obligatory in book-keeping, regulating the laws of dowry and guardianship, forbidding hasty burial, decreeing that every teacher must pass the state examination, and enacting the establishment of two or three Jewish schools in the electorate, the rescript continues: "In order to neglect nothing which may contribute to the education and the future welfare of the Jews, we permit, although we do not command, the Jewish youth of both sexes and all ages, like the Christian, to attend the Christian village and city ("Real und Normal") schools, especially in the electoral capital Mayence, and schools of all kinds." Further legislation beneficial to the Jews was checked by the outbreak of the French Revolution. From the capture of the fortress of Mayence on Oct. 21, 1792, by the French to its restoration to Germany by the terms of the Peace of Paris Nov. 3, 1814, the Jews of the city were free French citizens. The gates of the ghetto were removed on Sept. 12, 1798, by a decree of the municipal council. Members of the Mayence community were among the delegates sent to Paris in 1806 from the department of Mont Tonnerre, of which Mayence was the capital; the community sent delegates also to the Great Sanhedrin, held in the same city.

Interior of the Gemeinde Synagogue, Mayence.
(From a photograph.)

After civic liberty had been won, work on behalf of education and progress was undertaken. The regulation, introduced by Napoleon's decree of May 17, 1808, and providing that Jews must hold certificates of good character before being permitted to engage in trade, remained in force until 1847. After Mayence was incorporated with the grand duchy of Hesse June 16, 1816, full citizenship was guaranteed to the Jews therein by the law of Dec. 17, 1820, though this provision was not entirely kept. By the decree of Nov. 2, 1841, the community of Mayence, with the other communities of Hesse, was reorganized; on the establishment of the German empire they were granted full civic equality.

In spite of occasional outbreaks of mob violence the lives and the property of the Jews of Mayence were generally protected by law, and they held property under the same conditions as the Christians, with whom they lived peaceably. In the twelfth century they were made Kammerknechte of the empire, a status that entailed many hardships. They were oppressed by persecutions, forcible conversions, the humiliating Jews' oath, which Archbishop Conrad (1160–1200) exacted, and other measures. Emperor Otto IV. declared in 1209 that the empire had no claim to the Jews of the archbishopric of Mayence. The archbishops, who acted as protectors of the Jews of Germany, representing the emperor by virtue of their office of imperial

Social Condition.

chancellors, were not always lenient masters. The council held at Mayence in 1233 excommunicated Christians who associated with Jews, while the provincial synod held at Fritzlar in 1259 imposed the badge upon the Jews of Mayence, and issued inimical regulations, which were aggravated by Archbishop Peter in 1310. In 1295 Archbishop Gerhard, in consideration of a yearly payment of 112 Aachen heller, assigned his Jews to the city with the privilege of taxing them at will; Archbishop Gerlach renewed this agreement on Sept. 3, 1366. Mayence had its own Jews' law, which was not entirely unfavorable to them; but this did not protect them under the emperors Wenzel, Rupert, and Sigismund. In 1385 Archbishop Adolf remitted the Jews' tax and abolished the dice-tax which had been instituted in the Rhine provinces. The following centuries show an unbroken series of oppressive and exclusive measures as well as heavy taxation—the Jews being compelled to pay imperial, state, and municipal taxes, protection money, and especially the LEIBZOLL, of which the last-mentioned was not abolished until 1792.

In days of peace as well as in days of oppression and persecution the Jews of Mayence preserved and cultivated their literature. An academy founded by the family of KALONYMUS in the tenth century—which reached its zenith under R. Gershom and his contemporaries and pupils Judah ha-Kohen, Eliezer b. Isaac, Jacob b. Yaḳar, Isaac ha-Levi, Isaac b. Judah, and others—competed with that of Worms, sending its pupils into all countries. The religious, marital, social, and industrial life of the Jews of the Middle Ages was regulated by the decrees of the rabbinical synods held at Mayence in 1150, 1223, 1245, 1307, and 1381, as it had formerly been governed by the decrees of the French synod held at Troyes in the beginning of the twelfth century, and still earlier by the "regulations" ("taḳḳanot") of R. Gershom. The affairs of the community were directed, probably down to the end of the fourteenth or the beginning of the fifteenth century, by the "Judenrat," under the presidency of a BISHOP OF THE JEWS (called in the documents also "Jews' pope") appointed by the archbishop. Religious affairs were conducted by the rabbi and his college. After the reorganization the Jews of Mayence lived under simple regulations, rarely being without spiritual leaders, a well-attended yeshibah, and all the usual institutions of a well-ordered community.

A list of the most prominent scholars and rabbis down to the middle of the fifteenth century, and a complete list beginning with 1583, are given below:

Scholars and Rabbis. Members of the Kalonymus family; Gershom b. Judah, Me'or ha-Golah (c. 960–1028, or 1040); Simon b. Isaac ha-Gadol (beginning of the 11th century); Eliezer b. Isaac ha-Gadol (c. 1040); Judah ha-Kohen (author of a legal code; c. 1040); David b. Samuel ha-Levi (c. 1050); Abraham b. Judah ha-Kohen (c. 1060); Isaac b. Judah (c. 1080); Jacob b. Yaḳar (c. 1080); Isaac ha-Kohen ([b. Abraham?]; c. 1080); Isaac b. Eleazar ha-Kohen (1093); martyrs of the First Crusade (1096): David, Judah ha-Levi, Menahem b. David, Samuel b. Judah the younger, Samuel b. Judah ha-Kohen; Abraham b. Isaac ha-Kohen (c. 1100); Nathan b. Machir (c. 1100); Eliakim b. Joseph (c. 1130); Kalonymus b. Judah (c. 1140); Eliezer b. Nathan (c. 1150); Meshullam b. Kalonymus (c. 1150); Judah b. Kalonymus b. Moses (c. 1175); Moses b. Mordechai (c. 1175); Moses b. Solomon ha-Kohen (c. 1175); Solomon b. Moses ha-Kohen (c. 1200); Samuel b. Solomon (13th cent.); Baruch b. Samuel (c. 1220); Judah b. Moses ha-Kohen (c. 1250); Meïr b. Baruch of Rothenburg (1230–93); Yaḳar b. Samuel ha-Levi (later in Cologne, 1270); Abraham b. Meïr ha-Kohen (murdered in 1281); Jacob b. Isaac (d. 1318); Isaac b. David (d. 1329); Samuel b. Yaḳar (called "Bonfant"; ḥazzan; d. Sept. 23, 1345); Joseph b. Isaac of Thann (slain 1349); Eliezer b. Samuel ha-Kohen (d. 1357); Jacob of Nordhausen (c. 1365); Jehiel b. Moses ha-Levi (d. Nov. 14, 1380); Moses b. Jekuthiel ha-Levi (1381); Todros (c. 1400); Zalman Runkel (c. 1420); Jacob b. Moses ha-Levi (Maharil; c. 1355–1427); Moses Minz (left Mayence 1455); Judah Minz (brother of Moses; left Mayence; d. Padua 1508); Joshua Moses b. Solomon Luria (d. 1591); Reuben b. Solomon (d. 1598); Joseph (d. 1603); David b. Isaac (d. 1613); Eli Nathan b. Joseph Moses (d. 1631); Judah Löwe of Frankfort (1630–33); Löb Rofe (1634–44); Nathan, son of Isaac Jacob Bonn of Frankfort (1644–50); Saul Judah b. Moses Naphtali (1650–56); Simon Goldisch (1656–62); Jacob Simon (1662–68); Jacob of Ostrog (1668–74); Samuel Sanwil of Lublin (1675–78); David b. Aryeh Löb of Lida (1679–83); Wolf Traub (1683–87); Judah Löb b. Simon (1687–1714); Isaac Seckel b. Immanuel (1715–21); Bernhard Gabriel Eskeles (1721–23); Isaac Seckel Ethausen (1723–29); Bernhard Wiener (1730–32); Moses Brandeis (Moses Ḥarif; 1733–67); David (Tewele) Scheuer (1768–82); Noah Ḥayyim Ẓebi Berliner (1783–1800); Herz Scheuer (1800–10, and 1814–22); Samuel Wolf Levi (1810–14); Löb Ellinger (Schnadig; 1823–47); Joseph Aub (1853–66; later in Berlin; d. 1880); Benedict Cahn (until 1879; d. 1886); Marcus Lehmann (rabbi of the Religionsgesellschaft; 1854–90); Julius Fürst (until 1881); Siegmund Salfeld (since 1880); Jonas Bondi (rabbi of the Religionsgesellschaft since 1890).

Recent Developments. After the French period the conditions for a time were as they had been under the electorate; but in 1830 the Hessian government undertook to regulate the affairs of the Jewish community. The internal development of the community proceeded slowly. In 1836 instruction in the Jewish religion was made obligatory in the high schools. In 1853 R. Joseph Aub was called to the rabbinate, with R. Benedict Cahn as assistant rabbi and teacher of religion; and in the same year the new synagogue was dedicated. The reforms introduced in this synagogue caused a number of the Orthodox members of the community to form a separate congregation—the Religionsgesellschaft, which built its own synagogue and organized a school. It continued to participate in all the affairs of the community, and as few of the members of this separate congregation left it when the law of 1878 was promulgated, a large part of the communal taxes is remitted to it annually for its religious expenses. Mayence is the birthplace of Michael Creizenach, Isaac Bernays, Joseph Derenbourg, Ludwig Bamberger, and other notable men.

Following is a list of the synagogues and other communal institutions of Mayence: principal synagogue, dedicated in 1853 (see illustration); synagogue of the Religionsgesellschaft, dedicated in 1879 (see illustration); school, founded Nov. 11, 1880; elementary and religious school of the Religionsgesellschaft, founded in 1859; ritual bath (miḳweh), rebuilt in 1888; the old cemetery—first mentioned in 1286, closed in 1880 (see illustration); the new cemetery, opened in 1881 (see illustration); hospital and poorhouse, opened in 1904; various other charitable and religious societies, including a society for Jewish literature, a Zionist society, and a Bene Berit lodge. In April, 1904, while certain excavations were being made in the city, a remarkable building was discovered, which has been named the "House of Kalonymus."

The grand-ducal rabbinate of Mayence, in charge

of Dr. Siegmund Salfeld, includes the communities of the following places: Bodenheim, Bretzenheim-Finthen, Dalheim, Dolgesheim, Ebersheim-Harxheim, Essenheim, Guntersblum, Hahnheim, Kastel, Mayence, Mommenheim, Niederolm, Oberolm, and Oppenheim-Nierstein (where Jews have been living since the middle of the thirteenth century; see Kayserling, "Die Juden in Oppenheim," in "Monatsschrift," ix. 295 *et seq.*), Sörgenloch, and Weisenau.

The Rabbinate.

BIBLIOGRAPHY: Documents in the Allgemeines Reichsarchiv at Munich, the Kreisarchiv at Würzburg, the Hof- und Staatsarchiv at Darmstadt, the archives of the Jewish community at Mayence, and in the Mayence city library; Joannis, *Scriptores Rerum Moguntiacarum*, i. 526; Jaffé, *Monumenta Moguntina*; Gudenus, *Codex Diplomaticus*; Will, *Regesta Archiepiscop. Mogunt.*; Schunck, *Codex Diplomaticus*; Aronius, *Regesten*; Böhmer, *Fontes*, iv. 543; Neubauer-Stern-Baer, *Hebräische Berichte über die Judenverfolgung Während der Kreuzzüge*, in *Quellen zur Gesch. der Juden in Deutschland*, ii. 2 *et seq.*; Salfeld, *Martyrologium*; Schaab, *Diplomatische Gesch. der Juden in Mainz*, Mayence, 1855; Hegel, *Städtechroniken, Mainz II. Verfassungsgesch.* pp. 165 *et seq.*; Bodmann, *Rheingauische Alterthümer*, ii. 712 *et seq.*; Wiener, *Regesten*; Bresslau, *Zur Gesch. der Juden in Deutschland*, in Steinschneider, *Hebr. Bibl.* x. 169 *et seq.*; Carmoly, *Die Juden zu Mainz im Mittelalter*, in *Israelit*, 1865, 1866; Stern, *Quellenkunde zur Gesch. der Deutschen Juden*, Nos. 857-868; Carlebach, *Die Rechtlichen und Socialen Verhältnisse der Jüdischen Gemeinden Speyer, Worms und Mainz*, Leipsic, 1901; Stern, *König Ruprecht von der Pfalz in Seinen Beziehungen zu den Juden*, Kiel, 1898; Salfeld, *Bilder aus der Vergangenheit der Jüdischen Gemeinde Mainz*, Mayence, 1903; Leopold Rothschild, *Die Judengemeinden in Mainz, Speyer und Worms von 1349-1438*, Berlin, 1904; Bresslau, in *Zeit. für die Gesch. der Juden in Deutschland*, ii. 82 *et seq.*; Grätz, *Gesch.* vi. 96, 101; vii. 186, 374; viii. 252 *et seq.*, 273 *et seq.*; Stern, *Der Hochverratsprozess Gegen die Deutschen Juden im Anfange des 17. Jahrhunderts*, in *Königsberger Monatsblätter*, pp. 33 *et seq.*, Berlin, 1890. On the rabbis see Zunz; Güdemann; Kohn, *Mordechai ben Hillel*, Breslau, 1878; Michael, *Or ha-Hayyim*; Carmoly, *Zur Gesch. der Rabbiner in Mainz*, in Klein's *Schulbibliothek*, ii. 156 *et seq.*; *Memorbuch of the Community of Mayence, 1583-1847*.

D. S. SA.

MAYER, ABRAHAM: Belgian physician; born at Düsseldorf July 10, 1816; died at Antwerp March 1, 1899. After studying medicine at Bonn (M.D. 1839) he settled in Antwerp in 1848, where he practised as a physician until his death. He took an active part in public life and in the medical activities of his adopted country. For some years he was assistant surgeon in the Belgian regiment of the Hussars of the Guard; and he became a member of the board of medical inspectors to the schools at Antwerp, and president and vice-president of various medical societies in Belgium. Mayer contributed many essays to the medical journals of Belgium, including the following: "Un Cas de Mort par Suite de Brûlure (Perforation Duodénale)," 1866; "Un Cas d'Eclampsie Puerpérale au Commencement du Neuvième Mois de la Grossesse: Enfant né Vivant à Terme," 1868; "Quelques Observations sur les Hôpitaux de Londres," 1869; "Une Cause Insolite de l'Intoxication Saturne: par le Tabac à Priser," 1870; "Deux Cas d'Intoxication Puerpérale," 1878; "Une Note sur le Traitement du Choléra," 1885. Most of these were published in the proceedings of the Société de Médecine and the Société Médico-Chirurgicale, both of Antwerp.

BIBLIOGRAPHY: *Jew. Chron.* March 10, 1899; *Annales de la Société Médico-Chirurgicale d'Anvers*, pp. 89 *et seq.*, Antwerp, Feb., 1899.

S. F. T. H.

MAYER, CONSTANT: French painter; born at Besançon Oct. 4, 1832. He became a pupil at the Ecole des Beaux-Arts and of Léon Cogniet in Paris. In 1857 he went to America and settled in New York, but later returned to Paris, where he now (1904) resides. He is an associate of the National Academy of Design in New York and a member of the Société des Artistes Français of Paris; he became a member of the Legion of Honor in 1869 and is "Hors Concours" at the exhibitions of the Paris Salon. His subjects are genre and portraits. Among his paintings are: "Consolation" (1864); "Love's Melancholy"; "Maud Müller" (1867); "Episode in the Campaign of 1863" (1869); "Song of the Shirt" (1875); "Song of the Twilight" (1879); "Good News" (1882); "First Grief" (1885). Among the portraits painted by him are those of General Grant, General Sherman, and Mme. de Lizardi (exhibited in the Salon of 1903).

A. F. N. L.

MAYER, ELKAN: German army physician; born in Frankfort-on-the-Main (where his father was a physician), and took his degree at a German university. In 1753 he applied to the council of Frankfort for permission to practise, but the petition was refused. In 1760, however, he was appointed military physician of the imperial infantry regiment, under general master-of-ordnance Count von Macquard, whose regimental commander, Angelo de Pasquali, commended Mayer highly. Debates on the subject of the right of Jews to practise medicine took place for years between the council and the Jewish congregation.

BIBLIOGRAPHY: Landau, *Gesch. der Jüdischen Aerzte*, 1895, p. 124.

S. N. D.

MAYER, HENRY: American caricaturist; born at Worms July 18, 1868. Mayer is the son of a Jewish merchant of London, but was educated at Worms. In 1885 he went to Mexico, and subsequently to Texas. There he discovered his ability to draw, and developed his talent without the aid of a teacher. Mayer next went to Cincinnati and thence to Chicago, where he began his career as caricaturist and illustrator.

He has published most of his sketches, including the following: "The Autobiography of a Monkey" (1898); "In Laughland" and "Fantasies in Ha! Ha!" (1899); "Trip to Toyland" (1900); "The Adventures of a Japanese Doll" (1901). Mayer has contributed to "Fliegende Blätter" (Munich), "Black and White" and "Pall Mall Magazine" (London), "Life" and "Puck" (New York), "Le Rire" (Paris), and to many other publications. His cartoons on the "Dreyfus affair" in English periodicals attracted wide-spread attention.

BIBLIOGRAPHY: *Jew. Chron.* Oct. 29, 1899; *Brush and Pencil* (Chicago), June, 1901.

A. E. Ms.

MAYER, MORITZ: German rabbi; born at Dürckheim-on-the-Hardt, Germany, Dec. 16, 1821; died at New York Aug. 28, 1867. He studied law at Munich, and entered on the practise of his profession in his native city, when the revolution of 1848 broke out, and he, being forced to flee, emigrated to America. Arriving in New York, he taught at Dr. Lilienthal's institute up to 1851, when he was called as rabbi to Charleston, S. C., where he remained until 1856. Failing health and differences with his congregation owing to his radical views compelled him to leave Charleston; and he returned to New York, intending to practise law. For a short time he officiated as rabbi in Albany, and then, again returning to New York, he became secretary of the Grand Lodge of the Independent Order B'nai B'rith (1863), which office he held until his death.

Mayer contributed frequently to the Jewish press, and translated various German works into English; *e.g.*, Samuel Adler's catechism; Geiger's lectures on Jewish history; Ludwig Philipson's pamphlet on the Crucifixion; and Fanny Neuda's "Hours of Devotion."

Bibliography: *The American Israelite*, Sept. 13, 1867; *Allg. Zeit. des Jud.* 1867, pp. 800, 842.

A. D.

MAYER, SAMUEL: German rabbi and lawyer; born at Hechingen Jan. 3, 1807; died there Aug. 1, 1875. He studied at the Talmud Torah in his native town, entered the bet ha-midrash and the lyceum at Mannheim in 1823, and went to the University of Würzburg in 1826, where he attended at the same time the Talmudic lectures of Chief Rabbi Abraham Bing. Mayer then went to Tübingen, where he took his degree. In 1830 he was called to the rabbinate of Hechingen, which he occupied until his death. He took up also the study of law and was admitted to the bar in 1849. He was the only rabbi in Germany combining the offices of rabbi and lawyer. Mayer was a prolific writer; his chief work, the fruit of twelve years of labor, is entitled "Die Rechte der Israeliten, Athener und Römer, mit Rücksicht auf die Neuen Gesetzgebungen" (vol. i., "Das Oeffentliche Recht"; vol. ii., "Das Privatrecht," Leipsic, 1862–66; vol. iii., "Das Strafrecht," Treves, 1876). He edited the "Israelitisches Samstagsblatt" (1837) and the "Israelitischer Musenalmanach" (Dinkelsbühl, 1840). He wrote also "Gesch. der Israeliten in Hohenzollern-Hechingen" (published in "Orient, Lit." 1844).

Bibliography: Kayserling, *Bibl. Jüd. Kanzelredner*, ii. 166; *Allg. Zeit des Jud.* xxxix. 582 *et seq.*

S. M. K.

MAYER, SIGMUND: Austrian physician; born at Bechtheim, Rhein-Hessen, Dec. 27, 1842. He studied at the universities of Heidelberg, Giessen, and Tübingen (M.D. 1865) and took a postgraduate course at the universities of Heidelberg and Vienna, becoming privat-docent in the latter in 1869. In 1870 he removed to Prague, where he became privat-docent at the German university and assistant at the physiological institute. He was appointed assistant professor in 1872; became chief of the histological institute in 1880; and was appointed professor of histology in 1884.

Mayer has written many essays (about 60), which have been published in the medical journals of Austria and Germany, in the reports of the Vienna Imperial Academy of Sciences, in Stricker's "Handbuch der Lehre von den Geweben," and in Hermann's "Handbuch der Physiologie." He is the author also of "Histologisches Taschenbuch," Prague, 1887. He was one of the first to introduce the use of methylene blue in microscopy and to describe the chromaffin cells in the sympathetic nerve, the degeneration and regeneration of the nervous system, the sarcolysis, etc.

Bibliography: Pagel, *Biog. Lex.*

S. F. T. H.

MAYHEM: In English law, the offense of depriving a person of any limb, member, or organ by violence. The bearings of such an act in the rabbinical law are fully treated under Assault and Battery.

J. L. N. D.

MAYO, RAPHAEL ISAAC BEN AARON: Talmudical scholar of Smyrna; died in 1810. He was the author of the following works: "Sefer Shorashe ha-Yam," commentary on the Yad ha-Ḥazaḳah (3 vols., Salonica, 1806–15); "Darke ha-Yam," containing homilies and funeral sermons (*ib.* 1813); "Sefat ha-Yam," halakic decisions and responsa (*ib.* 1818); "Pe'at ha-Yam," a commentary on Beẓah, with a number of halakic rules appended (*ib.* 1832).

Bibliography: Steinschneider, *Cat. Bodl.* col. 2127 (where the author's name is given as "Maggio"); Zedner, *Cat. Hebrew Books Brit. Mus.* p. 515.

E. C. I. Br.

MAẒLIAḤ BEN ELIJAH IBN AL-BAẒAḲ: Italian Talmudist of the eleventh century. The surname, Ibn al-Baẓaḳ, the meaning of which is unknown, shows that Maẓliaḥ came from a family of Eastern Jews. Maẓliaḥ knew Arabic well. After having been dayyan in Sicily, he went to Pumbedita, where he attended the lectures of Hai Gaon; after Hai's death he returned to Europe. Maẓliaḥ at that time gave Samuel ha-Nagid an Arabic work entitled "Sirat R. Hai Gaon," in which he had recorded the most noteworthy features of Hai's life; this work is quoted by Moses ibn Ezra ("Kitab al-Muḥaḍarah wal-Mudhakarah," ch. vii.) and by Joseph ibn 'Aḳnin (commentary on Canticles). Maẓliaḥ relates in this work that he was particularly struck at the friendship which existed between Hai Gaon and the Catholicos, whom Hai did not hesitate to consult in regard to questions of exegesis.

A Maẓliaḥ was one of the teachers of Nathan b. Jehiel, who quotes him in his "'Aruk" (particularly *s.v.* אנפיקינון) and declares that he studied under him. Geiger and Kohut identified this Maẓliaḥ with Maẓliaḥ ben Elijah. Kohut even suggested that it was from his teacher that Nathan learned Hai's interpretations of Arabic and Persian words.

Bibliography: A. Geiger, *Jüd. Zeit.* ii. 301–304; Grätz, *Gesch.* 3d ed., vi. 3, 70; Kohut, preface to his edition of the *Aruch Completum*, p. xi.; Mortara, *Indice*, p. 38; Steinschneider, *Die Arabische Literatur der Juden*, § 85.

J. M. Sel.

MAẒLIAḤ, JUDAH B. ABRAHAM PADOVA: Italian Talmudist, cabalist, and poet; rabbi of Modena, where he died Aug. 10, 1728. He was the author of two works: "Tokaḥat Megullah" and "'Oẓerot Sheleg" (the latter cabalistic in nature); and of the following poems: רבון כל העולמים מאציל כל נאצל, Teḥinah; ואתה היודע ועד, an acrostic containing the words ושם שלע"ב ("the name of seventy-two letters"); and עולם הפוך, an epigram on human mortality, an epitaph in the cemetery at Pinale. Only a few of his many responsa have been printed.

Judah had two sons: **Manasseh Joshua** of Modena, brother-in-law of Isaiah Bassani (*c.* 1750), some of whose responsa have been preserved; and **Menahem Azariah,** rabbi of Florence (*c.* 1775), an authority in the Law and a prolific preacher, who also wrote various poems, many of which were liturgical. The genealogy of the family is traced to Abraham b. Samuel of Padua, who married in 1530.

Bibliography: Senior Sachs, הפליט, Nos. 12a, 20-32, 47; Zunz, *Literaturgesch.* pp. 447, 552; Landshuth, *'Ammude ha-'Abodah*, pp. 192 *et seq.*; Nepi-Ghirondi, *Toledot Gedole Yisrael*, pp. 163, 172, 239.

S. S. H. B.

MAZOVRA (MASSURIA). See Poland.

MAẒẒAH (plural, **Maẓẓot**): Bread that is free from leaven or other foreign elements. It is kneaded with water and without yeast or any other chemical effervescent substance, and is hastily prepared to prevent the dough from undergoing the process of spontaneous fermentation, which would make it "ḥameẓ" (leavened bread). The word is derived from the Hebrew root מצץ ("to compress" or "to extract"). "Maẓẓah," in the singular form, is found only in Leviticus (ii. 5, viii. 26) and Numbers (vi. 19); elsewhere it occurs in the plural. The maẓẓah was the primitive form of bread. The discovery of the leavening process not only resulted in an increase in the mass of the dough, but made the bread more palatable. Maẓẓah, however, still remained the poor man's bread, as he could not afford to wait even twenty-four hours for it to leaven; and it was called therefore "leḥem 'oni" (the bread of the poor; Deut. xvi. 3). Maẓẓah was necessary, also, when a meal was to be prepared at short notice for an unexpected guest; for example, at the reception of the angels by Abraham (Gen. xviii. 6), or at Sodom by Lot (Gen. xix. 3), or for Saul by the witch of Endor (I Sam. xxviii. 24). The usual form of the plain maẓẓah was that of a round cake ("ugah"); this is the usual form of bread eaten to-day in Syria and Palestine.

The Use of Maẓẓah.

The maẓẓah offered at sacrifices was of various forms—"leḥem" (lit. = "bread"), "ḥallah" (= "loaf"), "raḳiḳ" (= "wafer"); the latter two were mixed or spread with oil (Ex. xxix. 2). Maẓẓot were required to be absolutely pure, as neither leaven nor honey was permitted in connection with sacrifices (Lev. ii. 11). The reason assigned is that maẓẓah is a symbol of purity, while leaven represents the evil impulse of the heart (Ber. 17a). Maẓẓah was partaken of with the lamb on Passover eve (Ex. xii. 8) because the lamb was considered an offering to the Lord. The eating of maẓẓot during the seven days of the Passover festival is intended to recall the hurried departure from Egypt, which event must be commemorated (Ex. xii. 14, 17, 39; Deut. xvi. 4) on every anniversary.

A Symbol of Freedom.

The Zohar calls maẓẓah "naḥama 'illa'ah" (heavenly bread), an antidote to the Egyptian slavery and corruption and a symbol of freedom and idealism. Maẓẓah was to cure Israel and prepare him for the acceptance of the Torah (Zohar, Teẓawweh, p. 183b, Wilna, 1882).

Nevertheless, the eating of maẓẓah during Passover, unlike the prohibition against eating ḥameẓ, is not imperative; it is a voluntary act ("reshut"). That is, a Jew may abstain from eating both ḥameẓ and maẓẓah, except on the first eve, when the eating of maẓẓah is obligatory ("ḥobah"). This is deduced from the passage, "Six days thou shalt eat unleavened bread" (Deut. xvi. 8), though the other passages command that maẓẓot shall be eaten seven days (Pes. 120a). In accordance with this distinction, the maẓẓah of the first night is called "maẓẓat miẓwah" (= the "precept maẓẓah") or "maẓẓat

Making Maẓẓot.
(From a Passover Haggadah, Amsterdam, 1695.)

shemirah" (= the "observance maẓẓah," based on Ex. xii. 7); it must be specially prepared and preserved for Passover eve (Pes. 38b). The special care of the "shemirah" consists in watching the wheat during harvesting, milling, and baking, that it shall not become leavened, either by rain swelling the grains or dampening the flour, or by too much kneading and slow baking. The shemirah is used principally for the Seder nights, while the more pious use such maẓẓot every day of the Passover festival. The ordinary maẓẓah is prepared of "ḳemaḥ min ha-shuḳ" (flour purchased at the market), and the bakers are careful only during the process of kneading and baking. The ordinary maẓẓah may be used for the first night's meal, when eating maẓẓah is obligatory. Yet even the market flour must be made only of wheat, barley, spelt, oats, or rye (Pes. ii. 5), rice and a species of millet being excepted (Pes. 35a).

"Mayim She-Lanu."

On the theory that at night the sun underneath the earth warms the wells and rivers below and makes the water tepid (Pes. 94b), R. Judah ordered that the kneading for maẓẓah shall be done with "mayim she-lanu" (water that has "lodged" overnight at home and has been exposed to the cold night air). The aim is to have the water for kneading as cold as possible in order to prevent the fermentation of the dough (Shulḥan 'Aruk, Oraḥ Ḥayyim, 455, 2). Although not necessarily against the Law, it is the custom to omit salt or seasoning from the maẓẓah (*l.c.* 455, 5).

The size of each mass of dough for maẓẓah may not exceed one-tenth of an ephah, equal to 43⅕ medium-sized hens' eggs, and the time allowed for preparing it is the time required for a journey of a mile (= 2,000 cubits), that is, about twenty-seven minutes (*l.c.* 456, 1; 459, 2). However, a continuous kneading and frequent hand-washings in cold water may extend the time. According to R. Gamaliel, the preparation of the maẓẓah was performed by three women: one kneaded the dough, another formed the maẓẓah, and the third baked it (Pes. iii. 4).

PREPARATION OF MAẒẒOT.
(From Kirchner, "Jüdisches Ceremoniel," 1726.)

The thickness of the maẓẓah must not exceed the size of a closed fist, four fingers or four inches, which was the thickness of the showbread. A later custom was to make maẓẓah one finger thick ("Bet Hillel," Yoreh De'ah, No. 96). In modern times the maẓẓah is much thinner, varying from four to five maẓẓot to the inch, and is made in round form about twelve inches in diameter. In about 1875 maẓẓah-baking machinery was invented in England, and soon after introduced in America. Some rabbis opposed the innovation, claiming that the corners of the machine-made maẓẓah were trimmed round in a subsequent operation, thus prolonging the time and causing fermentation; as a result of their protest the form of the maẓẓah was changed to a square. Still, there are a great many, perhaps a majority, who use round, machine-made maẓẓot, while there are many pious ones who would use no other than hand-made maẓẓot. Eisenberg, at Kiev, Russia, recently invented a maẓẓah-machine capable of baking 15 poods (about 541 pounds) of dough in one or two hours ("Der Jud," 1902, No. 9).

Size and Shape.

The perforation of the maẓẓah, after being rolled into shape, and before baking, was for the purpose of keeping it from raising and swelling in baking. It appears that in the early centuries the perforation of the maẓẓah was quite artistic. In the house of R. Gamaliel the perforations of the maẓẓot represented figures. Evidently the perforating was done with an implement that looked like a comb, as the word "seriḳin" indicates. The figures were those of animals, flowers, etc. Artistic perforation was later prohibited, as it consumed too much time and caused fermentation. Baytus b. Zonin suggested stamping the maẓẓah with ready-made figured plates, but was opposed on the ground that no discrimination must be made in favor of any particular kind of perforation (Pes. 37a). R. Isaac b. Gayyat says the figures represented Greeks, doves, and ishes. Maimonides permits any fancy design if made by a professional baker, as he does it quickly ("Yad," Ḥameẓ u-Maẓẓah, v. 15). In later periods the perforating implement was a wheel, called the "reidel," provided with sharp teeth and attached to a handle. The perforator, usually a youth, would run his reidel through the maẓẓah in lines crossed at right angles and about one inch apart. The maẓẓah-machine has an automatic perforator that makes lines at intervals of a half inch.

The "Reidel."

The baking of pudding, fillings, or sponge-cake out of ordinary flour is prohibited during Passover for fear of fermentation in consequence of the delays in preparation. But it is permitted to make all kinds of pastry out of maẓẓah-flour, as no fermentation is possible after the flour is baked. For baking and cooking with maẓẓah-flour see COOKERY. Ordinary flour may be kneaded with pure fruit-juices, with eggs, or with honey, as no fermentation is possible with them. This is called "rich maẓẓah," and may be eaten on Passover, except on the first night, when the regular maẓẓah, or leḥem 'oni, is obligatory (Pes. 36a). In the early centuries maẓẓah-baking was done by the wife daily, for the household's use. In the Middle Ages preparations were made to bake maẓẓot thirty days before Passover, except the maẓẓah shemirah, which was baked in the afternoon of the 14th of Nisan, at the time when the Passover lamb was formerly sacrificed (Oraḥ Ḥayyim, 453, 4). Still later, when the community had a communal oven, it was incumbent on the "lord of the house" to superintend the maẓẓah-baking for his family (see "Am. Jew. Hist. Soc." ix. 70).

PREPARING MAẒẒOT.

(From Leusden, "Philologus Hebræo-Mixtus," Utrecht, 1657.)

In America maẓẓah-baking is an important industry. In New York city alone, in 1904, 10,000 barrels of flour were used in making about 1,700,000 pounds of maẓẓah, distributed among fifteen bakers, one of them making maẓẓah by hand, and one small bakery making maẓẓah shemirah. The larger bakeries commence work four or five months before Passover. New York supplies many cities in the United States and Canada with maẓẓah. Other large maẓẓah-making centers are Chicago, Pittsburg, Boston, Philadelphia, and Baltimore. Maẓẓot have become popular among non-Jews, who use them as tea-biscuits. R. Jacob Möln (d. 1420), in his "Sefer Maharil," mentions the custom, in baking maẓẓot, of starting the fire with the willows used for Hosha'na and for the lulab.

Maẓẓah-Baking as an Industry.

It is forbidden to eat maẓẓah on the day before Passover, in order that it may be more palatable on the evening of Passover. The three maẓẓah-cakes used at the Seder service on Passover eve are placed one on the other in a plate or in a threefold cover specially made for the occasion. The three maẓẓah-cakes are distinguished as "Kohen," "Levi," and "Israel." The fourth order of the Seder is Yaḥaz, in which the middle maẓẓah ("Levi") is broken into two parts, the larger being put aside as afiḳomen, with which the meal is finished; the smaller part is left between "Kohen" and "Israel." When the Haggadah is recited the maẓẓot are uncovered and exposed to view. The eighth order of the Seder is Maẓẓah; in it a piece of the "Kohen" and a piece of the "Levi" are eaten after the benedictions "Ha-Moẓi" and "Maẓẓah." The "Israel" is eaten during the tenth order, Korek, with the bitter herbs, as practised by Hillel.

At the Seder.

An ancient custom, which still prevails in some parts of the Orient and in Europe, is to keep a single maẓẓah hanging on the interior wall of the synagogue all the year in strict observance of the passage "That thou mayest remember the day when thou camest out of the land of Egypt all the days of thy life" (Deut. xvi. 3). See Afiḳomen; Blood Accusation; Leaven; Passover; Seder.

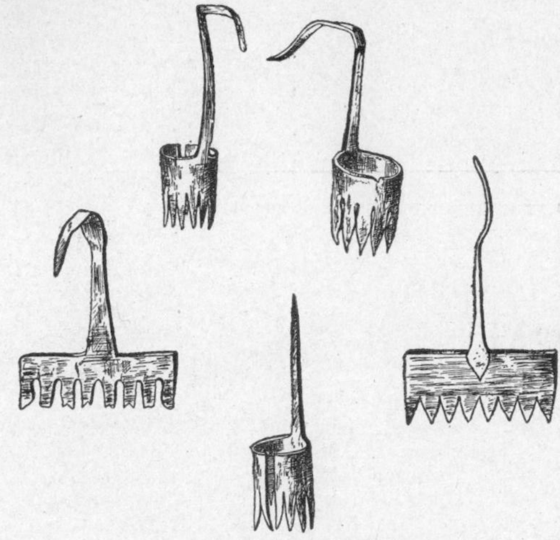

Implements for Marking Maẓẓot.
(From Frauberger.)

Bibliography: *Pes.* 35a-40a; Maimonides, *Yad*, *Ḥameẓ u-Maẓẓah*, v. and vi.; *Shulḥan 'Aruk*, *Oraḥ Ḥayyim*, 453-462, 471-482; Benzinger, *Arch.* pp. 85, 432, 451, 467; Rodkinson, *Maẓẓat Miẓwah wa-'Alilat ha-Dam*, Vienna, 1883; Stanislawska, *Sama de Hayye*, a manual of Maẓẓot, Berdychev, 1895.

J. J. D. E.

MAẒẒEBAH. See Stone and Stone-Worship.

McCAUL, ALEXANDER: English Christian missionary and author; born at Dublin May 16, 1799; died at London Nov. 13, 1863. He was educated at Trinity College, Dublin. Becoming interested in the Jews, he was sent as a missionary to Poland in 1821, where he studied Hebrew and German at Warsaw. In 1822 he went to interview the czar in regard to the conversion of the Jews. He continued to live at Warsaw for ten years, interesting the grand duke Constantine, the crown prince of Prussia, and Sir Henry Rose in his work. In 1837 he produced an elaborate attack upon Jewish legalism under the title "Old Paths"; it was published weekly for over a year. This created considerable interest among Jews, and was translated into several languages, including Hebrew ("Netibot 'Olam"). An answer in Hebrew ("Netibot Emet"), was published by Judah Middleman in 1847, a translation by Stanislaz Hoga having appeared in the preceding year. McCaul wrote vigorously agains the blood accusation, and refused the Protestan bishopric of Jerusalem, on the ground that it shoul be held by a Jew by birth, recommending M. S Alexander for that post. He became professor o Hebrew and rabbinical literature at King's College London.

Bibliography: *The Guardian* (London), Nov. 18, 1863; *Dic Nat. Biog.*

J.

MEAH. See Hammeah, Tower of.

MEAL-OFFERING: Comprehensive term fo all sacrifices from the vegetable world; to desig nate these in the Old Testament the Hebrew wor "minḥah" is used, which, as a probable derivativ of the Arabic verb "manaḥ" = "to give" properl signifies "gift" or "present." The desire of offerin to God oblations of vegetables or cereals is presup posed in the Bible to be as general a human one a that of pleasing God by animal sacrifices. The ea liest example of a meal-offering is u doubtedly the sacrifice that Cain te dered from the fruit of his field (Ge iv. 3-5). Gideon added to a mea offering maẓẓot made of an ephah c flour (סלת; Judges vi. 19). Maẓẓot were probabl also baked from the flour (קמח) that Hannah too to Shiloh (I Sam. i. 24); for it is not likely tha flour alone was sacrificed, it being in the unprepare state not an article of human food. A vegetab sacrifice is referred to also in the second member c the phrase זבח ומנחה (*ib.* ii. 29, iii. 14). Loaves c bread (ככרות לחם) were laid before God (*ib.* x. 3 Mention is made of their being placed in the san tuary of Yhwh at Nob (*ib.* xxi. 7). In the ter מנחת הערב (I Kings xviii. 29, 36) the second mem ber (הערב) is added not as a new distinction qual fying this מנחה as different from the others or as fixed regular institution, but merely in view of t preceding fixation of time, "and when midday w past." Leavened bread (חמץ) likewise was sacrifice (Amos iv. 5). Vegetable sacrifice is also designate as "minḥah" when it is connected with a than offering (Amos v. 22), a meat-offering (Isa. xix. 21 or a burnt offering (Jer. xiv. 12; Ps. xx. 2). T foregoing shows that cereal oblations are mention only sporadically in the early historical books.

Name and Early History.

The Law ordains: (*a*) as regards the material the meal-offering that it must consist, except in t case of the jealousy-offering (Num. v. 15), of fi flour (סלת; Lev. ii. 1), oil (*ib.*), salt (*ib.* verse 1 and incense (*ib.* verses 1 *et seq.*, 15 *et seq.*), whi leaven and honey must be kept strictly separate (verse 11), the latter probably because it ferment easily (comp. the Neo-Hebraic ביש = "to ferment," in Dalman, "Ar mäisch-Neuhebräisches Wörterb. Targum, Talmud, und Midrasch 1901, p. 86). (*b*) This material mig be offered in the following forms: (α) barley flo (קמח) without oil or incense was brought for the s called jealousy-offering (Num. v. 15); (β) fine flo (סלת), even in its original state, must have oil pour over it, and be sprinkled with incense, the last alo being lighted (Lev. ii. 1-3); (γ) the meal-offeri might consist of different kinds of cakes (vers

Regulations of the Law.

-7); (δ) the first-fruits of the field were offered in ıe shape of roasted ears or ground grains of fresh ɔrn (verse 14, where נרש כרמל is a later addition; ɔmp. König, "Syntax," § 333 t). It is an interest-ıg detail that the meal-offering which was baked ı a flat tin pan (מחבת) was broken into small ieces (פתים; Lev. ii. 6, vi. 14). (c) The meal-offer-ıgs, according to the purposes they served, might be ivided into two groups: (a) those offered alone as substitute in the case of the poor (Lev. v. 11 *et q.*) for the sin-offering; as the daily meal-offering ' tamid") of the priests (Ex. xl. 29; Lev. vi. 12-16; ɔmp. I Chron. ix. 31); and as the jealousy-offering Num. v. 15 *et seq.*), which "reminds of sin" (comp. ıe sheaf offered in recognition of the beginning of arvest [Lev. xxiii. 9 *et seq.*], the loaves of the Feast f Weeks [*ib.* xxiii. 16 *et seq.*], and the showbread *b.* xxiv. 5 *et seq.*]); and (β) meal-offerings added to ıe animal-offerings. These "musaf" offerings were lded to the thank-offering (Lev. vii. 11-13, etc.), ɔ the sacrifice of purification of the Israelites (Lev. :. 3) and of the lepers (*ib.* xiv. 10-20), and to the urnt offering (Num. xv. 1-16); and they were ɔmbined with a drink-offering. The unqualified atement that the unconsumed portion of the meal-ffering should belong to the priests (Lev. ii. 3) ·fers probably also to the accompanying meal-fferings (comp. Franz Delitzsch in Riehm's "Hand-örterb." cols. 1519b, 1520a). Not every burnt ffering, however, is to be supplemented by a meal-ffering, as Lev. xii. 6 shows.

BIBLIOGRAPHY: For the earlier views see Franz Delitzsch, in *Speiseopfer*, in Riehm's *Handwörterb. des Biblischen Al-terthums*; the later view of the history of vegetable sacri-fices is supported by Benzinger, *Arch.* §§ 62 *et seq.*; Baentsch, *Exodus Leviticus*, in *Handkommentar*, 1900; Bertholet, *Leviticus*, in *Kurzer Handkommentar*, 1901.

E. G. H. E. K.

ME'ASHA: **1.** Palestinian tanna, to whom one eference occurs in the Mishnah (Peah ii. 6), from 'hich it appears that he lived in the time of Hillel's escendants (comp. Heilprin, "Seder ha-Dorot," ii.).

2. Palestinian haggadist; grandson and pupil of OSHUA B. LEVI (Yer. Ber. ii. 3; Yer. Beẓah i. 6 *et l.*). From the few details concerning him it ap-ears that on Saturdays he used to have himself arried to the synagogue in order to preach (Yer. Beẓah *l.c.*), that he was not rich, and that he died uddenly in the time of AMMI (Ket. 85b). Me'asha s particularly noted for the vision which he is re-orted to have seen during a trance lasting three ays, and concerning which he said: "I have been ı a world of confusion where people who are hon-red here are held in contempt" (Ruth R. iii. 1). In 'es. 50a this vision is ascribed to JOSEPH B. JOSHUA . LEVI; Joseph was probably Me'asha's father. Ie'asha inferred from Isa. xxxiii. 15-17 that when ne shuts his eyes to things indecent he is worthy ɔ view the face of the Shekinah (Pesiḳ. R. 24 ed. Friedmann, p. 125a]; Derek Ereẓ i.; Lev. R. xiii. 13).

3. Palestinian amora of the fourth century; men-ioned as a companion of Samuel b. Isaac and Zera Yer. Ber. ii. 9 *et al.*). His halakic and haggadic entences are met with in both Talmudim.

BIBLIOGRAPHY: Bacher, *Ag. Pal. Amor.* iii. 614 *et seq.*, *et passim*; Heilprin, *Seder ha-Dorot*, ii.

S. S. M. SEL.

ME'ASSEFIM ("collectors"; from אסף = "to collect"; hence the name of the periodical "Ha-Me'assef" = "The Collector"): Name designating the group of Hebrew writers who between 1784 and 1811 published their works in the periodical "Ha-Me'assef," which they had founded. In 1782 Moses Mendelssohn's German translation of the Pentateuch had appeared. In the "bi'ur" or commentary which he added to this translation, he dwelt on the beauty of the Hebrew language, its wealth of imagery, and its adaptability for poetic expression. By his com-ments on Scripture, also, he largely stimulated He-brew, grammatical, and exegetic studies. The seeds he thus scattered bore fruit even in his lifetime. While reading and discussing Mendelssohn's Scrip-tural expositions, Isaac Abraham EUCHEL and Men-del BRESSLAU, who were at that time tutoring in the house of David Friedländer at Königsberg, con-ceived the idea of causing Hebrew as a literary lan-guage to be used more widely among the Jews. As-sured of the material support of Simon and Samuel Friedländer, they issued in the spring of 1783 an appeal to all Jews to assist in establishing a society for the study of Hebrew (Ḥebrat Doreshe Leshon 'Eber). The periodical "Ha-Me'assef" was projected as a rallying-point for all those who were inter-ested in and able to contribute to the work.

The undertaking met with a cordial reception in many quarters, especially in Berlin; Mendelssohn and even the aged Naphtali Hirz WESSELY prom-ising their support and contributing to "Ha-Me'as-sef," the former anonymously. The first number of the periodical was announced April 13, 1783, in a prospectus, "Naḥal ha-Besor," signed by Euchel, Bresslau, and Samuel and Simon Friedländer. The first volume appeared in 1784, being the earliest suc-cessful periodical published in Hebrew. The first three volumes were issued in monthly numbers at Königsberg (the frontispiece to vol. iii. being Naph-tali Herz Wessely's portrait); vols. iv.-vi. appeared in quarterly numbers at Königsberg and Berlin; vol. vii. (one number only) at Breslau; vol. viii. at Berlin; the first two numbers of vol. ix. at Altona, and the last two at Dessau; vol. x. (two numbers only) also at Dessau. The new "Collector" ("Aḥare ha-Me'assef" or "Ha-Me'assef he-Ḥadash"), edited by S. Cohen, may be regarded as a continuation of "Ha-Me'assef." Vol. i. appeared at Berlin in 1809; vol. ii. at Altona in 1810; and vol. iii. at Dessau in 1811.

In addition to articles on Hebrew prose and poetry "Ha-Me'assef" printed general scientific articles, in-teresting papers on mathematics and natural science, biographies of eminent Hebrew scholars, and articles on the history of the Roman emperors; responsa on religious questions, *e.g.*, on the speedy burial of the dead, have also been collected in its pages. The attitude of "Ha-Me'assef" was by turns Orthodox or Reform, according to the views of the collaborator. It was often very aggressive toward the strictly Or-thodox view, although Wessely had from the very beginning advised a purely objective point of view.

The principal collaborators on "Ha-Me'assef" were Ben Zeeb, Bras, Bresslau, Cohen, Dessau, Euchel, Franco-Mendez, Friedländer, Friedrichsfeld, Herz,

Joseph Hirsch, Lindau, Löwe, Löwisohn, Mendelssohn, Wessely, Witzhausen, and Wolfsohn.

See Biurists; Haskalah; Mendelssohn, Moses.

Bibliography: Fürst, *Bibl. Jud.* parts i.–iii.; Grätz, *Gesch.* xi. 131 *et seq.*; Lesser, *Register und Chronik der Gesellschaft der Freunde*, Berlin, 1842; Steinschneider, *Cat. Bodl.* col. 575; Zeitlin, *Bibl. Post-Mendels.* parts i. and ii.; *Allg. Zeit. des Jud.* 1837, p. 448; Israel Davidson, *The Beginnings of Periodical Literature*, Baltimore, 1900.

G. M. L. B.

MEASURES. See Weights and Measures.

MEAT-TAX: In Austria, as everywhere else, the Jewish communities imposed a tax on meat, the revenue from which was used for communal purposes. During the eighteenth century, however, the national government used this method of raising a revenue from the Jews in order to support educational institutions. Such was the case in Galicia after 1791. In the congregations belonging to the kingdom of Bohemia the meat-tax, with the tax on wine and fish, was used to compensate the government for the loss of revenue attending the abolition of the toleration-tax in 1782. It was about two kreutzer on one pound of meat and ten kreutzer on a goose. The tax was levied in such a way that the butchers had to give with every pound of meat a receipt for the payment of that duty, while in the case of fowl the shoḥeṭ was not permitted to kill unless the party requiring his services handed him such a receipt. This tax was farmed out to a contractor; he paid the government a fixed annual sum for the whole province and had his subcontractors in every town. The latter were almost invariably Jews, and exacted their money with merciless rigor. Those who attempted to evade the tax were heavily fined. The hardships entailed by the cruelty of these tax-farmers are vividly presented in Eduard Kulke's novels.

For the meat-tax in Russia see Korobka.

Bibliography: Stöger, *Gesetzliche Verfassung der Galizischen Judenschaft*, Lemberg, 1831; Scari, *Systematische Darstellung der in Betreff Juden in Mähren und Schlesien Erlassenen Gesetze*, Brünn, 1835.

D.

ME'ATI, HA- (המאתי): Family of translators which flourished at Rome in the thirteenth and fourteenth centuries.

Nathan b. Eliezer ha-Me'ati: Earliest known member of the family; called the "Prince of Translators" and the "Italian Tibbonide"; lived in Rome from 1279 to 1283. His native place seems to have been Cento, whence his name "Me'ati," which is the Hebrew equivalent of "Cento" (= 100). After acquiring many languages during his long wanderings, he settled at Rome, where he translated scientific and especially medical works from Arabic into Hebrew, to take the place, as he declared, of the medical literature of the Jews which had existed even at the time of Solomon but had been lost, and to silence the mockery of the Christians, who said that the Jews had no such literature. His translations are: (1) 'Ammar ben 'Ali al-Mausuli's "Al-Muntaḥib fi 'Ilaj al-'Ain," on the treatment of the eye; (2) the "Canon" of Avicenna; (3) the aphorisms of Hippocrates with Galen's commentary (Neubauer, "Cat. Bodl. Hebr. MSS." No. 1588); (4) the aphorisms of Maimonides, a selection from various authors, chiefly from Galen, published under th[e] title "Pirḳe Mosheh," Lemberg, 1804.

Many anonymous translations are attributed t[o] Me'ati, among them: (1) Razi's treatise on bleeding "Ma'amar be-Haḳḳazah"; (2) Zahrawi's "Kitab a[l-] Taṣrif" (Hebrew title, "Ẓeruf"); (3) Ibn Zuhr's "K[i]tab al-Aghdhiyah" (Hebrew title, "Sefer ha-Mez[o]not"); (4) an anonymous work on the causes of eclipses entitled "Ma'amar 'al Sibbot Liḳḳut ha-Me'orot."

Samuel ha-Me'ati: Son of Solomon ha-Me'at[i]. He concluded the translation of an extract fro[m] Galen's commentary to Hippocrates' work "O[n] Regimen in Acute Diseases," and, some time afte[r] 1306, the translation of a medical work by Ib[n] Zuhr.

Solomon ha-Me'ati: Son of Nathan b. Elieze[r] ha-Me'ati. He completed (1299) the translation, be[-]gun by his father, of Galen's commentary to Hip[-]pocrates' work "On Airs, Waters, and Places."

Bibliography: De Rossi, *Dizionario*, p. 53; Nepi-Ghirondi, *Toledot Gedole Yisrael*, p. 274; Carmoly, *Histoire des Médecins Juifs*, p. 84; Zunz, in Geiger's *Jüd. Zeit.* iv. 190; Steinschneider, *Cat. Bodl.* col. 2073; idem, *Hebr. Uebers.* pp. 59[-] 662, 663, 666, 670, 679, 701, 746; idem, in *Monatsschrift*, 189[-] xxxviii. 179; Vogelstein and Rieger, *Gesch. der Juden i[n] Rom*, i. 398 *et seq.*

J. I. Br.—I. E.

MEBORAK HA-NAGID. See Egypt.

MECHANIC. See Artisans; Labor; Maste[r] and Servant.

MECHNIKOV. See Novachovich, L.

MECIA (MATTHEW) DE VILADESTES Jewish chartographer of Majorca at the beginnin[g] of the fifteenth century. He was the author of [a] map, dated 1413, formerly in the convent of Val d[e] Cristo, near Segorbe, but now in the Bibliothèqu[e] Nationale at Paris. In it he gives special promi[-]nence to the navigation in African waters of Jacm[e] Ferrer, also of Majorca. It fills six sheets in Mar[-]cel's "Choix de Cartes et de Mappemondes des XIV[e] et XVe Siècles" (Paris, 1896). The map is base[d] upon the work of Jaffuda Cresques, the probabl[e] author of the atlas of Charles V. Mecia therefor[e] belonged to the Judæo-Catalan school of chartog[-]raphers. Don Miguel Bonet has discovered in th[e] archives of Majorca a permit of the governor's lieu[-]tenant allowing the "convert Macia" to debark i[n] Sicily. This is dated Jan. 20, 1401, and probabl[y] refers to Mecia.

Bibliography: E. T. Hamy, in *Comptes Rendus* of the *Académie des Inscriptions et Belles-Lettres*, 1902, p. 71.

J. G.

MECKLENBURG: Territory in North Ger[-]many; bounded on the north by the Baltic Sea. Formerly it constituted one duchy, but since 1701 i[t] has been divided into Mecklenburg-Schwerin an[d] Mecklenburg-Strelitz, forming two separate gran[d] duchies of the German empire. However, thei[r] governments are still intimately connected. Meck[-]lenburg-Schwerin has (1900) 607,770 inhabitants among whom are 1,763 Jews, divided into 36 con[-]gregations; Mecklenburg-Strelitz has 102,602 inhab[-]itants, including 331 Jews, divided into 6 congrega[-]tions. It is possible that the settlement of Jew[s] in Mecklenburg dates from 1243, when Brandenbur[g] expelled its Jews; but it is equally probable tha[t] the first Jewish settlers arrived from western Ger[-] nany, where the Jews were frequently persecuted. It is certain, however, that Jews lived in Mecklenburg as early as 1266, for in a document dated April 14, 1266, in which Henry I. (the Pilgrim) conferred upon Wismar the Lübeck rights, Jews are mentioned together with the private servants and officials of the prince. Thus Wismar seems to contain the oldest settlement of Jews in Mecklenburg. By and by they are heard of in other cities: in Boizenburg, 1267; Rostock, 1279; Cracow and Güstrow, 1325; Malchin, 1332; Schwerin (now the center of the Jewish communities in Mecklenburg), about 1340; Friedland and Parchim, 1350; Neubrandenburg, 1440.

Early Settlement.

The Jews of Mecklenburg were compelled to pay a considerable sum annually for the privilege of living there and for protection by the prince. The several estates looked with great disfavor upon their presence and never neglected an opportunity of injuring them. They had no right to own real estate, and their residence, as a rule, was confined to the most neglected quarters of the city they dwelt in. In Wismar, for instance, they inhabited the Altböterstrasse, which was called "Platea Judæorum"; here they had a synagogue, called "Domus Judæorum." Naturally their fate was bound up with that of their protector. Thus when Henry undertook a pilgrimage to Palestine, where he remained for twenty-four years in Mohammedan captivity, the Jews were expelled from Wismar (1290), and were not readmitted until the succession of Henry II. (the Lion-Hearted). During his reign a Jew named Nathan (1310)—was permitted to own real estate in Wismar. Under Albrecht II. their position changed for the worse; only two Jewish families were permitted to reside in Wismar, and they became subject to the jurisdiction of the city magistrates instead of to that of the prince, thus being exposed to the fanaticism and hatred of the people. Some Jews were admitted into Wismar in 1349, but they were expelled again in 1350, and since then and for 500 years thereafter there was no trace of Jewish residence there.

In the other cities matters were worse. Jews at Cracow and Güstrow suffered martyrdom three times within 167 years. A baptized Jewess accused her brother-in-law Eleazar of having desecrated the host; all the Jews were seized and burned, the synagogue was destroyed, and in its place was erected a "chapel of the Holy Blood" (1325). Two Christians of Rostock who were found guilty of having robbed and murdered a Jew and Jewess were punished with banishment only (1320). In 1350 the widespread accusation that the Jews had poisoned the wells was made in Mecklenburg, and nearly all the Jews there were driven out. They seem, however, to have resettled there within a few decades.

Mecklenburg's cruel treatment of the Jews reached its climax in 1492, in connection with a charge of desecrating the host. A Jew was accused of having persuaded a priest to become a convert to Judaism and of having induced him to steal the sacred host for the purpose of desecrating it. The matter being brought before the duke, he ordered all the Jews to be placed under arrest and brought to Sternberg. There they were subjected to horrible torture in order to extort from them a confession. But though they persistently denied the charge, the sentence to burn them alive was pronounced. On Oct. 24, 1492, twenty-four Jews and two Jewesses were taken to a hill near the city of Sternberg—since then called the "Judenberg"—where they died on the pyre. Those not burned were banished from the land. The prominent rabbis of the time declared the ban against any Jew who would settle in cruel Mecklenburg, and there is no evidence that any Jew settled there until the second half of the seventeenth century.

The Sternberg Burning.

In the meantime Protestantism had taken root in Mecklenburg, and religious fanaticism was no longer so rampant as in former days. Yet it was during the reign of the Catholic prince Christian I. (1658–1692) that the second movement of Jews to Mecklenburg began. In 1676 he called to his court the Jews Abraham Haym and Nathan Benedix of Hamburg, gave them special privileges, and granted them a tobacco monopoly, the first in Mecklenburg. At the intervention of the court Jews, Duke Frederick William abolished the poll-tax. But his successor, Charles Ludwig (1747–56), who had special political reasons for wishing to please the people, issued an edict that all unprivileged Jews should leave the land within four weeks; this left only about thirty "Schutzjuden" in Mecklenburg. The same prince called to his court the brothers Philip and Nathan Aaron, who became the real founders of the present Jewish communities in Mecklenburg. Through their influence the Jewish population there so increased that they were able in 1752 to call a convention to deliberate upon their religious needs. They decided, among other things, to request the chief rabbi of Frankfort-on-the-Oder to remove the ban of 1492 and to establish a Jewish tribunal. The latter, however, did not receive the sanction of the government, and was abolished (1755) by a rescript of the duke. In 1764 they held another convention, with the sanction of Duke Frederick the Pious, who vested in the rabbis the power of judges among the Jews. In 1765 one Marcus Moses graduated as a physician, and an edict of the duke permitted him to practise. This was the first graduation of a Jew in Mecklenburg. One Marcus Isaac (who distinguished himself during the occupation of Mecklenburg by Frederick the Great) and a certain Hirsch were the first in the commercial field; they began about this time to export wool, thus encouraging the raising of sheep, which occupation has greatly contributed to the prosperity of the country.

Under this mild government the community developed rapidly. Two synagogues were dedicated—one on Sept. 5, 1763, at Altstrelitz, the community of which numbered 130 families; the other at Schwerin in 1773. Still the populace was hostile toward the Jews and often insisted on the strict enforcement of the constitutional provisions by which the dukes of the Mecklenburg duchies pledged themselves to grant no privileges to Jewish settlers to the detriment of Christian citizens. Duke Frederick Francis I. was the first prince that earnestly desired their emancipation. On Feb. 22,

1811, the Jews petitioned him on that subject, and he consulted the estates at the following convention. They acknowledged the justice of the petition, but argued that the Jews were not as yet ready for emancipation. But Professor Tychsen of the University of Rostock, who was consulted on the matter, declared himself in favor of the petition. After some hesitation the duke finally decided in favor of the Jews, and issued, Feb. 22, 1813, a constitution which declared that his Jewish subjects, with their wives and children, were citizens of Mecklenburg; leaving future legislation to decide whether or not they were to be admitted to government positions. The Jews soon had an opportunity to show their gratitude; the Jewish youth enthusiastically responded to the duke's call to arms in 1813. But the reaction which set in after Waterloo and the ill-will of the states brought about a suspension of this law in 1815. In 1829 the Jews were first admitted to the practise of law, with the limitation that they could practise only in the city courts. Mecklenburg adopted in 1848 the "Grundrechte" (constitution) of the Frankfort Parliament abolishing all disabilities on account of religion, but repealed it two years later.

Their First Emancipation.

But times had changed. While in former days the people opposed the emancipation of the Jews, in 1867 the municipal boards of various cities in Mecklenburg petitioned the Reichstag for it, and a member of the Reichstag, Wigger by name, was the most ardent advocate of the passage of a law abolishing all disabilities based on differences of religion. The Reichstag passed that law by a large majority March 12, 1869, and King William of Prussia, as the head of the North German Federation, confirmed it July 3, 1869. With the passage of this law and its insertion in the constitution of the German empire in 1871, the last political disability resting on the Jews of Mecklenburg, as on Jews throughout the empire, was removed.

Bibliography: Donath, *Gesch. der Juden in Mecklenburg*, Leipsic, 1874.

D. I. War.

Of the internal conditions of the Mecklenburg Jewry during the first settlement, up to 1492, nothing is known. During the second settlement, in the seventeenth century, the community was too small to show any spiritual activity. The first sign of such is in the case of Nathan Aaron, who maintained Joshua Spira in his house as a chaplain. The first rabbi appointed by the duke was Jeremiah Israel (1763), whose chief duty consisted in acting as judge for the scattered communities of the duchies. He was succeeded by the above-mentioned Joshua Spira, author of "Panim Masbirot" (or "'Arba' Shiṭṭot li MeHaRISh"), novellæ and responsa (Frankfort-on-the-Oder, 1770).

During the latter part of the eighteenth and at the beginning of the nineteenth century the differences between R. Marcus Lazarus Jaffe and R. Joshua Falk Albu and their congregations frequently occupied the attention of the authorities. As these rabbis were Poles and not in sympathy with the educational movement which had won the allegiance of the Jews of Mecklenburg, as of other communities in Germany, an attempt was made about 1828 to establish in Güstrow a normal school where Jewish teachers might be trained, but the movement failed for lack of means. The congregation of Altstrelitz, however, established a parochial school, which at one time flourished under the famous German lexicographer Daniel Sanders.

Spiritual Activities.

The movement for emancipation which began about 1830 resulted in the foundation of a society for promoting the adoption of manual occupations by Jews (1836). Three years later the government took steps toward improving the condition of the Jews by giving them a constitution. An "Oberrath" was organized consisting of two government officials, the "Landrabbiner," and five representatives of the communities. The "Landrabbiner," who was required to have academic training, was to raise the intellectual standard of the congregation and introduce certain reforms. The first to hold this office was Samuel Holdheim, elected in 1840. He resigned in 1847 to take charge of the Berlin Reform congregation. He organized parochial schools and instituted Reform services; his reforms, however, were all of a moderate character, although they aroused considerable opposition.

A far stronger opposition was experienced by Holdheim's successor, David Einhorn (1847–53), when he blessed in the synagogue a child whose father refused to permit its circumcision. In the ensuing controversy Franz Delitzsch, then professor at Rostock, participated, publishing in a Rostock daily a series of articles to which Einhorn replied in very heated terms.

With Einhorn's resignation the government decided to strengthen the Orthodox party by calling Baruch Lipschütz, who was to effect a restoration of historic Judaism. The rigidity of his views, however, caused the government to dismiss him in 1858, when he was succeeded by another exponent of strict Orthodoxy, Solomon Cohn, who in 1876 was succeeded by the present (1904) incumbent, G. F. Feilchenfeld.

The smaller principality of Mecklenburg-Strelitz had a rabbi in the middle of the eighteenth century —Marcus Levin Süsskind, who published a German sermon preached at the dedication of the synagogue in 1763. He was succeeded by R. Sanwil of Brandenburg; the present (1904) incumbent, Jacob Hamburger, has officiated since 1852. The rabbinical author Judah Löb lived in Altstrelitz; his treatise on resurrection was translated by Professor Tychsen under the title "Die Auferstehung der Todten aus dem Gesetze Mosis Bewiesen" (1766). Later, Judah Löb was rabbi of Birnbaum, and then of Stockholm.

The University of Rostock had a famous Orientalist in Tychsen, who taught first in Bützow (1760) and then in Rostock (from 1779). A. T. Hartman, the opponent of the emancipation of the Jews, also taught in Rostock (1811–38). Among the prominent Jews who are natives of Mecklenburg may be mentoned: I. Marcus, alternate deputy to the Frankfort Parliament in 1848; the lexicographer Daniel Sanders; and the journalist Emil Jonas, translator of Scandinavian poetry into German. D.

MEDALS: Soon after the revival of the art of graving medals, about the middle of the fifteenth ntury, a few Jewish specimens were struck in ly, although the number was very small on ac- unt of the general oppression of the Jews at that riod. The number gradually increased during e eighteenth century, keeping pace with the im- ovement of Jewish conditions; and in the second lf of the nineteenth century, when the Jews had en emancipated in nearly all civilized countries, dals were struck so frequently that one or more peared nearly every year. The following list con- ns the principal Jewish medals known. Those ued in honor of comparatively unimportant pri- te persons and numerous miscellaneous and cab- stic medals are not included. The symbol ° desig- tes medals which are described in works mentioned the bibliography and * those in the illustrations.

503. Benjamin b. Elijah Beer: obverse, bust; reverse, inscription; 167 mm.
552.* ° Elias and Rica Delatas: bust on both sides; 49 mm.
556.* ° Gracia Nasi: engraved on one side only; bust; 66 mm.
559. Baptism of the Jew Michael of Prague: oval; obverse, baptism (in the Jordan); reverse, inscription; 82 × 69 mm.
570. Three hundredth anniversary of the alleged desecration of the host at Brussels: obverse, the Holy Sacrament; reverse, inscription; 39 mm.
570. *Idem*: obverse, the Holy Sacrament; reverse, escutcheon; 32 mm.
586. Participation of the Jews in the defense of Buda: obverse, smelting-furnace; reverse, inscription; 2 sizes, 41 and 47 mm. respectively.
711.* ° Conflagration in the ghetto of Frankfort: obverse, the fire; reverse, inscription; inscription about the edge; 44 mm.
735.° Eliezer ben Samuel Shmelka: obverse, bust; reverse, inscription.
738. Süss Oppenheimer's execution: obverse, bust; reverse, gallows; 38 mm.: "Schraub" medal; 42 mm.
745.* ° Edict of exile at Prague: obverse, audience; reverse, Solomon's Temple; 64 mm.
775.* ° Moses Mendelssohn: obverse, bust; reverse, skull and butterfly; 43 mm.
775. *Idem*: one-sided cast medallion; bust, skull, etc.; 99 mm.
781. Edict of Toleration by Emperor Joseph II.: obverse, bust; reverse, obelisk and genius; 45 mm.
782.* *Idem*: obverse, bust; reverse, clericals of the three confessions; 43 mm.
790.* Medal presented by the Hessian Jews to Landgrave Ludwig X.: obverse, man sacrificing; reverse, inscription; 37 mm.
790.° Medal presented by the Hessian Jews to the Landgravine Caroline Henrietta: obverse, palm-tree; reverse, inscription; three variants, 34, 34, and 29 mm. respectively.
791.* Wilhelmschule at Breslau: obverse, grafted trunk; reverse, inscription; two sizes, 18 and 11 mm. respectively.
793.* ° Daniel Itzig's seventieth birthday: obverse, bust; reverse, allegorical group; 52 mm.
303.° Lippmann Meyer's seventy-third birthday: obverse, bust; reverse, inscription; 38 mm.
803.* ° Marcus Herz: obverse, bust; reverse, Pallas; 41 mm.
305.* ° Emancipation of the Russian Jews: obverse, bust; reverse, man sacrificing; 46 mm.
306.* ° Napoleon and the Sanhedrin: obverse, bust; reverse, Napoleon and a Jew; 41 mm.
308.* ° Emancipation of the Westphalian Jews: obverse, thank-offering; reverse, two geniuses; 42 mm.
310. Building of the synagogue at Bordeaux: inscriptions on both sides; 35 mm.
816. Gershom Mendes Seixas: obverse, bust and inscription.
320. Four hundred and fiftieth anniversary of the alleged desecration of the host at Brussels: obverse, the Holy Sacrament; reverse, inscription; 32 mm.
324. Laying of the corner-stone of the synagogue at Munich: obverse, bust; reverse, engraved inscription; 26 mm.

1826. Dedication of the same synagogue: obverse, the synagogue; reverse, inscription; 39 mm.
1827. Court commission of the Dutch Jews: obverse, altar and symbols; reverse, plain; 59 mm.
1828. Giuditta Pasta: one-sided medallion; head; 113 mm.
1829. *Idem*: obverse, head; reverse, inscription; two variants, 43 and 35 mm.
1830. *Idem*: obverse, homage; reverse, inscription; 47 mm.
1830. Ludwig Börne: one-sided medallion; head; 159 mm.
1836.* Gabriel Riesser: obverse, allegorical group; reverse, inscription; 59 mm.
1836. Death of N. M. von Rothschild: obverse, head; reverse, inscription; 62 mm.
1836. Court commission of the Dutch Jews: observe, symbolic picture; reverse, plain; 47 mm.
1837. Elias Henschel and the Jews of Breslau: obverse, head; reverse, inscription; 39 mm.
1840. Montefiore and Crémieux at Damascus: obverse, audience; reverse, inscription; 43 mm.
1841. The king in the synagogue at Mastricht: obverse, the synagogue; reverse, inscription; 41 mm.
1841. Jewish Home for the Aged at The Hague: obverse, the building; reverse, inscription; 40 mm.
1841.* Jewish hospital at Hamburg (Solomon Heine): obverse, head; reverse, the building; two sizes, 45 and 12 mm. respectively.
1841.* Jewish loan institute at Hamburg: obverse, beehive; reverse, inscription; 45 mm.
1841.* Montefiore and the Jews of Hamburg: obverse, escutcheon; reverse, inscription; 42 mm.
1842. R. Solomon Herschell: obverse, bust; reverse, Torah scroll and inscription; 62 mm.
1843. Hebrew school at Birmingham; obverse, the building; reverse, inscription; 45 mm.
1843. First Jewish confirmation at Warsaw; obverse, seven-branched candlestick and tables of the Law; reverse, inscription; 42 mm.
1844. S. M. von Rothschild's seventieth birthday: obverse, head; reverse, escutcheon; 59 mm.
1846.* Isaac Bernays' jubilee: inscriptions on both sides; 51 mm.
1846. Rachel (Felix): obverse, head; reverse, inscription; 53 mm.
1847. Medal dedicated to Giacomo Meyerbeer by the Concordia Society: obverse, bust; reverse, inscription; 46 mm.
1848. Destruction of Rothschild's castle, Surenne: inscriptions on both sides; 69 mm.
1848. Medal given by the Italian Jews to B. d'Azeglio: obverse, bust; reverse, inscription; 51 mm.
1848. Daniel Manin: obverse, bust; reverse, homage of the people; 57 mm.
1850. Society for the Emancipation of the Oriental Christians and Jews: obverse, group; reverse, inscription; 62 mm.
1850. General de Meza: obverse, bust; reverse, trophy; 45 mm.
1850. August Neander: obverse, bust; reverse, inscription; 45 mm.
1851. Dr. Gruby: obverse, snake of Æsculapius; reverse, inscription; 50 mm.
1852. Orthodox synagogue at Frankfort: obverse, the synagogue; reverse, inscription; 39 mm.
1853. Engraver Samuel Jesi: obverse, head; reverse, inscription; 68 mm.
1854. Giacomo Meyerbeer: obverse, head; reverse, lyre; 41 mm.
1855. Medal presented by the Italian Jews to Albert Cohn: obverse, temple vessels; reverse, inscription; 55 mm.
1855. Similar medal presented to Ludwig Philippson.
1856. Laemmelschule at Jerusalem: obverse, palm-tree; reverse, inscription; 33 mm.
1858. Death of Rachel (Felix): obverse, head; reverse, inscription; 53 mm.; token, 23 mm.
1858 (?). M. G. Saphir: one-sided medal; bust; 47 mm.
1859. R. Henri Loeb's jubilee: obverse, bust; reverse, inscription; 59 mm.
1860. Right conferred upon the Austrian Jews to possess real estate: obverse, allegorical picture; reverse, inscription; 73 mm.
(*c.* 1860). Société J. R. Pereire, prize medal: obverse, Pereire teaching; reverse, inscription; 54 mm.
1861 (?). Historical painter B. Ullmann: one-sided medallion; bust; 123 mm.
1861. Synagogue at Cologne: obverse, the synagogue; reverse, interior view; 59 mm.

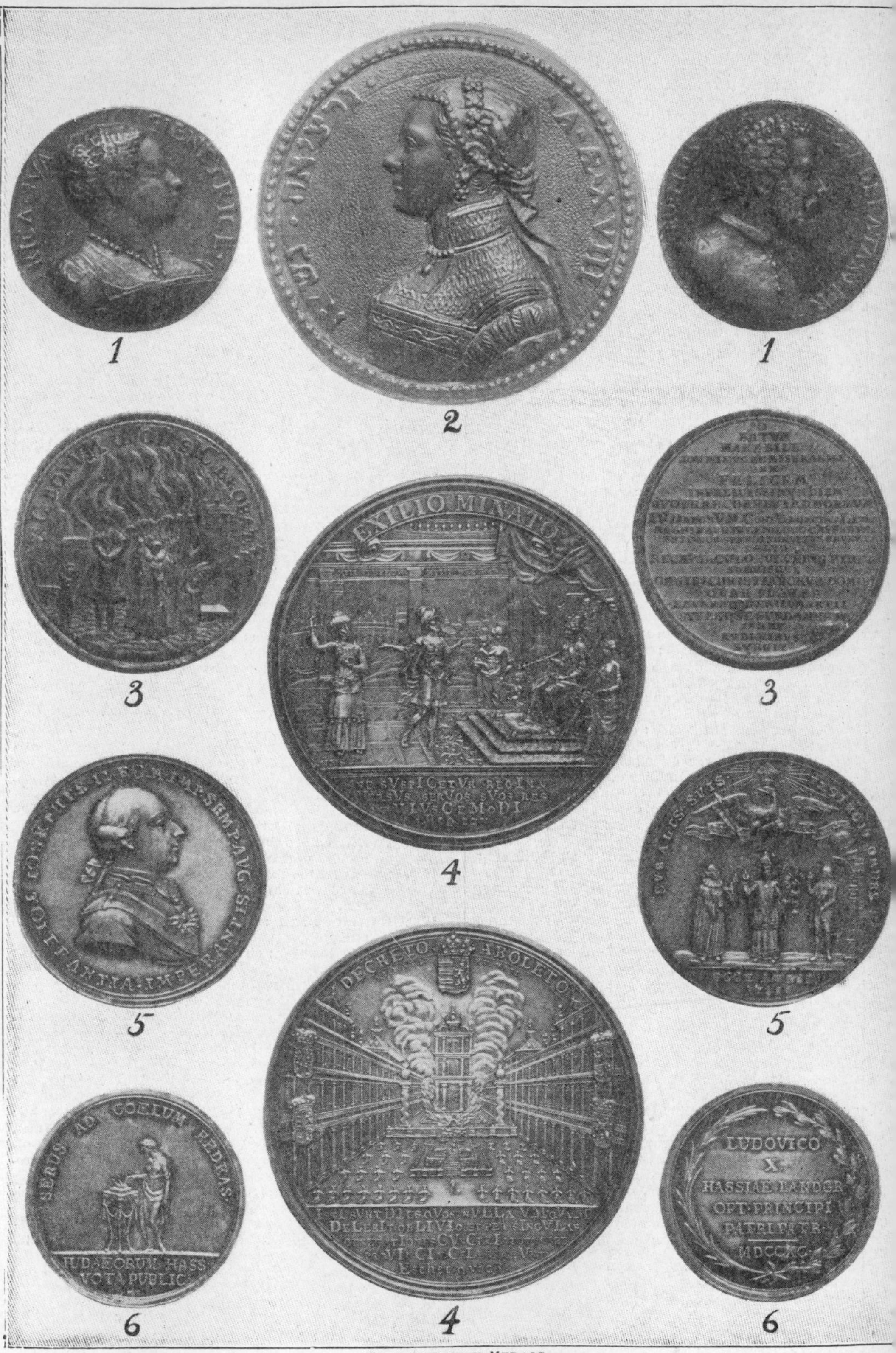

COMMEMORATIVE MEDALS.

1. Elias and Rica Delatas, 1552. 2. Gracia Nasi, 1556. 3. Conflagration at Frankfort-on-the-Main, 1711. 4. Edict of Exile fron Prague, 1745. 5. Edict of Toleration Issued by Emperor Joseph II., 1781. 6. Presented by Hessian Jews to the Landgrave Ludwig X., 1790.

(In the collection of Albert Wolf, Dresden.)

COMMEMORATIVE MEDALS.

7. Emancipation of Westphalian Jews, 1808. 8. Emancipation of Russian Jews by Alexander I., 1805. 9. Napoleon and Sanhedrin, 1806. 10. Marcus Herz, 1805. 11. Wilhelmschule at Breslau, 1791. 12. Daniel Itzig's Seventieth Birthday, 1793. 13. Moses Mendelssohn's "Phaedon," 1775.

(In the collection of Albert Wolf, Dresden.)

1861. Numismatist Oberndoerfer's seventieth birthday: obverse, bust; reverse, inscription; 40 mm.
1863. Preacher Mannheimer's seventieth birthday: obverse, bust; reverse, inscription; 50 mm.
1864. Moses and Judith Montefiore: obverse, busts of both; reverse, inscriptions; 68 mm.
1865. Jewish orphan asylum for boys at Amsterdam: obverse, allegorical group; reverse, building; 68 mm.
1867. Dr. M. H. Romberg: obverse, head; reverse, inscription; 62 mm.
1867. Joseph Wertheimer retiring from office: obverse, bust; reverse, inscription; 45 mm.
1867. Cantor Pereles' jubilee of office; inscriptions on both sides; 32 mm.
1868. Deputy Dr. Max Hirsch: octagon; obverse, bust; reverse, two hands; 25 mm.
1868. The astronomer H. Goldschmidt: obverse, three heads; reverse, allegorical figure; 69 mm.
1868.* Oppenheimer foundation at Hamburg; obverse, bust; reverse, building; 44 mm.
1870. Crémieux at Tours: obverse, head (on another an escutcheon); reverse, inscription; 46 mm.
1870. Franchetti's heroic death: two variants; (1) obverse, escutcheon; reverse, inscription; 33 mm.; (2) obverse, head; reverse, inscription; 24 mm.
1875. Synagogue at Pribram (Przibram): obverse, the synagogue; reverse, shield of David; 33 mm.
1875. Jubilee of the Portuguese synagogue at Amstérdam: obverse, escutcheon (pelican); reverse, inscription; 36 mm.
1876. Two hundredth anniversary of the Ḥebra Ḳaddisha, Gailingen: inscriptions on both sides; 34 mm.
1876. Death of the painter S. L. Verveer: obverse, bust; reverse, easel; 60 mm.
1877. Portuguese synagogue at Paris: obverse, tables of the Law; reverse, inscription; 28 mm.
1877. Salomon H. von Mosenthal's death: obverse, head; reverse, genius; 59 mm.
1879. Minister of Justice Godefroi: obverse, bust; reverse, inscription; 69 mm.
1879. Joseph Pizza's death: obverse, bust; reverse, masonic emblems; 42 mm.
1880. Medal presented by the officials of the Jewish community of Vienna to Ludwig August Frankl: obverse, head; reverse, escutcheon; 39 mm.
1880. R. E. A. Astruc's jubilee of office: obverse, bust; reverse, inscription; 55 mm.
1881. N. Montefiore: prize medal for military surgeons; obverse, field-hospital; reverse, escutcheon; 60 mm.
1881. Adolphe Crémieux's death: obverse, bust; reverse, inscription; 68 mm.
1881. Anti-Semitic movement at Berlin: four variants: (1) obverse, escutcheon; reverse, inscription; (2) obverse, caricature; reverse, sticks and hat; (3 and 4) inscriptions on both sides; 24 mm.
1881. Jubilee of the Edict of Toleration: obverse, bust; reverse, inscription; 30 mm.
1881. Adolf Sonnenthal's jubilee: obverse, bust; reverse, theater; 60 mm.; also in form of a thaler.
1881. Jubilee of the theater director Ch. Maurice: obverse, bust; reverse, inscription.
1882. Preacher Jellinek's jubilee of office: inscriptions on both sides; 44 mm.
1882. New synagogue at Frankfort: obverse, the synagogue; reverse, inscription; 36 mm.
1883. Prix Osiris: obverse, fencing - weapons; reverse, wreath; 34 mm.
1884. Architect Max Fleischer: obverse, bust; reverse, synagogue; 104 mm.
1884. Montefiore's one hundredth birthday; struck three times (London, Corfu, and Manchester): obverse, bust; reverse, inscription; 42, 41, and ? mm.
1884. Ignaz Kuranda: one-sided medallion; bust; 145 mm.
1886. Medal presented by the Jewish Aid Society at Luxemburg to Engenie Bloch: obverse, allegorical group; reverse, inscription; 50 mm.
1887. New synagogue at Munich: obverse, the synagogue; reverse, inscription; 40 mm.
1888. Founding of a Frankfort lodge: obverse, shield of David; reverse, tables of the Law; 25 mm.
1888. R. Abraham Alexander Wolf's sixtieth anniversary of office: obverse, bust; reverse, inscription; 38 mm.
1888. Numismatist Donebauer's death: obverse, bust; reverse, inscription; 58 mm.
1889. Gerson von Bleichröder: obverse, bust; reverse, escutcheon; 25 mm.
1889. Court choirmaster H. Levi: one-sided medallion; bust; 115 mm.
1889. Editors of the "Neue Freie Presse" (Bacher, Benedikt, and Werthner): obverse, three busts; reverse, newspaper; 85 mm.
1890. Liquidation of the Deutsch-Israelitische Gemeinde of Hamburg: obverse, Torah cabinet; reverse, allegorical group; 42 mm.
1890. Ludwig Barnay's jubilee: obverse, bust; reverse, inscription; 45 mm.
1890. M. R. von Mises' ninetieth birthday: obverse, bust; reverse, escutcheon; 45 mm.
1891. M. R. von Mises' death: obverse, bust; reverse, escutcheon; 40 mm.
1891. M. von Wilmersdoerffer's jubilee: obverse, bust; reverse, escutcheon; 49 mm.
1891. Prof. E. H. Kisch's fiftieth birthday: obverse, bust; reverse, Hygeia; 55 mm.
1892. Numismatist Adolph Meyers-Gedanensis: oval; obverse, bust; reverse, buildings; 71 × 57 mm.
1892. Prof. Th. Gomperz's sixtieth birthday: obverse, bust; reverse, allegorical group; 46 mm.
1893. Jubilee of the Nächstenliebe Society, Vienna: obverse, hands; reverse, inscription; 37 mm.
1893. State councilor T. M. C. Asser: obverse, bust; reverse, inscription; 65 mm.
1893. Preacher Adolf Jellinek's death: obverse, bust; reverse, inscription; 55 mm.
1894. Karl Marx: one-sided medallion; bust; 189 mm.
1894. Dr. Adolf Fischhof's death: obverse, bust; reverse, allegorical group; 55 mm.
1895. Jubilee of the factory of Ludwig Löwe: obverse, bust; reverse, allegorical figure; 56 mm.
1896. R. Isaac Elhanan Spektor: obverse, bust; reverse, chapel; 29 mm.
1896. Synagogue at Galatz: obverse, the synagogue; reverse, masonic emblems; 40 mm.
1896. Prof. Moritz Benedikt's jubilee: square plaque; bust; 60 × 44 mm.
1896. Charlotte Furtado-Heine: horticultural prize medal, founded by a will.
1897. Michael Fischhof, founder of "Austria": obverse, bust; reverse, view of city; 50 mm.
1897. Prof. Joseph Gruber's seventieth birthday; plaque; bust; 60 × 45 mm.
1897. Zionist leader Architect O. Marmorek: plaque; bust; 118 mm.
1898. Second Zionist Congress: obverse, allegorical group; reverse, inscription; 63 mm.
1899. Israelitische Religionsgesellschaft to Wilhelm Carl and Mathilde von Rothschild: obverse, interior view of synagogue; reverse, inscription; 40 mm.
1899. Reunion of the Frankfort Israelitische Realschule: obverse, view of city; reverse, inscription; 39 mm.
1899. Choir prize of the Religionsgesellschaft of Frankfort: obverse, interior view of synagogue; reverse, musical instruments; 39 mm.
1899. Prof. James Joseph Sylvester, prize medal for mathematics: obverse, bust; reverse, inscription; 56 mm.
1900. Stepney Jewish School: obverse, allegorical figure; reverse, inscription.
1900. Dr. K. Lippe's seventieth birthday: obverse, bust; reverse, flaming shield of David; 30 mm.
1900. Dr. Ludwig von Guttmann's death: obverse, bust; reverse, mine-inspector; 35 × 31 mm.
1900. Composer Carl Goldmark's seventieth birthday: obverse, bust; reverse, oak and laurel; 55 mm.
1900. *Idem*: plaque; bust; 200 × 155 mm.
1900. Fiftieth anniversary of the Stern Conservatorium: obverse, bust; reverse, allegorical figure; 42 mm.
1901. Salo Cohen, director of the Jewish community of Vienna: plaque; bust; 168 × 115 mm.
1901. Enlargement of the synagogue at Frankfort: obverse, old and new synagogues; reverse, inscription; 39 mm.
1902. Composer Ignaz Brüll: plaque; head; 200 × 135 mm.
1902. Virtuoso Alfred Grünfeld: plaque; head; 70 × 50 mm.
1903. Synagogue at Szegedin: obverse and reverse, building; 29 mm.
1903. Musician Siegfried Ochs: obverse, bust; reverse, lyre; 50 mm.
1904. Centenary of the Frankfort Philanthropin: obverse, sower; reverse, beehive; 50 mm.

1904. M. von Wilmersdörffer's death : plaque ; bust; 100 mm.
1904. Artist Joseph Israels' eightieth birthday.

For the names of Jews prominent as engravers of medals see JEW. ENCYC. v. 175, *s.v.* ENGRAVING AND ENGRAVERS.

BIBLIOGRAPHY: Mulder, *Eene Zeldzame Medaille*, Amsterdam, 1859; Schudt, *Jüdische Merckwürdigkeiten*, ii. 82; Wolf, *Eine Unbekannte Jüdische Medaille*, in *Monatsschrift*, 1894; idem, *Eine Medaille auf R. Elieser b. Samuel Schmelka*, ib. 1898; idem, *Das Jüdische Berlin Gegen Ende des Achtzehnten Jahrhunderts in Abbildungen und Medaillen*, in *Kaufmann Gedenkbuch*; idem, *Die Hamburger auf oder von Juden Geprägten Medaillen*, in *Mittheilungen für Jüdische Volkskunde*, No. xiii.; idem, *Zwei auf Judentaufen Bezügliche Medaillen*, in *Monatsschrift*, 1900; Zunz, *Eine Merkwürdige Medaille*, in *G. S.* iii.

A. A. W.

MEDEBA (modern name **Madeba**): A town east of the Dead Sea and a few miles south of Heshbon. It was wrested from the Moabites by Sihon, King of the Amorites (Num. xxi. 30); and after the conquest of Palestine it was assigned, together with the plain in which it lay, to the tribe of Reuben (Josh. xiii. 9, 16). During the war of the Ammonites against David, the Syrian allies of the former encamped at Medeba, which seems at that time to have been under Ammonite control (I Chron. xix. 6–15). Later it was seized by the Moabites again; for, according to the MOABITE STONE (line 8), "Omri annexed [all the land] of Medeba, and Israel occupied it, his days and half his son's days, forty years." This statement is confirmed by Isa. xv. 2, which mentions Medeba as a city of Moab, under whose control it remained until the Moabites were driven south of the Arnon by Jeroboam II.

During the Maccabean period John, brother of Jonathan and Simon Maccabeus, was murdered by a robber clan, led by Jambri or Ambri, who lived in Medeba, and who in revenge were ambushed and slain while taking part in a marriage procession near the town (I Macc. ix. 35–42; Josephus, "Ant." xiii. 1, §§ 2, 4). It was later taken by John Hyrcanus after a stubborn siege (*ib.* xiii. 9, § 1), and finally was captured by Alexander Jannæus, although Hyrcanus II. promised to restore it to Aretas, King of Arabia, (*ib.* xiii. 15, § 4; xiv. 1, § 4).

J. L. H. G.

Medeba, after lying desolate for some centuries, was reoccupied by a colony of Greek Christians about 1880; to this colony a smaller one of Latin Christians has since been added. In erecting the necessary buildings for this new occupation many beautiful mosaics which belonged to churches and monasteries of the fourth, fifth, and sixth centuries have been uncovered. Many of these may still be seen in hovels, stables, and farmyards. The most noteworthy of these is the mosaic map of Palestine, some remains of which may still be seen in the floor of the Greek church at Medeba. The discovery of this map was announced in Dec., 1896, but there is reason to believe that it had been known to a small circle of ecclesiastics for some time before this, and that when it was first discovered it was in a much better state of preservation than at present. Toward the end of 1896 efforts were made to make accurate charts of the remains of it and to give to the world some knowledge of this remarkable production. The publications in reference to it will be found in the bibliography at the end of this article.

The artistic and technical difficulties which the makers of the map had to overcome were very great, but they surmounted them with surprising success. Exact proportions and perspective were of course not attained, but the general relations of the sacred sites were graphically pictured; much valuable information as to the condition of the land at the time at which the mosaic was made (fifth or sixth century C. E.) is given, and the traditions then current concerning the location of Biblical sites found expression. Thus the statements of Eusebius and Jerome in their onomastica are illustrated and in some cases supplemented.

Jerusalem Map.

Jerusalem is pictured on the map as being bisected by a long colonnaded street. The wall of Jerusalem did not enclose the southern end of the two hills on which the city stands. After enclosing the Church of Mt. Zion on the site of the present Cœnaculum it turned sharply to the northeast. Traces of another wall, approximately on the line of the present one, are also visible; this latter wall is, no doubt, that built by Hadrian, while the extension which includes the Church of Mt. Zion pictures a period before the time of Eudoxia, who rebuilt the wall on the line of that of Nehemiah. This not only throws light on the topography of Jerusalem for that period, but helps to date the map. Prominent buildings like the Church of the Holy Sepulcher are pictured on the map with sufficient clearness to afford considerable information concerning their architecture at that time.

The makers of the mosaic were especially interested in Christian themes. They accordingly pictured the Sea of Galilee as bearing a ship containing the disciples, and Peter endeavoring to walk on the water (Matt. xiv. 25–31).

One easily recognizes on the map the names of many sites which are well known, such as Baitin (Bethel), Jifna, Jibia, Beer-sheba. Sites in southern Palestine and on the Philistine plain are given with considerable fulness. Gerar is shown close to Beer-sheba and to the west of it—a location which conflicts with the usual identification of Gerar with Umm Jarar, five miles to the south of Gaza. The Philistine Gath is placed near the site of the modern Ramleh.

On the south the map extends far enough to show Lower Egypt. Witnesses quoted as reliable by Father Cléopas, the librarian of the Convent of the Holy Sepulcher, said that they saw the mosaic some years before it was so badly mutilated and declared that they recognized Ephesus and Smyrna thereon. It would seem, therefore, that when intact the map included Asia Minor as well as Egypt.

Tradition in the fourth century was not always more reliable than it is now, a fact to which this map sometimes bears witness. For example, the thrashing-floor of Atad, which Gen. l. 10 places east of the Jordan, is on this map identified with Beth-hogla ("thrashing-floor of Atad, which is now Beth-hogla"). Beth-hogla, however, is the modern 'Ain (Ḳasr) Ḥajlah in the plain southeast of Jericho, west of the Jordan, where a Greek monastery is situated.

BIBLIOGRAPHY: Cléopas and Lagrange, *La Mosaïque Géographique de Madaba*, in *Rev. Bib.* April, 1897; Clermont-Ganneau, *Recueil d'Archéologie Orientale*, ii. 161 *et seq.*; *Pal. Explor. Fund, Quarterly Statement*, 1897, pp. 213 *et seq.* (Clermont-Ganneau); 1898, p. 251 (*idem*); 1898, p. 85 (Schick); 1898, pp. 177 *et seq.* (Mommert); Séjourné, *Médeba*, in *Revue Biblique*, 1892, i. 617-644; Bacher, in *J. Q. R.*, xiii.

E. G. H. G. A. B.

MEDES. See MEDIA.

MEDIA (Latin, *Media*; Greek, Μηδία; Old Persian, *Māda*; Hebr. מדי): Ancient name of a country which is located south and west of the Caspian Sea, and is associated with events in Jewish history. The confines of Media anciently embraced territory corresponding roughly to the present Azerbaijan, the southern borders of the Caspian, the province of 'Irak-'Ajami, and the districts of modern Persia which adjoin the mountains of Kurdistan and Luristan. In the Hebrew Scriptures Media and the Medes are mentioned more than a dozen times. The antiquity of the name is believed to be shown by its having been borne by Noah's grandson Madai, son of Japheth (Gen. x. 3 [A. V. 2]), who is commonly regarded as the progenitor of the Median race, Mount Ararat being within the ancient Median borders. From the Bible, furthermore, it is known that Israelites were placed in cities of the Medes by Shalmaneser, King of Assyria, after his conquest of Samaria (II Kings xvii. 6, xviii. 11); and Media is referred to under the form "Amada" or "Madai" in the records of this king and of Tiglath-pileser. Allusions to Media in connection with Persia are not rare in certain books of the Scriptures; and the laws of the Medes and Persians became a synonym for all that was fixed and unalterable (Esth. i. 3, 14, 18, 19; x. 2; Dan. v. 28, vi. 8, viii. 20). The part taken by Media and Elam, meaning Persia, in the overthrow of Babylon forms a portion of the prophecy of the elder Isaiah (Isa. xiii. 17, xxi. 2; comp. also Jer. xxv. 25). At Ecbatana, in the province of the Medes, moreover, was found the famous edict of Cyrus granting a decree for the building of the Temple at Jerusalem (Ezra vi. 2; I Esdras vi. 23). The same capital is prominent likewise in the Book of Judith (Judith i. 1 *et seq.*); and the ancient Median city Rhages figures elsewhere in this book and strikingly in the narrative of Tobit (Judith i. 5, 15; Tobit i. 14, v. 5, vi. 10). On the identification of "Darius the Median" and on Daniel's position under his rule (Dan. v. 28, vi. 8, viii. 20, ix. 1, xi. 1), see DANIEL; DARIUS.

In Bible.

With regard to Media as a factor in the world's history, the antiquity of the people as an Iranian nation is conceded, even though the existence of a so-called Median empire in very remote times may be open to some doubt. According to the fragments of Berosus of Babylon, however, the Median royal line extended back almost two thousand years before the time of Alexander the Great; and the historian Ctesias pretends to give a list of kings and their reigns running back nearly to 1000 B.C. For historic purposes, however, the story of Media begins with Dejoces (Δηϊόκης), whom Herodotus ("Hist." i. 16 *et seq.*) describes as the founder of the empire. This monarch is mentioned as "Dayaukku" in the inscriptions of Sargon: and he ruled over Media from 709 to 656 B.C. or, more exactly, from 700 to 647. He was succeeded by Phraortes (Old Persian, "Fravartish"), who extended the boundaries and sway of Media and ruled from 647 to 625. Phraortes in turn was followed by Cyaxares (Old Persian, "[H]uvaxshatara"; Babylonian, "Uvakuishtar"), whose reign (625–585 B.C.) formed the culmination of the Median ascendency. It was under this ruler, in alliance with Nabopalasar, King of Babylon, that the destruction of Nineveh and the overthrow of the Assyrian empire took place (*c.* 607–604 B.C.). His successor was Astyages (Bab. "Ishtuvegu"), whom Oriental tradition erroneously identifies with the legendary Azh-Dahak of Babylon. With the rule of Astyages (585–550 B.C.) came the decline and final overthrow of Media by Persia under CYRUS. The Median supremacy was lost sight of in the greater glory of Persia. Thenceforth the two nations came to be regarded as one, their names being often united and used interchangeably, although divisions were recognized. After the death of Alexander the Great, for example, Media Minor, which corresponds roughly to Azerbaijan, was distinguished from Media Major, which became a part of the Syrian empire; and, again, Media Major was later comprised in the Parthian domain and was finally included in the great empire of the Sassanians.

Ctesias' Account.

From the religious standpoint also Media is important because Zoroaster is believed to have arisen in that country; and the similarities between Zoroastrianism and Judaism are many and striking. See AVESTA; PERSIA.

BIBLIOGRAPHY: F. Justi, *Gesch. Irans von den Aeltesten Zeiten*, in Geiger and Kuhn, *Grundriss der Iranischen Philologie*, pp. 406–415, Strasburg, 1897; Rawlinson, *Five Great Monarchies of the Ancient Eastern World*, vols. iii.–iv., London, 1865; M. Duncker, *Gesch. des Alterthums*, Leipsic, 1877 (= *History of Antiquity*, Eng. transl. by E. Abbott, London, 1881); J. Oppert, *Le Peuple et la Langue des Mèdes*, Paris, 1879; Ed. Meyer, *Gesch. des Alterthums*, Stuttgart, 1884; idem, *Die Entstehung des Judenthums*, Halle, 1896.

G. A. V. W. J.

MEDIATOR (Greek, Μεσίτης): An agent that goes between; one who interposes between parties at variance; in particular, an intercessor between God and man. Judaism recognizes in principle no mediatorship between God and man. "The Lord alone did lead him [Israel], and there was no strange god with him" (Deut. xxxii. 12). "See now that I, even I, am he, and there is no god with me: I kill, and I make alive; I wound, and I heal" (*ib.* 39). "In his love and in his pity he redeems them; and he bare them and carried them" (Isa. lxiii. 9). "What nation is there so great, who hath God so nigh unto them, as the Lord our God is in all things that we call upon him for?" (Deut. iv. 7). When told by God that Israel should henceforth be led by an angel, Moses replied: "If thy presence go not with me, carry us not up hence" (Ex. xxxiii. 15). Still for the people the distance between the Deity and frail humanity was too great to be overcome by the spiritual effort of the multitude or of the common individual. Hence the prophet, believed to be in constant communion with God, is viewed in Scripture as the fit person to intercede on behalf of men in trouble. Thus Abraham is empowered by God to pray for pardon and restored health for

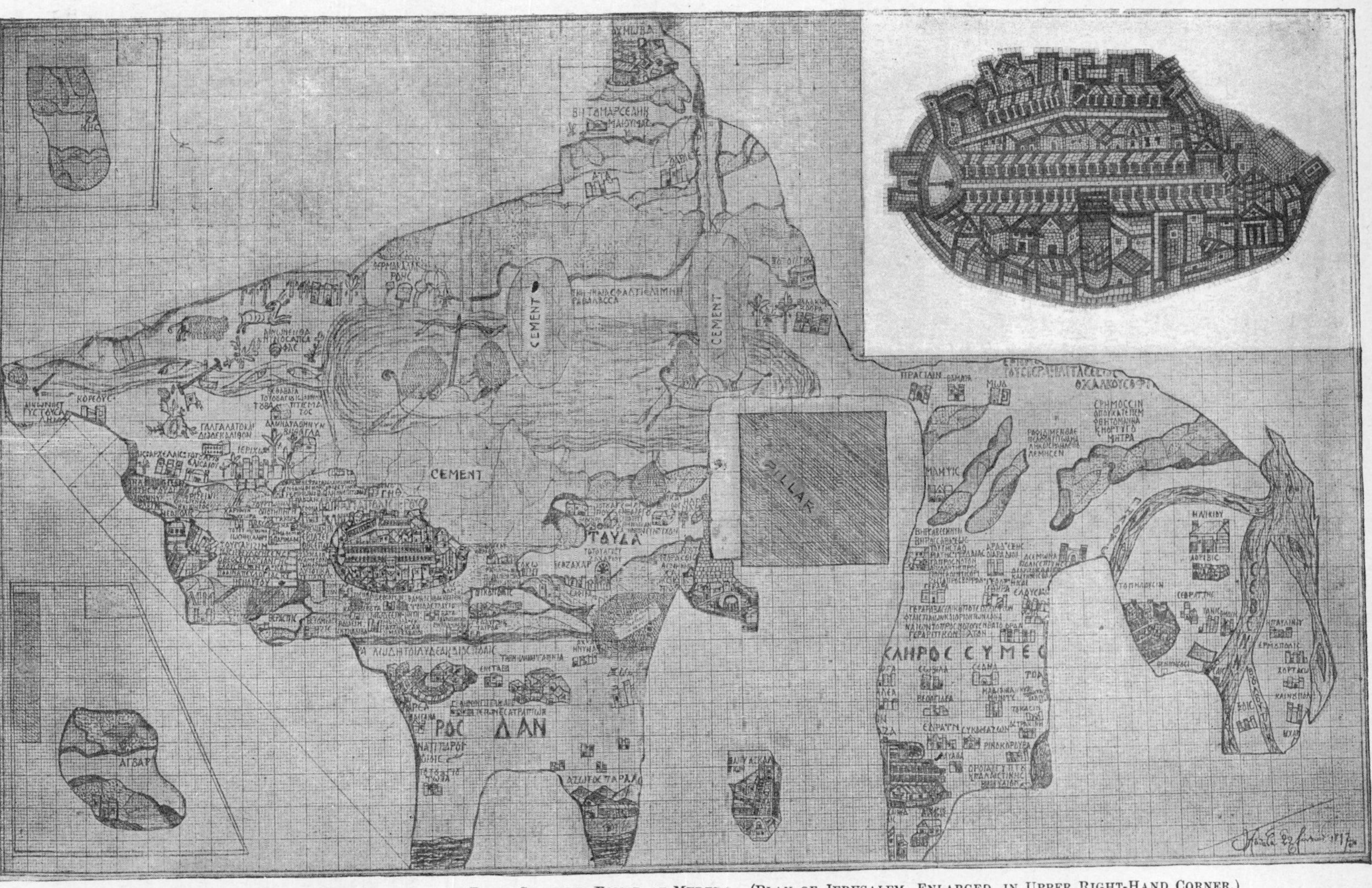

Mosaic Map of Palestine, Probably of the Fifth Century, Found at Medeba. (Plan of Jerusalem, Enlarged, in Upper Right-Hand Corner.)

Abimelech (Gen. xx. 7, 17; comp. *ib.* xviii. 23–33). Moses intercedes on behalf of Pharaoh and the Egyptians (Ex. viii. 5–8, 24–26; ix. 28–33; x. 17–18) and also on behalf of his own people (*ib.* xvii. 11, xxxii. 11; Deut. ix. 18); likewise Samuel (I Sam. vii. 5; xii. 19, 23; comp. Ps. xcix. 6), Jeremiah (Jer. xv. 1), and Job (Job xlii. 7; comp. Ezek. xiv. 14–20). Noah, Daniel, and Job save their generations by their righteousness.

In Apocryphal and Hellenistic Literature.

In the Apocryphal and Hellenistic literature the idea of mediatorship is more pronounced. Jeremiah is frequently mentioned as the one who "prayeth much for the people" (II Macc. xv. 14); "whose works are to this city [Jerusalem] as a firm pillar and whose prayers as a strong wall" (Apoc. Baruch, ii. 2; "Rest of the Words of Baruch," i. 2, ii. 3; comp. Jer. vi. 27; Pesiḳ. 115b). According to Tobit (iii. 26), angels bring the prayers of men before God's throne. Enoch is asked by the fallen angels to intercede for them (Enoch, xiii. 4–7). Abraham is described as interceding for the sinners in a state of suspense (Testament of Abraham, xiv.; comp. Luke xvi. 24). Moses was "the advocate of Israel who bent his knees day and night in prayer to make intercession for his people" (Assumptio Mosis, xi. 17, xii. 6). The Patriarchs in heaven were believed to be intercessors for the living (Philo, "De Execrationibus," § 9; Lam. R., Introduction, 25; comp. Josephus, "Ant." i. 13, § 3); for all the righteous souls (Sibyllines, ii. 331). Remarkable is the warning of Enoch to his children: "Say not our father stands before God and prays for us to be released from sin; for there is no person there to help any man that hath sinned" (Slavonic Enoch, liii. 1; comp. Isa. lxiii. 16).

In Rabbinical Literature.

In principle the Rabbis were against prayers to angels for intercession. Says R. Judan: "A man in trouble who has a great man for a patron stands at the door awaiting the answer the servants will bring, whether or not he will be permitted to approach him for aid. He who needs God's help ought not to ask the assistance of either Michael or Gabriel or any other angel, but should turn immediately to God; for whosoever shall call on the name of God shall be delivered" (Yer. Ber. ix. 13a, after Joel iii. 5 [A. V. ii. 32]). "However exalted the Most High is, let but a man enter His house and whisper a prayer and the Almighty listens as a friend to whom a secret is confided" (Yer. Ber. *l.c.*).

Nevertheless, to judge from the early Christian writers (Col. ii. 19; Origen, "Contra Celsum," i. 26, v. 6; Clement, "Stromata," vi. 5, 41; Aristides, "Apologue," xiv.), angels were often invoked by certain (Gnostic?) classes of Jews. The passage in Job xxxiii. 23 (comp. v. 1) also led the Rabbis to assume that angels plead for men at the throne of God (Yer. Ḳid. i. 61d). Shab. 12b reads: "He who prays in the Aramaic language will lack the aid of angels, whose language is Hebrew," while from Tosef., Ḥul. ii. 18 (comp. Mek., Yitro, Ex. xx. 4) it may be learned that angel-worship was not unknown in certain Jewish circles. And this led eventually, notwithstanding the opposition of many rabbinical authorities (see the passages in Zunz, "G. V." pp 147–149), to the introduction even into the liturg of prayers addressed to the angels and seeking thei mediation. The Ineffable Name, the divine attribute of mercy, the thirteen attributes of God (see MIDDOT), the holy throne, the gates of heaven and the Torah were also appealed to in the liturg (see Zunz, *l.c.*). A great sinner in the Talmu invokes the mountains and the stars to pray fo him ('Ab. Zarah 17a).

Especially was Michael invoked as intercessor fo the Jewish people (Dan. xii. 1; see Lücken, "Michael," 1898, pp. 11–25). Meṭaṭron (Mithra) also i frequently mentioned in Gnostic circles togethe with Michael as mediator of the Revelation (Sanh. 38b, with reference to Ex. xxiii. 21; Gen. R. v. comp. Tan., Mishpaṭim, ed. Buber, p. 12). Righteous souls also appear as intercessors (Tanna debe Eliyahu R. iii.).

The Rabbis, however, insisted upon not allowing God's absolute sovereignty and power to be infringed through the interference of angels. "The angels were created on the second day so that i should not be believed that they had a share in the creation of the world" (Gen. R. i., iii.). The Lord Himself, and no angel, or seraph, or other messenger of His, smote the Egyptians at the time of Israel's redemption from Egypt (Passover Haggadah; Mek., Bo, 7); though in the destruction of Sodom, Gabriel assisted (Gen. R. li. 3).

Moses the Mediator of the Law.

That the Law was given to the people or to Moses through angels is a belief ascribed to the Jews by Josephus ("Ant." xv. 15, § 3), by Paul (Gal. iii. 19; Heb. ii. 2), and by Stephen (Acts vii. 38, 53; comp. Apoc. Mosis, i.; Book of Jubilees, i. 27; Hermas, "Similitude," viii. 3, 3, where Michael is mentioned as mediator of the Book of the Law). Rabbinical teaching, on the other hand, consistently opposed the idea of such a mediatorship. "When the Lord spoke with Moses the angels who stood between them did not hear a word" (Num. R. xiv., end; comp. Sifre, Num. 58). Moses alone is viewed in rabbinical literature as the mediator ("sirsur" = "go-between") between God and Israel (Pesiḳ. R. vi.; Ex. R. iii. 6, vi. 3; Num. R. xi. 5). In Hellenistic literature also Moses is called "mediator," Μεσίτης (Philo, "De Vita Moysis," iii. 19; Assumptio Mosis, i. 14, iii. 12; Gal. iii. 19). The Samaritans call Moses the "Mesites" (see Baneth, "Marqah," 1888, p. 48), and he is actually invoked as intercessor by them (see "J. Q. R." viii. 604). At the same time the Midrash (Leḳaḥ Ṭob on Deut. xxxiii. 4) says: "No one knows the place where Moses is buried, so that no one should ever sacrifice at his grave, or worship him, or bring incense-offerings to him." "Wherefore criest thou to me?" (Ex. xiv. 15) is thus explained by the Rabbis: "There is no need of asking God concerning His children, as He Himself is in distress when His children suffer." "My children have already prayed to Me, and I have heard their prayer," said God to Moses (Ex. R. xxi.; Cant. R. i. 2; Mek., Beshallaḥ, 3).

Philo, however, speaks of "The Word" ("Logos") as the mediator between two worlds. "The Father who created the universe has given to His archangelic and most ancient Word a preeminent gift to stand on the confines of both; while separating the created things from the Creator he pleads before the immortal God on behalf of the mortal race which sins continually, and is the ambassador sent by the Ruler to the subject race. He exults in this office and boasts of it, saying: 'I stood in the midst between the Lord and you'" (Num. xvi. 48). From this it was but one step to claim for Jesus the same cosmic mediatorship, as Paul and his followers did while presenting him as the mediator of the new covenant and the restorer of the relations between man and God which had been broken through sin (I Tim. ii. 5; Heb. viii. 6, ix. 15, xii. 24). Against this teaching R. Akiba declares: "Happy are ye Israelites! Before whom do ye cleanse yourselves, and who cleanses you from sin? None but your Father in Heaven; for Scripture says: 'I shall sprinkle upon you clean waters, and ye shall be clean' (Ezek. xxxvi. 25), and 'Israel's hope ["miḳweh"] is the Lord' (Jer. xvii. 13). Like the miḳweh, 'the Fountain of Water,' so is the Lord the source of purification for all impurities" (Yoma viii. 9).

Philo's Logos.

Regarding the function of the priests, Judaism is also very outspoken in denying to any human being the power of conferring any blessing upon the people. The words "And they shall put my name upon the children of Israel, and I will bless them" (Num. vi. 27) are thus commented upon (Sifre, Num. 43; Num. R. xi., end): "Israel is not to believe that its blessing depends upon the priests, nor should the priests claim the power of blessing for themselves; but God alone is He who confers the blessing."

Maimonides in the fifth article of his creed lays especial stress upon prayer being offered exclusively to God and to no other being; and in his commentary (Sanh. xi.) he points out particularly that the angels should not be appealed to as mediators or intercessors between God and man. In the same manner Naḥmanides declares it wrong to pray to angels as intercessors (see his discourse "Torat Adonai," ed. Jellinek, pp. 30–31). Lipman of Mühlhausen in his "Nizzahon," pp. 12, 132, writes: "Our rabbis have rejected every kind of mediatorship, referring to the Scripture: 'Him alone shalt thou worship, and to him shalt thou cleave' (Deut. x. 20). Every appeal to intercessors leads to idolatry and to impurity." The remark of Abraham ibn Ezra (commentary on the Pentateuch, Introduction), "The angel that mediates between man and God is reason," is characteristic of the spirit of Judaism.

BIBLIOGRAPHY: Hamburger, *R. B. T.* ii. 138–142, s.v. *Mittel- oder Unmittelbarheit Gottes.*

K.

MEDICINE.—In Bible and Talmud: The ancient Hebrew regarded health and disease as emanating from the same divine source. "I kill, and I make alive; I wound, and I heal" (Deut. xxxii. 39), said the Lord through His servant Moses; and therefore they who minister to the health of their fellows are regarded as the messengers of God, as the executors of His will. Although YHWH is the physician of Israel (Ex. xv. 26), yet the practise of medicine is sanctioned by the Law: "If men strive together, and one smite another . . . and . . . he keepeth his bed . . . he shall pay for the loss of his time, and shall cause him to be thoroughly healed" (*ib.* xxi. 18–19). Joseph employed house physicians (Gen. l. 2); and Isaiah mentions especially a surgeon or wound-dresser (Isa. iii. 7). Among the Jews, unlike other primitive nations, the priests did not monopolize the art and science of healing. Moses assigned to them only the task of police supervision in cases of contagious diseases. The Bible does not mention a single instance of a priest having performed the functions of a physician. The Prophets, however, practised occasionally the art of healing. Elijah brought to life a child apparently dead (I Kings xvii. 17–22); and his disciple Elisha performed a similar miraculous cure (II Kings iv. 18–20, 34–35). A man of God restored the paralyzed hand of King Jeroboam (I Kings xiii. 4–6). Isaiah cured King Hezekiah of an inflammation by applying a plaster made of figs (II Kings xx. 7).

At a later period physicians were held in high esteem by the people, as may be gathered from Ben Sira: "Honor a physician with the honor due unto him for the uses which ye may have of him, for the Lord hath created him. . . . The Lord has created medicines out of the earth; and he that is wise will not abhor them. . . . And He has given men skill that He might be honored in His marvelous works. . . . My son, in thy sickness be not negligent; . . . give place to the physician; . . . let him not go from thee, for thou hast need of him" (Ecclus. [Sirach] xxxviii. 1–12). Afterward the status of the medical profession became still more exalted. The court of justice ("bet din") employed in certain cases the services of a physician ("rofe"), whose expert testimony was decisive in criminal matters. In cases of assault, for instance, it was his duty to give his opinion ("umdena") as to the danger to the life of the assaulted (Sanh. 78a; Giṭ. 12b). Corporal punishment was inflicted under the supervision of a physician (Mak. 22b). No physician was permitted to practise without a license from the local judicial council (B. B. 21a; Mak. 20b). Every city was required to have at least one physician; and to live in a city that had none was considered hazardous (Sanh. 17b).

The medical knowledge of the Talmudists was based upon tradition, the dissection of human bodies, observation of diseases, and experiments upon animals ("'issuḳ be-debarim"; Ḥul. 57b). When making their rounds physicians used to take their apprentices with them (Deut. R. x.). In the majority of cases the art of healing was transmitted from father to son (Yer. R. H. i. 3, 57b). The numerous medical aphorisms preserved in the Talmudim and Midrashim, and the fact that physicians took part in the discussion of many important religious questions by the Rabbis, indicate that the latter were not unacquainted with the science of medicine (Naz. 52a; Nid. 22b). That the demand upon the skill of physicians was considerable may be adduced from the statute law prohibiting the part owner of a house from renting his part to

Sources of Medical Knowledge.

a physician on account of the noise and disturbance caused by the visiting patients (B. B. 21a). Physicians received for their services comparatively large fees. A current saying was: "A physician who takes nothing is worth nothing" (B. Ḳ. 85a).

What was the sum total of medical knowledge possessed by the ancient Hebrews can not be stated definitely, for the reason that neither the Bible nor the Talmud contains medical treatises as such. The Mishnah mentions a medical book, "Sefer Refu'ot," which was attributed to King Solomon and expurgated by King Hezekiah (Pes. iv. 9), and the Talmud cites a treatise on pharmacology, "Megillat Sammanin" (Yoma 38a); but neither of these has been preserved. Medicine was an integral part of the religion of the Jews; and medical subjects are treated of or alluded to only in so far as they concern or elucidate some point of law.

Anatomy.

There are in the Bible but few direct references to the internal organs. Biblical poetry, however, abounds with expressions in which the names of such organs are used metaphorically, *e.g.*: "His archers compass me round about, he cleaveth my reins asunder, and doth not spare; he poureth out my gall upon the ground" (Job xvi. 13); "His vessels are full of healthy fluid, and the marrow of his bones is well moistened" (*ib.* xxi. 24, Hebr.); "I am weary; . . . my throat is dried" (Ps. lxix.). See ANATOMY.

The laws concerning clean ("ṭohorah") and unclean ("ṭum'ah") afford means for ascertaining in part the familiarity of the ancient Hebrews with certain branches of anatomy. According to the Mosaic law (Num. xix. 14), any one who comes in contact with a dead body or any part thereof, or who remains in a tent wherein a corpse is found, is considered infected ("unclean") for seven days. The Mishnah teaches that this tent-infection ("ṭum'at ohel") takes place in the presence either of a complete corpse, or of an anatomical unit or member ("eber"), *i.e.*, a bone covered with its soft parts. A bone stripped of its soft parts does not infect. Should, however, a collection of such bones, by either their bulk or number, represent more than half of the skeleton ("sheled"), their infecting power is equal to that of a complete corpse (Oh. i. *et seq.*). This law made it imperative that the number of bones in the human body should be ascertained. Oh. i.–viii. gives the number as 248; and the following bones are recognized and named: hand ("pissat ha-yad") 30; forearm ("ḳaneh") 2; elbow-joint ("marpeḳ") 2; arm 1; shoulder-joint ("kataf"), including shoulder-blade ("kanaf"), 4;

Osteology.

foot ("pissat ha-regel") 30; ankle-joint ("ḳarsol") 10; leg 2; knee-joint ("'arḳub"), including knee-cap ("piḳah") 5; thigh 1; hip-joint ("ḳoṭlit"), including head of femur ("buḳa de-iṭma") and innominate bone ("ḳeliboset"), 3; spinal column ("shedrah") made up of vertebræ ("ḥulyot") 18; ribs 11; breast-bone ("mafteaḥ shel-leb") 6; sacrum and coccyx ("'uḳaẓ") 6; and head 9, in which were recognized the vertex ("ḳederah"), two condyloid processes, the foramen magnum, the fontanels, maxillary bone, maxillary arch ("gabbot ha-zaḳan"), and the nasal bone ("'eẓem ha-ḥoṭam"). This enumeration gave rise to numerous disputes as to the number of bones constituting a normal skeleton. The disciples of R. Ishmael, in order to settle this question, obtained the body of a young harlot who had been put to death, and, having subjected it to prolonged boiling ("shelikah"), counted the bones and found the number of them to be 252 (Bek. 45a). Neither of the numbers given agrees with modern anatomical knowledge. The explanation of the discrepancy is to be found in the youthful age of the subject used, many of the bones not having become completely ossified; also the prolonged boiling caused them to be separated into their original component parts, so that the Talmudists counted the epiphysis and diaphysis as separate bones. As an expert osteologist is mentioned Theodos, a well-known physician (Naz. 52a).

Myology.

The Bible speaks of muscles under the general term "flesh" ("basar"). The abdominal muscles are mentioned in Job xl. 16. The psoas muscle is mentioned in the Talmud (Ḥul. 93a); and Rab Ḥisdai made the remarkable observation that the psoas in all clean animals, *i.e.*, those that chew the cud and whose hoofs are cleft, has two accessory muscles whose respective fibers run longitudinally and transversely (*ib.* 59a). Tendons are frequently mentioned under the term "giddim."

The salivary glands or "fountains" (Niddah 55b) are situated in the cavity of the mouth (Ab. R. N. xxxi.) and under the tongue (Lev. R. xvi.). The capacity of the pharynx ("bet ha-beli'ah") was found by experiment to be larger than it seems. A hen's egg can easily be swallowed whole (Yoma 80a). The esophagus ("wesheṭ") and larynx ("ḳaneh") have their respective origins in the pharynx. The structure of the esophagus is composed of two layers ("orot")—an outer, muscular one and an inner, serous one (Ḥul. 43a). The inner layer has longitudinal folds throughout its length, except at the upper part, which is called "tarbeẓ ha-wesheṭ" (*ib.* 43b). The lower portion of the inner layer is supplied with hair-like projections (*ib.* 44a).

The larynx ("ḳaneh," "gargeret") is composed of a large ring of cricoid cartilage ("ṭabba'at gedolah"), thyroid cartilage ("koba'," "piḳah shel-gargeret"), and the epiglottis ("shippuy koba'"; Ḥul. 18b). The trachea is composed of incomplete cartilaginous rings ("ḥulyot"), and membranous ones ("bene ḥulyah").

The alimentary canal of ruminating animals is thus described:

"The food passes from the mouth into the pharynx, thence into the esophagus ["isṭomka"], thence into the reticulum ["bet ha-kosot"], thence into the psalterium ["ha-masas" or "hemses"], thence into the abomasum ["karsa"], thence into the duodenum ["resh mayah"], thence into the small intestines ["kerukah ḳaṭṭinah"], thence into the blind gut ["sanya debe"], thence into the large intestines ["kerukit 'ubya"], thence into the rectum ["peṭaroka"], whence it makes its exit through the *sphincter ani* ["iskutha"]" (Lev. R. iii.).

According to R. Samuel, there are no hair-like projections ("milot") below the pylorus ("meẓar"). The gastro-intestinal tract throughout its length

·overed externally with the peritoneum ("ḳerum laf") except the posterior surface of the lower tion of the rectum ("ḥilḥolet"; Ḥul. 49b). The itoneum forms the greater omentum ("peder"), ich is attached to the greater curvature or "bow" ḳashta") of the stomach (*ib.* 50a) and the beging of the small intestines (*ib.* 93a).

'he liver is attached to the diaphragm ("ṭarpesha") a fold of the peritoneum (*ib.* 46a). It is united with the gall-bladder ("marah") by means of ırrow tube ("simpona"; *ib.* 48b). The pancreas onsidered an accessory organ of the liver, and is ed the "finger of the liver" ("eẓba' ha-kabed"). relations to the abdominal organs are described rectly (Tamid 31a). The anterior abdominal wall livided into an inner, peritoneal layer ("keres imit") and an outer, muscular one ("keres ḥiẓo-"). The spleen and kidneys are frequently tioned in Talmud and Midrash, but no descrip- is given (see below).

e Lungs l Heart.

'he lungs are composed of two "rows" ("'aru-"), right and left, divided vertically by a sep- ("ṭarpesh ha-leb") which rises from the pericardium ("kis ha-leb") and is attached to the spinal column. The large bronchi ("bet ha-simponot") enter respectively the inner side of each row (*ib.* 50a). ngside of the bronchi enter also the large bloodsels ("mizraḳim"; *ib.* 93b). The number of lobes ach lung is given correctly (*ib.* 47a). The pleura omposed of two layers, an outer, rough one crama 'illaya") and an inner, rose-colored one erama tatta'a," "kittuna de-warda"; *ib.* 46a). heart is composed of two ventricles ("ḥalal"), right being larger than the left (*ib.* 45b). It is ated to the left of the median line (Men. 37b). expressed a radical view for his time, namely, t the aorta ("ḳaneh shel-leb") contains blood, not (Ḥul. 45b). The large veins are called "weri-"; the small ones, "ḥuṭe dam."

'he brain is not mentioned in the Bible. Accord- to the Talmudists, it has two coats, an outer *dura mater*) and an inner coat (the *pia mater*), one being hard ("ḳashshish"), the other thin akkiḳ"). The spinal cord begins outside of the dyloid processes (Ḥul. 45a). The Zohar gives a ewhat more detailed description: "The skull tains three cavities in which the brain is lodged. m the brain issue thirty-two paths. These paths ad over the body connecting it with the brain" har on Lev. xxvi.).

The nerative rgans.

rom the laws relating to circumcision, flux, men- ation, etc., which are discussed at length in the le and especially in the Talmud, may be gath- some idea of the knowledge which the ancient s possessed concerning the anatomy of the gen- ive organs. Of the male genitals the anatom- parts are mentioned as follows: The scrotum ("kis") is divided by a septum into two sacculi (Bek. 40a); the testes ("beẓim," "ashakim") have two coats (Ḥul. 45a); each testicle has an appendix, the epididymis ("ḥuṭe beẓah"; . 75a); it is supplied with blood-vessels ("gide ad"; Ḥul. 93a) and nerves (*ib.* 45b), and it con- s a viscid fluid (Yeb. 75a). It was held that the spermatic fluid and the urine had each a separate canal for their exit (Bek. 44b).

Besides the uterus only the visible parts of the female generative organs ("reḥem"), there being many synonyms, are mentioned in the Bible. The Talmud mentions the following: *Mons veneris* (Hebr. "kaf tappuaḥ"; Yer. Yeb. 1–2); *vulva* ("'erwah"); *rima pudendorum* ("bet ha-setarim"; Niddah 66b); *vestibulum vaginæ* ("bet ḥiẓon"; *ib.* 41b); *orificium urethræ* ("lul"; *ib.* 17b); *hymen* ("betulim"); *ostium vaginæ* ("bet shinnayim"; *ib.* 46b); *vagina* ("bet toref," "bet ha-reḥem"; Shab. 64a); *septum vesico-vaginalis* ("gag prosdor"; Niddah 18a); *septum vagina-rectalis* ("karka prosdor"; *ib.*); *uterus* ("reḥem"; *ib.*); *canalis cervicis uteri* ("maḳor; *ib.* 41a); *cavum uteri* ("ḥeder" [*ib.* 17b]; "bet herayon" ['Ar. 7a]).

Embryology.

According to the Mosaic law (Lev. xii. 2–5), a woman after giving birth to a male child remained unclean for seven days thereafter; in the case of a female child, fourteen days. Then followed a period of purification—for a male thirty days, and for a female sixty-six days. According to the Mishnah, miscarriages fell under the same law, provided, however, the fetus ("shefir") was completely formed ("meruḳḳam") and its features were well differentiated ("mi-ẓorat adam"). Monstrosities and all fetuses not viable were exempt from the above-named law (Niddah iii.). This interpretation of the Biblical law served as an impetus to the Talmudists for the diligent study of embryology.

The esteem in which were held those who occupied themselves with this study is shown in the legend that King David devoted a great deal of his time to these investigations (Ber. 4a). R. Samuel, it is said, was able to tell the exact age of a fetus (Niddah 25b). The fetus, it was held, is completely formed at the end of the sixth week. Aba Saul, a grave-digger by occupation, but also an embryologist, describes an embryo at the end of the sixth week as follows: "Size, that of the locust; eyes are like two specks at some distance from each other, so are the nostrils; feet like two silken cords; mouth like a hair. . . . The soles are not well defined." He adds that the embryo should not be examined in water, but in oil, and only by sunlight (Niddah 25b). R. Samuel (*l.c.*) contended that it was impossible to differentiate the sex before the end of the fourth month, which, by the way, is the opinion of modern embryologists. At certain autopsies it was found that the male embryos were completely formed at the end of the forty-first day, and the female embryos at the end of the eighty-first day. The Rabbis contended that the autopsies had not been free from error (Niddah 30b). The soft parts are formed first, then the bones (Gen. R. xiv.). Monstrosities like cyclopia, monopsia, double back with double spinal column, and *artresia œsophagi* ("weshet aṭum"), etc., are mentioned (Niddah 23b, 24a, b).

The Bible identifies the blood with the soul (Gen. ix. 4). The Talmudists regard blood as the essential principle of life (Ḥul. 125a). The relation between strength and the development of muscles is mentioned in the Bible (Job xl. 16). The Talmudists noted the fact that the muscles change their form when in motion (Ḥul. 93a). Respiration is compared to burning. Expired air can not sustain life (Sanh. 77a). The life of all the organs of the body depends upon the heart (Yer. Ter. viii. 4). Each gland secretes a fluid peculiar to itself, although all the glands derive their material from the same source (Num. R. xv.). The difference in the structure of the teeth in herbivorous and carnivorous animals is noted (Ḥul. 59). Saliva, besides moistening the tongue, adds to the palatability of food (Num. R. xv.). The stomach performs a purely mechanical function, that of churning the food; it is compared to a mill. Digestion proper ("ikkul") is carried on in the intestines. The time occupied in digestion is not the same in all individuals. The end of the digestive period is made manifest by the return of a desire for food (Bek. 52b). Eating when the bowels are full is likened to the making of a fire in a stove from which the ashes have not been removed (*ib.* 55a). Normal defecation hastens digestion. Birds digest their food rapidly (Shab. 82a); dogs, slowly (Oh. xi. 7). The reasoning faculties are lodged in the brain (Yeb. 9a). The movements of the body depend upon the integrity of the spinal cord (Ḥul. 58). Rabbi Isaac holds that the liver elaborates blood (Shab. 82a).

Physiology.

There are numerous references to the influence of climate, customs, trade, etc., upon the development of the organism as a whole, and upon certain groups of muscles (Ab. R. N. xxxi.; Yeb. 103a; M. Ḳ. 25b).

The phenomena preceding the period of menstruation are described in detail (Niddah xi. 8). The menstrual fluid is considered by Rabbi Meïr as an extra nutritive material which is discharged periodically when of no use, but which is converted into milk during the period of lactation (*ib.*). Absence of menstruation indicates sterility. Fear and cold may arrest the flow (*ib.* 66).

That medicine was an integral part of the religion of Israel is made more evident from the pathological studies of the Rabbis than from any other branch of medical science. It is indeed remarkable that the Rabbis seem to have been the first to recognize practically what is at present the prevailing theory, namely, that the symptoms of all diseases are merely outward manifestations of internal changes in the tissues—a theory never advanced by their contemporaries, *e.g.*, Hippocrates and his disciples, and only vaguely hinted at by Galen ("De Locis Affectis," i., ch. ii.). Their pathological studies were a direct outgrowth of the law concerning the "flesh that is torn of beasts in the field," which becomes unfit ("ṭerefah") for food (Ex. xxii. 30 [A. V. 31]). Certain rules concerning this infection are enjoined upon those who come in contact with the flesh of an animal that "dieth of itself or is torn with beasts" (Lev. xxii. 8). The Talmudists went a step further, and declared that the word "unfit" included the flesh of animals afflicted with any disease which would have sooner or later caused the death of the animal (Ḥul. iii. 1).

Pathology.

In order, therefore, to determine the condition of the internal organs, each slaughtered animal was subjected to an autopsy; this is the practise even to-day. The pathological changes of the l[...] have been most diligently studied as to color, [...]sistency, cavities, and vegetable growths. Red[...] of the lungs indicates hyperemia (Ḥul. 47b[...] condition which is not fatal (*ib.* 46b); blue [...] light-green discoloration is not considered dan[...]ous (*ib.* 47b); black indicates that the object [...] begun to disintegrate ("laḳah"); and the pa[...] the lungs thus affected can not return to its [...]mal state. Bright yellow ("yaroḳ") is consid[...] the color indicative of the most fatal condition. [...] on inflating the lungs, it is found that air [...] not enter into a certain part of them ("oṭem[...] re'ah"), it is then important to find out whethe[...] obstruction is caused by pus or mucus ("mugla[...] the bronchi, which might have been expelled [...] coughing, or is due to thickening of the tissues. [...] the latter case the animal is unfit for food. Cas[...] degeneration ("re'ah she-yabeshah"), "in w[...] there is no blood and it crumbles under the n[...] makes the flesh of the animal unfit for food. [...]tening of the lung ("re'ah she-nitmasmesah") is f[...] In the case of an animal with collapsed lungs ("r[...] she-ẓameḳah") the following rule is given by [...] Talmud: if after they have been immersed in w[...] they can be inflated with air, the flesh of the an[...] is fit for food; if they can not be so inflated it is u[...] A pitcher-shaped cavity in the lung ("re'ah she-[...]pekah ke-ḳiton"), filled with fluid, renders the [...]mal unfit for food. An empty cavity ("re'ah [...] nimmoḳah") is not dangerous to life (*ib.*). [...] Rabbis speak of vegetable growths ("ẓemaḥim"[...] the lungs in connection with adhesions of the [...] to the thorax ("dofen"); and they describe se[...] forms, all of which are not considered dangero[...]

Perforation of the outer coat of the brain i[...] fatal; but the slightest perforation of the inner [...] is. Rabbi Jacob held that an injury of the s[...] cord is fatal; the editor of the Mishnah said t[...] is fatal only when the injury extends to more [...] one-half of its transverse diameter (Ḥul. iii. 1)[...] sheep that dragged its hind legs was diagnose[...] Rabbi Yemar as suffering from ischiagra ("[...]rona"); but Rabina contended that it was a para[...] due to the solution of continuity of the spinal [...] The sheep was killed, and the diagnosis of Ra[...] was corroborated (Ḥul. 51a). This is the only [...] on record in ancient literature where a diag[...] was made during life and was verified at a [...] mortem examination. Rabbi Levi saw one wh[...]fered from tremor of the head, and he remarked [...] the man was suffering from softening of the s[...] cord. Abaya said that such cases were not fata[...] the patients lost their reproductive functions (*i*[...]

Perforation of the heart is considered fatal. [...] other pathological changes of the heart are [...]tioned. A transverse division of the trachea i[...] considered fatal, provided it is less than one-ha[...] its circumference. Longitudinal wounds in [...] trachea heal quickly (*ib.* 45a, 54a, and 57b). [...] of substance is not considered fatal (*ib.* 18b). [...]foration of the esophagus is fatal, since the [...] may escape into the mediastinum (*ib.* 45b). [...]vulus is considered fatal (*ib.* 56b). Perforation o[...] stomach or of the intestines is fatal. Extirpati[...] the spleen in animals and in man is not consi[...]

l (Hul. 2). Rupture or wounding of the spleen onsidered fatal. Ablation of the uterus is men-ed and is not considered fatal (Bek. vi. 4). Atro- and abscess of the kidney are fatal (Ḥul. b). Accumulation of transparent fluid in the ıey is not fatal (*ib.* 53b).

he pathological changes in the liver mentioned in Talmud are: that in which the organ becomes and bloodless and "crumbles under the nails"; ess; and stone-like hardening. Extirpation of liver is not considered fatal if there is left intact part which surrounds the biliary duct and "that e from which the liver receives its vitality." ence of one testicle is mentioned, and the sub- is considered sterile (Bek. vi. 6). Hypertro- and atrophy of the testicles (*ib.* 40b), scrotal ia ("ruaḥ ba-ashakim"), and *elephantiasis scroti* sufferer being called "me'ushkan"; *ib.*) are also tioned. Various forms of hypospadias and epi-lias are described (Niddah 13a; Yeb. 76a). The ınah enumerates 140 pathological conditions h in the eyes of the Law make a man a "crip-" ("mum") and therefore unfit to perform any ious service in the Temple. Fifteen of these ribe various osteologic deformities of the head, e, and extremities (Bek. vii.). The rare cases of viduals having a tendency to hemorrhage are ed, and the fact that this affection is hereditary ted (Yeb. 64b).

ounds in different parts of the body, caused by rent weapons—sword, arrow, hammer, etc.—nentioned in the Bible (II Sam. ii. 23, iii. 27, iv. 6, . 14, xx. 10; Num. xxv. 8; Judges iii. 21, v. I Kings xxii. 34; II Chron. xxxv. 23; and often where). Inflammation and abscesses (Deut. lii. 27, 35), gangrene and putrid discharges (Ps. viii. 6; Prov. xii. 4, xiv. 30; II Macc. ix. 9) are referred to. Wounds were treated by the application of wine or oil, bandages or sutures (Isa. i. 5; Jer. viii. 22, xlvi. 11, li. 8; Deut. xxviii. 27). The sur-l operations mentioned in the Bible are those of CUMCISION and castration, the latter being pro-ed (Deut. xxiii. 1).

rgery.

uring the Talmudical period surgery attained gh degree of development. Many physicians ted themselves exclusively to it. Surgeons mmanim"; Sanh. 91b), when operating, used to a tunic over their dress (Kelim xxvi. 5). y used various surgical instruments (*ib.* xiii. 2). ajor operations the patients were given an an-etic or a sleeping-potion ("samme de-shinta"; . 83b). Venesection was extensively used upon healthy and the sick alike. Mar Samuel Yar-i went so far as to recommend its use once in y days (Shab. 129b). After the age of fifty section should be employed less frequently (Giṭ. It is not to be performed during inclement her; and a careful dietetic régime should be wed for some time after the operation (Shab.). Bleeding by means of leeches ("'aluḳah," ie shel mayim"; 'Ab. Zarah 12b) and by means of ing (the cup being called "ḳarna de-ummana"; . cliv. 2) is frequently mentioned. Dislocation arious joints ('Ab. Zarah 29), fractures, amputa-(Ker. 66a; Sem. 28; Shab. 66a), and trephining (Ket. 77b) are discussed in the Talmud. Artificial teeth, made of hard wood, gold, or silver, were used (Shab. 65a; Ned. 66b). Extirpation of the spleen was successfully performed upon man ('Ab. Zarah 44a). The following forms of castration are mentioned: *Amputatio membri*; *extirpatio testiculorum* (Deut. xxiii. 2 [A. V. 1]); subcutaneous stretching or cutting of the cord (Lev. xxii. 24; Bek. 39b); and obliteration of the testicle by means of gradual pressure. Intubation of the larynx was practised upon animals (the tube was called "ḳerumit shel ḳaneh"); and a plate ("ḥidduḳ shel ḳarweyah") was used in a case of loss of substance of the cranium. A uterine speculum was used (Niddah 66).

Operations.

The practise was adopted of freshening up the borders of old wounds in order that union might be effected (Ḥul. 77). The operation for imperforate anus in the new-born is described (Shab. 134b). Wounds exposed to air do not heal as readily as protected ones (Ḥul. 46). In an accident in which the abdominal viscera were protruding through a wound the reposition of the organs was effected automatically by frightening the patient, which caused the abdominal muscles to relax; after this the external wound was closed by sutures (Shab. 82a). Nasal polyps are said to cause *fetor ex ore* (Ket. 77). Crutches and various other orthopedic appliances are mentioned (Shab. 65a). Intestinal parasites and hydatids are frequently mentioned (Ḥul. 48a). Extraction of the fetus through an incision made in the abdomen was an operation known to the Talmudists (Niddah 40b). See BATHS, BATHING; CIRCUMCISION; MIDWIFE; MIRACLES; HEALTH LAWS.

BIBLIOGRAPHY: J. Bergel, *Die Medizin der Talmudisten*, Leipsic and Berlin, 1885; W. C. Bitting, *Biblical Medicine*, in *Tr. New York Medical Society*, 1891, viii. 367; F. Boerner and S. A. Wagner, *De Statu Medicinæ apud Veteros Ebræos*, Wittenberg, 1775; Brecher, *Der Aderlass im Talmud*, in *Prager Medizinische Wochenschrift*, 1896, pp. 228, 257; D. Carcassonne, *Essai Historique sur la Médecine des Hébreux Anciens et Modernes*, Montpellier, 1811; C. L. Craft, *Decas Theorematum ad Diætologam Biblicam Spectatitium*, Copenhagen, 1736; S. Csernowsky, *De Medicinæ apud Ebræos et Ægyptos Conditione*, Halle and Magdeburg, 1742; D. de Pomis, *De Medico Hebreo*, Venice, 1588; W. Ebstein, *Die Medizin im Alten Testament*, Stuttgart, 1901; C. E. Eschenbach, *Scripta Medico-Biblica*, Rostock, 1779; M. Fensdorf, *Ueber die Medizin der Alten Hebräer*, Bamberg, 1837; J. B. Friedrich, *Zur Bibel: Naturhistorische, Anthropologische, und Medicinische Fragmente*, Nuremberg, 1848; J. Jeoffroy, *Les Sciences Médicales chez Hébreux*, xxx. 697, 757, 769, Paris, 1880; Grünbaum, *Medycyna w Talmudzie. Pan. Towarz. Lek.* lxxx. 192, Warsaw, 1884; B. W. Gintzburger, *Disputatio Inauguralis qua Medicinam ex Talmudicis Illustratam*, Göttingen, 1743; Joachim Halpern (of Wilna), *Beiträge zur Gesch. der Talmudischen Chirurgie*, Breslau, 1869; J. M. B. Harden, *Notes on the Medicine of Moses*, in *Southern Medical and Surgical Journal*, iii. 257, Augusta, 1847; F. Hoffmann, *De Diætetica Sacræ Scripturæ Medicina*, in his *Opuscula Theol. Phys.-Med.* Halle, 1740; J. Hyrtl, *Das Arabische und Hebräische in der Anatomie*, Vienna, 1879; A. H. Israels, *Beiträge zur Talmudischen Medizin*, in *Janus*, ii. 330, 352, Breslau, 1847; idem, *De Keizersnede by Levenden, Volgens den Babylonischen Talmud*, Amsterdam, 1882; L. Kazenelson, *Anatomiya, Normalnaya i Patologicheskaya v Drevneyevreiskoi Pismennosti*, St. Petersburg, 1889; S. W. H. Kemper, *Biblical Medicine*, in *Indiana Journal of Medicine*, 1872-73, iii. 1, 47, 335; M. Levin, *Analecta Historica ad Medicinam Ebræorum*, Halle, 1798; S. Lizelius, *De Poetis Medicis Sacræ Scripturæ Interpretidus Commentatis*, Speyer, 1743; P. J. Müller, *Biblical Medicine*, Strasburg, 1785; J. H. Nebel, *Physiologicæ-Biblicæ Selecta Quadem Capita Breviter ac Strictim Illustrata*, Giessen, 1711; O. N. Nicolaus, *Meletema de Servis Josephi Medicis ad Gen. l. 1, 2*, Magdeburg, 1752; Oppler, *Einiges aus der Altjüdischen Medicin*, in *Deutsche Archiv für Medicinische Gesch.* iv. 62, Leipsic, 1881; G. L. Pasnoligo, *Della Condizione della Medica Scienza Presso il Popolo Ebreo*, n.d.; M. Pholis, *De Questione an Esau Fuerit Monstrum*, Wittenberg, 1669; I. M. Rabbinowicz, *La Médecine du Talmud*, Paris, 1880; Rittman, *Die Talmudische Medizin im Mittelalter*, in *Allg. Wiener Medicinische Zeitung*, 1868, xiii. 123; P. Schagen, *Specimen Anatomiæ Biblicæ*, Utrecht, 1750; J. D. Schleunitz, *Philologemata Medica, sive ad Medicinam et Res Medicas Pertinentia ex Ebrea et Huic Adfinibus Orientalibus Linguis Decerpta*, Halle and Magdeburg, 1758; J. J. Schmidt, *Biblischer Medicus*, Züllichau, 1743; J. H. Slevogtius, *Biblical Medicine*, Jena, 1699; C. D. Spivak, *Menstruation: A Summary of the Theories of the Ancients with Special Reference to the View Held by the Talmudists*, in *Medical Times*, Feb. 14, 1891; M. Steinschneider, *Schriften über Medicin in Bibel und Talmud und über Jüdische Aerzte*, in *Wiener Klinische Rundschau*, 1896; J. H. Walker, *On the State of Medical Art Among the Jews as Recorded in the Bible*, in *Midland Medical and Surgical Reporter*, ii. 163, 243, Worcester, 1830–1831; R. J. Wunderbar, *Biblisch-Talmudische Medizin*, 1857; Bumm, *Spuren der Griechischen Psychiatrie im Talmud*, 1901; Bennett, *Diseases of the Bible*, 1887; Burrell, *The Insane Kings of the Bible*, in *Am. Jour. of Insanity*, 1893, iv. 493; Bombaugh, *The Plagues and Pestilences of the Old Testament*, in *Johns Hopkins Medical Bulletin*, 1893, iv. 64; Carnault, *La Tuberculose Bovine et le Talmud*, in *Revue Scientifique*, 4th series, vol. xvii., Nos. 3, 75; Kotelman, *Die Geburtshilfe bei den Alten Hebräern*, Marburg, 1876; Ebstein, *Die Medizin im Neuen Testament und im Talmud*, Stuttgart, 1903; Ellis, *Biblical Obstetrics*, in *The Lancet*, i. 874, London, 1875; Preuss, *Der Arzt in Bibel und Talmud*, in *Virchow's Archiv*, vol. cxxxviii. 261; idem, *Materialien zur Geschichte der Alten Medizin: die Organe der Bauchhöhle nach Bibel und Talmud*, in *Allgemeine Medizinische Central-Zeitschrift*, 1898, pp. 489, 502, 514, 526; idem, *Die Erkrankungen der Haut*, ib. 1903, pp. 431, 455, 474; idem, *Der Tote und Seine Bestattung*, ib. 1901, Nos. 25, 26, 27; idem, *Die Männliche Genitalien und Ihre Krankheiten nach Bibel und Talmud*, in *Wiener Medizinische Wochenschrift*, 1898, pp. 570, 618, 662, 709, 1194, 1239; idem, *Biblisch-Talmudische Pathologie und Therapie*, in *Zeit. für Medizin*, xlv. 457; idem, *Chirurgisches in Bibel und Talmud*, in *Deutsche Zeit. für Chirurgie*, lix. 507; Ravitzki, *Ueber die Lehre der Superfœtatio und der Entstehungs-Ursache die Fœtus Compressus im Talmud*, in *Janus*, vi. 410, 461, 542; Rosenbaum, *Une Conference Contradictoire, Religieuse et Scientifique sur l'Anatomie et Physiologie des Organes Genitaux de la Femme à l'Ecole de Rami Fils de Samuel et de Rabbi Yitshac Fils de Rabbi Yehoudou, à la Fin du Deuxième Siècle*, Paris, 1901; Schapiro, *Obstetrique des Anciens Hébreux d'Après la Bible et le Talmud, Comparée avec la Tocologie Gréco-Romain*, in *La France Médicale*, 1904; idem, *Connaissance Medical de Mar Samuel*, in *R. E. J.* Paris, lxii., No. 83, p. 14; Pyasetski, *Medizina po Biblii i Talmudu*, St. Petersburg, 1903.

S. S. C. D. S.

——**In Post-Talmudic Times:** During the fifth and sixth centuries of the common era the sciences languished in the Orient owing in part to disturbed political conditions, to superstitions, and to the attention which was being paid to pseudo-sciences. The persecutions of the Jews under Honorius (in 404 and 419), Theodosius the Great (493), and Kobad in Persia (520) resulted in the promulgation of laws forbidding Jews to hold any office, to follow any handicraft or liberal art, or to practise medicine.

With the spread of Mohammedanism in the seventh century a great revival of the sciences took place in Asia Minor. The califs opened colleges which included medical schools at Bagdad, Kufah, and Bassora, and these were well equipped and were furnished with the best of teachers. Among both the teachers and the students were to be found many who bore Jewish names. Science then was free to all; but in 853 a law was promulgated in Bagdad which prohibited the Jews from teaching or studying medicine in any language other than Hebrew or Syriac. The Mohammedans, being able to fill all positions themselves, were no longer in need of the help of the Jews. The earliest Jewish physicians mentioned during the golden age under the Arabs were: Abu Ḥafṣah Yazid (*c.* 643), physician to the calif Omar, Mohammed's successor; MASARJAWAIH (Messer Jawait) in Bassora about 883, physician the calif Mu'awiyyah I., whom he induced to p cure translations of works written in foreign l guages, and who himself translated from the Syr into Arabic the pandects of Aaron the Archdeac upon medicinal plants and foods; Isḥaḳ ben Amr (d. 799; not to be confounded with the Kairw physician of the same name), who wrote a treatise poison; Sahl, called "Rabban al-Ṭabari," who li about 800 at Taberistan on the Caspian Sea, was eminent physician and mathematician, and transla into Arabic the "Almagest" of the Greek astro mer Ptolemy; his son ALI IBN SAHL IBN RABB AL-TABARI (ABU AL-ḤASAN), who lived at Irak ab 850, became a convert to Mohammedanism, and court physician to the califs Al-Mu'taṣim and Mutawakkil.

Harun al-Rashid (786–809) was the founder of university at Bagdad, the most flourishing insti tion of its time, possessing hospit a medical school, and holding m ical examinations. The professors cluded Joshua ben Nun (*c.* 800), a physician of h repute and translator, one of whose pupils was suf Ya'ḳub ibn Isḥaḳ (*c.* 850); much later HI ALLAH ABU AL-BARAKAT B. 'ALI B. MALKA, lived about 1150 and who pursued his studies un the greatest difficulties on account of the laws hibiting Jews from studying medicine (later he came a convert to Mohammedanism); Ibn Zakari (died at Aleppo 1190); Sa'ad al-Daulah, court p sician to the Mongolian khan Arghun (1284– when in Bagdad (killed in 1291 for not curing lord). The calif Ma'mun, Harun al-Rashid's (813–833), established the universities of Bassora Samarcand.

Bagdad.

After the beginning of the fourteenth century center of Mohammedan learning moved westw and no more Jewish physicians are met with in 'I after that date. The sciences followed the conq ing armies of the Arabs from Asia Minor thro Egypt and the Mediterranean countries of Afric Spain and southern France, to Sicily, and thenc Italy. Alexandria, Cairo, and Kairwan became seats of colleges with medical schools. At Kairw about 793 lived the Jewish physician Shammakh, poisoned the imam Idris by order of Harun al-Ras at Algiers, about 900, Isḥaḳ ibn 'Im court physician to the emir Ziy Allah II., and Isḥaḳ ibn 'Imran Younger, court physician to the Aghlabite emir, Ziyadat Allah 'Imran the Younger's successor was Isaac ben S mon ISRAELI (*c.* 832–932), who later became oc and physician to the Fatimite calif 'Ubaid Alla Mahdi at Kairwan. Israeli's works written in Ar were translated into Latin in 1087 by the monk stantine of Carthage, who claimed them as his o In 1515 they were reprinted in Latin in Ley under the title "Opera Omnia Isaci Judæi," the jects treated including fever, dietetics, urine, dr dropsy, therapeutics, and aliments; the last appeared in Hebrew under the title "Sefer Mis'adim." The Leyden edition contains not Israeli's works, but also those of other physic falsely attributed to Israeli (Steinschneider do

Egypt and Northern Africa.

if Israeli really existed). Israeli's pupil was Dunash ibn Tamim (Abu Sahl), also court physician (c. 950), who is said to have been a convert to Islam. Jewish physicians in Egypt were: Ephraim ibn al-Za'faran (d. 1068), celebrated through his library; Abu Sa'id ibn Ḥusain (Al-Ṭabib), about 1050; Abu Manṣur (c. 1125), one of the physicians of the calif Al-Ḥafiẓ; Nathanael Israeli (the Egyptian), at Cairo (c. 1150), court physician to the last Fatimite calif of Egypt and to the great Saladin; Abu al-Barakat (c. 1150); Abu al-Faḍa'il ibn al-Naḳid (d. 1189), a celebrated oculist; Abu al-Bayyan al-Mudawwar (d. 1184), also physician to Saladin, and David ben Solomon (1161–1241), connected with the hospital Al-Naṣiri in Cairo, both Karaite physicians; the Karaite Sadid b. Abi al-Bayyan (c. 1160); Abu Ja'far Joseph Nathanael Israel (c. 1175); and Abu al-Ma'ali, brother-in-law of Maimonides, also in the service of Saladin.

Maimonides.

In 1166 Maimonides himself (1135–1205) went to Egypt and settled in Fusṭaṭ. Born at Cordova, Spain, he left his native land on account of the disfranchisement of the Jews by the Mohammedan rulers. He became court physician to the sultan Saladin. Of the descendants of Maimonides the following were physicians: his son Abraham (1185–1254), his grandson David (1212–1300), also the two sons of the latter, Abraham Maimonides II. (1246–1310) and Solomon, all of whom held the office of nagid also. In Aleppo lived a pupil of Maimonides, Yusuf al-Sabti (d. 1226); while in Fez practised another pupil of his, Abu al-Ḥayyuj Yusuf. In Cairo lived 'Imran al-Isra'ili (1165–1239); Samuel Abu Naṣr ibn 'Abbas (c. 1165); Abu al-Ḥasan (d. 1251); Jacob b. Isaac (c. 1250); the Karaite Solomon Cohen and Al-Asad al-Maḥalli (about the end of the twelfth century); Ibn Abi al-Ḥasan al-Barkamani and the pharmacologist Abu al-Muna al-Kuhin al-'Aṭṭar (c. 1325); in Egypt, the encyclopedist Abu Manṣur al-Haruni (c. 1375); at Algiers, Simon ben Ẓemaḥ Duran (1360–1444); Samuel and his son Jacob (c. 1425); the Samaritan Abu Sa'id al-'Afif (c. 1450); Solomon ben Joseph (c. 1481), nagid of Egypt, and physician to the sultan Al-Malik al-Ashraf.

Spain.

When the Arabs crossed the Straits of Gibraltar the influx of culture from Arabia into Spain was important. Here again the califs supported the universities, as those of Cordova, Seville, and Toledo, and again Jewish physicians are found, *e.g.*: Hasdai Abu Yusuf ibn Shaprut (915–970), who lived in Cordova, was appointed physician to 'Abd al-Rahman III., and became prime minister to that calif, for whom he translated the works of Dioscorides into Arabic; Harun at Cordova (c. 975); Amram ben Isaac (d. 997) at Toledo; Jonah (Abu al-Walid Merwan ibn Janaḥ; at Cordova 995–1045). The physician Abu Bekr Mohammed ben Merwan ibn Zuhr (d. 1031 at Talabira) and his grandson, the celebrated Abu Merwan ibn Zuhr, who lived in Bagdad, Cairo, and Spain, are considered by many to have been Jews, but this has been frequently denied, and no positive proof of their Jewish descent has been presented. Abu Merwan was the most important physician of his time, opposing the Arabic physician Avicenna (980–1037), who in his "Canon" gave the "rules of medicine," superseding the works of Hippocrates and Galen, although he himself adopted the fundamental ideas of these two great physicians. Other Jewish physicians of note were: Judah ha-Levi (b. 1085); Sulaiman ibn al-Mu'allim, court physician to the calif Ali at Seville (1106–45); Abraham ibn Ezra (1092–1167) at Toledo; Maimonides, mentioned above; at Randa, Elias ibn al-Mudawwar (c. 1150); in Toledo, Jacob; in Aragon, Joseph Constantin; in Barcelona, Judah ben Isaac, Judah ben Joseph ibn al-Fakhkhar, court physician to Ferdinand III.; in Saragossa, Baḥiel ben Moses and his brother Solomon Baḥiel (c. 1225); in Madrid, Solomon ben David; in Gerona, Moses b. Naḥman (1194–1267) and Shem-Ṭob ben Isaac of Tortosa (1206–66). About 1250 lived Judah Moria; Ibrahim ben Sahl; Nathanael ben Joseph al-Maliḥ; Samuel Benveniste; Jacob ben Shushan; Joseph ibn Sason (d. at Toledo 1336); Abner of Burgos (1270–1348), a convert to Christianity; Samuel Ibn Waḳar (d. c. 1333), physician to King Alfonso XI.; Todros Abulafia; Abraham ben David Caslari (d. 1349); Vidal Crescas de Caslar (c. 1327); Eliezer Cohen ibn Ardot; Nissim ben Reuben Gerundi (at Barcelona 1340–80); Abraham ibn Machir; Abraham ibn Zarzal (d. at Toledo 1362); Shem-Ṭob ben Jacob; Meïr Alguadez (d. about 1415); Joseph ibn Vives (Joseph al-Lorqui); Solomon ben Abraham ibn Daud; Jacob of Toledo; Todros ibn Davor; Isaac b. Solomon; Abraham of Lerida, oculist to John II. of Aragon (c. 1470); in Catalonia, Gallab (Galled).

The Arabs had lost Spain forever, and the intolerance of the Christian rulers forced many Jewish physicians to leave that country. In 1335 the synod of Salamanca had declared that the Jewish physicians offered their services only to kill as many Christians as possible (Döllinger, "Die Juden in Europa," in "Akademische Vorträge"). In 1412 John II. prohibited Jews from practising in Spain. Some immigrated into France, *e.g.*, Judah ibn Tibbon, Joseph ben Isaac ben Ḳimḥi, Isaac ben Shem-Ṭob, Solomon ben Joseph ben Ayyub; some into Algiers, as Simon bar Ẓemaḥ Duran; and others into Italy, as Joshua ben Joseph Ibn Vives al-Lorqui (Hieronymus de Santa Fé) about 1400.

Portugal.

In Portugal lived Gedaliah ibn Yaḥya the Elder (c. 1300), physician to King Diniz; Solomon ben Moses Solomon; Moses, the physician to Ferdinand I. and John I.; Profiat Duran (c. 1400; he emigrated to Palestine); at Lisbon, Gedaliah ibn Yaḥya the Younger, physician to Alfonso V. (c. 1476; emigrated to Turkey); Joseph and Rodriquez, physicians to John II. of Portugal (1481–90), who were members of the commission appointed to examine Columbus' plans.

At the time the Jewish Arabic physicians were practising in Egypt, they are found in Sicily also. Shabbethai ben Abraham ben Joel (Donnolo) (913–982), who wrote a small work on pharmacology, which has been republished by Steinschneider, lived in Oria. From Sicily they came to southern Italy and settled in Salerno. The ancient University of Salerno is said to have been founded by the Benedictine monks of Monte Cassino in the sixth century, the monks being priests and physicians, as the rabbis of old. But it was not until the ninth century that it rose to prominence and became for the Occident what Bagdad had been for the Orient, the leading medical school. In 848 Joseph taught there, and in 855 Joshua, both Jewish physicians. In the eleventh century lectures are said to have been delivered in Greek, Arabic, Hebrew (with Elinus as teacher), and Latin. The medical school of Salerno became celebrated under the name of "Civitas Hippocratica." Elinus' successor as teacher of Hebrew was Copho, the editor of the "Compendium Salernitanum," the first medical encyclopedia. It is not known positively that both were Jews—Steinschneider thinks they were not—but tradition ascribes to them a Jewish origin, as it does to Copho II. (who wrote a book on the "Anatomica Porci"—which certainly makes the ascription dubious, dedicating it to Robert, eldest son of William the Conqueror). He was followed by Hillel ben Samuel of Verona (1220–95), who translated into Hebrew Brunó's work on surgery, known only under the title "Chirurgia Bruni ex Latina in Hebræam Translata."

Italy.

From Salerno the Jewish physicians can be traced through Italy. From this school proceeded: Hananeel of Amalfi; Abu al-Hakim of Turin; and FARAJ BEN SALIM (Faragut), who lived in Salerno about 1250. The last-named was physician to Charles of Anjou, King of Sicily, and was one of the first physicians who translated—not into Hebrew, but into Latin. Other physicians of note were: in Rome, Nathan ha-Me'ati, a noted translator, who rendered the "Canon" of Avicenna into Hebrew in 1279; Isaac, the court physician of Pope Boniface VIII.; Zerahiah ben Isaac ben Shealtiel of Barcelona (*c.* 1275); several members of the Anaw family (Benjamin, Abraham, Judah, Zedekiah, Jekuthiel, Menahem Rofe [about the fourteenth century]); Manuele and Angelus Manuele, physicians to Boniface IX.; Judah ben Solomon Nathan (En Bongodos); and Moses ben Isaac (Gajo) of Rieti (1388–1460); at Naples, Samuel ben Jacob of Capua, court physician to Charles II., and Isaac, court physician to King Robert of Anjou; at Palermo, David; at Verona, Michael ben Abraham; at Padua, Gentili da Foligno (died of the plague 1348); at Venice, Leo (*c.* 1330), and the following members of the Astruc family: Judah Solomon, Isaac Solomon, Abraham Solomon, Jacob Rofe, and many others.

As the school of Salerno grew in importance it was able to rely on its own pupils for teachers, and could, as Bagdad had done before it, discard Jewish assistance. The connection of the Jews with its further development diminished; in later years they did not exercise a great influence on the history of medicine in Italy, and their rôle became insignificant.

While the University of Salerno was flourishing, certain Jewish schools, where medicine also was taught, are said to have existed in the south of France. About the year 1000 Rabbi Abon was principal of the Jewish school at Narbonne; and one of his pupils founded the Jewish medical school at Montpellier (*c.* 1025). Independent of these unimportant schools, however, were the beginnings of the great universities of France—Paris, Narbonne, and Montpellier—which soon were to compete with Salerno. In Paris, always a seat of Orthodox Christian theology, a few Jewish physicians are met with at the end of the thirteenth century: Copin and Moses, Rabbi Isaac and his son Vital. In 1301 this school was closed to the Jews. In Montpellier, where the earliest professors are said to have taught at first in Arabic and Hebrew, the use of Latin was introduced in the twelfth century only, when the fame of that university was at its zenith. Among the teachers and pupils were: Isaac ben Abraham; his pupil Judah, whose pupil was Moses ben Naḥman; Jacob ha-Ḳaṭon, who was dean of the medical faculty; Meshullam the physician (1043–1108), a contemporary of Rashi; Samuel ibn Tibbon, the well-known translator; Jacob ben Abba Mari of Marseilles, later court physician to the German emperor Frederick II. at Naples; Judah ben Samuel ibn Tibbon (1120–1190), Moses ibn Tibbon (1230–85), and Jacob ben Machir ibn Tibbon, called Profatius Judæus, dean of the medical faculty about 1306 (this family produced three generations of eminent physicians; see IBN TIBBON); and Abraham ABIGDOR (b. 1350).

France.

Montpellier.

As at Bagdad and Salerno, so at Montpellier laws were promulgated against the Jews as teachers and practitioners of medicine, *e.g.*, in the edict of Count William in 1180; of the Council of Béziers in 1246, and of Alby in 1254. In 1293 a law was enacted punishing with three months' imprisonment Christian patients who accepted treatment from Jewish physicians. Philip of Arlois expelled Jewish physicians altogether from Montpellier in 1306. At the school of Marseilles were Shem-Ṭob ben Isaac of Tortosa (1206–66) and his son Abraham b. Shem-Ṭob. In southern France practised also Isḥanan Yarḥuni, Nathan ben Samuel, and the oculist Abraham of Aragon at Toulouse; in Narbonne, David CASLARI (*c.* 1275); at Avignon, Israel CASLARI (*c.* 1325). The councils of Avignon (1326 and 1337) and that of Rouergue also declared against Jewish physicians.

In 1350 the Jews were permitted to return to France; but a law was passed whereby only graduated and licensed physicians could practise. Again some names of Jewish doctors, especially as court physicians, are to be found, *e.g.*: Samuel and Meshullam ben Abigdor again at Montpellier; Elias of Arles (*c.* 1407) at Valence; Jacob Lunel and the surgeon Dolan Bellan at Carcassonne; Nathan Tauros (*c.* 1446) at Tarascon; Jekuthiel Judah ben Solomon and MOSES BEN JOSHUA (Maestre Vidal Blasom; died after 1362) at Narbonne; Crescas Salannas, Ḥayyim Bendig, Abraham Abigdor (*c.* 1402), Bendig of Caneto, Bellanti (*c.* 1415), Solomon Mordecai (*c.* 1431), Moses Carcassonne (*c.* 1468), all at Arles; Abraham ben Solomon and Abraham Astruc (*c.* 1446) of St. Maxim; Cohen (*c.* 1446) at Marseilles ("Revue des Etudes Juives," April and June, 1904, pp. 265 *et seq.*).

Recall of the Jews to France.

From France the Jewish physicians passed into Belgium, where in the fourteenth century are found Abraham le Mirre, Magister Sause, Lyon, Ely, Isaac of Amessi, and Jacob of Chambery.

In England at this time only three Jewish physi- ans call for mention: the young physician who as the last victim of the massacre at Lynn in 1190; aac Medicus of London (Jacobs, "The Jews of ngevin England," pp. 114, 340, London, 1893); and braham Motun of London (1260–90).

In Germany the influence of Jewish physicians at is time was small. Harun al-Rashid's great con- mporary was Charlemagne, in whose dominion are said to have practised the physi- cians Meshullam ben Kalonymus, Jo- seph ben Gorion, Moses ben Judah, odros of Narbonne, and Joseph ha-Levi. Under ouis the Bald a certain Zedekiah was court phy- cian. They were probably from the Orient. any Jews were living in Germany, a number of hom had migrated from Spain and France; but the niversities were founded comparatively late, and ey were not open to Jews. The Jews therefore udied Talmud and Cabala, and took no part in the naissance of science. Horowitz says that there are records of the Frankfort community before 1241; nd this is the most important German community. hat there must have existed Jewish physicians is own by the decree of the Council of Vienna of 267 forbidding Jews to treat Christian patients. uring the ravages of the plague in 1348 and 1349 ewish physicians were accused of having poisoned e wells; and at Strasburg a Jewish surgeon named alavignus was executed in 1348 for an alleged ime of this nature. The Jewish physicians of is period included the following: Jacob of Stras- urg at Frankfort (*c.* 1378); Baruch (*c.* 1390); the city hysician Solomon Pletsch of Ratisbon (1394), who ceived as stipend 36 florins and six yards of cloth nd was required to treat the servants of the city ouncil and the sick Jews; his successor, Isaac Fried- ch, who received only 20 florins; in Speyer, Lem- elin; in Schweidnitz, Abraham; in Bohemia, Simon; the Palatinate, Godliep; at Basel, Jossel, who held e office of city physician at an annual stipend of 5 silver pounds; Gutleben, his successor, who re- eived only 18 pounds; at Würzburg, Seligmann (*c.* 407), physician to Bishop John I.; his successor, ohn II., permitted a woman named Sarah to practise edicine in the bishopric of Würzburg, who, with e Jewess Zerlin (*c.* 1475), oculist at Frankfort-on- e-Main, was the earliest Jewish woman physician Germany of whom there is record.

Germany.

In addition to those above mentioned there were: Tirol, Rubein (*c.* 1432); in Graz, Niklas Unger . 1439); in Würzburg, Heylmann (*c.* 1450); Jacob en Jehiel Loans, physician to the emperor Frederick II. (*c.* 1450), who, with Obadiah Sforno, was Hebrew eacher of Reuchlin; Michael, surgeon to Frederick II.; at Frankfort, Solomon of Zynonge (*c.* 1450); is son Joseph (*c.* 1500); and Moses of Aschaffen- urg.

In the opening years of the sixteenth century per- ecutions of the Jewish physicians began. In 1509 ppeared Victor of Carben's "Opus Aureum ac Novum," the third part of which treats of Jewish physicians. In 1505 Lorenz of Bibra prohibited Jews from practising in Würzburg (the edict was eenacted in 1549). Up to 1517 the physicians who wished to practise in Vienna had to acknowledge under oath their belief in the "immaculate conception."

In 1422 Pope Martin V. in a bull exhorted all Christians to treat the Jews with kindness, and permitted the latter to practise medicine. But at the end of the fourteenth and at the beginning of the fifteenth century Jewish physicians found the greatest difficulty in practising medicine. Papal decrees and Church councils (as at Basel, 1434) decided against them. The Arabian influence in southern Europe had disappeared.

Hippocrates and Galen ruled supreme in the medical world up to the thirteenth century. The Arab physician Avicenna (980–1037) wrote his celebrated "Canon," which work took rank next to the writings of Hippocrates and Galen. But their works were translated into Arabic, a language which, in Europe, was known only to the Jews, who retranslated them into Hebrew and Latin, and thus held the key to medical science. Learning from these great scholars, the Jewish teachers and physicians wrote works of their own. They excelled in surgery and medicine (including ophthalmology), in therapeutics, pharmacology, and toxicology. The connection of the Jews with the drug-trade of the East helped them to contribute also to a practical knowledge of pharmacology at a time when every apothecary posed as a doctor; but with these branches of the true science of medicine there was during the first millennium of the common era combined also a knowledge of pseudo-science, astrology, and Cabala. Superstition was still an important factor. Against these pseudo-sciences Maimonides wrote. Astrology was to him not based on science, but on superstition; and in his works he warns against its use.

Retrospect from 622 to 1492.

——**In Modern Times:** Human anatomy, the basis of all medicine, had not been studied scientifically by the physicians of the Talmud (they seem only to have boiled human bodies as the physicians of other countries had done, and, counting the bones, to have come to erroneous conclusions), by Hippocrates, by Galen (who used monkeys for his subjects), by Avicenna, or by their respective followers. The Jewish and Mohammedan religions and the Christian Church were all opposed to a desecration of the human body such as proper anatomical investigations would have required. The German emperor Frederick II. (1212–56) permitted dissection; but Pope Boniface VIII. prohibited it.

Luigi Mondino de' Luzzi, professor at Bologna (d. there 1326), dissected three female bodies. From that time anatomy received, with little interruption, the attention it deserved, and medicine, from being a more or less pseudo-science, commenced to be a real science, although half a millennium had still to pass before it was entirely liberated from superstition.

While the popes, such as Eugenius IV., Nicholas V., Calixtus III., and the temporal sovereigns promulgated decrees against the Jews, they still employed Jewish physicians themselves. Many of these Jews became converts to Christianity, among them Josiah Lorki of Spain, physician to Benedict XIII.

Josiah took the name of "Hieronymus de Santa Fé," and became a great enemy of his former coreligionists, who gave him the name "the Calumniator." He persecuted especially Jewish physicians and apothecaries.

Italy.

There were, however, some important Jewish physicians in Italy, namely: Elijah Delmedigo (1460–97), professor at Padua and Florence; Obadiah Elias ben Judah at Tivoli; Isaac d'Albadi (1450) at Barletta; Joseph ha-Levi of Naples; Messer Leon of Mantua; his son Messer David of Naples; Judah (Laudadeus) de Blanis at Perugia (*c.* 1520); Abraham de Balmes (d. 1523) at Padua; Solomon Vidal of Venice at Corfu; Vidal Balso at Reggio; Vitale (*c.* 1550) and Bonajuto (*c.* 1610) Alatino at Spoleto; and Teodoro de Sacerdoti at the court of Julius III. Popes Paul II. and Alexander VI. favored Jewish physicians through privileges, *e.g.*, Samuel Ẓarfati and Isaac Ẓarfati (*c.* 1530), physicians to Pope Clement VII., whom Isaac saved from burial alive; Joseph ha-Kohen, physician to the doge Andrea Dorea of Venice (*c.* 1540); Obadiah Sforno (d. 1550 at Bologna), the Hebrew teacher of Reuchlin; Judah ibn Yaḥya at Bologna; Benjamin, also at Bologna; Raphael at Sarzena. Several important physicians were included in the Portaleone family, *e.g.*, Benjamin at Naples, his grandson David of Pavia, his great-grandson Abraham (1542–1612) at Mantua, and Isaac Cohen at Sienna. From these names it may be seen that while Jewish physicians were more or less prohibited by the popes from practising in the east of Europe, in Italy they flourished.

Bonet de Lates of Provence, when the Jews were expelled from that district in 1498, went to Rome as physician to Pope Leo X. He is well known also through the part he took during the Pfefferkorn persecutions. From Spain emigrated Judah Abravanel and Jacob Mantino. Judah Abravanel (Leo Hebræus) was minister at the court of Ferdinand and Isabella; expelled from Spain in 1492, he went to Italy. His brother lived as physician in Ferrara about 1549. Jacob Mantino settled in Rome as court physician to Pope Paul III. He acted also as ambassador of Charles V. at Venice. Paul IV. (1558) was a great persecutor of the Jews, enacting laws against them, some of which were repealed only in the nineteenth century, and on account of which many Jews emigrated to Turkey. During this period lived Juan Rodrigo de Castel-Branco, surnamed "Amatus Lusitanus" (1511–68), at Ancona and Salonica; David d'Ascoli, who defended the Jewish physicians in an essay published at Strasburg in 1559; David de Pomis (b. 1525 at Spoleto; d. at Venice 1588), also a great defender of his colleagues ("De Medico Hebræo Enarratio Apologica," Vienna, 1588). These were succeeded by the following: Moses ben Samuel Cases (*c.* 1600); Kalonymus ben Judah (*c.* 1575), Joseph Ḥameẓ, and Jacob Lombroso at Venice; Samuel Meldola at Mantua; David Ḥayyim Luria and three Cantarinis at Padua (Kalonymus, 1593–1631; Isaac Ḥayyim, 1644–1723; Judah, 1650–94); Ezekiel de Castro at Verona; Moses ben Jacob Cordovero at Leghorn; Jacob ben Isaac Zahalun at Ferrara, celebrated through his "Oẓar Ḥayyim" ("Thesaurus Vitæ") at Veni[ce] (1683); Hananiah ben Menahem Cases at Florence (1700); Isaac Cardoso, emigrated to Italy from Spai[n] where he had lived as a Marano; Manuele di Cesen[a] physician to Pope Sixtus V.

To the eighteenth century belong: Shabbethai Vi[ta] Marini of Padua; Isaac Lampronti (d. 1756); Isa[ac] Borgo; Mordecai Zahalun; Jacob Heilprin; Aar[on] Cases (d. 1767); Israel Gedaliah Cases (d. 1793), a[ll] of Ferrara; Solomon Levi and Isaac Levi Vali, [of] Verona; at Mantua, the Konia family: Josepl[h], Solomon, Moses Benjamin, Wolf, and Israel; [at] Leghorn, Isaac Foa, known also as a printer; Elia[s] Concile; Adam and his sons Jacob and Azaria[h] Ḥayyim Bondi; at Friaul, Isaac Luzzatto, 173[0]–1803; his brother Ephraim (b. 1729), who practise[d] for more than thirty years in London, and die[d] (1799) while traveling in Lausanne; Graziado Ne[ppi] (1759–1836), rabbi and physician at Cento, wh[o] belonged to the great French Sanhedrin of 1806.

France.

In France are to be found very few Jewish phys[i]cians during this period, as unbaptized Jews we[re] allowed only in papal Avignon. Pierre de Notre Dame (a baptize[d] Jew) at Arles (1500); Joseph Colon a[t] Perries; Mordecai Nathan and Joseph de Noves a[t] Avignon; Elias Montalto (d. at Paris 1615), cou[rt] physician to Maria de Medici, by whose order hi[s] body was embalmed and sent to Holland for buria[l] in a Jewish cemetery; his son Isaac, at Paris; a[t] Bordeaux, John Baptist de Silva (1686–1742), wh[o] had the best consulting practise in Europe, and wa[s] physician to Louis XIV., by whom he was knighted; at Nancy, Isaac Assur and Jacob Beer (*c.* 1775).

Though Jewish physicians were not allowed t[o] practise in France, their skill was so well know[n] that Francis I. (1515–47) during a severe sicknes[s] asked the Emperor of Germany for a Jewish physi[ci]an. When one arrived the king, thinking he was [a] Christian, sent him back. The king then asked th[e] Sultan of Turkey for another Jewish physician, wh[o] cured him (Cabanis, "Révolution de la Médecine," p. 128, Brussels, 1844).

In the Turkish Dominions.

While the Mohammedans lost Spain, they capture[d] Constantinople (1453), and Jewish physicians wer[e] allowed to practise in Turkey, as i[n] the other Mohammedan possessions. From Spain, Portugal, Italy, an[d] France Jews emigrated to Turkey. Among them were the following: i[n] Constantinople, Solomon Almoli (*c.* 1517); Josepl[h] Hamon; his son Moses (1490–1567), physician to Su[laiman] the Magnificent; and his grandson Josepl[h] (d. 1578); Ibn Yaḥya; Abraham ha-Levi ibn Migas[;] Abraham Nahmias; Leo Siaa (*c.* 1636); Israel Co[negliano] (*c.* 1680); Ephraim Penseri; Abraham be[n] Yaish; Abraham Samuel Solomon; and Isaac Jabe[z] (*c.* 1700); at Salonica, Samuel Uzziel (*c.* 1550); Abra[ham] Cohen (*c.* 1700); at Jerusalem, Elijah of Fer[r]ara (*c.* 1460); David ibn Shoshan, head of th[e] Sephardic yeshibah in 1552; Jacob ibn Amram[;] Jacob Aboab; and Samuel ha-Levi (*c.* 1625); th[e] physician Jacob Ḥayyim Ẓemaḥ was chief rabbi i[n] 1645. In Corfu lived Samuel Valerio (*c.* 1550)[;] in Zante, Jacob ben Uzziel (*c.* 1600); Abraha[m] Cohen (1670–1722).

In the Netherlands, which during this period was mostly under Spanish rule, Jewish physicians were few: Abraham ZACUTO (Zacutus Lusitanus), an emigrant from Portugal about 1600; at Amsterdam the BUENO family (Abraham, Ephraim Hezekiah, Jacob, Joseph, and Solomon); Balthazar de CASTRO (1620–87); somewhat later Joseph Israel MENDES; Samuel de Silva; Samuel Jeshurun; and Samuel de Mercado (*c.* 1650); Samuel de Misa (*c.* 1725); Johanan van Embden and Naphtali Herz (*c.* 1750).

In the Netherlands and England.

In England during this period there were very few Jewish physicians, *e.g.*, Elias Sabot (*c.* 1410); Rodrigo LOPEZ (b. 1525 in Portugal), court physician to Queen Elizabth 1580, for attempting to poison whom he was executed in 1594. When Cromwell permitted the Jews to settle openly in England there immigrated thither Abraham de Mercado about 1655; Joseph MENDES Bravo about 1675; Ephraim Isaac Abendana, in Cambridge and Oxford (d. 1710), and his brother Jacob (1630–95); David Nieto, in London (*c.* 1710); Jacob de Castro Sarmento, in London (1692–1762); Fernando Mendez (d. 1724); Isaac de Sequera Samuda (b. 1721); Israel Lyons (1739–75); Samuel Nunez (*c.* 1750); Joseph Hart Myers (1758–1823); Abraham Nonski (*c.* 1785; writer on vaccination); the three Schombergs (Isaac, d. 1781; Meïr Löw, d. 1761; and Ralph, d. 1792); Isaac Henriques Sequera (1738–1816); Abraham van Oven (d. 1778); Joshua van Oven (1766–1838); Solomon de Leon (*c.* 1775); George Gompertz Levisohn (d. 1797); Elias Friedberg; and a Doctor Jeremias (*c.* 1775).

While before 1500 there had been very few Jewish physicians in the German-speaking countries, in the later centuries many were to be found, among whom were especially the under-mentioned—in Frankfort-on-the-Main: Joseph bar Ephraim Levi (d. 1532); Abraham ben Joseph Levi (d. 1581); Jacob ben Samuel and Aaron (*c.* 1600); Shelomoh (d. about 1631); his son Löw Leo Shelomoh; Isaac Heln (d. 1654); Joseph Solomon DELMEDIGO (b. 1591 at Candia; practised in Candia, Cairo, Lithuania, Hamburg, Amsterdam, Frankfort-on-the-Main, Worms, and Prague, where he died 1655); his son-in-law Solomon BING (b. about 1615); Jonas ben Moses BONN; Abraham ben Isaac Wallach; Leo Simon; Abraham Heln (*c.* 1650); Benjamin Levi BUCHSBAUM (1645–1715); his sons Gutman Wolf (1678–1770) and Lipman (b. 1677); Amshel Gutman (d. 1743), son of Gutman Wolf; Issachar Bär Liebman (d. 1753); Anselm Schloss Beifuss (d. 1793); and Adolf Worms (d. 1812). In Hamburg are to be mentioned: Rodrigo de CASTRO (1550–1627), an eminent gynecologist; his sons Benedict de CASTRO (1597–1684), court physician to Queen Christina of Sweden, and Daniel (Andreas) de CASTRO (b. 1599), court physician to King Christian IV. of Denmark; Jacob ROSALES, who practised in Hamburg from 1637 to 1645; and Benjamin ben Immanuel Musaphia (1606–75). At Schaffhausen lived the physician David (*c.* 1550); at Mühlheim, Solomon ben Boaz; at Colmar and Rappoltsweiler, Judah Carmoly (1700–85); at Colmar, Anshel Meyer (*c.* 1750); at Coblenz, Emanuel Wallich (*c.* 1750); at Bingen, Abraham Bing (*c.* 1550), father of Solomon Bing of Hamburg; at Mayence, Selkeles Grotwahl (*c.* 1675) and his son Meier; Lippmann Levi and Phoebus Cohen (*c.* 1775); at Bonn (also at Neuwied), Benjamin Croneburg (*c.* 1750); Wolf and his two sons Heinrich and Solomon (also at Düren); at Düsseldorf, Gottschalk Lazarus van Geldern (1726–95) and his son Joseph (1765–96), Heine's grandfather; at Cologne, Naphtali ben Joseph Levi (*c.* 1625); at Metz, Isaac (*c.* 1650); Naphtali Herz; Solomon ben Baruch; Mayer and Isaac Wallich (*c.* 1700); Jacob Wallich; Marcus Cosman Gompertz Wolf; and Enoch Levin (*c.* 1750); the two brothers Willstadt (*c.* 1775); Elkan Isaac Wolf; and Jacob Aronsohn (*c.* 1790); at Hanover, Meier Cohen and Jacob Marx (*c.* 1775); at Bamberg, Adalbert Friedrich Markus (1753–1816). In the principalities of the Hapsburg family were only a few Jewish physicians; at Innsbruck, Lazarus (*c.* 1560); at Vienna, Isaac (Günzburg?) and his son Judah Löb Winckler (*c.* 1625; both left Vienna 1670 and settled in Posen); Joseph Oesterreicher (1756–1832). At Prague were: Isaac ben Joshua (*c.* 1550); Abraham KISCH (1720–1803); Jonas Mischel JEITELES (1735–1806) and his son Benedict (1762–1813); at Berlin, LIPPOLD (*c.* 1535), court physician to the elector Joachim II.; Hector, executed 1573 for having poisoned his master; Löbel (*c.* 1693); the dentist Veit Abraham (*c.* 1699); Marcus Eliezer BLOCH (1723–99); Aaron Solomon GUMPERZ (1723–69); Markus HERZ (1747–1803), husband of Henriette Herz; Georg Levison (d. 1797); at Königsberg, Isaac May and Michael Abraham (*c.* 1550); at Breslau, Zadok (*c.* 1775); at Lissa, Mordecaï Rofe.

Germany.

Although at the beginning of the eighteenth century conditions in Germany were not favorable for Jewish physicians, at the middle and end of the same century most of the Jewish practitioners received degrees from German universities. In 1700 the universities of Rostock and Wittenberg counseled Christians against employing Jewish physicians, who, they declared, were incompetent (meaning that they had not received a university education). In 1725 King Frederick William I. of Prussia prohibited Jews not having diplomas from practising medicine, and in 1745 appeared at Frankfort a book by Johann Helfrich Pfeil exposing the ignorance of Jewish physicians.

Medical Education of German Jews.

When the kings of Poland permitted Jews to settle in some parts of their dominions, physicians appeared there also. At Cracow lived Ezekiel (*c.* 1503); Isaac Jacob (d. about 1510), physician to King Sigismund I.; Solomon ben Nathan ASHKENAZI (1520–1602), physician to Sigismund II. and to the sultan Sulaiman II.; Solomon Luria in Lublin; Tobias COHN (1652–1729), who practised in Poland, Adrianople, Constantinople, and Jerusalem, and was court physician to five Turkish sultans; Jonas Casal (*c.* 1675), physician to John Sobieski; Philipp Lubelski at Cracow (1788–1879); Elias Pinschow (*c.* 1775); at Thorn, Morgenstern (*c.* 1567); at Posen, the Wincklers (the father Leo [Judah Löb] emigrated from Vienna about 1670); his sons Jacob and Isaac and his grandson Wolf, all four important physicians and leaders of the community; Levi Elias HIRSCHEL (1741–72).

In Poland.

In Moscow practised Magister Anton (Ehrenstein). The first Jewish physician in that city probably came from Rome. He was court physician under Ivan III. and was executed in 1485 by the servants of Prince Karakucza, whose son he had failed to cure. He was succeeded by LEO, who was executed in 1490, also for not having cured one of Ivan's sons. In the fifteenth century lived Solomon Calvaire; Stephan von GADEN, also court physician (executed in 1682). At St. Petersburg lived the court physician Antonio Ribeiro Sanchez (1699-1783). The greater number of Jewish physicians are found in the larger communities, *e.g.*, at Hasenpoth, Issachar Falkensohn BEHR (b. 1746), Judah ha-Levi Hurwicz, Jacob Löbschutz, David Abrahamson (*c.* 1775), Aaron Solomon Tobias (d. 1782), Lazar Isaac Kume (*c.* 1800); at Wilna, Löb Gordon (*c.* 1725); at Mitau, Elrich (d. 1809); at Bausk and Odessa, Eliezer Elias Löwenthal (*c.* 1775); also at Bausk, Lachmann.

Russia.

The foregoing lists of physicians are certainly not complete. There probably lived many a good Jewish practitioner whose name has not been recorded.

Review (1495-1800).

With very few exceptions the Jewish physicians of the period 1495-1800 did not excel. They were usually general practitioners, very often combining the offices of rabbi and physician. A few are cited as great consulting physicians, as the above-mentioned John Baptist de Silva of Paris and the gynecologist Rodrigo de Castro of Hamburg. Only a few left important medical works. As a rule their influence upon medicine was only slight. They suffered with their brethren expulsion from many countries. They were very often prohibited from practising among Christians and were allowed to follow their profession among their brethren only. The universities were often closed to them; and popes and princes issued edicts against them.

——**In Recent Times**: The French Revolution brought a great change in the status of Jewish physicians. Jews were admitted to citizenship in nearly every country of western Europe, and were permitted to study at all universities and to practise their profession. Even in Russia to-day (1904) there are many Jewish physicians to be found; but it is especially in Germany, Austria, and the United States that Jews have become prominent as general practitioners, specialists, university professors of medicine (since 1848), and medical journalists. It is only possible to enumerate some of those who have obtained prominence in medical circles during the nineteenth century, beginning with those who have died.

General Practitioners.

Physicians: Solomon Ludwig Steinheim (Altona, 1789-1866); Bernhard van Oven (London, 1797-1860); Martin Steinthal (Berlin, 1798-1892; at his death the oldest physician in Germany), reeditor of Hufeland's "Macrobiotik"; Daniel Peixotto (London, 1800-43); Hananeel de Leon (*ib.* *c.* 1825); J. L. Levinson (*ib.* 1800-74); Raphael KOSCH (Berlin, 1803-72); Jonathan Pereira (London, 1804-53); Maximilian HEINE (St. Petersburg, 1805-79), brother of Heinrich Heine; Johann JACOBY (Königsberg, 1805-77); Jonas GRÄTZER (Breslau, 1806-89); Moritz Rapoport (Lemberg, 1808-80); Isaac A. Franklin (London, 1812-80); David GRUBY (Paris, 1810-98), known through his free public lectures; Eleazar Meldola (London, 1810-79); Ludwig GÜTERBOCK (Berlin, 1814-95); Moritz Adolph Unna (Hamburg, 1813-88); Julius BARASCH (Bucharest, 1815-63); Sigismund Sutro (London, 1815-86); Jacob Eduard Polak (Vienna, 1818-91), court physician at Teheran to the Shah of Persia; Ferdinand FALKSON (Königsberg, 1820-1900), known through a lawsuit which was due to his marriage to a Christian woman; Samuel KRISTELLER (Berlin, 1820-1900); Hermann HIRSCHFELDT (Colberg, 1825-85), to whose memory a monument was erected at Colberg; Henry Behrend (London, 1828-93); Wilhelm LUBELSKI (Warsaw, 1832-90); Ernest Abraham HART (London, 1836-1898); and L. G. Gold (Odessa, d. 1902).

Deceased Specialists.

Anatomists: Friedrich Gustav Jacob HENLE (Göttingen, 1809-85), one of the leading anatomists of his time; Jacob HERZ (Erlangen, 1816-71), whose monument is to be seen in Erlangen—one of the three monuments erected to Jews in Germany, the other two being those of Moses Mendelssohn at Dessau, and Hermann Hirschfeldt at Colberg; Ludwik Maurycy HIRSCHFELD (Warsaw, 1816-1876); Siegmund SPITZER (Constantinople, 1839-1894), physician to Sultan 'Abd al-Majid.

Physiologists: Simone FUBINI (Palermo, 1841-98), friend and pupil of Moleschott; Ernst FLEISCHL VON MARXOW (Vienna, 1846-91); Moritz SCHIFF (Geneva, 1823-96); Gabriel Gustav VALENTIN (Bern, 1810-83), one of the leading physiologists of his age.

Microscopists: Gottlieb GLUGE (Brussels, 1812-1898), one of the pioneers of microscopy; Ludwik Mandl (Paris, 1812-81).

Embryologists: Robert REMAK (Berlin, 1815-65), the first Jewish privat-docent in Prussia, admitted to the Berlin faculty in 1847, and well known through his discoveries in neurology, embryology, and electrotherapy; Leopold SCHENK (Vienna, 1840-1892), well known through his theory.

Pathologists: Karl Friedrich CANSTATT (Erlangen, 1807-50), founder and editor of the well-known "Jahresbericht über die Fortschritte der Gesammten Medizin Aller Länder," begun in 1841 and continued after his death by Virchow; Julius COHNHEIM (Leipsic, 1839-84), author of the theory of emigration of white corpuscles as the origin of pus and of inflammation, and demonstrator of "Cohnheim's areas"; Felix Victor BIRCH-HIRSCHFELD (Leipsic, 1842-99); Moritz Heinrich ROMBERG (Berlin, 1795-1873), the eminent neurologist; Simon SAMUEL (Königsberg, 1835-99); Solomon STRICKER (Vienna, 1834-98), the founder of microtomy; Karl WEIGERT (Frankfort-on-the-Main, 1845-1904).

Clinicians: Jonas Freund (London, d. 1880), founder of the German Hospital, London; Heinrich JACOBSON (Berlin, 1826-90); Hermann LEBERT (Lewy) (Breslau, 1813-78); Ludwig TRAUBE (Berlin, 1818-76), the father of experimental pathology; Daniel Maduro Peixotto (New York, about 1850).

Surgeons: Michelangelo ASSON (Venice, 1802-77); Leopold von DITTEL (Vienna, 1815-98), who performed over 800 operations for calculus; Joseph GRUBER (*ib.* 1827-1900); Aaron JEITELES (Olmütz, 1799-

1878); Michel Lévy (Paris, 1809–72); Germain Sée (Paris, 1818–96); Lewis OPPENHEIM (London, 1832–1895); Julius WOLFF (Berlin, 1836–1902); Paul GÜTERBOCK (Berlin, 1844–97).

Gynecologist: David HAUSSMANN (Berlin, 1839–1895).

Pharmacologist: Hermann FRIEDBERG (Breslau, 1817–84).

Aurists: Joseph GRUBER (Vienna, 1827–1900) and Solomon Moos (Heidelberg, 1831–95).

Ophthalmologists: Isaac HAYS (Philadelphia, 1796–1879), editor of the "American Journal of Medical Science"; Ignaz HIRSCHLER (Budapest, 1823–91); John Zechariah Laurence (London, 1828–70); Aaron FRIEDENWALD (Baltimore, 1836–1902); Max LANDESBERG (New York, 1840–95); Ludwig MAUTHNER (Vienna, 1840–94), to whose memory a monument was erected in the arcades of Vienna University, the only monument dedicated to a Jew in Austria.

Laryngologists: Jacob GOTTSTEIN (Breslau, 1832–1895); Abraham KUHN (Strasburg, 1838–1900); Johann SCHNITZLER (Vienna, 1835–93); Elias HEYMAN (Stockholm, 1829–89); Karl Stoerk (Vienna, 1832–1899); Louis Elsberg (New York, 1836–85); Isaac MICHAEL (Hamburg, 1848–97); G. Ash (New York, d. 1902).

Neuropathist: Oscar BERGER (Breslau, 1844–85).

Dermatologists: Moriz KAPÓSI (Kohn) (Vienna, 1837–1902); Oskar SIMON (Breslau, 1845–82); Hermann von ZEISSL (Vienna, 1817–84), defender of the dual theory of syphilis.

Psychiatrist: Ludwig MEYER (Göttingen, 1827–1900).

Hygienists: Nikolaus Heinrich JULIUS (Hamburg, 1783–1862); Michel LÉVY (Paris, 1809–72); Levi Ali COHEN (Groningen, 1817–89).

Electrotherapist: Moritz Meyer (Berlin, 1821–93).

Balneologist: Gottfried Schmelkes (Teplitz, 1807–1870).

Biologist: Ludwig Lewin Jacobson (Copenhagen, 1783–1843).

Encyclopedists: Friedrich Jacob BEHREND (Berlin, 1803–89); Samuel GUTTMANN (Berlin, 1839–93).

Miscellaneous: Authority on forensic medicine: Johann Ludwig Caspar (Berlin, 1796–1864). Hydrotherapist: Ludwig F. FRÄNKEL (Berlin, 1806–1872). Dental surgeon: Ludwig Heinrich HOLLÄNDER (Breslau, 1833–97), one of the German pioneers of scientific dentistry.

Medical History and Journalism.

Historians of medicine: August HIRSCH (Berlin, 1817–94), still an undisputed authority; Abraham Hartog ISRAELS (Amsterdam, 1822–1883); Franz Romeo SELIGMANN (Vienna, 1808–79).

Journalists: Louis Posner (Berlin, 1815–68), editor of the "Berliner Klinische Wochenschrift"; Leopold WITTELSHÖFER (Vienna, 1818–89), editor of the "Wiener Medizinische Wochenschrift"; Paul GUTTMANN (Berlin, 1833–93), editor of the "Journal für Praktische Aerzte"; Julius GROSSER (Prenzlau, 1835–1901), editor of the "Deutsche Medizinal-Zeitung"; Louis WALDENBURG (Berlin, 1837–81), editor of the "Berliner Klinische Wochenschrift"; Johann Jacob (Joseph Isidor) SACHS (Nordhausen, 1803–46), publisher and editor of medical journals. The champion of homeopathy in Austria is Emil ALTSCHUL (Prague, 1812–65), who founded and published (1853) the first homeopathic magazine in Austria.

Of living physicians, the following list gives the names of some of the more important, especially of those who have held official positions:

Living Physicians in Europe.

Austria: The alienist Arnold PICK; the physiologist Sigmund MAYER; the pathologists Philipp Joseph PICK and Alfred Pribram, all four of Prague; the aural surgeon Adam POLITZER; the electrotherapists Moritz Benedikt and Gustav GÄRTNER; the pathologist Anton WEICHSELBAUM; the pediatrists Alois EPSTEIN and Max KASSOWITZ; the clinicians Moritz Heitler, Leopold OSER, Alois PICK, Wilhelm von WINTERNITZ, Emil ZUCKERKANDL; the dermatologist Isidor NEUMANN; the ophthalmologist Isidor SCHNABEL; Samuel von BASCH, body-physician to the emperor Maximilian of Mexico; the journalist Alexander FRÄNKEL; Leopold von SELIGMANN, retired colonel-surgeon of the Austrian army, all of Vienna; the balneologists Enoch Heinrich KISCH of Marienbad and Josef SEEGEN of Carlsbad.

Denmark: The pathologist Karl Julius SALOMONSEN of Copenhagen.

England: The ophthalmologist Richard LIEBREICH; the laryngologist Sir Felix SEMON; the pathologist Bertram Abrahams, all three of London; to these may be added the bacteriologist Waldemar HAFFKINE of Calcutta, India.

France: The inventor of color photography Gabriel LIPPMANN; the bacteriologist Alexander MARMOREK; the physician Anselme WEILL; the surgeon Marc SÉE; the clinicians Julius GOLDSCHMIDT, Georges HAYEM, and Louis Mandl; the laryngologists Benjamin Benno Loewenberg, Louis Lucien DREYFUS-BRISAC, all of Paris; the neurologists Hippolyte Bernheim of Nancy and Max NORDAU of Paris.

The number of Jewish physicians in **Germany** is very great: the anatomist Gustav SCHWALBE of Strasburg; the physiologists Julius BERNSTEIN of Halle, the brothers Hermann and Immanuel MUNK and Nathan ZUNTZ of Berlin, Isidor Rosenthal of Erlangen; the histologist Gustav Jacob BORN of Breslau; the pathologists Ludwig BRIEGER and Oskar ISRAEL of Berlin; the clinicians Imar BOAS and Wilhelm EBSTEIN of Göttingen, Albert FRÄNKEL and Julius LAZARUS of Berlin, Ludwig LICHTHEIM of Königsberg, Martin MENDELSOHN of Berlin, Oscar MINKOWSKI of Strasburg, Carl POSNER, Ottomar ROSENBACH, Hermann SENATOR, Georg Anton Solomon, all of Berlin; the dermatologists Gustav BEHREND, Heinrich KÖBNER, Oskar Lassar, Georg Richard LEWIN, all likewise of Berlin, Albert NEISSER of Breslau, Paul Gerson UNNA of Hamburg; the surgeons Robert KUTNER, James ISRAEL, William Levy, all of Berlin; the pediatrists Adolf BAGINSKY and Livius FÜRST of Berlin and Eduard Heinrich HENOCH of Dresden; the gynecologist Ernst FRÄNKEL of Breslau, Leopold and Theodor LANDAU of Berlin, Julius SCHOTTLÄNDER of Heidelberg, Paul ZWEIFEL of Leipsic; the neuropathists Hermann OPPENHEIM, Emanuel MENDEL, Albert MOLL, and Ernst Julius REMAK, all of Berlin; the bacteriologist Paul EHRLICH of Frankfort-on-the-Main; the orthopedist Leopold EWER of Berlin; the ophthalmologists Julius HIRSCHBERG of Berlin, Hermann L. COHN of Breslau, Ludwig L. LAQUEUR of Strasburg, Max Solomon of Berlin, Leopold WEISS of Heidelberg; the pharmacologists Max JAFFÉ of Königsberg, Oskar Matthias, Eugen LIEBREICH and Louis LEWIN of Berlin; the otologists Ludwig KATZ and Ludwig LÖWE of Berlin; the laryngologists Paul HEYMANN and B. FRÄNKEL of Berlin; the encyclopedist Albert EULENBURG of Berlin; the forensicist Adolf LESSER of Berlin; the hygienist Ernst Levy of Strasburg; the historian Julius Leopold PAGEL of Berlin; the anthropologist Abraham LISSAUER of Berlin.

Hungary: The neuropathist Otto Schwartzer von Babarcz; the oculist Nathaniel FEUER; the clinician Friedrich KORÁNYI, all of Budapest.

Italy: The specialist of forensic medicine Salvatore OTTOLENGHI of Sienna; the clinician Beniamino LUZZATTO of Padua; the great alienist Cesare LOMBROSO and the pathologist Pio FOÀ, both of Turin.

The Netherlands: The clinician Samuel Siegmund Rosenstein of Leyden.

Rumania: The physician Karpel Lippe.

Russia: Isaac DEMBO of St. Petersburg, author of "Ha-Sheḥiṭah weha-Bediḳah"; the ophthalmologist Max (Emanuel) MANDELSTAMM; the hygienist and court physician Joseph Vasilievich BERTENSOHN and his nephew Lev Bertensohn of St. Petersburg; the physician Joseph CHAZANOWICZ of Byelostok, founder of the Abarbanel Library at Jerusalem; the clinician W. Manassein of Kasan; Isidorus Brennson at Mitau. Of the physicians at present practising in Courland 19.2 per cent are Jews.

Switzerland: The pathologist Moritz ROTH of Basel.

Turkey: Elias COHEN Pasha of Constantinople.

United States: The first Jewish physician mentioned in colonial times in the United States is Jacob Lumbrozo, who practised about 1639 in Maryland.

In the United States.

The number of Jewish physicians in the United States to-day (1904) is very large, but only a few—mainly those who have acquired official positions—can be mentioned here: the general practitioners Mark Blumenthal, Simon Brainin, David A. D'Ancona, Julius Friedenwald, Boleslav Lapovski, Maurice T. Lewi, Samuel J. Meltzer, Alfred Meyer, William Moss, Max Rosenthal, Arthur F. Sampson, J. F. Schamberg, Lazarus Schöney, C. D. Spivak, Richard Stein, Jacob Teschner; the physiologist David Riesman; the pathologists Albert Abrams, Isaac Adler, Simon Flexner, and Bernard S. Talmey; the hydrotherapist Simon Baruch; the microscopist Isidore Berman; the surgeons G. W. Birkowitz, Nathan Jacobson, Howard Lilienthal, William Meyer, Joseph Ranschoff, and Lewis N. Steinbach; the jurisprudent N. E. Brill; the aurists William Cowen, M. D. Lederman, and Max Toeplitz; the gynecologists Joseph Brettauer, Louis Ladinsky, and S. Marx; the laryngologists Jacob da Silva Solis-Cohen, Max Freudenthal, and Emil Mayer; the clinicians Henry W. Bettmann, Solomon da Silva Solis-Cohen, Joseph and Julius Eichberg, Max Einhorn, A. A. Eshner, Joseph Oakland Hirschfelder, G. A. Knopf; the pediatrists S. Henry Dessau, Frederick Forchheimer, Henry Illoway, Abraham Jacobi, Henry Koplik, and Nathan Oppenheim; the dermatologists William Gottheil and Sigismund Lustgarten; the ophthalmologists Harry Friedenwald, Emil Gruening, Charles H. May, and H. Scharpringer; the neurologists Joseph Frankel, G. W. Jacoby, Bernhard Sachs, and William Leszynski; the biologist Jacques Loeb; the bacteriologist Milton Joseph Rosenau; and the dentists Leopold Greenbaum and John I. Hart.

BIBLIOGRAPHY: Carmoly, *Histoire des Médecins Juifs*, Brussels, 1844 (a book full of material, but often unreliable); Hyrtl, *Das Arabische und Hebräische in der Anatomie*, Vienna, 1879; Münz, *Ueber die Jüdischen Aerzte im Mittelalter*, Berlin, 1887; M. Horovitz, *Jüdische Aerzte in Frankfurt-am-Main*, Frankfort-on-the-Main, 1886; Landau, *Gesch. der Jüdischen Aerzte*, Berlin, 1895; Hirsch, *Biog. Lex.*; Pagel, *Biog. Lex.*; Steinschneider, *Wissenschaft und Charlatanerie Unter den Arabern im Neunten Jahrhundert*, in *Virchow's Archiv*, xxxvi.; idem, *Constantinus Africanus und Seine Arabischen Quellen*, ib. xxxvii.; idem, *Die Toxicologischen Schriften der Araber bis Ende des XII. Jahrhunderts*, ib. lii.; idem, *Ueber Medicin in Bibel und Talmud und über Jüdische Aerzte*, in *Wiener Klinische Rundschau*, 1896; idem, *Hebr. Uebers.*; idem, *Donnolo*, Berlin, 1868; idem, *Hebr. Bibl.*; idem, *Die Arabische Literatur der Juden*, Frankfort-on-the-Main, 1902; Wüstenfeld, *Die Academien der Araber und Ihre Lehrer*, Göttingen, 1837; idem, *Die Uebersetzungen Arabischer Werke in das Lateinische, seit den XI. Jahrhundert*, ib. 1877; idem, *Die Geschichtsschreiber der Araber und Ihre Werke*, ib. 1882; Haeser, *Lehrbuch der Geschichte der Medizin und der Epidemischen Krankheiten*, Jena, 1882; Aaron Friedenwald, *Jewish Physicians and the Contribution of the Jews to the Science of Medicine*, in *Publ. of the Gratz College, 1897*, Philadelphia, 1897; Vogelstein and Rieger, *Gesch. der Juden in Rom*, Berlin, 1895-96; Berliner, *Gesch. der Juden in Rom*, Frankfort-on-the-Main, 1893; Joseph Jacobs, *The Jews of Angevin England*, pp. 114, 340, London, 1893; idem, *Jewish Year Book*; Kayserling, *Zur Gesch. der Jüdischen Aerzte*, in *Monatsschrift*, vii. 165; Kaufmann, *Un Siècle de l'Existence d'une Famille de Juifs de Vienne et de Posen*, in *R. E. J.* xx. 275; Döllinger, *Die Juden in Europa*, in *Akademische Vorträge*, vol. i., Nördlingen, 1890; *Revue des Etudes Juives*, xli. 77-97, xlvii. 221-254, xlviii. 48-81, xcvi. 265-272.

J. F. T. H.

MEDINA: Second sacred city of Islam; situated in the Hijaz in Arabia, about 250 miles north of Mecca. It is celebrated as the place to which the Hegira (Mohammed's flight from Mecca) was directed, and as the capital and burial-place of Mohammed. According to Arabic tradition, Yathrib and the Hijaz were originally peopled with Amalekites, who were displaced by the Israelites. There are different accounts as to when this displacement was effected: some say that it occurred under Moses (comp. "Kitab al-Aghani," iv. 263); some, under Joshua; and some, under David, who it is stated resided in the Hijaz during Absalom's rebellion.

Jews may have settled in the Hijaz after the sack of Jerusalem by Nebuchadnezzar; and it is probable that they came in successive colonies, *e.g.*, after Pompey's attack upon Judea (64 B.C.), after Titus' conquest of Jerusalem (70 C.E.), and again after Hadrian's persecution of the Jews (in 136 C.E.; see ARABIA).

The Jews had a very rich and flourishing settlement at Yathrib and built strongholds in the city and vicinity. The principal families were the Banu Ḳainuḳa', the Banu Ḳuraiẓa, and the Banu al-Naḍir. The latter two were known as the "Al Kahinan," because they traced their descent from Aaron. In the fourth century Arab tribes from Yemen began to encroach upon the Jews in Medina. They were divided into two clans, the Banu Aus and the Banu Khazraj. By calling in outside assistance and treacherously massacring at a banquet the principal Jews, these Arab clans finally gained the upper hand at Medina toward the end of the fifth century (for date see "J. Q. R." vii. 175, note). From this time the Jews retired into the background for about a century. About four or five years before the Hegira the Jews took an active part in the battle of Bu'ath between the Banu Aus and the Banu Khazraj. The Banu Naḍir and the Banu Ḳuraiẓa fought with the Banu Aus, while the Banu Ḳainuḳa' were allied with the Banu Khazraj. The latter were defeated after a long and desperate battle.

Jewish Tribes at Medina.

It is probable that the presence of Jews in Medina did much to prepare the way for Mohammed's teaching. When the prophet first went to Medina he was inclined to be friendly toward the Jews. They were included in the treaty between him and the inhabitants of Medina. He also made certain concessions to them on the ground of religion, and adopted their ḳiblah—Jerusalem—in the hope of winning them to his cause. They, however, ridiculed him, and delighted in drawing him into arguments to expose his ignorance; so that his conciliatory attitude was soon changed to enmity. A few Jews were converted to Islam, among them Abdallah ibn Salam, whom Mohammed called the "servant of God," and of whose conversion the prophet made much.

Mohammed's Attitude Toward Jews of Medina.

Finally Mohammed began to use actual violence toward the Medina Jews. After the battle of Bedr a woman called Asma, said by some to be a Jewess, wrote satirical verses, and was killed in her sleep, probably with Mohammed's consent. Not long before, Abu 'Afak of the Banu Amr, who had been converted to Judaism, had been assassinated for having displeased Mohammed by writing verses ridiculing the new religion. Mohammed then seems to have decided to get rid of the Jews in a body, since they were a constant menace to his cause. He began with the Banu Ḳainuḳa', who were goldsmiths, and lived by themselves in a fortified suburb. He first summoned them to accept his religion, and they refused. Soon a pretext was found for an open attack. A Moslem girl was insulted by a Jew of the Banu Ḳainuḳa'; the Jew was killed by a Moslem, and the latter in turn was killed by the brothers of the murdered Jew. Mohammed immediately marched against the Banu Ḳainuḳa' and besieged them in their stronghold. After a siege of fifteen days they surrendered, and their lives were spared only at the urgent request of Abdallah ibn Ubai, the influential leader of the Arab opposition, whose pleading Mohammed dared not ignore. Being allowed to leave the country, they emigrated toward the north. Their departure weakened the Jews, who if they had been united might have withstood Mohammed's attacks.

Mohammed Attacks Jews.

About a month after the emigration of the Ḳainuḳa', Abu Sufyan, the leader of the Meccan opposition, visited Ḥuyayy of the Banu al-Naḍir, but, being refused admittance by him, spent the night with another influential man of the same tribe and obtained information from him concerning the state of Medina. Another Jewish poet was assassinated about this time at Mohammed's desire. This was Ka'b ibn al-Ashraf of the Banu Naḍir, who had been stirring up the Ḳuraish at Mecca by his verses after the battle of Bedr. Ibn Sanina, a Jewish merchant, was killed on the day after Ka'b; and the Jews now began to fear to leave their houses. In the summer of 625 Mohammed attacked and besieged the Banu al-Naḍir. There appears to have been no satisfactory pretext for the attack. Mohammed claimed that he had received a revelation telling him of the treachery of the Jews. After a siege of fifteen or twenty days Abdallah ibn Ubai prevailed on the Naḍir to surrender. They were exiled, being allowed to take their goods with them, and emigrated toward the north, settling in Khaibar and in Syria.

There were now left only the Banu Ḳuraiẓa, and Mohammed soon found a pretext to attack them. Some of the Jewish exiles, chief among them being the above-mentioned Ḥuyayy, had stirred up the Ḳuraish and other Arab tribes against Mohammed, and they persuaded the Banu Ḳuraiẓa to join them in their plans. Mohammed, however, succeeded in making the Jews and their Arab allies suspicious of each other; and the allies, who had been besieging Medina, suddenly departed in the midst of a storm, thus leaving the Ḳuraiẓa unsupported. Mohammed marched against them, claiming to have received a special revelation to that effect, and laid siege to their fortress, which was a few miles to the southeast of the city. They surrendered after a month's siege, without having risked a fight. Their fate was left to the decision of Sa'd ibn Mu'adh of the tribe of Aus, who, in spite of the pleading of his own tribe, condemned the men to death and the women and children to slavery. The sentence was executed; and 750 Jews were killed in cold blood. Ḥuyayy was the last to die, with his last breath denouncing Mohammed as an impostor. The prophet wished to make a beautiful woman of the tribe, by the name of Riḥanah, his wife, but, tradition says, she preferred to be his slave instead. Thus the last of the powerful Jewish tribes in Medina was destroyed. Neither Mohammed, however, nor his successor drove all the Jews out of the country. That extreme measure was taken by Omar, who claimed to have heard the prophet say that all Jews should be exiled. Medina is one of the Moslem cities that neither Jews nor Christians may enter. See Banu Ḳainuḳa'; Banu Ḳuraiẓa; Banu al-Naḍir.

Fate of Medina Jews.

Bibliography: Caussin de Perceval, *Essai sur l'Histoire des Arabes*, passim; Grätz, *Gesch.* iv. 66, 75 *et seq.*, 81-83; Hirschfeld, *Essai sur l'Histoire des Juifs de Médine*, in *R. E. J.* vii. 167 *et seq.*, x. 10 *et seq.*

J. M. W. M.

MEDINA: Prominent Jewish family, members of which lived during the sixteenth and seventeenth centuries chiefly in Turkey and Egypt. Most probably it took its name from one of the two Spanish cities named Medina.

The following is a genealogical tree of those members of the family whose relationship is established (the numbers in parentheses correspond to those given in the text):

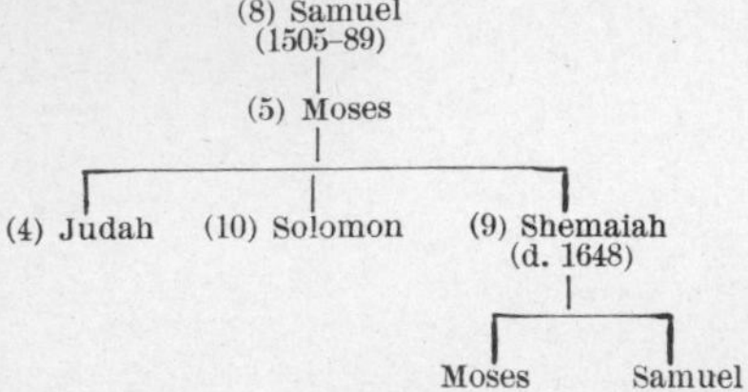

1. David b. Moses di Medina: Cabalistic author; flourished at the beginning of the eighteenth century. He wrote: "Nefesh Dawid" (Constantinople, 1736), a cabalistic commentary on the Pentateuch and the Five Scrolls; and "Ruaḥ Dawid we-Nishmat Dawid" (Salonica, 1747), in two parts, the first being a commentary on the part of the Zohar called "Iddera Rabba," and the second a cabalistic commentary on Canticles.

Bibliography: Benjacob, *Oẓar ha-Sefarim*, pp. 400, 544; Steinschneider, *Cat. Bodl.* s.v. *Samuel Medina*; Zedner, *Cat. Hebr. Books Brit. Mus.* p. 516.

2. Isaac Ḥayyim di Medina: Editor of a prayer-book for the congregation of Sienna, arranged and published by him with the cooperation of Jedidiah Levi under the title "Seder Zemirot," Leghorn, 1786.

Bibliography: Benjacob, *Oẓar ha-Sefarim*, p. 160; Zedner, *Cat. Hebr. Books Brit. Mus.* pp. 484, 516.

3. Jacob di Medina: Son of Isaac Ḥayyim (No. 2); author of liturgical poems published under the title "Yashir Yisrael" (Leghorn, 1805), and of a poem in the collection of congratulatory poems "'Et ha-Zamir" (*ib.* 1794 ?), published on the occasion of the wedding of E. M. Recanate.

Bibliography: Benjacob, *Oẓar ha-Sefarim*, pp. 232 (where "son of Moses" is erroneous, as the latter was only the co-editor), 434; Zedner, *Cat. Hebr. Books Brit. Mus.* pp. 475, 516, 651, s.v. *Recanate* (where the name "Medina" is missing), and p. 675, s.v. *Samuel b. Moses, the Priest*.

4. Judah di Medina (surname **Comprado** or **Conrado**): Son of Moses (No. 5); mentioned by Conforte as a scholar. His wealth aroused the enmity of a non-Jew, who killed him at the door of his own house. The Jews of Salonica seized the murderer, and hanged him at the scene of his crime.

Bibliography: Conforte, *Ḳore ha-Dorot*, pp. 43b, 50a; Steinschneider, *Cat. Bodl.* col. 3004.

5. Moses di Medina: Son of Samuel (No. 8); lived at Salonica. He is praised for his Talmudic learning and for the generous use which he made of his wealth in the interest of Hebrew literature. He published the responsa of his father and wrote a preface thereto. A list of his published works is given in Steinschneider, "Cat. Bodl." col. 3004 (see also Conforte, *l.c.* p. 43b).

6. Moses Medina: Talmudic scholar; lived at Constantinople, and later (*c.* 1650) at Jerusalem (see Conforte, "Ḳore ha-Dorot," p. 49a; Steinschneider, "Cat. Bodl." *s.v.* "Samuel Medina."

7. Moses Medina: Rabbi of the Portuguese congregation at London; contemporary of David Nieto. He wrote "Della Divina Providencia" (London, 1705), a defense of Nieto's work of the same title and published together with it.

Bibliography: Fürst, *Bibl. Jud.* ii. 339; Steinschneider, *Cat. Bodl.* No. 8910; Wolf, *Bibl. Hebr.* iii., No. 1593b.

8. Samuel b. Moses di Medina (RaShDaM): Talmudist and author; born 1505; died Oct. 12, 1589, at Salonica. He was principal of the Talmudic college of that city, which produced a great number of prominent scholars during the sixteenth and seventeenth centuries. His teachers were the noted Talmudists Joseph Taitazak and Levi ibn Ḥabib, and among his schoolmates were Isaac Adarbi, Joseph ibn Leb, and Moses Almosnino. While on a mission to Constantinople he met the noted grammarian Menahem di Lonsano, who studied under him for some time and who therefore speaks of him as his teacher (Conforte, "Ḳore ha-Dorot," ed. Cassel, p. 44a).

Among Samuel's many disciples who attained prominence were Abraham de Boton and Joseph ibn Ezra. He had a controversy with Joseph Caro and other rabbis at Safed, against whom he wrote a polemical letter ("Ketab Tokaḥah"; see Azulai, "Shem ha-Gedolim," *s.v.*). A grandson of his was Samuel Ḥayyun, author of "Bene Shemuel," novellæ and responsa (Salonica, 1613?).

Samuel's works include: "Ben Shemuel," Mantua, 1622, thirty sermons on various subjects, published with a preface by his grandson Shemaiah; "Ḥiddushim" (unpublished), novellæ on some Talmudic tractates (Benjacob, "Oẓar ha-Sefarim," p. 183); a collection of 956 responsa in four parts, of which the first two were published during the lifetime of the author (1578–87?) under the title "Pisḳe RaShDaM" (Benjacob, *l.c.* p. 491; Conforte, *l.c.* p. 38a, Cassel's note; Steinschneider, "Cat. Bodl." No. 7056). A complete edition of the last-named work was undertaken later by the author's son Moses, who added a preface (Salonica, 1594–97; new ed. *ib.* 1798).

Bibliography: Steinschneider, *Cat. Bodl.* No. 8909; Zedner, *Cat. Hebr. Books Brit. Mus.* s.v.

9. Shemaiah di Medina: Son of Moses (No. 5); born at Salonica; died at Venice June 3, 1648. Being compelled to leave Salonica owing to a quarrel with certain influential men of that city, he emigrated to Venice, where he occupied a very respected position as a member of the rabbinate. Jacob Frances wrote an elegy on his death.

Shemaiah was the author of many liturgical poems, concerning which see Steinschneider, "Cat. Bodl." *s.v.* He wrote also "Ma'amar al 'Onshe Gehinnom" (unpublished), a treatise on punishment in hell, dedicated to Isaac Aboab, Jr. A commentary on Proverbs (Nepi-Ghirondi, "Toledot Gedole Yisrael," pp. 323, 352, 358) has been ascribed to him, but whether correctly so is doubtful (see Steinschneider, *s.v.*). He also edited "Ben Shemuel," a collection of sermons by his grandfather Samuel, and "Bene Shemuel," the work of his relation Samuel Ḥayyun, to which two books he wrote prefaces.

Bibliography: *Ben Shemuel*, Preface, Mantua, 1622; Benjacob, *Oẓar ha-Sefarim*, pp. 283, 331, 469; Conforte, *Ḳore ha-Dorot*, Index; Steinschneider, *Cat. Bodl.* cols. 2516, 3004; Wolf, *Bibl. Hebr.* iii., Nos. 2195c-2196; Zedner, *Cat. Hebr. Books Brit. Mus.* p. 696.

10. Solomon di Medina: Son of Moses (No. 5); lived at Salonica. He was personally acquainted with David Conforte, who obtained from him some biographical data concerning his grandfather Samuel, and who speaks of him with respect. He was, however, dead when Conforte wrote his "Ḳore ha-Dorot" (1674–83; see Cassel's introduction, p. iv.), as the latter adds to Solomon's name the eulogy נ״ע.

Bibliography: Conforte, *Ḳore ha-Dorot*, p. 38a; Steinschneider, *Cat. Bodl.* col. 3004.

The following Medinas seem to belong to a different family:

Benjamin di Medina: Talmudist; died at Monastir, Turkey, about 1650. He was a pupil of Daniel Estrosa (see Michael, "Or ha-Ḥayyim," No. 789), and schoolmate of David Conforte (see the latter's "Ḳore ha-Dorot," p. 52b).

David di Medina: Rabbi in Cairo about 1650. He wrote an approbation to Mordecai Levi's "Darke No'am," published at Venice in 1697 (see Conforte, *l.c.* p. 52a; Michael, *l.c.* No. 749; Steinschneider, "Cat. Bodl." col. 2451, *s.v.* "Samuel Medina").

Samuel b. Isaac di Medina, a scribe (1491), is mentioned in Neubauer, Cat. Bodl. Hebr. MSS. No. 30, 2542.

D. H. M.

MEDINA, SIR SOLOMON DE: English army contractor about 1711. He was a wealthy Jew who went to England with William III., and who attained some notoriety by his extensive dealings with the English government of his day. "The Jew Medina," as he was popularly called, held a position of prominence in connection with the English forces. During the War of the Spanish Succession (1702–14) he accompanied the Duke of Marlborough on his campaigns, advanced him funds, and furnished provisions for the troops. He also established a system of expresses which outstripped those of the government, so that his agents were in possession of important news before it reached the ministers of the crown. His negotiations were made evident in an attack on the Duke of Marlborough in Parliament in 1711 for receiving from the Jew a yearly payment of £6,000. Marlborough replied that the money had been expended in obtaining trustworthy information. It was said of Medina that every British victory contributed as much to his wealth as to the glory of England. For his services he was knighted, being the first Jew in England to receive that honor. Sir Solomon de Medina was at one time the largest contributor to the Bevis Marks Synagogue, and he remained faithful to his coreligionists to the last. His descendants, however, eventually abandoned Judaism.

Bibliography: Picciotto, *Sketches of Anglo-Jewish History*, pp. 50, 58, 59; *Jew. World*, Feb., 1878; *Dict. Nat. Biog.*

J. G. L.

MEDINI, ḤAYYIM HEZEKIAH (known also under his initials חמח): Palestinian rabbinical writer; born at Jerusalem 1833; son of Rabbi Raphael Eliahu Medini. At the age of nineteen, on completing his studies in his native city, he received the rabbinical diploma. He then went to Constantinople, where for thirteen years he was a member of a rabbinical court. In 1866 he was called as chief rabbi to Kara-Su-Bazar in the Crimea. In 1889 Medini returned to Palestine, staying first at Jerusalem, and going in 1891 to Hebron, where he has since been acting chief rabbi.

Medini's works include: "Miktab le-Ḥizḳiyahu" (Smyrna, 1865), Talmudic studies and responsa; "Or Li" (*ib.* 1874), responsa; "Paḳḳu'ot Sadeh" (Jerusalem, 1900); "Sede Ḥemed," his chief work, an encyclopedic collection of laws and decisions in alphabetical order, twelve volumes of which have appeared since 1890 (Warsaw).

Bibliography: Nahum Sokolov, in *Sefer ha-Shanah*, Warsaw, 1900.

S. M. Fr.

MEGED YERAḤIM. See Periodicals.

MEGIDDO (מגדו; once **Megiddon** [מגדון, Zech. xii. 11]): Capital of one of the Canaanitish kings conquered by Joshua; assigned to Manasseh (Josh. xii. 21, xvii. 11; I Chron. vii. 29). Its Canaanitish inhabitants were only put to tribute, not driven out (Josh. xvii. 12–13; Judges i. 27–28). Megiddo is repeatedly referred to in Biblical history. It is mentioned in connection with Baana, one of Solomon's commissariat officers, who had to provision the king's household for one month in the year. Its fortifications, which were of ancient date (being mentioned in the inscription of Thothmes III.), were restored by Solomon (I Kings iv. 12, ix. 15). Ahaziah is said (II Kings ix. 27) to have died at Megiddo after he had escaped from Jehu; but in II Chron. xxii. 9 it is said that Ahaziah was found in Samaria, taken to Jehu, and slain. The most memorable occurrence connected with the city was the battle there or in the valley of Megiddo, between Pharaoh-nechoh and Josiah, in which the latter was slain (II Kings xxiii. 29–30; II Chron. xxxv. 22); "the mourning of Hadadrimmon in the valley of Megiddon" may have been on account of this battle (Zech. xii. 11; see Hadad). The same battle is mentioned by Herodotus (ii. 159), but under the name "Magdolum" instead of "Megiddo." The city is frequently mentioned in connection with Taanach (Josh. xii. 21, xvii. 11; Judges v. 19; I Kings iv. 12; I Chron. vii. 29), near the plain of Esdraelon; the expression in Deborah's song is "in Taanach on the waters of Megiddo."

Megiddo is mentioned on the El-Amarna tablets. Robinson ("Researches," iii. 177–300) identified the site of Megiddo with the modern Al-Lajjun, on the western border of the plain of Esdraelon. Other scholars have identified it with Al-Mujaidil, near Nazareth; with Majdal, near Acre; with Jida; and with Mujaddah, three miles south of Beth-shean.

J. M. Sel.

MEGILLAH: Name of a treatise in the Mishnah and in the Tosefta, as well as in the Babylonian and Jerusalem Talmuds. It is the tenth treatise in the mishnaic order Mo'ed, and includes four chapters, containing thirty-three paragraphs in all. Ch. i. 1–4 treats of the portion of the month Adar in which the Megillah is to be read, and, in case of a leap-year containing two months of Adar, it designates which month is to be chosen. The 15th of Adar, or in a leap-year the same day of the second Adar, is the day appointed for walled cities, and the 14th of Adar for unwalled cities and for villages. The inhabitants of the latter, however, when living in districts where they meet weekly in the neighboring city, may read the roll on the 13th, 12th, or 11th of Adar, if the gathering takes place on one of these days. Since this distinction is made between the two months of Adar of a leap-year, while both months are alike in all other respects, ch. i. 5–11 notes several other groups of objects and cases which differ from one another in one point only; one such group, *e.g.*, consists of the sacred books, the tefillin, and the mezuzah, the first two of which may be written in any language and script, but the last only in Hebrew and in square script. Greek is given the preference over all other foreign languages, since, according to R. Gamaliel, even the sacred books may be written in it.

Ch. ii. deals with the proper manner of reading the Megillah; with the language (mishnah 1), stating that those who do not understand Hebrew may read it in their own tongue; and with the problems whether it shall be read in whole or in part, which portions are to be read (mishnah 3) and at what time of the day. The statement that it may be read during the entire day is supplemented by the enumeration of many other regulations and customs which may be observed throughout the day if they are assigned to the daytime, or throughout the night if assigned to the night (mishnayot 5–6).

Ch. iii. discusses the sale of sacred objects, the synagogue and its furnishings, and the sacredness which still attaches in many respects to the ruins of a synagogue which has been destroyed (mishnayot 1–3). It further discusses the sections which are to be read on the Sabbaths in Adar in addition to the customary weekly sections, and what is to be read on each feast-day (mishnayot 4–6.). From the standpoint of contents this chapter does not belong to the treatise Megillah, being connected with it only by its fourth paragraph.

Ch. iv. begins with certain rules concerning the reading of the Megillah (mishnah 1a); then follow rules referring to other ritual readings from the Law and the Prophets (mishnayot 1b–2). One of these regulations holds that ten persons must be present at each reading; and in this connection many other religious ceremonies are enumerated as requiring the presence of ten persons (mishnah 3). Mishnah 4 defines the relation of the reader to the translator; mishnayot 5–7 determine who may read, who may lead in prayer, and which priest is entitled to lift up his hands for the blessing; mishnah 8 discusses unseemly dress of the prayer-leader and unseemly behavior regarding the tefillin; mishnah 9 enumerates incorrect expressions in prayer, designates the persons who must be silenced in public prayer, and contains various allusions to the views and customs of the sectarians ("minim") of the time; mishnah 10 enumerates the passages in the Torah which may be read but not translated, and the passages in the Prophets which may not be read as hafṭarot.

Interpolations and Digressions.

The sequence of chapters here given is that of the Palestinian Talmud in the manuscript of the Mishnah edited by Lowe, and is also the one found in most of the editions of the Mishnah, in the Tosefta, and in the codices of the Babylonian Talmud at Munich (MS. No. 140) and Oxford (Neubauer, "Cat. Bodl. Hebr. MSS." No. 366). The sequence of chapters in the printed editions of the Babylonian Talmud, on the other hand, corresponds with that of MS. Munich No. 95. Here the chapter cited above as the fourth, "Ha-ḳore et ha-megillah 'omed," precedes the chapter which has been designated as the third, "Bene ha-'ir." R. Hananeel offers a sequence differing from both; making "Ha-ḳore et ha-megillah 'omed" the second chapter, "Ha-ḳore et ha-megillah le-mafrea'" the third, and "Bene ha-'ir" the fourth.

Variations in MS.

The Tosefta to this treatise omits many of the passages contained in the Mishnah, but, on the other hand, it discusses in full detail much that is not found therein. Noteworthy is the enumeration of the passages in the Bible in which a euphemistic word is read instead of an objectionable one (iv. 39), while the condemnation of any translation of the Scriptures is also a striking feature (iv. 41).

The Gemara of the Babylonian Talmud contains in its first chapter, besides explanations of the various mishnayot, many important comments, of which the most interesting are: (1) on the origin of the final letters ך, ם, ן, ף, and ץ (pp. 2b–3a); (2) on the origin of the targumim, that of the Torah being ascribed to the proselyte Onḳelos, and that of the Prophets to Jonathan b. Uzziel (p. 3a; no targum of the Hagiographa seems to have been known at that time); (3) on the origin of Purim, which is said to have been originally merely a local festival at Shushan; the objections raised to its introduction that it might rouse the hatred of the Gentiles against the Jews; the hesitation at including the Book of Esther in the canon, and the reasons why it was finally admitted (p. 7a). The Gemara contains also the legend of the origin of the Septuagint (p. 9a, b). King Ptolemy called together seventy-two elders, assigned each one a separate house, and had them translate the Torah individually and without consultation. All these translations were found to agree absolutely, even to the changes made in certain passages. Pages 10b to 17a of the Gemara form a haggadic midrash to Esther.

Tosefta and Gemara.

The second chapter of the Gemara discusses the several mishnayot, gives an account of the origin of the Shemoneh 'Esreh prayer, and explains the sequence of the several benedictions. In the Gemara on ch. iii. the most noteworthy feature is the remark on the pronunciation of Hebrew current among the inhabitants of Bet-She'on, Bet-Ḥefa, and Tibonin, who confounded "alef" with "'ayin," and "he" with "ḥet." The Gemara to ch. iv. contains, in addition to the notes on the mishnayot, some important regulations regarding public worship. The Gemara of the Palestinian Talmud mentions certain other feast-days in the month of Adar, which were similar to Purim, including the Day of Trajan (טירוין), the 12th, and the Day of Nicanor, the 13th (i. 5). Especially noteworthy is the remark on the origin of square script and on the translation of Aquila (i. 9). The passage in the Palestinian Talmud on Aquila's version compels the assumption that "Onḳelos" in the Babylonian Talmud (3a) is merely a corruption of "Aquila," and that the reference in this latter Talmud also is to the Greek and not to the Aramaic translation.

S. S. J. Z. L.

MEGILLAH OF CAIRO. See EGYPT.

MEGILLAT ANTEYOKOS. See ANTIOCHUS, SCROLL OF.

MEGILLAT SETARIM ("Concealed Roll"): Name of a roll supposed to have been found in the bet ha-midrash of R. Ḥiyya, and which contained halakot recorded by him. Three passages from it, which are maxims of R. Ise b. Judah, are quoted by Abba Arika in the Talmud (Shab. 6b, 96b; B. M. 92a) with the introductory phrase: "I found a hidden roll in the bet ha-midrash of R. Ḥiyya."

According to Rashi (Shab. 6b), although it was not permissible to record halakot, the scholars were accustomed to write in rolls (which were then hidden) such sentences and maxims of various tannaim as were seldom repeated in the schools, and which were, therefore, liable to be forgotten; and he declares the Megillat Setarim was such a roll. This explanation is not satisfactory, however; for according to it R. Ḥiyya could not have been the only one to make such a roll, and yet no manuscript of this character by any other scholar is mentioned. Moreover, it is not easy to see how Rab could have had access to the scroll if it was kept in concealment merely because it was forbidden to write halakot. Rashi's assumption that the interdiction against recording halakot still existed at the time of R. Ḥiyya is wholly incorrect, for Judah ha-Nasi I. abrogated it by committing the MISHNAH to writing. R. Ḥiyya did not conceal his Megillah, therefore, because it contained halakot, but because of their nature, inasmuch as his roll comprised sentences which Judah ha-Nasi had excluded from his Mishnah, besides additions and emendations to Rabbi's Mishnah most of which were contrary to that author's opinions.

R. Ḥiyya hid his Megillah during Rabbi's lifetime that he might not offend him; but after Rabbi's death this reason no longer existed, and Rab was permitted to see the scroll. This explanation of the origin and contents of the Megillat Setarim is also indicated by its name, "concealed roll," which implies that there were rolls containing halakot which were not kept secret, among them Rabbi's Mishnah collection. This view also invalidates the assumption of Lebrecht ("Handschriften und Erste Ausgaben des Talmuds," p. 10), who, in reading "Megillat Sedarim" instead of "Megillat Setarim," infers that this roll contained the six orders ("sedarim") of the Mishnah.

BIBLIOGRAPHY: Weiss, *Dor*, ii. 198; Frankel, *Darke ha-Mishnah*, p. 218, note, Leipsic, 1859.

S. J. Z. L.

MEGILLAT TA'ANIT ("Scroll of Fasting"): A chronicle which enumerates thirty-five eventful days on which the Jewish nation either performed glorious deeds or witnessed joyful events. These days were celebrated as feast-days. Public mourning was forbidden on fourteen of them, and public fasting on all. In most of the editions this chronicle consists of two parts, which are distinct in language and in form, namely: (1) the text or the Megillat Ta'anit proper, written in Aramaic and containing merely brief outlines in concise style; (2) scholia or commentaries on the text, written in Hebrew. The days are enumerated, not in the chronological order of the events they commemorate, but in the sequence of the calendar, the Megillat Ta'anit being divided into twelve chapters, corresponding to the months of the year. Each chapter contains the memorial days of a single month, the first chapter dealing with those of the first month, Nisan, and so on to the twelfth chapter, which treats of those of the twelfth month, Adar.

Five Groups of Feasts.

The festal occasions which these days were intended to keep alive in the memory of the people belong to different epochs; and on this basis the days may be divided into five groups, namely: (1) pre-Maccabean; (2) Hasmonean; (3) ante-Sadducean; (4) ante-Roman; and (5) of the Diaspora, the last-named comprising memorial days admitted after the destruction of the Temple. There are also a few days which do not refer to any known historical event, and are, therefore, chronologically uncertain.

These memorial days did not become festivals by being incorporated and recorded in the Megillat Ta'anit, as J. Schmilg has attempted to prove ("Ueber die Entstehung und den Historischen Werth des Siegeskalenders Megillat Ta'anit," pp. 11-20), but had been known and celebrated by the people long before that time, as he himself is obliged to admit in the case of some of them; indeed, the celebration of these festivals or semi-festivals evidently existed as early as the time of Judith (Judith viii. 6). The compilers of the Megillat Ta'anit merely listed the memorial days and at the same time determined that the less important should be celebrated by a mere suspension of fasting, while public mourning was to be forbidden on the more important ones.

In an old baraita (Shab. 13b) the question as to the authorship of the work is answered as follows: "Hananiah b. Hezekiah of the Garon family, together with a number of others who had assembled for a synod at his house, compiled the Megillat Ta'anit." According to an account in the "Halakot Gedolot, Hilkot Soferim" (ed. Vienna, p. 104; ed. Zolkiev, p. 82c), the members of this synod were the "Ziḳne Bet Shammai" and "Ziḳne Bet Hillel," the eldest pupils of Shammai and Hillel. The Megillat Ta'anit must have been composed, therefore, about the year 7 of the common era, when Judea was made a Roman province to the great indignation of the Jews (comp. Schmilg, *l.c.* pp. 20-36). This calendar of victories was intended to fan the spark of liberty among the people and to fill them with confidence and courage by reminding them of the victories of the Maccabees and the divine aid vouchsafed to the Jewish nation against the heathen.

Authorship.

The scholium to Megillat Ta'anit, xii., end, evidently quoting an old baraita, says: "Eleazar b. Hananiah of the family of Garon together with his followers compiled the Megillat Ta'anit." This Eleazar is identical with the Zealot general Eleazar, who took a noteworthy part in the beginning of the revolt against the Romans, vanquishing the garrison at Jerusalem, as well as Agrippa's troops, and Menahem's Sicarian bands. According to this account, therefore, the Megillat Ta'anit was composed by the Zealots after the year 66 of the common era, during the revolution (Grätz, "Gesch." iii., note 26), although it is not necessary to correct the Talmudic account to agree with the scholium, and to read, as does Grätz, in Shab. 13b, "Eleazar b. Hananiah," instead of "Hananiah." On the other hand, the view of Schmilg (*l.c.*) that the scholium is incorrect is erroneous, since there is both internal and external evidence in favor of its authenticity. The account in the Talmud and that in the scholium may both be accepted, since not only Hananiah the father, but also Eleazar the son, contributed to the compilation of the work. Eleazar, one of the central figures in the war against the Romans, endeavored to strengthen the national consciousness of his people by continuing his father's work, and increased the number of memorial days in the collection, to remind the people how God had always helped them and had given them the victory over external and internal enemies.

Interpolations.

Eleazar did not, however, complete the work, and several days were subsequently added to the list which was definitely closed in Usha, as is proved by the fact that the 12th of Adar is designated as "Trajan's Day," and the 29th of that month as "the day on which the persecutions of Hadrian ceased" (comp. Brann in "Monatsschrift," 1876, p. 379). Furthermore, R. Simon b. Gamaliel, who was nasi at Usha, says in the baraita Shab. 13b: "If we should turn all the days on which we have been saved from some danger into holidays, and list them in the Megillat Ta'anit, we could not satisfy ourselves; for we should be obliged to turn nearly every day into a festival" (comp. Rashi *ad loc.*). This sentence clearly indicates that the work was definitely completed at Usha in the time of R. Simon, in order that no further memorial days might be added.

Hebrew Commentary.

The Hebrew commentary on the Megillat Ta'anit was written much later, the author, who did not live earlier than the seventh century, having before him the text of both the Talmudim as well as that of Bereshit Rabbah (comp. Brann, *l.c.* pp. 410–418, 445–451). The commentator collected those baraitot of the Talmud which contained comments on the Megillat Ta'anit, and jumbled them uncritically with accounts from other, unreliable sources. The references of Schmilg's (*l.c.* pp. 36–41) merely prove that the scholiast endeavored to make his work pass for a product of the tannaitic period. As a matter of fact, however, the Talmud knows only the Aramaic text, which alone is meant by the term "Megillat Ta'anit." This text, which had been committed to writing and was generally known ('Er. 62), was explained and interpreted in the same way as the Bible (Yer. Ta'an. ii. 66a). The many quotations from the Megillat Ta'anit in the Talmud are all taken from the Aramaic text and are introduced by the word "ketib" = "it is written," as in Ḥul. 129b; Meg. 5b; Ta'an. 12a and 18b; there is not a single quotation from the scholium. In Ta'an. 12a, the single passage, "bi-Megillat Ta'anit," from which Schmilg tries to prove that the Talmud quotes the scholium as well as the Megillat, is a later addition (comp. Brann, *l.c.* pp. 457 *et seq.*), and is not found in the Munich manuscript (comp. Rabbinowitz, "Ha-Meassef," iii. 63). Although the comments found in the scholium are mentioned in the Talmud, they are not credited to the Megillat Ta'anit, but are quoted as independent baraitot, so that the scholium took them from the Talmud, and not vice versa.

The Text and the Scholium.

As the text and the scholium of the Megillat Ta'anit are distinct in form and in language, so do they differ also in value. The text is an actual historical source, whose statements may be regarded as authentic, while its dates are reliable if interpreted independently of the scholium. The scholium, on the other hand, is of very doubtful historical value and must be used with extreme caution. Although it contains some old baraitot which are reliable, the compiler has mixed them with other, unhistorical, accounts and legends, so that even those data whose legendary character has not been proved can be credited only when they are confirmed by internal and external evidence.

Editions and Commentaries.

The Megillat Ta'anit is extant in many editions, and has had numerous commentaries. The best edition of the Aramaic and Hebrew text is that by A. Neubauer, which is based on the editio princeps and the Amsterdam edition of 1711, compared with the codex De Rossi (Parma MS. 117) and some fragments of a manuscript in the Bodleian Library, Oxford (Neubauer, "M. J. C." ii. 3–25, Oxford, 1895).

Of commentaries the following may be mentioned: Abraham b. Joseph ha-Levi, double commentary (Amsterdam, 1656); Judah b. Menahem, double commentary (Dyhernfurth, 1810); Johann Meyer, Latin translation published in his "Tractatus de Temporibus," etc. (Amsterdam, 1724). Derenbourg and Schwab have made French versions of the Aramaic text.

Bibliography: Grätz, *Gesch.* iii., notes 1, 26; J. Derenbourg, *Hist.* pp. 439–446; J. Schmilg, *Ueber Entstehung und Historischen Werth des Siegeskalenders Megillat Ta'anit*, Leipsic, 1874; J. Wellhausen, *Die Pharisäer und die Sadducäer*, pp. 56–63, Greifswald, 1874; Joel Müller, *Der Text der Fastenrolle*, in *Monatsschrift*, 1875, pp. 43–48, 139–144; M. Brann, *Entstehung und Werth der Megillat Ta'anit*, pp. 375–384, 410–418, 445–460, *ib.* 1876; P. Cassel, *Messianische Stellen des Alten Testaments*, Appendix, Berlin, 1885; Weiss, *Dor*, ii. 254–257; B. Rattner, in Rabbinowitz, *Ha-Meassef*, 1902, pp. 91–105; M. Schwab, *La Megillath Taanith*, in *Actes du Onzième Congrès International des Orientalistes*, pp. 199–259, Paris, 1898.

S. J. Z. L.

MEGILLAT YUḤASIN (= "Scroll of Genealogies"): A lost work to which several references are made in the Talmud and Mishnah. In Yeb. 49b Ben 'Azzai, in support of a point in law, says: "I found a 'Megillat Yuḥasin' in Jerusalem wherein it was written that . . . is a bastard born of a married woman." On the same page two other citations from the "Megillat Yuḥasin" occur: "The Mishnah of Rabbi Eliezer ben Jacob comprises but a ḳab, but it is choice"; and "Manasseh killed Isaiah." In Yer.

'a'an. iv. 2 and in Yeb. ii. the following occurs: They found a 'Megillat Yuḥasin' in Jerusalem, and herein it is written, 'Hillel was a descendant of)avid; Yannai, of Eli.'" From these allusions it eems that the "Megillat Yuḥasin" was a record of rincipal events, of genealogies, and of facts pertaining to the Law, haggadic and halakic. Pes. 62b nentions a "Sefer Yuḥasin," which may be identical vith the "Megillat Yuḥasin." It must have been a ecret book that was still extant at the beginning of he third century, for R. Johanan bar Nappaḥa reused to teach it to R. Simlai: "We do not teach it to he people of Lydda nd Nehardea." Later n the same century t became lost, and Rab laments the fact vith the words Pes. 62b): "Since he 'Sefer Yuḥasin' as been lost the trength of the ages has been veakened and the ight of their eyes limmed."

Rashi says the 'Sefer Yuḥasin" vas a history, but f it was the same as he "Megillat Yuḥasin," it must have ontained laws and amily records also. Eliakim Milzahagi, he author of "Sefer Rabiah," proposes the xplanation that the 'Megillat Yuḥasin" ontained genealgies, and the 'Sefer Yuḥasin" istory and laws, ut the exact nature f the work, lost ven in Talmudic imes, can not now e ascertained.

BIBLIOGRAPHY: Kohut, *Aruch Completum*, iv. 125, v. 76; Levy, *Neuhebr. Wörterb.* ii. 237, iii. 17; Hamburger, *R. B. T.* ii. 291; Benjacob, *Oẓar ha-Sefarim*, p. 216, No. 113; Zunz, *G. V.* p. 135; Eliakim Milzahagi, *Sefer Rabiah*, viii. 123.

E. C. S. J. L.

MEGILLOT, THE FIVE: The "five rolls" חמש מגלות)—Song of Solomon, Ruth, Lamentaions, Ecclesiastes, and Esther. At the time of the ormation of the canon of the Hagiographa these ive books were not regarded as a unit, nor is the ame "Megillah" as applied to them collectively ound either in the Talmud or in the Midrash. In the ldest two modes of arrangement of the Hagiographa, he Talmudic and the Masoretic, they do not follow ne another, at least in the order in which they tand in the first five editions of the Bible (comp. EW. ENCYC. iii. 144). During the Talmudic period nly the Esther roll was called "Megillah," as is hown by the treatise which bears that name; but since the word assumed the meaning of "a small roll," it was applied to the other four books when they were received into the liturgy in post-Talmudic times (Blau, "Althebräisches Buchwesen," pp. 66 *et seq.*). The sequence of the Song of Solomon and of Ecclesiastes, and probably of Esther, in the canon of the Hagiographa did not escape criticism (see JEW. ENCYC. iii. 149); and in the earliest arrangement Ecclesiastes seems to have stood at the end of the group (*ib.* 145a).

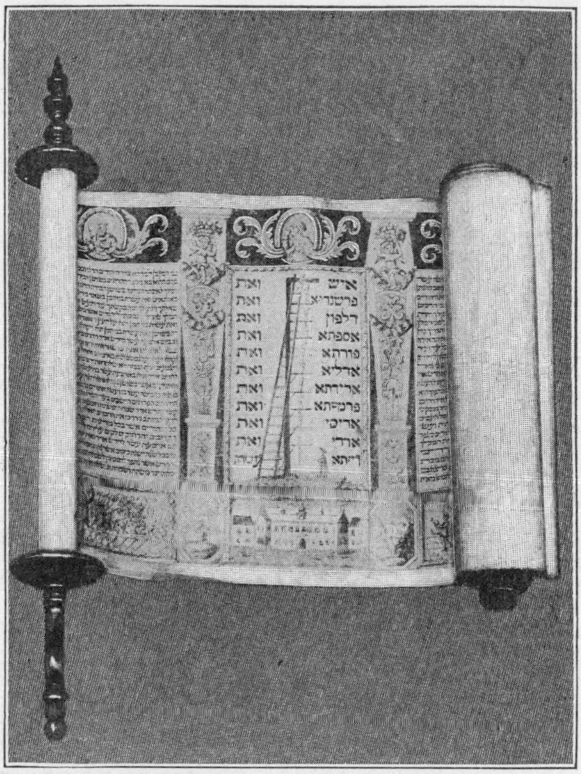

Megillat Esther, Dutch, Early Eighteenth Century.
(In the possession of Arthur E. Franklin, London.)

The oldest sources for the liturgy mention Ruth, Song of Solomon, Lamentations, and Esther, but not Ecclesiastes (Soferim xiv. 3). It is clear from Soferim xiv. 8, where the last-named roll is again ignored, that this is no chance omission. On the other hand, its name is found in the Maḥzor Vitry (p. 440, below): "The entire congregation while seated read the book [ספר, not מגלה] of Ecclesiastes [at the Feast of Tabernacles]." That this custom was of late development is shown by the fact that the entire congregation read—that the book was not read to them. At the time of the Mishnah only Esther was read publicly. In the Talmudic period Lamentations was read privately; while the other three megillot were admitted into the liturgy only in post-Talmudic days, Ecclesiastes being the last of all.

Liturgical usage necessitated manuscripts which should contain not only the Torah and the Hafṭarot from the Prophets, but also the Five Rolls. For the same reason the so-called Midrash Rabbah was gradually collected for the five Megillot as well as for the Torah. The allusions to the individual feasts which Müller ("Soferim," p. 187) finds in the Haggadah furnish no proof that the rolls in question were read at these particular festivals; for by the same process of reasoning it might be inferred from Yer. Meg., end, that the Song of Solomon instead of Ruth was read on the Feast of Pentecost. But Yalḳ., Ruth, 994, says: "Why is Ruth read at Pentecost? Because the Torah was given only through suffering." This statement is not found, however, in any of the parallel passages; and it is, therefore, evidently a later addition, and not an ancient mid-

Late Use in Liturgy.

rash. The late origin of this usage ("minhag") is reflected in the discussions of scholars up to the sixteenth century regarding the form of the benediction and other questions (Isserles, "Oraḥ Ḥayyim," p. 490, end; *idem*, Responsa, No. 35). Soferim xiv. 18 states that at the terminations of the festivals the proper rolls were read twice on the two evenings (Song of Solomon at the Passover; Ruth at Pente-

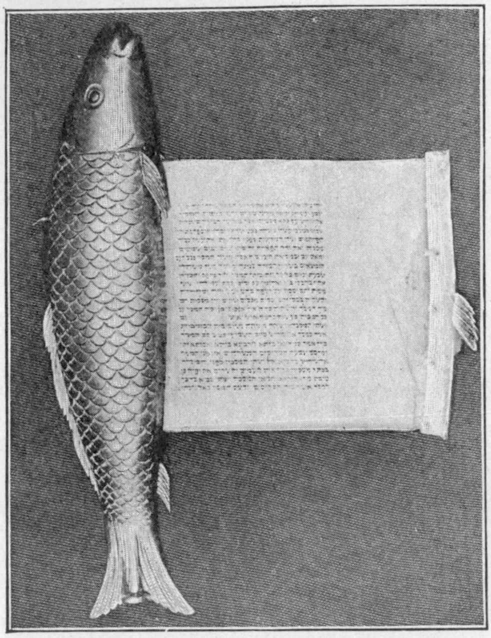

Silver Fish Forming Case for Scroll of Megillat Esther.
(In the possession of Arthur E. Franklin, London.)

cost), or on the Sabbath of each demi-festival, the latter being the custom among the people. It is now customary in Jerusalem to write the Five Rolls on parchment like the other Biblical books, and in reading them to pronounce over all the benediction which is generally used in the case of the roll of Esther, making the proper changes (see further on the Song of Solomon at Passover and Ruth at Pentecost, Maḥzor Vitry, ed. Hurwitz, pp. 304, 344).

Although the Feast of Purim was celebrated long before the present era (II Macc. xv. 36; Josephus, "Ant." xi. 6, § 13; comp. John v. 1), it is doubtful when the custom of reading the roll of Esther publicly was introduced; but it was at all events before the destruction of the Temple (Tosef., Meg. i. 6, where Zechariah ben ha-Ḳaẓẓab is quoted). Although the oldest tannaim are not mentioned in the rules for reading Esther, yet the detailed character of these regulations, and the fact that there is a special tractate on them, show that the usage was developed before the common era. On the other hand, the license allowed villagers on the day of reading, the discussions among scholars as to whether one was required to read only from ii. 5 or iii. 1 or iv. 1 (Meg. ii. 3; Tosef., Meg. ii. 9), together with many concessions as compared with the lessons from the Torah (*e.g.*, minors might read; *ib.* ii. 11, iv. 1),

The Roll of Esther.

and the fact that even in later times large scop was granted to popular custom, justify the con clusion that the origin of the reading of the roll o Esther must not be dated too remotely (Meg. 2a). The custom of reading it in the month of Ada had become general probably by the third centur of the common era, and had been sanctioned (Yer Meg. 70a, 2); but the public reading of the boo for those unable to read had apparently been in troduced a century before. In the third centur (*ib.* 73b, 28) the entire roll was usually read, bu only once and in the daytime (Meg. ii. 4, 5), whil during the persecution by Hadrian a scribe rea it at night (Tosef., Meg. ii. 4). In many place in Palestine it was read on two days (Yer. Sheḳ 46a, 8). The custom of reading in both the evenin and the morning, which now generally prevails was not established until the post-Talmudic perio (Soferim xxi. 8; comp. also Maḥzor Vitry, pp. 207 *e seq.*). The Karaites read the roll at the ends of th two Sabbaths which precede Purim, a reminiscenc

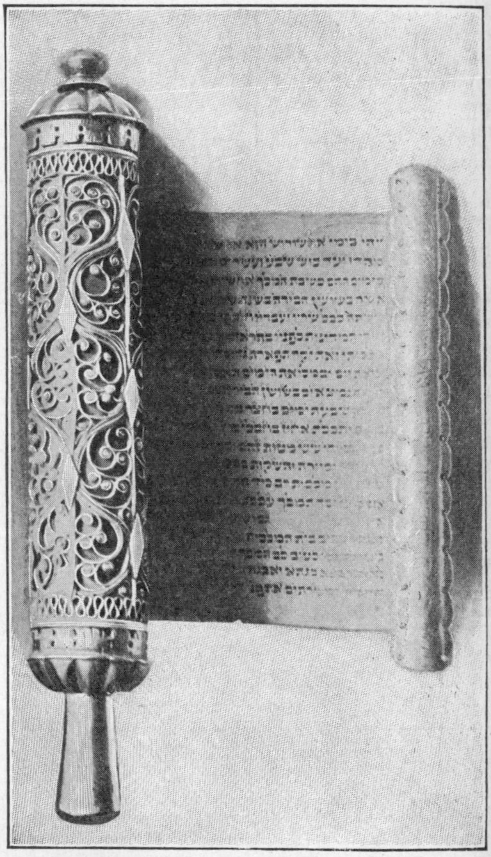

Silver Case Containing Scroll of Megillat Esther.
(In the possession of Maurice Herrmann, New York.)

of the original custom of reading it throughou Adar until the fifteenth. The Megillah was wrappe about a rod (the Maḥzor Vitry mentions two rods) and in the Middle Ages it was often illuminated.

In the Talmudic period Lamentations formed n part of the service; and, strictly speaking, it ha never become such. In Ta'an. 30a, below, the baraita states that on the Ninth of Ab the Bible may not be read nor the tradition studied, but that "Job, Lamentations, and the sections of Jeremiah which deal with calamity," may be recited. In post-Talmudic times, however, the custom of reading Lamentations had become general (Soferim xiv. 3). The book was also read responsively (Maḥzor Vitry, p. 226); and in many synagogues, because the Ninth of Ab is a day of mourning, only one light was lit by which it might be read (R. Asher, Ta'an. 9, end). The persecutions of the Crusades strongly influenced the gloom of Tish'ah be-Ab and its liturgy (see Maḥzor Vitry, p. 227, and Oraḥ Ḥayyim, § 554). See, also, ECCLESIASTES; ESTHER, BOOK OF; LAMENTATIONS; RUTH; and SONG OF SONGS.

Lamentations.

S. L. B.

MEHLSACK, ELIAKIM. See SAMILER, A. C.

MEIER, MORITZ HERMANN EDUARD: German philologist; born at Glogau, Silesia, Jan. 1, 1796; died at Halle Dec. 5, 1855. He was educated at the Graue Kloster in Berlin and at the universities of Breslau and Berlin (Ph.D. 1818). He embraced Christianity in 1817. In 1819 he became privat-docent in the University of Halle; in 1820, assistant professor at Greifswald; and in 1825, professor of ancient philology at Halle.

Of Meier's many works may be mentioned the following: (with Schömann) "Der Attische Process" (Halle, 1827), which received the prize from the Berlin Academy of Sciences; "De Gentilitate Attica," *ib.* 1835; "De Andocidis Oratione Contra Alcibiadem," *ib.* 1836; "De Crantoris Solensis Libro Deperdito," *ib.* 1840; "De Proxenio sive de Publico Græcorum Hospitio," *ib.* 1843; "Fragmentum Lexici Rhetorici," *ib.* 1844; "Die Privatschiedsrichter und die Oeffentlichen Dieten Athens," *ib.* 1846; "De Vita Lycurgi et de Lycurgi Orationum Reliquiis," *ib.* 1847. In 1832 he published (at Halle) an edition of Demosthenes' speech against Midias.

From 1828 Meier was coeditor of the "Allgemeine Litteraturzeitung." He edited also (from 1830 with Kämtz; from 1842 alone) the third section of Ersch and Gruber's "Allgemeine Encyklopädie der Wissenschaften und Künste," and from 1852 also the first section of that work. Eckstein and Haase published in Leipsic (1861-63) a collection of Meier's essays under the title "Opuscula Academica."

BIBLIOGRAPHY: G. Hertzberg, in *Allgemeine Deutsche Biographie*.

S. F. T. H.

ME'ILAH ("Trespass in Regard to a Holy Thing"): Treatise of Seder Ḳodashim in the Mishnah, Tosefta, and the Babylonian Talmud. In the Mishnaic order this treatise is the eighth, and contains six chapters comprising thirty-eight paragraphs in all. It deals chiefly with the exact provisions of the Law (Lev. v. 15-16) concerning the trespass-offering and the reparation which must be made by one who has used and enjoyed a consecrated thing. Its contents may be summarized as follows:

Ch. i.: Sacrifices in which trespass can occur; in what parts: in the most holy sacrifices ("ḳodshe ḳodashim") in all parts and in the partly holy ("ḳodashim ḳallim") in certain parts only. Cases in which trespass can occur and those in which it can not occur. Rule of R. Joshua that if the priests have once had the right to eat of a sacrifice no trespass can take place (§ 1). In this connection the question is raised whether there can be a trespass in the case of those parts of the sacrifice which have been removed from the sanctuary before the sprinkling of the blood (§§ 2-3). Effects of the sprinkling upon the sacrificial animal with regard to trespass (§ 4).

Ch. ii.: The time after which a trespass can take place in the various meat-offerings, the different offerings of food, the Pentecostal bread, and the showbread. Closely allied with this is the determination of the time after which the different sacrifices may be invalidated by certain errors, and the period after which one may become guilty of "piggul" (abomination), "notar" (leaving something over from the sacrifice), and "ṭame" (impurity) in connection with them (§§ 1-9).

In the Mishnah.

Ch. iii.: An enumeration of many things of which one may not partake, although if he does so, he is not guilty of trespass. This leads to a discussion of other regulations concerning certain of these things, as well as of the question whether and in what case one may be guilty of trespass in connection with objects belonging to or found upon certain consecrated things, such as grass in a consecrated field, the fruit of a consecrated tree (§ 6), and the foliage in a consecrated wood (§ 8).

Ch. iv.: The combination of various sacrifices in reckoning the minimum amount necessary to be used in order to constitute trespass (§§ 1-2). In this connection many more kinds of combinations are given with relation to other legal and ritual questions.

Ch. v.: Determination of a peruṭa, the smallest coin, as the minimum value which the use of holy objects must have to make one guilty of trespass. Discussion of the question whether the use made of a consecrated object must be worth a peruṭa or whether the amount of the object consumed by this usage must equal a peruṭa; in connection with which a distinction is made between different objects (§ 1). The commission of trespass by various persons successively upon the same object.

Ch. vi.: Cases in which the trespass has been committed by proxy. The principle is laid down that if the agent has acted precisely in accordance with his orders, the person who gave such orders is guilty of the trespass; but if the agent has not so acted, he himself is guilty of the trespass. Enumeration of different examples (§§ 1-5). Cases in which neither of the two is guilty of trespass and instances in which both trespass (§ 4).

In the Tosefta and Gemara.

In the Tosefta, Me'ilah is the seventh treatise and has but three chapters. These, however, contain all that is in the six chapters of the Mishnah, with a few omissions and amplifications.

The Gemara to this treatise is devoted almost exclusively to elucidations of the mishnayot, there being only one haggadah in the treatise, bearing on the story of BEN TEMALION.

There is no gemara of the Jerusalem Talmud to this treatise, nor in fact to any treatise of the order Ḳodashim (comp. Buber, "Die Angebliche Existenz eines Jerusal. Talmud zur Ordnung Kodaschim," in Berliner's "Magazin," 1878, pp. 100–105).

S. S. J. Z. L.

MEINEK, MOSES SÄKEL (called also **Moses Isaac ben Baruch of Redwitz**): German scholar and editor; lived at Offenbach at the beginning of the eighteenth century. He published in 1715, under his own name, Naphtali Pappenheim's "Teutsche Apothek," and in 1717 a riddle in Judæo-German verse composed by an anonymous author. This riddle was reproduced, with a German transcription, by Schudt in his "Jüdische Merckwürdigkeiten" (iv., continuation iii. 108–109), Schudt referring to Meinek as a printer. In 1722 Meinek edited the anonymous "Siyyumah ha-Parashiyyot meha-Torah," a guide for the reader of the Law. He was probably himself the author.

Bibliography: Steinschneider, *Cat. Bodl.* Nos. 3632, 3976, and col. 1944; Wolf, *Bibl. Hebr.* iii., No. 1572c, iv., No. 1547c; Benjacob, *Oẓar ha-Sefarim*, p. 419.

J. M. Sel.

MEÏR (MEÏR BA'AL HA-NES = "Meïr the miracle-worker"): Tanna of the second century (fourth generation); born in Asia Minor. The origin of this remarkable scholar, one of the most striking figures of his age, is wrapped in obscurity. According to a haggadah, he was a descendant of Nero, who, says a Jewish legend, escaped death at the time of his deposition and became subsequently a convert to Judaism (Giṭ. 56a). The mystery of Meïr's origin extends to his name, for according to the Talmud the name "Meïr" (="one who enlightens") was given to him because he instructed the wise in the Law ('Er. 13b); as to his original name, the Babylonian Talmud (*l.c.*) gives it as "Me'asha," but the Jerusalem Talmud seems not to know it. Sometimes he is called "Nehorai," the Aramaic equivalent of "Meïr." Meïr began to study very early in life. At first he entered the school of Akiba, but, finding himself not sufficiently prepared to grasp the lectures of that great master, he went to the school of Ishmael, where he acquired an extensive knowledge of the Law. He then returned to Akiba, who, recognizing his dialectical powers, ordained him over the heads of his other disciples ('Er. *l.c.*). This ordination, which was considered invalid on account of Meïr's youth, was confirmed by Judah ben Baba (Sanh. 14a; see Rashi *ad loc.*).

Ordained in Youth.

Unlike his master Akiba, Meïr seems to have kept aloof from the revolutionary movement of Bar Kokba. Nevertheless he suffered greatly from its consequences. His father-in-law, Hananiah ben Teradion, fell a martyr to the Hadrianic persecutions, and his sister-in-law was taken to Rome and sold to a keeper of a house of ill fame. A tale of her rescue by Meïr, though embellished with legend, may have a foundation in fact. Urged by his wife to attempt the rescue of her sister, who, she asserted, would rather forfeit her life than her virtue, Meïr journeyed to Rome. Attired as a wealthy Roman, he went to the house to which she had been taken, and asked to see her. "She is very beautiful," said the keeper, "but no man has as yet gained her favor." Overjoyed, Meïr offered him a large sum of money to permit her to be carried off. The keeper hesitated, fearing that it might cost him his head. "Fear not," said the rabbi; "when danger threatens thee say, 'Meïr's God, help me!'" Still the man hesitated. To convince him of the efficacy of his advice, Meïr approached a number of savage watch-dogs at the gate and by a mystic word made them cringe at his feet. His fears allayed, the keeper yielded ('Ab. Zarah 18a; Eccl. R. vii. 12).

During the Hadrianic persecutions Meïr lived abroad, but he returned to Judea after the repeal of the oppressive edicts, and took a prominent part in the reestablishment of the Sanhedrin in the city of Usha. Shortly afterward Simeon ben Gamaliel II. was elected patriarch, and Meïr was raised to the dignity of ḥakam, in which office he was charged with the duty of preparing the subjects to be discussed in the Sanhedrin. To his activity and influence was due the adoption of the laws known as the "Institutions of Usha." To his duties in connection with the Sanhedrin Meïr added the establishment of academies of his own in Bethsan, Ammaus near Tiberias, etc., where he successively lived and lectured. A wonderful feat of memory displayed by him on one of his travels is mentioned in the Talmud. On the eve of the Feast of Purim, Meïr found himself in a small Jewish community where no copy of the Book of Esther could be found; he thereupon wrote out the book from memory without a mistake (Tosef., Megillah, ii.).

At Usha.

Meïr infused new life into the development of the Halakah. He introduced the rule of testing the validity of a halakah on rational grounds. The dialectical power displayed by him in halakic discussion was so great that most of his hearers followed him with difficulty. "He was able," says the Talmud, "to give a hundred and fifty reasons to prove a thing legally clean, and as many more reasons to prove it unclean" ('Er. 13b). This excess of dialectics is given in the Talmud as the only reason why his halakot did not receive the force of law; the *pros* and *cons* offered by him were so nearly equal in strength that one never knew his real opinion on a subject. In the deduction of new halakot from the Biblical text Meïr used with great caution the hermeneutic rules established by his teacher Ishmael, regarding them as unreliable; and he rejected Aki-

Synagogue at the Alleged Tomb of Rabbi Meïr at Tiberias.
(From a photograph.)

a's method of deducing a new halakah from a eemingly superfluous particle in the Scriptural text Soṭah 17a; Sifre, Balaḳ, 131). Meïr's greatest erit in the field of the Halakah was that he connued the labors of Akiba in arranging the rich marial of the oral law according to subjects, thus aving the way for the compilation of the Mishnah y Judah ha-Nasi.

Meïr's haggadot won by far the greater populary; in this direction he was among the foremost.

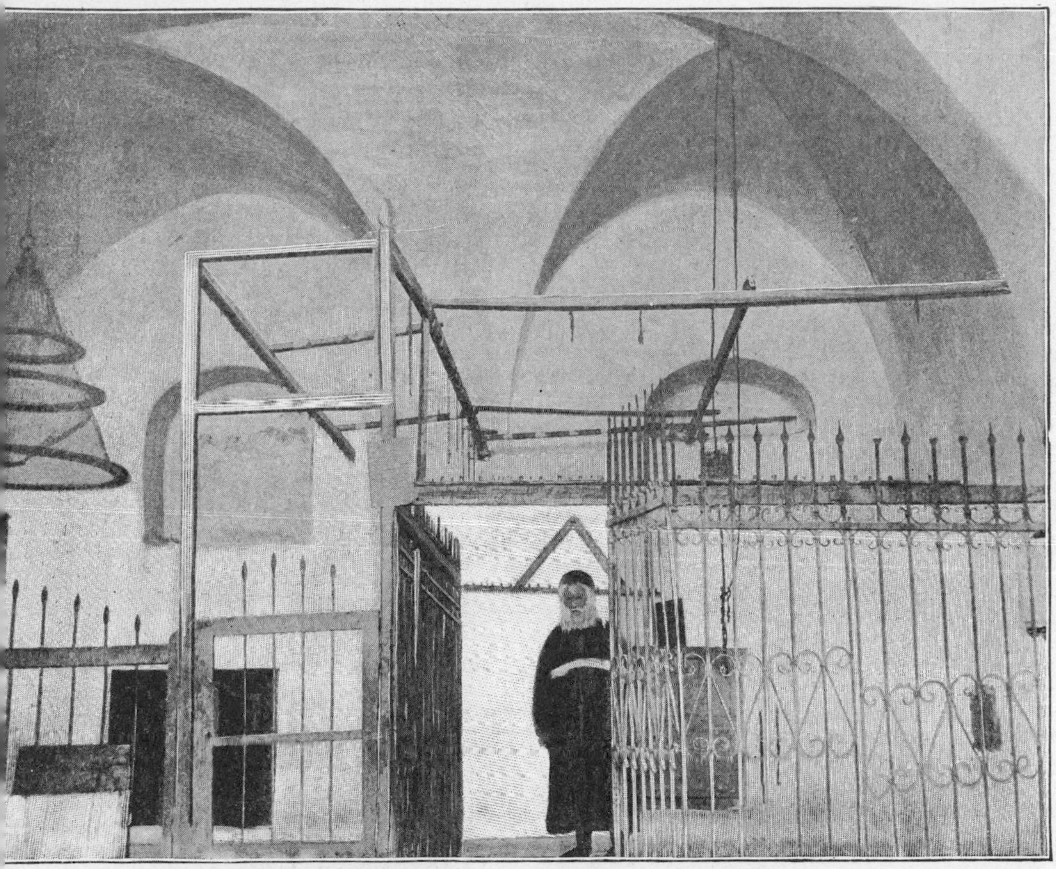

INTERIOR OF THE ALLEGED TOMB OF RABBI MEÏR AT TIBERIAS.
(From a photograph by Elkan N. Adler, London.)

Vell versed in the Greek and Latin literatures, he ould quote in his haggadic lectures fables, parables, and maxims which captivated his hearers. To popularize the Haggadah he wrote haggadic glosses on the margin of his Bible and composed idrashim. Both glosses and midrashim are no nger in existence, but they are quoted in the midashic literature, the former under the title "Torah hel Rabbi Meïr," or "Sifra shel Rabbi Meïr," and he latter, on the Decalogue, under the title "Midrash noki de-Rabbi Meïr" (Gen. R. ix. 5). To Meïr is ttributed also a collection of three hundred fables, hree of which are referred to in the Talmud (Sanh. 8b; see ÆSOP'S FABLES AMONG THE JEWS). mong those of Meïr's maxims that have found a

His Haggadah.

place with the traditional sayings of the Fathers are these: "Have little business, and be busied in the Torah"; "Be lowly in spirit to every man"; "If thou idlest from the Torah, thou wilt have many idlers against thee"; "If thou laborest in the Torah, He hath much to give unto thee" (Ab. iv. 14). Other maxims of his, on study and the fear of the Lord, have been transmitted by Johanan: "Learn the ways of the Lord with thy whole heart and with thy whole soul"; "Watch at the gates of the Law"; "Keep the Law in thy heart"; "Let the fear of the Lord be always before thine eyes and keep thy tongue from evil words"; "Cleanse and make thyself pure that thou mayest stand without sin before the Lord, and He will be with thee" (Ber. 17a).

An instance of Meïr's humility and love of peace is related in the Midrash. Among his hearers was a woman who never missed a lecture of his. Once, the discourse being more prolonged than usual, the woman returned home late in the evening. This infuriated her husband, who turned her out-of-doors and swore that he would not take her in until she had spat in Meïr's face. Refusing to do this, she lived separated from her husband. When Meïr was informed of the incident he went to the woman and, pretending to have a sore eye, requested her to spit in it to heal it (Lev. R., Deut. R.). Meïr was noted for his hatred of ignorance. "He that gives his daughter to an 'am ha-areẓ is as though he put her before a lion" (Pes. 56a). "He who leaves an 'am ha-areẓ in his house asleep and returns to find him awake may be sure the house has been polluted" (Ṭoh. 8a). Still he would rise before an old man, even if he were an 'am ha-areẓ (Yer. Bik. 65c).

Hatred of Ignorance.

Meïr's experience of the world was wide and varied, and the Haggadah records several of his social maxims: "Love the friend who admonishes thee and hate the one who flatters thee; for the former leads thee to life and the future world, while the latter puts thee out of the world." "Conciliate not thy friend in the hour of his passion; console him not when his dead is laid out before him; question him not in the hour of his vow; and strive to see him not in the hour of his disgrace" (Ab. R. N. xxix.; comp. *ib.* xxxvi. and Ab. iv. 18, where these maxims are given in the name of Simeon ben Eliezer). Meïr was fond of discoursing upon traveling. "When thou art in Rome do as the Romans do" (Gen. R. xlviii.). "Travelers should go in threes, for a single traveler is likely to be murdered; two are likely to quarrel; but three will always make their way in peace" (Eccl. R. iv.). Meïr exalts work and recommends parents to instruct their children in a clean trade (Ḳid. 82a). "He who does not work on week-days will end by being compelled to work even on Sabbaths; for idleness leads to misery, and misery to crime; and once a prisoner, the idler will be forced to labor even on the Sabbath" (Ab. R. N. xxi.). "It is not the trade followed but the merit of the workman which makes him rich or poor" (Ḳid. *l.c.*). Those who run after riches are reproved by Meïr in the following saying: "Man comes into the world with closed hands as though claiming ownership of everything; but he leaves it with hands open and limp, as if to show that he takes nothing with him. Yet if man has sought the best course in life, his reward awaits him beyond the grave; there he finds the table set for a feast of joy that will last through eternity" (Eccl. R. i.).

Maxims and Views.

Meïr's generosity and confidence in God are illustrated by the following details of his private life given in the Midrash (Eccl. R. ii. 18). By successfully following the calling of public scribe he earned three shekels a week. Of these two were spent on his household and one was given to poor fellow students. When asked why he did not save something for his children he answered, "If my children are good the Lord will provide for them, for it is said, 'I was young and I am old, yet I have never seen the righteous forsaken nor his seed demanding bread' [Ps. xxxvii. 25]. If my children are not good they deserve nothing, and it would be aiding the enemies of the Lord if I left them wealth." With all his piety, Meïr showed a spirit of great tolerance. He declared that a heathen who occupied himself with the Torah was as worthy of Judaism as a high priest, for it is said, "Ye shall therefore keep my statutes . . . which if a man do, he shall live in them" (Lev. xviii. 5). He explained this to mean that eternal happiness was not the heritage of the Jews exclusively (Sifra to Lev. *l.c.*). Thus Meïr is said to have lived on friendly terms with heathen scholars, with whom he had religious controversies; he was especially intimate with the Greek philosopher Euonymus of Gedara, to whom he paid a visit of condolence on the death of the latter's parents (Gen. R. lxv.; Lam. R., proem, 2).

Meïr's tolerance, however, is best shown by his attitude toward the apostate Elisha ben Abuyah (Aḥer), his teacher. Of all Elisha's colleagues he alone, perhaps in the hope of reclaiming him for Judaism, continued to associate with him and discuss with him scientific subjects, not heeding the remonstrances of some pious rabbis who regarded this association with some suspicion. Meïr's attachment for Elisha was so great that on the death of the latter he is said to have spread his mantle over his friend's grave. Thereupon, according to a legend, a pillar of smoke arose from it, and Meïr, paraphrasing Ruth iii. 13, exclaimed, "Rest here in the night; in the dawn of happiness the God of mercy will deliver thee; if not, I will be thy redeemer" (Ḥag. 15b). The same haggadah adds that at the death of Meïr smoke ceased to issue from Elisha's grave. Notwithstanding his tolerance, Meïr's treatment of the Samaritans was very severe; and he enacted several laws that were destined to widen the breach between them and the main body of Judaism (Ḥul. 6a). The Midrash (Gen. R. xv.; Pesiḳ. R. 23) reports several religious controversies between Meïr and Samaritan scholars concerning creation, resurrection, and similar subjects.

Relations with Aḥer.

The later part of Meïr's life was saddened by many misfortunes. In one day he lost two promising sons, who died suddenly on a Sabbath while he was at the house of study. A story is related in a midrash (quoted in Yalḳ., Prov. 964) of the fortitude shown on that occasion by Meïr's learned wife, Beruriah. Controlling her feelings, she withheld the knowledge of their death from her husband during the Sabbath in order that the day should not be profaned by weeping and lamentation, and on the conclusion of the Sabbath sought to console her husband with a parable. Shortly after the death of his sons Meïr lost his wife. According to a legend, she committed suicide after having been dishonored by one of her husband's pupils (Rashi to 'Ab. Zarah 18a).

The last years of Meïr's life were passed in Asia Minor. He was induced to leave Palestine because of the conflict that arose between him and the patriarch. The origin of this conflict was the change introduced by Simeon in the ceremonial of the Sanhedrin. Custom required its members to rise when the president, the judge, or the reader entered the academy. Simeon, having an exaggerated idea of his dignity, issued an order that the assembly should rise as a body only on his own entrance, while on the entrance of the judge only the first row, and on that of the reader only the second row, should rise. Meïr and Nathan (the judge) felt justly offended at this new arrangement and determined to show Simeon's unfitness for his office by puzzling him with difficult halakic questions which he would be unable to answer. Informed of this con

Opposes the Patriarch.

spiracy, Simeon expelled them from the Sanhedrin, but he could not prevent them from writing difficult questions and distributing them among its members. Compelled to readmit both Nathan and Meïr, he contrived that their names should not be recorded in the ordinances enacted by him. Nathan submitted, but Meïr continued to embarrass the patriarch by addressing to him difficult questions. When, at last, the patriarch threatened excommunication, he answered, "I do not care for your sentence unless you can prove to me on whom, on what grounds, and under what conditions excommunication may be imposed," and left the Sanhedrin (Yer. M. Ḳ. iii. 81a).

Meïr died somewhere in Asia Minor. "Bury me," said he to his pupils, "by the shore, that the sea which washes the land of my fathers may touch also my bones" (Yer. Kil., end). Though during life Meïr had many adversaries, after his death the tribute paid to his virtue and greatness was universal. "He opened the eyes even of the wise in the Law" is said of him in the Talmud ('Er. 13b). An amora said: "The Creator of the world knows that Meïr had not his equal in his time" (*ib.*). R. Jose, in pronouncing Meïr's funeral sermon at Sepphoris said: "He was a great man and a saint, and was humble withal" (Yer. Ber. ii. 56b). Of all the Tannaim, Meïr's name is most widely known among the people. In the house of every pious Jew there is a money-box hung on the wall in which the inmates deposit their alms for the poor of Palestine; this box is called "Meïr Ba'al ha-Nes Pushke."

BIBLIOGRAPHY: Heilprin, *Seder ha-Dorot*, vol. i.; Blumenthal, *Rabbi Meïr, Leben und Wirken*, Frankfort-on-the-Main, 1888; Revson, *Toledot Rabbi Meïr*, Warsaw, 1889; *Meïr Bat 'Ayin*, Tunis, 1899; Landsberg, in *Ha-Ẓofeh*, i. 87; Grätz, *Gesch.* iv. 130; Weiss, *Dor*, ii. 132; Bacher, *Ag. Tan.* ii. 2 *et seq.*; Braunschweiger, *Die Lehrer der Mishnah*, pp. 186 *et seq.*, Frankfort-on-the-Main, 1903.

J. I. BR.

MEÏR (MAESTRO BENDIG) OF ARLES. See BENDIG, MEÏR.

MEÏR BEN BARUCH HA-LEVI: Rabbi at Vienna from 1360 to 1390, a native of Fulda (Isserlein, "Terumat ha-Deshen," No. 81). His authority was acknowledged not only throughout Germany, but even by the Spanish rabbis (Isaac b. Sheshet, Responsa, No. 278). He acquired great celebrity through his introduction into Germany of the rabbinical system of ordination. Owing to persecutions, the number of competent rabbis had decreased, and persons unqualified were inducted into rabbinates. To prevent this Meïr issued an order to the effect that no Talmudical student should officiate as rabbi unless he had been ordained and had acquired the title of "morenu" (Isaac b. Sheshet, *l.c.* Nos. 268–272). At first the order provoked the opposition of many rabbis, who accused Meïr of a desire to rule; but they afterward accepted it. Later Meïr assumed authority over the French rabbis, and sent to France ISAIAH B. ABBA MARI with authority to appoint rabbis there.

Although Meïr left no work, it appears from Jacob Mölln, who frequently mentions him in his "Minhagim," that he collaborated with his contemporaries Abraham Klausner and Shalom of Neustadt in the compilation of a work on ritual customs. Two "teḥinnot" for the 10th of Adar and the 23d of Iyyar respectively are ascribed to Meïr.

BIBLIOGRAPHY: Auerbach, *Berit Abraham*, Preface, p. 6, Frankfort-on-the-Main, 1860; Grätz, *Gesch.* 3d ed., viii. 10 *et seq.*, 36; Weiss, *Dor*, v. 169 *et seq.*; Wolf, *Gesch. der Juden in Wien*, p. 14, Vienna, 1876.

G. M. SEL.

MEÏR CALW (CALVO; קאלוו): Biblical commentator; the country and year of his birth are unknown. As he quotes Levi b. Gershon it may be assumed that he lived not earlier than the fifteenth century. Meïr Calw was the author of a commentary on the Pentateuch entitled "Minḥah Ḥadashah," extracts from which were published by Heidenheim in one of his editions of the Pentateuch (Rödelheim, 1818–21).

BIBLIOGRAPHY: Benjacob, *Oẓar ha-Sefarim*, p. 339; Steinschneider, *Cat. Bodl.* col. 1695; Fürst, *Bibl. Jud.* i. 140.

D. M. SEL.

MEÏR OF CLISSON: French Talmudist of the first half of the thirteenth century. He is mentioned in an extract from "Pa'neaḥ Raza" (MS. Halberstam) on Gen. ii. 23 as a Bible commentator. Gross takes him to be identical with Meïr ben Baruch, who emigrated to Jerusalem in 1211 together with his brother the tosafist Joseph of Clisson and many other French rabbis.

BIBLIOGRAPHY: Gross, in *R. E. J.* vi. 128; idem, *Gallia Judaica*, p. 596.

S. S. A. PE.

MEÏR B. DAVID: Grammarian of the last third of the thirteenth century. He wrote, under the title "Hassagat ha-Hassagah," a criticism of Ibn Janaḥ's "Kitab al-Mustalḥaḳ." Meïr's work is known, however, only through passages quoted by Profiat Duran ("Ma'aseh Efod," pp. 116, 173). Joseph ibn Kaspi, who knew Meïr b. David personally, quotes, in his supercommentary on Ibn Ezra, an explanation which he heard from Meïr's lips (see Dukes, "Naḥal Ḳedumim," p. 9). Meïr is probably identical with the grammarian R. David, whose note on Job vii. 4 is quoted by Abraham Bedersi in his work on synonyms, "Ḥotam Toknit" (p. 189; comp. Introduction, p. x.).

T. W. B.

MEÏR BEN ELEAZAR (known also as **Meïr Lombard** [לונבורט, למברט] **ha-Darshan**): French liturgical poet of the first half of the thirteenth century. He wrote: (1) a series of poems to be recited on the seventh evening of Passover, some of which are arranged in alphabetical order; (2) a dirge beginning "Ẓiyyon ẓefirat pe'er," giving at the end in an acrostic "Meïr Ḥazaḳ"; (3) an alphabetical introduction to the Targum of Ex. xiii. 21, a passage which is read on the seventh day of Passover. The last-named poem is composed of six strophes, of four verses each, beginning with "It ḥazuta we-dugma." According to Landshuth ("'Ammude ha-'Abodah," p. 159), Meïr was the author of the dirge beginning "Aḥbirah millin," which is recited on the Ninth of Ab; but Zunz ("Literaturgesch." p. 360; Supplement, p. 38) ascribes it to Meïr of Rothenburg (comp. *ib.* p. 469).

G. M. SEL.

MEÏR BEN ELIAKIM: German liturgist; probably lived at Posen toward the end of the seventeenth century; author of "Meïr Elohim" (n.p., n.d.), a collection of Biblical passages to be recited on entering the synagogue, and ethical directions for prayer. Meïr says in this work that he wrote two "Menorot" containing collections of prayers, and Steinschneider thinks that the "Menorah" printed at Prague in 1696 may be one of them.

BIBLIOGRAPHY: Steinschneider, *Cat. Bodl.* col. 1697.
J. M. SEL.

MEÏR BEN ELIJAH OF NORWICH: English poet; flourished about 1260 at Norwich. One long elegiac poem and fifteen smaller ones by him are found in a Vatican manuscript, from which they were published by A. Berliner (London, 1887). It is possible that Meïr was a son of Elias Levesque (Jacobs and Wolf, "Bibl. Anglo-Jud." No. 102; A. Berliner, in "Hebräische Poesien von Meïr ben Eliah aus Norwich," Introduction). J.

MEÏR (MOSES MEÏR) B. EPHRAIM OF PADUA: Scribe and printer at Mantua; died in Nov., 1583. After practising various professions he settled in Mantua as a scribe. He was well versed in Talmud, and was a friend of Moses Provençal. There were forty-three of his scrolls among the Italian communities, the first being completed Oct. 23, 1541; the last was begun April 5, 1582. His standard scroll, which served as a model for his other work, was used by the community of Mantua, where it is still preserved. It contains a long colophon, in which all who gave him commissions and the dates of the completion of his scrolls are mentioned. For a time he wrote tefillin also. His method of writing gave rise to a learned controversy among the Italian rabbis, which was finally decided in his favor by R. Meïr KATZENELLENBOGEN. He was the author of a treatise on the "Taggin," and was likewise active as a teacher of the Bible, his system of instruction being praised by Abraham Portaleone. In 1556 he founded a printing establishment at Mantua, which was continued after his death, doing good service at a time when the Inquisition was active and Hebrew books were interdicted. He published, among other works, the first edition of the Zohar (1558-60), the Mishnah, the Shulḥan 'Aruk, Dei Rossi's "Me'or 'Enayim," the "Mishneh Torah," and the Talmudic treatises, all these being issued in handy volumes.

BIBLIOGRAPHY: Zunz, *Z. G.* pp. 252 *et seq.*; Mortara, *Indice*, p. 46; and especially D. Kaufmann, in *J. Q. R.* xi. 266 *et seq.*; *R. E. J.* xxxii. 130 *et seq.*
J. I. E.

MEÏR B. GEDALIAH OF LUBLIN. See LUBLIN, MEÏR B. GEDALIAH.

MEÏR BEN ISAAC OF ORLEANS: French liturgical poet and, possibly, Biblical commentator of the end of the eleventh century. Meïr and his son **Eleazar** are quoted in the commentary to I Chron. (xxix. 11) wrongly ascribed to Rashi. He composed several piyyuṭim, the best known of which are "Torah ha-Temimah" (a supplication interspersed with many Aramaic and Talmudic words and having the general rime in מה, and in which he expresses his horror of apostasy) and "Almanot Ḥayyot," a seliḥah for Yom Kippur. Both piyyuṭim are signed מאיר בר יצחק חזק and are acrostics containing the name "Eleazar." The second piyyuṭ was translated into German by Zunz ("S. P." p. 184). There is a seliḥah beginning "Mi yodea' yashub," referring to a massacre of 3,000 Jews by the Crusaders, which, though it is signed מאיר בר יצחק חזן and is an acrostic containing the name "Eleazar," is supposed by Zunz to have been composed a century later.

BIBLIOGRAPHY: Gross, *Gallia Judaica*, p. 33; Landshuth, *'Ammude ha-'Abodah*, p. 167; Zunz, *Literaturgesch.* p. 251.
J. M. SEL.

MEÏR B. ISAAC OF TRINQUETAILLE: French scholar of the twelfth century; a member of the family of Menahem Meïri of Perpignan. He was a native of Carcassonne, whence his father took him to Provence, where he soon became one of the most distinguished pupils of Abraham David (RaBaD) of Posquières. After settling at Trinquetaille, a suburb of Arles, he composed the following two works: "Sefer ha-'Ezer," a defense of Alfasi against the attacks of Zerahiah b. Isaac ha-Levi Gerondi; "Ḥibbur ha-Muḳẓeh," a treatise enumerating all the things that may not be touched on Sabbaths and feast-days.

BIBLIOGRAPHY: Gross, *Gallia Judaica*, p. 246; Isaac de Lattes, *Sha'are Ẓiyyon*, p. 72; Meïri, Introduction to the *Bet ha-Beḥirah*, p. 17b; Renan-Neubauer, *Les Rabbins Français*, p. 515.
J. S. K.

MEÏR IBN JAIR: Italian (?) Talmudist and grammarian of the sixteenth century. His family name seems to have been "Meïri"; for he is always mentioned under the name of "Meïr le-Bet Meïr" (= "Meïr of the house of Meïr"). He is called "Ibn Jair" because ן" יאיר is written after his name in the manuscript sources; it may, however, be an equivalent of "Meïr" or may mean "May his light continue." Meïr was the author of: "Yaïr Natib," or, according to Nepi-Ghirondi ("Toledot Gedole Yisrael," p. 255), "Meïr Natib" (Sabbionetta, 1553), a treatise on the law concerning the slaughtering of animals, frequently quoted by Ḥayyim Benveniste in his "Keneset ha-Gedolah"; a treatise on the eight conjugations in Hebrew grammar, under the title "Simane kol Shemonah Binyanim" (*ib.* 1554), a work which was afterward revised by the author and published under the title of "Diḳduḳ" (*ib.* 1597).

BIBLIOGRAPHY: Azulai, *Shem ha-Gedolim*, ii., s.v. *Yaïr Natib*; Steinschneider, *Cat. Bodl.* col. 1706.
G. M. SEL.

MEÏR BEN JOSEPH BEN MERWAN HA-LEVI: French scholar; flourished at Narbonne in the twelfth century; brother of the nasi R. Moses ben Joseph ben Merwan, and pupil of Isaac ben Merwan, head of the Narbonne academy in the early part of the twelfth century. He was held in great respect and associated with Abraham ben Isaac, ab bet din, who presided over the rabbinical college of Narbonne about 1165. According to the conjecture of Gross ("Gallia Judaica," p. 414), Meïr ben Joseph is identical with Meïr ben Jacob, who is mentioned, with the rabbinical scholars Todros ben Moses, Abraham ben Isaac, Moses ben Joseph Meshullam ben Nathan, and Moses ben Todros, at the end of a rabbinical responsum dated at Narbonne in the middle of the twelfth century.

BIBLIOGRAPHY: Abraham ben David, *Sefer ha-Kabbalah*; *Ahimaaz Chronicle*, p. 84; *Temim De'im*, p. 122; *Kol Bo*, No. 120; Benjamin Auerbach, Introduction to the *Sefer ha-Eshkol*, p. viii.
G. S. K.

MEÏR ḲADOSH (MEÏR BEN JEHIEL BRODA): Moravian Talmudist; born at Ungarisch-Brod in 1593. He is known for his "Megillat R. Meïr" (Cracow, 1632), in which he narrates an adventure which happened to him when he was fifteen years old, and on account of which he acquired the epithet "Ḳadosh" (= "saint" or "martyr"). In 1608 he left his native town with eight other students in order to attend a yeshibah in Poland. On the way he was kidnaped by the waywode of Auspitz, who kept him in prison for fifteen weeks, and endeavored to torture him into accepting Christianity. Meïr remained firm, and was finally ransomed by the Jews of Cracow and placed in the yeshibah of Moses Meisels.

BIBLIOGRAPHY: Steinschneider, *Cat. Bodl.* cols. 1701-1702.
D. M. SEL.

MEÏR HA-KOHEN: French scholar of the thirteenth century; born at Narbonne; died at Toledo, Spain, whither he had emigrated in 1263 (Israeli, "Yesod 'Olam," ii. 35, ed. Berlin, 1846). Meïr occupied himself particularly with the study of the Masorah; and, according to Menahem Meïri ("Ḳiryat Sefer"), he was one of the five rabbis who, by comparing a great number of manuscripts, endeavored to establish a correctly revised Pentateuch for France and Germany.

Meïr's identity has been frequently mistaken: Bartolocci ("Bibl. Rab. Magna," iv. 20) identifies him with the author of the "Haggahot Maimuniyyot," a German scholar of the end of the thirteenth century; Zunz ("Literaturgesch." p. 283), confounding him with Moses ha-Kohen of Lunel, attributes to him the "Hassagot," or strictures on Maimonides; while Carmoly ("Ha-Karmel," vii. 58) identifies him with Meïr Ẓarfati, the supposed author of a poem against the "Moreh," beginning with the words "Anshe minut" (comp. Steinschneider, "Hebr. Bibl." xiii.). It may be added that S. Sachs ("Cat. of the Günzburg Library," p. 46) attributes to Meïr ha-Kohen the "Sefer ha-Me'orot," which in reality is the work of Meïr b. Simeon.

BIBLIOGRAPHY: Gross, *Gallia Judaica*, p. 422; Renan-Neubauer, *Les Rabbins Français*, pp. 731-733.
G. M. SEL.

MEÏR BEN LEVI: Austrian Talmudist and Biblical commentator of the beginning of the eighteenth century; a native of Zolkiev. Under the title "Liḳḳuṭe Shoshannim" (Jessnitz, 1722), he compiled the comments and novellæ of the Geonim on the Pentateuch and arranged them in the order of the weekly lessons. Meïr afterward revised the work, and, having added thereto notes of his own, published it under the new title "Miḳsheh Zahab." From the preface to the second edition (Frankfort-on-the-Oder, 1733), the first edition seems to have been printed at Zolkiev (n.d.).

BIBLIOGRAPHY: Benjacob, *Oẓar ha-Sefarim*, p. 369; Steinschneider, *Cat. Bodl.* col. 1704.
G. M. SEL.

MEÏR OF OSTROWO. See MARGOLIOTH, MEÏR B. ẒEBI HIRSCH.

MEÏR OF ROTHENBURG (MEÏR B. BARUCH; frequently called in brief מור"ם מרוטנבורג or מוה"רם מרוט'**):** German tosafist, codifier, and liturgical poet; born at Worms about 1215; died in the fortress of Ensisheim, Alsace, May 2 (April 27 old style), 1293. He belonged to a family which was noted for its scholars; and in his responsa he designates about a dozen Talmudic authorities of his time as his relatives. The epitaph, still extant, of his father, who died (1275) at a very advanced age, praises the latter's extraordinary piety, eminent scholarship, brilliant gift of oratory, and great popularity. It may be assumed, therefore, that Meïr received his earliest instruction from his father, though his first teacher proper was Isaac b. Moses of Vienna, under whom, as well as under Samuel b. Menahem, he studied at Würzburg. Meïr studied at the French yeshibot also, his teachers there being Jehiel b. Joseph of Paris, Samuel b. Solomon of Falaise, and Samuel of Evreux. On his return to Germany he quickly gathered around him a band of devoted pupils, including many married men, who left their families for a time in order to listen to so brilliant a teacher.

It is difficult to determine Meïr's actual official position among the German rabbis of his time. Modern historians maintain that he was chief rabbi of Germany, elected by the communities and confirmed by Emperor Rudolph. It is very doubtful, however, whether at this time the office of chief rabbi existed in Germany; and even if it did, there is nothing to prove that Meïr occupied it. The designations "Chief" (Responsa, ed. Prague, No. 946), "Father of Rabbis," etc., merely indicate that on account of his great scholarship he was everywhere recognized as the spiritual leader, whose decrees and institutions were considered as authoritative. As far as is known, he officiated as rabbi in the following communities: Kostnitz, Augsburg, Würzburg, Rothenburg, Worms, Nuremberg, and Mayence. This order of enumeration is probably chronological; but nothing is known of Meïr's terms of office in the different cities. As he is generally called Meïr "of Rothenburg" (Rothenburg-on-the-Tauber), he probably stayed longest in that city. Meïr was well-to-do, perhaps rich; for, according to his own account, he had in his house at Rothenburg separate apartments for winter and summer, with an airy dining-room, and separate rooms for each of his pupils.

Official Activity.

Meïr's decisions in questions of taxation regulated the financial conditions of the Jewish communities of Germany. Thus he decided that no member of a community should be permitted to negotiate with the authorities in matters of taxation, as this might be detrimental to the community (*ib.* No. 134). When Emperor Rudolph presented his son Albrecht in 1282 with Austria, Styria, and Carinthia, the communities of those districts refused to pay their portion of the taxes to the federation of communities of the empire, on the ground that they now belonged to a different state. Meïr decided that the refusal of the communities to contribute to the general tax fund could be justified only if the emperor gave up those countries entirely without claiming any part of their revenues (*ib.* No. 131). Another important decision of Meïr's had reference to the ransom of Jews, who were frequently imprisoned at that time for the purpose of extorting money from them. He decided that the ransomed Jews must reimburse the community in every case; and that the latter, in case of need, was not only justified in taking, but was in duty bound to take, the property of the prisoners, even against their will, for ransom. He based his decision on the ground that in such cases the ransom was not a private matter, but concerned the Jewish communities, and that the individual ought therefore to be compelled to give up his property for his release, although he personally might prefer prison to poverty.

Meïr himself was soon to experience what life in prison meant. His seizure, imprisonment, and sad death have made too deep an impression on the Jews to be a matter for doubt; moreover, contemporaneous Christian writers confirm the chief incidents of the story. However, as some highly important points are not clear, it may be best to give here the following concise account: "R. Meïr b. Baruch was about to go abroad with his wife, his daughters, his sons-in-law, and all his family, and had proceeded as far as a city in the mountains of Lombardy, where he intended to stay until all his traveling companions had gathered about him, when suddenly the wicked Bishop of Basel passed through the city on his journey from Rome, accompanied by a baptized Jew named Kneppe [קינפפא]. The latter recognized Meïr and informed the bishop, who brought it about that the lord of that city, Count Meinhard of Görz, seized Meïr on the fourth of Tammuz [= June 28], 1286, and delivered him to Emperor Rudolph, who cast him into prison" (marginal glosses to folio 85 of the "Minhagbuch" of Worms, written in 1625, quoted by Lewysohn, "Sechzig Epitaphien," p. 36; comp. also S. Back, "R. Meïr ben Baruch," pp. 62 *et seq.*). Neither the object of his journey nor the actual reason for the imprisonment is given in any source; but modern historians have attempted various explanations.

Supposed Reasons for Imprisonment.

The condition of the Jews of Germany was such toward the end of the thirteenth century that they were not for a moment sure of their lives and property. Murder, pillage, arson, and extortion were of daily occurrence. Under these circumstances many Jews emigrated; and Palestine especially attracted the fugitives from Germany, as in that country very favorable conditions obtained for the Jews during the reign of the Mongolian khan Argun and his Jewish minister Sa'd al-Daulah. It is assumed that Meïr was leading such a band of emigrants, and that he was imprisoned by the government in order to put a stop to this movement, which, if continued, would have materially injured the imperial treasury.

The account of a young contemporary of Meïr, who was in very close relations with him, seems to indicate, however, that Meïr had entirely different reasons for emigrating. He says that the emperor demanded a great sum of money from the Jews, which the latter would not or could not pay, and that consequently their leader feared—and justly so, as the sequel showed—that the emperor would seize him as a hostage ("Ẓawwa'at R. Yehudah b. Asher," ed. Schechter, in "Bet Talmud," iv. 374). After his seizure Meïr was probably first taken to Wasserburg (ווישרבורג), a German locality that cannot now be identified, and then transferred to the fortress of Ensisheim in the district of Colmar, Upper Alsace. The Jewish communities of course did everything to secure the liberation of their greatest teacher; but the ransom demanded by the government—30,000 marks, according to one report—was such an exorbitant one that the negotiations dragged. A later authority, frequently well informed in matters of history (Solomon Luria, "Yam shel Shelomoh," to Giṭ. iv., No. 66), says that Meïr himself prevented any such high sum being paid for his liberation lest the government should repeat this expedient of imprisoning important men for the purpose of extorting money. He therefore remained in prison from June 28, 1286, until his death (1293). He bore his seven years of captivity heroically. In the beginning he was consoled by the hope of a speedy release; and later on he submitted in the thought that it was the will of God, whose ways are always just. Even in prison he was occupied solely with studying and teaching. He wrote, or revised, a large part of his works; and his responsa now took the place of oral instruction.

Meïr was a voluminous writer. His works include: (1) Tosafot to several Talmudic treatises. Passages are quoted therefrom to Berakot, Shabbat, 'Erubin, Yoma, Giṭṭin, Nedarim, Baba Ḳamma, Baba Meẓi'a, Baba Batra, Shebu'ot, Menaḥot, and Ḥullin.

Literary Activity.

The tosafot to Yoma in the editions are those of R. Meïr, and are the only tosafot of his that have been printed. (2) Responsa, of which various parts have appeared (Cremona, 1537; Prague, 1608; Lemberg, 1860; Berlin, 1891). (3) "Hilkot Berakot," or "Seder Berakot," regulations for the various formulas of blessings to be pronounced in performing certain actions. The book is frequently cited in the works of Meïr's pupils, and is probably identical with the "Birkot MaHaRaM," issued in 1558 in Riva di Trento. (4) "Hilkot Sheḥiṭah," regulations for the ritual slaughtering and subsequent examination ("bediḳah") of animals, in manuscript in the Bodleian Library, Oxford (Neubauer, "Cat. Bodl. Hebr. MSS." Nos. 1171, 2275). (5) "Hilkot Abelut," or "Hilkot Semaḥot," on mourning customs. This work, somewhat abbreviated, is included also in the "Mordekai" to Mo'ed Ḳaṭan; but in all the passages where the author speaks in the first person, the third person has been substituted, so that here Meïr's work appears everywhere in quotation. Judah b. Nathan ha-Levi edited and published this work under the title "Sefer Maḥaneh Lewiyyah," Leghorn, 1789. (6) "Halakot Pesuḳot," decisions on various subjects, in manuscript at the Bodleian (Neubauer, *l.c.* No. 781, 2a). This library contains also various collections of Meïr's decisions (Neubauer, *l.c.* Index). (7) "Pisḳe 'Erubin," short summary of the Talmudic-rabbinical regulation of the 'erub. (8) "Ḥiddushim," novellæ to various treatises of the Talmud. Azulai possessed a copy of this work. (9) Minhagim of ritual ceremonies in the synagogue, in manuscript in the Vatican and Bodleian libraries. (10) Treatise on the marital duties of husband and wife, in manuscript in the Vatican Library. (11) Commentary on the sixth order of the Mishnah, of which there have been published in Romm's edition of the Talmud (Wilna, 1897) the commentaries to the treatises Nega'im and Oholot, from an Oxford manuscript, and fragments of the rest from citations in Lippman Heller's Mishnah commentary. (12) Masoretic notes, in manuscript in the Vatican and Oxford libraries. It is not improbable that Meïr was the author also of the "Likkuṭe ha-Maimuni," found in the Austrian manuscript of the "Mordekai" (see MORDECAI B. HILLEL), and consisting of very brief extracts from Maimonides' "Yad," with occasional decisions by other authors referring to the subject or short remarks by the author himself. Meïr is not, however, the author of the cabalistic-ethical works "Sefer Emunot" and "Be'er Mayim Ḥayyim," which are ascribed to him by some scholars.

As Payyetan.

Meïr was also a voluminous liturgical poet, nineteen of his poems being included in the German Maḥzor. On account of his great authority as a Talmudist, his compositions were included even in the liturgy of the Day of Atonement and of the Ninth of Ab. Although Meïr was a German, he modeled his poems upon those of Judah ha-Levi, without, however, equaling them. Still his piyyuṭim show great command of language, and to a certain extent true poetic inspiration also. The best-known among his poems is his dirge on the public burning of Hebrew books at Paris in 1244, composed in the strophic rime of Judah ha-Levi's "Zionide," and rivaling its model in warmth of imagination and depth of feeling, though much inferior to it in purity of language and in versification. Meïr likewise wrote commentaries on earlier piyyuṭim, being probably encouraged to do so by his father, who himself wrote such comments (Zunz, "Ritus," pp. 195, 199).

The great authority which Meïr enjoyed during his life increased rather than lessened after his death. Aside from Rashi and Rabbenu Gershon, he is the only one upon whom the honorary title "Me'or ha-Golah" (= "Light of the Exile") has been conferred. It would be difficult to overestimate his influence on the development of the religious life of the Jews of Germany. He is also one among the few Germans whose authority extended far beyond the limits of their own country, and that not only during their lives—even Solomon ben Abraham ADRET, the greatest Spanish Talmudist, consulted Meïr on difficult questions—but also for generations afterward.

His Historical Importance.

Meïr's renowned pupil, ASHER BEN JEHIEL, introduced the teachings of his master into Spain and Portugal. The great influence which Meïr exercised upon the religious life of the Jews was chiefly personal, acting directly upon his pupils, who on their part endeavored to perpetuate the authority of their master. In addition to Asher ben Jehiel, especially noteworthy among Meïr's pupils were MORDECAI B. HILLEL and MEÏR HA-KOHEN, who were largely instrumental in establishing his authority through their widely circulated compendiums of the Law. Through the works of these pupils it is possible to form an opinion of Meïr's importance, although most of his works, with the exception of the responsa, either have perished or remain unpublished. The tosafot to Yoma, of which, as has been said above, Meïr is the author, show him to have been a most clear and logical thinker; and it is easy to see how his methods of Talmud study became the model for his pupil Asher b. Jehiel, who in his "Halakot" follows directly in his master's footsteps. These tosafot show also Meïr's fine insight into methods and system, as evidenced by his frequent references to the composition and methods of the Mishnah (comp., *e.g.*, Yoma 2a, catchword "Shibe'at," and *ib.* 73b, catchword "Yom ha-Kippurim").

Although Meïr was well versed in the works of his predecessors and studied them in detail, he was very independent in his views and often combated with vigor those of the old authorities. Meïr was the representative of uncompromising Talmudism, which looked upon the Talmud as the norm and rule of life. For this reason he was opposed to mysticism, which had flourished in Germany from the time of Eleazar of Worms, as well as to the philosophic trend of the Spanish school.

Tendencies.

It is especially noteworthy that he showed a marked independence of the superstition then prevailing in Germany among Jews as well as non-Jews. Thus he paid no regard to the "danger" of so-called pairs (see ZUGOT), *i.e.*, of using or partaking of things in pairs ("Tashbeẓ," No. 552); he trimmed his nails in the sequence of the fingers (*ib.* No. 560); and he advised that Jews might go bareheaded (*ib.* No. 549). He admitted that he knew nothing of eschatological secrets, of which the mystic books of his time were full (*ib.* No. 247), and declared emphatically against indiscriminate emigration to Palestine. Only those should go there, he claimed, who could support themselves well, and would be able to lead a holy life in the Holy Land (*ib.* Nos. 559–562). Where the Halakah, according to him, demanded onerous observance, this must be carried out; for he held that the Talmudic regulations must not become an object of derision, meaning thereby that they must be enforced by the authorities, so as not to lose their significance (Responsa, ed. Cremona, No. 194). Next to the Halakah, he assigned to religious practises a great authority, and endeavored to put them upon a firmer basis than their existing one. Meïr is cited as an authority for many religious customs of the house and the synagogue, as his influence gave stability to usages which hitherto had been variable.

In moral as well as ethical questions he inclined to the rigorous interpretation. The following sentence in one of his responsa is characteristic: "Cursed be the woman who has a husband and does not adorn herself; and cursed be the woman who has no husband and adorns herself" (Responsa, ed. Prague, No. 199). The question whether a lawyer could bring into court arguments which he was convinced were false, he answered as follows: "No Jew may become guilty of such an ignominious sin against truth and justice" (Responsa, ed. Cremona, No. 246). Meïr's importance lies in the fact, therefore, that he led the

German Jews away from the mysticism to which they were trending, and toward a rational, thorough study of the Talmud; also in that he endeavored to put their variable religious practises upon a firm basis, his principle being to decide religious questions in conformity with the conclusions at which he had arrived by independent study of the Talmud ("Tashbeẓ," No. 531).

When Meïr was imprisoned in Alsace, many of his relatives also went to that country, members of his family being found there for centuries (Neubauer, "La Famille de Meïr de Rothenburg," in "R. E. J." xii. 91-94). The WEIL family of southern Germany claimed Meïr as its ancestor; and there were also many Jews at Prague who designated themselves as ממשפחת מהר"א מרוטנבורג.

BIBLIOGRAPHY: S. Back, *R. Meïr ben Baruch*, Frankfort-on-the-Main, 1895; Carmoly, in Jost's *Annalen*, 1839, pp. 348-349; Duschak, in *Kokebe Yiẓḥaḳ*, xiii. 20-21; Grätz, *Gesch.* vii., Index; *idem*, in Wertheimer's *Jahrb. für Israeliten*, 1862-63, pp. 40-54; Güdemann, *Gesch.* i. 170-173; D. Kaufmann, *Die Grabsteine R. Meïr's von Rothenburg und Alexander Wimpfen's in Worms*, in *Monatsschrift*, xl. 126-130; idem, *ib.* pp. 185-188; Kohn, *Mardochai ben Hillel*, pp. 30-32, 85-88; Landshuth, *'Ammude ha-'Abodah*, pp. 160-161; I. Loeb, in *R. E. J.* xx. 21-22; Lewysohn, *Sechzig Epitaphien*, pp. 35-39; Steinschneider, *Cat. Bodl.* s.v.; Weiss, *Dor*, v. 75-77; Renan-Neubauer, *Les Rabbins Français*, pp. 452-461; Neubauer, *Cat. Bodl. Hebr. MSS.* Index; Wiener, *Regesten*; idem, in *Monatsschrift*, xii. 168-172; Zunz, *Literaturgesch.* pp. 357-362; idem, *S. P.* pp. 310-312 (contains translations of some of Meïr's piyyuṭim); idem, *Z. G.* Index.

S. S. L. G.

MEÏR BEN SAMUEL (RaM): French tosafist; born about 1060 in Ramerupt; died after 1135. His father was an eminent scholar. Meïr received his education in the Talmudical schools of Lorraine, his principal teachers being Isaac ben Asher ha-Levi and Eleazar ben Isaac of Mayence (Pardes, ed. Constantinople, p. 33a; comp. Neubauer in "Monatsschrift," 1887, p. 503), with whom he later carried on a correspondence ("Or Zarua'," ii. 75b; "Sefer ha-'Ittur," ed. Lemberg, i. 52).

Meïr married Rashi's second daughter, Jochebed, by whom he had three sons (Conforte, "Ḳore ha-Dorot," ed. Cassel, p. 14a), Samuel ben Meïr (RaSHBaM), Isaac ben Meïr (RIBaM), and Jacob ben Meïr (Rabbenu Tam), all of them well-known scholars. According to Gross, Meïr had also a fourth son, Solomon. Samuel ben Simḥah of Vitry, father of the tosafist Isaac the Elder, was Meïr's son-in-law. Meïr's son Isaac, the often-quoted tosafist, died in the prime of life, leaving seven children (see Rabbenu Tam, "Sefer ha-Yashar," ed. Vienna, No. 616, p. 72b; ed. Rosenthal, No. 41, p. 71). This loss distressed the father to such an extent that he felt indisposed to answer a halakic question addressed to him by his friend Eleazar ben Nathan of Mayence (*ib.*).

Meïr attained a very great age, and is sometimes designated as "the old" ("ha-yashish"; *ib.*; "Sefer Seder ha-Ḳabbalah," in Neubauer, "M. J. C." p. 184; Eliezer b. Nathan, p. 148a). From the fact that his grandson, Isaac ben Samuel, born about 1120, speaks of religious customs which he found conspicuous in his grandfather's house, and from other indications, it has been concluded that Meïr was still alive in 1135.

Meïr was one of the founders of the school of tosafists in northern France. Not only his son and pupil Rabbenu Tam ("Sefer ha-Yashar," ed. Vienna, No. 252, p. 27a), but also the tosafot (Tos. Ket. 103b; Tos. Ḳid. 15b, 59a; Tos. Men. 100a) quote his ritual decisions. It was Meïr ben Samuel who changed the text of the KOL NIDRE formula (see "Sefer ha-Yashar," ed. Vienna, No. 144, p. 17a). A running commentary on a whole passage of the Gemara (Men. 12a *et seq.*), written by him and his son Samuel in the manner of Rashi's commentary, is printed at the end of the first chapter of Menaḥot. Meïr composed also a seliḥah beginning "Abo lefaneka," which has been translated into German by Zunz ("Synagogale Poesie," p. 183), but which has no considerable poetic value (*idem*, "Literaturgesch." p. 254; Landshuth, "'Ammude ha-'Abodah," p. 168).

BIBLIOGRAPHY: Azulai, *Shem ha-Gedolim*, ed. Wilna, i. 118, No. 11; Grätz, *Gesch.* vi. 68-144; Gross, *Gallia Judaica*, pp. 304, 542, 635; D. Rosin, *Samuel ben Meïr als Schrifterklärer*, in *Jahresbericht des Jüdisch-Theologischen Seminars*, pp. 3 *et seq.*, Breslau, 1880; Weiss, *Dor*, iv. 336; idem, *Sefer Toledot Gedole Yisrael* (*Toledot R. Ya'aḳob ben Meïr*), p. 4, Vienna, 1883; Zunz, *Z. G.* p. 31; see also ISAAC BEN MEÏR OF NARBONNE; JACOB BEN MEÏR TAM; and SAMUEL BEN MEÏR.

G. M. Sc.

MEÏR B. SAMUEL OF SCZEBRSZYN: Hebrew author of the seventeenth century. In the disastrous years of 1648-49 he lived at Sczebrszyn, Russian Poland, an honored member of the community, whence he escaped, on its invasion by the Cossacks, to Cracow; there he published his "Ẓoḳ ha-'Ittim" (1650), an account, in Hebrew verse, of Jewish persecution during the Cossack uprising. This book was afterward published by Joshua b. David of Lemberg under his own name; Steinschneider was the first to discover this plagiarism. Meïr wrote also "Mizmor Shir," a Sabbath hymn, in Aramaic and Judæo-German (Venice, 1639).

BIBLIOGRAPHY: Gurland, *Le-Ḳorot ha-Gezerot*, iv. 3; Steinschneider, *Cat. Bodl.* No. 6324; Fürst, *Bibl. Jud.* ii. 345.

H. R. A. S. W.

MEÏR BEN SIMEON OF NARBONNE: Talmudist and controversialist; lived at Narbonne in the second half of the thirteenth century. He was a disciple of Nathan ben Meïr of Trinquetaille, and a contemporary of Naḥmanides, with whom he maintained a scientific correspondence. Meïr enjoyed a high reputation as a commentator. Asher ben David invokes his authority in his (Asher's) commentary on the thirteen attributes (יג" מדות); and the anonymous commentator on the Targum Onḳelos highly praises Meïr in his "Patshegen."

Meïr was the author of a controversial work entitled "Milḥemet Miẓwah" (Parma MSS. No. 2749). It is divided into five parts: (1) an account of a religious disputation held in 1245 before the bishop En Guillem de la Broa and in the presence of the Jewish notables of Narbonne and Capestang; (2) controversies with Christian ecclesiastics; (3) conversations of an apologetic nature, and explanations of Biblical passages concerning the Messiah and of Talmudical haggadot interpreted by Christians in favor of their belief; (4) commentary on the "Shema'" and on the thirteen attributes of God; and (5) letter on the "Sefer ha-Bahir," which work Meïr declares to be a forgery.

Another work by Meïr, entitled "Meshib Nefesh," defending the first chapter of Maimonides' "Yad ha-

Ḥazaḳah" against the attacks of an anonymous writer, is also extant in manuscript (MS. Ginzburg, No. 572, 10).

According to Neubauer ("Isr. Letterbode," iii. 57), Meïr is identical with the Meïr ben Simeon mentioned in a Talmudical compilation (Neubauer, "Cat. Bodl. Hebr. MSS." No. 1558, 2, § 665) and in other works, where he is sometimes called "Ha-Me'ili."

BIBLIOGRAPHY: Steinschneider, *Hebr. Bibl.* xvi. 44, 67; Neubauer, in *Archives des Missions*, 3d series, i. 556; Lubetzki, Introduction to *Sefer Hashlamah*; Gross, in *Monatsschrift*, 1874, p. 571; idem, *Gallia Judaica*, pp. 423-425; Renan-Neubauer, *Les Rabbins Français*, pp. 558 *et seq.*

S. S. I. BR.

MEÏR B. SOLOMON B. DAVID: Grammarian of the end of the thirteenth century. He wrote a short but interesting grammatical work, which is extant only in a manuscript formerly in the possession of Halberstam, but now in the Montefiore Library (No. 410, 3; see "R. E. J." xiv. 788). In the preface he states that the author of the Hebrew grammar entitled "Petaḥ Debarai" was his grandfather. Purposing to summarize some of the elements of Hebrew grammar, Meïr discusses, in seven chapters, transitive and intransitive verbs, the meaning of the "hif'il," the "pi'el," and the other derived stems, and the pronominal suffixes of the verbs. As he says in the preface, he intended thereby to prepare for his own use an aid to study, and to consider problems which had not been treated in the work of his grandfather, referred to above.

BIBLIOGRAPHY: W. Bacher, in *R. E. J.* x. 140 *et seq.*

T. W. B.

MEÏR BEN TODROS. See ABULAFIA.

ME'IRI, MENAHEM BEN SOLOMON: Provençal Talmudist and commentator; born at Perpignan in 1249; died there in 1306; his Provençal name was **Don Vidal Solomon.** He was a disciple of Reuben ben Ḥayyim of Narbonne. Me'iri is regarded as one of the most brilliant commentators of the Middle Ages. His works are clear and concise and bear the stamp of a scientific and logical mind. Me'iri was the author of many works, most of which are still extant. These are: a treatise on penitence entitled "Ḥibbur ha-Teshubah," or "Meshibat Nefesh," still extant in manuscript (MS. de Rossi, No. 1313); "Bet ha-Beḥirah," containing commentaries on most of the books of the Talmud, several of which were published, namely, those on Megillah (Amsterdam, 1769), Yebamot (Salonica, 1794), Shabbat (Leghorn, 1794), Nedarim, Nazir, and Soṭah (*ib.* 1795), Yoma (*ib.* 1760), Abot (with Me'iri's historical and literary introduction and a short biography of the author by G. Stern; Vienna, 1854); "Ḳiryat Sefer," a Masoretic work on the method of writing scrolls of the Law, in two parts (Smyrna, 1863-81); commentaries on the Bible, of which only those on Proverbs and the Psalms are extant (the former was published at Leiria, 1492; the latter is in manuscript; Neubauer, "Cat. Bodl." p. 69). Azulai mentions three other works by Me'iri which are no longer in existence: "Bet Yad," on the obligation of washing the hands before meals and in the morning; "Magen Abot"; and "Ohel Mo'ed." In the commentary on Sanhedrin, Me'iri quotes another work of his entitled "Ketab Dat," which, judging from the title, must have been a catechism.

Me'iri was too much of a philosopher himself to interdict the study of philosophy. Thus, when solicited by Abba Mari to give his adhesion to the excommunication launched against the secular sciences, Me'iri wrote him a letter in which he emphatically defended science, the only concession he made being to forbid the study of secular sciences by any one before he has thoroughly studied the Talmud.

BIBLIOGRAPHY: De Rossi, *Dizionario*, ii. 48; Azulai, *Shem ha-Gedolim*, i. 128; Steinschneider, *Cat. Bodl.* col. 1731; Shorr, in *Oẓar Neḥmad*, ii. 99; Stern, *Bet ha-Beḥirah*, Introduction; Geiger, in *He-Ḥaluẓ*, ii. 14; Carmoly, in *Orient*, i. 704; Renan-Neubauer, *Les Rabbins Français*, pp. 528 *et seq.*; Grätz, *Gesch.* vii. 256 *et seq.*; Gross, *Gallia Judaica*, pp. 461-462.

S. S. I. BR.

MEISACH, JOSHUA: Russian Hebrew author; born at Sadi, government of Kovno, 1848. Meisach has written and edited over one hundred works in Yiddish and Hebrew. He began his literary career in 1861 with the weekly "Ha-Karmel," since which year he has contributed to a great number of Hebrew and Yiddish periodicals, has edited the magazine "Gan Peraḥim" (i.-iii., Wilna-Warsaw, 1881-93), and has written various novels, essays, etc. Among these are the following: "Ha-Emunah we-Haskalah," essays (Wilna, 1874); "Miktabim mi-Sar shel Yam," essays (Warsaw, 1885-89); "Ṭefaḥ Megullah," criticisms (*ib.* 1886); "Bamat Yiẓḥaḳ," on the theater (*ib.* 1889); "Oẓar Ḥadash," anecdotes and narratives from the Talmud and the Midrash, alphabetically arranged (Wilna, 1898). Meisach now (1904) resides at Warsaw.

BIBLIOGRAPHY: *Sefer Zikkaron*, p. 68, Warsaw, 1888; Lippe, *Asaf ha-Mazkir he-Ḥadash*, p. 262; Zeitlin, *Bibl. Post-Mendels.* p. 235; *Ha-Yehudi*, 1904, No. 46.

H. R. A. S. W.

MEISEL: Bohemian family which became famous chiefly through Mordecai Marcus b. Samuel Meisel, "primate" of Prague. The family seems to have come originally from Cracow, to whose community Mordecai Meisel bequeathed large sums for charitable purposes; and there, toward the end of the sixteenth century, the printer **Menahem Nahum b. Moses Meisel** flourished. As early as 1477, however, the name of "Meisel" is mentioned in documents relating to Prague (Lieben, "Gal 'Ed," p. 15).

Frummet Meisel: Second wife of Mordecai Meisel; died Shebaṭ 23, 1625. She contributed with her husband to the building of the Meisel synagogue, and some of the gifts which they presented on the occasion of its dedication (see Mordecai Marcus MEISEL) are still exhibited on the anniversary of her death. On her tombstone she is described as a woman distinguished for piety and morality. It is furthermore stated that every synagogue of Prague possessed votive offerings of hers, the most noteworthy gift being a golden cup weighing 100 crowns; that she supported scholars liberally; and that she was hospitable and very philanthropic. David Gans likewise praised her noble character and her fidelity to her husband. It seems strange, then, to read in the "'Emeḳ ha-Baka" (ed. Wiener, p. 141), that she objected so strongly to the last will and testament of Mordecai Meisel that he divorced her while he lay dying. Although this statement has been often questioned, there must be some truth in it, for on her gravestone she is designated as the daughter of the famous elder Isaac Rofe (Lékarz), not as Meisel's wife.

Bibliography: Foges, *Altertümer der Prager Josefstadt*, Prague, 1882; Lieben, *Gal 'Ed*, ib. 1856; A. Kisch, *Das Testament Mardochai Meysels*, Frankfort-on-the-Main, 1893.

D. A. Ki.

Judah Löb ben Simḥah Bonim Meisel: Printer and author at Cracow in the seventeenth century. Meisel reopened, in 1663, the printing establishment of his father-in-law, Nahum Meisel, and continued it until 1670. The first work printed by him was Jacob Weil's "Sheḥiṭot u-Bediḳot"; the last one, the Eben ha-'Ezer and Ḥoshen ha-Mishpaṭ of the Shulḥan 'Aruk. Meisel was the author of a work entitled "Ṭa'ame ha-Massoret," a commentary on the Masorah, at the end of which there are some novellæ on the Talmud (Amsterdam, 1728).

Bibliography: Steinschneider, *Cat. Bodl.* cols. 1373, 2986; M. Zunz, *'Ir ha-Ẓedeḳ*, Supplement, p. 34, note.

J. M. Sel.

Mordecai Marcus Meisel (Miška Marek in Bohemian documents): Philanthropist and communal leader at Prague; son of Samuel Meisel; born at Prague 1528; died there March 13, 1601. The persecution of the Jews of Prague by the fanatical Ferdinand I. occurred while Mordecai was a youth. In 1542 and 1561 his family, with the other Jewish inhabitants, was forced to leave the city, though only for a time. The source of the great wealth which subsequently enabled him to become the benefactor of his coreligionists and to aid the Austrian imperial house, especially during the Turkish wars, is unknown. He is mentioned in documents for the first time in 1569, as having business relations with the communal director Isaac Rofe (Lékarz), subsequently his father-in-law. His first wife, **Eva,** who died before 1580, built with him the Jewish town-hall at Prague, which is still standing, as well as the neighboring Hohe Synagoge, where the Jewish court sat. With his second wife, Frummet, he built (1590–92) the Meisel synagogue, which was much admired by the Jews of the time, being, next to the Altneusynagoge, the metropolitan synagogue of the city; it still bears his name. The costly golden and silver vessels with which he and his wife furnished this building either were lost during the lawsuit over his estate or were burned during the conflagrations in the ghetto in 1689 (June 21) and 1754 (May 16). The only gifts dedicated by Meisel and his wife to this synagogue that have been preserved are a curtain ("paroket") embroidered with hundreds of pearls, a similarly adorned wrapper for the scroll of the Law, and a magnificent bronze ornament for the almemar. Jacob Segre, rabbi of Casale-Monferrato, celebrated the dedication of the synagogue in a poem which is still extant, and his contemporary David Gans, the chronicler of Prague, has described in his "Ẓemaḥ Dawid" the enthusiasm with which the Jewish population received the gift.

Tombstone of Mordecai Meisel at Prague.
(From Jerabék, "Der Alte Prager Judenfriedhof.")

Meisel enlarged the old Jewish cemetery of Prague by purchasing adjoining uncultivated land, on which he erected a house for washing the dead, a miḳweh, a bet ha-midrash, a Klaus, and a hospital (still in existence). He spent much money also in ransoming Jewish prisoners; paved the ghetto of

Prague, which had been much enlarged at that time; often provided clothing, of a uniform pattern, for all the poor of his community; presented large dowries every year at Ḥanukkah to two poor brides chosen by lot; lent large sums without interest to needy merchants; and provided for the widows and orphans of the community. He presented costly synagogal vessels and adornments to other communities, including those of Cracow, Posen, and Jerusalem. He presented and loaned altogether the sum of 20,000 thalers to the community of Posen when it was burned out June 11, 1590; gave generously to Christian philanthropies, contributing a considerable amount toward the completion of the Church of the Savior; and repeatedly lent large sums to the empress as well as to the emperor, being rewarded with considerable privileges, many of which affected the Meisel synagogue. This synagogue had a standard with an escutcheon; it might not be entered by any officer of the law; it was exempt from taxation for all time. Although Meisel had no children, the emperor granted him the right to dispose of his estate; but after his death the heirs were involved in difficulties as a result of this privilege. He had the right also to mint shekels for ritual purposes ("pidyon ha-ben" and "maḥaẓit ha-sheḳel"), and one of these coins, dated 1584, is still in existence.

His Benefactions.

Meisel's last will and testament, which he drew up in the presence of Chief Rabbi Löw (Judah Löw b. Bezaleel), the communal director Joachim Brandeis, and Meïr Epstein, leaving his estate to his two nephews, Samuel the Elder and Samuel the Younger, is still extant in manuscript. He was interred with the highest honors. Immediately after his burial the Bohemian treasury, at the instance of the emperor, confiscated his estate, consisting of 516,250 gulden in money together with many houses. Whatever was found was carried off; one of the chief heirs was tortured into revealing the hiding-place of what had been concealed, which also was claimed. Meisel's wealth and philanthropy have become proverbial among the Jews, and many anecdotes are connected with his name.

Bibliography: Lieben, *Gal 'Ed*; Foges, *Altertümer der Prager Josefstadt*; Hock-Kaufmann, *Die Familien Prags*, Presburg, 1892; A. Kisch, *Das Testament Mardochai Meysels*; idem, *Das Meiselbanner in Prag*, Prague, 1901.
D. A. Ki.

Moses b. Mordecai Meisel: Russian scholar and communal worker; born in Wilna about 1760; died in Hebron, Palestine, after 1838. He was shammash of the community in his native town and was in his younger days one of the followers of Elijah Gaon. Later he joined the Ḥasidim, but did not participate in the bitter controversies concerning them which disturbed the Polish Jewry in those times. He was a great admirer of Moses Mendelssohn and approved Solomon Dubno's bi'ur of Genesis (1783). There is also an approbation by Meisel of Samuel Gershoni's "Debar Shemuel" (Byelostok, 1814). He left Wilna for Palestine in 1813 and settled in Hebron. Dr. Löwe, who met him there in the summer of 1838, describes him as an old man well acquainted with German literature.

Meisel was the author of "Shirat Mosheh" (Shklov, 1788), a poem on the 613 precepts, each line beginning with a letter from the Ten Commandments. His son **Aryeh Löb** (d. 1835) was a leader among the Ḥasidim of Wilna.

Bibliography: Fuenn, *Ḳiryah Ne'emanah*, pp. 246-247, 288, Wilna, 1860; M. A. Ginzburg, *Debir*, pp. 47-48, Warsaw, 1883.
H. R. P. Wi.

Samuel Meisel (the elder): Nephew of Mordecai Marcus b. Samuel; born in 1585; died in 1630. He was wealthy and prominent in affairs. In 1616 he received an imperial privilege. The printing-press of Abraham Heide (Lemberger) was situated in his house. After Mordecai Meisel's death the settlement of his estate involved his family in a tedious suit with the government, and from the records of this suit is derived the information regarding the members of this family. One of the houses belonging to the estate was awarded, in 1610, to a nephew, **Jacob,** and his wife, Johanka; and three years later, King Matthias, successor of Rudolf II., gave the remaining real estate to another nephew, **Samuel Meisel** (the younger; d. 1625), son of Simon. The Meisel synagogue and other property were awarded to the Jewish community. As the state had confiscated all the money (more than 500,000 gulden) and most of the real estate, the family sued the community for the income from the synagogue, the baths, institutional buildings, etc., amounting to 800 florins a year. The rabbinate thereupon excommunicated the entirely impoverished family (*c.* 1670), and this led to indescribable persecutions and scandals. Decent burial was refused to **Marck,** son of the younger Samuel Meisel, in 1674, and the funeral cortège was insulted. His daughter was attacked in her house by the mob, and the family had to pay large sums in order to secure honorable burial for the heir **Joachim Meisel.** It did not appear until the final verdict rendered in this suit by the magistrate of Prague Sept. 13, 1684, that through the machinations of the notorious apostate Philipp Lang, chamberlain to the emperor until 1608, the record of Meisel's privileges had been secretly stricken from the official register in 1601, on the ground of their having been obtained by fraud, and that the sums subsequently paid to the widow and to the heirs, and the two houses given them, were alleged to have been merely gifts. The heirs, naturally, were not satisfied with this decision; but the great fire in the ghetto of Prague, in 1689, which destroyed the Meisel synagogue and the other buildings of the estate, terminated the controversy. The family flourished at Prague down to modern times; and branches of it are found at Warsaw, Budapest, Breslau, and Berlin.

Bibliography: A. Kisch, *Das Testament Mardochai Meysels*; Lieben, *Gal 'Ed*; Benedikt Foges, *Altertümer der Prager Josefstadt*.
D. A. Ki.

Wolf Alois Meisel: Hungarian rabbi; born at Roth-Janowitz July 16, 1815; died at Budapest Nov. 30, 1867. Owing to his father's conversion to Christianity, the family relations were so inharmonious that he reached the age of seventeen before he was able to begin definite preparation for the future. In 1832 he went to Hamburg, where he applied himself to the study of the Talmud and graduated from the gymnasium. He entered the University of Breslau in 1838, where he continued his study of the Talmud and attended lectures on rhetoric. In 1848 he was called to the rabbinate of Stettin, and on May 11, 1859, to that of Budapest. Here he was in constant conflict with his congregation owing to the state of transition, both in religion and in politics, through which the Hungarian Jews passed during his administration. His "Homilien über die Sprüche der Väter" (Stettin, 1851; Hungarian transl. by Bauer Márkfi Lörincz, Budapest, 1862) are models of Jewish pulpit-literature. His "Prinz und Derwisch," poems (Stettin, 1847; 2d ed., Budapest, 1860), and "Der Prüfstein," poems (published posthumously by the Meisel-Wohlthätigkeitsverein, Budapest, 1878), are translations. He died suddenly while preaching a sermon, which Simon Bacher and his son Wilhelm Bacher published in German and Hebrew under the title "Die Brunnen Isaak's" (*ib.* 1867).

BIBLIOGRAPHY: Kayserling, *W. A. Meisel; ein Lebens- und Zeitbild*, Leipsic, 1891; Venetianer, *A Zsidóság Szervezete*, pp. 496 *et seq.*; Büchler, *A Zsidók Torténete*, pp. 479 *et seq.*; *Pallas Lex.*; Hochmuth, *Leopold Löw*, pp. 208 *et seq.*, Leipsic, 1871.

S. L. V.

MEISEL SYNAGOGUE. See MEISEL, MORDECAI MARCUS; PRAGUE.

MEISELS, DOB BERUSH B. ISAAC: Polish rabbi and statesman; born in Szczekoeiny about 1800; died in Warsaw March 17, 1870. He was a scion of one of the oldest families in Cracow, and was brought up in Kamenetz, Podolia, where his father (d. 1832) was rabbi. After marrying the daughter of the wealthy Solomon Bornstein of Wielicka, he settled as a banker in Cracow, of which city he became rabbi in 1832. He occupied the rabbinate for nearly a quarter of a century, but was not recognized by the entire community, a considerable part of which adhered to his opponent, R. Saul Landau. Meisels always took a conspicuous part in the civic life of his place of residence; and in the stormy times of 1846 he was chosen one of the twelve senators of Cracow. In 1848 he was elected, with the aid of Catholic votes, to represent the city in the provisional Austrian Reichsrath, meeting at Kremsier. He took his seat among the radicals, and when the president expressed his surprise at seeing a rabbi seated on the "left," Meisels gave the reply: "Juden haben keine Rechte" (Jews have no right!).

In 1856 Meisels became rabbi of Warsaw, where he soon gained the respect and confidence of the entire population. In 1861, during the riots and excesses which preceded the outbreak of the second Polish insurrection, he did everything in his power to induce the Jews to sympathize with the cause of Poland. He accompanied the Archbishop of Warsaw to the funeral of the victims of the first outbreak and marched together with Father Wyszynski at the head of a delegation to the city hall. Later he was appointed by the Russian vice-regent a member of the provisional municipal council of Warsaw; but he remained loyal to the cause of the Polish patriots, thereby, it is believed, preventing massacres of Jews which some Polish leaders had planned and which the Russian government was not anxious to avert ("Allg. Zeit. des Jud." 1861, p. 227). Late in 1861 Meisels, together with **Dr. M. Jastrow**, wa arrested and thrown into prison; after severa months' confinement both were expelled fron the country. Meisels was invited to settle in London; but in 1862 he was permitted to return t Warsaw, where he remained until his death.

Meisels was the author of novellæ on the "Sefe ha-Miẓwot" of Maimonides, which appeared to gether with the text as "Ḥiddushe MaHaRDaM" (Warsaw, 1870). One of his sons, **Israel Meisels**, was dayyan in Cracow and rabbi of Siedlce, Poland from 1858 to 1867. He died in Cracow Nov. 17 1875, aged 58 ("Ha-Maggid," xix. 407). Another son, **Solomon Meisels**, was living in Vienna in 1871.

BIBLIOGRAPHY: B. D. Rabbinowicz, *Dobeb Sifte Yeshenim* Warsaw, 1870; Angelchik, *Ish Ḥayyil*, Cracow, 1871; Fuenn *Keneset Yisrael*, p. 185, Warsaw, 1886; Wettstein, *Toledo MaHaRaN* (biography of Ḥayyim N. Dembitzer), pp. 14 *et seq.*, Cracow, 1893; *Orient*, 1848, pp. 240, 348, 358; 1849, pp 15–16; *Allg. Zeit. des Jud.* 1861, pp. 177, 214, 228; 1862, p. 22 *Ha-Shaḥar*, viii. 504.

H. R. P. WI.

MEISELS, NAHUM. See CRACOW.

MEISSEN. See SAXONY.

MEKILTA (plural, **Mekilata**): The halakic midrash to Exodus. The name "Mekilta," which corresponds to the Hebrew "middah" (= "measure," "rule"), was given to this midrash because the Scriptural comments and explanations of the Law which it contains are based on fixed rules of Scriptural exegesis ("middot"; comp. TALMUD HERMENEUTICS). The halakic midrashim are in general called "middot," in contrast to the "halakot," or formulated laws; and an interpreter of the Midrash was termed "bar mekilan" = "a man of the rules" (Lev. R. iii.). Neither the Babylonian nor the Palestinian Talmud mentions this work under the name "Mekilta," nor does the word occur in any of the passages of the Talmud in which the other halakic midrashim, Sifra and Sifre, are named (Ḥag. 3a; Ḳid. 49b; Ber. 47b; etc.). It seems to be intended, however, in one passage (Yer. 'Ab. Zarah iv. 8), which runs as follows: "R. Josiah showed a mekilta from which he cited and explained a sentence." His quotation actually occurs in the Mekilta, Mishpaṭim (ed. Weiss, p. 106b). It is not certain, however, whether the word "mekilta" here refers to the work under consideration; for it possibly alludes to a baraita collection—which might also be designated a "mekilta" (comp. Pes. 48a; Tem. 33a; Giṭ. 44a)—containing the sentence in question. On the other hand, this midrash, apparently in written form, is mentioned several times in the Talmud under the title "She'ar Sifre debe Rab" = "The Other Books of the Schoolhouse" (Yoma 74a; B. B. 124b). A geonic responsum (Harkavy, "Teshubot ha-Geonim," p. 31, No. 66, Berlin, 1888) in which occurs a passage from the Mekilta (ed. Weiss, p. 41a) likewise indicates that this work was known as "She'ar Sifre debe Rab." The first person to mention the Mekilta by name was the author of the "Halakot Gedolot" (p. 144a, ed. Warsaw, 1874). Another geonic responsum

First Mention.

refers to it as the "Mekilta de-Ereẓ Yisrael" (Harkavy, *l.c.* p. 107, No. 229), probably to distinguish it from the Mekilta of R. SIMEON BAR YOḤAI, which was generally known in the Babylonian schools (Hoffnann, "Zur Einleitung in die Halachischen Midraschim," p. 36).

The author, or more correctly the redactor, of the Mekilta can not be definitely ascertained. R. Nissim b. Jacob, in his "Mafteaḥ" (to Shab. 106b), and R. Samuel ha-Nagid, in his introduction to the Talmud, refer to it as the "Mekilta de-Rabbi Yishmael," thus ascribing the authorship to Ishmael. Maimonides likewise says in the introduction to his Yad ha-Ḥazaḳah: "R. Ishmael interpreted from we'eleh shemot' to the end of the Torah, and this explanation is called 'mekilta.' R. Akiba also wrote a mekilta." This R. Ishmael, however, is neither an amora by the name of Ishmael, as Frankel assumed (Introduction to Yerushalmi, p. 105b), nor Rabbi's contemporary, Rabbi Ishmael b. R. Jose, as Gedaliah ibn Yaḥya thought ("Shalshelet ha-Ḳabbalah," p. 24a, Zolkiev, 1804). He is, on the contrary, identical with R. Ishmael b. Elisha, R. Akiba's contemporary, as is shown by the passage of Maimonides quoted above. The present Mekilta

Mekilta of R. Ishmael.

can not, however, be the one composed by R. Ishmael, as is proved by the reference to R. Ishmael's pupils and to other later tannaim. Both Maimonides and the author of the "Halakot Gedolot," moreover, refer, evidently on the basis of a tradition, to a much larger mekilta extending from Ex. i. to the end of the Pentateuch, while the midrash here considered discusses only certain passages of Exodus. It must be assumed, therefore, that R. Ishmael composed an explanatory midrash to the last four books of the Pentateuch, and that his pupils amplified it (Friedmann, "Einleitung in die Mechilta," pp. 64, 73; Hoffmann, *l.c.* p. 73). A later editor, intending to compile a halakic midrash to Exodus, took R. Ishmael's work on the book, beginning with ch. xii., since the first eleven chapters contained no references to the Law (Friedmann, *l.c.* p. 72; Hoffmann, *l.c.* p. 37). He even omitted passages from the portion which he took; but, by way of compensation, he incorporated much material from the other halakic midrashim, Sifra, R. Simeon b. Yoḥai's Mekilta, and the Sifre to Deuteronomy. Since the last two works were from a different source, he generally designated them by the introductory phrase, "dabar aḥar" = "another explanation," placing them after the sections taken from R. Ishmael's midrash. But the redactor based his work on the midrash of R. Ishmael's school; and the sentences of R. Ishmael and his pupils constitute the larger part of his Mekilta. Similarly most of the anonymous maxims in the work were derived from the same source; so that it, also, was known as the "Mekilta of R. Ishmael" ("Mekilta de-Rabbi Yishmael"). The redactor must have been a pupil of Rabbi, since the latter is frequently mentioned (comp. Abraham ibn David in "Sefer ha-Ḳabbalah," in Neubauer, "M. J. C." p. 57, Oxford, 1887, who likewise ascribes it to a pupil of Rabbi). He can not, however, have been R. Hoshaiah, as A. Epstein assumes ("Beiträge zur Jüdischen Alterthumskunde," p. 55, Vienna, 1887), and as might be inferred from Abraham ibn David's reference; for Hoshaiah is mentioned in the Mekilta (ed. Weiss, p. 30b). Rab (Abba Arika) therefore probably redacted the work, as Menahem ibn Zerah says in the preface to "Ẓedah la-Derek" (p. 14b). Rab, however, did not do this in Babylonia, as Weiss assumes ("Einleitung in die Mechilta," p. 19), but in Palestine, taking it after its completion to Babylonia, so that it was called the Mekilta of Palestine "Mekilta de-Ereẓ Yisrael").

Baraitot from the Mekilta are introduced in the Babylonian Talmud by the phrases "Tena debe R.

Quotations in the Talmud.

Yishmael" = "It was taught in the school of R. Ishmael," and in the Palestinian Talmud and the haggadic midrashim by "Teni R. Yishmael" = "R. Ishmael taught." Yet there are many baraitot in the Talmud which contain comments on Exodus, and which are introduced by the phrase "Tena debe R. Yishmael," but are not included in the Mekilta under discussion. These must have been included in R. Ishmael's original Mekilta, and the fact that they are omitted in this midrash is evidence that its redactor excluded many of the passages from R. Ishmael's work (comp. Hoffmann, *l.c.* p. 42).

The Mekilta begins with Ex. xii., this being the first legal section found in Exodus. That this is the beginning of the Mekilta is shown by the "'Aruk," *s.v.* טמא, and by the "Seder Tannaim we-Amora'im" (ed. Luzzatto, p. 12, Prague, 1839). In like manner R. Nissim proves in his "Mafteaḥ" (to Shab. 106b) that the conclusion of the Mekilta which he knew corresponded with that of the Mekilta now extant.

In the editions the Mekilta is divided into nine "massektot," each of which is subdivided into "parashiyyot." The nine massektot are as follows: (1) "Massekta de Pesḥa," covering the pericope "Bo" (quoted as "Bo"), Ex. xii. 1–xiii. 16, and containing an introduction, "petikta," and 18 sections; (2) "Massekta de-Wayeḥi Beshallaḥ" (quoted as "Besh."), *ib.* xiii. 17–xiv. 31, containing an introduction and 6 sections; (3) "Massekta de-Shirah" (quoted as "Shir"), *ib.* xv. 1–21, containing 10 sections; (4) "Massekta de-Wayassa'" (quoted as "Way."), *ib.* xv. 22–xvii. 7, containing 6 sections; (5) "Massekta de-'Amalek," consisting of two parts, (*a*) the part dealing with Amalek (quoted as "Am."), *ib.* xvii. 8–16, containing 2 sections, and (*b*) the beginning of the pericope "Yitro" (quoted as "Yitro"), *ib.* xviii. 1-27, also containing 2 sections; (6) "Massekta de-Baḥodesh" (quoted as "Baḥ."), *ib.* xix. 1–20, 26, containing 11 sections; (7) "Massekta de-Neziḳin," *ib.* xxi. 1–xxii. 23; and (8) "Massekta de-Kaspa," *ib.* xxii. 24–xxiii. 19; these last two massektot, which belong to the pericope "Mishpaṭim," contain 20 sections, consecutively numbered, and are quoted as "Mish."; (9) "Massekta de-Shabbeta," containing 2 sections, (*a*) covering the pericope "Ki Tissa" (quoted as "Ki"), *ib.* xxxi. 12–17, and (*b*) covering the pericope "Wayaḳhel" (quoted as "Wayaḳ."), *ib.* xxxv. 1–3. The Mekilta comprises altogether seventy-seven, or, if the two introductions be included, seventy-nine sections. All the editions, however, state at the end that there are eighty-two sections (comp. Weiss, *l.c.* p. 28; Friedmann, *l.c.* pp. 78–80).

Although the redactor intended to produce a halakic midrash to Exodus, the larger portion of the Mekilta is haggadic in character. From Ex. xii.

the midrash was continued without interruption as far as Ex. xxxiii. 19, *i.e.*, to the conclusion of the chief laws of the book, although there are many narrative portions scattered through this section whose midrash belongs properly to the haggadah.

Haggadic Elements.

Furthermore, many haggadot are included in the legal sections as well. The halakic exegesis of the Mekilta, which is found chiefly in the massektot "Bo," "Baḥ.," and "Mish.," and in the sections "Ki" and "Wayaḳ.," is, as the name "mekilta" indicates, based on the application of the middot according to R. Ishmael's system and method of teaching. In like manner, the introductory formulas and the technical terms are borrowed from his midrash (comp. Hoffmann, *l.c.* pp. 43–44). On the other hand, there are many explanations and expositions of the Law which follow the simpler methods of exegesis found in the earlier halakah (comp. Midrash Halakah).

The haggadic expositions in the Mekilta, which are found chiefly in "Beshallaḥ" and "Yitro," are in part actual exegeses, but the majority of them are merely interpretations of Scripture to illustrate certain ethical and moral tenets. Parables are frequently introduced in connection with these interpretations (*e.g.*, "Bo," ed. Weiss, p. 1b; "Besh.," pp. 36a, b, 37a), as well as proverbs (*e.g.*, "Bo," p. 2b; "Way.," p. 60b) and maxims (*e.g.*, the apothegm of the ancient Zeḳenim, "Besh.," p. 62b; "Shir," p. 46b). Especially noteworthy are the haggadot relating to the battles of the Ephraimites ("Besh.," p. 28b) and to Serah, Asher's daughter, who showed Joseph's coffin to Moses (*ib.* p. 29a), besides others, which are based on old tales and legends.

It must also be noted that some of the tannaim mentioned in the Mekilta are referred to only here and in Sifre, Num., which likewise originated in R. Ishmael's school (comp. Hoffmann, *l.c.* pp. 38–39). On the earlier editions of the Mekilta and the commentaries to it see Weiss, *l.c.* pp. 25–26, and Friedmann, *l.c.* pp. 12–14. The following are more recent critical editions: J. H. Weiss, "Mechilta" (with introduction and commentary), Vienna, 1865; M. Friedmann, "Mechilta de-Rabbi Ismael" (with introduction and commentary), *ib.* 1870.

Bibliography: Hirsch Chajes, *Iggeret Biḳḳoret*, p. 5a, Lemberg, 1840; Zunz, *G. V.* pp. 1–52, Frankfort-on-the-Main, 1892; Z. Frankel, *Hodegetica in Mischnam*, p. 308, Leipsic, 1859; *idem*, in *Monatsschrift*, 1853, pp. 388 *et seq.*; 1854, pp. 149–158, 191–196; J. H. Weiss, *Einleitung in die Mechilta*, pp. 16–35; M. Friedmann, *Einleitung in die Mechilta*, pp. 9–80; D. Hoffmann, *Zur Einleitung in die Halachischen Midraschim*, pp. 36–45, Berlin, 1887; L. A. Rosenthal, *Einiges über die Agada in der Mechilta*, in *Kohut Memorial Volume*, pp. 463–484, *ib.* 1897.

s. J. Z. L.

MEKILTA DE-RABBI SHIM'ON: Halakic midrash on Exodus from the school of R. Akiba. No midrash of this name is mentioned in Talmudic literature; but medieval authors refer to one which they call either "Mekilta de-R. Shim'on b. Yoḥai," or "Mekilta Aḥrita de-R. Shim'on," or simply "Mekilta Aḥeret" = "another mekilta." From it passages are cited, especially by Naḥmanides in his Pentateuchal commentary on Gen. xlix. 31; Ex. xiv. 19, xxi. 3, xxii. 12; Lev. xxiii. 24; and by R. Todros ha-Levi in his works "Sefer ha-Razim" and "Oẓar ha-Kabod" (MSS. in the Königliche Hof- und Staatsbibliothek, Munich; comp. M. H. Landauer in "Orient, Lit." 1845, vi. 182 *et seq.*). Until recently, aside from these quotations and some given by certain authors of the sixteenth century, as Elijah Mizraḥi in his commentary on Rashi's commentary on the Pentateuch, R. Shem-Ṭob b. Abraham in his "Migdal 'Oz" to Maimonides' "Yad," and R. Meïr ibn Gabbai in his "Tola'at Ya'aḳob" (p. 63b, Cracow, 1570), the only other extract of any length from the Mekilta de-R. Shim'on which was known was the one published by R. Isaac Elijah Landau from a manuscript of R. Abraham Halami, as an appendix to his edition of the Mekilta (Wilna, 1844). There were, therefore, various erroneous opinions regarding this lost work. Zunz ("G. V." p. 419, note *a*) considered it as a cabalistic work ascribed to R. Simeon b. Yoḥai. M. H. Landauer (*l.c.*) identified it with the Mekilta de-R. Yishmael, while J. Perles (in "Monatsschrift," 1858, pp. 145 *et seq.*) held that the medieval authors applied the name "Mekilta de-R. Shim'on" merely to his maxims which were included in the Mekilta de-R. Yishmael, since separate sentences could be called "mekilta". M. Friedmann was the first to maintain, in his introduction to the Mekilta of R. Ismael (pp. 54 *et seq.*, Vienna, 1870), that, in addition to R. Ishmael's work, there was a halakic midrash to Exodus by R. Simeon, which was called the "Mekilta de-R. Shim'on," and that this Mekilta formed part of the Sifre mentioned in Babli (Sanh. 86a; Ber. 47b; Meg. 28b; Ḳid. 49a; Sheb. 41b; Ḥag. 3a). This assumption of Friedmann's was subsequently confirmed by the publication of a geonic responsum (Harkavy, "Teshubot ha-Ge'onim," p. 107, No. 229, Berlin, 1888), where a baraita from the Sifre de-Be Rab to Exodus is quoted, which is the same passage as that cited by Naḥmanides from the Mekilta de-R. Shim'on b. Yoḥai, in his commentary on Ex. xxii. 12. This extract designates the work of R. Ishmael as the "Mekilta of Palestine," in contradistinction to R. Simeon b. Yoḥai's midrash. It is clear, therefore, that the Mekilta of R. Simeon was implied in the title Sifre de-Be Rab (comp. Hoffmann, "Einleitung in die Halachischen Midraschim," p. 46); and it is mentioned in the Midrash Tehillim (ed. Buber, Wilna, 1891), p. 252 (comp. Buber's note there), under the Hebrew name "Middot R. Shim'on b. Yoḥai." It is possible also that Simeon himself intended to refer to his midrash in his saying: "Learn my middot" (Giṭ. 67a). The Palestinian sources, the Yerushalmi and the haggadic midrashim, introduce baraitot from this Mekilta with the phrase, "Teni R. Shim'on" = "R. Simeon has taught" (comp. Friedmann, introduction to his edition of the Mekilta, pp. 55 *et seq.*; Hoffmann, *l.c.* p. 48). The phrase "Tena de-Be R. Shim'on" is extremely rare, however, in Babli where this midrash ranks as one of the "Sifre de-Be Rab" (Hoffmann, *l.c.* p. 50). Many sentences of R. Simeon are quoted there in the name of his son Eleazar, so that Hoffmann has very plausibly concluded (*l.c.* p. 51) that Eleazar edited his father's midrash.

The Mekilta de-R. Shim'on has disappeared; but some extracts from it have been preserved in the collection known as "Midrash ha-Gadol," as I. Lewy first pointed out ("Ein Wort über die Mechilta de

R. Simon"). These fragments have been collected by D. Hoffmann and published under the title "Mechilta des R. Simon b. Jochai" in the Hebrew monthly "Ha-Peles" (vols. i. to iv., *passim*).

This Mekilta compiled from the Midrash ha-Gadol preserves abundant material from the earliest Scriptural commentaries, quoting, for instance, a sentence from the "Doreshe Reshumot" on Ex. xxi. 12 ("Ha-Peles," iii. 258) which is found nowhere else. It contains also much from post-Talmudic literature (comp. Hoffmann, *l.c.* p. 387, note 19), for the collector and redactor of the Midrash ha-Gadol had a peculiar way of dressing sentences of such medieval authorities as Rashi, Ibn Ezra, "'Aruk," and Maimonides in midrashic garb and presenting them as ancient maxims (comp. Schechter, Introduction to "Midrash ha-Gadol," p. 13, Cambridge, 1902).

Bibliography: M. Friedmann, introduction to his edition of the *Mekilta*, pp. 51–73, Vienna, 1870; D. Hoffmann, *Einleitung in die Halachischen Midraschim*, pp. 45–51, Berlin, 1887; I. Lewy, *Ein Wort über die Mechilta des R. Simon*, Breslau, 1889.

s. J. Z. L.

MEKILTA LE-SEFER DEBARIM: A halakic midrash to Deuteronomy from the school of Rabbi Ishmael. No midrash by this name is mentioned in Talmudic literature, nor do the medieval authors refer to such a work. Although Maimonides says in his introduction to the Yad ha-Ḥazaḳah, "R. Ishmael explained from 'we-eleh shemot' to the conclusion of the Torah, that is, the Mekilta," he did not see this midrash, which also includes Deuteronomy, since he does not quote any Mekilta passages to that book of the Pentateuch in his 'Sefer ha-Miẓwot," although he draws upon the halakic midrashim in discussing most of the commandments. Maimonides probably knew, therefore, merely through an old tradition which he had heard that such a midrash by R. Ishmael existed.

But there are other circumstances which prove that there was once such a work. Many midrashic baraitot to Deuteronomy are introduced in the Talmud with the words "Tena debe R. Yishmael," and may be recognized in form and substance as Ishmael's midrashim (comp. Hoffmann, "Zur Einleitung in die Halachischen Midraschim," p. 77; *idem*, "Ueber eine Mechilta zu Deuteronomium," in the "Hildesheimer Jubelschrift," German part, pp. 83–98). B. B. 124b quotes a passage to a verse in Deuteronomy from the "She'ar Sifre de-Be Rab," a term by which the Mekilta de-Rabbi Yishmael is designated (comp. Hoffmann, *l.c.* p. 40). This clearly indicates that there was a midrash to Deuteronomy by R. Ishmael at the period of the Amoraim. This work, which was called also "Mekilta," disappeared at an early date, and was therefore unknown to the medieval authors. The editor of the Midrash ha-Gadol, however, knew it and included many passages from it in his collection. The citations from R. Ishmael's Mekilta to Deuteronomy which are contained in the Midrash ha-Gadol have been collected by D. Hoffmann and printed under the title "Liḳḳuṭe Mekilta: Collectaneen aus einer Mechilta" in the "Hildesheimer Jubelschrift," Hebr. part, pp. 3–32, and separately under the title "Liḳḳuṭe Batar Liḳḳuṭe: Neue Collectaneen aus einer Mechilta zu Deuteronomium" (Berlin, 1897). It appears from these passages that this midrash contained much valuable material from the earlier halakic exegetes. Especially noteworthy is the statement that R. Simon Gamaliel, together with R. Johanan b. Zakkai, addressed a circular letter to the Galileans and other communities ("Liḳḳuṭe Mekilta," p. 30), a statement which certainly antedates the parallel passage in Tosef., Sanh. ii. 6.

Hoffmann's collection of extracts from the Mekilta includes also many quotations from Maimonides' "Yad" (comp. Hoffmann, "Ueber eine Mechilta," p. 85, and his preface to the "Liḳḳuṭe Mekilta," p. 4). Aside from the passages included in the Midrash ha-Gadol, some fragments of the Mekilta have been preserved in the Cairo Genizah; these were discovered by Schechter and published by him in the "J. Q. R."

Bibliography: D. Hoffmann, *Zur Einleitung in die Halachischen Midraschim*, p. 77, Berlin, 1887; idem, *Ueber eine Mechilta zu Deuteronomium*, in *Jubelschrift zum Siebzigsten Geburtstag des Dr. Isr. Hildesheimer*, German part, pp. 83–98, Berlin, 1890.

s. J. Z. L.

MEḲIẒE NIRDAMIM: International society for the publication of old Hebrew books and manuscripts. It was established first at Lyck, Germany, in 1864, under the direction of Rabbi Nathan Adler, Sir Moses Montefiore, and Joseph Zedner (London), Albert Cohn (Paris), S. D. Luzzatto (Padua), M. Sachs (Berlin), Eliezer Lipman Silberman (Lyck), and M. Straschun (Wilna). It was reestablished at Berlin in 1885 under the supervision of Abraham Berliner (Berlin), Moses Ehrenreich (Rome), J. Derenbourg and David Ginsburg (Paris), S. J. Halberstam (Bielitz), A. Harkavy (St. Petersburg), M. Jastrow (Philadelphia), David Kaufmann (Budapest), and M. Straschun (Wilna).

The society has published the following works:

1864. 'Eṭ Sofer, by David Ḳimḥi.
1864–88. Paḥad Yiẓḥaḳ, by R. Isaac Lampronti, letters ח-ב. Lyck-Berlin.
1864–98. Teshubot ha-Ge'onim: one hundred and twenty responsa of the Geonim. Lyck.
1864–1902. Diwan le-R. Yehudah ha-Levi. Lyck-Berlin.
1866. Melammed ha-Talmidim, by Jacob Anatoli.
1866. Eben Sappir, by Jacob Safir.
1868. Pesiḳta ha-Yeshanah, attributed to Rab Kahana.
1868–71. Imre Shefer, by N. H. Wessely.
1871. Wikkuaḥ 'al ha-Ahabah, by Judah Abravanel.
1871. Sefer Toledot Rabbenu Yiẓḥaḳ Lampronṭi.
1871. Sefer ha-Musar, by Ephraim of Modena.
1874. Tagmule ha-Nefesh, by Hillel b. Samuel of Verona.
1874. Sefer ha-'Ibbur, by Abraham ibn Ezra.
1874. Perush 'al Shir ha-Shirim, by Moses ibn Tibbon.
1874. Yiḥuse Tanna'im we-Amora'im, by a contemporary of Rashi.
1881. Ha-Sarid weha-Paliṭ, by Saadia Gaon.
1881–83. Sefer Ḥasidim.
1882. Meteḳ Sefatayim, by R. Immanuel Frances.
1885. Perush 'al Sefer Yeẓirah, by Isaac Barcelona.
1885–87. Teshubot ha-Ge'onim.
1885–1904. Ḳobeẓ 'al Yad, a series of collected smaller works; collections of old documents.
1886. Tarshish, diwan of R. Moses b. Ezra.
1886–92. Maimonides, commentary on Seder Ṭohorot.
1887. Sefer ha-Galuy, by R. Joseph Ḳimḥi.
1887–92. Halakot Gedolot.
1888. Sefer Zikkaron, by Joseph Ḳimḥi.
1889. Ma'yan Gannim, commentary on Job, by Samuel b. Nissim Masnuth.
1889–93. Maḥzor Vitry, by R. Simḥah, pupil of Rashi.
1890. Yehudah Ya'aleh, by Judah Cologna and Isaac Hirschenson.
1891–92. Teshubot MaHaRaM, responsa of R. Meïr of Rothenburg.

1893–96. Sefer ha-Shorashim, by R. Jonah ibn Janaḥ.
1894. Midrash Zuṭa, on the five Megillot.
1895. Megillat Sedarim, by Abraham Brody.
1895. Seder ha-Ḥakamim.
1898. Minḥat Ḳena'ot, by R. Jehiel of Pisa.
1898. She'elot u-Teshubot she be-Sefer ha-Yashar le-Rabbenu Tam.
1899. Midrash ha-Torah, commentary on the Pentateuch, by Solomon Astruc of Barcelona.
1899. Kebod Ḥakamim, by David Messer Leon of Mantua.
1899–1901. Orḥot Ḥayyim, by Aaron ha-Kohen of Lunel.
1900. Tashlum Abudarham, Jose b. Jose's "Abodah" and other ritual poems, with notes by Abudarham.
1900–01. Midrash Sekel: Ṭob, by Menahem b. Solomon.
1902. Sefer ha-'Ittim, by Judah b. Barzilai of Barcelona.

Bibliography: H. D. Lippe, *Bibliographisches Lexicon*, i. 451 *et seq.*, Vienna, 1881; new series, i. 391, Vienna, 1899; *Verzeichniss der Schriften des Verein Meḳize Nirdamim*, 1885–95, 1896, 1898.
G. A. S. W.

MELAMMED ("teacher"): A term which in Biblical times denoted a teacher or instructor in general (*e.g.*, in Ps. cxix. 99 and Prov. v. 13), but which in the Talmudic period was applied especially to a teacher of children, and was almost invariably followed by the word "tinoḳot" (children; B. B. 21a). The Aramean equivalent was "makre dardeke" (*ib.*). The melammed was appointed by the community, and there were special regulations determining how many children he might teach, as well as rules governing the choice of applicants for the office and the dismissal of a melammed (*ib.*). These regulations were extended and augmented in the post-Talmudic period.

Besides the teachers appointed by the community there were others who were privately engaged by the parents of children; hence it became necessary to define accurately the mutual rights and duties of the melammed and of the parents. While giving instruction the melammed was not allowed to do any other work (Shulḥan 'Aruk, Ḥoshen Mishpaṭ, 333, 5). If he was ill, and therefore unable to teach for a time, as much was deducted from his wages as the lessons for that time would have cost (*ib.*); but if, on the other hand, the pupil was ill and could not take his lessons, the melammed received full payment (*ib.* 335, 1). The melammed was not allowed to punish his pupils too severely; and he had to teach both in the daytime and during part of the night (Shulḥan 'Aruk, Yoreh De'ah, 245, 10–11). He might not leave his pupils alone, nor neglect his duties; and he was required to be pious and to understand his vocation (*ib.* 245, 17). Only a married man might be a melammed (*ib.* 245, 20–21). In addition to these regulations many others concerning the melammed are given in Yoreh De'ah (*l.c.* and 246), as well as in Ḥoshen Mishpaṭ (*l.c.*), but some of them are not observed at present.

Regulations for Private Tutors.

A distinction is now made between the village melammed, who is engaged as a private tutor by a Jew living in a village, and who teaches the child in the house of its parents, and the melammed in a town, who teaches in his own home, which serves at the same time as a schoolroom (see Ḥeder). A distinction is likewise drawn between the "melammed dardeki" and the "melammed gemara." The former teaches children of both sexes to read and write Hebrew, and also a chapter or two of each weekly lesson from the Pentateuch, and he generally has one or more assistants (in German "behelfer"). The gemara melammed, on the other hand, teaches Bible and Talmud to the boys, and, when they are older, the Shulḥan 'Aruk as well. Searching questions are seldom asked concerning the melammed's pedagogical fitness; and it frequently happens, moreover, that parents, for charity's sake, send their children for instruction to persons who are unfit for any other vocation, but who possess more or less knowledge of the Talmud. As the profession of a melammed is not an enviable one, it is mostly practised by people who can not find any other employment. In Russia and Poland, therefore, the word "melammed" is, in slang, synonymous with "good-for-nothing" or "dolt." Among the Karaites, however, the term denotes, like "rab" among the Rabbinites, "teacher" and "master," and is regarded as a title of honor. Consequently there are among the Karaites many learned men who are called by the title "ha-melammed ha-gadol" (the great master), or merely "ha-melammed" (the master; comp. Pinsker, "Liḳḳute Ḳadmoniyyot," Index; Gottlober, "Biḳḳoret le-Toledot ha-Ḳara'im," pp. 195, 207, Wilna, 1865).

Bibliography: Lampronti, *Paḥad Yiẓḥaḳ*, s.v., in addition to the authorities cited in the article.
J. J. Z. L.

MELBOURNE: Capital of the British colony of Victoria. Attempts were made to hold services in Melbourne in the house of M. Lazarus in 1839 and in that of Solomon Benjamin in 1841; but the first congregation of the city was that entitled "The Holy Congregation of a Remnant of Israel," which was formed in 1844 with A. H. Hart as president. A synagogue, under the presidency of the above-mentioned Solomon Benjamin, was built on land granted by the government in 1847. The first minister was the Rev. Moses Rintel, a native of Edinburgh, who was called from Sydney to fill the position. In 1858 a trivial difference split the community and led to the formation of a so-called "Polish" section in opposition to the English congregation. The division was led by Rabbi Rintel himself, with whom the president had quarreled because the former had not been robed in his canonicals when attending the funeral of the wife of a leading member of the congregation. Rabbi Rintel began to hold services in a small hall in Lonsdale street, which was afterward abandoned for a new location in Stephen (Exhibition) street.

The existence of the second congregation, called the "Miḳra Yisrael," had the good effect of stimulating Judaism in Melbourne through the spirit of rivalry which was created between the two sections. In 1875 the "foreign," now known as the East Melbourne, congregation built a synagogue in Albert street, where it still continues to hold well-attended services. Rabbi Rintel arrived in Melbourne in 1847, and he continued in his work there till his death in 1880. During his later years he exercised a considerable influence over the community. In 1865 he utilized the hall in Lonsdale street for a Jewish denominational school, which was placed under the control of a Mr. Curtis. The school had a short ife, owing to the suppression of denominational by secular education.

The original congregation with its synagogue in Bourke street was looked upon for many years, and indeed is still regarded, as the leading Jewish religious organization. It was ministered to successively by the Revs. M. Rintel, A. Marks, A. F. Ornstein, Raphael Benjamin, and Dattnar Jacobson. Joseph Abrahams, present (1904) incumbent, arrived from London in 1884, and has helped in the establishment of the United Jewish Education Board, of which he is president as well as of the bet din of Victoria. In the latter position Abrahams has taken a firm stand on the admission of proselytes. In East Melbourne Rintel was succeeded by Revs. M. Grünbaum, A. D. Wolinski, I. Myers, and J. Lenzer. In 1873 the Bourke street congregation established a Hebrew denominational school, where both Hebrew and English subjects were taught. It was carried on with great success for about twenty years, after which time the congregation was compelled to close it on account of an insufficiency of funds.

Intimately connected with the Bourke street congregation and for many years regarded as the leading representative Jew of Victoria was the late Hon. Edward Cohen. Mayor of Melbourne on three occasions, he was elected by East Melbourne to the Legislative Assembly, continuing to represent this constituency till his death in 1877. His successor in Parliament was the late E. L. Zox, who also took a keen interest in synagogal and communal affairs, being at different times the president and treasurer of the Bourke street congregation. Among the living public men who maintain an interested connection with the synagogue is Sir Benjamin Benjamin.

The highest official position hitherto occupied by a Jew in Victoria was the attorney-generalship, held by the Hon. I. A. Isaacs during the Turner ministry from 1894 to 1899. His brother, J. I. Isaacs, was a member of Parliament, having been elected by the district of Owen in 1894. In addition to the above-named Jews who have sat or are still sitting in the Victorian Parliament, there are the Hon. N. Steinfeld of Ballarat, the Hon. Joseph Steinberg of Bendigo (ex-president of the Bendigo congregation), the Hon. F. J. Levien (whose parliamentary career has extended over a longer period than that of any other Jewish member and who was the first president of the Geelong congregation), Theo. Fink, B. J. Fink, and D. B. Lazarus, the last-named of whom was at one time an ardent supporter of the Jewish community in Bendigo.

The congregation of **St. Kilda,** a suburb of Melbourne, came into existence in the sixth decade of the nineteenth century. The synagogue was erected in 1872. For many years past the congregation has been composed for the most part of members of middle-class families in easy circumstances. The Michaelis family was for a long period among its chief supporters. The post of minister was held by E. Blaubaum from 1873 till his death (1904). He was co-editor of the "Jewish Herald," a fortnightly publication which chronicles the doings of Australian Judaism. In communal matters the St. Kilda congregation, as a rule, cooperates with the Melbourne institutions. In its district are situated the almshouses and Montefiore Hall. There is a federated board, appointed from the Bourke street, Albert street, and St. Kilda congregations, to deal with the question of mixed marriages—the most difficult of all the problems engaging the attention of the Melbourne community.

The oldest charitable institution in Melbourne is the Philanthropic Society, founded in 1856. In 1863 the Jewish Friendly Society was formed; it still does good work. A very useful society, founded in 1888, is known as the "Jewish Mutual Aid." It was the parent of the Sydney Mutual Aid, the object of both being to grant substantial loans without interest. The founders of the Melbourne society were P. Blashki, J. P., and the Rev. I. Myers; the son of the former founded the Sydney society.

J. D. I. F.

MELCHIOR, MORITZ GERSON: Danish merchant; born in Copenhagen June 22, 1816; died there Sept 19, 1884. At the age of twenty-four he entered the firm of Moses & Son G. Melchior, established by his grandfather. His father and one of his brothers, with whom he was associated in business, died a few years after, and left the management of the firm in his hands until, in 1850, he was joined by his younger brother **Moses Melchior** (b. Jan. 29, 1825, at Copenhagen). Together they enlarged the business greatly and founded a branch in Melbourne, Australia, in order to establish a market for Danish products.

Melchior filled several important public offices in Copenhagen. He was alderman from 1851 to 1869, a member of the Maritime and Commercial Court (Sö og Handelsretten) from 1862 to 1883, and a member of the Landsthing (Upper House) from 1866 to 1874. In 1861 he was one of the founders of the free-trade society, of which he later became the director. He was one of the founders also of Privatbanken (1857), and leader of the Chamber of Commerce (Grosserersocietetet) from 1873.

Within the Jewish community also Melchior was prominent; he was a member of its representative committee from 1849 to 1852, of which during the last year he was the leader.

Hans Christian Andersen (the well-known author of fairy tales) was often a guest in Melchior's house, where he spent his last days.

Bibliography: C. F. Bricka, *Dansk Biografisk Lexicon.*

S. F. C.

MELCHIOR, NATHAN GERSON: Danish physician; born in Copenhagen Aug. 2, 1811; died there Jan. 30, 1872; brother of Moritz G. and Moses Melchior. Nathan graduated from the University of Copenhagen in 1835. In 1836–37 he traveled, studying ophthalmology at the universities of Berlin, Leipsic, Dresden, and Prague, and on his return made the treatment of diseases of the eye his specialty. In 1842 he became a member of the Medical Society of Brussels, and in 1843 of that of Mechlin. During the war with Germany (1848–50) he served as an army surgeon at a lazaretto in Copenhagen. In 1853 the title of "professor" was conferred upon him; in 1855 he was appointed privat-docent in ophthalmology at Copenhagen University; two years later he became a member of the board of directors of the newly founded Ophthalmological Institute in Copenhagen; and in the same year he acted as vice-president of the ophthalmological congress at Brussels. In 1856 he was sent abroad by the king to study the means adopted by foreign countries against the contagious Egyptian eye-disease then ravaging a great part of Europe.

Melchior published a number of essays in Danish medical journals, among which may be mentioned "Et Tilfælde af Heldig Overskærelse af Musculus Rectus Internus paa begge Öjnene" and "Nogle Ord med Hensyn til Prof. Switzer's Bemærkninger om Operation for Skelen." To the "Annales d'Oculistique" he contributed (1844) an article entitled "Om Pupillens Dilatation i Sund og Sygelig Tilstand."

Bibliography: C. F. Bricka, *Dansk Biografisk Lexicon*; Erslew, *Almindeligt Forfatter-Lexicon*, Copenhagen, 1847.

s. F. C.

MELCHIZEDEK (מלכי־צדק = "king of righteousness"): King of Salem and priest of the Most High in the time of Abraham. He brought out bread and wine, blessed Abram, and received tithes from him (Gen. xiv. 18–20). Reference is made to him in Ps. cx. 4, where the victorious ruler is declared to be "priest forever after the order of Melchizedek." The story is neither an invention nor the product of a copyist's error, as Cheyne ("Encyc. Bibl.") thinks, but rests upon ancient Jerusalemic tradition (as Josephus, "B. J." vi. 10, affirms; comp. Gunkel, "Genesis," 1901, p. 261), "Zedek" being an ancient name of Jerusalem (probably connected with the Phenician Συδυκ = "Zedek" = "Jupiter"; comp. Shab. 156a, b; Gen. R. xliii.; Pesiḳ. R. 20; see Baudissin, "Studien zur Semitischen Religionsgesch." 1876, i. 14–15). Hence "'ir ha-ẓedeḳ" (Isa. i. 21, 26), "neweh ẓedeḳ" (Jer. xxxi. 23, l. 7), "sha'are ẓedeḳ" (Ps. cxviii. 19). The city's first king, accordingly, was known either as "Adoni Zedek" (Josh. x. 1 *et seq.*; comp. Judges i. 5–7, where "Adonizedek" is the correct reading) or as "Malkizedek." The fact that he united the royal with the priestly dignity, like all ancient (heathen) kings, made him a welcome type to the composer of the triumphal song (Ps. cx.).

But to the Jewish propagandists of Alexandria, who were eager to win proselytes for Judaism without submitting them to the rite of circumcision, Melchizedek appealed with especial force as a type of the monotheist of the pre-Abrahamic time or of non-Jewish race, like Enoch. Like Enoch, too, he was apotheosized. He was placed in the same category with Elijah, the Messiah ben Joseph, and the Messiah ben David (Suk. 52b, where "Kohenẓedeḳ" should be corrected to "Malkiẓedeḳ"). The singular feature of supernatural origin is ascribed to all four, in that they are described as being "without father and without mother, without descent, having neither beginning of days nor end of life, but made like unto the son of God abiding forever" (Heb. vii 2–3; comp. Ruth. R. v. 3, where the original text [see "Pugio Fidei," p. 125] referred also to Ps. cx. 4, Isa. liii. 2, and Zech. vi. 12, comp.

Type of Ancient Monotheism.

Yalḳ., Reubeni Bereshit, 9d; Epiphanius, "Hæresis," lv. 3). According to Midr. Teh. to Ps. xxxvii Abraham learned the practise of charity from Mechizedek. Philo speaks of him as "the logos, th priest whose inheritance is the true God" ("De Allgoriis Legum," iii. 26).

The Samaritans identified the city of Salem wit their sanctuary on Mount Gerizim (see LXX., Ge xxxiii. 18; comp. Eusebius, "Præparatio Evangelica," ix. 17).

The rabbis of later generations, rather antagonistic to the cosmopolitan monotheism of Alexandria identified Melchizedek with Shem, the ancestor c Abraham (Ned. 32b; Pirḳe R. El. xxiii.; Targ. t Gen. xiv. 4). A singular story is told of Melchizedek in the Ethiopian Book of Adam and Eve, which before it was turned into a Christian work, seems t have presented a strange combination of Jewish and Egyptian element emanating from a sect afterwar known as the Melchizedekites. Ther (iii. 13–21) Noah tells his son Shem before his death to take "Melchizedek, the son of Canaan, whom God had chosen from all generations c men, and to stand by the dead body of Adam after had been brought from the ark to Jerusalem as th center of the earth and fulfil the ministry befor God." The angel Michael then took away Me chizedek, when fifteen years of age, from his father and, after having anointed him as priest, brought hi to (Jerusalem) the center of the earth, telling hi father to share the mystery only with Shem, the so of Noah, while the Holy Spirit, speaking out of th ark when the body of Adam was hidden, greete Melchizedek as "the first-created of God." She went, carrying bread and wine, and, assisted by th angel, brought the body of Adam to its destinatior Melchizedek offered the bread and wine upon th altar they built near the place where Adam's bod was deposited, and then Shem departed, leaving th pure lad in his garment of skins under the so protection of the angel, no one on earth knowing of his whereabouts until, at last, Abraham me him. Compare also "Die Schatzhöhle" (Bezold transl. 1883, pp. 26–28), where the father of Me chizedek is called "Malki" and the mother "Yo Ẓedeḳ"; and see the notes to Malan's "Book c Adam and Eve" (1882, pp. 237–238). Against th opinion of Roensch (Das Buch der Jubiläen," 1874 p. 502), that the story of Melchizedek has been intentionally omitted from the Book of Jubilees, se Charles in his Commentary to Jubilees (xiii. 25). A remnant, probably, of these Melchizedekites appears in early Christian literature as a heretic sec which regarded Melchizedek as a great heavenl power and as a son of God, superior to Jesu (Epiphanius, "Hæresis," lv. 1–9; Hippolytus, "Refutatio Hæresium," vii. 36, x. 20; pseudo-Tertullian, 48; Augustinus, "De Hæresibus," 34; see als Herzog-Hauck, "Real-Encyc." *s.v.* "Monarchianismus").

The Melchizedekites.

Bibliography: Friedländer, *Antichrist*, 1901, pp. 88–89.

s. K.

MELDOLA: Ancient Sephardic family whos genealogy can be traced through sixteen genera

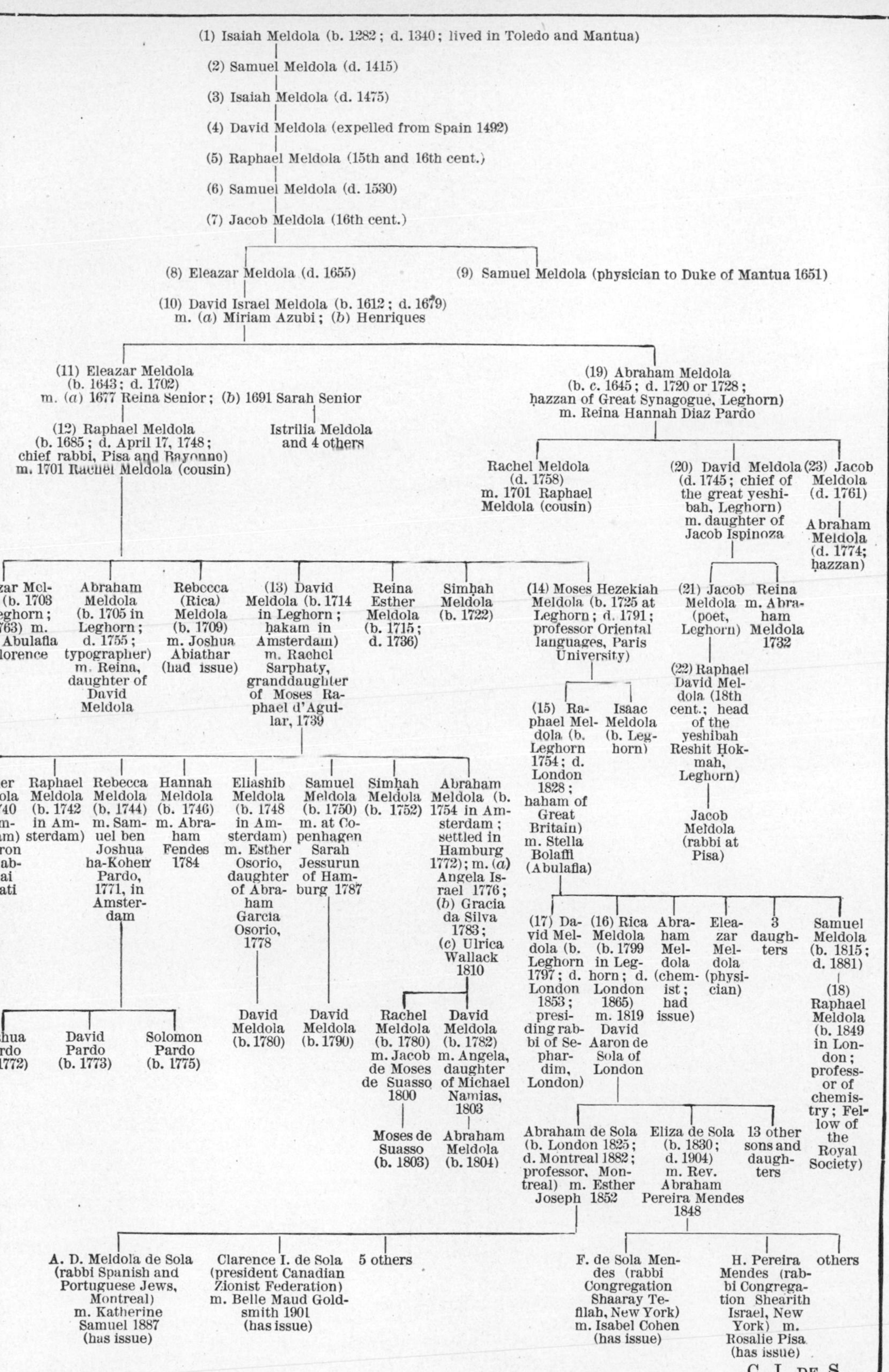

Genealogical Tree of the Meldola Family.

tions without a break to Isaiah Meldola of Toledo (born in 1282). Under Spanish names it long flourished in Toledo, and produced many men of note and of learning. The name "Meldola" seems to have been assumed when some of the family first established themselves in Italy, prior to the going of Isaiah Meldola to Mantua. One branch, however, took the name "Montalto"; and from this branch was descended the Portuguese Marano family of Montalto, including Elihu Montalto (physician to Marie de Medici, queen of Henry IV. of France, and counselor to Louis XIII.), as well as the painter G. S. D. Montalto.

Subjoined is the genealogical tree of the Meldola family. The numbers in parentheses correspond to those given in the text.

1. Isaiah Meldola: One of the sages of Castile; born in Toledo, Spain, 1282; died at Mantua, Italy, in 1340. He was ḥakam of Toledo after having previously served as dayyan. Owing to politico-religious troubles he left Spain for Italy, where some of his relatives had already settled, and he was appointed chief rabbi of Mantua and head of the college there.

2. Samuel Meldola: Son of Isaiah (No. 1); born in the earlier half of the fourteenth century; died in 1415. He succeeded his father as ḥakam of Mantua and as head of the college. He was distinguished as a preacher, and was the author of several theological works.

3. Isaiah Meldola: Son of Samuel (No. 2); born in Mantua toward the close of the fourteenth century; died 1475. He was ḥakam and dayyan, and was the author of "Ḥazon Yesha'yahu," a commentary on Isaiah, printed in Mantua. He also practised medicine and wrote a work on physiology.

4. David Meldola: Son of Isaiah Meldola (No. 3); born at Mantua in the early part of the fifteenth century; died about 1505. He went to Spain, where he made efforts to maintain the Spanish Jewish colleges, but returned to Italy in 1492. Rejoining his relatives in Mantua, he was received at court with favor. He devoted his declining years to the writing of a number of Jewish theological works.

5. Raphael Meldola: Son of David Meldola (No. 4); born about the middle of the fifteenth century; died during the earlier half of the sixteenth century. He was ḥakam of the Jewish community of Mantua, and also a court councilor.

6. Samuel Meldola: Son of Raphael Meldola (No. 5); born during the latter part of the fifteenth century; died 1530. He was physician to the Duke of Mantua, winning eminence by his skill as a practitioner; and he wrote a work on medicine. He was also ḥakam and dayyan of Mantua.

7. Jacob Meldola: Son of Samuel Meldola (No. 6); born about the beginning of the sixteenth century; died about 1580; one of the chief rabbis of Mantua. He was the father of two sons, Eleazar (No. 8) and Samuel (No. 9).

8. Eleazar Meldola: Elder son of Jacob Meldola (No. 7); born in the sixteenth century; died, according to most authorities, in 1655, but one authority places the date much earlier. He succeeded his father as ḥakam of Mantua, and was very distinguished as a preacher, his oratorical powers securing for him renown throughout Italy. A volume of h[is] orations was published in Venice.

9. Samuel Meldola: Italian physician; live[d] during the seventeenth century; younger son [o]f Jacob Meldola (No. 7) and brother of Eleazar Me[l]dola (No. 8). He was physician to the Duke [o]f Mantua, and was the author of a work on medicin[e] entitled "Refu'ot Te'alah." He devoted attentio[n] also to religious and metaphysical studies an[d] was the author of "Ḳeri'at Shema'" and "Deba[r] Shemuel."

10. David Israel Meldola: Son of Eleaza[r] Meldola (No. 8); born at Mantua 1612; died, accor[d]ing to most authorities, in 1679 at Florence, whil[e] one source gives an earlier date. He was traine[d] for the rabbinate in his native city, but on accou[nt] of the war, famine, and pestilence he fled to Flo[r]ence. He went thence to Leghorn, where he wa[s] head of the college for more than twenty year[s] and was then persuaded to return to Florence t[o] accept office as ḥakam and ab bet din.

Meldola was the author of a commentary on Scrip[t]ural passages, and of "Emunah Omen," a work o[n] the Jewish faith. He married Miriam Azubi, an[d] after her death espoused a grandniece of Elih[u] Montalto. He was survived by two sons: Eleaza[r] (No. 11), from whom springs the elder branch [o]f the family, and Abraham (No. 19), from whom i[s] descended the younger branch.

11. Eleazar Meldola: Elder son of David Isra[el] Meldola (No. 10); born 1643; died 1702 (one autho[r]ity states 1704). He went from Florence to Leghor[n] with his younger brother, and became head of th[e] Talmud Torah, and chief rabbi of Leghorn. He wa[s] noted as a grammarian and as the author of a wor[k] entitled "Halakah we-Haggadah." He married i[n] 1677 Reina Senior, daughter of Jacob Senior, b[y] whom he had seven children. After her death h[e] married (1691) Sarah Senior, by whom he had fiv[e] children.

12. Raphael Meldola: Italian rabbi; born a[t] Leghorn in 1685; died April 17, 1748; fifth child [o]f Eleazar Meldola (No. 11) by his wife Reina Senio[r]. He was originally named **Samuel Jacob Meldola**, but on his recovery from a dangerous illness h[is] name was changed to Raphael. He was electe[d] rabbi of Pisa in 1722. In 1729 he was elected t[o] succeed Isaac da Costa as chief rabbi of Bayonn[e] and St. Esprit, and he remained ḥakam of thes[e] congregations until 1741, when he returned to Leg[h]orn.

Meldola was the author of a large number of theo[]logical and ethical works, the most important bein[g] "Mayim Rabbim" (Amsterdam, 1737), and his re[]sponsa, in several volumes, which gained for him [a] European reputation, and which were afterwar[d] published by his son David in Amsterdam. H[e] wrote also a poem in honor of Mendelssohn's "Je[]rusalem." He married in 1701 Rachel Meldola, th[e] daughter of his uncle Abraham, by whom he ha[d] seven children. His third son, David (No. 13), an[d] his youngest son, Moses Hezekiah (No. 14), becam[e] very distinguished. His second son, Abraham, bor[n] in Leghorn 1705, was a noted typographer.

13. David Meldola: Third son of Rapha[el] Meldola (No. 12); born at Leghorn 1714; died (it said) at the age of 104. He went with his father to Bayonne, left that city in 1735, and settled in Amsterdam, where he undertook the publication of his father's works, as well as some of his own writings. He was appointed ḥakam of several of the religious societies and philanthropic organizations.

Meldola was the author of: "Mo'ed Dawid" (Amsterdam, 1740), an astronomical and mathematical work, including a poem giving the rules of the calendar (first published in the ritual work "Tefillat Yesharim," *ib.* 1740); "Dibre Dawid" (*ib.* 1753); "Darke Yesod ha-Limmud," on the methodology of the Talmud (*ib.* 1754); "Darke Dawid" (Amsterdam and Hamburg, 1793–95); and many others preserved in manuscript (Nepi-Ghirondi, "Toledot Gedole Yisrael," p. 79). He married in 1739 Rachel Sarphaty (or Sarfatti), daughter of Eliashib Nathanael Sarphaty of Amsterdam and granddaughter of Moses Raphael d'Aguilar, by whom he had eight children, born in Amsterdam. His youngest son, **Abraham,** born 1754, removed to Hamburg in 1772, and was the author of many works, including "Traduccion de las Cartos Mercantines y Manuales," Hamburg, 1784, and "Nova Grammatica Portugueza," Leipsic, 1785.

14. Moses Hezekiah Meldola: Youngest son of Raphael Meldola (No. 12); born at Leghorn 1725; died 1791. Though trained in the banking business, he abandoned commercial pursuits to follow a professional career. He won renown as a philologist, and was the author of a number of books on Semitic languages; he likewise attained to the rank of ḥakam and was appointed professor of Oriental languages in the University of Paris. He was the father of two sons, Raphael (No. 15) and Isaac.

15. Raphael Meldola: Elder son of Moses Hezekiah Meldola (No. 14); born in Leghorn 1754; died in London June 1, 1828; one of the most prominent members of the Meldola family. He received a thorough university training, both in theological and in secular branches, and displayed such remarkable talents that when only fifteen years old he was permitted to take his seat in the rabbinical college. He was preacher in Leghorn for some years, and in 1803 he obtained the title of rabbi.

Raphael Meldola.

In 1805 Meldola was elected haham of the Spanish and Portuguese Jews of Great Britain, and proved a worthy successor of Sasportas and Nieto. His name will ever be indissolubly associated with that of Bevis Marks, London. Possessed of a remarkably virile mind, he was a dominant factor in the British Jewry of his generation. He was the author of "Ḳorban Minḥah," "Ḥuppat Ḥatanim" (1796), and "Derek Emunah," published by his son after his death. He left several other works in manuscript. His scholarship attracted around him a circle in which were many of the most distinguished men of his day, including Benjamin D'Israeli and Isaac D'Israeli; and it is noteworthy that he opposed the policy which produced the famous rupture between the latter and the mahamad (see D'Israeli, Isaac). He maintained a literary correspondence with many of the most prominent Christian clergymen and scholars of his time; and his acquaintance with the Archbishop of Canterbury and the Canon of Windsor led to his being received by King George III.

Meldola married Stella Bolaffi (Abulafia), by whom he had four sons and four daughters.

16. Rica Meldola: Eldest daughter of Raphael Meldola (No. 15); born at Leghorn 1799; married (May 20, 1819) **David Aaron de Sola,** senior minister and preacher of Bevis Marks Synagogue, London, and became the mother of a large family. Of her sons, **Abraham de Sola** was professor of Semitic languages and literature in McGill University, Montreal, Canada, and rabbi of the Sephardic congregation in that city. He was the father of the Rev. **A. D. Meldola de Sola** and of **Clarence I. de Sola** of Montreal. One of Rica's daughters, **Eliza,** married the Rev. **Abraham P. Mendes** of Birmingham and London, England, and afterward of Newport, R. I. She was the mother of the Revs. F. de Sola Mendes and H. Pereira Mendes of New York.

17. David Meldola: Eldest son of Raphael Meldola (No. 15); born at Leghorn 1797; died in London 1853. He obtained the rabbinical degree at Leghorn, and after the death of his father was elected presiding officer of the bet din of the London Sephardic community. Although not given the title of haham, he was the acting chief rabbi from 1828 until his death. It was during his incumbency that the London Jewish community passed through the stormy period of the early Reform movement. Meldola was the founder, in conjunction with Moses Angel, of the London "Jewish Chronicle." A profound Hebraist and Talmudist, he was the author of a number of writings, including several works in manuscript on Jewish theology and prayers, besides elegies, orations, and poems in Hebrew.

18. Raphael Meldola: Son of **Samuel Meldola,** youngest son of Raphael Meldola (No. 15); English naturalist and chemist; born in London in 1849. In 1875 he was sent by the Royal Society to the Nicobar Islands in charge of an eclipse expedition. Since 1885 he has been professor of chemistry at the Finsbury Technical College. He has made many discoveries of important compounds and coal-tar dyes. He is the author of a large number of scientific works, among them the article on "Organic Chemistry" in the "Encyclopædia Britannica," and "The Chemistry of Photography," London, 1884; and he has translated and edited Weismann's "Studies in the Theory of Descent," published in 1882. In 1895 and 1896 he was president of the Entomological Society. Meldola has accomplished much for the diffusion of technical instruction, being a member of the Technical Instruction Committee of the Essex County Council. In recognition of his services to science he was elected fellow of the Royal Society.

The line of Abraham, younger son of David Israel Meldola (No. 10), is as follows:

19. Abraham Meldola: Chief ḥazzan of the

Great Synagogue, Leghorn; died 1720 or 1728. Meldola was the author of two works on "ḥazzanut" and Hebrew music. He married Reina Hannah, daughter of Jacob Diaz Pardo, by whom he had a daughter, **Rachel,** and two sons, David (No. 20) and Jacob (No. 23).

20. David Meldola: Elder son of Abraham Meldola (No. 19). He was ḥakam and chief of the great yeshibah at Leghorn, and was the author of several volumes of Hebrew poems. He married the daughter of Jacob Ispinoza, by whom he had a son, Jacob (No. 21), and a daughter, **Reina.**

21. Jacob Meldola: Italian poet; flourished during the eighteenth century; son of David Meldola (No. 20). He was also minister of the Leghorn synagogue.

22. Raphael David Meldola: Son of Jacob Meldola (No. 21); lived during the latter half of the eighteenth century. He was president of the Reshit Ḥokmah College, Leghorn, and gained celebrity as a poet and humorist. He published several volumes of verse. He was the father of **Jacob Meldola,** who occupied the rabbinate of Pisa some time in the nineteenth century.

23. Jacob Meldola: Younger son of Abraham Meldola (No. 19); died in 1761. He was a noted theologian, and the author of "Sefat Ḥayyim." His son, **Abraham Meldola** (d. 1774), was ḥazzan in Italy, and was the author of two volumes of discourses.

Bibliography: *Sefer Toledot Adam*, manuscript, part i., by Eleazar Meldola, Leghorn, beginning 1679; part ii., by Raphael Meldola, Leghorn, Pisa, and Bayonne, beginning 1702; part iii., by David Meldola, Amsterdam, beginning 1744; part iv., by Abraham Meldola, Hamburg, beginning 1772; supplemental part by David bar Raphael Meldola, London, 1828; *Dibre Dawid*, Preface and p. 139, Amsterdam, 1753; *Pedigree of the Meldola Family* from death of Isaiah Meldola, 1340, extracted from a book of about 400 verses from ancient manuscripts by R. Meldola; D. Meldola, *The Way of Faith*, Preface, London, 1848; Leon, *Histoire des Juifs de Bayonne*, p. 364, Paris, 1893; Gaster, *Hist. of Bevis Marks*, London, 1901; Henry S. Morais, *Eminent Israelites of the Nineteenth Century*, Philadelphia, 1880; *The Gentleman's Magazine* (London), Oct., 1828; *Jew. Chron.* July 25, 1851; *The Hebrew Observer* (London), March 11 and April 15, 1853; Lucien Wolf, *Old Jewish Families in England*, in *The Leisure Hour* (London), Aug., 1886; *The Occident* (Philadelphia), xi. 80, 213; *Israel* (London), June, 1899; April, 1901; *et seq.*

G. C. I. de S.

MELIḤAH ("salting"): The process of salting meat in order to make it ritually fit (kasher) for cooking. The prohibition against partaking of blood was extended by the Rabbis to include, under certain conditions, flesh containing blood (based on Gen. ix. 4; see Blood). Hence various regulations are prescribed in the rabbinic codes which tend toward the elimination of blood from the meat before it becomes fit for use. The prohibition against blood, however, applies only to the blood of mammals and birds, not to the blood of fishes or of locusts, and even in mammals and birds only the blood which is contained in the veins or which is congealed on the surface, or which has begun to flow from the meat, is forbidden; as long as the blood is a part of the meat it may be eaten. For instance, one may cut off a piece of raw meat, wash off all the blood that may have gathered on its surface, and eat it (Ker. 20b, 21a; Shulḥan 'Aruk, Yoreh De'ah, 67, 1). When, however, meat is to be used for cooking, during which process it will certainly discharge a great deal of its blood, it is necessary to salt it, in order to let the blood flow freely for a time before cooking it. Meat that is to be roasted over an open fire need not be salted, for all the blood that will be discharged during roasting will be consumed in the fire. The custom, however, is to salt it a little even in this case (Ḥul. 14a, and Tos., *s.v.* "We-Nasbin"; Yoreh De'ah, 76).

The Process.

In preparing meat for cooking the following process is observed: The meat is first soaked in water for about half an hour in order that the pores may be opened to emit the blood. If it is left in the water longer than twenty-four hours, both the meat and the vessel containing it become unfit for use, for the meat is then regarded as if it had been cooked (כבוש הרי הוא כמבושל), and meat cooked without previous salting is forbidden. It is customary not to use for any other purpose the vessel in which meat is soaked before salting, although if it is used (after it has been washed) the food cooked in it, even if placed in it hot, is permitted for food (Yoreh De'ah, 69, 1). The meat is next placed on a wicker basket, or on straw, or on a slanting board, and thickly salted on all sides. In the case of poultry the body should be opened and the entrails removed before it is salted. The meat is left in the salt for about an hour, or, if urgent, for about twenty minutes. The salt is then shaken off, and the meat is rinsed twice, after which it may be cooked (*l.c.* 69, 4–8). If the meat is cooked before the salt is washed off, the pot and all that it contains are forbidden, unless the quantity in the pot is sixty times greater than the quantity of the salt and the moisture of the blood upon it. If the meat is cooked before it is salted, the pot and all that it contains are forbidden, unless the quantity in the pot is sixty times greater than the piece of unsalted meat, and even then, according to some authorities, the piece itself is forbidden (*l.c.* 69, 9, 11; see also "Be'er Heṭeb").

Details.

Three days from the time the animal is slaughtered the meat does not discharge its blood through salting, and therefore may not be cooked except by roasting over an open fire. If, however, water has been poured over it during that time, it may be salted within three days from the time the water was poured over it, and may then be used in cooking (*l.c.* 69, 12, 13). The liver, because of the abundance of blood it contains, must be cut open and roasted before it may be cooked (Ḥul. 111a; Yoreh De'ah, 73). Before salting the head must be cut open and the brains removed; the horny parts of the legs must be removed (*l.c.* 71); the heart must be cut open; and it is also customary to open the large veins of the lungs before salting (*l.c.* 72).

Many pieces of meat, even if some are beef and some poultry, may be placed one on the top of the other in salting. Fish and meat, however, should not be salted together, for the fish, after discharging all its blood, will absorb the blood discharged by the meat (*l.c.* 70). The intestines should not be salted with other parts, although if this be done they may still be used in cooking (*l.c.* 75). Eggs found in the body of a fowl need salting, but must ot be salted with other meat (*l.c.* 75, 1, Isserles' loss).

BIBLIOGRAPHY: Maimonides, *Yad, Ma'akalot Asurot*, 6; Caro, *Shulḥan 'Aruk, Yoreh De'ah*, 69–78; *Roḳeaḥ*, §§ 410–431; *Kol Bo*, 103; *Or Zarua'*, i. 469–478; *Ḥokmat Adam*, §§ 30–35.

S. S. J. H. G.

MELLI: Family of scholars and rabbis that derived its name from Melli, an Italian village in the province of Mantua. The family can be traced back to the fifteenth century.

Eliezer Melli: Rabbi of Venice in the sixteenth century. He is mentioned in the responsa of Moses Provençal (No. 194).

Elijah ben Abraham Melli: The earliest known member of the family; rabbi of Parma in the second half of the fifteenth century. Among the Italian manuscript responsa in the possession of Mortara there is one of Elijah Melli's, addressed (1470) to Joseph Colon, concerning the divorcing of a baptized Jew. It was issued at Parma, where Melli was rabbi. Appended to it is the answer of Joseph Colon approving the bill of divorce.

Jehiel Melli: Rabbi of Mantua in the beginning of the seventeenth century; author of "Tapuḥe Zahab" (Mantua, 1623), an abstract of Elijah de Vidas' book on religious ethics, "Reshit Ḥokmah"; appended are annotations concerning ritual laws. It was published with the "Hanhagot" of Asher ben Jehiel by Melli's son-in-law, David Portaleone.

Phinehas Elijah ben Ẓemaḥ Elijah Melli: Rabbi in Mantua in the sixteenth century. He received the degree of chief rabbi Jan. 15, 1581. He was distinguished as a Talmudist, and is quoted by Lampronti ("Paḥad Yiẓḥaḳ," iv. 24) and Moses Provençal (Responsa, Nos. 97, 112). Responsum No. 231 of the 260 responsa of the Italian rabbis is his.

Ẓemaḥ Elijah b. Phinehas Elijah Melli: Rabbi in Mantua in the sixteenth century. He received the degree of chief rabbi on the same day as his father. Responsa of his, addressed to various contemporaries, are among the manuscripts in the possession of Mortara.

BIBLIOGRAPHY: Fuenn, *Keneset Yisra'el*, p. 560; Mortara, *Indice*, pp. 38–39; *Mosé*, v. 125, 379; vi. 134, 192, 264; Steinschneider, *Cat. Bodl.* col. 1280.

D. M. SEL.

MELO, DAVID ABENATAR: Rabbi and poet; born in Spain about 1550. His translation of some of the Psalms into Spanish verse brought him under the suspicion of the Inquisition, and he was imprisoned. When, after several years of torture, he was acquitted (1611), he left Spain and emigrated to Amsterdam. He soon gained a reputation as a stylist and scholar; became a member of the academy "De los Pintos"; and was finally appointed rabbi of the Portuguese synagogue Bet Yisrael in Amsterdam. There are many allusions in his verses to the tortures he underwent while imprisoned by the Inquisition.

BIBLIOGRAPHY: Kayserling, *Sephardim*, pp. 169 *et seq.*; De Barrios, *Insigne Jesiba de los Pintos*; idem, *Relacion de los Poetas*, p. 53; Wolf, *Bibl. Hebr.* iii. 177, 205, 1068.

G. W. M.

MELOL or MELUL (מילול), MOSES ḤAY: Compositor and translator in Leghorn (1777–93); son of Jacob Raphael Melol and brother of David Ḥayyim Melol. He translated or edited the "Sefer Azharot ha-Ḳodesh" and the Book of Ruth (Leghorn, 1777), and translated into Ladino "Seder Hattarat Nedarim," the ritual for dissolving an oath, "como suelen practicar en la Yesiba de Gemiluth Hasadim" (*ib.* 1792). **Mordecai Melol,** a relative of his, edited "Alegria de Purim" (*ib.* 1792).

BIBLIOGRAPHY: Ersch and Gruber, *Encyc.* section ii., part 28, p. 63; Kayserling, *Bibl. Esp.-Port.-Jud.* pp. 68, 92.

G. M. K.

MELS, ALFRED (pseudonym of **Martin Cohn**): German author; born at Berlin April 15, 1831; died at Summerdale, near Chicago, July 22, 1894. He studied at the University of Berlin, but in 1848 ran away to join the Foreign Legion of Algiers. He was severely wounded while on the way to Oran in charge of a detachment of recruits. Tiring of this life, he went to Paris, where he found literary employment with Alexandre Dumas.

In 1850 Mels as a private joined the rebel army of Sleswick-Holstein against Denmark, and at Idstadt was again wounded. Recovering, he returned to Paris as correspondent for various journals. Later he went to Madrid to become the editor of "Las Novedades." This position he resigned in order to join the Spanish army, in which he rose to the rank of captain. In 1864 Mels returned to Germany to become a contributor to the "Gartenlaube" and, later, to the "Daheim." In 1866 he published anonymously "Der Feldzug der Main-Armee," an account of the progress of the Prussian army operating in the vicinity of the Main in 1866. In 1869 he went to the Paris Exposition as representative of "Daheim" and "Ueber Land und Meer."

On the outbreak of the Franco-Prussian war Mels was appointed by the London "Times" one of its correspondents with the German army; but after the fall of Sedan he resigned in order to accompany Napoleon III. to Wilhelmshöhe. Thence he went to Vienna, where he became the feuilletonist of the "Wiener Tageblatt." In 1873 he published, under the nom de plume "Don Spavento," an exposé and a satirical criticism of Viennese journalists and their methods: "Typen und Silhouetten von Wiener Schriftsteller und Journalisten." From Vienna he went successively to Graz, Zurich, Paris, Italy, and Chicago.

Mels's best-known work is the comedy "Heine's Junge Leiden" (1872), which has been performed more than 2,000 times. An equal measure of success was achieved by "Der Neue Frühling" (1877), after two other plays, "Der Staatsanwalt" (1875) and "Das Letzte Manuscript" (1876), had been only moderately successful. Among Mels's other works are: "Erlebtes und Erdachtes" (1869); "Herzenskämpfe" (1869); "Gebilde und Gestalten" (1870); "Seltsame Schicksale" (1872); "Unsichtbare Mächte" (1875); and "Ferne Horizonte" (1876–78). Mels embraced Christianity in 1859.

BIBLIOGRAPHY: *Unsere Zeit*, i. 672–675; Bornmüller, *Schriftsteller-Lexikon*, 1882, p. 484; Franz Brümmer, *Deutsches Dichter-Lexikon*, 1876.

S. E. MS.

MELUN (Hebrew, מילאון, מליאון, מילון, or מיילאון): Principal town of the department Seine-et-Marne, France. There was a very important Jewish community here as early as the twelfth century. The scholars connected with the Talmudic school of the city took part in the synod held at Troyes about 1160 under the direction of Rashbam and R. Tam ("Kol Bo," No. 117, where חכמי מיליאון must be read instead of חכמי ליאון). A Jew of Melun, Vivant, was appointed in 1202 to collect the taxes of his coreligionists; another, Leo Crossius, obtained permission in 1204 to live at the Châtelet in Paris. In Dec., 1230, Saint Louis, King of France, together with the barons at a meeting held at Melun, promulgated the following decrees: (1) henceforth Jews will not be permitted to make contracts; (2) they will be considered the property of the barons in whose territory they live; (3) in cases of migration they may be forcibly returned to their former homes; (4) debts due to them shall become void if not collected within nine legal terms, and shall no longer bear interest; (5) the vouchers for their credits shall become worthless if not submitted to the barons before All Saints' Day.

The Jews occupied a special quarter at Melun, called "La Iviferie," which is mentioned in the documents of the years 1206, 1212, and 1218, preserved in the archives of Notre Dame of Melun. In a document dated Jan. 5, 1307, there is a reference to the sale of a house and barn, situated in the Jews' street, that had belonged to the Jew Donin and his nephews. Another document, of the year 1311, refers to the sale of a house situated in the manor of the "hopital S. Jean de Hierusalem, rue de la Iviferie, iouxte la maison qu'on appelle l'eschole aux Juifs." In the library of Melun there is a manuscript of the fourteenth century entitled "Breviarium Judaicum," being a maḥzor (partly unedited), according to the French ritual, for the holy-days of Rosh ha-Shanah and Yom Kippur (described in detail by M. Schwab in "R. E. J." xiii. 296–299). Like the Jews in other parts of France, those of Melun were forced in 1306 by King Philip the Fair to leave the city without hopes of ever returning.

The most prominent scholars of Melun include: (1) Meshullam b. Nathan, identical, according to Z. Kahn (*ib.* i. 236), with the Narbonne scholar of the same name. Meshullam is known to have gone in 1150 from Narbonne to Melun, where he soon acquired a high reputation. He corresponded with R. Tam and the most famous rabbis of his time. He is quoted in the tosafot to Beẓah (16a), 'Abodah Zarah (29b), and Pesaḥim (105a). (2) Nathan b. Meshullam, son of the preceding; was living at Etampes in 1180. (3) Jedidiah, teacher of Abraham ben Nathan of Lunel. (4) Menahem Sire Léon, or Messer Leon (13th cent.). (5) The tosafist David of Melun, and (6) his son Judah, who in 1225 directed the Talmud school and was one of the four French rabbis who took part in 1240 in the religious controversy at Paris against Nicholas Donin.

Bibliography: *Ordonnances des Rois de France*, i. 53; Depping, *Les Juifs dans le Moyen Age*, p. 125; Carmoly, *Itinéraires de la Terre Sainte*, p. 187; Zunz, *Z. G.* pp. 48, 53, 94; Renan-Neubauer, *Les Ecrivains Juifs Français*, p. 410; *R. E. J.* ii. 38, xiii. 299-300, xv. 234; Gross, *Gallia Judaica*, pp. 351-355.

G. S. K.

MELVILLE, LEWIS (LEWIS S. BENJAMIN): English author; born in 1874. He is the author of the following works: "Life of Thackeray" (1899); "Thackeray's Stray Papers" (1902); "In the World of Mimes" (1902); and "Introduction to Thackeray's Works" (1903–4). He is a contributor to the "Fortnightly Review," "The Bookman," "Temple Bar," and to other English periodicals.

Bibliography: *Literary Year-Book*, 1904.

J. I. L. B.

MEM: Thirteenth letter of the Hebrew alphabet; the meaning of the name is "water," the primitive shape of the letter resembling waves (see Alphabet). "Mem" has two forms: one for the beginning or middle of a word (מ), and one for the end (ם). Its numerical value (in post-Biblical writings) is 40. Being a labial, it interchanges in the Semitic group of languages with other labials, that is to say, with פ, ו, ב, and sometimes also with the liquids ר, נ, ל. In composition it appears as a prefix, denoting place, time, instrument, or agent, and is employed to form all participles except the "ḳal" and "nif'al," and numerous substantives.

T. M. Sel.

MEMEL: City in the district of Königsberg, East Prussia. It has a population of 19,796, including 1,214 Jews (1900). The earliest mention of the Jews of Memel occurs in connection with the adjournment of the diet by Duke Albrecht April 20, 1567, when he decreed their expulsion from the city. In 1664 the Great Elector granted the Dutch Jew Moses Jacobsohn de Jonge the right of residence in the city. De Jonge, who carried on an extensive business, was finally compelled by financial difficulties to leave, and after that Jews were permitted to enter only during the fairs. Furs and Hebrew books were important articles of trade. The Prussian edict of 1812 enabled the Jews again to settle in Memel and the extensive commerce in wood carried on with Russia attracted many Polish and Russian Jews, among others, to the city. The community was not organized until 1862, when the ḥebra ḳaddisha was established. The first rabbi was Dr. Isaac Rülf (1865–98), who established the parochial school and the hospital, as well as the method of religious instruction, and was actively interested in behalf of the Russian Jews. He was succeeded by Dr. Emanuel Carlebach.

Bibliography: Rülf, *Zur Gesch. der Juden in Memel*, in the first *Bericht der Israelitischen Religionsschule*, Memel, 1900.

D. H. V.

MEMOR-BOOK (German, "Memorbuch"): A manuscript list of localities or countries in which Jews have been persecuted, together with the names of the martyrs, and necrologies. Memor-books are devoted primarily to the learned and influential, although others may be included for special reasons, particularly Jews distinguished for their noble character, or who performed their duties toward the community with especial faithfulness or who gave or bequeathed gifts to its institutions. These memorials to the dead, which were intended to serve as inspirations to the living, were read wholly or in part at the memorial services (see Hazkarat Nesha

MOT). The so-called "memmern"—the reading of the lists of martyrs and of places of martyrdom—was heard in the synagogue on the Sabbath before the Ninth of Ab and on the Sabbath before Pentecost also.

Memor-book of Nuremberg.

The earliest memor-book extant is that of the community of Nuremberg. It was begun in 1296, and is so complete that it must have had predecessors which served as models for it. At all events, notwithstanding their name, the memor-books are not borrowed from the Christian Church, but are a product of Jewish piety; for it has always been customary in Israel to remember the dead, to pray and to present offerings for them, and to hand their names down to posterity. Indeed, the Christian Church adopted this custom, which developed into the ritual observance of All Souls' Day, from Judaism. Although the different memor-books occasionally show a resemblance to a certain form of literature produced by the Catholic Church—the diptychs borrowed from the Romans, the "libri vitæ" or "libri viventium" used until the Carolingian period, the later calendars, necrologies, and martyrologies—yet many passages in the Church Fathers indicate that the prayers for the dead were Jewish in origin, and date from the time of the Apostles, who were Jews (comp. Bautz, "Das Fegfeuer," p. 76, Mayence, 1883; Propst, "Liturgie der Ersten Drei Christlichen Jahrhunderte," pp. 304 *et seq.*).

After it had become customary to remember scholars, martyrs, benefactors, and others in prayers on the Sabbath and on feast-days, the names of the dead were entered in special books, with the formulas for the "hazkarah" or the "hashkabah" (see HAZKARAT NESHAMOT), generally beginning with the words: "Yizkor Elohim nishmat . . ." (May God remember the soul of . . .). These books contained, in addition to the general part—the introductory prayers and the names of the noble and beneficent—a simple list of the dead, with notes on their works and the sums spent for the repose of their souls. A list of localities and countries where persecutions had taken place either preceded the necrologies or was added to them.

Name.

The original name of the memor-book was taken from the Bible, and it was called either "Sefer Zikkaron" (= "Book of Remembrance," after Mal. iii. 16) or "Sefer ha-Zikronot" (= "Book of Commemorations"). The later title, "Sefer Hazkarat Neshamot" (= "Memorial Book of Souls"), was soon superseded by the general name "Memorial Book" or "Memor-Book," which was applied to similar works in Christian circles also. The names "pinkes" (= "book," from the Greek πίναξ), "Selbuch," and "Totenbuch" occur but seldom. The word "memor-book" (מימורבוך, ממערבוך, מאמרבוך) is derived from the Latin "memoria" (see Salfeld, "Martyrologium," p. xii., note 5).

So-Called Memor-Book of Mayence.

The memor-book of the community of Nuremberg, which was formerly designated by the misleading term "Memor-Book of Mayence," on the authority of Carmoly (in "Israelit," 1865, 1866), Grätz ("Gesch."), Neubauer (in "R. E. J." iv. 1 *et seq.*), and others, was begun in 1296 by a skilful scribe, Isaac b. Samuel of Meiningen, as a gift to be presented to the community of Nuremberg at the dedication of a new synagogue (Nov. 15, 1296). It was then taken to Mayence, where it was stolen and sold. Subsequently it was acquired by Carmoly, after whose death the Israelitische Religionsgesellschaft of Mayence obtained possession of it. It consists of three parts: (1) the first necrology of the community of Nuremberg, a list of deaths and of gifts from about 1280 to 1346; (2) the martyrologium, a list of martyrs from 1096 to 1349; and (3) the second necrology of the synagogue of Nuremberg, a memor-book and list of deaths and of gifts from 1373 to 1392. The entire work was edited by Salfeld (1896 and 1898); the necrologies by Stern and Salfeld ("Nürnberg im Mittelalter," pp. 95–205, Kiel, 1894–96); and the martyrology at Berlin, 1898, text, translation, introduction, etc.

Contents.

The first necrology, which was probably preceded by forty-four pages containing a history of the persecutions or a cycle of elegies, is prefaced by a prayer on the announcement of the New Moon; a benediction for the members of the community who undertake to keep the fast-day called "Sheni we-Ḥamishi we-Sheni"; a benediction for the benefactors and persons attending the synagogue; a prayer for the sick; and the "Ab ha-Rahamim," a prayer for the martyrs of Israel. This is followed by a poem referring to the book, the building, and the dedication of the synagogue, and closing with the words: "The names of the donors have been entered in the Book of the Beloved, who sleep in the grave." Then come the prayers, found in nearly all the memor-books, for the souls of the spiritual heroes of Israel and of individual benefactors, and the prayers for the dead ("yizkor"), in Hebrew and Old French, for the individual martyrs and the persecuted communities. The martyrology is introduced by a summary of the persecutions of 1096 to 1298, the names of the martyrs between 1096 and 1349, a list of cities and villages in which persecutions took place under Rindfleisch (1298) and Armleder (1336–39), and at the time of the Black Death (1348–49). The second necrology is introduced by the ritual for the New Moon and a prayer for the members of the community ("Misheberak," almost in the present form), to which are added the same lists and other material as in the first necrology.

As illustrations of the nature of the memor-book there follows a translation of the oldest portion thereof (*i. e.*, the portion which, amplified according as time and circumstance required, is common to all memor-books) and of two yizkor from the Hebrew and one from the Old French:

"The following souls are remembered [in prayer] on all Sabbaths of the year: Mar Solomon and Mistress Rachel, who have done much for the welfare of the community and have averted persecutions; our teacher R. Gershom, who by his teachings was the light of the eyes of the Israelites in the Diaspora; our teacher R. Simon the Great, who has done much for the communities and has averted persecutions; our teacher R. Solomon [b. Isaac, *i.e.*, Rashi], who through his commentaries was the light of the eyes of the Israelites in the Diaspora; our teacher R. Jacob and his brother R. Samuel, whose love spread the study of the Word of God in Israel; Mar Isaac and Mistress Bela, through whose efforts the toll was repealed at Coblenz; our teacher R. Meïr b. R. Baruch, who has spread the study of the Word of God in Israel."

"May God remember, as He has remembered the souls of Abraham, Isaac, and Jacob, the souls of all members of communities who have been killed, stoned, burned, strangled, slaughtered, drowned, broken on the wheel, hanged, or buried alive because they remained true to their belief in the One God. Since they have suffered this grievous pain, may God remember them, together with all pious men and women who rest in paradise. To this we respond: Amen!"

"May God remember, as He has remembered the souls of Abraham, Isaac, and Jacob, the souls of all members of communities who have striven for the welfare of the congregation, have averted persecutions, have secured the repeal of taxes, and have recovered scrolls of the Law from unworthy hands. Whether a pious gift has been vowed for them or not, may God remember them for their deeds."

"May God remember the soul of . . . together with the souls of Abraham, Isaac, and Jacob, because he bequeathed . . . to the cemetery (Rememra Dé spirteine . . . comme spirteine . . . ki ad layés . . . pour amour ki fesis, cil le memred . . .); because he did this, may God remember him together with the pious who dwell in paradise. Amen!"

The formulas in French were added later, probably after 1306, when a number of French exiles settled at Nuremberg.

Several of the extant memor-books, single lists from manuscripts and printed texts, as well as works dealing with the subject, have been used by Salfeld in his edition of the Nuremberg memor-book (see his "Martyrologium," pp. xxvi. *et seq.*), and a discussion of their form, contents, and importance for the history of scholars and of persecutions will be found there. The following list gives a survey of his material:

Hebrew Codex No. 45 of the Landes- und Universitäts-Bibliothek in Strasburg, pp. 15–16, with lists of the martyrs of Worms of 1096 and 1349.

Hebrew Codex No. 87 (42) of the municipal library, Hamburg, fols. 31 *et seq.*, with 165 places of persecution in 1298 *et seq.* (Salfeld, *l.c.* p. xxvii.).

Extract from a memor-book of 1313–14, formerly in the possession of Chief Rabbi Charleville-Versailles, containing a list of places in which persecutions occurred between 1298 and 1303 (Jellinek, "Kontres Hamkonen, Märtyrer- und Memorbuch," p. 9, Vienna, 1881).

Maḥzor, MS. Oxford, Neubauer, "Cat. Bodl. Hebr. MSS." No. 1108, with a list of places of the persecutions of 1349 (reprinted in "R. E. J." iv. 29).

Oxford MS., Neubauer, "Cat. Bodl. Hebr. MSS." No. 1171, with lists of 1349 (reprinted in "R. E. J." iv. 29, 30).

Codex Epstein in Vienna (formerly in the possession of Halberstam of Bielitz), prayer-book according to the German ritual, with a list of communities in which martyrdoms took place (first ed. "Isr. Letterbode," viii. 89; republished in "Martyrologium," p. 79; comp. also pp. xxiii., 272).

Wibel, translation of an old fragment of a Jewish martyrology ("Unschuldige Nachrichten auf das Jahr 1740"), dating from the second half of the fifteenth century.

Two anonymous memor-books of German communities ("Martyrologium," p. xxviii.).

Manuscript of Carmoly, in possession of Dr. Brann at Breslau (*ib.*).

Memor-books of the following places: Alsheim, eighteenth century; Bayersdorf, written in 1689; Bergheim-on-the-Erft, begun in 1677; Bingen, in 1787; Bödigheim, 1745; Bonn, 1725; Bretten, between 1716 and 1742; Coblenz, 1580; Deutz (Cologne), beginning with 1581; Dittigheim, 1746; Flörsheim, nineteenth century; Frankfort-on-the-Main (first entry 1627); Fürth, memor-book of the Neuschule, of the Waisenverein, of the Klaus, and of the Altschule (edited by Löwenstein in Geiger's "Zeitschrift," i. 274, ii. 91 *et seq.*); Gailingen, 1842; Gross-Gerau, seventeenth century; Hagenau, 1800; Hanau, part i., 1601; Kastel, 1785; Kirchhain, 1773; Kochendorf, 1732; Kreuznach, 1638; Kriegshaber; Mayence communal memor-books of 1583 and 1837, Krankenpflege-Verein No. 3, beginning of eighteenth century, and Religionsgesellschaft, 1853; Mannheim, 1784; Michelstadt, beginning of eighteenth century; Minden, beginning of seventeenth century; Nieder-Ehnheim; Nuremberg (necrology of 1349; ed. Lowe, "The Memor-Book of Nürnberg," London, 1881); Ober-Ehnheim; Oppenheim, 1795 (after an earlier copy); Partenheim, 1738; Pfersee (comp. Perles in "Monatsschrift," xxii. 503 *et seq.*); Rheinbach near Bonn, one necrology of 1650; Sontheim; Strasburg; Treves, 1664; Vienna; Weilmünster, 1708; Weisenau near Mayence, 1782 (after an earlier copy); Worms, i., ii., iii.; Xanten, on the lower Rhine, one part of 1776.

Many other valuable memor-books exist besides those used by Salfeld. That of Buttenwiesen has been edited by Lamm in "Monatsschrift," xlv. 540 *et seq.*, while those of Binswangen, Edenheim, Ehrenbreitstein (formerly called Thal; first entry 1647), Emden, Harburg (Swabia), Höchberg near Würzburg, Oettingen, Steppach, Wallerstein, Wittelshofen, and many others are still unedited. The memor-book of Misslitz belonging to the Klaus Synagogue of Zechariah Lewi of Vienna has been described by Kaufmann (in Berliner's "Magazin," xvii. 289 *et seq.*), who used also the one of Düsseldorf ("Aus Heinrich Heine's Ahnensaal," p. 274), while that of Mamelsdorf has been mentioned by Zunz ("Literaturgesch." p. 112) and others.

Further study on the subject, together with scientific editions of the memor-books, would probably yield valuable data for statistics, economics, genealogies of scholars and families, nomenclature, diplomatics, ritual, and liturgy, as well as for Jewish history in general. See MARTYROLOGY.

BIBLIOGRAPHY: Salfeld, *Martyrologium*, 1896–98; Stern and Salfeld, *Nürnberg im Mittelalter*, Kiel, 1894–96.

J. S. SA.

MEMORIAL DATES: Jewish communities, as a rule, have taken no note of birthdays of any of their members and only in rare cases of the dates of death. One of these cases is the anniversary of the day on which Gedaliah was assassinated (3d Tishri), upon which a fast is observed by Jews in all parts of the world; and on the 18th Iyyar (Lag be-'Omer) Jews living in Palestine visit the tomb of Simon ben Yoḥai, believing this date to be the anniversary of the latter's death. Jews of eastern Europe, furthermore, record the days on which eminent rabbis die, because on every "Jahrzeit" (anniversary of the day of death) they make it a practise to visit the graves of such rabbis, and to ask for their intercession in heaven.

Besides these "Jahrzeiten" there are a number of days which, although they have acquired a religious aspect, have also a historical significance, and are observed either by the Jews as a whole or by local communities. Thus the Ninth of Ab is observed as a fast-day, for on that day the Temple was twice destroyed. On the twenty-fifth of Kislew the Feast of Ḥanukkah begins, because on that day Judas Maccabeus consecrated anew the Temple at Jerusalem (165 B.C.).

The communities of Cologne, Worms, Mayence, and a few other cities in the Rhine district observed fast-days in memory of the martyrs who died during the First Crusade (Zunz, "Ritus," p. 127). Polish Jews fast on the 20th of Siwan on account of the Cossack atrocities of 1648 (see FASTING AND FAST DAYS). In Crete and Frankfort-on-the-Main as well as in certain communities in Egypt, special feasts or Purims are celebrated in commemoration of miraculous events. The Alexandrian Jews observed a memorial day in honor of the translation of the Bible into Greek (Philo, "Vita Mosis," ii., § 7; see also FESTIVALS).

In imitation of these memorial days sanctified by religion, other dates of Jewish interest have been recorded from time to time, and are used in calendars, almanacs, and at times in the Jewish press. In recent years large collections of notable dates have been made by Jewish scholars and historians, beginning with L. Zunz. The following list gives in calendric order the more important and interesting of these:

JANUARY.

1. Jair Ḥayyim Bacharach, German rabbi, died, 1702. Several thousand Jews killed by an earthquake at Safed and Tiberias, 1837.
2. Persecutions of Jews at Lauda and Bischofsheim, 1235.
3. "Neue Stättigkeit" for Frankfort-on-the-Main makes right of domicil perpetual, 1617. Rachel, French actress, died, 1858.
4. Moses Mendelssohn, philosopher and religious reformer, died, 1786. Wilhelm Beer, German astronomer, born, 1797.
5. Joseph Salvador, Jewish historian, born, 1796. Edward Lasker, German statesman, died, 1884.
6. First auto da fé held at Seville, 1481.
7. Disputation at Tortosa, Joseph Albo being one of the participants, 1413. Sir Julian Goldsmid, English member of Parliament, died, 1896.
8. Samuel Cahen, translator of the Bible into French, died, 1862.
9. Liebmann Adler, American rabbi, born, 1812.
10. David Nieto, haham of London, died, 1728. Poll-tax abolished in France, 1784.
11. Abraham Mapu, Russian Hebrew writer, born, 1808. Lelio della Torre, Italian Jewish theologian, born, 1805.
12. Edict of Juan II. of Castile, withdrawing civil jurisdiction from the Jews, confirmed, 1412.
13. Law of Baden forms Jews into special religious community with all privileges, 1809. Alexander I. of Russia issues edict removing Jews from villages to towns and cities in the governments of Moghilef and Vitebsk, 1825.
14. Hebrew books, confiscated under bull of Feb. 28, 1593, burned at Rome, 1601. Great fire in the Frankfort ghetto, 1711.
15. Leopold Dukes, Hungarian Jewish scholar, born, 1810.
16. Johann Jacob Raabe, translator of the Mishnah, born, 1711.
17. Marcus Herz, physician and philosopher, born, 1747.
18. Solomon Sulzer, reformer of synagogal music, died, 1890.
19. Marcus Herz, physician and philosopher, died, 1803. Isaac D'Israeli, English litterateur and father of the Earl of Beaconsfield, died, 1848.
20. Moritz Oppenheim, German painter of Jewish family life, born, 1800.
21. Jews expelled from France, 1306. Nathan Marcus Adler, chief rabbi of the British empire, died, 1890.
22. David Cassel, Jewish historian, died, 1893. English Zionist Federation founded, 1899.
23. Abraham ibn Ezra, Bible exegete and poet, died, 1167.
24. Ferdinand Julius Cohn, German botanist and zoologist, born, 1828. Isaac Artom, Italian statesman and senator, died, 1900.
25. Disputation at Paris on the Talmud, 1240.
26. First edition of the Hebrew Pentateuch printed at Bologna, 1482.
27. Jerome Napoleon grants full civil rights to Jews of Westphalia, 1808.
28. Lippold, master of the Brandenburg mint, executed, 1573. Theodor Benfey, German Sanskritist and philologist, born, 1809.
29. Abraham Furtado, president of the Sanhedrin summoned by Napoleon, died, 1817.
31. Henry III. issues regulations for English Jewry, 1253.

FEBRUARY.

1. Bogumil Dawison, German actor, died, 1872. Mass-meetings held at New York and London expressing sympathy with the persecuted Jews of the Russian empire, 1882. Perez Smolenskin, Russian Hebrew writer, died, 1885.
3. Felix Mendelssohn-Bartholdy, composer, born, 1809. Charles the Bourbon, King of Naples and of the two Sicilies, invites the Jews back for fifty years, 1740.
4. "Resettlement Day" in England. Oliver Cromwell grants Carvajal and other Jews right of residence, 1657. Joseph Süss Oppenheimer executed; many Jews driven from Württemberg in consequence, 1738.
5. Rashi on the Pentateuch, the earliest dated printed Jewish book, issued at Reggio, 1475. The disappearance of Father Tomaso (Thomas) gives rise to the Damascus Affair, 1840. Nehemiah Brüll, Jewish scholar, died, 1891.
6. Solomon Munk, French Arabic scholar, died, 1867. Elijah Benamozegh, Italian rabbi and cabalist, died, 1900.
8. Shabbethai Cohen (Shach), died, 1663. Berthold Auerbach, German novelist, died, 1882.
9. Opening of the Sanhedrin at Paris, 1807. Isaac Adolphe Crémieux, French statesman, died, 1880.
11. Societät Felix Libertate founded at Amsterdam, 1795.
12. Auto da fé at Toledo at which 740 Jews were reconciled, 1486. Ludwig Börne, German writer, died, 1837. Isaac Baer Levinsohn, the Mendelssohn of Russia, died, 1860.
13. Zacharias Frankel, Jewish scholar and theologian, died, 1875.
14. Two thousand Jews burned at Strasburg, 1349. Jews ordered to leave Vienna, 1670.
15. Carel Asser, Dutch jurist, born, 1780.
16. Emancipation of the Jews of Sweden, 1870. Commission appointed to revise the laws concerning the Jews of Russia, 1883.
17. Heinrich Heine, German poet, died, 1856.
18. "Ḥatti Humayun" issued, granting full civic rights to Turkish Jews, 1856. Congregation of the Holy Office declares forcible baptism of Jewish children by Christian nurses effective, 1705.
19. Peter Beer, Austrian educator, born, 1758. Henry IV. grants Jews of Speyer protection to life and property, 1090.
21. Johann Christopher Wolf, Christian bibliographer of Jewish books, born, 1683.
22. Johann Reuchlin, champion of the Jews and defender of the Talmud, born, 1455. Isaac Marcus Jost, Jewish historian, born, 1793.
23. Franz Delitzsch, Christian Hebraist, born, 1813. Sir George Jessel, master of the rolls, England, born, 1824.
24. Moritz Oppenheim, German painter of Jewish family life, died, 1882.
25. Bull of Nicholas V. prohibiting Christians from having social intercourse with Jews and Saracens, 1451.
26. Jews expelled from all Papal States except Rome and Ancona, 1659.
27. Benedict Spinoza, philosopher, died, 1677. Paulus Cassel, Jewish scholar and convert to Christianity, born, 1821.
28. Vincent Fettmilch and his chief accomplices executed, Frankfort, 1616. Berthold Auerbach, German novelist, born, 1812. Rachel, French actress, born, 1820.

MARCH.

1. About four thousand Jews burned at Worms, 1349.
4. Gregory IX. issues bill forbidding Christians to dispute on matters of faith with Jews, 1233. "Rights of Man" declared in Holland, 1795. Religious freedom proclaimed in Austria, 1849.
5. The states of Austria demand that no Jews be permitted to dwell there, 1460.
6. Massacre of Jews at Navarre, 1328.
7. Mordecai Jaffe, codifier of rabbinical law, died, 1612. Joseph Almanzi, bibliophile and poet, died, 1860.
9. Julius Fürst, Hebrew philologist and Jewish bibliographer, died, 1873.
10. Ignaz Moscheles, German composer, died, 1870.
11. Bull of Benedict XIII. against the Talmud and any Jewish books attacking Christianity, 1415. Edict giving the Jews of Prussia citizens' rights, 1812.
12. Judah Löb Bensew, Jewish grammarian and lexicographer, died, 1811. Ludwig Augustus Frankl, German writer and poet, died, 1893.
13. Aaron of Neustadt (surnamed Blumlein), uncle and chief instructor of Isserlein, died, 1421.
14. Mob attacks the Jewish quarter at Cordova, slaughtering many Jews and Maranos, 1473. Heyman Steinthal, linguist and philosopher, died, 1899. Ludwig Bamberger, German deputy and political economist, died, 1899.
15. Albert Cohn, Orientalist and philanthropist, died, 1879. Peddling prohibited in Rumania; 20,000 Jews are thus deprived of a livelihood, 1884.
16. Jews of York slay themselves in order to avoid baptism, 1190.

17. Napoleon institutes the system of consistories in France, 1808. Jacques-François-Fromenthal-Elie Halévy, composer, died, 1862. Judah P. Benjamin becomes secretary of war of the Confederacy of America, 1862.
18. Leopold Zunz, Jewish scholar, died, 1886.
19. Jews of Brest-Litovsk granted free trade and occupation and half of the tolls, 1527.
20. Riots in many cities of Germany, 1848.
21. Leo da Modena, Italian rabbi and author, died, 1648. Three Jews executed at Wilna on a false blood accusation, 1691.
22. Charter granted to Jews of England by Richard I., 1190. Jews permitted to return to Lithuania, 1503. Michael Beer, German poet, died, 1833.
23. Talmuds burned in Rome at the Feast of Pentecost, 1322. Naphtali Herz Wesel (Hartwig Wessely), died, 1805. Isaac Artom elected senator in Italy; first Jew to hold such an office, 1877.
24. Joseph Caro, codifier of rabbinical Judaism, died, 1575. Solomon Halberstam, Jewish scholar, died, 1900.
25. Joseph Almanzi, bibliophile and poet, born, 1801.
26. Isaac M. Wise, American Reform rabbi, died, 1900.
27. Wilhelm Beer, German astronomer, died, 1850.
28. Lazarus Bendavid, German philosopher and reformer, died, 1832. James Darmesteter, French Orientalist, born, 1849. Jews expelled from Moscow by order of the governor-general, 1891.
29. Meïr ben Todros ha-Levi Abulafia (RaMaH), nasi and Talmudist, died, 1244. Jews who served in Russian army permitted by edict to settle in Finland, 1858.
30. Moses ben Maimon (Maimonides), philosopher, born, 1135. Solomon Sulzer, reformer of synagogal music, born, 1804.
31. Edict of expulsion of Jews from Spain issued by Ferdinand and Isabella, 1492.

APRIL.

1. Disappearance of Esther Solymosi gives rise to a blood accusation at Tisza-Eszlár, 1882. Baroness Clara de Hirsch, philanthropist, died, 1899.
2. Jews expelled from Genoa, 1550.
3. Charles V. of Germany issues edict against blood accusations, 1544. Hirsch Kalischer, founder of modern Zionism, born, 1795.
4. Isaac da Fonseca Aboab, ḥakam at Amsterdam, died, 1693. Opening of the Anglo-Jewish Historical Exhibition in the Royal Albert Hall, London, 1887.
5. Moses Ephraim Kuh, first German Jewish poet, died, 1790.
6. Aaron Bernstein, German publicist, born, 1812.
7. Emancipation of the Jews of Prussia, 1848.
8. Ferdinand III. grants Bohemian Jews right of residence in all royal towns, 1648. One hundred and twenty-eight Jews killed by soldiers and populace at Bucharest as the result of a blood accusation, 1801.
10. Karl Isidor Beck, Austrian poet, died, 1879.
11. First anathema against Ḥasidim issued at Wilna, 1772. Ferdinand Lassalle, socialist agitator, born, 1825.
12. Jews of Cracow plundered and many murdered by soldiers, 1464.
13. Sabbato Morais, American rabbi, born, 1823. Edict of Nicholas I. founding agricultural colonies in Russia; general Jewish regulations issued in Russia, 1835.
14. Deutsch-Israelitischer Gemeindebund founded, 1869.
15. Dankmar Adler, American architect, died, 1900.
16. Menahem ben Jacob, poet and teacher at Worms, died, 1203.
17. Frederick the Great issues a "General-Privilegium" for the Prussian Jews, 1750. Pope Pius IX. issues edict to remove the walls of the Roman ghetto, 1848.
18. Charge of host desecration at Prague leads to massacre of Jews, 1389. Earl of Beaconsfield, English premier, died, 1881.
19. Massacre of Jews at Cordova by soldiers of Sulaiman ben al-Ḥakim, 1013. Jacob Emden, German rabbi, died, 1776.
20. Levi ben Gershon, philosopher and commentator, died, 1344. Proselyte Nicholas Anthoine burned at Geneva, 1632.
21. Baron Maurice de Hirsch, philanthropist, died, 1896.
22. Isaac Adolphe Crémieux, French statesman, born, 1796. Uriah Phillips Levy, American commodore, born, 1792.
23. Louis XIII. of France issues edict forbidding Christians, under penalty of death, to shelter Jews or converse with them, 1615. Elijah ben Solomon of Wilna, the "Gaon," born, 1720. Poll-tax in territories of Brunswick-Lüneburg abolished, 1803.
24. First recorded auto da fé held at Troyes, 1288.
25. Anti-Semitic league of Germany presents a petition with 255,000 signatures to Bismarck, 1881.
26. Dutch West India Company directs Peter Stuyvesant to allow Jews to dwell and trade in New Netherlands, 1655. Jews expelled from Russia and the Ukraine by Catherine, 1727.
27. Meïr of Rothenburg died, 1293. Anti-Semitic riot at Elizabethgrad begins a series of excesses against the Jews in South Russia, 1881.
29. Antony Samuel Adam-Salomon, French saulptor, died, 1881.
30. Decree ordering Jews to leave Spain publicly announced, 1492.

MAY.

1. Moses Isserles, Polish rabbi and code annotator, died, 1572. Johann Jacoby, German statesman, born, 1805. Sir Francis Henry Goldsmid, M.P., first English Jewish lawyer, born, 1808.
2. All the Jews of England thrown into prison, 1287. Giacomo Meyerbeer, composer, died, 1864.
3. Jews of Speyer massacred by the Crusaders, 1096.
4. Benjamin II., Rumanian traveler, died, 1864.
6. Ludwig Börne, German writer, born, 1786. Judah P. Benjamin, statesman and lawyer, died, 1884.
7. Attack on the Alcana (smaller Jewry) of Toledo by the enemies of Samuel ha-Levi; 1,200 injured, 1355.
8. Anti-Jewish riots in different parts of Russia, especially in Kiev, 1881.
10. Great auto da fé at Lisbon, 1682.
11. Bull of Benedict XIII. against Talmud and any Jewish books attacking Christianity, 1415. Abraham Geiger, Jewish scholar and theologian, born, 1810.
12. Massacre of the Jews of Worms by Crusaders, 1096. Synod of Vienna under Cardinal Guido orders Jews to wear pointed hats, 1267.
14. Solomon Munk, French Orientalist, born, 1803.
15. Bogumil Dawison, Polish-German actor, born, 1818. Russian "May Laws" issued, 1882.
16. Emancipation of the Jews of Holland, 1796. Heyman Steinthal, philosopher and linguist, born, 1823.
17. First Jewish school in Hungary opened at Alt-Ofen, 1784. William Steinitz, chess-player, born, 1836.
18. Anti-Jewish riots in Algeria, 1897.
19. Isaac Alfasi, Talmudic author, died, 1103.
20. Samuel Alatri, Italian philanthropist, died, 1889.
21. Thirty Jews burned at Bösing, near Presburg, 1529.
22. Martyrdom of Brussels Jews charged with host desecration, 1370. Israel ben Eliezer Ba'al Shem-Ṭob (BeSHT), founder of the sect Ḥasidim, died, 1760. Mordecai M. Noah, American diplomat and communal worker, died, 1851.
23. All the Jews of Austria seized, 1420.
24. Riot at Frankfort-on-the-Main on account of a Jewish pervert; 180 killed and Jewish quarters destroyed, 1241. Abraham Geiger, Jewish scholar and reformer, born, 1810.
25. Louis Philippe issues regulations for the internal organization of the French Jews, 1844.
26. Martyrdom of Jews at Blois, 1171.
27. Jews of Mayence massacred by Crusaders, 1096. Jacques-François-Fromenthal-Elie Halévy, composer, born, 1799.
29. Lelewel, Polish geographer and friend of Jews, died, 1861.
30. Massacre of Jews at Cologne by Crusaders, 1096. Ignaz Moscheles, German composer, born, 1794.

JUNE.

1. "Privilegium Fredericianum" issued by Duke Frederick II. of Austria, 1244.
2. Tolerance edict of Joseph II. of Austria issued, 1782. Grace Aguilar, English novelist and writer on Jewish history, born, 1816.
4. Outbreaks against Jews of Seville, 1391.
5. Jews of Rome forbidden to practise usury, 1570. Sir Julius Benedict, composer and conductor, died, 1885.
6. Henry II. imposes on Jews of Toledo a tax of 20,000 gold "dollars" (= $9,630,000), 1369.
7. Louis Jacoby, German engraver, born, 1828. David Kaufmann, Hebraist and Orientalist, born, 1852.
8. Riots at Posen lasting to July 4, on account of a false murder charge, 1696. Fanny von Arnstein, society leader at Vienna, died, 1818.
9. Jacob Tam, most prominent of French tosafists, died, 1171. Samuel Mohilever, rabbi and Zionist, died, 1898.
10. Six thousand Jews of Nemirov slaughtered by the Cossacks, 1648.
12. Jews of France ordered to wear a yellow badge, 1269.
15. Jews expelled from Genoese territory, 1567.
16. Many Jews murdered in Erfurt, 1221. Joseph Solomon de Medigo born, 1591.

17. Twenty-four wagon-loads of Talmuds and two hundred other manuscripts burned at Paris, 1244. Eighty Maranos imprisoned by Alexander VI. at Rome, 1503.
20. Four thousand Jews slain at Toledo, 1391. Cossacks slay thousands of Jews at Homel, Poland, 1767.
21. Rabbinical synod held at Ferrara, 1554. Jacques Offenbach, composer, born, 1819.
23. Martyrdom of Jews of Weissenburg, 1270.
24. Jews treacherously murdered at Tulchin by Cossacks, 1648. Edgar Mortara forcibly taken from his family, giving rise to the "Mortara Case," 1858.
25. Religious disputation before Louis IX. of France, 1240. Two hundred and fifty Jews murdered in Rothenburg-on-the-Tauber, 1298.
26. Lipmann Heller forced to leave his post as rabbi at Prague, 1629. Adolf Jellinek, Jewish scholar, born, 1821.
27. Jews of Xanten massacred by Crusaders, 1096. Joseph Israels, Dutch painter, born, 1824.
28. Meïr of Rothenburg imprisoned at Rotevil by Bishop Henry of Basel, 1286. Jew badge introduced into Venice, 1366.
29. Blood accusation at Xanten, 1891.
30. Edict forbidding Maranos to leave Portugal, 1557. Jews expelled from Prague, 1745.

JULY.

1. Elijah ben Samuel burned at Rome, 1298. Bernard Beer, German-Jewish scholar, died, 1861.
2. Anglo-Jewish Association founded, 1871.
3. Mansion House meeting in London protests against the outrages of the Damascus Affair, 1840. Religious freedom proclaimed in Germany, 1868. Theodor Herzl, Zionist leader, died, 1904.
4. Judah ben Asher, Talmudist, died, 1349. Isabella Nuñez Alvarez burned in auto da fé at Madrid, 1632.
5. Pope Innocent IV. issues bull against blood accusation, 1247.
6. Three hundred Jews murdered at Tarrega, Catalonia, 1348.
7. Gregory X. issues bull against blood accusation, 1274. Ludwig Chronegk, German theatrical manager and actor, died, 1891.
8. Seligmann Heller, German poet, born, 1831.
9. Julius Oppert, Orientalist, born, 1825. Lord Rothschild takes his seat as first Jewish peer in the British House of Lords, 1884.
11. Czarina Anne expels the Jews from Little Russia, 1740. E. H. Lindo, Jewish historian, died, 1865.
13. Godfrey of Bouillon takes Jerusalem, and nearly all the Jews there are slaughtered, 1099. Solomon Yiẓḥaki (Rashi), commentator, died, 1105. Berlin Congress inserts clause 44 into its treaty, 1878.
14. United Synagogue of London established by Act of Parliament, 1870.
15. Pope lays down principle that Jews were doomed to perpetual servitude because they had crucified Jesus, 1205. Royal decree expelling Jews from Portugal issued, 1508. Act permitting Jews to trade in New Netherlands issued, 1655.
16. Graziadio Isaiah Ascoli, Italian philologist, born, 1829.
17. Anti-Semitic riots at Neustettin, lasting two days, 1881.
18. Nathan Rothschild, founder of the London banking-house, died, 1836.
19. Thirty-eight Jews burned at Berlin, 1510.
20. Religious disputation at Barcelona, Naḥmanides defending Judaism, 1263.
21. Shabbethai ben Joseph Bass, founder of Jewish bibliography, died, 1718.
22. First expulsion of Jews from France, 1306. About 10,000 Jews slain at Polonnoye, near Jitomir, 1648.
23. Shabbethai Ẓebi, pseudo-Messiah, born, 1626.
24. Jean de Bloch, Russo-Polish financier, born, 1836.
25. Jews expelled from Vienna, 1670. Johann Christopher Wolf, bibliographer of Jewish books, died, 1739.
26. Pope Paul IV. establishes the ghetto at Rome, 1556. First sitting of the Assembly of Notables, 1806.
27. Benedict Spinoza excommunicated, 1656.
28. Emancipation in Hungary, 1849. Eduard Lasker secures the passing of the "Austritt-Gesetz," permitting persons in Prussia to sever connection with any religious community, 1876. Sir Moses Montefiore, philanthropist, died, 1885.
29. Max Nordau, writer and Zionist, born, 1849. Joseph Derenbourg, Orientalist, died, 1895.
30. Auto da fé at Toledo, 1488.
31. Little St. Hugh of Lincoln disappeared, 1255. Nachman Krochmal, Galician scholar, died, 1840.

AUGUST.

1. Mordecai ben Hillel killed during the massacre of Jews at Nuremberg, 1298. Two Jews elected to the National Assembly of Holland, 1797. Last auto da fé at which a Jew was burned held at Valencia, 1826.
2. Jews expelled from Spain, 1492. First Portuguese synagogue at Amsterdam dedicated, 1675.
3. Patent for Bohemia removes all Jewish disabilities, 1797. Carel Asser, Dutch jurist, died, 1836.
4. Samuel Cahen, translator of the Bible into French, born, 1796. Max Ring, German poet, born, 1817.
5. Great massacre of Jews at Barcelona, 1391. Maria Theresa, for an annual consideration of 3,000,000 gulden, suspends for a period of 10 years the edict expelling Jews from Austria, 1748.
6. Marcus Eliezer Bloch, naturalist, died, 1799.
7. Bolko I. of Silesia grants Jews "Privilegium Fredericianum," 1295.
8. Bull of Pius IV. permits Jews to lay aside the yellow hat on journeys, 1561. Jacob Christian Basnage, Christian historian of the Jews, born, 1653.
9. Jews settle in Pinsk and secure lands for synagogue and cemetery, 1506. Anti-Jewish riots at Frankfort; house of the Rothschilds attacked, 1819.
10. Leopold Zunz, Jewish scholar, born, 1794. Alexander I. of Russia prohibits foreign Jews from settling permanently in Russia, 1824.
11. Jonah Abravanel, Hebrew poet, died, 1667. Restriction on the use of Christian prænomens removed in Bohemia, 1836.
12. Naḥmanides visits Jerusalem, 1267. Jossel von Rosheim obtains from Charles V. an extension of the Alsatian privileges to the whole Holy Roman Empire, 1530. William Steinitz, chess-master, died, 1900.
13. Johannes Buxtorf II., Christian Hebraist, born, 1599.
14. Baruch Auerbach, educator and philanthropist, born, 1793.
15. Simon ben Asher, astronomer, died, 1342.
16. Johannes Buxtorf II., Christian Hebraist, died, 1664.
17. Papal edict forbids Jews to admit Christians into synagogue, 1592.
19. Michael Beer, German poet, born, 1800.
20. Maranos of the Basque Provinces ordered to leave the Jewish streets and to live among Christians, 1493.
21. Joseph Derenbourg, Orientalist, born, 1811.
22. Six thousand Jews slaughtered in Mayence, 1340.
24. Three thousand Jews slaughtered in Erfurt, 1349. Aaron Chorin (Choriner), Hungarian rabbi, died, 1844.
25. Samuel David Luzzatto, Italian Jewish scholar, born, 1800. David Gans, Jewish historian and mathematician, died, 1613.
28. "'Alenu" prayer forbidden in Prussia, 1703. Isaac Samuel Reggio, Jewish theological writer, died, 1855. Opening of the first Zionist Congress at Basel, 1897.
30. Ẓebi Ashkenazi, rabbi in London and Amsterdam, died, 1658.
31. Joseph Pichon of Seville, chief royal tax-gatherer, executed by order of Jewish judges, 1379. Ferdinand Lassalle, socialistic agitator, died, 1864.

SEPTEMBER.

1. Jews of Brest ordered to obey court of Rabbi Mendel Frank, 1531. Anti-Jewish riots at Frankfort-on-the-Main, under Fettmilch, 1614.
2. Jews of Holland declared by the National Assembly citizens of the Batavian republic, 1796.
3. Coronation massacre at London, 1189. James Joseph Sylvester, English mathematician, born, 1814. Anti-Jewish riots at Stockholm, 1852.
4. Michael Sachs, German rabbi, born, 1808.
5. Henrietta Herz, leader of Berlin salon, born, 1764.
6. Moses Mendelssohn, philosopher and religious reformer, born, 1729.
7. Hirsch (Heinrich) Graetz, Jewish historian, died, 1891.
8. Israelsky, accused of ritual murder at Konitz, acquitted, 1900.
9. Captain Alfred Dreyfus condemned a second time, 1899.
10. Jewish community founded at Berlin, 1671. Shabbethai Ẓebi, pseudo-Messiah, died, 1676.
11. Jewish Colonization Association founded by Baron de Hirsch, 1891.
12. David Oppenheim, bibliophile, died, 1736.
13. Johannes Buxtorf I., Christian scholar, died, 1629. Shabbethai Ẓebi embraces Mohammedanism, 1666.
14. Albert Cohn, Jewish scholar and philanthropist, born, 1814.
15. Akiba Eger the Elder, rabbi and Talmudic author, died, 1780. Giacomo Meyerbeer, composer, born, 1791.

16. Grace Aguilar, English novelist and writer on Jewish history, died, 1847.
17. Decree ordering Jews to leave France issued, 1394. Pedro Arbues, inquisitor, "the darling of Torquemada," died, 1485.
18. Jonathan Eybeschütz, rabbi and author, died, 1764. Sultan of Morocco grants religious liberty to Jews and Christians, 1880.
19. Mayer Rothschild, founder of the Frankfort banking-house, died, 1812. Capt. Alfred Dreyfus "pardoned," 1899.
20. Gedaliah Yaḥya, writer on history, died, 1487. Ghetto at Rome abolished, 1870.
22. Dedication of the Mayence synagogue, 1104.
24. Moses Sofer, rabbinical author, born, 1762.
27. Emancipation of the Jews of France, 1791.
28. First congregation founded at Stockholm, 1775.
29. Jews of Krems massacred, 1349. Fanny von Arnstein, society leader at Vienna, born, 1757. Samuel David Luzzatto, Italian Jewish scholar, died, 1865.
30. Zacharias Frankel, Jewish scholar and theologian, born, 1801.

OCTOBER.

1. About 7,000 Jews expelled from the government of Kiev, Russia, 1898.
2. Thousands of Jews killed at Lublin by Cossacks, 1656.
3. Blood-accusation riot at Galatz; ninety Jews injured and four synagogues destroyed, 1868. Moses Schreiber (Sofer), Orthodox leader and rabbi, died, 1839.
4. Emancipation of the Jews of Baden, 1862.
5. Jacques Offenbach, French composer, died, 1880.
6. Abraham Firkovich, Karaite scholar, born, 1787.
7. Eleazar of Brody, rabbi at Amsterdam, died, 1741.
8. Jacob Eduard Polack, physician to the Shah of Persia, died, 1891.
9. Casimir III., the Great, of Poland, grants Jews "Privilegium Fredericianum," 1333. Adolf Franck, French philosopher, born, 1809. Abraham Mapu, Russian Hebrew writer, died, 1867.
10. Elijah ben Solomon of Wilna, the "Gaon," died, 1797.
11. Ninety Jews massacred at Munich, 1285.
12. Akiba Eger, rabbi and Talmudic author, died, 1837.
13. Victor Emanuel emancipates the Jews of Rome, 1870. Leopold Löw, rabbi and critic, died, 1875.
14. Eduard Lasker, German politician, born, 1829.
15. Moritz Hartmann, Austrian poet, born, 1821.
16. Joseph Solomon del Medigo, physician and scientist, died, 1658. Jewish quarter of Kossow, Galicia, attacked; ten Jews killed, 1898.
17. Bull appointing Tomaso Torquemada inquisitor-general of Aragon, Valencia, and Catalonia, 1483. Senatorial decree grants privileges to baptized Jews in Russia, 1776.
18. Lazarus Bendavid, German philosopher and reformer, born, 1762.
19. James Darmesteter, French philologist, died, 1894. Giulio Bartolocci, Italian Christian student of Jewish literature, died, 1687.
20. Emin Pasha (Ed. Schnitzer), African traveler, killed, 1892.
21. Israelitische Theologische Lehranstalt of Vienna founded, 1893.
22. Roman Curia decides that a Jewish child once baptized must be brought up under Christian influences, 1587. Henriette Herz, leader of the Berlin salon, died, 1847.
23. Abraham Geiger, Jewish scholar and religious reformer, died, 1874. Inquisition at Rome refuses permission to Jews to put gravestones or inscriptions over their dead, 1625.
24. Moses Montefiore, philanthropist, born, 1784. Decree of Crémieux naturalizes the Jews of Algeria, 1870.
25. Asher ben Jehiel (Rosh), died, 1327.
26. Anti-Jewish riots at Cracow, 1407.
28. 'Abd al-Majid receives Moses Montefiore in regard to the Damascus Affair, 1840. Moses Naḥmanides, philosopher and commentator, died, 1270. Emanuel Deutsch, English Jewish Talmudic scholar, born, 1829.
29. Jews of Kur-Hessen granted full emancipation (first in Germany), 1833. Conference of Jewish notables of western Europe at Brussels, to discuss Rumanian question, 1872.
31. Jews expelled from Portugal, 1497. Heinrich Graetz, Jewish historian, born, 1817.

NOVEMBER.

1. Jews of England imprisoned by King John, 1210. Jews banished from England, 1290. Isidore Loeb, French Jewish scholar, born, 1839.
2. William II. of Germany receives a Zionist deputation headed by Dr. Theodor Herzl, at Jerusalem, 1898.
3. Third and final expulsion of the Jews from France, 1394. Ludwig Chronegk, German actor, born, 1837.
4. Auto da fé held at Seville, 1481. Felix Mendelssohn-Bartholdy, composer, died, 1847.
5. David Sassoon, Indian financier, died, 1864.
6. Firman issued by Sultan 'Abd al-Majid against blood accusation, 1840. Abraham Azulai, cabalistic author, died, 1643.
8. Rabbinical synod of Mayence regulates the payment of Jewish taxes, 1223. Peter Beer, educational writer, died, 1838.
10. David Einhorn, American Reform rabbi, born, 1809.
11. Sabbato Morais, American Orthodox rabbi, died, 1897.
12. Law regulating the adoption of family names by Jews in Austria, 1787.
13. Talmud burned at Kamenetz-Podolsk by the Frankists, 1757. Benjamin Peixotto, American diplomat, born, 1834.
15. Act passed by General Assembly of New York permitting Jews to omit "upon the faith of a Christian" from the oath of abjuration, 1727.
16. Riot at Paris; many Jews plundered, several killed, and the rest forced to flee, 1380. Jews executed for imaginary crime at La Guardia, 1491.
17. Simḥah Pinsker, Hebrew author, died, 1864.
18. First meeting of English Jewish Board of Deputies, 1760. "Lehrerseminar" founded at Berlin, 1840.
19. Emma Lazarus, American poetess, died, 1887.
20. Manasseh ben Israel, died, 1657. Anton Rubinstein, Russian composer and pianist, died, 1894. Isaac M. Jost, Jewish historian, died, 1860.
22. Solomon Maimon, German philosopher, died, 1800.
23. Leopold Kompert, ghetto poet and novelist, died, 1886.
24. Benedict Spinoza, philosopher, born, 1632.
27. Abraham ben David of Posquières (RaBaD III.), French Talmudic commentator, died, 1198. Sir Julius Benedict, English composer, born, 1804.
29. Jews of Augsburg massacred, 1349.
30. Bull of Honorius IV. to archbishops of York and Canterbury, against the Talmud, 1286. Anton Rubinstein, Russian composer and pianist, born, 1830.

DECEMBER.

1. Manuel Fernando de Villa Real, Portuguese Jewish statesman, executed by the Inquisition at Lisbon, 1652.
2. Ukase of Elizabeth expelling Jews from Great Russia, 1742.
3. Eduard Bendemann, German painter, born, 1811.
4. Opening of the Whitehall conference of English notables on the question of the readmission of Jews into England, 1586.
6. David Friedländer, religious reformer and scholar, born, 1750. Anselm Mayer von Rothschild, financier, died, 1855.
9. Jews expelled from Breslau, 1738. Nathan Ghazzati, warm adherent of Shabbethai Ẓebi, excommunicated, 1666. Baron Maurice de Hirsch, philanthropist, born, 1831.
10. Guildhall meeting protests against the persecution of Russian Jews by the "May Laws," 1890. Auto da fé held at Toledo; nine hundred Jews "reconciled," 1486.
11. Napoleon issues decree dividing the whole French empire into Jewish consistories, 1808.
12. Isaac Leeser, American Orthodox rabbi, born, 1806.
13. Moses ben Maimon (Maimonides), philosopher, died, 1204. Emperor Charles IV. makes an agreement with Rudolph IV. of Austria and John of Bohemia not to receive Jews expelled from Austria, and *vice versa*, 1360. Heinrich Heine, German poet, born, 1797.
14. Mattithiah Straschun, Talmudic scholar, died, 1885.
15. Ludwig Dessoir, German actor, born, 1810.
17. Three hundred Jews of Bychow, near Moghilef, slaughtered, 1659. Ḳalman Schulman, Russian Hebrew writer, died, 1898.
18. Jews expelled from Bohemia, 1744.
19. Poll-tax abolished in Austria, 1781.
20. Mefize Haskalah founded in Russia, 1863.
21. Benjamin Disraeli, afterward Earl of Beaconsfield, English premier, born, 1804. Adolf Sonnenthal, German actor, born, 1834. Emancipation of Jews of Austria, 1867.
22. Jacob Christian Basnage, Christian historian of the Jews, died, 1725.
23. Paulus (Selig) Cassel, Jewish scholar and convert to Christianity, died, 1892.
24. King Emanuel orders all Jews to leave Portugal, 1496. Anti-Semitic riots at Warsaw, lasting three days, 1881.

25. Johannes Buxtorf I., Christian Jewish scholar, born, 1564. David Friedländer, religious reformer and scholar, died, 1834. Jean de Bloch, Russo-Polish financier, died, 1901.
27. Judaizing followers of R. Zechariah of Kiev burned at Moscow, 1503. Eduard Bendemann, German painter, died, 1889.
28. Ludwig Philippson, Jewish publicist, born, 1811. Full civil rights and privileges granted to the Jews of Frankfort, 1811.
29. Ludwig Philippson, Jewish publicist, died, 1889. Jewish Emancipation Act passed in Hungary, 1867. Adolf Jellinek, Jewish scholar, died, 1893.
30. Jews of Granada, among them Joseph ibn Nagdila, massacred, 1061. Ludwig Dessoir, German actor, died, 1874.
31. Isaac Artom, Italian senator, born, 1829. Sampson Raphael Hirsch, Jewish theologian, died, 1888.

Bibliography: Zunz, *Die Monatstage des Kalenderjahres*, Berlin, 1872; M. Kayserling, *Sterbetage aus Alter und Neuer Zeit*, Prague, 1891; *Gedenkblätter: Hervorragende Jüdische Persönlichkeiten des 19. Jahrhunderts*, Leipsic, 1892; G. Deutsch, in *Deborah*, 1901 and 1902; idem, *Memorable Dates of Jewish History*, New York, 1904.

J. I. G. D.

MEMORIAL SERVICE: Prayer for the dead is mentioned as early as the last pre-Christian century (see II Macc. xii. 44), and a sacrifice for the dead, probably given in the form of charity, was known in Talmudic time (Sifre, Deut. 210; Hor. 6a). The reading of the chapter "Aḥare Mot" on the Day of Atonement suggested the idea of offering on that day a special prayer for the memory of the dead (comp. Pesiḳ. 174b with the interpolated sentence in Tan., Yelammedenu, Ha'azinu, and Kol-Bo, lxx.). Regarding the extension of the prayer for the dead to other holy days, see the literature in Bet Yosef, Ṭur Oraḥ Ḥayyim, 621; M. Brück, "Pharisäische Volkssitten und Ritualien"; L. Löw, "Gesammelte Schriften," i. 129, v. 29; I. Levi, "La Commémoration des Ames dans le Judaïsme," in "R. E. J." xxix. 43-60; Hamburger, "R. B. T." ii., *s.v.* "Seelenfeier"; Hazkarat Neshamot (in which article the memorial service for Orthodox congregations is treated).

Reform Judaism remolded the old liturgy, laying special stress on the idea of the immortality of the soul, thereby affording a source of comfort to mourners in their grief. In the new form, the memorial service, which dwells mainly on the awful solemnity of death and the hope of a future life, and which is written to a great extent in the vernacular, has become one of the most prominent and impressive features of the Day of Atonement. Among those who composed elaborate and solemn memorial service liturgies Leopold Stein and David Einhorn may be specially mentioned.

There is a certain uniformity in the Reform rituals with regard to the elements of which the memorial service consists: a recitation or intonation of the verses Ps. cxliv. 3-4, xc. 6, 3; Deut. xxxii. 29; Ps. xlix. 18 (A. V. 17), xxxvii. 3, xxxiv. 23 (A. V. 22), forms the introduction to a meditation dwelling on the fleetingness of life; this is followed by a psalm, like Ps. xxiii.; selected poems from Ibn Gabirol, Judah ha-Levi, and Baḥya ben Joseph, translated into the vernacular, lead up to the prayer for the memory of the departed, in which, finally, mention is made, as in the old "Hazkarat Neshamot," of the great martyrs of the past. In many congregations the death-roll for the year is read, and persons distinguished in Israel who died during that period are also remembered. The reciting of the "Ḳaddish" by the entire congregation closes the service, to which elaborate and befitting music lends great solemnity.

A. K.

MEMPHIS: City of ancient Egypt, situated about ten miles south of modern Cairo. "Memphis" is the Greek form of the Egyptian "Menfe," and is used in Hos. ix. 6, A. V., and in Isa. xix. 13, R.V., margin (comp. Judith i. 10). The Hebrew form is "Mof," and occurs in Hos. ix. 6; in all other places it has been corrupted to "Nof," which the versions, however, render correctly by "Memphis."

As the capital of Egypt, Memphis seems to be mentioned in Hos. ix. 6; Ezek. xxx. 13, 16 (where, however, some critics alter the name in accordance with the Septuagint); Cornill, by making certain corrections, reads it also in Ezek. xxx. 15 and Isa. xix. 13. Jer. ii. 16 places it parallel with other large Egyptian cities, especially of the Delta. According to Jer. xliv. 1, xlvi. 14, the Jews fleeing from the Babylonian war to Egypt had formed a colony there.

A part of Memphis, called "the White Wall" (later forming the citadel of the city; see Herodotus, iii. 91; Thucydides, i. 104), existed at a very early period, and the residences of many Egyptian kings of the third to the sixth dynasty were built near it. From its temple the city always retained the sacred name "Temple of Ptaḥ" ("Ḥat-ka-ptaḥ," whence, probably, the name "Egypt" has been taken). The civil name and an account of the development of the city are derived from the funeral pyramid of King Ppy (vocalized "Apopy"?) I. of the sixth dynasty, called "Men-nofer" = "good resting." Hence the later abbreviations "Menfe," "Menbe" ("Mempi" in Assyrian; Delitzsch, "Wo Lag das Paradies?" p. 314), etc. Other etymologies found in Greek writers are unwarranted.

Memphis remained from the sixth dynasty to the Arab conquest perhaps the first, certainly the second, city of Egypt; and it frequently was the capital. The Arabs, however, soon caused its depopulation by founding new capitals a little to the north of it, for which the stones from the ruins of Memphis were used so exhaustively that only a few traces, near modern Mitrahineh and the large necropoles on the border of the desert (the pyramids of Gizeh, etc.), bear witness to the former existence of the city.

E. G. H. W. M. M.

MEMPHIS: Largest city of the state of Tennessee in the United States of America. Although the year 1845 is designated as the date of the earliest settlement of Jews in Memphis, it appears that a few had lived there temporarily before that time. Among the most prominent of the earlier settlers was Joseph J. Andrews, a former resident of Charleston, S. C., and Philadelphia. In 1847, when his brother died, he donated several acres of land to the Israelites of Memphis to be used as a burial-ground. This caused his resident coreligionists to organize in 1850 a Hebrew Benevolent Society. Divine service was then held only on Rosh ha-Shanah and Yom ha-Kippurim.

By 1853 there was a considerable increase in the Jewish population, and a congregation was organized under the name "B'nai Israel," with M. Simon as president and Solomon Hess as secretary. A hall was leased in a building on Front street; and Jonas Levy, formerly of Little Rock, Ark., was engaged as ḥazzan and shoḥeṭ. A Hebrew school, under the direction of the Rev. L. Sternheimer, was established, and a lot was bought with $2,000 donated by Judah Touro in 1853. At the beginning of 1858 greater interest was manifested in communal affairs. A building, known as "The Farmers' and Mechanics' Bank," was purchased and dedicated (March 26, 1858) as a house of worship. At the same time the Rev. J. J. Peres was elected ḥazzan. In 1860 the Rev. Simon Tuska of Rochester, N. Y., was chosen as rabbi. His views were those of moderate Reform; but when an organ, a mixed choir, and family pews were introduced into the synagogue a considerable number of members seceded and formed (1862) an Orthodox congregation called "Beth-El Emess." The numerical strength of the B'nai Israel congregation was reduced; but the members held their own, and when, after the close of the Civil war, many Israelites from the West and the East settled in Memphis, most of them affiliated with the Reform congregation. Rabbi Tuska died suddenly on Dec. 30, 1870; and the congregation elected as his successor the Rev. M. Samfield, formerly rabbi of the B'nai Zion congregation, Shreveport, La. He was installed Aug. 15, 1871, and still (1904) occupies the rabbinate.

First Congregation.

Orthodox Congregation Formed.

Some years later a consolidation of the Beth-El Emess congregation with B'nai Israel was effected, and in 1883 a lot on Poplar street was bought for the site of a temple. The building was dedicated Jan. 18, 1884. Another Orthodox congregation, established in 1862, had no permanent place of worship until 1890, when the members bought a church and converted it into a synagogue, giving their organization the name of "Baron Hirsch Congregation." The number of members is at present (1904) eighty-five. Another orthodox congregation was founded in 1904, under the name of "Anshai S'fard," with a membership of fifty.

The number of Jews in Memphis is estimated at 2,500 in a total population of 120,000. The following societies are in existence: Hebrew Ladies' Benevolent Society, United Hebrew Relief Association, Young Ladies' Aid Society, Jewish Ladies' Aid Society (Orthodox), Young Men's Hebrew Association, Ladies' Salon Circle (literary), B'nai B'rith Lodge, Free Sons of Israel Lodge, Kesher shel Barzel Lodge, Zionist Society, Memphis Club (social). The majority of Jews are merchants, but many are engaged in various trades as tailors, shoemakers, tinners, printers, opticians, carpenters, barbers, engravers, watchmakers, painters, butchers, and manufacturers of clothing, caps, shirts, and mattresses. There are also a considerable number following the various professions, as lawyers, musicians, teachers, physicians, and journalists.

A. M. Sa.

MEMRA (= "Ma'amar" or "Dibbur," "Logos"): "The Word," in the sense of the creative or directive word or speech of God manifesting His power in the world of matter or mind; a term used especially in the Targum as a substitute for "the Lord" when an anthropomorphic expression is to be avoided.

——**Biblical Data:** In Scripture "the word of the Lord" commonly denotes the speech addressed to patriarch or prophet (Gen. xv. 1; Num. xii. 6, xxiii. 5; I Sam. iii. 21; Amos v. 1–8); but frequently it denotes also the creative word: "By the word of the Lord were the heavens made" (Ps. xxxiii. 6; comp. "For He spake, and it was done"; "He sendeth his word, and melteth them [the ice]"; "Fire and hail; snow, and vapors; stormy wind fulfilling his word" Ps. xxxiii. 9, cxlvii. 18, cxlviii. 8). In this sense it is said, "For ever, O Lord, thy word is settled in heaven" (Ps. cxix. 89). "The Word," heard and announced by the prophet, often became, in the conception of the seer, an efficacious power apart from God, as was the angel or messenger of God: "The Lord sent a word into Jacob, and it hath lighted upon Israel" (Isa. ix. 7 [A. V. 8], lv. 11); "He sent his word, and healed them" (Ps. cvii. 20); and comp. "his word runneth very swiftly" (Ps. cxlvii. 15).

——**In Apocryphal and Rabbinical Literature:** While in the Book of Jubilees, xii. 22, the word of God is sent through the angel to Abraham, in other cases it becomes more and more a personified agency: "By the word of God exist His works" (Ecclus. [Sirach] xlii. 15); "The Holy One, blessed be He, created the world by the 'Ma'amar'" (Mek. Beshallaḥ, 10, with reference to Ps. xxxiii. 6). Quite frequent is the expression, especially in the liturgy, "Thou who hast made the universe with Thy word and ordained man through Thy wisdom to rule over the creatures made by Thee" (Wisdom ix. 1; comp. "Who by Thy words causest the evenings to bring darkness, who openest the gates of the sky by Thy wisdom"; . . . "who by His speech created the heavens, and by the breath of His mouth all their hosts"; through whose "words all things were created"; see Singer's "Daily Prayer-Book," pp. 96, 290, 292). So also in IV Esdras vi. 38 ("Lord, Thou spakest on the first day of Creation: 'Let there be heaven and earth,' and Thy word hath accomplished the work"). "Thy word, O Lord, healeth all things" (Wisdom xvi. 12); "Thy word preserveth them that put their trust in Thee" (*l.c.* xvi. 26). Especially strong is the personification of the word in Wisdom xviii. 15: "Thine Almighty Word leaped down from heaven out of Thy royal throne as a fierce man of war." The Mishnah, with reference to the ten passages in Genesis (ch. i.) beginning with "And God said," speaks of the ten "ma'amarot" (= "speeches") by which the world was created (Abot v. 1; comp. Gen. R. iv. 2: "The upper heavens are held in suspense by the creative Ma'amar"). Out of every speech ["dibbur"] which emanated from God an angel was created (Ḥag. 14a). "The Word ["dibbur"] calleth none but Moses" (Lev. R. i. 4, 5). "The Word ["dibbur"] went forth from the right hand of God and made a circuit around the camp of Israel" (Cant. R. i. 13).

Personification of the Word.

——**In the Targum:** In the Targum the Memra figures constantly as the manifestation of the divine power, or as God's messenger in place of God Himself, wherever the predicate is not in conformity with the dignity or the spirituality of the Deity.

Instead of the Scriptural "You have not believed in the Lord," Targ. Deut. i. 32 has "You have not believed in the word of the Lord"; instead of "I shall require it [vengeance] from him," Targ. Deut. xviii. 19 has "My word shall require it." "The Memra," instead of "the Lord," is "the consuming fire" (Targ. Deut. ix. 3; comp. Targ. Isa. xxx. 27). The Memra "plagued the people" (Targ. Yer. to Ex. xxxii. 35). "The Memra smote him" (II Sam. vi. 7; comp. Targ. I Kings xviii. 24; Hos. xiii. 14; *et al.*). Not "God," but "the Memra," is met with in Targ. Ex. xix. 17 (Targ. Yer. "the Shekinah"; comp. Targ. Ex. xxv. 22: "I will order My Memra to be there"). "I will cover thee with My Memra," instead of "My hand" (Targ. Ex. xxxiii. 22). Instead of "My soul," "My Memra shall reject you" (Targ. Lev. xxvi. 30; comp. Isa. i. 14, xlii. 1; Jer. vi. 8; Ezek. xxiii. 18). "The voice of the Memra," instead of "God," is heard (Gen. iii. 8; Deut. iv. 33, 36; v. 21; Isa. vi. 8; *et al.*). Where Moses says, "I stood between the Lord and you" (Deut. v. 5), the Targum has, "between the Memra of the Lord and you"; and the "sign between Me and you" becomes a "sign between My Memra and you" (Ex. xxxi. 13, 17; comp. Lev. xxvi. 46; Gen. ix. 12; xvii. 2, 7, 10; Ezek. xx. 12). Instead of God, the Memra comes to Abimelek (Gen. xx. 3), and to Balaam (Num. xxiii. 4). His Memra aids and accompanies Israel, performing wonders for them (Targ. Num. xxiii. 21; Deut. i. 30, xxxiii. 3; Targ. Isa. lxiii. 14; Jer. xxxi. 1; Hos. ix. 10 [comp. xi. 3, "the messenger-angel"]). The Memra goes before Cyrus (Isa. xlv. 12). The Lord swears by His Memra (Gen. xxi. 23, xxii. 16, xxiv. 3; Ex. xxxii. 13; Num. xiv. 30; Isa. xlv. 23; Ezek. xx. 5; *et al.*). It is His Memra that repents (Targ. Gen. vi. 6, viii. 21; I Sam. xv. 11, 35). Not His "hand," but His "Memra has laid the foundation of the earth" (Targ. Isa. xlviii. 13); for His Memra's or Name's sake does He act (*l.c.* xlviii. 11; II Kings xix. 34). Through the Memra God turns to His people (Targ. Lev. xxvi. 90; II Kings xiii. 23), becomes the shield of Abraham (Gen. xv. 1), and is with Moses (Ex. iii. 12; iv. 12, 15) and with Israel (Targ. Yer. to Num. x. 35, 36; Isa. lxiii. 14). It is the Memra, not God Himself, against whom man offends (Ex. xvi. 8; Num. xiv. 5; I Kings viii. 50; II Kings xix. 28; Isa. i. 2, 16; xlv. 3, 20; Hos. v. 7, vi. 7; Targ. Yer. to Lev. v. 21, vi. 2; Deut. v. 11), through His Memra Israel shall be justified (Targ. Isa. xlv. 25); with the Memra Israel stands in communion (Targ. Josh. xxii. 24, 27); in the Memra man puts his trust (Targ. Gen. xv. 6; Targ. Yer. to Ex. xiv. 31; Jer. xxxix. 18, xlix. 11).

Like the Shekinah (comp. Targ. Num. xxiii. 21), the Memra is accordingly the manifestation of God. "The Memra brings Israel nigh unto God and sits on His throne receiving the prayers of Israel" (Targ. Yer. to Deut. iv. 7). It shielded Noah from the flood (Targ. Yer. to Gen. vii. 16) and brought about the dispersion of the seventy nations (*l.c.* xi. 8); it is the guardian of Jacob (Gen. xxviii. 20-21, xxxv. 3) and of Israel (Targ. Yer. to Ex. xii. 23, 29); it works all the wonders in Egypt (*l.c.* xiii. 8, xiv. 25); hardens the heart of Pharaoh (*l.c.* xiii. 15); goes before Israel in the wilderness (Targ. Yer. to Ex. xx. 1); blesses Israel (Targ. Yer. to Num. xxiii. 8); battles for the people (Targ. Josh. iii. 7, x. 14, xxiii. 3). As in ruling over the destiny of man the Memra is the agent of God (Targ. Yer. to Num. xxvii. 16), so also is it in the creation of the earth (Isa. xlv. 12) and in the execution of justice (Targ. Yer. to Num. xxxiii. 4). So, in the future, shall the Memra be the comforter (Targ. Isa. lxvi. 13): "My Shekinah I shall put among you, My Memra shall be unto you for a redeeming deity, and you shall be unto My Name a holy people" (Targ. Yer. to Lev. xxii. 12). "My Memra shall be unto you like a good plowman who takes off the yoke from the shoulder of the oxen"; "the Memra will roar to gather the exiled" (Targ. Hos. xi. 5, 10). The Memra is "the witness" (Targ. Yer. xxix. 23); it will be to Israel like a father (*l.c.* xxxi. 9) and "will rejoice over them to do them good" (*l.c.* xxxii. 41). "In the Memra the redemption will be found" (Targ. Zech. xii. 5). "The holy Word" was the subject of the hymns of Job (Test. of Job, xii. 3, ed. Kohler).

Mediatorship.

The Logos.

It is difficult to say how far the rabbinical concept of the Memra, which is used now as a parallel to the divine Wisdom and again as a parallel to the Shekinah, had come under the influence of the Greek term "Logos," which denotes both word and reason, and, perhaps owing to Egyptian mythological notions, assumed in the philosophical system of Heraclitos, of Plato, and of the Stoa the metaphysical meaning of world-constructive and world-permeating intelligence (see Reizenstein, "Zwei Religionsgeschichtliche Fragen," 1901, pp. 83–111; comp. Aall, "Der Logos," and the Logos literature given by Schürer, "Gesch." i. 3, 542–544). The Memra as a cosmic power furnished Philo the corner-stone upon which he built his peculiar semi-Jewish philosophy. Philo's "divine thought," "the image" and "first-born son" of God, "the archpriest," "intercessor," and "paraclete" of humanity, the "arch type of man" (see Philo), paved the way for the Christian conceptions of the Incarnation ("the Word become flesh") and the Trinity. The Word which "the unoriginated Father created in His own likeness as a manifestation of His own power" appears in the Gnostic system of Marcus (Irenæus, "Adversus Hæreses," i. 14). In the ancient Church liturgy, adopted from the Synagogue, it is especially interesting to notice how often the term "Logos," in the sense of "the Word by which God made the world, or made His Law or Himself known to man," was changed into "Christ" (see "Apostolic Constitutions," vii. 25-26, 34–38, *et al.*). Possibly on account of the Christian dogma, rabbinic theology, outside of the Targum literature, made little use of the term "Memra." See Logos.

Bibliography: Bousset, *Die Religion des Judenthums im Neutestamentlichen Zeitalter*, 1903, p. 341; Weber, *Jüdische Theologie*, 1897, pp. 180–184.

K.

MENAHEM: King of Israel 748–738 B.C.; son of Gadi. Zachariah, the son of Jeroboam II., had at the end of six months' reign been slain by Shallum, a usurper. Menahem went from Tirzah, one of the government fortresses, to Samaria, cut down the usurper, and occupied the throne (II Kings xv. 8-14). Immediately thereafter he smote Tiphsah because it refused to yield to him, and inflicted the most barbarous punishment upon the women of the city and its borders (*ib.* verse 16). This Tiphsah has been identified, by a slight change of letters, with En Tappuah (Josh. xvii. 7), a city on the borders of Ephraim and Manasseh.

It was in the reign of Menahem that the great Tiglath-pileser III. appeared on Israel's horizon: "There came against the land Pul, the King of Assyria; and Menahem gave Pul a thousand talents of silver, that his hand might be with him to confirm the kingdom in his hand. And Menahem exacted the money of Israel, even of all the mighty men of wealth, of each man fifty shekels of silver, to give to the king of Assyria. So the king of Assyria turned back, and stayed not there in the land" (*ib.* verses 19–20, R. V.). The identification of Pul with Tiglath-pileser III. is beyond dispute. Israel at this time had 60,000 men of wealth, and was too powerful a kingdom to yield to Assyria without a struggle.

Among the tributaries of Tiglath-pileser, as described in his own inscriptions, are found the following: Kushtashpi of the city of Kummukh; Raṣunnu of Gar-imeri (that is, Rezin of Aram-Damascus); Mi-ni-ḥi-im-mi of the city of Sa-mi-ri-na-ai (that is, Menahem of Samaria); and Hirum of the city of Ṣur (Tyre). From this reference it is possible to assign Menahem to a date about 748–738 B.C. His complete subjection to the King of Assyria seems to have occurred about the close of his reign, so that his son and successor was obliged to carry the burden of Assyria's tribute.

Menahem was the only king in this anarchic period of the Northern Kingdom who died a natural death.

E. G. H. I. M. P.

MENAHEM B. AARON IBN ZERAH: Spanish codifier; born in Navarre, probably at Estella, in the first third of the fourteenth century; died at Toledo July, 1385. His father, forced to leave France in 1306 through the expulsion of the Jews, went to Spain and settled in Estella, where Menahem passed his youth. In the massacre which took place in Estella in 1328, Menahem's parents and his four younger brothers were slain. Menahem himself was stricken to the ground, and lay all but dead from his wounds, when he was saved through the compassion of a knight, a friend of his father's. He then studied two years under Joshua ibn Shu'aib, after which he went to Alcala to join Joseph ibn al-'Aish, with whom he studied the Talmud and Tosafot. His chief teacher was Judah b. Asher, who went through the whole of the Talmud with him, with the exception of the third and fourth orders. In 1361 Menahem succeeded Joseph ibn al-'Aish as rabbi in Alcala, and held office for eight years, during which time he also taught the Talmud.

In consequence of the civil war which broke out in 1368, Menahem lost all his property, and he then went to Toledo, where Don Samuel Abravanel took him under his protection, and enabled him to continue his studies during the rest of his life. In honor and for the benefit of this protector Menahem wrote "Ẓedah la-Derek" (Ferrara, 1554). This work occupies a peculiar position among codes, and is in a certain sense unique. As the author states in the introduction (ed. Sabbionetta, p. 166), it is intended mainly for rich Jews who associate with princes and who, on account of their high station and their intercourse with the non-Jewish world, are not over-rigorous in regard to Jewish regulations. For such a class of readers a law-codex must not be too voluminous, but must contain the most essential laws, especially those that the higher classes would be inclined to overstep.

The "Ẓedah la-Derek" is divided into five parts (comprising altogether 372 sections), which may be summarized as follows: Part i.: The ritual and all that is related to it, as, for example, the regulations concerning phylacteries, ẓiẓit, etc. Part ii.: Laws concerning forbidden foods. Part iii.: Marriage laws. Part iv.: Sabbath and feast-days. Part v.: Fast-days and laws for mourning. As a supplement to the last part is a treatise on the Messiah and on the resurrection of the dead. Menahem sought to emphasize the ethical side of the Law in his work. He was not satisfied with merely stating the regulations like other religious codifiers: he tried also to give a reason for them. Deficient as the "Ẓedah la-Derek" is as a code, its author has succeeded remarkably well in bringing to light the religious element in the Jewish ceremonial. At the same time he is far removed from mysticism (comp. *ib.* ed. Sabbionetta, iv. 4, 1, p. 187), possessing an unusually wide mental horizon. Although his parents and brothers fell victims to religious hatred, he still maintained that the superiority of Israel as the "chosen people" is based upon their fulfilling God's word, and "that a non-Jew who lives in accordance with God's will is more worthy than a Jew who does not perform it" (*ib.* i. 1, 33, p. 39). In dogmatical questions Menahem was more inclined to a strictly Orthodox point of view than to a philosophical one, although he believed that the Biblical stories of the Creation and the Bible's teaching about the resurrection contained mysteries, which he did not venture to solve. In a Turin manuscript (A. iv. 37) are given laws by him on sheḥiṭah and bediḳah, perhaps excerpted from his larger work.

BIBLIOGRAPHY: Kayserling, *Gesch. der Juden in Spanien und Portugal*, i. 84; *Ẓedah la-Derek*, p. 16a; Almanzi-Luzzatto, *Abne Zikkaron*, pp. 14–16 (where the date of Menahem's death is given together with the inscription on his tomb: the Jewish chronographers place his death eleven years earlier); Steinschneider, *Cat. Bodl.* s.v.; Renan-Neubauer, *Ecrivains Juifs*, pp. 361 *et seq.*

S. S. L. G.

MENAHEM B. ABRAHAM. See BONAFOS, MENAHEM BEN ABRAHAM.

MENAHEM BEN ELIAKIM: German scholar of the fourteenth century; a native of Bingen. He was the author of "'Aruk Goren," a dictionary of the Talmud, with German translations of all the difficult words, particularly those taken from Arabic and Greek. The basis of this work is the "'Aruk" of Nathan ben Jehiel, from which Menahem made many extracts and to which he added new matter. The meaning of the title probably is "a condensed 'Aruk," but Wolf ("Bibl. Hebr." iv., No. 1426b) reads ערוך גוין = "Short 'Aruk," and the Latin translation "Aruch Breve" is given by Emden in "Ḳohelet Dawid" (No. 195d), although it does not correspond to the Hebrew ערוך גרן given by Isaac Metz. Wolf concluded that, in spite of the similarity of contents, the "'Aruk Goren" is not to be identified with the anonymous "'Aruk ha-Ḳaẓer."

BIBLIOGRAPHY: Steinschneider, *Jewish Literature*, p. 74; Zunz, *Z. G.* p. 120.

G. M. SEL.

MENAHEM ELIEZER BEN LEVI: Lithuanian Talmudist; born at Wilna; died at Minsk Dec. 23, 1816. After studying Talmud under Solomon of Vilkomir he settled at Minsk, where he became head of the yeshibah. His "Ya'ir Ḳinno," a commentary on Ḳinnim, which he wrote when still a young man, was much appreciated by Elijah Wilna:

"Menahem Eliezer was aided by Heaven to find the meaning of this difficult treatise, in which so many commentators have failed." After the death of Elijah Wilna his pupils requested Menahem Eliezer to write a commentary on their teacher's notes to the Shulḥan 'Aruk, Oraḥ Ḥayyim. This commentary he began, but did not finish. He was the author of works on the Pentateuch and on the Mishnah, of novellæ, and of responsa, none of which has been published.

Bibliography: Benzion Eisenstadt, *Rabbane Minsk*, p. 41; Fuenn, *Ḳiryah Ne'emanah*, pp. 205-206; Walden, *Shem ha-Gedolim he-Ḥadash*, p. 93.
H. R. M. Sel.

MENAHEM BEN ELIJAH: Turkish liturgist of the fifteenth century; a native of Kastoria. He composed the following piyyuṭim: (1) "Mah yaḳeru re'im be-ḳum ashmoret," a "petiḥah"; (2) "Me'on ehyeh asher ehyeh," a "tokaḥah"; both giving in acrostic the names of himself, his father, and his native town; (3) "He middot kol hodot le-baddeka milleta," a hymn consisting of twelve strophes, each beginning and ending with the letter "he"; (4) a "tefillah" entitled "Shirat ha-Yad ha-Ḥazaḳah" or "Malkiel." This piyyuṭ is peculiar in that, in addition to a short introduction, it consists of 140 lines of five words each. Every word in the first ten lines begins with מ; in the next ten lines, with נ; and so on to the end of the piyyuṭ, which therefore gives the full name מנחם בן כ״ר אליה ז״ל fifty times over.

Among the Egyptian fragments published by Neubauer in "J. Q. R." ix. 26-28 is a letter from a certain Menahem b. Elijah which refers to the Crusades. At the end of the letter the writer says that he had intended to go to Syria, but was detained through fear of the German army. As he speaks so often of Salonica, in the district of which Kastoria is situated, one might be tempted to identify him with the subject of this article; but Zunz concluded that the liturgist lived in the second half of the fifteenth century.

Bibliography: Zunz, *Literaturgesch.* p. 386; Supplement, p. 28.
G. M. Sel.

MENAHEM THE ESSENE: Prominent teacher of the Essene faction in the time of King Herod, about the middle of the first pre-Christian century. He was renowned for his prophetic powers. According to Josephus ("Ant." xv. 10, § 5), he was distinguished also for the saintliness of his life as well as for possessing knowledge of the future. Legend has it that when he saw young Herod going to school he clapped him on the back and addressed him as king, announcing to him that he would reign successfully, but without displaying the love and justice he ought toward men or the piety due to God, and that therefore his end would be one befitting his crimes. When afterward in the zenith of his power Herod recalled this strange prediction, he sent for Menahem and asked him how long his reign would be. As Menahem did not immediately answer, Herod urged him, asking whether his reign would last ten years; whereupon Menahem replied: "Yes, twenty; nay, thirty years." Pleased with this answer, Herod dismissed him with a clasp of the hand and thenceforth bestowed special honors upon the Essenes. This Menahem has been correctly identified with the one mentioned in the Mishnah as ab bet din and head of a school in association with Hillel ha-Nasi and as Shammai's predecessor; but the duumvirate of ab bet din and nasi is probably due to a misconstruction of history when the real issues between the Hasidæan or Pharisean and the Sadducean or Boethusian factions were no longer understood. A dim reminiscence of the relation of Menahem to Herod, however, has been preserved in a baraita, quoted in Ḥag. 16b, which states that "Menahem went out to join those serving the king, and eighty pairs of disciples attired in silk robes went with him." Another tradition is that he became an apostate (Yer. Ḥag. ii. 77d). The two traditions have been confounded and appear in two other forms also: according to one, Menahem was forced to leave the Pharisaic school, and when seen with his eighty pairs of disciples was told that they no longer had a share in the God of Israel; according to the other, he went from one degree ("middah") to another until he became a Gnostic (heretic ?). See, however, Grätz, "Gesch." iii. 213.

K.

MENAHEM BEN ḤELBO. See Ḳara, Joseph ben Simeon.

MENAHEM BEN JACOB BEN SOLOMON BEN SIMSON: German synagogal poet; died at Worms April 16, 1203. He was a member of an old family of Jewish scholars connected with that city. His great-grandfather Simson, who was living in Worms at the time of the First Crusade and was surnamed "Ha-Darshan," is quoted by Rashi on Isa. lviii. 14 and Amos vi. 3. One of Simson's sons, Samuel, is also quoted by Rashi ("Ha-Pardes," p. 33a). Jacob, another son of Simson, died at Worms during the First Crusade (1096). In his epitaph Menahem is called "teacher of the Law," "preacher," and "payyeṭan." A responsum of his addressed to the German Talmudist Eliezer ben Joel ha-Levi is preserved among the responsa of Judah ben Asher (p. 48a).

Menahem is known principally through his synagogal poetry. Zunz credits him with thirty-one poems—among them being examples of "Ma'arib," "Yoẓer," "Ofan," "Ahabah," "Sulat," "Reshut," "Ḳedushshah"—as well as with a number of "seliḥot." Among his elegies the following deserve mention: "Me'one Shamayim" (which found a place in the German ritual for the 9th of Ab); "Alelai Ki Ba'u Rega'" (on the martyrs of Blois, 1171, and of Boppard, 1195; part of it has been translated into German by Zunz, "S. P." p. 250); a seliḥah on the ten martyrs; a seliḥah commemorating the victims of a persecution in 1147 or 1190. Another seliḥah, beginning "Anah ha-Shem ha-Nikbad," has been translated by Zunz into German ("S. P." p. 263). Corresponding to the condition of the Jews during this period, a tone of gloom and despondency pervades his poetry.

It has been supposed that Menahem is identical with the synagogal poet Menahem ben Jacob de Luṭra, quoted in De Rossi, Parma MSS., No. 1274, and with Menahem of Luṭra (לוטרא), who produced a rimed compilation of the thirteen articles of faith (see "Catalogus Librorum Manuscriptorum civ. Lipsiensis," p. 295). It has been maintained that Menahem was born in Kaiserslautern, and that therefore he was called Menahem de Luṭra; this supposition, however, does not seem tenable.

BIBLIOGRAPHY: L. Lewysohn, in *Allg. Zeit. des Jud.* 1855, p. 215; *idem*, in *Monatsschrift*, 1856, p. 420; Landshuth, *'Ammude ha-'Abodah*, pp. 185 *et seq.*; L. Löwenstein, *Beiträge zur Gesch. der Juden in Deutschland*, i. 4, Frankfort-on-the-Main, 1895; Zunz, *Literaturgesch.* pp. 294 *et seq.*, 510.

J. M. Sc.

MENAHEM BEN JAIR: Leader of the SICARII. He was a grandson of Judas of Galilee, the founder of the Zealot party, of which the Sicarii were a branch. Menahem checked the lawlessness of the Sicarii, who, under his leadership, in 66 C.E., stormed the fortress of Masada and slew the Roman garrison. Later they entered the fortress of Antonia, after its garrison had been forced to retreat by the Zealots under Eleazar ben Ananias, and ruthlessly murdered the maimed and helpless left behind by the Romans. Exulting in his successes, Menahem now demanded the leadership of the Zealots, sought recognition as the Messiah, and led his men into still more cruel acts of violence. Eleazar ben Ananias, realizing that the Sicarii were a menace, turned the Zealots against Menahem, who fled to Ophla, but was captured and executed. He was succeeded by his brother Eleazar.

BIBLIOGRAPHY: Grätz, *Gesch.* 4th ed., iii. 432, 457 *et seq.*; Josephus, *B. J.* ii. 17, §§ 8-10.

D. S. J. L.

MENAHEM B. JOSEPH B. ḤIYYA: Gaon of Pumbedita 858-860. He was probably elected to the office of gaon rather on account of his father than for his own merit. He had a rival in the gaon Mar Mattithiah b. Rabbi, his superior in Talmudic lore, between whom and Menahem dissensions continued until the death of the latter.

BIBLIOGRAPHY: Sherira Gaon, *Responsa*, ed. Neubauer, p. 38; Grätz, *Gesch.* 3d ed., v. 231; Weiss, *Dor*, iv. 131; Heilprin, *Seder ha-Dorot*, ed. Maskileison, i. 181.

S. S. A. S. W.

MENAHEM BEN JOSEPH OF TROYES: Liturgical compiler; lived at Troyes in the thirteenth century, succeeding his father, JOSEPH ḤAZZAN BEN JUDAH, as ḥazzan. The Jewish liturgy is indebted to him for collecting the order of prayers which was used in the community of Troyes and which is often quoted under the title "Siddur Troyes" (Neubauer, "Cat. Bodl. Hebr. MSS." No. 1118; De Rossi, Parma MS. No. 403). His collection was arranged by his pupil Judah ben Eleazar, perhaps identical with the author of the commentary "Minḥat Yehudah" (written about 1313), which contains a quotation from Menahem's work.

BIBLIOGRAPHY: Gross, *Gallia Judaica*, p. 240; Steinschneider, *Jewish Literature*, p. 344, note 40a; S. D. Luzzatto, in G. I. Pollak, *Halikot Ḳedem*, p. 50, Amsterdam, 1847; Zunz, *Ritus*, pp. 28, 134; idem, *Literaturgesch.* pp. 221 *et seq.*

E. C. M. Sc.

MENAHEM B. JUDAH: Roman halakist of the twelfth century. There are few data regarding his life, neither the year of his birth nor that of his death being determined. It is known, however, that he was descended from a family of scholars. He is mentioned by Benjamin of Tudela; and he was personally acquainted with Joseph ibn Plat. The only known date in his history is 1166, in which yea he was director of the Talmudic academy at Rom Menahem's father, Judah b. Menahem, a young contemporary of Nathan, was a prolific liturgic poet, whose work is, for the most part, included i the Roman Maḥzor. Menahem Judah himself di not write, his studies being confined to the Halaka The names of two of his contemporaries are know Solomon b. Abraham and Abraham, called "Ezra b Mattathias," who were his colleagues on the rabbinical board.

Menahem's responsum referring to the benedictions at circumcision and delivered on the occasio of the visit of Joseph ibn Plat of southern Franc is the only one of his that has been preserved. It possible that he answered the question addresse by the mishnaic commentator Isaac b. Melchizede of Siponto to the "wise men of Rome"; in any cas the answer was delivered during his rabbinat Thus he may also be identical with the Menahe celebrated by Abraham ibn Ezra in the poem "Ḥadashim Ma'ase El" (ed. Rosin, "Reime und Gedichte," i. 124 *et seq.*). He was the father of a single son, **Moses.** There is ground for the assumptio that this Moses was identical with the author of t Roman "zulat" "Im Tekayyemu Miẓwotai," whic he dedicated to his son Menahem in an acrostic.

BIBLIOGRAPHY: Zunz, *Literaturgesch.* pp. 140, 173; Berline *Gesch. der Juden in Rom*, ii. 28; Gross, *Gallia Judaica*, 508; Vogelstein and Rieger, *Gesch. der Juden in Rom*, i. 2 227, 368.

S. H. B.—G. WE.

MENAHEM BEN MACHIR: German litu gist of the eleventh century; a native of Ratisbo His grandfather, also called Menahem b. Machi was a nephew of Gershom b. Judah, and he himse was a cousin of Isaac b. Judah, Rashi's teache He is quoted in Rashi's "Pardes" (21d, 33c) and i the "Liḳḳuṭe Pardes" (19b; comp. "Pisḳe Reḳanaṭi," No. 589). Menahem witnessed the Jewis massacres of 1096 in Germany and commemorat them in a number of seliḥot. His piyyuṭim includ "Adam be-ḳum," for the Esther fast (quoted in To to Ḥag. 11a); "Aḥalleh et pene Adonai," for Yo Kippur minḥah; "Amarer ba-beki," for the 17th Tammuz; "Lammah Adonai ta'amod" (in ten str phes); a "ḳinah" for the 9th of Ab, beginning "Eb a'orer"; five "yoẓerot," including one for the "N ḥamu" Sabbath and one for the "Shubah" Sabbat three "ofannim"; three "zulatot"; "Kehosha' elim," a "hosha'na" for the Sabbath of Tabernacle "Ma'arib," for the Feast of Tabernacles; "Nishmat to be recited on Simḥat Torah; and a "reshut" f Ḥatan Torah, to be recited on the same day. Mo of his piyyuṭim are alphabetically arranged, but a of them bear the author's signature.

BIBLIOGRAPHY: Landshuth, *'Ammude ha-'Abodah*, pp. 19 192; Zunz, *Literaturgesch.* pp. 158, 250.

A. M. SEL.

MENAHEM MANN BEN SOLOMON HA LEVI. See AMELANDER, MENAHEM MANN BE SOLOMON HA-LEVI.

MENAHEM MANUELE B. BARUC HA-LEVI: Polish rabbi and author; died in Le berg 1742. He was a descendant of R. Joseph Coh of Cracow (author of "She'erit Yosef"), of R. Isa Shrenzel, and of R. Saul Wahl. He occupied t office of dayyan in Lemberg under the presidency of R. Ḥayyim Rapoport.

Menahem was the author of "Zera' Baruk" (Wandsbeck, 1730), novellæ on some tractates of the Talmud. Another work of his was "'Emeḳ Halakah we-Ṭa'am Man" (Frankfort-on-the-Oder, 1745), consisting of two parts: (1) discourses on the Halakah; (2) explanations of the Haggadah. It contains also an approbation by R. Moses b. Aaron of Lemberg (given in 1735) and novellæ by Naphtali Herz Ashkenazi and Moses Ḥarif, both rabbis of Lemberg. According to a statement of the author in his preface to the "'Emeḳ Halakah," he wrote also a book entitled "'Abodat ha-Lewi" on the order Ḳodashim.

Menahem's signature as dayyan is found in documents and deeds inserted in the Lemberg memorbook.

BIBLIOGRAPHY: Buber, *Anshe Shem*, p. 142.

H. R. N. T. L.

MENAHEM MENDEL BEN BARUCH BENDET: Lithuanian Talmudist of the eighteenth century; born at Shklov; died in Palestine. He was a pupil of Elijah of Wilna, whose works he later helped to edit and publish. Elijah Gaon's commentaries on Proverbs, on the Shulḥan 'Aruk (Oraḥ Ḥayyim and Yoreh De'ah), on Abot, on the Sefer Yeẓirah, and on the Pesaḥ Haggadah, and his notes to the minor treatises, were published by him. After Elijah's death Mehahem Mendel went to Palestine and settled at Safed, where he became lecturer in Talmud in the bet ha-midrash established there in memory of Elijah of Wilna. He was the author of ten works, mystical in character, as yet unpublished (comp. Israel b. Samuel, "Pe'at ha-Shulḥan," Preface, Safed, 1836).

BIBLIOGRAPHY: Fuenn, *Ḳiryah Ne'emanah*, p. 102; Joshua Heshel Levin and Naḥman of Grodno, *'Aliyyot Eliyahu*, pp. 59, 67, Wilna, 1889.

E. C. M. SEL.

MENAHEM OF MERSEBURG (מרזיבורק): German author; lived between 1420 and 1450. Of his life few details are known. Jacob Weil (Responsa, No. 133) speaks of him as a great and prominent scholar; and he is mentioned also by Judah Minz, and by Solomon Luria in his commentary on the Talmud. Both of them identify him with Menahem Meïl Ẓedeḳ, while Azulai distinguishes between the two Menahems. According to Jacob Weil's allusions, Menahem must have lived in the first half of the fifteenth century.

Menahem wrote a collection of halakic notes ("nimuḳim"), which forms an appendix to Weil's responsa. This work, which was regarded as authoritative in all the communities in Saxony, deals with the rabbinical marriage laws, the civil code, and the taxation of the communities. In contrast to the meager scientific contributions of the German Jews of the period, who discussed little besides petty liturgical questions, Menahem's book shows his lively interest in all matters that concern Judaism. Of great practical importance was his ruling in reference to the "mi'un," or the decision that if a girl has been married during minority at the instance of her mother or brothers but not at the command of her father, she has the right, when she attains her majority, to dissolve the union without a bill of divorce. Menahem, considering this immoral, repealed the law by virtue of his authority; but in the following century his ruling was set aside, and the Talmudic law again went into force.

BIBLIOGRAPHY: Grätz, *Gesch.* viii. 137.

S. G. WE.

MENAHEM B. MICHAEL B. JOSEPH HA-ḲARA'I (called also **Menahem Girni ha-Goleh**): Karaite philosopher and poet; born in Babylon; a contemporary of Saadia. He corresponded with David al-Muḳammaṣ, whom he had met in Babylon, on philosophical subjects, and perhaps also regarding the Karaite "sheḥiṭah." Subsequently he went to Alexandria, whence he wrote to the Karaite community at Cairo asking aid. In his letter he touched also on philosophical topics, and quoted the Karaite philosopher Joseph al-Baṣir. Leaving Alexandria for Cairo, Menahem continued his correspondence with David al-Muḳammaṣ; for, although the latter was living in the same city, Menahem was restrained by poverty from approaching a man of such prominence. In one letter, written at Cairo, Menahem explained to David, in answer to the latter's reproach, that he believed both in the creation of the world and in the heavenly bodies.

Aside from the rules for slaughtering, written in verse, three of Menahem's piyyuṭim have been preserved in the Karaite siddur. Menahem is quoted as a grammarian in the "Sefer ha-Mibḥar" of Aaron b. Elijah the Elder, and probably also in the "'Eẓ ha-Ḥayyim" of Aaron b. Elijah the Younger. This Menahem must not be confounded with another who was likewise a contemporary of Saadia and who corresponded with the last-named in Arabic.

BIBLIOGRAPHY: Pinsker, *Liḳḳuṭe Ḳadmoniyyot*, p. 168; Appendix, pp. 45 *et seq.*; Steinschneider, *Cat. Leyden*, p. 186; Grätz, *Gesch.* 3d ed., v. 284; Mordecai b. Nisan, ed. Wolf, p. 130 (ed. Vienna, p. 13); Wolf, *Bibl. Hebr.* i. 762, iii. 684.

K. A. B.

MENAHEM B. MOSES TAMAR: Poet and commentator; probably a pupil of Mordecai COMTINO of Constantinople; flourished in the fifteenth and sixteenth centuries at Adrianople or Philippopolis. He wrote commentaries to the books of Proverbs, Ruth, and Esther, a supercommentary to Abraham ibn Ezra's commentary to the Pentateuch, and a Hebrew grammar entitled "Rashe Besamim." He furnished a noteworthy contribution to Hebrew poetry in his "Azharot" (comp. JEW. ENCYC. ii. 370–371), to which he wrote a commentary entitled "Tanḥumot El." He composed also other liturgical poems, including an imitation of Judah ha-Levi's "Zioniad," and a hymn for the commencement of Purim. It has not been proved—although the attempt has been made—that he is identical with Menahem b. Moses, the author of some liturgical poems found in the Roman Maḥzor, in the Maḥzor of Avignon, and in a manuscript of Abraham Bedersi's "Diwan," now in the British Museum.

BIBLIOGRAPHY: Steinschneider, *Cat. Leyden*, pp. 120 *et seq.* (comp. Zunz in *Zeit. für. Hebr. Bibl.* ix. 133) and pp. 139 *et seq.*; idem, *Hebr. Uebers.* p. 593; Zunz, *Literaturgesch.* p. 526; Landshuth, *'Ammude ha-'Abodah*, pp. 194 *et seq.*; Nepi-Ghirondi, *Toledot Gedole Yisrael*, p. 236; Luzzatto, *Naḥlat*, pp. 21, 51.

D. H. B.

MENAḤEM OBEL. See MOURNING.

MENAHEM BEN PEREZ OF JOIGNY: French tosafist and Biblical commentator of the twelfth century. Zadoc Kahn ("R. E. J." iii. 7) identifies him with Menahem the Saint mentioned in Tos. Ḥul. 11b; and he conjectures that Menahem was killed at Bray-sur-Seine in the massacre of 1190. Gross, however, thinks this assertion doubtful, and concludes that Menahem died about 1180. Menahem ben Perez took an active part in the synod which was assembled at Troyes under the direction of the two brothers R. Samuel b. Meïr and R. Jacob Tam.

As a tosafist, Menahem ben Perez is quoted in Tos. Ber. 39b, 40a; 'Er. 68a; B. M. 60a; Yoma 6a; Pes. 116a, and by later authorities. Asher b. Jehiel had before him Menahem's tosafot (Asheri, Yeb. 3a). As a Biblical commentator, he is quoted in the "Da'at Zeḳenim," p. 29a, and in the "Minḥat Yehudah," p. 33b. Menahem was the author of a work entitled "Massorah Gedolah" or "The Great Masorah" (still unpublished), in which he completed the work bearing the same title by R. Gershom Meor ha-Golah. Joseph the Zealous mentions Menahem's controversy with a priest ("R. E. J." *l.c.*).

BIBLIOGRAPHY: Grätz, in *Monatsschrift*, xxxvi. 19; Gross, *Gallia Judaica*, pp. 251-252.

S. S. M. SEL.

MENAHEM PORTO. See PORTO.

MENAHEM OF RECANATI. See RECANATI.

MENAHEM BEN SARUḲ (MENAHEM B. JACOB IBN SARUḲ): Spanish philologist of the tenth century. He was a native of Tortosa, and went, apparently at an early age, to Cordova, where he found a patron in Isaac, the father of the subsequent statesman Ḥasdai ibn Shaprut. At Isaac's death Menahem eulogized his protector's virtues in an inscription placed in the synagogue which had been built by Isaac at Cordova. He wrote also elegies on him, which were universally recited during the period of mourning. Menahem then returned to his native city, where he engaged in business.

Ḥasdai ibn Shaprut, however, recalled Menahem to Cordova and encouraged him to complete his life-work, a dictionary of the Hebrew language. In other ways also his new patron availed himself of his protégé's literary talents. Ḥasdai on his mother's death requested Menahem to compose a dirge; and when Ḥasdai addressed his questions to the king of the Chazars, Menahem was commissioned to write the letter, which has become an important historical document. Menahem, however, carried on his work amid great privations, as Ḥasdai did not prove a liberal patron.

The dictionary had scarcely been completed when an opponent to its author arose in Dunash ben Labraṭ, who had come to Spain from Fez, and who wrote a criticism on the work, which he prefaced by a eulogistic dedication to Ḥasdai. The slanders of personal enemies likewise seem to have aroused Ḥasdai's anger against Menahem to such a pitch that the latter, at the command of the powerful statesman, suffered bodily violence, his house being destroyed. In a touching letter to Ḥasdai (a valuable source from which most of these statements have been taken) Menahem, who probably died shortly afterward, complained of the wrong done him. He seems to have made some impression on his patron. Menahem himself had not replied to Dunash, but his pupils defended their teacher, and in response to Dunash's criticism wrote a detailed refutation which was marked by polemical acumen and exact grammatical knowledge. Judah b. David ḤAYYUJ, one of these three young scholars who so effectually defended their master, became the founder of scientific Hebrew grammar; another, Isaac ibn Gikatilla, was subsequently, as one of the most learned men of Lucena, the teacher of Abu al-Walid Merwan ibn Janaḥ. Thus the most flourishing period of Hebrew philology, whose chief representatives were Ḥayyuj and Ibn Janaḥ, began with Menahem ben Saruḳ.

Dispute with Dunash.

The place to be assigned to the "Maḥberet," as Menahem entitled his dictionary, has been briefly discussed elsewhere (see JEW. ENCYC. iv. 580, *s.v.* DICTIONARIES). This was the first complete lexical treatment of the Biblical vocabulary composed in Hebrew in which the view then prevailing, that there were both uniliteral and biliteral roots, was definitely systematized and worked out. This theory was set aside later by Menahem's own pupil, Ḥayyuj, who correctly assumed the triliteral character of Hebrew roots; but, because it was written in Hebrew, Menahem's dictionary remained for a long time the chief source of philological instruction for Jews who were unacquainted with Arabic, especially, therefore, for those in the Christian countries of Europe. Thus Rashi in the second half of the eleventh century refers to Menahem as a philological authority; Rashi's grandson, Jacob b. Meïr Tam, composed a work for the special purpose of vindicating Menahem against the attacks of Dunash; and (about 1140) Menahem b. Solomon composed in Italy a dictionary which was based for the most part on the "Maḥberet."

Characteristics of His Dictionary.

Regarding the grammatical importance of Menahem ben Saruḳ's work, it may be noted that, although he had no systematic knowledge of the forms of the language, and was unacquainted even with Saadia's grammatical works, yet he recognized throughout his lexicon that there are inviolable laws underlying the language, and that its forms and phenomena are subject to definite rules. This insight, which appears in the terminology he employs, bridges the apparent chasm between him and his pupil Ḥayyuj. As Menahem composed his work in Hebrew, he could not use the terminology of the Arabic grammarians; yet he tacitly adopted some of their terms, translating them into Hebrew, and explained some words, although without acknowledging it, on the analogy of kindred Arabic expressions. He avoids, however, any open comparison of the language of the Bible with that of the Koran, notwithstanding the precedent furnished him by Saadia and Ibn Ḳuraish, authors whom he quotes in his dictionary. He doubtless refrained from such comparison because of the narrow-minded religious prejudice which then prevented the Spanish Jews from engaging in such linguistic comparisons.

Menahem ben Saruk's dictionary was edited by Filipowski (London, 1854), and addenda from the Bern manuscript of the "Mahberet" were published by D. Kaufmann in "Z. D. M. G." xl. 367-409. The defense by Menahem's pupils was edited by S. G. Stern in "Liber Responsionum" (Vienna, 1870), where Menahem's letter to Hasdai ibn Shaprut (first edited by Luzzatto in "Bet ha-Ozar") is reprinted (pp. xxiii.-xxxvii.).

Editions.

BIBLIOGRAPHY: S. Gross, *Menahem b. Saruk*, Berlin, 1872; Bacher, in Winter and Wünsche, *Jüdische Litteratur*, ii. 145-149; idem, *Die Anfänge der Hebräischen Grammatik*, pp. 70-95; Dukes, *Beiträge zur Gesch. der Aeltesten Auslegung und Spracherklärung des A. T.* ii. 119 *et seq.*; Grätz, *Gesch.* 1st ed., v. 372 *et seq.*; Geiger, *Das Judenthum und Seine Gesch.* ii. 87 *et seq.*; *Jüdische Zeitschrift*, ix. 65, x. 81; Drachman, *Die Stellung und Bedeutung des Jehudah Hajjug in der Gesch. der Hebräischen Grammatik*, pp. 17-27, Breslau, 1885; Weiss, *Dor*, iv. 228-234; Steinschneider, *Cat. Bodl.* col. 1738.

T. W. B.

MENAHEM BEN SIMEON: French Biblical commentator at the end of the twelfth century; a native of Posquières and a pupil of Joseph Kimhi. The Bibliothèque Nationale, Paris (MS. No. 192, 1-2), contains Menahem's commentary to the books of Jeremiah and Ezekiel; the commentary to the former was completed in 1191; the commentary to the latter ends in the middle of ch. xl.

BIBLIOGRAPHY: Gross, *Gallia Judaica*, p. 450.

J. M. SEL.

MENAHEM B. SOLOMON B. ISAAC: Author of the "Sekel Tob" and the "Eben Bohan"; flourished in the first half of the twelfth century. The presence of twenty-five Italian glosses in his works indicates that he lived in Italy. The "Sekel Tob," written in 1139 at Rome, is a midrashic compilation on the Pentateuch. The substance of the old midrashim is quoted in smooth and ornate language, from which foreign words are excluded, the general method being that of Tobias b. Eliezer's "Lekah Tob," which is frequently quoted, both with and without acknowledgment. Menahem's sources, in addition to the Targumim, are the whole of the earlier midrashic literature as well as the literature of geonic mysticism. He interprets also halakic authors, especially Alfasi and R. Hananeel, explaining verses as well as single words literally, although he expressly states that the midrashic interpretation is deeper and more thorough. "Sekel Tob" is frequently quoted both for its exegesis and for its halakic decisions. In the Middle Ages it was still intact, but now only the portion from Gen. xv. 1 to Ex. xi. 2 (edited by Buber, Berlin, 1900) is in existence, in two separate manuscripts in the Bodleian Library. Fragments of his commentary to Leviticus are found in a Munich manuscript, and, according to Steinschneider, portions of a similar commentary to the Five Megillot are contained in a codex at Berlin.

Of Menahem's other work, the "Eben Bohan," only fragments are extant (Munich MS. No. 55). A part of it has been translated by Dukes, and it has been analyzed in detail by Bacher. This work, completed at Rome in 1143, in five months, was intended to prepare the author's three young sons for the study of the Bible. Menahem undertook to prepare for the first time in Hebrew a comprehensive manual of the Hebrew language and of Biblical exegesis. The work was divided into fifty parts; the first part, by far the largest and most valuable, was a dictionary of the Hebrew language; the other parts, now known only by their chapter-headings, dealt with grammar. The author follows chiefly Menahem b. Saruk; occasionally, and with diffidence, however, he advances his own views, and the entire conception of the form and contents of the work shows a certain degree of independence. It was intended, according to Bacher, to uphold Menahem b. Saruk's system against the teachings of Hayyuj and Ibn Janah, introduced about that time (1143) into Italy by Abraham ibn Ezra.

BIBLIOGRAPHY: Zunz, *Z. G.* pp. 71, 108; Bacher, *Die Hebr. Sprachwissenschaft* (Winter and Wünsche, *Die Jüdische Litteratur*, ii. 185); idem, *Bibelexegese* (*ib.* ii. 272); idem, *Einleitung zum Sechel Tob*, pp. i., lx., Berlin, 1900; Dukes, *Kobez 'al-Yad*, part 1, Esslingen, 1846; Kirchheim, in *Orient, Lit.* vii. 439; Steinschneider, *Hebr. Bibl.* xvii. 28 *et seq.*, 134 *et seq.*; Bacher, *Der Prüfstein des Menahem b. Salomo*, in *Grätz Jubelschrift*, pp. 94-115.

J. A. B.

MENAHEM OF TIKTIN (MaHaRaM TIKTIN; MENAHEM DAVID BEN ISAAC): Polish rabbi and author of the sixteenth century; pupil of Moses Isserles. Menahem occupied himself with emending and annotating various texts; his notes on the halakot of Isaac Alfasi and Mordecai b. Hillel have been published under the title "Haggahot Maharam Tiktin." These "haggahot" were first published by Menahem's son Asher (Cracow, 1597-1598), and have since been republished in the editions of Alfasi. According to Asher b. Menahem (preface to his edition of the "Haggahot"), Menahem wrote many other works, and particularly notes to the Targum, to the commentaries of Rashi and Nahmanides, to the prayers and piyyutim, to the Zohar and other cabalistic works.

BIBLIOGRAPHY: Fuenn, *Kiryah Ne'emanah*, p. 58; Fürst, *Bibl. Jud.* ii. 351-352; Steinschneider, *Cat. Bodl.* col. 1742.

E. C. M. SEL.

MENAHEM VARDIMAS BEN PEREZ THE ELDER: French tosafist and liturgist; died at Dreux 1224. The name "Vardimas," found in Talmud Babli (Shab. 118b) as a bye-name of Menahem bar Jose, was adopted by this tosafist probably to distinguish him from other persons bearing the name "Menahem." According to Gross, Menahem is identical with the person of the same name mentioned by Samuel of Falaise as having been his master, the epithet "Ha-Kadosh" given by Samuel meaning simply "the Pious" and not "the Martyr."

Menahem's authority in halakic matters is invoked by Moses of Coucy ("Semag," § 27) and by many others. He is mentioned among those who took part in the famous discussion on phylacteries, which, according to Gedaliah ibn Yahya ("Shalshelet ha-Kabbalah," p. 52a), was held in Menahem's house. In a manuscript commentary on the Pentateuch (Neubauer, "Cat. Bodl. Hebr. MSS." No. 270) Menahem is cited as a Biblical commentator. A liturgical poem of his on the sacrifice of Isaac is inserted in the ritual of Rosh ha-Shanah.

BIBLIOGRAPHY: Zunz, *Z. G.* pp. 53, 193; idem, *Literaturgesch.* p. 328; Neubauer, in *R. E. J.* xvii. 153; *idem*, in Geiger's *Jüdische Zeit.* ix. 218; Gross, *Gallia Judaica*, p. 173.

S. S. I. BR.

MENAHEM BEN ẒEBI: German rabbi; died at Posen (?) in 1724. He was the pupil of R. Heschel and of Aaron Samuel Kaidanover (author of "Birkat ha-Zebaḥ"). He wrote: "Ẓinẓenet Menaḥem" (Berlin, 1719), an elucidation of difficult passages in the Haggadah; "Leḥem Menaḥem," responsa, and explanations of various Talmudic passages; and "Ṭa'ame Menaḥem," on Rashi's commentary on the Pentateuch.

BIBLIOGRAPHY: Steinschneider, *Cat. Bodl.* No. 6372; Azulai, *Shem ha-Gedolim*, ii. 125.
E. C. A. S. W.

MENAHEM ZIONI (ẒIYYUNI) B. MEÏR OF SPEYER: Cabalist of the middle of the fifteenth century; author of the cabalistic commentary "Ẓiyyuni," from which he derives his name. He based his work upon Rashi and Naḥmanides, and especially upon the old cabalistic literature of the geonic period. The "Ẓiyyuni" is introduced by poems in alphabetic and acrostic order. The division Bereshit begins with a preface on the importance of the assumption of the creation of the world, and in support of this view the arguments of Maimonides are quoted at length. Short poems serve as transitions to the several parashiyyot, and in conclusion there is an acrostic poem, to which, in the second edition, another poem is added. The verse of Zioni quoted by Dukes ("Orient, Lit." iv. 798) from a manuscript chrestomathy constitutes the last stanza of this final poem. The book is frequently quoted in the Yalḳuṭ Re'ubeni. It was printed by Vincentio Conti at Cremona in 1559, in rabbinic script, and after this edition was burned (in the same year) by marauding Spanish soldiers, it was reprinted there in the following year. Menahem is not to be identified with Menahem Zion b. Meïr מלא דבר (as does Heidenheim, "Pijjutim und Pajtanim," p. 8), a payyeṭan of the twelfth century well known under the name of "Menahem b. Machir" (Zunz, "G. V." 2d ed., p. 405).

BIBLIOGRAPHY: Ph. Bloch, *Die Jüdische Mystik und Kabbala*, in Winter and Wünsche, *Die Jüdische Litteratur*, iii. 282; Zunz, *Z. G.* p. 105; Wolf, *Bibl. Hebr.* i. 774; Steinschneider, *Cat. Bodl.* col. 1742.
J. A. B.

MENAHEM-ZION BEN SOLOMON (generally called **Menahem-Ẓiyyon R. Zalman Gabbai's**): Polish rabbi and preacher; died at Altona in 1681. He was at first rabbi of Vladislav, government of Suwalki, Russian Poland, and then dayyan at Cracow. He wrote a work entitled "Neḥamot Ẓiyyon" (Frankfort-on-the-Main, 1677), a collection of twenty-two sermons.

BIBLIOGRAPHY: Wolf, *Bibl. Hebr.* i., No. 1451; Steinschneider, *Cat. Bodl.* col. 1733.
H. R. M. SEL.

MENAḤOT ("Meat-Offerings"): Treatise in the Mishnah, in the Tosefta, and in the Babylonian Talmud. It discusses chiefly the more precise details of the regulations governing the different kinds of meat-offering mentioned in Lev. ii. 5, 11–13; vi. 7–11; vii. 9, 10; xxiii. 13, 16; Num. v. 11 *et seq.*, vi. 13–20, xxviii., and xxix. In the Mishnaic order Ḳodashim this treatise is second. It is divided into thirteen chapters, containing ninety-three paragraphs in all.

Ch. i.: The intention requisite to make an offering valid; the omissions through which a meat-offering becomes "pasul" (unfit) or "piggul" (an abomination: if the person sacrificing intends to eat it after the allotted time, it becomes piggul; if he intends to eat it outside the place appointed for it, it becomes pasul); how the handful ("ḳomeẓ") is to be taken; the oil necessary for the ḳomeẓ, and the incense.

"Pasul" and "Piggul."

Ch. ii.: Further details concerning pasul and piggul, according to the different kinds of offerings; how the various parts of an offering affect one another in regard to piggul.

Ch. iii.: The circumstances under which a meat-offering remains kasher; how the parts of an offering, or how different offerings presented together, affect one another in regard to pasul. In this connection many other things are enumerated which render one another invalid, *e.g.*, the two sections of the law ("parashiyyot") in the mezuzah, or the four in the tefillin.

Ch. iv.: Continued enumeration of those things which do or do not render one another pasul (this affords an occasion to explain how the Israelites in the wilderness sacrificed and how the altar, the table, and the candlesticks were consecrated); the meat-offering of the high priest.

Mode of Sacrifice.

Ch. v.: Preparation of the meat-offerings; the offerings which need additional ingredients, and what these must be; what offerings must be brought near the altar ("haggashah") and what offerings must be waved ("tenufah"); what offerings must be both brought near the altar and waved; what offerings may be neither waved nor brought near.

Ch. vi.: Offerings from which only a handful is taken and offerings which are placed entire upon the altar; further details concerning the preparation of the meat-offering.

Ch. vii.: Regulations concerning the sacrifice of thanksgiving ("todah") and concerning the offering of the Nazarites. Here it is stated that the measures were changed, and that the new so-called "Jerusalem" measure was one-sixth larger than the old one, termed "midbari" (from the desert).

Ch. viii.: Whence the materials were taken for the different meat-offerings (here are mentioned the places which produced the best flour and the best oil); how the best oil and flour was obtained; where the best wine was found and how it was tested.

Ch. ix.: The different measures used in the Temple to measure the flour, the oil, and the wine for the various offerings; drink-offerings; the sacrifices for which drink-offerings were requisite; the laying of hands upon the sacrificial animal ("semikah"); the sacrifices in which this takes place, and who may perform the semikah.

Ch. x.: The wave-offering ("omer"); when and whence it was brought; the ceremonial observed in the cutting of it and how it was offered; the regulation introduced by R. Johanan b. Zakkai after the destruction of the Temple.

Wave-Offering.

Ch. xi.: The preparation of the pentecostal bread and of the showbread; the size of the loaves and when they may be eaten; the placing of the showbread on the table and the distribution of it among the priests.

Ch. xii.: Exemption from meat- and drink-offerings; the time after which exemption is no longer possible; offerings from which no one may be exempted; vows of meat- and drink-offerings; how the vow may be fulfilled.

Intention of Sacrifice.

Ch. xiii.: Regulations concerning vows of offerings which are not strictly defined; sacrifices vowed for the temple at Jerusalem may not be offered in the temple of Onias, or vice versa; the priests of the temple of Onias are not permitted to serve in the temple at Jerusalem. The conclusion of the chapter and of the treatise runs: "It is immaterial whether one sacrifices much or little so long as his mind is intent on God."

The order given above is that of the editions of the Mishnah and of many manuscripts of the Talmud (comp. the observation of R. Bezaleel Ashkenazi at the end of the "Shiṭṭah Meḳubbeẓet" on Menaḥot, in the Wilna edition of the Talmud, p. 109b). On the other hand, all the printed editions of the Talmud have the chapter beginning "R. Ishmael," given above as the tenth, in the sixth place, the remaining chapters occurring in the order given above. Special attention should be given to the account in the Tosefta to this treatise of the acts of greed and violence committed by the priests during the time of the Second Temple, which was destroyed because of their rapacity and mutual hatred (xiii. 18–22). The Gemara contains, in the third chapter, interesting observations on the forms of Hebrew letters and on the regulations for the writing of the Torah, of tefillin, and of the mezuzah, while in the fourth chapter are regulations concerning the ẓiẓit.

Special Passages.

The following passages also are specially noteworthy: p. 53a, b—an instance of the peculiar style of R. Ezra's haggadic exegesis; the tradition as to how God justified Himself to Abraham for the destruction of the Temple and the exile of the people; the comparing of Israel to an olive-tree; p. 99b—the attitude of R. Ishmael toward Greek culture; p. 109b—the account of the origin of the temple of Onias. The last passage is important enough to be repeated here: "At the hour of his death the high priest Simon the Just appointed his younger but learned son Onias to be his successor. Onias renounced his claim in favor of his elder brother Shimei. Onias, however, secretly grudged him his position and endeavored to supplant him. Consequently when Shimei, who was inexperienced in the priestly service, asked Onias to instruct him in its duties, the latter misled him into putting on a woman's cap and girdle to officiate in, and then told the priests that Shimei had promised his beloved to officiate in her cap and girdle on the day of his installation in office. When the priests threatened to kill Shimei for thus trifling with the service, he told them how the matter really stood. Thereupon the priests sought the death of Onias, but he fled to Egypt and there built his temple." There is no Jerusalem Gemara to Menaḥot. The Tosafot to Menaḥot (109b, reference word, "nizdamen") refers to Yerushalmi Yoma (v. 2), where the passage cited is found.

Bibliography: Isaiah di Trani, *Tosafot* (in the Warsaw edition of the Talmud, 1861, wrongly designated as "Ḥiddushim" of Solomon ben Adret).

s. J. Z. L.

MENAḲḲER. See Porging.

MENANDER: 1. Putative author of a collection of proverbs, in a Syriac manuscript in the British Museum, edited in 1862 by Land, and bearing the superscription, "The sage Menander said." Either this Menander was a real person, a Hellenistic Jew whose proverbs, probably written originally in Greek, are now extant only in this Syriac translation, or the name is a pseudonym, as Schürer assumes; similar collections of proverbs were frequently ascribed to the famous Attic comedian.

Frankenberg has recently proved that these Syriac sentences are of Jewish origin, and has pointed out numerous instances of relationship between them and sentences in the canonical Book of Proverbs and in Ecclesiasticus. A few sentences quoted from Land's edition may serve to make this kinship clear.

"Rejoice with thy children, O father, for these are the [true] joys" (p. 68, line 13; comp. Prov. x. 1; Ecclus. [Sirach] xxv. 7, xxx. 4). "Whosoever wrongeth his maid servant doth not escape the vengeance of God" (p. 71, line 5; comp. Ecclus. [Sirach] xli. 22).

"Whoever committeth adultery perisheth" (p. 69, line 12; comp. Prov. ii. 18, vii. 27).

"He who sleepeth at an untimely season hateth counsel and guidance; for such sleep bringeth death and destruction" (p. 66, line 3; comp. Prov. vi. 9-11, xix. 15, xx. 13). "If thou art about to take a wife, see that she hath no evil tongue, for a quarrelsome woman is hell, and an evil man is death" (p. 66, below; comp. Ecclus. [Sirach] xxv. 13, 19). "Fear God, and He shall save thee if thou shalt call upon Him in time of need" (p. 67, line 2; comp. Prov. xxiv. 16). "If thou sittest at meat with many, show them not thy filled purse, lest they borrow from thee without thought of repayment; or if thou remindest them, lest they provoke strife with thee, so that thou losest thy money and becomest their enemy" (p. 68, lines 7-9; comp. Ecclus. [Sirach] viii. 12; xxix. 4, 14). "Friendship is good and useful, since it endureth even to the house of death" (p. 72, line 10; comp. Ecclus. [Sirach] vi. 14, xxxvii. 2). "The heart of the fool rejoiceth in witchcraft, and the Chaldean art besotteth the understanding of the simple" (p. 70, line 6; comp. Ecclus. [Sirach] xxxi. 1). "Eat not with the wicked; for he filleth himself at thy table, and then speaketh evil of thee" (p. 70, below; comp. Ecclus. [Sirach] xi. 29). "Work diligently in youth, that thou mayest have wealth in thine age" (p. 71, lines 25 *et seq.*; comp. Prov. x. 22; Ecclus. [Sirach] xi. 10, 11). "Better one day under the sun than a hundred years in sheol" (p. 71, line 22; comp. Eccl. ix. 4). "Desirable are life, money, and the blessing of children; but of more worth is a good name" (p. 72, line 8; comp. Eccl. vii. 1).

The entire work consists of single disconnected sentences. There are no theoretical maxims on the value of wisdom, as in Proverbs and Ecclesiasticus, but only guides to practical life; concerning this there is hardly a theme in Menander that is not treated in the same spirit as in the two Biblical books. The ritual aspect of religion, however, is hardly mentioned.

The entire lack of Christian allusions in the collection may be held to confirm its Jewish origin. Pagan references are found only in the mention of Homer and in the rather long polemic against impious priests who despise their own gods and are gluttonous at banquets (p. 69). Frankenberg interprets this passage as referring to Jewish conditions, while Schürer regards it as a Gentile interpolation.

The only allusions to the date of composition point to the period of Roman rule, for gladiators are mentioned (p. 65, line 14) and crucifixion is declared to be the punishment for theft (p. 70, line 8), although the mention of priests and tithes implies the time of the Temple.

BIBLIOGRAPHY: Land, *Anecdota Syriaca*, i., Leyden, 1862; Frankenberg, *Die Schrift des Menander ein Produkt der Jüdischen Spruchweisheit*, in Stade's *Zeitschrift*, 1895, xv. 226-277; Schürer, *Gesch.* 3d ed., iii. 476-478.

2. Historian; a native of Ephesus; lived probably at the time when the kingdom and the school of Pergamos were at their zenith, whence he was called also "the Pergamonian"; apparently, one of the pupils of Eratosthenes (276-195 B.C.). Menander wrote a history of Phenicia, taking his material from the original documents in the archives at Tyre. As he mentions the fact that King Hiram had wood taken from the forests of Lebanon for the building of the Temple, he is cited by Josephus ("Ant." ix. 14, § 2) as a witness for the verity of Biblical history; and also in connection with Assyrian history Menander has a curious reference, unknown elsewhere, to the younger son of a certain Abdemon, who is said to have vanquished Solomon in guessing riddles (Josephus, "Contra Ap." i. 18; *idem*, "Ant." viii. 5, § 3).

BIBLIOGRAPHY: C. Müller, *Fragmenta Historicorum Græcorum*, iv. 445; Th. Reinach, *Textes d'Auteurs Grecs et Romains Relatifs au Judaïsme*, i. 44-46, Paris, 1895.

J. S. KR.

MENDE: Capital of the ancient county of Gévaudan; now chief town in the department of Lozère, France. In the twelfth century a Jewish community existed here, having a synagogue, whose ruins still (1904) remain. In 1307 a contention arose between Philip the Fair, King of France, and the Bishop of Mende on the question of the possessions of the Jews who had been expelled in the preceding year. In April, 1310, an arrangement between the king and the bishop was made by virtue of which Philip abandoned to the latter one-third of the confiscated goods of the Jews, as well as a house at Mende which had belonged to a Jew named Ferrier.

Other parts also of Gévaudan were inhabited by Jews in the Middle Ages, as **Marvejols** or **Marvège** (מרויש), where Jacob ha-Levi, the mystic, lived about 1203; **Villefort** (וילפורט), where the site of the old Jewish cemetery is still known ("Mémoires de la Société Royale des Antiquaires de France," viii. 334); and others. Even in their names several villages indicate the former residence of Jews there, as Salmon, formerly Salomon; Mont-David, Booz, Ruth, and Obed (*ib.* p. 320).

BIBLIOGRAPHY: Saige, *Les Juifs du Languedoc*, pp. 14, 101, 324; Depping, *Les Juifs dans le Moyen Age*, p. 133; Bédarride, *Les Juifs en France, en Italie, et en Espagne*, p. 227; F. André, *Notice sur les Juifs en Gévaudan*, in *Bulletin de la Société Historique de Lozère*, 1872, historical part, pp. 85-91; Gross, *Gallia Judaica*, p. 364.

D. S. K.

MENDEL: Name of a prominent Hungarian family which flourished in the latter half of the fifteenth century and in the first half of the sixteenth in Ofen (Buda). Members of three generations of it are known; namely, **Jacob, Israel,** and **Isaac Mendel,** who held the office of "Princeps Judæorum," "Supremus Judæorum," or "Præfectus Judæorum" between 1482 and 1539. This office, which seems to have existed only during that period, was created by King Matthias in order to give the Jews an accredited representative at court, who at the same time should be responsible for the payment of their taxes. The "Præfectus Judæorum" was empowered to impose fines and other penalties on the Jews. As an official of the crown he was exempted from wearing the Jews' hat.

BIBLIOGRAPHY: Kohn, *Magyar Zsidók Története*, pp. 216 et seq.; Engel, *Gesch. des Ungarischen Reiches*, i. 80 et seq.; Büchler, *A Zsidók Története Budapesten*, pp. 50 et seq.; Venetianer, *A Zsidóság Szerverete*, pp. 273 et seq., 326 et seq.

D. L. V.

MENDEL, EMANUEL: German physician; born at Bunzlau, Silesia, Oct. 28, 1839; educated at the universities of Breslau, Vienna, and Berlin (M.D. 1860). In 1861 he took charge of a private insane asylum at Pankow, near Berlin. He served as surgeon in the Franco-Prussian war (1870-71), and gained the Iron Cross. In 1871 he removed to Berlin and became privat-docent in psychiatry at the university, and in 1884 was made assistant professor. From 1877 to 1881 he was a member of the German Reichstag. He died June 23, 1907.

Mendel was collaborator in psychiatry on Eulenburg's "Realencyclopädie der Gesammten Heilkunde," Ebstein-Schwalbe's "Handbuch der Praktischen Medizin," and Tuke's "Journal of Mental Science." He wrote many essays in the medical journals, especially on psychiatry, and is editor of the "Neurologisches Centralblatt" and of the "Jahresbericht über Neurologie und Psychiatrie." Of his numerous works may be mentioned: "Progressive Paralyse der Irren," Berlin, 1880; "Die Manie," Vienna, 1881; and "Die Geisteskranken in dem Entwurf des Bürgerlichen Gesetzbuches für das Deutsche Reich," Berlin, 1889.

S. F. T. H.

MENDEL, HENRIETTE: Bavarian actress; born July 31, 1833; died at Munich Nov. 12, 1891. In early life she was noted for her beauty and histrionic talents. Having been created Baroness (Freifrau) of Wallersee in the peerage of Bavaria on May 19, 1859, she married, May 28, 1859, Duke Ludwig Wilhelm, eldest son of Duke Maximilian Joseph of Bavaria, who had renounced his rights of primogeniture in favor of his younger brother. The union was signally happy, and the issue of the marriage, Marie Luise, married Count Georg von Larisch. The baroness died after a protracted illness, and was buried according to the rites of the Catholic Church, in the city of Munich.

BIBLIOGRAPHY: *Almanach de Gotha*; *Allgemeine Zeitung*, Nov. 12-16, 1891.

S. A. M. F.

MENDEL, HERMANN: Music publisher and writer; born at Halle Aug. 6, 1834; died at Berlin Oct. 26, 1876. He received his musical education at Halle, Leipsic, and Berlin. In 1853 he entered the Berlin music-publishing house of Schlesinger, and later that of Bote & Bock. In 1862 he established a business of his own and conducted it until 1868, contributing at the same time to numerous periodicals, such as the "Echo," "Tonhalle," "Theaterdiener," "Berliner Montagszeitung," and "Deutsche Musikerzeitung," which last-named he conducted from its inception in 1870 until his death. He is best known as the projector of the celebrated "Musikalisches Konversations-Lexikon," which he began in 1870 with a large and distinguished staff of collaborators. At the time of his death, however, it had reached only the letter "M." As completed under the editorship of Dr. Reissmann, it consists of eleven volumes, and is one of the most comprehensive works of its kind. Prominent among the other publications of Mendel are his well-known biographies of Nicolai and Meyerbeer, and his edition of Mode's "Opernbibliothek," consisting of about ninety opera-libretti, with preface, etc.

BIBLIOGRAPHY: Grove, *Dictionary of Music and Musicians*; Riemann, *Musik-Lexikon*.

S. J. So.

MENDELSBURG, LEON: Russian teacher and writer; born at Hodava, Russian Poland, 1819; died at Warsaw March, 1897. He studied Talmud at Tomashov, where Phinehas-Mendel Heilprin exercised a beneficial influence on his education. In 1850 Mendelsburg was appointed government teacher at the Jewish public school in Novograd-Volhynsk; and in 1854 he was transferred to the rabbinical school at Jitomir, where he remained until the closing of that school by the government (July 1, 1873). He then settled in Koretz, and later removed to Warsaw. From 1850 Mendelsburg was a constant contributor in German to the "Allgemeine Zeitung des Judenthums," in which he published valuable papers on the life of the Jews in Russia. He published also "Dichtung und Warhheit" (Leipsic, 1862), a volume of sketches of Russo-Jewish life.

BIBLIOGRAPHY: Sokolow, *Sefer Zikkaron*, p. 72; *Ha-Ẓefirah*, 1897, p. 233.

H. R. J. G. L.

MENDELSOHN, JOSEPH: German author; born at Jever Sept. 10, 1817; died at Hamburg April 4, 1856. He was admitted at an early age to the Jewish free school at Hamburg, and in 1831 entered a printing establishment at Brunswick as an apprentice, remaining there as journeyman until 1839. On his return to Hamburg he devoted himself to literature, but shortly afterward, aided by Solomon Heine, he went to Paris for further study. In 1841 he returned to Hamburg and resumed his literary work.

Mendelsohn was the author of the following works: "Blüthen. Gedichte und Novellen eines Schriftsetzers" (Brunswick, 1839), with a preface by F. K. von Strombeck; "Pariser Briefe" (1841); "Wilde Blumen" (1842); "Ueberall Jesuiten" (1846); and some comedies from the French, including "Er Muss Aufs Land" (1845) and "Ein Weib aus dem Volke" (1846).

BIBLIOGRAPHY: Brümmer, *Lexikon Deutscher Dichter und Prosaisten*, ii. 29.

S. M. K.

MENDELSOHN, MARTIN: German physician; born at Posen Dec. 16, 1860; studied medicine at the universities of Leipsic and Berlin (M.D. 1885). After a year spent in Paris, where he took a postgraduate course, he established himself as a physician in Berlin, becoming assistant at the first medical clinic and later at the Charité Hospital. In 1895 he was admitted as privat-docent to the medical faculty of Berlin University, and received the title of professor in 1899.

Mendelsohn has collaborated on Eulenburg's "Realencyclopädie der Gesammten Heilkunde," and since 1894 has edited the "Zeitschrift für Krankenpflege." He has contributed many essays (about 100) to the medical journals, and is the author of: "Das Opium," Berlin, 1888; "Der Comfort des Kranken," *ib.* 1890 (2d ed. 1892); "Aerztliche Kunst und Medizinische Wissenschaft," Wiesbaden, 1893; "Einfluss des Radfahrens auf den Menschlichen Organismus," Berlin, 1896; "Krankenpflege für Mediziner," *ib.* 1899.

BIBLIOGRAPHY: Pagel, *Biog. Lex.*

S. F. T. H.

MENDELSOHN, SAMUEL: American rabbi and scholar; born in Shillelen, province of Kovno, Russia, March 31, 1850. He was educated at the rabbinical college, Wilna, at the rabbinic school, Berlin, and at Maimonides' College, Philadelphia, Pa. (1873). In 1883 he received the honorary degree of doctor of law from the University of North Carolina. Mendelsohn was rabbi of the Congregation Beth-El, Norfolk, Va., from 1873 to 1876, since which date he has served as rabbi of the Congregation Temple of Israel, Wilmington, N. C.

Mendelsohn has published "The Criminal Jurisprudence of the Ancient Hebrews" (Baltimore, 1891), in addition to several pamphlets and a large number of articles, on subjects of general Jewish interest and Talmudical research, in "Ha-Ẓofeh," the "Jewish Messenger," "Jewish Record," "South Atlantic Magazine," "American Israelite," and "Revue des Etudes Juives."

In 1879 he married Esther Jastrow, niece of the Rev. Dr. M. Jastrow. He has one son, **Charles Jastrow Mendelsohn**; the latter was fellow in classics in the University of Pennsylvania (1901–1903), where he also received the degree of doctor of philosophy in 1904. A.

MENDELSON, MORRITZ EMANUILOVICH: Polish physiologist and physician; born at Warsaw 1855. He studied medicine at the University of Warsaw, and received his doctor's degree from the University of Kharkov in 1884. From 1876 to 1887 he worked in various laboratories and clinics in Europe: at Berlin under Dubois-Reymond; at Erlangen under Rosenthal; and at Paris under Charcot and Mars of the Collége de France, where he was for some time assistant also. Since 1890 he has been privat-docent in physiology in the University of St. Petersburg.

Among the medical works of Mendelson the following may be mentioned: "Etude sur le Temps Perdu des Muscles," in "Publ. du Collége de France," 1879; "Recherches Cliniques sur la Periode d'Excitation Latente," in "Archives de Physiologie Normale," 1880; "Action de la Veratrine sur le Muscle," *ib.* 1883; "Excitabilité et Travail Mécanique du Muscle," in "Publ. de l'Académie des Sciences," Paris, 1883.

BIBLIOGRAPHY: *Entziklopedicheski Slovar*, xix. 82.

H. R. A. S. W.

MENDELSON, MOSES (called also **Moses ben Mendel Frankfort**): German Hebraist and writer of the eighteenth and nineteenth centuries; born in Hamburg; died there at an advanced age in 1861; a relative of Samson Raphael Hirsch.

Mendelson lived in his native city as a private scholar. He translated into Hebrew the first book of Campe's "Die Entdeckung Amerika's," entitling it "Meẓi'at ha-Areẓ ha-Ḥadashah" (Altona, 1807), and wrote a poem in honor of Ḥakam Isaac Bernays on the occasion of his installation at Hamburg (*ib.* 1822). His "Baḳḳashat ha-Lammedin," printed by Meïr Hesse, appeared anonymously (*ib.* 1829). He also published: "Shushan 'Edut, d. i. die Erklärung der Fünf Bücher Moshe's" (Stuttgart, 1840–42), two parts, containing the Book of Genesis and representing, according to his own statement, the fruit of thirty years' labor. The Hebrew introduction to the second section (pp. iii.–lxx.) consists of two treatises, "'Awon ha-Doresh ha-Yashan" and "'Awon ha-Doresh he-Ḥadash," in which in diverting fashion he scourges the old "darshanim" and the modern preachers. Mendelson wrote also "Die Synagoge zu Hamburg, Wie Sie War und Wie Sie Sein Soll" (Copenhagen, 1842), dedicated to the president of the German Jewish congregation of Hamburg.

Bibliography: Roest, *Cat. Rosenthal. Bibl.* p. 382; Fürst, *Bibl. Jud.* ii. 359.

S. M. K.

MENDELSSOHN: German family rendered illustrious by the philosopher and the musician. It can not verify its ancestry further back than the father of the philosopher, though there is a family tradition that it is descended from Moses Isserles.

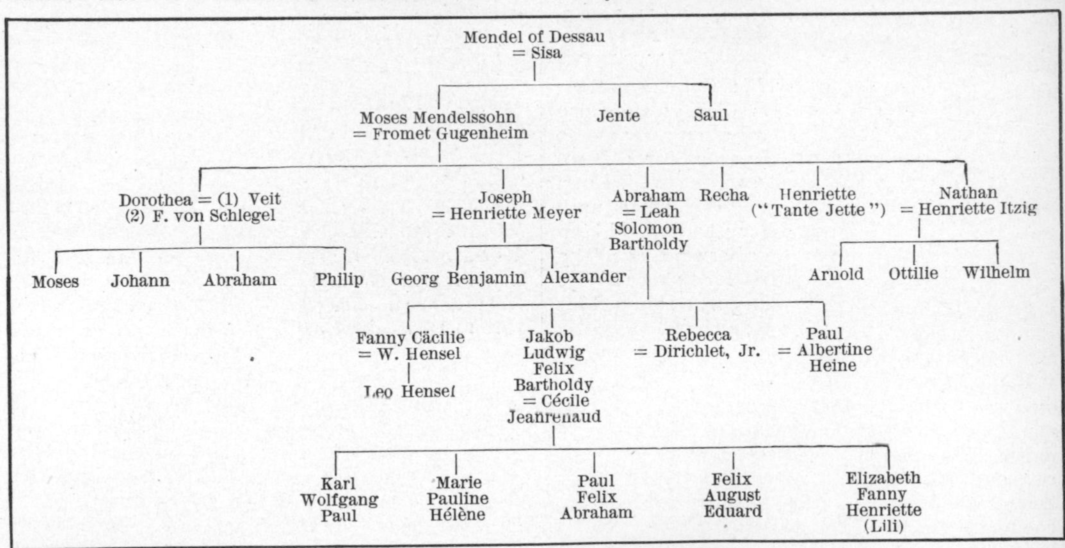

Mendelssohn Family Tree.

Bibliography: S. Hensel, *Die Familie Mendelssohn*, Berlin, 1879; Freudenthal, *Aus dem Heimat Mendelssohn*, Berlin, 1900.

J. I. G. D.

Abraham Mendelssohn: Second son of Moses Mendelssohn; born at Berlin Dec. 10, 1776; died there Nov. 19, 1835; father of Felix Mendelssohn-Bartholdy. In 1803 he became cashier in Foulds' banking-house at Paris; but a year later he returned to Hamburg and went into partnership with his brother Joseph. At the same time he married Leah Salomon, a granddaughter of Daniel Itzig, and was persuaded by his brother-in-law, who at baptism had adopted the name of Bartholdy, to call himself "Mendelssohn-Bartholdy." During the siege of Hamburg by the French, Abraham and his brother were obliged to leave the city on a foggy night secretly and in disguise. They went to Berlin and founded there the banking firm of Mendelssohn & Co., from which Abraham later retired. In the year 1813 he equipped several volunteers at his own expense, and in recognition of his efforts for the public welfare he was elected to the municipal council of Berlin.

Dorothea (Brendel) Mendelssohn: Eldest daughter of Moses Mendelssohn; born at Berlin on Dec. 24, 1764; died at Frankfort-on-the-Main on Aug. 3, 1839. On account of her superior intelligence and her somewhat masculine nature she was even in her youth the leader in the circle of her friends. Early in April, 1783, she married a Berlin banker named Veit, an honest, worthy man, but of limited education and not prepossessing in appearance. After fifteen years of a married life far from happy, Dorothea became acquainted with Friedrich von Schlegel, at the house of Henriette Herz, a friend of her youth, who had advised her a few years after her marriage to Veit to separate from him. Schlegel, at that time young, handsome, and already famous, was captivated by the brilliant intellect of Dorothea, seven years his senior, despite her lack of beauty. She deserted Veit for Schlegel, being disowned by her family. In 1799 Schlegel took her to Jena, where he was unsuccessful. She shared his troubles and endured his moods, and in 1802 traveled with him to Paris, where she became a Protestant and married him. Six years later, on the return journey, she, with her husband and her son Philip, went over to Catholicism at Cologne.

Dorothea paid a severe penalty for her relations

with Schlegel, and was often obliged to struggle against abject poverty. For several years she lived on the scanty income from her literary labors and from what her deserted husband sent her anonymously from time to time. In 1818 and 1819 she lived at Rome with her sons Johann and Philip Veit, who had become artists. The rest of her eventful, unhappy life was passed at Frankfort-on-the-Main, where Schlegel was councilor at the Austrian legation, and where, after his death (1829), she lived with her son Philip on a small pension.

While still Schlegel's mistress she had made a literary venture in the novel "Florentine," which was published by him anonymously (Lübeck and Leipsic, 1801), and which was considered the best production of the romanticists in the domain of fiction. Under Schlegel's name appeared her version of the old German metrical romance "Lother und Maller" (Frankfort-on-the-Main, 1805) and the translation of Madame de Staël's "Corinne" (Berlin, 1807). From Old French she translated the "Gesch. des Zauberers Merlin" in Schlegel's "Sammlung Romantischer Dichtungen" (Leipsic, 1804), and she furnished several articles, signed "D," for the magazine "Europa," which Schlegel edited. Later she exchanged the pen for the needle. "There are," she said, "too many books in the world; but I have never heard that there are too many shirts."

Bibliography: Reichlin-Meldegg, *Paulus und Seine Zeit*, Stuttgart, 1853, vol. ii., and the autobiography of Sulpice Boisserée, *ib.* 1862, containing many of Dorothea's letters; Kayserling, *Die Jüdischen Frauen*, p. 183; idem, *Dorothea von Schlegel*, in R. Prutz, *Deutsches Museum*, 1860, Nos. 49 *et seq.*; S. Hensel, *Die Familie Mendelssohn*, i. 45 *et seq.*, Berlin, 1879.

Fanny Mendelssohn: Eldest daughter of Abraham Mendelssohn; born at Hamburg Nov. 15, 1805; died there May 17, 1847. When very young she manifested an exceptional memory and talent for music. She, together with her brother Felix, received her musical training from Ludwig Berger and Zelter, while her education in other subjects was conducted by the philologist Karl Heyse, who was tutor in the Mendelssohn house. In the year 1829 she married the painter W. Hensel in Berlin. She was herself a composer, and many of her brother Felix's "Songs Without Words" are believed to be her work (Hensel, *l.c.* vols. i.-iii.).

D. M. K.

Felix Mendelssohn.

Felix Mendelssohn (full name, **Jakob Ludwig Felix Mendelssohn-Bartholdy**): German composer; born at Hamburg Feb. 3, 1809; died at Leipsic Nov. 4, 1847. He was a grandson of Moses Mendelssohn and a son of the banker Abraham Mendelssohn, who removed to Berlin in 1811. Felix received his early musical education from Ludwig Berger (piano), Zelter (thorough-bass and composition), and Henning (violin). At the age of ten he entered the Singakademie at Berlin as an alto, and in the following year composed the cantata "In Rührend Feierlichen Tönen" as well as several instrumental pieces.

The encouraging words of Cherubini, before whom Mendelssohn played while on a visit to Paris with his father in 1825, animated the young composer; on Aug. 6, 1826, he finished his overture to "Ein Sommernachtstraum" (A Midsummer Night's Dream, op. 21), which composition was publicly performed at Stettin in Feb., 1827. During this season Mendelssohn's opera "Die Hochzeit des Camacho" was produced at the Berlin Theater, but was soon withdrawn by Spontini, who at that time enjoyed almost unlimited authority as director of the opera, and is said to have had a personal antipathy to the young musician. During the following winter Mendelssohn began a propaganda in behalf of Bach's music, which culminated in the formation of a Bach Society and the publication of the masses of Bach as well as of all the church cantatas and other works of the great German composer.

On April 10, 1829, Mendelssohn left Berlin for London, where, in the following month, he made his début with much success at a concert of the Philharmonic Society. It was therefore from an English audience that he first received an acknowledgment of his genius. He gave five concerts in London, whence, in July, 1831, he set out upon a journey through Scotland, as a result of which he wrote one of his most beautiful overtures, "Die Hebriden" (The Hebrides, op. 26).

Always somewhat unpopular in Berlin, he, on his return to that city in 1833, failed in competition with Rungenhagen to obtain the conductorship of the Singakademie. In May of the same year, however, he was invited to conduct the Lower Rhine Musical Festival at Düsseldorf, in which city he remained as musical director until 1835, when he accepted the conductorship of the Gewandhaus orchestra in Leipsic, a body with which his name was thenceforth inseparably associated. The concerts given by this famous orchestra under Mendelssohn's leadership, and with the assistance of the eminent concert-master Ferdinand David, soon enjoyed a world-wide celebrity

Conductor of Gewandhaus Orchestra, Leipsic.

and contributed to make Leipsic the musical center of Germany. Mendelssohn's oratorio "Paulus" (St. Paul) was performed at the Lower Rhine festival held at Düsseldorf May 22–24, 1836.

On March 28, 1837, Mendelssohn married Cécile Charlotte Sophie Jeanrenaud. A few months later he left for England to conduct "Paulus" at the Birmingham festival. On his return he devoted all his energies to the Gewandhaus concerts. At the request of Frederick William IV. of Prussia, to whom several of his compositions were dedicated, Mendelssohn in 1841 went to Berlin to act as director of certain concerts which were to be given in connection with an academy of arts planned by the king. Finding, however, that the musicians and the public were more or less hostile to him, he resigned, remaining only at the special request of the king to arrange the music in the cathedral. The body of singers selected for that occasion afterward became famous as the "Domchor" (cathedral choir). During this visit Mendelssohn conducted also the music to "Antigone," which he had composed in compliance with the king's express desire.

In conjunction with Falkenstein, Keil, Kistner, Schleinitz, and Seeburg as directors, and Schumann, Hauptmann, David, Becker, and Pohlenz as teachers, Mendelssohn in 1842 organized the Conservatorium at Leipsic, which institution, under the patronage of the King of Saxony, was opened Jan. 16, 1843. During the summer of 1844 Mendelssohn revisited London, where he conducted the last five concerts given by the Philharmonic Society in that year. He took part also as a pianist in various other musical events of the season, everywhere receiving a most enthusiastic welcome. In 1846 he once more visited England, upon which occasion he conducted the first performance of his oratorio "Elias" (Elijah) at Birmingham (Aug. 26). On April 2, 1847, he conducted "Paulus" at Leipsic, and soon afterward again went to England, where he gave four performances of "Elias" at Exeter Hall, London, besides one at Manchester and another at Birmingham.

Organizes Leipsic Conservatorium.

On May 9 Mendelssohn returned to Germany. While he was at Frankfort the news of the sudden death of his sister Fanny, to whom he had been greatly attached, gave a serious shock to a constitution already enfeebled, and after visiting various health resorts the great composer returned in September to Leipsic, where about six weeks later he died. Baptized early in life, he was interred in Trinity Cemetery, Berlin.

Mendelssohn's best productions are the oratorios "Paulus" and "Elias," the greatest works of their kind since Haydn. Besides the opera "Die Hochzeit des Camacho," Mendelssohn left the unfinished opera "Lorelei," the operetta "Heimkehr aus der Fremde" (op. 89), and several other unpublished operatic compositions. Among his other works are four symphonies; the symphony-cantata "Lobgesang"; six concert-overtures; several concertos; chamber-music; and pianoforte and vocal compositions.

Bibliography: S. Hensel, *Die Familie Mendelssohn (1729-1847) nach Briefen und Tagebüchern*, Berlin, 1879; Carl Mendelssohn-Bartholdy, *Goethe und Felix Mendelssohn-Bartholdy (1821-1831)*, translated by M. E. von Glehn, London, 1872; F. Hiller, *Mendelssohn: Letters and Recollections*, translated by M. E. von Glehn, *ib.* 1874; Grove, *Dict. of Music and Musicians*, vol. ii., where a full list of Mendelssohn's compositions is given.

s. J. So.

Georg Benjamin Mendelssohn: German geographer; born in Berlin Nov. 16, 1794; died at Horchheim, near Coblenz, Aug. 24, 1874; son of Joseph Mendelssohn. As a child he went to Hamburg with his parents, but he began his studies at Berlin in 1811, although they were interrupted by the campaigns of 1813 and 1815. After 1828, being appointed privat-docent in geography and statistics at the University of Bonn, he gradually rose to the position of regular professor there. He edited the "Gesammelte Schriften" of his grandfather with a biographical sketch (Leipsic, 1843–45), and also published "Das Germanische Europa" (Berlin, 1836) as well as "Die Ständischen Institutionen im Monarchischen Staat" (Bonn, 1846).

Henriette (Sorel) Mendelssohn: Youngest daughter of Moses Mendelssohn; born at Berlin 1768; died there Nov. 9, 1831. She was a woman of broad interests, clear judgment, and exquisite manners; she remained unmarried, being, like her father, slightly deformed. She first devoted herself to teaching in her sister Recha's school in Altona, but in 1799 entered a Jewish family in Vienna as governess. After a few years, however, probably on the invitation of her brother Abraham, she went to Paris, where she was at the head of a boarding-school. Her modest apartments were the rendezvous of scholars and artists: Spontini, Madame de Staël, and Benjamin Constant were among her frequent visitors, while the two Humboldts, Von Eskeles of Vienna, and others visited her whenever they were in Paris. In the year 1812 she became governess to the daughter of Count Sebastiani and remained in the count's house until the marriage of her pupil to the Duke of Praslin, who became the murderer of his wife. Henriette, "the deepest and most thoughtful," as Rachel Levin called her, was indignant at her sister Dorothea's change of faith. Yet the course of action which she could not forgive in her sister, she later chose for herself, becoming not only a Catholic, but a bigot.

Bibliography: Kayserling, *Die Jüdischen Frauen*, pp. 197 *et seq.*; S. Hensel, *Die Familie Mendelssohn*, i. 55 *et seq.*

Joseph Mendelssohn: German banker; born at Berlin Aug. 11, 1770; died there Nov. 24, 1848; the eldest son of Moses Mendelssohn. He was highly talented, and was educated in the Talmud by Herz Homberg and in languages and science by Fischer, Engel (the tutor of the two Humboldts), and others. He attended the "Morgenstunden" given by his father, and the lectures on physics by Markus Herz and those on chemistry by Klaproth. He established himself at Hamburg, and afterward, together with his brother Abraham, founded the banking firm of Mendelssohn & Co. at Berlin. From early youth he was an intimate friend of Alexander von Humboldt, who came one day and said that his landlord had served a notice on him to vacate, which was very inconvenient for him because of his natural-history collections. Joseph listened in silence. On the

fternoon of the same day Humboldt received a let-
er saying he might live in his present house as
ng as he pleased, Mendelssohn having bought
e house and become his landlord.

Even in his latter years Mendelssohn busied him-
elf with literature and science. He published
Berichte über Rosseti's Ideen zu einer Neuen Er-
uterung des Dante und der Dichter Seiner Zeit"
Berlin, 1840) and "Ueber Zettelbanken" (*ib.* 1846).
is father's biography, published by his son G. B.
Mendelssohn, was largely Joseph's own work.

His son **Alexander** (died at Berlin Oct. 25, 1871)
as the last Jewish descendant of Moses Mendelsohn. He was at the head of the firm after his
ather's death. He
as a noble and un-
sually philanthropic
an, and was the
rst Jew to receive
e title of privy
ommercial councilor
Geheimer Commer-
enrath").

BLIOGRAPHY: Kayserling, *Moses Mendelssohn, Sein Leben und Wirken*, 2d ed., p. 451.

Karl Mendelssohn-Bartholdy: erman historian; orn Feb. 7, 1838, in eipsic; died Feb. , 1897, at Brugg, witzerland; son of elix Mendelssohn artholdy. He was ofessor of history Freiburg-im-Breisau.

Moses Mendelssohn (Moses ben enahem-Mendel; abbreviated **RaMBeaN**); German Philosopher, translator of e Bible, and commentator; the "third oses," with whom gins a new era in idaism. He was lled also, after his rthplace, **Moses essau,** with which name he signed his Hebrew and dæo-German letters; born at Dessau Sept. 6, 1729; ed at Berlin Jan. 4, 1786. Mendelssohn's father as a poor Torah scribe, whose exacting occupation d a marked influence on the delicate sense of form d the fine handwriting of his son. In spite of povty, the father carefully educated the child, whose st Hebrew teacher he was, although he later enged Rabbi Hirsch, the son of a Dessau dayyan, to struct him in the Talmud. The boy then continued s studies under the rabbi of Dessau, David FRÄNL, who introduced him to Maimonides' "Moreh Nekim." His unremitting application to his studies ought on an illness which left him with curvature the spine. In Oct., 1743, Mendelssohn went to Berlin, where Fränkel had been called as rabbi a few months earlier; but the desire for knowledge, which was being more and more awakened, could not be satisfied with the Talmud.

Early Influences.

A considerable influence was exerted upon the young Mendelssohn by a learned Pole, Israel Zamosz, who had been persecuted at home because of his liberal views. Zamosz instructed him in mathematics, and at the same time a young Jewish physician from Prague, Abraham KISCH, was his teacher in Latin. Mendelssohn had scarcely learned the principal rules of grammar when with his scanty earnings he bought a few of the Latin classics and an old Latin translation of Locke's "Essay Concerning the Human Understanding." This book, which had a profound influence on his future development, he tried with indescribable toil to decipher with the aid of a Latin dictionary. He found yet another teacher in Aaron Solomon GUMPERZ, a well-to-do Jewish medical student, who gave him lessons in French and English. Through him he acquired a taste for science and became interested in the Leibnitz-Wolffian philosophy. Gumperz, moreover, introduced him to several able young gymnasium teachers and to Maupertuis, the president of the Berlin Academy. After seven years of privation a better time came for Mendelssohn. A rich silk-manufacturer in Berlin, Isaac Bernhard (Bermann Zilz), engaged him in 1750 as tutor to his children; four years later he made him his bookkeeper, then his representative, and finally his partner.

(From the drawing by Daniel Chodowiecki.)

Occupation as Bookkeeper.

While conscientiously fulfilling his business duties, Mendelssohn continued unceasingly to acquire further knowledge. Without systematic schooling, almost without teachers and without guidance, he had attained great proficiency in languages, mathematics, philosophy, and poetry. "His integrity and philosophical mind make me anticipate in him a second Spinoza, lacking only his errors to be his equal," ran a letter of Oct. 16, 1754, written by Gotthold Ephraim Lessing, to whom Gumperz had introduced Mendelssohn as a good chess-player.

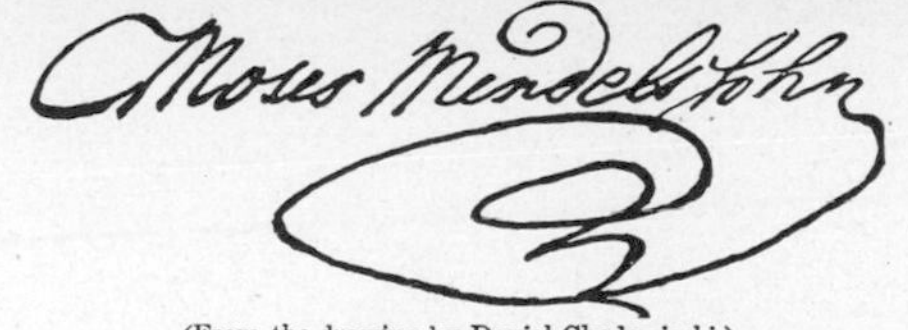

This acquaintance developed into a most intimate friendship and deeply influenced Mendelssohn's development. Lessing, only a few months his senior, was the most liberal of German authors and the most uncompromising opponent of every form of intolerance. In 1749 he had placed a noble-minded Jew upon the stage in his comedy "Die Juden," which may be regarded as the forerunner of "Nathan der Weise." The claim which had been advanced by certain anti-Jewish critics, that a Jew could not possibly be worthy of respect, drove Mendelssohn to defend the honor of his race in his first literary attempt in German, a letter to Gumperz, which brought him before the public. He was then introduced into the world of letters by Lessing, who, without Mendelssohn's knowledge, published a small book which the latter had given him to read. This work, which appeared anonymously in 1755, was the "Philosophische Gespräche," wherein Mendelssohn declared himself a disciple of the school of Leibnitz and, despite his antipathy for pantheism, took sides with Spinoza. In the same year was published at Danzig the anonymous satirical treatise "Pope ein Metaphysiker," called forth by a prize offered by the Berlin Academy, and written by Mendelssohn and Lessing, both of whom eagerly defended the teachings of Leibnitz. The names of the authors did not long remain hidden. Several academicians, with whom Mendelssohn was acquainted, greeted him with marked respect; and even the court was eager to know "the young Hebrew who wrote in German." Almost contemporaneously with the "Philosophische Gespräche" he wrote the "Briefe über die Empfindungen" (Berlin, 1755; translated into French by Thomas Abbt, Geneva, 1764), which contains a philosophy of the beautiful, and which forms the basis of all philosophic-esthetic criticism in Germany. On the advice of Lessing he then made a German version of the "Discours sur l'Inégalité Parmi les Hommes," a prize essay by Rousseau, whom he greatly admired. This translation, with explanatory notes and a dedicatory letter to "Magister" Lessing, appeared at Berlin in 1756.

Friendship with Lessing.

Through Lessing, Mendelssohn in 1755 made the acquaintance of the book-dealer Friedrich Nicolai, who in the course of a few months became his intimate friend, helping him in his study of modern languages and encouraging him to learn Greek. Together with Nicolai he took lessons from Rector Damm, who was known as a good Greek scholar; and in a short time he was able to read all the works of Plato in the original without assistance of any kind (G. Malkewitz, in "Vossische Zeitung," May 29, 1881, Supplement; G. A. Kohut, "Moses Mendelssohn and Rector Damm," New York, 1892). He and Nicolai also visited the "learned coffee-house," the meeting-place of a limited circle of scholars to which Mendelssohn belonged and in which each member read a mathematical or philosophical paper every fourth week. For this society Mendelssohn prepared a treatise containing observations "Ueber die Wahrscheinlichkeit" (On Probability), which he requested a fellow member to read for him, either out of modesty or because he stam mered. The substance of this paper was repeate in his "Morgenstunden."

Friendship with Nicolai.

When Nicolai projected the "Bibliothek de Schönen Wissenschaften und der Freien Künste" i 1756, Mendelssohn was asked to join its staff, an he soon became not only one of the most diliger collaborators, but the very soul of the whole unde taking. In this magazine he reviewed the lates works on esthetics and literature, and also publishe his own studies on esthetics. Mendelssohn, Le sing, and Nicolai began a correspondence on th subject, in which they discussed the purpose o tragedy, and the meaning of pity and fear and o terror and admiration. Upon this correspondence by which Mendelssohn influenced directly Le sing's "Laokoon," were based two treatises by th former which first appeared in the "Bibliothek, namely, "Die Hauptgrundsätze der Schönen Küns und Wissenschaften" and "Ueber das Erhabene un Naive in den Schönen Wissenschaften." Thes monographs—the first was translated into Italian b C. Ferdinandi (1779) and the other into Dutch b Van Goens (1769)—must be ranked among the mos important contributions to pre-Kantian esthetics.

Contributions to Criticism.

At the end of the first year Mendelssohn retire from the "Bibliothek," which Nicolai soon disco tinued, editing in its stead (after 175 the "Briefe die Neueste Literatu Betreffend." The "Literaturbriefe one of the most important publicatio of German journalism, were revol tionary in character. The criticism which Mendel sohn (upon whom a large part of the editorial wor devolved), together with Lessing, introduced wa positive, creative, and essentially German in chara ter. Mendelssohn's judgment was always impartia sound, and clear-sighted. He, the barely tolerate Jew, dared to use the columns of the "Literatu briefe" to criticize even the poems of Frederick th Great (1760). The review attracted much atte tion; and an unprincipled scribbler, Von Justi, wis ing to take revenge on the Jew and on the "Literatu briefe" (which had criticized a book of his as deserved), lodged a complaint against the journa The "Literaturbriefe" were condemned; and leger has it that Mendelssohn was ordered to appear b fore the king at Sans Souci. He is said to have e caped the difficulty by a witty simile which incline the king in his favor. "Whoever makes verses he said, "plays at ninepins; and whoever plays ninepins, be he king or peasant, must have the 'se ter-up' tell him how he bowls."

His Marriage.

Mendelssohn had good cause to be satisfied wi his position in life. He lived independently, ha faithful friends, and had already acquired a fortun small though it was. He now wished to have home of his own. In April, 1761, he went to Har burg, where he was welcomed by Christian a mirers, while the chief rabbi of th city, Jonathan Eybeschütz, greete him in a very flattering letter. The he became engaged to Fromet Guge heim (b. Oct. 6, 1737; d. at Hamburg March 1 1812), a plain, poor, and lowly girl, whom he ma ried in June, 1762. During his honeymoon he beg to work at the solution of a question proposed by the Berlin Academy of Sciences for a prize essay, "Ob die Metaphysischen Wissenschaften einer Solchen Evidenz Fähig Sind wie die Mathematischen." His monograph "Ueber die Evidenz der Metaphysischen Wissenschaften" received the prize of 50 ducats in June, 1763, and gained the victory over Thomas Abbt and Immanuel Kant, together with whose essays his was printed. A few months later (Oct., 1763) Mendelssohn received the privileges of a protected Jew. A very often-repeated legend tells that the privilege was given him upon the intercession of Marquis d'Argens, who said to the king: "A bad Catholic philosopher begs a bad Protestant philosopher to grant the privilege to a bad Jewish philosopher. There is too much philosophy in all this for justice not to be on the side of the request." At the same time the trustees of the Jewish community in Berlin honored him by exempting him from the payment of all Jewish taxes; and nine years later it passed a resolution that the "distinguished man" should be eligible to all positions in the community.

Partly owing to the "Literaturbriefe," of which he continued to be the chief collaborator until 1765, and partly because of the prize essay which had introduced him to philosophical circles, and also on account of his other literary works, his associations with poets and philosophers in Germany and Switzerland became more and more close. He stood in especially intimate relationship to the kindly and versatile young professor Thomas Abbt, in Frankfort-on-the-Oder, and to Rinteln, then "Consistorialrath" in Bückeburg. At the request of the former, who was constantly meditating upon death, Mendelssohn began a correspondence concerning the destiny of man, and on the soul and its fate after death. This correspondence, to which Mendelssohn himself published notes, was printed in Mendelssohn's "Gesammelte Schriften," v. 230-408, and in the third volume of Abbt's works. Abbt's questions and doubts confirmed his friend's decision, reached long before, to write on the immortality of the soul, and formed the basis of his chief philosophical work, "Phädon" (1767). This follows Plato's dialogue of the same name. Mendelssohn's argument is that in the body there must be at least one substance which is neither corporeal nor composite and which unites within itself all ideas and conceptions; the soul, as this self-existing, indivisible essence, can not be destroyed. The "Phädon" was the most widely read book of its time. Its special charm was its elegant and lucid style. Never before in Germany had philosophical questions been treated in such clear language; so that his contemporaries with justice called him the "German Plato." The "Phädon" is one of the best productions of classic German prose; it was reprinted fifteen times and translated into nearly all the European languages, while a number of Hebrew versions were made. The Crown Prince of Brunswick was so delighted with it that during a visit to his royal uncle in Berlin in the autumn of 1769, he invited the author to visit him at the castle, and expressed the wish that he might induce him to come to Brunswick.

His "Phädon."

Medal Struck in Honor of Mendelssohn's "Phädon."
(In the collection of F. Lobo, Philadelphia.)

The Count and Countess of Schaumburg-Lippe became well acquainted with Mendelssohn in Pyrmont, where he lived in 1773 on account of his health, and conversed with him about death and immortality. The Berlin Academy of Sciences proposed Mendelssohn as a regular member of the philosophical division, but Frederick the Great struck his name from the list, because the Empress Catherine of Russia also wished to be elected. The queen dowager, Luise Ulrika of Sweden, Frederick's talented sister, took pleasure in conversing with Mendelssohn. No stranger of importance who came to Berlin failed to pay his personal respects to the "German Socrates," as Mendelssohn was often called after the appearance of the "Phädon."

Controversy with Lavater.

Among those who corresponded with Mendelssohn and showed him great honor was Johann Kaspar Lavater, a preacher in Zurich, who visited the "Jew Moses" several times in 1763 and gave, in his "Physiognomik," a very interesting description of "this man with the Socratic soul." Lavater's most earnest wish was to convert the Jew who had spoken admiringly of Jesus (although with the limitation, "if Jesus of Nazareth had been content to remain only a virtuous man"), and who had demonstrated the immortality of the soul on the grounds of reason instead of the Bible. In 1769, therefore, Lavater translated the "Idées sur l'Etat Futur des Etres Vivants, ou Palingénésie Philosophique" of Charles Bonnet, a professor at Geneva, entitling his version "Untersuchung der Beweise für das Christenthum," and sent it to Mendelssohn with an introduction in which he challenged him "either to refute the book publicly, or, if he found it logical, to do what wisdom, love of truth, and honor required and what Socrates would have done if he had read the work and found it irrefutable." This rash step, distasteful to Bonnet and soon regretted by Lavater himself, made a painful impression upon the friends of Mendelssohn and upon all Berlin theologians, but it was most distressing to Mendelssohn himself. He, the avowed enemy of all religious disputes, owed it to his inmost conviction, to his honor, and to his reputation to make a public answer, after obtaining permission from the consistory. The latter willingly allowed him to reply, confiding in his "wisdom and modesty." Mendelssohn's answer is a model of Stoic calm and dialectic acuteness. He declared that his belief in the truths of his own religion was unshakable. "If I had changed my faith at heart," he says, "it would be most abject baseness not to wish to confess the truth according to my inmost conviction. If I were indifferent to both religions, and mocked or scorned all revelation, I should well know what wisdom would counsel, were conscience silent. What could keep me from it?" He declared, moreover, that Bonnet's book was not at all one which could convert him, and that he had read many other defenses of Christianity, written by Germans, which were far more thorough and philosophical. This "Schreiben an den Herrn Diaconus Lavater in Zürich" (Berlin, 1770; Hebrew translation with annotations by N. H. Wessely, edited by Solomon Fuchs, *ib.* 1892) was followed by the "Antwort an den Herrn Moses Mendelssohn zu Berlin," dated Feb. 14, 1770, with "Nacherinnerungen" by Mendelssohn (Berlin, 1770). Lavater regretted that he had involuntarily distressed "the most noble of men" and begged his forgiveness.

The dispute, however, continued. Although Bonnet regretted that he had been the innocent cause of Lavater's action, and although he assured Mendelssohn of his highest esteem, he tried to refute his arguments in a new edition which appeared in the same year, and claimed that "the Berlin Jew had copied his trashy statements from my foot-notes." Such a procedure impelled Mendelssohn to write his "Betrachtungen über Bonnets Palingenesie"; but the essay remained unfinished, and exists only as a sketch. In these observations as well as in letters to Lavater, to the Crown Prince of Brunswick, and to others, he expressed his views regarding the doctrines of Christianity. Meanwhile a succession of scribblers was meddling in the controversy, especially a Frankfort lawyer named J. B. Kölbele, who addressed to him two pamphlets (Frankfort-on-the-Main, 1770), in which spite and calumny rivaled each other. Mendelssohn made no reply. "Whoever is so obviously anxious to irritate me," he wrote to a friend, "ought to have much difficulty in succeeding." In this long controversy he found few defenders, although the theologian Semler in Halle and Professor Michaelis in Göttingen, as well as an anonymous citizen of Hamburg, who wrote "Dienstfreundliches Promemoria an die Welche Herrn Moses Mendelssohn Durchaus zum Christen Machen Wollen" (1771), and the satirist Lichtenberg in Göttingen, were his open partizans.

This controversy seriously affected Mendelssohn's health, and compelled him in 1771 to refrain for several months from all mental activity. In July of 1773 and 1774 he went to Pyrmont to regain his health, and there he won the friendship of the reigning prince and became acquainted with Herder, who satirically remarked that "Mordecai had as large a following as the grand vizier." After he had gradually regained his physical strength, Mendelssohn resolved to carry out a cherished plan of devoting more of his intellectual activity to the Jews and Judaism.

Acquaintance with Herder.

On account of his interest in philosophy and in German and esthetic literature, and owing to the failure of his first attempt to publish a weekly called "Ḳohelet Musar" (1750), he had somewhat neglected Jewish interests. In 1757 he had written a sermon on the victory of the Prussians at Rossbach, and a thanksgiving address after the battle of Leuthen, while six years later he prepared a sermon to celebrate the peace of Hubertsburg. The first of these addresses purported to have been delivered by Rabbi Fränkel, and the last by Rabbi Aaron Mosessohn in the synagogue at Berlin, and they had been published without Mendelssohn's name as author (Kayserling, "Dankpredigt und Danklieder von Moses Mendelssohn, zum Ersten Male Herausgegeben und mit Einleitung Versehen," Berlin, 1866). This sermon was translated into English at Philadelphia in 1763 ("Publ. of Am. Jew. Hist. Soc." i. 63, ii. 31, iii. 116; "Allg. Zeit. des Judenthums," lviii. 451). Besides these sermons, the first ones written and published in German by a Jew, Mendelssohn had annotated Ecclesiastes (Berlin, 1770) and written a commentary to the famous "Logic" of Maimonides, entitled "Millot ha-Higgayon." He gave the work to Samson Kalir, a Jewish scholar of Jerusalem, who had it printed (Frankfort-on-the-Oder, 1761) as his own work, but the second and all following editions appeared under Mendelssohn's name.

The controversy with Lavater opened the second period of Mendelssohn's activity, which was concerned chiefly with Judaism and the Jews. Being universally honored not only as a man, but as a metaphysician and German writer, he became, almost unconsciously, the chief representative of his coreligionists. When the Jews in Endingen and Lengnau (see Jew. Encyc. i. 1–2, *s.v.* Aargau), the only places in Switzerland in which they were then tolerated, were threatened with new restrictions in 1774, they appealed to Mendelssohn, asking him to intercede with Lavater. Distasteful as it was for him to have any further relations with his former opponent, he wrote him a letter asking him to do all he could for the Jews of Switzerland, and as a result their rights were protected. When in 1777 several hundred impoverished Jews were about to be expelled from Dresden, where Mendelssohn still had to pay the poll-tax, the president of the community turned to him, and he at once wrote a successful appeal to Freiherr von Ferber, from whom a year earlier he had received an oral assurance of esteem. At the request of the chief rabbi of Berlin, Hirschel Lewin, Mendelssohn compiled in German the "Ritualgesetze der Juden" on Jewish civil law (Berlin, 1778; 5th ed. 1826). Likewise, at the instance of his friend Klein, judge and later on professor, he ren-

Jewish Activities.

dered into pure German, instead of the former Yiddish, the formula of admonition which was spoken on taking the Jewish oath and which remained in force until 1869.

Mendelssohn, who in his feelings was both Jew and German, wished to teach his coreligionists the German language and thus to prepare them for German culture. For his own children he began to translate the Pentateuch into German; at the urgent request of Solomon DUBNO, however, who prepared a Hebrew commentary for the translation, he decided to publish it under his own name, and at his own expense, and a specimen soon appeared, entitled "'Alim li-Terufah" (Amsterdam, 1778). The undertaking was greeted with marked enthusiasm by the people, not only in Germany, but in Holland, France, and England, and was joyfully welcomed by such enlightened rabbis as Hirschel Lewin and his son Saul in Frankfort-on-the-Oder, while Hartwig Wessely and Joseph Haltern composed poems in honor of the translator. On the other hand, there were those who, like Raphael Kohen in Altona and his son-in-law Hirsch Janow, placed the German translation of the Pentateuch under a ban. Toward his opponents Mendelssohn displayed a philosophic calm; for he was opposed to all controversies and especially to those with theologians—"those pugnacious proclaimers of peace," as he called them. He knew only too well "how much opposition, hatred, and persecution are called forth at all times by the slightest innovation, no matter how beneficial." The King of Denmark and the princes and leading men of the kingdom were among the subscribers to his work. Early in March, 1780, the Book of Genesis appeared, to which Dubno had written the greater part of the commentary; but a few months later this collaborator, alienated by the opponents of Mendelssohn, left him, so that he himself was obliged to prepare the entire commentary to Exodus. As assistants for the remaining parts he obtained Hartwig Wessely, Aaron Jaroslav, and Herz Homberg. The whole Pentateuch was finished in 1783, and because of its remarkable merit it created a stir even in Christian circles. At the same time the translation of the Psalms appeared—the fruit of ten years' labor—first in German characters and then in Hebrew type with a Hebrew commentary by Joel Löwe. Mendelssohn's version of the Song of Solomon, which was found among his papers, was published in 1788 by Joel Löwe and Aaron Wolfson, with a Hebrew commentary.

Translation of the Bible.

The translation of the Pentateuch had an important effect in bringing the Jews to share in the progress of the age. It aroused their interest in the study of Hebrew grammar, which they had so long despised, made them eager for German nationality and culture, and inaugurated a new era in the education of the young and in the Jewish school system. At Mendelssohn's suggestion the Jüdische Freischule was founded at Berlin in 1781, the first organized Jewish school in Germany, after which many similar institutions were modeled. There, according to the system planned by him, instruction was given not only in the Bible and the Talmud, but also in technical branches and in German and French.

Influence on German Judaism.

Mendelssohn was also the first to advocate the emancipation of the Jews. When his coreligionists in Alsace, through their representative Cerfberr in Metz, requested him to prepare a petition for them to lay before the French council of state, he, seconded by Nicolai, persuaded his friend, the councilor of war, Chr. W. DOHM, to undertake the task. Thus originated the memorial "Ueber die Bürgerliche Verbesserung der Juden," which was the first monograph to discuss the question of emancipation scientifically, and in the drafting of which Mendelssohn appears personally to have had some share ("Zeitschrift für die Geschichte der Juden in Deutschland," v. 75 *et seq.*). The sensation produced by this work could not fail to call forth adverse criticism and new polemics against the Jews. Thereupon Mendelssohn induced his friend Markus Herz to translate the "Vindiciæ Judæorum" by the Amsterdam rabbi, MANASSEH BEN ISRAEL, from English into German (Berlin, 1782), and wrote for it a preface in which he replied to the critics of Dohm's work, remonstrated with Dohm himself, and energetically opposed the ban and the canon law. Attacks upon this preface appeared in periodicals and pamphlets. Cranz, the author of "Das Forschen nach Licht und Recht," who was supported by a certain Herr Mörschel, especially assailed Mendelssohn's principles and demanded a public reply. In answer Mendelssohn wrote his celebrated epoch-making work "Jerusalem, oder über Religiöse Macht und Judenthum" (Berlin, 1783; translated into Italian, Triest, 1799; into English by M. Samuels, London, 1838, and by Isaac Leeser, Philadelphia, 1852; into Hebrew by A. B. Gottlober, Jitomir, 1867, and by P. Smolenskin, Vienna, 1876).

Plea for Emancipation.

Mendelssohn's "Jerusalem," which shows frequent analogies with Spinoza's "Tractatus Theologico-Politicus," but reaches diametrically opposite results, deals in the first section with the relation of State and Church, both of which, though having different objects and methods, should promote human happiness. According to Mendelssohn, the Church has no right to own property, and Church law is essentially contradictory to the nature of religion. He again opposed energetically the right of ban and excommunication, and was the first, at least in Germany, to plead for the separation of Church and State, and for freedom of belief and conscience. In the second part he deals with Judaism, which, according to him, has, in contradistinction to Christianity, no dogma whose acceptance is necessary for salvation. With Leibnitz he differentiated between eternal truths, which are based on reason and not on supernatural revelation, and temporary, historical truths. Judaism is no revealed religion in the usual sense of the term, but only revealed legislation, laws, commandments, and regulations, which were supernaturally given to the Jews through Moses. Mendelssohn did not recognize miracles as evidences of eternal truths, nor did he formulate articles of faith; hence he did not say "I believe," but "I recog-

His "Jerusalem."

nize that to be true." "The spirit of Judaism is freedom in doctrine and conformity in action." Accordingly he very curiously defined the ceremonial law as "a kind of writ, living, quickening the mind and heart, full of meaning, and having the closest affinity with speculative religious knowledge." This is the indissoluble bond which is forever to unite all those who are born into Judaism. "What divine law has ordained can not be repealed by reason, which is no less divine," is Mendelssohn's reply to all those who wished to release the Jews from the Law by sophistry. "Jerusalem," on its appearance, met with little favor, yet Kant, then at the zenith of his reputation, called it an "irrefutable book" and regarded it as "the proclamation of a great reform, which, however, will be slow in manifestation and in progress," and which, as he wrote Mendelssohn, "will affect not only your nation, but others as well." A host of reviewers, among whom the Berlin theologians Zöllner, Uhle, and others, together with many insignificant scribblers, condemned "Jerusalem," while they decried its author as a rationalist or even as an atheist. The Jews were little more pleased. Since, on the one hand, he recognized the basal principle of Judaism to be freedom of thought and belief, and, on the other, placed its whole essence in the ceremonial law, both the Orthodox party and the reformers claimed him as their own. He was conservative by nature, and wished to abolish religious abuses, such as untimely burial; but he stood immovably upon the foundation of the ancestral religion. It was through no fault of his that his disciples took different roads, and that several of his children renounced Judaism after his death.

Tombstone of Moses Mendelssohn.
(From the drawing by Daniel Chodowiecki.)

Attitude Toward Reform.

On Feb. 15, 1781, Lessing, Mendelssohn's best and dearest friend, died. Though in his last years he had written to Mendelssohn but seldom, yet he had erected a noble monument to his friend in "Nathan der Weise," taking as the model for his hero Mendelssohn himself (Kayserling, "Moses Mendelssohn," 2d ed., p. 344, and the bibliography on "Nathan" on p. 342). After Lessing's death Mendelssohn formed a close friendship with the brother-in-law of Elise Reimarus in Hamburg, Mendelssohn's best woman friend. This was the young August von Hennings, who lived for a few years in Berlin as secretary of the legation and who visited Mendelssohn almost daily, afterward carrying on an active correspondence with him (for his letters see Kayserling, "Moses Mendelssohn," 1st ed., pp. 519 *et seq.*, and "Zeitschrift für die Geschichte der Juden in Deutschland," i. 111 *et seq.*). For a short time Mendelssohn was intimate with Herder, to whom he first disclosed his intention of writing a biography of Lessing. He afterward learned through Elise Reimarus that the philosopher F. H. Jacobi, an admirer of Bonnet and a friend of Lavater, had revealed this plan to her, and told her that Lessing in his later years had been an ardent disciple of Spinoza. A new struggle with another opponent confronted him, but before entering upon a contest with Jacobi, Mendelssohn, now weak and sickly, wished to set forth his own fundamental metaphysical beliefs and to refute pantheism. He did this in the lectures which he delivered for his children, for the two Humboldts, and for others, and which appeared under the title "Morgenstunden oder Vorlesungen über das Dasein Gottes" (Berlin, 1785; second enlarged edition, *ib.* 1786; translated into Italian, Triest, 1843; into Hebrew, Königsberg, 1845). Before Jacobi had received this work, he had already published his "Ueber die Lehren des Spinoza, in Briefen an Herrn Moses Mendelssohn," in which he recklessly attacked Mendelssohn. Despite his dislike for personal quarrels, the latter could not leave this challenge unanswered, and he replied in an article, "An die Freunde Lessings," in which he once more defended his friend. On the very day on which he took the manuscript to his publisher he caught cold, and a stroke of apoplexy brought his life to a close.

His "Morgenstunden."

The celebration of the hundredth anniversary of his birth, like that of his death, was general. The city of Dessau erected a monument to him, and one of his great-grandsons donated in his memory a scholarship-fund of 150,000 marks to the University of Berlin.

An incomplete collection of his works was published at Ofen 1819–21, and, in one volume, at Vienna 1838; the first complete edition, with a biography by Joseph Mendelssohn, which contains also many of Moses' letters, was published in conformity with the wishes of the family (Leipsic, 1843–45). A collection of his works on philosophy, esthetics, and apologetics was published by M. Brasch (Leipsic, 1880). There are several portraits of him by Graff, Frisch, Rode, and Chodowiecki.

Moses Mendelssohn left three sons, Joseph, Abraham, and Nathan, and three daughters, Dorothea, Recha, and Henriette, whose biographies, together with those of some of their children, are given here.

BIBLIOGRAPHY: Euchel, *Toledot Rambeman*, Berlin, 1786 (the first biography of Mendelssohn); Kayserling, *Moses Mendelssohn, Sein Leben und Seine Werke*, Leipsic, 1862 (2d ed. 1888); idem, *Moses Mendelssohn, Ungedrucktes und Unbekanntes von Ihm und über Ihn*, ib. 1883.

Nathan Mendelssohn: Youngest son of Moses Mendelssohn; born at Berlin Dec. 9, 1782; died there Jan. 9, 1852; married Henriette Itzig, youngest daughter of Daniel Itzig. He devoted himself to mechanics, and was the first German to pursue studies in this subject in England and France. He occupied a number of positions during his lifetime. From 1808 to 1813 he was a mechanician in Berlin; from 1813 to 1821, an officer in the militia; and from 1821 until 1825, a manufacturer in Silesia. He then became tax-collector in Glatz and Liegnitz, and in 1836 was appointed inspector of the chief mint in Berlin. Mendelssohn manufactured various instruments, some of which were of his own invention, and which much impressed Alexander von Humboldt by their excellence. At the instance of Humboldt he received a state subsidy for the construction of a dividing-machine which he completed in 1810.

Of a mechanical journal published by Mendelssohn, only a few numbers appeared. Until the end of his life he maintained an active interest in the promotion of industries and manufactures, as well as of art and science. He gave the first impulse to the foundation of the Polytechnic Society of Berlin, before which he lectured on photography, galvanoplastic art, electromagnetism, telegraphy, and kindred subjects.

BIBLIOGRAPHY: J. Löwenberg, in *Vossiche Zeitung* (Berlin), Oct. 7, 1883.

Rebecka Mendelssohn: Daughter of Abraham Mendelssohn; born at Hamburg April 11, 1811. She was distinguished for her keenness of intellect and her brilliant wit. She was a gifted linguist and acquired such an exact knowledge of Greek that even in her later years she could read Homer and Plato without difficulty. In May, 1832, she married Lejeune-Dirichlet, professor of mathematics at the University of Berlin, who had been introduced into Mendelssohn's house by Humboldt (Hensel, *l.c.* vols. i.–iii.).

Recha (Reikel) Mendelssohn: Second daughter of Moses Mendelssohn; born at Berlin 1766; married Mendel Meyer, the son of her father's intimate friend, the court-banker Nathan Meyer, in Mecklenburg-Strelitz. The marriage was not a happy one and was soon dissolved. Recha, a bright and clever but sickly woman, then established a boarding-school for girls in Altona, and later lived at Berlin in close association with her brother Abraham (Hensel, *l.c.* i. 55).

BIBLIOGRAPHY: Kayserling, *Moses Mendelssohn*, p. 538.

D. M. K.

MENDES (MENDEZ): Netherlandish family; one of the thirty prominent Jewish families which emigrated from Spain to Portugal under the leadership of the aged rabbi Isaac Aboab, and to which King John II. assigned the city of Oporto as a residence. Persecuted by the Inquisition, the Mendeses left Oporto and settled in Holland and England, emigrating later to America.

Gideon Mendes: Consul of the Netherlands in 1703 in the republic of Zale, Barbary, which had entered into a treaty with the Netherlands in 1651 (Koenen, "Geschiedenis," p. 210).

Isaac (Francisco) Mendes: A learned Jew who, with his parents and his brother **Mordecai (Christoval) Mendes,** went from Oporto to Amsterdam in 1598. Isaac was highly respected by the Senate of Amsterdam. Through his efforts, it is said, the second synagogue of Amsterdam, Neweh Shalom, was erected, and that without occasioning dissension in the community, despite Grätz's assertion to the contrary ("Gesch." ix. 518; Barrios, "Casa de Jacob," pp. 6 *et seq.*).

Isaac Mendes: Poet and musician; lived at Amsterdam about 1665; a friend of Daniel Levi de Barrios. About 100 years later another **Isaac Mendes** lived there, who copied "Danielillo ó Respuestas à los Christianos."

Joseph Israel Mendes: Physician; brother of **Abraham Israel Mendes**; died at Amsterdam Jan. 7, 1619.

Joseph Mendes Bravo: Physician; practised in London in 1663.

Moses (Fernando) Mendes: Physician; son of Maranos in Portugal; professor in the faculty of medicine at Coimbra, and physician to King John IV. of Portugal; died, according to some sources, in 1725, or, according to others, Nov. 26, 1724. When the king's daughter Catherine, wife of King Charles II. of England, became seriously ill in Castile on her way to London, Fernando was sent to her, and at her request he accompanied her to London and remained there as her physician. His brothers **Andreas** and **Antonio** went there with him. In London Fernando and his wife openly confessed Judaism, he taking the name of Moses. A daughter was born to him in the royal palace, to whom the queen was godmother, and who was named **Catherine** (Rachel) after her. In 1698 this daughter married Moses (Antonio) da Costa. In 1687 Mendes was elected a member of the Royal College of Physicians and Surgeons. See COSTA, ANDREA MENDES DA.

BIBLIOGRAPHY: Lindo, *History of the Jews in Spain*, p. 350; Kayserling, *Gesch. der Juden in Portugal*, p. 324; idem, *Sephardim*, p. 168; idem, *Bibl. Esp.-Port.-Jud.* p. 70; Gaster, *History of Bevis Marks*, pp. 12, 97 (with portrait), *et seq.*

D. M. K.

MENDES: One of the oldest Sephardic families. It continued in Spain and in Spanish possessions long after 1492, the year of the general expulsion. Many members of the family and its connections undoubtedly succeeded that year in joining the Jews of

Aquitaine. Others drifted to Holland, Italy, Turkey, etc. The French or Aquitaine branch settled chiefly in Bordeaux, Bayonne, and Came. It intermarried with such old families as Pereira, Da Costa, Gomez, Vaez, Osorio, Sola, Sespedes, Capote, Quiros, Henriques, Soares, Casado, Morro, Bonito, Fonsequa, Nunes, Corcho, Netto, etc. Among Bayonne notables of this family may be mentioned Edouard Mendes (member of the municipal council, president of the tribunal of commerce, chevalier of the Legion of Honor), Auguste Mendes ("inspecteur des postes"), and Elysée Mendes (member of the tribunal of commerce and of municipal council). The earliest Mendes tombstone now in existence in Bayonne is that of Rodrigues Mendes (1637).

The Holland branch produced some notable writers, such as David, son of Atalyah Franco Mendes (author of "Gemul 'Atalyah," "Ḥanukkat ha-Bayit," "Peri 'Eẓ Ḥayyim," "Teshu'ot Yisrael"), Samuel Rodrigues Mendes, and Samuel da Silva Mendes (authors or editors of editions of the Sephardic ritual on which the modern editions of David Levi, Meldola de Sola, Leeser, and Gaster are based).

The West-Indian or American branch springs from David Pereira Mendes, who fled from Spain to Bayonne and who arrived in Jamaica in 1786. He died the same year, leaving one son, Samuel. This son had twelve children, from one of whom, Isaac, were descended Joseph and Abraham. Joseph was the father of Isaac Philipe and four daughters. Abraham was the father of Frederick de Sola Mendes and Henry Pereira Mendes.

Abraham Pereira Mendes: English rabbi and educationist; born in Kingston, Jamaica, Feb. 9, 1825; died in New York April 18, 1893. He was the first master of the Beth Limud School of Kingston, but resigned in order to prepare in London, England, for the vocation of preacher and rabbi. He studied under Dr. Meldola, the dayyan, and the Rev. D. A. de Sola, "the learned ḥazzan" of the Sephardic community, and received his diplomas. He returned to Jamaica and became for a short time assistant to the Rev. Isaac Lopez, minister of the Kingston Sephardic congregation, but was soon called from that position to be the minister of the Montego Bay community. There he stayed until his wife's failing health compelled him, in 1851, to return to her milder native climate. Mendes was then elected minister and preacher in the Birmingham (Eng.) congregation, and remained there until 1858, when he removed to London, became head of the Neveh Zedek for six years, and established Northwick College, a school for Jewish youth. He continued meanwhile his ministerial duties and literary labors, and on the death of Haham Artom acted as preacher and dayyan for the Sephardic community of London. He was called to the ministry in the Newport (Rhode Island) congregation by the guardian congregation Shearith Israel of New York in 1883, and continued its minister until his death ten years later.

He was the first among the Sephardim to publish a volume of sermons in English (1855). He translated the Daily Prayer-Book of the German Jews (Valentine's edition), and finished the translation of the Festival and Holy Day Books left incomplete by the death of Rev. D. A. de Sola. He published, besides, "The Law of Moses," "Post-Biblical History of the Jews" (to fall of Jerusalem), "Interlineary Translation of the Prayer-Book" (German), and the Haggadah. He married Eliza, a daughter of Rev. D. A. de Sola of London.

A. H. P. M.

Frederick de Sola Mendes: American rabbi, author, and editor; born at Montego Bay, Jamaica, West Indies, July 8, 1850; son of R. Abraham Pereira Mendes. He was educated at Northwick College and at University College School, London, and at London University (B.A. 1869). Subsequently he went to Breslau, Germany, where he entered the university and studied rabbinics at the Jewish Theological Seminary. Mendes received the degree of Ph.D. from Jena University in 1871. Returning to England, he was licensed to preach as rabbi by Haham Benjamin Artom, in London, 1873; in the same year he was appointed preacher of the Great St. Helen's Synagogue of that city, but in December removed to New York, where he had accepted a call to the rabbinate of Shaaray Tefillah congregation (now the West End Synagogue); he entered upon his duties there Jan. 1, 1874. Mendes was one of the founders of the American Hebrew. In 1888 he took part in the Field-Ingersoll controversy, writing for the "North American Review" an article entitled "In Defense of Jehovah." In 1900 Mendes joined the staff of The Jewish Encyclopedia as revising editor and chief of the translation bureau, which positions he resigned Sept., 1902. Associated with Dr. Marcus Jastrow and Dr. Kaufmann Kohler, he is one of the revisers of the "New Bible Translation" in course of publication by the Jewish Publication Society. He has also translated "Jewish Family Papers: Letters of a Missionary," by "Gustav Meinhardt" (Dr. William Herzberg). Of his publications the following may be mentioned: "Child's First Bible"; "Outlines of Bible History"; "Defense not Defiance." He contributed also the article on the "Jews" to "Johnson's Encyclopedia." In 1903 he became for a time editor of "The Menorah," a monthly magazine.

Henry (Haim) Pereira Mendes: American rabbi; son of Abraham Pereira Mendes; born in Birmingham, England, April 13, 1852. He was educated at Northwick College (rabbinics), at University College (London), and at the University of the City of New York, taking the degree of M.D. He became minister of the Manchester (England) Sephardic congregation in 1874, and in 1877 was called to the Congregation Shearith Israel of New York, of which he is still (1904) the minister. In 1881 he was one of the founders of the New York Board of Ministers, and acted as its secretary from its foundation up to 1901, when he became president. He joined Dr. Morais in helping to establish the Jewish Theological Seminary in 1886, of which he became secretary of the advisory board and professor of history. On the death of Dr. Morais he became acting president of the faculty until the appointment of Dr. S. Schechter. In 1884, the centennial of the birth of Sir Moses Montefiore, he moved his congregation to convene the leading

Jews of New York to mark the event by some practical work: the outcome was the Montefiore Home for Chronic Invalids, established in the same year. He was made vice-president of the Gild for Crippled Children in 1896, and in 1901 established the Jewish branch of that gild. He promoted the formation of the Union of Orthodox Congregations of the United States and Canada (1897) and was subsequently elected its president. Mendes was one of the founders of the Young Women's Hebrew Association of New York (1902), of whose advisory board he is chairman.

In Zionism, Mendes stands specially for its spiritual aspect; he served as vice-president of the American Federation of Zionists and was a member of the Actions Committee of Vienna (1898–99). The degree of D.D. was conferred upon him by the Jewish Theological Seminary of America (1904).

In conjunction with his brother Frederick de Sola Mendes, and others, he was one of the founders of "The American Hebrew" (1879), to whose columns, as to those of the general press, he is a frequent contributor. He is the author of "Union Primer and Reading Book" (1882); "Jewish History Ethically Presented" (1895); "Looking Ahead," a plea for justice to the Jew (1900); "The Jewish Religion Ethically Presented" (1904). Among his other writings are: "In Old Egypt," stories about, but not from, the Bible; "Esther"; "Judas Maccabæus"; and many essays in periodical publications.

J. F. H. V.

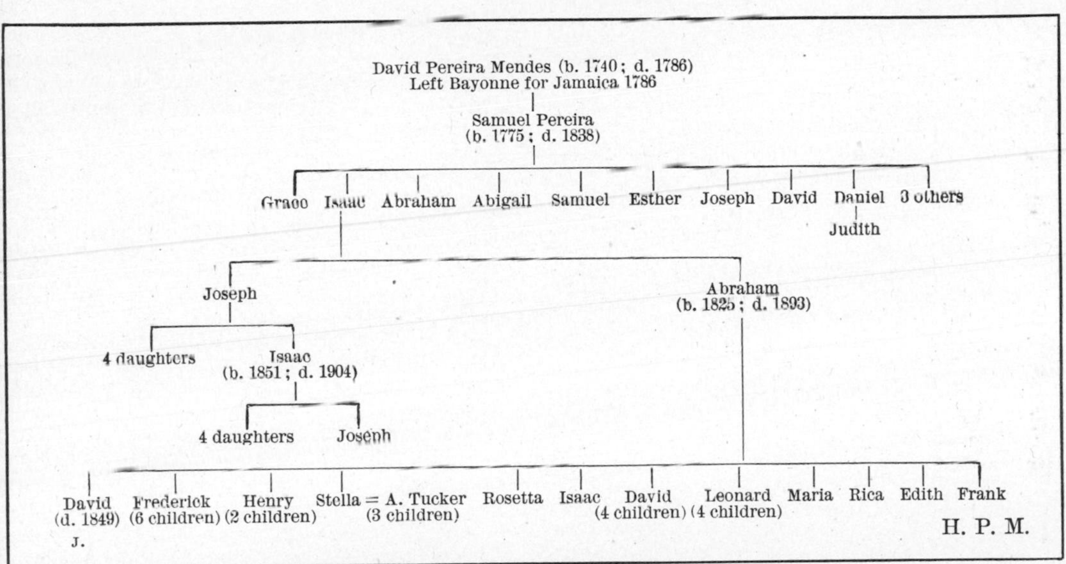

Mendes Pedigree.—American Branch.

MENDÈS, CATULLE: French poet, dramatist, and art critic; born at Bordeaux May 22, 1841. Educated in his native city, he went in 1859 to Paris, where he has since resided. In 1861 he founded the "Revue Fantaisiste" and in 1864 the "Parnasse," later "La République des Lettres." Since 1893 he has published an annual, under the title "L'Art au Théâtre," containing the articles on music and the drama which he has contributed during the year as critic to the "Journal."

Mendès is the author of a large number of works both in prose and in verse. A perfect stylist, he is nevertheless inclined to the sensual; his "Le Roman d'une Nuit," which appeared in the "Revue Fantaisiste" (1867), was condemned as an immoral novel, and Mendès was sentenced to a month's imprisonment and a fine of 500 francs for publishing it. Of his works may be cited: In verse: "Philomène," 1863; "Odelettes Guerrières," 1871; "La Colère d'un Franc-Tireur," 1872; "Le Soleil de Minuit," 1876; "Nouveaux Contes Epiques," 1885; "Les Vains Amours," 1896. Novels: "Histoires d'Amour," 1868; "Les 73 Journées de la Commune," 1871; "Les Folies Amoureuses," 1877; "Le Roi Vierge," 1881; "Les Monstres Parisiens," 1882–85; "Grand Magnet," 1888; "Rue des Filles-Dieu," 1893; "Le Chercheur de Tares," 1897. Most of these works have passed through several editions. Dramas: "La Part du Roi," 1872; "Justice," 1877; "Gwendoline," 1886; "Isoline," 1888; "Fiammette," 1889; "Médée," 1898. All his pieces have been produced at the theaters of Paris, and have been well received.

In 1894 Mendès received the cross of the Legion of Honor.

Bibliography: Curinier, *Dict. Nat.*; *La Grande Encyclopédie*; *Nouvelle Larousse Illustré*; *Meyers Konversations-Lexikon.*

S. F. T. H.

MENDES, DAVID FRANCO. See Franco.

MENDES, FRANCISCO: Portuguese Marano; physician to Don Affonso, brother of the cardinal infante; lived in Lisbon in the sixteenth century. The shoemaker Luis Diaz, who proclaimed himself to be the Messiah, induced Mendes to undergo circumcision at the age of thirty-seven and to confess Judaism (*c.* 1541) together with other converts. Diaz was burned at the first auto da fé held at Evora toward the end of 1542, Francisco Mendes escaping the same fate by flight.

BIBLIOGRAPHY: *Informatione Sommaria*, reprinted in Grätz, *Gesch.* 3d ed., ix. 551; *Historia da Inquisição*, p. 9, Lisbon, 1845.
G. M. K.

MENDES, MAURITS BENJAMIN DA COSTA: Dutch philologist; born at Amsterdam May 16, 1851; entered the Athenæum (now the University) there in 1867 and studied classic philology. An accident at gymnastics aggravated for two years the deafness from which he had suffered since his boyhood and caused him to give up his regular studies. Mendes established himself as a private master of classical languages and soon became known for his pedagogical capacity. Since 1891 he has been curator of manuscripts in the University library.

Mendes has applied himself to the study of Greek, especially of Homer. In collaboration with his friend Dr. van Leeuwen (since 1884 professor at Leyden) he published the so-called "Editio Batavorum" of Homer ("Ilias," 2 vols., Leyden, 1887–89; 2d ed. 1895-96; "Odyssea," 2 vols., 1890–92; 2d ed. 1897–1898). In this edition not only has the letter "digamma" been restored at the beginning of words in which the study of comparative grammar proves it to have been originally pronounced, but even the greater part of the results of the latest researches in Homeric grammar have been applied in reconstructing the text. For the use of Dutch schools the same collaborators published: "Attische Vormleer" (*ib.* 1877; 6th ed. 1901), an Attic grammar, and "Taaleigen der Homerische Gedichten" (*ib.* 1883; 4th ed. 1898; translated into German 1886, and into French 1887), a grammar of the Homeric idiom. Mendes himself wrote a Latin grammar (*ib.* 1885; 4th ed. 1899).

On Jan. 8, 1898, Mendes was nominated "doctor honoris causa" of Amsterdam University in recognition of his services in classical philology. As curator he published a catalogue of manuscripts, "De Handschriften der Stedelijke Bibliotheek met de Latere Aanwinsten" (Amsterdam, 1902).

From his youth Mendes has always had a great admiration for the stage. He is the author of many translations for the Dutch theater, and of some original comedies and plays, *e.g.*: "De Schuld" (1882); "Gravin Sarah" (1883); "Thuis Gebleven" (1883; 2d ed. 1892), "Zyn Model" (1888). His own reminiscences of the stage he collected in a volume entitled "Tooneelherinneringen" (Leyden, 1900), containing materials for the history of the Dutch stage during the second part of the nineteenth century. With the students of the universities of Amsterdam and Utrecht, Mendes prepared performances of the following classic plays: "Antigone" (1885) and "Œdipus Rex" (1891) of Sophocles; "Aulularia" of Plautus (1892).

Mendes' brother **Henri,** born 1845, a chess-problem composer of reputation, is a deaf-mute.

BIBLIOGRAPHY: Rössing, *Zondagsblad*, Dec. 26, 1897 (with portrait); *Mnemosyne*, 1898, xxvi. 205, 599.
S. E. SL.

MENDES (MENDEZ), MOSES: English poet and dramatist; born in London; died at Old Buckenham, Norfolk, Feb. 4, 1758; son of James Mendes, a stock-broker of Mitcham, Surrey, and grandson of Fernando Mendes. He was educated partly at St. Mary Hall, Oxford (M.A. 1750). Subsequently he engaged in stock-broking, and, having accumulated a fortune, he bought an estate at Old Buckenham, and devoted himself to literary pursuits.

His first effort was "The Double Disappointment," a ballad-opera, produced with considerable success at Drury Lane Theatre, March 18, 1746, and revived at Covent Garden March 22, 1759. "The Chaplet," a musical "entertainment," the words by Mendes and the score by Boyce, scored a great success Dec. 2, 1749, because of both its merit and the clever acting of Mrs. Clive as *Pastora.* "Robin Hood," produced at Drury Lane Dec. 13, 1750, and "The Shepherd's Lottery," played Nov. 19, 1751, were not successful.

Mendes' only prose work was "Henry and Blanch" (1745), a tale taken from the French of "Gil Blas." It was dramatized the same year by Thomson, and was produced at Drury Lane Theatre. Other works were: "The Seasons" (1751), written in imitation of Spenser; "The Battiad" (1751), a satire on Dr. William Battie, written in collaboration with Paul Whitehead and Schomberg; "The Squire of Dames," another poem in imitation of Spenser. Mendes also translated Maphæus' continuation of Vergil's "Æneid" (1767). His "The Blatant Beast" was not published until 1792, when it appeared in the "European Magazine." Mendes' verses betray the dilettante; his humor, the mechanical fun of the playhouse of his day.

Mendes' two sons dropped their father's name after his death, assuming that of "Head" by royal warrant. His grandson **Francis Bond Head** was created a baronet July 14, 1838.

BIBLIOGRAPHY: *European Magazine*, Oct., 1792, pp. 251 *et seq.*; *Dict. National Biography*, xxxvii. 248–249; *Jew. World*, Feb. 14, 1873.
J. E. Ms.

MENDES-NASI, FRANCISCO: Member of one of the richest and most respected Portuguese Marano families; died about 1536; husband of Beatrice de Luna. He owned a large banking-house in Lisbon, which had branches in Flanders and France, and which advanced money to Charles V. and other rulers. After Mendes-Nasi's death his brother **Diogo,** director of their Antwerp branch and husband of Beatrice de Luna's sister, was the richest Portuguese Marano, and, together with his sister-in-law, sacrificed great sums to prevent the introduction of the Inquisition into Portugal. Diogo died at Antwerp about 1545, leaving, like his brother, one daughter. A kinsman of both the Mendes was **Hector Mendes,** a very rich man, who, when asked by the King of Portugal what he called his own, replied: "The alms which I have given."

BIBLIOGRAPHY: Herculano, *Da Origem e Estabelecimento da Inquisiçao em Portugal*, ii. 159, Lisbon, 1854; Grätz, *Gesch.* ix. 366 *et seq.*; Kayserling, *Gesch. der Juden in Portugal*, pp. 211, 266 *et seq.*
D. M. K.

MENDESIA, GRACIA (called also **Beatrice de Luna**): Philanthropist; born about 1510, probably in Portugal; died at Constantinople 1569; member of the Spanish family of Benveniste. As a Marano she was married to her coreligionist Francisco Mendes-Nasi. After the early death of her husband, Gracia no longer felt secure in Portugal, where the introduction of the Inquisition had endangered her life and property; and together with her only daughter Reyna and several relatives, she fled in 1536 to Antwerp, where many Maranos were then sojourning and where her brother-in-law Diogo Mendes was manager of the branch of the Lisbon banking-house, which was soon transferred entirely to Antwerp.

At Antwerp.

Gracia did not feel at ease in the capital of Flanders, despite the esteem in which she was held; for she could not endure the equivocation, imposed upon all Neo-Christians, of appearing to be a good Catholic, and she longed for a place where she could openly avow her religion. All preparations had been made for departure, when her brother-in-law Diogo, who had married her younger sister, died (*c.* 1545). Being appointed in his will manager of the business and trustee of the entire property, which the rulers indebted to the house had claimed and confiscated under the cloak of religion, Gracia was obliged to remain for some troublous years in Antwerp. It was not until 1549 that she was able to go with her daughter, her widowed sister, and the latter's daughter to Venice. Here she met with new difficulties, occasioned by her own sister, for Gracia had been appointed by her brother-in-law guardian of his minor daughter and trustee of her property until her marriage. The younger sister, who was anxious to escape from Gracia's tutelage, betrayed the latter as a secret Jewess to the Venetian authorities, alleging that she intended to flee with her wealth to Turkey and there openly to avow Judaism. At the same time the sister employed an anti-Semitic Frenchman to denounce Gracia to the French government, within whose territory a large part of her wealth was invested. In consequence of these machinations the King of France as well as the Senate of Venice confiscated the property of the Mendes family, and imprisoned Gracia at Venice in order to prevent her flight. Her nephews, especially the energetic Joaõ Miguez (or Joseph Nasi, as he called himself as a Jew), who was also Gracia's son-in-law, took steps to liberate her and to save the fortune. They appealed to Sultan Sulaiman, explaining to him that a widow had the intention of bringing great treasures into the Turkish empire, but that the republic of Venice prevented her from doing so. Moses Hamon, physician to the sultan, also took the matter up, hoping that the heiress of the wealthy Gracia would marry his son. Thereupon a Turkish ambassador was despatched to Venice, with a mandate to the signoria to grant the captive Marano woman free passage to Turkey, together with her property and suite, and Gracia thus became unwittingly the cause of war between Venice and the Porte.

Causes War Between Venice and Turkey.

In spite of the sultan's mandate, the negotiations dragged over two years. Meanwhile Gracia was liberated (*c.* 1550) and immediately went to Ferrara, where she acknowledged herself to be a Jewess. In 1552 she settled with her daughter Reyna at Constantinople and there also openly confessed Judaism. Her sister soon followed her, and although the two had become reconciled, she still had many difficulties with her and with a nephew.

Her Charities.

Gracia was one of the noblest of women and was honored like a princess. She spent her large fortune in relieving her suffering coreligionists. She made great sacrifices to prevent the introduction of the Inquisition into Portugal, and was the guardian angel of the Maranos. The poet Samuel Usque, who dedicated to her his Portuguese work, "Consolaçam as Tribulaçoes de Ysrael," praises her as "the heart of her people." She relieved the impoverished Maranos in Flanders and other countries, protected them, and "gathered them together in obedience to the prescriptions of their ancient faith"; and in the words of Immanuel Aboab, "Whosoever should undertake to tell of the noble deeds and rare virtues of Donna Gracia would have to write entire books" ("Nomologia," p. 304). Gracia appealed to the sultan against the cruelties of the fanatical Pope Paul IV., who condemned many Portuguese Maranos to the stake, and contemporary rabbis praise the piety, philanthropy, and nobility of soul with which she founded synagogues and aided Jewish scholars. A synagogue which she built at Constantinople still bears her name.

Gracia betrothed her niece, Gracia Mendesia II., to her nephew Samuel Nasi; the portrait of this Gracia at the age of eighteen was engraved by Giovanni Paolo Poggini of Ferrara on a medal which is now preserved in the Cabinet of Medals, Paris.

Bibliography: Joseph Caro, *Abkat Rokel*, Responsum No. 80; Joseph ha-Kohen, *'Emek ha-Baka*, p. 116; Joseph ibn Leb, *Responsa*, i. 63b, ii. 26a; M. A. Levy, *D. Joseph Nasi, Herzog von Naxos*, Breslau, 1859; Grätz, *Gesch.* ix. 000 *et seq.*; idem, in *Wiener Jahrbuch*, 1857, pp. 7 *et seq.*; Kayserling, *Gesch. der Juden in Portugal*, p. 211; idem, *Die Jüdischen Frauen*, pp. 81 *et seq.*, 345 *et seq.*; see also Nasi, Joseph.

D. M. K.

MENDL, SIGISMUND FERDINAND: English politician; born 1866. He was educated at Harrow School and University College, Oxford, and in 1888 was admitted to the bar at the Inner Temple, London. After unsuccessfully contesting the Isle of Wight in 1892, and Plymouth in 1895, he was elected member of Parliament for Plymouth in the Liberal interest in 1898, serving until 1900.

Bibliography: *Who's Who*, 1902; Harris, *Jewish Year Book*, 1901-2.

J. M. W. L.

MENDLIN, JACOB WOLF: Russian Hebrew economist; born at Moghilef-on-the-Dnieper 1842. He was the first of the Hebrew writers to treat of economic questions in their application to the condition of the Jewish masses in Russia. About 1862 he went to Germany, where he studied the labor movement under Lassalle. This movement roused his ambition to go more deeply into the study of economics and cooperation.

In 1879 Mendlin made his first appearance as a writer in "Ha-Meliẓ," with an article on the economic condition of the Russian Jews; and since then he has contributed articles on the same and allied questions to "Ha-Ẓefirah," "Ha-Meliẓ," "Russkii Yevrei," "Voskhod," and "Ulei." Mendlin has also written: "Ba-Meh Niwwashea'" (St. Petersburg, 1883), four essays on the improvement of the economic condition of the Jews in Russia; "Meḳore ha-'Osher" (Odessa, 1898), a politico-economic study; and "Quellen fun Selbsthilfe" (in Yiddish), *ib.* 1894. In these writings Mendlin points to the mutual aid and cooperative organizations as the most effective means of improving the wretched condition of the Jewish masses in Russia. Mendlin also effected the founding of certain charitable institutions in the Jewish community of Odessa, where he is now (1904) living.

BIBLIOGRAPHY: *Khronika Voskhoda*, 1904, No. 15.

H. R. A. S. W.

MENDOZA, DANIEL (nicknamed "Star of Israel"): English pugilist; born 1763 in Whitechapel, London; died Sept. 3, 1836. Champion of England from 1792 to 1795, he was the founder of a distinct school of boxing which marks a period in the history of pugilism. In Miles's "History of British Boxing," London, n.d., the first period (1719–91) is described as "From the Championship of Fig to the Appearance of Daniel Mendoza" (i. 1–70). Mendoza entered the prize-ring April 17, 1787, at Barnet, where he defeated, in less than thirty minutes, Samuel Martin, a butcher of Bath. This victory led to his being matched against Richard Humphries, by whom he was defeated Jan. 9, 1788, at Odiham, Hampshire, after a contest that lasted twenty-nine minutes, and during which more skill and science were displayed than had been shown in any match hitherto in England. In another match, at Stilton, Huntingdonshire, May 6, 1789, Humphries in the twenty-second round dropped to the ground without being hit, and on a repetition of these tactics Mendoza was declared the conqueror. He fought a third battle with Humphries at Doncaster Sept. 29, 1790, and again defeated him. A popular ballad was composed on these encounters.

In 1791 Mendoza went on a sparring tour and, crossing over to Ireland, thrashed "Squire Fitzgerald," an amateur, who had expressed a desire to test his skill with the champion (Aug. 2, 1791). On his return to England Mendoza was matched against William Warr (sometimes called "Ward") of Bristol, whom he defeated in two encounters, at Smitham Bottom, near Croydon, May 14, 1792, and at Bexley Heath Nov. 12, 1794, respectively.

Mendoza was appointed sheriff's officer for the county of Middlesex in 1806, and later went on exhibition tours, the most successful being that made in the summer of 1819. After an absence of fourteen years from the ring, Mendoza was matched against Tom Owen, a Hampshire innkeeper, and met him July 20, 1820, at Banstead Downs. At this time Mendoza was in his fifty-seventh year, his opponent being six years younger. Owen, who had terribly "punished" his adversary, was declared the winner after twelve rounds. Advancing age and chagrin at his defeat led Mendoza to retire from the prize-ring, and to become the landlord of the "Admiral Nelson" in Whitechapel. It is clear that Mendoza introduced a more skilful method of defense than had been current before his time, and tended to make boxing more "scientific," a contest of skill rather than a struggle of brute force.

BIBLIOGRAPHY: *Boxiana: Sketches of Antient and Moder*
Pugilism, London, 1812; Miles, *Pugilistica*, vol. i., Londo
1880.

J. F. H. V.

MENE, MENE, TEKEL, UPHARSI
(מנא מנא תקל ופרסין): Words written by a mys
terious hand on the wall of Belshazzar's palace, an
interpreted by Daniel as predicting the doom of th
king and his dynasty. The incident is describe
as follows: Once when King Belshazzar was bar
queting with his lords and drinking wine fro
the golden vessels of the Temple of YHWH, a man
hand was seen writing on the wall certain myster
ous words. Frightened by the apparition, the kin
ordered his astrologers to explain the inscriptio
but they were unable to read it. Daniel was the
summoned to the royal palace; and the king prom
ised him costly presents if he would decipher th
inscription. Daniel read it "Mene, mene, teke
upharsin" and explained it to mean that God ha
"numbered" the kingdom of Belshazzar and brougl
it to an end; that the king had been weighed an
found wanting; and that his kingdom was divide
and given to the Medes and Persians (Dan. v. 1–28

The first question which presents itself to th
critic—namely, why could the inscription be dec
phered by Daniel only—engaged the attention of th
Talmudists, who advanced various answers. Ce
tain of them concluded that the Hebrew writin
had been changed in the time of Ezra, so that eve
the Jews that were found in the royal court coul
not read an inscription written in archaic character
But those who followed R. Simeon in maintainin
that the writing had not been changed found oth
solutions for the problem; *e.g.*, it was written in th
cryptographic combination of את בש, each letter
each pair being substituted by its companion, *e.g*
יטת יטת אדך פוג חמט; or the words were writte
thus: ממתום ננקפי אאלרן, one abov
the other, having to be read vert

Talmudical Explanations.

cally; or אנם אנם לקת ניסרפו, eac
word backward; or, again, אמ נמא
קתל פורסין, the first two letters of eac
word being transposed (Sanh. 22a). It is evide
that the author of the Book of Daniel meant that th
inscription was written in characters familiar to th
king and the wise men of Babylon, but that, as ofte
happens with ancient inscriptions, the transpositi
of certain letters baffled every attempt to deciph
them.

Various difficulties of the writing present the
selves also in Daniel's interpretation: *e.g.*, the rep
tition of מנא is not explained, and instead of th
plural ופרסין, the singular פרס without the co
junctive ו is translated. It is true that Theodoti
and Jerome, by giving three words only to verse 2
make it uniform with verses 26–28 (Theodotion rea
ing "Mane"), and that the Septuagint, though di
fering from Theodotion as to the meaning of th
words, has also only three words, which it transfe
to verse 17. Nevertheless the discrepancy in th
Masoretic text as well as the grammatical constru
tion of the words has greatly puzzled the mode
critics. It may be noted that the author cho
words which had a double meaning and that Dani
accordingly, gave the king a dual interpretatio

applying both meanings of the words. Thus he interpreted מנא as "to count" and "to finish"; תקל, to "weigh" and "to be wanting"; פרס, "to divide" and "Persia." The question now arises as to the grammatical construction of these words. According to Theodotion, Jerome, and Josephus ("Ant." x. 11, § 3), they are substantives; but according to the Septuagint they are verbs in the perfect passive, which, owing to their vocalization, are difficult of explanation.

Views of Modern Scholars.

Clermont-Ganneau, in a long article on this subject ("Journal Asiatique," series 8, viii. (1886), 36 *et seq.*), first advanced the opinion that they are names of weights, namely, a mina, a shekel, and a peras, which last-named in the Talmud means a half-mina (comp. the expression מנה ופרס in 'Eduy. iii. 3), and that ופרסין may be the dual form, "two half-minas." Thus the mina would be an allusion to Nebuchadnezzar; the shekel, which in value is a very small part of the mina, to Belshazzar; and the two half-minas to Media and Persia (comp. Ta'an. 21b). But as this interpretation does not show how the words predicted the fall of Babylon, Clermont-Ganneau admits the possibility of the first two words being verbs, but suggests that the ו of ופרסין should be affixed to the preceding word, which may be vocalized either תִּקְלוּ, "they weighed," or תְּקָלוּ, "weigh"; in either case having פרסין as its direct object.

Among the many other suggestions offered by modern scholars that of J. Marquart may be mentioned ("Fundamente Israelitischer und Jüdischer Geschichte," 1896, p. 73). He thinks that the legend of Belshazzar's vision is connected with that of HELIODORUS, and that possibly the writer of Dan. v. was of the Maccabean age. Marquart makes no emendation in the text of the passage in Daniel; but if his suggestion is well founded the sentence may be amended to read as follows: מחא מחא קטל פרש = "Smite, smite, slay, thou horseman!" As to the historicity of the inscription, Boissier points out that predictions written by a mysterious hand are referred to in a cuneiform tablet (see "Proc. Soc. Bibl. Arch." 1896, xviii. 237).

BIBLIOGRAPHY: Cheyne and Black, *Encyc. Bibl.*; D. Margoliouth, in Hastings, *Dict. Bible*; J. D. Prince, *Mene, Mene, Tekel, Upharsin*, Baltimore, 1893.

S. M. SEL.

MENELAUS (known also as **Onias**): High priest from 171 to about 161 B.C.; successor of Jason, the brother of Onias III. The sources are divided as to his origin. According to II Maccabees (iv. 23), he belonged to the tribe of Benjamin and was the brother of the Simeon who had denounced Onias III. to Antiochus IV. (Epiphanes) and revealed to the Syrians the existence of the treasure of the Temple; according to Josephus ("Ant." xii. 5), Menelaus was the brother of Onias III. and of Jason. Of these two conflicting statements the evidence is in favor of the former, first because it is unlikely that two brothers would be called by the same name, and secondly because the popular opposition to Menelaus in favor of Jason, though both belonged to the Hellenistic party, is more easily explained if the successor of Jason did not belong to the priestly family. It is possible that Josephus confounded Simeon, the brother of Menelaus, with Simeon, the father of Onias and Jason.

Although during the three years of his pontificate Jason had given many proofs of his attachment to the Hellenistic party—by building a gymnasium in Jerusalem and by introducing many Greek customs—the zealous Hellenists of the stamp of the Tobiads plotted his overthrow, suspecting him of partiality to traditional Judaism.

Hellenistic Tendencies.

At their head stood Menelaus, who professed the utmost contempt for the religion of his fathers and was ready to commit any crime in order to gratify his ambition. Having been sent to Antiochus to pay the annual tribute, he took the opportunity to outbid Jason and secure for himself the office of high priest. An officer named Sostrates was sent by Antiochus with a troop of Cyprian soldiers to subdue any opposition that might be attempted by the followers of the deposed high priest Jason and to collect at the same time the sum Menelaus had promised.

Menelaus' first act was to seize the sacred vessels in the Temple stores in order to meet the pecuniary obligations he had incurred. This sacrilegious act, which was regarded even by the Greeks as heinous, came to the ears of the deposed high priest Onias III., who publicly accused Menelaus of robbing the Temple. The latter, afraid of the consequences of this accusation, induced the king's lieutenant Andronicus, who had had his share of the plunder, to get rid of Onias before a formal complaint had been lodged with the king. Accordingly Onias was decoyed from the sanctuary at Daphne, in which he had sought refuge, and murdered. Menelaus continued to plunder the treasures of the Temple until the people were aroused and scenes of violence ensued, in which his brother Lysimachus met his death. He then brought before the king an accusation against the people of Jerusalem, that they were partizans of the Egyptians and persecuted him only because he was opposed to their party intrigues. This accusation caused the execution of several Jews who, although they proved beyond any doubt that Menelaus and Lysimachus had desecrated the Temple, were sentenced to death.

Meanwhile Jason had not abandoned his claims to the high-priesthood, and while (170) Antiochus was waging war against Egypt he succeeded in making himself master of Jerusalem and in forcing Menelaus to seek refuge in the citadel.

Conflict with Jason.

Antiochus regarded this proceeding as an affront upon his majesty, and, having been compelled by the Romans to leave Egypt, he marched against Jerusalem, massacred the inhabitants, and plundered the Temple; in this he is said to have been assisted by Menelaus.

According to II Maccabees, it was Menelaus who persuaded Antiochus to Hellenize the Jewish worship, and thereby brought about the uprising of the Judeans under the guidance of the Maccabees. During the first years of the restoration of the Jewish worship Menelaus still remained (though only nominally) high priest. He is said to have been put to death by Antiochus V. (Eupator) when the latter made definite concessions to the Jews, the reason assigned being that Menelaus, by his evil counsel, was indirectly responsible for the Jewish rebellion.

BIBLIOGRAPHY: *II Macc.* iv. 23 *et seq.*; Josephus, *Ant.* xii. 5; idem, *B. J.* i. 1, §§ 1-6; Grätz, *Gesch.* ii. 303 *et seq.*; Schürer, *Gesch.* i. 195 *et seq.*, 215; Büchler, *Die Tobiaden und Oniaden*, pp. 106 *et seq.*
S. I. BR.

MENEPHTHA. See MERNEPTAḤ.

MENGS, ANTON RAFAEL: Austrian painter; born in Aussig, Bohemia, March 12, 1728; died in Rome June 29, 1779; son of Ismael Israel MENGS. Anton Mengs was early destined for an artist's career; and his father with much strictness kept him to his studies, although the boy at first evinced but little inclination or ability for that calling. In 1741 he was taken to Rome, where he studied the old masters, and upon his return to Dresden (1744) he was honored by King Augustus III. with the title of court painter. He obtained the royal permission to return to Rome to complete his studies, and in 1748 his first large canvas, "The Holy Family," appeared. A beautiful peasant girl, Margareta Guazzi, who had posed as a model for this painting, won his heart; and in order to marry her he abandoned the Jewish faith and was admitted into the Roman Catholic Church. Mengs again visited Dresden in 1749, but returned to Rome in 1752, where he spent the greater part of his life, and where most of his important works were painted. In 1754 he became the first director of the newly founded Painters' Academy in that city.

Mengs was an eclectic who endeavored to blend the peculiar beauties of the old masters Raffael, Titian, and Correggio. His taste was exquisite, his groupings and compositions simple and noble, his drawing always correct; while his coloring, with regard to which he took Titian for his example, was strong and true. Though his paintings lack the originality of genius, their force and beauty give them rank among the foremost works of art.

In Rome Mengs painted the following large pictures: "Saint Eusebius Surrounded by Angels" (on the ceiling of the Celestine Monastery; 1757); "Apollo and the Nine Muses on Parnassus" (on a ceiling in Cardinal Albani's villa); "History Writing on the Shoulders of Time"; "A Meeting of the Gods"; "Cleopatra." In 1761 Mengs was called to Madrid by King Charles III. of Spain to decorate the ceiling of the dining-hall in the royal palace. He painted "The Apotheosis of Trajan" and "The Hall of Fame," which latter is considered his masterpiece. In Madrid he completed also "The Ascension of Christ" for the altar of a new Catholic church in Dresden. Various other paintings by Mengs are in the possession of the art-galleries of many European capitals. Berlin has a "Holy Family"; Vienna, "St. Joseph's Dream," "The Virgin," "The Infant Savior," "The Annunciation," and "Infanta Maria Theresa"; St. Petersburg, "Andromeda Liberated by Perseus"; Dresden, "Cupid Sharpening an Arrow"; Madrid, "Christ's Release from Calvary" and "Mary of Magdala."

The "Opere di Antonio-Raffaelle Mengs" (2 vols., Parma, 1780) has been translated into German (by G. F. Prange, Halle, 1786), English (London, 1796), and French (by Jansen, Ratisbon, 1782; Paris, 1786). A young Englishman named Webb, to whom Mengs had expressed his ideas on art, published them for his own under the title "Untersuchungen über die Schönheit" (Zurich, 1771), which act of plagiarism gained him considerable fame.

Mengs had twenty children, seven of whom outlived him. Of these, five daughters were adopted by King Charles III. of Spain, who also accorded pensions to Mengs's two sons. Mengs bequeathed his valuable collections of drawings, vases, and gypsoplasts to the royal academies of art in Madrid and Dresden. Empress Catherine II. of Russia erected a monument to his memory in St. Peter's Church, Rome, where he was interred.

BIBLIOGRAPHY: *Dictionnaire Universel Encyclopédique*; *Brockhaus Konversations-Lexikon*; *Meyers Konversations-Lexikon*; *Nouvelle Biographie Générale*; Woermann, *Ismael und Rafael Mengs*, in *Zeitschrift für Bildende Kunst*, vol. v., 1893.
S. F. C.

MENGS, ISMAEL ISRAEL: Danish portrait-painter; born in Copenhagen 1690; died in Dresden Dec. 26, 1765. He learned the art of miniature- and enamel-painting in Lübeck, and then traveled through Germany, Italy, and Austria, earning a scant livelihood until 1764, when he was appointed professor at the Academy of Art in Dresden, and court painter to King August III., from whom he received an annuity.

BIBLIOGRAPHY: C. F. Bricka, *Dansk Biografisk Lexicon*; Philip Weilbach, *Dansk Kunstnerlexikon*.
S. F. C.

MENKEN: American family, the first known member of which was Solomon Menken.

Jacob Stanwood Menken: American merchant; born in Cincinnati 1838; youngest son of Solomon Menken. With his brother Nathan Davis he entered the Union army, and was captain of Company B, 27th Ohio Infantry. He is (1904) a member of the Military Order of the Loyal Legion.

Nathan Davis Menken: American merchant; born 1837 at Cincinnati; died 1878 at Memphis, Tenn.; second son of Solomon Menken. He entered the Union army at the outbreak of the rebellion in 1861, and was captain of Company A, 1st Ohio Cavalry. He was commander of General Pope's body-guard, and took part in thirty-seven battles and skirmishes in West Virginia, being mentioned for his "distinguished and soldier-like bearing" as a member of the supporting force in Colonel Brodhead's report (March 27, 1862) of the battle of Kernstown, Va. ("War of the Rebellion, Official Records," first series, xii. 156, Washington, 1902). During the epidemic of yellow fever in Memphis in 1878 Menken assisted a number of his coreligionists to leave the city by supplying them with the necessary funds. He himself remained, and, while cooperating with the Howard Association of which he was a member, succumbed to the disease. Menken was also a member of the Military Order of the Loyal Legion.

Percival S. Menken: Eldest son of Jules A. Menken; born in Philadelphia 1865; educated at Columbia University (M.A., Ph.D., LL.B.). He is a member of the New York bar, and president of the Young Men's Hebrew Association of New York. For a number of years he was a trustee and secretary of the Jewish Theological Seminary Association, and in 1904 a director of the Jewish Theological Seminary of America. He died May 17, 1908.

S. Stanwood Menken: Eldest son of Nathan D. Menken; born in Memphis 1870. He is a member of the New York bar and is active in civic affairs. In 1897 he was nominated for judge of the City Court on the Citizens' Union ticket as well as on the People's ticket. In 1896 he founded the Hall of Records Association, to properly house the public records in New York city.

Solomon Menken: Born in Westphalia, Prussia, 1787; died in Cincinnati, Ohio, 1853. He was sent to New York in 1821 as supercargo in a sailing vessel belonging to his uncle, a banker and shipowner of Amsterdam. In 1819 he settled in Cincinnati, Ohio, and founded in that city about 1825 the first wholesale dry-goods house, that of Menken & Milius. His sons, **Jules A.** (born in New York 1836; died at Watch Point, Vt., 1890; first lieutenant in the Home Guards, Cincinnati, during the Rebellion), Nathan Davis, and Jacob Stanwood Menken (for the last two see above), were merchants in Cincinnati (from 1855 to 1861) and Jules A. and Nathan Davis in Memphis, Tenn. (as Menken & Co. from 1862 to 1888, and as J. S. Menken & Co. from 1888 to 1899).

Bibliography: Isaac Markens, *The Hebrews in America*, New York, 1888; H. S. Morais, *The Jews of Philadelphia*, Philadelphia, 1894; Simon Wolf, *The American Jew as Patriot, Soldier, and Citizen*, Philadelphia, 1895.

A. E. N. S.

MENKEN, ADA ISAACS: Anglo-American actress and writer; born June 15, 1835, at Milneburg, La.; died in Paris, France, Aug. 10, 1868. Her first appearance before the public was at the Opera-House, New Orleans, where she danced with her sister Josephine, the two being known as "The Theodore Sisters." From New Orleans Ada went to the Tacon Theater, Havana, as a dancer. Thence she went to Texas, where she had many thrilling experiences, among them being a capture by Indians. Next she tried her hand at literature, writing for various newspapers, and teaching languages.

In Aug., 1856, she was married to Alexander Isaacs Menken, publicly embracing Judaism; and she next played in Milman's "Fazio" at the Varieties, New Orleans, and at various theaters in the South and Middle West. While at Nashville (April 3, 1859) she was married to John C. Heenan, the prize-fighter, known also as the "Benicia Boy." With him she went to New York city, appearing at the National and the old Bowery theaters in "Soldiers' Danger" and "The French Spy." Next she joined the company of John E. Murdoch, with whom she went on tour, playing rôles entirely beyond her and even attempting *Lady Macbeth*.

She made her appearance in her best-known rôle, that of *Mazeppa*, at the Green Street Theater, Albany, N. Y., June 7, 1861. Her success was considerable, though the part was more acrobatic than histrionic. In Oct., 1861, she married R. H. Newell, better known as Orpheus C. Kerr. Her next step was to go to London, where on Oct. 3, 1864, she appeared at Astley's Theatre as *Mazeppa*. She failed to please, and went into temporary retirement, emerging Oct. 9, 1865, to play *Leon* in Brougham's "Child of the Sun." In the meantime she had divorced Newell and married James Barclay (Aug. 21, 1865). A year later she went to Paris, where she played at the Gaîté in Burgois and Dugué's "Les Pirates de la Savane" (Dec. 30).

Ada Menken published two books of poems: the first, "Memoirs" (1856), under the nom de plume "Indigena"; the second, "Infelicia," in 1868, dedicated "by permission" to Charles Dickens. She attracted considerable attention among English and French men of letters, *e.g.*, in London, Charles Dickens, Charles Reade, and Algernon C. Swinburne, and in Paris the elder Dumas, Théophile Gautier, and Victor Hugo.

Bibliography: *Era Almanac*, 1868; *Dict. National Biography*, xxxvii. 252; Appleton's *Encyc. American Biography*; *Memoirs* accompanying the 1888 edition of *Infelicia*.

J. E. Ms.

MENORAH: The holy candelabrum. For **Biblical Data** see Candlestick.

——**In Rabbinical Literature:** The Talmud

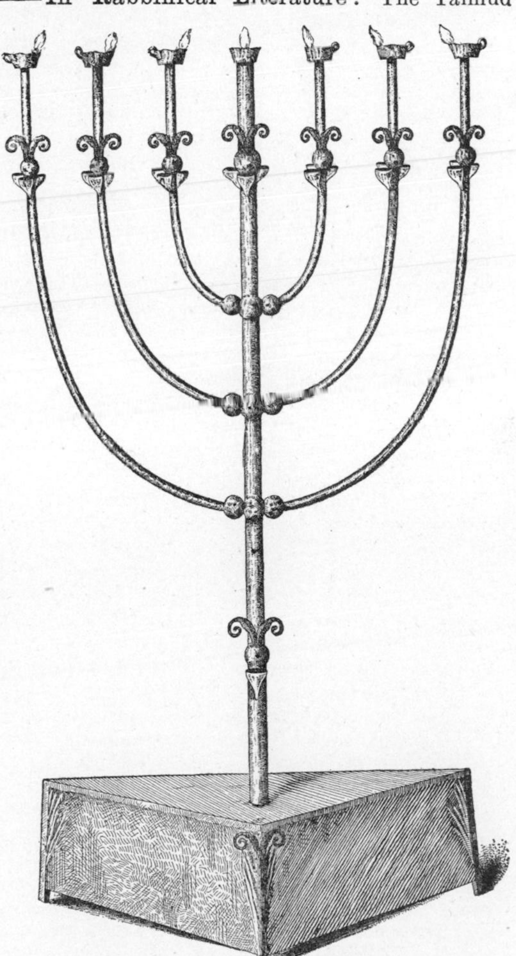

The Mosaic Menorah as Described in Rabbinical Literature.
(After a sketch by J. D. Eisenstein, New York.)

speaks only of the menorah made by Bezaleel for the Tabernacle in the time of Moses (Ex. xxxvii. 17 *et seq.*), which was later placed in the Temple

(Tosef., Soṭah, xiii., beginning), between the ten menorot made by Hiram for Solomon's Temple (I Kings vii. 49). Each of these menorot was one denarius in excess of the required weight ("kikkar") of the Mosaic menorah (Men. 29a).

The Mosaic menorah, according to the Talmud, stood 18 "ṭefaḥim" (1 ṭefaḥ = 4 inches), or 72 inches, high, divided as follows: 3 ṭefaḥim for the tripod, including a "peraḥ" (blossom in relief); 2 ṭefaḥim space; 1 ṭefaḥ for a "gebia'" (cup or vase), "kaftor" (knob), and peraḥ; 2 ṭefaḥim space; 1 ṭefaḥ for a kaftor and branch on each side of the center

A Modern Menorah.
(In the possession of Maurice Herrmann, New York.)

shaft and a kaftor above the joint; 1 ṭefaḥ space; 1 ṭefaḥ for a kaftor and branch on each side and a kaftor above; 1 ṭefaḥ space; 1 ṭefaḥ for a kaftor and branch on each side and a kaftor above; 2 ṭefaḥim space; 3 ṭefaḥim for a cluster of three gebi'ot, a kaftor, and a peraḥ on each of the branches and the center shaft (Men. 28b).

The gebia' is described as resembling an Alexandrian cup; the kaftor resembled the half of an apple; the peraḥ resembled a blossom carved on pillars. Altogether there were 22 gebi'im, 11 kaftorim, and 9 peraḥim (*ib.*; see accompanying illustration). Maimonides further explains that the gebia' was broad at the top and narrow at the bottom (probably in the style of a flower-vase); the kaftor was somewhat egg-shaped with pointed tops; the peraḥ looked like a dish with the brim doubled outward ("Yad," Bet ha-Beḥirah, iii. 1-11). The spread of the branches was 9 ṭefaḥim (36 inches), and there was the same measure for the tripod ("Shilṭe ha-Gibborim," ch. xxxi.).

The branches of the lamps had the apertures in which the wicks were placed turned toward the center lamp, which was known as "Ner ha-Ma'arabi" (= "the Western Lamp") because it was next to the branches on the east side (Rashi on Shab. 22b). For, according to the Talmud, the menorah was so placed that its two branches pointed toward the east and west respectively. A similar rule applied to all vessels in the Temple (Men. xi. 7), except the Ark. Maimonides, however, holds the opinion, also expressed in the Talmud, that the menorah, like the Ark, was placed at right angles to the length of the Temple, *i.e.*, pointing north and south and facing east and west. But this theory appears to be untenable. It was opposed by Abraham ibn Daud (RaBaD) and was strongly attacked in "Shilṭe ha-Gibborim" (xxxi. 26b).

Position.

The cleaning and refilling of the lamps, except the two most easterly, were performed by a priest every morning. If the priest found them extinguished, he relighted them. The two eastern lamps were left burning till after the morning service, and were then cleaned and refilled (Tamid iii. 9; Yoma 33a). The Ner ha-Ma'arabi, also called "Ner Elohim" (I Sam. iii. 3), was left burning all day and was refilled in the evening. It served to light all the lamps. The Ner ha-Ma'arabi contained no more oil than the other lamps, a half-log measure (1 log contains the liquid of six eggs), sufficient to last during the longest winter night (Men. 89a); yet by a miracle that lamp regularly burned till the following evening (*ib.* 86b). This miracle, however, ceased after the death of Simeon the Righteous, who was high priest forty years before the destruction of the Temple (Yoma 39b).

There was a ladder of three steps 9 ṭefaḥim high and 9 ṭefaḥim wide in front of the menorah. On the second step were placed the tongs, shovels, dishes, and oil. This ladder or stool was made by Bezaleel out of shittim-wood; but in Solomon's Temple it was made of marble. The priest ascended the steps to fix and light the lamps (Men. and Tamid *l.c.*).

The menorah depicted on Titus' arch is probably a representation of one of Solomon's menorot, but not of the Mosaic menorah, which was concealed by the priests prior to the destruction of the First Temple and of which all trace has since disappeared.

Symbolically the menorah represented the creation of the universe in seven days, the center light symbolizing the Sabbath. The seven branches are the seven continents of the earth and the seven heavens, guided by the light of God. The Zohar says "These lamps, like the planets above receive their light from the sun" ("Beha'aloteka," beginning).

Symbolic Significance.

The design of the menorah is used for a Mizraḥ picture. The seven words of Ps. cxiii. 3 respectively designate the seven branches. Some derive the design of the branches from a seven-verse chapter in the Psalms, or from the seven-verse prayer of R. Neḥunya ben ha-Kanah beginning with "Anna, bekoaḥ gedulot." A tablet with such a design is sometimes placed in front of the prayer-desk while others use the figure of the menorah as a ecoration for the Ark. Others again, in writing nulets, arrange a formula of seven letters and seven erses in the form of a menorah; and it was employed also on tombs. See AMULET (illustration); RT IN THE SYNAGOGUE; CANDLESTICK; MIZRAḤ.

BIBLIOGRAPHY: Bähr, *Symbolik des Mosaischen Cultus*, i. 534–543; Friedrich, *Symbolik der Mosaischen Stiftshütte*, pp. 157–158, Leipsic, 1841; Rofe, *Shilṭe ha-Gibborim*, ch. xxxi., Mantua, 1607; Isserles, *Torat ha-'Olah*, i., ch. xvi.; Kolbo, *Binyan Ariel*, p. 75, No. 259, ed. Vienna, 1883.

A. J. D. E.

MENORAH. See PERIODICALS.

MENSTRUATION: The first appearance of e menses is known to depend on various factors—imate, occupation, residence in towns, etc.—of hich racial affinities are the most important. Cliate is of unquestionable influence, the earliest age arying from eleven in hot to fifteen years in cold imates. Oppenheim, from an investigation of the me of the first menstruation in Bulgarian, Turkh, Armenian, and Jewish girls, concluded that race the most important factor; and Lebrun states at among 100 girls of Jewish and Slavonian exaction, the majority of the Jewish girls menstruted at thirteen, while only one Slavonian girl menruated at that age. Weissenberg presents statistics r Jewesses in South Russia from which it is seen at the first onset of menstruation was on the average at the age of fourteen; the earliest appearance as in one girl at the age of ten; and in one it was late as eighteen (Weissenberg, "Die Südrusschen Juden," p. 77).

F. Weber investigated the subject in St. Petersurg and found the following percentages, "early ppearance" representing cases of fifteen years of ge, and "late appearance" those of seventeen years:

	Russians.	Jewesses.	Germans.	Poles.	Finns.
rly appearance...	48.5	54.5	47.1	52.7	19.0
te appearance....	6.36	3.7	2.9	2.9	19.25

onsidering as "premature" those who had their rst menstruation at the age of twelve, and as "deyed" those at eighteen years, Weber found the llowing percentages:

	Russians.	Jewesses.	Germans.	Poles.	Finns.
emature..........	10.6	12.5	8.2	11.7	2.75
elayed............	2.86	1.2	3.8	2.9	0.0

appears from this that the first appearance of enstruation is much earlier in the Jewish and in e Slavonian girls than in the others.

Joachim's statistics for Hungary show that the rst menstruation takes place there as follows:

Magyar peasant girls....................	15 to 16 years.
Jewish girls	14 " 15 "
Slovak girls............................	16 " 17 "

tober ("Topographie et Histoire Médicale de Strassourg," p. 266, Paris, 1864) found that in Strasburg e first onset of menstruation was at about the me age in Jewish girls as in the non-Jewesses. n no case did he observe it to occur before the velfth year, and most had begun to menstruate etween fourteen and seventeen. But he based his opinion on only a few observations. Raciborski ("Traité de la Menstruation," p. 630, Paris, 1868) found that the first menstruation appeared in Jewesses at the average age of 14 years, 3 months, 25 days, as against 15 years, 3 months, 9 days in Slavonian girls.

From the investigations of M. Fishberg in New York it appears that the first menstruation appears in Jewish girls of that city at the average age of 12 years, 7 months. Of the 483 girls thus investigated 390 were immigrants mostly from eastern Europe, and 93 were natives, of foreign parentage. In the American-born girls the first menstruation appeared at the average age of 12 years, 1 month; and among the foreign-born girls the average age was 13 years, 2 months. The earlier onset of menstruation in the daughters of immigrants as compared with their mothers has been observed by Engelman in other immigrant peoples in the United States (see "Age of First Menstruation on the North American Continent" in "New York Medical Journal," lxxv. 221–228, 270–277). After a careful study of statistical evidence he concludes that as regards the time of functional development the American girls are "very much more precocious than those of other continents in the same region of the temperate zone, and more precocious than the peoples from whom they have sprung. It appears that the Jewish girls in the United States show similar characteristics when compared with their sisters in Europe. The cause of this precocity is to be looked for in the social and educational conditions surrounding Jewesses in the United States.

For laws concerning menstruation see NIDDAH.

BIBLIOGRAPHY: H. Ploss and Max Bartels, *Das Weib*, 7th ed., pp. 364–380; Weber, *Ueber Menstrualverhältnisse der Frauen in St. Petersburg*, in *St. Petersburger Medicinische Wochenschrift*, 1883, Nos. 41, 42, 43; Joachim, *Ungarische Zeitschrift*, iv., Nos. 20–28; A. Corre, *La Mère et l'Enfant dans les Races Humaines*, Paris, 1882.

J. M. FI.

MENZ, ABRAHAM JOSEPH BEN SIMON WOLF: Rabbi at Frankfort-on-the-Main at the beginning of the eighteenth century. He wrote an elementary text-book on mathematics entitled "Reshit Limmudim," in three parts: (1) "Kelale Handasah," the general rules of algebra; (2) "Yesodot ha-Gematriot," the elements of geometry; (3) "Yesod ha-Tekunah," on astronomy; the first part only has been published (Berlin, 1775). It contains the first book of Euclid, rearranged, with many original examples by the author.

BIBLIOGRAPHY: Steinschneider, *Cat. Bodl.* col. 702; Fürst, *Bibl. Jud.* ii. 368; Zeitlin, *Bibl. Hebr.* p. 238; Fuenn, *Keneset Yisrael*, i. 40; Benjacob, *Oẓar ha-Sefarim*, p. 542, No. 49.

D. S. J. L.

MEPHIBOSHETH: Only son of Jonathan, son of Saul, first king of Israel. The chronicler gives him the name of Merib-baal (I Chron. viii. 34), meaning, perhaps, "Ba'al contends." The relation of the two names is similar to that existing between Ish-bosheth = "man of shame," and Esh-baal = "man of Baal" (*ib.* verse 33). Upon the slaughter of Saul and his sons on Mt. Gilboa, the nurse in Jonathan's house fled with Mephibosheth, and in the flight the child fell and became a permanent cripple (II Sam. iv. 4). When David came to the throne his former love for Jonathan impelled him to inquire whether any of Saul's house remained alive, that he might show them kindness for the sake of his former bosom friend. Through Ziba, who had been a servant of Saul, he learned of the cripple Mephibosheth. David had him brought to Jerusalem, restored to him the estate of Saul, and made him a perpetual guest at the royal table (*ib.* ix. 1–8).

When David fled from Absalom this royal heir remained in Jerusalem—according to Ziba's story (*ib.* xvi. 3), that he might be ready to take the throne which was about to be restored to his father's house. On David's triumphal return to Jerusalem Mephibosheth went out to meet and greet him. He was unwashed and unkempt. When David questioned him concerning his reason for having remained behind, Mephibosheth threw the blame on Ziba, and as evidence of his own sincerity pointed out his unkempt state (*ib.* xix. 24–30). The king was evidently perplexed at the conflicting stories; and he decided that the estate of Saul should be divided equally between the questionable characters with whom he had to deal. Mephibosheth had a son, Micah (I Chron. viii. 34, 35).

E. G. H. I. M. P.

MEQUINEZ: Town in the interior of Morocco, about 35 miles west-southwest of Fez. It contains about 6,000 Jews in a total population of 50,000. But very little is known concerning the Jews there. The town was founded about 940 C.E. As was the case in other parts of Mauritania, it is probable that there were a few Jews in Mequinez before 1492, and that these were joined by many others at the time of the expulsion from Spain. It has been pointed out that of thirty family names in Mequinez at least eighteen, such as "Gozlan," "Toledano," "Pariente," "Sasportas," and "Verdugo," are Castilian in origin. Moreover, various customs, the mode of feminine dress, and the methods of preparing food, all seem to show the influence of the Spanish Middle Ages. Details of the history of the Mequinez Jews are accessible only for the years since the Alliance Israélite began to publish its bulletins. In 1878 the town suffered from a famine which ravaged all Morocco, and the Alliance Israélite, the Anglo-Jewish Association, and the Board of Deputies of London sent abundant relief to the suffering Jews. The following year the affliction was renewed through a drought and an epidemic, on which occasion Mequinez received relief from the Morocco Famine Relief Fund of London. According to the Bulletin of the Alliance for 1880, between 1864 and 1880 forty-two Jews in Mequinez were assassinated by Mohammedans. The appeal of the Alliance Israélite director of schools to the consular and diplomatic representatives of Morocco and the presence of one of these directors at Mequinez have helped to make the lives of the Jews there somewhat more secure.

Mequinez has nineteen synagogues, the oldest of which dates back 150 years. Each of these is named after its founder or else after the family which supports it (*e.g.*, the Synagogue of Mordecai Loubaton). The Alliance Israélite founded two schools (attendance 61 boys and 36 girls respectively) at Mequinez in 1901. There are also ten small Talmud Torahs, having about 800 pupils and known by the names of the teachers in charge of them. The custom o placing epitaphs upon graves is not general in Me quinez, except in the case of those who die withou leaving male issue. In Mequinez, as in almost a the Jewish communities of Morocco, it is not cus tomary to invest any one with the title of chie rabbi. Religious matters are placed in the hands c a triumvirate of dayyanim, the president of the pres ent (1904) triumvirate being R. Salomon Verdugc These three rabbis are assisted in the discharge c their duties by a "ma 'amad," or council of notables in case of necessity these constitute also a court c justice.

The revenues of the Jewish communal adminis tration are raised by means of a tax of one "douro (about 60 cents) per head for large cattle and on "peseta" (about 46⅔ cents) per head for small cattl and by contributions made by the wealthy familie on the approach of the important holy days. Thes sources of revenue enable the communal admini tration to contribute to the schools of the Allianc Israélite, support the rabbis and the poor of th city, provide for funerals, pay the poll-tax, mak gifts to the royal court and to the local authoritie on the occasion of great Arabian fêtes, and purchas the privilege of using the public roads.

There are two societies in this populous commu nity—the ḥebra ḳaddisha, which has charge of fune als, and the foundation of which dates back t ancient times, and the "ḥilluḳ," or the societ charged with the weekly distribution of money ar produce to the needy. The occupations of tl Jewish population embrace all classes of mecha ical labor and commerce. Some Jews are even en ployed as kitchen gardeners in the outskirts of tl town. The Jews of Mequinez occupy the Mella a walled ghetto containing 250 houses, all belongir to Jews. The streets are wide, but are not paved

From the standpoint of literature, Mequinez is tl most fruitful community of Morocco. It has ha at least thirteen rabbinical writers of note, of who the following belonged to the family of Verdug the dates of death in each case being given parentheses: Mordecai (1773); Moses (1783); Juda (1803); Mimun (1812); Raphael (1820); Peth hiah (1842); Jacob (1843); Joseph (1852). Of tl Toledano family there may be mentioned Ḥayyi (1782); Jacob (1802); Moses Ḥabib (middle of tl 19th cent.). David Hessin lived there toward tl end of the eighteenth century.

The 'Isawites, members of a fanatical Arab sec make annual pilgrimages to Mequinez to visit tl tomb of Abu 'Isa, the founder of the sect. On tl day of their arrival the gates of the Mellah are shu and the government of the town places a guard the to prevent the pilgrims from pillaging and mass cring its inhabitants. See MOROCCO.

BIBLIOGRAPHY: *Colonies Juives dans l'Afrique Romai* in *R. E. J.* 1902, No. 87; *Bulletins of the Alliance Israél Universelle*, 1861–1901; Hazan, *Ha-Ma'alot li-Shelomoh*, 32, 81, 90.

D. M. FR.

MERAB (מרב)**:** The elder of Saul's two daug ters (I Sam. xiv. 49; xviii. 17, 19). Saul formally fered Merab's hand to David with the condition th the latter should distinguish himself in the w with the Philistines. David did so, but Saul broke his promise by giving Merab to Adriel the Meholathite (*ib.* xviii. 19).

J. M. SEL.

MERARI, MOSES MENAHEM: Poet and chief rabbi of Venice in the seventeenth century. He was one of the rabbis who signed the decision in regard to the stores in Ferrara. A Hebrew poem ("Shir") of his is found in the "Ḥanukkat ha-Bayit" of Moses Ḥefeẓ (Venice, 1696).

BIBLIOGRAPHY: Fürst, *Bibl. Jud.* ii. 368; Mortara, *Indice*, p. 39; Nepi-Ghirondi, *Toledot Gedole Yisrael*, p. 253.

J. M. SEL.

MERCANTILE LAW. See COMMERCIAL LAW.

MERCY. See COMPASSION.

MERECH: Russian town in the government of Wilna. The earliest mention of Jews there is dated 1539, when a dispute was adjudicated (July 8) between a Jew named Konyuk and a Christian in regard to a debt of the former. In 1551 the Jews of Merech were named among those of fourteen other towns to be exempted from the special tax ("Serebshchizna") levied upon all inhabitants, with the exception of villagers and Jews, at the Polish diet held in that year (Nov. 27) at Wilna. Merech produced in the nineteenth century some noted Hebrew scholars, as Mordecai Melzer, Isaac b. Elijah Margolis (d. New York 1887), and his son Max Margolis, of the University of California.

BIBLIOGRAPHY: *Regesty i Nadpisi*, pp. 117, 203.

H. R. A. S. W.

MERIBAH (מריבה = "strife"): **1.** A place in Rephidim in the wilderness; called also "Massah and Meribah, because of the chiding of the children of Israel, and because they tempted the Lord" (Ex. xvii. 7). It is certainly this Meribah which is alluded to in Ps. xcv. 8. **2.** A place at Kadesh in the wilderness, the name occurring either as "Me Meribah" (= "the water of Meribah"; Num. xx. 13, 24) or as "Me Meribath-Kadesh" (= "the water of Meribah in Kadesh"; Num. xxvii. 14; Deut. xxxii. 51). The latter name appears as the southern limit of the land of Canaan in Ezek. xlvii. 19, xlviii. 28 (= "the waters of strife in Kadesh"). It must be said, however, that the Septuagint invariably translates the word "Meribah" by λοιδόρησις; and that the Targumim and the later commentators regard it as a common noun.

It may be seen that the two narratives which give the origin of the name differ only in that in Ex. xvii. 7 Moses is ordered by God to strike the rock, while in Num. xxvii. 14 he is ordered to speak to the rock, and for disobeying God's order is punished by not being allowed to enter into the promised land. Otherwise they are similar. It is for this reason that some critics regard the one narrative as a duplicate of the other.

S. M. SEL.

MERIDIAN, DATE-: Imaginary line fixed upon as the one along which the reckoning of the calendar day changes. East of this line the day is dated one day earlier than the west of it. The date-meridian involves many Jewish questions, such as fixing the Sabbath and the holy days in the Jewish calendar, counting the days of mourning, and dating documents. While in civil matters the Jews probably would be guided by the international date-line 180° from Greenwich, as agreed to by the geographers of many civilized nations, in religious matters the Jewish law can not recognize an imaginary date-line of recent origin which has not even been adopted by the majority of nations.

In the "Cuzari."

The question does not appear in the Talmud nor in the early rabbinical literature. It is first mentioned in the twelfth century in the "Cuzari" of Judah ha-Levi (ii. 20). Jerusalem is generally accepted as the navel, or center, of the world, as adduced from Ps. l. 2 (Tosef., Yoma, iii.; Yoma 564b). According to the "Cuzari," the Jewish date-line is 6 hours, or 90 degrees, east of Jerusalem, and 18 hours, or 270 degrees, west of Jerusalem. Judah ha-Levi's theory is based on the hypothesis that the date was fixed at midday when the sun was at its zenith, shedding light 90 degrees eastward and leaving 270 degrees westward to finish the day.

Jerusalem is in longitude 35° 13′ 25″ east of Greenwich, and according to this Judah ha-Levi's date-line would be in longitude 125° 13′ 25″ E., making China the Far East and separating it from Japan, which would be the Far West. Corea would be divided with Seoul (126° 35′ E.) to the west. Under the American date would come Kamchatka, eastern Siberia, and the whole of Australia. On the other hand, the Philippines, with Manila (120° 58′ 3″ E.), would come under the Asiatic date.

Phinehas Elijah, the author of "Sefer ha-Berit" (article iv., ed. Brünn, 1797), raised the question also regarding the latitudes near the north and south poles, where night and day may each cover six months. The author decided in that case to discard the sunlight as a distinction between night and day, and to figure 24 hours as a full day. As to the longitude he was aware that the Jews on the two hemispheres did not observe exactly the same day as Sabbath. He did not, however, attempt to locate the date-line.

Ḥayyim Selig Slonimski (d. May 15, 1904) published in "Ha-Ẓefirah," in 1874, an article addressed to the rabbinate and entitled "What Sabbath Shall the Jewish Traveler in the Far East Observe?" Several prominent rabbis took part in the discussion. R. Moses b. Ẓebi Lapidus of Raseyn, Russia, and R. Isaiah Meïr Kahana Schapiro of Czortkov, Galicia, accepted the meridian of Judah ha-Levi; Schapiro, however, marks it as passing through the Jordan instead of Jerusalem and thus moves the meridian about 20 miles eastward.

R. Benjamin Zeeb Wolf Weller of Yaroslav, Galicia, does not admit Judah ha-Levi's authority to establish a meridian and objects to any fixed date-line. In his opinion the method of dating must depend upon the order in which the countries were discovered. Hence far eastern Siberia, Japan, and Australia should retain the Asiatic or eastern date, while the Philippine Islands that were discovered from the American side should retain the American, or western, date.

R. Weller thinks that one crossing from land discovered from the Asiatic side to land discovered from the American side, or vice versa, must observe both his own Sabbath and that of his neighbors to make sure of the right date. The "natural" meridian, as R. Weller calls it, was criticized as impracticable, since discoveries of islands in the Pacific might be made from opposite coasts in such a way as to carry the Asiatic date farther west and the American date farther east. Slonimski, after reviewing the opinions of the rabbis, accepts Judah ha-Levi's view as to the location of the meridian at Jerusalem, which he advocates both from the Jewish-national and from the geographical standpoint. But he divides the distance equally, allowing 180 degrees on each side. According to his view, the date-line would be in longitude 145° 13′ 25″ west of Greenwich. Slonimski argues that by allowing an equal portion on either side of the meridian, the extreme difference from the meridian is but 12 hours, whereas Judah ha-Levi's division makes a difference of 18 hours. Besides, the equal division places the date-line in the most natural and convenient place in the Pacific, and gives the whole American continent, except a small part of Alaska near the Bering Strait, the same dating. This date-line, of course, excludes the Philippines, and even the Hawaiian Islands, from the American date, and the Jewish settlers on these islands ought to observe the American Sunday as the seventh day, or Sabbath.

Slonimski's Meridian-Line.

R. Samuel Mohilever of Byelostok coincides with Slonimski, holding, however, that any new Jewish settlement must accept the date adopted by the authorities of that place. But in case of dispute by the authorities regarding the correct date the Jewish settler must follow the Jewish date-line 180 degrees from Jerusalem. No change by the authorities thereafter can affect the date. Thus in the case of the Philippines, where the change of date occurred in the beginning of the year 1845, if the Jews living there prior to 1845 adopted the old date, they must follow it and keep Sunday as the Sabbath-day. This would apply also to Alaska, where the date was changed in 1867, when the United States purchased it from Russia. As to the Jewish traveler, Mohilever decided that privately he must observe his own Sabbath and in public he ought to observe also the Sabbath of the place he visits. But if the traveler intends to settle permanently in that place, he must adopt its date.

Halakic Points.

BIBLIOGRAPHY: Levi, *Dibre Ḥakamim*, Warsaw, 1876.

J.   J. D. E.

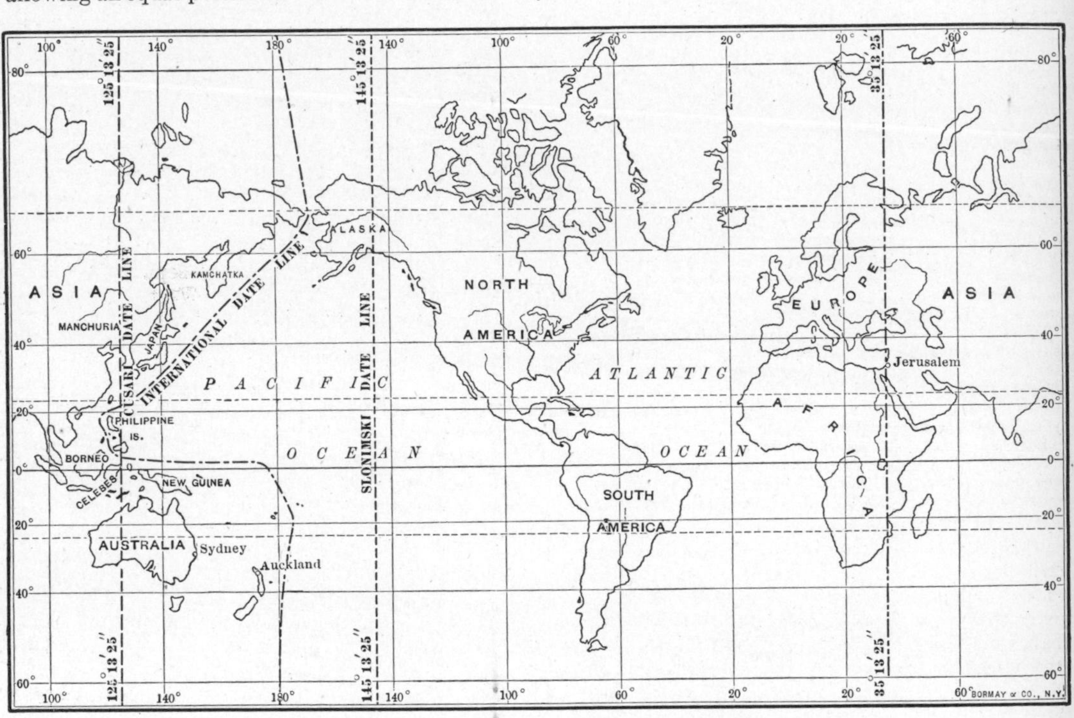

WORLD ON MERCATOR'S PROJECTION SHOWING DATE-MERIDIANS.

MERKABAH (lit. "chariot"): The Heavenly Throne; hence "Ma'aseh Merkabah," the lore concerning the heavenly Throne-Chariot, with especial reference to Ezek. i. and x. The conception of YHWH riding upon cherubim, or fiery cloud-birds, upon the heavens or the clouds, is certainly genuinely Hebrew (see Ps. xviii. 11 [A. V. 10]; Deut. xxxiii. 26; Ps. lxviii. 5 [A. V. 4]; Isa. xix. 1); hence His "war-chariot" (Hab. iii. 8 and Isa. lxvi. 15, Hebr.) and the name "chariot" for the ark with the cherubim (I Chron. xxviii. 18). Just as the Assyrian sun-chariot with its horses is employed in the legend of the ride of Elijah to heaven (II Kings ii. 11; comp. Enoch lxx. 2, lxxii. 5, lxxiii. 2), so did the prophet Ezekiel in his vision, probably suggested by Babylonian sculpture, see YHWH riding on the Throne-

Chariot when leaving the doomed Temple at Jerusalem (see Müller, "Ezechielstudien," 1895, pp. 8–11; Bertholet, "Das Buch Hezekiel," 1897, p. 12). To a later age Ezekiel's picture became a sacred mystery known by the term "Merkabah" as early as the time of Ben Sira (Ecclus. xlix. 8). The ancient Mishnah lays down the rule: "The Ma'aseh Merkabah should not be taught to any one except he be wise and able to deduce knowledge through wisdom ('gnosis') of his own" (Ḥag. ii. 1). Job beheld the throne of God, and his daughters sang the doxology of the Ma'aseh Merkabah (according to the Testament of Job, ed. Kohler, vii. 39, xi. 25; see Kohut Memorial Volume, pp. 282, 288). Quite characteristic is the story given in Tosef., Ḥag. ii. 1; Ḥag. 14b; Yer. Ḥag. ii. 77a:

"R. Eleazar ben 'Arak was riding on a mule behind R. Johanan b. Zakkai, when he asked for the privilege of being initiated into the secrets of the Merkabah. The great master demanded proof of his initiation into the gnosis, and when Eleazar began to tell what he had learned thereof, R. Johanan immediately descended from the mule and sat upon the rock. 'Why, O master, dost thou descend from the mule?' asked the disciple. 'Can I remain mounted upon the mule when the telling of the secrets of the Merkabah causes the Shekinah to dwell with us and the angels to accompany us?' was the answer. Eleazar continued, and, behold, fire descended from heaven and lit up the trees of the field, causing them to sing anthems, and an angel cried out, 'Truly these are the secrets of the Merkabah.' Whereupon R. Johanan kissed Eleazar upon the forehead, saying, 'Blessed be thou, O father Abraham, that hast a descendant like Eleazar b. 'Arak!' Subsequently two other disciples of R. Johanan b. Zakkai walking together said to each other: 'Let us also talk together about the Ma'aseh Merkabah'; and no sooner did R. Joshua begin speaking than a rainbow-like appearance [Ezek. i. 28] was seen upon the thick clouds which covered the sky, and angels came to listen as men do to hear wedding-music. On hearing the things related by R. Jose, R. Johanan b. Zakkai blessed his disciples and said: 'Blessed the eyes that beheld these things! Indeed I saw myself in a dream together with you, seated like the select ones [comp. Ex. xxiv. 11] upon Mount Sinai; and I heard a heavenly voice saying: "Enter the banquet-hall and take your seats with your disciples and disciples' disciples, among the elect, the highest ('third') class"'" (πνευματικοί; see Joël, "Blicke in die Religionsgeschichte," 1880, pp. 133–135).

Obviously this is a description of an ecstatic state in which pictures the mind forms seem realities (comp. Tosef., Meg. iv. 28 and Meg. 24—"With closed eyes they saw them"). The study of the Merkabah was theosophy; to the initiated the Ḥayyot and the Ofannim around the Heavenly Throne became beings that lived and moved before their eyes (see Joël, *l.c.* p. 152). It was in fact considered perilous to penetrate into these mysteries. "A youth who studied the 'Ḥashmal' [Ezek. i. 27, Hebr.] was consumed by the fire which sprang forth from it" (Ḥag. 13a; comp. Shab. 80a). Only the older men dared to be initiated into those mysteries. "I am not old enough," said R. Eleazar when R. Johanan b. Nappaḥa wished to instruct him in them. They were to be imparted in suggestions ("initial sentences," "rashe peraḳim") rather than in complete chapters (Ḥag. 13a). "The bird that flew over the head of Jonathan b. Uzziel as he studied them was consumed by the fire surrounding him" (Suk. 28a; comp. Meg. 3a). "Ben 'Azzai was seated meditating on the Torah, when, behold, a flame encircled him; the people told R. Aḳiba, and he went to Ben 'Azzai, saying, 'Art thou studying the mysteries of the Merkabah?'" (Cant. R. i. 10; Lev. R. xvi.). "In the future Ezekiel will come again and unlock for Israel the chambers of the Merkabah" (Cant. R. i. 4).

Symbolic Significance.

Glimpses of the mysteries of the Merkabah may be discerned in such rabbinical sayings as the following: "The angel Sandalfon towers above the rest of the angels the length of a five hundred years' journey; his feet touch the earth while his head reaches the holy Ḥayyot. He stands behind the Throne-Chariot binding wreaths for his Master" (Ḥag. 13b). To R. Ishmael b. Elisha is ascribed the saying that when offering the incense in the Temple as high priest he beheld the angel Akatriel ("the wreath-binding one"; Sandalfon?) seated on the Throne and asked him for a blessing (Ber. 7a; comp. Bacher, "Ag. Tan." i. 267). One of these great archangels is said to equal in size a third part of the world (Ex. R. iii.). Concerning the lion, the ox, the eagle, and the man as the four faces of the Ḥayyot, see Ḥag. 13b; on account of these four, which carry God's Throne-Chariot, the latter is called also "Tetramoulon" = "Quadriga" (Ex. R. iii. 3; comp. Jellinek, "B. H." iii. 92–95).

In the Enoch Literature.

The Merkabah mysteries, which remained the exclusive property of the initiated ones, the "Ẓenu'im" or "Ḥashsha'im" (see Essenes), have been preserved chiefly in the Enoch literature of the pre-Christian centuries, and in the "Hekalot" of the geonic time, known also as the "Merkabah" and "Enoch Books" (see Jellinek, "B. H." ii. 40–47, 114–117, and Introduction xiv.–xvii., xxx., xxxii.; iii. 83–108, 161–163, and Introduction xx.–xxv.; v. 170–190 and Introduction xli.–xliii.; Wertheimer, "Batte Midrashot," ii. 15–28; see Hekalot). Part of it has been embodied in the "payyeṭan-ḳedushshah" literature and has found its way also into other ancient apocrypha, such as the Testament of Abraham, the Ascensio Isaiæ, etc. Besides the descriptions of the seven heavens with their hosts of angels, and the various storehouses of the world, and of the divine throne above the highest heaven, the most remarkable feature is that the mysteries rest on the belief in the reality of the things seen in an ecstatic state brought about by ablutions, fasts, fervent invocations, incantations, and by other means. This is called "the Vision of the Merkabah" ("Ẓefiyat ha-Merkabah"), and those under this strange hallucination, who imagine themselves entering the Heavenly Chariot and floating through the air, are called "Yorede Merkabah" (= "those that go down into the ship-like chariot"; Jellinek, "B. H." iii. 90, 94 *et seq.*). In this chariot they are supposed to ascend to the heavens, where in the dazzling light surrounding them they behold the innermost secrets of all persons and things, otherwise impenetrable and invisible.

Particularly significant is the warrior-nature of the angels surrounding the Throne-Chariot; flames dart forth from their eyes; they ride upon fiery horses (comp. Zech. vi. 1–8) and are armed with weapons of fire (Jellinek, *l.c.*). In order to be allowed to pass these terrible beings the Merkabah-rider must provide himself with amulets or seals containing mysterious names ("Hekalot," *l.c.*

xvii.-xxii., xxx.), and in order to be able to step before the Throne he must recite certain prayers until God Himself addresses him, if he be worthy. The "Hekalot" mention especially either R. Aḳiba or R. Ishmael, and their associates of the Bar Kokba time, as types of the "Yorede Merkabah."

The central figure and chief actor in the theophany, however, is the "Prince of the Face," METAṬRON, the one next to the Throne, whose name, or whose seventy names, are like God's, and who is none else than Enoch translated to heaven and transformed into the highest angel. He is the one who imparted to man all the knowledge of heaven and of the past and the future (see especially Jellinek, *l.c.* v. 170–176), exactly as Enoch did in the Ethiopic and Slavonic Books of Enoch.

Concerning the origin of the Merkabah-ride, Jellinek ("B. H." iii. p. xxii.) expressed the opinion that Persian Sufism gave rise to its peculiar notions, and Bloch ("Monatsschrift," 1893, pp. 18–25, 69–74, 257–266, 305–311) endeavored to trace them all back to Arabic mysticism. But recent researches concerning the Mithra worship and the Mithra liturgy have cast altogether new light on the whole Merkabah lore. Mithra, the heavenly charioteer, with his Quadriga, a chariot drawn by four horses, who was worshiped in ancient Persia as the god of light and regarded in early Roman times as the prime mover of the world, formed of the four elements (Dio Chrysostomus, "Oratio," xxxvi.; see Cumont, "Die Mysterien des Mithra," 1903, pp. 87–88; Windischmann, "Zoroastrische Studien," 1863, pp. 309–312), was invoked under mysterious rites as the mediator between the inaccessible and unknowable Deity, in the ethereal regions of light, and man on earth (Cumont, *l.c.* pp. 95, 122). These rites bear such a striking resemblance to those by means of which the Merkabah-riders approached the Deity that there can scarcely be any doubt as to the Mithraic origin of the latter (see Dieterich, "Eine Mithrasliturgie," 1903, pp. 7–15). The only difference between them is that while the Mithra-worshipers, at least those of Roman times, had the coming forth of Mithra as the highest god their aim, the Merkabah-riders have the seeing of the Lord on high as their goal, Metaṭron-Mithra, the archangel, being the divine charioteer who ushers them into the presence of God. Otherwise there is the same hallucination at work which makes the ecstatic imagine that he is lifted up from the earth to heaven to see the sun, stars, and winds come forth from their places; to behold the sun (or sun-god) and the entire celestial household, the seven rulers of the celestial poles, or the archangels; and finally to gaze at the luminous youthful Mithra in all his beauty—the youthful Meṭaṭron of the Jewish mystics (see Cumont, *l.c.* pp. 117, 151, *et al.*).

Origin of the Conception.

Such spiritualistic experiences through mystic rites had their origin in Egypt rather than in Persia. Jamblichus ("De Mysteriis," iii. 4, 5) describes the optic and acoustic illusions under which the Egyptian mystic labored as if they were realities, and at the same time he states that in the ecstatic state brought about by magic songs and proper environment the soul is encompassed by a chariot of light and ether (αἰθεριωδές χαὶ αὐγοειδὲς ὀχημα), on which it beholds the heavenly things in the light reflected from above (iii. 14; see Von Harless, "Das Buch von der Aegyptischen Mysterien," pp. 53–54, 65–66). Neoplatonic ideas, accordingly, aided in rendering the Mithra worship the center of the mystic belief in which the world of antiquity sought relief during the period when the gods of classical antiquity were losing their authority and divinity; and Jewish wisdom, following the tendency of the age, embodied it, under the name of Enoch Meṭaṭron, as secret lore in its system (see METAṬRON).

Philo took the idea of the Merkabah with its charioteer Meṭaṭron and applied it to his Logos ("De Somniis," i. 25; "Quis Rerum Divinarum Heres Sit," §§ 42, 48; "De Profugis," § 19; "De Confusione Linguarum," § 28; "De Monarchia," i. 1; comp. Plato, "Phædrus," ii. 46). Maimonides ("Moreh Nebukim," iii. 1–7), in his antagonism to mysticism, went so far as to dissolve the whole Merkabah theophany of Ezekiel into mere physics, notwithstanding the rabbinical warning against disclosing these mysteries (see Pes. 119a). All the stronger, therefore, grew the zeal of the mystics, as is evidenced in the renewed form of the Cabala, which lent to the Merkabah lore and all the ecstatic visions and mystic operations connected therewith new life and vigor; of this the Book of RAZIEL and the later Cabala are ample proof. See MA'ASEH BERESHIT.

K.

MERNEPTAḤ (Greek, Μενεφθῆς): Egyptian king, the fourth of the 19th dynasty; a prominent figure in the discussions concerning the historicalness and chronology of Israel's exodus from Egypt. He was the son and successor of the famous Rameses II. (Sesostris), who is known to have built the cities enumerated in Ex. i. 11. Consequently, no conclusion seemed more certain than this: Rameses II. was the Pharaoh of the oppression; Merneptaḥ, that of the Exodus, which thus would date from the middle or end of the thirteenth century B.C. The discovery of the famous Israel inscription by Petrie ("Six Temples," plates 13–14) has now made this conclusion very doubtful. Line 27 in this inscription, a song of triumph over all foreign enemies of Egypt (Libyans, Hittites, Canaan, Ashkelon, Gezer, Yenu'ama), closes with the words: "Israel ["Y-s-ir(a)-'a-ra"] is annihilated [pulled out], without any [further] growth; Palestine has become like a widow [*i.e.*, helpless] for Egypt." These words, dating from the fifth year of Merneptaḥ, seem to point most naturally to Israel as settled in Palestine; though they have been construed as an allusion to the twelve tribes still wandering in the desert or still being held under bondage in Goshen.

Merneptaḥ reigned for at least twenty-five years, the first five of which were filled with desperate attacks on Egypt by Libyan tribes and by pirates from Europe and Asia Minor. Palestine and central Syria remained tributary, however. The buildings of the king (at Karnak, etc.) are not considerable. His mummy has recently been found at Thebes, and is now in the Museum at Cairo.

E. G. H. W. M. M.

MERODACH-BALADAN: King of Babylon (712 B.C.), who sent letters and a present to Hezekiah, King of Judah, when the latter had recovered from his sickness. Hezekiah, delighted with the courtesy, shows the messengers all his treasures, withholding nothing from them. Whereupon the prophet Isaiah, hearing of the visit, comes to Hezekiah and reproves him for the display he has made of his riches. He foretells the destruction of Hezekiah's kingdom, and the Babylonian captivity (Isa. xxxix.). In the parallel account in II Kings xx. 12-19 the name of this king is given as Berodach-baladan.

According to the Talmud, Baladan's face was changed to that of a dog, he being thereby compelled to abdicate the throne in favor of his son Merodach. Out of reverence, Merodach in all his edicts and ordinances added his name to that of his father in order to indicate that he really was only the representative of the latter (Sanh. 96b).

S. S. L. G.—A. PE.

MEROM: "The waters of Merom" is given in Josh. xi. 5 as the name of the place at which the hosts of the peoples of northern Palestine assembled to meet the invader Joshua and his army. Merom is now commonly identified with the modern Lake al-Ḥulah, about fifteen miles north of the Sea of Galilee, and it is described as being of the shape of a pear with the stem pointing southward. It is three miles wide in its broadest part, and nearly four miles long, from the swamps to the outlet into the River Jordan. The lake is seven feet above the level of the Mediterranean, and varies from ten to sixteen feet in depth. Not far from its southwestern shores there is a considerable plain which seems to be the most probable location of the great battle between Joshua and the North-Canaanitish allies. The commander-in-chief of these forces, gathered from all parts of northern Palestine and even from the Jordan valley, was Jabin, King of Hazor. The great multitude of warriors is compared in numbers with "the sand that is upon the seashore . . . with horses and chariots very many."

The only hint as to Joshua's method of attack is the statement that he came against the enemy suddenly, and fell upon them. This probably indicates a night march and early morning attack as at Gibeon (Josh. x. 9, 10). The Israelites smote them, put them to flight, and pursued them in every direction. Their horses were hamstrung, and their chariots were burned, while their cities and the whole country were laid waste. This last great battle so reduced opposition that Joshua was now ready to partition among the tribes of Israel for a permanent possession the land with its unconquered individual fortresses.

E. G. H. I. M. P.

MERON or **MIRON:** City of Galilee, situated on a mountain, three miles northwest of Safed and four miles south of Giscala, with which city it is almost always mentioned in the Talmud. One of the passages is: "One may eat olives [the product of the Sabbatical year] till the last ones disappear from the trees of Giscala and Meron" (Yer. Sheb. ix. 2). The ascent to Meron was so narrow that two persons could not walk abreast (R. H. 15a), and this description may well be applied to the Meroth fortified by Josephus ("Vita," § 37; "B. J." ii. 20, § 6). Meron is spoken of as a city inhabited by priests (Yer. Ta'an. iv. 5), a fact alluded to by Eleazar ha-Ḳalir in one of his piyyuṭim (comp. Rapoport in his preface to Shalom ha-Kohen's "Ḳore ha-Dorot," *s.v.* "Meron"). It is stated in the Midrash (Eccl. R. xi. 3) that a quarrel resulting in blows broke out between the people of Meron and those of Giscala on account of the remains of R. Eliezer b. Simeon, which each party desired to bury.

To-day Meron is represented by the village of Merun (called in Hebrew writings "Kefar Miron"), celebrated for its very ancient synagogue and for the tombs of some prominent tannaim. Benjamin of Tudela, who visited it, describes a cave there containing the tombs of HILLEL and Shammai and many of their disciples; and he states that R. Benjamin b. Japheth and R. Judah b. Beterah also were buried there. But Benjamin does not mention the tombs of R. Simeon b. Yoḥai and his son Eleazar. Samuel b. Samson, who was at Meron in 1230, speaks of the school and tomb of Simeon b. Yoḥai which he saw there, as well as of the tomb of Eleazar. At the foot of the mountain, Samuel states, are 336 other tombs, and outside of the village are the tombs of Simeon Ḥaṭufah and of the prophet Obadiah (Carmoly, "Itinéraires," pp. 133-134). There is now a magnificent bet ha-midrash enclosing the supposed tombs of Simeon b. Yoḥai and Eleazar, which have become the place of an annual festival, held on Lag be-'Omer, and called "Hillula de-R. Shim'on ben Yoḥai" in commemoration of the death of the supposed author of the Zohar.

Meron is not to be identified with Shimron-meron of Josh. xii. 20, as the latter is called by the Rabbis "Simonia" (Gen. R. lxxxi.; comp. LXX. *ad loc.*), and is the modern Simuniyyah, a village west of Nazareth (Robinson, "Researches," ii. 344). It may, however, be identical with Madon (Josh. xi. 1), which is rendered "Meron" in the Septuagint; and some scholars identify it with Meroz, mentioned in Judges v. 23.

BIBLIOGRAPHY: Benjamin of Tudela, *Itinerary*, ed. Asher, i. 45; Carmoly, *Itinéraires*, pp. 158 *et seq.*; Neubauer, *G. T.* pp. 228 *et seq.*; Robinson, *Researches*, ii. 444; Schwarz, *Tebu'ot ha-Areẓ*, pp. 223-224, Jerusalem, 1900.

J. M. SEL.

MERV: District town in Russian Central Asia, on the River Murgab. The town sprang up when the district was annexed to Russia in 1884. It has a total population of 8,727, including 486 Jews (1899). The old historic Merv is now utterly in ruins, and lies about eight miles east of the present town, adjoining the manufacturing settlement of Bairam Ali, in the imperial domain of the czar.

The Jews seem to have enjoyed greater religious liberty in old Merv than in many other cities. Dr. Wolff ("Mission to Bokhara," pp. 144, 148, New York, 1848), who was in Merv in 1831, and visited it again in 1844 when engaged on his well-known mission to Bokhara, speaks of the Jews there as being in great favor with the calif. They were permitted to maintain the Jewish faith and practises which they had been compelled to abandon at Meshed, where they were obliged to profess Mohammedanism.

O'Donovan, writing in 1882, before Merv was annexed to Russia, speaks of there being but seven Jewish families there. They were mostly engaged in trade, he states, and were treated with considerable tolerance; yet "they were not allowed to call themselves 'Moussai,' their religious name in these Eastern countries, but were compelled to style themselves 'Jedid,' which signifies a convert to the Mussulman faith" ("The Merv Oasis," ii. 129). A writer in the "Jewish Chronicle" (May 12, 1899) has a note regarding the Jews at Merv under the Russian rule. He states that they came from Meshed, which most of them left in 1840 to escape the alternatives of persecution or conformity to the Moslem faith. He adds, however, that "although they openly acknowledge their religion—for the Russian authorities put no impediments in their way in this respect—they live in dread, and meet for prayer in a cellar which is surrounded by a high wall. There is no Ark in the synagogue, and the scrolls of the Law are kept in a separate room, which can be entered only through a secret door. The Jedids have a dejected appearance and fear everybody. They earn a precarious living as artisans."

BIBLIOGRAPHY: O'Donovan, *The Merv Oasis*, 2 vols., London, 1882 (abridged, 1 vol., New York, 1884); Skrine and Ross, *The Heart of Asia*, pp. 349–356, London, 1899; Albrecht, *Russisch Centralasien*, pp. 37–69, Hamburg, 1896; Durrieux and Fauvelle, *Samarkand la Bien Gardée*, pp. 64–96, Paris, 1901.

H. R. A. V. W. J.

MERWAN HA-LEVI: French philanthropist of the second half of the eleventh century; one of the most prominent Jews of Narbonne, who devoted his time and fortune to that community. It seems that he was also in favor with the government, being thus enabled to check unfavorable measures against the Jews. He was the head of a family which produced several famous Jewish scholars, among whom were his son, R. Isaac of Narbonne, and his grandson, Nasi Moses ben Joseph of Narbonne.

BIBLIOGRAPHY: Gross, *Gallia Judaica*, p. 412.

G. A. PE.

MERZBACHER, ABRAHAM: German banker; born 1812 at Baiersdorf near Erlangen; died June 4, 1885, at Munich. He at first intended to follow a rabbinical career; but after an unsuccessful application for the office of rabbi in Ansbach, he settled as a banker in Munich. He was an enthusiastic champion of the moderate conservative Jewish party, and a member of the central committee of the Alliance Israélite Universelle.

Merzbacher was noted chiefly as a patron of Jewish science. He published at his own expense the work "Diḳduḳe Soferim," in 16 volumes, by Raphael Nathan Rabbinovicz (d. 1888). In the interest of this learned protégé and friend, Merzbacher collected one of the largest private Jewish libraries in the world, which now forms part of the city library of Frankfort-on-the-Main. S.

MESERITZ. See MIEDZYRZECZ.

MESHA: King of Moab, tributary to Ahab, King of Israel. He was a sheepmaster, and paid the King of Israel an annual tax consisting of the wool of 100,000 lambs and of 100,000 rams (II Kings iii. 4). He rebelled against Israel and refused to pay tribute; whereupon Jehoram, King of Israel, uniting his forces with those of Jehoshaphat, King of Judah, and of the King of Edom, marched round the southern end of the Dead Sea and invaded the Moabitish territory. That route was chosen, as is mentioned in the MOABITE STONE, because the cities north of the Arnon were fortified by Mesha.

The invading army suffering from want of water, the prophet Elisha, who was present, was consulted upon the suggestion of the King of Judah. He bade them dig trenches in the sandy soil, which were speedily filled with water. The Moabite army, seeing the rays of the sun reflected in the water, imagined that the enemies had quarreled and massacred one another; they made a reckless rush to spoil the camp, only to be repelled, routed, and put to flight with great loss, the few who escaped entering Kir-haraseth. The combined armies advanced into the land unopposed, "marred" the fields with stones, stopped up the cisterns and fountains, felled the forests, and beleaguered the fortress. With 700 warriors Mesha attempted to break through the enemy's lines. Utterly failing in this, and reduced to desperation, he went to the top of the wall, and, in full view of the invaders, offered his eldest son, who should have reigned in his stead, as a burnt offering to propitiate the wrath of his god Chemosh. In consequence of this "there came great wrath upon Israel"; and the Israelites, without pursuing their successes further, at once evacuated the country, leaving Mesha in undisturbed possession of it (*ib.* iii. 6–27). See MOABITE STONE.

E. G. H. C. L.

MESHA (Me'asha): Palestinian amora; lived in the third century at Lydda, in Judea. He seems to have lost his parents when a child, for he was brought up by his grandfather, the eminent haggadist Joshua b. Levi. At an early age he displayed fine intelligence. His grandfather was fond of hearing him recite on Fridays the Biblical portion for the week; and the Midrash relates of him that once in his childhood he became ill and remained in a trance for three days, and that when he recovered his father asked him where he had been all that time; to this Mesha replied that he had been in a confused world and that persons held in honor in this world were there disgraced (Ruth R. iii. 1). Only a few halakot and sayings of his have been preserved in the Talmud.

BIBLIOGRAPHY: Heilprin, *Seder ha-Dorot*, 1882, ii. 270; Bacher, *Ag. Pal. Amor.* i. 128, iii. 614.

S. S. A. S. W.

MESHERSHAYA BAR PAḲOD: Babylonian amora of the sixth and last generation; lived in Sura. In the persecution of Jews by Perozes (Firuz), King of Persia, Mershershaya was imprisoned and executed together with Amemar bar Mar Yanḳaï and the exilarch Huna Mar (469–470).

BIBLIOGRAPHY: Sherira Gaon, *Responsa*, ed. Neubauer, A 34; Heilprin, *Seder ha-Dorot*, 1889, i. 168.

S. S. A. S. W.

MESHULLAM BEN DAVID: German tosafist of the twelfth or of the first half of the thirteenth century. He was the son of the tosafist and liturgist David ben Kalonymus of Münzenburg, and he corresponded with R. Baruch ("Mordekai," Ket.

ii. 149), with Simḥah of Speyer (*ib.* Ḥul. vi. 657, x. 737), and with Isaac Or Zarua' (Ḥayyim Or Zarua', Responsa, Nos. 103, 121). Gross ("Gallia Judaica," p. 196) thinks that the Meshullam mentioned in "Mordekai," Ḥul. vi. 657, is Meshullam of Melun.

BIBLIOGRAPHY: A. Epstein, in *Monatsschrift*, xli. 468; Kohn, *Mardochai ben Hillel*, p. 141.
E. C. M. SEL.

MESHULLAM BEN ISAAC SALEM BEN JOSEPH: Italian poet; lived successively at Mantua and Venice at the end of the sixteenth century and at the beginning of the seventeenth. Like his father, he was a corrector in the Hebrew printing-offices at the above-named cities, which he often supplied with laudatory poems of his own composition. In addition to these, which were inserted at the head of several books, Meshullam was the author of three liturgical poems, namely: (1) "Ḳinah," an elegy on the conflagration at Mantua in 1610; (2) a poem on the Exodus from Egypt; and (3) a seliḥah forming a fourfold alphabetical acrostic.

BIBLIOGRAPHY: Steinschneider, *Cat. Bodl.* col. 1751; Zunz, *Literaturgesch.* p. 424.
G. I. BR.

MESHULLAM BEN ISRAEL: Talmudic scholar of the sixteenth and seventeenth centuries; author of "Mar'eh Meḳom ha-Dinim" (Cracow, 1647), an alphabetical index to the Shulḥan 'Aruk. Fürst ("Bibl. Jud." ii. 369) records that he was known also as "Phoebus," and says he died at Amsterdam in 1652 and was praised by David de Barrios.

BIBLIOGRAPHY: Steinschneider, *Cat. Bodl.* col. 1750.
E. C. M. SEL.

MESHULLAM BEN JACOB OF LUNEL: French Talmudist; died at Lunel in 1170. He directed a Talmudic school which produced several famous men, and was an intimate friend of Abraham b. Isaac, ab bet din of Narbonne, who addressed to him several responsa, and spoke of him in high terms. His Talmudic decisions are quoted in "Sefer ha-Terumot."

Meshullam was interested also in philosophy. According to Ibn Tibbon, whom he encouraged to translate Baḥya's "Al-Hidayah ila Fara'id al-Ḳulub" into Hebrew ("Ḥobot ha-Lebabot"), he wrote several works dealing with moral philosophy, advised and assisted other Jewish writers, and possessed a large library. Judah ibn Tibbon is never weary of praising Meshullam's zeal in investigating the various branches of knowledge.

BIBLIOGRAPHY: Gross, *Gallia Judaica*, p. 229.
S. S. A. PE.

MESHULLAM BEN JOEL HA-KOHEN: Galician Talmudist; died at Lemberg Sept. 25, 1809. At first rabbi at Zurawno (Galicia), he was called to Koretz to succeed his brother Isaac; he then went to Bolechow, and finally to Lemberg. Meshullam's Talmudic attainments are evident not only in his works, but also from the fact that the most famous among his contemporaries requested his responsa. One of these is contained in "Sha'ar ha-Hakanah" (Lemberg, 1794), the work of his ancestor Naphtali ha-Kohen, another in Elijah Gaon's "Shenot Eliyahu."

Meshullam was the author of "Pitḥe Niddah" (Lemberg, 1802), comments on the laws of Niddah. The book contains also a specimen of the author's work on the Pentateuch, entitled "Liḳḳuṭe Yom." One of his responsa is also found in "Zikron Kehunnah," a work by his brother Isaac.

BIBLIOGRAPHY: Buber, *Anshe Shem*, p. 171.
D. A. PE.

MESHULLAM BEN JONAH: Physician and translator of the thirteenth century. It appears that he lived in southern France. He occupied himself with medicine merely as a study, and seems never to have practised. At the desire of a friend named Ḥafeẓ or Shalem, Meshullam translated into Hebrew the medical work "Kitab al-Taẓrif," by Zahrawi. The translator's preface begins with a Hebrew poem in honor of Ḥafiẓ.

BIBLIOGRAPHY: Steinschneider, *Hebr. Uebers.* p. 745; Neubauer, *Cat. Bodl. Hebr. MSS.* No. 2120.
S. J. Z. L.

MESHULLAM BEN KALONYMUS BEN TODROS: French scholar of the twelfth and thirteenth centuries; nasi of Narbonne. Meshullam sided with Judah al-Fakhkhar in his attacks on the works of Maimonides and the philosophers. Nevertheless, he blamed Al-Fakhkhar for the excessive ardor with which the latter fought the Maimonists, saying that among the latter there were many great and pious Jews. In a letter which he wrote to Al-Fakhkhar, Meshullam particularly asked him to be indulgent toward David Ḳimḥi. Al-Fakhkhar yielded to his friend's request, assuring him that he would write nothing against Ḳimḥi.

BIBLIOGRAPHY: Geiger, in *Oẓar Neḥmad*, ii. 172; *idem*, in *Jüd. Zeit.* x. 285; Gross, *Gallia Judaica*, p. 408.
S. S. M. SEL.

MESHULLAM BEN MACHIR (DON BONET CRESCAS DE LUNEL): French scholar; settled at Perpignan, where he died in 1306. Abba Mari, who was a relative of Meshullam, lamented the latter's death in a letter of condolence which he sent to the community of Perpignan ("Minḥat Ḳena'ot," MS. No 132). Abba Mari also bewailed Meshullam's death in one of his liturgical pieces. Gross thinks that Meshullam b. Machir is to be identified with Sen Bonet de Lunel, who wrote a commentary on Ibn Ezra's Bible commentary.

BIBLIOGRAPHY: Gross, *Gallia Judaica*, pp. 289, 464; *idem*, in *R. E. J.* iv. 205; Renan-Neubauer, *Les Rabbins Français*, p. 694.
S. M. SEL.

MESHULLAM BEN NATHAN OF MELUN (called also **Meshullam of Narbonne**): French tosafist; born at Narbonne about 1120. He was a member of the rabbinical college of Narbonne and, with Abraham ben Isaac, ab bet din, and other rabbis, was one of the signatories of a responsum issued there about 1150 ("Teshubot ha-Rambam," p. 4, Leipsic, 1859; "Kol Bo," No. 20). Not long after 1150 Meshullam settled at Melun, where he acquired considerable authority and where he corresponded with some of the greatest rabbis of France, including those of Paris. He obtained the title of "Rab," which had an official character in northern France. Meshullam was rather indulgent in his decisions, which much displeased R. Tam. A polemical correspondence ensued between these two scholars, and Meshullam, in spite of his clever dialectics, was obliged to submit in fear of excommunication (comp. R. Tam, "Sefer ha-Yashar," pp. 72–76; Tos. to Pes. 105a; Beẓah 16a; 'Ab. Zarah 29b; "Mordekai," Shab. iv. 334 *et passim*). Gross (in "Monatsschrift," xvi. 290) and Kohn (*ib.* xxvi. 143) declared that Meshullam b. Nathan of Melun and Meshullam of Narbonne were two different persons, though Gross afterward surrendered this opinion and identified them. Gross conjectures also that this Meshullam may be identical with the Biblical commentator quoted in the commentary to Chronicles (II Chron. xiii. 2) wrongly attributed to Rashi (comp. Zunz, "Z. G." p. 71), and that it is he who is spoken of by Yom-Ṭob of Joigny ("Mordekai," Shab. i. 250).

BIBLIOGRAPHY: Gross, *Gallia Judaica*, pp. 352-353; Zadoc Kahn, in *R. E. J.* i. 235-238; Kohn, *Mardochai ben Hillel*, p. 141.

G. M. SEL.

MESHULLAM PHOEBUS BEN ISRAEL SAMUEL: Chief rabbi of Cracow; born about 1547; died at Cracow Oct. 17, 1617. Meshullam is first known as the head of a flourishing yeshibah at Brest-Litovsk, one of his pupils being Joel Sirḳes. The year of his arrival at Cracow is not recorded, but it is certain that he was there in 1605. He was a recognized authority in rabbinical matters and was consulted by Meïr Lublin (Responsa, No. 81) and by Sirḳes ("She'elot u-Teshubot ha-BaḤ," No. 102). A responsum of Meshullam to Joshua Falk ha-Kohen contains an explanation (to Niddah v. 1) which shows Meshullam to have possessed a thorough knowledge of anatomy and some knowledge of Latin ("She'elot u-Teshubot ha-BaḤ ha-Ḥadashot," No. 34). Two other responsa of his are extant (*ib.* No. 81 and "She'elot u-Teshubot Ge'one Batra'e," No. 44). Abraham Schrenzel in his "Etan ha-Ezraḥi" (Responsa, No. 29) mentions a work by Meshullam Phoebus entitled "Sefer Shemot Giṭṭin," a treatise on the proper names in a bill of divorce. From a manuscript in his possession Meshullam edited the responsa of Moses Minz (Cracow, 1617).

BIBLIOGRAPHY: J. M. Zunz, *'Ir ha-Ẓedeḳ*, pp. 49-52.

H. R. M. SEL.

MESHULLAM BEN SOLOMON (surnamed **En Vidas**): Poet; lived at the beginning of the thirteenth century. Although Jedaiah Bedersi, in his "Iggeret Hitnaẓẓelut," classes Meshullam among the Provençal poets, Meshullam's native country seems to have been Spain. According to Gross ("Gallia Judaica," p. 146), the name of the place דפאה, which is added to Meshullam's name in a Bodleian manuscript (Neubauer, "Cat. Bodl. Hebr. MSS." No. 1970, fol. 201), is to be corrected to דפיירה (= "Da Piera"). In a Florence manuscript Meshullam is designated as "En Vidas de Gerona."

Meshullam ranged himself with the Orthodox in their struggle against the philosophers. He directed his attacks chiefly against the translator of that work, Judah al-Ḥarizi, and wrote several satirical poems on the "Moreh Nebukim." These poems have been published by Steinschneider in the "Sammelband Kleiner Beiträge aus Handschriften" (i. 3). Meshullam was a poet of talent; indeed, Abraham Bedersi, in his review of the principal Hebrew poets, classes him before Benveniste. The greater part of his poetical productions are extant in manuscript (Neubauer, *l.c.*, and the Florence MS. cited above). See DAPIERA.

BIBLIOGRAPHY: Carmoly, in *Ha-Karmel*, vii. 40; Grätz, *Gesch.* vii. 52; Renan-Neubauer, *Les Rabbins Français*, p. 728; Gross, *Gallia Judaica*, p. 146.

G. I. BR.

MESHUMMAD. See APOSTASY.

MESHWI AL-'UKBARI: Founder of the Jewish sect **Al-'Ukbariyyah (Okbarites),** which derived its name from the city of 'Ukbara, near Bagdad, said to have been the place of residence of Meshwi. According to Ḳirḳisani, Meshwi lived after Ishmael Al-'Ukbari; his original name was Moses, but it was converted by his adversaries into Meshwi (= "one whose ideas are confused"). Meshwi differed in many points from both the Karaites and the Rabbinites. Because the Day of Atonement is termed in the Bible "Sabbath of Sabbaths" he affirmed that that feast must always occur on a Sabbath, which would make the Feast of Passover fall on Thursday. He ordered his followers to turn to the West in praying, instead of in the direction of the Temple. According to Meshwi, it was not allowable to offer sacrifices in the Temple on Sabbath. Contrary to the Biblical prohibition, Meshwi is said to have allowed his followers to eat fat. Hadassi ("Eshkol ha-Kofer," § 98), on the authority of David ibn Merwan al-Muḳammaṣ, gives the name of the founder of the sect as Moses of Baalbek, who is probably identical with Meshwi al-'Ukbari. From an obscure passage in the "Oẓar Neḥmad" of the Karaite Tobias ben Moses, Delitzsch concludes that Meshwi embraced Christianity in the later part of his life; but this is highly improbable, for the sect would not have survived the apostasy of its founder, and Meshwi still had followers at the time of Ḳirḳisani.

BIBLIOGRAPHY: Pinsker, *Liḳḳuṭe Ḳadmoniyyot*, i. 16, 43; ii. 88, 98; Fürst, *Gesch. des Karäert.* i. 85; Grätz, *Gesch.* v. 202; Gottlober, *Biḳḳoret le-Toledot ha-Ḳara'im*, p. 204; Harkavy, *Le-Ḳorot ha-Kittot be-Yisrael*, in Grätz, *Dibre Yeme Yisrael*, iii. 509.

S. I. BR.

MESOPOTAMIA. A wide region of western Asia which derived its name from its geographical position between the rivers Tigris and Euphrates. See ARAM; ASSYRIA; BABYLONIA.

MESQUITA: Castilian family, members of which, during the period of the Inquisition, found their way to Holland, England, and America.

David Bueno de Mesquita was one of the wealthy merchants of Amsterdam about the middle of the seventeenth century. The family Bueno de Mesquita still exists in England; in American history also the name appears at an early date. **Luis de Amesquita** is mentioned in the course of the trial of Gabriel of Granada by the Inquisition in Mexico (1642–45). From Obregon it is learned that **Luis de Mesquita** (alias De Amesquita Sarmiento) was a native of Segovia, Castile, and a citizen and merchant of Mexico. The name is found also in the West Indies. **Benjamin Bueno de Mesquita** is mentioned as a Portuguese merchant, resident in Jamaica, who petitioned the king for letters of denization in 1664; he appears to have lived there several years before the date mentioned. Banished from the island shortly after 1664, he went to New York. He was buried in that city, and his tombstone in the old cemetery on New Bowery is the oldest Jewish tombstone existing in New York; it bears the date of 1683. Other members of the same family remained in Jamaica, and their name is repeatedly met with at later dates; thus **Jacob Fernandes Mesquita** was naturalized there in 1740 and **Moses Mesquita** in 1749. **Abraham Bueno de Mesquita** was a resident of the island of Nevis early in the eighteenth century, though administration of his estate was granted in New York, to his daughter Blancha in 1715. Members of this family appear repeatedly in the records of the New York congregation, but the name disappears during the nineteenth century.

Bibliography: *Publications Am. Jew. Hist. Soc.* i. 91-92; v. 48-49, 112; vii. 102-103 (D. Fergusson, *Trial of Gabriel de Granada*); Obregon, *Epoca Colonial*, second series, p. 357, Mexico, 1895; *New York Hist. Soc. Col.* ii. 154; Graetz, *Hist.* vol. v.

A. L. Hü.

MESQUITA, MOSES GOMEZ DE: Haham of the Spanish and Portuguese Jews of England; born in 1688; died May 8, 1751. Mesquita was appointed haham in 1744, in succession to Isaac Nieto, who had resigned, and held the office until his death. He solemnized the second marriage of Isaac Nieto in 1747, and the marriage of his own daughter, in 1749, to Moses Cohen Dazevedo Ferme, who became haham in 1760.

Bibliography: Gaster, *Hist. of Bevis Marks*, pp. 130-131; *Cat. Anglo-Jew. Hist. Exh.* p. 49.

J. I. Co.

MESSENGER. See Agency, Law of.

MESSER, LEON (JUDAH BEN JEHIEL ROFE): Italian rabbi, physician, and philosopher; flourished in Mantua in the latter half of the fifteenth century. He is said to have been born in Naples. The name "Leon" is the usual equivalent of "Judah" and "Messer" (= "Maestro"), the title usually given to physicians. He was rabbi in Mantua, where he had a conflict with his colleague Joseph Colon, in consequence of which both were expelled from the city (1475). Leon wrote a text-book on logic entitled "Miklal Yofi" (see Luzzatto in "Kerem Ḥemed," v. 48), a grammar under the title "Libnat ha-Sappir," commentaries to the "Logic" and the "Ethics" of Aristotle, and a text-book of rhetoric under the title "Nofet Ẓufim." The last-mentioned is the only one of his works which has been printed; it was published in Mantua before 1480 and was reedited by Jellinek in 1863 (Vienna). The object of the work was both apologetic and propagandic. The author desired to demonstrate to the non-Jewish world that the Jews were not devoid of the literary sense, and he wished to prove to his coreligionists that Judaism is not hostile to secular studies, which contribute to a better appreciation of Jewish literature. His theories follow chiefly those of Cicero and Quintilian. The book, as is evident from the fact that it was not reprinted within 400 years, had only a small circle of readers, but within this circle it was highly appreciated. Azariah dei Rossi quotes Leon as a witness to the value of secular studies (ch. ii., in "Me'or 'Enayim," ed. Benjacob, i. 75, Wilna, 1863), and Joseph Solomon Delmedigo recommends the book to the Karaite Zarah ben Nathan (Geiger, "Melo Chofnajim," p. 19, Berlin, 1840). Messer Leon's son, **David,** also a physician of Mantua, is the author of "Tehillah le-Dawid," a book on philosophy, edited by his grandson Aaron ben Judah (Constantinople, 1577).

Bibliography: *Cat. Bodl.* cols. 1331-1332; Nepi-Ghirondi, *Toledot Gedole Yisrael*, p. 200; Wolf, *Bibl. Hebr.* iii. 333-334; De Rossi, *Dizionario*, ii. 7; Dukes, *Ehrensäulen*, pp. 55 *et seq.*, Vienna, 1837; Grätz, *Gesch.* viii. 243-244.

D.

MESSIAH (Hebr., "Ha-Mashiaḥ"; Aramaic, "Meshiḥa" = "anointed one"): The name or title of the ideal king of the Messianic age; used also without the article as a proper name—"Mashiaḥ" (in the Babylonian Talmud and in the midrash literature), like Χριστός in the Gospels. The Grecized Μεσσιας of the New Testament (John i. 41, iv. 25) is a transliteration of the Aramaic form, Aramaic being the spoken language of Palestine in the time of Jesus. "The Messiah" (with the article and not in apposition with another word) is, however, not an Old Testament expression, but occurs for the first time in apocalyptic literature. Similarly, in all probability the use of the word "Mashiaḥ" to denote the Messianic king is not found earlier than the apocalyptic literature. In the Old Testament the earliest use of the word is with Yhwh (or with a pronominal suffix referring to Yhwh) as a title of the ruling sovereign Meshiaḥ Yhwh ("God's anointed one"; I Sam. ii. 10, 35; xii. 3, 5; xvi. 6; xxvi. 9, 11, 16, 23, II Sam. i. 14, 16; xix. 21; II Chron. vi. 42; Ps. xviii. 51 [A. V. 50]; xx. 7 [A. V. 6]; cxxxii. 17 [applying to David]; Lam. iv. 20). In post-exilic times, the high priest, filling the place formerly occupied by the king, is spoken of as "ha-Kohen ha-Mashiaḥ" (the anointed priest; Lev. iv. 3, 5, 16; vi. 5), also (Dan. ix. 25, 26) as "Mashiaḥ Nagid" (an anointed one, a ruler) and simply "Mashiaḥ" (an anointed one), referring to Onias III. As the anointing of the high priest consecrated him above all his brethren to God's service and gave him immediate access to God (comp. Lev. viii. 12, xxi. 10-12; Zech. iii. 7), so the anointing of the king made him Meshiaḥ Yhwh, placed him in a special relationship to God, and established him as the one chosen by God to represent His rulership in Israel and to bear witness to His glory before the nations (comp. II Sam. vii. 8-11, 14; Isa. lv. 4; Ps. lxxxix. 4, 21-29). As "God's anointed one" the king was sacrosanct and inviolable (comp. I Sam. xxvi. 9). Hence the later applications of the title "Meshiaḥ Yhwh" in the Old Testament.

The Name.

In Isa. xlv. 1 Cyrus is called "God's anointed one," because God has called him and given him victory after victory for the distinct purpose of putting an end to the Babylonian kingdom and the worship of idols, of setting free exiled Israel, and thus introducing the new era of God's universal dominion. In Ps. cv. 15 the Patriarchs are called "God's anointed ones" because they are under the special protection of God and therefore inviolable. Finally, in Hab. iii. 13, Ps. xxviii. 8, lxxxiv. 10 (A. V.

9), and possibly in lxxxix. 39, 52 (A. V. 38, 51), the title is applied to Israel, God's chosen people. See ANOINTING.

"Mashiaḥ" (anointed one of God) in Ps. ii. 2, which was formerly thought to have Messianic reference, is now taken as referring either to a Hasmonean king or to Israel. The latter interpretation is that prevailing in the Midrash (comp. Midr. Rabbah and Tanḥuma, Emor; Yalḳuṭ, Toledot, near end; Midr. Shoḥer Ṭob, *ad loc.*), though the Messianic interpretation occurs in the eschatological description (Pesiḳ. Zuṭarta, Balaḳ).

But though the name is of later origin, the idea of a personal Messiah runs through the Old Testament. It is the natural outcome of the prophetic future hope. The first prophet to give a detailed picture of the future ideal king was Isaiah (ix. 1–6, xi. 1–10, xxxii. 1–5). Of late the authenticity of these passages, and also of those passages in Jeremiah and Ezekiel which give expression to the hope in a Messiah, has been disputed by various Biblical scholars (comp. Hackmann, "Die Zukunftserwartung des Jesaiah"; Volz, "Die Vorexilische Jahweprophetie und der Messias"; Marti, "Gesch. der Israelitischen Religion," pp. 190 *et seq.*; *idem*, "Das Buch Jesaia"; Cheyne, "Introduction to Isaiah," and edition and transl. of Isaiah in "S. B. O. T.").

The Ideal in Isaiah.

The objections of these scholars, however, rest principally on the hypothesis that the idea of the Messiah is inseparably bound up with the desire for universal dominion, whereas, in reality, this feature is not a characteristic of the Messianic hope until a later stage of its development. The ideal king to whom Isaiah looks forward will be a scion of the stock of Jesse, on whom will rest the spirit of God as a spirit of wisdom, valor, and religion, and who will rule in the fear of God, his loins girt with righteousness and faithfulness (xi. 1–3a, 5). He will not engage in war or in the conquest of nations; the paraphernalia of war will be destroyed (ix. 4); his sole concern will be to establish justice among his people (ix. 6b; xi. 3b, 4). The fruit of his righteous government will be peace and order throughout the land. The lamb will not dread the wolf, nor will the leopard harm the kid (xi. 8); that is, as the following verse explains, tyranny and violence will no longer be practised on God's holy mountain, for the land will be full of the knowledge of God as the water covers the sea (comp. xxxii. 1, 2, 16). The people will not aspire to political greatness, but will lead a pastoral life (xxxii. 18, 20). Under such ideal conditions the country can not but prosper, nor need it fear attack from outside nations (ix. 6a, xxxii. 15). The newly risen scion of Jesse will stand forth as a beacon to other nations, and they will come to him for guidance and arbitration (xi. 10). He will rightly be called "Wonderful Counselor," "Godlike Hero," "Constant Father," "Prince of Peace" (ix. 5).

This picture of the future fully accords with Isaiah's view, that the judgment will lead to a spiritual regeneration and bring about a state of moral and religious perfection; and it agrees also with the doctrine, which, in his bitter opposition to the alliances with Assyria and Egypt, he preached to his people—the doctrine, namely, that their so concern should be God and their sole reliance be c Him, for thus, and thus only, might they endure (vi 9; comp. also v. 4, viii. 13, xxx. 15). The prophe advocated a government which would be in co formity with God's will and be regulated by H laws of righteousness. In connection with Isaiah Messianic hope it remains to be observed that tl "Immanuel" passage, Isa. vii. 14, which is inte preted in Matt. i. 23 as referring to the birth Jesus, has, as Robertson Smith ("The Prophets Israel," pp. 271 *et seq.*, 426 *et seq.*) and others ha pointed out, no Messianic import whatever. T name has reference merely to even of the immediate present. He mea to give a token by which the truth his prophetic word may be teste saying that any young woman givi birth to a son in the near future will call him "I manuel" (= "God with us"), in remembrance of t withdrawal of the Syrian-Ephraimitic armies fro the country (v. 16). "'Almah" does not me "virgin" (as given in A. V. and other versions; t only word meaning this is "betulah"), but "a you woman sexually mature," whether married or u married; the article "ha-" of "ha-'almah" is t generic article.

The "Immanuel" Passage.

The idea of a personal Messiah is not met with aga until the time of Jeremiah and Ezekiel (the Messian picture of Micah v. 1, 3–8, as is proved by the fa that in it Israel and the Messiah hold dominion ov the nations, according to this view can not be pre-exilic product of prophecy; in fact, it mu have originated late in post-exilic times). Je miah's picture of the Messiah is not a detailed on but, like his future hope in general, it agrees in essentials with that of Isaiah. The Messiah will "a righteous sprout of David," who will establi just judgment and wise government in the countr and whose name will be יהוה צדקנו (= "God is o salvation"; xxiii. 5, 6; these t verses recur in almost the same fo in xxxiii. 15, 16, but in the latter ve the name is applied to Jerusalem, application which did not origina with Jeremiah. Ch. xxx. 9 *et seq.*, 21 does not cla consideration here, as it is of later origin).

In Jeremiah and Ezekiel.

In Ezekiel, the Messiah is a purely passive figu the only personal reference to him being in xvii. —"he will become a mighty cedar" (Hebr.). T regeneration of the people, like their restoration, exclusively the work of God.

But in xxxiv. 23 *et seq.*, xxxvii. 24 *et seq.*, whi passages date from exilic times, there is an entir new feature—the prophecy that David will be t king of the future state. As after the decline the Holy Roman Empire the saga arose of the retu of the emperor-hero Barbarossa, so, after the fall the nation, the Jews of the Exile dreamed of t coming of a second David, who would reestabli them as a glorious nation. So Ezekiel lays emp sis on the fact that the future Israel is to be a unit nation as it was under David of old. The hope the return of David is expressed also in the spuri passage mentioned above (Jer. xxx. 9) and in t gloss to Hos. iii. 5 ("and David their king"), and net with sporadically also in Neo-Hebraic apocalyp-ic literature (see below).

In post-exilic prophetic literature the hope in a Messiah is found only in the first two prophets of he post-exilic community, Haggai and Zechariah, nd in Deutero-Zechariah, ch. ix., which, probably, lates from the time of the Seleucids. Haggai and Zechariah see in Zerubbabel the promised "sprout f David"; but they state merely that he will re-build the Temple and attain great eminence as a uler (Hag. ii. 23; Zech. iii. 8, vi. 12).

Deutero-Zechariah's Messiah has much in com-mon with Isaiah's. He is described (Zech. ix. 9, 10) s a righteous Prince of Peace, who will rise from he ranks of the pious and oppressed, who will ride nto Jerusalem not in military splendor, but on an ss (comp. Jesus' entry into Jerusalem on an ass, nd also Ibn Ḳutaibah's account of Salman, the overnor of Medina at the time of the dissensions f the califs, who rode upon an ass in order to how his advocacy of peace). For, unlike worldly ulers, he will not maintain his dominion by the word—he will destroy all the instruments of var (if, instead of הכרתי, is read in accordance vith the LXX. הִכְרִת, 3d s. m.); but, by his ju-isdiction, which will extend to the ends of the arth, he will establish peace among the nations. Thus Deutero-Zechariah's conception of the Messiah ombines Isaiah's conception with the hope of world-ominion cherished by his own age.

The personal Messiah does not figure at all in the uture hope of Deutero-Isaiah, whose lofty univer-alism marks the final step in the development of the religious ideas of the Prophets.

Ideal of the Second Isaiah.

The salvation of mankind is the goal of history, and Israel's prerogative be-comes but the privilege of suffering for the good of the whole world. God as called Israel for the realization of His purpose oward man. Israel, and not an individual, is "the ervant of God" (Isa. xlii. 1–6, xlix. 1–6, l. 4–9, i. 13–liii. 12), through whom the regeneration of ankind will be accomplished, who will spread the ue religion among all nations, convert all men into illing servants of God, and lead all tongues to onfess Him (xlv. 23). Naturally, not the actual srael of the present is meant, but the ideal Israel f the future, risen to spiritual heights in conse-uence of his wonderful deliverance by God. For is high destiny Israel has been especially fitted by eason of the religious experience which God has ored up in him in the course of his history; and, y submitting, in accordance with God's will, to suf-ring and ignominy, he fulfils his mission and ad-ances toward his final goal. In Isa. ii. 1–4 and Micah iv. 1–4 there is the same picture of the Mes-anic future as in Deutero-Isaiah—Jerusalem as the eligious center of the world, whence salvation will adiate to all men—but contain the additional prom-e that universal peace will ensue in consequence ereof. In like manner the post-exilic prophets rito-Isaiah, Malachi, and Joel, and the post-exilic pocalypse of Isaiah, xxiv.–xxvii., have no personal Messiah. According to them, God Himself, without e instrumentality of a man, will redeem Israel from is present misery and bring about the new era of sal-vation. The conclusion, however, of Malachi (the authorship of which is doubtful) speaks of a mes-senger, Elijah, whom God will send to convert men and thus pave the way for His own coming.

As in the prophetic writings just enumerated, so in the Apocrypha of the Old Testament the figure of the Messiah has no prominence whatever. In I Maccabees there is a brief general ref-

In the Apocrypha.

erence to the promise given to David, that his throne would be reestablished (ii. 57), but Ecclesiasticus, Judith, Tobit, Baruch, II Maccabees, and the Wisdom of Solomon contain no mention of the Davidic hope. The Hellenistic author of the Wis-dom of Solomon is so thoroughly universalistic that the idea of a Messiah is precluded. His eschatolog-ical picture shows no nationalistic feature whatever.

The natural deduction from the facts thus far out-lined is that while from the time of the Prophets the belief in an ideal future determined the character and tendency of Jewish religious life and thought to such an extent that this belief may be called the special characteristic of the Jewish genius, still, in the periods thus far covered, the idea of a personal Messiah is far from having that general prominence which one would, at first, be inclined to assume. Further, it has been seen how Deutero-Isaiah her-alded Cyrus as the favorite of God, the hero called by God to introduce the new era of universal bliss. In like manner, no doubt, as Kampers has shown in his "Alexander der Grosse und die Idee des Welt-imperiums in Prophetie und Sage," the Jewish con-temporaries of Alexander the Great, dazzled by his glorious achievements, hailed him as the divinely appointed deliverer, the inaugurator of the period of universal peace promised by the Prophets. Proof of this is: (1) The legend related in

Alexander as Messiah.

Josephus ("Ant." xi. 8) and in the Talmud (Yoma 67b) of the audience of the high priest Jaddua (in the Tal-mud it is Simon the Just) with Alex-ander the Great in Gaza. Alexander recognizes in the high priest the man who had appeared to him in a dream, urging him to the conquest of Asia and promising him that he himself would lead his army and deliver the Persian kingdom into his hands; he prostrates himself to worship God, whose name he sees inscribed on the plate of gold on the high priest's cidaris, accompanies the high priest to Jeru-salem to sacrifice to God in His Temple, and is there shown the Book of Daniel, in which it is written that the Persian kingdom will be conquered by a Greek—a prophecy which Alexander applies to himself. (2) The various sagas which sprang up about Alexander, chiefly among the Jews in Alex-andria, and out of which the Alexander romance of pseudo-Callisthenes grew, the only explanation of which is that Alexander had once been the cen-tral figure in their future hope. (3) The apocalyp-tic traditions about Alexander the Great in medieval apocalyptic literature and also in the midrashic liter-ature—for example, the tradition (mentioned by Josephus) of Alexander imprisoning Gog and Magog behind the mountains of darkness in the far north. The version of this legend given by Jacob of Serug (521 C.E.) and in the Koran, sura 18 (comp.

Kampers, *l.c.* pp. 73, 76 *et seq.*) leaves no doubt that it was purely of apocalyptic origin.

But while all these hopes centering in Alexander the Great bear witness to the liberality and broad-mindedness of the Jews of that time, they, on the other hand, corroborate the conclusion, expressed above, that the hope in the Messiah had, as yet, no definite form and can not have been commonly an article of faith. This is true, not only of the time of Alexander the Great, but even as late as the first period of apocalyptic literature, and is proved by the absence of a personal Messiah in the oldest apocalyptic writing, the Book of Daniel, as well as in the oldest part of the Book of Enoch ("The Apocalypse of the Ten Weeks") and in the Book of Jubilees, which also date from the Maccabean period, apart from the fact, pointed out above, that in the contemporaneous apocrypha there is but vague reference to the Messiah. The "one of the likeness of man" ("ke-bar enash") of Dan. vii. 13 (Hebr.), to whom the rulership in the divine world-monarchy will be entrusted, is, according to the author's own explanation (vii. 18, 22, 27), the nation of God's holy ones (*i.e.*, the faithful Jews). These constitute the earthly representatives of God in the "civitas Dei," and in contrast to the other nations of the world, who are represented under the figures of animals, they are represented under the figure of a man in order to signify that in them the divine ideal of manhood has preserved itself most faithfully.

Rise of Popular Belief in a Personal Messiah.

Not until after the fall of the Maccabean dynasty, when the despotic government of Herod the Great and his family, and the increasing tyranny of the Roman empire had made their condition ever more unbearable, did the Jews seek refuge in the hope of a personal Messiah. They yearned for the promised deliverer of the house of David, who would free them from the yoke of the hated foreign usurper, would put an end to the impious Roman rule, and would establish His own reign of peace and justice in its place. In this way their hopes became gradually centered in the Messiah. As evidence that in the Roman period the Messianic hope had become universal among the Jews may be adduced: (1) Jesus' conviction that he was the Messiah, a conviction inspired in him by the current belief in a Messiah, as is shown by the fact that on his entry into Jerusalem the populace hailed him as such; (2) the testimony of Josephus ("B. J." vi. 5, § 4), Tacitus ("Hist." v. 13), and Suetonius (Vespasian, iv.) regarding the Messianic belief of the Jewish people at that time; (3) the fact that even in Philo's picture of the future, in spite of its moralistic tendency, the Messianic king has a place (comp. "De Præmiis et Pœnis," § 16). It may be noted in this connection that the "Prayer for the Coming of the Messiah," as the version of it given both in the Babylonian and in the Palestinian recensions of the Shemoneh 'Esreh shows (see Nos. 14 and 15 respectively), can not have become an integral part of the daily prayers later than the time immediately following the destruction of the Temple, for in that period the "Shemoneh 'Esreh" received its present form. Hillel's assertion (Sanh. 98b) that there would be no future Messia for Israel since the latter had had its Messiah in tl days of Hezekiah, can have no weight as a contra argument, as Hillel lived in the reign of Herc the Great, at the beginning of the period whic marks the development of the popular belief in tl Messiah.

As the future hopes of the Jews became Messian in character the figure of the Messiah assumed central and permanent place in apocalyptic liter ture: and as apocalyptic literature in general, the Messiah-concept in particular, embodies a mu titude of bizarre fantasies which can not possib be reconciled or woven into anything like a co nected picture. There are many factors which co tributed to this manifold and variegated imager Not only was all the Messianic and quasi-Messian material of the Scriptures collected, and out of i by means of subtle combinations, after the mann of the Midrash, a picture of the Messiah sedulous drawn, but everything poetical or figurative in t Prophets' descriptions of the future was taken a literal sense and expounded and dogmatized a cordingly. Many foreign elements, moreover, cre in at this time and became part of the general pc pourri of imagery relating to the Messiah. Th being the case, an exceedingly complex and dif cult question arises—where, in the Messiah-picture and, indeed, in the pictures of the future in genera

Development of Conception.

presented by apocalyptic literatur has one to deal with organic develo ment from prophetic ideas, and whe with foreign religious elements? present it is not possible to form final judgment in regard to the pla of origin of these foreign ideas. The materi from the Assyro-Babylonian religion and mytholog which has been offered in recent years by Assyri ogists shows what an involved question is present in this one point, and that a series of prelimina and exhaustive studies is necessary before a fin decision can be reached regarding it or the vario questions bound up with it. The one thing safe maintain in this connection is, perhaps, that, accor ing to the time at which the heterogeneous cha acter of the conceptions becomes noticeable in t literature, Alexandria must have had a promine part in the fusion of the native and foreign elemen since that city had been from the time of Alexa der the Great the seat of religious syncretism well as the intellectual metropolis of the civiliz world.

For the better understanding of the Messianic p tures in apocalyptic literature it is important point out that, although frequently interlaced, t distinct sets of ideas may be traced—the one concerned with this world, hence realistic and r tional; the other directed to the world to come, hen transcendent and universalistic. The Messiah p sents a correspondingly double character. Side side with the traditional idea of an earthly ki of the house of David is the new conception of heavenly preexistent Messiah, from which it follo that in regard to the question of the Messiah t older apocalyptic literature, as well as the young rabbinical branch, falls naturally into two group

In the Older Apocalyptic Literature. In the older apocalyptic literature the first book to be mentioned in which the Messiah figures as an earthly king is "The Vision of the Seventy Shepherds of the Book of Enoch" (ch. lxxxv.–xc.) of the time of John Hyrcanus (135–105 B.C.). The Messiah appears under the figure of a white bull at the conclusion of the world-drama (xc. 37 *et seq.*) and commands the respect and fear of all the heathen, who eventually become converted to God. Yet he does not take any actual rôle. It is God Himself who wards off the last attack of the heathen against Israel, gives judgment, and establishes the world-dominion of Israel. Second in this group come those parts of the Sibylline Books whose date, as Geffken's recent critical analysis has established ("Komposition und Entstehungszeit der Oracula Sibyllina," pp. 7–13), is about the year 83 B.C. The Messiah is pictured (verses 652-666) as a king sent by God from the rising of the sun, who will put an end to war all over the earth, inasmuch as he will destroy some peoples and make permanent treaties with the others; in all his actions he will be solicitous not to follow his own counsel, but to obey the commands of God. The writer then describes at length the attack by the heathen nations on the magnificent Temple of God and on the Holy Land, and the annihilation of the nations by God; the Last Judgment, with the ensuing conversion of the heathen to God; the establishment of God's eternal kingdom over all men and the reign of universal peace; but, strange to say, throughout the description there is no mention of the Messiah. In fact, in verses 781 *et seq.* the Israelites are spoken of as the prophets of God, the judges of mankind, and the just kings who will put an end to the sway of the sword upon earth.

In the Psalms of Solomon. "The Vision of the Seventy Shepherds" and Sibyllines, iii. 652 *et seq.* say nothing whatever about the lineage of the earthly Messiah, but in the Psalms of Solomon (xvii.), which were called forth by the conquest of Jerusalem by Pompey (63 B.C.), he is designated as the "son of David," who will appear at a time known only to God. These Psalms (*l.c.*) contain a more detailed description of his personality and of his reign than any other writing of that period. The Messiah will first crush the unjust rulers and rid Jerusalem of, and destroy, the impious heathen. Then he will gather the scattered ones of Israel, distribute them through the land according to their tribes, and found his own kingdom of peace and justice. No wicked person will be tolerated in his kindgom nor will foreigners be allowed to dwell there. He will subject the heathen nations to his rule, glorify the Lord before the whole world, and make Jerusalem pure and holy as of old, so that the nations will come from the ends of the earth to witness God's glory. The description which follows of his righteous reign shows the influence of Isa. xi. 1 *et seq.* Free from sin, strong in the divine fear, and filled with the spirit of God, of valor, and of justice, he will tend the flock of the Lord faithfully, hold the higher officers in check, and make sinners cease by the power of his word, so that injustice and tyranny will not be practised in the land. He will not rely upon horses and warriors, nor heap up gold and silver to wage war, nor keep armies. In God alone will he place his trust, and his strength will be in Him.

In the Apocalypse of Baruch (70–100 C.E.) the earthly Messiah will appear at the close of the fourth (*i.e.*, the Roman) world-empire and destroy it. The last ruler of the empire will, after his hosts have been destroyed, be brought in chains before the Messiah on Mount Zion, and there, after the impiousness of his rule has been pointed out to him, he will be put to death by the Messiah's own hand. Of the other nations, those hostile to Israel will be put to the sword and the remainder subjected to the rule of the Messiah, who will establish himself on the throne of his kingdom, inaugurate the reign of morality and bliss, and hold dominion until the end of time, that is, until the consummation of the present world (xxix. 3, xxxix. 5–xl. 3, lxxii.–lxxiii. 4. Ch. xxx. 1 is to be taken, with Volz ["Jüdische Eschatologie," pp. 37, 203], as Christian interpolation).

In the Testaments of the Patriarchs. The Testament of Levi (ch. viii. and xviii.) shows a unique conception of the Messiah. He is not, as in the Testament of Judah (see below) and according to the popular belief, a descendant of David, but a priestly king of the tribe of Levi. His character and activity are altogether spiritual. The pouring out of the spirit and knowledge of the Lord over all mankind and the cessation of sin and evil will be the fruit of his ideal priesthood, which will last for all eternity. He himself will open the doors of paradise, cast aside the sword threatening Adam, and give the saints to eat of the tree of life. He will chain up Belial and will give his children power to trample on the evil spirits. The picture of the Messiah in the Testament of Judah (ch. xxiv.), although far more brief, resembles, in its spiritual character and in its universalistic tendency, that in the Testament of Levi. The sole mission of the Messiah will be the regeneration of mankind, and his kingdom will be one of justice and salvation for the whole world. If, as Bousset sought to prove ("Zeitschrift für die Neutestamentliche Wissenschaft," i. 193 *et seq.*), the Testaments of the Twelve Patriarchs date mainly from the time of the Maccabees, then the Messiah-conception of the Testament of Levi is easily accounted for; the author expects that the future Savior will be a prince of the reigning priestly house of the Maccabees.

The Heavenly Messiah. The oldest apocalypse in which the conception of a preexistent heavenly Messiah is met with is the Messiological section of the Book of Enoch (xxxvii.–lxxi.) of the first century B.C. The Messiah is called "the Son of Man," and is described as an angelic being, his countenance resembling a man's, and as occupying a seat in heaven beside the Ancient of Days (xlvi. 1), or, as it is expressed in ch. xxxix. 7, "under the wings of the Lord of spirits." In ch. xlviii. 3, 6, xlix. 2b it is stated that "His name was called before the Lord of spirits before the sun and the signs of the zodiac were created, and before the stars of heaven were made"; that "He was chosen and hidden with God before the world was created, and will remain in His presence forevermore" (comp. also lxii. 6); and that "His glory will last from eternity unto eternity and his might from generation unto generation" (that "his name" in xlviii. 3 means really "son of man" is evident from verse 6; comp. the similar use of "Shem YHWH" for "YHWH" in Isa. xxx. 27). He is represented as the embodiment of justice and wisdom and as the medium of all God's revelations to men (xlvi. 3; xlix. 1, 2a, 3). At the end of time the Lord will reveal him to the world and will place him on the throne of His glory in order that he may judge all creatures in accordance with the end to which God had chosen him from the beginning. When he rises for the judgment all the world will fall down before him, and adore and extol him, and give praise to the Lord of spirits. The angels in heaven also, and the elect in the Garden of Life, will join in his praise and will glorify the Lord. "He will judge all hidden things, and no one will be able to make vain excuses to him"; he will judge also Azazel, with all his associates and all his hosts. The wicked ones of the earth, especially all kings and potentates, he will give over to damnation, but for the just and chosen ones he will prepare eternal bliss, and he will dwell in their midst for all eternity (xlv. 3, 4; xlvi. 4–6; xlviii. 4–10; xlix. 4; li. 3; lv. 4; lxi. 7–lxii. 14).

It is worthy of special note that in the appendix to the Messiological section of Enoch, the latter himself is the Son of Man = Messiah (lxxi. 14), and, as in the Slavonic Book of Enoch and the Hebrew Book of Enoch (see JEW. ENCYC. i. 676, *s.v.* APOCALYPTIC LITERATURE), as well as throughout rabbinical literature, Enoch is identical with METAṬRON = *Μετάθρονος* or *Μετατύρανος* (*i.e.*, the highest, ministering spirit, who stands next to God and represents His rulership over the universe), so there is an important connecting-link between the conception of the Son of Man = Messiah, and the Logos, which appears repeatedly in Philo in place of the earthly future king (comp., *e.g.*, his interpretation of "ẓemaḥ," Zech. vi. 12, in "De Confess." § 14; see MEMRA). The Fourth Book of Ezra (about 100 C.E.) presents both the preexistent and the earthly Messiah. The latter is seen in ch. vii. 28, xi. 37–46, xii. 31–34, where the Messiah is represented as the Lion "who will spring from the seed of David," will destroy the fourth (*i.e.*, the Roman) world-monarchy, will rule 400 years till the end of the Messianic interim, and then will die, together with all men. The former appears in the vision of the man rising from the sea (ch. xiii.). Here, as in the Messiological section, the Messiah is described as "one resembling a man" and is called "ille homo" or "ipse homo" (verses 3, 12). The statement is made also (under the influence of Dan. vii. 13) that he "flew with the clouds of heaven." Other points of contact with the Messiological Book are: the statement that "he is the one whom the Most High has reserved for many ages to deliver creation" (verse 26); the reference to his being hidden with God (verse 52)—"Even as no one can fathom nor learn what is in the depths of the sea, so none of the inhabitants of earth can see My son nor his escort [*i.e.*, the host of angels who will accompany him when he appears upon earth], unless it be at the appointed hour"; and, finally, the obvious reference to his preexistence in heaven, where the promise is given to Ezra, "Thou wilt be taken from among men [to heaven] and wilt dwell with My son and with thy comrades until the end of time" (xiv. 9).

Whether the Messiah in Sibyllines v. 415–430, where he is called "a blessed man coming from heaven," is the preexistent or the earthly Messiah can not be determined. In the Assumptio Mosis, however (*c.* 4 B.C.), it may be concluded, on the ground of the identification of the Son of Man = Messiah with Enoch = Meṭaṭron in Enoch lxxi. 14, that it is the preexistent Messiah who is referred to (x. 2), for it is stated that, at the end of the last tribulation, when God's dominion will be established over all creation, "the hands of the angel who stands in the highest place will be filled, and he will immediately avenge them [Israel] on their enemies." As the author of the Fourth Book of Ezra (xiii.), as well as the author of the Messiological Book, evidently had Dan. vii. 13 in mind when he described the preexistent Messiah, it may be mentioned here that, while the Messianic interpretation of this passage prevails in the rabbinic literature (the oldest example is the Messianic tradition in Sanh. 98a, for which Joshua b. Levi is mentioned as authority), the Greek text of Dan. vii. 13 presents not only the Messianic interpretation of "Bar Nash," but unmistakably also, in *καὶ ὡς παλαιὸς ἡμερῶν παρῆν* added after *ὡς υἱὸς ἀνθρώπου ἤρχετο*, the conception of the preexistent Messiah.

In Rabbinic Literature.

Moreover, contrary to the view held by many, that all the passages concerning the Son of Man = Messiah in the Book of Enoch and IV Ezra are of Christian origin, it may be pointed out that the phrase "Bar Nash" (= "Son of Man") must have been a common name for an angel of the highest order among the Palestinian Jews of the first Christian centuries. Yer. Yoma v. relates that, when reference was made in the bet ha-midrash to Simon the Just's having, every year of the forty during which he was high priest, been accompanied into the Holy of Holies on the Day of Atonement by an "aged one," veiled and garbed in linen (*i.e.*, by a heavenly being; comp. the "labush ha-badim" in Ezek. ix. 1, 3 *et al.*), R. Abbahu objected: "Does not the prohibition, 'No man shall be present in the Tabernacle when the high priest enters the sanctuary,' extend to those of whom it is said, 'the appearance of their countenance was that of a man's countenance'?" (Lev. xvi. 17; Ezek. i. 10). Whereupon the rejoinder was made: "Who says that that being was Bar Nash? It was the All Holy Himself." It may be noted in passing that this haggadah is of importance for the Greek text of Dan. vii. 13 as well as for the identification of the Son of Man = Messiah with Enoch = Meṭaṭron.

In the rabbinical apocalyptic literature the conception of an earthly Messiah is the prevailing one, and from the end of the first century of the common era it is also the one officially accepted by Judaism. As proof of this may be given: (1) "The Prayer for the Coming of the Messiah," mentioned above, in

ıich the Messiah is called "descendant of David."
The information given in the second century by stin ("Dialogus cum Tryphone," ch. xlix.) and the author of "Philosophumena" (ix. 30). Both ·iters state expressly that, contrary to the belief the Christians, the Jews emphasize the human gin of the Messiah, and the author of "Philosophu-·na" adds that they expect him to be descended ·m David. (3) The liturgy of later times, which, e the Daily Prayer, calls him the descendant of ·vid throughout. His mission is, in all essential ·pects, the same as in the apocalypses of the older riod: he is to free Israel from the power of e heathen world, kill its ruler and destroy his sts, and set up his own kingdom of peace ·mp. the descriptions of him in JEW. ENCYC. 675, *s.v.* APOCALYPTIC LITERATURE, NEO-HE-·AIC).

The conception of the preexistent Messiah is met th in Pesiḳ. R. xxxiii., xxxvi. (pp. 152b, 162, ed. iedmann; comp. Yalḳ. i. 339). In accordance with the Messiological section of Enoch the former of these two passages says: "At the beginning of the creation of the world was born the King Messiah, who mounted into God's oughts before the world was made"; and in the ter passage it is related that God contemplated the ·ssiah and his works before the creation of the ·rld and concealed him under His throne; that ·tan, having asked God who the Light was under s throne, was told it was the one who would ·ing him to shame in the future, and, being then al-·wed, at his request, to see the Messiah, he trembled ·d sank to the ground, crying out, "Truly this the Messiah who will deliver me and all hea-·n kings over to hell." God calls the Messiah ·phraim, my righteous Messiah."

Heavenly Preexistence.

The preexistent Messiah is presented also in the ·ggadah (Pes. 54a; Ned. 39a; Yalḳ. i. 20; *et al.*), ·ere the name of the Messiah is included among the ·ven things created before the world was made, and ·ere he is called "Yinnon," reference being made Ps. lxxii. 17 (which passage probably was in the ·nd of the author of the Messiological section of ·ioch when writing xlviii. 3). That, contrary to ·e view of Weber ("Jüdische Theologie," 2d ed., 355) and others, it is actual preexistence which is ·eant here, and not predestination, is evident from ·e additional remark—"According to another view, ·ly the Torah and the Throne of Glory were [actu-·y] created; as to the other [five] things the inten-·n was formed to create them" (Yalḳ., *l.c.*; in re-·rd to "the name of the Messiah" compare the ·mment above to Enoch, xlviii. 3). Finally, the ·eexistence of the Messiah in paradise is minutely ·scribed in "The Revelation of R. Joshua b. Levi" ·e JEW. ENCYC. i. 680), in Midrash Konen (Jelli-·k, "B. H." ii. 29), and in "Seder Gan Eden" (*ib.* . 132 *et seq.*, 195). In the first two, regardless of e apparent anomaly, the preexistent Messiah is ·lled "Messiah ben David."

The conception met with in the rabbinical litera-·re of an earthly preexistence of the Messiah must · distinguished from that of his heavenly preexist-·ce. It occurs in various forms, representing, probably, different stages of development. First, he is expected to lead a hidden life and then to step forth suddenly. (On this conception of the sudden, unexpected appearance of the Messiah comp. Matt. xxiv. 27, 43–44, where it is said that the Messiah will come like a thief in the night or like a flash of lightning.) This is the conception of him in Ex. R. i. and in Tan., Shemot, both of which say that as Moses, the first deliverer, was reared at the court of Pharaoh, so the future deliverer will grow up in the Roman capital; in agreement with this, in the Agadat ha-Mashiaḥ (Jellinek, *l.c.* iii. 142) it is said that the Messiah will suddenly be revealed to Israel in Rome. Then, again, the Messiah is represented as born, but not yet revealed. This conception appears as early as the second century in Justin Martyr's "Dialogus cum Tryphone" (ch. viii.), and in accordance with it is the passage Sanh. 98b, where R. Joshua ben Levi is quoted as saying that the Messiah is already born and is living in concealment at the gates of Rome. In Targ. Yer. to Micah iv. 8 the Messiah is on the earth, but because of the sins of the people he is still in hiding. Finally, the Messiah is thought of as born at a certain time in the past. This is the case in Yer. Ber. ii., which states that the Messiah was born at Bethlehem on the day the Temple was destroyed, and in the Apocalypse of Zerubbabel (see JEW. ENCYC. i. 682), which declares he was born in the days of King David and is dwelling in Rome.

Earthly Preexistence.

The notion, traceable to Ezek. xxxiv. 23 *et al.*, that David himself is the Messiah, is another variation of the conception of earthly preexistence. It occurs in the apocalyptic fragment of the "Siddur" of R. Amram (see JEW. ENCYC. i. 678, *s.v.* APOCALYPTIC LITERATURE, 2) and in Yer. Ber. ii. The latter states that whether the King Messiah belongs to the living or to the dead, his name is David.

Finally, there must be mentioned a Messianic figure peculiar to the rabbinical apocalyptic literature —that of Messiah ben Joseph. The earliest mention of him is in Suk. 52a, b, where three statements occur in regard to him, for the first of which R. Dosa (*c.* 250) is given as authority. In the last of these statements only his name is mentioned, but the first two speak of the fate which he is to meet, namely, to fall in battle (as if alluding to a well-known tradition). Details about him are not found until much later, but he has an established place in the apocalypses of later centuries and in the midrash literature—in Saadia's description of the future ("Emunot we-De'ot," ch. viii.) and in that of Hai Gaon ("Ṭa'am Zeḳenim," p. 59). According to these, Messiah b. Joseph will appear prior to the coming of Messiah b. David; he will gather the children of Israel around him, march to Jerusalem, and there, after overcoming the hostile powers, reestablish the Temple-worship and set up his own dominion. Thereupon ARMILUS, according to one group of sources, or GOG AND MAGOG, according to the other, will appear with their hosts before Jerusalem, wage war against Messiah b. Joseph, and slay him. His corpse, according to one group, will lie unburied in the streets of Jerusalem; according to the

Messiah ben Joseph.

other, it will be hidden by the angels with the bodies of the Patriarchs, until Messiah b. David comes and resurrects him (comp. JEW. ENCYC. i. 682, 684 [§§ 8 and 13]; comp. also Midr. Wayosha' and Agadat ha-Mashiaḥ in Jellinek, "B. H." i. 55 *et seq.*, iii. 141 *et seq.*).

When and how this Messiah-conception originated is a question that has not yet been answered satisfactorily. It is not possible to consider Messiah b. Joseph the Messiah of the Ten Tribes. He is nowhere represented as such; though twice it is mentioned that a part of the Ten Tribes will be found among those who will gather about his standard. There is a possibility, however, as has been repeatedly maintained, that there is some connection between the Alexander saga and the Messiah b. Joseph tradition, for, in the Midrash, on the strength of Deut. xxxiii. 17, a pair of horns, with which he will "strike in all directions," is the emblem of Messiah b. Joseph (comp. Pirḳe R. El. xix.; Gen. R. lxxv.; Num. R. xiv.; *et al.*), just as in the apocalyptic Alexander tradition in the Koran (referred to above) the latter is called "The Double-Horned" ("Dhu al-Ḳarnain"). See also ESCHATOLOGY; JESUS; JUDAISM.

BIBLIOGRAPHY: R. Smend, *Alttestamentliche Religionsgesch.*; W. Nowack, *Die Zukunftshoffnung Israels in der Assyrischen Zeit*; Hühn, *Die Messianischen Weissagungen*; Fr. Giesebrecht, *Der Knecht Jahwe's in Deutero-Jesaia*; Schürer, *Gesch.* 3d ed., ii. 29; W. Bousset, *Die Religion des Judentums im Neutestamentlichen Zeitalter*, part 3, ch. ii.-v.; part 6, pp. 474 *et seq.*; P. Volz, *Jüdische Eschatologie von Daniel bis Akiba*, §§ 34-35; H. J. Holtzmann, *Lehrbuch der Neutestamentlichen Theologie*, i. 68-85; W. Baldensperger, *Die Messianisch-Apokalyptischen Hoffnungen des Judentums*; F. Weber, *Jüdische Theologie auf Grund des Talmud*, etc., ch. xxii.-xxiii.; G. H. Dalman, *Der Leidende und der Sterbende Messias*; idem, *Die Worte Jesu*, pp. 191 *et seq.*; Kampers, *Alexander der Grosse und die Idee des Weltimperiums in Prophetie und Sage*; B. Beer, *Welchen Aufschluss Geben die Jüdischen Quellen über den "Zweigehörnten" des Korans?* in *Z. D. M. G.* ix. 791 *et seq.*

J. M. BU.

MESSIAH, FALSE. See PSEUDO-MESSIAH.

MESSIANIC PROPHECY. See PROPHETS.

MESSIANIC YEAR. See CALENDAR.

MESSINA: Italian city, "at the point of Sicily, on the strait called Lunir, which divides Calabria from Sicily" ("Itinerary" of Benjamin of Tudela). Its Jewish community may have been founded even before the destruction of the Second Temple, although it is first mentioned in the letters of Gregory I. After a long silence the sources again refer to it, in connection with a royal decree of 1129, and about 1170 Benjamin of Tudela found 200 Jews there on his return from the Holy Land. The Jews of Messina had the same constitution, rights, and taxes as all the other Sicilian communities, though their lot may have been somewhat harder because the archbishop claimed a certain authority over them.

In 1347 several Jews were executed on the false charge of ritual murder, and their heads were publicly exposed; a marble inscription, "a monument to the faithless Jews," was subsequently placed in the cathedral to commemorate the event. On a similar occasion, in 1475, the Jews averted a riot only by the payment of a large sum of money. In 1492 they were expelled from Messina, as well as from the entire island, though thirty-seven years before, in 1455, they had in vain attempted to emigrate.

Messina occupied an exceptional position in virt of being the seat of the highest court of appeal f all the Jews of Sicily; and in 1439 Moses Ḥef (Bonavoglio, who, as the representative of seve teen communities, had induced King Alfonso V in 1430 and 1431, to repeal ordinances unfavoral to the Jews) was made chief justice ("naggid") the supreme court. Being at the court in Nap when appointed, he deputed his brother to act as h proxy; the latter accordingly was invested with t new dignity in the synagogue of Palermo. Mos Ḥefeẓ died in 1447. Messina itself was not subje to the jurisdiction of the new chief justice, b formed a judicial district of its own.

The Messina community must have been one the largest on the island, judging from the tax- turns. In addition to the imposts levied equal upon all the communities, it was required to fu nish, after 1347, the standards for the galleys of t commanding officer. Wine and meat also we taxed. In 1170 the community numbered only 2 persons, but in 1453 there were 180 families there about 3 per cent of the total population. It h several synagogues, one in the suburb of San Phil There fragments of an inscription of the year 440 a said to have been found, but the reference is probab to one of much later date, in honor of a certa "Moses" (?) who built a synagogue or some simi structure. A considerable number of Jews livi in the vicinity of Messina endeavored to evade t taxes and imposts of the community, and con quently were excluded by a royal decree of 13 from its rights and privileges.

Little is known of the intellectual life of the Je of Messina. About 1300 Abraham Abulafia, cabal and magician, had two pupils there—Abraham a Nathan; some time later Aaron Facassi (Favi) o ciated there as rabbi, and pronounced a sentence excommunication upon a physician named Aar (1340), which sentence was repealed by the gover ment. Moses Ḥefeẓ (referred to above) officiated rabbi about 1430, and succeeded in having the Je released from compulsory attendance at Christi sermons.

The scholars of Messina who edited the man script of Naḥmanides' commentary on the Pen teuch, on which the Naples 1490 edition was base are of somewhat later date. The Jewish physicia of Messina include Naccon de Fariono and Aar (1367), Moses Spagnuolo and Bulfarachio (137 Moses Yabe (1383), Joseph Factas and Gaudio (139 Benedetto da S. Marco "Lugrossu" and Machalu Ayculino (1404), Isaac de Bonavoglia (1425), Vileh Saccas (1432), Aaron de Sacerdotu de Girachi a Raba (1448), Moses de la Bonavoglia (1477), a Vitali Aurifici. There were a number of Turki scholars of the sixteenth century who bore the s name "Messini."

BIBLIOGRAPHY: Zunz, *Z. G.* passim; Bartolomeo e Giuse Lagumina, *Codice Diplomatico dei Guidei di Sicilia*, pass

G. I. E.

MESSING: Prussian family, members of whi in the nineteenth century settled in the Unit States of America.

Joseph Messing: Talmudist, exegete, a rabbi; born at Argenau, Prussia, April 30, 18 died in London, England, March 20, 1880. The only rabbinates he held were those of Gostyn and Witkowo, Posen. Messing was the author of: twelve homilies on Ḥanukkah (Breslau, 1862); "Gal Na'ul" (1864), a commentary on Megillah, containing a prefatory notice by Sir Moses Montefiore; "Abne Shayish" (1868), a commentary on the tractate Abot; "Perush'al Haggadah" (1869), a commentary on the Haggadah; and "Arono shel Yosef" (1876) on Bible exegesis.

Three sons of Joseph Messing, who received their training under Guttmacher at Grätz, and Öttinger and Zunz at Berlin, were called to fill prominent pulpits in the United States.

Aaron Messing: Eldest son of Joseph Messing; born 1843; rabbi at Mecklenburg (1859–67), New York (1867–70), San Francisco (1871–91). In 1891 Messing was called to the rabbinate of B'nai Sholom Temple, Chicago, which he still (1904) occupies. He has founded not less than twelve congregations and twenty-three Sunday-schools in Nevada, Oregon, and California. Messing is the author of several popular Sabbath-school text-books, especially "A Hebrew Primer" and "The Jewish Catechism."

Mayer Messing: Second son of Joseph Messing; born 1843. He is the oldest rabbi in continuous service with one congregation in the United States, having been minister to the Indianapolis Hebrew Congregation for thirty-seven years, since Oct. 21, 1867.

Henry Messing: Third son of Joseph Messing; born March 10, 1848. He has been rabbi of the United Hebrew Congregation, St. Louis, Mo., since March 8, 1878.

Abraham Joseph Messing: Youngest son of Aaron Messing; born Aug. 4, 1873, at Chicago, Ill.; was graduated from the Hebrew Union College in 1897, and has been rabbi of Temple Beth-Or, Montgomery, Ala., since Sept. 1, 1897.

Bibliography: Lippe, *Bibliographisches Lexikon*, pp. 319–321; Winter and Wünsche, *Die Jüdische Litteratur*, iii. 824; *American Jewish Year Book*, 1903-4, pp. 81, 92.

A. S.

METALS: Although Deut. viii. 9 describes the Promised Land as one rich in ore, Palestine itself was really almost without metals, which had to be imported from neighboring countries. The passage in question is therefore taken by certain scholars to refer not to Palestine proper, but to Bashan, the present Hauran, whose rocks contain as much as 20 per cent of iron—hence the name "basalt." Nothing is known of mining among the Hebrews themselves (see Mines and Mining); the description in Job xxviii., which shows a full knowledge of the technical process, probably refers to Egypt, which had engaged in mining on the Sinaitic Peninsula from earliest times. The existence of these mines in Sinai may account for the fact that the Jerusalem Pentateuch Targum translates "the wilderness of Zin" (Num. xiii. 21; xxxiv. 3, 4) by "mountain of iron." Josephus ("B. J." iv. 8, § 2; comp. Malala's "Chronicle," xviii. 182), however, places "the iron mountain" in Trachonitis and not in the vicinity of Sinai (comp. Derenbourg in "R. E. J." viii. 275). Another "mountain of iron" is mentioned (Suk. iii. 1); but this was in the vicinity of Jerusalem, and received its name not from its richness in iron, but from the fact that its rocks were hard as iron. Robinson ("Researches," i. 512) has shown that the country about the Red Sea is likewise entirely without iron deposits.

Sources of the Metals.

The Hebrews were aware of the existence of gold at Havilah, Ophir, and Uphaz; and they obtained the precious metal from these districts either by means of their own ships, as under Solomon (I Kings ix. 28) and Jehoshaphat (*ib.* xxii. 49), or through the markets of Tyre, where silver, iron, tin, and lead were brought (Ezek. xxvii. 12), probably by traders from Tarshish (*ib.* xxxviii. 13). Tarshish is mentioned as being under Tyrian dominion (Isa. xxiii. 10); but its location and even the meaning of its name are still disputed points. The same doubt attaches to two cities, Betah and Berothai, conquered by David, from which he "took exceeding much brass" (II Sam. viii. 8; in I Chron. xviii. 8 these cities are Tibhath and Chun). Copper utensils came also from Javan (which here probably means Cyprus), Tubal, and Meshech (Ezek. xxvii. 13). According to the ideas of the time, the people of the last-named country lived in the far north; and the expression "iron from the north" occurs in Jer. xv. 12. This iron seems to have been an especially good variety. The Rabbis mention the excellent Indian iron ('Ab. Zarah 16a; Ab. R. N., Recension A, xxviii.) and the Indian swords (Tan., Wa'etḥanan, 6). Since the Oriental trade was chiefly in the hands of the Phenicians, the Israelites could thus become directly acquainted with the metals and had opportunity to obtain possession of them.

A general name for "metal" does not occur in the Bible, but the following species are mentioned: gold, silver, copper, iron, tin, lead, antimony or stibium, and electrum.

Gold ("zahab," connected with the root "ẓahab," "to shine"): The various Biblical terms (see Gold) employed to designate the color or the degree of purity of different varieties of the metal are in part identical with the terms used in the Talmud (Yer. Yoma iv. 41d; a little different in Yoma 44b) to characterize seven varieties: (1) good gold (with reference to Gen. ii. 12; comp. "good gold from Ophir"; Targum Sheni to Esth. ii. 1, ed. Lagarde, p. 227); (2) pure gold, *i.e.*, such gold as can be put into the fire without losing weight (the golden lamp of the Tabernacle is said to have been put into the fire eighty times without losing weight); (3) fine gold ("zahab sagur"; comp. I Kings vi. 20); (4) "zahab mufaz," which, according to one explanation, looks like burning brimstone, and according to another and probably more correct explanation is so called from the place in which it was found (Solomon's throne was covered with this kind of gold; see I Kings x. 18); (5) unalloyed gold; (6) spun gold ("zahab shaḥuṭ"), flexible as wax (the emperor Hadrian is said to have had a piece of the size of an egg; Diocletian, one as large as a Gordian denarius); (7) Parvaim gold (II Chron. iii. 6), probably so called from an Arabian district. In the Babylonian Talmud gold of Ophir occupies the third place in the list; and "mufaz" gold is—apparently correctly—connected with "paz" (comp. Cant. v. 15). The word occurs with the same meaning in the Talmud (Giṭ. 11b, 58a). If "ufaz" (Jer. x. 9; Dan. x. 5) is not a proper name, it is likewise probably connected with the same root. Some commentators, referring to Targum, Peshiṭta, and manuscripts of the Septuagint, consider it to be corrupted from "Ofir." Almost all the names for gold here mentioned occur in I Kings x. Perhaps "eshkar" (Ps. lxxii. 10; Ezek. xxvii. 15) should also be connected with "sagur"; in Assyrian "hurasu sakru" means "massive" or "solid gold" (Delitzsch, "Assyrisches Handwörterbuch," p. 499b); and "sagur" and "eshkar" may be synonymous (Cheyne, in "Proc. Soc. Bibl. Arch." 1899, xxi. 246; comp. Barth in "Programm des Berliner Rabbinerseminars," p. 32, Berlin, 1901). The Assyrian "hurasu" explains the Hebrew "haruẓ" (Prov. viii. 10, xii. 27); the latter is used poetically for gold and really means "decided," *i.e.*, "declared a unit of value," which gold had been for a long time. Moreover, the Greek χρυσός (= "gold") is said to come from the Hebrew (perhaps Phenician; see "R. E. J." xvi. 276) word "haruẓ" (Bochart, "Hierozoicon," ii. 534; H. Lewy, "Die Semitischen Fremdwörter im Griechischen," p. 59). Poetically "ketem" (Lam. iv. 1; Job xxviii. 19, xxxi. 24, etc.) is used, and appears also in connection with "paz." The expression "beẓer" occurs only twice (Job xxii. 24, 25), and is usually interpreted to mean "bars of gold." The meaning "gold in rings" is also accepted for it (Hoffmann, in "Zeitschrift für Assyriologie," 1887, p. 48). "Ophir"—that is, gold of Ophir—is its parallel; and the writer of the Book of Job (Job *l.c.*) says that both of these kinds of gold shall be as of no value to those who fear God. In the Talmud "seething gold" is also mentioned ("zahab roteaḥ"; Sanh. 92b). See also GOLD for Biblical passages.

Silver ("kesef"): This metal derives its name from its pale color. The denominative "hiksif" means "make pale" ("kasaf," like the Arabic "kasaf," = "desiderare"), although in Job xxii. 25 a comparison seems to be made between silver and something shining. The Greek ἀργύριον (= Latin "argentum") likewise goes back to ἀργός ("white"). "Kesef" was, in addition, a term for money in general among the Hebrews (see below). Silver has its veins (Job xxviii. 1). It is not found on the surface, nor in river-beds, like gold; but it must be taken with hard labor from the depths of the mountain. Strangely enough, the Septuagint translates "kasifya," in Ezra viii. 17, according to the meaning of the root: ἐν ἀργυρίου τόπῳ, "place of silver," that is, Ctesiphon.

Copper ("neḥoshet"): The Hebrews probably knew copper only in its natural state, and not as bronze, which is copper alloyed with tin, unless the copper ore was found mixed with tin. According to one hypothesis, the Biblical-Hebraic "sefer" means "brass" or "bronze" ("J. Q. R." xv. 102). The term ברונזא ("bronze") occurs only in a late Jewish work ("Seder ha-Dorot," *s.v.* דוד, following "Shalshelet ha-Ḳabbalah," ed. Amsterdam, p. 8b), where the metals collected by David for the building of the sanctuary are enumerated (comp. Eusebius, "Præparatio Evangelica," ix. 4). Bronze tablets are mentioned in I Macc. viii. 22; xiv. 18, 26; and in ANTIOCH tablets of the same metal informed the Jews of their rights. The altar was covered with copper, which did not melt, although fire was continually burning upon it (Lev. R. vii.; Tan., Terumah, 11). A bronze serpent (Num. xxi. 9; II Kings xviii. 4) is mentioned, and the proper name "Nehushta" (II Kings xxiv. 8), the hyssop represented in bronze (Parah xii. 5), and shells of bronze (κόγχη; Yelammedenu, in "'Aruk," *s.v.* קונכי) are noteworthy. See COPPER.

Iron ("barzel," "parzel"): The mountains of Palestine contained iron ore (Deut. viii. 9). Its value was less than silver and more than stones (Isa. lx. 17). As was also the case in early times among the Greeks and Romans, iron was little used by the Hebrews; and it is mentioned only four times in the first four books of Moses (see IRON). Many understand the word "paldah" (Nah. ii. 4) to mean "steel," a preparation of iron; but the correctness of this interpretation is uncertain. Iron can be broken in pieces with a hammer. In this it is a symbol of the Torah, which has numerous attributes and characteristics (Suk. 52a; see Tos. *ib.*). A teacher of the Law must be as hard as iron (Ta'an. 4a). To forge and harden iron it must be put red-hot into cold water (Shab. 41a). Iron was heated on coal; and there are halakic regulations for doing this on the Sabbath (*ib.* 130a). Iron as well as lead was used on the yokes of animals (Kelim xiv. 4, 5). The Rabbis were acquainted with the magnetic stone which attracts iron (Soṭah 47a, "eben sho'ebet").

Tin ("bedil," from a root meaning "to separate"): The name itself indicates that the metal is not a pure one, but consists of parts separated from other metals, perhaps the lead in bars of silver (so Delitzsch on Isa. i. 25, where the word is used in the plural with "sigim"; Ibn Ezra rightly observes that no other names of metals occur in the plural); compare the Latin "stannum" (Pliny, "Historia Naturalis," xxxiv. 47); German, "werk"; and English, "alloy." That "bedil" denotes some particular metal is evident from passages like Num. xxxi. 22 and Ezek. xxii. 18, 20; xxvii. 12, where it is mentioned along with other metals; and according to the Septuagint this metal was κασσίτερος = "tin," a translation which Luther has throughout his version. Among the Romans, until the fourth century, tin was called "plumbum album." The Jews were probably acquainted with tin through the Phenicians, who brought it from their European colonies (from Britain [?]; see Gutschmid, "Kleine Schriften," ii. 55). The instrument used in summoning the people to synagogue in Babylonia was of tin (Pethahiah of Regensburg, p. 14, ed. London, 1856). Beautiful tin Seder platters are still in existence.

Lead ("'oferet"; Aramaic and Neo-Hebrew in Mishnah and Talmud, "abar," "abra"): Lead is mentioned in Num. xxxi. 22; Ezek. xxii. 18, 20; also in Ezek. xxvii. 12, where it is referred to as an export of Tarshish. Lead was obtained direct from the mines (Ḥul. 8a). It is the symbol of weight (Ex. xv. 10). Tradition relates that the river-beds near Jerusalem were lined with lead (Letter of Aristeas, ed. Wendland, § 90; comp. "Seder ha-Dorot," i. 115, Warsaw, 1891). White lead (Persian, "sapidag" [see "Z. D. M. G." l. 6, 43]; Syriac, "aspedka") occurs in the "Halakot Gedolot" and elsewhere in the literature of the Geonim as "alsefidag" (see Kohut, "Aruch Completum," iv. 82). A wire of lead ("petilah shel abar"; Sanh. 52a) was used in killing those condemned to death by fire. The eaves of houses were made of lead (Miḳ. vi. 8).

Antimony or **Stibium** ("puk" = "eye-paint" [comp. "Z. D. M. G." v. 236]; now called "kuḥl" in the Orient; hence the verb "kaḥal" [Ezek. xxiii. 40]; often mentioned in the Talmud and Midrash [*e.g.*, Shab. viii. 3]): One spoke of "enlarging" the eyes with paint (Jer. iv. 30, R. V.) or of painting them (II Kings ix. 30). The meaning of Isa. liv. 11 is disputed. According to Saadia, paint is meant here also; thus the meaning would be that the stones shine like women's eyes. More modern scholars read "nofek." Wisdom xiii. 14 interprets it to mean that on feast-days the faces of the gods were colored red with minium.

Electrum: A translation given by many for "ḥashmal" (Ezek. i. 4, viii. 2); the English versions have AMBER. Bochart ("Hierozoicon," iii. 893) takes it to be the aurichalcum of the ancients. The Talmud has a haggadic interpretation for it (Ḥag. 13a; comp. Munk in "Guide des Egarés," ii. 229). Omitting "ḥashmal" as not being the name of a metal, Moses Cohen (on Ibn Ezra on Isa. i. 25) says that there are seven kinds of metals mentioned in the Bible.

Metals in the Talmud.

A general name for metals, "matteḳet" (plural, "mattakot"; Kelim xiii. 7, xiv. 1; Ḥul. i. 6), from the root "matak" — "natak" (Targ. to I Kings vii. 16, 23), is first found in the post-Biblical literature of the Jews. מטיל occurs in the Middle Ages ("R. E. J." xliii. 83). Roman "metalla" in Spain are mentioned in I Macc. viii. 3. By way of punishment Jews were often exiled to Roman "metalla," *i.e.*, mines. A rather comprehensive word is גרומי ("broken pieces of iron"; Jastrow, "Dictionary," p. 266), from which גרומני (B. B. 89b; comp. "Halakot Gedolot," ed. Hildesheimer, p. 421) would seem to mean "iron-monger." Other names for metals which occur are the following:

Argentum or **Argentarium** (Latin): Table-silver; occurs often in the Midrash (Krauss, "Lehnwörter," ii. 126). A similar word is "chrysargyrum," a kind of money (see below).

Arsenicon (Greek): A chemical element which occurs naturally together with sulfur and metals. In the Talmud (Ḥul. 88b), Syriac, and Arabic it is called "zarnikh."

Asimon (Greek, *ἄσημον*): In Mishnah, Talmud, and Midrash, an unstamped (silver) coin (Krauss, *l.c.* p. 86). The word may, however, be related to the Syriac "sema," which means simply "silver" (Payne Smith, "Thesaurus Syriacus," p. 2494). By "asem" the Egyptians indicated a compound of gold and silver (Greek, *ἤλεκτρον*); and the Septuagint translates the Hebrew "ḥashmal" (see above) similarly.

From tannaitic times dates a regulation forbidding the making of weights out of "ba'aẓ" (see below), lead, tin (*κασσίτερος*), and other metals, because they gradually wear away to the disadvantage of the buyer (Tosef., B. B. v. 9 [ed. Zuckermandel, p. 405]; B. B. 89b); in the text of the "Halakot Gedolot," p. 421, אספרדא also is found among the forbidden metals. Still Immanuel Löw reads more correctly אלספידאג (= "white lead"; see above) instead of אלא אספרדא.

Ba'aẓ: This metal, mentioned above, is probably a kind of tin (comp. Kelim xxx. 3; Targ. to Ezek. xxii. 18, and Targ. Yer. to Num. xxxi. 22). Ba'aẓ ranks above lead and *κασσίτερος* (Men. 28b). It is doubtful whether "abaẓa" (Targum for "bedil") is related to it (see commentators on Kelim x. 2). Ba'aẓ was used for sealing documents (Targ. to Jer. xxxii. 11, 14).

Ḥalḳoma (Greek, *χάλκωμα*): Brass or copper; mentioned often in the Targum (Krauss, *l.c.* p. 299); especially bows of brass are mentioned (comp. the cognomen "Haliḳopri" = *χαλκοπάρειος* = "the man with a brazen face" (Krauss, *l.c.* p. 251). A similar analogy was: "A scholar is firm as iron" (Ta'an. 4a). Corinthian brass, celebrated in antiquity (קלונית), is mentioned in the Talmud (Krauss, *l.c.* p. 543), as well as by Josephus ("Vita," § 13). The Syrian translates Ezra viii. 27 similarly. *Χαλκολίβανον*, in Rev. i. 15, ii. 18, can hardly mean anything else than "brass of Lebanon."

Gruti (Greek, *γρύτη*): Pieces of metal (Krauss, *l.c.* p. 183). Perhaps the above-mentioned גרומי came from it (comp. *γρυτοπώλης* = "dealer in old iron," in Wilcken, "Ostraka," i. 381).

Ḥararah (Kelim xi. 3): Lumps of metal after casting.

Karkemisha: An Aramaic word of unknown origin, occurring in the Targum (Targ. Yer. to Num. xxi. 22; Job xix. 24), and meaning "lead."

Milela (Ket. 67a): Gold ore as broken in the mine (Jastrow, *l.c.* p. 793).

Niska: A bar of gold or silver; occurs a dozen times in the Babylonian Talmud (Jastrow, *l.c.* p. 917). According to J. Halévy (in "M. Soc. Ling." xi. 73), "niska" is Sanskrit, and means "money-bag." The Greek *βῶλος* also indicates "lumps" or "bars" (Krauss, *l.c.* p. 141; comp. the Greek *μύδρος* = Latin "massa" in Blümner, "Technologie," iv. 219).

For sheet metal there was likewise a term from the Greek, פיטלון (*πέταλον*; Krauss, *l.c.* p. 441), for which "ṭas" is used elsewhere. Still unworked pieces are called "golemim" (Kelim xii. 6).

'Eshet and **'Ashashit**: Especially frequent terms (Kohut, *l.c.* vi. 281; Jastrow, *l.c.* p. 1127), meaning "lumps" or "plates" or something similar (comp. Yoma 34b). Plates of iron were warmed (for the high priest); iron plates are spoken of also in 'Ab. Zarah 16a. It is therefore natural to connect these words with the Biblical Hebrew "'eshet" (Ezek. xxvii. 19) = "hard iron"; since the idea "hard" seems certainly to be contained in it. In Men. 28b it is stated that the lamp of the sanctuary might be made of "'eshet" as well as of gold; but "'eshet" can not mean "iron," since it is classed above silver, unless indeed iron on account of its rarity was more valued than silver or even than gold. The metal must also have cast a reflection; for the lamp itself ("candela") is called "'ashasit." The plates, whether of iron, silver, or gold, must, therefore, have been highly polished, somewhat like the ancient mirrors.

Obryzon (Greek, *ὄβρυζον*): Pure gold; a term occurring once in the Targum (Krauss, *l.c.* p. 14), and used also in Syriac and Arabic. Χρυσάργυρον, money called "gold-silver," occurs also in rabbinical writings (Krauss, *l.c.* p. 298).

Paliza (Arabic, "falaz"; but see Fraenkel, *l.c.* p. 153): A kind of bronze. Samuel (in the 3d cent.) bought a golden dish which was offered him as bronze (B. Ḳ. 113b).

Stomoma (Latin, from the Greek στόμωμα; in Ber. 62b, אסטמא): A term meaning sometimes the tempering of iron, sometimes steel itself. The expression is found also in Syriac, Mandæan, and Arabic; the genuine Arabic is "shaburkan" (Löw, in Krauss, *l.c.* p. 120; according to a passage quoted there, tin was also so tempered. Concerning the method see Blümner, *l.c.* iv. 343). Jäger, Reichenow, and Frenzel, in "Handbuch der Zoologie," etc. (ii. 510, Breslau, 1880), state that the art of changing iron to steel was practised by the Jews.

Sulfate of Iron: Used for ink; χάλκανθος = "vitriol"; often mentioned by the Rabbis (Krauss, *l.c.* p. 549).

Marteka: Silver-slag (Giṭ. 69b).

Manufacture.

For the working of metals the Hebrews had to rely wholly on the Phenicians, as the history of the building of Solomon's Temple indicates. In Saul's time the Hebrews had armorers who were very unpopular with the Philistines (I Sam. xiii. 19, 20); and at the fall of Jerusalem smiths and locksmiths ("ḥaras" and "masger"; II Kings xxiv. 14) are mentioned.

The tools used were: the hammer or ax ("pa'am"; Isa. xli. 7; comp. ἄκμων in Sirach [Ecclus.] xxxviii. 33; other tools are mentioned, *ib.* xxxviii. 13, xlviii. 17; also "maḳḳabah" in Isa. li. 1; "paṭṭish," *ib.* xli. 7; and "halmut" in Judges v. 26); tongs ("melkaḥayim"; Isa. vi. 6); hatchet ("garzen"; Siloam inscription and Deut. xix. 5; this makes the word "barzel" in II Kings vi. 5 mean "tongs," whereas it usually denotes only "iron"); bellows ("mappuaḥ"; Jer. vi. 29; comp. Isa. liv. 6); fining-pot ("maẓref") for silver and a (melting) furnace ("kur") for gold (Prov. xvii. 3), whence the designation "furnace," for Egypt (Deut. iv. 20; comp. Isa. xlviii. 10), is derived. A prophecy of Ezekiel's (Ezek. xxii. 18-22) rests wholly on the technical process of metal-casting.

In Talmudic times there was used the anvil ("saddan" = "block"; Gen. R. x.), the "base" ("taḥtit"; Kelim xvii. 17) for forging, which was beaten upon with a hammer. "To beat with the hammer" ("makah ba-paṭṭish") is a very frequent expression in rabbinical literature. In the opinion of the Rabbis, tongs ("ẓebet") were created directly by God as the final act of creation (Ab. v. 6); compare the tongs ("yattukin" and "parakin" in Kelim xii. 3) used in metal-casting. There were used also the spade ("ḳardom," in Ps. lxxiv. 5, 6; comp. Ab. iv. 5), the shovel ("mara" = μάῤῥον), the ax ("ḥaẓina"), and the hammer ("ḳornos" = κέαρνος). For grinding a peculiar tool was used ("mashḥezet"; Kelim xvii. 17; comp. "yaḥad" in Prov. xxvii. 17). Iron sledges ("masreḳot shel barzel"; Ber. 61b; comp. Giṭ. 57b) are mentioned as instruments of torture.

The passage quoted from Ezekiel (xxii. 18-22) illustrates the manipulation of metals. The ore was gathered and thrown into the furnace, and the fire was blown to melt it ("natak," substantive, "hittuk").

To rid the cast of slag ("sig," "sigim") the metal was refined again in the fire ("ẓaraf," "zaḳaḳ").

Manipulation.

To aid the process of melting, a kind of soap ("bar," "barit" = "sal alkali," "potash"; see Luzzatto on Isa. i. 25) was thrown into the furnace. Hence a distinction was made between unrefined silver ("kesef sigim" is probably the term; Ezek. xxii. 18) and refined silver ("kesef mezuḳḳaḳ" in I Chron. xxix. 4, or "ẓaruf" in Ps. xii. 7). After the metal had been purified it was tested ("baḥan"). Smelters and gold-workers in general were called "refiners" ("ẓorefim"; Neh. iii. 32; comp. *ib.* verse 31); there were also ironsmiths ("ḥarashe barzel"; II Chron. xxiv. 12) and coppersmiths ("ḥarash neḥoshet"; I Kings vii. 14). Copper could be worked in various ways; there were shining copper (yellow bronze?; "neḥoshet muẓhab" in Ezra viii. 27), polished copper ("neḥoshet ḳalal" in Ezek. i. 7; Dan. x. 6), and probably gilded copper also.

Perhaps certain places in Palestine derived their names from the foundries existing therein, *e.g.*, "Zarephat" (I Kings xvii. 9) and "Misrephoth" (Josh. xi. 8, xiii. 6). Malleable metals, such as gold, were made into plates (רקע) from which were cut threads or wires ("ḳiẓẓeẓ petilim"; Ex. xxxix. 3). The important art of soldering was also known ("debeḳ"; Isa. xli. 7). At the time of Solomon there was a special place for casting ("yaẓaḳ"; comp. "muẓẓaḳ" in Job xi. 15). For the sanctuary "scoured" copper ("moraṭ"; I Kings vii. 45, 46) was used, while for the Tabernacle in the wilderness the metal was not cast, but hammered into shape (comp. "miḳshah"). As the excavations at Mycenæ show, this process was known before casting, and was in use even in prehistoric times. The Hebrews knew also how to make gold and silver articles by incrustation ("ẓafah," "ḥafah").

Ornaments of gold and silver are frequently mentioned in the Bible (see Costume). The Hebrews had metal mirrors ("mar'ot"; Ex. xxxviii. 8; comp. Blümner, *l.c.* iv. 265). Several metal articles recorded in the Bible and Mishnah are mentioned together in Kelim xi. 8; *e.g.*, weapons (helmet, lance, νικών, greaves, cuirass), women's ornaments ("golden city," *i.e.*, a kind of crown with an image of Jerusalem), necklaces ("catellæ"), nose-rings, finger-rings with or without seals, metal threads, etc. Besides, there were the sword ("ḥereb," "sayif"), knife, dagger ("pugio"), sickle, scissors, hair-curlers (καλλιγραφῶν), etc. (Kelim xiii. 1, 2). The mortar ("maktesh"; Prov. xxvii. 22) was usually of copper, probably for sanitary reasons, because copper does not rust; the pestle (Biblical "'eli"; Aramaic, "bukna"), of iron. The iron pestle breaks the copper mortar ("asita"; Niddah 36b). Mention should also be made of: the hoe ("mafselet"), the cutting-knife (σμίλη = Hebr. "sakkin," "magrefah"), the metal funnel (πρόχοος = "aparkas"; Kelim xiv., end), and the furnace and hearth of metal (*ib.* v. 11). From this last arises

Ornaments, Weapons, and Utensils.

the expression "copper bottom" of the furnace (*ib.* viii. 3).

The wealth of the Patriarchs in gold and silver is often emphasized (Gen. xiii. 2, xxiv. 22). According to a legend, Abraham built himself a high iron tower (Soferim ix.). The Israelites took articles of silver and gold with them out of Egypt (Ex. xi. 2, xii. 35); and the Midrash on this passage (Tan., Bo, 8) states that they melted the idols of the Egyptians into lumps of metal. For the golden calf and for the Tabernacle the precious metal was used in large quantities. Many fabulous stories are told of the wealth of Korah, as also of that of Joseph. David's and Solomon's wealth in gold has already been spoken of. Solomon's throne was especially costly (I Kings x. 18). On the other hand, some of the later Jewish kings were so poor that they often used copper instead of gold. The copper pillars of Solomon's Temple are said to have been taken to Rome; but those taken could have been only from Herod's Temple. Benjamin of Tudela, who saw them in Rome, states that on the day of mourning for Jerusalem they wept and exuded sweat. Moreover, the pillars of the Temple (Herod's) are described as of silver, gold, copper, tin (בדיל), and iron ("Seder ha-Dorot," ed. Warsaw, i. 92a). Antiochus IV. stole much gold and silver from the Second Temple (I Macc. i. 21-24); and Herod the Great enriched himself by plundering the alleged graves of the kings (Josephus, "Ant." vii. 15, § 3; xvi. 7, § 1). All the gates of Herod's Temple were of gold with the exception of the Nicanor Gate, the copper on which, however, shone like gold (Mid. ii. 3). It is said that Nicanor had copper gates made in Alexandria for the Temple, and that they reached Palestine only by a miracle (Yoma 38a; Yer. Yoma ii. 4). At the time of Herod, Menahem, the president of the Sanhedrin, brought eighty men in golden breastplates before the king (Ḥag. iii. 2). The Roman general Crassus took away a golden beam from the Temple of Jerusalem (Josephus, *l.c.* xiv. 7, § 1). The cymbals in the Temple at Jerusalem deserve mention (Ps. cl. 5; Sheḳ. v. 1, צלצל) as being made of metal. A golden grape-vine was placed on the gate of the Temple (Mid. iii. 8).

History.

Miscellaneous Conditions.

The high priest John, *i.e.*, King John Hyrcanus, did away with "the noise of hammering" in Jerusalem (Ma'as. Sh. v. 15; otherwise interpreted in M. Ḳ. 11a). There are halakic regulations as to whether neighbors were required to endure the noise of hammering (see "Paḥad Yiẓḥaḳ," *s.v.* אומנות חבירו). Founders or gold-workers figure in later times also (*ib. s.v.* אומניות). When the table service broke at the court of King Jannæus it was replaced by the gold-workers in Jerusalem (*ib.*). Women liked to wear golden ornaments; hence it is said that "goldsmiths have much to do with women" (Ḳid. 82a). R. Ishmael b. Elisha had a golden tooth made for a Jewish maiden (Tosef., Nedar, 66b). Earth instead of gold was put into the chest of Naḥum of Gimzo. B. Joshua b. Hananiah was a maker of needles (Yer. Ber. 7d; Yer. Ta'an. 67d; see "'Aruk," *s.v.* פחמי). The teachers with the cognomen "Nappaḥa" were probably blacksmiths. The word "paṭṭish" (= "hammer") occurs also as a proper name; in the Talmud it has a symbolical meaning. At the time of Bar Kokba there were many Jewish smiths, and at Sichnim metal-workers were especially numerous (Grätz, "Gesch." 3d ed., iv. 136, 145). The workshops of the goldsmiths are mentioned in the time of the Mishnah (Tosef., Kelim, middle extract, vii. 10). At Jerusalem the gold-workers seem to have formed a separate gild ("zahabim"; Tosef., Suk. iv. 6). The word "ṭarsiyyim" was formerly translated "ironsmith" (Schürer, "Gesch." 3d ed., ii. 65, note 212).

In the Middle Ages.

In the Middle Ages there were makers of metal implements (Abraham, "Jewish Life in the Middle Ages," Index, London, 1896). It is interesting to note that Jews took part in the Bristol copper trade (*ib.*). The Jews engaged extensively in coinage also (see Minters). Strangely enough, the writings on alchemy in the Middle Ages circulated under the name of Moses; the word מי זהב (Gen. xxxvi. 39), really a proper noun, was explained to mean "the one who changes copper into gold" (Ibn Ezra, *ad loc.*; comp. a work on מי זהב in Steinschneider, "Hebr. Uebers." No. 577). Miriam, Moses' sister, is said to have been the discoverer of the chemical known as bain-marie (see Jew. Encyc. i. 329, *s.v.* Alchemy). A Jew taught the English how to smelt copper ("Tr. Jew. Hist. Soc. Eng." iii. 12). In northern Africa the Jews were the only locksmiths, goldsmiths, metal-founders, and minters (see Africa). An Italian traveler of the sixteenth century relates that the greater number of Karaites in Jerusalem had for a long time been metal-founders ("Jerusalem," v. 86). From the very beginning Jews took an active part in the art of printing; and in some instances the Rabbis themselves cast the type for the printing of their own works (*ib.* v. 286). Toward the end of the eighteenth century there were in Berlin many Jewish die-sinkers and engravers (see "Kaufmann Gedenkbuch," pp. 629-653; comp. "Mitteilungen . . . für Jüdische Volkskunde," ix. 12 *et seq.*). The word "Ghetto" is said to have been derived from the Venetian mint, beside which the Jews lived.

Halakic Bearing.

Just as on the occasion of the war with Midian the Bible established laws of cleanliness in regard to metals, so later in rabbinical literature metal vessels are discussed in their relation to the Levitical laws of cleanliness. Metal vessels, whether flat or hollow, become unclean (vessels of other materials, if flat, do not become unclean); if they break they become clean; but when mended the earlier uncleanness returns (Kelim xi. 1). Each metal dish which has a particular name may become unclean (*ib.* 2). If clean iron is united with unclean iron, the larger constituent decides as to purity (*ib.* 4). All implements of war, all ornaments worn by women may become unclean in so far as they have a hollowed part, thus constituting a vessel (*ib.* 8). The rule that a firmly fitting cover protects from uncleanness does not apply to ba'aẓ (see above) and lead, because the cover only lies on top, but does not close the vessel hermetically (*ib.* x. 2). If metal vessels which have become unclean from contact with a corpse receive the purificative sprinkling, then break and are melted together and resprinkled, all on the same day, they, in the opinion of some, become clean (*ib.* xiv. 7). But these rules become lost in a sea of details, and further information on the subject must be obtained from the codes (Maimonides, "Yad," etc.). See KELIM.

Value of Metals.

In the only passage in the Bible in which an almost complete list of the metals is given their order of value is as follows: gold, silver, copper, iron, tin, and lead (Num. xxxi. 22). Generally, however, in the Bible, as also on the Egyptian monuments, silver is named before gold, to which metal it was preferred, owing to the greater difficulty in obtaining it. However, in estimating Solomon's wealth, it is said of silver that "it was nothing accounted of." Consequently, even at that early time gold must have been estimated at its true value (I Kings x. 21).

From the Talmudic description of the lamp (Men. 28b) the following classification of the metals according to their value results, beginning with the most precious: "'eshet" (see above), gold, silver, ba'aẓ (see above), lead, tin (*κασσίτερος*). The spears of the Hasmonean kings were of iron plated with ba'aẓ (*ib.*); hence iron stood at the foot of the list, but only in regard to value. In respect to usefulness it stood high among the Jews. Among the Greeks and Romans iron is always ranked above tin and lead (Blümner, *l.c.* iv. 8). The coinage of Oriental peoples rests on a gold basis; that of the Phenicians and the Greeks on a silver one; that of the Romans on one of copper (*ib.*). The Bible fixes silver as the medium of exchange (Levy, "Gesch. der Jüdischen Münzen," p. 8); so that in the matter of money, as in other things, the Hebrews were dependent on the Phenicians (comp. Schürer, *l.c.* ii. 53). A mishnah in this connection is instructive (B. M. iv. 1). It states which metal is to be regarded as a commodity, which as coin. "Silver buys gold (that is, as soon as the buyer has the gold coins—the commodity—in his hands, he must pay for them with silver coins); gold, however, will not buy silver. Silver will buy copper; but not vice versa. Stamped money ("maṭbea'") will buy asimon; but not vice versa."

Among the figures of speech in the Bible in which metals occur, there is the elaborate symbolism of Dan. ii. and vii., where the kingdoms of the earth are compared to metals. This idea was thoroughly exploited throughout the Middle Ages (see Driver, "Daniel," pp. 94–97, Cambridge, 1900); comp. Ex. R. xxxv. 5: "Gold is Babylon; silver is Media; copper is Greece; iron is not mentioned either at the time of the First or of the Second Temple, since it symbolizes Edom [Rome], which had destroyed the Temple; hence Edom can bring God no present in the Messianic kingdom." Iron is the symbol of war (Mek., Yitro; Tosef., B. Ḳ. vii. 6); the relation between gold and copper altars should be judged accordingly (Midr. Tadshe, xi.). A phallus was made of copper, or of gold (Ezek. xvi. 17; Isa. lvii. 8). According to Philo, who developed at length the symbolism of metals, gold denoted wisdom (*σοφία*; Philo, "De Leg. Alleg." ed. Mangey, i. 25) or reason (*idem*, "De Vita Moysis" iii. 4); copper denoted perception (*αἴσθησις*; *ib.*). From this Bähr ("Symbolik des Mosaischen Cultus," i. 280) tried in vain to prove the existence of an elaborate symbolism of metals among the Hebrews. Maimonides says of the Sabians that they associated a particular metal with each of the planets and made their statues to the latter of the appropriate metal (Chwolson, "Ssabier und Ssabismus," ii. 658 *et seq.*). In ALCHEMY "moon" is equivalent to silver; "sun," to gold. In the Midrash iron is the symbol of war (Mek., Yitro, 11; B. Ḳ. vii. 6). The golden altar in the sanctuary symbolized the soul; the copper one, the body (Midr. Tadshe, xi.). "A scholar who is not hard as iron is no scholar" (Ta'an. 4a); R. Sheshet was such a hard scholar (Men. 95b). A scholar appears to an idiot like a golden pitcher; if he has spoken to the idiot once he seems like a silver pitcher; and if he derives benefit from the fool he is only an earthen one (Shab. 52b). The strict ban was called "iron fate" ("gizra de-farzela"; B. Ḳ. 81b).

Symbolic Meaning.

In sorcery and superstition the metals were important agents. If any one was bitten by a mad dog he was to drink out of a copper tube for twelve months; in a severe case he was to use a golden one (Yoma 84a). Just as imprecations were usually written on leaden tablets in Rome (R. Wünsch, "Sethianische Verfluchungstafeln aus Rom," Leipsic, 1898), so the Jews wrote, and still write, their AMULETS preferably on metal tablets. Coins or gold ornaments were put in the shoes or clothing of a bridegroom, with the idea that gold would take away the power of witchcraft (responsum quoted in Glassberg's "Zikron Berit la-Rishonim," p. 149, Berlin, 1892). If copper, iron, tin, lead, or any other kind of metal is thrown into the fire and some of the pretended stone of wisdom is rubbed off and mixed with the metal, gold refined seven times will come out of the fire ("Kerem Ḥemed," ii. 48; Glassberg, *l.c.* p. 204). Even to-day Jews give heed to the so-called "tekufah." Water may be kept from becoming poisonous if it comes in contact with iron (S. Landau, in "Aruch," p. 1665; Grünbaum, "Gesammelte Aufsätze zur Sprach- und Sagenkunde," pp. 102, 144, Berlin, 1901; "R. E. J." xli. 47). For sorcery with metals see also "Sefer Yuḥasin," ed. London, p. 234a.

In Yemen to-day most people wear iron bands on their arms and feet and claim to feel strengthened thereby. The children wear around their necks a thick band of seven kinds of iron ("Eben Safir," p. 58b, Lyck, 1866). With this should be compared the metal amulets ("lamina") representing the serpent of Moses, which a sect of Jews wore early in the common era (Philastrius, "Hæres," § 21). In an apocryphal work ascribed to Ham, prescriptions on copper plates are spoken of (Fabricius, "Codex Apocr. N. T." i. 301). Indeed, Korah is said to have engaged in chemistry (Grünbaum, "Neue Beiträge zur Semitischen Sprach- und Sagenkunde," p. 171).

BIBLIOGRAPHY: De Wette, *Lehrbuch der Hebräisch-Jüdischen Archäologie*, §§ 105, 106, Leipsic, 1814; Rosenmüller, *Biblische Alterthumskunde*, iv. 1, 58; Movers, *Phönizier*, iii. 1, 27; Burton, *The Gold Mines of Midian*, London, 1878; *Globus*, xxxv. 282; Kinzler, *Biblische Naturgeschichte*, 9th ed.; Blümner, *Technologie und Terminologie der Gewerbe und Künste bei Griechen und Römern*, vol. iv., section 1, Leipsic, 1886; Bähr, *Symbolik des Mosaischen Cultus*, i. 258–295, Heidelberg, 1837; E. Meyer, *Gesch. des Alterthums*, i. 226; Blau, *Das Altjüdische Zauberwesen*, p. 157; *Z. D. P. V.* ii. 101.

J. S. Kr.

MEṬAṬRON (Hebr. מטטרון; Greek, Μητάτωρ; Latin, "Metator"): Name of an angel found only in Jewish literature. Elisha b. Abuyah, seeing this angel in the heavens, believed there were "two powers" or divinities (Ḥag. 15a, above). When God wept over the destruction of the Temple, Meṭaṭron fell on his face and said: "I will weep; but weep not Thou." God answered and said: "If thou wilt not suffer Me to weep, I will go whither thou canst not come, and there will I lament" (Lam. R., Introduction, § 24; comp. Jer. xiii. 17). Meṭaṭron bears the Tetragrammaton; for Ex. xxiii. 21 says, "My name is in him." Yet he may not be worshiped; for the same passage says, "Exchange Me not for him" (dialogue between a heretic and a Babylonian teacher, in Sanh. 38b, below; Targ. Yer. to Ex. xxiv. 1 has Michael instead of Meṭaṭron).

Moses begs Meṭaṭron to intercede with God for him, that he may not die; but the angel answers: "It is useless; for I heard the words behind the veil, 'Thy prayer will not be answered'" (both editions of Tan., Wa'etḥanan, 6). When God sorrowed for the death of Moses, Meṭaṭron fell down before Him and consoled Him (Grünhut, "Liḳḳuṭim," v. 105a), and when Moses died, this angel with three others, "the princes of wisdom," cared for him (Targ. Yer. to Deut. xxxiv. 6). The early commentators with good reason identified the prince of the world (Ḥul. 60a; Zeb. 16b; Sanh. 94a) with Meṭaṭron (Joël, "Blicke in die Religionsgesch." i. 124 *et seq.*). God instructs children in the Torah during the last quarter of the day; Meṭaṭron, during the first three-quarters ('Ab. Zarah 3b). It was this angel who caused Shamḥazai to say before the Flood, "God will destroy the world" (Yalḳ. i., § 44). He is, moreover, Enoch, the great scribe (Targ. Yer. to Gen. v. 24; in Ḥag. 15a he is likewise represented as a scribe).

These statements, found in the earlier sources, contain all the characteristic traits ascribed to Meṭaṭron in the later mystical works. The latter call him the "prince of the presence" (Jellinek, "B. H." ii., pp. xvi., 55 *et seq.*, v. 171; "Responsen der Gaonen," ed. Harkavy, No. 373, p. 372; comp. Isa. lxiii. 9), and "prince of the ministering angels" (Jellinek, *l.c.* v. 172). He is the "mighty scribe" (*ib.* ii. 68), the lord of all the heavenly hosts, of all treasures, and of secrets (*ib.* ii. 114, v. 174), and bears the lesser divine name (*ib.* ii. 61, 114, 117; v. 175). The Zohar defines his nature exactly by declaring that he is little lower than God (after Ps. viii. 6; Yalḳ. Ḥadash, 7, No. 51; comp. especially Jellinek, *l.c.* v. 174). He is identical in all respects with Enoch; the "Hekalot" (*ib.* v. 170–190), in which he is the chief personage, is called also "The Book of Enoch" (comp. *ib.* ii., p. xvi. and vi. 58: "Enoch whose name is Meṭaṭron").

In Later Records.

In the Apocrypha likewise Enoch appears as the heavenly scribe (Book of Jubilees, iv. 23; II Enoch liii. 2), although elsewhere he is called Michael (Ascensio Isaiæ, ix. 21), while, as noted above, Targ. Yer. to Ex. xxiv. 1 substitutes the name of Michael for Meṭaṭron, which is found in the other sources. In the Hebrew writings Meṭaṭron fills the rôle of Enoch in the Apocrypha in bearing witness to the sins of mankind. Since both sources represent him as a youth, it may be assumed that the first versions of the Hebrew mystical works, though they received their present form in the geonic period, originated in antiquity, so that the conception of Meṭaṭron must likewise date from an early period.

Identical with Enoch.

The views regarding the source of this conception differ widely. The name "Meṭaṭron," which, as stated above, occurs only in Hebrew writings, is in itself striking. The derivation from the Latin "metator" (= "guide") is doubtless correct, for Enoch also is represented as a guide in the apocryphal work which bears his name; and the Hebrew Book of Enoch, in which, however, reference to Meṭaṭron is constantly implied, says: "He is the most excellent of all the heavenly host, and the guide [Meṭaṭron] to all the treasuries of my [God]" (B. H. ii. 117).

Mysticism prefers obscurity, and intentionally chooses a foreign word instead of the well-known name of Enoch. Kohut identifies Meṭaṭron with the Zoroastrian Mithra; but probably only a few traits were borrowed from the latter. Sachs, Grünbaum, Weinstein, and others think that Meṭaṭron is identical with Philo's Logos; but L. Cohn, the eminent Philonist, contradicts this view. M. Friedländer, on the other hand, takes Meṭaṭron to be, both in name and in nature, none other than Horus, the "frontier guardian" and "surveyor of the frontier" of the early Gnostics. These divergent views clearly indicate that Meṭaṭron combines various traits derived from different systems of thought. Grunwald (in "Jahrb. für Jüdische Gesch. und Literatur," 1901, pp. 127 *et seq.*) has yet another solution for the problem of Meṭaṭron. The ancients had already noticed that the numerical value of the letters in the word "Meṭaṭron" corresponded with those of the word "Shaddai" (= 314), and "Meṭaṭron" is also said to mean "palace" ("metatrion"), and to be connected with the divine name מקום ("place"), etc.

Views as to Origin.

In medieval mysticism Meṭaṭron plays the same rôle as in antiquity and in the period of the Geonim (passages in Schwab, *s.v.*), thus furnishing a further proof of the tenacity and stability of mystic and superstitious conceptions.

Bibliography: W. Bousset, *Die Religion des Judenthums im Neutestamentlichen Zeitalter*, pp. 247, 348, Berlin, 1903; Buttenwieser, in Jew. Encyc. i. 677 *et seq.* (Meṭaṭron-Enoch); M. Friedländer, *Der Vorchristliche Jüdische Gnosticismus*, pp. 102 *et seq.*, Göttingen, 1898; M. Grünbaum, *Gesammelte Aufsätze zur Sprach- und Sagenkunde*, pp. 74, 124, 194, Berlin, 1901; M. Grunwald, *Ein Altes Symbol in Neuer Beleuchtung*, in *Jahrb. für Jüdische Gesch. und Literatur*, iv. 127, Berlin, 1901; *idem*, in *Mitteilungen der Gesellschaft für Jüdische Volkskunde*, x. 138; *Yalḳ. Ḥadash*, pp. 66b *et seq.*, Nos. 1, 2, 9, 10, 12, 15, 16, 22, 23, 25, 68a; Nos. 43 *et seq.*, 68b; Nos. 59, 72; M. Joël, *Blicke in die Religionsgesch.* i. 124 *et seq.*; L. Ginzberg, Jew. Encyc. iii. 461b (Meṭaṭron-Enoch); A. Kohut, *Jüdische Angelologie und Dämonologie*, pp. 36 *et seq.*, Leipsic, 1866; *idem*, in *Magyar Zsidó Szemle*, 1884, i. 98–100; M. Sachs, *Beiträge zur Sprach- und Alterthumsforschung*, i. 108, Berlin, 1852; M. Schwab, *Vocabulaire de l'Angélologie*, p. 170; Weinstein, *Zur Genesis der Agada*, part ii., *Die Alexandrinische Agada*, Göttingen, 1901; comp. L. Cohn in *Monatsschrift*, xlvii. 89–96; Zunz, *G. V.* 2d ed., p. 179.

J. L. B.

METEMPSYCHOSIS. See Transmigration of Souls.

METER IN THE BIBLE: The question whether the poetical passages of the Old Testament show signs of regular rhythm or meter is yet unsolved; the question involves principally Psalms, Proverbs, Job, and most of the prophetical books, with many songs and speeches contained in the historical books. The subject of strophic arrangement is not treated here, since it relates as much to the divisions of thought as to those of metrical form (see Parallelism).

State of the Question.

No one can establish the metrical character of the whole of this literature, and no one can successfully deny that it is metrical in part. The former of these statements will be generally accepted; for those who wish to find meter in the Old Testament are obliged to make many emendations of the text. As the second statement is often controverted, the appeal must be made to a trained and unprejudiced ear (not eye). The case might rest on a single Psalm, the 54th, which is as metrical throughout as some familiar English poems. The following translation of verse 3 imitates accurately the flow of the original:

"O my God! by Thy name now redeem me,
And by all Thine omnipotence free me."

The rime is unessential, though it is perfect in the Hebrew. The important matter is the regularity of movement, indicated by the symbol 3 + 3, which means that the verse consists of two equal stichoi separated by a cesura, each stichos having three tones. The movement may be termed either "rhythmical" or "metrical," for the two are identical, as Sievers has shown ("Studien zur Hebräischen Metrik," p. 25, Leipsic, 1901). It is just as erroneous to call such a Hebrew verse a hexameter as it would be to apply that term to its English equivalent; it is convenient to call each tone-section a foot, but even that designation must be explained as referring to rhythm, not to syllabic division. That which gives these feet their metrical character is not the accent, which only marks, not makes, the rhythm; it is the flow of time, as measured in waves or pulse-beats recurring at regular intervals. The time being equal, it matters not whether the syllables in the different feet are alike in number or not. In the example given they happen to correspond; each foot has the form × × –́ except that the two riming feet are of the form × × –́ ×.

Collocations of Regular Accent.

Every kind of foot in this psalm is frequently met with in English poetry; take, for example

Ps. liv. 3, 4: × × –́, × × –́ ×, × –́. (Comp. Tennyson: "That he shouts with his sister at play.")
Ps. liv. 8, 4: –́ × ×, × × × –́. (Comp. "All in the valley of death.")

There are but three more variations in the psalm: –́ ×, × –́ ×, –́, which all occur in two consecutive lines from Coleridge's "Christabel":

–́ × –́ –́ × × –́
"Is the night chilly and dark?"
× –́ × –́ × –́ × –́
"The night is chilly but not dark."

This same measure (3 + 3) holds in Psalms liv., lxvii., and lxxxii., and it is a curious coincidence that verse 5 in each is extended to 3 + 3 + 3 tones, while nearly all the other verses have 3 + 3. Psalm c. begins with a single 3, has a triple 3 in verses 3 and 4, and ends, as does Psalm lxxxii., with a kind of Alexandrine. The remaining feet are 3 + 3. All these are short psalms, but several long ones are almost as strictly regular (*e.g.*, Ps. lxxx., lxxxi., lxxxv., xci.). Others follow prevailingly the scheme 4 + 4 (*e.g.*, Ps. xlvi., liii.), and there are still other combinations, as 2 + 2, 3 + 2, and 4 + 3.

Outside the Psalms there are many poems and long sections either completely or measurably regular, as Deut. xxxii., Ex. xv., Isa. xli. 1-10, and large portions of the Book of Job. But the great majority of the Psalms are very irregular, and some of them defy all metrical rules (*e.g.*, Ps. xlv., lv., lxiv., lxxi., lxxxvi., xcv., cii.). The common practise is to be censured, which, by conjectural emendation, alters the text in such cases to fit the assumed meter. Conjectures that approve themselves on critical grounds give, to be sure, one more sign of their correctness when they smooth rough meters; but no metrical system thus far proposed has proved satisfactory. An example or two may serve to soften the apparent dogmatism of this judgment. One of the most elaborate metrical systems is that of Sievers (1901), who analyzes 93 poems. Of these, 20 are psalms, but not a single rhythmically difficult psalm is included. Baethgen's commentary on the Psalms (3d ed., 1904) attempts to give some metrical account of each of the 150 Psalms. In the case of those noted above as difficult (and of many more) he frankly admits the difficulty, often confesses that it is insoluble, and in most other cases offers conjectures resting on an assumed regularity of the meter, whereas the very question at issue is whether any such regularity can be shown.

So far as the evidence extends at present, it can only be asserted that the Hebrew poets were acquainted with meter, and employed it very freely, changing at will from one form to another, within the same composition, but making the substance of their thought so far paramount over its form that they were often unwilling to wait for a perfect rhythmical expression.

History of the Question.

Metrical systems published before the nineteenth century are so mingled with subjective fancies that none of them is now worth considering; they were all patiently examined and thoroughly refuted by J. L. Saalschütz ("Von der Form der Hebräischen Poesie," Königsberg, 1825). J. J. Bellermann's little book on the subject ("Versuch über die Metrik der Hebräer," Berlin, 1813) is sound in principle, and its only important defects relate to the "moræ" (units of time) and the "sheva." Saalschütz corrected these defects, but erred in contending for a rhythm that descends (–́ × ×. –́ ×, etc.) instead of one that ascends (× –́, × × –́, etc.). Ernst Meier ("Die Form der Hebräischen Poesie," Tübingen, 1853) returned to Bellermann, and reduced the matter to greater simplicity through his folk-lore studies. His contribution has been unduly belittled, even by Kuenen; its chief mistake was in applying to all poetry what is true only of a part. Julius Ley ("Grundzüge des Rhythmus in der Hebräischen Poesie," Halle, 1875) supplied that defect by a fundamental investigation which gave a scientific basis to the whole subject. His system was cumbersome at first (1866), but he improved it under the criticism of thirty-five years. Bickell held the untenable theory that Hebrew meter is syllabic, like the Syriac, and is written uniformly in regular trochees or iambi. Hubert Grimme ("Psalmenprobleme," Freiburg, 1902) built avowedly on Ley's basis, but added a new doctrine of the moræ which is an improvement on the old, but which he has not been able to establish. In his earlier work he held correctly that the structure of the feet may vary in the same composition; at present he holds the opposite theory and employs it freely in textual emendations. Sievers was the first to trace out thoroughly the relations of Hebrew metrics to general metrics. That part of his system possesses permanent value; but its practical application is marred by the attempt at an impossible simplicity and symmetry which derives every foot from the anapest.

Bibliography: In addition to works mentioned in the body of the article, Ewald, *Die Dichter des Alten Bundes*, part 1, Göttingen, 1835; Gustav Bickell, *Carmina Veteris Testamenti Metrice*, Innsbruck, 1882; Kuenen, *Einleitung*, part 3, Leipsic, 1894; Charles A. Briggs, *The Study of Holy Scripture*, pp. 355-426, New York, 1899; Nivardus Schlögl, *De Metrica Veterum Hebræorum*, Vienna, 1899; Eduard König, *Stilistik, Rhetorik, Poetik*, pp. 313-360, Leipsic, 1900.

J. W. H. C.

METHODOLOGY. See Talmud.

METROLOGY. See Weights and Measures.

METUENTES (lit. "fearing"): Term used in the Latin inscriptions by Juvenal for Jewish proselytes. It corresponds to the Greek term *σεβόμενοι τὸν Θεόν*, which occurs in Josephus ("Ant." xiv. 72, ed. Niese) and in Acts x. 2, 22; xiii. 16, 26, 43, 50; xvi. 14; xvii. 4, 17; xviii. 7, and to the Hebrew "Yire Yhwh," which, at an early date, likewise seems to have denoted proselytes (see II Kings xvii. 28, xxxii. 33). In the Psalms the expression is used for the whole body of pious persons outside the house of Israel (Ps. cxv. 11, cxviii. 4, cxxxv. 20; comp. Esth. ix. 27; Isa. lvi. 6), or perhaps for certain Gentiles who had adopted some of the Jewish customs, notably the observance of the Sabbath and abstention from forbidden meat. Paul refers to such at Antioch, Thyatira, Thessalonica, and Athens. About the Black Sea a large number of inscriptions have been discovered relating to "worshipers of the Most High God" who were also of the same class, though possibly their Judaic practises were not so pronounced as in the cases nearer Palestine (see Hypsistarians). A mocking crucifix found on the Palatine Hill at Rome has the expression ΣΕΒΕΤΕ ΘΕΟΝ (see Jew. Encyc. ii. 222, *s.v.* Ass-Worship). Mek., Mishpaṭim explains Isa. lvi. 6 as "those who fear Heaven." See Proselyte.

Bibliography: Schürer, *Gesch.* 2d ed., iii. 103-105; idem, *Die Juden im Bosporanischen Reiche*, etc., in *Sitzungsberichte der Berliner Akademie*, 1897, pp. 200-225; Bernays, *Die Gottesfürchtigen bei Juvenal*, in *Gesammelte Schriften*.

S. J.

METURGEMAN ("interpreter"): With the return of the exiles from captivity the religious instruction of the people was put into the hands of the Levites (Neh. viii. 7-9; II Chron. xvii. 8, 9; xxxv. 3). These functionaries were called מבינים ("teachers"). In all probability the language of instruction was still Hebrew (Friedmann, "Onkelos," p. 81, to the contrary). How long the Levites continued in the office of teachers and how long the Hebrew language remained intelligible to the masses are unknown; but at a later time, when Aramaic had become the vernacular, and religious instruction had ceased to be the exclusive privilege of the priesthood, the Levitic מבין ("teacher") gave way to the lay מתורגמן ("interpreter," "translator"), called also תורגמן or מתרגם. The official was paid probably by the community (comp. Pes. 50b; Rashi *ad loc.*). This seems, however, not to have been always the case, since the Halakah speaks also of a minor acting as meturgeman.

The weekly lesson from the Pentateuch and the Prophets was read by a member of the congregation, and the meturgeman had to translate into the vernacular the Pentateuchal lesson verse by verse; from the Prophets he translated three verses at a time. While the reader of the Hebrew text was forbidden to recite by heart, the meturgeman was not permitted to read his translation from a book, or to look at the Hebrew text when translating, in order that the people should not think that the translation was contained in the text. The meturgeman was also forbidden to raise his voice higher than that of the reader of the text. He did not limit himself to a mere literal translation, but dilated upon the Biblical contents, bringing in haggadic elements, illustrations from history, and references to topics of the day. This naturally required much time, to gain which the weekly lesson had to be short, so that the Pentateuch was finished only in a cycle of three or three and one-half years; while the portion from the Prophets was frequently abbreviated.

The free handling of the text, which frequently changed the translation into a sermon or homily, gave the meturgeman ample opportunity to introduce his subjective views into the lesson; and with the multiplication of sects this became distasteful to the Rabbis. The increase in the opposition to the meturgeman led to the fixation of the Targumim and to the demand that the meturgeman keep strictly to mere translation. But a mere translation satisfied neither the public, who had known the text from early school-days, nor the meturgeman, who was deprived of an opportunity to parade his knowledge and to display his oratorical gifts. As a consequence the "darshan," or preacher, was introduced; and the literal translation fell gradually into disuse.

While the meturgeman as Bible interpreter was a purely Palestinian institution, as interpreter of the Mishnah he was known also in Babylonia, where he was called Amora. The head of the academy, while seated, would tell him in Hebrew and in a low voice the outline of his lecture; and the meturgeman would in a lengthy popular discourse explain it in the vernacular to the audience. It is noteworthy that the meturgeman, whether explaining Bible or Mishnah, was not held in much esteem by the public; and in Talmud and Midrash he is frequently referred to with contempt. See also Targum.

Bibliography: A. Hübsch, in *Ben Chananja*, v. 77 *et seq.*; A. Berliner, *Targum Onkelos*, ii. 73 *et seq.*, Berlin, 1890; M. Friedmann, *Onkelos*, pp. 81 *et seq.*

S. S. C. L.

METZ: German fortified city in Lorraine; it has a population of 58,462, including 1,451 Jews. According to ancient chronicles, Jews had settled in Metz in the year 221; they enjoyed municipal freedom, and lived on very good terms with the Christians. It is stated also that when St. Eucaire, Bishop of Toul, had undertaken to convert the Jews, the emperor Julian, who was at Metz at the time, condemned the bishop to prison for his untimely zeal. Under the Merovingians and Carlovingians there were Jews at Metz, engaged as agriculturists, merchants, artisans, and especially as goldsmiths and physicians. Jews and Christians formed intimate friendships; the clergy dined in the homes of the Jews, and more than one intermarriage resulted from this friendly intercourse.

Early Conditions.

The cordiality of these relations was increased by the efforts made by the Church councils to disturb it. At a council held at the monastery of St. Arnould at Metz May 1, 888, at which Balbodus, Archbishop of Trèves, presided, and which was attended by Dadou, Bishop of Verdun; Arnold, Bishop of Toul; and Robert, Bishop of Metz, on the complaint of the dean of the cathedral Jews were forbidden to drink or eat with, or to marry, Christians.

Ancient Synagogue at Metz.
(From Frauberger.)

These vexations lasted but a short time; under the successors of Charles the Bald, Jews might own real estate, and this would lead to the supposition that they had other municipal rights. Bishop Adalberon in 945 commanded David, a Jew of the diocese of Metz, to restore to the monastery of St. Glossinde a vineyard of which he had secured possession. This Adalberon, who occupied the episcopal see until 984, was always very favorable to the Jews, who revered him. According to the chronicles, at his death "the Jews wept aloud; and mourned and lamented." Some years later they showed similar feeling at the obsequies of another virtuous and tolerant archbishop—Mattard. The dukes of Lorraine also took them under their protection and treated them with the greatest consideration. Thanks to this social peace, they devoted themselves to study, and among them were scholars called "the sages of Lorraine" (חכמי לותר); celebrated rabbis, such as R. Simon ha-Gadol, R. Machir, Leontin, R. Eliezer (the author of the "Sefer Yere'im"), and especially Rabbenu Gershom Me'or ha-Gadol.

Period of Persecution.

Persecutions, especially during the Crusades, scattered the Jews of Metz. Those who afterward returned found a refuge there, for which they were obliged to pay thirty-four deniers, levied on them when they entered the city. Nevertheless, in 1365 they were expelled by the magistrates, who assigned their presence as the cause of the destruction by lightning of twenty-two houses. In 1567, after France had taken possession of Metz, some Jewish families were again admitted with the consent of the marshal of Vieilleville, and less than thirty years later they were organized into a community.

Under French Rule.

In 1595 they met in general assembly and elected a communal board, to which they delegated all power and all authority in everything concerning administration and police, and the jurisdiction of civil cases. Of the six men composing this council the following three were rabbis: Isaac, son of Lazare Levy; Joseph Levy; and Solomon, son of Gershon Zay. The proceedings of this assembly, as well as those of the election, were submitted for the approval of the higher authorities, who on July 12, 1595, "by the grace of God, and with the consent of his majesty, and of Monsieur, the Duke of Epergnan," recognized those elected as the official representatives and the regularly appointed intermediaries of the Jewish community of Metz.

The community developed in influence and numbers; in 1614 it numbered 500; in 1624 there were 120 families, consisting of more than 600 individuals. The rabbi at that time was Moses Cohen of Prague. His nomination was confirmed by the Duke de Valette, peer and colonel-general of France and commanding general of the king in the city and citadel of Metz, "to undertake the above-mentioned charge and functions of rabbi." A fact that should be noticed is that throughout the Middle Ages the nomination of the rabbi required ratification by the state. In 1650 the rabbi was Moses Nerol; contrary to custom, and for some unknown reason, the council of the community did not ask the government to confirm his nomination. Louis XIV., during his visit to Metz Sept. 25, 1657, visited the synagogue and gave audience to the council of the trustees of the community as well as to the rabbi. The same day he signed letters patent for the privileges of the Jews, in which he warned them that in the future they would not be allowed to choose a rabbi without obtaining his consent.

As early as March 24, 1603, and Oct. 18, 1605, Henry IV. had granted the Jews letters patent, according to which he "took them under his protection, and permitted them to trade according to their franchises, liberties, and ancient customs." These letters patent were maintained, and the Jews' privileges were even increased, by Louis XIII. (Jan. 24, 1632), by Louis XIV., and by Louis XV. (July 9, 1718). Louis XIII. "rewarded them for their devotion and charity," and granted them a new law to remove all difficulties between them and the inhabitants of the city, in consideration of the services they had rendered the garrison of Metz during the civil wars. The letters patent granted by Louis XIV. and Louis XV. were ratified and registered by the Parliament of Metz (Sept. 3, 1718). Those of May 7, 1777, gave the Jews still greater liberties and spoke of them as citizens of the land. In 1782, when the Count of Provence, afterward Louis XVIII., went to Metz, he visited the synagogue, and the chief rabbi, Lion Asser (Aryeh Loeb ben Asher), in the name of the community, assured him of his homage and bestowed upon him the priestly benediction. This made a profound impression upon the count, and those about him were astonished to hear him praise the Jew. "Jew or Christian," he said, "what is the difference? I honor virtue wherever it is found."

Interior of an Old Synagogue at Metz.
(From Frauberger.)

The French Revolution was greeted with enthusiasm by the Jews of Metz. In 1792 the chief rabbi himself, Uri Cohen, already advanced in years, offered an example of patriotism by tendering his services for the defense of the city. It was he, also, who, after the victory of Valmy, set out at the head of the defenders of Thionville and, with Rolley, mayor of Metz, led them before the Ark, where, in an enthusiastic speech, he extolled the bravery of the Jews and declared the country had the right to count upon the cooperation of all its citizens. During the Reign of Terror the synagogue was closed, the sacred utensils used in the services were put under seal, and the courtyard was used for a pasture; the tombstones were taken from the cemetery and used for building purposes.

By the decrees of 1806 and of March 7, 1808, the Jewish creed was officially recognized, and in the creation of the seven consistories and grand rabbinates the district of Metz and the community of the city of Metz are mentioned.

In Recent Times.

The first chief rabbi was Mayer Charleville, who was followed by Joseph Gougenheim, Wittersheim, Aaron Worms, Lyon Lambert, and Lippmann. After the war of 1870 Lippmann, who was unwilling to surrender his allegiance to France, resigned his post. He was subsequently made chief rabbi at Lille. During this period Louis Morhange, formerly professor at the rabbinical school in Metz, served as chief rabbi until the installation of Bigard. In 1885 the latter was succeeded by Isaac Weill, who in 1890 succeeded Arnold Aron as chief rabbi at Strasburg. His successors at Metz were Adolphe Ury and the present (1904) incumbent, Nathan Netter.

By the royal decree of 1824 the rabbinical school that was transferred to Paris in 1859 was established at Metz. The synagogue was erected in 1840 and dedicated in 1845. The community possesses communal schools, an infant school, a hospital, a maẓẓah bakery, and numerous charitable societies, including a society of young people, which is recognized by the state and which gives aid without distinction as to creed.

BIBLIOGRAPHY: A. Cahen, *Les Rabbins de Metz*, in *R. E. J.* xii. 295; Schwab, *Répertoire*.
D. A. U.

METZ, ISAAC: German scholar; lived at Hamburg in the first half of the nineteenth century. He compiled a catalogue, entitled "Ḳehillat Dawid," of David Oppenheimer's library (translated into Latin by Lazar Embden, Hamburg, 1826). To this catalogue Jacob Goldenthal added an index (Leipsic, 1845). Metz published also an edition of Judah ha-Levi's "Cuzari" (Hanover, 1836), based upon the Venice 1547 and 1594 editions.

BIBLIOGRAPHY: Steinschneider, *Cat. Bodl.* col. 1752; Zeitlin, *Bibl. Post-Mendels.* pp. 238-239.
D. S. MAN.

METZLER-LÖWY, PAULINE: Austrian contralto singer; born at Theresienstadt, Bohemia, Aug. 31, 1853. At the age of seven she entered the Prague Conservatorium, where she studied for four years. Graduating with honors, she immediately received an engagement at the theater in Altenburg. Her principal rôles at this time were in Gluck's "Orpheus," *Alcazene* in "Il Trovatore," and *Nancy* in "Martha." In 1875 she went to Leipsic at the invitation of Friedrich Hasse, then manager of the Stadttheater there, and after her début was at once permanently engaged. Here she remained for twelve years, singing with extraordinary success under three successive managers, Friedrich Hasse, Angelo Neumann, and Max Staegemann. She frequently appeared also at concerts and in oratorio at Hamburg, Bremen, Leipsic, Brunswick, and other cities, her appearance at the musical festival of the Allgemeiner Deutscher Musikverein in 1886 being especially memorable in this connection.

In 1881 Pauline Löwy married the piano-teacher Ferdinand Metzler. Since her retirement from the operatic stage (June 12, 1887) she has devoted herself principally to concert performances and later (from 1897) exclusively to vocal instruction.

BIBLIOGRAPHY: Bernhard Vogel, in *Musikalisches Wochenblatt*, pp. 468-470, Leipsic, 1888; Riemann, *Musik-Lexikon*.
S. J. So.

MEXICO. See SOUTH AND CENTRAL AMERICA.

MEYER, ADOLPH: American congressman; born at New Orleans, La., Oct. 19, 1842. He was a student at the University of Virginia when the Civil war broke out; and in 1862 he entered the Confederate army, serving until the close of the war on the staff of Brig.-Gen. John S. Williams of Kentucky, and holding finally the position of assistant adjutant-general.

After the war Meyer was largely engaged in the cultivation of sugar and cotton and in financial and commercial pursuits in New Orleans. In 1879 he was elected colonel of the First Regiment of the Louisiana State National Guard, and in 1881 was appointed brigadier-general to command the First Brigade, embracing all the uniformed corps of the state. He was elected as a Democrat to represent the First District of Louisiana in the Fifty-second Congress, and successively reelected up to the (1904) Fifty-eighth Congress. Meyer served on the committees on Naval Affairs and District of Columbia. He died March 8, 1908.

BIBLIOGRAPHY: *Biographical Congressional Directory*, p. 692, Washington, 1903.
A.

MEYER, ALBERT: Danish tenor singer; born Oct. 29, 1839, at Sorö, Zealand. In 1860 he sang in the chorus of the Royal Theater, Copenhagen, where he received instruction from H. Rung. He subsequently appeared at several concerts, and had just received his first rôle in "The Hunter's Bride" ("Jægerbruden") at the Royal Theater, when the war between Denmark and Germany broke out (1864) and he was called to serve in the army. Upon his return in 1865 he gave a concert which procured for him the means for a year's study under Lamperti in Milan. In 1866 he received an engagement at Folketheatret in Copenhagen, where he remained as a soloist until 1873, when he decided to devote his whole time to giving instruction in singing. He wrote "Theoretisk-Praktisk Sangskole," which presents a theoretical-practical singing method based upon physiological studies of the human voice, and which appeared in Copenhagen, 1874, with a preface by Professor Panum. After a visit to the conservatories in Berlin, Leipsic, Brussels, and Paris, Meyer opened in 1876 a similar institution in Copenhagen.

In 1882 he was appointed conductor of the chorus of the Copenhagen Synagogue, for which he compiled "Synagogekorets Melodier ved Sabbathsgudstjenesten" (Copenhagen, 1892), melodies for use at the Sabbath services, among which are some compositions of his own.

BIBLIOGRAPHY: C. F. Bricka, *Dansk Biografisk Lexicon*.
S. F. C.

MEYER, ANNIE (née **Nathan**): American writer; born in New York city Feb. 19, 1867. She early revealed literary gifts, and articles from her pen appeared in "The Critic," "Harper's Bazar," "Lippincott's Magazine," and "The Bookman." The best-known of her shorter stories is "Vorbei." Some of her tales depict phases of Jewish life.

In 1887 she married Dr. Alfred Meyer. Her first books were "Helen Brent, M.D." and "My Park Book" (New York, 1899). Her most notable production is a novel, "Robert Annys, Poor Priest" (New York, 1901). She also edited "Woman's Work" (1898), the standard book on the subject.

Mrs. Meyer has further distinguished herself as an organizer, public lecturer, and woman of affairs. She was chairman of the Committee on Literature at the World's Fair Congress at Chicago, and was at one time vice-president of an anti-woman suffrag movement. Her most valued communal service was in connection with the founding of Barnard College—the first women's college in New York. It was her energy that gathered together its promoters and secured the collection of funds for the first year. See also NATHAN.

A. M. H. H.

MEYER, ARTHUR: French journalist; born at Havre 1846. When still a youth he went to Paris and bought and edited the "Revue de Paris," which, however, was soon discontinued. For nearly twenty years he reported for "Le Gaulois" and "Paris Journal," becoming, in 1868, part owner of the former, which he made the organ of the Bonapartists. When Prince Louis died in 1879 Meyer left the "Gaulois" and bought the "Paris Journal," soon afterward "Le Gaulois," and finally the "Clairon." The three papers he then merged under the name of the "Gaulois," and made it the main organ of the Clerical-Monarchic party. Meyer was one of the most vehement adversaries of Captain Dreyfus.

BIBLIOGRAPHY: *Nouveau Larousse Illustré.*

S. F. T. H.

MEYER, DAVID AMSEL: Danish financier; born in Copenhagen Jan. 18, 1753; died there Aug. 30, 1813. Meyer started in business for himself at a very early age, and during the period of general prosperity in the last decade of the eighteenth century his operations increased greatly, extending to transoceanic countries. On the death of his brother, who had for some time been his partner, Meyer associated himself with his nephew S. S. Trier, and founded the firm of Meyer & Trier, which occupied a prominent position in the world of finance. Several times the house had to face severe crises, as in 1795, when a fire devastated Copenhagen, and in 1799, when a general financial panic occurred. The firm, however, sustained no material injury to its commercial interests.

In 1806 Meyer criticized the way in which the finances of the country were being administered, and he especially denounced the reckless issue of unsecured paper currency. During the depression of the money market due to the Napoleonic wars, he was summoned by King Frederick VI. (1808), who consulted him on financial matters of state. Meyer is said to have exercised a great deal of influence on legislation in those days; and, in common with other unofficial advisers of the king, he had to bear his share of popular hatred, perhaps not unmixed with envy. During a financial crisis in 1811 Meyer acted as the agent of the government in endeavoring to avert pecuniary disaster. Enormous sums were placed at his disposal; and it was left to him to decide whether applicants for funds desired the money for legitimate business purposes or for speculation, and to grant or refuse the requests accordingly. The Danish merchants did not long submit to his arbitration, but sought other means of raising capital.

During the latter part of the year 1811 Meyer retired from active business, and in 1812 his firm received a letter of thanks from the king for its "arduous and self-sacrificing work in accordance with our will and desire." At the same time he received the title of "Hofraad."

Meyer left a fortune of 300,000 rigsbankdaler ($150,000), of which sum he bequeathed 200,000 kroner ($50,000) to Jewish schools and charities in Copenhagen, while the remainder was distributed among various other educational and charitable institutions.

BIBLIOGRAPHY: Nathanson, *Hofraad David Amsel Meyer's Levnet*, Copenhagen, 1816; C. F. Bricka, *Dansk Biografisk Lexicon.*

S. F. C.

MEYER, EDVARD: Danish journalist and author; born Aug. 6, 1813, in Copenhagen; died there Aug. 4, 1880. He was the son of very poor parents and received little or no education during his boyhood, which he spent in a Jewish charitable institution. At the age of fourteen he was apprenticed to a wood-turner in Kjöge, and spent several years at this trade. In 1837 he established a weekly journal, the "Kallundborg Ugeblad," which in 1839 was incorporated with another paper. In 1841 Meyer returned to Copenhagen, where he started a humorous weekly, "Friskytten," and later a sensational daily, "Flyveposten," which latter for some years yielded him an annual income of nearly 50,000 Danish crowns. After many vicissitudes Meyer ended his days as he had begun them—in a Jewish charitable institution.

Of his many writings may be mentioned: "Poetisk Nyscpulver" (Copenhagen, 1826); "Conversation" (*ib.* 1839), four pamphlets; "Danske Folkesange" (*ib.* 1839), Danish popular melodies; "Digte og Eventyr" (*ib.* 1842), poems and fairy-tales.

BIBLIOGRAPHY: C. F. Bricka, *Dansk Biografisk Lexicon*; *Erslew's Forfatter-Lexicon.*

S. F. C.

MEYER, ERNST: Danish genre painter; born May 11, 1797, at Altona, Sleswick-Holstein; died in Rome Feb. 1, 1861. He studied at the Academy of Arts and in Lorentzen's Malerskole ("painters' school") in Copenhagen, and became, in 1814, a pupil of the Modelskolen, where he was twice awarded a silver medal (1816 and 1818). One of his first paintings was "Gretchen Kneeling Before the Holy Virgin," which was exhibited at the Academy of Arts in 1818 and which received much favorable comment.

Meyer aspired to become a historical painter, but after an unsuccessful attempt he abandoned this branch of the art. He spent three years (1821–24) in Munich, and then went to Rome, where he met Thorwaldsen, the sculptor, who was the animating spirit of the circle of Danish artists there.

Of Meyer's paintings the following may be mentioned: "Scene at a Well near a Capuchin Monastery," 1827; "A Neapolitan Fisher Family" (bought by Prince Christian Frederick), 1833; "A Fisherman Observing the Wind" and "Parents Leading Their Son to the Cloister" (painted between 1833 and 1837), both of which are now in Thorwaldsen's Museum. His most famous painting was "Sailors Landing Travelers at Capri," which was exhibited at the Copenhagen Academy of Arts in 1837 and became so popular that Meyer made several copies of it.

BIBLIOGRAPHY: C. F. Bricka, *Dansk Biografisk Lexicon.*

S. F. C.

MEYER, FRIEDERICH CHRISTIAN: Jewish convert to Christianity; born at Hamburg in the second half of the seventeenth century; died in Belgium about 1738. After having been baptized at Bremen, he became a missionary and traveled for thirty years. He was the author of the following works: (1) "Licht zu Erleuchten die Juden," exalting the glory of Jesus (Leipsic, 1711); (2) "Me'irat 'Enayim," a pamphlet written in German, in which the author draws a parallel between Moses and Jesus, showing the supremacy of the latter (Amsterdam, 1713); (3) "Der Abscheuliche Mord Christi," in which he endeavors to demonstrate that the duration of the exile of the Jews can be attributed only to the crucifixion of Jesus (Hamburg, 1719); (4) "Vera Immanuelis Generatio," written in Hebrew and demonstrating the divinity of Jesus from the Prophets, especially from Isa. vii. 14.

BIBLIOGRAPHY: *Sammlung von Alten und Neuen Theologischen Sachen*, 1723, p. 628; Wolf, *Bibl. Hebr.* iii., No. 1897b.

D. I. Br.

MEYER, LEOPOLD: Danish physician; born in Copenhagen Nov. 1, 1852. After graduating from the university of that city (M.D. 1880) he went abroad to study obstetrics, and on his return became privat-docent in gynecology at his alma mater. In 1897 he was appointed professor of obstetrics and children's diseases in the same university.

Of Meyer's writings the following may be mentioned: "Det Normale Svangerskab, Födsel, og Barselseng," Copenhagen, 1882 (2d ed. 1891); "Menstruationsprocessen og dens Sygelige Afvigelser," *ib.* 1890; "Den Förste Barnepleje," *ib.* 1891. Since 1890 Meyer has been associate editor of the "Bibliothek for Læger," the leading Danish medical journal.

BIBLIOGRAPHY: Caröe and Selmer, *Den Danske Lægestand*; C. F. Bricka, *Dansk Biografisk Lexicon*.

S. F. C.

MEYER, LOUIS: Polish poet; born in the village of Sluzewo (Sluzhew), government of Warsaw, Russian Poland, 1796; died March 25, 1869. He was sent in 1810 by his father to Berlin, where he prepared himself for a business career, at the same time manifesting an unusual talent for poetry. In 1816 he returned to Poland, where he established himself in business, but still found ample time to continue his studies and to write German verse. In 1861 he was elected member of the County Assembly, which, however, on account of the Polish insurrection, did not convene.

Meyer's collected writings were published under the title "Hinterlassene Deutsche Schriften eines Polnischen Juden," Berlin, 1871. The book contains epic and dramatic poetry, pictures from Jewish life, and some aphorisms in prose.

BIBLIOGRAPHY: *Hinterlassene Deutsche Schriften*, etc.

H. R.

MEYER, LUDWIG: German psychiatrist; born at Bielefeld Dec. 27, 1827; died at Göttingen Feb. 8, 1900. He studied medicine at the universities of Bonn, Würzburg, and Berlin (M.D. 1852), and became assistant at the Charité Hospital in the last-named city. Later he held the post of physician at the insane asylum in Schwetz, and was appointed chief physician at the city hospital, Hamburg, in 1856. In 1866 he became professor of psychiatry at the University of Göttingen, and director of the insane asylum connected with this university, which positions he continued to hold until his death.

Meyer founded with Griesinger in 1867 "Das Archiv für Psychiatrie." He wrote more than one hundred essays for the medical journals. He was an authority on psychiatry, and many hospitals have been built and furnished according to his suggestions and plans; among them are those of Hamburg, Göttingen, St. Urban, and Marburg.

BIBLIOGRAPHY: Pagel, *Biog. Lex.*; Hirsch, *Biog. Lex.*; A. Cramer, in *Deutsche Medizinische Wochenschrift*, Feb. 22, 1890, p. 140.

S. F. T. H.

MEYER, LUDWIG BEATUS: Danish author; born in Gandersheim, Brunswick, Jan. 3, 1780; died in Copenhagen July 28, 1854. From 1802 to 1805 he lived in the latter city as a private teacher, being subsequently appointed tutor in the family of Count Schimmelmann. In 1810 he became a naturalized citizen of Denmark, and entered the service of the government as chief of the bureau of the national debt. He resigned his appointment in 1821, receiving the title of professor.

Meyer now devoted his time exclusively to writing, his first work, "Haandbog i den Tyske Poetiske Literatur," appearing in Copenhagen in 1828. In 1837 he published a voluminous glossary of all foreign words and phrases occurring in the Danish language. This lexicon, which was entitled "Kortfattet Lexicon over Fremmede, i det Danske Skrift- og Omgangssprog Forekommende Ord, Kunstudtryk, og Talemaader," has, under the name of "Meyer's Fremmedordbog," become one of the leading authorities among Danish lexicographical works, and has passed through several editions (Copenhagen, 1837, 1841, 1899–1900).

BIBLIOGRAPHY: *Salmonsen's Store Illustrerede Konversations-Lexicon*.

S. F. C.

MEYER, MORITZ: German physician; born at Berlin Nov. 10, 1821; died there Oct. 30, 1893. After studying at the universities of Heidelberg, Halle, and Berlin (M.D. 1844), he settled in Berlin in 1845, where he practised until his death. Meyer was a specialist in diseases of the nerves and in the use of electricity in their treatment. During his researches he invented the "Meyersche Unterbrecher," an instrument used in examining the reaction of muscles and nerves. He is the author of a well-known work entitled "Die Electricität in Ihrer Anwendung auf Practische Medizin" (Berlin, 1854; 4th ed. 1883). He furthermore wrote several articles on the paralysis induced by the constant use of snuff.

BIBLIOGRAPHY: Pagel, *Biographisches Lexikon*.

S. F. T. H.

MEYER, M. WILHELM: German astronomer; born at Brunswick Feb. 15, 1853. He first engaged in the book-trade, but soon gave it up and pursued astronomical studies at the universities and observatories at Göttingen, Leipsic, and Zurich. In 1876 he established himself as privat-docent at Zurich; in 1877 he became a member of the staff of the observatory at Geneva, and in 1882 he lectured on astronomy at the Geneva University. In 1883 he removed to Vienna, and thence to Berlin, where he became (1888) director of the "Urania," a society for the popularizing of natural science, whose organ, "Himmel und Erde," he has edited since 1889. Together with Schwalbe he edited Diesterweg's "Populäre Himmelskunde" (18th ed., Berlin, 1893). He has published: "Die Königin des Tages und Ihre Familie" (Vienna, 1885); "Die Entstehung der Erde und des Irdischen" (Berlin, 1888); "Mussestunden eines Naturfreundes" (*ib.* 1891), etc.

BIBLIOGRAPHY: *Meyers Konversations-Lexikon.*

S.

MEYER, RACHEL: German authoress; born in Danzig March 11, 1806; died in Berlin Feb. 8, 1874. A few years after the death of her sister Frederika, she married the latter's husband. While devoting herself to charity and teaching, she found time to entertain noted men and to continue her own self-education. The publication of her first book, written while superintending the instruction of her children, was retarded by the death of a son. It appeared in Berlin in 1853 under the title "Zwei Schwestern"; it deals with the triumph of love over self and is an idealistic exposition of the marital relation. Her husband's business necessitated his removing to Vienna; here Rachel met Kompert and August Frankl, and here she produced her sketch of Vienna life entitled "Wider die Natur." Another work, entitled "Rachel" (Vienna, 1859), is a novel describing the life of the great actress Rachel. "In Banden Frei" (Berlin, 1869), her last novel, is a character study of her friend Lina Davidson. Rachel spent her last years in Berlin, with her daughters. Despite her idealism she was practical, and shortly before her death wrote a sketch of Stephenson, the inventor, with the express purpose of fostering in her nephew the practical spirit.

BIBLIOGRAPHY: Kayserling, *Die Jüdischen Frauen*, pp. 248–253.

S. S. J. L.

MEYER, SAMUEL: German rabbi; born in Hanover Feb. 26, 1819; died there July 5, 1882. He studied Talmud in his native city and at Frankfort-on-the-Main, and attended the University of Bonn. In 1845 he was chosen successor to Nathan Adler as district rabbi of Hanover and Lüneburg. He carried out in 1847 the plan, already projected by Adler, of founding a teachers' seminary in Hanover. Besides a few sermons he published "Gesch. des Wohlthätigkeits-Vereins der Synagogen-Gemeinde Hannover" (Hanover, 1862), and edited some unpublished poems of Abraham ibn Ezra, which he had discovered ("Orient, Lit." 1842).

BIBLIOGRAPHY: Steinschneider, *Hebr. Bibl.* vi. 32.

S. M. K.

MEYER, SARA (BARONIN VON GROTTHUSZ): German authoress, and leader of a salon; born in Berlin in the latter half of the eighteenth century; died at Oranienburg Dec. 11, 1828. She wrote many stories, dramas, and political and moral essays in German and French, her French work being especially well received. Among her many friends were Goethe, Lessing, and Schiller. Most of their letters to her were accidentally burned, only twenty-one letters from Goethe, written in the years 1797–1815, being saved; these were published by Varnhagen von Ense.

Sara Meyer was light-minded, susceptible to flattery, conceited, and lacked moral stamina. After severing her first marriage-ties she was baptized and married Baron von Grotthusz. Her younger sister, **Mariane,** after the death of Prince Reuss, Austrian ambassador to the Prussian court, was found to be his lawful wife. She never bore the title of princess, but resided in Vienna as **Frau von Eybenburg** (from 1799). Like her sister, she was well educated, but wrote indifferently. She left in manuscript a number of sketches of well-known characters.

BIBLIOGRAPHY: Kayserling, *Die Jüdischen Frauen*, pp. 216–219.

S. S. J. L.

MEYER, VICTOR: German chemist; born in Berlin Sept. 8, 1848; died in Heidelberg in 1897. He was inclined toward literature and the stage, when a visit to his elder brother, then studying chemistry at Heidelberg, turned his thoughts into another channel, and he decided to become a chemist. He thoroughly prepared himself in mathematics and natural science in one of the gymnasiums of Berlin, spent one semester at the University of Berlin, and studied for some time with A. W. Hofmann. In 1865 he entered the University of Heidelberg, in whose faculty there were such men as Helmholtz, Kirchhoff, and Bunsen. The last-named made him his private assistant. In 1868 he returned to Berlin to increase under Bayer his knowledge of organic chemistry.

When only twenty-three years old he was appointed assistant professor at the Stuttgart Polytechnic School, and in 1872 was called to Zurich as the successor of Wislicenus. His brilliant work in Switzerland (1872–85), both in the laboratory and in the lecture-room, attracted students from many countries.

In 1885 he received a call from the University of Göttingen, and spent three years in reorganizing the laboratories there. In 1889 he was invited to Heidelberg, his alma mater, to succeed Bunsen. The latter regarded him as the brightest and most promising of the many eminent men who had studied under him, and it was his wish on his retirement that Meyer should be appointed as his successor.

Meyer's fame as a lecturer was world-wide; and his ingenuity and skill in devising and manipulating experiments, combined with his personal magnetism, attracted many hearers. Meyer's remarkable insight is illustrated by his discovery and studies of the thiophene group (1882). He discovered and described the type of oximes (1882), investigated the nitro- (1872), nitroso-, isonitroso-, and iodo-compounds (1892), and studied the organic derivatives of ammonia, and with these the stereochemistry of nitrogen. He published his important researches on the esterification of the acids of the aromatic series (1894–95).

Of great value are his investigations in physical chemistry, particularly those of vapor densities (1878–80) and the study of high temperatures. Together with Jacobson he wrote an excellent textbook on organic chemistry ("Lehrbuch der Organischen Chemie," 2 vols., Leipsic, 1891–95). Of his other works may be mentioned: (with Langer) "Pyrochemische Untersuchungen," Brunswick, 1885; "Die Thiophengruppe," *ib.* 1888; "Chemische Probleme der Gegenwart," Heidelberg, 1890; "Ergebnisse und Ziele der Stereochemischen Forschung," 1890; (with Treadwell) "Tabellen zur Qualitativen Analyse," 3d ed., Berlin, 1891; "Aus Natur und Wissenschaft," Heidelberg, 1892; "Märztage im Kanarischen Archipel," *ib.* 1893.

Meyer's unceasing and confining work ultimately shattered his nervous system; and in a fit of dejection he took his own life.

Bibliography: *Meyers Konversations-Lexikon*; *Zeitschrift für Anorganische Chemie*, xvi.; *Naturwissenschaftliche Rundschau*, xii., Nos. 43, 44; H. Goldschmidt, *Zur Erinnerung an Victor Meyer*, Heidelberg, 1897.

s. J. G. L.

MEYERBEER, GIACOMO: German composer; born at Berlin Sept. 5, 1791; died at Paris May 2, 1864. His real name was **Jakob Liebmann Beer**; but he changed it when his grandfather promised to leave him his fortune on condition that the composer prefix the name "Meyer" to his patronymic. He received his early instruction in music from Franz Lauska and Muzio Clementi, and at the age of seven made his début as a pianist in one of Patzig's pupils' concerts (Oct. 14, 1800), playing the D Minor Concerto by Mozart. He then studied theory under Zelter, and later under Bernard Anselm Weber, director of the Berlin Opera, with whom he remained until 1810, in which year he went to Darmstadt to study for two years under Abbé Vogler.

Giacomo Meyerbeer.

In 1811 he wrote the oratorio "Gott und die Natur," the score of which so pleased the Grand Duke of Hesse that he appointed Meyerbeer composer to the court. The first performance of the work took place May 8, 1811, at the Singakademie, Berlin. Two operas, "Jephtha's Gelübde" and "Abimelek, oder die Beiden Khalifen," which Meyerbeer had written, were produced at the Royal Opera-House, Munich, in 1813. Soon afterward he gave a piano recital at Vienna, achieving a complete success.

Early Works.

In 1815 Meyerbeer went to Venice in order to familiarize himself with Italian melody and vocalization. He now set to work writing in the Italian vein, and met with instantaneous success, his four operas composed at this time being received with immense enthusiasm. In 1823, while engaged on "Il Crociato in Egitto," the composer went to Berlin, where he unsuccessfully endeavored to arrange for a performance of his three-act opera "Das Brandenburger Thor." In 1824 "Il Crociato" was produced at Venice with very great success; and two years later Meyerbeer accepted an invitation to Paris to witness a performance of the same opera. Thenceforth he became wholly identified with the French school of opera. On Nov. 21, 1831, his "Robert le Diable" was produced at the Grand Opera, Paris; and within a year the libretto had been translated into nearly every European language, and performances had been given in every important city. This opera was followed (Feb. 20, 1836) by "Les Huguenots," an opera which was at first received with somewhat less favor than "Robert le Diable," but which ultimately came to be regarded as greatly its superior.

After the production of "Les Huguenots" at Berlin, Meyerbeer was called to that city by King Frederick William IV. as general musical director; and there he composed his opera "Das Feldlager in Schlesien," which, however, was not successfully produced until Jenny Lind, whom Meyerbeer had introduced to the Berlin public, assumed the rôle of *Vielka.* In the summer of 1846, at the request of the Princess of Prussia, Meyerbeer composed the incidental music to the drama "Struensee," written by his brother Michael Beer; and on Sept. 19 following, this work, the music of which ranks among his best productions, was performed at the Royal Theater, Berlin. After visits to Vienna and London in 1847, Meyerbeer returned to Berlin, where he produced Richard Wagner's "Rienzi." Two years later "Le Prophète," the libretto of which had been completed by Scribe in 1842, was produced at the Grand Opera, Paris (April 16, 1849), and, like its predecessors, "Robert le Diable" and "Les Huguenots," soon made the circuit of the globe.

Despite failing health Meyerbeer produced "L'Etoile du Nord" at the Opéra Comique (1854), and four years later "Dinorah ou le Pardon de Ploermel." Neither of these operas, however, met with the favorable reception accorded to Meyerbeer's previous Parisian productions. In 1862 he represented German music at the opening of the London International Exhibition with his "Overture in the Form of a March." Upon his return to Berlin he resumed his work upon "L'Africaine," on which he had been engaged since 1838. For years the difficulty of getting a satisfactory cast had prevented the production of this opera; and several other circumstances hindered its performance dur-

"L'Africaine."

ing the composer's lifetime. In April, 1864, he returned for the last time to Paris, to superintend the preparatory rehearsals of this opera; but in the midst of his labors he died, and the opera was not produced until May 28, 1865. In accordance with Meyerbeer's last wishes his body was taken to Berlin for burial; but imposing funeral obsequies were held in Paris also.

Compositions.

Of Meyerbeer's compositions besides those already mentioned, the following deserve special notice: the monodrama "Thevelinden's Liebe," for soprano solo and chorus with clarinet obligato; "Romilda e Costanza" (1815); "La Semiramide Riconosciuta" (1819); "Emma di Resburgo" (1819); "Margherita d'Anjou" (1820); "L'Esule di Granada" (1822); seven sacred cantatas of Klopstock, for quartet unaccompanied; choruses to Æschylus' "Eumenides"; "Der Genius der Musik am Grabe Beethoven's," for soli and chorus; "Freundschaft," for 4-part male chorus; Psalm xci., for eight voices, composed for the choir of the Berlin Cathedral; "Fackeltänze," for brass orchestra, composed for the weddings of the King of Bavaria (1846) and of the Princesses Charlotte (1850) and Anne (1853) of Bavaria; grand march for the Schiller Centenary Festival. 1859; Coronation March for King William I. (1863); also a large number of songs with pianoforte accompaniment, among which "Le Moine" (for bass) and "Das Fischermädchen" are perhaps the most popular.

Meyerbeer received medals and other distinctions from almost every civilized government. He steadfastly adhered to Judaism throughout his life. He was ever ready to assist his fellow artists irrespective of creed; and in his will he made provision for a similarly beneficent disposition of his wealth. He set aside, for instance, 10,000 thalers (the Meyerbeer-Stiftung), the interest of which he directed to be used in providing traveling fellowships for promising students of music.

BIBLIOGRAPHY: Hermann Mendel, *Giacomo Meyerbeer*, Berlin, 1868; H. Blaze de Béry, *Meyerbeer, Sa Vie, Ses Œuvres et Son Temps*; M. Joël, *Worte Gesprochen an der Bahre Meyerbeers*, Breslau, 1864; Grove, *Dictionary of Music and Musicians*; Fétis, *Biographie Universelle des Musiciens*.

S. J. So.

MEYSELS, BERISCH (BAER). See MEISELS, DOB BERUSH B. ISAAC.

MEYUḤAS (מיוחס): Oriental Jewish family which gave several rabbinical writers to Jerusalem and Constantinople.

Abraham ben Samuel Meyuḥas: Rabbi in Turkey in the eighteenth century; author of "Sedeh ha-Areẓ," in three parts, the first two being homilies on the Pentateuch (Salonica, 1784–98) and the third containing responsa on the four parts of the Shulḥan 'Aruk, collectanea, and Talmudic annotations (Leghorn, 1788). In the preface Meyuḥas asserts that he wrote the following commentaries: "Digle Ahabah," on Isaac Luria's "Derek 'Eẓ ha-Ḥayyim"; "Ha-Ma'or ha-Ḳaṭon," on Ḥayyim Vital's "'Eẓ Ḥayyim"; "Siaḥ ha-Sadeh," on Isaac Luria's "Sefer ha-Kawwanot." Fürst ("Bibl. Jud." ii. 347) ascribes to this Meyuḥas the work entitled "Bene Abraham," responsa and homilies, and "Ḳontres," containing the laws of Giṭṭin (Constantinople, 1773); the responsa and homilies, however, are those of **Abraham ben Judah Meyuḥas;** while the "Ḳontres" was written by **Nathan Meyuḥas.**

BIBLIOGRAPHY: Benjacob, *Oẓar ha-Sefarim*, p. 567, No. 302; Zedner, *Cat. Hebr. Books Brit. Mus.* pp. 536–537.

M. SEL.

Moses Mordecai Joseph Meyuḥas: Son of Raphael Meyuḥas ben Samuel; born 1738; died 1806. He succeeded Yom-Ṭob al-Ghazi as chief rabbi of Jerusalem (1801–6). In 1799, on the approach of Bonaparte's army, which already had taken Jaffa, Meyuḥas assembled the Jews of Jerusalem and delivered a patriotic speech, after which he seized a pickax and commenced to dig a trench, his coreligionists immediately following his example. He was the author of three Hebrew works: "Sha'ar ha-Mayim," notes on the Shulḥan 'Aruk, and responsa (Salonica, 1768); "Birkot ha-Mayim," novellæ, religious laws, and responsa (*ib.* 1789); "Mayim Sha'al," on the same subjects as the "Sha'ar ha Mayim" (*ib.* 1799).

M. FR.

Raphael ben Samuel Meyuḥas: Chief rabbi of Jerusalem and head of the yeshibah there; flourished about the middle of the eighteenth century. He was the author of the following works, all published at Salonica: "Minḥat Bikkurim," halakic and haggadic novellæ on several treatises of the Talmud (1752); "Peri ha-Adamah," novellæ on the four divisions of Maimonides' "Yad" (1752); "Pene ha-Adamah," homilies on the "parashiyyot" of the Pentateuch (1752); "Mizbaḥ Adamah," novellæ on the four parts of the Shulḥan 'Aruk (1777).

BIBLIOGRAPHY: Azulai, *Shem ha-Gedolim*, ii., s.v. *Mizbaḥ Adamah*; Fürst, *Bibl. Jud.* ii. 347; Zedner, *Cat. Hebr. Books Brit. Mus.* p. 536.

M. SEL.

Samuel Ḥayyim Meyuḥas: Chief rabbi of Constantinople from 1836 to 1839; died some years after the latter date. He was the author of a volume of responsa entitled "Shemen ha-Mishḥah" (Constantinople, 1840).

BIBLIOGRAPHY: Azulai, *Shem ha-Gedolim*; Hazan, *Ha-Ma'alot li-Shelomoh*; Franco, *Histoire des Israélites de l'Empire Ottoman*; Walden, *Shem ha-Gedolim he-Ḥadash*.

J. M. FR.

MEZA (MESA): A family of Amsterdam distinguished for the number of its members that filled rabbinic offices.

Abraham Ḥayyim de Jacob de Solomon de Meza: Member of the Talmud Torah 'Eẓ Ḥayyim in Amsterdam, and author of a sermon, delivered in Portuguese on the day of solemn devotion, "Sermão Moral . . . na Occasião de Hum Dia Solemne de Oração . . . em 4 Nisan 5507 = 15 Março 1747," Amsterdam, 1747.

David de Abraham Ḥayyim de Jacob de Solomon de Meza: Son of Abraham de Meza; died in Amsterdam after 1793. He published: "Sermão da Liberdade, Pregado na K. K. de Talmud Torah em 28. Yjar 5527," Amsterdam, 1767; "Sermão Moral, Preg. . . . em S. Emor, 13 Yjar 5532," *ib.* 1767; "Sermão Moral Sobre o Pezo do Peccado, Preg. em S. Qui Tetsè 9 Elul 5546," *ib.* 1786. He prepared also a new edition of "Paraphrasis Caldayca en los Cantares de Selomoh como Tambien los Apophthegmas de Aboth," *ib.* 1766. Several Hebrew songs of his are to be found in the collection of poems "Shir Emunim," edited by Moses de Piza, *ib.* 1793.

David de Jacob de Meza: Son of the editor **Jacob de Meza;** member of the Talmud Torah 'Eẓ Ḥayyim. Many of his responsa are contained in the compilation "Peri 'Eẓ Ḥayyim," *ib.* 1741.

Solomon de Isaac de Meza: Physician and ḥakam; born at Amsterdam; died there in 1742. He was a disciple of Solomon de Oliveyra and David de Pina, the latter of whom initiated him in the science of medicine. He was a member of the rabbinate of the Spanish-Portuguese community in Amsterdam. In conjunction with his colleagues Solomon Ayllon, David Mendes da Silva, and others, he signed the famous rabbinical decision in favor of the Shabbethaian Nehemiah Ḥayyun (1711). A year after his death the catalogue of his library was published (Amsterdam, 1743). He wrote under the title "Shulḥan Shelomoh" an unimportant disquisition concerning the Sabbath-day's journey from a village near Amsterdam (*ib.* 1725). After his death appeared his "Meditaçoens Sacras ou Sermoens Varios" (part i., *ib.* 1764).

BIBLIOGRAPHY: Kayserling, *Bibl. Esp.-Port.-Jud.* p. 71; Carmoly, *Histoire des Médecins Juifs*, p. 226; D. Henriques de Castro, *Catalogue de Vente*, p. 118; Grätz, *Gesch.* x., p. xciii.; Zedner, *Cat. Hebr. Books Brit. Mus.* p. 537.

G. M. K.

MEZA, CHRISTIAN JACOB THEOPHILUS DE: Danish physician and author; born in Copenhagen Nov. 26, 1756; died there April 6, 1844. He was a son of the physician Christian de Meza, together with whom he embraced Christianity in 1783. In the same year he graduated as M.D. from the University of Copenhagen, and became a member of the Royal Medical Society. From 1784 until his death he practised medicine in Elsinore.

Meza published in the medical journals numerous essays, of which the following may be mentioned: "De Graviditate Mixta Observatio," in "Acta Regiæ Societatis Med. Hafniensis," i. 442–450; "Relatio Febris Tertianæ Intermittentis Epidemicæ Anno 1784 Grassantis," in "Observationes Medico-Practicæ Quinque," ii. 197–213; "En Sjælden og Abnormal Tvillingfödsel," in "Bibliothek for Læger," 1821, ix. 41–43 (appeared afterward in "Bulletin des Sciences Médicales," Jan., 1830, and in "American Journal of the Medical Sciences," No. 12, 1830).

Meza wrote also a drama, "Dormon og Vilhelmine," which was produced at the Royal Theater, Copenhagen, in 1796.

Meza's son, **Christian Julius de Meza** (1792–1865), was a general in command of a division of the Danish army during the war with Germany (1864).

BIBLIOGRAPHY: C. F. Bricka, *Dansk Biografisk Lexicon*; *Erslew's Forfatter-Lexicon.*

G. F. C.

MEZA, CHRISTIAN JULIUS FREDERIK (SOLOMON) DE: Danish physician; born in Amsterdam Sept. 4, 1727; died in Copenhagen June, 1800. Meza, who was the son of a Portuguese rabbi, Abraham de Meza, studied medicine in Amsterdam, and later at the University of Utrecht (M.D. 1749). After further study in Hamburg he went (1753) to Copenhagen, where he took up the practise of medicine.

In 1769 Meza published in French a treatise on hygiene entitled "De l'Education des Enfants tant Physique que Morale." Another work of Meza's, entitled "Tentamen Historiæ Medicæ" (1795), was severely criticized in Germany.

In 1772 he became a member of the newly founded medical society of Copenhagen. He was popularly called "Jödedoktoren," and was generally respected in Copenhagen, where he was for a long time the only Jewish physician. In 1783, after the death of his wife, Meza, together with a son and a daughter, embraced Christianity.

BIBLIOGRAPHY: C. F. Bricka, *Dansk Biografisk Lexicon*; Nathanson, *Jódernes Stilling i Danmark*, Copenhagen, 1870.

S. F. C.

MEZEI, ERNEST: Hungarian deputy and journalist; born at Satoralja-Ujhely, Hungary, in May, 1851. He completed his school career partly in his native city and partly in Kaschau, and then took a course in law and philosophy at the University of Budapest. While still a student he entered upon a journalistic career, contributing leaders to the "Ellenör." In 1874 he became one of the founders of the "Egyetértés," the representative organ of the extreme opposition, the so-called Independent party; and he has been on its editorial staff ever since. In 1878 he was nominated as deputy for the district of Gyoma, being warmly recommended by Louis Kossuth, but failed to secure election. In 1881 he was elected deputy for the city of Miskolcz.

During this period sprang up the celebrated Tisza-Eszlár blood accusation, which gave rise to an intense anti-Semitic agitation. Mezei made the affair the basis of an interpellation addressed to the minister of justice, which called forth exciting scenes in the House of Deputies. During the consideration of the bill on mixed marriages between Christians and Jews he made several pointed speeches against the anti-Semites.

Mezei is active also in the literary field, having published many scattered poems and sketches of travel, as well as "Olasz Bolyongások" (1877), a narrative of rambles through Italy. Occasionally he contributes to the periodicals articles on current questions relating to the Jews. In a lecture entitled "Zionismus als Nationale Idee," delivered before the Hungarian Jewish Literary Society, he took a firm stand in opposition to the attempt to place over against the religious world-mission of Judaism a Jewish national propaganda.

S. G. W.

MEZEI, MORITZ: Hungarian jurist and deputy; born at Satoralja-Ujhely Jan. 17, 1836. He studied law in Budapest, and even as a student took an active part in the efforts to restore the Hungarian constitution and emancipate the Hungarian Jews. He was the chief founder of the National Judæo-Hungarian Society in 1861, and edited its journal, the "Izraelita Közlöny." The spirit of Hungarian nationalism which pervaded his writings caused him to be court-martialed by the governor, Count Moritz Pálffy; but for a royal proclamation of amnesty issued on the occasion of the recovery of Queen Elizabeth he would have been condemned. He was obliged, however, to resign his editorial position. In 1864, by the permission of the king, he began the practise of law at Budapest, although the legal profession had not hitherto been opened to the Jews. Three years later he was able to resume his journalistic advocacy of Jewish emancipation, and in 1868 was appointed secretary of the congress convened by Baron Eötvös for the regulation of Hebrew communal affairs. In 1892 he was elected president of the organization which secured recognition of the Jewish religion in Hungary, and in 1893 he was elected to the Hungarian Parliament by the Jewish district of Budapest (Leopoldstadt). Mezei is also vice-president of the Hebrew congregational district of Budapest.

BIBLIOGRAPHY: Venetianer, *A Zsidóság Szervezete*, p. 498; *Pallas Lex.*

S. L. V.

MEZEY, FRANZ: Hungarian jurist and author; born at Acsad Feb. 5, 1860. His parents had destined him for a rabbinical career, but after reaching maturity and becoming a thorough Hebrew scholar, he took up the study of jurisprudence and was admitted to the bar at Budapest. As a writer and speaker his abilities were devoted to the cause of Judaism even in his student days. In 1883 he was the mainstay of the defense in the Tisza-Eszlár affair as the representative of the Hungarian Jews, and for the past two decades, as secretary of the Jewish chancery ("Landeskanzlei"), he has been their chief source of inspiration toward advancement in religious and educational matters. He was one of the founders of the Hungarian Jewish Literary Society, and, with Wilhelm Bacher, edited its year-book; from 1891 to 1895 he was coeditor of the "Magyar Zsidó Szemle" with Ludwig Blau. He has also contributed to the "Nemzeti Ujság" and the "Jogtudomany i Kozlony." Mezey is (1904) secretary and attorney of the ḥebra ḳaddisha of Budapest, which has attained, under his management, a membership of 10,000.

BIBLIOGRAPHY: Szinnyei, *Magyar Irók.*

S. L. V.

MEZUZAH (מזוזה; lit. "door-post"): Name given to a rectangular piece of parchment inscribed with the passages Deut. vi. 4-9 and xi. 13-21, written in twenty-two lines according to the same rules as those for the Torah and tefillin. The parchment is rolled up and inserted in a wooden or metal case or tube. This is affixed, in a slanting position, to the upper part of the right-hand door-post, so that the upper part is inward and the lower part outward, and about a handbreadth from the outer edge of the door-post. On the outer side of the top of the parchment is inscribed the name of God, שדי; and an opening is left in the case opposite this word, which opening is protected by a piece of glass. The material on which the mezuzah may be written is as carefully prescribed as is that for a scroll of the Law (Massek. Soferim i. 1; Asheri to Alfasi, "Sefer Torah"; Shulḥan 'Aruk, Yoreh De'ah, 271; Yer. Megillah i. 9; Shab. 108a; Mas. Mezuzah, ed. Kirchheim, i. 1); but while a scroll must always be written from a copy, the mezuzah may be written from memory (Men. 32b). Both selections mentioned above must be contained therein; and if even one letter is missing the mezuzah may not be used (Men. 28a). Generally the text is written in twenty-two lines equally spaced. The pious touch and kiss this part of the mezuzah as they pass through the door. The mezuzah is obligatory for every building used as a residence; and its fastening to the door-post is accompanied by the usual formula of benediction: "Blessed art Thou our God, King of the world, who hast sanctified us by Thy commandments and hast commanded us to fasten the mezuzah." On entering and leaving the house the pious touch the mezuzah (at "Shaddai") with the hand, and recite the prayer: "May God keep my going out and my coming in from now on and ever more."

שמע ישראל יהוה אלהינו יהוה אחד ואהבת את
יהוה אלהיך בכל לבבך ובכל נפשך ובכל מאדך והיו
הדברים האלה אשר אנכי מצוך היום על לבבך ושננתם
לבניך ודברת בם בשבתך בביתך ובלכתך בדרך
ובשכבך ובקומך וקשרתם לאות על ידך והיו לטטפת
בין עיניך וכתבתם על מזזות ביתך ובשעריך
והיה אם שמע תשמעו אל מצותי אשר אנכי
מצוה אתכם היום לאהבה את יהוה אלהיכם ולעבדו
בכל לבבכם ובכל נפשכם ונתתי מטר ארצכם בעתו
יורה ומלקוש ואספת דגנך ותירשך ויצהרך ונתתי
עשב בשדך לבהמתך ואכלת ושבעת השמרו לכם
פן יפתה לבבכם וסרתם ועבדתם אלהים אחרים
והשתחויתם להם וחרה אף יהוה בכם ועצר את
השמים ולא יהיה מטר והאדמה לא תתן את יבולה
ואבדתם מהרה מעל הארץ הטבה אשר יהוה נתן לכם
ושמתם את דברי אלה על לבבכם ועל נפשכם וקשרתם
אתם לאות על ידכם והיו לטוטפת בין עיניכם ולמדתם
אתם את בניכם לדבר בם בשבתך בביתך ובלכתך
בדרך ובשכבך ובקומך וכתבתם על מזוזות ביתך
ובשעריך למען ירבו ימיכם וימי בניכם על האדמה
אשר נשבע יהוה לאבתיכם לתת להם כימי השמים
על הארץ

Mezuzah Scroll.

The mezuzah brings blessings to him that touches it; but it must not be touched with unclean hands. It is inspected from time to time to make sure of its correctness. It may not be given to a non-Jew, lest it be not treated with due respect (see Men. iii. 7, 33b; Maimonides, "Yad," Tefillin, i., v., vi.; Yoreh De'ah, 285–291).

The obligation of the mezuzah is derived from the words: "And thou shalt write them on the door-posts of thy house and within thy gates." The Rabbis considered the mezuzah of equal importance with the tefillin and ẓiẓit (Men. 43b; Pes. 113b; comp. Shab. 23b, 32b).

Origin and Significance.

The antiquity of the mezuzah is attested by Josephus (*c.* 37–100 C.E.), who speaks of its employment ("Ant." iv. 8, § 13) as an old and well-established custom. Inscribed with passages of the Torah which emphasize the unity of God, His providence, and the resulting duty of man toward Him, the mezuzah is an emblematic representation of Israel's belief and practise. Thus Josephus says in speaking of the mezuzah (*l.c.*): "The greatest benefits of God are to be written on the doors . . . in order that His benevolent providence may be made known everywhere"; and Maimonides adds ("Yad," Tefillin, vi. 13): "By the commandment of the mezuzah man is reminded, when coming or going, of the unity of God, and is aroused to the love of Him. He is awakened from his slumber and his vain worldly thoughts to the knowledge that nothing endures in eternity like the knowledge of the Rock of the World. This contemplation brings him back to himself and leads him on the right path."

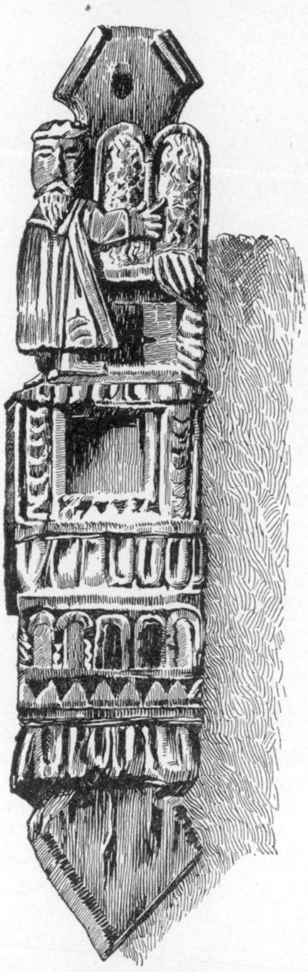

Wooden Case for Mezuzah.
(In the possession of F. David, Cassel.)

In Talmudic times a protective power, especially in warding off evil spirits, was attributed to the mezuzah.

Superstitious Conception.

This appears in such anecdotes as those of Artaban and Abba Arika (see ARTABAN V.; comp. Yer. Peah i. 1, 15d; Gen. R. xxxv. 3) and of Onḳelos ('Ab. Zarah 11a; comp. also Targ. to Cant. viii. 3; Men. 32b, 33b). In the Middle Ages, under the influence of the Cabala, not only passages from the Bible treating of God's watchfulness over His people (Ps. cxxi. 7 *et seq.*), but also various names of angels were added to the original contents of the mezuzah. שדי was explained to represent the initials of שומר דלתות (דירות) ישראל, after a cabalistic interpretation of Job xxii. 17, 25 (comp. "Kol Bo," 101, 4). At the bottom of the blank side the words כוזו במוכסז כוזו are written, which, according to אב"גד, *i.e.*, every letter standing for the next preceding, reads: יהוה אלהינו יהוה. Some, when leaving home on business bent, invoke God by the mysterious words "Kozo bemuksaz Kozo," declaring that in His name they are about to go forth, and petitioning for success. Against the additions to the mezuzah Maimonides raised his voice. He says ("Yad," Tefillin, v. 4): "There is no harm in writing שדי on the outside; but those who write on the inside the names of angels, or holy names, or verses, or other formula, are of those who will have no share in the future world. For these fools not only defeat in this manner the fulfilment of a great commandment which has for its end the remembrance of the unity of God, and the love of Him and worship of Him, but turn it into an amulet for their selfish interest, believing in their foolish hearts that it can be made to serve the preservation of transitory worldly goods." Maimonides' view prevailed, and the additions were eliminated.

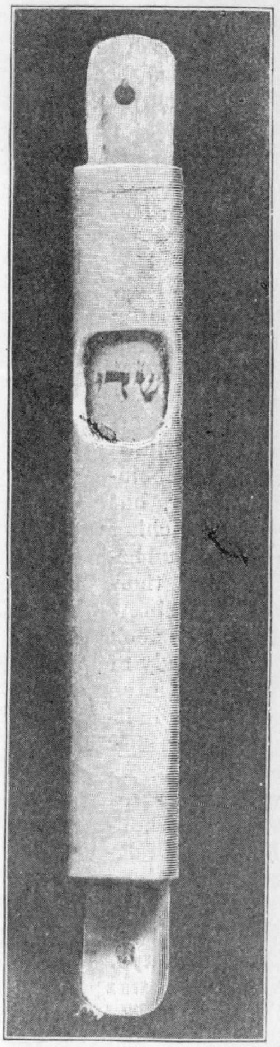

Glass Cylinder Containing Mezuzah.

The Mohammedans likewise place over the doors and windows of their dwellings as well as of their shops the name of God, or their profession of faith, or some maxim, or a verse of the Koran, or a short invocation (comp. Lane, "Account of the Manners and Customs of the Modern Egyptians," 3d ed., i. 7, 22, 320); and a similar custom seems to have prevailed among the ancient Egyptians (comp. Wilkinson, "Manners and Customs of the Ancient Egyptians," 1878, i. 361; and Huetius, "Demonstratio Evangelica," p. 58).

BIBLIOGRAPHY: Dassorius, *De Ritibus Mezuzæ*, in Ugolino, *Thesaurus*, xxi.; Bodenschatz, *Kirchliche Verfassung der Heutigen Juden*, iv. 19-24; Leopold Löw, *Gesammelte Werke*, ii. 81-84.

A. I. M. C.

MHUSHILKAR, REUBEN EZEKIEL: Beni-Israel soldier. He enlisted in the 19th Regiment Native Infantry Jan. 15, 1849, was made jemidar Oct. 1, 1861, and promoted subahdar Jan. 1, 1870. He was present at the battles of Multan, Gujarat, the Punjab (awarded medal and two clasps), Rajghur, Mungrowlee, Sindwah, and Kurai in central India (medal); served in Afghanistan from 1878 to 1880 (medal and clasp); and retired March 6, 1881.

J. J. Hy.

MICAH (מיכה): **1.** Prophet; author of the sixth book in the collection known as "The Twelve Minor Prophets" (Mic. i. 1). The name of the prophet appears to be a shortened form of מיכיה, "Micaiah" (= "Who is like Yhwh?"), and is so written in Jer. xxvi. 18 (comp. also Micah No. 2). The only data concerning Micah are those given in the superscription of the book bearing his name. He was a Morasthite; that is to say, a native of Moresheth-gath (Mic. i. 14); and he prophesied in the days of Jotham, Ahaz, and Hezekiah, kings of Judah—a period covering at the most fifty-nine years (756–697 B.C.). In the above-cited passage of Jeremiah, however, only the reign of Hezekiah is given as the period of Micah's activity.

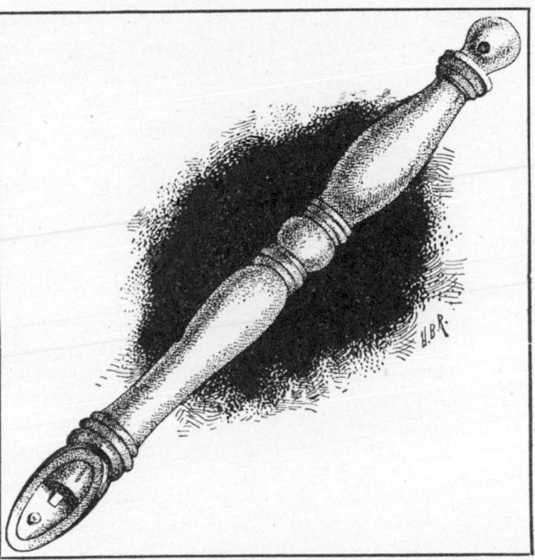
Mezuzah Case.
(After Picart.)

Pseudo-Epiphanius ("Opera," ii. 245) makes Micah an Ephraimite. Confounding him with Micaiah, son of Imlah (I Kings xxii. 8 *et seq.*), he states that Micah, for his inauspicious prophecy, was killed by order of Ahab through being thrown from a precipice, and was buried at Morathi (Maroth?; Mic. i. 12), near the cemetery of Enakim ('Ενακεὶμ, Septuagint rendering of בכו; *ib.* i. 10). According to "Gelilot Ereẓ Yisrael" (quoted in "Seder ha-Dorot," i. 118, Warsaw, 1889), Micah was buried in Chesil, a town in southern Judah (Josh. xv. 30).

2. Biblical Data: A resident of Mount Ephraim who, having stolen 1,100 pieces of silver from his mother, restored them to her on hearing her curses at the theft. The mother had dedicated the silver to Yhwh; and she accordingly gave 200 pieces to a founder, who made a molten image which was placed in Micah's house. Micah thus established a house of idols with an ephod and teraphim, and consecrated one of his sons to be his priest (Judges xvii. 1–5). In the course of time a young Levite named Jonathan, son of Gershon, happened to come to the house, and he was appointed by Micah as his priest (*ib.* xvii. 7–13). The image, together with the priest, was captured by the Danites, who set it up at Dan, where it continued to be an object of worship as long as the Tabernacle was at Shiloh (*ib.* xviii.; see Jonathan No. 1). In Judges xvii. 1, 4, the name "Micah" appears in the form מיכיהו.

S. M. Sel.

——**In Rabbinical Literature:** Micah is identified by the Rabbis with Sheba, son of Bichri, and with Nebat, the father of Jeroboam (Sanh. 101b). His name, derived by them from נתמכמך, is interpreted as meaning "the crushed one," an appellation due to a miracle which happened to him. According to a haggadah, the Israelites, when unable to complete the tale of bricks required from them by the Egyptians, were compelled to put their children in the brickwork in place of the bricks that were lacking. Moses withdrew one child (Micah), already crushed, and revived him; but, as God had foretold, he grew up to be an idolater (Tan., Yelammedenu, Ki Tissa; comp. Rashi to Sanh. *l.c.*).

The Rabbis all agree that Micah was among those who crossed the Red Sea with Moses; but they differ with regard to his idol. According to Sanh. 103b and Tan., Yelammedenu (*l.c.*), Micah had the idol with him; but according to Ex. R. (xli. 1) he took with him only the silver of which the idol was afterward made. A passage in Pesaḥim (117a) seems to support the latter opinion. There is also a tradition that it was Micah who made the golden calf in the wilderness, and in the following manner: Moses, in order to bring Joseph's coffin to the surface of the Nile, wrote on a splinter עלי שור (= "Come up, ox"; Joseph being compared to an ox; see Deut. xxxiii. 17) and threw it into the water. Micah found the splinter, and, later, when Aaron cast the gold into the fire (Ex. xxxii. 24), threw the splinter after it. As a result a calf came out (Tan., Yelammedenu, *l.c.*; see also Jew. Encyc. iii. 509a, *s.v.* Calf, Golden).

Micah, though an idolater, was praised for his hospitality to travelers. Gareb, where his idol was set up, was three miles distant from Shiloh, where the Tabernacle stood; and the smoke of the two altars mingled on account of their proximity. The angels wished to throw down the idol; but God said to them, "Leave it alone; for Micah offers bread to travelers." Micah is even supposed to have a share in the future world (Sanh. 103b); it is for this reason that his name is twice written "Micaiah" (see Micah No. 2, Biblical Data), that is, with a part of the Tetragrammaton, like the names of the just (Num. R. x. 14).

S. S. M. Sel.

——**Critical View:** The narrative of Micah's idol, the historical basis of which is undoubted, was apparently written with the object of showing the origin of the temple of Dan (comp. I Kings xii. 29).

At the same time it throws much light on the state of the Yhwh cult and of the Levites in the time of the Judges. The author expressly points out that Micah was a worshiper of Yhwh, for whose cult he had his private shrine with a regular priestly service. Although the laws of Yhwh forbade the erection of any shrine besides the one in the chosen place and the making of any image of Him (Ex. xx. 4 *et passim*; Deut. xii. 5 *et seq.*), Micah, evidently ignorant of the Law, not only set up engraved and molten images representing the divinity he worshiped, but added other idols, the teraphim for instance. The narrative further shows that the Levites, being deprived of a share in the land, had to wander from place to place, accepting the office of family priest in order to procure a livelihood.

The account itself presents many difficulties in regard to its construction. Besides several discrepancies in the text there are absolute contradictions. Thus in Judges xvii. 7 the Levite is a young man who lived in the neighborhood of Micah, while in the following verse he is a wandering Levite. There is also a discrepancy between verses 19 and 27 of ch. xviii. and between verses 30 and 31 of the same chapter concerning the duration of the cult of the idol at Dan. According to Oort, Wellhausen, and Kuenen, the text has received many interpolations, with the object of throwing contempt upon the cult of Dan. On the other hand, Vatke ("Alttestamentliche Theologie," 1835, p. 268) and Berthau, followed by other critics, recognize two parallel narratives united by a redactor. While there is some disagreement as to the component parts of the two versions, Budde's division seems to be the most acceptable; he holds, namely, that the first narrative consists of Judges xvii. 1, 5, 8–11a, 12, beginning, 13; xviii. 1, part of 2, 3b, 4b–6, 8–10, part of 11, 12, part of 13, 14, 16, 18a, 19–29, 31; and that the intervening verses form the second narrative. Budde is of opinion that the first narrative belongs to E; but he does not find sufficient grounds for ascribing the second to J. Moore thinks that the first version belongs to J. In the second version (*ib.* xviii. 30) the cult at Dan is indicated as having lasted "till the day of the captivity of the land," which is supposed by Moore to refer to the deportation by Tiglath-pileser (734 B.C.).

Besides the above-mentioned discrepancies certain points remain unsettled by the critics. Ḳimḥi explains the discrepancy between verses 3 and 4 of Judges xvii. by suggesting that the 200 shekels were an additional artisan's fee, while the whole amount of the silver was used in the fabrication of the idol. Kuenen, however, thinks that the author intended to show that the mother broke her vow, and that Micah desired to throw contempt on the idol cult of Dan. Further, the critics do not explain precisely the name of Micah's residence, nor the phenomenon of a Levite descended from Judah. Wellhausen's opinion that the term לוי means not a Levite, but one exercised in the cult of a divinity, is shown by the context to be an erroneous one. Halévy's theory is that the whole narrative belongs to one author, whose object was to show the origin of both temples, that of Beth-el and that of Dan, and who twice mentions Mount Ephraim, meaning thereby Beth-el (comp. Josh. xvi. 1). Thus Beth-el, having previously been the place of a private shrine which was subsequently transported to Dan, became, like Dan, the place of a public temple. The Judah from whom the Levite was descended (Judges xvii. 7) was not the patriarch, but the ancestor of a Levite family (comp. Neh. xii. 8; in Ezra ii. 40 הודויה may be an anagram of יהודה). The residence of a Levite at Beth-lehem, which was not among the cities allotted to the Levites, shows that a temple of Yhwh with a Levitical service existed there (comp. Judges xix. 18). The author points out that the Levite was of the tribe of Levi, namely, a descendant of Moses, in whose name a suspended "nun" was interpolated by the Masorites out of respect for the lawgiver (see Jonathan No. 1). With regard to the apparent discrepancy between verses 30 and 31 of Judges xviii., the word הארץ in verse 30 was corrected to הארן by Ḳimḥi, then by Hävernick, Hengstenberg, and Bleek, the passage thus reading "till the deportation of the Ark," referring to the capture of the Ark in the battle with the Philistines described in I Sam. iv. 4, 11. This renders possible a perfect agreement between the two verses.

Bibliography: J. Halévy, in *R. E. J.* xxi. 207–217; Moore, *Judges*, pp. 366 *et seq.*; idem, *Judges*, notes to ch. xvii.–xviii., in *Polychrome Bible*, Eng. ed.
S. M. Sel.

3. Son of Merib-baal (I Chron. viii. 34, 35; ix. 40, 41) or Mephibosheth (II Sam. ix. 12; A. V. "Micah"; R. V. "Mica"), and grandson of Jonathan. **4.** Head of the Uzziel branch of the Kohathite Levites in the time of David (I Chron. xxiii. 20; xxiv. 24, 25). **5.** A Reubenite; ancestor of the prince of that tribe, Beerah, whom Tiglath-pileser carried into captivity (*ib.* v. 5–6). **6.** Contemporary of Josiah, and father of Abdon, one of Josiah's messengers to Huldah (II Chron. xxxiv. 20). In the parallel account of II Kings xxii. 12 he is called "Micaiah," and his son's name is given as "Achbor." **7.** A Levite of the family of Asaph whose descendants lived in Jerusalem (I Chron. ix. 15; Neh. xi. 17, 22). **8.** A Simeonite; father of Ozias, one of the rulers of Bethulia (Judith vi. 15).

E. G. H. M. Sel.

MICAH, BOOK OF.—Biblical Data: The sixth book in the collection known as "The Twelve Minor Prophets"; it is ascribed to Micah the Morasthite (see Micah No. 1). It consists of seven chapters, the contents of which are as follows: Ch. i.: The idolatry of Samaria and Jerusalem are denounced; the prophet laments their fall and exhorts the people to mourning. Ch. ii.: Denunciation of oppression; prediction of the punishment of the people therefor; the restoration of Israel foretold. Ch. iii.: The prophet reproves first the princes for their cruelty, then the false prophets, who are the cause of all the evil. He again reproves the princes for their oppression, which, he says, will cause the ruin of Jerusalem. Ch. iv.: In poetical language the restoration of Jerusalem and of the glory of the house of the Lord and the victory of Israel over the other nations are foretold. Ch. v.: Prediction that a powerful king of Judah will vanquish the other nations, particularly Ashur, and will destroy idolatry. Ch. vi.: Israel is reproved for its sins, particularly its injustice; its punishment is prophesied. Ch. vii.: The lack of righteous men and the corruption of Israel are lamented; the prophet comforts Israel, promising that it will be restored to its land and will triumph over its enemies.

——**Critical View:** With regard to the period of Micah's activity, it has been remarked under MICAH (No. 1) that there is a difference between the superscription of the Book of Micah, where it is said that Micah began his prophetical career in the days of Jotham, and Jer. xxvi. 18, where his prophecies are confined to Hezekiah's reign. But a closer examination of the prophecies themselves may lead to the acceptance of a period between the two; for it is evident from Mic. i. 2 *et seq.* that Micah prophesied before the fall of Samaria, which, contrary to II Kings xviii. 10, took place under the reign of Ahaz, as may be inferred from a comparison between II Kings xviii. 13 and the cuneiform inscriptions (see HEZEKIAH, CRITICAL VIEW). Hence it may be concluded that Micah prophesied as early as the reign of Ahaz; but nothing in his prophecies shows that they were pronounced earlier than that period. It does not follow, however, that the above-cited passage of Jeremiah really conflicts with this view; for it may be that Hezekiah's reign is mentioned alone either because it was more important than that of his predecessors or because the redaction of Micah's prophecies possibly took place during the rule of that king.

As the opening words of the book, "Hear, all ye people!" are the same as those terminating the prophecy of Micaiah, the son of Imlah (I Kings xxii. 28), it may be that the latter was identified with Micah by the compiler of the Book of Kings, as he was later by pseudo-Epiphanius (see MICAH No. 1). The termination of Micaiah's prophecy with the identical words of the beginning of the Book of Micah seems to indicate in the former an allusion to the latter (comp. end of II Chron. with beginning of Ezra). Hengstenberg ("Christologie des Alten Testaments," i. 475) and Keil ("Lehrbuch der Historisch-Kritischen Einleitung in die Schriften des Alten Testaments," §§ 92, 93), however, suppose that the words of Micaiah in I Kings (*l.c.*) were added later, in the eighth century B.C.

Contents and Unity.

With regard to the division of the contents modern critics do not agree. Some divide them into three parts, ch. i.–ii.; iii.–v.; vi.–vii.; others, into two main divisions: prophetic-political, ch. i.–v.; and reflective, ch. vi.–vii. The question arises whether the whole of the book was written by Micah. It is generally accepted that the first three chapters, apart from ii. 12–13, belong to him. He begins with announcing the divine judgment upon Samaria and Judah (ch. i.), and then states the reason for that judgment (ii.–iii.). The two verses ii. 12–13 are considered by Stade and Kuenen as of the exilic, and by Wellhausen as of the post-exilic, period; and Micah's authorship of them is denied by all the critics. Ch. iv.–v., which refer to the Messianic time, seem to have emanated from some other hand, for the following reasons: (1) the contrast of these chapters with iii. 12; (2) the nature of certain verses—for instance, "and thou shalt come to Babylon" (iv. 10)—shows clearly that they were not pronounced by Micah (comp. Hartmann, "Das Buch Micha Neu Uebersetzt und Erklärt," 1800); (3) the ideas set forth in certain passages (*e.g.*, iv. 11–13, v. 9–13) were not current in the time of Micah. Ch. vi.–vii. 6, representing YHWH's controversy with Israel, the denunciation of the corruption of the people, and the prophet's lament over the decay of the Israelites, might from their contents proceed from Micah; but vii. 7 and the following verses are considered by most of the critics as spurious, inasmuch as the fall of Jerusalem, which is foretold in the preceding chapter, is here stated as having already taken place (comp. Driver, "Introduction," pp. 310 *et seq.*).

Other theories concerning the composition of the book are advanced, among which that of Elhorst, in his "De Profetie van Micha" (1891), is the most peculiar. He thinks that, owing to a misunderstanding on the part of the transcriber, the arrangement of the chapters is a confused one, and that the true order should be: i.; ii. 1–5; iii. 1–5; ii. 6–11; iii. 6–11; ii. 12 *et seq.*; iii. 12; vi. 1–5; vii. 1–6; vi. 6–16; vii. 13, 7–12, 14–20; iv. 1–8; v. 1–7; iv. 9–14; v. 8–14. He admits, however, that iv. 9–14 and v. 8 are post-exilic. This arrangement is plausible to a certain extent, but the location of iii. 12 after ii. 13 and of vii. 13 before vii. 7 is impossible. Finally, it may be remarked that the words of iv. 1–3 are identical with those of Isa. ii. 2 4, and that most probably they were interpolated later by the transcriber.

Style.

Micah's language is classical. With regard to rhetorical peculiarity he stands between Hosea and Isaiah, but nearer to the latter than to the former; for although, like the former, he is sometimes abrupt, he is similar to the latter in the mingling of mildness and strength, of gentleness and elevation. Another point of similarity between Micah and Isaiah is the frequent use of paronomasia (comp. Mic. i. 10–15, ii. 4), with the difference that Isaiah's scope is greater than that of Micah, who in his prophecies lingers among the towns of the maritime plain, wherein was his birthplace. As to his message, Micah, like Isaiah, attacks the false prophets (*ib.* iii. 6–8; comp. Isa. xxix. 10 *et seq.*), but he goes even further than Isaiah in warning against the overvaluation of sacrifices (Mic. vi. 6–8; comp. Isa. i. 11 *et seq.*), and in showing that the family of David must lose the throne before the most perfect scion will be born (Mic. v. 1 *et seq.*; comp. Isa. xi. 1 *et seq.*).

BIBLIOGRAPHY: Baudissin, *Einleitung in die Bücher des Alten Testaments*, 1901, sections 132 *et seq.*; Cornill, *Einleitung*, section 2, pp. 182 *et seq.*; Nowack, *Erklärung des Zwölfprophetenbuches*, in *Handkommentar zum Alten Testament*, 1897; G. A. Smith, *The Twelve Minor Prophets*, in *The Expositor's Bible*.

S. M. SEL.

MICHA (מיכא): **1.** Son of Mephibosheth (see MICAH No. 3). **2.** One of the Levites who sealed the covenant with Nehemiah (Neh. x. 11).

E. G. H. M. SEL.

MICHAEL (מיכאל): One of the archangels ("one of the chief princes"; Dan. x. 13), who is also represented as the tutelary prince of Israel (*ib.* x. 21, xii. 1). The signification of the name (= "Who is like El"?) was recognized by the Talmudists, who found an allusion to it in Ex. xv. 11 (מי כמכה) and in Deut. xxxiii. 26 (אין כאל), combining the first word of the former passage with the second of the latter (Num. R. ii. 9). According to Simeon b. Laḳish, however, the names of the angels were brought by the Jews from Babylon (Yer. R. H. 54d; Gen. R. xlviii. 9). Upon the basis of the above-cited passages from the Book of Daniel (where Michael is represented first as helping Daniel in his dispute with the angel of Persia and then as helping Israel in time of trouble—that is, in the Messianic time—and where he is styled "your prince") Michael is specially designated in early Jewish writings and very frequently in the Book of Enoch as "the prince of Israel" (שרם של ישראל), and in later Jewish writings, particularly in cabalistic works, as "the advocate of the Jews." It is for this reason that he is represented as the angel of forbearance and mercy (Enoch, xl. 3) who taught Enoch the mysteries of clemency and justice (*ib.* lxxi. 2).

Israel's Advocate.

Being the prince or advocate of Israel, Michael had to fight with the princes of the other nations (comp. Dan. x. 13) and particularly with Samael, Israel's accuser. His enmity with Samael dates from the time when the latter was thrown down from heaven. Samael took hold of the wings of Michael, whom he wished to bring down with him in his fall; but Michael was saved by God (Pirḳe R. El. xxvi.). The Rabbis declare that Michael entered upon his rôle of defender at the time of the Patriarchs. Thus, according to Eliezer b. Jacob, it was Michael who rescued Abraham from the furnace into which he had been thrown by Nimrod (Gen. R. xliv. 16). It was Michael, the "one that had escaped" (Gen. xiv. 13), who told Abraham that Lot had been taken captive (Pirḳe R. El. *l.c.*), and who protected Sarah from being defiled by Abimelech (*ib.*). He announced to Sarah that she would bear a son (comp. Gen. xviii. 10); and he rescued Lot at the destruction of Sodom (B. M. 86b; comp. Gen. R. l. 2). Michael prevented Isaac from being sacrificed by his father by substituting a ram in his place ("Yalḳ. Reubeni," section "Wayera"), and saved Jacob, while yet in his mother's womb, from being killed by Samael (Midr. Abkir, in Yalḳ., Gen. 110). Later Michael prevented Laban from harming Jacob (Pirḳe R. El. xxxvi.). It was Michael, too, who wrestled with Jacob and who afterward blessed him (Targ. pseudo-Jonathan to Gen. xxxii. 25; Pirḳe R. El. xxxvii.). The Midrash Abkir (*l.c.* 132) thus graphically describes the scene of the wrestling: "At the break of day companies of angels came, saying, 'Michael, the hour of singing in praise of the Lord has arrived.' Michael began to implore Jacob to cease wrestling, saying he was afraid the angels might burn him (Michael) for omitting to take part in the heavenly chorus. When Michael finally struck Jacob's thigh he was blamed by God for having caused a blemish in God's priest. Michael applied to his companion Raphael, who healed Jacob's wound. Then God appointed Michael to be the defender of Israel" (comp. "David," No. 13, "Yalḳ. Ḥadash," where it is said that Michael's appointment took place when Solomon had built the Temple). Michael saved Asenath, daughter of Shechem by Dinah, from being killed by Jacob's sons (Pirḳe R. El. xxxviii.), and Tamar from being burned (Targ. pseudo-Jonathan and Targ. Yer. to Gen. xxxviii. 25).

Wrestles with Jacob.

Michael exercised his function of advocate of Israel at the time of the Exodus also, when Satan accused the Israelites of idolatry and declared that they were consequently deserving of death by drowning in the Red Sea (Ex. R. xviii. 5). But according to Midr. Abkir (Yalḳ., Ex. 241), when 'Uzza, the tutelar angel of Egypt, summoned Michael to plead before God, Michael remained silent, and it was God Himself who defended Israel. Michael led the Israelites during their forty years' wandering in the wilderness (Abravanel to Ex. xxiii. 20). Legend makes him the teacher of Moses; so that the Israelites are indebted to their advocate for the supreme good of the Torah. This fact is alluded to in Deut. R. xi. 6 in the statement that Michael declined to bring Moses' soul to God on the ground that he had been Moses' teacher. It is clearly stated in Apoc. Mosis, i. that Moses received the two tables through the mediation of Michael. In the Book of Jubilees (i. 27, ii. 1) the angel who is said to have instructed Moses on Mount Sinai and to have delivered to him the tables of the Law is most probably Michael.

Teacher of Moses.

Michael destroyed the army of Sennacherib (Ex. R. xviii. 5). He endeavored also to prevent Israel from being led into captivity by Nebuchadnezzar and to save the Temple from destruction; but the sins of the people were so great that he was powerless to carry his purposes into effect. "Michael, thy nation has sinned," God said. "Save them for the sake of the good men which they still have," Michael answered. "I will burn Israel with his good men," God replied (Yoma 77a; comp. Zohar, Ex. col. 414). According to Yalḳ., Lam. 1009, Michael and Gabriel pleaded for the Israelites, who, however, were doomed, and the two angels were themselves compelled to set the Temple on fire. In later writings Michael is represented as refuting also on this occasion the accusations of Samael (Zohar, Mishpaṭim). There is a legend which seems to be of Jewish origin, and which was adopted by the Copts, to the effect that Michael was first sent by God to bring Nebuchadnezzar against Jerusalem, and that Michael was afterward very active in freeing his nation from Babylonian captivity (Amélineau, "Contes et Romans de l'Egypte Chrétienne," ii. 142 *et seq.*). According to most of the rabbis, Michael saved Hananiah and his companions from the furnace (Gen. R. xliv. 16). Michael was very active in the time of Esther: "The more Haman accused Israel on earth, the more Michael defended Israel in heaven" (Esth. R. iii. 8). It was Michael who reminded Ahasuerus that he was Mordecai's debtor (Targ. to Esth. vi. 1); and there is a legend that Michael appeared to the high priest Hyrcanus, promising him assistance (comp. Josephus, "Ant." xiii. 10, § 3).

Michael will continue his advocacy to the very end; and he will contend with Samael for the liberation of Israel from Edom or Rome ("Yalḳ. Ḥadash," "Galut," No. 11). Samael will be subdued by Michael; but when the latter asks God to help Israel, God will say, "Israel should turn toward Me, be it only as far as the point of a needle." When Israel turns toward the Lord, his advocate, Michael, will plead in his favor (Pesiḳ. R. 44 [ed. Friedmann, p. 185a]). According to Ex. R. (xviii. 5), Michael and Gabriel will have the charge of vindicating Israel against Edom; but Rabbi's opinion is that Michael alone will act. He will, besides, cleanse Israel from the wicked people ("Otot ha-Mashiaḥ," in Jellinek, "B. H." ii. 61). It was Michael's fight with Samael (with the devil in Assumptio Mosis, x.) which gave rise to the well-known legend of Michael and the dragon. This legend is not found in Jewish sources except in so far as Samael or Satan is called in the Cabala "the primitive serpent" ("naḥash ha-ḳadmoni").

Continuous Guardianship.

The idea that Michael was the advocate of the Jews became so prevalent that in spite of the rabbinical prohibition against appealing to angels as intermediaries between God and His people, Michael came to occupy a certain place in the Jewish liturgy. Apart from the word סניגר, which occurs frequently and which refers to Michael, there are two prayers beseeching him as the prince of mercy to intercede in favor of Israel: one composed by Eliezer ha-Ḳalir (Bartolocci, "Bibl. Rab. Magna," i. 192 *et seq.*), and the other by Judah b. Samuel he-Ḥasid (MS. De Cambrai No. 946, fol. 110). But appeal to Michael seems to have been more common in ancient times. Thus Jeremiah is said (Baruch Apoc. Ethiopic, ix. 5) to have addressed a prayer to him. "When a man is in need he must pray directly to God, and neither to Michael nor to Gabriel" (Yer. Ber. ix. 13a).

The conception of Michael as an advocate always interceding on behalf of Israel gave rise to another idea, that of his being a high priest making atonement for his people. Ezra recognized the place of the altar by seeing there one on which Michael, the great prince, was in the act of sacrificing (Zeb. 62a; comp. Men. 110a). The fourth heaven is called "Zebul" (זבול) because it contains the heavenly Jerusalem, the Temple, and the altar on which Michael, the great prince, sacrifices (Ḥag. 12b). A different statement is given in "Seder Gan 'Eden" (Jellinek, *l.c.* iii. 137), which places Michael in the upper heaven called "'Arabot" (ערבות; comp. Midr. Abkir in Yalḳ., Gen. 132). This idea was afterward greatly developed by the cabalists. Michael is identified with Melchizedek ("Yalḳ. Ḥadash," "Mal'akim," No. 19); and the words "and the priest shall pronounce him clean" (Lev. xiii. 23) are explained in the "Tiḳḳune Zohar" (fol. 2b) as referring to Michael, the high priest, acting as the representative of clemency. Michael, the high priest, is the standard-bearer of God (Joseph Gikatilla, "Sha'are Orah," p. 60c). The institution of tithes is ascribed to Michael (Targ. pseudo-Jonathan to Gen. xxxii. 25); and his place is appointed in the east, with the tribe of Levi ("Midr. Konen," in Jellinek, *l.c.* ii. 39).

Michael as High Priest.

With regard to the nature of the offerings which Michael brings to the altar, one opinion is that they are the souls of the just, while according to another they are fiery sheep (Tos. to Men. 110a). The former opinion, which has become prevalent in cabalistic writings ("Seder Gan 'Eden," *l.c.*; "Yalḳ. Ḥadash," "Neshamot," No. 31; "Reshit Ḥokmah," ch. iii.), explains the important position occupied by Michael in Jewish eschatology. The idea that Michael is the Charon of individual souls, which is common among Christians, is not found in Jewish sources, but that he is in charge of the souls of the just appears in many Jewish writings. In the Testament of Abraham (Robinson, "Texts and Studies," ii. 2, Cambridge, 1893), which is Jewish, it is said that Michael was ordered by God to bring Abraham's soul to Him. He had a discussion with Samael over the soul of Moses (Deut. R. xi. 6; "Midr. Peṭirat Mosheh," in Jellinek, *l.c.* vi. 75 *et seq.*; comp. Jude 9). According to the Zohar (Gen., col. 303), Michael accompanies the souls of the pious and helps them to enter the gates of the heavenly Jerusalem. In "Midr. ha-Ne'elam" ("Zohar Ḥadash," p. 19c), however, it is said that Michael and his host are stationed at the gates of the heavenly Jerusalem and give admittance to the souls of the just. Michael's function is to open the gates also of justice to the just (comp. Baruch Apoc. Ethiopic, ix. 5). David was not admitted there till the Temple was built by Solomon; then he was introduced by Michael ("Yalḳ. Ḥadash," "David," No. 13). At the resurrection Michael will sound the trumpet, at which the graves will open and the dead will rise ("Otot ha-Mashiaḥ," in Jellinek, *l.c.* ii. 61–62; comp. Dan. xii. 1). It is in this sense that the Falashas mention Michael in their prayer ("Prières des Falashas," ed. J. Halévy, pp. 48–49, Ethiopic text). There is another haggadah to the effect that when the Messiah comes Michael and Gabriel will place themselves at the entrance of paradise and in the name of God greet the just (Jellinek, *l.c.* vi. 148). Michael's residence will be in a range of seven mountains, surrounded by a grove of fragrant trees, among which one will be particularly distinguished for its beauty. The highest of the seven mountains will be the seat of the Lord, and the most fragrant tree, which will be inaccessible to any human being till the Day of Judgment, will be given to the pious (Enoch, xxiv.–xxv. 5). Contrary to Dan. xii. 2, it is said in "Otiyot de-R. 'Aḳiba," *s.v.* זרבבל (in Jellinek, *l.c.* iii. 28), that at the advent of the Messiah, God will give the keys of hell to Michael and Gabriel, who will bring the souls of the wicked into paradise.

Michael as Guide of Souls.

Michael's Mount.

It is quite natural that, owing to his position with regard to the Jews, Michael should be represented in the Haggadah as the most prominent of the archangels. He is called by Daniel (Dan. xii. 1) "the great prince," and his greatness is described at length in later Jewish writings. He was one of the seven archangels first created (Enoch, xc. 21–22; Targ. Yer. to Deut. xxxiv. 6 gives only six), but among these seven four excel, and Michael is the chief of the four. Both he and Gabriel are called "great princes"; but Michael is higher in rank than

Gabriel (Ber. 4b; Yoma 37a). He is the viceroy of God, who rules over the world (Enoch, lxix. 14 *et seq.*), and wherever Michael appears the Shekinah also is to be found (Ex. R. ii. 8). Michael is on the right of God's throne, while Gabriel is on the left ("Haggadat Shema' Yisrael," in Jellinek, *l.c.* v. 166; Targ. to Job xxv. 2; Enoch, xl. 9). Four armies of angels sing in praise of the Lord, the first being that of Michael at the right hand of God (Pirḳe R. El. iv.; "Hekalot," in Jellinek, *l.c.* ii. 43–44). A similar tradition is given in "Seder Gan 'Eden" (*l.c.* p. 138): Michael's place is by the first river, Pison, while Gabriel's is by the second, Gihon. It is Michael who, on account of his occupying the first place near God, receives the prayers of men from the angels and presents them to God (Baruch Apoc. Slavonic, xii.). His position makes him the companion of METAṬRON (Zohar, i. 149b).

Michael and Gabriel.

As an angel of nature, Michael is represented as of the element of water, on account of which he is the prince of water, while Gabriel is the prince of fire ("'Ammudeha Shib'ah," p. 49c; "Berit Menuḥah," 37a; and elsewhere). This is probably the origin of the haggadah that when Solomon married Pharaoh's daughter, Michael drove into the bed of the sea a stick around which slime gathered and on which, later, Rome was built (Cant. R. i. 6). In Sanh. 21b and Shab. 56b, however, this is ascribed to Gabriel, owing to a confusion which occurs also in Targ. to Job xxv. 2, where Michael is called the prince of fire. Michael is really the prince of snow, which is the element of water (Deut. R. v. 12); and he is also the angel of silver, while Gabriel is the angel of gold ("Yalḳ. Ḥadash," "Mal'akim," No. 75). Michael presides over the planet Mercury and consequently over Wednesday (Abraham Avenar, in Münster, "Calendar Hebræorum," Basel, 1527). The same statement is given in the Hebrew manuscripts Paris No. 602 (fol. 142a) and No. 603 (fol. 125a), both containing cabalistic formulas. But it would more befit Michael to preside over Saturn and be the angel of Saturday; and this position is ascribed to him in "Sefer Razi'el," pp. 8a, 17b. He presides over the second solar period ("teḳufah") and over the south wind, which blows during that season (*ib.* 7a; Paris MS. No. 602, fol. 122a). He is the third of the "figure equivalents" ("Ḳeneh Binah," p. 19a); and in enchantment his name is pronounced to charm reptiles ("Sefer Razi'el," p. 4a). See ANGELOLOGY.

BIBLIOGRAPHY: A. Kohut, *Jüdische Angelologie*, pp. 24 *et seq.*, in *Abhandlungen für die Kunde des Morgenlandes*, iv., No. 3; W. Lüken, *Michael*, Göttingen, 1898; M. Schwab, *Vocabulaire de l'Angélologie*, s.v. מיכאל, Paris, 1897.

J. M. SEL.

——**In Arabic Literature:** Michael is called in Arabic literature "Mika'il" or (in the Koran) "Mikal." He is one of the four archangels, and, according to Arabic tradition, he occupies a similar position among the Jews to that occupied by Gabriel among the Arabs; that is to say, he is their peculiar guardian. In the Koran Michael is mentioned once only, in sura ii. 92. In his commentary on verse 91 of that sura, Baiḍawi relates that on one occasion Omar went into a Jewish school and inquired concerning Gabriel. The pupils said he was their enemy, but that Michael was a good angel, bringing peace and plenty. In answer to Omar's question as to the respective positions of Michael and Gabriel in God's presence, they said that Gabriel was on His right hand and Michael on His left. Omar exclaimed at their untruthfulness, and declared that whoever was an enemy to God and His angels, to him God would be an enemy. Upon returning to Mohammed, Omar found that Gabriel had forestalled him by revealing the same message, which is contained in verse 92. The commentators state with reference to sura xi. 72 that Michael was one of the three angels who visited Abraham.

In Arabic tradition Michael always appears as second to Gabriel. When God is creating Adam He sends first Gabriel and then Michael to fetch the clay out of which man is to be formed. Both are restrained by the earth's protests; only Israfil pays no heed to them. When Adam and Eve are expelled from paradise, Gabriel is sent to the former, and Michael to the latter, to impart comfort. On his death-bed Mohammed stated that Gabriel would be the first and Michael the second to pray over him.

It is unusual for Michael to be sent independently, as in the story of St. George, where Michael is commissioned to destroy the brazen statue in which St. George is to be burned alive (Zotenberg, "Chronique d'Abu Djafer . . . Tabari," i. 30, 73; ii. 61; iii. 213, Paris, 1867–71). At the last day Michael will be one of the four angels who will survive after every other creature has been destroyed.

BIBLIOGRAPHY: The commentaries of Baiḍawi and Zamakhshari on the *Koran*; Hughes, *Dict. of Islam*, s.v.; Mas'udi, *Les Prairies d'Or*, ed. Barbier de Menard, Index; Weil, *Biblical Legends of the Mussulmans*, p. 37, New York, 1846.

J. M. W. M.

MICHAEL ḤASID. See JEHIEL MICHAEL BEN JUDAH LÖB.

MICHAEL, HEIMANN JOSEPH: Hebrew bibliographer; born at Hamburg April 12, 1792; died there June 10, 1846. He showed great acuteness of mind in early childhood, had a phenomenal memory, and was an indefatigable student. He studied Talmudics and received also private instruction in all the branches of a regular school education. He was a born bibliophile, and began to collect valuable works when still a boy of twelve. With his progress in Hebrew literature his love for books increased also, the result of which was his magnificent library of 860 manuscripts and 5,471 printed works, covering all branches of Hebrew literature. There were few books in his collection which he had not read; and he undertook the preparation of a full catalogue of it. As far as he accomplished this task, it was the foundation of the "Oẓerot Ḥayyim, Katalog der Michael'schen Bibliothek," Hamburg, 1848.

Michael took an interest not only in Jewish literature, but in all the intellectual movements of the day, as is shown by the large number of contemporary books and leaflets found in his library. He never wrote directly for publication; but many scholars applied to him for information, and this he never withheld. His correspondence with Leopold Dukes, Franz Delitzsch, Wolf Heidenheim, Rapoport, Luzzatto, Gesenius, Lebrecht, Akiba, Eger, and Leopold Zunz is of great literary interest. Michael's only independent work was "Or ha-Ḥayyim" (Frankfort-on-the-Main, 1891), a comprehensive bibliographical and literary-historical dictionary of rabbinical literature, edited by his son, with preface by A. Berliner; it covers, however, only a few letters of the alphabet.

Bibliography: Zunz, *Z. G.* p. 244, Berlin, 1845; *Oẓerot Ḥayyim*, Preface, Hamburg, 1848; *Allg. Zeit. des Jud.* 1846, p. 224.

S. I. War.

MICHAEL, ISAAC: German laryngologist; born at Hamburg Nov. 16, 1848; died there Jan. 7, 1897. He studied at the universities of Heidelberg, Leipsic, Berlin, and Würzburg (M.D. 1873), became assistant at the throat, and later at the ear, dispensary of the University of Vienna, and in 1876 returned to Hamburg, where he practised until his death. His works include "Gesang- und Registerbildung" (Hamburg, 1887) and "Gesch. des Aerztlichen Vereins von Hamburg" (*ib.* 1896). He translated Mackenzie's "Hygiene of the Vocal Organs" (*ib.* 1889).

Bibliography: Pagel, *Biographisches Lexikon.*

S. F. T. H.

MICHAEL JESOFOVICH: Senior of the Jews of Lithuania under King Sigismund I. of Poland; born at Brest-Litovsk about the middle of the fifteenth century; died there between 1530 and 1533. Michael, like his brothers Abraham and Isaac, was among the most prominent tax-collectors and leaseholders in Lithuania during the last quarter of the fifteenth and the first quarter of the sixteenth century. Exiled with the other Jews of Lithuania by Alexander Jagellon in 1495, he emigrated with his brothers to Poland. His brother Abraham embraced Christianity and soon returned to Lithuania; but Michael remained true to his religion, and did not again set foot in his native city until 1503, when permission to return was given to the expelled Jews.

King Sigismund I., by a decree dated Wilna, Feb. 27, 1514, appointed Michael to the newly created seniorship over the Jews of Lithuania. In his capacity as senior he not only was to serve as mediator between the Jews and the king, but was also empowered to judge and to punish the Jews, in keeping with the rights granted to them, and to impose a fine or even a term of emprisonment on the guilty. Michael evinced his piety by attempting to force the Karaite Jews of Lithuania to conform to the doctrines of rabbinical law; but the Karaites, who possessed a charter of privileges granted them by Grand Duke Witold, refused to acknowledge Michael's authority, and the matter was decided in their favor by the king.

This appointment, while it shows the favorable attitude of Sigismund toward his Jewish subjects, was actuated in the main by his desire to insure a thorough and prompt collection of the taxes imposed on the Jewish communities, and to reward the valuable services rendered to the crown by Michael and his brother Abraham. On the whole, however, the office of senior was honorary and nominal, since the concentration of the powers of the several communities in the hands of one person of the same religion was antagonistic to the traditions of the Lithuanian Jews. While it is true that soon after his appointment Michael excommunicated Itzko and Berek, two Jews of Brest, as traitors against God and the king (the said Jews having been sentenced to excommunication with Prince Michael Krinsky), and ordered the excommunication "to be announced by trumpets," it does not follow that Michael was invested with extraordinary judicial powers, since he was merely carrying out an order of the king, and similar excommunications had been proclaimed before (Bershadski, "Litovskiye Yevrei," p. 358). The fact that Michael was authorized by the king to employ a doctor (rabbi) shows that he himself was not a rabbi, and was not privileged according to Jewish law to assume the functions of one. Documents of a later date no longer refer to him as the senior, but apply to him the title of "fiscal agent to the king."

His Commercial Activity.

Michael's commercial enterprises covered a period of almost half a century, and were intimately connected with the prosperity of the country. He took an active part in the affairs of his brother Abraham even before the expulsion of the Jews from Lithuania, and formed in 1487 with his brother Isaac a partnership which continued for forty years. In documents of 1516 and of subsequent date Michael is mentioned as collector of the king's taxes of Lithuania and as farmer of the salt- and wax-taxes of Brest. In 1520 he was granted the farming of the customs duties of Vladimir and Lutsk; and in 1522 he farmed the wax- and weights-taxes in Moghilef. Soon after this he leased the inns of Vitebsk for a period of three years, and a year later he leased the inns and farmed the taxes of Brest, Dorogitz, Grodno, Byelsk, Lutsk, and Vladimir. In 1524 he farmed, in partnership with Michael Shpis, the customs duties of the entire duchy of Lithuania. From 1525 to 1529 he extended his operations to the farming of the taxes of Minsk and Novgorod. Aside from the collection of taxes and duties, Michael carried on also an extensive business in various articles of merchandise, such as cloth. Not content with all this, he with the king's consent advanced money and goods to the king's officers, protecting himself by liens on their salaries, while the king received for his good offices a certain share of the profits ("Dokumenty i Regesty," No. 1, vol. viii.). The extremely valuable services rendered by Michael to his sovereign and the influence of his immense financial interests finally led the king to raise him to the hereditary nobility with the coat of arms of Leliva, formerly belonging to George Gyebovich, regent of Smolensk (*ib.*, No. 96).

The extent of Michael's property may be gathered from a document which refers to the division in 1527 of the estate, real and personal, belonging to him and to his brother Isaac, and which enumerates their respective possessions (*ib.*, No. 119).

After Michael's death his son Abraham was confirmed (March 15, 1533) in the privileges granted to the former ("Regesty," No. 261).

Bibliography: *Russko-Yevreiski Arkhiv*, vol. ii., *passim*; Bershadski, *Litovskiye Yevrei*, p. 358; Kraushar, *Historya Zydów w Polsce*, ii. 49; Grätz, *Gesch.* Hebrew ed., vii. 313.

H. R.

MICHAEL, MAX: German painter; born in Hamburg March 23, 1823; died at Berlin March 24, 1891. He studied art first at the Kunst-Akademie in Dresden, then for five years at Paris, after which he spent twenty years at Rome and Venice. In these cities he produced his first work, "Country Girl Writing" (1866), now in the Ravené Gallery, Berlin. In 1870 he returned to Berlin, and five years later was appointed professor of painting in the Royal Academy. He held this office until his death. Other works of his are: "Girls' School in the Sabine Mountains," in the Kunsthalle, Hamburg; "The Visit of the Cardinal to the Monastery"; "Job Disputing with His Friends"; "Bertini Painting an Altar-Piece in the Monastery of the Camaldolites."

BIBLIOGRAPHY: *Jew. Chron.* April 3, 1891, p. 9; Singer, *Allgemeines Künstler Lexikon*, Frankfort-on-the-Main, 1899.

S. F. T. H.

MICHAEL BEN MOSES COHEN: Palestinian rabbi and liturgist; lived at Jerusalem in the seventeenth century. He wrote "Moreh Ẓedeḳ" (Salonica, 1655), an index to the laws contained in the Shulḥan 'Aruk, Ḥoshen Mishpaṭ, showing where they may be found in other works of the Poseḳim as well as in the responsa of later rabbis. There is also ascribed to him another work, "'Et le-Ḥenenah" (Venice, 1708), prayers to be recited at the western wall of the ancient Temple, with additions by the author's son Moses. According to Nepi-Ghirondi ("Toledot Gedole Yisrael," p. 228), however, Michael only revised and edited that work.

BIBLIOGRAPHY: F. Delitzsch, *Gesch. der Jüdischen Poesie*, pp. 56-57; Fürst, *Bibl. Jud.* i. 182; Steinschneider, *Cat. Bodl.* No. 3271; idem, *Jewish Literature*, p. 242.

A. M. SEL.

MICHAEL, MOSES GERSON: American merchant and capitalist; born Aug. 15, 1862, at Jefferson, Ga. At an early age he graduated as B.E. from the University of Georgia with highest honors, and shortly afterward entered with his brother **Simon** upon a commercial career at Athens, Ga. Here he has amassed a fortune in the dry-goods trade.

Michael has been an influential factor in the development of northeastern Georgia, having been identified with a number of large industrial enterprises. He holds the rank of lieutenant-colonel in the state militia, and was aide-de-camp to Governor Candler during his administration. He is a member of the Democratic executive committee of the Eighth Congressional District, and a potent factor in the councils of the party.

For a number of years Michael has been superintendent of the Jewish Sabbath-school at Athens, which he makes his peculiar charge.

A. H. E. C.

MICHAEL BEN SHABBETHAI (called also **Magister Zematus**): Rabbi of Rome in the sixteenth century. In a decision of 1539 his signature reads "Michael b. Shabbethai זמט," the last word being the name of a place in Africa whence probably Michael's ancestors originated, and becoming when Latinized "Zematus." Michael was a prominent cabalist and as such was the teacher of Ægidius of Viterbo and of Widmanstadt (Perles, "Studien," pp. 186, 189). Elijah di Nola (1555) speaks of Michael as the possessor of an excellent collection of cabalistic works (Perles, *l.c.* p. 217).

BIBLIOGRAPHY: Vogelstein and Rieger, *Gesch. der Juden in Rom*, ii. 92, 99, 260.

K. M. SEL.

MICHAEL BEN SHABBETHAI COHEN BALBO (called also **Michael Cohen of Crete**): Greek scholar, Hebrew poet, and preacher; born March 27, 1411. A manuscript preserved in the Vatican (No. 305) contains several works of his, namely: a poem composed in 1453 on the occasion of the capture of Constantinople by Mohammed the Conqueror and the cessation of the war; another poem (1456), lamenting his father's death; a homiletic commentary on Ps. xxviii.; and three sermons preached by Michael in Khania in 1471, 1475, and 1477 respectively. Vatican MS. No. 254 contains an account of a disputation ("wikkuaḥ") between Michael Cohen and Moses Cohen Ashkenazi on metempsychosis ("gilgul"). Zunz ("Additamenta," p. 320) is doubtful whether to identify the former with Michael b. Shabbethai or with Michael b. Elijah Cohen, copyist of Vatican MSS. Nos. 345 and 346 (fourth part). Steinschneider doubts the correctness of the name Michael b. Elijah. According to Assemani, the commentary on Averroes' commentary to Aristotle's "Physics" (i.-vi.), contained in the former manuscript, was made by a pupil of Michael Cohen of Crete. Wolf ("Bibl. Hebr." i., No. 1413), however, ascribes the commentary to Michael Cohen, calling him a disciple of Averroes. Wolf thinks also that the author of the account of the disputation is Michael b. Moses ha-Kohen, who, in collaboration with Abraham Samuel of Sofia, wrote the "Moreh Ẓedeḳ."

A work entitled "Sha'are Raḥamim" (Vatican MS. No. 30, 8), which is a supercommentary on Maimonides' commentary on the eleventh chapter of Sanhedrin, and a commentary on Ibn Ezra's hymn beginning "Eḥad lebaddo be-en samuk," both bear the name of Michael Cohen as author, who is supposed by Steinschneider to be identical with the subject of this article.

BIBLIOGRAPHY: Steinschneider, *Hebr. Uebers.* p. 120; *idem*, in *Mosé*, iv. 303 *et seq.*, v. 267 *et seq.*

J. M. SEL.

MICHAELIS, JOHANN DAVID: Christian Orientalist and polyhistor; born at Halle Feb. 27, 1717; died at Göttingen Aug. 22, 1791; grand-nephew of Johann Heinrich Michaelis. He was educated at the university of his native city, and made scientific journeys in England and Holland, returning to lecture at Halle on Semitic languages and Bible exegesis. For nearly half a century he was professor at Göttingen University (he became assistant professor in 1746 and professor in 1750), where he lectured chiefly on Old Testament exegesis, Hebrew antiquities, Mosaic law, and the Semitic languages.

Besides writing a Hebrew grammar (1745) and a supplement to Hebrew lexicons (1784-92), Michaelis translated and commented upon the whole of the Old Testament (1769-83). He was also one of the first to write an introduction to the Old Testament (1787). His work on the Mosaic law ("Das Mosaische Recht," 1770-75) was one of the earliest cientific treatments of Jewish antiquities. Many f his essays on this subject appeared in the "Orienalische Bibliothek," edited by him from 1771 to 791.

IBLIOGRAPHY: *Allgemeine Deutsche Biographie.*

T. J.

MICHAELIS, JOHANN HEINRICH: German Christian theologian and Hebraist; born at lletterberg July 26, 1668; died at Halle March 10, 738. He studied Ethiopic under Ludolf at Frankort-on-the-Main, and became assistant professor of riental languages at Halle in 1699 and professor f theology in 1709. His chief work was a text of ne Hebrew Bible founded on Jablonski, but with a omparison of nineteen printed editions and five anuscripts of Erfurt. This was published in 720 at Frankfort-on-the-Main and was reprinted roughout the eighteenth century. Some of his itical annotations were published separately in the me year. Michaelis wrote also a Hebrew grammar 702); and two works on Hebrew accents (1696, 700), the latter of which, "Institutio de Accentibus rosaicis et Metricis," went through five further litions, and was for a long time the standard auority on the subject. He composed also the Latin anslation of the Ethiopic psalter published by Luolf.

IBLIOGRAPHY: *Allgemeine Deutsche Biographie.*

T. J.

MICHAELMAS GEESE. See BARNACLE-OOSE.

MICHAL (מוכל; lit. "rivulet"): The younger of ne two daughters of Saul, probably by Ahinoam Sam. xiv. 49–50). David, then a boy of about xteen, was to have married her sister Merab; but ne latter having been given to another, and Michal aving fallen in love with David, Saul consented the marriage of the two last-named, not insisting n the customary dowry ("mohar"), but requiring hat David kill a hundred Philistines. David killed ouble this number; and Michal became his wife (*ib.* viii. 17–28).

Michal was instrumental in saving her husband hen her father, in a fit of anger, attempted to kill im. She lowered him through the window and, to eceive and delay the king's messengers, substituted ne of her teraphim in his place. On her stratagem eing discovered she declared that David had threatned her with death if she did not let him go (*ib.* xix. 1–17). After David's escape Saul bestowed Michal pon Phalti ben Laish of Gallim (*ib.* xxv. 44). It ould appear, however, that she was still regarded s the lawful wife of David; for at his earliest opportunity he claimed her from Saul's son, Ish-boheth (II Sam. iii. 13–15), through Abner.

One incident, however, occurred which caused neir relations to be greatly strained and which robably resulted in a separation. The Ark of the ord having been brought to Zion, David indulged a joyful religious dance, for which he was severe- criticized by his wife (*ib.* vi. 16, 20). Either beause of this incident or owing to several other auses combined, they never lived together again. ccording to one tradition, Michal spent her reaining years in bringing up the five children of er sister Merab (*ib.* xxi. 8, if the reading מרב be accepted instead of מיכל); according to another, she returned to Phalti ben Laish and lived as his protegée, though not as his wife (Targ. to Ruth iii. 3).

David seems not to have had any children by Michal (II Sam. vi. 23), though some authorities (*e.g.*, Rashi and Cheyne) claim that Ithream was the result of their union, and that "Eglah," the name of his supposed mother (*ib.* iii. 5), like "Michal," is merely a corrupted form of her real name, which must have been Abigail.

This Biblical story has inspired J. L. Gordon with the subject for his popular "Ahabat Dawid u-Mikal," which has been published in many editions.

J. J. S. R.

MICHEL JUD (usually called "Wealthy Michel"): A public character prominent in his day for wealth and influence; born about the end of the fifteenth century at Derenburg, near Halberstadt; died in 1549. He was described as of imposing appearance and eloquent of speech, and was regarded as an illegitimate son of one of the counts of Regenstein. His wife, Merle, was the daughter of Joseph of Schleusingen. Michel, being well-mannered, was received by princes and nobles, who courted him on account of his wealth. The elector Joachim of Brandenburg, Duke Friedrich of Liegnitz, and Landgrave Philip of Hesse were among those who maintained relations with him. On July 25, 1529, Duke Erich the Elder of Brunswick-Lüneburg, ignoring the wishes of the magistrates of the city of Hanover, granted Michel permission "to build a house in the new city in the suburbs of Hanover" and to dwell therein with his wife, his children, and his servants. Besides the house in Hanover, Michel owned one in Derenburg, one in Frankfort-on-the-Oder, and one in Berlin. He was in the good graces of the elector Joachim II., who on Feb. 27, 1544, sanctioned the jointure settled by Michel on his wife. From Duke Erich Michel received important commercial privileges, and his business relations extended from France to Silesia and Poland. He played an important part in the imperial diets also. In 1548 he appeared at the Diet of Augsburg in very costly garments, wearing heavy gold chains around his neck, riding on a richly caparisoned horse, and accompanied by a retinue of ten or twelve servants, all Jews. Shortly afterward he was taken captive by Magdeburg knights on Brandenburg territory, but escaped, and on his accusation the knights were taken to Torgau and condemned to death by order of Joachim II. Count Ulrich of Regenstein, who hated Michel and is said to have published a pamphlet against him, was forced by Joachim to sign a treaty favorable to him on May 15, 1549. Michel died a few days later as the result of a fall down a flight of stairs.

BIBLIOGRAPHY: *Von Michel Juden Todt*, Marbach, June 6, 1549; Boysen, in *Hist. Magazin*, v. 45; Raumer, *Hist. Taschenbuch*, 3d series, ii. 279 *et seq.*; *Monatsschrift*, x. 239, xiv. 425, xvi. 388; Wiener, *Zur Geschichte der Juden in Hannover*, in the *Jahrbuch für die Gesch. der Juden und des Judenthums*, i. 187; L. Geiger, *Zeitschrift*, ii. 340, 372.

D. M. K.

MICHELSON, ALBERT A.: American physicist; born at Strelno, in the district of Bromberg, Prussia, Dec. 19, 1852. His father, **Samuel Michelson,** emigrated to the United States and settled in

San Francisco, where Albert Michelson received his early education. After leaving the high school he entered the United States Naval Academy, at Annapolis, Md., and graduated in 1873. For the purpose of extending his studies he went to Germany in 1880, entered the University of Berlin, and remained there for a short time. From Berlin he went to Heidelberg University and studied there until 1881. In that year Michelson resigned from the United States naval service and went to Paris, where he entered the Collège de France and the Ecole Polytechnique (1882). On his return to the United States he accepted the chair of physics at the Case School, Cleveland, Ohio, which position he resigned for the chair of physics at Clark University, Worcester, Mass. (1889). There he remained until, three years later, he was called to the professorship in physics at the University of Chicago. This office he still holds (1904).

Michelson has received the degrees of Ph.D. (hon.) from Stevens Institute, D.Sc. from Cambridge (Eng.), and LL.D. from Yale. He is a member of the National Academy of Sciences, a foreign member of the Royal Society (London), a corresponding member of the Academy of Sciences of the Institute of France, and a member of the International Committee on Weights and Measures. He was awarded the Rumford medal by the Royal Institution of Great Britain. His international scientific reputation is largely due to his determination of the velocity of light and to other experiments in the domain of optics which were marked by a high degree of accuracy. He designed a new form of spectroscope, and has largely contributed to the scientific journals the results of his researches on light.

A. F. H. V.

Temple Beth El, Detroit, Michigan.
(From a photograph.)

MICHIGAN: One of the Western states of the United States of America. There are no records of the settlement of Jews in Michigan prior to the year 1848, when about a dozen families of Bavarian Jews settled in Detroit. Within a decade a few of the original settlers had traveled to the so-called "copper country" in the upper peninsula of Michigan, where not a few laid the foundation of a comfortable fortune by peddling in the mining districts. The first Jewish organization in the state was the Beth El Society, out of which grew Congregation Beth El of Detroit. This was founded Sept. 22, 1850, by ten adult males, exactly the number required to form a minyan. The last of these charter members, Solomon Bendit, died at St. Clair, Mich., in the fall of 1902.

From 1850 until the first great influx of Russian Jews into America (1882) the Jewish population of Michigan grew gradually, being especially augmented by the relatives of the early settlers. Up to this time the Jews of Michigan were predominantly of German extraction, but the immigration of 1883 not only more than doubled the number of Jews resident in the state, but gave to the Russian and Polish Jews a large numerical majority. To-day, of the total number of the Jews of the state at least 65 per cent are of Russian or Polish nativity or extraction. In 1883 the Hebrew Relief Society of Detroit, assisted by the Baron de Hirsch Committee, settled a colony of Russian Jews near Bad Axe, Mich. About half of the original settlers are still there, having become successful and prosperous farmers.

There are no exact statistics of the Jews resident in Michigan, but data carefully compiled render it possible to estimate the number at 16,000 (out of a total population of 2,450,000), of which 12,000 must be credited to Detroit.

There are regularly organized congregations at **Detroit** (9), **Grand Rapids** (2), **Kalamazoo** (2), **Bay City** (2), **Alpena, Port Huron, Saginaw, Jackson, Battle Creek, Lansing,** and **Hancock;** and a number of cities support religious schools and cemeteries. The total value of real estate held by congregations in the state is about $300,000. Reform congregations at Detroit, Kalamazoo, Grand Rapids, and Bay City support regularly ordained rabbis, while some of the smaller cities have the ministrations of these same rabbis through a well-organized system of circuit preaching; others engage rabbis or rabbinical students for the high holy days.

All the large cities of the state have the usual benevolent societies, but, excepting in Detroit, there are none that have occasion to do any considerable work. At Detroit, however, the United Jewish Charities (organized Nov., 1899) carries on practically every phase of philanthropic work. It dedicated in Sept., 1903, a new and thoroughly equipped building of its own. About $18,000 is annually expended by the Jews of Michigan in organized philanthropy. See Detroit.

All the principal lodges are represented in the cities of Michigan, notably the B'nai B'rith, Kesher shel Barzel, Brith Abraham, and Free Sons of Israel.

There are social clubs in Detroit, Kalamazoo, Grand Rapids, and Bay City, and educational organizations exist in the larger cities. Of these the most noteworthy are the Talmud Thora Association of Detroit, which owns a modern and splendidly equipped school-building; the Jewish Woman's Club of Detroit; and the Temple Literary Society of Kalamazoo. One Jewish newspaper, the "Jewish American," of Detroit, is published in Michigan. It is edited by Rabbi Leo M. Franklin.

Quite a number of Jews in Michigan have held public offices of importance. Among those at present (1903) in office are Charles C. Simons, state senator; Bernard Ginsburg, vice-president of the Municipal Lighting Commission of Detroit; Albert Kahn, art commissioner of Detroit; Samuel Folz, mayor of Kalamazoo; and M. Bloomrosen, mayor of Manistique.

A. L. M. F.

MICHMASH (מכמש): A town of Benjamin, east of Beth-aven (I Sam. xiii. 2 *et passim*; Neh. xi. 31). The form "Michmas" (מכמס) occurs in Ezra ii. 27 and in Neh. vii. 31, according to which the name may mean "hidden." Michmash is particularly known as the scene of the war between the Philistines and Saul and Jonathan (I Sam. xiii.-xiv.; see JONATHAN No. 2); and it is praised in the Mishnah for its excellent wheat (Men. viii. 1).

J. M. SEL.

MICROCOCCUS PRODIGIOSUS ("the microbe of miracles"; known also as **the Microbe of Bleeding Hosts**): A microscopical organism, first mentioned in 1819 by an Italian doctor, Vincenzo Sette, who observed it on polenta, a sort of Italian maize pudding, and gave it the strange name of *Zaogalactina imetropha* (from ζάω = "I live"; γαλαχτινή = "gelatin"; ἧμαι = "I am placed upon"; τροφή = "food"); afterward called *Monas prodigiosa* by Ehrenberg (1848); *Micrococcus prodigiosus* by Cohn (1872); and *Bacillus prodigiosus* by Flügge (1886). It does not belong to the *Infusoria*, as Ehrenberg believed, but is a short, roundish bacterium, varying from about one half to one thousandth of a millimeter in size, motile, and bearing a variable number of cilia. It multiplies by simple division and forms no spores. Its colonies emit a disagreeable trimethylamin smell and generally produce a blood-red coloring-matter (sometimes pink, sometimes brownish). Cultures of this bacterium can be observed on gelatin, milk, meat, and other articles of food, especially on boiled potatoes (Fig. 1), on bread, and on wafers (Figs. 2, 3).

Its germs, though not very common, exist here and there in atmospheric dust, and are thus capable of accidentally producing "blood-spots" on different substances. These spots were formerly interpreted as indicating the wrath of Heaven; and they gave rise to the belief in miracles of "bleeding hosts," "bleeding bread," etc. Errera witnessed (1882) the "miracle" make its appearance unexpectedly on loaves of bread on which he was cultivating a certain fungus for phytochemical study. A well-known case is the epidemic in 1843 of "blood-spots" on the bread produced in the military bake-houses of Paris. The German naturalist Ehrenberg mentions (in "Ber. der Berl. Ak. der Wiss." 1848, p. 350; 1849, p. 106) a series of similar "miracles." A very characteristic one happened near Padua, Italy, in 1819, where Sette discovered its cause in the growth of the *Zaogalactina*. Another was observed by Ehrenberg in Berlin in 1848. Many of these "miracles" are of interest in connection with the subject of the desecration of the sacred hosts, the Jews having often been accused of transfixing those in which the microbes had appeared (see BRUSSELS; HOST, DESECRATION OF).

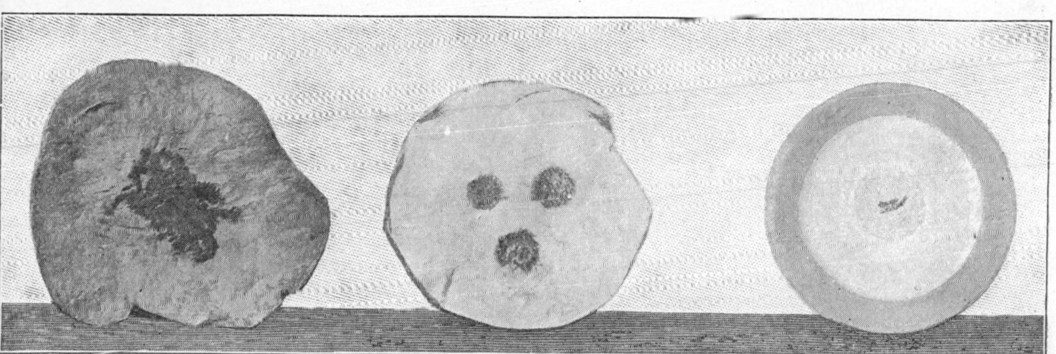

CULTURES OF MICROCOCCUS PRODIGIOSUS ON (1) POTATO AND ON (2 AND 3) WAFERS.

The Myth of Host-Desecration.

It may be assumed that many of the stories of blood-miracles had no material basis, and were mere inventions; but as the *Micrococcus prodigiosus* grows quite easily on wafers, it is not unlikely that some accusations had their origin in the actual appearance of red spots on sacred hosts which had been kept damp and become exposed to atmospheric dust. Besides, other bacteria produce similar red spots, *e.g.*, *Bacillus kiliensis* Migula, *B. plymouthensis* Migula, *B. ruber* Cohn, and *Sarcina rubra* Menge; and other lower organisms, *e.g.*, *Saccharomyces glutinis*, on starch, potatoes, and bread; *Euglena sanguinea*, on standing waters, etc. Again, in other cases, red dust from ferruginous soils and precipitated by a shower may have produced so-called "blood-rain" or "blood-stains."

Nor must it be forgotten that the Christian belief in transubstantiation lent special force to any superstition which associated the idea of blood with that of the sacred host. It is reported that this belief, which was at first much contested, became general only after the "miracle" of 1264 at Bolsena. A priest who doubted the real presence of Christ in the bread of communion suddenly saw "drops of blood" falling on his linen garment. This was considered a decisive proof; and Pope Urban IV. immediately ordered the event to be solemnized by the institution of Corpus Christi Day.

It is possible also, according to a passage of Lucian quoted by Ferdinand Cohn, that the Pythagorean prohibition against eating beans was due to the fact that bloodlike spots had been observed on cooked beans which had been preserved for some time. Perhaps the Jewish custom of placing some iron in contact with every dish, on four days of the year, in order to prevent the fall of blood, supposed to drop from heaven into the food (see Teḳufah), may also have originated in some such case of accidental blood-red spots.

Bibliography: Vincenzo Sette, *Memoria Storico-Naturale sull' Arrossimento Straordinario di Alcune Sostanze Alimentose Osservato Nella Provincia di Padova l'Anno 1819*, Venice, 1824; Ehrenberg, *Monas (?) Prodigiosa*, in *Berichte der Berliner Akademie der Wissenschaften*, 1848, p. 349; idem, *Fortsetzung der Beob. des Sogen. Blutes im Brode als Monas Prodigiosa*, ib. 1848, p. 354; idem, *Fernere Mittheilungen über Monas Prodigiosa*, ib. 1849, p. 101; Ferdinand Cohn, *Ueber Blutähnliche Färbungen Durch Mikroskopische Organismen*, in *Mittheilungen der Schlesischen Gesellschaft für Vaterländische Cultur*, 1850, p. 39; idem, *Brief an Ehrenberg über Monas Prodigiosa auf Gekochten Bohnen und das Verbot des Bohnenessens bei den Pythagoräern*, in *Berichte der Berliner Akademie der Wissenschaften*, 1850, p. 5; idem, *Blut auf Speisen, Hostien* (in his *Die Mikroskopische Welt*, in *Die Gegenwart*, xi. 808); Flügge, *Die Mikroorganismen*, 2d ed., 1886, p. 284; W. Migula, *System der Bakterien*, ii. 845, Jena, 1900.

J. L. Er.

MICROCOSM (Greek, *μικρός*, small; *κόσμος*, universe): Philosophical term applied to man when contrasted with the universe, which, in this connection, is termed the macrocosm. The idea of an analogy between man and the universe was expressed by the ancient Greek philosophers like Pythagoras, Plato, Aristotle, and especially by the Stoics, who developed it in connection with their doctrine of *πνεῦμα*. They considered the universe to be an animated being resembling a man and, like him, made up of a body and a soul. From this idea, exaggerated and developed, proceeded the doctrine of microcosm and macrocosm, according to which man is a universe in little, and the universe a man in great.

Man a Universe in Little.

The soul of man, which forms a part of the universal soul, is to his body what the universal soul is to the universe; and the rational part of the soul performs in man the same functions as the universal intellect in the universe. From this assimilation of man to the universe resulted the prevailing belief in a mutual influence exercised by each on the other.

The doctrine of man's being a microcosm penetrated early into Jewish literature. It is found, though only in a haggadic form, in the Abot de-Rabbi Natan (ch. xxxi.), where every part of man's body is compared with a certain object. The hair represents the forest; the bones, woods; the lungs are the wind; the loins, counselors; the stomach, a mill; the knees, horses; when erect the man resembles the mountain, when recumbent the plain. Less fantastic analogies between man and the universe are given by Israeli ("Sefer ha-Yesodot," ed. Fried, p. 59), Saadia (commentary on the "Sefer Yeẓirah," iv. 1), and Shabbethai Donolo (commentary on Gen. i. 26). To them man is a microcosm owing to the correspondence of the four humors of which his body is made up to the four elements which constitute the universe: the blood corresponds to the air; the phlegm, to water; the black bile, to earth; and the yellow bile, to fire. Ibn Gabirol expounds in his "Meḳor Ḥayyim" (iii., § 6) the theory of microcosm and macrocosm in its metaphysical sense.

The Four Humors and the Four Elements.

"As the intellect," he says, "which is the most sublime and the most simple of all the substances of the microcosm, is not attached directly to the body, but has for intermediaries the animal soul and the ethical spirit, so the most sublime and the most simple substances of the macrocosm must have intermediaries by means of which they are attached to corporeality." In another passage of the same work (iii., § 44) Gabirol says: "If thou wishest to form an idea of the construction of the universe, thou hast only to observe the construction of the human body, in which thou mayest find an analogy." Very original analogies between man and the heavenly spheres are given by Baḥya ("Ma'ani al-Nafs"; Hebr. version by I. Broydé, ch. xiii., Paris, 1894). As there are nine spheres, one contained within the other, so is the human body constituted of nine various substances entering one into another; namely: the bones, which contain the marrow; the vessels and the veins, which contain the blood; the flesh; the skin; the hair; and the nails.

Baḥya's Analogies.

To the twelve signs of the zodiac of the heavenly sphere correspond the twelve apertures in the human body, six to the right, and six to the left: the eyes, the ears, the nostrils, the mouth, the breasts, the navel, and the two other openings. As every sign of the zodiac is supervised by a power proceeding from the universal soul and returning to it, so is every limb of the human body governed by one of the powers of the soul. As the destinies of all living beings and natural phenomena are regulated by the seven planets, so the maintenance and good order of the human body depend on the seven powers of the soul, combined with the physical faculties of man. As the stars are constituted of bodies and souls that have a visible influence on the animal and vegetable kingdoms, so the human body is provided with seven physical powers by means of which it grows and maintains itself. To the seven intellectual powers of the heavenly spheres correspond the five senses with the faculties of perception and understanding, the first five resembling the five planets, and the last two the sun and the moon.

The comparison between man and the universe is the central idea of the philosophical work of Joseph ibn Ẓaddiḳ entitled "'Olam Ḳaṭan" (The Microcosm). To it are devoted the end of the first division and the whole second division of the book. There is nothing in the world, says Ibn Ẓaddik, that does not find a parallel in man. In him are found the four elements and their characteristics; for he passes from heat to cold, from moisture to dryness. He participates in the nature of minerals, vegetables, and animals; he comes into being and passes out of being like the minerals; nourishes and reproduces himself like the plants; has feeling and life like the animals. Further, he presents analogies to the characteristics of things: his erect figure resembles that of the terebinth; his hair, grass and vegetation; his veins and arteries, rivers and canals; and his bones, the mountains. In addition, he possesses the characteristics of the animals: he is brave like a lion, timid like a hare, patient like a lamb, and cunning like a fox. Moses ibn Ezra, in his "'Arugat ha-Bosem," says that man is called microcosm because he resembles the macrocosm in his composition, derivation, and creation. With the spread of the Peripatetic philosophy, in the twelfth century, the doctrine of microcosm, which entered Jewish philosophy through the Arabian Neoplatonists, and especially through the encyclopedists known as "the Brethren of Sincerity" (comp. Dieterici, "Die Anthropologie der Araber," pp. 41 *et seq.*). lost all its significance. Maimonides is concerned only with the original Aristotelian idea from which the doctrine evolved, namely, that the whole universe is one organic body, and that it has the properties of a living being, possessing life, motion, and a soul, but he does not seem to believe in the niceties of the analogy between the human body and the universe as established by the Neoplatonists (see "Moreh Nebukim," i., chap. lxxii.). However, the doctrine became prominent in the Cabala. "The human body," says the Zohar, "is the model of all the creations; it unites all the earthly and celestial worlds" (iii. 135a). In another passage it is said: "The human figure unites all that is above and all that is below; therefore the Ancient of Ancients has chosen it for His form" (iii. 141b). In "Tiḳḳune Zohar" man is regarded as a microcosm, and, viewed in his relation to the macrocosm, considered as the great universal ideal man or ADAM ḲADMON. It is probably through the influence of the Cabala that the doctrine of the microcosm came into great favor among the philosophers of the Renaissance like Bruno, Paracelsus, and others, who held that in man's nature is found the sum of all the cosmic forces. He is able to understand the material world, because he unites in his body the finest essence of all the material things; and as an intellectual being of sidereal origin, he has the faculty of conceiving the world of intellectual forms through the spark of the divine infused into his nature.

Joseph ibn Ẓaddiḳ.

In the Cabala.

BIBLIOGRAPHY: Fried, *Sefer ha-Yesodot*, p. 59; Jellinek, edition of Ibn Ẓaddiḳ's *'Olam Ḳaṭan*, Intro.; Bloch, in Winter and Wünsche, *Die Jüdische Litteratur*, ii. 729; Steinschneider, *Hebr. Uebers.* p. 407; Kaufmann, *Attributenlehre*, p. 5; Munk, *Guide des Egarés*, i., chap. lxxii., note; Karppe, *Etudes sur l'Origine et la Nature du Zohar*, pp. 452 *et seq.*; Joël, *Beiträge zur Gesch. der Philosophie*, i. 29.

J. I. BR.

MIDDLEMAN, JUDAH: English rabbi of the first half of the nineteenth century. He was the author of "Netibot Emet," a work written in defense of the traditions of the Talmud against the attacks, in "Old Paths" ("Netibot 'Olam"), of the Rev. Alexander McCaul. Only the first part of the "Netibot Emet" was published, in 1847, under the title "Paths of Truth," an English translation by M. H. Breslau appearing in the same year.

BIBLIOGRAPHY: Jacobs and Wolf, *Bibl. Anglo-Jud.* p. 107.

J. I. Co.

MIDDOT: Treatise in the Mishnah; tenth in the order Ḳodashim. It deals with the dimensions and the arrangement of the Temple, and is divided into five chapters containing thirty-four paragraphs in all.

Ch. i.: The night-watches in the sanctuary. The priests kept guard in three places, the Levites in twenty-one (§ 1). These watches were controlled by the captain of the Temple ("ish har ha-bayit"). When this official passed the priest or the Levite on guard, the latter was required to rise. If he failed to do so, the captain addressed him; and if it became evident that the guard was asleep, the captain struck him with his staff. The captain had also the option of burning the sleeping watchman's coat. The other guards then jested at the expense of the sleeper and shouted: "A Levite is beaten and his clothes are burned because he has fallen asleep at his post" (§ 2). The gates of the hill of the Temple. On the eastern gate was a representation of Susa, the Persian capital, in token of the Persian supremacy (§ 3). The gates of the inner court (§§ 4-5). In the northeastern part of the forecourt was a cell in which the Hasmoneans preserved the altar-stones which were consecrated during the reign of the Greek (Syrian) kings (§ 6). The "place of the hearth" ("bet ha-moḳed") was a large hall with an arched ceiling. Around the walls were stone benches upon which the older priests rested, the younger ones sleeping on the floor (§§ 7-8). While a Levite kept watch outside, a priest within locked the doors, put the bunch of keys in a place hollowed out for them, and covered them with a marble slab, on which he lay down to sleep (§ 9).

Ch. ii.: The dimensions of the Temple hill: 500 cubits square (§ 1). All who ascended the hill kept to the right excepting mourners and those under a ban, who walked on the left, that they might be distinguished from the rest. Those who met the grief-stricken greeted them with the words, "May He who dwelleth in this house comfort thee"; while to one under a ban they wished reconciliation with his friends and the consequent removal of the ban (§ 2). Within the walls of the Temple hill was a railing which had been broken in thirteen places by heathen kings, but had been restored. Height and breadth of the steps and of the gates of the Temple. All the doors with the exception of those of the gate of Nicanor were covered with gold (§ 3). Dimensions of the space allotted to women in the inner court. From this court the men's court was reached by a flight of fifteen steps, corresponding to the fifteen "songs of degrees" in the Psalms (Ps. cxx.-cxxxiv.); and on these steps the priests stood while singing (§ 5). Under the forecourt were cells in which the Levites kept their musical instruments. Enumeration of the thirteen gates of the forecourt (§ 6).

Ch. iii.: Dimensions of the altar of burnt offerings. This at first was only twenty-five cubits square, but was afterward enlarged to thirty-two cubits (§ 1). The stones of the altar might not be hewn with an iron tool or changed in any way. The reason assigned for this is noteworthy, and is at the same time an explanation of Ex. xx. 25. The weapon which shortens human life and causes early death is of iron, while the altar serves to prolong the life of man by expiating sin; hence it is not fitting that this destructive metal should be used on the altar (§ 4). Arrangement of the place, on the north side of the altar, for killing the sacrificial animals (§ 5). The laver between the porch and the altar (§ 6). The porch, the golden grape-vine with its golden tendrils, leaves, and grapes (§§ 7-8; comp. Ḥul. 90b, where R. Isaac b. Naḥmani remarks that this mishnah—Mid. iii. 8—was one of the passages in which the wise had spoken words of exaggeration and hence were not to be taken literally).

Ch. iv.: Detailed description of that part of the Temple called "hekal," of its entrances—one of which, according to Ezek. xliv. 2, was never used —doors, chambers, steps, and balustrades.

Ch. v.: Description of the inner court and of its chambers. In this court was a hall built of square stones and called "lishkat ha-gazit," where the Great Sanhedrin met and decided all matters touching the priesthood. One of its chief duties was to examine the genealogy of each individual priest and to determine his fitness for service in the Temple. The priest in whom a blemish was discovered wrapped himself in black garments and left the Temple, but he in whom no fault was found clothed himself in white, entered the Temple, and took his place among the other priests. Whenever it happened that all the priests who were examined on a single day were without blemish, that day was celebrated as a holiday. There is no Gemara to this treatise. See also TEMPLE.

S. S. J. Z. L.

MIDDOT: THE SEVEN, OF HILLEL. See TALMUD HERMENEUTICS.

MIDDOT, SHELOSH-'ESREH: The thirteen forms of mercy, enumerated in Ex. xxxiv. 6-7, whereby God rules the world. According to the explanation of Maimonides ("Moreh Nebukim," i. 52), which is confirmed by the Sifre (Deut. 49 [ed. Friedmann, p. 85]), these middot must not be regarded as qualities inherent in God, but merely as so many attributes of His activity, by which the divine governance appears to the human observer to be controlled. In the Sifre, however, these attributes are not called "middot," which may mean "quality" as well as "rule" and "measure" (comp. Ab. v. 10-15), but "derakim" (ways), since they are the ways of God which Moses prayed to know (Ex. xxxiii. 13), and which God, according to the traditional explanation of Ex. xxxiv. 6-7, proclaimed to him. The number thirteen is adopted from the Talmudic and rabbinic tradition, while the Karaites count only nine, ten, or eleven middot (comp. Aaron b. Elijah, "Keter Torah," *ad loc.*, Eupatoria, 1866). The rabbinical school indeed agrees that the middot number thirteen and that they are contained in Ex. xxxiv. 6-7, but with which word they begin and with which they conclude are moot questions. According to Tobiah ben Eliezer, Midrash Leḳaḥ Ṭob, *ad loc.*, ed. Buber, Wilna, 1884; R. Jacob Tam, in Tos. R. H. 17b, catchword "Shelosh-'Esreh Middot"; Abraham ibn Ezra in his commentary, *ad loc.*; Asher b. Jehiel; and Kalonymus, "Meshoret Mosheh," ed. Goldenthal, p. 14, Leipsic, 1845, the thirteen middot begin with the first

Division.

"Adonai," in verse 6, and end with the word "we-naḳeh" in verse 7. The single attributes are contained in the verses as follows:

(1) "Adonai," compassion before man sins; (2) "Adonai," compassion after man has sinned (comp. R. H. 17b); (3) "El," mighty in compassion to give all creatures according to their need; (4) "Raḥum," merciful, that mankind may not be distressed; (5) "Ḥanun," gracious if mankind is already in distress; (6) "Erek appayim," slow to anger; (7) "Rab ḥesed," plenteous in mercy; (8) "Emet," truth; (9) "Noẓer ḥesed la-alafim," keeping mercy unto thousands (comp. the explanation of Samuel b. Meïr in "Da'at Zeḳenim," *ad loc.*); (10) "Nose 'awon," forgiving iniquity; (11) "Nose pesha'," forgiving transgression; (12) "Nose ḥaṭa'ah," forgiving sin; (13) "We-naḳeh," and pardoning.

According to R. Nissim (quoted in Tos. R. H., *l.c.*), Isaac Alfasi, and others, the thirteen middot begin only with the second "Adonai," since the first one is the subject of "wa-yiḳra" (and he proclaimed). To secure the number thirteen, some count "noẓer ḥesed la-alafim" as two (Nissim in Tos. *l.c.*), while others divide "erek appayim" into two, since forbearance is shown both to the good and to the wicked (comp. the gloss on Tosafot, *l.c.* and Ibn Ezra, *l.c.*), and still others end the thirteenth middah with "lo yenaḳeh" (he does not pardon; Maimonides, "Pe'er ha-Dor," p. 19b, Lemberg, 1859), this being considered a good quality, since through punishment man is moved to repentance, after which he is pardoned and pure (comp. Yoma 86a; Aaron b. Elijah, *l.c.*; and "'Ez ha-Ḥayyim," ch. xcii.). Others term "we-naḳeh lo yenaḳeh" a single middah, the thirteenth being, in their opinion, "poḳed 'awon abot 'al-banim" (visiting the iniquity of the fathers upon the children), "this being regarded as compassionate since the transgressor is not punished immediately" (Maimonides, *l.c.*; Aaron b. Ḥayyim, *l.c.*; comp. also "Da'at Zeḳenim").

The general usage is based on the view of Leḳaḥ Ṭob, R. Tam, and Ibn Ezra, and the various recitations of the thirteen middot begin with the first "Adonai" after "wa-yiḳra," and conclude with

Liturgical Usage.

"we-naḳeh." They must not be recited by only one person in prayer (Shulḥan 'Aruk, Oraḥ Ḥayyim, 565, 5), but by an entire congregation, which must consist of ten persons at least ("minyan"). They are recited on every holy day—not on the ordinary Sabbaths—when the Torah scroll is taken from the Ark, and it is also customary that on the fast-days on which Ex. xxxii. 11-14 and xxxiv. 1-10 are read, the reader stops at the word "wa-yiḳra" in order that the congregation may recite the thirteen middot, after which he continues his reading. The thirteen middot are very frequently recited in penitential prayers, in some of which they have even been hypostatized and are invoked, as inferior celestial beings, to aid the prayers of Israel and to present them before God. This is especially the case in the seliḥah of the eve of the New-Year, which is repeated at the morning service on the Day of Atonement, and which begins with the words "Shelosh 'esreh middot," and in the pizmon of Amittai b. Shephatiah for the fifth day of repentance, which is recited also at the evening service on the Day of Atonement, and in which the "middat ha-raḥamim" (compassion) is particularly invoked. On fast-days as well as during the week before the New-Year (the so-called seliḥot days), and on the days between the New-Year and the Day of Atonement, called the days of repentance, many penitential prayers ("seliḥot") are recited in addition to the usual daily prayers. After every such petition the thirteen middot are recited with their introductory prayer, the well-known "El Melek yosheb," which runs as follows: "Almighty King, sittest on the throne of mercy, showing forth Thy compassion, and forgiving the sins of Thy people by ever taking away their former guilt, ofttimes granting pardon unto sinners and forgiveness to the transgressors, making manifest Thy goodness both to body and to soul, nor punishing them according to their iniquity; Almighty One, as Thou hast taught us to recite the thirteen [middot], so remember now the thirteenfold covenant, as Thou didst in former days proclaim it to the modest one [Moses], even as it is written . . ." (then follow the verses Ex. xxxiv. 5-7a and 9b). The importance attributed to the thirteen middot in this prayer and the potency ascribed to the recitation of them in the penitential prayer are based upon an overliteral and partially erroneous interpretation of a passage from the Talmud, which runs as follows (R. H. 17b): "After God had proclaimed the thirteen middot to Moses, He told him: 'As often as Israel shall offend, thus shall they do in My presence, and I will forgive them.' Rab Judah says that a covenant was made that the thirteen middot should not be without effect." The phrase "thus shall they do" was understood as requiring the recitation of the thirteen middot in the same way as God had proclaimed them to Moses, while the words of Rab Judah were interpreted to imply that even the mention of the thirteen middot in prayer should not be without effect. In reality, however, the first sentence does not read "yomeru," recite, but "ya'asu," act, and, according to the correct explanation of R. Isaiah Horowitz in "Shene Luḥot ha-Berit" (Amsterdam, 1698, p. 333a), the passage means that if one acts according to the pattern of these middot and shows himself compassionate, merciful, and forgiving toward his fellow creatures, God also will be compassionate and merciful toward him and will forgive his sins (comp. the aphorism of Raba, R. H. 17a, and the remark in Sifre, *l.c.*, that the middot are the ways of God, in which, according to Deut. xi. 22, mankind should walk). In like manner, the words of Rab Judah really denote that if the thirteen middot are the rules of life and conduct, not mere formulas, they will not be inefficacious. The exercise and practise of these virtues cause God to treat man with mercy and compassion, for according to human actions, both in degree and in kind, divine recompense is measured (Soṭah 8b). If this correct interpretation of the Talmudic passage in question be adopted, the importance attributed to the recitation of the thirteen middot lacks all justification.

s. J. Z. L.

MIDDOT: THE THIRTEEN, OF R. ISHMAEL. See TALMUD HERMENEUTICS.

MIDIAN AND MIDIANITES: Midian was the son of Abraham and Keturah. His five sons, Ephah, Epher, Hanoch, Abidah (R.V. "Abida"), and Eldaah, were the progenitors of the Midianites (Gen. xxv. 1-4; I Chron. i. 32-33). The term "Midian" (מדין), which seems to be derived from the Arabic root דין (= "place of judgment"), denotes also the nation of the Midianites, the plural form, מדינים, occurring only in Gen. xxxvii. 28, 36 (in the latter passage מדנים seems to be a scribal error for מדינים) and Num. xxv. 17, xxxi. 2. Their geographical situation is indicated as having been to the east of Palestine; Abraham sends the sons of his concubines, including Midian, eastward (Gen. xxv. 6). But from the statement that Moses led the flocks of Jethro, the priest of Midian, to Mount Horeb (Ex. iii. 1), it would appear that the Midianites dwelt in the Sinaitic Peninsula. Later, in the period of the Kings, Midian seems to have occupied a tract of land between Edom and Paran, on the way to Egypt (I Kings xi. 18). Midian is likewise described as in the vicinity of Moab: the Midianites were beaten by the Edomite king Hadad "in the field of Moab" (Gen. xxxvi. 35), and in the account of Balaam it is said that the elders of both Moab and Midian called upon him to curse Israel (Num. xxii. 4, 7). Further evidences of the geographical position of the Midianites appear in a survey of their history.

Geographical Position.

In the time of Moses the Midianites are first mentioned as having had a priest by the name of Reuel or JETHRO, who became afterward Moses' father-in-law. Toward the close of the forty years' wandering of the children of Israel in the wilderness, the Midianites were allied with the Moabites in the attempt to exterminate the Israelites. For this reason Moses was ordered by God to punish the Midianites. Moses, accordingly, despatched against them an army of 12,000 men, under Phinehas the priest; this force defeated the Midianites and slew all their males, including their five kings, Evi, Rekem, Zur, Hur, and Reba. It may be noted that these five princes of Midian are called by Joshua (xiii. 21) the vassals of Sihon, the king of the Amorites. It is possible that Sihon had previously conquered Midian and made it a dependency, and that after his death the Midianites recovered their independence. The Israelitish soldiers set on fire all the cities and fortresses of the Midianites, carried the women and children into captivity, and seized their cattle and goods. The Israelites were afterward ordered by Moses to slay every Midianite male child and every woman, sparing only the female children (Num. xxxi. 2-18). It appears from the same account that the Midianites were rich in cattle and gold. The narrative shows that each of the five Midianite tribes was governed by its own

Wars.

king, but that all acted together against a common enemy; that while a part of each tribe dwelt in cities and fortresses in the vicinity of Moab, another part led a nomadic life, living in tents and apparently remote from the seat of the war. For, after the Midianites had been "exterminated" by the army of Phinehas, they reappear some hundreds of years later, in the time of Gideon.

The Biblical account of the battle between the Midianites and Gideon (Judges vi.–viii.) asserts that the Israelites suffered at the hands of the Midianites for a space of six years. The Midianites seem to have been then a powerful and independent nation; they allied themselves with the Amalekites and the children of the East, and they oppressed the Israelites so severely that the last-named were obliged to seek refuge in caves and strongholds; they destroyed their crops and reduced them to extreme poverty (*ib.* vi. 1–6). The allied army of Midianites and Amalekites encamped in the valley of Jezreel (*ib.* vi. 33) after having crossed the Jordan. Gideon with his army encamped by the fountain of Harod, the Midianite army being to the north of him. With 300 men Gideon succeeded in surprising and routing them, and they fled homeward across the Jordan in confusion (*ib.* vii. 1–24). A point worth noting is that here only two Midianite kings, Zebah and Zalmuna, and two princes, Oreb and Zeeb, are mentioned (*ib.* vii. 25; viii. 3, 5, 10, 12, 18, 21). This would show that only two tribes bore the name "Midianites," while the remaining three probably were merged with other Arabic tribes, their kinsmen, and perhaps partly with the Israelites also. Midian is stated to have been "subdued before the children of Israel, so that they lifted up their heads no more" (*ib.* viii. 28). In fact, aside from allusions to this victory (Ps. lxxxiii. 10, 12; Isa. ix. 4, x. 6; Hab. iii. 7), Midian is not mentioned again in sacred history except in Judith ii. 16, where the term "Midianites" seems to be a mistake for "Arabians."

The first recorded instance of a Midianite tribe surrendering its identity by attaching itself to another people appears in Judges i. 16. In this instance, which occurred in the period of the Judges, the Kenites, descendants of Jethro the Midianite, attached themselves to the Israelites in the wilderness of Judah, south of Arad. Later, in the time of Tiglath-pileser (745–727 B.C.), a tribe, called in the cuneiform inscriptions "Ḥayapa" and identified by Friedrich Delitzsch ("Wo Lag das Paradies?" p. 304) with the tribe of Ephah, is said to have dwelt in the northern part of the Hejaz. Isaiah (lx. 6) speaks of Midian and Ephah as of two distinct peoples. The second son of Midian, Epher, is identified by Knobel with the Ghifar, an Arabic tribe which, in the time of Mohammed, had encampments near Medina. Traces of the Midianites existed in post-Biblical times. Ptolemy ("Geography," vi. 7) mentions a place called Modiana, on the coast of Arabia; according to his statement of its position, this place may be identified with the Madyan of the Arabic geographers, in the neighborhood of 'Ain 'Una, opposite the extremity of the Sinaitic Peninsula, and now known under the name of "Magha 'ir Shu'aib" (= "the caves of Shu'aib" ["Jethro"]).

BIBLIOGRAPHY: Cheyne and Black, *Encyc. Bibl.*; Sir Richar Burton, *The Gold Mines of Midian*, London, 1878; iden *The Land of Midian Revisited*, ib. 1879.

S. M. SEL.

MIDRASH (מדרש, from the root דרש, "t study," "to investigate"): A term occurring a early as II Chron. xiii. 22, xxiv. 27, though perhap not in the sense in which it came to be used late and denoting "exposition," "exegesis," especiall that of the Scriptures. In contradistinction to li eral interpretation, subsequently called "peshaṭ (comp. Geiger's "Wiss. Zeit. Jüd. Theol." v. 244 the term "midrash" designates an exegesis which going more deeply than the mere literal sense, a tempts to penetrate into the spirit of the Scriptures to examine the text from all sides, and thereby t derive interpretations which are not immediatel obvious. The Talmud (Sanh. 34b) compares thi kind of midrashic exposition to a hammer whic awakens the slumbering sparks in the rock. Th divergence between midrash and peshaṭ increase steadily; and, although the consciousness of thi divergence may not have increased in a proportion ate degree, contrary to the view of Geiger (*l.c.* pp 53 *et seq.*, 234 *et seq.*; comp. Weiss, "Dor Dor, i. 167 *et seq.*) and others, it was never wholly ob scured. The confession of Rab Kahana (Shab. 63a that although he knew the entire Talmud by th time he was eighteen, it was many years later be fore he learned the principle that a Bible verse ca never lose its evident and literal meaning, is no to be taken as an indication of the general state o Bible study in his time; on the contrary, Ra Kahana wishes to indicate thereby that he was a exception to the rule. Raba's statement in Yeb 24a likewise proves that a distinction was made be tween midrash and peshaṭ. At the most it can b proved that in some cases the Midrash was based o a peculiar interpretation of the literal meaning thus, Sifra, Tazria', Neg. ix. 14 remarks in regar to the sentence "We-im be-'enaw 'amad ha-neteḳ (Lev. xiii. 37), "En li ella be-'ene 'aẓmo be-'ene beno, etc.; this shows that "be-'enaw" was explained a "in his eyes," an interpretation which certainl does not contradict the statement that the differenc between midrash and peshaṭ was recognized.

The Bible exegesis of the Rabbis which had moralizing or edifying tendency must be distin guished from that which was of a legal nature: th former is known as MIDRASH HAGGADAH; the lat ter, as MIDRASH HALAKAH. Exegesis from an eth ical or devotional point of view admits of more free dom than hermeneutics aiming at the determinatio of legal maxims. This is true not only because th imagination has freer play in the former, and reaso in the latter, but also because halakic exegesis since it is intended for practical guidance and i more far-reaching in its results, is bound mor closely by certain laws and principles (comp. th different view of Hirschfeld in "Halachische Exe gese," p. 13).

As concerns the origin of the Midrash, Maimonide ("Sefer ha-Miẓwot," Hilkot "Shoresh," 2) held tha the Midrash was a product of the Halakah; Naḥmani des, on the contrary, that the former was the sourc of the latter. It is impossible to decide whethe either one was correct. Only this much can be sai priori, that there are certain expositions which could not have been evolved through mere theoretical speculation. Any other conclusions on the subject must be based on a consideration of the various circumstances which favored the origin and development of the Midrash.

Origin of the Midrash.

In the first place, any application of theory to practise demands a more recondite interpretation than does the mere explanation of the literal meaning. A general law demands special exposition in order to deal with the complications which frequently arise in daily life. Even Moses was obliged to seek instruction in several instances (Lev. x. 16, xxiv. 12, Num. xv. 34; the expressions "to expound unto them according to the mouth of the Lord" and "because it was not declared what should be done unto him" in the second and third of these passages respectively being especially noteworthy; see Krochmal, "Moreh Nebuke ha-Zeman," p. 13). But even if the Midrash gave rise to the Halakah in certain cases in which an "investigation" of the Law became necessary for a practical decision, there were in all probability many more instances in which a legal basis, often difficult to find, was sought for certain rules which had arisen from the exigencies of life. That there were many such cases in which the Halakah was a subsequent justification of an accomplished fact, though they are not always specifically noted, is shown by the well-known sentence of the Mishnah (Ḥag. 10a), "Miḳra mu'aṭ, halakot merubbot," by the sentence of R. Johanan (Yer. Ber. 4c), "Kol milla di-la mehawwera mesammekin lah min atrin saggin," and by the remark "Ḳera asmakta be'alma," which is frequently found in connection with very important rules, such as the determination of weights (Ber. 41b, Yer. Pes. 15a). Retroactive justification is to be seen in many of the cases when one and the same halakah is variously deduced by different tannaim ("mishma'ot dorshin"), and where the Amoraim feel themselves compelled to assume a material difference, as in Pes. 84a, where no less than eight explanations are attempted.

Great as was this twofold influence of actual practise on the origin and development of the Midrash, it must be borne in mind that speculation for its own sake in the obligatory study of the Law (Deut. vi. 7; Josh. i. 8) was likewise a factor; for this exclusive and continued study probably contributed much to the search for other interpretations than the merely literal one. The exegetes endeavored to find everything expressed in the Law; and Philo's view that there were no superfluous words in Scripture, and that everything had a meaning ("De Profugis," § 458), dominated not only the allegorical exegesis of Alexandria, but also to a large extent the Midrash, even though no other connection existed between the two. On the rules by which the exegetes were guided in making these deductions see MIDRASH HALAKAH and TALMUD.

The history of the Midrash may be divided into three periods: (1) of the Soferim; (2) of the Tannaim; and (3) of the Amoraim. (1) Midrashim ascribed to Biblical persons (Ber. 31b; Yeb. 77a *et passim*) are haggadic aphorisms and may be recognized as such. Noteworthy is Sheḳ. vi. 8, "Zeh Midrash she-darash Yehoyada' Kohen Gadol" (This is the Midrash which Jehoiada the High Priest taught), a statement which, however, can not lay claim to historical value.

Historical View.

The real date of the origin of the Midrash in question appears to be the period of the Soferim, the writers or scribes (Ḳid. 31a; Yer. Sheḳ. 48c), whose activity is summed up in the sentence, "So they read in the book, in the law of God, distinctly, and made them to understand" (Neh. viii. 8); however this verse is to be explained (Ned. 37b; Yer. Meg. 74d; "Responsen der Geonim," ed. Harkavy, p. 217), it certainly indicates that the Soferim were much more than mere translators. Alleged traces of their Midrash, closely based upon the Bible, are Neg. xii. 5 *et seq.*; Soṭah viii. 1 *et seq.*; Ma'as. Sh. v. 7 *et seq.* According to Krochmal (*l.c.*), the Soferim indicated which were their interpretations by means of peculiar script and certain signs (dots, ḳere and ketib, full and defective writings); accordingly such midrashim as Sifra, Emor, ix. 3; *ib.* Shemini, v. 8; *ib.* Behar, iv. 4; Mek., Mishpaṭim, 3, would belong to them; and even though the later explanations of these signs and this peculiar script are not established by tradition, but are in general controvertible and doubtful (comp. Sanh. 4a), the great age of some of the interpretations is indicated by the Septuagint; *e.g.*, Ex. xxii. 7; Lev. xxiii. 11, xxxiii. 40; Deut. xxv. 5 (comp. Frankel, "Ueber den Einfluss der Palästinensischen Exegese auf die Alexandrinische Hermeneutik," pp. 89 *et seq.*; Hoffmann, "Zur Einleitung in die Halachischen Midraschim," p. 74).

(2) The beginning of the second period likewise is shrouded in obscurity. Of the "zeḳenim ha-rishonim," whose date can not be definitely determined, three midrashim have been preserved, Sifra, Wayiḳra, Ḥobah, xii. 1; *ib.* Meẓora', ix. 12; Mek., Amalek, 2; likewise a few midrashim by Judah b. Ṭabbai and Simon b. Sheṭaḥ, both of whom lived in the first century B.C. (Mek., Mishpaṭim, 20; Tosef., Sanh. viii. 3; Mak. 5b; Yer. Sanh. 22b). The opposition of the Sadducees, who rejected the oral law, and who were attacked by Ṭabbai and Sheṭaḥ, naturally led to an attempt to base the oral law on Scripture, thus encouraging midrashic exegesis. The well-known interpretation of the passage "an eye for an eye" (Ex. xxi. 24), contradicting the view of the Sadducees, who wished to apply the Law literally, gives evidence of a free and profound conception of the Biblical text even at that early date. In the following period Shemaiah and Abṭalion are mentioned as "darshanim gedolim" (Pes. 70; comp. Mek., Beshallaḥ, 3). The seven rules of exposition propounded by Hillel—of whom, as of his opponent Shammai, only a few midrashim, all simple in character, have been preserved (Sifra, Shemini, ix. 5; *ib.* Neg. ix. 16; Yer. Pes. 33a; Tosef., 'Er. iv. 7; Shab. 19a; Ḳid. 43a)—presuppose a very extensive Midrash; and a like inference is to be drawn from the attempt of Hananiah b. Hezekiah b. Garon to harmonize the contradictions between Ezekiel and the Pentateuch. The explanation in Sifre, Deut. 294, transmitted in the name of Hananiah's son, and also mentioned in the passage Mek., Baḥodesh, 7, is perhaps a fragment of this

same Midrash. On the Mishnah of R. Akiba see Jew. Encyc. *s.v.*

(3) In regard to the Midrash of the Amoraim the Babylonians employed more simple methods than the Palestinians, as Frankel correctly says ("Mebo," 31b), though Weiss objects to this view ("Bet ha-Talmud," i. 69, note 4). But the exegesis of the Palestinian Amoraim was more simple than the Palestinian. For the midrashim of this period which have been preserved see Midrash Halakah.

Bibliography: Abraham b. David, exposition of the *Baraita de-Rabbi Yishma'el* in his commentary on the *Sifra*; Abudarham, *ib.* pp. 35 *et seq.*, Warsaw, 1877; Aaron ibn Ḥayyim, *Middot Aharon*; Algazi, *Yabin Shemu'ah*; B. Auerbach, *Ha-Ẓofeh 'al Darke ha-Mishnah*, Frankfort-on-the-Main, 1861; Bacher, *Die Aelteste Terminologie der Jüdischen Schriftauslegung*, Leipsic, 1899; J. Ḥagiz, *Teḥillat Ḥokmah*, Amsterdam, 1709; Dobschütz, *Die Einfache Bibelexegese der Tannaim*, Halle-on-the-Saale, 1893; Derenbourg, *Hist.* pp. 393–395; Frankel, *Darke ha-Mishnah*; idem, *Ueber Palästinensische und Alexandrinische Schriftforschung*, Breslau, 1854; idem, *Ueber den Einfluss der Palästinensischen Exegese auf die Alexandrinische Hermeneutik*; M. Plungian, *Talpiyyot*, 1849; Geiger, *Wiss. Zeit. Jüd. Theol.* v. 53 *et seq.*, 234; Levi b. Gershon, *Sha'are Ẓedeḳ*, reprinted in *Berit Ya'aḳob*, Leghorn, 1840; *Sefer ha-Peli'ah*, pp. 74 *et seq.*, Koret, 1784; Hamburger, *R. B. T.* s.v. *Talmudische Schriften*; D. Hoffmann, *Zur Einleitung in die Halachischen Midraschim*, Berlin, 1886–87; *idem*, in *Jüdische Presse*, 1892, Supplement, pp. 18 *et seq.*; idem, in *Berliner Festschrift*, 1903, pp. 55 *et seq.*; Hirschfeld, *Die Halachische Exegese*, 1840, reviewed in *Orient, Lit.* 1841; *idem*, in *Monatsschrift*, xxviii. 368–374; I. Horowitz, *Torah she-be'al-Peh*; A. L. J. Jehuda, *Kiẓẓur Kelale ha-Gemarah*; Ibn Musa, in the collection *Me-Harare Nemerim*, Venice, 1599; Joshua ha-Levi, *Halikot 'Olam*; J. S. Kaempf, *Mamtiḳ Sod*, Prague, 1861; S. Klein, *Mi-Pene Ḳosht*, Frankfort-on-the-Main 1861; J. Caro, *Kelale ha-Gemarah*; Ch. Kases, *Ḳin'at Soferim*, 1740; Königsberger, *Die Quellen der Halacha*, Berlin, 1890; N. Krochmal, *Moreh Nebuke ha-Zeman*, pp. 13 *et seq.*; Malbim, *Ayyelet ha-Shaḥar*, Introduction to his commentary on the *Sifra*; Malachi Cohen, *Yad Mal'aki*; J. Mecklenburger, *Ha-Ketab weha-Ḳabbalah*; S. Rapoport, *Dibre Shalom we-Emet*, Prague, 1861; Rashi, commentary on *Middot*; Kobak, *Jeschurun*, vi. 38 *et seq.*; Saadia, commentary on *Middot*, reprinted by Schechter in *Bet Talmud*, iv. 235 *et seq.*; by Müller, in Saadia's collected works, vol. ix., Paris; Samuel Valenci, in *Me-Harare Nemerim*; Scherschawski printed an old exposition to *Middot* in *Ha-Karmel*, viii. 213 *et seq.*; S. Serillo, *Kelale Shemuel*; Samson of Chinon, *Sefer Keritot*; Schwarz, *Die Hermeneutische Analogie*, reviewed in *R. E. J.* xxxvi.; idem, *Der Hermeneutische Syllogismus*; Moses Solomon, *Netib Mosheh*, Vienna, 1896; Strack, *Midrash*, in Herzog-Plitt, *Real-Encyc.* ix. 507 *et seq.*; Eliezer Trietsch, *Sheb Shema'teta*; Weber, *System der Altsynagogalen Palästinischen Theologie*, 1880, xix. *et seq.*; Weiss, *Gesch. der Tradition*; Zunz, *G. V.* pp. 37 *et seq.*

J. S. Ho.

MIDRASH HAGGADAH: The subject will be treated under the following headings:

General Statement.
Special Divisions:
A. Midrash Haggadah in the tannaitic midrashim, etc.
- 1. Mekilta.
- 2. Sifra.
- 3. Sifre to Numbers.
- 4. Sifre to Deuteronomy.

B. The purely haggadic midrashim.
- I. The earliest exegetical midrashim.
  - 1. Bereshit Rabbah.
  - 2. Ekah Rabbati.
- II. The homiletic midrashim.
  - 1. Pesiḳta.
  - 2. Wayiḳra Rabbah.
  - 3. Tanḥuma Yelammedenu.
  - 4. Pesiḳta Rabbati.
  - 5. Debarim Rabbah.
  - 6. Bemidbar Rabbah.
  - 7. Shemot Rabbah.
  - 8. Agadat Bereshit.
  - 9. We-Hizhir (Hashkem).
- III. The exegetical midrashim to Canticles, Ruth, Ecclesiastes, and Esther.
  - 1. Shir ha-Shirim Rabbah.
  - 2. Midrash Ruth.
  - 3. Midrash Ḳohelet.
  - 4. Midrash Megillat Esther.
- IV. The other exegetical midrashim not dealing with the Pentateuch. (For Midrash Shemu'el, Midrash Mishle, Midrash Tehillim see the several articles.)
  - 1. Midrash Yeshayah.
  - 2. Midrash Yonah.
  - 3. Midrash Iyyob.
- V. Special haggadic works.
  - 1. Pirḳe R. Eli'ezer.
  - 2. Seder Eliyahu.
  - (Other haggadic works referred to the article Midrashim, Smaller.)
- VI. Yalḳuṭ Shim'oni, Yalḳuṭ ha-Makir, and Midrash ha-Gadol.

Midrash Haggadah embraces the interpretation, illustration, or expansion, in a moralizing or edifying manner, of the non-legal portions of the Bible (see Haggadah; Midrash; Midrash Halakah). The word "haggadah" (Aramaic, "agada") means primarily the recitation or teaching of Scripture; in a narrower sense it denotes the exegetic amplification of a Biblical passage and the development of a new thought based thereupon. Like the formula "maggid ha-Katub" (= "the Scripture teaches"), frequently found in the ancient writings, the noun "haggadah" (plural, "haggadot") probably had at first a general application, but at an early date was restricted to denote a non-halakic explanation (comp. Bacher, "Ag. Tan." 2d ed., pp. 461 *et seq.*). The word then came to be used in a more general sense, designating not the haggadic interpretation of single passages, but haggadic exegesis in general, the body of haggadic interpretations—in fine, everything which does not belong to the field of the Halakah. The haggadic Midrash, which confined itself originally to the exposition of Scripture text, was developed in its period of florescence into finished discourses. "The Haggadah, which is intended to bring heaven down to the congregation, and also to lift man up to heaven, appears in this office both as the glorification of God and as the comfort of Israel. Hence religious truths, moral maxims, discussions concerning divine retribution, the inculcation of the laws which attest Israel's nationality, descriptions of its past and future greatness, scenes and legends from Jewish history, comparisons between the divine and Jewish institutions, praises of the Holy Land, encouraging stories, and comforting reflections of all kinds form the most important subjects of these discourses" (Zunz, "G. V." 1st ed., pp. 349 *et seq.*).

Connotation of Haggadah.

The opening words of this quotation are a paraphrase of a famous sentence in which the Haggadah was praised by the old haggadists themselves. "If thou wishest to know Him at whose word the world came into being, then learn the Haggadah, for through it thou shalt know the Holy One, praised be He, and follow His ways" (Sifre to Deut. xi. 22). Indeed, the Haggadah, being exegesis from a religious and ethical standpoint, undertook to influence the mind of man and to induce him to lead a religious and moral life, "that he might walk in the ways of God." In conformity with the conditions of its time, it neither could nor would limit itself to the simple interpretation of Scripture, but included in its ever-widening circle of discussions and reflections on the Scripture text the highest thoughts of religious philosophy, mysticism, and ethics. It interpreted all the historical matter contained in the Bible in such a religious and national sense that the heroes of the olden time became prototypes, while the entire history of the people of Israel, glorified in the light of Messianic hopes, was made a continual revelation of God's love and justice. For this reason the importance for modern Jewish science of the study of the Haggadah can not be overestimated.

Object of Haggadah.

The entire wealth of the haggadic Midrash has

been preserved in a series of very different works, which, like all the works of traditional literature, are the resultant of various collections and revisions, and the contents of all of which originated a long time before they were reduced to writing. The first traces of the midrashic exegesis are found in the Bible itself (see MIDRASH); while in the time of the Soferim the development of the Midrash Haggadah received a mighty impetus, and the foundations were laid for public services which were soon to offer the chief medium for the cultivation of Bible exegesis. Much Midrash Haggadah, often mixed with foreign elements, is found in the Apocrypha, the Pseudepigrapha, the works of Josephus and Philo, and the remaining Judæo-Hellenistic literature; but haggadic exegesis reached its highest development in the great epoch of the Mishnaic-Talmudic period, between 100 and 500 C.E., when all its different branches were fully worked out. The Haggadah of the Amoraim is the continuation of that of the Tannaim; and, according to Bacher, there really is no difference between the Amoraim and the Tannaim with reference to the Haggadah.

Development of Haggadah.

The final edition of the Mishnah, which was of such signal importance for the Halakah, is of less significance for the Haggadah, which, in form as well as in content, shows the same characteristics in both periods. It may be said in particular, that in the field of the Haggadah the century after the completion of the Mishnah may be fairly compared with the century before its completion, as regards not only the wealth of the extant material and the number of the authors to be considered, but also the independence and originality of the subject-matter treated (comp. Bacher, "Ag. Pal. Amor." vol. i., pp. viii. *et seq.*).

A story told in Yer. Hor. iii. 48b indicates the great extent of the haggadic exegesis and its general popularity at this time. When the aged Ḥanina b. Ḥama saw the people of Sepphoris flocking to the school of R. Benaiah, and heard that it was to hear R. Johanan deliver a discourse there, he exclaimed, "Praised be God that He permits me to behold the fruit of my labors during my lifetime. I have taught him the entire Haggadah, with the exception of that on Proverbs and Ecclesiastes." In another passage, in a conversation between the patriarch Judah I. and Ishmael b. Jose, the story is told of R. Ḥiyya, that, lost in thought, he read through the whole Book of Psalms from the haggadic standpoint (Yer. Kil. ix. 32b; Gen. R. xxxiii.). During the third and at the beginning of the fourth century the masters of Halakah were also the representatives of the Haggadah; but side by side with them appeared the haggadists proper ("rabbanan di-Agadta," "ba'ale Agada"), who subsequently became more and more prominent, attracting with their discourses more hearers than the halakists. The highest product of the Haggadah, the public discourse drawing upon all the arts of midrashic rhetoric—sentence, proverb, parable, allegory, story, etc.—now received its final form. The ancient sentence "We-kullehon yesh lahem miḳra we-yesh lahem mashal we-yesh lahem meliẓah" (For each of them there is Bible text, a proverb, and a saying; comp. Cant. R. i. 1) may be applied to these products of haggadic rhetoric. The epigoni of the Haggadah flourished in the fourth and at the beginning of the fifth century, and were followed by the anonymous haggadists who preserved and revised the immense haggadic material. Creative haggadic activity ceases with the end of the Talmudic period. The post-amoraic and the geonic period is the epoch of the collectors and revisers, during which the haggadic midrashim were reduced to writing, receiving the form in which they have been handed down more or less unchanged. Sometimes the results of the Midrash Haggadah—specific deductions on the one hand, general precepts, sentences, and maxims on the other, obtained by a study of the Biblical books from the religio-ethical or historical side, or by penetration into the spirit of Scripture—were collected in special works, forming special branches of the Haggadah, such as ethical Haggadah, historical Haggadah, Cabala, etc.

Divisions of Haggadah.

At other times single Scriptural interpretations, haggadic sentences, and stories of all kinds, which originated or were used in the course of some halakic discussion—and this was often the case—were included when that discussion was reduced to writing; and it is for this reason that the Mishnah, Tosefta, and both Talmuds contain so much haggadic material. Or, finally, the mass of haggadic matter was collected and edited in the exegetic midrashim proper—the midrashim par excellence, which formed either running haggadic commentaries to the single books of the Bible, or homiletic midrashim, consisting of discourses actually delivered on the Sabbath and festival lessons or of revisions of such discourses.

The following discussion of individual midrashic works will be restricted to the most important productions in the field of the Midrash Haggadah proper; for the ethical and historical Haggadah, and such as is included in halakic works, see ABOT; APOCALYPSE; APOCALYPTIC LITERATURE; APOCRYPHA; CABALA; DEREK EREẒ RABBAH; ETHICS; etc. Similarly, as regards the Targumim containing or reflecting the Midrash Haggadah, reference must be made to the articles on the various targumim. It may be regarded as characteristic of the midrashim proper that they are anonymous—that is, the name of the editor who made the final revision is unknown; accordingly, haggadic works whose authors are known (*e.g.*, R. Tobias b. Eliezer's "Leḳaḥ Ṭob"; R. Menahem b. Solomon's "Sekel Ṭob"), and the haggadic commentaries of a later period, such as that published by Buber under the title "Midrash Agada" (Vienna, 1894), must likewise be excluded from this review. Haggadic exegesis was, as mentioned above, assiduously cultivated in the period of its florescence by the most eminent rabbis, some of whom are praised in particular as being "learned in the Haggadah" ("baḳi ba-Agada"); and it became a special branch of traditional science for the "scholars of the Haggadah" ("rabbanan di-Agadta").

Students of the Haggadah.

It was the subject of study in the schools and furnished an inexhaustible supply of material for the sermons and discourses which were delivered on Sabbaths and feast-days, and which followed the Scripture lesson and formed a part of public worship, or could be separated from it at need. Opportunity, moreover, often arose, both on joyous and on sad occasions, to resort to haggadic expositions for words of comfort or of blessing, for farewell discourses, etc.

References to the arrangement of the Haggadah, to connected haggadic discourses, to the writing down of single haggadic sentences, and even to books of the Haggadah, are extant even from early times. Thus R. Simon b. Pazzi was an editor of the Haggadah ("mesadder Agadta") during the time of R. Joshua b. Levi (comp. Ber. 10a). The latter, a Palestinian amora of the first half of the third century, who was also a famous haggadist, was the author of the sentence explaining the phrase "works of God" in Ps. xxviii. 5 as referring to the haggadot (Midr. Teh. *ad loc.*); he, as well as his pupil R. Ḥiyya b. Abba, severely censures the reducing of haggadot to writing and the use of written haggadot, for it was in general considered that the prohibition against writing down the "words of the oral law" referred not only to halakot, but also to haggadot; for the latter in particular might be the expression of private opinions and interpretations which, not being under control of the schools, were likely to lead to abuses. The severity of this censure indicates that it was not a question of writing down single haggadot merely. R. Joshua b. Levi himself says that he once looked into a haggadic work ("sifra di-Agadta"), and he quotes numerical interpretations therefrom (Yer. Shab. xvi. 15c; Soferim xvi.); a "Haggadah-book of the school" is mentioned by R. Jacob bar Aḥa, the contemporary of Judah I. (Sanh. 57b); and it is said of R. Johanan and R. Simeon b. Laḳish, the contemporaries of R. Joshua b. Levi, that they read a Haggadah-book on the Sabbath. They regarded such collections as demanded by the times, and paraphrasing Psalm cxix. 126 they declared that it were better to repeal an interdiction (*i.e.*, that against writing down the oral law, which they referred to the Haggadah) than to allow the Torah to be forgotten in Israel (Giṭ. 60a; Tem. 14b).

R. Johanan, who always carried a Haggadah with him, is the author of the saying, "A covenant has been made: whoever learns the Haggadah from a book does not easily forget it" (Yer. Ber. v. 9a). There are other scattered allusions to haggadic works in Talmudic-midrashic literature. There must also have been collections of legends and stories, for it is hardly conceivable that the mass of haggadic works should have been preserved for centuries by word of mouth only. These scattered allusions merely show, however, that the beginnings of the written Haggadah date very far back; very little is known of the nature of the old Haggadah-books, and it is impossible to determine what traces they left in the old Midrash literature. Much material from the various early midrashic collections, which gradually increased in numbers, was doubtless incorporated in the exegetic midrashim which have been preserved; and the latter clearly indicate the nature of the early exegesis, the "manner of discourse of antiquity"; but only the herein mentioned tannaitic midrashim—the Mekilta, Sifre, and Sifra, containing Haggadah mixed with Halakah—date in their earliest component parts from the second century, having been definitively edited in the post-tannaitic time. The purely haggadic-exegetic midrashim were edited at a much later time, after the completion of the Talmud. One may, as Bacher says, "speak in a certain sense of the completion of the haggadic Midrash as one speaks of the completion of the Talmud, although the works belonging to this class continued to be produced for five centuries or more after that time."

It is of the utmost importance, in considering the several midrash works, to emphasize the fundamental difference in plan between the midrashim forming a running commentary to the Scripture text and the homiletic midrashim. In order to avoid repetitions later on, brief reference must here be made to the connection of the midrashic homilies with the Scripture lessons, which were delivered at the public worship on the Sabbath and on feast-days after the Sedarim and Pesiḳta cycle; to the structure of the homilies; to the nature of the proems which occupy such an important position in the entire midrash literature; to the halakic exordia, the formulas, etc.

Exegetic and Homiletic Midrash.

When the scholars undertook to edit, revise, and collect into individual midrashim the immense haggadic material of centuries, they followed the method employed in the collections and revisions of the halakot and the halakic discussions; and the one form which suggested itself was to arrange in textual sequence the exegetical interpretations of the Biblical text as taught in the schools, or the occasional interpretations introduced into public discourses, etc., and which were in any way connected with Scripture; and since the work of the editor was often merely that of compilation, the existing midrashim betray in many passages the character of the sources from which they were taken. This was the genesis of the midrashim which are in the nature of running haggadic commentaries to single books of the Bible, as Bereshit Rabbah, Ekah Rabbati, the midrashim to the other Megillot, etc.

But even the earliest of these works, Bereshit Rabbah, is essentially different in its composition from the tannaitic midrashim in that the several "parashiyyot" (sections) are introduced by proems. These are characteristic of a different class of midrashim, the homiletic, in which entire homilies and haggadic discourses as delivered during public worship or in connection with it were collected and edited, and which accordingly do not deal in regular order with the text of a book of the Bible, but deal in separate homilies with certain passages, generally the beginnings of the lessons. These lessons were either the pericopes of the Pentateuch divided according to the three-year cycle-reading of the Torah as customary in Palestine and on which the division of the Pentateuch into from 154 to 175 "sedarim" is based, or the Pentateuchal and prophetic sections as assigned in accordance with the Pesiḳta cycle to the various feast-days and special Sabbaths (*e.g.*, the Sabbaths of mourning and of comforting from the 17th of Tammuz to the end of the Jewish calendar year). These may be designated respectively as **sedarim homilies** and as **pesiḳta homilies.** The Sedarim homilies are the homilies to the pericopes of the Sedarim cycle—of which one has been preserved in the Tanḥuma Midrashim, although it is not a collection to the entire cycle, *i.e.*, to the entire Pentateuch—and to individual books of the Pentateuch in Shemot Rabbah (in part), Wayiḳra Rabbah, Bemidbar Rabbah (beginning with ch. xv.), Debarim Rabbah, etc. The Pesiḳta homilies are the homilies to the Scripture sections according to the Pesiḳta cycle, as found in the Pesiḳta edited by Solomon Buber and in the Pesiḳta Rabbati: the designation is applied also to the homilies on lessons of the Pesiḳta cycle in the Tanḥumas and other Pentateuch midrashim. In brief, the arrangement and division of the Pentateuch midrashim, with the exception of Bereshit Rabbah, it is generally recognized, is based on the Palestinian three-year cycle, with the sedarim of which its sections correspond almost throughout. These midrashim therefore contain homilies to the Sabbath lessons of the three-year cycle together with a number of homilies intended for the feast-days and Sabbaths of the Pesiḳta cycle (Theodor, in "Monatsschrift," 1885, pp. 356 *et seq.*).

Sedarim and Pesikta Homilies.

The sedarim and pesiḳta homilies are clear and comprehensive in structure, although this may not be recognized in the midrash editions, in which the homilies are often not properly arranged. In the Pesiḳta, Wayiḳra Rabbah, etc., the homilies begin with several proems; in the Tanḥumas (with considerable differences in various parts and in the different recensions), the Pesiḳta Rabbati, Debarim Rabbah, and Bemidbar Rabbah, a halakic exordium more or less systematically precedes the proems. The latter are followed by the exposition proper, which, however, covers only a few of the first verses of the Scripture lesson; the first verse (or the first part thereof) of the lesson is generally discussed more fully than the remaining verses. The homilies generally close with verses from the Bible prophesying Israel's auspicious future. This is the common form of the homilies in all the homiletic midrashim; it allows, however, of the utmost freedom of treatment and execution in its various parts. The proems, which are the clearest evidence of the existence of a deliberate technical arrangement in the haggadic midrashim, constitute both in name ("petiḥah") and in nature an introduction to the exposition of the lesson proper; to this, however, they lead up by means of the interpretation of an extraneous text, the proemial text, which must not be taken from the lesson itself; and the proems may be as different in structure and finish as in contents. The proems are either simple, consisting of a simple exposition of the proem-text, often amplified by quotations, parables, etc., and connected throughout, or at least at the end, with the lesson or with the initial verse thereof, or composite (see Jew. Encyc. iii. 62, *s.v.* Bereshit Rabbah), consisting of different interpretations of the same extraneous verse, by one or by various authors, and connected in various ways, but always of such a nature that the last interpretation, the last component part of the proem, leads to the interpretation of the lesson proper. The direct transition from the proem to the lesson is often made by means of a formula common to all the proems of the homily, wherewith the proem is brought to a logical and artistic conclusion. Exegetic material for use in the proems, especially the composite ones, which are often very extensive, was always at hand in abundance; and the art of the haggadist appeared in the use he made of this material, in the interesting combination, grouping, and connection of the several sentences and interpretations into a uniform structure so developed that the last member formed the fitting introduction to the exposition of the lesson proper. There are many formulas ("Ketib," "Hada hu di-ketib" [הה ד], "Zeh she-amar ha-katub" [זש"ה]) with which the proem-text is introduced, which may, however, also appear without formula, as often in Bereshit Rabbah and in the Pesiḳta; and the final formulas, which frequently are very rigid in form, as in the Pesiḳta, are likewise very numerous.

The Proems.

The various midrash works are differentiated by the relation of the simple to the compound proems—the structure of the latter, their development into more independent haggadic structures, the use of the various formulas, etc. By the method of selecting extraneous texts for the proems so many non-Pentateuchal, especially Hagiographic, verses were expounded, even in early times, in the proems to the Pentateuch homilies and interpretations, that these homilies became mines for the collectors of the non-Pentateuch midrashim. Many extensive interpretations which are found in connection with Scripture passages in those midrashim are merely proems from various homilies, as often appears clearly in the final proem-formulas retained. In such cases these formulas offer the surest criterion for proving the dependence of one midrash upon another. While proems are characteristic of all the homiletic midrashim—and it was due to the popularity of this form of the old homilies that proems were added also to the parashiyyot of the Bereshit Rabbah, although this old midrash is a running commentary on the Scripture text—yet the practise of prefacing the haggadic discourse with the discussion of a simpler halakic question is observed only in a part of those midrashim. The halakic exordium begins in the Tanḥumas with the words, "Yelammedenu rabbenu" (Let our teacher teach us). This formula gave rise to the name "Yelammedenu," by which this midrash and an earlier version of it were frequently designated; the same formula occurs in the Pesiḳta Rabbati. In Debarim Rabbah the word "halakah" is used, the question proper beginning in most of the exordia with "Adam mi-Yisrael." The word "halakah" instead of the formula "yelammedenu rabbenu" is used also in the part of Bemidbar Rabbah which is derived from the Tanḥuma. The interpretations which follow the proems and the halakic exordium in the halakic midrashim are confined, as mentioned above, to some of the first verses of the lesson.

In some homilies the proems are equal in length

to the interpretations proper, while in others they are much longer. Even if the editors of the midrashim combined the proems of different authors from the various homilies they had at hand, it yet seems strange that they should have been able to select for each homily several proems, including some very long ones, while they could find only a limited number of interpretations to the lessons, these interpretations, furthermore, covering only a few verses. The disproportion between the proems and the interpretations has not yet been satisfactorily explained, in spite of various attempts to do so.

The character of the exposition in the exegetic midrashim like Bereshit Rabbah has been discussed in Jew. Encyc. iii. 63, *s.v.* Bereshit Rabbah.

Character of Exegesis.

Here the literal and textual explanation is not yet in contrast to the Midrash Haggadah, as it often was in the time of the scientific exegesis. The old midrash contains many Scriptural interpretations which are exegetic in the truest sense of the word, affording a deep insight into the contemporary attitude toward the Scripture. But the haggadic midrash is the well-spring for exegesis of all kinds, and the simple exposition of Scripture is more and more lost in the wide stream of free interpretation which flowed in every direction.

Zunz has divided the Haggadah into three groups, following the old designations which were subsequently summed up in the word פרד"ס: (1) interpretation of the Scripture text according to its literal meaning; (2) development of the thought in any desired form, with a free use of the text; (3) discussion of the mysteries of religion and the supersensuous worlds (comp. "G. V." p. 59). The words of Zunz, the master of midrash study, in his chapter "Organismus der Hagada," may serve to close the first, general part of the present survey: "Definite rules were as impossible for this exegesis as rules of rhetoric for the Prophets; the thirty-two 'middot' postulated by Eliezer ha-Gelili were in part categories deduced from former works, which remained unobserved in the later Haggadah, and in part merely sentences given for the purpose of determining the literal meaning, and not intended to be applied in haggadic exegesis. For the power of this exegesis lay not in literal interpretation and in natural hermeneutics, . . . but in the unhampered application of the contents of the Bible to contemporary views and needs; everything that was venerated and beloved by the present generation was connected with the sacred though limited field of the past. This method of free exegesis was manifested in many ways: the obvious sense of the Biblical passage was followed; or the inner meaning of the text, to the exclusion of the literal sense, was considered; or recourse was had to the traditional haggadah (מסורת אגדה); or the results of the Masorah were taken into account. . . . But this liberty wished neither to falsify Scripture nor to deprive it of its natural sense, for its object was the free expression of thought, and not the formulation of a binding law" ("G. V." pp. 325 *et seq.*).

Bibliography: Zunz, *G. V.* Berlin, 1832 (the basic work for the study of the midrash literature); Weiss, *Dor*, ii. 200 *et seq.*, iii. 252 *et seq.*; Bacher, *Ag. Tan.* i. 451-475; idem, *Ag. Pal. Amor.* i., pp. vii. *et seq.*; iii. 500-514; Theodor, *Zur Composition der Agadischen Homilien*, in *Monatsschrift*, 1879; idem, *Die Midraschim zum Pentateuch und der Dreijährige Palästinische Cyclus*, in *Monatsschrift*, 1885-1887; Bloch, *Studien zur Aggadah*, ib. 1885.

A. Midrash Haggadah in the Tannaitic (Halakic-Haggadic) Midrashim — Mekilta, Sifra, and Sifre. For the name, composition, origin, and edition of these midrashim see special articles and Midrash Halakah.

1. The Mekilta: The Midrash to Exodus generally known under this name, and which originated in R. Ishmael's school, begins with Ex. xii., the first legal section in the book—on the Passover and the institution of the Passover festival. The exegesis is continued, with the omission of a few verses, down to xxiii. 19, the end of the principal laws dealt with in the book, to which are added two shorter passages on the law referring to the Sabbath—xxxi. 12-17 and xxxv. 1-3. It appears from this that the editor of the Mekilta intended to compile a halakic midrash. But as the exegesis is in the nature of a running commentary to these passages without regard to whether the subject under discussion is legal or historical in nature, and as much haggadic matter is mingled with the halakic interpretations, it appears from a comparison of all the haggadic passages with the halakic passages that the larger part of the Mekilta is really haggadic in nature; *e.g.*, nearly one-half of the exegesis in Bo to Ex. xii. 1 *et seq.* is haggadic. Beshallaḥ (ed. Friedmann, pp. 23b-56b) is, with a few exceptions, haggadic throughout; so is nearly the whole of Yitro (pp. 56b-74a), with the exception of a few verses, where even the exposition of the Decalogue contains only a small amount of halakic matter. But Mishpaṭim throughout and the exegesis of xxxi. 12 *et seq.* and xxxv. 1 *et seq.* are halakic, including only a few haggadic interpretations. (The Mekilta is divided not according to the Biblical pericopes, but into massektot and parashiyyot.) The following are simple exegetic explanations such as frequently precede the haggadic elaboration. To xiii. 17: נחם has only the meaning "to lead" (not "to comfort"), like נחית in Ps. lxxvii. 21 and וינחם in Ps. lxxviii. 14. To xiii. 18: וחמשים means "armed" (comp. Josh. i. 14), or ("dabar aḥar") "equipped" (comp. *ib.* iv. 12), or "one out of five," or, according to others, "one out of fifty." To xiii. 20: סכת is the name of a place, like איתם; R. Akiba says, "סכת means the clouds of the glory of God [which surrounded them like a hut]," etc. To xiv. 7: ושלישים means "heroes" (comp. Ezek. xxiii. 23 *et seq.*). To xiv. 8: "And the children of Israel went ביד רמה" denotes that they went with uncovered heads (*i.e.*, as free men), or that the power of Israel was above that of Egypt. To xiv. 27: איתנו means "his strength" (comp. Num. xxiv. 21). To xiii. 19: פקד יפקד is interpreted homiletically as referring to both past and future: "God remembered you in Egypt, He will remember you at the Red Sea; He remembered you by the sea, He will remember you also in the desert; He remembered you in the desert, He will remember you also by the brook of Arnon; He remembered you in this world, He will remember you also in the future world." The editor of the Mekilta had such a wealth of haggadic material at his disposal that he was enabled to compile entire parashiyyot to single verses, as to xiv. 15 and xv. 1 (two parashiyyot); xv. 2, 11; xx. 2. See MEKILTA.

Two passages may be translated here as specimens of the haggadah of the Mekilta:

To Ex. xvii. 11: *And it came to pass, when Moses held up his hand, that Israel prevailed: and when he let down his hand Amalek prevailed.* Did the hands of Moses help Israel to victory or did they destroy Amalek? Neither; but as long as he pointed his hand upward [heavenward] the Israelites looked up to and believed in Him who had commanded Moses to do thus, and the Holy One, praised be He, vouchsafed to them marvels and victory (comp. R. H. iii. 8). Similarly: "And the Lord said unto Moses, Make thee a fiery serpent" [Num. xxi. 8]. Can the serpent kill and make alive again? No; but so long as Moses did thus, the Israelites looked upon it and believed in Him who had thus commanded Moses, and the Holy One, praised be His name, gave them healing. Similarly: "And the blood shall be to you for a token . . . " [Ex. xii. 13]. R. Eliezer said: "What mean the words, 'And Israel prevailed,' or 'And Amalek prevailed'? So long as Moses kept up his hand he reminded Israel that they would be victorious through the word of the Torah, which was to be revealed by him."

To Ex. xx. 17 *et seq.* (conclusion of the Decalogue): In what way were the Ten Commandments given? Five on one table and five on the other. There it is written: "I am the Eternal One, thy God," and opposite to it, "Thou shalt not kill." Scripture teaches that the person who sheds blood lessens the image of the King [the prototype of God for man]: simile of an earthly king who came into a province and erected statues and images, and minted coins; subsequently he overturned the statues, broke the images, destroyed the coins, and lessened the image of the king. Similarly, the person who sheds blood is adjudged to have lessened the image of the king, for it is written: "Whoso sheddeth man's blood, by man shall his blood be shed; for in the image of God made he man" [Gen. ix. 6]. It is written, "Thou shalt have no other gods," and opposite to it, "Thou shalt not commit adultery." Scripture teaches that whosoever practises idolatry is adjudged to have committed adultery behind God's back, as it is written, "A wife that committeth adultery, which taketh strangers instead of her husband . . . " [Ezek. xvi. 32]. It is written, "Thou shalt not take the name of the Lord thy God in vain," and opposite to it, "Thou shalt not steal." Scripture teaches that whosoever steals will finally swear falsely also, as it is written, "Will ye steal, murder, and commit adultery, and swear falsely?" [Jer. vii. 9]. It is written, "Remember the Sabbath, to keep it holy," and opposite to it, "Thou shalt not bear false witness." Scripture teaches that whosoever desecrates the Sabbath testifies that God did not create the world and rest on the seventh day; but whosoever keeps the Sabbath testifies that God created the world in six days and rested on the seventh, as it is written, "Therefore ye are my witnesses, saith the Lord" [Isa. xliii. 12]. It is written, "Honor thy father and mother," and opposite to it, "Thou shalt not covet." Scripture teaches that whosoever lusteth will finally beget a son who will curse his father and mother and will honor him who does not honor his father. Therefore the Ten Commandments were given, five on one table and five on the other. This is the view of R. Ḥanina b. Gamaliel. The sages say: "Ten were on one table and ten on the other."

2. The Sifra: The Sifra, or **Torat Kohanim,** originating in the school of R. Akiba, with additions belonging in part to the school of R. Ishmael, and finally edited by R. Ḥiyya, "provides, in so far as it has been preserved intact, the text of the Book of Leviticus with a running halakic commentary which explains or turns almost every word into a source for a halakic maxim" (Hoffmann, "Zur Einleitung in die Halachischen Midraschim," p. 21). It contains only a small proportion of haggadic matter, of which the most significant parts are to Lev. viii. 1-x. 7 (on the dedication of the Tabernacle; ed. Weiss, pp. 40c–46b), to Lev. xviii. 1-5 (*ib.* pp. 85c–86d), to some verses in the beginning of the pericope "Ḳedoshim" (Lev. xix. 1-3, 15-18), to Lev. xxii. 32 *et seq.*, to the blessings and punishments announced in Lev. xxvi. 3-46 (*ib.* pp. 110c–112c). The following is a translation of the important passage, to Lev. xix. 17-18, containing Akiba's and Ben 'Azzai's sentences on the fundamental principle of Judaism:

Thou shalt not hate thy brother. One might take this to mean, Thou shalt not curse him, nor strike him, nor box his ears; therefore it is written, "in thy heart," which indicates that here merely such hatred as is harbored in silence is meant. And wherefore does it follow that when you have reproved him four or five times you shall continue to reprove him? Because it is written הוכח תוכיח. This might be taken to mean in case you reprove him and his countenance changes [shows shame]. Therefore it is written, "that thou sin not on his account." R. Ṭarfon said, "By worship! [*i.e.*, "by God"] there is no one in our time who is able to reprove." R. Eleazar b. Azariah said, "By worship! there is no person in our time who would accept a reproof." R. Akiba said, "By worship! there is no one in our time who understands how to reprove." R. Johanan b. Nuri said, "I call heaven and earth to witness that Akiba was lashed by R. Gamaliel more than four or five times because I complained of him. And yet I know that he loved me all the more on that account."

Thou shalt not take vengeance. What is meant by taking vengeance? When one person says to another, "Lend me your sickle," and he will not lend it; then on the following day the latter says to the former, "Lend me your ax," whereupon he replies, "I will not lend it to you because you would not lend me your sickle."

Thou shalt not be resentful. What is meant by being resentful? When one person says to another, "Lend me your ax," and he will not lend it; then on the following day the latter says to the former, "Lend me your sickle," whereupon he says, "Here it is; I am not like you, who refuses to lend me your ax." Therefore is it written, "Thou shalt not take vengeance," and "Love thy neighbor as thyself." R. Akiba says, "This is the great principle in the Torah." Ben 'Azzai says, "'This is the book of the generations of man' [Gen. v. 1, Hebr.], which is a still greater principle."

3. Sifre to Numbers: Sifre to Numbers and Deuteronomy is not, as it exists in current editions and as it was formerly considered, a uniform work, but is in both of its parts a combination of two midrashim of different character and different origin. Sifre to Numbers is in its main part a midrash of the school of R. Ishmael, like the Mekilta (comp. Hoffmann, *l.c.* p. 52). Beginning with ch. v. 1, it forms a running halakic commentary down to vi. 21; then it goes on to viii. 1-4, 23-26; ix. 1-14; x. 1-10; xv. 1-40; xviii. 1-32; xix. 1-22; xxvi. 52-56; xxvii. 8-11; xxviii. 1 *et seq.*; xxx. 2-17; xxxi. 17-20, 22-24; xxxv. 9-33. Haggadic are the comments to vi. 22-27 (priest's blessing); vii. 1-18, 84-89 (presents and sacrifices of princes); x. 9, 10, 29-34 (on Hobab), 35 *et seq.* (ויהי בנסע); xi. 1-xii. 16 (on the complaints of Miriam, Aaron, and the people against Moses); xv. 41 *et seq.*; xxv. 1 *et seq.* (Israel's sojourn in Shittim), 12 *et seq.*; xxvii. 1-7 (on the daughters of Zelophehad), 12-25 (command given to Moses to go up into Mount Abarim, etc.); xxxi. 1-16 (campaign against Midian), 21. It appears from this list that many passages are not commentated in Sifre to Numbers (*i.e.*, the beginning down to iv. 49; vii. 19-83; viii. 5-22; ix. 15-23; x. 11-28; xxv. 14-19; xxvi. 1-51, 57-65; xxix. 1-11, 14-34; xxxi. 25-xxxii. 41; xxxiii. 1-xxxv. 8; xxxvi. 1-43); nor is there, strangely enough, any haggadic treatment in this midrash to the long historical passages relating to the sending out of the spies (xiii. and xiv.), to the revolt of Korah, with its consequences (xvi. and xvii.), to all the historical matter in pericope חקת beginning with xx. 1, and to the story of Balak and Balaam (xxii. 2-xxiv. 25). It is possible that Sifre to Numbers has not been handed down in its complete form, or that the collector did not have access to haggadic material for all passages. Some passages of the comment on the priest's blessing (vi. 22 *et seq.*) may be quoted:

The Lord bless thee [with goods] and keep thee [in their possession]. R. Nathan says, "May He bless thee with goods and protect thee in thy body." R. Isaac says, "May He protect thee from the evil impulse, as it is written, 'For the Lord shall be thy confidence, and shall keep thy foot from being taken'" [Prov. iii. 26]. Another explanation ("dabar aḥar"): And may He so protect thee that others shall have no power over thee, as it is written, "The sun shall not smite thee by day nor the moon by night" [Ps. cxxi. 6]; and it is written, "Behold, he that keepeth Israel shall neither slumber nor sleep" [*ib.* 4]; and it is written, "The Lord is thy keeper: the Lord is thy shade upon thy right hand" [*ib.* 5]; and it is written, "The Lord shall keep thee from all evil" [*ib.* 7]; and it is written, "The Lord shall keep thy going out and thy coming in" [*ib.* 8]. Another explanation: May He protect thee from all demons, as it is written, "For he shall give his angels charge over thee, to keep thee in all thy ways" [Ps. xci. 11]. Another explanation: He shall protect thee, He shall keep the covenant of thy fathers, as it is written, "The Lord thy God shall keep unto thee the covenant and the mercy which he sware unto thy fathers" [Deut. vii. 12]. Another explanation: He shall protect thee, He shall keep for thee the end [*i.e.*, of sorrows, the time of redemption], as it is written, "The burden of Dumah [Edom]. He calleth to me out of Seir, Watchman, what of the night? . . . The watchman said, The morning cometh, and also the night" [Isa. xxi. 11 *et seq.*].

Another explanation: He shall protect thee: He shall protect thy soul in the hour of death, as it is written, "But the soul of my Lord shall be bound in the bundle of life" [I Sam. xxv. 29]. One might think that this applied to sinners as well as to the pious, therefore it is written: "The souls of thy enemies, them shall he sling out, as out of the middle of a sling" [*ib.*]. Another explanation: He shall keep thee: He shall keep thy foot from hell, as it is written, "He will keep the feet of his saints" [I Sam. ii. 9]. Another explanation: He will keep thee in this world, as it is written, "But they that wait upon the Lord shall renew their strength; they shall mount up with wings as eagles" [Isa. xl. 31].

The Lord make his face shine upon thee. May He open thy eyes. R. Nathan says, "That is, the light of the Shekinah, as it is written, 'Arise, shine; for thy light is come; . . . for, behold, the darkness shall cover the earth, and gross darkness the people: but the Lord shall arise upon thee' [Isa. lx. 1-2]; and as it is written, 'God be merciful unto us, and bless us; and cause his face to shine upon us' [Ps. lxvii. 2 (A. V. 1)]; and as it is written, 'God is the Lord, which hath shewed us light' [Ps. cxviii. 27]. Another explanation: May He give light—that is, the light of the Torah, as it is written, 'For the commandment is a lamp; and the Law is light'" [Prov. vi. 23].

The Lord be gracious unto thee (ויחנך) in thy wishes, as it is written, "[I] will be gracious to whom I will be gracious" [Ex. xxxiii. 19]. Another explanation: May He grant thee favor (חנך) in the eyes of the people, as it is written, "But the Lord was with Joseph, and shewed him mercy, and gave him favor in the sight of the keeper of the prison" [Gen. xxxix. 21]. Another explanation: May He favor thee with knowledge, insight, understanding, good conduct, and wisdom. Another explanation: May He show favor to thee and give thee grace (יחנך) by the study of the Torah, as it is written, "She shall give to thine head an ornament of grace [חן]," and "For they shall be an ornament of grace unto thy head, and chains about thy neck" [Prov. iv. 9 and i. 9].

4. Sifre to Deuteronomy: This Sifre is as fragmentary in regard to the haggadah as Sifre to Numbers, and leads to the same conclusions arrived at regarding the latter midrash. The haggadah constitutes about four-sevenths of the Sifre to Deuteronomy, and is divided into two groups, which include between them the halakic exposition. This midrash therefore consists of three parts: (1) the first haggadic part to i. 1–30, iii. 23–29, vi. 4–9, xi. 10–32; (2) the halakic exposition to Deut. xii. 1 (in pericope ראה)–xxvi. 15 (in pericope תבוא); (3) second haggadic part to xxxi. 14 (beginning of the seder according to the seder cycle), xxxii. and xxxiii. (the sedarim and pericopes האזינו and וזאת הברכה). Halakic matter is found also in the first haggadic part, especially to vi. 8 *et seq.* and xi. 13; similarly there are haggadic expositions in the halakic portion, as to xiii. 18–xiv. 2, xv. 4, xvii. 19, xviii. 12 *et seq.*, xx. 3 *et seq.*, xxiii. 5 *et seq.*, xxvi. 5 *et seq.* According to Hoffmann's investigations the middle halakic portion is a midrash of R. Akiba's school, while the two haggadic portions belong to R. Ishmael's school. Following are translations of two passages:

Deut. xi. 13: *To love the Lord your God.* Perhaps thou sayest: I study the Torah that I may become rich and be called "rabbi," and receive reward. Therefore it is written, "to love the Lord your God; all that you do you shall do only for love [Hebr.]." *And to serve him.* That is, to study the Torah. Or is real work meant? It is written, "And the Lord God took the man, and put him into the garden of Eden to dress it and to keep it" [Gen. ii. 15]. What kind of work was there at that time, and what was there to keep? You conclude therefrom that "to dress" means "to learn," and "to keep" means "to observe the commandments"; and as the service at the altar is called "service," so learning is called a "service" [to God]. Another explanation: "To serve Him" refers to prayer. Thou sayest, Perhaps by "prayer" service is meant; and therefore it is written, "with all your heart." Is there then a service of the heart? When it is written, therefore, "and to serve him with all your heart," prayer is meant.

Deut. xi. 26: *Behold, I set before you this day a blessing and a curse.* Because it is written, "I have set before you life and death, blessing and cursing" [xxx. 19], the Israelites will perhaps say, Since God has shown us two ways, the way of life and the way of death, we will choose whichever way we please. Therefore it is written, "Therefore choose life, that both thou and thy seed may live" [*ib.*]. A man sat at a crossing, where two roads lay before him—one smooth in the beginning and full of thorns at the end, and one thorny at the beginning and smooth at the end; and he taught the travelers and said to them: "You see this path, which is smooth at the beginning? Two or three steps you will walk easily, and then you will come to thorns. You see that other path, full of thorns at the beginning? Two or three steps you will walk through thorns, and then you will reach the clear road." Thus Moses spake to Israel: "You see the sinners, that they are happy? Two or three days their happiness lasts in this world, but in the end they are cast out; as it is written, 'For there shall be no reward to the evil man' [Prov. xxiv. 20]; and as it is written, 'And behold the tears of such as were oppressed,' etc. [Eccl. iv. 1]; and as it is written, 'The fool foldeth his hands,' etc. [*ib.* iv. 5]; and as it is written, 'The way of the wicked is as darkness' [Prov. iv. 19]. You see the pious, how hard is their way in this world? For two or three days they toil, but finally they shall rejoice, as it is written, 'To do thee good at thy latter end' [Deut. viii. 16]; and as it is written, 'Better is the end of a thing than the beginning thereof' [Eccl. vii. 8]; and as it is written, 'For I know the thoughts that I think toward you' [Jer. xxix. 11]; and as it is written, 'Light is sown for the righteous' [Ps. xcvii. 11]; and as it is written, 'The path of the just is as the shining light'" [Prov. iv. 18]. R. Joshua b. Ḳarḥa said: "A king prepared a meal, and had invited all the guests; his friend sat among them, and thought to take a good portion, but he had no understanding. When the king saw that he had no understanding, he took his hand and laid it upon the good portion." Similarly it is written, "The Lord is the portion of mine inheritance and of my cup . . . The lines are fallen to me in pleasant places . . . I will bless the Lord, who hath given me counsel" [Ps. xvi. 5-7].

From quotations found in old authors and from longer extracts in the Yalḳuṭ and the Midrash ha-Gadol, three other tannaitic midrashim are known, namely, the Mekilta of R. Simeon to Exodus and Sifra Zuṭa to Numbers (both of R. Akiba's school) and the Mekilta to Deuteronomy (of R. Ishmael's school); probably they also contained much haggadic matter.

Bibliography: Zunz, *G. V.* pp. 46 *et seq.*, 84 *et seq.*; Z. Frankel, *Darke ha-Mishnah*, 1859, pp. 307 *et seq.*; Weiss, *Dor*, ii. 225 *et seq.*; Brüll, in *Grätz Jubelschrift*, pp. 179 *et seq.*; Hoffmann, *Zur Einleitung in die Halachischen Midraschim*; idem, *Likkute Mekilta*, in *Hildesheimer Jubelschrift*; idem, *Neue Collectaneen*; Lewy, *Ein Wort über die Mechilta des R. Simon*; Bacher, *Ag. Tan.* i. 235, ii. 78. See also the introductions to Weiss's edition of the *Sifra*, 1862, and to Friedmann's edition of the *Mekilta*, 1870. The review given above is based chiefly on Hoffmann's researches.

B. The Purely Haggadic Midrashim.—I. The Earliest Exegetical Midrashim—Bereshit Rabbah and Ekah Rabbati.

1. Bereshit Rabbah: This midrash, which occupies the first position among the midrashim in virtue of its age and importance, has been discussed in Jew. Encyc. iii. 62 *et seq.* As was said there, the opinion handed down by nearly all the old authors that R. Hoshaiah, an amora of the first generation, living in Palestine in the third century, was the author of Bereshit Rabbah, may be interpreted to mean that R. Hoshaiah was responsible for the work in its original form; as such it was a running commentary (a form that originated in the tannaitic time), collecting and combining, verse by verse, according to a certain system, the various comments to Genesis, and forming a necessary supplement to the tannaitic midrashim to the other books of the Pentateuch. That there had been no similar halakic-haggadic midrash to Genesis is likely because in the composition of the tannaitic midrashim, Mekilta, Sifra, etc., the collection of the halakic comments was probably the chief object in view, and Genesis contains only a small portion of legal matter. The tannaitic character of Bereshit Rabbah, as well as the antiquity of the sources it must have used, appears from the fact, among others, that it contains more than fifty controversies between R. Judah and R. Nehemiah. The author of the old Halakot Gedolot, furthermore, ranged Bereshit Rabbah with the tannaitic midrashim, Sifra, Sifre, and Mekilta. Bereshit Rabbah is entirely distinct in its composition from the other purely haggadic Pentateuch midrashim, like Wayiḳra Rabbah, the Tanḥumas, etc., which are homiletic midrashim, and do not comment upon the Scripture text consecutively; on the other hand, Bereshit Rabbah in certain respects differs also from most of the tannaitic midrashim—Mekilta, Sifre to Numbers, and Sifre to Deuteronomy—which are, as has been seen, fragmentary in execution, while Bereshit Rabbah is (with the exception of a few passages not adapted to haggadic treatment) a running commentary, verse by verse, on the Book of Genesis from beginning to end.

The chief difference in composition between the tannaitic midrashim and Bereshit Rabbah lies in the fact that the parashiyyot into which the latter is divided, begin, with a few exceptions, with proems, such as are always found at the beginning of the homilies collected in the homiletic midrashim. Bereshit Rabbah, therefore, presents a combination of the form of the running commentary with that of the homily complete in itself (Tanḥuma and Pesiḳta homilies). Although the original commentary on Genesis may have been divided into parashiyyot with rudimentary proems (see Bereshit Rabbah)—traces of such proems appear also in the tannaitic midrashim—yet the addition of the many artistic proems found in the existing form of the commentary was doubtless the work of a later time, when the Bereshit Rabbah received its present form. By the addition of a mass of haggadic material from the time of the Amoraim it became a large and important midrash to Genesis; and this was called "Bereshit Rabbah," perhaps, to distinguish it from the original form or from intermediate, but less comprehensive, amplifications.

Characteristics.

The date of the redaction of Bereshit Rabbah is difficult to determine exactly; but it is probably not much later than that of the Jerusalem Talmud. Zunz holds that it was collected and edited in the sixth century. The more recent conjecture, that it was not edited until the end of the seventh, or possibly not until the beginning of the second half of the eighth, century, can not be maintained. Even after the redaction many interpretations may have been added, and the proems increased in number and amplified; the midrash, beginning with the pericope "Wayishlaḥ," contains lengthy passages possessing the characteristics of the later Haggadah.

The editing of Bereshit Rabbah does not seem to have been entirely completed, as appears from the pericopes "Wayiggash" and "Wayeḥi" (for a further discussion of this subject, as well as for the number of the parashiyyot, their arrangement according to the open and closed sections in the Scripture text, and in part according to the beginnings of the sedarim, the proems, the character and extent of the exposition, etc., see Bereshit Rabbah). Attention has also been drawn to the disproportion between the extent of the parashiyyot which now form the pericope "Bereshit" of the midrash and the length of the remaining part of the work; that pericope alone constitutes more than one-fourth of the midrash and contains twenty-nine parashiyyot, several of which deal only with a few, and in some cases only with single, verses. This portion may have been taken from another and a larger haggadic work on Genesis that remained incomplete, and from which the midrash may have derived also the name "Bereshit Rabbah."

The designation "Rabbah" was then applied to the midrashim to the other books of the Pentateuch, as Wayiḳra Rabbah, Shemot Rabbah, etc., which were copied, with Bereshit Rabbah, even in (later) manuscripts, this collection then being called "Midrash Rabbot" (*i.e.*, "Midrash of the Rabbot"), to which the midrashim most in use during divine service—to Canticles, Ruth, Esther, Lamentations, and Ecclesiastes—were subsequently added. Thus the Venice edition of 1545, in which the midrashim to the Pentateuch and to the Five Rolls were for the first time printed together, has on the title-page of the first part the words "Midrash Rabbot 'al Ḥamishshah Ḥumshe Torah" (Midrash Rabbah to the Five Books of the Torah), and on that of the second part "Midrash Ḥamesh Megillot Rabbeta" (Midrash Rabbah of the Five Megillot). The editio princeps of the midrashim to the Pentateuch (Constantinople, 1512) begins with the words "Be-shem El atḥil Bereshit Rabba" (In the name of God I shall begin Bereshit Rabbah), and the title of the editio prin-

Title.

ceps of the midrashim to the Five Rolls (Pesaro, 1519) reads "Midrash Ḥamesh Megillot" (Midrash of the Five Megillot).

Still more inexact and misleading is the term "Midrash Rabbah to the Five Books of the Pentateuch and the Five Rolls," as found on the title-page of the two parts in the much-used Wilna edition. After Zunz, it is not necessary to point out that the Midrash Rabbah consists of ten entirely different midrashim. On the manuscript of the Bereshit Rabbah and some of the other rabbot to the Pentateuch see Theodor in "Monatsschrift," xxxvii. 170 *et seq.* To these must be added the manuscript of Bereshit Rabbah in MSS. Orient. 4°, No. 32, in the Landesbibliothek in Stuttgart. According to Solomon Schechter, there are not even six manuscripts of the rabbot to the Pentateuch and the Five Rolls in existence (comp. Midrash ha-Gadol, Preface, xi.). The following is an extract from the first proem of parashah 9 and the interpretations to Gen. i. 26, directed against the Christian view finding support for the doctrine of the Trinity in this passage, and other interesting interpretations showing the use of foreign words in Bereshit Rabbah; the text followed is that of Theodor's critical edition.

And God said, Let us make man, etc. R. Johanan quotes the verse אחור וקדם צרתני וגו' [Ps. cxxxix. 5] and says: "If man is worthy of it, he enjoys two worlds, as it is written, 'Thou hast made me for afterward [the future world] and for formerly [this world],' but if not, then he will have to give an accounting, as it is written, 'And [thou hast] laid thine hand upon me'" [*ib.*]. R. Jeremiah b. Eleazar said, "When the Holy One, praised be He, created the first man, He created him as a hermaphrodite [ἀνδρόγυνος], as it is written, 'Male and female created he them'" [Gen. v. 2]. R. Samuel b. Naḥman said, "When the Holy One, praised be He, created the first man, He created him with a double face [πρόσωπος], and then cut him into halves and gave him two backs, one here, the other there." [This coincides with Plato's doctrine that man was originally androgynous and had two faces; Philo also frequently expresses the view that the ideal man was born as a man-woman.] He was interrupted, "It is written there, 'And he took אחת מצלעותיו'" [Gen. ii. 21]. He answered, "It means one of his 'sides' [not ribs], as it is written, ולצלע המשכן" ['And for the second side of the tabernacle'; Ex. xxvi. 20]. R. Tanḥuma, in the name of R. Bene Benaiah and R. Berechiah and R. Eleazar, said, "He created him as a golem [Adam in the primal state], who reached from one end of the world to the other, as it is written, 'Thine eyes did see my substance'" [Ps. cxxxix. 16]. R. Joshua b. Nehemiah and R. Judah b. Simeon, in the name of R. Eleazar, said, "He created him so that he filled the whole world, from east to west [also reflecting a Philonic view], as it is written, 'Thou hast formed me אחור וקדם [= 'behind, *i.e.*, westward and eastward'], from north to south,' as it is written, 'From the one side of heaven unto the other'" [Deut. iv. 32]. R. Eleazar said, "אחור; *i.e.*, as the last one in the creation of the last [sixth] day; וקדם; *i.e.*, and the first in the creation of the last day." This corresponds with R. Eleazar's view, who said, "Let the earth bring forth the living creature [Gen. i. 24; this is said in connection with the creation of the sixth day], that is, the spirit of the first man." R. Simeon b. Laḳish said, "אחור; *i.e.*, as the last in the creation of the last day; וקדם; *i.e.*, and as the first one in the creation of the first day." This corresponds with R. Simeon b. Laḳish's view, who said, "And the spirit of God moved [Gen. i. 2], that is, the spirit of the first man," as it is written, "And the spirit of the Lord shall rest upon him," etc. [Isa. xi. 2]. R. Naḥman said, "As the last one after all the created works, and as the first one at the judgment" [compare Gen. vii. 23]. R. Samuel b. Tanḥuma said, "In praising the Lord also he comes last, as it is written, 'Praise ye the Lord from the heavens' [Ps. cxlviii. 1]; and then, 'Praise the Lord from the earth,' etc. [*ib.* verse 7]; and then, 'Kings of the earth,'" etc. [*ib.* verse 11]. R. Simlai said, "As he praises only after the animals and birds [comp. *ib.* verses 10, 11 *et seq.*], so he was created after the animals and birds; first [it is written] 'And God said: Let the waters bring forth abundantly,' etc. [Gen. i. 20], and last, 'Let us make man,'" etc.

And God said, Let us make man, etc. With whom did He take counsel? R. Joshua b. Levi said, "He consulted the works of the heaven and the earth, like a king who has two counselors [σύγκλητος], without whose consent he does nothing." R. Samuel b. Naḥman said, "He took counsel with the work of every day of creation, like a king who has a coregent [συγκάθεδρος], without whose consent he does nothing." R. Ammi said, "He took counsel with his heart. . . ." R. Berechiah said, "When the Holy One, praised be He, was about to create the first man, He foresaw that both the pious and the wicked would descend from him. He said, 'If I create him, then the wicked will descend from him; if I do not create him, how can the pious descend from him?' What did the Holy One, praised be He? He removed the path of the sinner from His face, and created the attribute of mercy ["middat ha-raḥamim"], as it is written, 'The Lord knoweth [makes known] the way of the righteous; but the way of the ungodly shall perish'" [Ps. i. 6]. R. Ḥanina did not say thus, but: "When He was about to create the first man He took counsel with the angels. He said to them, 'Let us make man.' They said to Him: 'What is his nature?' He said to them, 'Righteous men shall descend from him. . . .' But He did not reveal to them that the ungodly should descend from him. For if He had revealed to them that the ungodly should descend from him, then the attribute of justice ['middat ha-din'] would not have consented that he should be created." R. Simeon said: "When the Holy One, praised be He, was about to create the first man the angels divided into groups; some of them said, 'Let him be created'; the others said, 'Do not let him be created, as it is written: "Mercy and truth are met together; righteousness and peace have kissed"' [Ps. lxxxv. 11]. Mercy said, 'Let him be created, for he will do works of mercy.' Truth said, 'Let him not be created, for he is full of deceit.' Benevolence said, 'Let him be created, for he will bestow benefits.' Peace said, 'Let him not be created, for he is full of quarrels.' What did the Holy One, praised be He? He took Truth and cast her upon the ground. Then the angels said, 'Lord of the World, why do you curse your Truth? Let Truth rise up from earth, as it is written, "Truth shall spring out of the earth"'" [*ib.* verse 12].

R. Huna the Elder of Sepphoris said, "While the angels were disputing and discussing with one another, the Holy One, praised be He, created him." R. Huna, in the name of R. Aibu, said, "He created him with circumspection, for He created first the things necessary for his life [the same thought and a parable similar to the following are found also in Philo]. Then the angels spoke before the Holy One, praised be He: 'Lord of the World, what is man that Thou art mindful of him? and the son of man that Thou visitest him? Why should this sorrow be created?' Then He said to them, 'Why have all sheep and oxen been created, the fowl of the air and the fish of the sea—why have these been created? A castle with all good things, and there are no guests; what pleasure has the owner who takes his fill?' Then the angels said, 'O Lord our Lord, how excellent is Thy name in all the earth! Do what seems best to Thee'" [Ps. viii. 5-10 (A. V. 4-9)]. R. Joshua of Shiknin, in the name of R. Levi, said, "He took counsel with the souls of the pious. . . ." R. Samuel b. Naḥman, in the name of R. Jonathan, said, "When Moses wrote down the Torah, he noted therein the creative work of each day; when he reached the verse, 'And God said, Let us make man,' he said, 'Lord of the World, why dost Thou give cause for attack to the "minim" [heretics]?' But He said to him, 'Write; let him err who will.' The Holy One, praised be He, said to him, 'Moses, shall I not produce great and small ones from the man whom I create? Then when the great one comes to ask permission from the small one, and says, "Why do I need to ask permission from the small one?" then the small one shall say to him, "Learn from thy Creator, who created the upper and the lower beings, and when He was about to create man took counsel with the angels!"'"

R. Liya said: "It is not the question here of taking counsel; it is as a king who, walking before the gate of the palace [παλάτιον], saw a block of stone [βυλάριον]. He said, 'What shall we do with this?' Some said, 'Use it for public baths [δημόσια]'; others said, 'Use it for private baths [πριουᾶτος].' But the king said, 'I will make a statue [ἀνδριάς] of it; who shall hinder me?'" The minim asked R. Simlai: "How many gods have created the world? What means בראשית ברא אלהים?" He answered, "It does not say בראו אלהים [the verb in the plural], but ברא אלהים." R. Simlai said, "Where you find a sentence for the minim, there you will find beside it its refutation." They asked him, further, "What means God by נעשה אדם?" Then he said to them, "Read what follows from it. It does not say ויבראו אלהים את האדם, but ויברא" [the verb in the singular; Gen. i. 27]. R. Hoshaiah said, "When the Holy One, praised be He, created the first man the angels erred and would have said before him 'Holy!' It is as a king who sat with a governor [ἔπαρχος] in a coach of state [καρροῦχα]. The people wished to cry 'Domine' before the king, but they did not know which was he. What did the king? He pushed the governor out of the coach, and then they recognized the king. So the angels erred when the Holy One, praised be He, created the first man. What did the Holy One, praised be He? He put him into a deep sleep [comp. Gen. ii. 21], and all then recognized that it was a man."

2. Ekah Rabbati: The midrash to Lamentations, one of the oldest Palestinian midrashim, has been discussed in Jew. Encyc. v. 85 *et seq.* Here it may briefly be repeated that Ekah Rabbati begins with a collection of thirty-six proems, which are followed by the commentary to Lamentations, verse by verse, together with numerous stories. The midrash has many parallel passages to Yerushalmi which were probably not taken directly from the latter, for old collections were probably the common source for Ekah Rabbati, Bereshit Rabbah, and the Pesiḳta. It may be assumed with certainty that Ekah Rabbati was edited some time after the final edition of Yerushalmi, and that Bereshit Rabbah also must be considered to be older, but it has been by no means proved, as Zunz assumes for various reasons, that the entire work was not finished before the second half of the seventh century. For all details, as well as for another midrash to Lamentations published by Buber in the Midrash Zuṭa, see Ekah Rabbati. The following is from the beginning of the exposition to Lam. i. 1, after the text of the Wilna (1899) edition of Buber (pp. 21a *et seq.*):

How [איכה = "Ekah"] *doth the city sit solitary.* Three prophets used the expression איכה in their prophecies—Moses, Isaiah, and Jeremiah. Moses said, "How can I myself alone bear . . ." [Deut. i. 12]; Isaiah said, "How is the faithful city become an harlot!" [i. 21]; Jeremiah said, "How doth sit solitary." R. Levi said: "It is like a noble woman [matron] who had three friends: one of them saw her in her honor; another saw her in her abandon; and the third one saw her in her sorrow. Moses saw them [the Israelites] in their honor [their happiness], and said, 'How can I myself alone bear'; Isaiah saw them in their abandon, and said, 'How is become a harlot'; Jeremiah saw them in their sorrow, and said, 'How doth sit solitary'" [R. Eleazar and R. Johanan interpreted איכה as two words—אי and כה]. R. Eleazar said, "Where [איה] is the 'so' [כה] which He spoke to Moses—'So shall thy seed be'" [Gen. xv. 5]; and R. Johanan said, "Where [איה] is the 'so' [כה] which He spake to Moses, 'Thus shalt thou say to the house of Jacob'" [Ex. xix. 3]. R. Judah and R. Nehemiah: R. Nehemiah said, "איכה is merely the expression for wailing, as it is written [Gen. iii. 9], 'And the Lord God called unto Adam and said unto him, איכה'" [interpreted as אוי לכה = 'wo unto thee']. R. Judah said, "איכה is the term for reproof, as it is written, 'How [איכה] do ye say, We are wise!'" [Jer. viii. 8]. Ben Azzai was asked, and they said to him, "Say to us a word concerning the Roll of Lamentations." He said to them [playing on the letters of the word איכה], "Israel went into exile only after it had denied the Only One of the world [א], the ten words [י], the circumcision which had been commended after twenty generations [*i.e.*, to Abraham, who lived twenty [כ] generations after Adam], and the five books [ה] of the Torah."

Doth sit solitary [בדד]. R. Berechiah, in the name of R. Abdima of Ḥaifa: "Like a king who had a son whom he arrayed in magnificent garments when he fulfilled the will of his father; but when the king was angry with him he let him wear soiled [בדוּרים] garments. So with Israel; as long as he fulfilled the will of God he was clothed magnificently, as it is written, 'I clothed thee also with רקמה'" [Ezek. xvi. 10]. R. Simlai said: "That is purple; Akylas translated it 'garments embroidered in colors [= ποικιλτά]'; but when they angered him he made them wear soiled garments." R. Joshua b. Levi said, "The Holy One, praised be He, said to Israel, 'So long as you did My will I allowed you to live secure, apart [בדד], as it is written, "Israel then shall dwell in safety alone" [Deut. xxxiii. 28]; but when you transgressed My will, then I banished you to unclean places, as it is written, "He [the leper] shall dwell alone [בדד]; without the camp shall his habitation be"'" [Lev. xiii. 46]. Why is the Roll of Lamentations composed according to the alphabet? In order that the lamenters may recite it fluently. Another explanation: I thought to bless you from "alef" to "taw," as it is written, "If [אם] you walk in my commandments . . . upright" [קוממיות, Lev. xxvi. 3-13; *i.e.*, this section, containing the divine blessings, begins with א, in the word אם, and ends with ת, in the word קוממיות]. When was the Roll of Lamentations recited? R. Judah says, "In the days of Jehoiakim." R. Berechiah b. Nehemiah said, "Do people weep for a person before he has died? It was rather written down in the days of Jehoiakim and recited after the destruction of the Temple."

II. The Homiletic Midrashim: As it is customary nowadays to distinguish between festival and Sabbath sermons, so in antiquity there were collections of homilies, haggadic discourses on the Scripture sections intended as lessons for the feast-days and special Sabbaths, as well as on the Sabbatical pericopes of the three-year cycle—either on the pericopes of the entire Pentateuch (hence covering the entire cycle) or on the pericopes from single books of the Pentateuch. Such collections are the Pesiḳta (erroneously ascribed to Rab Kahana, and called also "Pesiḳta de-Rab Kahana"), the Pesiḳta Rabbati, Wayiḳra Rabbah, the Tanḥuma Midrashim, Debarim Rabbah, Bemidbar Rabbah (beginning with parashah 15), Shemot Rabbah, etc. The nature of the homilies has been sketched above; they begin with several proems, to which is added the exposition, which generally covers only a few of the first verses and verse-texts of the lesson in question, ending with a Messianic or other comforting verse. The halakic exordium preceding the proems is peculiar to Tanḥuma, Pesiḳta Rabbati, Debarim Rabbah, and Bemidbar Rabbah (part ii.). The homilies in Wayiḳra have the same form as those in the Pesiḳta.

1. The Pesiḳta de-Rab Kahana: This Pesiḳta exists in only one edition, that of Solomon Buber (Lyck, 1868); it consists of 33 (or 35) homilies on the lessons forming the Pesiḳta cycle: the Pentateuchal lessons for special Sabbaths (Nos. 1-6) and for the feast-days (Nos. 7-12, 23, 27-32), the prophetic lessons for the Sabbaths of mourning and comforting (Nos. 13-22), and the penitential sections "Dirshu" and "Shubah" (Nos. 24, 25; No. 26 is a homily entitled "Seliḥot"). According to the arrangement in this edition the homilies fall into three groups: Pentateuchal, Prophetic, and Tishri, "pisḳot" (discourses on the lessons). An unnumbered "other pisḳah" to Isa. lxi. 10, after two manuscripts, is printed after No. 22; similarly No. 29, after a manuscript, is designated with No. 28 as "another pisḳah" for Sukkot, and the pisḳah on pp. 194b *et seq.*, recognizable as spurious by the halakic exordium, and also printed after a manuscript, is designated with No. 30 as another version of the pisḳah for Shemini. Pisḳot Nos. 12 and 32 each consist really of two homilies. But the second homily in No. 27 (pp. 174b *et seq.*) does not belong to the Pesiḳta.

The various manuscripts differ not only in regard to the above-mentioned second pisḳot and to other and longer passages, but also in regard to the arrangement of the entire collection, which began, in a manuscript which is defective at the beginning, with the homilies to prophetical lessons Nos. 13–22 and 24–25. These twelve homilies are designated by an old abbreviation as דש"ח נו"ע אר"ק שד"ש. Another manuscript, entitled "Hafṭarah Midrash," contains only these homilies, with the exception of next to the last one. Entire homilies of the Pesiḳta have been taken over, or sometimes worked over, into the Pesiḳta Rabbati; there are also a number of Pesiḳta homilies in the Tanḥuma Midrashim. Wayiḳra Rabbah also contains some of the homilies found in Pesiḳta. The parashiyyot 20, 27–30 in Wayiḳra Rabbah are, with the exception of a few differences, the same as pisḳot Nos. 27, 9, 8, 23, 28 of the Pesiḳta. Zunz takes the Pesiḳta to be dependent on Wayiḳra Rabbah, assigning this midrash to the middle of the seventh century, but the Pesiḳta to the year 700. Weiss, while emphasizing still more strongly the dependence of Pesiḳta on Wayiḳra Rabbah, takes it to be nearly as old as Bereshit Rabbah; he thinks that the Pesiḳta took for its sources Bereshit Rabbah, Wayiḳra Rabbah, Ekah Rabbah, and Shir ha-Shirim Rabbah. But other authorities regard the Pesiḳta as the earliest midrash collection.

Undoubtedly the Pesiḳta is very old, and must be classed together with Bereshit Rabbah and Ekah Rabbah. But the proems in the Pesiḳta, developed from short introductions to the exposition of the Scripture text into more independent homiletic structures, as well as the mastery of form apparent in the final formulas of the proems, indicate that the Pesiḳta belongs to a higher stage of midrashic development. The nature of certain Pentateuch lessons, intended apparently for the second feast-days (not celebrated in Palestine), still calls for investigation, as well as the question as to the time at which the cycle of the twelve prophetic lessons designated by דש"ח, etc., came into use; this cycle is not mentioned in Talmudic times, but is subsequently stated to have been ordained or prescribed in the Pesiḳta. For further details and quotations of passages see PESIḲTA.

2. Wayiḳra Rabbah: Wayiḳra Rabbah is generally classed among the oldest midrashim; it consists of thirty-seven parashiyyot and as many homilies, twenty-two of which belong to the Sabbath lessons of the sedarim cycle in the Book of Leviticus (according to various statements regarding this cycle), and five to feast-day lessons of the Pesiḳta cycle, taken from Leviticus. To certain of the lessons belong two homilies each: parashahs i. and ii. each contains a homily to Lev. i. 1; parashahs iv. and v. each one to Lev. iv. 1; and parashahs xx. and xxi. each one to the Pesiḳta lesson Lev. xvi. 1. As mentioned above, the five homilies on the feast-day lessons in parashahs xx., xxvii.–xxx. are identical with five pisḳot in the Pesiḳta. Buber, contrary to all manuscripts, has erroneously printed also Wayiḳra Rabbah, parashah xxi., as a continuation of pisḳah No. 27 (pp. 174b *et seq.*). The inclusion of the seven other parashiyyot may be due to another partly different arrangement of the sedarim cycle, just as there are, on the other hand, no homilies in Wayiḳra Rabbah to certain passages in Leviticus now known as commencements of sedarim. Wayiḳra Rabbah (section 3) contains an interesting statement in regard to the variations in the sedarim cycle and the general custom of introducing the exposition by a proem; R. Ḥanina b. Abba, when he came to a place where a pericope began with Lev. ii. 3, was asked which verse he used for the proem. The proems are more independent in structure, as in the Pesiḳta, with which Wayiḳra Rabbah has much in common regarding also the use of the final formulas for the proems.

The frequent use of proverbs ("be-matla amerin," "matla amer") is characteristic of this midrash: "If you have knowledge, what do you lack? If you lack knowledge, what do you possess?" (parashah i. 6). "Whoever lends on interest destroys his own and other property" (iii. 1). "She plays the coquette for apples, and divides among the sick" (*ib.*). "Whoever leases one garden eats birds; whoever leases two gardens is eaten by birds" (*ib.*). "Where the master hangs up his weapon there the common herdsman hangs up his water-jug" (iv. 1). "If one knot is unraveled, then two knots are unraveled" (xiv. 3). "Whoever eats palm-cabbage is wounded by the palm-thorn" (xv. 8). "Do not care for the good pup of a bad dog, much less for the bad pup of a bad dog" (xix. 6; comp. "Monatsschrift," 1881, p. 509). See WAYIḲRA RABBAH.

3. Tanḥuma Yelammedenu: While Wayiḳra Rabbah is a homily collection to a single book of the Pentateuch—Leviticus—the midrash Tanḥuma is a collection covering the entire Pentateuch, arranged according to the sedarim cycle, as appears from most of the Tanḥuma homilies which have been preserved; it contains also homilies to the feast-day and Sabbath lessons of the Pesiḳta cycle. The order of the Tanḥuma homilies is as follows: halakic exordium; several proems; exposition of the first verses; Messianic conclusion. The work derives its name "Yelammedenu" from the formula "Yelammedenu rabbenu" (Let our teacher teach us), with which the halakic exordium begins; it is generally cited under this name, especially in the "'Aruk." It is called "Midrash Tanḥuma" by many old authors. A number of its proems bear the name of R. Tanḥuma, and the sentence "Thus R. Tanḥuma expounded [or preached]" is added to several larger sections. The author of Yalḳuṭ Shim'oni, however, cites two midrash works, one under the title "Yelammedenu" and the other under that of "Tanḥuma." Furthermore, the midrash Tanḥuma, which has been frequently reedited since the Constantinople edition of 1520–22, and the midrash which Solomon Buber published in 1885 from manuscripts, in so far as the parts to Genesis and Exodus are concerned are seen to be special collections. Variations in text, evidence for which is furnished by the two editions mentioned, as well as by quotations and extracts found in many writings, and by the fact that the work is known under various titles, can not be explained by assuming that the different collections now possessed—to which must be added Debarim Rabbah—or those formerly used were different revisions and extracts from the "original" Yelammedenu.

If this mythical haggadic work was the common

source for such different collections, containing entirely different homilies to many of the lessons, it must have been very voluminous and heterogeneous. One is justified in assuming that even if the Yelammedenu had covered the entire Pentateuch it would have contained only one homily to each seder. But if the homilies consisting of halakic introductions, proems, and expositions to some verses be designated as typical Tanḥuma homilies, modeled on the form of the Tanḥuma Yelammedenu (for the increasing popularity of sermons must have given rise to a great number of such homilies), then the existence of collections of entirely different homilies, but modeled on this type and called "Tanḥuma midrashim," is easily explainable. Or perhaps works were compiled by omitting a number of homilies from an earlier collection (Yelammedenu) and adding others having the same form together with various other selections; instances of this kind can be seen in the parts to Genesis and Exodus in the extant two Tanḥuma midrashim. Bacher assumes ("Ag. Pal. Amor." iii. 502 *et seq.*) that R. Tanḥuma b. Abba, one of the foremost haggadists of the fourth century—of whom more proems have been preserved than of any other author and with whom the haggadic activity of Palestine was, in a sense, brought to an end—undertook to collect and edit the haggadic Scripture interpretations according to the pericopes, of both the sedarim and the Pesiḳta cycle; although the haggadic works he collected are no longer extant, the two pesiḳtot and the Tanḥuma midrashim were based on them. According to Bacher, these midrashim contain not only passages from the original Tanḥuma, but passages from the other midrashim to the Pentateuch and to the Five Rolls, even Bereshit Rabbah and Wayiḳra Rabbah having drawn directly or indirectly from the same source. This is a far-reaching hypothesis. Zunz believed that he "did not detract from the Yelammedenu" by assigning its author to the first half of the ninth century. This view can not now be accepted. According to Brull, the Yelammedenu was completed by the middle of the eighth century, and recognized as an authority, to which R. Aḥa of Shabḥa refers in the "She'eltot"; Brüll thinks it was "composed about 650–720" (Brüll's "Jahrb." viii. 127 *et seq.*). Yelammedenu is quoted as early as Saadia's time. The references to the rivers Tiber and Ticinus do not prove that the Tanḥuma was compiled in Italy.

Tanḥuma comprises 158 homilies in Buber's edition, and 161 in the other editions (in which it still shows in part the original division); Nos. 129 and 132 are homilies to the sedarim and the Pesiḳta cycle. The part to Deuteronomy has been preserved very imperfectly. Tanḥuma was divided according to the pericopes of the one-year cycle when that cycle was in general use. See TANḤUMA.

4. Pesiḳta Rabbati: The Pesiḳta Rabbati is a collection of homilies on the Pentateuchal and prophetic lessons, the special Sabbaths, etc.; it was probably called "rabbati" (the larger) to distinguish it from the earlier Pesiḳta. In common with the latter it has five entire pisḳot—No. 15 ("Ha-Ḥodesh"), No. 16 ("Korbani Laḥmi"), No. 17 ("Wayehi ba-Ḥazi"), No. 18 ("Omer"), No. 32 ("Aniyyah So'arah"), and the larger part of No. 14 ("Para"); but otherwise it is very different from the Pesiḳta, being in every respect like the Tanḥuma midrashim. In Friedmann's edition (Vienna, 1880) it contains, in forty-seven numbers, about fifty-one homilies, part of which are combinations of smaller ones; seven or eight of these homilies belong to Ḥanukkah, and about seven each to the Feast of Weeks and New-Year, while the older Pesiḳta contains one each for Ḥanukkah and the Feast of Weeks and two for New-Year. Pesiḳta Rabbati contains also homilies to lessons which are not paralleled in the Pesiḳta. There are also various differences between these two Pesiḳtot in regard to the feast-day lessons and the lessons for the Sabbaths of mourning and of comforting. The works are entirely different in content, with the exception of Nos. 15–18, 33, the part of No. 14, and some few minor parallels above mentioned. The Pesiḳta contains no halakic exordiums or proems by R. Tanḥuma. But in the Pesiḳta Rabbati there are not less than twenty-eight homilies with such exordiums having the formula "Yelammedenu Rabbenu," followed by proems with the statement "kak pataḥ R. Tanḥuma"; two homilies, Nos. 38 and 45, the first of which is probably defective, have the Yelammedenu without proems with "kak pataḥ," etc.

Some of the homilies have more than one proem by R. Tanḥuma. The pisḳot taken from the Pesiḳta have of course no Yelammedenu or Tanḥuma proems; the first part of pisḳah No. 14, which does not belong to the Pesiḳta, has at the beginning two halakic introductions and one proem of R. Tanḥuma. Homilies Nos. 20–24, which together form a midrash to the Decalogue, are without these introductions and proems. Only three of the homilies for the Sabbaths of mourning and comforting have such passages, namely, Nos. 29, 31, 33; but they are prefixed to those homilies, beginning with No. 38 (except No. 46, which is of foreign origin), which have the superscription "Midrash Harninu"—a name used to designate the homilies for New-Year to the Feast of Tabernacles which the old authors found in the Pesiḳta Rabbati. The present edition of the Pesiḳta Rabbati, which ends with the homily for the Day of Atonement, is doubtless defective; the older Pesiḳta has also vrrious homilies for Sukkot, Shemini 'Aẓeret, and the Feast of the Torah. Some of the homilies also, as Nos. 19, 27, 38, 39, 45, are defective. Pesiḳta Rabbati therefore appears to be a composite, the homilies of the older Pesiḳta, perhaps, being added later. It is said above that No. 46 is a foreign addition; here Ps. xcii. 1 is interpreted as an acrostic למשה (ascribed to Moses), and there is also a passage from the Midrash Konen; other passages also may have been added, as the passage in No. 20, which is elsewhere quoted in the name of the "Pirḳe Hekalot" and of "Ma'aseh Bereshit" (comp. also Jellinek, "Bet ha-Midrash," i. 58). No. 36 was considered doubtful on account of its contents; No. 26 is peculiar, referring not to a Scripture passage but to a verse or a parable composed by the author. The diction and style are very fine in many passages. In the beginning of the first homily, which shows the characteristics of the "genuine" portions of the Pesiḳta Rabbati, in the proems of R. Tanḥuma following the halakic exordium, the year 845 is indicated as the date of composition of the work; there are no grounds for regarding the date as a gloss (see PESIKTA RABBATI).

In the appendix to the Friedmann edition four homilies are printed from a manuscript, Nos. 1 and 2 of which have yelammedenus and proems. The midrash referred to here is a later, shorter midrash for the feast-days, designated as "New Pesiḳta," and frequently drawing upon the Pesiḳta Rabbati; it has been published by Jellinek in "Bet ha-Midrash," vi. 36–70.

5. Debarim Rabbah: Debarim Rabbah contains twenty-five homilies and two fragments of homilies on sections of Deuteronomy which are known for the larger part as lessons of the sedarim cycle. Homilies on the Pesiḳta lessons of Deut. xiv. 22 and xxv. 17 are not included in this midrash. Debarim Rabbah has been fully analyzed in JEW. ENCYC. iv. 487, where it has been said that it contains a much more complete collection of Tanḥuma homilies in a much more original form than does the Midrash Tanḥuma in Buber's and the earlier editions; and it must be again especially noticed here that in Debarim Rabbah all homilies begin with halakic exordiums (preceded by the word "halakah" instead of the yelammedenu formula), while the portion of Midrash Tanḥuma to Deuteronomy does not have that introduction in either edition. The proems in Debarim Rabbah are quite independent structures; while the old sources, as Yerushalmi, Bereshit Rabbah, and Wayiḳra Rabbah, are used, a freer rendering is often noticeable, as well as the endeavor to translate Aramaic passages into Hebrew. Zunz ascribes the midrash to about the year 900. See DEBARIM RABBAH.

6. Bemidbar Rabbah: This midrash is, in its earlier portions, beginning with the pericope "Beha'aloteka," not an independent midrash, but an extract from Tanḥuma, giving, with some variations and additions, the text of the earlier editions rather than that of Buber's edition. The word "halakah" instead of "yelammedenu Rabbenu" is added to the halakic exordiums in the editions, as in Debarim Rabbah; some of the homilies in Bemidbar Rabbah are without the halakic exordiums found in Tanḥuma. The thirty homilies which are found here in parashiyyot xv.–xxii. (see BEMIDBAR RABBAH), are on the whole identical with Tanḥuma (the earlier editions, from "Beha'aloteka" to the end); noteworthy among the interpolations is parashah xviii., No. 21 (remarkable on other grounds also), which is not found in the manuscripts of Tanḥuma, but which was added to the editio princeps of Tanḥuma (Constantinople, 1520–22) from Bemidbar Rabbah. To the Tanḥuma homilies to Numbers, beginning with ch. viii., was added a later haggadic elaboration of Num. i.–vii., which, according to Zunz, is not older than the twelfth century; it is laid out on such a large scale that, covering only the pericopes "Bemidbar" and "Naso," it takes up nearly three-fourths of the Midrash Bemidbar Rabbah. The exposition of "Naso" is, again, more than three times as long as that of "Bemidbar"; in it the method of revising and elaborating the old Tanḥuma homilies may still be seen; in the pericope "Naso" nearly all traces of the old arrangement have been swept away by the new Haggadah. It is doubtful whether the midrash in both pericopes is the work of the same author, and it is improbable that originally it formed a part of a haggadic work which dealt in a similar way with the entire Book of Numbers. The extent of the development of the Midrash Haggadah in the course of the centuries, from the epoch of the tannaitic midrashim down to the period that produced the Bemidbar Rabbah to Num. ch. i.–vii., appears on comparing the exegesis to Num. vii. 1 *et seq.*, which is so brief that only one verse relating to the gifts of the princes on the second day is expounded, with that in Bemidbar Rabbah, in which the haggadist gave a twelvefold ingenious and suggestive exposition of the same gifts. See BEMIDBAR RABBAH.

7. Shemot Rabbah: The Midrash to Exodus, containing in the editions fifty-two parashiyyot, is likewise not uniform in its composition. In parashiyyot i.–xiv. the proems are almost invariably followed by the running commentary on the entire seder or other Scriptural division (the beginnings of the sedarim are distinguished by an asterisk):

(1) Parashah i., on *Ex. i. 1–ii. 25; (2) par. ii. and iii., on *Ex. iii. 1–iv. 17; (3) par. iv. and v., Nos. 2–8, on *Ex. iv. 18–26; (4) par. v., Nos. 1, 9–23, on Ex. iv. 27–vi. 1; (5) par. vi., on *Ex. vi. 2–12; (6) par. vii., on Ex. vi. 13 *et seq.*; (7) par. viii., on Ex. vii. 1 *et seq.* (a Tanḥuma homily); (8) par. ix., on *Ex. vii. 8–25; (9) par x., on Ex. vii. 26–viii. 15; (10) par. xi., on *Ex. viii. 16–ix. 12; (11) par. xii., on Ex. ix. 13–35; (12) par. xiii., on *Ex. x. 1–20; (13) par. xiv., on Ex. x. 21–29 (there is no exposition nor, in the Tanḥuma midrashim, any homily to *Ex. xi. 1).

Shemot Rabbah, beginning with parashah xv., contains homilies and homiletical fragments to the first verses of the Scripture sections. Many of the homilies are taken from the Tanḥumas, though parashiyyot xv., xvi.–xix., xx., xxx., and others show that the author had access also to homilies in many other sources. In the editions the text is sometimes abbreviated and the reader referred to such collections, as well as to the Pesiḳta; in parashah xxxix. the entire exposition of the Pesiḳta lesson Ki Tissa (Ex. xxx. 11) has been eliminated in this fashion. Such references and abbreviations were doubtless made by later copyists. There is an interesting statement in parashah xliv. regarding the manner of treating a proem-text from the Psalms for the homily to Ex. xxxii. 13. The assumption is justified that Shemot Rabbah down to Ex. xii. 1, with which section the Mekilta begins, is based on an earlier exegetical midrash, constituting, perhaps, the continuation of Bereshit Rabbah. This would explain the fact that in the first part there are several parashiyyot to the open and closed Scripture sections, and that several expressions recall the terminology of the tannaitic midrash. Zunz ascribes the composition of the entire work to the eleventh or twelfth century; although, immediately following Bereshit Rabbah in the collection of the rabbot, it "is separated from the latter by 500 years" ("G. V." p. 256).

8. Aggadat Bereshit: Aggadat Bereshit is a collection of homilies to a number of sedarim of Genesis, notable for its artistic composition. In Buber's edition (Cracow, 1903) it contains 83 homilies in 84 chapters (really 83, since 82 and 83 form one chapter); each homily, down to ch. lxxxi., is in three sections, so arranged that the first one connects with a seder from Genesis, the second with a prophetic section (which may be regarded as the hafṭarah to this seder), and the third with a psalm (which, perhaps, was recited during worship on the Sabbath for which this seder was a lesson). The several homilies are combined from proemial passages generally connected with extraneous texts. Twenty-six of the twenty-eight sections of Genesis are known as sedarim from old lists; Gen. vi. 5 and xviii. 25, to which the homilies in ch. i. and xxii. belong, and to which there are homilies in the Tanḥuma midrashim (to Gen. xviii. 25 in ed. Buber), were probably beginnings of sedarim according to a different division of the sedarim cycle. Hence the Aggadat Bereshit contains the haggadic material for twenty-eight Sabbaths, on which, according to the three-year sedarim cycle, the following passages were read (the Roman numerals between parentheses indicate the corresponding peraḳim in the Tanḥuma): (1) Gen. vi. 5 with Ezek. xxxviii. 10 and Ps. li. (ch. i.–iii.); (2) Gen. viii. 1 with Jer. xxxi. 19 and Ps. xvii. (iv.–vi.); (3) Gen. viii. 15 with Micah vii. 9 and Ps. xvii. (vii.–ix.); (4) Gen. ix. 18 with Micah vii. 9 and Ps. xxvii. (x.–xii.); (5) Gen. xv. 1 with Isa. i. 1 and Ps. xxvii. (xiii.–xv.); (6) Gen. xvii. 1 with Jer. xxxiii. 25 and Ps. cx. (xvi.–xviii.); (7) Gen. xviii. 1 with Mal. iii. 19 and Ps. cx. (xix.–xxi.); (8) Gen. xviii. 25 with Mal. iii. 18 and Ps. cx. (xxii.–xxiv.); (9) Gen. xx. 1 with Judges ix. 22 and Ps. cx. (xxv.–xxvii.); (10) Gen. xxi. 1 with I Sam. ii. 21 and Ps. cx. (xxviii.–xxx.); (11) Gen. xxii. 1 with Judges iii. 1 and Ps. cxii. (xxxi.–xxxiii.); (12) Gen. xxiv. 1 with I Kings i. 1 and Ps. cxxi. (xxxiv.–xxxvi.); (13) Gen. xxv. 19 with I Kings i. 1 and Ps. cxxi. (xxxvii.–xxxix.); (14) Gen. xxvii. 1 with I Sam. ii. 22 and Ps. lxv. 10 (xl.–xlii.); (15) Gen. xxvii. 28 with Micah v. 6 and Ps. cxxi. (xliii.–xlv.); (16) Gen. xxviii. 10 with Hosea xii. 13 and Ps. cxxi. (xlvi.–xlviii.); (17) Gen. xxix. 31 with I Sam. i. 1 and Ps. cxxi. (xlix.–li. 1); (18) Gen. xxx. 22 with I Sam. i. 11 and Ps. cxxi. (lii.–liv.); (19) Gen. xxxii. 4 with Ob. i. 1 and Ps. cxxi. (lv.–lvii.); (20) Gen. xxxvii. 1 with Ob. i. 1 and Ps. cxxix. (lviii.–lx.); (21) Gen. xxxviii. 1 (correctly so after a MS.) with Isa. xl. 27 and Ps. cxxix. (lxi.–lxiii.); (22) Gen. xxxix. 1 (so the MS.) with Isa. xl. 27 and Ps. cxxix. (lxiv.–lxvi.); (23) Gen. xli. 1 with Hag. i. 1 and Ps. cxxix. (lxvii.–lxix.); (24) Gen. xlii. 1 with Isa. xlix. 14 and Ps. cxxix. (lxx.–lxxii.); (25) Gen. xliii. 13 with Jer. ii. 4 and Ps. lxxvi. (lxxiii.–lxxv.); (26) Gen. xliv. 18 with I Kings xviii. 36 and Ps. lxxvi. (lxxvi.–lxxviii.); (27) Gen. xlvi. 28 with I Kings xviii. 36 and Ps. lxxvi. (lxxix.–lxxxi.); (28) Gen. xlix. 1 with Isa. xlviii. 12 (lxxxii.–lxxxiii., belonging together, and lxxxiv.; there is no Psalm exposition for this passage.)

Sedarim and Homilies.

The collection is not complete, beginning only with Gen. vi. 5; there are no homilies to a large number of sedarim of Genesis, and the ending is defective. The assumption that the prophetic sections in Aggadat Bereshit are hafṭarot to the respective sedarim according to the three-year cycle is in part supported by the list of the sedarim hafṭarot which has been published by Büchler, from a manuscript source, in the "Jewish Quarterly Review" (1894, vi. 39 *et seq.*); here, as in Aggadat Bereshit, the sedarim Gen. xv. 1, xxi. 1, xxvii. 28, xxviii. 10, xxx. 22, xxxii. 4 have assigned to them the hafṭarot Isa. i. 1, I Sam. ii. 21, Micah v. 6, Hosea xii. 13, I Sam. i. 11, Ob. i. 1. After Büchler's statements, the difference in the hafṭarot to the other sedarim does not seem strange. But it is curious that several prophetic sections, as I Kings i. 1, xviii. 36, Isa. xl. 27, Ob. i. 1, Micah vii. 9, Malachi iii. 18, are repeated. The Psalms which are expounded in Aggadat Bereshit present a problem that has not yet been explained. Ps. xvii. occurs twice, xxvii. twice, lxxvi. three times, cx. five times, cxxi. seven times. As is the case with the above-mentioned prophetical sections, the sedarim in which the same Psalm is used are, with one exception, consecutive, the treatment being always a different one and displaying not a little of the art of midrashic exegesis.

The contents of Aggadat Bereshit were taken, for the greater part, from Tanḥuma, and there are many signs to indicate a late date of composition of the midrash; nor is it quoted, according to Buber, by the old authors. The author of this work must have been living in a country where Greek was freely spoken; he uses Greek words not found in other midrashim—as in ch. xi., הלפים (ἀλπίς)—words for which he could easily have substituted equivalent Hebrew expressions. The word instanced, a ἅπαξ λεγόμενον, was recognized to be Greek even by Menahem di Lonsano, who first edited this midrash at the end of the collection "Shete Yadot" (Venice, 1618).

9. We-Hizhir (Hashkem): Although the discussion of the purely haggadic Pentateuch midrashim does not belong to this article, yet a brief mention of a work known to the old authors indifferently as **Midrash we-Hizhir** or **Midrash Hashkem** is required here. It took its halakic portion from the Talmudic sources, the baraita on the building of the Tabernacle, the "She'eltot," and the "Halakot Gedolot," the "She'eltot" also being arranged according to the one-year cycle and being in its minor portions especially dependent on Tanḥuma. The first part of the Munich codex, after which the work was published (by I. M. Freimann, under the title "We-Hizhir," part i., Leipsic, 1873; part ii., Warsaw, 1880), is doubtless somewhat defective. It begins with a haggadic passage, which, belonging to Ex. viii. 16 ("Wa-yomer hashkem ba-boker"), is found also in the earlier editions of Tanḥuma (ed. Stettin, *s.v.* "Wa'era," no. 14).

The work was called "Hashkem" after the second word in this introductory sentence. In the editions as well as in the codex this first passage, as well as the beginning of the following haggadic passage to Ex. ix. 22, included in both Tanḥumas in the pericope "Wa'era," is erroneously combined with a passage to Ex. x. 21—which also, perhaps, was taken from Tanḥuma—as belonging to the pericope "Bo." The midrash was called by other authors "We-Hizhir," after the standing formula "We-hizhir ha-Ḳadosh, baruk Hu," with which nearly all the pericopes in the midrash as now extant begin, and which is occasionally found at the beginning of a new section in the middle of the pericope. No one, however, quotes Hashkem and We-Hizhir together as two different works. "The halakic expositions refer in 'Bo' to the tefillin; in 'Beshallaḥ' to the rest on the Sabbath and the 'dine 'erub'; in 'Yitro' to the commandments connected with the Decalogue; in 'Mishpaṭim' to the requirements of the judge; in 'Terumah' to the priestly gift; in 'Wayaḳhel' to the Sabbath; in 'Wayiḳra' to slaughtering; in 'Ẓaw' to the oath and the testimony of witnesses; in 'Shemini' to the 'hilkot terefot'; in 'Tazria'' to the 'dine yoledot'; in 'Meẓora'' to the 'dine ṭum'ah'; in 'Aḥare' and 'Ḳedoshim' to forbidden marriages; in 'Beḥuḳḳotai' to vows; in 'Bemidbar' to the 'dine bekor'" (Zunz, "G. S." iii. 258). The haggadic portions are those mentioned above; also part i., pp. 4a *et seq.* (from the Mekilta); pp. 19a *et seq.* (from Tanḥuma, ed. Buber, and Mekilta); p. 22b (from Mekilta); p. 76b (after Tanḥuma); pp. 115a *et seq.*, 121b (after Tanḥuma); p. 128b (after Tanḥuma, ed. Buber); part ii., pp. 34b *et seq.* (from Wayiḳra Rabbah, ix.); p. 128b (from Sifra), etc.

The midrash, which ends in the edition with the halakic passage (to Num. v. 11 *et seq.*) והזהיר הקב"ה שכל מי שמקנא לאשתו וכו', is probably defective at the end as well as in some other passages (following the manuscript), and it can not be determined whether it covered Numbers only or Numbers and Deuteronomy. Several passages quoted by the old authors, but not found in the edition, may have been included in the missing portion of the work. Zunz, who closely examined the manuscript after which the edition was subsequently printed (*l.c.* pp. 251 *et seq.*), comes to the conclusion that We-Hizhir and Hashkem are one and the same work. This view must be unhesitatingly accepted (comp. also Geiger's "Jüd. Zeit." 1875, pp. 95 *et seq.*). The fact that some passages quoted by the old authors from the Midrash Hashkem do not correspond entirely with the edition, and that some are not found in it at all, does not prove that these are two different works (as Freimann, Buber, and Grünhut assume). The differences are not important, and both differences and omissions may be due to variations in the copies or to different revisions. The work, which is quoted as early as the middle of the eleventh century as a recognized authority, is assigned by Zunz to the tenth century. The assumption of the editor expressed even in the title, that Ḥefeẓ Alluf is the author of the work, lacks support. The quotations from Hashkem by the old authors have been collected by Grünhut ("Sefer ha-Liḳḳuṭim," part i.).

See Midrashim, Smaller, for the Midrash **Abkir** (which probably covered Genesis and Exodus, and of which extracts are preserved in the Yalḳuṭ), for **Tadshe** (based on Gen. i. 11), for **Wayissa'u** (on Gen. xxxv. 5), for **Wayosha'** (on Ex. xiv. 30–xv. 18), for the **Midrash of the Ten Commandments,** and for **Esfa** (on Num. xi. 16).

III. The Exegetical Midrashim to Canticles, Ruth, Ecclesiastes, and Esther: The midrashim to the Five Rolls, which, like the Rabbot to the Pentateuch, are entirely separate midrashic works, are, as mentioned above, printed together in the editio princeps, Pesaro, 1519, under the title "Midrash Ḥamesh Megillot"; in the Venice edition, 1545, the word "Rabbeta" was added to the title. The sequence of the midrashim with the names given to them in the paginal superscriptions of the Venice edition (as in the editio princeps) is as follows: (1) "Shir ha-Shirim Rabbah" (called "Rabbati" in the editio princeps, and, at the end, "Midrash Shir ha-Shirim"); (2) "Midrash Ruth" (at the end, "Midrash Megillat Ruth"); (3) "Midrash Megillat Esther" (at the end, "Midrash Aḥashwerosh"); (4) "Ekah Rabbati" (at the end, "Midrash Ekah Rabbati"); (5) "Midrash Ḳohelet" (at the end, "Nishlam Midrash Ḥamesh Megillot"). Hence the words "Rabbah" and "Rabbati" are added to two only of the midrashim, each of the three others being called merely "Midrash." The five works collected here were, perhaps, the most popular midrashim to the rolls used during divine service; other midrashim to the rolls have, in part, been published recently. The very old midrash Ekah Rabbati has been discussed above; the remaining four are treated below.

1. Shir ha-Shirim Rabbah, or **Midrash Shir ha-Shirim** (called also **Midrash** or **Aggadat Ḥazit,** after the proem-verse Prov. xxii. 29, quoted in the beginning): Shir ha-Shirim Rabbah is an exegetical midrash to Canticles, in which the author collected and edited, verse by verse, following the Biblical text, the wealth of material at his disposal. Canticles was made the subject of midrashic interpretation at a very early date; Akiba declared it to be "most holy," taking it as an allegorical glorification of the relation between God and Israel. Rules for its exposition occur in the midrashim to i. 12. and ii. 4. "Canticles must not be interpreted to the shame [that is, erotically] but to the glory of Israel"; to i. 1, "Where the word 'king' stands God [or, according to another view, Israel as a whole] is meant." Some passages were explained as glorifications of the exodus from Egypt, the revelation of the Temple, etc. The numerous interpretations of single verses in the Seder 'Olam, Sifre, Mekilta, and the Talmud follow this old allegorical method of interpretation. Much of this interpretation is found in Shir ha-Shirim Rabbah, taken directly or indirectly from those old sources. But not all the comments are so old. The compiler of the Shir ha-Shirim Rabbah, who intended to compile a running midrash to Canticles, took—as has often been remarked in connection with the exegetic midrashim—the expositions for the single verses wherever, and in whatever connection, he found these verses explained.

There is a remarkable variation in the extent and character of the several expositions; there are clearly recognizable proems from older homilies; whole sermons, with many variations of texts, on several verses; and short, disconnected explanations of single words and sentences, the expositions to the same or similar verse-parts being repeated here two or three times, as in other old midrashim. Shir ha-Shirim Rabbah is dependent on the Pesiḳta and Wayiḳra Rabbah as well as on Yerushalmi and Bereshit Rabbah. The proems borrowed from these works may be recognized by the final formulas, which also were borrowed. More than one-fourth of Shir ha-Shirim is directly borrowed from Yerushalmi and the three old midrashim mentioned. Mishnah passages and baraitot are quoted very frequently. The five proems in the beginning of the midrash each close with the same sentence, taken from Seder 'Olam. The author has, of course, used also other sources that are no longer extant. The longer passages, as those to Cant. iii. 9–10, iv. 1–4, and others, are, perhaps, taken from these sources, or they may be the work of the author himself; they contain interpretations of several verses, and most of them consist of several variations of the same theme (presented, however, in a way different from that found in the variations of the earlier midrashim), in which entire sentences are frequently repeated verbatim, and in some of which many passages from the Mishnah, etc., are quoted.

In the editions these passages are, almost invariably, wrongly divided, making a survey of them difficult. They belong, doubtless, to a later period of the midrash—*i.e.*, the time after the edition of Bereshit Rabbah, Wayiḳra Rabbah, and the Pesiḳta. The words "Sidra Tinyana" are inserted between the comments to Cant. ii. 7 and ii. 8; in the sedarim cycle there are no sedarim for Canticles. Two other midrashim to Canticles, lost for centuries, are now known—the Aggadat Shir ha-Shirim, published by Solomon Schechter (Cambridge, 1896; also by Buber in "Midrash Zuṭa," pp. 1–41), and the Midrash Shir ha-Shirim, published by Grünhut (1897). For these midrashim and their relation to the Shir ha-Shirim Rabbah discussed here see Song of Songs, Midrashim to.

2. Midrash Ruth: Midrash Ruth (so called in the editio princeps and the Venice edition) contains comments, haggadic sentences, etc., following the sequence of the text, and is divided into eight parashiyyot, beginning at Ruth i. 1, i. 2, i. 18, i. 22, ii. 10, iii. 8, iii. 14, iv. 18. The midrash begins with a passage called a "petiḥta," consisting of six proems, and a lengthy exposition of an old haggadic rule (probably taken from Bereshit Rabbah or Wayiḳra Rabbah and found in other midrashim), "which has been brought back from the Exile" and which declares that a time of sorrow is referred to wherever a Biblical story begins with the words "It happened in the days of." There are also proems to parashiyyot iii., iv., vi., and viii. Parashah ii. begins with a composite exposition to I Chron. iv. 21–23; parashah v. with an exposition to I Chron. xi. 13–18 taken from Yerushalmi. Midrash Ruth has borrowed from Yerushalmi, Bereshit Rabbah, Pesiḳta, Wayiḳra Rabbah, etc., and, perhaps, from Babli also; it has several passages in common with the Midrash Ḳohelet, as, *e.g.*, to Ruth iii. 13, the story of R. Meïr and his teacher Elisha ben Abuyah, which, probably, was not taken directly from its source, Yer. Ḥag. ii. 77b, c.

Among the other longer passages may be mentioned the sixfold interpretation ("shet shittin") of R. Johanan, referring to David, Solomon, Hezekiah, Manasseh, the Messiah, and to Boaz himself Boaz's words to Ruth in ii. 14. The passage "Famine came ten times into the world," found in Bereshit Rabbah xxv. (40), 64 to Gen. v. 29 (xii. 10), xxvi. 1, is quoted in connection with Ruth i. 1 ("there was a famine"), and is here further worked out with reference to Elimelech. An inexact reference to Bereshit Rabbah occurs in the editions, in a defective passage toward the end of the work. In this passage, to Ruth iv. 18, there must have been the interpretation of the writing of the word תולדות which is quoted by Abravanel in "Yeshu'ot Meshiḥo" (ed. Königsberg, p. 55b) from the Midrash Ruth, and which is found also in Leḳaḥ Ṭob to Ruth *ib.* In regard to this interpretation a copyist has referred the reader to Bereshit Rabbah xii. (6); and in connection with the words פרץ פרץ there must have been added to the interpretation of אלה and ואלה (found also in Bereshit Rabbah, ch. xii. [3]) that concerning the doubling of names; the latter is similarly added in Bereshit Rabbah, ch. xxx. (4) and is found alone *ib.* ch. xxxviii. (12), ending in both passages with the words "bisseru she-Yishma'el 'oseh teshubah," which the copyist quotes as the conclusion of his abbreviated reference.

The midrash to Ruth published by Buber in the "Midrash Zuṭa" (pp. 45–56) is entirely different in arrangement and execution; it begins with a short proem by R. Tanḥuma and contains a brief exposition according to the sequence of the text. See Ruth Rabbah.

3. Midrash Ḳohelet (so called in the editio princeps and the Venice edition): The Midrash Ḳohelet, or Ecclesiastes, was divided, probably, according to the sedarim of the Biblical book; it contained, aside from extensive borrowings from Yerushalmi, proems from Bereshit Rabbah, Ekah Rabbati, Wayiḳra Rabbah, Pesiḳta, and Shir ha-Shirim Rabbah, which make up a large portion of the work. But the author of the Midrash Ḳohelet takes many passages from Babli as well, quotes from the "Sayings of the Fathers" with the reference "Abot," and refers to smaller treatises by name, betraying thereby conclusively the relatively late date of composition of this midrash. Zunz designates this midrash as "a work of the later epoch." But it is difficult to agree with him, especially as regards Yelammedenu, when he adds: "Many passages from the abovementioned haggadot to Canticles, Ruth, and Ecclesiastes have been incorporated in Yelammedenu, Debarim Rabbah, Pesiḳta Rabbati, and Shemot Rabbah; they occupy a middle position between the last-named and the earlier haggadah." See Ḳohelet Rabbah (in which comp. statement in regard to the other midrash to Ecclesiastes printed in Buber's "Midrash Zuṭa," pp. 83–144).

4. Midrash Megillat Esther (so called in the editio princeps and in the Venice edition): This midrash consists of six parashiyyot introduced by one or more proems, beginning with Esth. i. 1, i. 4, i. 9, i. 13, ii. 1, and ii. 5. After this there is hardly any trace of a further division. As the division is not carried out systematically, so the exposition appears to be incomplete. The midrash borrows from Yerushalmi, Bereshit Rabbah, Wayiḳra Rabbah, and from other sources, and has some points of similarity with the expositions to Esther in Babli. Especially noteworthy is the story of Mordecai's dream and prayer, and of Esther's prayer and her appearance before the king, recognized at an early date as an interpolation from "Yosippon." Bacher's assumption that the passage is not a later addition, but was taken by the author of the Midrash Esther from a Hebrew apocryphon to the Book of Esther, can not be accepted in view of the literal agreement of that passage with "Yosippon." In JEW. ENCYC. v. 241, *s.v.* ESTHER RABBAH, aside from the Midrash Abba Gorion, another haggadic exposition to Esther is referred to, which was printed in Buber's "Sammlung Agadischer Commentare," etc., pp. 55–82. Entirely independent of this work is a South-Arabic midrash compilation to Esther, also printed by Buber ("Agadische Abhandlungen," etc., Cracow, 1897); this work borrows especially from Babli, the Pirḳe Rabbi Eli'ezer, and from Alfasi and Maimonides. The midrash to the roll of Esther printed at Constantinople in 1519 and edited by C. M. Horowitz in his "Sammlung Kleiner Midraschim" (1881) is also a later composition. Gaster published still another midrash, which he considers the oldest midrash to Esther, in the Kohut Memorial Volume (1897, pp. 167–177). See ESTHER RABBAH. The following are some passages from this midrash, which has been included in the Rabbot collection; they are taken from the exposition to Esth. ii. 5 and 7:

In Shushan there was a certain Jew [*Yehudi*]. The expression איש teaches that Mordecai was as important in his time as Moses had been in his time, of whom it is said, "Now the man [והאיש] Moses was very meek" [Num. xii. 3]. As Moses stood in the breach, of whom it is written, "Therefore he said that he would destroy them, had not Moses his chosen stood before him in the breach" [Ps. cvi. 23], so also Mordecai, of whom it is written, "[He] accepted of the multitude of his brethren, seeking the wealth of his people" [Esth. x. 3]. As Moses taught Israel the Torah, as it is written, "Behold, I have taught you statutes and judgments" [Deut. iv. 5], so Mordecai also, as it is written, "words of peace and truth" [Esth. ix. 30], and "truth" means the "Torah," as it is written, "Buy the truth, and sell it not" [Prov. xxiii. 23].

Whose name was Mordecai. In speaking of the wicked the name is placed first: "Nabal is his name" [I Sam. xxv. 25]; "Sheba, the son of Bichri by name" [II Sam. xx. 21]; but in the case of the pious the word "name" stands first: "and his name was Manoah" [Judges xiii. 2]; "and his name was Kish" [I Sam. ix. 1]; "and his name was Saul" [*ib.* ix. 2]; "and his name was Elkanah" [*ib.* i. 1]; "and his name was Boaz" [Ruth ii. 1]; "and his name was Mordecai"; because they resemble their Maker, as it is written, "But by my name JEHOVAH was I not known to them" [Ex. vi. 3].

Yehudi. Why, since he was a Benjamite, was he called a "Yehudi" [comp. Esth. ii. 5]? Because he confessed the name of the One God before the whole world, as it is written, "But Mordecai bowed not, nor did him reverence" [Esth. iii. 2]. Was he quarrelsome and one who transgresses the commands of the king? No; but when Ahasuerus had commanded that every one should bow down to Haman, the latter graved an image of an idol in his heart, in order that the people might thus bow down to the idol; and when Haman saw that Mordecai did not bow before him, he was very wroth. But Mordecai said, "There is a Lord who is above all; how shall I leave Him and bow down to an idol?" And because he confessed the name of the One God, he was called "Yehudi" [*i.e.*, יהודי means יחידי = "confessor of the unity of God"]. Others say he was as great as Abraham in his time. As our father Abraham allowed himself to be cast into the fiery furnace [comp. the story in Bereshit Rabbah, xxxviii., end], thus leading men to recognize the Holy One, praised be He, as it is written, "and the souls that they had gotten in Haran" [Gen. xii. 5; according to the midrash the proselytes who were led by Abraham to recognize God are meant; comp. Sifre, Deut. 32; Gen. R. xxxix.], so men recognized the greatness of the Holy One, praised be He, in the days of Mordecai, as it is written, "And many of the people of the land became Jews" [Esth. viii. 17]. He confessed the name of the One God and sanctified Him, therefore he was called "Jehudi."

And he brought up Hadassah. As the myrtle [הדסה] is sweet of smell and bitter of taste, so Esther was sweet for Mordecai and bitter for Haman. For she had neither father nor mother. R. Phinehas and R. Ḥama b. Gorion, in the name of Rab: "Was she a 'shetuḳit' [child whose origin must be concealed]? No; but when her mother became pregnant with her, her father died, and when she was born her mother died." R. Berechiah, in the name of R. Levi: "The Holy One, praised be He, said to Israel, 'You weep and say, Orphans are we, without father [comp. Lam. v. 3]. By your life, the redeemer, whom I will send to you out of Media, shall be without father and mother, as it is written, "For she had neither father nor mother."'"

IV. The Remaining Exegetical Midrashim not Dealing with the Pentateuch: For the midrashim to Samuel, the Psalms, and Proverbs see SAMUEL, PSALMS, and PROVERBS, MIDRASH TO.

1. Midrash Yeshayah: This midrash is mentioned by Abravanel, Abraham Portaleone, and the author of the midrash commentary "Mattenot Kehunnah" (to Wayiḳra Rabbah, section 29, and Bemidbar Rabbah, section 16). But no extract from this midrash is found either in Yalḳuṭ Shim'oni or in Yalḳuṭ Makiri.

2. Midrash Yonah: The midrash to the Book of Jonah, read on the Day of Atonement as hafṭarah during the Minḥah prayer, contains a haggadic version of this prophetical book. In the editions the work consists of two parts; the second part, in which the story of Jonah is allegorically referred to the soul, beginning with the words "Wa-yomer Adonai la-dag," is reprinted in Jellinek, "Bet ha-Midrash" (i. 102 *et seq.*). This part is merely a literal translation from the Zohar (comp. *ib.* p. xx.); it is not found in the version printed by C. M. Horowitz (after a Codex De Rossi) in the "Sammlung Kleiner Midraschim" (Berlin, 1881). The first part, the midrash proper, is found also in the Yalḳuṭ to Jonah (part ii., §§ 550–551), with the exception of a few missing passages and with several variations; but here the Pirḳe Rabbi Eli'ezer is given as the source (for some passages, Yerushalmi and Babli).

Jellinek assumes that the first part of the Midrash Jonah was compiled subsequently to Yalḳuṭ. But as many passages which the Yalḳuṭ has in common with the Midrash Jonah—*e.g.*, the penitential prayer given in Jellinek, "Bet ha-Midrash" (i. 99) and the description of Nineveh's grandeur there—are not found in Pirḳe Rabbi Eli'ezer; and as, furthermore, the author of the Yalḳuṭ probably did not find all this material in the Pirḳe Rabbi Eli'ezer, he must have taken his quotations from a midrash which was substantially identical with the Midrash Jonah (*i.e.*, with the first part). The author of this midrash borrowed nearly the whole of ch. x. from the Pirḳe Rabbi Eli'ezer, and borrowed also from Yerushalmi and Babli. The version of the Codex De Rossi begins with the passage which in the Midrash Jonah is found in connection with iii. 3 *et seq.*; the extracts borrowed by the latter from Babli and Yerushalmi and inserted in the course of its commentary to this passage and later are missing in the Codex De Rossi. Then follows the end of part i. of the midrash, into which ch. x. of the Pirḳe Rabbi Eli'ezer has been interpolated. It concludes with the exposition of some verses—Deut. iv. 31, Micah vii. 18, and others. It may be noted, finally, that in a compilation included in the earlier editions of Tanḥuma to the pericope "Wayiḳra" (ed. Stettin, *ib.* § 8), which dates from a later time, ch. x. of the Pirḳe Rabbi Eli'ezer was also included.

3. Midrash Iyyob: It can be doubted no longer that the old authors possessed a midrash to the Book of Job. Extracts with express reference to the source Midrash Iyyob are found to Job i. 14 (in the Yalḳuṭ Makiri to Isa. lxi. 11), to Job i. 6 (in a MS. commentary of Rashi to Job), to Job i. 1 and iv. 12 (in a MS. Maḥzor commentary; both these commentaries are in the possession of Abraham Epstein, in Vienna; comp. "Ha-Ḥoḳer," i. 325), to Job vii. 9 (in the "Recanati" to Gen. iii. 24), to Job ii. 1 ([?]; in the "Recanati"—according to the statement in "Rab Pe'alim," p. 34), to Job iv. 10 (in Yalḳ. Shim'oni, ii. 897). The extracts found in the Yalḳuṭ Makiri to Ps. li. 7 and Ps. cxlvi. 4 with the source-reference "Midrash" and referring to Job iii. 3 and xxxviii. 1, are, perhaps, likewise taken from the Midrash Iyyob, as are many passages in the Job commentaries of Samuel b. Nissim Masnuth ("Ma'-yan Gannim," Berlin, 1889) and Isaac b. Solomon (Constantinople, 1545). The extracts and quotations from Midrash Iyyob have been collected by Wertheimer ("Leḳeṭ Midrashim," Jerusalem, 1903; comp. also Zunz, "G. V." p. 270; Brüll's "Jahrb." v.–vi. 99).

According to Zunz, there are also evidences of the existence of midrashim to Ezra and Chronicles (*ib.* p. 271). For the **Midrash al Yithallel,** to Jer. ix. 22 and to the Hallel Midrash, see MIDRASHIM, SMALLER.

V. Special Haggadic Works: 1. Pirḳe (de) Rabbi Eli'ezer: This work, consisting of fifty-four chapters, is quoted by the ancient authors either under this name or—especially by the author of the "'Aruk"—as **Baraita de Rabbi Eli'ezer.** It is not an exegetical or homiletical midrash like the midrashim discussed so far, although it contains occasional expositions, as to Jonah i. and ii. (in ch. x.) and to passages in Esther (in ch. xlix. and l.); but it describes in lucid Hebrew, often having recourse to Biblical phraseology and poetic diction different from that of most of the other midrashim, the most important events of the Pentateuch—the works of God as revealed in the Creation and in the ancient history of Israel. The plan of the work, as Weiss has happily stated ("Dor," iii. 290), is outlined in the words which the author puts into the mouth of R. Eliezer b. Hyrcanus—whose fortunes and the recognition he received from R. Johanan b. Zakkai are related in the introductory chapters, i. and ii. —at the beginning of the discourse: "'Who can utter the mighty acts of the Lord? who can shew forth all his praise?' [Ps. cvi. 2]. Is there one in the world able to utter God's mighty acts and to proclaim His praise? Even the angels are not able to do so. We may speak only of one part of His deeds, namely, what He has done and will do, in order that the name of the Lord may be glorified by His creatures," etc.

In ch. iii.–xi. the creative acts of the several days are treated haggadically. Ch. iii. begins with the things created before the world—the Torah, hell, paradise, etc.; ch. iv. deals with the "ḥayyot" and the angels; in ch. vi.–viii. the author connects with the creative acts of the fourth day details in regard to the planets, the signs of the zodiac, calendric science, and intercalation; ch. ix., on the creative acts of the fifth day, connects with the above-mentioned chapter on Jonah, who fled before God on the fifth day.

The haggadah on the creation of man in ch. xi. connects with ch. xii.–xxi., dealing with Adam and his descendants (note particularly ch. xiii., on the envy of the angels at the creation of man; *ib.* and part of ch. xiv., on Samael; ch. xv., on the angels who warn man from the path of evil; ch. xvi., on the deeds of love which God showed to Adam; ch. xvii., on comforting the mourning; ch. xviii., on Sabbath rest; ch. xx., on Adam at the end of the first Sabbath and on Habdalah). Ch. xxiii. and xxiv. deal with Noah, his sons and descendants; ch. xxv.–xxxi., with Abraham; ch. xxxii.–xxxv., with Isaac; ch. xxxvi.–xxxvii., with Jacob; ch. xxxviii.–xxxix., with Joseph (ch. xxix., on circumcision, and ch. xxxiii., on benevolence and resurrection); ch. xl.–xlvii., with Moses, the revelation of the Law, the Exodus, Amalek, and the golden calf (comp. ch. xliii., on penitence, and ch. xlvi., on the Day of Atonement). Connected with these chapters, probably, are ch. xlviii., on the release from Egypt and on Moses; ch. xlix. and l., on Amalek's descendants, Haman, and Titus (together with comments to the Book of Esther); and ch. li., on future redemption. Ch. lii. deals with seven divine miracles; ch. liii. and liv. deal with the sin of the evil tongue—slander and calumny. Aaron's and Miriam's calumny against Moses (Num. xii. 1 *et seq.*) is also mentioned here; the last chapter of the work closes with the account of Miriam's punishment.

It is hardly probable that this is the original ending of this haggadic work, which evidently was planned on a very large scale, "since a writer who goes so extensively into all the details of the Pentateuch will hardly have laid down his pen with the story of the leprosy of Moses' sister" (comp. Zunz, "G. V." pp. 271 *et seq.*). The incompleteness of the work, or the failure to carry out the original plan, is evident from other facts also. Ch. xxvii., xxxiv., xxxv., xl., and xliii. end with the final sentences of the first five of the Eighteen Benedictions respectively; the endings of ch. xlvi., li., liv. correspond with the three following benedictions of that prayer. This seems to point to the existence of a connective thread, which is broken at the end of the work. In ch. xiv. the haggadah of God's ten appearances on earth is recounted (comp. Mekilta to Ex. xix. 11; Sifre, Num. 93; Gen. R. xxxviii. and xlix.; Ab. R. N., ed. Schechter, pp. 96, 102), and the same subject is treated in detail in ch. xxiv., xxv., xxxix., xl., xli., xlvi., liv.; while the eighth appearance is discussed only in the last chapter. But it can not be demonstrated from the quotations which are found in the works of old writers, especially R. Nathan, that the midrash ever extended any further; it probably remained incomplete (comp. Zunz, *l.c.* p. 273).

No further proofs are required now to show that R. Eliezer b. Hyrcanus was not the author of the work. Aside from many indications recalling the productions of the geonic period, the interesting passage in ch. xxx., omitted in some editions, explicitly referring to the building of the mosque on the site of the Temple, and the allusions to the deeds of the califs, clearly indicate that the author lived under Arabic rule. According to Zunz, the work can not have been composed before the eighth century. It was used by Ḳalir, is mentioned by R. Nissim (*c.* 1030), and is often quoted since Rashi and the "'Aruk." The author was doubtless a Palestinian. There are various other versions of the story of R. Eliezer b. Hyrcanus narrated in ch. i. and ii., namely, in Gen. R. xlii.; Ab. R. N., recension A, ch. vi.; recension B, ch. xiii.; Tan., Lek Leka, 30 (ed. Buber); and elsewhere (comp. the list in Horowitz, "Bibl. Haggadica," i., No. 1, pp. 1 *et seq.*; Pirḳe Rabbi Eli'ezer, ch. xxxix.-xli., is printed after a Codex De Rossi, *ib.* No. ii., pp. 21-25). An extract or a revision of the Pirḳe Rabbi Eli'ezer, ch. iii.-vi., ix., xi., was published by Horowitz, after a codex in the British Museum, in the collection "Sammlung Kleiner Midraschim" (pp. iv.-x., Berlin, 1881). On the important chapters vi.-viii. (on calendric science) compare Zunz, "G. S." iii. 242, and Epstein, "Beiträge zur Jüdischen Alterthumskunde," pp. 21 *et seq.*

2. Seder Eliyahu, or **Tanna debe Eliyahu:** This work derived its name, its division into **Seder Eliyahu Rabbah** and **Seder Eliyahu Zuṭa,** and perhaps more or less of its contents, from an old work mentioned in the Talmud (Ket. 106a), where it is said that it was revealed to Rab Anan, a pupil of Rab in the third century, by the prophet Elijah, and that it included Seder Eliyahu Rabbah and Seder Eliyahu Zuṭa. Seven of the nine halakic and haggadic passages mentioned in different treatises of the Talmud with the formula "Tanna debe Eliyahu" are found in the Seder Eliyahu. The work as now known was composed in the second half of the tenth century; this is evident from the dates (which must not be regarded as interpolations or as having been changed) in ch. ii., vi., and xxxi. of the Seder Eliyahu Rabbah (ed. Friedmann, pp. 7, 37, and 163 respectively). The purpose of the book is clearly expressed in the haggadic interpretation to Gen. iii. 24 at the beginning of the work ("Let man guard the way [of life] and the tree of life [the Torah]"—that is, let him glorify the Torah and study the Law) as well as in the exhortation to practise all virtues and pious works, which the author understands the term "derek ereẓ" to denote. To this are added some expositions and interpretations—in part very extended—of the statutes, which, in a measure, transform the Seder Eliyahu into an exegetical midrash.

Among the stories included those are most characteristic of the work in which the author speaks through the mouth of the prophet Elijah; furthermore, many parables, maxims, prayers, and exhortations enliven the discourse. The unprejudiced ethics of the work and the attitude of the Israelites toward the non-Israelites appear in the sentence, "I call heaven and earth to witness that, whether Israelite or non-Israelite, whether man or woman, whether male or female slave, the Holy Spirit rests upon man according to his deeds" (p. 48), and in many other fine passages, as pp. 36, 65, 81, 88, 140 (comp. Theodor in "Monatsschrift," 1900, pp. 554, 558). The work is written in pure Hebrew, the diction of many passages is notably beautiful, and the style is fluent though frequently verbose; it is not always easy to follow the train of thought and to find the real connection between the several passages. The division into chapters is frequently merely an external one, and the several chapters vary greatly in length. R. Nathan says in the "'Aruk" (*s.v.* סדר [3]) that the Seder Eliyahu Rabbah has three "gates" and thirty chapters, and the Seder Eliyahu Zuṭa twelve chapters; but there is no quotation from the work in the "'Aruk." In the Venice edition of 1598, which was printed from a codex of the year 1186, the first part contains thirty-one chapters and the second part twenty-five chapters; Zunz, however, has shown ("G. V." p. 117) that ch. xv.-xxv. of the Seder Eliyahu Zuṭa are a later compilation. In the Friedmann edition (Vienna, 1902), after a Vatican manuscript of the year 1073, part i. has been carefully divided into twenty-nine chapters, while part ii. closes with ch. xv. of the Venice edition.

Liberal Character of the Work.

The last chapter may be recognized as spurious. In a Codex De Rossi published by Horowitz (*l.c.* i., No. ii., pp. 3-19), Eliyahu Zuṭa has only twelve chapters.

The two editions of the entire work, the numerous extracts from it in Yalḳuṭ Shim'oni, and the Seder Eliyahu Zuṭa according to the Codex De Rossi vary in many points, appearing in parts to be different versions.

The work fared badly in the edition published by R. Samuel b. Moses Heida, with a prolix cabalistic commentary (Prague, 1677). This edition goes beyond all attempted reconstructions of modern midrash criticism; the text has been worked over, interpolated, and interspersed with entirely extraneous elements, and is designated as a "new version" ("nusḥa ḥadasha"), destined to supplant the text of the Venice edition, the chapters of which, printed in smaller type, head the chapters of this edition. See TANNA DEBE ELIYAHU.

For a number of special haggadic works, which vary greatly in content and which constitute, in part, a distinct class of literature, such as **Dibre ha-Yamim sihel Moseh, Midrash Eleh Ezkerah, Midrash 'Eser Galliyot, Midrash Ma'ase Torah, Meir Petirat Aharon, Midrash we-Yeterot, Meir Petirat Moseh, Meir Ta'ama, Midrash Temurah,** etc., as well as for the collections of similar works, see MIDRASHIM, SMALLER.

VI. Yalḳuṭ Shim'oni, Yalḳuṭ ha-Makiri, and Midrash ha-Gadol: A brief reference to these three works, more fully discussed under their respective titles, may here be given. As in the case of the entire midrash literature, the author of the Yalḳuṭ Shim'oni—a broadly planned midrashic thesaurus to the twenty-four books of the Bible, combining all the products of the Midrash, Halakah, and Haggadah, and which could easily furnish material for midrashic compendiums to the several books of the Bible—is unknown, or, rather, the identity of the Simeon after whom the midrash is called has not yet been definitely determined. The words "Sefer Yalḳuṭ ha-Niḳra Shim'oni" occur on the title-page of the first part of the work in the editio princeps (Salonica, 1526–27; part ii., *ib.* 1521). At the end of the first part, in the editio princeps only, is a valuable appendix, introduced by the remark that R. Simeon ha-Darshan edited it after having composed the work.

According to the statement on the title-page of the Venice edition, 1566, "Rabbenu Shimeon, the head of the 'Darshanim' of Frankfort," composed the Yalḳuṭ. In this edition the corrector has taken the liberty of changing the readings of the Yalḳuṭ according to the text of printed midrash editions (comp. Theodor in "Monatsschrift," 1895, pp. 390, 484 *et seq.*; comp. also the paragraph numbers in part ii. of the editio princeps and the sequence of the prophetic and hagiographic books according to the Yalḳuṭ). The writer of the preface in the edition of Frankfort-on-the-Oder, 1709, designates the author more explicitly as "R. Shimeon of Frankfort-on-the-Main." But it is not certain either that his name was "R. Shimeon" or that the author was a native of Frankfort-on-the-Main. Zunz's view that the date of composition of the Yalḳuṭ Shim'oni remains to be determined is to be accepted ("G. V." p. 299; Epstein, in "Ha-Ḥoḳer," i. 85 *et seq.*, 133 *et seq.*; Brüll's "Jahrb." v.–vi. 221 *et seq.*). The extracts in the Yalḳuṭ are often contracted and changed to afford a more suitable connection with the respective verses of the Biblical text; the names of the authors also are abbreviated, especially in the first part. It is furthermore evident that different manuscripts of the same midrash, etc., were used in the different parts of the work. But it must be emphasized, in answer to many accusations of both earlier and more recent times, that the Yalḳuṭ does not arbitrarily alter readings, but reproduces the text according to the manuscripts which the author or his collaborators had at hand. The readings of the Yalḳuṭ are of great critical value, especially when compared with the readings of other manuscripts, or when the latter are supported by the authority of the Yalḳuṭ (comp. Theodor in "Monatsschrift," 1900, p. 383).

In the editio princeps of the Yalḳuṭ the sources are always given in the text, not in the margin. The reference to the sources was doubtless made by the compiler himself, who freely drew upon nearly the entire Talmudic-midrashic literature, the above-mentioned tannaitic midrashim (including Seder 'Olam, Baraita on the Tabernacle, etc.), the two Talmuds, the exegetic and homiletic midrashim, and, with few exceptions, the remaining haggadic works; an exact list of the sources is given in Zunz, "G. V." p. 298. It must be noted here that the following Rabbot are not used: Shemot Rabbah, Bemidbar Rabbah, the midrashim to Ecclesiastes and Esther. The midrash to Ecclesiastes published by Buber in Midrash Zuṭa, Abba Gorion, and other haggadot to Esther, have been used.

Machir b. Abba Mari's Yalḳuṭ ha-Makiri is doubtless a later work than the Yalḳuṭ Shim'oni; the following portions of it have recently been published: to Isaiah (ed. Spira, Berlin, 1894, not complete); to the Psalms (ed. Buber, Berdychev, 1899); to Proverbs (ed. Grünhut, 1902, defective at the beginning and supplemented in "Sefer ha-Liḳḳuṭim," part vi.); a codex in the British Museum, defective at the beginning and the end, contains the Yalḳuṭ ha-Makiri to the Twelve Minor Prophets. In the prefaces of the Yalḳuṭ ha-Makiri to Isaiah and the Psalms, similar in wording, the author adds to his name the names of his ancestors for several generations back; but otherwise nothing is known either about the time in which he lived or about his home and the circumstances of his life. The Codex Leyden, however (after which the Yalḳuṭ ha-Makiri to Isaiah was printed), contains a note referring to its sale, and dated 1415. From the above-mentioned prefaces it is known that Machir b. Abba Mari's work included the books of Jeremiah, Ezekiel, and Job also; hence it did not cover the entire Bible, as did the Yalḳuṭ Shim'oni; nor were so many sources used as for that work, the compiler having taken hardly anything from the smaller midrashim.

The sources are invariably noted in the text at the beginning of the extracts, which are given entire, and without abbreviation of names, being therefore more exact than the extracts given in the other Yalḳuṭ. The versions of the midrash works used in Yalḳuṭ ha-Makiri are, in part, different from those used in the Yalḳuṭ Shim'oni; the titles of the works likewise are differently given in the two collections; *e.g.*, "Torat Kohanim" and "Midrash Tehillim" in the Yalḳuṭ Shim'oni, and "Sifra" and "Shoḥer Ṭob" in Yalḳuṭ ha-Makiri. The author of the latter cites also from Shemot Rabbah, Bemidbar Rabbah, Ḳohelet Rabbah, and Esther Rabbah, designating the last-named as "Midrash Ahasuerus"; he does not seem to have known the Pesiḳta Rabbati. As different manuscripts were used for the two collections, they vary, as regards many of the readings, both from each other and from other midrash texts, these variations constituting the greatest value these collections possess.

While both of the two Yalḳuṭ works entirely ignore the Targumim, the works on mysticism, and the works of rabbinical literature, the Midrash ha-Gadol extracts from the "'Aruk," from Rashi, Ibn Esra, and Maimonides, and from the works of other rabbis, as appears from the part to Genesis published by Schechter (Cambridge, 1902; comp. Preface, p. xiii.). The anonymous author, who freely quotes Talmudic sentences and discussions, as well as expositions, from the halakic and haggadic midrashim, changing, transposing, and commingling them as required, nowhere gives his source, unlike the authors of the two Yalḳuṭs. The above-mentioned publications by Lewy and Hoffmann on the tannaitic midrashim that had entirely disappeared, as well as the notes of the editor to many passages of the edited part, give an idea of the treasures contained in the Midrash ha-Gadol.

Bibliography: See the special articles on the various works here treated.

S. J. T.

MIDRASH HALAKAH ("investigation of the Halakah"): Strictly speaking, the verification of the traditionally received Halakah by identifying its sources in the Bible and by interpreting these Scriptural passages as proofs of its authenticity. The term is applied also to the derivation of new halakot and legal enactments from the Bible, either by means of a correct interpretation of the obvious meaning of the Scriptural words themselves or by the application of certain hermeneutic rules (see TALMUD). The phrase "Midrash Halakah" was first employed by Nachman Krochmal (in his "Moreh Nebuke ha-Zeman," p. 163), the Talmudic expression being "Midrash Torah" = "investigation of the Torah" (Ḳid. 49b). Since all halakic interpretations were regarded as corresponding to the real meaning of the Scriptural texts concerned in each case, it was held that a correct elucidation of the Torah carried with it the proof of the Halakah and the reason for its existence. In the Midrash Halakah three divisions may be distinguished: (1) the midrash of the older Halakah, that is, the midrash of the Soferim and the Tannaim of the first two generations; (2) the midrash of the younger Halakah, or the midrash of the Tannaim of the three following generations; (3) the midrash of several younger tannaim and of a large number of amoraim who did not interpret a Biblical passage as an actual proof of the Halakah, but merely as a suggestion or a support for it ("zeker le-dabar"; "asmakta").

The Term.

The Midrash of the Older Halakah: The early Halakah sought only to define the compass and scope of individual laws, asking under what circumstances of practical life a given rule was to be applied and what would be its consequences. The earlier Midrash, therefore, aims at an exact definition of the laws contained in the Scriptures by an accurate interpretation of the text and a correct determination of the meaning of the various words. The form of exegesis adopted is frequently one of simple lexicography, and is remarkably brief. A few examples will serve to illustrate the style of the older Midrash Halakah. It translates the word "ra'ah" (Ex. xxi. 8) "displease" (Mek., Mishpaṭim, 3 [ed. Weiss, p. 85a]), which is contrary to the interpretation of R. Eliezer (Ḳid. 19b). From the expression "be-miksat" (Ex. xii. 4), which, according to it, can mean only "number," the older Halakah deduces the rule that when killing the Passover lamb the slaughterer must be aware of the number of persons who are about to partake of it (Mek., Bo, 3 [ed. Weiss, p. 5a]). Similarly the prohibition against eating the Passover lamb uncooked is derived from the word "na" (Ex. xii. 9), which, it is declared, can signify only "raw" (Mek., Bo, 6 [ed. Weiss, p. 8b]). The statement that the determination of the calendar of feasts depends wholly on the decision of the nasi and his council is derived from Lev. xxiii. 37, the defectively written "otam" (them) being read as "attem" (ye) and the interpretation, "which ye shall proclaim," being regarded as conforming to the original meaning of the phrase (R. H. 25a). When two different forms of the same word in a given passage have been transmitted, one written in the text ("ketib"), and the other being the traditional reading ("ḳere"), the Halakah, not wishing to designate either as wrong, interprets the word in such a way that both forms may be regarded as correct. Thus it explains Lev. xxv. 30—where according to the ḳere the meaning is "in the walled city," but according to the ketib, "in the city which is not walled"—as referring to a city that once had walls, but no longer has them ('Ar. 32b). In a similar way it explains Lev. xi. 29 (Ḥul. 65a). According to Krochmal (*l.c.* pp. 151 *et seq.*), the ketib was due to the Soferim themselves, who desired that the interpretation given by the Halakah might be contained in the text; for example, in the case of "otam" and "attem" noted above, they intentionally omitted the ו.

Examples of Style of the Older Halakah.

Another example of the methods of the older Halakah is found in Num. ix. 10 *et seq.*, where it is ordained that if a man at the time of the Passover be unclean from contact with a corpse, or if he be "in a journey afar off" ("be-derek reḥoḳah"), he shall keep the feast on the same day of the following month. In this passage no mention is made of any other defilement. The Halakah, however, assumes that one who is unclean, even though he has not touched a corpse, may not partake of the feast. Justification for this interpretation is found in a dot which occurs over the final ה of the word "reḥoḳah," and which shows according to the older Midrash that the ה must be omitted in interpreting the word, and accordingly Sifre, Num. 69 (ed. Friedmann, p. 18a) makes the word refer to the man ("ish"), and not to the journey ("derek") ("ish raḥoḳ welo derek reḥoḳah," Yer. Pes. ix. 2), and interprets that in some way he is "afar off from the temple," *i.e.*, that on account of his uncleanness he is forbidden to enter it. This interpretation is found in the Jerusalem Targum also. According to Geiger ("Urschrift," p. 186), the dot was placed over the ה at a later time, as in the case of the ו mentioned above. As a matter of fact, all these interpretations and explanations are elucidations of the Biblical text and do not depart from the obvious meaning of the words as they were understood by the exegesis of the time. Hence the old versions are frequently found to agree with the older midrashic Halakah. Thus, for example, the midrashic explanation of Ex. xxii. 6 (Mek., Mishpaṭim, 15 [ed. Weiss, p. 97b]) agrees with that of the Septuagint, as does the explanation of "mi-moḥarat ha-shabbat" (Lev. xiii. 15) as meaning "from the morrow after the feast" (Men. 65b).

The Midrash of the Younger Halakah: The younger Halakah did not confine itself to the mere literal meaning of single passages, but sought to draw conclusions from the wording of the texts in question by logical deductions, by combinations with other passages, etc. Hence its midrash differs from the simple exegesis of the older Halakah. It treats the Bible according to certain general principles, which in the course of time became more and more amplified and developed (see TALMUD); and its interpretations depart further and further from the simple meaning of the words. A few examples will illustrate this difference in the method of interpretation between the older and the younger Halakah. It was a generally accepted opinion that the first Passover celebrated in Egypt, that of the Exodus, differed from those which followed it, in that at the first one the prohibition of leavened bread was for a single day only, whereas at subsequent Passovers this restriction extended to seven days. The older Halakah (in Mek., Bo, 16 [ed. Weiss, 24a]), represented by R.

Jose the Galilean, bases its interpretation on a different division of the sentences in Ex. xiii. than the one generally received; connecting the word "ha-yom" (= "this day"), which is the first word of verse 4, with verse 3 and so making the passage read: "There shall no leavened bread be eaten this day." The younger Halakah reads "ha-yom" with verse 4, and finds its support for the traditional halakah by means of the principle of "semukot" (collocation); that is to say, the two sentences, "There shall no leavened bread be eaten," and "This day came ye out," though they are separated grammatically, are immediately contiguous in the text, and exert an influence over each other (Pes. 28b, 96b). What the older Halakah regarded as the obvious meaning of the words of the text, the younger infers from the collocation of the sentences.

Contrast with Earlier Halakah.

The wide divergence between the simple exegesis of the older Halakah and the artificiality of the younger is illustrated also by the difference in the method of explaining the Law, cited above, in regard to uncleanness. Both halakot regard it as self-evident that if a man be unclean, whether it be from contact with a corpse or from any other cause, he may not share in the Passover (Pes. 93a). The younger Halakah, despite the dot over the ה, reads "reḥoḳah" and makes it refer to "derek," even determining how far away one must be to be excluded from participation in the feast. In order, however, to find a ground for the halakah that those who are unclean through contact with other objects than a corpse may have no share in the Passover, it explains the repetition of the word "ish" in this passage (Lev. ix. 10) as intending to include all other cases of defilement.

Despite this difference in method, the midrashim of the older and of the younger Halakah alike believed that they had sought only the true meaning of the Scriptures. Their interpretations and deductions appeared to them to be really contained in the text; and they wished them to be considered correct Biblical expositions. Hence they both have the form of Scriptural exegesis, in that each mentions the Biblical passage and the halakah which is given in explanation of it, or, more correctly speaking, which is derived from it.

It is to a law stated in this form—*i.e.*, together with the Biblical passage from which it is derived—that the name midrash is applied, whereas one which, though ultimately based on the Bible, is cited independently as an established statute is called a halakah. Collections of halakot of the second sort are the Mishnah and the Tosefta; compilations of the first sort are the halakic midrashim. This name they receive to distinguish them from the haggadic midrashim, since they contain halakot for the most part, although there are haggadic portions in them.

Abstract and Midrash Halakah.

In these collections the line between independent Halakah and Midrash Halakah is not sharply drawn. Many mishnayot in the Mishnah and in the Tosefta are midrashic halakot, *e.g.*, Ber. i. 3, 5; Bek. i. 4, 7; Ḥul. ii. 3, viii. 4; Tosef., Zeb. i. 8, xii. 20. On the other hand, the halakic midrashim contain independent halakot without statements of their Scriptural bases, *e.g.*, Sifra, Wayiḳra, Ḥobah, i. 9–13 (ed. Weiss, p. 16a, b). This confusion is explained by the fact that the redactors of the two forms of halakot borrowed passages from one another (Hoffmann, "Zur Einleitung in die Halach. Midraschim," p. 3).

Since the halakic Midrashim had for their secondary purpose the exegesis of the Bible, they were arranged according to the text of the Pentateuch. As Genesis contains very little matter of a legal character, there was probably no halakic midrash to this book. On the other hand, to each of the other four books of the Pentateuch there was a midrash from the school of R. Akiba and one from the school of R. Ishmael, and these midrashim are still in great part extant. The halakic midrash to Exodus from the school of R. Ishmael is the MEKILTA, while that of the school of R. Akiba is the Mekilta of R. Simeon b. Yoḥai, most of which is contained in

The Two Schools.

the Midrash ha-Gadol (comp. I. Lewy, "Ein Wort über die Mechilta des R. Simon," Breslau, 1889). A halakic midrash to Leviticus from the school of R. Akiba exists under the name "Sifra" or "Torat Kohanim." There was one to Leviticus from the school of R. Ishmael also, of which only fragments have been preserved (comp. Hoffmann, *l.c.* pp. 72–77). The halakic midrash to Numbers from the school of R. Ishmael is the "Sifre"; while of that of the school of R. Akiba, the Sifre Zuṭa, only extracts have survived in the Yalḳuṭ Shim'oni and in the Midrash ha-Gadol (comp. *ib.* pp. 56–66). The middle portion of the Sifre to Deuteronomy forms a halakic midrash on that book from the school of R. Akiba, while another from the school of R. Ishmael has been shown by Hoffmann to have existed (D. Hoffmann, "Liḳḳuṭe Mekilta, Collectaneen aus einer Mechilta zu Deuteronomium," in "Jubelschrift zum 70. Geburtstag des Dr. I. Hildesheimer," Hebrew part, pp. 1–32, Berlin, 1890; *idem*, "Ueber eine Mechilta zu Deuteronomium," *ib.* German part, pp. 83–98; *idem*, "Neue Collectaneen," etc., 1899).

This assignment of the several midrashim to the school of R. Ishmael and to that of R. Akiba respectively, however, is not to be too rigidly insisted upon; for the Sifre repeats in an abbreviated form some of the teachings of the Mekilta, just as the Mekilta included in the Midrash ha-Gadol has incorporated many doctrines from Akiba's midrash (comp. Hoffmann, *l.c.* p. 93). Midrashic halakot are found also scattered through the two Talmuds; for many halakic baraitot which occur in the Talmuds are really midrashic, recognizable by the fact that they mention the Scriptural bases for the respective halakot, often citing the text at the very beginning. In the Jerusalem Talmud the midrashic baraitot frequently begin with "Ketib" (= "It is written"), followed by the Scriptural passage. From the instances of midrashic baraitot occurring in the Talmud which are not found in the extant midrashim, the loss of many of the latter class of works must be inferred (Hoffmann, "Zur Einleitung," p. 3).

The Midrash of Several Younger Tannaim and of a Large Number of Amoraim: The Midrash which the Amoraim use when deducing tannaitic halakot from the Scriptures is frequently very artificial; and its interpretations are in great part so divergent from the obvious meaning of the words that they can not be considered as Scriptural exegesis in any sense. In like manner there are many explanations by the younger tannaim which can by no means be regarded as actual interpretations. These occur chiefly as expositions of such halakot as were not based on Scripture but which it was desired to connect with or support by a word in the Bible. The Gemara often says of the interpretations of a baraita: "The Biblical passage should be merely a support." Of this class are many of the explanations in the Sifra (comp. Tos. B. B. 66a, *s.v.* "miklal") and in the Sifre (comp. Tos. Bek. 54a, *s.v.* "ushne"). The tanna also often says frankly that he does not cite the Biblical word as proof ("re'aya"), but as a mere suggestion ("zeker"; lit. "reminder") of the halakah, or as an allusion ("remez") to it (Mek., Bo, 5 [ed. Weiss, p. 7b]; Sifre, Num. 112, 116 [ed. Friedmann, pp. 33a, 36a]).

BIBLIOGRAPHY: Z. Frankel, *Hodegetica in Mischnam*, pp. 11-18, 307-314, Leipsic, 1859; A. Geiger, *Urschrift*, pp. 170-197, Breslau, 1857; D. Hoffmann, *Zur Einleitung in die Halachischen Midraschim*, Berlin, 1888; Nachman Krochmal, *Moreh Nebuke ha-Zeman*, section 13, pp. 143-183, Lemberg, 1863; H. M. Pineles, *Darkah shel Torah*, pp. 168-201, Vienna, 1861; I. H. Weiss, *Dor*, i. 68-70 *et passim*, ii. 42-53.

J. J. Z. L.

MIDRASH MISHLE. See PROVERBS, MIDRASH TO.

MIDRASH SHEMUEL. See SAMUEL, MIDRASH TO.

MIDRASH TANHUMA. SEE TANHUMA.

MIDRASH TEHILLIM. See PSALMS, MIDRASH TO.

MIDRASHIM, SMALLER: A number of midrashim exist which are smaller in size, and generally later in date, than those dealt with in the articles MIDRASH HAGGADAH and MIDRASH HALAKAH. The chief of these are:

1. Midrash Abkir: This midrash, the extant remains of which consist of more than fifty excerpts contained in the Yalkuṭ and a number of citations in other works, dealt, according to all accessible evidence, only with the first two books of the Pentateuch. It derived its name from the formula אמן בימינו כן יהי רצון with which all these homilies closed, according to the testimony of R. Eleazar of Worms in a manuscript commentary on the prayer-book, and according to a codex of De Rossi. It is possible that these religious discourses were arranged in the order of the sedarim of Genesis and Exodus, the beginnings of the sedarim being Gen. i. 1, ii. 4, iii. 22, vi. 9, xii. 1, xvii. 1, xviii. 1, xxii. 1, xxvii. 1, xliv. 18; Ex. iii. 1, xvi. 4, and xxv. 1, to which belong the excerpts in Yalḳ., Gen. 4, 17, 34, 50, 63, 81, 82, 96, 120, 150, and in Yalḳ., Ex. 169, 258, and 363. If it may be assumed that in these homilies of the Midrash Abkir the expositions are not confined to the first verses, the fact that certain passages are not connected with the beginning of any seder need cause no surprise.

The language of this midrash is pure Hebrew, while its contents and discussions recall the works of the later haggadic period. As in the Pirḳe Rabbi Eli'ezer, angels are frequently mentioned (comp. the excerpts in Yalḳ. 132, 234, 241, and 243). Shemaḥsai and Azael, according to the account in the Midrash Abkir, descended to earth to hallow the name of God in a degenerate world, but could not withstand the daughters of man. Shemaḥsai was entrapped by the beauty of Istahar, who, through the marvelous might of the Divine Name, which she had elicited from him, ascended to heaven. As a reward for her virtue she was placed among the Pleiades, while the angel did penance before the Flood, and in punishment of his seduction of the daughters of men was suspended head downward between heaven and earth. Azael, however, still wanders unreformed among mortals, and through dress and adornment seeks to mislead women (Jellinek, "B. H." iv., pp. ix. *et seq.*). The version of this story in Yalḳ. 44 (on Gen. vi. 2) concludes: "Therefore do the Israelites offer as a sacrifice on the Day of Atonement a ram [sic] to the Eternal One that He may forgive the sins of Israel, and a ram [sic] to Azazel that he may bear the sins of Israel, and this is the Azazel that is referred to in the Torah." This passage of the midrash explains the words of Yoma 67b: "According to the school of R. Ishmael, Azazel is he who atones for the deed of Usa and Azael." It is to be noted that in the editio princeps of the Yalḳuṭ (Salonica, 1526-27) the source of the legend of the fallen angels (in § 44) as well as of the legend concerning the temptation of R. Mattithiah b. Ḥeresh by Satan (in § 161), who was successfully resisted by the pious hero, is simply the ordinary midrash, not the Midrash Abkir. The latter legend is found also in the Midrash of the Ten Commandments (Jellinek, *l.c.* i. 79) and in Tanḥuma (ed. Buber, "Ḥuḳḳat," Addenda, § 1).

In several other excerpts from the Yalḳuṭ, which, according to later editions, are derived from the Midrash Abkir, the source is indicated in the first edition merely by the word "Midrash," as in § 241, which discusses the legend of Usa, the patron of Egypt; here "Midrash" apparently means "Midrash Wayosha'" (Jellinek, *l.c.* i. 39 *et seq.*). Yalḳ. 235 (on Ex. xiv. 24) relates that the Egyptian magicians JANNES AND JAMBRES obtained wings by their art and soared to heaven, but were dashed down into the sea by the angel Michael. It can not be determined, however, whether this passage belongs to the fragment excerpted from the Midrash Abkir in Yalḳ. 234. This midrash was at all events known to the author of the "Shemot Rabbah," and was used or cited in the following works among others: the "Leḳaḥ Ṭob" of R. Tobias b. Eliezer, the "Ha-Roḳeaḥ" of Eleazar ben Judah of Worms, the "Pa'aneaḥ Raza," the "Ketab Tamim" of Moses Talḳu, the "Kad ha-Ḳemaḥ" of Baḥya ben Asher, a manuscript commentary by a grandson of R. Samuel of Speier, and the Yalḳuṭ Re'ubeni. The entire midrash was likewise known to Azariah dei Rossi (comp. "Me'or 'Enayim," ed. Wilna, p. 455) and to Abraham ibn Akra. The extracts in the Yalḳuṭ, which had been listed almost completely by Zunz, were collected by Buber in "Ha-Shaḥar," xi. (reprinted separately, Vienna, 1883) and by Simon Chones in "Rab Pe'alim," pp. 133 *et seq.* The legend of the two angels was also reprinted by Jellinek, *l.c.* iv. 127 *et seq.* Jannes and Jambres are mentioned also in Men. 85a and "Shemot Rabbah," 9.

BIBLIOGRAPHY: Zunz, *G. V.* p. 282; Abraham Wilna, *Rab Pe'alim*, ed. Chones, pp. 22 *et seq.*, 133 *et seq.*, Wilna, 1894; Buber, *Yeri'ot Shelomoh*, pp. 9 *et seq.*; Neubauer, in *R. E. J.* xiv. 109; Brüll's *Jahrb.* v., vi. 98 *et seq.* On the name of the midrash see especially Brüll, *l.c.* i. 146; Chones, *l.c.* p. 27; on the legend of the angels Shemaḥsai and Azael see *Enoch*, vi. *et seq.* in Kautzsch, *Pseudepigraphen*, ii. 238 *et seq.*, 275; *Targ. Yer.* on *Gen.* vi. 4; *Pirke R. El.* xxii.; *Midr. Peṭirat Mosheh*, in Jellinek, *B. H.* i. 129; Recanati on *Gen.* iv 4, vi. 2; Jellinek, *l.c.* ii. 86, v., pp. xlii., 172; Epstein, *Bereshit Rabbati*, p. 21; Brüll's *Jahrb.* i. 145 *et seq.*

2. Midrash Al Yithallel: A midrash containing stories from the lives of the wise Solomon, the mighty David, and the rich Korah, illustrating Jer. ix. 22. The text has been published according to a manuscript at Munich by Jellinek ("B. H." vi. 106–108), and according to a manuscript from Yemen by Grünhut ("Sefer ha-Liḳḳuṭim," i. 20 *et seq.*), with valuable references to sources and parallels. With the story of Solomon may be compared the passage cited in Jellinek (*l.c.* ii. 86 *et seq.*, from the "'Emeḳ ha-Melek"); the history of David is similar to the midrash of Goliath (*ib.* iv. 140 *et seq.*); and that of Korah to the passage in the Midrash Tehillim (ed. Buber on Ps. i. 15).

BIBLIOGRAPHY: Jellinek, *B. H.* iv., p. xiii.; vi., pp. xxvi. *et seq.*

3. Midrash 'Aseret ha-Dibrot: A midrash which dates, according to Jellinek, from about the tenth century, and which is devoted entirely to the Feast of Weeks, being actually called in a Vatican manuscript "a haggadah for Shabu'ot." Its author seeks to inculcate the doctrines of the Decalogue by citing pertinent tales of a moral and religious nature; and he employs, in addition to much material from unknown sources, many passages from treatises on the Creation, revelation, and similar topics, which he introduces with the phrase "ameru ḥakamim" (the sages say); he seldom cites his authorities. He writes in a lucid Hebrew style. The separate commandments are prefaced by a general introduction based on Ps. cvi. 2: "Who can utter the mighty acts of the Lord? who can shew forth all his praise?" This verse is explained, with reference to Pirḳe R. El. iii., as follows: "Even the angels are unable to recount His mighty acts; only faintly may be shown what He hath created and what shall come to pass, that the name of the King of all kings, the Holy One, blessed be He! may be praised and honored."

After a few sentences follows the haggadah of the strife of the letters, which contended with each other for the honor of forming the beginning of Creation. The victor in this contest was the letter "bet," the initial of the word בראשית, while "alef" was comforted by the promise that with it, as the first letter of אנכי, the revelation of the Ten Commandments should begin (comp. the recension of the Midrash of the Alphabet in Jellinek, "B. H." iii. 50 *et seq.*; Gen. R. i., ed. Theodor, p. 9). The word אנכי is explained as a noṭariḳon and as Egyptian (comp. Shab. 105a; Pesiḳ. 109a). This section is followed by a mystic and cosmological discussion of the magnitude of the world, of the waters above and below the firmament, and of the seven heavens (comp. "Seder Rabbah de-Bereshit" in Wertheimer, "Batte Midrashot," i. 9, 22 *et seq.*). The introduction then makes excursus on the modesty of Moses, which gained for him the honor of God's revelation of the Torah; on the pre-existence of the Torah, and on God's invitation to the Gentiles to accept it, which they all refused; and on the pledges which God required of Israel to ḳeep the Torah, these pledges being their children (comp. Cant. R. to Cant. i. 3). In the discussion of the several commandments (דיבור ראשון, etc., to דיבור תשיעי, which are included in the editions of this midrash) only the first and sixth commandments, which have no story attached to them, are treated at any length in haggadic fashion. In the case of the other commandments, legends form the principal part of the discussion, and are arranged as follows: commandment ii., the mother and her seven children, the limping Jew; commandment iii., one who never swore; commandment iv., the pious man and the cow; Joseph, who kept holy the Sabbath-day, the emperor and R. Joshua b. Hananiah, Tinnius Rufus and Rabbi Akiba; commandment v., three examples of the love of children, the child and the Book of Genesis; commandment vii., the temptation of Mattithiah b. Ḥeresh, Rabbi Meïr and the wife of his host, Mattaniah's wife and death; the history of Saul, who by the help of Elijah was reunited with his wife after a long separation; commandment viii., Solomon and the thief, the merchant and the thievish innkeeper; commandment ix., the son of the publican Baya.

BIBLIOGRAPHY: Zunz, *G. V.* pp. 142, 144; Jellinek, *B. H.* i., p. xviii.; text of the *Midrash*, ib. pp. 62–90; Benjacob, *Oẓar ha-Sefarim*, p. 301; Horowitz, *Uralte Tosefta's*, v. 66 *et seq.*; Wertheimer, *Batte Midrashot*, ii. 8, 20. On another recension of this midrash in the *Ḥibbur ha-Ma'asiyyot*, Verona, 1647, which contains a story on the honor due the Torah, as well as on a דרש עשרת הדברות, and which is contained in a manuscript of historical miscellanies, comp. Epstein in *Ha-Ḥoḳer*, i. 67; *Maḥzor Vitry*, Introduction, p. 183. Winter and Wünsche's *Die Jüdische Litteratur*, i. 669 *et seq.*, contains a translation of some fragments of another midrash to the Ten Commandments, attributed to Saadia Gaon (comp. Eisenstadter, *Arabischer Midrasch zu den Zehn Geboten*, Vienna, 1868; see also Weiss, *Dor*, iv. 152).

4. Dibre ha-Yamim shel Mosheh: This midrash, which is written in pure Hebrew, and which is in many portions a mere cento of verses from the Bible in close imitation of Biblical style, presents a history of the life of Moses embellished with many legends which must be very old, since the same or similar stories are found as early as Josephus ("Ant." ii. 9, §§ 2 *et seq.*).; viz., the stories of the wise men's prophecy to the king of the birth of a child who some day will destroy the power of the Egyptians (in the midrash the interpretation of a dream replaces the prophecy; comp. also Targ. Yer. 1 to Ex. i. 15), upon which prophecy followed the command of the king to cast the male children of the Israelites into the river; the crown which the king places upon Moses' head, and which the latter casts to the earth (in the midrash Moses is described as taking the crown from the king's head); Moses as leader of the Israelites in a war against the Ethiopians, his use of the ibis in combating the snakes that have made his way dangerous, and the love of the king's daughter for him (according to the midrash Moses enters the camp of the Ethiopian king קיקנוס, upon whose death he marries the latter's widow, and, overcoming the dangers due to the snakes, captures the long-besieged city). For other older sources which agree in part with this midrash and differ from it in some respects, see MOSES IN RABBINICAL LITERATURE.

According to Jellinek ("B. H." ii., p. viii.), the life of Moses was originally treated in detail in a chronicle which employed sources still older. This work was incorporated in the well-known collection of legends entitled "Sefer ha-Yashar"; and from this the Yalḳuṭ took extracts which agree with the "Sefer ha-Yashar" and not with the present Chronicle of Moses. At a later time, however, a shorter recension of the older chronicle was made, which is the one now existing. It was published at Constantinople in 1516, at Venice in 1544, and elsewhere, and was reprinted by Jellinek (*l.c.* ii. 1–13). Extracts were made from the chronicle by the author of the "Midrash Wayosha'"; and it was one of the sources of the "Shemot Rabbah"; it was likewise cited in the "'Aruk," by Ibn Ezra (who rejects it as apocryphal) on Ex. ii. 22, and by Samuel ben Meïr on Numbers xii. 1.

BIBLIOGRAPHY: Zunz, *G. V.* p. 145; *Rab Pe'alim*, p. 45; Jellinek, *B. H.* ii., pp. vii. *et seq.*

5. Midrash Eleh Ezkerah: This midrash receives its name from the fact that a seliḥah for the Day of Atonement, which treats the same subject and begins with the words "Eleh ezkerah," recounts the execution of ten famous teachers of the Mishnah in the time of the persecution by Hadrian. The same event is related in a very ancient source, Ekah Rabbati on Lam. ii. 2, ed. Buber, p. 50b (comp. also Midr. Teh. on Ps. ix. 13, ed. Buber, p. 44b). According to the Midrash Eleh Ezkerah, a Roman emperor commanded the execution of the ten sages of Israel to expiate the guilt of the sons of Jacob, who had sold their brother Joseph—a crime which, according to Ex. xxi. 16, had to be punished with death. The names of the martyrs are given here, as in the seliḥah already mentioned (varying in part from the Ekah Rabbati and the Midrash Tehillim), as follows: R. Simeon b. Gamaliel, R. Ishmael the high priest, R. Akiba, R. Ḥanina b. Teradion, R. Judah b. Baba, R. Judah b. Dama, R. Ḥuzpit, R. Hananiah b. Ḥakinai, R. Jeshebeab, and R. Eleazar b. Shammua'.

Although this midrash employs other sources, borrowing its introduction from the Midrash Konen, and the account of the conversation of Rabbi Ishmael with the angels in heaven probably from the "Hekalot," it forms, nevertheless, a coherent work. It was edited, on the basis of a Hamburg codex, by Jellinek (Leipsic, 1853, and in his "B. H." ii. 64–72), and, according to another manuscript, by Chones, in the "Rab Pe'alim" (pp. 157–160). A second and a third recension of the midrash were edited, on the basis of manuscript sources, in "B. H." (vi. 19–35), and a fourth is contained in the Spanish liturgical work "Bet Ab" (Leghorn, 1877). According to Jellinek, "the fourth recension is the oldest, since it has borrowed large portions from the 'Hekalot'; next to this stand the second and the third; while the youngest is the first, which, nevertheless, has the advantage of real conformity with the spirit of the race and represents this the best of all." The martyrdom of the ten sages is also treated in the additions to the "Hekalot" ("B. H." v. 167 *et seq.*) and in the ḳinah for the Ninth of Ab.

BIBLIOGRAPHY: Zunz, *G. V.* p. 142; Jellinek, *B. H.* ii., pp. xxiii. *et seq.*; v., p. xli.; vi., pp. xvii. *et seq.*; Benjacob, *Oẓar ha-Sefarim*, p. 299. On the problem of the synchronism of the ten martyrs see Grätz, *Gesch.* iv. 175 *et seq.*, and *Monatsschrift*, i. 314 *et seq.* A German translation by P. Möbius appeared in 1854.

6. Midrash 'Eser Galiyyot: This midrash treats of the ten exiles which have befallen the Jews, counting four exiles under Sennacherib, four under Nebuchadnezzar, one under Vespasian, and one under Hadrian. It contains also many parallels to the Seder 'Olam, ch. xxii. *et seq.* A citation of the commentator R. Hillel on Sifre ii. 43 (ed. Friedmann, p. 82a) justifies the inference that the Midrash 'Eser Galiyyot originally stood at the end of the Seder 'Olam; and it is also possible that Abraham ben David likewise drew material from it, for an older edition of his "Sefer ha-Ḳabbalah" includes this midrash. The haggadah at the beginning of the midrash, to the effect that the Jews had suffered ten exiles, was cited, with the formula "Our teachers have taught," by R. Ẓemaḥ Gaon in his letter addressed to the community of Kairwan in the latter part of the ninth century. The midrash has been edited by Jellinek ("B. H." iv. 133–136) and, with valuable notes, by Grünhut ("Sefer ha-Liḳḳuṭim," iii. 2–22). A later recension which "cares little about haggadic chronology, but much about haggadic embellishment," was printed in "B. H." v. 113–116.

BIBLIOGRAPHY: Jellinek, *B. H.* iv., p. xii.; v., p. xxxv.; Grünhut, *ib.* 5–13; Brüll, in *Ben Chananja*, 1866, p. 125; Epstein, *Eldad ha-Dani*, pp. 7, 17; Ratner, Introduction to the *Seder 'Olam*, pp. 49, 123, and notes on the same work, pp. 48a, 51a, 56a.

7. Midrash Esfah: This midrash, which as yet is known only from a few excerpts in Yalḳuṭ and two citations in "Sefer Raziel" and "Ha-Roḳeaḥ," receives its name from Num. xi. 16: "Gather unto me ["Esfah-li"] seventy men of the elders of Israel." In Yalḳ. i, § 736 is found a citation relating to the same verse, which can not be traced to any other midrash, and is doubtless taken from Midrash Esfah. To this midrash may possibly be referred a passage in the "Halakot Gedolot" (ed. Warsaw, p. 283b) and a fragment on Num. xvii. 14, xx. 1–3, in Wertheimer, "Batte Midrashot," iii. 8–10, which agrees in its concluding words with the excerpt in Yalḳ., Num. 763 on Num. xx. 3 (found also *ib.* 262, on Ex. xvii. 2, which begins with the same words). The name of the midrash shows that it must have begun with Num. xi. 16. The other excerpts in the Yalḳuṭ from the Midrash Esfah, §§ 737, 739, 742, 764, 773, and 845, are based on Num. xi. 24, xii. 3–7, xii. 12, xxi. 9, xxvi. 2 (found also *ib.* 684, on Num. i. 2, which begins with the same words), and Deut. vi. 16; the extent of the midrash, however, can not be determined.

The interesting extract in Yalḳ., Num. on Num. xi. 16 names the seventy elders in two of its recensions (a third recension of this passage is furnished by a Vatican manuscript); and one of these versions concludes with a noteworthy statement which justifies the inference that the midrash was taught in the academy of Ḥanina Gaon by Rabbi Samuel, brother of Rabbi Phinehas. It would seem, therefore, that the midrash was composed in Babylon in the first half of the ninth century.

BIBLIOGRAPHY: Zunz, *G. V.* pp. 279 *et seq.*; Chones, *Rab Pe'alim*, pp. 36 *et seq.*; Rapoport, *Kerem Ḥemed*, vi.; Weiss, *Dor*, iv. 41, 216; Buber, in *Keneset Yisrael*, i.; Müller, *Einleitung in die Responsa*, 1891, p. 73; Wertheimer, *Batte Midrashot*, Introduction, pp. 5 *et seq.* The excerpts from the Midrash Esfah have been collected by Buber (*l.c.*) and by Chones (*l.c.* pp. 147–153; comp. Buber, *Yeri'ot Shelomoh*, pp. 13 *et seq.*).

8. Midrash Hallel. See PSALMS, MIDRASH TO.

9. Midrash Leku Nerannena. This midrash, which is cited in the Maḥzor Vitry (§ 296, p. 334) and of which a few fragments are still preserved, seems to have been a homily ("pesiḳta") for the Feast of Ḥanukkah.

BIBLIOGRAPHY: Epstein, *Ha-Ḥoḳer*, i. 65 *et seq.*

10. Midrash Ma'aseh Torah: This midrash contains compilations of doctrines, regulations of conduct, and empirical rules, arranged in groups of three to ten each and taken from various works. It is frequently found in manuscript, and has been edited at Constantinople (1519), Venice (1544), Amsterdam (1697), and elsewhere, while it has appeared more recently in Jellinek's "B. H." (ii. 92–101) and is contained also in the "Kol Bo" (§ 118), where it frequently deviates from the Amsterdam edition even in the arrangement of its sentences. The fact that this midrash is ascribed to the patriarch R. Judah ha-Nasi (Rabbenu ha-Ḳadosh) receives its explanation from the fact that the Ma'aseh Torah is merely another recension of the similar midrash found in the edition of Schönblum (in his collection "Sheloshah Sefarim Niftaḥim," Lemberg, 1877) and in Grünhut's "Sefer ha-Liḳḳuṭim" (iii. 33–90). This latter midrash begins in both editions with the teachings which Rabbenu ha-Ḳadosh taught his son, and the work is accordingly called "Pirḳe de-Rabbenu ha-Ḳadosh" or "Pirḳe Rabbenu ha-Ḳadosh" in the two editions and in the manuscripts on which they are based.

The editions in question comprise two different recensions. In the text of Schönblum the number of numerical groups is 24; and at the beginning stands the strange order 6, 5, 4, 3, followed by the numbers 7–24. On the other hand, in Grünhut's text, which is based on a defective manuscript, the order of the "peraḳim" proceeds naturally from 3 to 12 (or 13), but the rest are lacking; and, quite apart from this divergence in the method of grouping, even within the numerical groups the two editions differ strikingly in the number and occasionally also in the wording of individual passages. In an Oxford codex of the Maḥzor Vitry a passage occurring in both editions (ed. Schönblum, p. 33a; ed. Grünhut, p. 35) is cited as being in the Pesiḳta; and it is also stated that it treats of a series of from 3 to 10 objects (comp. the introduction to the Maḥzor Vitry, p. 179; Tos. Ber. 8b; 'Er. 19a).

A similar collection, probably more ancient in origin, was edited by Horowitz in the "Kebod Ḥuppah," Frankfort-on-the-Main, 1888, the work being based on a codex of De Rossi of the year 1290. This compilation is named the "Ḥuppat Eliyahu" or the "Sheba' Ḥuppot," on account of its opening words, "Seven canopies will God set up for the righteous in the world to come" (comp. B. B. 75a). This haggadah agrees for the most part with the Ma'aseh Torah and the Pirḳe Rabbenu ha-Ḳadosh, and presents the numerical groupings up to the number 24, arranged without much order; on the whole, it harmonizes more closely with the Pirḳe. According to Horowitz, the "Ḥuppat Eliyahu" was revised and expanded into the "Huppat Eliyahu Rabbah."

The "Ḥuppat Eliyahu" was edited as far as No. 16 by R. Israel Alnaqua at the end of his "Menorat ha-Ma'or"; and this portion of the compilation, together with other extracts from this work, was appended by Elijah de Vidas to his "Reshit Ḥokmah" (comp. Schechter, "Monatsschrift," 1885, pp. 124 *et seq.*, 234). Alnaqua mentions also among the sources which he used "Ḥuppat Eliyahu Zuṭa we-Rabbah," which were evidently merely parts of the same work. From them were probably derived the two extracts in paragraphs 201 and 247 of the "Menorat ha-Ma'or" of Isaac Aboab, which are cited as occurring in the "Ḥuppat Eliyahu Rabbah" and the "Ḥuppat Eliyahu Zuṭa." Alnaqua was, furthermore, the compiler of many maxims beginning with the words לעולם, גדול, and גדולה, and forming the "Or 'Olam" at the end of his "Menorat ha-Ma'or." This collection was likewise incorporated by De Vidas in his work, and has been reprinted by Jellinek ("B. H." iii. 109–130) as the "Midrash le-'Olam" and "Midrash Gadol u-Gedolah."

The "Ma'aseh Torah" formed the model for the rich collection of Elijah Wilna which bears the same name, and which appeared at Warsaw in 1804 with the additions of his son Abraham.

BIBLIOGRAPHY: Zunz, *G. V.* pp. 284 *et seq.*; Chones, *Rab Pe'alim*, pp. 59 *et seq.*, 87 *et seq.*; Benjacob, *Oẓar ha-Sefarim*, pp. 337 *et seq.*, 357 *et seq.*; Grünhut, *Sefer ha-Liḳḳuṭim*, iii., Introduction, pp. 17 *et seq.* Abundant material regarding this midrash has been collected by Horowitz; but the numerical relations of the midrashim require thorough investigation.

11. Midrash Peṭirat Aharon: A midrash based on Num. xx. 1 *et seq.*, and describing the lack of water experienced by the children of Israel after the death of Miriam and the events at the rock from which water was obtained. It likewise treats of Num. xx. 24 *et seq.*, recounting the death of Aaron. Aaron, escorted by the people, ascended the mountain with Moses and Eleazar. There a cavern opened which Moses invited his brother to enter; in it were a table, a burning lamp, and a couch surrounded by angels. With gentle words Moses addressed Aaron, whose fate was to be happier than his own; for Aaron was to be buried by his brother, and his honor was to be inherited by his children. Aaron then lay down upon the couch, and God took him to Himself. When Moses left the cavern it vanished; but at his prayer, his assertion that Aaron was dead being disbelieved, the mountain opened again and the high priest was seen resting on the couch (see JEW. ENCYC. i. 4a, *s.v.* AARON; and on the beginning of the midrash, which is based on Zech. xi. 8, comp. Ta'an. 9a and Sifre, Deut. 305). Authorities are nowhere cited, but several statements are introduced by the formula ואז"ל (*i.e.*, ואמרו ז"ל). The midrash was edited at Constantinople (1516), Venice (1544), and elsewhere, and has been reprinted by Jellinek ("B. H." i. 91–95).

BIBLIOGRAPHY: Zunz, *G. V.* p. 146; Jellinek, *B. H.* i., p. xix.

12. Midrash Peṭirat Mosheh: This midrash describes in great detail the last acts of Moses and his death, at which the angels and God Himself were present. There are several recensions of it. The first, published at Constantinople in 1516 (Venice, 1544, and elsewhere; also in Jellinek, "B. H." i. 115–129), begins with a brief exegesis by R. Samuel Naḥmani and R. Tanḥuma of the first verse of the pericope "We-zot ha-berakah" (Deut. xxxiii. 1, xxxiv. 12), closing with its last verses, and doubtless intended for Simḥat Torah. The real content of the midrash is a haggadic treatment of Deut. xxxi. 14 *et seq.*, supplemented by an exegesis of Deut. iii. 23 *et seq.*, and is filled with somewhat tedious dialogues between God and Moses, who is represented as unwilling to die. All his tears and entreaties were in vain, however; for God commanded all the princes of heaven to close the gates of prayer. In the last days of his life, until the 7th of Adar, Moses interpreted the Torah to Israel; and on the day of his death, according to R. Ḥelbo, he wrote thirteen Torahs, of which twelve were for the twelve tribes, and the best was for the Ark of the Covenant (*ib.* xxxi. 24 *et seq.*; comp. Pesiḳ. p. 197a; Deut. R., Wayelek, end.; Midr. Teh. on Ps. xc.); some say that Gabriel descended, and took the Torah from the hands of Moses, bearing it through each heaven to show the piety of its scribe, and that the souls of the holy read from this Torah on Mondays and Thursdays and on festivals. This is followed by a long section beginning with R. Josiah's account of the honors which Moses rendered Joshua, and the service which he did him in the last days of his life. Especially noteworthy here is the poetic prayer of Joshua beginning עורו רנו שמי השמים העליונים.

After this the close of Moses' life is depicted, a bat ḳol giving warning with increasing insistence of the hours, even of the seconds, that remained for him. This enumeration of the hours and the conventional formula יצתה בת קול are important for the determination of the dependence of the additions in Deut. R. xi. and the second recension on the original version. Early in the midrash the angels Gabriel and Zangaziel, "the scribe of all the sons of heaven," are mentioned; but in the last hours of the life of Moses it is Samael, the head of the Satans, whose activity is most conspicuous as he watches for the passing of the soul, while Michael weeps and laments. At last Samael receives the command to bring the soul of Moses, but flees in terror before his glance. Again he appears with a drawn sword before Moses, but he has to yield before the "shem ha-meforash," carved on the staff of the leader of Israel. The last moment approaches, however, and God Himself appears to receive Moses' soul. The three good angels accompany Him to prepare a resting-place for Moses, whose soul at length is taken in the kiss of death. See Moses in Rabbinical Literature.

Other Recensions.

Large portions of this midrash are contained in Deut. R., ed. Wilna, xi. 4, 7, 8, 9 (?), and 10, where they must be regarded as later additions. The entire passage represented by paragraphs 9 and 10 of Deut. R. xi. is found also, combined in the same manner, in Yalḳ., Deut. 940 (on Deut. xxxi. 14), where the Midrash Peṭirat Mosheh is given as the source. Sifre 305 contains an exquisite little haggadah on Moses and the angel of death (comp. Pesiḳ. p. 199b; Deut. R. xi. 5). A long citation from the beginning of the midrash is also contained in a homily in Tan., Wa'etḥanan, 6 (on Deut. iii. 26), treating of the same theme, the death of Moses.

A second recension is based on Prov. xxxi. 39, and is considered by Jellinek, but probably incorrectly, to be the older. It was edited by him in "B. H." vi. 71–78, and has an entirely different beginning from that which is found in the other recension (comp. Deut. R. xi. 3). As it is based upon a defective manuscript, the manner in which this introduction was connected with the original midrash can not be determined; but what follows the missing portion does not differ essentially from that found in the first recension, although it is somewhat shorter and is changed in arrangement. Moses' lament that he may never taste the fruits of the land receives a long explanatory addition to the effect that he grieved not for the products of the earth, but because he would be unable to fulfil the divine commands pertaining to Palestine.

A third recension or revision of the midrash was published by Gaulmyn (Paris, 1692), together with a Latin translation and the first recension. In the "Assumptio Mosis" the manuscript ends abruptly before the account of the assumption from which that work receives its name. According to Schürer, this concluding portion must have related to the dispute of the archangel Michael with Satan, mentioned in Jude 9.

Bibliography: Zunz, *G. V.* p. 146; Jellinek, *B. H.* i., p. xxi.; vi., pp. xxi. *et seq.*; Schürer, *Gesch.* 3d ed., iii. 217 *et seq.*

13. Midrash Ṭa'ame Ḥaserot we-Yeterot: This midrash, which has been edited most completely by Wertheimer (Jerusalem, 1899), gives haggadic explanations not only of the words which are written defective or plene, as the title of the work implies, but also of a great number of those which are not read as they are written (comp. on the ketib in Wertheimer's ed., Nos. 8, 11, 13, 19, 21–30, 37, 51, 89, 106, 111, 118, 124, 125, 127–129, 131, 134, 138–140, 181, and No. 12 on a word which is read without being written). There are likewise notes on names and words which are read differently in different places (*e.g.*, in Nos. 17, 20, 123, 126, 141, 142, 164, 172), on the ἅπαξ λεγόμενον שמיכה, Judges iv. 18 (No. 108), on the peculiar writing of certain words (*e.g.*, No. 133 on למרבה, Isa. ix. 6, and No. 163 on ההלכוא, Josh. x. 24), and on the suspended letters in Judges xviii. 30, Ps. lxxx. 14, and Job xxxviii. 15 (Nos. 112–114). The midrash may be termed, therefore, a Masoretic one, although it frequently deviates from the Masorah. The haggadic interpretations are derived for the most part from scattered passages in the Talmud and in the Midrashim, while the arrangement is capricious, the individual words being arranged neither according to the order of the alphabet nor according to the sequence of the books of the Bible. In the different manuscripts and editions of it this midrash varies considerably, not only in the number and arrangement of the passages which it discusses, but also in the wording of individual interpretations. It is cited under its present title in the Tosafot (Ber. 34a), in the "Sefer Miẓwot Gadol" of Moses of Coucy, and by Asher ben Jehiel, while it is called "Midrash Ḥaserot we-Yeterot" by Solomon Norzi. A brief

מעשה עשרה הרוגי מלכות ז״לה״ה

ואלו הן רבן שמעון בן גמליאל ור׳ ישמעאל בן אלישע
כהן גדול ור׳ עקיבא בן יוסף ור׳ יהודה בן בבא ור׳

PAGE FROM MIDRASH ELEH EZKERAH, CONSTANTINOPLE (?), 1620.

(From the Sulzberger collection in the Jewish Theological Seminary of America, New York.)

extract from this work enumerating the words to be written "defective" or "plene," but omitting the reason therefor, is contained in the Maḥzor Vitry, § 518, pp. 656 *et seq.*

To the Masoretic midrashim belong also the explanations of passages read and not written or written and not read which have been edited from an old grammatical and Masoretic miscellany in the "Manuel du Lecteur" of Joseph Derenbourg (Paris, 1871), and in Jacob Saphir's "Eben Sappir" (ii. 218 *et seq.*, Mayence, 1874), and reprinted by Jellinek in his "B. H." (v. 27–30).

BIBLIOGRAPHY: The midrash on the reasons for words written "defective" and "plene" was edited by Berliner on the basis of a Munich manuscript in his *Peleṭat Soferim*, Hebrew section, pp. 36 *et seq.*, Breslau, 1872; by Wertheimer on the basis of a Genizah manuscript in the *Batte Midrashot*, i. 32 *et seq.*, iii. 1 *et seq.*; and on the basis of a codex of De Rossi in the edition mentioned in the text; comp. Berliner, *l.c.* German section, pp. 34 *et seq.*; the introductions of Wertheimer in the various editions; Zunz, *G. V.* p. 284; *Rab Pe'alim*, pp. 65 *et seq.*; Buber in *Ha-Shaḥar*, iv.

14. Midrash Tadshe (called also **Baraita de-Rabbi Pineḥas b. Ya'ir**): This small midrash begins with an interpretation of Gen. i. 11: "And God said, Let the earth bring forth" ("Tadshe ha-areẓ"). "Why," asked R. Phinehas, "did God decree that grass and herbs and fruits should grow upon the third day, while light was not created until the fourth? To show His infinite power, which is almighty; for even without the light He caused the earth to bring forth [while now He creates all manner of trees and plants through the operation of the light]." The name of the author occurs twice (ed. Epstein, pp. xxi., xxxi.); and the midrash closes with the words "'ad kan me-dibre R. Pineḥas ben Ya'ir." No other authors are named. This midrash is peculiar in several respects, varying in many statements from other midrashim; and, although written in pure Hebrew, it contains numerous expressions which are not found elsewhere, such as חג העומר, חג השופרות, כוכבים שרועים (= "planets," p. xix.). The structure of the midrash is very loose.

The Midrash Tadshe is in the main symbolic in tendency, and it plays much on groups of numbers. Section 2 contains a symbolization of the Tabernacle; and, according to Epstein, the central idea of the midrash is the theory of three worlds—earth, man, and the Tabernacle. Section 10 contains a mystic explanation of the numbers mentioned in connection with the offerings of the princes (comp. Num. vii. 12 *et seq.*). Combinations and parallelisms based on the number ten are found in sections 5 and 15; on seven, in 6, 11, and 20; on six, in 20; on five, in 7; on four, in 20; on three, in 12, 18, etc. Desultory expositions of Gen. ii. 17; iii. 3, 14 *et seq.*; Num. vii. 12 *et seq.*, 84 *et seq.*; Lev. xiii. 2, xiv. 34; Lam. i. 1, *et seq.*; Num. iv. 3, xxvii. 7; and Deut. xxxii. 12, are contained in sections 7, 10, 17, 20, 21, and 22. Especially noteworthy is section 8, on "the ages of the pious," the Patriarchs, the Matriarchs, and the twelve sons of Jacob, giving also the dates of their births. In this list the months are not designated as Nisan, etc., but as "the first," "the second," etc. The dates for Zebulun and Benjamin are lacking in the present text, but are given in a citation by Baḥya and in the Yalḳuṭ, where, however, the months are named and not numbered. The length of life ascribed to the sons of Jacob agrees with that given in the Seder 'Olam Zuṭa; but only the Book of Jubilees gives the days and months of their births, and even it does not state the length of their lives (comp. Jubilees, xxviii. and xxxii., where, however, some dates differ from those given in the midrash). On the other hand, section 6 of the Midrash Tadshe is in entire agreement with the Book of Jubilees (ii., iii., iv., vii., x., xii., xiv., xv., and xxxiii.) in its statement that twenty-two varieties of things were created in the world—seven on the first day; one on the second; four on the third; three on the fourth; three on the fifth; and four on the sixth—and that these twenty-two varieties correspond to the twenty-two generations from Adam to Jacob (and to the twenty-two letters of the alphabet).

Analogies with the Book of Jubilees.

Epstein has drawn attention to other striking analogies between this midrash and the Book of Jubilees, especially to the strange theory of Rabbi Phinehas b. Jair (p. xxxi.) that Adam was created in the first week, and that Eve was formed in the second week, from his rib; this serving as the foundation for the rule of purification given in Lev. xii. 2 *et seq.*, with which Jubilees, iii. 8 is to be compared. On these grounds, Epstein advances the hypothesis that in this and many other passages the author of the Midrash Tadshe used the Book of Jubilees, which existed at that time in Hebrew and was much larger in scope than at present, and was ascribed, "on account of its Essenic tendency," to Rabbi Phinehas b. Jair, who was famous for his great piety. It is hardly probable, however, that the present Book of Jubilees is incomplete; and a much more plausible view of Epstein's is that which regards the Midrash Tadshe as the work of Rabbi Moses ha-Darshan. Either on account of its beginning, or for some other reason, R. Phinehas b. Jair was regarded as the author of this midrash, and Num. R. xiii. 10 and xiv. 12, 18 contain several expositions and maxims from it cited under the name of that tanna. The midrash, from which Yalḳuṭ excerpted several passages and which has been cited by various authors, has been edited according to manuscript sources by Jellinek ("B. H." iii. 164–193) and by Epstein ("Beiträge zur Jüdischen Alterthumskunde," Vienna, 1887).

The Midrash Tadshe must not be confused with another baraita bearing the title "Baraita de-Rabbi b. Jair," which deals with gradations of virtues, the highest of which causes its possessor to share in the holy spirit (comp. Soṭah, end, and parallels).

BIBLIOGRAPHY: Zunz, *G. V.* p. 280; *Rab Pe'alim*, pp. 114 *et seq.*; Jellinek, *B. H.* iii., pp. xxxiii. *et seq.*; vi. p. xxix.; Epstein, *l. c.* pp. i.-xiv.; idem, *Le Livre des Jubilés, Philon et le Midrash Tadsche*, in *R. E. J.* xxi. 80 *et seq.*, xxii. 1 *et seq.*; Weiss, *Dor.* iv. 216; Kautzsch, *Pseudepigraphen*, ii. 37; Bacher, *Ag. Tan.* ii. 497, 499; Grünhut, *Sefer ha-Liḳḳuṭim*, ii. 20b.

15. Midrash Temurah (called by Me'iri **Midrash Temurot**): A small midrash consisting of three chapters. It develops the view that God in His wisdom and might has created all things on earth as contrasted pairs which mutually supplement each other. Life is known only as opposed to death, and death as opposed to life; and, in like manner, if all were foolish or wise, or rich or poor, it would not be known that they were foolish or wise, or rich or poor. "Therefore God created man and woman, beauty and deformity, fire and water, iron and wood, light and darkness, heat and cold, food and famine, drink and thirst, walking and lameness, sight and blindness, hearing and deafness, sea and land, speech and dumbness, activity and repose, pain and pleasure, joy and sorrow, health and sickness," and the like. In ch. iii. the antitheses given in Eccl. iii. 1 *et seq.* are enumerated and are paralleled with Ps. cxxxvi. Ch. i., which contains an interesting anthropological passage, and ch. ii. begin with pseudepigraphical interpretations ascribed by the midrash to Rabbis Ishmael and Akiba; the latter appear, consequently, as joint authors of the midrash.

According to Jellinek, the Midrash Temurah was composed in the first half of the thirteenth century, since it drew upon Ibn Ezra and upon Galen's dialogue on the soul, even though it is cited by Me'iri and Abraham Abulafia. It was first edited by Azulai (Leghorn, 1786), being appended to the second part of his "Shem ha-Gedolim"; and it has been reprinted by Jellinek ("B. H." i. 106–114).

Bibliography: Zunz, *G. V.* p. 118; *Rab Pe'alim*, pp. 123 *et seq.*; Jellinek, *B. H.* i., pp. xx. *et seq.*

16. Midrash Wa-Yekullu: A midrash named after Gen. ii. 1 ("Wa-Yekullu ha-Shamayim"). It contained both halakic and haggadic material, and doubtless covered several books of the Pentateuch; but it now exists only in citations by various authors after the middle of the twelfth century. In "Ha-Rokeaḥ," §§ 192, 209, 320, and 324, passages from it are quoted as belonging to Gen. xix. 24, to the pericopes Beḥuḳḳotai and Beha'aloteka and to Deut. ii. 31. Judging from the first and fourth of these citations, the Midrash Wa-Yekullu was a homiletic one, since Tanḥuma on Gen. xix. and on Deut. ii. 31, as well as Deut. R. on the latter passage, likewise contains homilies. The midrash must have derived much material from the Tanḥuma-Yelammedenu, since some of the few fragments that have been preserved agree more or less accurately with passages from the Tanḥuma or with excerpts in Yalḳuṭ from Yelammedenu. The midrash seems also to have been called "Wayekullu Rabbah." The citations from it are collected in Grünhut's "Sefer ha-Liḳḳuṭim," ii. 16b *et seq.*

Bibliography: Zunz, *G. V.* p. 281; idem, *G. S.* iii. 252; *Rab Pe'alim*, pp. 52 *et seq.*; Grünhut, *Sefer ha-Liḳḳuṭim*, Introduction, pp. 13 *et seq.*

17. Midrash Wayissa'u: This small midrash, "the heroic legend of the sons of Jacob," is based on Gen. xxxv. 5 and xxxvi. 6, and recounts the story of the wars of Jacob and his sons against the kings of the Amorites and against Esau and his army. The beginning of its version of the former story is as follows: "Our teachers said that although they did not pursue after them this time, yet seven years later all the kings of the Amorites gathered themselves together against the sons of Jacob." That the legends contained in the Wayissa'u are very old may be inferred from the Book of Jubilees, xxxiv., xxxvii. *et seq.*, and from the Testament of Judah (Kautzsch, "Pseudepigraphen," ii. 97 *et seq.*, 102 *et seq.*, 471 *et seq.*); the midrash betrays its relationship to these old pseudepigraphical writings in many details. The war against the Amorites is treated at greater length in the "Sefer ha-Yashar," pericope "Wayishlaḥ." The midrash itself is contained in Yalḳ., Gen. 133, and is mentioned by Naḥmanides on Gen. xxxiv. 13, as "Sefer Milḥamot Bene Ya'aḳob."

The text has been edited according to the Yalḳuṭ by Jellinek ("B. H." iii. 1–5), and by Chones (in his edition of "Rab Pe'alim," pp. 153 *et seq.*), and by Charles in his edition of the Book of Jubilees, Appendix II., Oxford, 1895.

Bibliography: Zunz, *G. V.* p. 145; *Rab Pe'alim*, pp. 54 *et seq.*; Jellinek, *B. H.* iii., pp. ix. *et seq.*

18. Midrash Wayosha': A midrash based on Ex. xiv. 30–xv. 18. It is an exposition in the style of the later haggadah and seems to have been intended for the "Shirah" Sabbath or for the seventh day of the Passover. Entire sections are taken verbatim from the Tanḥuma, such as the passage on Ex. xv. 3 from Tan., Bo, and on xv. 5 from Ḥuḳḳat, beginning. With the story in the exposition of Ex. xiv. 30, concerning Satan, who appeared before Abraham and Isaac as they went to the sacrifice, may be compared the addition in Tan., Wayera, ed. Stettin, No. 22; Yalḳ., Ex. §§ 98–99, end; and "Sefer ha-Yashar," end of pericope "Wayera." The midrash on Ex. xv. 2, 7 also contains extracts from the Chronicle of Moses, the passage on Usa, the genius of Egypt, agreeing word for word with the excerpt in Yalḳ., § 241. Here the first edition has merely "Midrash," while other editions give the Midrash Abkir as the source, although it is doubtful whether this haggadah ever occurred in that work.

The sections begin for the most part with the words "ameru ḥakamim," though Rabbi Joshua ben Levi and Rabbi Samuel b. Naḥmani are occasionally given as the authors. In the exposition of xv. 18 on the sorrows and the redemption in the Messianic time, the terrible figure of King Armilus is described, and it is said that he will slay the Messiah of the race of Joseph, but will himself be slain by the Messiah who is the son of David (comp. Suk. 52a); God will then gather together the scattered remnant of Israel and hold the final judgment; and the wonderful beauty of a new world full of joy and happiness is revealed.

The Midrash Wayosha' was first published at Constantinople in 1519 (Metz, 1849, and elsewhere), and has been reprinted by Jellinek ("B. H." i. 35–57).

Bibliography: Zunz, *G. V.* p. 282; *Rab Pe'alim*, p. 55; Jellinek, *B. H.* i., p. xvii.; Benjacob, *Oẓar ha-Sefarim*, p. 299.

The more recent collections of small midrashim mentioned in this article and in Midrash Haggadah are the following: A. Jellinek, "B. H." parts i.–iv., Leipsic, 1853–57; parts v.–vi., Vienna, 1873–78; Ḥayyim M. Horowitz, "Agudat Agadot," etc., Berlin, 1881; *idem*, "Bet 'Eḳed ha-Agadot: Bibliotheca Haggadica," 2 parts, Frankfort-on-the-Main, 1881; *idem*, "Kebod Ḥuppah," *ib.* 1888; *idem*, "Tosefta Attiḳta: Uralte Tosefta's," i.–v., *ib.* 1889–90; S. A. Wertheimer, "Batte Midrashot," i.–iv., Jerusalem, 1893–97; *idem*, "Leḳeṭ Midrashim," *ib.* 1903; L. Grünhut, "Sefer ha-Liḳḳuṭim, Sammlung Aelterer Midraschim," etc., i.–vi., *ib.* 1898–1903; comp. also Abraham Wilna, "Rab Pe'alim," ed. Chones, pp. 133 *et seq.*; H. L. Strack, in Herzog-Hauck, "Real-Encyc." *s.v.* "Midrasch."

In these collections, especially in Jellinek's "Bet ha-Midrash," there are many small midrashim, either edited there for the first time or reprinted, as well as a number of works under other names, a discussion of which belongs rather to an article on mystic literature. The following treatises, however, may be mentioned here, the titles being given for the most part according to Jellinek:

(1) Agadat Mashiaḥ (Haggadah of the Messiah; *ib.* iii. 141 *et seq.*). (2) Baraita Ma'ase Bereshit (in Chones' addenda to Abraham Wilna's "Rab Pe'alim," pp. 47 *et seq.*); also Seder Rabbah de-Bereshit (in Wertheimer, *l.c.* i. 1–31). (3) Gan 'Eden we-Gehinnom (Paradise and Hell; *ib.* v. 42 *et seq.*). (4) Ma'aseh R. Yehoshua' b. Levi (History of R. Joshua b. Levi; *ib.* ii. 48 *et seq.*). (5) Midrash Konen (in "B. H." ii. 23–39); Be-Ḥokmah Yasad (Divine Wisdom; *ib.* v. 63–69); Masseket Gehinnom (Tractate of Gehenna; *ib.* i. 147–149). (6) Milḥamot ha-Mashiaḥ (War of the Messiah; *ib.* vi. 117 *et seq.*). (7) Nisterot R. Shim'on b. Yoḥai (Mysteries of R. Simeon b. Yoḥai; *ib.* iii. 78 *et seq.*). (8) Otiyot de-Rabbi Akiba (Alphabetical Midrash of R. Akiba; first and second recensions in "B. H." iii. 12–64; comp. *ib.* v. 31–33; vi., p. xl.; Wertheimer, *l.c.* ii. 23 *et seq.*; and see AKIBA BEN JOSEPH, ALPHABET OF); Hekalot Rabbati (Great Hekalot; in "B. H." iii. 83–108); Masseket Hekalot (Tractate Hekalot; *ib.* ii. 40–47; comp. also *ib.* i. 58 *et seq.*, iii. 161 *et seq.*, vi. 109 *et seq.*); and "Baraita Ma'ase Merkabah" (in Wertheimer, *l.c.* ii. 15–25). (9) Otiyot Mashiaḥ (Signs of the Messiah; *ib.* ii. 58–63). (10) Pirḳe Mashiaḥ (Sections Concerning the Messiah; *ib.* iii. 68 *et seq.*). (11) Seder Gan 'Eden (Description of Paradise; *ib.* ii. 52 *et seq.*; second recension, *ib.* iii. 131–140; additions, *ib.* 194–198). (12) Sefer Eliyahu (Apocalypse of Elijah; *ib.* iii. 65 *et seq.*). (13) Sefer Zerubbabel (Book of Zerubbabel; *ib.* ii. 54–57; comp. also Wertheimer, *l.c.* ii. 25 *et seq.*, 29 *et seq.*).

E. C. J. T.

MIDWIFE.—Biblical Data: Midwives are referred to in the Bible as having been employed among the Hebrews at an early period; thus Rachel and Tamar were assisted by midwives (Gen. xxxv. 17, xxxviii. 28). They were called in, however, only in rare cases. For instance, the delivery of Rachel is expressly stated to have been a difficult one, and Tamar was delivered of twins. But in general midwives were dispensed with. Thus in Egypt, where the Hebrews multiplied rapidly (Ex. i. 7, 12), the names of only two midwives are recorded, Shiphrah and Puah; and it is stated that the Hebrew women, unlike the Egyptians, "are delivered ere the midwives come in unto them" (*ib.* i. 15, 19). Sometimes the necessary service was rendered by friends or relatives (I Sam. iv. 20).

The general Hebrew term for "midwife" is מילדת (plural, מילדות); but the word חיות (Ex. i. 19), also, is interpreted by Rashi to denote midwives, like the Aramaic חייתא. The word אבנים (*ib.* i. 16), which is the dual form of אבן (= "two stones"), has given rise to some difficulty. The Targumim and the later commentators, as Rashi and David Ḳimḥi, interpret it as "the delivery-stool," while Ibn Janaḥ, Joseph Ḳimḥi, and Parḥon, followed by some modern commentators, as Eichhorn and Knobel, render it "the womb." Gesenius ("Th."), rejecting the idea that delivery-stools existed in Egypt at such an early period (comp. Ploss, "Das Weib," 2d ed., pp. 197, 232), translates "the stone bath."

Although it is not stated what were the functions of a midwife after the delivery, yet the services enumerated in Ezek. xvi. 4 were most probably rendered by her.

J. M. SEL.

——**In Rabbinical Literature:** The midwife is generally designated by חיה, חיתא (a term applied also to the lying-in woman) and by חכמה (= "the wise woman"; comp. the French "sage-femme"), but from Lev. R. xxvii. 7 it seems that the term מחבלתא is also applied to the midwife (comp. Gen. R. lx. 3). Besides tying the umbilical cord (Shab. 128b), she performed two other duties, as may be inferred from the Talmudic passage Soṭah 11b. It is here implied that "Shiphrah" and "Puah" (see MIDWIFE, BIBLICAL DATA) were not the real names of the midwives, but only indicated their functions; the former meaning "the one who trims the child," and the latter, "the one who talks to the child," or, according to R. Hananeel, "the one who whispers"; that is to say, the midwife whispered in the woman's ear in order to facilitate parturition.

The question whether the delivery-stool was in use in Egypt during the Biblical period is answered by the Rabbis in the affirmative; for they translate אבנים "delivery-stool," giving various reasons for so doing (Soṭah *l.c.*). The Talmudic interpretation of משבר (Hosea xiii. 13) also is "delivery-stool."

A midwife, when called to assist a woman in labor, is allowed to profane the Sabbath, if necessary, in the discharge of her duties (Shab. *l.c.*; Yer. Shab. xviii. 3); and all concessions are granted to her as to one engaged in saving human life.

Although many physicians studied obstetrics, and rabbis who were acquainted with that science (Samuel, among others) were consulted on certain occasions with regard to the ritual cleanness or uncleanness of the mother, yet it does not appear from the Talmud that men were ever called to assist a woman in her delivery. It is also difficult to say whether in the Talmudic times midwives were specially trained for their profession or whether they gained their knowledge of it merely by watching the operations of others. The term חכמה, however, would seem to indicate that they were well trained.

Midwives, as appears from the Talmud, were called to assist not only women, but even domestic animals (Ḥul. 43a).

BIBLIOGRAPHY: Wilhelm Ebstein, *Die Medizin in Neuen Testament und im Talmud*, pp. 213 *et seq.*, Stuttgart, 1903; L. Kotelmann, *Die Geburtshilfe der Alten Hebräer*, 1876.

S. S. M. SEL.

MIECZYSLAV III. See POLAND.

MIEDZYBOZ (MEDZHIBOZH): Russian town in the government of Podolia; it has a total population of 5,100, including 3,400 Jews. Among the latter there are 1,009 artisans and 57 day-laborers. There are the usual charitable organizations. About 300 families were assisted in 1898 with fuel, and were given aid for Passover. A Jewish community existed at Miedzyboz as early as the sixteenth century, but in the course of the Cossack uprising under Chmielnicki it was destroyed. A few years later the census (1661) of the district of

Podolia showed that Miedzyboz had only a few Jewish houses, including two inns; these were exempted from taxation by privilege. During the war between Russia and Poland for the possession of Little Russia, the Jews of Miedzyboz were again put to the sword (1664). About 1740 the founder of Ḥasidism, Israel b. Eliezer BA'AL SHEM-ṬOB, settled there, and began to disseminate his teachings.

BIBLIOGRAPHY: *Regesty i Nadpisi*, i. 426, 453, 464, St. Petersburg, 1899; S. Dubnow, *Yevreiskaya Istoriya*, ii. 428, Odessa, 1897.

H. R. S. J.

MIEDZYRZECZ (MESERITZ or **MEZHIRECHYE):** Town in the government of Siedlce, Russian Poland; near Warsaw. It has (1904) a population of 13,681, of whom 9,000 are Jews. The first Jewish settlement dates probably from the sixteenth century, its members coming from Germany and especially from Frankfort-on-the-Main. The Jews control all the business of the town. The making of bristles for the German export trade, via Leipsic, is one of its important industries, in which many Jewish workmen are employed. Moses Michel Migdal introduced this enterprise.

The synagogue, a very imposing stone structure, with a seating capacity of approximately 3,000, was built about 1800; Count Potocki, who formerly owned the town, is said to have contributed a large sum toward its erection. The bet ha-midrash was built in 1859. Miedzyrzecz has several minor congregations, a Talmud Torah, and a yeshibah (founded by Bendet Barg; d. 1891). Many Jews from Miedzyrzecz settled in the Holy Land, among them being Ẓebi Hirsch Fischbein (d. Jerusalem 1870) and David Janower. Both contributed to the founding of a Talmud Torah in Jerusalem. The colonists of Yesod ha-Ma'alah, near Safed, in 1885, were all from Miedzyrzecz.

The following is a list of the rabbis of Miedzyrzecz: **Ẓebi Hirsch b. Abbusch** of Frankfort-on-the-Main (d. 1734); **Isaac b. Ẓebi Hirsch** (d. 1771); **Löb of Frankfort; Naḥman b. Elijah; Ephraim Eliezer Ẓebi b. Ẓeeb Harlap** (Eliezer Harlap; d. 1849; a descendant of Gedaliah ibn Yaḥya; he was a cabalist and left many manuscripts, some of which have been published under the title "Migdenot Eliezer"; in its introduction he traces his descent from King David); **Yom-Ṭob Lippe Heilpern** (author of "'Oneg Yom-Ṭob," responsa); **Joshua Löb Diskin** (d. Jerusalem 1898); **Simḥah Samuel** (author of "Mesharet Mosheh," novellæ on Maimonides' "Yad"; d. 1865); **Israel Isser Shapiro** of Augustow (d. 1895); **Naḥman Baer Shapiro** (son of Israel Isser).

Miedzyrzecz has had several authors of note. **Abraham Dob Berusch Flohm,** maggid, was the author of "Ḥesed le-Abraham," on the Haggadah (1836). He corrected for the press all the manuscripts of Jacob, the maggid of Dubno. **Jacob David Biederman** was the author of annotations on "Torat Kohanim"; he became rabbi of Kozenitz, a small town near Miedzyrzecz. **Moses Ḥayyim Triwaks** (b. 1868) was the author of "Nod Dema'ot" (Warsaw, 1888) and "Naḥalat Mosheh" (1890). There is a congregation in New York city whose members are mostly natives of Miedzyrzecz.

H. R. J. D. E.

MIELZINER, MOSES: American rabbi and author; born at Schubin, province of Posen, Germany, Aug. 12, 1828; died at Cincinnati Feb. 18, 1903. His father, **Benjamin,** rabbi in his native town, gave him the first instruction in Talmudic literature, while he received his secular education from L. I. Braunhart, a man of superior gifts, who, after having been a pupil of Heinrich Heine in the course founded by the Culturverein in Berlin, was appointed principal of the Jewish school in Schubin in 1835, and remained there until his death in his ninety-eighth year in 1904. In 1843 Mielziner was sent to Exin, where he attended the yeshibah of the aged rabbi Wolf Klausner, and in 1845 he went to Berlin in pursuit of further secular education, attending at the same time the Talmudic course of Rabbi J. J. Oettinger. Having prepared himself privately for academic studies, he entered the University of Berlin in 1848, and remained there until 1852, when Samuel HOLDHEIM, who took a great interest in him, recommended him to Waren in Mecklenburg as teacher and preacher. The Orthodox reaction introduced by the "Landrabbiner" Lüpschitz in 1853 forced Mielziner, much to the regret of his congregation ("Allg. Zeit. des Jud." 1854, p. 527; 1857, p. 369), to resign his position. He went to Denmark, where his brother Solomon was minister in Aalborg, and soon obtained a position at Randers in 1854. In 1857 he was called as principal of the religious school to Copenhagen, where he remained until 1865, when he was called to the rabbinate of the Congregation Anshe Chesed in New York ("New Yorker Staats-Zeitung," 1865, No. 215). When this congregation was absorbed by the Beth-El congregation, he opened a private school, which he conducted until 1879, when he received a call as professor of Talmud and rabbinical literature from the Hebrew Union College in Cincinnati. Upon the death of Isaac M. WISE March 26, 1900, he became president of this institution, and held this position until his death.

Moses Mielziner.

Mielziner was not a voluminous writer. Apart from several sermons which he published, the first of which was delivered in Waren, 1854, he wrote "Die Verhältnisse der Sklaven bei den Hebräern," Copenhagen, 1859, this being the thesis for which he received the degree of Ph.D. from the University of Giessen. This book appeared also in an English translation under the title "Slavery Among the Ancient Hebrews," Cincinnati, 1895. As a result of his lectures at the college he published: "Jewish Law of Marriage and Divorce," Cincinnati, 1884; "Introduction to the Talmud," *ib.* 1894; second edition, New York, 1903; and "Legal Maxims of the Talmud," *ib.* 1898. Mielziner edited a Danish almanac for the year 5622 = 1862–63, and "A Selection from the Psalms for School and Family," Cincinnati, 1890. He also contributed to the "Allgemeine Zeitung des Judenthums," "Ben Chananja," the "American Israelite," and "Die Deborah," and wrote articles for the "Year-Book of the Central Conference of American Rabbis" and for THE JEWISH ENCYCLOPEDIA.

Mielziner married in 1861 Rosette Levald of Copenhagen, and of the seven children who survived him, one, **Leo,** is an artist, living in Paris, and another, **Jacob,** is a rabbi at Helena, Mont.

BIBLIOGRAPHY: *American Israelite*, Feb. 26, 1903; *Allg. Zeit. des Jud.* 1903, pp. 271–273; *Program of the Hebrew Union College*, 1903, and *Beretning om den Jödiske Religionsskole's Virksomhed i de Forlöbne 50 Aar*, Copenhagen, 1904.

A. D.

MIESES: A family of German and Austrian scholars of the nineteenth century, of which the following are prominent members:

Fabius Mieses: Galician litterateur and philosopher; born at Brody Oct. 31, 1824; died at Leipsic Oct. 10, 1898. Up to his fifteenth year he studied Hebrew literature exclusively. At an early age he gave signs of great intellectual power, and was hailed as a genius. In the house of his father-in-law, I. Mieses, a scholar living in Dresden, he met, besides Rapoport and other Maskilim, his future teacher, M. Schöngut, who initiated him into the study of philosophy, and with whom he used to converse in Hebrew during their regular daily walks. At the same time he assiduously applied himself to the study of German, French, Italian, Latin, mathematics, and astronomy. In 1846 his German essay "Gegenwart und Vergangenheit im Judenthume" appeared in Fürst's "Orient"; and from that time he became assistant editor of and a regular contributor to that paper. In 1878 he published (at Lyck) a didactic poem entitled "Ha-Emunah weha-Tebunah," treating of Darwinism and its opponents. By this production he gained for himself a prominent and lasting place among Hebrew poets.

Mieses was a prolific writer. Besides frequently contributing to various Hebrew and German periodicals, he wrote the following independent works: "Ha-Ḳabbalah weha-Ḥasidut" (Breslau, 1866; Odessa, 1871); "Ḳorot ha-Filusufiyah ha-Ḥadashah" (Leipsic, 1887), a history of modern philosophy from Kant to Mieses' own time; "Shirim" (Cracow, 1891), a collection of miscellaneous poems; "Die Bibel der Vernunft" (Leipsic, 1895). Upon this last work rests his chief claim to fame, as it is the first and only one of its kind which was written in the Hebrew tongue. Mieses was opposed to all religious reforms.

BIBLIOGRAPHY: E. Günzig, *Toledot F. Mieses*, Cracow, 1890; *Keneset Yisrael*, p. 118, Warsaw, 1887.

S. I. WAR.

Isaac Mieses: Austrian writer; born at Lemberg 1802; died in 1883. A very talented boy, he acquired at an early age a knowledge of the Talmud and kindred works. Later on he devoted himself mainly to philosophy. He removed to Thorn when nearly sixty years of age.

His works include the following: "Beitrag zur Würdigung der Wirren im Judentum," Leipsic, 1845; "Zofnath Paneach: Darstellung und Kritische Beleuchtung der Jüdischen Geheimlehre," in two parts, Cracow, 1862; "Benedict Spinoza und Sein Verhältniss zum Kriticismus," in "Zeitschrift für Exacte Philosophie," vol. iii.; and many other scientific essays published in various periodicals.

BIBLIOGRAPHY: E. Ginzig, *Toledot Fabius Mieses*, Cracow, 1890.

S. A. H. R.

Jacques Mieses: German journalist and chess master; born at Leipsic Feb. 27, 1865; educated at the universities of his native city and Berlin, where he studied mainly the natural sciences. When seventeen years of age he won the first prize at the annual tournament of one of the Berlin chess clubs, and then for some time devoted himself chiefly to theoretical chess and problems. Of the latter he is generally admitted to be one of the leading solvers. Since 1888 he has participated in most of the international tournaments, at each of which he has gained prizes:

1888. Nuremberg.	1900. Paris.
1888. Leipsic.	1901. Monte Carlo.
1889. Breslau.	1902. Hanover.
1899. London.	

At the tourney held at Cambridge Springs, Pa., in 1904, he was placed eighth, tying with Pillsbury.

Mieses is the author of the following works on chess: "Kleines Lehrbuch des Schachspiels" (Leipsic); "Schachmeister-Partieen" (*ib.*); and, with C. von Bardeleben, "Lehrbuch des Schachspiels" (*ib.* 1894). He edits also the chess columns of the "Berliner Tageblatt," "Leipziger Neueste Nachrichten," and "Zur Guten Stunde."

BIBLIOGRAPHY: *The Hastings Chess Tournament*, 1895, ed. Cheshire, p. 361, London, 1896; C. T. Blanchard, *Examples of Chess Master-Play*, second series, p. 117, London, 1894.

S. A. P.

Judah Löb Mieses: One of the most prominent Maskilim of Galicia; died at Lemberg 1831. He was a man of wealth and education, and made his house the center of a literary circle. He encouraged and aided Isaac Erter and other young men who showed eagerness for knowledge and self-culture, and he offered them the use of his valuable library.

Mieses was a fluent Hebrew writer and a strong opponent of Ḥasidism. He was the author of "Ḳin'at ha-Emet" (Vienna, 1828; 2d ed., Lemberg, 1879), containing an introduction and three dialogues between Maimonides and Solomon of Chelm, author of "Merkebet ha-Mishneh" (Salonica, 1777). In this work Mieses pleads for pure Judaism free from all superstitious belief in spirits, dreams, demons, witchcraft, metempsychosis, etc., which in the course of time had obscured the light of the sublime religion. He sharply criticizes the ẓaddiḳ for spreading the grossest superstition among the Ḥasidim, and for exploiting the credulity of the ignorant masses. The author evinces a wide acquaintance with Jewish and general literature; and he appends to his book, under the title "Liḳḳuṭe Peraḥim," extracts from the writings of Judah ha-Levi, Ibn Ezra, Ḳimḥi, Albo, Abravanel, Joseph Delmedigo, and others, in support of his own views. He wrote also additions to David Caro's "Tekunat ha-Rabbanim" (2d ed., Lemberg, 1879; see JEW. ENCYC. iii. 582, *s.v.* CARO, DAVID).

BIBLIOGRAPHY: Benjacob, *Oẓar ha-Sefarim*, p. 530; *Bikkure ha-'Ittim*, xi. 126–142, Vienna, 1830; Fürst, *Bibl. Jud.* ii. 377; Geiger, *Melo Chofnajim*, pp. xlviii., 51, and Hebrew text, p. 6, Berlin, 1840; Grätz, *Gesch.* xi. 425–426, 488, Leipsic, 1870; *Kerem Ḥemed*, pp. 124–134, Vienna, 1833; Letteris, in Erter, *Gesammelte Schriften*, p. v., Vienna, 1864; Zeitlin, *Bibl. Post-Mendels.* p. 239.

D. S. MAN.

MIGAS, IBN. See Ibn Migas.

MIGGO: An Aramaic word contracted from "min gaw" (= "from within"), meaning to proceed from the content of a sentence or circumstance, and designating originally a conclusion based on analogy. It is used in this sense in B. M. 5b. If it be assumed that one has transgressed a commandment, and has taken money or property which does not belong to him, it follows that he may be suspected with regard to an oath, and that he is likely to commit perjury. Such a conclusion, however, is valid only when the breaking of a venial commandment is inferred from the violation of an important one, and not conversely (comp. Tos. B. M. *l.c.*, catch-word "de-ḥashid"). Another example of the use of "miggo" in this sense occurs in Suk. 7a, where, from the assumption that a ledge is considered a wall in the case of a booth, the conclusion is drawn that a ledge is likewise a wall so far as the Sabbath is concerned. The Hebrew equivalent for the Aramaic "miggo" in this sense is "mittok," a contraction of "min tok" (= "from within"). An example of the use of this term occurs in Beẓah 12a, where, from the fact that work is permissible on a holiday when it is necessary for a livelihood, it is inferred that it is allowed also when it is not necessary for subsistence: "Mittok she-hutterah le-ẓorek hutterah nami shello le-ẓorek."

Later the expression "miggo" was frequently used as a legal term, connoting "for this reason." When, for instance, a defendant or a plaintiff who bases his statements on a given assertion is known to have other and better reasons for his complaint or his defense, he is believed on the ground of the assertion made, and it is assumed that he has spoken only the truth; for had he wished to perjure himself he would have alleged better reasons. Thus the expression "The defendant (or the plaintiff) has a miggo" signifies that he was in a position to produce more convincing grounds for his statements; and in like manner, the formula "His case is decided on account of a miggo" signifies that he is believed for this reason.

Bases of Legal Argument.

The Mishnah does not contain the word "miggo," but a similar idea is expressed in the sentence "ha-peh she-asar hu ha-peh she-hittir" (= "the mouth which has bound has loosed"). An application of this principle occurs in Ket. 15b: "When one says, 'This field belonged to thy father, but I have bought it from him,' he is believed; for, had he wished to appropriate what was not his, he would not have called attention to the fact that the land had previously belonged to another."

Miggo is not, however, conclusive proof, but only evidence of probability. If two parties present their opposing statements to a judge who can not decide which is true, and if one party has a miggo, the fact that he did not plead other arguments which he might have alleged is allowed to decide the matter and results in a favorable judgment for him. The miggo is valid, therefore, only when it must be admitted that the party in question omitted the presentation of other pleas within his power in good faith and not for some ulterior reason. If, on the other hand, the latter motive is to be assumed, the miggo is absolutely invalid. An example may make this clearer. A entrusts B with a given object. If B asserts that the object so given him was destroyed through no fault of his, he is obliged to take the oath prescribed by the Bible, in spite of the fact that he has a miggo—namely, he might deny that A had given him the object in question. But in the case in question B did not avail himself of this plea, only because he did not have the audacity to deny a fact known to A and because he preferred to tell a falsehood which was not known by his opponents to be such (comp. Asheri to Shebu. 45a).

The miggo is, furthermore, subject to many limitations. Thus it is invalid when the better plea of the party in question is an unusual one, or one of an incriminating character, or one which is known only to lawyers. It is invalid also when the court recognizes the assertion made to be false (comp. Tos. B. B. 30a, *s.v.* לאו). Neither is the miggo valid when the assertion made is suspected to be based on error, although the defendant or the plaintiff believes he is speaking the truth. When, for example, a wife declares that her husband died in battle, she is not believed simply because she has a miggo—namely, she might have averred that he died elsewhere than in battle. The miggo can find no application here, because the woman's veracity has not been questioned, the point at issue being whether or not she was mistaken and thought that her husband died on the field, whereas he was only severely wounded (Yeb. 115a).

Limitations.

Bibliography: Z. Frankel, *Der Gerichtliche Beweis nach Mosaisch-Talmudischem Rechte*, pp. 437-474, Berlin, 1846; Fink, *Miggo als Rechtsbeweis im Babylonischen Talmud*, Breslau, 1891.

s. J. Z. L.

MIGRATION: Removal from one region to another. Ever since the Exile, Jews have been forced to wander from country to country, and a full history of their migrations would be almost identical with a complete history of that people.

In the first century the center of Jewish population, taking the whole spread of the Diaspora, was probably somewhere about Tarsus. In the twelfth century it had moved to the neighborhood of Troyes because of the migration of the Jews to Rome, to Spain, to Gaul, to England, and to Germany. By the middle of the sixteenth century, owing to the expulsion and migrations from western Europe, the center of Jewish population had moved over to Poland. It is impossible here to deal with these movements in detail, but the forcible migration of Jews to Babylonia in Bible times, whence they spread to Persia, and, it has been conjectured, even up to Caucasia, is a typical instance of such movements. Expulsion from England removed 16,000 Jews; that from Spain is reckoned to have spread more than 300,000 over the lands bordering the Mediterranean. The medieval history of the German Jews consists almost entirely of wholesale movements of communities from one town to another. Unfortunately in few of these instances are any numerical details available. It was only recently that new conditions enable some estimate to be made of the numbers of Jews forced through migration from their native countries.

In recent times a new kind of migration has taken place, due partly to economic causes and partly to persecution, which can be traced in some detail for the past quarter of a century. The chief countries from which emigration has taken place are Russia, Galicia, and Rumania; the chief countries of immigration, England and the United States. J.

From Russia.

The emigration of Jews from Russia increased remarkably in the seventies and became widespread in the eighties of the nineteenth century. That until then the emigration movement was but slight is evidenced by the fact that between the years 1821–70 only 7,550 Jewish emigrants from Russia and Russian Poland set out for the United States, at that time the most important objective point, and in the decade 1871–80 no less than 41,057 came from Russia alone.

The direct cause which led to the largely increased emigration may be found in the anti-Jewish riots which occurred in the early eighties. Maddened by fear after these riots, the Jewish population, including not a few professional men, formed regular emigrant companies. These removed to Germany, Austro-Hungary, England, France, the United States, and Palestine. There are no exact figures at hand to show the extent of that first emigration movement. The emigration from Russia to the United States, which amounted, on the average, to no more than 4,100 persons a year even in the decade 1871-80, reached in the decade 1881-90 an annual average of 20,700. The following table gives the number of Russian Jews who emigrated to the United States during the several years of this decade according to the figures of the United States Immigration Commission and of the United Hebrew Charities respectively:

Year.	From Russia.	From Other Countries.	Year.	From Russia.	From Other Countries.
1881..........	8,193	......	1886.........	17,309	29,658
1882..........	17,497	14,310	1887.........	28,944	27,468
1883..........	6,907	......	1888.........	31,256	31,363
1884..........	15,122	......	1889.........	31,889	23,962
1885..........	16,603	19,611	1890.........	33,147	34,303

However, while the riots of 1881 were the immediate cause of the increased emigration, the true cause was undoubtedly the very unfortunate economic condition of the Jewish population in Russia, and the riots merely supplied the stimulus. The pioneers were scarcely settled in their new homes when their friends and relatives followed them. The relations between the Pale of Settlement and the countries whither the emigrants moved became more intimate, and because of the more favorable economic conditions in these countries the emigration to them increased. The fluctuations in the separate years covering the period may be explained mainly by the fluctuations in the commercial prosperity of these lands.

The new and repressive measures inaugurated by the Russian government in the early nineties resulted in another increase of Jewish emigration. In 1891 and 1892 occurred the administrative expulsion of the Jews from Moscow and a similar expulsion from the villages and hamlets outside the Pale. It is estimated that there were expelled in this manner more than 400,000 persons. This mass of people rushed to the already overcrowded cities and towns of the Pale, and naturally enough could find no room there. As a result of this those who were expelled by the administration either emigrated themselves or crowded out others from the Pale, and the latter in their turn had to emigrate. The average number of Jewish immigrants to the United States, by far the greater part of whom were from Russia, was in the nineties more than double the number in the preceding decade. For the single years the immigration was as follows:

Year.	From Russia.	From Other Countries.	Year.	From Russia.	From Other Countries.
1891..........	42,145	69,139	1896.........	45,137	28,118
1892..........	76,417	60,325	1897.........	22,750	20,684
1893..........	35,626	32,943	1898.........	27,221	27,409
1894..........	36,725	22,108	1899.........	24,275	......
1895..........	33,232	32,077	1900.........	37,011	......

In Russia the emigration took place from every part of the Pale and from Poland, but the greater numbers came from the provinces which are nearest the boundary, such as Volhynia, Podolia, Kiev, Grodno, Kovno, Suwalki, etc.

BIBLIOGRAPHY: *Voskhod*; G. M. Price, *Russkiye Yevrei v Amerikye*, St. Petersburg, 1893; *Alien Immigration, Reports to the Board of Trade*, London, 1893.

E. C. L. Wy.

Austria and Rumania.

Statistics of the emigration of Jews from Austria and Rumania are accessible for the decade 1890–1900. These are obtained by subtracting the Jewish population of the former date from that of the end of the century. The increase in the Jewish population of Austria during that period was 81,594, but the excess of births over deaths was 186,352, showing that 104,758 had migrated from Austria. The majority of these went from Galicia; and by the same process it is shown that 108,949 Jews left that province, some of them going to other parts of Austria ("Oesterreichische Statistik," lxvi., pp. xxxii.–xxxiii., Vienna, 1902).

If the same method be applied to Rumania, from data supplied by J. Jacobs in "The Jewish Chronicle," Aug. 21, 1885, and by W. Bambus in Bloch's "Oesterreichische Wochenschrift," 1902, p. 678, it would appear that between 1877 and 1894 the Jewish population increased 26,919, whereas the excess of births over deaths for that period ran to 69,193, showing that in those seventeen years 42,274 Rumanian Jews had emigrated. This number must have increased considerably in the last decade, during which persecution in Rumania has been more severe.

As regards the countries to which these emigrants from Russia, Galicia, and Rumania wend their way, it must be borne in mind that most of the Continental countries rigidly enforce the restrictions forbidding the Jews of eastern Europe to settle within their boundaries, yet, notwithstanding these restrictions, it has been reckoned that nearly 30,000 have settled in Germany since 1875 ("Ha-Maggid," 1903, No. 19). Nevertheless, there have been practically only two asylums for the Jews of the new Exodus, Great Britain and the United States, though numbers have gone to South Africa; but during the Boer war the emigration to South Africa stopped on account of the limitations prescribed by the Cape Parliament against immigration. It is still uncertain at the present time whether the new law will actually stop the migration of Jews to South Africa. A few of the emigrants have been transported by the Jewish Colonization Association to the Argentine Republic (see AGRICULTURAL COLONIES).

England and United States.

So far as immigration to England is concerned there is difficulty in ascertaining the number, as no statistics of religion are taken there. A conservative estimate ("Jewish Chronicle," Feb. 7, 1902) reckoned the number of alien Jews in London as 55,000, five-sevenths of whom were Russian Poles. The total Jewish immigration during the past twenty years has probably not exceeded 100,000 for all the British Isles, of which 80,000 came directly from Russia.

For the United States fuller details can be given, as records have been kept at the chief ports of entry—New York, Philadelphia, and Baltimore—since the great exodus in 1881. Between that year and 1884 74,310 Jews were recorded as reaching the United States, though details no longer exist as to their provenience. From 1884 to October, 1903, the United Hebrew Charities recorded the nationalities of all Jewish immigrants landing at Castle Garden and Ellis Island, and furnish the following figures:

Nationality.	Total.	Percentage.	Nationality.	Total.	Percentage.
Russians	406,657	65.36	Dutch	524	.08
Austrians	158,609	25.49	Swedes	380	.06
Rumanians	36,099	5.80	French	354	.05
Germans	15,469	2.48	Danes	225	.04
English	2,273	.36			
Turks	1,534	.24	Total	622,124	

Besides these, up to 1903 there have come in at Philadelphia 50,264 and at Baltimore 28,487, making a grand total of 775,181 of Jewish immigrants actually counted since 1881, of whom it may be conjectured more than 500,000 were Russians, 180,000 were Austrians, and 50,000 were Rumanians.

Altogether during the quarter of a century from 1881 to 1904 there has probably been a migration of Jews numbering close on a million souls, of whom, so far as the imperfections of the records enable one to estimate, about 850,000 have gone to America, 100,000 to England, 30,000 to Germany, and 20,000 have been scattered throughout the rest of Europe. Of these 200,000 came from Galicia, 100,000 from Rumania, and the remaining 700,000 from Russia. Apart from these great streams of migration there is a natural ebb and flood of young men seeking their fortunes in most of the European communities and almost all quarters of the globe. Their numbers are somewhat larger in proportion than those of the rest of the population, owing to their international relationships; but in the more settled communities like those of Holland, France, England, and the United States, where there is no active persecution, there is little tendency toward emigration.

Among the results of migration of which notice will have to be taken in all statistical inquiries are the ages and sexes of the migrants. It has been reckoned that whereas in Russia persons between the ages of 14 and 45 form 45 per cent of the Jewish population, they constitute 70 per cent of those who migrate to America. So, too, while there are 95 Jews to 100 Jewesses in Russia, there are said to be 134 Jews as against 100 Jewesses among those emigrating ("Ha-Ẓefirah," 1903, No. 62). This is confirmed by the records of the United Hebrew Charities in New York, between 1884 and 1902, which show that the immigrants consisted of 222,202 males, 155,000 females, and 197,351 children.

This tends to make the death-rate of any population consisting of Russian Jewish refugees very low, owing to the fact that so many of them are of the ages between 14 and 45, and at the same time renders the marriage-rate very high, as so many of the Jewish immigrants are between 20 and 30, the favorite age for marriage; but it must be borne in mind that there are three men to two women in the stream of migration.

S. J.

MIGUES, JOÃO. See NASI, JOSEPH (JOÃO MIGUES).

MIHAILENI: Small town in the district of Dorogoi, Rumania. It was formerly called Vladeni and Tirgu-Nou, and was founded in 1792 by a number of Jews under an agreement with the proprietor of the domain. This agreement was confirmed by a decree of Prince Alexander Constantine Moruzi, dated May 30 of the same year. Besides certain personal advantages, the founders obtained the right to use gratuitously the grounds necessary for a synagogue, a bath, and a cemetery.

When the town came into the possession of Prince Michel Sturza in 1835, he made it the capital of the district of Dorogoi. Actuated by a desire to change the terms of the original agreement, he persecuted the inhabitants, especially the Jews, cruelly beating one of their leading men and imprisoning his son. Later, however, a law was enacted under which all artisans who should settle in the city were to be exempt for five years from the payment of rent for property held by emphyteusis.

The law of 1838, framed by a commission which included seven representatives of the Jewish community, provided that the large synagogue and two small ones, an oratory, and the bath should be exempt from rent. Because of such measures the Jewish population gradually increased. The number of Jewish taxpayers increased from 60 in 1803 to 129 in 1820; the census of 1831 reported 747 Jews and 72 Christians; and that of 1859 showed 2,472

Jews and 1,812 Christians. The Jewish population reached its maximum in 1886, when there were 2,855 Jews as compared with 1,075 Christians. The city was, however, neglected by the authorities, and began to decline. In spite of an excess of births and the fact that many Jews expelled from neighboring villages took refuge in Mihaileni, the number of Jews continued to diminish. According to the census of 1899 there were only 2,446 Jews in Mihaileni; and this number has decreased considerably on account of emigration since 1900.

The income of the Jewish community, which amounts to 18,000 francs annually, is derived from a tax on meat, poultry, unleavened bread, and from certain other fees, including those from the bath. The Jews support a rabbi and four shoḥeṭim. The Talmud Torah of former years has been transformed into a modern school; but ten ḥadarim have been closed. In addition to the large synagogue, built when the city was founded, there are eleven small synagogues or oratories, and the community possesses also a benevolent association and a Zionist society.

BIBLIOGRAPHY: T. Codrescu, *Uricarul*, viii. 152, ix. 12; *Buletinul Moldovei*, March 16, 1839; N. Filipescu-Dubau, *Dictionarul Geografic al Judetului Dorohoi*, p. 218; *Fraternitatea*, 1882, p. 345; *Calendarul Israelit-Illustrat pe 5564*, Bucharest, 1903; M. Schwarzfeld, *Excursiuni Critice Asupra Istoriei Evreilor*, ib. 1888, pp. 16-17.

G. E. SD.

MI-KAMOKAH ("Who is like unto Thee?"): Opening words of the verse Ex. xv. 11, which, with verse 18 of the same chapter ("Adonai Yimlok," etc.), is regularly employed as a response in the evening and morning services between the SHEMA' and the SHEMONEH 'ESREH. Normally, as on week-days and ordinary Sabbaths, these verses are chanted to the melody-type in the free employment of which the particular service is intoned (comp. ḤAZZANUT). In one case, indeed, the setting of "Mi-Kamokah" may have itself determined the intonation of the whole of the service in which it finds a place. This is the evening service of the Days of Penitence (New-Year to Day of Atonement), the traditional intonation of which is much later in style than that of any of the other services of the northern Jews. It differs from them very notably in its tonality also, which is that of the ordinary modern major mode, while the other services utilize scale-forms, surviving only in the early medieval plain-song of the Church, or in the folk-song of eastern Europe. This penitential setting is accordingly designated when "Mi-Kamokah" is itself quoted as an ancient melody; and it is given in the accompanying transcription.

MI-KAMOKAH

To the use of "Mi-Kamokah" as a response is due also the introduction of the more recent custom into the northern liturgies according to which certain melodies, usually of post-medieval adoption, sung in the synagogue or in the home on special occasions, have come to be utilized as representative themes, and chanted as such not only with "Mi-Kamokah" and the opening verses of Ps. cxviii. (see HALLEL), but also with other passages utilized on previous days as anticipatory references to the occasion. As an example may be cited the practise customary on the last Sabbath in the month, when the day of the ensuing new moon is announced to the melody representative of any festival or fast which may occur in the approaching month.

The first such melody utilized as a representative theme was probably that of MA'OZ ẒUR, the domestic hymn on the festival commemorating the triumph of the Maccabees, whose name, it was traditionally held, was itself compounded of the initial letters of the response "Mi-Kamokah ba-elim Adonai"; so that the introducer of the custom saw an eponymous connection between the text of the response and the melody.

According to recent practise, "Mi-Kamokah" and the accompanying passages are chanted on special occasions to the following melodies, considered as representative of the respective occasions, viz.:

Festivals (including intermediate Sabbaths):

Passover......ADDIR HU.
Pentecost.....AḲDAMUT or else Yeẓib Pitgam.
Tabernacles..."Lulab" chant (see HALLEL).

Feast of Dedication (Ḥanukkah)....Ma'oz Ẓur.
Sabbaths in the 'Omer weeks....Lekah Dodi of same.
Sabbaths between the fasts of Tammuz and Ab.....'Eli Ẓiyyon.
At a circumcision..A melody specially introduced by the mohel into the morning service at references to "the covenant."

Bibliography: The traditional melodies are collected in Baer, *Ba'al Tefillah*, Nos. 26, 28, 30, 48b-51, 384-398, 533-535, 735-745, 974-977, 1050-1052, Frankfort-on-the-Main, 1883; Cohen and Davis, *Voice of Prayer and Praise*, Nos. 25, 50, 132-134, 189, 292 and 294, London, 1899.
A. F. L. C.

MIḲMAṢ, DAVID IBN MERWAN. See David ibn Merwan al-Muḳammaṣ.

MIḲWA'OT ("Baths"; called **Mikwot** by the Geonim, in the "'Aruk," and in the Mishnah, ed. Lowe): Treatise in the Mishnah and the Tosefta in the order Ṭohorot. The legal code of the Pentateuch prescribes a bath for lepers (Lev. xiv. 9) and for persons suffering from certain other diseases (*ib.* xv.). The bath, according to the rabbinical interpretation of Lev. xiv. 9, must hold at least forty seahs (= 268.29 liters), and must be of such a size that the person who is to be cleansed may immerse his whole body (Ḥag. 11a). The water may be from a spring or a river, or it may be rain-water, but it must not be drawn. The treatise Miḳwa'ot deals with a more exact definition of the rules upon these subjects. In most of the editions of the Mishnah as well as in the Tosefta this treatise is the sixth in the order Ṭohorot; but in the edition of the Babylonian Talmud it is the seventh, and in the editions of the Mishnah of 1559 and 1606 it stands first in this order. It is divided into ten chapters, containing seventy-one paragraphs in all.

Kind of Water.

Ch. i.: There are six grades of bodies of water so far as cleansing and purification are concerned. The lowest in value is water from a pond, ditch, cistern, or cavern, as well as standing water which has flowed from a mountain. These waters, under certain circumstances, cause uncleanness, but they may, nevertheless, be lawfully used for washing the hands and also for making dough (§§ 1-5). Water still flowing from a mountain is a grade higher, for it can never become unclean; and it may therefore be used in preparing the priestly heave-offering of dough (§ 6). Next in ascending order is a body of water which contains forty seahs, and is therefore suitable for ritual baths and for the purification of vessels. Still higher in grade is a spring to which other water drawn from some source is added, and which in certain respects resembles a body of water and in others a spring (§ 7). A yet higher grade of water is that from a mineral spring, which cleanses even while flowing; and the highest of all is pure spring-water, which may also be used for the ritual sprinkling (§ 8; comp. Lev. xiv. 5-6; Num. xix. 17).

Impurities.

Ch. ii.: When one has bathed and is uncertain whether he has performed the ceremony correctly, or when he is in doubt as to the size of the miḳweh, or when, on being measured, the bath is found to be of insufficient size, the person bathing is not considered clean (§§ 1-2). When drawn water renders the miḳweh unclean, even though it is doubtful whether it fell into the bath (§ 3). Three logs of water drawn intentionally render the miḳweh unfit, but if unintentionally drawn they do not have this effect, even though such water has been preserved in a vessel (§§ 4-9). Regulations concerning a miḳweh of water and clay, and the degree of fluidity of the clay which requires that the latter be taken into account (§ 10).

Ch. iii.: Additional regulations concerning drawn water. How a miḳweh made unfit by drawn water may be rendered fit again (§§ 1-2). The method of reckoning drawn water derived from several vessels, and other methods of reckoning considered in connection therewith (§§ 3-4).

Ch. iv.: How rain-water may be led into a miḳweh and not be considered drawn water (§§ 1-3). On the mixing of rain-water and drawn water before they reach the miḳweh (§ 4). Cases in which a conduit of stone is considered a vessel, so that the water in it is regarded as drawn water. Of the conduit of Jehu at Jerusalem (§ 5).

Flowing Water.

Ch. v.: Cases in which a spring resembles a miḳweh, its water having cleansing properties when collected in a pool ("ashboran"), but not while it flows (§§ 1-3). Whether the sea may be considered a miḳweh and whether, even while flowing, it cleanses (§ 4). Flowing or dripping water, and what objects may be used to stop the flow (§ 5). Regarding a wave of the sea which contains forty seahs, and other bodies of water (§ 6).

Ch. vi.: Of holes and rifts connected with a miḳweh (§ 1). Of dipping several objects at once (§ 2). Of reservoirs lying near one another (§ 3). Cases in which drawn water does not make the miḳweh unfit (§ 4). Of large vessels standing in the miḳweh or in the sea (§§ 5-6). Of the connection of miḳwa'ot with each other (§§ 7-9). Of pipes fixed in bath-houses (§§ 10-11).

Ch. vii.: Things which may make up the measure of forty seahs, such as ice, snow, and hail, and things which may not, although they do not make the miḳweh unfit (§§ 1-2). Cases in which the miḳweh becomes unfit through a change of color in the water (§§ 3-5). Of bathing in a miḳweh which contains exactly forty seahs (§§ 6-7).

Ch. viii.: The baths in the land of Israel, even in its heathen cities, are clean and fit for use; but the heathen baths in other lands are to be considered clean only in one respect (§ 1). The bathing of those who have certain diseases, and how such persons are to bathe (§§ 2-5).

Use of Miḳweh.

Ch. ix.: Enumeration of things which, if they touch the bather, render the bath ineffectual (§§ 1-4). Things which have a similar effect with regard to the bath in case they come in contact with objects dipped in the water (§§ 5-6).

Ch. x.: Detailed regulations concerning the dipping of objects which are to be cleansed (§§ 1-5; comp. Num. xxxi. 23). Regarding the purification of water by contact ("hashakah") with the water of the bath (§ 6). Of unclean foods and drinks which defile and of the method of reckoning them (§§ 7–8).

In the Tosefta the treatise Miḳwa'ot is divided into seven chapters. Especially interesting in the Tosefta are the discussions between R. Ṭarfon and R. Akiba concerning the bath of Jabneh. Noteworthy also is the discussion between JOSE THE GALILEAN and Akiba in which R. Ṭarfon expressed his respect for Jose (viii. 11).

S. J. Z. L.

MIḲWEH (rabbinic Hebrew, **miḳwah;** plural, **miḳwa'ot**): Literally, a "collection," a "collected mass," especially of water (Gen. i. 10; Ex. vii. 19; Lev. xi. 36; comp. Isa. xxii. 11). Because of the use made of this word in connection with ritual purification (Lev. xi. 36), it has become the term commonly used to designate the ritual bath. In all cases of ritual impurity it was necessary for the person or object to be immersed in a bath built in accordance with the rules laid down by the Rabbis (see ABLUTION; BATHS; PURITY). Since the Dispersion the custom of observing the laws of purity has on the whole fallen into desuetude, except in the case of the impure woman (see NIDDAH). With regard to her the laws are still observed in most Orthodox communities, and therefore the ritual miḳweh is still a necessary institution there. Some observant Jews, especially among the Ḥasidim, immerse themselves in the miḳweh in cases also of impurity other than niddah.

Jewish Bath of the Sixteenth Century.
(From Philipp von Allendorf, "Der Juden Badstub," 1535.)

In order to be ritually fit for use, the miḳweh must contain sufficient water to cover entirely the body of a man of average size. The Rabbis estimated that the miḳweh should be 3 cubits long, 1 cubit wide, and 1 cubit deep (= 44,118.375 widths of the thumb; Shulḥan 'Aruk, Yoreh De'ah, 201, 1), containing 40 se'ahs of water ('Er. 4b; Yoma 31a; *et al.*; comp. Pes. R. 82b). The se'ah is described as a measure holding 144 eggs (Num. R. xviii. 17), *i.e.*, 24 logs (= 24 pints = 3 gallons approximately; see WEIGHTS AND MEASURES), so that the miḳweh must contain at least 120 gallons of water.

Size and Contents.

The water of the miḳweh must come from a natural spring or from a river that has its source in a natural spring (Sifra to Lev. xi. 36). A tank filled by the rain may be used as a miḳweh, although some authorities forbid the use of a pool which is full of water in the rainy season and dried up in the summer (Maimonides, "Yad," Miḳwa'ot, iii. 1–3; Yoreh De'ah, 201, 2, Isserles' gloss). A miḳweh derived from snow, ice, or hail is regarded by the authorities as ritually fit for use, although there is a difference of opinion with regard to the manner of melting the snow (Miḳ. vii. 1; Yoreh De'ah, 201, 30; comp. SHaK and "Pitḥe Teshubah," *ad loc.*; see also "Ḥatam Sofer" on Yoreh De'ah, 200, 213).

The water contained in the miḳweh must not have passed through a vessel of such a form that it can hold objects placed in it. Pipes open on both sides are not regarded as vessels in the accepted meaning (Miḳ. iv. 1; "Yad," *l.c.* vi. 1, 2). In large cities, where the water-supply comes through underground pipes and where water is measured by meters, many points involving legal technicalities must be observed in the construction of a miḳweh. In order to observe these the following is the process followed by some rabbis in the building of a miḳweh in a large city: A small miḳweh, with a capacity of 40 se'ahs, is built near a large tank, and a conduit is made from the smaller tank that leads to an opening in the larger. The small tank or miḳweh is first filled with snow or ice; when the snow or ice fills it to the brim the aperture leading into the large tank is opened, and water is poured over the ice or snow and passes into the large tank. Thus the original miḳweh is made from snow or ice, about the ritual fitness of which there is no doubt, and then as much water is added as is needed (Yoreh De'ah, 201, 36; "Resp. Rosh," 30, 31; Caro, "Abḳat Rokel," pp. 50, 51, 56; "Noda' bi-Yehudah," 2d series, Yoreh De'ah, 136, 137; "Ḥatam Sofer," *ib.* 198, 199, 203, 204, 206; Berlin, "Meshib Dabar," ii. 38).

If three logs (= pints) of water be poured into a miḳweh which does not have the prescribed measure of water, the miḳweh becomes unfit for ritual use, even though the 40 se'ahs are later completed in a legitimate manner. In such a case, the miḳweh has to be emptied and then refilled in the prescribed way. If, however, the miḳweh has the required measure, water from other sources may be poured into it without impairing its ritual fitness (Miḳ. iii.; "Yad," *l.c.* v.; Yoreh De'ah, 201, 15 *et seq.*).

The ritual bath always formed one of the most important institutions of a Jewish community (see Abrahams, "Jewish Life in the Middle Ages," p. 73). In urgent cases it was permitted even to sell a synagogue in order to erect a miḳweh (Berlin, "Meshib Dabar," ii. 45).

A. J. H. G.

MILAN (Latin, **Mediolanum**): Capital of Lombardy, and the largest commercial city of Italy. Jews settled there under Roman rule and were persecuted even in the early Christian period. Ambrose, the patron saint of the city, was their inveterate enemy, and hoped to become a martyr by the destruction of a synagogue. In 388, when the emperor Theodosius commanded a bishop to rebuild a synagogue which he had bidden some monks to destroy, Ambrose called Theodosius a Jew, and attacked him so bitterly that he countermanded his order. An inscription commemorates his hatred of the Jews

Jewish Bath of the Sixteenth Century.
(From a contemporary print.)

(Giulini, "Memorie Spettanti alla Storia di Milano," vi. 162). The records of the following centuries mention Jews in Lombardy as large landowners. At Milan, in the tenth century, there was a mint-master named Gideon who was probably a Jew. During the period of the great wars and the rapid rise of the Italian cities the Jews seem to have been excluded therefrom, yet commerce and banking, which were in the hands of Jews in other countries, were so skilfully carried on by the Lombards that all competition seemed undesirable, especially when complicated by religious antipathies. During the great persecution of heretics in 1320 the podestà was obliged to promise to expel all Jews, and not to readmit any to the city or to the bishopric in opposition to the wishes of the archbishop, nor were they allowed to return to the territory of Milan before the fifteenth century. On Jan. 23, 1452, in consideration of the payment of a large sum of money, the Jews of Milan received from the pope, through the intercession of the duke, permission to build synagogues, to celebrate their feasts, and to intermarry, yet the granting of these privileges was excused in ambiguous phrases, and the Jews were compelled to wear the yellow badge.

Expelled in 1320.

The holocaust of the Jews at Trent in 1475 aroused hatred against their coreligionists in the territory of Milan, and this was fanned by the speeches of Bernardinus of Feltre. Although the dukes tried to protect the Jews, the latter seem to have been expelled from the city, so that the confirmation of the privileges granted by Pope Paul III. in 1541, the search of the Inquisition for interdicted Hebrew books in 1554 and 1566, as well as the repeated decrees of expulsion issued by Philip II. and Philip III., applied only to the communities in other cities of the dukedom, Alessandria and Cremona being the most important of these. Then no Jews were living at Milan, although some did reside in the neighboring cities of Padua and Lodi.

When Milan came under Austrian rule in 1714 Jews seem to have settled there again. They were subject to the same laws as their coreligionists in Mantua. The interdiction against the forcible baptism of Jewish children, issued in 1765 and 1768, and still extant, was renewed by the Austrian laws of 1803 and 1817. The remarkable growth of Milan after 1848 brought many Jews to the city, especially from Piedmont, Mantua, and the Papal States, and the community, which had formerly belonged to Mantua, became autonomous. In 1857 it numbered 500 persons, and in 1901 about 2,000, to whom may be added many Jews who are not publicly known as such.

Under Austrian Rule.

The following persons may be mentioned among the prominent Jews of Milan: Joachim Basevi (an eminent lawyer, counsel for Andreas Hofer), and the senators Tullo Massarani and Graziadio Ascoli. Of the rabbis the most prominent have been Moses Menahem Coen (Rapoport), who took part in the dispute regarding the miḳweh at Rovigo, and, in the nineteenth century, Mosè Mazliaḥ Ariani and Alessandro da Fano.

Bibliography: Ersch and Gruber, *Encyc.* s.v. *Juden*, ii. 27, 147 *et seq.*; *Educatore Israelita*, iii. 107 *et seq.*
G. I. E.

MILCAH (מלכה): **1.** Daughter of Haran, and wife of her uncle Nahor (Gen. xi. 29). She bore eight sons, the youngest of whom was Bethuel, father of Rebekah (*ib.* xxii. 21-23). Ibn Ezra commentary on Gen. xi. 29) thinks that Haran, Milcah's father, was a different person from Haran, Abraham's brother, and consequently that Milcah's husband was not her uncle. **2.** Fourth daughter of Zelophehad (Num. xxvi. 33).

E. G. H. M. Sel.

MILCOM. See Moloch.

MILES OF MARSEILLES, or **SAMUEL BEN JUDAH BEN MESHULLAM** (surnamed **Barbaveira**): Provençal physician and philosopher; born at Marseilles 1294. In some manuscripts he is designated by the name "Bongodos," the Provençal equivalent of "Ben Judah." From early youth he devoted himself to the study of science and philosophy. While still young he left his native place for Salon, where he studied astronomy under the direction of Abba Mari Senior Astruc de Noves. In 1322 he is met with at Beaucaire as a prisoner together with other Jews in the tower of Rodorte. Later he sojourned successively at Murcia, Tarascon, Aix, and Montélimar.

Miles became known through his Hebrew translations from the Arabic of scientific and philosophical works. These include: (1) "Ha-She'elot ha-Dibriyyot meha-Derushim Asher le-Filusufim," translation of questions or dissertations concerning some obscure points in the commentary of Averroes on certain parts of the "Organon," finished May 8,

1320; (2) translation of the Middle Commentary of Averroes on Aristotle's "Ethics," completed at Beaucaire Feb. 9, 1321; (3) translation of the commentary of Averroes on Plato's "Republic," finished Sept. 3, 1321, at Beaucaire, in the tower of Rodorte; (4) translation of the compendium made by Averroes of Aristotle's "Organon," completed at Tarascon Dec. 13, 1329; (5) translation of the text of the figures 30 and 31 of the treatise of Euclid on the five bodies (in completion of the translation of Kalonymus, where these figures are wanting), finished Aug. 23, 1335; (6) commentary on the "Almagest," parts i.-iii.; (7) translation of a compendium of the "Almagest" by Abu Mohammed Jabar ibn Aflaḥ, translated from the Arabic into Hebrew by Jacob ben Machir and corrected by Miles, finished Dec. 17, 1335, at Aix; (8) "Ma'amar Alexander ha-Firdusi," treatise of Alexander of Aphrodisias on the soul, translated from the Greek into Arabic by Isḥaḳ ibn Ḥunain, finished July 4, 1340, at Montélimar; (9) translation of the astronomical works of the vizier Abu Abdallah Mohammed ibn Mu'adh of Seville, in two parts: (1) treatise in seven chapters on the eclipse of the sun July 3, 1079; (2) "Iggeret be-'Ammud ha-Shaḥar," treatise on the aurora; (10) "Ma'amar be-Tenu'at ha-Kokabim ha-Ḳayyamim," treatise on the movement of the fixed stars by Abu Isḥaḳ al-Zarkala.

Bibliography: Zunz, *G. S.* iii. 189; Munk, *Mélanges*, p. 489; Neubauer, in *R. E. J.* ix. 215; Kaufmann, *ib.* xiii. 300 *et seq.*; Renan, *Averroès et l'Averroïsme*, p. 191; Renan-Neubauer, *Les Ecrivains Juifs Français*, pp. 207 *et seq.*; Steinschneider, *Hebr. Uebers.* pp. 131, 138, 152, 222; Gross, *Gallia Judaica*, p. 379.

G. I. Br.

MILHAU, JOSEPH BEN MOSES (called also **Joseph Moscat**): French scholar and liturgical poet; lived at Carpentras in the second half of the eighteenth century. He was the author of a work entitled "Oẓerot Yosef" (Leghorn, 1783), a commentary on Rashi's and Elijah Mizraḥi's commentaries on the Pentateuch, and of a poem recited at Avignon at the circumcision ceremony. Zunz ("Z. G." p. 470) says that "Joseph of Milhau of the eighteenth century" composed several liturgical poems; and, indeed, the Maḥzor of Avignon contains other pieces of his. But in Jost's "Annalen," i. 341, Zunz attributes those poems to the Joseph of Milhau who in 1751 was a member of the rabbinical college and who was apparently another person than the subject of this article.

Bibliography: Gross, *Gallia Judaica*, p. 345; Steinschneider, *Cat. Bodl.* col. 1513; Zunz, in *Allg. Zeit. des Jud.* iii. 682.

S. M. Sel.

MILHAU, MOSES BEN MICHAEL: French scholar and poet; lived at Carpentras in the second half of the eighteenth century. Moses Milhau seems to have been the father of Joseph b. Moses Milhau, as may be concluded from the genealogy given by the latter in his work. Milhau was the author of: "Mishpaṭ Emet," a philosophical essay on Job, a kind of theodicy; "Maṭṭeh Mosheh," a rimed paraphrase of Ruth, with philosophical reflections; and "Iggeret ha-Neḥamah," a rimed work purposing to console the reader in his sadness; all three works being published at Leghorn in 1787. A poem entitled "Mizmor Shir le-Napoleon" (Paris, 1806) was composed in honor of Napoleon I. by a Moses Milhau, who is identified by Zedner ("Cat. Hebr. Books Brit. Mus." p. 544) with the subject of this article; but if the latter was the father of Joseph of Milhau, it is not likely that he was still living in the beginning of the nineteenth century.

Bibliography: Fürst, *Bibl. Jud.* ii. 378; Gross, *Gallia Judaica*, p. 345.

S. M. Sel.

MILHAUD (Latin, Amiliavum; Hebrew, אמיל״ב, מיליי״אב): Village in the department of Gard, France. In Renan-Neubauer, "Les Rabbins Français," p. 665, its name is given as אאלב. It has been erroneously confounded with Millau (the ancient Æmilianum or Amilbanum) in the department of Aveyron, where there probably never was a Jewish community. There are no documents to indicate the status of the Jewish community of Milhaud in the Middle Ages. Whatever it may have been, the Jews established there were expelled in 1306. They sought refuge in the Comtat-Venaissin, chiefly at Carpentras, where many of their descendants were living in the sixteenth, seventeenth, and eighteenth centuries. The name "Milhaud," "Milhau," or "Milliaud" is still a common one among the Jews of southern France.

The scholars of Milhaud include: Don Dieulosal; Abraham ben Reuben ben Joseph ben Joshua Amilabi (14th cent.); Moses מולאבי; Gabriel המילייאבי, translator and commentator of the medical work "Tabula Super Vita Brevis," by Arnauld de Villeneuve; Maestre Bonenfant or Hezekiah of Milhaud, author of the medical work "Gabriel" (16th cent.); Immanuel ben Gad; Joseph of Milhau, member of the rabbinical college of Carpentras; David of Milhau; Moses ben Michael; and Joseph of Milhau (called also "Joseph Muscat"), author of a commentary on Rashi entitled "Oẓerot Yosef" (18th cent.).

Bibliography: Zunz and Carmoly, in *Israelitische Annalen*, 1839, pp. 196, 341; Zunz, *Ritus der Synagoge von Avignon*, in *Allg. Zeit. des Jud.* 1839, p. 1786; idem, *Z. G.* p. 470; *R. E. J.* ix. 216, xii. 197-220; Gross, *Gallia Judaica*, pp. 343-346; Renan-Neubauer, *Les Ecrivains Juifs Français*, pp. 577, 762.

G. S. K.

MILK (Hebrew, "ḥalab"; Aramaic, "ḥelba"): A common article of food among the ancient Hebrews.—**Biblical Data**: Palestine is praised in the Bible as a "land flowing with milk and honey" (Ex. iii. 8 *et al.*), milk representing the common necessities of life, and honey referring to luxuries. In Isa. lv. 1, milk is coupled with wine to denote a similar idea (comp. Ezek. xxv. 4). The Israelites used the milk of goats (Deut. xxxii. 14) and the milk of sheep (Prov. xxvii. 27). Cows' milk is rarely mentioned (comp. Deut. *l.c.*), probably because of its scarcity owing to the unsuitability of the mountainous country of Palestine for pasturing large cattle. Milk was received in buckets (Job xxi. 24) and kept in skins (Judges iv. 19), and was used as a refreshing drink at meals (Gen. xviii. 8).

Milk was supposed to give whiteness to the teeth (*ib.* xlix. 12), and was employed as a simile for the whiteness of the human body (Lam. iv. 7; comp. Cant. v. 12). Deborah refers to milk ("ḥem'ah" in parallelism to "ḥalab") as "a cup of the nobles"

(Judges v. 25); and in several other texts it is spoken of as one of the most delicious beverages (comp. Cant. iv. 11, v. 1). Ben Sira counts milk among "the principal things for the whole use of man's life" (Ecclus. [Sirach] xxxix. 26). The abundance which the Israelites will enjoy in Messianic times is pictured in the figure that the hills of Palestine will flow with milk (Joel iv. [A. V. iii.] 18; comp. Isa. vii. 22). Cream or butter ("ḥem'ah") is also used as a figure denoting abundance (Isa. *l.c.*; Job xx. 17), and is frequently mentioned with milk (Gen. xviii. 8; Deut. xxxii. 14; Judges v. 25; Prov. xxx. 33; *et al.*). See CHEESE; FOOD.

S. J. H. G.

——**In Rabbinical Literature:** Although regarded as a pleasant beverage (Ket. 111a; "Agadat Shir ha-Shirim," ed. Schechter, p. 187, note, Cambridge, 1896), milk was probably used more by the poorer classes of the community than by the rich (Ḥul. 84a; Yalḳ., Prov. 961). It was especially used as food for infants (Seder Eliyahu Zuṭa, ed. Friedmann, p. 195, Vienna, 1903; comp. Heb. v. 12; I Cor. iii. 2; I Peter ii. 2). A mixture of milk and honey was regarded as a delicious drink (Cant. R. iv. 22). One is counseled against drinking beer or wine after milk (M. Ḳ. 11a). In a figurative sense milk was used to denote whiteness and purity (Gen. R. xcviii. 15; Cant. R. v. 10). One who wishes his daughter to be fair should feed her in her youth on young birds and on milk (Ket. 59b). Milk is one of the five things (three, in Yalḳ., Isa. 480) to which the Torah was compared (Deut. R. vii. 3; comp. Ḳimḥi's commentary on Isa. lv. 1). On this account some maintain that the custom arose of eating food prepared with milk on the festival of Shabu'ot ("Kol Bo," 52; comp. Shulḥan 'Aruk, Oraḥ Ḥayyim, 494, 3, Isserles' gloss; see SHABU'OT). He who devotes himself to the study of the Law will be greeted in the future world with sixty cups of milk, besides many other delicious beverages ("Agadat Shir ha-Shirim," p. 84, note).

Halakah.

The permission to drink milk was regarded by the Rabbis as an exception ("ḥiddush"), since it was held that the milk of mammals is derived from decomposed blood (Nid. 9a), and is furthermore something separated from a living animal and therefore to be included in the general prohibition against eating anything that comes from the living ("dabar min ha-ḥai"; Bek. 6b). The milk of an unclean animal is forbidden in accordance with the general rule, "that which comes from the unclean is unclean; from the clean, clean" (*ib.* 5b; comp. Gen. xxxii. 16). It is forbidden also to use the milk of an animal suffering from a visible malady which causes the animal to be ritually unfit for food ("ṭerefah"), or that of an animal found, after the ritual slaughtering, to have suffered from such a disease as late as three days before its death (Ḥul. 112b; comp. *ib.* 11a, Tos., *s.v.* "Atya"; Maimonides, "Yad," Ma'akalot Asurot, iii. 16; Shulḥan 'Aruk, Yoreh De'ah, 81).

Milk bought from a non-Jew is forbidden, the apprehension being that the non-Jew in his carelessness or from a desire to improve it may have mixed with it some forbidden ingredient. If, however, a Jew has been present at the milking, the milk may be used. Different customs prevail with regard to the use of butter bought from a non-Jew; and even with regard to milk and cheese later authorities are more lenient ('Ab. Zarah 29b, 35b; "Yad," *l.c.* iii. 12–17; Yoreh De'ah, 115; see CHEESE). The process of curdling milk was effected in Talmudic times either by rennet ("ḳebah," 'Ab. Zarah, *l.c.*) or by the juice of leaves or roots ('Orlah i. 7).

Milk is one of the three beverages which, if left uncovered overnight, should not be used, because it is possible that a serpent may have left its venom therein. In places where serpents are not found, this apprehension does not exist (Ter. viii. 4, 5; Yalḳ., Judges, 45; "Yad," Roẓeaḥ, xi. 7; Yoreh De'ah, 116, 1; comp. "Pitḥe Teshubah," *ad loc.*). Milk is also one of the seven beverages that make articles of food liable to receive impurity (Maksh. vi. 4; see PURITY).

Milk and Meat.

The Rabbis did not hesitate to admit their inability to assign a reason for the prohibition against eating meat with milk ("basar be-ḥalab"), and they accordingly labeled it as "ḥiddush," an exception, a unique law (Pes. 44b; Ḥul. 108a; comp. Rashi and Tos. *ad loc.*). Maimonides says in this connection: "Meat boiled with milk is undoubtedly gross food, and makes overfull. But I think that it was probably prohibited because it was somehow connected with idolatry, forming perhaps part of the services at a heathen festival." This latter theory he supports by the fact that in Exodus the prohibition against seething a kid in its mother's milk is mentioned twice in connection with the festivals ("Moreh," iii. 48).

Basing their opinions on an ancient tradition, the Rabbis explained the thrice-repeated prohibition against seething the kid in its mother's milk (Ex. xxiii. 19, xxxiv. 26; Deut. xiv. 21) as referring to three distinct prohibitions—(1) against cooking meat and milk together; (2) against eating such a mixture; and (3) against deriving any benefit from such a mixture (Ḥul. 115b; comp. there the various attempts made to find Biblical support for the prohibition against eating meat with milk). It is curious to note in this connection that Onḳelos, a most literal translator, renders the passages in all the three places by "ye shall not eat meat with milk" (לא תיכלון בשר בחלב; comp. LXX. to Ex. xxxiv. 26). The expression "kid" was accepted to be a generic term including all mammals and, according to some, even birds (Ḥul. 113a). The prevalent opinion, however, is that the prohibition against eating poultry with milk is of rabbinic origin merely (Maimonides, "Yad," Ma'akalot Asurot, ix. 4; Shulḥan 'Aruk, Yoreh De'ah, 87, 3). Fish and locusts as well as eggs are excluded from the prohibition (Ḥul. 103b, 104a; Beẓah 6b).

The prohibition against eating meat with milk was extensively elaborated by the Rabbis, who provided for every possible occurrence. Not only was the eating of meat with milk forbidden, but also the eating of meat that had a taste of milk, or vice versa; for "the taste of forbidden food is forbidden as the food itself" (טעם כעיקר; Ḥul. 98b, 108a; Pes. 44b; 'Ab. Zarah 67b; *et al.*). If a piece of meat that had become forbidden as food because it had absorbed milk to an extent which made the taste of the latter appreciable in it was cooked with other meat in a pot, all that the pot contained was forbidden, unless the contents were sixty times as great as the prohibited piece. It was not sufficient that there should be in the pot sixty times as much meat as the quantity of milk absorbed in the piece of meat; for with regard to meat and milk the principle was that the forbidden piece became in itself a "carcass," *i.e.*, a forbidden object; and when it could not be recognized, it was necessary that the taste of it should be annihilated (חתיכה נעשית נבילה; Yoreh De'ah, 92, 4; comp. Isserles' gloss, where the principle is extended to all kinds of forbidden food).

Cooking-Vessels.

A pot in which meat has been cooked should not be used for cooking milk, and vice versa. If such a pot be so used within twenty-four hours after it has been used with milk or meat respectively, everything that is in it becomes ritually unfit, unless the contents of the pot are sixty times as much as the pot itself. If the second cooking takes place twenty-four hours or more after the first, the contents of the pot are permitted for use; for the food which the pot has absorbed in the first cooking has by that time lost its agreeable taste, and the general rule is that any vessel which communicates an offensive taste (נותן טעם לפגם) does not render food ritually unfit for use. The pot itself, however, should not be used either with meat or with milk (Yoreh De'ah, 93, 1; comp. SHaK *ad loc.*).

Food prepared with milk and food in which meat is an ingredient should not be eaten at the same meal. The general custom is to wait six hours between a meal at which meat has been eaten and one at which food prepared with milk is to be eaten, although custom varies in this particular, some persons waiting one hour only. There is no need to wait at all after eating food prepared with milk; it is necessary only to see that there is none of the food left on the hands, and also to wash the mouth before partaking of meat. It is forbidden to place meat upon the table at the same time with food prepared with milk, lest by mistake both be eaten together. In the households of observing Jews not only are there two separate sets of dishes and of kitchen utensils, but different table-cloths are used for meals consisting of food prepared with milk and those at which meat is eaten (Yoreh De'ah, 88, 89). As bread is eaten with meat it is not permitted to prepare it with milk unless the form and size of the loaf or cake are different from those of ordinary bread (*ib.* 96). See DIETARY LAWS; FOOD.

A. J. H. G.

MILL AND MILLSTONE. See FLOUR.

MILLAUD (ARTHUR PAUL DAVID), ALBERT: French journalist and playwright; born at Paris in 1836; died there Oct. 22, 1892; son of Moïse MILLAUD. When only eighteen years of age he published a volume of poems which met with considerable success. In 1869 he joined the staff of the "Figaro," for which he originated the style of feuilletonism which it has since adopted. To the "Figaro" he contributed a number of witty and sarcastic poems and sketches, published under the pseudonyms "Baron Grimm" and "La Bruyère." Later these were published collectively under the title "Petite Némesis."

For the stage Millaud wrote, often in collaboration with others, a great number of excellent pieces, mostly in a sarcastic vein, the leading rôles of which were played generally by Madame Judic. Of these plays the following may be mentioned: "Madame l'Archiduc" (1874); "Niniche" (1878); "La Femme à Papa" (1879); "Lili" (1882); "Mam'zelle Nitouche" (1883); "Le Remords d'Anatole" (1885). In his younger days Millaud, together with Abel Auerbach, founded the "Revue de Poche," and later the "Gazette de Hollande," but neither of these ventures proved successful.

BIBLIOGRAPHY: *Jew. Chron.* Jan. 9, 1885; *Nouveau Larousse Illustré.*

S. F. C.

MILLAUD, EDOUARD: French barrister and statesman; born at Tarascon, Bouches-du-Rhône, Sept. 27, 1834; educated at Lyons, and there admitted to the bar in 1856. Taking an active part in politics, he was an opponent of the imperial government and became attorney-general for Lyons after the overthrow of Napoleon III. He resigned in 1871; but in the same year he was elected to the Assembly as a member of the Extreme Left, was reelected in 1876 and in 1877, always belonging to the Republican Union, of which political club he was one of the founders. In 1880 he was elected to the Senate, and in 1891 and 1900 was reelected. Being a good speaker, Millaud has taken a prominent part in the debates of the Upper House and has been a member of several commissions. In 1886 he became secretary of public works in the cabinet of Freycinet, and in the following year in that of Goblet, resigning in 1887.

Millaud has written several essays on jurisprudence, including medical jurisprudence, in the professional journals, and is the author of: "Etude sur l'Orateur Hortensius," 1859; "De la Réorganisation de l'Armée," 1867; "Devons-Nous Signer la Paix?" 1871.

BIBLIOGRAPHY: Curinier, *Dict. Nat.*; *Nouveau Larousse Illustré.*

S. F. T. H.

MILLAUD, MOÏSE-POLYDORE: French journalist and banker; born at Bordeaux Aug. 27, 1813; died at Paris 1871. The son of a poor Jewish tradesman, he received but a meager education, and entered a bailiff's office as clerk. He applied himself to literature from his youth, and at the age of twenty established a small newspaper, "Le Lutin." In 1836 he went to Paris and founded "Le Gamin de Paris," the first newspaper to be sold at the doors of theaters, and "Le Négociateur," concerned entirely with commercial matters. Although neither was financially successful, he gained valuable training from them. In 1839 he founded "L'Audience," devoted exclusively to the news of the law courts, which was very prosperous until 1845; and he was the leading competitor of the "Gazette des Tribunaux." On Feb. 24, 1845, he established "La Liberté," which strongly supported the cause of Prince Louis Napoleon. After the insurrection of June the paper was suppressed. Together with Mirès, his compatriot, he started an industrial and financial sheet, "Le Journal des Chemins de Fer," which became a power in matters of speculation and finance. Availing themselves of the popularity of Lamartine, the two collaborators established the paper "Le Conseiller du Peuple," and founded the two banking institutions Caisse des Actions Réunies and Caisse des Chemins de Fer, from which Millaud retired in favor of Mirès in 1853, after each had cleared 3,000,000 francs. The Caisse Générale des Actionnaires and the purchase of the rights of Girardin in "La Presse" proved less fortunate than the two preceding ventures. In 1863 he conceived the idea of starting a daily paper at the price of 5 centimes, and established "Le Petit Journal," which was a signal success. He was the founder also of "Le Journal Illustré," "Le Soleil," and "Le Journal des Voyageurs."

In 1859, in collaboration with Clairville, Millaud made his first essay in dramatic literature, and produced a three-act light comedy, "Ma Mère et Mon Ours," which had a great success. During the Second Empire, Millaud gave superb entertainments; but finally he lost the greater part of his large fortune.

Bibliography: *La Grande Encyclopédie*; *Nouveau Larousse Illustré*.

S. J. Ka.

MILLENNIUM: The reign of peace, lasting one thousand years, which will precede the Last Judgment and the future life. The concept has assumed especial importance in the Christian Church, where it is termed also "chiliasm," designating the dominion of Jesus with the glorified and risen saints over the world for a thousand years. Chiliasm or the idea of the millennium is, nevertheless, older than the Christian Church; for the belief in a period of one thousand years at the end of time as a preliminary to the resurrection of the dead was held in Parseeism. This concept is expressed in Jewish literature in Enoch, xiii., xci. 12–17; in the apocalypse of the ten weeks, in Apoc. Baruch, xl. 3 ("And his dominion shall last forever, until the world doomed to destruction shall perish"); and in II Esdras vii. 28–29. Neither here nor in later Jewish literature is the duration of this Messianic reign fixed. It is clear, however, that the rule of the Messiah was considered as an interregnum, from the fact that in many passages, such as Pes. 68a, Ber. 34b, Sanh. 91b and 99a, Shab. 63a, 113b, and 141b, a distinction is made between ימות המשיח and עולם הבא, although it must be noted that some regarded the Messianic rule as the period of the fulfilment of the prophecies, while others saw in it the time of the subjugation of the nations.

Messianic Period an Interregnum.

There are various views regarding the duration of this kingdom, and there is considerable confusion in traditional literature on this point, one and the same opinion being often quoted as held by different authorities. According to the two baraitot in Sanh. 99a, the Messianic kingdom is to last for 40, or 70, or 365, or 400, or even for 7,000 years. In the opinion of others its period is to equal the time from the creation of the world, or else from Noah, to the "present" day. Similar statements, often merely ascribed to other authors, are found in Yalḳ. 806. Sanh. 97a quotes Abaye and an old baraita, which is found also in 'Ab. Zarah 9a, to the effect that the Messianic period comprises two of the six millenniums of the world, while R. Ḳeṭina and a baraita make the interesting statement that the 6,000 years of the world will be concluded by the seventh thousand of the Messianic kingdom. In the passage in Yalḳuṭ already quoted, this same view is ascribed to two tannaim of the second century. Both of these chronologies are based on the calculation found in Ps. xc. 4 ("For a thousand years in thy sight are but as yesterday"), a comparison of which with the account of Creation formed the basis for the 6,000 years of the duration of the world, while the Sabbath corresponded to the seventh thousand, that of the Messiah.

The calculation of 6,000 or 7,000 years is found, according to Lagarde ("Mittheilungen," iv. 315), as early as the Greek translators of the Pentateuch, whom he places about 280 B.C., and is given also in Enoch, xxxiii. The idea of the Messianic interregnum was later incorporated in this form in Revelation (ch. xx.). When Jesus has conquered the serpent, representing the hostile anti-Christian world, the martyrs of the faith will be raised from the dead and will rule with him for 1,000 years as a band of kingly priests. This period is to be followed by the Last Judgment and the creation of a new heaven and a new earth. The concept of the Messianic kingdom, which is here described merely as a reign of peace, is elaborated more fully in the eschatological descriptions of apocalyptic literature (as in Papias), in the Epistle of Barnabas, and in the writings of Justin. Barnabas follows the Jewish theory that the world is to exist unchanged for 6,000 years, and that at the beginning of the Sabbatical or seventh millennium the son of God will appear, although, unlike Papias, he regards this event as purely spiritual. The view of Justin ("Dial. cum Tryph." cxiii.) concerning the Messianic kingdom is nationalistic in coloring, being influenced, according to Hamburger, by the insurrection of Bar Kokba. After the middle of the second century of the common era these ideas fell into abeyance, until the Montanists arose in Asia Minor (*c.* 160–220) and revived the ancient hopes, declaring, however, that their city of Pepuza was to be the site of the future Jerusalem and the center of the millennial kingdom. In the Greek Church chiliasm was displaced entirely by Origen's Neoplatonic mysticism, and was kept alive only in the Oriental branches of that communion.

Found in Revelation.

Bibliography: Corrodi, *Kritische Gesch. des Chiliasmus*; A. Harnack, *Millennium*, in *Encyc. Brit.*; Semisch, *Chiliasmus*, in Herzog-Plitt, *Real-Encyc.*; Hamburger, *R. B. T.* s.v. *Chiliasmus*; Schürer, *Gesch.* 2d ed., ii. 457 *et seq.*; F. Weber, *Jüdische Theologie*, 2d ed., pp. 371–373.

J. A. B.

MILLET: An important species of grain which grows chiefly in sandy regions. In Arabia, Italy, and elsewhere a bread, excellent when fresh, is made of it, and also of the species *Panicum italicum* Linn. The grain is mentioned but once in the Bible, in Ezek. iv. 9: "Take thou also unto thee wheat, and barley, and beans, and lentils, and millet, and fitches, and put them in one vessel, and make thee bread thereof." Since this passage was evidently intended to enumerate all the kinds of grain used for making bread, millet ("doḥan") was included; but it is practically impossible to decide which variety the prophet meant. Rosenmüller and others preferred to translate "doḥan" by "Indian millet," because the Arabic "dukhn" was shown by Forskål to have this meaning, although Furrer had already pointed out that panicum likewise bears the same name; it is best to translate "doḥan" by "millet," especially if the Biblical "sorah" be rendered "sorghum" (Isa. xxviii. 25, A. V., "wheat"; with which Sachau compares the שורה [*i.e.*, "durrah" = "broom-corn"] of an inscription at Zenjirli; comp. Post, "Flora of Syria, Palestine, and Sinai," p. 854, Beirut, 1896), and to use "panicum" as a translation of "pereg," which is first found in the Mishnah. The Syrians, misled by their word "peragga," have traced this Mishnaic word to the "pannag" of Ezek. xxvii. 17. The Septuagint and the Vulgate, followed by the English versions, incorrectly translate "nisman" (Isa. xxviii. 25) by "millet."

Mishnah.

In Mishnaic times millet of two kinds, rice, and sesame constituted a separate category of cultivated plants, which were grouped between grain and pulse, although rice and millet more closely approached the former (Löw, "Pflanzennamen," p. 102; Sheb. ii. 7; Yer. Sheb. 34a, 10; Sifra, Behar, 105c; R. H. 13b; Ḥal. i. 4; Mek., Bo, 8b, 12; 9a, 27; Sifre, i. 110, 146; ii. 105; Yer. Peah i. 16c, 23; Mek., Deut. i. 14; Hoffmann). Dioscorides discusses the four kinds of plants in the same sequence. In spite of the fact that rice and millet are kinds of grain, they were not included among the recognized species ('Er. 81a; Pes. 35a; Ber. 37a; "Halakot Gedolot," ed. Hildesheimer, p. 54; Maimonides, "Yad," Berakot, v. 10; "Kesef Mishne," *ad loc.*).

Foreign names for millet occur in rabbinical works, *e.g.*: "hirse," "hirsen" ("'Aruk ha-Ḳaẓer"; "Lebush," Oraḥ Ḥayyim, 208, 8; Isaac Tyrnau; *et passim*), "arzan hindi" (Bacher, "Sefer ha-Shorashim," No. 879), "dokhn" (Maimonides), "ḍurra" ("Birke Yosef," Oraḥ Ḥayyim, 205), "mil," "miglio" (D. Ḳimḥi, "Zunz Jubelschrift," Hebrew part, p. 97; Rashi), "panis," "panitz" (Rashi, and A. Berliner, "Festschrift," p. 248), "panizo" ("Paḥad Yiẓḥaḳ," *s.v.*).

BIBLIOGRAPHY: Beckmann, *Beiträge*, ii. 543; Rosenmüller, *Biblische Naturgesch.* i. 84; Ibn Safir, *Eben Sappir*, i. 40a; Wönig, *Die Pflanzen im Alten Aegypten*, pp. 173 *et seq.*, Leipsic, 1886.

J. I. Lö.

MILMAN, HENRY HART: Historian; born in London Feb. 10, 1791; died there Sept. 24, 1868. His career at Oxford was a brilliant one. He first became known through his dramatic poems "Fazio" (1815), "Fall of Jerusalem," "Martyr of Antioch," and others. In 1830 he published his "History of the Jews," a work which brought down on him the censure of the Church. This history is aggressively rationalistic; it treats the Jews as an Oriental tribe, and all miracles are either eliminated or evaded. He was nevertheless presented with a piece of plate by some representative Jews in recognition of his sympathetic attitude. His history was republished in 1863 and 1867.

Dean Milman was appointed Dean of St. Paul's in 1849. He was the first to translate Sanskrit epics into English. He edited Gibbon in 1838, and Horace in 1849. His ecclesiastical and theological sympathies were very liberal, as is shown by his "History of Latin Christianity" (1855), in which also occur several sympathetic references to the Jews.

BIBLIOGRAPHY: *Dictionary of National Biog.*

J. S. J. L.

MILSAHAGI, ELIAKIM. See SAMILER, A. G.

MILWAUKEE: Metropolis of the state of Wisconsin. The oldest congregation of Milwaukee, Bene Jeshurun, was organized in 1855 by Löbl Rindskopf, Leopold Newbauer, Solomon Adler, Emanuel Silverman, and others of the first Jewish settlers in the city. At the outset the congregation had as ḥazzanim Messrs. Alexander, Lasker, and Marcus Heiman in the order named, and it then came under the guidance of Rabbis Isidor Kalisch, M. Falk, Elias Epstein, Emanuel Gerechter, and Victor Caro, the present (1904) incumbent. On Oct. 18, 1869, under the leadership of David Adler and Henry Friend, a new congregation named "Emanu-El" was organized, which was incorporated Feb. 17, 1870. After a short period of service by M. Schulhof as ḥazzan, Rabbis E. M. V. Brown, M. Spitz, Isaac S. Moses, Sigmund Hecht, and Julius H. Meyer were successively the spiritual guides of the congregation. There are four other incorporated congregations.

A federation of Jewish charities was effected in Jan., 1903, the income of the new organization being about $12,000. Out of this sum the following local charities are supported: the Hebrew Relief Association; the Settlement; the Jewish Hospital Association; the Ladies' Relief Sewing Society; and the Sisterhood of Personal Service. From this source, also, the contributions of Milwaukee Jews to national Jewish charities are made.

In a total population of 300,000 there are about 8,000 Jews.

A. J. H. M.

MI-MIZRAḤ UMI-MA'ARAB. See PERIODICALS.

MIN (pl. **Minim**): Term used in the Talmud and Midrash for a Jewish heretic or sectarian. Its etymology is obscure, the most plausible among numerous explanations being that given by Bacher, namely, that it is derived from the Biblical מין (= "species"), which has received in post-Biblical Hebrew the signification of "sect"; and just as "goy," which in the Bible has only the meaning of "nation," took later the sense of "non-Jew," so "min" received also the signification of "sectary." As expressly stated by R. Naḥman (Ḥul. 13b), the term "min" is applied only to a Jewish sectary, not to a non-Jew. It is variously used in the Talmud and the Midrash for the Samaritan, the Sadducee, the Gnostic, the Judæo-Christian, and other sectaries, according to the epoch to which the passage belongs. Yerushalmi states that there were, at the time of the destruction of the Temple, no less than twenty-four kinds of minim (Yer. Sanh. x. 5). Thus the min who (the Midrash states) derided Alexander the Great for rising before the Jewish high priest Simon the Just (Lev. R. xiii.) was undoubtedly a Samaritan. The minim referred to in Berakot ix., on whose account the custom was established of closing the benedictions with the words "from eternity to eternity" in order to emphasize the existence of more than one world, were undoubtedly Sadducees, who, as known, denied the existence of another world. In passages referring to the Christian period, "minim" usually indicates the Judæo-Christians, the Gnostics, and the Nazarenes, who often conversed with the Rabbis on the unity of God, creation, resurrection, and similar subjects (comp. Sanh. 39b). In some passages, indeed, it is used even for "Christian"; but it is possible that in such cases it is a substitution for the word "Noẓeri," which was the usual term for "Christian."

Various Applications of the Term.

During the first century of Christianity the Rabbis lived on friendly terms with the minim. Rabbi Eliezer, who denied to the heathen a share in the future life, is said to have discoursed with the Judæo-Christian Jacob of Kefar Sekanya and to have quietly listened to the interpretation of a Biblical verse he had received from Jesus ('Ab. Zarah 16b; Eccl. R. i. 8). Ben Dama, a nephew of R. Ishmael, having been bitten by a snake, allowed himself to be cured by means of an exorcism uttered by the min Jacob, a Judæo-Christian. These friendly feelings, however, gradually gave way to violent hatred, as the minim separated themselves from all connection with the Jews and propagated writings which the Rabbis considered more dangerous to the unity of Judaism than those of the pagans. "The writings of the minim," says R. Ṭarfon, "deserve to be burned, even though the holy name of God occurs therein, for paganism is less dangerous than 'minut'; the former fails to recognize the truth of Judaism from want of knowledge, but the latter denies what it fully knows" (Shab. 116a).

On the invitation of Gamaliel II., Samuel ha-Ḳaṭan composed a prayer against the minim which was inserted in the "Eighteen Benedictions"; it is called "Birkat ha-Minim" and forms the twelfth benediction; but instead of the original "Noẓerim" (= "Nazarenes"; see Krauss in "J. Q. R." v. 55; comp. Bloch, "Die Institutionen des Judenthums," i. 193) the present text has "we-la-malshinim" (="and to the informers"). The cause of this change in the text was, probably, the accusation brought by the Church Fathers against the Jews of cursing all the Christians under the name of the Nazarenes. It was forbidden to partake of meat, bread, and wine with the min. Scrolls of the Law, tefillin, and mezuzot written by a min were burned (Giṭ. 45b; Yer. Shab. 14b; 'Ab. Zarah 40b; Shulḥan 'Aruk, Oraḥ Ḥayyim, 39, 1; *ib.* Yoreh De'ah, 281, 1). An animal slaughtered by a min was forbidden food (Ḥul. 13a). The relatives of the min were not permitted to observe the laws of mourning after his death, but were required to assume festive garments and rejoice (Sem. ii. 10; Yoreh De'ah, 345). The testimony of the min was not admitted in evidence in Jewish courts (Shulḥan 'Aruk, Ḥoshen Mishpaṭ, 34, 22); and an Israelite who found anything belonging to one who was a min was forbidden to return it to him (see Ḥoshen Mishpaṭ, 266, 2).

Prayer Against Minim.

According to Maimonides ("Yad," Teshubah, iii.) the term "min" is applied to five classes of heretics: to those who deny the existence of God and His providence; to those who believe in two or in more than two gods; to those who ascribe to God form and figure; to those who maintain that there existed before the creation of the world something besides God; and to those who worship stars, planets, or other things in order that these may act as intermediaries between them and the Master of the World.

Bibliography: Sachs, in *Orient, Lit.* ii. 825; Dreifus, *ib.* iv. 204, vi. 620; Kirchheim, *ib.* v. 1; Jost, *Gesch. des Judenthums und Seiner Sekten*, i. 414; Grätz, *Gnosticismus und Judenthum*, Krotoschin, 1846, *passim*; M. Friedländer, *Der Vorchristliche Jüdische Gnosticismus*, Göttingen, 1898, *passim*; Bacher, in *R. E. J.* xxxviii. 38; Israel Lévi, *ib.* xxxviii. 204; Schürer, in *Theologische Literaturzeitung*, 1899, No. 6; Goldfahn, in *Monatsschrift*, xix. 163; J. Derenbourg, in *R. E. J.* xiv. 30; Krauss, in *J. Q. R.* ix. 515.

J. I. Br.

MINDEN, JUDAH (LÖB) B. JOEL: German lexicographer; lived at Berlin in the sixth decade of the eighteenth century. In 1760 he published there, with the approbation of the rabbinates of Berlin and Halberstadt, the first Hebrew dictionary produced by a Jew and using German as the medium of translation; it was, as Zunz says ("G. V." p. 451), "the initial attempt to introduce the High German language into the national literature." The title "Millim le-Eloah" (comp. Job xxxvi. 2) was chosen for it, "because it explains the words of the divine writings," while its first word (מלים) hints at the author's name (מנני יהודה ליב מינדען). The book, which is based on David Ḳimḥi's dictionary, contains also additions from the Concordance, as well as discussions of the grammatical functions of the letters. In 1765 Minden published a new edition of Musafia's "Zeker Rab" as a supplement to his own work.

Bibliography: Steinschneider, *Cat. Bodl.* col. 1344; idem, *Bibliographisches Handbuch*, pp. 93, 98; Roest, *Cat. Rosenthal. Bibl.* Hebrew part, No. 1108.

T. W. B.

MINDEN, LÖB B. MOSES: Cantor and poet; born at Selichow (from which he is called also **Judah b. Moses Selichower**), in Lesser Poland, in the seventeenth century; died at an advanced age at Altona or Hamburg May 26, 1751. He acted as ḥazzan at Minden-on-the-Weser, whence his name "Minden." He was the author of "Shire Yehudah," Hebrew songs with German translations and music. One of these begins: "Ihr lieben Brüder und Gesellen, die da sitzen und zechen," and another, "Hört zu, ihr Leut, gedenkt an die Zeit." In an epilogue to this work (Amsterdam, 1696) he exhorts the rabbis not to allow conversation in the synagogue. He wrote also "Zemer wa-Shir," which was printed by Solomon London, Frankfort-on-the-Main, 1714.

Bibliography: Steinschneider, *Cat. Bodl.* cols. 643, 1361, No. 4064; Roest, *Cat. Rosenthal. Bibl.* p. 816; Appendix, pp. 211 *et seq.*
H. R. M. K.

MINERBI, HIRSCHEL DE: Count of Oscarre; Italian diplomat; descendant of a wealthy and illustrious Jewish family of Triest; born April 25, 1838; educated at the University of Padua, where he received his degree in law in 1864. He then went to Italy, and entered the government service in 1867, being first sent to Paris, later in turn to Bern, Constantinople, London, Brussels, and finally to London again, where he remained until he withdrew from the service. Before he retired to private life he set aside the sum of 80,000 lire which he directed to be used as a nucleus for the foundation of an institute for the benefit of the widows and orphans of diplomatists.

s. V. C.

MINES AND MINING: Mines did not exist in the land inhabited by the Israelites. In the description of Palestine in Deut. viii. 9, it is true, the words "whose stones are iron and out of whose hills thou mayest dig brass" seem to refer to mining; but it is doubtful whether this passage is to be taken literally. The writer may have only meant that the stones were like iron in hardness. Here and there, however, superficial deposits of iron ore, such as pea ore or meadow ore, are to be found. In the Wadi Ajlun there are even thin deposits of red iron ore; but whether these were perhaps worked in some primitive manner is unknown. Traces of iron-mines and of ancient copper-works are found in the Lebanon. Possibly the words in Deuteronomy refer to this territory, though it was never inhabited by the Israelites.

The author of Job xxviii. betrays a more exact knowledge of mining. In verses 4, 7, 8 he refers to the passages and galleries which run crosswise with many sharp turns, following the labyrinthine course of the vein of ore. Verse 3 refers to the miner's light, which, according to Diodorus (iii. 11), the workers in Egyptian mines used to wear fastened to their foreheads. Verse 5 refers to the process of breaking the stone by making it intensely hot and then pouring water on it. This process also is mentioned by Diodorus. Verse 10 refers to the cleaving of a rock in which a vein of ore ran through it in a fissure. Water burst from the fissure, and the flow was stopped by closing up the gap. Perhaps the writer's knowledge of the subject came from Egyptian sources.

The rich gold-mines of which Diodorus (*l.c.*) speaks were on the boundary between Egypt and Naṣb, but more likely in this passage the allusion is to the copper-works of the Egyptians on the Sinaitic Peninsula. Traces of extensive mining operations are still to be seen in the wadis Maghara and Naṣb, in the heaps of rubbish, the piles of slag, and the ruined passages. The inscriptions found on the rocks there intimate that the ore was excavated even before the time of Cheops (the builder of the great pyramid), under King Snefru. Mining was not carried on by regular miners, but by slaves, convicts, prisoners of war, etc. The author of Job xxviii. must in some way have become acquainted with such mines, and have used the picture with poetical freedom for a general illustration of human skill in obtaining precious metals. See Metals.

E. G. H. W. N.

MINHAG. See Custom.

MINḤAH PRAYER: The afternoon devotional service of the Jewish liturgy. The term is probably derived from Elijah's prayer at "the time of the offering of the evening ["minḥah"] sacrifice" (I Kings xviii. 36). Minḥah is one of the three daily services referred to in Dan. vi. 10. Tradition credits the patriarchs Abraham, Isaac, and Jacob with the authorship of the morning, afternoon, and evening prayers respectively (Ber. 26b). That Isaac was the original author of Minḥah is deduced from the verse, "And Isaac went out to meditate in the field at the eventide" (Gen. xxiv. 63).

Divisions.

Minḥah proper, otherwise known as "Minḥah Gedolah" (major) begins at six and one-half hours of the day (12.30 P.M.); "Minḥah Ḳeṭannah" (minor), at nine and one-half hours of the day (3.30 P.M.); and they both end at sunset (6 P.M.). "Pelag" (split or semi-) Minḥah divides the "Minḥah Ḳeṭannah" in half at ten and three-quarter hours of the day (4.45 P.M.; Ber. iv. 1, 26a). Sunset is calculated to occur at the twelfth hour of the day (6 P.M.); no attention is paid to variations in the length of day and of night according to the seasons, but each is reckoned as containing exactly twelve hours.

The distinction between Minḥah Gedolah and Minḥah Ḳeṭannah corresponds to a division of activities into important and unimportant; it being forbidden to enter upon one of either class after the beginning of the corresponding Minḥah; this rule was made as a precaution against any undertaking being continued after the limit of the time fixed for prayer (Shab. i. 2, 9a). Accordingly, one must not commence a large business transaction or sit down to a banquet after 12.30 P.M., nor begin a small transaction or partake of an ordinary meal after 3.30 P.M., without having previously recited the Minḥah prayer. The semi-Minḥah is a special division made by Rabbi Judah, who sets the limit of the "Minḥah" time at one and one-quarter hours before sunset.

It appears that some made it a practise to pray both at Minḥah Gedolah and Minḥah Ḳeṭannah. R. Maẓliaḥ did so; but Asheri rules against him, inasmuch as there is an additional Minḥah known as "ne'ilah," which is confined to Yom-Kippur and special fast-days (Asheri, Rule iv., § 13). The Shulḥan 'Aruk allows one to say the Minḥah prayer twice, provided one Minḥah is recited as an obligation ("ḥobah") and the other as a voluntary act ("reshut"). This, however, is allowed only to men of extraordinary devotion; this rule being supported by the words of Isaiah: "To what purpose is the multitude of your sacrifices unto me?" (Shulḥan 'Aruk, Oraḥ Ḥayyim, 234, 1).

Minḥah consists of Ps. cxlv., "'Amidah," "Taḥnun" (except on Fridays), and "'Alenu." When there is a quorum of ten ("minyan") the leader repeats the standing prayer ("'Amidah") aloud, and recites the "Ḳaddishim." On Saturdays and on fast-days a portion of the Pentateuch is read in public before the "'Amidah." When time presses, the leader recites aloud only the first part of the prayer, through "Ḳedushshah" ("thrice holy"), and the rest is said silently with the assembly.

The third meal on Saturdays is eaten between Minḥah and Ma'arib or evening prayer. Formerly, a maggid sometimes preached in the synagogue after Minḥah. In the nineteenth century, when the people became more busy in worldly affairs, it was difficult for them to assemble in the afternoon and again in the evening; hence the Minḥah prayer was postponed to very near sunset in order that it might be followed by Ma'arib after a short interval.

On the relation of the Minḥah prayer to the sacrifices in the Temple see PRAYER.

BIBLIOGRAPHY: Dembitz, *Jewish Services in Synagogue and Home*, pp. 76-81, 332, Philadelphia, 1898.

J. J. D. E.

He was the author of the Talmudic commentary "Be'erot Yiẓḥaḳ."

Joseph ben Isaac Minir: Rabbi at Constantine; died before 1408; son of Isaac ben Joseph Minir; for ten years a pupil of Isaac ben Sheshet, who esteemed him highly for his scholarship.

Moses Minir: Edited Hebrew works at Venice in 1593.

Shem-Ṭob Minir: Contemporary of Joseph Caro; was living at Constantinople in 1569.

BIBLIOGRAPHY: Isaac ben Sheshet, *Responsa*, Nos. 79 *et seq.*, 123, 126, 396; *Oẓar Neḥmad*, ii. 99; *He-Ḥaluẓ*, ii. 26, iv. 85; Conforte, *Ḳore ha-Dorot*, p. 36b; Zunz, *Literaturgesch.* p. 504; Kayserling, *Gesch. der Juden in Spanien*, i. 78 *et seq.*, 88.

G. M. K.

MINIS: American family especially prominent in the South. Its founder, Abraham Minis, went from England to America in 1733. The family tree is as follows:

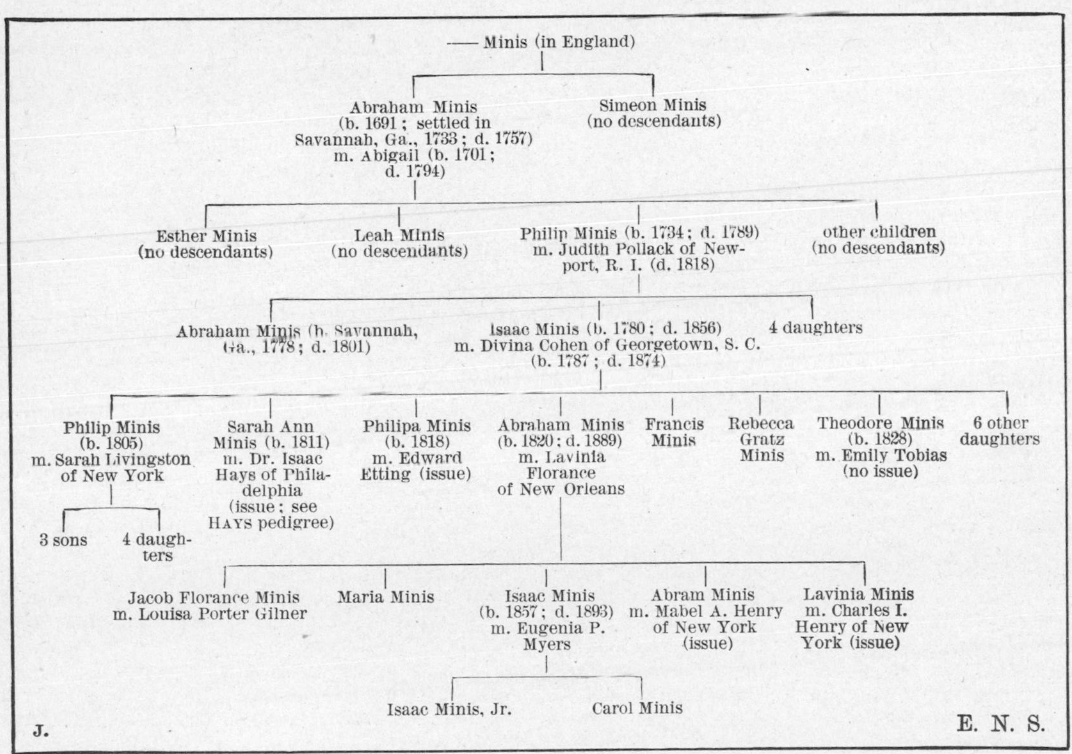

PEDIGREE OF THE MINIS FAMILY.

MINIR (מניר): Family of scholars of Tudela, members of which are met with in the East and in Italy.

Abraham ben Joseph Minir (probably a brother of Isaac ben Joseph Minir); **Acah (Isaac) ben Ḥayyim** and his son **Abraham Minir;** and **Shem-Ṭob ben Samuel Minir** were prominent members of the community of Tudela in 1363.

Isaac ibn Minir: Contemporary of Isaac ben Sheshet.

Isaac ben Joseph Minir: Commentator and liturgical poet; pupil of Yom-Ṭob ben Abraham of Seville, and contemporary of Solomon ben Adret.

Abraham Minis: One of the earliest settlers in the colony of Georgia; born *c.* 1696; died 1757. He arrived at Savannah with the group of Jewish colonists which came from England July 11, 1733, shortly after Oglethorpe. Abraham was accompanied by his wife Abigail, his daughters Leah and Esther, and his brother Simeon. He seems to have been a man of means. Some of the family silver he brought with him is still in possession of his descendants; and several pieces bear his crest. Abraham's name appears among those of the few Jewish grantees mentioned in the general conveyance of town lots and farms executed in Dec., 1733, and which is virtually the earliest deed in the colony. He soon became a merchant, and is mentioned as such in Savannah as early as 1737.

When many of the colonists, both Jew and Gentile, left Georgia about 1740, owing to the illiberal policy of the trustees, Minis was one of the few Jews who remained; he is mentioned in the trustees' minutes of that period. His widow died in 1794.

Simeon Minis: Brother of Abraham Minis; also one of the original settlers. His name appears in the records as late as 1743, when he received an allotment of land.

Philip Minis: Son of Abraham Minis; born at Savannah July 11, 1734 (being the first white male child born in the colony of Georgia); died 1789. He was a successful merchant at the outbreak of the American Revolution. An ardent patriot, he advanced considerable sums to the Revolutionary cause, mainly in connection with the payment of the troops. His name appears in the "Journal of the Continental Congress." In 1778 Congress directed the payment to him of several thousands of dollars, advanced to the "acting paymaster and commissary to the Virginia and North Carolina troops in the State of Georgia." When, in Sept., 1779, the French auxiliaries besieged Savannah, Minis acted as guide through the woods, and was consulted as to the best place for landing. He also volunteered to act as a patriot guide thereafter. In 1780 the British passed their famous "Disqualifying Act," whereby certain persons were disqualified from holding office, because of their prominence in the "rebel cause." The name of Philip Minis is one of the 150 names appearing in this list.

After the Revolution Minis took a lively interest in congregational affairs at Savannah. On the reestablishment of the congregation in 1786 he became parnas or president of the Mickva Israel congregation in that city.

David Minis: A member of the family who was prominent in masonic affairs as early as 1757. He was among those who, on behalf of the order, waited on Governor Ellis with an address of welcome in that year.

Judith (Judy) Minis (*née* **Judith Pollack**): Wife of Philip Minis; died 1818. She and her mother were both prominent patriots. On this account both were confined to their dwelling after the taking of Savannah, and were finally ordered to leave the town.

Among the soldiers of the Georgia line in the Revolution are also found the names of **William Minis** and **James Minis,** presumably members of the same family.

Isaac Minis: Son of Philip and Judith Minis; said to have been born in 1780, in a cave near Charleston, S. C., while that city was besieged and while Savannah was in the hands of the British; died 1856. He served as a private in the War of 1812 in Capt. William Bullock's company of artillery, 1st Regiment Georgia Militia.

Abraham Minis: Son of Isaac Minis; born at Savannah 1820; died 1889. He was physically disqualified from serving in the field at the outbreak of the Civil war. Though disapproving of secession, he, after hostilities commenced, espoused the Confederate cause, and filled a position in the commissary's office at Savannah. He also subscribed liberally to the issue of Confederate bonds.

Isaac Minis: Son of Abraham Minis; born at Savannah 1857; died 1893. He was an active member of the Georgia Hussars for many years, until his death.

Abraham Minis: Son of Abraham Minis; born 1859. He joined the Georgia Hussars in 1881, and became first lieutenant. At the outbreak of the Spanish-American war he requested assignment to a cavalry regiment, but as no cavalry was called from Georgia he had no opportunity for active service. Later he was appointed quartermaster (with the rank of captain) of the 1st Regiment of Georgia Cavalry, of which body he is now (1904) adjutant.

Bibliography: Charles C. Jones, *Hist. of Georgia*, vol. i.; *idem*, in *Pub. Am. Jew. Hist. Soc.* i. 5; George White, *Historical Collections of Georgia*, pp. 98, 102, 104, 339, New York, 1855; *Occident*, i. 247, 381; George Gilman Smith, *The Story of Georgia*, pp. 517, 619, 627, Macon, 1900; George White, *Statistics of Georgia*, in *Journal of the Transactions of the Trustees of Georgia*, p. 418, Wormloe, 1896; W. B. Stevens, *History of Georgia*, vol. i., 1847; *Georgia Gazette*, March 12, 1789; Leon Hühner, *The Jews of Georgia in Colonial Times*, in *Pub. Am. Jew. Hist. Soc.* x.; idem, *The Jews of Georgia in the American Revolution*; Charles P. Daly, *Settlement of the Jews in North America*, pp. 68–73, New York, 1893; Isaac Markens, *The Hebrews in America*, p. 49, New York, 1888; *Journals of Continental Congress*, 1778; Herbert Friedenwald, in *Pub. Am. Jew. Hist. Soc.* i. 67.

A. L. Hü.

MINKOVSKY, PHINEHAS: Russian cantor; born at Byelaya Tzerkov April, 1859. His father, Mordecai, a descendant of Yom-Ṭob Lipmann Heller, was cantor in the great synagogue of Byelaya Tzerkov, and he himself was a singer in his father's choir. After having studied the Bible and Talmud under different teachers, Minkovsky continued his Talmudical studies alone in the bet ha-midrash of his native town. At the age of eighteen he began to study Russian and German, and he mastered these two languages. His first teacher in vocal music was his father; later he studied it under Nisan Spivak (Nisan Belzer or Nisan Berdychever), and finally he went to Vienna, where he continued under Robert Fuchs, now (1904) director of the Conservatorium of Vienna, from whom he obtained a diploma as singer. From 1888 Minkovsky was successively cantor at Kishinef, Kherson, Lemberg, Odessa (in the great synagogue), New York (in the synagogue Ḳehal 'Adat Yeshurun), and in 1892 he was called back to Odessa, where he is now cantor in the Broder Synagogue. He has written "Die Entwicklung der Synagogalen Liturgie bis nach der Reformation des 19jahrhunderts" (Odessa, 1902). Minkovsky has contributed to many Hebrew periodicals and to "Die Wahrheit."

H. R. B. Ei.

MINKOWSKI, OSCAR: German physician; born at Alexoten, near Kovno, Russia, Jan. 13, 1858; educated at the universities of Freiburg, Strasburg, and Königsberg (M.D. 1881). He became assistant at the medical clinic of Königsberg University in 1882 and privat-docent in 1885. Removing to Strasburg in 1888, he was appointed assistant professor at the university there in 1891. In 1900 he became chief physician at the General Hospital at Cologne.

Minkowski is a contributor to Leyden's "Handbuch der Ernährungstherapie," Nothnagel's "Handbuch der Speziellen Pathologie und Therapie," Liebreich's "Encyklopädie der Therapie," and Lubarsch and Ostertag's "Ergebnisse der Allgemeinen Therapie." Besides contributing many essays to the medical journals, he has written: "Untersuchungen über den Diabetes Mellitus nach Exstirpation des Pankreas," Leipsic, 1893; and "Untersuchungen zur Physiologie und Pathologie der Harnsäure," *ib.* 1898.

BIBLIOGRAPHY: Pagel, *Biog. Lex.*

S. F. T. H.

MINNEAPOLIS: Chief commercial city of the state of Minnesota. In 1900 it had in a total population of 202,718 a Jewish community of about 6,000 souls. The first Jewish settlers were Germans, Bohemians, and Russians, who went there between the years 1865–70, there being among them one Ralph Rees, still living, who came in 1866, and who was for many years the most active member of the community. In 1876 about a dozen families rented a hall for worship and engaged the Rev. Mr. Schreiber as minister. In 1878 the congregation was permanently organized and incorporated, and shortly after a frame structure was erected as a synagogue on leased ground now situated in the very center of the business district. Such was the beginning of the present Jewish Reform Congregation Shaarei Tov. About five years later the synagogue was enlarged and moved to its present site, Fifth avenue and Tenth street south. Henry Iliowizi then became the rabbi of the congregation and remained here eight years. His successors have been: Rabbi S. Marks, two years; A. Friedman, seven years; and S. N. Deinard, the present (1904) incumbent, who was elected in 1901. The congregation dedicated a new synagogue in 1903.

The great bulk of Russian and Rumanian Jews, who are now the predominating element of the community, have come since 1882. The first congregations organized by them were the Adath Yeshurun, which existed for about seven years, and the Rumanian Hebrew Congregation Sons of Abraham, both in 1888. In 1890 the Congregation Beth Midrash Haggadol was started, but two years later was dissolved and succeeded by the Congregation Keneseth Israel, which built its present synagogue in 1894. This congregation, the leading Orthodox one, maintains a Hebrew Free School (daily) with about 70 pupils, and a Sunday-school attended mostly by girls. With the congregation are connected a Ḥebra Tillim, a Ḥebra Mishnah, and a Ḥebra Gemarah. Other Orthodox congregations are: Mikra Kodesh Nusaḥ Sfard; Congregation Anshe Tavrig; Adath Yeshurun (reorganized in 1903); and South Side Hebrew Congregation Agudath Ahim. They all own their houses of worship. The spiritual head of the Orthodox portion of the community was, until 1901, Rabbi I. Yaffey, who has been succeeded by Rabbi M. S. Silber.

Charitable Organizations.

The following organizations attend to communal charity: the Hebrew Ladies' Benevolent Society, composed of members of the Jewish Reform congregation; Sisters of Peace; Russian Hebrews Charity Association; Biḳḳur Ḥolim of the North Side; Biḳḳur Ḥolim of the South Side; and Haknasat Orḥim (free temporary shelter for strangers)—the last five conducted and maintained by the Orthodox Jews.

Before there was any established congregation in Minneapolis, the first few Jewish settlers bought a small tract of land about four miles from the center of the city, and organized themselves into what is now known as the Montefiore Burial Association. It is not connected with any congregation, although its membership is composed of those who affiliate with the Reform congregation. In addition there are now the Adath Yeshurun Cemetery Association; the Minneapolis City Lodge O. B. A. Cemetery Association; and the Hennepin County Lodge O. B. A. Cemetery Association.

Jewish secret fraternal organizations are particularly numerous in Minneapolis: one lodge of the I. O. B. B. with about 70 members; five lodges of the O. B. A. with a total membership of 1,250; two lodges of the Sons of Benjamin; one of the Free Sons of Israel; Mendelssohn Camp, M. W. A.; Baron Hirsch Camp, W. W.; and one Jewish lodge of each of the following: Modern Samaritans, Bankers' Union, Knights and Ladies of Security, Loyal Mystic Legion of America, Supreme Court of Honor, and Modern Brotherhood of America.

Zionism is represented by the Ohave Zion Kadimah and the American Daughters of Zion. There are several literary and social organizations.

The professions are represented by nine lawyers (one of whom, Simon Meyers, was in the state legislature from 1897 to 1899) and six physicians; three Jewish names are on the faculty list of the University of Minnesota: Robert Kolliner, professor at the University Law School; S. N. Deinard, of the chair of Semitics; and Lilian Cohen, instructor of chemistry. Dr. George J. Gordon is on the faculty of the Hamline Medical College.

A. S. N. D.

MINNESOTA: One of the northwestern states of the American Union. It has a Jewish population of about 13,000, distributed in the following cities: **Minneapolis,** the largest city of the state, 6,000; **St. Paul,** the capital city, 5,000; **Duluth,** 1,000; and about 1,000 scattered over the rest of the state, where from 5 to 20 Jewish families may be found in most towns of 3,000 or more inhabitants.

The three brothers Samuels, English Jews, who as early as 1852 had an Indian trading-post at Taylor Falls, on the Minnesota side of the St. Croix River, seem to have been the first Jewish settlers. One of the brothers, Morris Samuels, was captain in the Union army during the Civil war. Another Jew known to have been engaged in trading with the Indians in those early pioneer days was Isaac Marks, who had his residence in Mankato, and a trading-post about twelve miles from that place.

About 1857 some Jews went to St. Paul and engaged in general business, which likewise consisted mostly in trading with the Indians. The first Jewish organization was not effected till 1871, when the present Mt. Zion congregation of St. Paul came into existence. At that time Minneapolis had only a very few Jews. Since then, however, the Twin Cities have had an extraordinary growth in population, and the Jewish communities in them have grown in proportion, especially since 1882. Of late years several Jews of St. Paul have greatly prospered in business, and are now recognized factors in the commercial life of that city, so that while the Jewish community of Minneapolis is the larger in point of numbers, that of St. Paul is the wealthier and more influential.

In political and general communal activity the Jews of Minnesota have so far achieved little distinction, though T. N. Cardozo of St. Paul was as early as 1855 appointed United States commissioner, and Joseph Oppenheim of St. Paul was early in the eighties a member of the state legislature for two consecutive terms.

About 30 Jews from Minnesota were in the United States service during the Spanish-American war, one of them, Albert Steinhauser of New Ulm, being captain of Company A, 12th Minnesota Volunteer Infantry (see "American Jewish Year Book," 5661).

There are 17 organized congregations in the state, to wit: 7 in Minneapolis; 7 in St. Paul; and 3 in Duluth; one in each city—namely, Mt. Zion of St. Paul, Shaarei Tov of Minneapolis, and Emanuel of Duluth—belonging to the Reform wing of Judaism, while all the others retain the Orthodox ritual. These three have within the last two years dedicated new and handsomely built houses of worship. There is an I. O. B. B. lodge in each of the three cities, the one in St. Paul having been organized in 1871, and the one in Duluth in 1904. In the Twin Cities many lodges of the other Jewish fraternal orders, particularly of the O. B. A., are in flourishing condition. Zionism is well represented in St. Paul, where a Zionist society with a large membership of young men and young women maintains a well-appointed club-house.

"The Jewish Progress" of the Twin Cities, a weekly in English, is issued at Minneapolis.

A. S. N. D.

MINOR, SOLOMON ZALKIND: Russian rabbi and author; born at Wilna 1827; died there Jan. 21, 1900. He received his elementary education from his father, R. Jekuthiel, a well-known Talmudist. At the age of twelve Minor took up the study of Biblical and rabbinical subjects, but without the aid of a teacher. In 1849 the rabbinical seminary at Wilna was established, and Minor was among its first graduates. In 1854 he became instructor in Talmud and rabbinical literature in that institution, and in 1856 was appointed special adviser on Jewish affairs in the office of the governor-general of Wilna. Among the sermons he delivered in German at that time in the Wilna seminary may be mentioned "Der Rabbiner und der Lehrer" (Wilna, 1858). It pictures the ideal rabbi as a devoted guardian of the spiritual interests of his flock and as the advocate of his people. In 1860 Minor was appointed rabbi at Minsk; and for the next nine years he lived a life of conspicuously beneficent activity. Owing to his efforts a Sabbath-school and a night-school for artisans were opened (1861), and a library for the Jewish community was established (1862). In 1869 Minor was called to Moscow, where a Jewish congregation had recently been formed. There he succeeded in obtaining from the government the right to establish an independent Jewish religious organization, a right which the community of Moscow had, till then, never enjoyed. At the same time he received permission to build a synagogue and other communal institutions, such as a Hebrew free school, an industrial school, and an orphan asylum. He also taught the Jewish religion at the high school for girls in Moscow.

In his younger days Minor delivered his sermons in German, but at Minsk and Moscow he delivered them in Russian, and frequently had many Christians among his hearers. Indeed, Minot was the first Russian rabbi to preach in the vernacular; and his sermons have since served as models for synagogal discourses in Russia. They consisted largely of elucidations of the principles of Judaism, explanations of historical events concerning the Jews, and homilies on the duties of the Jews as Russian citizens. Minor was a friend of Count Leo Tolstoy, whose studies in Hebrew and in the Old Testament he directed. In 1891, when the expulsion of Moscow Jews began, Minor, owing to his too open expressions of sympathy for his people, was banished by the governor-general to his native town, Wilna, where he remained in seclusion until his death.

Minot's sermons have been published (3 vols., Moscow, 1875–89). He was the author of: "Rabbi Ippolit Lutostanski" (Moscow, 1879), directed against Lutostanski's anti-Semitic book "The Jews and the Talmud"; an outline of the history of the Jewish people, after the German of M. Elkan (Moscow, 1880; 2d ed., 1881); "Poslye Pogromov" (*ib.* 1882), on the anti-Jewish riots in Russia; and "Biblia Ob Utotrebleniye Vina" (*ib.* 1889), on the teaching of the Bible in regard to alcoholic beverages. Minor wrote articles for the Russian supplement to "Ha-Karmel" (1866, Nos. 11–25), and for "Yevreiskaya Biblioteka" (vol. iv.), and was a constant contributor to other Hebrew and Russian periodicals. He also corresponded with many of the prominent Maskilim of his time.

BIBLIOGRAPHY: Sokolov, *Sefer ha-Shanah*, ii. 288, Warsaw, 1901; *Voskhod*, 1900, No. 5; *Sistematitsheski Ukazatel*, s.v.

H. R. J. G. L.

MINORCA. See BALEARIC ISLES.

MINORITY. See MAJORITY.

MINSK (formerly **Mensk**): Russian city; capital of the government of the same name. Of the history of its Jewish community very little is known. In 1576 King Stephen Bathori granted the Jews of Minsk the privilege of engaging in trade or commerce of any kind. At the end of the sixteenth century the Minsk Jews, sharing the lot of their brethren in other parts of the country, were expelled from Lithuania. In 1606, however, Jews are again found in Minsk, owning shops. In the same year King Sigismund III. confirmed the decree of expulsion; but within ten years (1616) he annulled it, and reestablished the privileges granted by Stephen Bathori. Moreover, in 1625 Sigismund granted the Jewish community permanent possession of the tracts of land occupied by the synagogue and the cemetery. Subsequently (1629) he permitted them to own stores; but they were not allowed to build houses. King Ladislaus IV., in response to a petition of the Minsk Jews, confirmed the privileges granted by his predecessors. In addition he allowed them to "acquire lots and to build shops on them, as well as to buy old shops." They were still precluded from building houses, though they might own such if they came into their possession for debts. Ladislaus also left in their possession the brick-built synagogue, which he exempted from taxation; and he gave permission for founding a new Jewish cemetery.

In 1629 the superior of the Minsk Monastery of Peter and Paul brought before the civil court a complaint against the Jews of Minsk, charging them with having attacked the monastery during the baptism of a Jew. In 1648 another complaint of a similar character was made. On this occasion the waywode severely reprimanded the Jews, threatening them with prosecution if such a thing should again occur. In 1670 King Michael ordered the Minsk judicial starost not to allow unauthorized officials to judge the Jews and not to hinder the latter from appealing to the king or to the royal court, as they were subject only to the jurisdiction of the starost. During the second half of the eighteenth century the taxpayers of the Minsk Jewish community repeatedly sent representatives to the chief Lithuanian exchequer court in Grodno with complaints against the elders of the Minsk ḳahal. The elders were charged with depleting the public revenues and with defrauding the taxpayers among the middle classes.

On Jan. 1, 1896, the Jews of Minsk numbered 43,658. There were about forty synagogues and numerous houses of prayer. Five of the synagogues belong to the Jewish community, the others being controlled by separate congregations or belonging to private individuals. Among the numerous yeshibot the more important are: Blumke's yeshibah, the Little Yeshibah, and the yeshibah at the Synagogue of the Water-Carriers. The personnel of the Talmud Torah consists of eight "melammedim" and four instructors in general subjects; out of the 334 pupils only 106 studied these subjects. The expenditure of the Talmud Torah amounted to 4,355 rubles (1885). In 1879 a Jewish trade-school was established in Minsk with locksmiths' and carpenters' departments; instruction was offered also in general subjects, in Hebrew, and in religion. In 1885 the school had 112 apprentices, and it expended 5,912 rubles. The Jewish hospital, founded in 1829, has accommodations for seventy patients; its expenses amounted in 1885 to 8,068 rubles. The Jewish poorhouse, with eighty beds, had an expenditure of 5,356 rubles in the same year. Besides, there are many charitable associations, of which the more important are: a society for the assistance of students of the Talmud, with an expenditure of 3,000 rubles (1885); a society for the assistance of indigent sick, with an expenditure of 1,500 rubles (1885); and a society (founded about 1820) for the distribution of bread among the poor, with an expenditure of 3,310 rubles (1884).

H. R. M. R.

The following are the names of the Jews of Minsk who obtained particular prominence:

DISTRICT RABBIS.

Moses Zeeb b. Judah, author of "Ḳol Yehudah."
Menahem Mendel, son of the preceding.
Asher b. Löb, tosafist.
Isaac Abraham (held office 1749-55; d. 1776).
Raphael b. Jekuthiel Lifländer (1756-66).
Samuel of Indur (held office till 1777, when the district rabbinate was abolished by the government).

LOCAL RABBIS.

Moses (d. 1696), son of the martyr Mordecai, who was killed in Lublin Aug. 11, 1636.
Löb Ba'al ha-Tosefot (d. about 1708).
Löb b. Asher, author of "Sha'agat Aryeh."
Jehiel b. Solomon Heilprin (d. about 1742), author of "Seder ha-Dorot."
Moses b. Jehiel Heilprin, succeeded his father about 1744.
Joseph b. Simḥah Rapoport.
Gershon Ḥarif (1778-93).
Israel b. Löb Mirkes (d. about 1813).
Samuel Segal (d. Dec. 27, 1818).
Israel b. Ḥayyim Heilprin (d. 1836).
Isaac b. Naphtali Hirz Pines (d. 1836), chief of the bet din.
Judah Löb de Boton, son-in-law of Isaac Abigdor, author of "Pardes Rimmonim."
Zeeb Wolf b. Moses (dayyan; d. 1848).
Judah Löb b. Abraham (d. 1851).
David Tebele b. Moses, author of "Bet Dawid" (d. 1861).
Moses Ẓebi, appointed rabbi by the government.
Moses Samuel Pines (d. 1862), chief of the bet din.
Baruch b. Ẓebi, Saul b. Solomon, Ḥayyim Lipschitz, Joel Ḥarif, } dayyanim.
Aryeh b. Jacob (d. 1866), chief rabbi; author of "Be'er Heṭeb."
Moses Judah Löb (d. 1889), son-in-law of David Tebele.
Jeroham Judah Löb Pearlman ben Solomon, Russian rabbi; born in Brest 1835; died in Minsk 1896. He was one of the greatest rabbis of his time, and was surnamed "Gadol" (great one) on account of his prominence in the world of Talmudical scholarship. At the age of thirty he became rabbi of Seltz, near Brest, where he remained till 1871, when he was called to occupy the office of rabbi in Pruzan, government of Grodno. After the death of the two rabbis of Minsk, R. Gershon Tanḥum and R. Aryeh of Umen, the congregation of that city decided to appoint him as its rabbi (1883); and he occupied the rabbinate till his death (Benzion Eisenstadt, "Rabbane Minsk wa-Ḥakameha," pp. 24, 62, Wilna, 1899).
Eliezer Rabinowitz, chief rabbi.
Isaac b. David Tebele, Jacob b. Meïr, } assistant rabbis.
Abraham Haneles, appointed by the government.

PRESIDENTS OF YESHIBOT.

Aryeh Löb b. Ẓebi Horwitz, author of "Margenita Ṭaba."
Aryeh Löb b. Asher, author of "Sha'agat Aryeh."
Raphael b. Jekuthiel.
Joshua Heshel, author of "Maẓmiaḥ Yeshu'ah" and "Yeshu' be-Rosh"; died in Jerusalem.
Dob Isaac b. Ẓebi Meïr (d. 1851).
Israel Michael Jeshurun (d. 1851).
Abraham b. Joshua Evenzik (d. 1859).
Issachar Bär, surnamed "the diligent" ("Masmid"; d. 1879).
Gershon Tanḥum b. Elijah Benzion (d. 1881).
Solomon b. Saul Levin.
Mandel, Ber of Krasni, } instructors at the yeshibah.
Abraham b. Asher Anshel, author of "'Ammude ha-Yemini."

PROMINENT PREACHERS.

Moses b. Judah, author of "Eben Shoham," who was later (1764) appointed preacher in London, where he published that work.
Israelit, Israel Asher b. Ozer, Russian preacher; born about 1806; died in Minsk June 6, 1896. He was popularly known as the "Grodnoer Maggid" and was the preacher of the Jewish community in Minsk for more than fifty-five years. Besides being an able preacher he was an indefatigable communal worker and very charitable. His simple life and his untiring exertions in behalf of the poor endeared him to all classes of the population. Numerous stories are still related in Minsk about his merciful exertions to release men who were unjustly impressed for military service in the last years of the reign of Nicholas I. as "poimaniki" or substitutes for others ("Aḥiasaf," 5696, p. 312).

Abraham b. Zechariah Hamburg.
Joshua Isaac b. Jehiel, author of "'Emeḳ Yehoshua'."
Abraham Abele Rosens, author of "Maḥazeh Abraham."
H. R. P. Wi.

AUTHORS, SCHOLARS, AND OTHERS.

Bampi, Issachar, author of a book "on Jewish customs."
Broyde, Aaron (d. 1897), one of the directors of the Government Bank at Minsk; he was honored with various medals.
Eliasberg, Judah Bezaleel (d. 1845).
Eger, Samuel, son of Akiba Eger.
Jolles, Isaiah Zechariah (d. 1853), author of "'Et le-Dabber" and "Dober Mesharim."
Kaplan, Jacob, corrected and added notes to the "Ereẓ Ḳedumim."
Levanda, L., Hebrew-Russian writer.
Luria, Jacob Aaron, honored by Nicholas I. with a medal for useful work in the Jewish community.
Luria, David, son of the preceding; contributor to the Hebrew periodicals of his time.
Libowitz (1758–1853), the miracle-worker; an intimate friend of Elijah Wilna.
Maskileison, Abraham b. Judah Löb (d. July 19, 1848), author of "Maskil le-Etan" and other works.
Maskileison, Naphtali (d. 1898), son of the preceding; publisher of the "Seder ha-Dorot," with his own critical notes and additions.
Menahem Eliezer b. Levi (d. 1817), author of "Ya'ir Ḳinno."
Rabinowitz, Eliezer Lipman (d. 1887), an eminent Talmudic scholar, and owner of a famous library.
Rapoport, Jekuthiel Süssel (d. 1872), member of the rabbinical committee appointed by the government.
Solomonov, Mordecai (d. 1897), author of many novellæ on Talmudical subjects.
Solomon, Menahem b. Elijah, author of novellæ on all parts of the Talmud.

PIONEERS OF "HASKALAH."

Brill, Joseph, Hebrew writer.
Haneles, Abraham, rabbi appointed by the government.
Horowitz, poet.
Kaplan, Israel, author of "Le-Torah we-Da'at."
Nofet, J. Zeeb, superintendent of the Jewish trade-school.
Sirkin, Joshua, prominent Zionist.
Sirotkin, Abraham, author.
Wohlman, Israel Mendel, ex-editor of the "Ha-Kokabim."

PHILANTHROPISTS.

Blimowitz, Bär; Eliasberg, Lipman; Eliasberg, Samuel Jonah; Ettinger, Hillel; Goldberg, David; Jolles, Zusman; Luria, Ḥayyim; Luria, Samuel; Pollak, Benjamin; Pollak, Moses; Ragovin, Uriah; Rapoport, Akiba; Simḥowitz, Mordecai; Sliasberg, Solomon; Solomonov, Moses Ẓebi; Zeldowitz, Bär; and Zeldowitz, Baruch.
H. R. N. T. L.

MINSKI, NIKOLAI MAKSIMOVICH: Russian poet and writer; born at Glubokoye, government of Wilna, in 1855. At the age of twelve Nikolai removed to Minsk and entered the local classical gymnasium (graduated in 1875). The town of his gymnasium course supplied him with his pseudonym "Minski," whereas his real family name is **Wilenkin**. He began his literary career in 1876, and at once attracted attention by his highly artistic poem "Na Rodinye." This appeared in the best Russian journal, "Vyestnik Yevropy," in which Minski has published most of his poems. "Na Rodinye" is an inspired poetical response to the sufferings of the Bulgarian people when the Russo-Turkish war was at its height. The period of Minski's elementary studies corresponded with that distinguished by the intense striving of Russian society for progress and enlightenment, and those auspicious years were important also for the Russian Jewry. The stimulating influence of the times was also reflected in the Jewish circle in which the future poet-philosopher lived and studied. He obtained his higher education in the department of law of the University of St. Petersburg, graduating in 1879 with the degree of bachelor of law. In that same year he published his best poem, "Byelyya Nochi," which reflects the spiritual life of the contemporary youth with its restlessness and its dreams. The characteristic feature of his poetry is its pessimistic mood; it exhibits a desire to lay bare the misery of life. Very frequently Minski is the poet of sorrow, but this sorrow is impersonal and concerns some hated problem. The first volume of his writings appeared in 1887 and was received with high praise by the critics, who nevertheless pointed out the defects of his verses. A second edition of his book was soon called for. In 1889 Minski wrote a historical drama, "Osada Tulchina," which shows an unusual clearness in character-drawing, a plot of absorbing interest, and an intimate knowledge of the history of the time, besides beauty of style. The drama describes in a characteristic manner the struggle of three peoples—the Jews, Poles, and Little-Russians. Others of Minski's writings likewise are of significance to Jews. In 1879–80 he published in the Russo-Jewish journal "Razsvyet" a series of war feuilletons under the signature "Nord-West," written after the manner of Börne's "Parisian Letters." In these writings he attacked fiercely the enemies of Judaism. In the more recent period of his literary activity, beginning with the nineties of the nineteenth century, Minski has turned from Jewish life and its interests, and has devoted himself to literary philosophy, tinged strongly with Christian mysticism (see Brockhaus, and also Skabichevski's "Istoria Noveishei Russkoi Literatury").

BIBLIOGRAPHY: *Entziklopedicheski Slovar*, vol. vi., St. Petersburg, 1892; *Bolshaya Entziklopediya*, vol. v., *ib.* 1901.
H. R. N. R.

MINTERS: Persons authorized to strike coinage on behalf of a government. As early as 555 a certain Priscus struck coins at Châlons ("R. E. J." x. 237). One Gideon was minter at Milan in the tenth century. In 1181 three Jews at Winchester were apparently fined for minting, though the reading of the document on which the statement is based is ambiguous (Jacobs, "Jews of Angevin England," p. 73). Several "short-cross" pennies exist of the twelfth and thirteenth centuries with names of moneyers which may be Jewish, as David of London, Isaac of York, Samuel, Simon, and Solomon of Canterbury; but it is doubtful whether these were really Jews (*ib.* pp. 392–396). A certain number of German coins of the twelfth century with Hebrew inscriptions have been found (see Aronius, "Regesten," Nos. 351, 389). A certain Jew, Jehiel, is mentioned as mint-master on one of the coins of Bishop Otto of Würzburg; another held a similar position in Treves (Lamprecht, "Deutsches Wirthschaftsleben," ii. 1452, 1472). Earlier than this a Jew named Schlom was mint-master to Leopold V. of Austria. He appears to have been murdered during the Third Crusade (Scherer, "Rechtsverhältnisse der Juden," i. 121 *et seq.*). In Hungary the early minters appear to have been exclusively Jews (Kohn, "A Zsidók Tostenete Magrarorszagan," i. 240); and there are a number of Polish coins with Hebrew inscriptions (see NUMISMATICS). J.

MINYAN (מנין): Literally, "count"; the quorum necessary for public worship. The smallest congregation which is permitted to hold public worship is one made up of ten men, boys over thirteen years being for this, as for other religious purposes, counted as men. See Bar Mizwah.

The minimum of ten is evidently a survival in the Synagogue from the much older institution in which ten heads of families made up the smallest political subdivision. In Ex. xviii. Moses, on the advice of Jethro, appoints chiefs of tens, as well as chiefs of fifties, of hundreds, and of thousands. In like manner there were the decurio among the Romans and the tithingman among the early English.

The rule is laid down in the Mishnah thus (Megillah iv. 3): "They do not [1] 'divide' over the Shema' [Hear, O Israel], [2] nor pass before the Ark, [3] nor lift their hands, [4] nor read from the Law, [5] nor conclude with the Prophets, [6] nor arrange the standing and sitting, [7] nor say the benedictions of the mourners or the consolation of the mourners, [8] nor the benedictions of the bridegrooms, [9] nor use God's name in preparing for grace after meals, with less than ten."

The references in this rule are to: [1] The invocation "Bless ye" ("Bareku") with its response, which, with or without a "Ḳaddish" preceding it, is recited before the first benediction of Shema' in the evening and morning service. [2] The repetition of the prayer proper, *i.e.*, the Eighteen or Seven Benedictions, by the leader, and including the responsive Ḳedushshah. [3] The priestly blessing (Num. vi. 24-26). [4] The reading from the Scroll and benedictions before and after the lesson. [5] The hafṭarah with like benedictions. [6] Some ancient funeral ceremonies. [7] Likewise forms no longer in use. About these it is said (Ket. 8a, b) that the mourners are not counted among the ten. [8] The seven benedictions spoken at a wedding, or at any meal of the bridegroom and bride within a week from the wedding. [9] The sentence "Let us bless *our God*, from whose wealth we have eaten," instead of "Let us bless Him from whose," etc., with which latter words grace is begun when three or more have eaten at the same table (Ber. viii. 3). The distinctions there suggested between ten and eleven, or between ten and a hundred, have not been followed in practise.

The Babylonian Talmud, in commenting on this section of the Mishnah, finds the Scriptural authority for ten men constituting a congregation in the words (Num. xiv. 27): "How long shall I bear with this evil congregation which murmur against me?" which it refers to the scouts who were sent to spy out the land of Canaan, twelve in all, two of whom, Caleb and Joshua, were faithful, and only ten "evil."

Eligible for Quorum.

All male Israelites of the proper age, unless they are under the ban, or have openly severed their connection with their brethren by professing a hostile creed, are counted among the needful ten even though they are notorious and habitual sinners (Oraḥ Ḥayyim, 55, 12).

It is suggested (Ber. 47 and Yer. Ber. vii. 3) that while slaves or boys under thirteen are not counted in minyan, one slave or one minor boy may be admitted along with nine qualified men—at least when the boy is nearly of full age (a budding boy); and an example in an analogous case is given (Ber. 48a) of two prominent rabbis counting a boy as one of the three men necessary for saying grace after meals, it having been ascertained that he had ideas about God and prayer. The codes are somewhat divided on this subject: public service should be carried on with nine men and one infant only in "case of need," that is, if the attendance of a tenth man is not expected for that service (Oraḥ Ḥayyim, 55). Usage varies: in some synagogues nine adults and a boy over twelve years of age are deemed adequate for minyan; yet in the usage of other synagogues they are not adequate.

While women may, in certain contingencies, take an active part in public service, by reading parts of the weekly lesson (Megillah 23a; allowed by all the codes, but rarely, if ever, carried out in practise), none of the authorities speaks of counting women in the minyan.

The ten men include the leader. They and he should meet in one room or enclosure; Maimonides (Hil. Tefillah, viii.) discusses how the ten may be distributed in two adjoining rooms without destroying the quorum; but they must be within hearing of each other.

In the same chapter Maimonides explains as the advantage of reciting the prayer with minyan: that it is sure to be heard; and, following the Talmudic passages below, the other codes concur.

Presence of the Shekinah.

It was the firm belief of the sages that wherever ten Israelites are assembled, either for worship or for the study of the Law, the Shekinah (Divine Presence) "dwells" among them. Thus (Abot iii. 6): "R. Ḥalafta, the man of Kefar-Ḥananiah, says: When ten men sit down together to study the Law [another reading has it: "to act as judges"], the Presence dwells among them; for it is said (Ps. lxxxii. 1): God ["Elohim"] standeth in the congregation of God ["El."]." A baraita (Ber. 6a) puts it plainly: "Whence do we know that the Holy and Blessed One is found at the synagogue; or that when ten men say prayers together the Presence dwells among them?" It answers each of these questions with the verse of the psalm quoted above; it being understood that the word "'edah" (congregation) means ten or more Israelites meeting for a religious purpose. And the words in Solomon's prayer (I Kings viii. 28), "to hearken to the song and to the prayer," are shown by Abba Benjamin (Ber. *ib.*) to mean that man's prayer is best heard at the synagogue, for where men sing, there also they should pray. Both in the Mishnah and in the baraita quoted, consolation is held out to those who for study or prayer meet in smaller numbers—even to one who meditates or prays alone; but the stress is put upon the merits and sacredness of the minyan. The codifiers, such as Maimonides, his annotators, and the author of the Shulḥan 'Aruk, and many popular writers, have unitedly given strength to this sentiment, and have thus, for more than a thousand years, made the daily attendance at public worship, morning and evening, the rule among both men and boys in Israel.

The treatise Soferim, written in Babylonia in the seventh century, contains a passage (x. 7) often interpreted as asserting that in Palestine at that time seven men were allowed to hold public services. Correctly interpreted it refers to the repeating of "Ḳaddish" and "Bareku" at the synagogue for the benefit of late comers, and declares that in Palestine such a repetition is permitted only when seven (according to others, when six) men are present who have not yet heard these responsive readings. In modern times various authorities (*e.g.*, the Rabbinical Conference at Breslau, the "Oberrath" in Mecklenburg (1847), and Naphtali Ẓebi Judah Berlin in Woloshin) have declared the public worship permissible without the presence of minyan.

A. L. N. D.

MINZ (**מינץ**): Family of rabbis and scholars, deriving its name from the town of Mayence and founded in the fifteenth century. The family tree is as follows:

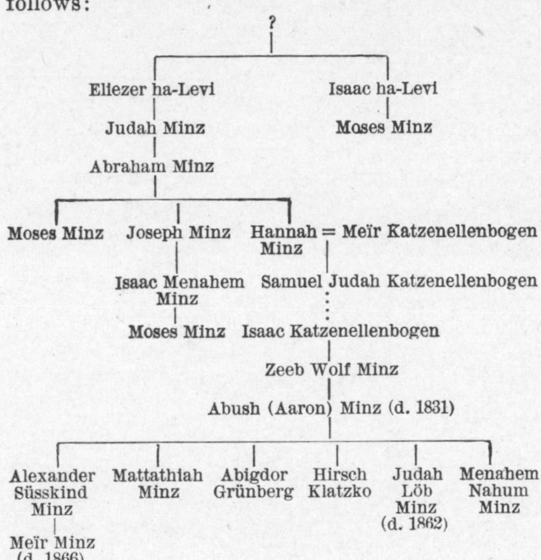

Judah b. Eliezer ha-Levi Minz (Minzi), the progenitor of the most prominent branch of the family, settled, or was born, in Italy in the fifteenth century. His cousin Moses b. Isaac ha-Levi Minz (Minzi) was a rabbi in Germany. The name "Minz," however, appears to have been borne by others in Italy who were not related to Judah Minz; for Joseph Colon (Responsa, No. 2) speaks of Joshua and Solomon, sons of an Abraham Minz who had formerly lived under the Duke of Milan and then removed to another town in Lombardy in order to avoid paying his part of the 13,000 gold pieces which the Jews of Milan had pledged themselves to pay the duke. Asher b. Perez Minz of Naples was related, perhaps, to the German branch of the Minz family. The last known direct male descendant of Judah Minz was **Moses b. Isaac Menahem Minz,** a descendant in the fourth generation.

At the beginning of the sixteenth century the Minz family of Padua united with that of Katzenellenbogen through the marriage of the daughter of Abraham ben Judah Minz to Meïr Katzenellenbogen of Padua. The descendants of this alliance emigrated afterward to Germany and then to Russia, and Zeeb Wolf b. Isaac, in Russia, a descendant of the tenth generation, assumed the name of Minz. From him is descended the present family of Minz.

Bibliography: Eisenstadt-Wiener, *Da'at Ḳedoshim*, part iii., pp. 82-86; Nepi-Ghirondi, in *Kerem Ḥemed*, iii. 91; Mortara, *Indice*, p. 39.

Abraham ben Judah ha-Levi Minz: Italian rabbi; flourished at Padua in the first half of the sixteenth century; father-in-law of Meïr Katzenellenbogen. Minz studied chiefly under his father, Judah Minz, whom he succeeded as rabbi and head of the yeshibah of Padua. According to Ibn Yaḥya ("Shalshelet ha-Ḳabbalah," p. 51a, Amsterdam, 1697), it was with Abraham Minz that Jacob Pollak had the quarrel which ended in their excommunicating each other; according to most other authorities, the quarrel was with Judah Minz (see Jacob Pollak). Ibn Yaḥya further says that the Italian rabbis believe that Pollak and Abraham Minz died on the same day (according to David Gans in 1530; according to Halberstam in 1541). Minz was the author of a number of decisions that were printed with those of R. Lewa of Ferrara (Venice, 1511). He was the author also of "Seder Giṭṭin wa-Ḥaliẓah," a treatise on divorce and ḥaliẓah, printed with the responsa of his father and of his son-in-law (*ib.* 1553).

Bibliography: Nepi-Ghirondi, in *Kerem Ḥemed*, iii. 91; Michael, *Or ha-Ḥayyim*, No. 114; Mortara, in *Mosé*, v. 307; idem, *Indice*, p. 39; Steinschneider, *Cat. Bodl.* col. 632.

E. C. M. Sel.

Asher ben Perez Minz: German printer; typesetter in Azariah b. Joseph's printing establishment in Naples, where was printed, in 1491, the Hebrew translation of Avicenna's "Canon." Wolf ("Bibl. Hebr." i., No. 366), following Bartolocci, read מניצא ("mi-Nizza" = "of Nizza") instead of מינצא ("Minẓa").

Bibliography: De Rossi, *Annales*, p. 179; Steinschneider, *Cat. Bodl.* col. 2841.

Judah ben Eliezer ha-Levi Minz: Italian rabbi; born about 1408; died at Padua in 1508. He was the most prominent rabbi of his time. He officiated as rabbi of Padua for forty-seven years, during which time he had a great number of pupils, among whom were his son Abraham Minz and the latter's son-in-law Meïr Katzenellenbogen. In a quarrel he had with Elijah Delmedigo he was supported by Elijah Mizraḥi (comp. Joseph Solomon Delmedigo, "Maẓref la-Ḥokmah," p. 3b; *idem*, "Elim," p. 29; Mizraḥi, Responsa, No. 56). It appears from Solomon Luria's responsa (No. 6) that Minz was the author of a number of ordinances ("taḳḳanot") at Padua. According to Ghirondi, he was professor of philosophy at the University of Padua. Ghirondi further states that in recognition of Minz's services as professor the authorities of the university placed his portrait, with an appreciative inscription, in the hall of the university, over the staircase. But it is very likely that Ghirondi confounded Minz with Elijah Delmedigo or Abraham de Balmes, both of whom lectured on philosophy before Christian audiences. In the sack of Padua soon after Minz's death almost all of his writings were destroyed. Joseph b. Abraham Minz, his grandson, discovered sixteen of his responsa, and these were published (Venice, 1553) by Meïr Katzenellenbogen, who printed in the same volume his own responsa and the "Seder Giṭṭin wa-Ḥaliẓah" of Abraham Minz. These responsa have been edited, and supplemented with an extended commentary and preface, by Johanan ben Moses Preschel (Munkacs, 1898). Judah's responsa, though scanty, afford interesting information on the history of his age and on Jewish customs in Padua.

BIBLIOGRAPHY: Fuenn, *Keneset Yisrael*, p. 412; Frankel, in *Orient, Lit.* vii. 520 *et seq.*; Grätz, *Gesch.* 3d ed., viii. 253 *et seq.*; Michael, *Or ha-Ḥayyim*, No. 1020; Nepi-Ghirondi, *Toledot Gedole Yisrael*, pp. 122-124; Preschel, in the preface to his edition of Minz's responsa; Steinschneider, *Cat. Bodl.* col. 1344.

Meïr ben Alexander Süsskind Minz: Galician scholar; born Oct. 6, 1814; died May 22, 1866. Having acquired a thorough knowledge of Hebrew, the Talmud, and of several European languages, Meïr Minz devoted himself to the defense of Judaism. He wrote: "Ein Wort zur Zeit" (1848); "Lelewels Kampf um Recht"; "Die Judenfeinde."

BIBLIOGRAPHY: Eisenstadt-Wiener, *Da'at Ḳedoshim*, part iii., p. 85.

Moses ben Isaac ha-Levi Minz: German rabbi of the fifteenth century; contemporary of Israel Isserlein, whom he frequently consulted. He was successively rabbi at Mayence, Landau, Bamberg, and Posen. In his responsa (No. 114) he mentions a certain Jacob Margolioth of לוקו (Lucca?), and refers to a case of divorce in Posen in 1444 (Steinschneider gives 1474). Fränkel ("Zeitschrift," iii. 387) doubts that Moses ever was at Posen. He suggests that פוזנו (Posen) is a printer's mistake for פיזרו (Pesaro). Moses' responsa (Cracow, 1617) mention also Joseph Colon, Israel Isserlein, and his cousin Judah Minz. Responsum No. 46 contains a dispute over a philological point with Eliezer Treves (comp. M. Wiener in "Monatsschrift," xvi. 390).

BIBLIOGRAPHY: Azulai, *Shem ha-Gedolim*, i. 140; Conforte, *Kore ha-Dorot*, p. 27b; Fürst, *Bibl. Jud.* ii. 380; Steinschneider, *Cat. Bodl.* cols. 1946-1947.

D. M. SEL.

MIPHKAD (מפקד; R. V. **HAMMIPHKAD**): Name of a gate mentioned in connection with the repair of the wall of Jerusalem by Nehemiah (Neh. iii. 31). It seems that this gate was not in the wall of Jerusalem, but that the part of the wall facing it was to the east, between the Horse Gate and the Sheep Gate. Indeed, it is not mentioned among the gates of Jerusalem in Neh. xii. 31 *et seq.* The word מפקד designates in Ezek. xliii. 21 the place near the Temple where the sin-offering was burned, and it seems to mean "an appointed place," to which the name of this gate may refer. But, while the Septuagint renders שער המפקד by πύλη τοῦ Μαφεκάδ, Jerome translates it by "porta judicialis," which induces Lightfoot ("Horæ Hebraicæ," ii. 27) to suggest that it may refer either to the hall of judgment in the Prætorium or to the east gate of the Temple. Barclay ("City of the Great King," p. 156), however, identifies the gate Miphkad with the "high gate of Benjamin" (Jer. xx. 2), locating it at the west end of the bridge which crosses the Tyropæon.

S. M. SEL.

MIRABEAU, GABRIEL HONORÉ RIQUETI, COMTE DE: French statesman of the revolutionary era; born at Bignon March 9, 1749; died at Paris April 2, 1791. Sent by De Calonne on a secret mission to Prussia, he became acquainted at Berlin with several distinguished Jews belonging to the circle of Henriette HERZ, and associated much with DOHM, the author of "Ueber die Bürgerliche Verbesserung der Juden." Recognizing the advantage which France might derive from the Jews, Mirabeau wrote, and published in London (1787), his "Sur Moses Mendelssohn, sur la Réforme Politique des Juifs et en Particulier sur la Révolution Tentée, en Leur Faveur, en 1753, dans la Grande Bretagne." When he was elected deputy from Provence to the States General, and one of his Jewish friends of Aix asked what he would do in the Assembly, he replied, "I will make a human being of you." True to this promise, he seized every opportunity to plead for the emancipation of the Jews, being, together with the Abbé Grégoire and the pastor Rabaud-Saint-Etienne, one of their most zealous advocates. Several times he took up their cause before the National Assembly: on Aug. 17, 1789, he proposed, in the name of the "Committee of Five," the "Declaration of the Rights of Man"; on Aug. 22 he eloquently attacked religious intolerance, and he was the first to protest against the institution of a dominant state church—"Nothing should dominate except justice; nothing should dominate but the rights of each man, to which all else is subject." On Dec. 24, in speaking in favor of the admission of Jews to civil and military offices, he said: "I have heard with astonishment the honorable speaker [H. de Baumetz] state that the Jews perhaps do not desire the civil and military offices to which you declare them eligible, and draw therefrom the specious conclusion that it would be a gratuitous and ill-advised generosity on your part to pronounce them fit for such positions. . . . In a government such as you are establishing all men must be equal; you must exclude all who are not equal or who refuse to become so. The petition which the Jews, however, have laid before this Assembly contradicts the statement of the gentleman who has just spoken."

Like all who at that time took the part of the Jews, Mirabeau found his motives misinterpreted, being accused of accepting bribes from the Jews and of deriving benefit from ministerial appointments; but he never allowed himself to be moved from his purpose. While Mirabeau in 1787 was already in favor of the emancipation of the Jews, he expected that, like other acts of the doctrinaires then in power, it would embitter the people against the Jacobins and lead to a moderate constitutional government. This appears clearly from the secret correspondence in which he furnished the king with reports of the proceedings of the National Assembly and with directions in regard to the policy to be pursued by the court ("Correspondance Entre le Comte de Mirabeau et le Comte de la Marck . . . Publiée par M. A. de Bacourt," ii. 374-377, Paris, 1851; Oncken, "Das Zeitalter der Revolution, des Kaiserreiches und der Befreiungskriege," i. 340, Berlin, 1884).

BIBLIOGRAPHY: J. Weyl, *Discours Prononcé à l'Occasion de la Cérémonie Commemorative Célébrée au Temple Israélite de Marseille*, p. 20; Halphen, *Recueil des Lois*, pp. 192-193; Léon Kahn, *Les Juifs à Paris*, p. 61; idem, *Les Juifs de Paris Pendant la Révolution*, pp. 16, 56, 58.

D. S. K.

MIRACLE (אות ,מופת ,פלא; lit. "wonder" or "sign"): An event which can not be explained by ordinary natural agencies, and which, therefore, is taken as an act of a higher power.

Miracles are by no means identical with myths. Myths are primitive or pagan personifications (or rather deifications) of the powers, or forms of nature, represented as acting like human beings. Miracles, on the contrary, place all things in nature under the control of a higher power, which uses them as means of working out its holier designs; they are, therefore, essentially monotheistic. It is true, however, that ancient myths have frequently been transformed in support of the monotheistic idea into miracles performed by prophet or saint (see Steinthal, "Mythe und Religion").

In the Bible every occurrence which contrasts with the ordinary happenings of life is counted a miracle or wonder. It is by the wonders which the Lord did in Egypt (Ex. iii. 20, vii. 3, xi. 9; Deut. iv. 34, vi. 22, vii. 19, xxvi. 8, xxix. 2; Judges vi. 13; Jer. xxxii. 20, 21; Ps. lxxviii. 43, cvi. 7) that His power was made known. He alone "does wonders" (Ex. xv. 11; Ps. lxxii. 18, lxxxvi. 10); there is nothing "too wonderful" (Gen. xviii. 14; Jer. xxxii. 17, 27 [A. V. "too hard"]) for Him. He worked wonders for Israel as for no other nation (Ex. xxxiv. 10; Josh. iii. 5). But He works wonders without number in the natural world also (Job v. 9, xxxvii. 14; Ps. cvii. 24). As a matter of fact, every occurrence in nature is, in the Biblical view, an act of God. He sends the rain and causes the thunder (Job xxxvii. 4-6); "He bringeth out the stars by number" (Isa. xl. 26, Hebr.); every work of creation is an act of His providence (Ps. civ.). Yet only an uncommon or inexplicable event makes man ponder and see "the finger of God" (Ex. viii. 15); God must "make a new thing" in order to make men know that He rules (Num. xvi. 30). The rain, hail, fire, and brimstone that are treasured up in the heavens must come down in an unusual time and quantity to destroy the evil-doers (Gen. xx. 24; Ex. ix. 22-24; Josh. x. 11; comp. Ps. xviii. 13 [A. V. 12]; Job xxxvii. 6, xxxviii. 22); the waters of the sea and the river must leave the place assigned to them to show His might (Ex. xiv. 21-27; Josh. iii. 13-16); and sun, moon, and stars must be stayed in their course to show that God battles for Israel (Josh. x. 10-14; Judges v. 20).

The miracles of the Bible are performed either directly by the Deity—to manifest His punitive justice, as in the cases of Sodom, of Egypt, of the Canaanites or Assyrians, or of individuals, such as Abimelech, Korah, Uzza, and others (Gen. xix. 24; Ex. viii.-xiv.; Josh. vi.-x.; II Kings xix. 35; Gen. xii. 17; Num. xvii.; II Sam. vi. 7), or to protect His chosen ones, as in the furnishing of water, bread, and meat to Israel in the wilderness (Ex. xv. 23, xvii. 7; Num. xii. 31), to Samson and Elijah (Judges xv. 19; I Kings xvii. 6, xix. 5)—or by the messengers of God in order to prove their divine calling (Ex. iv. 1-17; Deut. xxxiv. 11; II Kings ii.-vi.). Every theophany, in fact, is a miracle (Ex. xvi. 7-13, xxi. 17-19; Judges vi. 21-22), and accordingly the revelation of the Lord on Sinai is the greatest of miracles (Deut. iv. 32-36). A literal belief in the Torah, therefore, necessarily implies a belief in the miracles told therein.

Belief in Miracles.

Nevertheless, the Torah itself lays down the principle that miracles are no test of the truth of the thing for which their testimony is invoked. The Deuteronomic law says: "If a prophet arise among you who giveth a sign or wonder, and the sign or wonder comes to pass, but he desires to lead you into idolatry, thou shalt not hearken to that prophet, for the Lord your God trieth you whether you truly love the Lord your God" (Deut. xiii. 2-4, Hebr. [A. V. 1-3]). This is a plain statement that miracles do not prove a religious truth, as they are performed also in the cause of untruth.

Miracle has justly been called "des Glauben's liebstes Kind" (the dearest child of faith). The belief in God's omnipotence and all-encompassing providence necessitates at a certain stage of religious consciousness the belief in miracles, that is, in supernatural help in times of great stress or peril. To deny the possibility of miracles appears to the believing soul to be tantamount to a denial of the absolute omnipotence of God. "Is anything impossible to God?" "Is the Lord's hand waxed short?" (Gen. xviii. 14, Hebr.; Num. xi. 23) are questions asked ever anew by helpless man. Talmudic Judaism, therefore, accepts all the miracles related in the Bible, but at the same time it does not emphasize belief in them as fundamental to the faith. What Paul says of the Jews, "they seek signs while the Greeks seek wisdom" (I Cor. i. 22, Greek), is certainly not true of the representatives and exponents of Judaism. Miracles, which occupy so conspicuous a place in the New Testament and in the history of Christianity, are viewed as matters of secondary importance throughout the rabbinical literature.

Talmudic Judaism.

The Talmudic sages made the very possibility of miracles a matter of speculation, stating that "when God created the world He made an agreement that the sea would divide, the fire not hurt, the lions not harm, the fish not swallow persons singled out by God for certain times, and thus the whole order of things changes whenever He finds it necessary" (Gen. R. v. 4; Ex. R. xxi. 6). This view removes some of the objections to miracles as involving an interruption of the order of creation and as an admission of the insufficiency of the first creative act. In the same spirit the Rabbis, in the Mishnah (Ab. v. 6; comp. Ab. R. N., Text B, xxxvii. [ed. Schechter, p. 95]; Sifre, Deut. 355; Pirḳe R. El. xix.; Targ. Yer. to Num. xxii. 28), enumerate the things created at dusk on the Sabbath of the week of creation, and that would appear in due time as miraculous works: the mouth of the earth (Num. xvi. 30); the mouth of the well (*ib.* xxi. 17); the mouth of the ass (*ib.* xxii. 28); the bow (Gen. ix. 13); the manna; the rod (Ex. iv. 17); the tables of the Law; and so on. The underlying idea of these utterances is that miracles, instead of being interruptions of the divine order of things, are in reality foreordained by the creative wisdom and appear only to man as something new.

The Rabbis prescribe benedictions to be recited when approaching places made memorable by miraculous events (Ber. ix. 1, 53b–54a); they speak of miracles which occurred continuously during the time of the Temple (Ab. v. 5; Yoma 21a, b); they knew of saints to whom, as to the Prophets of old, miracles were of daily occurrence ("melummadim be-nissim"; Ta'an. 21–25; Ḥul. 7a; see Essenes). Nevertheless, they pay little heed to the power of miracles. Simeon b. Shetaḥ threatened Onias the saint with excommunication for his demonstrative appeal to God to send down the rain in a miraculous manner (Ta'an. iii. 8). When asked by the Romans, "If your God is as omnipotent as you claim, why does He not destroy the idols?" the Jewish sages replied, "Shall God destroy sun, moon, and stars on account of the fools that worship them? The world goes on in its order, and the idolaters shall meet with their doom" ('Ab. Zarah iv. 7). When Pappus and Lulianus were asked by their Roman executioners, "Why does your God not save you as He did the three youths in Nebuchadnezzar's time?" they replied, "We are probably not worthy of such a miracle" (Ta'an. 18b).

The current belief of the Talmudic time is that only former generations, because of their greater piety, were worthy of miracles occurring on their account (Ber. 4a, 20a; Sanh. 94b). "One should by no means incur perils while relying for safety upon the occurrence of a miracle" (Pes. 50b; Ta'an. 20b; Ket. 61b). That miracles should not be invoked as testimony in favor of one religious opinion as against another is the principle asserted in a halakic controversy between R. Eliezer and R. Joshua (B. M. 59b; "The Torah is not in heaven that the decision should be made there"). The daily wonders of divine providence are extolled by some rabbis above the Biblical miracles: "Greater is the miracle that occurs when a sick person escapes from perilous disease than that which happened when Hananiah, Mishael, and Azariah escaped from the fiery furnace" (Ned. 41a). The wonder of the support of a family in the midst of great distress is as great as the wonder of the parting of the Red Sea for Israel (Pes. 118a).

The medieval Jewish philosophers endeavored as much as possible to bring the Biblical miracles within the sphere of natural occurrences, without, however, denying the possibility of miracle in general. Saadia, while accepting every word of the Torah as divine, insisted that the truth of the Bible rests upon reason, and wherever the Bible seems to be in conflict with reason the words must be taken in a metaphorical sense ("'Emunot we-De'ot," ii. 44, 68); he therefore substituted for the speech of the serpent (Gen. iii. 1) and of Balaam's ass (Num. xxii. 28) that of the angel (Ibn Ezra to Gen. iii. 1). Maimonides, while maintaining against the Aristotelian view of the unalterable law of necessity ruling nature the absolute freedom of the Creator which makes miracle possible, finds at the same time in the rabbinical utterances quoted above (Gen. R. v. and Ab. v. 6) support for his view that the Creator implanted the powers of miracle in nature, so that in reality God did not effect any change after creation ("Moreh," ii. 25, 29, and comment to Ab. v. 6; comp. Joël, "Moses Maimonides," 1876, p. 77; Lipmann Heller to Ab. *l.c.*). With finer acumen Gersonides discussed the problem of miracles in the last part of his "Milḥamot" (see Levi ben Gershon), ascribing them to the divine intelligence which foreordains all things, but denying the actuality of the performance within a given time. This is opposed by Crescas, who nevertheless takes miracles as prearranged in the divine plan of creation ("Or Adonai," iii. i. 5). In the "Yad" (Yesode ha-Torah, viii. 1–3) Maimonides declares that the belief in Moses and his law was based on the actual revelation of God on Sinai and by no means on the miracles performed; since miracles may be the work of witchcraft and of other non-divine agencies, they can not be accepted as proof. This position is taken also by Albo ("'Iḳḳarim," i. 18).

Consequently miracles are never adduced in support of the faith by Jewish writers; and Mendelssohn, in his answer to Bonnet, who referred to the miracles of the New Testament as proof of the truth of Christianity, was perfectly justified in declaring in the name of Judaism that miracles may be appealed to in support of every religion and that therefore they can not serve as proof of any (Mendelssohn, "Gesammelte Schriften," iii. 123 *et seq.*, 311). Modern historical research can no longer, says Joël (see "Jahrb. für Jüdische Gesch. und Litteratur," 1904, pp. 70–73), view the narratives of the Bible in the same light as did the medieval thinkers who could not discriminate between the objectivity of the facts narrated and the subjectivity of the narrator.

Bibliography: *Das Wunder in Seinem Verhältnisse zur Religion*, in *Jüdisches Literaturblatt*, i. 77–93.

K.

MIRANDA, LALLA: Australian singer; born in Melbourne 1876. Both of her parents were singers, and she herself sang in public when only thirteen years of age. After completing her musical education in Europe, under Mdlle. de Garette, and Madame Richard of the Grand Opera, Paris, she sang for three consecutive years at the opera-houses of Amsterdam and Rotterdam. Later she appeared at the Théâtre de la Monnaie, Brussels, and in 1900 sang in "Rigoletto" at the opera, Covent Garden, London.

Bibliography: Harris, *Jewish Year Book*, 1901–2.

J. M. W. L.

MIRELS, MESHULLAM ZALMAN BEN DAVID (NEUMARK): German rabbi; born about 1620 at Vienna; died Nov. 28, 1706, at Altona. When, in 1670, the Jews were expelled from Vienna, he and his son Zeeb Wolf and other members of the Mirels family emigrated to Berlin. A few years later (1678) Mirels was elected chief rabbi ("ab bet din") of the communities Altona, Hamburg, and Wandsbeck, which position he held until his death. He was the father of a large family, ramified through Poland and Lithuania, and lived to see the fifth generation. His daughter Sarah was the wife of Ẓebi Ashkenazi (Ḥakam Ẓebi) and the mother of Jacob Emden.

One responsum written by Mirels is found in the collection "Eben ha-Shoham." See also Jew. Encyc. i. 474, *s.v.* Altona.

Bibliography: Jacob Emden, *Megillat Sefer*, ed. Kahana, pp. 10, 13, Warsaw, 1888; Dembitzer, *Kelilat Yofi*, i., 8a, 91b, 92a, Cracow, 1888; Fuenn, *Keneset Yisrael*, p. 328.

D. S. Man.

MIRELS, ẒEBI HIRSCH BEN AARON: German Talmudist; rabbi of Schwerin in the middle of the eighteenth century. He received his early education in London. After studying at various yeshibot he became rabbi at Wreschen, Poland, and shortly after was appointed rabbi to the congregation at Schwerin. He was the author of "Mispar Ẓeba'am" (Berlin, 1787), a pilpulistic treatise on the Talmud, in two parts—"Pinnot Ẓeba'aw" and "Ereẓ Ẓebi."

Bibliography: Fuenn, *Keneset Yisrael*, i. 285; Walden, *Shem ha-Gedolim he-Ḥadash*, i. 39; Steinschneider, *Cat. Bodl.* col. 2757; Fürst, *Bibl. Jud.* ii. 380.

E. C. S. J. L.

MIRÈS, JULES ISAAC: French financier; born at Bordeaux Dec. 9, 1809; died at Marseilles in 1871. A broker in 1848, he became, after the February Revolution of that year, director of the gas company of Arles. Subsequently he bought the "Journal des Chemins de Fer" and founded the "Conseiller du Peuple," which became quite popular through Lamartine's contributions. Together with Millaud, Mirès organized the "Caisse des Chemins de Fer," of which he became sole director in 1853. In 1851 he bought "Le Pays" and "Le Constitutionnel." He undertook colossal works at Marseilles, including the construction of a harbor and of a new quarter of the city, and the installation of a system of illumination by gas. In 1860 he obtained the concession for the construction of the Roman railroads and for the negotiation of the Turkish loan. On July 11, 1861, he was sentenced to five years' imprisonment and to the payment of a fine of 3,000 francs, but he succeeded in getting this verdict set aside on April 21, 1862, and was rehabilitated by the court of Douai. Toward the end of 1869 Mirès was sentenced to six months' imprisonment and fined 3,000 francs on account of his pamphlet "Un Crime Judiciaire," attacking the expert Monginot and the judges who had tried his suit against the firm of Pereire.

Miriam.
(From the Sarajevo Haggadah of the fourteenth century.)

He contributed several financial articles to "Le Constitutionnel" and "La Presse," and published a number of pamphlets, including "Aperçus Financiers" (1868) and "Mémoires Judiciaires" (in his own defense).

He was decorated by Napoleon III. with the ribbon of the Legion of Honor in 1860. His daughter married a French nobleman.

Bibliography: Vapereau, *Dictionnaire des Contemporains*; *La Grande Encyclopédie*.

S. J. Ka.

MIRIAM.—Biblical Data: Prophetess; daughter of Amram and sister of Moses and Aaron (I Chron. vi. 3; Ex. xv. 20; Num. xxvi. 59). When Moses was left at the river Miriam watched from a distance until Pharaoh's daughter took him up, whereupon she proposed to the princess to find a Hebrew nurse; the princess assenting to this, Miriam returned with her mother (Ex. ii. 4–7). After the Israelites had crossed the Red Sea Miriam sang a song of triumph, in which all the women joined (Ex. xv. 20–21). Miriam and Aaron spoke against Moses on account of the Cushite woman whom he had married, whereupon God summoned Moses, Aaron, and Miriam to the tabernacle of the congregation, reproved her, and punished her with leprosy. She was healed through the prayers of Moses, but was obliged to remain without the camp of the Israelites for seven days, although the people did not proceed until she had returned (Num. xii.). Miriam died in the desert at Kadesh, where she was buried (Num. xx. 1). In Micah vi. 4 she is mentioned, with Moses and Aaron, as a leader of the people.

S. J. Z. L.

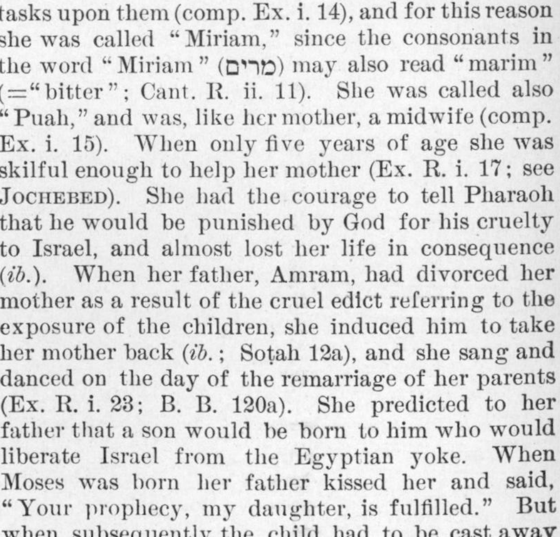

——In Rabbinical Literature: Miriam was born at the time when the Egyptians began to embitter the lives of the Israelites by imposing arduous tasks upon them (comp. Ex. i. 14), and for this reason she was called "Miriam," since the consonants in the word "Miriam" (מרים) may also read "marim" (="bitter"; Cant. R. ii. 11). She was called also "Puah," and was, like her mother, a midwife (comp. Ex. i. 15). When only five years of age she was skilful enough to help her mother (Ex. R. i. 17; see Jochebed). She had the courage to tell Pharaoh that he would be punished by God for his cruelty to Israel, and almost lost her life in consequence (*ib.*). When her father, Amram, had divorced her mother as a result of the cruel edict referring to the exposure of the children, she induced him to take her mother back (*ib.*; Soṭah 12a), and she sang and danced on the day of the remarriage of her parents (Ex. R. i. 23; B. B. 120a). She predicted to her father that a son would be born to him who would liberate Israel from the Egyptian yoke. When Moses was born her father kissed her and said, "Your prophecy, my daughter, is fulfilled." But when subsequently the child had to be cast away her parents upbraided her and asked what would now be the outcome of her prophecy. Miriam therefore went to the river (Ex. ii. 4) to see how her prophecy would be fulfilled (Ex. R. i. 26; Soṭah 12b–13a).

Miriam is said to have had also the following names: Ephrath, Helah, Naarah, Azubah, Jerioth, Zohar, Zereth, Ethan, and Aharhel (comp. I Chron. ii. 18, iv. 5–8), which were given to her on special occasions (Ex. R. i. 21; Soṭah 11b–12a). She was married to Caleb b. Jephunneh, or b. Hezron, to whom she bore Hur (comp. I Chron. ii. 18–21). Then she fell ill (hence her name "Helah") and was thereupon left by her husband (hence the name "Azubah"). Subsequently she regained her health, became again like a young woman (hence the name "Naarah"), and was taken back by her husband (Ex. R. *l.c.*). Miriam was the ancestress of King David, and of Bezaleel, who made the Tabernacle and its vessels. Bezaleel's wisdom (comp. Ex. xxxi. 3) is said to have been due to his grandmother Miriam (Ex. R. xlviii. 6). To have so illustrious a descendant was Miriam's reward for not obeying Pharaoh (comp. Ex. i. 21; Ex. R. *l.c.*). When Miriam talked against Moses (comp. Num. xii.) she did not intend to slander him; she wished him to live with his wife and raise children (Deut. R. vi. 6). But when she was punished with leprosy, and had to remain without the camp, God honored her by officiating as priest Himself (Zeb. 102a). The Israelites waited for her seven days (Num. xii. 15; Soṭah 9b), for she had once waited for Moses by the river (Ex. ii. 4).

Her Names.

Miriam is regarded as the savior of Israel (Ex. R. xxvi. 1). For her sake a marvelous well accompanied the Israelites, a rock from which water flowed. This well disappeared after Miriam's death (Ta'an. 9a). It was subsequently shown in the sea (Shab. 35a). Miriam, like Moses and Aaron, died by a kiss from God (M. Ḳ. 28a), for the angel of death could not take her; and worms did not touch her body (B. B. 17a). Another legend says that Miriam, like Moses and Aaron, died on account of the water of strife ("me meribah"; comp. Num. xx. 7–13). This seems inconsistent, for, according to the Bible as well as the legends, water became scarce only after Miriam's death, with the disappearance of the well (Lev. R. xxxi. 5 and commentaries *ad loc.*).

S. J. Z. L.

MIRKES, SOLOMON ZALMAN BEN JUDAH LÖB: Lithuanian Talmudist of the eighteenth century; a native of Mir, government of Minsk. He published at Königsberg in 1769 his "Derush," a funeral oration on the death of R. Abraham, chief rabbi of Frankfort-on-the-Main. In 1771 he was rabbi of Frankfort-on-the-Oder, where he published in that year his two works: "Sharsheret ha-'Abotot," containing novellæ, decisions, and discussions upon Talmudic matters, and "Shulḥan Shelomoh," a compendium of the Shulḥan 'Aruk, Oraḥ Ḥayyim, according to the Aḥaronim.

Bibliography: Fürst, *Bibl. Jud.* ii. 380; Zedner, *Cat. Hebr. Books Brit. Mus.* p. 726.

H. R. M. Sel.

MIRROR: An object having a nearly perfect reflecting surface. In ancient times mirrors were invariably made of metal; in Egypt, of polished brass. It is no doubt this kind of mirror to which reference is made in Ex. xxxviii. 8 and in Job xxxvii. 18. Reflections might also be seen in still water (Prov. xxvii. 19). In the enumeration of women's ornaments in Isa. iii. 23, hand-mirrors seem to be included; but this is somewhat doubtful. References to mirrors occur in the Apocrypha (Ecclus. [Sirach] xxii. 11) and in the New Testament (I Cor. xxxiii. 12).

The Rabbis were acquainted with the use of mirrors, sometimes employing metal (Kelim xxx. 2). On the Sabbath it was not allowable to look into a mirror unless it was fixed on a wall (Shab. 149a). It would appear that later there was a tendency to forbid men to view themselves in mirrors, as this was regarded as effeminate (see Levy, "Neuhebr. Wörterb." i. 236). Nevertheless, the members of Rabbi's family were allowed to do so (Yer. Shab. vi. 7) because they were "close to the government."

The modern Jews of eastern Europe have a number of superstitions in regard to mirrors the exact origin of which it is difficult to trace. Mirrors are covered when a person dies. The angel of death will be seen if one looks into a mirror at such a time. If a mirror is broken, seven years of poverty will result; this is a general superstition, and not confined to Jews. In Galicia it is supposed that if one puts a mirror in front of a sleeping man with a candle between them, the sleeper will follow a person whither the latter wills. If the sleeper strikes one under these circumstances, the person stricken will not live more than a year. J.

MI-SHEBERAK. See Sacrifice.

MISHLE SINDABAR. See Sindabar.

MISHNAH (construct state, **Mishnat**): A noun formed from the verb "shanah," which has the same meaning as the Aramaic "matnita," derived from "teni" or "tena." The verb "shanah," which originally meant "to repeat," acquired in post-Biblical Hebrew the special force of "to teach" and "to learn" that which was not transmitted in writing but only orally; the development of connotation being due to the fact that the retention of teachings handed down by word of mouth was possible only by frequent recitation.

"Mishnah," the derivative of the verb "shanah," means therefore: (1) "instruction," the teaching and learning of the tradition, the word being used in this sense in Ab. iii. 7, 8; and (2) in a concrete sense, the content of that instruction, the traditional doctrine as it was developed down to the beginning of the third century of the common era. "Mishnah" is frequently used, therefore, to designate the law which was transmitted orally, in contrast to "Miḳra," the law which is written and read (*e.g.*, B. M. 33a; Ber. 5a; Ḥag. 14a; 'Er. 54b; Ḳid. 30a; Yer. Hor. iii. 48c; Pes. iv. 130d; Num. R. xiii.; and many other passages); and the term includes also the halakic midrashim, as well as the Tosefta or explanatory additions to the Mishnah (Ḳid. 49b; see Baraita). In this wider sense the word was known to the Church Fathers, who, however, regarded it as the feminine form of "mishneh," analogous to "miḳneh" and "miḳnah," and supposed that it signified "second teaching" (comp. "'Aruk," *s.v.* שהיא שנייה לתורה), translating it by *δευτέρωσις* (see the passages in Schürer, "Gesch." 3d ed., i. 113).

The Name.

The term "mishnah" connotes also (3) the sum and substance of the teachings of a single tanna (*e.g.*, Giṭ. 67a; Yeb. 49b, 50a: "mishnat R. Eliezer b. Ya'aḳob" = "the teachings of R. Eliezer b. Jacob"; comp. Rashi *ad loc.*); or it may mean (4) the view of a tanna in regard to some one matter (*e.g.*, Men. 18a: "mishnat R. Eliezer" = "the view of R. Eliezer," and the expressions "mishnah rishonah" = "the earlier view," and "mishnah aḥaronah" = "the later view," Ḥag. 2a; Ket. v. 29d; M. Ḳ. iii. 83b). It may furthermore denote (5) a single tenet (*e.g.*, B. M. 33b; Hor. 13b; B. Ḳ. 94b; Shab. 123b), being in this sense parallel to the expression HALAKAH (on the difference between the two see Frankel, "Hodegetica in Mischnam," p. 8). It is used also for (6) any collection of such tenets, being thus applied to the great Mishnaic collections ("Mishnayot Gedolot") of R. Akiba, R. Ḥiyya, R. Hoshaiah, and Bar Ḳappara, in Lam. R., Introduction, and in Cant. R. viii. 2 (comp. Yer. Hor. iii. 48c; Eccl. R. ii.).

Finally the name "Mishnah" is applied particularly to (7) the collection of halakot made by R. Judah ha-Nasi I. (generally called "Rabbi"), which constitutes the basis of the Talmud, and which, with many additions and changes, has been transmitted to the present time. In Palestine this collection was called also "Halakot," as in Yer. Hor. iii. 48c; Ber. i. 53c; Lev. R. iii. (comp. Frankel, *l.c.* p. 8). The designation "Talmud" is likewise applied to R. Judah ha-Nasi's Mishnah (Yer. Shab. v. 1, 7b; Beẓah ii. 1, 61b; Yeb. viii. 9a; comp. also Frankel, *l.c.* p. 285; O. H. Schorr in "He-Ḥaluẓ," 1866, p. 42; A. Krochmal in the introduction to "Yerushalayim ha-Benuyah," p. 6; Oppenheim, "Zur Gesch. der Mischna," p. 244).

The "Mishnah of R. Judah," however, is not to be regarded as a literary product of the third century, nor R. Judah as its author. It is, on the contrary, a collection which includes almost the entire material of the oral doctrine as developed from the period of the earliest halakic exegesis down to that of the fixed and crystallized halakot of the early third century. Judah ha-Nasi, who was the redactor of this work, included in his compilation the largest and most important portion of the earlier collections that he had at hand, and fortunately preserved, for the most part without change, the traditional teachings which he took from older sources and collections; so that it is still possible to distinguish the earlier from the later portions by their form and mode of expression.

Development of the Mishnah.

In order to obtain a correct conception of the Mishnah, as well as of its value and importance, it is necessary to consider its relation to preceding collections of similar content as well as the general development of the oral doctrine from the earliest midrash of the Soferim down to the time when the Halakah received its final form.

According to a reliable tradition, contained in the Letter of Sherira Gaon (Neubauer, "M. J. C." p. 15) and confirmed by other sources (Hoffmann, "Die Erste Mischna," pp. 6-12), the earliest form of discussion of halakic regulations was the Midrash (see MIDRASH HALAKAH); and vestiges of such halakot may still be found in the Mishnah.

In addition to this form of the Midrash, which connects the halakic interpretation with the Scriptural passage on which it is based, the independent, definitive Halakah, apart from Scripture, was used in very early times in certain cases, and collections of such halakot were compiled (comp. Hoffmann, *l.c.* p. 11, note 2). As early as the time of the Second Temple the definitive Halakah was used more frequently than the midrashic form, the change having begun, according to geonic accounts, as early as the time of Hillel and Shammai (comp. Hoffmann, *l.c.* pp. 12–14). Although it can not be assumed that a collection of halakot, arranged in six orders, was undertaken when this change was made, or that Hillel himself edited a Mishnah, as Lerner has attempted to show (Berliner's "Magazin," 1886, pp. 1–20), it is probable that the material of the Mishnah first began to be collected at the time of the "Ziḳne Bet Shammai" and "Ziḳne Bet Hillel," the elder pupils of Shammai and Hillel. The beginnings of the present Mishnah may be found in this first mishnah collection, which in the completed text is termed "Mishnah Rishonah" (Sanh. iii. 4; 'Eduy. vii. 2; Giṭ. v. 6; Nazir vi. 1). A large portion of this first Mishnah is still preserved in its original form, notwithstanding the many changes to which it was subjected by the Tannaim; for many portions can be proved to have been redacted, in the form which they now bear, at the time of the schools of Shammai and Hillel, while the Temple was still standing (comp. Hoffmann, *l.c.* pp. 15–20; *idem*, "Bemerkungen zur Kritik der Mischna," in Berliner's "Magazin," 1881, pp. 170 *et seq.*).

This first collection of the Mishnah and its separation from the Midrash were intended, on the one hand, to reduce the traditional Halakah to a shorter form, and, on the other, to fix the disputed halakot as such; of these disputed halakot there were then but few. The isolation of the Halakah from the Midrash not only resulted in a shorter and more definite form, but also removed many differences then existing. Indeed in many cases the divergency had been merely one of form, the proof and the derivation from Scripture being differently stated for the same halakah by different teachers. This earliest Mishnah was intended to afford the teachers both a norm for their decisions and a text-book for their classes and discourses, and thus to preserve the uniformity of teaching. It did not accomplish this purpose entirely, however; for when the political disorders and the fall of the Jewish state diverted attention from careful doctrinal studies, many halakot of the Mishnah were forgotten, and their wording became a subject of controversy. Since, moreover, in addition to these differences each tanna taught the first Mishnah according to his own conception of it, the one Mishnah and the one doctrine developed into many mishnayot and many doctrines (Sanh. 88b; Soṭah 47b). This multiplication occurred during the period of the later "Bet Hillel" and "Bet Shammai" (comp. Letter of Sherira Gaon, *l.c.* pp. 4, 9; Hoffmann, *l.c.* p. 49).

The Synod of Jabneh.

To avert the danger which threatened the uniformity of doctrine, the synod of Jabneh was convened (Tosef., 'Eduy. i. 1; comp. Letter of Sherira Gaon, *l.c.* p. 5; Dünner, "Einiges über Ursprung und Bedeutung des Traktates Eduyot," in "Monatsschrift," 1871, pp. 37 *et seq.*), and under the presidency of Gamaliel II. and Eleazar b. Azariah it undertook to collect the ancient halakot, to examine and determine their wording, and to discuss and decide their differences; thus there arose the collection 'Eduyot (Ber. 28a). This compilation, that in its original form was much larger than the treatise that now bears its name, included all the halakot which were then known, whether controverted or not, and was in a certain sense a revision of the first Mishnah. Even in the present form of the treatise there are many "'eduyot" which are expressly said to have modified the earlier Mishnah; and there are many others, not so characterized, which must likewise be regarded as modifications of the Mishnah as redacted for the first time. But neither the first Mishnah nor its revision, the 'Eduyot collection, was arranged topically or systematically. It is true, a geonic responsum, which was printed in "Sha'are Teshubah," No. 187 (Leipsic, 1858) and erroneously ascribed to Sherira (comp. Harkavy, "Einleitung zu den Teschubot Hageonim," pp. x. *et seq.*), refers to six orders of the Mishnah said to date from the time of Hillel and Shammai, as does also the "Seder Tanna'im we-Amora'im" (ed. Luzzatto, p. 7), but this statement, which is probably based on Ḥag. 14a, is untrustworthy.

Divisions of Earliest Mishnah.

The earliest Mishnah, however, must have been divided in some way, possibly into treatises, although such a division, if it existed, was certainly arranged formally and not topically like the present tractates and orders. The several halakot were grouped together by a common introductory phrase, which served as the connecting-link, as may be inferred from various traces of this old method of grouping still to be seen in the Mishnah, especially in the last treatises of the order Mo'ed. These phrases (comp. Oppenheim, *l.c.* p. 270) referred for the most part to the similarity or the contrast between two or more halakot. Moreover, the name of the author or of the transmitter was often used as the connecting-link for the various halakot, as is evident from the treatise 'Eduyot in its present form (Dünner, *l.c.* pp. 62–63; A. Krochmal, in "He-Ḥaluẓ," ii. 81–82).

The 'Eduyot collection, which now became the basis for the discourses delivered in the schools, was the means of preserving the uniformity of teaching; but, as the mass incorporated in it was difficult to handle, there was a growing need for a methodical arrangement. R. Akiba, therefore, undertook a sifting of this traditional material, and made a mishnaic collection which he edited systematically by arranging the different subjects in different treatises, and perhaps also by combining the various treatises into orders. In the present Mishnah this collection is often mentioned in contradistinction to the first Mishnah (Sanh. iii. 4, and elsewhere; comp. Frankel, *l.c.* p. 210; Hoffmann, *l.c.* p. 38).

The passage Ab. R. N. xviii. 1 indicates that Akiba arranged his Mishnah according to topics (comp. Oppenheim, *l.c.* pp. 237 *et seq.*); and a like inference is to be drawn from the expression "tiḳḳen" (Yer. Sheḳ. v. 1), which does not mean "to correct," as A. Krochmal supposed ("Yerushalayim ha-Benuyah," pp. 34b–35a), but "to arrange," "to redact," the same word being applied to the work of Judah ha-Nasi in the redaction of his Mishnah (Yeb. 64b). Similarly the term "sidder," meaning "to arrange," is applied both to Akiba's work (Tosef., Zab. i. 5) and to that of R. Judah ha-Nasi (Yer. Pes. iv. 30d), thus justifying the conclusion that Akiba's method of division and arrangement of the Mishnah was the same as that followed by Judah ha-Nasi. Two treatises are definitely known to have been included in their present form in Akiba's Mishnah, in which they even bore their present names. R. Meïr mentions the treatise 'Uḳẓin by name in Hor. 13b; and R. Jose in like manner names the treatise Kelim (Kelim, end): both of these tannaim, who antedated Judah ha-Nasi, undoubtedly designated by these names the treatises Kelim and 'Uḳẓin as included in the Mishnah of their teacher Akiba.

Mishnah of R. Akiba.

R. Akiba's treatment of the old Mishnah in editing his own Mishnah collection was entirely arbitrary. He excluded many of the halakot contained in the original text; and those which he accepted he endeavored to found upon some text, explaining their phraseology, and tracing their origin, but striving most of all to present the Halakah in short, clear, and explicit form (comp. Tosef., Zab. i. 5). Many halakic sentences which he included called for more detailed explanation. For the sake of brevity, however, and to aid his pupils in memorizing the Mishnah, he omitted the required explanations and made an additional collection containing the comments to the Mishnah, thus laying the foundation for the Tosefta (comp. Letter of Sherira Gaon, *l.c.* p. 16; Frankel, *l.c.* p. 306; Oppenheim, *l.c.* p. 270).

Akiba's method, which reduced the halakic collections to an orderly system, soon found imitators; and nearly every tannaitic head of a school, who, in virtue of his position, had a mishnaic collection, sooner or later adopted Akiba's method of dividing and arranging the material. R. Meïr especially followed this system, availing himself of it when the increasing number of new halakot, discovered and established by Akiba's pupils, rendered a new mishnaic collection necessary. In this compilation he included the larger portion of Akiba's Mishnah, but also drew upon other existing collections, such as that of Abba Saul (comp. Lewy, "Ueber Einige Fragmente aus der Mischna des Abba Saul," Berlin, 1876). He likewise incorporated many old halakot known in the schools but excluded by Akiba. He frequently cited the opinions of Akiba, without naming him, as "setam" and therefore authoritative for halakic decisions; but sometimes, when the opinion of the majority was opposed to Akiba's view, he designated the former as "setam" and binding for the Halakah (comp. Oppenheim, *l.c.* p. 315).

R. Meïr's collection had a wide circulation, although it was not able to displace the other compilations. As every tanna at the head of a school, however, had, as stated above, his own mishnaic collection in which the halakot of preceding teachers as well as their controversies were differently expounded, the uniformity in teaching which the redactors of the Mishnah had desired and which had almost been attained was again lost; for there were as many different teachings as there were Mishnah collections. There was good ground, therefore, for the complaint that the religious world was thrown into disorder by the teachers who gave halakic decisions according to their own mishnaic collections (Soṭah 22a), since a clear and reliable Halakah could not be found in any individual compilation (Shab. 138b, 139a).

To remedy this evil and to restore uniformity of teaching, Judah ha-Nasi undertook his collection, arrangement, and redaction of the Mishnah, which work has survived to the present time. He followed his own method so far as the selection and presentation of the material were concerned, but adopted the systems of Akiba and Meïr in regard to the division and arrangement. This Mishnah was intended to serve practical purposes and to be an authority in deciding religious and legal questions. Judah often gives, therefore, the opinion of a single teacher, where he regards it as the correct one, in the name of "the sages" ("ḥakamim") (Ḥul. 85a); and in order that the opinion of a single scholar may prevail as final, he ignores the fact that this view was controverted by many others. At times he, without mentioning his name, quotes his own opinion as "setam," to record it as authoritative (comp. Oppenheim, *l.c.* p. 347, No. 16). Frequently, too, he explains or limits the earlier Halakah (see Yer. Hor. i. 46a), and endeavors to find a compromise in the case of disputed halakot, or he himself decides the cases in which the halakah is to follow one opinion and in which the other (comp. Frankel, *l.c.* pp. 195 *et seq.*).

R. Judah ha-Nasi.

In addition to the practical purpose of restoring and preserving uniformity of halakic doctrine and of providing for teachers an authority for their decisions, Judah ha-Nasi had another purely theoretical object in view; namely, the preservation of the teachings of the ancients, except those which he regarded as relatively unimportant or which he considered to have been preserved in some other place in his collection. This fact explains many peculiarities of the Mishnah, which were regarded as shortcomings by those who considered it a legal code. The following are some of these peculiarities: Judah ha-Nasi quotes the opinion of a single authority even when invalidated, and he quotes the original view of a scholar even after such scholar had himself retracted it (Ḥul. 32b; comp. Oppenheim, *l.c.* p. 344). He quotes also a given halakah in one passage as being controverted ("maḥloket") and in another passage as authoritative ("setam"), or vice versa; and he cites contradictory teachings in different places. All these peculiarities are due to the fact that Judah wished to preserve the ancient teachings; and to attain this object more completely he included in his Mishnah, in addition to the collections of Akiba and Meïr, which formed his chief sources, the major portion of all the other mishnayot (Yer. Shab. xvi. 15c); according to a later account, he used in all thirteen collections (Ned. 41a). He dealt independently with his material; for while he frequently made no changes in the wording or form of the old Mishnah, and even included old halakot which had long since been refuted, he altered various others (comp. Hoffmann, "Bemerkungen zur Kritik der Mischna," in Berliner's "Magazin," 1881, pp. 127 *et seq.*). He expounded many of the old halakot ('Ar. iv. 2; Sanh. ix. 3; Yer. Sanh. 27a; comp. Oppenheim, *l.c.* p. 347), following certain rules (Yer. Ter. i. 2, 40c), and endeavoring to determine the text of the old Mishnah (Yer. Ma'as. Sh. v. 1, 55d; comp. Letter of Sherira Gaon, *l.c.* pp. 9–10; Frankel, *l.c.* p. 214). The less-known halakot, as well as those which the pupils of Akiba had propounded, were interpreted by Judah ha-Nasi according to his conception of them. In this way he impressed upon his Mishnah the stamp of uniformity, and gave it the appearance of a work thoroughly revised, if not new; and his compilation displaced its predecessors by its inclusion of the major portion of their contents with the exception of those halakot which appeared to him untenable, or to which he had alluded in some other passage of his Mishnah.

Because of his personal prominence and his dignity as patriarch (comp. J. S. Bloch, "Einblicke," etc., pp. 59 *et seq.*), his Mishnah soon became the only one used in the schools, and was known to teachers and students alike, Judah thereby attaining his object of restoring uniform teachings. Whereas the exposition of the various halakot given by the Tannaim and called "[Tannaitic] Talmud," had been used hitherto in preference to the dry mishnaic collections (comp. Letter of Sherira Gaon, *l.c.* pp. 18–19), most of the teachers now resorted to R. Judah's Mishnah, which included both the halakot themselves and the expository tannaitic Talmud (this fact explains the application of the name "Talmud" to his Mishnah; B. M. 33a; Yer. Shab. xvi. 15c). Interest in this work was so highly esteemed that a haggadist said: "The study of the Mishnah is equal to sacrifice" (Lev. R. vii.). Every pupil was supposed, as a matter of course, to be familiar with the Mishnah of R. Judah ha-Nasi; and when any one propounded a sentence which was to be found in it, his hearers exclaimed, "What! do we not learn that ourselves from the Mishnah?" According to R. Joshua b. Levi, "The Mishnah is a firm iron pillar"; and none may stray from it (*ib.* xxi.). "The passage, Num. xv. 31, 'He hath despised the word of the Lord,' denotes him who does not consider the Mishnah" (baraita quoted by Isaac Alfasi in his compendium to Sanh. x.). It was considered the only authority for legal decisions. R. Johanan said, "The correct halakic decision is always the one which is declared in the Mishnah to be incontrovertible" ("Halakah ki-setam Mishna"; Yeb. 42b, and parallel passages); and the most conclusive refutation of a sentence was to prove that it was contradicted by the Mishnah. If a decision was accidentally made contrary to the

The Authoritative Mishnah.

Mishnah, the decision at once became invalid (Sanh. 6a, 33a; Ket. 84a, 100a). The Amoraim regarded the Mishnah as the Tannaim did the Scripture; and many of them interpreted and expounded it (comp. Bacher "Ag. Bab. Amor." p. 33, note 207 on Rab). Even subsequently, when the collections which were made by the pupils of Judah ha-Nasi were widely used, his Mishnah remained the sole authority. In cases where the Mishnah conflicted with the Baraita, the former was considered decisive (Suk. 19b; B. Ḳ. 96b), while there is but a single example to show that the Gemara preferred the Baraita in such a disputed case (see Jew. Encyc. ii. 516a, *s.v.* Baraita). Some amoraim, such as Ilfa and Simeon b. Laḳish, even regarded the later collections as unnecessary and useless, since their entire contents were included by implication in the Mishnah, and all questions could be explained from it without the aid of the subsequent compilations (Yer. Kil. i. 6, 27a; Yer. B. Ḳ. v. 5a; Yer. Ḳid. iii. 64b; Ta'an. 22a; comp. Oppenheim, *l.c.* pp. 344–345). Another sentence, likewise derogatory to these later collections, says: "If Rabbi has not taught it, how does R. Ḥiyya [the collector of the baraitot] know it?"

This Mishnah, however, has not been preserved in the form in which Rabbi redacted it; for, as stated above, it was subjected to many changes, and received numerous additions before it reached its definitive form. Notwithstanding the superiority of Rabbi's Mishnah to its predecessors, it had many defects, some of which may still be seen in the present Mishnah. Though Rabbi himself subsequently renounced many of his Mishnaic opinions, as his views changed in the course of time, he retained such discarded opinions in his Mishnah as he had held them in his younger days (B. M. 44a; 'Ab. Zarah 52b; Yer. 'Ab. Zarah iv. 44a). Occasionally he recorded one decision as authoritative in one passage of his Mishnah, considering it the correct view, and, deciding later in favor of an opposite opinion, he in another place gave this also as authoritative without retracting or suppressing his former view (Sheb. 4a). These shortcomings would not have been serious, since Rabbi did not intend to furnish a mere halakic code, if he had not failed to include in his collection many halakot which were taught in his school and which were, therefore, highly important, not only for halakic decision, but also for a knowledge of tradition in general. He furthermore excluded his own halakot and the points of divergence between him and his contemporaries. These omissions were the most serious defects in his Mishnah for his pupils, since, being a compendium of the entire traditional instruction, it must have seemed incomplete inasmuch as it did not include the teachings of the last tannaim, whose legal decisions should certainly have been incorporated in it if it was to serve as an authoritative code. Rabbi's pupils R. Ḥiyya, R. Hoshaiah, Levi, and Bar Ḳappara began, therefore, even during Rabbi's lifetime and with his knowledge, to make additions and emendations to his Mishnah. Rabbi, who was aware of the deficiencies of his work, probably approved many of these corrections (comp. Oppenheim, *l.c.* pp. 344 *et seq.*), and added some himself (Yer. Ket. iv. 29a, b). Most of the changes, however, were such as were contrary to his views, and were consequently concealed from him by his pupils (see Megillat Setarim; comp. Weiss, "Dor," ii. 191).

Modifications of the Text.

Thus arose new collections by R. Ḥiyya, R. Hoshaiah, and Bar Ḳappara, which were called "Mishnayot Gedolot," since they were more voluminous than Rabbi's collection. As these new compilations imperiled the uniformity of teaching, which was possible only through the existence of a Mishnah familiar to all teachers, the "Debe Rabbi" (the scholars of Rabbi's school) undertook a revision of his Mishnah, probably long after his death. They made various changes and a large number of additions in agreement with current demands; and in this form the Mishnah has been transmitted to the present time. The majority of the additions made by the Debe Rabbi betray their later origin, although some of them are known to be supplementary only by statements in the Gemara. For instance, the discussion between R. Hezekiah and R. Johanan, in Men. 104b, indicates that the passage in the present Mishnah (Men. xiii. 2), beginning "Rabbi omer," is a later addition of which Hezekiah and Johanan did not know. The same is true of Mishnah Sanh. ix. 2, since the R. Simeon there mentioned is Rabbi's son, as is shown by Yerushalmi (*ad loc.* 27a, b). Mishnah 'Ab. Zarah ii. 6, where a decision of Judah ha-Nasi is quoted, also comes in this category, since it refers to Judah II., grandson of Judah ha-Nasi I., the original redactor of the Mishnah (comp. Tos. 'Ab. Zarah 36a, *s.v.* "Ashor"). In general, all the passages in which something concerning Rabbi is related, or something which he did either alone (Sheb. vi. 4) or together with his colleague (Oh. xviii. 19), must be regarded as later accretions (comp. Frankel, *l.c.* pp. 215 *et seq.*); and the same statement holds good of all the passages in which Rabbi's opinion is quoted after that of other tannaim. On the other hand, there are passages concluding with "dibre Rabbi" (the words of Rabbi), which are not necessarily additions; for Rabbi may in such instances have quoted his own opinion anonymously as setam, as he frequently did, and the words "dibre Rabbi" may have been added by later editors. Various sentences of the Tosefta also found their way into the Mishnah (comp. Hoffmann, *l.c.* pp. 156 *et seq.*). Many of these are haggadic in nature, such as those at the end of the treatises Makkot, 'Uḳẓin, Ḳinnim, Ḳiddushin, and Soṭah, as well as many sentences in the treatise Abot, which must be regarded as accretions. The later origin of many of these sentences is at once indicated by the name of the author, as in the cases of R. Joshua b. Levi, who belonged to the first generation of Amoraim ('Uḳẓin, end); Simon, son of Judah ha-Nasi (Ab. ii. 2); and Hillel, grandson of Judah ha-Nasi (*ib.* ii. 4 *et seq.*; comp. Lipmann Heller in Tos. Yom-Ṭob, *ad loc.*). Aside from these additions, the Debe Rabbi emended the phraseology and single words of the Mishnah (comp. Yer. Ḳid. iii. 64c), even as Rabbi himself had done (comp. B. M. iv. 1; 'Ab. Zarah iv. 4, and the Babylonian and Palestinian Gemaras, *ad loc.*).

Many of Rabbi's own emendations have been preserved in the different readings of Yerushalmi and Babli, although the differences between these two versions are not all due to his changes, as Rapoport assumes ("Kerem Ḥemed," vii. 157–167); for most of the differences not due to philological causes must be ascribed to the different mishnaic schools. In addition to the Debe Rabbi, later amoraim also emended the Mishnah if the received reading seemed untenable. These emendations were then incorporated into the Mishnah; those made by the Babylonian amoraim into the Mishnah which was taught in the Babylonian schools; and those made by the Palestinian amoraim into the Mishnah as taught in the Palestinian schools. Thus, in 'Ab. Zarah i., the Mishnah in the Palestinian Talmud was corrected according to the Gemara (Yer. 'Ab. Zarah i. 39d), while the Mishnah in the Babylonian Talmud retained its original reading. Sometimes—curiously enough—the Mishnah of the Palestinian Talmud was corrected to harmonize with the results of the discussion in the Babylonian Talmud, and vice versa (comp. O. H. Schorr in "He-Ḥaluẓ," vi. 32–47; Frankel, "Mebo," pp. 19a–22a), although only a few of these emendations, of which there are many in the Talmud—introduced by the phrases "sami mi-kan" = "omit from here," or "ḥasuri miḥasra" = "something missing," or "teni kak" = "teach thus"—found their way into the Mishnah itself. Many of the amoraim objected to corrections in the Mishnah, holding that the phraseology chosen by the ancients in their mishnaic collections should be retained unchanged (Yer. Nazir i. 51a).

Babylonian and Palestinian Mishnah.

The Mishnah is written in a peculiar kind of Hebrew, which is far more different from the Hebrew of the earlier books of the Old Testament than from that of some of the later ones and which is, therefore, correctly designated as "Neo-Hebraic." This language was spoken by the people of Palestine as late as the second century of the common era, but was cultivated especially by the scholars; so that it was called "leshon ḥakamim" = "the speech of the wise." It contains many old Hebraic terms which were preserved in popular speech, although they are not found in the Bible, as well as numerous foreign elements, especially from Aramaic, Greek, and Latin; the scholars being forced to adopt these loan-words as terms for objects and concepts which were formerly unknown and for which there were no designations in the Hebrew vocabulary. Foreign words were especially used to designate implements borrowed from foreign peoples (comp. Weiss, "Mishpaṭ Leshon ha-Mishnah," pp. 1–7; A. Geiger, "Lehrbuch zur Sprache der Mischna," pp. 1–3); and these borrowed terms were so Hebraized as to be taken by many for native words.

From the first there were various opposing opinions regarding the problems when and by whom the Mishnah was reduced to writing. According to the Letter of Sherira Gaon (*l.c.* pp. 2, 9, 12), Judah ha-Nasi himself performed this task; and this view is supported by Rabbenu Nissim b. Jacob (in the preface to his "Sefer ha-Mafteaḥ," ed. J. Goldenthal, p. 3a, Vienna, 1847), Samuel Nagid (in his "Mebo ha-Talmud"), Maimonides (in the introduction to his commentary on the Mishnah and in the preface to the Yad ha-Ḥazaḳah), Meïri (in his "Bet ha-Beḥirah"), and a commentary on Pirḳe Abot (pp. 6a, 8b, 9a, Vienna, 1854); and many other medieval authors, as well as some modern scholars (comp. Strack, "Einleitung in den Talmud," p. 54), hold the same opinion. Rashi, on the other hand (see his commentary on Shab. 13b; 'Er. 62b; B. M. 33a; Suk. 28b; Ket. 19b), with some tosafists and other medieval and modern authors (comp. Strack, *l.c.* p. 55), held not only that the Mishnah was not reduced to writing by Rabbi himself, but that even the later amoraim did not have it in written form. He maintained that it, together with the Gemara, was written by the Saboraim. This view is based principally on the passage Giṭ. 60b, which declares that it was forbidden to record halakot, as well as on certain other statements of the Amoraim (comp. *e.g.*, Tan., Ki Tissa, ed. Buber, pp. 59b *et seq.*), which draw a distinction between the Bible as being a written doctrine and the Mishnah as a system of teaching which is not and may not be reduced to writing. It is, however, extremely unlikely that such a systematized collection, dealing with problems so numerous and so diverse, could have been transmitted orally from generation to generation; and this improbability is increased by the fact that in the Talmud remarks concerning "resha" and "sefa" (the "first" and the "last" cases provided for in a single paragraph) are frequently added to Mishnah quotations, a fact explicable only on the assumption that the text of the Mishnah was definitely fixed in writing.

The Written Text.

It must be assumed, therefore, that Rabbi himself reduced the Mishnah to writing in his old age, transgressing in a way the interdiction against recording halakot, since he deemed this prohibition liable to endanger the preservation of the doctrine. He did not abrogate this interdiction entirely, however; for the oral method of instruction continued, the teacher using the written Mishnah merely as a guide, while the pupils repeated the lesson orally. Thus the distinction between "miḳra" (the law to be read) and "mishnah" (the oral teaching) was retained (comp. "Paḥad Yiẓḥaḳ," *s.v.* "Mishnah," pp. 219 *et seq.*; Frankel, "Hodegetica in Mischnam," pp. 217–218; Brüll, "Einleitung," ii. 10–13; Weiss, "Dor," p. 216).

The Mishnah has been transmitted in four recensions: (1) the manuscripts and editions of the mishnayot; (2) the Babylonian Talmud, in which the several mishnayot are separated by the Gemara in those treatises which have it, while in the treatises which have no Gemara they follow in sequence; (3) the Palestinian Talmud, in which the Gemara follows each entire chapter of the Mishnah, the initial words of the mishnaic sentences to be expounded being repeated (of this version only the first four orders and chapters i.–iv. of the treatise Niddah of the sixth order are extant); (4) "the Mishnah on which the Palestinian Talmud rests," published by W. H. Lowe in 1883 after the Mishnah manuscript (Add. 470, 1) in the library of the University of Cambridge. On the relation of the first three editions to one another see above (comp. A. Krochmal, "Yerushalayim ha-Benuyah," Introduction, pp. 10–14; Frankel, *l.c.* pp. 219–223; Weiss, *l.c.* ii. 313). The relation of the fourth version to the preceding three has not yet been thoroughly investigated.

Division into Orders. The Mishnah is divided into six main parts, called orders (Aramaic, "sedarim," plural of "seder"; Hebr. "'arakin," plural of "'erek"), the ששה סדרי משנה (as in B. M. 85b) or the שש ערכי משנה (Pesiḳ., ed. Buber, 7a; Cant. R. vi. 4) being therefore frequently mentioned. The abbreviated name ש"ס ("shas") was formed from the initial letters of ששה סדרים (Ḥag. 3a, 10a; M. Ḳ. 10b). Each order contains a number of treatises, "massektot" (Mishnah, ed. Lowe, fol. 32a; Midr. Teh. to Ps. civ.) or "massekot" (Mishnah, ed. Lowe, fol. 69a), plural of "masseket," or "massektiyyot" (Cant. R. vi. 9), the singular of which is "massekta." Each treatise is divided into chapters, "peraḳim" (singular, "pereḳ") (Ned. 8a; Ḥag. 9a; Men. 99b), and each chapter into paragraphs or sentences, "mishnayot," or "halakot" in the Palestinian Talmud (see above).

The six orders are first mentioned by R. Ḥiyya (B. M. 85b), and represent the original division. A division into five orders is nowhere mentioned, although Geiger ("Einiges über Plan," etc., p. 487), misinterpreting the Midrash passage Num. R. xiii., considers only five orders to be enumerated there. Ulla (Meg. 28b), when he alludes to those who teach and learn only four orders, does not imply that the Mishnah was divided into four orders, but refers merely to those who study only four. This conclusion is confirmed by a conversation in which Simeon b. Laḳish communicates to a man who has studied only the first four orders a sentence belonging to the sixth order (Meg. 28b). The geonic tradition ("Sha'are Teshubah," No. 143) which refers to seven orders of the Mishnah seems to include the "Small Treatises" ("Massektot Ḳeṭannot"; Hoffmann, *l.c.* pp. 98–99). The names of the orders are old, and are mentioned by Simeon b. Laḳish (Shab. 31a), who enumerates them, according to his interpretation of Isa. xxxiii. 6, in the following sequence: Zera'im, Mo'ed, Nashim, Neziḳin, Ḳodashim, Ṭohorot. This is the original order, which is found also in Num. R. xiii. There are other enumerations with different sequences. R. Tanḥuma has the following in Yalḳ., Ps. xix.: Nashim, Zera'im, Ṭohorot, Mo'ed, Ḳodashim, Neziḳin. He gives another series in Num. R. xiii.: Nashim, Zera'im, Mo'ed, Ḳodashim, Ṭohorot, Neziḳin. As R. Tanḥuma evidently does not intend to give the actual sequence but only to explain the verses as referring to the orders of the Mishnah, he adapts his enumeration of the orders to the sequence of the verses. That Simeon b. Laḳish's sequence is the correct one may be proved also from other sources. For example, Ta'an. 24b has: "In the days of Rab Judas they went in their studies only as far as the order Neziḳin; but we study all six orders." The parallel passage reads: "We have proceeded in our studies as far as 'Uḳẓin" (the end of the sixth order Ṭohorot). It is clear from Meg. 28b that formerly only four orders were studied, of which Neziḳin formed the conclusion (according to Ta'an. 24a, where the shorter course of study in former times is mentioned in another form of expression). That the treatise 'Uḳẓin of the order Ṭohorot was the end of the sixth order is shown by Ber. 20a. It is seen, therefore, that the order Neziḳin is always mentioned as the fourth, and the order Ṭohorot as the sixth and last, thus conforming to the sequence of Simeon b. Laḳish (comp. Brüll, *l.c.* ii. 15; Weiss, *l.c.* iii. 186). Isaac ibn Gabbai, author of the mishnaic commentary "Kaf Naḥat," has, consequently, no grounds for his reversal of the arrangement of the orders (comp. Lipmann Heller, *l.c.* Preface); nor is there any foundation for the attempt of Tobias Cohn to reverse the sequence ("Aufeinanderfolge der Mischna Ordnungen," in Geiger's "Jüd. Zeit." iv. 126 *et seq.*). For a justification of the accepted sequence see the introduction of Maimonides to his commentary on the Mishnah; Frankel, *l.c.* p. 254; Brüll, *l.c.* ii. 15–16. It can not be ascertained whether Rabbi himself originated this sequence, or whether the orders were thus discussed in the academies. Isaac Alfasi and Asher b. Jehiel apply the Talmudic passage "En seder le-Mishnah" (= "Rabbi observed no definite sequence in the Mishnah") to the orders as well, and infer that this arrangement did not originate with Rabbi himself. Other authorities, however, assert that the passage "En seder le-Mishnah" refers only to the treatises, and not to the orders; for here Rabbi himself observed a definite series (comp. Lipmann Heller, *l.c.*; *idem,* commentary on Soṭah ix. 1). This view seems to be the correct one, since Simeon b. Laḳish, who was in his youth a pupil of Rabbi (Yer. Beẓah v. 2, 63a), refers to this sequence of the orders as being well known. The names of the several orders, which are frequently mentioned in the Talmud (Suk. 4b; Shab. 54b; Meg. 7a; Nid. 8a; Bek. 30b), were selected according to the subject of most of the treatises belonging to them.

Earlier Divisions. The division of the Mishnah into treatises is a very old device, the collections upon which Rabbi drew being also arranged in this same way. II Esd. xiv. 44–46 mentions, in addition to the twenty-four written books of the Old Testament, seventy other books which may not be written down, having been given by God to Moses for oral communication to the elders of the people. According to an assumption of Ginsberg's, which is supported by a comparison of the passage in Esdras with its parallel in the Tan., Ki Tissa (ed. Buber, pp. 58b–59a), these seventy books are the seventy treatises of the oral teachings, and hence of the Mishnah. The number seventy may be obtained by counting either the seven small treatises (comp. R. Kirchheim, Preface to his edition of them, Frankfort-on-the-Main, 1851), or, as Ginsberg obtains it, the halakic midrashim Sifra and Sifre, the first of which was divided into nine parts. In any case, it is evident that the division into treatises is a very old one, and that Rabbi arranged his Mishnah in conformity with it, although, as has been said, the present division is not the original one which he adopted, but has been subjected to many changes.

Sixty-three treatises are now extant, although the traditional number is only sixty, as Cant. R. vi. 9

says, "Sixty queens, these are the sixty treatises of the halakot." The three "babot," or gates, at the beginning of the order Neziḳin formed originally only a single treatise, which also was called "Neziḳin" (B. Ḳ. 102a; B. M. 10a, b; Lev. R. xix.), and which was divided into three treatises on account of its size. Makkot was originally a dependent treatise combined with Sanhedrin, of which it formed the end (comp. Maimonides' introduction to his commentary on the Mishnah). The names of the treatises, which were derived mostly from the contents, but occasionally from the initial letter, are old, being known to the Amoraim, and in part even to the Tannaim.

The following treatises are mentioned by name in the Talmud: Baba Ḳamma and Baba Meẓi'a (B. Ḳ. 102a); Bekorot (Beẓah 20a); Berakot (B. Ḳ. 30a); 'Eduyot under the name "Beḥirta" (Ber. 27a) as well as under its own name (Ber. 28a); Kelim (Mishnah Kelim, end); Keritot (Sanh. 65a); Ketubot (Soṭah 2a); Ḳiddushin (Ḳid. 76b); Ḳodashim (B. M. 109b); Makkot (Sheb. 2b); Menaḥot (Men. 7a); Middot (Yoma 16a); Nazir and Nedarim (Soṭah 2a); Oholot under the name "Ahilot" ('Er. 79a); Rosh ha-Shanah (Ta'an. 2a); Shebu'ot (Sheb. 2b); Tamid (Yoma 14b); Terumot (Pes. 34a); 'Uḳẓin (Hor. 13b); Yoma (Yoma 14b); and Zebaḥim under the name "Sheḥitat Ḳodashim" (B. M. 109b). The names of the treatises have, however, been subjected to various changes, and have, in some cases, been replaced by later terms. Thus the earlier name "Mashḳin" gave way to the later "Mo'ed Ḳaṭan"; "Zebaḥim" was substituted for "Sheḥiṭat Ḳodashim"; and "Sheḥiṭat Ḥullin" was abbreviated to "Ḥullin" (on the names comp. A. Berliner in "Ha-Misderonah," i. 20 *et seq.*, 40 *et seq.*; see also Frankel, *l.c.* p. 255; Brüll, *l.c.* ii. 18–20). The treatises belonging to each order deal with similar subjects, or have some other bond of relationship which causes them to be placed in a given order. Although there are some tractates, such as Nazir (comp. Naz. 2a) and Berakot, which apparently do not belong to the order in which they are included, a closer examination reveals the reason for their inclusion (comp. Maimonides' introduction to his commentary on the Mishnah; Brüll, *l.c.* ii. 17–18; Weiss, *l.c.* ii. 207; Geiger, *l.c.* p. 486).

The Treatises.

It is a harder task to define the principle on which the treatises are arranged within the various orders; and this difficulty is increased by the existence of many different sequences, especially since it is uncertain which of these is the oldest. According to the Letter of Sherira Gaon (*l.c.* pp. 12–13), Rabbi observed no definite sequence, but discoursed on each massekta singly without reference to the other treatises, changing their arrangement at will. This statement is supported by 'Ab. Zarah 7a, which states that for two treatises there was no definite order in the Mishnah—an assertion which is all the more trustworthy since it is recognized as a principle in making halakic decisions as well. It appears, on the other hand, from various passages in the Talmud (*e.g.*, Sheb. 2b; Soṭah 2a; Ta'an. 2a), that even at an early period a certain arrangement of the several treatises within their respective orders was followed, and it is necessary, therefore, to adopt Hoffmann's view (in Berliner's "Magazin," 1890, pp. 322–323) that a definite sequence was gradually developed and observed in the course of instruction in the Palestinian and Babylonian academies. The teachers of these schools arranged their material on pedagogic lines, and in interpreting an order of the Mishnah they selected the longest treatise for the beginning of the lesson, when the minds of their pupils were still fresh, and then passed on to the smaller tractates. Likewise in Maimonides' sequence, which was the one generally adopted, the treatises from the second to the sixth order are arranged according to length, as Geiger has remarked ("Einiges über Plan," etc., in Geiger's "Wiss. Zeit. Jüd. Theol." ii. 480 *et seq.*); and this principle is evident in the first order likewise (Hoffmann, *l.c.* p. 323; Geiger, *l.c.* p. 402). Maimonides' sequence seems, therefore, to have been the same as that adopted in the Palestinian and Babylonian academies, and hence was the original one (for other reasons for this sequence see Maimonides' introduction to his commentary on the Mishnah; Frankel, *l.c.* pp. 255–264; Brüll, *l.c.* ii. 20–27).

The Chapters.

The division of the several treatises into chapters as well as the sequence of these chapters was the work of Rabbi himself (Letter of Sherira Gaon, *l.c.* p. 13). The portion discussed each day constituted an independent pereḳ; and this term was, therefore, applied elsewhere to a single discourse also (Ber. 11b; 'Er. 36b; on a statement in the "Seder Tanna'im we-Amora'im," to the effect that the Saboraim divided the treatises into chapters, see M. Lerner, "Die Aeltesten Mischna-Compositionen," in Berliner's "Magazin," 1886, p. 3, note 1). Generally speaking, the original division and sequence of the chapters have been preserved, as appears from various passages of the Talmud (R. H. 31b; Suk. 22b; Yeb. 9a; Ket. 15a; Niddah 68b; Zeb. 15a). The names of the chapters taken from the initial letters are likewise old, and some of them are mentioned even in the Talmud (B. M. 35b; Niddah 48a). In the course of time, however, various changes were made in the division, sequence, and names of the chapters; thus, for example, the division of Tamid into seven chapters is not the original one. On other variations in sequence see Frankel, *l.c.* pp. 264–265, and on the changes in the names see Berliner in "Ha-Misderonah," i. 40b.

There are altogether 523 chapters in the Mishnah, divided as follows: Zera'im 74 (Bikkurim 3), Mo'ed Ḳaṭan 88, Nashim 71, Neziḳin 73 (Abot 5), Ḳodashim 91, Ṭohorot 126. Some authorities reckon 524 chapters by adding a sixth chapter to Abot, while others count 525 by adding a sixth chapter to Abot and a fourth chapter to Bikkurim.

The division of the chapters into paragraphs, which is likewise very old, has not been preserved in its original form, the different recensions of the present Mishnah having a different division (comp. Frankel, *l.c.* p. 265). The several paragraphs are mostly cast in the form of the fixed Halakah without a Scripture passage (see MIDRASH HALAKAH), although Weiss (*l.c.* ii. 211, notes 1–6) has enumerated 217 passages in which the Halakah is given together with the Scriptural text on which it is based, hence assuming the form of the Midrash. Some of these midrashic sentences in the Mishnah have the form of the earliest exegesis of the Soferim (comp. Frankel, *l.c.* p. 5), and there are also many passages modeled on the tannaitic Talmud (comp. Weiss, *l.c.* ii. 209–210).

The following is the list of the mishnaic orders with their treatises, according to Maimonides, the deviations in both Talmudim being given at the end of each order (for details see separate articles under the names of the respective orders and treatises; and on variations in certain editions of the Mishnah comp. Strack, *l.c.* pp. 9–12):

Orders and Treatises.

I. The order **Zera'im** ("Seeds") contains the following eleven treatises: (1) Berakot ("Blessings"), divided into nine chapters; deals with the rules for the daily prayer, and other prayers and blessings. (2) Pe'ah ("Corner"); eight chapters; deals with the regulations concerning the corners of the field (Lev. xix. 9, 10; xxiii. 22; Deut. xxiv. 19–22), and with the rights of the poor in general. (3) Demai ("Doubtful"); seven chapters; deals chiefly with various cases in which it is not certain whether the offering of the fruit has been given to the priests. (4) Kilayim ("Of Two Sorts"; "Heterogeneous"); nine chapters; deals chiefly with rules regarding forbidden mixtures (Lev. xix. 19; Deut. xxii. 9–11). (5) Shebi'it ("Sabbatical Year"); ten chapters; deals with the regulations concerning the seventh year (Ex. xxiii. 11; Lev. xxv. 1–8; Deut. xv. 1 *et seq.*). (6) Terumot ("Offerings"); eleven chapters; deals with the laws regarding the offering to be given to the priest (Num. xviii. 8 *et seq.*; Deut. xviii. 4). (7) Ma'aserot or Ma'aser Rishon ("Tithes" or "First Tithes"); five chapters; deals with the prescription regarding the tithe to be given to the Levites (Num. xviii. 21–24). (8) Ma'aser Sheni ("Second Tithe"); five chapters; deals with the rules concerning the tithe or its equivalent which was to be eaten at Jerusalem (Deut. xiv. 22–26). (9) Ḥallah ("Cake"); four chapters; deals with the laws regarding the heave-offering of dough to be given to the priests (Num. xv. 18–21). (10) 'Orlah ("Foreskin of the Trees"); three chapters; deals chiefly with the regulations of Lev. xix. 23–25. (11) Bikkurim ("First-Fruits"); three chapters; deals with the laws in Ex. xxiii. 19; Deut. xxvi. 1 *et seq.*

In many editions of the Mishnah, even early ones like those of Naples 1492, and of Riva 1559, as well as in most of the editions of the Babylonian Talmud, a fourth chapter to the eleventh treatise, which does not belong to the Mishnah, has been added (comp. the gloss in the Wilna edition of the Talmud, p. 87b). The sequence of the treatises of this first order in both the Talmudim corresponds with that of Maimonides.

II. **Mo'ed** ("Festivals") includes the following twelve treatises: (1) Shabbat ("Sabbath"); twenty-four chapters; deals with the laws regarding the seventh day as a day of rest (Ex. xvi. 23 *et seq.*, xx. 8–11, xxiii. 12, xxxiv. 21, xxxv. 2–3; Deut. v. 12–15). (2) 'Erubin ("Mingling"); ten chapters; deals with the means by which inconvenient regulations regarding the Sabbath may be legally obviated. (3) Pesaḥim ("Passover Festivals"); ten chapters; deals with the prescriptions regarding the Passover and the paschal sacrifice (Ex. xii., xiii. 6–8, xxiii. 15, xxxiv. 15 *et seq.*; Lev. xxiii. 5 *et seq.*; Num. ix. 2–14, xxviii. 16 *et seq.*). (4) Sheḳalim ("Shekels"); eight chapters; treats chiefly of the poll-tax of a half-shekel for each male, prescribed in Ex. xxx. 12–16, and which was devoted to defraying the expenses of the services of the Temple. (5) Yoma ("Day"), called also "Kippurim" or "Yom ha-Kippurim" (= "Day of Atonement"); eight chapters; deals with the prescriptions regarding worship and fasting on the Day of Atonement (Lev. xvi., xxiii. 26–32). (6) Sukkah or Sukkot ("Booth"); five chapters; deals with the regulations concerning the Feast of Tabernacles, the Tabernacle, and the garland on it (Lev. xxiii. 34–36; Num. xxix. 12 *et seq.*; Deut. xvi. 13–16). (7) Beẓah ("Egg"; so called from the first word, but originally termed, according to its subject, "Yom-Ṭob" = "Feast-Day"); five chapters; deals chiefly with the rules to be observed on the feast-days. (8) Rosh ha-Shanah ("New-Year Feast"); four chapters; deals chiefly with the regulation of the calendar by the new moon, and with the services on the New-Year. (9) Ta'anit ("Fasting"); four chapters; deals chiefly with the special fast-days in times of drought or other untoward occurrences. (10) Megillah ("Esther Scroll"); four chapters; contains chiefly regulations and prescriptions regarding the reading of the scroll of Esther at Purim, and the reading of other passages in the synagogue. (11) Mo'ed Ḳaṭan ("Half-Feasts"; originally called "Mashḳin," after its initial word); three chapters; deals with the regulations concerning the intermediate feast-days, or the days between the first two and the last two days of Pesaḥ and Sukkah. (12) Ḥagigah ("Feasting"); three chapters; deals among other things with the manner of observance of the three principal feasts.

In the Babylonian Talmud the treatises of the order Mo'ed are arranged as follows: Shabbat, 'Erubin, Pesaḥim, Beẓah, Ḥagigah, Mo'ed Ḳaṭan, Rosh ha-Shanah, Ta'anit, Yoma, Sukkah, Sheḳalim, and Megillah; while the sequence in the Palestinian Talmud is Shabbat, 'Erubin, Pesaḥim, Yoma, Sheḳalim, Sukkah, Rosh ha-Shanah, Beẓah, Ta'anit, Megillah, Ḥagigah, and Mo'ed Ḳaṭan.

III. **Nashim** ("Women") contains the following seven treatises: (1) Yebamot ("Widows Obliged to Contract a Levirate Marriage"); sixteen chapters; deals chiefly with the rules for the levirate marriage and of the Ḥaliẓah, whereby the widow is enabled to contract another marriage (Deut. xxv. 5–10). (2) Ketubot ("Marriage Contracts"); thirteen chapters; deals chiefly with the mutual duties and rights of husband and wife. (3) Nedarim ("Vows"); eleven chapters; deals with the regulations concerning vows (Num. xxx. 2–17). (4) Nazir ("Nazarite"; called also "Nezirut" = "Nazariteship"); nine chapters; deals chiefly with the prescriptions regarding the Nazarite vows (Num. vi. 1–21). (5) Giṭṭin ("Documents"; "Bills of Divorce"); nine chapters; deals chiefly with the laws for the dissolution of marriage (Deut. xxiv. 1–4). (6) Soṭah ("Woman Suspected of Adultery"); nine chapters; deals chiefly with rules concerning a woman suspected of infidelity (Num. v. 11–31). (7) Ḳiddushin ("Betrothal"); four chapters; discusses the question how, by what means, and under what conditions a legal marriage may be contracted.

In the Babylonian Talmud the sequence of the treatises in this order is as follows: Yebamot, Ketubot, Ḳiddushin, Giṭṭin, Nedarim, Nazir, and Soṭah. In the Palestinian Talmud the sequence is: Yebamot, Soṭah, Ketubot, Nedarim, Giṭṭin, Nazir, and Ḳiddushin.

IV. **Neziḳin** ("Injuries"; called also "Yeshu'ot" = "Deeds of Help," as in Num. R. xiii.) contains the following ten treatises: (1) Baba Ḳamma ("First Gate"); ten chapters; deals chiefly with injuries and compensation for damages. (2) Baba Meẓi'a ("Middle Gate"); ten chapters; deals chiefly with the laws relating to sales, leases, objects found, and usury. (3) Baba Batra ("Last Gate"); ten chapters; deals chiefly with the rights of sale, the ownership of real estate, and the rights of succession. (4) Sanhedrin ("Court of Law"); eleven chapters; deals chiefly with judicial procedure and criminal law. (5) Makkot ("Blows," "Punishments"); three chapters; deals chiefly with the regulations concerning the number of stripes imposed as punishment by law (Deut. xxv. 1–3). (6) Shebu'ot ("Oaths"); eight chapters; deals chiefly with the rules regarding different oaths (Lev. v. 4 *et seq.*). (7) 'Eduyot, or 'Ediyyot ("Evidences"); eight chapters; contains the testimony of later teachers regarding statements of earlier authorities, a large part of this material being contained in other portions of the Mishnah as well. (8) 'Abodah Zarah ("Idolatrous Worship"); five chapters; deals chiefly with the regulations concerning the attitude of the Jews toward idolatry and idolaters. (9) Abot, or Pirḳe Abot ("Sayings of the Fathers"); five chapters; contains maxims and aphorisms. A sixth chapter called "Pereḳ Ḳinyan ha-Torah" (= "Acquisition of the Law") was subsequently added to this treatise, but it does not belong to the Mishnah. (10) Horayot, or Hora'ot ("Decisions"); three chapters; deals chiefly with such religious and legal decisions as had been made through error.

The sequence of these treatises is as follows in the Babylonian Talmud: Baba Ḳamma, Baba Meẓi'a, Baba Batra, 'Abodah Zarah, Sanhedrin, Makkot, Shebu'ot, Horayot, 'Eduyot, and Abot. The usual sequence is observed in the Mishnah of the Palestinian Talmud.

V. **Ḳodashim** ("Holy Things") contains the following eleven treatises: (1) Zebaḥim ("Sacrifice"; originally called "Sheḥiṭat Ḳodashim" = "Slaughtering of the Holy Animals"; B. M. 109b); fourteen chapters; deals chiefly with the laws regarding sacrifices (Lev. i. *et seq.*). (2) Menaḥot ("Meat-Offering"); thirteen chapters; deals chiefly with the rules concerning meat-offerings (Lev. ii.; v. 11–13; vi. 7–16; vii. 9–10; xiv. 10–20; xxiii. 13, 16; Num. v. 11 *et seq.*, vi. 13–20, xv. 24, xxviii., xxix.). (3) Ḥullin ("Profane"; called also "Sheḥiṭat Ḥullin" = "Slaughtering of Non-Consecrated Animals"); twelve chapters; deals chiefly with the laws for slaughtering and with other rules relating to the eating of meat. (4) Bekorot ("First-Born"); nine chapters; deals chiefly with the regulations concerning the various firstlings (Ex. xiii. 2, 12 *et seq.*; Lev. xxvii. 26 *et seq.*; Num. viii. 16–18, xviii. 15–17; Deut. xv. 19 *et seq.*). (5) 'Arakin ("Estimations"); nine chapters; deals chiefly with the prescriptions regarding the ransom of those who have been dedicated to God (Lev. xxvii. 2 *et seq.*). (6) Temurah ("Exchange"); seven chapters; deals chiefly with the laws regarding the exchange of a dedicated animal (Lev. xxvii. 10, 33). (7) Keritot ("Extirpations"); six chapters; deals among other subjects with the punishment by excommunication ("karet"), which is frequently mentioned in the Old Testament. (8) Me'ilah ("Trespass"); six chapters; deals with the rules concerning trespass in the case of a dedicated object (Num. v. 6–8). (9) Tamid ("The Daily Morning and Evening Burnt Offering"); deals among other subjects with the regulations for the daily sacrifice (Ex. xxix. 38–42; Num. xxviii. 2–8). In the editions of the Mishnah, Tamid is divided into seven chapters, excepting in Löwe's edition, where it has but six; while Levi b. Gershon (RaLBaG) enumerates only five chapters for Tamid in the introduction to his commentary on the Pentateuch. (10) Middot ("Measures"); five chapters; describes the apartments and furniture of the Temple. (11) Ḳinnim ("Birds' Nests"); three chapters; deals with the prescriptions regarding the offering of doves (Lev. i. 14–17, v. 1 *et seq.*, xii. 8).

In the Babylonian Talmud the sequence of the treatises of this order is as follows: Zebaḥim, Menaḥot, Bekorot, Ḥullin, 'Arakin, Temurah, Keritot, Me'ilah, Ḳinnim, Tamid, and Middot.

VI. **Ṭohorot** ("Purifications") contains the following twelve treatises: (1) Kelim ("Utensils"); thirty chapters; deals chiefly with the regulations concerning the different kinds of uncleanness of vessels (Lev. xi. 32 *et seq.*; Num. xix. 14 *et seq.*, xxxi. 20 *et seq.*). (2) Oholot, or Ahilot ("Tents"); eighteen chapters; deals chiefly with the laws regarding the deflement occasioned by a corpse (Num. xix. 14–20). (3) Nega'im ("Leprosy"); fourteen chapters; deals with the rules concerning the various kinds of leprosy (Lev. xiii., xiv.). (4) Parah ("Red Heifer"); twelve chapters; deals with the regulations concerning the red heifer and the purificative ashes obtained from it (Num. xix.). (5) Ṭohorot ("Purities"; euphemistic for "Impurities"); ten chapters; deals with minor deflements. (6) Miḳwa'ot, or Miḳwot ("Ritual Baths"); ten chapters; deals with the regulations concerning the bathing of the defiled (Lev. xiv. 8, xv. 5 *et seq.*). (7) Niddah ("Menstruous Woman"); ten chapters; deals with the laws concerning the defilement caused by menstruation (Lev. xii., xv. 19 *et seq.*). (8) Makshirin ("Predisposings"; called also "Mashḳin" = "Liquids"); six chapters; deals with the rule which declares that an object is defiled by contact with anything unclean only in case it was wet beforehand (Lev. xi. 34, 37, 38). (9) Zabim ("Sufferers from Discharges"); five chapters; deals with the rules in Lev. xv. (10) Ṭebul Yom ("He Who Has Taken a Ritual Bath on That Same Day"); four chapters; deals chiefly with the effect produced upon an entire object which has come in contact with a "ṭebul yom," who, according to Lev. xv. 5, is unclean until sundown, even though this contact has been only partial. (11) Yadayim ("Hands"); four chapters; deals chiefly with the deflement and cleansing of the hands. (12) 'Uḳẓin ("Stems"); three chapters; deals chiefly with the relation of the fruit to the stems, skins, and seeds, with reference to deflement, uncleanness of the fruit affecting the stems, skins, and seeds, and vice versa.

In the Babylonian Talmud the sequence of the treatises in Ṭohorot is as follows: Niddah, Kelim, Oholot, Nega'im, Parah, Ṭohorot, Miḳwa'ot, Makshirin, Zabim, Ṭebul Yom, Yadayim, and 'Uḳẓin.

Editions and Commentaries.

The Mishnah is extant in many editions, although only the earlier ones can be mentioned here: first edition, Naples, 1492, fol., with the Hebrew commentary of Maimonides; Venice, Justiniani, 1546–50, fol.; Venice, 1549, 4to, with the commentary of Obadiah Bertinoro; Riva di Trento, 1559, fol., with the commentaries of Maimonides and Obadiah; Sabbionetta and Mantua, 1559–63, 4to; Venice, 1606, fol., with the same two commentaries.

Many commentaries on the Mishnah have been written. Maimonides wrote one in Arabic with a general introduction on the history, origin, and arrangement of the Mishnah. This commentary, which was translated into Hebrew several times, is printed in many editions of the text. The Arabic original of several treatises has recently been published, in addition to that of the entire sixth order, edited by Derenbourg (comp. the enumeration in Strack, *l.c.* p. 113 and Appendix); the Hebrew translation, which is faulty in many passages, being corrected to agree with it.

Asher b. Jehiel of Germany (d. Toledo 1327) wrote a commentary on the first and sixth orders, which was first printed in the Amsterdam edition of the Talmud, 1714–16, and in the Frankfort-on-the-Main edition, 1720–21. R. Samson of Sens also wrote a commentary on the same orders, which is printed in most of the editions of the Talmud. R. Obadiah Bertinoro (end of 15th cent.) wrote a commentary on the entire Mishnah, which is printed in most editions. The commentaries "Tosefot Yom-Ṭob" by Yom-Ṭob Lipmann Heller (1579-1654) and "Tif'eret Yisrael" by Israel Lipschütz are likewise printed in many editions of the Mishnah. The following commentaries may also be mentioned: "Kaf Naḥat," by Isaac ibn Gabbai, printed in the Venice edition of the Mishnah, 1609, and in some other editions; "'Eẓ ha-Ḥayyim" (Leghorn, 1653 *et seq.*), by Jacob Ḥagiz; "Ḳab we-Naḳi," by Elisha b. Abraham, in ed. Amsterdam, 1697, 1698, etc.; "Zera' Yiẓḥaḳ," by Isaac b. Jacob Ḥayyut, Frankfort-on-the-Oder, 1739; "Sefer Bet Dawid," Amsterdam, 1739; "Melo Kaf Naḥat," by Senior Phoebus b. Jacob, in ed. Offenbach, 1737; Berlin, 1832–34; "Sefer Mishnat Rabbi Natan," on Zera'im (Frankfort-on-the-Main, 1862), by Nathan Adler; and "Liḳḳuṭe ha-Mishnah" (Breslau, 1873), by Shraga Phoebus Frenkel.

Translations.

Of the translations of the Mishnah the following may be mentioned: (1) "Mischna sive Totius Hebræorum Juris, Rituum, Antiquitatum ac Legum Oralium Systema cum Clarissimorum Rabbinorum Maimonidis et Bartenoræ Commentariis Integris; Quibus Accedunt Variorum Auctorum Notæ ac Versiones in Eos Quos Ediderunt Codices; Latinitate Donavit ac Notis Illustravit Guilielmus Surenhusius," Amsterdam, 1698–1703, 6 vols., fol.; the text in Hebrew and Latin, with the commentaries of Maimonides and Obadiah Bertinoro in a Latin translation. (2) "Mishnayot," Berlin, 1832–34, 6 parts, 4to. (3) Vocalized Hebrew text of the Mishnah, with German translation in Hebrew letters. (4) The commentary "Melo Kaf Naḥat," and (5) a brief German introduction with notes, published by the Gesellschaft von Freunden des Gesetzes und der Erkenntniss, generally known as "Jost's translation." (6) Johann Jacob Rabe, "Mischnah, oder der Text des Talmuds Uebersetzt und Erläutert," 6 parts, 4to, Onolzbach, 1760–1763. A new edition of the vocalized Hebrew text with a German translation has been undertaken by D. Hoffmann and E. Baneth, of which several parts have appeared. An Italian translation by Vittorio Castiglione is likewise in course of publication (1904).

Bibliography: *Letter of Sherira Gaon*, ed. Neubauer, in *M. J. C.* pp. 3–41, Oxford, 1887; Maimonides, introduction to his commentary on the Mishnah, printed in many editions of the Talmud after the treatise *Berakot*; Z. Frankel, *Hodegetica in Mischnam*, Leipsic, 1859; J. Brüll, *Mebo ha-Mishnah*, part i., Frankfort-on-the-Main, 1876; part ii., *ib.* 1885; S. J. Rapoport, in *Kerem Ḥemed*, vii. 157–167; A. Krochmal,

Toledot R. Yehudah ha-Nasi, in *He-Ḥaluẓ*, ii. 75-83; idem, *ib.* iii. 118-124; *idem*, preface to his *Yerushalayim ha-Benuyah*, Lemberg, 1867; O. H. Schorr, in *He-Ḥaluẓ*, 1866, pp. 41-44; vi. 32-47; Z. Frankel, *Introductio in Talmud Hierosolymitanum*, pp. 19a-22a, Breslau, 1870; Joachim Oppenheim, *Zur Gesch. der Mischna*, in *Bet Talmud*, ii. 143-151, 172-179, 237-245, 269-273, 304-315, 343-355 (also reprinted separately, Presburg, 1882); A. Geiger, *Einiges über Plan und Anordnung der Mischna*, in Geiger's *Wiss. Zeit. Jüd. Theol.* 1836, ii. 474-492; idem, *Lehrbuch zur Sprache der Mischna*, Breslau, 1845; Isaac Lampronti, *Paḥad Yiẓḥaḳ*, s.v. *Mishnah*; W. Landsberg, *Plan und System in der Aufeinanderfolge der Einzelnen Mischnas*, in *Monatsschrift*, 1873, pp. 208-215; Tobias Cohn, *Aufeinanderfolge der Mischnaordnungen*, in Geiger's *Jüd. Zeit.* 1866, iv. 126-140; Dünner, *Veranlassung, Zweck und Entwickelung der Halakischen und Halakischexegetischen Sammlungen Während der Tannaimperiode im Umriss Dargestellt*, in *Monatsschrift*, 1871, pp. 137 *et seq.*, 158 *et seq.*, 313 *et seq.*, 363 *et seq.*, 416 *et seq.*, 449 *et seq.*; idem, *R. Jehuda Hanasi's Anteil an Unserer Mischna*, ib. 1872, pp. 161 *et seq.*, 218 *et seq.*; idem, *Einiges über Ursprung und Bedeutung des Traktates Edoyot*, ib. 1871, pp. 33-42, 59-77; D. Hoffmann, *Die Erste Mischna und die Controversen der Tannaim*, Berlin, 1882; idem, *Bemerkungen zur Kritik der Mischna*, in Berliner's *Magazin*, 1881, pp. 121-130, 169-177; 1882, pp. 96-105, 152-163; 1884, pp. 17-30, 88-92, 126-127; M. Lerner, *Die Aeltesten Mischna-Compositionen*, ib. 1886, pp. 1-20; J. Derenbourg, *Les Sections et les Traités de la Mischna*, in *R. E. J.* 1881, iii. 205-210; A. Berliner, in *Ha-Misderonah*, i. 20 *et seq.*, 40 *et seq.*; J. S. Bloch, *Einblicke in die Gesch. der Entstehung der Talmudischen Literatur*, Vienna, 1884; I. H. Weiss, *Dor*, ii. 182-184, 207-217; idem, *Mishpaṭ Leshon ha-Mishnah*, ib. 1867; L. A. Rosenthal, *Ueber den Zusammenhang der Mischna; Ein Beitrag zu Ihrer Entstehungsgesch.* Strasburg, 1891-92; idem, *Die Mischna, Aufbau und Quellenscheidung*, ib. 1903.

E. C. J. Z. L.

MISHNEH TORAH. See Moses b. Maimon.

MISSISSIPPI: One of the southern states of the United States of America; admitted to the Union in 1817. In 1682 La Salle took possession of the territory for the King of France. It passed to England in 1763, was ceded to Spain in 1781, and to the United States in 1798. In 1724 a law was passed in France by which "Jews were expelled, and no other religion [than the Roman Catholic] was tolerated." When the Spaniards took possession in 1781, a more tolerant government was established. It seems that there were a few Jews in the Natchez district at the close of the eighteenth century. At any rate, in Natchez a tombstone has been found bearing the name of Harris and the date 1828; and there are indications that of the several people of that name one had lived in the city a number of years prior to his death.

It was about 1840 that the Jews had become sufficiently numerous to found congregations; the establishment of cemeteries usually preceded the formation of religious organizations. In 1849 three pedlers came to **Woodville.** One of them, Henry Burgance, died the same year. Loath to have their companion buried with Christians, the other two, Jacob Cohen and Jacob Schwarz, bought a small piece of land for $50 and founded a cemetery; this is still used. Similarly the few Jews who settled at **Grand Gulf** bought a cemetery, which they abandoned when, owing to frequent inroads of the Mississippi River, they moved to **Port Gibson;** the Jews of **Natchez** bought their cemetery in 1840, and organized Congregation B'nai Israel in 1843; **Jackson** organized a cemetery in 1854 and Congregation Beth Israel a few years later; **Meridian** purchased a cemetery in 1868, and organized Congregation Beth Israel in 1869. In **Columbus** a B'nai B'rith lodge was founded in 1872, a cemetery in 1875, and Congregation B'nai Israel in 1879.

Early Congregational Activity.

Remarkable, and speaking well for Jewish zeal, is the fact that almost all congregations were founded by a few men. For example, **Vicksburg** (1843) could not have contained more than 10 Jewish families; Natchez (also 1843) had no more; Meridian (1869) organized with 8 men; Woodville held services on Rosh ha-Shanah, 1860, when but 7 families lived there. **Brookhaven** now has but about 20; **Canton,** about 25; Columbus, 20; **Summit,** about 10; yet all these places have organized congregations. Some of these congregations began as Orthodox; those organized in the seventies and after were Reform from the start. Now (1904) all those mentioned above are Reform. Early in the eighties, however, a few Orthodox Jews settled here and there, and formed "minyanim" for the holy days. Meridian first organized an Orthodox congregation (Ohel Jacob) in 1894; Vicksburg followed in 1900; these are at present the only places supporting a shoḥeṭ. Orthodox services were held in **Laurel** in 1901 and 1903.

In addition to the places mentioned above there are small communities with congregations in **Brownsville, Greenwood,** and **Lexington.**

Except in the Natchez district (Natchez, Vicksburg, Woodville, and Port Gibson), most of the congregations lie within a limited strip of land running east and west about the middle of the state. Very few Jews live south of 32° or north of 33° 30′ N. lat.

In almost every instance Jews entered the state to transact mercantile business. Thus, coming in contact with Gentiles, and being isolated from their coreligionists, fast friendships were formed with those of other religious views, and to-day the members of the two faiths mingle freely. During the Mexican war there were too few Jews living in the state to call for notice of their services; in the Civil war, however, Jew and Christian fought side by side. Federal soldiers displaced and mutilated tombstones in Jewish as well as in Christian cemeteries, thus effacing many records which would now be of great interest. Quite a number of Jews attained to the rank of captain; and there is no camp of Confederate Veterans in the larger places that does not include some Jewish members.

Communal Life.

Bibliography: *American Jewish Year Book*, 1901; *The Owl* (New Orleans), Aug., 1901; Franklin L. Riley, *Hist. of Mississippi*, Richmond, Va., 1900.

A. W. Wi.

MISSOURI: One of the central states of the United States; admitted to the Union in 1821. While yet a territory it was inhabited by Jewish settlers, the earliest of whom were the Bloch family. The Jewish communities of the state are as follows:

St. Louis: Jews began to settle here shortly after 1830. At the present time there are six permanent and several temporary places of worship. The Reform congregations are: Shaare Emeth, Temple Israel, B'nai El, and United Hebrew. These four congregations aggregate about 800 families. Of the Orthodox bodies there are: B'nai Emunah, Tifereth Israel, and the Beth Hamidrash Hagadol.

All the Orthodox organizations have their places of worship on the north side of the city. Tifereth Israel was founded in 1899; its present membership is 160, and it has a Talmud Torah where 200 children receive daily instruction in Hebrew after public-school hours. The Rev. S. Rosenberg is rabbi.

The oldest of the Reform congregations are the B'nai El and the United Hebrew. The latter was established in 1838. It held its first services in a private residence, and its first synagogue was built in 1858. Dr. Illoway was then rabbi. In 1881 a new synagogue was erected at Twenty-first and Olive streets. The membership is 146. Dr. H. J. Messing has been rabbi since 1878. The Sabbath-school has 80 pupils. The congregation has a United Hebrew ladies' aid society, consisting of 80 members; and a young people's literary circle.

Congregations.

The B'nai El congregation was founded in 1852 by a consolidation of two previously existing religious organizations. Its synagogue, built in 1883, is at Chouteau avenue and Eleventh street; present membership, 150. The Sabbath-school numbers about 100 pupils. The Jastrow prayer-book is used. The rabbi (since 1877) is Dr. Spitz; he is also publisher and editor of "The Jewish Voice," established in 1888. The congregation has a ladies' aid society of about 100 members, and a young people's society of about the same number.

Congregation Shaare Emeth was organized in 1866 with 83 members. It worshiped first at the Harmonia Club on Market street. Its present synagogue, on the corner of Lindell boulevard and Vandeventer avenue, was erected in 1897; present membership, 289. The Sabbath-school has an attendance of 246 pupils. Dr. Samuel Sale has been rabbi since 1887. Associated with the congregation is a ladies' auxiliary society.

Temple Israel congregation was organized in 1886. Its synagogue is on the corner of Pine and Twenty-eighth streets; present membership, 250. It has Saturday and Sunday services. Dr. Leon Harrison, rabbi since 1891, conducts services also in the United Charities building on Friday nights for residents of the Russo-Jewish quarter. This voluntary office was established by the Social Settlement League. Besides the regular religious instruction of the young, Temple Israel has a confirmation and postgraduate class, a Bible class for women, and an alumni association.

The following are the chief Jewish philanthropic societies and institutions in St. Louis: The oldest Jewish benevolent society of the city, probably the oldest in the West, is the Hebrew Benevolent Society, instituted in 1842. It was legally incorporated in 1847; present membership, 66. It has the character of a mutual benefit society. There is also a fraternal benefit association under the name of "Progressive Order of the West" (founded 1896), with sixteen lodges, thirteen of which are in the city; the total membership is 1,008 males and 848 females.

The first systematic relief of the Jewish poor was begun in 1871. The influx of needy Jews after Chicago's great conflagration made a union of charitable activities necessary. Later on the large immigration of Russo-Jewish refugees made such union still more needful. The United Hebrew Relief Society then became the leading charitable organization of the Jewish community. The late Rev. Isaac Epstein was president for many years, and Dr. Messing vice-president from 1878. There were, besides, three other benevolent societies. All of them were in 1897 merged into one common association under the name of "United Jewish Charities"; each retained, however, its own distinct existence as to officers and the particular scope of charitable work for which it had been founded; all relief is dispensed at the main office of the United Charities. This institution has its own building (erected 1901) on the corner of Ninth and Carr streets. Since its erection all the Jewish charitable and educational societies of the city have joined the union; of these are to be mentioned: the Home for Aged and Infirm Israelites; the Jewish Hospital; and the Hebrew Free and Industrial School, founded in 1879 by Dr. Messing. In this school over 400 children receive religious instruction twice a week, and of this number 200 girls are taught domestic arts and industrial branches three times a week. The industrial department has recently been put under the management of the Sisterhood of Personal Service.

Educational and Charitable Institutions.

The pupils in the Jewish Alliance night-school (present enrolment 460) receive instruction four times a week in the elementary English branches, and free reading-rooms and a library are open to them. The Alliance and the Free School societies have recently been consolidated.

The Jewish Hospital was founded in 1900 and dedicated in 1902; it occupies a lot of 200 feet fronting Delmar boulevard; free treatment is given to all poor applicants. It has also a training-school for nurses. The Home for Aged and Infirm Israelites was established in 1880; it is located on Jefferson avenue.

The Jews of St. Louis number about 40,000 in a total population of 575,238.

Kansas City: The Reform congregation B'nai Jehudah, organized in 1870, was incorporated in 1872, with 36 members. The present rabbi is Dr. Harry H. Mayer; membership, 190. The Sabbath-school has 165 pupils and 8 assistant teachers. Free religious instruction is given to the children of non-members, mainly of poor parents, on Saturday afternoons. There are the usual two Sabbath services only. The synagogue is on the corner of Eleventh and Oak streets. There are about six congregations of the Orthodox persuasion, two of which have their own synagogues: the Keneseth Israel with 110, and the Gomel Chesed with 90, members. The other Orthodox societies worship in rented halls. The various benevolent organizations of the Jewish community were within the last two years confederated as the United Jewish Charities, with a board of directors. The charitable, educational, and industrial work of its several departments is carried on in a rented building on East Fifteenth street.

The Jewish residents of the city number about 8,000 in a total population of 163,752.

St. Joseph: The Jewish settlement at St. Joseph dates from about 1850. The congregation was established in 1859 with 7 members; in 1861 the membership was 20, when an old church building was bought and transformed into a synagogue. This was burned a year later. A new site, on the corner of Sixth and Jule streets, was purchased, on which the present synagogue was erected in 1866. The present rabbi, Dr. Isaac Schwab, has held the office since 1879. The congregation has a membership of 59. The Ladies' Benevolent Society, with a present membership of 60, is an important charitable factor in the Jewish community. There is also an Orthodox congregation composed of Jews from eastern Europe. By their exemplary thrift these later comers have risen from lowly beginnings to fair competencies, and in 1900 succeeded in building a synagogue of their own. There is a Hebrew school where daily instruction is given, and a ladies' benevolent society is connected with the congregation. The minister is S. Kanter. There are 75 members, and about as many more families not affiliated with the congregation, making a total of about 800 persons in the Orthodox section of the community. The whole Jewish population of the city may fairly be figured at 1,200 in a total population of 102,979.

Other Towns: There are a number of other towns of the state with Jewish populations averaging from 12 to 25. In others, again, the number is larger, as may be seen from the accompanying list. **Columbia,** 9 families; total number of individuals, 31. **Chillicothe,** 14 families, aggregating 50 individuals; there is a benevolent society. **Hannibal,** 12 families. **Joplin,** 38 families, representing a total of about 150 persons; a ladies' aid society. **Jefferson City,** 8 families, a total of 34 souls; there is a synagogue. **Moberly,** 16 persons. **Sedalia,** 16 families, aggregating 60 persons; a benevolent society. **Springfield,** 25 families, with about 100 individuals; a congregation and place of worship, with Friday evening services; a ladies' benevolent society.

A. I. SCH.

MITAU: Capital of the government of Courland, Russia; situated about 20 miles from Riga on the Drixa, an arm of the River Aa. The castle of Mitau was founded by the German Knights in 1263; and the town itself received its charter in 1435. Under the rule of the Knights, Jews were not permitted to reside in Mitau. In the sixteenth century, when Mitau was already Polish territory, Jewish merchants carried on a more or less extensive business in the city; yet even then they were not recognized as permanent residents, and they had not the right to organize a community; and in the next century, after the Cossacks' uprising (1648), the Christians of Mitau finally caused their expulsion from the city. The Jew Bär ben ha-Ḳadosh Rabbi Benjamin, whose father was killed in Lithuania during the Cossacks' uprising, was court jeweler (1730) under Duke Ferdinand, and stood high in the esteem of the Knights. He made numerous gifts to the Jewish community, among them a funeral carriage and a coffin, which were still preserved in the middle of the nineteenth century. A concession for a cemetery was granted in 1730 to the Jews of Mitau by the duke on the application of their representative Isaac ben Judah; and a ḥebra ḳaddisha was founded in the same year. Ẓebi Hirsch Ḥarif (d. 1738), son of Rabbi Moses of Lemberg, and an eminent Talmudic scholar, acted as rabbi of the community. Duke John Biron, Ferdinand's successor (1737), was friendly toward the Jews and transacted business in partnership with his court Jew Lipman (Levi). At that time there was a considerable number of Jewish residents in Mitau; under the name of "Schutzjuden" they lived in a separate quarter called the "Judengasse," now the Doblen'sche Strasse.

The Jew Meyer Kreslawe was given permission to open a Jewish inn in the center of the city. This was known as "Hotel de Jerusalem." It still existed in the middle of the nineteenth century, being then owned by H. Michelsohn.

Eighteenth Century.

The successor of Ẓebi Hirsch Ḥarif was another prominent rabbi, Samuel ben Elkanah (d. 1742), author of the responsa collection "Meḳom Shemuel." He was probably followed by Jekuthiel ha-Kohen (d. 1775), father of Raphael ha-Kohen of Hamburg, and a descendant on his mother's side of Mordecai Jaffe, author of the "Lebushim." He held the title "Rabbi of the Province of Livland." His son David Ezekiel Jekuthiel (d. 1823) succeeded him as rabbi of the community. When Duke Ernst Biron was banished to Siberia in 1741, the knights of Courland attempted to expel the Jews from Mitau; and in 1760 the Diet passed a resolution forbidding Lithuanian and Polish Jews to sojourn in Mitau for more than a day or two (see JEW. ENCYC. iv. 312b, *s.v.* COURLAND). With Biron's return from exile in 1762 the condition of the Jews improved; and his son and successor, Duke Peter, was also favorably inclined toward them.

In 1784 a prominent Jew of Mitau, Kalman Borkum, laid the foundation of a synagogue, which was erected entirely at his expense. Both he and his brother Samson were very active in promoting the welfare of the Mitau community, and were strenuous champions in defense of the rights of the Courland Jews against the German merchants. The son-in-law of Kalman Borkum, Dr. Elrich (d. 1809), was a native of Russia, and came to Mitau (1770) from Vilkomir, Lithuania, where he had practised as government and city physician and had received the title of court councilor. Markus HERZ, husband of Henriette HERZ, visited Mitau in 1775. Judah ben Mordecai ha-Levi Hurwitz, a prominent physician and scholar, practised medicine in Mitau for a time.

Notwithstanding the influence of prominent Jews at court, and in spite of the liberal views introduced from Berlin into German Courland, the Jews of Mitau did not enjoy the rights accorded to the Christians, and often suffered from official abuses and from the enmity of the German merchants. This is evident from the fact that in 1795 the members of the Jewish community of Mitau submitted a memorandum to the knights of Courland assembled at the Diet, in which they gratefully acknowledged the protection hitherto extended to them, and asked for relief from their uncertain legal condition. The petition was signed by the elders Aaron Lipman and Isaac Moses Eides and by other prominent Jews representing the community. Among the latter were David Levi, Joseph Sholem, Joseph Kirschner, Marcus Jacob, Marcus Hirsch, Simon Abraham, and Abraham Danziger. In reply to this petition to the Diet submitted Jan. 13, 1795, the duke expressed an opinion favorable to the proposal that Jews be permitted to settle in Courland. However, before the duke had an opportunity to act in regard to the Jews, Courland was annexed to Russia (March 16, 1795). Catherine II., also, was very favorably disposed toward the Courland Jews, some of whom were among the early Jewish residents in St. Petersburg. When Emperor Paul visited Mitau in 1797, representatives of the Jewish community were received by him in audience. In 1810 the Empress of Russia gave an audience to a Jewish deputation, and appointed Bär Seelig Klein and Samuel Kandauer as court factors. By a ukase of May 12, 1797, the Jews of Courland received the same rights as the Jews of Lithuania and Poland. Their privileges were further extended by Alexander I. in 1805.

In 1835 the Jewish population of Mitau was 4,987; in 1850, only 4,189. The decrease was due to the migration in 1840 of 863 Jews of Mitau to the South-Russian colonies, and also to the ravages of the cholera epidemic in 1848. The income from the meat-tax in 1850 was 8,010 rubles, and from the candle-tax, 2,183 rubles. The Jewish population of Mitau at that time included 1 banker (who was an honorary citizen), 5 merchants of the second gild, 49 merchants of the third gild, 48 merchant families, 85 house and real-estate owners, 45 tailors, 30 shoemakers, 28 capmakers, 25 milliners, 18 tinsmiths, 6 polishers, 6 glaziers, 4 painters, 4 watchmakers, 4 engravers, 2 opticians, 4 umbrella-makers, 3 cotton-spinners, 3 furriers, 3 cigarmakers, 2 dyers, 2 beltmakers, 4 turners, 1 brushmaker, 3 pipe-decorators, 2 bookbinders, 1 tortoise-shell worker, 2 basketmakers, 1 gold-plater, 12 expressmen and drivers, 12 butchers, 6 innkeepers and cooks. There were also a number of hucksters, hostlers, horse-dealers, servants, day-laborers, porters, stone-crushers, woodcutters, water-carriers, etc. There were no Christian porters in Mitau at that time; and for many years the moving of furniture was done by the Jews.

Occupations.

The first Jewish government school in Mitau was established in 1850 with one Jewish and one Christian teacher, a Jewish private school having existed there since 1824. In 1850 there were in Mitau a Talmud Torah (founded in 1805), 10 licensed Jewish private schools, a poorhouse, a synagogue, and two houses of prayer. The ḥebra ḳaddisha was founded, as has been said, in 1730; a ḥebra biḳḳur ḥolim in 1770; Jewish Women's Society in 1840; Prisoners' Aid Society in 1829; Artisans' Association in 1815; and a number of Jewish learned societies during the early half of the nineteenth century.

In 1853 the income and expenditures of the Jewish community amounted to 1,200 rubles. The Jewish artisans were represented in the city council by two delegates from among their number; the Jewish charities were managed by a committee elected by the community; the Jews were represented on the school commission by one rabbi and one merchant; and S. Waggenheim was attached to the governor's office in the capacity of "learned Jew."

Prominent among the Mitau Jews of the nineteenth century were the Sterns, Friedliebs, Rubinsteins, Traugotts, and Marcus Erben. Besides the rabbis already mentioned reference should be made to Elihu, son of David Ezekiel; Israel David Friedman (probably also a son of David), who erected a synagogue at his own expense, and who died in Mitau in 1843; Ephraim Israel Jacobson, dayyan (d. 1831); Moses Enoch Feiertag, dayyan (d. 1848); Hirsch Rabinovich (died in the second half of the nineteenth century); Mendel Israelsohn (d. 1861), assistant rabbi, honorary citizen, and member of the rabbinical commission of 1852; and Solomon Pucher (d. 1899), appointed government rabbi in 1862. Reuben Joseph WUNDERBAR, author of a history of the Jews of Livland and Courland, and Adolph EHRLICH were natives of Mitau.

Prominent Persons.

The Jews of Mitau were more akin in language, manners, and dress to the Jews of Germany than to those of Poland and Lithuania. Notwithstanding, however, their higher culture, they were never held in favor by the Germans of Courland, who in the last quarter of the nineteenth century were strongly influenced by the anti-Semitic movement of Germany. The nationalistic movement of the Lets, the native population of Courland, and their growing activity in commercial and social affairs, have unfavorably affected the prosperity of the Jewish community in Mitau. Moreover, the improved railroad facilities have made Mitau practically a suburb of Riga, which has attracted to itself most of the business once belonging to the former. On the construction of the Riga-Dünaburg railroad many of the prominent Jewish merchants of Mitau removed to Riga.

In 1904 Mitau had 8,402 Jews in a total population of about 35,000. See COURLAND.

BIBLIOGRAPHY: Wunderbar, *Gesch. der Juden in den Provinzen Liv- und Kurland*, Mitau, 1853.

H. R.

MITER: A head-dress; one of the sacred garments of the priests. The high priest's miter was designated as "miẓnefet," and was made of fine linen, to which the diadem ("ẓiẓ") of pure gold, inscribed with the title "Holiness to the Lord," was fastened by means of a purple cord (Ex. xxviii. 4, 39; xxxix. 31).

The miter of the ordinary priests was called "migba'ah"; but the term is found only in the plural form, "migba'ot." These miters were also known by the compound name "pa'are ha-migba'ot," and were likewise of fine linen (*ib.* xxviii. 40, xxxix. 28). That "pa'are" (from "pe'erim"; sing. "pe'er") is not an adjective, but a noun, is evident from the expression "pa'are pishtim" = "miters of linen, worn by the priests" (Ezek. xliv. 18). Indeed, the use of the "pe'er" was not restricted to priests. It was a head-covering of distinction for a bridegroom and for the daughters of Zion (Isa. iii. 20, lxi. 10). Being a personal ornament, it was removed during periods of mourning (*ib.* lxi. 3; Ezek. xxiv. 17, 23).

The priestly miters are not described in the Bible, yet the name "miẓnefet," like "ẓanif," the miter which the prophet saw placed on Joshua the high priest (Zech. iii. 5), suggests a turban wound around the head. The term used to denote the miters of the common priests ("migba'ot," derived from "gebia'" = "cup") suggests a covering of conical shape, fitted tightly on the head, and the verb "we-ḥabashta" (Ex. xxix. 9) seems to point to the same. "Pe'er" may be translated "a beautiful bonnet"; and the "pa'are ha-migba'ot" worn by the priests may have been bonnets with a conical extension.

Josephus' description of the miter of the high priest and of that of the ordinary priests ("Ant." iii. 7, §§ 3, 6) appears to be confused; but it might be elucidated by a study of the rabbinical literature on the subject. The Mishnah makes no distinction between "miẓnefet" and "migba'ot," and calls the miter of the common priest likewise "miẓnefet" (Yoma vii. 5, 25a). The miter of the high priest was shorter, to allow room on the forehead for the diadem, which was two finger-breadths wide and reached from ear to ear (Suk. 5a), a space being left for the phylacteries (Zeb. 19a *et seq.*). A baraita says that the high priest wore a woolen cap, to which was attached the diadem (Ḥul. 138a). Perhaps this cap served as an underlining for the miẓnefet. The miters were all made of six-cord threads (Maimonides, "Yad," Kele ha-Miḳdash, viii. 1, 2). The code of Moses of Coucy ("Semag," No. 173) and later authorities agree that the miter of the common priests was not coiled around like a turban, but was rather a stiff, conical hat graduating to a point at the top. Ibn Ezra, in his commentary, says the miẓnefet was like a woman's bonnet and the migba'ah like a man's hat (fez). All authorities are unanimous in their opinion that the miẓnefet of the high priest was much smaller, covering only about one-half of his head. It was made of fine linen, twined around the head many times.

Symbolically the miter and the rest of the priest's vesture, like the sacrifices, represented certain sins to be forgiven. Using another symbol, R. Ḥanina said: "Let the miter on high combat the high spirit of the arrogant" ('Ar. 16a).

Bibliography: Isserles, *Torat ha-'Olah*, ii. § 44; Rofe, *Shilṭe ha-Gibborim*, ch. xlv.; Lipschütz, *Tif'eret Yisrael*, introduction to *Mo'ed*, p. 39a; Azariah dei Rossi, *Me'or 'Enayim*, ch. xlix., l.; Braunius, *De Vestitu Sacerdotum Hebræorum*, pp. 517 *et seq.*, Amsterdam, 1680; Bähr, *Symbolik des Mosaischen Cultus*, ii. 110-115, Heidelberg, 1874.

J. — J. D. E.

MITNAGGEDIM (lit. "opponents"): Title applied by the Ḥasidim to their opponents, *i.e.*, to the Orthodox Jews of the Slavonic countries who have not become adherents of Ḥasidism (see Jew. Encyc. vi. 254, *s.v.* Ḥasidim). The latter have in course of time accepted that title, and "mitnagged" now means not necessarily an active or even a passive opponent of Ḥasidism, but simply a non-Ḥasid. An alternative title for "mitnagged" is "'Olam'sher Yid" (= "Jew of the world"), not in the sense of being worldly, but meaning one who belongs to the great mass of the Jews of the world who are not Ḥasidim.

J. — P. Wi.

MITRANI. See Trani.

MITZKUN, DAVID MOSES: Russian Hebraist; born May, 1836; died in Wilna July 23, 1887. He was a writer of Hebrew prose and poetry, and maintained himself chiefly by teaching Hebrew. A collection of his Hebrew poems entitled "Kinnor Dawid" was published at Wilna in 1863.

Bibliography: Kohner, *Ḥeḳer Dabar*, pp. 5-25, Warsaw, 1865; Fuenn, in *Ha-Karmel*, iii., No. 50; *Ha-Asif*, 1887, iv. 27.

H. R. — J. S. R.

MI'UN: A Hebrew word signifying "refusal, denial, or protest"; used technically by the Rabbis to denote a woman's protest against a marriage contracted for her during her minority; also the annulment of such a marriage.

A marriage contracted for a girl minor by her father was regarded as valid; and it necessitated the formality of a divorce if separation was desired (see Daughter; Majority; Marriage). If, however, the minor was divorced or widowed after she had been given in marriage by her father, and then, while still in her minority, married again, or, in the case of the father's death, was given in marriage by her brothers or by her mother, even when her consent was obtained, such a marriage was not valid until she reached the age of maturity. During her minority she might at any time declare her aversion to her husband and leave him without a geṭ (Yeb. 107a). Nor was any formal declaration on her part necessary. If she in any manner showed her disapproval of the marriage contracted for her, or if she accepted betrothal-money ("ḳiddushin") from another man, she was released from the bonds of the marriage previously contracted in her behalf (Yeb. 108a; Maimonides, "Yad," Gerushin, xi. 3; Shulḥan 'Aruk, Eben ha-'Ezer, 155, 3).

The usual procedure in regard to mi'un was that the minor said, in the presence of two witnesses, "I do not wish to live with my husband . . .," or used some other phrase denoting the same idea, and thereby became released (Yeb. 108a). Originally it was the custom to make out a so-called "geṭ mi'un," in which the minor declared, "I do not like him; he does not please me; I do not wish to remain with him as his wife." This was subsequently abolished, and the following practise was introduced: The two men before whom such a declaration was made prepared a document, which, however, was not necessary for the minor's remarriage, since she became free as soon as she had made the declaration (Yeb. 107b, 108a). This document, as given by Maimonides ("Yad," *l.c.* xi. 11, and with a few unimportant variations in "Or Zarua'," i. 687), reads as follows:

Form of Mi'un.

"On . . . [day of the week], the . . . day of the month . . . , in the year . . . according to the . . . era, . . . , daughter of . . . , protested before us and said, 'My mother [or my brothers] deceived me and gave me in marriage [or betrothed me] to . . . , son of . . . , and now I declare before you that I do not desire him, and that I will not stay with him.' We have examined this . . . and are satisfied that the girl is yet a minor, and have written and signed and given [this] to her as a document and a clear proof.

. . . ., witness. . . . ., witness."

If the marriage was contracted for the girl before she had reached the age of six, or after that age without her consent, the formality of mi'un was not necessary. If the marriage took place with her consent when she was between the ages of six and ten, mi'un was necessary if she showed signs of intelligence and of appreciation of the symbols of marriage. After ten, mi'un was necessary even if the girl manifested no signs of intelligence (Yeb. 107b; Giṭ. 65a; "Yad," *l.c.* xi. 7; Eben ha-'Ezer, 155, 2). Since mi'un was regarded as an annulment of marriage, and not merely as a separation, like divorce, the girl might afterward marry any of the relatives of her presumptive husband, and he any of her relatives. She might marry a kohen, or might remarry her previous husband, even though she had been married to another after mi'un (Yeb. 108a; "Yad," *l.c.* xi. 16, 17; Eben ha-'Ezer, 155, 10; see DIVORCE).

Antiquity of Custom.

The institution of mi'un seems to have been of very early origin. The Rabbis speak of it as a well-established custom, although some of them look upon it with disfavor. Bet Shammai restricted mi'un to betrothed minors, and prohibited it after marriage had already taken place (Yeb. 107a). Bar Ḳappara includes mi'un among the things which one should avoid (*ib.* 109a); and one is therefore advised against associating oneself with witnesses for the purposes of mi'un ("Yad," *l.c.* x. 16). In the Middle Ages some of the rabbis vigorously objected to the marriage of minors, giving as one of their reasons the desire to make mi'un impossible (Tos., Yeb. 109a, *s.v.* "Wayitraḥeḳ"; "Haggahot Maimuni" to "Yad," *l.c.* xi. 1; "Or Zarua'," i. 686; Eben ha-'Ezer, 155, 1, Isserles' gloss).

In the fifteenth century R. Menahem of Merseburg wished to abolish the institution of mi'un altogether; and while he did not secure for his decree unanimous adoption, the sentiment against the marriage of young children, which became stronger in later times, and the diffidence with which the Rabbis approached a case of mi'un on account of the conflicting opinions, caused this institution to become almost obsolete (see Judah Minz, Responsa, No. 13, Fürth, 1766; Eben ha-'Ezer, 155, 22, Isserles' gloss; and "Pitḥe Teshubah," *ad loc.*; see also MAJORITY).

BIBLIOGRAPHY: Löw, *Die Lebensalter*, pp. 179-184, Szegedin, 1875; Duschak, *Das Mosaisch-Talmudische Eherecht*, pp. 142-143, Vienna, 1864; Mielziner, *The Jewish Law of Marriage and Divorce*, § 36, Cincinnati, 1884; Saalschütz, *Das Mosaische Recht*, p. 807, note, Berlin, 1853; Weill, *La Femme Juive*, part i., ch. iii., iv., Paris, 1874.

E. C. J. H. G.

MIXED MARRIAGE. See INTERMARRIAGE.

MIZMOR LE-DAWID (lit. "A Psalm of David"): The superscription to Ps. xxix., chanted on Sabbaths before the evening service, and at morning service while the scroll of the Law is being returned to the Ark. Settings by modern composers are in most cases utilized in the morning service by the Ashkenazim, there being among them no recognized traditional melody. The Sephardic synagogues, however, possess an ancient chant, of Peninsular origin, which, in its melodic outline, and in its extensive use of the third and fifth degrees of the scales as the reciting notes, and particularly the former as the closing one, characteristically illustrates the general tone of their traditional melodies and intonations (comp. LEKAH DODI; 'ET SHA'ARE RAẒON). The transcription here given exhibits the employment of both strains of the chant.

MIZMOR LE-DAWID

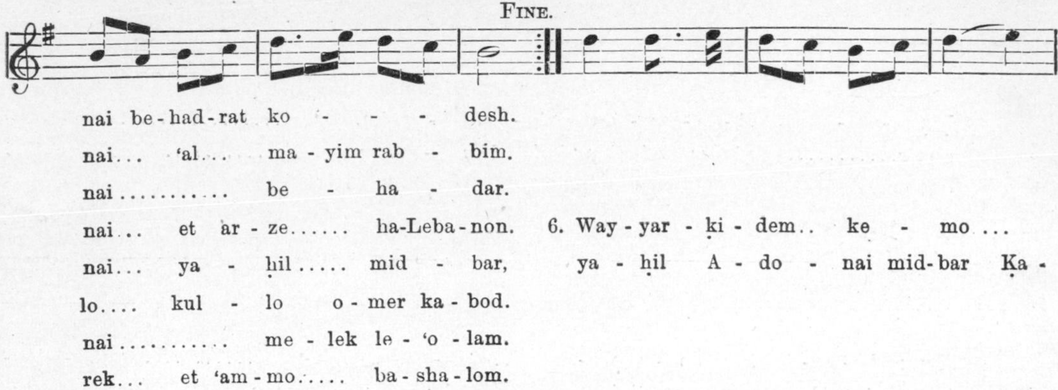

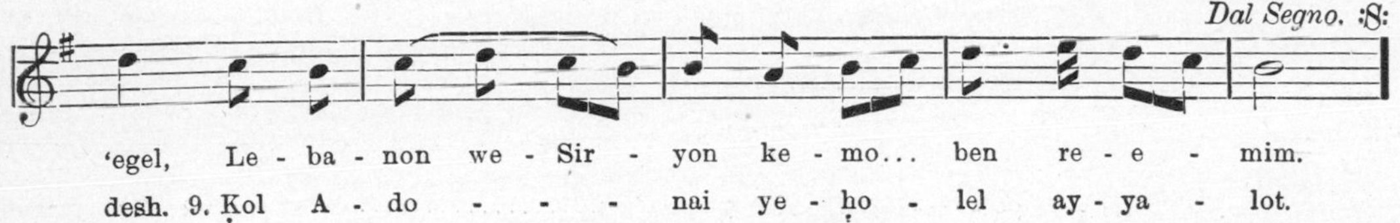

Bibliography: De Sola and Aguilar, *Ancient Melodies of the Liturgy of the Spanish and Portuguese Jews*, No. 13, London, 1857; Cohen and Davis, *Voice of Prayer and Praise*, No. 16, London, 1899.

A. F. L. C.

MIZMOR SHIR LE-YOM HA-SHABBAT (lit. "A Psalm, a Song for the Sabbath Day"): The superscription to Ps. xcii., chanted with Ps. xciii. before the commencement of evening service on Sabbaths (including festivals falling on that day) in the "Pesuḳe de-Zimrah" of the early part of morning service on Sabbaths and festivals (see Liturgy), and (without Ps. xciii.) after the Reading of the Law at Sabbath afternoon service. There is, strangely enough, no general musical tradition for the psalm in the northern uses. The modern ḥazzanim and choir-masters have produced numerous settings (choral and solo) for it. A noteworthy composition by Franz Schubert for verses 1 to 8, designed for special festival occasions, is included in Sulzer's "Schir Zion" (i. No. 6). This setting is written for barytone solo, soli quartet, and chorus, and has been introduced by Georg Henschel at the London Symphony Concerts.

Ordinarily, in the northern ritual, the psalm is read by the congregation, and the concluding verses, from No. 12, are then intoned by the ḥazzan in an elaborate melismatic recitative, of the character shown in the transcription commencing "Ẓaddiḳ ka-tamar" (comp. the similar passage in Sulzer's "Schir Zion," ii.).

MIZMOR SHIR LE-YOM HA-SHABBAT

ẒADDIḲ KA-TAMAR

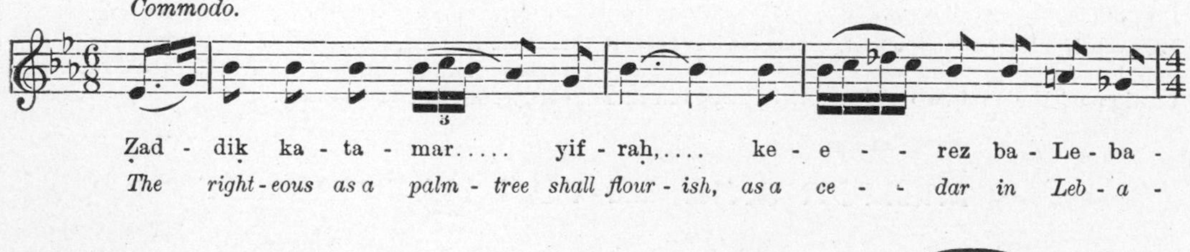

In the Spanish and Portuguese tradition there is preserved for the Sabbath Psalm an ancient chant of exceptional beauty and interest, which is utilized in England also in the synagogues of the Reform and the German and Polish rites. It has been effectively scored, as the Psalm of the day in the Temple service, by Sir Edward Elgar in his oratorio "The Apostles," which was produced at the Birmingham Musical Festival of 1903. The first strain (marked A in the transcription), the pair of simple musical phrases employed for ordinary verses, is very antique in character; and the secondary strain (marked B), even if a later addition to it, also must have originated under Moorish influence. The ornamental figuration of the first two and parallel phrases in this secondary strain is of true Oriental character, and appears frequently in Arab songs, as, for instance, those founded on the "Oriental chromatic" scale given by Bourgault-Ducoudray in "Trente Mélodies Populaires de Grèce et d'Orient," Paris, 1876, particularly No. 2 (quoted also by Ambros, in his "Gesch. der Musik," and by others), No. 17, and the more modern No. 29. But it is important to note that this figure, and also that of the third phrase in the same strain, frequently occur in the traditional melody of the Jews of Teutonic and Slavonic lands as well as of those around the Levant (comp. Jew. Encyc. iii. 247, *s.v.* Birkat Kohanim [the Polish melody]; Geshem [melody A]; Ne'ilah; and especially Music, Synagogal).

MIZMOR SHIR LE-YOM HA-SHABBAT

ṬOB LE-HODOT

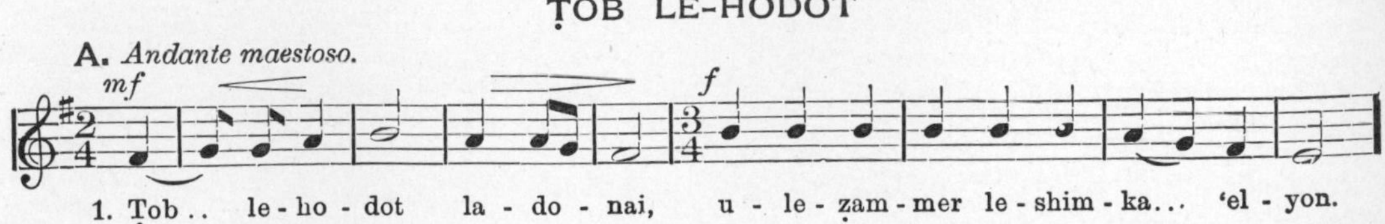

The rest of the Psalm similarly, all verses being chanted to A, except v. 9 and vv. 14, 15, which are set to B.

Bibliography: De Sola and Aguilar, *Ancient Melodies of the Liturgy of the Spanish and Portuguese Jews*, No. 8 (gives also the traditional ending for Ps. xciii.), London, 1857; Baer, *Ba'al Tefillah*, Nos. 368, 369, 373, Frankfort-on-the-Main, 1883; Salaman and Verrinder, *Music of the West London Synagogue of British Jews*, vol. i.; Pauer and Cohen, *Traditional Hebrew Melodies*, No. 2, London, 1896; Cohen and Davis, *Voice of Prayer and Praise*, No. 20, London, 1899.

A. F. L. C.

MIZPAH (MIZPEH; מצפה): Name of several places in Palestine. It is derived from צפה (= "to look"), on account of which it is translated in certain instances by the Septuagint σκοπιά and ὅρασις, and by the Targumim סכותא (Gen. xxxi. 49). Except in Hosea v. 1, "Mizpah" always occurs with the definite article prefixed; "Mizpeh" occurs three times with the article—(1) in Josh. xv. 38, where it designates a town of Judah; (2) in Josh. xviii. 26, where it is applied to a town of Benjamin; and (3) in II Chron. xx. 24, where it probably signifies a watch-tower in the wilderness—and twice in the construct state; namely, in Judges xi. 29 ("Mizpeh of Gilead") and in I Sam. xxii. 3 ("Mizpeh of Moab").

Mizpah is first mentioned in the Bible in connection with the meeting of Jacob and Laban on Mount Gilead, where the heap of stones which they erected as a witness, and which was called by Jacob "Galeed" and by Laban "Jegar-sahadutha," was called "Mizpah" also, for the stated reason, "the Lord watch between me and thee" (Gen. *l.c.*). This Mizpah is most probably identical with the Mizpeh of Gilead (see above), which, according to Schwarz ("Das Heilige Land," pp. 17, 183), is the same as Ramath-mizpeh of Gad (Josh. xiii. 26), and which he identifies with the modern village of Al-Ṣuf in the eastern mountain-range of Gilead.

The most important of the places bearing the name of "Mizpah" was that in Palestine, which on several occasions was the seat of assemblies at which the Israelites discussed their affairs, *e.g.*, in the time of Jephthah (Judges xi. 11), and during the war of Israel with Benjamin (*ib.* xx. 1). Samuel, also, summoned Israel to Mizpah (I Sam. vii. 5–6, 11, 16); and, finally, in the time of the Maccabees, Mizpah (Μασσηφά) appears again as a place of solemn assembly (I Macc. iii. 46). From the foregoing it would appear that at Mizpah a shrine for the worship of Yhwh existed; but there is a diversity of opinion as to the location of the place.

Mizpah in Palestine.

There is no doubt that, since it is mentioned with Geba of Benjamin, the Mizpah which Asa fortified against the attacks of the King of Israel (I Kings xv. 22; II Chron. xvi. 6) was the Mizpah of Benjamin, which was called "Mizpeh" in Josh. xviii. 26 (see above), and which was over against Jerusalem. It was also this Mizpah which became the seat of the governor Gedaliah after the destruction of the Temple (II Kings xxv. 23; Jer. xl. 6 *et seq.*, xli. 1); for when Ishmael went forth from Mizpah he met certain people journeying from Shiloh to Jerusalem. W. F. Birch concludes that the other Mizpahs indicated as places of assembly are also identical with the same town of Benjamin ("Pal. Explor. Fund," 1881, pp. 91 *et seq.*; 1882, pp. 260 *et seq.*). Finally may be mentioned the opinion of Conder ("Handbook to Bible," p. 277, London, 1879), who identifies Mizpah with Nob. The Mizpeh of Judah (Josh. xv. 38; see above) is in the Shefelah or lowlands, mentioned as lying between Dilean and Jokthe-el, neither of which places has been identified. Schwarz (*l.c.* p. 74) identifies Mizpeh with Tel al-Safiyah, the Alba Specula of the Middle Ages (comp. Robinson, "Researches," ii. 363 *et seq.*).

Land of Mizpah.

There was also a whole tract of land called "the land of Mizpah" ("ereẓ ha-Miẓpah") or "the valley of Mizpeh" ("biḳ'at Miẓpeh"), mentioned in connection with the battle between Joshua and Jabin, King of Hazor, which took place at the waters of Merom (Josh. xi. 3, 8). The topography indicated, "under Hermon in the land of Mizpeh" and "unto great Zidon and unto Misrephoth-maim, and unto the valley of Mizpeh eastward," taken in connection with Josh. xi. 17, suggests that the land or valley of Mizpah is to be identified with the valley of the Lebanon or the Cœle-Syria of the Greek writers. The Mizpeh of Moab (see above) is mentioned only once (I Sam. xxii. 3), as the residence of the King of Moab, to whose care David consigned his parents.

J. M. SEL.

MIZRAḤ: Hebrew term denoting the rising of the sun, the east (Num. xxi. 11; Ps. l. 1); also used to designate an ornamental picture hung on the eastern wall of the house, or in front of the reading-desk in the synagogue, and applied to the row of seats in the synagogue on either side of the Ark. The custom of turning toward the east while at prayer, observed by the Jews living west of Palestine, is of great antiquity (Dan. vi. 11; comp. I Kings viii. 38; Ber. 28b; see EAST). The Jews of Palestine prayed with their faces turned westward (Suk. 51b). In later times opinion varied on this subject. While some of the rabbis, claiming that the Divine Presence ("Shekinah") is everywhere, maintained that it makes little difference in which direction one's face is turned in prayer, others were of the opinion that the Divine Presence is especially located in the west, and that therefore one should turn westward. R. Sheshet positively objected to the custom of praying while facing the east because the Minim prayed in that direction (B. B. 25a). The custom, however, predominated and was formulated in a baraita reading as follows: "One who is outside of Palestine should turn toward Palestine; in Palestine, toward Jerusalem; in Jerusalem, toward the Temple; and in the Temple, toward the Holy of Holies" (Ber. 30a; Yer. Ber. iv. 5).

In accordance with this injunction, synagogues are so constructed that the Ark may be placed in the direction of Palestine, and that the people may turn toward it in prayer (Maimonides, "Yad," Tefillah, xi. 2; Shulḥan 'Aruk, Oraḥ Ḥayyim, 94, 1-3). In places east of Palestine, the Ark is placed in the west and the door opposite to it in the east (Tosef., Meg. iii. 14; Rosh, *ib.* iii. 12; Ber. 6a; Tos. *s.v.* "Aḥure"; "Yad," *l.c.*; comp. Oraḥ Ḥayyim, 150, 5 and Isserles' gloss; "Ḥatam Sofer," *ib.* 27).

In spite of the objection of the medieval rabbis to the presence of any object of art in the synagogue, there were still some figures and pictures retained (see ART). In many synagogues and in almost every bet ha-midrash of modern times an ornamental picture, usually bearing the inscription "From the rising of the sun unto the setting thereof, the name of the Lord is praised" (Ps. cxiii. 3, Hebr.), is hung in front of the reading-desk, which latter is near the Ark. Many other passages, and even whole psalms, are added, and frequently are artistically strung together so as to form the likeness of the menorah or of some animal. One of the later authorities ("Ḥatam Sofer," Yoreh De'ah, 127) forbids the engraving of the above-cited passage around a picture of the sun in one of the eastern windows of the synagogue (comp. "Sefer Ḥasidim," ed. Wistinetzki, § 1625). No one, however, seems to raise any objection to the mizraḥ, which is found in synagogues and in many homes.

BIBLIOGRAPHY: Dembitz, *Jewish Services in Synagogue and Home*, pp. 65, 199, Philadelphia, 1898; Hamburger, *R. B. T.* ii. 1144.

A. J. H. G.

MIZRAḤI: Family living in the Orient, to which belong some well-known rabbinical authors. There are two main branches: one in Constantinople, and the other in Jerusalem. The name "Mizraḥi" signifies "an Oriental," and is used as a surname by many Persian Jews who have settled in Turkey.

Abraham ben Baruch Mizraḥi: Shoḥeṭ at Jerusalem in the seventeenth and eighteenth centuries. He was the author of "Zikkaron li-Bene Yisrael," containing laws pertaining to ritual slaughtering. It was printed with Moses Ventura's "Yemin Mosheh," Amsterdam, 1718.

BIBLIOGRAPHY: Fürst, *Bibl. Jud.* ii. 381; Steinschneider, *Cat. Bodl.* col. 702.

Absalom ben Moses Mizraḥi: Oriental scholar of the fourteenth century. Abraham de Balmes in his "Miḳneh Abraham" (in the chapter on prosody) quotes a work by Mizraḥi entitled "Imre Shefer." This work was published by Carmoly, under the title "Ḳabbalah 'al Meleket ha-Shir" (Paris, 1841), from a Paris manuscript, in which it is indicated that it was composed in 1391. Among the models which Mizraḥi gives is the letter of Ibn Pulgar to Abner of Burgos, which Mizraḥi styles "shir meyuḥas" (noble poem, that is, a poem arranged in Mosaic style).

BIBLIOGRAPHY: L. Dukes, in *Orient, Lit.* iv. 435, vii. 808; Fuenn, *Keneset Yisrael*, p. 70; Steinschneider, *Jewish Literature*, p. 177.

Elijah ben Abraham (Re'em), Mizraḥi: Turkish rabbi and mathematician; born at Constantinople about 1455; died there 1525 or 1526. Mizraḥi was a pupil in Talmud and rabbinics of Elijah ha-Levi, who was known for his mild attitude toward the Karaites, whom he taught the Talmud (Mizraḥi, Responsa, Nos. 41, 57). But it appears from a letter of Elijah Capsali (see Grätz, "Gesch." 3d ed., viii. 448) that Mizraḥi studied also under Judah Minz of Padua, who warned him not to throw himself headlong into the quarrel between Joseph Colon and Moses Capsali. From this letter it is evident also that Elijah Mizraḥi is not to be identified, as he is by Conforte ("Ḳore ha-Dorot," p. 29a) and Azulai ("Shem ha-Gedolim," i. 22), with Elijah Parnes, who is mentioned in Colon's responsa, and who is called by Elijah Capsali a corrupt forger (comp. Zunz's notes to the "Itinerary" of Benjamin of Tudela, ed. Asher, ii. 40).

A TYPICAL MIZRAḤ.

(In the possession of Maurice Herrmann, New York.)

While still a young man, Mizraḥi distinguished himself as a Talmudist and as an authority in rabbinical matters, on which he was consulted by many rabbis even in the lifetime of Moses Capsali. Although he was very religious, yet he devoted a part of his time to the study of the secular sciences, particularly to mathematics and astronomy, which he studied under Mordecai Comtino (see letter of Delmedigo in Geiger, "Melo Ḥofnayim," p. 12). Mizraḥi for some time earned a livelihood by teaching Talmud, mathematics, astronomy, and other sciences; but owing to his weak constitution the work proved too hard for him (Mizraḥi, Responsa, No. 56). Though it would appear from his mathematical works that he read the Greek authors, it can not be said with certainty whether he read them in the original or in an Arabic translation. It is evident, however, that he was master of at least one, if not both, of these two languages. At the death of Moses Capsali (*c.* 1495), Mizraḥi succeeded him as grand rabbi or ḥakam bashi of the Ottoman empire, which office he held till his death. Like his predecessor, Mizraḥi had a seat in the divan assigned to him by the sultan beside the mufti and above the patriarch of the Christians. The work "Me'ora'ot 'Olam" (Constantinople, 1756) contains several legends in connection with Mizraḥi and the sultan (Nepi-Ghirondi, "Toledot Gedole Yisrael," p. 267).

Studies Mathematics.

Mizraḥi, who had previously written against the Karaites and who had entered into polemics with Elijah Bashyaẓi (comp. the introduction to the latter's "Adderet Eliyahu"), changed his attitude toward them after he had become ḥakam bashi. Like his master, Elijah ha-Levi, he favored the idea of teaching the Talmud to the Karaites, provided the latter would abstain from reviling it. When the zealots, aiming at the destruction of every means of reconciliation between the Rabbinites and the Karaites, made so many restrictions with regard to the latter and threatened with excommunication those who would not observe them, Mizraḥi was not in Constantinople. When he returned he was indignant at the restrictions; he declared that it was the duty of the Rabbinites to consider the Karaites as Jews, and that Elijah ha-Levi and Eliezer Capsali, whose piety nobody doubted, were of the same opinion (Mizraḥi, Responsa, No. 57). He was opposed also to certain innovations of the cabalists with regard to the interpretation of the Bible (*ib.* No. 1).

The following are Mizraḥi's rabbinical and exegetical works: "Tosefe Semag" (Constantinople, 1520), novellæ on Moses of Coucy's "Sefer Miẓwot Gadol," afterward published with the text under the title "Ḥiddushim" (*ib.* 1541); "Sefer ha-Mizraḥi" (Venice, 1527), a supercommentary on Rashi's commentary on the Pentateuch; "She'elot u-Teshubot," a collection of responsa in two parts: part i., containing 100 responsa (Constantinople, 1546); part ii., containing 39 responsa, printed with the responsa of Elijah ibn Ḥayyim under the title "Mayim 'Amuḳḳim" (Venice, 1647). Mizraḥi himself considered his commentary on Rashi the most important of his works (Responsa, Nos. 5, 78). Besides showing Rashi's Talmudic and midrashic sources, he endeavors to elucidate all obscure passages, thus defending him from the strictures of the later commentators, particularly Naḥmanides. The work was published after Mizraḥi's death by his son Israel, a fact which makes it possible to fix the approximate date of the author's death; for in Jan., 1525, he was still alive (comp. Benjamin Zeeb, Responsa, No. 284). A compendium made by Jacob Marcaria (?) was published under the title "Ḳiẓẓur Mizraḥi" (Riva di Trenta, 1561), and later one by Isaac ha-Kohen of Ostrog, entitled "Mattenat 'Ani" or "Ḳiẓẓur Mizraḥi" (Prague, 1604–9). Many commentaries and strictures were written on Mizraḥi's commentary, among the former being: "To'afot Re'em," by Mordecai Carvallo, and "Ḥayye Yiẓḥaḳ," by his son Isaac Carvallo (printed together, Leghorn, 1761); Eliakim Gatigno's "To'afot Re'em" (Smyrna, 1766); Isaac Ḥaddad's "Ḳarne Re'em" (Leghorn, 1768); Joseph of Milhau's (Muscat's) "Oẓerot Yosef" (*ib.* 1783); and Moses Toledano's "Meleket ha-Ḳodesh" (*ib.* 1803). Among the critics were Samuel Edels ("Ḥiddushe Maharsha," Hanau, 1716) and Samuel Ẓarfati ("Nimmuḳe Shemu'el," Amsterdam, 1718).

His Works.

Mizraḥi's mathematical works are "Sefer ha-Mispar" (Constantinople, 1534), on arithmetic, and a commentary to Ptolemy's "Almagest" (no longer extant), of which Mizraḥi was very proud, no commentary having been previously written on that work. He says (Responsa, No. 5) that, owing to the importance of the science of astronomy, the study of which is considered as a "miẓwah" (good deed), he occupies himself daily with writing a commentary on the "Almagest." According to Delmedigo (*l.c.*), Mizraḥi wrote also a commentary on Euclid's "Elements." The "Sefer ha-Mispar" is in three books, divided into "gates" ("she'arim"), which are subdivided into chapters. Book i. consists of three gates, treating respectively of the four functions in (1) whole numbers, (2) fractions, and (3) mixed numbers. Book ii., also of three gates, treats of (1) the four functions in astronomical fractions, (2) the extraction of the square and cube roots, and (3) proportion. Book iii. is divided into two parts, the first containing arithmetical and the second geometrical problems. Each series of problems consists of two classes treated in two chapters, the first being problems that are solved with, and the second those that are solved without, the help of the rule of three. In the introduction, Mizraḥi speaks of the relation between theology, mathematics, and the natural sciences, remarking that, while theology is in no sense concrete, the other two sciences are. He says also that mathematics is like a bridge by which one may pass from one science to the other, and that therefore special attention should be paid to it. Mizraḥi based this work mainly on Ibn Ezra's "Sefer ha-Mispar"; and twenty-one out of the 100 problems which it contains are almost literally copied from the latter. He employed Greek and Arabic works also, often quoting Nicomachus of Gerasa, Euclid, and Heron of Alexandria. From the Arabs he took

Mathematical Works.

material for his observations on fractions, extraction of the square root, and quadratic equations.

An abridgment of Mizraḥi's work and of Abraham b. Ḥiyya's "Sefer Ẓurat ha-Areẓ" was made by Sebastian Münster, to be used as a text-book by his pupils. This abridgment was published with a Latin translation by Schreckenfuchs (Basel, 1546), through which Mizraḥi came to the knowledge of European scholars, his original work having become rare. A similar work attributed to Mizraḥi was published at Lemberg (1807) under the title "Meleket ha-Mispar." It contains at the end lessons in chess. In answer to a question by Count Boncompagni of Rome as to whether a Jewish writer would occupy himself with the summation of the series $1^3+2^3+3^3+ \ldots +n^3$, Steinschneider translated into Italian the parts of the "Sefer ha-Mispar" relating to the question, together with the introduction ("Brani dell' Aritmetica d'Elia Misrachi," pp. 43–67, Rome, 1866). According to Delambre ("Histoire de l'Astronomie du Moyen-Age," p. 212, Paris, 1819), Mizraḥi was the first to treat of the extraction of the cube root. It is true that Delambre ascribed to him a much earlier epoch than that in which he lived; for, considering Mizraḥi as later than Ibn Yunus (d. 1008), he placed him in the twelfth century.

Bibliography: Conforte, *Ḳore ha-Dorot*, p. 31a; Fuenn, *Keneset Yisrael*, p. 116; *idem*, in *Ha-Karmel*, iv. 214 *et seq.*; Fürst, *Bibl. Jud.* ii. 381 *et seq.*; Grätz, *Gesch.* 3d ed., ix. 30 *et seq.*; Steinschneider, *Cat. Bodl.* cols. 946 *et seq.*; idem, *Jewish Literature*, pp. 118, 121, 189; idem, *Hebr. Uebers.* pp. 508, 524; *idem*, in *Abhandlungen zur Gesch. der Mathematik*, ix. 477, Leipsic, 1899; G. Wertheim, *Die Arithmetik des Elia Misrachi*, Brunswick, 1896.

Israel ben Elijah Mizraḥi: Turkish Talmudist; lived at Constantinople in the sixteenth century. He edited his father's "Sefer ha-Mizraḥi" (Venice, 1527), adding to it a preface in which he asked the readers, in case they were unable to understand certain passages, not to criticize his father, but to apply to him (Israel) for explanation. A responsum of Mizraḥi's is found in "Abḳat Rokel" (No. 180). He corresponded with Abraham Treves, the author of "Birkat Abraham."

Bibliography: Azulai, *Shem ha-Gedolim*, i. 115; Fuenn, *Keneset Yisrael*, p. 698.

Israel Meïr ben Joseph Mizraḥi: Palestinian rabbi; head of the yeshibah of Jerusalem in the first half of the eighteenth century. He distinguished himself as a rabbinical scholar at an early age, and although he died when still young, he left important works. In 1727 he was sent to Constantinople to collect alms; and there he published his responsa collection "Peri ha-Areẓ," followed by a "Ḳontres" containing novellæ to Maimonides' "Yad" and its commentaries. He wrote also "Ner Mizraḥi," a commentary on Elijah Mizraḥi's novellæ to the "Semag," and "Tif'eret Yisrael," sermons. Both of these works remain unpublished.

Bibliography: Fuenn, *Keneset Yisrael*, p. 699; Fürst, *Bibl. Jud.* ii. 382; Steinschneider, *Cat. Bodl.* col. 1168.

E. C. M. Sel.

Raphael Abraham Shalom Mizraḥi (better known as **Rab Sharabi**): Rabbi in Jerusalem; born at Yemen; died in 1777. He enjoyed the reputation of being the most learned cabalist of his time, while his fervent piety, which, according to the historians, recalled that of the famous Isaac Luria of Safed and which has become proverbial, secured for him the position of president of the yeshibah Ḳahal Ḳadosh Ḥasidim.

Of Sharabi's writings on the Cabala the principal ones are "Reḥobot ha-Nahar" and "Derek Shalom."

Sharabi's son **Isaac Mizraḥi Sharabi** (d. at Jerusalem in 1803) bore the same high reputation for piety as his father, whom he succeeded at the yeshibah.

Bibliography: Azulai, *Shem ha-Gedolim*, s.v.; Hazan, *Ha-Ma'alot li-Shelomoh*, pp. 20, 47, 93, 103.

S. S. M. Fr.

Reuben ben Hananiah Mizraḥi: Rabbi of Constantinople in the seventeenth and eighteenth centuries; a descendant of Elijah Mizraḥi. He was the author of "Ma'yan Gannim" (Constantinople, 1721), a work containing decisions upon ritual matters and homilies on the Pentateuch, with a preface by Aaron Hamon. In the preface are mentioned the following works by Mizraḥi, which are still unpublished: "Be'er Mayim Ḥayyim," commentary on the Zohar; "Nozelim Min Lebanon," commentary on the "Tiḳḳunim"; "Peri 'Eẓ Ḥayyim," commentary on Maimonides' "Yad"; "Kappot Temarim," commentary on Midrash Rabbah; "'Arbe Naḥal," commentary on Pirḳe Abot and Esther; "'Eẓ Abot," responsa; "Ketem Paz," commentary on the Ṭurim Oraḥ Ḥayyim and Eben ha-'Ezer; and novellæ on the Talmud.

Bibliography: Benjacob, *Oẓar ha-Sefarim*, p. 350, No. 1706; Fürst, *Bibl. Jud.* ii. 382; Nepi-Ghirondi, *Toledot Gedole Yisrael*, pp. 312–314; Steinschneider, *Cat. Bodl.* col. 2139.

E. C. M. Sel.

MIZRAIM. See Egypt.

MIẒWAH. See Commandment.

MNEMONICS (Hebrew, "simanim" = "signs"): Certain sentences, words, or letters used to assist the memory. Such aids are employed in the Mishnah, in both Talmuds, and in the Masorah, as well as by the Geonim and by the teachers of the Law during the Middle Ages. In this article only the Talmudic mnemonics will be discussed, together with those employed by the later teachers of the Law. For Masoretic signs and their use see Masorah. The mnemonics employed in the Talmud may be divided into the following two groups:

Formed of Sentences.

(1) Mnemonics which are formed from a Scriptural passage, a mishnah, a halakic sentence, or a proverb or maxim taken from life or from nature. These simanim, which are introduced by the word "we-simanak" (= "and let thy sign be"), stand invariably after the halakic sentences for which they serve as signs; and it is usually stated who invented and used them. Many originated with the Babylonian amora R. Naḥman b. Isaac, who employed them with special frequency. They occur very often in 'Abodah Zarah, Ḥullin, and Shabbat, as well as in Bekorot, 'Erubin, Yebamot, Ta'anit, and the remaining treatises. Mnemonics are used to prevent confusion where for any reason it might easily occur. Thus Ps. cxxxix. 5a ("Thou hast set me behind and before") is employed as a mnemonic for 'Ab. Zarah 8a, to show that in the enumeration of heathen feasts the Mishnah "goes from the

end toward the beginning," and that the feasts which were celebrated later are mentioned first; it might be supposed that the Mishnah had followed the order of the seasons in which the several festivals occurred. In like manner, when there is a difference between two things which are apparently alike, a sign is employed to avoid possible confusion (see several examples in Ḥul. 62b–63a). These simanim are used especially to keep the authors of divergent teachings distinct. Thus, for example, in Ḥul. 46a, where it is said that R. Ḥiyya used to throw away the liver, while R. Simon, the son of R. Judah ha-Nasi, used to eat it, the saying "ashirim meḳammeẓin " (= "the rich are economical ") is employed, inasmuch as the rich R. Simon b. R. Judah was frugal and did not wish to throw away the liver. If two or more scholars bear the same name, a sign is used to show which one of them is meant.

To Distinguish Authorship.

Thus in Pes. 114a, where it is said that the R. Isaac who in halakic sentences is called "Shema'ata " is R. Isaac b. Aḥa, the phrase "shema'uni aḥai " (I Chron. xxviii. 2) is used as a sign, *i.e.*, the son of Aḥa is one of the Shema'ata to whom halakic sentences belong.

(2) A wholly different kind of sign, found in the mnemonic sentences which are composed of single words each of which is a catchword for a halakic sentence, a teaching, or an opinion; or of the names of the authors and together with words made up of single letters either of the authors' names or of the catchwords characteristic of the sentences, or again of both. There are only a few examples of these sentences which have any meaning, most of them making no sense. With one exception (Zeb. 7b), they all stand before the sentences which they are to impress on the memory, and are never introduced by "we-simanak," but by "siman," which word stands sometimes before and sometimes after the mnemonic term.

Single Words.

Mnemonics, however, are often found without the word "siman " to designate their character (*e.g.*, Shebu. 35a; Sanh. 83a), and have thus sometimes been wrongly considered as parts of the halakic sentences, as in Meg. 31a (comp. N. Brüll in his "Jahrb." ii. 119). On the other hand, there is a case (B. B. 113) where the mnemonic term was lost, and the introductory word "siman " was then supposed to be the name of an amora (comp. J. Brüll, "Die Mnemotechnik des Talmuds," p. 18).

These mnemonics, which are nearly all anonymous, designate the order of succession of the sentences which are to follow, or of the transmitters of the sentence about to be given, or even how many times and in what passages the name of the same transmitter occurs in the treatise under discussion. A few examples may be given. In Ḥul. 4a the sayings of R. Manasseh which occur in the treatise are comprised in a single sentence which itself contains a regulation concerning circumcision. In Ḥul. 11a different amoraim of various periods give different reasons for one fundamental law. Out of single letters taken from the names of these authors is formed the mnemonic sentence "zeman shebaḥ mekannesh," denoting that time collects that which is good; *i.e.*, in this case time has not caused the excellent sayings of the amoraim of different times to be forgotten. Occasionally these mnemonics show that something is missing in the Talmud (comp. Tos., Men. 20a, *s.v.* "Sheken "). With the exception of 'Arakin, Beẓah, Ḥagigah, Me'ilah, Rosh ha-Shanah, Sukkah, Tamid, and Temurah, such simanim are found in all the treatises of the Babylonian Talmud. It is probable, however, that in the treatises just cited there were likewise simanim which were afterward lost, especially since many mnemonics are missing in the present editions of the Talmud which were to be found in earlier copies (comp. N. Brüll, *l.c.* ii. 62 *et seq.*).

Means of Preserving Halakot.

These mnemonics were used by students as early as the period in which the Halakah was still handed down only orally. The prohibition against committing halakot to writing did not apply to these simanim; and they thus furnished aids to the memory.

Most of the mnemonics, however, appear to have originated after the Talmud had been collected and arranged, but was not yet reduced to writing. Many of them presuppose the order of succession of the sentences, and contain the entire Talmud in stenographic signs. When the Talmud was written down these mnemonic notes were used as a basis for the work. After its completion the signs were retained, since they were of great assistance to many pupils who still had to memorize the Talmud, owing to the lack of written copies. They were inserted in the text likewise because they were very useful as superscriptions and indexes, since a passage in the Talmud could be more precisely referred to by means of them (comp. N. Brüll, *l.c.* ii. 61). Similarly the Geonim and the teachers of the Law during the Middle Ages employed such sentences to formulate their legal decisions (comp. Brüll, *l.c.* p. 66, note 105). Mnemonics were also invented to indicate the order of succession of the treatises, or of the chapters of individual tractates, as well as of the weekly readings from the Pentateuch (see R. Bezaleel Ashkenazi at the end of the "Shiṭṭah Meḳubbeẓet " on Men., and Judah of Modena in "Leb ha-Aryeh," ii. 2). Such is the sign "zeman naḳaṭ," employed by Maimonides in his introduction to the Mishnah to indicate the sequence of the six mishnaic orders, and which means "time has preserved," *i.e.*, "has preserved the literary products of ancient times." Furthermore, each letter of these two words indicates the name of an order of the Mishnah and the place of such order among its fellows; thus, "zayin " = "Zera'im "; "mem " = "Mo'ed "; "nun " = "Nashim "; etc. See also ABBREVIATIONS.

BIBLIOGRAPHY: S. J. Rapoport, in *Kerem Ḥemed*, vi. 252 *et seq.*; J. Brüll, *Die Mnemotechnik des Talmuds*, Vienna, 1864; N. Brüll, in his *Jahrb.* ii. 59-67, Frankfort-on-the-Main, 1876.

T. J. Z. L.

MOAB (Hebrew, מואב; LXX. Μωάβ; Assyrian, "Mu'aba," "Ma'ba," "Ma'ab"; Egyptian, "Muab"): District and nation of Palestine. The etymology of the word is very uncertain. The earliest gloss is found in the Septuagint, Gen. xix. 37, which explains the name, in obvious allusion to the account of Moab's parentage, as ἐκ τοῦ πατρός μου. Other etymologies which have been proposed regard it as a corruption of מי אב = "seed of a father," or as a participial form from יאב = "to desire," thus connoting "the desirable (land)." The latest explanation is by Hommel ("Verhandlungen des Zwölften Internationalen Orientalisten-Congresses," p. 261, Leyden, 1904), who regards "Moab" as an abbreviation of "Immo-ab" = "his mother is his father."

According to Gen. xix. 30-38, Moab was the son of Lot by his elder daughter, while Ammon was Moab's half-brother by a similar union of Lot with his younger child. The close ethnological affinity of Moab and Ammon which is thus attested (comp. also Judges iii. 13; II Chron. xx. 22; Isa. xi. 14; Jer. xxvi. 21) is confirmed by their subsequent history, while their kinship with the Hebrews is equally certain, and is borne out by the linguistic evidence of the Moabite Stone. They are also mentioned in close connection with the Amalekites (Judges iii. 13), the inhabitants of Mount Seir (II Chron. xx. 22; Ezek. xxv. 8), the Edomites (Ex. xv. 15; Ps. lx. 10 [A. V. 8]; Isa. xi. 14; Jer. xxv. 21), the Canaanites (Ex. xv. 15), the Sethites (Num. xxiv. 17), and the Philistines (Ps. lx. 10 [A. V. 8]; Isa. xi. 14).

Geography. Moab occupied a plateau about 3,000 feet above the level of the Mediterranean, or 4,300 feet above the Dead Sea, and rising gradually from north to south. It was bounded on the west by the Dead Sea and the southern section of the Jordan; on the east by Ammon and the Arabian desert, from which it was separated by low, rolling hills; and on the south by Edom. The northern boundary varied, but in general it may be said to have been represented by a line drawn some miles above the northern extremity of the Dead Sea. In Ezek. xxv. 9 the boundaries are given as being marked by Beth-jeshimoth (north), Baal-meon (east), and Kiriathaim (south). That these limits were not fixed, however, is plain from the lists of cities given in Isa. xv.-xvi. and Jer. xlviii., where Heshbon, Elealeh, and Jazer are mentioned to the north of Beth-jeshimoth; Medeba, Beth-gamul, and Mephaath to the east of Baal-meon; and Dibon, Aroer, Bezer, Jahaz, and Kir-hareseth to the south of Kiriathaim. The principal rivers of Moab mentioned in the Bible are the Arnon, the Dimon or Dibon, and the Nimrim. The limestone hills which form the almost treeless plateau are generally steep but fertile. In the spring they are covered with grass; and the table-land itself produces grain. In the north are a number of long, deep ravines, and Mount Nebo, famous as the scene of the death of Moses (Deut. xxxiv. 1-8). The rainfall is fairly plentiful; and the climate, despite the hot summer, is cooler than that of western Palestine, snow falling frequently in winter and in spring. The plateau is dotted with hundreds of rude dolmens, menhirs, and stone-circles, and contains many ruined villages, mostly of the Roman and Byzantine periods. The land is now occupied chiefly by Bedouins, who render the district by no means the safest in Palestine.

History. At the time of the Hebrew invasion the Moabites seem to have been so powerful that conflict with them was avoided (Deut. ii. 9; Judges xi. 15; II Chron. xx. 10), although the Israelites defeated and slew Sihon, the Amorite king of Heshbon, who himself had conquered a former king of Moab (Num. xxi. 21-31; Deut. ii. 24-35). Moab, on the other hand, under its king Balak, meditated a resistance to the invaders which it dared not carry out (Num. xxii.-xxiv.; Deut. xxiii. 4; Judges xi. 25). After the conquest the Moabite territory was allotted to the tribe of Reuben (Josh. xiii. 15-21; comp. Num. xxxii. 37-38). The Moabites seem to have submitted to the control of the Hebrews for a time, until Eglon, King of Moab, with the help of the Ammonites and the Amalekites, succeeded in conquering them, and ruled over them eighteen years. At the end of this period a Benjamite named Ehud obtained access to Eglon and treacherously assassinated him, whereupon the Hebrews arose and slaughtered 10,000 Moabites (Judges iii. 12-30). A few years later Saul waged a war, apparently of little importance, against them and their allies (I Sam. xiv. 47). David also subdued them and made them tributary (II Sam. viii. 1-2, 11-12; I Chron. xviii. 2, 11), although it is noteworthy that even before this time a Moabite named Ithmah was one of his generals (I Chron. xi. 46).

After the death of Ahab the Moabites under Mesha rebelled against Jehoram, who allied himself with Jehoshaphat, King of Judah, and with the King of Edom. At the direction of Elisha the Israelites dug a series of ditches between themselves and the enemy, and during the night these channels were miraculously filled with water which was as red as blood. Deceived by the crimson color into the belief that their opponents had attacked one another, the Moabites became overconfident and were entrapped and utterly defeated at Ziz, near Engedi (II Kings iii.; II Chron. xx., which states that the Moabites and their allies, the Ammonites and the inhabitants of Mount Seir, mistook one another for the enemy, and so destroyed one another). According to Mesha's inscription on the Moabite Stone, however, he was completely victorious and regained all the territory of which Israel had deprived him. The battle of Ziz is the last important date in the history of the Moabites as recorded in the Bible. In the year of Elisha's death they invaded Israel (II Kings xiii. 20), and later aided Nebuchadnezzar in his expedition against Jehoiakim (*ib.* xxiv. 2).

Although allusions to Moab are frequent in the prophetical books (*e.g.*, Isa. xxv. 10; Ezek. xxv. 8-11; Amos ii. 1-3; Zeph. ii. 8-11), and although two chapters of Isaiah (xv.-xvi.) and one of Jeremiah (xlviii.) are devoted to the "burden of Moab," they give little information about the land. Its prosperity and pride, which brought on the Moabites the wrath of Yhwh, are frequently mentioned (Isa. xvi. 6; Jer. xlviii. 11, 29; Zeph. ii. 10); and their contempt for Israel is once expressly noted (Jer. xlviii. 27). From this time Moab disappears as a nation; and in Neh. iv. 7 the Arabians instead of the Moabites are the allies of the Ammonites (comp. I Macc. ix. 32-42; Josephus, "Ant." xiii. 13, § 5; xiv. 1, § 4).

References to the religion of Moab are scanty. The Moabites were polytheists like the other early Semites; and they induced the Hebrew invaders to join in their sacrifices (Num. xxv. 2; Judges x. 6).

Their chief god was CHEMOSH (Jer. xlviii. 7, 13), so that they are even called the "people of Chemosh" (Num. xxi. 29; Jer. xlviii. 46). At times, especially in dire peril, human sacrifices were offered to him, as by Mesha, who gave up his son and heir to him (II Kings iii. 27). Nevertheless, Solomon built, for this "abomination of Moab," on the hill before Jerusalem, a "high place" (I Kings xi. 7) which was not destroyed until the reign of Josiah (II Kings xxiii. 13). The Moabite Stone also mentions (line 17) a female counterpart of Chemosh, Ishtar- (or Ashtar-) Chemosh, and a god Nebo (line 14), the well-known Babylonian divinity, while the cult of Baal-peor (Num. xxv. 5; Ps. cvi. 28) or Peor (Num. xxxi. 16; Josh. xxii. 17) seems to have been marked by sensuality. Since the Moabites had opposed the invasion of Palestine, they, like the Ammonites, were excluded from the congregation unto the tenth generation (Deut. xxiii. 3-4; comp. Neh. xiii. 1-3). This law was violated during the Exile, however; and Ezra and Nehemiah sought to compel a return to the ancient custom of exclusion (Ezra ix. 1-2, 12; Neh. xiii. 23-25). The exilian usage had had royal sanction: the harem of Solomon included Moabite women (I Kings xi. 1). On the other hand, the fact that the marriages of the Beth-lehem-judah Ephrathites Chilion and Mahlon to the Moabite women Orpah and Ruth (Ruth i. 2-4), and the marriage of the latter, after her husband's death, to Boaz (*ib.* iv. 10, 13), who was the great-grandfather of David, are mentioned with no shade of reproach, shows that the law had fallen into abeyance at a comparatively early period and had become a mere priestly restriction.

Religion.

In the Nimrud clay inscription of Tiglath-pileser the Moabite king Salmanu (perhaps the Shalman who sacked Beth-arbel [Hos. x. 14]) is mentioned as tributary to Assyria. Sargon II. mentions on a clay prism a revolt against him by Moab together with Philistia, Judah, and Edom; but on the Taylor prism, which recounts the expedition against Hezekiah, Kammusu-Nadbi (Chemosh-nadab), King of Moab, brings tribute to Sargon as his suzerain. Another Moabite king, Muẓuri ("the Egyptian" ?), is mentioned as one of the subject princes at the courts of Esar-haddon and Assurbanipal, while Kaashalta, possibly his successor, is named on cylinder B of Assurbanipal.

In Assyrian and Babylonian Inscriptions.

In the Egyptian inscriptions Moab is mentioned once, on the base of one of six colossal figures at Luxor, where Rameses II. (*c.* 1300 B.C.) includes "Mu'ab" in the list of his conquests. See MOABITE STONE.

BIBLIOGRAPHY: Tristram, *The Land of Moab*, London, 1874; George Adam Smith, *Historical Geography of the Holy Land*, ib. 1897; Clermont-Ganneau, *Recueil d'Archéologie Orientale*, ii. 185-234, Paris, 1889; Baethgen, *Beiträge zur Semitischen Religionsgeschichte*, Berlin, 1888; Smith, *Rel. of Sem.* Edinburgh, 1894.

J. L. H. G.

MOABITE STONE: Name usually given to the only known surviving inscribed monument of ancient Moab. It was discovered in 1868 at Dhiban, the ancient DIBON, four miles north of the River Arnon. When first seen by Europeans (including a German missionary named Klein) it was an inscribed slab of black basalt 3½ feet long by 2 feet wide. The Arabs of the neighborhood, dreading the loss of such a talisman, broke the stone into pieces; but a squeeze had already been obtained by Clermont-Ganneau, and most of the fragments were recovered and pieced together by him. The reconstructed monument is now, together with the squeeze, in the museum of the Louvre in Paris.

The inscription consists of thirty-four lines containing about 260 words and is well engraved in old Hebrew (Phenician) characters. It was written about 860 B.C. in the name of MESHA, the King of Moab. The translation of the first two-thirds of the inscription is as follows:

"I am Mesha, son of Chemosh . . . (?), King of Moab, the Dibonite. My father reigned over Moab thirty years, and I became king after my father, and I made this high place for Chemosh in קרחה, the high place of deliverance, because he had delivered me from all that attacked me, and because he had made me see my desire upon all my enemies. Omri, King of Israel, oppressed Israel many days because Chemosh was angry with his land; and his son succeeded him, and he also said, 'I will oppress Moab.' In my days he said this, and I saw my desire upon him, and Israel was humbled with everlasting humiliation. Omri had taken possession of the land of Medeba and [his people] occupied it during his days and half the days of his son, forty years; but Chemosh restored it in my days. . . . And the men of Gad had occupied the land of Ataroth for a long time, and the King of Israel had built up Ataroth for himself. And I fought against the city and took it, and I slew all the people from the city, a sight for the eyes of Chemosh and of Moab. . . . And Chemosh said to me, 'Go, take Nebo against Israel.' And I went by night and fought against it from the break of dawn until noon, and I took it and slew all [that were in] it, seven thousand men and boys and women and girls and maid servants; for to Ashtor-Chemosh I had devoted it. And I took from there the vessels of YHWH and brought them before Chemosh. And the King of Israel had fortified Jahaz and occupied it while he was at war with me, and Chemosh drove him out from before me. And I took of Moab two hundred, all its chiefs, and I attacked Jahaz and took it, in order to add it to Dibon."

In the rest of the inscription Mesha tells of restoring and fortifying cities that rightfully belonged to Moab, of building a palace for himself, and of constructing reservoirs for water.

The inscription is by far the most important yet found in Palestine. It has added essentially to the scanty knowledge of the history and religion of Moab itself, and has thrown light on the fortunes of Israel east of the Jordan, as well as upon the foreign relations of the dynasty of Omri. The character of the language of Moab is also pretty fairly indicated.

In regard to the last point it may be noticed that the inflections depart but very seldom from those of classical Hebrew. The masculine plural ends in "-in" instead of "-im," and there is an ifte'al verb-stem. "Waw" consecutive with the first person imperfect is regularly followed by the cohortative or subjunctive. The vowel-letter ה is used for the pronominal suffix of both genders.

In matters of religion Moab is seen to furnish a close parallel to Israel. Chemosh here bears exactly the same political relation to his people as Jehovah does to His (comp. Num. xxi. 29; Judges xi. 24). In both nations religion is the basis of a fiercely intense patriotism (comp. II Kings iii. 27), and the king is the nearest representative of the Deity in executing all His will. The vivid picture given of the border war-

Religious and Historical Importance.

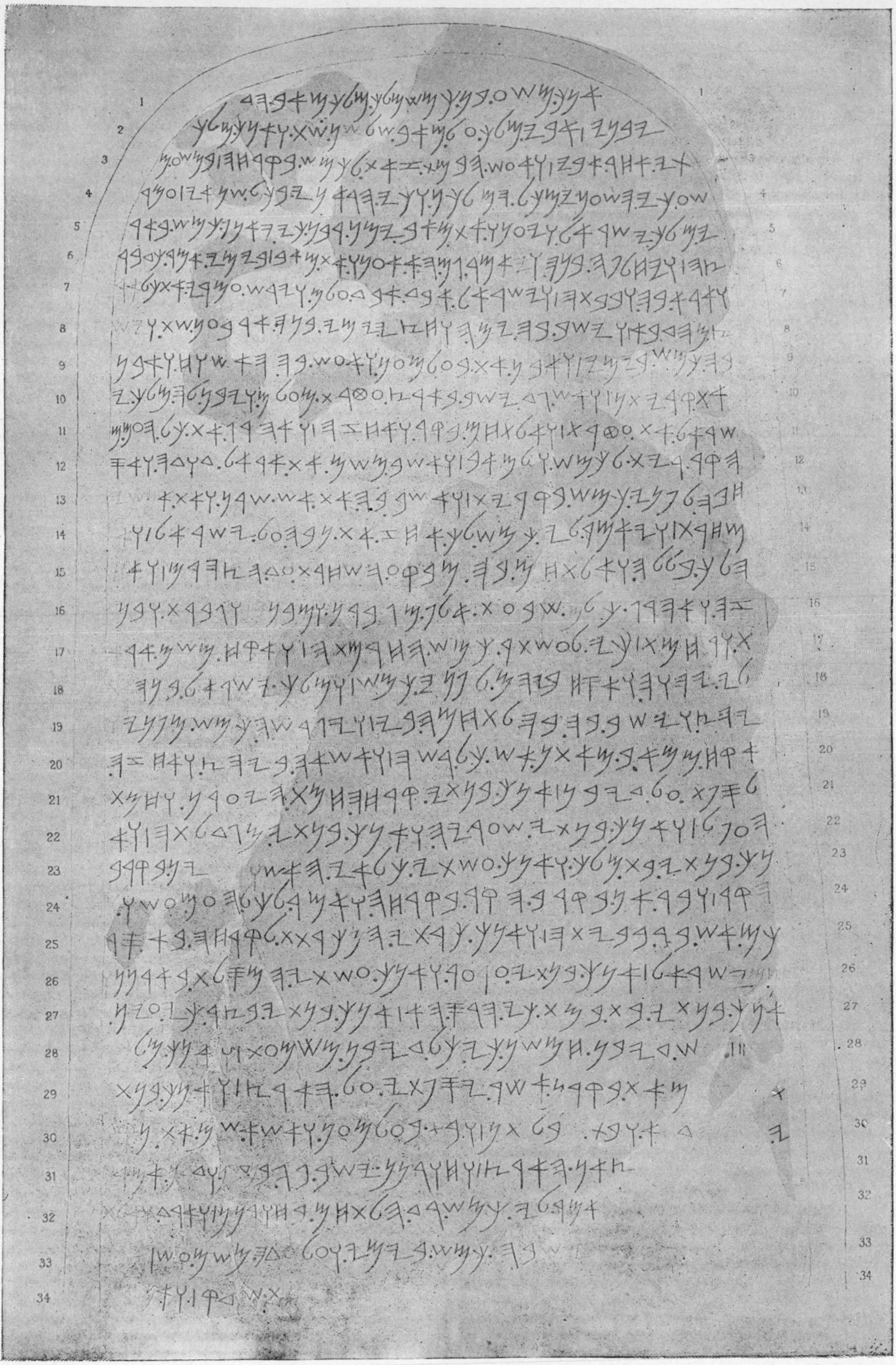

Inscription on the Moabite Stone.

(After Smend and Socin.)

fare between Moab and Israel helps one to understand the bitter hostility of each people toward the other, and the race hatred to which Judah became heir after the fall of the Northern Kingdom. Of Israel's history it is learned that the warlike Gadites had absorbed the tribe of Reuben, and that they upheld the banner of Israel east of the Jordan. A clearer idea is obtained of the epoch-making deeds of Omri, under whom, in spite of the wars with Damascus, a large portion of Moab was annexed and the whole kingdom forced to pay an enormous tribute (comp. II Kings iii. 4); but after his day Israel gradually lost its hold upon Moab, which was thus left to its habitual repose, and, like wine, "settled on his lees" (Jer. xlviii. 11).

The literature in connection with the Moabite stone is quite large. Inasmuch as the elucidation of the language of the inscription is continually progressing, the later treatises are the most valuable for practical purposes. Translations with notes were given in 1870 by Clermont-Ganneau, Nöldeke, Ginsburg, Schlottmann, and Derenbourg, and in 1871 by Wright. Recent discussions give results based on reexamination and closer criticism of the text. It may be noted that an attempt to disprove the authenticity of the stone was recently made by A. Löwy (Berlin, 1903). The most important of the later studies are cited in the bibliography.

BIBLIOGRAPHY: Smend and Socin, *Die Inschrift des König's Mesa*, 1886; Clermont-Ganneau, *La Stèle de Mesa*, in *Journal Asiatique*, Jan., 1887; Nordlander, *Die Inschrift des Königs Mesa*, 1896; Lidzbarski, *Ephemeris für Semitische Epigraphie*, 1900; comp. Driver, *Mesha*, in Cheyne and Black, *Encyc. Bibl.*

J. J. F. McC.

MOBILE. See ALABAMA.

MOCATTA: An Anglo-Jewish family which can be traced back to one of the earliest of the resettlers in England.

David Mocatta: English architect; born in London 1806; died May 1, 1882; son of Moses Mocatta, translator of "Faith Strengthened." Having shown in early youth a leaning to art pursuits, he made the choice of architecture as a profession, and studied for many years in Italy under competent masters, returning to England to practise his profession. He was engaged on many important buildings, and was frequently employed by the directors of the London, Brighton, and South Coast Railway. On the death of his father he succeeded to an ample fortune, which was subsequently increased to a considerable extent by property bequeathed to him by his brother **Benjamin Mocatta.** When the late Sir John Soane bequeathed his collection to the nation, David Mocatta was appointed a trustee, Sir John having been one of his teachers before he left Italy.

Mocatta was one of the original Council of Founders of the West London Reform Synagogue. He had been directing architect of the temporary synagogue in Burton street, and he likewise superintended the construction of the building in Margaret street. On the death of Sir Francis Goldsmid he became chairman of the council of the congregation. He was a member of the council of the University College Hospital, and of the Cancer Hospital. He married the eldest daughter of Alexander Goldsmid, brother of Sir Isaac Lyon Goldsmid.

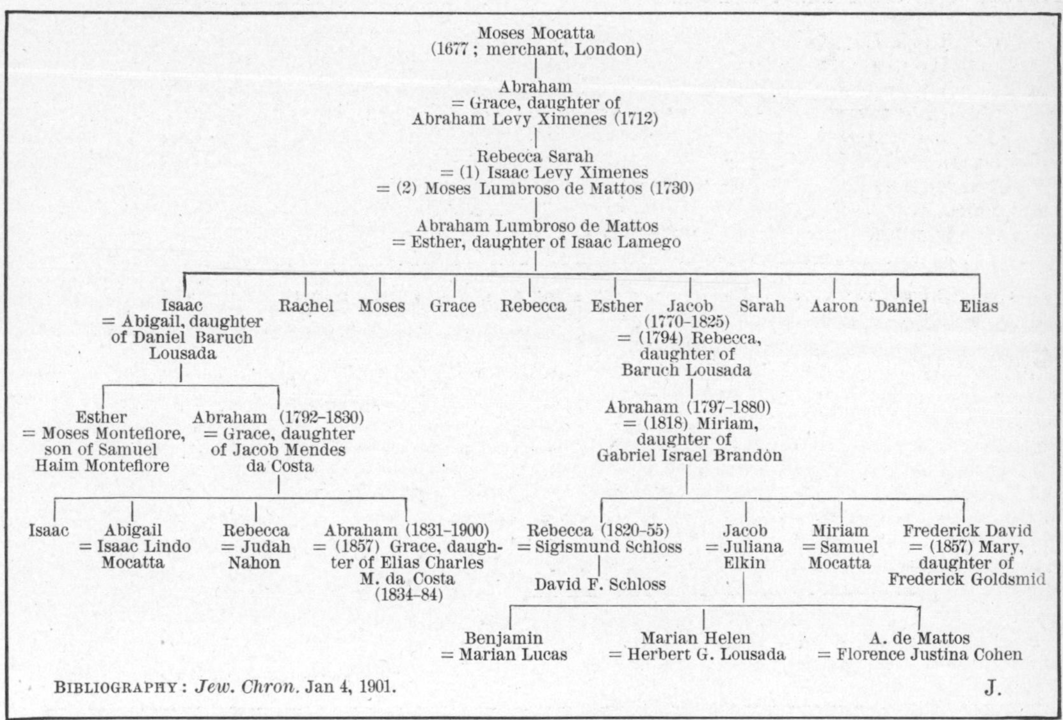

MOCATTA PEDIGREE.

Bibliography: *Jew. Chron.* May 5, 1882 · *The Times*, May 4, 1882.

J. I. H.

Frederick David Mocatta: English philanthropist and communal worker; born in London Jan. 15, 1828; retired from the firm of Mocatta & Goldsmid, bullion-brokers to the Bank of England, in 1874, and devoted himself almost exclusively to the study of charitable and social questions. The condition of the working classes of all creeds, the improvement of their dwellings, and the administration of charity with a view to promoting the independence of the poor on the lines of the Charity Organization Society, are some of the principal subjects that have engaged his attention. His philanthropic work is conducted on certain well-defined principles, foremost among them being the unification and systematic organization of charity so as to prevent the undue multiplication of institutions. He acted as chairman of the committee appointed to effect the union of the Jews' Hospital and Orphan Asylum. In 1871 a Jewish Workhouse was started, which was subsequently amalgamated under his presidency with the Hand-in-Hand Asylum. He has been active also in abrogating the voting system in Jewish charitable institutions.

Frederick David Mocatta.

Mocatta is a vice-president of the Anglo-Jewish Association; served as a member of the Rumanian and Russo-Jewish committees; and in 1882 was deputed by the Mansion House Committee to proceed to the various Continental centers in which the refugees from persecution were congregated. In 1895 Mocatta reorganized the Jewish Home for Incurables. At the beginning of his seventieth year he was presented with a testimonial from over 200 philanthropic, literary, and other institutions of which he was a member.

Mocatta was specially interested in the promotion of Jewish learning, having been one of the most active members in the Society of Hebrew Literature. Among works partly or wholly subventioned by him may be mentioned Zunz, "Zur Geschichte und Literatur" and "Literaturgeschichte der Synagogalen Poesie"; Berliner, "Juden in Rom"; Jacobs, "Sources of Spanish Jewish History"; the English translation of Graetz, "History of the Jews"; etc. He himself was the author of "The Jews and the Inquisition," London, 1877, of which German, Hebrew, and Italian translations have appeared. In 1900 he was elected president of the Jewish Historical Society of England. He died Jan. 16, 1905.

Bibliography: *Young Israel*, March, 1897; *Jew. Chron.* Jan. 15, 1897; *Jewish Year Book*, 5661, pp. 304–305.

J. G. L.

Isaac Lindo Mocatta: Author; born in London 1818; died at Reading 1879. His early life was passed in the business pursuits which he carried on in South America. He likewise spent three years in Australia. On settling in England he interested himself in Jewish charitable work. Later in life, like his father before him, he devoted himself to writing. His two best-known works are entitled: "Moral Biblical Gleanings" (London, 1872), illustrating moral principles by Biblical examples, and "The Jewish Armory" (Brighton, 1877, privately printed). Some of the Sabbath readings issued by the Jewish Association for the Diffusion of Religious Knowledge were from his pen. He designed and printed some ingenious pictorial representations of moral truths. His secular works include "Times and Places," London, n.d., and various pamphlets on social subjects.

Bibliography: *Jewish Chronicle*, November 21, 1879.

Moses Mocatta: Broker, author, and communal worker; born in London February, 1768; died September, 1857. He was connected with the most influential Sephardic families of his day. His sister **Rachel** was the mother of Sir Moses Montefiore. For many years he was a partner in the firm of Mocatta & Goldsmid (bullion-brokers to the Bank of England), which had been founded by his father. He retired from business in middle life and devoted himself to study and to communal work. He was a diligent student of Hebrew, and well read in Biblical and Jewish literature. The "Hebrew Review" (1846) as well as the works of Grace Aguilar found in him a generous patron. Theological controversy was a subject which particularly interested him. His "Faith Strengthened" (1851) is a translation from the Hebrew of the famous "Ḥizzuḳ Emunah" of Isaac ben Abraham of Troki. His other translation, entitled "The Inquisition and Judaism" (1845), was a contribution to controversial literature, and comprised a sermon on Isa. xlii. 22 addressed to Jewish martyrs on the occasion of an auto da fé at Lisbon in 1705, and a reply to the sermon by E. Vero (a posthumous work of the author of the "Secret History of the Inquisition"). The sermon was translated from the Portuguese, and the reply from the Spanish. Moses Mocatta compiled also "The Wisdom of Solomon; a Selection from Proverbs and Ecclesiastes in Hebrew, with a Corrected Version on Parallel Lines" (1834).

As a communal worker Moses Mocatta rendered conspicuous service to the Shaaré Tikva schools and other institutions of the Spanish and Portuguese Congregation. When the schism of 1841 occurred Mocatta was one of those members of Bevis Marks who seceded from the parent community, and helped to establish the West London Synagogue of British Jews, his considerable knowledge of Hebrew and Jewish literature proving of great value to the new movement.

Bibliography: *Jewish Chronicle*, Oct. 2, 1857; Jan. 4, 1901; *Leisure Hour*, July, 1886.

J. I. H.

MOCH, JULES: French officer; colonel of the 130th Regiment of Infantry; born at Sarrelouis Aug. 4, 1829; died at Paris Aug. 8, 1881. On completing his classical studies at the lycée of Metz, he entered the military school of Saint-Cyr (1849) and was appointed sublieutenant of infantry in 1851. Moch took part in the campaigns in the Crimea (1855–56) and in Syria (1860–61), and in the occupation of Rome (1863-67); in the Franco-Prussian war (1870–71) he was commander of the battalion of the 3d Regiment, which had the mournful distinction of firing the last shots of the war, and took an honorable part in the battle of Sedan (Sept., 1870). During the interval between the Crimean and Syrian campaigns he was tutor at the school of Saint-Cyr, to which he returned later on as examiner.

After the conclusion of the Franco-Prussian war Moch published in the military journals a number of articles on the reorganization of the army. He was one of the founders and also vice-president of the Assembly of Officers (known later on as the "Military Club"), whose official organ was "Le Bulletin" (now the "Revue du Cercle Militaire"). Moch was a chevalier of the Legion of Honor, officer of the Academy, commander of the Order of Charles III. of Spain and of Nisham-el-Istikhar (Tunis), and was decorated with the stars of the Order of Nisan-i-Medjidie and the Order of Pope Pius IX. Moch openly professed Judaism.

BIBLIOGRAPHY: Gaston Moch, *Sedan; les Derniers Coups de Feu*, Paris, 1885; Zadoc Kahn, *Souvenirs et Regrets*, pp. 121–125, Paris, 1898.

S. J. KA.

MOD'AI: Family of Turkish authors.

Ḥayyim Mod'ai (the Elder): Rabbinical author; born at Safed 1709; died there 1784. He was sent by the Safed community to Europe to collect ḥaluḳḳah. From 1755 to 1776 he lived at Constantinople, returning in his old age to Safed. He left a number of manuscripts, two of which have been published—"Ṭib Giṭṭin," a treatise on divorce (Jerusalem, n.d.), and "Sefer Ḥayyim le-'Olam," responsa, 2 vols. (Smyrna, 1785).

Ḥayyim Mod'ai (the Younger): Rabbinical author; grandson of Ḥayyim Mod'ai the Elder; lived at Smyrna in the middle of the nineteenth century. His "Sefer Memar Ḥayyim," responsa, was printed with his grandfather's "Sefer Ḥayyim le-'Olam" (Smyrna, 1879). He also edited Said Leon's "Yissad ha-Melek," homilies (*ib.* 1866).

Nissim Mod'ai: Printer; lived at Smyrna in the middle of the nineteenth century. He was in partnership with Jacob Ashkenazi. The "Ḳiryat Sefer" of Moses Cohen Na'ar is among the works printed by Mod'ai and Ashkenazi.

BIBLIOGRAPHY: Hazan, *Ha-Ma'alot li-Shelomoh*, pp. 31, 39, 90.

D. M. FR.

MODEL, MARX: Court Jew to Margrave William Frederick of Brandenburg-Ansbach (1703–1723). From 1691 Model and his family were exempt from the payment of duties on the goods which they imported, and in the same year were given the privilege of printing the Talmud. The margrave protected him by several decrees, and ordered the authorities to take the necessary measures to collect debts due to him "so that Model may surely be able to help us."

Model sometimes used his influence in favor of his coreligionists, but he was very domineering, especially as an elder of the community of Fürth. He threatened them with imprisonment and heavy fines if they should refuse to carry out his orders.

Like all court Jews, Model had to suffer much from the hatred and jealousy of his rivals. Elhanan Fränkel (see HANAU, ẒEBI HIRSCH) was one of his most dangerous and embittered enemies. Fränkel tried several times, especially in 1711, to turn the margrave against Model and to have the latter imprisoned on the charge of dishonesty; but the court Jew and his family kept their place at court, while Fränkel became involved in a serious charge and was ruined.

About 1716 Model was denounced for having participated in defrauding the public revenues. Although he was not convicted, his reputation became so much damaged by the long investigation that he and some of the family retired from court, and others emigrated into the county of Pfalz-Neuburg.

BIBLIOGRAPHY: Haenle, *Gesch. der Juden im Ehemaligen Fürstentum Ansbach*, passim.

D. A. FE.

MODENA: City in central Italy; formerly the capital of the duchy of Modena. Of its Jewish community, which has been, during the last few centuries, one of the most important in Italy, there is no record until a comparatively late date. Although Jews were living in the territory of Modena as early as the year 1000, no reference to them as dwelling in the city itself occurs before 1450. There, as in so many other places, they seem at first to have been bankers who established themselves in Modena with the approval of the dukes of Ferrara, and they were treated exactly like the other Jews in the duchy. On the extinction of the house of Ferrara in 1598, the duchy did not come under the control of the States of the Church, but of a collateral branch of the house of Este. The Jews of Modena did not suffer to the same extent, therefore, as their coreligionists elsewhere, although they were subject to all the hardships of the ecclesiastical laws.

The Jewish community increased considerably in the seventeenth century, when it occupied an important position because of its rabbis and of the studies which were pursued there. Prominent among its scholars of this period was Abraham Joseph Solomon GRAZIANO (d. 1685). Cabalistic thought predominated; and the community was one of the first to introduce the daily penitential services שומרים לבקר. The political status of the Jews remained uncertain, with the exception of a temporary improvement during the French Revolution; and the Jews were not emancipated until the city was incorporated with the kingdom of Italy in 1861. In 1845 Cesare Rovighi of Modena edited the first Italian Jewish periodical, the "Rivista Israelitica," which was published at Parma.

The following rabbis and scholars of Modena may be mentioned. Fifteenth century: Samuel of Modena, corresponded with Joseph Colon (Responsa, No. 128). Sixteenth century: Gershom b. Moses; Abraham b. Daniel Modena (1543), author of many liturgical prayers; Baruch Abraham da Spoleto b. R. Pethahiah (1584). Seventeenth century: Gershom b. Israel Chezigin, Menahem b. Elhanan Cases, Moses Israel Foà b. Vardama, Judah b. Jacob Poggetto, Abraham Rovigo b. Michael Raphael, Moses David Valle, Elijah Usili, Meshullam Levi, Naḥman b. Naḥman b. Joseph, Joseph Melli b. Joseph Israel,

David b. Elijah Ravenna, the above-named Abraham Joseph Solomon Graziano (1685), Aaron Berechiah Modena, Ephraim b. Elijah da Ostra, Abraham Jedidiah b. Menahem Samson Basilea. Eighteenth century: Judah Maẓliaḥ Padua (-1722), Manasseh Joshua Padua (1728), Ephraim Coen (1728), David Coen b. Abraham Isaac, Jacob Ḥayyim b. Reuben Yaḥya, Moses b. Levi, Abraham Ḥai b. Menahem Grassini, Abraham Vita Sinigaglia b. Solomon Jedidiah, Solomon Jedidiah, Abraham Vita II., Moses Elijah b. Solomon Jedidiah (d. 1849), Ishmael Coen b. Abraham Isaac, Ephraim b. Joseph Gallico. Nineteenth century: Elishama Meïr Padovani, Solomon Nissim, Solomon Teglio, Moses Ehrenreich, Solomon Jonah, Guiseppe Cammeo.

Since 1900 the monthly "L'Idea Sionista" has been published at Modena by Carlo Conigliani, professor of law in the university there. At present (1904) the Jews of the city number about 1,200 in a total population of 64,941.

BIBLIOGRAPHY: Ersch and Gruber, *Encyc.* section ii., part 27, p. 156, s.v. *Juden*; *R. E. J.* xx. 35 *et seq.*; Mortara, *Indice*, passim.

G. I. E.

MODENA: An Italian family the most distinguished members of which are:

Aaron Berechiah Modena. See AARON BERECHIAH BEN MOSES BEN NEHEMIAH OF MODENA.

David ben Abraham Modena: Supposed author of the anonymous Hebrew Italian school dictionary "Dabar Ṭob" (Venice, 1596, 1606), in three parallel columns in Hebrew, Italian, and German. The existence of the author and the book is, however, called in question.

BIBLIOGRAPHY: Fürst, *Bibl. Jud.* i. 198; Wolf, *Bibl. Hebr.* i. 288; Steinschneider, *Cat. Bodl.* col. 855.

David Zacuto b. Mazzal Ṭob Modena: Italian scholar of the nineteenth century; popular preacher and teacher at Modena. He wrote a number of didactic, religious, and casuistic works in Hebrew and Italian, including: (1) "Zeker Dawid," on customs of circumcision, two parts (Leghorn, n.d.); (2) Limmude Adonai," fundamental principles of religion for children, with Italian translation, three parts (Reggio, 1814, 1824); (3) responsa to the four Ṭurim; (4) commentary to the prayer-book and the Maḥzor according to the Italian ritual; (5) "Shelal Dawid," notes to the Pentateuch; and 300 sermons. Only the first three of these works have been printed.

BIBLIOGRAPHY: Nepi-Ghirondi, *Toledot Gedole Yisrael*, p. 78; Benjacob, *Oẓar ha-Sefarim*, passim.

Judah Aryeh Modena. See LEON (JUDAH ARYEH) OF MODENA.

Pomona Modena: Mother of Abraham b. Daniel, who wrote over 1,000 liturgical prayers between 1536 and 1552, in which he celebrated her as a pious woman. These prayers are contained in the Codex Bislichis 72. Pomona Modena was versed in the Talmud, and David of Imola addressed a detailed Talmudic responsum to her.

BIBLIOGRAPHY: Zunz, *Literaturgesch.* p. 535; Benjacob, *Oẓar ha-Sefarim*, p. 494; Kayserling, *Die Jüdischen Frauen*, p. 140.

G. I. E.

MODIANO, JOSEPH SAMUEL: Turkish rabbinical author; lived at Salonica at the end of the eighteenth century. He belonged to a family originally from Modena, Italy, the descendants of which are prominent in financial and industrial enterprise in Salonica. He corresponded with Ḥayyim ben David Abulafia, rabbi of Smyrna. Modiano published two works—"Uryan Telitai" (Salonica, 1795) and "Rosh Mashbir," responsa (2 vols., *ib.* 1821 and 1840). The former is a collection of novellæ on various Talmudic treatises by Naḥmani, Ibn Migash, Yom-Ṭob b. Abraham, R. Samuel Isaac of Salonica (18th cent.), and by Modiano himself. The latter work was published posthumously.

BIBLIOGRAPHY: Hazan, *Ha-Ma'alot li-Shelomoh*, p. 90; Azulai, *Shem ha-Gedolim*, s.v. *Uryan Telitai.*

D. M. FR.

MODIGLIANI, ELIA: Italian traveler, naturalist, and author; born at Florence June 13, 1861; graduated at Pavia in 1883. From early youth he showed a marked inclination for natural science and a special fondness for travel. He visited the Malay Peninsula and returned with a very rich collection of specimens, which he presented to the museums of Genoa, Florence, and Rome. Among his numerous published works may be mentioned his "Ricerche sulla Grotta di Bergeggi"; "L'Isola di Nias"; "Un Viaggio all' Isola di Nias," Milan and Treves, 1890; and "L'Isola delle Donna."

BIBLIOGRAPHY: De Gubernatis, *Diz. Biog.*

S. V. C.

MODIN (MODA'IM, MODI'IM, MODEÏN, MODI'IT). See MATTATHIAS MACCABEUS.

MODON, SIMSON HA-KOHEN: Poet; born in Mantua Aug. 1, 1679; died there June 10, 1727. He received a thorough education and was recognized as an accomplished linguist. He was one of those sent by the congregation in Mantua to do homage to Emperor Charles VI. at Vienna, where he acquitted himself most creditably and gained the emperor's good-will. Encouraged by David Finzi, rabbi of Mantua, he devoted himself to the writing of poetry; Finzi added some of his own poems to the collection "Ḳol Musar," published by Modon at Mantua in 1725 (Lemberg, 1845). Others of his poems are "Keter Torah" (Venice, 1721); "Ẓir ha-Ẓirim" (*ib.* 1722), an elegy on his teacher Judah Brill; and "Shigyon Shimshon." The last is a poem of three hundred lines, each commencing with the letter ש. He also compiled a rabbinical encyclopedia, arranged alphabetically, and called "Sefer Zikronot"; this and the "Shigyon Shimshon" are in manuscript.

BIBLIOGRAPHY: Steinschneider, *Cat. Bodl.* col. 2636; Fürst, *Bibl. Jud.* ii. 386; Samuel della Volta, in *Kerem Ḥemed*, ii. 113 *et seq.*; *Allg. Zeit. des Jud.* 1838, p. 216; Mortara, *Indice*, p. 41; Benjacob, *Oẓar ha-Sefarim*, p. 159, No. 185.

S. S. J. L.

MODONA, LEONELLO: Italian Orientalist; born at Cento in 1841; educated at the Istituto degli Studi Superiori of Florence. Besides compiling several library catalogues he has written: "L'Uomo e la Natura"; "La Safo Storica e il Mito di Safo e Faone"; "La Leggenda Cristiana del Mito della Caduta degli Angeli in Rapporto a Due Tavolette del Museo Britannico"; "Sara Copia Sullam"; "Di una Edizione del Sidur Tefilot."

BIBLIOGRAPHY: De Gubernatis, *Diz. Biog.*

S. V. C.

MO'ED ("Feasts"): Name of an order of the Mishnah and the Tosefta both in Babli and in Yerushalmi. The name "Mo'ed," which is mentioned in the Talmud itself (Suk. 4b), is applied to this order because all the treatises belonging to it contain regulations and rules regarding the Sabbath and the feast-days. It is the second order in the Mishnah (Shab. 31a), and is divided into twelve treatises containing altogether eighty-eight chapters. The following are the names of the treatises: Shabbat, 'Erubin, Pesaḥim, Sheḳalim, Yoma, Sukkah, Beẓah, Rosh ha-Shanah, Ta'anit, Megillah, Mo'ed Ḳaṭan, and Ḥagigah. On their contents and their sequence in the order Mo'ed, as well as on the single instance where the order is enumerated as the third in the Mishnah, see MISHNAH.

In the editions of Babli the Palestinian Gemara to Sheḳalim is printed together with that treatise, no Babylonian Gemara to it being now extant, and none, in all probability, having ever existed. The Palestinian Gemara is lacking to ch. xxi.-xxiv. of the treatise Shabbat.

BIBLIOGRAPHY: Frankel, *Hodegetica in Mischnam*, pp. 258-259, Leipsic, 1859.

S. J. Z. L.

MO'ED ḲAṬAN ("Smaller Festival"): Treatise in the Mishnah, in the Tosefta, and in the Babylonian and Jerusalem Talmuds. It deals principally with the regulations concerning the semi-feasts, or intermediary festivals, which are termed "mo'ed" and are the days between the first two and the last two days of the feasts of Passover and Sukkot. The treatise receives its name from this designation, with the addition of "Ḳaṭan" to distinguish it from the whole Seder Mo'ed (I. Derenbourg, in "R. E. J." xx. 136 *et seq.*). In the manuscript of the Mishnah edited by Lowe and in the "'Aruk" of Nathan ben Jehiel, Mo'ed Ḳaṭan is called "Mashkin" from its opening word, signifying "they water, give to drink." In the Mishnah of the Seder Mo'ed it is the eleventh treatise, and is divided into three chapters, which contain twenty-four paragraphs in all.

Contents.

Ch. i.: What agricultural work may be undertaken on the intermediary festivals (§§ 1-4). In connection with the rule that the irrigating ditches may be repaired if they are injured, it is stated that municipal water-works and canals, as well as public streets, may be put in good condition, and in general any labor necessary for the public welfare may be performed (§ 2b). The treatise contains also regulations for the avoidance of mourning on these days (§ 5); for digging graves and sepulchers and preparing coffins (§ 6); for marriage (§ 7); for sewing (all may sew as usual, except tailors, who must take irregular stitches; § 8); for erecting an oven and a hand-mill (§ 9); for constructing balustrades; and for making repairs (§ 10).

Ch. ii.: Rules for pressing olives or wine and garnering fruit (§§ 1-3), for purchasing houses, slaves, and cattle (§ 4), and for selling fruits, clothes, and utensils (§ 5).

Ch. iii.: Enumeration of the occasions upon which a man may cut his hair and wash his clothes during the intermediary festivals (§§ 1-2); what one may write during these days (documents of all kinds), and what may not be written (*e.g.*, promissory notes, books, etc.; §§ 3-4). The feast-days interrupt a period of mourning and end it altogether; but if the mourning has not yet begun, they are not reckoned as part of it, while the Sabbath, on the contrary, is included in the period of mourning and does not terminate it (§ 5). Enumeration of the feasts which resemble the Sabbath in this respect (§ 6), and the mourning ceremonies observed in the intermediary festivals; with a description of how the women are to sing the dirges on these days (§§ 7-8) and, in connection with this, how the dirges are to be sung at the New Moon, on Ḥanukkah, and on Purim (§ 9).

Tosefta and Gemaras.

The Mishnah to this treatise, like its Tosefta, which is divided into two chapters, contains much important matter relating to Jewish social life, such as information regarding furniture and tools, housework and agriculture, public institutions, and mourning customs.

The Gemaras of both Talmuds explain the several mishnayot. In the first chapter the Babylonian Gemara contains also a number of tales, proverbs, and benedictions, which give examples of the picturesque style of the Rabbis. In the third chapter, besides the explanations of the individual mishnayot, the Babylonian Gemara contains detailed regulations concerning the different forms of the BAN and its removal (pp. 15a-17b), as well as narratives of remarkable incidents which took place when certain teachers died or were buried (p. 25a, b), and legends concerning the manner in which death overtook them (p. 28a). Here are also found interesting specimens of dirges and funeral orations delivered in Hebrew and showing traces of paronomasia and rime (p. 25b), besides Raba's citation of examples of wailing songs sung by the hired mourning-women in the vernacular at Shekanẓib (p. 28b).

Especial mention should be made of the enumeration of modifications which had taken place in the course of time in many of the usages connected with mourning and burial (p. 27a, b). All these changes were made for the sake of the poor, who could not afford the luxury of the old customs. The sums expended in the preparation of the body were so large that the relatives often left the corpse unburied because they could not meet the enormous outlay. It was not until after Rabban Gamaliel had been buried in simple linen garments that this custom became general. At a later period simplicity was carried still further, and the cheapest coverings were used for the burial of the dead (p. 27b).

S. S. J. Z. L.

MOGADOR (or **SUERAH**): Seaport of Morocco, on the Atlantic; founded by Sidi Mohammed ibn Abdallah in 1759. It has a total population of 29,000, including 10,000 Jews. Mogador is divided into three parts: the Ḳaṣbah, where the governor, some Mohammedans, the European officials, and a number of Jewish merchants reside; the Medinah, or city, of the Moors; and the Mellah, or Jewish quarter, which has two fortified gates. The Medinah contains the old Jewish quarter, called "Al-Mellaḥ al-Ḳadim" (the old Mellah). In 1807 the governor, Ibn 'Abd al-Ṣaddiḳ, found it necessary for the security of the Jews to found the present Mellah. The condition of the Jews has always been better in Mogador than in many other parts of the empire, as the sultans—especially those of the Sherifian dynasty—in many instances favored them. An exception, however, was made in this respect by the sultan Muley Yazid, who in order to convert ten Jews of Mogador tortured them for ten days by repeatedly hanging them head downward in a dry cistern and bastinadoing them. When the news of the death of Muley Yazid came, some of them had expired and one had embraced Islam; the rest were set free.

The Sherifs encouraged the commerce of the Jews in every possible way by granting them privileges and loans; this condition lasted until the end of the government of Muley al-Ḥassan, when the European merchants began to give protection to their Moroccan agents. When the French navy, in 1846, bombarded Mogador, the Arab tribes of the neighborhood suddenly attacked the city and pillaged the houses of Jews and Mohammedans, dishonoring the women, and killing many of the inhabitants. Those who could escape fled as far as the city of Morocco in order to find a shelter. When peace was restored, they returned to Mogador in a condition of abject poverty. In 1860, again, when Spanish war-ships were sent to Morocco, the Jews left the city and fled to the southern province of Haha, where they were protected by the governor. The mission of Sir Moses Montefiore to Morocco brought about a better state of affairs for the Jews of Mogador and resulted in the abolition of the bastinado. The condition of the Jews of Mogador to-day, however, is still far from being secure.

The commerce of the city, mostly with England, France, and Germany, lies chiefly in the hands of the Jews, so that the Mohammedans are compelled to suspend business on the Jewish Sabbaths and holy days. Religious matters and also civil cases are decided by a board of three rabbis, and Jewish congregational affairs by a committee of seven members of the community, chosen annually. The Mellah is represented in civic and political affairs by a sheik, who is installed by the government and is responsible to it for the regular payment of the Jewish tax, which amounts to 250 "doros." The expenses of the Jewish community, including the salaries of the rabbis and charity for the poor, are met by a meat-tax, a tax on imported and exported merchandise, and by donations from a French and an English shipping company by whose ships the Jews have agreed to export their merchandise. The community has a bet ha-midrash, a French and an English school for boys (founded respectively in 1862 and 1864), and two English schools for girls, one, founded in 1887, being supported by the Anglo-Jewish Association, the other being a private school.

Since its foundation the community has had the following rabbis: Yaḥya, from Agadir; Jacob Bibaz, from Rabat; Abraham Coriat, author of "Sefer Zekut Abot" (went to Leghorn in 1793); Ḥayyim Pinto (d. 1846); David ibn al-Ḥazzan (d. 1828); Joseph ben Jacob Almaliḥ, called Joseph al-Kabir (d. Jerusalem 1837); Abraham Coriat II., author of "Sefer Berit Abot"; Joseph ben Aaron ALMALIḤ; Abraham ibn 'Aṭṭar (d. 1882); Moses Cohen (emigrated to the city of Morocco); and Abraham Sabah (d. 1903). The present (1904) rabbis of Mogador are Judah ben Maniel, Mas'ud Knafo, and Joseph ibn 'Aṭṭar.

D. M. KN.

MOGHILEF (MOHILEV): 1. Capital of the government of the same name in White Russia; situated on the Dnieper. Though the city was well known as an important trading center as early as the fourteenth century, the first mention of Jews there occurs in a document dated 1522, wherein King Sigismund awards a lease, for a period of three years, of the various taxes of Moghilef to MICHAEL JESOFOVICH, the noted merchant of Brest. This lease was renewed three years later, and subsequently taken up by the Jesofovich family and other Jewish merchants, as appears from a number of documents. Toward the end of the sixteenth century Jews had probably settled in Moghilef in considerable numbers, although there are no documents extant to show that they had a well-organized community at that time. In 1583 AFFRAS RACHMAELOVICH, a prominent Jewish merchant of Moghilef, carried on an import and export trade with Riga and Lublin. The presence of a considerable number of Jews in Moghilef at the end of the sixteenth century is attested also by the petition, dated March 5, 1585, of the burghers of the city to King Stephen Bathori praying that Jews might be prohibited from settling in Moghilef, since they would be a serious menace to the prosperity of the Christian merchants. The king promised to grant the request of the burghers; but in spite of this the agents of the Jewish tax-farmers continued their business in Moghilef, as is shown by certain lawsuits brought by them in 1589 against some Christian merchants for selling spirituous liquors without a license. In a document dated Jan. 31, 1597, a Jew, Avram Rubinovich, is mentioned as residing on Pokrovsky street. A Jewish community seems to have existed in Moghilef for some time prior to 1621, in which year the local gild of butchers passed resolutions making it illegal for Christian as well as Jewish members of the gild to buy cattle outside of the city, and requiring Christian butchers who wished to sell kasher meat to do business in certain places where the Jewish butchers were established. In the following year the municipal council of Moghilef borrowed from the Jew Gabriel Samuelovich and his wife, Rukhana Itzkhakovna, 100 Lithuanian kop groschen for a term of ten years, and as security gave to Gabriel a house belonging to the city, situated on Nikolski street.

Community in 1621.

The growing antagonism on the part of the Christian merchants, provoked by the competition of the Jews, caused the former to make repeated complaints to the king, and finally led to the promulgation of an edict (July 23, 1626) by Sigismund III., whereby all Jews owning houses on the market-place were ordered to remove to the street on which their prayer-house was situated, "in order to prevent the conflicts due to the residence of Jews and Christians on the same streets." Equivalent areas were assigned to the Jews on the Jewish street. This edict was confirmed by Ladislaus IV. (March 8, 1633), who also prohibited the Jews from building baths and breweries within the city limits. This and other documents show that the populace was being incited against the Jews by the burghers and the clergy. In 1639 the burghers reported to the city council that a Christian servant who had been employed for ten years by the Jewess Lyuba Josefova, had died under suspicious circumstances and that the Jews had buried her without giving notice of the funeral to her relatives. The investigation revealed that the deceased had been drinking heavily in the monastery and had fallen unconscious in the street near the house; that Lyuba with the aid of the servant's sister had carried her into the house, where she died soon after; and that the son of the deceased, accompanied by other relatives, had buried her, a fact corroborated by numerous witnesses. Other unfounded accusations were repeatedly made against the Jews of Moghilef, especially as to their responsibility for the frequent conflagrations occurring in the city.

Conflicts with Citizens.

The enmity toward the Jews found expression in a riot which occurred on the Jewish New-Year's Day, Sept. 21, 1645. Led by the burgomaster, Roman Rebrovich, an armed mob attacked the Jews, who had gone to the River Dnieper for the observance of the religious custom of "Tashlik"; the mob wounded men and women, robbed them of their jewelry, and attempted to throw them into the river. The case was carried to Prince Radziwil, the chief marshal of the duchy of Lithuania, whose influence enabled the burgomaster to escape punishment. This incident, one of many, throws light on the popular attitude toward the Jews a few years before the uprising under Chmielnicki. The Jews of Moghilef apparently escaped the first fury of Chmielnicki's Cossacks in 1648; and they benefited in the following year by the renewal of the charter of privileges granted to many Lithuanian communities by King John Casimir (Feb. 17).

Synagogue at Moghilef, Russia.
(After a photograph.)

The security of the Moghilef community was, however, of short duration. In 1654 the city was annexed to Russia, and by order of the czar Aleksei Mikhailovich in response to a petition of the Moghilef burghers the Jews were commanded to leave (Sept. 15, 1654). In spite of this order they remained in Moghilef (probably as the result of bribery of the local officials), but they paid dearly for so doing. In 1655 most of them were massacred by the Russian soldiers outside of the city walls, where the Jews had assembled by order of the Russian commander Poklonski (see Jew. Encyc. iv. 286b, *s.v.* Cossacks' Uprising). The only Jews spared were those who had not yet left the city, and who, fearing a similar fate, had declared their readiness to accept baptism. The Father Superior Orest, commenting on this incident in his memoirs, laments the fact that after the war, when the danger to the Jews had passed, most of the converts returned to Judaism, only a tenth part of them remaining Christians.

Expelled 1654.

In 1656 Moghilef was again under Polish rule; and the old charter of privileges was renewed by King John III. In the memoirs of Orest, referred to above, mention is made also of Shabbethai Ẓebi (whom Orest calls "Sapsai Gershonovich").

The first rabbi of Moghilef and of "the Russian province" of whom record is preserved in Jewish documents, was Mordecai Süsskind Ruttenburg, who was living in Moghilef in 1686, as appears from his responsa (i. 44b; Amsterdam, 1746). He was probably among the first (if not the first) of the rabbis of the Moghilef community after permission was given the Jews in 1678 to reside anywhere in the city. For the next century the Jews of Moghilef remained secure under the protection of the Polish crown, with the exception of the period covered by the Swedish war, when Moghilef was for a time on the battle-ground between the Swedes and the Russians. Orest describes in his memoirs the entry of Peter the Great into Moghilef, when the Jewish inhabitants together with the rest came to welcome him, and presented him with a live sturgeon.

With the partition of Poland in 1772 Moghilef became a part of the Russian empire. Catherine II. visited the city in 1780 and was received by the Jews with expressions of joy. They decorated the public square with flowers and erected an arch bearing the inscription "We rejoice as in the days of King Solomon." They also engaged a band of music to play in the daytime and in the evening. During the successive reigns of Catherine, Paul, and Alexander the prosperity of the community increased. The Jewish merchants of Moghilef

Under Russian Rule.

were especially prominent as traders in timber, hemp, and grain, which were sold in Riga, where a number of Jews of Moghilef settled later. Important commercial relations were maintained also by way of the Dnieper with Kiev and Kherson. Toward the middle of the nineteenth century and later the Jewish merchants of Moghilef became prominent also as government contractors, and carried on an extensive trade with Moscow.

In 1897 the Jews of Moghilef numbered 19,398 in a total population of 43,106. The city had two synagogues and about forty houses of prayer; thirty-five ḥadarim and three yeshibot; a Jewish hospital and a number of dispensaries; Jewish elementary schools for boys and girls; a Talmud Torah; and the usual Jewish charitable organizations. By far the greater portion of the Jews of Moghilef are artisans earning scanty wages. Since the construction of the railroad, which did not touch Moghilef, the prosperity of the city has declined.

BIBLIOGRAPHY: *Regesty*, vol. i., *s.v.*; *Russko Yevreiski Arkhiv*, i., *s.v.*; Levontin, in *Keneset Yisrael*, i. 794; Mstislavski, in *Voskhod*, 1886, ix. and x.

H. R. J. G. L.

2. City in the government of Podolia, Russia; situated on the Dniester; it has a population of 22,093, of whom 14,000 are Jews. The latter include 3,306 artisans and 131 day-laborers; 61 are employed in the shops and factories. The Jewish children are taught in fifty-eight ḥadarim (700 pupils), in the Jewish school with its industrial department (140), in a private school for girls (68), and in the city school (130, the total being 320). Among the charitable institutions is a hospital. In 1897 there was founded a loan association which lends small sums of money without interest to petty traders and artisans. A society for aiding the poor, founded in 1899, gives special attention to supplying artisans with proper tools and to aiding them to dispose of their wares. Poverty is steadily increasing, leading to increased emigration. During the war between the Russians and the Poles many Jews of Moghilef were killed by the Cossacks and the Russian troops (1664).

BIBLIOGRAPHY: *Sion*, 1861, No. 30; *Voskhod*, 1898, No. 2; 1899, Nos. 7 and 56; 1900, No. 54; 1901, Nos. 58 and 68; *Regesty i Nadpisi*, vol. i., No. 1021, St. Petersburg, 1899.

H. R. S. J.

INTERIOR OF A SYNAGOGUE AT MOGHILEF, RUSSIA.
(After a photograph.)

MOGHRABI (MAGHRABI), JOSEPH AL-. See JOSEPH BEN JUDAH IBN 'AḲNIN.

MOGULESKO, SIGMUND (SELIG): American comedian; born in Kalorausk, Bessarabia, Dec. 16, 1858; now residing in New York. He possessed a fine voice from early youth, and was the favorite "meshorer" or choir-singer with several well-known ḥazzanim. He went to Bucharest, Rumania, while very young, and for some years studied there at the Conservatory of Music. He joined GOLDFADEN soon after the organization of the Yiddish theater, and since that time has been recognized as the best comedian on the Yiddish stage. He traveled with various companies over Russia, Austria, Rumania, and England. He went to the United

States about the year 1886, since when, except for an interruption of three years through illness, he has followed his profession to the present time (1904). He is known also as a leading composer of music for the Yiddish stage.

BIBLIOGRAPHY: Hapgood, *Spirit of the Ghetto*, pp. 138, 150 *et seq.*, New York, 1902; Seifert, *Die Yiddische Bühne*, vol. ii. (*Geschichte von Yiddischen Theater*), New York, 1897.

S. P. Wi.

MOHAMMED: Founder of Islam and of the Mohammedan empire; born at Mecca between 569 and 571 of the common era; died June, 632, at Medina. Mohammed was a posthumous child and lost his mother when he was six years old. He then came under the guardianship of his grandfather 'Abd al-Muṭṭalib, who at his death, two years later, left the boy to the care of his son Abu Ṭalib, Mohammed's uncle. The early years of Mohammed's life were spent among the Banu Sa'd, Bedouins of the desert, it being the custom at Mecca to send a child away from home to be nursed. From the stories told of these early years it would appear that even then he showed symptoms of epilepsy which greatly alarmed his nurse. It has been stated that the boy was once taken on a caravan journey to Syria, and that he there came in contact with Jews and Christians. But he could very easily have become acquainted with both at Mecca; hence this theory is not necessary to explain his knowledge of Jewish and Christian beliefs. When Mohammed was twenty-five years old Abu Ṭalib obtained for him an opportunity to travel with a caravan in the service of Ḥadijah, a wealthy widow of the Ḳuraish, who offered Mohammed her hand on his return from the expedition. Six children were the fruit of this union, the four daughters surviving their father. Ḥadijah, although fifteen years his senior, was, as long as she lived, Mohammed's faithful friend and sympathizer.

Early Years.

G. M. W. M.

Mohammed's religious activity began with the fortieth year of his life. The Islamic tradition assigns as the beginning of this new career a sudden marvelous illumination through God. The Koran, however, the most authentic document of Islam, whose beginnings are probably contemporaneous with Mohammed's first sermons, speaks of this revelation on the "fateful night" rather vaguely in a passage of the later Meccan period, while the earlier passages give the impression that Mohammed himself had somewhat hazy ideas on the first stages of the revelation which culminated in his occasional intercourse with God, through the mediation of various spiritual beings. Small wonder that his pagan countrymen took him to be a "kahin," *i.e.*, one of those Arab soothsayers who, claiming higher inspiration, uttered rimed oracles similar to those found in the earliest suras. Historical investigations, however, show that Mohammed must not be classed with those pagan seers, but with a sect of monotheistic visionaries of whose probable existence in southern Arabia, on the borderland between Judaism and Christianity, some notice has come down in the fragment of an inscription recently published in "W. Z. K. M." (1896, pp. 285 *et seq.*). This fragment ascribes to God the attribute of vouchsafing "revelation" (?) and "glad tidings" ("bashr," *i.e.*, "gospel" or "gift of preaching"), meaning probably the occasional visionary illumination of the believer. As the same inscription contains other religious concepts and expressions which parallel those in the Koran, Mohammed may well be associated with this religious tendency. The name of this South-Arabian sect is not known; but the "Ḥanifs" of the Islamic tradition belonged probably to them, being a body of monotheistic ascetics who lived according to the "religion of Abraham" and who bitterly inveighed against the immoral practises of paganism.

South-Arabian Visionaries.

Islam in its earliest form certainly did not go far beyond the tenets of these men. Mohammed condemns idolatry by emphasizing the existence of a single powerful God, who has created and who maintains heaven and earth: but he condemns still more emphatically the vices born of idolatry, namely, covetousness, greed, and injustice to one's neighbor; and he recommends prayer and the giving of alms as a means of purifying the spirit and of being justified at the divine judgment. This gospel includes nothing that was not contained in Judaism or in Christianity, nor anything of what constituted the fundamental difference between the two. Islam, however, did not undertake to bridge the gulf between them. Mohammed's teaching, on the contrary, was at first expressly directed against the Arab pagans only; and even in the later Meccan period it refers to its consonance with the doctrines of the "men of the revelation," *i.e.*, Jews and Christians. Nothing is more erroneous than to assume that the watchword of the later Islam, "There is no God but Allah, and Mohammed is His prophet," was characteristic of the very beginning of the religious movement inaugurated by Mohammed: not the belief in dogmas, but the recognition of ethical obligations, was the object of his mission to his countrymen. That meant that the Arab prophet strove to gain in every believer an ally to help him to wage war upon the corruptions of the day. Mohammed's political astuteness, which was a signal characteristic of his Medina period, is apparent even in the organization of the first community. Its members were mostly poor but intellectually eminent Ḳuraish like Ali, Abu Bakr, Zubair, 'Abd al-Raḥman ibn 'Auf, Sa'd ibn Abi Waḳḳaṣ, Othman, and others. They, being in the execution of their religious duties under Mohammed's personal supervision, soon grew to be so dependent upon him that their tribal consciousness—the strongest instinct in the social life of the ancient Arabs—was gradually superseded by the consciousness of being Moslems, the community thus developing into a small state with Mohammed as its chief. Hence in time sharp conflicts arose between the powerful Meccans, the sheiks of the leading families, and Mohammed. For years they had suffered him as a harmless dreamer, a soothsayer, a magician, and even as one possessed of demons; then, when his prediction in regard to the imminent judgment of God remained unfulfilled, they had mocked him; but when the community grew—even

The First Moslems.

eminent personages like Ḥamzah swearing by Islam—they grew hostile and began to persecute him and his adherents, their action culminating in the ostracism of Mohammed's family, the Banu Hashim. Restricted in his missionary activity, and separated from a large part of the faithful who had sought refuge in Christian Abyssinia, the prophet lost heart. His preaching, in so far as its nature can be gathered from the Koran, was filled with references to the persecutions to which the earlier messengers of God had been subjected, and to their final rescue by Him; and it emphasized "raḥmah"—*i.e.*, mercy shown to the good, and long-suffering to the wicked—as being God's chief attribute. Various dogmatic-theosophic discussions were added, among them being the first protests against the Christian doctrine of the son of God. The teachings of Islam, which at first had been merely a body of precepts, developed more and more into a regular system which reflected in its chief tenets the later Judaism.

When the leading families of Mecca revoked the ban pronounced against the Banu Hashim, which had been maintained for nearly three years, they might well have believed that Mohammed's political importance at Mecca was destroyed. The prophet himself perceived, especially after the death of his protector Abu Ṭalib and of his (Mohammed's) wife Ḥadijah, that his native city was not the proper place in which to carry out his communal ideas; and he cast about for a locality better adapted to his purposes. After various unsuccessful attempts to find a following among neighboring tribes, he happened to meet, during the annual festival of the temple at Mecca, six people from Yathrib (Medina); the Arab inhabitants of this city had come into close contact with monotheistic ideas through their long sojourn among the Jewish tribes which had been the original masters of the city, as well as with several Christian families. These men, being related to Mohammed on his mother's side, took up the cause of the prophet, and were so active in its behalf among their people that after two years seventy-five believers of Medina went to Mecca during the festival and proclaimed in the so-called "'aḳabah," or war assembly, the official reception of Mohammed and his adherents at Mecca into the community of Yathrib. The consequence was that within a short time all the Moslems removed to Medina; and the prophet himself, as the last one, closed the first period of Islam by his hasty departure, as in flight ("Hegira"; Sept., 622).

The Hegira (622).

Mohammed's entry into Medina marks the beginning of an almost continuous external development of Islam, which as a religion, it is true, lost in depth and moral content, and crystallized into dogmatic formulas, but as a political entity achieved increasing success through the eminent political ability of the prophet himself. The Arab inhabitants of Medina, the tribes of Aus and Khazraj, all joined the religion of the prophet within two years from the Hegira. Political differences, however, arose between them, especially after Mohammed had reserved for himself exclusively the office of judge; and these differences led to the formation of a moderate party of opposition, the Munafij, or weak believers, who often, and without detriment to his cause, restrained the prophet's impetuosity. But the propaganda came to a halt among the numerous Jews living in the city and the surrounding country, who were partly under the protection of the ruling Arab tribes, the Banu 'Auf, Al-Ḥarith, Al-Najjar, Sa'idah, Jusham, Al-Aus, Tha'labah, and partly belonged to such large and powerful Jewish tribes as the Banu Ḳuraiẓa, Al-Naḍir, Ḳainuḳa'. In the first year of the Hegira Mohammed was apparently on friendly terms with them, not yet recognizing their religion to be different from his; indeed, they were included in a treaty which he made with the inhabitants of Medina shortly after his arrival among them. The prophet and his adherents borrowed from these Jews many ritual customs, as, for instance, the regularity and formality of public prayers, fasting—which later on, following the Christian example, was extended to a whole month—the more important of the dietary laws, and the "ḳiblah" (direction in which one turns during prayer) toward Jerusalem, which was subsequently changed to the ḳiblah toward Mecca. But the longer Mohammed studied the Jews the more clearly he perceived that there were irreconcilable differences between their religion and his, especially when the belief in his prophetic mission became the criterion of a true Moslem.

The Jews, on their side, could not let pass unchallenged the way in which the Koran appropriated Biblical accounts and personages; for instance, its making Abraham an Arab and the founder of the Ka'bah at Mecca. The prophet, who looked upon every evident correction of his gospel as an attack upon his own reputation, brooked no contradiction, and unhesitatingly threw down the gauntlet to the Jews. Numerous passages in the Koran show how he gradually went from slight thrusts to malicious vituperations and brutal attacks on the customs and beliefs of the Jews. When they justified themselves by referring to the Bible, Mohammed, who had taken nothing therefrom at first hand, accused them of intentionally concealing its true meaning or of entirely misunderstanding it, and taunted them with being "asses who carry books" (sura lxii. 5). The increasing bitterness of this vituperation, which was similarly directed against the less numerous Christians of Medina, indicated that in time Mohammed would not hesitate to proceed to actual hostilities. The outbreak of the latter was deferred by the fact that the hatred of the prophet was turned more forcibly in another direction, namely, against the people of Mecca, whose earlier refusal of Islam and whose attitude toward the community appeared to him at Medina as a personal insult which constituted a sufficient cause for war. The Koran, in order to lead its adherents to the belief that side by side with the humane precepts of religion were others commanding religious war ("jihad"), even to the extent of destroying human life, had to incorporate a number of passages enjoining with increasing emphasis the faithful to take up the sword for their faith. The earlier of these passages enunciated only the right of defensive action, but later ones emphasized the duty of taking the offen-

Relation to Jews.

sive against unbelievers—*i.e.*, in the first place, the people of Mecca—until they should accept the new faith or be annihilated. The prophet's policy, steadily pursuing one object, and hesitating at no means to achieve it, soon actualized this new doctrine.

G. H. G.

Mohammed's first attacks upon the Meccans were of a predatory nature, made upon the caravans, which, as all classes had a financial interest in them, were the very life of the city. The early expeditions were of comparatively little importance; and the battle of Badr in the second year of the Hegira was the first encounter of really great moment. In this battle the Moslems were successful and killed nearly fifty of the Ḳuraish, besides taking prisoners. This battle was of supreme importance in the history of Islam. The prophet had preached the doctrine that war against the unbelievers was a religious duty; and now he could claim that God was on his side. His power was consolidated; the faith of the wavering was strengthened; and his opponents were terrified. The die was cast; Islam was to be a religion of conquest with the sword. After the battle of Badr, Mohammed dared to manifest his hostility to the Jews openly. A Jewess, named Asma, who had written satirical verses on the battle of Badr, was assassinated, by command of Mohammed, as she lay in bed with her child at the breast. The murderer was publicly commended the next day by the prophet. A few weeks later Abu 'Afak, a Jewish poet whose verses had similarly offended, was likewise murdered. It is said that Mohammed had expressed a desire to be rid of him. These were single instances. The prophet soon found a pretext for attacking in a body the Banu Ḳainuḳa', one of the three influential Jewish tribes at Medina. They were besieged in their stronghold for fifteen days, and finally surrendered. Mohammed was prevented from putting them all to death only by the insistent pleading in their behalf of Abdallah b. Ubai, the influential leader of the opposition whom Mohammed did not dare offend. Instead, the whole tribe was banished, and its goods were confiscated. The prophet was thus enabled to give material benefits to his followers.

First Raids.

Medina now enjoyed a few months of comparative quiet, disturbed only by a few unimportant marauding expeditions. The third year of the Hegira was marked by the assassination of a third Jewish poet, Ka'b b. al-Ashraf, who by his verses had stirred up the Ḳuraish at Mecca against Mohammed. The prophet prayed to be delivered from him; and there was no lack of men eager to execute his wishes. The circumstances attending the murder were particularly revolting. At about the same time a Jewish merchant, Abu Sanina by name, was murdered, and the Jews complained to Mohammed of such treacherous dealing. A new treaty was concluded with them, which, however, did not greatly allay their fears. Some months after these events (Jan., 625) occurred the battle of Uḥud, in which the Meccans took revenge for their defeat at Badr. Seventy-four Moslems were killed in the fight; Mohammed himself was badly wounded; and the prophet's prestige was seriously affected. The Jews were especially jubilant, declaring that if he had claimed Badr to be a mark of divine favor, Uḥud, by the same process of reasoning, must be a proof of disfavor. Various answers to these doubts and arguments may be found in the Koran, sura iii.

Death to Jewish Poets.

Mohammed now needed some opportunity to recover his prestige and to make up for the disappointment of Uḥud. He found it the next year in an attack upon the Banu al-Naḍir, another of the influential Jewish tribes in the vicinity of Medina. A pretext was easily invented. Mohammed had visited the settlement of the tribe to discuss the amount of blood-money to be paid for the murder of two men by an ally of the Jews, when he suddenly left the gathering and went home. He is said by some to have declared that the angel Gabriel had revealed to him a plot of the Banu al-Naḍir to kill him as he sat among them. The latter were immediately informed that they must leave the vicinity. They refused to obey; and Mohammed attacked their stronghold. After a siege lasting more than a fortnight, and after their date-trees had been cut down—contrary to Arabian ethics of war—the Jewish tribe surrendered and was allowed to emigrate with all its possessions, on condition of leaving its arms behind (Sprenger, "Das Leben des Moḥammad," iii. 162; "Allg. Zeit. des Jud." pp. 58, 92). The rich lands thus left vacant were distributed among the refugees who had fled with Mohammed from Mecca and who had hitherto been more or less of a burden on the hospitality of the people of Medina. The prophet was thus able both to satisfy his hatred against the Jews and materially to strengthen his position.

Attacks the Banu al-Naḍir.

In the fifth year of the Hegira the Banu Ḳuraiẓa, the last Jewish tribe remaining in the neighborhood of Medina, were disposed of. Again the direct cause for attack was a matter of policy. The Ḳuraish of Mecca, whose caravans were constantly being harassed by the Moslems and by other disaffected tribes including the Jews, had formed the project of uniting their forces against Mohammed. The leader of this enterprise was the able and vigorous Abu Sufyan of Mecca. The allies encamped before Medina and engaged in what is known as "the battle of the trenches," so called from the manner in which Medina was protected from attack. The Moslems succeeded in keeping the Banu Ḳuraiẓa out of the fight by making them and the allies mutually suspicious, and the allies finally withdrew without having accomplished their purpose. The Moslems also were disappointed in having no plunder, so that Mohammed felt called upon to provide a diversion. The allies had scarcely departed, the Moslems had not yet laid down their arms, when the prophet claimed to have received a communication from Gabriel bidding him march instantly against the Banu Ḳuraiẓa. The last-named, who had no time to prepare for a long siege, retired to their castles, and surrendered after two weeks, trusting to escape as their kinsmen of the Banu Ḳainuḳa' and the Banu al-Naḍir had done. Their fate was left to the decision of Sa'ad b. Mu'adh, who, although of the tribe of Aus, the allies of the Ḳuraiẓa, felt bitter toward them on account of their supposed treachery toward the Moslems. He decided that all the men should be killed, the women and children sold as slaves, and the property divided among the army. The carnage began the next morning, and between 600 and 700 victims were beheaded beside the trenches in which they were to be buried. Mohammed refers to the siege of Medina and the massacre of the Jews in sura xxxiii.

Destroys the Banu Ḳuraiẓa.

There were now no more Jews in the vicinity of Medina, but those at Khaibar continued to annoy the prophet. Abu al-Ḥuḳaiḳ of the Banu al-Naḍir, who had settled at Khaibar, was suspected of inciting the Bedouins to plunder the Moslems. Accordingly five men of the Banu Khazraj were sent secretly and murdered him. Usair, who succeeded him as chief of Khaibar, was likewise assassinated at Mohammed's command. In the sixth year of the Hegira Mohammed made a treaty with the Ḳuraish, at Ḥudaibiyah, whither he had proceeded with some of his followers with the intention of making the pilgrimage to Mecca. The Ḳuraish objected to his entering the city, and this treaty was made instead. It provided for a cessation of hostilities for ten years. In the same year Mohammed sent embassies to the rulers of the six surrounding states inviting them to embrace Islam, but the King of Abyssinia was the only one who sent a favorable reply. In the next year the prophet attacked the Jews of Khaibar in order to reward with the rich plunder of that place the followers who had accompanied him to Ḥudaibiyah. The Jews were conquered after a brave resistance, and their leader, Kinanah, was killed. Mohammed married the chief's young wife on the battle-field; and a very rich booty fell into the hands of the Moslems. Some Jews were still left at Khaibar, but merely as tillers of the soil, and on condition of giving up one-half the produce. They remained until Omar banished all Jews from the country. The Jews of the Wadi al-Ḳura, of Fadak, and of Taima were still left; but they surrendered before the end of the year. An attempt on the life of Mohammed was made at Khaibar by a Jewish woman named Zainab, who, in revenge for the death of her male relatives in battle, put poison in a dish prepared by her for the prophet. One of Mohammed's followers who partook of the food died almost immediately afterward; but the prophet, who had eaten more sparingly, escaped. He, however, complained of the effects of the poison to the end of his life.

Attacks Jews of Khaibar.

During the twenty-five years of his union with Ḥadijah Mohammed had no other wife; but scarcely two months had elapsed after her death (619) when he married Sauda, the widow of Sakran, who, with her husband, had become an early convert to Islam and who was one of the emigrants to Abyssinia. At about the same time Mohammed contracted an engagement with 'A'ishah, the six-year-old daughter of Abu Bakr, and married her shortly after his arrival at Medina. 'A'ishah was the only one of his wives who had not been previously married; and she remained his favorite to the end. After his death she exercised great influence over the Moslems. In his married life, as well as in his religious life, a change seems to have come over Mohammed after his removal to Medina. In the space of ten years he took twelve or thirteen wives and had several concubines: even the faithful were scandalized, and the prophet had to resort to alleged special revelations from God to justify his conduct. Such was the case when he wished to marry Zainab, the wife of his adopted son Zaid. Two of his wives were Jewesses: one was the beautiful Riḥanah of the Banu Ḳuraiẓa, whom he married immediately after the massacre of her husband and other relatives; the other was Safya, the wife of Kinanah, whom, as stated above, Mohammed married on the battle-field of Khaibar. None of these wives bore him any children. Mohammed built little huts for his wives adjoining the mosque at Medina, each wife having her own apartment. At his death there were nine of these apartments, corresponding to the number of his wives living at that time. Mohammed's daughter Faṭimah, by Ḥadijah, married Ali and became the mother of Ḥasan and Ḥusain.

His Domestic Life.

The last three years of Mohammed's life were marked by a steady increase of power. In the eighth year of the Hegira (630) he entered the city of Mecca as a conqueror, showing great forbearance toward his old enemies. This event decided his eventual supremacy over the whole of Arabia. Other conquests extended his authority to the Syrian frontier and as far south as Ṭa'if; and in the following years embassies poured in from the different parts of the peninsula bringing the submission of the various tribes. Mohammed's death occurred in the eleventh year of the Hegira, after he had been ill with a fever for over a week. He was buried where he died, in the apartment of 'A'ishah; and the spot is now a place of pilgrimage.

BIBLIOGRAPHY: Grimme, *Mohammed*; M. Hartmann, in *Allg. Zeit. des Jud.* lviii. 66-68, 79-80, 89-92, 102-104; Ibn Hisham, *Das Leben Mohammeds*, ed. Wüstenfeld, Göttingen, 1858; W. Muir, *The Life of Mahomet*, London, 1877; A. Sprenger, *Das Leben und die Lehre des Mohammad*, Berlin, 1869. See also ISLAM; KORAN.

G. M. W. M.

MOHEL. See CIRCUMCISION.

MOHILEWER, SAMUEL: Russian rabbi and Zionist; born in Hluboka, government of Wilna, April 25, 1824; died in Byelostok June 10, 1898. His father, Judah Löb, educated him not only in Hebrew, but also in secular subjects, and Mohilewer became in consequence an advocate of the introduction of European culture among his people. Ordained in his eighteenth year, he occupied the rabbinates successively of his native town (1848-56), Szaki (1856-60), Suwalki (1860-68), Radom (1868-83), and Byelostok (1883-98). With a keen eye for the practical needs of his people, Mohilewer devoted his energies and his fortune to Zionism. In 1875, on the occasion of the celebration of the ninetieth birthday of Sir Moses Montefiore, Mohilewer openly declared himself in favor of the colonization of Palestine. After the great persecution of the Jews in 1881 he accompanied the Russian refugees as far as Lemberg and suggested to the Emigration Committee that they be sent to the Holy Land. On his return in 1882 he founded the first Chovevei Zion Society in Warsaw. In the same year, and again in 1886, he undertook journeys to western Europe to win adherents for the movement. In Paris, with the help of Zadoc Kahn and M. Erlanger, he succeeded in gaining the support of Baron Edmond de Rothschild, who commissioned him to select a number of Russian Jewish families as colonists. Their colony, Ekron, prospered at first, but when the colonists in 1888 were influenced by agitators to stop work, that year being a Shemiṭṭah year, economic failure became imminent. At this juncture Mohilewer and other prominent Russian rabbis stepped in, and reassured the colonists of the religious propriety of resuming work. On another occasion, in 1889, when quarrels arose between the administration and the population of the colony Rishon le-Ẓiyyon, Mohilewer acted as arbitrator. In 1896 he again favored the non-observance of the Shemiṭṭah year. In 1890 he went to Palestine himself to inspect the colonies, and from this journey gained "new hope for a brighter future for Israel as soon as Israel shall take the right path and every Jew shall consider the honor of the nation rather than his own personal advantage." During his stay in Palestine Mohilewer, backed by certain wealthy Russian Zionists, bought 1,556 acres of land near Jaffa and founded the colony Rehoboth (see Jew. Encyc. i. 250, *s.v.* Agricultural Colonies in Palestine). In 1891, hearing of the intention of Baron de Hirsch to found colonies, he again went to Paris and urged, though unsuccessfully, the choice of Palestine instead of the Argentine Republic as the land of Jewish colonization.

Samuel Mohilewer.

Favors Palestine Colonization.

In the Zionist movement as outlined at the first Basel Congress in 1897 Mohilewer took a prominent part as leader of the Russian Zionists. His influence and activity in the propagation of this movement were remarkable. As the condition of his health had prevented him from attending the first Basel Congress, he had sent a letter of greeting in Hebrew, full of wise and practical advice.

The day before his death Mohilewer wrote a circular letter to all friends of Zion, recommending the foundation of the Jewish Colonial Bank and the colonization of Palestine, and at the same time urging again the idea of unity. This last letter may be regarded as containing his testament to his people. Among his posthumous works are a collection of responsa, commentaries on Ḥoshen Mishpaṭ, and sermons. His Hebrew treatise entitled "Massa Polen," concerning the condition of the Jews in Poland, appeared in a German journal in 1872.

Mohilewer's son, **Joseph,** also a Zionist, was elected to the rabbinate of Byelostok in 1902.

Bibliography: *Allg. Zeit. des Jud.* 1898, No. 24 (*Der Gemeindebote*, p. 4); Makel (I. Nissenbaum), *Rabbenu Shemuel Mohileber*, Berdychev, 1898; I. Nissenbaum, *Luaḥ Ahiasaf*, 1898, p. 289; *Ha-Meliẓ*, 1898, No. 27, p. 5; *Jüdischer Volkskalender*, 1897-98, p. 109; 1898-99, p. 202; *Die Welt*, 1897, vol. i., No. 3; W. Bambus, in *Zion*, vol. iv., No. 6, Berlin, 1898.

H. R. M. Sc.

MOHR, ABRAHAM MENDEL. See Muhr, Abraham.

MOINESHTI: Small town in Moldavia, district of Bakau. The census of 1820 reported forty-two Jewish taxpayers in the town, who constituted the larger part of the population. The Jews are engaged in exploiting the petroleum-wells which abound in that region. In 1860 the Jew Wolf Lazarovici installed the first petroleum-refinery, and six years later he built a paraffin-factory. The town and the district passed later into the hands of the Theiler brothers, naturalized Jews, who developed scientifically the output of petroleum and paraffin, and gave a remarkable impetus to the industry in that region.

In spite of the fires which periodically devastated the town, the Jews of Moineshti were prosperous until 1880, when the expulsion of a large number of Jews from the neighboring villages increased the Jewish population of Moineshti, but diminished its prosperity. In this town the first group of Rumanian emigrants and colonists was recruited for Palestine in 1882. From that time the poverty of the community increased, and Jews of Moineshti were among the emigrants to America after the latter part of 1899. The emigration from the town continues steadily, and the Jewish population is much decreased in numbers since the census of 1899 reported 2,363 Jews resident there. The community is organized and derives its revenues from a tax of 20 centimes per kilo on kasher meat and 20 centimes per head on poultry, from the money collected at a bath owned by the community, and from a tax on unleavened bread. The community supports a rabbi and three shoḥeṭim, and gives aid to the poor and sick, in addition to maintaining the Passover relief fund. There are three synagogues at Moineshti, a school for boys, one for girls, two charitable societies, and a Zionist society.

Bibliography: Ortensia Racovitza, *Dictionar Geografic al Jud. Bacau*, pp. 32, 367-368, 543-544, Bucharest, 1895; *Fraternitatea*, 1882, iv. 269-270; *Calendarul Israelit Illustrat pe 5664.*

G. E. Sd.

MOÏSE: American Jewish family descended from **Abraham Moïse,** who was born in Alsace and emigrated to the West Indies, where he married a member of a Jewish family of St. Eustace. He amassed great wealth, but in 1791 was compelled to flee on account of the insurrection of the slaves. With his wife, Sarah, and his sons, Aaron, Benjamin (d. unmarried), Cherie, and Hyam, he reached South Carolina. Three other sons and two daughters were born to him in Charleston, S. C.

A. Welborne Moïse: Eldest son of Aaron Moïse, the lawyer and editor; born in 1846. After serving as page in the United States House of Representatives from 1857 to 1861, he entered the service of the Confederacy and served through the war with distinction, being promoted for bravery.

After the surrender he studied law, practised for a time in Richmond, Va., and then went West.

Aaron Moïse: Elder son of the founder of the family; cashier of the Bank of the State of South Carolina. He married Sarah Cohen of Kingston, Jamaica, by whom he had nine children. He studied medicine, but did not follow it as a profession.

Aaron Moïse: Lawyer and editor; born in Charleston, S. C., 1820; died in Richmond, Va., 1880. He was appointed clerk in the United States Treasury in 1853, which position he resigned in 1861, when he went to Nashville, Tenn., and was appointed captain in a Tennessee regiment. Three months later he was called to Richmond and made chief clerk in the auditor's office of the Confederate government. After the war he took up the practise of law, which he continued until his death.

Abraham Moïse: Lawyer; born 1799, the first of the family born in America; died 1869. He married Caroline, granddaughter of Meyer Moses, and left two sons (**Charles H.** and **Edwin W.**) and one daughter. His brother **Isaac** married Hetty Lopez, descendant of the Newport family of Lopez. Isaac died early, leaving three sons—**Isaac**, **Edwin**, and **David**—and four daughters. All three sons served throughout the Civil war on the Confederate side. David afterward studied law, and was judge of one of the courts of New Orleans at the time of his death.

Abram Moïse: Succeeded his father as cashier of the Bank of Charleston, S. C., which position he retained until his death; died without issue. He married Louise Lopez, a member of the Newport family of Lopez.

Camillus Moïse: Son of Aaron Moïse; died at the age of twenty-seven while serving in the Mexican war.

Cherie Moïse: Third son of Abraham Moïse, the founder of the family. He married Hetty Cohen of Charleston, S. C. Their daughter **Cordelia** (b. 1809; d. 1869) was known for her gift of poetry. She wrote a number of the hymns used by the Portuguese congregation of Charleston.

Columbus Moïse: Son of Aaron Moïse; born in Charleston, S. C., 1809; died in Virginia 1871. He married a daughter of D. C. Levy of Philadelphia, Pa. For thirty-five years he was president of the principal bank of New Orleans, La. He was postmaster of that city, and was chosen by its citizens to receive Gen. Zachary Taylor on his return from the battle of Buena Vista. He was granted a large tract of land in Florida for services rendered in the Indian war. Columbus Moïse wrote many short poems, one of which was sung at the laying of the cornerstone of the Portuguese synagogue in Charleston, S. C.

Columbus Moïse: Son of Columbus Moïse; born in New Orleans, La., 1855; died in Kansas City, Mo., 1895. He was city attorney of East Las Vegas, N. M., regent of the Territorial College, master in chancery of the United States Court of New Mexico, and chief justice of New Mexico. He wrote a number of short stories and poems, contributing to "Harper's Magazine," the "Century Magazine," and other periodicals, under the nom de plume "C. Esiom."

Edwin Warren Moïse: Son of Hyam and Cecilia Moïse; born at Charleston, S. C., 1811; died in New Orleans, La., 1868. After being educated as a physician at Charleston Medical College, he went to Woodville, Miss., where he practised his profession with great success. In 1840 he removed to New Orleans, studied law there, and for many years practised at the bar of Louisiana. He was elected for a number of consecutive terms to the State House of Representatives, of which he was speaker for many years; later he was appointed United States district attorney, and in 1861 was made judge of the Confederate States Court in Louisiana. Under the administration of Governor Wycliffe he became attorney-general of the state. He was a secessionist of the Calhoun school, an acknowledged leader in the Democratic party of Louisiana, and was closely identified with the history of the state during the Civil war. Two of his sons, **Harry** and **Theodore S.**, are identified with various railroad enterprises; the latter is now (1904) superintendent of the Georgia Central Railroad. Another son, **E. W. Moïse**, resides in California, where he is well known as a financier.

Edwin Warren Moïse: Son of Abraham and Caroline Moïse; born May 21, 1832, in Charleston, S. C.; died in Sumter, S. C., Dec. 9, 1902. He married Esther Lyon of Petersburg, Va., in 1854. In 1856 he opened a law-office in Columbus, Ga. When the Civil war began he organized a company of 120 men, 50 of whom he mounted and equipped at an expense of $10,000—the whole of his fortune. This company bore his name until it became Company A, 7th Confederate Cavalry, with Moïse as its captain; in 1863 he became major of the regiment, and was in command of it at the end of the war; he had not received his colonel's commission, but he had been recommended for promotion after the battle of Burgess' Mills, and the recommendation had been approved by General Lee. He fought in all the battles of the army of northern Virginia under General Lee, was slightly wounded at Gettysburg, had three horses killed under him in the battles below Petersburg, and was with Hampton in his raid and capture of Kilpatrick's camp. With 200 of his men he built the dams at Hatch's Run which protected Lee's left flank against Grant, and at Smithfield, N. C., in 1865, he performed the service of burning the bridges in the retreat of Generals Hampton and Butler from Bentonville to Raleigh. He surrendered with Gen. Joseph Johnston at Greensboro, N. C.

Edwin Moïse emerged from the war penniless and settled in Sumter, S. C., where he practised law with success. He was largely instrumental in redeeming South Carolina from radical rule in 1876, giving up his practise to cooperate with Hampton for that purpose. He was nominated as adjutant- and inspector-general of his state on the same ticket with Hampton, receiving more votes than his leader. Reelected in 1878, he served four years and declined renomination in 1880. He gave the whole of his first term's salary to the public schools of his state. He was a delegate to the Reconstruction Convention in 1865, was presidential elector in 1880, and was repeatedly sent as a delegate to various state conventions.

His son, **Marion Moïse** (b. June 15, 1855, at Sullivan's Island, S. C.), was educated at the Virginia Military Institute and South Carolina College. He was elected intendant of the city of Sumter, S. C., in 1884, serving two terms, and was chosen state senator from Sumter county in 1886, serving four years. He is now (1904) prominent as a lawyer at Sumter. He married (1877) Isabel de Leon of Charleston, S. C.

Hyam Moïse: Fourth son of Abraham Moïse; born at Port-au-Prince 1755; died 1811. He married Cecilia Wolfe of Charleston, S. C., by whom he had two sons—**Theodore Sydney** and **Edwin Warren.**

Jacob Moïse: Youngest son of the founder of the family; died in 1837. He married Rebecca Cohen, of Charleston, S. C., and settled in Augusta, Ga.; they were the first Jewish family there. His eldest daughter, **Sarah Ann,** showed literary ability at the early age of twelve. She married T. W. Dinkins, an editor, and is known for her stories, sketches, poems, and for numerous contributions to the Jewish press. Her youngest brother, **Howard,** served through the Civil war on the Confederate side. He was wounded three times and was made deaf by exposure and by the bombardment of Fort Sumter. He helped to build the batteries on Morris Island in 1860. He now lives (1904) in Sumter, S. C.

A. L. C. H.

Penina Moïse: Daughter of Abraham Moïse, who settled in Charleston, S. C., in 1791; born April 23, 1797, at Charleston; died Sept. 13, 1880. Her father died when she was about twelve years of age, and the helpless condition of the large family he left compelled her to give up school at that age. She gave early promise of literary ability, and her verse soon became known throughout the South. In 1833 she published a collection of poems entitled "Fancy's Sketch-Book," which was favorably received. From that time on she became a regular contributor to the publications of her day. Among the periodicals to which she contributed may be mentioned the "Washington Union," "The Home Journal of New York," "The Boston Daily Times," "Heriot's Magazine," "The New Orleans Commercial Times," "Godey's Lady's Book," "The Occident," and the "Charleston Courier." She contributed also several articles to the first copy of the "Charleston Book," a well-known publication in its day. Her contributions to the daily press were frequently of a humorous character. As a poet she was so highly esteemed that her fellow citizens looked to her for the celebration of every local event of importance.

An ardent Jewess, Penina Moïse wrote much on topics affecting her race. She took a lively interest in communal affairs, and was for years the superintendent of the Sabbath-school of the Charleston synagogue. During this period she wrote many hymns and religious pieces. Her book of hymns has been in use in the Congregation Beth Elohim of Charleston and in other Southern congregations.

In 1854, during the epidemic of yellow fever in South Carolina, she devoted herself to caring for the victims, whom she nursed irrespective of creed. Just before the outbreak of the Civil war her sight began to fail. The war compelled her to leave Charleston, but at its close she returned with her sister, Rachel Moïse, and opened a school which became widely known. Finally she lost her sight completely and met with other misfortunes as well.

Bibliography: *Appleton's Encyc. of American Biography;* Mrs. S. A. Dinkins, in *American Jews' Annual,* 1885; Isaac Markens, *The Hebrews in America,* p. 59, New York, 1888; M. Kayserling, *Die Jüdischen Frauen,* Leipsic, 1879; Charlotte Adams, in *The Critic,* xv. 327.

A. L. Hü.

Theodore Sydney Moïse: Elder brother of the attorney-general of that name; born in Charleston, S. C., 1806; died in Natchitoches, La., July 2, 1883. He married Cecilia F. Moses, granddaughter of Meyer Moses of Revolutionary times; by her he had one daughter, who married her cousin, Charles H. Moïse. Theodore Moïse was an artist of ability. His portraits are found in many homes in South Carolina, Mississippi, Louisiana, and Kentucky (where he painted a portrait of the beautiful Sallie Ward, a famous Kentucky belle of that day). In 1836 he removed from Charleston to Mississippi, and afterward to New Orleans, La. He served during the Civil war on the staff of General Herbert of Louisiana, and his ingenuity contributed to the planning of the fire-rafts which were used to repel the Federal fleet. His second wife, Mathilde Vaughn, bore him six sons: **Robert** (entered the Catholic priesthood); **Charles; "Brother Ambrose"** (head of the Christian Brothers' College in St. Paul, Minn.; won the gold medal offered during the World's Fair at Chicago for the best epic on the discovery of America); and three others who became prominent lawyers, one of them, **James C. Moïse,** being at the time of his death (1901) judge of the criminal court of New Orleans.

A. L. C. H.

MOÏSEVILLE. See Agricultural Colonies in the Argentine Republic.

MOKAMES, DAVID AL-. See David (Abu Sulaiman) ibn Merwan al-Muḳammaṣ.

MOKIAḤ, MORDECAI. See Mordecai Mokiaḥ.

MOLAD. See Calendar.

MOLDAVIA. See Rumania.

MOLE: Traditional rendering of the Hebrew "ḥaparparah" (Isa. ii. 20). Some give "mole" as the translation also of "ḥoled" (Lev. xi. 29), which is, however, generally assumed to mean Weasel. "Tinshemet," which the Septuagint, the Vulgate, and the Targum take for some kind of mole, is commonly admitted to mean either a lizard (Lev. xi. 3) or some kind of bird (*ib.* verse 18).

The mole proper (*Talpa*) does not occur in Palestine. The animal which would answer the description of Isa. ii. 20 is the mole-rat (*Spalax typhlus*), which is common about ruins, loose débris, and stone-heaps, and which in external appearance resembles the mole.

The Talmud has for the mole the terms "tinshemet" (Ḥul. 63a) and "ishut" (Kelim xxi. 3; comp. Targ. to Lev. xi. 30). The mole is described as having no eyes (comp. Aristotle, "History of Animals," iv. 8, 2, and Pliny, "Historia Naturalis," xi. 37, 52) and as being destructive to grain and plants (M. Ḳ. 6b). In Ber. 57b (comp. Tos. to M. Ḳ. 6b) קרפראי, which Rashi explains by "talpa," is mentioned alongside of the bat and weasel, whose appearance in dreams is a bad omen.

Bibliography: Tristram, *Nat. Hist.* p. 120; Lewysohn, *Z. T.* p. 101.

E. G. H. I. M. C.

MOLIN, JACOB BEN MOSES HA-LEVI. See Mölln, Jacob ben Moses.

MOLINA, ISAAC: Egyptian rabbi of the sixteenth century; a native of Venice. He had a controversy with Joseph Caro on the subject of R. Gershom's "taḳḳanot" (comp. Caro, Responsa on Eben ha-'Ezer). There is also a responsum of Molina in Caro's "Abḳat Rokel," No. 130, the following number being Caro's answer. Molina collected all the responsa of Asher b. Jehiel and some of other rabbis into one volume, which he entitled "Besamim Rosh," providing it with notes and with a preface (Berlin, 1793). In his preface he claims to have written responsa and novellæ on the Talmud and on Maimonides' "Yad."

Bibliography: Azulai, *Shem ha-Gedolim*, i. 106; Conforte, *Ḳore ha-Dorot*, p. 36b; Fürst, *Bibl. Jud.* ii. 387; Steinschneider, *Cat. Bodl.* col. 1139.

E. C. M. Sel.

MOLITOR, JOSEPH FRANZ: German Christian cabalist; born June 8, 1779, in Ober Ursel, in the Taunus; died in Frankfort-on-the-Main March 23, 1860. Early in life he interested himself in the philosophy of Kant, Fichte, and Schelling, writing under the influence of the last-named's teachings "Ideen zu einer Künstlichen Dynamik der Geschichte" (1805). In the same year he published his "Ueber den Wendepunkt des Antiken und Modernen," which shows the influence of Baader's theosophy. "Ueber die Philosophie der Modernen Welt" came out in 1806. About this time Prince von Dalberg founded an institution for the uplifting of Judaism, and Molitor became teacher there. Becoming interested in the various phases of Judaism, he began the study of Hebrew and Aramaic, then Talmud, and later, actuated by an insight into the Cabala he had received from the Jewish cabalist Metz in 1813, he turned his attention to the study of the Zohar, to which henceforth he devoted himself entirely. He wrote the first volume of his "Philosophie der Geschichte oder über die Tradition" in 1824, as a result of his cabalistic studies. The second volume (1834) contains a compendium of the Cabala and a reference to the need of divine revelation. This was followed by a third volume (1839), containing a general account of paganism, Christianity, and Judaism, and a discussion of the Jewish laws of impurity. The fourth volume of this work, published in 1853, shows the relation of the Cabala to Christianity. The fundamental object of this work is to show the superiority of cabalistic mysticism over that of the Christian, and that Christianity is Judaism obscured by a false mysticism.

Bibliography: *Allg. Deutsche Biog.*, s.v.; *La Grande Encyclopédie*, s.v.; *Allg. Zeit.* 1860, Supplement to April 21; J. E. Erdmann, *Grundriss der Gesch. der Philologie*, 3d ed., vol. ii., pp. 506 *et seq.*

S. S. J. L.

MOLKO, SOLOMON: Marano cabalist; born a Christian in Portugal about 1500; died at Mantua in 1532. His baptismal name probably was **Diogo Pires.** He held the post of secretary in one of the higher courts of his native country. When the adventurer David Reubeni came ostensibly on a political mission from Khaibar, in Africa, to Portugal, Molko wished to join him, but was rejected. He then circumcised himself, though without thereby gaining Reubeni's favor, and emigrated to Turkey. Highly

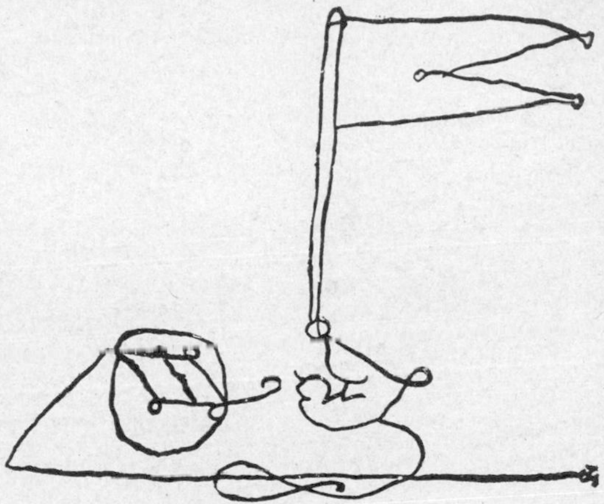

Autograph of Solomon Molko.
(After a manuscript in the possession of the Alliance Israélite Universelle.)

endowed, but a visionary and believer in dreams, he studied the Cabala with Joseph Taytazak and became acquainted with Joseph Caro. He then wandered, as a preacher, through Palestine, where he achieved a great reputation and announced that the Messianic kingdom would come in 1540. In 1529 Molko published a portion of his sermons under the title "Derashot," or "Sefer ha-Mefo'ar." Going to Italy, he was opposed by prominent Jews, who feared that he might mislead their coreligionists, but he succeeded in gaining the favor of Pope Clement VII. and of some Judeophile cardinals at Rome. He is said to have predicted to the pope a certain flood which inundated Rome and various other places. After his many cabalistic and other strange experiments, Molko felt justified in proclaiming himself the Messiah, or his precursor. In company with David Reubeni, whom he came across in Italy, he went in 1532 to Ratisbon, where the emperor Charles V. was holding a diet. On this occasion Molko carried a flag with the inscription מכבי (abbreviation for "Who among the mighty is like unto God?"). The emperor imprisoned both Molko and Reubeni, and took them with him to Italy. In Mantua an ecclesiastical court sentenced Molko to death by fire. At the stake the emperor offered to pardon him on condition that he return to the Church, but Molko refused, asking for a martyr's death.

Bibliography: Grätz, *Gesch.* 3d ed., ix. 234 *et seq.*, note 5; Neubauer, *M. J. C.* ii.; Vogelstein and Rieger, *Gesch. der Juden in Rom.*

S. P. B.

MOLL, ALBERT: German physician; born at Lissa May 4, 1862; educated at the universities of

Breslau, Freiburg, Jena, and Berlin (M.D. 1885). During the following two years he took postgraduate courses at Vienna, Budapest, London, Paris, and Nancy, and in 1887 established himself as a neuropathologist in Berlin. In 1894 he visited the leading medical institutions of eastern Europe, and in 1898 those of North America.

Moll has written several essays in the medical journals, and is the author of: "Der Hypnotismus," Berlin, 1889 (3d ed. 1895); "Die Konträre Sexualempfindung," *ib.* 1891 (3d ed. 1899); "Der Rapport in der Hypnose," Leipsic, 1892; "Untersuchungen über die Libido Sexualis," *ib.* 1897; "Das Nervöse Weib," *ib.* 1898; and "Medizinische Ethik," *ib.* 1900.

s. F. T. H.

MÖLLN (MOLIN): Name of a family of Mayence. The name מולין, which, according to D. Kaufmann ("Der Grabstein des R. Jacob ben Moses ha-Levi," in "Monatsschrift," xlii. 26), is to be read "Molin" rather than "Mölln," is not intended to indicate the place from which Moses came, but is a personal name, as is evidenced by the fact that one of the sons of MaHaRIL is called simply "Molin," after the name of his grandfather. "Molin" is usually considered to be a pet name for "Moses"; the correctness of this theory, however, is doubted by Salfeld ("Martyrologium," p. 406).

Jacob ben Moses Mölln (MaHaRIL): Rabbi and teacher of Mayence; born about 1365; died in 1427. The fact that he is termed "Maharil," "Mahari Segal," or "Mahari Mölln" has caused much confusion. His father's name being Moses, his own name was really R. Jacob b. Moses ha-Levi. He was a pupil of R. Shalom of Austria, rabbi at Wiener-Neustadt, and won a reputation even in his youth for Talmudic learning and piety, while in problems of ceremonial law his responsa were sought. At Mayence he attracted many pupils, the most noteworthy of whom was Jacob Weil (MaHaRIN; rabbi at Nuremberg, Augsburg, and Erfurt), whose responsa were considered authoritative. Mölln and his teacher were the first two rabbis to bear the title "Morenu," which was at that time applied to scholars in order to put an end to the abuses practised by unauthorized persons in performing marriage ceremonies or in granting divorces (comp. in regard to this point David Gans, "Ẓemaḥ Dawid," ed. Offenbach, 30a, *s.v.* מהרי"ל).

Mölln lived during the period of the Hussite wars, which brought misery upon the Jews of the Rhine, of Thuringia, and of Bavaria, all of whom appealed to him to intercede with God for them. Accordingly he sent messengers to the neighboring communities (which were in their turn to commission others), urging them to institute a general season of fasting and prayer. The German communities, obeying the call, fasted for seven days (Sept., 1421). Soon afterward the imperial army and the mercenaries mobilized at Saaz, dispersed, and the very soldiers who had threatened the Jews now came to them to beg bread and received food from them (comp. G. Pollak, "Halikot Ḳedem," pp. 79 *et seq.*; Grätz, "Gesch." 2d ed., viii. 136; Zunz, "S. P." p. 48).

Jacob Mölln was considered the greatest authority of his time. Communities far and wide sought his advice; and his discourses and responsa, in which he emphasized the importance of tradition, and in general followed Alexander Süsslein ha-Kohen (d. 1349), the author of the "Aguddah" frequently mentioned in the codes, were regarded as authoritative in the congregations and exerted a decisive influence, not only on his contemporaries, but also on later teachers. His death occurred before he could publish his responsa, which he had collected carefully, but a part of them appeared at Venice, 1549, and frequently later. His chief work is the "Sefer ha-Maharil" or "Minhagim," published by his pupil Zalman of St. Goar at the request of his contemporaries. This book is frequently quoted in the codes and commentaries, and has become a valuable source for later scholars. In addition to sermons, regulations of the ceremonial law, and textual comments, it contains a detailed description of religious observances and rites within and without the synagogue, and outlines, therefore, a faithful picture of the life of the German Jews. It was first published, with various additions, at Sabbionetta, in 1556, and frequently later. It exerted great influence on the Jews of central Europe, being largely responsible for the high esteem accorded to religious tradition ("minhag") in the communities. Mölln frowns upon any changes, and demands implicit obedience to the time-honored observances, even in regard to the liturgical melodies and the piyyuṭim (comp. R. Moses Isserles to Oraḥ Ḥayyim, 619). According to tradition he composed most of the synagogal hymns, and his "Minhagim" actually contain many references to the use of certain melodies. A third work, "Bi'urim" to Yoreh De'ah, is extant in manuscript (comp. Wolf, "Bibl. Hebr." i. 604).

Works.

Bibliography: Grätz, *Gesch.* 2d ed., viii. 136; Winter and Wünsche, *Die Jüdische Litteratur*, ii. 498 *et seq.*, 661 *et seq.*, iii. 515; Güdemann, *Gesch.* iii. 17, 111; *Or ha-Ḥayyim*, Frankfort-on-the-Main, 1891, pp. 497 *et seq.*

s. E. N.

Moses ben Jekuthiel ha-Levi Mölln: Rabbi in Mayence in the second half of the fourteenth century. In two ordinances concerning the administration of the three communities, Speyer, Worms, and Mayence ("Taḳḳanot ShUM"), dated respectively 1381 and 1386, his signature appears first (see Moses Minz, Responsa, ed. Lemberg, 1851, p. 11b; Neubauer, "Cat. Bodl. Hebr. MSS." No. 820). A responsum of his, dated 1369, is preserved among the responsa of his son MaHaRIL (ed. Hanau, 1610, No. 233), who succeeded him in the rabbinate of Mayence.

Of Mölln's other children are known by name: **Jekuthiel, Simon, Gumprecht,** and two daughters, **Simḥah** and **Bonlin** or **Bonchin.**

Bibliography: Güdemann, *Gesch.* iii. 17; Michael, *Or ha-Ḥayyim*, No. 1121.

D. M. Sc.

MOLO, FRANCISCO: Dutch financier and statesman; lived in the seventeenth century. In 1679 he settled in Amsterdam as financial agent of John III., King of Poland, a fact which hardly agrees with De Barrios' statement ("Panegyrico al Laureado Juan Tercero, Rey de Polonia") that

Molo was a Spanish Jew. He was held in high esteem on account of his ability in financial matters; and in recognition of the services which he had rendered to the Dutch state, he was exempted for two years from the payment of taxes. Molo's influence with the States General was so great that through his mediation Louis XIV. was enabled to conclude the treaty of Ryswick (1697).

BIBLIOGRAPHY: Koenen, *Geschiedenis der Joden in Nederland*, p. 219, Utrecht, 1843; Lamberti, *Mémoires*, i. 11, Amsterdam, 1757; Wagenaar, *Vaderlandsche Historie*, xvi., p. 321, *ib.* 1757.

D. M. SEL.

MOLOCH (MOLECH).—Biblical Data: In the Masoretic text the name is "Molech"; in the Septuagint "Moloch." The earliest mention of Molech is in Lev. xviii. 21, where the Israelite is forbidden to sacrifice any of his children to Molech. Similarly, in Lev. xx. 2–5, it is enacted that a man who sacrifices his seed to Molech shall surely be put to death. Then, curiously, it is provided that he shall be cut off from the congregation. In I Kings xi. 7 it is said that Solomon built a high place for Molech in the mountain "that is before Jerusalem." The same passage calls Molech an Ammonite deity. The Septuagint as quoted in the New Testament (Acts vii. 43) finds a reference to Moloch in Amos v. 26; but this is a doubtful passage. In II Kings xxiii. 10 it is stated that one of the practises to which Josiah put a stop by his reform was that of sacrificing children to Molech, and that the place where this form of worship had been practised was at Topheth, "in the valley of the children of Hinnom." This statement is confirmed by Jer. xxxii. 35. From II Kings xxi. 6 it may be inferred that this worship was introduced during the reign of Manasseh. The impression left by an uncritical reading of these passages is that Molech-worship, with its rite of child-sacrifice, was introduced from Ammon during the seventh century B.C.

——**Critical View:** The name "Molech," later corrupted into "Moloch," is an intentional mispointing of "Melek," after the analogy of "bosheth" (comp. Hoffmann in Stade's "Zeitschrift," iii. 124). As to the rites which the worshipers of Molech performed, it has sometimes been inferred, from the phrase "pass through the fire to Molech," that children were made to pass between two lines of fire as a kind of consecration or februation; but it is clear from Isa. lvii. 5 and Jer. xix. 5 that the children were killed and burned. The whole point of the offering consisted, therefore, in the fact that it was a human sacrifice. From Jer. vii. 31 and Ezek. xx. 25, 26, it is evident that both prophets regarded these human sacrifices as extraordinary offerings to YHWH. Jeremiah declares that YHWH had not commanded them, while Ezekiel says YHWH polluted the Israelites in their offerings by permitting them to sacrifice their first-born, so that through chastisement they might know that YHWH was YHWH. The fact, therefore, now generally accepted by critical scholars, is that in the last days of the kingdom human sacrifices were offered to YHWH as King or Counselor of the nation and that the Prophets disapproved of it and denounced it because it was introduced from outside as an imitation of a heathen cult and because of its barbarity. In course of time the pointing of "Melek" was changed to "Molech" to still further stigmatize the rites.

Nature of the Worship.

The motive for these sacrifices is not far to seek. It is given in Micah vi. 7: "Shall I give my first-born for my transgression, the fruit of my body for the sin of my soul?" In the midst of the disasters which were befalling the nation men felt that if the favor of YHWH could be regained it was worth any price they could pay. Their Semitic kindred worshiped their gods with offerings of their children, and in their desperation the Israelites did the same. For some reason, perhaps because not all the priestly and prophetic circles approved of the movement, they made the offerings, not in the Temple, but at an altar or pyre called "Tapheth" (LXX.), erected in the valley of Hinnom (comp. W. R. Smith, "Rel. of Sem." 2d ed., p. 372). "Tapheth," also, was later pointed "Topheth," after the analogy of "bosheth." In connection with these extraordinary offerings the worshipers continued the regular Temple sacrifices to YHWH (Ezek. xxiii. 39).

Motive of Sacrifices.

Babylonian Cylinder Representing Sacrifice of a Child.
(From Menant, "Glyptique Orientale.")

From the fact that I Kings xi. 7 calls Molech the "abomination of the children of Ammon" it was formerly assumed that this worship was an imitation of an Ammonite cult. But so little is known of the Ammonite religion that more recent scholarship has looked elsewhere for the source. Because of the mention in II Kings xvii. 31 of Adrammelech (= Adar-malik) and Anammelech (=Anu-malik) as gods of Sepharvaim transplanted to Samaria, it has been inferred that this form of worship was borrowed from Babylonia (comp. Bäthgen, "Beiträge zur Semitischen Religionsgesch." pp. 238 *et seq.*). This view rests on the supposition that "Sepharvaim" is equal to "Sippar," which probably is not the case. Even if it were, Anu and Adar were not gods of Sippar; Shamash was god of that city. From this verse, therefore, a Babylonian or Assyrian origin can not be demonstrated.

Support for this view has been sought also in Amos v. 26. If, as is probable, Siccuth and Chiun in that passage are names or epithets of Babylonian deities (comp. CHIUN), the use of "Melek" in connection with these affords no sound basis for argument. The whole passage may be, as Wellhausen and Nowack believe, a late gloss introduced on account of II Kings xvii. 31, and is in any case too obscure to build upon. Furthermore, there is no evidence that the sacrifice of the first-born was a feature of the worship of Babylonian deities. Because child-sacrifice was a prominent feature of the worship of the Phenician Malik-Baal-Kronos, Moore (in Cheyne and Black, "Encyc. Bibl.") seeks to prove that the worship of Moloch was introduced from Phenicia. The evidence of its existence in Phenicia and her colonies is especially strong. Diodorus Siculus (xx. 14) tells how the Carthaginians in a siege sacrificed two hundred boys to Kronos. Burning was an important feature of the rite.

BIBLIOGRAPHY: W. R. Smith, *Rel. of Sem.* 2d ed., pp. 372 *et seq.*; Bäthgen, *Beiträge zur Semitischen Religionsgesch.* 1888, pp. 237 *et seq.*; Moore, *The Image of Moloch*, in *Jour. Bib. Lit.* 1897, xvi. 161 *et seq.*; M. J. Lagrange, *Etudes sur les Religions Sémitiques*, 1903, pp. 99-109.

S. G. A. B.

MOMBACH, JULIUS LAZARUS: Musician and composer; born in Pfungstadt 1813; died at London, England, Feb. 8, 1880. In 1828 he went to London and received a good musical education under Enoch Eliasson. On the election of Simon Ascher to the position of reader at the Great Synagogue, Mombach entered the choir. Subsequently he became director of the choir, and held this position till his death. He took part in all the services at the Great Synagogue for a period of fifty-two years; and threw all his energy into the task of improving the musical portion of the service. He acquired the reputation of a skilful pianist, and of a clever composer of synagogue music. Nearly all the music in use in the German synagogues of England and the English colonies was composed by him.

Mombach's services as choirmaster were sought on almost every occasion of special importance in the history of the London and chief provincial synagogues; and many of the readers in English and colonial synagogues owed their training to him. He taught the singing of ḥazzanut to the students of Jews' College; was a member of the Committee for the Diffusion of Religious Knowledge; and directed the singing of the senior pupils of the Sabbath classes of the Association for Religious Instruction. For several years he conducted the concerts at the Jewish Workingmen's Club, Aldgate.

BIBLIOGRAPHY: *Jew. Chron.* and *Jew. World*, Feb. 13, 1880.

J. G. L.

MOMMSEN, CHRISTIAN MATTHIAS THEODOR: Jurist, archeologist, and historian; born Nov. 30, 1817, at Garding, Sleswick-Holstein; died Nov. 1, 1903, at Charlottenburg, near Berlin. His most important work is his "Römische Gesch." (vol. i., 9th ed., Berlin, 1903; vols. ii., iii., 8th ed., 1889; vol. v., 3d ed., 1886; vol. iv. was not published). In vol. iii. he treats exhaustively the position and influence of the Jews in the Roman empire; and in vol. v. he devotes a chapter headed "Judäa und die Juden" to the spiritual and religious development of Judaism in the Persian, Greek, and Roman periods.

As a member of the Prussian Diet (1873-82) and of the German Reichstag (1881-84), Mommsen belonged to the Liberal party and strongly opposed the anti-Semitic movement. In his pamphlet "Auch ein Wort über Unser Judentum" (1881), which was written in reply to Treitschke's arguments in "Ein Wort über Unser Judentum," he warmly pleaded for tolerance and humanity, and argued that the Jewish element in the German empire is a wholesome one. He was among the first who signed the declaration of German notables (Nov. 12, 1880) in which Jew-baiting ("Judenhetze") was designated a "national disgrace." The passage in his "Römische Gesch." (iii. 350), "Auch in der alten Welt war das Judentum ein wirksames Ferment des Kosmopolitismus und der nationalen Dekomposition und insofern ein vorzugsweise berechtigtes Mitglied in dem cäsarischen Staate, dessen Politik doch eigentlich nichts als Weltbürgertum, dessen Volkstümlichkeit im Grunde nichts als Humanität war," having been misunderstood and misinterpreted by the anti-Semites, was omitted by Mommsen in a later edition.

Mommsen was an active member of the Verein zur Abwehr des Antisemitismus (founded 1891) until his death. He also declared himself against the accusation of ritual murder. In a prefatory letter to Errera's "Les Juifs Russes" (see JEW. ENCYC. v. 203, *s.v.* ERRERA, LEO-ABRAM) he expressed the hope "that the statesmen of a great empire and the sovereign arbiter of Europe may no longer be dominated by the blind action of a resuscitated Torquemada."

BIBLIOGRAPHY: *Brockhaus Konversations-Lexikon*; *Mittheilungen aus dem Verein zur Abwehr des Antisemitismus*, 1893, p. 177; 1894, p. 55; 1897, p. 387; 1903, pp. 345, 381; Hermann Vogelstein, in *Allg. Zeit. des Jud.* 1904, pp. 103-106.

D. S. MAN.

MONASTIR: Capital of Rumelia, European Turkey; 400 miles west of Constantinople; the ancient **Vitolia.** It has a population of 65,000, including 6,000 Jews. There are no documents referring to Jews in Monastir before the arrival of the Spanish exiles in 1492. In the middle of the sixteenth century there was a Talmudic school in Monastir which was under the direction of R. Joseph ibn Leb, the author of four volumes of responsa (see "Ḳore ha-Dorot," ed. Cassel, p. 37b). In 1863 a terrible fire swept over the city; 1,008 out of the 2,080 houses and shops that were burned belonged to Jews. In 1884 there were 4,000 Jews in Monastir. In 1900 the Jews were accused of ritual murder in connection with the disappearance of an Orthodox Bulgarian, sixty years of age.

The affairs of the community are administered by a chief rabbi ("ḥakam bashi"; officially recognized by a decree of the sultan), a bet din or religious court, and a council of notables; from the taxes levied by the last-named the chief rabbi, the judges, and the schools are supported, and the poor relieved. There are three synagogues and five batte midrashot; a large Talmud Torah with 250 children; a boys' school with 150 pupils, founded in 1895, and subsidized by the Alliance Israélite Universelle and the Anglo-Jewish Association; a girls' school with 110 pupils, also aided by the Alliance; and day-nurseries that care for about 120 infants. Its two ḥebra ḳaddishahs date back to the first settlement of the Jews in the city. The occupations followed by the community are as follows: 600 merchants, including bankers; 150 cobblers; 150 tailors; 150 blacksmiths; 50 tinsmiths; 250 porters; and 150 dealers in old clothes (in which the Jews have the monopoly). The Jewish workmen belong to unions. Formerly they lived in "cortijos," or groups of houses enclosed by a wall, but most of these have been destroyed by the frequent fires. Down to the beginning of the last century the Monastir Jews put no inscriptions on their tombstones.

The following have occupied the rabbinate of Monastir: Joseph Jacob Israel (*c.* 1768); Joseph Israel (*c.* 1790); Jacob Joseph Israel (1854–89; author of "Yismaḥ Mosheh," a book of devotions in Judæo-Spanish, published by his grandson; Belgrade, 1896); Abraham Levi of Janina (1896–98).

BIBLIOGRAPHY: M. Schwab, *Histoire des Israélites*, p. 238; *Bulletin All. Isr.* 1884, 1900, 1901; M. Franco, *Histoire des Israélites de l'Empire Ottoman*, p. 206; *El Avenir di Salonica*, Dec. 31, 1902; Jacob Joseph Israel, *Yismaḥ Mosheh*, Belgrade, 1896.

D. M. FR.

MONATSSCHRIFT FÜR DIE GESCHICHTE UND WISSENSCHAFT DES JUDENTHUMS: The oldest and most important monthly devoted to the science of Judaism. It was founded by Zacharias FRANKEL in Dresden in the year 1851, in continuation of his "Zeitschrift für die Religiösen Interessen des Judenthums," which had been suppressed in 1846. Frankel believed that the objects striven for in the contest of 1848 had been attained, and that the Jews no longer had separate political interests. He therefore considered that the time had arrived for them to undertake a scientific investigation of their history and literature.

The first seventeen volumes of the "Monatsschrift" were edited by Frankel, who was succeeded by the historian Heinrich GRAETZ. The latter edited vols. xviii. to xxxvi. inclusive, being assisted by Pinkus Frankl of Berlin in vols. xxxiii. to xxxv. Publication was stopped in 1887, but was resumed in 1892, with M. Brann and David Kaufmann as joint editors (vols. xxxvii. to xliii.). Upon Kaufmann's death (1899) Brann became sole editor. Since Jan., 1904, the "Monatsschrift" has appeared as the organ of the Gesellschaft zur Förderung der Wissenschaft des Judenthums.

The "Monatsschrift" was first published in Dresden. Some volumes were then issued at Krotoschin and some at Berlin; but the greatest number appeared in Breslau. A complete table of contents for the first seventeen volumes is appended to vol. xvii., and a similar table for the years 1869 to 1887 is given at the end of vol. xxxvi. This table has been published separately also.

BIBLIOGRAPHY: *Monatsschrift*, vol. i., Preface; S. P. Rabbinowitz, *Zacharias Frankel* (in Hebrew), pp. 143 *et seq.*, Warsaw, 1898. An exhaustive criticism, by Atlas, of vol. xxxiii. appears in *Ha-Asif*, ii. 432-450.

S. P. WI.

MONCALVO (מונקלוו): Small town in the province of Alessandria, Piedmont, Italy. Jews settled there after their expulsion from France. The community, like those of Asti and Fossano, long retained the old French ritual, and still uses the German Maḥzor with several additions from the French rite. The history of the community is similar to that of the other communities of Savoy. In 1866 it contained 220 persons, including a large number of artisans engaged in various trades, but it is now considerably smaller. It formerly had various philanthropic societies and foundations, ritual institutions, etc. Joseph Lattes (d. 1880) officiated for a time as rabbi.

BIBLIOGRAPHY: Luzzatto, in *Halikot Ḳedem*, p. 51; idem, *Mebo le-Maḥzor*, p. 7; Zunz, *Ritus*, p. 64; *Corriere Israelitico*, iv. 315.

G. I. E.

MOND, LUDWIG: English chemist; born at Cassel, Germany, March 7, 1839; educated at the Polytechnic School, Cassel, and at the universities of Marburg and Heidelberg. In 1862 he went to England and engaged in the Le Blanc soda industry, introducing his process for recovering sulfur from alkali waste. In 1873 he established, in partnership with T. T. Brunner, at Winnington, Northwich, Cheshire, the manufacture of ammonia soda by the Solvay process, which he has perfected; and the works there now constitute the largest alkali establishment in the world. Mond has patented many inventions of great scientific and commercial importance. He also founded and endowed the Davy-Faraday Research Laboratory of the Royal Institution in 1896.

Mond has held various high scientific positions. He is fellow of the Royal Society; a vice-president of the Royal Institution; vice-president of the Chemical Society; ex-president of the Society of Chemical Industry; and ex-president of the chemical section of the British Association for the Advancement of Science (1896). He has written numerous papers and addresses which have been published in the transactions and proceedings of these societies and institutions.

BIBLIOGRAPHY: *Who's Who*, 1904; *Jewish Year Book*, 1903.

J. G. L.

MONDAY AND THURSDAY PRAYER. See LITURGY.

MONEY.—Biblical Data: I. As far back as the history of Israel can be traced, gold and silver were used as standards of value and mediums of exchange, and, as the Egyptian tribute-lists show, they were thus employed in Canaan even before the Israelites inhabited it. The general use of the word "kesef," meaning "silver," to designate money shows that silver was the prevailing medium of exchange. Up to the time of the Exile, and even later, the metals were not coined, but were weighed (Ex. xxii. 16; II Sam. xviii. 12; I Kings xx. 39; see NUMISMATICS). The scales and weights were carried about with the precious metal in a bag attached to the girdle (Deut. xxv. 13 *et seq.*; Isa. xlvi. 6; Prov. xvi. 11). An adulteration or debasement of the value of the precious metals by means of certain alloys seems not to have occurred; at least the practise was not given any thought, and warnings are uttered only against false measures (Deut. *l.c.*; Lev. xix. 36).

To disprove the opinion that during the whole period before the Exile coined money was unknown—that is, money under state control in regard to weight, purity, etc.—the passage in I Sam. ix. 8 is cited. Here it is related that Saul's slave gave him the fourth part of a shekel of silver, which he had with him. The conclusion, however, that this is a reference to coined money is too hasty. The only inference to be drawn is that at the time when the author of I Sam. ix. lived silver pieces of a certain weight may have existed and that they were cast into certain shapes known to every one, in order to obviate the necessity of weighing them at each transaction. Perhaps the name for "talent" ("kikkar" = "ring") is derived from such forms, since Egyptian documents show that it was quite usual to cast the metals into such rings or into bars. These forms were not found among the Assyrians, who, however, used wedge-shaped pieces of gold, which are mentioned in Josh. vii. 21.

The Shekel.

For money, as for weight, the shekel was the standard unit, the pieces of metal being either fractions or multiples of the shekel. The struggle between the Egyptian decimal system and the sexagesimal method of the Babylonians first made itself felt in regard to weights of gold and silver. The Phenicians were probably the mediators; and a mina of 50 shekels was established as a standard. According to certain indications, the relative value of gold to silver was as 10 to 1. Later, in consequence of the great increase in the supply of silver, the relative value was as 40 to 3. This may, perhaps, have affected the possibility of introducing the sexagesimal system.

The gold shekel originally weighed $\frac{1}{60}$ of a mina. The silver shekel, to have had an equal value, must have weighed $\frac{40}{3} \times \frac{1}{60} = \frac{2}{9}$ of a mina. As this would have been impracticable for use, it was decided to make a smaller piece, one more suitable for circulation. Two methods presented themselves: (1) either the silver equivalent of the gold shekel could be divided into ten parts, in which case a silver shekel of $\frac{2}{90} = \frac{1}{45}$ of a shekel of weight would result; or (2) the silver equivalent could be divided into fifteen parts, in which case a silver shekel would weigh $\frac{2}{135}$ of a mina.

The Mina.

When the decimal system made its way into use, the gold mina as well as the silver mina was reckoned at 50 such shekels. Consequently there was (1) the Babylonian silver mina, equivalent to $\frac{50}{45} = \frac{10}{9}$ of a mina of weight; (2) the Phenician silver mina, equivalent to $\frac{100}{135} = \frac{20}{27}$ of a mina of weight.

In the earlier system of Babylonian silver values (which was used also in the Lydian and Persian kingdoms) the silver shekel was divided into thirds, sixths, and twelfths, whereas in the Phenician system it was divided into halves, fourths, eighths, etc.

The Phenician silver shekel is found among the Jews also. This is proved by the fact that they had the same method of division: the quarter-shekel appears in I Sam. ix. 8; the half-shekel is the Temple-tax in the Priestly Code. The shekels of the Maccabean period which have been preserved vary between 14.50 and 14.65 gr., which is exactly $\frac{2}{135}$ of the large "common" (see WEIGHTS AND MEASURES) Babylonian mina. The mina accordingly weighed 727.7 gr., and the talent 43,659 kg.

In the Persian period the Babylonian shekel, equivalent to one-tenth of the mina of weight, came into use, since Nehemiah (x. 33 [A. V. 32]) assessed the Temple-tax at one-third of a shekel. This Persian system of coinage had the small mina as a basis.

The Siglos.

The unit was the siglos, which corresponded to one-half of a Babylonian shekel. The relation between it and the Jewish one was 3 to 8. It was considered as the one-hundredth part of a mina and not the fiftieth. It amounted to 5.61–5.73 gr.; the mina, to 561–573 gr.; and the talent to 33,660–34,380 kg. In the Maccabean period the Phenician silver shekel was again in use. Consequently the Temple-tax was again a half-shekel (Matt. xvii. 24, 27).

II. Coined money did not come into use among the Jews until the time of the Persians. In the Old Testament, Persian darics (A. V. "drams") are mentioned in Ezra viii. 27 and I Chron. xxix. 7 as "adarkon," and in Ezra ii. 69 and Neh. vii. 70–72 as "darkemon." They weighed 8.40 gr., thus corresponding almost exactly to one-sixtieth of the Babylonian light mina. The corresponding silver coin was one-twentieth of the daric; which, perhaps, was meant by the term "shekel" in Neh. v. 15, x. 33. See NUMISMATICS.

BIBLIOGRAPHY: Benzinger, *Hebräische Archäologie*, pp. 189–198; Madden, *Coins of the Jews*, London, 1881; Nowack, *Lehrbuch der Hebräischen Archäologie*, 1894; Herzfeld, *Handelsgeschichte der Juden des Alterthums*, Brunswick, 1879, pp. 171–185; F. de Saulcy, *Recherches sur la Numismatique Judaïque*, 1854; Levy, *Geschichte der Jüdischen Münzen*, 1862.

E. G. H. W. N.

——**In Rabbinical Literature:** In conformity with the unvarying usage of the Mosaic law, the Mishnah (B. M. iv. 1) treats both gold and copper coins as commodities when they come to be exchanged for silver coins (see ALIENATION); but the Gemara upon this section gives a glimpse into the history of the battle of the gold and silver standards, which raged with varying fortunes from the days of Hillel and Shammai, in King Herod's time, to the compilation of the Mishnah by Rabbi. The latter's leading disciple, R. Ḥiyya, addresses him: "Rabbi, you teach us now in your old age that gold [as a commodity] gives title to silver; but when you were young you taught us the contrary!" In the discussion that follows the Mishnah is referred to (Ma'as. Sh. ii. 7). The school of Shammai says: "A man must not turn shekels into gold denarii [for transport of second tithe to Jerusalem]." The school of Hillel permitted it. The former school seemed to look on gold as a commodity, at least as compared with silver; the latter school was willing, for this purpose, at least, to treat both alike as money, if not to give gold a preference over silver. The Hillelites seemingly yielded to the Roman influence of their time, which maintained the gold standard.

The gold denarius passed generally for twenty-five silver denarii—that is, 6¼ shekels. It is urged in favor of gold as the true money that it was usual in the redemption of the first-born son for the father to give a gold denarius to the kohen, and for the latter to return five zuz, or silver denarii, in change, though the rate of exchange between silver and gold at the time might be such as to make the former worth either more or less than twenty-five of the latter. Another point is made in a responsum by R. Ḥiyya himself, that a loan made in gold may be recovered in gold, though it has risen in exchange value, without violating the law against usury (B. M. 44b–45b). Rabbi, as most of the intervening patriarchs, was one of Hillel's descendants, and naturally followed his teachings. It was probably a change in the Roman currency laws and in the habits of business which induced him in his later years to reestablish the old silver standard among the Jews.

S. L. N. D.

MONEY-LENDING. See Usury.

MONIES, DAVID: Danish portrait and genre painter; born in Copenhagen June 3, 1812; died there April 29, 1894. He was admitted to the school of the Academy of Arts in 1824, and was twice (1827 and 1832) awarded silver medals for meritorious work. In 1830 he began painting, producing and exhibiting portraits of eminent contemporaries.

In 1833 Monies produced "En Kunstner som spöger med en Bondepige." In 1835 he went to Munich, and in the following year 400 rix-dollars per annum was awarded to him from the public funds to enable him to continue his studies abroad. In 1848 he was elected a member of the Danish Academy of Arts, and in 1859 he received the title of professor. Among other paintings by Monies, the following may be mentioned: "To Börn ved et Vandlöb," 1838; "Erindring fra Danseboden," 1849; "Konfirmanden"; "Pengebrevet"; "En Skovtur" (in the royal gallery at Copenhagen). Monies essayed also historical painting, and his "Episode af Troppernes Hjemkomst," 1850, vividly expresses the feeling of joy mingled with sadness which animated the Danish people on the occasion of the homecoming of the troops after the Three Years' war. This painting is in the museum in Frederiksborg Castle. Monies was less fortunate in the large pictures in which he depicted scenes from the history of the Jewish people.

Bibliography: C. F. Bricka, *Dansk Biografisk Lexicon*; Weilbach, *Nyt Kunstnerlexicon*.

S. F. C.

MONIS, JUDAH: American scholar. Hannah Adams in her "History of the Jews" says that he was born in Algiers about 1683, and that he died in Northborough, Mass., in 1764; while Josiah Quincy in his "History of Harvard University" gives the year of his birth as 1680 and that of his death as 1761. Little is known of his early career. He is said to have received his education in Italy, and to have emigrated to Boston in the early part of the eighteenth century (Adams, *l.c.*). The first event of his life of which there is authentic record is his baptism (March 27, 1722) in the College Hall at Cambridge, Mass. After that he was an active and energetic worker in the cause of his new faith, although he observed throughout his life the Jewish Sabbath. He held the appointment of instructor in Hebrew at the university from 1722 till 1759, when, on the death of his wife, he resigned and removed to Northborough.

On the occasion of his baptism, after the sermon of the officiating clergyman, he delivered a discourse in which he formulated and defended his confession of faith. The title of this address (printed by S. Kneeland for O. Henchman "at the Corner Shop on the South Side of the Town House," Boston, 1722) is: "The Truth, Being a Discourse which the Author delivered at his Baptism, Containing Nine Principal Arguments the Modern Jewish Rabbins do make to prove the Messiah is yet to Come; With the Answers to each . . . not only according to the Orthodox Opinion, but even with the Authority of their own Authentick Rabbins of Old, and Likewise, With the Confession of his Faith, at the Latter End. Dedicated to the Jewish Nation and Prefac'd by the Reverend Increase Mather, D.D." Monis was the author also of two short essays, both treating of the same subject as his address.

In 1735 he published in Boston the first Hebrew grammar printed in America. It bore the title: "Dickdook Leshon Gnebreet. A Grammar of the Hebrew Tongue, Being an Essay To bring the Hebrew Grammar into English to Facilitate the Instruction of all those who are desirous of acquiring a clear idea of this Primitive Tongue by their own studies; In order to their more distinct Acquaintance with the Sacred Oracles of the Old Testament, according to the Original. And Published more especially for the Use of the Students of Harvard College at Cambridge, in New England."

Bibliography: Joseph Lebovich, *Judah Monis*, in *Jewish Comment*, Baltimore, Aug. 22, 1902; Hannah Adams, *History of the Jews*, London, 1818; Josiah Quincy, *History of Harvard University*, Cambridge, Mass., 1840; G. A. Kohut, in *American Journal of Semitic Languages*, xiv. 217 *et seq.*; *Publ. Am. Jew. Hist. Soc.*, i. 10, 423; x. 32.

T. F. T. H.

MONOGAMY: In Judaism the Law tolerated though it did not enact polygamy; but custom stood higher than the Law. From the period of the return from the Babylonian Exile, monogamy became the ideal and the custom of Jewish married life. That monogamy was the ideal may be seen from several facts. Not only does the narrative of Genesis, containing the story of the first man and woman, point to monogamy, but Gen. ii. 24 is best explained in the same sense. So, too, in the story of the Flood, in which the restoration of the human race is depicted, the monogamous principle is assumed. Also the polygamous marriages of some of the patriarchs are felt by the narrator (J) to need excuse and apology, as being infringements of a current monogamous ideal. Even more unmistakable is the monogamous ideal displayed in the Wisdom literature. The "Golden A B C of the Perfect Wife" in Prov. xxxi. 10–31 is certainly monogamous; in fact, throughout the Book of Proverbs "monogamy is assumed" (Toy, "Proverbs," p. xii.; comp. Cheyne, "Job and Solomon," p. 136). Ben Sira, moreover, as well as Tobit, confirms this conclusion (comp. History of Susanna 23, 69), though, while Ben Sira's view of woman is lower on the whole than that of the canonical Proverbs, Tobit's is quite as high as the highest ideal. Job is monogamous. So is the Song of Solomon. Harper gives a most convincing argument in this sense in his edition of the Song of Solomon (Cambridge, 1902; comp. especially pp. xxxi. and xxxiv.).

Monogamy the Jewish Ideal.

From another side the monogamous ideal is illustrated by the prophetic use of marriage as typical of the relation between God and Israel. In this sense monogamy becomes the corollary of the divine Unity (comp. Hamburger, "R. B. T." i., *s.v.* "Vielweiberei"). It is a commonplace of prophetic imagery to describe God as the husband and Israel as the bride (comp. Hosea, *passim*; the exquisite passage Jer. ii. 2; also *ib.* iii. 14, xxxi. 32), in contrast to idolatry, which is typical of impure married life (Isa. liv. 5, and many other passages). Infidelity toward God is expressed under the figure of whoredom (see Driver on Deut. xxxi. 16). The same figure of the relation of God to Israel passed over to the later Judaism; and a similar figure is prominent in Christianity also.

As to the Law, the facts have already been treated in part under Bigamy. Monogamy was not legally enforced. In the case of the Levirate Marriage, monogamy was legally invaded; otherwise, polygamy was merely tolerated and not set up as a laudable rule. But on the other hand the Law made several provisions which are of a nature to act as bars to polygamy. By positively prohibiting an Israelite eunuch-class (Deut. xxiii. 1) the possibility of the large Oriental harem was much diminished (see, however, Eunuch). Royal license in the matter of polygamy is denounced (Deut. xvii. 17), and in later times it is chiefly the un-Jewish Herod who is represented as having a large harem. The high priest, in the traditional explanation of Lev. xxi. 13, was restricted to one wife (Yoma i. 1; Yeb. 59a; Maimonides, "Yad," Issure Biah, xvii. 13). Perhaps the most effective deterrent of polygamy was the equality of rights established among a man's wives if he took more than one. The law of Ex. xxi. 10, "if he take himself another wife, her food, her raiment, and her duty of marriage, he shall not diminish," must in ancient as in medieval times have made polygamy unattractive, if not impossible, except to the very wealthy (comp. Luckock, "History of Marriage," 1894, pp. 13 *et seq.*). Again, the law of inheritance, by which the child of a second and favorite wife could not be preferred to the child of a less-beloved wife, must have stood as a bar to a second marriage. This law (Deut. xxi. 15), by its use of the terms "hated" and "beloved" of the two wives, also gives incidentally the main social objection to polygamy, namely, the difficulty of maintaining under a polygamous régime cordial relations within the home (Nowack, "Hebräische Archäologie," i. 159). It is certain that polygamy did not largely prevail in Israel (*ib.* 158). Until strict monogamy generally established itself after the Exile, the Jew had for the most part only one wife, with, perhaps, a secondary consort of lower status (a similar custom is revealed by the code of Hammurabi; see Johns in Hastings, "Dict. Bible," extra vol., p. 599a).

Legal Aspects.

It was the consideration of the difficulty of maintaining a happy home-life that practically abrogated polygamy among the Jews after the Exile. The ideal of Jewish family life is very high in the Wisdom literature; and the ideal continually rose with subsequent centuries. Güdemann rightly sees in this argument the strongest evidence of the monogamous condition of the Jews for centuries before monogamy was legally enforced (comp. Güdemann, "Das Judenthum," 1902, pp. 7 *et seq.*). It may be clearly seen from Ps. cxxviii., in which the domestic happiness of the monogamist God-fearer is depicted. This psalm has thus been appropriately introduced into the Church marriage service, as well as into the Synagogue processional for the Bridegroom of the Law.

That polygamy survived into the Christian era is, however, asserted by Josephus ("Ant." xvii. 1, § 2); and he himself ("Vita," § 75) seems to have had one wife in Palestine and another in Egypt (comp. Löw, "Gesammelte Schriften," iii. 47). Such a practise is forbidden by a baraita in Yeb. 37a; and this prohibition is (with certain limitations) introduced into the Shulḥan 'Aruk (Eben ha-'Ezer, ii. 11). The Talmud certainly does not enact monogamy (see Bigamy); and as far as the Law is concerned, Justin Martyr ("Dial. cum Tryph." § 134) is not wrong in asserting that in his time (2d cent. C.E.) Jews were permitted to have four or five wives. But it is very doubtful whether they availed themselves of the permission. Frankel ("Grundlinien des Mosaisch-Talmudischen Eherechts," 1860) maintains the prevalence of monogamy; and his view was not seriously shaken by the criticisms of Löw (*l.c.* pp. 48 *et seq.*), who does not contest Frankel's main position, but merely adduces some evidence to show that Frankel's conclusion was perhaps stated without sufficient reserve. It is not necessary to examine the details further here; for the main fact remains that the general impression made by the Talmudic evidence is altogether favorable to Frankel's contention (comp. the statement of Amram in "The Jewish Law of Divorce," 1897, p. 76, note 3: "There are many indications in the Mishnah that monogamy was the rule and polygamy the exception"; he cites Yeb. ii. 9, 10—on which Frankel also lays stress—where the presumption that a messenger bringing a document of divorce from foreign parts had assisted in divorcing the woman because he wished to marry her himself, is rebutted by the fact that he had a wife living at the time). It is, however, on the general impression that one relies in adopting the view of Frankel. Edersheim ("Hist. of the Jewish Nation," 1896, p. 272) is equally emphatic.

Josephus and the Talmud.

The Jewish law reached the Middle Ages with polygamy permitted, but not much practised. Theoretically a man might have several wives if he wished, for R. Ami's view to the contrary does not seem to have been accepted (Yeb. 65a, below). So in his codification of the Jewish law, Maimonides ("Yad," Ishut, xiv.; comp. Shulḥan 'Aruk, Eben ha-'Ezer, i. 9) makes it lawful for man to contract many simultaneous marriages. But this must not be taken to represent the personal opinion of Maimonides, especially if the letter attributed to him concerning the French (Provençal) rabbis be authentic. In that letter Maimonides scornfully attacks the practise of bigamy with an abusive vigor certainly unusual with him (on this letter see Kobak's "Jeschurun," iii. 46-55). The law, as laid down in the Talmud and codified by Maimonides, required, however, that the husband should not only insure to each wife adequate maintenance (each wife could claim a separate domicile), but should also secure for each full conjugal rights. Such

The Middle Ages.

restrictions are essentially foreign to a polygamous condition.

It may be inferred that, except in the case of childlessness, very few European Jews in the Middle Ages were other than monogamous. It must be remembered that in the Jewish view the purpose of marriage was not to satisfy carnal desires, but to raise up a family; hence it was not uncommon that a man was permitted and even urged to take a second wife when this purpose was unfulfilled. It is open to question whether a simultaneous marriage or a divorce of the first wife would be the more humane or expedient course; but while the Jewish theory as to the purpose of marriage prevailed, one or other course was natural in case of the wife's sterility. At all events when R. Gershom at the beginning of the eleventh century succeeded with the utmost ease in making monogamy the law for Western Jews, he was merely formalizing current practise (comp. Güdemann, "Gesch." i. 11, ii. 165, iii. 116; Abrahams, "Jewish Life in the Middle Ages," ch. vii.). Graetz's arguments to show that polygamy prevailed in Europe in R. Gershom's time are refuted by Harkavy in the Hebrew edition of Graetz (iii. 367, note קי״א). On R. Gershom's celebrated ḥerem see Bigamy and Gershom b. Judah.

Monogamy Becomes Jewish Law.

In Mohammedan parts of Europe, as well as in the Orient generally, the law of monogamy was not, and is not, formally accepted. Occasional cases of bigamy are found in Spain as late as the fourteenth century (for a case in 1322 comp. Kayserling in "Monatsschrift," 1865, pp. 390-391, and add the evidence from the Responsa of Isaac b. Sheshet, 1901, § 20). But it may be doubted whether any clear cases can be produced of such marriages except for specific reasons which the Jewish theory of marriage regarded as adequate (comp., for instance, RaSHBA's testimony in Ṭur Eben ha-'Ezer). The objection in the Orient to Gershom's rule turned on this very point as well as on the levirate difficulty. That even in the Orient bigamy was against the sentiment of many may be seen from the customary undertaking (included in the ketubah) by the husband that he will not take a second wife. The insertion of such a clause is termed "customary" in the Ṭur Eben ha-'Ezer, § 119, near end (comp. Abrahams, *l.c.* p. 120, and Jew. Encyc. vii. 476, *s.v.* Ketubah). Thus in the East a voluntary promise often replaced what was law in the West. No doubt cases of bigamy still occur among Eastern Jews (see references in Westermarck, "History of Human Marriage," Index, *s.v.* "Jews"); but such cases are surprisingly rare. In addition to the citations in Kalisch (Commentary on Leviticus, ii. 374), the following may be quoted: "As a rule, the Oriental Jews are practically monogamists" (Lucy Garnett, "The Women of Turkey," 1891, p. 12); "Bigamy [in Morocco] is also legal, though uncommon" (Budgett Meakin, "The Moors," 1902, p. 443); "They [the Yemenites] rarely marry more than one wife" (M. Thomas, "Two Years in Palestine and Syria," 1900, p. 40). For similar statements as to Teheran and Safed see "Revue des Ecoles de l'Alliance Israélite Universelle," No. 2, p. 166; No. 3, p. 195. It is indeed to the schools, now so beneficently established in most parts of the East, that one must look for a complete legalization of what is after all the ordinary rule and custom in regard to monogamy.

Conditions in the Orient.

J. I. A.

MONOTHEISM: The belief in one God. The French writer Ernest Renan has propounded the theory that the monotheistic instinct was a Semitic trait, and that therefore the universal belief that it was characteristic of the Hebrews alone must be modified. But later research into Semitic origins has demonstrated the untenability of Renan's contention. Robertson Smith has summed up the matter with the statement that "what is often described as a natural tendency of Semitic religion toward ethical monotheism is in the main nothing more than a consequence of the alliance of religion with monarchy" ("Rel. of Sem." p. 74; Montefiore, "Hibbert Lectures," p. 24; Schreiner, "Die Jüngsten Urtheile über das Judenthum," p. 7). The Hebrews alone of all the Semitic peoples reached the stage of pure monotheism, through the teachings of their prophets; however, it required centuries of development before every trace of idolatry disappeared even from among them, and before they stood forth as a "unique people on earth," worshipers of the one God and of Him alone.

In Hebrew tradition the origin of the belief in the one God is connected with the religious awakening of the patriarch Abraham. Later legends describe circumstantially how Abraham reached this belief (Beer, "Leben Abrahams nach Auffassung der Jüdischen Sage"; see Abraham). Though the tradition contains without doubt the kernel of the truth, modern criticism holds that the Hebrew tribes were brought to a clear realization of the difference between their God and the gods of the surrounding nations through the work and teachings of Moses. The acceptance of the pure monotheistic belief by the whole people was a slow process at best; how slow, many statements in the historical and prophetical books of the Bible prove amply. Throughout the period of the first commonwealth there was constant reversion to idolatry on the part of the people (comp. Judges ii. 11-13, 17, 19; iii. 7; viii. 33; x. 6, 10, 13; I Sam. viii. 8, xii. 10; I Kings ix. 9, xiv. 9, xvi. 31; II Kings xvii. 7, xxii. 17; Isa. ii. 8, x. 11, xxxi. 7; Jer. i. 16; vii. 9, 18; ix. 13; xi. 10, 13, 17; xii. 16; xiii. 10; xvi. 11; xix. 4-5, 23; xxii. 9; xxxii. 29, 35; xliv. 3, 5, 15; Hos. ii. 7, iii. 1, iv. 17, viii. 4, xi. 2; Ps. cvi. 36; II Chron. vii. 22; xxiv. 18; xxviii. 2, 25; xxxiii. 7; xxxiv. 25). Forgetful of their obligation to worship Yhwh and Him alone, the people followed after the "ba'alim"; the "bamot" and the "asherot" dotted the land; frequently, too, the Israelites confounded the worship of Yhwh with the worship of Baal.

Rise of the Belief.

Monolatry.

In the development of religious belief in Israel there are indications of a growth through various stages before the conception of absolute uncompromising monotheism was reached. Down to the eighth-century prophets, the religion of the people was monolatrous rather than monotheistic; they considered YHWH to be the *one* God and *their* God, but not the one and only God. He was the national God of Israel as Chemosh was the god of Moab and Milkom the god of Ammon (Num. xxi. 29; Judges xi. 24; I Kings xi. 33). He was not yet the God of all the nations and of the universe. The existence of other gods was not definitively denied; even the second commandment does not disclaim the existence of other gods; it merely forbids Israel to bow down to them or serve them (comp. Deut. iv. 19). There was, in truth there could be, no other God in Israel; but this, it is held, did not affect the reality of the gods of other nations; though, in comparison with the might and glory of YHWH, they were weak and powerless. A very early poem has the words, "Who is like unto thee, O Lord, among the gods?" (Ex. xv. 11)—a sufficient indication that the idea that there were other gods was in the writer's mind. In a later psalm there is a reminiscence of this early state of thought—"There is none like unto thee among the gods" (Ps. lxxxvi. 8, R. V.).

As among other Semitic peoples (Smith, *l.c.* p. 91), so, too, in early Israel the closest relationship was supposed to subsist between the Deity, the land, and the people. YHWH was the God not only of Israel the people (II Sam. vii. 23; I Kings viii. 59), but of the land of Israel; He could be approached nowhere else (comp. the story of Naaman, II Kings v. 15); the great conception of His omnipresence as held by the author of the 139th Psalm was not yet reached. Thus when David was compelled by his enemies to flee he complained bitterly: "They have driven me out this day that I should not cleave unto the inheritance of the Lord, saying, Go, serve other gods" (I Sam. xxvi. 19, R. V.); and the prophet Hosea speaks of the domain of the Israelites as "God's land" (ix. 3). The triple relationship of God, people, and land is forcibly expressed in as late a passage as the prayer of the Deuteronomist, "Look down from thy holy habitation, from heaven, and bless thy people Israel, and the land which thou hast given us" (Deut. xxvi. 15).

God, Land, and People.

In Israel, then, and in Israel's land YHWH was sole God. Even this preparatory stage to universal monotheism was not reached until centuries after the occupation of the land; there was a syncretism of religious cults; the people were tolerant of the local ba'alim; Jeroboam was able to set up the calf-gods at Dan and Bethel without arousing a great outcry.

YHWH alone in the land, the land YHWH's alone, the worship of no other god to be tolerated in the land—this was the program of the zealous prophet Elijah, and in his activity there was a decided step forward to the recognition of YHWH alone as the God of Israel. For Elijah it was YHWH only or nothing; "How long halt ye between two opinions? if the Lord be God, follow him; but if Baal, then follow him" (I Kings xviii. 21). Monolatry reaches its supreme expression in Elijah: "YHWH is God" is the watchword of his activity; there is room for none other in Israel.

From this attitude of Elijah it was but a step to pure monotheism; the belief is found in full flower in the speeches of the great eighth-century prophets; the genius of Amos and his successors carried the conception of the "oneness" of YHWH to its uttermost limit, although even in their time the people did not reach this height of thought; it was only after the return from the Babylonian exile that the monotheistic belief was a positive possession of the people as well as of the great spirits to whom the truth was first vouchsafed.

The modern view of the development of religious thought in Israel is that the conception of pure monotheism was reached through three channels—through the recognition of God in nature and in history, and through the belief in the ethical character or holiness of God. When YHWH was recognized as the Creator of heaven and earth and all that in them is (comp. Amos v. 8, ix. 6), when the appellation "the Lord of the heavenly hosts" was given Him (Amos iv. 13, v. 27, Hebr.), when the whole earth was spoken of as being full of His glory (Isa. vi. 3), then there was room for no other god; for the conception of God as the Lord and Creator of nature carried with it, as a necessary corollary, the belief that there was no god beside Him (Jer. x. 11). The great conceptions of the Prophets that YHWH punishes wrong-doing not only in Israel but in other nations (Amos i.-ii.), that He is the arbiter of the destinies of such other nations (*ib.* ix. 7), that He uses heathen kings as instruments of punishment or salvation, as when Isaiah speaks of the Assyrian monarch as "the rod of God's anger," when Jeremiah points to the Babylonian king as the instrument whereby God will punish Jerusalem, and when deutero-Isaiah refers to Cyrus as God's anointed—all this involves the conclusion that there was no god but YHWH, for His dominion extended not only over Israel, but over the nations of the earth also, and His guiding hand directed the course of kings and peoples in the working out of their history.

True Monotheism.

But the conception of the holiness of YHWH (Isa. v. 16, vi. 3; Hab. i. 13), the recognition of His ethical character, led more than anything else to monotheism, as Kuenen has pointed out ("Hibbert Lectures," 1882, p. 127). As long as YHWH was looked upon as only the national God, it was a question of the supremacy of the strongest as between Him and the national gods of other peoples. But when God was presented primarily in His ethical character and worshiped as the God of holiness, there was no longer any measure of comparison. If YHWH was the holy God, then the other gods were not. Here was an entirely new element; YHWH as the moral governor of men and nations was absolutely unique; the gods of the nations were "elilim" (= "nothings"; Isa. ii. 8, 18, 20; x. 10-11; xix. 1, 3; xxxi. 7; Hab. ii. 18; Ezek. xxx. 13), "vanity" (Jer. ii. 5, viii. 19, x. 15, xvi. 19, xviii. 15; Isa. xliv. 9, lix. 4), "lies" (Amos ii. 4; Hab. ii. 18; Jer. xxix. 31), "abomination" (Hos. ix. 10; Jer. iv. 1, vii. 30, xiii. 27, xxxii. 34; Ezek. v. 11; vii. 20; xx. 7-8, 30; Isa. xliv. 19).

The doctrine of absolute monotheism is preached in the most emphatic manner by Jeremiah (x. 10; xiv. 22; xxiii. 36; xxxii. 18, 27) and the Deuteronomist (iv. 35, 39), but the Biblical teaching on the subject may be said to have culminated in Isaiah of Babylon. YHWH, though in a peculiar sense the God of Israel, is still the God of all the world. This prophet's standpoint is uncompromising: "I, even I, am the Lord; and beside me there is no savior" (xliii. 11); "I am the first, and I am the last; and besides me there is no God" (xliv. 6, xlviii. 12); "that they may know from the rising of the sun to the setting thereof that there is none besides me; I am God and there is none else" (xlv. 6, Hebr.). In the post-exilic psalms and such other portions of the Bible as were produced during the second commonwealth—Proverbs, Job, Song of Songs, Ecclesiastes, Daniel—the belief in the one God and in Him alone is positively assured. Not only in Palestine was monotheism now the sure possession of the Jewish people, but it may be said that the Judaism of the Diaspora is conscious of itself as the bearer of the monotheistic doctrine and as being therein distinguished from all its surroundings (comp. Friedländer, "Gesch. der Jüdischen Apologetik," p. 217). In proof of this latter statement many passages can be cited from the apocryphal and the pseudepigraphical writings. "Let them [the nations] know thee, as we also have known thee, that there is no God but only thou, O God" (Ecclus. xxxvi. 5; comp. also xliii. 28); "neither is there any God besides thee, that careth for all" (Wisdom of Solomon xii. 13); "O Lord, Lord God, the Creator of all things, . . . who alone art King and gracious, who alone suppliest every need, who alone art righteous and almighty and eternal" (II Macc. i. 24–25; comp. Ep. Jer. 5, in Kautzsch, "Apokryphen," i. 226; Aristeas Letter, 134: *ib.* ii. 16; Sibyllines, Proem, 7, 15, 54; iii. 584 *et seq.*, v. 76 *et seq.*: *ib.* i. 184, 196, 207; comp. also Josephus, "Ant." iv. 8, § 5).

Culmination in Isaiah.

The spread of Christianity with its doctrine of the divinity of its founder called forth a number of expressions from the Jewish sages touching the subject of the absolute unity of God; thus a commentary on the first commandment reads, "A king of flesh and blood has a father and a brother; but God says, 'With Me it is not so; "I am the first" because I have no father, and "I am the last" because I have no brother; and "besides me there is no God," because I have no son'" (Ex. R. xxix. 5). A similar expression is used in explanation of Ecclus. iv. 8 ("There is one alone, and there is not a second"): "he hath neither child nor brother; but hear, O Israel, the Lord is our God, the Lord is One" (Deut. R. ii. 33). There can be little doubt that such a saying as "Whoever draws out the pronunciation of the word 'one' [in the Shema'], his days and years will be lengthened" is of similar import (Ber. 13b); the emphasizing of the unity was the particular characteristic of the faithful in a world of dualistic and trinitarian propaganda. As long as a man refused allegiance to other gods he was looked upon as a Jew; "whoever denies the existence of other gods is called a Jew" (Meg. 13a).

Talmudic Attitude.

The unity of God was a revealed truth for the Jew; there was no need of proofs to establish it; it was the leading tenet of the faith; nor is any attempt at such proof found until the time of the medieval Jewish philosophers, who, in building up their systems of religious philosophy, devoted considerable space to the consideration of the attributes of God, especially of His unity. Proofs for the unity are given at length by Saadia ("Emunot we-De'ot," i. 7), Maimonides ("Moreh," ii. 1), Gersonides ("Milḥamot Adonai," iii. 3), and Ḥasdai Crescas ("Or Adonai," iii. 4).

The belief in the unity was formulated by Maimonides as the second of the thirteen articles of the faith known as the Maimonidean Creed: "I believe that the Creator, Blessed be His name, is One, and that no unity is like His in any form, and that He alone is our God, who was, is, and ever will be." Solomon ibn Gabirol expressed the idea in another manner in his great liturgical poem "Keter Malkut": "Thou art One, the first great Cause of all; Thou art One, and none can penetrate—not even the wise in heart—the mystery of Thy unfathomable unity; Thou art One, the Infinitely Great." This statement of belief found constant expression in the liturgy, as in the Minḥah service for Sabbath afternoon ("Thou art One and Thy name is One"), and in such liturgical poems as the "Adon 'Olam" ("He is One and there is no second, to compare to Him or associate with Him") and the "Yigdal" ("He is One and there is no unity like His unity . . . His unity is unending").

The profession of the unity is the climax of the devotion of the greatest of the holy days, the Day of Atonement. At death it is the last word to fall from the Jew's lips and from the lips of the bystanders. This has been Judaism's great contribution to the religious thought of mankind, and still constitutes the burden of its Messianic ideal, the coming of the day when all over the world "God shall be One and His name One" (comp. Zech. xiv. 9). See SHEMA'.

J. D. P.

MONREAL: City in Navarre, situated three miles from Pamplona; to be distinguished from a city of the same name in Aragon. A small number of Jews lived here in a "Juderia." In 1320 the Jews of Pamplona, who were threatened by the shepherds, fled to Monreal and, supported by the brave D. Alfonso of Aragon, united with their co-believers in defending themselves against the pursuing herdsmen; 170 of them were, however, killed. In 1366 there were fourteen Jews in Monreal; in 1380 the Jews paid taxes to the local abbot; in 1477 their number had become so small that they held divine worship in a private house. D. Juze Orabuena, chief rabbi of Navarre and body-physician to the king, received houses in the Monreal Juderia as a present from the king.

BIBLIOGRAPHY: Usque, *Consolaçam*, p. 182a; Ibn Verga, *Shebet Yehudah*, p. 6; Joseph ha-Kohen, *'Emeḳ ha-Baka*, p. 61; Kayserling, *Gesch. der Juden in Spanien*, i. 36; Grätz, *Gesch.* viii.; Jacobs, *Sources*, Nos. 1465, 1571; *Boletin Acad. Hist.* xxiii. 142; *R. E. J.* xxvii. 275.

S. M. K.

MONSTER. See LEVIATHAN.

MONTAGU, HYMAN: English numismatist and lawyer; died in London Feb. 18, 1895; son of Samuel Moses (having later assumed the name of

Montagu); educated at the City of London School. Articled to a firm of lawyers, he passed his final examination with distinction, and established himself as an expert in bankruptcy law. In early life a collector of beetles, he afterward took up coin-collecting, which he pursued with enterprising industry, becoming a numismatist of the highest rank. He presented a valuable collection of coins to the British Museum.

His principal works on numismatics are: (1) "Catalogue, with Illustrations, of a Collection of Milled English Coins Dating from the Reign of George I. to that of Queen Victoria" (1890); (2) "The Copper, Tin, and Bronze Coinage, and Patterns for Coins of England from the Reign of Elizabeth to that of Queen Victoria" (1885–93). His collection of Greek coins was especially noteworthy; and the sale catalogue of it became the standard work on the subject. He was the author of many essays on coinage, contributed to the publications of learned societies, and was a fellow of the Society of Antiquaries.

Montagu compiled the catalogue of coins for the Anglo-Jewish Historical Exhibition, London, 1887, for which, too, he wrote an introductory essay on Jewish coins and medals. He was for many years honorary secretary of Jews' College and a member of the education committee of that institution. He was also honorary solicitor for the industrial committee of the Stepney Jewish and the Board of Guardians schools, and a member of the committee of the Aged Needy Society.

BIBLIOGRAPHY: *Jew. Chron.* and *Jew. World*, Feb. 22, 1895.

J. G. L.

MONTAGU, SIR SAMUEL, Bart.: English banker and communal worker; born at Liverpool Dec. 21, 1832; son of Louis Samuel, his name, "Montagu Samuel," having been in his early boyhood reversed by his parents. He went to London in 1847, and in 1853 founded the firm of Samuel Montagu & Co., foreign bankers, in Leadenhall street, afterward in Old Broad street.

In the Jewish community of London Montagu has been a prominent figure. For over a quarter of a century he has been connected with the Jewish Board of Guardians, the Board of Deputies, the United Synagogue, and other Jewish institutions. In 1870 he established and became president of the Jewish Working Men's Club. He has also been greatly interested in the building of new synagogues. In 1875 he founded, in conjunction with Lord Rothschild, the first industrial Jewish school in Jerusalem. In 1882, at the instance of the Mansion House (Russo-Jewish) Committee, of which he became treasurer, he went to Brody to inspect the emigration to America. In 1884 he visited the United States to inspect the Jewish agricultural colonies there. In 1886, Montagu visited several towns in Russian Poland and Russia proper, but was ordered by the Russian government to leave Moscow within twenty-four hours. In 1890 he merged the various ḥebras in the East End of London in the Federation of Synagogues, of which he became the first president.

In the general community Sir Samuel is or has been a justice of the peace for London and Hampshire; deputy lieutenant for the Tower Hamlets; member of the Gold and Silver Commission (1887–1890); and member of Parliament in the Liberal interest for the Whitechapel Division of the Tower Hamlets (1885–1900). He was created a baronet by Mr. Gladstone in 1894. In Oct., 1900, he contested unsuccessfully the parliamentary seat for Central Leeds. He has taken great interest in the proposal to introduce decimal coinage into England.

BIBLIOGRAPHY: *Banker's Magazine*, Sept., 1888; *Jew. Chron.* Aug. 5, 1892; Sept. 28, 1900.

J. G. L.

MONTALBAN: City in Aragon; not to be confused with Montalban in Castile, in the archbishopric of Toledo, which was also inhabited by Jews. Montalban possessed a Jewish community as early as the fourteenth century. In 1306 the governor of the place received permission to admit ten Jewish families which had been expelled from France. He was then given charge of the Jews and was empowered to adjust all their litigations. At the disputation in Tortosa the Montalban community was represented by Abu Ganda. A certain Jacob of Montalban died a martyr at Ancona in 1556.

BIBLIOGRAPHY: Isaac b. Sheshet, *Responsa*, § 510; *Shebeṭ Yehudah*, p. 68; *R. E. J.* xi. 153; Jacobs, *Sources*, Nos. 759, 1095, 1197.

J. M. K.

MONTALTO, FILOTHEO ELIAU (ELIJAH): Portuguese physician; born at Castello Branco in the middle of the sixteenth century; died at Tours, France, in 1616. According to Kayserling ("Die Juden in Navarra," p. 146), Montalto was a brother of the physician Amatus Lusitanus; but this supposition is not sufficiently corroborated to make it probable.

Montalto was brought up by his Marano parents in the Jewish religion, and to this he remained faithful during his entire life. Having graduated as physician, he left his native country, where he was always exposed to the rigors of the Inquisition, and went to Italy. He settled first at Leghorn (*c.* 1598), and several years later at Venice. In the latter city he made the acquaintance of Concino Concini, on whose recommendation he was invited by Maria de Medici to come as physician to the French court. Montalto had declined many high positions in Italy—chief among them being that of successor to the renowned Mercurial in the University of Padua—because he feared that if he accepted them he would not be able to perform his religious obligations. In accepting Maria de Medici's invitation, therefore, he made it a condition that he should have complete religious freedom, and be exempt from any service on Saturday, although the rabbis of Venice decided that in cases of emergency he might travel on that day.

Montalto, who became a general favorite, was appointed councilor; and he remained at the French court until his death, which occurred suddenly while he was accompanying Louis XIII. to Tours. Maria de Medici caused the body to be embalmed, and sent it, accompanied by Morteira and certain of Montalto's relatives, to Amsterdam for burial.

Montalto was considered a high authority, not

only in medicine but in all branches of science. Among his numerous works on medicine the most important were: (1) "Optica Intra Philosophiæ et Medicinæ Aream de Visu, de Visus Organo et Objecto Theor. Accurate Complectens" (Florence, 1606); (2) "Archipathologia in Qua Internarum Capitis Affectionum, Essentia, Causæ Signa, Præsagia, et Curatio Accuratissima Indagine Disseruntur" (Paris, 1614; St. Gervais, 1618; Nuremberg, 1686); (3) "Consultationes Medicæ Itemque de Sensu et Sensato Super Aristotelem" (1614). Montalto was the author also of the following polemical works, still extant in manuscript: (1) "Sobre el Capitulo 53 de Ezayas é Outros Textos da Sagrada Escritura," divided into three parts (Columbia University [New York] MS.); (2) "Livro Fayto . . . em Que Mostra a Verdade de Diversos Textos, e Cazos, Que Alegão as Gentilidades para Confirmar Suas Seictas" (Wolf, "Bibl. Hebr." iii. 104); (3) "Razonamiento del Señor H. M . . . . em Paris, por Mandado del Rey Enrique IV. Delante de los Mayores Teologos y Doctores de Su Corte."

BIBLIOGRAPHY: Barrios, *Relacion de los Poetas y Escritores Españoles de la Nacion Judayca*, p. 55; Manasseh ben Israel, *Miḳweh Yisrael*, p. 57; Grätz, *Gesch.* ix. 485-490; Kayserling, *Bibl. Esp.-Port.-Jud.* p. 73.

D. I. BR.

MONTANA: One of the northwestern states of the American Union. It was organized as a territory in 1864, and admitted as a state in 1889. It has the following Jewish communities: **Helena,** the capital of the state, with a benevolent association founded in 1872 and a congregation, Emanu-El, founded in 1887. Its rabbi is Jacob Mielziner. Helena has also a social club and a ladies' auxiliary society. **Butte,** with two congregations. Of the older, the B'nai Israel, founded in 1897, the present rabbi is Harry Weiss; the community has a Hebrew benevolent association founded in 1881. **Anaconda,** with a congregation, B'nai Israel. A.

MONTAUBAN, R. ELIEZER. See DAUPHINÉ.

MONTE DI PIETÀ. See PAWNBROKERS.

MONTEFIORE: Anglo-Jewish family which derives its name from a town in Italy. In 1856 there were three towns so named in the Pontifical States, but from which of the three the family came is not definitely known. As far back as 1630 the Montefiores were settled at Ancona as merchants. From Ancona they, or some of them, seem to have gone to Leghorn. Thither, about the end of the seventeenth or the commencement of the eighteenth century, **Judah Montefiore** went, and was taken into business by his uncle, **Isach Vita Montefiore.** Judah married a daughter of the Medinas, by whom he had four sons. The third son, **Moses Vita (Haim) Montefiore,** married, in 1752, Esther Hannah, daughter of Massahod Racah, a Moorish merchant of Leghorn. Moses had seventeen children. The third, **Samuel,** married Grace, daughter of Abraham Mocatta, and became the grandfather of Haim Guedalla. The fourth, **Joseph Elias,** was the father of Sir Moses Montefiore. The seventh, **Eliezer,** married a granddaughter of Simon Barrow of Amsterdam, and emigrated to the West Indies. He became the father of Joseph Barrow Montefiore (1803–93) and Jacob Montefiore (1801–95), both of whom were among the early pioneers of Australia. But the most notable was the sixth son, Joshua, who had seven children by a second marriage.

Abraham Montefiore: Stock-broker; born in London 1788; died at Lyons 1824; son of Joseph Elias Montefiore and brother of Sir Moses Montefiore, with whose commercial career he was afterward identified. He first adopted a trade and was apprenticed to Mr. Flower, silk-merchant of Watling street. In the silk trade he realized a small fortune, but being ambitious to push forward more rapidly, he joined his brother Moses in business; the firm of Montefiore Brothers thus formed carried on business in Shorters' court, Throgmorton street.

Montefiore was exceptionally fortunate on the Stock Exchange and left behind him a very large fortune. In 1824 he died at Lyons, on his way home from Cannes, whither he had gone for the reestablishment of his health. He was twice married: by his first wife, a daughter of George Hall of the London Stock Exchange, he had one daughter, Mary, who married Benjamin Mocatta; and by his second wife, Henrietta Rothschild, he had two sons and two daughters.

BIBLIOGRAPHY: L. Wolf, *Life of Sir Moses Montefiore*, pp. 13, 15, 18, 25, London, 1885.

Charlotte Montefiore: Authoress; born in London 1818; died there July 2, 1854. She took an active part in the Jewish Ladies' Benevolent Loan and Visiting Society as well as in the Jewish Emigration Society, of which she was one of the founders. She was the active friend of the Jews' Free School, the Jews' Infant School, the West Metropolitan School, and of many other educational establishments. Her reading was extensive, especially in moral and ethical philosophy. She was a contributor to many publications calculated to improve and elevate Jewish youth. For the "Cheap Jewish Library" she wrote "The Way to Get Rich," "The Birthday," "Caleb Asher," etc.; she wrote also "A Few Words to the Jews" (London, 1851).

BIBLIOGRAPHY: *Jew. Chron.* July 14, 1854; Kayserling, *Die Jüdischen Frauen*, pp. 275-276.

Claude Goldsmid Montefiore: English scholar and philanthropist; younger son of Nathaniel Montefiore; born in 1858. He was educated at Balliol College, Oxford, where he obtained a first class in the classical final examination, and where he came under the influence of Jowett and T. H. Green. Intended originally for the ministry of the Reform congregation of England, he studied theology in Berlin, but finding himself unable to sympathize with the arrest of the Reform Movement, he devoted himself instead to scholarly and philanthropic pursuits. He nevertheless continued to be a spiritual teacher and preacher, though in a lay capacity, and published a volume of sermons, in conjunction with Israel Abrahams, entitled "Aspects of Judaism" (London, 1894). In 1886 he was selected by the Hibbert trustees to deliver the Hibbert course of lectures for 1892 ("The Origin of Religion as Illustrated by the Ancient Hebrews"). In these lectures Montefiore made a permanent contribution to the science of theology. In 1896 he published the

Montefiore Pedigree.

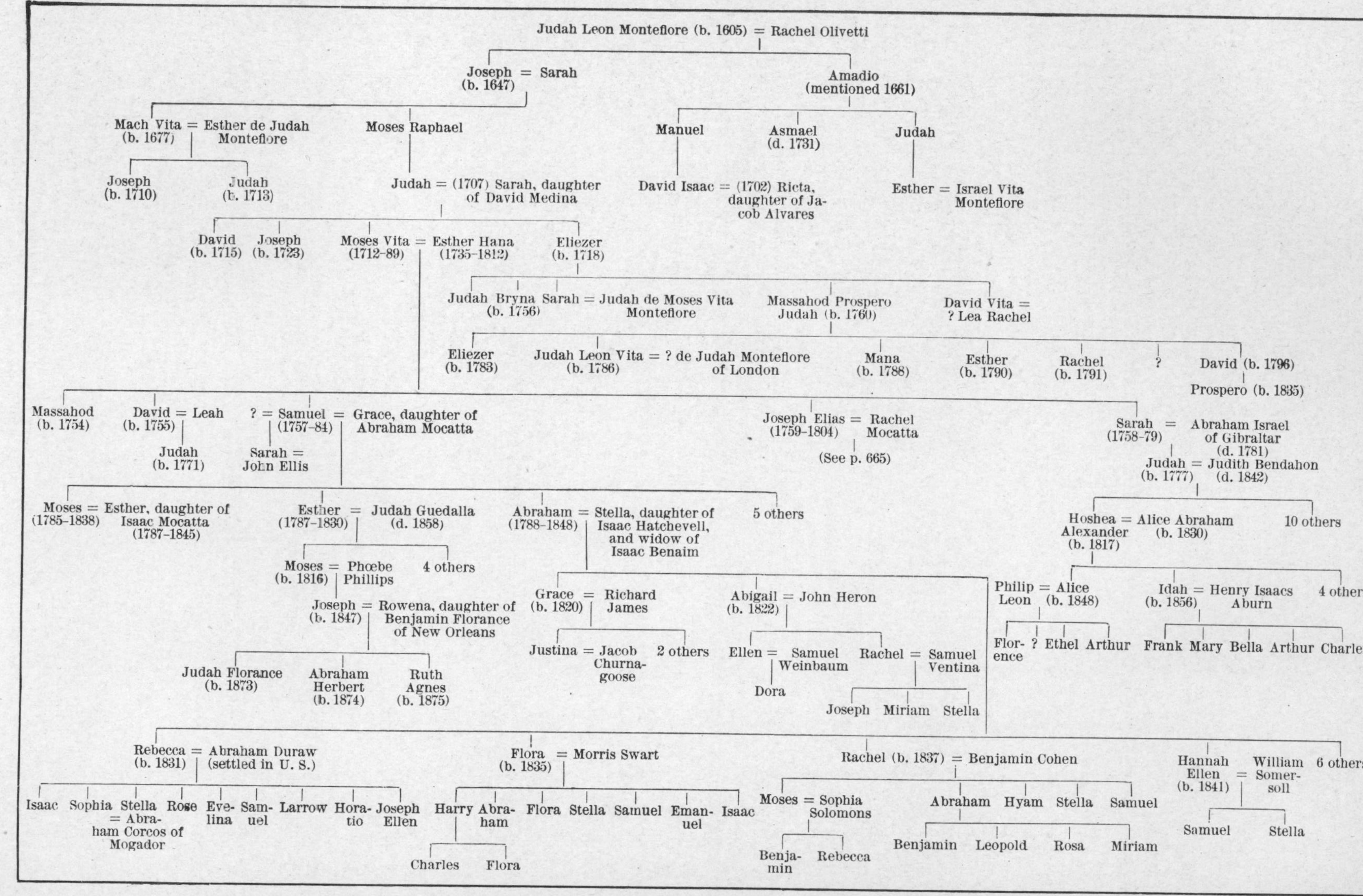

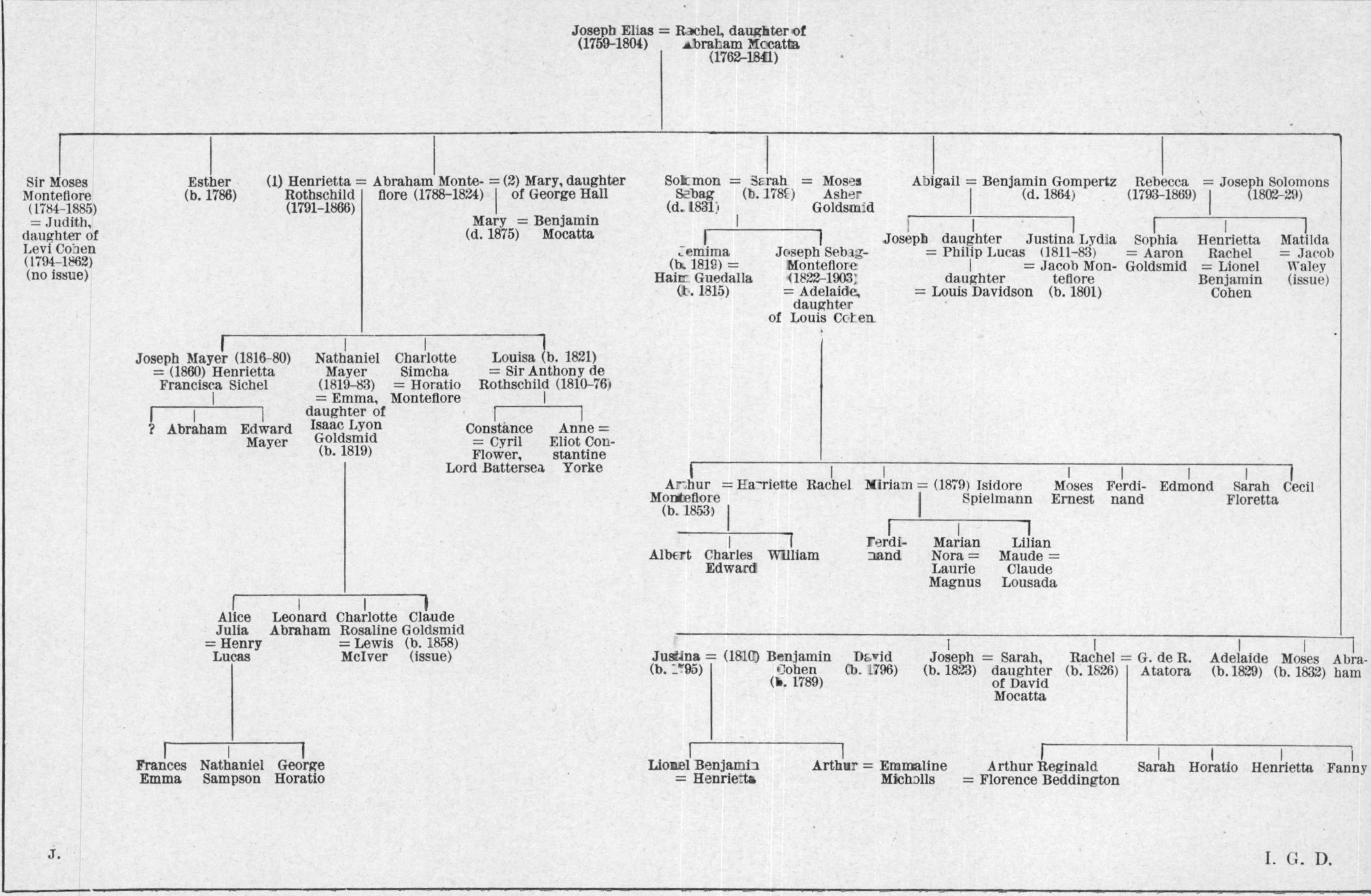
Joseph Elias = Rachel, daughter of Abraham Mocatta
(1759–1804) (1762–1841)
Sir Moses Montefiore (1784–1885) = Judith, daughter of Levi Cohen (1794–1862) (no issue)
Esther (b. 1786)
(1) Henrietta Rothschild (1791–1866) = Abraham Montefiore (1788–1824) = (2) Mary, daughter of George Hall
Mary (d. 1875) = Benjamin Mocatta
Solomon Sebag (d. 1831) = Sarah (b. 1789) = Moses Asher Goldsmid
Jemima (b. 1819) = Haim Guedalla (b. 1815)
Joseph Sebag-Montefiore (1822–1903) = Adelaide, daughter of Louis Cohen
Abigail = Benjamin Gompertz (d. 1864)
Joseph
daughter = Philip Lucas
daughter = Louis Davidson
Justina Lydia (1811–83) = Jacob Montefiore (b. 1801)
Rebecca (1793–1869) = Joseph Solomons (1802–29)
Sophia = Aaron Goldsmid
Henrietta Rachel = Lionel Benjamin Cohen
Matilda = Jacob Waley (issue)
Joseph Mayer (1816–80) = (1860) Henrietta Francisca Sichel
? Abraham
Edward Mayer
Nathaniel Mayer (1819–83) = Emma, daughter of Isaac Lyon Goldsmid (b. 1819)
Charlotte Simcha = Horatio Montefiore
Louisa (b. 1821) = Sir Anthony de Rothschild (1810–76)
Constance = Cyril Flower, Lord Battersea
Anne = Eliot Constantine Yorke
Arthur Montefiore (b. 1853) = Harriette
Rachel
Miriam = (1879) Isidore Spielmann
Moses Ernest
Ferdinand
Edmond
Sarah Floretta
Cecil
Albert
Charles Edward
William
Ferdinand
Marian Nora = Laurie Magnus
Lilian Maude = Claude Lousada
Alice Julia = Henry Lucas
Leonard Abraham
Charlotte Rosaline = Lewis McIver
Claude Goldsmid (b. 1858) (issue)
Frances Emma
Nathaniel Sampson
George Horatio
Justina (b. 1795) = (1810) Benjamin Cohen (b. 1789)
David (b. 1796)
Joseph (b. 1823) = Sarah, daughter of David Mocatta
Rachel (b. 1826) = G. de R. Atatora
Adelaide (b. 1829)
Moses (b. 1832)
Abraham
Lionel Benjamin = Henrietta
Arthur = Emmaline Micholls
Arthur Reginald = Florence Beddington
Sarah
Horatio
Henrietta
Fanny
J.
I. G. D.

first volume of his "Bible for Home Reading," forming a commentary on the Bible with moral reflections from the standpoint of the "higher criticism"; the second volume appeared in 1899. In 1890 Montefiore founded and edited, in conjunction with Israel Abrahams, the "Jewish Quarterly Review," a journal that stood on the very highest level of contemporary Jewish scholarship, and in which numerous contributions from his pen have appeared.

Montefiore is one of the leading authorities on questions of education; he was for some time a member of the School Board for London, and he is (1904) president of the Froebel Society and the Jews' Infant School, London, and a member of numerous other educational bodies. Montefiore has been mainly instrumental in enabling Jewish pupil teachers at elementary schools to enjoy the advantages of training in classes held for the purpose at the universities; he is on the council of Jews' College and of the Jewish Religious Education Board. He ranks as one of the leading philanthropists in the Anglo-Jewish community and holds office in various important bodies. He was elected president of the Anglo-Jewish Association in 1895, and he is a prominent member of the Council of the Jewish Colonization Association.

Montefiore has shown great sympathy with all liberal tendencies in Jewish religious movements in London and is president of the recently formed Jewish Religious Union. He was president of the Jewish Historical Society in 1899-1900.

BIBLIOGRAPHY: J. Jacobs, in *Young Israel*, June, 1897.

J. G. L.

Sir Francis Abraham Montefiore (Bart.): English communal worker and Zionist; son of Joseph M. Montefiore, president of the Board of Deputies; born Oct. 10, 1860. In 1886 he took up the baronetcy previously held by Sir Moses Montefiore. He became high sheriff of the county of Kent in 1894, and of Sussex in 1895. He is chairman of the executive committee of the English Zionist Federation and has represented the English section at recent Zionist congresses. Montefiore was recently elected chairman of Elders of the Spanish and Portuguese congregation.

BIBLIOGRAPHY: *Jewish Year Book* (London), 5659 (=1898-1899).

J. V. E.

Jacob Montefiore: Merchant; born in Bridgetown, England, Nov. 23, 1801; died Nov. 3, 1895. He entered into business with his brother Moses, and when in the early thirties the movement for the financing of Australian colonization from London was incepted Montefiore, who had been connected with the Colonial produce trade, became active in the various public schemes as a member of the South Australian Colonization Association, organized to settle South Australia on the Wakefield system. He was also appointed member of the first board of commissioners entrusted by the British government with the administration of the colony. He visited the colony in the year 1843 and again in 1854. His reception on his first visit by the governor, Sir George Grey, and the people was enthusiastic. During his visit to South Australia in 1843 he acted as an agent for the Rothschilds, at the same time holding a partnership with his brother **Joseph Barrow** in the firm of Montefiore Brothers of London and Sydney. The township of Montefiore, at the confluence of the Bell and MacQuarrie rivers, in Wellington Valley, was founded by the brothers, and they contributed actively to the establishment there of places of worship for all denominations. The organization of the Bank of Australasia was largely due to their efforts. In Adelaide there is a hill named after them. In 1885, at the request of the directors of the Art Union Gallery of Adelaide, Jacob sat for the artist B. S. Marks, the portrait being hung in that gallery.

J. T. Se.

Jacob Isaac Levi Montefiore: Australian merchant; son of Isaac Levi and Esther Hannah Levi (daughter of Eliezer Montefiore); born at Bridgetown, Barbados, Jan. 11, 1819; died at Norwood, London, 1885. In 1837 he proceeded to Sydney, where he assumed his mother's maiden name. There he became one of the leading merchants and took an active part in the development of the city. In 1857 he was nominated a member of the first legislative council of the colony of New South Wales. He acted as president of the chamber of commerce, and was for many years a director of the Bank of Australasia. In 1876 he left Australia and settled in England, where he became a director of the Queensland National Bank, the Queensland Investment Company, and several other important commercial undertakings. One of his brothers is **Edward Levi Montefiore,** a member of the financial house of Cahen d'Anvers et Cie., and another, **George Levi Montefiore,** of Brussels, is a member of the Belgian Senate; both are still living (1904).

BIBLIOGRAPHY: *Jewish World*, Jan. 30 and Feb. 2, 1885.

J. I. H.

Joseph Barrow Montefiore: Merchant; son of Eliezer Montefiore; born in London June 24, 1803; died at Brighton, England, Sept. 4, 1893. In 1826, during the mayoralty of Sir William Magnay, he became one of the twelve "Jew brokers" in the city of London, purchasing the privilege for £1,500. He did not remain long in the city, but seized a favorable opportunity of emigrating to Australia, where several members of his family were already settled. In New South Wales he traded in partnership with his brother and made many fortunate speculations in town allotments. He helped to found the township of Montefiore and the Bank of Australasia, and was one of the chief agents in the organization of the Jewish congregation in Sydney. In 1832 he obtained a grant of land from the government for a Jewish burial-place. At the same time he helped to organize the society which developed into the Sydney Hebrew Congregation. On retiring from business Montefiore settled in London and joined the Reform Congregation.

BIBLIOGRAPHY: *Jew. Chron.* and *Jew. World*, Sept., 1893.

Joseph Elias Montefiore: Son of Moses Vita (Haim) Montefiore; born in London 1759; married Rachel Mocatta (1783). He became the father of three sons and five daughters, the eldest son being Sir Moses Montefiore. The second son, Abraham, was twice married, and by his second wife, Henrietta Rothschild, became the father of Joseph Mayer (father of Sir Francis Montefiore), Nathaniel (father of Claude G. Montefiore), Charlotte (d. 1854; author of "A Few Words to the Jews"), and **Louisa** (afterward **Lady Anthony de Rothschild).** The third son, **Horatio** (1798–1867), became a merchant in London, and was one of the principal founders of the London Reform Community (1841). He married a daughter of David Mocatta, by whom he had six sons and six daughters. The youngest of these sons, **Emanuel Montefiore** (b. 1842), became a lieutenant-colonel in the Royal Artillery, assistant secretary of the London Charity Organization Society, commandant of the Jewish Lads' Brigade, and a member of the council of the West London Reform Synagogue.

Of the daughters of Joseph Montefiore the eldest, **Sarah,** married Solomon Sebag of London; she became the mother of Joseph Sebag, afterward Sir Joseph Sebag-Montefiore (1822–1903), who had three sons—**Arthur** (father of **Robert Sebag-Montefiore), Cecil,** and **Edmund.** Sarah had also five daughters: **Jemima** (married Haim Guedalla), **Esther** (died prematurely), **Abigail** (wife of Benjamin Gompertz, the mathematician), **Rebecca** (married Joseph Salomons, brother of the late Sir David Salomons), and **Justina** (married Benjamin Cohen, father of Arthur Cohen and Lionel Benjamin Cohen).

Bibliography: Lucien Wolf, *Life of Sir Moses Montefiore*, London, 1883; *Jew. Chron.* April 28, 1876.

J. I. H.

Joseph Mayer Montefiore: English communal worker; nephew of Sir Moses Montefiore; born in London May 10, 1816; died there Oct. 9, 1880. In 1844 he was elected a member of the Board of Deputies, London, as one of the representatives of the Spanish-Portuguese congregation. He retired from the office in 1853, but was reelected in 1857. In 1858 he became vice-president of the board, acting as president during the absence abroad of Sir Moses, whom he succeeded, Oct., 1874. Montefiore was elected treasurer of the Spanish-Portuguese Synagogue in 1846, and warden in 1851. He was a liberal subscriber to and took much interest in the charitable and educational institutions connected with the congregation. He was a director of the Alliance Insurance Company for twenty-three years, and acted for some years as director of the National Provincial Bank of Ireland. He was a justice of the peace and deputy-lieutenant for Sussex, and served as high sheriff of that county in 1870.

Bibliography: *Jew. Chron.* and *Jew. World*, Oct. 15, 1880.

Sir Joseph Sebag-Montefiore: Stock-broker; son of Solomon Sebag and Sarah, eldest sister of Sir Moses Montefiore; born in 1822; died at London Jan. 18, 1903. On succeeding (1885) to the estate of his maternal uncle he assumed the name of Montefiore by royal license. He was one of the leading members of the London Stock Exchange, on which he amassed a large fortune.

He was a justice of the peace for Kent and the Cinque Ports and lieutenant of the city of London; and in 1889 he served as high sheriff for Kent. He was for many years a leading member of the Spanish-Portuguese congregation and was president of the elders of that body. In 1895 he became president of the Board of Deputies, after having been vice-president for many years; and in 1896 he was appointed by the King of Italy Italian consul-general in London. He was knighted in 1896.

Bibliography: *Jew. Chron.* May 22, 1896; *Jewish Year Book* (London), 5659 (=1898–99).

Joshua Montefiore: English lawyer, soldier, and journalist; born in London Aug. 10, 1762; died at St. Albans, Vt., June 26, 1843. After graduating at Oxford he studied law and was admitted to the bar in 1784. While practising in London he attained considerable success as an author, his "Commercial Dictionary" being regarded as the standard work of its kind. In 1791 he joined a band of adventurers under Moses Ximenes, who purposed establishing a colony on the coast of Africa; Montefiore took charge of the military side of the expedition. The party occupied the Island of Bulama and raised the British flag; but after several conflicts with the natives, they were compelled to withdraw. Of this early attempt at African colonization he has left a lively account. Before the settlement was broken up Montefiore attempted to establish schools for the children of his companions. On his return to England he declined the honor of knighthood and entered the army as a captain, being the first Jew to hold a military commission in England. He was present as an officer of the York Light Infantry at the taking of Martinique and Guadalupe in 1809. After serving in various parts of the world, he resigned his commission and emigrated to the United States; for some time he published and edited in New York "Men and Measures," a weekly political journal; he afterward took up his residence at St. Albans, Vt.

Montefiore published: "Commercial Dictionary" (1803); "Commercial and Notarial Precedents" (1804); "Trader's Compendium"; "United States Trader's Compendium"; "Law of Copyright"; "Synopsis of Mercantile Laws" (1830); "Law and Treatise on Bookkeeping" (1831); "Laws of Land and Sea" (1831).

Bibliography: *Jew. World*, Oct. 31, 1884; L. Wolf, *Centennial Biog. of Sir Moses Montefiore*, London, 1884; *Cyclopedia of American Biog.*

Lady Judith Montefiore: Wife of Sir Moses Montefiore; daughter of Levi Barent Cohen; born in London in 1784; died Oct. 1, 1862. She was an accomplished linguist and musician. She married Moses Montefiore in 1812. For thirteen years they lived at New Court, Saint Swithin's Lane, London. Her prudence and intelligence influenced all her husband's undertakings, and when he retired from business the administration of his fortune in philanthropic endeavors was largely directed by her. Lady Montefiore accompanied her husband in all his foreign missions up to 1859, and was the beneficent genius of his memorable expeditions to the Holy Land, Damascus, St. Petersburg, and Rome. By her linguistic abilities she was enabled to materially assist her husband in his self-imposed tasks. During the journey to Russia, in 1846, she was indefatigable in her efforts to alleviate the misery she saw everywhere around her. The wife and daughter of the Russian governor paid her a ceremonious visit and expressed the admiration she had inspired among all classes. Her sympathies were greatly widened by travel; two journals of some of these travels were published anonymously by her. The last years of her life were spent alternately in London and Ramsgate. At her death Sir Moses founded in her memory the Judith Montefiore College at the latter place.

BIBLIOGRAPHY: Lucien Wolf, *Life of Sir Moses Montefiore*, pp. 189-212; Morais, *Eminent Israelites*, pp. 240-242; *Jew. Chron.* Oct. 3, 1862; Kayserling, *Die Jüdischen Frauen*, pp. 272-275, 308; L. Loewe, *Diaries of Sir Moses and Lady Montefiore*, 1890.

J. G. L.

Leonard Montefiore: English author and philanthropist; brother of Claude G. Montefiore; born in London May 4, 1853; died at Newport Sept. 6, 1879; educated at Balliol College, Oxford, where he came under the influence of Jowett, T. H. Green, and of his fellow student Arnold Toynbee. Even before he left college he had contributed to some of the principal periodicals, as "The Nineteenth Century" and "The Fortnightly Review," and was at the time of his death devoting himself to the study of the German struggle for emancipation, on which he published some preliminary essays. Montefiore was associated with many philanthropic movements, especially with the movement for women's emancipation. His "Literary Remains" were privately printed by his family after his death (1880).

BIBLIOGRAPHY: Memoir in his *Literary Remains*; *Athenæum* and *Examiner*, Sept. 13, 1879; *Women's Union Journal*, Nov., 1879; *Jew. Chron.* and *Jew. World*, Sept. 12, 1879.

J.

Sir Moses Montefiore in 1818.
(From a sketch by Dighton.)

Sir Moses Montefiore (Bart.): English philanthropist; born in Leghorn, Italy, Oct. 28, 1784; died at Ramsgate, England, July 25, 1885. Moses Ḥayyim Montefiore and his wife, both of Leghorn, settled in London in the middle of the eighteenth century. One of their seventeen children, Joseph Elias Montefiore, took his young wife, Rachel, daughter of Abraham Lumbroso de Mattos Mocatta, on a business journey to Leghorn, where their eldest child, Moses, the subject of this article, was born. On their return they lived at Kennington, where Moses went to school and was apprenticed to a provision merchant. Later he entered a counting-house in the city of London, and ultimately became one of the twelve Jewish brokers then licensed by the city. His career was not entirely unchequered by adversity. In 1806 he was deceived by a man whom he had trusted in a large transaction in Exchequer bills, and had to ask for time in which to settle certain obligations. This his high character and popularity enabled him to secure. His brother Abraham joined him in business; and they remained in partnership till 1816. Moses married (1812) Judith, daughter of Levi Barent Cohen. Levi Barent Cohen was an Ashkenazi, and it was a sign of indifference, on the part of the Montefiores, to current prejudice that, although they belonged to the London Sephardim, they married German Jewesses. Moses lived in New Court, close to his friend Rothschild; and the brothers Montefiore, as the brokers of that financial genius, became wealthy men. Moses was able to retire from the Stock Exchange in 1821; and in 1824 he assisted in founding the Alliance Assurance Company, of which he was the first president. He was among the founders of the Imperial Continental Gas Association, which extended gas-lighting to the principal European cities; and he was one of the original directors (1825) of the Provincial Bank of Ireland, which gained for him the honorary freedom of Londonderry. For a short time he was also a director of the South Eastern Railway. In 1836 he was made a Fellow of the Royal Society; and in 1837 he was elected sheriff of the city of London, being the second Jew to fill that office (see SALOMONS, Sir David). In the same year he was knighted by Queen Victoria on her accession. He had become acquainted with her in 1834, while she was staying at Broadstairs with her mother, the Duchess of Kent, to whom he had been able to show courtesy by placing at her disposal the secluded grounds of his house near that seaside resort. In 1846 he was created a baronet, and in 1847 became high sheriff for Kent. He was a deputy lieutenant and a magistrate in more than one jurisdiction. At an earlier period of his life (1810–

Jewish Broker.

Dignities.

1814) he had been captain in the Surrey local militia and practised assiduously the bugle calls and drill. In part he owed his stately bearing to these early days of military training.

While Sir Moses was winning wealth and social distinction, he was living the life of a most pious and observant Jew. His diaries record his regular attendance at the synagogue, his scrupulous performance of the functions of a member of the ancient Society of Lavadores, which made it a sacred duty to perform the last rites for members of the synagogue; and they show also that under great difficulties he strictly complied with the dietary laws as well as with those which enjoin rest and forbid travel upon Sabbaths and festivals. In pursuance of inflexible principle, he resisted all attempts at congregational reform. The following is an account in his own language of his life in 1820:

"With God's blessing, rise, say prayers at 7 o'clock. Breakfast at 9. Attend the Stock Exchange, if in London, 10. Dinner, 5. Read, write, and learn, if possible, Hebrew and French, 6. Read Bible and say prayers, 10. Then retire. Monday and Thursday mornings attend the Synagogue. Tuesday and Thursday evenings for visiting." "I attended," he says on another occasion, "many meetings at the City of London Tavern, also several charitable meetings at Bevis Marks, in connection with the Spanish and Portuguese Synagogue; sometimes passing the whole day there from ten in the morning till half-past eleven at night (Jan. 25, 1820), excepting two hours for dinner in the committee-room; answered in the evening 350 petitions from poor women, and also made frequent visits to the Villa Real School."

He cooperated also with the Rothschilds and the Goldsmids in the movement for parliamentary emancipation of the Jews. In 1814 he became treasurer of the Sephardic Synagogue in London, and in due course passed through all its highest offices, being six times warden-president. From 1838 to 1874 he was president of the Board of Deputies of British Jews; and on his retirement £12,000 was subscribed as a testimonial to him and was used by his wish in aid of building industrial dwellings at Jerusalem. His time in office was vigorously employed in the relief of his suffering brethren.

Seven times Sir Moses Montefiore visited Palestine, in 1827, 1838, 1849, 1855, 1857, 1866, and 1875; being accompanied by his wife each time before her death in 1862, and making the last journey when he was ninety-one years old. Another regular companion was Dr. L. Loewe, who became his literary executor. In the Holy Land he endowed hospitals and almshouses, set on foot agricultural enterprises, planted gardens, and built synagogues and tombs. He not only gave bounteously of his own means, but administered public and private subventions, among others a fund bequeathed by Judah Touro of New Orleans, who left $50,000 to be applied, as Sir Moses thought fit, for the benefit of the Jews in the Holy Land. The events of these journeys were carefully narrated in his own diaries and in those of Lady Montefiore, some of which have been published in full, while others have unfortunately been destroyed, though not till extracts from them had been printed. Besides passing references to interesting personages whom the travelers met, the diaries furnish incidentally a history of the gradual development of the means of travel. In their early adventures the courageous couple encountered serious dangers; even in England they were shot at, presumably by highwaymen, on the Dover Road. But they were not deterred by the fears of slavery and imprisonment which then beset travelers in the East, or by breaking ice or by wolves in Russia. On one of his journeys (1840) Sir Moses obtained from the Sultan of Turkey a firman denouncing the inveterate charge of ritual murder brought against the Jews. He obtained promises of friendliness from two czars (1846 and 1872), crossed the desert of the Atlas and at the age of seventy-nine won for his brethren the favor of the Sultan of Morocco; made an unsuccessful journey to Rome to obtain the return to his parents of the boy Mortara (1858), and went to Rumania (1867), where he presented himself at an open window to a mob at the imminent risk of his life. It was at the age of seventy-six that he went to the office of the London "Times" after midnight, with a letter soliciting relief for the Christians of Syria. His own contribution was £200, and he collected over £20,000. The affection which his magnetic personality and his native goodness inspired can not be exaggerated. In Palestine

Visits to Palestine.

Visits Morocco.

M. Montefiore

(From a photograph when 100 years old.)

his brethren flocked to kiss the hem of his garment. On his entering into his one hundredth year (Nov. 8, 1883) Queen Victoria, Albert Edward Prince of Wales, and many hundreds of his most distinguished fellow citizens sent telegrams of congratulation. The birthday was a public festival at Ramsgate, where he passed the evening of his days.

His Popularity.

Sir Moses was buried at Ramsgate, near the synagogue he had founded, side by side with his wife in the mausoleum which he had erected for the purpose, a reproduction of the building known as the Tomb of Rachel on the Bethlehem road. By his will (proved at £370,000) he directed the continuance of many and various charities, and among others added to the endowment of the Montefiore College and Library, Ramsgate, which he had first established in memory of his wife. The college is now devoted to a few learned men who spend their days in the study of the Law. For a time an institution for younger students was also maintained, but the trustees in lieu thereof make an annual subvention to Jews' College, London.

Sir Moses Montefiore had no children; but the baronetcy was revived by the crown in favor of Francis Montefiore, grandson of Abraham, Sir Moses' brother and partner; while his seat at Ramsgate was by his will entailed upon Joseph Sebag (afterward Sir Joseph Sebag-Montefiore), son of Sir Moses' sister.

BIBLIOGRAPHY: *The Times* (London), Oct. 22, 23, 1883; July 29, 1885; *Jew. Chron.* Aug. 28, 1885; June 13, 20, 1902; L. Loewe, *Diaries of Sir Moses and Lady Montefiore*, 1890; Israel Davis, *Sir Moses Montefiore: a Biographical Sketch*, 1884; Lucien Wolf, *Sir Moses Montefiore: a Centennial Biography*, London, 1884; Lady Judith Montefiore, *Diary of a Visit to Egypt* (privately printed, n.d.); Liebermann, *Internationales Montefiore-Album*, 1884; Ḥayyim Guedalla, *Keter Shem Ṭob*, 1887.

J. I. DA.

SYNAGOGUE AND TOMB OF SIR MOSES MONTEFIORE, RAMSGATE, ENGLAND.
(From a photograph.)

Nathaniel Montefiore: English communal worker; second son of Abraham Montefiore and Henrietta, daughter of Mayer A. de Rothschild; born in London 1819; died there 1883. He married Emma, the youngest daughter of Sir Isaac Lyon Goldsmid. He was trained for the medical profession at Guy's Hospital and was elected a member of the Royal College of Surgeons in 1858. He did not establish a practise, but used his medical knowledge for the benefit of the inmates of the Beth Holim Hospital, an ancient charity of the Spanish-Portuguese Jews of London of which he was treasurer for over a quarter of a century. He filled also numerous other communal offices. He was president of the Jewish and General Literary Institution, in Leadenhall street, which was known as "Sussex Hall"; president of the Jews' Infant Schools; and president of the Jews' Emigration Society. But most of his communal work was in connection with the Spanish-Portuguese congregation, to which most members of his family belonged. He served as senior warden of the congregation, president of the board of elders, president of the Gates of Hope school, and representative of the congregation on the Board of Deputies. He was buried in the Balls Pond Cemetery of the West London Reform Synagogue, by the side of his son Leonard.

Bibliography: *Jew. Chron.* and *Jew. World*, March 30, 1883.

J. I. H.

MONTÉLIMAR (Hebrew, איימר or מונטיל אדמר): A city of the department of the Drôme, France. A large number of Jews lived here from the beginning of the fourteenth century. They possessed a synagogue in the Rue du Puits-Neuf, formerly the Rue de la Juiverie, as well as a school situated near the Porte Saint-Martin, a cemetery, and a slaughter-house, the privilege of maintaining the latter being ratified by the Dauphin Louis in 1455.

The condition of the Jews of Montélimar was comparatively prosperous. The following were the principal men among them during the fourteenth and fifteenth centuries: Solomon, Isaac Maignan, Lionel de Livron, Josse Nercas, Isaac de Lattes, Solomon Massip, Isaac Saul de Mornas, and Bonsenhor Bonafossa. In 1339 and 1340 Samuel ben Judah of Marseilles revised at Montélimar his Hebrew version (made in 1324) of the "Treatise on the Soul" by Alexander Aphrodisius, a work which had been translated from Greek into Arabic by Isaac ibn Hunain.

In 1439 the lords of Montélimar required the Jews of the city to wear the badge, from which the toleration of the consuls had hitherto exempted them; and this decree was renewed two years later by Jean de Poitiers, Bishop of Valence. In 1453 the Jews were commanded to attend Christian worship, and a preacher was appointed to convert them to Christianity. After this the Jewish community gradually lost its importance; and in 1468 it contained but seven families, which, on account of accusations—admitted to be false by the parliament of Grenoble—were maltreated by the inhabitants and expelled from the city in that year.

Bibliography: De Costou, *Histoire de Montélimar*, 1878, i. 516, ii. 579; Gross, *Gallia Judaica*, pp. 319, 381; *R. E. J.* ix. 237.

G. S. K.

MONTEZINOS, ANTONIO DE (AARON LEVI): Marano traveler of the seventeenth century. He claimed that while journeying in South America about 1641 near Quito, Ecuador, he met with savages who practised Jewish ceremonies and recited the Shema' and who were of the tribe of Reuben. He met other savages of the tribe of Levi. Going to Holland in 1644 he told this story to Manasseh ben Israel; the latter repeated it to Thomas Thorowgood, by whom it was printed in his "Jews in America," pp. 1-9 *et seq.* It was also published by Manasseh ben Israel in his "Hope of Israel," pp. 1-7.

Bibliography: L. Wolf, *Menasseh ben Israel's Mission to Oliver Cromwell*, pp. xxiv.; xxvii., 154.

D. J.

MONTEZINOS LIBRARY: Division of the library of the Portuguese Rabbinical Seminary 'Eẓ Ḥayyim at Amsterdam, Holland. It was bequeathed in 1889 by D. R. Montezinos (b. Dec. 6, 1829), the well-known bibliophile of that city, and was dedicated on April 10, 1891, after the seminary had enlarged its structure in order to accommodate the valuable collection.

The Montezinos Library consists of 20,000 volumes of Hebraica and Judaica, including a number of incunabula and about seventy volumes of responsa. Besides, it contains more than 1,000 pamphlets and about 300 portraits of Jewish celebrities. The collection includes a number of very rare Hebraica and Judaica, several of which are not recorded by Jewish bibliographers. Among its manuscripts are to be found a few by Isaac Cohen Belinfante, Isaac Sasportas, and David Franco Mendes.

Montezinos, who for some time was in charge of the 'Eẓ Ḥayyim library, supervised the arrangement of the entire library of the seminary, when his collection was added to it.

J. I. G. D.

MONTGOMERY. See Alabama.

MONTH (Hebrew, "yeraḥ," "ḥodesh"; plural, "yeraḥim," "ḥodashim"): A unit of time; the period between one new moon and another. According to the account of Creation in Genesis, it was decreed that the "lesser light" should "rule the night" and serve "for signs and for seasons" (Gen. i. 14). The Psalmist also says, "He appointed the moon for seasons" (Ps. civ. 19). In round numbers thirty days constituted a month, as is evident from the Flood narrative, counting 150 days for five months from the 17th of the second to the 17th of the seventh month (Gen. vii. 11, 24; viii. 4); and the mourning period, reckoned as a full month in Deut. xxi. 13, is elsewhere fixed at thirty days. That twelve months constituted a year also is evident from the Flood narrative (Gen. viii. 5-13).

Undoubtedly there was an occasional interpolation of an extra month to correct the lunar year to the solar cycle; and it is evident from the fact that the festivals named in given months—such as Passover, Pentecost, and Tabernacles—all had to do with crops, and therefore solar seasons, that this correction to solar time is of the highest antiquity. The relation of the months to the signs of the zodiac is a further evidence that the solar-lunar year was employed.

From the first Babylonian exile the Jews adopted the Babylonian names of the months (R. Ḥanina, in Yer. R. H. i. 2). Prior to the Exile the months were designated partly by names and partly by numbers. Thus Nisan was called "Abib" (Ex. xii. 2), Iyyar = "Ziw" (I Kings vi. 1, 37), Tishri = "Yeraḥ ha-Etanim" (*ib.* viii. 2), and Ḥeshwan = "Yeraḥ Bul" (*ib.* 6, 38). The Babylonian name "Ara-aḥ-sham-nu" means the eighth month = ירח־שמיני. According to Ḳimḥi, מרחשון is transposed from ירח־שמון(י). The pronoun "Mar" was at a later period sometimes dropped, leaving the name "Ḥeshwan."

The following names of the months are mentioned in post-exilic Biblical writings: Kislew, the seventh month, and Shebaṭ, the eleventh month, in Zech. i. 7, vii. 1; Kislew, Nisan, and Elul in Neh. i. 1, ii. 1, vi. 15; Nisan, Siwan, Ṭebet, and Adar, the twelfth month, in Esth. ii. 16, iii. 7, viii. 9. The months Tishri, Marḥeshwan, Iyyar, Tammuz, and

Ab are not mentioned in the Bible, but are found in the Talmud. Tishri is characterized as the month of the birth of the Patriarchs; Ṭebet, as the month of marriages (Meg. 13a); Nisan, as the month of coronations (Shab. 87b); Adar, as that of rejoicing; and Ab as the month of mourning (Ta'an. 26b, 29a). In the Middle Ages Elul became the month of repentance. See ALMANAC; CALENDAR; NEW MOON; ZODIAC.

TABLE OF THE JEWISH MONTHS.

	Hebrew Names.	Assyrian Names.	No. of Days.	During 20th Cent. First of Month Occurs Between	Constellations of Zodiac Corresponding to the Months.
1.	תשרי Tishri	Tash-ri-tu	30	Sept. 6–Oct. 5	מאזנים Libra.
2.	מרחשון Marḥeshwan	A-ra-aḥ-sham-nu.	29-30	Oct. 6–Nov. 4	עקרב Scorpio.
3.	כסלו Kislew	Ki-si-li-mu	29-30	Nov. 4–Dec. 3	קשת Sagittarius.
4.	טבת Ṭebet	Ṭi-bi-tu	29	Dec. 4–Jan. 2	גדי Capricornus.
5.	שבט Shebaṭ	Sha-ba-ṭu	30	Jan. 2–Jan. 31	דלי Aquarius.
6.	אדר Adar	Ad-da-ru	29-30	Feb. 1–March 2	דגים Pisces.
	אדר שני We-Adar (Leap-Year)	Arḥu-na-ak-ru Ad-da-ru.	29	March 3–March 13	
7.	ניסן Nisan	Ni-sa-an-nu	30	March 13–April 11	טלה Aries.
8.	אייר Iyyar	A-a-ru	29	April 12–May 11	שור Taurus.
9.	סיון Siwan	Si-ma-nu	30	May 11–June 9	תאומים Gemini.
10.	תמוז Tammuz	Du-mu-zu	29	June 10–July 9	סרטן Cancer.
11.	אב Ab	A-bu	30	July 9–Aug. 7	אריה Leo.
12.	אלול Elul	U-lu-lu	29	Aug. 8–Sept. 6	בתולה Virgo.

BIBLIOGRAPHY: Benzinger, *Arch.* pp. 198–203; Epstein, *Mi-Ḳadmoniyyot ha-Yehudim*, i. 1–30, Vienna, 1887; Levensohn, ילקוט ריב״ל, p. 62, Warsaw, 1878; Weiss and Friedmann, *Bet Talmud*, ii. 20, 54, 248.

A. J. D. E.

MONTI, ANDREA DI. See JOSEPH ẒARFATI.

MONTICELLI: Small town in the province of Piacenza, northern Italy, with a Jewish community dating from the expulsion of the Jews from the duchy of Milan in 1597. The first settlers were the Soavi and Sforni families of Cremona. The community brought its German ritual from Lombardy, and has retained it until the present time. A society for nursing and for study, entitled "Ḥebrat Biḳḳur Ḥolim," founded in the sixteenth century, is also still in existence. In 1865 the Jewish inhabitants numbered 143; but in 1901 they had become reduced to 32. Flaminio Servi officiated as rabbi in 1863.

BIBLIOGRAPHY: *Corriere Israelitico*, v. 338.

G. I. E.

MONTORO, ANTON DE: Spanish poet of the fifteenth century; born in Montoro 1404; died after March, 1477; son of Fernando Alfonso de Baena Ventura, and a near relative of the poet Juan Alfonso de Baena. His vocation was that of a "ropero"; he calls himself "el Ropero" or "Aljabibe," both signifying a dealer in old clothes. When advanced in years he was baptized, but despite his baptism he remained a Jew at heart throughout his life; and in a poem to a magistrate in Cordova, his place of residence, he laments that, driven by hunger, he had had to break the oath of his ancestors and buy pork, as he found no other meat in the butcher's shop. Even in his old age he took a lively interest in his persecuted coreligionists. Thus he addressed a pathetic complaint to King Henry IV. in reference to the plundering of the houses of the Maranos of Carmona in 1474.

Anton de Montoro, who was welcomed by the noblest families of Cordova, and whose verse was valued highly by some of the best poets of his time, as by the Marquis de Santillana, Juan de Mena, etc., was treated with contumely by poets of his own race. At sixty-five he wrote a poem to Queen Isabella in which he complains that he is still treated as a Jew and called "the old, contemptible Jew." Commendador Roman, who posed as a pious Christian, taunted Montoro with the fact that his father had been a ḥazzan; Juan de Valladolid, Rodrigo Cota, and others scorned him because of his former faith. He was in high favor with D. Pedro de Aguilar and with his son D. Alonso Fernandez de Aguilar, the noble protector of the Maranos, whom he celebrated in several poems. After the persecution of the Maranos in March, 1473, Anton de Montoro, who was also made to suffer under this calamity, found protection and refuge with D. Alonso de Aguilar. He settled in Seville, but soon returned to Cordova, where, old and weak, he made his will March, 1477, and soon afterward died. His poems were collected by Emil Cotarelo y Mori, and published with an excellent introduction and valuable notes under the title "Cancionero de Anton de Montoro" (Madrid, 1900).

BIBLIOGRAPHY: Kayserling, *Sephardim*, pp. 85 *et seq.*; *R. E. J.* xliii. 261 *et seq.*; Grätz, *Gesch.* viii. 306.

J. M. K.

MONTPELLIER (Hebrew, מונטפשליר or מונפשליר): Capital of the department of Hérault, a part of the old province of Languedoc, France. It is sometimes called also "Har Ga'ash" = "Mountain of Trembling," "Har ha-Niḳra Pissulano" = "Mount Pessulanus," or simply "Har" = "Mountain." In the Middle Ages Montpellier was divided into two distinct cities, one being the capital of the Guillems, and the other the fief of the bishops of Maguelone. One of the most important communities of Languedoc existed here from the second half of the eleventh century. Through their relations with their coreligionists all over the world, the Jews of Montpellier helped enormously to build up the commerce of the city; and they at the same time contributed largely to the development of the school of medicine established there in the twelfth century. Guillem VIII., Lord of Montpellier, granted them in 1180 the right to practise medicine; and the kings of

Aragon and Majorca, James I and James II., merely added (in 1272 and 1281 respectively) the proviso that the Jewish physicians must pass the regular examinations before exercising their profession. The progress made by these Jewish physicians was such that in 1300, according to Astruc ("Mémoires pour Servir à l'Histoire de la Faculté de Médecine de Montpellier," p. 168), the Jew Jacob b. Machir, called "Don Profiat" (Latin, "Profatius Judæus"), was appointed regent of the faculty of medicine. James I. interested himself in the Jews on many occasions, especially in 1252, 1266, and 1268, and confirmed them in all the privileges which they had enjoyed under his predecessors.

School of Medicine.

These fortunate conditions changed in 1292, when Bérenger of Frédol, Bishop of Maguelone, ceded to King Philip the Fair of France the Jews then living in his territory. They were expelled in 1306, but returned to Montpellier in 1319, having been recalled by King Sancho, who protected them in 1320 against the fury of the Pastoureaux. On demand of the consuls, King John of France compelled the Jews in 1363 to wear the Jews' badge. In 1368 the same consuls forbade them to drink or to draw water from any well other than that which had been assigned to them ("Petit Thalamus," pp. 166–167). Finally, a royal edict issued on Sept. 17, 1394, put an end to the existence of the Jewish community of Montpellier.

In the sixteenth century a number of Marano fugitives from Spain fled to Montpellier. The physician Felix Platter of Basel, who resided in the city from 1552 to 1559, knew several of these Maranos, whom he mentions by name and whose customs he describes (autobiography of Felix Platter, ed. Fechter, Basel, 1840). In the seventeenth century some Jews from the Comtat-Venaissin joined the Spanish refugees. The parliament of Toulouse authorized them at first to remain at Montpellier for one month only in each of the four seasons; but thanks to the tolerance of the consuls, the assistance of the Marquis of Grave, proprietor of the markets of Pont-Juvénal, and, especially, the protection of Louis Basil of Bernage, commissary of Languedoc, the Jews, in spite of the most bitter complaints of the Christian merchants, established themselves definitely in the city. In the beginning of the nineteenth century the Jewish community numbered 105 persons.

The site of the Jewish quarter was often changed. At first it was near the synagogue and the Jewish baths (traces of which still exist in Rue Barralerie No. 1), extending northward as far as the tolerance of the kings of Majorca permitted. The Jews acquired some houses near the square of Castel-Maton, and spread themselves as far as the right side of Rue Vieille-Intendance. By order of the Duke of Anjou in 1365 they were restricted to the Rue de la Vacherie ("Vacaria"), near the gate of La Saunerie. In this street was the synagogue which the Bishop of Montpellier permitted the community, on the representations of Hélias of Loan and Samuel Caylli, to erect in 1387, in consideration of the payment of 400 pounds Tours currency. Finally, in the beginning of the sixteenth century the Jews established themselves in the blind alley of the Vieux Consulat, called "Juiverie" or "Juzétarie," which has now disappeared.

Jewish Quarter.

The Jews owned successively two cemeteries. One of these was situated between the gates of La Saunerie and St. Guillem. In 1263 James I. presented it to the Cistercians of Valmagne, who established a theological college there. The other cemetery was in the suburb of Villefranche, between the present seminary and Boutonnet. It was sold in 1306 by Philip the Fair; but in 1319, by permission of King Sancho, the Jews of Montpellier repurchased it. In 1287 James I. permitted the Jews to establish their own slaughter-house. A police regulation of 1364 forbade the Christian butchers to sell or to permit the sale of meat to the Jews ("Petit Thalamus," p. 166).

Benjamin of Tudela, who visited Montpellier in 1165, speaks in terms of the highest praise of the scholars of that city, who devoted themselves to the study of the Talmud. The Jewish school was a very important one. It was compared to the Sanhedrin of Jerusalem ("Har ha-Bayit"; "Temim Deim," No. 7) and to the great school of Granada ("Rimmon Sefarad"; Neubauer, "Cat. Bodl. Hebr. MSS." p. 17), and was sometimes called "the Holy Mountain," "the Mother of Israel" ("Har ha-Ḳodesh," "Em le-Yisrael"; Solomon ben Adret, Responsa, i. 418). This school issued the first anathema against the writings of Maimonides. In 1232 Rabbi Solomon b. Abraham together with two of his pupils, Jonah b. Abraham Gerundi and David b. Saul, prohibited the "Moreh Nebukim." He even went so far as to invoke the ecclesiastical authorities against his adversaries and to denounce Maimonides' work as impious and injurious to the Christian faith. But the only result was that the adversaries of Maimonides were declared to be calumniators; and it is said that some of them were condemned to have their tongues burned.

Rabbinical Schools.

After a time, however (1303–6), the battle against Maimonides' writings waged afresh. The chief author of the new attack was another rabbi of Montpellier, Abba Mari of Lunel. Two of his partizans, Todros of Beaucaire and Simeon b. Joseph, called "En Duran of Lunel," signed, together with twenty-four notables of the community of Montpellier, the letter which he addressed to Solomon ben Adret of Barcelona. But Abba Mari found even at Montpellier bitter opponents, in the above-mentioned Jacob b. Machir, in the physician Solomon of Lunel, in Judah b. Moses ibn Tibbon, and especially in Jedaiah ben Abraham BEDERSI, one of Maimonides' most enthusiastic admirers. The controversy was carried on bitterly by both sides, and it was stopped only by the cruel persecutions attendant on the expulsion of the Jews from France by Philip the Fair in 1306.

In addition to those that have been referred to above, the following scholars of Montpellier should be mentioned here: Abraham b. David of Posquières (RABaD III.), Moses b. Samuel ibn Tibbon, Judah (Aryeh) Harari, Elijah, Levi b. Abraham of Villefranche, Reuben b. Isaac, Aaron b. Joseph ha-

Levi, and Abraham Bonet b. Meshullam b. Solomon Abigdor.

In 1902 there were from thirty to thirty-five Jewish families in Montpellier, subject to the authority of the consistory of Marseilles.

BIBLIOGRAPHY: Astruc, *Mémoires pour Servir à l'Histoire de la Faculté de Médecine de Montpellier*, pp. 7 *et seq.*; D'Aigrefeuille, *Histoire de Montpellier*, 2d ed., iii. 518; Germain, *Histoire de la Commune de Montpellier*, i., Introduction and pp. 61, 240; ii. 420; iii. 92, 107, 246 *et seq.*; Dom Vaissète, *Hist. Générale du Languedoc*, ii. 151, 418; iii. 28, 119; Renan-Neubauer, *Les Rabbins Français*, pp. 514, 593-623, 647-695; Grätz, *Gesch.* vii. 38 *et seq.*; Carmoly, *Hist. des Médecins Juifs*, pp. 73, 90; Saige, *Les Juifs du Languedoc*, pp. 100, 102, 128, 308-319, 326; Gariel, *Ser. Praes.* part i., p. 436; Bédarride, *Les Juifs en France*, pp. 226, 236, 465-466, 539-542; Depping, *Les Juifs dans le Moyen Age*, pp. 132-133; *R. E. J.* xix. 259, xxii. 264, xxiii. 265, xxiv. 272, xxxiii. 283, xxxiv. 276, xxxv. 91; Gross, *Gallia Judaica*, pp. 322-335; S. Kahn, *Les Ecoles Juives et la Faculté de Médecine de Montpellier*, pp. 6 *et seq.*; L. Guiraud, *Recherches Topographiques sur Montpellier au Moyen Age*, in *Mémoires de la Société Archéologique de Montpellier*, 2d series, i. 208-213.

S. S. K.

MONTREAL: Metropolis of the Dominion of Canada, situated on an island in the St. Lawrence River; the most important center of Jewish population in British North America. In 1901 the Jewish population of Montreal was 6,790. Owing to the large influx of settlers from eastern Europe since that date the present (1904) Jewish population is about 15,000 in a total population of 370,000, including the suburbs. For the history of its community see JEW. ENCYC. iii. 524 *et seq.*, *s.v.* CANADA. In religious, philanthropic, and educational work the Jews of Montreal have shown much activity, and their communal organizations are numerous and important. The first congregation was founded in 1768, but it was not until 1858 that the community had grown sufficiently large to support a second synagogue. In 1882 a third congregation was formed, and between that year and the present (1904) the growth of the community has been so rapid that eleven other congregations have been organized; some of these have a large membership, and possess commodious synagogues, while some have hardly passed the formative stage. In the western part of the city are the places of worship of the congregation of Spanish and Portuguese Jews, Shearith Israel (organized in 1768); of the English, German, and Polish congregation, Shaar Hashamayim (1858); and of Temple Emmanuel (1882). Other congregations are the B'nai Jacob (Russian; 1885), the Beth David (Rumanian; 1888), the Shaaré Tefilla (Austro-Hungarian; 1892), and the Chevra Kadisha (1893). The more recently established congregations are: the Beth Hamidrash Hagadol, Chevra Shass (1894), the Aavath Achim (1896), the K. K. Ohel Moshé (1902), the Chevra Tillim (1902), the Beth Israel, Chevra Shass (1903), the K. K. Adath Jeshurun (Galician; 1903), the Kether Torah (1903), and the Tifereth Israel (1904). All the congregations are Orthodox with the exception of Temple Emmanuel, whose founders introduced Reform when the congregation was organized.

Congregations.

The secular education of Jewish children in the Province of Quebec is provided for by a bill passed by the legislature in 1903. By the "Provincial Education Act" Protestant and Catholic school commissioners maintain separate public schools. Previous to 1903 Jews were given the option of contributing their taxes to either the Protestant or Catholic panel. Generally they paid their taxes into the former, and sent their children either to the Protestant public schools or to Jewish schools subsidized by the commissioners. So long as the number of Jewish pupils formed but a small ratio of those attending, there were no difficulties, but with the growth of the population serious differences arose. The law attributed the tax to the landlord, whether paid by him or by the tenant, and as the ratio of Jewish landowners was small, this led to the claim that the Jewish contribution to the tax was not in proportion to the number of Jewish pupils attending the schools of the Protestant Board. Although the Protestant commissoners continued to receive Jewish pupils at their schools, they declined to acknowledge any obligation to educate children of the Jewish faith whose parents were not owners of immovable property subject to taxation for school purposes; and they claimed the right to refuse to receive Jewish pupils in the event that the schools should become too crowded.

Education.

A crisis was provoked when a scholarship won by a Jewish pupil was withheld by the Protestant commissioners. The case was carried into the courts in 1903, and the validity of the Protestant commissioners' contention was judicially established. Vigorous measures were promptly taken to alter an act which was so opposed to the full civil rights secured to the Jews by the act of 1831. Public opinion was unanimous in demanding that the anomalies of the law should be corrected. A committee of the Jewish Educational Rights Movement, representative of every section of the community, waited on the government, and with the cooperation of the Protestant commissioners a law was passed in April, 1903, enacting that all Jews were to pay their taxes into the Protestant panel and enjoy equal rights with the Protestants in the schools under the Protestant commissioners. A conscience clause was provided protecting Jewish children in their religious observances.

In addition to those that attend the ordinary public schools a large number of Jewish children are educated at the school attached to the Baron de Hirsch Institute; they receive instruction in Hebrew and in secular subjects, the cost in the case of the latter being assumed by the Protestant Board. A night-school is also connected with the Baron de Hirsch Institute. The Talmud Torah Association (founded 1896) maintains a large school for the training of children in Jewish religion and history and in the Hebrew language. Instruction in these subjects is imparted also in the several schools supported by the congregations.

The Jewish philanthropic organizations of Montreal are numerous. The excellent work performed by The Baron de Hirsch Institute and Hebrew Benevolent Society in relieving distress and assisting immigrants has been mentioned in the article CANADA, referred to above. Other associations which have performed important charitable work are the Ladies' Hebrew Benevolent Society (founded 1877), the Ladies' Chevra Kadisha (1878), the Hebrew Sick Benefit Association (1892), the Hebrew Benevolent Loan Society (1893), the Hebrew Young Ladies' Sewing Society (with Diet Dispensary; 1894), the Hebrew Ladies' Aid Society (1894), the Charity Society of the Chevra Tillim (1898), and the Jewish Endeavor Sewing School (1902). Several of the congregations maintain their own aid societies and sewing circles.

Organizations.

Montreal is the headquarters of the Federation of Zionist Societies of Canada, and in 1904 supported six local branches of the movement. Among other communal organizations are four lodges of the Independent Order of the Sons of Benjamin, the Montreal Lodge of B'nai B'rith, the Zion Cadet Corps and Jewish Lads' Brigade, the Montefiore Club, the Maimonides Literary Circle, the Gereuth Circle, the Young Men's Hebrew Association, and the Montreal Branch of the Jewish Theological Seminary; the Anglo-Jewish Association maintained a branch in Montreal from 1881 to 1891, and the Kesher Shel Barzel supported a lodge from 1872 to 1890. In 1895 the Montreal Chovevei Zion Society No. 2 purchased 4,000 "duman" of land in Palestine, east of the Jordan, for colonization; this land, however, was afterward transferred to other hands. Several other philanthropic and literary societies established in the earlier days of the community have been replaced in their activities by later organizations.

BIBLIOGRAPHY: *Statutes of Province of Quebec*, 1903; *Jewish Year-Book* (London), 1903; Ville-Marie, *Montreal Past and Present*, Sandham, 1870; *Gazetteer of Montreal*, 1892.

A. C. I. DE S.

MONUMENTS IN THEIR BEARING ON BIBLICAL EXEGESIS: For centuries the evidence of the authenticity of the Old Testament Scriptures had to be sought from within; of contemporaneous external testimony there was practically nothing. All this is now changed. The civilized nations by whom Israel was surrounded have risen, as it were, from the dead, and there is at hand as much information about the culture of Egypt and western Asia in the Mosaic age as about the culture of Athens in the age of Pericles. The books of the Old Testament are taking their place as part of a vast and ever-increasing literature which explains and illustrates them and at the same time affords the only sure and certain test of their veracity.

The belief that the use of writing for literary purposes was of comparatively late date has been swept away forever. There were schools and libraries in Egypt and Babylonia long before Abraham was born. Under the dynasty of Hammurabi or Amraphel, the contemporary of Abraham (Gen. xiv. 1), Babylon was the center of a great literary movement. Old literary works were reedited, and new poets and writers arose who cast the ancient legends and traditions of the country into literary form. In Egypt there was already an extensive literature, and "The Proverbs of Ptah-ḥotep," of which there is now a copy in the Louvre, Paris, was written in the time of the Old Empire or at least as early as 3,000 B.C.

The Mosaic age, accordingly, belongs to a late epoch in the history of Oriental literature; and there is no need for surprise at finding that it was emphatically an age of readers and writers, of schools and students, of books and correspondence. The cuneiform tablets discovered in 1887 at Tell el-Amarna in Egypt have shown that from one end of the civilized world to the other letters were being constantly sent, sometimes on the most trivial of matters; that Canaan was the center of the correspondence; and that it was carried on in the language and script of Babylonia. As the language of Babylonia was not that of most of the writers it is evident that schools must have existed throughout the civilized world of the East in which the foreign language and writing were taught and learned, as well as libraries in which Babylonian books and the native archives could be preserved. Indeed, among the El-Amarna tablets fragments of Babylonian literary works have been found, some of which were used for purposes of study. Fragments of dictionaries have also been discovered. When it is remembered that among the correspondents of the Egyptian court are Bedouin sheiks and a Canaanitish lady, an idea may be formed of the extent to which education had spread. At all events Moses could have written the Law, and some at least of the Israelites could have read what was written. Moreover, there was plenty of material in the libraries of Canaan, not to speak of those of Egypt and Babylonia, with the help of which the historian could have compiled a truthful history of the past. Urusalim, or Jerusalem, and Gezer, more especially, are prominent in the El-Amarna letters.

El-Amarna Tablets.

From the Babylonian inscriptions it has been learned that in the Abrahamic age Canaan was a province of the Babylonian empire, and that colonies of "Amorites," as its inhabitants were called, were settled in Babylonia itself. One of the witnesses to a contract dated in the reign of Hammurabi's grandfather is an "Amorite," the son of Abiramu or Abram. For some years Babylonia had been under the domination of Elam, and Eri-aku or Arioch, the son of an Elamite prince, had been established at Larsa in the south of the country, but Hammurabi in the thirty-second year of his reign at last succeeded in shaking off the Elamite supremacy and in ruling over a united Babylonian empire. The Babylonian monuments have proved that the migration of Abraham was no isolated or unusual event; and they have further proved that the political position described in Gen. xiv. is in strict accordance with fact. They have also shown that Babylon was at the time under the rule of kings who belonged to the western branch of the Semitic race, who revered the god Samu (Sumu) or Shem, and who spoke a language resembling those of Canaan and southern Arabia rather than that of Babylonia. Canaanites were settled in Babylonia; and among them are found the names of Abram (Abi-ramu), Jacob (Ya'ḳub-ilu), and Joseph (Yasupu-ilu).

In the sixteenth century B.C. Canaan passed from the Babylonians to the Egyptians. The kings of the eighteenth dynasty made it an Egyptian province, so that Canaan became for a while the political brother of Mizraim and Cush. The same close intercourse which in the Abrahamic age had existed between Canaan and Babylonia now existed between Canaan and Egypt. In Egypt itself the land of Goshen has been rediscovered by Professor Naville. It lay in the Wadi Tumilat on the southeastern border of the Delta, in touch with Asia, and separate from the cultivated land of Egypt proper. The Pharaoh Me(r)neptaḥ states that it had been handed over as pasturage to "foreign" herdsmen from the south of Canaan. Naville has discovered the site of Pithom also, now Tell el-Maskhuṭa, in the district of Succoth (Thukut) and on the edge of the land of Goshen. It was built by Rameses II., and the store-chambers have been found in which provisions were laid up for the soldiers and travelers who passed into Asia. Rameses II. was the builder also of the city of Rameses (Ex. i. 11), an account of which is given in a papyrus. Zoan, moreover, was restored by him and made one of the residences of the court.

Canaan Under the Egyptians.

Rameses I., the grandfather of Rameses II., was the founder of the nineteenth dynasty and the representative of a national reaction against the Semitic tendencies of the kings who had immediately preceded him. The Canaanitish officials who had held high places at court were driven away, and the Semitic form of religion which had been introduced by the Pharaoh himself was suppressed. In accordance with this policy, every effort was made to weaken the Semitic settlers who still remained in Egypt. An explanation is thus afforded of the treatment of the Israelites; they were turned into royal bondsmen, and the male children were destroyed. The massacre is referred to in a hymn of victory in honor of Me(r)neptaḥ, the son and successor of Rameses II., which was discovered by Flinders Petrie at Thebes. Here it is said that "the seed" of the "I-s-r-a-i-l-u," or Israelites, had been destroyed, so that the women of Khar or Edom were left, "like the widows of Egypt," without husbands. The hymn was written just after the defeat of the Libyan hordes who had invaded the Delta in the fifth year of Me(r)neptaḥ; and, while all the other peoples mentioned in it have a country assigned to them, the Israelites alone are without local habitation. They must therefore already have left Egypt and not as yet been settled in Palestine. The Exodus was probably effected under cover of the Libyan invasion; Me(r)neptaḥ states that the invaders had encamped at the western extremity of the land of Goshen, where they were in contact with "the foreign" herdsmen, while three years later an Egyptian official writes to the Pharaoh that the district had been deserted and that he had accordingly allowed a fresh body of herdsmen from Edom to occupy it. It may be added that the geographical background of the Exodus as described in the Pentateuch is the eastern Delta as it was in the time of the nineteenth dynasty, and at no subsequent date, and that even the name of Moses appears as "Messu" or "Messui" in the Egyptian inscriptions of that period. There was a Messui, for example, who was governor of Ethiopia in the reign of Me(r)neptaḥ.

The conquest of southern Palestine by a king of Aram-naharaim in the early days of the Judges has been explained by the El-Amarna tablets, from which it has been learned that Aram-naharaim, or Mitanni as it was called by its inhabitants, interfered from time to time in the internal politics of Canaan. The King of Jerusalem refers to its intrigues in his letters to the Egyptian court, and Rameses III., the contemporary of Othniel, includes Mitanni among his enemies.

A flood of light has been thrown upon the later history of Jerusalem by the Assyrian monuments. The Biblical chronology, so long the despair of historians, has been corrected by means of the synchronisms established between Assyrian and Israelitish history. Shalmaneser II. (858–823 B.C.) made repeated attacks on Hamath and Damascus, and in 853 defeated a league which had been formed by Hamath, Arvad, Ammon, and other states under the leadership of Hadadezer of Damascus, the Ben-hadad of the Old Testament. The decisive battle took place at Ḳarḳar, among the allies being Ahab of Israel, who contributed 2,000 chariots and 10,000 men. Twelve years later Jehu of Beth-omri or Samaria is met with, paying tribute to the Assyrian king. His envoys are represented on a black obelisk now in the British Museum. The capture of Damascus by Assyria in 804 (when Samaria again paid tribute to the Assyrian conqueror) had doubtless much to do with the successes of Jeroboam II. (II Kings xiv. 25, 28). The older Assyrian dynasty was overthrown in April, 745, and the throne seized by Pul, who took the name of Tiglath-pileser III. The Assyrian army was reorganized, and a new policy was entered upon, that of uniting the whole of western Asia under the rule of Nineveh. In 738 tribute was paid to Assyria by Menahem of Samaria and Rezon of Damascus; and the appeal of Ahaz for help in 734 gave Tiglath-pileser a further opportunity of asserting his suzerainty over Palestine. Rezon was blockaded in his capital, while Samaria, Ammon, Moab, and Philistia were overrun. In 732 Damascus was taken, Rezon put to death, and his kingdom placed under an Assyrian prefect. Pekah had already been murdered, and Hoshea, an Assyrian nominee, placed upon the throne, a fine of 10 (?) talents of gold and 1,000 of silver being exacted from him. After this Tiglath-pileser held an assembly of the subject princes; among them was Ahaz, to whom the Assyrian scribes give his full name of Jeho-ahaz (see II Kings xvi. 10). Tiglath-pileser died in Dec., 727, and was succeeded as king by Ulula, who took the name of Shalmaneser IV. The revolt of Hoshea caused him to besiege Samaria; but before the siege was ended he died (Dec., 722), and another usurper, Sargon, made himself king. Sargon soon captured Samaria, and carried the upper and military classes into captivity. The captives amounted in all to 27,280 persons, but only fifty chariots were found in the city. Samaria was now placed under an Assyrian governor.

Biblical Chronology.

The death of Shalmaneser had allowed the Babylonians to recover their independence under a "Chaldean" from the Persian Gulf, Merodach-baladan by name. For some years Sargon was too much occupied in fighting against his northern neighbors to turn to the south. But by 711 B.C. his hands were free, and Merodach-baladan accordingly began to look for allies. An embassy was sent to Hezekiah, and an anti-Assyrian league was formed in the west between Judah, Edom, Moab, and Egypt, of which Ashdod (at that time under the suzerainty of Judah, like the rest of Philistia) was the head. But Sargon moved too rapidly for the allies. Ashdod was taken by the tartan or commander-in-chief; the states of southern Syria were compelled once more to pay tribute; and Sargon himself invaded Babylonia. In 709 he entered Babylon in triumph, and Merodach-baladan fled to his ancestral domains.

Sargon was murdered in 705 B.C., and his son Sennacherib succeeded him in the following July. In 701 the revolt of Hezekiah and the neighboring princes, who had trusted to Egyptian help, brought Sennacherib to Palestine. The Sidonian king fled to Cyprus; Ammon, Moab, and Edom submitted; Judah was wasted with fire and sword, and Hezekiah alone held out behind the strong walls of Jerusalem. He was, however, compelled to restore to Ekron its former ruler, whom he had imprisoned in Jerusalem in consequence of his faithfulness to Assyria. Tirhakah of Egypt indeed came to Hezekiah's assistance, but was defeated at Eltekeh, and Hezekiah vainly endeavored to buy off his offended suzerain by numerous presents, which included, according to Sennacherib, 30 talents of gold, 800 talents of silver, his Arab body-guard, his daughters, singing men and singing women, and furniture inlaid with ivory. The Jewish king was shut up in his capital, "like a bird in a cage," but suddenly, for reasons which Sennacherib naturally does not state, the Assyrian forces were withdrawn and the rebellious vassal remained unpunished. Sennacherib had to content himself with the presents sent to him at Lachish—the capture and plunder of which are represented in a bas-relief now in the British Museum—and with the spoil of the country districts, 200,150 Jews being carried into captivity.

Assyriological Evidence.

Sennacherib was murdered by two of his sons in Dec., 681 B.C.; but a battle soon afterward near Malatiyeh placed the crown on the head of Esar-haddon, who formally ascended the throne at Nineveh in May, 680. Esar-haddon adopted a policy of conciliation, one result of which was that Judah returned to its allegiance, and the name of Manasseh appears among his tributaries. Babylon, which had been destroyed by Sennacherib, was restored and made one of the capitals of the empire (see II Chron. xxxiii. 11). The conquest of Egypt was effected by Esar-haddon and completed by his successor, Assurbanipal, in whose reign Thebes, the No-amon of Nah. iii. 8 (R. V.), was razed to the ground.

The inscriptions of Nebuchadnezzar and his successors which have been thus far found contain but few references to political events, and therefore do not touch directly upon the Old Testament. The invasion of Egypt by Nebuchadnezzar, however, is mentioned as taking place in the thirty-seventh year of his reign (see Jer. xliii. 10–13), and there exists a very full account of the conquest of Babylonia by Cyrus, and of the peaceful occupation of Babylon by his general Gobryas. Belshazzar, the eldest son of Nabonid, the last Babylonian king, is also named in the inscriptions; he seems to have been in command of the Babylonian army, and he is found acting as a wool-merchant and paying tithes to the temple of the sun-god at Sippara. The restoration of the various exiles in Babylonia with the images of their gods (or, in the case of the Jews, their sacred vessels) is alluded to by Cyrus in a proclamation issued by him shortly after his occupation of Babylon.

Outside the cuneiform inscriptions the most important illustration of Old Testament history comes from the inscription of the Moabite king Mesha which was discovered at Diban or Dibon in 1868. In this reference is made to the "oppression" of Moab by Omri and Ahab, and to its successful revolt under Mesha and still more successful war against Israel. Mesha describes also his restoration of the ruined Moabite towns, as well as of his capital, with the help of Israelitish captives. See MOABITE STONE; also ASSYRIOLOGY; BABYLONIA; SILOAM INSCRIPTION.

E. C. A. H. S.

MONZON: Town near Lerida in the ancient kingdom of Aragon, Spain. It had a considerable Jewish community, the members of which were engaged in business, especially money-lending. In 1260 Solomon de Daroca was one of the wealthiest Jews in Monzon; he was probably also a farmer of the taxes. He often advanced large sums of money to the court, and received as security the taxes of the Jewries of Monzon and Lerida. In 1262 he appears as leaseholder of the salt-works of Arcos (Jacobs, "Sources," Nos. 221, 249, 336 *et seq.*).

When the Jews of Aragon were called upon to render King James II. pecuniary assistance in his war against Sicily, the Jews of Monzon, by a special agreement with the king, were exempted from contributing. During the bitter persecution of the Jews of Aragon in 1349 the Jews of Monzon fasted and prayed and fortified themselves within the Jewry, which they did not leave until the danger had passed. According to Jewish chronicles, a general massacre of the Monzon Jews took place on the middle days of a certain Passover festival. Some Jews were engaged in playing blind man's buff, when a quarrel arose between them and certain Christians who were passing by. In order to avenge themselves on the Jews, the Christians lodged a complaint against them with the justice, who believed their statements. Without, however, awaiting the results of an investigation the people fell upon the Jews and caused terrible bloodshed, while many children were forcibly baptized ("Shebeṭ Yehudah," p. 39). This massacre occurred probably in 1391, in which year several Jews in Monzon submitted to baptism.

Among the richest Jews in Monzon at that time were the Zaportas, of which family several members were converted. Louis Zaporta's daughter married a son of the first duke of Villahermosa. Jaime Ram, the son of Rabbi Ram (the word "Ram" being formed perhaps of the initial letters of "Rabbi Abraham [or Aaron] Monzon"), was considered one of the leading jurists of his time. The Jewish community of Monzon, which in the beginning of the fifteenth century paid 350 sueldos in taxes, was represented at the Tortosa disputation by Don Joseph ha-Levi and R. Yom-Ṭob Carcosa. The study of the Talmud was pursued with zeal at Monzon; and the rabbinical college there was recognized by Solomon b. Adret as among the foremost of the day. At Monzon lived En-Parid Saladin, who was among Isaac ben Sheshet's opponents when the latter was rabbi in Saragossa; Judah Alshech; Ḥayyim Emtabuch (?), who corresponded with Isaac ben Sheshet; the industrious translator Elijah Ḥabillo; and others.

Bibliography: Rios, *Hist.* ii. 146; iii. 82, 91; Isaac b. Sheshet, *Responsa*, Nos. 314 *et seq.*, 481, 483, 495 *et seq.*, 507; *Shebeṭ Yehudah*, p. 68; Joseph ha-Kohen, *'Emeḳ ha-Baka*, p. 66.
D. M. K.

MONZON, ABRAHAM (the Elder): Rabbi of the latter part of the sixteenth century; died at Constantinople. He was a pupil of Bezaleel Ashkenazi, and on account of his knowledge and acumen was called by his contemporaries "Sinai we-'Oḳer Harim" = "Polyhistor, and Eradicator of Mountains." He officiated as rabbi first in Egypt, but later went to Constantinople, where he remained until his death. He was an excellent scribe, and wrote many Torah scrolls, which are still extant in Egypt. He was also the author of a large number of decisions and responsa, which are included in great part in the collections of Samuel of Medina (ii. 175 *et seq.*), Solomon ben Abraham Cohen (ii. 5; iii. 2, 20 *et seq.*), Abraham de Boton (Nos. 28, 29), and Joseph di Trani (i. 104, 121, 122, 144; ii. 40). Other responsa of his, as well as his novellæ, his collections of "derashot," and his defense of Vital against Menahem di Lonsano, still exist in manuscript.

Bibliography: Conforte, *Ḳore ha-Dorot*, p. 41b; Azulai, *Shem ha-Gedolim*, i. 13; Fürst, *Bibl. Jud.* ii. 388.
E. C. M. K.

MONZON, ABRAHAM (the Younger): Rabbinical and Talmudic scholar of the middle of the sixteenth century. He was originally from Tetuan in Morocco, where he was engaged in commerce. He left that city and settled successively in Algiers, Oran, and Cairo. At Cairo a generous patron enabled him to devote his time to study, while Jonah Nabon of Jerusalem was one of his correspondents. Monzon was the author of the following works, all of which exist in manuscript: "Toẓe'ot Ḥayyim," a reply to the "'Eẓ ha-Ḥayyim" of Ḥayyim Abulafia; "Eshel Abraham," a collection of responsa; "Shulḥan Shabbat," a commentary on the Talmudic treatise Shabbat; and "'Eẓ ha-Da'at," a commentary on the Yoreh De'ah.

Bibliography: Azulai, *Shem ha-Gedolim*, ii. 152; Hazan, *Ha-Ma'alot li-Shelomoh*, p. 5.
E. C. M. K.—M. Fr.

MOON.—Biblical Data: The most common Hebrew word for the moon is "yeraḥ," the root of which is probably akin to "araḥ," so that the meaning of the term would be "the wanderer." Poetically, it is called, on account of its whiteness, "lebanah," a term occurring in the Bible three times only (Cant. vi. 10; Isa. xxiv. 23, xxx. 26). The word "ḥodesh," which also occurs thrice (I Sam. xx. 5 and 18; II Kings iv. 23), as its meaning indicates, denotes the New Moon. In the narrative of the Creation, the moon is indicated, without any special name, as one of the two great luminaries. Relatively to the sun, it is "the lesser light to rule the night"; and it is to serve together with the sun for signs, seasons, days, and years (Gen. i. 14, 16). In Ps. civ. 19 it is expressly stated that the moon was created in order to indicate the seasons. Its course, like that of the sun, was stopped by the divine will (Josh. x. 13).

Like the other celestial bodies, the moon was believed to have an influence on the universe. Its injurious influence on man is referred to in Ps. cxxi. 6, which passage probably refers to the blindness which, according to Eastern belief, results from sleeping in the moonlight with uncovered face (Carne, "Letters from the East," p. 77). It was also believed that the moon caused epilepsy (comp. the Greek *σεληνιαζόμενος* and the Latin "lunaticus"; Matt. iv. 24). On the other hand, there are "precious things put forth by the moon" (Deut. xxxiii. 14); that is to say, the growth of certain plants is influenced by it. Steuernagel, however, thinks the allusion is to the dew.

The moon was regarded by all Oriental nations as a divinity, whose worship was forbidden to the Israelites (Deut. xvii. 3). Nevertheless, the latter practised for a long time the cult of the "queen of heaven," making sacrifices to her (Jer. vii. 18, xliv. 17). Kissing the hand on seeing the moon, an act of adoration, is referred to in Job xxxi. 26–27. The moon-shaped ornaments which adorned the necks of the Midianite camels in the time of Gideon (Judges viii. 21, 26) and the "round tires like the moon" of the Israelitish women (Isa. iii. 18) were probably results of the same idolatrous tendency. The moon is frequently used in figurative language: it is the emblem of beauty (Cant. vi. 10) and of eternity (Ps. lxxii. 5, 7; lxxxix. 37). Its eclipse (Isa. xiii. 10, xxiv. 23; Joel ii. 10) and its turning to blood (*ib.* ii. 31) are tokens that the day of God's wrath is near. The light of the moon will be as the light of the sun when Yhwh shall have restored His people to their former state (Isa. xxx. 26). See Calendar; Month.

——**In Rabbinical Literature:** Referring to Gen. i. 16, where the moon and sun are first called "the two great lights" and the moon is then styled "the lesser light," R. Simeon b. Pazzi declared that at the time of the Creation the moon was of the same size as the sun. The moon then objected that it would not be decorous for two kings to use one crown, whereupon God diminished her size. In reply to the moon's question "Ought I to be punished for having spoken reasonable words?" God consoled her by promising that she also should reign in the daytime; and on her objecting that the light of a candle in the daytime was useless, God promised her that the Jews should count the years after the moon. The latter again objecting that the sun served a similar purpose, God consoled her with the idea that certain righteous men would bear the same epithet ("the smaller one"), *e.g.*, Jacob (Amos vii. 5), David (I Sam. xvii. 14), and Samuel ha-Ḳaṭon. The moon, however, remained disconsolate, and God therefore required that a he-goat be sacrificed on the first of every month as a sin-offering for His having diminished the moon's size (Ḥul. 60b). According to R. Johanan, God required that sin-offering for having caused the moon to encroach on the domain of the sun. God appeased the complaints of the moon also by surrounding her with a host of stars, like a veritable queen (Pesiḳ. R. 15; Gen. R. vi. 3-4). R. Ḥanina thinks that at first the sun alone was created to give light, and that God subsequently created the moon because He foresaw that the sun and moon would be worshiped like gods, and He said: "If when they are two, rivaling each other, they are considered as divinities, how would it be if the sun were alone?" (*ib.* vi. 1). The orbit of the moon is, like that of the sun, in the second heaven (*ib.* vi. 9; comp. Heller, "Tosafot Yom-Ṭob" to R. H. ii. 6).

There is a disagreement between R. Judah and the other rabbis as to the setting of the moon and the sun. According to the former, after setting they continue their route above the celestial vault; and it is for this reason that in summer the springs are colder than the surface of the earth. The Rabbis argued that, after setting, both moon and sun travel below the vault and consequently under the earth; and this is why in the winter the springs are not as cold as the surface of the earth (Gen. R. vi. 8). The reason why the Jews count the days of the year by the moon is that, like the moon, which reigns both in the daytime and at night, the Jews have both this world and the future one (*ib.* vi. 2). On this account the eclipse of the moon is considered by the Rabbis as a bad sign for the Jews. The eclipse of the moon and stars is caused by four kinds of sin: (1) forgery, (2) false witness, (3) breeding small cattle in Palestine (for they spoil the land), and (4) cutting down fruit-trees (Suk. 29a). The fact of women spinning their wool or flax by the light of the moon is mentioned several times in the Talmud (Soṭah vi. 1 [= p. 31a]; Giṭ. 89a; *et passim*).

The moon, on account of its monthly reappearance, is considered as the emblem of Israel; the latter, like the moon, undergoing several phases through persecution without being destroyed. Therefore the reappearance of the moon is sanctified, like the entrance of the Sabbath or festivals, by the recitation of benedictions known in the liturgy as "Ḳiddush ha-Lebanah" or "Birkat ha-Lebanah." See New Moon, Blessing of.

S. M. Sel.

MOOS, SOLOMON: German otologist; born at Randegg, near Constance, Germany, July 15, 1831; died at Heidelberg July 15, 1895; educated at the universities of Prague, Vienna, and Heidelberg (M.D. 1856). He settled in Heidelberg and was admitted to the medical faculty of the university there in 1859. In 1866 he was appointed assistant professor. From 1875 he practised otology, and he was elected assistant professor of that science in 1891. He founded the otological clinic hospital and dispensary at Heidelberg, of which he remained chief surgeon and director until his death.

Moos wrote many essays and monographs on his specialty, and conjointly with Knapp founded in 1868 the "Archiv für Augen- und Ohrenheilkunde," which journal now appears in Wiesbaden under the title "Zeitschrift für Ohrenheilkunde." He translated Toynbee's "Diseases of the Ear" under the title "Lehrbuch der Ohrenkrankheiten" (Würzburg, 1863).

Of his works may be mentioned: "Klinik der Ohrenkrankheit," Vienna, 1866; "Anatomie und Physiologie der Eustachischen Röhre," Wiesbaden, 1875; "Meningitis Cerebrospinalis Epidemica," 1881; "Ueber Pilzinvasion des Labyrinths im Gefolge von Einfacher Diphtherie," Wiesbaden, 1887; "Ueber Pilzinvasion des Labyrinths im Gefolge von Masern," *ib.* 1888; "Histologische und Bakterielle Untersuchungen über Mittelohrerkrankungen bei den Verschiedenen Formen der Diphtherie," *ib.* 1890.

Moos was one of the leading otologists of his time. He succeeded in demonstrating that in various infectious diseases microorganisms enter the labyrinth, causing disturbances in the auditory organs and in the equilibrium.

Bibliography: Pagel, *Biog. Lex.*

S. F. T. H.

MORAIS, HENRY SAMUEL: American writer and minister; born May 13, 1860, at Philadelphia, Pa.; educated at private and public schools of that city. He received his religious instruction from his father, Sabato Morais. For about twelve years he was a teacher in the schools of the Hebrew Education Society and in the Hebrew Sabbath-schools of Philadelphia. Morais was the principal founder and for the first two years managing editor of the "Jewish Exponent." He edited also "The Musical and Dramatic Standard" (Philadelphia) and "The Hebrew Watchword and Instructor" (*ib.*), and has been a frequent contributor to the Jewish and general press of the United States; he was on the reportorial and special staff of the "Philadelphia Public Ledger" almost four years.

Morais has been successively acting minister of the Mikve Israel congregation in Philadelphia (1897-98) and minister of the Adath Yeshurun congregation, Syracuse, N. Y. (1899-1900 and again 1902-3), and of the Jeshuat Israel congregation at Newport, R. I. (1900-1). He is the author of: "Eminent Israelites of the Nineteenth Century," Philadelphia, 1880; "The Jews of Philadelphia," *ib.* 1894, the most important local history of the Jews in America thus far published; and of various pamphlets.

Bibliography: Markens, *The Hebrews in America*, pp. 231-232, New York, 1888.

A. I. G. D.

MORAIS, SABATO: American rabbi; born at Leghorn, Italy, April 13, 1823; died at Philadelphia Nov. 11, 1897. He was the elder son and the third of nine children of **Samuel** and Bona Morais. The Morais family came originally from Portugal, being probably among the large number of Jews who fled thence from the Inquisition. At the time of Sabato's birth Italy was in the thick of her great struggle for freedom. Samuel Morais was an ardent republican, at one time undergoing imprisonment for his political views; and his father, Sabato Morais, was prominently identified with the political movements of his day. Upon young Sabato early rested the responsibility of aiding in the support of the family. While still a child he earned a little by teaching

Hebrew hymns and prayers to other children, meantime pursuing his own studies under Rabbis Funaro, Curiat, and others, and then under his Hebrew master, Rabbi Abraham Baruch Piperno, and gaining honorable mention in belles-lettres under Prof. Salvatore de Benedetti. In addition to Hebrew and Italian, he acquired familiarity with Aramaic, French, and Spanish. He remained at his home studying and teaching until 1845, when he went to London to apply for the vacant post of assistant ḥazzan of the Spanish and Portuguese congregation in that city. Owing to his unfamiliarity with English he was unsuccessful and returned to his home; but in the following year (1846) he accepted an invitation to become Hebrew master of the Orphans' School of the same congregation. Here he remained five years, meantime perfecting himself in English. During this period he formed a close friendship with Joseph Mazzini; and that patriot's struggle for Italian freedom was warmly seconded by Morais.

Early Years.

Sabato Morais.

In 1850, owing to the withdrawal of Isaac Leeser, the pulpit of the Mickve Israel congregation at Philadelphia, Pa., became vacant, and Morais was an applicant for the post. He arrived in Philadelphia on March 17, 1851, and was elected April 13 following, the synagogue services in the interval being conducted by him. In 1855 he married Clara Esther Weil, who died in 1872, leaving seven children. From the date of his installation as ḥazzan until his death his influence was a continually growing power for conservative Judaism. The synagogue now occupied by the Mickve Israel congregation was built and consecrated during his incumbency. Though his ministry covered the period of greatest activity in the adaptation of Judaism in America to changed conditions, he, as the advocate of Orthodox Judaism, withstood every appeal in behalf of ritualistic innovations and departures from traditional practise, winning the esteem of his opponents by his consistency and integrity. His sermons covered a wide scope of thought and action; and he showed the loftiness of his spirit when, in spite of congregational opposition to the expression of his views during the American Civil war, he continued, both in prayer and in his discourses, to show his warm sympathy with the cause of the slave. In appreciation of his attitude during these trying times the Union League Club of Philadelphia placed him on the roll of its honorary members.

Elected Ḥazzan in Philadelphia.

When, in 1867, Maimonides College was established in Philadelphia, Morais was made professor of the Bible and of Biblical literature; and he held the chair during the six years that the college existed. For a number of years thereafter he felt the urgent need of an institution for the training of Jewish ministers on historical and traditional lines; and the declarations of the Pittsburg Conference in 1885 urged him to immediate action. After a considerable agitation of the subject he succeeded, in conjunction with a few others, in establishing (Jan., 1886) the Jewish Theological Seminary at New York. He was at once made president of the faculty and professor of Bible, holding both posts until his death. Unquestionably the establishment of the seminary constitutes Morais' most lasting influence upon Judaism in America. The directors of that body have fittingly recognized his memory by naming the chair of Biblical literature and exegesis "the Sabato Morais professorship." In 1887 the University of Pennsylvania conferred upon him the honorary degree of doctor of laws, he being the first Jew so honored by that institution.

Aids in Founding the Theological Seminary.

In addition to the work which he did in official positions, Morais was most active in religious, educational, and charity matters. The Hebrew Sunday-School, Society, the Hebrew Education Society of Philadelphia, and the Young Men's Hebrew Association of that city numbered him among their most steadfast friends. In his own home he gathered about him a small band of young men whom he instructed in Hebrew, Talmud, and Jewish history, and in whom he inspired a zealous love for Judaism which has had a very marked effect upon the character not only of his pupils, but of the community at large. The strong conservatism of the Jews of Philadelphia and the warm interest in the higher things of Judaism evinced by the younger men of that city may be in a large measure directly traced to the influence of Sabato Morais. He was greatly interested in the Alliance Israélite Universelle, and was in constant correspondence with rabbis and scholars in Europe and the Orient. Through his friend Chevalier Emanuel Felice Veneziani, the almoner of Baron de Hirsch, he was enabled to secure timely aid for the agricultural colonies in New Jersey and was the representative of Baron de Hirsch in the Carmel Colony.

His Multifarious Activity.

When the Russo-Jewish exodus began, in 1882, and Russian Jews in large numbers settled in Philadelphia, Morais immediately became their friend. Although unable to speak their language, his perfect familiarity with Hebrew as a living tongue gave him a ready means of communication. Among Gentiles also he was widely known and esteemed, and was very frequently called upon to address public assemblies.

Besides his sermons, he contributed to Jewish literature much in the form of addresses to various Jewish organizations and of theological, polemical, literary, and critical articles for the Jewish press at home and abroad. He wrote classic Hebrew in prose and in verse with ease and elegance. Among his later works are: a translation of the "Prolegomena to a Grammar of the Hebrew Language," by S. D. Luzzatto (in "Fifth Biennial Report of the Jewish Theological Seminary"); "An Essay on the Jew in Italy" (in "Second Biennial Report" of the same); "Italian Jewish Literature" (in "Publications of Gratz College," 1897). His translation of the Book of Jeremiah for the Bible of the Jewish Publication Society of America was completed shortly before his death.

Bibliography: Morais, *The Jews of Philadelphia*, Philadelphia, 1894; memoir by H. S. Morais in *Sixth Biennial Report of the Jewish Theological Seminary Association*, New York, 1896.

A. C. L. S.

MORATA, OLYMPIA FULVIA. See Heidelberg.

MORAVIA: Austrian province, formerly part of the kingdom of Bohemia, containing 44,255 Jews in a total population of 2,437,706 (1900). The first historical notice of Jews in Moravia is found in the toll law of Raffelstetten (Jew. Encyc. ii. 322), which mentions Jews who came from Moravia (Dudik, i. 381). This, however, does not prove conclusively that Jews lived in Moravia in the beginning of the tenth century, for its regulations applied probably to traveling merchants who went to Moravia chiefly to buy slaves (Thietmar's "Chronicon," vi. 36, in Pertz, "Monumenta Germaniæ Scriptores," iii. 821; "Vita Sancti Adalberti," in Pertz, *ib.* iv. 586 and 600; Dudik, iv. 211). Jews must have lived in Moravia in the eleventh century, for Cosmas of Prague, the Bohemian chronicler (1040-1125), refers to them on various occasions. He gives the somewhat improbable report that, in 1096, when the Jews, having heard of the approach of the Crusaders, desired to emigrate, Duke Bretislav issued an order for the confiscation of all property belonging to the Jews; for, he said, "they have made their money in the country, and therefore should leave it there" (Pertz, "Scriptores," ix. 103-104; Dudik, iv. 216; D'Elvert, "Zur Geschichte der Juden in Mähren," p. 49, Brünn, 1895; Grätz, "Gesch." vi. 94, 3d ed.). Cosmas reports also that Duke Ladislaus (1109-25) ordered that thereafter (1124) no Christian should serve a Jew, because a certain Jew had taken holy relics from the altar of a church and had thrown them into a sewer. For this crime the Jews were forced to pay 1,000 pounds of gold and 3,000 pounds of silver as ransom (Pertz, *l.c.* ix. 128).

Early Traces.

The attempt which had been made by the territorial lords to wrest from the emperor jurisdiction over the Jews especially affected Bohemia also, as King Ottocar II. (Margrave of Moravia from 1247 and King of Bohemia 1253-78), after the death of Duke Frederick II. of Austria in 1246, claimed succession to the latter's possessions, in which the ducal jurisdiction had been proclaimed in 1244 (Jew. Encyc. ii. 322). In his charter of March 29, 1254, Ottocar promulgated the same law that Frederick had proclaimed for Austria, but omitted the limit of the rate of interest, and added the prohibition against accepting Church vestments as pledges and the provision that a Christian who accuses a Jew of child-murder, and who can not support his charge with the testimony of three Christians and three Jews, shall be punished as the Jew would have been punished. This last provision is identical with one in the bull of Innocent IV. of the same year (Jirecek, "Codex Juris Bohemici," i. 131-143; Roessler, "Prager Stadtrecht," pp. 177-187). A second charter, granted 1268, confirms that of 1254 and adds that, except in the presence of two sworn city officials, the Jews of Brünn shall not be permitted to receive a pledge after nightfall, nor to buy horses or cattle on which there rests a suspicion of theft. They were required to contribute one-fourth of the cost of maintaining the city's fortifications. The last provision was a concession to the rising hostility of the cities against the Jews, a hostility which affected the Jews of Moravia as those of other countries of western Europe until the beginning of the nineteenth century. An undated document promulgated by Ottocar exempts the Jews for one year from all taxes "because they have been mulcted by foreign lords, and because we shall soon derive profit from them, they being of our exchequer" ("Cod. Dipl. Mor." iv. 17-22; Dudik, viii. 232).

The animosity of the Church, which allied itself with the cities against the princes, did not affect the Jews in Moravia at that time. Bishop Bruno of Olmütz did not attend the council of Vienna (Jew. Encyc. ii. 323), held in 1267, which passed resolutions hostile to the Jews; and he absented himself, as Dudik thinks (vi. 40), probably on account of the Jews who were favored by the king in the charter issued the following year. The passing of the country into the hands of the Hapsburgs did not produce any change. King Rudolf ordered (1278) that the Jews of Olmütz, like those of Brünn, should contribute to the city's expenses ("Cod. Dipl. Mor." iv. 218, v. 267; Dudik, viii. 235).

Under the Hapsburgs.

Olmütz must have had an important congregation in the twelfth century, for Isaac of Durbalo in his notes to the Maḥzor Vitry quotes a decision which he had heard in that city (Maḥzor Vitry, p. 388, Berlin, 1896-97). The Rindfleisch riots, which started in Franconia in 1298, spread also to Bohemia and Moravia. The Jews intended to flee, but King Wenzel II. (1283-1305) would not permit it. "He spared their lives, but took from them immense wealth" (Chronicle of Königsaal, in Dudik, viii. 218). Perhaps this is an exaggerated report of the sums exacted by the same king for confirming the charter of Ottocar II. about 1300.

While Bishop Bruno of Olmütz became hostile to the Jews, and in a report to Pope Gregory XII. in 1273 complained that they were guilty of violating the Church canons by keeping Christian servants and by accepting Church vestments as pledges, and that they were exploiters of the country as usurers and tax- and mint-farmers, the cities became more favorably disposed toward them, since the kings had ordered that they might be taxed for municipal purposes. Iglau asked even for the privilege of keeping Jews, and the Iglauer "Stadtrecht" restricted to Maundy Thursday the prohibition that Jews may not appear in public during Holy Week (Pertz, "Leges," iii. 426). When King John (1310-46) came to Brünn in 1311 the Jews participated in the festivities, and met the king outside of the city limits (Dudik, xi. 103). In 1322 King Charles IV. gave permission to the Bishop of Olmütz to allow one Jew to settle in each of his four cities, including KREMSIR.

A great change occurred in the fifteenth century, due partly to the general hostility then manifested toward the Jews in the cities, and partly to local conditions, as the country was the prey of warring factions owing to the Hussite movement, and the Jews were accused of favoring the rebels. The first expulsion occurred in Iglau in 1426; and it was probably due to the influence of the Franciscan friar John of CAPISTRANO on the young king Ladislaus Posthumus (1440–57) that the Jews were later expelled from Brünn, Znaim, Olmütz, and Neustadt ("Luaḥ," ed. by Epstein, Brünn [1887, or 5648]; Willibald Müller, pp. 12–17). The king gave them only four months' time to find another home. The citizens of the places from which the Jews were expelled were compelled to pay their debts to the latter, but without interest; and they received, moreover, the synagogue cemeteries and baths; but they had to pay the king an annual tribute equal to the amount which had been collected from the Jews in the form of taxes. Occasional expulsions occurred during the sixteenth century, as in Hradisch, 1514, and in Neutitschein and Sternberg, 1562. The edicts of expulsion against all Jews of the kingdom of Bohemia promulgated by Ferdinand I. in 1541 and 1557 were not carried into effect. The Jews expelled from the cities settled in small towns under the protection of the feudal lords, although the records of their activities and sufferings are very meager until the Thirty Years' war, when the Jews came into greater prominence. Ferdinand II., although a bigot, treated the Jews comparatively well, because he needed the revenues derived from their taxation to wage his wars and because he concentrated all his efforts to crush Protestantism in his dominions. By a charter, dated Oct. 15, 1629, he permits Jews to visit fairs even in the cities where they have no right of residence; he promises not to exact more than the sum of 12,000 florins annually, and forbids that they be taxed by any one but their lords, to whom, moreover, they shall pay no more than the usual tribute. Further, it was expressly stipulated that they should not have to pay more toll than the legal rate. Still it would seem that these laws were never strictly enforced, for as early as 1635 the "Landtshauptmann" (governor), Cardinal von Dietrichstein, had to admonish the royal cities to allow the Jews free passage. Cities and states continued to lay complaints before the emperor that the Jews adulterate spices, misrepresent the quality of the fabrics, woolen goods, and hides they deal in, buy stolen goods, seduce Christian women, and "take the scanty bread from the mouths of Christians." Nevertheless, Ferdinand II. (1657) and Leopold I. (1659) reconfirmed the charter of 1629, and especially their right to frequent the fairs in the cities in which they had no right of residence (Müller, pp. 19–31). The expulsion of the Jews from Vienna in 1670 brought a great many of them to Moravia, and possibly the growth of the congregation of Nikolsburg dates from that period. The newcomers were heavily taxed, and, notwithstanding the solemn promise made by Ferdinand II. in 1629 that they should not be taxed beyond the limit stated in his charter, they were continuously harassed with "special" and extraordinary imposts by the imperial treasury, by their lords, and by the cities to which they went on business, and were constantly deprived of the means of earning a livelihood.

Expulsions.

Right to Attend Fairs.

The emperor, while in need of the taxes paid by the Jews, had to consider the wishes of the states and the cities which complained of the constant increase in the Jewish population, and it was repeatedly stipulated that only those Jews who had lived there in 1657 might transmit their right of residence to their children. Still the emperor Charles VI. not only confirmed their privileges (May 13, 1723), but even reduced their annual taxes from 12,000 to 8,000 florins, renewed their right to visit all fairs, and allowed them to enter the crafts. These favors seem to have aroused the enmity of the states, for on Sept. 15, 1726, the emperor proclaimed a law decreeing that in any Jewish family only one son should be allowed to marry (FAMILIANTEN GESETZ), and on Dec. 8, 1726, the Jews were driven into ghettos, having been compelled to sell all their houses and to accept others which were assigned to them. The reason for these harsh measures seems to have been religious fanaticism, for the edict of the emperor refers specifically to the fact that the Jewish houses were near the church and that the object of the tyrannical measure was "die ungehinderte Uebung des Cultus divini." The destruction of the synagogue of AUSSEE in 1722, upon the false accusation that the Jews had assaulted the Catholic priest who attempted to convert them to Christianity, may have given occasion for the promulgation of that law. The Bishop of Olmütz, to whose diocese the priest belonged and who was particularly anxious to save him from the punishment which he had incurred by disturbing the peace of a synagogue, reported that the Jews of Rausnitz had mocked at the rites of the Catholic Church. This report, which was written May 6, 1727, seems to have had a decisive effect, for on June 27, 1727, the order to separate the Jewish houses from those of the Christians was finally issued. Further hostile measures were planned. The Jews should be compelled to wear beards and a distinctive costume; they should not be locksmiths or goldsmiths; foreign Jews should not be tolerated in the country, and private synagogues should not be permitted. These propositions were submitted to the "Landesrabbiner" Issachar Berush Eskeles, who curiously enough took occasion to ask the government to issue a prohibition against shaving with a razor, but at the same time declared himself against the distinctive costume and against the order to compel the Jews to wear beards (Schram, "Ein Buch für Jeden Brünner," iii. 39, Brünn, 1903; Müller, pp. 68–72).

Segregated in Ghettos.

A time of severe trial for the Jews of Moravia began with the reign of Maria Theresa (1740–80). As soon as war broke out the Jews were accused of aiding the enemy. General von Seherr, the com-

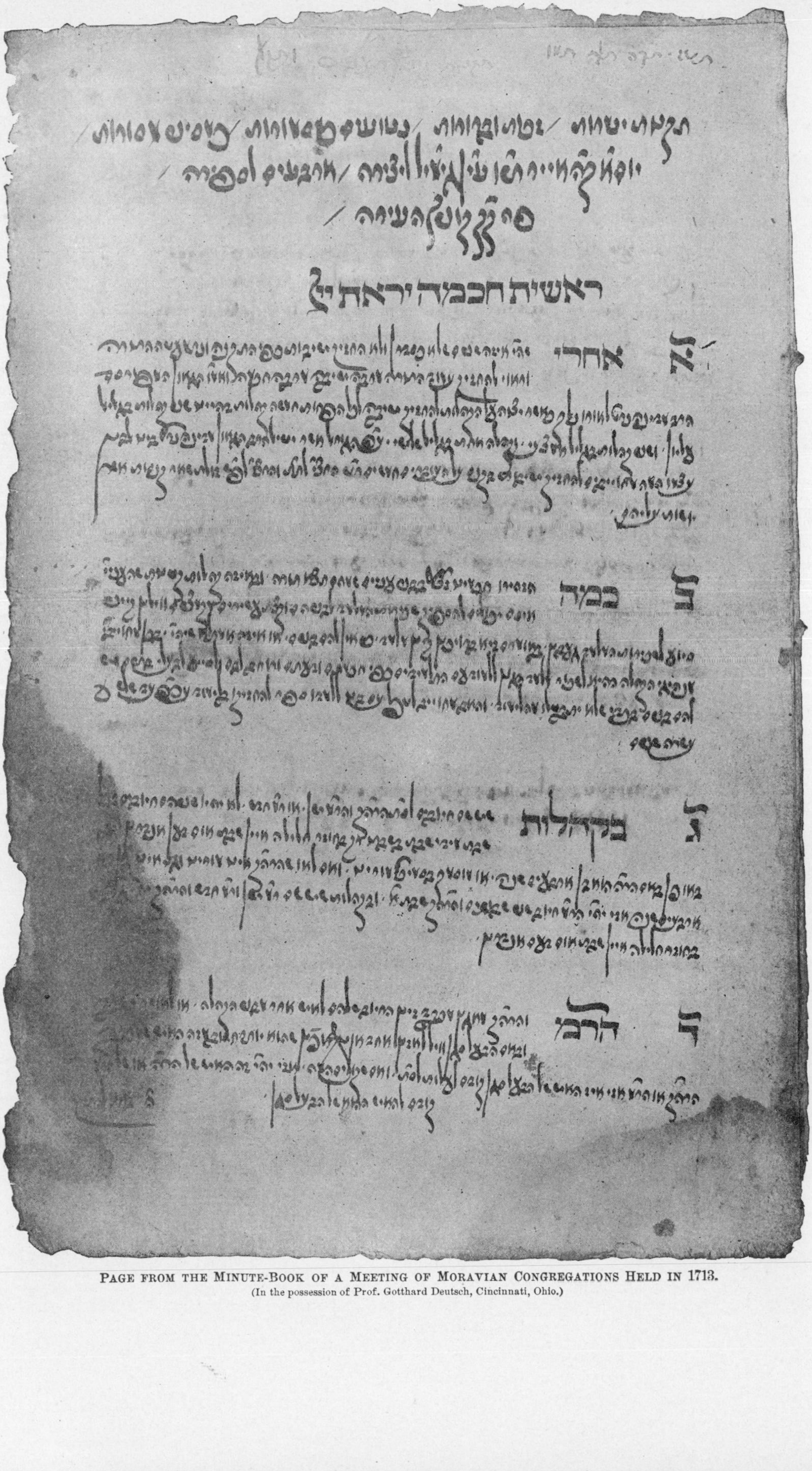

ראשית חכמה יראת יי

א׳ אחרי

ב׳ בכמה

ג׳ בקהלות

ד׳ הרבה

PAGE FROM THE MINUTE-BOOK OF A MEETING OF MORAVIAN CONGREGATIONS HELD IN 1713.
(In the possession of Prof. Gotthard Deutsch, Cincinnati, Ohio.)

mander of the fortress of Brünn, gave orders that no Jew be admitted into the city, no matter what passport he held. On March 14, 1742, he ordered also that the Jews of Moravia should pay within six days the sum of 50,000 florins under penalty of massacre and pillage. Upon the intercession of Baron Diego d'AGUILAR and of the "Landesrabbiner" Eskeles, the empress repealed this order temporarily; but the Jews had to pay the amount afterward.

In the Seven Years' War.

The second war between Frederick the Great and Maria Theresa brought still greater trouble upon the Jews, and the empress, influenced by the persistent report of a conspiracy of the Jews with the Prussians, ordered the expulsion of the former from the kingdom of Bohemia within six months. For the province of Moravia this edict was promulgated Jan. 2, 1745 (Trebitsch, "Ḳorot ha-'Ittim," pp. 17b *et seq.*; D'Elvert, *l.c.* pp. 1901 *et seq.*; Grätz, "Gesch." 3d ed., x. 355; Kaufmann, "Barthold Dowe Burmania," in "Grätz Jubelschrift," pp. 279–313, Breslau, 1887). Efforts made by the Jews, who were supported not only by some foreign powers, as the Netherlands and the Hamburg Senate ("Oesterreichische Wochenschrift," 1902, p. 137), but even by the local authorities, induced the empress to grant a temporary suspension of the cruel law (May 15, 1745). Later a further suspension was granted which permitted the Jews to remain ten years, and finally the entire edict was relegated to obscurity. The imperial office ("Hofkanzlei") expressly stated in 1762 that the suspicion of high treason under which the Jews had suffered had never been proved ("Allg. Zeit. des Jud." 1887, p. 678). But the attitude of the empress did not become any more favorable to the Jews. Immediately after the edict of expulsion had been revoked she considered the suggestion of a Jew named David Heinrich Lehmann of Prague to put a tax on ETROGIM, and demanded of the Jews of the Bohemian kingdom an annual sum of 40,000 florins for the privilege of importing this fruit, of which tax the Jews of Moravia were to pay five-twelfths. The impossibility of collecting this exorbitant sum led to a reduction of the amount in 1746 to 4,000 florins; and in 1748, when the Jews were given permission to remain another ten years in the province, this tax, like all other Jewish special taxes, was abolished, and the Jews of Moravia were called on to pay annually a "Schutzgeld" of 87,000 florins during the first five years, and of 76,700 florins during the next five years. In 1752, when the first five years had expired, the tax was increased to 90,000 florins, but in 1773 it was reduced to 82,200. For the empress the ten-year limit was evidently merely a means of saving herself from the embarrassment of a direct repeal of the edict of expulsion, and she ordered at once a compilation of the existing statutes regulating the affairs of the Jews of Moravia. Alois von SONNENFELS was ordered to prepare a translation of the old Jewish constitution as it had grown out of the deliberations of the periodical assemblies ("Shay Taḳḳanot," 311 articles). The product of his labors was the "General-Polizei-Prozess- und Kommerzialordnung für die Judenschaft des Markgrafthums Maehren," published in 1754. In its attempt at regulating all details of congregational life it is typical of the spirit of institutionalism prevailing in Austria. It states who has the right to confer the title of "Reb" (Ḥaber) and of "doppelter Reb" (Morenu), makes it the duty of the "Landesrabbiner" to assign to the other rabbis which "so-called Masechte" they should teach during the coming term, regulates the marriage fees of the rabbi, ḥazzan, and sexton, and contains several very humiliating regulations, *e.g.*, that the "Landesrabbiner" should every other year pronounce the "great ban" against thieves and receivers of stolen goods. This law contains also a civil code and a constitution of the Jewish congregations. The empress was very fond of interfering in every detail of government. Thus she revised personally the cost of the elections of the elders for the province in 1758 (G. Wolf, in Wertheimer's "Jahrbuch," vol. x., pp. 14 *et seq.*); she had a census of the Jewish families taken in 1754, and limited the number of all Jewish families in the province to 5,106 (Von Scari, p. 3; D'Elvert, *l.c.* p. 177).

The "General-ordnung" of 1754.

Under Joseph II.

Under the reign of JOSEPH II. (1780–90) conditions were considerably improved. Although most of the officials and the city councils did not favor it, he issued his "Toleranzpatent" in Brünn on Feb. 13, 1782. Limitation of the number of Jewish families remained, but the number was increased to 5,400. The "Schutzgeld" was abolished, but the Jews still had to pay special taxes—namely, a family tax of five florins annually for each head of a family, and an impost on every article of consumption—so that the treasury should not lose the 82,200 florins paid theretofore by the Jews of the province. From the surplus of these taxes a fund was created which still exists as the "Maehrisch-Juedischer Landesmassafonds." The tax on articles of consumption was especially burdensome, and its method of levy led to constant quarrels and accusations. The dues on cattle and fowl were levied when they were killed, but fish had to be carried from the market to the revenue office, and a receipt for two kreutzer had to be shown when the collector appeared in the house, which he did very often during the Friday night meal. Similar vexatious measures were applied in the case of wine which the Jews used for their own households. These conditions remained almost unchanged until 1848.

Under Francis II. further restrictions were added: an edict of 1803 prohibited the Jews from dealing in flour and grain; and an edict of 1804 required that Jews should not be permitted to buy any cattle in the markets, unless they could prove that they needed it for the purposes of retail trade as butchers or feeders, or could show a written order from a butcher for whom they acted as agents. When the Reichstag of Kremsir proclaimed freedom of religion the Catholic clergy protested, and the cities and villages where Jews had not been before tolerated also opposed the new policy. The city of Sternberg, whence Jews had been expelled in 1562, passed a resolution that it would never allow a Jew to settle there ("Allg. Zeit. des Jud." 1849, p. 506). In the village of Raitz as late as 1861 the mayor would not allow a Jewish family to settle. In other cities where Jews had been living from times immemorial, the population arose against them when they left the ghetto and opened stores in the part of the city formerly not open to them. This was the case in Trebitsch, Pirnitz, Strassnitz, and Olmütz in 1850 ("Allg. Zeit. des Jud." 1850, pp. 296, 314, 339, 359). But after the proclamation of the constitution of Dec. 20, 1867, the old restrictions were entirely removed, and the Jewish population shifted from its former habitations to the cities, especially to the larger ones from which it had been excluded; so that when, in accordance with the law of March 21, 1890, the new congregational districts were formed by the minister of worship (June 15, 1891), of the previous fifty-two congregations twelve were dissolved, while ten new ones were formed, among which are the largest, namely, Brünn, Olmütz, and Mährisch Ostrau.

Present Constitution.

A peculiarity of Moravia is the fact that it still has (1904) twenty-five Jewish settlements which are regular townships, as they used to be up to 1848, when almost every Jewish settlement was governed as a political community ("Jüdisches Volksblatt," Vienna, June 24, 1904). These communities have been required since 1884 to have separate boards for religious and municipal affairs (D'Elvert, *l.c.* p. 207); their members are those living within the old ghetto confines, so that in many instances the community counts more Christians than Jews, while the majority of the latter live in "the Christian city." The "Landesmassafonds" (to which fines and other revenues were later added) for assisting poor congregations which through excessive special taxes fell into debt, is now used exclusively for the assistance of needy congregations and congregational officials. It was handed over to the Jews in 1868, and is administered by a board of eleven members, chosen by the congregations. It amounted when first given over to the Jews, to 911,846 florins, and in 1903, to 2,201,404 kronen ($440,000). A convention of rabbis, teachers, and congregational officers, called together by the government in the city of Brünn Oct. 30, 1868, to consider the question of religious instruction and especially that of preparatory theological education, did not reach any definite results ("Allg. Zeit. des Jud." 1868, pp. 939 *et seq.*).

Another peculiar Moravian institution was that of the Landesrabbiner, which, according to the "Generalordnung" of 1754, existed "at all times" in Nikolsburg. The "Landesrabbiner" was nominated by the six representatives of the congregations—those situated in each of the six districts ("Kreis") sending one elector—and appointed by the government. Those known to have held the office are: Judah Loew ben Bezaleel, Yom-Ṭob Lipmann Heller, Menahem Mendel Krochmal, Gershon Ashkenazi, David Oppenheimer, Gabriel Eskeles, his son Issachar Berush Eskeles, who however, held the office merely nominally, as he was in the banking business in Vienna. After him the office was held by Aaron Lemberger (Lwow; 1753–57); he lived in conflict with the local rabbi Gershon Pollitzer, who succeeded him as "Landesrabbiner" (1758–72); Schmelke Horowitz, called Samuel Herschel Lewi (1774–78); Gershon Chajes (1780–89); Mordecai Benet (1789–1829); Nehemiah Trebitsch (1832–42); Samson Raphael Hirsch (1847–51). Hirsch was the last regularly elected "Landesrabbiner." After his resignation Abraham Placzek was appointed by the government as temporary "Landesrabbiner," which office he held until his death in 1884. During his last years his son Baruch Placzek was made his assistant. An attempt to provide for the office of the "Landesrabbiner" in the law regulating the affairs of the Jews of Austria March 21, 1890, failed, but the minister declared that the present law had not abolished the office. Still it was not revived, although the present (1904) incumbent, Baruch Placzek, is given that title by the government. His recent application to have Solomon Funk of Boskowitz appointed as his successor was not granted ("Oesterreichische Wochenschrift," 1904, p. 190).

Many famous rabbis occupied the rabbinical seat in Nikolsburg and in other cities of Moravia, among whom may be mentioned, apart from those already noted, Shabbethai Kohen, Nathan Adler, and Eleazar Loew, who made Moravia a seat of Talmudic learning; a number of Talmudic authors are natives of the province or have lived there, as Eliezer Nin of Nikolsburg, Samuel Loew of Boskowitz, Naphtali Hirsch Spitz, and others. The modern Haskalah movement had some devotees there, as Joseph Fleisch in Rausnitz; and the science of Judaism had also a number of representatives, among whom may be mentioned: Leopold Loew, Ad. Jellinek, Moritz Steinschneider, Isaac Hirsch Weiss, Nehemias Bruell, and David Kaufmann. A printing-office opened in Brünn during the latter part of the eighteenth century by a convert named Neumann did not produce anything remarkable.

Distinguished Rabbis.

While in the seventeenth and the eighteenth century complaints were constantly made that the strictest rules against the increase of the Jewish population were without avail, the Jewish population decreased in the ten years from 1890 to 1900 from 45,524 to 44,255, though the general population of the province during the same time increased by 160,000.

Bibliography: Dudik, *Maehrens Allgemeine Geschichte*, Brünn, 1860–89; D'Elvert, *Zur Geschichte der Juden in Mähren und Oesterreichisch-Schlesien*, Brünn, 1895; Willibald Müller, *Beiträge zur Geschichte der Mährischen Judenschaft*, Olmütz, 1903; Abraham Trebitsch, *Ḳorot ha-'Ittim*, Brünn, 1801; Löw, *Das Mährische Landesrabbinat seit Hundert Jahren*, in *Gesammelte Schriften*, vol. ii., pp. 165 *et seq.*, Szegedin, 1890; Benjamin Fränkel, in *Ḳobeẓ 'al Yad* of the Meḳiẓe Nirdamim, Berlin; Von Scari, *Systematische Darstellung der in Betreff der Juden in Mähren . . . Erlassenen Gesetze* . . . , Brünn, 1835.

D.

END OF VOL. VIII.